# HOLT
# ELEMENTS OF
# LITERATURE®

## Fifth Course

### ESSENTIALS OF
### AMERICAN LITERATURE

ILLINOIS EDITION

**HOLT, RINEHART AND WINSTON**

A Harcourt Education Company

Orlando • **Austin** • New York • San Diego • London

**Cover**
**Photo Credits:** (Inset) *The Fourth of July, 1916* (detail) by Frederick Childe Hassam (1859–1935). Oil on canvas. 36 × 26 in. © Christie's Images/SuperStock.
(Background) Front Cover only. Tickertape parade. Index Stock Imagery/*PictureQuest.*

Acknowledgments appear on pages 1455–1458, which are an extension of the copyright page.

Printed in the United States of America

ISBN 0-03-092574-6

3 4 5 6 048 08 07

# English Language Arts Learning Standards

The following chart lists the Illinois **English Language Arts Learning Standards.** While you are in grade 11, you are expected to achieve five major **goals** in reading, literature, writing, listening and speaking, and research. Each goal and its parts are spelled out in a set of standards. Each **standard** appears in a yellow box below the goal. Below the standard is an explanation of its meaning. To the right of the standard, you will find an example of how *Elements of Literature* helps you master that standard.

## GOAL 1, READING:
### Read with understanding and fluency.

**Reading 1.A.** Apply word analysis and vocabulary skills to comprehend selections.

**1.A.5a** Identify and analyze new terminology applying knowledge of word origins and derivations in a variety of practical settings.

Many words used in math, science, and political science have Greek or Latin origins. Applying a knowledge of words origins will help you become a more fluent reader.

EXAMPLE: Applying Knowledge of Word Origins

For help in applying word-origin knowledge in practical settings, see pages 543–544 on Greek and Latin roots used in math and science, and pages 949–950 on terms used in political science and history. In addition, the Vocabulary Skills index on page 1465 serves as a handy guide to the full range of vocabulary exercises contained in this textbook.

**1.A.5b** Analyze the meaning of abstract concepts and the effects of particular word and phrase choices.

Understanding abstract concepts and the relationships between words will help you to comprehend what you read and to learn to use words and phrases effectively.

EXAMPLE: Analyzing Effects of Word Choices

The Vocabulary Development exercise at the top of page 788 focuses directly on the effects of words by helping you compare their connotations. Additionally, this textbook contains many exercises that help you use analogies to understand gradations of meaning. (See, for instance, pages 187–188 and 788–789.)

**Reading 1.B.** Apply reading strategies to improve understanding and fluency.

### 1.B.5a Relate reading to prior knowledge and experience and make connections to related information.

To master this skill, you will learn how to connect the texts you read to what you know or have experienced in your own life.

**EXAMPLE:** Making Connections

This textbook contains "Political Points of View" features, which include a range of documents on specific topics. For example, the selections in the feature on World War II include a poem, comments, memoirs, reportage, a speech, a letter, and diary excerpts. Introductory and analysis pages (pages 907–908 and 958–959) help you relate the selections to your prior knowledge of World War II.

### 1.B.5b Analyze the defining characteristics and structures of a variety of complex literary genres and describe how genre affects the meaning and function of the texts.

To master this skill, you will distinguish the unique features of different kinds of literature and understand how literary form can influence the ideas expressed in the text.

**EXAMPLE:** Analyzing Literary Genres

Throughout this book are features that teach the unique characteristics of various genres of literature. For instance, you will learn about poetry and its forms, such as the dramatic monologue (page 657) and the villanelle (page 1142). Many Before You Read features focus on specific literary elements, such as theme, character, allusion, and figures of speech.

### 1.B.5c Evaluate a variety of compositions for purpose, structure, content and details for use in school or at work.

You will learn how to evaluate a variety of texts, not only in terms of their message but also in terms of their purpose, structure, and supporting details.

**EXAMPLE:** Evaluating Public Documents

On pages 1345–1348 in the World of Work handbook, you'll find definitions and tips on how to analyze consumer documents (such as warranties and contracts), workplace documents (such as memos and procedure manuals), and persuasive works (such as policy statements, political platforms, speeches, and debates).

### 1.B.5d Read age-appropriate material with fluency and accuracy.

A major goal of Illinois' state standards is ensuring that you can readily take in what you read. All of the selections in this textbook were chosen to help you read well at an eleventh-grade level.

**EXAMPLE:** Reading Fluently and Accurately

This textbook provides a wealth of reading instruction. For tips on improving all of your reading skills, see the Reading Matters handbook on pages 1331–1344.

**Reading 1.C.** Comprehend a broad range of reading materials.

**1.C.5a  Use questions and predictions to guide reading across complex materials.**

To improve reading comprehension, you will learn to approach reading selections with questions in mind or with predictions about what you'll read.

**EXAMPLE:** Making Predictions

The Reading Skills section on page 175 shows how a suspenseful story, such as "The Devil and Tom Walker," makes you want to keep guessing what's coming. The section guides you on how to record your predictions and how to adjust your predictions as necessary.

---

**1.C.5b  Analyze and defend an interpretation of text.**

Literature and documents can often be interpreted in more ways than one. Response and Analysis questions under the heading "Thinking Critically" often ask you to interpret an element of a text and to give evidence from the text that supports your interpretation.

**EXAMPLE:** Supporting an Interpretation

The Thinking Critically questions for Tim O'Brien's short story "Speaking of Courage" provide a good "how-to" guide for using details from a text to support your analysis and interpretation. Question 8, for example, requires you to relate your interpretation of a symbol to the story's historical context (page 970).

---

**1.C.5c  Critically evaluate information from multiple sources.**

To master this standard, you will learn skills for analyzing and evaluating a variety of texts of different lengths and genres. These texts also represent different eras and countries.

**EXAMPLE:** Evaluating Information from Multiple Sources

The Political Points of View features ask you to evaluate texts as varied as poems, news reports, letters, and speeches. On page 487, for example, you are asked to evaluate the power and clarity of what is said about slavery in autobiographical excerpts, spirituals, and a newspaper article.

---

**1.C.5d  Summarize and make generalizations from content and relate them to the purpose of the material.**

For this standard, you'll need to find, understand, and sum up the most important points in a selection. You'll also need to make generalizations—broad statements that can be deduced from the details of a selection.

**EXAMPLE:** Summarizing and Generalizing

For help in summarizing a poem, see the Reading Skills section on page 401. For help in summarizing narrative and expository text, see pages 1337–1338 in the Reading Matters handbook. For help in making a generalization, see the Reading Skills section on page 215.

**1.C.5e** Evaluate how authors and illustrators use text and art across materials to express their ideas (e.g., complex dialogue, persuasive techniques).

This standard covers the ways authors and artists communicate with their audience, especially how they draw attention to key ideas and images.

**EXAMPLE:** Evaluating a Text Feature

An author's use of text might include complex dialogue and persuasive techniques. For a review of the meaning of persuasion and persuasive techniques, see the Literary Focus on page 81, Reading Skills on pages 232–233, and "Persuasion" on page 1390. For dialogue, see "Dialogue" on page 1384 and the Literary Focus on page 1064.

**1.C.5f** Use tables, graphs and maps to challenge arguments, defend conclusions and persuade others.

To meet this standard, you will need to understand how to read and use various kinds of tables, graphs, charts, and maps.

**EXAMPLE:** Using Visuals

See "Visuals" on pages 1361–1362 in the Writer's Handbook for definitions and examples of bar graphs, line graphs, tables, spreadsheets, pictures, charts, and time lines. The exercise on page 1362 provides practice in analyzing a specific body of information in order to create the type of visual that best represents the data.

## GOAL 2, LITERATURE:
## Read and understand literature representative of various societies, eras and ideas.

**Literature 2.A.** Understand how literary elements and techniques are used to convey meaning.

**2.A.5a** Compare and evaluate oral, written or viewed works from various eras and traditions and analyze complex literary devices (e.g., structures, images, forms, foreshadowing, flashbacks, stream of consciousness).

To help you master this standard, this textbook presents the essentials of American literature, from colonial times to the present. This book also includes several "Literature of the Americas" selections—works by authors from Central and South America. You will also learn about the literary devices that make these works compelling.

**EXAMPLE:** Analyzing Literary Devices

For quick definitions of the literary devices included in this standard, see the Handbook of Literary and Historical Terms on pages 1379–1398. Use the Literary Skills section of the Index on pages 1463–1465 to locate additional explanations and examples.

**2.A.5b** Evaluate relationships between and among character, plot, setting, theme, conflict and resolution and their influence on the effectiveness of a literary piece.

Making connections between literary elements will help you understand and appreciate literature. A Literary Focus feature often appears on the Before You Read pages at the beginning of selections. This feature alerts you to an element, such as plot or theme, that is especially important in the selection you are about to read.

**EXAMPLE:** Evaluating Literary Elements

The Literary Focus feature on page 719 alerts you to the importance of setting and characterization in William Faulkner's short story "A Rose for Emily." The Response and Analysis questions (page 729) invite discussion of additional literary elements, such as conflict, foreshadowing, narrator, and symbol.

**2.A.5c** Analyze the development of form (e.g., short stories, essays, speeches, poetry, plays, novels) and purpose in American literature and literature of other countries.

You will learn how different kinds of literature—and the reasons for writing it—developed as part of the literary tradition of different countries.

**EXAMPLE:** Analyzing Form and Purpose

The introductory material for each collection explains the historical and literary changes associated with certain eras and movements. For example, the introduction to the American Romantic period (pages 157–173) includes a time line of events from 1790 through 1860, "Political and Social Milestones" (including the Gold Rush and education reform), an essay comparing American Romanticism with that of Europe, and representative artworks from the era.

**2.A.5d** Evaluate the influence of historical context on form, style and point of view for a variety of literary works.

To help you meet this standard, this textbook is arranged chronologically. Each collection includes an introductory essay that sets the historical context for the selections that follow.

**EXAMPLE:** Evaluating Historical Context

To help you understand the literature in Collection 4, "The Rise of Realism: The Civil War to 1914," the introductory essay covers such topics as slavery, the war in literature, and the rise of realism.

**Literature 2.B.** Read and interpret a variety of literary works.

### 2.B.5a Analyze and express an interpretation of a literary work.

To understand a literary work, you must be able to develop your own ideas about it and express those ideas to others. For help in mastering this standard, use the Before You Read and Response and Analysis pages that appear throughout the textbook.

**EXAMPLE:** Interpreting a Literary Work

The Writing Workshop "Analyzing a Novel" (page 870) and the Listening and Speaking Workshop "Presenting a Literary Analysis" (page 878) allow you to analyze literary works and express your interpretation in written and oral forms.

### 2.B.5b Apply knowledge gained from literature as a means of understanding contemporary and historical economic, social and political issues and perspectives.

Most literature, though grounded in historical eras, reveals thoughts and experiences that transcend time and place. You should be able to use literature as a window to the past and to the world around you.

**EXAMPLE:** Linking Literature with Issues

The "Political Points of View: Civil Disobedience" feature (pages 232–248) that accompanies Collection 2, "American Romanticism," discusses civil disobedience—a topic that is still relevant to twenty-first century society. This feature guides you in examining the issue as it was addressed by Henry David Thoreau, Mohandas K. Gandhi, and Martin Luther King, Jr., and in evaluating the relevance of their views today.

## GOAL 3, WRITING:
## Write to communicate for a variety of purposes.

**Writing 3.A.** Use correct grammar, spelling, punctuation, capitalization and structure.

### 3.A.5 Produce grammatically correct documents using standard manuscript specifications for a variety of purposes and audiences.

This standard focuses on editing, proofreading, and publishing. By mastering these parts of the writing process, you will learn to create documents with increased credibility and impact.

**EXAMPLE:** Polishing Documents

Grammar Link features help you with specific grammatical problems, and each Writing Workshop includes a revising section that suggests ways to correct errors and improve your content and style. (See page 432, for example.) For quick reference, use the Language Handbook (pages 1400–1437): It provides instruction in grammar, usage, and mechanics.

**Writing 3.B.** Compose well-organized and coherent writing for specific purposes and audiences.

**3.B.5** Using contemporary technology, produce documents of publication quality for specific purposes and audiences; exhibit clarity of focus, logic of organization, appropriate elaboration and support and overall coherence.

To help you master this standard, this textbook provides workshops in writing, media, and listening and speaking that walk you through every stage of creating written, multimedia, and oral documents. Each workshop outlines techniques appropriate for a specific purpose and audience.

**EXAMPLE:** Using Contemporary Technology

The "Designing Your Writing" feature (pages 1359–1361) provides information on page design and type to help you with electronic publishing. In addition, the Media Workshop "Analyzing and Using Media" (pages 1314–1321) helps you analyze both print and electronic media and then produce your own multimedia presentation.

**Writing 3.C.** Communicate ideas in writing to accomplish a variety of purposes.

**3.C.5a** Communicate information and ideas in narrative, informative and persuasive writing with clarity and effectiveness in a variety of written forms using appropriate traditional and/or electronic formats; adapt content, vocabulary, voice and tone to the audience, purpose and situation.

You will master a variety of writing modes by completing the Writing Workshops in this book. Instruction includes focusing your writing according to the context.

**EXAMPLE:** Writing in a Variety of Forms

See, for example, the following Writing Workshops and Mini-Workshops:

**Persuasion:** "Writing an Editorial" (page 138)

**Narrative:** "Writing a Short Story" (page 338)

**Informative:** "Analyzing Literature" (page 739) and "Analyzing Nonfiction" (page 1127)

**3.C.5b** Write for real or potentially real situations in academic, professional and civic contexts (e.g., applications, job applications, business letters, resume, petitions).

This standard focuses on learning writing skills you'll need throughout life. Much of your success will depend on your ability to understand and create real-life documents such as letters and applications. This textbook offers instruction on these types of writing.

**EXAMPLE:** Writing for Real Situations

Writing Workshops throughout this textbook assist you with writing for academic purposes. "The World of Work" (pages 1345–1350) gives instruction on both reading and writing in professional and real-world documents. This section not only explains what to put into job applications, résumés, and workplace documents but also gives tips on formatting these documents and on including databases, graphics, and spreadsheets.

## GOAL 4, LISTENING AND SPEAKING:
### Listen and speak effectively in a variety of situations.

**Listening and Speaking 4.A.** Listen effectively in formal and informal situations.

**4.A.5a** Use criteria to evaluate a variety of speakers' verbal and nonverbal messages.

It is important that you have standards on which to base your judgements of speeches and presentations. How a speaker delivers his or her message can be as important as what he or she has to say.

**EXAMPLE:** Evaluating Verbal and Nonverbal Messages

The Listening and Speaking Workshops in this textbook teach you verbal and nonverbal techniques you can use in your own speeches and presentations. You can use your knowledge of those techniques to evaluate other speakers.

**4.A.5b** Use techniques for analysis, synthesis, and evaluation of oral messages.

To master this standard, you will learn ways to listen critically to the messages you hear.

**EXAMPLE:** Evaluating Oral Messages

The Listening and Speaking Workshop "Presenting and Evaluating Speeches" (pages 146–149) gives specific instruction on how to spot logical fallacies and propaganda in persuasive speeches.

**Listening and Speaking 4.B.** Speak effectively using language appropriate to the situation and audience.

**4.B.5a** Deliver planned and impromptu oral presentations, as individuals and members of a group, conveying results of research, projects or literature studies to a variety of audiences (e.g., peers, community, business/industry, local organizations) using appropriate visual aids and available technology.

This skill requires you to give effective presentations to inform others. By mastering this skill, you'll be able to present information whether you have been given time for preparation or not. You'll also be able to use presentation tools to support your message.

**EXAMPLE:** Presenting Your Views

The questions found in the Response and Analysis pages following each selection can serve as the basis for impromptu group discussions. The Media Workshop "Analyzing and Using Media" (pages 1314–1321) is especially helpful for designing a multimedia presentation that employs modern technology.

**4.B.5b**  Use speaking skills to participate in and lead group discussions; analyze the effectiveness of the spoken interactions based upon the ability of the group to achieve its goals.

This standard requires you to work within a group and to lead effective classroom discussions toward a common goal. You will also learn to evaluate discussion in terms of its effectiveness.

**EXAMPLE:** Participating in Groups

The Listening and Speaking Workshop "Presenting and Evaluating Speeches" (pages 146–149) gives tips on active listening and speaking that apply equally well to formal speaking situations and to group discussions.

---

**4.B.5c**  Implement learned strategies to self-monitor communication anxiety and apprehension (e.g., relaxation and transference techniques, scripting, extemporaneous outlining, repetitive practice).

Preparing well for an oral presentation can help you overcome nervousness and communicate more effectively. Such preparation includes learning techniques and strategies for overcoming anxiety and for appropriate practice and rehearsal.

**EXAMPLE:** Using Strategies to Reduce Anxiety

The Listening and Speaking Workshops suggest various strategies to use in preparing for specific types of oral presentations. For example, "The Natural Sound" on page 623 explains what to put on note cards and how to arrange them to help you speak in a natural manner.

---

**4.B.5d**  Use verbal and nonverbal strategies to maintain communication and to resolve individual, group and workplace conflict (e.g., mediation skills, formal and informal bargaining skills).

Both regular conversations and conflict situations require verbal and nonverbal skills. Mastery of this standard will help you manage conflict in personal and professional situations.

**EXAMPLE:** Maintaining Communication

The Techniques charts on pages 435 and 623 instruct you to consider verbal and nonverbal strategies, such as language, tone, gestures, and facial expressions, when addressing an audience. These strategies can be useful in resolving conflict in both formal and informal speaking situations.

## GOAL 5, RESEARCH:
## Use the language arts to acquire, assess and communicate information.

**Research 5.A.** Locate, organize, and use information from various sources to answer questions, solve problems and communicate ideas.

**5.A.5a** Develop a research plan using multiple forms of data.

Before researching, you will create a plan that includes looking for information in many different kinds of sources.

**EXAMPLE:** Planning Your Research

The Writing Workshop "Reporting Historical Research" (pages 602–621) includes an Information Resources chart (page 604) that lists both print and nonprint sources and where to find them.

**5.A.5b** Research, design and present a project to an academic, business or school community audience on a topic selected from among contemporary issues.

You will create and deliver written and oral messages on real-world topics to audiences both in and out of school.

**EXAMPLE:** Selecting an Issue for a Project

The "Writing an Editorial" workshop (page 138) and the analysis pages at the ends of Political Points of View features can help you choose a contemporary issue. For example, see the Writing prompts about freedom and equality on page 114 or the Listening and Speaking prompts about civil disobedience on page 248.

**Research 5.B.** Analyze and evaluate information acquired from various sources.

**5.B.5a** Evaluate the usefulness of information, synthesize information to support a thesis, and present information in a logical manner in oral and written forms.

In both speaking and writing, you will use solid information from a variety of trusted sources. You should present this information in a clear and sensible way.

**EXAMPLE:** Usefulness of Information

On page 605 of the Writing Workshop "Reporting Historical Research" is instruction on determining the reliability and validity of sources as well as using information from all relevant perspectives. Consult "Develop an Outline" in the same workshop (page 608) for effective organizational patterns.

**5.B.5b** Credit primary and secondary sources in a form appropriate for presentation or publication for a particular audience.

You will use appropriate conventions to credit the sources from which you gather information. Your sources should consist of both firsthand, original information (letters, autobiographies, historical documents) and secondary information about or derived from those firsthand sources (encyclopedias, biographies, history books).

EXAMPLE: Crediting Sources

The Writing Workshop "Reporting Historical Research" (pages 602–621) provides detailed instruction on documenting sources. See especially the guidelines for giving credit within a paper (page 610) and "Sample Works Cited Entries" (pages 611–613). Examples range from standard reference works, such as books and magazine articles, to nonstandard reference works, such as interviews, film or video recordings, and material accessed through the Internet.

**Research 5.C.** Apply acquired information, concepts and ideas to communicate in a variety of formats.

**5.C.5a** Using contemporary technology, create a research presentation or prepare a documentary related to academic, technical or occupational topics and present the findings in oral or multimedia formats.

You will use current technology to research, create, and give presentations in a variety of forms and for different purposes.

EXAMPLE: Contemporary Technology

The Media Workshop "Analyzing and Using Media" (pages 1314–1321) gives useful instruction on selecting and using media to maximize the impact of your presentations. For example, instructions let you know that text slides should use six or fewer lines with six words per line so that your audience can easily absorb the information on the slide.

**5.C.5b** Support and defend a thesis statement using various references including media and electronic resources.

You'll use audio and video materials as well as Internet resources as evidence and examples to support the ideas you form about a topic.

EXAMPLE: Defending a Thesis

The Writing Workshops provide guidance on establishing a thesis statement and developing support. (See, for example, pages 608 and 871.) "Sample Works Cited Entries" (pages 611–613) gives examples of media and electronic resources.

# Taking the PSAE

You probably have been taking national and statewide **standardized tests** throughout your school career. These tests become increasingly important as you approach graduation and think about applying to college.

In Illinois, eleventh-graders currently are required to take the **Prairie State Achievement Examination (PSAE).** The PSAE in reading measures your ability to read and understand literature, informational materials, and real-world documents. The PSAE in reading also measures what you know about writing skills by giving you short passages for you to edit.

Specifically, the test measures your mastery of the following reading and writing skills.

Read to understand by
- using reading strategies
- using vocabulary strategies
- identifying and analyzing literary elements
- experiencing a variety of reading selections

Write to communicate effectively by
 presenting ideas in a clear and coherent manner
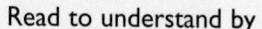 using correct grammar, spelling, and punctuation

In addition to the PSAE, you may take other standardized tests before you graduate from high school. The pages that follow give you some hints for improving your scores not only on the PSAE, but also on other important standardized tests.

These pages are designed to help you become familiar with what you'll find on the reading portion of the PSAE and to give you practice in responding to similar items. The practice items in this textbook are similar to those on the PSAE but are not identical in format. For instance, the exam may contain longer reading passages.

# Tips for Taking Multiple-Choice Tests

Multiple-choice questions are the type most commonly found on standardized tests. Teachers and other education professionals suggest these tips for success:

**Watch your time.** Quickly skim the test to see how many sections there are. Estimate how long you can afford to spend on each section and on each item in each section.

**Read everything carefully.** Stay focused and alert as you read, and do not skip anything. Pay special attention to the **directions,** which tell you what to do; the literary and informational **reading passages;** and **each question in full,** including all answer choices. Some of the questions on the PSAE in reading offer four choices for each answer. Other questions offer five choices for each answer.

**There are no trick questions.** Do not waste time wondering what a question "really" means. However, do look closely for words that limit the correct answer choice.

• *Not* and *except* require you to choose an answer that is false or opposite in some way.

• *Always* and *never* signal that a choice applies in all or no situations.

**Trust yourself.** Carefully read the question and try to predict the right answer. Then, read each of the answer choices to see whether one of them matches your prediction. If the answer is not apparent, try the following:

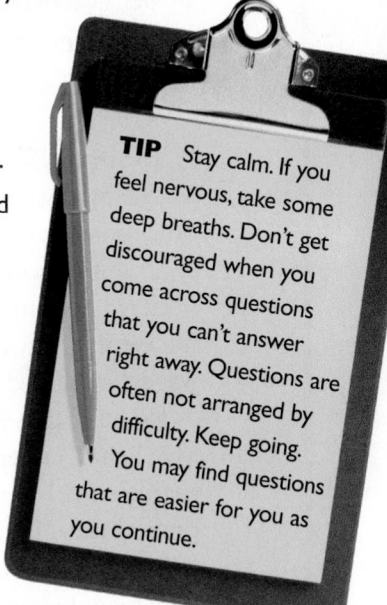

**TIP** Stay calm. If you feel nervous, take some deep breaths. Don't get discouraged when you come across questions that you can't answer right away. Questions are often not arranged by difficulty. Keep going. You may find questions that are easier for you as you continue.

• Read the entire question with only the first answer choice, as if the other choices did not exist. Do this with each choice in turn. As you study the choices, look for key phrases or ideas that you can recall from the passage.

• Eliminate answer choices that are obviously wrong. Then, make an informed guess about the choices that remain.

If you still cannot decide on the correct choice, mark the question for later review. Then, move on to other questions.

**Mark answers carefully.** First, be careful to match each question number on the test with the same number on your answer form. Then, double-check to make sure that you have correctly recorded your intended answer choice for each question.

**Review your work.** If you have time, go back to answer any question that you skipped. Erase any stray marks you have made on your answer form.

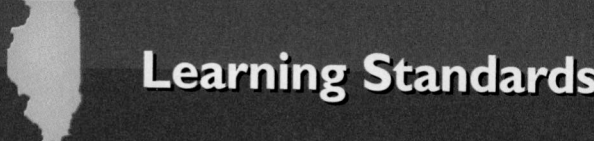
# Taking Part One of the PSAE in Reading

The PSAE includes the ACT Assessment Reading Test. The ACT is a national college admissions test. This part of the ACT contains fictional and informational passages that vary in difficulty. Each passage is followed by multiple-choice questions. The questions measure your ability to

- identify main ideas
- identify important details
- recognize comparisons
- identify cause-and-effect relationships
- determine word meanings
- make generalizations
- draw conclusions
- recognize tone

Below are a sample reading passage and questions like those on the ACT component of the PSAE. The explanation that follows each question will help you understand the correct answer.

**DIRECTIONS:** The reading passage is followed by several questions. Read the passage. Then, choose the best answer to each question and fill in the answer on your answer document. You may refer to the passage as often as needed.

**PROSE NONFICTION:** This passage is taken from Mark Twain's autobiographical narrative *Life on the Mississippi.*

The boat [*Paul Jones*] backed out from New Orleans at four in the afternoon. . . . Mr. Bixby, my chief, "straightened her up," plowed her along past the sterns of the other boats that lay at the Levee, and then said, "Here, take her; shave those steamships as close as you'd peel an apple." I took the wheel, and my heartbeat
5   fluttered up into the hundreds. . . . In half a minute I had a wide margin of safety intervening between the *Paul Jones* and the ships; and within ten seconds more I was set aside in disgrace. . . .

Now and then Mr. Bixby called my attention to certain things. Said he, "This is Six-Mile Point." I assented. It was pleasant enough information, but I could not see the
10   bearing of it. I was not conscious that it was a matter of any interest to me. Another time he said, "This is Nine-Mile Point." Later he said, "This is Twelve-Mile Point." They were all about level with the water's edge; they all looked about alike to me; they were monotonously unpicturesque. I hoped Mr. Bixby would change the subject. But no; he would crowd up around a point, hugging the shore with affection, and then
15   say: "The slack water ends here, abreast this bunch of China trees; now we cross over." So he crossed over. He gave me the wheel once or twice, but I had no luck. I either

came near chipping off the edge of a sugar-plantation, or I yawed too far from shore, and so dropped back into disgrace again and got abused.

The watch was ended at last, and we took supper and went to bed. At mid-
20   night the glare of a lantern shone in my eyes, and the night watchman said:

"Come, turn out!"

And then he left. I could not understand this extraordinary procedure; so I presently gave up trying to, and dozed off to sleep. Pretty soon the watchman was back again, and this time he was gruff. I was annoyed. I said:

25   "What do you want to come bothering around here in the middle of the night for? Now, as like as not, I'll not get to sleep again to-night."

The watchman said:

"Well, if this ain't good, I'm blessed."

The "off-watch" was just turning in, and I heard some brutal laughter
30   from them, and such remarks as "Hello, watchman! ain't the new cub turned out yet? He's delicate, likely. . . ."

About this time Mr. Bixby appeared on the scene. Something like a minute later I was climbing the pilot-house steps with some of my clothes on and the rest in my arms. Mr. Bixby was close behind, commenting. Here was
35   something fresh—this idea of getting up in the middle of the night to go to work. It was a detail in piloting that had never occurred to me at all. I knew that boats ran all night, but somehow I had never happened to reflect that somebody had to get up out of a warm bed to run them. . . .

It was a rather dingy night, although a fair number of stars were out. The
40   big mate was at the wheel, and he had the old tub pointed at a star and was holding her straight up the middle of the river. The shores on either hand were not much more than half a mile apart, but they seemed wonderfully far away and ever so vague and indistinct. The mate said:

"We've got to land at Jones's plantation, sir."

45   The vengeful spirit in me exulted. I said to myself, "I wish you joy of your job, Mr. Bixby; you'll have a good time finding Mr. Jones's plantation such a night as this; and I hope you never *will* find it as long as you live."

Mr. Bixby said to the mate:

"Upper end of the plantation, or the lower?"

50   "Upper."

"I can't do it. The stumps there are out of water at this stage. It's no great distance to the lower, and you'll have to get along with that."

"All right, sir. If Jones don't like it, he'll have to lump it, I reckon."

And then the mate left. My exultation began to cool and my wonder to
55   come up. Here was a man who not only proposed to find this plantation on such a night, but to find either end of it you preferred. . . .

# Learning Standards

1. A good title for this passage is:
   A. Steering a Mississippi Steamboat.
   B. Learning the Mississippi River.
   C. Becoming a Pilot on the Mississippi River.
   D. Ways of Making Conversation.

**EXPLANATION:** To answer this main-idea question, you must choose the answer that best covers the most important details in the passage. You can eliminate answers that are too general, like A and B, or not relevant at all, like D. The details in the passage specifically focus on Twain's first experiences as a cub pilot. **The correct answer is C.**

2. Mr. Bixby tells Twain the names of points and other details about the river because:
   F. he is filling the time with idle conversation.
   G. he loves the river and every detail about it.
   H. he likes the sound of his own voice.
   J. he knows that a would-be pilot needs to learn about locations, currents, and so on.

**EXPLANATION:** This question requires an inference based on details in the passage. While it is possible that F, G, or H may be true, details near the end of the passage imply that a good steamboat pilot is able to find any location along the river. Mr. Bixby has begun to teach Twain about the river. **The correct answer is J.**

3. In lines 3–4, "shave those steamships as close as you'd peel an apple" means that Twain should:
   A. steer the boat wide, well clear of all other ships.
   B. steer a course that passes quite near each of the other ships.
   C. scrape the other boats lightly as he steers the *Paul Jones* past them.
   D. bounce the *Paul Jones* off the other ships as he steers.

**EXPLANATION:** This question requires you to understand figurative language. When Mr. Bixby tells Twain what to do, he uses a simile. He compares the act of steering the ship to peeling an apple. You must use common sense and context when you interpret figurative language. Clearly, it is not a good idea for a pilot to hit other ships, so C and D can be eliminated. Choice A contains a safer course of action for a pilot. However, steering well clear of another ship is not consistent with the idea of "closeness" suggested in the act of peeling an apple. **The correct answer is B.**

4. As it is used in line 19, the word *watch* means:
   F. a ship's clock.
   G. a work period.
   H. a telescope.
   J. a watchman.

**EXPLANATION:** To determine the correct meaning, you must study the context of the word. Line 19 and the lines before it indicate that a "watch" is a period of time spent observing the course of the ship. **The correct answer is G.**

**5.** In lines 19–38, when Twain is awakened in the middle of the night, the new aspect of piloting he learns is that:

 **A.** night watchmen like to play jokes on novice pilots.

 **B.** older crew members laugh harshly at new members.

 **C.** experienced pilots test the patience of novice pilots.

 **D.** steamboats must be piloted by night as well as by day.

**EXPLANATION:** Be sure to review all of the lines cited in a question. At first, Twain is mystified by being awakened. He assumes that he is the victim of thoughtlessness or a joke until Mr. Bixby sets him straight. Twain directly states the effect of this experience, the lesson he learned, in lines 34–38. **The correct answer is D.**

**6.** In line 39, the word *dingy* means:

 **F.** crazy.

 **G.** dark and hazy.

 **H.** a ship's small boat.

 **J.** none of the above

**EXPLANATION:** Only one choice makes sense in combination with the context clues "although a fair number of stars were out" and "vague and indistinct." **The correct answer is G.**

**7.** In line 45, Twain "exults," or delights, because:

 **A.** the mean part of him wants Mr. Bixby to fail.

 **B.** no one could find a specific landing on such a murky night.

 **C.** every place along the river looks the same to Twain.

 **D.** Twain doesn't like Mr. Jones.

**EXPLANATION:** Choice D can be eliminated; nothing in the passage suggests that Twain even knows Mr. Jones. While C is true according to the second paragraph of the passage, it is not relevant in this situation. Having already read the entire passage, you also know that B is false—a good pilot can tell where he is. The context clue "vengeful spirit" tells you **the correct answer is A.**

**8.** In lines 54–56, Twain's "wonder" comes up because:

 **F.** it is really a beautiful night after all.

 **G.** he has come to admire the mate greatly.

 **H.** he is awed by Mr. Bixby's abilities as a riverboat pilot.

 **J.** he is envious of the easy way Mr. Bixby and the mate get along.

**EXPLANATION:** Most of the choices have no direct relevance to the passage. The passage makes it clear that Twain is awed to learn not only that Mr. Bixby can find *two* landings on Mr. Jones's plantation but also that he can choose the best one for that night's conditions. **The correct answer is H.**

**9.** Taking the passage as a whole, the most important thing Twain learned on his first day as a novice pilot was that piloting a steamboat:

**A.** is filled with romance and excitement.

**B.** requires getting up for night watches.

**C.** requires hard work and study of the river.

**D.** brings a high rate of pay.

**EXPLANATION:** The passage says nothing about pay, so you can eliminate D; and Twain's first day is anything but romantic and exciting, so you can eliminate A. While he does learn that he will have to work at night, the more important thing he learns is how much work and study of the Mississippi have gone into Mr. Bixby's skills. **The correct answer is C.**

**10.** Twain's tone in this autobiographical narrative is mainly:

**F.** dull and factual.

**G.** excited and confused.

**H.** lacking in all feeling.

**J.** emotional yet factual.

**EXPLANATION:** Choices F and H are wrong, since Twain does report his feelings, which are sometimes very strong. Choice G seems attractive. However, "excited and confused" is not an accurate description of Twain's *main* tone. **The correct answer is J.**

On the first day of the PSAE in reading, you will also complete the ACT Assessment English Test. It contains multiple-choice questions that test your knowledge of standard punctuation, grammar, usage, sentence structure, writing strategies, organization, and style. Each question is followed by four choices.

In the section that follows, you will find a sample passage accompanied by multiple-choice questions that test your knowledge of writing conventions and skills. The explanation following each question will help you understand the right answer.

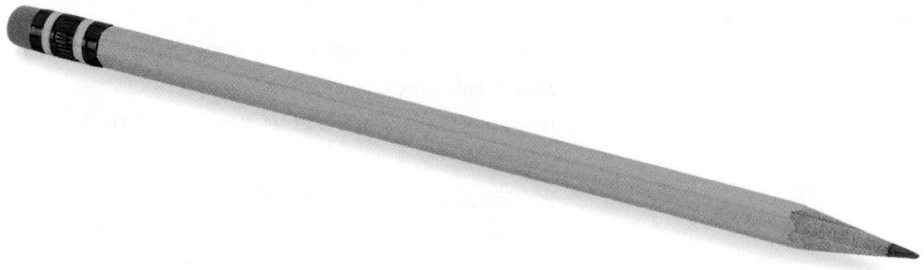

**DIRECTIONS:** In the passage on the next page, certain words and phrases are underlined and numbered. In each item that follows, you will find alternatives for the underlined part. In most cases, you are to choose the answer that best expresses the idea, makes the statement appropriate for standard written English, or is worded most consistently with the style and tone of the passage as a whole. If you think the original version is best, choose "NO CHANGE."

For each question, choose the alternative you consider best and fill in the answer on your answer document. Read the passage through once before you begin to answer the questions that accompany it. For some of the questions, you must read beyond the underlined part to determine the answer. Be sure that you have read far enough ahead before you choose an alternative.

### Eyes of an Era

Civil War photographers struggled with heavy <u>equipment. Stray bullets,</u> rain, mud, insects,
<br>1

foliage, wandering livestock, and frozen hands. In the field, <u>processing photographs were</u>
<br>2

complicated and messy work. Many pictures were ruined when they were washed in

<u>streams. Debris</u> could stick to the gummy image.
<br>3

Most Civil War photographers and their work fell into obscurity after the war. Hundreds

of glass negatives were sold for use as greenhouse windows. Decades later, many of the glass

plates ended up in <u>gas masks. They were worn</u> by soldiers during World War I.
<br>4

---

**I. A.** NO CHANGE
**B.** equipment, stray bullets,
**C.** and stray bullets
**D.** like stray bullets

**EXPLANATION:** Be sure to read far enough ahead. The words *heavy equipment, stray bullets, rain,* and so on, are part of a series of things that made work difficult for Civil War photographers. Items in a series are separated by commas. **The correct answer is B.**

**2. F.** NO CHANGE
**G.** processing photograph were
**H.** processing photographs is
**J.** processing photographs was

**EXPLANATION:** Choices F and G have subject-verb agreement errors. Choice H does not have a subject-verb agreement error, but it does create inconsistent verb tenses. **The best answer is J.**

**3. A.** NO CHANGE
  **B.** streams, although debris
  **C.** streams, where debris
  **D.** streams, whenever debris

**EXPLANATION:** Choice A is not the best choice, since it leaves two strongly related ideas as separate sentences. B and D do not connect the ideas logically. Choice C connects the ideas by adding a subordinate detail about what caused the pictures to be ruined. **The best answer is C.**

**4. F.** NO CHANGE
  **G.** gas masks, and they were worn
  **H.** gas masks worn
  **J.** gas masks, they were worn

**EXPLANATION:** Choice F is poor, since the ideas in the sentences can be joined to better show their relationship. Even though G joins them, it does not do so effectively. J contains a punctuation error. **The best answer is H.**

# Taking Part Two of the PSAE in Reading

On the second day of the PSAE in reading, you will take ACT's WorkKeys *Reading for Information* test. This test contains short reading passages and multiple-choice questions. The passages are arranged in order of increasing difficulty. They include memos, policies, procedures, and regulations taken from business and government sources. The questions measure your ability to

- identify main ideas
- identify important details
- understand word meanings

- apply instructions
- apply information
- apply reasoning

In the section that follows, you'll find informational passages like those on the WorkKeys test. Each is followed by a question. Be sure to read all five choices before you choose your answer.

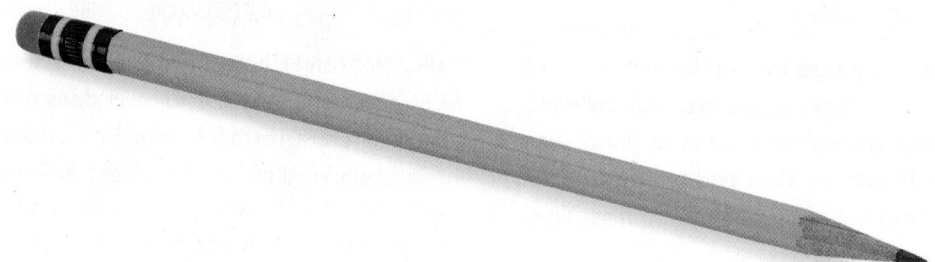

**DIRECTIONS:** Read the information in each box, and answer the question that follows it.

---

*BUZZ Magazine:* **Join the Buzzards! Be Current!**

Subscribe to *BUZZ Magazine* today and you'll know the latest about your favorite stars. Our **HOT** magazine includes personal stories as well as photos you'll want for your own walls. Impress your friends! For only $31.00, you can receive the next 12 buzz-packed issues. Buy them on the newsstand and you'll pay $51.00. **Can you use $20?**

**An extra-special offer.** Get an autographed picture of your favorite star. Just mail the coupon below along with your check or money order. Subscribe now!

---

1. The group that *Buzz Magazine* is targeting with this advertisement is most likely:
   A. senior citizens.
   B. teens.
   C. married people with families.
   D. single men and women.
   E. business owners.

**EXPLANATION:** Study the ad, while considering each answer option. Remember that you are looking for the *best* answer. While people of any age and situation might follow entertainment news, the appeals in this ad—appeals to being current and to belonging to a group—are clearly not directed at seniors (A). C, D, and E are possible but can also be eliminated, since nothing in the ad seems designed to appeal to such specific groups. That leaves teens as the likeliest target of the ad. **The correct answer is B.**

---

The SureFocus digital camera is guaranteed to be free of defects in material or workmanship under normal use for a period of one (1) year from the date of purchase. Equipment covered by the warranty will be repaired by SureFocus Repair Members WITHOUT CHARGE, except for insurance, transportation, and handling charges. A copy of this warranty card and proof of purchase must be enclosed when returning equipment for warranty service. The warranty does not apply in the following cases:

! the camera has been damaged through abuse or neglect

! leaking batteries or other liquids have caused damage to the camera

! unauthorized repair technicians have attempted to service the camera

---

2. You did not damage your camera in any way, but it still doesn't work. If you are returning it for repair, what must you include in your package?
   A. The camera
   B. The sales slip or other proof of purchase
   C. A copy of the warranty card
   D. A, B, and C
   E. A, B, C, and a check for handling charges

**EXPLANATION:** The warranty specifically states that you must include a copy of the warranty card and proof of purchase, together with the equipment you are returning. Although you will be expected to pay handling charges, the warranty says nothing about sending a check in your original package. **The correct answer is D.**

**BodyFitness Membership Contract**

Member agrees to the following terms:

1. The monthly membership fee will be paid by the tenth of each month for a full year. A charge of 5 percent will be added to late payments.
2. Members who discontinue membership will be required to pay all past-due charges and to pay for the remaining months of the membership.
3. After one year, membership may be renewed on a month-to-month basis.

**3.** What happens if you must move to another city seven months after you sign this contract?
   **A.** You can transfer your membership to a BodyFitness Gym in your new location.
   **B.** BodyFitness Gym will assess a small fee for canceling your membership.
   **C.** You must still pay for the remaining five months of the contract.
   **D.** BodyFitness Gym will cancel the contract at no additional cost to you.
   **E.** You will be refunded for the balance of the current month.

**EXPLANATION:** The terms given in the contract require payment of a full year's membership; no exceptions or transfers of membership are mentioned. In fact, the second item under "Member agrees to the following terms" specifically states that those who "discontinue membership" must pay for "the remaining months of the membership." **The correct answer is C.**

**Notice 97–60 Education IRAs**

Parents, grandparents, other family members, friends, and a child him/herself may contribute to the child's Education IRA, provided that the total contributions for the child during the taxable year do not exceed the $500 limit. Amounts deposited in the account grow tax-free until distributed, and the child will not owe tax on any withdrawal from the account if the child's qualified higher education expenses at an eligible educational institution for the year equal or exceed the amount of the withdrawal.... Amounts withdrawn from an Education IRA that exceed the child's qualified higher education expenses in a taxable year are generally subject to income tax....

**4.** What is one way to avoid paying tax on a withdrawal from an Education IRA?
   **A.** Take out more than your qualified education expenses.
   **B.** Take out less than your qualified education expenses.
   **C.** Deposit up to $500 toward your qualified education expenses.
   **D.** Deposit less than $500 toward your qualified education expenses.
   **E.** Ask a parent to waive the tax.

**EXPLANATION:** C and D are incorrect; they involve the deposit limit. E is incorrect, since it is not a condition in the notice. Two statements reveal that withdrawing more than the qualified expenses will generally result in tax. Therefore, take out less to avoid the tax. **The correct answer is B.**

# Taking a Writing Test

Sometime during your school career, you may be asked to compose a coherent, well-written paper in response to a writing prompt. You may be given only one writing prompt, not a choice. The prompt may require you to write either an expository or a persuasive essay. Most writing tests are designed to check your mastery of the following writing skills:

Write to communicate effectively by
- considering your purpose for writing
- addressing the needs of a specific audience
- presenting ideas in a clear and coherent manner
- supporting your ideas with specific examples and details
- using correct grammar, spelling, and punctuation

To help you focus your essay-writing practice, take a look at the characteristics of an excellent paper presented on the next page. These characteristics are followed by descriptions of a paper that would receive the highest scores, based on a scoring rubric. A **scoring rubric** consists of sets of statements that enable essay readers to rank essays from 6 to 1, for example, with 6 being the highest score in the areas of Focus, Elaboration, Organization, and Integration. Conventions are usually graded less strictly since the essay is often viewed as a first draft. The Conventions score may be a 1, for example, if the errors seriously interfere with communication or a 2 if the errors are few and do not interfere with communication.

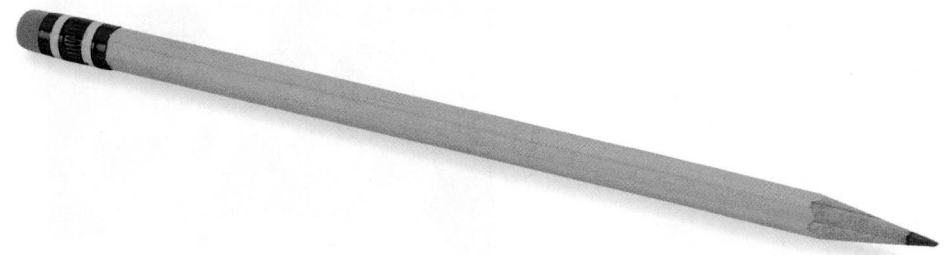

# CHARACTERISTICS OF AN EXCELLENT PAPER

**Focus:** *How clearly does the essay present and sustain a clear position or main idea?*
The opening clearly establishes the subject or position and hooks the reader. The essay is purposeful and logical throughout. An effective closing ties the important points together.

**Elaboration:** *How well is the position or main idea supported and explained?*
All major points are fully developed and evenly supported by details. Supporting details are specific, accurate, and credible (believable). The writer uses multiple strategies such as examples, explanations, comparisons, or cause and effect. Word choice is powerful and specific.

**Organization:** *How clear is the essay's plan, and how logically does it flow?*
The essay has a clear beginning, middle, and end. The points are logically interrelated. All paragraphs are appropriate and purposeful. Organization is also evident at the sentence level, in the way the writer connects each sentence with the next. The writer uses varied sentence structures and word choice to achieve coherence.

**Integration:** *How effectively does the essay as a whole respond to the prompt?*
The paper is fully developed for the writer's grade level. The focus is clear and purposeful, and supporting details are well-balanced. Sentences and paragraphs fit smoothly together. Any errors in conventions are minor and do not interfere with communication.

**Conventions:** *How well does the essay observe the conventions of standard written English?*
The paper shows correct sentence structure (few or no run-on sentences or fragments), mastery of subject-verb agreement, correct use of pronouns, and correct punctuation, capitalization, and spelling. Any errors are minor and few in number in proportion to the amount written.

# STEPS FOR TAKING A WRITING TEST

Here are steps for responding to a writing prompt.

**STEP 1**  **Analyze the prompt and do your prewriting.** Read the prompt carefully. The paragraph at the top defines your writing task. The numbered steps suggest how to proceed. Then, use the page provided in the test booklet to brainstorm and organize your ideas. Make sure you have a strong opening and closing.

**STEP 2**  **Write your essay.** As you write, make each sentence and each idea as clear as you can. Use relevant details or examples to support each main point or argument you make.

**STEP 3**  **Edit and revise.** Review the entire essay. Look for places where changes will make your sentences flow more smoothly. Eliminate unnecessary repetition. Improve your word choices. Make changes as neatly as possible.

**STEP 4**  **Proofread one last time.** Take your last few minutes to read for errors in grammar, usage, spelling, punctuation, and capitalization. Correct them neatly.

# A SAMPLE WRITING PROMPT

Here is a sample prompt for a persuasive essay.

> Some school districts are debating whether to hold athletic practices only after school. Imagine that your school district is also debating this issue. Choose a position, and write a persuasive paper that tells the school board where you stand on the issue.
>
> You should:
> 1. Take a few minutes to develop a basic plan for the contents of your paper.
> 2. State your position on when athletic practices should or should not be held.
> 3. Give reasons supporting your position on the issue.
> 4. Correct any errors in grammar, usage, spelling, and punctuation.

## PREWRITING: ORGANIZING YOUR IDEAS

The writing prompt asks you to take a position. Notice what the options are, and decide where you stand. Then, brainstorm a variety of reasons that support your position. Choose only the strongest reasons to use in your essay. Be sure that you fully explain each reason. Here is a rough outline one student used to organize a persuasive essay in response to the prompt on page IL27.

> **Issue:** Limiting Sports Practice to After School
>
> **My Position:** Practice should not be only after school.
>
> **Reasons:** Limiting practice this way would exclude many people from participating (my friend Paloma).
>
> It would prevent some students from realizing their talents (my experience with volleyball).
>
> It would limit an important source of exercise (health issue).
>
> It would be a negative for the school (would decrease chances of winning games/events; would limit student involvement).

## WRITING: GETTING IT DOWN ON PAPER

You have a good head start because you know roughly what you are going to say and how you are going to organize your ideas. In your introductory paragraph, be sure to include a clear **thesis statement.** In the body of your essay, use **details** to support each paragraph's **main idea.** End with a concluding paragraph that ties your entire essay together.

## REVISING AND PROOFREADING: POLISHING YOUR ESSAY

Be sure to allow some time for revising and polishing your work. You probably will not have time to recopy your essay, but you can neatly mark changes and corrections that improve it and make it flow more smoothly.

## ONE WRITER'S RESPONSE

Here is how one student responded to the writing prompt on page IL27. The response contains a good opening and closing, clearly identifies a position on the issue, uses reasons and examples to develop its arguments, and contains no errors in usage or mechanics. It is well done for the limited time allowed.

### "No" to Only After-School Practices

Having only after-school practices might sound like a good idea—that is, until you consider that such a policy would result in some students not having the opportunity to participate. With that loss of opportunity come other negative consequences for students and for the school. For these reasons, I believe we should reject an only after-school practice policy.

After school, many students must ride the bus to get home. Also, quite a few students have part-time jobs, tutoring, or other responsibilities after school. My friend Paloma is a good example. After school, Paloma, who is on the track team, has to take care of her little brother. In effect, limiting practice to after school would make it difficult or impossible for students like Paloma to participate in school-sponsored sports.

"Does it matter if some students can't play sports?" you might ask. I would answer that it matters a lot to those particular students. We have all heard the news reports about students not getting enough exercise and about how lack of exercise can lead to health problems. Well, for students at our school, playing sports is a major source of needed exercise. For some students, it is the only source. In addition to the health benefits of playing sports, there are also emotional benefits. Playing sports can make students feel successful, fulfilled, and part of something bigger. It can help them realize their talents. I know that it did all of this for me when I played volleyball last season. The point is, if we adopt an only after-school practice policy, then many students would potentially lose the benefits that school-sponsored sports are meant to provide.

This issue matters not only to individual students but also to the school. Some of our best players cannot practice every day after school. Losing those players might mean losing more games and events. Remember Paloma? She happens to be a championship relay runner, a runner who has helped take our school to victory many times. The issue of losing games aside, I believe that the most important consequence for the school is lack of participation and school spirit. As a school, we should have as many students as possible involved in school sports—whether as participants or as fans going to watch their friends and schoolmates.

I feel that there are too many negative consequences to adopting a policy that restricts sports practice to after-school hours. Therefore, we should reject it. Having at least some practice time during school would allow the school to include more students in its sports programs.

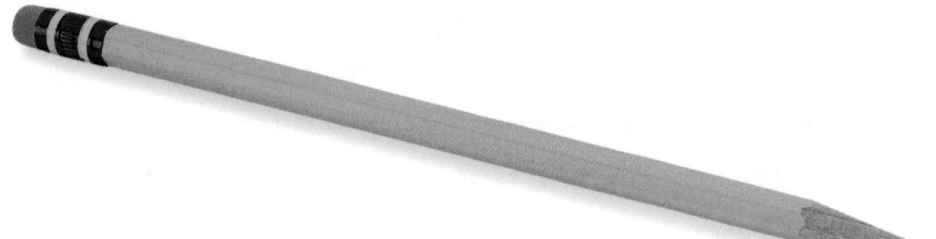

# Preparing to Take Tests

You have taken practice tests, and now you are ready to take the PSAE. However, you feel you may get nervous moments before the test. What do you do? The section below offers strategies you can use to combat your nerves and to prepare yourself mentally and physically.

## THE NIGHT BEFORE

- Review any test-taking notes you might have. Be familiar with the types of questions you will encounter.

- Prepare your materials. Get together everything you will need for your test, such as forms of identification, sharp pencils, scratch paper, or anything else you will need.

- Get plenty of sleep. Go to bed at your usual time. If you are nervous, try reading a magazine or listening to soothing music.

## THE MORNING OF THE TEST

- Eat breakfast. Even if you feel nervous, your brain will need energy. Avoid sugary foods that could make you sleepy later.

- Double check to make sure you have everything you need for the test.

- Leave in plenty of time to get to the testing site. You don't want to feel rushed when you arrive.

## DURING THE TEST

- Stay calm. Remind yourself that you have prepared carefully and can expect to do well.

- Keep breathing. Breathing deeply helps keep you calm and supplies the brain with oxygen.

- Check the time periodically. You want to make sure that you have enough time to finish the sections of the test.

# HOLT
# ELEMENTS OF
# LITERATURE

## Fifth Course

### ESSENTIALS OF
### AMERICAN LITERATURE

# HOLT
# ELEMENTS OF
# LITERATURE®

## Fifth Course

### ESSENTIALS OF
### AMERICAN LITERATURE

**HOLT, RINEHART AND WINSTON**

A Harcourt Education Company

Orlando • **Austin** • New York • San Diego • Toronto • London

**Cover**
**Photo Credits:** (Inset) *The Fourth of July, 1916* (detail) by Frederick Childe Hassam (1859–1935). Oil on canvas. 36 x 26 in. ©Christie's Images/SuperStock.
(Background) Front Cover only. Tickertape parade. Index Stock Imagery/*PictureQuest.*

Acknowledgments appear on pages 1455–1458, which are an extension of the copyright page.

ISBN 0-03-042418-6

5  6  048  07

# Program Authors

**Dr. Kylene Beers** is the senior program author for *Elements of Literature*. A former middle school teacher who is now a senior reading researcher in the School Development program at Yale University, Dr. Beers has turned her commitment to helping struggling readers into the major focus of her research, writing, speaking, and teaching. She is the author of *When Kids Can't Read: What Teachers Can Do* and *Aliteracy: The Glitch in Becoming a Nation of Readers*. From 1999 to 2006, she was the editor of the National Council of Teachers of English (NCTE) literacy journal *Voices from the Middle*. Additionally, Dr. Beers is the co-editor of *Into Focus: Understanding and Creating Middle School Readers*. Having authored chapters in numerous books and articles in *English Journal, Journal of Adolescent and Adult Literacy, School Library Journal, Middle Matters,* and *Voices from the Middle*, she is a recognized authority on struggling readers, who speaks both nationally and internationally. Dr. Beers has served as the chair of the National Adolescent Literacy Coalition (2005–2007) and has served as a member of the review boards for *English Journal, The ALAN Review,* the Special Interest Group on Adolescent Literature of the International Reading Association, and the Assembly on Literature for Adolescents of the NCTE. She is the 2001 recipient of the Richard W. Halle Award given by NCTE for outstanding contributions to middle school literacy.

**Dr. Lee Odell** helped establish the pedagogical framework for writing, listening, and speaking for *Elements of Literature*. Dr. Odell is Professor of Composition Theory and Research and, since 1996, Director of the Writing Program at Rensselaer Polytechnic Institute. He began his career teaching English in middle and high schools. More recently he has worked with teachers in grades K–12 to establish a program that involves students from all disciplines in writing across the curriculum and for communities outside their classrooms. Dr. Odell's most recent book (with Charles R. Cooper) is *Evaluating Writing: The Role of Teachers' Knowledge About Text, Learning, and Culture*. He is past chair of the Conference on College Composition and Communication and of NCTE's Assembly for Research.

# Writers

**Gary Q. Arpin** received his doctorate from the University of Virginia, where he taught for several years before taking a position with Western Illinois University at Macomb. He has written articles on John Berryman and other American poets and has published a book, *John Berryman: A Reference Guide*.

**John Malcolm Brinnin,** author of six volumes of poetry that have received many awards, was a member of the American Academy and Institute of Arts and Letters. He was a critic of poetry, a biographer of poets, and director of New York's famous Poetry Center. His teaching career included terms at Vassar College, the University of Connecticut, and Boston University, where he succeeded Robert Lowell as Professor of Creative Writing and Contemporary Letters. In addition to other works, Mr. Brinnin wrote *Dylan Thomas in America: An Intimate Journal* and *Sextet: T. S. Eliot & Truman Capote & Others*.

**Kathleen Daniel** has edited and directed middle school and secondary literature and language programs for over forty years, specializing in literature anthologies. She currently works as a writer, editor, and educational consultant.

**Thomas Hernacki** holds a doctorate in English from Columbia University. His dissertation explores "the poetics of place" in the works of Wallace Stevens. Dr. Hernacki is an educational writer specializing in modern and contemporary literature, particularly American poetry. In the 1970s, he contributed to Northrop Frye's archetype-based literature series, *Uses of the Imagination*. Over the past two decades, Dr. Hernacki has directed the editorial development of numerous literature and composition textbooks.

**Rose Sallberg Kam** holds a master's degree in English from California State University, Sacramento, and a master's in biblical studies from the Graduate Theological Union, Berkeley. She taught secondary English for seventeen years, has been a freelance writer of educational materials for more than twenty years, and is the author of *Their Stories, Our Stories: Women of the Bible*.

**John Leggett** is a novelist, biographer, and teacher. He went to the Writers' Workshop at the University of Iowa in the spring of 1969, expecting to work there for a single semester. In 1970, he assumed temporary charge of the program, and for the next seventeen years he was its director. Mr. Leggett's novels include *Wilder Stone, The Gloucester Branch, Who Took the Gold Away?, Gulliver House*, and *Making Believe*. He is also the author of the highly acclaimed biography *Ross and Tom: Two American Tragedies* and of a biography of William Saroyan, *A Daring Young Man*. Mr. Leggett lives in California's Napa Valley.

**Fannie Safier,** a former teacher, has written and edited language arts materials for over thirty-five years.

**Mairead Stack** holds a master's degree in English from New York University. A former teacher, she has edited and written educational materials for literature and language arts for more than twenty years.

**Susan Allen Toth** studied at the University of California at Berkeley and received her doctorate from the University of Minnesota. She is an adjunct professor and a writer-in-residence at Macalester College in St. Paul, Minnesota. Dr. Toth has written *Blooming: A Small-Town Girlhood* about her childhood in Ames, Iowa; *Ivy Days: Making My Way Out East* about her experiences at Smith College in Northampton, Massachusetts; and *How to Prepare for Your High-School Reunion and Other Mid-Life Musings*. She contributes articles to many periodicals and newspapers, including *Harper's Magazine, McCall's*, and *The New York Times*.

## Senior Program Consultant

**Carol Jago** teaches English at Santa Monica High School, in Santa Monica, and directs the California Reading and Literature Project at UCLA. Her classroom experience began with middle school and has included journalism, remedial reading and writing, and honors and advanced placement. She has written a weekly education column for the *Los Angeles Times* and edits the quarterly journal of the California Association of Teachers of English, *California English*. She is the author of several books, including a series on contemporary writers in the classroom: *Alice Walker in the Classroom, Nikki Giovanni in the Classroom*, and *Sandra Cisneros in the Classroom*. She is also the author of *With Rigor for All: Teaching the Classics to Contemporary Students; Beyond Standards: Excellence in the High School English Classroom; Cohesive Writing: Why Concept Is Not Enough; Classics in the Classroom: Designing Accessible Literature Lessons;* and *Papers, Papers, Papers: An English Teacher's Survival Guide*.

# CONTENTS IN BRIEF

## COLLECTION 1

# Encounters and Foundations to 1800

## FORGING A NEW NATION

# COLLECTION 2

# American Romanticism: 1800–1860

## IMAGINATION AND THE INDIVIDUAL

## COLLECTION 3

# American Masters: Whitman and Dickinson

## CELEBRATE THE PEOPLE, CELEBRATE THE SELF

# COLLECTION 4

# The Rise of Realism
# The Civil War to 1914

## FROM CONFLICTS TO NEW FRONTIERS

# The Moderns
# 1914–1939

## REDEFINING THE AMERICAN DREAM

## MIDCENTURY VOICES

# THE HARLEM RENAISSANCE

# Contemporary Literature 1939 to Present

## NEW VOICES, NEW VISIONS

## CONTEMPORARY FICTION

# CONTEMPORARY NONFICTION

# CONTEMPORARY POETRY

## CONTEMPORARY DRAMA

# Resource Center

# SELECTIONS BY ALTERNATIVE THEMES

Selections are listed here in alternative theme groupings.

# INNOCENCE AND EXPERIENCE

# LIFE AND LOSS

## THE POWER OF NATURE

## THE QUEST AND THE PERILOUS JOURNEY

## REALMS OF DARKNESS

## THE SEARCH FOR IDENTITY

## SEARCH FOR MEANING, TESTS OF FAITH

## TRICKSTERS AND ROGUES

## WAR

## WHAT IS A HERO?

# SELECTIONS BY GENRE

## FICTION

# DRAMA

# POETRY

## NARRATIVE POEM

## SONNETS

## SPIRITUALS

## VILLANELLE

# NONFICTION AND INFORMATIONAL TEXT

## APHORISMS

## EULOGY

## HISTORY

## INTERVIEWS

## INTRODUCTION

## JOURNAL

## LETTERS

## MEMOIRS

## NEWSPAPER ARTICLES

## SKILLS

### LITERARY SKILLS

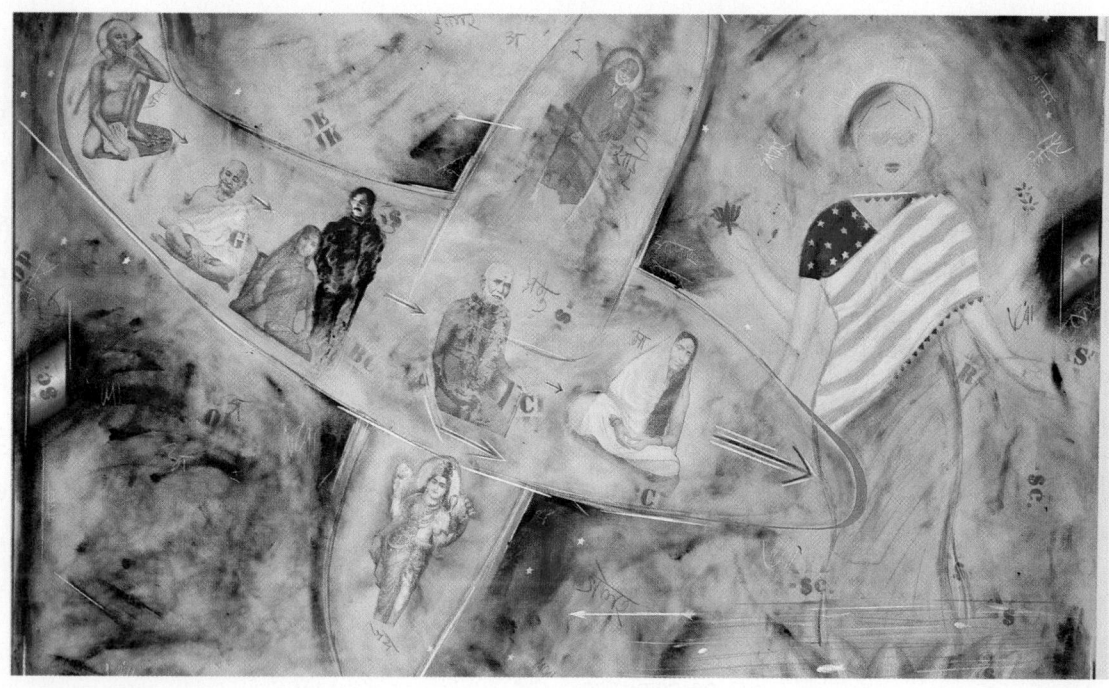

# READING SKILLS

# WORKSHOPS

## WRITING WORKSHOPS

## MINI-WORKSHOPS

## LISTENING AND SPEAKING WORKSHOPS

## MEDIA WORKSHOP

# FEATURES

## A CLOSER LOOK

## COMPARING POINTS OF VIEW

## CRITICAL COMMENTS

## PRIMARY SOURCES

## REFLECTING ON THE LITERARY PERIOD

# GRAMMAR LINK

# LANGUAGE HANDBOOK

# SKILLS REVIEW

# THE WORLD OF WORK

# WRITER'S HANDBOOK

# TEST SMARTS

# *Elements of Literature* on the Internet

## TO THE STUDENT

At the *Elements of Literature* Internet site, you can analyze the work of professional writers and learn the inside stories behind your favorite authors. You can also build your word power and analyze messages in the media. As you move through *Elements of Literature,* you will find the best online resources at **go.hrw.com.**

Here's how to log on:

**1.** Start your Web browser, and enter **go.hrw.com** in the Address or Location field.

**2.** Note the keyword in your textbook.

**INTERNET**

**Speeches**

Keyword: LE7 11-1

**3.** Enter the keyword and click "go."

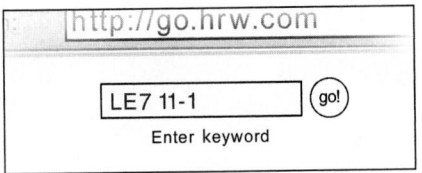

## FEATURES OF THE SITE

### More About the Writer
Author biographies provide the inside stories behind the lives and works of great writers.

### More Writer's Models
Interactive Writer's Models present annotations and reading tips to help you with your own writing. Printable Professional Models and Student Models provide you with quality writing by real writers and students across the country.

### Interactive Reading Model
Interactive Reading Workshops guide you through high-interest informational articles and allow you to share your opinions through pop-up questions and polls.

### Vocabulary Practice
Interactive vocabulary-building activities help you build your word power.

### Projects and Activities
Projects and activities help you extend your study of literature through writing, research, art, and public speaking.

### Speeches
Video clips from historical speeches provide you with the tools you need to analyze elements of great speechmaking.

### Media Tutorials
Media tutorials help you dissect messages in the media and learn to create your own multimedia presentations.

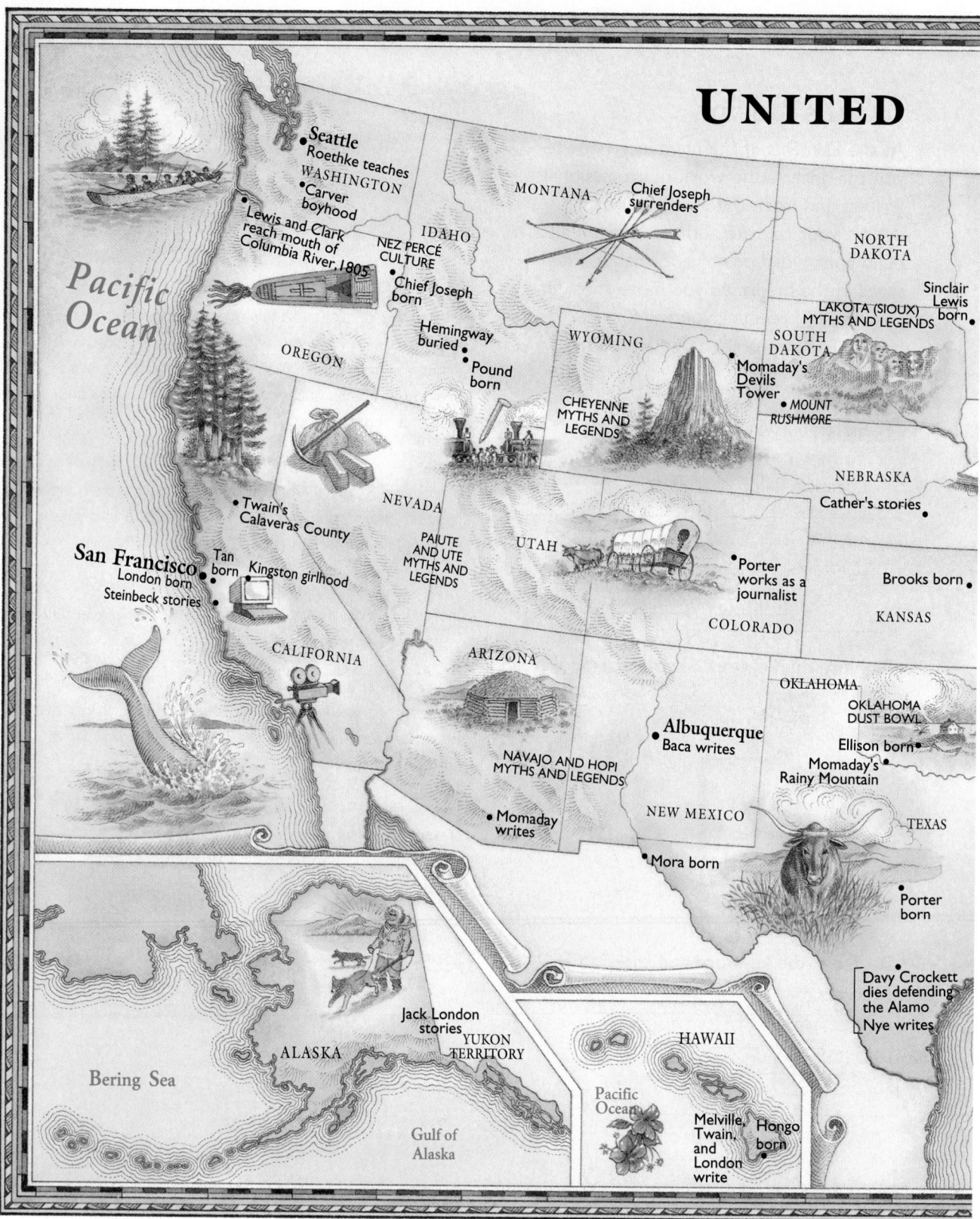

# UNITED

Pacific Ocean

**Seattle**
Roethke teaches
WASHINGTON
Carver boyhood

Lewis and Clark reach mouth of Columbia River, 1805

IDAHO

NEZ PERCÉ CULTURE

Chief Joseph born

Hemingway buried

Pound born

OREGON

MONTANA

Chief Joseph surrenders

WYOMING

CHEYENNE MYTHS AND LEGENDS

NORTH DAKOTA

Sinclair Lewis born

LAKOTA (SIOUX) MYTHS AND LEGENDS

SOUTH DAKOTA

Momaday's Devils Tower

MOUNT RUSHMORE

NEBRASKA

Cather's stories

Twain's Calaveras County

NEVADA

PAIUTE AND UTE MYTHS AND LEGENDS

UTAH

Porter works as a journalist

Brooks born

KANSAS

**San Francisco**
London born
Steinbeck stories

Tan born

Kingston girlhood

CALIFORNIA

ARIZONA

NAVAJO AND HOPI MYTHS AND LEGENDS

Momaday writes

COLORADO

**Albuquerque**
Baca writes

NEW MEXICO

Mora born

OKLAHOMA

OKLAHOMA DUST BOWL

Ellison born

Momaday's Rainy Mountain

TEXAS

Porter born

Davy Crockett dies defending the Alamo

Nye writes

Jack London stories

YUKON TERRITORY

ALASKA

Bering Sea

Gulf of Alaska

HAWAII

Pacific Ocean

Melville, Twain, and London write

Hongo born

A42

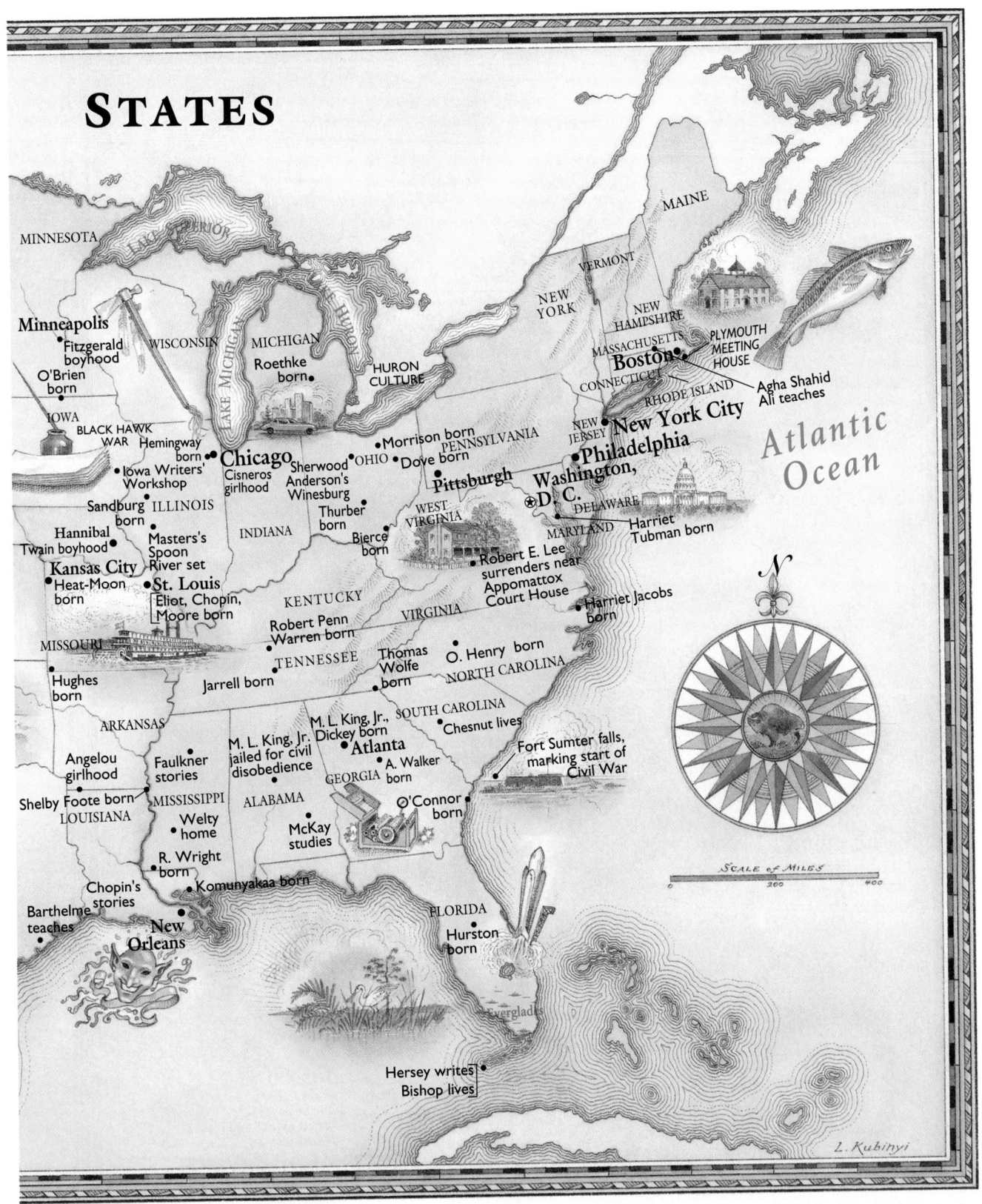

# STATES

MINNESOTA

**Minneapolis**
• Fitzgerald
  boyhood
• O'Brien
  born

WISCONSIN

MICHIGAN
• Roethke
  born

HURON
CULTURE

LAKE SUPERIOR

LAKE MICHIGAN

LAKE HURON

MAINE

VERMONT

NEW YORK

NEW HAMPSHIRE

MASSACHUSETTS

CONNECTICUT

RHODE ISLAND

PLYMOUTH
MEETING
HOUSE

**Boston**
Agha Shahid
Ali teaches

IOWA

BLACK HAWK
WAR    Hemingway
         born
• Iowa Writers'
  Workshop
• Sandburg
  born

ILLINOIS

• Masters's
  Spoon
  River set

**Chicago**
Cisneros
girlhood

Sherwood
Anderson's
Winesburg
• Thurber
  born

OHIO
• Morrison born
• Dove born

INDIANA

Bierce
born

WEST
VIRGINIA

• Morrison born
• Dove born

PENNSYLVANIA

NEW
JERSEY

**New York City**

**Philadelphia**

**Washington,**
**D. C.**

DELAWARE

MARYLAND

**Pittsburgh**

Harriet
Tubman born

Robert E. Lee
surrenders near
Appomattox
Court House

Hannibal
Twain boyhood

**Kansas City**
Heat-Moon
born

**St. Louis**
Eliot, Chopin,
Moore born

KENTUCKY

VIRGINIA

Robert Penn
Warren born

Harriet Jacobs
born

MISSOURI

• Hughes
  born

TENNESSEE

Jarrell born

Thomas
Wolfe
born

O. Henry  born

NORTH CAROLINA

SOUTH CAROLINA

Chesnut lives

Atlantic
Ocean

ARKANSAS

• Angelou
  girlhood

Faulkner
stories

M. L. King, Jr.
jailed for civil
disobedience

M. L. King, Jr.,
Dickey born

**Atlanta**
• A. Walker
  born

GEORGIA

Fort Sumter falls,
marking start of
Civil War

N

Shelby Foote born
LOUISIANA

MISSISSIPPI
• Welty
  home

ALABAMA

McKay
studies

•O'Connor
 born

• R. Wright
  born

• Komunyakaa born

FLORIDA

Chopin's
stories

Barthelme
teaches

**New**
**Orleans**

• Hurston
  born

Everglades

SCALE of MILES
0        200        400

Hersey writes
Bishop lives

L. Kubinyi

**A43**

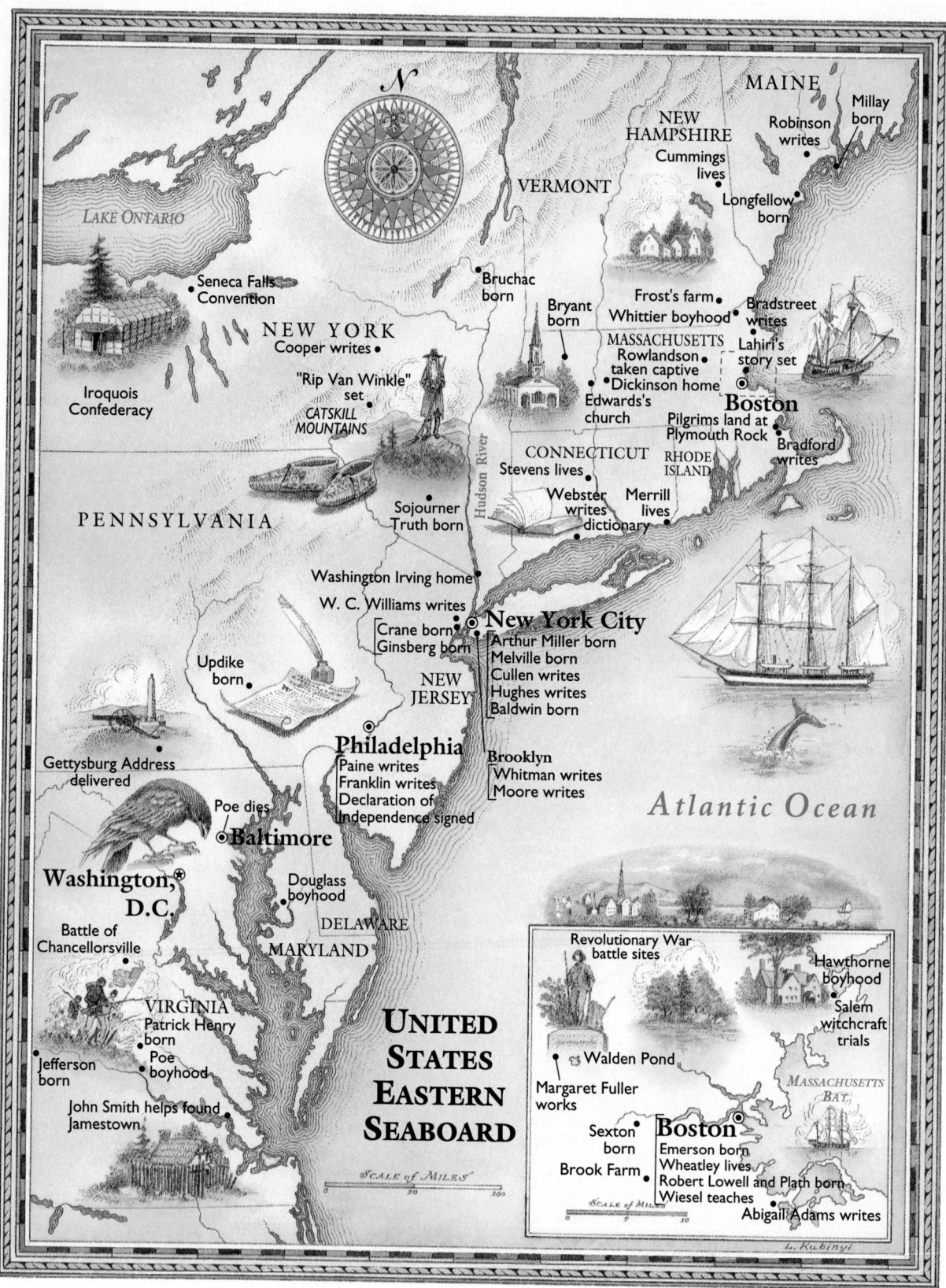

MAINE

NEW HAMPSHIRE

VERMONT

Robinson writes

Millay born

Cummings lives

Longfellow born

Bruchac born

Frost's farm

Whittier boyhood

Bradstreet writes

Bryant born

MASSACHUSETTS

Lahiri's story set

LAKE ONTARIO

Seneca Falls Convention

NEW YORK

Cooper writes

Rowlandson taken captive

Dickinson home

Boston

Iroquois Confederacy

"Rip Van Winkle" set

CATSKILL MOUNTAINS

Edwards's church

Pilgrims land at Plymouth Rock

Bradford writes

CONNECTICUT

RHODE ISLAND

Stevens lives

Sojourner Truth born

Hudson River

Webster writes dictionary

Merrill lives

PENNSYLVANIA

Washington Irving home

W. C. Williams writes

Crane born

Ginsberg born

New York City

Arthur Miller born

Melville born

Cullen writes

Hughes writes

Baldwin born

NEW JERSEY

Updike born

Philadelphia

Paine writes

Franklin writes

Declaration of Independence signed

Brooklyn

Whitman writes

Moore writes

Atlantic Ocean

Gettysburg Address delivered

Poe dies

Baltimore

Washington, D.C.

Battle of Chancellorsville

Douglass boyhood

DELAWARE

MARYLAND

UNITED STATES EASTERN SEABOARD

VIRGINIA

Patrick Henry born

Poe boyhood

Jefferson born

John Smith helps found Jamestown

SCALE of MILES

0    50    100

Revolutionary War battle sites

Hawthorne boyhood

Salem witchcraft trials

Walden Pond

Margaret Fuller works

MASSACHUSETTS BAY

Sexton born

Brook Farm

Boston

Emerson born

Wheatley lives

Robert Lowell and Plath born

Wiesel teaches

Abigail Adams writes

SCALE of MILES

0    5    10

L. Rubinyi

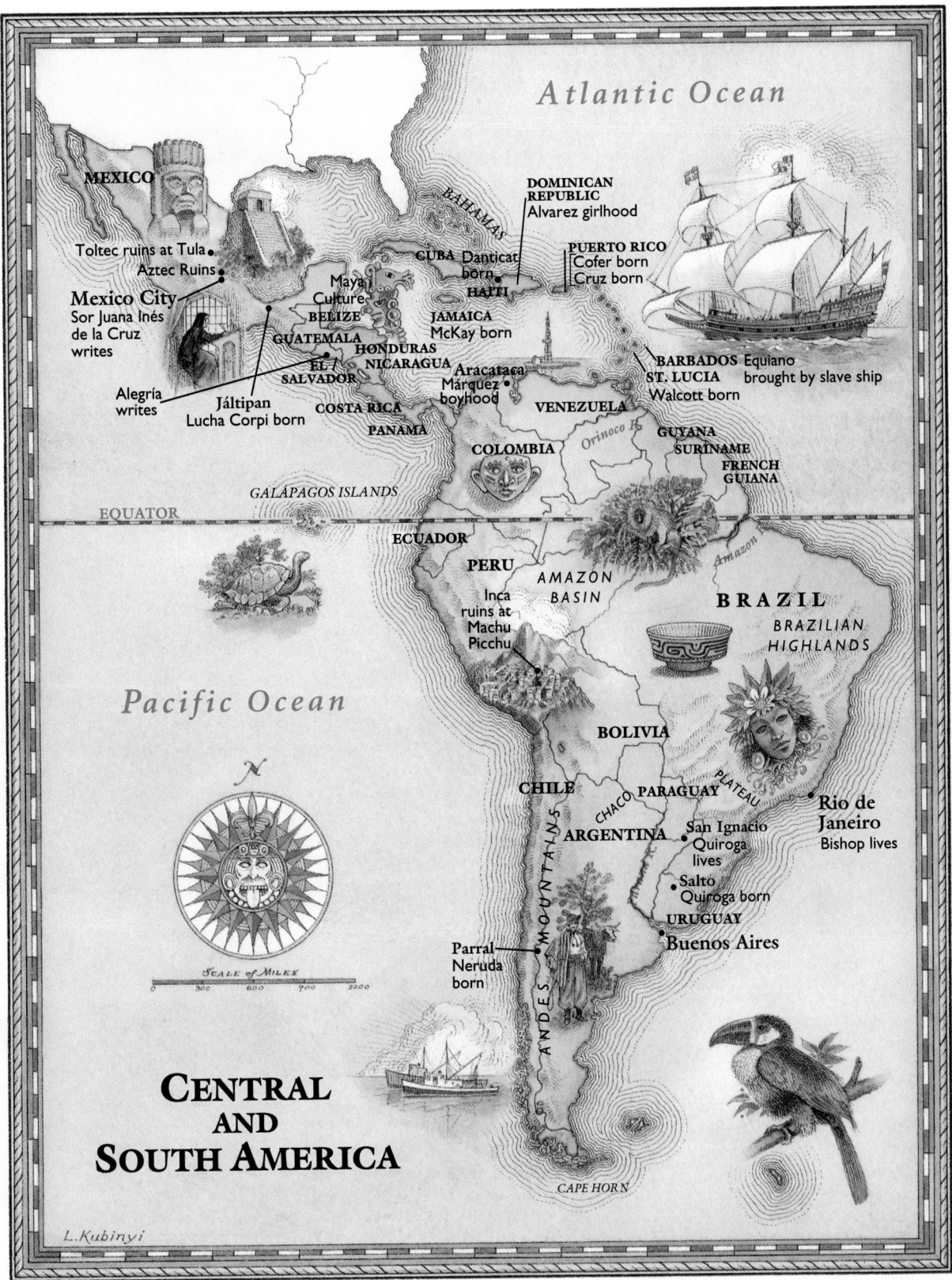

*Atlantic Ocean*

MEXICO

Toltec ruins at Tula
Aztec Ruins

**Mexico City**
Sor Juana Inés
de la Cruz
writes

Alegría
writes

Jáltipan
Lucha Corpi born

Maya
Culture

BELIZE

GUATEMALA

EL
SALVADOR

HONDURAS

NICARAGUA

COSTA RICA

PANAMA

BAHAMAS

CUBA Danticat
born

HAITI

JAMAICA
McKay born

DOMINICAN
REPUBLIC
Alvarez girlhood

PUERTO RICO
Cofer born
Cruz born

BARBADOS Equiano
ST. LUCIA brought by slave ship
Walcott born

Aracataca
Márquez
boyhood

VENEZUELA

COLOMBIA

*Orinoco R.*

GUYANA
SURINAME
FRENCH
GUIANA

*GALÁPAGOS ISLANDS*

EQUATOR

ECUADOR

PERU

Inca
ruins at
Machu
Picchu

*AMAZON
BASIN*

*Amazon*

**B R A Z I L**

*BRAZILIAN
HIGHLANDS*

BOLIVIA

CHILE

ANDES MOUNTAINS

CHACO

PARAGUAY

*PLATEAU*

ARGENTINA

San Ignacio
Quiroga
lives

Salto
Quiroga born

URUGUAY

Buenos Aires

**Rio de
Janeiro**
Bishop lives

*Pacific Ocean*

N

SCALE of MILES
0  300  600  900  1200

Parral
Neruda
born

CAPE HORN

**CENTRAL
AND
SOUTH AMERICA**

L. Kubinyi

Indian petroglyphs, or rock carvings, at Newspaper Rock, Indian Creek State Park, Utah.

# Encounters and Foundations to 1800

## *Forging a New Nation*

For we must consider that we shall be as a city upon a hill, the eyes of all people are upon us. So that if we shall deal falsely with our God in this work we have undertaken, and so cause Him to withdraw His present help from us, we shall be made a story and a byword through the world. . . .

—John Winthrop, from a sermon delivered aboard the *Arbella*, on the way to New England, spring 1630

**go.hrw.com**

**INTERNET**

Collection
Resources

Keyword: LE7 11-1

1

# Encounters and Foundations to 1800

## LITERARY EVENTS

**1490** | **1700**

**1605, 1615** Spain's Miguel de Cervantes publishes his novel *Don Quixote* in two parts

**1605–1606** England's William Shakespeare writes *King Lear* and *Macbeth*

**1620–1647** William Bradford writes *Of Plymouth Plantation*

**1650** Anne Bradstreet's *The Tenth Muse Lately Sprung Up in America* is published in England

**1682** Mary Rowlandson's captivity narrative is published

**1719** England's Daniel Defoe publishes *Robinson Crusoe*, considered one of the first English novels

**1726** England's Jonathan Swift publishes the satiric novel *Gulliver's Travels*

**1728** William Byrd writes *The History of the Dividing Line*

**1741** Jonathan Edwards delivers his vivid sermon "Sinners in the Hands of an Angry God"

**1749** England's Henry Fielding publishes the novel *The History of Tom Jones*

**1754, 1763** John Woolman publishes antislavery essays

## POLITICAL AND SOCIAL EVENTS

**1490** | **1700**

**1492** Christopher Columbus lands on an island in the Caribbean

**c. 1500** Mohawk leader Dekanawida establishes the Iroquois Confederacy

**1517** Protestant Reformation starts in Germany

**1521** Aztec Empire falls to Spanish army

**1528–1536** Spanish explorer Álvar Núñez Cabeza de Vaca lands in Florida and spends eight years walking through modern-day Texas, New Mexico, and Arizona

**1607** Settlement founded at Jamestown, Virginia

**1620** *Mayflower* Pilgrims land at Plymouth

**c. 1630** Great Migration of Puritans to New England begins

**1632–1638** Mughal emperor Shah Jahan builds Taj Mahal in northern India

**1675** Metacomet's war on Massachusetts colonies begins

**1687** England's Isaac Newton explains laws of motion and gravity in *Principia Mathematica*

**1690** Slavery exists in all English colonies in North America

**1692** Twenty people are executed in witch trials in Salem, Massachusetts

**1700** About 251,000 European settlers live in what is now the United States

**1721** Smallpox epidemic hits Boston

**1729** German composer Johann Sebastian Bach completes the oratorio *St. Matthew Passion*

**1740–1745** The Great Awakening is touched off by a traveling English preacher

**1742** George Frideric Handel's *Messiah* is first performed, in Dublin, Ireland

**1748** France's Montesquieu publishes *The Spirit of Laws,* a study of government later reflected in the U.S. Constitution

**Arresting a witch in the streets of Salem.**

The Granger Collection, New York.

COMMON SENSE:
ADDRESSED TO THE
INHABITANTS
A M

**1755** England's Samuel Johnson publishes his monumental *Dictionary of the English Language*

**1762** Benjamin Franklin's sister-in-law Anne Franklin becomes first woman printer in New England

**1771** Benjamin Franklin begins to write his *Autobiography*

**1773** Phillis Wheatley publishes *Poems on Various Subjects, Religious and Moral*

**1775** Patrick Henry demands liberty from British rule, at the Virginia Convention

**1776** Thomas Paine publishes *Common Sense*

**1785** Thomas Jefferson publishes *Notes on the State of Virginia*

**1787–1788** *The Federalist,* a series of essays by Alexander Hamilton, James Madison, and John Jay, urges voters to approve the U.S. Constitution

**1789** Olaudah Equiano publishes *The Interesting Narrative of the Life of Olaudah Equiano*

**1798** England's Samuel Taylor Coleridge publishes *The Rime of the Ancient Mariner,* a long Romantic poem

**1752** Benjamin Franklin's experiments with a kite and a key prove that lightning is a manifestation of electricity

**1763** French and Indian War officially ends as British gain control of most French North American territory

**1765** American colonists hold Stamp Act Congress to protest a direct British tax (British repeal tax in 1766)

**Stamp from Stamp Act, 1765.**

Negative number 41127. © Collection of The New-York Historical Society.

**1773** Boston Tea Party occurs in Boston Harbor

**April 19, 1775** First shots of American Revolution are fired at Lexington and Concord, Massachusetts

**July 4, 1776** Second Continental Congress adopts Declaration of Independence

**October 1781** American Revolutionary War ends as British surrender at Yorktown, Virginia (peace treaty signed in 1783)

**1781–1788** America is governed under Articles of Confederation

**1787** Austrian composer Wolfgang Amadeus Mozart finishes the opera *Don Giovanni*

**1789** George Washington is inaugurated as first president under U.S. Constitution

**George Washington.**

**1789** French Revolution begins

**1790** First census in America sets population at about 3.9 million

**1792** New York Stock Exchange is organized

**1793** Invention of cotton gin leads to increase in slave labor

**1796** English physician Edward Jenner develops smallpox vaccine

**1799** Napoleon Bonaparte becomes dictator of France

**1800** Library of Congress is established

**1800** Washington, D.C., is named capital of the United States

# Political and Social

## Clash of Cultures

**D**uring the 1490s, when the great wave of European exploration of the Americas started, numerous groups of American Indians were living all over North America. These societies were diverse, and each had its own long history. Most were made up of a few thousand people. (The Aztec Empire, in what is now Mexico, was the largest Native American civilization in the fifteenth century, with millions of people living within its borders.)

What's important to remember is that there were people on this continent when the Europeans arrived; descendants of those original people are still here, and their traditions remain. In 1994, for example, the Pequots—whom the English met when they arrived in what is now Connecticut, Rhode Island, and Massachusetts—donated ten million dollars to the new National Museum of the American Indian in Washington, D.C., to promote and save native cultures.

Native Americans and a Puritan in a village (19th century).

## Puritan Dominance

**I**n many respects the American character has been shaped by the moral, ethical, and religious convictions of the Puritans. In 1620, just before Christmas, the first and most famous group of these English Puritans landed on the tip of Cape Cod. They were followed ten years later by about seven hundred more Puritan settlers. By 1640, as many as twenty thousand English Puritans had sailed to what they called New England.

Although the real commerce of the Puritans was with heaven, they were competent in the business of the world as well. It is important to remember that the founding of a new society in North America was a business venture as well as a spiritual one. For the Puritans the everyday world and the spiritual world were closely intertwined.

# Milestones to 1800

*The First Thanksgiving* by Jennie Augusta Brownscombe.

*Reverend Jonathan Edwards* (detail) (1703–1758) B.A. 1720, M.A. 1723 by Joseph Badger. Oil on canvas.

Yale University Art Gallery, Bequest of Eugene Phelps Edwards.

## Rise of Rationalism and Independence

**B**eginning in Europe near the end of the seventeenth century, a group of philosophers and scientists began calling themselves rationalists. This marked the start of the Age of Reason, which soon had a growing influence in America. These rationalists believed that people can discover truth by using their own reason rather than relying on only religious faith or intuition. Along with a homegrown American sense of practicality, the ideas of these European thinkers inspired many of the triumphs of eighteenth-century American life. The great by-product of rationalism in America was the mind-set that resulted in the Declaration of Independence and the American Revolution.

*The Declaration of Independence, 4 July 1776*, by John Trumbull (1756–1843). Oil on canvas.

Yale University Art Gallery, Trumbull Collection.

# Encounters and Foundations to 1800

*by* Gary Q. Arpin

PREVIEW

## Think About ...

The United States is a land of immigrants. The first people began entering North America on foot many thousands of years ago. Then people came in wooden sailing ships. Later millions were brought against their will in the stifling holds of slave ships. Millions of others, lacking money for better accommodations, endured weeks of discomfort in the cramped, uncomfortable steerage sections of passenger or merchant ships.

As you read about this period, look for answers to these questions:

- What effect did European settlement have on American Indians—the people who already lived on this vast continent?

- Who were the Puritans, and what were their beliefs about human nature?

- How did rationalism differ from Puritanism, and what effect did rationalism have on the new American political system?

**SKILLS FOCUS**

Collection introduction (pages 6–19) covers **Literary Skills** Evaluate the philosophical, political, religious, ethical, and social influences of a historical period.

About five hundred years ago European explorers first set foot on land in our hemisphere. In some ways their voyages must have seemed as daring and ultimately triumphant as Neil Armstrong's first steps on the moon in 1969. However, European feet were not the first to tread on American soil. American Indians lived here for thousands of years before the first Europeans stumbled across what they called the New World. As J. H. Parry states in his book *The Spanish Seaborne Empire*, "Columbus did not discover a new world; he established contact between two worlds, both already old."

## Forming New Relationships

The first interactions between Europeans and American Indians largely involved trading near various harbors and rivers of North America. As the English began to establish colonies on these new shores, a mutual curiosity and increasing interdependence grew between the cultures. The Europeans relied on the American Indians to teach them survival skills, such as how to make canoes and

*Jacques Cartier's Discovery of the St. Lawrence River* (1957) by Thomas H. Benton.
Tempera on canvas (7′ × 6′).

*Black Cloud, a Cherokee Chief* (1836) by George Catlin. Oil on canvas.

The Granger Collection, New York.

shelters, how to fashion clothing from buckskin, and how to plant their crops. At the same time and in exchange, the American Indians were eager to acquire European firearms, textiles, and steel tools.

In the early years of European settlement, American Indians vastly outnumbered the colonists. Historians estimate that in 1600, the total American Indian population of New England alone was from 70,000 to 100,000 people—more than the English population of New England would be two centuries later.

## Battling New Diseases

The arrival of the European settlers had a deadly impact on Native Americans. Because the ancestors of American Indians probably crossed the ancient land bridge from Asia to North America during the Ice Age, their descendants weren't exposed to the diseases that had wracked Europe over the centuries. When European settlers made contact with Native Americans, the settlers unwittingly exposed them to diseases to which they had no immunity. These diseases, especially smallpox, sometimes killed off a village's entire population.

Here is how William Bradford (1590–1657), who was elected governor of Plymouth Colony thirty times, described the horrors of smallpox visited upon the American Indians:

> 66 For want of bedding and linen and other helps . . . they fall into a lamentable condition as they lie on their hard mats, the pox breaking and mattering and running one into another, their skin cleaving by reason thereof to the mats they lie on. When they turn them, a whole side will flay off at once as it were, and they will be all of a gore blood, most fearful to behold. And then being very sore, what with cold and other distempers, they die like rotten sheep. 99

—*Of Plymouth Plantation 1620–1647*

Against enormous odds some Native Americans managed to survive the epidemics. Many of these survivors, however, were eventually forced to vacate their land and homes by settlers, who, now able to survive on their own, no longer needed the American Indians' friendship and guidance. Historian Francis Jennings writes bitterly of the effects of the European settlements:

> 66 Europeans did not find a wilderness here; rather, however involuntarily, they made one. Jamestown, Plymouth, Salem, Boston, Providence, New Amsterdam, Philadelphia—all grew upon sites previously occupied by Indian communities. So did Quebec and Montreal and Detroit and Chicago. The so-called

*Columbus did not discover a new world; he established contact between two worlds, both already old.*

—J.H. Parry, *The Spanish Seaborne Empire* (1966)

settlement of America was a resettlement, a reoccupation of a land made waste by the diseases and demoralization introduced by the newcomers. **99**

—*The Invasion of America* (1975)

## Explorers' Writings

The first detailed European observations of life on this vast continent were recorded in Spanish and French by explorers of the fifteenth and sixteenth centuries. These writings open a window onto a time when the so-called New World was the focus of the dreams and desires of an entire era. Christopher Columbus (c. 1451–1506), Francisco Vásquez de Coronado (c. 1510–1554), and many other explorers described the Americas in a flurry of eagerly read letters, journals, and books. Hoping to receive funding for further expeditions, the explorers emphasized the Americas' abundant resources, the peacefulness and hospitality of the inhabitants, and the promise of unlimited wealth to be gained from fantastic treasuries of gold.

### ■ Cabeza de Vaca's Expedition

In 1528, only thirty-six years after Columbus first sighted a flickering fire on the beach of San Salvador, a Spaniard named Álvar Núñez Cabeza de Vaca (c. 1490–1557) landed with an expedition (he was its treasurer) on the west coast of what is now Florida. Cabeza de Vaca and others left the ship and marched inland. They did not return. Their fleet waited an entire year for them, then departed for Mexico, giving up the explorers for dead. Lost in the Texas Gulf area, Cabeza de Vaca and his companions wandered for the next eight years in search of other Europeans who would help them to get home. Cabeza de Vaca's narrative of his journeys through what is now Texas is a gripping adventure story. It is also a firsthand account of the habits of some of the American Indians in what is now the southwestern United States: what they ate (very little), how they housed themselves, and what their religious beliefs were. Cabeza de Vaca also provides the first account of some animals and plants that the Europeans had never known existed.

Cabeza de Vaca and his shipmates were alternately captives and companions of the various

*Cabeza de Vaca in the Desert* (1906) by Frederic Remington. Oil on canvas.

Courtesy Frederic Remington Art Museum, Ogdensburg, New York.

Native American peoples they encountered on their long trek. Here is part of his report of the expedition's experiences with a people in the Gulf Coast area, who are struggling to survive a famine:

> 66 Their support is principally roots, of two or three kinds, and they look for them over the face of all the country. The food is poor and gripes the persons who eat it. The roots require roasting two days: Many are very bitter, and withal difficult to be dug. They are sought the distance of two or three leagues, and so great is the want these people experience, that they cannot get through the year without them. Occasionally they kill deer, and at times take fish; but the quantity is so small and the famine so great, that they eat spiders and the eggs of ants, worms, lizards, salamanders, snakes, and vipers that kill whom they strike; and they eat earth and wood, and all that there is, the dung of deer, and other things that I omit to mention; and I honestly believe that were there stones in that land they would eat them. 99

> —*La relación* (*The Report*)

## A CLOSER LOOK: SOCIAL INFLUENCES

### The Salem Witchcraft Trials

INFORMATIONAL TEXT

During the cold, dreary winter of 1691–1692, the daughter and the niece of Samuel Parris, a minister in Salem, Massachusetts, began to dabble in magic. By February the two girls started having seizures. Lesions appeared on their skin, and it seemed as if they were being choked by invisible hands. A doctor diagnosed the girls as victims of malicious witchcraft.

Urged to name those responsible for bewitching them, the girls accused Sarah Good and Sarah Osborne, two unpopular women from the village, and Tituba, a slave whom Samuel Parris had brought back from Barbados. During the subsequent trial the girls writhed and moaned and behaved as if they were being choked. Based on this "evidence," Sarah Good was condemned to death. In an attempt to save her own life, Tituba confessed to being a witch. She claimed that there was a coven of witches in Massachu-

setts and testified that she had seen several names written in blood in the Devil's book. The witch hunt had begun.

Zealous ministers like Cotton Mather argued that the epidemic of witchcraft proved beyond a doubt that New England was a holy place, since the Devil was so interested in it. Mather and others demanded that all witches be rooted out and severely punished. Hundreds of people from Salem and other eastern Massachusetts towns came forward to testify that they were victims of witchcraft.

Before long the prisons were overcrowded, and a special court was established in Salem. Within the next ten months about 150 people in this small community were accused of witchcraft. Neighbors, especially those with long-standing quarrels, turned on one another. Between June and September nineteen people were hanged, and one man, Giles Corey, who had refused to plead either innocent or guilty, was crushed to death under a pile of stones.

# The Puritan Legacy

Central to the development of the American literary tradition have been the writings of the Puritans of New England. *Puritan* is a broad term, referring to a number of Protestant groups that, beginning about 1560, sought to "purify" the Church of England, which since the time of Henry VIII (who reigned from 1509 to 1547) had been virtually inseparable from the country's government. Like other Protestant reformers on the European continent, English Puritans wished to return to the simpler forms of worship and church organization that are described in the Christian Scriptures. For them religion was first of all a personal, inner experience. They did not believe that the clergy or the government should or could act as an intermediary between the individual and God.

The examination of Sarah Good at the Salem witchcraft trials.

What really happened at Salem? Many historians believe that Salem experienced a mass hysteria, a sort of shared delusion. Still others have suggested that a more restrictive form of government recently imposed on the Massachusetts Bay Colony, in addition to new economic pressures in the colony's towns, may have led to bitterness, aggression, and outright paranoia. Perhaps the strict society of Puritan New England finally erupted under the strain of its repression. A recent theory proposes that fear of unusual or powerful nonconformists—particularly women—may have led to an attempt to constrain their behavior. Statistics show that the majority of the "witches" were unmarried women between the ages of forty and sixty, eccentric and independent loners with abrasive personalities. Some of them may have been "cunning folk," that is, midwives or people with unusual healing abilities and knowledge of herbal remedies. Some of these were women who could potentially come into their fathers' inheritances and therefore may have been seen as threats to male power.

The Salem trials fascinate to this day. They are the subject of one of the great American plays, Arthur Miller's *The Crucible* (1953). Set in 1692 Salem, *The Crucible* draws parallels between the Salem witch trials and the 1950s hunt for Communists in the U.S. government conducted by Senator Joseph McCarthy.

Many Puritans suffered persecution in England. Some were put in jail and whipped, their noses slit and their ears chopped off. Some fled England for Holland. A small group in Holland, fearing that they would lose their identity as English Protestants, set sail in 1620 for what was advertised as the New World. There they hoped to build a new society patterned after God's word.

## Puritan Beliefs: Sinners All?

For a people who were so convinced that they were right, the Puritans had to grapple with complex uncertainties. At the center of Puritan theology was an uneasy mixture of certainty and doubt. The certainty was that because of Adam and Eve's sin of disobedience, most of humanity would be damned for all eternity. However, the Puritans were also certain that God in his mercy had sent his son Jesus Christ to earth to save particular people.

The doubt centered on whether a particular individual was one of the saved (the "elect") or one of the damned (the "unregenerate").

How did you know if you were saved or damned? As it turns out, you did not know. A theology that was so clear-cut in its division of the world between saints and sinners was fuzzy when it came to determining which were which. There were two principal indications of the state of your soul, neither of them completely certain. You were saved by the grace of God, and you could *feel* this grace arriving in an intensely emotional fashion. The inner arrival of God's grace was demonstrated by your outward behavior. After receiving grace, you were "reborn" as a member of the community of saints, and you behaved like a saint. People hoping to be among the saved examined their inner lives closely for signs of grace and tried to live exemplary lives. Thus, American Puritans came to value self-reliance, industriousness, temperance, and simplicity. These were, coincidentally, the ideal qualities needed to carve out a new society in a strange land.

*Mrs. Freake and Baby Mary* (1674).

The Granger Collection, New York.

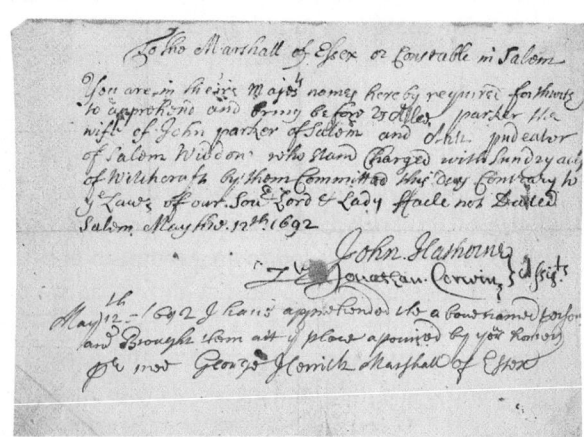

Warrant for the arrest of Ann Pudeator, accused of witchcraft (1692).

Courtesy Peabody Essex Museum, Salem, Massachusetts.

*The Puritan Deacon Samuel Chapin* (1899) by Augustus Saint-Gaudens. Bronze model.

James Graham & Sons, Inc. New York.

Page from *The Day of Doom* by Michael Wigglesworth.

## Puritan Politics: Government by Contract

In the Puritan view a covenant, or contract, existed between God and humanity. This spiritual covenant was a useful model for worldly social organization as well: Puritans believed that people should enter freely into agreements concerning their government. On the *Mayflower*, for example, in 1620, the Puritans composed and signed the Mayflower Compact, outlining how they would be governed once they landed. In this use of a contractual agreement, they prepared the ground for American constitutional democracy.

On the other hand, because the Puritans believed the saintly elect should exert great influence on government, their political views tended to be undemocratic. There was little room for compromise. In 1692, the witchcraft hysteria in Salem, Massachusetts, resulted in part from fear that the community's moral foundation was threatened and therefore its political unity was also in danger.

- The Bible provided a
  model for Puritan
  writing. The Puritans
  viewed each individ-
  ual life as a journey
  to salvation. Puritans
  looked for direct
  connections between
  biblical events and
  events in their own
  lives.
- Diaries and histories
  were the most com-
  mon forms of literary
  expression in Puritan
  society; in them
  writers described the
  workings of God.
- Puritans favored a
  plain style of writing.
  They admired clarity
  of expression and
  avoided complicated
  figures of speech.

# The Bible in America

The Puritans read the Bible as the story of the creation, fall, wanderings, and rescue of the human race. Within this long and complex
narrative, each Puritan could see connections to events in his or her
own life or to events in the life of the community. Each Puritan was
trained to see life as a pilgrimage, or journey, to salvation. Each
Puritan learned to read his or her life the way a literary critic reads
a book.

The Puritans believed that the Bible was the literal word of God.
Reading the Bible was a necessity for all Puritans, as was the ability
to understand theological debates. For these reasons the Puritans
placed great emphasis on education. Thus, Harvard College, originally intended to train Puritan ministers for the rapidly expanding
colony, was founded in 1636, only sixteen years after the first
Pilgrims had landed. Just three years later the first printing press
in the American Colonies was set up.

Their beliefs required the Puritans to keep a close watch on both
their spiritual and their public lives. This focus of the Puritan mind
greatly affected their writings. Diaries and histories were important
forms of Puritan literature because they were used to record the
workings of God.

# The Age of Reason: Tinkerers and Experimenters

By the end of the seventeenth century, new ideas that had been
fermenting in Europe began to present a challenge to the unshak-
able faith of the Puritans.

The Age of Reason, or the Enlightenment, began in Europe with
the philosophers and scientists of the seventeenth and eighteenth
centuries who called themselves rationalists. **Rationalism** is the
belief that human beings can arrive at truth by using reason, rather
than by relying on the authority of the past, on religious faith, or
on intuition.

The Puritans saw God as actively and mysteriously involved in
the workings of the universe; the rationalists saw God differently.
The great English rationalist Sir Isaac Newton (1642–1727), who
formulated the laws of gravity and motion, compared God to a
clockmaker. Having created the perfect mechanism of this universe,
God then left his creation to run on its own, like a clock. The
rationalists believed that God's special gift to humanity is reason—
the ability to think in an ordered, logical manner. This gift of reason
enables people to discover both scientific and spiritual truth.
According to the rationalists, then, everyone has the capacity to
regulate and improve his or her own life.

While the theoretical background for the Age of Reason took shape in Europe, a homegrown practicality and interest in scientific tinkering or experimenting was already thriving in the American Colonies. From the earliest Colonial days, Americans had to be generalists and tinkerers; they had to make do with what was on hand, and they had to achieve results.

## The Smallpox Plague

The unlikely hero of America's first foray into scientific exploration was the strict Puritan minister Cotton Mather (1663–1728), who was interested in natural science and medicine.

In April 1721, a ship from the West Indies docked in Boston Harbor. This was not unusual, for trade with the West Indies was one of the foundations of New England economic life. This ship was different, though. For in addition to its cargo of sugar and molasses, this ship carried smallpox.

Title page of the *Bay Psalm Book* (1640).

The Granger Collection, New York.

Hornbook used to teach the alphabet to children.

Rare Book Department, Free Library of Philadelphia.

**The Rationalist Worldview**

- People arrive at truth by using reason rather than by relying on the authority of the past, on religion, or on nonrational mental processes, such as intuition.

- God created the universe but does not interfere in its workings.

- The world operates according to God's rules, and through the use of reason, people can discover those rules.

- People are basically good and perfectible.

- Since God wants people to be happy, they worship God best by helping other people.

- Human history is marked by progress toward a more perfect existence.

# FAST FACTS

## Political Highlights

- The Mohawk leader Dekanawida establishes the Iroquois Confederacy around 1500, uniting Native American peoples who used to be rivals.

- The *Mayflower* Pilgrims adopt the Mayflower Compact and land at Plymouth, Massachusetts, in 1620.

- Mounting tension between the colonists and the British Empire results in the Revolutionary War (1775–1783).

- The Second Continental Congress adopts the Declaration of Independence on July 4, 1776.

In the seventeenth and eighteenth centuries, smallpox was one of the scourges of life, just as AIDS and the Ebola virus are today. The disease spread rapidly, disfigured its victims, and was often fatal. The outbreak in Boston in 1721 was a major public-health problem. What was to be done?

## ■ An Unlikely Cure

At the time of the smallpox epidemic, Cotton Mather was working on what would be the first scholarly essay on medicine written in America. In his opening sentences he reveals his Puritan perspective: "Let us look upon sin as the cause of sickness." Mather's religious point of view did not, however, prevent him from seeking cures for specific diseases. He had heard of a method, devised by a Turkish physician, for dealing with smallpox. The method seemed illogical, but it apparently worked. It was called inoculation. In June 1721, as the smallpox epidemic spread throughout Boston, Mather began a public campaign for inoculation.

Boston's medical community was violently opposed to such an experiment, especially one invented by a Muslim. The debate was vigorous, raging all summer and into the fall. Controversy developed into violence: In November, Mather's house was bombed.

Despite such fierce opposition, Mather succeeded in inoculating

nearly 300 people. By the time the epidemic was over, in March of the following year, only 6 of these people had died. Of the almost 6,000 other people who contracted the disease (nearly half of Boston's population), about 850 had died. The evidence, according to Mather's figures, was clear: Whether or not inoculation made much sense to scientists, it worked.

## ■ A Practical Approach to Change

The smallpox controversy illustrates two interesting points about American life in the early eighteenth century. First, it shows that contradictory qualities of the American character often existed side by side. Puritan thinking was not limited to a rigid and narrow interpretation of the Bible; a devout Puritan like Mather could also be a practical scientist.

Mather's experiment also reveals that a practical approach to social change and scientific research was necessary in America. The frontier farmer with little access to tools shared a problem with the scientist who had few books and a whole new world of plants and animals to catalog. American thought had to be thought in action: Improving the public welfare required a willingness to experiment, to try things out, no matter what the authorities might say.

## Deism: Are People Basically Good?

Like the Puritans, the rationalists discovered God through the medium of the natural world, but in a different way. Rationalists thought it unlikely that God would choose to reveal himself only at particular times to particular people. It seemed much more reasonable to believe that God had made it possible for *all* people at *all* times to discover natural laws through their God-given power of reason.

This outlook, called **deism** (dē′iz′əm), was shared by many eighteenth-century thinkers, including many founders of the American nation. American deists came from different religious backgrounds, but they avoided supporting specific religious groups. They sought instead the principles that united all religions.

Deists believed that the universe was orderly and good. In contrast to the Puritans, deists stressed humanity's goodness. They believed in the perfectibility of every individual through the use of reason. God's objective, in the deist view, was the happiness of his creatures. Therefore, the best form of worship was to do good for others. There already existed in America an impulse to improve people's lives, as Cotton Mather's struggle to save Boston from smallpox illustrates. Deism elevated this impulse to one of the nation's highest goals. To this day social welfare is still a political priority and still the subject of fierce debate.

The American struggle for independence was justified largely by appeals to rationalist principles. The arguments presented in the Declaration of Independence are based on rationalist assumptions about the relations between people, God, and natural law.

## Self-made Americans

Most of the literature written in the American Colonies during the Age of Reason was, understandably, rooted in reality. This

*What then is ... this new man? ... He is an American, who, leaving behind him all his ancient prejudices and manners, receives new ones from the new mode of life he has embraced, the new government he obeys, and the new rank he holds. ... [In America] individuals of all nations are melted into a new race of men, whose labors ... will one day cause great changes in the world.*

—Michel-Guillaume Jean
    de Crèvecoeur,
    *Letters from an American
    Farmer* (1782)

*Thomas Jefferson* (1805)
by Rembrandt Peale. Oil on canvas.

Collection of The New-York Historical Society, negative
number 6003, accession number 1867.306.

was an age of pamphlets, since most literature was intended to serve practical or political ends. Following the Revolutionary War (1775–1783), the problems of organizing and governing the new nation were of the highest importance.

The unquestioned masterpiece of the American Age of Reason is *The Autobiography* by Benjamin Franklin (page 69). Franklin used the autobiographical narrative, a form common in Puritan writing, and omitted its religious justification. Written in clear, witty prose, this account of the development of the self-made American provided the model for a story that would be told again and again. In the twentieth century it appeared in F. Scott Fitzgerald's novel *The Great Gatsby* (1925). It is still found in the countless biographies and autobiographies of self-made men and women that appear on the bestseller lists today.

*Benjamin Franklin.* Drawing by David Levine.

Reprinted with permission from *The New York Review of Books.* Copyright © 1967 NYREV, Inc.

## R E V I E W

## Talk About . . .

Turn back to the Think About questions at the start of the introduction to this period (page 6), and discuss your views.

## Write About . . .

### Contrasting Literary Periods

**Who are we? Answers then and now.** Consider what you've learned about the dominant philosophical and religious beliefs in early America. The **Puritans** believed that the world was fallen and that people were sinners who could be redeemed only through the grace of God. The **rationalists** believed that the universe was basically good and that doing good for others was the best way to worship God. How do people today regard the universe and human nature itself? Write a brief essay explaining whether you find evidence of Puritanism and rationalism in American society today.

# Native American Oral Traditions

J oseph Bruchac (1942–    ) was born in Saratoga Springs, New York, and was raised there by his grandfather, a member of the Abenaki people. Bruchac has edited several anthologies of poetry and has written short stories, poems, and novels, many of which incorporate myths from the Abenaki heritage.

"The Sky Tree" is a creation myth of the **Huron,** a Native American people of the eastern woodlands, the region around the Great Lakes and toward the Atlantic Ocean. The Huron lived in villages along the St. Lawrence River, where they competed in the fur trade with the peoples of the Iroquois League. Rivalry with the Iroquois League and European settlers gradually forced the Huron west into the north central United States and Canada and then into Kansas and Oklahoma.

"The Earth Only" comes from the oral tradition of the **Teton Sioux,** a North American Plains Indian people who are sometimes called the Dakota. The Sioux led a nomadic life, following the buffalo and traveling in established cycles across the rolling plains of what is now Minnesota, North Dakota, and South Dakota. The Sioux offered intense resistance to the westward expansion of the United States.

Shield cover, once the property of Pretty Bear, a Crow chief.

Courtesy, National Museum of the American Indian, Smithsonian Institution. (20/7130). Photograph by Carmelo Guadagno.

"Coyote Finishes His Work" has been handed down through the tradition of the **Nez Perce,** a Native American people of the Plateau culture who lived in what is now Idaho, Oregon, and Washington. The French coined the name *nez percé,* meaning "pierced nose," because some of the people wore nose pendants. Following the establishment of the Oregon Trail and aggravated by the mania of the nineteenth-century gold rush, fierce conflicts erupted over the Nez Perce land. In 1877, the Nez Perce leader, Chief Joseph, surrendered to federal troops with the now famous words "I will fight no more forever."

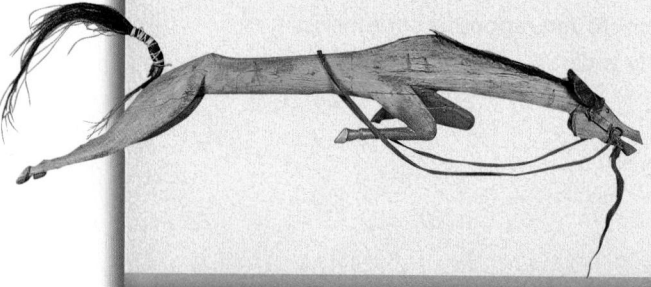

Teton Sioux horse sculpture.

Museum of the South Dakota State Historical Society.

## The Sun Still Rises . . . ◆ The Sky Tree ◆ The Earth Only ◆ Coyote Finishes His Work

### Make the Connection
#### Quickwrite ✏️

People have always asked questions about the origins of the world and about their place in the natural order of things. To answer their questions, people have told themselves stories. The stories, which are almost always connected with religious rituals, explain the world the people live in and their traditions. These stories, called **myths,** also comfort people when they are afraid and give them a sense of cultural identity. Take some notes on myths you are familiar with. What do they explain to people? What comfort might they offer?

### Literary Focus
#### Archetypes

Most myths contain archetypes. An **archetype** (är′kə·tīp′) is an old imaginative pattern that has appeared in literature throughout the ages. The tree in the Huron myth here is an archetype—that of the life-giving tree. Coyote in the Nez Perce myth is an archetype—that of the trickster hero. Archetypes cross cultural and national boundaries.

   Archetypes can be plots (the death of the hero, boy wins girl, the quest), characters (the trickster, the savior, the rescued maiden), or images (a place where people never die, a golden cup, hoarded treasure). The life-giving tree is an archetypal image found in Native American myths as well as in Norse and Middle Eastern myths. The trickster hero is a character archetype found in African and Scandinavian myths and in modern fiction (and comics).

> An **archetype** is an old imaginative pattern that appears across cultures and is repeated through the ages. An archetype can be a character, a plot, or an image.
>
> *For more on Archetype, see the Handbook of Literary and Historical Terms.*

### Reading Skills 📖
#### Understanding Cultural Characteristics

In reading works by members of different cultures, it is important to recognize differences in literary traditions. Since American Indian literature was handed down orally by storytellers, these pieces lose some of their power in written form. As you read, try to imagine each piece being spoken by a skilled storyteller to an eager audience—or, better yet, read each piece aloud.

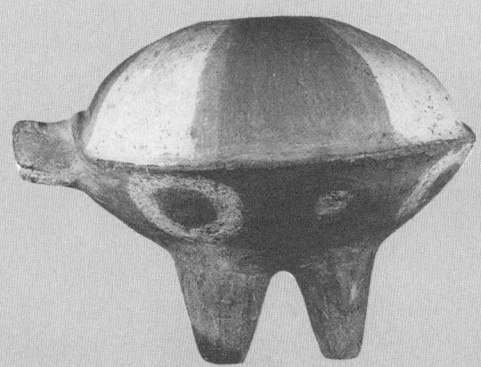

Quapaw ceramic turtle-effigy vessel (late Mississippian period, A.D. 1300–1500).

The University Museum, University of Arkansas, Fayetteville.

**SKILLS FOCUS**

**Literary Skills**
Understand archetypes.

**Reading Skills**
Understand cultural characteristics.

# The Sun Still Rises in the Same Sky: Native American Literature

Joseph Bruchac

Few peoples have been as appreciated and, at the same time, as misrepresented as the many different cultures today called American Indian or Native American. Images of Indians are central to mainstream America, from Longfellow's misnamed epic poem *The Song of Hiawatha* (which actually tells the story of the Chippewa hero Manabozho, not the Iroquois Hiawatha) to the "cowboys and Indians" tradition of movies about the Old West. Yet it's only recently that the authentic literary voices of Native Americans have received serious attention. Native American literature has been a living oral tradition, but it was never treated with the same respect as European, or Western, literature. But Western literature itself has its roots firmly planted in the oral tradition—such ancient classics as the *Odyssey*[1] and *Beowulf*,[2] long before they were written down, were stories kept alive by word of mouth. The vast body of American Indian oral literature, encompassing dozens of epic narratives and countless thousands of stories, poems, songs, oratory, and chants, was not even recognized by Western scholars until the late 1800s. Until then, it was assumed that Native Americans had no literature.

Part of the problem scholars had in recognizing the rich traditions of American Indian literature was translating the texts from hundreds of different languages—a task often best done by Native Americans themselves. Over the decades, various American Indian writers—N. Scott Momaday, Louise Erdrich, Simon J. Ortiz, and Leslie Marmon Silko, among others—have revitalized Native American literature by combining their fluency in English with a deep understanding of their own languages and traditions.

We can make some important generalizations about American Indian oral traditions. First of all, Native American cultures use stories to teach moral lessons and convey practical information about the natural world. A story from the Abenaki people of Maine, for example, tells how Gluskabe catches all of the game animals. He is then told by his grandmother to return the animals to the woods. They will die if they are kept in his bag, she tells him, and if they do die, there will be no game left for the people to come. In this one brief tale, important, life-sustaining lessons about greed, the wisdom of elders, and game management are conveyed in an entertaining and engaging way.

American Indian literature also reflects a view of the natural world that is more inclusive than the one typically seen in Western literature. The Native American universe is not dominated by human beings. Animals and humans are often interchangeable in myths and folk tales. Origin myths may even feature animals as the instruments of creation.

All American Indian cultures also show a keen awareness of the power of metaphor. Words are as powerful and alive as the human breath that carries them. Songs and chants can make things happen—call game animals, bring rain, cure the sick, or destroy an enemy. For Native Americans, speech, or oratory—often relying on striking similes drawn from nature—is a highly developed and respected literary form.

Passed on from generation to generation, oral traditions preserve historical continuity. But these traditions are also, like the Native American peoples themselves, tenacious, dynamic, and responsive to change. The American Indian worldview is not that of a progressive straight line, but of an endless circle. This cyclical nature of existence is reflected both in the natural world itself, with its changing seasons and cycles of birth, death, and rebirth, and in Native American ceremonies repeated year after year. Each summer, for example, the Lakota people have their Sun Dance. In pre-Columbian times, they went to the Sun Dance on foot; after the coming of the Spanish, they rode horses to the annual event. Today, the Lakota arrive by automobile. While a European eye might see the technology of transport as the important point of this anecdote, to a Lakota the issue of changing transportation is unimportant. It is, after all, only a different way of getting to the same place. The sun still rises in the same sky.

---

1. ***Odyssey***: ancient Greek epic poem, attributed to Homer.
2. ***Beowulf***: epic poem composed in Old English between A.D. 700 and 750.

# The Sky Tree

In the beginning, Earth was covered with water. In Sky Land, there were people living as they do now on Earth. In the middle of that land was the great Sky Tree. All of the food which the people in that Sky Land ate came from the great tree.

The old chief of that land lived with his wife, whose name was Aataentsic,° meaning "Ancient Woman," in their longhouse near the great tree. It came to be that the old chief became sick, and nothing could cure him. He grew weaker and weaker until it seemed he would die. Then a dream came to him, and he called Aataentsic to him.

"I have dreamed," he said, "and in my dream I saw how I can be healed. I must be given the fruit which grows at the very top of Sky Tree. You must cut it down and bring that fruit to me."

Aataentsic took her husband's stone ax and went to the great tree. As soon as she struck it, it split in half and toppled over. As it fell, a hole opened in Sky Land, and the tree fell through the hole. Aataentsic returned to the place where the old chief waited.

"My husband," she said, "when I cut the tree, it split in half and then fell through a great hole. Without the tree, there can be no life. I must follow it."

Then, leaving her husband, she went back to the hole in Sky Land and threw herself after the great tree.

---

°**Aataentsic** (ä′tä·ent′sik).

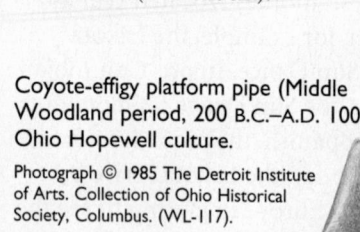

Coyote-effigy platform pipe (Middle Woodland period, 200 B.C.–A.D. 100). Ohio Hopewell culture.

Photograph © 1985 The Detroit Institute of Arts. Collection of Ohio Historical Society, Columbus. (WL-117).

Navajo sand painter at Hubbell Trading Post, Ganado, Arizona.

As Aataentsic fell, Turtle looked up and saw her. Immediately Turtle called together all the water animals and told them what she had seen.

"What should be done?" Turtle said.

Beaver answered her. "You are the one who saw this happen. Tell us what to do."

"All of you must dive down," Turtle said. "Bring up soil from the bottom, and place it on my back."

Immediately all of the water animals began to dive down and bring up soil. Beaver, Mink, Muskrat, and Otter each brought up pawfuls of wet soil and placed the soil on Turtle's back until they had made an island of great size. When they were through, Aataentsic settled down gently on the new Earth, and the pieces of the great tree fell beside her and took root.

—from the Huron tradition,
*retold by* Joseph Bruchac

# The Earth Only

| Wica'hcala kin | The old men |
| heya'pelo' | say |
| maka' kin | the earth |
| lece'la | only |
| tehan yunke'lo | endures |
| eha' pelo' | You spoke |
| ehan'kecon | truly |
| wica' yaka pelo' | You are right. |

—composed by Used-as-a-Shield (Teton Sioux), translated in 1918

# Coyote Finishes His Work

From the very beginning, Coyote was traveling around all over the earth. He did many wonderful things when he went along. He killed the monsters and the evil spirits that preyed on the people. He made the Indians, and put them out in tribes all over the world because Old Man Above wanted the earth to be inhabited all over, not just in one or two places.

He gave all the people different names and taught them different languages. This is why Indians live all over the country now and speak in different ways.

He taught the people how to eat and how to hunt the buffalo and catch eagles. He taught them what roots to eat and how to make a good lodge and what to wear. He taught them how to dance. Sometimes he made mistakes, and even though he was wise and powerful, he did many foolish things. But that was his way.

Coyote liked to play tricks. He thought about himself all the time, and told everyone he was a great warrior, but he was not. Sometimes he would go too far with some trick and get someone killed. Other times, he would have a trick played on himself by someone else. He got killed this way so many times that Fox and the birds got tired of bringing him back to life. Another way he got in trouble was trying to do what someone else did. This is how he came to be called Imitator.

Coyote was ugly too. The girls did not like him. But he was smart. He could change himself around and trick the women. Coyote got the girls when he wanted.

One time, Coyote had done everything he could think of and was traveling from one place to another place, looking for other things that needed to be done. Old Man saw him going along and said to himself, "Coyote has now done almost everything he is capable of doing. His work is almost done. It is time to bring him back to the place where he started."

So Great Spirit came down and traveled in the shape of an old man. He met Coyote. Coyote said, "I am Coyote. Who are you?"

Old Man said, "I am Chief of the earth. It was I who sent you to set the world right."

"No," Coyote said, "you never sent me. I don't know you. If you are the Chief, take that lake over there and move it to the side of that mountain."

"No. If you are Coyote, let me see you do it."

Coyote did it.

"Now, move it back."

Coyote tried, but he could not do it. He thought this was strange. He tried again, but he could not do it.

Chief moved the lake back.

Coyote said, "Now I know you are the Chief."

Old Man said, "Your work is finished, Coyote. You have traveled far and done much good. Now you will go to where I have prepared a home for you."

Then Coyote disappeared. Now no one knows where he is anymore.

Old Man got ready to leave, too. He said to the Indians, "I will send messages to the earth by the spirits of the people who reach me but whose time to die has not yet come. They will carry messages to you from time to time. When their spirits come back into their bodies, they will revive and tell you their experiences.

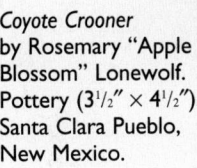

Coyote Crooner by Rosemary "Apple Blossom" Lonewolf. Pottery ($3\frac{1}{2}'' \times 4\frac{1}{2}''$). Santa Clara Pueblo, New Mexico.

"Coyote and myself, we will not be seen again until Earthwoman is very old. Then we shall return to earth, for it will require a change by that time. Coyote will come along first, and when you see him, you will know I am coming. When I come along, all the spirits of the dead will be with me. There will be no more Other Side Camp. All the people will live together. Earthmother will go back to her first shape and live as a mother among her children. Then things will be made right."

Now they are waiting for Coyote.

—from the Nez Perce tradition,
*retold by* Barry Lopez

# Response and Analysis

## The Sun Still Rises . . .

### Reading Check

1. Why did scholars have problems recognizing the traditions of Native American literature?
2. What three generalizations does Bruchac make about American Indian oral traditions?
3. Identify three comparisons Bruchac makes between American Indian and Western views of the world.

### Thinking Critically

4. What does Bruchac's **title** suggest?
5. What does the emphasis on oral literature tell you about Native American cultures?

## The Sky Tree

### Reading Check

1. According to this myth, what was the world like in the beginning?
2. What happens when Aataentsic cuts the tree?
3. How does this myth explain the origin of the earth as we know it today?

### Thinking Critically

4. Would the people who told this myth feel hostile or supportive toward the natural world? Why?
5. What aspects of the settings in this **myth** are **archetypes**? What other stories have used the same archetypes?

## The Earth Only

### Thinking Critically

1. What does the idea repeated in the last three lines of this chant signify about the position of old men in this culture?

2. What profound philosophical comment does "The Earth Only" make by what it leaves out? In other words, what does *not* endure?

## Coyote Finishes His Work

### Reading Check

1. What aspects of life on earth are explained in this myth?
2. **Metamorphoses,** or shape changes, are common in myths of all cultures. What metamorphoses take place in this myth?
3. What does this myth promise for the future?

### Thinking Critically

4. Old Man says that when he returns, earth "will require a change." What do you think he means?
5. What does the **archetype** of the Earth-mother in this story reveal about the Nez Perce vision of nature?

Sand painting representing storm, lightning, and the four seasons, by Michael Tsosie.

## WRITING

### Learning Lessons

Each of these selections offers insights into an aspect of human experience. In an **essay,** analyze the myths. First, discuss these topics: what "The Sky Tree" reveals about the origins of the earth and our relationship to nature; what "The Earth Only" reminds us about our life on earth; and what "Coyote Finishes His Work" promises for the future. Then, explain how these myths relate to what Bruchac says about Native American myths in his essay. Finally, present your own thoughts on the universal, cross-cultural appeal of myths like these.

# Anne Bradstreet
## (1612–1672)

**W**ho could have guessed that the writer who would begin the history of American poetry would be an immigrant teenage bride? This fact seems less far-fetched when we know something about the life of the young woman who came from England to America when the Colonies were no more than a few villages precariously perched between the ocean and the wilderness.

Shakespeare was still alive when Anne Bradstreet was born, and like many budding poets, she found in Shakespeare, and in other great English poets, sources of inspiration and technique that would one day run like threads of gold through the fabric of her own work. However, what most determined the course of Anne Bradstreet's life was not a poetic influence but a religious one.

Anne Bradstreet was born into a family of Puritans. She accepted their reformist views as naturally as most children accept the religious teachings of a parent. When she was about sixteen, she married a well-educated and zealous young Puritan by the name of Simon Bradstreet. Two years later, in 1630, Simon, Anne, and Anne's father journeyed across the Atlantic to the part of New England around Salem that would become known as the Massachusetts Bay Colony. There her father and then her husband rose to prominence, each serving as governor of the colony, while Anne kept house first in Cambridge, then Ipswich, and finally in Andover. She raised four boys and four girls and, without seeking an audience or publication, found time to write poems.

Bradstreet's poems might never have come to light had it not been for John Woodbridge, her brother-in-law and a minister in Andover. In 1648, he went to England and, in 1650, without consulting the author herself, published Bradstreet's poems in London under the title *The Tenth Muse Lately Sprung Up in America.*

In one stroke an obscure wife and mother from the meadows of New England was placed among the nine Muses of art and learning sacred to the ancient Greeks. In itself this was embarrassing enough, but in the middle of the seventeenth century, the real arrogance was that a woman would aspire to a place among the august company of established male poets. *The Tenth Muse* fared better with critics and the public than Anne expected (later even the learned Puritan minister Cotton Mather praised her work), and she felt encouraged to write for the rest of her life.

Today Anne Bradstreet is remembered not for her elaborate earlier poems, which focus on public events, but for a few simple, personal lyrics on such topics as the birth of children, the death of grandchildren, her love for her husband, her son's departure for England, and her own illnesses and adversities. In a letter to her children just before she died, she wrote, "Among all my experiences of God's gracious dealings with me I have constantly observed this, that He hath never suffered me long to sit loose from Him, but by one affliction or other hath made me look home, and search what was amiss."

*Anne Bradstreet* (detail) (1948) by Harry Grylls. Stained glass.

Reproduced by kind permission of the vicar and church wardens of St. Botolph's Church, Boston, England.

# Here Follow Some Verses upon the Burning of Our House, July 10, 1666

## Make the Connection

### Quickwrite 🖉

This poem is a response to a terrible personal loss. The event that is the focus of the poem took place hundreds of years ago, but it could be a story in today's newspapers. In trying to work through her loss, this poet portrays an internal debate, a dialogue between herself and her soul. As you read, notice the points at which Bradstreet questions her own thoughts and emotions. Note also your own responses: How would you deal with the destruction of a home? Before you read, take some notes on what your response might be if all the material things you hold dear went up in flames.

## Literary Focus

### The Plain Style

In their style of writing, as well as in their manner of worship, the Puritans favored the plain and unornamented. Though the style used by Puritan writers now seems hard to read, in the 1600s it was considered simple and direct. This **plain style** emphasized uncomplicated sentences and the use of everyday words from common speech.

The Puritan plain style differed greatly from the ornate "high style" that was in fashion in England at the time—a style that used classical allusions, Latin quotations, and elaborate figures of speech, as in this example from the poet and Anglican clergyman John Donne:

> First, for the incomprehensibleness of God, the understanding of man hath a limited, a determined latitude; it is an intelligence able to move that sphere which it is fixed to, but could not move a greater:

> I can comprehend *naturam naturatam,* created nature, but for that *natura naturans,* God himself, the understanding of man cannot comprehend.

Although Bradstreet uses figurative language in her poetry, her writing is still influenced by strong, simple Puritan style and diction. Rather than narrating a straightforward account of the burning of her house, Bradstreet records her journey from grief to spiritual solace. Present too in the poem is Bradstreet's realization that her love of material things is in danger of eclipsing her love of things divine.

---

The **plain style** is a way of writing that stresses simplicity and clarity of expression.

*For more on Plain Style, see the Handbook of Literary and Historical Terms.*

---

## Reading Skills

### Analyzing Text Structures: Inversion

In order to accommodate the demands of **meter** and **rhyme,** poets through the centuries have used **inversion.** In an inversion the words of a sentence or phrase are wrenched out of normal English syntax, or word order: for example, "In silent night when rest I took" instead of "In silent night when I took rest." As you read Bradstreet's poem, pay close attention to her use of inversion. Then, go through the poem line by line, and rewrite it so that these words appear in normal order.

**SKILLS FOCUS**

**Literary Skills**
Understand the characteristics of plain style.

**Reading Skills**
Understand the use of inversion. Rewrite inverted text in normal order.

# Here Follow Some Verses upon the Burning of Our House, July 10, 1666

## Anne Bradstreet

In silent night when rest I took
For sorrow near I did not look
I wakened was with thund'ring noise
And piteous shrieks of dreadful voice.
5 That fearful sound of "Fire!" and "Fire!"
Let no man know is my desire.
I, starting up, the light did spy,
And to my God my heart did cry
To strengthen me in my distress
10 And not to leave me succorless.°
Then, coming out, beheld a space
The flame consume my dwelling place.
And when I could no longer look,
I blest His name that gave and took,°
15 That laid my goods now in the dust.
Yea, so it was, and so 'twas just.
It was His own, it was not mine,
Far be it that I should repine;
He might of all justly bereft
20 But yet sufficient for us left.
When by the ruins oft I past
My sorrowing eyes aside did cast,
And here and there the places spy
Where oft I sat and long did lie:
25 Here stood that trunk, and there that chest,
There lay that store I counted best.
My pleasant things in ashes lie,
And them behold no more shall I.
Under thy roof no guest shall sit,
30 Nor at thy table eat a bit.
No pleasant tale shall e'er be told,
Nor things recounted done of old.
No candle e'er shall shine in thee,
Nor bridegroom's voice e'er heard shall be.

35 In silence ever shall thou lie,
Adieu, Adieu, all's vanity.
Then straight I 'gin my heart to chide,
And did thy wealth on earth abide?
Didst fix thy hope on mold'ring dust?
40 The arm of flesh didst make thy trust?
Raise up thy thoughts above the sky
That dunghill mists away may fly.
Thou hast an house on high erect,
Framed by that mighty Architect,
45 With glory richly furnished,
Stands permanent though this be fled.
It's purchased and paid for too
By Him who hath enough to do.
A price so vast as is unknown
50 Yet by His gift is made thine own;
There's wealth enough, I need no more,
Farewell, my pelf,° farewell my store.
The world no longer let me love,
My hope and treasure lies above.

---

**52. pelf** *n.:* wealth or worldly goods (sometimes used as a term of contempt).

*Cover for a chair seat,* (1725–1750) owned by the Bradstreet family. Cotton and linen twill (fustian), embroidered with wool. 54 × 44 cm (21¼ × 17⁵⁄₁₆ in.).

---

**10. succorless** (suk′ər • lis) *adj.:* without aid or assistance; helpless.

**14. that gave and took:** allusion to Job 1:21, "The Lord gave, and the Lord hath taken away; blessed be the name of the Lord."

# Response and Analysis

## Thinking Critically

**1.** In this poem, Bradstreet first narrates an incident and then moves on to draw conclusions from it. What do you think is the turning point of the poem?

**2.** Where does Bradstreet get her inner strength to face the loss of her house? How do you think someone today might deal with the same situation? Look back at your Quickwrite notes for ideas. ✏️

**3.** Bradstreet speaks of another "house" in an **extended metaphor** at the end of the poem. What is this house, who is its architect, and how is it better than the house she has lost?

**4.** *Pelf*—a word designating riches or worldly goods—is usually used only when the riches or goods are considered to be slightly tainted, ill-gotten, or stolen. Why do you suppose Bradstreet uses such a bitter word in line 52 to describe her own cherished treasures?

**5.** Using your "noninverted" version of the poem as a starting point, write a paraphrase of the entire poem. (A **paraphrase** is a restatement of a text in your own words.) 📖

## Extending and Evaluating

**6.** Some readers have felt that by so lovingly enumerating her losses, Bradstreet is crying out to heaven in a way that unconsciously reveals more attachment to her earthly possessions than she would admit to. On the other hand, what Bradstreet does not reveal in this poem is significant: Hundreds of books, as well as her papers and all her unpublished poems, were also lost in the fire. Using specific examples from the text, explain why you are, or are not, convinced that the speaker means what she says.

## Literary Criticism

**7.** Think about the major Puritan beliefs as you re-read this poem. What philosophical beliefs about God and the purpose of human life are reflected in Bradstreet's poem?

## WRITING

### Trials and Tribulations

In the Book of Job from the Bible, Job endures great misery, yet he is still able to say, "The Lord gave, and the Lord hath taken away; blessed be the name of the Lord" (Job 1:21). Bradstreet expresses a similar attitude in her poem; twice she checks herself from mourning over the loss of her beloved possessions. The first instance is in lines 14–20; the second begins with line 37. In a brief **essay,** discuss Bradstreet's attitude toward earthly suffering and the providence of God. Cite details from the poem to support your analysis.

## LISTENING AND SPEAKING

### Oral Performance

Get together with a partner, and practice reading Bradstreet's poem aloud. Pay close attention to the meter, the inexact rhymes, and the pronunciation of unfamiliar words. Then, present an oral performance of the poem. Decide who will speak at what point, which words to emphasize, and how to use body language to enhance the reading.

# Literature of the Americas

## Mexico

Courtesy of Schalkwijk/Art Resource, NY. Museo Nacional de Historia, Castillo de Chapultepec, Mexico City, D.F., Mexico.

*Sister Juana Inés de la Cruz* (1750) by Miguel Cabrera (1695–1768). Oil on canvas.

### Sor Juana Inés de la Cruz
#### (1651–1695)

Even as a child growing up in a Mexican village, Juana Ramirez de Asbaje displayed an extraordinary love of learning. At six, she begged her mother to dress her as a boy and send her to the university in Mexico City. Her request was denied, so the child threw herself into reading in her grandfather's library—a world of books that in the seventeenth century was generally available only to men. Young Juana was hard on herself; she cut off her hair if she failed to learn Latin grammar according to her own schedule.

At sixteen, Juana was presented at the court of the Spanish viceroy in Mexico City, where she charmed everyone, according to reports. She served as a lady-in-waiting for four years, then abruptly entered a convent, taking the name Sor (Sister) Juana Inés de la Cruz. Her career is summed up by Octavio Paz (1914–1998), the Nobel Prize–winning poet from Mexico who wrote a critical study of Sor Juana's life and work:

> 66 There was nothing ordinary about her person or her life. She was exceptionally beautiful, and poor. She was the favorite of a Vicereine [wife of a viceroy] and lived at court, courted by many; she was loved and perchance she loved. Abruptly she gives up worldly life and enters a convent—yet far from re-nouncing the world entirely, she con-verts her cell into a study filled with books, works of art, and scientific in-struments and transforms the convent locutory [room for conversation] into a literary and intellectual salon. She writes love poems, verses for songs and dance tunes, profane comedies, sacred poems, an essay in theology, and an autobio-graphical defense of the right of women to study and cultivate their minds. She becomes famous, sees her plays per-formed, her poems published, and her genius applauded in all the Spanish do-minions, half the Western world. Then suddenly she gives up everything; sur-renders her library and collections; re-nounces literature; and finally, during an epidemic, after ministering to stricken sisters in the convent, dies at the age of forty-six. 99

# Before You Read

## World, in hounding me . . .

### Make the Connection
#### Quickwrite ✎

To *hound* means to "chase or follow; nag." Consider the title of this poem. What does it mean when the world hounds you? Write down your first thoughts on the significance of the poem's title.

### Literary Focus
#### Sonnet

The **sonnet** is a fourteen-line lyric poem that is built around a strict structure. Sor Juana's sonnet is a **Petrarchan sonnet,** a form popularized in the fourteenth century by the Italian poet Petrarch. The Petrarchan sonnet is divided into two parts: an eight-line octave (from the Latin *octo,* meaning "eight"), with the rhyme scheme *abba abba,* and a six-line sestet (from the Latin *sex,* meaning "six"), with the rhyme scheme *cde cde* or *cdc dcd.* (The letters simply indicate a rhyming sound: Each line that ends with one rhyming sound is marked "a," each line that ends with another rhyming sound is marked "b," and so on.) In a strict Petrarchan sonnet the octave poses a question or states an idea, and the sestet then answers the question or restates the poet's point more forcefully.

You might ask why some poets choose to follow such tough rules. Perhaps these poets enjoy the challenge of expressing their ideas within strict forms. Robert Frost, a great American poet, said that writing poetry without paying attention to structure is like playing tennis without the net.

### Background

In her time, Sor Juana was called "the tenth muse from Mexico," just as Anne Bradstreet was called "the tenth muse lately sprung up in America." Although both poets possessed a strong creative force, the personal lives of Bradstreet and Sor Juana were vastly different. Bradstreet was fundamentally a private person, a Puritan wife and mother, who wrote poems but did not seek publication. Sor Juana, although a devout Catholic nun, had served at court, acquired the education of a scholar, written plays and song lyrics, and presided over a salon—a regular gathering of distinguished literary and intellectual guests.

Octavio Paz considered Sor Juana's poems to be among "the most elegant and refined in Spanish. Few poets in our language equal her, and those who surpass her can be counted on the fingers of one hand." Her style is an example of Spanish baroque writing in the Americas, with its intricate verse forms, its interplay of the intellectual and the sensual, and its verbal dexterity and wit. In 1974, at a ceremony in Mexico, Sor Juana was awarded the title First Feminist of the Americas.

In the following poem by Sor Juana, the word *vanity* plays an important role. It means an empty pursuit that is characterized by conceit and is ultimately worthless. For Sor Juana the word would also have carried echoes of the powerful exclamation of the preacher at the beginning of Ecclesiastes in the Bible: "Vanity of vanities; all is vanity."

**SKILLS FOCUS**

**Literary Skills**
Understand the characteristics of a Petrarchan sonnet.

A **sonnet** is a rhymed fourteen-line poem, usually written in iambic pentameter.

*For more on Sonnet, see the Handbook of Literary and Historical Terms.*

# World, in hounding me …

## Sor Juana Inés de la Cruz

*translated by* **Alan S. Trueblood**

> World, in hounding me, what do you gain?
> How can it harm you if I choose, astutely,
> rather to stock my mind with things of beauty,
> than waste its stock on every beauty's claim?
> 5     Costliness and wealth bring me no pleasure;
> the only happiness I care to find
> derives from setting treasure in my mind,
> and not from mind that's set on winning treasure.
>     I prize no comeliness.° All fair things pay
> 10 to time, the victor, their appointed fee
> and treasure cheats even the practiced eye.
>     Mine is the better and the truer way:
> to leave the vanities of life aside,
> not throw my life away on vanity.

°**comeliness** *n.:* beauty.

# En perseguirme, mundo …

## Sor Juana Inés de la Cruz

> En perseguirme, mundo, ¿qué interesas?
> ¿En qué te ofendo, cuando sólo intento
> poner bellezas en mi entendimiento
> y no mi entendimiento en las bellezas?
> 5     Yo no estimo tesoros ni riquezas;
> y así, siempre me causa más contento
> poner riquezas en mi pensamiento
> que no mi pensamiento en las riquezas.
>     Y no estimo hermosura que, vencida,
> 10 es despojo civil de las edades,
> ni riqueza me agrada fementida,
>     teniendo por mejor, en mis verdades,
> consumir vanidades de la vida
> que consumir la vida en vanidades.

SOR JVANA INES DE LA CRVZ

# Response and Analysis

## Thinking Critically

1. The first four lines of "World, in hounding me . . ." consist of two **rhetorical questions**—questions that are asked for effect. Rhetorical questions don't need to be answered because the answers are obvious. Restate Sor Juana's opening questions in your own words.

2. The word *treasure* is used in different ways in lines 7 and 8. What kind of treasure is Sor Juana referring to in each of these lines?

3. In lines 9–11, Sor Juana uses **personification** in talking about "fair things," "time," and "treasure." How does she personify these three nonhuman things? Restate these lines in your own words.

4. How would you state the **theme** of the poem? Which words or lines convey the theme most clearly for you?

5. How closely has Sor Juana followed the structure of the **Petrarchan sonnet**? (See the Literary Focus on page 32.) To answer this question, focus first on the original Spanish. Then, analyze the English translation.

## Extending and Evaluating

6. How effective is the poem's title in conveying the speaker's attitude toward the world? How does it compare with your own point of view? (Check your Quickwrite notes.)

## WRITING

### Comparing Literature

Religion strongly influenced Sor Juana's and Anne Bradstreet's writings. Sor Juana, however, was from Latin America and had a Catholic background, while Bradstreet was from New England and had a Puritan background. Re-read Bradstreet's poem "Here Follow Some Verses upon the Burning of Our House, July 10, 1666" (page 29). In a brief essay, **compare and contrast** the two poems, including the use of the word *vanity* in each. Before you write, gather your details in a chart like the one that follows. Remember to use specific quotations from the poems to support your ideas.

|                   | Sor Juana | Bradstreet |
| ----------------- | --------- | ---------- |
| Topic             |           |            |
| Theme             |           |            |
| Use of metaphor   |           |            |
| Use of rhyme      |           |            |
| Key words in poem |           |            |

# Mary Rowlandson
## (c. 1636–c. 1711)

From June 1675 to August 1676, the Wampanoag chief, Metacomet, called King Philip by the colonists, carried out a series of bloody raids on Colonial settlements in what is now called King Philip's War. This conflict was the natural result of growing encroachments by the settlers on American Indian land. The native people of New England had been forced into ever more restricted areas, and although they had sold the land, they rejected conditions stipulating that they could no longer hunt on it. To them "selling" meant selling the right to share the land with the buyers, not selling its exclusive ownership.

Matters came to a head when Metacomet's former assistant, who had given information to the colonists, was killed by his own people. His killers were tried and hanged by the Puritans. This was too much for Metacomet to bear, and two weeks later the most severe war in the history of New England began. Its tragic result was the virtual extinction of the indigenous way of life in the region. Among the war's victims was Mary Rowlandson, the wife of the Congregational minister of Lancaster, a frontier town that was located thirty miles west of Boston. In February 1676, she and her three children were carried away by a Wampanoag raiding party that wanted to trade hostages for money. After eleven weeks and five days of captivity, Rowlandson's ransom was paid.

Not long after the family's reunion, which included the return of their two surviving children, the Rowlandsons resettled in Wethersfield, Connecticut. In 1678, Mary's husband, Joseph, died, and the following year she married Capt. Samuel Talcott, a wealthy landowner. Mary Rowlandson lived in Wethersfield until her death, around 1711.

Rowlandson's story was horrific, but it is important to realize that her captors were only slightly better off than their prisoners. Virtually without food, the Wampanoag were chased from camp to camp by Colonial soldiers. Their captives, they thought, were the only currency with which to buy supplies and food. In a graphic passage, Rowlandson describes the lengths to which the Wampanoag were driven by their hunger, eating horses, dogs, frogs, skunks, rattlesnakes, and even tree bark. "They would pick up old bones," she wrote, "and cut them to pieces at the joints, and if they were full of worms and maggots, they would scald them over the fire to make the vermin come out, and then boil them, and drink up the liquor. . . . They would eat horse's guts, and ears, and all sorts of wild birds which they could catch. . . . I can but stand in admiration," she concluded, "to see the wonderful power of God in providing for such a vast number of our enemies in the wilderness, where there was nothing to be seen."

Rowlandson's narrative not only presents a terrifying and moving tale of frontier life but also provides insight into how the Puritans viewed their lives—with a characteristic double vision. For Rowlandson, as for other Puritans, events had both a physical and a spiritual significance. She did not want merely to record her horrifying experience; she wished to demonstrate how it revealed God's purpose. The full title of her narrative (as published in 1682) illustrates this intention: *The Sovereignty and Goodness of God, Together with the Faithfulness of His Promises Displayed: Being a Narrative of the Captivity and Restauration of Mrs. Mary Rowlandson.*

# Before You Read

## from A Narrative of the Captivity . . .

### Make the Connection
#### Quickwrite ✏️

Who hasn't listened with rapt attention to stories of people enduring life-threatening circumstances—a flood, a plane crash on a snowy mountain, an earthquake, or captivity as a hostage? Perhaps our fascination with such stories comes from wondering how we would survive if we were put to the same test. In your notebook, write your thoughts on what might help a person survive a life-threatening situation.

### Literary Focus
#### Allusions

The Puritans regarded biblical captivity narratives, such as that of the enslavement of the Israelites by the ancient Egyptians, as allegories representing the Christians' liberation from sin through the intervention of God's grace. Rowlandson views her experiences as a repetition of the biblical pattern and uses **allusions** to reflect her own situation. Through apt quotations from the Bible, Rowlandson places her experiences in the context of the ancient biblical captivities.

**SKILLS FOCUS**

**Literary Skills**
Understand allusions.

**Reading Skills**
Understand chronological order.

> An **allusion** is a reference to someone or something well known from history, literature, religion, politics, sports, science, or some other branch of culture.
>
> *For more on Allusion, see the Handbook of Literary and Historical Terms.*

**go.hrw.com**

**INTERNET**

**Vocabulary Practice**

Keyword: LE7 11-1

### Reading Skills 🏊
#### Analyzing Text Structures: Chronological Order

As you read, keep track of events and their impact on Rowlandson by taking notes in a three-column chart. Use the first column to list events in **chronological order** (also called time or sequential order). Use the second column to note where Rowlandson links her sufferings with those of people in the Bible. Use the third column to record her comments about her captors in relation to some of the events. In those comments, be sure to note Rowlandson's **word choice,** especially her use of emotional language. You will have more entries in the first column than in either of the other two.

| Events in chrono-logical order | References to Bible | Comments about captors |
|---|---|---|
| | | |

### Vocabulary Development

**tedious** (tē′dē·əs) *adj.*: tiring; dreary.

**lamentable** (lam′ən·tə·bəl) *adj.*: regrettable; distressing.

**entreated** (en·trēt′id) *v.*: asked sincerely; begged.

**afflictions** (ə·flik′shənz) *n. pl.*: pains; hardships.

**plunder** (plun′dər) *n.*: goods seized, especially during wartime.

**melancholy** (mel′ən·käl′ē) *adj.*: sad; sorrowful.

**savory** (sā′vər·ē) *adj.*: appetizing; tasty.

**bewitching** (bē·wich′iŋ) *v.* used as *adj.*: enticing; irresistible.

*In the opening part of her narrative, Mary Rowlandson describes the attack on Lancaster, in which twelve people were killed and twenty-four taken captive, and the assault on her own house. During the raid, Mary and her six-year-old child Sarah, whom she refers to as her "babe," were wounded. The first part of this selection recounts Mary's move from Princeton to Braintree, Massachusetts, two days after the raid in Lancaster.*

# *from* A Narrative of the Captivity . . .

## Mary Rowlandson

### The Move to an Indian Village on the Ware River, Near Braintree (February 12–27)

The morning being come, they prepared to go on their way. One of the Indians got up upon a horse, and they set me up behind him, with my poor sick babe in my lap. A very wearisome and <u>tedious</u> day I had of it; what with my own wound, and my child's being so exceeding sick, and in a <u>lamentable</u> condition with her wound. It may be easily judged what a poor feeble condition we were in, there being not the least crumb of refreshing that came within either of our mouths from Wednesday night to Saturday night, except only a little cold water. This day in the afternoon, about an hour by sun, we came to the place where they intended, *viz.*[1] an Indian town, called Wenimesset, norward of Quabaug. . . . I sat much alone with a poor wounded child in my lap, which moaned night and day, having nothing to revive the body, or cheer the spirits of her, but instead of that, sometimes one Indian would come and tell me one hour, that your master will knock your child in the head, and then a second, and then a third, your master will quickly knock your child in the head.

This was the comfort I had from them, miserable comforters are ye all, as he said.[2] Thus

---

1. *viz.:* abbreviation for the Latin word *videlicet,* for "namely."

2. **he said:** The biblical allusion is to Job 16:2. In the passage cited, Job addresses those who try to console him. God had severely tested Job's faith by causing Job to lose his children and his money and to break out in boils all over his body.

---

**Vocabulary**
**tedious** (tē′dē·əs) *adj.:* tiring; dreary.
**lamentable** (lam′ən·tə·bəl) *adj.:* regrettable; distressing.

nine days I sat upon my knees, with my babe in my lap, till my flesh was raw again; my child being even ready to depart this sorrowful world, they bade me carry it out to another wigwam (I suppose because they would not be troubled with such spectacles) whither I went with a very heavy heart, and down I sat with the picture of death in my lap. About two hours in the night, my sweet babe like a lamb departed this life, on February 18, 1675. It being about six years and five months old. It was nine days from the first wounding, in this miserable condition, without any refreshing of one nature or another, except a little cold water. I cannot but take notice, how at another time I could not bear to be in the room where any dead person was, but now the case is changed; I must and could lie down by my dead babe, side by side all the night after. I have thought since of the wonderful goodness of God to me, in preserving me in the use of my reason and senses, in that distressed time, that I did not use wicked and violent means to end my own miserable life. In the morning, when they understood that my child was dead they sent for me home to my master's wigwam: (by my master in this writing, must be understood Quanopin, who was a Sagamore,[3] and married King Philip's wife's sister; not that he first took me, but I was sold to him by another Narragansett Indian, who took me when first I came out of the garrison). I went to take up my dead child in my arms to carry it with me, but they bid me let it alone: There was no resisting, but go I must and leave it. When I had been at my master's wigwam, I took the first opportunity I could get, to go look after my dead child: When I came I asked them what they had done with it. Then they told me it was upon the hill: Then they went and showed me where it was, where I saw the ground was newly digged, and there they told me they had buried it: There I left that child in the wilderness, and must commit it, and myself also in this wilderness condition, to him who is above all. God having taken away

this dear child, I went to see my daughter Mary, who was at this same Indian town, at a wigwam not very far off, though we had little liberty or opportunity to see one another. She was about ten years old, and taken from the door at first by a Praying Ind.[4] and afterward sold for a gun. When I came in sight, she would fall aweeping; at which they were provoked, and would not let me come near her, but bade me be gone; which was a heart-cutting word to me. I had one child dead, another in the wilderness, I knew not where, the third they would not let me come near to: "Me (as he said) have ye bereaved of my Children, Joseph is not, and Simeon is not, and ye will take Benjamin also, all these things are against me."[5] I could not sit still in this condition, but kept walking from one place to another. And as I was going along, my heart was even overwhelmed with the thoughts of my condition, and that I should have children, and a nation which I knew not ruled over them. Whereupon I earnestly entreated the Lord, that He would consider my low estate, and show me a token for good, and if it were His blessed will, some sign and hope of some relief. And indeed quickly the Lord answered, in some measure, my poor prayers: For as I was going up and down mourning and lamenting my condition, my son came to me, and asked me how I did; I had not seen him before, since the destruction of the town, and I knew not where he was, till I was informed by himself, that he was amongst a smaller parcel of Indians, whose place was about six miles off; with tears in his eyes, he asked me whether his sister Sarah was dead; and told me he had seen his sister Mary; and prayed me, that I would not be troubled in reference to

---

4. **Praying Ind.:** American Indians who converted to Christianity were known as praying Indians. The Colonial assemblies allowed these converts to live in self-governing towns.
5. **Me . . . against me:** Rowlandson quotes Jacob's lament in Genesis 42:36. Jacob had only his youngest son, Benjamin, at home.

**Vocabulary**

**entreated** (en·trēt'id) v.: asked sincerely; begged.

---

3. **Sagamore** (sag'ə·môr') n.: secondary chief in the hierarchy of several American Indian peoples.

himself. . . . I cannot but take notice of the wonderful mercy of God to me in those afflictions, in sending me a Bible. One of the Indians that came from Medfield fight, had brought some plunder, came to me, and asked me, if I would have a Bible, he had got one in his basket. I was glad of it, and asked him, whether he thought the Indians would let me read. He answered, yes: So I took the Bible, and in that melancholy time, it came into my mind to read first the 28th chapter of Deuteronomy,[6] which I did, and when I had read it, my dark heart wrought on this manner, that there was no mercy for me, that the blessings were gone, and the curses come in their room, and that I had lost my opportunity. But the Lord helped me still to go on reading till I came to Chapter 30 the seven first verses, where I found, there was mercy promised again, if we would return to Him by repentance; and though we were scattered from one end of the earth to the other, yet the Lord would gather us together, and turn all those curses upon our enemies. I do not desire to live to forget this Scripture, and what comfort it was to me. . . .

## The Fifth Remove

The occasion (as I thought) of their moving at this time, was, the English Army, it being near and following them: For they went, as if they had gone for their lives, for some considerable way, and then they made a stop, and chose some of their stoutest men, and sent them back to hold the English Army in play while the rest escaped: And then, like Jehu,[7] they marched on furiously, with their old, and with their young: Some carried their old decrepit[8] mothers, some carried one, and some another. Four of them carried a great Indian upon a bier; but going through a thick wood with him, they were hindered, and could make no haste; whereupon they took him upon their backs, and carried him, one at a time, till they came to Bacquaug River. Upon a Friday, a little after noon we came to this river. When all the company was come up, and were gathered together, I thought to count the number of them, but they were so many, and being somewhat in motion, it was beyond my skill. In this travel, because of my wound, I was somewhat favored in my load; I carried only my knitting work and two quarts of parched meal: Being very faint I asked my mistress to give me one spoonful of the meal, but she would not give me a taste. They quickly fell to cutting dry trees, to make rafts to carry them over the river: and soon my turn came to go over: By the advantage of some brush which they had laid upon the raft to sit upon, I did not wet my foot (which many of themselves at the other end were midleg deep) which cannot but be acknowledged as a favor of God to my weakened body, it being a very cold time. I was not before acquainted with such kind of doings or dangers. "When thou passeth through the waters I will be with thee, and through the Rivers they shall not overflow thee," Isaiah, 43:2. A certain number of us got over the river that night, but it was the night after the Sabbath before all the company was got over. On the Saturday they boiled an old horse's leg which they had got, and so we drank of the broth, as soon as they thought it was ready, and when it was almost gone, they filled it up again.

The first week of my being among them, I hardly ate anything; the second week, I found my stomach grow very faint for want of something; and yet it was very hard to get down their filthy trash: but the third week, though I could think how formerly my stomach would turn

---

6. **28th chapter of Deuteronomy:** In Deuteronomy 28, Moses warns that God will bless those who obey Him and curse those who do not.
7. **Jehu** (jē′hoō′): Israelite king of the ninth century B.C. Jehu was said to be a "furious driver" (2 Kings 9:20), and Rowlandson's allusion here is to the speed and fury with which her captors moved away from the English army.
8. **decrepit** *adj.:* run-down; worn out by age or use.

---

**Vocabulary**

**afflictions** (ə·flik′shənz) *n. pl.:* pains; hardships.
**plunder** (plun′dər) *n.:* goods seized, especially during wartime.
**melancholy** (mel′ən·käl′ē) *adj.:* sad; sorrowful.

against this or that, and I could starve and die before I could eat such things, yet they were sweet and savory to my taste. . . .

## The Sixth Remove

We traveled on till night; and in the morning, we must go over the river to Philip's crew. When I was in the canoe, I could not but be amazed at the numerous crew of pagans that were on the bank on the other side. When I came ashore, they gathered all about me, I sitting alone in the midst: I observed they asked one another questions, and laughed, and rejoiced over their gains and victories. Then my heart began to fail: And I fell aweeping which was the first time to my remembrance, that I wept before them. Although I had met with so much affliction, and my heart was many times ready to break, yet could I not shed one tear in their sight: but rather had been all this while in a maze, and like one astonished: But now I may say as, Psalm 137:1, "By the rivers of Babylon, there we sat down: yea, we wept when we remembered Zion." There one of them asked me, why I wept, I could hardly tell what to say: Yet I answered, they would kill me: "No," said he, "none will

---

**Vocabulary**

**savory** (sā′vər·ē) *adj.:* appetizing; tasty.

## A CLOSER LOOK: SOCIAL INFLUENCES

### Captivity Narratives

INFORMATIONAL TEXT

*A Narrative of the Captivity, Sufferings, and Removes of Mrs. Mary Rowlandson* was one of the most widely read prose works of the seventeenth century. It was especially popular in England, where people were eager for lurid tales of native inhabitants of the Americas. Rowlandson's story went through at least thirty editions, and it inspired a mass of imitations that were often partially or purely fictional. These "captivity" stories became one of the most widely produced forms of entertainment in America, but they had a tragic side effect: They contributed to the further deterioration of relations between American Indians and colonists.

Between the seventeenth and nineteenth centuries, as settlers moved westward and occupied American Indian lands, tensions between the two groups increased. American Indians, in retaliation for various injustices, raided settlements and took captives to ransom, enslave, or sell to the French or to other native peoples. These captives didn't necessarily suffer grim fates: Some captives actually chose to remain with their captors and were adopted by them; a few married American Indi-ans and never expressed any desire to return to their original homes. Many of those who escaped or were ransomed recorded their experiences when they returned home. Eventually thousands of captivity tales—of varying quality and accuracy—sprouted up all over the country. Scarcely any first editions of these books remain, as they were literally read and re-read to shreds by an eager public.

**From Providence to propaganda.** Because early captivity narratives were almost all told from the limited first-person point of view, they often failed to mention settlers' actions that may have provoked American Indian aggression. Typically seventeenth-century captivity narratives begin with a brief description of a raid and the rounding up of hostages; they then focus on the gritty details of the day-to-day struggle for survival. The captives in these early narratives generally accept their condition as a punishment sent by God to test their faith, and any relief from their suffering is always evidence of divine Providence, not sympathy from their captors. By the eighteenth century, continuing animosity between settlers and American Indians, aggravated by the French and Indian War, led to a different kind of captivity narrative, one that was an undisguised ex-

hurt you." Then came one of them and gave me two spoonfuls of meal to comfort me, and another gave me half a pint of peas; which was more worth than many bushels at another time. Then I went to see King Philip, he bade me come in and sit down, and asked me whether I would smoke it (a usual compliment nowadays amongst saints and sinners) but this no way suited me. For though I had formerly used tobacco, yet I had left it ever since I was first taken. It seems to be a bait, the devil lays to make men lose their precious time: I remember with shame, how formerly, when I had taken two or three pipes, I was presently ready for another, such a bewitching thing it is: But I thank God, He has now given me power over it; surely there are many who may be better employed than to lie sucking a stinking tobacco pipe.

Now the Indians gather their forces to go against North Hampton: Overnight one went about yelling and hooting to give notice of the design. Where upon they fell to boiling of groundnuts, and parching of corn (as many as had it) for their provision: And in the morning away they went. During my abode[9] in this place,

---

9. **abode** (ə•bōd′) *n.*: stay.

**Vocabulary**

**bewitching** (bē•wich′iŋ) *v.* used as *adj.*: enticing; irresistible.

---

pression of hatred toward American Indians. No longer were captivity narratives instructive tales of physical and spiritual survival in the wilderness; now they were inflammatory propaganda, assertions of European superiority.

### Sensationalism and stereotypes.

By the early nineteenth century, propaganda had turned into pure sensationalism. Journalists and authors of lurid fiction, gifted at manipulating the fantasies and prejudices of the reading public, revised the original narratives. They pulled out all the stops, using melodramatic plot devices and long passages of grisly detail. The public eagerly read these penny dreadfuls (the popular term for cheap magazines with tales of horror and crime), shuddering with mixed fascination and horror at fictional tales of American Indian atrocities and the suffering of innocent captives. The tawdriness of these publications didn't go unnoticed by more educated readers. Many actual nineteenth-century captives were reluctant to publish their stories, afraid that by association with sleazy popular magazines, their experiences would not be taken seriously.

Some historians have argued that captivity narratives, by advancing the stereotype of the "savage Indian," made it easier for settlers to justify occupation of American Indian lands. By

*Native American Sachem* (detail) (c.1700). Oil on canvas (33¹/₈″ × 30¹/₈″).

the late nineteenth century, with the "Indian threat" a thing of the past, captivity narratives gradually became less popular. Unfortunately, though, stereotypes of the "bad" Indian and the "virtuous" European settler remained in the popular imagination well into the twentieth century, appearing in countless western novels, Hollywood movies, and television programs.

Philip spoke to me to make a shirt for his boy, which I did, for which he gave me a shilling: I offered the money to my master, but he bade me keep it: And with it I bought a piece of horseflesh. Afterward he asked me to make a cap for his boy, for which he invited me to dinner. I went, and he gave me a pancake, about as big as two fingers; it was made of parched wheat, beaten, and fried in bear's grease, but I thought I never tasted pleasanter meat in my life. There was a squaw who spoke to me to make a shirt for her *sannup*,[10] for which she gave me a piece of bear. Another asked me to knit a pair of stockings, for which she gave me a quart of peas: I boiled my peas and bear together, and invited my master and mistress to dinner, but the proud gossip, because I served them both in one dish, would eat nothing, except one bit that he gave her upon the point of his knife. . . .

## The Move to the Ashuelot Valley, New Hampshire

But instead of going either to Albany or homeward, we must go five miles up the river, and then go over it. Here we abode awhile. Here lived a sorry Indian, who spoke to me to make him a shirt. When I had done it, he would pay me nothing. But he living by the riverside, where I often went to fetch water, I would often be putting of him in mind, and calling for my pay: At last he told me if I would make another shirt, for a papoose not yet born, he would give me a knife, which he did when I had done it. I carried the knife in, and my master asked me to give it him, and I was not a little glad that I had anything that they would accept of, and be pleased with. When we were at this place, my master's maid came home, she had been gone three weeks into the Narragansett country, to fetch corn, where they had stored up some in the ground: She brought home about a peck and half of corn. This was about the time that their great captain, Naananto, was killed in the Narragansett country. My son being now about a mile from me, I asked liberty to go and see him, they bade me go, and away I went: but quickly lost myself, traveling over hills and through swamps, and could not find the way to him. And I cannot but admire at the wonderful power and goodness of God to me, in that, though I was gone from home, and met with all sorts of Indians, and those I had no knowledge of, and there being no Christian soul near me; yet not one of them offered the least imaginable miscarriage to me. I turned homeward again, and met with my master, he showed me the way to my son. . . .

But I was fain[11] to go and look after something to satisfy my hunger, and going among the wigwams, I went into one, and there found a squaw who showed herself very kind to me, and gave me a piece of bear. I put it into my pocket, and came home, but could not find an opportunity to broil it, for fear they would get it from me, and there it lay all that day and night in my stinking pocket. In the morning I went to the same squaw, who had a kettle of groundnuts boiling; I asked her to let me boil my piece of bear in her kettle, which she did, and gave me some groundnuts to eat with it: And I cannot but think how pleasant it was to me. I have sometime seen bear baked very handsomely among the English, and some like it, but the thoughts that it was bear, made me tremble: But now that was savory to me that one would think was enough to turn the stomach of a brute creature.

One bitter cold day, I could find no room to sit down before the fire: I went out, and could not tell what to do, but I went in to another wigwam, where they were also sitting round the fire, but the squaw laid a skin for me, and bid me sit down, and gave me some groundnuts, and bade me come again: and told me they would buy me, if they were able, and yet these were strangers to me that I never saw before. . . . ■

10. *sannup* (san′up′) *n.:* husband.

11. **fain** *adj.:* archaic word meaning "glad; ready."

# Response and Analysis

## Reading Check

1. List in **chronological order** the main events of Rowlandson's narrative.

2. How is Rowlandson treated by her captors?

3. Find details that reveal that Rowlandson's captors are themselves desperate to find food.

## Thinking Critically

4. What conflicting attitudes, if any, does Rowlandson reveal toward her captors? Do you think her attitude changes as the narrative progresses? Explain.

*I hated at 1st then likes hor*

5. The Puritans' habit of seeing spiritual meanings in their experiences helped them find significance in even minor events. Describe at least two **allusions** to biblical stories that Rowlandson makes during her captivity. In what specific ways does each of these biblical stories resemble Rowlandson's experiences?

*Psalms and quotes - onom*

6. Rowlandson's narrative was enormously popular in England. What reasons can you propose for its popularity? What aspects of Rowlandson's narrative might have promoted stereotyped and hostile views toward American Indians?

## Extending and Evaluating

7. Despite her efforts to be accurate, Rowlandson's narrative is full of **subjective reporting.** Instead of using neutral language, she relies on emotionally loaded words—words with strong positive or negative **connotations.** Select any extract from Rowlandson's narrative, and find the emotionally loaded words or phrases that reveal her attitude toward her captors. What words or phrases does Rowlandson use that a detached, objective historian would *not* use?

*She things she says as subjective reporting / connotations are: look of page 38*

## WRITING

### Survival Skills

In his classic work of psychology, *Man's Search for Meaning,* Viktor Frankl, a survivor of the Nazi concentration camps of World War II, claims that survival in the camps depended less on physical endurance and general health than on an internal sense that the experience, no matter how horrifying, had some ultimate meaning for the prisoner. Those who had strong religious faith, committed political views, or even just a strong love of family were far more likely to survive, both physically and mentally. In a brief **essay,** identify and discuss Mary Rowlandson's ultimate source of strength. How does her story compare with other captivity stories you've read or seen dramatized on TV? Be sure to provide details from Rowlandson's account in your response.

*Puritain vision & talks about god a lot and relates him to her daily life*

---

## Vocabulary Development

### Synonyms

Match each Vocabulary word from the list below with the word that is closest in meaning. When you have finished matching, find the place in the text where the Vocabulary word is underlined. Can its synonym be substituted for Mary Rowlandson's original word, or are there subtle distinctions between the meanings of the two words?

| | |
|---|---|
| 1. tedious | asked |
| 2. lamentable | delicious |
| 3. entreated | enchanting |
| 4. afflictions | hardships |
| 5. plunder | loot |
| 6. melancholy | sad |
| 7. savory | tiresome |
| 8. bewitching | unfortunate |

**SKILLS FOCUS**

**Literary Skills**
Analyze allusions.

**Reading Skills**
Analyze chronological order.

**Writing Skills**
Write an essay analyzing a narrative.

**Vocabulary Skills**
Understand synonyms.

**go. hrw .com**

**INTERNET**
Projects and Activities
Keyword: LE7 11-1

# Jonathan Edwards
## (1703–1758)

**D**espite his fire-and-brimstone imagery, Jonathan Edwards was not merely a stern, zealous preacher. He was a brilliant, thoughtful, and complicated man. Science, reason, and observation of the physical world confirmed Edwards's deeply spiritual vision of a universe filled with the presence of God.

Edwards's abilities were recognized early. Groomed to succeed his grandfather as pastor of the Congregational Church in Northampton, Massachusetts, Edwards entered Yale when he was only thirteen. When his grandfather died in 1729, Edwards mounted the pulpit and quickly established himself as a strong-willed and charismatic pastor.

Edwards's formidable presence and vivid sermons helped to bring about the religious revival known as the Great Awakening. This revival began in Northampton in the 1730s and, during the next fifteen years, spread throughout the Eastern Seaboard. The Great Awakening was marked by waves of conversions that were so intensely emotional as to amount at times to mass hysteria.

The Great Awakening began at a time when enthusiasm for the old Puritan religion was declining. To offset the losses in their congregations, churches had been accepting growing numbers of "unregenerate" Christians—people who accepted church doctrine and lived upright lives but who had not confessed to being born again in God's grace, and so were not considered to be saved.

Edwards became known for his extremism as a pastor. In his sermons he didn't hesitate to accuse prominent church members by name of relapsing into sin. Edwards's strictness eventually proved to be too much for his congregation, and in 1750, he was dismissed from

*Reverend Jonathan Edwards* (1750–1755) by Joseph Badger. Oil on canvas (28½″ × 22″).

his prestigious position as pastor of Northampton. After rejecting a number of pastorships offered to him, Edwards relocated to the raw and remote Mohican community of Stockbridge, Massachusetts. After eight years of missionary work in virtual exile, shared with his wife, Sarah, Edwards was named president of the College of New Jersey (later called Princeton University). Three months after assuming this position, he died of a smallpox inoculation—a modern medical procedure that, ironically, had been promoted by the fierce Puritan minister Cotton Mather.

Intellectually, Edwards straddled two ages: the modern, secular world exemplified by such men as Benjamin Franklin (page 67) and the religious world of his zealous Puritan ancestors. He believed (like Franklin) in reason and learning, the value of independent intellect, and the power of the human will. On the other hand, he believed (like Mather) in the lowliness of human beings in relation to God's majesty and in the ultimate futility of merely human efforts to achieve salvation. Edwards, as "the last Puritan," stood between Puritan America and modern America. Tragically, he fit into neither world.

# Before You Read

## *from* Sinners in the Hands of an Angry God

### Make the Connection
#### Quickwrite ✏️

Many people would agree that fear is one of the most powerful motivators of human behavior. Fear of injury makes us buckle our seat belts. Fear of failure makes us study or work harder. Edwards and other pastors used harsh warnings in their sermons to make "sinners" understand the precariousness of their situation by actually *feeling* the fear and horror of their sinful state. Do you think fear is a great motivator? Take a few moments to write about what motivates you and whether you would use fear to motivate someone else.

### Literary Focus
#### Figures of Speech

**Figures of speech** describe one thing in terms of another, very different thing. Although Edwards's belief in eternal damnation is literal, he uses figures of speech to compare God's wrath to ordinary, everyday things that his listeners could relate to and understand.

> **Figures of speech** are words or phrases that compare one thing to another, unlike thing.
>
> *For more on Figures of Speech, see the Handbook of Literary and Historical Terms.*

### Background

This is Edwards's most famous sermon, which he delivered on a visit to the congregation at Enfield, Connecticut, in 1741. The "natural men" he was trying to awaken were those in the congregation who had not been "born again," meaning they had not accepted Jesus as their savior. Edwards was influenced by the work of the English philosopher John Locke (1632–1704). Locke believed that everything we know comes from experience, and he emphasized that understanding and feeling were two distinct kinds of knowledge. (To Edwards the difference between these two kinds of knowledge was like the difference between reading the word *fire* and actually being burned.) Edwards's sermon had a powerful effect; several times he had to ask his shrieking and swooning audience for quiet.

### Vocabulary Development

**provoked** (prə·vōkt′) *v.* used as *adj.*: angered.

**appease** (ə·pēz′) *v.*: calm; satisfy.

**constitution** (kän′stə·too′shən) *n.*: physical condition.

**contrivance** (kən·trī′vəns) *n.*: scheme; plan.

**inconceivable** (in′kən·sēv′ə·bəl) *adj.*: unimaginable; beyond understanding.

**omnipotent** (äm·nip′ə·tənt) *adj.*: all-powerful.

**abhors** (ab·hôrz′) *v.*: scorns; hates.

**abominable** (ə·bäm′ə·nə·bəl) *adj.*: disgusting; loathsome.

**ascribed** (ə·skrībd′) *v.*: regarded as coming from a certain cause.

**induce** (in·doos′) *v.*: persuade; force; cause.

**Literary Skills**
Understand figures of speech.

**INTERNET**
Vocabulary Practice
Keyword: LE7 11-1

*from*

# Sinners in the Hands of an Angry God

### Jonathan Edwards

So that, thus it is that natural men[1] are held in the hand of God, over the pit of hell; they have deserved the fiery pit, and are already sentenced to it; and God is dreadfully <u>provoked</u>, His anger is as great toward them as to those that are actually suffering the executions of the fierceness of His wrath in hell, and they have done nothing in the least to <u>appease</u> or abate[2] that anger, neither is God in the least bound by any promise to hold them up one moment: The devil is waiting for them, hell is gaping for them, the flames gather and flash about them,  and would fain[3] lay hold on them, and swallow them up; the fire pent up in

> **❶**
> Note how Edwards uses **parallelism** in these lines: "The devil is waiting for them, hell is gaping for them, the flames gather and flash about them."
> **❓** *How does the parallel structure build a sense of horror?*

---

1. **natural men:** people who have not been "reborn."
2. **abate** *v.:* reduce in amount or intensity.
3. **fain** *adv.:* archaic word meaning "happily" or "gladly."

---

**Vocabulary**

**provoked** (prə·vōkt′) *v.* used as *adj.:* angered.
**appease** (ə·pēz′) *v.:* calm; satisfy.

*The Progress of Sin* (detail) (1744) by Benjamin Keach.

Sinclair Hamilton Collection. Department of Rare Books and Special Collections. Princeton University Library.

their own hearts is struggling to break out: And they have no interest in any Mediator,[4] there are no means within reach that can be any security to them.

In short, they have no refuge, nothing to take hold of; all that preserves them every moment is the mere arbitrary will, and uncovenanted, unobliged forbearance[5] of an incensed[6] God.

The use of this awful subject may be for awakening unconverted persons in this congregation. This that you have heard is the case of every one of you that are out of Christ. ❷ That world of misery, that lake of burning brimstone, is extended abroad under you. There is the dreadful pit of the glowing flames of the wrath of God; there is hell's wide gaping mouth open; and you have nothing to stand upon, nor anything to take hold of; there is nothing between you and hell but the air; it is only the power and mere pleasure of God that holds you up.

You probably are not sensible of this; you find you are kept out of hell, but do not see the hand of God in it; but look at other things, as the good state of your bodily <u>constitution</u>, your care of your own life, and the <u>means</u> you use for your own preservation. But indeed these things are nothing; if God should withdraw His hand, they would avail no more to keep you from falling, than the thin air to hold up a person that is suspended in it.

Your wickedness makes you as it were heavy as lead, and to tend downward with great weight and pressure toward hell; and if God should let you go, you would immediately sink and swiftly descend and plunge into the bottomless gulf, and your healthy constitution, and your own care and prudence, and best <u>contrivance</u>, and all your righteousness, would

❷

❓ *Whom does Edwards address in his sermon, and what does he hope it will accomplish?*

have no more influence to uphold you and keep you out of hell, than a spider's web would have to stop a fallen rock.... ❸

The wrath of God is like great waters that are dammed for the present; they increase more and more, and rise higher and higher, till an outlet is given; and the longer the stream is stopped, the more rapid and mighty is its course, when once it is let loose. It is true, that judgment against your evil works has not been executed hitherto; the floods of God's vengeance have been withheld; but your guilt in the meantime is constantly increasing, and you are every day treasuring up more wrath; the waters are constantly rising, and waxing more and more mighty; and there is nothing but the mere pleasure of God that holds the waters back, that are unwilling to be stopped, and press hard to go forward. If God should only withdraw His hand from the floodgate, it would immediately fly open, and the fiery floods of the fierceness and wrath of God, would rush forth with <u>inconceivable</u> fury, and would come upon you with <u>omnipotent</u> power; and if your strength were ten thousand times greater than it is, yea, ten thousand times greater than the strength of the stoutest, sturdiest devil in hell, it would be nothing to withstand or endure it.

The bow of God's wrath is bent, and the arrow made ready on the string, and justice bends the arrow at your heart, and strains the bow, and it is nothing but the mere pleasure of God, and that of an angry God, without any promise or obligation at all, that keeps the arrow one moment from being made drunk

❸

Edwards uses a **metaphor** here to dramatize human powerlessness: People who think they can escape Hell on their own have as little chance of doing so as a spider's web has of stopping a falling rock.

---

**Vocabulary**

**constitution** (kän′stə·tōō′shən) *n.*: physical condition.

**contrivance** (kən·trī′vəns) *n.*: scheme; plan.

**inconceivable** (in′kən·sēv′ə·bəl) *adj.*: unimaginable; beyond understanding.

**omnipotent** (äm·nip′ə·tənt) *adj.*: all-powerful.

---

4. **Mediator:** Jesus Christ. In general, one who intervenes between two parties in conflict.

5. **forbearance** *n.*: tolerance or restraint.

6. **incensed** *v.* used as *adj.*: angered; enraged.

with your blood. ❹  Thus all you that never passed under a great change of heart, by the mighty power of the Spirit of God upon your souls; all you that were never born again, and made new creatures, and raised from being dead in sin, to a state of new, and before altogether unexperienced light and life, are in the hands of an angry God. However you may have reformed your life in many things, and may have had religious affections,[7] and may keep up a form of religion in your families and closets,[8] and in the house of God, it is nothing but His mere pleasure that keeps you from being this moment swallowed up in everlasting destruction. However unconvinced you may now be of the truth of what you hear, by and by you will be fully convinced of it. ❺  Those that are gone from being in the like circumstances with you, see that it was so with them; for destruction came suddenly upon most of them; when they expected nothing of it, and while they were saying, peace and safety: Now they see, that those things on which they depended for peace and safety, were nothing but thin air and empty shadows.

The God that holds you over the pit of hell, much as one holds a spider, or some loathsome insect over the fire, abhors you, and is dreadfully provoked: His wrath toward you burns like fire; He looks upon you as worthy of nothing else but to be cast into the fire; He is of purer eyes than to bear to have you in His sight; you are ten thousand times more abominable in His eyes than the most hateful venomous serpent is in ours. ❻  You have offended Him infinitely more than

❹
Edwards uses a **metaphor** to describe God's wrath. Explain this metaphor in your own words.

❺
**?** What main point does Edwards want his listeners to understand? Who or what does he say will convince them?

❻
**?** What two creatures does Edwards compare sinners to in this passage?

7. **affections** *n. pl.:* feelings.
8. **closets** *n. pl.:* rooms for prayer and meditation.

ever a stubborn rebel did his prince; and yet it is nothing but His hand that holds you from falling into the fire every moment. It is to be ascribed to nothing else, that you did not go to hell the last night; that you was suffered to awake again in this world, after you closed your eyes to sleep. And there is no other reason to be given, why you have not dropped into hell since you arose in the morning, but that God's hand has held you up. There is no other reason to be given why you have not gone to hell, since you have sat here in the house of God, provoking His pure eyes by your sinful wicked manner of attending His solemn worship. Yea, there is nothing else that is to be given as a reason why you do not this very moment drop down into hell. ❼

O sinner! Consider the fearful danger you are in: It is a great furnace of wrath, a wide and bottomless pit, full of the fire of wrath, that you are held over in the hand of that God, whose wrath is provoked and incensed as much against you, as against many of the damned in hell. You hang by a slender thread, with the flames of divine wrath flashing about it, and ready every moment to singe it, and burn it asunder;[9] and you have no interest in any Mediator, and nothing to lay hold of to save yourself, nothing to keep off the flames of wrath, nothing of your own, nothing that you ever have done, nothing that you can do, to induce God to spare you one moment. . . . ❽

❼
Here Edwards repeats one of his **main ideas:** that the only reason his listeners have not fallen into the fires of Hell is that God has held them up.

❽
**?** How does Edwards use **repetition** to increase the emotional effect of his sermon?

9. **asunder** *adv.:* into pieces.

**Vocabulary**
**abhors** (ab·hôrz′) *v.:* scorns; hates.
**abominable** (ə·bäm′ə·nə·bəl) *adj.:* disgusting; loathsome.
**ascribed** (ə·skrībd′) *v.:* regarded as coming from a certain cause.
**induce** (in·do͞os′) *v.:* persuade; force; cause.

It is *everlasting* wrath. It would be dreadful to suffer this fierceness and wrath of Almighty God one moment; but you must suffer it to all eternity. There will be no end to this exquisite horrible misery. When you look forward, you shall see a long forever, a boundless duration before you, which will swallow up your thoughts and amaze your soul; and you will absolutely despair of ever having any deliverance, any end, any mitigation, any rest at all. You will know certainly that you must wear out long ages, millions of millions of ages, in wresting and conflicting with this almighty merciless vengeance; and then when you have so done, when so many ages have actually been spent by you in this manner, you will know that all is but a point to what remains. So that your punishment will indeed be infinite. Oh, who can express what the state of a soul in such circumstances is! All that we can possibly say about it gives but a very feeble, faint representation of it; it is inexpressible and inconceivable: For "who knows the power of God's anger?" ❾

How dreadful is the state of those that are daily and hourly in the danger of this great wrath and infinite misery! But this is the dismal case of every soul in this congregation that has not been born again, however moral and strict, sober and religious, they may otherwise be. Oh, that you would consider it, whether you be young or old! There is reason to think, that there are many in this congregation now hearing this discourse that will actually be the subjects of this very misery to all eternity. We know not who they are, or in what seats they sit, or what thoughts they now have. It may be they are now at ease, and hear

❾ What details in Edwards's description help his listeners understand the concept of eternity?

In Memory of 4 Children of Capt. JOHN & Mrs. JANE GULIKE who are here Interr'd Viz JOHN GULIKER Junr who died o 3d Augt 1770 Aged 13 Day

all these things without much disturbance, and are now flattering themselves that they are not the persons, promising themselves that they shall escape. If we knew that there was one person, and but one, in the whole congregation that was to be the subject of this misery, what an awful thing would it be to think of! If we knew who it was, what an awful sight would it be to see such a person! How might all the rest of the congregation lift up a lamentable and bitter cry over him! But, alas! Instead of one, how many is it likely will remember this discourse in hell? And it would be a wonder if some that are now present should not be in hell in a very short time, even before this year is out. And it would be no wonder if some persons that now sit here, in some seats of this meetinghouse, in health, quiet, and secure, should be there before tomorrow morning. Those of you that finally continue in a natural condition, that shall keep out of hell longest, will be there in a little time! Your damnation does not slumber; it will come swiftly and, in all probability, very suddenly upon many of you. You have reason to wonder that you are not already in hell. It is doubtless the case of some whom you have seen and known that never deserved hell more than you, and that heretofore appeared as likely to have been now alive as you. Their case is past all hope; they are crying in extreme misery and perfect despair. But here you are in the land of the living and in the house of God, and have an opportunity to obtain salvation. What would not those poor damned hopeless souls give for one day's opportunity such as you now enjoy!

And now you have an extraordinary opportunity, a day wherein Christ has thrown the door of mercy wide open, and stands in calling and crying with a loud voice to poor sinners; a day wherein many are flocking to him, and pressing into the kingdom of God. Many are daily coming from the east, west, north, and south; many that were very lately in the same miserable condition that you are in are now in a happy state, with their hearts filled with love to him who has loved them and washed them from their sins in his own blood, and rejoicing in hope of the glory of God. How awful is it to be left behind at such a day! To see so many others feasting, while you are pining and perishing! To see so many rejoicing and singing for joy of heart, while you have cause to mourn for sorrow of heart, and howl for vexation of spirit! How can you rest one moment in such a condition? . . . **10**

**10**

**?** *What comparison does Edwards make between those who have accepted Christ's love and those who have not?*

Therefore, let everyone that is out of Christ now awake and fly from the wrath to come. The wrath of Almighty God is now undoubtedly hanging over a great part of this congregation: let everyone fly out of Sodom.[10] "Haste and escape for your lives, look not behind you, escape to the mountain, lest you be consumed."[11]

---

10. **Sodom:** in the Bible, a city so wicked that God destroyed it, sparing only one man, Lot, and his family.
11. **"Haste and escape . . . lest you be consumed":** from Genesis 19:17, the words spoken by an angel of God to Lot, warning him to flee Sodom and never look back.

# Response and Analysis

## Reading Check

1. Find the direct statement in which Edwards sets forth the **purpose** of his sermon.

2. According to the sermon, what keeps sinners out of the fiery "pit of hell"?

3. Identify the three famous **figures of speech** that Edwards develops in the fourth through seventh paragraphs. What things is he comparing in each one?

## Thinking Critically

4. What references in the sermon reveal Edwards's implicit philosophical beliefs about divine mercy?

5. What **images** and **figures of speech** might have helped Edwards's listeners to *feel* the peril of their sinful condition?

6. Edwards struck fear into the hearts of his listeners in order to persuade them to act to avoid everlasting torment. Which specific **metaphors** and **similes** in the sermon were probably the most persuasive?

7. At the end of his sermon, what do you think Edwards means when he says that the "door of mercy" is wide open? What effect might this hope of God's mercy have had on his listeners?

## Extending and Evaluating

8. If you had a chance to respond to Edwards, what would you say?

9. Edwards believed that fear was a great motivator, yet many philosophers and politicians have disagreed. For example, President Franklin Delano Roosevelt, in his first inaugural address, made this famous comment about fear: "The only thing we have to fear is fear itself." What do you think of the use of fear as a motivator? Before you answer, look back at your Quickwrite notes. What motivation might work better than fear? ✏️

## WRITING

### The Tone of the Time

Edwards's fiery words were delivered to the congregation of a church he was visiting. What is Edwards's **tone**, or attitude toward his audience, and what effect does this attitude have on his listeners? Consider how Edwards's sermon would differ if he had chosen a different style or diction. Write a brief **essay** in which you analyze Edwards's tone and then consider what would happen if that tone were different. Would the sermon be as effective?

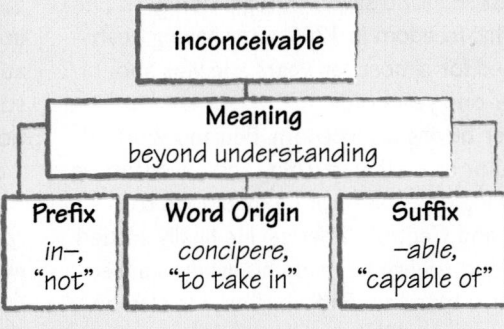

### Vocabulary Development
#### Prefixes and Suffixes

provoked    contrivance    abominable

appease    omnipotent    ascribed

constitution    abhors    induce

Just a few letters tacked onto the beginning of a word (a **prefix**) or the end of a word (a **suffix**) can change its meaning and often its part of speech. When you find an unfamiliar word, look for prefixes and suffixes that provide clues to how the base form of the word changes. Keep in mind that –s, –ed, and –ing are inflectional suffixes (suffixes that indicate the tense or case of a word rather than changing its meaning). Fill out a chart like the one below for each remaining Vocabulary word. Consult a dictionary to find the origins of words and the meanings of prefixes and suffixes.

| inconceivable | | |
| --- | --- | --- |
| **Meaning** *beyond understanding* | | |
| **Prefix** *in–*, "not" | **Word Origin** *concipere*, "to take in" | **Suffix** *–able*, "capable of" |

**SKILLS FOCUS**

**Literary Skills**
Analyze figures of speech.

**Writing Skills**
Write an essay analyzing tone.

**Vocabulary Skills**
Understand prefixes and suffixes.

**INTERNET**

Projects and Activities

Keyword: LE7 11-1

# Olaudah Equiano
## (c. 1745–1797)

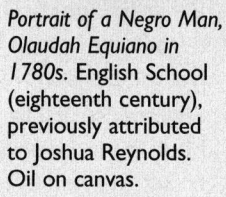

Olaudah Equiano (ō·lōō′dä ek′wē·än′ō) was the first African writer to reach a sizable audience of American readers. A member of the Ibo people, Equiano was born in a part of West Africa that is now Nigeria. When he was only eleven years old, Equiano, along with his sister, was kidnapped from his home by African raiders involved in the slave trade. Over a period of six or seven months, during which he and his sister were separated, the slave traders took Equiano to a series of way stations. When he reached the coast, Equiano was put aboard one of the infamous slave ships bound for Barbados, an island in the West Indies, in the Caribbean. There was a great demand for slaves to work on the sugar plantations in the Caribbean. In his narrative, Equiano vividly describes this cruel and horrifying part of the slave route, which was known as the Middle Passage.

After a short stay in Barbados, Equiano was sold to a British military officer, who gave him the name Gustavus Vassa, after a Swedish king. Equiano served with this officer during the Seven Years' War between England and France and gained great skill as a seaman. In time a Quaker merchant from Philadelphia purchased Equiano. From his own profitable business ventures while managing his master's business, Equiano saved enough money to purchase his freedom in 1766, after having been enslaved for almost ten years. He was about twenty-one years old.

After buying his freedom, Equiano worked as a sailor and led an exciting and adventurous life, sailing on exploratory expeditions to the Arctic and Central America. He finally settled in England, where he made his living as a free servant, a musician, and a barber. He also became active in the antislavery movement. In 1781, the captain of the *Zong*, which was transporting more than four hundred Africans to Jamaica, threw a third of the shackled captives overboard in order to collect the insurance. In 1783, Equiano was instrumental in bringing this atrocity to the attention of the public and the British naval authorities. When the abolition of the slave trade became a hotly debated issue in the English Parliament, Equiano actively campaigned against slavery, writing letters to officials and newspapers and visiting abolitionist leaders.

Equiano's autobiography, published in England in 1789, was titled *The Interesting Narrative of the Life of Olaudah Equiano, or Gustavus Vassa, the African*. Reprinted in New York in 1791, the book—considered the first great black autobiography—proved popular with readers in the United States as well as abroad. The author's account of the horrors he suffered struck a responsive chord with northern abolitionists. In 1792, Equiano married an Englishwoman, Susanna Cullen.

Though Equiano traveled widely, he never returned to the United States. Nor did he ever again see his native Africa, to which he dreamed of returning. He defined himself, to the end of his life, simply as "the African."

*Portrait of a Negro Man, Olaudah Equiano in 1780s*. English School (eighteenth century), previously attributed to Joshua Reynolds. Oil on canvas.

Royal Albert Memorial Museum, Exeter, Devon, UK/Bridgeman Art Library.

# Before You Read

## from The Interesting Narrative of the Life of Olaudah Equiano

### Make the Connection
#### Quickwrite ✏️

The first Africans in the Americas were unwilling immigrants who arrived on slave ships before 1600. Between the seventeenth and nineteenth centuries, about ten million people were captured in Africa and shipped to North and South America and the islands of the West Indies, where they were sold as slaves.

Before you read Equiano's account, make a KWL chart like the one below. Fill out the first two columns—what you already know about slavery and the slave trade in the eighteenth century and what you'd like to learn about it. Leave the third column blank.

| K<br>What I<br>Know | W<br>What I Want<br>to Know | L<br>What I<br>Learned |
|---|---|---|
| | | |

### Literary Focus
#### Autobiography

Equiano's **autobiography** was one of the first of a number of slave narratives, so called because they were firsthand accounts written by ex-slaves. The publication of these narratives was encouraged by abolitionists in the nineteenth century to fuel the crusade against slavery.

> An **autobiography** is a firsthand account of the writer's own life.
>
> *For more on Autobiography, see the Handbook of Literary and Historical Terms.*

### Reading Skills
#### Making Inferences About an Author's Beliefs

An **inference** is an educated guess based on what you already know and what you learn from reading a text. To make an inference, you look beyond what's being stated directly in a text and think about what is implicit, or hinted at. As you read, be alert for phrases or passages that give you insight into an author's beliefs about a subject. What do you think are Equiano's philosophical or fundamental beliefs about human cruelty?

### Vocabulary Development

**assailant** (ə·sāl′ənt) *n.*: attacker.

**distraction** (di·strak′shən) *n.*: mental disturbance or distress.

**apprehensions** (ap′rē·hen′shənz) *n. pl.*: feelings of anxiety or dread.

**alleviate** (ə·lē′vē·āt′) *v.*: relieve; reduce.

**interspersed** (in′tər·spʉrst′) *v.* used as *adj.*: placed at intervals.

**commodious** (kə·mō′dē·əs) *adj.*: spacious.

**consternation** (kän′stər·nā′shən) *n.*: confusion resulting from fear or shock.

**improvident** (im·präv′ə·dənt) *adj.*: careless; not providing for the future.

**avarice** (av′ə·ris) *n.*: greed.

*Slave Deck of the* Albanoz (1843–1847) by Lt. Francis Meynell. Watercolor on paper.
© National Maritime Museum, London.

*from* The Interesting
Narrative *of the* Life *of*
Olaudah Equiano

Olaudah Equiano

# Kidnapped

**M**y father, besides many slaves, had a numerous family of which seven lived to grow up, including myself and a sister who was the only daughter. As I was the youngest of the sons I became, of course, the greatest favorite with my mother and was always with her; and she used to take particular pains to form my mind. I was trained up from my earliest years in the art of war, my daily exercise was shooting and throwing javelins, and my mother adorned me with emblems after the manner of our greatest warriors. In this way I grew up till I was turned the age of 11, when an end was put to my happiness in the following manner. Generally when the grown people in the neighborhood were gone far in the fields to labor, the children assembled together in some of the neighbors' premises to play, and commonly some of us used to get up a tree to look for any assailant or kidnapper that might come upon us, for they sometimes took those opportunities of our parents' absence to attack and carry off as many as they could seize. One day, as I was watching at the top of a tree in our yard, I saw one of those people come into the yard of our next neighbor but one to kidnap, there being many stout young people in it. Immediately on this I gave the alarm of the rogue[1] and he was surrounded by the stoutest of them, who entangled him with cords so that he could not escape till some of the grown people came and secured him.

But alas! ere long it was my fate to be thus attacked and to be carried off when none of the grown people were nigh. One day, when all our people were gone out to their works as usual and only I and my dear sister were left to mind the house, two men and a woman got over our walls, and in a moment seized us both, and without giving us time to cry out or make resistance they stopped our mouths and ran off with us into the nearest wood. Here they tied our hands and continued to carry us as far as they could till night came on, when we reached a small house where the robbers halted for refreshment and spent the night. We were then unbound but were unable to take any food, and being quite overpowered by fatigue and grief, our only relief was some sleep, which allayed our misfortune for a short time. The next morning we left the house and continued traveling all the day. For a long time we had kept to the woods, but at last we came into a road which I believed I knew. I had now some hopes of being delivered, for we had advanced but a little way before I discovered some people at a distance, on which I began to cry out for

---

1. **rogue** *n.*: rascal; scoundrel.

---

**Vocabulary**
**assailant** (ə·sāl′ənt) *n.*: attacker.

assistance: But my cries had no other effect than to make them tie me faster and stop my mouth, and then they put me into a large sack. They also stopped my sister's mouth and tied her hands, and in this manner we proceeded till we were out of the sight of these people.

When we went to rest the following night they offered us some victuals, but we refused it, and the only comfort we had was in being in one another's arms all that night and bathing each other with our tears. But alas! we were soon deprived of even the small comfort of weeping together. The next day proved a day of greater sorrow than I had yet experienced, for my sister and I were then separated while we lay clasped in each other's arms. It was in vain that we besought them not to part us; she was torn from me and immediately carried away, while I was left in a state of <u>distraction</u> not to be described. I cried and <u>grieved</u> continually, and for several days I did not eat anything but what they forced into my mouth. At length, after many days' traveling, during which I had often changed masters, I got into the hands of a chieftain in a very pleasant country. This man had two wives and some children, and they all used me extremely well and did all they could to comfort me, particularly the first wife, who was something like my mother. Although I was a great many days' journey from my father's house, yet these people spoke exactly the same language with us. This first master of mine, as I may call him, was a smith, and my principal employment was working his bellows,[2] which were the same kind as I had seen in my vicinity. They were in some respects not unlike the stoves here in gentlemen's kitchens, and were covered over with leather; and in the middle of that leather a stick was fixed, and a person stood up and worked it in the same manner as is done to pump water out of a cask with a hand pump. I believe it was gold he worked, for it was of a lovely bright yellow color and was worn by the women on their wrists and ankles. . . .

Soon after this my master's only daughter and child by his first wife sickened and died, which affected him so much that for some time he was almost frantic, and really would have killed himself had he not been watched and prevented. However, in a small time afterward he recovered and I was again sold. I was now carried to the left of the sun's rising, through many different countries and a number of large woods. The people I was sold to used to carry me very often when I was tired either on their shoulders or on their backs. I saw many convenient well-built sheds along the roads at proper distances, to accommodate the merchants and travelers who lay in those buildings along with their wives, who often accompany them; and they always go well armed.

From the time I left my own nation I always found somebody that understood me till I came to the seacoast. The languages of different nations did not totally differ, nor were they so copious[3] as those of the Europeans, particularly the English. They were therefore easily learned, and while I was journeying thus through Africa I acquired two or three different tongues. In this manner I had been traveling for a considerable time, when one evening, to my great surprise, whom should I see brought to the house where I was but my dear sister! As soon as she saw me she gave a loud shriek and ran into my arms—I was quite overpowered: Neither of us could speak, but for a considerable time clung to each other in mutual embraces, unable to do anything but weep. Our meeting affected all who saw us, and indeed I must acknowledge, in honor of those sable destroyers of human rights, that I never met with any ill-treatment or saw any offered to their slaves except tying them, when necessary, to keep them from running away.

When these people knew we were brother and sister they indulged us to be together, and

3. **copious** *adj.:* here, wordy.

2. **bellows** *n.:* device that produces a strong air current, used for blowing fires.

**Vocabulary**
**distraction** (di·strak′shən) *n.:* mental disturbance or distress.

the man to whom I supposed we belonged lay with us, he in the middle while she and I held one another by the hands across his breast all night; and thus for a while we forgot our misfortunes in the joy of being together: But even this small comfort was soon to have an end, for scarcely had the fatal morning appeared when she was again torn from me forever! I was now more miserable, if possible, than before. The small relief which her presence gave me from pain was gone, and the wretchedness of my situation was redoubled by my anxiety after her fate and my apprehensions lest her sufferings should be greater than mine, when I could not be with her to alleviate them. . . .

I did not long remain after my sister. I was again sold and carried through a number of places till, after traveling a considerable time, I came to a town called Tinmah in the most beautiful country I had yet seen in Africa. It was extremely rich, and there were many rivulets which flowed through it and supplied a large pond in the center of town, where the people washed. Here I first saw and tasted coconuts, which I thought superior to any nuts I had ever tasted before; and the trees, which were loaded, were also interspersed amongst the houses, which had commodious shades adjoining and were in the same manner as ours, the insides being neatly plastered and whitewashed. Here I also saw and tasted for the first time sugar cane. Their money consisted of little white shells the size of the fingernail. I was sold here for 172 of them by a merchant who lived and brought me there. I had been about two or three days at his house when a wealthy widow, a neighbor of his, came there one evening, and brought with her an only son, a young gentleman about my own age and size. Here they saw me; and, having taken a fancy to me, I was bought of the merchant, and went home with them. Her house and premises were situated close to one of those rivulets I have mentioned, and were the finest I ever saw in Africa: They were very extensive, and she had a number of slaves to attend her. The next day I was washed and perfumed, and when mealtime came I was led into the presence of my mistress, and ate and drank before her with her son. This filled me with astonishment; and I could scarce help expressing my surprise that the young gentleman should suffer me, who was bound, to eat with him who was free; and not only so, but that he would not at any time either eat or drink till I had taken first, because I was the eldest, which was agreeable to our custom. Indeed everything here, and all their treatment of me, made me forget that I was a slave. The language of these people resembled ours so nearly that we understood each other perfectly. They had also the very same customs as we. There were likewise slaves daily to attend us, while my young master and I with other boys sported with our darts and bows and arrows, as I had been used to do at home. In this resemblance to my former happy state I passed about two months; and I now began to think I was to be adopted into the family, and was beginning to be reconciled to my situation, and to forget by degrees my misfortunes, when all at once the delusion vanished; for without the least previous knowledge, one morning early, while my dear master and companion was still asleep, I was wakened out of my reverie to fresh sorrow, and hurried away even amongst the uncircumcised.

Thus at the very moment I dreamed of the greatest happiness, I found myself most miserable; and it seemed as if fortune wished to give me this taste of joy only to render the reverse more poignant. The change I now experienced was as painful as it was sudden and unexpected. It was a change indeed from a state of bliss to a scene which is inexpressible by me, as it discovered to me an element I had never before beheld and till then had no idea of, and wherein such instances of hardship and cruelty continually occurred as I can never reflect on but with horror. . . .

## Vocabulary

**apprehensions** (ap′rē·hen′shənz) *n. pl.:* feelings of anxiety or dread.

**alleviate** (ə·lē′vē·āt′) *v.:* relieve; reduce.

**interspersed** (in′tər·spʉrst′) *v.* used as *adj.:* placed at intervals.

**commodious** (kə·mō′dē·əs) *adj.:* spacious.

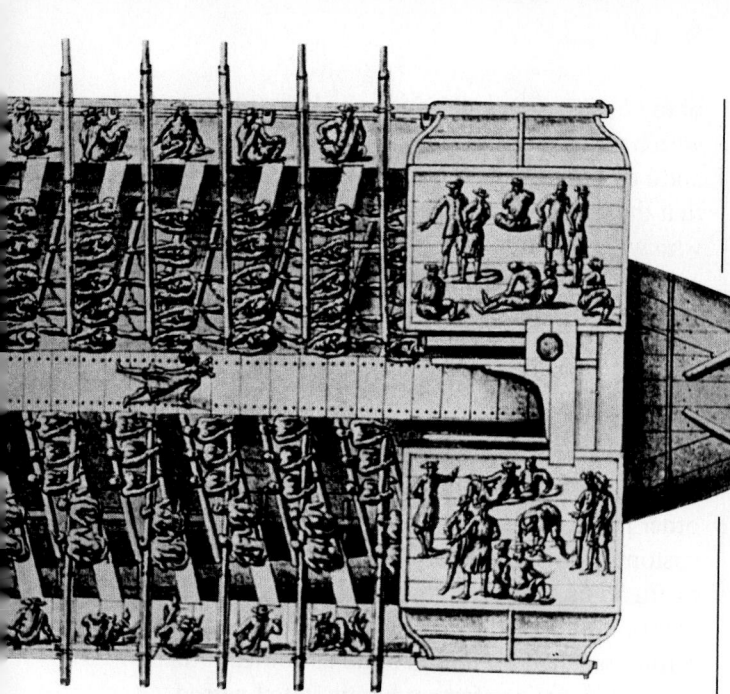

A slave ship manned by captives.

## The Slave Ship

The first object which saluted[4] my eyes when I arrived on the coast was the sea, and a slave ship which was then riding at anchor and waiting for its cargo. These filled me with astonishment, which was soon converted into terror when I was carried on board. I was immediately handled and tossed up to see if I were sound by some of the crew, and I was now persuaded that I had gotten into a world of bad spirits and that they were going to kill me. Their complexions too differing so much from ours, their long hair and the language they spoke (which was very different from any I had ever heard) united to confirm me in this belief. Indeed such were the horrors of my views and fears at the moment that, if ten thousand worlds had been my own, I would have freely parted with them all to have exchanged my condition with that of the meanest[5] slave in my own country. When I looked round the ship too and saw a large furnace or copper boiling and a multitude of black people of every description chained together, every one

of their countenances[6] expressing dejection and sorrow, I no longer doubted of my fate; and quite overpowered with horror and anguish, I fell motionless on the deck and fainted. When I recovered a little I found some black people about me, who I believed were some of those who had brought me on board and had been receiving their pay; they talked to me in order to cheer me, but all in vain. I asked them if we were not to be eaten by those white men with horrible looks, red faces, and loose hair. They told me I was not, and one of the crew brought me a small portion of spirituous liquor in a wineglass, but being afraid of him I would not take it out of his hand. One of the blacks therefore took it from him and gave it to me, and I took a little down my palate, which instead of reviving me, as they thought it would, threw me into the greatest consternation at the strange feeling it produced, having never tasted such any liquor before. Soon after this the blacks who brought me on board went off, and left me abandoned to despair.

I now saw myself deprived of all chance of returning to my native country or even the least glimpse of hope of gaining the shore, which I now considered as friendly; and I even wished for my former slavery in preference to my present situation, which was filled with horrors of every kind, still heightened by my ignorance of what I was to undergo. I was not long suffered to indulge my grief; I was soon put down under the decks, and there I received such a salutation in my nostrils as I had never experienced in my life: So that with the loathsomeness of the stench and crying together, I became so sick and low that I was not able to eat, nor had I the least desire to taste anything. I now wished for the last friend, death, to relieve me; but soon, to my grief, two of the white men offered me eatables,

---

4. **saluted** *v.:* met.
5. **meanest** *adj.:* lowest.

6. **countenances** *n. pl.:* faces.

**Vocabulary**

**consternation** (kän′stər·nā′shən) *n.:* confusion resulting from fear or shock.

and on my refusing to eat, one of them held me fast by the hands and laid me across, I think, the windlass,[7] and tied my feet while the other flogged[8] me severely. I had never experienced anything of this kind before, and although, not being used to the water, I naturally feared that element the first time I saw it, yet nevertheless could I have got over the nettings I would have jumped over the side, but I could not; and besides, the crew used to watch us very closely who were not chained down to the decks, lest we should leap into the water: And I have seen some of these poor African prisoners most severely cut for attempting to do so, and hourly whipped for not eating. This indeed was often the case with myself. In a little time after, amongst the poor chained men I found some of my own nation, which in a small degree gave ease to my mind. I inquired of these what was to be done with us; they gave me to understand we were to be carried to these white people's country to work for them. I then was a little revived, and thought if it were no worse than working, my situation was not so desperate: But still I feared I should be put to death, the white people looked and acted, as I thought, in so savage a manner; for I had never seen among my people such instances of brutal cruelty, and this not only shown toward us blacks but also to some of the whites themselves. One white man in particular I saw, when we were permitted to be on deck, flogged so unmercifully with a large rope near the foremast[9] that he died in consequence of it; and they tossed him over the side as they would have done a brute. This made me fear these people the more, and I expected nothing less than to be treated in the same manner. I could not help expressing my fears and apprehensions to some of my countrymen: I asked them if these people had no country but lived in this hollow place (the ship): They told me they did not, but came from a distant one. "Then,"

said I, "how comes it in all our country we never heard of them?" They told me because they lived so very far off. I then asked where were their women? Had they any like themselves? I was told they had: "And why," said I, "do we not see them?" They answered, because they were left behind. I asked how the vessel could go? They told me they could not tell, but that there were cloths put upon the masts by the help of the ropes I saw, and then the vessel went on; and the white men had some spell or magic they put in the water when they liked in order to stop the vessel. I was exceedingly amazed at this account and really thought they were spirits. I therefore wished much to be from amongst them for I expected they would sacrifice me: But my wishes were vain, for we were so quartered that it was impossible for any of us to make our escape.

While we stayed on the coast I was mostly on deck, and one day, to my great astonishment, I saw one of these vessels coming in with the sails up. As soon as the whites saw it they gave a great shout, at which we were amazed; and the more so as the vessel appeared larger by approaching nearer. At last she came to an anchor in my sight, and when the anchor was let go I and my countrymen who saw it were lost in astonishment to observe the vessel stop, and were now convinced it was done by magic. Soon after this the other ship got her boats out, and they came on board of us, and the people of both ships seemed very glad to see each other. Several of the strangers also shook hands with us black people, and made motions with their hands, signifying I suppose we were to go to their country; but we did not understand them. At last, when the ship we were in had got in all her cargo, they made ready with many fearful noises, and we were all put under deck so that we could not see how they managed the vessel.

But this disappointment was the least of my sorrow. The stench of the hold[10] while we were on the coast was so intolerably loathsome that it was dangerous to remain there for any time, and

---

7. **windlass** (wind′ləs) *n.:* device used to raise and lower heavy objects, like a ship's anchor.
8. **flogged** *v.:* beat with a rod or whip.
9. **foremast** *n.:* mast closest to the bow, or front, of a ship.

10. **hold** *n.:* enclosed area below a ship's deck, where cargo is usually stored.

some of us had been permitted to stay on the deck for the fresh air; but now that the whole ship's cargo were confined together it became absolutely pestilential.[11] The closeness of the place and the heat of the climate, added to the number in the ship, which was so crowded that each had scarcely room to turn himself, almost suffocated us. This produced copious perspirations, so that the air soon became unfit for respiration from a variety of loathsome smells, and brought on a sickness among the slaves, of which many died, thus falling victims to the improvident avarice, as I may call it, of their purchasers. This wretched situation was again aggravated by the galling of the chains, now become insupportable, and the filth of the necessary tubs,[12] into which the children often fell and were almost suffocated. The shrieks of the women and the groans of the dying rendered the whole a scene of horror almost inconceivable. Happily perhaps for myself I was soon reduced so low here that it was thought necessary to keep me almost always on deck, and from my extreme youth I was not put in fetters.[13] In this situation I expected every hour to share the fate of my companions, some of whom were almost daily brought upon deck at the point of death, which I began to hope would soon put an end to my miseries. Often did I think many of the inhabitants of the deep much more happy than myself. I envied them the freedom they enjoyed, and as often wished I could change my condition for theirs. Every circumstance I met with served only to render my state more painful, and heighten my apprehensions and my opinion of the cruelty of the whites. One day they had taken a number of fishes, and when they had killed and satisfied themselves with as many as they thought fit, to our astonishment who were on the deck, rather than give any of them to us to eat as we expected, they tossed the remaining fish into the sea again, although we begged and prayed for some as well as we could, but in vain;

and some of my countrymen, being pressed by hunger, took an opportunity when they thought no one saw them of trying to get a little privately; but they were discovered, and the attempt procured them some very severe floggings.

One day, when we had a smooth sea and moderate wind, two of my wearied countrymen who were chained together (I was near them at the time), preferring death to such a life of misery, somehow made through the nettings and jumped into the sea: Immediately another quite dejected fellow, who on account of his illness was suffered to be out of irons, also followed their example; and I believe many more would very soon have done the same if they had not been prevented by the ship's crew, who were instantly alarmed. Those of us that were the most active were in a moment put down under the deck, and there was such a noise and confusion amongst the people of the ship as I never heard before, to stop her and get the boat out to go after the slaves. However two of the wretches were drowned, but they got the other and afterward flogged him unmercifully for thus attempting to prefer death to slavery. In this manner we continued to undergo more hardships than I can now relate, hardships which are inseparable from this accursed trade. Many a time we were near suffocation from the want of fresh air, which we were often without for whole days together. This and the stench of the necessary tubs carried off many.

During our passage I first saw flying fishes, which surprised me very much: They used frequently to fly across the ship and many of them fell on the deck. I also now first saw the use of the quadrant; I had often with astonishment seen the mariners make observations with it, and I could not think what it meant. They at last took notice of my surprise, and one of them, willing to increase it as well as to gratify my curiosity, made me one day look through it.

---

11. **pestilential** adj.: deadly; harmful.
12. **necessary tubs:** toilets.
13. **fetters** n. pl.: shackles or chains for the feet.

**Vocabulary**

**improvident** (im·präv′ə·dənt) adj.: careless; not providing for the future.
**avarice** (av′ə·ris) n.: greed.

The clouds appeared to me to be land, which disappeared as they passed along. This heightened my wonder, and I was now more persuaded than ever that I was in another world and that everything about me was magic. At last we came in sight of the island of Barbados, at which the whites on board gave a great shout and made many signs of joy to us. We did not know what to think of this, but as the vessel drew nearer we plainly saw the harbor and other ships of different kinds and sizes, and we soon anchored amongst them off Bridgetown. Many merchants and planters now came on board, though it was in the evening. They put us in separate parcels and examined us attentively. They also made us jump, and pointed to the land, signifying we were to go there. We thought by this we should be eaten by these ugly men, as they appeared to us; and when soon after we were all put down under the deck again, there was much dread and trembling among us, and nothing but bitter cries to be heard all the night from these apprehensions, insomuch that at last the white people got some old slaves from the land to pacify us. They told us we were not to be eaten but to work, and were soon to go on land where we should see many of our countrypeople. This report eased us much; and sure enough soon after we were landed there came to us Africans of all languages.

We were conducted immediately to the merchant's yard, where we were all pent up together like so many sheep in a fold without regard to sex or age. As every object was new to me everything I saw filled me with surprise. What struck me first was that the houses were built with stories, and in every other respect different from those in Africa: But I was still more astonished on seeing people on horseback. I did not know what this could mean, and indeed I thought these people were full of nothing but magical arts. While I was in this astonishment one of my fellow prisoners spoke to a countryman of his about the horses, who said they were the same kind they had in their country. I understood them though they were from a distant part of Africa, and I thought it odd I had not seen any horses there; but afterward when I came to converse with different Africans I found they had many horses amongst them, and much larger than those I then saw.

We were not many days in the merchant's custody before we were sold after their usual manner, which is this: On a signal given (as the beat of a drum) the buyers rush at once into the yard where the slaves are confined, and make choice of that parcel they like best. The noise and clamor with which this is attended and the eagerness visible in the countenances of the buyers serve not a little to increase the apprehensions of the terrified Africans, who may well be supposed to consider them as the ministers of that destruction to which they think themselves devoted. In this manner, without scruple,[14] are relations and friends separated, most of them never to see each other again. I remember in the vessel in which I was brought over, in the men's apartment there were several brothers who, in the sale, were sold in different lots; and it was very moving on this occasion to see and hear their cries at parting. O, ye nominal Christians! might not an African ask you, Learned you this from your God who says unto you, Do unto all men as you would men should do unto you? Is it not enough that we are torn from our country and friends to toil for your luxury and lust of gain? Must every tender feeling be likewise sacrificed to your avarice? Are the dearest friends and relations, now rendered more dear by their separation from their kindred, still to be parted from each other and thus prevented from cheering the gloom of slavery with the small comfort of being together and mingling their sufferings and sorrows? Why are parents to lose their children, brothers their sisters, or husbands their wives? Surely this is a new refinement in cruelty which, while it has no advantage to atone for it, thus aggravates distress and adds fresh horrors even to the wretchedness of slavery. ■

---

14. **scruple** *n.*: unease or doubt arising from difficulty in determining what is right.

# Phillis Wheatley:
# A Revolutionary Woman

**A**ll the odds were stacked against her— she was an African held in slavery, she was young, and she was female. But Phillis Wheatley (c. 1753–1784) published her first poem when she was barely thirteen, and by the time she was twenty years old she had developed a reputation as a poet whose work was praised by George Washington and Thomas Jefferson (page 97).

When Phillis Wheatley was about seven or eight years old, she, like Olaudah Equiano, was stolen from her home in West Africa. She arrived in America onboard a slave ship in 1761. At first, of course, she spoke no English. But she was purchased by the Wheatley family of Boston to assist Mrs. Susanna Wheatley and was treated kindly. Pleased to find this young woman intelligent and eager to learn, the Wheatleys provided her with an excellent education, equal to that of any free person in Boston at the time.

Susanna Wheatley arranged the London publication of a volume of Phillis's poems in 1773; the book received generally encouraging reviews, and it was read widely in England, France, and the American Colonies. Around this time, Phillis was given her freedom, though she chose to remain with the Wheatleys. When they died, she married John Peters, a freeman, in 1778.

Wheatley's poems imitate the style popular in the poetry of her time: She uses a Latinate vocabulary, inversions, and elevated diction. The stanza on page 63 is from her poem to the earl of Dartmouth, who had just been appointed secretary of state in charge of the American Colonies (1772). Dartmouth, she hopes, will be open to the colonists' grievances.

*Phillis Wheatley* (1773). Frontispiece of *Poems* by Phillis Wheatley. Engraving.

The Granger Collection, New York.

Wheatley's life ended on a tragic note. Her married life was filled with personal, financial, and familial hardships. Wheatley bore three children, but none of them survived. When she herself was sick and poor, the same society that had lavished attention on her as a kind of "sideshow attraction"—an enslaved woman who could write lofty poetry—abandoned her to a position of powerlessness and anonymity. She died in her early thirties, destitute and grieving, without having published another book of poems. Since her death, however, her poems have been reprinted and, in the twentieth century, have again attracted lavish attention. Today Phillis Wheatley is praised as a true pioneer—the first African American poet.

# *from* To the Right Honorable William, Earl of Dartmouth, His Majesty's Principal Secretary of State for North America, etc.

## Phillis Wheatley

    Should you, my lord, while you peruse my song,
Wonder from whence my love of *Freedom* sprung,
Whence flow these wishes for the common good,
By feeling hearts alone best understood,
5    I, young in life, by seeming cruel fate
Was snatch'd from *Afric's* fancy'd happy seat:
What pangs excruciating must molest,
What sorrows labor in my parent's breast?
Steel'd was that soul and by no misery mov'd
10    That from a father seiz'd his babe belov'd:
Such, such my case. And can I then but pray
Others may never feel tyrannic sway?

# Honoring African Heritage

## Halimah Abdullah

Ignoring the creaking of rusting amusement rides behind him, Ahsana Adae kept his gaze focused ahead, toward the horizon, where the gray expanse of overcast sky met the brackish waves.

"When I look out across those waters," Mr. Adae said, "I feel like walking across them back home."

For Mr. Adae and others who gathered in Coney Island on June 14 for a ceremony known as the Tribute to the Ancestors of the Middle Passage celebration, the ocean view represented a symbolic connection to their African ancestors' voyages here.

For four hundred years, millions of Africans were enslaved and transported across the Atlantic. Experts estimate that one third died on their journeys.

"The Atlantic Ocean is the largest single graveyard in the world, with over thirty million people buried in that ocean," said Zala Chandler, a professor of English and black and women's studies at Medgar Evers College and an organizer of the event.

"We're paying tribute to both those who died during that African holocaust and the survivors," she said of the celebration, now in its eighth year. "We ask that those present receive the blessings of those lost spirits."

Mr. Adae said he hoped that by setting adrift a photo of his great-grandparents, the children of slave mothers, they would symbolically return to their mothers' homelands.

"It's important for us to do these things to regain a sense of pride," he said. "Every other race that I know of is proud of who they are.

Spectators at the Middle Passage Monument, Riverbank State Park, New York City.

So it's about us learning to like ourselves. We have to learn that our African heritage is nothing to be ashamed of."

The gathering, swathed in colorful African prints, paid tribute through song, dance, and prayers. Some participants sat quietly in beach chairs facing the waves, reflecting.

"We as a people need to really take some time out and look at what happened during the Middle Passage," one participant, Tony Akeem, said. "We need to think about what they must have gone through."

As a solemn drumbeat sounded, the group proceeded to the water's edge and cast flowers, fruit, and pictures of dead relatives along the waves, offering whispered prayers. A scratched sepia° photo bobbed wildly as the current carried it toward open waters.

"The real story there," Mr. Akeem said, "is in the bottom of that briny deep."

—*The New York Times,* June 22, 1997

°**sepia** *adj.:* dark reddish brown.

# Response and Analysis

## Reading Check

1. How was Equiano treated by his captors and owners while he was held in slavery in West Africa?

2. Under what circumstances was Equiano twice parted from his sister?

3. How did some Africans onboard the ship try to escape life in bondage?

4. Why did the ship's crew keep Equiano on deck most of the time?

## Thinking Critically

5. Fill in the third column of the KWL chart that you made in your Quick-write. Has your understanding of slavery and the slave trade changed? Did the article "Honoring African Heritage" add to your understanding? (See the **Connection** on page 64.) Explain your responses.

6. Equiano was "handled and tossed up" by some of the crew as soon as he was taken onboard. Why? What would have happened to him if the crew had found him unsatisfactory?

7. Look back at the notes you took while reading. What **inferences** did you make about Equiano's beliefs? Why do you think Equiano described the flogging of a crew member?

8. What is the basic contradiction between the crew's main goal and their treatment of the captives?

## Extending and Evaluating

9. What characteristics of Equiano's **autobiography** distinguish it from the poem by Phillis Wheatley (see the **Connection** on page 62)? How does the message in his autobiography differ from that in Wheatley's poem?

10. How do you account for the depth of human cruelty described in parts of this autobiography? What current events reveal a similar capacity for cruelty in human nature?

## WRITING

### Teach Your Children Well

Create a **book** for children that will teach them about some aspect of the African American heritage—perhaps something that you've just learned from Equiano's account. Research your topic, and report your findings in clear, easy-to-read language for children. You might even want to write in poetic form. (You may illustrate your book if you wish.)

### Vocabulary Development

#### Getting Information

| | |
|---|---|
| assailant | commodious |
| distraction | consternation |
| apprehensions | improvident |
| interspersed | avarice |

This chart organizes some basic information about the word *alleviate*. With a partner or small group, use a dictionary to make similar charts for the other Vocabulary words.

| alleviate |
|---|
| **Meaning** *make more bearable; lighten* |
| **Origin** *ad–, "to" + levis, "light"* |
| **Synonyms** *relieve; lessen; reduce* |
| **Sample Sentence** *This painkiller will alleviate the patient's suffering.* |

**SKILLS FOCUS**

**Literary Skills** Analyze the characteristics of an autobiography.

**Reading Skills** Analyze inferences about an author's beliefs.

**Writing Skills** Write a book for children about African American heritage.

**Vocabulary Skills** Create semantic charts.

# Vocabulary Development

## Context Clues

A word's **context**—the words and sentences that surround it—often gives clues to the word's meaning. Look at this example from *The Interesting Narrative of the Life of Olaudah Equiano*.

> "Some of us used to get up a tree to look for any <u>assailant</u> or kidnapper that might come upon us, for they sometimes took those opportunities of our parents' absence to attack and carry off as many as they could seize." (page 55)

You can infer from the context that an assailant is a "kidnapper" or someone who would "attack" and "carry off" someone. The context has given you an **example** of an assailant.

You will find many different types of context clues in your reading. An example is one type of clue. Here are three other common types to look for:

1. **Definition or restatement.** Look for an actual definition or a rephrasing of the word in more familiar terms.

   As a child, Equiano was trained to shoot and throw <u>javelins</u>, or light spears.

   "Light spears" is the definition of *javelins*.

2. **Synonyms.** Look for clues indicating that an unfamiliar word is similar in meaning to a familiar word or phrase.

   The closest relations were deprived of the comfort of companionship and separated from their <u>kindred</u>.

   *Kindred* is a synonym for "closest relations."

3. **Contrast.** An unfamiliar word may sometimes be contrasted with a more familiar word or concept.

   Sleep was Equiano's only relief from his overpowering <u>fatigue</u>.

   *Fatigue* is contrasted with the word *sleep*. Since sleep was Equiano's "only relief," you can infer that *fatigue* means "exhaustion" or "weariness."

## PRACTICE

**SKILLS FOCUS**

**Vocabulary Skills**
Use context clues to determine the meaning of words.

For each of the other Vocabulary words, construct a sentence that gives the meaning of the word in a context clue. Model your sentences after the sentences above. Include a definition or rephrasing of the word in more familiar terms.

| | | |
|---|---|---|
| distraction | interspersed | improvident |
| apprehensions | commodious | avarice |
| alleviate | consternation | |

# Benjamin Franklin
## (1706–1790)

*Benjamin Franklin* (1777) after Jean Baptiste Greuze. Oil on canvas ($28^5/_8'' \times 22^5/_8''$).

F ew people have been so energetically devoted to improvement as Benjamin Franklin. Born in Boston, one of seventeen children, he rose from poverty to eminence even though he had to leave school early in order to work. By the time he was twenty-four, Franklin was a prosperous merchant, owner of a successful print shop, and publisher of *The Pennsylvania Gazette*. He helped found the Academy of Philadelphia (which became the University of Pennsylvania), the American Philosophical Society, and the first public library in America. Franklin was a scientist and an important inventor: His research, especially on electricity, resulted in his election to England's Royal Society. In addition, he invented an open heating stove (called a Franklin stove), bifocal eyeglasses, a type of harmonica, and a rocking chair that could swat flies.

Franklin also possessed uncommon talents as a diplomat and negotiator, and he used these skills in the service of his state and his country. Franklin lived in London in the 1750s and '60s, representing the interests of Pennsylvania as an agent of the Pennsylvania Assembly. A decade later he was back in London lobbying for the Colonies in their dispute with Britain, hoping to bring about a reconciliation that would prevent war. Franklin's wit and charm made him enormously popular in London for many years; he once said that he was invited out to dinner there six nights a week. But by 1774, when he was sixty-eight, the stress between Britain and the Colonies had become too great. The king's Privy Council publicly attacked Franklin for his policies, and the British press called him an "old snake." Franklin finally relinquished his hopes for peace and sailed for America in 1775.

When Franklin arrived home, he was greeted with news that the first battles of the Revolutionary War had been fought at Lexington and Concord, Massachusetts. "The shot heard round the world" had been fired. After helping to draft the Declaration of Independence in 1776, Franklin left for Paris to negotiate the treaty that brought the French into the war on America's side.

In Paris, Franklin was even more popular than he had once been in England. He played the role of the sophisticated but homespun American to the hilt. When the Revolution was over, he helped negotiate the peace. In 1787, Franklin served as a member of the Constitutional Convention. His death three years later was cause for international mourning.

Franklin's practicality, like the success story of his life, is typically American, but it has not been universally admired throughout the nation's history. The American novelist Herman Melville deplored Franklin's lack of imagination: "Jack-of-all-trades, master of each and mastered by none—the type and genius of his land. Franklin was everything but a poet."

## Make the Connection
### Quickwrite ✏️

From founding a nation to flying to the moon, Americans have always believed in the possibility of progress. Progress, however, can be measured in many ways—technological, financial, educational, social, and even spiritual. Just as Benjamin Franklin invented devices to improve the quality of life in America, he also tried to invent a moral "machine" to improve the quality of his own character. Today a walk through a bookstore or a glance at TV commercials quickly reveals that self-improvement is still a hot topic. Jot down the titles of any self-help books you know of or of TV self-help programs that you have seen. Why do you think so many of these books and programs are popular?

## Reading Skills
### Making Inferences 📖

One of the pleasures of reading an autobiography is getting to know the writer's personality, as well as his or her philosophical beliefs and attitudes—in other words, what makes the writer "tick." In many cases, though, writers don't directly reveal this information. Readers need to look beneath the surface of the text to **infer,** or use clues to guess, the writer's implicit, or suggested but unstated, beliefs.

As you read this excerpt from *The Autobiography,* jot down any words or phrases that help you infer Franklin's attitudes and beliefs. For example, how do you think Franklin felt about being self-reliant and practical?

## Background

Franklin began *The Autobiography* when he was sixty-five and continued working on it intermittently for years, although he never finished it and it was not published during his lifetime. When Franklin was a teenager, he was apprenticed to his older brother James, who printed a Boston newspaper. Disputes arose between the brothers, and the younger Franklin fled Boston for Philadelphia to escape from a second, secret indenture, or contract of service, that his brother had forced him to sign. This selection begins with Franklin's arrival in Philadelphia.

### Vocabulary Development

**arduous** (är′joo·əs) *adj.:* difficult.

**rectitude** (rek′tə·tood′) *n.:* correctness.

**facilitate** (fə·sil′ə·tāt′) *v.:* make easier.

**subsequent** (sub′si·kwənt) *adj.:* following.

**eradicate** (ē·rad′i·kāt′) *v.:* eliminate.

**SKILLS FOCUS**

**Reading Skills**
Make inferences about a writer's beliefs.

**go. hrw .com**

**INTERNET**

Vocabulary Practice
•
More About Benjamin Franklin
•

Keyword: LE7 11-1

Odometer used by Benjamin Franklin to measure postal routes.

From the Historical and Interpretive Collections of The Franklin Institute, Philadelphia, PA.

*Benjamin Franklin Drawing Electricity from the Sky* (c. 1805) by Benjamin West.
Oil on paper on canvas (13¼″ × 10″).

## *from* The Autobiography

### Benjamin Franklin

*Second Street, North from Market Street, with Christ Church, Philadelphia* (1799) by W. Birch & Son. Colored line engraving.

## Arrival in Philadelphia

I have been the more particular in this description of my journey, and shall be so of my first entry into that city, that you may in your mind compare such unlikely beginnings with the figure I have since made there. I was in my working dress, my best clothes being to come round by sea. I was dirty from my journey; my pockets were stuffed out with shirts and stockings, and I knew no soul nor where to look for lodging. I was fatigued with traveling, rowing, and want of rest, I was very hungry; and my whole stock of cash consisted of a Dutch dollar, and about a shilling in copper. The latter I gave the people of the boat for my passage, who at first refused it, on account of my rowing; but I insisted on their taking it. A man being some-

times more generous when he has but a little money than when he has plenty, perhaps through fear of being thought to have but little.

Then I walked up the street, gazing about till near the market house I met a boy with bread. I had made many a meal on bread, and, inquiring where he got it, I went immediately to the baker's he directed me to, in Second Street, and asked for biscuit, intending such as we had in Boston; but they, it seems, were not made in Philadelphia. Then I asked for a three-penny loaf, and was told they had none such. So not considering or knowing the difference of money, and the greater cheapness nor the names of his bread, I bade him give me three-penny worth of any sort. He gave me, accordingly, three great puffy rolls. I was surprised at the quantity, but took it, and, having no room in my pockets, walked off with a roll under each arm, and eating the other. Thus I went up Market Street as far as Fourth Street, passing by the door of Mr. Read, my future wife's father; when she, standing at the door, saw me, and thought I made, as I certainly did, a most awkward, ridiculous appearance. Then I turned and went down Chestnut Street and part of Walnut Street, eating my roll all the way, and, coming round, found myself again at Market Street wharf, near the boat I came in, to which I went for a draft[1] of the river water; and, being filled with one of my rolls, gave the other two to a woman and her child that came down the river in the boat with us, and were waiting to go farther.

Thus refreshed, I walked again up the street, which by this time had many clean-dressed people in it, who were all walking the same way. I joined them, and thereby was led into the great meetinghouse of the Quakers[2] near the market. I sat down among them, and, after looking round awhile and hearing nothing said, being very drowsy through labor and want of rest the preceding night, I fell fast asleep, and continued so till the meeting broke up, when one was kind enough to rouse me. This was, therefore, the first house I was in, or slept in, in Philadelphia. . . .

## Arriving at Moral Perfection

It was about this time I conceived the bold and arduous project of arriving at moral perfection. I wished to live without committing any fault at

*Tolerate no uncleanliness in body, clothes, or habitation.*

Drawing by David Levine. Reprinted with permission from *The New York Review of Books.* Copyright © 1973 NYREV, Inc.

any time; I would conquer all that either natural inclination, custom, or company might lead me into. As I knew, or thought I knew, what was right and wrong, I did not see why I might not always do the one and avoid the other. But I soon found I had undertaken a task of more difficulty than I had imagined. While my care was employed in guarding against one fault, I was often surprised by another; habit took the advantage of inattention; inclination was sometimes too strong for reason. I concluded, at length, that the mere speculative conviction that it was our interest to be completely virtuous,[3] was not sufficient to prevent our slipping; and that the contrary habits must be broken, and good ones acquired and established, before we can have any dependence on a steady, uniform rectitude of conduct. For this purpose I therefore contrived the following method.

In the various enumerations of the moral virtues I had met with in my reading, I found the catalog more or less numerous, as different writers included more or fewer ideas under the same name. Temperance, for example, was by some confined to eating and drinking, while by others it was extended to mean the moderating every other pleasure, appetite, inclination, or passion, bodily or mental, even to our avarice and ambition. I proposed to myself, for the sake of clearness, to use rather more names, with fewer ideas annexed to each, than a few names with more ideas; and I included under thirteen

---

3. **virtuous** *adj.:* morally excellent; pure.

---

**Vocabulary**
**arduous** (är′joo·əs) *adj.:* difficult.
**rectitude** (rek′tə·tood′) *n.:* correctness.

---

1. **draft** *n.:* gulp or swallow.
2. **Quakers:** members of the Religious Society of Friends, a Christian group founded in the seventeenth century.

names of virtues all that at that time occurred to me as necessary or desirable, and annexed to each a short precept,[4] which fully expressed the extent I gave to its meaning.

These names of virtues, with their precepts, were:

1. **Temperance.** *Eat not to dullness; drink not to elevation.*

2. **Silence.** *Speak not but what may benefit others or yourself; avoid trifling[5] conversation.*

3. **Order.** *Let all your things have their places; let each part of your business have its time.*

4. **Resolution.** *Resolve to perform what you ought; perform without fail what you resolve.*

5. **Frugality.** *Make no expense but to do good to others or yourself; i.e., waste nothing.*

6. **Industry.** *Lose no time; be always employed in something useful; cut off all unnecessary actions.*

7. **Sincerity.** *Use no hurtful deceit; think innocently and justly, and, if you speak, speak accordingly.*

8. **Justice.** *Wrong none by doing injuries, or omitting the benefits that are your duty.*

9. **Moderation.** *Avoid extremes; forbear resenting injuries so much as you think they deserve.*

10. **Cleanliness.** *Tolerate no uncleanliness in body, clothes, or habitation.*

11. **Tranquility.** *Be not disturbed at trifles, or at accidents common or unavoidable.*

## I wished to live without committing any fault at any time.

Drawing by David Levine. Reprinted with permission from *The New York Review of Books.* Copyright © 1973 NYREV, Inc.

12. **Chastity.** *Rarely use venery[6] but for health or offspring, never to dullness, weakness, or the injury of your own or another's peace or reputation.*

13. **Humility.** *Imitate Jesus and Socrates.[7]*

My intention being to acquire the habitude of all these virtues, I judged it would be well not to distract my attention by attempting the whole at once, but to fix it on one of them at a time; and, when I should be master of that, then to proceed to another, and so on, till I should have gone through the thirteen; and, as the previous acquisition of some might facilitate the acquisition of certain others, I arranged them with that view, as they stand above. *Temperance* first, as it tends to procure that coolness and clearness of head, which is so necessary where constant vigilance was to be kept up, and guard maintained against the unremitting[8] attraction of ancient habits, and the force of perpetual temptations. This being acquired and established, *silence* would be more easy; and my desire being to gain knowledge at the same time that I improved in virtue, and considering that in conversation it was obtained rather by the use of the ears than of the tongue, and therefore wishing to break a habit I was getting into of prattling, punning, and joking, which only made me acceptable to trifling com-

---

6. **venery** (ven′ər·ē) *n.:* sex.
7. **Socrates** (säk′rə·tēz′) (470?–399 B.C.): Greek philosopher who is said to have lived a simple, virtuous life.
8. **unremitting** *adj.:* not stopping; persistent.

**Vocabulary**
**facilitate** (fə·sil′ə·tāt′) *v.:* make easier.

---

4. **precept** *n.:* rule of moral conduct; principle.
5. **trifling** *adj.:* unimportant; shallow.

pany, I gave *silence* the second place. This and the next, *order,* I expected would allow me more time for attending to my project and my studies. *Resolution,* once become habitual, would keep me firm in my endeavors to obtain all the subsequent virtues; *frugality* and *industry* freeing me from my remaining debt, and producing affluence and independence, would make more easy the practice of *sincerity* and *justice,* etc., etc. Conceiving then, that, agreeably to the advice of Pythagoras[9] in his Golden Verses, daily examination would be necessary, I contrived the following method for conducting that examination.

I made a little book, in which I allotted a page for each of the virtues. I ruled each page with red ink, so as to have seven columns, one for each day of the week, marking each column with a letter for the day. I crossed these columns with thirteen red lines, marking the beginning of each line with the first letter of one of the virtues, on which line, and in its proper column, I might mark, by a little black spot, every fault I found upon examination to have been committed respecting that virtue upon that day.

I determined to give a week's strict attention to each of the virtues successively. Thus, in the first week, my great guard was to avoid every[10] the least offense against *temperance,* leaving the other virtues to their ordinary chance, only marking every evening the faults of the day. Thus, if in the first week I could keep my first line, marked T, clear of spots, I supposed the habit of that virtue so much strengthened, and its opposite weakened, that I might venture extending my attention to include the next, and for the following week keep both lines clear of spots. Proceeding thus to the last, I could go through a course complete in thirteen weeks, and four courses in a year. And like him who, having a garden to weed, does not attempt to eradicate all the bad herbs at once, which would exceed his reach and his strength, but works on one of the beds at a time, and, having accom-

**Form of the Pages**

| Temperance | | | | | | | |
|---|---|---|---|---|---|---|---|
| Eat not to dullness. Drink not to elevation. | | | | | | | |
| | S | M | T | W | T | F | S |
| T | | | | | | | |
| S | | | | | | | |
| O | | | | | | | |
| R | | | | | | | |
| F | | | | | | | |
| I | | | | | | | |
| S | | | | | | | |
| J | | | | | | | |
| M | | | | | | | |
| Cl | | | | | | | |
| T | | | | | | | |
| Ch | | | | | | | |
| H | | | | | | | |

plished the first, proceeds to a second, so I should have, I hoped, the encouraging pleasure of seeing on my pages the progress I made in virtue, by clearing successively my lines of their spots, till in the end, by a number of courses, I should be happy in viewing a clean book, after a thirteen weeks' daily examination. . . . ■

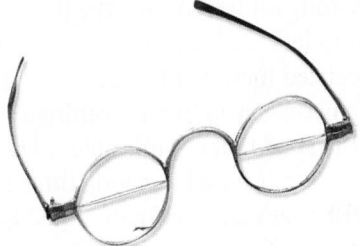

**Vocabulary**

**subsequent** (sub′si·kwənt) *adj.:* following.

**eradicate** (ē·rad′i·kāt′) *v.:* eliminate.

---

9. **Pythagoras** (pi·thag′ə·rəs): Greek philosopher and mathematician of the sixth century B.C.

10. **every:** archaic for "even."

*Behind Benjamin Franklin's project for achieving moral perfection lies what seems to be a common human impulse—the need to simplify life, to get at the root of what's fundamental to us. In 1986, Robert Fulghum published some thoughts of his own about how to live a full and happy life. The book became a bestseller.*

# from All I Really Need to Know I Learned in Kindergarten

## Robert Fulghum

Each spring, for many years, I have set myself the task of writing a personal statement of belief: a Credo. When I was younger, the statement ran for many pages, trying to cover every base, with no loose ends. It sounded like a Supreme Court brief, as if words could resolve all conflicts about the meaning of existence.

The Credo has grown shorter in recent years—sometimes cynical, sometimes comical, sometimes bland—but I keep working at it. Recently I set out to get the statement of personal belief down to one page in simple terms, fully understanding the naive idealism that implied. . . .

I realized then that I already know most of what's necessary to live a meaningful life—that it isn't all that complicated. *I know it.* And have known it for a long, long time. Living it—well, that's another matter, yes? Here's my Credo:

All I really need to know about how to live and what to do and how to be I learned in kindergarten. Wisdom was not at the top of the graduate-school mountain, but there in the sandpile at Sunday school. These are the things I learned:

> Share everything.
> Play fair.
> Don't hit people.
> Put things back where you found them.
> Clean up your own mess.
> Don't take things that aren't yours.
> Say you're sorry when you hurt somebody.
> Wash your hands before you eat.
> Flush.
> Warm cookies and cold milk are good for you.
> Live a balanced life—learn some and think some and draw and paint and sing and dance and play and work every day some.
> Take a nap every afternoon.
> When you go out into the world, watch out for traffic, hold hands, and stick together.
> Be aware of wonder. Remember the little seed in the Styrofoam cup: The roots go down and the plant goes up and nobody really knows how or why, but we are all like that.
> Goldfish and hamsters and white mice and even the little seed in the Styrofoam cup—they all die. So do we.
> And then remember the Dick-and-Jane books and the first word you learned—the biggest word of all—LOOK.

. . . Think what a better world it would be if we all—the whole world—had cookies and milk about three o'clock every afternoon and then lay down with our blankies for a nap. Or if all governments had as a basic policy to always put things back where they found them and to clean up their own mess.

And it is still true, no matter how old you are—when you go out into the world, it is best to hold hands and stick together.

## *from* Poor Richard's Almanack

### Make the Connection

**Quickwrite** ✏️

TV talk shows, radio call-in programs, newspaper columns, how-to books, inspirational speakers—sometimes today's world seems to overflow with people who want to give advice. Dispensing wisdom—or at least reflections on one's own experience—has become an American industry. Why do you think so many readers and listeners flock to advice givers? Make a list of three pieces of advice you would give to an incoming freshman at your school.

### Literary Focus

**Aphorisms**

An **aphorism** is a brief, cleverly worded statement that makes a wise observation about life. Aphorisms grow out of speeches, sermons, religious texts such as the Bible ("Love your neighbor"), poems and stories, advertisements, and most commonly, the expressions of ordinary people in ordinary situations.

Aphorisms can serve many purposes. They entertain, especially through their humor, wit, and wordplay; they instruct, suggesting ways to overcome obstacles, solve problems, and achieve success; and they inspire, often providing a kind of moral uplift. Aphorisms can also **satirize,** using humor to mock and criticize the way things are. They can address any subject—from war and peace to the fleas on a dog.

> An **aphorism** is a brief, cleverly worded statement that makes a wise observation about life.
>
> *For more on Aphorisms, see the Handbook of Literary and Historical Terms.*

### Background

With the publication of *Poor Richard's Almanack* in 1732, Franklin found his biggest publishing success, and he continued to publish his almanac for twenty-five years. Almost every house had an almanac. Almanacs calculated the tides and the phases of the moon, forecast the weather for the next year, and even provided astrological advice. Many almanacs also supplied recipes, jokes, and aphorisms. Poor Richard was an imaginary astrologer with a critical wife named Bridget. One year Bridget wrote the aphorisms to answer those her husband had written the year before on female idleness. Another time Bridget included "better" weather forecasts so that people would know the good days for drying their clothes.

Franklin's practicality shows itself not only in the content of his almanacs but also in the way he put them together: He took his wit and wisdom wherever he found it. He printed old sayings translated from other languages, lifted some aphorisms from other writers, and adapted others from popular and local sources. An American to the core, Franklin never hesitated to rework what he found to suit his own purposes. For example, for the 1758 almanac, Franklin skimmed all his previous editions to compose a single speech on economy. This speech, called "The Way to Wealth," has become one of the best known of Franklin's works. It has been mistakenly believed to be representative of Poor Richard's wisdom. Poor Richard often called for prudence and thrift, but he just as often favored extravagance.

**SKILLS FOCUS**

**Literary Skills**
Understand aphorisms.

**INTERNET**

**More About Benjamin Franklin**

Keyword: LE7 11-1

# from Poor Richard's Almanack

## Benjamin Franklin

1. Love your neighbor; yet don't pull down your hedge.

2. If a man empties his purse into his head, no man can take it away from him. An investment in knowledge always pays the best interest.

3. Three may keep a secret if two of them are dead.

4. Tart words make no friends; a spoonful of honey will catch more flies than a gallon of vinegar.

5. Glass, china, and reputation are easily cracked and never well mended.

6. Fish and visitors smell in three days.

7. He that lieth down with dogs shall rise up with fleas.

8. One today is worth two tomorrows.

9. A truly great man will neither trample on a worm nor sneak to an emperor.

10. A little neglect may breed mischief; for want of a nail the shoe was lost; for want of a shoe the horse was lost; for want of a horse the rider was lost; for want of the rider the battle was lost.

11. If you would know the value of money, go and try to borrow some; he that goes a-borrowing goes a-sorrowing.

12. He that composes himself is wiser than he that composes books.

13. He that is of the opinion that money will do everything may well be suspected of doing everything for money.

14. If a man could have half his wishes, he would double his troubles.

15. 'Tis hard for an empty bag to stand upright.

16. A small leak will sink a great ship.

17. A plowman on his legs is higher than a gentleman on his knees.

18. Keep your eyes wide open before marriage, half shut afterward.

19. Nothing brings more pain than too much pleasure; nothing more bondage than too much liberty.

Panel from an engraving for Benjamin Franklin's *Poor Richard Illustrated* (c. 1800).

The Granger Collection, New York.

# Response and Analysis

## *from* The Autobiography

### Reading Check

1. What was Franklin's condition in life when he arrived in Philadelphia?
2. What does Franklin say must happen before people can depend on correct moral behavior?
3. Why does Franklin place temperance first on his list?
4. How many "courses" of his list of virtues does Franklin plan to go through in one year?

### Thinking Critically

5. What **inferences** can you make about Franklin's attitudes and beliefs, based on his plan to achieve moral perfection? If Franklin were alive today, what modern causes might he support? Explain.
6. Franklin writes about "arriving at moral perfection" just as he had earlier written about his arrival in the city of Philadelphia. What does this similarity in his language reveal about Franklin's philosophical assumptions?

### Extending and Evaluating

7. Compare Robert Fulghum's list of things learned in kindergarten (see the **Connection** on page 74) to Franklin's list of virtues. Which list do you think would be more useful to people today? In general, how does Franklin's scheme for moral perfection compare with the self-help books available today? Be sure to refer to your Quickwrite notes. 🖊

### Literary Criticism

8. Reactions to *The Autobiography* have sometimes been negative. Read the following comment by satirist Mark Twain. What is Twain's **tone** in this paragraph—that is, his attitude toward Ben Franklin?

> [Franklin had] a malevolence which is without parallel in history; he would work all day and then sit up nights and let on to be studying algebra by the light of a smoldering fire, so that all the boys might have to do that also, or else have Benjamin Franklin thrown upon them. Not satisfied with these proceedings, he had a fashion of living wholly on bread and water, and studying astronomy at mealtime—a thing which has brought affliction to millions of boys since, whose fathers had read Franklin's pernicious biography.
>
> —Mark Twain

The word *pernicious* (pər·nish′əs), in the last sentence, means "deadly." What elements of Franklin's autobiography is Twain attacking? How do you feel about Twain's grumblings?

## *from* Poor Richard's Almanack

### Thinking Critically

1. Poor Richard's aphorisms often succeed because of their **implied metaphors,** or metaphors that do not state explicitly the two things being compared. Re-read aphorisms 4, 7, 15, and 16. Then, identify what each of the following images might mean: a spoonful of honey, lying down with dogs, an empty bag, a small leak.
2. Many of Poor Richard's aphorisms convey moral lessons. Choose one of the aphorisms, and restate it in your own words, explaining its moral lesson.
3. Which of the aphorisms reveals a healthy skepticism and humor about human nature?

**INTERNET**

Projects and Activities

Keyword: LE7 11-1

## WRITING

### Becoming Virtuous

Using your Quickwrite notes, write a short handbook titled *Surviving Freshman Year.* Create **aphorisms** to make your advice short and memorable.

### Comparing Texts

In an **essay,** compare and contrast Franklin with Jonathan Edwards (page 44). Be sure to consider each man's goals in life and the philosophy behind those goals. Are these Americans alike in any ways?

# Grammar Link

### Linking It Up: Coordinating Conjunctions

Here's one way to describe one of Benjamin Franklin's projects for self-improvement:

> Benjamin Franklin knew that arriving at moral perfection would be difficult. He was willing to give it a try.

Here's a better way to express the same information:

> Benjamin Franklin knew that arriving at moral perfection would be difficult, yet he was willing to give it a try.

In the second example, the writer combined two related thoughts into a single sentence with a connective word—in this case, the coordinating conjunction *yet.* A **coordinating conjunction** joins words or word groups that are used in the same way. Separating two thoughts into two sentences is not incorrect; there are times when short, simple sentences sound best. However, using coordinating conjunctions to combine two thoughts into one sentence can result in more graceful syntax, or sentence structure.

| Some Connective Words and What They Indicate | |
| --- | --- |
| **Conjunction** | **Indicates** |
| and | similarity, addition |
| but | opposition, contrast |
| yet | opposition, contrast |
| or | choice |
| nor | negation |
| so | cause and effect, result |
| for | explanation |

**SKILLS FOCUS**

**Grammar Skills**
Use coordinating conjunctions.

All the words in the chart above function as coordinating conjunctions, but some can also function as other parts of speech.

For example, *for* is a preposition in the sentence *We went to the store for apples.* However, the word *for* is a coordinating conjunction in the sentence *We went to a store downtown, for the store on our block was closed.* To combine two related sentences into a single sentence, you will need to select an appropriate coordinating conjunction.

PRACTICE

Combine each pair of sentences into one sentence by using the most appropriate coordinating conjunction from the chart. Make necessary revisions so that the resulting sentence reads smoothly.

1. Benjamin Franklin was practically penniless when he arrived in Philadelphia. He was able to buy some rolls.
2. Franklin wished to achieve moral perfection. He devised a book in which he could record his transgressions and his progress.
3. Franklin wanted to avoid wrongdoing. He thought self-improvement was important.

## Apply to Your Writing

Take out a writing assignment you are working on now or have already completed. Use coordinating conjunctions to combine any short, choppy sentences that have a clear relationship to one another.

▶ **For more help, see Combining by Coordinating Ideas, 10c, in the Language Handbook.**

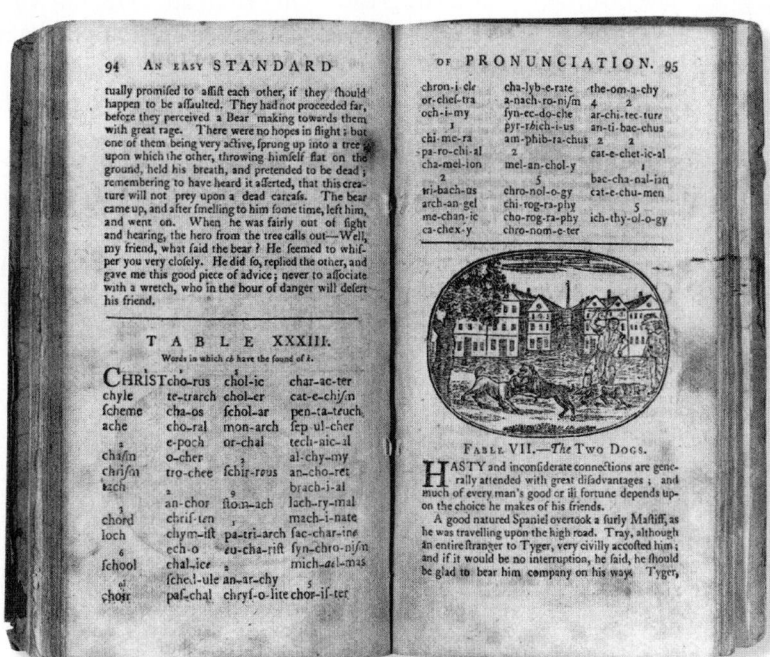

*The American Spelling Book by Noah Webster.*

# Patrick Henry

**(1736–1799)**

*Patrick Henry* (1820–1830), attributed to Asahel L. Powers. Oil on canvas.
© The Shelburne Museum, Shelburne, Vermont.

**O**ne fiery act can catapult someone from obscurity to fame. That is what happened to Patrick Henry, a young representative who stood up in the Virginia House of Burgesses one day in 1765. He delivered a dynamic, thundering speech against the hated Stamp Act, with which the British Parliament instituted taxes on all newspapers and public documents. For the ten years following his declaration of resistance, Henry—a tall, lank, somber-looking man who favored the kind of clothing a preacher might wear—was recognized as one of the most persuasive figures in Virginia politics.

Henry had not always been so successful. Born in a frontier region of Virginia, he was raised in a cultured but modest environment. During his youth the country was undergoing the religious revival known as the Great Awakening, and young Patrick often accompanied his mother to hear the sermons of the traveling preachers. Later, as a young man, he made several unsuccessful stabs at farming and merchant life before discovering his love of oratory and his true calling: the law.

In 1765, the twenty-nine-year-old lawyer was chosen to represent his region in the Virginia House of Burgesses. Henry's speech against the Stamp Act was the first of the two most famous speeches in American Colonial history. The second, his famous "liberty or death" speech, came ten years later in 1775 as the Colonies were nearing the breaking point with England. Following the Boston Tea Party in December 1773, the British had closed the port of Boston and instituted other harsh measures referred to by the colonists as the Intolerable Acts. When the First Continental Congress protested these acts, the British Crown relieved the Colonies of taxation on a number of conditions. One condition was that the colonists fully support British rule and contribute toward the maintenance of British troops in America, whose numbers were increasing greatly. On March 20, 1775, the Virginia House of Burgesses held a convention in St. John's Episcopal Church in Richmond to decide how to respond to the growing British military threat. George Washington and Thomas Jefferson (page 97) were both present.

On March 23, after several speeches in favor of compromise with the British, Patrick Henry rose to defend his resolution to take up arms. Later, a clergyman who was present recalled that during Henry's speech he felt "sick with excitement." As the speech reached its climax, Henry is said to have grabbed an ivory letter opener and plunged it toward his chest at the final word *death*.

Henry persuaded the delegation. The Virginia Convention voted to arm its people against England. On April 19, 1775, the Battle of Lexington, Massachusetts, ignited the Revolutionary War.

## Speech to the Virginia Convention

### Make the Connection
#### Quickwrite ✏️

Words shape us; they make us who we are. The American dream, as we loosely call our aspirations toward freedom, self-reliance, and self-creation, is defined in large part by the words of the men and women who helped shape America in its early years. Blood and suffering resulted from Henry's famous impassioned cry "give me liberty, or give me death!" yet his words generate pride to this day. Write a few sentences about what liberty means to you.

### Literary Focus
#### Persuasion

**Persuasion** is a form of speaking or writing that aims to convince an audience to take a specific action. A good persuasive speaker or writer appeals to both head and heart—or **logic** and **emotion**—to win over an audience. To be persuasive, a writer or speaker must provide reasons to support a particular opinion or course of action. In the final analysis, audiences are often won over by the speaker's ability to address their concerns as much as by forceful arguments and a powerful personality.

> **Persuasion** is a form of discourse that uses logical and emotional appeals to convince another person to think or act in a certain way.
>
> *For more on Persuasion, see the Handbook of Literary and Historical Terms.*

### Reading Skills 📖
#### Recognizing Modes of Persuasion

Patrick Henry uses two modes of **persuasion:** appeals to **reason** and appeals to **emotions** or values. As you read, track these types of appeals in a two-column chart. In the left column, list Henry's logical appeals for wanting war. In the right column, write down his emotional appeals. As you take notes, mark a star next to those appeals that you find most effective. Mark an X next to appeals that strike you as deceptive or faulty.

### Background

Although Henry's 1775 speech is one of the most famous in all American oratory, no manuscript of it exists. William Wirt, a biographer of Henry, pieced together the traditionally accepted text forty years after it was delivered, using notes of people who were present at the speech. As you read Henry's speech, try to envision the physical surroundings where it was delivered: a church in eighteenth-century Richmond, Virginia, on an early spring day. Try also to imagine the manner in which Henry delivered his speech.

SKILLS FOCUS

**Vocabulary Development**

**solace** (säl′is) *v.*: comfort.

**insidious** (in·sid′ē·əs) *adj.*: sly; sneaky.

**martial** (mär′shəl) *adj.*: warlike.

**supplication** (sup′lə·kā′shən) *n.*: plea; prayer.

**avert** (ə·vurt′) *v.*: prevent; turn away.

**spurned** (spurnd) *v.*: rejected.

**inviolate** (in·vī′ə·lit) *adj.*: uncorrupted.

**adversary** (ad′vər·ser′ē) *n.*: opponent.

**vigilant** (vij′ə·lənt) *adj.* used as *n.*: those who are watchful.

**inevitable** (in·ev′i·tə·bəl) *adj.*: not avoidable.

**Literary Skills**
Understand the characteristics of persuasion.

**Reading Skills**
Recognize modes of persuasion, including appeals to reason and appeals to emotion.

go.hrw.com

**INTERNET**

**Vocabulary Practice**

Keyword: LE7 11-1

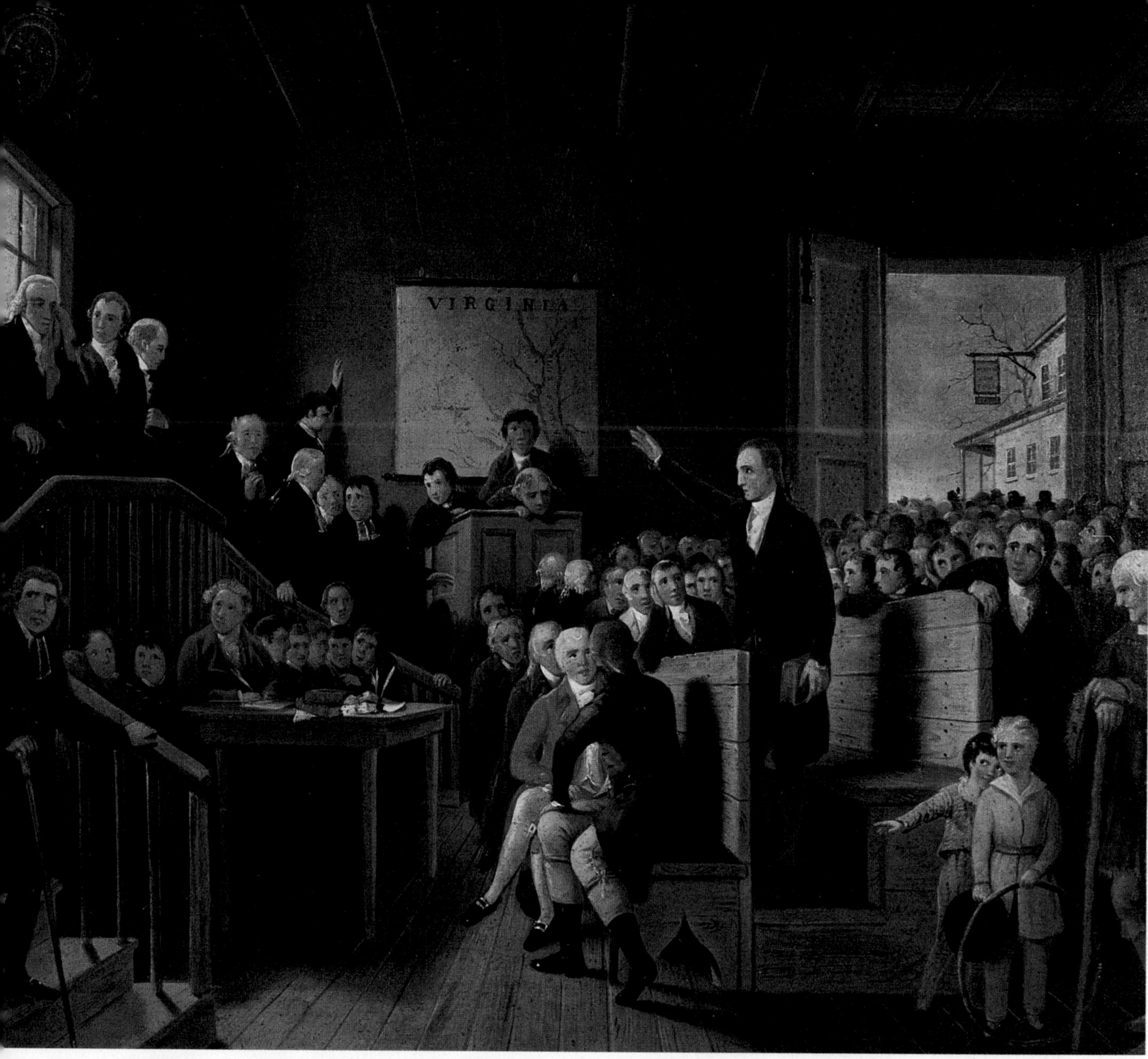


Virginia Historical Society, Richmond, Virginia.

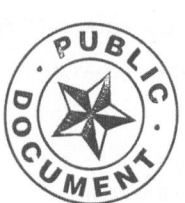

*Patrick Henry Arguing the Parson's Cause* (c. 1830), attributed to George Cooke. Oil on canvas.

# Speech to the Virginia Convention

PUBLIC DOCUMENT

## Patrick Henry

Mr. President:[1] No man thinks more highly than I do of the patriotism, as well as abilities, of the very worthy gentlemen who have just addressed the House. But different men often see the same subject in different lights; and, therefore, I hope that it will not be

1. **Mr. President:** Peyton Randolph (1721–1775), president of the Virginia Convention.

thought disrespectful to those gentlemen, if, entertaining[2] as I do, opinions of a character very opposite to theirs, I shall speak forth my sentiments freely and without reserve. This is no time for ceremony. ❶ The question before the House is one of awful moment[3] to this country. For my own part I consider it as nothing less than a question of freedom or slavery; and in proportion to the magnitude of the subject ought to be the freedom of the debate. It is only in this way that we can hope to arrive at truth, and fulfill the great responsibility which we hold to God and our country. Should I keep back my opinions at such a time, through fear of giving offense, I should consider myself as guilty of treason toward my country, and of an act of disloyalty toward the majesty of heaven, which I revere above all earthly kings. ❷

Mr. President, it is natural to man to indulge in the illusions of hope. We are apt to shut our eyes against a painful truth, and listen to the song of that siren, till she transforms us into beasts.[4] Is this the part of wise men, engaged in a great and arduous struggle for liberty? Are we disposed to be of the number of those who, having eyes, see not, and having ears, hear not, the things which so nearly concern their temporal salvation? For my part, whatever anguish of spirit it may cost, I am willing to know the whole truth; to know the worst and to provide for it.

❶ In his opening remarks, Henry makes a respectful appeal to his audience. He anticipates their objections to what he is about to say.
**?** *What effect might his appeal have on his audience?*

❷ **?** *Simply put, how does Henry describe the question or debate that is before the Convention?*

I have but one lamp by which my feet are guided; and that is the lamp of experience. I know of no way of judging of the future but by the past. And judging by the past, I wish to know what there has been in the conduct of the British ministry for the last ten years, to justify those hopes with which gentlemen have been pleased to solace themselves and the House? Is it that insidious smile with which our petition[5] has been lately received? Trust it not, sir; it will prove a snare to your feet. Suffer not yourselves to be betrayed with a kiss. Ask yourselves how this gracious reception of our petition comports[6] with these warlike preparations which cover our waters and darken our land. Are fleets and armies necessary to a work of love and reconciliation? Have we shown ourselves so unwilling to be reconciled, that force must be called in to win back our love? Let us not deceive ourselves, sir. These are the implements of war and subjugation;[7] the last arguments to which kings resort. ❸

I ask gentlemen, sir, what means this martial array, if its purpose be not to force us to submission? Can gentlemen assign any other possible motives for it? Has Great Britain any enemy, in this quarter of the world, to call for all this accumulation

❸ Henry asks his listeners to look back on past experiences. He lists the recent actions of King George III and the English army to support his **main idea**—that the colonists are mistaken in thinking that the British are ready to compromise.

---

2. **entertaining** *v.:* having in mind; considering.
3. **awful moment:** great importance.
4. **listen . . . beasts:** In Greek mythology, the sirens are sea maidens whose seductive singing lures men to wreck their boats on coastal rocks. In the *Odyssey*, Circe, an enchanter, transforms Odysseus's men into swine after they arrive at her island home. Henry's allusion combines these two stories.

---

5. **our petition:** The First Continental Congress had recently protested against new tax laws. King George III had withdrawn the laws conditionally, but the colonists were unwilling to accept his conditions.
6. **comports** *v.:* agrees.
7. **subjugation** *n.:* conquest; domination.

---

**Vocabulary**

**solace** (säl′is) *v.:* comfort.
**insidious** (in·sid′ē·əs) *adj.:* sly; sneaky.
**martial** (mär′shəl) *adj.:* warlike.

of navies and armies? No, sir, she has none. They are meant for us; they can be meant for no other. They are sent over to bind and rivet upon us those chains which the British ministry have been so long forging. And what have we to oppose to them? Shall we try argument? Sir, we have been trying that for the last ten years. Have we anything new to offer on the subject? Nothing. We have held the subject up in every light of which it is capable; but it has been all in vain. Shall we resort to entreaty and humble supplication? What terms shall we find which have not been already exhausted? Let us not, I beseech you, sir, deceive ourselves longer. ❹ Sir, we have done everything that could be done, to avert the storm which is now coming on. We have petitioned; we have remonstrated;[8] we have supplicated; we have prostrated ourselves before the throne, and have implored its interposition[9] to arrest the tyrannical hands of the ministry and Parliament. Our petitions have been slighted; our remonstrances have produced additional violence and insult; our supplications have been disregarded; and we have been spurned, with contempt, from the foot of the throne. In vain, after these things, may we indulge the fond[10] hope of peace and reconciliation. There is no longer any room for hope. If we wish to be free—if we mean to preserve inviolate those inestimable privileges for which we have been so long contending—if we mean not basely to abandon the noble struggle in which we have been so long engaged, and which we have pledged ourselves never to abandon until the glorious object of our contest shall be obtained, we must fight! I repeat it, sir, we must fight! An appeal to arms and to the God of Hosts is all that is left us! ❺

They tell us, sir, that we are weak; unable to cope with so formidable[11] an adversary. But when shall we be stronger? Will it be the next week, or the next year? Will it be when we are totally disarmed, and when a British guard shall be stationed in every house? Shall we gather strength by irresolution and inaction? Shall we acquire the means of effectual resistance, by lying supinely on our backs, and hugging the delusive[12] phantom of hope, until our enemies shall have bound us hand and foot? Sir, we are not weak, if we make a proper use of the means which the God of nature hath placed in our power. Three millions of people, armed in the holy cause of liberty, and in such a country as that which we possess, are invincible by any force which our enemy can send against us. Besides, sir, we shall not fight our battles alone. There is a just God who presides over the destinies of nations; and who will raise up friends to fight our battles for us. The battle, sir, is not to the strong alone; it is to the vigilant, the active, the brave. Besides, sir, we have no election.[13] If we were base[14] enough to desire it, it is now too late to retire from the contest. There is no retreat, but in submission and slavery! Our chains are forged! Their clanking may be heard on the plains of Boston! The war is inevitable—

❹
Note Henry's use of **rhetorical questions,** or questions asked for effect with no answer anticipated.

❓ *How do these questions help anticipate the arguments of his opponents?*

❺
❓ *What **appeals to reason** does Henry make in this paragraph? What does he want the colonists to understand?*

---

8. **remonstrated** *v.:* objected; complained.
9. **interposition** *n.:* intervention; stepping in to try to solve the problem.
10. **fond** *adj.:* foolishly optimistic.
11. **formidable** *adj.:* powerful; difficult to defeat.
12. **delusive** *adj.:* deceptive; misleading.
13. **election** *n.:* choice.
14. **base** *adj.:* showing little courage, honor, or decency.

---

**Vocabulary**

**supplication** (sup′lə·kā′shən) *n.:* plea; prayer.
**avert** (ə·vʉrt′) *v.:* prevent; turn away.
**spurned** (spʉrnd) *v.:* rejected.
**inviolate** (in·vī′ə·lit) *adj.:* uncorrupted.
**adversary** (ad′vər·ser′ē) *n.:* opponent.
**vigilant** (vij′ə·lənt) *adj.* used as *n.:* those who are watchful.
**inevitable** (in·ev′i·tə·bəl) *adj.:* not avoidable.

and let it come! I repeat it, sir, let it come! ❻

It is in vain, sir, to extenuate[15] the matter. Gentlemen may cry peace, peace—but there is no peace. The war is actually begun! The next gale that sweeps from the north will bring to our ears the

15. **extenuate** *v.*: weaken.

❻
**?** What fiery language and **loaded words** does Henry use in this paragraph? What effect do you think his words would have had on the audience?

clash of resounding arms! Our brethren are already in the field! Why stand we here idle? What is it that gentlemen wish? What would they have? Is life so dear, or peace so sweet, as to be purchased at the price of chains and slavery? Forbid it, Almighty God! I know not what course others may take; but as for me, give me liberty, or give me death! ❼

❼
To wrap up his speech, Henry uses a final strong **appeal to emotion.**
**?** What makes his conclusions so powerful?

# Response and Analysis

## Reading Check

1. According to the first two paragraphs of this speech, why is Henry speaking out?

2. In the third paragraph, what facts does Henry offer to convince his listeners that Great Britain will not respond to peaceful petitions?

3. In the fourth paragraph, what facts does Henry offer to prove that the colonists have tried everything and that war is now the only solution?

4. According to the fifth paragraph, what answers does Henry give to those who say that the colonists cannot win the war?

5. In the sixth paragraph, how does Henry wrap up his argument?

## Thinking Critically

6. Review your two-column chart, noting especially the appeals you starred and those you marked with an X. What made these appeals powerful or weak? Explain whether you are more convinced by Henry's appeals to **reason** or his appeals to **emotion.**

7. In the fourth paragraph, what **metaphors** does Henry use to describe the coming war?

8. Henry makes use of the **rhetorical question**—a question that is asked for effect. Rhetorical questions, which are often used in **persuasion,** presume that the audience agrees with the speaker on the answers and so no answer is expected or required. Find the series of rhetorical questions in the fifth paragraph of this speech. How does this technique make Henry's speech more persuasive?

9. Because his audience knew the Bible, as well as classical mythology, Henry knew he could count on certain **allusions** to produce emotional effects. Look up the classical or biblical passages that Henry alludes to in each of the following statements from his speech. How would each allusion relate to the conflict in Virginia in 1775? Could any of them relate to life today? Explain.

   • "We are apt to . . . listen to the song of that siren, till she transforms us into beasts." (*Odyssey*, Books 10 and 12)

   • "Are we disposed to be of the number of those who, having eyes, see not, and having ears, hear not, the things which so nearly concern their temporal salvation?" (Ezekiel 12:2)

**SKILLS FOCUS**

**Literary Skills**
Analyze the use of persuasion.

**Reading Skills**
Analyze modes of persuasion, including appeals to reason and appeals to emotion.

**Writing Skills**
Write an essay comparing and contrasting a speech with a sermon.

**Vocabulary Skills**
Understand synonyms.

**INTERNET**
Projects and Activities
Keyword: LE7 11-1

- "Suffer not yourselves to be betrayed with a kiss." (Luke 22:47–48)
10. An **assertion** is a statement that declares a position on some issue or topic. What assertions would you make about Patrick Henry's arguments that the Colonies should arm for war? How will you back up your assertions? Be sure to discuss your assertions in class.

## Extending and Evaluating

11. Look back at your Quickwrite notes on your feelings about liberty. Do you think liberty is more important than life itself? Explain your answers. 🖉

## WRITING

### Politician Versus Preacher

In a brief essay, **compare and contrast** Patrick Henry's speech with Jonathan Edwards's sermon "Sinners in the Hands of an Angry God" (page 46). Consider the specific ways in which the speech and sermon are alike and the ways they are different. Use the following chart to help organize your material:

| Elements of the Oration | Edwards | Henry |
|---|---|---|
| Speaker's purpose and audience | | |
| Main idea | | |
| Appeals to reason and emotion | | |
| Use of metaphors | | |
| Use of rhetorical questions | | |
| Overall effectiveness | | |

## Vocabulary Development

### In Other Words

| | |
|---|---|
| solace | spurned |
| insidious | inviolate |
| martial | adversary |
| supplication | vigilant |
| avert | inevitable |

Replace the underlined word or words below with a word from the list above.

1. The British failed to respond to the plea of the Colonies.
2. Henry thought a warlike confrontation was impossible to avoid.
3. Some colonists found comfort in ignoring the danger signs.
4. The watchful will outwit their opponent.
5. Henry believed that the true plans of the British were underhanded.
6. We must try to turn away the approaching troops.
7. The British rejected with contempt the colonists' attempts to compromise.
8. Henry would fight to keep his rights sacred and protected.

# Thomas Paine
## (1737–1809)

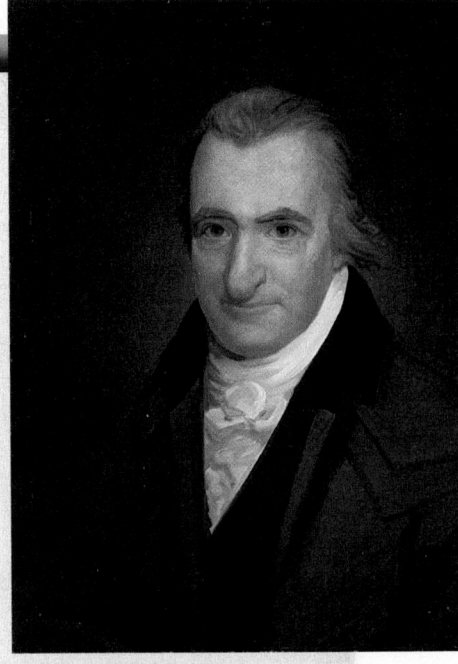

*Thomas Paine* (1806–1807) by John Wesley Jarvis. Oil on canvas.

Image © 2005 Board of Trustees, National Gallery of Art, Washington, D.C. Gift of Marian B. Maurice.

The most persuasive writer of the American Revolution came from an unlikely background. Thomas Paine, the poorly educated son of a corset maker, was born in England and spent his first thirty-seven years drifting through occupations—corset maker, grocer, tobacconist, schoolteacher, tax collector. In 1774, Paine was dismissed from his job as a tax collector for attempting to organize the employees in a demand for higher wages (an unusual activity in those days). Like many others at that time and since, he came to America to make a new start.

With a letter of introduction from Benjamin Franklin (page 67), whom he had met in London, Paine went to Philadelphia, where he worked as a journalist. In the conflict between England and the Colonies, he quickly identified with the underdog. In January 1776, he published the most important written work in support of American independence: *Common Sense,* a forty-seven-page pamphlet that denounced King George III as a "royal brute" and asserted that a continent should not remain tied to an island. The pamphlet sold a half-million copies—in a country whose total population was roughly two and a quarter million.

After the Revolution, Paine lived peacefully in New York and New Jersey until 1787, when he returned to Europe. There he became involved once more in radical revolutionary politics, supporting the French Revolution. In 1791, he began to compose *The Rights of Man,* a reply to the English statesman Edmund Burke's condemnation of the French revolt. *The Rights of Man* was an impassioned defense of republican government and a call to the English people to overthrow their king. Although he was living in France at the time, Paine was tried for treason in England and banned from the country. Safe in France from English law, he was briefly celebrated as a hero of the French Revolution, but Paine was soon imprisoned for being a citizen of an enemy nation (England). James Monroe, the American minister to France at the time, gained his release in 1794 by insisting that Paine was an American citizen.

Paine's final notable work, *The Age of Reason,* was published in two parts, the first in 1794 and the second in 1796. Expounding the principles of deism (page 18), the book was controversial in America. Americans did not fully understand Paine's ideas and thought he was an atheist—that he did not believe in God. When Paine returned to America in 1802, he was a virtual outcast, scorned as a dangerous radical and nonbeliever. He was stripped of his right to vote, had no money, and was continually harassed. When he died in New York in 1809, he was denied burial in consecrated ground. His body was buried on his farm in New Rochelle.

Even in death, though, Thomas Paine was not allowed to rest. In 1819, an English sympathizer named William Cobbett dug up Paine's body and removed it and the coffin to England, intending to erect a memorial to the author of *The Rights of Man.* No monument was ever built. The last record of Paine's remains shows that the coffin and the bones were acquired by a furniture dealer in England in 1844.

# *from* The Crisis, No. 1

## Make the Connection
### Quickwrite

At various times in life, we have to make personal sacrifices for a common cause. The early American colonists were urged to do just that by Thomas Paine in *The Crisis, No. 1*. Record your thoughts on the crucial decision facing the colonists: Should they kneel as British subjects or stand together as Americans? Try to identify the conflicts this posed for the colonists.

## Literary Focus
### Style

A writer's **style** is the distinctive way in which he or she uses language. Style is largely determined by **sentence structure, word choice,** and use of **figurative language** and **imagery.** Paine uses a combination of styles: Direct, common speech is mixed with heightened expressions that are sharpened by dramatic rhetorical techniques. Paine says that he speaks "in language as plain as A, B, C," yet he also includes such lofty declarations as "What we obtain too cheap, we esteem too lightly."

> **Style** is the distinctive way in which a writer uses language.
>
> *For more on Style, see the Handbook of Literary and Historical Terms.*

## Reading Skills
### Recognizing Modes of Persuasion

A good writer of **persuasion** advances his or her argument by using a variety of appeals. By citing evidence, facts, and statistics, a writer can appeal to **logic,** or the reason of the audience. By using loaded words, figurative language, and personal experiences, the writer can arouse the **emotions** of the audience.

In *The Crisis,* watch especially for these two literary techniques—an **analogy** that compares the king with a thief and an **anecdote** about a tavern keeper and his child. As you read, write down the extent to which each technique appeals to both reason and emotion.

## Background

In 1776, Paine joined the Continental army as it retreated across New Jersey to Philadelphia. The exhausted and demoralized army was heavily outnumbered by the enemy. As he traveled with the army, Paine began writing a series of sixteen pamphlets called *The American Crisis,* commenting on the war and urging Americans not to give up the fight. The first of these pamphlets was read to General George Washington's troops in December 1776, a few days before the army recrossed the Delaware River to attack the British-held city of Trenton, New Jersey.

## Vocabulary Development

**tyranny** (tir′ə·nē) *n.:* cruel use of power.

**consolation** (kän′sə·lā′shən) *n.:* comfort.

**celestial** (sə·les′chəl) *adj.:* divine; perfect.

**impious** (im′pē·əs) *adj.:* irreverent.

**ravage** (rav′ij) *n.:* violent destruction.

**relinquished** (ri·liŋ′kwishd) *v.:* given up.

**pretense** (prē·tens′) *n.:* false claim.

**dominion** (də·min′yən) *n.:* rule.

**eloquence** (el′ə·kwəns) *n.:* forceful, fluent, and graceful speech.

**perseverance** (pʉr′sə·vir′əns) *n.:* persistence.

**SKILLS FOCUS**

**Literary Skills**
Understand the characteristics of style.

**Reading Skills**
Recognize modes of persuasion, including appeals to logic, appeals to emotion, and analogy.

go. hrw .com

**INTERNET**

**Vocabulary Practice**

Keyword: LE7 11-1

Colonial campfire reenactment, Valley Forge, Pennsylvania.

(Swords) The Granger Collection, New York.

# *from* The Crisis, No. 1

## Thomas Paine

These are the times that try men's souls. The summer soldier and the sunshine patriot will, in this crisis, shrink from the service of his country; but he that stands it NOW, deserves the love and thanks of man and woman. Tyranny, like hell, is not easily conquered; yet we have this consolation with us, that the harder the conflict, the more glorious the triumph. What we obtain too cheap, we esteem[1] too lightly; 'tis dearness only that gives everything its value. Heaven knows how to put a proper price upon its goods; and it would be strange indeed, if so celestial an article as FREEDOM should not be highly rated. Britain, with an army to enforce her tyranny, has declared that she has a right (*not only to* TAX) but "to BIND *us in* ALL CASES

---

1. **esteem** *v.:* value; hold in high regard.

**Vocabulary**

**tyranny** (tir′ə·nē) *n.:* cruel use of power.
**consolation** (kän′sə·lā′shən) *n.:* comfort.
**celestial** (sə·les′chəl) *adj.:* divine; perfect.

WHATSOEVER,"[2] and if being *bound in that manner,* is not slavery, then is there not such a thing as slavery upon earth. Even the expression is impious, for so unlimited a power can belong only to God. ❶

Whether the independence of the continent was declared too soon, or delayed too long, I will not now enter into as an argument; my own simple opinion is, that had it been eight months earlier, it would have been much better. We did not make a proper use of last winter, neither could we, while we were in a dependent state. However, the fault, if it were one, was all our own; we have none to blame but ourselves. But no great deal is lost yet; all that Howe[3] has been doing for this month past, is rather a ravage than a conquest, which the spirit of the Jerseys[4] a year ago would have quickly repulsed, and which time and a little resolution will soon recover. ❷

I have as little superstition in me as any man living, but my secret opinion has ever been, and still is, that God Almighty will not give up a people to military destruction, or leave them unsupportedly to perish, who have so earnestly and so repeatedly sought to avoid the calamities of war, by every decent method which wisdom

❶ **?** How does Paine try to persuade the colonists not to shrink from the tough struggle ahead?

❷ **?** What **reasons** does Paine give to persuade the colonists that all is not lost, even after their recent defeats?

could invent. Neither have I so much of the infidel[5] in me, as to suppose that he has relinquished the government of the world, and given us up to the care of devils; and as I do not, I cannot see on what grounds the king of Britain can look up to heaven for help against us: A common murderer, a highwayman,[6] or a housebreaker, has as good a pretense as he .... ❸

I once felt all that kind of anger, which a man ought to feel, against the mean[7] principles that are held by the Tories:[8] A noted one, who kept a tavern at Amboy,[9] was standing at his door, with as pretty a child in his hand, about eight or nine years old, as I ever saw, and after speaking his mind as freely as he thought was prudent, finished with this unfatherly expression, *"Well! Give me peace in my day."* Not a man lives on the continent but fully believes that a separation must sometime or other finally take place, and a generous parent should have said, *"If there must be trouble let it be in my day, that my child may have peace";* and this single reflection, well applied, is sufficient to awaken every man to duty. Not a place upon earth might be so happy as America. Her situation is remote from all the wrangling world, and she has nothing to do but

❸ **?** What **appeals to emotion** does Paine use here to rally the colonists against the English king? Look especially at the **loaded words.**

---

2. **to bind ... whatsoever:** In response to Colonial protests over the Stamp Act (which taxed all commercial and legal documents in the Colonies), Parliament repealed the act on March 17, 1766. On the same day, it passed the Declaratory Act, which stated that Parliament had the right "to make laws . . . to bind the Colonies and people of America . . . in all cases whatsoever."
3. **Howe:** Sir William Howe, commander in chief of the British forces in America during the Revolution.
4. **Jerseys:** New Jersey was at this time divided into East Jersey and West Jersey.

5. **infidel** *n.:* unbeliever.
6. **highwayman** *n.:* thief who patrolled the highways and robbed travelers.
7. **mean** *adj.:* low.
8. **Tories:** those who supported British rule in the American Colonies.
9. **Amboy:** Perth Amboy, New Jersey.

---

**Vocabulary**

**impious** (im′pē·əs) *adj.:* irreverent.
**ravage** (rav′ij) *n.:* violent destruction.
**relinquished** (ri·liŋ′kwishd) *v.:* given up.
**pretense** (prē·tens′) *n.:* false claim.

to trade with them. A man can distinguish himself between temper and principle, and I am as confident, as I am that God governs the world, that America will never be happy till she gets clear of foreign dominion. Wars, without ceasing, will break out till that period arrives, and the continent must in the end be conqueror; for though the flame of liberty may sometimes cease to shine, the coal can never expire. ❹

America did not, nor does not want[10] force; but she wanted a proper application of that force. Wisdom is not the purchase of a day, and it is no wonder that we should err at the first setting off. From an excess of tenderness, we were unwilling to raise an army, and trusted our cause to the temporary defense of a well-meaning militia.[11] A summer's experience has now taught us better; yet with those troops, while they were collected, we were able to set bounds to the progress of the enemy, and—thank God!—they are again assembling. I always consider militia as the best troops in the world for a sudden exertion, but they will not do for a long campaign. Howe, it is probable, will make an attempt on this city;[12] should he fail on this side the Delaware, he is ruined: If he succeeds, our cause is not ruined. He stakes all on his side against a part on ours; admitting he succeeds, the consequence will be, that armies from both ends of the continent will march to assist their suffering friends in the middle states; for he cannot go everywhere; it is impossible. I consider Howe the greatest enemy the Tories have; he is bringing a war into their country, which, had it not been for him and partly for themselves, they had been clear of. Should he now be expelled, I wish with all the devotion of

❹ What powerful **emotional appeal** does Paine use here to convince Americans that they must get rid of foreign domination?

a *Christian*, that the names of Whig[13] and Tory may never more be mentioned; but should the Tories give him encouragement to come, or assistance if he come, I as sincerely wish that our next year's arms may expel them from the continent, and that congress appropriate their possessions to the relief of those who have suffered in well doing. A single successful battle next year will settle the whole. America could carry on a two years' war by the confiscation of the property of disaffected[14] persons; and be made happy by their expulsion. Say not that this is revenge, call it rather the soft resentment of a suffering people, who, having no object in view but the *good* of *all*, have staked their *own all* upon a seemingly doubtful event. Yet it is folly to argue against determined hardness; eloquence may strike the ear, and the language of sorrow draw forth the tear of compassion, but nothing can reach the heart that is steeled with prejudice. ❺

❺ What does Paine suggest be done with the Tories, the colonists who sympathize with the British?

Quitting this class of men, I turn with the warm ardor[15] of a friend to those who have nobly stood, and are yet determined to stand the matter out: I call not upon a few, but upon all; not on *this* state or *that* state, but on *every* state; up and help us; lay your shoulders to the wheel; better have too much force than too little, when so great an object is at stake. Let it be told to the future world, that in the depth of winter, when nothing but hope and virtue could survive, that the city and the country, alarmed at one

---

10. **want** *v.*: lack.
11. **militia** *n.*: By "militia," Paine means an army of citizens quickly raised to meet an emergency. An army would be better equipped and well trained.
12. **this city:** Philadelphia.

---

13. **Whig:** The Whigs were colonists who supported the Revolution.
14. **disaffected** *adj.*: disloyal, especially toward the government.
15. **ardor** *n.*: emotional warmth; passion.

---

**Vocabulary**

**dominion** (də·min′yən) *n.*: rule.
**eloquence** (el′ə·kwəns) *n.*: forceful, fluent, and graceful speech.

Reenactment of a redcoat musket firing, Trenton, New Jersey.

common danger, came forth to meet and to repulse it. Say not that thousands are gone, turn out your tens of thousands;[16] throw not the burden of the day upon Providence, but "*show your faith by your works*,"[17] that God may bless you. It matters not where you live, or what rank of life you hold, the evil or the blessing will reach you all. The far and the near, the home counties and the back, the rich and the poor, will suffer or rejoice alike. The heart that feels not now, is dead: The blood of his children will curse his cowardice, who shrinks back at a time when a little might have saved the whole, and made *them* happy. (I love the man that can smile at trouble; that can gather strength from distress; and grow brave by reflection.) 'Tis the business of little minds to shrink; but he whose heart is firm, and whose conscience approves his conduct, will pursue his principles unto

death. My own line of reasoning is to myself as straight and clear as a ray of light. Not all the treasures of the world, so far as I believe, could have induced me to support an offensive war, for I think it murder; but if a thief breaks into my house, burns and destroys my property, and kills or threatens to kill me, or those that are in it, and to *"bind me in all cases whatsoever,"* to his absolute will, am I to suffer it? What signifies it to me, whether he who does it is a king or a common man; my countryman, or not my countryman; whether it be done by an individual villain or an army of them? If we reason to the root of things we shall find no difference; neither can any just cause be assigned why we should punish in the one case and pardon in the other. Let them call me rebel, and welcome, I feel no concern from it; but I should suffer the misery of devils, were I to make a whore of my soul by swearing allegiance to one whose character is that of a sottish,[18] stupid, stubborn, worthless, brutish man. I conceive likewise a horrid idea in receiving mercy from a being, who at the last day shall be shrieking to the rocks and mountains to cover him, and fleeing with terror from the orphan, the widow, and the slain of America. **6**

> **6**
>
> **?** What strong **emotional arguments** does Paine use here to demonize the British king?

There are cases which cannot be overdone by language, and this is one. There are persons too who see not the full extent of the evil which threatens them; they solace[19] themselves with hopes that the enemy, if he succeeds, will be merciful. Is this the madness of folly, to expect mercy from those who have refused to do justice; and even mercy, where conquest is the object, is only a trick of war; the cunning of the fox is as murderous as the violence of the wolf; and we ought to guard equally against both. Howe's first object is partly by threats and partly by promises, to terrify or seduce the people to

---

16. **thousands . . . tens of thousands:** "Saul hath slain his thousands, and David his ten thousands" (1 Samuel 18:7).
17. **show . . . works:** "Show me thy faith without thy works, and I will show thee my faith by my works" (James 2:18).

18. **sottish** (sät′ish) *adj.:* stupid or foolish from too much drinking.
19. **solace** *v.:* comfort; soothe.

deliver up their arms and to receive mercy. The ministry recommended the same plan to Gage,[20] and this is what the Tories call making their peace, *"a peace which passeth all understanding,"*[21] indeed! A peace which would be the immediate forerunner of a worse ruin than any we have yet thought of. Ye men of Pennsylvania, do reason upon these things! Were the back counties to give up their arms, they would fall an easy prey to the Indians, who are all armed; this perhaps is what some Tories would not be sorry for. Were the home counties to deliver up their arms, they would be exposed to the resentment of the back counties, who would then have it in their power to chastise[22] their defection[23] at pleasure. And were any one state to give up its arms, *that* state must be garrisoned[24] by Howe's army of Britains and Hessians[25] to preserve it from the anger of the rest. Mutual fear is the principal link in the chain of mutual love, and woe be to *that* state that breaks the compact. Howe is mercifully inviting you to barbarous destruction, and men must be either rogues or fools that will not see it. I dwell not upon the powers of imagination; I bring reason to your ears; and in language as plain as A, B, C, hold up truth to your eyes. ❼

I thank God that I fear not. I see no real cause for fear. I know our situation well and can see the way out of it. While our army was collected, Howe dared not risk a battle, and it is no credit to him that he decamped from the White Plains, and waited a mean opportunity to ravage the defenseless Jerseys;[26] but it is great credit to us, that, with a handful of men, we sustained an orderly retreat for near an hundred miles, brought off our ammunition, all our field pieces, the greatest part of our stores, and had four rivers to pass. None can say that our retreat was precipitate,[27] for we were near three weeks in performing it, that the country[28] might have time to come in. Twice we marched back to meet the enemy, and remained out till dark. The sign of fear was not seen in our camp, and had not some of the cowardly and disaffected inhabitants spread false alarms through the country, the Jerseys had never been ravaged. Once more we are again collected and collecting, our new army at both ends of the continent is recruiting fast, and we shall be able to open the next campaign with sixty thousand men, well armed and clothed. This is our situation, and who will may know it. By perseverance and fortitude we have the prospect of a glorious issue; by cowardice and submission, the sad choice of a variety of evils—a ravaged country—a depopulated city—habitations without safety, and slavery without hope—our homes turned into barracks and bawdyhouses for Hessians, and a future race to provide for, whose fathers we shall doubt of. Look on this picture and weep over it! And if there yet remains one thoughtless wretch who believes it not, let him suffer it unlamented. ❽

> ❼
>
> Paine says he brings reason to the colonists' ears.
>
> ❓ Which of his arguments here are based on **reason**? Which are **emotional**?

> ❽
>
> ❓ What final **emotional** and **logical appeals** does Paine use to persuade his readers to maintain the struggle and not give up?

---

20. **Gage:** Gen. Thomas Gage, head of the British forces in America before Gen. Howe took over.
21. **a peace ... understanding:** ironic echo of Paul's epistle to the Philippians (Philippians 4:7).
22. **chastise** *v.:* criticize severely; punish.
23. **defection** *n.:* desertion; abandonment.
24. **garrisoned** *v.:* supplied with troops.
25. **Hessians** (hesh′ənz): German troops, mostly from the region of Hesse, hired to fight on the British side.

26. **White Plains ... Jerseys:** Howe had defeated George Washington at White Plains, New York, in 1776 but had failed to press his advantage.
27. **precipitate** (prē·sip′ə·tit) *adj.:* sudden; unexpected.
28. **country** *n.:* the local people. Paine uses the term to refer to local volunteers.

---

**Vocabulary**

**perseverance** (pʉr′sə·vir′əns) *n.:* persistence.

# Response and Analysis

## Reading Check

1. Paine opens with a powerful emotional appeal. In the third paragraph, what reasons does he give for his confidence that God will favor the Americans and not the British?

2. Re-read the fourth paragraph and the anecdote about the tavern keeper at Amboy. Why does Paine view the Tory tavern keeper's harmless remark as "unfatherly"?

3. What powerful **emotional appeal** does Paine make at the end of this part of his essay to describe the choices facing the colonists?

**SKILLS FOCUS**

**Literary Skills**
Analyze a writer's style.

**Reading Skills**
Analyze modes of persuasion, including appeals to logic, appeals to emotion, and analogy.

**Writing Skills**
Write an essay analyzing a persuasive essay.

**Vocabulary Skills**
Analyze synonyms.

**INTERNET**

Projects and Activities

Keyword: LE7 11-1

## Thinking Critically

4. What is Paine's main **purpose** in writing this essay? In your opinion, what details supporting that purpose are most powerful?

5. The pamphlet opens with two famous **images** (page 89). What kinds of people does Paine identify with summer and sunshine? Why are these images appropriate?

6. Explain the meaning of Paine's **metaphor** "Mutual fear is the principal link in the chain of mutual love" (page 93). Do you agree or disagree with this idea, and why?

*Common Sense,* pamphlet by Thomas Paine.
Courtesy National Park Service, Museum Management Program and Guilford Courthouse National Military Park.

7. An **analogy** is a comparison between two things that are alike in certain respects. Analogies are used often in **argument** and **persuasion** to demonstrate the logic of one idea by showing how it is similar to another accepted idea. Analogies can be tricky, though, because few ideas or situations are completely alike in all aspects. What analogy does Paine draw when he talks about the thief (page 92)? What point is he making, and how might an opponent answer?

8. One of Paine's persuasive strategies is to anticipate and then refute possible **counterclaims,** or opposing arguments, to his ideas. For example, on page 91, he anticipates criticism when he writes, "Say not that this is revenge." Find another example of this persuasive strategy, and then evaluate Paine's rebuttal of its potential counterclaim.

## Extending and Evaluating

9. "Not a place upon earth might be so happy as America. Her situation is remote from all the wrangling world, and she has nothing to do but to trade with them. . . . I am . . . confident . . . that America will never be happy till she gets clear of foreign dominion" (pages 90–91). Evaluate these words from Paine's pamphlet. Considering the world as it is today, how would you reply to Paine?

10. Review your Quickwrite notes about the difficult decisions that colonists faced. If you were a colonist reading this excerpt from *The Crisis,* would you be persuaded to continue the fight for liberty? Why or why not?

11. Paine's essay is full of memorable and moving statements. Find some that could be used to encourage people to face the kinds of conflicts that threaten the peace today.

# WRITING

## Taking It Apart

Write an **essay** in which you first sum up the main points of Paine's essay and then identify the logical and emotional appeals he provides to support those points. Before you write, review your responses to the questions asked in the margins of the essay itself. Then, gather your details in a chart like the following one:

Main Points:

Key Statements:

Emotional Appeals:

1.

2.

3.

Logical Appeals:

1.

2.

3.

## Vocabulary Development

### Synonyms

Choose the *best* synonym (word or words that have the same or similar meaning) for each item.

1. CELESTIAL:
   - **a.** disastrous
   - **c.** fake
   - **b.** heavenly
   - **d.** ordinary

2. DOMINION:
   - **a.** house
   - **c.** agreement
   - **b.** slavery
   - **d.** reign

3. TYRANNY:
   - **a.** oppression
   - **c.** anger
   - **b.** justice
   - **d.** skill

4. IMPIOUS:
   - **a.** greedy
   - **c.** unfriendly
   - **b.** holy
   - **d.** disrespectful

5. PRETENSE:
   - **a.** claim
   - **c.** calm
   - **b.** tension
   - **d.** reality

6. RAVAGE:
   - **a.** construction
   - **c.** damage
   - **b.** stronghold
   - **d.** enrichment

7. RELINQUISHED:
   - **a.** found
   - **c.** won
   - **b.** abandoned
   - **d.** surrounded

8. PERSEVERANCE:
   - **a.** sloth
   - **c.** resistance
   - **b.** determination
   - **d.** harshness

9. CONSOLATION:
   - **a.** aggression
   - **c.** hindrance
   - **b.** comfort
   - **d.** misery

10. ELOQUENCE:
    - **a.** prejudice
    - **c.** powerful speech
    - **b.** slang
    - **d.** bad behavior

# Introduction **Comparing Points** *of* **View**

## Freedom and Equality

You will be reading the four selections listed above in this Comparing Points of View feature on freedom and equality. In the top corner of the pages in this feature, you'll find three stars. Smaller versions of the stars appear next to the questions on page 106 that focus on freedom and equality. At the end of the feature (page 114), you'll compare these points of view.

### Examining the Issue: Freedom and Equality

Today freedom and equality are guaranteed for you and people of all races, religions, and genders, according to the laws of the United States. Every citizen is guaranteed equal and fair treatment under the laws and the freedom to openly express ideas. Every citizen is also guaranteed the right to vote. However, this was not always the case. When the Declaration of Independence was written, only white males could vote. Many groups in our country have had to fight long and hard to gain equality and the right to vote.

### Make the Connection

#### Quickwrite ✐

Take a few minutes to write about what freedom and equality mean to you. Are these rights something you take for granted, or do you hold them precious? Comment on how you regard freedom and equality.

### Reading Skills ✍

#### Comparing Main Ideas Across Texts

When you compare texts, first identify the main ideas of each text, and then identify the key details that support each main idea. As you read the following documents, on pages 99–113, fill in a chart like this one:

Pages 96–114 cover
**Literary Skills**
Analyze points of view on a topic.

**Reading Skills**
Compare main ideas across texts.

| Selection | Main Idea | Key Supporting Details |
|-----------|-----------|------------------------|
|           |           |                        |
|           |           |                        |

# Thomas Jefferson
## (1743–1826)

*Thomas Jefferson* (1791) by Charles Willson Peale. Oil on canvas.

In 1962, at a White House dinner honoring forty-nine Nobel Prize winners, President John F. Kennedy hailed his guests as "the most extraordinary collection of talent, of human knowledge, that has ever been gathered together at the White House, with the possible exception of when Thomas Jefferson dined alone." President Kennedy was exaggerating only slightly.

Thomas Jefferson, the brilliant and versatile third president of the United States, was an accomplished statesman, architect, botanist, paleontologist, linguist, and musician. He displayed the range of interests that we associate with the eighteenth-century mind at its best.

Jefferson was born in the red clay country of what is now Albemarle County, Virginia. Jefferson's father, a surveyor and magistrate, died when Thomas was fourteen, but he had provided his son with an excellent classical education and an estate of five thousand acres. After attending the College of William and Mary, Jefferson became a lawyer, a member of the Virginia House of Burgesses, and a spokesperson for the rights of personal liberty and religious freedom. In 1774, he wrote a pamphlet called *A Summary View of the Rights of British America*, a call for the rejection of parliamentary authority. Two years later the Second Continental Congress chose him to help draft the Declaration of Independence.

During the Revolution, Jefferson served for a time as governor of Virginia. When the British invaded Virginia, he retired to Monticello, the home he had designed, and devoted himself to his family and to scientific research. During this time he also composed most of his *Notes on the State of Virginia*. Shortly after Jefferson's beloved wife Martha died in 1782, he returned to public life, in part as an escape from his private grief. He served as minister to France, secretary of state, and vice president and then served as president from 1801 to 1809.

A determined opponent of federal power, Jefferson embodied the principles of what would come to be called Jeffersonian democracy. He believed in the rights of individuals and states to govern themselves as much as possible. He strove to keep power vested in the agrarian backbone of the country. He also expanded the country enormously in 1803: The Louisiana Purchase doubled the size of the United States, adding land that would later be divided into part or all of fifteen states. As for Jefferson's presidential style, he avoided public displays and wore simple clothes: A president, he thought, should neither act nor look like a king.

After his presidency, Jefferson retired once again to Monticello. He devoted his energy to the establishment of the University of Virginia, planning its courses of study and designing many of its buildings. In 1826, both Jefferson (at eighty-three) and the former president John Adams (at ninety) became gravely ill. Both hoped to live to see the fiftieth anniversary of the independence they had done so much to ensure. Jefferson died on the morning of July 4, several hours before Adams, whose last words were "Thomas Jefferson still survives."

# Before You Read

## *from* The Autobiography: The Declaration of Independence

### Points *of* View

Without a doubt the cornerstone of the American dream is the ideal of freedom. The words of the Declaration of Independence are a ringing affirmation of freedom. However, Jefferson knew that freedom's twin is responsibility—every kind of liberty we enjoy has to be balanced by an equal amount of personal responsibility.

### Literary Focus

#### Parallelism

**Parallelism** is the repeated use of sentences, clauses, or phrases with identical or similar structures. For example, when Jefferson cites the truths that are "self-evident," he begins each clause with *that*. He also begins a long series of paragraphs with the words *He has*. Jefferson's use of parallelism creates a stately **rhythm,** or **cadence,** in the Declaration. Listen for this cadence as you read passages aloud.

**SKILLS FOCUS**

**Literary Skills**
Analyze points of view on a topic. Understand the use of parallelism.

**Parallelism,** or parallel structure, is the repetition of grammatically similar words, phrases, clauses, or sentences.

*For more on Parallel Structure, see the Handbook of Literary and Historical Terms.*

go. hrw .com

**INTERNET**

Vocabulary Practice
•
More About Thomas Jefferson
•

Keyword: LE7 11-1

### Background

Four other writers worked with Jefferson on the draft of the Declaration that was submitted to Congress: John Adams of Massachusetts, Roger Sherman of Connecticut, Robert Livingston of New York, and Benjamin Franklin of Pennsylvania. Few changes were made by these other writers, but Congress insisted on major alterations. Jefferson was upset by what he called "mutilations" of his document.

In *The Autobiography,* Jefferson chronicled the alterations Congress made. The underlined passages in the Declaration show the parts omitted by Congress from the original. The words added by Congress appear in the margins.

### Vocabulary Development

**prudence** (prōō′dəns) *n.:* sound judgment.

**transient** (tran′shənt) *adj.:* temporary.

**constrains** (kən·strānz′) *v.:* forces.

**expunge** (ek·spunj′) *v.:* erase; remove.

**candid** (kan′did) *adj.:* unbiased; fair.

**abdicated** (ab′di·kāt′id) *v.:* given up responsibility for.

**confiscation** (kän′fis·kā′shən) *n.:* seizure of property by authority.

**magnanimity** (mag′nə·nim′ə·tē) *n.:* nobility of spirit.

**renounce** (ri·nouns′) *v.:* give up.

**acquiesce** (ak′wē·es′) *v.:* accept quietly.

*In June 1776, the Second Continental Congress appointed a five-person committee including Thomas Jefferson to write a document declaring the Colonies' independence from Britain. By signing the Declaration, a full-scale rebellion was launched against Britain, but tension also mounted within the newly formed United States. John Dickinson, one of Pennsylvania's representatives to the Second Continental Congress, led the conservative opposition to the Declaration and refused to sign the document, alleging that the colonists were not ready for such a fight. In the excerpt from his autobiography below, Jefferson explains some of the problems with the original draft of the document, of which he was the main author.*

# *from* The Autobiography:
# The Declaration of Independence

## Thomas Jefferson

Thomas Jefferson. Fragment of white marble.
The Maryland Historical Society, Baltimore, Maryland.

Congress proceeded the same day to consider the Declaration of Independence, which had been reported and lain on the table the Friday preceding, and on Monday referred to a committee of the whole. The pusillanimous[1] idea that we had friends in England worth keeping terms with, still haunted the minds of many. For this reason, those passages which conveyed censures[2] on the people of England were struck out, lest they should give them offense. The clause too, reprobating[3] the enslaving the inhabitants of Africa, was struck out in complaisance[4] to South Carolina and Georgia, who had never attempted to restrain the importation of slaves, and who, on the contrary, still wished to continue it. Our northern brethren also, I believe, felt a little tender under those censures; for though their people had very few slaves themselves, yet they had been pretty considerable carriers of them to others. The debates, having taken up the greater parts of the 2d, 3d, and 4th days of July, were, on the evening of the last, closed; the Declaration was reported by the committee, agreed to by the House, and signed by every member present, except Mr. Dickinson. As the sentiments of men are known not only by what they receive, but what they reject also, I will state the form of the Declaration as originally reported. The parts struck out by Congress shall be distinguished by a black line drawn under them; and those inserted by them shall be placed in the margin, or in a concurrent column.

---

1. **pusillanimous** (pyo͞o′si·lan′ə·məs) *adj.:* cowardly; lacking courage.
2. **censures** *n. pl.:* strong, disapproving criticisms.
3. **reprobating** *v.:* disapproving; condemning.
4. **complaisance** *n.:* desire to please.

# A Declaration by the Representatives of the United States of America, in General Congress Assembled

When, in the course of human events, it becomes necessary for one people to dissolve the political bands which have connected them with another, and to assume among the powers of the earth the separate and equal station to which the laws of nature and of nature's God entitle them, a decent respect to the opinions of mankind requires that they should declare the causes which impel them to the separation.

We hold these truths to be self-evident: that all men are created equal; that they are endowed by their creator with inherent and inalienable rights;[1] that among these are life, liberty, and the pursuit of happiness; that to secure these rights, governments are instituted among men, deriving their just powers from the consent of the governed; that whenever any form of government becomes destructive of these ends, it is the right of the people to alter or to abolish it, and to institute new government, laying its foundation on such principles, and organizing its powers in such form, as to them shall seem most likely to effect their safety and happiness. Prudence, indeed, will dictate that governments long established should not be changed for light and transient causes; and accordingly all experience hath shown that mankind are more disposed to suffer while evils are sufferable, than to right themselves by abolishing the forms to which they are accustomed. But when a long train of abuses and usurpations,[2] begun at a distinguished[3] period and pursuing invariably the same object, evinces[4] a design to reduce them under absolute despotism,[5] it is their right, it is their duty to throw off such government, and to provide new

certain

---

1. **inalienable** (in·āl′yən·ə·bəl) **rights:** rights that cannot be taken away.
2. **usurpations** (yo͞o′sər·pā′shənz) *n. pl.:* acts of unlawful or forceful seizure of property, power, rights, and the like.
3. **distinguished** *v.* used as *adj.:* clearly defined.
4. **evinces** *v.:* indicates; makes clear.
5. **despotism** *n.:* rule by a tyrant or king with unlimited power.

---

**Vocabulary**

**prudence** (pro͞o′dəns) *n.:* sound judgment.
**transient** (tran′shənt) *adj.:* temporary.

guards for their future security. Such has been the patient sufferance of these colonies; and such is now the necessity which constrains them to expunge their former systems of government. The history of the present king of Great Britain is a history of unremitting injuries and usurpations, among which appears no solitary fact to contradict the uniform tenor of the rest, but all have in direct object the establishment of an absolute tyranny over these states. To prove this, let facts be submitted to a candid world for the truth of which we pledge a faith yet unsullied by falsehood.

*alter*

*repeated*

*all having*

He has refused his assent[6] to laws the most wholesome and necessary for the public good.

He has forbidden his governors to pass laws of immediate and pressing importance, unless suspended in their operation till his assent should be obtained; and, when so suspended, he has utterly neglected to attend to them.

He has refused to pass other laws for the accommodation of large districts of people, unless those people would relinquish the right of representation in the legislature, a right inestimable[7] to them, and formidable to tyrants only.[8]

He has called together legislative bodies at places unusual, uncomfortable, and distant from the depository of their public records, for the sole purpose of fatiguing them into compliance with his measures.

He has dissolved representative houses repeatedly and continually for opposing with manly firmness his invasions on the rights of the people.

He has refused for a long time after such dissolutions to cause others to be elected, whereby the legislative powers, incapable of annihilation, have returned to the people at large for their exercise, the state remaining, in the meantime, exposed to all the dangers of invasion from without and convulsions within.

He has endeavored[9] to prevent the population of these states; for that purpose obstructing the laws for naturalization[10] of foreigners,

---

6. **assent** *n.:* agreement.
7. **inestimable** *adj.:* invaluable; priceless.
8. **formidable . . . only:** causing fear only to tyrants.
9. **endeavored** *v.:* attempted; tried.
10. **naturalization** *n.:* process by which foreigners become citizens.

---

**Vocabulary**

**constrains** (kən·strānz′) *v.:* forces.
**expunge** (ek·spunj′) *v.:* erase; remove.
**candid** (kan′did) *adj.:* unbiased; fair.

refusing to pass others to encourage their migrations hither, and
raising the conditions of new appropriations of lands.

He has suffered the administration of justice totally to cease in some
of these states refusing his assent to laws for establishing judiciary
powers.

obstructed / by

He has made our judges dependent on his will alone for the tenure[11]
of their offices, and the amount and payment of their salaries.

He has erected a multitude of new offices, by a self-assumed power
and sent hither swarms of new officers to harass our people and eat out
their substance.

He has kept among us in times of peace standing armies and ships
of war without the consent of our legislatures.

He has affected to render the military independent of, and superior
to, the civil power.

He has combined with others[12] to subject us to a jurisdiction foreign to our constitutions and unacknowledged by our laws, giving his
assent to their acts of pretended legislation for quartering large bodies
of armed troops among us; for protecting them by a mock trial from
punishment for any murders which they should commit on the
inhabitants of these states; for cutting off our trade with all parts of the
world; for imposing taxes on us without our consent; for depriving us
[ ] of the benefits of trial by jury; for transporting us beyond seas to be
tried for pretended offenses; for abolishing the free system of English
laws in a neighboring province,[13] establishing therein an arbitrary
government, and enlarging its boundaries, so as to render it at once an
example and fit instrument for introducing the same absolute rule into
these states; for taking away our charters, abolishing our most valuable
laws, and altering fundamentally the forms of our governments; for
suspending our own legislatures, and declaring themselves invested
with power to legislate for us in all cases whatsoever.

in many cases

colonies

He has abdicated government here withdrawing his governors, and
declaring us out of his allegiance and protection.

by declaring us out of his
protection, and waging war
against us.

He has plundered our seas, ravaged our coasts, burnt our towns, and
destroyed the lives of our people.

He is at this time transporting large armies of foreign mercenaries[14]
to complete the works of death, desolation, and tyranny already begun

---

11. **tenure** *n.:* length of time that an office is held.
12. **others** *n. pl.:* members of British Parliament and their supporters and agents.
13. **neighboring province:** Quebec in Canada.
14. **mercenaries** *n. pl.:* professional soldiers hired to serve in foreign armies.

---

**Vocabulary**
**abdicated** (ab′di·kāt′id) *v.:* given up responsibility for.

---

with circumstances of cruelty and perfidy[15] [ ] unworthy the head of a civilized nation. scarcely paralleled in the most barbarous ages, and totally

He has constrained our fellow citizens taken captive on the high seas, to bear arms against their country, to become the executioners of their friends and brethren, or to fall themselves by their hands.

He has [ ] endeavored to bring on the inhabitants of our frontiers, the merciless Indian savages, whose known rule of warfare is an undistinguished destruction of all ages, sexes, and conditions of existence. excited domestic insurrection among us, and has

He has incited treasonable insurrections of our fellow citizens, with the allurements of forfeiture and confiscation of our property.

He has waged cruel war against human nature itself, violating its most sacred rights of life and liberty in the persons of a distant people

---

**15. perfidy** *n.:* betrayal of trust.

---

**Vocabulary**
**confiscation** (kän′fis·kā′shən) *n.:* seizure of property by authority.

---

*The Declaration of Independence, 4 July 1776* (detail) by John Trumbull (1756–1843). Oil on canvas.
Yale University Art Gallery, Trumbull Collection.

who never offended him, captivating and carrying them into slavery in another hemisphere, or to incur miserable death in their transportation thither. This piratical warfare, the opprobrium[16] of infidel powers, is the warfare of the CHRISTIAN king of Great Britain. Determined to keep open a market where MEN should be bought and sold, he has prostituted his negative[17] for suppressing every legislative attempt to prohibit or to restrain this execrable commerce. And that this assemblage of horrors might want no fact of distinguished die,[18] he is now exciting those very people to rise in arms among us, and to purchase that liberty of which he has deprived them, by murdering the people on whom he also obtruded them: thus paying off former crimes committed against the LIBERTIES of one people, with crimes which he urges them to commit against the LIVES of another.

In every stage of these oppressions we have petitioned for redress[19] in the most humble terms: Our repeated petitions have been answered only by repeated injuries.

A prince whose character is thus marked by every act which may define a tyrant is unfit to be the ruler of a [ ] people who mean to be free. Future ages will scarcely believe that the hardiness of one man adventured, within the short compass of twelve years only, to lay a foundation so broad and so undisguised for tyranny over a people fostered and fixed in principles of freedom.

Nor have we been wanting in attentions to our British brethren. We have warned them from time to time of attempts by their legislature to extend a jurisdiction over these our states. We have reminded them of the circumstances of our emigration and settlement here, no one of which could warrant so strange a pretension: that these were effected at the expense of our own blood and treasure, unassisted by the wealth or the strength of Great Britain: that in constituting indeed our several forms of government, we had adopted one common king, thereby laying a foundation for perpetual league and amity with them: but that submission to their parliament was no part of our constitution, nor ever in idea, if history may be credited: and, we [ ] appealed to their native justice and magnanimity as well as to the ties of our common

Writing materials used at the signing of the Declaration of Independence, Independence Hall, Philadelphia, Pennsylvania.

free

an unwarrantable / us

have
and we have conjured[20] them by

---

16. **opprobrium** (ə·prō′brē·əm) *n.*: shameful conduct.
17. **negative** *n.*: veto.
18. **fact of distinguished die:** clear stamp or mark of distinction. Jefferson is being sarcastic here.
19. **redress** *n.*: correction for a wrong done.
20. **conjured** (kən·joord′) *v.*: solemnly called upon.

---

**Vocabulary**
**magnanimity** (mag′nə·nim′ə·tē) *n.*: nobility of spirit.

kindred to disavow these usurpations which were likely to interrupt our connection and correspondence. They too have been deaf to the voice of justice and of consanguinity,[21] and when occasions have been given them, by the regular course of their laws, of removing from their councils the disturbers of our harmony, they have, by their free election, reestablished them in power. At this very time too, they are permitting their chief magistrate to send over not only soldiers of our common blood, but Scotch and foreign mercenaries to invade and destroy us. These facts have given the last stab to agonizing affection, and manly spirit bids us to <u>renounce</u> forever these unfeeling brethren. We must endeavor to forget our former love for them, and hold them as we hold the rest of mankind, enemies in war, in peace friends. We might have been a free and a great people together; but a communication of grandeur and of freedom, it seems, is below their dignity. Be it so, since they will have it. The road to happiness and to glory is open to us too. We will tread it apart from them and <u>acquiesce</u> in the necessity which denounces[22] our eternal separation [ ]!

We, therefore, the representatives of the United States of America in General Congress assembled, [ ] do in the name, and by the authority of the good people of these states reject and renounce all allegiance and subjection to the kings of Great Britain and all others who may hereafter claim by, through or under them; we utterly dissolve all political connection which may heretofore have subsisted between us and the people or parliament of Great Britain: And finally we do assert and declare these colonies to be free and independent states, and that as free and independent states, they have full power to levy war, conclude peace, contract alliances, establish commerce, and to do all other acts and things which independent states may of right do.

And for the support of this declaration, [ ] we mutually pledge to each other our lives, our fortunes, and our sacred honor.

The Declaration thus signed on the 4th, on paper, was engrossed[23] on parchment, and signed again on the 2d of August.

---

*(margin notes)*

would inevitably

We must therefore

and hold them as we hold the rest of mankind, enemies in war, in peace friends.

appealing to the supreme judge of the world for the rectitude of our intentions,

colonies, solemnly publish and declare, that these united colonies are, and of right ought to be free and independent states; that they are absolved from all allegiance to the British crown, and that all political connection between them and the state of Great Britain is, and ought to be, totally dissolved;

with a firm reliance on the protection of divine providence,

---

21. **consanguinity** (kän′saŋ·gwin′ə·tē) *n.:* kinship; family relationship.
22. **denounces** (dē·nouns′iz) *v.:* archaic for "announces, proclaims."
23. **engrossed** *v.:* written in final draft.

---

**Vocabulary**

**renounce** (ri·nouns′) *v.:* give up.
**acquiesce** (ak′wē·es′) *v.:* accept quietly.

# Response and Analysis

## Reading Check

1. What truths does Jefferson consider self-evident?

2. What is the **main idea** or the main argument of the Declaration of Independence? What are the key facts that support this main argument?

## Thinking Critically

3. What changes made in the text show a desire not to make an absolute break with the English people? Why do you think it would be important that the new nation maintain its "consanguinity," or close kinship, with the English people?

4. A famous and controversial omission in the Declaration of Independence is the section condemning the king of England for enslaving Africans. Find the section on slave trade that was omitted. According to Jefferson, what political concerns prompted the omission of this passage?

5. Find at least two passages in the Declaration that use **parallelism.** What is the effect of the parallel structure on the *idea* of the passage?

6. The Declaration opens with a rational statement of its purpose. In a document with such radical intent, it is not surprising that supporting details often use emotionally laden language. Find at least five details in the document that use **loaded words** to cite factual support. What emotions are revealed in the use of charged language?

## Literary Criticism

7. **Political approach.** Which changes seem to have been made to the Declaration for stylistic reasons, such as brevity or clarity, and which changes for political reasons?

In your opinion, was the Declaration a more powerful argument for freedom and equality in Jefferson's original words, or did the changes strengthen its impact?

## WRITING

### Freedom at What Cost?

Americans are fond of saying "It's a free country," yet freedom has responsibilities that go along with it. Write a brief **essay** explaining how freedom can bring both gains and losses.

## Vocabulary Development

### True or False?

Answer true or false to each of the following statements, and briefly explain your answer.

1. A person showing <u>prudence</u> often makes rash judgments.

2. A person displaying <u>magnanimity</u> would be disliked.

3. A <u>transient</u> moment is one that flies by.

4. A person who <u>constrains</u> another is a liberator.

5. A leader who has <u>abdicated</u> a post no longer occupies that post.

6. If you <u>renounce</u> chocolate, you give it up.

7. <u>Confiscation</u> of a thing leads to its disappearance.

8. If you wanted someone's agreement, you would want him or her to <u>acquiesce.</u>

9. A fair person is often also <u>candid.</u>

10. You would <u>expunge</u> something that you found unpleasant.

**SKILLS FOCUS**

**Literary Skills**
Analyze points of view on a topic. Analyze the use of parallelism.

**Writing Skills**
Write an essay analyzing a political point of view.

**Vocabulary Skills**
Demonstrate word knowledge.

# Vocabulary Development

## Terms Used in Political Science and History

English is a language full of borrowings—that is, words that have origins in other languages. Many English words come originally from Latin or from Old English, a Germanic language that traveled to England with the Anglo-Saxons in the fifth century. Other words are derived from Greek, French, Spanish, and various Native American languages.

Many English words relating to law, politics, history, and education are borrowed from Latin (or Greek by way of Latin). In reading political documents such as the Declaration of Independence (page 100) and the Declaration of Sentiments (page 112), you will encounter many terms that are derived from one of these languages.

**Tracing a word's history.** To learn the history of a word's origin and development—its **etymology**—the best place to look is a dictionary. Most dictionaries include a bracketed etymology after a word's pronunciation and part-of-speech designation. In the introduction to a dictionary, you will usually find an explanation of the organization, symbols, and abbreviations used in that dictionary's etymologies. Here's the beginning of a dictionary entry for the word *tyrant*:

> **ty·rant** (tī′rənt) *n.* [[ME *tirant* < OFr *tiran, tirant* (with *–t* after ending *–ant* of prp.) < L *tyrannus* < Gr *tyrannos*]] **1** an absolute ruler; specif., in ancient Greece, etc., one who seized sovereignty illegally; usurper **2** a cruel, oppressive ruler; despot **3** any person who exercises authority in an oppressive manner; cruel master

The etymology of *tyrant* shows that the English word derives from (<) the Middle English word *tirant,* which in turn comes from the Old French *tiran* or *tirant.* The Old French words come from the Latin word *tyrannus,* which derives from the Greek word *tyrannos.*

Learning a word's etymology can help you recognize related words. For example, knowing the origin of *tyrant* should help you figure out the meaning of *tyranny* and *tyrannical.*

### PRACTICE

Work with a partner, and use a dictionary to research the etymologies and meanings of the following political and historical terms. You can record your information in a chart like the one below:

**constitution    judiciary    colonies    insurrection    vassal**
**covenant    sanction    abdicate    democracy    abolish**

| Word | Etymology | Meaning |
|---|---|---|
|  |  |  |

**SKILLS FOCUS**

**Vocabulary Skills**
Understand the etymology of terms used in political science and history.

# Connected Readings

## Freedom and Equality

You have just read the Declaration of Independence, and you have considered the views it expresses about freedom and equality. Each of the next three selections you will be reading—by Dekanawida, Abigail Adams, and Elizabeth Cady Stanton—presents another point of view on freedom and equality. As you read each selection, continue to fill out the chart that you began for the Declaration of Independence (see page 96). Write down the main idea of each selection and its supporting details. After you have read these selections, answer the questions on page 114, which ask you to compare all four selections. Your chart will help in the discussion.

*Not-o-way, or the Thinker, an Iroquois Chief* (1835–1836) by George Catlin.

## Points of View

### Before You Read

Before Revolutionary patriots put pen to paper to draft the U.S. Constitution in 1787, Colonial leaders such as Thomas Jefferson and Benjamin Franklin studied other systems of government, including an example flourishing close to home: the Iroquois Confederacy. This political group had what Jefferson and Franklin were searching for—a constitution infused with the basic principles of democracy and federalism.

The Iroquois Confederacy, also known as the League of Five Nations, was a union of the Senecas, Cayugas, Onondagas, Oneidas, and Mohawks (the Tuscaroras joined later). Around 1500, so the legend goes, a Mohawk visionary named Dekanawida convinced the nations to unite in order to establish peace and to protect "life, property, and liberty." Thanks to the constitution they created, the confederacy became a formidable power. By 1750, it numbered about fifteen thousand people, and Iroquois hunters and warriors ranged over one million square miles.

**The oldest living constitution.** The Iroquois Constitution, which still governs the Iroquois today, is regarded as the world's oldest living constitution. It gives member peoples equal voice in the nations' affairs, spells out a system of checks and balances, and guarantees political and religious freedom. Most amazing by European standards of that time, the Iroquois Constitution grants extensive political power to women, who hold the right to nominate and impeach chiefs.

**The strength of five arrows.** The Iroquois Constitution survives as a brilliant American political and literary work, filled with rich symbolism. Dekanawida had envisioned a huge evergreen "Tree of Peace" whose spreading roots represented the five nations of the Haudenosaunee (Iroquois). After unification of the nations, a symbolic tree was planted. An eagle atop the Tree of Peace, clutching five arrows, symbolizes the Iroquois Confederacy—and it's the image we see pictured on the back of the U.S. quarter.

In 1988, to mark the bicentennial of the U.S. Constitution, Congress passed a joint resolution stating that "the confederation of the original Thirteen Colonies into one republic was influenced by the political system developed by the Iroquois Confederacy, as were many of the democratic principles which were incorporated into the Constitution itself." Like five arrows bound together, the Iroquois political and literary legacy is entwined forever with the ideals that continue to shape American life.

---

## POLICY STATEMENT

# *from* The Iroquois Constitution
## Dekanawida

### Tree of Great Peace

I am Dekanawida and with the Five Nations' Confederate Lords I plant the Tree of the Great Peace. I plant it in your territory, Adodarhoh, and the Onondaga Nation, in the territory of you who are Firekeepers.

I name the tree the Tree of the Great Long Leaves. Under the shade of this Tree of the Great Peace we spread the soft white feathery down of the globe thistle as seats for you, Adodarhoh, and your cousin Lords.

We place you upon those seats, spread soft with the feathery down of the globe thistle, there beneath the shade of the spreading branches of the Tree of Peace. There shall you

sit and watch the Council Fire of the Confederacy of the Five Nations, and all the affairs of the Five Nations shall be transacted at this place before you, Adodarhoh, and your cousin Lords, by the Confederate Lords of the Five Nations.

Roots have spread out from the Tree of the Great Peace, one to the north, one to the east, one to the south, and one to the west. The name of these roots is The Great White Roots and their nature is Peace and Strength.

If any man or any nation outside the Five Nations shall obey the laws of the Great Peace and make known their disposition to the Lords of the Confederacy, they may trace the Roots to the Tree and if their minds are clean and they are obedient and promise to obey the wishes of the Confederate Council, they shall be welcomed to take shelter beneath the Tree of the Long Leaves.

We place at the top of the Tree of the Long Leaves an Eagle who is able to see afar. If he sees in the distance any evil approaching or any danger threatening he will at once warn the people of the Confederacy.

## Leaders

The Lords of the Confederacy of the Five Nations shall be mentors of the people for all time. The thickness of their skin shall be seven spans—which is to say that they shall be proof against anger, offensive actions, and criticism. Their hearts shall be full of peace and goodwill and their minds filled with a yearning for the welfare of the people of the Confederacy. With endless patience they shall carry out their duty and their firmness shall be tempered with a tenderness for their people. Neither anger nor fury shall find lodgment in their minds and all their words and actions shall be marked by calm deliberation.

## Clans

The lineal descent of the people of the Five Nations shall run in the female line. Women shall be considered the progenitors of the Nation.

Tree of Peace.

They shall own the land and the soil. Men and women shall follow the status of the mother.

## Symbols

Five arrows shall be bound together very strong and each arrow shall represent one nation. As the five arrows are strongly bound this shall symbolize the complete union of the nations. Thus are the Five Nations united completely and enfolded together, united into one head, one body, and one mind. Therefore they shall labor, legislate, and council together for the interest of future generations.

## War and Peace

I, Dekanawida, and the Union Lords, now uproot the tallest pine tree and into the cavity thereby made we cast all weapons of war. Into the depths of the earth, down into the deep underearth currents of water flowing to unknown regions we cast all the weapons of strife. We bury them from sight and we plant again the tree. Thus shall the Great Peace be established and hostilities shall no longer be known between the Five Nations but peace to the United People.

## Points *of* View

### Before You Read

Abigail Smith suffered poor health as a child and so was given no formal education, but she grew up to be an intelligent woman and a voracious reader. In 1764, she married John Adams, who was later to become second president of the United States. During their marriage, John Adams was appointed as a delegate to the First Continental Congress. Later his diplomatic duties in Europe kept him away from home for years at a time, except for occasional short visits. During this time, Abigail Adams managed the family farm in Braintree, Massachusetts; raised four children (including future president John Quincy Adams); and wrote her husband more than three hundred letters, which today serve as a significant record of early American life. On March 31, 1776, Abigail wrote to her husband about the anticipated Declaration of Independence, urging him to consider the situation of women in the Colonies.

LETTER

# Letter to John Adams

## Abigail Adams

Abigail Adams.

March 31, 1776

I long to hear that you have declared an independency—and by the way in the new Code of Laws which I suppose it will be necessary for you to make I desire you would Remember the Ladies, and be more generous and favorable to them than your ancestors. Do not put such unlimited power into the hands of the Husbands. Remember all Men would be tyrants if they could. If particular care and attention is not paid to the Ladies we are determined to foment[1] a Rebellion, and will not hold ourselves bound by any Laws in which we have no voice, or Representation.

That your Sex are Naturally Tyrannical[2] is a Truth so thoroughly established as to admit of no dispute, but such of you as wish to be happy willingly give up the harsh title of Master for the more tender and endearing one of Friend. Why then, not put it out of the power of the vicious and the Lawless to use us with cruelty and indignity with impunity.[3] Men of Sense in all Ages abhor[4] those customs which treat us only as the vassals[5] of your Sex. Regard us then as Beings placed by providence under your protection and in imitation of the Supreme Being make use of that power only for our happiness.

*A Adams*

---

1. **foment** *v.:* stir up.
2. **tyrannical** *adv.:* harsh, cruel, unjust.
3. **impunity** *n.:* freedom from punishment or harm.
4. **abhor** *v.:* turn away from in disgust; detest.
5. **vassals** *n. pl.:* servants; subjects.

## Points *of* View

### Before You Read

Elizabeth Cady (1815–1902) was studying law in her father's office when she became aware of the inequalities that women lived with (including the fact that she was not permitted to go to college or to obtain a law license). In 1840, Cady married abolitionist and lawyer Harry Stanton. (The promise to obey was omitted from her wedding vows.) The two reformers spent their honeymoon in London at the World Anti-Slavery Convention. There she met Lucretia Mott, another active women's rights advocate. The women were denied admission to the London convention solely because of their gender. As a result, the two began to plan a women's rights convention. This historic convention was eventually held in 1848 in Seneca Falls, New York, where Stanton lived with her husband and children. At the convention, Stanton read the Declaration of Sentiments to the assembled participants. Modeled on Jefferson's Declaration of Independence, Stanton's version called for women to be given both voting rights and equal treatment under the law.

POLICY STATEMENT / SPEECH

# *from* Declaration of Sentiments of the Seneca Falls Woman's Rights Convention

## Elizabeth Cady Stanton

When, in the course of human events, it becomes necessary for one portion of the family of man to assume among the people of the earth a position different from that which they have hitherto occupied, but one to which the laws of nature and of nature's God entitle them, a decent respect to the opinions of mankind requires that they should declare the causes that impel them to such a course.

We hold these truths to be self-evident: that all men and women are created equal; that they are endowed by their Creator with certain inalienable rights; that among these are life, liberty, and the pursuit of happiness; that to secure these rights governments are instituted, deriving their just powers from the consent of the governed. . . .

The history of mankind is a history of repeated injuries and usurpations on the part of man toward woman, having in direct object the establishment of an absolute tyranny over her. To prove this, let facts be submitted to a candid world.

He has never permitted her to exercise her inalienable right to the elective franchise.[1]

He has compelled her to submit to laws, in the formation of which she had no voice.

He has withheld from her rights which are given to the most ignorant and degraded[2] men—both natives and foreigners.

Having deprived her of this first right of a citizen, the elective franchise, thereby leaving her without representation in the halls of legislation, he has oppressed her on all sides.

---

1. **inalienable right to the elective franchise:** right to vote, which cannot be taken away.
2. **degraded** *adj.:* disgraced; corrupted.

Elizabeth Stanton and Susan B. Anthony, another advocate for women's rights.

He has made her, if married, in the eye of the law, civilly dead.

He has taken from her all right in property, even to the wages she earns.

He has made her, morally, an irresponsible being, as she can commit many crimes with impunity, provided they be done in the presence of her husband. In the covenant[3] of marriage, she is compelled to promise obedience to her husband, he becoming, to all intents and purposes, her master—the law giving him power to deprive her of her liberty, and to administer chastisement.[4]

He has so framed the laws of divorce, as to what shall be the proper causes, and in case of separation, to whom the guardianship of the children shall be given, as to be wholly regardless of the happiness of women—the law, in all cases, going upon a false supposition of the supremacy of man, and giving all power into his hands.

After depriving her of all rights as a married woman, if single, and the owner of property, he has taxed her to support a government which recognizes her only when her property can be made profitable to it.

He has monopolized nearly all the profitable employments, and from those she is permitted to follow, she receives but a scanty remuneration.[5] He closes against her all the avenues to wealth and distinction which he considers most honorable to himself. As a teacher of theology, medicine, or law, she is not known.

He has denied her the facilities for obtaining a thorough education, all colleges being closed against her.

He allows her in Church, as well as State, but a subordinate position, claiming Apostolic[6] authority for her exclusion from the ministry, and, with some exceptions, from any public participation in the affairs of the Church.

He has created a false public sentiment by giving to the world a different code of morals for men and women, by which moral delinquencies which exclude women from society, are not only tolerated, but deemed of little account in man.

He has usurped the prerogative[7] of Jehovah himself, claiming it as his right to assign for her a sphere of action, when that belongs to her conscience and to her God.

He has endeavored, in every way that he could, to destroy her confidence in her own powers, to lessen her self-respect, and to make her willing to lead a dependent and abject[8] life.

Now, in view of this entire disfranchisement[9] of one half the people of this country, their social and religious degradation—in view of the unjust laws above mentioned, and because women do feel themselves aggrieved, oppressed, and fraudulently deprived of their most sacred rights, we insist that they have immediate admission to all the rights and privileges which belong to them as citizens of the United States . . .

---

3. **covenant** *n.:* binding agreement; compact.
4. **chastisement** *n.:* punishment.
5. **remuneration** *n.:* payment.
6. **Apostolic:** of the Pope; papal.
7. **prerogative** *n.:* exclusive right or privilege.
8. **abject** *adj.:* hopeless.
9. **disfranchisement** *n.:* act of taking away the rights of citizenship, especially the right to vote.

# Analysis Comparing Points of View

## Freedom and Equality

The questions on this page ask you to analyze the views on freedom and equality in the preceding four selections.

Thomas Jefferson . . . . . . . . . . *from* **The Autobiography: The Declaration of Independence**

Dekanawida . . . . . . . . . . . . . *from* **The Iroquois Constitution**

Abigail Adams . . . . . . . . . . . **Letter to John Adams**

Elizabeth Cady Stanton . . . . . *from* **Declaration of Sentiments**

### Thinking Critically

1. Review the chart you made analyzing each document's **main ideas** (see page 96). Now consider the historical period and context in which each document was written, and add another column to the chart identifying the **purpose** behind each of the documents.

2. These powerful documents were not written to spare feelings. Discuss the effectiveness of each document. Do you see any flaws in their reasoning? Explain your responses.

3. Has the passage of time made any of the writers' points of view irrelevant or questionable, or are their ideas timeless? How do their ideas compare with your own? (Look back at your Quickwrite notes from page 96.)

## WRITING

### Evaluating the Documents

Review the selections about freedom and equality that you've just read. First, examine each piece separately, and evaluate the clarity and strength of the author's argument. Next, consider the texts as a group, and think about the various points of view represented. Note especially those points of view that are in agreement or disagreement. Then, write a brief **essay** evaluating the documents. Do you consider the pieces powerful documents? Taken together, are they an effective grouping? Be sure to use examples from the texts to support your points.

### How Equal?

"All men are created equal" are perhaps the most famous words of the Declaration of Independence or of any document in American history. What do you think the statement really meant to Jefferson and the men who revised his draft—considering that they went on to form a government in which slavery was legal, women could not vote, and Native Americans were called merciless savages? Write an **editorial** in which you analyze your ideas about freedom and equality. Do you feel that some people in America, in fact, are not yet equal?

▶ **Use "Writing an Editorial," pages 138–145, for help with this assignment.**

SKILLS
FOCUS

Pages 96–114
cover
**Literary Skills**
Analyze and
compare points
of view on a
topic.

**Reading Skills**
Compare main
ideas across texts.

**Writing Skills**
Write an essay
evaluating
documents. Write
an editorial.

# Reflecting *on the* Literary Period

## Encounters and Foundations to 1800

The selections in this feature were written during the same literary period as the other selections in Collection 1, and they share many of the same ideas and concerns. The Focus Question will guide your reading and help you reflect on important aspects of the period.

The Granger Collection, New York.

### Think About...

Early European explorers and settlers in the Americas undertook long and difficult journeys with a variety of different goals. Some hoped to find a faster trade route to China; others hoped to find an earthly paradise and rivers filled with gold. Puritans, like William Bradford, believed they were on a spiritual journey to salvation. What these newcomers didn't expect to find, however, was a large and flourishing American Indian population.

As interest in the new land shifted from exploration to settlement, Europeans began to see America as a place where resources were plentiful and people could improve their lot. The promise of land ownership and religious freedom brought permanent settlers to America—forever changing the American Indian way of life. These early settlements shaped the future of American history and literature. What the explorers, Puritans, and early Southerners like William Byrd share in their writing is a desire to convey the special quality of life in America, to show how they feel living in a new land, encountering native cultures, and facing new experiences.

SKILLS
FOCUS

### Focus Question

As you read each selection, keep in mind this Focus Question and take notes to help you answer it at the end of the feature:
How did the attitudes and beliefs of early settlers in America not only help them endure hardships but also shape their interactions with the native inhabitants?

Pages 115–136 cover **Literary Skills** Evaluate the philosophical, political, religious, ethical, and social influences of a historical period.

## Reflecting *on the* Literary Period • Before You Read

# *from* La Relación

**Meet the Writer** **Alvar Núñez Cabeza de Vaca** (c. 1490–c. 1560) was born in Spain to a noble family. He took his unusual name (meaning "head of a cow") from an ancestor who had once helped the Spanish win a battle by marking an unguarded mountain pass with a cow's skull. Cabeza de Vaca joined the army in his teens and was a member of an expedition that set sail in June 1527 for Florida. The journey was dogged by misfortunes: Two ships were wrecked; men deserted; many died. Finally, Cabeza de Vaca and a small party were shipwrecked on a narrow island off the coast of Texas. *La Relación* reveals the great hardships these men endured between 1528 and 1537 as they walked across Texas, New Mexico, and Arizona before reaching Mexico.

**Background** During the sixteenth century, Spain sent several expeditions to explore, conquer, and colonize North America. Fortunately, some narratives of these expeditions have survived. *La Relación,* first published in 1542, is an extraordinary document of American exploration. Written as a report to the king after Cabeza de Vaca's return to Spain in 1537, *La Relación* is more than a travel document: Cabeza de Vaca identifies twenty-three Indian groups and describes their languages, rituals, diets, and migrations. He also argues against the brutal Spanish slave trade and urges respect for the Indians as fellow human beings.

---

**CONNECTING TO THE**
**Focus Question**

The Spanish conquistadors hoped to conquer North America, find its treasures, and claim all for Spain. As you read, consider this question: How might Cabeza de Vaca's hopes and expectations have changed as a result of his experiences on the expedition and interactions with American Indians?

---

Explorer Alvar Núñez Cabeza de Vaca and men trekking American terrain.

*In 1527, Cabeza de Vaca was second-in-command of a disastrous five-ship expedition to establish a colony in "Florida." After two ships went down in a hurricane and more than two hundred men drowned or deserted, the expedition landed in 1528 near present-day Tampa, Florida. The commander and his men wandered for six months in Florida, exhausted by hunger, disease, and Indian attacks. Finally, they built barges in an attempt to reach Mexico by sea. Most of the barges were lost, but Cabeza de Vaca's landed on an island off the coast of Texas. In this section of his narrative, Cabeza de Vaca describes an encounter with the Karankawa on what is thought to have been Galveston Island, Texas.*

# *from* La Relación

## Alvar Núñez Cabeza de Vaca
*translated by* **Cyclone Covey**

### Chapter 19

#### The Indians' Hospitality before and after a New Calamity

As the sun rose next morning, the Indians appeared as they promised, bringing an abundance of fish and of certain roots which taste like nuts, some bigger than walnuts, some smaller, mostly grubbed[1] from the water with great labor.

That evening they came again with more fish and roots and brought their women and children to look at us. They thought themselves rich with the little bells and beads we gave them, and they repeated their visits on other days.

Being provided with what we needed, we thought to embark again. It was a struggle to dig our barge out of the sand it had sunk in, and another struggle to launch her. For the work in the water while launching, we stripped and stowed our clothes in the craft.

Quickly clambering in and grabbing our oars, we had rowed two crossbow shots from shore when a wave inundated[2] us. Being naked and the cold intense, we let our oars go. The next big wave capsized the barge. The Inspector [Solís][3] and two others held fast, but that only carried them more certainly underneath, where they drowned.

A single roll of the sea tossed the rest of the men into the rushing surf and back onto shore half-drowned.

We lost only those the barge took down; but the survivors escaped as naked as they were born, with the loss of everything we had. That was not much, but valuable to us in that bitter November cold, our bodies so emaciated we could easily count every bone and looked the very picture of death. I can say for myself that from the month of May I had eaten nothing but corn, and that sometimes raw. I never could bring myself to eat any of the horse-meat at the time our beasts were slaughtered; and fish I did not taste ten times. On top of everything else, a cruel north wind commenced to complete our killing.

The Lord willed that we should find embers while searching the remnants of our former fire. We found more wood and soon had big fires raging. Before them, with flowing tears, we prayed for mercy and pardon, each filled with pity not only for himself but for all his wretched fellows.

---

1. **grubbed:** dug from.
2. **inundated** (in′ən·dāt′id): covered over or engulfed.
3. **Solís:** Alonzo de Solís.

At sunset the Indians, not knowing we had gone, came again with food. When they saw us looking so strangely different, they turned back in alarm. I went after them calling, and they returned, though frightened. I explained to them by signs that our barge had sunk and three of our number drowned. They could see at their feet two of the dead men who had washed ashore. They could also see that the rest of us were not far from joining these two.

The Indians, understanding our full plight, sat down and lamented[4] for half an hour so loudly they could have been heard a long way off. It was amazing to see these wild, untaught savages howling like brutes in compassion for us. It intensified my own grief at our calamity and had the same effect on the other victims.

When the cries died down, I conferred with the Christians about asking the Indians to take us to their homes. Some of our number who had been to New Spain warned that the Indians would sacrifice us to their idols.[5] But death being surer and nearer if we stayed where we were, I went ahead and beseeched[6] the Indians. They were delighted. They told us to tarry[7] a little while, then they would do as we wished.

Presently thirty of them gathered loads of wood and disappeared to their huts, which were a long walk away; while we waited with the remainder until near nightfall. Then, supporting us under our arms, they hurried us from one to another of the four big fires they had built along the path. At each fire, when we regained a little warmth and strength, they took us on so swiftly our feet hardly touched ground.

Thus we made their village, where we saw they had erected a hut for us with many fires inside. An hour later they began a dance celebration that lasted all night. For us there was no joy, feasting, or sleep, as we waited the hour they should make us victims.

In the morning, when they brought us fish and roots and acted in every way hospitably, we felt reassured and somewhat lost our anxiety of the sacrificial knife. ∎

---

4. **lamented** (lə·ment′id): cried out in sorrow.
5. **New Spain . . . idols:** New Spain was the Spanish colonial territory in the Americas that would eventually include Mexico, portions of Central and South America, the largest Caribbean islands, the Bahamas, the Philippines, Florida, and the southwestern United States. In Mexico, the Spanish conquistador Hernando Cortés and his men had encountered Aztecs who practiced human sacrifice.
6. **beseeched:** begged.
7. **tarry:** wait.

# Response and Analysis

## Reading Check

1. What happens to the Spaniards after they decide to launch their barge and embark again on their journey?

2. Why are some of the Spaniards fearful of being taken to the Karankawas' homes?

## Thinking Critically

3. Consider Cabeza de Vaca's description of the Spaniards' physical state after the barge disaster. What words convey their desperate plight? What impression do these words create?

4. What can you **infer,** or reasonably guess, about Cabeza de Vaca's attitude toward the Karankawa from his commentary about their response to the Spaniards' misfortune? Cite passages from the selection that support your inferences.

5. Using details from the selection, respond to **Connecting to the Focus Question** on page 116.

# *from* **Of Plymouth Plantation**

**Meet the Writer** **William Bradford** (1590–1657) was the son of a prosperous farmer in Yorkshire, England. Inspired by his reading of the Bible and by the sermons of a Puritan minister, Bradford began attending the meetings of a small group of Nonconformists and joined them in 1606. In 1608, under increasing pressure of persecution, the Nonconformists crossed the North Sea to Holland. In 1620, the Nonconformists sailed for America in order to found a community where they would be free to worship and live according to their beliefs. They landed at Plymouth; the following year, Bradford was elected governor of the Plymouth Colony. Bradford proved to be an exemplary leader, and he went on to be elected governor of the colony no fewer than thirty times.

As the Plymouth Colony prospered and grew, it also gradually disintegrated as a religious community despite Bradford's efforts to hold it together. The ideal of the "city on the hill," the Pilgrims' dream of an ideal society founded on religious principles, gradually gave way to the realities of life in the new land.

**Background** In 1630, Bradford began to write his annual account of the Plymouth settlement, which he hoped would inspire future generations to carry on the Pilgrims' ideals. The first nine chapters of Bradford's history were copied into the Plymouth church records, but the entire manuscript was lost when British troops plundered the church during the Revolutionary War. Almost a century later, Governor Bradford's vellum-bound volume was discovered in the library of the bishop of London. *Of Plymouth Plantation* was first published in 1856 by the Massachusetts Historical Society. The manuscript was finally returned to the United States in 1897 and can be seen today in Boston.

---

### CONNECTING TO THE
### Focus Question

Bradford wrote his history in part to inspire younger Puritans to respect the older generation for overcoming difficulties in the settlement of New England. As you read, ask yourself: What difficulties did the Puritans encounter from their natural surroundings? What seems to be their attitude about the role Native Americans played in helping them?

1620  1920
SIXTEEN PILGRIMS
LED BY
MYLES STANDISH WILLIAM BRADFORD
STEPHEN HOPKINS AND EDWARD TILLEY
ENCAMPED ON THE SHORE OF THIS POND
FOR THEIR SECOND NIGHT ON AMERICAN SOIL
NOVEMBER 16 1620
OLD STYLE
DRANK THEIR FIRST NEW ENGLAND WATER
THREE MILES NORTHEAST FROM HERE AT THE
PILGRIM SPRING
FOUND THE PRECIOUS INDIAN CORN TWO
MILES SOUTHWEST FROM HERE AT
CORN HILL
PROVINCETOWN TERCENTENARY COMMISSION

*from* **Of Plymouth Plantation**

## William Bradford

### *from* Chapter 9

#### Of their Voyage, and how they Passed the Sea; and of their Safe Arrival at Cape Cod

**September 6 [1620].** These troubles[1] being blown over, and now all being compact together in one ship, they put to sea again with a prosperous wind, which continued divers[2] days together, which was some encouragement unto them; yet, according to the usual manner, many were afflicted with seasickness. And I may not omit here a special work of God's providence. There was a proud and very profane[3] young man, one of the seamen, of a lusty,[4] able body, which made him the more haughty;[5] he would always be condemning the poor people in their sickness and cursing them daily with grievous execrations;[6] and did not let to tell them that he hoped to help to cast half of them overboard before they came to their journey's end, and to make merry with what they had; and if he were by any gently reproved,[7] he would curse and swear most bitterly. But it pleased God before they came half seas over, to smite this young man with a grievous disease, of which he died in a desperate manner, and so was himself the first that

---

1. **troubles:** the return of the *Speedwell* to England and the transfer of her passengers to the *Mayflower*.
2. **divers** (diʹvərz): many.
3. **profane:** irreverent.
4. **lusty:** energetic; robust.
5. **haughty** (hôtʹē): proud; disdainful of something or someone.
6. **execrations** (ekʹsi·krāʹshanz): angry words; curses.
7. **reproved:** reprimanded.

*Landing of the Pilgrims at Plymouth* (1803) by Michel Felice Corne. Oil on canvas.
Courtesy of Pilgrim Hall Museum, Plymouth, Massachusetts.

was thrown overboard. Thus his curses light on his own head, and it was an astonishment to all his fellows for they noted it to be the just hand of God upon him.

After they had enjoyed fair winds and weather for a season, they were encountered many times with crosswinds and met with many fierce storms with which the ship was shroudly[8] shaken, and her upper works made very leaky; and one of the main beams in the midships was bowed and cracked, which put them in some fear that the ship could not be able to perform the voyage. So some of the chief of the company, perceiving the mariners to fear the sufficiency of the ship as appeared by their mutterings, they entered into serious consultation with the master and other officers of the ship, to consider in time of the danger, and rather to return than to cast themselves into a desperate and inevitable peril. And truly there was great distraction and difference of opinion amongst the mariners themselves; fain[9] would they do what could be done for their wages' sake (being now near half the seas over) and on the other hand they were loath[10] to hazard their lives too desperately. But in examining of all opinions, the master and others affirmed they knew the ship to be strong and firm underwater; and for the buckling of the main beam, there was a great iron screw the passengers brought out of Holland, which would raise the beam into his place; the which being done, the carpenter and master affirmed that with a post put under it, set firm in the lower deck and otherways bound, he would make it sufficient. And as for the decks and upper works, they would caulk them as well as they could, and though with the working of the ship they would not long keep staunch,[11] yet there would otherwise be no great danger, if they did not overpress her with sails. So they committed themselves to the will of God and resolved to proceed.

---

8. **shroudly** (shrōōd′lē): shrewdly, used here in its archaic sense of "wickedly."
9. **fain:** archaic for "gladly."
10. **loath:** reluctant.
11. **staunch:** watertight.

In sundry[12] of these storms the winds were so fierce and the seas so high, as they could not bear a knot of sail, but were forced to hull[13] for divers days together. And in one of them, as they thus lay at hull in a mighty storm, a lusty young man called John Howland, coming upon some occasion above the gratings was, with a seele[14] of the ship, thrown into sea; but it pleased God that he caught hold of the topsail halyards[15] which hung overboard and ran out at length. Yet he held his hold (though he was sundry fathoms underwater) till he was hauled up by the same rope to the brim of the water, and then with a boathook and other means got into the ship again and his life saved. And though he was something ill with it, yet he lived many years after and became a profitable member both in church and commonwealth. In all this voyage there died but one of the passengers, which was William Butten, a youth, servant to Samuel Fuller, when they drew near the coast.

But to omit other things (that I may be brief) after long beating at sea they fell with that land which is called Cape Cod;[16] the which being made and certainly known to be it, they were not a little joyful. After some deliberation had amongst themselves and with the master of the ship, they tacked about and resolved to stand for the southward (the wind and weather being fair) to find some place about Hudson's River[17] for their habitation. But after they had sailed that course about half the day, they fell amongst dangerous shoals and roaring breakers, and they were so far entangled therewith as they conceived themselves in great danger; and the wind shrinking upon them withal, they resolved to bear up again for the Cape and thought themselves

---

12. **sundry:** some.
13. **hull:** to float without using the sails.
14. **seele** (sēl): sudden lurch to one side.
15. **halyards** (hal′yərdz): ropes for raising a sail.
16. **Cape Cod:** They sighted Cape Cod at daybreak on November 9, 1620.
17. **Hudson's River:** They were trying for Manhattan Island. Henry Hudson had made his voyage in 1609 and had claimed the area for the Dutch, but the English did not recognize the Dutch claim.

happy to get out of those dangers before night overtook them, as by God's good providence they did. And the next day they got into the Cape Harbor[18] where they rid in safety. . . .

Being thus arrived in a good harbor, and brought safe to land, they fell upon their knees and blessed the God of Heaven who had brought them over the vast and furious ocean, and delivered them from all the perils and miseries thereof, again to set their feet on the firm and stable earth, their proper element. . . .

> **I**f they looked behind them, there was the mighty ocean . . . to separate them from all the civil parts of the world. . . .

But here I cannot but stay and make a pause, and stand half amazed at this poor people's present condition; and so I think will the reader, too, when he well considers the same. Being thus passed the vast ocean, and a sea of troubles before in their preparation (as may be remembered by that which went before), they had now no friends to welcome them nor inns to entertain or refresh their weather-beaten bodies; no houses or much less towns to repair to, to seek for succor.[19] It is recorded in Scripture[20] as a mercy to the Apostle and his shipwrecked company, that the barbarians showed them no small kindness in refreshing them, but these savage barbarians, when they met with them (as after will appear) were readier to fill their sides full of arrows than otherwise. And for the season it was winter, and they that know the winters of that country know them to be sharp and violent, and subject to cruel and fierce storms, dangerous to travel to known places, much more to search an unknown coast. Besides, what could they see but a hideous and desolate wilderness, full of wild beasts and wild men—and what multitudes there might be of them they knew not. Neither could they, as it were, go up to the top of Pisgah[21] to view from this wilderness a more goodly country to feed their hopes; for which way soever they turned their eyes (save upward to the heavens) they could have little solace or content in respect of any outward objects. For summer being done, all things stand upon them with a weather-beaten face, and the whole country, full of woods and thickets, represented a wild and savage hue. If they looked behind them, there was the mighty ocean which they had passed and was now as a main bar and gulf to separate them from all the civil parts of the world. . . .

What could now sustain them but the Spirit of God and His grace? May not and ought not the children of these fathers rightly say: "Our fathers were Englishmen which came over this great ocean, and were ready to perish in this wilderness; but they cried unto the Lord, and He heard their voice and looked on their adversity,"[22] etc.? "Let them therefore praise the Lord, because He is good: And His mercies endure forever." "Yea, let them which have been redeemed of the Lord, show how He hath delivered them from the hand of the oppressor. When they wandered in the desert wilderness out of the way, and found no city to dwell in, both hungry and thirsty, their soul was overwhelmed in them. Let them confess before the Lord His lovingkindness and His wonderful works before the sons of men."[23]

---

18. **Cape Harbor:** now called Provincetown Harbor. The sea voyage from England had taken sixty-five days.
19. **succor** (suk′ər): aid.
20. **Scripture:** In the Acts of the Apostles (Chapter 28), Paul tells how the shipwrecked Christians were helped by the "barbarous people" of Malta.

---

21. **Pisgah** (piz′gə): mountain from which Moses first viewed the Promised Land.
22. **they cried . . . their adversity:** paraphrase of Deuteronomy 26:7.
23. **Let them . . . the sons of men:** paraphrase of Psalm 107.

*from* **Chapter 11**

### The Starving Time

**[1620–1621].** But that which was most sad and lamentable was, that in two or three months' time half of their company died, especially in January and February, being the depth of winter, and wanting houses and other comforts; being infected with the scurvy and other diseases which this long voyage and their inaccommodate condition had brought upon them. So as there died sometimes two or three of a day in the foresaid time, that of 100 and odd persons, scarce fifty remained. And of these, in the time of most distress, there was but six or seven sound persons who to their great commendations, be it spoken, spared no pains night nor day, but with abundance of toil and hazard of their own health, fetched them wood, made them fires, dressed them meat, made their beds, washed their loathsome clothes, clothed and unclothed them. In a word, did all the homely and necessary offices for them which dainty and queasy stomachs cannot endure to hear named; and all this willingly and cheerfully, without any grudging in the least, showing herein their true love unto their friends and brethren; a rare example and worthy to be remembered. Two of these seven were Mr. William Brewster, their reverend Elder, and Myles Standish,[24] their Captain and military commander, unto whom myself and many others were much beholden in our low and sick condition. And yet the Lord so upheld these persons as in this general calamity they were not at all infected either with sickness or lameness. And what I have said of these I may say of many others who died in this general visitation, and others yet living; that whilst they had health, yea, or any strength continuing, they were not wanting to any that had need of them. And I doubt not but their recompense is with the Lord.

---

24. **Myles Standish (c. 1584–1656):** a soldier who had been hired to handle the colonists' military affairs. Not a member of the Puritan congregation, he still became a most steadfast ally.

But I may not here pass by another remarkable passage not to be forgotten. As this calamity fell among the passengers that were to be left here to plant, and were hasted ashore and made to drink water that the seamen might have the more beer, and one[25] in his sickness desiring but a small can of beer, it was answered that if he were their own father he should have none. The disease began to fall amongst them also, so as almost half of their company died before they went away, and many of their officers and lustiest men, as the boatswain, gunner, three quartermasters, the cook and others. At which the Master was something strucken and sent to the sick ashore and told the Governor he should send for beer for them that had need of it, though he drunk water homeward bound.

But now amongst his company there was far another kind of carriage in this misery than amongst the passengers. For they that before had been boon companions in drinking and jollity in the time of their health and welfare, began now to desert one another in this calamity, saying they would not hazard their lives for them, they should be infected by coming to help them in their cabins; and so, after they came to lie by it, would do little or nothing for them but, "if they died, let them die." But such of the passengers as were yet aboard showed them what mercy they could, which made some of their hearts relent,[26] as the boatswain (and some others) who was a proud young man and would often curse and scoff at the passengers. But when he grew weak, they had compassion on him and helped him; then he confessed he did not deserve it at their hands, he had abused them in word and deed. "Oh!" (saith he) "you, I now see, show your love like Christians indeed one to another, but we let one another lie and die like dogs." Another lay cursing his wife, saying if it had not been for her he had never come this unlucky voyage, and anon cursing his fellows, saying he had done

---

25. **one:** Bradford himself.
26. **relent:** soften.

*Pilgrims' First Winter, 1620.*
The Granger Collection, New York.

this and that for some of them; he had spent so much and so much amongst them, and they were now weary of him and did not help him, having need. Another gave his companion all he had, if he died, to help him in his weakness; he went and got a little spice and made him a mess of meat once or twice. And because he died not so soon as he expected, he went amongst his fellows and swore the rogue would cozen[27] him, he would see him choked before he made him any more meat; and yet the poor fellow died before morning.

27. **cozen** (kuz′ən): cheat.

## Indian Relations

All this while the Indians came skulking about them, and would sometimes show themselves aloof off, but when any approached near them, they would run away; and once they stole away their tools where they had been at work and were gone to dinner. But about the 16th of March, a certain Indian came boldly amongst them and spoke to them in broken English, which they could well understand but marveled at it. At length they understood by discourse[28] with him,

28. **discourse:** conversation.

**William Bradford**   125

The Pilgrims' treaty with Chief Massasoit in William Bradford's house at Plymouth Colony, March 1621.
The Granger Collection, New York.

that he was not of these parts, but belonged to the eastern parts where some English ships came to fish, with whom he was acquainted and could name sundry of them by their names, amongst whom he had got his language. He became profitable to them in acquainting them with many things concerning the state of the country in the east parts where he lived, which was afterward profitable unto them; as also of the people here, of their names, number and strength, of their situation and distance from this place, and who was chief amongst them. His name was Samoset.[29] He told them also of another Indian whose name was Squanto,[30] a native of this place, who had been in England and could speak better English than himself.

Being, after some time of entertainment and gifts dismissed, a while after he came again, and five more with him, and they brought again all the tools that were stolen away before, and made way for the coming of their great Sachem, called

Massasoit.[31] Who, about four or five days after, came with the chief of his friends and other attendance, with the aforesaid Squanto. With whom, after friendly entertainment and some gifts given him, they made a peace with him (which hath now continued this 24 years)[32] in these terms:

1. That neither he nor any of his should injure or do hurt to any of their people.

2. That if any of his did hurt to any of theirs, he should send the offender, that they might punish him.

3. That if anything were taken away from any of theirs, he should cause it to be restored; and they should do the like to his.

4. If any did unjustly war against him, they would aid him; if any did war against them, he should aid them.

29. **Samoset** (sam′ə·set′)(1590?–1655): a Pemaquid from Maine.
30. **Squanto** (skwän′tō)(1585?–1622): one of the few survivors of the Pawtuxet(pô·tuks′it), an Algonquian(al·gäŋ′kē·an) people. He later joined Massasoit's Wampanoags(wäm′pa·nō′agz).

31. **Massasoit** (mas′ə·soit′) (c. 1580–1661): sachem (chief) of the Wampanoags, who lived in the area that became Rhode Island and southern Massachusetts.
32. **With whom . . . this 24 years:** The treaty was kept faithfully until the reign of Massasoit's younger son, Metacomet, (met′ə·com′it)(1639?–1676), also known to the colonists as King Philip.

5. He should send to his neighbors confederates[33] to certify them of this, that they might not wrong them, but might be likewise comprised[34] in the conditions of peace.

6. That when their men came to them, they should leave their bows and arrows behind them.

After these things he returned to his place called Sowams, some 40 miles from this place, but Squanto continued with them and was their interpreter and was a special instrument sent of God for their good beyond their expectation. He directed them how to set their corn, where to take fish, and to procure other commodities, and was also their pilot to bring them to unknown places for their profit, and never left them till he died. He was a native of this place, and scarce any left alive besides himself. He was carried away with divers others by one Hunt, a master of a ship, who thought to sell them for slaves in Spain. But he got away for England and was entertained by a merchant in London, and employed to Newfoundland and other parts, and lastly brought hither into these parts by one Mr. Dermer, a gentleman employed by Sir

---

33. **confederates**(kən·fed′ər·its): allies; persons who share a common purpose.
34. **comprised:** included.

Ferdinando Gorges and others for discovery and other designs in these parts. . . .

## First Thanksgiving

They began now to gather in the small harvest they had, and to fit up their houses and dwellings against winter, being all well recovered in health and strength and had all things in good plenty. For as some were thus employed in affairs abroad, others were exercised in fishing, about cod and bass and other fish, of which they took good store, of which every family had their portion. All the summer there was no want; and now began to come in store of fowl, as winter approached, of which this place did abound when they came first (but afterward decreased by degrees). And besides waterfowl there was great store of wild turkeys, of which they took many, besides venison, etc. Besides they had about a peck of meal a week to a person, or now since harvest, Indian corn to that proportion. Which made many afterward write so largely of their plenty here to their friends in England, which were not feigned but true reports.[35] ■

---

35. **Which made . . . true reports:** Although the specific day of the Plymouth colonists' first Thanksgiving is not known, it occurred in the fall of 1621. For three days, Massasoit and almost a hundred of his men joined the Pilgrims, feasting and playing games.

# Response and Analysis

## Reading Check

1. Why did the Mayflower return to Cape Cod?
2. During the first winter, how many of the Pilgrims survived?

## Thinking Critically

3. At what points in his history does Bradford give inner, spiritual significance to outward events?
4. Consider the treaty drawn up with Massasoit (Chapter 11), and explain whether or not you feel its terms were equally favorable to both parties. What seems to be Bradford's attitude toward the Wampanoag?

5. Using details from the selection, respond to **Connecting to the Focus Question** on page 119.

## Extending and Evaluating

6. Think about the challenges faced by present-day immigrants who have come to America in search of liberty, peace, or prosperity. In what ways might the Puritans' experiences and struggles be relevant to contemporary pioneers or refugees?

# Huswifery

**Meet the Writer** Born in Leicestershire, England, **Edward Taylor** (1642?–1729) was raised in a family that held dissenting views about many of the practices of the Church of England. Feeling more and more uncomfortable in the religious climate of his country, where the Act of Uniformity was contributing to the persecution of Puritans, he determined to seek the freedom that other Nonconformists had found in Colonial America. In 1668, Taylor sailed for Boston. After attending Harvard, Taylor accepted a call in 1671 to become pastor of a church in Westfield, Massachusetts. Taylor stayed in Westfield for the rest of his life.

Taylor wrote an enormous amount of poetry, but he allowed only a portion of one poem to be published during his lifetime. For many years, his brilliant poems moldered in the archives of Yale Library, to which Taylor's grandson had donated them. The publication in 1939 of *The Poetical Works of Edward Taylor* was another instance in American literature when buried poetic treasure was discovered. Taylor could have had little notion that his poems, which he had scrupulously put away, would outlive him with a radiance bright enough to penetrate the darkness of two centuries of obscurity.

**Background** *Huswifery* (huz′wif′ər•ē) is an archaic spelling of *housewifery,* which means "the care and management of a household." It suggests the whole range of domestic responsibility, as well as the qualities of thrift and orderliness. A *housewife* also came to be the name for a small sewing kit.

---

### CONNECTING TO THE
### Focus Question

As you read Taylor's poem, consider how it reflects the Puritans' belief that each aspect of their identity was shaped by God and that all their emotions, thoughts, desires, and behavior should be directed toward God's service. How might these beliefs have helped the Puritans maintain the intensity of their religion as they adjusted to life in the American wilderness?

Views of the Irish Linen Industry, (1783) plate 6, by William Hincks.
American Textile History Museum, Lowell, MA.

# Huswifery

## Edward Taylor

Make me, O Lord, thy Spinning Wheel complete.
    Thy Holy Word my Distaff° make for me.
Make mine Affections thy Swift Flyers neat
    And make my Soul thy holy Spool to be.
5     My Conversation make to be thy Reel
    And reel the yarn thereon spun of thy Wheel.

Make me thy Loom then, knit therein this Twine:
    And make thy Holy Spirit, Lord, wind quills:°
Then weave the Web thyself. The yarn is fine.
10    Thine Ordinances° make my Fulling Mills.°
    Then dye the same in Heavenly Colors Choice,
    All pinked° with Varnished° Flowers of Paradise.

Then clothe therewith mine Understanding, Will,
    Affections, Judgment, Conscience, Memory,
15 My Words, and Actions, that their shine may fill
    My ways with glory and thee glorify.
    Then mine apparel shall display before ye
    That I am Clothed in Holy robes for glory.

**2. distaff** (dis′taf′): On spinning wheels, the distaff is a stick around which fibers are wound before they are spun into thread. Flyers help govern the rate of spinning. The finished thread is wound upon a reel, or spool.

**8. quills:** a loom's spools or bobbins, on which thread is wound before weaving.

**10. ordinances** (ôrd′n·əns′is): religious rules and laws. **Fulling Mills:** Fulling, or milling, is the term used for the processing of raw wool cloth through a combination of washing, heating, and compressing. The cloth is processed in fulling mills to preshrink and treat the individual fibers, thereby enhancing its appearance in finished fabrics.
**12. pinked:** decorated. **varnished:** embellished.

# Response and Analysis

## Thinking Critically

1. The poet states his main **metaphor** in the first line. What does he ask the Lord to make him?

2. Describe the specific ways that Taylor extends his central **metaphor**. First, list the implements and materials used in spinning and weaving; then, next to each item, list the spiritual experiences that Taylor compares to the act of spinning and weaving.

3. Re-read the last two lines of the poem. What transformation does the speaker want to see in his life?

4. Huswifery can mean "thrift," or making the most of what one has. Who is practicing the art of huswifery in this poem?

5. Using details from the poem, respond to **Connecting to the Focus Question** on page 128.

## Extending and Evaluating

6. Readers sometimes have difficulty understanding Taylor's poetry. Briefly explain what you think might make "Huswifery" difficult to read. Consider the poet's use of language and his references to religious ideas that may be different from your own. Use specific examples from the poem to support your answer.

## *from* The History of the Dividing Line

**Meet the Writer** **William Byrd**
(1674–1744) was born in Virginia, the son of a
wealthy landowner and merchant, but he was
educated in England, where he spent half his life.
Byrd preferred London, with its elegant homes,
witty conversation, and gambling tables. During
his visits to Westover, his 2,000-acre home in
Virginia, he tried to keep alive both his social
and intellectual life.

Byrd is in many ways a representative figure
of the Southern writers of the Colonial period. In
addition to the Puritan tradition of New England,
there was another literary tradition in the American Colonies—that of the Southern planters, also
known as the Cavaliers, a group of people whose
background and social views varied from those of
the Puritans. New England was settled largely by
those in conflict with British intellectual, theological, and social life; Virginia was settled by those in
harmony with that life. By and large, the fervent,
short-haired puritanical Roundheads went to
New England; the aristocratic, long-haired,
worldly Cavaliers—like Byrd—went to Virginia.

William Byrd was truly a Renaissance man. He
translated Greek and Latin works, composed
poetry, and wrote about mathematics. Writing a
generation before Thomas Jefferson, Byrd
displayed the same intellectual curiosity that his
fellow Virginian would exemplify later. Byrd's
library at Westover contained almost 4,000
volumes and was rivaled in his time only by
Cotton Mather's library in New England.

**Background** In 1728, Byrd joined a survey
expedition of the disputed boundary line between
Virginia and North Carolina and began writing *The
History of the Dividing Line.* By then, more than a
century had passed since the first English settlers
reached Virginia. Byrd's *History* is far more than
a simple record of the expedition. Witty and
elegantly written, it is filled with philosophical
observations and barbed comments on American
Colonial life. *The History* was found among Byrd's
personal papers after his death and wasn't
published until 1841.

### CONNECTING TO THE
### Focus Question

As you read, pay close attention to Byrd's
point of view about the first colonists, their
expectations of life in North America, and
their relations with Native Americans. In
Byrd's view, what qualities and attitudes of
the Virginia colonists proved to be obstacles
to their success?

The ancestral home of the Byrd family of Virginia.
The Granger Collection, New York.

# *from* The History of the Dividing Line

## William Byrd

### Early Virginia Colonies

As it happened some ages before to be the fashion to saunter to the Holy Land and go upon other Quixote adventures,[1] so it was now grown the humor to take a trip to America. The Spaniards had lately discovered rich mines in their part of the West Indies, which made their maritime neighbors eager to do so too. This modish frenzy, being still more inflamed by the charming account given of Virginia by the first adventurers, made many fond of removing to such a Paradise.

Happy was he, and still happier she, that could get themselves transported, fondly expecting their coarsest utensils in that happy place would be of massy[2] silver.

This made it easy for the Company to procure[3] as many volunteers as they wanted for their new colony, but, like most other undertakers who have no assistance from the public, they starved the design by too much frugality; for, unwilling to launch out at first into too much expense, they shipped off but few people at a time, and those but scantily provided. The adventurers were, besides, idle and extravagant

---

1. **Quixote** (kē·hō′tē) **adventures:** foolish adventures, like those taken by the mad hero of Miguel de Cervantes's novel *The Ingenious Gentleman Don Quixote de la Mancha.*

(above) Arrival of the English in Virginia, (1585–88), by Theodore de Bry, Service Historique de la Marine, Vincennes, France.

2. **massy:** weighty.
3. **procure:** to gain; obtain; acquire.

*The Plantation* (1825). Unknown American artist. Oil on wood (19⅛" x 29½").

The Metropolitan Museum of Art, Gift of Edgar William and Bernice Chrysler Garbisch, (1963) (63.201.3). Photograph © 1984 The Metropolitan Museum of Art.

and expected they might live without work in so plentiful a country.

These wretches were set ashore not far from Roanoke Inlet, but by some fatal disagreement or laziness were either starved or cut to pieces by the Indians.

Several repeated misadventures of this kind did for some time allay[4] the itch of sailing to this new world, but the distemper broke out again about the year 1606. Then it happened that the Earl of Southampton and several other persons eminent[5] for their quality and estates were invited into the Company, who applied themselves once more to people the then almost abandoned colony. For this purpose they em-

barked about an hundred men, most of them reprobates[6] of good families and related to some of the Company who were men of quality and fortune.

The ships that carried them made a shift to find a more direct way to Virginia and ventured through the capes into the Bay of Chesapeake. The same night they came to an anchor at the mouth of Powhatan, the same as James River, where they built a small fort at a place called Point Comfort.

This settlement stood its ground from that time forward, in spite of all the blunders and disagreement of the first adventurers and the many calamities that befell the colony afterward.

4. **allay** (ə·lāʹ): lessen; relieve.
5. **eminent** (emʹə·nənt): well known for excellence; important; outstanding.

6. **reprobates** (repʹrə·bāts'): people without any sense of duty or decency.

The six gentlemen who were first named of the Company by the Crown and who were empowered to choose an annual president from among themselves were always engaged in factions and quarrels, while the rest detested work more than famine. At this rate the colony must have come to nothing had it not been for the vigilance and bravery of Captain Smith,[7] who struck a terror into all the Indians round about. This gentleman took some pains to persuade the men to plant Indian corn, but they looked upon all labor as a curse. They chose rather to depend upon the musty provisions that were sent from England; and when they failed they were forced to take more pains to seek for wild fruits in the woods than they would have taken in tilling the ground. Besides, this exposed them to be knocked in the head by the Indians and gave them fluxes[8] into the bargain, which thinned the plantation very much. To supply this mortality, they were reinforced the year following with a greater number of people, amongst which were fewer gentlemen and more laborers, who, however, took care not to kill themselves with work. These found the first adventurers in a very starving condition but relieved their wants with the fresh supply they brought with them. From Kecoughtan[9] they extended themselves as far as Jamestown, where, like true Englishmen, they built a church that cost no more than fifty pounds and a tavern that cost five hundred.

## Intermarriage

They had now made peace with the Indians, but there was one thing wanting to make that peace lasting. The natives could by no means persuade themselves that the English were heartily their friends so long as they disdained[10] to intermarry with them. And, in earnest, had the English consulted their own security and the good of the colony, had they intended either to civilize or convert these gentiles,[11] they would have brought their stomachs to embrace this prudent[12] alliance.

The Indians are generally tall and well proportioned, which may make full amends for the darkness of their complexions. Add to this that they are healthy and strong, with constitutions untainted by lewdness and not enfeebled by luxury. Besides, morals and all considered, I cannot think the Indians were much greater heathens than the first adventurers, who, had they been good Christians, would have had the charity to take this only method of converting the natives to Christianity. For, after all that can be said, a sprightly lover is the most prevailing[13] missionary that can be sent amongst these or any other infidels.

Besides, the poor Indians would have had less reason to complain that the English took away their land if they had received it by way of a portion with their daughters. Had such affinities been contracted in the beginning, how much bloodshed had been prevented and how populous[14] would the country have been, and, consequently, how considerable! Nor would the shade of the skin have been any reproach at this day, for if a Moor may be washed white in three generations, surely an Indian might have been blanched in two.

The French, for their parts, have not been so squeamish[15] in Canada, who upon trial find abundance of attraction in the Indians. Their late grand monarch thought it not below even the dignity of a Frenchman to become one flesh with this people and therefore ordered 100

---

7. **Captain Smith:** John Smith (c. 1580–1631) helped found Jamestown, Virginia, the first permanent English settlement in America.
8. **fluxes** (fluks′es): dysentery; severe diarrhea.
9. **Kecoughtan** (kē′kō′tan): present-day site of Hampton, Virginia.
10. **disdained:** refused; disapproved; scorned.

11. **gentiles** (jen′tīlz′): here, nonbelievers. Historically, among Christians, *gentile* meant a pagan or nonbeliever. (*Gentile* comes from a Latin word meaning "foreigner.") The term is more commonly used by Jews to refer to those who are not Jewish.
12. **prudent:** well thought out; cautious.
13. **prevailing:** convincing.
14. **populous** (päp′yoo·ləs): crowded with people.
15. **squeamish:** easily offended.

Pocahontas and Captain John Smith who was freed by Indians and taken into tribe by Powhatan, from "The Story of Pocahontas and Captain John", (detail), by Elmer Boyd Smith, Boston: Houghton, 1906, 18 x 23 cm, Picture Collection, The Branch Libraries, Astor, Lenox and Tilden Foundations.

livres[16] for any of his subjects, man or woman, that would intermarry with a native.

By this piece of policy we find the French interest very much strengthened amongst the savages and their religion, such as it is, propagated[17] just as far as their love. And I heartily wish this well-concerted scheme don't hereafter give the French an advantage over His Majesty's good subjects on the northern continent of America.

### The Native Religion

In the evening we examined our friend Bearskin concerning the religion of his country, and he explained it to us without any of that reserve to which his nation is subject. He told us he believed there was one supreme god, who had several subaltern[18] deities under him. And that this master god made the world a long time ago. That he told the sun, the moon, and stars their business in the beginning, which they, with good

looking-after, have faithfully performed ever since. That the same power that made all things at first has taken care to keep them in the same method and motion ever since. He believed that God had formed many worlds before he formed this, but that those worlds either grew old and ruinous or were destroyed for the dishonesty of the inhabitants. That God is very just and very good, ever well pleased with those men who possess those godlike qualities. That he takes good people into his safe protection, makes them very rich, fills their bellies plentifully, preserves them from sickness and from being surprised or overcome by their enemies. But all such as tell lies and cheat those they have dealings with he never fails to punish with sickness, poverty, and hunger and, after all that, suffers them to be knocked on the head and scalped by those that fight against them.

He believed that after death both good and bad people are conducted by a strong guard into a great road, in which departed souls travel together for some time till at a certain distance this road forks into two paths, the one extremely level and the other stony and mountainous. Here the good are parted from the bad by a flash of lightning, the first being hurried away to the right, the other to the left. The right-hand road leads to a charming, warm country, where the spring is everlasting and every month is May; and as the year is always in its youth, so are the people, and particularly the women are bright as stars and never scold. That in this happy climate there are deer, turkeys, elks, and buffaloes innumerable, perpetually fat and gentle, while the trees are loaded with delicious fruit quite throughout the four seasons. That the soil brings forth corn spontaneously, without the curse of labor, and so very wholesome that none who have the happiness to eat of it are ever sick, grow old, or die. Near the entrance into this blessed

---

16. **livres** (lē′vərz): former French monetary unit worth about a pound of silver.
17. **propagated** (prop′ə·gāt′id): transmitted or spread.
18. **subaltern** (sub·ôl′·tərn): subordinate; of inferior rank or position.

land sits a venerable[19] old man on a mat richly woven, who examines strictly all that are brought before him, and if they have behaved well, the guards are ordered to open the crystal gate and let them enter into the land of delight.

The left-hand path is very rugged and uneven, leading to a dark and barren country where it is always winter. The ground is the whole year round covered with snow, and nothing is to be seen upon the trees but icicles. All the people are hungry yet have not a morsel of anything to eat except a bitter kind of potato, that gives them the dry gripes[20] and fills their whole body with loathsome ulcers that stink and are insupportably painful. Here all the women are old and ugly, having claws like a panther with which they fly upon the men that slight their passion. For it seems these haggard old furies[21] are intolerably fond and expect a vast deal of cherishing. They talk much and exceedingly shrill, giving exquisite pain to the drum of the ear, which in that place

of the torment is so tender that every sharp note wounds it to the quick. At the end of this path sits a dreadful old woman on a monstrous toadstool, whose head is covered with rattlesnakes instead of tresses, with glaring white eyes that strike a terror unspeakable into all that behold her. This hag pronounces sentence of woe upon all the miserable wretches that hold up their hands at her tribunal. After this they are delivered over to huge turkey buzzards, like harpies,[22] that fly away with them to the place above mentioned. Here, after they have been tormented a certain number of years according to their several degrees of guilt, they are again driven back into this world to try if they will mend their manners and merit a place the next time in the regions of bliss.

This was the substance of Bearskin's religion and was as much to the purpose as could be expected from a mere state of nature, without one glimpse of revelation or philosophy. It contained, however, the three great articles of natural religion: the belief of a god, the moral distinction between good and evil, and the expectation of rewards and punishments in another world. ∎

---

19. **venerable** (ven′ər·ə·bəl): respected; esteemed for age or distinguished character.
20. **dry gripes:** stomach cramps.
21. **furies:** violent, vengeful women. In Greek and Roman mythology, the Furies are fierce avenging spirits.

22. **harpies:** evil mythological creatures with women's heads and birds' wings and legs.

# Response and Analysis

### Reading Check

**1.** What reasons does Byrd suggest for the failure of the first Virginia settlements?

**2.** What, according to Byrd, are the three basic religious beliefs of Bearskin, the American Indian guide?

### Thinking Critically

**3.** Describe Byrd's **tone**—his attitude toward his subject, the people he mentions, and his intended audience. Does the tone remain consistent throughout, or does it change? Cite passages to support your answer.

**4.** What examples of **satire**—the use of ridicule to expose the shortcomings of people or institutions—do you find in Byrd's account of the early settlers of Virginia? What personal qualities do you think Byrd admired?

**5.** Using details from the selection, respond to **Connecting to the Focus Question** on page 130.

### Extending and Evaluating

**6.** What issues, events, or attitudes in American society today do you think would be good topics for **satire**?

# Reflecting *on the* Literary Period

## Encounters and Foundations to 1800

The following questions ask you to compare and analyze the selections in this feature and respond to the Focus Question. Where possible, cite passages from the selections to support your answers.

Alvar Núñez Cabeza de Vaca . . . . . . . . . . . . . . . . . . . . . . . . . . . . *from* **La Relación**

William Bradford . . . . . . . . . . . . . . . . . . . . . . . *from* **Of Plymouth Plantation**

Edward Taylor . . . . . . . . . . . . . . . . . . . . . . . . . . . . . . . . . . . . . . . . . . **Huswifery**

William Byrd . . . . . . . . . . . . . . . . . . *from* **The History of the Dividing Line**

### Comparing Literature

1. Each selection in this feature offers a perspective on life in a new land. What common **themes** or ideas are evident throughout these writings?

2. Cabeza de Vaca and William Bradford both write about their encounters with American Indians. What do you find both similar and different about the experiences they describe? What attitudes toward American Indians are reflected in their writings?

3. How does William Byrd's description of the early settlers in Virginia compare with William Bradford's description of the Puritans in New England? Why might Byrd's observations on the first Virginia settlements be less reliable than Bradford's on the Plymouth Colony?

4. Consider Byrd's remarks on intermarriage, on the New England colonists, and on American Indian theology. What attitudes toward religion do these remarks reveal? How do Byrd's attitudes compare to those of Puritan writers, such as William Bradford and Edward Taylor?

5. Although both Bradford and Byrd were writing about colonial America, they each convey a very different **tone**. Which writer do you think sounds more modern? What are some characteristics of the writing that give it a more recognizable, contemporary tone?

**SKILLS FOCUS**

Pages 115–136 cover
**Literary Skills**
Evaluate the philosophical, political, religious, ethical, and social influences of a historical period.

### RESPONDING TO THE
## Focus Question

Review your notes and responses related to the Focus Question for this feature. Using details from the selections, write your answer to the question.
How did the attitudes and beliefs of early settlers in America not only help them endure hardships but also shape their interactions with the native inhabitants?

**FICTION**

## Hope in a New World

Set in seventeenth-century New England, *Hope Leslie* by Catharine Maria Sedgwick tells the story of an independent, freethinking young woman living in a repressive Puritan society. Determined to follow her own principles, she battles the injustices suffered by the Native Americans and champions the independence of women. The novel centers around Hope's friendship with Magawisca, the passionate and articulate daughter of a Pequot chief. Through their friendship, Hope and Magawisca transcend the restrictive boundaries of their cultures.

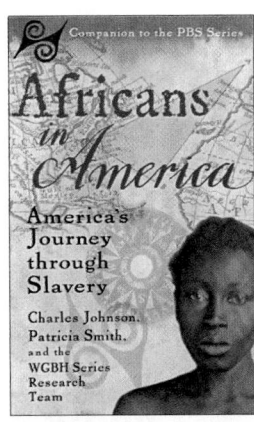

**FICTION / NONFICTION**

## A New Perspective

*Africans in America* by Charles Johnson and Patricia Smith chronicles the history of slavery in America. Smith's vivid narrative—which uses diaries, letter excerpts, and historical documents—is coupled with Johnson's fictional histories to bring a new perspective to the slave experience, one told from the African point of view.

For another fictional perspective on Africans in America, read Johnson's *Middle Passage.* A National Book Award winner, this novel tells the story of a newly freed slave who stows away on a ship without realizing it is a slave ship bound for Africa.

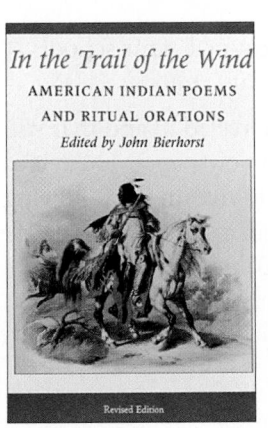

**POETRY**

## Guiding Voices

*In the Trail of the Wind: American Indian Poems and Ritual Orations,* edited by John Bierhorst, tells the history of the original inhabitants of our land through their own rich oral tradition. These songs, dreams, and prayers from Indian cultures of North and South America paint a vivid picture of peoples both ancient and living.

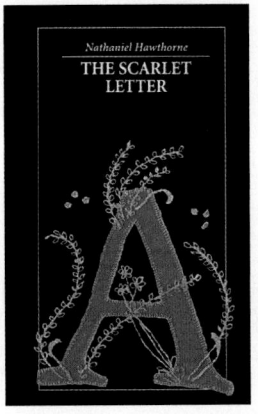

**FICTION**

## Puritan Principles

A famous fictional account of the Puritan era is Nathaniel Hawthorne's powerful novel *The Scarlet Letter,* which examines the consequences of private sin and public penance. It touches on many familiar conflicts in literature—emotion versus reason, love versus hate, and the individual versus society.

**This title is available in the HRW Library.**

# Writing an Editorial

**Writing Assignment**
**Write an editorial that conveys a well-defined perspective and a tightly reasoned argument.**

**W**hen you read Patrick Henry's famous speech to the Virginia Convention, you probably noted the strength and eloquence of the arguments he used to try to persuade his peers to take up arms against Great Britain. In this workshop you'll get to try your hand at using language to persuade others to take a particular action on an issue by writing an **editorial** for your school newspaper.

# Prewriting

## Choose a Specific Issue

**Add Incite to Insight** Inciting people to riot is a crime. Inciting them to think is not—at least not in free societies. Editorial writers incite people to think about controversial **issues**—topics about which people disagree—for the **purpose** of convincing readers that a particular stand on the issue is the correct one. As a "guest editor" for your school newspaper, encourage your readers to think about and agree with the position you support on an issue that concerns them. To find an issue, try these strategies.

- Talk to friends and classmates about issues that concern them.

- Read editorials or letters to the editor in local, state, and national newspapers or magazines or online.

- Attend meetings of your school's student council, your school district's board of education, or your local city council.

   Make a list of several issues that you're interested in and that you believe would interest readers of your school newspaper. Then, create a ratings chart and rate each issue from one to five on the following criteria: 1) it is narrow enough to be argued in a short editorial, 2) each side can make a strong case for its position, 3) people have strong feelings about the issue. Choose the issue with the highest total of points to defend or attack in an editorial.

## Analyze Your Audience

**The Object of Your Persuasion** To write effective editorials, first become familiar with your **audience**—the readers of your school newspaper. Here are some questions you can use.

- **How much do my readers know?** If your issue is unfamiliar, fill readers in on its basic points. If the issue is front-page news, assume your readers know about it.

**SKILLS FOCUS**

**Writing Skills**
Write an editorial.
Choose a topic.
Analyze the
audience.

- **What are the concerns of readers who disagree with my position?**
Anticipate that some readers will disagree with your views. What will their counterarguments be and how can you address them?

## Plan Your Thesis

**Make Your Point** The **thesis** of an editorial is a statement of the writer's basic opinion on the issue. Plan your thesis by jotting down an **opinion statement,** one or two sentences that identify the issue and state your perspective on it. Here is an example of an opinion statement one student wrote for an editorial opposing a curfew law for teenagers.

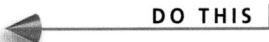

[issue]       [opinion]

The city's new curfew law for teenagers should be repealed.

## Gather and Shape Support

**Convince Me!** In order to persuade your audience, you must explain to them why your opinion is valid. Back up your opinion statement with the **reasons** for your opinion. Each of these reasons should appeal to readers' sense of logic, to their emotions, or to their ethical beliefs. Support your reasons with relevant **evidence**—precise and pertinent facts, statistics, examples, anecdotes, and expert opinions. If the connection between a reason and its supporting evidence is not self-evident, elaborate upon the evidence, showing how it connects to the reason. When you support the reasons for your opinion with evidence and elaboration of that evidence, you form **sustained arguments.** Take a look at the chart below to see one student's support of his opinion statement and an analysis of that support.

**DO THIS**

**TIP** If your opinion statement suggests that a certain action should be taken, you might issue a **call to action** in the conclusion of your editorial. For example, the student opposed to the curfew law calls upon readers to contact their city council members and ask that the law be repealed.

**Opinion Statement:** The city's new curfew law for teenagers should be repealed.

| Reason | Evidence | Analysis |
|---|---|---|
| The law will have no effect on crime. | Teenage crime makes up only 11 percent of the city's total; Dr. Chang says statistics show most teen crime occurs between 4 and 9 p.m. | Evidence consists of facts, some cited by expert. Appeal is to logic. |
| The law further burdens an already overburdened police force. | Police chief says, "The curfew won't do a thing, except to make officers waste their time enforcing it." Only 5 percent of officers support the law. A poll of officers shows that 93 percent think more officers and equipment are needed, not a new law. | Evidence consists of expert opinions and facts. Appeal is mostly to logic, but also to emotions and ethics. |

*(continued)*

(continued)

| School activities often require later hours than curfew allows. | Sports teams and school-sponsored clubs often get back late from competitions and conventions. Activities like Bowl-a-Thon, which has raised $17,000 for charity, require late hours. | Evidence consists of examples. Appeal is to logic, emotions, and ethics. |
| --- | --- | --- |

**The Art of Persuasion**  Shape your support in a persuasive and sophisticated way by using **rhetorical devices,** techniques writers use to enhance their arguments and make their writing effective. Here are some rhetorical devices you can use in your editorial.

## RHETORICAL DEVICES AND EXAMPLES

| | |
| --- | --- |
| **Repetition** is the repeated use of a word, phrase, or clause more than once for emphasis. | The curfew law should be **repealed—repealed** immediately in fairness to the community, the police, and the students. |
| **Parallelism** is the repetition of the same grammatical form to express equal, or parallel, ideas. A noun is paired with a noun, a phrase with a phrase, a clause with a clause, and so on. | This week, the Riverdale High School student council had to cancel its annual charity Bowl-a-Thon—**not because of a lack of interest, not because of a shortage of funds, and not because of a failure to sign up enough enthusiastic volunteers.** |
| **Rhetorical questions** are questions that are not meant to be answered but are asked for effect. | **Should students who are out late because of such events be jailed or fined? Should such school activities be dropped?** |
| **Argument by analogy** draws a parallel between basically dissimilar events or situations. | If the curfew law aims to reduce youth crime, it mistakenly targets the wrong hours. **It's much like shutting the corral gate after the horses have escaped.** |

## Organize Your Support

**Right This Way**  The body paragraphs of your editorial should develop each of the reasons in your argument by presenting and elaborating on evidence. Most writers arrange their reasons from strongest to weakest when they want to grab the attention of the audience and from weakest to strongest when they want to leave readers with the strongest possible impression. Some writers use a combination such as beginning with the second strongest reason, going next to the third strongest, and ending with the strongest. Use the pattern you think will have the greatest impact on your audience.

**SKILLS FOCUS**

**Writing Skills**
Organize your support. Use rhetorical devices.

**PRACTICE & APPLY 1**  Use the instruction in this section to develop an editorial for your school newspaper. Choose an issue that is important to you and others.

# Revising

## Evaluate and Revise Your Editorial

**The Editorial Touch**  An editorial is a serious piece of writing. When you write one, you want people to pay attention to what you have to say. Therefore, because you want everything about your editorial to contribute to its persuasive effect, you need to evaluate and revise it carefully. The guidelines in the chart below and in the chart on the next page will help you.

> **First Reading: Content and Organization**  An editorial succeeds or fails first on the basis of its content. How the editorial is organized affects readers' understanding of that content. Evaluating and revising the content and organization of your editorial is an integral part of the process of producing an effective editorial. Use the tips in the chart below to evaluate and revise the content and organization of your editorial.

> **PEER REVIEW**
>
> Give your editorial to a peer to read. He or she may be able to offer hints on how to elaborate on your evidence.

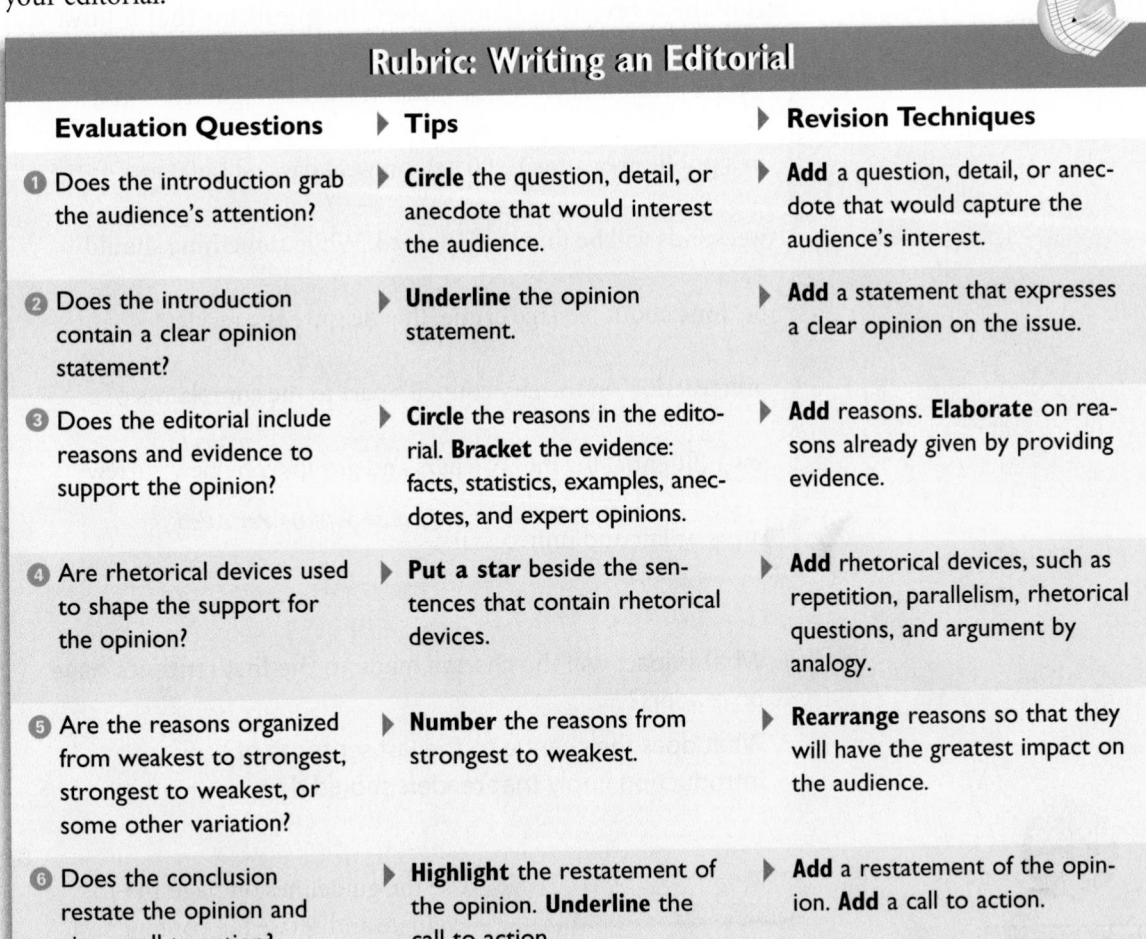

### Rubric: Writing an Editorial

| Evaluation Questions | ▶ Tips | ▶ Revision Techniques |
|---|---|---|
| ❶ Does the introduction grab the audience's attention? | ▶ **Circle** the question, detail, or anecdote that would interest the audience. | ▶ **Add** a question, detail, or anecdote that would capture the audience's interest. |
| ❷ Does the introduction contain a clear opinion statement? | ▶ **Underline** the opinion statement. | ▶ **Add** a statement that expresses a clear opinion on the issue. |
| ❸ Does the editorial include reasons and evidence to support the opinion? | ▶ **Circle** the reasons in the editorial. **Bracket** the evidence: facts, statistics, examples, anecdotes, and expert opinions. | ▶ **Add** reasons. **Elaborate** on reasons already given by providing evidence. |
| ❹ Are rhetorical devices used to shape the support for the opinion? | ▶ **Put a star** beside the sentences that contain rhetorical devices. | ▶ **Add** rhetorical devices, such as repetition, parallelism, rhetorical questions, and argument by analogy. |
| ❺ Are the reasons organized from weakest to strongest, strongest to weakest, or some other variation? | ▶ **Number** the reasons from strongest to weakest. | ▶ **Rearrange** reasons so that they will have the greatest impact on the audience. |
| ❻ Does the conclusion restate the opinion and give a call to action? | ▶ **Highlight** the restatement of the opinion. **Underline** the call to action. | ▶ **Add** a restatement of the opinion. **Add** a call to action. |

**Second Reading: Style** Now, concentrate on your editorial's style, or the way you expressed yourself. In persuasive writing, your style should be direct and clear. Avoid **euphemisms,** or indirect, pleasant ways of referring to things that some people might find unpleasant, distasteful, or disturbing. Examples include *garden of memories* for *cemetery* and *previously owned* for *used.* Use the guidelines in the chart below to find and replace euphemisms in your editorial.

## Style Guidelines

| Evaluation Question | ▶ Tip | ▶ Revision Technique |
|---|---|---|
| ● Are euphemisms used in place of more direct terms? | ▶ **Circle** words and phrases used to avoid describing unpleasant things in direct terms. | ▶ **Replace** each euphemism with a more direct word. |

## ANALYZING THE REVISION PROCESS

Study these revisions, and answer the questions that follow.

> Under the new law, anyone under the age of eighteen found
>
> in a public area after 10:00 P.M. on weekdays or 11:00 P.M. on
>
> **replace** weekends will be fined or ~~detained~~. *jailed* While something should
>
> be done about teenage crime, the measure is a reckless
>
> overreaction on the city council's part to the complaints of a
>
> few influential business owners and groups. *Because* The new curfew
>
> **add** law is unfair and unnecessary, *it should be repealed.*

### Responding to the Revision Process

1. What impact will the change made to the first sentence have on readers?

2. What does the change to the last sentence of the introduction imply that readers should do?

**SKILLS FOCUS**

**Writing Skills**
Revise for content and style.

**PRACTICE & APPLY** 3 Use the guidelines on page 143 to evaluate and revise the content and organization of your editorial. Then, use the guidelines above to evaluate its style, replacing any euphemisms.

# Publishing

## Proofread and Publish Your Editorial

**One More Check** Since the issue at the heart of your editorial is important to you, you want to be sure that the editorial is free of errors. When you chose an issue and wrote an editorial on it, you assumed a position of authority on that issue. If you want your audience to accept your authority, don't undermine it by leaving careless mistakes in grammar, usage, or mechanics uncorrected.

**Go Public** To persuade readers, you first have to reach them. Here are some ways you can take your editorial to a wider audience.

- Submit your editorial to the editor of the editorial page of your school or local newspaper. Check the submission guidelines to make sure your piece meets the paper's criteria.

- If your issue is a specialized one, look for periodicals that cover that field, including newsletters and online magazines. A magazine or newsletter might wish to reformat your editorial as a feature article or a letter to the editor.

- You can also reach a wide audience by publishing your editorial on the Internet. Post your editorial to an Internet newsgroup related to your issue.

- Conduct panel discussions of the issues you and your classmates wrote about in your editorials, exchanging editorials with the members of the panel as the starting point of the discussion.

## Reflect on Your Editorial

**Learn from the Process** Professional editorial writers have daily practice in refining their craft. To refine yours, reflect on the process of writing an editorial by writing short responses to the following questions.

- In what ways is writing an editorial different from writing an expository piece, such as an explanation of a law?

- What constructive advice on improving your editorial were you offered by your peers? What effect did your resulting revisions have on the impact of your editorial?

- Did writing your editorial change your understanding of the issue you wrote about? Explain.

**PRACTICE & APPLY** 4 Using the guidelines on this page, proofread your editorial for errors in the conventions of standard American English grammar, usage, and mechanics. Then, publish and reflect on your editorial.

> **TIP** Errors that confuse readers and prevent them from following an argument are especially destructive in an editorial. As you proofread, check to see that you have followed the **conventions** of standard American English. Look for ambiguous pronoun references, which occur when a pronoun can refer to more than one antecedent. For more on **ambiguous pronoun references,** see Clear Pronoun Reference, 4j, in the Language Handbook.

**SKILLS FOCUS**

**Writing Skills**
Proofread, especially for clear pronoun references.

# Presenting and Evaluating Speeches

## Speaking Assignment

**Adapt your written editorial for a persuasive speech and deliver it to an audience. Then, listen to and evaluate the persuasive speeches of others.**

**E**ffective **persuasive speeches** incorporate the same techniques that are used to write editorials. A speech, though, allows you to use your voice and body as well as words to make your point. In this workshop you will learn how to use the techniques of persuasion in a speech and how to listen to and evaluate the persuasive speeches of others.

## Adapt Your Editorial

**Part by Part**  A persuasive speech consists of the same introduction, body, and conclusion arrangement your written editorial had. However, you might need to make alterations to each of these parts of your editorial so they will be better suited for a speech.

- The **introduction** to an effective persuasive speech is dramatic. Consider using a thought-provoking literary quotation, a touching anecdote that illustrates an aspect of the issue you're dealing with, or a reference to an authority on the subject of your speech. Then, state your **distinct perspective** on the issue in a strong but simple opinion statement, perhaps even repeating it for dramatic effect and impact.

- The **body** of a persuasive speech supports the opinion statement and must consist of **solid reasoning.** To fit within your time limits, choose only the most effective reasons from your written editorial based on the makeup of your audience. For example, an audience composed exclusively of classmates might respond favorably to reasons that appeal to their emotions. An audience of city council members might respond best to reasons that appeal to logic or ethics.

- The **conclusion** to an effective speech should be memorable. First, summarize the main points and restate your opinion directly. Finally, call the audience to action, using specific language.

**Take the Right Approach**  There are two basic ways to organize the body of a persuasive speech—deductively or inductively. You can use either to make sure that your speech is coherent and focused.

- **The Deductive Approach**  Deductive reasoning moves from general to specific. State your opinion in the introduction, and give specific reasons and evidence in the body of the speech.

- **The Inductive Approach**  Inductive reasoning moves from specific to general. You present the reasons and evidence (the specifics) for your opinion at the beginning and build to your opinion statement (the general) in the conclusion.

**TIP**  Keep in mind that your reasoning will be evaluated as you present your speech. Therefore, you should avoid faulty logic and the use of propaganda. For more on **logical fallacies and propaganda,** see page 149.

**SKILLS FOCUS**

**Listening and Speaking Skills**
Present and evaluate a persuasive speech.

**The Artful Speaker** The same rhetorical devices you used in your written editorial—**repetition, parallelism, rhetorical questions,** and **argument by analogy**—can be equally effective in your speech.

Another rhetorical device you can use is irony, especially effective in speaking because you can use your voice to communicate tone, or attitude. **Irony** is the contrast between expectation and reality. For example, the writer of the Writer's Model that begins on page 141 makes the point that the city council *expected* the curfew to reduce teen crime when the *reality* is that most teen crimes are committed before the curfew even begins. In a speech, this writer could use his voice to make the irony clear to the audience.

Another effective device in persuasive speaking is to frame one or more of your arguments as a **syllogism,** a formula for presenting an argument in which you show that two premises—a major and a minor premise—lead to a single, inescapable conclusion. Here are the parts of a syllogism with examples.

**Reference Note**
For more on **rhetorical devices,** see page 140.

**Major Premise**  The purpose of the 10:00 P.M. curfew for teens is to reduce teen crime.

**Minor Premise**  Most teen crime occurs between 4:00 and 9:00 P.M.

**Conclusion**  The curfew will have little effect on teen crime.

Once you set up your major and minor premises, you might find it effective to allow the audience to draw the inevitable conclusion for themselves, perhaps prompting them to do so by asking them for the conclusion. For example, the speaker adapting the editorial on the teen curfew might ask, "Now, how much is the curfew going to affect teen crime?" This technique also makes the irony of the situation clear.

## Present Your Speech

**Special Delivery** Because your persuasive speech is on an issue about which you care deeply, consider delivering it as a **formal** speech. Write your speech out completely, and practice it until you have it memorized. On your written speech, note the pitch and volume that you intend to use at various points in the speech. Do the same thing for gestures, pauses, and eye contact. Also, don't forget to adopt a serious **tone** while presenting your appeals by avoiding slang, colloquialisms, or contractions. For more on **delivery techniques,** see page 435. For more on **verbal** and **nonverbal techniques,** see page 623.

**Listening and Speaking Skills**
Use rhetorical devices. Practice delivery techniques.

**INTERNET**
Speeches
Keyword: LE7 11-1

**PRACTICE & APPLY** 5  Use the instructions in this section to adapt your written editorial into a persuasive speech. Practice the speech until you have it memorized. Then, deliver it to an audience.

# Evaluate a Persuasive Speech

**The Critical Ear**   Critical listeners are able to make informed and wise **judgments** regarding issues they are faced with every day. The first step in being a critical listener is to know the type of persuasive speech you are listening to. The type of speech is revealed in the speaker's opinion statement. Here are the four basic types of persuasive speeches.

1. A speech that proposes a fact argues that a thesis can be seen as true or false. An opinion statement such as "The new standardized tests required by the state assure school accountability" is a **proposition of fact.** The speaker can argue that this thesis is true or false.

2. A speech that proposes a policy attempts to get the audience to support a particular plan of action. An opinion statement such as "Developing alternatives to fossil fuels should be a national priority" is a **proposition of policy.**

3. A speech that proposes a problem tries to persuade an audience that a specific problem exists and is serious enough to warrant action. An opinion statement such as "Our city's sewage system poses a health hazard to citizens" is a **proposition of problem.**

4. A speech that proposes a value argues the relative merit of a person, place, or thing. You can't prove a proposition of value, but you can provide evidence to support your belief. An opinion statement such as "A person who avoids jury duty is a poor citizen" is a **proposition of value.** The value word in the thesis is "poor."

The language used to argue the first three types of persuasive speeches is the language of reason. The reasons you present for your opinion appeal to the listener's sense of logic, and your proof consists of hard evidence such as statistics and expert testimony. The speech is organized so that reasons that appeal to listeners' emotions or ethics are clearly secondary to the reasons that appeal to logic.

The language used to argue a proposition of value can appeal to the emotions or ethics. The emotional and ethical appeals used might outweigh the factual proof or evidence. A speech arguing a proposition of value is usually organized for dramatic effect.

**TIP**   Once you've identified the speaker's purpose and which type of speech you're listening to, evaluate the speaker's **diction** (word choice) and **syntax** (sentence structure). Be wary of speakers who use elaborate diction and sentence structure to present simple concepts and speakers who use simple words and sentence structure to present complex ideas. They might be trying to make a weak argument sound convincing.

**Beware Logical Fallacies and Propaganda**   Most effective persuasive arguments are based on reasons and evidence. A critical listener recognizes when a speaker is using fallacious reasoning or propaganda to get the audience on his or her side of the issue.

The chart below provides definitions and examples of different types of faulty logic and propaganda. When you listen to a persuasive speech, be on the lookout for them.

## LOGICAL FALLACIES AND PROPAGANDA TECHNIQUES

| | |
|---|---|
| An **overgeneralization** is based on too little evidence or evidence that ignores exceptions. | Adults just want to deny teenagers their rights. Otherwise, the curfew law would not have been approved. |
| **False causality** assumes one event caused another because one happened before the other. | Councilman Jay Jones proposed the curfew after his store was robbed. The robbery is the reason he proposed it. |
| A **false analogy** draws an invalid conclusion from a comparison that is weak or unreasonable. | The city council understands modern teenagers about as well as most people understand the theory of relativity. |
| A **red herring** is something that takes a listener's attention away from the real issue or point. | The curfew law is the city council's attempt to usurp parents' authority. |
| An **attack *ad hominem*** means attacking a person associated with the issue instead of the issue itself. | Mr. Lee, a longtime member of the city council, is well known for his dislike of children in general and teenagers in particular. |
| The **bandwagon effect** encourages listeners to act or think a certain way because everyone else is. | The student council, the football and basketball teams, and the entire cheerleading squad oppose the curfew. So should you. |

**PRACTICE & APPLY** 6   Following the instructions above, listen to and evaluate the persuasive speeches of your peers. Then, provide polite feedback.

One way to better understand a piece of literature is to compare it with literature from an earlier or later period. The following two poems share certain qualities; they also show differences that can be attributed in part to the time period in which each poem was written.

"To My Dear and Loving Husband" by Puritan poet Anne Bradstreet (1612–1672) was published in 1678, six years after her death. Edna St. Vincent Millay (1892–1950), a famous poet from the modern period, published "Love is not all" in 1931. As you read, think about how these poems' messages and styles reflect the circumstances of the two poets—a pioneer who wrote within a strict religious tradition and a woman in post–World War I America who experimented with new freedoms from tradition and authority.

DIRECTIONS: Read the following poems. Then, read each multiple-choice question that follows, and write the letter of the best answer.

# To My Dear and Loving Husband
## Anne Bradstreet

If ever two were one, then surely we.
If ever man were loved by wife, then thee;
If ever wife was happy in a man,
Compare with me, ye women, if you can.
5   I prize thy love more than whole mines of gold
Or all the riches that the East doth hold.
My love is such that rivers cannot quench,
Nor ought° but love from thee, give recompense.°
Thy love is such I can no way repay,
10  The heavens reward thee manifold,° I pray.
Then while we live, in love let's so persevere°
That when we live no more, we may live ever.

**8. ought** *n.:* archaic word meaning "anything." **recompense** *n.:* repayment.

**10. manifold** *adv.:* in many ways.

**11. persevere** *v.:* pronounced so last two syllables rhyme with *ever.*

**SKILLS FOCUS**

Pages 150–153 cover
**Literary Skills**
Compare and contrast works from different literary periods.

# Love is not all

Edna St. Vincent Millay

Love is not all: it is not meat nor drink
Nor slumber nor a roof against the rain;
Nor yet a floating spar to men that sink
And rise and sink and rise and sink again;
5   Love can not fill the thickened lung with breath,
Nor clean the blood, nor set the fractured bone;
Yet many a man is making friends with death
Even as I speak, for lack of love alone.
It well may be that in a difficult hour,
10   Pinned down by pain and moaning for release,
Or nagged by want past resolution's power,
I might be driven to sell your love for peace,
Or trade the memory of this night for food.
It well may be. I do not think I would.

# Collection 1: Skills Review
## Comparing Literature

1. In "To My Dear and Loving Husband," the speaker describes her love for her husband using **imagery** relating to —
   A  wealth and nature
   B  thirst and hunger
   C  water and air
   D  gold and diamonds

2. The speaker in Bradstreet's poem states that her love for her husband is —
   F  less than her love of wealth and comfort
   G  greater than her love for God
   H  less than the love other women feel for their husbands
   J  as strong, if not stronger, than any other woman's love

3. Bradstreet's poem ends with a **paradox**—an apparent contradiction that reveals a truth. Which of the following items explains this paradox?
   A  People who are no longer alive on earth can be alive forever in heaven.
   B  People who don't love each other on earth will love each other in heaven.
   C  People should love each other while they're alive because life is short.
   D  People who don't love each other will not live forever.

4. In "Love is not all," the speaker compares love to what it is not and what it cannot do. Which of these points does the speaker make in lines 1–6?
   F  Love cannot let you down.
   G  Love cannot fill material needs or cure sickness.
   H  Love is less important than friendship.
   J  Love cannot last forever.

5. What **paradox** does the speaker in "Love is not all" point out in lines 1–8?
   A  Love is painful yet it makes us happy.
   B  Loving oneself is more important than loving other people.
   C  Love cannot save lives yet people can die without it.
   D  It is more important to love people than to heal them.

6. In Millay's poem, which statement best describes the speaker's **attitude** toward love?
   F  The speaker believes that love will not let a person down.
   G  The speaker thinks peace is more important than love.
   H  The speaker thinks love fills an essential need.
   J  The speaker thinks love isn't worth the trouble.

7. A major stylistic difference between the two poems is —

    A  Bradstreet's poem rhymes and Millay's poem does not

    B  Millay uses more religious imagery than Bradstreet

    C  Millay's language is more contemporary than Bradstreet's

    D  only Bradstreet's poem is addressed to a "you"

8. Which statement *best* describes the contrast in **tone** between the two poems?

    F  Bradstreet's tone is spiritual, and Millay's tone is playful.

    G  Bradstreet's tone is loving, and Millay's tone is regretful.

    H  Bradstreet's tone is pessimistic, and Millay's tone is optimistic.

    J  Bradstreet's tone is devoted, and Millay's tone is spiteful.

9. Which of the following statements *best* expresses the shared **theme** of the two poems?

    A  Love makes life easier to bear.

    B  Love is always painful.

    C  Women love men more than men love women.

    D  Love cures everything.

10. What is one way that each poem reflects the time period in which it was written?

    F  Bradstreet's poem reveals her Puritan devotion to God while Millay's poem addresses more earthbound concerns.

    G  Bradstreet's poem questions a woman's place in society while Millay's poem uses romantic imagery.

    H  Bradstreet's poem uses elaborate figures of speech while Millay's poem does not.

    J  Bradstreet's poem praises love, but Millay sees it only as troublesome.

## Essay Question

In an essay, compare and contrast these two love poems, paying particular attention to the elements of theme and tone. Address the following questions in your essay: What is each speaker's **tone**—sincere, cynical, sarcastic, tragic, ironic, or something else? Are the poems—in terms of **content** and **theme**—more similar to one another or different? Could Bradstreet's poem have been written by a twentieth-century poet? Could Millay's poem have been written by a Puritan? Why or why not? Could either poem have been written by a man?

# Collection 1: Skills Review
## Vocabulary Skills

**Context Clues**

DIRECTIONS: Use the context clues in the following sentences to help you identify the meanings of the underlined Vocabulary words.

1. When Mary Rowlandson felt melancholy, or sad, she often turned to the Bible for comfort. In this sentence, melancholy means —
   A   joyful
   B   sorrowful
   C   boring
   D   angry

2. Only by sleeping next to his sister could Equiano alleviate his fears. In this sentence, alleviate means —
   F   increase
   G   confirm
   H   relieve
   J   clarify

3. Edwards believed that God was provoked and that the people who had irritated God should seek forgiveness. In this sentence, provoked means —
   A   pleased
   B   weakened
   C   angered
   D   pacified

4. Benjamin Franklin's goal of rectitude was based on his ideas for proper moral conduct. In this sentence, rectitude means —
   F   strength
   G   wealth
   H   correctness
   J   harmony

5. According to Patrick Henry, the colonists should see Britain as an adversary, not as a protector. In this sentence, adversary means —
   A   friend
   B   companion
   C   champion
   D   enemy

6. Patrick Henry believed that war with Britain was inevitable and urged his countrymen to be ready to fight. In this sentence, inevitable means —
   F   foolish
   G   reasonable
   H   confusing
   J   unavoidable

7. Devoted to the colonists' cause, Thomas Paine spurned the idea that they could ever be happy under British rule. In this sentence, spurned means —
   A   developed
   B   rejected
   C   revised
   D   supported

8. The colonists vowed to reject and renounce the government of the Colonies by British rule. In this sentence, renounce means —
   F   deny
   G   encourage
   H   avenge
   J   support

**SKILLS FOCUS**

**Vocabulary Skills**
Use context clues to determine the meanings of words.

# Collection 1: Skills Review
## Writing Skills

**Test Practice** DIRECTIONS: Read the following paragraph from a draft of a student's editorial. Then, read the questions below it. Choose the best answer to each question.

(1) Last week the president of the local school board, Melinda C. Patterson, proposed a mandatory uniform policy for all public schools in the city. (2) Other states have rejected such a policy. (3) Such a policy is ridiculous! (4) A mandatory uniform policy denies parents the right to choose their children's clothing. (5) Moreover, the school district will probably have to furnish uniforms for the students who can't afford them. (6) That will be a misuse of funds, especially when school buildings are crumbling, teachers are grossly underpaid, and parents are losing faith in public schools.

1. Which sentence could replace sentence 3 to better convey the writer's perspective, or opinion?
   - **A** Ms. Patterson's proposal has merit and should be adopted.
   - **B** Ms. Patterson's proposal will deny parents their rights.
   - **C** Ms. Patterson's proposal will cost taxpayers too much.
   - **D** Ms. Patterson's proposal should be rejected by the board.

2. What evidence could the writer add to support the idea in sentence 5?
   - **F** School uniforms lower the social pressure students feel to fit in with their peers by dressing a certain way.
   - **G** School uniforms will impose a heavy financial burden on the students' families.
   - **H** School uniforms have been successful in decreasing disciplinary problems.
   - **J** School uniforms cost approximately fifty dollars per student, so the potential cost to taxpayers could be four million dollars.

3. Which of the following rhetorical devices does the writer use to enhance the effectiveness of sentence 6?
   - **A** a rhetorical question
   - **B** an analogy
   - **C** repetition
   - **D** parallelism

4. Which sentence should be deleted or moved to another paragraph to improve the coherence of the passage?
   - **F** 1  **H** 4
   - **G** 2  **J** 5

5. To adapt this passage to include in a persuasive speech, the speaker might
   - **A** use only emotional appeals to convince an audience
   - **B** eliminate reasons that address listeners' concerns
   - **C** cut out the conclusion to keep within the time limits of the presentation
   - **D** enliven the introduction to capture the audience's attention

**SKILLS FOCUS**

**Writing Skills**
Write an editorial.

The Museum of Fine Arts, Houston. Museum purchase with funds provided by the Agnes Cullen Arnold Endowment Fund.

*Indian Pass* (1847) by Thomas Cole. Oil on canvas (40¹/₁₆″ × 29³/₄″).

# American Romanticism
# 1800–1860

## *Imagination and the Individual*

We will walk on our own feet;

we will work with our own hands;

we will speak our own minds.

—Ralph Waldo Emerson

**go.hrw.com**

**INTERNET**

Collection
Resources

Keyword: LE7 11-2

# American Romanticism
## 1800–1860

### LITERARY EVENTS

**1792** England's Mary Wollstonecraft publishes *A Vindication of the Rights of Woman*

**1798** William Wordsworth and Samuel Taylor Coleridge publish *Lyrical Ballads,* a landmark of English Romanticism

**1817** William Cullen Bryant publishes "Thanatopsis"

*The Deerslayer* **(detail), illustrated by N. C. Wyeth (1925).**

**1820** Washington Irving publishes *The Sketch Book*

**1823** James Fenimore Cooper publishes *The Pioneers*

**1828** Noah Webster publishes a landmark dictionary of American English

**1830** Oliver Wendell Holmes publishes "Old Ironsides"

**1833** John Greenleaf Whittier publishes *Justice and Expediency,* in which he calls for the abolition of slavery

**1835** France's Alexis de Tocqueville publishes *Democracy in America,* a noted study of U.S. political and social institutions

### POLITICAL AND SOCIAL EVENTS

**1791** First ten amendments, or Bill of Rights, is added to U.S. Constitution

**1794** Eli Whitney's improved cotton gin increases U.S. cotton cultivation and expands demand for slave labor

**1800** U.S. population is 5.3 million

**1800** Washington, D.C., becomes U.S. capital

**1803** President Thomas Jefferson negotiates Louisiana Purchase from France, more than doubling U.S. territory

**1810** Miguel Hidalgo y Costilla launches the Mexican war of independence from Spain

**1814** In War of 1812, British burn much of Washington, D.C.

**1814** Francis Scott Key, commemorating the War of 1812, writes "The Star-Spangled Banner"

**1815** Napoleon I of France is defeated at Waterloo and subsequently exiled

**1819** Simón Bolívar, South American independence leader, becomes Gran Colombia's first president

**1820–1821** Missouri is admitted as a slave state, Maine as a free state, in Missouri Compromise

**1822** Liberia is founded on west coast of Africa as a settlement for freed U.S. slaves

**1824** Peru assures its independence by defeating Spain at Ayacucho

**1825** Erie Canal is opened, connecting Great Lakes and Atlantic Ocean

**1826** Thomas Jefferson and John Adams die on same day, July 4

**c. 1830** Underground Railroad, a secret system for helping fugitive slaves reach safety, is organized

**1836** Thomas Cole completes *The Oxbow,* an early Hudson River school Romantic landscape painting

**1837** Queen Victoria of England is crowned

**1838** U.S. Army forces Cherokees out of Georgia on long Trail of Tears to Oklahoma

*Trail of Tears* **by Robert Lindneux.**

**1841** Ralph Waldo Emerson publishes his first collection, *Essays,* including "Self-Reliance" and "The Over-Soul"

**1845** Margaret Fuller publishes *Woman in the Nineteenth Century,* the first full-length study of women's position in American society

**1845** Edgar Allan Poe publishes *The Raven and Other Poems*

**1848** James Russell Lowell publishes *The Biglow Papers,* satirical poems opposing the Mexican War and written in a Yankee dialect

**1850** Nathaniel Hawthorne publishes *The Scarlet Letter*

**1851** Herman Melville publishes *The Whale,* or *Moby-Dick*

**1854** Henry David Thoreau publishes *Walden*

**1855** Walt Whitman publishes the first edition of his book of poems, *Leaves of Grass*

**1858** Emily Dickinson begins to copy her poems into bound booklets

**1858** Henry Wadsworth Longfellow publishes *The Courtship of Miles Standish*

**1840** U.S. population is 17.1 million

**1841** Brook Farm undertakes experiment in cooperative living

**1842** By Treaty of Nanking, China cedes Hong Kong to Great Britain and opens five ports to foreign trade

**1845** Alexander Cartwright formulates rules to regulate modern game of baseball

**1845** United States annexes Texas (leads to war with Mexico, 1846–1848)

**1846** Famine in Ireland due to potato-crop failure causes increased emigration from Ireland to United States

**1848** Lucretia Mott and Elizabeth Cady Stanton organize first women's-rights convention in the United States in Seneca Falls, New York

**1849** California gold rush begins as thousands of gold miners travel to Sacramento area

**1851** *The New York Times* is founded

**1854** Modern Republican party is organized to oppose the extension of slavery

**1854** Commodore Matthew Perry opens two Japanese ports to U.S. trade

**1857** U.S. Supreme Court's *Dred Scott* decision antagonizes antislavery forces

**1858** After Indian revolt against British East India Company rule, British government takes over administration of India

**1858** Abraham Lincoln and Stephen A. Douglas stage a noted series of seven debates as candidates for the Illinois seat in the U.S. Senate

**Title page from a gold-mining manual (detail) (1849).**

**Lincoln-Douglas debate (1858).**

**American Romanticism: 1800–1860**     **159**

# Political and Social

## Westward Ho! The Louisiana Purchase, 1803

The biggest land deal in history, the Louisiana Purchase, was settled between France and the United States in 1803. President Thomas Jefferson negotiated the purchase of all the land between the Mississippi River and the Rocky Mountains and the Gulf of Mexico and Canada for fifteen million dollars. At a cost of about four cents an acre, the area of the United States was immediately doubled, and a century of westward expansion was launched.

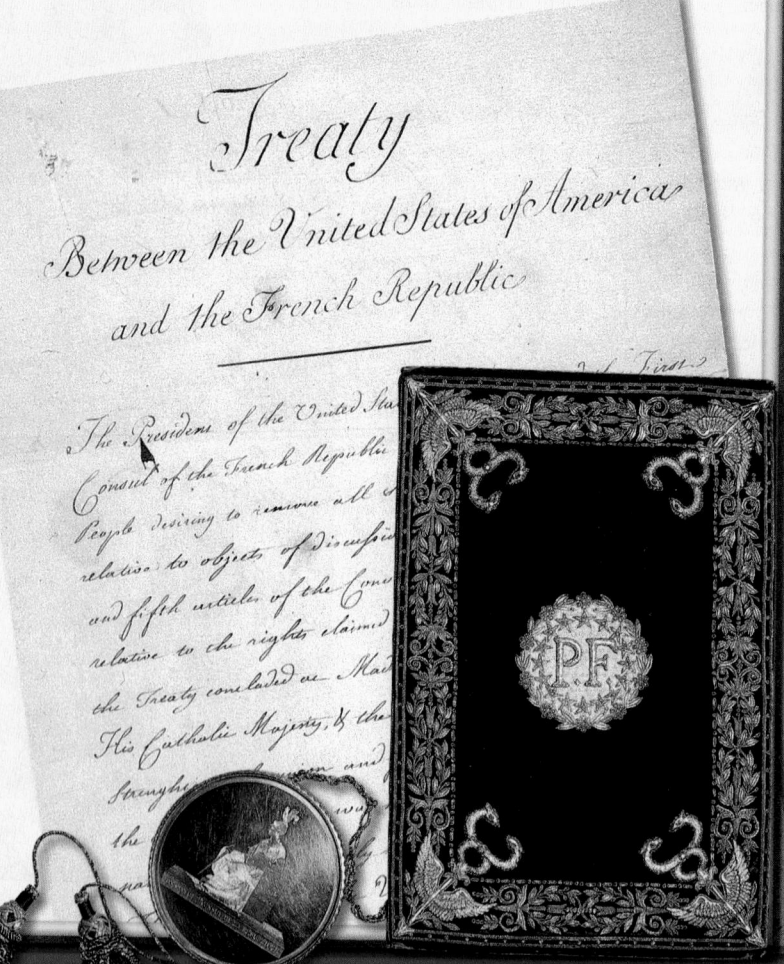

## The Gold Rush, 1849

In 1848, gold was discovered at Sutter's Mill in California. By 1849, tens of thousands of Americans traveled west, hoping to strike it rich. Gold rushes continued through the rest of the century, from Colorado to Alaska. The rush for gold left many prospectors with broken lives and dreams, but it also led to the founding of new towns and cities all across the country and to the building of the first transcontinental railroads.

# Milestones 1800–1860

## Education and Reform

New England was long known for its interest in self-improvement and intellectual inquiry. In 1826, the lyceum (lī·sē′əm) movement began in Millbury, Massachusetts. Lyceum organizations had a number of goals, including educating adults, training teachers, establishing museums, and instituting social reforms. A typical part of a lyceum program was a course of winter lectures. One of the most popular speakers was Ralph Waldo Emerson.

The reform movement was also centered in New England. Horace Mann fought to improve public education. Dorothea Dix sought to relieve the horrible conditions in institutions for the mentally ill. William Lloyd Garrison and other abolitionists struggled to put an end to slavery. Feminists like Elizabeth Peabody, Margaret Fuller, and Emma Willard campaigned for women's rights.

The abounding interest in social causes stirred up ideas both reasonable and crackpot. Numerous utopian projects—plans for creating a more perfect society—were developed. In 1840, Emerson wryly remarked that every man who could read had plans in his pocket for a new community. Emerson was speaking from personal experience, for he was a member of one of the most influential of these idealistic groups, the Transcendentalists.

(Above and below) Gold prospectors, c. 1850.

Emerson lecturing in Concord, Massachusetts.

# American Romanticism
## 1800–1860

*by* Gary Q. Arpin

## PREVIEW

## Think About ...

By the beginning of the nineteenth century, Americans had forged an independent nation, but they had not yet created their own cultural identity. A new generation of writers, who called themselves Romantics and Transcendentalists, took the first giant steps in that direction. Even today we feel the effects of the monumental changes these writers brought about in the ways that Americans view themselves, their society, and the world of nature.

As you read about this time period, think about these questions:

- What were the values of the Romantics, and how did these values affect the American imagination?

- Who were the Transcendentalists, and how do their beliefs still influence American life?

- What darker side of human life was recognized by some major American Romantics?

**SKILLS FOCUS**

Collection introduction (pages 162–173) covers **Literary Skills** Evaluate the philosophical, political, religious, ethical, and social influences of a historical period.

The journey—there is probably no pattern so common in all of narrative literature, from the Bible to Homer's *Odyssey* to films like *The Wizard of Oz* and *Star Wars*. Very early in *The Autobiography* (page 69), Benjamin Franklin describes an important American journey: a personal quest in which the young Ben leaves his home in Boston and travels to Philadelphia. The significance of Franklin's journey is clear: It is a declaration of independence, a move away from his family, toward a new city where he might prosper. It is, in other words, a quest for opportunity. Without stretching the metaphor greatly, we can see in Franklin's journey an expression of both his personal goals and the goals of eighteenth-century America: a reaching out for independence, prosperity, and commerce.

Franklin wrote about his journey to Philadelphia in 1771. In 1799, the American writer Charles Brockden Brown described a very different journey to Philadelphia in his Romantic novel *Arthur Mervyn*. In this tale the hero, a young farm boy, leaves his home in the country for Philadelphia. Instead of finding a place of promise where he can make his dreams come true, the boy is plunged into a

*Emigrants Crossing the Plains* (detail) (1867) by Albert Bierstadt. Oil on canvas (67″ × 102″).

National Cowboy Hall of Fame and Western Heritage Center, Oklahoma City, Oklahoma.

plague-ridden urban world of decay, corruption, and evil. The Philadelphia of this novel is no city of promise; it is an industrial hell.

The journeys described in Franklin's autobiography and Brown's *Arthur Mervyn* make clear the differences between the views of the rationalists and those of the Romantics. To Franklin and other rationalists the city was a place to find success and self-realization. To the Romantic writers who came after Franklin, the city was far from the seat of civilization; it was often a place of shifting morals and, worse, corruption and death.

The characteristic Romantic journey is to the countryside, which Romantics associated with independence, moral clarity, and healthful living. Sometimes, as shown in the works of writers like Edgar Allan Poe (page 277), the Romantic journey is a psychological voyage to the country of the imagination. Whatever the destination of the Romantic journey, it is a flight both *from* something and *to* something.

## The Romantic Sensibility: Celebrating Imagination

In general, **Romanticism** is the name given to those schools of thought that value feeling and intuition over reason. The first rumblings of Romanticism were felt in Germany in the second half of the eighteenth century. Romanticism had a strong influence on

A tenement-house alley gang.

## A CLOSER LOOK: SOCIAL INFLUENCES

### The City, Grim and Gray

INFORMATIONAL TEXT

In the first half of the nineteenth century, the largest American cities were Boston, Philadelphia, Baltimore, Charleston, and, largest of all, New York. Between 1820 and 1840, the population of New York more than doubled, from 124,000 to 312,000 people. In the 1830s, the first tenements were built—buildings where a bathtub might be shared by four hundred people and eight or more people might live in a single room without furniture. The soundtrack to this scene might be provided by the bloodcurdling screeches of chickens being slaughtered indoors for the night's meal.

The city streets were fouled with droppings from the main source of transportation: horses. When a horse collapsed or was injured, it was left to die on the curbside. Its body might remain on the street for days or weeks at a time. Given such conditions, it's no surprise that disease was rampant. In Manhattan during the summer of 1832, one third of the city's population—those who could afford to leave—left the city to escape a cholera epidemic that killed an average of one hundred people a day.

There were twenty thousand homeless children on the streets of New York. Some worked in sweatshops, some sold toothpicks or newspapers, and others turned to petty crime. If the children lived to be twenty, they were

literature, music, and painting in Europe and England well into the nineteenth century. But Romanticism came relatively late to America, and as you will see in this chapter, it took different forms.

Romanticism, especially in Europe, developed in part as a reaction against **rationalism.** In the sooty wake of the Industrial Revolution, with its squalid cities and wretched working conditions, people had come to realize the limits of reason. The Romantics believed that the imagination was able to discover truths that the rational mind could not reach. These truths were usually accompanied by powerful emotion and associated with natural, unspoiled beauty. To the Romantics, imagination, individual feelings, and wild nature were of greater value than reason, logic, and cultivation. The Romantics did not flatly reject logical thought as invalid for all purposes; but for the purpose of art, they placed a new premium on intuitive, "felt" experience.

To the Romantic mind, poetry was the highest embodiment of the imagination. Romantic artists often contrasted poetry with science, which they saw as destroying the very truth it claimed to seek. Edgar Allan Poe, for example, called science a "vulture" with wings of "dull realities," preying on the hearts of poets.

*Street Scene in New York, Winter* (1855) by Hippolyte Victor Valentin Sebron (1801–1879). Oil on canvas (29¼″ × 42½″).

Chateau Blerancourt, Picardy, France.
© Giraudon/Bridgeman Art Library.

lucky; disease, accidents, exposure, violence, and starvation took most of them long before that time.

Crime and violence were no strangers to the city. Waterfront gangs often included "pirates" who would kill for next to nothing. On the infamous Cherry Street, fifteen thousand sailors were robbed in a single year. There were even riots on the streets: In 1834, men opposed to the abolition of slavery burned down homes, churches, and a school, trying to destroy free African Americans and their supporters.

There was one bright spot in this picture of squalor and degradation, though: talk in the 1840s of constructing a huge city park for "health and recreation." It was the poet William Cullen Bryant's idea—a dream of bringing the countryside to a city wracked with poverty, illness, and crime. New Yorkers would have to wait until after the Civil War for their oasis: Central Park would not become a completed reality until 1876.

Illustration by Wilfred Satty for Edgar Allan Poe's short story "The Fall of the House of Usher."

> *They who dream by day are cognizant of many things which escape those who dream only by night.*
>
> —Edgar Allan Poe

## Romantic Escapism: From Dull Realities to Higher Truths

The Romantics wanted to rise above "dull realities" to a realm of higher truth. They did this in two principal ways. First, the Romantics searched for exotic settings in the more "natural" past or in a world far removed from the grimy and noisy industrial age. Sometimes they discovered this world in the supernatural realm or in old legends and folklore. For example, you'll find a story by Washington Irving on page 177 that is based on the old European legend of a man who sells his soul to the devil for worldly riches.

Second, the Romantics tried to reflect on the natural world until dull reality fell away to reveal underlying beauty and truth. This second Romantic approach is evident in many lyric poems. In a typical Romantic poem the speaker sees an ordinary object or scene. A flower found by a stream or a bird flying overhead brings the speaker to some important, deeply felt insight, which is then recorded in the poem. This process is similar to the way the Puritans drew moral lessons from nature. The difference is one of emphasis and goal. The Puritans' lessons were defined by their religion. In nature the Puritans found the God they knew from the Bible. The Romantics, on the other hand, found a less clearly defined divinity in nature. Their contemplation of the natural world led to a more generalized emotional and intellectual awakening.

## The American Novel and the Wilderness Experience

During the Romantic period, the big question about American literature was: Would American writers continue to imitate the English and European models, or would they finally develop a distinctive literature of their own? While the Romantic poets of the period were still staying close to traditional forms, American novelists were discovering that the subject matter available to them was very different from the subjects available to European writers. America provided a sense of limitless frontiers that Europe, so long settled, simply did not possess. Thus, the development of the American novel coincided with westward expansion, with the growth of a nationalist spirit, and with the rapid spread of cities. All these factors tended to reinforce the idealization of frontier life. A geography of

> ### Characteristics of American Romanticism
>
> - Values feeling and intuition over reason
> - Places faith in inner experience and the power of the imagination
> - Shuns the artificiality of civilization and seeks unspoiled nature
> - Prefers youthful innocence to educated sophistication
> - Champions individual freedom and the worth of the individual
> - Reflects on nature's beauty as a path to spiritual and moral development
> - Looks backward to the wisdom of the past and distrusts progress
> - Finds beauty and truth in exotic locales, the supernatural realm, and the inner world of the imagination
> - Sees poetry as the highest expression of the imagination
> - Finds inspiration in myth, legend, and folklore

the imagination developed, in which town, country, and frontier would play a powerful role in American life and literature—as they continue to do today.

We can see how the novel developed in America by looking at the career of James Fenimore Cooper (1789–1851). Cooper explored uniquely American settings and characters: frontier communities, American Indians, backwoodsmen, and the wilderness of western New York and Pennsylvania. Most of all he created the first American heroic figure: Natty Bumppo (also known as Hawkeye, Deerslayer, and Leatherstocking). Natty was a heroic, virtuous, skillful frontiersman whose simple morality, love of

Title page of *The Deerslayer,* illustrated by N. C. Wyeth (1925).

nature, distrust of town life, and almost superhuman resourcefulness mark him as a true Romantic hero.

### ■ A New Kind of Hero

Most Europeans had an image of the American as unsophisticated and uncivilized. This was a stereotype that Ben Franklin, when he lived in France, took great pains to demonstrate was unfair and untrue. Cooper and other Romantic novelists who followed him, though, took no such pains. Instead, by creating such heroes as Natty Bumppo they turned the insult on its head. Virtue, the Romantics implied, was in American innocence, not in European sophistication. Eternal truths were waiting to be discovered not in dusty libraries, crowded cities, or glittering court life, but in the American wilderness that was unknown and unavailable to Europeans.

Cooper's Natty Bumppo is a triumph of American innocence and an example of one of the most important outgrowths of the early American novel: the American Romantic hero. Here was a new kind of heroic figure, one quite different from the hero of the Age of Reason. The rationalist hero—exemplified by a real-life figure such as Ben Franklin—was worldly, educated, sophisticated, and bent on making a place for himself in civilization. The typical hero

---

## Characteristics of the American Romantic Hero

- Is young or possesses youthful qualities
- Is innocent and pure of purpose
- Has a sense of honor based not on society's rules but on some higher principle
- Has a knowledge of people and life based on deep, intuitive understanding, not on formal learning
- Loves nature and avoids town life
- Quests for some higher truth in the natural world

of American Romantic fiction, on the other hand, was youthful, innocent, intuitive, and close to nature. By today's standards the hero was also hopelessly uneasy with women, who were usually seen (by male writers, at least) to represent civilization and the impulse to "domesticate."

Today Americans still create Romantic heroes; the twentieth-and twenty-first-century descendants of Natty Bumppo are all around us. They can be found in dozens of pop-culture heroes—the Lone Ranger, Superman, Luke Skywalker, Indiana Jones—and any number of other western, detective, and fantasy heroes.

Harrison Ford in the movie
*Raiders of the Lost Ark* (1981).

*It has been a matter of marvel to my European readers, that a man from the wilds of America should express himself in tolerable English. I was looked upon as something new and strange in American literature. . . .*

—Washington Irving

Daniel Day-Lewis as Natty Bumppo in the movie
*The Last of the Mohicans* (1992).

# American Romantic Poetry: Read at Every Fireside

The American Romantic novelists looked for new subject matter and new themes, but the opposite tendency appears in the works of the Romantic poets. Like Franklin, these Romantic poets wanted to prove that Americans were not unsophisticated hicks. They attempted to prove this by working solidly within European literary traditions rather than by crafting a unique American voice. Even when they constructed poems with American settings and subject matter, the American Romantic poets used typically English themes, meter, and imagery. In a sense they wrote in a style that a cultivated person from England who had recently immigrated to America might be expected to use.

In fact, the Fireside Poets—as the Boston group of Henry Wadsworth Longfellow (page 194), John Greenleaf Whittier, Oliver Wendell Holmes, and James Russell Lowell was called—were, in their own time and for many decades afterward, the most popular poets America had ever produced. They were called Fireside Poets because their poems were read aloud at the fireside as family entertainment. They were also sometimes called Schoolroom Poets, because their poems were for many years memorized in every American classroom.

Limited by their literary conservatism, the Fireside Poets were unable to recognize the poetry of the future, which was being written right under their noses. Whittier's response in 1855 to the first volume of a certain poet's work was to throw the book into the fire. Ralph Waldo Emerson's response was much more farsighted. "I greet you," Emerson wrote to this maverick new poet Walt Whitman, "at the beginning of a great career."

## The Transcendentalists: True Reality Is Spiritual

At the heart of America's coming-of-age were the Transcendentalists, who were led by Ralph Waldo Emerson (page 203). **Transcendental** refers to the idea that in determining the ultimate reality of God, the universe, the self, and other important matters, one must transcend, or go beyond, everyday human experience in the physical world.

For Emerson, Transcendentalism was not a new philosophy but "the very oldest of thoughts cast into the mold of these new times." That "oldest of thoughts" was idealism, which had already been explained by the Greek philosopher Plato in the fourth century B.C. Idealists said that true reality was found in ideas rather than in the world as perceived by senses. Idealists sought the permanent reality that underlies physical appearances. The Americans who called themselves Transcendentalists were idealists but in a broader, more

*I was simmering, simmering, simmering; Emerson brought me to a boil.*

—Walt Whitman

*Ralph Waldo Emerson. Drawing by David Levine.*

Reprinted with permission from *The New York Review of Books.* Copyright ©1968 NYREV, Inc.

practical sense. Like many Americans today, they also believed in human perfectibility, and they worked to achieve this goal.

### ■ Emerson and Transcendentalism: The American Roots

Though Emerson was skeptical of many of the Transcendentalists' ideas and projects, he was the most influential and best-known member of the group, largely because of his lectures and books. As developed by Emerson, Transcendentalism grafted ideas from Europe and Asia onto a homegrown American philosophical stem. Its American roots included Puritan thought, the beliefs of the eighteenth-century religious revivalist Jonathan Edwards (page 44), and the Romantic tradition exemplified by William Cullen Bryant (page 189).

The Puritans believed that God revealed himself to people through the Bible and through all aspects of the physical world. Jonathan Edwards, for example, described a moving mystical experience in his "Personal Narrative": "Once as I rode out into the woods for my health . . . I had a view that for me was extraordinary, of the glory of the Son of God. . . . I felt an ardency of soul to be, what I know not otherwise how to express, emptied and annihilated; to lie in the dust, and to be full of Christ alone." This native mysticism—also typical of Romanticism—reappears in Emerson's thought. "Every natural fact," Emerson wrote, "is a symbol of some spiritual fact."

### ■ Emerson's Optimistic Outlook

Emerson's mystical view of the world sprang not from logic but from intuition. Intuition is our capacity to know things spontaneously and immediately through our emotions rather than through our reasoning abilities. Intuitive thought—the kind Emerson believed in—contrasts with the rational thinking of someone like Benjamin Franklin. Franklin did not gaze on nature and feel the presence of a Divine Soul; Franklin looked at nature and saw something to be examined scientifically and used to help humanity.

An intense feeling of optimism was one product of Emerson's belief that we can find God directly in nature. God is good, and God works through nature, Emerson believed. Therefore, even the natural events that seem most tragic—disease, death, disaster—can be explained on a spiritual level. Death is simply a part of the cycle of life. According to Emerson, we are capable of evil because we are separated from a direct, intuitive knowledge of God. But if we simply trust ourselves—that is, trust in the power each of us has to know God directly—then we will realize that each of us is also part of the Divine Soul, the source of all good.

Emerson's sense of optimism and hope appealed to audiences who lived in a period of economic downturns, regional strife, and

---

### A Transcendental View of the World

- Everything in the world, including human beings, is a reflection of the Divine Soul.

- The physical facts of the natural world are a doorway to the spiritual or ideal world.

- People can use their intuition to behold God's spirit revealed in nature or in their own souls.

- Self-reliance and individualism must outweigh external authority and blind conformity to custom and tradition.

- Spontaneous feelings and intuition are superior to deliberate intellectualism and rationality.

---

*I unsettle all things. No facts are to me sacred; none are profane; I simply experiment, an endless seeker, with no Past at my back.*

—Ralph Waldo Emerson

## FAST FACTS

### Philosophical Views

- A movement called Romanticism cele-brates feeling over reason, imagination over science, and nature over civilization. The Romantics also champion freedom and the development of the individual spirit.

- A group of Romantics called the Transcenden-talists believes that everything in the physi-cal world is a reflection of the Divine Soul.

- Another group of Romantic writers explores the conflict between good and evil, the effects of guilt and sin, and the destructive underside of appearances.

### Social Influences

- The lyceum move-ment furthers American education, self-improvement, and cultural development.

- Reform movements begin for women's rights, child labor, temperance, and the abolition of slavery involving many Americans in social activism.

- Utopian planners attempt to turn idealized visions of human potential into practical realities.

conflict over slavery. Your condition today, Emerson seemed to tell his readers and listeners, may seem dull and hopeless, but it need not be. If you discover the God within you, he suggested, your lives will partake of the grandeur of the universe.

## The Dark Romantics

Emerson's idealism was exciting for his audiences, but not all the writers and thinkers of the time agreed with Transcendentalist thought. "To one who has weathered Cape Horn as a common sailor," Herman Melville wrote scornfully of Emerson's ideas, "what stuff all this is."

Some people think of Nathaniel Hawthorne, Herman Melville, and Edgar Allan Poe as anti-Transcendentalists, because their views of the world seem so profoundly opposed to the optimistic views of Emerson and his followers. But these Dark Romantics, as they are known, had much in common with the Transcendentalists. Both

*Edgar Allan Poe* by Tony Bailey.

groups valued intuition over logic and reason. Both groups, like the Puritans before them, saw signs and symbols in all events—as Anne Bradstreet found spiritual significance in the fire that destroyed her house (page 29).

The Dark Romantics didn't disagree with Emerson's belief that spiritual facts lie behind the appearances of nature; they just did not think that those facts are necessarily good or harmless. Emerson, they felt, had taken the ecstatic, mystical elements of Puritan thought and ignored its dark side—its emphasis on Original Sin, its sense of the innate wickedness of human beings, and its notions of predestination. The Dark Romantics came along to correct the balance. Their view of existence developed from both the mystical and the melancholy aspects of Puritan thought. In their works they explored the conflict between good and evil, the psychological effects of guilt and sin, and even madness in the human psyche. Behind the pasteboard masks of social respectability, the Dark Romantics saw the blankness and the horror of evil. From this imaginative, unflinching vision they shaped a uniquely American literature.

> *That blue-eyed darling Nathaniel knew disagreeable things in his inner soul. He was careful to send them out in disguise.*
>
> —D. H. Lawrence on Hawthorne

# REVIEW

## Talk About . . .

Turn back to the Think About section found at the start of this introduction to American Romanticism (page 162). Discuss your responses to the questions posed there.

## Write About . . .

### Contrasting Literary Periods

**Romantic heroes today.** Review the characteristics of the Romantic hero on page 168. How does this type of hero compare with the characters who play major roles in literature and movies today? Do you find evidence of the Romantic hero in the ways that today's prominent public figures (for example, politicians) are packaged for popular culture? Write a paragraph or two in response to these questions.

# Washington Irving
## (1783–1859)

Many people in Europe and England felt that America would never develop a literary voice of its own. But then came Washington Irving, the youngest and not too well educated son of a pious hardware importer and his amiable wife. Irving, who was from New York City, had a genius for inventing comic fictional narrators. (In fact, he did not sign his real name to his work until he was over fifty.) The first of these narrators Irving called Jonathan Oldstyle, Gent.—a caricature of those British writers who could not accept the simple values of the new nation.

Irving's second invented narrator was called Diedrich Knickerbocker. Irving pretended that Knickerbocker was the author of a book called *A History of New York, from the Beginning of the World to the End of the Dutch Dynasty*. The mysterious Knickerbocker is supposed to have left the manuscript to his landlord in payment of back rent. This fake and comical history, in which the entire American past is ridiculed, established Washington Irving as the foremost New York satirist.

All this time Irving was enjoying the literary societies that were popular then in New York. His interest in law, which he practiced half-heartedly, was lukewarm. In 1815, he was sent off by his father to Liverpool, England, to look after the failing overseas branch of the family business. Irving found the business beyond repair, but he loved the British literary scene and stayed abroad for seventeen years. He was particularly attracted to the works of the Romantic novelist Sir Walter Scott (1771–1832), who gave Irving advice that was to make his reputation. Scott told the younger writer to read the German Romantics and find inspiration in folklore and legends.

Now Irving decided against putting further energy into business and its "sordid, dusty, soul-killing way of life." He would give himself entirely to writing. In 1817, Irving began to write the first drafts of stories based on German folk tales. These were narrated by yet another of Irving's comic voices, Geoffrey Crayon, and the stories were collected under the title *The Sketch Book* (1819–1820). This book carried Irving to the summit of international success.

Even though Irving borrowed openly from a European past, he brought to his material a droll new voice, as inflated as a preacher's or a politician's at one moment and self-mocking the next. It was a voice the new nation recognized as its own.

Irving gave his country its first international literary celebrity. This was a role Irving enjoyed exploiting to the fullest. He had always loved parties and people and praise. Now he had access to the literary circles of the world. It was a remarkable achievement for the unpromising child of a middle-class American family.

His next book, *Tales of a Traveller* (1824), which included "The Devil and Tom Walker," met with such unfavorable reviews that Irving stopped writing fiction altogether. He never again wrote anything that matched the success of the two great comic tales in *The Sketch Book*. Today we remember Irving for Rip Van Winkle, who slept through the American Revolution, and the Headless Horseman, who plagued the lovelorn Yankee schoolteacher Ichabod Crane in the dreamy glen of Sleepy Hollow, in New York's lush Hudson Valley.

*Washington Irving* (1809) by John Wesley Jarvis. Oil on wood panel (33″ × 26″).

Historic Hudson Valley, Tarrytown, New York.

# Before You Read

## The Devil and Tom Walker

### Make the Connection

Many cultures tell tales of characters bargaining with the devil in order to get what they think they want. You might know some of these stories, most of which offer a moral lesson about pride, greed, or just plain stupidity. Washington Irving's Tom Walker demonstrates all three of these characteristics in his dealings with the devil, or Old Scratch. The devil's unusual name comes from the Old German word *scraz*, which means "goblin."

### Literary Focus
#### Mood

Mood—the overall feeling or atmosphere of a story, play, or poem—may be the most difficult literary element to define. After all, mood is intangible; you can't point to mood in a text.

In order to identify a story's mood, start with the **setting.** Pay close attention to the details of time and place, and ask yourself how the setting makes you feel. Look carefully at the writer's **word choice.** For example, is a tree *budding* or *rotting*? Then, consider the **plot.** Does it end happily, or does it present a bitter or tragic outlook on life?

The mood of most stories can be identified with one or two adjectives: *gloomy, romantic, threatening,* and so on. Remember that even though you may sense several moods in some stories one dominant feeling (humor in the midst of horror, for example) will usually prevail.

> The **mood** of a story, play, or poem is its overall feeling or atmosphere.
>
> *For more on Mood, see the Handbook of Literary and Historical Terms.*

### Reading Skills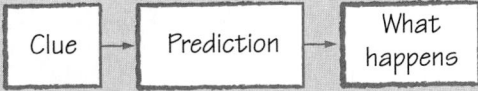
#### Making Predictions

When you make an inference about a text, you make an educated guess based on clues in the text and on your own knowledge and experience. A **prediction** is a special type of inference—an educated guess about what will happen later. Not all predictions turn out to be accurate, and adjusting them is an essential part of active reading. As you read "The Devil and Tom Walker," take notes in chart form. Identify a clue that suggests or foreshadows what may happen further along in the story. Then, make a prediction based on the clue. Later, note what actually happens. How often did the writer surprise you?

```
┌───────┐     ┌────────────┐     ┌──────────┐
│ Clue  │ ──▶ │ Prediction │ ──▶ │  What    │
│       │     │            │     │ happens  │
└───────┘     └────────────┘     └──────────┘
```

### Background

"The Devil and Tom Walker" is an American version of the archetypal story of Faust, the sixteenth-century German philosopher who sells his soul to the devil for knowledge and power. An **archetype** (är′kə·tīp′) is an original or fundamental imaginative pattern that is repeated through the ages. An archetype can be a plot, an event, a character, a setting, or an object. The story of a person who sells his or her soul to the devil for worldly gain is an archetypal plot. The most famous and influential version of the tale is *Faust,* a play by Johann Wolfgang von Goethe (1749–1832). Each retelling of the Faustian legend puts a different spin on the story, and the ending may change: The Faust character, for example, may face eternal flames, find forgiveness and love, or somehow cleverly beat the devil.

**SKILLS FOCUS**

**Literary Skills**
Understand mood.

**Reading Skills**
Make predictions.

**INTERNET**

Vocabulary Practice

Keyword: LE7 11-2

## Vocabulary Development

**prevalent** (prev′ə·lənt) *adj.*: widely existing; frequent.

**stagnant** (stag′nənt) *adj.*: not flowing or moving.

**precarious** (pri·ker′ē·əs) *adj.*: uncertain; insecure; risky.

**impregnable** (im·preg′nə·bəl) *adj.*: impossible to capture or enter by force.

**melancholy** (mel′ən·käl′ē) *adj.*: sad; gloomy.

**obliterate** (ə·blit′ər·āt′) *v.*: erase or destroy.

**avarice** (av′ə·ris) *n.*: greed.

**resolute** (rez′ə·lo͞ot′) *adj.*: determined; resolved; unwavering.

**parsimony** (pär′sə·mō′nē) *n.*: stinginess.

**superfluous** (sə·pʉr′flo͞o·əs) *adj.*: more than is needed or wanted; useless.

# The DEVIL and TOM WALKER

## Washington Irving

A few miles from Boston in Massachusetts, there is a deep inlet, winding several miles into the interior of the country from Charles Bay, and terminating in a thickly wooded swamp or morass. On one side of this inlet is a beautiful dark grove; on the opposite side the land rises abruptly from the water's edge into a high ridge, on which grow a few scattered oaks of great age and immense size. Under one of these gigantic trees, according to old stories, there was a great amount of treasure buried by Kidd the pirate.[1] The inlet allowed a facility to bring the money in a boat secretly and at night to the very foot of the hill; the elevation of the place permitted a good lookout to be kept that no one was at hand; while the remarkable trees formed good landmarks by which the place might easily be found again. The old stories add, moreover, that the devil presided at the hiding of the money, and took it under his guardianship; but this, it is well known, he always does with buried treasure, particularly when it has been ill-gotten. Be that as it may, Kidd never returned to recover his wealth; being shortly after seized at Boston, sent out to England, and there hanged for a pirate.

---

1. **Kidd the pirate:** William Kidd (1645?–1701), known as Captain Kidd, a famous pirate in the late 1690s.

About the year 1727, just at the time that earthquakes were <u>prevalent</u> in New England, and shook many tall sinners down upon their knees, there lived near this place a meager,[2] miserly fellow, of the name of Tom Walker. He had a wife as miserly as himself: They were so miserly that they even conspired to cheat each other. Whatever the woman could lay hands on, she hid away; a hen could not cackle but she was on the alert to secure the new-laid egg. Her husband was continually prying about to detect her secret hoards, and many and fierce were the conflicts that took place about what ought to have been common property. They lived in a forlorn-looking house that stood alone, and had an air of starvation. A few straggling savin trees,[3] emblems of sterility, grew near it; no smoke ever curled from its chimney; no traveler stopped at its door. A miserable horse, whose ribs were as articulate as the bars of a gridiron, stalked about a field, where a thin carpet of moss, scarcely covering the ragged beds of puddingstone,[4] tantalized and balked his hunger; and sometimes he would lean his head over the fence, look piteously at the passerby, and seem to petition deliverance from this land of famine.

The house and its inmates had altogether a bad name. Tom's wife was a tall termagant,[5] fierce of temper, loud of tongue, and strong of arm. Her voice was often heard in wordy warfare with her husband; and his face sometimes showed signs that their conflicts were not confined to words. No one ventured, however, to interfere between them. The lonely wayfarer shrunk within himself at the horrid clamor and clapperclawing;[6] eyed the den of discord askance;[7] and hurried on his way, rejoicing, if a bachelor, in his celibacy.

One day that Tom Walker had been to a distant part of the neighborhood, he took what he considered a shortcut homeward, through the swamp. Like most shortcuts, it was an ill-chosen route. The swamp was thickly grown with great gloomy pines and hemlocks, some of them ninety feet high, which made it dark at noonday, and a retreat for all the owls of the neighborhood. It was full of pits and quagmires,[8] partly covered with weeds and mosses, where the green surface often betrayed the traveler into a gulf of black, smothering mud: There were also dark and <u>stagnant</u> pools, the abodes of the tadpole, the bullfrog, and the watersnake, where the trunks of pines and hemlocks lay half drowned, half rotting, looking like alligators sleeping in the mire.

Tom had long been picking his way cautiously through this treacherous forest; stepping from tuft to tuft of rushes and roots, which afforded <u>precarious</u> footholds among deep sloughs;[9] or pacing carefully, like a cat, along the prostrate trunks of trees; startled now and then by the sudden screaming of the bittern, or the quacking of wild duck rising on the wing from some solitary pool. At length he arrived at a firm piece of ground, which ran out like a peninsula into the deep bosom of the swamp. It had been one of the strongholds of the Indians during their wars with the first colonists. Here they had thrown up a kind of fort, which they had looked upon as almost <u>impregnable</u> and had used as a place of refuge for their squaws and children. Nothing remained of the old Indian fort but a few embankments, gradually sinking to the level of the surrounding earth, and already

---

2. **meager** *adj.:* thin.
3. **savin trees:** juniper trees.
4. **puddingstone** *n.:* rock consisting of pebbles embedded in cement.
5. **termagant** (tur'mə·gənt) *n.:* quarrelsome, scolding woman.
6. **clapperclawing** *v.* used as *n.:* scratching or clawing with the fingernails.
7. **askance** *adv.:* with a sideways glance.

---

8. **quagmires** *n. pl.:* areas of land with soft, muddy surfaces; bogs.
9. **sloughs** (slo͞oz) *n. pl.:* swamps or marshes, usually parts of inlets.

---

**Vocabulary**

**prevalent** (prev'ə·lənt) *adj.:* widely existing; frequent.
**stagnant** (stag'nənt) *adj.:* not flowing or moving.
**precarious** (pri·ker'ē·əs) *adj.:* uncertain; insecure; risky.
**impregnable** (im·preg'nə·bəl) *adj.:* impossible to capture or enter by force.

overgrown in part by oaks and other forest trees, the foliage of which formed a contrast to the dark pines and hemlocks of the swamp.

It was late in the dusk of evening when Tom Walker reached the old fort, and he paused there awhile to rest himself. Anyone but he would have felt unwilling to linger in this lonely, melancholy place, for the common people had a bad opinion of it, from the stories handed down from the time of the Indian wars, when it was asserted that the savages held incantations here, and made sacrifices to the evil spirit.

Tom Walker, however, was not a man to be troubled with any fears of the kind. He reposed himself for some time on the trunk of a fallen hemlock, listening to the boding cry of the tree-toad, and delving with his walking staff into a mound of black mold at his feet. As he turned up the soil unconsciously, his staff struck against something hard. He raked it out of the vegetable mold, and lo! a cloven[10] skull, with an Indian tomahawk buried deep in it, lay before him. The rust on the weapon showed the time that had elapsed since this deathblow had been given. It was a dreary memento of the fierce struggle that had taken place in this last foothold of the Indian warriors.

"Humph!" said Tom Walker, as he gave it a kick to shake the dirt from it.

"Let that skull alone!" said a gruff voice. Tom lifted up his eyes, and beheld a great black man seated directly opposite him, on the stump of a tree. He was exceedingly surprised, having neither heard nor seen anyone approach; and he was still more perplexed on observing, as well as the gathering gloom would permit, that the stranger was neither Negro nor Indian. It is true he was dressed in a rude half-Indian garb, and had a red belt or sash swathed round his body; but his face was neither black nor copper color, but swarthy and dingy, and begrimed with soot, as if he had been accustomed to toil among fires and forges. He had a shock of coarse black hair, that stood out from his head in all directions, and bore an ax on his shoulder.

He scowled for a moment at Tom with a pair of great red eyes.

"What are you doing on my grounds?" said the black man, with a hoarse, growling voice.

"Your grounds!" said Tom, with a sneer, "no more your grounds than mine; they belong to Deacon Peabody."

"Deacon Peabody be d—d," said the stranger, "as I flatter myself he will be, if he does not look more to his own sins and less to those of his neighbors. Look yonder, and see how Deacon Peabody is faring."

Tom looked in the direction that the stranger pointed, and beheld one of the great trees, fair and flourishing without, but rotten at the core, and saw that it had been nearly hewn through, so that the first high wind was likely to blow it down. On the bark of the tree was scored the name of Deacon Peabody, an eminent man, who had waxed[11] wealthy by driving shrewd bargains with the Indians. He now looked around, and found most of the tall trees marked with the name of some great man of the colony, and all more or less scored by the ax. The one on which he had been seated, and which had evidently just been hewn down, bore the name of Crowninshield; and he recollected a mighty rich man of that name, who made a vulgar display of wealth, which it was whispered he had acquired by buccaneering.[12]

"He's just ready for burning!" said the black man, with a growl of triumph. "You see I am likely to have a good stock of firewood for winter."

"But what right have you," said Tom, "to cut down Deacon Peabody's timber?"

"The right of a prior claim," said the other. "This woodland belonged to me long before one of your white-faced race put foot upon the soil."

"And pray, who are you, if I may be so bold?" said Tom.

---

10. **cloven** *adj.:* split.

11. **waxed** *v.:* become or grown.
12. **buccaneering** *v.* used as *n.:* robbery at sea; piracy.

**Vocabulary**

**melancholy** (mel′ən·kal′ē) *adj.:* sad; gloomy.

"Oh, I go by various names. I am the wild huntsman in some countries; the black miner in others. In this neighborhood I am known by the name of the black woodsman. I am he to whom the red men consecrated this spot, and in honor of whom they now and then roasted a white man, by way of sweet-smelling sacrifice. Since the red men have been exterminated by you white savages, I amuse myself by presiding at the persecutions of Quakers and Anabaptists;[13] I am the great patron and prompter of slave dealers, and the grand master of the Salem witches."

---

13. **Quakers and Anabaptists:** In Puritan New England, where this story is set, Quakers were known primarily for their pacifism and refusal to take oaths, and Anabaptists were known for their opposition to infant baptism.

"The upshot of all which is, that, if I mistake not," said Tom, sturdily, "you are he commonly called Old Scratch."

"The same, at your service!" replied the black man, with a half-civil nod.

Such was the opening of this interview, according to the old story; though it has almost too familiar an air to be credited. One would think that to meet with such a singular personage, in this wild, lonely place, would have shaken any man's nerves; but Tom was a hard-minded fellow, not easily daunted, and he had lived so long with a termagant wife, that he did not even fear the devil.

It is said that after this commencement they had a long and earnest conversation together, as Tom returned homeward. The black man told him of great sums of money buried by Kidd the

pirate, under the oak trees on the high ridge, not far from the morass. All these were under his command, and protected by his power, so that none could find them but such as propitiated[14] his favor. These he offered to place within Tom Walker's reach, having conceived an especial kindness for him; but they were to be had only on certain conditions. What these conditions were may be easily surmised, though Tom never disclosed them publicly. They must have been very hard, for he required time to think of them, and he was not a man to stick at trifles when money was in view. When they had reached the edge of the swamp, the stranger paused. "What proof have I that all you have been telling me is true?" said Tom. "There's my signature," said the black man, pressing his finger on Tom's forehead. So saying, he turned off among the thickest of the swamp, and seemed, as Tom said, to go down, down, down, into the earth, until nothing but his head and shoulders could be seen, and so on, until he totally disappeared.

When Tom reached home, he found the black print of a finger burnt, as it were, into his forehead, which nothing could obliterate.

The first news his wife had to tell him was the sudden death of Absalom Crowninshield, the rich buccaneer. It was announced in the papers with the usual flourish, that "A great man had fallen in Israel."[15]

Tom recollected the tree which his black friend had just hewn down, and which was ready for burning. "Let the freebooter[16] roast," said Tom. "Who cares!" He now felt convinced that all he had heard and seen was no illusion.

He was not prone to let his wife into his confidence; but as this was an uneasy secret, he willingly shared it with her. All her avarice was awakened at the mention of hidden gold, and she urged her husband to comply with the black man's terms, and secure what would make them wealthy for life. However Tom might have felt disposed to sell himself to the devil, he was determined not to do so to oblige his wife; so he flatly refused, out of the mere spirit of contradiction. Many and bitter were the quarrels they had on the subject; but the more she talked, the more resolute was Tom not to be damned to please her.

At length she determined to drive the bargain on her own account, and if she succeeded, to keep all the gain to herself. Being of the same fearless temper as her husband, she set off for the old Indian fort toward the close of a summer's day. She was many hours absent. When she came back, she was reserved and sullen in her replies. She spoke something of a black man, whom she met about twilight hewing at the root of a tall tree. He was sulky, however, and would not come to terms: She was to go again with a propitiatory offering, but what it was she forbore to say.

The next evening she set off again for the swamp, with her apron heavily laden. Tom waited and waited for her, but in vain; midnight came, but she did not make her appearance: Morning, noon, night returned, but still she did not come. Tom now grew uneasy for her safety, especially as he found she had carried off in her apron the silver teapot and spoons, and every portable article of value. Another night elapsed, another morning came; but no wife. In a word, she was never heard of more.

What was her real fate nobody knows, in consequence of so many pretending to know. It is one of those facts which have become confounded by a variety of historians. Some asserted that she lost her way among the tangled mazes of the swamp, and sank into some pit or slough; others, more uncharitable, hinted that she had eloped with the household booty, and

---

14. **propitiated** (prō·pish′ē·āt′id) *v.*: gained the goodwill of.

15. **A great man had fallen in Israel:** popular expression, drawn from the Bible (2 Samuel 3:38), to refer to the death of a prominent member of the community.

16. **freebooter** *n.*: pirate.

---

**Vocabulary**

**obliterate** (ə·blit′ər·āt′) *v.*: erase or destroy.
**avarice** (av′ə·ris) *n.*: greed.
**resolute** (rez′ə·lōōt′) *adj.*: determined; resolved; unwavering.

made off to some other province; while others surmised that the tempter had decoyed her into a dismal quagmire, on the top of which her hat was found lying. In confirmation of this, it was said a great black man, with an ax on his shoulder, was seen late that very evening coming out of the swamp, carrying a bundle tied in a check apron, with an air of surly triumph.

The most current and probable story, however, observes, that Tom Walker grew so anxious about the fate of his wife and his property, that he set out at length to seek them both at the Indian fort. During a long summer's afternoon he searched about the gloomy place, but no wife was to be seen. He called her name repeatedly, but she was nowhere to be heard. The bittern alone responded to his voice, as he flew screaming by; or the bullfrog croaked dolefully from a neighboring pool. At length, it is said, just in the brown hour of twilight, when the owls began to hoot, and the bats to flit about, his attention was attracted by the clamor of carrion crows[17] hovering about a cypress tree. He looked up, and beheld a bundle tied in a check apron, and hanging in the branches of the tree, with a great vulture perched hard by, as if keeping watch upon it. He leaped with joy; for he recognized his wife's apron, and supposed it to contain the household valuables.

"Let us get hold of the property," said he, consolingly to himself, "and we will endeavor to do without the woman."

As he scrambled up the tree, the vulture spread its wide wings, and sailed off, screaming, into the deep shadows of the forest. Tom seized the checked apron, but, woeful sight! found nothing but a heart and liver tied up in it!

Such, according to this most authentic old story, was all that was to be found of Tom's wife. She had probably attempted to deal with the black man as she had been accustomed to deal with her husband; but though a female scold is generally considered a match for the devil, yet in this instance she appears to have had the worst

of it. She must have died game, however; for it is said Tom noticed many prints of cloven feet stamped upon the tree, and found handfuls of hair, that looked as if they had been plucked from the coarse black shock of the woodman. Tom knew his wife's prowess by experience. He shrugged his shoulders, as he looked at the signs of a fierce clapperclawing. "Egad," said he to himself, "Old Scratch must have had a tough time of it!"

Tom consoled himself for the loss of his property, with the loss of his wife, for he was a man of fortitude. He even felt something like gratitude toward the black woodman, who, he considered, had done him a kindness. He sought, therefore, to cultivate a further acquaintance with him, but for some time without success; the old black legs played shy, for whatever people may think, he is not always to be had for calling for: He knows how to play his cards when pretty sure of his game.

At length, it is said, when delay had whetted Tom's eagerness to the quick, and prepared him to agree to anything rather than not gain the promised treasure, he met the black man one evening in his usual woodman's dress, with his ax on his shoulder, sauntering along the swamp, and humming a tune. He affected to receive Tom's advances with great indifference, made brief replies, and went on humming his tune.

By degrees, however, Tom brought him to business, and they began to haggle about the terms on which the former was to have the pirate's treasure. There was one condition which need not be mentioned, being generally understood in all cases where the devil grants favors; but there were others about which, though of less importance, he was inflexibly obstinate. He insisted that the money found through his means should be employed in his service. He proposed, therefore, that Tom should employ it in the black traffic; that is to say, that he should fit out a slave ship. This, however, Tom resolutely refused: He was bad enough in all conscience; but the devil himself could not tempt him to turn slave trader.

Finding Tom so squeamish on this point, he did not insist upon it, but proposed, instead,

---

17. **carrion crows** *n. pl.:* crows that feed on decaying flesh.

that he should turn usurer;[18] the devil being extremely anxious for the increase of usurers, looking upon them as his peculiar[19] people.

To this no objections were made, for it was just to Tom's taste.

"You shall open a broker's shop in Boston next month," said the black man.

"I'll do it tomorrow, if you wish," said Tom Walker.

"You shall lend money at two percent a month."

"Egad, I'll charge four!" replied Tom Walker.

"You shall extort bonds, foreclose mortgages, drive the merchants to bankruptcy—"

"I'll drive them to the d—l," cried Tom Walker.

"You are the usurer for my money!" said black legs with delight. "When will you want the rhino?"[20]

"This very night."

"Done!" said the devil.

"Done!" said Tom Walker. So they shook hands and struck a bargain.

A few days' time saw Tom Walker seated behind his desk in a countinghouse in Boston.

His reputation for a ready-moneyed man, who would lend money out for a good consideration, soon spread abroad. Everybody remembers the time of Governor Belcher,[21] when money was particularly scarce. It was a time of paper credit. The country had been deluged with government bills; the famous Land Bank[22] had been established; there had been a rage for speculating; the people had run mad with schemes for new settlements, for building cities in the wilderness; land jobbers[23] went about

with maps of grants, and townships, and Eldorados,[24] lying nobody knew where, but which everybody was ready to purchase. In a word, the great speculating fever which breaks out every now and then in the country, had raged to an alarming degree, and everybody was dreaming of making sudden fortunes from nothing. As usual the fever had subsided; the dream had gone off, and the imaginary fortunes with it; the patients were left in doleful plight, and the whole country resounded with the consequent cry of "hard times."

At this propitious time of public distress did Tom Walker set up as usurer in Boston. His door was soon thronged by customers. The needy and adventurous, the gambling speculator, the dreaming land jobber, the thriftless tradesman, the merchant with cracked credit; in short, everyone driven to raise money by desperate means and desperate sacrifices hurried to Tom Walker.

Thus Tom was the universal friend of the needy, and acted like a "friend in need"; that is to say, he always exacted good pay and good security. In proportion to the distress of the applicant was the hardness of his terms. He accumulated bonds and mortgages; gradually squeezed his customers closer and closer; and sent them at length, dry as a sponge, from his door.

In this way he made money hand over hand, became a rich and mighty man, and exalted his cocked hat upon 'Change.[25] He built himself, as usual, a vast house, out of ostentation;[26] but left the greater part of it unfinished and unfurnished, out of parsimony. He even set up a carriage in the fullness of his vainglory, though he nearly starved the horses which drew it; and as

---

18. **usurer** *n.*: one who lends money at excessive rates of interest.
19. **peculiar** *adj.*: here, special or particular.
20. **rhino** *n.*: slang for "money."
21. **Governor Belcher:** Jonathan Belcher (1681?–1757) was governor of the Massachusetts Bay Colony from 1730 to 1741.
22. **Land Bank:** loan system by which the province advanced money in exchange for mortgages on land. When the bank was outlawed, many people faced financial ruin.
23. **land jobbers** *n. pl.*: people who buy and sell land for profit.

24. **Eldorados:** Spanish word meaning "the gilded"; places of fabulous wealth.
25. **cocked hat upon 'Change:** Tom's cocked hat was a three-corner hat worn at the time. *'Change* is short for "the Exchange," a place where merchants and stockbrokers meet to do business.
26. **ostentation** *n.*: showy display.

**Vocabulary**

**parsimony** (pär′sə·mō′nē) *n.*: stinginess.

the ungreased wheels groaned and screeched on the axletrees, you would have thought you heard the souls of the poor debtors he was squeezing.

As Tom waxed old, however, he grew thoughtful. Having secured the good things of this world, he began to feel anxious about those of the next. He thought with regret on the bargain he had made with his black friend, and set his wits to work to cheat him out of the conditions. He became, therefore, all of a sudden, a violent churchgoer. He prayed loudly and strenuously, as if heaven were to be taken by force of lungs. Indeed, one might always tell when he had sinned most during the week, by the clamor of his Sunday devotion. The quiet Christians who had been modestly and steadfastly traveling Zionward,[27] were struck with self-reproach at seeing themselves so suddenly outstripped in their career by this new-made convert. Tom was as rigid in religious as in money matters; he was a stern supervisor and censurer of his neighbors, and seemed to think every sin entered up to their account became a credit on his own side of the page. He even talked of the expediency of reviving the persecution of Quakers and Anabaptists. In a word, Tom's zeal became as notorious as his riches.

Still, in spite of all this strenuous attention to forms, Tom had a lurking dread that the devil, after all, would have his due. That he might not be taken unawares, therefore, it is said he always carried a small Bible in his coat pocket. He had also a great folio Bible on his countinghouse desk, and would frequently be found reading it when people called on business; on such occasions he would lay his green spectacles in the book, to mark the place, while he turned round to drive some usurious bargain.

Some say that Tom grew a little crackbrained in his old days, and that, fancying his end approaching, he had his horse new shod, saddled and bridled, and buried with his feet uppermost; because he supposed that at the last day the world would be turned upside down; in which case he should find his horse standing ready for mounting, and he was determined at the worst to give his old friend a run for it. This, however, is probably a mere old wives' fable. If he really did take such a precaution, it was totally superfluous; at least so says the authentic old legend, which closes his story in the following manner:

One hot summer afternoon in the dog days, just as a terrible black thunder gust was coming up, Tom sat in his countinghouse, in his white linen cap and India silk morning gown. He was on the point of foreclosing a mortgage, by which he would complete the ruin of an unlucky land speculator for whom he had professed the greatest friendship. The poor land jobber begged him to grant a few months' indulgence. Tom had grown testy and irritated, and refused another day.

"My family will be ruined and brought upon the parish," said the land jobber. "Charity begins at home," replied Tom. "I must take care of myself in these hard times."

"You have made so much money out of me," said the speculator.

Tom lost his patience and his piety. "The devil take me," said he, "if I have made a farthing!"

Just then there were three loud knocks at the street door. He stepped out to see who was there. A black man was holding a black horse, which neighed and stamped with impatience.

"Tom, you're come for," said the black fellow, gruffly. Tom shrank back, but too late. He had left his little Bible at the bottom of his coat pocket, and his big Bible on the desk buried under the mortgage he was about to foreclose: Never was sinner taken more unawares. The black man whisked him like a child into the saddle, gave the horse the lash, and away he galloped, with Tom on his back, in the midst of the thunderstorm. The clerks stuck their pens behind their ears, and stared after him from the windows. Away went Tom Walker, dashing

---

27. **Zionward:** toward Zion, or Heaven.

**Vocabulary**

**superfluous** (sə·pʉr'flōō·əs) *adj.*: more than is needed or wanted; useless.

down the streets, his white cap bobbing up and down, his morning gown fluttering in the wind, and his steed striking fire out of the pavement at every bound. When the clerks turned to look for the black man, he had disappeared.

Tom Walker never returned to foreclose the mortgage. A countryman, who lived on the border of the swamp, reported that in the height of the thunder gust he had heard a great clattering of hoofs and a howling along the road, and running to the window caught sight of a figure, such as I have described, on a horse that galloped like mad across the fields, over the hills, and down into the black hemlock swamp toward the old Indian fort; and that shortly after a thunderbolt falling in that direction seemed to set the whole forest in a blaze.

The good people of Boston shook their heads and shrugged their shoulders, but had been so much accustomed to witches and goblins, and tricks of the devil, in all kinds of shapes, from the first settlement of the colony, that they were not so much horror-struck as might have been expected. Trustees were appointed to take charge of Tom's effects. There was nothing, however, to administer upon. On searching his coffers,[28] all his bonds and mortgages were found reduced to cinders. In place of gold and silver, his iron chest was filled with chips and shavings; two skeletons lay in his stable instead of his half-starved horses, and the very next day his great house took fire and burnt to the ground.

Such was the end of Tom Walker and his ill-gotten wealth. Let all griping money brokers lay this story to heart. The truth of it is not to be doubted. The very hole under the oak trees whence he dug Kidd's money is to be seen to this day; and the neighboring swamp and old Indian fort are often haunted in stormy nights by a figure on horseback, in morning gown and white cap, which is doubtless the troubled spirit of the usurer. In fact the story has resolved itself into a proverb, and is the origin of that popular saying, so prevalent throughout New England, of "The Devil and Tom Walker." ■

---

28. **coffers** *n. pl.:* containers for money and valuables.

# Response and Analysis

## Reading Check

1. Fill out a graph like the following one to show the elements that make up the **plot** of this story. Add as many key events as you think are necessary.

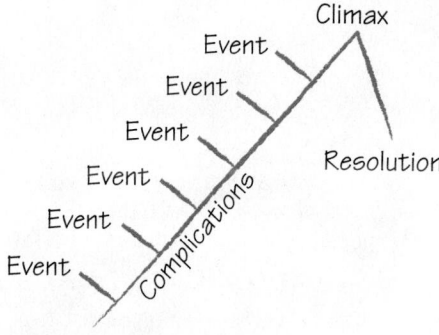

Climax

Event

Event

Event

Event

Event

Event

Complications

Resolution

Basic situation (conflict)

## Thinking Critically

2. Usually we look for surprises in stories; we would be disappointed if a story turned out just the way we predicted. What did you predict would happen to Tom and his wife? Did any particular detail or event in the story surprise or shock you?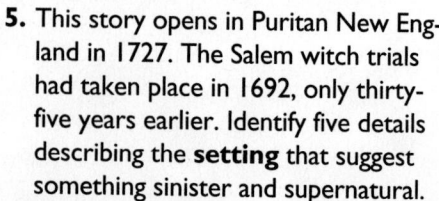

3. Irving's **characters** in this story are one-dimensional people who represent one or two character traits. In fact, Mrs. Tom Walker is a stereotype of the nagging wife, still a source of comedy today. What character traits are represented by Tom Walker? Why do you think Mrs. Walker met with such a nasty end?

4. In stories about the devil, this character takes on many forms. Look back at the first description of the devil, on page 179. What details suggest at once that he comes from a region of hellfire? What details refer to the devil's special dealings in America?

5. This story opens in Puritan New England in 1727. The Salem witch trials had taken place in 1692, only thirty-five years earlier. Identify five details describing the **setting** that suggest something sinister and supernatural.

6. How does the physical **setting** of the story reflect the moral decay of the characters and, indeed, of the whole society presented in this story?

7. A **tragedy** is a story about the fall of a great person. A **satire** is a story that mocks some human folly. Plots built on bargains with the devil are often tragic, as in the story told by Christopher Marlowe about Dr. Faustus. If Irving's story is a satire, what human follies is Irving mocking? What details in the story reveal that Irving was specifically critical of the values held by the Puritans of Boston?

8. How would you describe the **mood,** or atmosphere, created in the story? What details help to create that mood?

9. As the narrator tells the story—which certainly has its gruesome and fearful aspects—what **tone** prevails? Is it comic, frightening, bitter, romantic, or something else? Find details from the story that support your response.

10. Irving's story opens in 1727 in Boston, Massachusetts. What if the story were set in another time and place? Consider the following questions:

    • Would the theme remain the same?

    • Who would the characters be?

    • What bargain would they drive with the devil?

    • What would the devil look like, and where would he hang out?

**SKILLS FOCUS**

**Literary Skills**
Analyze mood.

**Reading Skills**
Review predictions.

**Writing Skills**
Write an essay analyzing how a work is representative of Romanticism.

**Vocabulary Skills**
Use context clues to determine the meanings of words.

## Extending and Evaluating

11. This story was first published in 1824, long before people's consciousness had been raised about the cruelty of viewing other people as stereotypes. It was a time, for example, when women characters were housewives, when African Americans were looked down on, and when American Indians were feared as "savages." These views are reflected in Irving's story. How do you feel about reading literature like this today?

# WRITING

## Literary Criticism

Review the characteristics of American Romanticism on page 167. In a brief **essay,** describe the characteristics of this story that make it an example of American Romanticism. At the end of your essay, respond to these questions: How would a contemporary American writer be likely to handle the same plot—say, Stephen King? Would the story's tone change?

## Vocabulary Development
### Context Clues

Respond to each numbered item below. Then, indicate the context clues that give you hints to the meaning of the underlined words in each sentence.

1. If a swampy terrain is filled with stagnant pools, are mosquitoes likely to be prevalent there?
2. Why would it be superfluous for an inexperienced soldier to storm an impregnable fortress?
3. Is someone whose heart is filled with avarice more likely to show parsimony or to make a charitable donation?
4. Name three pleasant things that might help you obliterate a melancholy feeling.
5. If you faced a long and precarious climb up a mountain, why would you want a partner who was especially resolute?

# Vocabulary Development

## Analogies

A kind of comparison called an **analogy** often appears as a logic problem on standardized tests. An analogy begins with a related pair of words or phrases. The goal is to identify a second pair of words with a similar relationship.

LARGE : GIGANTIC ::

a. depressed : happy      c. round : square

b. noisy : excited        d. tired : weary

The colon (:) stands for the phrase "is related to." The double colon (::) can be read as "in the same way that." Thus, you'd read the above analogy question like this: "*Large* is related to *gigantic* in the same way that . . ."

**Finding the connection.** Now you have to do two things: Identify the relationship of the first word pair as precisely as possible, and choose a second pair whose relationship is most similar to that of the first pair. In the example above, you could say, "*Large* is similar in meaning to *gigantic*." *Is similar in meaning to* is the relationship. Next, check to see which answer choices include a pair of words whose meanings are

**SKILLS FOCUS**

**Vocabulary Skills**
Analyze word analogies.

similar. The only choice that contains words with similar meanings is d. The word *tired* is similar in meaning to *weary*.

**Classifying analogies.** Most analogies can be classified into one of about ten relationships. Here are three types of analogy relationships. (For other types of analogies, see pages 788 and 1046.)

| Type | Relationship | Example |
|------|-------------|---------|
| Synonym | is similar in meaning to | SMART : CLEVER |
| Antonym | is opposite in meaning of | GREED : GENEROSITY |
| Characteristic | is characteristic of | LOYAL : PATRIOT |

**Test-taking strategies.** Keep the following guidelines in mind when doing analogies in which you have to choose a second pair of words with the same relationship as the first pair:

1. Look for a second pair with a clear, precise relationship.
2. Compare the relationship, not the words.
3. Know the precise denotation, or dictionary definition, of words. Consult a dictionary frequently when dealing with unfamiliar words.

## PRACTICE 1

Using the information given in the chart above, identify the type of relationship that exists in each of the following word pairs:

1. NOISE : SOUND
2. TRIVIAL : IMPORTANT
3. FREEZING : ICE
4. CARNIVOROUS : TIGER
5. COURAGE : TIMIDITY
6. WONDER : AWE

## PRACTICE 2

Select the lettered word pair that best expresses a relationship similar to that of the capitalized word pair. (In each capitalized pair, the first word is from "The Devil and Tom Walker.")

1. INTERIOR : EXTERIOR ::
   a. beautiful : gorgeous
   b. tired : sleepy
   c. immense : small
   d. smoke : chimney

2. GLOOMY : DISMAL ::
   a. soothing : irritating
   b. cautious : careless
   c. meek : humble
   d. quiet : noisy

3. CONFIDENCE : TRUST ::
   a. illusion : reality
   b. contradiction : agreement
   c. determination : unease
   d. authenticity : truth

4. DESPERATE : HOPELESS ::
   a. strict : stern
   b. rich : poor
   c. unlucky : fortunate
   d. miserable : joyous

# William Cullen Bryant

(1794–1878)

*William Cullen Bryant* (1833) by James Frothingham. Oil on canvas (21″ × 17½″).

Museum of Fine Arts, Boston. Gift of Maxim Karolik for the M. and M. Karolik Collection of American Paintings, 1815–1865 (62.271). Photograph © 2007 Museum of Fine Arts, Boston.

**P**oetry is a lonely occupation but not a solitary one. Poets of any consequence rarely write in isolation from the influence of their predecessors or from the influence of other poets of their own time. When William Cullen Bryant was still an adolescent, he read a book of poems that would change his life: *Lyrical Ballads,* published in 1798 by his great English contemporaries William Wordsworth and Samuel Taylor Coleridge. This volume of poetry and theory focused the expression and much of the philosophy of the Romantic era. The book was a powerful source of inspiration for poets who wanted to replace conventional poetic diction with the common speech of their own time. Bryant was one of these poets—the first mature American Romantic, the country boy who translated the messages of English Romanticism into his native tongue.

Two other important factors supported the influence of English Romanticism on Bryant's poetry. One factor was Bryant's own growing attraction to the philosophy of deism (page 18), which held that divinity could be found in nature. The other factor was the geography of his surroundings, which placed Bryant in immediate contact with everything that supported this philosophy.

By the time of Bryant's birth, western Massachusetts was no longer a Colonial frontier but a widely settled countryside. Over the next hundred years and more, its farms, steepled towns, and mountain forests would be the homes of many poets. These writers would find in their surroundings metaphors to express their sense of correspondence between human life and the life of nature. After Bryant, the same New England seasons would turn for Herman Melville and Emily Dickinson and later for Robert Frost and Richard Wilbur. All these poets were intimate with the shadows and whispers of the Berkshires and the adjacent Green Mountains. All would make their own small plot of ground part of the permanent landscape of American poetry.

Bryant was born in Cummington, Massachusetts. His father was a physician, and his mother came from a family of clergy. Bryant's literary gifts were evident from an early age: By the age of nine, he was already writing poetry and had earned a reputation as a prodigy.

Bryant was tutored for a career as a lawyer, but with the publication of "Thanatopsis," his literary future was assured. In his late twenties he moved to New York City and for many years played the triple role of editor, critic, and poet.

Bryant became not only a famous literary figure but also an influential voice in religion and politics. An outspoken liberal, Bryant supported social reform, free speech, and the growing movement for the abolition of slavery. He was also one of the founders of the Republican party, which, in his lifetime, would produce one of America's greatest presidents, Abraham Lincoln. When Bryant died, at the age of eighty-three, he was a millionaire and so widely honored at home and abroad that he had become a kind of national monument, the widely acknowledged father of American poetry.

# Before You Read

## Thanatopsis

### Make the Connection

Romantic poets looked to nature for lessons—lessons that we too can learn by looking around us. One of the ever-present lessons of nature is the organic cycle of birth, growth, death, and rebirth. Think of some of the ways that nature reminds us of this recurring cycle. Do you find this aspect of nature disturbing or comforting?

### Literary Focus
#### Theme

Bryant composed the first version of "Thanatopsis" when he was only sixteen years old, during solitary walks in the woods. Despite his youth, though, or perhaps because of it, he tackled the most serious questions a poet can explore: What happens to us after we die, and how should we think or feel about death? Bryant's answers to these questions represent the **theme** of this poem—its central insight into human experience. As you read "Thanatopsis," pay special attention to lines 17–72, where the "still voice" of Nature speaks. What spiritual "teachings" does Nature offer?

> The **theme** of a literary work is the insight it offers into human experience.
>
> *For more on Theme, see the Handbook of Literary and Historical Terms.*

### Reading Skills
#### Reading Inverted Sentences

In order to maintain his **meter** and create certain sound effects, Bryant makes use of **inversion**—a reversal or rearranging of the usual word order in sentences. The usual word order in English sentences is subject, then verb, and then object or complement. In lines 17–19, Bryant reverses this order: "Yet a few days, and thee / The all-beholding sun shall see no more / In all his course." The normal word order would be "Yet a few days, and thee shall see no more the all-beholding sun in all his course." *Thee* is the subject, *see* is the verb, and *sun* is the object. If you're having trouble understanding a line or passage, look for the subject and the verb, and then restate the sentence in normal English word order.

### Background

*Thanatopsis* is a word Bryant coined by joining two Greek words, *thanatos,* "death," and *opsis,* "sight." The new word is defined by the poem: a way of looking at and thinking about death.

# Thanatopsis

## William Cullen Bryant

To him who in the love of Nature holds
Communion with her visible forms, she speaks
A various language; for his gayer hours
She has a voice of gladness, and a smile
5   And eloquence of beauty, and she glides
Into his darker musings, with a mild
And healing sympathy, that steals away
Their sharpness, ere he is aware. When thoughts
Of the last bitter hour come like a blight
10  Over thy spirit, and sad images
Of the stern agony, and shroud, and pall,°
And breathless darkness, and the narrow house,°
Make thee to shudder, and grow sick at heart;—
Go forth, under the open sky, and list°
15  To Nature's teachings, while from all around—
Earth and her waters, and the depths of air—
Comes a still voice.—
              Yet a few days, and thee
The all-beholding sun shall see no more
In all his course; nor yet in the cold ground,
20  Where thy pale form was laid, with many tears,
Nor in the embrace of ocean, shall exist
Thy image. Earth, that nourished thee, shall claim
Thy growth, to be resolved to earth again,
And, lost each human trace, surrendering up
25  Thine individual being, shalt thou go
To mix forever with the elements,
To be a brother to the insensible rock
And to the sluggish clod, which the rude swain°
Turns with his share,° and treads upon. The oak
30  Shall send his roots abroad, and pierce thy mold.

   Yet not to thine eternal resting place
Shalt thou retire alone, nor couldst thou wish
Couch more magnificent. Thou shalt lie down
With patriarchs of the infant world—with kings,
35  The powerful of the earth—the wise, the good,
Fair forms, and hoary seers° of ages past,
All in one mighty sepulcher. The hills
Rock-ribbed and ancient as the sun,—the vales
Stretching in pensive quietness between;

**8.** Ere *means "before." What does Nature do for those who communicate with her?*

**11. pall** (pôl) *n.:* coffin cover.
**12. narrow house:** grave.

**14. list** *v.:* archaic for "listen."

**17.** *Here the voice of Nature begins to speak. When you get to line 30, sum up Nature's advice to those who think sad thoughts of death.*

**28. rude swain:** uneducated country youth.
**29. share** *n.:* short for "plowshare."

**36. hoary seers:** white-haired prophets.
**37.** *A sepulcher is a burial place. What does Nature say to those who fear the solitude of death?*

40   The venerable woods—rivers that move
     In majesty, and the complaining brooks
     That make the meadows green; and, poured round all,
     Old Ocean's gray and melancholy waste,—
     Are but the solemn decorations all
45   Of the great tomb of man. The golden sun,
     The planets, all the infinite host of heaven,
     Are shining on the sad abodes of death,
     Through the still lapse of ages. All that tread
     The globe are but a handful to the tribes
50   That slumber in its bosom.—Take the wings
     Of morning,° pierce the Barcan wilderness,°
     Or lose thyself in the continuous woods
     Where rolls the Oregon,° and hears no sound,
     Save his own dashings—yet the dead are there:
55   And millions in those solitudes, since first
     The flight of years began, have laid them down
     In their last sleep—the dead reign there alone.
     So shalt thou rest, and what if thou withdraw
     In silence from the living, and no friend
60   Take note of thy departure? All that breathe
     Will share thy destiny. The gay will laugh
     When thou art gone, the solemn brood of care
     Plod on, and each one as before will chase
     His favorite phantom; yet all these shall leave
65   Their mirth and their employments, and shall come
     And make their bed with thee. As the long train
     Of ages glides away, the sons of men,
     The youth in life's fresh spring, and he who goes
     In the full strength of years, matron and maid,
70   The speechless babe, and the gray-headed man—
     Shall one by one be gathered to thy side,
     By those, who in their turn shall follow them.

      So live, that when thy summons comes to join
     The innumerable caravan, which moves
75   To that mysterious realm, where each shall take
     His chamber in the silent halls of death,
     Thou go not, like the quarry slave at night,
     Scourged to his dungeon, but, sustained and soothed
     By an unfaltering trust, approach thy grave,
80   Like one who wraps the drapery of his couch
     About him, and lies down to pleasant dreams.

**45.** *What decorates the "tomb of man"?*

**51. Take … morning:** allusion to Psalm 139:9: "If I take the wings of the morning . . ."
**Barcan wilderness:** desert near Barca (now al-Marj), in Libya, North Africa.
**53. Oregon:** early name for the Columbia River, which flows between Washington and Oregon.

**57.** *What examples does the speaker use to explain that the dead are everywhere?*

**72.** *What comfort does Nature offer in lines 58–72?*

**73.** *The speaker's voice resumes here. When you get to the end of the poem, sum up the speaker's message in lines 73–81.*

# Response and Analysis

## Thinking Critically

1. As the poem opens, Nature is **personified** as someone who speaks "a various language." How does Nature speak to us in our "gayer hours"? How does Nature respond to our "darker musings"?

2. Lines 17–30 have a sad, tragic **tone.** Describe the shift in tone that occurs in line 31. What **metaphors** and **images** in this section of the poem reinforce the change in tone?

3. After Nature's speech (lines 17–72), the human speaker's voice resumes for the concluding section, or summing up. In your own words, summarize the speaker's advice in lines 73–81. What **images** does the poet make you see in these lines?

4. Do you find this speaker's attitude toward death comforting or disturbing, or do you have some other reaction? Explain.

5. How does "Thanatopsis" reveal the Romantic conviction that the universe, far from operating like a machine, is really a living organism that undergoes constant cyclical changes? How does the human speaker feel about this view of the universe?

## Extending and Evaluating

6. Today many readers view a poem like "Thanatopsis" as simply a period piece with only historical interest, yet Bryant's intent was to offer serious spiritual counsel. Does Bryant's poem still speak to us today? Or are his musings no longer meaningful? Give reasons for your opinion.

## Literary Criticism

7. Some readers think this poem expresses a traditional notion of an afterlife in heaven. Others find in it a very untraditional view of an afterlife, in which people rejoin the great chain of Nature instead of ascending to a heavenly realm. Which interpretation strikes you as a more valid reading of the poem's **theme**?

## WRITING

### A Puritan Writes to a Romantic

How might Anne Bradstreet (page 27) or Jonathan Edwards (page 44) have reacted to Bryant's meditation on death? Write a **letter** from Bradstreet or Edwards to Bryant, conveying a Puritan reaction to "Thanatopsis." In your letter, be sure to cite specific lines from the poem.

## LISTENING AND SPEAKING

### Performing a Poem

Working with a partner, present an oral reading of "Thanatopsis." One reader can take the part of the human speaker (lines 1–17 and 73–81), and the other can be the voice of Nature (lines 17–72). As you rehearse, pay attention to where sentences begin and end, since the poem has many run-on lines and sentences that end in the middle of a line. To avoid a singsong rhythm, stop only at punctuation marks (pause briefly at commas, and stop at periods). Before you perform, be sure you have identified lines in the poem that use **inverted syntax.**

**SKILLS FOCUS**

**Literary Skills**
Analyze theme.

**Reading Skills**
Recognize inverted sentences.

**Writing Skills**
Write a letter reacting to a poem.

**Listening and Speaking Skills**
Present an oral reading of a poem.

# Henry Wadsworth Longfellow

## (1807–1882)

Longfellow was and still is the most popular poet America has ever produced. With the possible exception of Robert Frost (page 790), no twentieth-century poet has ever become a household name, let alone achieved the kind of recognition suggested by the word *popular*.

Longfellow's immense popularity was based largely on his appeal to an audience hungry for sermons and lessons. That audience wanted assurances that their cherished values would prevail over the new forces of history

Henry Wadsworth Longfellow. Photograph by Julia Margaret Cameron.
Courtesy of George Eastman House.

—such as industrialization—that were threatening to destroy them. The values Longfellow endorsed were positive forces in the making of the American character, but his tendency to leave these values unexamined led to poetry that often offered easy comfort at the expense of illumination.

Born in Portland, Maine, Longfellow was never far from the rocks and splashing waves of the Atlantic Coast or from the cultural and religious influences of the well-to-do families who lived north of Boston. Longfellow's early interest in foreign languages and literature led him naturally to an academic career. He attended Bowdoin College (where Nathaniel Hawthorne was one of his classmates) and then pursued three additional years of study in France, Spain, Italy, and Germany. When Longfellow returned, he joined the Bowdoin faculty, married, and began to write a series

of sketches about his experiences abroad.

During a second European trip in 1835, Longfellow's young wife died of a miscarriage. When he returned to America, the young widower became a professor of French and Spanish at Harvard; seven years later he married Frances (Fanny) Appleton, whom he had met in Europe after his first wife's death. He settled into eighteen years of happily married life, fathering six children and producing some of his most celebrated poetry, much of it based on American legends, such as *Evangeline* (1847) and *The Song of Hiawatha* (1855).

By 1854, Longfellow had devoted himself to writing full time. Seven years later, though, a second tragedy struck: His wife, Frances, died in a fiery accident at home, when a lighted match or hot sealing wax ignited her summer dress. Longfellow tried to save her, smothering the flames with a rug, and was badly burned himself.

Longfellow now devoted himself to his work with a religious and literary zeal. By the end of his long and productive life, he had become for Americans the symbolic figure of the Poet: wise, graybearded, haloed with goodness, and living in a world of undiminished romance. Two years after his death, Longfellow's marble image was unveiled in the Poets' Corner in London's Westminster Abbey. He was the first American to be so honored.

# Before You Read

## The Tide Rises, the Tide Falls

### Make the Connection

Think of how nature repeats its cycles over and over again: Summer turns to winter and returns again; day follows night and returns again; the tide rises and falls and rises again. Then, think of individual human lives. Are our lives like these endlessly repeated cycles of the natural world, or is a human life different?

### Literary Focus

#### Meter: A Pattern of Sounds

**Meter** is a pattern of stressed and unstressed syllables in poetry. **Scanning** a poem means marking the stressed syllables with one symbol ( ′ ) and the unstressed syllables with another ( ˘ ).

A metrical unit of poetry is called a **foot**. A foot always contains at least one stressed syllable and usually one or more unstressed syllables. A common type of foot is the **iamb** (ī′amb′)—an unstressed syllable followed by a stressed syllable. The meter of

"The Tide Rises, the Tide Falls" is essentially iambic. Read this line aloud, stressing the syllables marked with the stress symbol.

˘ ′  ˘ ′  ˘ ′  ˘ ′
Along / the sea- / sands damp / and brown

Poets often vary their metrical patterns to avoid a mechanical, singsong effect. In this poem's first line, notice how Longfellow avoids a purely iambic meter by pairing two stressed syllables. This kind of metrical foot is called a **spondee**.

Read the entire poem aloud to hear how the rise and fall of its rhythm mimics the rise and fall of the tide.

> **Meter** is a pattern of stressed and unstressed syllables in poetry.
>
> *For more on Meter, see the Handbook of Literary and Historical Terms.*

Portion of the original manuscript of "The Cross of Snow" by Henry Wadsworth Longfellow.

**SKILLS FOCUS**

**Literary Skills**
Understand meter.

*Meditation by the Sea* (early 1860s) by an unidentified American artist. Oil on canvas (13⅝" × 19⅝") (34.6 cm × 49.8 cm).

# The Tide Rises, the Tide Falls

## Henry Wadsworth Longfellow

The tide rises, the tide falls,
The twilight darkens, the curlew° calls;
Along the sea-sands damp and brown
The traveler hastens toward the town,
5     And the tide rises, the tide falls.

Darkness settles on roofs and walls,
But the sea, the sea in the darkness calls;
The little waves, with their soft, white hands,
Efface° the footprints in the sands,
10     And the tide rises, the tide falls.

The morning breaks; the steeds in their stalls
Stamp and neigh, as the hostler° calls;
The day returns, but nevermore
Returns the traveler to the shore,
15     And the tide rises, the tide falls.

**2. curlew** (kur′lo͞o′) *n.:* large, brownish shore-bird with long legs.

**9. efface** (ə·fās′) *v.:* wipe out; erase.

**12. hostler** (häs′lər) *n.:* person who takes care of horses.

## The Cross of Snow

### Make the Connection
#### Quickwrite ✏

Romantic poets often use aspects of nature to express emotions that might be too painful or personal to state directly. In this poem, Longfellow takes a dramatic scene in nature and transforms it into a powerful **image** conveying intense grief. Think of an image from nature that you could use to describe or represent a feeling of great sorrow. Set up your comparison like a **metaphor:** "Grief is . . ." Then, explore in a few sentences how grief is like the image you have chosen.

### Literary Focus
#### Sonnet

"The Cross of Snow" is a **sonnet,** a fourteen-line rhymed poem usually written in **iambic pentameter.** *Iambic pentameter* means that a line of poetry contains five **iambs.** An iamb is an unstressed syllable followed by a stressed syllable, as in the word *repose.*

   The sonnet is one of the oldest and most enduring poetic forms in world literature. Two of its early masters were the Italian poet Petrarch (1304–1374) and the English playwright William Shakespeare (1564–1616). In later periods the sonnet was taken up by writers such as John Milton, William Wordsworth, John Keats, Elizabeth Barrett Browning, Edna St. Vincent Millay, John Berryman, Robert Frost, and Robert Lowell.

   Two principal forms of the sonnet have been used in English. In the **Elizabethan,** or **Shakespearean, sonnet** there are three four-line groups, called **quatrains,** which are followed by two rhyming lines, called a **couplet.**

   The **Petrarchan,** or **Italian, sonnet** is composed of two groups: The first eight lines are called the **octave,** and the last six lines are called the **sestet.** Longfellow, who knew Italian literature well, used the Italian form of the sonnet for "The Cross of Snow." (For another example of a Petrarchan sonnet, see Sor Juana Inés de la Cruz's "World, in hounding me . . ." on page 33.)

### Background

"I shall win this lady, or I shall die," Longfellow had written of Fanny Appleton, his second wife, who kept him waiting seven years before she agreed to marry him. Longfellow wrote "The Cross of Snow" eighteen years after Fanny died in a fire. Three years later Longfellow died without having shown the poem to anyone. Discovered among his papers, it was published four years later and immediately became one of his most famous poems. Longfellow had a large audience waiting to read everything he wrote. Why, then, do you think Longfellow chose to keep this sonnet private?

Frances "Fanny" Appleton.

**Literary Skills**
Understand the characteristics of Elizabethan and Petrarchan sonnets.

*Mount of the Holy Cross–Colorado* (1873). Tinted photograph by William Henry Jackson.

# The Cross of Snow

## Henry Wadsworth Longfellow

In the long, sleepless watches of the night,
   A gentle face—the face of one long dead—
   Looks at me from the wall, where round its head
   The night lamp casts a halo of pale light.
5  Here in this room she died; and soul more white
   Never through martyrdom of fire was led
   To its repose; nor can in books be read
   The legend of a life more benedight.°
There is a mountain in the distant West
10  That, sun-defying, in its deep ravines
   Displays a cross of snow upon its side.
Such is the cross I wear upon my breast
   These eighteen years, through all the changing scenes
   And seasons, changeless since the day she died.

**8. benedight** (ben′ə·dīt′) *adj.*: archaic for "blessed."

*In the following article a critic discusses Longfellow's place in American literature. The title "Return to Gitche Gumee" is a reference to a famous line from Longfellow's epic poem* The Song of Hiawatha. *Gitche Gumee is thought to be Lake Superior.*

# Return to Gitche Gumee

## J. D. McClatchy

Hiawatha wooing Minnehaha, from a Currier and Ives print by John Cameron (1867).

When Henry Wadsworth Longfellow was in England in 1868 to receive an honorary degree from Cambridge University, Queen Victoria invited him to tea. She was a great admirer of his work and found his company delightful. When she accompanied the poet to the door and watched him walk down the long palace corridor, she saw something slightly disconcerting. "I noticed," she confided to her diary that night, "an unusual interest among the attendants and servants. I could scarcely credit that they so generally understood who he was. When he took leave, they concealed themselves in places from which they could get a good look at him as he passed. I have since inquired among them, and am surprised and pleased to find that many of his poems are familiar to them. No other distinguished person has come here that has excited so peculiar an interest."

Monarch and manservant, curate[1] and carpetbagger, the whole world read Longfellow. He outsold Browning and Tennyson. In the White House, Lincoln asked to have Longfellow's poems recited to him, and wept.

When the emperor of Brazil made a state visit to the United States, his only request was to have dinner with Longfellow. The poet's seventieth birthday, in 1877, was a day of national celebration, commemorated by parading schoolchildren around the country. It was proclaimed on that day that "there is no man living for whom there is so universal a feeling of love and gratitude, and no man who ever wore so great a fame so gently and simply."

His popularity marked a literary milestone. It could be said that Longfellow was our first professional poet. Not

---

1. **curate** *n.:* clergyman.

only was he able to make a living from his writing but he worked carefully to establish for American poetry a cultural eminence. He was both professor and balladeer; that is to say, he had literary qualities that rarely coincide and from either sideline are usually sneered at. He had an authority based on learning and allusion, gaining for his work an intellectual respect. And he had a narrative gift both sweeping and canny, along with a near perfect ear, that made his work memorable and gave it an enormous popular appeal. . . .

And then, less than half a century after Longfellow's death, the modernist braves circled and shot him down like a dazed buffalo. Ezra Pound (who, by the way, was Longfellow's grandnephew) and T. S. Eliot were determined to rid the poetic landscape of mawkishness.[2] Narrative was out and the skewered, ego-bound lyric was in. Moralizing was out and psychologizing was in. The elegant and delicate were derided, the fragmented and confessional applauded. Meter and rhyme were considered fustian,[3] and the

The death of Minnehaha, from a Currier and Ives print by John Cameron (1867).

broken line or free-verse effusion[4] was all the rage. Longfellow was officially declared kitsch.[5] . . .

Longfellow is not a poet of startling originality, not a Whitman or Dickinson. But he is a much better poet than is now supposed. Yes, he will seem sentimental at times, but from how many Victorian poems would we not nowadays want to snip off the last few, homilizing[6] lines? Still, re-reading his best lyrics, one is struck by the twilit, ghostly melancholy of his lost paradises. The moon glides along the damp mysterious chambers of the air, and somber

houses are hearsed with plumes of smoke. And the grand narrative poems of his *Tales of a Wayside Inn* sequence have a dramatic thrust and vivid portraiture that can evoke one's first, enthralled experiences with stories, the high adventurous romance of those books that helped shape our desires and still abide in our memories. If Longfellow has long since been consigned to your dusty top shelf, it may be time to take him down. You won't just be opening a book; you'll encounter a world sometimes thought lost, but actually as near as a dream.

—from *The New York Times*
October 22, 2000

---

2. **mawkishness** *n.:* excessive sentimentality.
3. **fustian** (fus'chən) *adj.:* pompous; overblown.
4. **effusion** *n.:* unrestrained outpouring of feeling.
5. **kitsch** *adj.:* marked by bad taste.
6. **homilizing** *v.* used as *adj.:* moralizing.

# Response and Analysis

## The Tide Rises, the Tide Falls

### Thinking Critically

1. Look closely at each stanza. What does each stanza tell you about the passage of time?

2. "Footsteps on the sands of time" is a common expression referring to our mortality and to the passage of time. In the second stanza a similar image appears. What does this **image** suggest has happened to the traveler?

3. What words in the third stanza hint at the traveler's fate? How does the image of the lively horses contrast with what probably has happened to the traveler?

4. In the second stanza the poet **personifies** the sea and the waves—that is, he gives the sea and the waves attributes of a human being. What words personify the sea and the waves? Do these images create a disturbing effect or a gentle, comforting feeling? Explain.

5. Longfellow was a master craftsman. Identify the places where he uses **alliteration,** or the repetition of consonant sounds. How would you describe the emotional effect of these sounds—are they soothing, haunting, upsetting, or something else?

6. Read the poem aloud. How does the **meter** of the poem sound like the rising and falling movement of the tides?

Henry Wadsworth Longfellow in his study in the house in Cambridge, Massachusetts.

7. At the end of the poem, the tide continues to rise and fall, although the human traveler does not return. How does this contrast reveal the poem's **theme**—its central insight into the relationship between human life and nature?

8. Do you think this is a poem about one specific traveler, or could it be seen as a drama about everyone's life? Explain.

### Literary Criticism

9. How does this poem reflect the Romantics' view of nature and death? How would you compare Longfellow's attitude with William Cullen Bryant's in "Thanatopsis" (page 191)?

**SKILLS FOCUS**

**Literary Skills**
Analyze meter and the characteristics of Petrarchan sonnets.

**Writing Skills**
Write an essay comparing and contrasting two poems. Write a poem using an image from nature.

**INTERNET**

**Projects and Activities**

Keyword: LE7 11-2

# The Cross of Snow

## Thinking Critically

1. The phrase "watches of the night" usually refers to the rounds made by a guard. What does the phrase mean in line 1?

2. The image "martyrdom of fire" in line 6 might confuse readers who do not know that Longfellow's wife died in a fire. (A martyr is a person who dies for his or her faith. Many early Christian martyrs were burned to death.) What is Longfellow suggesting about his wife's character by using this powerful **image**? What other image reinforces this characterization of his wife as saintly?

3. Explain how *sun-defying* (line 10) suggests conditions of weather and geology that might actually produce a permanent cross of snow on the side of a mountain. How does the poet relate this idea to his own feelings of grief?

4. Why might Longfellow have chosen to use a cross as the **symbol** of his grief?

## Literary Criticism

5. In his article on Longfellow (see the **Connection** on page 199), J. D. McClatchy says that Queen Victoria was surprised that her servants read Longfellow. What universal human experiences do you think Longfellow has expressed in these two poems that might account for his popularity?

# WRITING

## Comparing Poems

In a brief **essay,** compare and contrast the attitudes toward death in "The Tide Rises, the Tide Falls" and "The Cross of Snow." How important is it that one poem is about an unnamed traveler—probably standing for everyone—while the other is about a specific person?

## An Image of Grief

Refer to your Quickwrite notes, and write a brief **poem** in which you use an image from nature to stand for an experience of grief. ✎

## Literary Focus

### What Is a Sonnet?

☑ A sonnet has fourteen lines arranged in a specific pattern. It uses a set rhyme scheme.

☑ The typical rhyme scheme in a Petrarchan, or Italian, sonnet is *abba, abba, cde, cde.*

☑ The usual rhyme scheme in a Shakespearean sonnet is *abab, cdcd, efef, gg.*

☑ The first part of a sonnet usually introduces a subject. The last group of lines makes a comment on the subject. When you read a sonnet, look for the subject and the comment on the subject.

• Longfellow chose to write "The Cross of Snow" in the form of a **Petrarchan sonnet.** Identify the **rhyme scheme** of the sonnet. What question or idea does the **octave** (lines 1–8) present? What answer or response does the **sestet** (lines 9–14) offer?

• This sonnet is written in **iambic pentameter.** This is the most common meter used in English poetry because it sounds the most like ordinary speech. Where does Longfellow vary his iambic pentameter?

List of characters from *Tales of a Wayside Inn.*

# Ralph Waldo Emerson
## (1803–1882)

**S**hortly before the poet Walt Whitman died, he honored a man whose ideas had influenced him profoundly throughout his own long and controversial career. "America in the future," he wrote, "in her long train of poets and writers, while knowing more vehement and luxurious ones, will, I think, acknowledge nothing nearer [than] this man, the actual beginner of the whole procession."

"This man" was Ralph Waldo Emerson. Emerson expressed, better than anyone before him, the advantages of a young land—its freedom from the old, corrupt, and dying thought and the customs of Europe; its access to higher laws directly through nature rather than indirectly, through books and the teachings of the past; its energy; and its opportunity to reform the world.

Emerson was one of those rare writers who appealed both to intellectuals and to the general public. His influence on the popular mind—thanks to the thousands of lectures he gave throughout the United States—was strong. Although Emerson had something of a reputation for being hard to understand, his lectures were usually quite accessible. "I had heard of him as full of transcendentalisms, myths, and oracular gibberish," Herman Melville wrote a friend after hearing Emerson lecture. "To my surprise, I found him quite intelligible." Melville added wryly, "To say truth, they told me that that night he was unusually plain."

Despite Emerson's great influence, it is difficult even to classify what kind of writer he was. *Essayist* is too limited a term, and *philosopher* is too broad. The best term, perhaps, is *poet*—a poet whose best work was not always in verse.

"I am born a poet," Emerson wrote to his fiancée, Lydia Jackson, in 1835, "of a low class without doubt, yet a poet. That is my nature and vocation. My singing, be sure, is very 'husky,' and is for the most part in prose. Still am I a poet in the sense of a perceiver and dear lover of the harmonies that are in the soul and in matter. . . ."

## The Burden of Expectation

Emerson was born in Boston in 1803 to a family that was cultured but poor. When he was not quite eight years old, his father, a Unitarian minister, died of tuberculosis. His mother, left with six growing children to care for, opened a boardinghouse.

In the lives of the Emerson children, their father's place was taken by an aunt, Mary Moody Emerson. She was a strict Calvinist who emphasized self-sacrifice and whose enormous energy drove the Emerson boys to achievement. "She had the misfortune," Emerson later wrote, "of spinning with a greater velocity than any of the other tops."

Every step of Emerson's life had been laid out for him from an early age. He was to go to Harvard and become a minister, like the eight generations of Emersons before him. Emerson uncomfortably obeyed. His life was a series of attempts to establish his own identity against this background of expectation.

## Young Rebel

Emerson entered Harvard at fourteen. He was an indifferent student, although he read widely in philosophy and theology. Upon graduation,

*Ralph Waldo Emerson* (c. 1867) by William Henry Furness, Jr. Oil on canvas (45³/₄″ × 36³/₁₆″). Acc. no.: 1899.8

Courtesy of the Pennsylvania Academy of the Fine Arts, Philadelphia. Gift of Horace Howard Furness.

Emerson took a job at a school run by his brother and prepared himself, with many doubts, for the Unitarian ministry. In 1829, at the age of twenty-five, he accepted a post at Boston's Second Church; that same year he married Ellen Tucker, a beautiful but fragile seventeen-year-old already in the early stages of tuberculosis. Seventeen months later Ellen died.

Emerson's grief coincided with a growing disbelief in some of the central doctrines of his religion. In June 1832, he shocked his congregation by resigning from the ministry and setting off on an extended tour of Europe. There he met and conversed with the Romantic poets William Wordsworth and Samuel Taylor Coleridge, as well as other influential writers.

### Emerson's "New Pulpit"

Returning to the United States in late 1833, Emerson settled in Concord, Massachusetts, and soon married Lydia Jackson. He began to supplement his meager income by giving lectures and found in that occupation "a new pulpit," as he once wrote. Emerson's view was distinctively American in that he denied the importance of the past: "Let us unfetter ourselves of our historical associations and find a pure standard in the idea of man."

The last phrase points to Emerson's focus on humanity. Individual men and women were part of this "idea of man" in the same way that individual souls were part of a larger entity, which Emerson later called the Over-Soul. The idea of nature also corresponded to the "idea of man"—both were part of a universal whole in which people could see their souls reflected.

Over the years, Emerson's influence grew. In 1837, he excited students at Harvard with the lecture now known as "The American Scholar." In the speech, Emerson demanded that American scholars free themselves from the shackles of the past. "Our day of dependence," he declared, "our long apprenticeship to the learning of other lands, draws to a close."

A year later Emerson was invited back to Harvard to speak to a group of divinity students. His speech, "Divinity-School Address," called for a rejection of institutional religion in favor of a personal relation with God. Religious truth, Emerson said, is "an intuition. It cannot be received at secondhand." The lecture so outraged Harvard authorities (who heard in it a denial of the divinity of Jesus) that three decades passed before Emerson was allowed to speak there again.

### Twilight of an Idol

With the author's growing fame, Concord increasingly became a destination for truth-seeking young people who looked to Emerson as their guru. The young responded to Emerson's predictions that they were on the verge of a new age; intellectuals responded to his philosophical ideas about the relations among humanity, nature, and God; and society as a whole responded to his optimism.

That optimism was dealt a severe blow in 1842, when Emerson's son Waldo died of scarlet fever at the age of five. By nature a rather reserved man, Emerson had found in Waldo someone to whom he could show his love spontaneously. At the child's death he shrank into an emotional shell from which he never emerged. "How can I hope for a friend," he wrote in his journal, "who have never been one?"

In later years, Emerson suffered from a severe loss of memory and had difficulty recalling the most ordinary words. This affliction resulted in his increasing public silence, and when he did appear in public, he read from notes.

In the autumn of 1881, Walt Whitman paid Emerson a visit of respect and was asked to dinner. Whitman wrote that Emerson, "though a listener and apparently an alert one, remained silent through the whole talk and discussion. A lady friend [Louisa May Alcott] quietly took a seat next to him, to give special attention. A good color in his face, eyes clear, with the well-known expression of sweetness, and the old clear-peering aspect quite the same." Six months later Emerson was dead.

# Before You Read

## from Nature

### Make the Connection
**Quickwrite** ✏️

Emerson was exhilarated by nature's beauty and grandeur. In the presence of nature, Emerson felt he was in tune with his better self and in harmony with eternal things. How do you feel about nature? Jot down your thoughts on anything that nature has taught or revealed to you.

### Literary Focus
**Imagery**

In this essay, Emerson the poet helps Emerson the philosopher. Here Emerson *shows* us scenes of nature that have moved him; he doesn't just *tell* us how he feels. As you read, look for **imagery,** or descriptive language that appeals to your senses. How do the images help you share the writer's experiences?

> **Imagery** is the use of language to evoke a picture or a concrete sensation of a person, a thing, a place, or an experience.
> *For more on Imagery, see the Handbook of Literary and Historical Terms.*

### Reading Skills 📖
**Monitoring Your Reading**

As you read these essays, look for key passages that state or suggest a **main idea.** If a statement puzzles you, try to **paraphrase** it, or restate it in your own words. Check the footnotes, and use a dictionary to look up the definitions of difficult words. Above all, read the essay more than once, and be sure to ask questions of the text.

### Background

In his introduction to the book *Nature,* from which the following chapter is taken, Emerson offers a clue to his underlying purpose when he encourages his contemporaries to look directly at nature:

> Our age is retrospective. It builds the sepulchers [tombs] of the fathers. It writes biographies, histories, and criticism. The foregoing generations beheld God and nature face to face; we, through their eyes. Why should we not also enjoy an original relation to the universe? Why should we not have a poetry and philosophy of insight and not of tradition, and a religion by revelation to us, and not the history of theirs?

In his quest for original religious insight and a uniquely American literary expression, Emerson inspired the American renaissance. In *Nature* he made it clear to those who wished to see that the magnificent American landscape itself could be the basis for spiritual rebirth.

### Vocabulary Development

**admonishing** (ad·män′ish·iŋ) v. used as *adj.:* gently warning.

**integrate** (in′tə·grāt′) v.: unify.

**perennial** (pə·ren′ē·əl) *adj.:* persistent; constant.

**blithe** (blīth) *adj.:* carefree.

**occult** (ə·kult′) *adj.:* hidden.

**SKILLS FOCUS**

**Literary Skills**
Understand the use of imagery. Analyze an author's philosophical beliefs.

**Reading Skills**
Monitor reading by identifying main ideas and paraphrasing.

go.
hrw.
.com

**INTERNET**

Vocabulary Practice
•
More About Ralph Waldo Emerson
•
Keyword: LE7 11-2

# *from* Nature

## Ralph Waldo Emerson

To go into solitude, a man needs to retire as much from his chamber[1] as from society. I am not solitary while I read and write, though nobody is with me. But if a man would be alone, let him look at the stars. The rays that come from those heavenly worlds, will separate between him and vulgar things. One might think the atmosphere was made transparent with this design, to give man, in the heavenly bodies, the perpetual presence of the sublime.[2] Seen in the streets of cities, how great they are! If the stars should appear one night in a thousand years, how would men believe and adore; and preserve for many generations the remembrance of the city of God which had been shown! But every night come out these envoys[3] of beauty, and light the universe with their admonishing smile. ❶

The stars awaken a certain reverence, because though always present, they are always inaccessible; but all natural objects make a kindred impression, when the mind is open to their influence. Nature never wears a mean appearance. Neither does the wisest man extort all her secrets, and lose his curiosity by finding out all her perfection. Nature never became a toy to a wise spirit. The flowers, the animals, the mountains, reflected all the wisdom of his best hour, as much as they had delighted the simplicity of his childhood.

When we speak of nature in this manner, we have a distinct but most poetical sense in the mind. We mean the integrity of impression made by manifold[4] natural objects. It is this which distinguishes the stick of timber of the woodcutter, from the tree of the poet. The charming landscape which I saw this morning, is indubitably[5] made up of some twenty or thirty farms. Miller owns this field, Locke that, and Manning the woodland beyond. But none of them owns the landscape. There is a property in the horizon which no man has but he whose eye can integrate all the parts, that is, the poet. This is the best part of these men's farms, yet to this their warranty deeds[6] give no title. ❷

To speak truly, few adult persons can see nature. Most persons do not see the sun. At least they have a very superficial seeing. The sun illuminates only the eye of the man, but shines into the eye and the heart of the child. The lover of nature is he whose inward and outward senses are still truly adjusted to each other; who has retained the spirit of infancy even into the era of manhood. His intercourse with heaven and earth, becomes part of his daily food. In the presence of nature, a wild delight runs through the man, in spite of real sorrows. ❸ Nature says—he is my creature, and

❶ **According to this first paragraph, how would people respond if the stars came out only one night every thousand years?**

❷ **What can the poet's eye do when he or she looks at nature?**

❸ **How does Emerson define the "lover of nature"?**

---

1. **chamber** *n.:* room.
2. **sublime** *adj.* used as *n.:* something that inspires awe. Here, Emerson refers to the divine.
3. **envoys** *n. pl.:* messengers.
4. **manifold** *adj.:* many and varied.
5. **indubitably** *adv.:* without a doubt.
6. **warranty deeds** *n. pl.:* legal documents showing ownership of property.

**Vocabulary**

**admonishing** (ad·män′ish·iŋ) *v.* used as *adj.:* gently warning.
**integrate** (in′tə·grāt′) *v.:* unify.

maugre[7] all his impertinent griefs, he shall be glad with me. Not the sun or the summer alone, but every hour and season yields its tribute of delight; for every hour and change corresponds to and authorizes a different state of the mind, from breathless noon to grimmest midnight. Nature is a setting that fits equally well a comic or a mourning piece. In good health, the air is a cordial[8] of incredible virtue. Crossing a bare common, in snow puddles, at twilight, under a clouded sky, without having in my thoughts any occurrence of special good fortune, I have enjoyed a perfect exhilaration. Almost I fear to think how glad I am. In the woods too, a man casts off his years, as the snake his slough,[9] and at what period soever of life, is always a child. In the woods, is perpetual youth. Within these plantations of God, a decorum[10] and sanctity reign, a perennial festival is dressed, and the guest sees not how he should tire of them in a thousand years. In the woods, we return to reason and faith. There I feel that nothing can befall me in life—no disgrace, no calamity (leaving me my eyes), which nature cannot repair. Standing on the bare ground—my head bathed by the blithe air, and uplifted into infinite space—all mean egotism vanishes. I become a transparent eyeball. I am nothing. I see all. The currents of the Universal Being circulate through me; I am part or particle of God. The name of the nearest friend sounds then foreign and accidental. To be brothers, to be acquaintances—master or servant, is then a trifle and a disturbance. I am the lover of uncontained and immortal beauty. In the wilderness, I find something more dear and connate[11] than in streets or villages. In the tranquil landscape, and especially in the distant line of the horizon, man beholds somewhat[12] as beautiful as his own nature. **❹**

The greatest delight which the fields and woods minister, is the suggestion of an occult relation between man and the vegetable. I am not alone and unacknowledged. They nod to me and I to them. The waving of the boughs in the storm, is new to me and old. It takes me by surprise, and yet is not unknown. Its effect is like that of a higher thought or a better emotion coming over me, when I deemed I was thinking justly or doing right. **❺**

Yet it is certain that the power to produce this delight, does not reside in nature, but in man, or in a harmony of both. It is necessary to use these pleasures with great temperance. For, nature is not always tricked[13] in holiday attire, but the same scene which yesterday breathed perfume and glittered as for the frolic of the nymphs, is overspread with melancholy today. Nature always wears the colors of the spirit. To a man laboring under calamity, the heat of his own fire hath sadness in it. Then, there is a kind of contempt of the landscape felt by him who has just lost by death a dear friend. The sky is less grand as it shuts down over less worth in the population. **❻** ∎

> **❹ ?** What does Emerson think and feel when he stands in the woods?

> **❺ ?** What is the greatest delight the fields and woods give us, according to Emerson?

> **❻ ?** What does Emerson say about how our own moods can affect the way we look at nature?

---

7. **maugre** (mô′gər) *prep.:* archaic for "in spite of; despite."
8. **cordial** (kôr′jəl) *n.:* medicine, food, or drink that stimulates the heart.
9. **slough** (sluf) *n.:* outer layer of a snake's skin, which is shed periodically.
10. **decorum** *n.:* orderliness.
11. **connate** *adj.:* having the same nature.

12. **somewhat** *pron.:* something.
13. **tricked** *v.:* dressed up.

---

**Vocabulary**

**perennial** (pə·ren′ē·əl) *adj.:* persistent; constant.
**blithe** (blīth) *adj.:* carefree.
**occult** (ə·kult′) *adj.:* hidden.

# Before You Read

## *from* Self-Reliance

### Make the Connection

As citizens of a bold, young nation, Americans have always taken tremendous pride in their personal liberty. Emerson nourished this individualistic creed with his essay "Self-Reliance." What associations do you make with the word *self-reliance*? How does *self-reliance* differ from *selfishness* and *self-centeredness*?

### Literary Focus
#### Figures of Speech

Emerson said he was "born a poet" who sang "for the most part in prose." One sign of his poetic nature is the way he uses figures of speech in his philosophical arguments. **Figures of speech** are imaginative comparisons of things that are basically unlike. Emerson often compares abstract ideas to ordinary things or events—such as when he says, "Society is a joint-stock company." Here Emerson compares society to a business where the shareholders or owners are held personally liable.

**SKILLS FOCUS**

**Literary Skills**
Understand figures of speech.

**Reading Skills**
Interpret difficult figures of speech.

**go.hrw.com**

**INTERNET**

Vocabulary Practice
•
More About Ralph Waldo Emerson
•
Keyword: LE7 11-2

> A **figure of speech** is a word or phrase that describes one thing in terms of another, very different thing. Figures of speech are not meant to be taken literally. The most common figures of speech are **simile, metaphor, personification,** and **symbol.**
>
> *For more on Figure of Speech, see the Handbook of Literary and Historical Terms.*

### Reading Skills
#### Understanding Figures of Speech

In a good figure of speech, a characteristic of one thing helps us see the other, unlike thing in a new, imaginative way. Some of Emerson's figures of speech are difficult and require re-reading and analysis. When you come across a figure of speech—especially a complex one—ask yourself, "What do these two things have in common?" and "Why has the writer chosen this particular comparison?"

> ### Vocabulary Development
>
> **conviction** (kən·vik′shən) *n.:* fixed or strong belief.
>
> **imparted** (im·pärt′id) *v.:* revealed.
>
> **manifest** (man′ə·fəst′) *adj.:* plain; clear.
>
> **transcendent** (tran·sen′dənt) *adj.:* excelling; surpassing.
>
> **integrity** (in·teg′rə·tē) *n.:* sound moral principles; honesty.

*Long Island Farmer Husking Corn* (1833–1834) by William Sidney Mount. Oil on canvas mounted on panel (20⁷⁄₈″ × 16⁷⁄₈″).

The Long Island Museum of American Art, History and Carriages. Gift of Mr. and Mrs. Ward Melville, 1975.

# *from* Self-Reliance

## Ralph Waldo Emerson

There is a time in every man's education when he arrives at the conviction that envy is ignorance; that imitation is suicide; that he must take himself for better, for worse, as his portion; that though the wide universe is full of good, no kernel of nourishing corn can come to him but through his toil bestowed on that plot of ground which is given to him to till. The power which resides in him is new in nature, and none but he knows what that is which he can do, nor does he know until he has tried. Not for nothing one face, one character, one fact makes much impression on him, and another none. This sculpture in the memory is not without preestablished harmony. ❶ The eye was placed where one ray should fall, that it might testify of that particular ray. We but half express ourselves, and are

> ❶
> Emerson believes that each person has unique talents and passions that can be discovered only on one's own.
> ❓ What does he mean by "this sculpture in the memory"?

**Vocabulary**
**conviction** (kən·vik′shən) *n*.: fixed or strong belief.

ashamed of that divine idea which each of us represents. It may be safely trusted as proportionate[1] and of good issues, so it be faithfully imparted, but God will not have his work made manifest by cowards. A man is relieved and gay when he has put his heart into his work and done his best; but what he has said or done otherwise, shall give him no peace. It is a deliverance which does not deliver. In the attempt his genius deserts him; no muse befriends; no invention, no hope. ❷

Trust thyself: Every heart vibrates to that iron string. Accept the place the divine Providence has found for you; the society of your contemporaries, the connection of events. Great men have always done so and confided themselves childlike to the genius of their age, betraying their perception that the absolutely trustworthy was seated at their heart, working through their hands, predominating[2] in all their being. And we are now men, and must accept in the highest mind the same transcendent destiny; and not minors and invalids in a protected corner, not cowards fleeing before a revolution, but guides, redeemers, and benefactors, obeying the Almighty effort, and advancing on Chaos and the Dark. . . . ❸

These are the voices which we hear in solitude, but they grow faint and inaudible as we enter into the world. Society everywhere is in conspiracy against the manhood of every one of its members. Society is a joint-stock company in which the members agree for the better securing of his bread to each shareholder, to surrender the liberty and culture of the eater. The virtue in most request is conformity. Self-reliance is its aversion.[3] It loves not realities

> ❷
> **?** According to Emerson, when is a person relieved and happy?

> ❸
> **?** Who or what should every person trust?

and creators, but names and customs. ❹

Whoso would be a man must be a non-conformist. He who would gather immortal palms[4] must not be hindered by the name of goodness, but must explore if it be goodness. Nothing is at last sacred but the integrity of your own mind. Absolve[5] you to yourself, and you shall have the suffrage of the world. . . . ❺

A foolish consistency is the hobgoblin of little minds, adored by little statesmen and philosophers and divines. With consistency a great soul has simply nothing to do. He may as well concern himself with his shadow on the wall. Speak what you think now in hard words, and tomorrow speak what tomorrow thinks in hard words again, though it contradict everything you said today—"Ah, so you shall be sure to be misunderstood"—Is it so bad then to be misunderstood? Pythagoras was misunderstood, and Socrates, and Jesus, and Luther, and Copernicus, and Galileo, and Newton,[6] and every pure and wise spirit that ever took flesh. To be great is to be misunderstood. . . . ❻ ■

> ❹
> **?** What is the opposite, or "aversion," of self-reliance?

> ❺
> **?** According to Emerson, what must a person be?

> ❻
> **?** What does Emerson say about "foolish consistency"?

---

4. **he who . . . immortal palms:** he who would win fame. In ancient times, palm leaves were carried as a symbol of victory or triumph.
5. **absolve** *v.:* pronounce free from guilt or blame.
6. **Pythagoras . . . Newton:** people whose contributions to scientific, philosophical, and religious thought were ignored or suppressed during their lifetimes.

**Vocabulary**

**imparted** (im·pärt′id) *v.:* revealed.
**manifest** (man′ə·fəst) *adj.:* plain; clear.
**transcendent** (tran·sen′dənt) *adj.:* excelling; surpassing.
**integrity** (in·teg′rə·tē) *n.:* sound moral principles; honesty.

---

1. **proportionate** *adj.:* having a correct relationship between parts; balanced.
2. **predominating** *v.* used as *adj.:* having influence or power.
3. **aversion** *n.:* object of intense dislike or opposition.

# Response and Analysis

## from Nature

### Reading Check

1. Review each paragraph of the essay. Then, write down one statement from each paragraph that you think sums up the **main idea** of that paragraph. You should have six main ideas.

### Thinking Critically

2. In the first paragraph, Emerson says that our attitude toward the stars would change if they appeared only once every thousand years. What point is Emerson making about nature with this striking example?

3. What do you think Emerson means in the third paragraph by a "poetical sense" of looking at nature?

4. Emerson's **image** of a "transparent eyeball" in the fourth paragraph is one of the most famous passages in all of his works. (See the caricature on this page.) In your own words, tell how you interpret Emerson's image. What effect does this unusual image have on you?

5. "Nature always wears the colors of the spirit," Emerson says in the sixth paragraph. What does Emerson mean by this statement? How does the statement demonstrate Emerson's Romantic beliefs?

### Extending and Evaluating

6. "To speak truly," Emerson says, "few adult persons can see nature." Emerson sees children as having the advantage over adults when it comes to experiencing nature directly. Do you agree with Emerson? What do people seem to lose as they grow older?

7. Emerson's expectations of nature were immense, and they formed the basis of his philosophy. How would his views of nature be received today? Be sure to check your Quickwrite notes for your own thoughts about nature.

8. Implicit in the fourth paragraph is the assumption that city life can't help us feel the "currents of the Universal Being." How do you feel about this assumption?

Caricature of Emerson by Christopher Pearce Cranch from *Illustrations of the New Philosophy.*

## from Self-Reliance

### Thinking Critically

1. In the first paragraph, what do you think Emerson means by "that divine idea which each of us represents"? How does this philosophical assumption influence the entire essay?

2. Describe what Emerson compares to these things and events: planting corn, an iron string, a joint-stock company, a shadow on the wall.

*Dover Plains, Dutchess County, New York* (1848) by Asher Brown Durand. Oil on canvas (42½″ × 60½″).

National Museum of American Art/Smithsonian Institution/Art Resource, NY: Gift of Thomas M. Evans and Museum Purchase through the Smithsonian Collections Acquisition Program.

## Extending and Evaluating

3. Do you think that there is too little or too much emphasis on self-reliance and individualism in America today? What might Emerson think of today's focus on the individual?

4. "The virtue in most request is conformity," Emerson says. A paraphrase of this sentence might read: "The virtue that is most often demanded of us is that we conform to what someone else thinks." What is your opinion of this belief? Do you think this belief holds true today? Is conformity always a negative? Explain your responses.

## WRITING

### Sage Sayings

Emerson's work is filled with memorable sayings, called **aphorisms** (af′ə·riz′əmz). These are short statements that express wise or clever observations about life, such as "Trust thyself: Every heart vibrates to that iron string." Pick an aphorism from one of Emerson's writings, and write a **reflective essay** on what that saying means to you. In your essay, consider whether the statement needs updating to apply to today's world. Be sure to quote the aphorism in your essay and to tell which work of Emerson's it comes from.

▶ Use "Writing a Reflective Essay," pages 426–433, for help with this assignment.

### Analyze Emerson's Philosophy

In an **essay,** analyze one of Emerson's philosophical beliefs, about either nature or self-reliance. Be sure to use passages from the essays to support your analysis. Follow this structure:

- Tell in your own words what the philosophical belief is.

- Quote passages to support your summary.

- Make an assertion or statement of your own about the belief, and provide details to explain or support your assertion.

### Vocabulary Development
#### Yes or No?

Answer yes or no to the following questions, and justify your answers:

1. If you wanted to integrate a classroom, would you divide it into parts?

2. Is someone with perennial happiness often happy?

3. Would a jury that arrives at the conviction that a man is innocent pronounce him guilty?

4. Is an admonishing remark comforting?

5. Would you trust a person with integrity?

6. If a song gives you a transcendent feeling, does it make you joyful?

7. When you're feeling blithe, are you weighed down with worry?

8. Would a secret be imparted by you to someone you don't trust?

9. Is occult information common knowledge?

10. If you have a manifest intention, can people recognize it easily?

# Henry David Thoreau
## (1817–1862)

On July 4, 1845 (the date was apparently accidental), a young man ended a three-year stay at the house of a friend and moved to a cabin on the shores of Walden Pond in Massachusetts. He was almost twenty-eight years old and, to all appearances, a failure. He had lasted only two weeks as a schoolteacher (he refused to whip a child, then a mandatory form of punishment); his public lectures had been uninspiring; the woman to whom he had proposed marriage had turned him down; and he had little interest in the family business. Despite his impressive Harvard education, he had not realized his literary ambitions.

If ever a person looked like a self-*unmade* man, a man who had squandered the advantages of intelligence, education, and the friendship of brilliant and successful people, it was Henry David Thoreau. On top of all his other problems, Thoreau was difficult to get along with. Three days before Thoreau went to Walden, Nathaniel Hawthorne (page 249) wrote to a New York publisher that Thoreau was "tedious, tiresome, and intolerable." Hawthorne added, "And yet he has great qualities of intellect and character."

Even his closest friends had doubts about Thoreau. "He seemed born for great enterprise and for command," Ralph Waldo Emerson said years later at Thoreau's funeral, "and I so much regret the loss of his rare powers of action, that I cannot help counting it a fault in him that he had no ambition. Wanting this, instead of engineering for all America, he was

Henry David Thoreau (1856).
Photograph by Benjamin D. Maxham.

the captain of a huckleberry party."

What Emerson failed to see, and what Thoreau knew (or hoped) all along, was that by leading a berry-picking party on a jaunt in the woods he could "engineer for all America" in the most profound way. This paradox is at the center of Thoreau's life and work.

### The Student Who Wouldn't Wear Black

Thoreau was born in Concord, Massachusetts, in 1817. His father was a moderately successful manufacturer of pencils. His mother took in boarders, among them the sister of Emerson's wife, thus establishing the relationship between the two families. As a boy, Thoreau tramped the woods and fields around Concord, often with a fishing rod and seldom with a gun.

Thoreau entered Harvard in 1833 and graduated four years later. Independent and eccentric even then, he attended chapel in a green coat, "because," he wrote, "the rules required black." Thoreau never ranked higher than the middle of his class, but he was extremely well read. He became thoroughly familiar with English literature and with the German philosophers who provided many of the underpinnings of Transcendentalism.

After returning to Concord and teaching school, Thoreau went to New York in 1843, but he pined for his hometown. After six months of struggling, he gave up and returned to Concord. A friend proposed that Thoreau and he sail to Europe and work their way across the Continent, but Thoreau turned him down. He appeared to be floundering, but in fact he knew what he was doing: Thoreau's voyage would be inward, and it would depart from Walden Pond, where Emerson had offered him the use of some land.

## Walden: Life in Its Essence

The experiment at Walden Pond was an attempt to rediscover the grandeur of a simple life led close to nature. Though only two miles from town, Walden offered a focus for Thoreau's contemplative urge. "I wish to meet the facts of life," he wrote in his journal, "the vital facts, which are the phenomena or actuality the gods meant to show us . . . and so I came down here."

This private confrontation was to Thoreau's mind the truly heroic enterprise of his time. "I am glad to remember tonight as I sit by my door," he wrote on the evening of July 7, "that I too am at least a remote descendant of that heroic race of men of whom there is a tradition. I too sit here on the shore of my Ithaca, a fellow wanderer and survivor of Ulysses."

When he looked toward town, Thoreau saw his fellow citizens so caught up in making a living that they had become one-dimensional. "The mass of men," as one of the most famous sentences in *Walden* puts it, "lead lives of quiet desperation." He hoped to wake them up and show them that the heroic enterprise of confronting the "vital facts of life" lay literally in their own backyards.

*Walden*—one of the most well-known works ever produced in America—owes much of its artistic success to Thoreau's blending of style and content. He looked to nature, rather than to the stylists of the past, for a model. To Thoreau a style that imitated nature would speak fundamental spiritual truths. Thoreau wished to build sentences "which lie like boulders on the page, up and down or across; which contain the seed of other sentences, not mere repetition, but creation; which a man might sell his grounds and castles to build."

## Thoreau the Protester

It was while he was at Walden that Thoreau's other famous act took place. As a protest against the Mexican War, which he and many others saw as an attempt to extend American slaveholding territory, Thoreau refused to pay his poll tax and spent a night in jail as a result. While at Walden and again in 1851 (after the Fugitive Slave Act had been passed), Thoreau helped fugitives escaping slavery make their way to Canada. In 1859, he was one of the first defenders of John Brown, the radical abolitionist who staged a famous raid on the federal arsenal at Harpers Ferry in Virginia.

Thoreau remained at Walden for a little more than two years. In 1847, he left the cabin and moved back into the Emersons' house in exchange for a few hours a day of odd jobs and gardening. During the next few years he worked on *Walden* (which was published in 1854) and essays such as "Resistance to Civil Government" (page 235). The latter, delivered as a lecture in 1848 and published as an essay in 1849, had little immediate influence, but few essays have had such an overwhelming long-term effect on human history. It was especially important in helping to inspire the passive resistance used by Mohandas K. Gandhi in India and later by Martin Luther King, Jr., in the United States.

Thoreau moved back into his parents' house in 1848 and lived there the rest of his life. He supported himself by making pencils, taking odd jobs (he was an excellent carpenter, mason, and gardener), and doing survey work on the land around Concord. Thoreau became a kind of local record keeper, a fount of knowledge about the amount of rainfall and snowfall and the first days of frost. He could predict to the day when each wildflower in the area would bloom.

In 1860, Thoreau caught a cold, and it soon became clear that beneath the cold lay incurable tuberculosis. He faced his coming death with great calm. The town constable, Sam Staples (who had jailed Thoreau for refusing to pay his poll tax), told Emerson that he "never saw a man dying with so much pleasure and peace."

"Henry, have you made your peace with God?" his aunt is said to have asked him toward the end. "Why, Aunt," he replied, "I didn't know we had ever quarreled."

## *from* Walden, or Life in the Woods

### Make the Connection

A temporary move to a site on a large pond in Concord, Massachusetts, resulted in a work of literature that has become an American classic. Thoreau moved to Walden because he wanted to find out what life is. That is a question people still ask; it is something people the world over have always asked, when they have the leisure to think about it. As you read, imagine yourself in the woods near this pond. How would you have responded to a life that offered little more in excitement than a battle between ants, no company other than the visit of a bird?

### Literary Focus
#### Metaphor

A **metaphor** is a figure of speech that makes an imaginative comparison between two unlike things. A metaphor is direct; unlike a simile it does not use a specific word of comparison, such as *like, as, than,* or *resembles.* Thoreau's metaphors are highly visual. They are drawn from nature and from simple, everyday things that he and his audience are familiar with. To be sure you understand the points that Thoreau is making with his metaphors, try to **paraphrase** each metaphor you encounter—that is, try to explain what is being compared to what.

> A **metaphor** is a figure of speech that makes a comparison between two unlike things without using a specific word of comparison, such as *like, as, than,* or *resembles.*
>
> *For more on Metaphor, see the Handbook of Literary and Historical Terms.*

### Reading Skills
#### Making Generalizations About a Writer's Beliefs

Active readers can often make generalizations about a writer's beliefs, based on specific information they get from a text. A **generalization** is a type of **inference** in which a conclusion is drawn from explicit examples in the text. For example, after reading Thoreau, you might make this generalization: Thoreau believed people should eliminate unnecessary complexity and lead lives focused on what matters most to them.

As you read *Walden,* take notes in the form of a double-entry journal. In the left column, list Thoreau's explicit ideas. In the right column, make generalizations about Thoreau's beliefs that you think logically follow from his views.

### Vocabulary Development

**pertinent** (pʉrt′′n·ənt) *adj.*: to the point; applying to the situation.

**encumbrance** (en·kum′brəns) *n.*: burden; hindrance.

**impervious** (im·pʉr′vē·əs) *adj.*: resistant; incapable of being penetrated.

**temporal** (tem′pə·rəl) *adj.*: temporary.

**superficial** (soo′pər·fish′əl) *adj.*: not profound; shallow.

**effete** (e·fēt′) *adj.*: sterile; unproductive.

**incessantly** (in·ses′ənt·lē) *adv.*: without stopping.

**derision** (di·rizh′ən) *n.*: ridicule; contempt.

**tumultuous** (too·mul′choo·əs) *adj.*: noisy and disorderly; stormy.

**ethereal** (ē·thir′ē·əl) *adj.*: not earthly; spiritual.

**SKILLS FOCUS**

**Literary Skills**
Understand metaphor.

**Reading Skills**
Make generalizations about a writer's beliefs.

**INTERNET**

Vocabulary Practice
•
More About Henry David Thoreau
•

Keyword: LE7 11-2

*from*

# Walden, or Life in the Woods

## Henry David Thoreau

*I went to the woods because I wished to live deliberately,
to front only the essential facts of life,
and see if I could not learn what it had to teach, and not,
when I came to die, discover that I had not lived.*

## from **Economy**

When I wrote the following pages, or rather the bulk of them, I lived alone, in the woods, a mile from any neighbor, in a house which I had built myself, on the shore of Walden Pond, in Concord, Massachusetts, and earned my living by the labor of my hands only. I lived there two years and two months. At present I am a sojourner in civilized life again.

I should not obtrude my affairs so much on the notice of my readers if very particular inquiries had not been made by my townsmen concerning my mode of life, which some would call impertinent, though they do not appear to me at all impertinent, but, considering the circumstances, very natural and pertinent. Some have asked what I got to eat; if I did not feel lonesome; if I was not afraid; and the like. Others have been curious to learn what portion of my income I devoted to charitable purposes; and some, who have large families, how many poor children I maintained. I will therefore ask those of my readers who feel no particular interest in me to pardon me if I undertake to answer some of these questions in this book. In most books, the *I*, or first person, is omitted; in this it will be retained; that, in respect to egotism, is the main difference. We commonly do not remember that it is, after all, always the first person that is speaking. I should not talk so much about myself if there were anybody else whom I knew as well. Unfortunately, I am confined to this theme by the narrowness of my experience. Moreover, I, on my side, require of every writer, first or last, a simple and sincere account of his own life, and not merely what he has heard of other men's lives; some such account as he would send to his kindred from a distant land; for if he has lived sincerely, it must have been in a distant land to me. Perhaps these pages are more particularly addressed to poor students. As for the rest of my readers, they will accept such portions as apply to them. I trust that none will stretch the seams in putting on the coat, for it may do good service to him whom it fits. . . .

By the middle of April, for I made no haste in my work, but rather made the most of it, my house was framed and ready for the raising. I had already bought the shanty of James Collins, an Irishman who worked on the Fitchburg Railroad, for boards. James Collins's shanty was considered an uncommonly fine one. When I called to see it he was not at home. I walked about the outside, at first unobserved from within, the window was so deep and high. It was of small dimensions, with a peaked cottage roof, and not much else to be seen, the dirt being raised five feet all around as if it were a compost heap. The roof was the soundest part, though a good deal warped and made brittle by the sun. Doorsill there was none, but a perennial passage for the hens under the door board. Mrs. C. came to the door and asked me to view it from the inside. The hens were driven in by my approach. It was dark, and had a dirt floor for the most part, dank, clammy, and aguish,[1] only here a board and there a board which would not bear removal. She lighted a lamp to show me the inside of the roof and the walls, and also that the board floor extended under the bed, warning

---

1. **aguish** (āʹgyoo·ish) *adj.*: likely to cause ague, or fever and chills.

---

**Vocabulary**

**pertinent** (purtʹn·ənt) *adj.*: to the point; applying to the situation.

me not to step into the cellar, a sort of dust hole two feet deep. In her own words, they were "good boards overhead, good boards all around, and a good window"—of two whole squares originally, only the cat had passed out that way lately. There was a stove, a bed, and a place to sit, an infant in the house where it was born, a silk parasol, gilt-framed looking glass, and a patent new coffee mill nailed to an oak sapling, all told. The bargain was soon concluded, for James had in the meanwhile returned. I to pay four dollars and twenty-five cents tonight, he to vacate at five tomorrow morning, selling to nobody else meanwhile: I to take possession at six. It were well, he said, to be there early, and anticipate certain indistinct but wholly unjust claims on the score of ground rent and fuel. This he assured me was the only encumbrance. At six I passed him and his family on the road. One large bundle held their all—bed, coffee mill, looking glass, hens—all but the cat; she took to the woods and became a wild cat, and, as I learned afterward, trod in a trap set for woodchucks, and so became a dead cat at last.

I took down this dwelling the same morning, drawing the nails, and removed it to the pond side by small cartloads, spreading the boards on the grass there to bleach and warp back again in the sun. One early thrush gave me a note or two as I drove along the woodland path. I was informed treacherously by a young Patrick that neighbor Seeley, an Irishman, in the intervals of the carting, transferred the still tolerable, straight, and drivable nails, staples, and spikes to his pocket, and then stood when I came back to pass the time of day, and look freshly up, unconcerned, with spring thoughts, at the devastation; there being a dearth of work, as he said. He was there to represent spectatordom, and help make this seemingly insignificant event one with the removal of the gods of Troy.[2]

I dug my cellar in the side of a hill sloping to the south, where a woodchuck had formerly dug his burrow, down through sumac and blackberry roots, and the lowest stain of vegetation, six feet square by seven deep, to a fine sand where potatoes would not freeze in any winter. The sides were left shelving, and not stoned; but the sun having never shone on them, the sand still keeps its place. It was but two hours' work. I took particular pleasure in this breaking of ground, for in almost all latitudes men dig into the earth for an equable temperature. Under the most splendid house in the city is still to be found the cellar where they store their roots as of old, and long after the superstructure has disappeared posterity remark its dent in the earth. The house is still but a sort of porch at the entrance of a burrow.

At length, in the beginning of May, with the help of some of my acquaintances, rather to improve so good an occasion for neighborliness than from any necessity, I set up the frame of my house. No man was ever more honored in the character of his raisers[3] than I. They are destined, I trust, to assist at the raising of loftier structures one day. I began to occupy my house on the 4th of July, as soon as it was boarded and roofed, for the boards were carefully featheredged and lapped,[4] so that it was perfectly impervious to rain, but before boarding I laid the foundation of a chimney at one end, bringing two cartloads of stones up the hill from the pond in my arms. I built the chimney after my hoeing in the fall, before a fire became necessary for warmth, doing my cooking in the mean-

---

2. **the gods of Troy:** Thoreau loved classical allusions. Here he humorously compares taking down a little cabin to the destruction of the great ancient city of Troy. In the *Aeneid* by Virgil, the conquering Greeks carry off the images of the Trojan gods after the fall of Troy.

3. **raisers** *n.:* Thoreau's helpers included the Transcendentalist writers Ralph Waldo Emerson (page 203), Bronson Alcott, and William Ellery Channing; hence the reference in the next sentence to raising loftier structures one day.

4. **featheredged and lapped:** The edges were cut at an angle and overlapped.

while out of doors on the ground, early in the morning: which mode I still think is in some respects more convenient and agreeable than the usual one. When it stormed before my bread was baked, I fixed a few boards over the fire, and sat under them to watch my loaf, and passed some pleasant hours in that way. In those days, when my hands were much employed, I read but little, but the least scraps of paper which lay on the ground, my holder, or tablecloth, afforded me as much entertainment, in fact answered the same purpose as the *Iliad*.[5]

It would be worth the while to build still more deliberately than I did, considering, for instance, what foundation a door, a window, a cellar, a garret, have in the nature of man, and perchance never raising any superstructure until we found a better reason for it than our <u>temporal</u> necessities even. There is some of the same fitness in a man's building his own house that there is in a bird's building its own nest. Who knows but if men constructed their dwellings with their own hands, and provided food for themselves and families simply and honestly enough, the poetic faculty would be universally developed, as birds universally sing when they are so engaged? But alas! we do like cowbirds and cuckoos, which lay their eggs in nests which other birds have built, and cheer no traveler with their chattering and unmusical notes. Shall we forever resign the pleasure of construction to the carpenter? What does architecture amount to in the experience of the mass of men? I never in all my walks came across a man engaged in so simple and natural an occupation as building his house. . . .

Before winter I built a chimney, and shingled the sides of my house, which were already impervious to rain, with imperfect and sappy shingles made of the first slice of the log, whose edges I was obliged to straighten with a plane.

I have thus a tight shingled and plastered house, ten feet wide by fifteen long, and eight-foot posts, with a garret and a closet, a large window on each side, two trapdoors, one door at the end, and a brick fireplace opposite. The exact cost of my house, paying the usual price for such materials as I used, but not counting the work, all of which was done by myself, was as follows; and I give the details because very few are able to tell exactly what their houses cost, and fewer still, if any, the separate cost of the various materials which compose them—

| | | |
|---|---|---|
| Boards, | $ 8 03 ½ | Mostly shanty boards |
| Refuse shingles for roof and sides, | 4 00 | |
| Laths, | 1 25 | |
| Two secondhand windows with glass, | 2 43 | |
| One thousand old brick, | 4 00 | |
| Two casks of lime, | 2 40 | That was high |
| Hair, | 0 31 | More than I needed |
| Mantle-tree iron, | 0 15 | |
| Nails, | 3 90 | |
| Hinges and screws, | 0 14 | |
| Latch, | 0 10 | |
| Chalk, | 0 01 | |
| Transportation, | 1 40 | I carried a good part on my back |
| In all, | $28 12 ½ | |

. . . Before I finished my house, wishing to earn ten or twelve dollars by some honest and agreeable method, in order to meet my unusual expenses, I planted about two acres and a half of light and sandy soil near it chiefly with beans, but also a small part with potatoes, corn, peas, and turnips. The whole lot contains eleven acres, mostly growing up to pines and hickories, and was sold the preceding season for eight dollars and eight cents an acre. One farmer said that it was "good for nothing but to raise cheeping squirrels on." I put no manure whatever on this land, not being the owner, but merely a

---

5. the *Iliad*: Homer's epic about the Greek siege of Troy.

**Vocabulary**
**temporal** (tem′pə·rəl) *adj.*: temporary.

squatter, and not expecting to cultivate so much again, and I did not quite hoe it all once. I got out several cords of stumps in plowing, which supplied me with fuel for a long time, and left small circles of virgin mold, easily distinguishable through the summer by the greater luxuriance of the beans there. The dead and for the most part unmerchantable wood behind my house, and the driftwood from the pond, have supplied the remainder of my fuel. I was obliged to hire a team and a man for the plowing, though I held the plow myself. My farm outgoes for the first season were, for implements, seed, work, etc., $14.72½. The seed corn was given me. This never costs anything to speak of, unless you plant more than enough. I got twelve bushels of beans, and eighteen bushels of potatoes, beside some peas and sweet corn. The yellow corn and turnips were too late to come to anything. My whole income from the farm was

| | | |
|---|---:|---|
| | $23 44, | |
| Deducting the outgoes, | 14 72 | ½ |
| There are left, | $ 8 71 | ½ |

beside produce consumed and on hand at the time this estimate was made of the value of $4.50—the amount on hand much more than balancing a little grass which I did not raise. All things considered, that is, considering the importance of a man's soul and of today, notwithstanding the short time occupied by my experiment, nay, partly even because of its transient character, I believe that that was doing better than any farmer in Concord did that year. . . .

## *from* Where I Lived, and What I Lived For

. . . I went to the woods because I wished to live deliberately, to front only the essential facts of life, and see if I could not learn what it had to teach, and not, when I came to die, discover that I had not lived. I did not wish to live what was not life, living is so dear; nor did I wish to practice resignation, unless it was quite necessary. I wanted to live deep and suck out all the marrow of life, to live so sturdily and Spartan-like[6] as to put to rout all that was not life, to cut a broad swath and shave close, to drive life into a corner, and reduce it to its lowest terms, and, if it proved to be mean, why then to get the whole and genuine meanness of it, and publish its meanness to the world; or if it were sublime, to know it by experience, and be able to give a true account of it in my next excursion. For most men, it appears to me, are in a strange uncertainty about it, whether it is of the devil or of God, and have *somewhat hastily* concluded that it is the chief end of man here to "glorify God and enjoy him forever."[7]

Still we live meanly, like ants; though the fable tells us that we were long ago changed into men; like pygmies we fight with cranes;[8] it is error upon error, and clout upon clout, and our best virtue has for its occasion a superfluous and evitable[9] wretchedness. Our life is frittered away by detail. An honest man has hardly need to count more than his ten fingers, or in extreme cases he may add his ten toes, and lump the rest. Simplicity, simplicity, simplicity! I say, let your affairs be as two or three, and not a hundred or a thousand; instead of a million count half a dozen, and keep your accounts on your thumbnail. In the midst of this chopping sea of civilized life, such are the clouds and storms and quicksands and thousand-and-one items to be allowed for, that a man has to live, if he would not founder and go to the bottom and not make his port at all, by dead reckoning, and

---

6. **Spartan-like:** like the Spartans, the hardy, frugal, and highly disciplined citizens of the ancient Greek city-state Sparta.
7. **glorify . . . forever:** answer to catechism question "What is the chief end of man?"
8. **the fable . . . cranes:** In a Greek fable, Zeus changes ants into men. In the *Iliad*, Homer compares the Trojans to cranes fighting with pygmies.
9. **superfluous and evitable:** unnecessary and avoidable.

he must be a great calculator indeed who succeeds. Simplify, simplify. Instead of three meals a day, if it be necessary eat but one; instead of a hundred dishes, five; and reduce other things in proportion. Our life is like a German Confederacy,[10] made up of petty states with its boundary forever fluctuating, so that even a German cannot tell you how it is bounded at any moment. The nation itself, with all its so-called internal improvements, which, by the way are all external and superficial, is just such an unwieldy and overgrown establishment, cluttered with furniture and tripped up by its own traps, ruined by luxury and heedless expense, by want of calculation and a worthy aim, as the million households in the land; and the only cure for it, as for them, is in a rigid economy, a stern and more than Spartan simplicity of life and elevation of purpose. It lives too fast. Men think that it is essential that the *Nation* have commerce, and export ice, and talk through a telegraph, and ride thirty miles an hour, without a doubt, whether *they* do or not; but whether we should live like baboons or like men, is a little uncertain. If we do not get out sleepers,[11] and forge rails, and devote days and nights to the work, but go to tinkering upon our *lives* to improve *them,* who will build railroads? And if railroads are not built, how shall we get to heaven in season? But if we stay at home and mind our business, who will want railroads? We do not ride on the railroad; it rides upon us. Did you ever think what those sleepers are that underlie the railroad? Each one is a man, an Irishman, or a Yankee man. The rails are laid on them, and they are covered with sand, and the cars run smoothly over them. They are sound sleepers, I assure you. And every few years a new lot is laid down and run over; so that, if some have the pleasure of riding on a rail, others have the misfortune to be ridden upon. And when they run over a man that is walking in his sleep, a supernumerary[12] sleeper in the wrong position, and wake him up, they suddenly stop the cars, and make a hue and cry about it, as if this were an exception. I am glad to know that it takes a gang of men for every five miles to keep the sleepers down and level in their beds as it is, for this is a sign that they may sometime get up again. . . .

## *from* Solitude

. . . Some of my pleasantest hours were during the long rainstorms in the spring or fall, which confined me to the house for the afternoon as well as the forenoon, soothed by their ceaseless roar and pelting; when an early twilight ushered in a long evening in which many thoughts had time to take root and unfold themselves. In those driving northeast rains which tried the village houses so, when the maids stood ready with mop and pail in front entries to keep the deluge out, I sat behind my door in my little house, which was all entry, and thoroughly enjoyed its protection. In one heavy thunder-shower the lightning struck a large pitch pine across the pond, making a very conspicuous and perfectly regular spiral groove from top to bottom, an inch or more deep, and four or five inches wide, as you would groove a walking stick. I passed it again the other day, and was struck with awe on looking up and beholding that mark, now more distinct than ever, where a terrific and resistless bolt came down out of the harmless sky eight years ago. Men frequently say to me, "I should think you would feel lonesome down there, and want to be nearer to folks, rainy and snowy days and nights especially." I am tempted to reply to such—This whole earth which we inhabit is but a point in space. How far apart, think you, dwell the two most distant inhabitants of yonder star, the breadth of whose disk cannot be appreciated by our instruments?

---

10. **German Confederacy:** At the time Thoreau was writing, Germany was not yet a unified nation.
11. **sleepers** *n. pl.:* British usage for "railroad ties," so called because they lie flat.

---

12. **supernumerary** (so͞o′pər·no͞o′mə·rer′ē) *adj.:* additional; unnecessary.

**Vocabulary**
**superficial** (so͞o′pər·fish′əl) *adj.:* not profound; shallow.

*Quaker Ladies* (1956) by Andrew Wyeth. Watercolor and drypoint.

Why should I feel lonely? Is not our planet in the Milky Way? This which you put seems to me not to be the most important question. What sort of space is that which separates a man from his fellows and makes him solitary? I have found that no exertion of the legs can bring two minds much nearer to one another. What do we want most to dwell near to? Not to many men surely, the depot, the post office, the barroom, the meetinghouse, the schoolhouse, the grocery, Beacon Hill, or the Five Points, where men most congregate, but to the perennial source of our life, whence in all our experience we have found that to issue, as the willow stands near the water and sends out its roots in that direction. This will vary with different natures, but this is the place where a wise man will dig his cellar. . . .

## *from* The Bean Field

Meanwhile my beans, the length of whose rows, added together, was seven miles already planted, were impatient to be hoed, for the earliest had

Heaven knows. This was my curious labor all summer—to make this portion of the earth's surface, which had yielded only cinquefoil, blackberries, johnswort, and the like, before, sweet wild fruits and pleasant flowers, produce instead this pulse.[14] What shall I learn of beans or beans of me? I cherish them, I hoe them, early and late I have an eye to them; and this is my day's work. It is a fine broad leaf to look on. My auxiliaries are the dews and rains which water this dry soil, and what fertility is in the soil itself, which for the most part is lean and effete. My enemies are worms, cool days, and most of all woodchucks. The last have nibbled for me a quarter of an acre clean. But what right had I to oust johnswort and the rest, and break up their ancient herb garden? Soon, however, the remaining beans will be too tough for them, and go forward to meet new foes. . . .

It was a singular experience that long acquaintance which I cultivated with beans, what with planting, and hoeing, and harvesting, and threshing, and picking over and selling them—the last was the hardest of all—I might add eating, for I did taste. I was determined to know beans. When they were growing, I used to hoe from five o'clock in the morning till noon, and commonly spent the rest of the day about other affairs. Consider the intimate and curious acquaintance one makes with various kinds of weeds—it will bear some iteration in the account, for there was no little iteration in the labor—disturbing their delicate organizations so ruthlessly, and making such invidious distinctions with his hoe, leveling whole ranks of one species, and sedulously cultivating another. That's Roman wormwood—that's pigweed—that's sorrel—that's pipergrass—have at him, chop him up, turn his roots upward to the sun, don't let him have a fiber in the shade, if you do

grown considerably before the latest were in the ground; indeed they were not easily to be put off. What was the meaning of this so steady and self-respecting, this small Herculean labor, I knew not. I came to love my rows, my beans, though so many more than I wanted. They attached me to the earth, and so I got strength like Antaeus.[13] But why should I raise them? Only

---

13. **Antaeus** (an·tē′əs): in Greek mythology the giant who draws strength from the earth, his mother.

---

14. **pulse** *n.*: beans, peas, and other edible seeds of plants having pods.

**Vocabulary**
**effete** (e·fēt′) *adj.*: sterile; unproductive.

he'll turn himself t'other side up and be as green as a leek in two days. A long war, not with cranes, but with weeds, those Trojans who had sun and rain and dews on their side. Daily the beans saw me come to their rescue armed with a hoe, and thin the ranks of their enemies, filling up the trenches with weedy dead. Many a lusty crest-waving Hector,[15] that towered a whole foot above his crowding comrades, fell before my weapon and rolled in the dust. . . .

## *from* Brute Neighbors

. . . One day when I went out to my woodpile, or rather my pile of stumps, I observed two large ants, the one red, the other much larger, nearly half an inch long, and black, fiercely contending with one another. Having once got hold they never let go, but struggled and wrestled and rolled on the chips incessantly. Looking farther, I was surprised to find that the chips were covered with such combatants, that it was not a *duellum*, but a *bellum*,[16] a war between two races of ants, the red always pitted against the black, and frequently two red ones to one black. The legions of these Myrmidons[17] covered all the hills and vales in my wood yard, and the ground was already strewn with the dead and dying, both red and black. It was the only battle which I have ever witnessed, the only battlefield I ever trod while the battle was raging; internecine[18] war; the red republicans on the one hand, and the black imperialists on the other. On every side they were engaged in deadly combat, yet without any noise that I could hear, and human soldiers never fought so resolutely. I watched a couple that were fast locked in each other's embraces, in a little sunny valley amid the chips, now at noonday prepared to fight till the sun went down, or life went out. The smaller red champion had fastened himself like a vise to his adversary's front, and through all the tumblings on that field never for an instant ceased to gnaw at one of his feelers near the root, having already caused the other to go by the board; while the stronger black one dashed him from side to side, and, as I saw on looking nearer, had already divested him of several of his members. They fought with more pertinacity than bulldogs. Neither manifested the least disposition to retreat. It was evident that their battle cry was "Conquer or die." In the meanwhile there came along a single red ant on the hillside of this valley, evidently full of excitement, who either had dispatched his foe, or had not yet taken part in the battle; probably the latter, for he had lost none of his limbs; whose mother had charged him to return with his shield or upon it.[19] Or perchance he was some Achilles, who had nourished his wrath apart, and had now come to avenge or rescue his Patroclus.[20] He saw this unequal combat from afar—for the blacks were nearly twice the size of the red—he drew near with rapid pace till he stood on his guard within half an inch of the combatants; then, watching his opportunity, he sprang upon the black warrior, and commenced his operations near the root of his right foreleg, leaving the foe to select among his own members; and so there were three united for life, as if a new kind of attraction had been invented which put all other locks and cements to shame. I should not have wondered by this time to find that they had their respective musical bands stationed on some eminent chip, and playing their national airs the while, to excite the slow and cheer the dying combatants. I was myself excited somewhat even as if they had been men.

---

15. **Hector:** In the *Iliad*, Hector is the Trojan prince killed by the Greek hero Achilles.
16. **not a** *duellum,* **but a** *bellum:* not a duel, but a war.
17. **Myrmidons:** Achilles' soldiers in the *Iliad*. *Myrmex* is Greek for "ant."
18. **internecine** (in′tər·nē′sin) *adj.:* harmful to both sides of the group.

19. **return . . . upon it:** echo of the traditional charge of Spartan mothers to their warrior sons: in other words, return victorious or dead.
20. **Achilles . . . Patroclus** (pə·trō′kləs): In the *Iliad*, Achilles withdraws from the battle at Troy but rejoins the fight after his friend Patroclus is killed.

**Vocabulary**

**incessantly** (in·ses′ənt·lē) *adv.:* without stopping.

The more you think of it, the less the difference. And certainly there is not the fight recorded in Concord history, at least, if in the history of America, that will bear a moment's comparison with this, whether for the numbers engaged in it, or for the patriotism and heroism displayed. For numbers and for carnage it was an Austerlitz or Dresden.[21] Concord Fight! Two killed on the patriots' side, and Luther Blanchard wounded! Why here every ant was a Buttrick— "Fire! for God's sake fire!"—and thousands shared the fate of Davis and Hosmer.[22] There was not one hireling there. I have no doubt that it was a principle they fought for, as much as our ancestors, and not to avoid a three-penny tax on their tea; and the results of this battle will be as important and memorable to those whom it concerns as those of the Battle of Bunker Hill, at least.

I took up the chip on which the three I have particularly described were struggling, carried it into my house, and placed it under a tumbler on my windowsill, in order to see the issue. Holding a microscope to the first-mentioned red ant, I saw that, though he was assiduously gnawing at the near foreleg of his enemy, having severed his remaining feeler, his own breast was all torn away, exposing what vitals he had there to the jaws of the black warrior, whose breastplate was apparently too thick for him to pierce; and the dark carbuncles of the sufferer's eyes shone with ferocity such as war only could excite. They struggled half an hour longer under the tumbler, and when I looked again the black soldier had severed the heads of his foes from their bodies, and the still living heads were hanging on either side of him like ghastly trophies at his saddlebow, still apparently as firmly fastened as ever, and he was endeavoring with feeble struggles, being without feelers and with only the remnant of a leg, and I know not how many other wounds, to divest himself of them; which at length, after half an hour more, he accomplished. I raised the glass, and he went off over the windowsill in that crippled state. Whether he finally survived that combat, and spent the remainder of his days in some Hôtel des Invalides,[23] I do not know; but I thought that his industry would not be worth much thereafter. I never learned which party was victorious, nor the cause of the war; but I felt for the rest of that day as if I had had my feelings excited and harrowed by witnessing the struggle, the ferocity and carnage, of a human battle before my door. . . .

In the fall the loon (*Colymbus glacialis*) came, as usual, to molt and bathe in the pond, making the woods ring with his wild laughter before I had risen. At rumor of his arrival all the Milldam sportsmen are on the alert, in gigs and on foot, two by two and three by three, with patent rifles and conical balls and spyglasses. They come rustling through the woods like autumn leaves, at least ten men to one loon. Some station themselves on this side of the pond, some on that, for the poor bird cannot be omnipresent; if he dive here he must come up there. But now the kind October wind rises, rustling the leaves and rippling the surface of the water, so that no loon can be heard or seen, though his foes sweep the pond with spyglasses, and make the woods resound with their discharges. The waves generously rise and dash angrily, taking sides with all waterfowl, and our sportsmen must beat a retreat to town and shop and unfinished jobs. But they were too often successful. When I went to get a pail of water early in the morning I frequently saw this stately bird sailing out of my cove within a few rods.[24] If I endeavored to overtake him in a boat, in

---

21. **Austerlitz or Dresden:** major battles of the Napoleonic Wars.
22. **Luther . . . Hosmer:** All these men fought at the Battle of Concord, the first battle of the Revolutionary War. Maj. John Buttrick led the minutemen who defeated the British. Isaac Davis and David Hosmer were the two colonists killed.
23. **Hôtel des Invalides** (ō·tel′ dez an′vä·lēd′): Home for Disabled Soldiers, a veterans' hospital in Paris, France. The body of Napoleon I (1769–1821) is buried there.
24. **rods** *n. pl.*: one rod measures 16½ feet.

*Common Loon* (1833) by John James Audubon. Watercolor, graphite, gouache, pastel.
Collection of The New-York Historical Society, accession number 1863.17.306.

order to see how he would maneuver, he would dive and be completely lost, so that I did not discover him again, sometimes, till the latter part of the day. But I was more than a match for him on the surface. He commonly went off in a rain.

As I was paddling along the north shore one very calm October afternoon, for such days especially they settle onto the lakes, like the milkweed down, having looked in vain over the pond for a loon, suddenly one, sailing out from the shore toward the middle a few rods in front of me, set up his wild laugh and betrayed himself. I pursued with a paddle and he dived, but when he came up I was nearer than before. He dived again, but I miscalculated the direction he would take, and we were fifty rods apart when he came to the surface this time, for I had helped to widen the interval; and again he laughed long and loud, and with more reason than before. He maneuvered so cunningly that I could not get within half a dozen rods of him. Each time, when he came to the surface, turning his head this way and that, he coolly surveyed the water and the land, and apparently chose his course so that he might come up where there was the widest expanse of water and at the greatest distance from the boat. It was surprising how quickly he made up his mind and put his resolve into execution. He led me at once to the widest part of the pond, and could not be driven from it. While he was thinking one thing in his brain, I was endeavoring to divine his thought in mine. It was a pretty game, played on the smooth surface of the pond, a man against a loon. Suddenly your adversary's checker disappears beneath the board, and the problem is to place yours nearest to where his will appear again. Sometimes he would come up unexpectedly on the opposite side of me, having apparently passed directly under the boat. So long-winded was he and so unweariable, that when he had swum farthest he would immediately plunge again, nevertheless; and then no wit could divine where in the deep pond, beneath the smooth surface, he might be speeding his way like a fish, for he had time and ability to visit the bottom of the pond in its deepest part. It is said that loons have been caught in the New York lakes eighty feet beneath the surface, with hooks set for trout—though Walden is deeper than that. How surprised must the fishes be to see this ungainly visitor from another sphere speeding his way amid their schools! Yet he appeared to know his course as surely underwater as on the surface, and swam much faster there. Once or twice I saw a ripple where he approached the surface, just put his head out to reconnoiter, and instantly dived again. I found that it was as well for me to rest on my oars and wait his reappearing as to endeavor to calculate where he would rise; for again and again, when I was straining my eyes over the surface one way, I would suddenly be startled by his unearthly laugh behind me. But why, after displaying so much cunning, did he invariably betray himself the moment he came up by that loud laugh? Did not his white breast enough betray him? He was indeed a silly loon, I thought. I could commonly hear the plash of the water when he came up, and so also detected him. But after an hour he seemed as fresh as ever, dived as willingly, and swam yet farther than at first. It was surprising to see how serenely he sailed off with unruffled breast when he came to the surface, doing all the work with his webbed feet beneath. His usual note was this demoniac laughter, yet somewhat like that of a waterfowl; but occasionally, when he had balked me most successfully and come up a long way off, he uttered a long-drawn unearthly howl, probably more like that of a wolf than any bird; as when a beast puts his muzzle to the ground and deliberately howls. This was his looning—perhaps the wildest sound that is ever heard here, making the woods ring far and wide. I concluded that he laughed in derision of my efforts confident of his own resources. Though the sky was by this time overcast, the pond was so smooth that I could see where he broke the surface when I did not hear him. His white breast, the stillness of the air, and the smoothness of the water were all against him. At length, having come up fifty rods off, he uttered one of those prolonged howls, as if calling on the god of loons to aid him, and immediately there came a wind from the east and rippled the surface, and filled the whole air with misty rain, and I was impressed as if it were the prayer of the loon answered, and his god was angry with me; and so I left him disappearing far away on the tumultuous surface. . . .

## from Conclusion

. . . I left the woods for as good a reason as I went there. Perhaps it seemed to me that I had several more lives to live, and could not spare any more time for that one. It is remarkable how easily and insensibly we fall into a particular route, and make a beaten track for ourselves. I had not lived there a week before my feet wore a path from my door to the pond side; and though it is five or six years since I trod it, it is still quite distinct. It is true, I fear, that others may have fallen into it, and so helped to keep it open. The surface of the earth is soft and impressible by the feet of men; and so with the paths which the mind travels. How worn and dusty, then, must be the highways of the world, how deep the ruts of tradition and conformity! I did not wish to take a cabin passage, but rather to go before the mast and on the deck of the world, for there I could best see the moonlight amid the mountains. I do not wish to go below now.

I learned this, at least, by my experiment:

---

**Vocabulary**

**derision** (di·rizh′ən) n.: ridicule; contempt.
**tumultuous** (to͞o·mul′cho͞o·əs) adj.: noisy and disorderly; stormy.

That if one advances confidently in the direction of his dreams, and endeavors to live the life which he has imagined, he will meet with a success unexpected in common hours. He will put some things behind, will pass an invisible boundary; new, universal, and more liberal laws will begin to establish themselves around and within him; or the old laws be expanded, and interpreted in his favor in a more liberal sense, and he will live with the license of a higher order of beings. In proportion as he simplifies his life, the laws of the universe will appear less complex, and solitude will not be solitude, nor poverty poverty, nor weakness weakness. If you have built castles in the air, your work need not be lost; that is where they should be. Now put the foundations under them. . . .

Some are dinning in our ears that we Americans, and moderns generally, are intellectual dwarfs compared with the ancients, or even the Elizabethan men. But what is that to the purpose? A living dog is better than a dead lion.[25] Shall a man go and hang himself because he belongs to the race of pygmies, and not be the biggest pygmy that he can? Let everyone mind his own business, and endeavor to be what he was made.

Why should we be in such desperate haste to succeed and in such desperate enterprises? If a man does not keep pace with his companions, perhaps it is because he hears a different drummer. Let him step to the music which he hears, however measured or far away. It is not important that he should mature as soon as an apple tree or an oak. Shall he turn his spring into summer? If the condition of things which we were made for is not yet, what were any reality which we can substitute? We will not be shipwrecked on a vain reality. Shall we with pains erect a heaven of blue glass over ourselves, though when it is done we shall be sure to gaze still at the true ethereal heaven far above, as if the former were not? . . .

The life in us is like the water in the river. It may rise this year higher than man has ever known it, and flood the parched uplands; even this may be the eventful year, which will drown out all our muskrats. It was not always dry land where we dwell. I see far inland the banks which the stream anciently washed, before science began to record its freshets. Everyone has heard the story which has gone the rounds of New England, of a strong and beautiful bug which came out of the dry leaf of an old table of apple-tree wood, which had stood in a farmer's kitchen for sixty years, first in Connecticut, and afterward in Massachusetts—from an egg deposited in the living tree many years earlier still, as appeared by counting the annual layers beyond it; which was heard gnawing out for several weeks, hatched perchance by the heat of an urn. Who does not feel his faith in a resurrection and immortality strengthened by hearing of this? Who knows what beautiful and winged life, whose egg has been buried for ages under many concentric layers of woodenness in the dead dry life of society, deposited at first in the alburnum[26] of the green and living tree, which has been gradually converted into the semblance of its well-seasoned tomb—heard perchance gnawing out now for years by the astonished family of man, as they sat round the festive board—may unexpectedly come forth from amidst society's most trivial and handselled[27] furniture, to enjoy its perfect summer life at last!

I do not say that John or Jonathan[28] will realize all this; but such is the character of that morrow which mere lapse of time can never make to dawn. The light which puts out our eyes is darkness to us. Only that day dawns to which we are awake. There is more day to dawn. The sun is but a morning star. ■

---

25. **A living dog . . . lion:** Ecclesiastes 9:4.

26. **alburnum** *n.:* sapwood, soft wood between the inner bark and the hard core of a tree.
27. **handselled** *v.* used as *adj.:* given as a mere token of good wishes; therefore, of no great value in itself.
28. **John or Jonathan:** John Bull and Brother Jonathan were traditional personifications of England and the United States, respectively.

**Vocabulary**

**ethereal** (ē·thir′ē·əl) *adj.:* not earthly; spiritual.

*Don Henley (of the rock group the Eagles) founded the Walden Woods Project to protect a part of Walden Woods under threat of real estate development. Here Henley talks about how Thoreau and Emerson contributed to his "spiritual awakening" and his commitment to the preservation of Walden Woods.*

INFORMATIONAL TEXT

# *from* Heaven Is Under Our Feet

## Don Henley

I honestly don't remember when I was first introduced to the works of Henry David Thoreau or by whom. It may have been my venerable high school English teacher, Margaret Lovelace, or it may have been one of my university professors. I was lucky enough to have a few exceptional ones and that is sometimes all a kid needs—just one or two really good teachers can make all the difference in the world. It can inspire and change a life. . . .

Thoreau's writing struck me like a thunderbolt. Like all great literature, it articulated something that I knew intuitively, but could not quite bring into focus for myself. I loved Emerson, too, and his essay "Self-Reliance" was instrumental in giving me the courage to become a songwriter. The works of both men were part of a spiritual awakening in which I rediscovered my hometown and the beauty of the surrounding landscape, and, through that, some evidence of a "Higher Power," or God, if you like. This epiphany brought great comfort and relief. . . .

. . . [T]here has been a great deal of curiosity, speculation, and, in some quarters, skepticism bordering on cynicism, as to how and why I came to be involved in the movement to preserve the stomping grounds of Henry David Thoreau and his friend and mentor, Ralph Waldo Emerson. What, in other words, is California rock and roll trash doing meddling around in something as seemingly esoteric and high-minded as literature (pronounced "LIT-tra-chure"), philosophy, and history—the American Transcendentalist Movement and all its ascetic practitioners. Seems perfectly natural to me. American Literature, like the air we breathe, belongs—or should belong—to everybody. . . . The great halls of learning may keep Thoreau's literature and principles alive, but they will be of little help in fortifying the well from whence they sprang.

. . . Unfortunately, the focus of preservation efforts has come to rest on the pond and its immediate surroundings. That is all well and good, except that there remain approximately two thousand six hundred acres that are inside the historic boundaries of Walden Woods and deserve protection as well. Thoreau did not live *in* Walden Pond; he lived beside it. The man did not walk on water, he walked several miles a day through the woods, and his musings and writings therein figure at least as prominently in his literature as Walden Pond does. In other words, the width and breadth of his inspiration, the scope of his legacy is not limited to one sixty-two-acre pond, and it is absurd to think so. Walden Woods is not a pristine, grand tract of wilderness, but it is still, for the most part, exceedingly beautiful and inspiring. It is, for all intents and purposes, the cradle of the American environmental movement and should be preserved for its intrinsic, symbolic value or, as Ed Schofield, Thoreau Society president, so succinctly put it, "When Walden goes, all the issues radiating out from Walden go, too. If the prime place can be disposed of, how much easier to dispose of the issues it represents." Otherwise, we might just as well turn all our national parks, our monuments to freedom and independence, into theme parks and shopping malls.

# Response and Analysis

## Reading Check

1. According to the second paragraph in "Economy," why has Thoreau decided to write about his life?

2. How does Thoreau answer the questions implied in the title "Where I Lived, and What I Lived For"?

3. What arguments does Thoreau present in "Solitude" to demonstrate that he is not lonely in his isolated cabin?

4. What satisfactions does Thoreau find in the labor of raising beans in "The Bean Field"?

## Thinking Critically

5. Thoreau's **metaphors** are highly visual. Though they're clever and original, they aren't far-fetched. Thoreau takes his comparisons from nature and from other things he and his audience are familiar with, such as clothes and sailing. To be sure you understand Thoreau's figures of speech, **paraphrase** the following metaphors:

   a. "As for the rest of my readers, they will accept such portions as apply to them. I trust that none will stretch the seams in putting on the coat, for it may do good service to him whom it fits." (page 217)

   b. "I wanted to live deep and suck out all the marrow of life." (page 220)

   c. "If a man does not keep pace with his companions, perhaps it is because he hears a different drummer. Let him step to the music which he hears, however measured or far away." (page 228)

6. A **parable** is a very brief story that teaches a moral or ethical lesson. What do you think is the lesson of the parable involving the bug in the wood table at the conclusion of *Walden*?

7. What do you think Thoreau means in his final paragraphs by these words: "Only that day dawns to which we are awake"?

## Extending and Evaluating

8. Review the double-entry journal you kept as you read *Walden*. What **generalizations** can you make about Thoreau's beliefs? For example, you might make a generalization about Thoreau's beliefs on technological progress, based on what he says about railroads and other inventions.

Thoreau's journals and a writing box.

# WRITING

## How Romantic?

In a brief **essay,** evaluate evidence of the Romantic point of view in *Walden*—for instance, the emphasis on intuition, the power of nature, and individual autonomy. In your opinion, is Thoreau a Romantic, or can you identify strong non-Romantic strains in his thinking? (Review the characteristics of Romanticism on page 167.) Be sure to quote from *Walden* to support your evaluation.

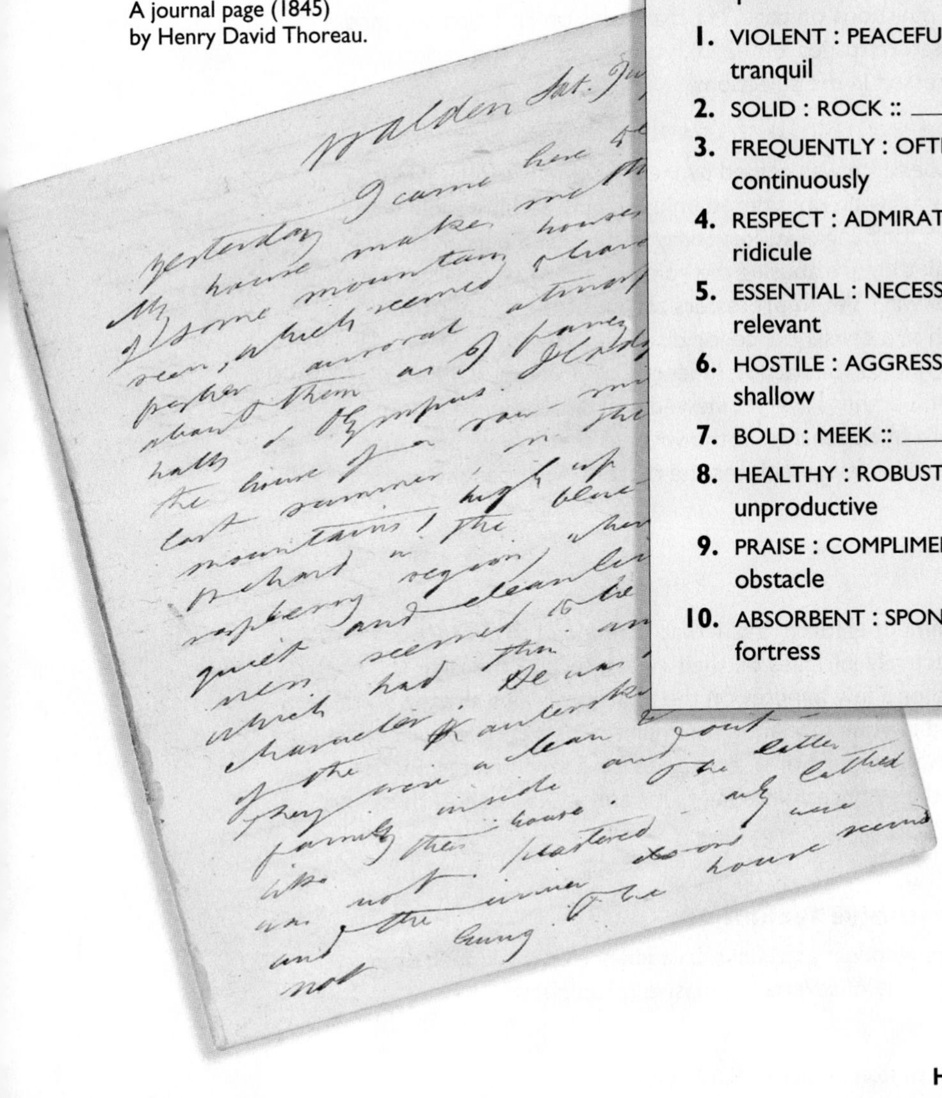

A journal page (1845) by Henry David Thoreau.

## Vocabulary Development
### Analogies

In an analogy two pairs of words have the same relationship. For example, in each pair the words could be synonyms or antonyms, or one word could describe a characteristic or be an example of the other word. Fill in each blank below with the Vocabulary word that completes the analogy. (For more help with analogies, see pages 187, 788, and 1046.)

| | |
|---|---|
| pertinent | effete |
| encumbrance | incessantly |
| impervious | derision |
| temporal | tumultuous |
| superficial | ethereal |

 1. VIOLENT : PEACEFUL :: _____ : tranquil

 2. SOLID : ROCK :: _____ : heaven

 3. FREQUENTLY : OFTEN :: _____ : continuously

 4. RESPECT : ADMIRATION :: _____ : ridicule

 5. ESSENTIAL : NECESSARY :: _____ : relevant

 6. HOSTILE : AGGRESSIVE :: _____ : shallow

 7. BOLD : MEEK :: _____ : eternal

 8. HEALTHY : ROBUST :: _____ : unproductive

 9. PRAISE : COMPLIMENT :: _____ : obstacle

10. ABSORBENT : SPONGE :: _____ : fortress

# Introduction **Comparing Points** *of* **View**
## Civil Disobedience

You will be reading the three selections listed above in this Comparing Points of View feature on civil disobedience. In the top corner of the pages in this feature, you'll find three stars. Smaller versions of the stars appear next to the questions on page 241 that focus on civil disobedience. At the end of the feature (pages 247–248), you'll compare the various points of view expressed in the selections.

### Examining the Issue: Civil Disobedience

The phrase *civil disobedience* was coined by Henry David Thoreau when he chose to disobey a law he considered unjust. Think about people who hold rallies, boycotts, or hunger strikes today to protest a perceived injustice. Do you think they are abusing the role of citizens or fulfilling that role in a responsible way? When protesters accept beatings, imprisonment, or even death as a consequence for disobeying laws they view as unjust, are they criminals or patriots? Henry David Thoreau, Mohandas K. Gandhi, and Martin Luther King, Jr., viewed civil disobedience as an important expression of citizenship. In the writings that follow, each man attempts to explain to his fellow citizens the reasons he chose the path of civil disobedience.

### Make the Connection

#### Quickwrite ✏️

Sometimes a government enforces a law that is intended to protect or benefit people but actually infringes on their rights, such as the right to free speech. Reflect for a few minutes on the policies or laws already existing or proposed in your school or community (for example, curfews, dress codes, or smoking regulations). Freewrite for a few minutes on what you think are the strongest arguments for and against one of these policies or laws.

### Reading Skills

#### Recognizing Persuasive Techniques

Speakers and writers who want to move an audience to think, feel, or act in a certain way make use of several persuasive techniques:

**SKILLS FOCUS**

Pages 232–248 cover
**Literary Skills**
Analyze points of view on a topic.

**Reading Skills**
Recognize persuasive techniques (logical, ethical, and emotional appeals).

- **Logical appeals** consist of facts, examples, and well-reasoned arguments.

  *Because 85 percent of the taxpayers are senior citizens and do not have school-age children, they should not be expected to pay for academic expenses. The school budget should be cut.*

- **Ethical appeals** are arguments based on widely accepted values or moral standards.

  *America has a long-standing tradition in which every taxpayer is obliged to support the education of our young people. If it were not for the help of all taxpayers, our young people would not get the future they deserve.*

- **Emotional appeals** consist of language and anecdotes that arouse strong feelings.

  *Senior taxpayers are sick and tired of seeing their taxes used to support expensive nonacademic programs like wrestling.*

As you read the selections that follow, note examples of each of these persuasive techniques.

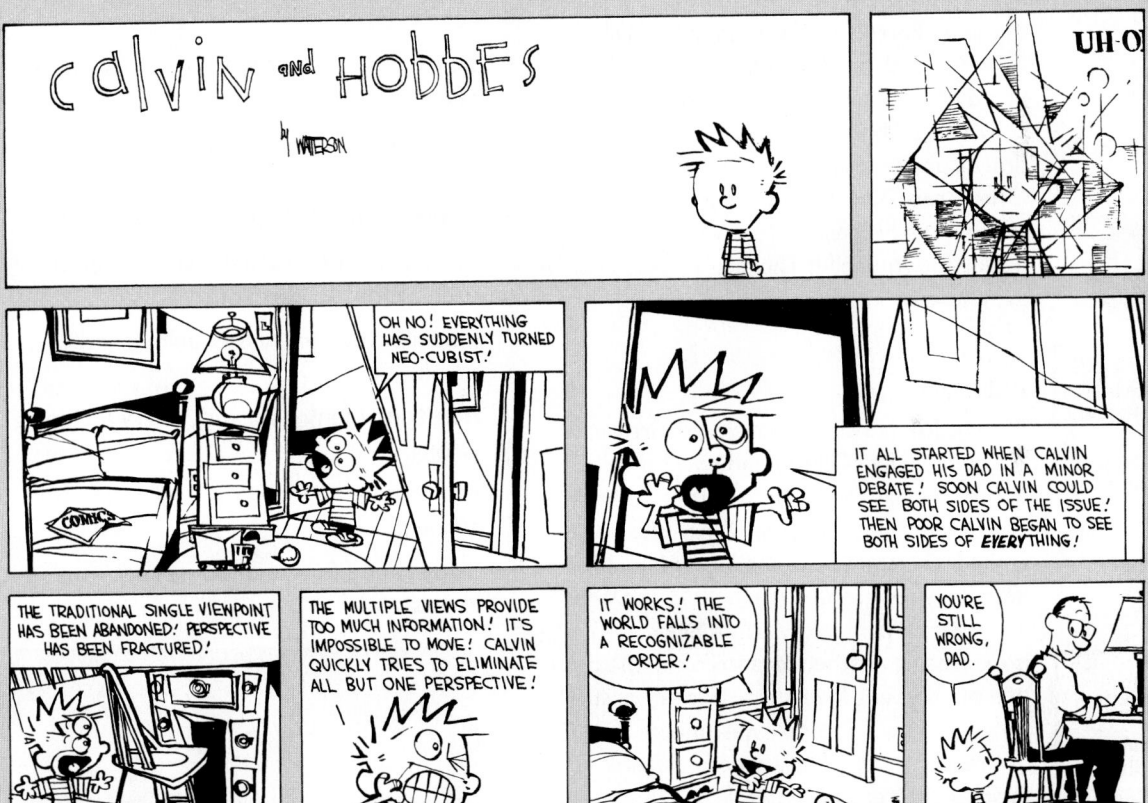

# *from* Resistance to Civil Government

## Points *of* View

In July 1846, Thoreau's stay at Walden Pond was interrupted by a night in jail. Thoreau was arrested because he refused on principle to pay a tax to the state. He refused to pay the tax because he was opposed to the U.S. war with Mexico, which he believed was an excuse to expand America's slave-holding territory. The police in Concord offered to pay the tax for Thoreau, but he refused that also. He was forced, therefore, to spend the night in jail. Thoreau might have spent more time there, except that someone, probably his aunt, paid the tax for him. This night in jail was the inspiration for the essay known as "Resistance to Civil Government" or "Civil Disobedience." Some people have suggested that the essay shows that Thoreau merely wanted to withdraw from life and all its hard questions. Others see Thoreau's action as the logical outcome of his beliefs. You will have to decide for yourself if Thoreau's position is admirable or not.

**SKILLS FOCUS**

**Literary Skills**
Analyze points of view on a topic. Understand paradox.

## Literary Focus

### Paradox

A **paradox** is a statement that expresses the complexity of life by showing how opposing ideas can be both contradictory and true at the same time. When the poet Emily Dickinson wrote the line "Much Madness is divinest Sense" (page 404), she was expressing a paradox. William Shakespeare is expressing another paradox when he has one of his young lovers say, "Parting is such sweet sorrow." Paradox was one of Thoreau's favorite literary devices; look for it as you read his essay.

**go.
hrw
.com**

**INTERNET**

**Vocabulary
Practice**

•

**More About
Henry David
Thoreau**

Keyword: LE7 11-2

---

A **paradox** is a statement that appears to be self-contradictory but that actually reveals a kind of truth.

*For more on Paradox, see the Handbook of Literary and Historical Terms.*

---

## Vocabulary Development

**expedient** (ek·spē′dē·ənt) *n.*: convenience; means to an end.

**perverted** (pər·vʉrt′id) *v.*: misdirected; corrupted.

**posterity** (päs·ter′ə·tē) *n.*: generations to come.

**alacrity** (ə·lak′rə·tē) *n.*: promptness in responding; eagerness.

**inherent** (in·hir′ənt) *adj.*: inborn; built-in.

**eradication** (ē·rad′i·kā′shən) *n.*: utter destruction; obliteration.

**insurrection** (in′sə·rek′shən) *n.*: rebellion; revolt.

**penitent** (pen′i·tənt) *adj.*: sorry for doing wrong.

**effectual** (e·fek′chōō·əl) *adj.*: productive; efficient.

**impetuous** (im·pech′ōō·əs) *adj.*: impulsive.

*from* **Resistance to Civil Government**

Henry David Thoreau

I heartily accept the motto—"That government is best which governs least";[1] and I should like to see it acted up to more rapidly and systematically. Carried out, it finally amounts to this, which also I believe—"That government is best which governs not at all"; and when men are prepared for it, that will be the kind of government which they will have. ❶ Government is at best but an expedient; but most governments are usually, and all governments are sometimes, inexpedient. The objections which have been brought against a standing army, and they are many and weighty, and deserve to prevail, may also at last be brought against a standing government. The standing army is only an arm of the standing government. The government itself, which is only the mode which the people have chosen to execute their will, is equally liable to be abused and perverted before the people can act through it. Witness the present Mexican war, the work of comparatively a few individuals using the standing government as their tool; for, in the outset, the people would not have consented to this measure.[2] ❷

This American government—what is it but a tradition, though a recent one,

> ❶
> Thoreau opens his essay with a radical **paradox:** "That government is best which governs not at all."
>
> **?** *What does Thoreau mean?*

> ❷
> Thoreau uses **logic** in providing an example of the problems with government.
>
> **?** *What is the example?*

endeavoring to transmit itself unimpaired to posterity, but each instant losing some of its integrity? It has not the vitality and force of a single living man; for a single man can bend it to his will. It is a sort of wooden gun to the people themselves; and, if ever they should use it in earnest as a real one against each other, it will surely split. But it is not the less necessary for this; for the people must have some complicated machinery or other, and hear its din, to satisfy that idea of government which they have. Governments show thus how successfully men can be imposed on, even impose on themselves, for their own advantage. It is excellent, we must all allow; yet this government never of itself furthered any enterprise, but by the alacrity with which it got out of its way. *It* does not keep the country free. *It* does not settle the West. *It* does not educate. ❸ The character inherent in the American people has done all that has been accomplished; and it would have done somewhat more, if the government had not sometimes got in its way. For government is an expedient by which men would fain[3] succeed in letting one another alone; and, as has been said, when it is most expedient, the governed are most let alone by it. Trade and commerce, if they were not made of India rubber, would never manage to bounce over the obstacles which legislators are continually putting in their way; and, if one

> ❸
> Thoreau uses an **emotional appeal** in citing what the government does *not* do.
>
> **?** *What does government not do?*

---

1. **That . . . least:** This statement, attributed to Thomas Jefferson, was the motto of the New York *Democratic Review,* which had published two of Thoreau's essays.

2. **this measure:** On May 9, 1846, President James K. Polk received word that Mexico had attacked U.S. troops. He then asked Congress to declare war, which it did on May 13. Some Americans, including Thoreau, thought the war was unjustified. Because Thoreau would not pay taxes to support the war, he went to jail.

3. **fain** *adv.:* archaic for "gladly; willingly."

**Vocabulary**

**expedient** (ek·spē′dē·ənt) *n.:* convenience; means to an end.

**perverted** (pər·vurt′id) *v.:* misdirected; corrupted.

**posterity** (päs·ter′ə·tē) *n.:* generations to come.

**alacrity** (ə·lak′rə·tē) *n.:* promptness in responding; eagerness.

**inherent** (in·hir′ənt) *adj.:* inborn; built-in.

were to judge these men wholly by the effects of their actions, and not partly by their intentions, they would deserve to be classed and punished with those mischievous persons who put obstructions on the railroads.

But, to speak practically and as a citizen, unlike those who call themselves no-government men, I ask for, not at once no government, but *at once* a better government. Let every man make known what kind of government would command his respect, and that will be one step toward obtaining it.

After all, the practical reason why, when the power is once in the hands of the people, a majority are permitted, and for a long period continue, to rule, is not because they are most likely to be in the right, nor because this seems fairest to the minority, but because they are physically the strongest. But a government in which the majority rule in all cases cannot be based on justice, even as far as men understand it. Can there not be a government in which majorities do not virtually decide right and wrong, but conscience?—in which majorities decide only those questions to which the rule of expediency is applicable? Must the citizen ever for a moment, or in the least degree, resign his conscience to the legislator? Why has every man a conscience, then? I think that we should be men first, and subjects afterward. It is not desirable to cultivate a respect for the law, so much as for the right. The only obligation which I have a right to assume, is to do at any time what I think right. . . . ❹

It is not a man's duty, as a matter of course, to devote himself to the eradication of any, even the most enormous wrong; he may still properly have other concerns to engage him; but it is his duty, at least, to wash his hands of it, and, if he gives it no thought longer, not to give it practically his support. If I devote myself to other pursuits and contemplations, I must first see, at least, that I do not pursue them sitting upon another man's shoulders. I must get off him first, that he may pursue his contemplations too. See what gross inconsistency is tolerated. I have heard some of my townsmen say, "I should like to have them order me out to help put down an insurrection of the slaves, or to march to Mexico—see if I would go"; and yet these very men have each, directly by their allegiance, and so indirectly, at least, by their money, furnished a substitute. The soldier is applauded who refuses to serve in an unjust war by those who do not refuse to sustain the unjust government which makes the war; is applauded by those whose own act and authority he disregards and sets at nought; as if the State were penitent to that degree that it hired one to scourge it while it sinned, but not to that degree that it left off sinning for a moment. Thus, under the name of order and civil government, we are all made at last to pay homage to and support our own meanness. After the first blush of sin, comes its indifference and from immoral it becomes, as it were, *un*moral, and not quite unnecessary to that life which we have made. . . . ❺

I meet this American government, or its representative the State government, directly, and face to face, once a year, no more, in the person of its tax gatherer; this is the only mode in which a man situated as I am necessarily meets it; and it then says distinctly, Recognize me; and the simplest, the most effectual, and, in the present posture of affairs, the indispensablest mode of treating with it on this head, of expressing your

> ❹
> **?** **What conflict does Thoreau see between majority rule and individual conscience?**

> ❺
> **?** **What ethical appeals does Thoreau make in this paragraph?**

---

**Vocabulary**

**eradication** (ē·rad′i·kā′shən) *n*.: utter destruction; obliteration.

**insurrection** (in′sə·rek′shən) *n*.: rebellion; revolt.

**penitent** (pen′i·tənt) *adj*.: sorry for doing wrong.

**effectual** (e·fek′chōō·əl) *adj*.: productive; efficient.

little satisfaction with and love for it, is to deny it then. My civil neighbor, the tax gatherer, is the very man I have to deal with—for it is, after all, with men and not with parchment that I quarrel—and he has voluntarily chosen to be an agent of the government. How shall he ever know well what he is and does as an officer of the government, or as a man, until he is obliged to consider whether he shall treat me, his neighbor, for whom he has respect, as a neighbor and well-disposed man, or as a maniac and disturber of the peace, and see if he can get over this obstruction to his neighborliness without a ruder and more impetuous thought or speech corresponding with his action? I know this well, that if one thousand, if one hundred, if ten men whom I could name—if ten *honest* men only—aye, if *one* HONEST man, in this State of Massachusetts, *ceasing to hold slaves,* were actually to withdraw from this copartnership, and be locked up in the county jail therefor, it would be the abolition of slavery in America. For it matters not how small the beginning may seem to be: What is once well done is done forever. . . . ❻

I have paid no poll tax[4] for six years. I was put into a jail once on this account, for one night; and, as I stood considering the walls of solid stone, two or three feet thick, the door of wood and iron, a foot thick, and the iron grating which strained the light, I could not help being struck with the foolishness of that institution which treated me as if I were mere flesh and blood and bones, to be locked up. I wondered that it should have concluded at length that this was the best use it could put me to, and had never thought to avail itself of my

> ❻
> **?** What **emotional appeal** does Thoreau make in this paragraph? Do you think he is correct about one person being able to change the system?

services in some way. I saw that, if there was a wall of stone between me and my townsmen, there was a still more difficult one to climb or break through, before they could get to be as free as I was. I did not for a moment feel confined, and the walls seemed a great waste of stone and mortar. I felt as if I alone of all my townsmen had paid my tax. They plainly did not know how to treat me, but behaved like persons who are underbred. In every threat and in every compliment there was a blunder; for they thought that my chief desire was to stand the other side of that stone wall. I could not but smile to see how industriously they locked the door on my meditations, which followed them out again without let or hindrance, and *they* were really all that was dangerous. As they could not reach me, they had resolved to punish my body; just as boys, if they cannot come at some person against whom they have a spite, will abuse his dog. I saw that the State was half-witted, that it was timid as a lone woman with her silver spoons, and that it did not know its friends from its foes, and I lost all my remaining respect for it, and pitied it. . . . ❼

The night in prison was novel and interesting enough. The prisoners in their shirt sleeves were enjoying a chat and the evening air in the doorway, when I entered. But the jailer said, "Come, boys, it is time to lock up"; and so they dispersed, and I heard the sound of their steps returning into the hollow apartments. My roommate was introduced to me by the jailer, as "a first-rate fellow and a clever man." When the door was locked, he showed me where to hang my hat, and how he managed matters there. The rooms were white-

> ❼
> **?** Why might Thoreau include this **anecdote** about the boys and the dog? What is the purpose of the comparison of the state to a woman with her silver spoons?

---

4. **poll tax:** fee some states and localities required from each citizen as a qualification for voting. It is now considered unconstitutional in the United States to charge such a tax.

---

**Vocabulary**

**impetuous** (im·pech′o͞o·əs) *adj.*: impulsive.

washed once a month; and this one, at least, was the whitest, most simply furnished, and probably the neatest apartment in the town. He naturally wanted to know where I came from, and what brought me there; and, when I had told him, I asked him in my turn how he came there, presuming him to be an honest man, of course; and, as the world goes, I believe he was. "Why," said he, "they accuse me of burning a barn; but I never did it." As near as I could discover, he had probably gone to bed in a barn when drunk, and smoked his pipe there; and so a barn was burnt. He had the reputation of being a clever man, had been there some three months waiting for his trial to come on, and would have to wait as much longer; but he was quite domesticated and contented, since he got his board for nothing, and thought that he was well treated.

He occupied one window, and I the other; and I saw, that, if one stayed there long, his principal business would be to look out the window. I had soon read all the tracts that were left there, and examined where former prisoners had broken out, and where a grate had been sawed off, and heard the history of the various occupants of that room; for I found that even here there was a history and a gossip which never circulated beyond the walls of the jail. Probably this is the only house in the town where verses are composed, which are afterward printed in a circular form, but not published. I was shown quite a long list of verses which were composed by some young men who had been detected in an attempt to escape, who avenged themselves by singing them.

I pumped my fellow prisoner as dry as I could, for fear I should never see him again; but at length he showed me which was my bed, and left me to blow out the lamp.

It was like traveling into a far country, such as I had never expected to behold, to lie there for one night. It seemed to me that I never had heard the town clock strike before, nor the evening sounds of the village; for we slept with the windows open, which were inside the grat-

ing. It was to see my native village in the light of the middle ages, and our Concord was turned into a Rhine stream, and visions of knights and castles passed before me. They were the voices of old burghers that I heard in the streets. I was an involuntary spectator and auditor of whatever was done and said in the kitchen of the adjacent village inn—a wholly new and rare experience to me. It was a closer view of my native town. I was fairly inside of it. I never had seen its institutions before. This is one of its peculiar institutions; for it is a shire town.[5] I began to comprehend what its inhabitants were about. ❽

In the morning, our breakfasts were put through the hole in the door, in small oblong square tin pans, made to fit, and holding a pint of chocolate, with brown bread, and an iron spoon. When they called for the vessels again, I was green enough to return what bread I had left; but my comrade seized it, and said that I should lay that up for lunch or dinner. Soon after, he was let out to work at haying in a neighboring field, whither he went every day, and would not be back till noon; so he bade me good day, saying that he doubted if he should see me again.

When I came out of prison—for someone interfered, and paid the tax—I did not perceive that great changes had taken place on the common, such as he observed who went in a youth, and emerged a tottering and gray-headed man; and yet a change had to my eyes come over the scene—the town, and State, and country—greater than any that mere time could effect. I saw yet more distinctly the State in which I lived. I saw to what extent the people among whom I lived could be trusted as good neighbors and friends; that their friendship was for summer

❽ ? To what does Thoreau compare his night in jail? How does he explain his unusual comparison?

---

5. **shire town:** town where a court sits, like a county seat.

weather only; that they did not greatly purpose to do right; that they were a distinct race from me by their prejudices and superstitions, as the Chinamen and Malays are; that, in their sacrifices to humanity, they ran no risks, not even to their property; that, after all, they were not so noble but they treated the thief as he had treated them, and hoped, by a certain outward observance and a few prayers, and by walking in a particular straight though useless path from time to time, to save their souls. This may be to judge my neighbors harshly; for I believe that most of them are not aware that they have such an institution as the jail in their village. ❾

> ❾
> **?** Why does Thoreau criticize his neighbors so harshly?

It was formerly the custom in our village, when a poor debtor came out of jail, for his acquaintances to salute him, looking through their fingers, which were crossed to represent the grating of a jail window, "How do ye do?" My neighbors did not thus salute me, but first looked at me, and then at one another, as if I had returned from a long journey. I was put into jail as I was going to the shoemaker's to get a shoe which was mended. When I was let out the next morning, I proceeded to finish my errand, and, having put on my mended shoe, joined a huckleberry party, who were impatient to put themselves under my conduct; and in half an hour—for the horse was soon tackled[6]—was in the midst of a huckleberry field, on one of our highest hills, two miles off; and then the State was nowhere to be seen.

---

6. **tackled** *v.:* harnessed.

This is the whole history of "My Prisons." . . .

The authority of government, even such as I am willing to submit to—for I will cheerfully obey those who know and can do better than I, and in many things even those who neither know nor can do so well—is still an impure one: To be strictly just, it must have the sanction and consent of the governed. It can have no pure right over my person and property but what I concede to it. The progress from an absolute to a limited monarchy, from a limited monarchy to a democracy, is a progress toward a true respect for the individual. Is a democracy, such as we know it, the last improvement possible in government? Is it not possible to take a step further toward recognizing and organizing the rights of man? There will never be a really free and enlightened State, until the State comes to recognize the individual as a higher and independent power, from which all its own power and authority are derived, and treats him accordingly. I please myself with imagining a State at last which can afford to be just to all men, and to treat the individual with respect as a neighbor; which even would not think it inconsistent with its own repose, if a few were to live aloof from it, not meddling with it, nor embraced by it, who fulfilled all the duties of neighbors and fellow men. A State which bore this kind of fruit, and suffered it to drop off as fast as it ripened, would prepare the way for a still more perfect and glorious State, which also I have imagined, but not yet anywhere seen. ❿ ■

> ❿
> Thoreau sums up his political ideas about ideal government.
> **?** What does he envision as a truly just government?

# Response and Analysis

## Reading Check

1. Explain what Thoreau finds wrong with majority rule. What does he say is the only obligation he has the right to assume?

2. What does Thoreau predict about slavery in America?

3. Why was Thoreau put in jail? What were his feelings about the government while he was in jail?

4. At the end of the essay, what qualities does Thoreau envision in an ideal "perfect and glorious State"?

## Thinking Critically

5. Identify the opposing ideas, and then explain the truth contained in each of these **paradoxes:**

   a. "I saw that, if there was a wall of stone between me and my towns-men, there was a still more difficult one to climb or break through, before they could get to be as free as I was." (page 238)

   b. "I felt as if I alone of all my towns-men had paid my tax." (page 238)

6. How are Thoreau's perceptions of his fellow citizens changed by his night in jail?

7. What point is Thoreau making by telling us that he got his shoe fixed and led the huckleberry party on the day he was released?

## Extending and Evaluating

8. Which of Thoreau's arguments did you find convincing, and which did you disagree with? What would be the effect on civil order if each person always followed his or her own conscience? Explain.

9. When Thoreau accepted release from jail (because someone else paid his tax), did he become just like the people he criticized—those who opposed the Mexican War and the expansion of slavery but supported it indirectly with their tax money? If he wanted to make a truly courageous and effective protest, should he have insisted on staying in jail? Explain your response.

## Literary Criticism

10. From what you know about American Romanticism (pages 162–173), would you say that the assumptions and values that Thoreau reveals in this essay are fundamentally Romantic? Explain.

11. What influences of Emerson can you find in Thoreau's "Resistance to Civil Government"?

## WRITING

### Taking a Stand 🖉

What issue is important in your community today? Select an issue you feel strongly about, and write an **essay** using "Resistance to Civil Government" as your model. Argue for or against a particular solution to the issue. (Be sure to check your Quickwrite notes.) Be aware of the kinds of appeals you are using: Emotional appeals can be powerful, but logical ones will provide stronger support. Use a chart like the one below to organize your essay:

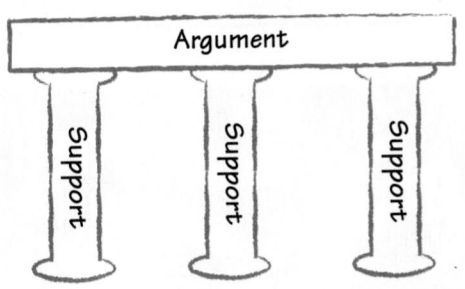

**SKILLS FOCUS**

**Literary Skills**
Analyze points of view on a topic. Analyze paradox.

**Writing Skills**
Write a persuasive essay.

**Vocabulary Skills**
Create semantic maps. Clarify word meanings.

**go.hrw.com**

**INTERNET**

**Projects and Activities**

Keyword: LE7 11-2

## Vocabulary Development

### Etymology

expedient          eradication
perverted          insurrection
posterity          penitent
alacrity           effectual
inherent           impetuous

You can learn the history of a word, or its **etymology,** by checking a good dictionary. Information about a word's etymology is usually found in brackets or parentheses before the word's definition(s). Make an etymology map like the one below for the remaining Vocabulary words in the list. In the "Related Words" box, list as many words as you can with the same origin.

| Word |
| --- |
| **insurrection** |

| Etymology |
| --- |
| from L *insurgere* |
| *in–,* = "in; upon" + *surgere,* "to rise" |

| Meaning |
| --- |
| rising up against authority; rebellion |

| Related Words |
| --- |
| insurgent, surge, resurgent, resurrect |

## Language and Style

### Determining the Precise Meanings of Words

1. "After the first blush of sin," writes Thoreau on page 237, "comes its indifference and from immoral it becomes, as it were, *unmoral.* . . ."

   a. The word *indifference* can mean "neutrality" or "apathy." What is the difference between the two meanings? Which meaning does the word *indifference* have in Thoreau's sentence?

   b. How is *unmoral* different from *immoral*?

2. Thoreau was arrested because he did not pay a "poll tax."

   a. The word *poll* comes from a Middle English word for "top of the head." Usage has added other meanings, including the sense of "individual" ("one head"). What do you think a poll tax is?

   b. What do the words *poll* and *pollster* mean today? How are they related to the sense of "head"?

Center of Concord village a few years after Thoreau met Emerson.

Courtesy Concord Free Public Library.

# Connected Readings

## Civil Disobedience

Mohandas K. Gandhi ...... *from* **On Nonviolent Resistance**

Martin Luther King, Jr. ..... *from* **Letter from Birmingham City Jail**

You have just read Thoreau's "Resistance to Civil Government" and considered the views it expresses about civil disobedience. The next two selections—by Mohandas K. Gandhi and Martin Luther King, Jr.—present other points of view on civil disobedience. After you read these two selections, you'll find questions on pages 247–248 asking you to compare all three selections.

## Points *of* View

### Before You Read

Mohandas K. Gandhi (1869–1948), leader of India's fight for independence from British rule, is considered the father of his country. As a young lawyer, Gandhi worked for the rights of Indians living under the racist and repressive government of South Africa. From the 1920s to the mid-1940s, he led a prolonged *satyagraha* (noncooperation) campaign for Indian independence from the rule of Great Britain. Though Gandhi was often arrested and imprisoned for his actions, he urged his followers to hold to the principles of nonviolent resistance even in the face of violent tactics by those in power. After independence was granted by the British crown, Gandhi, himself a Hindu, fought desperately, and in the end ineffectively, to ease the religious tension between India's Muslims and Hindus. In 1948, Gandhi was assassinated by a Hindu fanatic.

Today Mohandas K. Gandhi (also called Mahatma, meaning "Great Soul") has assumed mythic stature as the embodiment of the principle of civil disobedience, or noncooperation with unjust laws.

The following is an excerpt from a 1916 speech on the principle of *satyagraha* and its use in the fight against the South African government. The speech was made to Gandhi's Hindu supporters after a prayer meeting at Kochrab Ashram in India, the retreat that served as Gandhi's first headquarters.

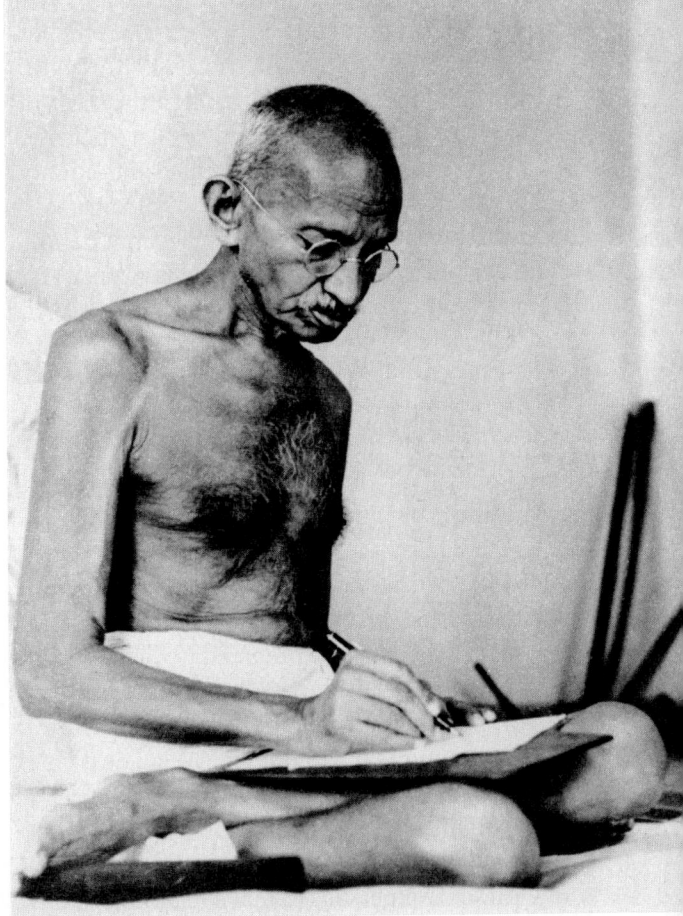

Mahatma Gandhi (August 1942).

PUBLIC · DOCUMENT

# *from* On Nonviolent Resistance

## Mohandas K. Gandhi

There are two ways of countering injustice. One way is to smash the head of the man who perpetrates injustice and to get your own head smashed in the process. All strong people in the world adopt this course. Everywhere wars are fought and millions of people are killed. The consequence is not the progress of a nation but its decline. . . . Pride makes a victorious nation bad-tempered. It falls into luxurious ways of living. Then for a time, it may be conceded, peace prevails. But after a short while, it comes more and more to be realized that the seeds of war have not been destroyed but have become a thousand times more nourished and mighty. No country has ever become, or will ever become, happy through victory in war. A nation does not rise that way; it only falls further. In fact, what comes to it is defeat, not victory. And if, perchance, either our act or our purpose was ill-conceived, it brings disaster to both belligerents.

But through the other method of combating injustice, we alone suffer the consequences of our mistakes, and the other side is wholly spared. This other method is *satyagraha*. One who resorts to it does not have to break another's head; he may merely have his own head broken. He has to be prepared to die himself suffering all the pain. In opposing the atrocious laws of the Government of South Africa, it was this method that we adopted. We made it clear to the said Government that we would never bow to its outrageous laws. No clapping is possible without two hands to do it, and no quarrel without two persons to make it. Similarly, no State is possible without two entities, the rulers and the ruled. You are our sovereign, our Government, only so long as we consider ourselves your subjects. When we are not subjects, you are not the sovereign either. So long as it is your endeavor to control us with justice and love, we will let you to do so. But if you wish to strike at us from behind, we cannot permit it. Whatever you do in other matters, you will have to ask our opinion about the laws that concern us. If you make laws to keep us suppressed in a wrongful manner and without taking us into confidence, these laws will merely adorn the statute books. We will never obey them. Award us for it what punishment you like; we will put up with it. Send us to prison and we will live there as in a paradise. Ask us to mount the scaffold and we will do so laughing. Shower what sufferings you like upon us; we will calmly endure all and not hurt a hair of your body. We will gladly die and will not so much as touch you. But so long as there is yet life in these our bones, we will never comply with your arbitrary laws.

TWENTY CENTS                                    JUNE 30, 1937

# TIME

### THE WEEKLY NEWSMAGAZINE

MOHANDAS KARAMCHAND GANDHI
"I wish to wrestle with the snake."

Martin Luther King, Jr., being booked for loitering as his stunned wife, Coretta, looks on (1958).

## Points *of* View

### Before You Read

Martin Luther King, Jr., the brilliant and eloquent leader of the U.S. civil rights movement in the 1960s, was inspired by the ideas of both Thoreau and Gandhi. King's courageous commitment to nonviolence and passive resistance captured the attention and respect of the nation. In April 1963, he led a campaign in Birmingham, Alabama, to end racial segregation at lunch counters and discrimination in hiring. While King and his supporters were on a peaceful march toward city hall, the police turned fire hoses on them and then arrested them. On April 16, 1963, while serving his sentence for marching without a permit, King wrote this open letter explaining his philosophy of nonviolent resistance.

### OPEN LETTER

# *from* Letter from Birmingham City Jail
## Martin Luther King, Jr.

You express a great deal of anxiety over our willingness to break laws. This is certainly a legitimate concern. Since we so diligently urge people to obey the Supreme Court's decision of 1954 outlawing segregation in the public schools, it is rather strange and paradoxical to find us consciously breaking laws. One may well ask, "How can you advocate breaking some laws and obeying others?" The answer is found in the fact that there are two types of laws: there are

just and there are unjust laws. I would agree with Saint Augustine that "An unjust law is no law at all."

Now what is the difference between the two? How does one determine when a law is just or unjust? A just law is a man-made code that squares with the moral law or the law of God. An unjust law is a code that is out of harmony with the moral law. . . .

An unjust law is a code inflicted upon a minority which that minority had no part in enacting or creating because they did not have the unhampered right to vote. Who can say that the legislature of Alabama which set up the segregation laws was democratically elected? Throughout the state of Alabama all types of conniving methods are used to prevent Negroes from becoming registered voters and there are some counties without a single Negro registered to vote despite the fact that the Negro constitutes a majority of the population. Can any law set up in such a state be considered democratically structured?

These are just a few examples of unjust and just laws. There are some instances when a law is just on its face and unjust in its application. For instance, I was arrested Friday on a charge of parading without a permit. Now there is nothing wrong with an ordinance which requires a permit for a parade, but when the ordinance is used to preserve segregation and to deny citizens the First Amendment privilege of peaceful assembly and peaceful protest, then it becomes unjust.

I hope you can see the distinction I am trying to point out. In no sense do I advocate evading or defying the law as the rabid segregationist would do. This would lead to anarchy. One who breaks an unjust law must do it *openly, lovingly* (not hatefully as the white mothers did in New Orleans when they were seen on television screaming, "nigger, nigger, nigger"), and with a willingness to accept the penalty. I submit that an individual who breaks a law that conscience tells him is unjust, and willingly accepts the penalty by staying in jail to arouse the conscience of the community over its injustice, is in reality expressing the very highest respect for law.

Martin Luther King, Jr., in Birmingham City Jail, November 3, 1963.

# Analysis Comparing Points of View

## Civil Disobedience

The questions on this page ask you to analyze the views on civil disobedience that were expressed in the preceding three selections.

Henry David Thoreau . . . . . *from* **Resistance to Civil Government**

Mohandas K. Gandhi . . . . . . *from* **On Nonviolent Resistance**

Martin Luther King, Jr. . . . . . *from* **Letter from Birmingham City Jail**

### Thinking Critically

1. In "Resistance to Civil Government," what does Thoreau mean by saying that he must not pursue his own interests while "sitting upon another man's shoulders. . . . I must get off him first" (page 237)? What details from the speech and letter show that Gandhi and King held this same idea?

2. Look back over the three texts, and list in chart form the **logical, ethical,** and **emotional appeals** you find in each one. Which of these arguments do you think is the most effective? Which is weakest?

| Kind of Appeal | Thoreau | Gandhi | King |
|---|---|---|---|
| Logical | | | |
| Ethical | | | |
| Emotional | | | |

3. King and Gandhi drew their inspiration from Thoreau, who argues that if one honest man truly protested slavery and went willingly to jail for his belief, "it would be the abolition of slavery" (page 238). Explain how that single night in jail serves as the "small beginning" that expanded the campaigns of King and Gandhi?

4. Each writer you have read had specific ideas about the consequence of disobeying laws. Consider the following statements:

   a. "I did not for a moment feel confined, and the walls seemed a great waste. . . ." (Thoreau)

   b. "Send us to prison and we will live there as in a paradise." (Gandhi)

   c. "[Stay] in jail to arouse the conscience of the community. . . ." (King)

   What do these statements assume about the power of ideas and moral action versus the power of walls and physical punishment?

5. Consider the consistency of the political assumptions underlying Thoreau's essay, King's letter, and Gandhi's speech. What do all three writers believe about these questions:

a. What is the ultimate source of any government's power?

b. What makes a practice or a law just or unjust?

c. What ways of resisting injustice are appropriate?

d. Must someone accept the consequences for acts of civil disobedience?

*The Problem We All Live With* (1964) by Norman Rockwell.
Photo courtesy of The Norman Rockwell Museum, Stockbridge, Massachusetts.

## WRITING

### Resisters All

Prepare and present a brief **research report** on some aspect of the history of civil disobedience or nonviolent resistance. You might do further research on one of the writers represented in this feature (Thoreau, Gandhi, King) or report on other leaders of civil disobedience movements around the world, such as Cesar Chavez (United States), Leo Tolstoy (Russia), Rosa Parks (United States), Lech Walesa (Poland), Aung San Suu Kyi (Myanmar, formerly Burma), or Nelson Mandela (South Africa). In your report, evaluate the effectiveness of using civil disobedience to resolve issues involving massive repression and resulting in violent retaliation.

▶ Use **"Reporting Historical Research," pages 602–621, for help with this assignment.**

## LISTENING AND SPEAKING

### Civil Disobedience Today

Are the principles endorsed by Thoreau, King, and Gandhi still relevant in the twenty-first century? Could these principles lead to a resolution of the violent political conflicts in the world today? Debate this issue with a classmate or with teams of classmates.

Girls leaving an elementary school in New Orleans, escorted by U.S. marshals (1960).

# Nathaniel Hawthorne
## (1804–1864)

**N**athaniel Hawthorne was an unusually handsome man, with a loving and beloved wife. By midlife he had earned recognition as a writer and won the admiration of his contemporaries. Nevertheless, he became increasingly dissatisfied, remote, and disappointing to his friends. It was as if his dark insights into the human heart had cast gloom into his own. His fiction, which has survived the changing tastes of many generations and is more admired today than when it was written, is fueled by an awareness of the guilt that accompanies a Puritan conscience. This shadow of guilt appears to have darkened Hawthorne's life.

The source of darkness is thought to lie in Hawthorne's illustrious ancestors. William Hathorne, a serious soldier and judge, came to the Massachusetts Bay Colony in 1630. Hawthorne describes him in the preamble to *The Scarlet Letter* as the "bearded, sable-cloaked, and steeple-crowned progenitor." William Hathorne's son, John, was also a judge. During the Salem witch trials of 1692, he played a minor role in sentencing nineteen of the accused to death.

By 1804, however, the year of Hawthorne's birth in Salem, the family had lost its wealth and renown. His own father, a sea captain, died during a voyage and left his grief-stricken wife with three young children to raise and few resources beyond the charity of relatives.

### Prisoner of the Dismal Chamber

Hawthorne (who added the *w* to the family name to ensure a broad *a* in its pronunciation)

*Nathaniel Hawthorne* (1840) by Charles Osgood. Oil on canvas.

Peabody Essex Museum, Salem, Massachusetts.
Photo by Mark Sexton (121.459).

attended schools in Salem and college at Bowdoin in Maine. Here, by his own judgment, he was an idle student, "rather choosing to nurse my own fancies than to dig into Greek roots." He chewed tobacco, played cards, drank wine at the taverns, and avoided intellectual company in favor of pleasure. After graduation, Hawthorne wrote to his sister Elizabeth, "I shall never make a distinguished figure in the world, and all I hope or wish is to plod along with the multitude." There is good reason to believe that this was an ironic statement, concealing an ambition that burned intensely.

Returning to Salem, Hawthorne set himself up in what he called the "dismal chamber," a room on the third floor of the family house. He kept himself a virtual prisoner there for the next twelve years, until he had learned the craft of fiction. In 1837, Hawthorne emerged to publish a collection of stories, *Twice-Told Tales.* They offer a vision of the human heart as a lurking place for the secrets of past sins. The book won Hawthorne just enough success to encourage further work.

Over the next few years, Hawthorne courted and became engaged to Sophia Peabody, and he briefly joined the utopian experiment in communal living at Brook Farm. Neither the shoveling of manure nor the endless, lofty discussions of the Transcendentalists appealed to him. After their marriage in 1842, the Hawthornes moved into the Old Manse in Concord, where Emerson had lived before them. Hawthorne often walked with Thoreau and Emerson, but no warm friendship resulted from these meetings.

## A Novel with No "Cheering Light"

Making only the barest living from his stories, Hawthorne had to accept a political appointment as surveyor to the Salem customhouse in 1846. The job freed him from financial worry, but he hated the work. In 1849, he lost the job. Despite this loss and the simultaneous death of his mother, he somehow found the energies for his masterwork, *The Scarlet Letter.* It was, he said, "positively a hell-fired story, into which I found it almost impossible to throw any cheering light."

The novel is set in Puritan Boston during the mid–seventeenth century. The title refers to a cloth letter *A* that the narrator finds in a customhouse, along with documents outlining the tragic story of Hester Prynne, who bore an illegitimate child. Refusing to name the baby's father, she was sentenced to wear the scarlet *A* (for *adultery*) on her breast. The tale is one of sin and redemption and the tragic consequences of hypocrisy and concealed guilt.

The novel's publication in 1850 brought Hawthorne wide acclaim, some money, and the admiration and friendship of Herman Melville. Another great novel, *The House of the Seven Gables,* appeared the following year.

## Out of Harmony with His Times

In 1853, President Franklin Pierce—Hawthorne's old friend from his days at Bowdoin—offered Hawthorne the post of U.S. consul at Liverpool. Hawthorne and his family lived in Europe for seven years. As an expatriate, however, he found his creativity dwindling, and he became inexplicably dejected. Even Hawthorne's return to America in 1860 was oddly cheerless. After his years abroad, he was disenchanted with both the Europe where he had been and the America from which he now felt estranged. His old friend Pierce, for whom he had written a campaign biography in 1852, had been defeated for reelection. Abraham Lincoln was in the White House, and with the onset of the Civil War, Hawthorne felt out of harmony with his times.

Back in Concord, Hawthorne found himself unable to complete the several fiction projects he had promised his publisher. His health declined. On the night of May 18, 1864, while on a trip with Pierce, Hawthorne died in a New Hampshire hotel room.

Emerson felt that Hawthorne, no longer able to endure his solitude, "died of it." After attending Hawthorne's funeral, Emerson also noted in his journal that he was sorry he hadn't known Hawthorne better. Emerson recorded this sadly ironic anecdote: "One day, when I found him on the top of his hill, in the woods, he paced back the path to his house, and said, *'This path is the only remembrance of me that will remain.'*"

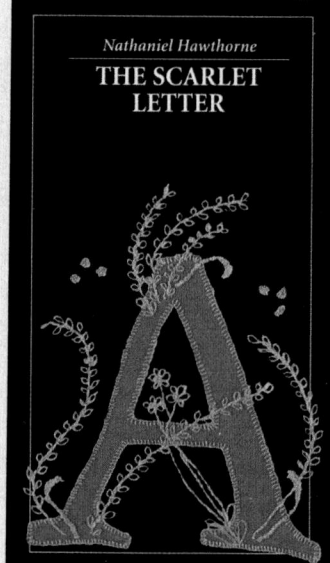

Nathaniel Hawthorne
THE SCARLET LETTER

# Before You Read

## Dr. Heidegger's Experiment

### Make the Connection
#### Quickwrite ✏️

Suppose you were given the chance to be very young again and to start your teenage years over. Would you relive your life differently, or do you think you would make the same mistakes? Jot down your thoughts on what people would do if they were given a second chance.

### Literary Focus
#### Allegory

Some stories and poems have two levels of meaning—literal and allegorical. An **allegory** is a literary work in which characters, settings, and events stand for abstract ideas or moral qualities. In some famous allegories, characters are named for the qualities they stand for: Hope, Worldly Wiseman, Little Faith, and so on. Hawthorne does not go this far, but he makes clear what his characters represent.

To recognize Hawthorne's allegory, pay close attention to the way he describes his characters. Allegorical characters are often one-dimensional, since they are meant to represent only a particular aspect of human nature. Look carefully, too, for a moral. The didactic, or instructive, purpose of most allegories is not intended to be obscure: The writer *wants* you to get the message. In some allegories the moral is so obvious that the reader is practically banged over the head with it. Hawthorne, however, is more subtle.

> An **allegory** is a story or poem in which characters, settings, and events stand for abstract ideas or moral qualities.
>
> *For more on Allegory, see the Handbook of Literary and Historical Terms.*

### Reading Skills 📖
#### Identifying Details

To interpret the allegorical meaning of Hawthorne's story, take notes on the characters and how Hawthorne describes them. Watch what they say and how they behave during the course of the story. As you review the story, fill out a **character chart** like this one:

| Characters | Key Descriptions | Actions and Words | What Character Represents |
|---|---|---|---|
| Mr. Medbourne | | | |
| Colonel Killigrew | | | |
| Mr. Gascoigne | | | |
| Widow Wycherly | | | |

### Vocabulary Development

**venerable** (ven′ər·ə·bəl) *adj.*: worthy of respect, usually by reason of age.

**infamous** (in′fə·məs) *adj.*: having a bad reputation; disgraceful.

**ponderous** (pän′dər·əs) *adj.*: very heavy.

**veracious** (və·rā′shəs) *adj.*: honest; truthful.

**effervescent** (ef′ər·ves′ənt) *adj.*: bubbling up; foaming.

**imputed** (im·pyo͞ot′id) *v.*: credited; assigned.

**delusion** (di·lo͞o′zhən) *n.*: false belief or opinion.

**deferential** (def′ər·en′shəl) *adj.*: showing respect or courteous regard.

**effaced** (ə·fāst′) *v.*: erased; wiped out.

**transient** (tran′shənt) *adj.*: temporary; passing quickly or soon.

**SKILLS FOCUS**

**Literary Skills**
Understand the characteristics of allegory.

**Reading Skills**
Identify details.

**INTERNET**

**More About Nathaniel Hawthorne**

Keyword: LE7 11-2

# Dr. Heidegger's EXPERIMENT

## Nathaniel Hawthorne

That very singular man, old Dr. Heidegger, once invited four venerable friends to meet him in his study. There were three white-bearded gentlemen, Mr. Medbourne, Colonel Killigrew, and Mr. Gascoigne, and a withered gentlewoman, whose name was the Widow Wycherly. They were all melancholy old creatures, who had been unfortunate in life, and whose greatest misfortune it was that they were not long ago in their graves. Mr. Medbourne, in the vigor of his age, had been a prosperous merchant, but had lost his all by a frantic speculation, and was now little better than a mendicant.[1] Colonel Killigrew had wasted his best years, and his health and substance, in the pursuit of sinful pleasures, which had given birth to a brood of pains, such as the gout,[2] and diverse other torments of soul and body. Mr. Gascoigne was a ruined politician, a man of evil fame, or at least had been so, till time had buried him from the knowledge of the present generation and made him obscure instead of infamous. As for the Widow Wycherly, tradition tells us that she was a great beauty in her day; but, for a long while past, she had lived in deep seclusion, on account of certain scandalous stories, which had prejudiced the gentry[3] of the town against her. It is a circumstance worth mentioning, that each of these three old gentlemen, Mr. Medbourne, Colonel Killigrew, and Mr. Gascoigne, were early lovers of the Widow Wycherly, and had once been on the point of cutting each other's throats for her sake. And, before proceeding farther, I will merely hint, that Dr. Heidegger and all his four guests were sometimes thought to be a little beside themselves; as is not unfrequently the case with old people, when worried either by present troubles or woeful recollections. ❶

"My dear old friends," said Dr. Heidegger, motioning them to be seated, "I am desirous of your assistance in one of those little experiments with which I amuse myself here in my study."

If all stories were true, Dr. Heidegger's study must have been a very curious place. It was a dim, old-fashioned chamber, festooned[4] with cobwebs, and besprinkled with antique dust. Around the walls stood several oaken book-cases, the lower shelves of which were filled with rows of gigantic folios, and black-letter quartos, and the upper with little parchment-covered

> ❶ The narrator explains that the guests had all "been unfortunate in life."
>
> ❓ What has happened to each guest?

---

4. **festooned** v. used as adj.: decorated in draping curves.

**Vocabulary**

**venerable** (ven'ər·ə·bəl) adj.: worthy of respect, usually by reason of age.

**infamous** (in'fə·məs) adj.: having a bad reputation; disgraceful.

---

1. **mendicant** (men'di·kənt) n.: beggar.
2. **gout** n.: painful disease of the joints.
3. **gentry** n.: people of high social standing.

duodecimos.[5] Over the central bookcase was a bronze bust of Hippocrates,[6] with which, according to some authorities, Dr. Heidegger was accustomed to hold consultations, in all difficult cases of his practice. In the obscurest corner of the room stood a tall and narrow oaken closet, with its door ajar, within which doubtfully appeared a skeleton. Between two of the bookcases hung a looking glass, presenting its high and dusty plate within a tarnished gilt frame. Among many wonderful stories related of this mirror, it was fabled that the spirits of all the doctor's deceased patients dwelt within its verge,[7] and would stare him in the face whenever he looked thitherward. The opposite side of the chamber was ornamented with the full-length portrait of a young lady, arrayed in the faded magnificence of silk, satin, and brocade, and with a visage[8] as faded as her dress. Above half a century ago, Dr. Heidegger had been on the point of marriage with this young lady; but, being affected with some slight disorder, she had swallowed one of her lover's prescriptions, and died on the bridal evening. The greatest curiosity of the study remains to be mentioned: It was a ponderous folio volume, bound in black leather, with massive silver clasps. There were no letters on the back, and nobody could tell the title of the book. But it was well known to be a book of magic; and once, when a chambermaid had lifted it, merely to brush away the dust, the skeleton had rattled in its closet, the picture of the young lady had stepped one foot upon the floor, and several ghastly faces had peeped forth from the mirror while the brazen head of Hippocrates frowned, and said— "Forbear!"[9]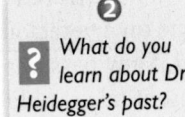

**2** *What do you learn about Dr. Heidegger's past?*

---

5. **folios ... black-letter quartos ... duodecimos:** books of different sizes. A folio is a large book made of one large printer's sheet folded once to form four pages; a black-letter quarto (from the Latin word *quarto,* meaning "fourth") is a smaller book made of a printer's sheet folded twice to form eight pages, with text set in a heavy, ornamental typeface; and a duodecimo (from the Latin *in duodecimo,* meaning "in twelve") is a smaller book made from a printer's sheet folded to form twelve pages.
6. **Hippocrates** (hi·päk′rə·tēz′): Greek physician (460?–377? B.C.) widely regarded as the father of medicine.
7. **verge** *n.:* border; boundary; enclosed area.

8. **visage** *n.:* face.
9. **forbear** *v.:* stop; cease.

**Vocabulary**
**ponderous** (pän′dər·əs) *adj.:* very heavy.

Such was Dr. Heidegger's study. On the summer afternoon of our tale, a small round table, as black as ebony, stood in the center of the room, sustaining a cut glass vase, of beautiful form and elaborate workmanship. The sunshine came through the window, between the heavy festoons of two faded damask curtains, and fell directly across this vase, so that a mild splendor was reflected from it on the ashen visages of the five old people who sat around. Four champagne glasses were also on the table.

"My dear old friends," repeated Dr. Heidegger, "may I reckon on your aid in performing an exceedingly curious experiment?"

Now Dr. Heidegger was a very strange old gentleman, whose eccentricity had become the nucleus for a thousand fantastic stories. Some of these fables, to my shame be it spoken, might possibly be traced back to mine own veracious self; and if any passages of the present tale should startle the reader's faith, I must be content to bear the stigma of a fiction-monger.[10] ❸

> ❸
> **?** What details in this paragraph might make you doubt the truth of the story?

When the doctor's four guests heard him talk of his proposed experiment, they anticipated nothing more wonderful than the murder of a mouse in an air pump, or the examination of a cobweb by the microscope, or some similar nonsense, with which he was constantly in the habit of pestering his intimates. But without waiting for a reply, Dr. Heidegger hobbled across the chamber, and returned with the same ponderous folio, bound in black leather, which common report affirmed to be a book of magic. Undoing the silver clasps, he opened the volume, and took from among its black-letter pages a rose, or what was once a rose, though now the green leaves and crimson petals had assumed one brownish hue, and the ancient flower seemed ready to crumble to dust in the doctor's hands.

"This rose," said Dr. Heidegger, with a sigh, "this same withered and crumbling flower, blos-

somed five and fifty years ago. It was given me by Sylvia Ward, whose portrait hangs yonder; and I meant to wear it in my bosom at our wedding. Five and fifty years it has been treasured between the leaves of this old volume. Now, would you deem it possible that this rose of half a century could ever bloom again?"

"Nonsense!" said the Widow Wycherly, with a peevish[11] toss of her head. "You might as well ask whether an old woman's wrinkled face could ever bloom again."

"See!" answered Dr. Heidegger.

He uncovered the vase, and threw the faded rose into the water which it contained. At first, it lay lightly on the surface of the fluid, appearing to imbibe[12] none of its moisture. Soon, however, a singular change began to be visible. The crushed and dried petals stirred, and assumed a deepening tinge of crimson, as if the flower were reviving from a deathlike slumber; the slender stalk and twigs of foliage became green; and there was the rose of half a century, looking as fresh as when Sylvia Ward had first given it to her lover. It was scarcely full-blown; for some of its delicate red leaves curled modestly around its moist bosom, within which two or three dewdrops were sparkling. ❹

> ❹
> **?** Why is the rose important to the old doctor? What supernatural event occurs when the faded rose is immersed in the water?

"That is certainly a very pretty deception," said the doctor's friends; carelessly, however, for they had witnessed greater miracles at a conjurer's show. "Pray how was it effected?"

"Did you never hear of the 'Fountain of Youth,'" asked Dr. Heidegger, "which Ponce de León,[13] the Spanish adventurer, went in search of, two or three centuries ago?"

---

10. **stigma of a fiction-monger:** mark of disgrace on a liar.

11. **peevish** *adj.:* hard to please; irritable.
12. **imbibe** *v.:* absorb.
13. **Ponce de León:** Spanish explorer Juan Ponce de León (1460?–1521), who sought the fabled Fountain of Youth in Florida.

**Vocabulary**

**veracious** (və·rā′shəs) *adj.:* honest; truthful.

"But did Ponce de León ever find it?" said the Widow Wycherly.

"No," answered Dr. Heidegger, "for he never sought it in the right place. The famous Fountain of Youth, if I am rightly informed, is situated in the southern part of the Floridian peninsula, not far from Lake Macaco. Its source is overshadowed by several gigantic magnolias, which, though numberless centuries old, have been kept as fresh as violets, by the virtues of this wonderful water. An acquaintance of mine, knowing my curiosity in such matters, has sent me what you see in the vase."

"Ahem!" said Colonel Killigrew, who believed not a word of the doctor's story, "and what may be the effect of this fluid on the human frame?"

"You shall judge for yourself, my dear colonel," replied Dr. Heidegger. "And all of you, my respected friends, are welcome to so much of this admirable fluid, as may restore to you the bloom of youth. For my own part, having had much trouble in growing old, I am in no hurry to grow young again. With your permission, therefore, I will merely watch the progress of the experiment."

While he spoke, Dr. Heidegger had been filling the four champagne glasses with the water of the Fountain of Youth. It was apparently impregnated with an effervescent gas, for little bubbles were continually ascending from the depths of the glasses and bursting in silvery spray at the surface. As the liquor diffused[14] a pleasant perfume, the old people doubted not that it possessed cordial and comfortable properties; and, though utter skeptics as to its rejuvenescent[15] power, they were inclined to swallow it at once. But Dr. Heidegger besought them to stay a moment.

"Before you drink, my respectable old friends," said he, "it would be well that, with the experience of a lifetime to direct you, you should draw up a few general rules for your guidance, in passing a second time through the perils of youth. Think what a sin and shame it would be, if, with your peculiar advantages, you should not become patterns of virtue and wisdom to all the young people of the age!" **❻**

The doctor's four venerable friends made him no answer, except by a feeble and tremulous[16] laugh; so very ridiculous was the idea that, knowing how closely repentance treads behind the steps of error, they should ever go astray again.

"Drink, then," said the doctor, bowing. "I rejoice that I have so well selected the subjects of my experiment."

With palsied[17] hands, they raised the glasses to their lips. The liquor, if it really possessed such virtues as Dr. Heidegger imputed to it, could not have been bestowed on four human beings who needed it more woefully. They looked as if they had never known what youth or pleasure was, but had been the offspring of Nature's dotage,[18] and always the gray, decrepit, sapless, miserable creatures, who now sat stooping round the doctor's table, without life enough in their souls or bodies to be animated even by the prospect of growing young again. They drank off the water, and replaced their glasses on the table.

Assuredly there was an almost immediate improvement in the aspect of the party, not unlike what might have been produced by a glass of generous wine, together with a sudden glow of cheerful sunshine, brightening over all their visages at once. There was a healthful suffusion[19] on their cheeks, instead of the ashen hue that had made them look so corpselike. They gazed at one another, and fancied that some magic power had really begun to smooth away

---

14. **diffused** *v.:* spread out; scattered widely.
15. **rejuvenescent** (ri·jōō′və·nes′ənt) *adj.:* causing renewed youthfulness.

---

16. **tremulous** *adj.:* shaking; quivering.
17. **palsied** *v.* used as *adj.:* affected by uncontrollable shaking.
18. **dotage** *n.:* feebleness that comes from old age; senility.
19. **suffusion** *n.:* spreading out of glow or color; blush.

**Vocabulary**

**effervescent** (ef′ər·ves′ənt) *adj.:* bubbling up; foaming.
**imputed** (im·pyōōt′id) *v.:* credited; assigned.

the deep and sad inscriptions which Father Time had been so long engraving on their brows. The Widow Wycherly adjusted her cap, for she felt almost like a woman again.

"Give us more of this wondrous water!" cried they, eagerly. "We are younger—but we are still too old! Quick!—give us more!"

"Patience, patience!" quoth Dr. Heidegger, who sat watching the experiment, with philosophic coolness. "You have been a long time growing old. Surely, you might be content to grow young in half an hour! But the water is at your service."

Again he filled their glasses with the liquor of youth, enough of which still remained in the vase to turn half the old people in the city to the age of their own grandchildren. While the bubbles were yet sparkling on the brim, the doctor's four guests snatched their glasses from the table, and swallowed the contents at a single gulp. Was it delusion? Even while the draft[20] was passing down their throats, it seemed to have wrought a

change on their whole systems. Their eyes grew clear and bright; a dark shade deepened among their silvery locks; they sat around the table, three gentlemen of middle age and a woman, hardly beyond her buxom prime.

"My dear widow, you are charming!" cried Colonel Killigrew, whose eyes had been fixed upon her face, while the shadows of age were flitting from it like darkness from the crimson daybreak.

The fair widow knew, of old, that Colonel Killigrew's compliments were not always measured by sober truth; so she started up and ran to the mirror, still dreading that the ugly visage of an old woman would meet her gaze. Meanwhile, the three gentlemen behaved in such a manner, as proved that the water of the Fountain of Youth possessed some intoxicating qualities; unless, indeed, their exhilaration of spirits were merely a lightsome dizziness, caused by the

---

20. **draft** *n.*: serving of a drink; large swallow.

**Vocabulary**

**delusion** (di·loo′zhən) *n.*: false belief or opinion.

sudden removal of the weight of years. Mr. Gascoigne's mind seemed to run on political topics, but whether relating to the past, present, or future, could not easily be determined, since the same ideas and phrases have been in vogue these fifty years. Now he rattled forth full-throated sentences about patriotism, national glory, and the people's right; now he muttered some perilous stuff or other, in a sly and doubtful whisper, so cautiously that even his own conscience could scarcely catch the secret; and now, again, he spoke in measured accents, and a deeply deferential tone, as if a royal ear were listening to his well-turned periods. Colonel Killigrew all this time had been trolling forth a jolly bottle song and ringing his glass in symphony with the chorus, while his eyes wandered toward the buxom figure of the Widow Wycherly. On the other side of the table, Mr. Medbourne was involved in a calculation of dollars and cents, with which was strangely intermingled a project for supplying the East Indies with ice, by harnessing a team of whales to the polar icebergs.

As for the Widow Wycherly, she stood before the mirror, curtsying and simpering[21] to her own image, and greeting it as the friend whom she loved better than all the world beside. She thrust her face close to the glass, to see whether some long-remembered wrinkle or crow's-foot had indeed vanished. She examined whether the snow had so entirely melted from her hair, that the venerable cap could be safely thrown aside. At last, turning briskly away, she came with a sort of dancing step to the table. ❻

"My dear old doctor," cried she, "pray favor me with another glass!"

> ❻
> **?** How does each elderly subject in the experiment behave after his or her metamorphosis, or change in form?

21. **simpering** *v.* used as *adv.*: smiling in a silly, self-conscious manner.

**Vocabulary**
**deferential** (def'ər·en'shəl) *adj.*: showing respect or courteous regard.

"Certainly, my dear madam, certainly!" replied the complaisant[22] doctor. "See! I have already filled the glasses."

There, in fact, stood the four glasses, brimful of this wonderful water, the delicate spray of which, as it effervesced from the surface, resembled the tremulous glitter of diamonds. It was now so nearly sunset, that the chamber had grown duskier than ever; but a mild and moon-like splendor gleamed from within the vase, and rested alike on the four guests and on the doctor's venerable figure. He sat in a high-backed, elaborately carved, oaken armchair, with a gray dignity of aspect that might have well befitted that very Father Time, whose power had never been disputed, save by this fortunate company. Even while quaffing[23] the third draft of the Fountain of Youth, they were almost awed by the expression of his mysterious visage.

But, the next moment, the exhilarating gush of young life shot through their veins. They were now in the happy prime of youth. Age, with its miserable train of cares, and sorrows, and diseases, was remembered only as the trouble of a dream, from which they had joyously awoke. The fresh gloss of the soul, so early lost, and without which the world's successive scenes had been but a gallery of faded pictures, again threw its enchantment over all their prospects. They felt like new-created beings, in a new-created universe.

"We are young! We are young!" they cried, exultingly.

Youth, like the extremity of age, had effaced the strongly marked characteristics of middle life, and mutually assimilated[24] them all. They were a group of merry youngsters, almost maddened with the exuberant frolicsomeness of their years. The most singular effect of their gaiety was an impulse to mock the infirmity and decrepitude of which they had so lately been the victims. They laughed loudly at their old-fashioned attire, the wide-skirted coats and flapped waistcoats of the young men, and the ancient cap and gown of the blooming girl. One limped across the floor, like a gouty grandfather; one set a pair of spectacles astride of his nose and pretended to pore over the black-letter pages of the book of magic; a third seated himself in an armchair and strove to imitate the venerable dignity of Dr. Heidegger. Then all shouted mirthfully, and leaped about the room. The Widow Wycherly—if so fresh a damsel could be called a widow—tripped up to the doctor's chair, with a mischievous merriment in her rosy face.

"Doctor, you dear old soul," cried she, "get up and dance with me!" And then the four young people laughed louder than ever, to think what a queer figure the poor old doctor would cut.

"Pray excuse me," answered the doctor, quietly. "I am old and rheumatic,[25] and my dancing days were over long ago. But either of these gay young gentlemen will be glad of so pretty a partner."

"Dance with me, Clara!" cried Colonel Killigrew.

"No, no, I will be her partner!" shouted Mr. Gascoigne.

"She promised me her hand, fifty years ago!" exclaimed Mr. Medbourne.

They all gathered round her. One caught both her hands in his passionate grasp—another threw his arm about her waist—the third buried his hand among the glossy curls that clustered beneath the widow's cap. Blushing, panting, struggling, chiding, laughing, her warm breath fanning each of their faces by turns, she strove to disengage herself, yet still remained in their triple embrace. Never was there a livelier picture of youthful rivalship, with bewitching beauty for the prize. Yet, by a strange deception, owing to the duskiness of the chamber, and the antique dresses which they still wore, the tall mirror is said to have reflected the figures of the three old, gray, withered grandsires, ridiculously contend-

---

22. **complaisant** *adj.*: willing to please.
23. **quaffing** *v.* used as *adj.*: deeply drinking.
24. **assimilated** *v.*: absorbed.

---

25. **rheumatic** *adj.*: suffering from rheumatism, or inflammation or pain of the joints.

**Vocabulary**

**effaced** (ə·fāst′) *v.*: erased; wiped out.

ing for the skinny ugliness of a shriveled grandam. ❼

But they were young: Their burning passions proved them so. Inflamed to madness by the coquetry[26] of the girl-widow, who neither granted nor quite withheld her favors, the three rivals began to interchange threatening glances. Still keeping hold of the fair prize, they grappled fiercely at one another's throats. As they struggled to and fro, the table was overturned, and the vase dashed into a thousand fragments. The precious Water of Youth flowed in a bright stream across the floor, moistening the wings of a butterfly, which, grown old in the decline of summer, had alighted there to die. The insect fluttered lightly through the chamber, and settled on the snowy head of Dr. Heidegger.

"Come, come, gentlemen!—come, Madam Wycherly," exclaimed the doctor, "I really must protest against this riot."

They stood still, and shivered; for it seemed as if gray Time were calling them back from their sunny youth, far down into the chill and darksome vale of years. They looked at old Dr. Heidegger, who sat in his carved armchair, holding the rose of half a century, which he had rescued from among the fragments of the shattered vase. At the motion of his hand, the four rioters resumed their seats; the more readily, because their violent exertions had wearied them, youthful though they were.

"My poor Sylvia's rose!" ejaculated Dr. Heidegger, holding it in the light of the sunset clouds. "It appears to be fading again."

And so it was. Even while the party were looking at it, the flower continued to shrivel up, till it became as dry and fragile as when the doctor had first thrown it into the vase. He shook off the few drops of moisture which clung to its petals.

"I love it as well thus, as in its dewy freshness," observed he, pressing the withered rose to his withered lips. While he spoke, the butterfly

**❼**
Recall the description of each character when he or she was young, given at the beginning of the story.

**?** How are the subjects all repeating the follies of their youth?

fluttered down from the doctor's snowy head, and fell upon the floor. ❽

His guests shivered again. A strange chillness, whether of the body or spirit they could not tell, was creeping gradually over them all. They gazed at one another, and fancied that each fleeting moment snatched away a charm, and left a deepening furrow where none had been before. Was it an illusion? Had the changes of a lifetime been crowded into so brief a space, and were they now four aged people, sitting with their old friend, Dr. Heidegger?

"Are we grown old again, so soon?" cried they, dolefully.

In truth, they had. The Water of Youth possessed merely a virtue more transient than that of wine. The delirium[27] which it created had effervesced away. Yes! they were old again. With a shuddering impulse, that showed her a woman still, the widow clasped her skinny hands before her face, and wished that the coffin lid were over it, since it could be no longer beautiful.

"Yes, friends, ye are old again," said Dr. Heidegger, "and lo! the Water of Youth is all lavished on the ground. Well—I bemoan it not; for if the fountain gushed at my very doorstep, I would not stoop to bathe my lips in it—no, though its delirium were for years instead of moments. Such is the lesson ye have taught me!"

But the doctor's four friends had taught no such lesson to themselves. They resolved forthwith to make a pilgrimage to Florida, and quaff at morning, noon, and night, from the Fountain of Youth. ❾ ∎

**❽**
The **climax** of the story is about to take place.

**?** How might the fates of the rose and the butterfly foreshadow the fates of the four guests?

**❾**
**?** What do you learn about the foolish foursome at the story's **resolution**?

---

26. **coquetry** n.: flirtatious attitude.

---

27. **delirium** n.: temporary state of extreme mental excitement, characterized by restlessness, confused speech, and hallucinations.

---

**Vocabulary**

**transient** (tran'shənt) adj.: temporary; passing quickly or soon.

## The Search for Eternal Youth

INFORMATIONAL TEXT

What is the greatest quest in the world? Many writers would answer, "The quest to conquer age and death." Thus, Dr. Heidegger's attempt to reverse the aging process is only one of many stories built on this archetypal plot.

In Greek mythology the gifted musician Orpheus is so devastated by the sudden death of his wife, Eurydice, that he descends into the dark underworld in hopes of persuading Hades, the king of the underworld, to release her. The price Orpheus pays for tampering with death is immeasurable; after being granted an opportunity to retrieve his wife, Orpheus botches the job and spends a lonely existence in the wild land of Thrace until his own horrible death. In the ancient Irish legend of Oisín, a young man who is allowed to live in Tír na nóg (the Land of Youth) asks if he can visit the real world again for just one day. Oisín disobeys a prohibition against touching the earth and instantly withers into an ancient man. The power of these early stories was twofold: They spoke to a common fear of death and aging (a particularly legitimate fear in a time when one's life expectancy was about half what it is today), and they tapped into the human desire to live forever. Nathaniel Hawthorne's tale of an afternoon spent in a doctor's study is another retelling of this well-established tradition.

### The original Fountain of Youth.

Without question the real-life adventures of Ponce de León (1460?–1521) were a great source of inspiration for "Dr. Heidegger's Experiment." You may have heard of this Spanish explorer who went on a quest for the Fountain of Youth—the legendary fountain whose waters were said to restore youth and vitality to whoever drank from them. Although the fountain was believed to be in Bimini in the Bahamas, Ponce de León's journey landed him in what is now Florida; it was Ponce de León who gave this state its name, which means "abounding in flowers." Ironically, instead of discovering the Fountain of Youth, the famed explorer encountered the opposite: He was killed in Florida by a Seminole arrow. Not even his death, however, could quell people's hope that a formula or potion for eternal life might still exist somewhere. Even as late as the twentieth century, a number of health spas with names like Fountain of Youth have cropped up throughout the United States. The spas, not some magic potion, seem to be offering the same bright promise of external youth that once lured Ponce de León into parts unknown.

### The tradition continues.

The archetypal quest-for-youth story extends throughout the nineteenth and twentieth centuries. It is found in Oscar Wilde's *The Picture of Dorian Gray* (1891), about a well-heeled gentleman whose attic contains the secret of his apparent agelessness. It is also found in Ray Bradbury's *Something Wicked This Way Comes* (1962), in which a man is given the opportunity to become as young as he likes. In these stories and others the characters who test the limits of fate are given more or less than they bargained for. Most often the results are tragic; at other times the characters receive a hard-learned lesson or an unforeseen fate. Whatever the outcome, such stories almost always point out the foolishness of refusing to accept what nature dictates. The stories may even suggest that old age is nothing to be feared: Who is to say, after all, that the greatest sorrow of Dr. Heidegger's four guests is that they have reached old age? Perhaps the true sorrow is their failure to embrace what just might have been the best years of their lives.

# Response and Analysis

## Reading Check

1. Imagine that you are Dr. Heidegger and your experiment is over. Summarize the facts of your experiment and the results. Be sure to answer the following questions: *What* happened? *Where* did it happen? To *whom* did it happen?

## Thinking Critically

2. Hawthorne makes it clear that each of Dr. Heidegger's ancient (and unlikable) guests represents a particular human vice or weakness. Identify what each **character** represents. Then, cite at least three details in the story that support your interpretation. Be sure to refer to your character chart.

3. The **setting** of this story is important. What details describing the doctor's study suggest the supernatural?

4. What is the story behind the painting in Dr. Heidegger's study? What does the painting and its story suggest about Dr. Heidegger's motivations for his experiments?

5. During the experiment, what does the mirror reflect? What do you think this mirror **symbolizes** in the story?

6. At the story's end, have the guests learned anything from the experience? How do you know?

7. What does Dr. Heidegger prove by his experiment? What has he learned?

8. An **archetype** is an original or fundamental imaginative pattern—it could be a character, a story plot, a setting, or an object. Archetypes appear across cultures and have been repeated through the ages. The Fountain of Youth is an archetype that has been used in many stories over the years. (See *A Closer Look* on page 260.) How does Hawthorne's use of this archetype reveal his views of human nature?

## WRITING

### Analyze the Moral

When Dr. Heidegger kisses the withered rose, he says, "I love it as well thus." What does he mean? How does this statement connect with the moral lesson of the **allegory**? Answer these questions in a brief **essay.**

### A Second Chance?

Refer to the notes you took before you read the story, and write a brief **response** to Hawthorne. Do you agree with his view of human nature, or do you think most people would use a second chance more wisely? Give at least one good reason to support your opinion.

---

## Vocabulary Development

### Context Clues

Explain why the underlined words are used incorrectly in each sentence below:

1. Dr. Heidegger easily lifted the light and ponderous book.

2. The widow imputed her good reputation to the gossips who scandalized her.

3. He lied so often that everyone considered him veracious.

4. The infamous colonel was well respected by the others.

5. It was easy to read the effaced inscription.

6. Mr. Gascoigne was a ruined politician and a venerable citizen.

7. The colonel received deferential treatment because of his sinful past.

8. The transient effects of the liquor never went away.

9. The doctor relied on observation, fact, and delusion.

10. Because it was effervescent, the liquor did not bubble up in the glass.

---

**SKILLS FOCUS**

**Literary Skills**
Analyze allegory.

**Reading Skills**
Identify details.

**Writing Skills**
Write an essay analyzing a moral lesson. Write a response to a story.

**Vocabulary Skills**
Use context clues to demonstrate word knowledge.

# Before You Read

## The Minister's Black Veil

### Make the Connection

The narrator of this story remarks that the "saddest of all prisons" is a person's "own heart." As you read this story, think about the world today. Do people still carry guilt for secret sins committed in the past? Can these guilty secrets isolate people from others and even from parts of themselves?

### Literary Focus
#### Symbol

A **symbol** is something that has meaning in itself but also stands for something more than itself. Hawthorne—indeed, all the dark Romantics—used symbolism as a technical strategy in his writing. As the title suggests, Hawthorne's central symbol in this story is a "horrible black veil," a "dismal shade" that separates its wearer from the world.

> A **symbol** is a person, a place, a thing, or an event that has meaning in itself and also stands for something beyond itself.
>
> *For more on Symbol, see the Handbook of Literary and Historical Terms.*

**SKILLS FOCUS**

**Literary Skills**
Understand symbolism.

**Reading Skills**
Make inferences.

### Reading Skills
#### Drawing Inferences

When you read, you make inferences all the time. When you make an **inference** about a character or an event, you are making an educated guess based on clues in the text and on your own knowledge and experience. When you come to Goodman Gray's line "Our parson has gone mad!" (page 264), stop and write down three inferences you could make, explaining why the minister has draped his face with the black material ordinarily used by mourners.

**INTERNET**

Vocabulary Practice

•

More About Nathaniel Hawthorne

•

Keyword: LE7 11-2

### Background

Like much of Hawthorne's best work, this story is set in the time of his Puritan ancestors, an era he said was "characterized by . . . gloom and piety."

Hawthorne added the following note to the story: "Another clergyman in New England, Mr. Joseph Moody, of York, Maine, who died about eighty years since, made himself remarkable by the same eccentricity that is here related of the Reverend Mr. Hooper. In this case, however, the symbol had a different import. In early life he had accidentally killed a beloved friend; and from that day till the hour of his own death, he hid his face from men."

By adding the subtitle "A Parable" to this story, Hawthorne indicates the importance of the story's moral theme. A **parable** is a short, usually simple story, based on events from ordinary life, from which a moral lesson is drawn.

### Vocabulary Development

**semblance** (sem'bləns) *n.*: outward appearance.

**obscurity** (əb·skyoor'ə·tē) *n.*: darkness.

**iniquity** (i·nik'wi·tē) *n.*: wickedness.

**ostentatious** (äs'tən·tā'shəs) *adj.*: deliberately attracting notice.

**sagacious** (sə·gā'shəs) *adj.*: wise; keenly perceptive.

**portend** (pôr·tend') *v.*: signify.

**pensively** (pen'siv·lē) *adv.*: thinking deeply or seriously.

**antipathy** (an·tip'ə·thē) *n.*: strong dislike.

**plausibility** (plô'zə·bil'ə·tē) *n.*: believability.

**resolute** (rez'ə·lōōt') *adj.*: determined.

# The Minister's BLACK VEIL

## A Parable

"He has changed himself into something awful, only by hiding his face."

## Nathaniel Hawthorne

The sexton[1] stood in the porch of Milford meetinghouse, pulling lustily at the bell rope. The old people of the village came stooping along the street. Children, with bright faces, tripped merrily beside their parents, or mimicked a graver gait, in the conscious dignity of their Sunday clothes. Spruce[2] bachelors looked sidelong at the pretty maidens, and fancied that the Sabbath sunshine made them prettier than on weekdays. When the throng had mostly streamed into the porch, the sexton began to toll the bell, keeping his eye on the Reverend Mr. Hooper's door. The first glimpse of the clergyman's figure was the signal for the bell to cease its summons.

"But what has good Parson Hooper got upon his face?" cried the sexton in astonishment.

All within hearing immediately turned about, and beheld the semblance of Mr. Hooper, pacing slowly his meditative[3] way toward the meetinghouse. With one accord they started, expressing more wonder than if some strange minister were coming to dust the cushions of Mr. Hooper's pulpit.

"Are you sure it is our parson?" inquired Goodman[4] Gray of the sexton.

"Of a certainty it is good Mr. Hooper," replied the sexton. "He was to have exchanged pulpits with Parson Shute of Westbury; but Parson Shute sent to excuse himself yesterday, being to preach a funeral sermon."

The cause of so much amazement may appear sufficiently slight. Mr. Hooper, a gentlemanly person of about thirty, though still a bachelor, was dressed with due clerical neatness, as if a careful wife had starched his band, and

---

1. **sexton** *n.:* church officer or employee whose duties may include maintenance, ringing the bells, and digging graves.
2. **spruce** *adj.:* neat in appearance.

3. **meditative** *adj.:* deeply thoughtful.
4. **Goodman:** form of polite address similar to *mister.*

**Vocabulary**
**semblance** (sem′bləns) *n.:* outward appearance.

brushed the weekly dust from his Sunday's garb. There was but one thing remarkable in his appearance. Swathed about his forehead, and hanging down over his face, so low as to be shaken by his breath, Mr. Hooper had on a black veil. On a nearer view, it seemed to consist of two folds of crape,[5] which entirely concealed his features, except the mouth and chin, but probably did not intercept his sight, farther than to give a darkened aspect to all living and inanimate[6] things. With this gloomy shade before him, good Mr. Hooper walked onward, at a slow and quiet pace, stooping somewhat and looking on the ground, as is customary with abstracted[7] men, yet nodding kindly to those of his parishioners who still waited on the meetinghouse steps. But so wonder-struck were they, that his greeting hardly met with a return.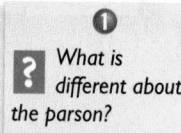

**?** What is different about the parson?

"I can't really feel as if good Mr. Hooper's face was behind that piece of crape," said the sexton.

"I don't like it," muttered an old woman, as she hobbled into the meetinghouse. "He has changed himself into something awful, only by hiding his face."

"Our parson has gone mad!" cried Goodman Gray, following him across the threshold.

A rumor of some unaccountable phenomenon had preceded Mr. Hooper into the meetinghouse, and set all the congregation astir. Few could refrain from twisting their heads toward the door; many stood upright, and turned directly about; while several little boys clambered upon the seats, and came down again with a terrible racket. There was a general bustle, a rustling of the women's gowns and shuffling of the men's feet, greatly at variance[8] with that hushed repose which should attend the entrance of the minister. But Mr. Hooper appeared not to notice the perturbation[9] of his people. He entered with an almost noiseless step, bent his head mildly to the pews on each side, and bowed as he passed his oldest parishioner, a white-haired great-grandsire, who occupied an armchair in the center of the aisle. It was strange to observe, how slowly this venerable man became conscious of something singular in the appearance of his pastor. He seemed not fully to partake of the prevailing wonder, till Mr. Hooper had ascended the stairs, and showed himself in the pulpit, face to face with his congregation, except for the black veil. That mysterious emblem was never once withdrawn. It shook with his measured breath as he gave out the psalm; it threw its obscurity between him and the holy page, as he read the Scriptures; and while he prayed, the veil lay heavily on his uplifted countenance. Did he seek to hide it from the dread Being whom he was addressing?

Such was the effect of this simple piece of crape, that more than one woman of delicate nerves was forced to leave the meetinghouse. Yet perhaps the pale-faced congregation was almost as fearful a sight to the minister, as his black veil to them.

Mr. Hooper had the reputation of a good preacher, but not an energetic one: He strove to win his people heavenward, by mild persuasive influences, rather than to drive them thither, by the thunders of the Word. The sermon which he now delivered, was marked by the same characteristics of style and manner, as the general series of his pulpit oratory. But there was something, either in the sentiment of the discourse itself, or in the imagination of the auditors, which made it greatly the most powerful effort that they had ever heard from their pastor's lips. It was tinged, rather more darkly than usual, with the gentle gloom of Mr. Hooper's temperament. The subject had reference to secret sin,

---

5. **crape** *n.*: kind of black cloth worn as a sign of mourning; from the French word *crêpe*.
6. **inanimate** *adj.*: lifeless.
7. **abstracted** *adj.*: lost in thought.
8. **at variance:** not in agreement.

---

9. **perturbation** *n.*: state of alarm.

---

**Vocabulary**
**obscurity** (əb·skyoor′ə·tē) *n.*: darkness.

and those sad mysteries which we hide from our nearest and dearest, and would fain conceal from our own consciousness, even forgetting that the Omniscient[10] can detect them. A subtle power was breathed into his words. Each member of the congregation, the most innocent girl, and the man of hardened breast, felt as if the preacher had crept upon them, behind his awful veil, and discovered their hoarded iniquity of deed or thought. Many spread their clasped hands on their bosoms. There was nothing terrible in what Mr. Hooper said; at least, no violence; and yet, with every tremor of his melancholy voice, the hearers quaked. An unsought pathos[11] came hand in hand with awe. So sensible were the audience of some unwonted attribute in their minister, that they longed for a breath of wind to blow aside the veil, almost believing that a stranger's visage[12] would be discovered, though the form, gesture, and voice were those of Mr. Hooper. ❷

❷ How does the veil affect the sermon and the congregation?

At the close of the services, the people hurried out with indecorous[13] confusion, eager to communicate their pent-up amazement, and conscious of lighter spirits, the moment they lost sight of the black veil. Some gathered in little circles, huddled closely together, with their mouths all whispering in the center; some went homeward alone, wrapped in silent meditation; some talked loudly, and profaned[14] the Sabbath day with ostentatious laughter. A few shook their sagacious heads, intimating[15] that they could penetrate the mystery; while one or two affirmed that there was no mystery at all, but only that Mr. Hooper's eyes were so weakened by the midnight lamp, as to require a shade. After a brief interval, forth came good Mr. Hooper also, in the rear of his flock. Turning his veiled face from one group to another, he paid due reverence to the hoary[16] heads, saluted the middle-aged with kind dignity, as their friend and spiritual guide, greeted the young with mingled authority and love, and laid his hands on the little children's heads to bless them. Such was always his custom on the Sabbath day. Strange and bewildered looks repaid him for his courtesy. None, as on former occasions, aspired to the honor of walking by their pastor's side. Old Squire Saunders, doubtless by an accidental lapse of memory, neglected to invite Mr. Hooper to his table, where the good clergyman had been wont[17] to bless the food, almost every Sunday since his settlement. He returned, therefore, to the parsonage, and, at the moment of closing the door, was observed to look back upon the people, all of whom had their eyes fixed upon the minister. A sad smile gleamed faintly from beneath the black veil, and flickered about his mouth, glimmering as he disappeared.

"How strange," said a lady, "that a simple black veil, such as any woman might wear on her bonnet, should become such a terrible thing on Mr. Hooper's face!"

"Something must surely be amiss with Mr. Hooper's intellects," observed her husband, the physician of the village. "But the strangest part of the affair is the effect of this vagary,[18] even on a sober-minded man like myself. The black veil, though it covers only our pastor's face, throws its influence over his whole person, and makes him ghostlike from head to foot. Do you not feel it so?"

"Truly do I," replied the lady; "and I would not be alone with him for the world. I wonder he is not afraid to be alone with himself!"

"Men sometimes are so," said her husband.

___

16. **hoary** *adj.:* white or gray, as with age.
17. **wont** *adj.:* accustomed.
18. **vagary** *n.:* odd, unexpected action.

**Vocabulary**
**iniquity** (i·nik′wi·tē) *n.:* wickedness.
**ostentatious** (äs′tən·tā′shəs) *adj.:* deliberately attracting notice.
**sagacious** (sə·gā′shəs) *adj.:* wise; keenly perceptive.

___

10. **the Omniscient:** the all-knowing God.
11. **pathos** *n.:* feelings of pity, sympathy, and sorrow.
12. **visage** *n.:* face.
13. **indecorous** *adj.:* improper; lacking good taste.
14. **profaned** *v.:* showed disrespect for.
15. **intimating** *v.* used as *adj.:* indirectly suggesting.

*The Sermon* (1886) by Julius Gari Melchers. Oil on canvas.

The afternoon service was attended with similar circumstances. At its conclusion, the bell tolled for the funeral of a young lady. The relatives and friends were assembled in the house, and the more distant acquaintances stood about the door, speaking of the good qualities of the deceased, when their talk was interrupted by the appearance of Mr. Hooper, still covered with his black veil. It was now an appropriate emblem. The clergyman stepped into the room where the corpse was laid, and bent over the coffin, to take a last farewell of his deceased parishioner. As he stooped, the veil hung straight down from his forehead, so that, if her eyelids had not been closed forever, the dead maiden might have seen his face. Could Mr. Hooper be fearful of her glance, that he so hastily caught back the black veil? A person, who watched the interview be-

tween the dead and living, scrupled[19] not to affirm, that, at the instant when the clergyman's features were disclosed, the corpse had slightly shuddered, rustling the shroud[20] and muslin cap, though the countenance retained the composure of death. A superstitious old woman was the only witness of this prodigy.[21] From the coffin, Mr. Hooper passed into the chamber of the mourners, and thence to the head of the staircase, to make the funeral prayer. It was a tender and heart-dissolving prayer, full of sorrow, yet so imbued with celestial[22] hopes, that the music

---

19. **scrupled** *v.:* hesitated.
20. **shroud** *n.:* cloth used to wrap a body for burial.
21. **prodigy** *n.:* something extraordinary or inexplicable.
22. **celestial** *adj.:* heavenly.

of a heavenly harp, swept by the fingers of the dead, seemed faintly to be heard among the saddest accents of the minister. The people trembled, though they but darkly understood him, when he prayed that they, and himself, and all of mortal race, might be ready, as he trusted this young maiden had been, for the dreadful hour that should snatch the veil from their faces. The bearers went heavily forth, and the mourners followed, saddening all the street, with the dead before them, and Mr. Hooper in his black veil behind.

"Why do you look back?" said one in the procession to his partner.

"I had a fancy," replied she, "that the minister and the maiden's spirit were walking hand in hand."

"And so had I, at the same moment," said the other. ❸

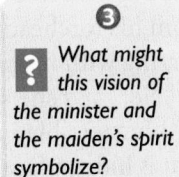

❸ What might this vision of the minister and the maiden's spirit symbolize?

That night, the handsomest couple in Milford village were to be joined in wedlock. Though reckoned a melancholy man, Mr. Hooper had a placid cheerfulness for such occasions, which often excited a sympathetic smile, where livelier merriment would have been thrown away. There was no quality of his disposition which made him more beloved than this. The company at the wedding awaited his arrival with impatience, trusting that the strange awe, which had gathered over him throughout the day, would now be dispelled. But such was not the result. When Mr. Hooper came, the first thing that their eyes rested on was the same horrible black veil, which had added deeper gloom to the funeral, and could <u>portend</u> nothing but evil to the wedding. Such was its immediate effect on the guests, that a cloud seemed to have rolled duskily from beneath the black crape, and dimmed the light of the candles. The bridal pair stood up before the minister. But the bride's cold fingers quivered in the tremulous[23] hand of the bridegroom, and her deathlike paleness caused a whisper, that the maiden who had been buried a few hours before, was come from

23. **tremulous** *adj.*: trembling.

her grave to be married. If ever another wedding were so dismal, it was that famous one, where they tolled the wedding knell.[24] After performing the ceremony, Mr. Hooper raised a glass of wine to his lips, wishing happiness to the new-married couple, in a strain of mild pleasantry that ought to have brightened the features of the guests, like a cheerful gleam from the hearth. At that instant, catching a glimpse of his figure in the looking glass, the black veil involved his own spirit in the horror with which it overwhelmed all others. His frame shuddered— his lips grew white—he spilt the untasted wine upon the carpet—and rushed forth into the darkness. For the Earth, too, had on her Black Veil. ❹

❹ How does the black veil affect the wedding?

The next day, the whole village of Milford talked of little else than Parson Hooper's black veil. That, and the mystery concealed behind it, supplied a topic for discussion between acquaintances meeting in the street, and good women gossiping at their open windows. It was the first item of news that the tavern keeper told to his guests. The children babbled of it on their way to school. One imitative little imp covered his face with an old black handkerchief, thereby so affrighting his playmates, that the panic seized himself, and he well nigh lost his wits by his own waggery.[25]

It was remarkable, that, of all the busybodies and impertinent people in the parish, not one ventured to put the plain question to Mr. Hooper, wherefore he did this thing. Hitherto, whenever there appeared the slightest call for such interference, he had never lacked advisers, nor shown himself averse to be guided by their judgment. If he erred at all, it was by so painful a degree of self-distrust, that even the mildest

24. **If . . . wedding knell:** reference to Hawthorne's story "The Wedding Knell." A knell is the ringing of a bell.
25. **waggery** *n.*: joke.

**Vocabulary**

**portend** (pôr·tend′) *v.*: signify.

censure[26] would lead him to consider an indifferent action as a crime. Yet, though so well acquainted with this amiable[27] weakness, no individual among his parishioners chose to make the black veil a subject of friendly remonstrance.[28] There was a feeling of dread, neither plainly confessed nor carefully concealed, which caused each to shift the responsibility upon another, till at length it was found expedient to send a deputation[29] of the church, in order to deal with Mr. Hooper about the mystery, before it should grow into a scandal. Never did an embassy so ill discharge its duties. The minister received them with friendly courtesy, but became silent, after they were seated, leaving to his visitors the whole burden of introducing their important business. The topic, it might be supposed, was obvious enough. There was the black veil, swathed round Mr. Hooper's forehead, and concealing every feature above his placid mouth, on which, at times, they could perceive the glimmering of a melancholy smile. But that piece of crape, to their imagination, seemed to hang down before his heart, the symbol of a fearful secret between him and them. Were the veil but cast aside, they might speak freely of it, but not till then. Thus they sat a considerable time, speechless, confused, and shrinking uneasily from Mr. Hooper's eye, which they felt to be fixed upon them with an invisible glance. Finally, the deputies returned abashed to their constituents, pronouncing the matter too weighty to be handled, except by a council of the churches, if, indeed, it might not require a general synod.[30]

**❺** *What happens when the church sends a delegation to talk to Mr. Hooper?*

But there was one person in the village, unappalled by the awe with which the black veil had impressed all beside herself. When the deputies returned without an explanation, or even venturing to demand one, she, with the calm energy of her character, determined to chase away the strange cloud that appeared to be settling round Mr. Hooper, every moment more darkly than before. As his plighted[31] wife, it should be her privilege to know what the black veil concealed. At the minister's first visit, therefore, she entered upon the subject, with a direct simplicity, which made the task easier both for him and her. After he had seated himself, she fixed her eyes steadfastly upon the veil, but could discern nothing of the dreadful gloom that had so overawed the multitude: It was but a double fold of crape, hanging down from his forehead to his mouth, and slightly stirring with his breath.

"No," said she aloud, and smiling, "there is nothing terrible in this piece of crape, except that it hides a face which I am always glad to look upon. Come, good sir, let the sun shine from behind the cloud. First lay aside your black veil: Then tell me why you put it on."

Mr. Hooper's smile glimmered faintly.

"There is an hour to come," said he, "when all of us shall cast aside our veils. Take it not amiss, beloved friend, if I wear this piece of crape till then."

"Your words are a mystery too," returned the young lady. "Take away the veil from them, at least."

"Elizabeth, I will," said he, "so far as my vow may suffer me. Know, then, this veil is a type and a symbol, and I am bound to wear it ever, both in light and darkness, in solitude and before the gaze of multitudes, and as with strangers, so with my familiar friends. No mortal eye will see it withdrawn. This dismal shade must separate me from the world: Even you, Elizabeth, can never come behind it!"

**❻** *Why is this a key passage in the story?*

"What grievous affliction hath befallen you," she earnestly inquired, "that you should thus darken your eyes forever?"

---

26. **censure** *n.:* expression of strong disapproval or criticism.
27. **amiable** *adj.:* friendly; likable.
28. **remonstrance** *n.:* protest; complaint.
29. **deputation** *n.:* group of representatives.
30. **synod** (sin′əd) *n.:* governing body of a group of churches.

---

31. **plighted** *v.* used as *adj.:* promised.

> **Her eyes were fixed insensibly on the black veil,**
>
> **when, like a sudden twilight in the air, its terrors fell around her.**

"If it be a sign of mourning," replied Mr. Hooper, "I, perhaps, like most other mortals, have sorrows dark enough to be typified by a black veil."

"But what if the world will not believe that it is the type of an innocent sorrow?" urged Elizabeth. "Beloved and respected as you are, there may be whispers, that you hide your face under the consciousness of secret sin. For the sake of your holy office, do away this scandal!"

The color rose into her cheeks, as she intimated the nature of the rumors that were already abroad in the village. But Mr. Hooper's mildness did not forsake him. He even smiled again—that same sad smile, which always appeared like a faint glimmering of light, proceeding from the obscurity beneath the veil.

"If I hide my face for sorrow, there is cause enough," he merely replied; "and if I cover it for secret sin, what mortal might not do the same?"

And with this gentle, but unconquerable obstinacy,[32] did he resist all her entreaties. At length Elizabeth sat silent. For a few moments she appeared lost in thought, considering, probably, what new methods might be tried, to withdraw her lover from so dark a fantasy, which, if it had no other meaning, was perhaps a symptom of mental disease. Though of a firmer character than his own, the tears rolled down her cheeks. But, in an instant, as it were, a new feeling took the place of sorrow: Her eyes were

fixed insensibly on the black veil, when, like a sudden twilight in the air, its terrors fell around her. She arose, and stood trembling before him.

"And do you feel it then at last?" said he mournfully.

She made no reply, but covered her eyes with her hand, and turned to leave the room. He rushed forward and caught her arm.

"Have patience with me, Elizabeth!" cried he passionately. "Do not desert me, though this veil must be between us here on earth. Be mine, and hereafter there shall be no veil over my face, no darkness between our souls! It is but a mortal veil—it is not for eternity! Oh! you know not how lonely I am, and how frightened to be alone behind my black veil. Do not leave me in this miserable obscurity forever!"

"Lift the veil but once, and look me in the face," said she.

"Never! It cannot be!" replied Mr. Hooper.

"Then, farewell!" said Elizabeth.

She withdrew her arm from his grasp, and slowly departed, pausing at the door, to give one long, shuddering gaze, that seemed almost to penetrate the mystery of the black veil. But, even amid his grief, Mr. Hooper smiled to think that only a material emblem had separated him from happiness, though the horrors which it shadowed forth, must be drawn darkly between the fondest of lovers. ❼

From that time no attempts were made to

---

**7**

**?** What is the result of the encounter between Elizabeth and Mr. Hooper?

---

32. **obstinacy** *n.*: stubbornness; willfulness.

**Nathaniel Hawthorne** 269

remove Mr. Hooper's black veil, or, by a direct appeal, to discover the secret which it was supposed to hide. By persons who claimed a superiority to popular prejudice, it was reckoned merely an eccentric whim, such as often mingles with the sober actions of men otherwise rational, and tinges them all with its own semblance of insanity. But with the multitude, good Mr. Hooper was irreparably a bugbear.[33] He could not walk the streets with any peace of mind, so conscious was he that the gentle and timid would turn aside to avoid him, and that others would make it a point of hardihood to throw themselves in his way. The impertinence of the latter class compelled him to give up his customary walk, at sunset, to the burial ground; for when he leaned <u>pensively</u> over the gate, there would always be faces behind the gravestones, peeping at his black veil. A fable went the rounds, that the stare of the dead people drove him thence. It grieved him, to the very depth of his kind heart, to observe how the children fled from his approach, breaking up their merriest sports, while his melancholy figure was yet afar off. Their instinctive dread caused him to feel, more strongly than aught else, that a preternatural[34] horror was interwoven with the threads of the black crape. In truth, his own <u>antipathy</u> to the veil was known to be so great, that he never willingly passed before a mirror, nor stooped to drink at a still fountain, lest, in its peaceful bosom, he should be affrighted by himself. This was what gave <u>plausibility</u> to the whispers, that Mr. Hooper's conscience tortured him for some great crime, too horrible to be entirely concealed, or otherwise than so obscurely intimated. Thus, from beneath the black veil, there rolled a cloud into the sunshine, an ambiguity of sin or sorrow, which enveloped the poor minister, so that love or sympathy could never reach him. It was said, that ghost and fiend consorted with him there. With self-shudderings and outward terrors, he walked continually in its shadow, groping darkly within his own soul,

or gazing through a medium that saddened the whole world. Even the lawless wind, it was believed, respected his dreadful secret, and never blew aside the veil. But still good Mr. Hooper sadly smiled, at the pale visages of the worldly throng as he passed by. **8**

**8**
? What do the villagers think is the reason their pastor wears the veil?

Among all its bad influences, the black veil had the one desirable effect, of making its wearer a very efficient clergyman. By the aid of his mysterious emblem—for there was no other apparent cause—he became a man of awful power, over souls that were in agony for sin. His converts always regarded him with a dread peculiar to themselves, affirming, though but figuratively, that, before he brought them to celestial light, they had been with him behind the black veil. Its gloom, indeed, enabled him to sympathize with all dark affections. Dying sinners cried aloud for Mr. Hooper, and would not yield their breath till he appeared; though ever, as he stooped to whisper consolation, they shuddered at the veiled face so near their own. Such were the terrors of the black veil, even when Death had bared his visage! Strangers came long distances to attend service at his church, with the mere idle purpose of gazing at his figure, because it was forbidden them to behold his face. But many were made to quake ere they departed! Once, during Governor Belcher's[35] administration, Mr. Hooper was appointed to preach the election sermon. Covered with his black veil, he stood before the chief magistrate, the council, and the representatives, and wrought so deep an impression, that the legislative measures of that year, were characterized by

---

33. **bugbear** *n.:* source of irrational fears.
34. **preternatural** *adj.:* abnormal; supernatural.

---

35. **Governor Belcher's:** Jonathan Belcher (1681?–1757) was governor of the Massachusetts Bay Colony from 1730 to 1741.

---

**Vocabulary**
**pensively** (pen′siv·lē) *adv.:* thinking deeply or seriously.
**antipathy** (an·tip′ə·thē) *n.:* strong dislike.
**plausibility** (plô′zə·bil′ə·tē) *n.:* believability.

all the gloom and piety of our earliest ancestral sway. ❾

In this manner Mr. Hooper spent a long life, irreproachable[36] in outward act, yet shrouded in dismal suspicions; kind and loving, though unloved, and dimly feared; a man apart from men, shunned in their health and joy, but ever summoned to their aid in mortal anguish. As years wore on, shedding their snows above his sable veil, he acquired a name throughout the New England churches, and they called him Father Hooper. Nearly all his parishioners, who were of mature age when he was settled, had been borne away by many a funeral: He had one congregation in the church, and a more crowded one in the churchyard; and having wrought so late into the evening, and done his work so well, it was now good Father Hooper's turn to rest.

Several persons were visible by the shaded candlelight, in the death chamber of the old clergyman. Natural connections he had none. But there was the decorously grave, though unmoved physician, seeking only to mitigate[37] the last pangs of the patient whom he could not save. There were the deacons, and other eminently pious members of his church. There, also, was the Reverend Mr. Clark, of Westbury, a young and zealous divine, who had ridden in haste to pray by the bedside of the expiring minister. There was the nurse, no hired handmaiden of death, but one whose calm affection had endured thus long, in secrecy, in solitude, amid the chill of age, and would not perish, even at the dying hour. Who, but Elizabeth! And there lay the hoary head of good Father Hooper upon the death-pillow, with the black veil still swathed about his brow and reaching down over his face, so that each more difficult gasp of his faint breath caused it to stir. All through life that piece of crape had hung between him and the world: It had separated him from cheerful brotherhood and woman's love, and kept him in that saddest of all prisons, his own heart; and still it lay upon his face, as if to deepen the gloom of his darksome chamber, and shade him from the sunshine of eternity. ❿

For some time previous, his mind had been confused, wavering doubtfully between the past and the present, and hovering forward, as it were, at intervals, into the indistinctness of the world to come. There had been feverish turns, which tossed him from side to side, and wore away what little strength he had. But in his most convulsive struggles, and in the wildest vagaries of his intellect, when no other thought retained its sober influence, he still showed an awful solicitude lest the black veil should slip aside. Even if his bewildered soul could have forgotten, there was a faithful woman at his pillow, who, with averted eyes, would have covered that aged face, which she had last beheld in the comeliness of manhood. At length the death-stricken old man lay quietly in the torpor[38] of mental and bodily exhaustion, with an imperceptible pulse, and breath that grew fainter and fainter, except when a long, deep, and irregular inspiration[39] seemed to prelude the flight of his spirit.

The minister of Westbury approached the bedside.

"Venerable Father Hooper," said he, "the moment of your release is at hand. Are you ready for the lifting of the veil, that shuts in time from eternity?"

Father Hooper at first replied merely by a feeble motion of his head; then, apprehensive, perhaps, that his meaning might be doubtful, he exerted himself to speak.

"Yea," said he, in faint accents, "my soul hath a patient weariness until that veil be lifted."

"And is it fitting," resumed the Reverend Mr. Clark, "that a man so given to prayer, of such a

❾ How does the veil affect Mr. Hooper?

❿ What do we learn about Elizabeth, whom Hooper has loved?

---

36. **irreproachable** *adj.:* blameless.
37. **mitigate** *v.:* make less painful.

38. **torpor** *n.:* dull or sluggish state.
39. **inspiration** *n.:* inhaling.

*There he sat, shivering with the arms of death around him, while the black veil hung down . . .*

blameless example, holy in deed and thought, so far as mortal judgment may pronounce; is it fitting that a father in the church should leave a shadow on his memory, that may seem to blacken a life so pure? I pray you, my venerable brother, let not this thing be! Suffer us to be gladdened by your triumphant aspect, as you go to your reward. Before the veil of eternity be lifted, let me cast aside this black veil from your face!" ⓫

> ⓫
> **?** What reasons does Reverend Clark give for lifting the black veil?

And thus speaking, the Reverend Mr. Clark bent forward to reveal the mystery of so many years. But, exerting a sudden energy, that made all the beholders stand aghast, Father Hooper snatched both his hands from beneath the bedclothes, and pressed them strongly on the black veil, resolute to struggle, if the minister of Westbury would contend with a dying man.

"Never!" cried the veiled clergyman. "On earth, never!"

"Dark old man!" exclaimed the affrighted minister, "with what horrible crime upon your soul are you now passing to the judgment?"

Father Hooper's breath heaved; it rattled in his throat; but, with a mighty effort, grasping forward with his hands, he caught hold of life, and held it back till he should speak. He even raised himself in bed; and there he sat, shivering with the arms of death around him, while the black veil hung down, awful, at that last moment, in the gathered terrors of a lifetime. And yet the faint, sad smile, so often there, now

seemed to glimmer from its obscurity, and linger on Father Hooper's lips.

"Why do you tremble at me alone?" cried he, turning his veiled face round the circle of pale spectators. "Tremble also at each other! Have men avoided me, and women shown no pity, and children screamed and fled, only for my black veil? What, but the mystery which it obscurely typifies, has made this piece of crape so awful? When the friend shows his inmost heart to his friend; the lover to his best beloved; when man does not vainly shrink from the eye of his Creator, loathsomely treasuring up the secret of his sin; then deem me a monster, for the symbol beneath which I have lived, and die! I look around me, and, lo! on every visage a Black Veil!" ⓬

> ⓬
> This is the **climax** of the story.
> **?** What does Hooper say has made the veil so awful?

While his auditors shrank from one another, in mutual affright, Father Hooper fell back upon his pillow, a veiled corpse, with a faint smile lingering on the lips. Still veiled, they laid him in his coffin, and a veiled corpse they bore him to the grave. The grass of many years has sprung up and withered on that grave, the burial stone is moss-grown, and good Mr. Hooper's face is dust; but awful is still the thought, that it moldered beneath the Black Veil! ∎

**Vocabulary**

**resolute** (rez′ə·lōōt′) *adj.:* determined.

# Response and Analysis

## Reading Check

1. How does the congregation respond at first to Mr. Hooper's black veil? Why?

2. In a single afternoon, Hooper presides at both a funeral and a wedding. How do people react to the presence of the veil at each event?

3. What explanation does Hooper give to Elizabeth, his fiancée, for wearing the veil? What arguments against wearing the veil does she make?

## Thinking Critically

4. Briefly describe Hooper's **character** as revealed in the story's opening paragraphs. What does the congregation's attitude toward him seem to have been before the appearance of the veil?

5. Explain the narrator's remark on page 271 about the human heart being the "saddest of all prisons." Do you agree or disagree? Do you think this observation refers only to Hooper, or is it true of everyone in the story? Explain your response.

6. **Tone** is the attitude a writer takes toward a subject. Would you describe this narrator's tone as neutral or emotional? (Think particularly of the words the narrator uses in referring to the veil.) Write down words and phrases that contribute to the story's tone.

7. Trace the progression of Elizabeth's responses to the veil. How do you explain her changing attitudes?

8. On his deathbed, Hooper says, "I look around me, and, lo! on every visage a Black Veil!" What does Hooper mean? In what ways is Hooper's veil a **symbol**?

9. Look for evidence in the story that suggests more than one **symbolic meaning** for the black veil. What are some of these meanings?

10. Does Hooper's veil have any positive effects during his long life? Use details from the story to support your answer.

11. Why do you think the villagers bury Hooper without removing the veil?

12. What would you say is the moral lesson of this **parable**—the **theme,** or insight it provides about our human existence?

## Extending and Evaluating

13. Edgar Allan Poe said that Hooper wore the veil because "a crime of dark dye (having reference to the 'young lady') has been committed." What do you think Poe is referring to? Do you think the story would be more effective if Hawthorne had revealed precisely why Hooper wears the veil? Explain.

## WRITING

### Behind the Veil: Analyzing the Story

In a brief **essay,** analyze the way that the black veil functions in this story. Trace Hooper's use of the veil and its effects on him and people in the community. Using the inferences you made while reading, follow the effects of the veil right through to its shocking appearance on Hooper's face on his deathbed. Conclude with your interpretation of what the black veil **symbolizes.**

### Comparing Literature

In a brief **essay,** compare and contrast the attitudes revealed in Hawthorne's story to attitudes held by Puritans such as Jonathan Edwards (see "Sinners in the Hands of an Angry God," page 46). Consider especially attitudes toward sin, guilt, and the conditions necessary for salvation. How do you think Hawthorne felt about the tenets of Puritanism?

**SKILLS FOCUS**

**Literary Skills**
Analyze symbolism.

**Reading Skills**
Make inferences.

**Writing Skills**
Write an essay analyzing a symbol. Write an essay comparing and contrasting authors' attitudes.

**Vocabulary Skills**
Create semantic charts. Use context clues to understand archaic words.

**INTERNET**

Projects and Activities

Keyword: LE7 11-2

Illustration by Elenore Plaisted Abbott for "The Minister's Black Veil," from the 1900 edition of *Twice-Told Tales.*

## Vocabulary Development
### Word Charts

Fill out a chart like the one below for each of the Vocabulary words. Use a dictionary to find basic information about each word.

| semblance | portend |
| obscurity | pensively |
| iniquity | antipathy |
| ostentatious | plausibility |
| sagacious | resolute |

| Word | sagacious |
|---|---|
| Definition | wise; keenly perceptive |
| Origin | L sagax, "wise, forseeing"; akin to sagire, "to perceive acutely" |
| Related words | sagacity, sage |
| Sample sentence | Mrs. Keller was a shrewd and sagacious business-woman. |

## Language and Style
### Understanding Archaic Language

If modern readers have trouble with Hawthorne, it is usually because of his **archaic,** or old-fashioned, language. **Context clues** (page 66) can often help you figure out unfamiliar vocabulary. Which word or words in each of the following passages from the story are rarely used today? Rephrase each passage in Modern English. Are any of these words still in use today but with different meanings?

- "So sensible were the audience of some unwonted attribute in their minister . . ." (page 265)

- "A superstitious old woman was the only witness of this prodigy." (page 266)

- ". . . He well nigh lost his wits by his own waggery." (page 267)

- ". . . having wrought so late into the evening . . ." (page 271)

# Grammar Link

## Avoiding Sentence Fragments and Run-on Sentences: Respecting Boundaries

Just because a group of words looks like a sentence does not mean it is one. It may be a sentence fragment or a run-on sentence.

### Sentence Fragments

A **sentence** is a group of words that has a **subject** and a **verb** and expresses a complete thought. A **sentence fragment** lacks one of these elements. It may be missing a subject or a verb or both, or the fragment may depend on a nearby sentence to make sense. The following items are examples of fragments:

> Roused the fears of the congregation. [no subject]
> Even on his deathbed. [not a complete thought]

Although sentence fragments are acceptable in informal writing and dialogue, you should avoid using them in formal writing. There are two ways to correct a fragment.

1. Add the missing subject or verb.

   The black veil roused the fears of the congregation. [subject added]

2. Rewrite the fragment to make it a complete sentence. (Sometimes this involves connecting the fragment to a neighboring sentence.)

   Reverend Hooper wore the veil even on his deathbed. [subject and predicate added]

### Run-on Sentences

While a fragment is not a complete thought, a **run-on sentence** contains two or more complete thoughts running into one another, without respect for boundaries. There are two common types of run-on sentences: A **fused sentence** has no punctuation at all between its complete thoughts. A **comma splice** has only a comma between the two complete thoughts.

> The sexton rang the bell the people walked toward the church. [fused sentence]
> The sexton rang the bell, the people walked toward the church. [comma splice]

There are several ways to fix a run-on sentence.

1. Turn the run-on sentence into two or more separate sentences.

   The sexton rang the bell. The people walked toward the church.

SKILLS FOCUS

**Grammar Skills**
Revise run-on sentences and sentence fragments.

Nathaniel Hawthorne    275

**2.** Add a **coordinating conjunction** (*and, but, or, nor, for, so, yet*), and if the run-on sentence is a fused sentence, add a comma before the conjunction.

The sexton rang the bell**,** and the people walked toward the church.

**3.** Separate the complete thoughts with a semicolon.

The sexton rang the bell**;** the people walked toward the church.

**4.** Add a **subordinating conjunction** (such as *because, although, until,* or *when*) and, if necessary, a comma before the conjunction.

The sexton rang the bell while the people walked toward the church.

**5.** Use a semicolon and a conjunctive adverb.

The sexton rang the bell**;** consequently, the people walked toward the church.

**PRACTICE**

In the following items, indicate whether each example is a **sentence fragment** (SF), a **fused sentence** (FS), or a **comma splice** (CS). Then, correct each sentence fragment or run-on sentence, using whichever method you think works best.

**1.** At the beginning of Hawthorne's story, readers probably suspect that Mr. Hooper wears the veil because he has committed a sin, by the end they may not be so sure.

**2.** Hooper refuses to remove the veil. Although Elizabeth, his fiancée, begs him to lift it and let her see his face.

**3.** On his deathbed, Hooper insists that he sees a black veil. Covering every human face.

**4.** Some readers may view Hooper as morally courageous others may view him as arrogant and obsessive.

## Apply to Your Writing

Re-read a current writing assignment or a piece of writing that you've already completed. Can you find any sentence fragments or run-on sentences? If so, revise each of them according to what you have learned.

**For more help, see Obstacles to Clarity, 9d–e, in the Language Handbook.**

# Edgar Allan Poe
## (1809–1849)

"The want of parental affection," wrote Poe, "has been the heaviest of my trials." Edgar Allan Poe was, indeed, most unfortunate in his parents. His father, David Poe, was a mediocre traveling actor who drank heavily. His mother, Elizabeth Arnold, was a talented actress who was deserted by her husband when Edgar was still a baby. She died on tour in Richmond, Virginia, leaving Edgar virtually an orphan before his third birthday.

The boy was taken in by John and Frances Allan, a charitable and childless couple in Richmond. John Allan, an ambitious and self-righteous merchant, became Edgar's guardian (and the source of the writer's middle name). He provided generously for Edgar's early education, but he never formally adopted the boy.

Although Frances Allan was kind to Edgar, the boy grew up feeling both the lack of a natural father and the disapproval of his foster father. John Allan made no secret of his disappointment in Edgar—in his idleness, in his indifference to business life, and in his literary ambitions. Surely Allan's criticism added to Edgar's growing moodiness.

### Breaking Away

At seventeen, Edgar entered the University of Virginia. He did well in his studies but was resentful of the meager allowance Allan gave him. When he tried to earn extra money by gambling, he went deep into debt. On discovering this, Allan refused to help his foster son and instead withdrew him from college.

After an especially bitter quarrel with Allan, Poe ran off to Boston to make his own way in the world. There, in 1827, he published a small volume of poems, *Tamerlane*. The book did not attract much attention, and Poe could find no other work. In despair he joined the army. He was promoted to the rank of sergeant major, but he disliked the enlisted man's life and appealed to Allan for help. At the request of his wife, who was dying, Allan interceded for Poe (for the last time) and agreed to help him enter the U.S. Military Academy at West Point. Poe's motive in going to the academy was probably to please his foster father.

While waiting to get into the academy, Poe published a second book of poems, *Al Aaraaf,* in 1829 and received his first real recognition as a writer. The next year, while at West Point, Poe learned that Allan (now a widower) had remarried and that the woman was young enough to have children. Since this appeared to end all hope of becoming Allan's heir, Poe had himself dismissed from West Point.

### Exploring the Darkness and the Depths

Poe moved in with an aunt, Maria Poe Clemm, in Baltimore, Maryland. In 1835, he married her thirteen-year-old daughter, Virginia. The difference in their ages and Virginia's poor health resulted in a very odd marriage, but need and a strong sense of family drew the three housemates together.

Poe supported his family by working as an editor at various magazines. He wrote when he could find the time, completing his only full-length novel, *The Narrative of Arthur Gordon Pym,* several years after his marriage. It was his short stories, however, that had the greatest effect on other writers.

In "The Gold Bug" and in the tales built around the intuitive sleuth C. Auguste Dupin, "The Purloined Letter" and "The Murders in the Rue Morgue," Poe laid the foundations for the modern detective story. In fact, he inspired Sir Arthur Conan Doyle to create Sherlock Holmes. In tales such as "The Tell-Tale Heart" and "The Cask of Amontillado," Poe inspired the Russian novelist Fyodor Dostoyevsky

(1821–1881) to explore the criminal mind.

Poe was a master of the psychological thriller. His tales of the ghastly and the grotesque are peopled with distraught narrators, deranged heroes, and doomed heroines, yet his purpose in creating such characters was not to present readers with convincing likenesses of human beings—nor merely to shock and frighten. Instead, Poe wanted to take us behind the curtain that separates the everyday from the incredible. He wanted to leave behind the sunlit, tangible, rational world and discover the unsettling truth that lies in the dark, irrational depths of the human mind.

### Small Triumphs and Great Tragedy

Poe produced a considerable body of work in spite of humiliating poverty and a serious drinking problem. The slightest amount of alcohol made him senseless, yet he drank to escape a reality he found agonizing. Publication of his poem "The Raven" in 1845 brought Poe some fame at last, but financial security still eluded him.

When Virginia died of tuberculosis in 1847, Poe and "Muddy" (Virginia's mother) were left alone. Poe grew more unstable. He pursued romance relentlessly, always looking for someone to "adopt" him. In 1849, on his way home after a visit to Virginia to see a woman he hoped to marry, Poe disappeared. A week later, he was found in a Baltimore tavern—delirious and in cheap clothing that was not his, wet through from a raging storm. Four days later, having passed in and out of delirium, Poe died, leaving critics to argue endlessly about this final mystery. What happened during those last days in Baltimore?

### For Independent Reading

For more of Poe's horror stories, read these titles:

- "William Wilson"
- "The Oval Portrait"

## A CLOSER LOOK: SOCIAL INFLUENCES

Edgar Allan Poe. Drawing by David Levine.

**INFORMATIONAL TEXT**

### Poe the Pop Icon

Can you guess what Edgar Allan Poe has in common with Elvis Presley, Marilyn Monroe, the Beatles, and Michael Jordan? Like all of the above, Poe is a legend of popular culture. Consider these facts:

- Poe's works have been translated into virtually every language.

- Such popular writers as Stephen King and Ray Bradbury point to Poe as their literary forefather.

- The Mystery Writers of America annually honors great achievements in mystery writing with the Edgar—the equivalent of an Oscar or an Emmy.

- Poe has been immortalized in the popular arts, on everything from posters, buttons, and coffee mugs to bumper stickers and T-shirts.

- Poe has been "ushered" into pop culture through dozens of film adaptations, including *The Masque of the Red Death, The Black Cat, The Tomb of Ligeia,* and *The Pit and the Pendulum.*

Keep your eye out for Poe. He may be closer than you think.

# The Pit and the Pendulum

## Make the Connection
### Quickwrite ✏️

Here is Edgar Allan Poe's famous story of confinement in an extraordinary prison cell in Toledo, Spain, during the brutal Spanish Inquisition. Poe's story is powerful for many reasons, one being its point of view. It is the prisoner himself who tells this story. Given this fact, do you already know at the outset that he will survive the torture—or could he possibly die?

The other powerful device in the story is the form of torture itself, which gradually takes on symbolic meaning. Before you read the story, freewrite for a few minutes about one of your fears and the images you associate with it.

## Literary Focus
### Symbolic Meaning

When we read, we often sense that a story means more than what simply happens on the surface level. For instance, if a young girl in a story is in conflict with her parents over wearing certain earrings, we suspect that those earrings represent something important to her—perhaps her self-expression or independence. A **symbol** is a concrete object, a person, a place, or an action that works on at least two levels: It functions as itself, and it also suggests a deeper meaning. As you read "The Pit and the Pendulum," consider what elements may have broader symbolic significance.

> The **symbolic meaning** of a story emerges from an overall interpretation of the story's individual symbols.
>
> *For more on Symbol, see the Handbook of Literary and Historical Terms.*

The Granger Collection, New York.

## Reading Skills
### Retelling

Good readers sometimes stop at key points in a story in order to retell what has happened so far. Try this retelling strategy with Poe's story. You'll find boxed questions at certain points in the story. Stop at these points, and retell the key events that have taken place so far. Focus also on causes and their effects. Ask yourself, "What has *caused* this event to happen?" and "What is the *effect* of this action?"

## Background

The Spanish Inquisition was a kind of religious court set up by the Catholic Church and the monarchy in Spain during the fifteenth century to accuse and punish those who

**SKILLS FOCUS**

**Literary Skills**
Understand symbolic meaning.

**Reading Skills**
Retell key events.

**INTERNET**

Vocabulary Practice
•
More About Edgar Allan Poe
•

Keyword: LE7 11-2

failed to comply with the church or royal authority. Poe may have gotten the idea for this story from a book by Juan Antonio Llorente. Poe read a review of this book, which contains the following passage:

> 66 The Inquisition was thrown open, in 1820, by the orders of the Cortes of Madrid. Twenty-one prisoners were found in it. . . . Some had been confined three years, some a longer period, and not one knew perfectly the nature of the crime of which he was accused. One of these prisoners had been condemned and was to have suffered on the following day. His punishment was to be death by the Pendulum. The method of thus destroying the victim is as follows: The condemned is fastened in a groove, upon a table, on his back; suspended above him is a Pendulum, the edge of which is sharp, and it is so constructed as to become longer with every movement. The wretch sees this implement of destruction swinging to and fro above him, and every moment the keen edge approaching nearer and nearer. 99

## Vocabulary Development

**imperceptible** (im′pər·sep′tə·bəl) *adj.:* not clear or obvious to the senses or mind.

**ponders** (pän′dərz) *v.:* thinks deeply.

**lucid** (lo͞o′sid) *adj.:* clearheaded; not confused.

**tumultuous** (to͞o·mul′cho͞o·əs) *adj.:* violent; greatly agitated or disturbed.

**insuperable** (in·so͞o′pər·ə·bəl) *adj.:* incapable of being overcome.

**prostrate** (präs′trāt′) *adj.:* lying flat.

**potent** (pōt′′nt) *adj.:* powerful or effective.

**lethargy** (leth′ər·jē) *n.:* abnormal drowsiness.

**proximity** (präk·sim′ə·tē) *n.:* nearness.

**averted** (ə·vʉrt′id) *v.:* turned away; prevented.

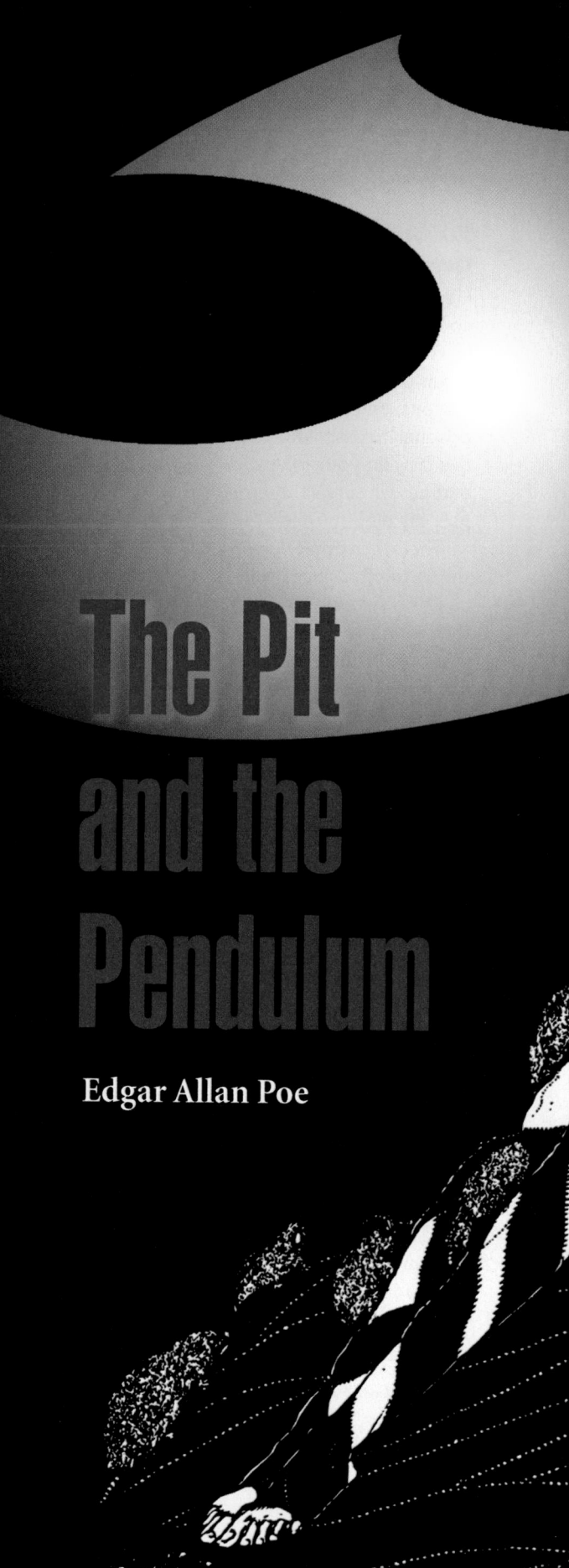

# The Pit and the Pendulum

**Edgar Allan Poe**

# Any horror but this!

I was sick—sick unto death with that long agony; and when they at length unbound me, and I was permitted to sit, I felt that my senses were leaving me. The sentence—the dread sentence of death—was the last of distinct accentuation which reached my ears. After that, the sound of the Inquisitorial voices seemed merged in one dreamy, indeterminate hum. It conveyed to my soul the idea of *revolution*[1]— perhaps from its association in fancy[2] with the burr of a mill wheel. This only for a brief period, for presently I heard no more. Yet for a while, I saw—but with how terrible an exaggeration! I saw the lips of the black-robed judges. They appeared to me white—whiter than the sheet upon which I trace these words—and thin even to grotesqueness; thin with the intensity of their expression of firmness—of immovable resolution—of stern contempt of human torture. I saw that the decrees of what to me was Fate were still issuing from those lips. I saw them writhe with a deadly locution.[3] I saw them fashion the syllables of my name; and I shuddered because no sound succeeded.[4] I saw, too, for a few moments of delirious horror, the soft and nearly imperceptible waving of the sable draperies which enwrapped the walls of the apartment. And then my vision fell upon the seven tall candles upon the table. At first they wore the aspect of charity and seemed white, slender angels who would save me; but then, all at once, there came a most deadly nausea over my spirit, and I felt every fiber in my frame thrill as if I had touched the wire of a galvanic battery, while the angel forms became meaningless specters, with heads of flame, and I saw that from them there would be no help. And then there stole into my fancy, like a rich musical note, the thought of what sweet rest there must

1. **revolution** *n.*: rotation; turning motion.
2. **fancy** *n.*: imagination.
3. **locution** (lō·kyōō'shən) *n.*: utterance; statement.
4. **succeeded** *v.*: followed.

**Vocabulary**

**imperceptible** (im'pər·sep'tə·bəl) *adj.*: not clear or obvious to the senses or the mind.

be in the grave. The thought came gently and stealthily, and it seemed long before it attained full appreciation; but just as my spirit came at length properly to feel and entertain it, the figures of the judges vanished, as if magically, from before me; the tall candles sank into nothingness! Their flames went out utterly; the blackness of darkness supervened; all sensations appeared swallowed up in a mad rushing descent, as of the soul into Hades. Then silence, and stillness, and night were the universe.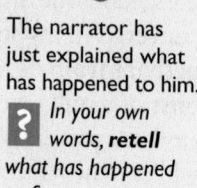

❶
The narrator has just explained what has happened to him. *In your own words*, **retell** *what has happened so far.*

I had swooned;[5] but still will not say that all of consciousness was lost. What of it there remained I will not attempt to define, or even to describe; yet all was not lost. In the deepest

slumber—no! In delirium—no! In a swoon—no! In death—no! Even in the grave all *is not* lost. Else there is no immortality for man. Arousing from the most profound of slumbers, we break the gossamer web of *some* dream. Yet in a second afterward (so frail may that web have been), we remember not that we have dreamed. In the return to life from the swoon, there are two stages: first, that of the sense of mental or spiritual; second, that of the sense of physical existence. It seems probable that if, upon reaching the second stage, we could recall the impressions of the first, we should find these impressions eloquent in memories of the gulf beyond. And that gulf is—what? How at least shall we distinguish its shadows from those of the tomb? But if the impressions of what I have termed the first stage are not, at will, recalled, yet, after long interval, do they not come unbidden, while we marvel whence they come? He who has never swooned is not he who finds

---
5. **swooned** *v.:* fainted.

## A CLOSER LOOK: POLITICAL INFLUENCES

### The Inquisition: Power, Greed, and Suffering

INFORMATIONAL TEXT

King Ferdinand and Queen Isabella of Spain had political as well as religious motives for establishing the Spanish Inquisition in 1478. The Catholic monarchs wished to regain control over a fragmented country that had been ruled for centuries by the Moors (Muslims from North Africa) and that had a large population of influential Jews, many of whom had converted to Christianity. By finding Spanish Jews and Muslims guilty of converting to Christianity not out of true religious conviction but from a desire to keep their lands and property, the monarchy used the Inquisition to seize the converts' wealth and destroy their influence. The methods of the Inquisition included imprisonment, torture, confiscation of property, and public execution. At its height, from 1483 to 1498, a Dominican priest, Tomás de Torquemada, presided over thousands of trials and about

two thousand burnings at the stake. These burnings were preceded by a public religious ceremony, called an auto-da-fé (Portuguese for "act of faith"), in which the accused was marched in procession into a church, a Mass was held, and the death sentence was read. Then the convicted person was handed over to the state authorities for execution.

The Inquisition was temporarily halted in 1808, when Napoleon's army invaded and defeated Spain. General Lasalle commanded the French troops who seized the city of Toledo. Napoleon proclaimed his older brother king of Spain, but in 1813, he was ousted by the Spanish with British aid. The Spanish monarchy was restored and with it the Inquisition, which persisted in a limited form in Spain and Latin America until 1834.

strange palaces and wildly familiar faces in coals that glow; is not he who beholds floating in midair the sad visions that the many may not view; is not he who ponders over the perfume of some novel flower; is not he whose brain grows bewildered with the meaning of some musical cadence which has never before arrested his attention.

Amid frequent and thoughtful endeavors to remember, amid earnest struggles to regather some token of the state of seeming nothingness into which my soul had lapsed, there have been moments when I have dreamed of success; there have been brief, very brief, periods when I have conjured up remembrances which the lucid reason of a later epoch assures me could have had reference only to that condition of seeming unconsciousness. These shadows of memory tell, indistinctly, of tall figures that lifted and bore me in silence down—down—still down—till a hideous dizziness oppressed me at the mere idea of the interminableness of the descent. They tell also of a vague horror at my heart, on account of that heart's unnatural stillness. Then comes a sense of sudden motionlessness throughout all things; as if those who bore me (a ghastly train!) had outrun, in their descent, the limits of the limitless, and paused from the wearisomeness of their toil. After this I call to mind flatness and dampness; and then all is *madness*—the madness of a memory which busies itself among forbidden things. ❷

❷ What has the narrator dreamed, and what does he realize at this moment?

Very suddenly there came back to my soul motion and sound—the tumultuous motion of the heart and, in my ears, the sound of its beating. Then a pause in which all is blank. Then again sound, and motion, and touch—a tingling sensation pervading my frame. Then the mere consciousness of existence, without thought—a condition which lasted long. Then, very suddenly, *thought,* and shuddering terror, and earnest endeavor to comprehend my true state. Then a strong desire to lapse into insensibility. Then a rushing revival of soul and a suc-

cessful effort to move. And now a full memory of the trial, of the judges, of the sable draperies, of the sentence, of the sickness, of the swoon. Then entire forgetfulness of all that followed; of all that a later day and much earnestness of endeavor have enabled me vaguely to recall.

So far, I had not opened my eyes. I felt that I lay upon my back, unbound. I reached out my hand, and it fell heavily upon something damp and hard. There I suffered[6] it to remain for many minutes, while I strove to imagine where and *what* I could be. I longed, yet dared not, to employ my vision. I dreaded the first glance at objects around me. It was not that I feared to look upon things horrible, but that I grew aghast lest there should be *nothing* to see. At length, with a wild desperation at heart, I quickly unclosed my eyes. My worst thoughts, then, were confirmed. The blackness of eternal night encompassed me. I struggled for breath. The intensity of the darkness seemed to oppress and stifle me. The atmosphere was intolerably close. I still lay quietly, and made effort to exercise my reason. I brought to mind the Inquisitorial proceedings and attempted from that point to deduce my real condition. The sentence had passed; and it appeared to me that a very long interval of time had since elapsed. Yet not for a moment did I suppose myself actually dead. Such a supposition, notwithstanding what we read in fiction, is altogether inconsistent with real existence—but where and in what state was I? The condemned to death, I knew, perished usually at the autos-da-fé, and one of these had been held on the very night of the day of my trial. Had I been remanded to my dungeon, to await the next sacrifice, which would not take place for many months? This I at once saw could not be. Victims had been in immediate

---

**6. suffered** *v.*: allowed; tolerated.

**Vocabulary**

**ponders** (pän′dərz) *v.*: thinks deeply.
**lucid** (lōō′sid) *adj.*: clearheaded; not confused.
**tumultuous** (tōō·mul′chōō·əs) *adj.*: violent; greatly agitated or disturbed.

The Metropolitan Museum of Art, H. O. Havemeyer Collection, Bequest of Mrs. H. O. Havemeyer, 1929 (29.100.6). Photograph ©1992 The Metropolitan Museum of Art.

*View of Toledo* (1608) by El Greco (Domenikos Theotokopoulos) (Greek, 1541–1614). Oil on canvas. 47³/₄ × 42³/₄ in. (121.3 × 108.6 cm).

demand. Moreover, my dungeon, as well as all the condemned cells at Toledo, had stone floors, and light was not altogether excluded.

A fearful idea now suddenly drove the blood in torrents upon my heart, and for a brief period I once more relapsed into insensibility. Upon recovering, I at once started to my feet, trembling convulsively in every fiber. I thrust my arms wildly above and around me in all di-rections. I felt nothing; yet dreaded to move a step, lest I should be impeded by the walls of a *tomb*. Perspiration burst from every pore and stood in cold, big beads upon my forehead. The agony of suspense grew at length intolerable, and I cautiously moved forward, with my arms extended and my eyes straining from their sockets in the hope of catching some faint ray of light. I proceeded for many paces; but still all was blackness and vacancy. I breathed more freely. It seemed evident that mine was not, at least, the most hideous of fates. ❸

And now, as I still continued to step cautiously onward, there came thronging upon my recollection a thousand vague rumors of the horrors of Toledo. Of the dungeons there had been strange things narrated—fables I had always deemed them—but yet strange, and too ghastly to repeat, save in a whisper. Was I left to perish of starvation in the subterranean world of darkness; or what fate, perhaps even more fearful, awaited me? That the result would be death, and a death of more than customary bitterness, I knew too well the character of my judges to doubt. The mode and the hour were all that occupied or distracted me.

My outstretched hands at length encountered some solid obstruction. It was a wall, seemingly of stone masonry—very smooth, slimy, and cold. I followed it up, stepping with all the careful distrust with which certain antique narratives had inspired me. This process, however, afforded me no means of ascertaining the dimensions of my dungeon, as I might make its circuit and return to the point whence I set out without being aware of the fact, so perfectly uniform seemed the wall. I therefore sought the knife which had been in my pocket when led into the Inquisitorial chamber, but it was gone; my clothes had been exchanged for a wrapper of coarse serge. I had thought of forcing the blade in some minute crevice of the masonry, so as to identify my point of departure. The difficulty, nevertheless, was but trivial; although, in the disorder of my fancy, it seemed at first insuperable. I tore a part of the hem from the robe and placed the fragment at full length and at right angles to the wall. In groping my way around the prison, I could not fail to encounter this rag upon completing the circuit. So, at least, I thought; but I had not counted upon the ex-

❸
The narrator now is relieved that "the most hideous of fates" is not for him.

❓ *What is this fate? How does the narrator come to realize that this punishment is not his?*

tent of the dungeon, or upon my own weakness. The ground was moist and slippery. I staggered onward for some time, when I stumbled and fell. My excessive fatigue induced me to remain prostrate; and sleep soon overtook me as I lay.

Upon awaking and stretching forth an arm, I found beside me a loaf and a pitcher with water. I was too much exhausted to reflect upon this circumstance, but ate and drank with avidity.[7] Shortly afterward, I resumed my tour around the prison and, with much toil, came at last upon the fragment of the serge. Up to the period when I fell, I had counted fifty-two paces, and upon resuming my walk, I had counted forty-eight more—when I arrived at the rag. There were in all, then, a hundred paces; and, admitting two paces to the yard, I presumed the dungeon to be fifty yards in circuit. I had met, however, with many angles in the wall, and thus I could form no guess at the shape of the vault, for vault I could not help supposing it to be.

I had little object—certainly no hope—in these researches; but a vague curiosity prompted me to continue them. Quitting the wall, I resolved to cross the area of the enclosure. At first, I proceeded with extreme caution, for the floor, although seemingly of solid material, was treacherous with slime. At length, however, I took courage and did not hesitate to step firmly—endeavoring to cross in as direct a line as possible. I had advanced some ten or twelve paces in this manner when the remnant of the torn hem of my robe became entangled between my legs. I stepped on it and fell violently on my face.

In the confusion attending my fall, I did not immediately apprehend a somewhat startling circumstance, which yet, in a few seconds afterward and while I still lay prostrate, arrested my attention. It was this—my chin rested upon the

---

7. **avidity** (ə·vid′ə·tē) *n.:* great eagerness.

**Vocabulary**
**insuperable** (in·sōō′pər·ə·bəl) *adj.:* incapable of being overcome.
**prostrate** (präs′trāt′) *adj.:* lying flat.

floor of the prison, but my lips and the upper portion of my head, although seemingly at a less elevation than the chin, touched nothing. At the same time, my forehead seemed bathed in a clammy vapor, and the peculiar smell of decayed fungus arose to my nostrils. I put forward my arm, and shuddered to find that I had fallen at the very brink of a circular pit, whose extent, of course, I had no means of ascertaining at the moment. Groping about the masonry just below the margin, I succeeded in dislodging a small fragment and let it fall into the abyss. For many seconds I hearkened to its reverberations as it dashed against the sides of the chasm in its descent; at length, there was a sullen plunge into water, succeeded by loud echoes. At the same moment, there came a sound resembling the quick opening and as rapid closing of a door overhead, while a faint gleam of light flashed suddenly through the gloom and as suddenly faded away.

## I had fallen at the very brink of a circular pit . . .

I saw clearly the doom which had been prepared for me, and congratulated myself upon the timely accident by which I had escaped. Another step before my fall, and the world had seen me no more. And the death just avoided was of that very character which I had regarded as fabulous and frivolous in the tales respecting the Inquisition. To the victims of its tyranny, there was the choice of death with its direst physical agonies or death with its most hideous moral horrors. I had been reserved for the latter. By long suffering, my nerves had been unstrung, until I trembled at the sound of my own voice and had become in every respect a fitting subject for the species of torture which awaited me.

Shaking in every limb, I groped my way back to the wall; resolving there to perish rather than risk the terrors of the wells, of which my imagination now pictured many in various positions about the dungeon. In other conditions of mind, I might have had courage to end my misery at once, by a plunge into one of these abysses; but now I was the veriest[8] of cowards. Neither could I forget what I had read of these pits—that the *sudden* extinction of life formed no part of their most horrible plan. ❹

Agitation of spirit kept me awake for many long hours, but at length I again slumbered. Upon arousing, I found by my side, as before, a loaf and a pitcher of water. A burning thirst consumed me, and I emptied the vessel at a draft. It must have been drugged; for scarcely had I drunk before I became irresistibly drowsy. A deep sleep fell upon me—a sleep like that of death. How long it lasted of course I know not; but when, once again, I unclosed my eyes, the objects around me were visible. By a wild, sulfurous luster,[9] the origin of which I could not at first determine, I was enabled to see the extent and aspect of the prison.

In its size I had been greatly mistaken. The whole circuit of its walls did not exceed twenty-five yards. For some minutes this fact occasioned me a world of vain trouble; vain indeed, for what could be of less importance, under the terrible circumstances which environed me, than the mere dimensions of my dungeon? But my soul took a wild interest in trifles, and I busied myself in endeavors to account for the error I had committed in my measurement. The truth at length flashed upon me. In my first attempt at exploration I had counted fifty-two paces, up to the period when I fell; I must then have been within a pace or two of the fragment of serge; in fact, I had nearly performed the circuit of the vault. I then slept, and upon awaking, I must have returned upon my steps—thus supposing the circuit nearly double what it actually was.

> ❹
> **Retell** what has happened to the narrator since he awakened in the dungeon. What effect does the discovery of the pit have on the narrator?

---

8. **veriest** (ver′ē·ist) *adj.*: greatest.
9. **sulfurous** (sul′fər·əs) **luster:** glow like that of burning sulfur, which produces a blue flame. The word *sulfurous* also suggests the fires of hell.

My confusion of mind prevented me from observing that I began my tour with the wall to the left and ended it with the wall to the right.

I had been deceived, too, in respect to the shape of the enclosure. In feeling my way I had found many angles and thus deduced an idea of great irregularity; so potent is the effect of total darkness upon one arousing from lethargy or sleep! The angles were simply those of a few slight depressions, or niches, at odd intervals. The general shape of the prison was square. What I had taken for masonry seemed now to be iron, or some other metal, in huge plates, whose sutures or joints occasioned the depression. The entire surface of this metallic enclosure was rudely daubed[10] in all the hideous and repulsive devices to which the charnel[11] superstition of the monks has given rise. The figures of fiends in aspects of menace, with skeleton forms, and other, more really fearful images, overspread and disfigured the walls. I observed that the outlines of these monstrosities were sufficiently distinct, but that the colors seemed faded and blurred, as if from the effects of a damp atmosphere. I now noticed the floor, too, which was of stone. In the center yawned the circular pit from whose jaws I had escaped; but it was the only one in the dungeon. ❺

❺ **?** What causes the narrator to be confused about the size and shape of his cell? Now that he sees his surroundings more clearly, how is he affected?

All this I saw indistinctly and by much effort: for my personal condition had been greatly changed during slumber. I now lay upon my back, and at full length, on a species of low framework of wood. To this I was securely bound by a long strap resembling a surcingle.[12] It passed in many convolutions about my limbs and body, leaving at liberty only my head, and my left arm to such extent that I could, by dint of much exertion, supply myself with food from an earthen dish which lay by my side on the floor. I saw, to my horror, that the pitcher had been removed. I say to my horror, for I was consumed with intolerable thirst. This thirst it appeared to be the design of my persecutors to stimulate—for the food in the dish was meat pungently seasoned.

Looking upward, I surveyed the ceiling of my prison. It was some thirty or forty feet overhead and constructed much as the side walls. In one of its panels a very singular figure riveted my whole attention. It was the painted figure of Time as he is commonly represented, save[13] that, in lieu of[14] a scythe, he held what, at a casual glance, I supposed to be the pictured image of a huge pendulum, such as we see on antique clocks. There was something, however, in the appearance of this machine which caused me to regard it more attentively. While I gazed directly upward at it (for its position was immediately over my own), I fancied that I saw it in motion. In an instant afterward the fancy was confirmed. Its sweep was brief and of course slow. I watched it for some minutes somewhat in fear, but more in wonder. Wearied at length with observing its dull movement, I turned my eyes upon the other objects in the cell.

A slight noise attracted my notice, and looking to the floor, I saw several enormous rats traversing it. They had issued from the well which lay just within view to my right. Even then, while I gazed, they came up in troops, hurriedly, with ravenous eyes, allured by the scent of the meat. From this it required much effort and attention to scare them away. ❻

It might have been half an hour, perhaps even an hour (for I could take but

❻ The narrator has just given a detailed description of his cell.
**?** Describe what he has seen.

---

10. **daubed** *v.:* painted crudely or unskillfully.
11. **charnel** *adj.:* suggesting death. A charnel house is a tomb or place where bones of the dead are deposited.
12. **surcingle** (sʉr′siŋ′gəl) *n.:* strap that binds a saddle or a pack to a horse's body.

13. **save** *conj.:* except.
14. **in lieu** (lo͞o) **of:** instead of.

**Vocabulary**

**potent** (pōt′′nt) *adj.:* powerful or effective.
**lethargy** (leth′ər·jē) *n.:* abnormal drowsiness.

**In the center yawned the circular pit
from whose jaws I had escaped . . .**

imperfect note of time), before I again cast my eyes upward. What I then saw confounded and amazed me. The sweep of the pendulum had increased in extent by nearly a yard. As a natural consequence its velocity was also much greater. But what mainly disturbed me was the idea that it had perceptibly *descended*. I now observed—with what horror it is needless to say—that its nether extremity[15] was formed of a crescent of glittering steel, about a foot in length from horn to horn; the horns upward, and the under edge evidently as keen as that of a razor. Like a razor also, it seemed massy and heavy, tapering from the edge into a solid and broad structure above. It was appended to a weighty rod of brass, and the whole *hissed* as it swung through the air.

I could no longer doubt the doom prepared for me by monkish ingenuity in torture. My cognizance[16] of the pit had become known to the Inquisitorial agents—*the pit*, whose horrors had been destined for so bold a recusant[17] as myself—*the pit*, typical of hell and regarded by rumor as the ultima Thule[18] of all their punishments. The plunge into this pit I had avoided by the merest of accidents, and I knew that surprise, or entrapment into torment, formed an important portion of all the grotesquerie of these dungeon deaths. Having failed to fall, it was no part of the demon plan to hurl me into the abyss, and thus (there being no alternative) a different and a milder destruction awaited me.

---

15. **nether extremity:** lower end.
16. **cognizance** (käg′nə·zəns) *n.:* awareness.
17. **recusant** (rek′yoo·zənt) *n.:* person who stands out stubbornly against an established authority.
18. **ultima Thule** (ul′ti·mə thoo′lē): most extreme. The term is Latin for "northernmost region of the world."

Milder! I half smiled in my agony as I thought of such application of such a term.

What boots it[19] to tell of the long, long hours of horror more than mortal, during which I counted the rushing vibrations of the steel! Inch by inch—line by line—with a descent only appreciable at intervals that seemed ages—down and still down it came! Days passed—it might have been that many days passed—ere it swept so closely over me as to fan me with its acrid breath. The odor of the sharp steel forced itself into my nostrils. I prayed—I wearied heaven with my prayer for its more speedy descent. I grew frantically mad and struggled to force myself upward against the sweep of the fearful scimitar.[20] And then I fell suddenly calm and lay smiling at the glittering death, as a child at some rare bauble.

There was another interval of utter insensibility; it was brief; for, upon again lapsing into life, there had been no perceptible descent in the pendulum. But it might have been long—for I knew there were demons who took note of my swoon and who could have arrested the vibration at pleasure. Upon my recovery, too, I felt very—oh! inexpressibly—sick and weak, as if through long inanition.[21] Even amid the agonies of that period, the human nature craved food. With painful effort I outstretched my left arm as far as my bonds permitted and took possession of the small remnant which had been spared me by the rats. As I put a portion of it within my lips, there rushed to my mind a half-formed thought of joy—of hope. Yet what business had *I* with hope? It was, as I say, a half-formed thought—man has many such, which are never completed. I felt that it was of joy—of hope; but I felt also that it had perished in its formation. In vain I struggled to perfect—to regain it. Long suffering had nearly annihilated all my ordinary powers of mind. I was an imbecile—an idiot.

---

19. **what boots it:** of what use is it.
20. **scimitar** (sim′ə·tər) *n.:* sword with a curved blade, used mainly by Arabs and Turks.
21. **inanition** (in′ə·nish′ən) *n.:* weakness from lack of food.

The vibration of the pendulum was at right angles to my length. I saw that the crescent was designed to cross the region of the heart. It would fray the serge of my robe—it would return and repeat its operations—again—and again. Notwithstanding its terrifically wide sweep (some thirty feet or more) and the hissing vigor of its descent, sufficient to sunder these very walls of iron, still the fraying of my robe would be all that, for several minutes, it would accomplish. And at this thought I paused. I dared not go further than this reflection. I dwelt upon it with a pertinacity[22] of attention—as if, in so dwelling, I could arrest[23] *here* the descent of the steel. I forced myself to ponder upon the sound of the crescent as it should pass across the garment—upon the peculiar thrilling sensation which the friction of cloth produces on the nerves. I pondered upon all this frivolity until my teeth were on edge.

Down—steadily down it crept. I took a frenzied pleasure in contrasting its downward with its lateral velocity. To the right—to the left—far and wide—with the shriek of a damned spirit! to my heart, with the stealthy pace of the tiger! I alternately laughed and howled, as the one or the other idea grew predominant.

Down—certainly, relentlessly down! It vibrated within three inches of my bosom! I struggled violently—furiously—to free my left arm. This was free only from the elbow to the hand. I could reach the latter, from the platter beside me, to my mouth, with great effort, but no farther. Could I have broken the fastenings above the elbow, I would have seized and attempted to arrest the pendulum. I might as well have attempted to arrest an avalanche!

Down—still unceasingly—still inevitably down! I gasped and struggled at each vibration. I shrunk convulsively at its every sweep. My eyes followed its outward or upward whorls with the eagerness of the most unmeaning despair; they closed themselves spasmodically at the descent, although death would have been a relief, oh,

how unspeakable! Still I quivered in every nerve to think how slight a sinking of the machinery would precipitate that keen, glistening ax upon my bosom. It was *hope* that prompted the nerve to quiver—the frame to shrink. It was *hope*— the hope that triumphs on the rack—that whispers to the death-condemned even in the dungeons of the Inquisition.

I saw that some ten or twelve vibrations would bring the steel in actual contact with my robe, and with this observation there suddenly came over my spirit all the keen, collected calmness of despair. For the first time during many hours—or perhaps days—I *thought*. It now occurred to me that the bandage, or surcingle, which enveloped me, was *unique*. I was tied by no separate cord. The first stroke of the razor-like crescent athwart any portion of the band would so detach it that it might be unwound from my person by means of my left hand. But how fearful, in that case, the proximity of the steel! The result of the slightest struggle, how deadly! Was it likely, moreover, that the minions[24] of the torturer had not foreseen and provided for this possibility? Was it probable that the bandage crossed my bosom in the track of the pendulum? Dreading to find my faint and, as it seemed, my last hope frustrated, I so far elevated my head as to obtain a distinct view of my breast. The surcingle enveloped my limbs and body close in all directions—*save in the path of the destroying crescent.* ❼

Scarcely had I dropped my head back into its original position when there flashed upon my mind what I cannot better describe than as the unformed half of that idea of deliverance to which I had previously alluded, and of which a moiety[25] only floated indeterminately through my brain when I raised food to my burning lips.

❼ **Retell** what has happened to the narrator since he first saw the rats coming out of the pit.

---

22. **pertinacity** (pʉrt''n·as'ə·tē) *n.*: stubborn persistence.
23. **arrest** *v.*: stop.

24. **minions** *n. pl.*: servants; followers.
25. **moiety** (mɔi'ə·tē) *n.*: part.

**Vocabulary**
**proximity** (präk·sim'ə·tē) *n.*: nearness.

The whole thought was now present—feeble, scarcely sane, scarcely definite—but still entire. I proceeded at once, with the nervous energy of despair, to attempt its execution.

For many hours the immediate vicinity of the low framework upon which I lay had been literally swarming with rats. They were wild, bold, ravenous—their red eyes glaring upon me as if they waited but for motionlessness on my part to make me their prey. "To what food," I thought, "have they been accustomed in the well?"

They had devoured, in spite of all my efforts to prevent them, all but a small remnant of the contents of the dish. I had fallen into a habitual seesaw or wave of the hand about the platter; and, at length, the unconscious uniformity of the movement deprived it of effect. In their voracity, the vermin frequently fastened their sharp fangs in my fingers. With the particles of the oily and spicy viand which now remained, I thoroughly rubbed the bandage wherever I could reach it; then, raising my hand from the floor, I lay breathlessly still.

At first, the ravenous animals were startled and terrified at the change—at the cessation of movement. They shrank alarmedly back; many sought the well. But this was only for a moment. I had not counted in vain upon their voracity. Observing that I remained without motion, one or two of the boldest leaped upon the framework and smelled at the surcingle. This seemed the signal for a general rush. Forth from the well they hurried in fresh troops. They clung to the wood—they overran it and leaped in hundreds upon my person. The measured movement of the pendulum disturbed them not at all. Avoiding its strokes, they busied themselves with the anointed bandage. They pressed—they swarmed upon me in ever accumulating heaps. They writhed upon my throat; their cold lips sought my own; I was half stifled by their thronging pressure; disgust for which the world has no name swelled my bosom and chilled, with a heavy clamminess, my heart. Yet one minute, and I felt that the struggle would be over. Plainly I perceived the loosening of the bandage. I knew that in more than one place it must be already

severed. With a more than human resolution I lay *still.*

Nor had I erred in my calculations—nor had I endured in vain. I at length felt that I was *free.* The surcingle hung in ribbons from my body. But the stroke of the pendulum already pressed upon my bosom. It had divided the serge of the robe. It had cut through the linen beneath. Twice again it swung, and a sharp sense of pain shot through every nerve. But the moment of escape had arrived. At a wave of my hand my deliverers hurried tumultuously away. With a steady movement—cautious, sidelong, shrinking, and slow—I slid from the embrace of the bandage and beyond the reach of the scimitar. For the moment, at least, *I was free.* ❽

❽ Why does the narrator rub the binding with the meat? What effect does this have on his situation?

*Free!*—and in the grasp of the Inquisition! I had scarcely stepped from my wooden bed of horror upon the stone floor of the prison when the motion of the hellish machine ceased, and I beheld it drawn up, by some invisible force, through the ceiling. This was a lesson which I took desperately to heart. My every motion was undoubtedly watched. Free!—I had but escaped death in one form of agony to be delivered unto worse than death in some other. With that thought I rolled my eyes nervously around on the barriers of iron that hemmed me in. Something unusual—some change which at first I could not appreciate distinctly—it was obvious, had taken place in the apartment. For many minutes of a dreamy and trembling abstraction, I busied myself in vain, unconnected conjecture. During this period, I became aware, for the first time, of the origin of the sulfurous light which illumined the cell. It proceeded from a fissure, about half an inch in width, extending entirely around the prison at the base of the walls, which thus appeared, and were, completely separated from the floor. I endeavored, but of course in vain, to look through the aperture.

As I arose from the attempt, the mystery of the alteration in the chamber broke at once

A scene from "The Pit and the Pendulum," illustrated by John Byam Shaw.

upon my understanding. I had observed that, although the outlines of the figures upon the walls were sufficiently distinct, yet the colors seemed blurred and indefinite. These colors had now assumed and were momentarily assuming, a startling and most intense brilliance that gave to the spectral and fiendish portraitures an aspect that might have thrilled even firmer nerves than my own. Demon eyes, of a wild and ghastly vivacity, glared upon me in a thousand directions where none had been visible before, and gleamed with the lurid luster of a fire that I could not force my imagination to regard as unreal.

*Unreal!*—even while I breathed, there came to my nostrils the breath of the vapor of heated iron! A suffocating odor pervaded the prison! A deeper glow settled each moment in the eyes that glared at my agonies! A richer tint of crimson diffused itself over the pictured horrors of blood. I panted! I gasped for breath! There could be no doubt of the design of my tormenters— oh! most unrelenting! oh! most demoniac of men! I shrank from the glowing metal to the center of the cell. Amid the thought of the fiery destruction that impended, the idea of the coolness of the well came over my soul like balm. I rushed to its deadly brink. I threw my straining vision below. The glare from the enkindled roof illumined its inmost recesses. Yet for a wild moment did my spirit refuse to comprehend the meaning of what I saw. At length it forced—it wrestled its way into my soul—it burned itself in upon my shuddering reason.—Oh! for a voice to speak!—oh! horror! —oh! any horror but this! With a shriek, I rushed from the margin and buried my face in my hands—weeping bitterly.

The heat rapidly increased, and once again I looked up, shuddering as with a fit of the ague.[26] There had been a second change in the cell— and now the change was obviously in the *form*. As before, it was in vain that I at first endeavored to appreciate or understand what was taking place. But not long was I left in doubt. The Inquisitorial vengeance had been hurried by my

twofold escape, and there was to be no more dallying with the King of Terrors. The room had been square. I saw that two of its iron angles were now acute[27]—two, consequently, obtuse.[28] The fearful difference quickly increased with a low rumbling or moaning sound. In an instant the apartment had shifted its form into that of a lozenge.[29] But the alteration stopped not here— I neither hoped nor desired it to stop. I could have clasped the red walls to my bosom as a garment of eternal peace. "Death," I said, "any death but that of the pit!" Fool! Might I not have known that *into the pit* it was the object of the burning iron to urge me? Could I resist its glow? Or if even that, could I withstand its pressure? And now, flatter and flatter grew the lozenge, with a rapidity that left me no time for contemplation. Its center, and of course its greatest width, came just over the yawning gulf. I shrank back—but the closing walls pressed me resistlessly onward. At length, for my seared and writhing body, there was no longer an inch of foothold on the firm floor of the prison. I struggled no more, but the agony of my soul found vent in one loud, long, and final scream of despair. I felt that I tottered upon the brink—I averted my eyes— ❾

❾
**?** What third crisis does the narrator face after he escapes from his "bed of horror"?

There was a discordant hum of human voices! There was a loud blast as of many trumpets! There was a harsh grating as of a thousand thunders! The fiery walls rushed back! An outstretched arm caught my own as I fell, fainting, into the abyss. It was that of General Lasalle. The French army had entered Toledo. The Inquisition was in the hands of its enemies. ∎

27. **acute** *adj.*: of less than 90 degrees.
28. **obtuse** *adj.*: of more than 90 degrees and less than 180 degrees.
29. **lozenge** *n.*: diamond shape.

**Vocabulary**
**averted** (ə·vʉrt′id) *v.*: turned away; prevented.

26. **ague** (ā′gyo͞o′) *n.*: chills.

# Response and Analysis

## Reading Check

1. The retellings you did while reading the story should help you fill out a story map like the one below. Add as many events as you think are necessary.

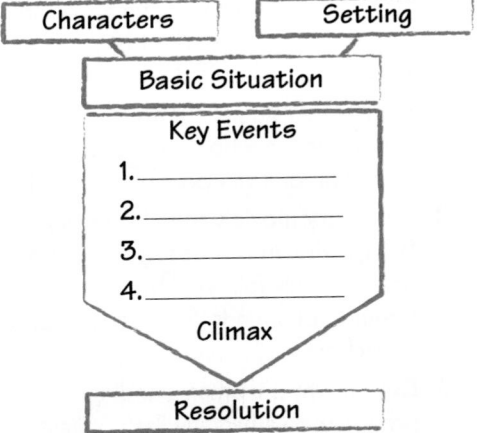

Characters

Setting

Basic Situation

Key Events

1._____

2._____

3._____

4._____

Climax

Resolution

## Thinking Critically

2. The **setting** of this story may be its most unforgettable element. List at least six of its horrible details. Did any of these horrors tap into the fear you described in your Quickwrite notes?

3. Some critics read Poe's text **symbolically,** as the story of a man who dies and almost loses his soul in the pit of hell but is saved at the end by God. See if the story works with this symbolic interpretation. Consider the following items:

   • The man, above all, fears falling into the pit. What could the pit symbolize?

   • What does a pendulum suggest to you, and what does an old man with a scythe represent? What connection might there be between these two symbols and the scythe on the pendulum in Poe's story?

   • Rats are often used as symbols of death and decay. How does the prisoner's response to these rats—especially when they crawl over him—suggest that he might see them in this way?

   • What sounds are usually associated with Judgment Day, at the end of the world? Do you hear these sounds at the story's end?

   Do you think this symbolic reading makes sense, or is it stretching the meaning of a simple horror story too far? Explain.

4. Stories of imprisonment and torture often explore **themes** of power and its abuse. What comment do you think Poe may be making about the political, religious, and social situation in the historical period in which this story takes place?

## Extending and Evaluating

5. Did General Lasalle's arrival seem an exceptionally lucky coincidence to you? If so, did the last-minute rescue lessen the story's credibility or your enjoyment of the story? Explain your opinion.

## WRITING

### The Story as Springboard

On page 282, you read a brief feature about the political situation in Spain during the fifteenth century. These details shed some interesting light on Poe's brutal story. Select a topic that is featured in the story or in **A Closer Look,** and write a **research report.** You might focus on one of these topics:

• the Spanish Inquisition
• the Moors in Spain during the Middle Ages
• the Jewish presence in Spain in the Middle Ages
• El Greco (see the art on page 284)

Before you begin, formulate a series of questions about the topic you choose. As you find the answers to those broad questions, make decisions that will narrow the focus of your research.

▶ **Use "Reporting Historical Research," pages 602–621, for help with this assignment.**

SKILLS
FOCUS

**Literary Skills**
Analyze symbolic meaning.

**Reading Skills**
Retell key events.

**Writing Skills**
Write a historical research report. Write an updated horror story.

**Vocabulary Skills**
Use context clues to determine the meanings of words.

# WRITING

## Terror Today

"The Pit and the Pendulum" is a classic psychological horror story. Do you think the events in the story—or something like them—could take place today? Fill out a chart like the following one for help organizing your thoughts:

|  | Poe's Story | Updated Story |
|---|---|---|
| Setting (when and where?) |  |  |
| Protagonist (What is his or her crime?) |  |  |
| Punishment |  |  |
| Opponents or jailers |  |  |
| Rescuers |  |  |

Then, write your own modern retelling.

▶ **Use "Writing a Short Story," pages 338–345, for help with this assignment.**

## Vocabulary Development
### Using Context Clues

Justify your responses to each numbered item below. Then, indicate the context clues in each sentence that gave you hints to the meaning of each underlined word. When you've identified the context clues in the sentences, go back to Poe's story, and write down any context clues he gives for the underlined Vocabulary words.

1. Why would simple, lucid instructions help someone who <u>ponders</u> the operation of a videocassette recorder?

2. A mystery movie's soundtrack begins faintly, with an almost <u>imperceptible</u> noise, quickly followed by shocking, <u>tumultuous</u> sounds. Suggest examples of each type of sound.

3. Explain why a woman standing in <u>proximity</u> to a blinding flash of light would have <u>averted</u> her eyes.

4. Why might desperate people facing an <u>insuperable</u> enemy lie <u>prostrate</u> on the ground?

5. Name three <u>potent</u> smells that would rouse you from a summer afternoon's <u>lethargy</u>.

Illustration by Wilfred Satty for "The Fall of the House of Usher" by Edgar Allan Poe.

# Vocabulary Development

## Greek, Latin, and Anglo-Saxon Affixes in Math and Science

Prefixes and suffixes are examples of **affixes,** word parts that are attached to the beginning or end of a base word or root to make a new word. Knowing some frequently used affixes can help you quickly unlock the meanings of some difficult words.

**Prefixes** are added to the beginning of a base word and always change its meaning. The following chart shows prefixes commonly used in mathematical and scientific terms:

| Latin Prefixes | Meanings | Examples |
|---|---|---|
| co–, col–, com– | with; together | coefficient, collide, compute |
| circum– | around | circumvent, circumnavigate |
| di–, dis– | away; lack of | disinfect, dilute |
| re– | again; back | research, reproduce |
| **Greek Prefixes** | **Meanings** | **Examples** |
| ant–, anti– | against; opposing | antibiotic, antidote |
| hypo– | under; below | hypothesis, hypodermic |
| micro– | enlarging; small | microscope, microorganism |
| **Anglo-Saxon Prefixes** | **Meanings** | **Examples** |
| mis– | badly or wrongly; not | misdiagnose, miscalculate |
| over– | too much | overdose, overestimate |
| un– | not | unconscious, unknown |

*(continued)*

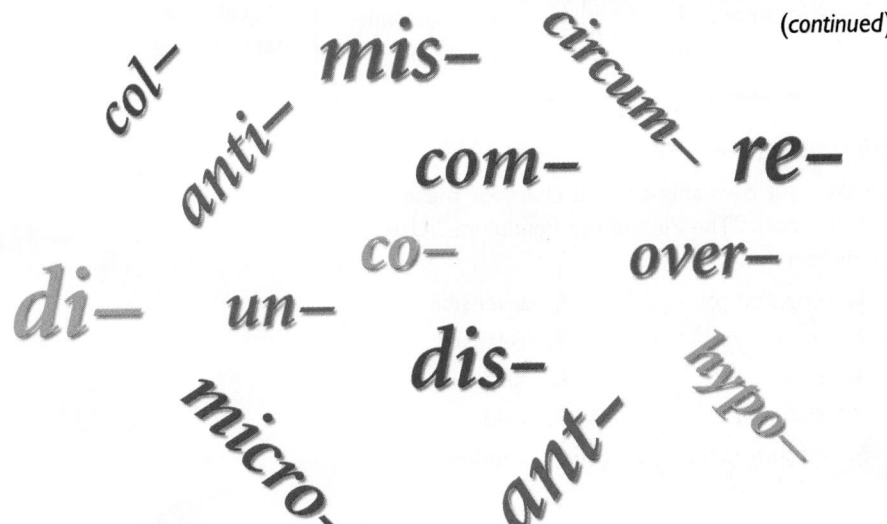

**Vocabulary Skills**
Use Latin, Greek, and Anglo-Saxon affixes to infer meanings of scientific and mathematical terms.

**Suffixes** are added to the end of a base word or root. **Inflectional suffixes,** like –ed and –ing, usually just change the tense, the person, or the number of a word (generally a verb). **Derivational suffixes,** like the ones listed below, change the meaning of a root or base word. This chart shows suffixes commonly used in math and science:

| Greek and Latin Suffixes | Meanings | Examples |
|---|---|---|
| –ance, –ence | state or quality of being | buoyance, turbulence |
| –able, –ible | able to; likely to | malleable, combustible |
| –tion | action of; condition of | respiration, condensation |
| –ous | full of | igneous, deciduous |
| –cy | condition of; state of | accuracy, currency |
| –ity | state of; condition of | possibility, regularity |
| **Anglo-Saxon Suffixes** | **Meanings** | **Examples** |
| –ness | quality or state of being | consciousness, sickness |
| –dom | state of being; rank of or domain of | kingdom, wisdom |
| –ly | like; characteristic of | internally, regressively |
| –less | lacking; without | motionless, bloodless |

This chart shows one way in which you can do an affix analysis to get at the meaning of a difficult word:

| Word | Prefix + Its Meaning | Base/Root Word + Its Meaning | Suffix + Its Meaning | Meaning of Word |
|---|---|---|---|---|
| unconsciousness | un–, "not" | conscious, "knowing; feeling" | –ness, "quality or state of being" | the state of not knowing or feeling |

**PRACTICE**

Make your own affix-analysis chart for these words from "The Pit and the Pendulum." Use a dictionary for help.

1. cognizance
2. intensity
3. alteration
4. sulfurous
5. circumstance

6. insensibility
7. relapsed
8. disorder
9. evidently
10. limitless

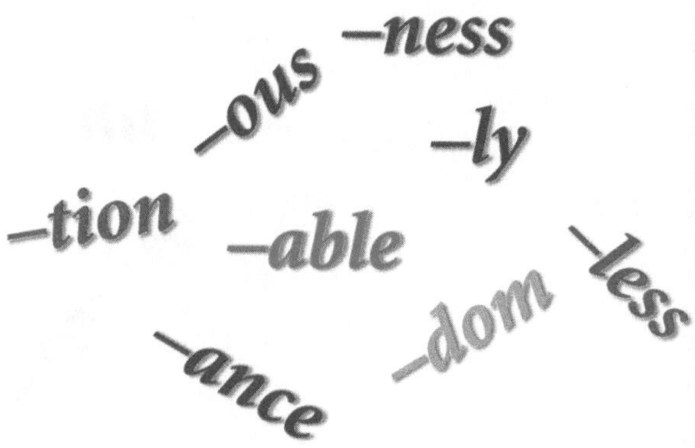

–ous  –ness
–ly
–tion  –able
–ance  –dom  –less

# Before You Read

## The Raven

### Make the Connection

"The Raven"—one of the most famous poems ever written—is a narrative poem with a story line that leads the reader from curiosity to horror. The poem explores one aspect of the dark side of human nature— what Poe himself called "that species of despair which delights in self-torture." In the jargon of psychology, the narrator projects or puts onto the bird whatever his own wild imagination dredges up.

### Literary Focus
#### Sound Effects

One of the reasons "The Raven" electrified the public is that it's catchy in the way a song can be. Like many songs, the poem has evocative rhythms, clever rhymes, alliteration, and other pleasing sound effects. These devices make you want to read the poem aloud or listen to it being read aloud. You want to hear not only the story but also the *sound* of the story.

As you read or listen, bear in mind that literary sound effects—just like movie sound effects—have a purpose. What is Poe trying to accomplish with the sound effects he creates in "The Raven"?

### Background

When "The Raven" was first published, in 1845 in a New York newspaper, it was a hit—an enormous popular success with the same kind of impact that a new CD might have today. Back then it seemed as if everyone was reading "The Raven," reciting it, and talking about it. As a result of the poem's success, Poe's name became a household word—yet he received only about ten dollars for his work.

**SKILLS FOCUS**

**Literary Skills**
Understand sound effects in poetry.

go.
hrw.
.com

**INTERNET**

More About Edgar Allan Poe

Keyword: LE7 11-2

# The Raven

## Edgar Allan Poe

Once upon a midnight dreary, while I pondered, weak and weary,
Over many a quaint and curious volume of forgotten lore—
While I nodded, nearly napping, suddenly there came a tapping,
As of someone gently rapping, rapping at my chamber door—
5  " 'Tis some visitor," I muttered, "tapping at my chamber door—
    Only this and nothing more."

Ah, distinctly I remember it was in the bleak December;
And each separate dying ember wrought its ghost upon the floor.
Eagerly I wished the morrow;—vainly I had sought to borrow

10  From my books surcease° of sorrow—sorrow for the lost Lenore—
For the rare and radiant maiden whom the angels name Lenore—
    Nameless *here* for evermore.

And the silken, sad, uncertain rustling of each purple curtain
Thrilled me—filled me with fantastic terrors never felt before;

15  So that now, to still the beating of my heart, I stood repeating
" 'Tis some visitor entreating° entrance at my chamber door—
Some late visitor entreating entrance at my chamber door;—
    This it is and nothing more."

Presently my soul grew stronger; hesitating then no longer,

20  "Sir," said I, "or Madam, truly your forgiveness I implore;°
But the fact is I was napping, and so gently you came rapping,
And so faintly you came tapping, tapping at my chamber door,
That I scarce was sure I heard you"—here I opened wide the door;—
    Darkness there and nothing more.

25  Deep into that darkness peering, long I stood there wondering, fearing,
Doubting, dreaming dreams no mortal ever dared to dream before;
But the silence was unbroken, and the stillness gave no token,
And the only word there spoken was the whispered word, "Lenore?"
This I whispered, and an echo murmured back the word, "Lenore!"

30      Merely this and nothing more.

Back into the chamber turning, all my soul within me burning,
Soon again I heard a tapping somewhat louder than before.
"Surely," said I, "surely that is something at my window lattice;°
Let me see, then, what thereat is, and this mystery explore—

35  Let my heart be still a moment and this mystery explore;—
    'Tis the wind and nothing more!"

**10. surcease** *n.:* end.

**16. entreating** *v.:*
begging; asking.

**20. implore** *v.:* plead; ask.

**33. lattice** *n.:* shutter or
screen formed by strips
or bars overlaid in a criss-
cross pattern.

Open here I flung the shutter, when, with many a flirt and flutter,
In there stepped a stately Raven of the saintly days of yore;°
Not the least obeisance° made he; not a minute stopped or stayed he;
40    But, with mien° of lord or lady, perched above my chamber door—
Perched upon a bust of Pallas° just above my chamber door—
    Perched, and sat, and nothing more.

Then this ebony bird beguiling° my sad fancy into smiling,
By the grave and stern decorum of the countenance it wore,
45    "Though thy crest be shorn and shaven, thou," I said, "art sure no craven,
Ghastly grim and ancient Raven wandering from the Nightly shore—
Tell me what thy lordly name is on the Night's Plutonian shore!"°
    Quoth the Raven "Nevermore."

Much I marveled this ungainly° fowl to hear discourse so plainly,
50    Though its answer little meaning—little relevancy bore;
For we cannot help agreeing that no living human being
Ever yet was blessed with seeing bird above his chamber door—
Bird or beast upon the sculptured bust above his chamber door,
    With such name as "Nevermore."

55    But the Raven, sitting lonely on the placid bust, spoke only
That one word, as if his soul in that one word he did outpour.
Nothing farther then he uttered—not a feather then he fluttered—
Till I scarcely more than muttered "Other friends have flown before—
On the morrow *he* will leave me, as my Hopes have flown before."
60        Then the bird said "Nevermore."

Startled at the stillness broken by reply so aptly spoken,
"Doubtless," said I, "what it utters is its only stock and store
Caught from some unhappy master whom unmerciful Disaster
Followed fast and followed faster till his songs one burden bore—
65    Till the dirges of his Hope that melancholy burden bore
    Of 'Never—nevermore.'"

But the Raven still beguiling my sad fancy into smiling,
Straight I wheeled a cushioned seat in front of bird, and bust and door;
Then, upon the velvet sinking, I betook myself to linking
70    Fancy unto fancy, thinking what this ominous bird of yore—
What this grim, ungainly, ghastly, gaunt, and ominous bird of yore
    Meant in croaking "Nevermore."

**38. Raven . . . of yore:** *Of yore* is an obsolete way of saying "of time long past." Poe's allusion is to 1 Kings 17:1–6, which tells of the prophet Elijah being fed by ravens in the wilderness.
**39. obeisance** (ō·bā′səns) *n.:* gesture of respect.
**40. mien** (mēn) *n.:* manner.
**41. Pallas:** Pallas Athena, the Greek goddess of wisdom.
**43. beguiling** *v.* used as *adj.:* deceiving.
**47. Plutonian shore:** Pluto is the Greek god of the underworld—the land of darkness—called Hades (hā′dēz′). Hades is separated from the world of the living by several rivers; hence, the mention of a shore.
**49. ungainly** *adj.:* unattractive.

This I sat engaged in guessing, but no syllable expressing
To the fowl whose fiery eyes now burned into my bosom's core;
75 This and more I sat divining,° with my head at ease reclining
On the cushion's velvet lining that the lamplight gloated o'er,
But whose velvet-violet lining with the lamplight gloating o'er,
      *She* shall press, ah, nevermore!

Then, methought, the air grew denser, perfumed from an unseen censer
80 Swung by seraphim° whose footfalls tinkled on the tufted floor.
"Wretch," I cried, "thy God hath lent thee—by these angels he hath sent thee
Respite—respite and nepenthe° from thy memories of Lenore;
Quaff,° oh quaff this kind nepenthe and forget this lost Lenore!"
      Quoth the Raven "Nevermore."

85 "Prophet!" said I, "thing of evil!—prophet still, if bird or devil!—
Whether Tempter sent, or whether tempest tossed thee here ashore,
Desolate yet all undaunted,° on this desert land enchanted—
On this home by Horror haunted—tell me truly, I implore—
Is there—*is* there balm in Gilead?°—tell me—tell me, I implore!"
90       Quoth the Raven "Nevermore."

"Prophet!" said I, "thing of evil!—prophet still, if bird or devil!
By that Heaven that bends above us—by that God we both adore—
Tell this soul with sorrow laden if, within the distant Aidenn,°
It shall clasp a sainted maiden whom the angels name Lenore—
95 Clasp a rare and radiant maiden whom the angels name Lenore."
      Quoth the Raven "Nevermore."

"Be that word our sign of parting, bird or fiend!" I shrieked, upstarting—
"Get thee back into the tempest and the Night's Plutonian shore!
Leave no black plume as a token of that lie thy soul hath spoken!
100 Leave my loneliness unbroken!—quit the bust above my door!
Take thy beak from out my heart, and take thy form from off my door!"
      Quoth the Raven "Nevermore."

And the Raven, never flitting, still is sitting, *still* is sitting
On the pallid° bust of Pallas just above my chamber door;
105 And his eyes have all the seeming of a demon's that is dreaming,
And the lamplight o'er him streaming throws his shadow on the floor;
And my soul from out that shadow that lies floating on the floor
      Shall be lifted—nevermore!

**75. divining** v. used as *adj.*: guessing; supposing.

**80. seraphim** *n. pl.*: highest of the nine ranks of angels.
**82. nepenthe** (nē·pen'thē) *n.*: sleeping potion that people once believed would relieve pain and sorrow.
**83. quaff** *v.*: drink heartily.
**87. undaunted** *adj.*: unafraid.
**89. Is . . . Gilead:** literally, Is there any relief from my sorrow? Poe paraphrases a line from Jeremiah 8:22: "Is there no balm in Gilead?" Gilead was a region in ancient Palestine known for its healing herbs, such as balm, a healing ointment.
**93. Aidenn:** Arabic for "Eden; Heaven."

**104. pallid** *adj.*: pale.

# Poe's Process: Writing "The Raven"

INFORMATIONAL TEXT

Several years after the hugely successful publication of "The Raven," Poe wrote an essay describing how he composed it. He described the writing of the poem as though he were solving a mathematical puzzle. Here are the first stages of Poe's writing process:

1. He decided he wanted to write a poem with a melancholy effect.
2. Then he decided that the melancholy would be reinforced by the refrain "Nevermore" (he liked its sound) and that a raven would utter the refrain. (Before he settled on a raven, though, he considered an owl and even a parrot.)
3. Finally, he decided his subject would be what he thought was the most melancholy subject in the world: a lover mourning for a beautiful woman who has died.

Now Poe was ready to write. The first stanza he wrote, he claimed, was the climactic one, lines 85–90. From there he set about choosing his details: the interior space in which the lover, who is a student, and the raven are brought together; the tapping that introduces the raven; the fact that the night is stormy rather than calm; and the action of the raven alighting on the bust of Pallas.

Then Poe goes on to describe his writing process:

❝ The raven addressed, answers with its customary word, 'Nevermore'—a word which finds immediate echo in the melancholy heart of the student, who, giving utterance aloud to certain thoughts suggested by the occasion, is again startled by the fowl's repetition of 'Nevermore.'

"One more time."

The student now guesses the state of the case, but is impelled, as I have before explained, by the human thirst for self-torture, and in part by superstition, to propound such queries to the bird as will bring him, the lover, the most of the luxury of sorrow, through the anticipated answer 'Nevermore.' ...

It will be observed that the words 'from out my heart' involve the first metaphorical expression in the poem. They, with the answer 'Nevermore,' dispose the mind to seek a moral in all that has been previously narrated. The reader begins now to regard the raven as emblematical [symbolic]—but it is not until the very last line of the very last stanza, that the intention of making him emblematical of *Mournful and never ending Remembrance* is permitted distinctly to be seen. ... ❞

# Response and Analysis

## Reading Check

1. What is the **setting**—the time and place—of the poem?

2. Trace the main events of the story, starting with the rap on the door (stanza 1) and ending with the raven's sitting on the sculpture above the chamber door (stanza 18). Include the questions the narrator asks the raven.

## Thinking Critically

3. How does the significance of the word *nevermore* change each time it is spoken? Though the speaker says his beloved will be nameless, he uses her name in lines 28–29, 82–83, and 94–95. How does the raven's answer to the speaker's queries keep reminding you of her?

4. How would you describe the **mood,** or feeling, created by the **setting**? Which **images** in the beginning of the poem help create this mood?

5. In line 101, what do you think the speaker means when he begs the bird, "Take thy beak from out my heart"?

6. The speaker's **tone,** or attitude toward his visitor, changes as the raven gradually turns from a slightly comic figure into a demonic one. Trace these changes in tone. Is there any evidence suggesting that the speaker is going mad? Explain.

7. What, in your opinion, does the raven **symbolize**? Why do you suppose Poe chose a raven to carry this meaning, rather than a chicken, an owl, a parrot, or any other bird? (For Poe's thoughts on "The Raven," see the **Primary Source** on page 302.)

## Extending and Evaluating

8. Look back at the **Primary Source** where the first three steps of Poe's writing process for "The Raven" are outlined. How do you evaluate the results of Poe's intention to write "a poem with a melancholy effect"?

## Literary Focus

### Interpreting Sound Effects

In writing "The Raven," Poe deliberately set out to produce an original verse form and to create novel effects using rhyme and alliteration.

The poem is a virtuoso performance in the use of **internal rhyme**—rhyme that occurs within the lines or repetition of an end rhyme within a line. "Dreary" and "weary" in line 1 prepare us for a pattern of internal rhyming sounds. "Napping," "tapping," and "rapping" in lines 3–4 make us expect more. Some of the rhymes are ingenious. Not many writers, for example, would think of rhyming "window lattice" with "what thereat is" (lines 33–34).

The technique of **alliteration** (the repetition of a consonant sound) is sometimes used to create **onomatopoeia**—the use of words with sounds that actually echo their sense. Often alliteration is used merely to create a striking sound effect; at times it becomes so exaggerated that we might even wonder if Poe is mocking himself. A good example of the excessive use of alliteration is in line 71, where the hard *g* is repeated four times, almost resulting in a tongue twister: "this grim, ungainly, ghastly, gaunt, and ominous bird of yore."

- What other examples of internal rhyme can you find?

- Where in lines 13–18 and 37–42 is alliteration used to create onomatopoeia?

SKILLS FOCUS

**Literary Skills**
Analyze sound effects in poetry.

**INTERNET**

Projects and Activities

Keyword: LE7 11-2

# Before You Read

## Eldorado

### Make the Connection
### Quickwrite ✏

The poem you are about to read is about a quest for Eldorado, a mythical land of great wealth. What quests do people take today to find great wealth? What are the results of some of those quests? Take notes on your responses to these questions.

### Literary Focus
### Archetype

The quest for a place of fabulous wealth is an archetype. Throughout history and literature this search for a golden land has been repeated, with different characters and varying endings. America itself once took on the aura of a paradise on earth. Europeans who were fleeing starvation or persecution imagined America as a place where the streets were paved with gold. From *Paradise Lost* to *The Wizard of Oz,* the message of this enduring archetype seems to be that as long as people can imagine a land where money practically grows on trees, they will continue to search for it.

gold dust, which would then be rinsed from his body in Lake Guatavita. During the ceremony, emeralds and other precious stones would be thrown into the depths of the lake. The conquistadors became convinced that if only they could find it, a country of vast riches would be theirs. Eldorado was never found.

In 1849, the year in which this poem was written, Eldorado took on a new meaning. The discovery of gold in California convinced thousands of Americans that a land of golden opportunity was at hand. Thus began the great rush that would take the gold seekers to the vicinity of Sutter's Mill and the muddy streets of San Francisco.

Behind this poem, then, lie both the legend passed on by the frustrated conquistadors and the reality reported in the daily newspapers. For Poe, though, Eldorado was predominantly an idea, as it remains for us today. "Eldorado" speaks to a universal human hope that somewhere lies a great, good place, the land of our hearts' desires.

**SKILLS FOCUS**

**Literary Skills**
Understand the use of archetype.

An **archetype** is an original, imaginative pattern that appears across cultures and is repeated through the ages. An archetype can be a character, a plot, a setting, or an object.

*For more on Archetype, see the Handbook of Literary and Historical Terms.*

**INTERNET**

More About Edgar Allan Poe

Keyword: LE7 11-2

### Background

*El Dorado* is Spanish for "the gilded one." The term is associated with the conquistadors, who had heard repeatedly about a ruler who lived in what is now Colombia. Every year the ruler would be covered in

# Eldorado

## Edgar Allan Poe

    Gaily bedight,°
    A gallant knight,
In sunshine and in shadow,
    Had journeyed long,
5     Singing a song,
In search of Eldorado.

    But he grew old—
    This knight so bold—
And o'er his heart a shadow
10    Fell as he found
    No spot of ground
That looked like Eldorado.

    And, as his strength
    Failed him at length,
15   He met a pilgrim shadow—
    "Shadow," said he,
    "Where can it be—
This land of Eldorado?"

    "Over the Mountains
20    Of the Moon,°
Down the Valley of the Shadow°
    Ride, boldly ride,"
    The shade replied,
"If you seek for Eldorado!"

---

1. **bedight** *adj.:* archaic for bedecked; dressed.
20. **Mountains of the Moon:** legendary source of the Nile River.
21. **Valley of the Shadow:** The "valley of the shadow of death" is mentioned in Psalm 23.

(Opposite and right), Gold sculpture showing the ceremony in Lake Guatavita that started the search for Eldorado.

# Response and Analysis

## Reading Check

1. Paraphrase what happens to the knight in the first two stanzas of the poem.
2. What directions does the shadow give the knight?

## Thinking Critically

3. The response the shadow makes to the knight is **ambiguous,** or open to interpretation. Explain what you think the shadow's answer really means.
4. How do the meanings of the word *shadow* change from stanza to stanza? How do these changes reflect a shift in the poem's **tone**—the attitude the speaker reveals about the quest?
5. The characters of the knight and the shadow have a **symbolic** meaning. What types of persons, attitudes, or values might these two characters represent?
6. This poem is based on an **archetypal** story pattern: the quest or perilous journey taken to find something of great value. According to the pilgrim shadow, what will be the result of this quest for the land of Eldorado?
7. Refer to the notes about quests that you wrote for the Quickwrite. What contemporary Eldorados are people searching for? How do their quests compare with the quest in "Eldorado"?

## Extending and Evaluating

8. Suppose this questing knight is a symbol of the poet himself. What then would the fate of this knight and his quest mean, in terms of Poe's feelings about his poetry?

## WRITING

### Comparing Poems

In a brief **essay,** compare "Eldorado" with "The Raven." Before you write, gather your details in a chart like the following one. Be sure to quote lines from the poems to support your comparison.

|  | The Raven | Eldorado |
|---|---|---|
| What raven symbolizes | | |
| What Eldorado symbolizes | | |
| Fate of main character | | |
| Theme of poem | | |
| Mood created by poem | | |

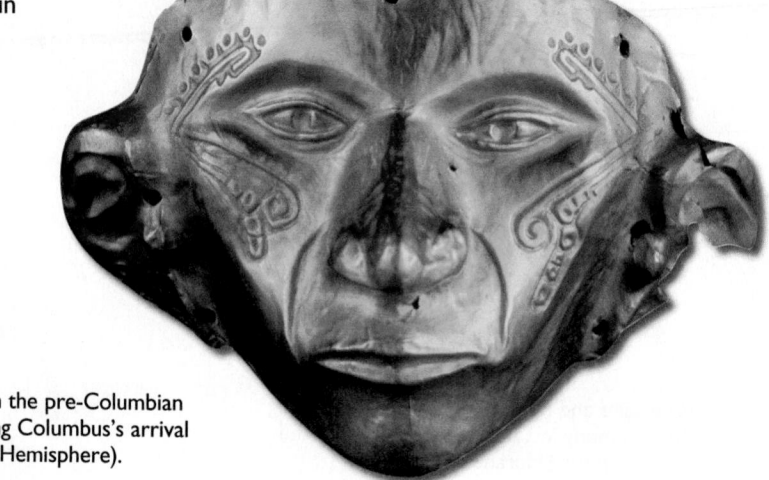

Gold mask from the pre-Columbian period (predating Columbus's arrival in the Western Hemisphere).

# Reflecting *on the* Literary Period

## American Romanticism: 1800–1860

The selections in this feature were written during the same literary period as the other selections in Collection 2, and they share many of the same ideas and concerns. The Focus Question will guide your reading and help you reflect on important aspects of the period.

*Cathedral Forest* (detail) by Albert Bierstadt, Private Collection.

## Think About . . .

Instead of celebrating logic and reason as the way to truth, the Romantics placed primary importance on imagination as the means to give expression to the feelings and intuitions that make each individual unique. Nothing is more characteristic of Romanticism than its defense of individual potential and its claim for individual freedom. This expansive spirit was well suited to the nineteenth-century United States—a new nation that was expanding geographically, economically, and politically.

   Certain subjects became characteristic of Romantic literature, such as the study of nature as a means to self-knowledge. In "The Chambered Nautilus," Oliver Wendell Holmes compares the life of a sea creature to the progress of the human soul. The Romantic emphasis upon intuition and the individual's interior world of intense feeling leads in Edgar Allan Poe's work to an interest in the irrational elements of the human mind. In his novel *Moby-Dick*, Herman Melville finds in the mysteries of nature and human nature a mixture of both good and evil.

SKILLS FOCUS

### Focus Question

As you read each selection, keep in mind this Focus Question and take notes to help you answer it at the end of the feature:
   According to Romantic views, how do the power of the imagination, individual feelings, and nature help us discover truths about ourselves that may elude the rational mind?

Pages 307–336 cover **Literary Skills** Evaluate the philosophical, political, religious, ethical, and social influences of a historical period.

# Reflecting *on the* Literary Period • **Before You Read**

## The Chambered Nautilus

**Meet the Writer** A descendant of Anne Bradstreet, **Oliver Wendell Holmes** (1809–1894) was born into a distinguished family in Cambridge, Massachusetts. After briefly studying law, he became bored and turned to medicine. He taught at Harvard, where he lectured on anatomy and physiology and served as dean of the medical school. He was an enthusiastic spokesperson for progress in medicine, and he is credited with coining the word *anesthesia* ("without feeling").

Holmes, who considered writing an avocation for most of his life, found time to write medical treatises, novels with medical themes, humorous essays, and many poems. He and his friends founded the magazine *The Atlantic Monthly,* to which he contributed a series of lively essays

eventually collected as *The Autocrat of the Breakfast Table* (1858). Holmes is usually grouped with James Russell Lowell, Henry Wadsworth Longfellow, and John Greenleaf Whittier, who were known as the Fireside Poets because they wrote on subjects geared for a family audience and their work was often read aloud at the fireside.

Holmes is remembered today for his wit, his wordplay, and his genial temperament. It is impossible to forget the gentleness and humor of a man who, beginning his practice as a young physician, hung out a sign saying GRATEFUL FOR SMALL FEVERS.

**Background** The chambered, or pearly, nautilus is a snaillike sea creature of the South Pacific and Indian Oceans. This mollusk grows year by year from the size of a tiny bead to the size of a pumpkin. As it grows, the nautilus creates new chambers of shell to house its body. The name *nautilus,* from a Greek word meaning "sailor," came from an old belief that the creature could actually use its shell as a ship in which it sailed. The nautilus interested the scientist in Holmes, but it also touched the poet in him.

The first three stanzas of the poem are a meditation upon the life and death of the nautilus. In the next to last stanza, the poet begins an **apostrophe** (a direct address to someone or something that is not present).

---

**CONNECTING TO THE**
### Focus Question

As you read the poem, consider this question: How do the speaker's observations reflect Romantic beliefs in the bond that exists between the natural and human world and in the individual's potential for spiritual growth?

---

# The Chambered Nautilus

## Oliver Wendell Holmes

This is the ship of pearl, which, poets feign,°
   Sails the unshadowed main,—
   The venturous bark that flings
On the sweet summer wind its purpled wings
In gulfs enchanted, where the siren° sings,
   And coral reefs lie bare,
Where the cold sea maids° rise to sun their streaming hair.

Its webs of living gauze no more unfurl;
   Wrecked is the ship of pearl!
   And every chambered cell,
Where its dim dreaming life was wont to dwell,
As the frail tenant shaped his growing shell,
   Before thee lies revealed,—
Its irised° ceiling rent,° its sunless crypt unsealed!

5

10

**1. feign** (fān): archaic for "imagine."

**5. siren** (sī′rən): in Greek mythology, one of a group of sea maidens whose seductive singing lures sailors to wreck their ships on coastal rocks.
**7. sea maids:** mermaids or sea nymphs.

**14. irised** (ī′risd): iridescent; rainbowlike. Iris is the Greek goddess of the rainbow. **rent:** torn.

15 Year after year beheld the silent toil
    That spread his lustrous coil;
    Still, as the spiral grew,
He left the past year's dwelling for the new,
Stole with soft step its shining archway through,
20     Built up its idle door,
Stretched in his last-found home, and knew the old no more.

Thanks for the heavenly message brought by thee,
    Child of the wandering sea,
    Cast from her lap, forlorn!
25 From thy dead lips a clearer note is born
Than ever Triton blew from wreathèd horn!°
    While on mine ear it rings,
Through the deep caves of thought I hear a voice that sings:—

Build thee more stately mansions, O my soul,
30     As the swift seasons roll!
    Leave thy low-vaulted past!
Let each new temple, nobler than the last,
Shut thee from heaven with a dome more vast,
    Till thou at length art free,
35 Leaving thine outgrown shell by life's unresting sea!

**26. than ... wreathèd**
(rēth'id) **horn:** echoes a line
from "The World Is Too
Much with Us," a sonnet by
English poet William
Wordsworth (1770–1850):
"Or hear old Triton blow his
wreathèd horn." In Greek
mythology, Triton is a sea god,
often represented as blowing a
trumpet made from a conch
shell. *Wreathèd* means
"coiled" or "spiral-shaped."

# Response and Analysis

## Thinking Critically

**1.** What **images** in the first stanza help you picture the nautilus sailing?

**2.** In stanza 3, the poet uses a **metaphor** comparing the nautilus to a person who changes homes. What details describe how this happens year after year?

**3.** What do you think the speaker means by "the heavenly message" (line 22)?

**4.** Step by step, explain the **extended metaphor** comparing the life span of the nautilus and the progress of the human soul. Explain the "stately mansions" (line 29), the "low-vaulted past" (line 31), "each new temple" (line 32), the "outgrown shell" (line 35), and the "unresting sea" (line 35).

**5.** Using details from the poem, respond to **Connecting to the Focus Question** on page 308.

## Extending and Evaluating

**6.** "The Chambered Nautilus" is one of the most enduring poems in American literature. (Abraham Lincoln is said to have known it by heart.) Why do you think this poem has endured? Do you think it will still be read one hundred years from now? Explain your reasons.

# The Fall of the House of Usher

**Meet the Writer** For **Edgar Allan Poe** (1809–1849), the intensity of imagination provides an escape from the exterior, physical world and a passage to an inner world that operates from a different reality. "The Fall of the House of Usher," which has been called "the definitive tale of horror," illustrates Poe's unique contribution to American literature—his exploration of the dark, often irrational world of the human mind.

Poe wrote "The Fall of the House of Usher" during the most productive period of his career. He was at the time working at *Burton's Gentleman's Magazine,* to which he contributed the story. While at *Burton's,* Poe published a collection of stories in two volumes: *Tales of the Grotesque and Arabesque,* which included "Usher." Although *Tales* was praised by reviewers, it took three years to sell out the edition of 750 copies, and the publishers retained the profits.

(For more information about Edgar Allan Poe, see page 277.)

**Background** A rotting mansion, mysterious illnesses, strange sounds, a person buried alive: Poe uses all of these Gothic details—and more—in "The Fall of the House of Usher" to create an **atmosphere** or mood of dread and menace.

The term *Gothic* is used to describe a kind of novel that sprang up in Germany in the late 1700s and early 1800s. These eerie novels summoned up the mysterious atmosphere suggested by old castles and cathedrals whose dank dungeons and secret passageways might have witnessed any number of sinister or even supernatural events.

Notice how Poe begins to build his mood in the very first paragraph of this story, with its hissing *s* sounds and powerful sensory images. In stories of terror like this, the world of reason disintegrates as the protagonist is swept into the strange, irrational depths of his own being.

---

**CONNECTING TO THE**
**Focus Question**

In "The Fall of the House of Usher," Poe's narrator makes a perilous journey into the underworld of the mind and is nearly destroyed by it. As you read, consider this question: How does Poe portray the interior world of Roderick Usher's fantasy and explore the inner workings of his imagination?

---

# The Fall of the House of Usher

## Edgar Allan Poe

*Son cœur est un luth suspendu;*
*Sitôt qu'on le touche il résonne.*[1]
　　　　　　　*—De Béranger*

During the whole of a dull, dark, and soundless day in the autumn of the year, when the clouds hung oppressively low in the heavens, I had been passing alone, on horseback, through a singularly dreary tract of country; and at length found myself, as the shades of the evening drew on, within view of the melancholy House of Usher. I know not how it was—but, with the first glimpse of the building, a sense of insufferable gloom pervaded[2] my spirit. I say insufferable; for the feeling was unrelieved by any of that half-pleasurable, because poetic, sentiment, with which the mind usually receives even the sternest natural images of the desolate or terrible. I looked upon the scene before me—upon the mere[3] house, and the simple landscape features of the domain—upon the bleak walls—upon the vacant eyelike windows—upon a few rank sedges[4]—and upon a few white trunks of decayed trees—with an utter depression of soul which I can compare to no earthly sensation more properly than to the afterdream of the reveler upon opium—the bitter lapse into everyday life—the hideous dropping off of the veil. There was an iciness, a sinking, a sickening of the heart—an unredeemed dreariness of thought which no goading of the imagination could torture into aught[5] of the sublime. What was it—I paused to think—what was it that so unnerved me in the contemplation of the House of Usher? It was a mystery all insoluble; nor could I grapple with the shadowy fancies that crowded upon me as I pondered. I was forced to fall back upon the unsatisfactory conclusion, that while, beyond doubt, there *are* combinations of very simple natural objects which have the power of thus affecting us, still the analysis of this power lies among considerations beyond our depth. It was possible, I reflected, that a mere different arrangement of the particulars of the scene, of the details of the picture, would be sufficient to modify, or perhaps to annihilate its capacity for sorrowful impression; and, acting upon this idea, I reined my horse to the precipitous brink of a black and lurid tarn[6] that lay in unruffled luster by the dwelling, and gazed down—but with a shudder even more thrilling than before—upon the remodeled and inverted images of the gray sedge, and the ghastly tree stems, and the vacant and eyelike windows.

Nevertheless, in this mansion of gloom I now proposed to myself a sojourn[7] of some weeks. Its proprietor, Roderick Usher, had been one of my boon companions in boyhood; but many years had elapsed since our last meeting. A letter, however, had lately reached me in a distant part of the country—a letter from him—which, in its wildly importunate nature, had admitted

---

1. *Son coeur . . . il résonne:* "His heart is a suspended lute; / Whenever one touches it, it resounds." From "Le Refus" ("The Refusal") by Pierre-Jean de Béranger (1780–1857).
2. **pervaded** (pər·vā'did): spread throughout.
3. **mere** (mir): lake.
4. **sedges:** grasslike plants that grow in watery ground.
5. **aught** (ôt): anything.
6. **tarn:** small but deep mountain lake. Its waters are dark from the decomposition of vegetation and because there is no circulation.
7. **sojourn** (sō'jʉrn): short stay.

of no other than a personal reply. The MS.[8] gave evidence of nervous agitation. The writer spoke of acute bodily illness—of a mental disorder which oppressed him—and of an earnest desire to see me, as his best, and indeed his only personal friend, with a view of attempting, by the cheerfulness of my society, some alleviation of his malady. It was the manner in which all this, and much more, was said—it was the apparent *heart* that went with his request—which allowed me no room for hesitation; and I accordingly obeyed forthwith what I still considered a very singular summons.

Although, as boys, we had been even intimate associates, yet I really knew little of my friend. His reserve had been always excessive and habitual. I was aware, however, that his very ancient family had been noted, time out of mind, for a peculiar sensibility of temperament, displaying itself, through long ages, in many works of exalted art, and manifested, of late, in repeated deeds of munificent yet unobtrusive charity, as well as in a passionate devotion to the intricacies, perhaps even more than to the orthodox and easily recognizable beauties, of musical science. I had learned, too, the very remarkable fact, that the stem of the Usher race, all time-honored as it was, had put forth, at no period, any enduring branch; in other words, that the entire family lay in the direct line of descent, and had always, with very trifling and very temporary variation, so lain. It was this deficiency, I considered, while running over in thought the perfect keeping of the character of the premises with the accredited character of the people, and while speculating upon the possible influence which the one, in the long lapse of centuries, might have exercised upon the other—it was this deficiency, perhaps, of collateral issue,[9] and the consequent undeviating transmission, from sire to son, of the patrimony with the name, which

had, at length, so identified the two as to merge the original title of the estate in the quaint and equivocal[10] appellation of the "House of Usher"—an appellation which seemed to include, in the minds of the peasantry who used it, both the family and the family mansion.

I have said that the sole effect of my somewhat childish experiment—that of looking down within the tarn—had been to deepen the first singular impression. There can be no doubt that the consciousness of the rapid increase of my superstition—for why should I not so term it?—served mainly to accelerate the increase itself. Such, I have long known, is the paradoxical law of all sentiments having terror as a basis. And it might have been for this reason only, that, when I again uplifted my eyes to the house itself, from its image in the pool, there grew in my mind a strange fancy—a fancy so ridiculous, indeed, that I but mention it to show the vivid force of the sensations which oppressed me. I had so worked upon my imagination as really to believe that about the whole mansion and domain there hung an atmosphere peculiar to themselves and their immediate vicinity—an atmosphere which had no affinity with the air of heaven, but which had reeked up from the decayed trees, and the gray wall and the silent tarn—a pestilent and mystic vapor, dull, sluggish, faintly discernible,[11] and leaden-hued.

Shaking off from my spirit what *must* have been a dream, I scanned more narrowly the real aspect of the building. Its principal feature seemed to be that of an excessive antiquity. The discoloration of ages had been great. Minute fungi overspread the whole exterior, hanging in a fine tangled webwork from the eaves. Yet all this was apart from any extraordinary dilapidation. No portion of the masonry had fallen; and there appeared to be a wild inconsistency between its still perfect adaptation of parts, and the crumbling condition of the individual

---

8. **MS.:** abbreviation for "manuscript."
9. **collateral issue:** relatives, such as cousins, who share the same ancestors but who are not in a direct line of descent.

10. **equivocal** (ē·kwiv′ə·kəl): having more than one meaning.
11. **discernible** (di·sʉrn′ə·bəl): noticeable.

stones. In this there was much that reminded me of the specious[12] totality of old woodwork which has rotted for long years in some neglected vault, with no disturbance from the breath of the external air. Beyond this indication of extensive decay, however, the fabric gave little token of instability. Perhaps the eye of a scrutinizing[13] observer might have discovered a barely perceptible fissure, which, extending from the roof of the building in front, made its way down the wall in a zigzag direction, until it became lost in the sullen waters of the tarn.

Noticing these things, I rode over a short causeway to the house. A servant-in-waiting took my horse, and I entered the Gothic archway of the hall.[14] A valet, of stealthy step, thence conducted me, in silence, through many dark and intricate passages in my progress to the *studio* of his master. Much that I encountered on the way contributed, I know not how, to heighten the vague sentiments of which I have already spoken. While the objects around me—while the carvings of the ceilings, the somber tapestries of the walls, the ebon blackness of the floors, and the phantasmagoric[15] armorial trophies which rattled as I strode, were but matters to which, or to such as which, I had been accustomed from my infancy—while I hesitated not to acknowledge how familiar was all this—I still wondered to find how unfamiliar were the fancies which ordinary images were stirring up. On one of the staircases, I met the physician of the family. His

> *T*he discoloration of ages had been great. Minute fungi overspread the whole exterior, hanging in a fine tangled webwork from the eaves.

countenance, I thought, wore a mingled expression of low cunning and perplexity. He accosted me with trepidation and passed on. The valet now threw open a door and ushered me into the presence of his master.

The room in which I found myself was very large and lofty. The windows were long, narrow, and pointed, and at so vast a distance from the black oaken floor as to be altogether inaccessible from within. Feeble gleams of encrimsoned light made their way through the trellised panes, and served to render sufficiently distinct the more prominent objects around; the eye, however, struggled in vain to reach the remoter angles of the chamber, or the recesses of the vaulted and fretted[16] ceiling. Dark draperies hung upon the walls. The general furniture was profuse,[17] comfortless, antique, and tattered. Many books and musical instruments lay scattered about, but failed to give any vitality to the scene. I felt that I breathed an atmosphere of sorrow. An air of stern, deep, and irredeemable gloom hung over and pervaded all.

Upon my entrance, Usher arose from a sofa on which he had been lying at full length, and greeted me with a vivacious[18] warmth which had much in it, I at first thought, of an overdone cordiality—of the constrained effort of the *ennuyé*[19] man of the world. A glance, however, at his countenance, convinced me of his perfect sincerity. We sat down; and for some moments, while he spoke not, I gazed upon him with a feeling half of pity, half of awe. Surely, man had never before so terribly altered, in so brief a

---

12. **specious** (spē′shəs): seemingly sound, but not really so.
13. **scrutinizing** (skrōōt′ʼn·īz′iŋ): carefully observant.
14. **Gothic . . . hall:** The hallway looked like a Gothic arch—high, pointed, and elaborately carved.
15. **phantasmagoric** (fan·taz′mə·gôr′ik): images appearing to change rapidly, like the events in a dream.

16. **fretted:** carved in an ornamental architectural design.
17. **profuse** (prō·fyōōs′): abundant.
18. **vivacious** (vī·vā′shəs): cheerful; lively.
19. *ennuyé* (än·nwē·ā′): French for "bored" or "jaded."

period, as had Roderick Usher! It was with difficulty that I could bring myself to admit the identity of the wan being before me with the companion of my early boyhood. Yet the character of his face had been at all times remarkable. A cadaverousness[20] of complexion; an eye large, liquid, and luminous beyond comparison; lips somewhat thin and very pallid,[21] but of a surpassingly beautiful curve; a nose of a delicate Hebrew model, but with a breadth of nostril unusual in similar formations; a finely molded chin, speaking, in its want of prominence, of a want of moral energy; hair of a more than weblike softness and tenuity;[22] these features, with an inordinate[23] expansion above the regions of the temple, made up altogether a countenance not easily to be forgotten. And now in the mere exaggeration of the prevailing character of these features, and of the expression they were wont to convey, lay so much of change that I doubted to whom I spoke. The now ghastly pallor of the skin, and the now miraculous luster of the eye, above all things startled and even awed me. The silken hair, too, had been suffered to grow all unheeded, and as, in its wild gossamer texture, it floated rather than fell about the face, I could not, even with effort, connect its arabesque[24] expression with any idea of simple humanity.

In the manner of my friend I was at once struck with an incoherence—an inconsistency; and I soon found this to arise from a series of feeble and futile struggles to overcome an habitual trepidancy—an excessive nervous agitation. For something of this nature I had indeed been prepared, no less by his letter, than by reminiscences of certain boyish traits, and by conclusions deduced from his peculiar physical conformation and temperament. His action was alternately vivacious and sullen. His voice varied rapidly from a tremulous indecision (when the animal spirits seemed utterly in abeyance) to that species of energetic concision—that abrupt, weighty, unhurried, and hollow-sounding enunciation—that leaden, self-balanced and perfectly modulated guttural utterance, which may be observed in the lost drunkard, or the irreclaimable eater of opium, during the periods of his most intense excitement.

It was thus that he spoke of the object of my visit, of his earnest desire to see me, and of the solace he expected me to afford him. He entered, at some length, into what he conceived to be the nature of his malady. It was, he said, a constitutional and a family evil, and one for which he despaired to find a remedy—a mere nervous affection,[25] he immediately added, which would undoubtedly soon pass. It displayed itself in a host of unnatural sensations. Some of these, as he detailed them, interested and bewildered me; although, perhaps, the terms, and the general manner of the narration had their weight. He suffered much from a morbid acuteness of the senses; the most insipid[26] food was alone endurable; he could wear only garments of certain texture; the odors of all flowers were oppressive; his eyes were tortured by even a faint light; and there were but peculiar sounds, and these from stringed instruments, which did not inspire him with horror.

To an anomalous[27] species of terror I found him a bounden slave. "I shall perish," said he, "I *must* perish in this deplorable folly. Thus, thus, and not otherwise, shall I be lost. I dread the events of the future, not in themselves, but in their results. I shudder at the thought of any, even the most trivial, incident, which may operate upon this intolerable agitation of soul. I have, indeed, no abhorrence of danger, except in its absolute effect—in terror. In this unnerved—in this pitiable condition—I feel that the period will sooner or later arrive when I must abandon life and reason together, in some struggle with the grim phantasm, FEAR."

---

20. **cadaverousness:** paleness or gauntness, as a corpse.
21. **pallid:** pale.
22. **tenuity** (tə·noo′ə·tē): fineness; lack of substance.
23. **inordinate** (in·ôr′də·nit): excessive.
24. **arabesque** (ar′ə·besk′): strangely mixed; fantastic.

---

25. **affection:** ailment; disorder.
26. **insipid** (in·sip′id): bland; without flavor.
27. **anomalous** (ə·näm′ə·ləs): abnormal.

I learned, moreover, at intervals, and through broken and equivocal hints, another singular feature of his mental condition. He was enchained by certain superstitious impressions in regard to the dwelling which he tenanted, and whence, for many years, he had never ventured forth—in regard to an influence whose supposititious[28] force was conveyed in terms too shadowy here to be restated—an influence which some peculiarities in the mere form and substance of his family mansion, had, by dint of long sufferance, he said, obtained over his spirit—an effect which the *physique* of the gray walls and turrets, and of the dim tarn into which they all looked down, had, at length, brought about upon the *morale* of his existence.

He admitted, however, although with hesitation, that much of the peculiar gloom which thus afflicted him could be traced to a more natural and far more palpable[29] origin—to the severe and long-continued illness—indeed to the evidently approaching dissolution—of a tenderly beloved sister—his sole companion for long years—his last and only relative on earth. "Her decease," he said, with a bitterness which I can never forget, "would leave him (him the hopeless and the frail) the last of the ancient race of the Ushers." While he spoke, the lady Madeline (for so was she called) passed slowly through a remote portion of the apartment, and, without having noticed my presence, disappeared. I regarded her with an utter astonishment not unmingled with dread—and yet I found it impossible to account for such feelings.

> *He was enchained by certain superstitious impressions in regard to the dwelling which he tenanted, and whence, for many years, he had never ventured forth—*

A sensation of stupor[30] oppressed me, as my eyes followed her retreating steps. When a door, at length, closed upon her, my glance sought instinctively and eagerly the countenance of the brother—but he had buried his face in his hands, and I could only perceive that a far more than ordinary wanness had overspread the emaciated fingers through which trickled many passionate tears.

The disease of the lady Madeline had long baffled the skill of her physicians. A settled apathy, a gradual wasting away of the person, and frequent although transient affections of a partially cataleptical[31] character, were the unusual diagnosis. Hitherto she had steadily borne up against the pressure of her malady, and had not betaken herself finally to bed; but, on the closing in of the evening of my arrival at the house, she succumbed (as her brother told me at night with inexpressible agitation) to the prostrating power of the destroyer; and I learned that the glimpse I had obtained of her person would thus probably be the last I should obtain—that the lady, at least while living, would be seen by me no more.

For several days ensuing, her name was unmentioned by either Usher or myself: And during this period I was busied in earnest endeavors to alleviate the melancholy of my friend. We painted and read together; or I listened, as if in a dream, to the wild improvisations of his

---

28. **supposititious** (sə·päz′ə·tish′əs): supposed; assumed; hypothetical.
29. **palpable** (pal′pə·bəl): obvious; perceivable.

30. **stupor** (stoo′pər): state of mental dullness; loss of the senses.
31. **cataleptical** (kat′ə·lep′tik·əl): Catalepsy is an emotional condition, associated with disorders such as epilepsy and schizophrenia, which may cause the victim to lose sensation and the ability to move the limbs, or even the entire body. In a cataleptic attack, Madeline could be as stiff as a corpse.

speaking guitar. And thus, as a closer and still closer intimacy admitted me more unreservedly into the recesses of his spirit, the more bitterly did I perceive the futility of all attempt at cheering a mind from which darkness, as if an inherent positive quality, poured forth upon all objects of the moral and physical universe, in one unceasing radiation of gloom.

I shall ever bear about me a memory of the many solemn hours I thus spent alone with the master of the House of Usher. Yet I should fail in any attempt to convey an idea of the exact character of the studies, or of the occupations, in which he involved me, or led me the way. An excited and highly distempered ideality[32] threw a sulfureous[33] luster over all. His long improvised dirges will ring forever in my ears. Among other things, I hold painfully in mind a certain singular perversion and amplification of the wild air of the last waltz of Von Weber.[34] From the paintings over which his elaborate fancy brooded, and which grew, touch by touch, into vaguenesses at which I shuddered the more thrillingly, because I shuddered knowing not why—from these paintings (vivid as their images now are before me) I would in vain endeavor to educe more than a small portion which should lie within the compass of merely written words. By the utter simplicity, by the nakedness of his designs, he arrested and overawed attention. If ever mortal painted an idea, that mortal was Roderick Usher. For me at least—in the circumstances then surrounding me—there arose out of the pure abstractions which the hypochondriac contrived to throw upon his canvas, an intensity of intolerable awe, no shadow of which felt I ever yet in the contemplation of the certainly glowing yet too concrete reveries of Fuseli.[35]

One of the phantasmagoric conceptions of my friend, partaking not so rigidly of the spirit of abstraction, may be shadowed forth, although feebly, in words. A small picture presented the interior of an immensely long and rectangular vault or tunnel, with low walls, smooth, white, and without interruption or device. Certain accessory points of the design served well to convey the idea that this excavation lay at an exceeding depth below the surface of the earth. No outlet was observed in any portion of its vast extent, and no torch, or other artificial source of light was discernible; yet a flood of intense rays rolled throughout, and bathed the whole in a ghastly and inappropriate splendor.

I have just spoken of that morbid[36] condition of the auditory nerve which rendered all music intolerable to the sufferer with the exception of certain effects of stringed instruments. It was, perhaps, the narrow limits to which he thus confined himself upon the guitar, which gave birth, in great measure, to the fantastic character of his performances. But the fervid *facility* of his *impromptus*[37] could not be so accounted for. They must have been, and were, in the notes, as well as in the words of his wild fantasias (for he not unfrequently accompanied himself with rhymed verbal improvisations), the result of that intense mental collectedness and concentration to which I have previously alluded as observable only in the moments of the highest artificial excitement. The words of one of these rhapsodies I have easily remembered. I was, perhaps, the more forcibly impressed with it, as he gave it, because, in the under or mystic current of its meaning, I fancied that I perceived, and for the first time, a full consciousness on the part of Usher, of the

---

32. **distempered ideality:** mental derangement.
33. **sulfureous** (sul·fyoor′ē·əs): hellish; infernal. Poe's description probably comes from the yellowish color of sulfur, which is associated with the fires of hell.
34. **Von Weber:** Carl Maria von Weber (1786–1826), German Romantic composer.

35. **Fuseli:** Johann Heinrich Füssli (1741–1825), Swiss painter who lived in England and is known for scenes of horror and the supernatural.
36. **morbid:** diseased; unhealthy.
37. **impromptus** (im·prämp′tōōz′): spontaneous performances.

tottering of his lofty reason upon her throne. The verses, which were entitled "The Haunted Palace," ran very nearly, if not accurately, thus:

### I

In the greenest of our valleys,
    By good angels tenanted,
Once a fair and stately palace—
    Radiant palace—reared its head.
In the monarch Thought's dominion—
    It stood there!
Never seraph[38] spread a pinion[39]
    Over fabric half so fair.

### II

Banners yellow, glorious, golden,
    On its roof did float and flow;
(This—all this—was in the olden
    Time long ago)
And every gentle air that dallied,
    In that sweet day,
Along the ramparts plumed and pallid,
    A winged odor went away.

### III

Wanderers in that happy valley
    Through two luminous windows saw
Spirits moving musically
    To a lute's well-tunéd law,
Round about a throne, where sitting
    (Porphyrogene!)[40]
In state his glory well befitting,
    The ruler of the realm was seen.

### IV

And all with pearl and ruby glowing
    Was the fair palace door,
Through which came flowing, flowing, flowing,
    And sparkling evermore,
A troop of Echoes whose sweet duty

    Was but to sing,
In voices of surpassing beauty,
    The wit and wisdom of their king.

### V

But evil things, in robes of sorrow,
    Assailed the monarch's high estate;
(Ah, let us mourn, for never morrow
    Shall dawn upon him, desolate!)
And, round about his home, the glory
    That blushed and bloomed
Is but a dim-remembered story
    Of the old time entombed.

### VI

And travelers now within that valley,
    Through the red-litten[41] windows, see
Vast forms that move fantastically
    To a discordant melody;
While, like a rapid ghastly river,
    Through the pale door,
A hideous throng rush out forever,
    And laugh—but smile no more.

I well remember that suggestions arising from this ballad led us into a train of thought wherein there became manifest an opinion of Usher's which I mention not so much on account of its novelty (for other men have thought thus), as on account of the pertinacity with which he maintained it. This opinion, in its general form, was that of the sentience[42] of all vegetable things. But, in his disordered fancy, the idea had assumed a more daring character, and trespassed, under certain conditions, upon the kingdom of inorganization.[43] I lack words to express the full extent, or the earnest *abandon* of his persuasion. The belief, however, was connected (as I have previously hinted) with the gray stones of the home of his forefathers. The conditions of the sentience had been here, he

---

38. **seraph** (ser′əf): angel.
39. **pinion** (pin′yən): wing.
40. **Porphyrogene** (pôr·fir′ə·jēn): Poe coined this word from *porphyrogenite*, the name once used to refer to royalty in Byzantine times. (The Greek word *porphyros* means "purple.") *Porphyrogene* means "one born to the purple" or "one of royal blood."

---

41. **red-litten:** red-lighted; Poe coined this archaic-sounding term.
42. **sentience** (sen′shəns): consciousness.
43. **kingdom of inorganization:** world of inorganic objects.

imagined, fulfilled in the method of collocation of these stones—in the order of their arrangement, as well as in that of the many *fungi* which overspread them, and of the decayed trees which stood around—above all, in the long undisturbed endurance of this arrangement, and in its reduplication in the still waters of the tarn. Its evidence—the evidence of the sentience—was to be seen, he said (and I here started as he spoke), in the gradual yet certain condensation of an atmosphere of their own about the waters and the walls. The result was discoverable, he added, in that silent, yet importunate and terrible influence which for centuries had molded the destinies of his family, and which made *him* what I now saw him—what he was. Such opinions need no comment, and I will make none.

Our books—the books which, for years, had formed no small portion of the mental existence of the invalid—were, as might be supposed, in strict keeping with this character of phantasm. We pored together over such works as the *Ververt et Chartreuse* of Gresset; the *Belphegor* of Machiavelli; the *Heaven and Hell* of Swedenborg; *The Subterranean Voyage of Nicholas Klimm* by Holberg; the Chiromancy of Robert Flud, of Jean D'Indaginé, and of De la Chambre; the *Journey into the Blue Distance* of Tieck; and *The City of the Sun* of Campanella. One favorite volume was a small octavo edition of the *Directorium Inquisitorum*, by the Dominican Eymeric de Gironne; and there were passages in Pomponius Mela, about the old African Satyrs and Ægipans,[44] over which Usher would sit dreaming for hours. His chief delight, however, was found in the perusal of an exceedingly rare and curious book in quarto Gothic—the manual of a forgotten church—the *Vigiliae Mortuorum*[45] secundum *Chorum Ecclesiae Maguntinae*.

I could not help thinking of the wild ritual of this work, and of its probable influence upon the hypochondriac, when, one evening, having informed me abruptly that the lady Madeline was no more, he stated his intention of preserving her corpse for a fortnight (previously to its final interment), in one of the numerous vaults within the main walls of the building. The worldly reason, however, assigned for this singular proceeding, was one which I did not feel at liberty to dispute. The brother had been led to his resolution (so he told me) by consideration of the unusual character of the malady of the deceased, of certain obtrusive and eager inquiries on the part of her medical men, and of the remote and exposed situation of the burial ground of the family. I will not deny that when I called to mind the sinister countenance of the person whom I met upon the staircase,[46] on the day of my arrival at the house, I had no desire to oppose what I regarded as at best but a harmless, and by no means an unnatural, precaution.[47]

At the request of Usher, I personally aided him in the arrangements for the temporary entombment. The body having been encoffined, we two alone bore it to its rest. The vault in which we placed it (and which had been so long unopened that our torches, half smothered in its oppressive atmosphere, gave us little opportunity for investigation) was small, damp, and entirely without means of admission for light; lying, at great depth, immediately beneath that portion of the building in which was my own sleeping apartment. It had been used, apparently, in remote feudal times, for the worst purposes of a dungeon-keep,[48] and, in later days, as a place of deposit for powder, or some other highly combustible substance, as a portion of its floor, and the whole interior of a long archway through which we reached it, were carefully sheathed with copper. The door, of

---

44. *Ververt et Chartreuse . . . Satyrs and Ægipans:* The books, authors, and subjects listed have to do with mysticism, magic, and horror.
45. *Vigiliae Mortuorum:* Latin for "vigil of the dead."
46. **person . . . staircase:** the physician.
47. **harmless . . . precaution:** Usher wishes to be sure his sister's body will not be dissected by doctors. At the time, bodies were sometimes stolen and sold to medical students for dissection and study.
48. **dungeon-keep:** underground prison.

massive iron, had been, also, similarly protected. Its immense weight caused an unusually sharp grating sound, as it moved upon its hinges.

Having deposited our mournful burden upon tressels within this region of horror, we partially turned aside the yet unscrewed lid of the coffin, and looked upon the face of the tenant. A striking similitude[49] between the brother and sister now first arrested my attention; and Usher, divining, perhaps, my thoughts, murmured out some few words from which I learned that the deceased and himself had been twins, and that sympathies of a scarcely intelligible nature had always existed between them. Our glances, however, rested not long upon the dead—for we could not regard her unawed. The disease which had thus entombed the lady in the maturity of youth, had left, as usual in all maladies of a strictly cataleptical character, the

---

49. **similitude** (sə·mil′ə·tōōd′): likeness.

mockery of a faint blush upon the bosom and the face, and that suspiciously lingering smile upon the lip which is so terrible in death. We replaced and screwed down the lid, and, having secured the door of iron, made our way, with toil, into the scarcely less gloomy apartments of the upper portion of the house.

And now, some days of bitter grief having elapsed, an observable change came over the features of the mental disorder of my friend. His ordinary manner had vanished. His ordinary occupations were neglected or forgotten. He roamed from chamber to chamber with hurried, unequal, and objectless step. The pallor of his countenance had assumed, if possible, a more ghastly hue—but the luminousness of his eye had utterly gone out. The once occasional huskiness of his tone was heard no more; and a tremulous quaver, as if of extreme terror, habitually characterized his utterance. There were times, indeed, when I thought his unceasingly agitated mind was laboring with some oppressive secret, to divulge which he struggled for the necessary courage. At times, again, I was obliged to resolve all into the mere inexplicable vagaries[50] of madness, for I beheld him gazing upon vacancy for long hours, in an attitude of the profoundest attention, as if listening to some imaginary sound. It was no wonder that his condition terrified—that it infected me. I felt creeping upon me, by slow yet certain degrees, the wild influences of his own fantastic yet impressive superstitions.

It was, especially, upon retiring to bed late in the night of the seventh or eighth day after the placing of the lady Madeline within the dungeon, that I experienced the full power of such feelings. Sleep came not near my couch—while the hours waned and waned away. I struggled to reason off the nervousness which had dominion over me. I endeavored to believe that much, if not all of what I felt, was due to the bewildering influence of the gloomy furniture of the room—of the dark and tattered draperies,

which, tortured into motion by the breath of a rising tempest, swayed fitfully to and fro upon the walls, and rustled uneasily about the decorations of the bed. But my efforts were fruitless. An irrepressible tremor gradually pervaded my frame; and, at length, there sat upon my very heart an incubus[51] of utterly causeless alarm. Shaking this off with a gasp and a struggle, I uplifted myself upon the pillows, and, peering earnestly within the intense darkness of the chamber, harkened—I know not why, except that an instinctive spirit prompted me—to certain low and indefinite sounds which came, through the pauses of the storm, at long intervals, I knew not whence. Overpowered by an intense sentiment of horror, unaccountable yet unendurable, I threw on my clothes with haste (for I felt that I should sleep no more during the night), and endeavored to arouse myself from the pitiable condition into which I had fallen, by pacing rapidly to and fro through the apartment.

I had taken but few turns in this manner, when a light step on an adjoining staircase arrested my attention. I presently recognized it as that of Usher. In an instant afterward he rapped, with a gentle touch, at my door, and entered, bearing a lamp. His countenance was, as usual, cadaverously wan—but, moreover, there was a species of mad hilarity in his eyes—an evidently restrained *hysteria* in his whole demeanor.[52] His air appalled me—but anything was preferable to the solitude which I had so long endured, and I even welcomed his presence as a relief.

"And you have not seen it?" he said abruptly, after having stared about him for some moments in silence—"you have not then seen it?—but, stay! you shall." Thus speaking, and having carefully shaded his lamp, he hurried to one of the casements, and threw it freely open to the storm.

The impetuous fury of the entering gust nearly lifted us from our feet. It was, indeed, a

---

50. **vagaries** (vā′gə·rēz): whims.

51. **incubus** (in′kyo͞o·bəs): nightmare. In medieval times, it was believed that nightmares were caused by demons (incubi) who tormented the sleeping.
52. **demeanor** (di·mēn′ər): behavior; conduct.

tempestuous yet sternly beautiful night, and one wildly singular in its terror and its beauty. A whirlwind had apparently collected its force in our vicinity; for there were frequent and violent alterations in the direction of the wind; and the exceeding density of the clouds (which hung so low as to press upon the turrets of the house) did not prevent our perceiving the lifelike velocity with which they flew careering from all points against each other, without passing away into the distance. I say that even their exceeding density did not prevent our perceiving this—yet we had no glimpse of the moon or stars—nor was there any flashing forth of the lightning. But the under surfaces of the huge masses of agitated vapor, as well as all terrestrial objects immediately around us, were glowing in the unnatural light of a faintly luminous and distinctly visible gaseous exhalation which hung about and enshrouded the mansion.

*Huge masses of agitated vapor...were glowing in the unnatural light of a faintly luminous...gaseous exhalation which hung about and enshrouded the mansion.*

"You must not—you shall not behold this!" said I, shudderingly, to Usher, as I led him, with a gentle violence, from the window to a seat. "These appearances, which bewilder you, are merely electrical phenomena not uncommon—or it may be that they have their ghastly origin in the rank miasma of the tarn.[53] Let us close this casement—the air is chilling and dangerous to your frame. Here is one of your favorite romances. I will read, and you shall listen;—and so we will pass away this terrible night together."

The antique volume which I had taken up was the *Mad Trist* of Sir Launcelot Canning;[54]

but I had called it a favorite of Usher's more in sad jest than in earnest; for, in truth, there is little in its uncouth and unimaginative prolixity[55] which could have had interest for the lofty and spiritual ideality of my friend. It was, however, the only book immediately at hand; and I indulged a vague hope that the excitement which now agitated the hypochondriac, might find relief (for the history of mental disorder is full of similar anomalies) even in the extremeness of the folly which I should read. Could I have judged, indeed, by the wild overstrained air of vivacity with which he harkened, or apparently harkened, to the words of the tale, I might well have congratulated myself upon the success of my design.

I had arrived at that well-known portion of the story where Ethelred, the hero of the *Trist*, having sought in vain for peaceable admission into the dwelling of the hermit, proceeds to make good an entrance by force. Here, it will be remembered, the words of the narrative run thus:

"And Ethelred, who was by nature of a doughty[56] heart, and who was now mighty withal, on account of the powerfulness of the wine which he had drunken, waited no longer to hold parley with the hermit, who, in sooth, was of an obstinate[57] and maliceful turn, but, feeling the rain upon his shoulders, and fearing the rising of the tempest, uplifted his mace outright, and, with blows, made quickly room in the plankings of the door for his gauntleted hand; and now pulling therewith sturdily, he so cracked, and ripped, and

---

53. **rank miasma** (mī·az′mə′) . . . **tarn:** The decomposing matter of the tarn could have given rise to swamp gas or electrical discharges, resulting in frightening optical illusions.

54. ***Mad Trist* of Sir Launcelot Canning:** a book invented by Poe for this story.

55. **prolixity** (prō·liks′ə·tē): wordiness.

56. **doughty** (dout′ē): courageous.

57. **obstinate** (äb′stə·nət): stubborn.

tore all asunder, that the noise of the dry and hollow-sounding wood alarumed and reverberated throughout the forest."

At the termination of this sentence I started, and for a moment, paused; for it appeared to me (although I at once concluded that my excited fancy had deceived me)—it appeared to me that, from some very remote portion of the mansion, there came, indistinctly, to my ears, what might have been, in its exact similarity of character, the echo (but a stifled and dull one certainly) of the very cracking and ripping sound which Sir Launcelot had so particularly described. It was, beyond doubt, the coincidence alone which had arrested my attention; for, amid the rattling of the sashes of the casements, and the ordinary commingled noises of the still increasing storm, the sound, in itself, had nothing, surely, which should have interested or disturbed me. I continued the story:

"But the good champion Ethelred, now entering within the door, was sore enraged and amazed to perceive no signal of the maliceful hermit; but, in the stead thereof, a dragon of a scaly and prodigious[58] demeanor, and of a fiery tongue, which sate in guard before a palace of gold, with a floor of silver; and upon the wall there hung a shield of shining brass with this legend enwritten—

Who entereth herein, a conqueror hath bin;
Who slayeth the dragon, the shield he shall win;

And Ethelred uplifted his mace, and struck upon the head of the dragon, which fell before him, and gave up his pesty breath, with a shriek so horrid and harsh, and withal so piercing, that Ethelred had fain to close his ears with his hands against the dreadful noise of it, the like whereof was never before heard."

Here again I paused abruptly, and now with a feeling of wild amazement—for there could be no doubt whatever that, in this instance, I did actually hear (although from what direction it proceeded I found it impossible to say) a low and apparently distant, but harsh, protracted, and most unusual screaming or grating sound—the exact counterpart of what my fancy had already conjured up for the dragon's unnatural shriek as described by the romancer.

Oppressed, as I certainly was, upon the occurrence of this second and most extraordinary coincidence, by a thousand conflicting sensations, in which wonder and extreme terror were predominant, I still retained sufficient presence of mind to avoid exciting, by any observation, the sensitive nervousness of my companion. I was by no means certain that he had noticed the sounds in question; although, assuredly, a strange alteration had, during the last few minutes, taken place in his demeanor. From a position fronting my own, he had gradually brought round his chair, so as to sit with his face to the door of the chamber; and thus I could but partially perceive his features, although I saw that his lips trembled as if he were murmuring inaudibly. His head had dropped upon his breast—yet I knew that he was not asleep, from the wide and rigid opening of the eye as I caught a glance of it in profile. The motion of his body, too, was at variance with this idea—for he rocked from side to side with a gentle yet constant and uniform sway. Having rapidly taken notice of all this, I resumed the narrative of Sir Launcelot, which thus proceeded:

"And now, the champion, having escaped from the terrible fury of the dragon, bethinking himself of the brazen shield, and of the breaking up of the enchantment which was upon it, removed the carcass from out of the way before him, and approached valorously over the silver pavement of the castle to where the shield was upon the wall; which in sooth tarried not for his full coming, but fell down at his feet upon the silver floor, with a mighty great and terrible ringing sound."

No sooner had these syllables passed my lips, than—as if a shield of brass had indeed, at the moment, fallen heavily upon a floor of silver—I

---

**58. prodigious** (prō·dij′əs): of great size and power.

became aware of a distinct, hollow, metallic, and clangorous, yet apparently muffled reverberation. Completely unnerved, I leaped to my feet; but  the measured rocking movement of Usher was undisturbed. I rushed to the chair in which he sat. His eyes were bent fixedly before him, and throughout his whole countenance there reigned a stony rigidity. But, as I placed my hand upon his shoulder, there came a strong shudder over his whole person; a sickly smile quivered about his lips; and I saw that he spoke in a low, hurried, and gibbering murmur, as if unconscious of my presence. Bending closely over him, I at length drank in the hideous import of his words.

"Not hear it?—yes, I hear it, and *have* heard it. Long—long—long—many minutes, many hours, many days, have I heard it—yet I dared not—oh, pity me, miserable wretch that I am!— I dared not—I *dared* not speak! *We have put her living in the tomb!* Said I not that my senses were acute? I *now* tell you that I heard her first feeble movements in the hollow coffin. I heard them— many, many days ago—yet I dared not—*I dared not speak!* And now—tonight—Ethelred—ha! ha!—the breaking of the hermit's door, and the death cry of the dragon, and the clangor of the shield!—say, rather, the rending of her coffin, and the grating of the iron hinges of her prison, and her struggles within the coppered archway of the vault! Oh whither shall I fly? Will she not be here anon? Is she not hurrying to upbraid me for my haste? Have I not heard her footstep on the stair? Do I not distinguish that heavy and horrible beating of her heart? *Madman!*"—here he sprang furiously to his feet, and shrieked out his syllables, as if in the effort he were giving up his soul—"*Madman! I tell you that she now stands without the door!*"

As if in the superhuman energy of his utterance there had been found the potency[59] of a spell—the huge antique panels to which the speaker pointed, threw slowly back, upon the instant, their ponderous and ebony jaws. It was the work of the rushing gust—but then without those doors there *did* stand the lofty and enshrouded figure of the lady Madeline of Usher. There was blood upon her white robes, and the evidence of some bitter struggle upon every portion of her emaciated[60] frame. For a moment she remained trembling and reeling to and fro upon the threshold—then, with a low moaning cry, fell heavily inward upon the person of her brother, and in her violent and now final death agonies, bore him to the floor a corpse, and a victim to the terrors he had anticipated.

59. **potency** (pōt′n·sē): strength; power.
60. **emaciated** (ē·mā′shē·āt′id): unusually thin.

From that chamber, and from that mansion, I fled aghast. The storm was still abroad in all its wrath as I found myself crossing the old causeway. Suddenly there shot along the path a wild light, and I turned to see whence a gleam so unusual could have issued; for the vast house and its shadows were alone behind me. The radiance was that of the full, setting, and blood-red moon, which now shone vividly through that once barely discernible fissure, of which I have before spoken as extending from the roof of the building, in a zigzag direction, to the base. While I gazed, this fissure rapidly widened—there came a fierce breath of the whirlwind—the entire orb of the satellite burst at once upon my sight—my brain reeled as I saw the mighty walls rushing asunder—there was a long tumultuous shouting sound like the voice of a thousand waters—and the deep and dank tarn at my feet closed sullenly and silently over the fragments of the "*House of Usher.*" ∎

# Response and Analysis

## Reading Check
1. Imagine that you are telling a friend about this story. List the main events in chronological order.

## Thinking Critically
2. Roderick's studio is reached "through many dark and intricate passages." What does this fact suggest about his state of mind?
3. Why do you think Poe made Roderick and Madeline *twins*—not just brother and sister?
4. The narrator's rationality becomes suspect during the course of the tale. What evidence can you find that the narrator's state of mind may be deteriorating? How does this uncertainty about the narrator's objectivity affect your response to the story?
5. What do you think is happening at the end of the story, when Madeline Usher appears? Support your response with evidence from the story.
6. Poe said that the poem "The Haunted Palace" is meant to suggest a disordered brain. How might the whole story be read as an allegory of a journey into the human mind? (An **allegory** is a story or poem that can be read on one level for its literal meaning and on a second level for its symbolic meaning.) What could the final *fall* of the house represent?
7. Using details from the selection, respond to **Connecting to the Focus Question** on page 311.

## *from* Moby-Dick

**Meet the Writer** It is the central irony of **Herman Melville's** (1819–1891) career that his triumphant achievement, now widely recognized as one of the greatest American novels, was almost wholly ignored while its author was alive. As a result, Melville spent the last third of his life in poverty and despair, thinking himself a failure.

Melville was born into a distinguished Boston family. But his father went bankrupt in 1830, suffered an emotional breakdown, and died when young Melville was twelve. Faced with a grim life in his family's house, he took to the sea in 1839 as cabin boy on a merchant ship. A whaling expedition to the South Seas followed in 1841. A year and a half later, Melville jumped ship at the Marquesas Islands. After a month, Melville signed on to an Australian ship, which he deserted in a semimutiny at Papeete. He roamed the islands of Tahiti and Moorea before joining a whaler to Honolulu and then enlisting as a seaman on a U.S. Navy frigate. When his ship docked at Boston in October 1844, a career's worth of seagoing adventure had ended. Ishmael, the young narrator of *Moby-Dick,* surely voices Melville's own sentiments when he says, "A whale ship was my Yale College and my Harvard."

In less than two years, Melville produced a book of slightly fictionalized travel memoirs, *Typee,* that became an immediate success. With the publication of four other semiautobiographical sea tales between 1847 and 1850, Melville became one of the most popular authors of the day.

In the fall of 1850, Melville bought a farm near Pittsfield, Massachusetts. Nathaniel Hawthorne, who lived in nearby Lenox, responded to Melville's admiration, and they saw much of each other. Hawthorne's example encouraged Melville, who was writing *Moby-Dick*—a book that would both exploit his whaling experience and, on a far more ambitious plane, seek the ultimate truth of human existence.

When he finished *Moby-Dick* in July 1851, Melville sensed that he had taken a great risk and won. Yet for all Melville's bright expectations, *Moby-Dick* was a failure. Critics and readers alike were either puzzled or indifferent, and Melville finally had to admit that his literary career had foundered. Melville continued to hope for a change in his fortunes, and in the next six years he published three poorly received novels.

Around 1886, Elizabeth, Melville's wife, came into a small inheritance that allowed her husband to begin work on a book that would become another masterpiece. This was *Billy Budd.* When Melville died on September 28, 1891, the novella lay unwanted in his desk drawer. In 1924, thirty-three years later, it was published and acclaimed. Near the desk where Melville had composed it, a note was found. It read, "Keep true to the dreams of thy youth."

**Background** *Moby-Dick* is the story of the fateful voyage of the *Pequod,* a whaling ship commanded by the mysterious and obsessive Captain Ahab. Throughout the novel, Ahab relentlessly pursues Moby-Dick, the white whale that years before had taken off his leg. The officers and crew are an assortment of men from all over the world: South Pacific islanders, Massachusetts Indians, and more. The harpooners are Queequeg, Tashtego, and Daggoo; the first, second, and third mates are Starbuck, Stubb, and Flask, respectively. The narrator of the novel, Ishmael, has joined the voyage as a common sailor. The book opens with one of the most famous sentences in literature—"Call me Ishmael."

---

### CONNECTING TO THE
### Focus Question

Melville's Ahab is driven to understand the truth and to discover the meaning of existence. As you read, consider this question: How might Ahab's struggle against the white whale be viewed as humankind's struggle against the mysteries of life that elude understanding?

The Sperm Whale in a Flurry from 'The Whale Fishery,' published by Currier & Ives (colour lithograph), by Louis Ambroise Garneray, (1783–1857) (after).
©Peabody Essex Museum, Salem, Massachusetts, USA.

*The quarter-deck is a center of dramatic action in* Moby-Dick. *Here Ahab calls the men to assemble on the deck and reveals his secret purpose—to track down and kill the great white whale. He binds the crew—even Starbuck, the reluctant first mate—to his relentless pursuit. The whaling voyage, which was to be an ordinary business venture, becomes instead the instrument of Ahab's vengeance.*

# *from* **Moby-Dick**

## Herman Melville

### The Quarter-Deck
*(Enter Ahab: Then all.)*

It was not a great while after the affair of the pipe,[1] that one morning shortly after breakfast,

---

1. **affair of the pipe:** Ahab had thrown his pipe overboard one evening when he realized that he had no business with "this thing that is meant for sereneness."

Ahab, as was his wont, ascended the cabin gangway to the deck. There most sea captains usually walk at that hour, as country gentlemen, after the same meal, take a few turns in the garden.

Soon his steady, ivory stride was heard, as to and fro he paced his old rounds, upon planks so familiar to his tread, that they were all over dented, like geological stones, with the peculiar mark of his walk. Did you fixedly gaze, too, upon

that ribbed and dented brow; there also, you would see still stranger footprints—the footprints of his one unsleeping, ever-pacing thought.

But on the occasion in question, those dents looked deeper, even as his nervous step that morning left a deeper mark. And, so full of his thought was Ahab, that at every uniform turn that he made, now at the mainmast and now at the binnacle,[2] you could almost see that thought turn in him as he turned, and pace in him as he paced; so completely possessing him, indeed, that it all but seemed the inward mold of every outer movement.

"D'ye mark him, Flask?" whispered Stubb; "the chick that's in him pecks the shell. 'Twill soon be out."

The hours wore on—Ahab now shut up within his cabin; anon, pacing the deck, with the same intense bigotry of purpose in his aspect.

It drew near the close of day. Suddenly he came to a halt by the bulwarks,[3] and inserting his bone leg into the auger hole there, and with one hand grasping a shroud, he ordered Starbuck to send everybody aft.

"Sir!" said the mate, astonished at an order seldom or never given on shipboard except in some extraordinary case.

"Send everybody aft," repeated Ahab. "Mastheads, there! Come down!"

When the entire ship's company were assembled, and with curious and not wholly unapprehensive faces were eyeing him, for he looked not unlike the weather horizon when a storm is coming up, Ahab, after rapidly glancing over the bulwarks, and then darting his eyes among the crew, started from his standpoint; and as though not a soul were nigh him resumed his heavy turns upon the deck. With bent head and half-slouched hat he continued to pace; unmindful of the wondering whispering among the men; till Stubb cautiously whispered to Flask, that Ahab must have summoned them there for the purpose of witnessing a pedestrian feat. But this did not last long. Vehemently pausing, he cried—

"What do ye do when ye see a whale, men?"

"Sing out for him!" was the impulsive rejoinder[4] from a score of clubbed[5] voices.

"Good!" cried Ahab, with a wild approval in his tones; observing the hearty animation into which his unexpected question had so magnetically thrown them.

"And what do ye next, men?"

"Lower away, and after him!"

"And what tune is it ye pull to, men?"

"A dead whale or a stove[6] boat!"

More and more strangely and fiercely glad and approving grew the countenance of the old man at every shout; while the mariners began to gaze curiously at each other, as if marveling how it was that they themselves became so excited at such seemingly purposeless questions.

But, they were all eagerness again, as Ahab, now half-revolving in his pivot hole, with one hand reaching high up a shroud, and tightly, almost convulsively grasping it, addressed them thus—

"All ye mastheaders have before now heard me give orders about a white whale. Look ye! d'ye see this Spanish ounce of gold?"—holding up a broad bright coin to the sun—"it is a sixteen-dollar piece, men. D'ye see it? Mr. Starbuck, hand me yon top-maul.[7]

While the mate was getting the hammer, Ahab, without speaking, was slowly rubbing the gold piece against the skirts of his jacket, as if to heighten its luster, and without using any words was meanwhile lowly humming to himself, producing a sound so strangely muffled and inarticulate that it seemed the mechanical humming of the wheels of his vitality in him.

Receiving the top-maul from Starbuck, he advanced toward the mainmast with the hammer uplifted in one hand, exhibiting the gold with the other, and with a high raised voice exclaiming: "Whosoever of ye raises me a white-headed

---

2. **binnacle:** upright stand holding the ship's compass.
3. **bulwarks:** above-deck part of a ship's side.
4. **rejoinder:** answer.
5. **clubbed:** united.
6. **stove:** with a hole smashed in it.
7. **top-maul:** heavy wooden hammer.

PEHE NU-E: MOBY DICK, the only known picture of Moby Dick drawn during Herman Melville's lifetime, late 19<sup>th</sup> century, wood engraving. The Granger Collection, New York.

whale with a wrinkled brow and a crooked jaw; whosoever of ye raises me that white-headed whale, with three holes punctured in his starboard fluke[8]—look ye, whosoever of ye raises me that same white whale, he shall have this gold ounce, my boys!"

"Huzza! huzza!" cried the seamen, as with swinging tarpaulins they hailed the act of nailing the gold to the mast.

"It's a white whale, I say," resumed Ahab, as he threw down the top-maul; "a white whale. Skin your eyes for him, men; look sharp for white water; if ye see but a bubble, sing out."

All this while Tashtego, Daggoo, and Queequeg had looked on with even more intense interest and surprise than the rest, and at the mention of the wrinkled brow and crooked jaw they had started as if each was separately touched by some specific recollection.

"Captain Ahab," said Tashtego, "that white whale must be the same that some call Moby-Dick."

"Moby-Dick?" shouted Ahab. "Do ye know the white whale then, Tash?"

"Does he fantail[9] a little curious, sir, before he goes down?" said the Gay-Header deliberately.

---

8. **starboard fluke:** right-hand side of the whale's tail.

9. **fantail:** spread the tail like a fan.

"And has he a curious spout, too," said Daggoo, "very bushy, even for a parmacety,[10] and mighty quick, Captain Ahab?"

"And he have one, two, tree—oh! good many iron in him hide, too, Captain," cried Queequeg disjointedly, "all twiske-tee be-twisk, like him—him——" faltering hard for a word, and screwing his hand round and round as though uncorking a bottle—"like him—him——"

"Corkscrew!" cried Ahab, "aye, Queequeg, the harpoons lie all twisted and wrenched in him; aye, Daggoo, his spout is a big one, like a whole shock of wheat, and white as a pile of our Nantucket wool after the great annual sheepshearing; aye, Tashtego, and he fantails like a split jib in a squall. Death and devils! men, it is Moby-Dick ye have seen—Moby-Dick—Moby-Dick!"

"Captain Ahab," said Starbuck, who, with Stubb and Flask, had thus far been eyeing his superior with increasing surprise, but at last seemed struck with a thought which somewhat explained all the wonder. "Captain Ahab, I have heard of Moby-Dick—but it was not Moby-Dick that took off thy leg?"

"Who told thee that?" cried Ahab; then pausing, "Aye, Starbuck; aye, my hearties all round; it was Moby-Dick that dismasted me; Moby-Dick that brought me to this dead stump I stand on now. Aye, Aye," he shouted, with a terrific, loud, animal sob, like that of a heart-stricken moose; "Aye, aye! it was that accursed white whale that razeed[11] me; made a poor pegging lubber[12] of me for ever and a day!" Then tossing both arms, with measureless imprecations[13] he shouted out: "Aye, aye! and I'll chase him round Good Hope and round the Horn, and round the Norway Maelstrom, and round perdition's flames before I give him up. And this is what ye have shipped for, men! to chase that white whale on both sides of land, and over all sides of earth, till he spouts black blood and rolls fin out. What say ye, men, will ye splice[14] hands on it, now? I think ye do look brave."

"Aye, aye!" shouted the harpooners and seamen, running closer to the excited old man: "a sharp eye for the White Whale; a sharp lance for Moby-Dick!"

"God bless ye," he seemed to half sob and half shout. "God bless ye, men. Steward! Go draw the great measure of grog.[15] But what's this long face about, Mr. Starbuck; wilt thou not chase the White Whale? Art not game for Moby-Dick?"

"I am game for his crooked jaw, and for the jaws of Death too, Captain Ahab, if it fairly comes in the way of the business we follow; but I came here to hunt whales, not my commander's vengeance. How many barrels will thy vengeance yield thee even if thou gettest it, Captain Ahab? It will not fetch thee much in our Nantucket market."

"Nantucket market! Hoot! But come closer, Starbuck; thou requirest a little lower layer. If money's to be the measurer, man, and the accountants have computed their great counting-house the globe, by girdling it with guineas, one to every three parts of an inch; then, let me tell thee, that my vengeance will fetch a great premium *here*!"

"He smites his chest," whispered Stubb, "what's that for? Methinks it rings most vast, but hollow."

"Vengeance on a dumb brute!" cried Starbuck, "that simply smote thee from blindest instinct! Madness! To be enraged with a dumb thing, Captain Ahab, seems blasphemous."

"Hark ye yet again—the little lower layer. All visible objects, man, are but as pasteboard masks. But in each event—in the living act, the undoubted deed—there, some unknown but still reasoning thing puts forth the moldings of its features from behind the unreasoning mask. If

---

10. **parmacety** (pär′mə·sed′ē): slang for "spermaceti" (a sperm whale).

11. **razeed** (rā·zēd′): to razee is to make a wooden warship lower by removing the upper deck. Here, Ahab means that the whale reduced him to this low state.

12. **lubber:** big, slow, clumsy person.

13. **imprecations** (im′pri·kā′shənz): curses.

14. **splice:** join.

15. **grog:** watered-down liquor drunk by sailors.

man will strike, strike through the mask! How can the prisoner reach outside except by thrusting through the wall? To me, the White Whale is that wall, shoved near to me. Sometimes I think there's naught beyond. But 'tis enough. He tasks me; he heaps me; I see in him outrageous strength, with an inscrutable[16] malice sinewing it. That inscrutable thing is chiefly what I hate; and be the White Whale agent, or be the White Whale principal, I will wreak that hate upon him. Talk not to me of blasphemy, man; I'd strike the sun if it insulted me. For could the sun do that, then could I do the other; since there is ever a sort of fair play herein, jealousy presiding over all creations. But not my master, man, is even that fair play. Who's over me? Truth hath no confines. Take off thine eye! More intolerable than fiends' glarings is a doltish stare! So, so; thou reddenest and palest; my heat has melted thee to anger-glow. But look ye, Starbuck, what is said in heat, that thing unsays itself. There are men from whom warm words are small indignity. I meant not to incense thee. Let it go. Look! see yonder Turkish cheeks of spotted tawn—living, breathing pictures painted by the sun. The pagan leopards—the unrecking and unworshipping things, that live; and seek, and give no reasons for the torrid life they feel! The crew, man, the crew! Are they not one and all with Ahab, in this matter of the whale? See Stubb! he laughs! See yonder Chilean! he snorts to think of it. Stand up amid the general hurricane, thy one tossed sapling cannot, Starbuck! And what is it? Reckon it. 'Tis but to help strike a fin; no wondrous feat for Starbuck. What is it more? From this one poor hunt, then, the best lance out of all Nantucket, surely he will not hang back, when every foremast-hand has clutched a whetstone? Ah! constrainings seize thee; I see! the billow lifts thee! Speak, but speak!—Aye, aye! thy silence, then, *that* voices thee. *(Aside)* Something shot from my dilated nostrils, he has inhaled it in his lungs. Starbuck now is mine; cannot oppose me now, without rebellion."

*Sailors-Companion to the Tailors* (detail) (mid-19th century). Unsigned, attributed to John Cranch. Oil on wood panel. Peabody Essex Museum, Salem, Massachusetts (M16265).

"God keep me!—keep us all!" murmured Starbuck lowly.

But in his joy at the enchanted, tacit[17] acquiescence of the mate, Ahab did not hear his foreboding invocation; nor yet the low laugh from the hold; nor yet the presaging vibrations of the winds in the cordage; nor yet the hollow flap of the sails against the masts, as for a moment their hearts sank in. For again Starbuck's downcast eyes lighted up with the stubbornness of life; the subterranean laugh died away; the winds blew on; the sails filled out; the ship heaved and rolled as before. Ah, ye admonitions and warnings! Why stay ye not when ye come? But rather are ye

---

16. **inscrutable** (in·skro͞ot'ə·bəl): mysterious.

17. **tacit** (tas'it): implied but not expressed openly.

Whalers capturing a sperm whale in the South Pacific, (1847), engraving.
The Granger Collection, New York.

predictions than warnings, ye shadows! Yet not so much predictions from without, as verifications of the foregoing things within. For with little external to constrain us, the innermost necessities in our being, these still drive us on.

"The measure! the measure!" cried Ahab.

Receiving the brimming pewter, and turning to the harpooneers, he ordered them to produce their weapons. Then ranging them before him near the capstan,[18] with their harpoons in their hands, while his three mates stood at his side with their lances, and the rest of the ship's company formed a circle round the group; he stood for an instant searchingly eyeing every man of his crew. But those wild eyes met his, as the bloodshot eyes of the prairie wolves meet the eye of their leader, ere he rushes on at their head in the trail of the bison; but, alas! only to fall into the hidden snare of the Indian.

"Drink and pass!" he cried, handing the heavy charged flagon to the nearest seaman. "The crew alone now drink. Round with it, round! Short drafts—long swallows, men; 'tis hot as Satan's hoof. So, so; it goes round excellently. It spiralizes in ye; forks out at the serpent-snapping eye. Well done; almost drained. That way it went, this way it comes. Hand it me—here's a hollow! Men, ye seem the years; so brimming life is gulped and gone. Steward, refill!

"Attend now, my braves. I have mustered ye all round this capstan; and ye, mates, flank me with your lances; and ye, harpooneers, stand there with your irons; and ye, stout mariners, ring me in, that I may in some sort revive a noble custom of my fisherman fathers before me. O men, you will yet see that—— Ha! boy, come back? bad pennies come not sooner. Hand it me. Why, now, this pewter had run brimming again, wert not thou St. Vitus's imp[19]—away, thou ague!

"Advance, ye mates! Cross your lances full before me. Well done! Let me touch the axis." So saying, with extended arm, he grasped the three level, radiating lances at their crossed center; while so doing, suddenly and nervously twitched them; meanwhile, glancing intently from Starbuck to Stubb, from Stubb to Flask. It seemed as though, by some nameless, interior volition,[20] he would fain have shocked into them the same fiery emotion accumulated within the Leyden jar[21] of his own magnetic life. The three mates quailed before his strong, sustained, and mystic aspect. Stubb and Flask looked sideways from him; the honest eye of Starbuck fell downright.

"In vain!" cried Ahab; "but, maybe, 'tis well. For did ye three but once take the full-forced shock, then mine own electric thing, *that* had perhaps expired from out me. Perchance, too, it would have dropped ye dead. Perchance ye need it not. Down lances! And now, ye mates, I do

18. **capstan:** similar to a winch; a large cylinder, usually on a ship's deck, around which cables are wound to lift heavy objects such as anchors and weights.

19. **St. Vitus's imp:** Saint Vitus is the patron saint of people ill with chorea, a nervous disorder characterized by irregular, jerking movements. An imp is a mischievous child or young demon. Ahab is complaining that the steward's clumsiness caused the pitcher of grog to be spilled.

20. **volition** (vō·lish′ən): will.

21. **Leyden jar:** device for storing electrical charges.

appoint ye three cupbearers to my three pagan kinsmen there—yon three most honorable gentlemen and noblemen, my valiant har-pooneers. Disdain the task? What, when the great Pope washes the feet of beggars, using his tiara for ewer?[22] Oh, my sweet cardinals! your own condescension, *that* shall bend ye to it. I do not order ye; ye will it. Cut your seizings and draw the poles, ye harpooneers!"

Silently obeying the order, the three har-pooneers now stood with the detached iron part of their harpoons, some three feet long, held, barbs up, before him.

"Stab me not with that keen steel! Cant[23] them; cant them over! know ye not the goblet end? Turn up the socket! So, so; now, ye

cupbearers, advance. The irons! take them; hold them while I fill!" Forthwith, slowly going from one officer to the other, he brimmed the harpoon sockets with the fiery waters from the pewter.

"Now, three to three, ye stand. Commend the murderous chalices! Bestow them, ye who are now made parties to this indissoluble league. Ha! Starbuck! but the deed is done! Yon ratifying sun now waits to sit upon it. Drink, ye harpooneers! drink and swear, ye men that man the deathful whaleboat's bow—Death to Moby-Dick! God hunt us all, if we do not hunt Moby-Dick to his death!" The long, barbed steel goblets were lifted; and to cries and maledictions[24] against the White Whale, the spirits were simultaneously quaffed down with a hiss. Starbuck paled, and turned, and shivered. Once more, and finally, the replenished pewter went the rounds among the frantic crew; when, waving his free hand to them, they all dispersed; and Ahab retired within his cabin. ■

---

22. **tiara for ewer:** literally, "crown for a pitcher"; a reference to the practice of the pope washing the feet of the poor on Holy Thursday in imitation of Jesus' washing the feet of his disciples.
23. **cant:** overturn or tilt.

24. **maledictions** (mal′ə·dik′shunz): curses.

# Response and Analysis

## Reading Check

1. Why does Ahab meet with his crew? What does he order the mates to do with their lances?

2. What do you learn about Moby-Dick's appearance from Ahab's dialogue with his crew?

## Thinking Critically

3. Explain Ahab's famous **metaphor** comparing visible objects to "pasteboard masks" (page 332). What do you think he means when he says "strike through the mask"?

4. What **symbolic** meaning might the white whale have? Recall Ahab's comment that the white whale "is that wall. . . . Sometimes I

think there's naught beyond" (page 333). What might the ship and crew symbolize?

5. What can you **infer** about Ahab's **character** when he says, "Talk not to me of blasphemy, man; I'd strike the sun if it insulted me" (page 333)?

6. Using details from the selection, respond to **Connecting to the Focus Question** on page 328.

## Extending and Evaluating

7. Who are Ahab and Ishmael in the Bible? Look up Ahab's story in I Kings 16:29–22:40 and Ishmael's story in Genesis 16:8–15; 21:9–21. Why do you think Melville chose those names?

# Reflecting *on the* Literary Period

## American Romanticism: 1800–1860

The following questions ask you to compare and analyze the selections in this feature and respond to the Focus Question. Where possible, cite passages from the selections to support your answers.

Oliver Wendell
Holmes . . . . . . . . . . . . . . . . . . . . . . . . . . .**The Chambered Nautilus**

Edgar Allan Poe . . . . . . . . . . . . . . . . .**The Fall of the House of Usher**

Herman Melville . . . . . . . . . . . . . .**The Quarter-Deck** *from* **Moby-Dick**

### Comparing Literature

1. How do the selections in this feature illustrate the Romantic emphasis on inner experience and the power of the imagination?

2. Consider the attitude toward nature expressed in "The Chambered Nautilus" and in "The Quarter-Deck." What do these works reveal about each writer's response to the natural world?

3. How do Edgar Allan Poe and Herman Melville use **symbols**—people, places, things, or events that stand for something more than themselves— in order to examine complex human psychology?

4. The journey is an important motif in literature. Examine the motif of the journey in "The Fall of the House of Usher" and in "The Quarter-Deck." What do you find both similar and different about each author's use of this narrative pattern?

5. **Style** refers to a writer's characteristic way of writing—the choice of words, arrangement of words in sentences, and relationship of sentences to one another. Select a passage from two of the works in this feature, and describe each author's style. Point out essential similarities and differences.

**SKILLS FOCUS**

Pages 307–336 cover **Literary Skills** Evaluate the philosophical, political, religious, ethical, and social influences of a historical period.

### RESPONDING TO THE
## Focus Question

Review your notes and responses related to the Focus Question for this feature. Using details from the selections, write your answer to the question.

According to Romantic views, how do the power of the imagination, individual feelings, and nature help us discover truths about ourselves that may elude the rational mind?

**FICTION**

## Death to Moby-Dick!

A literary masterpiece of the Romantic era, Herman Melville's *Moby-Dick* is the epic tale of a man's obsession that is both dark and tragic. Captain Ahab, the strange captain of the whaling ship *Pequod,* has one goal in life: to destroy the white whale that cost him his right leg. *Billy Budd,* another masterwork written by Melville, is the story of an innocent, young sailor aboard the H.M.S. *Indomitable* who inadvertently kills John Claggart, the ship's master-at-arms, who is envious of Billy.

**FICTION**

## The Face of One Long Dead

Longfellow's "The Cross of Snow" is a poem of mourning for a lost love whose absence still haunts the speaker. For another treatment of this theme, read Emily Brontë's classic novel *Wuthering Heights.* Inspired by many of the same Romantic poets that influenced Longfellow, Brontë's novel chronicles a tragic love of such intensity that it transcends even death.

**This title is available in the HRW Library.**

**NONFICTION**

## On America's Highways

Thoreau went to Walden Pond to experience the simplicity of nature in his own corner of America. In *Blue Highways: A Journey into America,* William Least Heat-Moon does the exact opposite—he hits the asphalt and travels the back roads of America. In the faces of people, in the beauty of the landscape, and in the small towns with names like Bear Wallow, Mud Lick, and Love Joy, Heat-Moon celebrates the human spirit and the American way of life.

**NONFICTION**

## Nature Revisited

Emerson deeply loved the natural world. He believed that in the presence of nature "a wild delight" would fill a person "in spite of real sorrows." What can renew us when we find sorrow in nature? Rachel Carson's *Silent Spring,* written in 1962, chronicles the dire effects of pesticides on songbird populations across America. This meticulously researched book helped launch environmental campaigns and ecological movements that are still active today.

# Writing a Short Story

**Writing Assignment**
Write a short story of at least 1,500 words with an interesting plot and well-developed characters.

If a minister begins wearing an unexplained black veil, how will his congregation respond? If a man makes a bargain with the devil about the fate of his soul, can he escape the consequences? As you've seen in this chapter, Nathaniel Hawthorne and Washington Irving answer these questions in **short stories**—short, fictional narratives that create imaginative worlds in very few pages. In this workshop you will learn how to develop a story idea into an interesting short story—to make readers cry, laugh, or shriek in terror.

# Prewriting

## Consider Audience, Purpose, and Tone

**Have You Heard the One About . . . ?** The kind of story you will write will be short enough for your readers—or **audience**—to complete in one sitting. When you write a short story, your **purpose** is a literary one—that is, you use language creatively to express an idea. The attitude you have toward your readers and your subject establishes your **tone,** which may be serious, comic, or ironic.

## Explore Story Ideas

**"What if . . . ?" Situations** Many authors say that their best ideas for short stories come from real life—from a news story, an interesting-looking person, or an everyday situation. To find a story idea, try looking around and making note of your observations. Next, brainstorm a "What if?" question about each news event, person, or situation you have recorded. Then, choose the most interesting idea for your short story.

## Imagine Characters and Setting

**Who?** Once you have a story idea, imagine the people who will appear in the story—the **characters,** or the fictional individuals that have human traits (even if the characters are animals). Your short story will usually have one or more main characters and perhaps one or two secondary characters. Because believable characters act and behave in stories the way people do in real life, use **concrete sensory details** in making the characters come to life. To help you create complex characters, write responses to the following analysis questions for each character.

**SKILLS FOCUS**

**Writing Skills**
Write a short story. Create characters, setting, and plot.

● **What is the character's appearance?** How does he or she speak and move? Does this character have distinctive actions and gestures?

- **How does the character behave?** What actions or reactions could help develop and reveal information about the character?

- **What motivates the character?** What is important to this person? What does he or she want?

**Where?** As you develop your characters, also develop the times and places—or the **settings**—for their actions and speech. Locate the scenes in your short story in specific places with unique sights, sounds, and smells, which you will describe, again using concrete sensory details. Limit the number of settings in your story to one or two places to avoid confusing your reader. Here is how one writer used sensory language to make one of the settings of her short story immediately recognizable for the reader.

> They walked into the permanent sausage-and-potato-salad smell of the restaurant.

## Plot Your Story

**Make Trouble** To keep your readers interested in the situation, characters, and setting you've chosen, something has to happen. The sequence of events in a short story is called the **plot**. To develop a plot for your story, answer the questions in the chart below. One writer's responses to the questions appear in the right-hand column.

### QUESTIONS FOR DEVELOPING PLOT

| Questions | Examples |
|---|---|
| 1. **What's the conflict—the problem in the story?** The conflict can be **external,** in which a character struggles against an outside force such as another character or the environment; or it can be **internal,** in which a character struggles against his or her own feelings. | Leticia and her best friend Jennifer have a misunderstanding. Jennifer has decided she won't go to college after all, and Leticia doesn't understand her reasons. |
| 2. **What happens next?** The characters' actions or decisions complicate the plot. They make up the **rising action** that advances the plot toward the climax. | Leticia begins to change; she has a new friend and a new hairstyle. She tells Jennifer she wants everything to be new. Jennifer thinks Leticia wants a new best friend, too. |
| 3. **Will things like this go on forever?** The **climax,** or crisis point, is usually the moment when the outcome of the conflict is imminent. | Leticia apologizes for saying she wanted everything to be new, but Jennifer tells her she doesn't need her sympathy. |
| 4. **What happens to the characters at the end?** The resolution of the conflict is the **denouement,** the results or significance of the story's events for the characters. | Jennifer explains that she wants to help her dad with the restaurant. It's a choice she has made. Leticia realizes that things change, even friendships. |

**As It Happens**  Decide when to vary the **pace** in your short story—the rate at which you relate events. For example, you can build suspense by lingering over details that describe a character or setting, or you can create tension by speeding up the narrative. Although you'll present most plot events in **chronological order,** you may sometimes skip forward in time (**flash-forward**) or backward (**flashback**). In either case, give readers time clues to make sure you don't lose them.

**Put Words in Their Mouths**  Let the characters speak for themselves. **Dialogue**—characters' actual words—can help move the plot forward and develop a character's personality. While dialogue shows a character's spoken words, **interior monologue** shows unspoken thoughts and attempts to mimic the flow of thoughts, feelings, and memories through a character's mind.

**TIP**  To distinguish dialogue from regular prose, use quotation marks to enclose people's exact words. For more on **using quotation marks,** see Quotation Marks, 13c–d, in the Language Handbook.

## Choose a Point of View

**See It My Way**  The perspective from which a writer tells a story is called its **point of view.** The term *point of view* refers to two separate but related ideas: *who* tells the story and *how much* he or she knows. As a general rule, maintain a consistent point of view throughout your story. Choose from the following points of view.

- **First person**  The narrator, usually a character in the story, tells only what he or she knows and experiences.

- **Third person (limited)**  The narrator is not a character but tells the story from the perspective of one of the story's characters, describing only what that one character knows and experiences.

- **Third person (omniscient)**  The narrator is not a character in the story. The narrator can tell the story from the perspective of any character and include the thoughts and feelings of any character. Using this point of view allows the narrator to **shift perspectives** from one character to another in the short story.

## Consider Style

**How You Say It**  To add interest to your story, enhance your **style**—how you express yourself in writing. Using stylistic devices, such as **figures of speech** (similes, metaphors, or personification), adds to the rhetorical and aesthetic impact of your story—that is, they help you to write more effectively and to make your story more appealing to readers. Other stylistic devices you may use include **imagery** (language that evokes a picture or feeling) and **irony** (a contrast between appearances and reality).

**SKILLS FOCUS**

**PRACTICE & APPLY 1**  Develop a short story idea by planning a setting, plot, and characters; choosing a point of view; and considering ways to use stylistic devices.

**Writing Skills**
Choose a point of view.
Create style.

# Writing

## Writing a Short Story

### A Writer's Framework

**Beginning**

- Engage readers' attention.
- Give details about the setting.
- Introduce the main characters, and establish the point of view.
- Set the plot in motion with an event or situation that initiates conflict.

**Middle**

- Develop the characters through specific actions, dialogue, description, and concrete sensory details.
- Introduce plot complications through conflict.
- Add stylistic devices—figures of speech, imagery, or irony.

**End**

- Develop the plot intensity to a climax.
- Resolve the conflict.
- Reveal the final outcome.
- Make the significance of the events clear to readers.

### A Writer's Model

Keep the Change

Standing in her bedroom by her bookshelf filled with keepsakes, Leticia turned and threw a blue stuffed dog on her bed. Her dorm room wouldn't have much space, and she would only be able to take a few things when she and her best friend, Jennifer, left for college in a couple of months. The phone rang. "Hey, Leticia. What are you doing?"

"I'm cleaning stuff out. Are you taking your softball trophies?"

"I'm not going," said Jennifer offhandedly.

Startled, Leticia replied, "But you have to go! You have a scholarship!"

"A scholarship won't help my dad run the restaurant now. Since his illness, he can't do it himself."

Leticia hung up the phone. "Now everything is ruined," she wailed to herself. "Who will be my roommate?" Leticia remembered how Jennifer had recently danced around and sung, "Goodbye, smoke! Goodbye, carving knife! Goodbye, scale!" Jennifer didn't complain about her job at her father's restaurant, the Bar-B-Q Shack, but she had skipped around like someone let out of prison. Leticia began to cry.

As the weeks went on, Leticia's excitement returned. Megan Greene, the most popular girl in school, called her to say that since they were going to the same college, they should get to know each other.

Even though Megan had hardly spoken to Leticia in high school, Leticia now found herself actually shopping with Megan. "Going to

*(continued)*

**BEGINNING**
Setting
Engaging opener
Main characters
Third-person point of view, limited

Dialogue

External conflict

**MIDDLE**
Interior monologue

Figurative language
Plot complication

Irony

*(continued)*

**Interior monologue**
**Sensory details**

**Plot complication**

**Conflict developed through dialogue**

**END**

**Sensory details**

**Climax**

**Conflict resolved**
**Final outcome revealed**

**Imagery**

**Significance**

college sure does change things—and people," Leticia thought as Megan even whisked her off to a salon to get her floppy bangs and straight hair transformed into a sleek, flattering cut. As soon as Megan left her, Leticia started for the Bar-B-Q Shack, but Jennifer didn't seem that happy to see her.

"New haircut. What's the occasion?" Jennifer asked.

"It's the new me! When I get to college I want everything to be new!" Leticia replied.

"Then you'd better not hang out with an old friend like me."

"Oh, Jennifer! I didn't mean that."

"But I did. Leave me alone."

Leticia was confused. She walked down to the high school and wandered around to think. She sat on the bench where she and Jennifer used to talk at lunch, and looked at their old homeroom where Jennifer had finally made her understand algebra. She remembered showing off her new hairstyle. Leticia blushed. How could she have been so insensitive?

The next morning Leticia waited for Jennifer at the door of the Bar-B-Q Shack. Swallowing hard, she said, "Jennifer, I'm sorry."

Jennifer opened the door and turned on the lights. They walked into the permanent sausage-and-potato-salad smell of the restaurant.

"For what? I told you to stay away."

"For saying I wanted everything to be new. I was so insensitive."

Jennifer turned on the cash register and then looked Leticia straight in the eye. "You and Megan Greene just go on to college. I don't need your sympathy."

"But I thought you wanted to go, too," pleaded Leticia.

"I did, but then I realized there were other things I'd rather do—like help my dad run the restaurant for a while." Jennifer smiled, a genuine smile. "I guess I can be happy where I am."

Jennifer cracked a roll of quarters. A ray of sun forced its way through the Bar-B-Q Shack's smoky windows, illuminating the quarters as they cascaded from Jennifer's hand into the change drawer.

"I guess we all have to make our own change," said Leticia finally.

**INTERNET**

**More Writer's Models**

Keyword: LE7 11-2

**PRACTICE & APPLY 2** Using the framework on page 341 and the model above as guides, write your short story. Introduce your characters and plot quickly. Add plot complications, and use stylistic devices.

# Revising

## Evaluate and Revise Your Draft

**Look Again** Your favorite short story writers work hard on their stories. Most of them revise their drafts again and again before the stories are ready to be published. You, too, will benefit from revising. First, polish your story by using the guidelines below to evaluate and revise your content and organization. Then, use the guidelines on page 344 to evaluate and revise your story's style.

**PEER REVIEW**

Before you finish revising your story, exchange it with a peer. Ask for feedback on your character and plot development and your use of stylistic devices.

▶ **First Reading: Content and Organization** Use the chart below to look for ways to improve upon the content and organization of your story. Keep in mind your story's purpose and intended audience as you answer the questions.

### Rubric: Writing a Short Story

| Evaluation Questions | ▶ Tips | ▶ Revision Techniques |
|---|---|---|
| ❶ Does the story's beginning name the main characters and initiate the conflict? Does it give details about the setting? | ▶ **Draw a box** around the names of the characters. **Highlight** the event or situation that initiates the conflict. **Bracket** the sentence that gives details about the setting. | ▶ **Add** the main characters to the beginning. **Reword** to include a conflict to set the plot in motion. **Add** a sentence that gives details about the setting. |
| ❷ Does the story have a clear point of view? Is the point of view developed consistently? | ▶ **Label** the point of view in the margin with *I* for first person, *3L* for third person limited, or *3O* for third person omniscient. **Underline** phrases in your story that indicate the point of view. | ▶ **Add** phrases that clearly indicate the point of view. **Delete** any information that the narrator would not reasonably know, especially for a first-person or a third-person-limited narrator. |
| ❸ Is the plot developed with complications shown by specific actions and events? | ▶ **Number** each plot complication, and **label** in the margin whether the complication is a specific action or event. | ▶ **Add** actions or events that show a clear sequence to develop the plot. |
| ❹ Does the story use dialogue, interior monologue, and concrete sensory details to create complex characters? | ▶ **Draw a dotted line** under sentences that show a character's spoken words or thoughts. **Put parentheses** around any concrete sensory details. | ▶ **Add** dialogue or interior monologue to make characters more complex. **Elaborate** on characters with concrete sensory details. |
| ❺ Does the story use stylistic devices, such as figures of speech, imagery, or irony? | ▶ **Circle** each figure of speech, use of imagery, or use of irony. | ▶ **Replace** dull sentences with more lively ones that use figures of speech, imagery, or irony. |

*(continued)*

*(continued)*

| | | |
|---|---|---|
| ❻ Does the story's end include a climax? Does it resolve the story's conflict and show the significance of the events? | ▸ **Put a star** by the sentences that show a climax. **Bracket** the sentences that resolve the conflict. **Highlight** the sentence that shows the significance of the events. | ▸ **Reword** the end to include a climax. **Add** sentences that resolve the conflict. **Elaborate** with a sentence that shows the significance of the events. |

▷ **Second Reading: Style** Next, evaluate the style of your short story. Strong, precise adjectives help establish your story's **tone** and help readers visualize the fictional world you are creating—the characters, setting, and events. Using tired, worn-out, or vague adjectives such as *good* or *big* will detract from the effectiveness of your writing. Your short story will be more dramatic if you exchange tired adjectives for fresh, precise ones.

## Style Guidelines

| Evaluation Question | ▸ Tip | ▸ Revision Technique |
|---|---|---|
| ● Do precise adjectives help readers visualize characters, setting, and events? | ▸ **Bracket** all vague adjectives such as *good* or *big*. | ▸ **Replace** vague adjectives with precise adjectives. |

### ANALYZING THE REVISION PROCESS
Study these revisions, and answer the questions that follow.

add/delete

"Going to college sure does change things—and people,"
Leticia thought ~~about all that was changing~~ as Megan, ~~who hoped to turn Leticia into another her,~~ even whisked her off to a salon to

replace

get her ~~dull~~ *floppy* bangs and straight hair transformed into a ~~pretty~~ *sleek, flattering* cut.

### Responding to the Revision Process

1. Why did the writer replace some information with the information in quotation marks?

2. Why did the writer delete the phrase about Megan?

3. Why did the writer replace words in the last line?

**Writing Skills**
Revise for content and style.

**PRACTICE & APPLY 3** Revise the content, organization, and style of your story. Use specific descriptions of character and setting, and a clear sequence of events in the plot.

# Publishing

## Proofread and Publish Your Story

**Picture Perfect**   Before final publication of their stories, professional authors often examine galley proofs to make sure that their stories are error-free. You also should look at the final draft of your story, or its "galley proof," to be certain that it doesn't contain distracting mistakes.

**Get the Word Out**   A short story is more than just a school assignment. It is a creative way to share your imagination with others. Try a few of these publishing suggestions.

- Send your story to a younger class, and ask that class to critique your short story based on the elements of short fiction that they have been discussing in their literature class.

- Exchange a set of your class's short stories with a high school in another country. Discuss what is gained and lost in the translation between cultures.

- Illustrate your story, and submit it to your school's literary magazine or newspaper.

- Submit your story to an annual short story contest. Ask a librarian to help you identify several.

- As a class, develop criteria for evaluating short stories. Then, swap stories with a classmate and write brief reviews of one another's stories, using the criteria that you developed.

## Reflect on Your Story

**Hindsight Is 20/20**   Write a short response to each of the following questions. Keep the answers in your portfolio, along with the final version of your story.

- If you wanted to tell the short story again, this time from another point of view, what changes would you need to make and why?

- What part of your story—such as plot, characters, or style—was the most satisfying for you to write? least satisfying? Explain why.

- If you were answering the question, "What is your short story about?" for a potential reader, how would you describe the significance of events in the story?

**PRACTICE & APPLY 4**   Follow the suggestions above to proofread, publish, and reflect on your story. Remember to check for the conventions of American English, especially the proper sequence of verb tenses in your short story.

**TIP**   Proofreading will help you follow the **conventions** of American English. Make sure that your verb tenses follow the right sequence, especially if you are describing events both from the past and from the present. For more on **sequence of tenses,** see Tenses and Their Uses, 3b–c, in the Language Handbook.

**COMPUTER TIP**

You can use a computer to insert graphics or visuals into the final draft of your short story. For information on **graphics and visuals,** see Designing Your Writing in the Writer's Handbook.

**SKILLS FOCUS**

**Writing Skills**
Proofread, especially for correct sequence of tenses.

**Test Practice**  The following two poems are about a woman in Greek mythology—Helen of Troy. The wife of King Menelaus of Sparta (Sparta was one of the great city-states of ancient Greece), Helen was said to be the most beautiful woman in the world. Helen ran off with (or in some versions was abducted by) Paris, a handsome prince from the city of Troy in Asia Minor. The enraged husband, Menelaus, with many other Greek warriors, attacked Troy to get Helen back. The resulting Trojan War lasted ten years. Edgar Allan Poe (1809–1849) first published "To Helen" in 1831 and then again, in a slightly revised version, in 1845. The poet H. D. (1886–1961) published "Helen" in 1924.

DIRECTIONS: Read the following poems. Then, read each multiple-choice question that follows, and write the letter of the best response.

# To Helen
### Edgar Allan Poe

Helen, thy beauty is to me
   Like those Nicéan barks of yore,
That gently, o'er a perfumed sea,
   The weary, way-worn wanderer bore
5    To his own native shore.°

On desperate seas long wont to roam,
   Thy hyacinth° hair, thy classic face,
Thy Naiad° airs have brought me home
   To the glory that was Greece,
10    And the grandeur that was Rome

Lo! in yon brilliant window-niche
   How statuelike I see thee stand,
The agate lamp° within thy hand!
   Ah, Psyche,° from the regions which
15    Are Holy Land!

**5. Nicéan...shore:** Nicaea was a Greek colony. **barks:** ships. **wanderer:** Odysseus from Homer's epic. Poe scholars have never found an adequate explanation for "Nicéan" (since Odysseus traveled home by ships from Phaeacia) and think Poe used the word to contribute to the music of the poem.
**7. hyacinth** (hī′ə·sinth′) *n.* used as *adj.:* curly, like the petals on a hyacinth flower.
**8. Naiad** (nā′ad′): nymphlike. In Greek mythology, the Naiads were water nymphs believed to have healing powers.
**13. agate lamp:** lamp made of agate, a semi-precious stone associated with immortality.
**14. Psyche** (sī′kē): mortal woman whose great beauty captivated the god of love, Cupid.

**SKILLS FOCUS**

Pages 346–349 cover
**Literary Skills**
Compare and contrast works from different literary periods.

# Helen

H. D.

All Greece hates
the still eyes in the white face,
the luster as of olives
where she stands,
5   and the white hands.

All Greece reviles
the wan face when she smiles,
hating it deeper still
when it grows wan and white,
10   remembering past enchantments
      and past ills.

Greece sees unmoved,
God's daughter,° born of love,
the beauty of cool feet
15   and slenderest knees,
could love indeed the maid,
only if she were laid,
white ash amid funereal cypresses.

**13. God's daughter:** Helen was a daughter of Zeus, the king of the gods. She was conceived when Zeus (in the form of a swan) seduced the mortal Leda.

1. In the first two lines of Poe's poem, the main poetic device is —

   **A** personification

   **B** simile

   **C** symbol

   **D** metaphor

2. In line 4 of Poe's poem, the main poetic device is —

   **F** personification

   **G** alliteration

   **H** onomatopoeia

   **J** simile

3. In Poe's first two stanzas the speaker is saying that Helen's beauty makes him —

   **A** feel weary and desperate

   **B** long to travel by sea

   **C** feel angry

   **D** feel as if he is returning home

4. In the third stanza of Poe's poem, what is Helen compared to?

   **F** A lamp

   **G** Greece

   **H** A statue

   **J** Rome

5. In H. D.'s poem, Helen's eyes are compared to —

   **A** water

   **B** olives

   **C** ash

   **D** cypresses

6. In H. D.'s poem, how do the Greek people feel about Helen?

   **F** They pity her because she is a victim.

   **G** They condemn her for causing the Trojan War.

   **H** They forgive her for her past misdeeds.

   **J** They are jealous of her beauty.

7. In the second stanza of H. D.'s poem, Helen grows increasingly pale because —

   **A** she knows she is growing old

   **B** she is angry at the Greeks' attitude toward her

   **C** she thinks she will be murdered and buried among cypresses

   **D** she is troubled by memories of her past

8. In the third stanza of "Helen," the speaker is saying that the people of Greece can love Helen —
   F despite the trouble she has caused
   G because they feel sorry for her
   H only when she is dead
   J because she is "God's daughter"

9. In contrast to Poe's poem, the overall **tone** in H. D.'s poem is —
   A bitter while Poe's tone is romantic
   B adoring while Poe's tone is bitter
   C envious while Poe's tone is ironic
   D reserved while Poe's tone is humorous

10. Unlike Poe's poem, H. D.'s poem depicts Helen as —
    F a symbol of classic beauty
    G a victim of male domination
    H an object of societal hatred
    J an ordinary woman

## Essay Question

In an essay, compare and contrast these two poems. Pay particular attention to each poet's attitude toward feminine beauty and its effects. Be sure to consider how Poe's poem reflects some of the key characteristics of American Romanticism (see page 167) and how H. D.'s poem goes against them.

# Collection 2: Skills Review
## Vocabulary Skills

**Test Practice**

**Analogies**

DIRECTIONS: For each of the following items, choose the lettered pair of words that expresses the relationship most similar to the relationship between the pair of capitalized words.

1. BLITHE : CAREFREE ::
   A  biased : fair
   B  joyful : depressed
   C  anxious : worrisome
   D  lazy : powerful

2. STAGNANT : FLOWING ::
   F  rough : coarse
   G  difficult : puzzling
   H  vigorous : lively
   J  drowsy : alert

3. TUMULTUOUS : RIOT ::
   A  hilarious : grievance
   B  courageous : hero
   C  timid : clown
   D  cold : sun

4. AVARICE : GREED ::
   F  generosity : bitterness
   G  fear : courage
   H  pride : self-respect
   J  honesty : deceitfulness

5. EFFERVESCENT : SODA ::
   A  sour : lemon
   B  slippery : gravel
   C  dry : water
   D  fragrant : metal

6. TRANSIENT : ETERNAL ::
   F  annual : yearly
   G  clear : hazy
   H  immense : large
   J  brilliant : shiny

7. EFFACED : CREATED ::
   A  preserved : saved
   B  ignored : disregarded
   C  trapped : freed
   D  honored : respected

8. INIQUITY : WICKEDNESS ::
   F  fragility : youthfulness
   G  reality : boldness
   H  purity : filth
   J  honesty : truthfulness

**SKILLS FOCUS**

**Vocabulary Skills**
Analyze word analogies.

# Collection 2: Skills Review
## Writing Skills

DIRECTIONS: Read the following excerpt from a draft of a short story and the questions below it. Choose the best answer to each question, and mark your answers on your own paper.

(1) "My dad's going to ground me forever," Sean told his best friend Anthony. (2) They stood there inspecting the damage to the side of Sean's dad's new extended-cab pickup truck. (3) The door on the passenger's side had a big dent in it where Sean had scraped a tree. (4) The two boys walked from the front to the back of the truck, leaning over several times to squint at the dent, trying to see if it might disappear if they viewed it from a certain angle.

(5) "Maybe you could tell your dad that it got bumped in the parking lot and you didn't see who did it," Anthony suggested.

1. To add characterization to the passage, which of the following could the writer add after sentence 3?

   A "I'm so stupid for denting Dad's truck," Sean thought.

   B The metallic blue paint was scratched for about four inches.

   C Anthony's mother called him on his cell phone at that moment.

   D Just then, Sean's father pulled up into the driveway.

2. The best way to add interest to the plot and slow down the pace of the story would be to

   F contrast the different upbringings that Sean and Anthony had

   G flashback to the day Sean's dad bought the new truck

   H describe the neighborhood in which Sean lives

   J tell about the methods used to fix dents and scratches

3. Which adjective could replace the word *big* in sentence 3 to improve the precision of the writing?

   A large          C small

   B plate-sized    D full

4. If the writer wanted to establish a humorous tone in the paragraph, he could

   F describe the two boys' appearances in clear detail

   G add language that further depicts the apprehensive mood

   H write with a more lighthearted and relaxed vocabulary

   J include dialogue between Sean and his father

5. Which of the following sentences would add to the story's conflict?

   A "I'm glad you were with me when this happened, Anthony."

   B "I'm lucky that I didn't have a fatal crash, like so many teens."

   C "That's the last time I'll back up without looking in the mirrors."

   D "That *would* be a nice way out, but I've never lied to my dad before."

SKILLS FOCUS

**Writing Skills**
Write a story.

# American Masters

## *Whitman and Dickinson*

### *Celebrate the People,*
### *Celebrate the Self*

If you want me again look for me

under your boot-soles.

—Walt Whitman

This is my letter to the World

That never wrote to Me—

—Emily Dickinson

go.
hrw
.com

**INTERNET**

Collection
Resources

Keyword: LE7 11-3

# American Masters
## Whitman and Dickinson

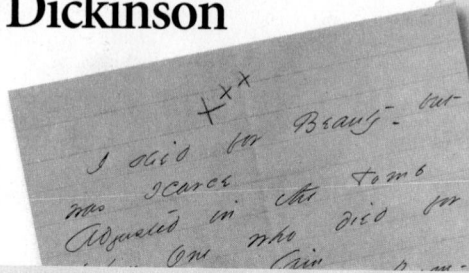

O CAPTAIN! MY CAPTAIN!
BY WALT WHITMAN.

I.

O CAPTAIN! my captain! our fearful trip is done,
The ship has weathered every rack, the prize we sought is won,
The port is near, the bells I hear, the people all exulting,
While follow eyes the steady keel, the vessel grim and daring;
    But O heart! heart! heart!
        Leave you not the little spot,
    Where on the deck my captain lies,
        Fallen cold and dead.

II.

...in! my captain! rise up and hear the bells,
...for you the flag is flung, for you the bells,
...quets and ribboned wreath...
...ng;
...all. $1

---

**1810**     **1850**

**1819** Walt Whitman is born in Long Island, New York (his home, as it looks today, is pictured at far right, page 355)

**1830** Emily Dickinson is born in Amherst, Massachusetts

**1831** Edgar Allan Poe publishes third volume of *Poems,* including "To Helen"

**1836** Ralph Waldo Emerson publishes *Nature*

**1848** In New Orleans, Whitman first encounters the vast American landscape

**1848** Dickinson spends a year at Mount Holyoke Female Seminary

**1850** Nathaniel Hawthorne publishes *The Scarlet Letter,* which sells four thousand copies in ten days

**1851** Herman Melville publishes *Moby-Dick; or The Whale*

**1852** Harriet Beecher Stowe publishes *Uncle Tom's Cabin*

**1854** Henry David Thoreau publishes *Walden*

**1855** Walt Whitman publishes first edition of *Leaves of Grass;* Emily Dickinson visits Philadelphia and Washington, perhaps meeting a married clergyman whom she has fallen in love with

Leaves
of
Grass.

**1861** Civil War begins

**Harriet Beecher Stowe.**

**Portrait of Private George A. Stryker, New York Regiment.**

**1862** Dickinson begins correspondence with Thomas Wentworth Higginson; Whitman travels to Virginia and begins caring for Civil War wounded; Abraham Lincoln issues Emancipation Proclamation

**1863** Louisa May Alcott publishes *Hospital Sketches,* about her experiences as Civil War nurse

**1864** Dickinson is treated for eye disease in Boston

**1865** Civil War ends; Lincoln is assassinated; Whitman publishes *Drum-Taps,* including elegy for Lincoln, "When Lilacs Last in the Dooryard Bloom'd"

**1869** Dickinson is no longer leaving her house in Amherst (the house is pictured above, as it looks today)

**First printing of some of Dickinson's poems.**.

**1870** Higginson is one of the few visitors to Amherst whom Dickinson meets in person

**1873** Whitman moves to Camden, New Jersey

**1876** Alexander Graham Bell patents the telephone

**1879** Thomas Alva Edison invents the incandescent lamp

**1882** Ralph Waldo Emerson dies

**1884** Mark Twain publishes *Adventures of Huckleberry Finn*

**1886** Emily Dickinson dies of a kidney disease

**1890** Dickinson's *Poems* published by Higginson and Mabel Loomis Todd

**1892** Whitman publishes *Leaves of Grass,* Deathbed Edition; Whitman dies of a stroke

# American Masters
## Whitman and Dickinson

*by* John Malcolm Brinnin

PREVIEW

## Think About ...

Walt Whitman and Emily Dickinson are the two writers at the core of American literature who most fully lived out Emerson's call for *self-reliance,* yet they did so in vastly different ways. They looked deeply into nature and described their visions with burning intensity. They both found ways to be immersed in the world and isolated from it. They both created original styles. They both found the divine in the everyday.

As you read about Whitman and Dickinson, think about these questions:

- Where do you find poetry in American life today?
- Is poetry important to people?

**SKILLS FOCUS**

Collection introduction (pages 356–359) covers **Literary Skills** Evaluate genres and traditions in American literature.

The two greatest American poets of the nineteenth century were so different from each other, both as artists and as personalities, that only a nation as varied in character as the United States could possibly contain them.

Walt Whitman worked with bold strokes on a broad canvas; Emily Dickinson worked with the delicacy of a miniaturist. Whitman was sociable and loved company, a traveler; Dickinson was private and shy, content to remain in one secluded spot throughout her lifetime.

While both poets were close observers of people and life's daily activities, the emphasis they gave to what impressed them was so distinct as to make them opposites. Whitman was the public spokesman of the masses and the prophet of progress. "I hear America singing," he said, and he joined his eloquent voice to that chorus. Dickinson was the obscure homebody, peering through the curtains of her house in a country town, who found in nature metaphors for the spirit and recorded them with no hope of an audience. Whitman expected that his celebration of universal brotherhood and the bright destiny of democracy would be carried like a message into the future. Dickinson expected nothing but a box in a dusty attic for the poetry that was her "letter to the World."

Introduction to the London edition of *Leaves of Grass*, 1861. Autograph manuscript.

Revisions made by Walt Whitman to his poem "O Captain! My Captain!"

Manuscript for "I died for Beauty" by Emily Dickinson.

## Two Seams in the Fabric

Whitman's career might be regarded as another American success story—the story of a pleasant young man who drifted into his thirties, working at one job after another, never finding himself until, at his own expense, he boldly published *Leaves of Grass* (1855). The book made him famous around the world. Dickinson's career as a poet began after her death. It is one of those ironies of history in which a writer dies unknown, only to have fame thrust upon her by succeeding generations.

Whitman and Dickinson represent two distinct seams in the fabric of American poetry, one slightly uneven and the other carefully measured and stitched tight. Whitman was as extravagant with words as he was careless with repetition and self-contradiction. Aiming for the large, overall impression, he filled his pages with long lists as he strained to catalog everything in sight. His technique is based on **cadence**—the long, easy sweep of sound that echoes the Bible and the speeches of orators and preachers. This cadence is the basis for his **free verse**—poetry without rhyme or meter.

Dickinson, on the other hand, wrote with the precision of a diamond cutter. Extremely careful in her choice of words, she aimed to evoke the feelings of things rather than simply name them. She was always searching for the one right phrase that would fix a thought in the mind. Her technique is economical, and her neat stanzas are controlled by the demands of rhyme and the meters she found in her hymn book.

## Models for Future Poets

As the history of our poetry shows, both modes of expression have continued to be used by American writers. Both poets have served as models for later poets who have been drawn to the visions Dickinson and Whitman fulfilled and the techniques they mastered. Poetry as public speech written in the cadences of free verse remains a part of our literature; poetry as private observation, carefully crafted in rhyme and meter, still attracts young writers who tend to regard poems as experiences rather than statements.

The coequal importance of the two poetic methods has never been more clearly affirmed than in the following words by the American poet Ezra Pound (see page 648). Pound speaks for himself here as a poet who admired the tightness of Dickinson and disliked the expansiveness of Whitman. Nevertheless, he offers in this poem a blessing that represents the feeling of every poet who has envied the gemlike artistry of Dickinson and the all-embracing power of Whitman. A *pact* is an agreement. Pacts are usually made between people or groups or between nations who have quarreled with each other and are in the process of making up.

## A Pact

I make a pact with you, Walt Whitman—
I have detested you long enough.
I come to you as a grown child
Who has had a pig-headed father;
I am old enough now to make friends.
It was you that broke the new wood,
Now is a time for carving.
We have one sap and one root—
Let there be commerce between us.

—Ezra Pound

*Walt Whitman.* Drawing by David Levine.

Reprinted with permission from *The New York Review of Books.* Copyright © 1970 NYREV, Inc.

The "new wood" Pound writes of is Whitman's new brand of poetry—free verse, a poetry not bound by any rules of rhyme or meter. Pound may not have liked Whitman's style, but, he says, all of our writing comes from one root and is fed by the same sap. We can learn from Whitman.

Whitman and Dickinson together mark a turning point in American poetry.

## REVIEW

### Talk About ...

Turn back to the Think About section at the start of this introduction to Walt Whitman and Emily Dickinson (page 356). Get together with a classmate, and discuss your views on the questions posed there.

### Write About ...

**What do they mean?** A quotation from Walt Whitman and a quotation from Emily Dickinson appear on page 353, at the start of this introduction. Read each quotation carefully. Then, write a paragraph reflecting on the two quotations. You can comment on what you think each poet means by the quotation, or you can express your own feelings about what each poet says—even if your feelings are confused!

*Emily Dickinson.* Drawing by David Levine.

Reprinted with permission from *The New York Review of Books.* Copyright © 1963 NYREV, Inc.

# Walt Whitman
## (1819–1892)

Less than a hundred years after the United States was founded, the new nation found its voice in a poet who spoke to all the world. His name was Walt Whitman, and he struck a note in literature that was as forthright, as original, and as deeply charged with democracy's energies as the land that produced him.

### Student of the World

Whitman was born on May 31, 1819, to parents of Dutch and English descent. They kept a farm in West Hills, Long Island, in what is today the town of Huntington. His father's ancestors had come from England only twenty years after the landing of the *Mayflower* and had settled in Connecticut. On his mother's side his ancestors were among the early immigrants from Holland who settled on Manhattan Island and along the Hudson River. Whitman and his seven brothers and sisters were able to assume their essential American-ness with an uncommon confidence. They knew their American grandparents, and they grew up in circumstances that allowed them both the communal experience of country life and the urban experience of a new city, Brooklyn, on its way to becoming a metropolis.

Here young Walter went to school until he was eleven. He then worked as an office clerk and printer's assistant, and for a time he taught school. On weekends spent along the beaches and in the woods of Long Island, Whitman read Sir Walter Scott, the Bible, Shakespeare, Homer, Dante, and ancient Hindu poetry. He never became a scholar; he never went to college.

Before Whitman was twenty, his feeling for the written word and his fascination with the boomtown atmosphere of Brooklyn led him to journalism. After ten years of that, he took a kind of working vacation—a difficult overland trip by train, horse-drawn coach, and riverboat to New Orleans. There he put his journalistic talent to work for the *Crescent* and his own talent for observation to work for himself. After a few months he returned to New York by way of the Great Lakes and a side trip to Niagara Falls. By this time, Whitman had added to his limited sense of America the experience of a wilderness surrendering its vastness to civilization. He also had become acquainted with the entirely alien culture that French Catholic New Orleans represented to him.

Back in Brooklyn, Whitman accepted an offer to serve as editor of the *Brooklyn Freeman*. For the next six or seven years he supplemented his income as a part-time carpenter and building contractor. All this while he was keeping notebooks and quietly putting together the sprawling collection of poems that would transform his life and change the course of American literature.

### The Making of a Masterpiece

In 1855, Whitman published his collection at his own expense under the title *Leaves of Grass*. Since the book was too boldly new and strange to win the attention of reviewers or readers who had fixed ideas about poetry, its publication went all but unnoticed. To stir up interest, he sent samples to people whose endorsement he thought might be useful. One of these samples reached Ralph Waldo Emerson, who at once wrote to Whitman the most important letter Whitman would ever receive:

Concord, Massachusetts, 21 July, 1855

Dear Sir—I am not blind to the worth of the wonderful gift of *Leaves of Grass*. I find it the most extraordinary piece of wit and wisdom that America has yet contributed. I am very happy in reading it, as great power makes us happy. It meets the demand I am always making of what seemed the sterile and stingy Nature, as if too much handi-work, or too much lymph in the temperament, were making our Western wits fat and mean.

I give you joy of your free and brave thought. I have great joy in it. I find incomparable things said incomparably well, as they must be. I find the courage of treatment which so delights us, and which large perception only can inspire.

I greet you at the beginning of a great career, which yet must have had a long foreground somewhere, for such a start. I rubbed my eyes a little, to see if this sunbeam were no illusion; but the solid sense of the book is a sober certainty. It has the best merits, namely, of fortifying and encouraging.

I did not know until I last night saw the book advertised in a newspaper that I could trust the name as real and available for a post-office. I wish to see my benefactor, and have felt much like striking my tasks and visiting New York to pay you my respects.

R. W. Emerson

The "long foreground" of which Emerson wrote had not been the careful, confident period of preparation to which many poets devote themselves before they are ready to publish. Instead, it had been a precarious existence. Journalism had kept Whitman going financially, but not even the editorials he wrote for the *Brooklyn Eagle* had brought him distinction. On the surface at least, his "long foreground" of preparation had been a mixture of hack work and jack-of-all-trades ingenuity.

By the time he was ready to declare himself a poet and to publish the first version of his book, Walt Whitman was unique. *Leaves of Grass* is a masterpiece that Whitman was to expand and revise through many editions. Its process of growth did not end until the ninth, "deathbed" edition was published in 1891,

thirty-six years after its first appearance. It is a spiritual autobiography that tells the story of an enchanted observer who says who he is at every opportunity and claims what he loves by naming it. "Camerado," he wrote, "this is no book / Who touches this touches a man."

### In the Crowd, but Not of It

The figure we know today as Walt Whitman was conceived and created by the poet himself. Whitman endorsed his image and sold it to the public with a promoter's skill worthy of P. T. Barnum, the great show manager of the nineteenth century. At first glance that figure is a bundle of contradictions. Whitman seems to have had the theatrical flair of a con artist and the selfless dignity of a saint; the sensibility of an artist and the carefree spirit of a hobo; the blustery egotism of a braggart and the demure shyness of a shrinking violet. On second glance these contradictions disappear: Walt Whitman was everything he seemed to be. The figure he so carefully crafted and put on display was not a surrogate but the man himself.

"One would see him afar off," wrote the great naturalist John Burroughs, "in the crowd but not of it—a large, slow-moving figure, clad in gray, with broad-brimmed hat and gray beard—or, quite as frequently, on the front platform of the street horse-cars with the driver. . . . Whitman was of large mold in every way, and of bold, far-reaching schemes, and is very sure to fare better at the hands of large men than of small. The first and last impression which his personal presence always made upon one was of a nature wonderfully gentle, tender, and benignant. . . . I was impressed by the fine grain and clean, fresh quality of the man. . . . He always had the look of a man who had just taken a bath."

If there is a side of Whitman that today we would associate with image building, or self-promotion, there is nothing in his poetry to suggest that it was anything but the product of

The Walt Whitman House in Camden, New Jersey. Whitman lived here from 1884 until his death.

the kind of genius that permanently changes the history of art. He modified standard, king's-English diction and abandoned traditional rhyme schemes and formal meters in favor of the rhythms and speech patterns of free verse.

### Everything Under the Sun

The result was poetry that could sing and speak of everything under the sun. Its sweep was easy, and its range was broad. Suddenly poetry was no longer a matter of organized word structures that neatly clicked shut at the last line; instead, it was a series of open-ended units of rhythm that flowed one into the other and demanded to be read in their totality.

"Whitman throws his chunky language at the reader," writes the critic Paul Zweig. "He cajoles and thunders; he chants, celebrates, chuckles, and caresses. He spills from his capacious American soul every dreg of un-Englishness, every street sound thumbing its nose at traditional subject matter and tone. Here is Samson pulling the house of literature down around his ears, yet singing in the ruins."

Walt Whitman had invented a way of writing poetry that perfectly accommodated his way of seeing. His form is loose enough to allow for long lists and catalogs abundant in detail; it is also flexible enough to include delicate moments of lyricism as well as stretches of blustering oratory. This form served Whitman as observer and prophet—as a private man tending the wounded in the hospital wards of the Civil War and as the public man who gave voice to the grief of a nation in his great elegy for the slain Abraham Lincoln, "When Lilacs Last in the Dooryard Bloom'd."

### An American Epic

When Whitman died, in 1892, he had met a great personal goal. He had enlarged the possibilities of American poetry to include the lyricism of simple speech and the grand design of the epic.

How is *Leaves of Grass* like an epic? Who is its hero? What is its action? The hero is the poet, and he is a hero not of the ancient past but of the future. As in all epics the action takes the form of a journey. In *Leaves of Grass*, the journey is the one the speaker takes as he becomes a poet:

> I am the poet of the Body and I am the
>     poet of the Soul . . .
> I am the poet of the woman the same as
>     the man . . .
> I am not the poet of goodness only, I do
>     not decline to be the poet of wickedness
>     also. . . .

By the end of his epic journey, which even takes him down into a kind of hell, the poet has also been transformed. The "I" has become identified with every element in the universe and has been reborn as something divine. The poet has become the saving force that Whitman believed was the true role of the American poet.

Nothing quite like it had ever been done in America before.

# Before You Read

## I Hear America Singing

### Make the Connection
### Quickwrite ✏️

This famous poem appears near the beginning of *Leaves of Grass* and introduces one of the poet's major themes—the tremendous variety and individuality in American life. Whitman celebrates the American enterprise, in all its forms, through the varied carols, or songs, of men and women who take pride in their occupations. Why do you think a poet who celebrates America would focus on *work* songs? List a few of the jobs you would expect to be celebrated in an American epic written today.

### Literary Focus
### Catalog

One of the most obvious characteristics of Whitman's poetry is his frequent use of **catalogs**—long lists of related things, people, or events. By selecting and naming items in this way, Whitman expresses his unbounded love for everything and everyone in the world. He also, by means of the catalog, creates a kind of rhythm built on the repetition of certain sentence patterns. To hear the effect of cataloging, read aloud this poem and others in this Whitman collection.

*Construction of the Dam* (1937) by William Gropper. Mural study, Department of the Interior, National Park Service.

© Smithsonian American Art Museum, Washington, D.C./Art Resource, NY.

**SKILLS FOCUS**

**Literary Skills**
Understand the use of catalogs in poetry.

> A **catalog** is a list of things, people, or events.
>
> *For more on Catalog, see the Handbook of Literary and Historical Terms.*

**INTERNET**

**More About Walt Whitman**

Keyword: LE7 11-3

# I Hear America Singing

## Walt Whitman

I hear America singing, the varied carols I hear,
Those of mechanics, each one singing his as it should be blithe and strong,
The carpenter singing his as he measures his plank or beam,
The mason singing his as he makes ready for work, or leaves off work,
The boatman singing what belongs to him in his boat, the deckhand singing on the
      steamboat deck,
5
The shoemaker singing as he sits on his bench, the hatter singing as he stands,
The wood-cutter's song, the plowboy's on his way in the morning, or at noon
      intermission or at sundown,
The delicious singing of the mother, or of the young wife at work, or of the girl sewing
      or washing,
Each singing what belongs to him or her and to none else,
10  The day what belongs to the day—at night the party of young fellows, robust, friendly,
Singing with open mouths their strong melodious songs.

# Response and Analysis

## Thinking Critically

1. Name the people the speaker hears in lines 2–8. According to line 9, what does each person sing?

2. What Whitman has in mind here are not the actual work songs associated with various trades and kinds of physical labor but something more subtle. What would you say is the real **theme** of this poem—what is the speaker saying about the American people?

3. A feeling of acceptance, even contentment, runs through many of these voices. Considering the long hours and low pay of laborers in the nineteenth century, would you say Whitman is romanticizing or idealizing the lot of workers? Instead, do the songs express a positive and realistic aspect of American life? Explain your response, and support it with specific references to the poem.

4. Imagine the kinds of singing Whitman would hear if he were alive today. In what ways might these work songs be different from those he heard in his own time? In what ways would they be the same? Before you answer, review your Quickwrite notes.

5. The **catalog** in this poem uses **parallel structures** to create a kind of rhythm. What parallel structures can you find repeated in the poem? Read them aloud to hear the rhythm they create.

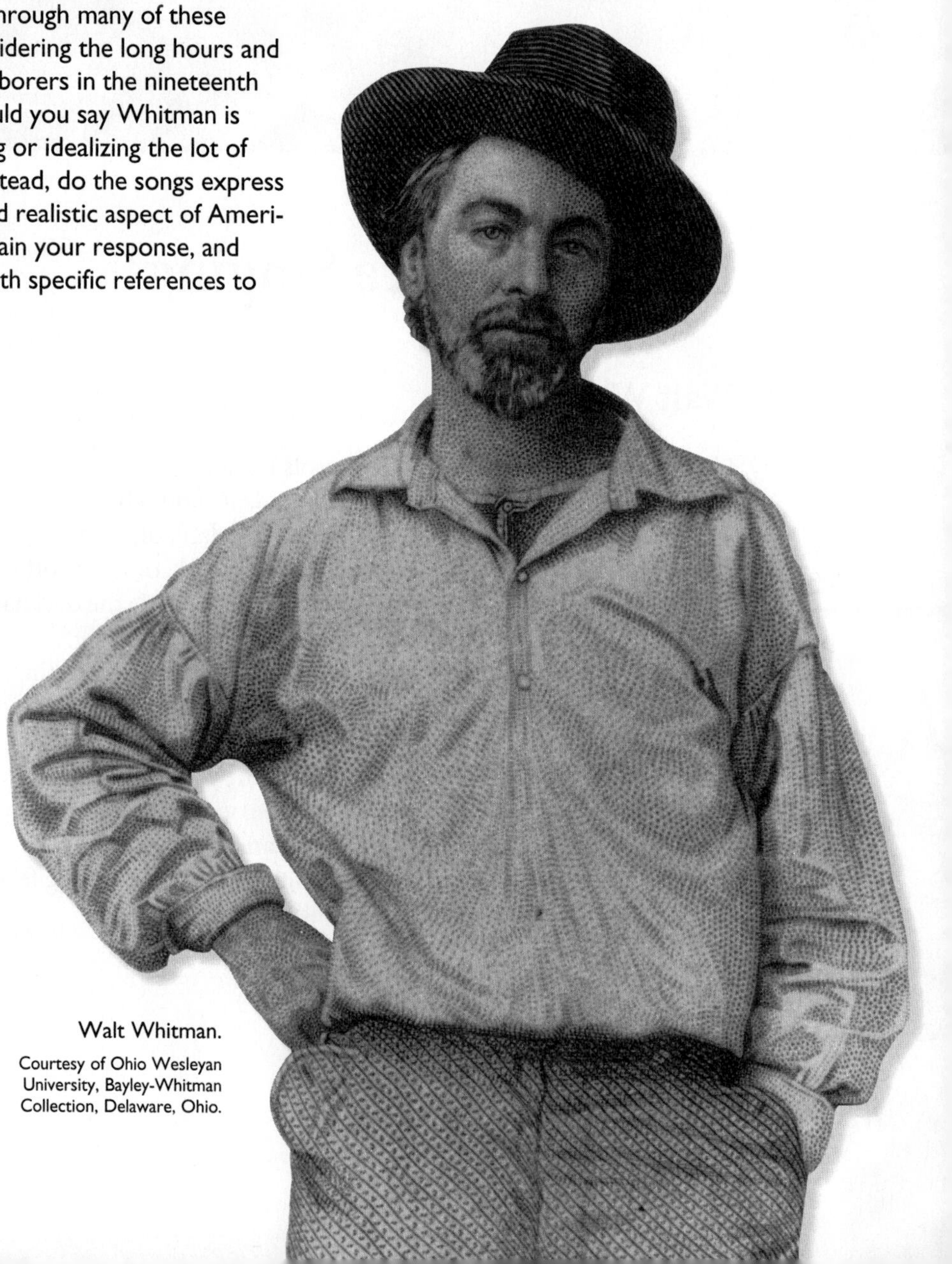

Walt Whitman.

Courtesy of Ohio Wesleyan University, Bayley-Whitman Collection, Delaware, Ohio.

# Before You Read

## from Song of Myself, Numbers 10 and 33

### Make the Connection

Whitman tries to feel what other people feel, to step into their lives, even to become the person or thing he is talking about. Perhaps you have experienced this blend of imagination and empathy—the ability to share in another's thoughts or feelings—which is at the heart of *Song of Myself.* The poem juxtaposes a wide variety of scenes and emotions in movielike glimpses into the broad American scene. Each experience—whether real or fictional, or a bit of both—provides Whitman with an opportunity for empathy, a chance to feel joy (as in number 10) or to share in heroic suffering (as in number 33).

As you read, look for words and phrases that reveal Whitman's ability to feel empathy with people quite different from himself.

### Literary Focus
#### Free Verse

Today we are so used to poetry written in free verse that we take it for granted. In Whitman's time, however, Americans preferred poetry that was like that being written in England: They expected a poem to show strict concern for **meter** and **rhyme.** Thus, Whitman's sprawling lines were revolutionary, as was his daring use of American slang, foreign words, and words he occasionally made up to suit his purpose. Whitman's free verse is said to have been inspired by the roll and sweep of passages from the King James Bible and even by the measured cadence of Emerson's essays.

**Free verse** is poetry that is written without regular rhyme schemes and meter. It is not really free at all. Whitman abandoned meter and regular rhyme schemes, but he made full use of these other traditional elements of poetry:

- **alliteration**—the repetition of similar consonant sounds
- **assonance**—the repetition of similar vowel sounds
- **imagery**—the use of language to evoke visual pictures, as well as sensations of smell, hearing, taste, and touch
- **onomatopoeia**—the use of words whose sounds echo their meaning (such as *buzz*)
- **parallel structure**—the repetition of phrases, clauses, or sentences that have the same grammatical structure

Most important, when you read Whitman's lines aloud, you hear **cadence,** the musical run of words that rises and falls as the poet sings the song. As you can hear in Whitman's poems, cadence does not depend on a strict count of stressed and unstressed syllables.

Poets who, like Whitman, choose to write in cadence have nothing but their own sense of balance and proportion to tell them when a line should end and when it should continue. They must rely completely on their own sense of spacing and timing and on their own feeling about what sounds right. In Whitman's poems, lines can be any length at all—three syllables or thirty syllables.

> **Free verse** is poetry that does not conform to a regular meter or rhyme scheme.
>
> *For more on Free Verse, see the Handbook of Literary and Historical Terms.*

**SKILLS FOCUS**

**Literary Skills**
Understand the characteristics of free verse.

**INTERNET**

More About
Walt Whitman

Keyword: LE7 11-3

# *from* Song of Myself

## Walt Whitman

### 10

Alone far in the wilds and mountains I hunt,
Wandering amazed at my own lightness and glee,
In the late afternoon choosing a safe spot to pass the night,
Kindling a fire and broiling the fresh-kill'd game,
5    Falling asleep on the gather'd leaves with my dog and gun by my side.

The Yankee clipper is under her sky-sails,° she cuts the sparkle and scud,°
My eyes settle the land, I bend at her prow or shout joyously from the deck.

The boatmen and clam-diggers arose early and stopt for me,
I tuck'd my trowser-ends in my boots and went and had a good time;
10    You should have been with us that day round the chowder-kettle.

I saw the marriage of the trapper in the open air in the far west, the bride was a red girl,
Her father and his friends sat near cross-legged and dumbly smoking, they had moccasins to
      their feet and large thick blankets hanging from their shoulders,
On a bank lounged the trapper, he was drest mostly in skins, his luxuriant beard and curls
      protected his neck, he held his bride by the hand,
She had long eyelashes, her head was bare, her coarse straight locks descended upon her
      voluptuous limbs and reach'd to her feet.

15    The runaway slave came to my house and stopt outside,
I heard his motions crackling the twigs of the woodpile,
Through the swung half-door of the kitchen I saw him limpsy° and weak,
And went where he sat on a log and led him in and assured him,
And brought water and fill'd a tub for his sweated body and bruis'd feet,
20    And gave him a room that enter'd from my own, and gave him some coarse clean clothes,
And remember perfectly well his revolving eyes and his awkwardness,
And remember putting plasters on the galls° of his neck and ankles;
He stayed with me a week before he was recuperated and pass'd north,
I had him sit next me at table, my fire-lock lean'd in the corner.

---

6. **sky-sails** *n.:* small sails atop a square-rigged mast.    **scud** *n.:* windblown sea spray or foam.
17. **limpsy** *adj.:* limp; exhausted.
22. **galls** *n. pl.:* sores.

*Lost on the Prairie* (1837) by Alfred Jacob Miller. Watercolor on paper (9¼″ × 13½″).

Stark Museum of Art, Orange, Texas.

A Ride for Liberty—The Fugitive Slaves (c. 1862) by Eastman Johnson. Oil on board (22″ × 26¼″).
The Brooklyn Museum of Art, Gift of Miss Gwendolyn O. L. Conkling (40.59.A).

# *from* Song of Myself

## Walt Whitman

### *from* 33

I understand the large hearts of heroes,
The courage of present times and all times,
How the skipper saw the crowded and rudderless wreck of the
    steam-ship, and Death chasing it up and down the storm,
How he knuckled tight and gave not back an inch, and was faithful
    of days and faithful of nights,

And chalk'd in large letters on a board, *Be of good cheer, we will not*
5     *desert you;*
How he follow'd with them and tack'd with them three days and
    would not give it up,
How he saved the drifting company at last,
How the lank loose-gown'd women look'd when boated from the
    side of their prepared graves,
How the silent old-faced infants and the lifted sick, and the sharp-
    lipp'd unshaved men;
10 All this I swallow, it tastes good, I like it well, it becomes mine,
I am the man, I suffer'd, I was there.°

The disdain and calmness of martyrs,
The mother of old, condemn'd for a witch, burnt with dry wood,
    her children gazing on,
The hounded slave that flags in the race, leans by the fence,
    blowing, cover'd with sweat,
The twinges that sting like needles his legs and neck, the
15     murderous buckshot and the bullets,
All these I feel or am.

I am the hounded slave, I wince at the bite of the dogs,
Hell and despair are upon me, crack and again crack the
    marksmen,

**1–11. I understand . . . I was there:** This stanza was inspired by an incident that occurred in 1853. According to reports in the New York *Weekly Tribune* of January 21, 1854, the ship *San Francisco* sailed from New York City on December 22, 1853, destined for South America. A violent storm hit the ship several hundred miles out of port, washing many passengers overboard. The captain of another ship helped rescue the survivors. A copy of the newspaper story was found among Whitman's papers after his death.

I clutch the rails of the fence, my gore dribs,° thinn'd with the ooze of my skin,

20   I fall on the weeds and stones,
The riders spur their unwilling horses, haul close,
Taunt my dizzy ears and beat me violently over the head with whip-stocks.

Agonies are one of my changes of garments,
I do not ask the wounded person how he feels, I myself become the wounded person,
25   My hurts turn livid upon me as I lean on a cane and observe.

I am the mash'd fireman with breast-bone broken,
Tumbling walls buried me in their debris,
Heat and smoke I inspired,° I heard the yelling shouts of my comrades,

I heard the distant click of their picks and shovels,
30   They have clear'd the beams away, they tenderly lift me forth.

I lie in the night air in my red shirt, the pervading hush is for my sake,
Painless after all I lie exhausted but not so unhappy,
White and beautiful are the faces around me, the heads are bared of their fire-caps,
The kneeling crowd fades with the light of the torches.

35   Distant and dead resuscitate,
They show as the dial or move as the hands of me, I am the clock myself.

I am an old artillerist, I tell of my fort's bombardment,
I am there again.

Again the long roll of the drummers,
40   Again the attacking cannon, mortars,
Again to my listening ears the cannon responsive.

I take part, I see and hear the whole,
The cries, curses, roar, the plaudits for well-aim'd shots,
The ambulanza° slowly passing trailing its red drip,

45   Workmen searching after damages, making indispensable repairs,
The fall of grenades through the rent roof, the fan-shaped explosion,
The whizz of limbs, heads, stone, wood, iron, high in the air.

Again gurgles the mouth of my dying general, he furiously waves with his hand,
He gasps through the clot *Mind not me—mind—the entrenchments.*

# Response and Analysis

## Song of Myself, Number 10

### Thinking Critically

1. In the five stanzas of this poem, the **speaker** observes and participates in five American scenes. Describe the scene in each stanza. What emotion does each scene evoke?

2. Identify at least three **images** of sight, sound, or touch in the poem that are most vivid to you.

3. **Tone** is the attitude a writer takes toward a subject. A writer can change tone by manipulating language. Whitman changes the **tone** of this poem in the fourth and fifth scenes. Identify the tone of the first three scenes. Then, tell how the tones of the fourth and fifth scenes are different. What effect do you think the poet hoped to create by changing tones?

4. Read this **free-verse** poem aloud. What repetitions of sentence patterns help to create a **cadence**—a rhythmic rise and fall of your voice as the lines are spoken aloud? How does the sound of the poem contribute to its meaning?

5. In the last scene the "runaway slave" is one of thousands who entrusted their lives to those who would help them escape. What do you think this stanza shows about the speaker's relationship with his guest?

## from Song of Myself, Number 33

### Thinking Critically

1. As in number 10, the **speaker** in number 33 observes and participates in several American scenes. Identify the scenes, and describe the emotions they evoke in the speaker.

2. One of Whitman's most famous lines is found in number 33. At what moments does the speaker restate the point that "I am the man, I suffer'd, I was there"? What is the effect of these restatements?

3. To see how Whitman uses various poetic devices in his poems, fill out a chart like the following one. Quote lines from the poem that illustrate his use of these devices.

| Poetic Device | Quotations |
|---|---|
| Alliteration | |
| Assonance | |
| Imagery | |
| Onomatopoeia | |
| Parallel structure | |

4. How would you describe the speaker's **tone** in this song? In other words, how does he feel about the heroes he describes?

5. Find examples of very long lines and very short lines. Read the poem aloud to feel the effects of these long and short lines. How do they force you to vary your rate of reading and your emphasis?

6. Based on the scenes in this section of *Song of Myself,* how do you think Whitman defines heroism?

7. If you were to add a contemporary hero (or heroes) to this poem, whom would you choose? Why?

# Before You Read

## from Song of Myself, Number 52

### Make the Connection

In this final section, Whitman restates some of the themes that run through *Song of Myself*. The poet weaves these themes in and out of this final verse, like a composer filling a song with familiar refrains. Since the most insistently present element throughout *Song of Myself* is the mind and spirit of the speaker himself, this passage is highly personal. True to his nature, Whitman mocks his own egotism. True to his confidence in himself, he also proclaims his importance—and his inescapability.

### Reading Skills 📖
**Comparing Themes Across Texts**

The final section of *Song of Myself* is not only the poet's farewell to the reader but also a **coda**—a summing up and restatement of the themes of the entire poem. As you read this concluding section a second time, write down your observations of how particular lines and phrases echo themes you've already encountered in the Whitman poems you've read.

**Reading Skills**
Compare themes across texts.

go.hrw.com

**INTERNET**
**More About Walt Whitman**
Keyword: LE7 11–3

# from Song of Myself

## Walt Whitman

### 52

The spotted hawk swoops by and accuses me, he complains
　　　of my gab and my loitering.

I too am not a bit tamed, I too am untranslatable,
I sound my barbaric yawp over the roofs of the world.

The last scud° of day holds back for me,
5　　It flings my likeness after the rest and true as any on the shadow'd wilds,
　　It coaxes me to the vapor and the dusk.

　　I depart as air, I shake my white locks at the runaway sun,
　　I effuse° my flesh in eddies, and drift it in lacy jags.

　　I bequeath myself to the dirt to grow from the grass I love,
10　　If you want me again look for me under your boot-soles.

---

4. **scud** *n.*: windblown mist and low clouds.
8. **effuse** *v.*: spread out.

You will hardly know who I am or what I mean,
But I shall be good health to you nevertheless,
And filter and fiber your blood.

Failing to fetch me at first keep encouraged,
15   Missing me one place search another,
I stop somewhere waiting for you.

# Response and Analysis

## Thinking Critically

**1.** How does Whitman show his connection to the natural world in this section of *Song of Myself*? For example, what qualities does he say he shares with the spotted hawk?

**2.** What might Whitman mean by line 10: "If you want me again look for me under your boot-soles"?

**3.** As Whitman departs (lines 7–8), what happens to him, and what does he become? Explain in your own words his final bequest (line 9).

**4.** How can Whitman be "good health" to the reader (line 12)?

**5.** What verb tense does Whitman use in this poem and in other parts of *Song of Myself*? How would the effect of the poem have been different if the speaker had used a different verb tense?

**6.** The first line of *Song of Myself* is "I celebrate myself, and sing myself" (see page 436), and the last line is "I stop somewhere waiting for you." Taking into account all that you have learned of the poet's character and the range of his poetry, tell what you think the last words of number 52 reveal about Whitman's purpose in writing *Song of Myself*.

**7.** Re-read the Whitman poems, and review your reading notes. Then, sum up the **themes** restated in number 52, the coda to *Song of Myself*.

**8.** You've already studied some of the American poets who preceded Whitman—Longfellow (page 194), Bryant (page 189), Poe (page 277)—as well as other Romantics. Based on what you know about the work of these earlier poets, what do you think Whitman means when he describes his own poetry as his "barbaric yawp" (line 3)?

*From Williamsburg Bridge* (1928) by Edward Hopper.

**SKILLS FOCUS**

**Reading Skills**
Compare themes across texts.

Union hospital at Fair Oaks, Virginia (1862). Photograph by James F. Gibson.

# Before You Read

## A Sight in Camp in the Daybreak Gray and Dim

### Make the Connection

A common emotional focus in Whitman's poetry is empathy—an understanding so intimate that the feelings and thoughts of other people are actually experienced by someone else. In the following poem, Whitman's empathy extends to the wounded of the Civil War. If you have ever felt that you actually *shared* the pain or sorrow of another person, you have felt empathy.

### Literary Focus
#### Symbol

In literature a **symbol** is a person, a place, a thing, or an event that functions as itself and as something broader than itself as well. A writer rarely makes a symbol obvious by directly stating what it means. Most symbols are more subtle; you as the reader must make inferences about their wider meanings.

In this poem, Whitman sees three faces. After you read the poem the first time, go back and re-read it. What could each of these faces symbolize?

> A **symbol** is a person, a place, a thing, or an event that functions as itself as well as something broader.
>
> *For more on Symbol, see the Handbook of Literary and Historical Terms.*

### Background

In December 1862, Whitman traveled to Virginia to care for his brother George, who had been wounded at the First Battle of Fredericksburg. Though George's injuries were minor, Whitman stayed on to assist the staffs of hospitals who were caring for the wounded. Whitman comforted and fed the injured and dying men, cleaned and bandaged their wounds, read to them, and wrote letters home to their families. By the end of the war, Whitman had probably met thousands of soldiers.

SKILLS FOCUS

**Literary Skills**
Understand symbolism.

go.
hrw
.com

**INTERNET**

**More About Walt Whitman**

Keyword: LE7 11-3

*Wounded Drummer Boy* (c. 1862–1865) by William Morris Hunt. Oil on canvas (14″ × 19¼″).

# A Sight in Camp in the Daybreak Gray and Dim

## Walt Whitman

A sight in camp in the daybreak gray and dim,
As from my tent I emerge so early sleepless,
As slow I walk in the cool fresh air the path near by the hospital tent,
Three forms I see on stretchers lying, brought out there untended lying,
5   Over each the blanket spread, ample brownish woolen blanket,
Gray and heavy blanket, folding, covering all.

Curious I halt and silent stand,
Then with light fingers I from the face of the nearest the first just lift the blanket;
Who are you elderly man so gaunt and grim, with well-gray'd hair, and flesh all sunken
        about the eyes?
10   Who are you my dear comrade?

Then to the second I step—and who are you my child and darling?
Who are you sweet boy with cheeks yet blooming?

Then to the third—a face nor child nor old, very calm, as of beautiful yellow-white ivory;
Young man I think I know you—I think this face is the face of the Christ himself,
15   Dead and divine and brother of all, and here again he lies.

*The following extracts are from Whitman's "memoranda book," which he called* Specimen Days.

# *from* Specimen Days

## The Inauguration

**March 4, 1865**—The President[1] very quietly rode down to the Capitol in his own carriage, by himself, on a sharp trot, about noon, either because he wished to be on hand to sign bills, or to get rid of marching in line with the absurd procession, the muslin temple of liberty, and pasteboard monitor. I saw him on his return, at three o'clock, after the performance was over. He was in his plain two-horse barouche,[2] and looked very much worn and tired; the lines, indeed, of vast responsibilities, intricate questions, and demands of life and death, cut deeper than ever upon his dark brown face; yet all the old goodness, tenderness, sadness, and canny shrewdness, underneath the furrows. (I never see that man without feeling that he is one to become personally attached to, for his combination of purest, heartiest tenderness, and native western form of manliness.) By his side sat his little boy, of ten years. There were no soldiers, only a lot of civilians on horseback, with huge yellow scarves over their shoulders, riding around the carriage. (At the inauguration four years ago, he rode down and back again surrounded by a dense mass of armed cavalrymen eight deep, with drawn sabers; and there were sharpshooters stationed at every corner on the route.) I ought to make mention of the closing levee[3] of

Saturday night last. Never before was such a compact jam in front of the White House— all the grounds filled, and away out to the spacious sidewalks. I was there, as I took a notion to go—was in the rush inside with the crowd—surged along the passageways, the Blue and other rooms, and through the great East Room. Crowds of country people, some very funny. Fine music from the Marine band, off in a side place. I saw Mr. Lincoln, dressed all in black, with white kid gloves and a claw-hammer coat, receiving, as in duty bound, shaking hands, looking very disconsolate, and as if he would give anything to be somewhere else.

## The Real War Will Never Get in the Books

And so goodbye to the war. I know not how it may have been, or may be, to others—to me the main interest I found (and still, on recollection, find) in the rank and file of the armies, both sides, and in those specimens amid the hospitals, and even the dead on the

---

1. **The President:** Abraham Lincoln. He would be assassinated in April, just a month after Whitman wrote this.
2. **barouche** (bə·rōōsh′) *n.:* four-wheeled, horse-drawn carriage.
3. **levee** *n.:* reception.

field. To me the points illustrating the latent personal character and eligibilities of these States, in the two or three millions of American young and middle-aged men, North and South, embodied in those armies—and especially the one-third or one-fourth of their number, stricken by wounds or disease at some time in the course of the contest—were of more significance even than the political interests involved. (As so much of a race depends on how it faces death, and how it stands personal anguish and sickness. As, in the glints of emotions under emergencies, and the indirect traits and asides in Plutarch, we get far profounder clues to the antique world than all its more formal history.)

Future years will never know the seething hell and the black infernal background of countless minor scenes and interiors (not the official surface courteousness of the generals, not the few great battles), of the Secession war; and it is best they should not—the real war will never get in the books. In the mushy influences of current times, too, the fervid atmosphere and typical events of those years are in danger of being totally forgotten. I have at night watched by the side of a sick man in the hospital, one who could not live many hours. I have seen his eyes flash and burn as he raised himself and recurred to the cruelties on his surrendered brother, and mutilations of the corpse afterward. (See, in the preceding pages, the incident at Upperville—the seventeen killed as in the description, were left there on the ground. After they dropped dead, no one touched them—all were made sure of, however. The carcasses were left for the citizens to bury or not, as they chose.)

Such was the war. It was not a quadrille[4] in a ballroom. Its interior history will not only never be written—its practicality, minutiae of deeds and passions, will never be even suggested. The actual soldier of 1862–1865, North and South, with all his ways, his incredible dauntlessness, habits, practices, tastes, language, his fierce friendship, his appetite, rankness, his superb strength and animality, lawless gait, and a hundred unnamed lights and shades of camp, I say, will never be written—perhaps must not and should not be.

The preceding notes may furnish a few stray glimpses into that life, and into those lurid interiors, never to be fully conveyed to the future. The hospital part of the drama from 1861 to 1865, deserves indeed to be recorded. Of that many-threaded drama, with its sudden and strange surprises, its confounding of prophecies, its moments of despair, the dread of foreign interference, the interminable campaigns, the bloody battles, the mighty and cumbrous and green armies, the drafts and bounties—the immense money expenditure, like a heavy-pouring constant rain—with, over the whole land, the last three years of the struggle, an unending, universal mourning wail of women, parents, orphans—the marrow of the tragedy concentrated in those Army Hospitals—(it seemed sometimes as if the whole interest of the land, North and South, was one vast central hospital, and all the rest of the affair but flanges)—those forming the untold and unwritten history of the war—infinitely greater (like life's) than the few scraps and distortions that are ever told or written. Think how much, and of importance, will be—how much, civic and military, has already been—buried in the grave, in eternal darkness.

*Walt Whitman*

---

4. **quadrille** (kwə·dril′) *n.*: French dance for four couples.

*Like Walt Whitman, Louisa May Alcott (1832–1888) nursed wounded soldiers in Washington, D.C., hospitals during the Civil War. The army thought that female nurses would improve the morale of the wounded men, even though critics said that the work was "indecent" for women and fretted that women would flirt with the soldiers. Alcott's nursing ended quickly, when she contracted typhoid from unsanitary hospital conditions, and she was never again completely well. Her* Hospital Sketches, *based on her letters home and published in 1863, proved the critics wrong about female nurses.*

*The daughter of an impractical Massachusetts philosopher named Bronson Alcott, Louisa had worked hard from childhood to support her mother and three sisters. She tried sewing, teaching in country schools, working as a domestic, and writing potboiler fiction before she became a Civil War nurse.* Hospital Sketches *brought her some fame, and she went on to write several well-known autobiographical novels, starting with the still beloved* Little Women *(1868–1869). The success of* Little Women *enabled her to write in her journal, "Paid up all the debts . . . thank the Lord!"*

*The first excerpt begins when forty ambulances of wounded men are brought to the hospital where Alcott is working.*

# *from* Hospital Sketches

## Louisa May Alcott

The first thing I met was a regiment of the vilest odors that ever assaulted the human nose, and took it by storm. . . . The worst of this affliction was [that] everyone had assured me that it was a chronic weakness of all hospitals, and I must bear it. I did, armed with lavender water, with which I so besprinkled myself and premises, that, like my friend, Sairy, I was soon known among my patients as "the nurse with the bottle." Having been run over by three excited surgeons, bumped against by migratory coal-hods,[1] water pails, and small boys; nearly scalded by an avalanche of newly filled teapots, and hopelessly entangled in a knot of colored sisters coming to wash, I progressed by slow stages upstairs and down, till the main hall was reached, and I paused to take breath and a survey. There they were! "our brave boys," as the papers justly call them, for cowards could hardly have been so riddled with shot and shell, so torn and shattered, nor have borne suffering for which we have no name, with an uncomplaining fortitude,[2] which made one glad to cherish each as a brother. In they came, some on stretchers, some in men's arms, some feebly staggering along propped on rude crutches, and one lay stark and still with covered face, as a comrade gave his name to be recorded before they carried him away to the dead house. All was hurry and confusion; the hall was full of these wrecks of humanity, for the most exhausted

---

1. **coal-hods** *n. pl.*: buckets used to pour coal onto a fire.
2. **fortitude** *n.*: strength; courage.

could not reach a bed till duly ticketed and registered; the walls were lined with rows of such as could sit, the floor covered with the more disabled, the steps and doorways filled with helpers and lookers-on; the sound of many feet and voices made that usually quiet hour as noisy as noon; and, in the midst of it all, the matron's motherly face brought more comfort to many a poor soul than the cordial draughts[3] she administered, or the cheery words that welcomed all, making of the hospital a home.

The sight of several stretchers, each with its legless, armless, or desperately wounded occupant, entering my ward, admonished me that I was there to work, not to wonder or weep; so I corked up my feelings, and returned to the path of duty, which was rather "a hard road to travel" just then. The house had been a hotel before hospitals were needed, and many of the doors still bore their old names; some not so inappropriate as might be imagined, for my ward was in truth a *ballroom*, if gunshot wounds could christen it. Forty beds were prepared, many already tenanted by tired men who fell down anywhere, and drowsed till the smell of food roused them. Round the great stove was gathered the dreariest group I ever saw—ragged, gaunt and pale, mud to the knees, with bloody bandages untouched since put on days before; many bundled up in blankets, coats being lost or useless; and all wearing that disheartened look which proclaimed defeat, more plainly than any telegram of the Burnside blunder.[4] I pitied them so much,

I dared not speak to them, though, remembering all they had been through since the rout at Fredericksburg, I yearned to serve the dreariest of them all. Presently, Miss Blank tore me from my refuge behind piles of one-sleeved shirts, odd socks, bandages and lint; put basin, sponge, towels, and a block of brown soap into my hands, with these appalling directions:

"Come, my dear, begin to wash as fast as you can. Tell them to take off socks, coats and shirts, scrub them well, put on clean shirts, and the attendants will finish them off, and lay them in bed."

If she had requested me to shave them all, or dance a horn-pipe on the stove funnel, I should have been less staggered; but to scrub some dozen lords of creation at a moment's notice, was really—really—. However, there was no time for nonsense, and, having resolved when I came to do everything I was bid, I drowned my scruples[5] in my washbowl, clutched my soap manfully, and, assuming a businesslike air, made a dab at the first dirty specimen I saw, bent on performing my task *vi et armis*[6] if necessary. I chanced to light on a withered old Irishman, wounded in the head, which caused that portion of his frame to be tastefully laid out like a garden, the bandages being the walks, his hair the shrubbery. He was so overpowered by the honor of having a lady wash him, as he expressed it, that he did nothing but roll up his eyes, and bless me, in an irresistible style which was too much for my sense of the ludicrous; so we laughed together . . .

*L. M. Alcott.*

---

3. **cordial draughts** (kôr′jəl drafts): chiefly British for "doses of medicine or liquor used to stimulate the heart."
4. **Burnside blunder:** Ambrose Everett Burnside (1824–1881) was a Union general in the American Civil War. The "blunder" refers to Burnside's failed attack at the Battle of Fredericksburg. Burnside was relieved of his command following this crushing defeat.

5. **scruples** *n. pl.:* doubts or misgivings about what is right and what is wrong.
6. *vi et armis:* Latin phrase meaning "by force and arms."

# Response and Analysis

## Thinking Critically

1. Describe the scene you see in "A Sight in Camp . . ." What feelings are immediately evoked by the poem's **setting**?

2. What question does the speaker repeat in the poem?

3. What do you think the old man and the "sweet boy" **symbolize** to the speaker?

4. What does the speaker think the third face is? How would you explain what the speaker means in line 15? (Keep in mind that this is a civil war, in which "brother" kills "brother.")

5. The point of the poem is never openly stated; that is, it remains implicit. How would you make the poet's **message** explicit?

6. In Whitman's poems we sometimes seem to be overhearing a man's conversation with himself. How would you describe the **tone** of this poem? What main elements of the poem support your description?

7. How does Whitman's **tone** in this poem compare with his tone in the excerpt from *Specimen Days*? (See the **Primary Source** on page 377.) How does it compare with Alcott's tone in the excerpt from *Hospital Sketches*? (See the **Connection** on page 379.)

8. Paul Zweig, one of Whitman's biographers, says that Whitman had a genius for the single line, "the verbal snapshot." Find at least five **images** in any of his poems that you think make particularly unusual and evocative verbal snapshots.

(Above) Surgeon at work at the rear during an engagement. Illustration by Winslow Homer for *Harper's Weekly*, July 12, 1862.

SKILLS FOCUS

**Literary Skills**
Analyze symbolism.

go. hrw .com

**INTERNET**

**Projects and Activities**

Keyword: LE7 11-3

**Walt Whitman** 381

# WRITING

## 1. Reading Nature

Nature is a major element in Whitman's writing, as it is in the writings of the Transcendentalists. In a brief essay, **compare and contrast** Whitman's "reading" of nature with Emerson's *Self-Reliance* (page 209) or Thoreau's *Walden* (page 216). You may want to create a chart to organize your ideas and reveal your points of comparison more clearly. Focus your comparison by asking and answering a specific question about the selections, such as

- What does nature *teach* the author?

- Is nature a source of *comfort* or *anxiety* to the author?

- What aspects of *self* does nature enable the author to understand?

- What aspects of the *divine* or the *sublime* does nature enable the author to understand?

## 2. My Walt Whitman

Write a free-verse **poem** in the tradition of Walt Whitman, using one of the poems you have read as a model. Consider beginning with one of Whitman's openers, such as "I hear America singing" or "I understand the large hearts of heroes." When you write in free verse (see page 367), you are not restricted to the use of rhymes and regular meters. However, you will want to use **imagery** and **sound effects** (alliteration, repetition, parallel structure), as well as one or more of Whitman's techniques: catalogs, rolling cadences, and changes of voice that result in a specific tone.

## 3. A Close Look

In a **critical essay,** analyze the Whitman poems you have read. Focus on analyzing one aspect of Whitman's poems that

interests you: perhaps his **themes,** his everyday **diction,** his use of **catalogs,** his use of **free verse,** his **commonplace subject matter,** or his celebration of the **ordinary person** as hero. Open your essay with a thesis statement that clearly states your main idea. Be sure to use evidence from the poems to support your main points. When you quote directly from a poem, be sure to use quotation marks and to indicate the poem you are citing.

## 4. You Hear America Singing

How does Whitman's America differ from the America you know? How have social, historical, religious, and ethical influences changed from his time to yours? Reflect upon your own life, and then create a catalog of items that describe America as you see it today. Using that catalog as a starting point, write a **reflective essay** on the experiences you have had and the people and places that have influenced your life. How does America look in your eyes?

▶ Use "Writing a Reflective Essay," pages 426–433, for help with this assignment.

# LISTENING AND SPEAKING

## Performance

Prepare a public reading of Whitman's poems. You will have to decide when you will use solo readers and when you will use a chorus. For some poems you might want to use musical accompaniment. Be sure to ask your audience to evaluate your performance.

**SKILLS FOCUS**

**Writing Skills**
Write an essay comparing and contrasting literary works. Write a free-verse poem. Write a critical essay analyzing poems. Write a reflective essay about a personal experience.

**Listening and Speaking Skills**
Prepare and present a public reading of a poem.

# Vocabulary Development

## Multiple-Meaning Words

Many English words that are spelled the same have multiple meanings and sometimes different pronunciations. For example, the noun *desert,* with stress on the first syllable, means "dry, barren, sandy region." The verb *desert,* with stress on the second syllable, means "abandon," as in this line from Whitman's *Song of Myself,* number 33.

"*Be of good cheer, we will not desert you*"

Often, however, words carry multiple meanings even when pronunciation and the part of speech don't change. Suppose, for example, that someone asks for a *roll.* Depending on the situation, the person might be requesting a class list, a cylinder of cloth, a piece of bread, a flight maneuver, or a rapid drumbeat. To understand which meaning is intended, you must pay attention to the word's **context**—the surrounding words and sentences. Which meaning of *roll* does Whitman intend in this line from *Song of Myself,* number 33?

"Again the long roll of the drummers"

**Using a dictionary.** When you look up a word like *desert* or *roll,* you will find separate entries (or parts of an entry) for the word's use as a verb and as a noun. Some dictionaries start with the word's oldest meaning and end with its most recent meaning. Other dictionaries start with the modern meanings and then list old, rare, or obsolete meanings.

**Studying origins.** Word origins usually appear in brackets at the beginning of a dictionary entry. Some words have the same origin for all of their meanings. Other words, such as *desert* (dez′ərt) and *desert* (di·zʉrt′) have different origins—it is an accident of language history that the words ended up with the same spelling. Read the lines below by Louisa May Alcott, and note her use of the word *pale.* Then, study the chart. Which meaning of the word *pale* did Alcott intend?

"Round the great stove was gathered the dreariest group I ever saw—ragged, gaunt and pale, mud to the knees, with bloody bandages untouched since put on days before . . ."

| Word | Origin | Present Meaning |
|------|--------|-----------------|
| 1. pale | Latin *pallidus,* "pale" | of a colorless complexion; wan |
| 2. pale | Latin *palus,* "stake" | narrow, pointed stake; picket |

**PRACTICE**

1. Use a dictionary to look up the origin and different meanings of all five words listed below. Then, choose two of the words. Use each of them in two different contexts to show its different meanings.

   **a.** sound     **d.** form

   **b.** bank     **e.** room

   **c.** limbs

2. Read the line below from Whitman's *Song of Myself,* number 33. Then, choose the lettered sentence that uses *hand* in the same sense as Whitman uses the word.

   "Again gurgles the mouth of my dying general, he furiously waves with his hand. . . ."

   **a.** Please give me a hand with this shoveling.

   **b.** The hired hand was plowing the field.

   **c.** Let's play another hand of bridge.

   **d.** He asked her for her hand in marriage.

   **e.** My hand aches from writing.

**SKILLS FOCUS**

**Vocabulary Skills**
Understand multiple-meaning words.

# Pablo Neruda

## (1904–1973)

**P**ablo Neruda was born and educated in Chile. Neruda wrote that he went out "hunting poems" as a child, and he received his first acclaim as a poet at the age of sixteen, when he won first prize in a poetry competition. By the age of twenty, he was already regarded as a young poet with great promise. In addition to enjoying an enormously full and diverse life as a writer, Neruda served as a diplomat and a member of the Chilean senate for several years. He also lived in exile from his homeland when the Chilean right-wing government outlawed his socialist political party and terminated his position in the senate. Before resettling on Isla Negra in Chile, in 1953, Neruda lived in many countries around the world, including Burma (now called Myanmar), Italy, Spain, France, Mexico, Russia, and China. In 1971, he was awarded the Nobel Prize in literature. Known for his diverse range of poetic styles and voices, Neruda is celebrated for his humanism, his call for peace and equality, and his love and respect for the natural elements of the world. His poems are questions, riddles, political shouts, observations, homages, and introspective movements toward truth. Like Whitman, he influenced and inspired many of the great poets of the twentieth century. Here is what Neruda wrote about poetry:

> **66** Poetry is like bread, and it must be shared by everyone, the men of letters and the peasants, by everyone in our vast, incredible, extraordinary family of man. **99**

### For Independent Reading

For more poems by Pablo Neruda, try these unusual odes, a form Neruda particularly enjoyed:

- "Ode to Walt Whitman"
- "Ode to My Socks"
- "Ode to the Cat"

## Full Powers

### Make the Connection

Like many great writers, Pablo Neruda was deeply inspired by Walt Whitman's *Leaves of Grass.* A year before his death, Neruda made the following remarks:

> ❝ I was barely fifteen when I discovered Walt Whitman, my primary creditor. I stand here among you today still owing this marvelous debt that has helped me to live.
>
> To renegotiate this debt is to begin by making it public, by proclaiming myself the humble servant of the poet who measured the earth with long, slow strides, pausing everywhere to love and to examine, to learn, to teach, and to admire. . . . Clearly, he feared neither mortality nor immortality, nor did he attempt to define the boundaries between pure and impure poetry. He is the first absolute poet, and it was his intention not only to sing but to impart his vast vision of the relationships of men and of nations. In this sense, his obvious nationalism is part of an organic universality. He considers himself indebted to happiness and sorrow, to advanced cultures and primitive societies. . . . In Whitman's poetry the ignorant are never humbled, and the human condition is never derided.
>
> We are still living in a Whitmanesque epoch. . . . The bard complained of the all-powerful European influence that continued to dominate the literature of his time. In fact, it was he, Walt Whitman, in the persona of a specific geography, who for the first time in history brought honor to an American name. ❞

### Reading Skills

#### Comparing and Contrasting Poems

In many ways, Whitman and Neruda are cut from the same cloth, even though they emerged from different cultures years apart. Read Neruda's poem twice. After the second reading, jot down **images** or phrases that remind you of lines from any of the poems in *Song of Myself.*

**SKILLS FOCUS**

**Reading Skills**
Compare and contrast poems.

# Plenos poderes

## Pablo Neruda

A puro sol escribo, a plena calle,
a pleno mar, en donde puedo canto,
sólo la noche errante me detiene
pero en su interrupción recojo espacio,
5  recojo sombra para mucho tiempo.

El trigo negro de la noche crece
mientras mis ojos miden la pradera
y así de sol a sol hago las llaves:
busco en la oscuridad las cerraduras
10  y voy abriendo al mar las puertas rotas
hasta llenar armarios con espuma.

Y no me canso de ir y de volver,
no me para la muerte con su piedra,
no me canso de ser y de no ser.

15  A veces me pregunto si de donde
si de padre o de madre o cordillera
heredé los deberes minerales,

los hilos de un océano encendido
y sé que sigo y sigo porque sigo
20  y canto porque canto y porque canto.

No tiene explicación lo que acontece
cuando cierro los ojos y circulo
como entre dos canales submarinos,
uno a morir me lleva en su ramaje
25  y el otro canta para que yo cante.

Así pues de no ser estoy compuesto
y como el mar asalta el arrecife
con cápsulas saladas de blancura
y retrata le piedra con la ola,
30  así lo que en la muerte me rodea
abre en mí la ventana de la vida
y en pleno paroxismo estoy durmiendo.
A plena luz camino por la sombra.

# Full Powers

## Pablo Neruda

*translated by* **Ben Belitt** *and* **Alastair Reid**

I write in the clear sun, in the teeming street,
at full sea-tide, in a place where I can sing;
only the wayward night inhibits me,
but, interrupted by it, I recover space,
5  I gather shadows to last me a long time.

The black crop of the night is growing
while my eyes meanwhile take measure of the
   meadows.
So, from one sun to the next, I forge the keys.
In the darkness, I look for the locks
10  and keep on opening broken doors to the sea,
for it to fill the wardrobes with its foam.

And I do not weary of going and returning.
Death, in its stone aspect, does not halt me.
I am weary neither of being nor of non-being.

15  Sometimes I puzzle over origins—
was it from my father, my mother, or the
   mountains

that I inherited debts to minerality,
the fine threads spreading from a sea on fire?
And I know that I keep on going for the going's
   sake,
20  and I sing because I sing and because I sing.

There is no way of explaining what does happen
when I close my eyes and waver
as between two lost channels under water.
One lifts me in its branches toward my dying,
25  and the other sings in order that I may sing.

And so I am made up of a non-being,
and, as the sea goes battering at a reef
in wave on wave of salty white-tops
and drags back stones in its retreating wash,
30  so what there is in death surrounding me
opens in me a window out to living,
and, in the spasm of being, I go on sleeping.
In the full light of day, I walk in the shade.

# Response and Analysis

## Thinking Critically

1. In the first stanza, why might the night inhibit the speaker from writing?

2. What could the "keys" in line 8 unlock for the speaker? What do you think he means by "night" and "darkness" in the second stanza?

3. In line 14, what does the speaker mean by "I am weary neither of being nor of non-being"? Explain.

4. What could the speaker mean by his "debts to minerality" (line 17)?

5. Why does the speaker "keep on going," according to lines 19–20?

6. Why might the poem be titled "Full Powers"? What is the source of the speaker's creative powers?

## WRITING

### Comparing and Contrasting Poems

Look back at the notes you took on your second reading of "Full Powers." Based on these notes, write a brief **essay** comparing and contrasting "Full Powers" with the songs in *Song of Myself.* Here are some general points to focus on: the poets' use of **imagery**, their attitudes toward death, and their views of themselves in relation to others. In your essay, cite lines or passages from the poems to support your comparisons.

# Emily Dickinson
## (1830–1886)

A brief outline of Emily Dickinson's life reads like the plot of a story destined to become a legend. Once upon a time there was born to a religious and well-to-do New England family a daughter, whom they named Emily. As a child, she was lively, well behaved, and obedient; she took pleasure in the busy household of which she was a part and in the seasonal games, parties, and outings of a village snowy cold in winter and brilliantly green and flowering in summer.

At home Emily learned to cook and sew. When she was old enough, she was sent to a school where strict rules did not dampen the girls' high spirits as they enjoyed the entertainments of boarding-school life. Emily took part in these, but not always with as much enthusiasm as she might have. As she said many years later, something sad and reserved in her nature made her "a mourner among the children."

To her family and friends everything about the young Dickinson seemed normal. No one doubted that she would grow gracefully into womanhood, make a good marriage, and settle into a village life of churchgoing, holiday gatherings, and neighborly harmony. Then something happened in her life, something that has been the subject of speculation for decades.

When Dickinson was twenty-four years old, her father, who had become a U.S. congressman, took her with him to Washington, D.C., and then on to Philadelphia. The journey seems to have marked the start of a turning point in her life. Her father may have taken her with him because she had fallen in love with someone she could never marry. This person might have been a married lawyer, older than Emily, a man who would die that year of tuberculosis.

Whatever happened, it seems likely that in the course of the journey, Emily fell in love with someone else: Charles Wadsworth, who was also married and who was pastor of the Arch Street Presbyterian Church in Philadelphia. Letters to Wadsworth show that Dickinson saw him as a "muse," someone who could inspire her, someone she could love passionately in her imagination.

In 1862, Wadsworth took up a new assignment in San Francisco. His leaving seems to have caused a great crisis in Dickinson's life: "I sing," she wrote around this time, "as the boy does by the burying ground, because I am afraid."

## The Recluse of Amherst

The young woman quietly and abruptly withdrew from all social life except that involving her immediate family. Within a few years, dressed always in white—like the bride she would never become—she had gone into a state of seclusion. Her only activities were household tasks and the writing of poems that she either kept to herself or sent as valentines, birthday greetings, or notes to accompany the gift of a cherry pie or a batch of cookies.

Around the time that Wadsworth was preparing to move to California, Dickinson sent a few of her poems to Thomas Wentworth Higginson. As an editor of *The Atlantic Monthly*, Higginson had been encouraging the work of younger poets. Higginson never became a substitute for Wadsworth, but he did serve as a kindly, distant "teacher" and "mentor." Eventually Dickinson gave up hope of ever finding a wider audience than her few friends and relatives. About 1861, she wrote "I'm Nobody! Who are you? / Are you—Nobody—too?"

During her lifetime, Emily Dickinson published no more than a handful of her typically brief poems. She seemed to lack all concern for an audience, and she went so far as to

(Opposite) Portrait by Barry Moser.

instruct her family to destroy any poems she might leave behind after her death. Still, she saw to it that bundles of handwritten poems were carefully wrapped and put away in places where, after her death, friendly, appreciative, and finally astonished eyes would find them. The poems were assembled and edited by different family members and friends; they were then published in installments so frequent that readers began to wonder when they would ever end.

Then, in 1955, a collection called *The Poems of Emily Dickinson* was finally made available. This was the devoted work of Thomas H. Johnson, a scholar who, unlike Dickinson's earlier editors, refrained from making "presentable" entities of poems whose punctuation, rhyme schemes, syntax, and word choice were frequently baffling. Instead, he attempted to remain faithful to the original manuscript.

As a result of Johnson's research, whole generations of readers who had grown up on Dickinson poems were faced with new versions of those poems, versions that sometimes rescued Dickinson's originals from the tamperings of her first editors. Sometimes these originals made emphases that, in the interest of "smoothness," those editors had overlooked.

Here is an example of how one stanza was changed by the original editors. Johnson's version is first:

> We passed the School, where Children strove
> At Recess—in the Ring—
> We passed the Fields of Gazing Grain—
> We passed the Setting Sun—

This is how the early editor changed it:

> We passed the school where children played
> Their lessons scarcely done;
> We passed the fields of gazing grain,
> We passed the setting sun.

## The Secret of Genius

When Dickinson died, at the age of fifty-five, hardly anyone knew that the strange, shy woman in their midst was a poet whose sharp and delicate voice would echo for generations to come. Some seventy years after her death, when the quarrels among her relatives who had inherited her manuscripts had died down and all her poems were finally published, she was recognized as one of the greatest poets America, and perhaps the world, had produced.

The self-imposed restrictions of Dickinson's actual life were more than matched by her ability to see the universal in the particular and vice versa. She perceived the relationship between a drop of dew and a flood, between a grain of sand and a desert. These perceptions helped her make metaphors that embraced experiences far beyond the limited compass of Amherst village life.

Still, no matter how far her imagination ranged, Dickinson never denied those experiences their truth as aspects of a cycle of existence important in itself. When an Amherst neighbor's barn caught fire and lit up the sky, it was a real barn at the edge of a real pasture, and its loss became a matter of local anguish. These local actualities did not prevent Dickinson from regarding the incident as a reminder of ultimate doom, of the biblical prophecies of destruction of the earth by fire.

Behind the now famous legend of Emily Dickinson, and the plays and novels that have romanticized and sentimentalized her life, is a woman whose genius made its own rules, followed its own commands, and found its own fulfillment. Emily Dickinson's life as a recluse may have been richer, more varied, and—in the satisfactions that come with the exercise of natural talent—even happier than the lives of those around her. In the prospect of history, we can see that the untold secret of Emily Dickinson's emotional life is secondary to the great secret of her genius, the secret that destiny would not let her keep.

## The Soul selects her own Society

This poem is about making choices and the mysterious instinct that leads each one of us to prefer certain things and cherish certain people above all others. In Dickinson's view this instinct has less to do with the discriminations of the mind than with the yearnings of that spiritual part of us that some call the soul. How do you think most people select their friends—with their minds (thoughts), with their souls (feelings), or with a combination of the two?

### Literary Focus
**Slant Rhyme**

Not long ago exact rhyme was part of every poet's craft. **Exact rhyme** occurs when the accented syllables and all following syllables of two or more words share identical sounds, as in the words *free* and *bee* or *mixture* and *fixture*. Today exact rhyme is still the most familiar aspect of sound in poetry. Over the years, however, exact rhyme has fallen out of favor with many poets. One reason is that many poets feel that the exact rhymes in English have been used over and over again. Another reason is that imposed rhymes can act as a constraint and can limit expression. As a solution some poets have abandoned rhyme altogether. Other poets, like Dickinson, use slant rhyme.

**Slant rhyme** is a close, but not exact, rhyming sound. Word pairs like *society/majority* or *nerve/love* are examples of slant rhymes. Slant rhyme makes many readers uncomfortable—in the way that a sharp or flat note would disturb a listener who wasn't expecting it.

> **Slant rhyme** is a close, but not exact, rhyming sound.
>
> *For more on Slant Rhyme, see the Handbook of Literary and Historical Terms.*

# The Soul selects her own Society

## Emily Dickinson

The Soul selects her own Society—
Then—shuts the Door—
To her divine Majority—
Present no more—

5   Unmoved—she notes the Chariots—pausing—
At her low Gate—
Unmoved—an Emperor be kneeling
Upon her Mat—

I've known her—from an ample nation—
10  Choose One—
Then—close the Valves of her attention—
Like Stone—

## If you were coming in the Fall

### Make the Connection

Poetry is called metaphysical when the simplest thoughts and emotions are described using fantastic and often highly intellectual **imagery** and **figures of speech.** In metaphysical poetry, private emotions, such as unfulfilled love, take on the importance of great and profound events. See if you think this poem qualifies as metaphysical.

# If you were coming in the Fall

## Emily Dickinson

If you were coming in the Fall,
I'd brush the Summer by
With half a smile, and half a spurn,
As Housewives do, a Fly.

5    If I could see you in a year,
I'd wind the months in balls—
And put them each in separate Drawers,
For fear the numbers fuse—

If only Centuries, delayed,
10   I'd count them on my Hand,
Subtracting, till my fingers dropped
Into Van Dieman's Land.°

If certain, when this life was out—
That your's and mine, should be
15   I'd toss it yonder, like a Rind,
And take Eternity—

But, now, uncertain of the length
Of this, that is between,
It goads me, like the Goblin Bee—
20   That will not state—it's sting.

**12. Van Dieman's** (dē′mənz) **Land:** former name of Tasmania, an island that is a state of Australia.

*Autumn: October. Hillside, Noonday, Glen Cove, Long Island* (1860) by John La Farge.
Oil on canvas (31.75 × 24.13 cm).

Museum of Fine Arts, Boston. Bequest of Mrs. Henry Lee Higginson, Sr., 35.1166. Photograph © 2007 Museum of Fine Arts, Boston.

*The editors of Dickinson's poems, feeling that the poet's original works needed improvements, frequently altered them. Usually the editors' goal was to make Dickinson's poems more traditionally poetic—that is, to provide conventional rhymes and rhythms and to get rid of what they thought were awkward phrasings and punctuation. Here is a copy of "If you were coming in the Fall" with the alterations Dickinson's original editors made. Describe the kinds of changes the editors made, and evaluate them. In your opinion, why was each change made? How do the changes affect the poem? Why did Dickinson write the poem the way she did? Which changes corrected grammatical errors?*

If you were coming in the Fall,
I'd brush the Summer by
With half a smile, and half a spurn,
As Housewives do, a Fly.

5   If I could see you in a year,
I'd wind the months in balls—
And put them each in separate Drawers,
*Until their time befalls.*
For fear the numbers fuse—

If only Centuries, delayed,
10  I'd count them on my Hand,
Subtracting, till my fingers dropped
Into Van Dieman's Land.

If certain, when this life was out—
That your's and mine, should be
15  I'd toss it yonder, like a Rind,
*taste*
And take Eternity—

     *all ignorant*
But, now, uncertain of the length
*time's uncertain wing*
Of this, that is between,
It goads me, like the Goblin Bee—
20  That will not state—it's sting.

# Response and Analysis

## The Soul selects her own Society

### Thinking Critically

1. Dickinson uses **personification,** attributing human feelings, thoughts, or attitudes to a soul. What does the soul do in the last stanza of the poem?

2. *Majority* has at least two meanings: "the greater part of something" and "having reached full legal age." An older, obsolete meaning of *majority* is "superiority." What do you think *majority* means in this poem? What kind of person does the adjective *divine* suggest?

3. Do you think the phrase "Valves of her attention" is derived from organic things (valves of the heart) or mechanical ones (valves of a faucet)? What do you picture happening here?

4. Dickinson's early editors changed the word *Valves* to *lids* in line 11. How does this change the **metaphor**? How does it change what you see?

5. Look at the **meter** of lines 10 and 12. How does their rhythmical pattern differ from the corresponding lines in the first and second stanzas? What is the effect of this difference?

6. Dickinson gave very few of her poems titles. (The titles in this text are the first lines of the poems.) Her early editors called this poem "Exclusion." In what ways does this title apply? In what ways is it a limiting title?

7. An example of **slant rhyme** in this poem occurs in the third stanza, where Dickinson rhymes *stone* with *one*. Why is it important that the word *stone* be emphasized? To hear the difference, imagine that Dickinson had ended her poem with the words "And be done."

Find another example of slant rhyme in this poem.

8. Do you think the "soul selects her own society" in the strict way that is described in the poem? Do you think that most people make choices the way the speaker in this poem does? Explain your response.

## If you were coming in the Fall

### Thinking Critically

1. How would you describe the speaker's situation? How does she feel about it?

2. What two things are being compared in the **simile** in the first stanza?

3. In the second stanza, what domestic articles are the months compared to? Why does the speaker put them in separate drawers?

4. Van Dieman's Land, besides being the old name of Tasmania, also refers to those places on the globe farthest away from the United States. Given this information, how would you **paraphrase** the third stanza?

5. How would you describe the speaker's **tone** in the first four stanzas? How does the tone change in the fifth stanza, where her exaggerations disappear? What goads, or pushes, her against her will?

6. In folklore a goblin is a tormenting creature. What might Dickinson be suggesting when she says that the bee is a goblin and will not "state" its sting?

7. Do you think the hopes expressed in this poem are fairly common, or are they rare or odd? Explain your responses.

**SKILLS FOCUS**

**Literary Skills**
Analyze exact rhyme and slant rhyme.

## Tell all the Truth but tell it slant

**Make the Connection**

**Quickwrite** ✏

Dickinson's famous line "Tell all the Truth but tell it slant" may reveal her method of survival as well as the essence of her own poetry. What do you think it would mean to tell the truth "slant"? Is truth told slant the same as a lie? Jot down your thoughts.

# Tell all the Truth but tell it slant

## Emily Dickinson

Tell all the Truth but tell it slant—
Success in Circuit° lies
Too bright for our infirm Delight
The Truth's superb surprise
As Lightning to the Children eased
With explanation kind
The Truth must dazzle gradually
Or every man be blind—

2. **circuit** *n.:* indirect path.

**INTERNET**
**More About**
**Emily Dickinson**
Keyword: LE7 11-3

*Rooms by the Sea* (1951) by Edward Hopper. Oil on canvas.

Yale University Art Gallery, Bequest of Stephen Clark, B.A., 1903.

## Apparently with no surprise

### Make the Connection
#### Quickwrite ✎

Dickinson had only to look out her window to see the powers of nature at work. In her poetry she uses deceptively innocent observations about birds, flies, and flowers to reveal deep and sometimes disturbing ideas about life and death. Think about nature for a few minutes: Do you think nature is nurturing and helpful, or is it threatening and hostile? Create a double-column chart in which you write evidence of nature's benevolence in one column and evidence of nature's destructiveness in the other.

### Literary Focus
#### Tone

A writer's attitude toward a subject, or even toward an audience, is called **tone.** Tone is most often revealed by word choice. Tone can be described in a single word: *optimistic, pessimistic, sarcastic, playful, loving, awed,* and so on. We cannot say we have understood any piece of literature until we have understood, or heard, its tone.

> **Tone** is the attitude a writer takes toward the subject of a work, the characters in it, or the audience.
>
> *For more on Tone, see the Handbook of Literary and Historical Terms.*

# Apparently with no surprise

## Emily Dickinson

Apparently with no surprise
To any happy Flower
The Frost beheads it at its play—
In accidental power—
The blonde Assassin passes on—
The Sun proceeds unmoved
To measure off another Day
For an Approving God.

# Before You Read

## Success is counted sweetest

### Make the Connection
#### Quickwrite ✏️

In 1862, Dickinson sent this poem along with three others to Thomas Wentworth Higginson, a literary critic and editor for *The Atlantic Monthly,* to ask his advice about her poems. It is one of several poems that shows Dickinson's feelings about success and her struggles with the values of the world. Write down some of your own thoughts about success. How do you think people who always encounter failure feel?

### Background

Literary scholars debate Dickinson's lack of interest in publishing and in public recognition. This poem, included in *A Masque of Poets,* is one of the poems that Dickinson did publish during her lifetime. Ironically many readers thought it was written by Ralph Waldo Emerson (page 203).

# Success is counted sweetest

## Emily Dickinson

Success is counted sweetest
By those who ne'er succeed.
To comprehend a nectar°
Requires sorest° need.

5   Not one of all the purple Host°
Who took the Flag today
Can tell the definition
So clear of Victory

As he defeated—dying—
10   On whose forbidden ear
The distant strains of triumph
Burst agonized and clear!

*Taps* (detail) (c. 1907–1909) by Gilbert Gaul. Oil on canvas (32¾″ × 43″).

Collection of the Birmingham Museum of Art, Birmingham, Alabama. Gift of John Meyer.

---

3. **nectar** *n.:* name for the drink of the Greek and Roman gods; also, a term applied to any delicious beverage.
4. **sorest** *adv.:* deepest; most extreme.
5. **purple host:** royal army.

# Response and Analysis

## Tell all the Truth but tell it slant

### Thinking Critically

1. Look back at your Quickwrite notes. How would you define the word *slant* as it is used in the poem? How is telling something "slant" different from lying?

2. Explain the meaning of *circuit* (line 2) in the context of the poem. What is "Too bright for our infirm Delight" (line 3)?

3. Lines 5 and 6 provide an example to illustrate the poet's point about truth. As is typical of Dickinson's **style,** she omits several words in these lines. How would you rephrase the lines to make a full sentence?

4. According to the last two lines, why must the truth be told "slant"? How would you define *dazzle* and *blind* here?

5. What **metaphor** is implied in line 7? What is "Truth" being compared to?

### Extending and Evaluating

6. Do you agree with the poet's message? In what way can this lyric be seen as a reference to the way poetry works?

## Apparently with no surprise

### Thinking Critically

1. What is the "blonde Assassin"?

2. How are the flower, the frost, and the sun **personified** in this poem? What kind of person does each seem to be compared to?

3. A **pun** is a play on words, based on the multiple meanings of a single word or on words that sound alike but mean different things. What pun do you find in line 6? How would you explain it?

4. According to the speaker, how does God feel about the flower's beheading? How do you think the speaker feels?

5. What word would you use to describe the **tone** of this poem: *optimistic, pessimistic, awed, defiant*? Be sure to find details in the poem to support your response.

6. How does this speaker's attitude toward nature differ from Emerson's attitude in the excerpt from his essay *Nature* (page 206)? Is either point of view supported by the chart you made before reading the poem? Explain.

### Extending and Evaluating

7. What do you think is the **theme** of this poem? Do you find the theme shocking, reassuring, or something else? Explain.

## Success is counted sweetest

### Thinking Critically

1. According to the speaker, who is likely to count success as sweetest? Do you think the poet is accurate in describing the feelings of people who fail? Be sure to review your Quickwrite notes.

2. Purple is a color associated with bloodshed in battle (the Purple Heart medal is given to soldiers wounded or killed in action). It is also a color associated with royalty and nobility. What do you think is the "purple Host" in line 5?

3. Whose ear is mentioned in line 10? Why is the ear "forbidden"?

4. Describe the **image** you see in the last stanza. How could this image be extended to refer to other situations in life? Explain.

5. Have you ever been like the soldier in the last stanza—in agony because someone else is proclaimed winner? What other circumstances in life (other than a wartime battle) could this situation be applied to? (Could it describe the feelings of a poet who could not publish her work?)

**SKILLS FOCUS**

**Literary Skills**
Analyze tone.

## Because I could not stop for Death

### Make the Connection

Like many other metaphors in Dickinson's poetry, the one in this poem "tames" or "domesticates" the most awesome and inevitable of human experiences—death. The literal elements of the metaphor are simple: Dying is compared to an unexpected ride in a horse-drawn carriage.

### Literary Focus

**Irony**

The success of this poem depends on **irony**, on gradual comprehension, and on a light-hearted, witty tone that contrasts with the subject of the story being told. In this poem what seems to be a pleasant carriage ride turns into a trip of eternal significance. As you read, pay careful attention to details which give the poem an ironic twist.

In general, **irony** is a discrepancy between appearances and reality, between what seems suitable or appropriate and what actually happens.

*For more on Irony, see the Handbook of Literary and Historical Terms.*

### Reading Skills

**Summarizing a Text**

Dickinson uses time in an unusual way in this poem. It will help, as you read, to pause at the end of each stanza and note *when* the events are occurring.

**SKILLS FOCUS**

Pages 401–403 cover
**Literary Skills** Understand irony.
**Reading Skills** Summarize a text.

**INTERNET**

More About Emily Dickinson

Keyword: LE7 11-3

# Because I could not stop for Death

## Emily Dickinson

Because I could not stop for Death—
He kindly stopped for me—
The Carriage held but just Ourselves—
And Immortality.

5 We slowly drove—He knew no haste
And I had put away
My labor and my leisure too,
For His Civility—

We passed the School, where Children strove
10 At Recess—in the Ring—
We passed the Fields of Gazing Grain—
We passed the Setting Sun—

Or rather—He passed Us—
The Dews drew quivering and chill—
15 For only Gossamer,° my Gown—
My Tippet—only Tulle°—

We paused before a House that seemed
A Swelling of the Ground—
The Roof was scarcely visible—
20 The Cornice°—in the Ground—

Since then—'tis Centuries—and yet
Feels shorter than the Day
I first surmised the Horses' Heads
Were toward Eternity—

---

**15. gossamer** *n.:* thin, soft material.
**16. tippet . . . tulle:** shawl made of fine netting.
**20. cornice** *n.:* molding at the top of a building.

*Open Window With Curtain* by Linda Fennimore.

## I heard a Fly buzz— when I died

One of Dickinson's most brilliantly original works, this poem begins with such boldness and continues with such quick shifts of attention that we may not stop to think about what we are hearing—a voice from the dead. Write down what you would expect someone to sense at the time of death—that ultimate moment when we cannot "see to see."

# I heard a Fly buzz— when I died

## Emily Dickinson

I heard a Fly buzz—when I died—
The Stillness in the Room
Was like the Stillness in the Air—
Between the Heaves of Storm—

5    The Eyes around—had wrung them dry—
And Breaths were gathering firm
For that last Onset—when the King
Be witnessed—in the Room—

I willed my Keepsakes—Signed away
10   What portion of me be
Assignable—and then it was
There interposed a Fly—

With Blue—uncertain stumbling Buzz—
Between the light—and me—
15   And then the Windows failed—and then
I could not see to see—

## Much Madness is divinest Sense

### Make the Connection

Since her death, Dickinson has often been portrayed as an eccentric recluse. In fact, Dickinson lived as many other great poets (and quite a few "ordinary" people) have lived—deliberately choosing solitude for contemplation, reading, and writing.

### Literary Focus
**Paradox**

A **paradox** is a statement that seems to be self-contradictory. For example, when Juliet says "Parting is such sweet sorrow," she uses a paradox: She is sad to be leaving Romeo, but kissing him goodbye (over and over again) is very sweet. The very title of this poem states an interesting paradox.

> A **paradox** is a statement that appears to be self-contradictory but reveals a kind of truth.
>
> *For more on Paradox, see the Handbook of Literary and Historical Terms.*

## Much Madness is divinest Sense

### Emily Dickinson

Much Madness is divinest Sense—
To a discerning Eye—
Much Sense—the starkest Madness—
'Tis the Majority
In this, as All, prevail—
Assent—and you are sane—
Demur—you're straightway dangerous—
And handled with a Chain—

*Path with Grass Border* (detail) (1956) by Jean Dubuffet. Oil on canvas cutout with sand, earth, and pebbles. Dubuffet was a French artist who coined the term *art brut,* or "outsider art."

© 2005 Artists Rights Society (ARS), New York/ADAGP, Paris.

**SKILLS FOCUS**

**Literary Skills**
Understand paradox.

# "I sing . . . because I am afraid"

*In 1862, Emily Dickinson sent the editor and critic Thomas Wentworth Higginson a letter and four poems, asking for critical help. Dickinson saw him as a mentor, and they corresponded for several years. Four years after Dickinson's death, Higginson assisted Mabel Loomis Todd (a friend of Austin Dickinson, Emily's brother) in editing Dickinson's poems. The following excerpts are from two of Dickinson's letters. The first was written after Dickinson asked Higginson for some criticism, which she referred to as "surgery."*

April 26, 1862

Mr. Higginson,—Your kindness claimed earlier gratitude, but I was ill, and write today from my pillow.

Thank you for the surgery; it was not so painful as I supposed. I bring you others, as you ask. . . .

You asked how old I was? I made no verse, but one or two, until this winter, sir.

I had a terror since September, I could tell to none; and so I sing, as the boy does of the burying ground, because I am afraid.

You inquire my books. For poets, I have Keats, and Mr. and Mrs. Browning. For prose, Mr. Ruskin, Sir Thomas Browne, and the Revelations. I went to school, but in your manner of the phrase had no education. When a little girl, I had a friend who taught me Immortality; but venturing too near, himself, he never returned. Soon after my tutor died, and for several years my lexicon was my only companion. Then I found one more, but he was not contented I be his scholar, so he left the land.

You ask of my companions. Hills, sir, and the sundown, and a dog large as myself, that my father bought me. They are better than beings because they know, but do not tell; and the noise in the pool at noon excels my piano.

I have a brother and sister; my mother does not care for thought, and father, too busy with his briefs to notice what we do. He buys me many books, but begs me not to read them, because he fears they joggle the mind. They are religious, except me. . . .

But I fear my story fatigues you. I would like to learn. Could you tell me how to grow, or is it unconveyed, like melody or witchcraft?

You speak of Mr. Whitman. I never read his book, but was told that it was disgraceful. . .

*In the second excerpt, Dickinson responds to Higginson's request for her picture.*

July 1862

Could you believe me without? I had no portrait, now, but am small, like the wren; and my hair is bold, like the chestnut bur; and my eyes, like the sherry in the glass, that the guest leaves. Would this do just as well?

It often alarms father. He says death might occur, and he has molds [photographs] of all the rest, but has no mold of me. . . .

*E. Dickinson*

# Response and Analysis

## Because I could not stop for Death

### Thinking Critically

1. How many passengers are in Death's carriage? Who are they?

2. How is Death **personified**? What are his human characteristics?

3. What three things do the riders pass in the third stanza?

4. What is significant about the sun passing the carriage in the fourth stanza? How does the temperature now change?

5. What has the speaker surmised, or guessed, in the last stanza?

6. How would you paraphrase the first two lines in a way that emphasizes their **irony**? What word in line 2 tells you that the tone is ironic?

7. In the second stanza, *civility* means "politeness; good manners." How does this kind of behavior on the part of both Death and the speaker extend the **irony** of the first stanza?

8. The fifth stanza is a riddle in itself. What is the house that is nearly buried?

9. Do you think the concluding stanza introduces a **tone** of terror, because the speaker has suddenly realized she will ride on forever, conscious of being dead? Or is the poem really an expression of trust and even triumph? Explain your response.

### Literary Criticism

10. The critic Alfred Kazin said of the last stanza of this poem: "What that famous Eternity is, we cannot say." Do you agree with Kazin? What do *you* think Dickinson meant by the "Eternity" the horses were going toward?

*New England Cemetery—Augusta, Maine* (1997) by Fred Danziger (20″ × 23″).

**SKILLS FOCUS**

**Literary Skills**
Analyze irony and paradox.

**Reading Skills**
Summarize a text.

## I heard a Fly buzz—when I died

### Thinking Critically

1. How would you **paraphrase** the first stanza—that is, how would you rephrase it in your own words?

2. According to the second and third stanzas, how have the speaker and those around her prepared for death?

3. Whom are the dying person and those around her expecting to find in the room? What appears instead, and why is this **ironic**?

4. In line 4, Dickinson uses the word *heaves* to refer to the behavior of storms. Why is *heaves* an appropriate word to describe what is happening in this poem?

5. How does the poet use pauses and specific words in lines 12–13 to make the appearance of the fly dramatic and lively?

6. In the third stanza, what portion of the speaker is "assignable"? What portion, by implication, is *not* assignable?

7. What does the phrase "the Windows failed" (line 15) mean?

8. What **tone** do you hear in this poem? Why might Dickinson insert the fly into this deathbed scene? (Refer to your notes about the expectations most people have about death and dying.) 🖉

## Much Madness is divinest Sense

### Thinking Critically

1. What is the meaning of the two **paradoxes,** or apparent contradictions, in the first three lines?

2. The word *assent* means "agree to." The word *demur* means "hesitate; object." What does the "Majority" say about those who assent and those who demur? In what situations in life might someone be considered dangerous because he or she demurred?

3. What do you think is the poem's **theme**? (Consider what the speaker thinks about the individual's proper relationship to society.)

4. Dickinson liked to use dashes—a mark of punctuation her first editors removed. How do dashes help emphasize certain ideas in this poem?

5. What would you say is Dickinson's **tone** in this poem? What similarities do you notice to other poems in this collection?

# In the season of change

## Teresa Palomo Acosta

If E. Dickinson and I had been friends,
we would have each owned a treasure chest
filled with doilies for laying under our silverware,
for showing off atop our china cabinets.
5   For softening the scars in the 300-year-old dining room tables
we would have inherited
from our great-grandmothers.

But our bisabuelas° never met,
exchanged glances or
10   sat next to each other in church.
And I only discovered E. Dickinson
in the few pages she was allowed
to enter in my high school literature texts.

Only years later did
15   I finally pore over her words,
believing that
her songs held
my name inscribed within.
And that they might fill the air
20   with the ancient signs of kinship
that women can choose to pass along.

And thus left on our own,
E. Dickinson and I
sat down at the same table,
25   savoring her rhubarb pie and my cafecito°
chatting and chismeando°
and trading secrets
despite decrees demanding silence between us:

women from separate corners of the room.

*Two Girls Talking*
by Pierre-Auguste Renoir
(15.3″ × 20.1″).

---

**8. bisabuelas** (bēs·ä·bwä′läs) *n. pl.:* great-grandmothers.
**25. cafecito** (kä′fä·sē′tô) *n.:* little cup of coffee.
**26. chismeando** (chēs·mä·än′dô) *adj.:* gossiping.

# Emily Dickinson

## Linda Pastan

We think of her hidden in a white dress
among the folded linens and sachets
of well-kept cupboards, or just out of sight
sending jellies and notes with no address
5  to all the wondering Amherst neighbors.
Eccentric as New England weather
the stiff wind of her mind, stinging or gentle,
blew two half-imagined lovers off.
Yet legend won't explain the sheer sanity
10  of vision, the serious mischief
of language, the economy of pain.

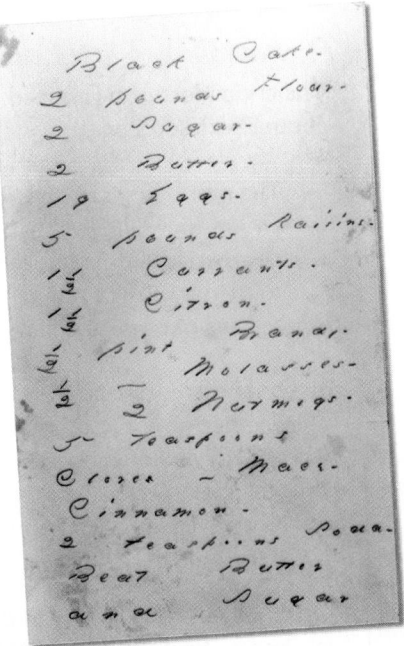

Dickinson's handwritten recipe for black cake.

# Emily Dickinson

## Gary Smith

I've defended you against the many
who have made a madcap of you—
citing the middle years, how feverishly
you paced the house in bridal whites,
5  the longing of every poem you wrote—
how easily they spill into nothing.
We like to own the poets we keep—
to mother each word like obsessions.
Your company is not easily kept—
10  too soon, too soon you retire to bed.
A peevish old maid worrying Puritans.
If heaven had been given to you in gold,
before singing your hymns of praise,
you would have discovered copper within.

Emily Dickinson's bedroom window.

# WRITING

## 1. Analyzing Dickinson

The critic Northrop Frye had this to say about Dickinson's poetry:

> The most cursory glance at Emily Dickinson will reveal that she is a deeply religious poet, preoccupied, to the verge of obsession, with the themes of death and immortality.

In a brief **essay,** discuss this comment, and tell whether or not you agree with it and why. At the end of your essay, explain how you feel about Dickinson's themes and the tone she reveals in talking about them.

## 2. Echoes of Dickinson

On pages 408–409, you read three poems inspired by Emily Dickinson. Write a **poem** of your own—either one addressed to Dickinson or one that treats one of the subjects that engaged Emily Dickinson: love and loss, the life of the spirit, death and immortality, the nature of nature, or the power of imagination. You might even use one of Dickinson's lines as your opener and try out Dickinson's style of punctuation and capitalization.

**SKILLS FOCUS**

**Writing Skills**
Write an essay analyzing a critical comment. Write a poem. Write an essay comparing and contrasting poems by two poets.

**Listening and Speaking Skills**
Present a performance using a prepared script.

**Grammar Skills**
Understand and use subordinating conjunctions.

## 3. Comparing Poems

In a brief **essay,** compare and contrast one of Dickinson's poems with a poem by another poet. You might choose a work by an earlier poet, such as "Upon the Burning of Our House" by Anne Bradstreet (page 29), or "Thanatopsis" by William Cullen Bryant (page 191), or "The Cross of Snow" by Henry Wadsworth Longfellow (page 198). Look for poems that have something in common—a similar subject or theme. Before you write, collect your points of comparison and contrast in a chart like the one below:

|  | Dickinson Poem | Other Poem |
|---|---|---|
| Subject matter |  |  |
| Theme |  |  |
| Tone |  |  |
| Figures of speech |  |  |

# LISTENING AND SPEAKING

### Dickinson Onstage

With a partner or a small group, prepare a script for a performance called *An Evening with Emily Dickinson.* Let Dickinson tell about her life, her views of poetry and language, and her feelings about nature, faith, and eternity. Include readings of selected poems. You might want to include Teresa Palomo Acosta's poem "In the season of change" (see the **Connection** on page 408), Linda Pastan's poem "Emily Dickinson" (see the **Connection** on page 409), or Gary Smith's poem "Emily Dickinson" (see the **Connection** on page 409). Present your performance for the class.

# Grammar Link

## Using Subordinating Conjunctions: Showing Relationships

When you write, part of your job is to clarify the relationships between ideas. In the following example sentence the two clauses are joined with the coordinating conjunction *and*. As you will see, this conjunction fails to indicate the relationship between the two parts of the sentence.

> Emily Dickinson published only a handful of poems during her lifetime, <u>and</u> she is now considered one of the most important American poets.

By using a **subordinating conjunction** instead of a coordinating conjunction, you can join the same clauses in a way that clearly conveys the relationship between ideas.

> <u>Although</u> Emily Dickinson published only a handful of poems during her lifetime, she is now considered one of the most important American poets.

A subordinating conjunction is a linking word (or group of words) that connects two complete ideas by making one of the ideas subordinate, or less important than the other. A subordinate clause is sometimes called a **dependent clause** because it can't stand on its own as a sentence—it depends on an independent clause to express a complete thought. A subordinating conjunction may come between two clauses, or it may appear at the beginning of a sentence.

When you're writing sentences with subordinate clauses, choose a subordinating conjunction that pinpoints the precise relationship you want to convey between the two ideas (cause, purpose, time, contrast, comparison, and so on). Here are some possibilities:

Some subordinate clauses begin with a **relative pronoun** (*that, which, who, whom, whose*) rather than a subordinating conjunction.

Basket at Emily Dickinson's window.

| Some Common Subordinating Conjunctions | | |
| --- | --- | --- |
| although | in order to | that |
| as | rather than | unless |
| because | since | until |
| before | so that | when |
| even if | than | while |

Rewrite these sentences, replacing *and* with a subordinating conjunction that more precisely explains the relationship between the two clauses.

1. Dickinson's early editors altered her poems, and they wanted to make her work more conventionally poetic.

2. Readers did not get a chance to read what Dickinson actually wrote, and Thomas H. Johnson published a new edition of her poetry in 1955.

3. Dickinson's punctuation, rhymes, syntax, and diction were often baffling, and Johnson restored her poems to their original form.

## Apply to Your Writing

Look through a current writing assignment or a work that you've already completed. Can you find any sentences in which the relationship between the clauses is vague? If so, try replacing coordinating conjunctions with subordinating conjunctions that express your meaning more clearly.

▶ **For more help, see Combining by Subordinating Ideas, 10d, in the Language Handbook.**

Center of Amherst, Massachusetts (c. 1875), Dickinson's hometown, by George A. Thomas.

Amherst Historical Society, Amherst, Massachusetts.

# Reflecting *on the* Literary Period

## American Masters: Whitman and Dickinson

This feature contains additional selections by Walt Whitman and Emily Dickinson. The Focus Question will guide your reading and help you reflect on important aspects of their work.

*A Road in Fontainbleu Forest* by Abbott Handerson Thayer. (1849–1921) © The Sullivan Collection. Oil on canvas.

## Think About...

Among nineteenth-century American writers, two poets—Walt Whitman and Emily Dickinson—stand out today as masters. In their own time, one was considered a renegade, and the other was a complete unknown. Yet the works of these two poets completely changed the face of American poetry.

Whitman and Dickinson had very different experiences of the world and brought different styles to their work. Whitman displayed a public persona and saw himself as connected to everyone and everything. In his poems, he identifies himself with laborers, runaway slaves, mothers, and different aspects of nature. Dickinson, on the other hand, was shy and private and focused on a world in which she was predominantly a spectator. Her limited contact with society led her to write about such things as her garden, her wanderings, and her own personal struggles with love and grief. Though these poets expressed their creative spirits in different ways, together they represent a turning point in American poetry.

**SKILLS FOCUS**

Pages 413–424 cover **Literary Skills** Evaluate genres and traditions in American literature.

### Focus Question

As you read each selection, keep in mind this Focus Question and take notes to help you answer it at the end of the feature:

How are Walt Whitman's and Emily Dickinson's public versus private experiences of the world reflected in their poetry?

*from* **Song of Myself, Number 6**

# When I Heard the Learn'd Astronomer

# A Noiseless Patient Spider

**Meet the Writer** **Walt Whitman** (1819–1892) was a curious mixture of the home-spun and the theatrical: He had the earthy spirit of the born democrat but the self-dramatizing disposition of an aristocratic dandy. Whitman's two-sided image of himself is a clue to his poetry. Much of it has the simplicity of folk literature. The greater part of Whitman's poetry, however, escapes all categories and demands to be read with the same attention that we give to the most sophisticated poetry in our language.

(For more information about Walt Whitman, see page 360.)

**Background** Although Whitman wrote a number of prose works, his collection of poems *Leaves of Grass* became a lifelong occupation as he continued to add poems that recorded his most essential experiences. The first edition of *Leaves of Grass* (1855)—which included *Song of Myself*—was ninety-five pages long. By the time the ninth edition of *Leaves of Grass* was printed, Whitman had become the "representative poet," the man who identified himself with everyone and everything under the sun.

---

**CONNECTING TO THE**
**Focus Question**

Through his poems, Whitman emphasizes a connection not only to other people but also to nature. As you read, consider this question: In what ways do Whitman's poems portray a connection between the poet and society as a whole? between the poet and different aspects of nature?

---

*Apple Picking* (1878) by Winslow Homer. Terra Foundation for American Art, Chicago, U.S.A.

*In* Song of Myself, *Whitman presents the philosophical notion that everyone is part of the whole of nature. In number 6, he uses grass to symbolize humankind's relationship to the universe.*

# *from* Song of Myself

## Walt Whitman

### 6

A child said *What is the grass?* fetching it to me with full hands;
How could I answer the child? I do not know what it is any more than he.

I guess it must be the flag of my disposition, out of hopeful green stuff woven.

Or I guess it is the handkerchief of the Lord,
5    A scented gift and remembrancer designedly dropt,
Bearing the owner's name someway in the corners, that we may see and remark,
       and say *Whose?*

Or I guess the grass is itself a child, the produced babe of the vegetation.

Or I guess it is a uniform hieroglyphic,°
And it means, Sprouting alike in broad zones and narrow zones,
10   Growing among black folks as among white,
Kanuck, Tuckahoe, Congressman, Cuff,° I give them the same, I receive them
      the same.

And now it seems to me the beautiful uncut hair of graves.

Tenderly will I use you curling grass,
It may be you transpire from the breasts of young men,
15   It may be if I had known them I would have loved them,
It may be you are from old people, or from offspring taken soon out of their
      mothers' laps,
And here you are the mothers' laps.

---

    **8. hieroglyphic** (hī′ər·ō′glif′ik): picture symbol used
in a writing system to represent sounds or words.
  **11. Kanuck** (kə·nuk′), **Tuckahoe ... Cuff:** Kanuck,
Tuckahoe, and Cuff are slang terms, now considered offensive, for the following people: a French
Canadian, an inhabitant of the Virginia lowlands,
and an African American.

*The Nooning* (1872) by Winslow Homer. (American, 1836–1910) Oil on canvas. 1947.1.
Wadsworth Atheneum Museum of Art, Hartford, CT. The Ella Gallup Sumner and Mary Catlin Sumner Collection Fund.

The grass is very dark to be from the white heads of old mothers,
Darker than the colorless beards of old men,
20   Dark to come from under the faint red roofs of mouths.

O I perceive after all so many uttering tongues,
And I perceive they do not come from the roofs of mouths for nothing.

I wish I could translate the hints about the dead young men and women,
And the hints about old men and mothers, and the offspring taken soon out of
    their laps.

25   What do you think has become of the young and old men?
And what do you think has become of the women and children?

They are alive and well somewhere,
The smallest sprout shows there is really no death,
And if ever there was it led forward life, and does not wait at the end to arrest it,
30   And ceas'd the moment life appear'd.

All goes onward and outward, nothing collapses,
And to die is different from what any one supposed, and luckier.

*Although elsewhere Whitman is both admiring of and receptive to science, in "When I Heard the Learn'd Astronomer," he seems to disdain the astronomer's scientific knowledge in favor of his own intuitive, even mystical response to the stars.*

# When I Heard the Learn'd Astronomer

## Walt Whitman

When I heard the learn'd astronomer,
When the proofs, the figures, were ranged in columns before me,
When I was shown the charts and diagrams, to add, divide, and measure them,
When I sitting heard the astronomer where he lectured with much applause in
    the lecture room,
5   How soon unaccountable I became tired and sick,
Till rising and gliding out I wander'd off by myself,
In the mystical moist night air, and from time to time,
Look'd up in perfect silence at the stars.

*"A Noiseless Patient Spider" epitomizes the yearning for universal love, which gives Whitman's view of democracy a mystical character. The poet throws filament after filament—line after line, poem after poem—hoping to connect with readers.*

# A Noiseless Patient Spider

## Walt Whitman

A noiseless patient spider,
I mark'd where on a little promontory it stood isolated,
Mark'd how to explore the vacant vast surrounding,
It launch'd forth filament, filament, filament, out of itself,
5   Ever unreeling them, ever tirelessly speeding them.

And you O my soul where you stand,
Surrounded, detached, in measureless oceans of space,
Ceaselessly musing, venturing, throwing, seeking the spheres to connect them,
Till the bridge you will need be form'd, till the ductile anchor hold,
10   Till the gossamer thread you fling catch somewhere, O my soul.

# Response and Analysis

## *from* Song of Myself, Number 6

### Thinking Critically

1. How does the **image** of the grass as "the hair of graves" contribute to Whitman's idea that "there is really no death" (line 28)? Cite words and phrases from the poem to support your response.

2. Find at least three **parallel structures,** or repetitions of words or groups of words, in the poem. How does this repetition help create **cadence**—a rhythmic rise and fall of your voice as the lines are spoken aloud? How does the sound of the poem contribute to its meaning?

### Extending and Evaluating

3. Whitman states in this poem that to die is "luckier" than what people think. Briefly explain what you think Whitman means by this. Would you agree or disagree with his statement? Why?

## When I Heard the Learn'd Astronomer

### Thinking Critically

1. How does the audience's reaction to the astronomer's lecture differ from the speaker's reaction?

2. The speaker is not enjoying a lecture that he had presumably wanted to attend. What do you think might have been the reason for such an unexpected reaction?

3. In terms of the conflict between reality and imagination, what is the significance of the poem's final line? What do you think the speaker gained from watching the stars in "perfect silence" that he couldn't get from the astronomer's lecture?

### Extending and Evaluating

4. What do you think is the **theme,** or insight about life, that Whitman reveals in "When I Heard the Learn'd Astronomer"? Do you agree or disagree with his insight?

## A Noiseless Patient Spider

### Thinking Critically

1. What **analogy,** or comparison, does Whitman draw between the spider and his own soul?

2. What **tone,** or attitude toward his subject, does Whitman have about the spider? In what ways does he reveal this attitude?

### Extending and Evaluating

3. Whitman emphasizes both the isolation of the spider and of the human soul. How might this **image** of an isolated self in search of a connection with the universe reflect Whitman's view of life? Do you agree with Whitman's view? Why or why not?

• • •

Using details from the poems, respond to **Connecting to the Focus Question** on page 414.

The Granger Collection, New York.

**Walt Whitman**   **419**

## My life closed twice before its close

## This is my letter to the World

## I taste a liquor never brewed

**Meet the Writer**  **Emily Dickinson**
(1830–1886) wrote over seventeen hundred
poems that celebrate nature, describe love,
and personify death. The great mystery of Emily
Dickinson is that she could describe life so
insightfully when she herself remained closed
off from the world. (By the late 1860s, she refused to leave her family's property.) It is as
though she lived outside of life in order to
obtain a unique, unclouded view of it. Dickinson's
poetry leaves no doubt that she lived an intense
inner life.

(For more information about Emily Dickinson,
see page 389.)

(For more information about Emily Dickinson,
see page 389.)

---

**CONNECTING TO THE**
**Focus Question**

As you read, consider these questions: What
private triumphs, fears, and disappointments
might Dickinson's poems address? How
might they also relate to broader themes
experienced by people everywhere?

---

*The following poem deals with loss, which Dickinson experienced much of.
"My life closed twice before its close" could be referring to any number of peo-
ple in her life: from the loss of two older male friends, Charles Wadsworth and
Samuel Bowles, to the loss of her parents.*

# My life closed twice before its close

## Emily Dickinson

My life closed twice before its close—
It yet remains to see
If Immortality unveil
A third event to me

5   So huge, so hopeless to conceive
As these that twice befell.
Parting is all we know of heaven,
And all we need of hell.

*Emily Dickinson did not write her poetry for money or recognition. In "This is my letter to the World," Dickinson seems to be able to see into the future and know that her work would one day be read by "Hands" she could not see.*

# This is my letter to the World

### Emily Dickinson

This is my letter to the World
That never wrote to Me—
The simple News that Nature told—
With tender Majesty

5   Her Message is committed
To Hands I cannot see—
for love of Her—Sweet—countrymen
Judge tenderly—of Me

George Inness (American, 1825–1894). *Saco Ford: Conway Meadows.* Oil on canvas, 1876. Gift of Ellen W. Ayer.
Mount Holyoke College Art Museum, South Hadley, Mass.

*Some critics believe that Dickinson is making fun of Emerson in the following poem. Like Emerson's poem "Bacchus," this poem compares a poet's feeling of inspiration to the feeling of intoxication some get when drinking liquor. However, in contrast to Emerson's serious tone, Dickinson's is humorous.*

# I taste a liquor never brewed

## Emily Dickinson

I taste a liquor never brewed—
From Tankards scooped in Pearl—
Not all the Vats upon the Rhine°
Yield such an Alcohol!

5   Inebriate° of Air—am I—
And Debauchee° of Dew—
Reeling—thro endless summer days—
From inns of Molten Blue—

When "Landlords" turn the drunken Bee
10   Out of the Foxglove's° door—
When Butterflies—renounce their "drams"—
I shall but drink the more!

Till Seraphs° swing their snowy Hats—
And Saints—to windows run—
15   To see the little Tippler°
Leaning against the—Sun—

**3. Rhine:** an allusion to the Rhine River in Germany, an area that is noted for fine wine and beer.
**5. inebriate:** (in·ē′brē·it′): drunk.
**6. debauchee** (deb′ô·shē′): person who overindulges in pleasures.

**10. foxglove's:** A foxglove is a kind of plant with cuplike flowers.

**13. seraphs:** angels of the highest order.
**15. tippler:** drinker.

## My life closed twice before its close

### Thinking Critically

1. How would you describe the **tone** of this poem? Find details in the poem to support your response.

2. The specific events that twice "closed" Dickinson's life are not mentioned. What suggests that they were a kind of death?

3. The last two lines talk about the suffering caused by parting and how it is "all we need of hell." In what way is parting also "all we know of heaven"?

## This is my letter to the World

### Thinking Critically

1. Dickinson once wrote to a friend: "A letter always feels to me like immortality because it is the mind alone" that one encounters, without the physical presence of the person. How might this sense of immortality be related to her speaking of her poetry as "my letter to the World" (line 1)?

2. Dickinson says the message of her poetry is "The simple News that Nature told" (line 3), that is "committed / To Hands I cannot see" (lines 5–6). How does this develop the idea about a letter and the world introduced in lines 1–2?

3. In line 8, Dickinson asks that she be judged "tenderly" by her readers. How is this related to the "tender Majesty" in line 4?

### Extending and Evaluating

4. In this poem, Dickinson talks about leaving, in essence, a legacy for the world. Do you think she was successful in passing along her contribution to the world? Explain.

## I taste a liquor never brewed

### Thinking Critically

1. What is being compared in this poem? Why is the comparison so striking?

2. Who do you think are the "Landlords" in stanza 3? What details in the poem suggest a **tone,** or attitude, of defiance?

3. Where is the "little Tippler," or drinker, in the last stanza? What is significant about the last word in the poem?

### Extending and Evaluating

4. Many readers see this poem, at least in part, as a description of the inspiration that drives artists to create. What other human activities or emotions could it pertain to?

• • •

Using details from the poems, respond to **Connecting to the Focus Question** on page 420.

*Mourning Picture* (1890) by Edwin Romanzo Elmer. (American, 1850–1923) Oil on canvas. 27¹⁵/₁₆ × 36 in.; 70.9613 × 91.44 cm. SC1953:129.

Smith College Museum of Art, Northampton, Massachusetts. Purchased.

(Opposite) *Passion Flowers and Hummingbirds* (about 1870–83) by Martin Johnson Heade. (American, 1819–1904) Museum of Fine Arts, Boston. Gift of Maxim Karolik for the M. and M. Karolik Collection of American Paintings, 1815–1865. 47.1138. Oil on canvas. 39.37 × 54.93 cm (15½ × 21⅝ in.).

Photograph © 2007 Museum of Fine Arts, Boston.

### REVIEW

# Reflecting *on the* Literary Period

## American Masters: Whitman and Dickinson

The following questions ask you to compare and analyze the selections in this feature and respond to the Focus Question. Where possible, cite passages from the selections to support your answers.

Walt Whitman ......................... from **Song of Myself, Number 6**

.............. **When I Heard the Learn'd Astronomer**

......................... **A Noiseless Patient Spider**

Emily Dickinson................... **My life closed twice before its close**

........................ **This is my letter to the World**

........................ **I taste a liquor never brewed**

### Comparing Literature

1. Whitman and Dickinson had differing views about their places in society. How does their poetry reveal their respective attitudes about interacting with society?

2. Whitman and Dickinson both write about their observations of nature. What is similar about their view of nature? What is different?

3. In *Song of Myself*, number 6, and "My life closed twice before its close," what insights about death do Whitman and Dickinson discuss? How do their views about dying differ?

4. In "A Noiseless Patient Spider" and "I taste a liquor never brewed," what circumstances or experiences do the poets seem to suggest are necessary to generate poetry?

5. In "A Noiseless Patient Spider," Whitman wants to connect with the world. How does Dickinson's "This is my letter to the World" express a similar desire? How are the two poets' aspirations different?

**SKILLS FOCUS**

Pages 413–424 cover
**Literary Skills**
Evaluate genres and traditions in American literature.

### RESPONDING TO THE
## Focus Question

Review your notes and responses related to the Focus Question for this feature. Using details from the selections, write your answer to the question.

How are Walt Whitman's and Emily Dickinson's public versus private experiences of the world reflected in their poetry?

### POETRY
## Legacy in Latin America

Who's the most popular U.S. poet in Latin America? The answer is probably Walt Whitman. One of his greatest admirers was the Cuban poet José Martí, who introduced Whitman's work to Spanish-speaking audiences at the turn of the century. Whitman's influence on Martí's own verse is evident in *José Martí: Major Poems,* a bilingual edition with English translations by Elinor Randall, edited by Philip Foner.

### FICTION
## Meet the Marches

Meg, Jo, Beth, and Amy—to those who grew up with Louisa May Alcott's classic *Little Women,* these names conjure images of four spirited New England girls bound together through comedy and tragedy. This enduring story, whose events closely resemble those of Alcott's own life, offers up an unforgettable portrait of the four March sisters, who must grow up in a hurry after their father is sent to fight in the Civil War.

### NONFICTION
## Beholder of Mysteries

"I am no scientist," Annie Dillard says of herself. "I am a wanderer with a background in theology and a penchant for quirky facts." In *Pilgrim at Tinker Creek,* Dillard draws on her experiences in an isolated Virginia valley to create a memorable reflection on life, death, and the mysteries of nature.

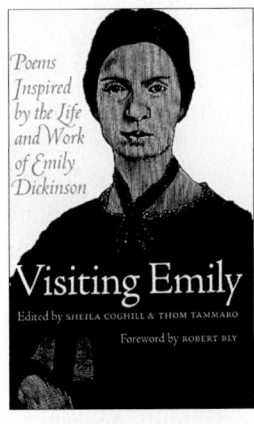

### POETRY
## A Tribute to Emily

Something about Emily Dickinson— her shadowy reclusiveness, her fierce, driven poems —has captured people's imaginations in a way few other writers have. *Visiting Emily,* edited by Sheila Coghill and Thom Tammaro, is a collection of poems inspired by the life and work of Emily Dickinson, featuring such poets as Richard Wilbur, Robert Bly, and Adrienne Rich. Some are in imitation of Dickinson's style; others are tributes to the woman herself.

# Writing a Reflective Essay

**Writing Assignment**
Write a reflective essay in which you explore an experience from your life and share its significance with readers.

Some discoveries that you read about, such as the detection of a distant solar system, make headlines around the globe. Other discoveries are smaller and more personal, such as Emily Dickinson's discovery that "The Soul selects her own Society—." Writing a **reflective essay** leads to discoveries, too. When you write about an experience from your life—the white-water rafting trip you took this summer or your first driving lesson—you explore the meaning of the experience and your beliefs about life in general.

## Prewriting

### Consider Your Purpose

**Sense of Purpose** Before you start thinking of your life experiences, think about why you are writing so that you can pick the best experience. Your **purpose** in writing a reflective essay is to express and explore your thoughts and feelings. You'll not only discover and share the **significance** of the experience you describe, but you'll also go beyond the specifics to show how it compares and connects to the beliefs you hold important and to the ideas you have about life.

### Choose an Experience

**Sifting Through Memories** Think back on the experiences that have been important in your life. The experience you write about might be something as simple as feeding a pet or overhearing a conversation; however, it must be an experience that has taught you something about yourself or the world. For example, feeding a pet may have taught you responsibility and compassion for all living things. Journals, diaries, and photo albums are good places to look for significant experiences. You might also try reading published reflective essays, such as memoirs or biographies, for ideas. Think of your **audience** when selecting an experience to explore—be sure you'll feel comfortable sharing the experience with the people who will be reading your essay.

### Reflect on Meaning

**The Heart of the Matter** Once you've chosen an experience to explore, spend some time reflecting not only on what the experience meant to you at the time it occurred, but also on what it means to you now. As a springboard for reflection, ask yourself the questions in the left-hand column of the chart on the next page. Look also at one

**Writing Skills**
Write a reflective essay. Choose an experience and reflect on its meaning. Gather details.

student's answers in the right-hand column. These answers are based on her experience doing community service at a retirement center.

## REFLECTION QUESTIONS

| Questions | Answers |
|---|---|
| **What did I feel during this experience? What did I feel when I thought about it shortly afterwards? How do I feel about it now?** | At first I felt dread and disappointment at having to spend my spring break doing community service. Later, I felt pleasantly surprised. When I think about it now, I feel grateful. |
| **What did I learn about others and myself from this experience?** | I learned that you can find friends in unexpected places and that you might find that you have things in common with people who seem very different from you. |
| **How did this experience influence what I believe about people or life in general? How have my beliefs changed or developed since then?** | I came to believe that life is unpredictable—something you don't want to do may end up being something you enjoy. Since then, I try to keep an open mind about new situations. |

**Sum It All Up**  Answer the questions in the chart above. Then, write a sentence that sums up the significance of your experience. This sentence will appear at the end of your essay, but writing down your ideas now will remind you of the larger meaning you want to convey to readers. Every detail you include in your essay should help communicate the importance of the experience. The following example shows what the student writer learned while working in a retirement center.

**DO THIS**

I've gained a new belief: Life is unpredictable, and sometimes an experience brings you a surprise—a new perspective.

## Recall and Record Details

**A Detailed Account**  Now, gather the details that will bring the experience to life and will convince your readers that it is significant. First, list the individual events that made up the experience. Here are some suggestions to help you recall as many events as you can.

- Close your eyes and visualize the experience.

- Discuss your experience with a friend or family member. Talking about it may help to bring it all back.

- Allow yourself to daydream by looking through photos or souvenirs of the experience.

Next, add details to your list that provide a more complete picture of each event that made up the experience. Use **narrative and descriptive**

**TIP**  Try to **balance** how much time you spend relating each event, and try to connect each event to **general** or **abstract ideas** about life.

details that flesh out the sequence of events by describing the people involved and the places where the events took place. The following chart gives explanations and examples of these types of details.

## ADDING NARRATIVE AND DESCRIPTIVE DETAILS

| Types of Details | Examples |
|---|---|
| **Narrative details**<br><br>• tell the actions, thoughts, and feelings of the people involved<br><br>• include **dialogue,** words spoken by people involved in the experience, and **interior monologue,** your internal flow of thoughts | "Are you in there, Mrs. Anderson?" I called, after knocking on her open door at the Summerdale Retirement Center.<br><br>All I could think was, "This is going to be a long week." |
| **Descriptive details**<br><br>• describe **appearances** of people involved<br><br>• describe the **setting**<br><br>• use **sensory language** that appeals to the five senses (sight, hearing, smell, taste, and touch) | Mrs. Anderson had curly hair, smooth skin, and eyes crinkled with age. The staff at the center had decorated the hallways for the Fourth of July. On the door hung a huge, white straw hat with shiny red and blue strings of stars and red, white, and blue streamers. |

## Arrange the Details

**Truth and Consequences**  Once you've recalled the events and details of your experience, decide how you'll organize them. Often, reflective essays use **chronological order**—the order in which events occurred. Within that order, though, writers may arrange details **spatially** or in **order of importance** to describe a person or a place.

Look at the following example to see how one writer organized her essay to give an early hint at the significance of her experience and to create a sense of how her reflections have deepened over time. Notice that she plans to start her essay in the present and then use a **flashback** to skip backward in time. She'll use chronological order within the flashback to recount the experience. Finally, she'll conclude her essay with further reflection and some thoughts on life in general.

Begin with most recent visit to the center. → Flashback to first day I went to the center. → Event 1: Secretary asks me to get Pierre, the parrot. → Event 2: Meet Mrs. Anderson. We share stories. → Relate the significance of the experience.

**PRACTICE & APPLY 1**  Choose an experience to write about, think about its significance, and write a sentence that expresses that significance. Then, recall, record, and arrange details that will make the experience come alive for readers.

# Writing

## Writing a Reflective Essay

### A Writer's Model

A Spring Break Surprise

"Are you in there, Mrs. Anderson?" I called, after knocking on her open door at the Summerdale Retirement Center. The staff at the center had decorated the hallways for the Fourth of July. On Mrs. Anderson's door hung an enormous white straw hat, its brim wrapped with shiny red and blue strings of stars, its crown trailing red, white, and blue streamers. I let the streamers run through my fingers as I remembered how much I'd learned from the person inside the room.

"Why, Amy!" she laughed. "Is that you coming back to see me?"

Even though it was midsummer, Mrs. Anderson still remembered me. A week at the retirement center had not been my first choice of recreation for my spring break. Unfortunately, however, the fall before I'd gotten a ticket for failure to yield right of way. In my court appearance, the judge had assigned me, instead of a hefty fine, twelve hours of community service to be completed within a four-month period. Of course my schoolwork had kept me so busy that my only time to fulfill this requirement was during my spring break. I was not at all happy with the prospects for the week's entertainment.

The day I first arrived at the center, the secretary said, "Sign our volunteer register first. Then, get Pierre out of his cage."

Pierre, I found out, was the pet parrot kept in a cage by the front office. He had beautiful blue and green feathers on his back, yellow breast feathers with streaks of orange, golden feet, and a wicked-looking

**INTRODUCTION**
Attention-grabbing anecdote

Descriptive details

Hint at significance

Dialogue

Background information

Narrative details

**BODY**
Event one of flashback

Descriptive details

*(continued)*

*(continued)*

**Narrative details**

**Interior monologue**

**Event two of flashback**

**Descriptive details**

**Narrative details**

black eye. He talked. He also nipped my ear, cracked sunflower seeds into my shirt pocket, and dug his claws into my shoulder. The residents, however, loved him. My volunteer job, the secretary told me, was to carry this cranky, unpleasant bird on my shoulder around the halls, stopping to talk to residents who were outside their rooms or in the recreation areas. All I could think was, "This is going to be a long week."

On that first day, however, I also met Mrs. Amelia Anderson. She had curly hair, smooth skin, and eyes crinkled with age. Even though she sat in a wheelchair most of the time because of her chronic back trouble, she had a cheerful personality and sweet smile. She reminded me of my grandmother, who had died the preceding year. When I told her why I was at the center, she clucked her tongue in sympathy. "I know just how you feel," she said.

It seems that Mrs. Anderson had had an experience similar to mine when she was in her twenties. She'd also failed to yield the right of way, but in her case, her carelessness had caused a wreck in rush-hour traffic at a busy intersection. The police officer had given her a ticket, despite her protests.

We began to laugh over our similar experiences, especially since she told me that, as an adult, she had been given no choice but to pay the fine. I should feel lucky, she said, because all I had to do was dodge Pierre's flapping feathers. From that moment on, we became friends. We really didn't even need Pierre to start our conversations. Every day we shared stories about our families. She was interested in my friends and schoolwork, and I in turn became interested in her life as a former high school teacher.

**CONCLUSION**

**Significance of experience**

**Statement about life**

Now when I think of my time with Mrs. Anderson and the friendship we developed, I realize I've gained a new belief: Life is unpredictable and sometimes an experience brings you a surprise—a new perspective. I now try to keep an open mind about meeting unfamiliar people and facing new situations. Where I had once been uninterested in, maybe even dismissive of, older people, I now know that they can make interesting, valuable friends.

**INTERNET**

**More Writer's Models**

Keyword: LE7 11-3

**PRACTICE & APPLY** 2 Using the framework on page 429 as a guide, write the first draft of your reflective essay. Refer to the Writer's Model beginning on that same page to give you ideas for writing your own work.

# Revising

## Evaluate and Revise Your Draft

**Did I Say That?** Not even professional writers get everything right the first time. The revision process gives you the chance to make your writing as clear and as interesting as you can make it. To polish your writing, read through your paper at least twice. Using the guidelines below, read first for content and organization. Then, use the guidelines on page 432 to read your essay for style, concentrating on letting your personality show through your writing.

> **First Reading: Content and Organization** Use the chart below to look for ways to improve the content and organization of your reflective essay. Ask yourself the questions in the left-hand column. Then, use the middle column for practical tips. To revise your paper, use the suggestions in the right-hand column.

> **PEER REVIEW**
>
> Ask a peer to review your essay by using the guidelines in this section for content, organization, and style. He or she may have ideas about where you should include additional narrative or descriptive details. Carefully consider his or her suggestions.

### Rubric: Writing a Reflective Essay

| Evaluation Questions | ▶ Tips | ▶ Revision Techniques |
|---|---|---|
| ❶ Does the introduction capture readers' attention? | ▶ **Bracket** any attention-getting anecdote, question, or interesting statement. | ▶ **Add** an anecdote, a question, or an interesting statement. |
| ❷ Does the introduction give a hint about the significance of the experience? | ▶ **Underline** the sentence or sentences in the introduction that hint at the significance of the experience. | ▶ **Add** a sentence or two that hints at the significance of the experience. |
| ❸ Are the specific events of the experience presented clearly and in an order that makes sense? | ▶ **Number** each event. If the events are not presented clearly or in a logical order, revise. | ▶ **Add** missing events, or **delete** events that do not relate to the experience. **Rearrange** events to make the chronology clear to the reader. |
| ❹ Do narrative and descriptive details describe the people, places, and events? | ▶ **Circle** the sentences that help readers imagine the events, people, and places. | ▶ **Add** details that clarify the experience, including details about what people do, say, or think, and **add** sensory details. |
| ❺ Does the conclusion make the significance of the experience clear? Does it include a final statement that connects the experience to life in general? | ▶ **Star** the sentence that relates the meaning of the experience. **Double star** the statement that relates ideas about life in general. | ▶ **Add** a sentence that states the importance of the experience, or **revise** sentences so that they clearly convey the importance. **Add** a sentence that makes a generalization about life. |

> **Second Reading: Style** Just as you would be completely your-self when speaking with a friend, you should also let your individual voice emerge in your writing. **Voice** is the individual way in which you express yourself. Since your purpose in writing a reflective essay is to express your thoughts and feelings, your audience will accept and sometimes even expect you to use **colloquial expressions**—the infor-mal words and phrases of conversational language. However, it takes practice to strike a balance between being yourself and confusing your readers with expressions they're unfamiliar with. In your second read-ing, practice including colloquial expressions effectively by following the guidelines in the chart below.

## Style Guidelines

| Evaluation Question | ▶ Tip | ▶ Revision Technique |
|---|---|---|
| ● Does the essay sound stuffy? Are there places where appropriate colloquial expressions could make it sound more natural? | ▶ **Highlight** any words or expressions that seem overly formal or unnatural. | ▶ **Replace** overly formal words and phrases with colloquial expressions that sound more natural. |

### ANALYZING THE REVISION PROCESS
Study these revisions, and answer the questions that follow.

replace

Unfortunately, however, the ~~previous autumn~~ *fall before* I'd gotten a

add

ticket, *for failure to yield right of way.* In my court appearance, the judge had assigned me,

replace, add

instead of a ~~substantial penalty,~~ *hefty fine* community service to be *twelve hours of*

completed within a four-month period.

### Responding to the Revision Process

1. How do the additions improve the paragraph?

2. How does replacing "previous autumn" with "fall before" and "substantial penalty" with "hefty fine" improve the voice of the writing?

**SKILLS FOCUS**

**Writing Skills**
Revise for content and style.

**PRACTICE & APPLY** 3 Follow the guidelines above and on the previous page to evaluate and revise the content, organization, and style of your reflective essay. Also, look at the revision example above for ideas on how to revise your draft. You might also conduct a peer-editing session with a classmate.

# Publishing

## Proofread and Publish Your Essay

**Checkmate or Checkmark?** Have you ever gotten a scratch on your watch? Although the watch works just fine, the little imperfection in its appearance may bother you so much that you get it fixed or replaced. Similarly, when people read your reflective essay, you want them to focus on your experience and its meaning, not on imperfections in grammar, punctuation, or spelling. Proofread your paper individually, collaboratively, or both. Keep proofreading until your essay is error-free.

**Let Me Tell You All About It** Don't keep your experience to yourself! Try one or more of the ideas below to share your reflective essay with an audience.

- If other people were involved in the experience, send them a copy of your essay.

- Submit your essay to your high school's literary magazine or Web site.

- Stage a group reading of your essay at your school or community library. Invite family and friends to attend. For more on **presenting a reflection,** see page 434.

- Collect the reflective essays you and your peers wrote. Use publishing software to make a professional-looking collection. Title the collection and place it in your school library.

## Reflect on Your Essay

**If I Had to Do It All Over Again** Reflecting on your writing process will help you to improve your writing and analytical skills. Write a short response to each of the following questions. Keep your answers in your portfolio, along with the final version of your essay.

- How did you choose an experience for your essay? Do you think you made a good choice? Why or why not?

- Did writing about the experience change your thoughts and feelings about it? Explain.

- What would you do differently if you were to write another reflective essay?

**PRACTICE & APPLY** Proofread your paper to ensure that it is the best that it can be. Then, consider your publishing options, and choose one to get your essay out to an audience. Finally, take some time to reflect upon what you have learned in this workshop by answering the reflection questions.

**TIP** When you proofread your paper, make sure that it conforms to the **conventions** of standard American English. For example, make sure that the dialogue you use in your reflection is punctuated correctly. For more on **using quotation marks,** see Quotation Marks, 13c–d, in the Language Handbook.

**COMPUTER TIP**

For more on **creating professional-looking documents,** see Designing Your Writing in the Writer's Handbook.

**SKILLS FOCUS**

**Writing Skills**
Proofread, especially for correct use of quotation marks.

# Presenting a Reflection

**Speaking Assignment**
**Adapt your reflective essay into an oral presentation, and deliver it to an audience.**

In the Writing Workshop for this chapter, you shared your thoughts and feelings about an experience, which allowed your audience to see how you drew meaning from that experience. Presenting your reflection orally, however, can give it a different feel by allowing your voice and body to express your emotions, to give voice to the people involved in your experience, and to bring events to life.

## Adapt Your Reflective Essay

**Bring It to Life**  While your essay relied on words alone, your presentation can use words as well as visuals, sounds, and actions to convey your experience and its significance. Your **purpose,** however, will be the same as in your essay—to express and explore your thoughts and feelings about an experience. Use the following suggestions to adapt your essay for an effective presentation.

- **Don't tell if you can show.**  Instead of describing actions or appearances, for instance, act them out. For example, bring the people in your narrative to life by speaking their **dialogue** in a way that captures their unique voices. In addition, use **visual** and **sound effects,** such as props, graphics, or music, to enhance your descriptions. For example, the student who wrote the essay that begins on page 429 used an overhead projector to show photos of the retirement center, Mrs. Anderson, and Pierre. She also played an audio recording of Pierre's squawks.

- **Strike a balance between showing the events and expressing their meaning.**  Your audience will not understand why the experience is important to you unless you tell them. Narrate the events in chronological order, acting out details when you can, but also explain the events' significance. Help listeners clearly see the comparisons you are drawing between your experience and broader themes that show the beliefs or general ideas you've gained about life.

- **Use clear, forceful, interesting language.**  If you must describe, rather than show, relate **concrete images** that appeal to the five senses, or use **figurative language,** letting a metaphor or simile draw a comparison between what you're describing and something familiar.

**TIP**  Don't overwhelm your audience with too many effects. Evaluate when to use them in order to achieve the greatest effect.

**SKILLS FOCUS**

**Listening and Speaking Skills**
Adapt a reflective essay into an oral presentation.

## Plan Your Delivery and Rehearse

**Make a Note**  To deliver your presentation extemporaneously—without reading or memorizing it word-for-word—create note cards. Note cards should be brief and to the point. Each card should remind you of one event that makes up your experience plus any visual or sound effects, dialogue, actions, or thoughts and feelings you will use to describe the event.

**Delivering the Goods** How you say something is often as important as what you say. When you give a presentation, let both your voice and your body speak for you. Use the following chart to tailor your verbal and nonverbal delivery techniques to your audience and purpose.

## DELIVERY TECHNIQUES

### Verbal Techniques

**Language:** For the most part, use **standard American English** so that your presentation will be clear. However, you may use appropriate **informal expressions** for effect; for example, to reflect the personality of a person involved in your experience.

**Tone:** Vary your tone of voice to fit the events you're narrating or to portray another person's voice. Use a light tone if the events are funny and a somber tone if the events are serious.

**Volume:** Vary the volume of your voice to fit the mood of the events, but make sure you always speak loudly enough to be heard.

### Nonverbal Techniques

**Eye contact:** Draw your audience into the story by making eye contact with as many members as possible. This gives each listener the idea that you are speaking directly to him or her, and that you want that person to hear and understand you clearly.

**Gestures:** When acting out events, make sure that your gestures are natural and that they give a sense of what's happening—without distracting the audience.

**Facial expressions:** Let your feelings about the events show on your face. Use facial expressions to portray people in your experience.

**Acting the Part** How will you remember what you're going to say? How will you present your visuals without fumbling, or play music without breaking the flow of your presentation? The only way to achieve command of the text and create skillful artistic staging is to practice. Try one or more of the following rehearsal strategies.

- **Rehearse your presentation in front of a mirror.** Watch yourself to see if your gestures and facial expressions look natural.

- **Rehearse your presentation for family or friends.** Ask them for feedback—both compliments on what you've done well and suggestions on how to improve.

- **Videotape your rehearsals.** After you have rehearsed, critically view the video, taking notes on where you may need to improve.

**SKILLS FOCUS**

**Listening and Speaking Skills**
Use effective verbal and nonverbal techniques. Rehearse and deliver the presentation.

**PRACTICE & APPLY 5** Adapt your reflective essay for an oral presentation. Prepare note cards to aid you in your presentation. After practicing your delivery, present your reflection to an audience.

**Test Practice**  Some poets claim that all poetry is about other poetry. Certainly it is true that many poems are written to imitate or respond to other poems.

The following poems were written by two poets who lived in very different times. The first poem is by Walt Whitman (1819–1892). Whitman wrote poetry that was considered radical in its time because, for one thing, it sang of things that were not usually considered poetic. For another thing it was written without any care for perfect rhymes and *dum-de-dum* rhythms.

The second poem was written by Jimmy Santiago Baca (1957–    ) nearly one hundred years after Whitman's death. Clearly Baca was thinking of Whitman's *Song of Myself* when he wrote *his* poem about *himself*. Evident in this poem is the fact that Baca had a troubled childhood. In his young adulthood he even spent time in prison.

DIRECTIONS: Read the two poems. Then, read each multiple-choice question that follows, and write the letter of the best answer.

# *from* Song of Myself
Walt Whitman

## 1

I celebrate myself, and sing myself,
And what I assume you shall assume,
For every atom belonging to me as good belongs to you.

I loaf and invite my soul,
5   I lean and loaf at my ease observing a spear of summer grass.

My tongue, every atom of my blood, form'd from this soil, this air,
Born here of parents born here from parents the same, and their
    parents the same,
I, now thirty-seven years old in perfect health begin,
Hoping to cease not till death.

10   Creeds and schools in abeyance,°
Retiring back a while sufficed at what they are, but never forgotten,
I harbor for good or bad, I permit to speak at every hazard,
Nature without check with original energy.

**10. abeyance** *n.:* temporary suspension; inactivity.

**SKILLS FOCUS**

Pages 436–439 cover
**Literary Skills**
Compare and contrast works from different literary periods.

# Who Understands Me but Me

Jimmy Santiago Baca

They turn the water off, so I live without water,
they build walls higher, so I live without treetops,
they paint the windows black, so I live without sunshine,
they lock my cage, so I live without going anywhere,
5    they take each last tear I have, I live without tears,
they take my heart and rip it open, I live without heart,
they take my life and crush it, so I live without a future,
they say I am beastly and fiendish, so I have no friends,
they stop up each hope, so I have no passage out of hell,
10    they give me pain, so I live with pain,
they give me hate, so I live with my hate,
they have changed me, and I am not the same man,
they give me no shower, so I live with my smell,
they separate me from my brothers, so I live without brothers,
15    who understands me when I say this is beautiful?
who understands me when I say I have found other freedoms?

*(continued)*

I cannot fly or make something appear in my hand,
I cannot make the heavens open or the earth tremble,
I can live with myself, and I am amazed at myself, my love, my beauty,
20  I am taken by my failures, astounded by my fears,
I am stubborn and childish,
in the midst of this wreckage of life they incurred,
I practice being myself,
and I have found parts of myself never dreamed of by me,
25  they were goaded out from under rocks in my heart
when the walls were built higher,
when the water was turned off and the windows painted black.
I followed these signs
like an old tracker and followed the tracks deep into myself,
30  followed the blood-spotted path,
deeper into dangerous regions, and found so many parts of myself,
who taught me water is not everything,
and gave me new eyes to see through walls,
and when they spoke, sunlight came out of their mouths,
35  and I was laughing at me with them,
we laughed like children and made pacts to always be loyal,
who understands me when I say this is beautiful?

---

**1.** In *Song of Myself,* number 1, the speaker's **attitude** toward himself is *best* described as —

 **A** self-hatred

 **B** mild curiosity

 **C** joyful wonder

 **D** pessimism

**2.** Which of the following lines in *Song of Myself,* number 1, gives the *best* example of the speaker's love of life?

 **F** "And what I assume you shall assume"

 **G** "I celebrate myself, and sing myself"

 **H** "I harbor for good or bad"

 **J** "I lean and loaf at my ease"

**3.** Which statement *best* expresses the speaker's relationship with other people in *Song of Myself,* number 1?

 **A** The speaker and other people are one and the same.

 **B** The speaker feels alienated from other people.

 **C** The speaker feels angry at other people.

 **D** The speaker wants to control other people.

**4.** In line 1 of "Who Understands Me but Me," "they" most likely refers to —

   **F** the speaker's best friends

   **G** an oppressive society

   **H** irresponsible teachers

   **J** a loving family

**5.** At the end of Baca's poem, the speaker's **attitude** is *best* described as —

   **A** hopeless

   **B** remorseful

   **C** triumphant

   **D** exhausted

**6.** Which of the following statements *best* expresses the **contrast** in **tone** between the two poems?

   **F** Whitman's tone is humorless, and Baca's tone is playful.

   **G** Whitman's tone is judgmental, and Baca's tone is joyous.

   **H** Whitman's tone is joyous, and Baca's tone is determined.

   **J** Whitman's tone is loving, and Baca's tone is dreary.

**7.** Which of the following statements expresses a shared **theme** of these two poems?

   **A** Technology has damaged the natural world.

   **B** The speakers celebrate the miracle of one's own self.

   **C** Society cannot dominate the individual.

   **D** Not all people are worthy of respect.

**8.** Which statement accurately describes a **contrast** between the two selections?

   **F** Whitman's poem condemns society; Baca's poem does not.

   **G** Whitman's speaker identifies himself with the world of nature; Baca's speaker does not.

   **H** Whitman's poem is written in free verse; Baca's poem is not.

   **J** Whitman's poem celebrates the human spirit; Baca's poem does not.

## Essay Question

In an essay, compare and contrast these two poems, paying close attention to each poem's **theme, style,** and **tone.** Be sure to consider how each poet deals with these topics: the speaker's relationship to nature, his relationship to people, and his relationship with himself.

# Collection 3: Skills Review
## Vocabulary Skills

**Test Practice**

**Multiple-Meaning Words**

DIRECTIONS: Choose the sentence in which the underlined word is used in the same way as it is used in each of the following quotations from Walt Whitman.

1. "The carpenter singing his [carol] as he measures his plank or <u>beam</u> . . ."
   A  The <u>beam</u> of sunlight on the ocean made the waves sparkle.
   B  This <u>beam</u> is a major support in the building's framework.
   C  The radio station can <u>beam</u> its signal for miles.
   D  The happy baby loved to <u>beam</u> at the silly adults.

2. "In the late afternoon choosing a safe <u>spot</u> to pass the night . . ."
   F  He scrubbed and scrubbed, but the <u>spot</u> would not come out.
   G  Can you <u>spot</u> the boat drifting off in the distance?
   H  Would you care for a <u>spot</u> of tea?
   J  She chose to pitch the tent on a <u>spot</u> of soft grass.

3. "You should have been with us that day <u>round</u> the chowder-kettle. . . ."
   A  He could tell that the smooth, <u>round</u> melon was ripe.
   B  The boxer was ready to fight another <u>round</u>.
   C  Just <u>round</u> up to the nearest dollar, and forget the change.
   D  The scouts gathered <u>round</u> the campfire to roast marshmallows.

4. "The courage of <u>present</u> times and all times . . ."
   F  It is my honor to <u>present</u> Walt Whitman.
   G  It's better to live in the <u>present</u> than to dwell in the past.
   H  She wrapped the <u>present</u> with beautiful blue paper.
   J  The officers were ordered to <u>present</u> their credentials.

5. "All this I swallow, it tastes good, I like it <u>well</u>, it becomes mine. . . ."
   A  The tears began to <u>well</u> in his eyes.
   B  A toddler fell into the <u>well</u> and was quickly rescued.
   C  After they dried off, they all felt <u>well</u> and good.
   D  That book is a <u>well</u> of information.

6. "The hounded slave that <u>flags</u> in the race, leans by the fence . . ."
   F  People hung <u>flags</u> in their windows after the tragedy.
   G  His strength <u>flags</u> when he doesn't eat properly.
   H  The scholar put <u>flags</u> in the textbook he was studying.
   J  The young woman beside the stalled car <u>flags</u> us down for help.

**SKILLS FOCUS**

**Vocabulary Skills**
Understand multiple-meaning words.

# Collection 3: Skills Review

## Writing Skills

**Test Practice** DIRECTIONS: Read the following paragraph from a draft of a student's reflective essay. Then, answer the questions below.

(1) My twin sister, Natasha, and I used to engage in unceasing hostilities. (2) We would fight over everything: clothes, bathroom space, chores, *everything*. (3) Then, the week after we turned fifteen, we got news that changed our lives. (4) Natasha had been feeling sick for a while, and medical tests determined that she had leukemia. (5) The type of leukemia she had held a strong chance of survival, but it would require chemotherapy and some sacrifice and determination from our family. (6) The thought of losing my sister made me reevaluate our relationship.

1. Which sentence could the writer add to communicate the significance of the experience?
   A  Leukemia is a terrible form of cancer.
   B  Just because two people are twins doesn't make them close.
   C  Natasha's leukemia made me realize how trivial our fights were.
   D  Siblings should never fight.

2. To make a connection between the experience and life in general, which sentence could the writer add?
   F  I learned that life is too precious to waste fighting over nothing.
   G  I learned to love my sister and appreciate her.
   H  I learned how the doctors planned to treat my sister's cancer.
   J  I learned to value different people's points of view.

3. To include more narrative details, the writer could
   A  contrast her appearance with her sister's
   B  describe the house where she and her sister live

   C  use sensory language to describe the clothing they share
   D  describe her thoughts and feelings after hearing the bad news

4. To add a colloquial expression and maintain an informal voice, which sentence could replace sentence 1?
   F  My twin sister, Natasha, and I used to abominate each other.
   G  My twin sister, Natasha, and I used to fight incessantly.
   H  My twin sister, Natasha, and I never used to get along.
   J  My twin sister, Natasha, and I used to quarrel ceaselessly.

5. If the writer were presenting the passage as a reflective presentation, she could adapt the essay by
   A  acting out emotions rather than describing them
   B  providing only the details that show action and not meaning
   C  speaking with a lighthearted tone
   D  writing the essay word for word on note cards

**SKILLS FOCUS**

**Writing Skills**
Write a reflective essay.

*Home, Sweet Home* (1863) by Winslow Homer (1836–1910).
Oil on canvas (21½″ × 16½″).

# The Rise of REALISM

## The Civil War to 1914

### From Conflicts to New Frontiers

A man said to the universe:

"Sir, I exist!"

"However," replied the universe,

"The fact has not created in me

A sense of obligation."

—Stephen Crane

**INTERNET**

Collection Resources

Keyword: LE7 11-4

# The Rise of Realism
## The Civil War to 1914

**c. 1850** Sojourner Truth, abolitionist and women's rights advocate, dictates *Narrative of Sojourner Truth*

**Sojourner Truth (1797–1883), abolitionist.**
© National Portrait Gallery, Smithsonian Institution/Art Resource, NY.

**1852** Harriet Beecher Stowe publishes an influential novel about slavery, *Uncle Tom's Cabin*

**1856** France's Gustave Flaubert publishes a classic realistic novel, *Madame Bovary*

**1856** Herman Melville publishes *The Piazza Tales*, short stories including "Bartleby the Scrivener"

**1867** Mark Twain publishes *The Celebrated Jumping Frog of Calaveras County and Other Sketches*

**Mark Twain Riding the Celebrated Jumping Frog by W. J. Welch. Woodcut.**

**1868–1869** Louisa May Alcott publishes a popular novel about growing up, *Little Women*

**1869** Bret Harte publishes the short story "The Outcasts of Poker Flat"

**1869** Russian author Leo Tolstoy completes his panoramic novel *War and Peace*

**1850** Fugitive Slave Act imposes stiff penalties on anyone helping a person escape enslavement

**early 1850s** Susan B. Anthony and Elizabeth Cady Stanton become co-leaders of U.S. women's rights movement

**1858** The Sepoy Rebellion, a large-scale uprising against British rule in India, ends

**1859** England's Charles Darwin explains his groundbreaking theory of evolution in *Origin of Species*

**Abraham Lincoln (1863). Photograph by Alexander Gardner.**

**April 1861** First shots of Civil War are fired

**July 1861** Confederate troops defeat Union forces at Bull Run in Virginia, in the first major battle of the Civil War

**1862** Homestead Act promises 160 acres of land to new settlers

**November 1863** President Abraham Lincoln delivers the Gettysburg Address at the dedication of a Civil War cemetery

**April 9, 1865** Confederate surrender at Appomattox Court House in Virginia ends Civil War

**April 14, 1865** President Lincoln is assassinated in Ford's Theatre, Washington, D.C.

**1865** The Thirteenth Amendment to the U.S. Constitution, outlawing slavery, is ratified

**1867** The United States purchases Alaska from Russia

## 1880

**1879** Henry James publishes the novel *Daisy Miller,* a study of European and American manners

**1879–1880** Russian novelist Fyodor Dostoyevsky publishes *The Brothers Karamazov*

**1885** William Dean Howells publishes the realistic novel *The Rise of Silas Lapham*

**1894** Kate Chopin publishes *Bayou Folk*

**Kate Chopin.**
The Missouri Historical Society, St. Louis.

**1895** Stephen Crane publishes *The Red Badge of Courage*

**1896** Paul Laurence Dunbar publishes *Lyrics of Lowly Life*

**Paul Laurence Dunbar.**

## 1900

**1903** Jack London publishes a novel about sled dogs in Alaska, *The Call of the Wild*

**1903** W.E.B. DuBois publishes his influential book of essays, *The Souls of Black Folk*

**1910** Edwin Arlington Robinson publishes a collection of poems, *The Town Down the River*

**1913** Willa Cather publishes the novel *O Pioneers!*

## 1880

**1870** John D. Rockefeller founds the Standard Oil Company of Ohio

**1876** Sioux soldiers defeat U.S. forces under Gen. George A. Custer on the Little Bighorn in Dakota Territory

**1876** Alexander Graham Bell patents the first telephone

**1878** Thomas Edison patents the first phonograph

**1881** Clara Barton organizes the American Red Cross

**1881** Booker T. Washington founds Tuskegee Institute

**1886** Statue of Liberty is dedicated

**1890** Two hundred Sioux are killed by soldiers at Wounded Knee, South Dakota

**1896** Athens, Greece, is the site of the first modern Olympic Games

**1898** The United States annexes Hawaii

## 1900

***Black Rock, a Two-Kettle(?) Chief* (1832) by George Catlin.**

**1901** Queen Victoria of England dies

**1905** Albert Einstein formulates his theory of relativity

**1913** Henry Ford introduces conveyor-belt technology to mass-produce automobiles

445

# Political and Social

## The Civil War, 1861–1865

From the firing on Fort Sumter to the Confederate surrender at Appomattox four years later, the Civil War divided the United States. Four years of destruction and bloodshed awakened Americans to a dark side of the national character. By the war's end more than 600,000 soldiers had died, nearly as many as in all the other wars combined that this country has fought. The South faced economic devastation, with its farms in ruins. The Union was preserved, but a fragile republic now had to find a future.

*The Second Minnesota Regiment at Mission Ridge, November 25, 1863 (1906) by Douglas Volk.*
Minnesota Historical Society.

Harriet Tubman (far left) with a group of people she helped escape from slavery.

## The End of Slavery

A major cause of the Civil War was the hotly debated issue of slavery, which fiercely divided the country. In 1863, President Lincoln's Emancipation Proclamation freed the slaves in states that had seceded from the Union. The Thirteenth Amendment formally abolished slavery in 1865, but the fight for freedom and equality for blacks had just begun.

## Westward Expansion

**B**eginning in the 1860s, huge numbers of people moved west. The Homestead Act of 1862 promised 160 acres of land free of charge to anyone (including emancipated slaves) who would cultivate it for five years. People flocked west hoping to find their fortunes on the frontier as farmers, miners, and ranchers. The tide of settlers became a surge when the first transcontinental railroad was completed in 1869. Also contributing to the expansion in the West was the massive influx of immigrants from Europe—almost fourteen million immigrants arrived in the United States between 1860 and 1900. The West was changed forever. The settlers transformed the landscape—the open range disappeared, along with its herds of buffalo—and thrust the American Indians into crisis. The Indian Appropriation Act of 1871 nullified all treaties with the American Indians and forced native peoples to fight for their ancestral lands. Nothing, however, could stop the relentless migration of settlers.

*The Connecticut Settlers Entering the Western Reserve* (19th century) by Howard Pyle. Oil on canvas.

# The Rise of Realism
## The Civil War to 1914

*by* Gary Q. Arpin

**PREVIEW**

## Think About ...

Americans have fought only one civil war, but that tragedy cut deep into the heart of the nation. Reactions to the grim casualties of the war, as well as to the rapid urban expansion, inspired writers and artists to abandon their Romantic ideals. A new movement was created, called realism.

As you read about this time period, look for answers to these questions:

- How and when did American writers and poets respond to the Civil War?
- What are the basic characteristics of realism?
- What did the naturalist writers believe?

**SKILLS FOCUS**

Collection introduction (pages 448–461) covers **Literary Skills** Evaluate the philosophical, political, religious, ethical, and social influences of a historical period.

On the evening of April 12, 1861, Walt Whitman attended the opera at the Academy of Music in Manhattan. After the opera he was walking down Broadway toward Brooklyn when, as he later wrote, "I heard in the distance the loud cries of the newsboys, who came presently tearing and yelling up the street, rushing from side to side even more furiously than usual. I bought an extra and crossed to the Metropolitan Hotel . . . where the great lamps were still brightly blazing, and, with a crowd of others, who gathered impromptu, read the news, which was evidently authentic."

The news that Whitman and the others read so avidly was of the Confederate attack on Fort Sumter, the opening shots of the Civil War. Thus solemnly began, for one of the few American poets or novelists who would witness it firsthand, the greatest cataclysm in U.S. history.

## Slavery Divides the Country

What had brought the country to the point of the Civil War? It had but "a single cause," asserted the historian James Ford Rhodes in 1913, and that cause was slavery. Today historians acknowledge additional causes of the war, such as the economic differences between the South and the North, but slavery lay at the heart of this conflict.

*Evening Gun Fort Sumter* (detail) (1864) by John Gadsby Chapman. Painted in Rome after a sketch made by Chapman's son Conrad Wise Chapman. Oil on board.

From the personal accounts of people held in slavery—such as Frederick Douglass and Harriet A. Jacobs—we learn firsthand about the horrors and injustices of slavery. Increasing numbers of Northerners viewed slaveholding as a monstrous violation of the basic American principle of equality, but Southerners wanted to preserve the institution of slavery. The conflict reached a fever pitch and erupted at Fort Sumter. As soldiers went off to battle, emotions ran high through a divided country.

## A Response to the War: Idealism

In Concord, Massachusetts, home of Ralph Waldo Emerson, Henry David Thoreau, Nathaniel Hawthorne, and many other intellectual leaders of the nation, army volunteers met in 1861 at the bridge that Emerson had immortalized in "Concord Hymn," his famous poem about the beginning of the American Revolution. Emerson had for decades warned that this day would come if slavery were not abolished. Now that the day had arrived, he was filled with patriotic fervor. He watched the Concord volunteers march to Boston, and he visited a navy yard, declaring that "sometimes gunpowder smells good."

Photograph by Mathew Brady.

Cooper-Hewitt National Design Museum, Smithsonian Institution; Gift of Charles Savage Homer, Jr., 1912-12-100.

*Soldier Giving Water to a Wounded Companion* (1864) by Winslow Homer (American, 1836–1910). Charcoal, white chalk, brush and white gouache on green wove paper, mounted on cardboard. 36.5 cm × 49.6 cm (14³⁄₈ × 19¹⁄₂ in.).

Emerson had great respect for the Southern will to fight, however, and he suspected, quite rightly, that the war would not be over in a few months, as some people had predicted. When the Concord volunteers returned a few months later from the First Battle of Bull Run (July 1861), defeated and disillusioned, many of them unwilling to reenlist, Emerson maintained his conviction that the war must be pursued.

## A Reality of the War: Appalling Suffering

Late in 1862, Walt Whitman traveled to Virginia to find his brother George, who had been wounded in battle. After George was nursed back to health, Whitman remained in Washington off and on, working part time and serving as a volunteer hospital visitor, comforting the wounded and writing to their loved ones. The condition of the wounded was appalling. Many of the injured had to remain on the battlefield for two or three days until the camp hospitals had room for them. Antiseptics were primitive, as were operating-room techniques. A major wound meant amputation or even death.

Whitman estimated that in three years as a camp hospital volunteer, he visited tens of thousands of wounded men. "I am the man," he had written in "Song of Myself," "I suffer'd, I was there," and now he *was* there, in the real heart of America. In his poems he had presented a panoramic vision of America; now America passed

> *Future years will never know the seething hell and the black infernal background of the countless minor scenes and interiors . . . and it is best they should not— the real war will never get in the books.*
>
> —Walt Whitman

**The Rise of Realism: The Civil War to 1914**

*Young Soldier: Separate Study of a Soldier Giving Water to a Wounded Companion* (1861) by Winslow Homer. Oil, gouache, and black crayon on canvas (36 cm × 17.5 cm).

Cooper-Hewitt, National Design Museum, Smithsonian Institution. Gift of Charles Savage Homer, Jr., 1912-12-110.

through the hospital tents in the form of wounded men from every state in the Union and the Confederacy. Nevertheless, out of the horror that he viewed, Whitman was able to derive an optimistic vision of the American character, of "the actual soldier of 1862–65 . . . with all his ways, his incredible dauntlessness, habits, practices, tastes, language, his fierce friendship, his appetite, rankness, his superb strength—and a hundred unnamed lights and shades."

## A Result of the War: Disillusionment

The war that strengthened Whitman's optimism served at the same time to justify Herman Melville's pessimism. Melville's poems about the war, collected in *Battle-Pieces and Aspects of the War* (1866), were often dark and foreboding. Of the elation following the firing on Fort Sumter, Melville wrote:

> O, the rising of the People
>     Came with the springing of the grass,
> They rebounded from dejection
>     After Easter came to pass.
> And the young were all elation
>     Hearing Sumter's cannon roar. . . .
> But the elders with foreboding
>     Mourned the days forever o'er,
> And recalled the forest proverb,
>     The Iroquois' old saw:
> *Grief to every graybeard*
>     *When young Indians lead the war.*

Melville was fascinated by the war, but he never wrote a novel about it. The poems in *Battle-Pieces,* based on newspaper accounts of the battles as well as visits to battlefields, record the heroism and futility of the fighting on both sides and demonstrate respect for Southern soldiers as well as Northern troops. In some of Melville's best poems, though, there is a sense of human nature being stripped bare, revealing not the heroism and strength that Whitman found, but rather humanity's basic evil.

Civil War ambulance.

## Eyes of an Era

Television's close-up coverage of modern warfare has made the thick of battle a common sight on the nightly news, but during the American Civil War, photographs were the closest thing to newscasts. By the latter part of the 1800s, technical advances began to allow for truly mobile photographers. As a result, the Civil War became the first war to be fully documented in pictures. Cameras went on the march, up in observation balloons, and to sea on battleships.

Cameras of the time could not capture motion; charging troops and thrusting bayonets came out as hazy blurs. However, cameras richly recorded the preparations and the aftermath of war. After battles, photographers roamed the killing fields, shooting pictures while wearing handkerchiefs across their faces to block the stench of death. They captured the war's still lifes—fields and forests filled with dead soldiers; blasted cities and landscapes; and scenes inside prisons, hospitals, and camps.

The most famous of these war photographers was Mathew Brady (1823?–1896). Brady was among the first photographers to bring portable darkrooms to combat zones. Though Brady helped to inspire Civil War photography, he often employed courageous photographers, such as Alexander Gardner and Timothy O'Sullivan, to take their cameras onto the battlefields.

Gardner came closer than anyone else to capturing an actual battle scene when he set his camera on a ridge overlooking the Battle of Antietam in Maryland in 1862. He recognized that "verbal representations" of the war "may or may not have the merit of accuracy; but photographic presentments of them will be accepted by posterity with an undoubting faith."

Alexander Gardner (seated) and his portable darkroom.

O'Sullivan was one of the most fearless and brilliant of Brady's assistants. When bridge builders whom O'Sullivan was photographing were targeted by enemy sharpshooters, he calmly continued taking pictures while men screamed and fell.

Photographers struggled with heavy equipment, stray bullets, rain, mud, insects, foliage, wandering livestock, and frozen hands. Processing photographs in the field was complicated and messy: Many pictures were ruined when they were washed in streams, where debris could stick to the gummy image.

Sadly, most Civil War photographers and their work fell into obscurity after the war. Hundreds of glass negatives were sold for use as greenhouse windows, and decades later many of the glass plates ended up in gas masks worn by soldiers in World War 1.

*The Harriet Tubman Series* (1939–1940), No. 9, by Jacob Lawrence. Hardboard (12″ × 17⅞″).

*Harriet Tubman dreamt of freedom ("Arise! Flee for your life!") and in the visions of the night she saw the horsemen coming. Beckoning hands were ever motioning her to come, and she seemed to see a line from the land of slavery to the land of freedom.*

## The War in Literature

Although many works of historical interest—soldiers' letters and diaries, as well as journalistic writings—came out of the war, works of literary significance were rare, prompting the question, Why did an event of such magnitude result in such a scanty literary output?

Modern readers think that one byproduct of a war is literary accounts, largely in the form of novels and poems by participants in the war. Modern writers like Ernest Hemingway went to war intending to return with the material for novels. This was not the case with the Civil War. Few major American writers saw the Civil War first-hand. Emerson was in Concord during most of the war, "knitting socks and mittens for soldiers," as he wrote to his son, and "writing patriotic lectures." Thoreau, who had been a fervent abolitionist, died in 1862, and Hawthorne died two years later. Emily Dickinson remained in Amherst, Massachusetts, and the country's grief over the war seems not to have informed her poetry. Of the younger generation of writers, William Dean Howells, Henry James, and Henry Adams were abroad.

Perhaps most important, the traditional literary forms of the time were inadequate to express the horrifying details of the Civil War. The literary form most appropriate for handling such strong material—the **realistic novel**—had not yet been fully developed in the United States. Thus, the great novel of the war, *The Red Badge of Courage,* had to wait to be written by a man who was not born until six years after the war had ended: Stephen Crane.

## The Rise of Realism

One of the most enduring subjects of prose fiction has been the exploits of larger-than-life heroes. Born of the chivalric romance, the **Romantic novel** presents readers with lives lived idealistically—beyond the level of everyday life. The heroes and heroines of the novels of James Fenimore Cooper, for example, engage in romantic adventures filled with courageous acts, daring chases, and exciting escapes.

In America the great fiction writers of the mid–nineteenth century, Edgar Allan Poe, Nathaniel Hawthorne, and Herman Melville, shared an aversion to simple realism. These writers used romance

Woman freed from slavery, learning to read.
Leib Image Archives, York, Pennsylvania.

*With malice toward none; with charity for all; with firmness in the right, as God gives us to see the right, let us strive on to finish the work we are in; to bind up the nation's wounds; to care for him who shall have borne the battle, and for his widow, and his orphan—to do all which may achieve and cherish a just and lasting peace, among ourselves, and with all nations.*

—President Abraham Lincoln, Second Inaugural Address, March 4, 1865

Children in Mullen's Alley, off Cherry Street, New York City (c. 1888). Photograph by Jacob Riis.

not simply to entertain readers but to reveal truths that would be hidden in a realistic story that limited itself to what actually could happen.

After the Civil War, however, a new generation of writers came of age. They were known as realists, writers who aimed at a "very minute fidelity" to the common course of ordinary life. Their subjects were drawn from the slums of the rapidly growing cities, from the factories that were rapidly replacing farmlands, and from the lives of far-from-idealized characters—poor factory workers, corrupt politicians, and even prostitutes.

## Realism Takes Root in Europe

Realism was well entrenched in Europe by the time it began to flower in the United States. It developed in the work of such writers as Daniel Defoe, George Eliot, Anthony Trollope, Honoré de Balzac, Stendhal, Gustave Flaubert, and Leo Tolstoy. These writers tried to represent faithfully the environment and the manners of everyday life: the way ordinary people lived and dressed and the things they thought and felt and talked about.

Realism was not simply concerned with recording wallpaper patterns, hairstyles, or the subjects of conversations. It sought also to explain *why* ordinary people behave the way they do. Realistic novelists often relied on the emerging sciences of human and animal behavior—biology, psychology, and sociology—as well as on their own insights and observations.

## American Regionalism: Brush Strokes of Local Color

In America, realism had its roots in **regionalism,** literature that emphasizes a specific geographic setting and that makes use of the speech and manners of the people who live in that region. Sarah Orne Jewett, Kate Chopin, Harriet Beecher Stowe, Bret Harte, and Charles W. Chesnutt are noted early regionalists who recorded the peculiarities of customs, speech, and temperament in the different parts of a rapidly expanding nation. (Regionalism flourished again in the 1920s and 1930s, especially in the South, and is still an important aspect of American literature.)

While regional writers strove to be realistic in their depiction of speech patterns and manners, they were often unrealistic—even sentimental—in their depiction of character and social environment. For example, the Southern writer Thomas Nelson Page, who wrote popular post–Civil War novels about the South before the war, stressed the romantic "moonlight and magnolia" environment

> ### Elements of Realism
>
> - Rejection of the idealized, larger-than-life hero of Romantic literature
> - Detailed depiction of ordinary characters and realistic events
> - Emphasis on characters from cities and lower classes
> - Avoidance of the exotic, sensational, and overly dramatic
> - Use of everyday speech patterns to reveal class distinctions
> - Focus on the ethical struggles and social issues of real-life situations

> *The only reason for the existence of a novel is that it does attempt to represent life.*
>
> —Henry James

*Coming and Going of the Pony Express* (1900) by Frederic Remington.
Oil on canvas (26″ × 39″).

> *All modern American literature comes from one book by Mark Twain called Huckleberry Finn.*
>
> —Ernest Hemingway

at the expense of the realities of a social world that relied on slavery. Realism as a literary movement in the United States went far beyond regionalism in its concern for accuracy in portraying social conditions and human motivation.

Mark Twain is the best-known example of a regional writer whose realism far surpassed local bounds. Although he first established his reputation as a regional humorist, Twain evolved into a writer whose comic view of society became increasingly satiric. His best novel, *Adventures of Huckleberry Finn* (1884), describes the moral growth of a comic character in an environment that is at the same time physically beautiful and morally repugnant. *Huckleberry Finn* combines a biting picture of some of the injustices inherent in pre–Civil War life with a lyrical portrait of the American landscape.

# Realism and Naturalism: A Lens on Everyday Life

## ■ "Smiling Realism"

The most active proponent of realism in American fiction was William Dean Howells, editor of the influential magazine *The Atlantic Monthly*. In both his fiction and his critical writings, Howells insisted that realism should deal with the lives of ordinary people, be faithful to the development of character even at the expense of action, and discuss the social questions perplexing Americans. Howells's "smiling realism" portrayed an America where people may act foolishly but where their good qualities eventually win out.

Other realistic novelists viewed life as a much rougher clash of contrary forces. The Californian Frank Norris, for example, agreed with Howells that the proper subject for fiction was the ordinary person, but he found Howells's fiction too strait-laced and narrow. It was, Norris said, "as respectable as a church and proper as a deacon." Norris was an earthier writer, interested in the impact of large social forces on individuals. His best-known novel, *The Octopus* (1901), is about the struggles between wheat farmers and the railroad monopoly in California. Norris was not the first to use the novel to examine social institutions with the aim of reforming them; Harriet Beecher Stowe's novel *Uncle Tom's Cabin* (1852) had been published

> ### Elements of Naturalism
>
> - Attempt to analyze human behavior objectively, as a scientist would
> - Belief that human behavior is determined by heredity and environment
> - Sense that human beings cannot control their own destinies
> - Sense of life as a losing battle against an uncaring universe

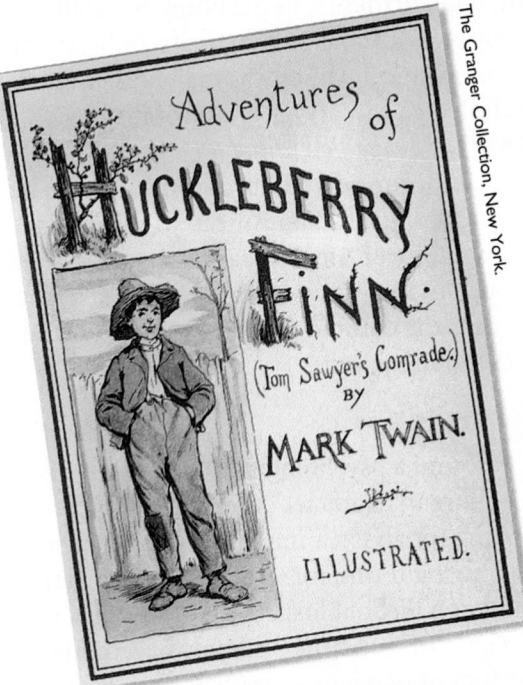

The Granger Collection, New York.

Original edition of Mark Twain's *Adventures of Huckleberry Finn* (1885).

Advertisement for Harriet Beecher Stowe's antislavery novel *Uncle Tom's Cabin* (1852).

### Political Highlights

- Civil War (1861–1865) results in the loss of more than 600,000 men and a reunited but bitter republic.

- Slavery, a leading cause of the Civil War, is abolished in 1865.

- Abraham Lincoln is assassinated in Ford's Theatre, Washington, D.C., on April 14, 1865.

### Philosophical Views

- Romanticism is overtaken by more realistic attitudes toward art and life.

- Advances in sociology and psychology lead to growing interest in analyzing everyday life and the behavior of society as a whole.

### Social Influences

- Reformers and muckraking journalists expose abuses in industries such as mining and meatpacking.

- Large numbers of immigrants from Europe settle in American cities.

- In 1908, Henry Ford introduces the Model T, an invention that will drastically change the landscape and reshape the American way of life.

before the Civil War and, according to Lincoln (and many historians), played a part in bringing about the war. But *Uncle Tom's Cabin* was more melodrama than realistic fiction.

### ■ Grim Naturalism

Norris is generally considered a **naturalist.** Following the lead of the French novelist Émile Zola, naturalists relied heavily on the emerging scientific disciplines of psychology and sociology. In their fiction, the naturalists attempted to dissect human behavior with as much objectivity as a scientist would use. For naturalists, human behavior was determined by forces beyond the individual's power, especially by biology and environment. The naturalists tended to look at human life as a grim losing battle. Their characters usually have few choices. In the eyes of some naturalist writers, human beings are totally subject to the natural laws of the universe; like animals, they live crudely, by instinct, unable to control their own destinies.

## Psychological Realism: Inside the Human Mind

### ■ Exploring Motivation

On the other hand, the New York–born Henry James, considered America's greatest writer of the psychological novel, concentrated principally on fine distinctions in character motivation. James was a realist, but no realist could be further from the blunt, naturalistic view that people were driven by animal-like instincts. In his finely tuned studies of human motivation, James was mainly interested in complex social and psychological situations. Many of his novels, including *Daisy Miller* (1879) and *The Portrait of a Lady* (1881), take place in Europe, because James considered European society to be both more complex and more sinister than American society. He frequently contrasts innocent, eager Americans with sophisticated, more manipulative Europeans. In a typical James novel a straightforward American confronts the complexities of European society and either defeats or is defeated by them.

### ■ Examining Characters in Crisis

Stephen Crane was as profound a psychologist as James, but his principal interest was the human character at moments of stress. For James the proper setting for an examination of human behavior under pressure was the drawing room; for Crane it was the battlefield, the streets of a slum, or a lifeboat lost at sea. Although Crane is sometimes referred to as a naturalist, he is probably best thought of as an **ironist;** he was the first of many modern American writers— later including Ernest Hemingway and Kurt Vonnegut, Jr.—to juxtapose human illusions with the indifference of the universe. Of all the nineteenth-century realists, only Crane could describe a stabbing death (in his story "The Blue Hotel") in this coolly cynical manner: "[The blade] shot forward, and a human body, this citadel of virtue, wisdom, power, was pierced as easily as if it had been a melon." It would take this sensibility to get the "real war" in the books at last.

## Endings and Beginnings

The period from around the turn of the century up to 1914 saw the continuation of many nineteenth-century trends and, at the same time, the early flowerings of modernism. Some writers worked to sustain earlier visions of America, such as Edwin Arlington Robinson, with his classic New England characters. Others, like Willa Cather, reminded readers of the heroic struggle to settle the vanishing frontier. Still, the currents of realism and naturalism evoked by the Civil War continued to dominate American literature.

In the period between the end of the Civil War and the outbreak of World War I in 1914, the American nation was transformed from an isolated, rural nation to an industrialized world power. Even these changes would soon be dwarfed, however. World War I would rock the world and shake people's faith in humanity. Idealism would turn to cynicism, and thinkers and writers called modernists would seek new literary forms for exploring the social and spiritual upheavals wrought once again by war.

> *[Crane's] importance lies not only in those few works of his which completely come off, like "The Open Boat," but in his constantly seeking the primitive facts, the forbidden places, the dangerous people.*
>
> —Alfred Kazin

**REVIEW**

# Talk About ...

Turn back to the Think About questions at the start of this introduction to the period (page 448), and discuss your views.

# Write About ...

## Contrasting Literary Periods

**The Romantics and the realists.** The shift from Romanticism to realism brought about new literary forms, new styles, and, most important, new attitudes in writers and readers. Write a brief essay in which you compare and contrast the basic attitudes and beliefs of the Romantic writers with those of the realist writers. Consider, for example, the writers' subjects, characters, and attitudes toward human nature and their views on the purpose of literature.

# Introduction **Comparing Points** *of* **View**

## Slavery

You will be reading the five selections listed above in this Comparing Points of View feature on slavery. In the top corner of each page of this feature, you'll find three stars. Smaller versions of the stars appear next to the questions on pages 470 and 477 that focus on this political issue. At the end of the feature (page 487), you'll compare the various points of view on slavery expressed in the selections.

### Examining the Issue: Slavery

The fact that slavery could flourish in a nation so fervently dedicated to the ideals of equality and freedom is perhaps the greatest paradox, or seeming contradiction, in our nation's history. It would take the upheaval of civil war to confront this American paradox and force a change.

Slavery is an issue that makes clear the close relationship between the personal and the political. The laws governing the slave system were not mere technicalities. They defined people, determined the course of their lives, and controlled all their relationships. As you read the selections in this section, note how, for the writers, the political is personal.

### Reading Skills

### Comparing Points of View Across Texts

The readings in this section describe several ways by which human beings opposed the horrors of slavery. In order to compare these points of view, make a chart like the one below. For each reading, note how slavery is opposed, and then describe the writer's point of view.

**SKILLS FOCUS**

Pages 462–487 cover
**Literary Skills**
Analyze points of view on a topic.

**Reading Skills**
Compare points of view across texts.

| Selection | Opposition to Slavery | Point of View |
|---|---|---|
| *Narrative of the Life of Frederick Douglass* | Endures beating; complains to "master"; fights Covey | Defiant resistance revives dignity and hope for freedom. |

# Frederick Douglass
## (1817?–1895)

Frederick Douglass was born into slavery in Talbot County, on the Eastern Shore of Maryland, and was separated from his mother soon after his birth. "The practice of separating children from their mothers," wrote Douglass years later, "and hiring the latter out at distances too great to admit of their meeting, except at long intervals, is a marked feature of the cruelty and barbarity of the slave system. But it is in harmony with the grand aim of slavery, which, always and everywhere, is to reduce man to a level with the brute. It is a successful method of obliterating from the mind and heart of the slave all just ideas of the sacredness of *the family*."

Since birth records were not kept for children born into slavery, Douglass was never sure of his exact age. "Genealogical trees do not flourish among slaves," he was to remark ironically later. Although Douglass received no formal education, he did teach himself to read with the help, at first, of members of the household he served. Later these same people became furious when they saw Douglass reading a book or a newspaper; education, they decided, was incompatible with being enslaved.

When Douglass was about twenty-one, he satisfied his hunger for freedom by escaping to Massachusetts, where he married and soon started to make public speeches in support of the abolitionist cause. He changed his last name from Bailey to Douglass, after the hero of the Romantic novel *The Lady of the Lake* by Sir Walter Scott.

In 1845, Douglass went to England, largely because of the danger he faced as a fugitive, especially after the publication that same year of his autobiography *Narrative of the Life of Frederick Douglass, an American Slave.* In England he mobilized antislavery sentiment and became independent when British friends collected around seven hundred dollars to purchase his freedom.

When he returned to the United States, in 1847, Douglass founded a newspaper, the *North Star.* (The name was chosen because escapees used this star as a guide north.) In his newspaper, Douglass championed the abolition of slavery. In 1855, he published a revised version of his life story, titled *My Bondage and My Freedom.* Escape narratives, like earlier captivity stories (page 37), were enormously popular, and Douglass's were widely read and very influential in the abolitionist cause.

When the Civil War began, Douglass worked ardently for the Underground Railroad, the secret network of abolitionists that helped many people held in slavery escape to the North. He also energetically helped to recruit black soldiers for the Union armies.

Continuing to write and lecture after the war, Douglass argued that the surest way to rehabilitate his tragically scarred people was through education. In 1881, he published yet another version of his autobiography, titled *The Life and Times of Frederick Douglass.* Today Douglass is revered for the courage with which he insistently proclaimed his profoundly humane values, and he is admired for the quiet eloquence of his writing style.

# Before You Read

## *from* Narrative of the Life of Frederick Douglass

### Points *of* View
#### Quickwrite ✏️

While he was still enslaved, Frederick Douglass fought to assert his human rights and defend his dignity against a brutal social institution. His courageous action became a turning point in his life. Think of other heroic men and women who have fought against slavery, and jot down the qualities or attitudes you admire in them.

### Literary Focus
#### Metaphor

Writers and poets use **metaphors** to make creative comparisons. Near the end of the selection, Douglass uses a metaphor that compares his triumph over Mr. Covey to resurrection from the dead: "It was a glorious resurrection, from the tomb of slavery, to the heaven of freedom." The metaphor adds a spiritual dimension to the story by connecting a physical victory to a victory of the soul.

**Literary Skills**
Analyze points of view on a topic. Understand metaphor.

**Reading Skills**
Analyze a writer's purpose.

**INTERNET**

Vocabulary Practice
•
More About Frederick Douglass
•
Keyword: LE7 11-4

---

> A **metaphor** is a figure of speech that makes a comparison between two unlike things without the use of a specific word of comparison, such as *like, as, than,* or *resembles.*
>
> *For more on Metaphor, see the Handbook of Literary and Historical Terms.*

### Reading Skills 📖
#### Analyzing a Writer's Purpose

In many cases, writers combine several modes of expression—such as description, narration, exposition, and persuasion—in order to accomplish their purpose. Douglass's writing provides a good example. He does not rely on *persuasion* to prove that slavery is dehumanizing. Instead, he *describes* the life of a slave and *narrates* his experiences in order to persuade readers to take action against slavery.

### Background

In the following selection, Douglass provides a graphic account of a critical incident that occurred when he was sixteen years old. Earlier in his narrative he explains to his readers "how a man was made a slave"; now he sets out to explain "how a slave was made a man." At the time, Douglass was "owned" by a man named Thomas, who had rented Douglass's services out for a year to a man named Covey.

---

### Vocabulary Development

**intimated** (in′tə·māt′id) *v.*: stated indirectly; hinted.

**comply** (kəm·plī′) *v.*: obey; agree to a request.

**interpose** (in′tər·pōz′) *v.*: put forth in order to interfere.

**afforded** (ə·fôrd′id) *v.*: gave; provided.

**solemnity** (sə·lem′nə·tē) *n.*: seriousness.

**render** (ren′dər) *v.*: make.

**singular** (siŋ′gyə·lər) *adj.*: remarkable.

**attributed** (ə·trib′yo͞ot·id) *v.*: thought of as resulting from.

**expiring** (ek·spīr′iŋ) *v.* used as *adj.*: dying.

# *from* Narrative of the Life of Frederick Douglass

**Frederick Douglass**

## The Battle with Mr. Covey

I have already intimated that my condition was much worse, during the first six months of my stay at Mr. Covey's, than in the last six. The circumstances leading to the change in Mr. Covey's course toward me form an epoch[1] in my humble history. You have seen how a man was made a slave; you shall see how a slave was made a man. On one of the hottest days of the month of August, 1833, Bill Smith, William Hughes, a slave named Eli, and myself, were engaged in fanning wheat.[2] Hughes was clearing the fanned wheat from before the fan, Eli was turning, Smith was feeding, and I was carrying wheat to the fan. The work was simple, requiring strength rather than intellect; yet, to one entirely unused to such work, it came very hard.

About three o'clock of that day, I broke down; my strength failed me; I was seized with a violent aching of the head, attended with extreme dizziness; I trembled in every limb. Finding what was coming, I nerved myself up, feeling it would never do to stop work. I stood as long as I could stagger to the hopper with grain. When I could stand no longer, I fell, and felt as if held down by an immense weight. The fan of course stopped; everyone had his own work to do; and no one could do the work of the other, and have his own go on at the same time.

Mr. Covey was at the house, about one hundred yards from the treading yard where we were fanning. On hearing the fan stop, he left immediately, and came to the spot where we were. He hastily inquired what the matter was. Bill answered that I was sick, and there was no one to bring wheat to the fan. I had by this time crawled away under the side of the post-and-rail fence by which the yard was enclosed, hoping to find relief by getting out of the sun. He then asked where I was. He was told by one of the hands.

He came to the spot, and, after looking at me awhile, asked me what was the matter. I told him as well as I could, for I scarce had strength to speak. He then gave me a savage kick in the side, and told me to get up. I tried to do so, but fell back in the attempt. He gave me another kick, and again told me to rise. I again tried, and succeeded in gaining my feet; but, stooping to get the tub with which I was feeding the fan, I again staggered and fell. While down in this situation, Mr. Covey took up the hickory slat with which Hughes had been striking off the half-bushel measure, and with it gave me a heavy blow upon the head, making a large wound, and the blood ran freely; and with this again told me to get up. I made no effort to comply, having now made up my mind to let him do his worst. In a short time after receiving this blow, my head grew better. Mr. Covey had now left me to my fate.

At this moment I resolved, for the first time, to go to my master, enter a complaint, and ask his protection. In order to [do] this, I must that afternoon walk seven miles; and this, under the circumstances, was truly a severe undertaking. I was exceedingly feeble; made so as much by the kicks and blows which I received, as by the severe fit of sickness to which I had been subjected. I, however, watched my chance, while Covey was looking in an opposite direction, and started for St. Michael's. I succeeded in

---

1. **epoch** (ep′ək) *n.:* noteworthy period of time.
2. **fanning wheat:** separating out usable grain.

*The Life of Frederick Douglass* (1938–1939), No. 10, by Jacob Lawrence. "The master of Douglass, seeing he was of a rebellious nature, sent him to a Mr. Covey, a man who had built up a reputation as a 'slave breaker.' A second attempt by Covey to flog Douglass was unsuccessful. This was one of the most important incidents in the life of Frederick Douglass: He was never again attacked by Covey. His philosophy: A slave easily flogged is flogged oftener; a slave who resists flogging is flogged less." (17⅞″ × 12″).

getting a considerable distance on my way to the woods, when Covey discovered me, and called after me to come back, threatening what he would do if I did not come. I disregarded both his calls and his threats, and made my way to the woods as fast as my feeble state would allow; and thinking I might be overhauled by him if I kept the road, I walked through the woods, keeping far enough from the road to avoid detection, and near enough to prevent losing my way.

I had not gone far before my little strength again failed me. I could go no farther. I fell down, and lay for a considerable time. The blood was yet oozing from the wound on my head. For a time I thought I should bleed to death; and think now that I should have done so, but that the blood so matted my hair as to stop the wound. After lying there about three quarters of an hour, I nerved myself up again, and started on my way, through bogs and briers, barefooted and bareheaded, tearing my feet sometimes at nearly every step; and after a journey of about seven miles, occupying some five hours to perform it, I arrived at master's store. I then presented an appearance enough to affect any but a heart of iron. From the crown of my head to my feet, I was covered with blood. My hair was all clotted with dust and blood; my shirt was stiff with blood. My legs and feet were torn in sundry places with briers and thorns, and were also covered with blood. I suppose I looked like a man who had escaped a den of wild beasts, and barely escaped them.

In this state I appeared before my master, humbly entreating him to interpose his authority for my protection. I told him all the circumstances as well as I could, and it seemed, as I spoke, at times to affect him. He would then walk the floor, and seek to justify Covey by saying he expected I deserved it. He asked me what I wanted. I told him, to let me get a new home; that as sure as I lived with Mr. Covey again, I should live with but to die with him; that Covey would surely kill me; he was in a fair way for it.

Master Thomas ridiculed the idea that there was any danger of Mr. Covey's killing me, and said that he knew Mr. Covey; that he was a good man, and that he could not think of taking me from him; that, should he do so, he would lose the whole year's wages; that I belonged to Mr. Covey for one year, and that I must go back to him, come what might; and that I must not trouble him with any more stories, or that he would himself *get hold of me*. After threatening me thus, he gave me a very large dose of salts, telling me that I might remain in St. Michael's that night (it being quite late), but that I must be off back to Mr. Covey's early in the morning; and that if I did not, he would *get hold of me*, which meant that he would whip me.

I remained all night, and, according to his orders, I started off to Covey's in the morning (Saturday morning), wearied in body and broken in spirit. I got no supper that night, or breakfast that morning. I reached Covey's about nine o'clock; and just as I was getting over the fence that divided Mrs. Kemp's fields from ours, out ran Covey with his cowskin, to give me another whipping. Before he could reach me, I succeeded in getting to the cornfield; and as the corn was very high, it afforded me the means of hiding. He seemed very angry, and searched for me a long time. My behavior was altogether unaccountable. He finally gave up the chase, thinking, I suppose, that I must come home for something to eat; he would give himself no further trouble in looking for me. I spent that day mostly in the woods, having the alternative before me—to go home and be whipped to death, or stay in the woods and be starved to death.

That night, I fell in with Sandy Jenkins, a slave with whom I was somewhat acquainted. Sandy had a free wife who lived about four miles from Mr. Covey's; and it being Saturday,

**Vocabulary**

**interpose** (in′tər·pōz′) v.: put forth in order to interfere.
**afforded** (ə·fôrd′id) v.: gave; provided.

he was on his way to see her. I told him my circumstances, and he very kindly invited me to go home with him. I went home with him, and talked this whole matter over, and got his advice as to what course it was best for me to pursue. I found Sandy an old advisor.[3] He told me, with great <u>solemnity</u>, I must go back to Covey; but that before I went, I must go with him into another part of the woods, where there was a certain *root,* which, if I would take some of it with me, carrying it *always on my right side,* would <u>render</u> it impossible for Mr. Covey, or any other white man, to whip me. He said he had carried it for years; and since he had done so, he had never received a blow, and never expected to while he carried it. I at first rejected the idea, that the simple carrying of a root in my pocket would have any such effect as he had said, and was not disposed to take it; but Sandy impressed the necessity with much earnestness, telling me it could do no harm, if it did no good. To please him, I at length took the root, and, according to his direction, carried it upon my right side. This was Sunday morning.

I immediately started for home; and upon entering the yard gate, out came Mr. Covey on his way to meeting. He spoke to me very kindly, made me drive the pigs from a lot nearby, and passed on toward the church. Now, this <u>singular</u> conduct of Mr. Covey really made me begin to think that there was something in the *root* which Sandy had given me; and had it been on any other day than Sunday, I could have <u>attributed</u> the conduct to no other cause than the influence of that root; and as it was, I was half inclined to think the *root* to be something more than I at first had taken it to be. All went well till Monday morning. On this morning, the virtue of the *root* was fully tested.

Long before daylight, I was called to go and rub, curry, and feed the horses. I obeyed, and was glad to obey. But while thus engaged, while in the act of throwing down some blades from

---

3. **an old advisor:** someone who can offer good advice.

the loft, Mr. Covey entered the stable with a long rope; and just as I was half out of the loft, he caught hold of my legs, and was about tying me. As soon as I found what he was up to, I gave a sudden spring, and as I did so, he holding to my legs, I was brought sprawling on the stable floor. Mr. Covey seemed now to think he had me, and could do what he pleased; but at this moment—from whence came the spirit I don't know—I resolved to fight; and, suiting my action to the resolution, I seized Covey hard by the throat; and as I did so, I rose. He held on to me, and I to him. My resistance was so entirely unexpected, that Covey seemed taken all aback. He trembled like a leaf. This gave me assurance, and I held him uneasy, causing the blood to run where I touched him with the ends of my fingers. Mr. Covey soon called out to Hughes for help. Hughes came, and, while Covey held me, attempted to tie my right hand. While he was in the act of doing so, I watched my chance, and gave him a heavy kick close under the ribs. This kick fairly sickened Hughes, so that he left me in the hands of Mr. Covey.

This kick had the effect of not only weakening Hughes, but Covey also. When he saw Hughes bending over with pain, his courage quailed.[4] He asked me if I meant to persist in my resistance. I told him I did, come what might; that he had used me like a brute for six months, and that I was determined to be used so no longer. With that, he strove to drag me to a stick that was lying just out of the stable door. He meant to knock me down. But just as he was leaning over to get the stick, I seized him with both hands by his collar, and brought him by a

---

4. **quailed** *v.:* faltered.

**Vocabulary**

**solemnity** (sə·lem′nə·tē) *n.:* seriousness.
**render** (ren′dər) *v.:* make.
**singular** (siŋ′gyə·lər) *adj.:* remarkable.
**attributed** (ə·trib′yo͞ot·id) *v.:* thought of as resulting from.

*The Life of Frederick Douglass* (1938–1939), No. 9, by Jacob Lawrence. "Transferred back to the eastern shore of Maryland, being one of the few Negroes who could read or write, Douglass was approached by James Mitchell, a free Negro, and asked to help teach a Sabbath School. However, their work was stopped by a mob who threatened them with death if they continued their class—1833." (12″ × 17⅞″).

Hampton University Museum, Hampton, Virginia. © 2005 The Jacob and Gwendolyn Lawrence Foundation, Seattle/Artists Rights Society (ARS), New York.

sudden snatch to the ground. By this time, Bill came. Covey called upon him for assistance. Bill wanted to know what he could do. Covey said, "Take hold of him, take hold of him!" Bill said his master hired him out to work, and not to help to whip me; so he left Covey and myself to fight our own battle out. We were at it for nearly two hours. Covey at length let me go, puffing and blowing at a great rate, saying that if I had not resisted, he would not have whipped me half so much. The truth was, that he had not whipped me at all. I considered him as getting entirely the worst end of the bargain; for he had drawn no blood from me, but I had from him. The whole six months afterward, that I spent with Mr. Covey, he never laid the weight of his finger upon me in anger. He would occasionally say, he didn't want to get hold of me again. "No," thought I, "you need not; for you will come off worse than you did before."

This battle with Mr. Covey was the turning point in my career as a slave. It rekindled the few expiring embers of freedom, and revived within me a sense of my own manhood. It recalled the departed self-confidence, and inspired me again with a determination to be free. The gratification afforded by the triumph was a full compensation for whatever else might follow, even death itself. He only can understand the deep satisfaction which I experienced, who has himself repelled by force the bloody arm of slavery. I felt as I never felt before. It was a glorious resurrection,[5] from the tomb of slavery, to the heaven of freedom. My long-crushed spirit rose, cowardice departed, bold defiance took its place; and I now resolved that, however long I might remain a slave in form, the day had passed forever when I could be a slave in fact. ■

---

**5. resurrection** *n.*: coming back to life.

**Vocabulary**
**expiring** (ek·spīr′iŋ) *v.* used as *adj.*: dying.

# Response and Analysis

## Reading Check

1. What action did Douglass take after Covey struck him? What did Thomas order Douglass to do?

2. Explain how Sandy Jenkins helped Douglass.

## Thinking Critically

**SKILLS FOCUS**

3. The root Douglass carried was thought to have supernatural powers. What made him think the root was magical? What did he discover was more powerful than the root?

4. Based on this account, how would you **characterize** the young Frederick Douglass? Did he possess any of the qualities or attributes you noted in the Quickwrite? Explain. ✏️

5. Explain the **metaphor** implied in this line: "It [the battle with Covey] rekindled the few expiring embers of freedom." How is the metaphor related to the idea of rebirth?

6. At the end of the selection, Douglass distinguishes between being "a slave in form" and "a slave in fact." How does this distinction support the **theme** of this selection?

7. Think about Douglass's **purpose** in writing this narrative. Consider Douglass's **style,** including his objectivity and restraint in describing painful incidents. How does Douglass win over an audience that might be uneasy at the idea of a black man's fighting a white man? 📖

## Literary Criticism

8. **Political approach.** In every period of history, certain conditions and events shape the character of people who live during that time. How was Douglass influenced by slavery, and in what ways

does his story influence the institution of slavery?

## WRITING

### Douglass Writes Back

American literature abounds with writers who have championed principles of freedom—such as Jefferson, Paine, Emerson, and Thoreau. Write a **letter** in which Douglass responds to one of these writers. Have Douglass express his views on slavery and then comment on the author's writings and beliefs.

### Vocabulary Development
#### Context Clues

| intimated | afforded | singular |
| comply | solemnity | attributed |
| interpose | render | expiring |

Look back at the selection now, and see if there are any clues in the **context** (the surrounding sentences) that would help you figure out the meaning of each underlined Vocabulary word. Record your findings in a chart like this one:

> curry

⬇

> **Meaning:** comb and groom

⬇

> **Clues:** "I was called to go and rub, curry, and feed the horses." Curry must be something done to a horse.

⬇

> **Possible meaning from context:** He is rubbing and feeding the horses; perhaps he is washing and combing them as well.

---

go.
hrw
.com

**INTERNET**

Projects and Activities

Keyword: LE7 11-4

# Harriet A. Jacobs
## (1813?–1897)

**S**lave, fugitive, abolitionist, author, and mother—Harriet A. Jacobs led an extraordinary life. Born into slavery in Edenton, North Carolina, Jacobs was orphaned when she was only six years old. She was then taken into the home of her first mistress and trained as a house servant. There Jacobs learned how to read and write—vital skills usually forbidden to slaves. When her mistress died, Jacobs was "willed" to her mistress's young niece and sent to live at the home of Dr. James Norcom.

As a teenager, Jacobs was subjected to repeated harassment by her second owner, Dr. Norcom. Furious at her refusals of his advances, he sent her away to do hard labor as a plantation slave and then threatened to do the same to her two young children. Luckily Jacobs escaped from the plantation and found shelter with sympathetic relatives and friends, both black and white.

In her grandmother's house in Edenton, she found the safest place of all, a tiny crawl space above a storeroom. Jacobs hid there for seven years—reading (mainly the Bible), writing, sewing, and catching treasured glimpses of her children. All she ever wanted, she said, was freedom and a home for her children and herself. In 1842, Jacobs escaped to New York City, where she found work as a nursemaid and was eventually reunited with her children. She spent the next ten years as a fugitive, but in 1852, she finally gained her freedom.

Jacobs began writing the story of her life in 1853 and published it herself in 1861, using the pen name Linda Brent. *Incidents in the Life of a Slave Girl, Written by Herself* is an emotionally charged personal account and a fierce

indictment of the slave system. Jacobs wrote on the title page:

**❝** Northerners know nothing at all about Slavery. They think it is perpetual bondage only. They have no conception of the depth of *degradation* involved in that word, *Slavery;* if they had, they would never cease their efforts until so horrible a system was overthrown. **❞**

After the publication of her book, Jacobs became active in the abolitionist movement. During the Civil War she worked tirelessly to relieve the poverty and suffering of other former slaves. Jacobs distributed clothes and supplies, raised money, and helped to establish schools and orphanages in Philadelphia, New York, Washington, D.C., Alexandria, and Savannah.

Although Jacobs's writing at times resembles the popular melodramas of her day, her story nevertheless retains an authentic power. *Incidents in the Life of a Slave Girl*—its raw facts of experience told with skill and honesty—provides modern readers with a chilling first-hand look at the particular plight of someone who was both a woman and a slave.

# Before You Read

## *from* Incidents in the Life of a Slave Girl

### Points *of* View

The most obvious influence in Harriet Jacobs's life was slavery. It established her identity, ruled her daily existence, controlled her family life, and dominated her ideas and emotions. Jacobs was not only a slave, though; she was also a woman and a mother. Her autobiography brings us this additional perspective on the dehumanizing effects of slavery.

### Literary Focus
#### Internal and External Conflict

**Conflict** is central to Jacobs's narrative. She experienced **external conflicts** when she escaped from her furious owner and tried to avoid recapture. In a larger context her life can be seen as one long struggle against the slave system.

Jacobs's **internal conflicts** were just as intense (for example, she pondered whether she dared abandon her children or involve her friends). These internal conflicts also had a direct influence on how her external conflicts were resolved.

### Background

Harriet Jacobs's autobiography is an authentic historical narrative. She used language and dialect that were typical of her time but would be considered offensive by today's readers. Although *Incidents in the Life of a Slave Girl* is nonfiction, Jacobs used made-up names for the characters. The narrator, who says she is writing her autobiography, is called Linda Brent. Dr. James Norcom, the slaveholder who pursued Jacobs for years, is called Dr. or Mr. Flint.

### Vocabulary Development

**malice** (mal′is) *n.:* ill will; desire to harm.

**fervently** (fʉr′vənt·lē) *adv.:* with intense feeling.

**unnerve** (un·nʉrv′) *v.:* cause to lose one's courage.

**provocation** (präv′ə·kā′shən) *n.:* something that stirs up action or feeling.

**distressed** (di·strest′) *adj.:* suffering; troubled.

**cunning** (kun′iŋ) *adj.:* sly or crafty.

**compelled** (kəm·peld′) *v.:* driven; forced.

**impulse** (im′puls′) *n.:* sudden desire or urge.

**SKILLS FOCUS**

**Literary Skills**
Analyze points of view on a topic.
Understand internal and external conflict.

**Conflict** is the struggle between opposing forces or characters in a story. Conflict can be **internal** (a character struggles with conscience, for example) or **external** (a character struggles with another person or with society).

*For more on Conflict, see the Handbook of Literary and Historical Terms.*

go.hrw.com

**INTERNET**

**Vocabulary Practice**

Keyword: LE7 11-4

# *from* Incidents in the Life of a Slave Girl

## Harriet A. Jacobs

### The Flight

**M**r. Flint was hard pushed for house servants, and rather than lose me he had restrained his malice. I did my work faithfully, though not, of course, with a willing mind. They were evidently afraid I should leave them. Mr. Flint wished that I should sleep in the great house instead of the servants' quarters. His wife agreed to the proposition, but said I mustn't bring my bed into the house, because it would scatter feathers on her carpet. I knew when I went there that they would never think of such a thing as furnishing a bed of any kind for me and my little one. I therefore carried my own bed, and now I was forbidden to use it. I did as I was ordered. But now that I was certain my children were to be put in their power, in order to give them a stronger hold on me, I resolved to leave them that night. I remembered the grief this step would bring upon my dear old grandmother; and nothing less than the freedom of my children would have induced me to disregard her advice. I went about my evening work with trembling steps. Mr. Flint twice called from his chamber door to inquire why the house was not locked up. I replied that I had not done my work. "You have had time enough to do it," said he. "Take care how you answer me!"

I shut all the windows, locked all the doors, and went up to the third story, to wait till midnight. How long those hours seemed, and how fervently I prayed that God would not forsake[1] me in this hour of utmost need! I was about to risk everything on the throw of a die; and if I failed, Oh what would become of me and my poor children? They would be made to suffer for my fault.

At half past twelve, I stole softly downstairs. I stopped on the second floor, thinking I heard a noise. I felt my way down into the parlor, and looked out of the window. The night was so intensely dark that I could see nothing. I raised the window very softly and jumped out. Large drops of rain were falling, and the darkness bewildered me. I dropped on my knees, and breathed a short prayer to God for guidance and protection. I groped my way to the road, and rushed toward the town with almost lightning speed. I arrived at my grandmother's house, but dared not see her. She would say, "Linda,[2] you are killing me," and I knew that would unnerve me. I tapped softly at the window of a room occupied by a woman who had lived in the house several years. I knew she was a faithful friend, and could be trusted with my secret. I tapped several times before she heard me. At last she raised the window, and I whispered, "Sally, I have run away. Let me in, quick." She opened the door softly, and said in low tones, "For God's sake, don't. Your grandmother is trying to buy you and de chillern. Mr. Sands was here last week. He tole her he was going away on business, but he wanted her to go ahead about buying you and de chillern, and he would help her all he could. Don't run away, Linda. Your grandmother is all bowed down wid trouble now."

I replied, "Sally, they are going to carry my children to the plantation tomorrow; and they will never sell them to anybody so long as they have me in their power. Now, would you advise me to go back?"

"No, chile, no," answered she. "When dey finds you is gone, dey won't want de plague ob de chillern; but where is you going to hide? Dey knows ebery inch ob dis house."

---

2. **Linda:** Jacobs's made-up name for herself (see Background, page 472).

---

**Vocabulary**

**malice** (mal′is) *n.*: ill will; desire to harm.
**fervently** (fur′vənt·lē) *adv.*: with intense feeling.
**unnerve** (un·nurv′) *v.*: cause to lose one's courage.

---

1. **forsake** *v.*: abandon; give up.

African American
schoolchildren, New Bern,
North Carolina (c. 1862).
(Inset) Advertisement for the
capture of an escaped slave (1835).

$100 REWARD!

RANAWAY

From the undersigned, living on Current
River, about twelve miles above Doniphan,
in Ripley County, Mo., on 2nd of March, 1860, A NE
GRO MAN, about 30 years old, weighs about
160 pounds; high forehead, with a scar on it; had on brown pants and coat
very much worn, and an old black wool hat; shoes size No. 11.

The above reward will be given to any person who may apprehend this
negro, or of the State, and fifty dollars if apprehended in this State outside of Ripley county, or $25 if taken in Ripley county.
APOS TUCKER.

I told her I had a hiding place, and that was all it was best for her to know. I asked her to go into my room as soon as it was light, and take all my clothes out of my trunk, and pack them in hers; for I knew Mr. Flint and the constable[3] would be there early to search my room. I feared the sight of my children would be too much for my full heart; but I could not go out into the uncertain future without one last look. I bent over the bed where lay my little Benny and baby Ellen. Poor little ones! Fatherless and mother-less! Memories of their father came over me. He wanted to be kind to them; but they were not all to him, as they were to my womanly heart. I knelt and prayed for the innocent little sleepers. I kissed them lightly, and turned away.

As I was about to open the street door, Sally laid her hand on my shoulder, and said, "Linda, is you gwine all alone? Let me call your uncle."

"No, Sally," I replied, "I want no one to be brought into trouble on my account."

I went forth into the darkness and rain. I ran on till I came to the house of the friend who was to conceal me.

Early the next morning Mr. Flint was at my grandmother's inquiring for me. She told him she had not seen me, and supposed I was at the plantation. He watched her face narrowly, and said, "Don't you know anything about her running off?" She assured him that she did not. He went on to say, "Last night she ran off without the least provocation. We had treated her very kindly. My wife liked her. She will soon be found and brought back. Are her children with you?" When told that they were, he said, "I am very glad to hear that. If they are here, she cannot be far off. If I find out that any of my niggers have had anything to do with this damned business, I'll give 'em five hundred lashes." As he started to go to his father's, he turned round and added, persuasively, "Let her be brought back, and she shall have her children to live with her."

The tidings[4] made the old doctor rave and storm at a furious rate. It was a busy day for them. My grandmother's house was searched from top to bottom. As my trunk was empty, they concluded I had taken my clothes with me. Before ten o'clock every vessel northward bound was thoroughly examined, and the law against harboring[5] fugitives was read to all on-board. At night a watch was set over the town. Knowing how distressed my grandmother would be, I wanted to send her a message; but it could not be done. Everyone who went in or out of her house was closely watched. The doctor said he would take my children, unless she be-came responsible for them; which of course she willingly did. The next day was spent in search-ing. Before night, the following advertisement was posted at every corner, and in every public place for miles round:

$300 REWARD! Ran away from the sub-scriber,[6] an intelligent, bright mulatto[7] girl, named Linda, 21 years of age. Five feet four inches high. Dark eyes, and black hair inclined to curl; but it can be made straight. Has a de-cayed spot on a front tooth. She can read and write, and in all probability will try to get to the Free States. All persons are forbidden, under penalty of the law, to harbor or employ said slave. $150 will be given to whoever takes her in the state, and $300 if taken out of the state and delivered to me, or lodged in jail.

Dr. Flint

---

3. **constable** *n.:* officer of the law, ranking just below sheriff.

4. **tidings** *n. pl.:* news.
5. **harboring** *v.* used as *n.:* providing protection or shelter.
6. **subscriber** *n.:* literally, the person whose name is "written below"; that is, Dr. Flint.
7. **mulatto** *adj.:* of mixed black and white ancestry.

---

**Vocabulary**

**provocation** (präv′ə‧kā′shən) *n.:* something that stirs up action or feeling.
**distressed** (di‧strest′) *adj.:* suffering; troubled.

*Jacobs (Linda) passed a terrifying week in hiding. Then one night she heard her pursuers nearby. Afraid of capture, she rushed out of her friend's house and concealed herself in a thicket, where she was bitten by a poisonous reptile. Determined not to give up, Jacobs adopted the motto "Give me liberty, or give me death." With the aid of her friend Betty, she found shelter with the sympathetic wife of a local slaveholder. The woman urged Jacobs never to reveal who had helped her, and she hid the fugitive in a small upstairs storeroom.*

## Months of Peril

I went to sleep that night with the feeling that I was for the present the most fortunate slave in town. Morning came and filled my little cell with light. I thanked the heavenly Father for this safe retreat. Opposite my window was a pile of feather beds. On the top of these I could lie perfectly concealed, and command a view of the street through which Dr. Flint passed to his office. Anxious as I was, I felt a gleam of satisfaction when I saw him. Thus far I had outwitted him, and I triumphed over it. Who can blame slaves for being cunning? They are constantly compelled to resort to it. It is the only weapon of the weak and oppressed against the strength of their tyrants.

I was daily hoping to hear that my master had sold my children; for I knew who was on the watch to buy them. But Dr. Flint cared even more for revenge than he did for money. My brother William, and the good aunt who had served in his family twenty years, and my little Benny, and Ellen, who was a little over two years old, were thrust into jail, as a means of compelling my relatives to give some information about me. He swore my grandmother should never see one of them again till I was brought back. They kept these facts from me for several days. When I heard that my little ones were in a loathsome jail, my first impulse was to go to them. I was encountering dangers for the sake of freeing them, and must I be the cause of their death? The thought was agonizing. My benefactress[8] tried to soothe me by telling me that my aunt would take good care of the children while they remained in jail. But it added to my pain to think that the good old aunt, who had always been so kind to her sister's orphan children, should be shut up in prison for no other crime than loving them. I suppose my friends feared a reckless movement on my part, knowing, as they did, that my life was bound up in my children. I received a note from my brother William. It was scarcely legible, and ran thus: "Wherever you are, dear sister, I beg of you not to come here. We are all much better off than you are. If you come, you will ruin us all. They would force you to tell where you had been, or they would kill you. Take the advice of your friends; if not for the sake of me and your children, at least for the sake of those you would ruin."

Poor William! He also must suffer for being my brother. I took his advice and kept quiet. My aunt was taken out of jail at the end of a month, because Mrs. Flint could not spare her any longer. She was tired of being her own housekeeper. It was quite too fatiguing to order her dinner and eat it too. My children remained in jail, where brother William did all he could for their comfort. Betty went to see them sometimes, and brought me tidings. She was not permitted to enter the jail; but William would hold them up to the grated window while she chatted with them. When she repeated their prattle,[9] and told me how they wanted to see their ma, my tears would flow. Old Betty would exclaim, "Lors, chile! what's you crying 'bout? Dem young uns vil kill you dead. Don't be so chick'n-hearted! If you does, you vil nebber git thro' dis world." ∎

---

8. **benefactress** *n.:* woman who gives aid.
9. **prattle** *n.:* chatter; babble.

---

**Vocabulary**

**cunning** (kun′iŋ) *adj.:* sly or crafty.
**compelled** (kəm·peld′) *v.:* driven; forced.
**impulse** (im′puls′) *n.:* sudden desire or urge.

# Response and Analysis

## Reading Check

1. Why did Jacobs finally decide to escape?

2. What did Jacobs ask Sally to do for her at dawn?

3. What did Jacobs's grandmother tell Dr. Flint about the escape?

4. What did Dr. Flint assume Jacobs would try to do?

5. What advice did Jacobs receive from her brother William?

## Thinking Critically

6. How would you describe Jacobs's **character**? Find details in the text that reveal her character traits.

7. Describe how Jacobs resolved one of her **internal conflicts**. How did her decision affect the **external conflict** she faced?

8. Cite specific passages in Jacobs's narrative that illustrate the religious influences that affected Jacobs and her decisions.

## Extending and Evaluating

9. Explain Jacobs's **purpose** in writing and publishing her story. Judging from this excerpt, do you think she achieved her purpose? Why or why not?

10. Jacobs's writing has been criticized as resembling too much the melodramatic novels popular in her time. Do you think her story rings true, or do you find parts of it sentimental? How might you change the language or alter her word choice to update the selection?

## Literary Criticism

11. **Political approach.** Frederick Douglass (page 463) and Harriet Jacobs narrate two different episodes of slave life. Compare and contrast their situations, their actions, their emotions, and their opinions. How do their attitudes and views contribute to their credibility? In other words, what do they believe, and do you believe them?

## WRITING

### Across the Lines

Imagine that Jacobs escaped to the North and sent a written message back to one of the characters in the excerpt—Sally, Betty, her grandmother, the woman who hid her in the storeroom, or Dr. Flint. Write the **message,** explaining Jacobs's motivations, expressing her feelings, and describing her plans and hopes for the future.

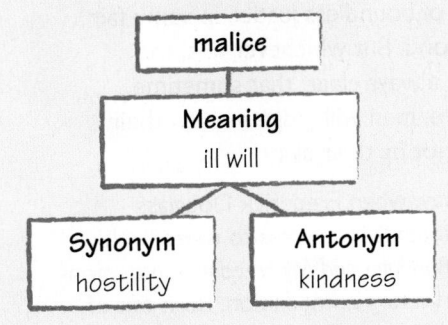

## Vocabulary Development
### Mapping Meanings

Create a word map like the one below for each of the remaining Vocabulary words. (Not all words will have an antonym.)

malice    provocation    compelled
fervently    distressed    impulse
unnerve    cunning

malice

Meaning
ill will

Synonym
hostility

Antonym
kindness

**SKILLS FOCUS**

**Literary Skills**
Analyze points of view on a topic. Analyze internal and external conflict.

**Writing Skills**
Write a message or letter from the point of view of a character.

**Vocabulary Skills**
Create semantic maps with synonyms and antonyms.

Harriet A. Jacobs    477

# Connected Readings

## Slavery

Frederick Douglass . . . . . . . . *from* **My Bondage and My Freedom**

Spirituals . . . . . . . . . . . . . . . **Go Down, Moses/Follow the Drinking Gourd/
Swing Low, Sweet Chariot**

*Commonwealth* and
*Freeman's Record* . . . . . . . . . **The Most Remarkable Woman of This Age**

You have just read selections from the autobiographies of Frederick Douglass and
Harriet A. Jacobs describing their experiences of slavery. The next three selections
you will be reading—another piece by Douglass, some spirituals, and an article about
Harriet Tubman—present other views on slavery. As you read, ask yourself how the
experiences and views expressed in the selections are alike and how they are different. At the end, on page 487, you'll find questions asking you to compare
all five selections in this Comparing Points of View feature on slavery.

## Points *of* View

### Before You Read

In this excerpt from *My Bondage and My Freedom*,
Frederick Douglass writes eloquently about the
songs of slavery—compositions later called
sorrow songs by the African American writer
W.E.B. DuBois. In his 1903 book *The Souls of
Black Folk,* DuBois made the following comments
about sorrow songs:

> ❝ Through all the sorrow of the Sorrow
> Songs there breathes a hope—a faith in
> the ultimate justice of things. The minor
> cadences of despair change often to triumph
> and calm confidence. Sometimes it is faith
> in life, sometimes a faith in death, sometimes
> assurance of boundless justice in some fair
> world beyond. But whichever it is, the
> meaning is always clear: that sometime,
> somewhere, men will judge men by their
> souls and not by their skins. ❞

In the same way, when Frederick Douglass
describes his intense responses to those "wild
notes" in *My Bondage and My Freedom,* he demonstrates how a literary composition, born out of
hard real-world experience, can ultimately have
a political impact.

African American girl picking cotton on a Georgia
plantation (1895).

# *from* My Bondage and My Freedom

## Frederick Douglass

**S**laves are generally expected to sing as well as to work. A silent slave is not liked by masters or overseers. *"Make a noise, make a noise,"* and *"bear a hand"* are the words usually addressed to the slaves when there is silence amongst them. This may account for the almost constant singing heard in the southern states. . . . On allowance day, those who visited the great house farm were peculiarly excited and noisy. While on their way, they would make the dense old woods, for miles around, reverberate with their wild notes. These were not always merry because they were wild. On the contrary, they were mostly of a plaintive[1] cast, and told a tale of grief and sorrow. In the most boisterous outbursts of rapturous sentiment, there was ever a tinge of deep melancholy.[2] I have never heard any songs like those anywhere since I left slavery, except when in Ireland. There I heard the same *wailing notes,* and was much affected by them. It was during the famine of 1845–1846. In all the songs of the slaves, there was ever some expression in praise of the great house farm; something which would flatter the pride of the owner, and, possibly, draw a favorable glance from him.

. . . I cannot better express my sense of them now, than ten years ago, when, in sketching my life, I thus spoke of this feature of my plantation experience:

". . . The hearing of those wild notes always depressed my spirits, and filled my heart with ineffable[3] sadness. The mere recurrence, even now, afflicts my spirit, and while I am writing

*Frederick Douglass* (detail) (c. 1844), attributed to Elisha Hammond. Oil on canvas (27½″ × 22½″).

National Portrait Gallery, Smithsonian Institution. Courtesy Art Resource, New York.

these lines, my tears are falling. To those songs I trace my first glimmering conceptions of the dehumanizing character of slavery. I can never get rid of that conception. Those songs still follow me, to deepen my hatred of slavery, and quicken my sympathies for my brethren in bonds. If anyone wishes to be impressed with a sense of the soul-killing power of slavery, let him go to Colonel Lloyd's plantation, and, on allowance day, place himself in the deep, pine woods, and there let him, in silence, thoughtfully analyze the sounds that shall pass through the chambers of his soul, and if he is not thus impressed, it will only be because 'there is no flesh in his obdurate[4] heart.' "

---

1. **plaintive** *adj.:* mournful; sad.
2. **melancholy** *n.:* sadness; gloom.
3. **ineffable** *adj.:* too great to be expressed; indescribable.

---

4. **obdurate** *adj.:* without sympathy; pitiless.

*The Cotton Pickers* (1876) by Winslow Homer. Oil on canvas (24 × 38⅛ in.).

## Points *of* View

### Before You Read

The moving and intensely emotional songs known as spirituals developed largely from the oral traditions of Africans held in slavery in the South before the Civil War. Spirituals, like other kinds of folk literature and music, were composed by anonymous artists and passed on orally. They often combine African melodies and rhythms with elements of white southern religious music.

Even though individuals probably composed the spirituals, the ideas and the language came from a common group of images and idioms. As the songs were passed from generation to generation by word of mouth, lines were changed and new stanzas were added, so that numerous versions of a particular spiritual might exist.

Spirituals were concerned above all with issues of freedom: spiritual freedom in the form of salvation and literal freedom from the shackles of slavery. The biblical Moses delivered the ancient Israelites from slavery in Egypt. Many

people during the time of slavery were therefore called Moses by those longing for deliverance. Harriet Tubman, for example, used Moses as her code name with the Underground Railroad. A Methodist minister named Francis Asbury was also known as Moses, and according to some scholars, the spiritual "Go Down, Moses" is really a plea for Asbury's help.

Some of the songs were code songs, or signal songs—that is, songs with details that provided runaways with directions, times, and meeting places for their escapes. For example, in "Follow the Drinking Gourd," the drinking gourd refers literally to the shell of a vegetable related to the squash or melon, dried and hollowed out for drinking. Slaves, however, knew that the drinking gourd was also the Big Dipper, a group of stars. Two stars in the bowl of the Big Dipper point to the North Star—and the direction of freedom.

# Go Down, Moses

Go down, Moses,
Way down in Egypt land
Tell old Pharaoh
To let my people go.

5   When Israel was in Egypt land
Let my people go
Oppressed so hard they could not stand
Let my people go.

Go down, Moses,
10  Way down in Egypt land
Tell old Pharaoh,
"Let my people go."

"Thus saith the Lord," bold Moses said,
"Let my people go;
15  If not I'll smite your firstborn dead
Let my people go."

Go down, Moses,
Way down in Egypt land,
Tell old Pharaoh,
20  "Let my people go!"

# Follow the Drinking Gourd

When the sun comes back and the first
    quail calls,
    Follow the drinking gourd,
For the old man is a-waiting for to carry
    you to freedom
    If you follow the drinking gourd.

[Refrain]

5  Follow the drinking gourd,
    Follow the drinking gourd,
For the old man is a-waiting for to carry
    you to freedom
    If you follow the drinking gourd.

The river bank will make a very good road,
10    The dead trees show you the way,
Left foot, peg foot traveling on
    Follow the drinking gourd.

[Refrain]

The river ends between two hills,
    Follow the drinking gourd.
15  There's another river on the other side,
    Following the drinking gourd.

[Refrain]

Where the little river meets the great big
    river,
    Follow the drinking gourd.
The old man is a-waiting for to carry you
    to freedom,
20    If you follow the drinking gourd.

[Refrain]

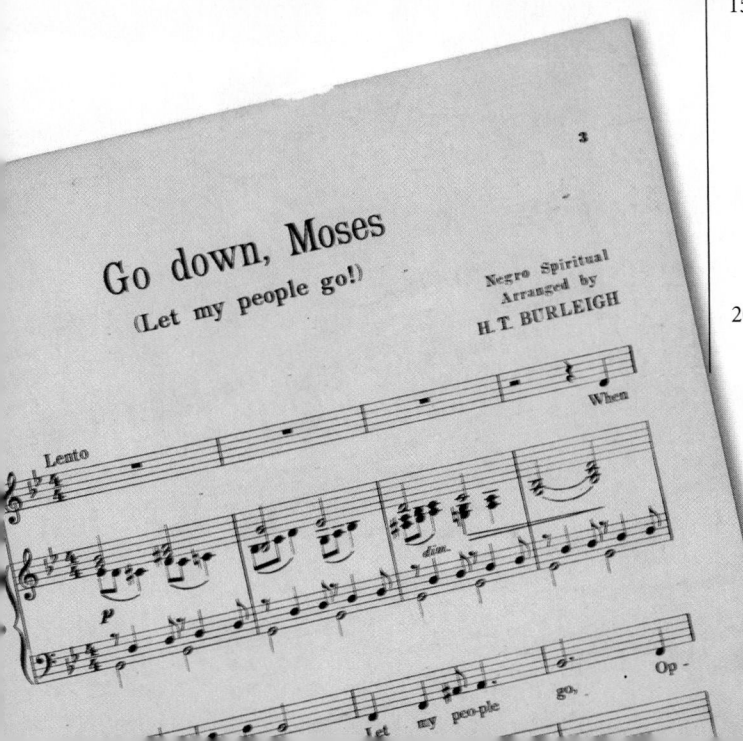

# Swing Low, Sweet Chariot

Swing low, sweet chariot,
Coming for to carry me home,
Swing low, sweet chariot,
Coming for to carry me home.

5    I looked over Jordan and what did I see
Coming for to carry me home,
A band of angels, coming after me,
Coming for to carry me home.

If you get there before I do,
10   Coming for to carry me home,
Tell all my friends I'm coming too,
Coming for to carry me home.

Swing low, sweet chariot,
Coming for to carry me home,
15   Swing low, sweet chariot,
Coming for to carry me home.

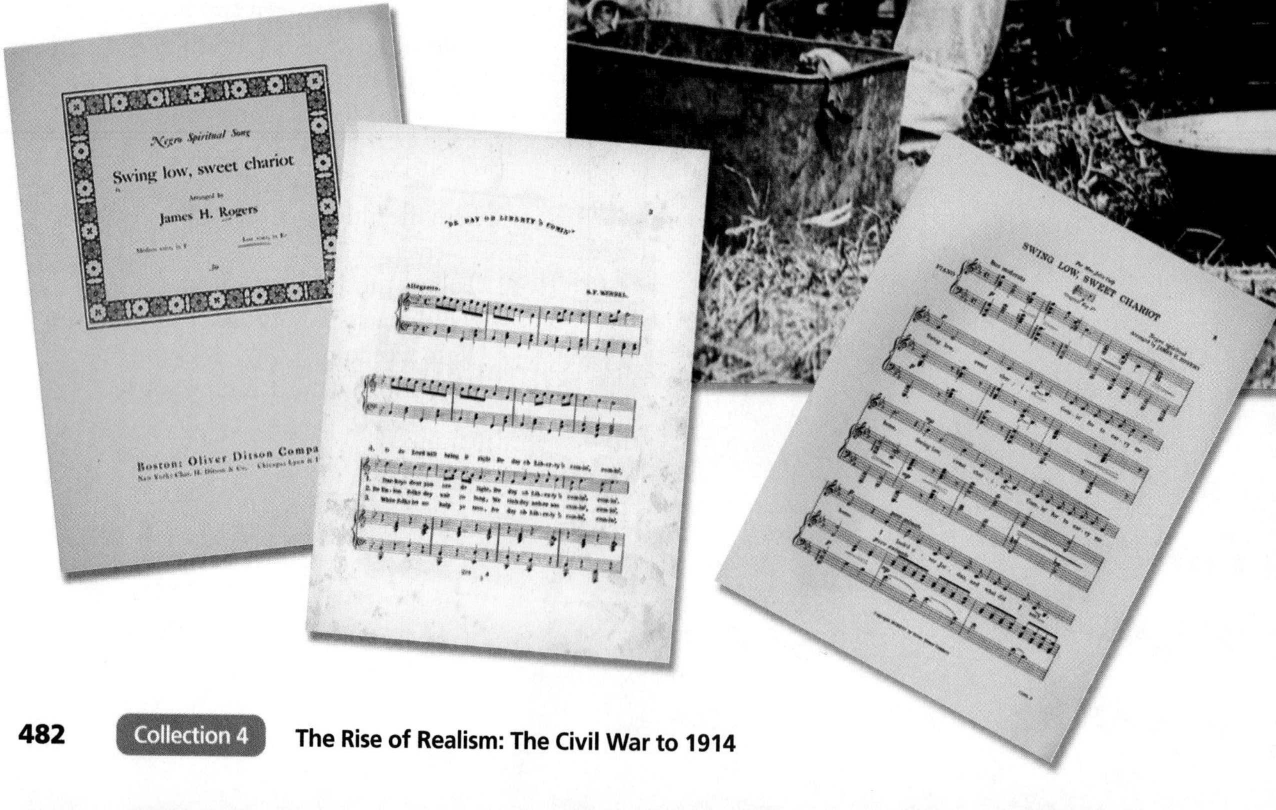

Harriet Tubman (c. 1860s).

These people were formerly held in slavery.

## Points *of* View
### Before You Read

The most famous "conductor" on the Underground Railroad, a secret system organized to help fugitive slaves escape to free states, was Harriet Tubman, herself an escaped slave. Tubman, who went by the code name Moses, made nineteen dangerous journeys back into slave territory, rescuing more than three hundred people from bondage in the 1850s. When the Civil War broke out, she not only tended to wounded soldiers but also served as a scout and a spy, once leading more than 750 people to safety. She was never captured.

The following selection, which is based on interviews with Tubman, appeared in regional newspapers in 1863 and 1865.

# The Most Remarkable Woman of This Age

from *Commonwealth*, July 17, 1863, and *Freeman's Record*, March 1865

Magee house (c. 1855) in Canesto, New York, a safe house on the Underground Railroad.

Harriet Tubman, the famous fugitive slave from Maryland, risks her life sneaking into slave territory to free slaves. Slaveholders posted a forty thousand dollar reward for the capture of the "Black Moses."

One of the teachers lately commissioned by the New England Freedmen's Aid Society is probably the most remarkable woman of this age. That is to say, she has performed more wonderful deeds by the native power of her own spirit against adverse circumstances than any other. She is well known to many by the various names which her eventful life has given her, Harriet Garrison, Gen. Tubman, and so on, but among the slaves she is universally known by her well-earned title of Moses—Moses the deliverer. She is a rare instance, in the midst of high civilization and intellectual culture, of a being of great native powers, working powerfully, and to beneficent[1] ends, entirely untaught by schools or books.

Her maiden name was Araminta Ross.[2] She is the granddaughter of a native African, and has not a drop of white blood in her veins. She

---

1. **beneficent** (bə·nef′ə·sənt) *adj.:* showing kindness or charity.
2. **Araminta Ross** (1820?–1913): Tubman was also known as Araminta Greene; she was the daughter of Benjamin Ross and Harriet Greene.

was born in 1820 or 1821, on the Eastern Shore of Maryland. Her parents were slaves, but married and faithful to each other, and the family affection is very strong. . . .

She seldom lived with her owner, but was usually "hired out" to different persons. She once "hired her time," and employed it in the rudest farming labors, ploughing, carting, driving the oxen, and so on, to so good advantage that she was able in one year to buy a pair of steers worth forty dollars.

When quite young, she lived with a very pious mistress; but the slaveholder's religion did not prevent her from whipping the young girl for every slight or fancied fault. Araminta found that this was usually a morning exercise; so she prepared for it by putting on all the thick clothes she could procure to protect her skin. She made sufficient outcry, however, to convince her mistress that her blows had full effect; and in the afternoon she would take off her wrappings, and dress as well as she could. When invited into family prayers, she preferred to stay on the landing, and pray for herself. "And I prayed to God," she says, "to make me strong and able to fight and that's what I've allers prayed for ever since."

In her youth she received a severe blow on her head from a heavy weight thrown by her master at another slave, but which accidentally hit her. The blow produced a disease of the brain which was severe for a long time, and still makes her very lethargic.[3] . . . She was married about 1844 to a free colored man named John Tubman, but never had any children. Owing to changes in her owner's family, it was determined to sell her and some other slaves; but her health was so much injured that a purchaser was not easily found. At length she became convinced that she would soon be carried away, and she decided to escape. Her brothers did not agree with her plans, and she walked off alone, following the guidance of the brooks, which she had observed to run North. . . .

She remained two years in Philadelphia working hard and carefully hoarding her money. Then she hired a room, furnished it as well as she could, bought a nice suit of men's clothes, and went back to Maryland for her husband. But the faithless man had taken to himself another wife. Harriet did not dare venture into her presence, but sent word to her husband where she was. He de-clined joining her. At first her grief and anger were exces-sive. . . . But finally she thought . . . "if he could do without her, she could without him," and so "he dropped out of her heart," and she deter-mined to give her life to brave deeds. Thus all personal aims died out of her heart; and with her simple brave motto, "I can't die but once," she began the work which has made her Moses—the deliverer of her people. Seven or eight times she has returned to the neigh-borhood of her former home, always at the risk of death in the most terrible forms, and each time has brought away a company of fugitive slaves, and led them safely to the free States, or to Canada. Every time she went, the dangers increased. In 1857, she brought away her old parents, and, as they were too feeble to walk, she was obliged to hire a wagon, which added greatly to the perils of the journey. In 1860, she went for the last time, and among her troop was an infant whom they were obliged to keep stupefied with laudanum[4] to prevent its outcries. This was at the period of great excitement, and Moses was not safe even in New York State; but her anx-ious friends insisted upon her

---

3. **lethargic** *adj.*: abnormally drowsy; sluggish.

4. **laudanum** *n.*: solution of opium in alcohol.

taking refuge in Canada. So various and interesting are the incidents of the journeys, that we know not how to select from them. She has shown in them all the characteristics of a great leader: courage, foresight, prudence, self-control, ingenuity, subtle perception, command over others' minds. . . .

She always came in the winter when the nights are long and dark, and people who have homes stay in them. She was never seen on the plantation herself, but appointed a rendezvous[5] for her company eight or ten miles distant, so that if they were discovered at the first start she was not compromised.[6] She started on Saturday night; the slaves at that time being allowed to go away from home to visit their friends—so that they would not be missed until Monday morning. Even then they were supposed to have loitered on the way, and it would often be late on Monday afternoon before the flight would be certainly known. If by any further delay the advertisement was not sent out before Tuesday morning, she felt secure of keeping ahead of it; but if it were, it required all her ingenu-

ity to escape. She resorted to various devices; she had confidential friends all along the road. She would hire a man to follow the one who put up the notices, and take them down as soon as his back was turned. She crossed creeks on railroad bridges by night; she hid her company in the woods while she herself, not being advertised, went into the towns in search of information. . . .

The expedition was governed by the strictest rules. If any man gave out, he must be shot. "Would you really do that?" she was asked. "Yes," she replied, "if he was weak enough to give out, he'd be weak enough to betray us all, and all who had helped us; and do you think I'd let so many die just for one coward man." "Did you ever have to shoot anyone?" she was asked. "One time," she said, "a man gave out the second night. His feet were sore and swollen; he couldn't go any further. He'd rather go back and die, if he must." They tried all arguments in vain, bathed his feet, tried to strengthen him; but it was of no use, he would go back. Then she said, "I told the boys to get their guns ready, and shoot him. They'd have done it in a minute; but when he heard that, he jumped right up and went on as well as anybody."

When going on these jour-

Graue Mill in Oak Brook, Illinois, a stop on the Underground Railroad.

neys, she often lay alone in the forests all night. Her whole soul was filled with awe of the mysterious Unseen Presence, which thrilled her with such depths of emotion that all other care and fear vanished. Then she seemed to speak with her Maker "as a man talketh with his friend"; her childlike petitions had direct answers, and beautiful visions lifted her up above all doubt and anxiety into serene trust and faith. No man can be a hero without this faith in some form; the sense that he walks not in his own strength, but leaning on an almighty arm. Call it fate, destiny, what you will, Moses of old, Moses of today, believed it to be Almighty God.

---

5. **rendezvous** (rän′dā·vōō′) *n.*: meeting place.
6. **compromised** *v.*: laid open to danger.

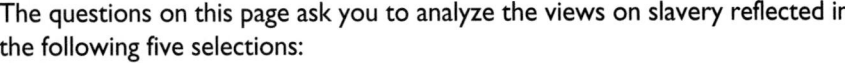

# Analysis Comparing Points of View

## Slavery

The questions on this page ask you to analyze the views on slavery reflected in the following five selections:

Frederick Douglass .... *from* **Narrative of the Life of Frederick Douglass**

Harriet A. Jacobs ...... *from* **Incidents in the Life of a Slave Girl**

Frederick Douglass .... *from* **My Bondage and My Freedom**

Spirituals ............. **Go Down, Moses / Follow the Drinking Gourd / Swing Low, Sweet Chariot**

*Commonwealth* and
*Freeman's Record* ...... **The Most Remarkable Woman of This Age**

### Thinking Critically

1. What assumptions about slavery did you infer from the narratives of Frederick Douglass and Harriet Jacobs?

2. Compare the forms of resistance to slavery that each of these readings describes. Which form of resistance do you think was the most effective? Explain your opinion.

3. Consider the readings in this Comparing Points of View feature and the genre in which each is written. What qualities do the autobiographies have that make them different from the newspaper article and the spirituals? In which readings do you find the political message the most clear and powerful? Explain.

4. Do you think that reading and discussing these historical narratives and spirituals can have an effect on a contemporary understanding of slavery? Why or why not?

### WRITING

#### Historical Research

Write a one- or two-page **research report** about one aspect of slavery exposed in these readings. You might consider, for example, the treatment of slave children, fugitive slave laws, or the Underground Railroad. A vast amount of material has been written about slavery, so remember that it is essential to limit your topic.

▶ **Use "Reporting Historical Research," pages 602–621, for help with this assignment.**

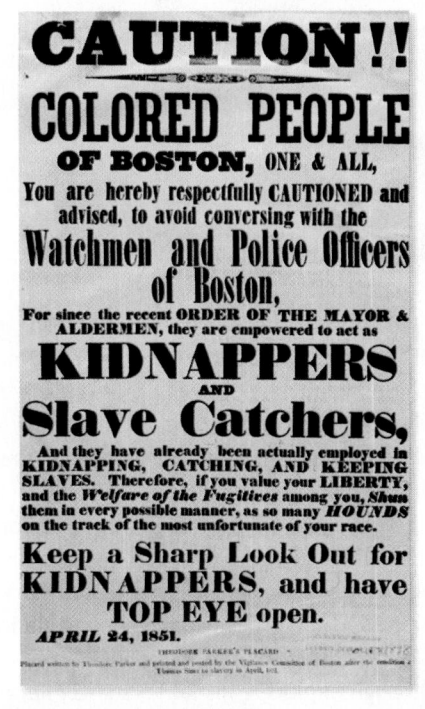

Placard issued by the Vigilance Committee of Boston in 1851.

SKILLS FOCUS

Pages 462–487 cover
**Literary Skills**
Analyze and compare points of view on a topic.

**Reading Skills**
Compare points of view across texts.

**Writing Skills**
Write a historical research report.

# Ambrose Bierce

(1842–1914?)

*Ambrose Bierce* by J.H.E. Partington (1843–1899). Oil on canvas.

The Huntington Library, Art Collections, and Botanical Gardens, San Marino, California/SuperStock.

**A**mbrose Bierce infused his writing with an attitude of scorn for all the sentimental illusions human beings cling to. His dark vision of life centers on warfare and the cruel joke it plays on humanity. This bleak vision assures Bierce's place in our literary history.

Bierce was born in 1842, the tenth of thirteen children in the family of an eccentric and unsuccessful farmer named Marcus Aurelius Bierce. The Bierces lived in a log cabin in Meigs County, Ohio. Bierce was educated primarily through exploring his father's small library.

At nineteen, Bierce joined the Ninth Indiana Volunteers and saw action at the bloody Civil War battles of Shiloh and Chickamauga. He was also part of General Sherman's march to the sea in 1864. Bierce was once severely wounded and was cited for bravery no fewer than fifteen times.

At the war's end, Bierce reenlisted, but several years in the peacetime army left him discouraged about his prospects. He left the army and joined his brother Albert to work at the United States Mint in San Francisco.

He began to contribute caustically witty short pieces to the city's weeklies.

A growing reputation as a muckraking reporter brought Bierce the editorship of the San Francisco *News Letter* and the acquaintance of the literary community, including Mark Twain (page 523). When the financier Collis P. Huntington, head of the Southern Pacific Railroad, asked Bierce's price for silence on the railroad's tax fraud case, Bierce is said to have replied, "My price is about seventy-five million dollars, to be handed to the treasurer of the United States." Bierce's disillusionment with the deceit and greed of his times continued to spur his pen and earned him the nickname "Bitter Bierce."

Bierce married in 1871 and moved to England, where he spent the next four years editing and contributing to humor magazines and making his first attempts at fiction. On his return to San Francisco in 1876, he wrote a regular column. This was the most active and fruitful time of Bierce's life. He became the witty scholar and literary dictator of the West Coast, but he never achieved wide recognition for his stories.

*The Devil's Dictionary,* first published in 1906 as *The Cynic's Word Book,* was more successful. In his dictionary, Bierce offered a collection of definitions filled with irony and sardonic humor. He defined war as a "byproduct of the arts of peace," and peace as "a period of cheating between two periods of fighting." A cynic was a person who "sees things as they are, not as they ought to be. Hence the custom among the Scythians of plucking out a cynic's eyes to improve his vision."

In 1913, when Bierce was lonely and weary of his life, he asked his few friends to "forgive him in not perishing where he was." He set off for Mexico to report on or join in its revolution. "Goodbye," he wrote. "If you hear of my being stood up against a Mexican stone wall and shot to rags please know that I think it a pretty good way to depart this life. It beats old age, disease, or falling down the cellar stairs." No further word was ever heard from him.

# An Occurrence at Owl Creek Bridge

## Make the Connection

Can we ever really understand the complexities of the human mind? What's real? What's imaginary? When someone we love is late or missing, we can conjure up the details of disaster in a few seconds and make ourselves sick with worry. Imagine, then, the extremes to which the human imagination might go if a person were threatened with imminent death. What thoughts might pass through his or her mind?

## Literary Focus
### Point of View

In the different sections of Bierce's story, watch for these variations in **point of view:** (1) **omniscient,** in which the narrator seems to know everything about all the characters or events; (2) **objective,** in which the narrator reports without comment, much as a camera would record a scene; and (3) **third-person-limited,** in which the narrator zooms in on the thoughts and feelings of a single character.

> **Point of view** is the vantage point from which a writer tells a story.
>
> *For more on Point of View, see the Handbook of Literary and Historical Terms.*

## Reading Skills
### Analyzing Sequence of Events

As you read Bierce's story, make a list of the major events in the order in which they're presented in the story. After you've finished reading, put the events in chronological order on a time line, showing the order in which they actually happened. Think about why Bierce chose to relate the events of the story out of sequence.

## Background

The belief that life will prove gratifying and will reward our virtues is so strong that it has become a main current in storytelling. This romantic notion, however, has its inevitable counterpart in realism and naturalism—fiction that conforms to the truth as it is experienced rather than as we would like it to be.

Bierce's no-punches-pulled story is set in the Deep South during the Civil War (1861–1865). The horrors of war serve as only an external setting for the landscape that *really* interests the writer. That landscape is the inside of the mind of a man condemned to death.

## Vocabulary Development

**sentinel** (sent′'n·əl) *n.:* guard; sentry.

**deference** (def′ər·əns) *n.:* respect.

**perilous** (per′ə·ləs) *adj.:* dangerous.

**encompassed** (en·kum′pəst) *v.* used as *adj.:* surrounded; enclosed.

**oscillation** (äs′ə·lā′shən) *n.:* regular back-and-forth movement.

**pivotal** (piv′ət·'l) *adj.:* central; acting as a point around which other things turn.

**appalling** (ə·pôl′iŋ) *adj.:* frightful.

**gyration** (jī·rā′shən) *n.:* circular movement; whirling.

**abrasion** (ə·brā′zhən) *n.:* scrape.

**malign** (mə·līn′) *adj.:* harmful; evil.

**SKILLS FOCUS**

**Literary Skills**
Understand point of view.

**Reading Skills**
Analyze a sequence of events.

**INTERNET**

**Vocabulary Practice**

Keyword: LE7 11-4

# An Occurrence at Owl Creek Bridge

## Ambrose Bierce

### I

A man stood upon a railroad bridge in northern Alabama, looking down into the swift water twenty feet below. The man's hands were behind his back, the wrists bound with a cord. A rope closely encircled his neck. It was attached to a stout cross-timber above his head, and the slack fell to the level of his knees. Some loose boards laid upon the sleepers[1] supporting the metals of the railway supplied a footing for him and his executioners—two private soldiers of the Federal army, directed by a sergeant who in civil life may have been a deputy sheriff. At a short remove[2] upon the same temporary platform was an officer in the uniform of his rank, armed. He was a captain. A sentinel at each end of the bridge stood with his rifle in the position known as "support," that is to say, vertical in front of the left shoulder, the hammer resting on the forearm thrown straight across the chest—a formal and unnatural position, enforcing an erect carriage of the body. It did not appear to be the duty of these two men to know what was occurring at the center of the bridge; they merely blockaded the two ends of the foot planking that traversed it.

Beyond one of the sentinels nobody was in sight; the railroad ran straight away into a forest for a hundred yards, then, curving, was lost to view. Doubtless there was an outpost farther along. The other bank of the stream was open ground—a gentle acclivity[3] topped with a stockade of vertical tree trunks, loopholed for rifles, with a single embrasure through which protruded the muzzle of a brass cannon

---

1. **sleepers** *n. pl.:* railroad ties.
2. **remove** *n.:* distance.
3. **acclivity** *n.:* uphill slope.

**Vocabulary**
**sentinel** (sent'′n • əl) *n.:* guard; sentry.

---

commanding the bridge. Midway of the slope between bridge and fort were the spectators—a single company of infantry in line, at "parade rest," the butts of the rifles on the ground, the barrels inclining slightly backward against the right shoulder, the hands crossed upon the stock. A lieutenant stood at the right of the line, the point of his sword upon the ground, his left hand resting upon his right. Excepting the group of four at the center of the bridge, not a man moved. The company faced the bridge, staring stonily, motionless. The sentinels, facing the banks of the stream, might have been statues to adorn the bridge. The captain stood with folded arms, silent, observing the work of his subordinates, but making no sign. Death is a dignitary who when he comes announced is to be received with formal manifestations of respect, even by those most familiar with him. In the code of military etiquette, silence and fixity[4] are forms of deference.

The man who was engaged in being hanged was apparently about thirty-five years of age. He was a civilian, if one might judge from his habit, which was that of a planter. His features were good—a straight nose, firm mouth, broad forehead, from which his long, dark hair was combed straight back, falling behind his ears to the collar of his well-fitting frock coat. He wore a moustache and pointed beard, but no whiskers; his eyes were large and dark gray, and had a kindly expression which one would hardly have expected in one whose neck was in the hemp. Evidently this was no vulgar assassin. The liberal military code makes provision for hanging many kinds of persons, and gentlemen are not excluded.

The preparations being complete, the two private soldiers stepped aside and each drew away the plank upon which he had been standing. The sergeant turned to the captain, saluted, and placed himself immediately behind that officer, who in turn moved apart one pace. These movements left the condemned man and the sergeant standing on the two ends of the same plank, which spanned three of the crossties of the bridge. The end upon which the civilian stood almost, but not quite, reached a fourth. This plank had been held in place by the weight of the captain; it was now held by that of the sergeant. At a signal from the former, the latter would step aside, the plank would tilt and the condemned man go down between two ties. The arrangement commended itself to his judgment as simple and effective. His face had not been covered nor his eyes bandaged. He looked a moment at his "unsteadfast footing," then let his gaze wander to the swirling water of the stream racing madly beneath his feet. A piece of dancing driftwood caught his attention, and his eyes followed it down the current. How slowly it appeared to move! What a sluggish stream!

He closed his eyes in order to fix his last thoughts upon his wife and children. The water, touched to gold by the early sun, the brooding mists under the banks at some distance down the stream, the fort, the soldiers, the piece of drift—all had distracted him. And now he became conscious of a new disturbance. Striking through the thought of his dear ones was a sound which he could neither ignore nor understand, a sharp, distinct, metallic percussion like the stroke of a blacksmith's hammer upon the anvil; it had the same ringing quality. He wondered what it was, and whether immeasurably distant or nearby—it seemed both. Its recurrence was regular, but as slow as the tolling of a death knell.[5] He awaited each stroke with impatience and—he knew not why—apprehension. The intervals of silence grew progressively longer; the delays became maddening. With their greater infrequency the sounds increased in strength and sharpness. They hurt his ear like the thrust of a knife; he feared he would shriek. What he heard was the ticking of his watch.

He unclosed his eyes and saw again the water below him. "If I could free my hands," he thought, "I might throw off the noose and

---

4. **fixity** *n.:* steadiness; motionlessness.

---

5. **knell** *n.:* sound of a bell ringing slowly.

---

**Vocabulary**
**deference** (def′ər·əns) *n.:* respect.

spring into the stream. By diving I could evade the bullets and, swimming vigorously, reach the bank, take to the woods, and get away home. My home, thank God, is as yet outside their lines; my wife and little ones are still beyond the invader's farthest advance."

As these thoughts, which have here to be set down in words, were flashed into the doomed man's brain rather than evolved from it, the captain nodded to the sergeant. The sergeant stepped aside.

## II

Peyton Farquhar was a well-to-do planter, of an old and highly respected Alabama family. Being a slave owner and, like other slave owners, a politician, he was naturally an original secessionist[6] and ardently devoted to the Southern cause. Circumstances of an imperious[7] nature, which it is unnecessary to relate here, had prevented him from taking service with the gallant army that had fought the disastrous campaigns ending with the fall of Corinth,[8] and he chafed[9] under the inglorious restraint, longing for the release of his energies, the larger life of the soldier, the opportunity for distinction. That opportunity, he felt, would come, as it comes to all in wartime. Meanwhile he did what he could. No service was too humble for him to perform in aid of the South, no adventure too perilous for him to undertake if consistent with the character of a civilian who was at heart a soldier, and who in good faith and without too much qualification assented to at least a part of the frankly villainous dictum[10] that all is fair in love and war.

One evening while Farquhar and his wife were sitting on a rustic bench near the entrance to his grounds, a gray-clad soldier rode up to the gate and asked for a drink of water. Mrs. Farquhar was only too happy to serve him with her own white hands. While she was fetching the water, her husband approached the dusty horseman and inquired eagerly for news from the front.

"The Yanks are repairing the railroads," said the man, "and are getting ready for another advance. They have reached the Owl Creek bridge, put it in order, and built a stockade on the north bank. The commandant has issued an order, which is posted everywhere, declaring that any civilian caught interfering with the railroad, its bridges, tunnels, or trains will be summarily[11] hanged. I saw the order."

"How far is it to the Owl Creek bridge?" Farquhar asked.

"About thirty miles."

"Is there no force on this side the creek?"

"Only a picket post half a mile out, on the railroad, and a single sentinel at this end of the bridge."

"Suppose a man—a civilian and student of hanging—should elude the picket post and perhaps get the better of the sentinel," said Farquhar, smiling, "what could he accomplish?"

The soldier reflected. "I was there a month ago," he replied. "I observed that the flood of last winter had lodged a great quantity of driftwood against the wooden pier at this end of the bridge. It is now dry and would burn like tow."

The lady had now brought the water, which the soldier drank. He thanked her ceremoniously, bowed to her husband, and rode away. An hour later, after nightfall, he repassed the plantation, going northward in the direction from which he had come. He was a Federal scout.

## III

As Peyton Farquhar fell straight downward through the bridge, he lost consciousness and was as one already dead. From this state he was awakened—ages later, it seemed to him—by the pain of a sharp pressure upon his throat,

---

6. **secessionist** *n.:* one who favored the separation of Southern states from the Union.
7. **imperious** *adj.:* urgent.
8. **Corinth:** Union forces under Gen. William S. Rosecrans (1819–1898) took Corinth, Mississippi, on October 4, 1862.
9. **chafed** *v.:* became impatient.
10. **dictum** *n.:* statement; saying.

---

11. **summarily** *adv.:* without delay.

---

**Vocabulary**
**perilous** (per'ə·ləs) *adj.:* dangerous.

followed by a sense of suffocation. Keen, poignant agonies seemed to shoot from his neck downward through every fiber of his body and limbs. These pains appeared to flash along well-defined lines of ramification[12] and to beat with an inconceivably rapid periodicity. They seemed like streams of pulsating fire heating him to an intolerable temperature. As to his head, he was conscious of nothing but a feeling of fullness—of congestion. These sensations were unaccompanied by thought. The intellectual part of his nature was already effaced; he had power only to feel, and feeling was torment. He was conscious of motion. Encompassed in a luminous cloud, of which he was now merely the fiery heart, without material substance, he swung through unthinkable arcs of oscillation, like a vast pendulum. Then all at once, with terrible suddenness, the light about him shot upward with the noise of a loud plash; a frightful roaring was in his ears, and all was cold and dark. The power of thought was restored; he knew that the rope had broken and he had fallen into the stream. There was no additional strangulation; the noose about his neck was already suffocating him and kept the water from his lungs. To die of hanging at the bottom of a river!—the idea seemed to him ludicrous. He opened his eyes in the darkness and saw above him a gleam of light, but how distant, how inaccessible! He was still sinking, for the light became fainter and fainter until it was a mere glimmer. Then it began to grow and brighten, and he knew that he was rising toward the surface—knew it with reluctance, for he was now very comfortable. "To be hanged and drowned," he thought, "that is not so bad; but I do not wish to be shot. No; I will not be shot; that is not fair."

He was not conscious of an effort, but a sharp pain in his wrist apprised[13] him that he was trying to free his hands. He gave the struggle his attention, as an idler might observe the feat of a juggler, without interest in the outcome. What splendid effort!—what magnificent, what superhuman strength! Ah, that was a fine endeavor! Bravo! The cord fell away; his arms parted and floated upward, the hands dimly

---

12. **flash . . . ramification:** spread out rapidly along branches from one point.

13. **apprised** *v.:* informed.

---

**Vocabulary**

**encompassed** (en·kum′pəst) *v.* used as *adj.:* surrounded; enclosed.

**oscillation** (äs′ə·lā′shən) *n.:* regular back-and-forth movement.

seen on each side in the growing light. He watched them with a new interest as first one and then the other pounced upon the noose at his neck. They tore it away and thrust it fiercely aside, its undulations resembling those of a water snake. "Put it back, put it back!" He thought he shouted these words to his hands, for the undoing of the noose had been succeeded by the direst pang that he had yet experienced. His neck ached horribly; his brain was on fire; his heart, which had been fluttering faintly, gave a great leap, trying to force itself out at his mouth. His whole body was racked and wrenched with an insupportable anguish! But his disobedient hands gave no heed to the command. They beat the water vigorously with quick, downward strokes, forcing him to the surface. He felt his head emerge; his eyes were blinded by the sunlight; his chest expanded convulsively, and with a supreme and crowning agony his lungs engulfed a great draft of air, which instantly he expelled in a shriek!

He was now in full possession of his physical senses. They were, indeed, preternaturally[14] keen and alert. Something in the awful disturbance of his organic system had so exalted and refined them that they made record of things never before perceived. He felt the ripples upon his face and heard their separate sounds as they struck. He looked at the forest on the bank of the stream, saw the individual trees, the leaves, and the veining of each leaf—saw the very insects upon them: the locusts, the brilliant-bodied flies, the gray spiders stretching their webs from twig to twig. He noted the prismatic colors in all the dewdrops upon a million blades of grass. The humming of the gnats that danced above the eddies of the stream, the beating of the dragonflies' wings, the strokes of the water spiders' legs, like oars which had lifted their boat—all these made audible music. A fish slid along beneath his eyes, and he heard the rush of its body parting the water.

He had come to the surface facing down the stream; in a moment the visible world seemed to wheel slowly round, himself the pivotal point, and he saw the bridge, the fort, the soldiers upon the bridge, the captain, the sergeant, the two privates, his executioners. They were in silhouette against the blue sky. They shouted and gesticulated, pointing at him. The captain had drawn his pistol, but did not fire; the others were unarmed. Their movements were grotesque and horrible, their forms gigantic.

---

14. **preternaturally** *adv.:* extraordinarily; abnormally.

**Vocabulary**

**pivotal** (piv′ət·'l) *adj.:* central; acting as a point around which other things turn.

Suddenly he heard a sharp report[15] and something struck the water smartly within a few inches of his head, spattering his face with spray. He heard a second report, and saw one of the sentinels with his rifle at his shoulder, a light cloud of blue smoke rising from the muzzle. The man in the water saw the eye of the man on the bridge gazing into his own through the sights of the rifle. He observed that it was a gray eye and remembered having read that gray eyes were keenest, and that all famous marksmen had them. Nevertheless, this one had missed.

A counterswirl had caught Farquhar and turned him half round; he was again looking into the forest on the bank opposite the fort. The sound of a clear, high voice in monotonous singsong now rang out behind him and came across the water with a distinctness that pierced and subdued all other sounds, even the beating of the ripples in his ears. Although no soldier, he had frequented camps enough to know the dread significance of that deliberate, drawling, aspirated chant; the lieutenant on shore was taking a part in the morning's work. How coldly and pitilessly—with what an even, calm intonation, presaging,[16] and enforcing tranquility in the men—with what accurately measured intervals fell those cruel words:

"Attention, company! . . . Shoulder arms! . . . Ready! . . . Aim! . . . Fire!"

Farquhar dived—dived as deeply as he could. The water roared in his ears like the voice of Niagara, yet he heard the dulled thunder of the volley and, rising again toward the surface, met shining bits of metal, singularly flattened, oscillating slowly downward. Some of them touched him on the face and hands, then fell away, continuing their descent. One lodged between his collar and neck; it was uncomfortably warm and he snatched it out.

As he rose to the surface, gasping for breath, he saw that he had been a long time underwater; he was perceptibly farther downstream—nearer to safety. The soldiers had almost finished reloading; the metal ramrods flashed all at once in the sunshine as they were drawn from the barrels, turned in the air, and thrust into their sockets. The two sentinels fired again, independently and ineffectually.

The hunted man saw all this over his shoulder; he was now swimming vigorously with the current. His brain was as energetic as his arms and legs; he thought with the rapidity of lightning.

"The officer," he reasoned, "will not make that martinet's[17] error a second time. It is as easy to dodge a volley as a single shot. He has probably already given the command to fire at will. God help me, I cannot dodge them all!"

An appalling plash within two yards of him was followed by a loud, rushing sound, *diminuendo*,[18] which seemed to travel back through the air to the fort and died in an explosion which stirred the very river to its deeps! A rising sheet of water curved over him, fell down upon him, blinded him, strangled him! The cannon had taken a hand in the game. As he shook his head free from the commotion of the smitten water, he heard the deflected shot humming through the air ahead, and in an instant it was cracking and smashing the branches in the forest beyond.

"They will not do that again," he thought; "the next time they will use a charge of grape.[19] I must keep my eye upon the gun; the smoke will apprise me—the report arrives too late; it lags behind the missile. That is a good gun."

Suddenly he felt himself whirled round and round—spinning like a top. The water, the banks, the forests, the now distant bridge, fort, and men—all were commingled and blurred. Objects were represented by their colors only;

---

15. **report** *n.:* explosive noise.
16. **presaging** *v.* used as *adj.:* forewarning; predicting.

17. **martinet's:** A martinet is a disciplinarian of military rigidity.
18. ***diminuendo*** (də·min′yo͞o·en′dō) *adj.:* decreasing in loudness.
19. **charge of grape:** cannon charge of small iron balls, called grapeshot.

**Vocabulary**
**appalling** (ə·pôl′iŋ) *adj.:* frightful.

circular horizontal streaks of color—that was all he saw. He had been caught in a vortex and was being whirled on with a velocity of advance and gyration that made him giddy and sick. In a few moments he was flung upon the gravel at the foot of the left bank of the stream—the southern bank—and behind a projecting point which concealed him from his enemies. The sudden arrest of his motion, the abrasion of one of his hands on the gravel, restored him, and he wept with delight. He dug his fingers into the sand, threw it over himself in handfuls, and audibly blessed it. It looked like diamonds, rubies, emeralds; he could think of nothing beautiful which it did not resemble. The trees upon the bank were giant garden plants; he noted a definite order in their arrangement, inhaled the fragrance of their blooms. A strange, roseate light shone through the spaces among their trunks, and the wind made in their branches the music of aeolian harps.[20] He had no wish to perfect his escape—was content to remain in that enchanting spot until retaken.

A whiz and rattle of grapeshot among the branches high above his head roused him from his dream. The baffled cannoneer had fired him a random farewell. He sprang to his feet, rushed up the sloping bank, and plunged into the forest.

All that day he traveled, laying his course by the rounding sun. The forest seemed interminable; nowhere did he discover a break in it, not even a woodsman's road. He had not known that he lived in so wild a region. There was something uncanny[21] in the revelation.

By nightfall he was fatigued, footsore, famishing. The thought of his wife and children urged him on. At last he found a road which led him in what he knew to be the right direction. It was as wide and straight as a city street, yet it seemed untraveled. No fields bordered it, no dwelling anywhere. Not so much as the barking of a dog suggested human habitation. The black bodies of the trees formed a straight wall on both sides, terminating on the horizon in a point, like a diagram in a lesson in perspective. Overhead, as he looked up through this rift in the wood, shone great golden stars looking unfamiliar and grouped in strange constellations. He was sure they were arranged in some order which had a secret and malign significance. The wood on either side was full of singular noises, among which—once, twice, and again—he distinctly heard whispers in an unknown tongue.

His neck was in pain and lifting his hand to it he found it horribly swollen. He knew that it had a circle of black where the rope had bruised it. His eyes felt congested; he could no longer close them. His tongue was swollen with thirst; he relieved its fever by thrusting it forward from between his teeth into the cold air. How softly the turf had carpeted the untraveled avenue—he could no longer feel the roadway beneath his feet!

Doubtless, despite his suffering, he had fallen asleep while walking, for now he sees another scene—perhaps he has merely recovered from a delirium. He stands at the gate of his own home. All is as he left it, and all bright and beautiful in the morning sunshine. He must have traveled the entire night. As he pushes open the gate and passes up the wide white walk, he sees a flutter of female garments; his wife, looking fresh and cool and sweet, steps down from the veranda to meet him. At the bottom of the steps she stands waiting, with a smile of ineffable[22] joy, an attitude of matchless grace and dignity. Ah, how beautiful she is! He springs forward with extended arms. As he is about to clasp her, he feels a stunning blow upon the back of the neck; a blinding white light blazes all about him with a sound like the shock of a cannon—then all is darkness and silence!

Peyton Farquhar was dead; his body, with a broken neck, swung gently from side to side beneath the timbers of the Owl Creek bridge. ■

---

22. **ineffable** *adj.*: indescribable; unspeakable.

**Vocabulary**

**gyration** (jī·rā′shən) *n.*: circular movement; whirling.
**abrasion** (ə·brā′zhən) *n.*: scrape.
**malign** (mə·līn′) *adj.*: harmful; evil.

---

20. **aeolian** (ē·ō′lē·ən) **harps:** stringed instruments that are played by the wind. Aeolus is the god of the winds in Greek mythology.
21. **uncanny** *adj.*: eerie; weird.

# Response and Analysis

## Reading Check

1. State the situation Peyton Farquhar faces in Part I.

2. Part II of the story is a flashback. List its events in **chronological order.** Be sure to explain who visits Peyton Farquhar and what plan Farquhar conceives as a result of this visit.

3. **Summarize** in one sentence what Farquhar imagines in Part III.

## Thinking Critically

4. What **point of view** does the writer use in Part III of the story, which occurs within the few seconds before Farquhar dies? Why is this point of view particularly appropriate?

5. Bierce's **style** is to tell his story out of **chronological order.** How might the impact of the story be different if the events were revealed in order?

6. In this story the Civil War serves as a backdrop; Bierce's main intent is to examine the psychology of someone in a life-or-death situation. What does this story imply about human psychology in the face of death?

## Extending and Evaluating

7. Did you think the outcome of this story was credible and powerful, or did you think the surprise ending cheated the reader? Explain.

## Literary Criticism

8. **Philosophical approach.** The critics Cleanth Brooks and Robert Penn Warren have said that Bierce's story depends too much on a quirk of human psychology and is thus a mere "case study" that does not reveal anything important about human nature, as good fiction does. Do you agree? Why or why not?

## WRITING

### Owl Creek Bridge: The Movie

Write a **memorandum** to a film producer outlining your plans for adapting Bierce's story into a movie. Point out scenes where you would use each of the following techniques: (a) close-up shot; (b) moving-camera shot; (c) quick cut to new scene; (d) fast motion; (e) slow motion; (f) fuzzy image; and (g) sound effects. (The story was made into an award-winning film in 1962 in France.)

### Vocabulary Development

**Synonyms and Antonyms**

| | | |
|---|---|---|
| sentinel | oscillation | abrasion |
| deference | pivotal | malign |
| perilous | appalling | |
| encompassed | gyration | |

A **synonym** is a word that has the same, or almost the same, meaning as another word. An **antonym** has the opposite, or nearly the opposite, meaning of another word. Find the Vocabulary word from the list above that answers each of the following questions:

1. What word is a synonym for *rotation?*

2. What word is an antonym for *safe?*

3. What word is a synonym for *crucial?*

4. What word is a synonym for *lookout?*

5. What word is an antonym for *disrespect?*

6. What word is a synonym for *scratch?*

7. What word is a synonym for *shocking?*

8. What word is a synonym for *encircled?*

9. What word is an antonym for *harmless?*

10. What word is a synonym for *vibration?*

# Introduction Comparing Points of View

## The Civil War

You will be reading the seven selections listed above in this Comparing Points of View feature on the Civil War. In the top corner of each page in this feature, you'll find three stars. Smaller versions of the stars appear next to the questions on page 510 that focus on the Civil War. At the end of the feature (pages 518–519), you'll compare the various points of view expressed in the selections.

### Examining the Issue: The Civil War

During the American Civil War many families, especially in the border states, had friends and relatives in both the North and the South. For such families the Civil War was a profoundly personal conflict. What drove supporters of both sides to carry on, despite devastation to themselves and their families? In the readings that follow, you will find surprising similarities in the ways Northerners and Southerners viewed this terrible conflict in American history.

### Make the Connection

#### Quickwrite ✏️

The United States was not even one hundred years old when the Civil War began. Neither the North nor the South anticipated how long the war would last and how many lives would be lost before it ended. How would you feel if the United States found itself in a similar controversy today? How would your ideas about what unites the states change? Write a few sentences about your thoughts.

**SKILLS FOCUS**

Pages 498–519 cover
**Literary Skills**
Analyze points of view on a topic.

**Reading Skills**
Use prior knowledge.

### Reading Skills 📖

#### Using Prior Knowledge

Make a KWL chart in which you write down what you already know about the Civil War and what you want to know. Fill out what you have learned after you've read the selections that follow.

| K What I Know | W What I Want to Know | L What I Learned |
|---|---|---|
| | | |

# Stephen Crane
## (1871–1900)

**S**tephen Crane was the youngest of the fourteen children of a Methodist minister and his devout wife. Although frail as a child, Stephen grew up—in upstate New York—yearning to become a baseball star. He attended Lafayette College and Syracuse University before deciding to try earning a living as a writer.

When Crane was about sixteen, he took a job at his brother's news agency in New Jersey. Later, working as a reporter in New York City, Crane was drawn to the city's underside. What he called his "artistic education" on the Bowery (Skid Row) left him hungry and often ill.

Crane's first significant fiction, *Maggie: A Girl of the Streets* (1893), was a somber, shocking novel based on his explorations of the city's slums and saloons. This novel revealed Crane as a pioneer of **naturalism**—a literary movement that dissected human instincts and behavior and examined the society that "conditioned" people to turn out as they did. Crane borrowed seven hundred dollars to have it printed. Subsequently the unsold copies lay piled in his room—it was an impossibly grim novel for readers at the time.

Crane's apparent failure with *Maggie* was followed by a triumph—a short novel titled *The Red Badge of Courage* (1895). Using an impressionistic technique, Crane filtered the events of the novel through the eyes of Henry Fleming, a young soldier in the Civil War. (In fiction, **impressionism** is a technique whereby the writer gives us not objective reality but one character's impression of that reality.) Though Crane had never been in battle, he equated war with football. He

wrote, "The psychology is the same. The opposing team is the enemy tribe."

*The Red Badge of Courage* made Crane a celebrity and a national expert on war. He was seen as epitomizing the adventurous war correspondent, living a sensational life, writing about it, and delighting in shocking conservative readers.

Crane had a knack for interweaving his fiction with his real-life experiences. When he sailed from Florida in 1896 to cover a gun-running operation in Cuba, he was shipwrecked and endured a thirty-hour struggle with the sea. The result was his superb story "The Open Boat" (1898).

Before this ill-fated journey, Crane had taken up with a hotel hostess, Cora Taylor. The oddly matched couple later went off to Greece as war correspondents and eventually settled in England. All these adventures were taking their toll on Crane's ever-delicate health. Still he continued to travel and write. In 1899, he produced his second volume of poems, *War Is Kind*. Tuberculosis was sapping his strength, though, and he died in June 1900, at the age of twenty-eight.

## For Independent Reading

For more adventures by Crane, try

- "The Open Boat" (short story)
- *The Red Badge of Courage* (novel)

# Before You Read

## A Mystery of Heroism

### Points of View

**Quickwrite** ✏️

Imagine this scene: In the midst of the frightful noise and bloody destruction of a Civil War battlefield, a soldier suddenly decides to jump up and run straight into the enemy line to get something. To his fellow soldiers it is an impulse that seems simply crazy, but could he be a hero?

The above scene is the one Crane describes in this story. Although he never experienced the war himself, Crane had read firsthand accounts of the mayhem of Civil War battlefields, where often one soldier would escape death and another would die by the merest chance. Dazed by battle, soldiers often struggled later to explain their actions.

Before you read, jot down your thoughts about what makes someone a hero during war. Then, as you read, think about Crane's view of heroism.

### Literary Focus

**Situational Irony**

**Situational irony** occurs when what actually happens differs from what one expects will happen. For example, suppose a heroic soldier is wounded as he battles through war-torn terrain to rescue a fallen comrade—only to find out that the comrade is quite safe and never needed help. The irony of the situation shocks—or at least surprises—both the hero and the reader.

**Literary Skills**
Analyze points of view on a topic. Understand situational irony.

**INTERNET**

Vocabulary Practice
•
More About Stephen Crane
•

Keyword: LE7 11-4

> **Situational irony** takes place when there is a discrepancy between what is expected to happen and what actually happens.
>
> *For more on Irony, see the Handbook of Literary and Historical Terms.*

### Background

In war the military chain of command makes it possible for an army to function. When reading stories about war, you can better understand not only the military action but also the relationships between soldiers by knowing the different military ranks. Here are the ranks mentioned in "A Mystery of Heroism," from highest to lowest:

Colonel
Lieutenant Colonel
Major
Captain
Lieutenant
Sergeant
Private

### Vocabulary Development

**conflagration** (kän′flə·grā′shən) *n.*: huge fire.

**stolidity** (stə·lid′ə·tē) *n.*: absence of emotional reactions.

**ominous** (äm′ə·nəs) *adj.*: threatening; menacing.

**gesticulating** (jes·tik′yoo·lāt′iŋ) *v.* used as *adj.*: gesturing, especially with the hands and arms.

**provisional** (prə·vizh′ə·nəl) *adj.*: temporary; serving for the time being.

**retraction** (ri·trak′shən) *n.*: withdrawal.

**indolent** (in′də·lənt) *adj.*: lazy.

**blanched** (blancht) *v.* used as *adj.*: drained of color.

# A Mystery of Heroism

## Stephen Crane

The dark uniforms of the men were so coated with dust from the incessant wrestling of the two armies that the regiment almost seemed a part of the clay bank which shielded them from the shells. On the top of the hill a battery[1] was arguing in tremendous roars with some other guns, and to the eye of the infantry, the artillerymen, the guns, the caissons,[2] the horses, were distinctly outlined upon the blue sky. When a piece was fired, a red streak as round as a log flashed low in the heavens, like a monstrous bolt of lightning. The men of the battery wore white duck trousers, which somehow emphasized their legs, and when they ran and crowded in little groups at the bidding of the shouting officers, it was more impressive than usual to the infantry.

Fred Collins of A Company was saying: "Thunder, I wisht I had a drink. Ain't there any water round here?" Then somebody yelled: "There goes th' bugler!"

As the eyes of half of the regiment swept in one machinelike movement, there was an instant's picture of a horse in a great convulsive leap of a death wound and a rider leaning back with a crooked arm and spread fingers before his face. On the ground was the crimson terror of an exploding shell, with fibers of flame that seemed like lances. A glittering bugle swung

---

1. **battery** *n.*: set of heavy guns.
2. **caissons** (kā′sənz) *n. pl.*: ammunition wagons.

clear of the rider's back as fell headlong the horse and the man. In the air was an odor as from a conflagration.

Sometimes they of the infantry looked down at a fair little meadow which spread at their feet. Its long, green grass was rippling gently in a breeze. Beyond it was the gray form of a house half torn to pieces by shells and by the busy axes of soldiers who had pursued firewood. The line of an old fence was now dimly marked by long weeds and by an occasional post. A shell had blown the well house to fragments. Little lines of gray smoke ribboning upward from some embers indicated the place where had stood the barn.

From beyond a curtain of green woods there came the sound of some stupendous scuffle as if two animals of the size of islands were fighting. At a distance there were occasional appearances of swift-moving men, horses, batteries, flags, and, with the crashing of infantry, volleys were heard, often, wild and frenzied cheers. In the midst of it all, Smith and Ferguson, two privates of A Company, were engaged in a heated discussion, which involved the greatest questions of the national existence.

The battery on the hill presently engaged in a frightful duel. The white legs of the gunners scampered this way and that way and the officers redoubled their shouts. The guns, with their demeanors of stolidity and courage, were typical of something infinitely self-possessed in this clamor of death that swirled around the hill.

One of a "swing" team was suddenly smitten quivering to the ground and his maddened brethren dragged his torn body in their struggle to escape from this turmoil and danger. A young soldier astride one of the leaders swore and fumed in his saddle and furiously jerked at the bridle. An officer screamed out an order so violently that his voice broke and ended the sentence in a falsetto[3] shriek.

The leading company of the infantry regiment

*The Hornet's Nest* (1895) by Thomas Corwin Lindsay. Oil on canvas.

was somewhat exposed and the colonel ordered it moved more fully under the shelter of the hill. There was the clank of steel against steel.

A lieutenant of the battery rode down and passed them, holding his right arm carefully in his left hand. And it was as if this arm was not at all a part of him, but belonged to another man. His sober and reflective charger[4] went slowly. The officer's face was grimy and perspiring and his uniform was tousled as if he had been in direct grapple with an enemy. He smiled grimly when the men stared at him. He turned his horse toward the meadow.

---

4. **charger** *n.:* horse trained for battle.

---

**Vocabulary**

**conflagration** (kän′flə·grā′shən) *n.:* huge fire.
**stolidity** (stə·lid′ə·tē) *n.:* absence of emotional
   reactions.

---

3. **falsetto** *n.* used as *adj.:* artificially high voice.

Cincinnati Museum Center-Cincinnati Historical Society Library.

Collins of A Company said: "I wisht I had a drink. I bet there's water in that there ol' well yonder!"

"Yes; but how you goin' to git it?"

For the little meadow which intervened was now suffering a terrible onslaught of shells. Its green and beautiful calm had vanished utterly. Brown earth was being flung in monstrous handfuls. And there was a massacre of the young blades of grass. They were being torn, burned, obliterated. Some curious fortune of the battle had made this gentle little meadow the object of the red hate of the shells and each one as it exploded seemed like an imprecation[5] in the face of a maiden.

The wounded officer who was riding across this expanse said to himself: "Why, they couldn't shoot any harder if the whole army was massed here!"

A shell struck the gray ruins of the house and as, after the roar, the shattered wall fell in fragments, there was a noise which resembled the flapping of shutters during a wild gale of winter. Indeed the infantry paused in the shelter of the bank, appeared as men standing upon a shore contemplating a madness of the sea. The angel of calamity[6] had under its glance the battery upon the hill. Fewer white-legged men labored about the guns. A shell had smitten one of the pieces, and after the flare, the smoke, the dust, the wrath of this blow was gone, it was possible to see white legs stretched horizontally upon the ground. And at that interval to the rear, where it is the business of battery horses to stand with their noses to the fight awaiting the command to drag their guns out of the destruction or into it or wheresoever these incomprehensible humans demanded with whip and spur—in this line of passive and dumb spectators, whose fluttering hearts yet would not let them forget the iron laws of man's control of them—in this rank of brute soldiers there had been relentless and hideous carnage. From the ruck[7] of bleeding and prostrate[8] horses, the men of the infantry could see one animal raising its stricken body with its forelegs and turning its nose with mystic and profound eloquence toward the sky.

Some comrades joked Collins about his thirst. "Well, if yeh want a drink so bad, why don't yeh go git it?"

"Well, I will in a minnet if yeh don't shut up."

A lieutenant of artillery floundered his horse straight down the hill with as great concern as if it were level ground. As he galloped past the colonel of the infantry, he threw up his hand in swift salute. "We've got to get out of that," he roared angrily. He was a black-bearded officer, and his eyes, which resembled beads, sparkled

---

5. **imprecation** *n.*: curse.

6. **calamity** *n.*: disaster; misfortune.
7. **ruck** *n.*: mass; crowd.
8. **prostrate** *adj.*: lying flat on the ground.

like those of an insane man. His jumping horse sped along the column of infantry.

The fat major standing carelessly with his sword held horizontally behind him and with his legs far apart, looked after the receding horseman and laughed. "He wants to get back with orders pretty quick or there'll be no batt'ry left," he observed.

The wise young captain of the second company hazarded[9] to the lieutenant colonel that the enemy's infantry would probably soon attack the hill, and the lieutenant colonel snubbed him.

A private in one of the rear companies looked out over the meadow and then turned to a companion and said: "Look there, Jim." It was the wounded officer from the battery, who some time before had started to ride across the meadow, supporting his right arm carefully with his left hand. This man had encountered a shell apparently at a time when no one per-ceived him and he could now be seen lying face downward with a stirruped foot stretched across the body of his dead horse. A leg of the charger extended slantingly upward precisely as stiff as a stake. Around this motionless pair the shells still howled.

There was a quarrel in A Company. Collins was shaking his fist in the faces of some laugh-ing comrades. "Dern yeh! I ain't afraid t' go. If yeh say much, I will go!"

"Of course, yeh will! Yeh'll run through that there medder, won't yeh?"

Collins said, in a terrible voice: "You see, now!" At this <u>ominous</u> threat his comrades broke into renewed jeers.

Collins gave them a dark scowl and went to find his captain. The latter was conversing with the colonel of the regiment.

"Captain," said Collins, saluting and standing at attention. In those days all trousers bagged at the knees. "Captain, I want t' git permission to go git some water from that there well over yonder!"

The colonel and the captain swung about simultaneously and stared across the meadow. The captain laughed. "You must be pretty thirsty, Collins?"

"Yes, sir; I am."

"Well—ah," said the captain. After a moment he asked: "Can't you wait?"

"No, sir."

The colonel was watching Collins's face. "Look here, my lad," he said, in a pious[10] sort of a voice. "Look here, my lad." Collins was not a lad. "Don't you think that's taking pretty big risks for a little drink of water?"

"I dunno," said Collins, uncomfortably. Some of the resentment toward his companions, which perhaps had forced him into this affair, was beginning to fade. "I dunno wether 'tis."

The colonel and the captain contemplated him for a time.

"Well," said the captain finally.

"Well," said the colonel, "if you want to go, why go."

Collins saluted. "Much obliged t' yeh."

As he moved away, the colonel called after him. "Take some of the other boys' canteens with you an' hurry back now."

"Yes, sir. I will."

The colonel and the captain looked at each other then, for it had suddenly occurred that they could not for the life of them tell whether Collins wanted to go or whether he did not.

They turned to regard Collins, and as they perceived him surrounded by <u>gesticulating</u> comrades, the colonel said: "Well, by thunder! I guess he's going."

Collins appeared as a man dreaming. In the midst of the questions, the advice, the warnings, all the excited talk of his company mates, he maintained a curious silence.

---

10. **pious** *adj.*: seemingly virtuous.

**Vocabulary**

**ominous** (äm′ə·nəs) *adj.*: threatening; menacing.
**gesticulating** (jes·tik′yoo·lāt′iŋ) *v.* used as *adj.*: gesturing, especially with the hands and arms.

---

9. **hazarded** *v.*: risked saying.

They were very busy in preparing him for his ordeal. When they inspected him carefully, it was somewhat like the examination that grooms give a horse before a race; and they were amazed, staggered by the whole affair. Their astonishment found vent in strange repetitions.

"Are yeh sure a-goin'?" they demanded again and again.

"Certainly I am," cried Collins, at last furiously.

He strode sullenly[11] away from them. He was swinging five or six canteens by their cords. It seemed that his cap would not remain firmly on his head, and often he reached and pulled it down over his brow.

There was a general movement in the compact column. The long animal-like thing moved slightly. Its four hundred eyes were turned upon the figure of Collins.

"Well, sir, if that ain't th' derndest thing. I never thought Fred Collins had the blood in him for that kind of business."

"What's he goin' to do, anyhow?"

"He's goin' to that well there after water."

"We ain't dyin' of thirst, are we? That's foolishness."

"Well, somebody put him up to it an' he's doin' it."

"Say, he must be a desperate cuss."

When Collins faced the meadow and walked away from the regiment, he was vaguely conscious that a chasm, the deep valley of all prides, was suddenly between him and his comrades. It was provisional, but the provision was that he return as a victor. He had blindly been led by quaint emotions and laid himself under an obligation to walk squarely up to the face of death.

But he was not sure that he wished to make a retraction even if he could do so without shame. As a matter of truth he was sure of very little. He was mainly surprised.

It seemed to him supernaturally strange that he had allowed his mind to maneuver his body into such a situation. He understood that it might be called dramatically great.

However, he had no full appreciation of anything excepting that he was actually conscious of being dazed. He could feel his dulled mind groping after the form and color of this incident.

Too, he wondered why he did not feel some keen agony of fear cutting his sense like a knife. He wondered at this because human expression had said loudly for centuries that men should feel afraid of certain things and that all men who did not feel this fear were phenomena, heroes.

He was then a hero. He suffered that disappointment which we would all have if we discovered that we were ourselves capable of those deeds which we most admire in history and legend. This, then, was a hero. After all, heroes were not much.

No, it could not be true. He was not a hero. Heroes had no shames in their lives and, as for him, he remembered borrowing fifteen dollars from a friend and promising to pay it back the next day, and then avoiding that friend for ten months. When at home his mother had aroused him for the early labor of his life on the farm, it had often been his fashion to be irritable, childish, diabolical, and his mother had died since he had come to the war.

He saw that in this matter of the well, the canteens, the shells, he was an intruder in the land of fine deeds.

He was now about thirty paces from his comrades. The regiment had just turned its many faces toward him.

From the forest of terrific noises there suddenly emerged a little uneven line of men. They fired fiercely and rapidly at distant foliage on which appeared little puffs of white smoke. The

---

11. **sullenly** *adv.*: in a resentful manner; sulkily.

**Vocabulary**

**provisional** (prə·vizh'ə·nəl) *adj.*: temporary; serving for the time being.

**retraction** (ri·trak'shən) *n.*: withdrawal.

spatter of skirmish firing was added to the thunder of the guns on the hill. The little line of men ran forward. A color sergeant fell flat with his flag as if he had slipped on ice. There was hoarse cheering from this distant field.

Collins suddenly felt that two demon fingers were pressed into his ears. He could see nothing but flying arrows, flaming red. He lurched from the shock of this explosion, but he made a mad rush for the house, which he viewed as a man submerged to the neck in a boiling surf might view the shore. In the air, little pieces of shell howled and the earthquake explosions drove him insane with the menace of their roar. As he ran, the canteens knocked together with a rhythmical tinkling.

As he neared the house, each detail of the scene became vivid to him. He was aware of some bricks of the vanished chimney lying on the sod. There was a door which hung by one hinge.

Rifle bullets called forth by the insistent skirmishers came from the far-off bank of foliage. They mingled with the shells and the pieces of shells until the air was torn in all directions by hootings, yells, howls. The sky was full of fiends who directed all their wild rage at his head.

When he came to the well, he flung himself face downward and peered into its darkness. There were furtive silver glintings some feet from the surface. He grabbed one of the canteens and, unfastening its cap, swung it down by the cord. The water flowed slowly in with an indolent gurgle.

And now as he lay with his face turned away, he was suddenly smitten with the terror. It came upon his heart like the grasp of claws. All the power faded from his muscles. For an instant he was no more than a dead man.

The canteen filled with a maddening slowness in the manner of all bottles. Presently he recovered his strength and addressed a screaming oath to it. He leaned over until it seemed as if he intended to try to push water into it with his hands. His eyes as he gazed down into the well

*Charge of VMI Cadets at New Market* (1914) by Benjamin West Clinedinst. Oil on canvas (18″ × 23″).
Virginia Military Institute, Lexington, Virginia.

shone like two pieces of metal and in their expression was a great appeal and a great curse. The stupid water derided[12] him.

There was the blaring thunder of a shell. Crimson light shone through the swift-boiling smoke and made a pink reflection on part of the wall of the well. Collins jerked out his arm and canteen with the same motion that a man would use in withdrawing his head from a furnace.

---

12. **derided** *v.*: mocked.

---

**Vocabulary**
**indolent** (in′də·lənt) *adj.*: lazy.

He scrambled erect and glared and hesitated. On the ground near him lay the old well bucket, with a length of rusty chain. He lowered it swiftly into the well. The bucket struck the water and then turning lazily over, sank. When, with hand reaching tremblingly over hand, he hauled it out, it knocked often against the walls of the well and spilled some of its contents.

In running with a filled bucket, a man can adopt but one kind of gait. So through this terrible field over which screamed practical angels of death Collins ran in the manner of a farmer chased out of a dairy by a bull.

His face went staring white with anticipation—anticipation of a blow that would whirl him around and down. He would fall as he had seen other men fall, the life knocked out of them so suddenly that their knees were no more quick to touch the ground than their heads. He saw the long blue line of the regiment, but his comrades were standing looking at him from the edge of an impossible star. He was aware of some deep wheel ruts and hoof prints in the sod beneath his feet.

The artillery officer who had fallen in this meadow had been making groans in the teeth of the tempest of sound. These futile cries, wrenched from him by his agony, were heard only by shells, bullets. When wild-eyed Collins came running, this officer raised himself. His face contorted and blanched from pain, he was about to utter some great beseeching cry. But suddenly his face straightened and he called: "Say, young man, give me a drink of water, will you?"

Collins had no room amid his emotions for surprise. He was mad from the threats of destruction.

"I can't," he screamed, and in this reply was a full description of his quaking apprehension. His cap was gone and his hair was riotous. His clothes made it appear that he had been dragged over the ground by the heels. He ran on.

The officer's head sank down and one elbow crooked. His foot in its brass-bound stirrup still stretched over the body of his horse and the other leg was under the steed.

But Collins turned. He came dashing back. His face had now turned gray and in his eyes was all terror. "Here it is! Here it is!"

The officer was as a man gone in drink. His arm bended like a twig. His head drooped as if his neck was of willow. He was sinking to the ground, to lie face downward.

Collins grabbed him by the shoulder. "Here it is. Here's your drink. Turn over! Turn over, man, for God's sake!"

With Collins hauling at his shoulder, the officer twisted his body and fell with his face turned toward that region where lived the unspeakable noises of the swirling missiles. There was the faintest shadow of a smile on his lips as he looked at Collins. He gave a sigh, a little primitive breath like that from a child.

Collins tried to hold the bucket steadily, but his shaking hands caused the water to splash all over the face of the dying man. Then he jerked it away and ran on.

The regiment gave him a welcoming roar. The grimed faces were wrinkled in laughter.

His captain waved the bucket away. "Give it to the men!"

The two genial,[13] skylarking[14] young lieutenants were the first to gain possession of it. They played over it in their fashion.

When one tried to drink, the other teasingly knocked his elbow. "Don't, Billie! You'll make me spill it," said the one. The other laughed.

Suddenly there was an oath, the thud of wood on the ground, and a swift murmur of astonishment from the ranks. The two lieutenants glared at each other. The bucket lay on the ground empty. ■

---

13. **genial** *adj.*: friendly; cheerful.
14. **skylarking** *v.* used as *adj.*: frolicking; playful.

---

**Vocabulary**

**blanched** (blancht) *v.* used as *adj.*: drained of color.

Stephen Crane     **507**

## Before You Read

# War Is Kind

### Points of View

When you think of antiwar protests, what images come to mind—shouting crowds bearing placards, flamboyant speakers? Antiwar protests can also be quiet, intimate, and—when given poetic form—timeless, as demonstrated by this poem written more than one hundred years ago.

### Literary Focus
### Verbal Irony

**Verbal irony,** or saying one thing but meaning something completely different, is the most common type of irony. It can take the form of **understatement,** such as "Michael Jordan? Oh, he's a pretty good ballplayer." Verbal irony can take the form of **exaggeration:** "This sour milk smells great!" It can also descend to **sarcasm:** "The police officer stopped the speeder and asked, 'Where's the fire?'" A speaker who uses verbal irony usually expects the audience to understand from the context, the tone, or the obvious facts that the speaker means the opposite of what is being said.

**SKILLS FOCUS**

**Literary Skills**
Analyze points of view on a topic.
Understand verbal irony.

> **Verbal irony** occurs when someone says one thing but really means something completely different.
>
> *For more on Irony, see the Handbook of Literary and Historical Terms.*

**go.
hrw
.com**

**INTERNET**

**More About Stephen Crane**

Keyword: LE7 11-4

*The Young Widow* (1844) by Edward Killingworth Johnson.

# War Is Kind

## Stephen Crane

Do not weep, maiden, for war is kind.
Because your lover threw wild hands
    toward the sky
And the affrighted steed ran on alone,
Do not weep.
5  War is kind.

Hoarse, booming drums of the
    regiment,
Little souls who thirst for fight,
These men were born to drill and die.
The unexplained glory flies above them,
Great is the Battle-God, great, and
10      his Kingdom—
A field where a thousand corpses lie.

Do not weep, babe, for war is kind.
Because your father tumbled in the yellow
    trenches,

Raged at his breast, gulped and died,
15  Do not weep.
War is kind.

Swift blazing flag of the regiment,
Eagle with crest of red and gold,
These men were born to drill and die.
20  Point for them the virtue of slaughter,
Make plain to them the excellence of
    killing
And a field where a thousand corpses lie.

Mother whose heart hung humble as
    a button
On the bright splendid shroud of your son,
25  Do not weep.
War is kind.

# Response and Analysis

## A Mystery of Heroism

### Reading Check

1. What "heroic" task does Collins want to perform?
2. What does Collins do when the wounded officer asks for water?
3. How much of the water in the bucket does Collins drink?

### Thinking Critically

4. What do you think is Collins's **motive** for his daring act? In what sense might the "mystery" in the title of the story refer to Collins's motivation?

5. There is a good deal of "rank" in this short story—lieutenants, a captain, a major, a lieutenant colonel, and a colonel. Collins, however, is a private. How is his low rank significant?

6. Crane draws our attention to the legs of men in white duck (linen) trousers. Why might Crane emphasize this **image**?

7. Find two or three examples in this story showing that Crane believes war **personifies** machines and dehumanizes people. What do you think of this interpretation of war?

8. What **situational irony** occurs at the end of the story? What is its significance?

**SKILLS FOCUS**

**Literary Skills**
Analyze points of view on a topic. Analyze situational irony.

**Writing Skills**
Write an essay comparing two works by the same author.

**Vocabulary Skills**
Demonstrate word knowledge.

## War Is Kind

### Thinking Critically

1. Explain why the refrain "Do not weep. / War is kind" is an example of **verbal irony.**

2. How are the images of war presented in the second and fourth stanzas different from the image of war presented in the rest of the poem?

3. What do you think the "unexplained glory" in line 9 is? Why is it "unexplained"?

4. How would you characterize the overall **tone** of the poem?

### Literary Criticism

5. **Political approach.** Compare the **political views** of the Civil War in "A Mystery of Heroism" and "War Is Kind." Which piece do you think provides a stronger argument against war? How does it do so?

## WRITING

### The Irony of War

Expand on your comparisons of these selections in a brief **essay.** Respond to these questions: In what sense can anyone in the story or in the poem be considered a hero? How does Crane use irony in the story and in the poem to reveal his true attitude toward war? Be sure to cite specific examples. (Check your Quickwrite notes.) 🖊

---

### Vocabulary Development
**Yes or No**

Be sure you can justify your yes or no responses to the following questions.

1. Would an <u>indolent</u> person be called a couch potato?

2. If you saw smoke in the sky, would you suspect a <u>conflagration</u>?

3. Does someone who is scared have a <u>blanched</u> complexion?

4. Do people rejoice at <u>ominous</u> news?

5. Does a <u>provisional</u> official remain in office for life?

6. Is <u>stolidity</u> during a crisis a sign of self-discipline?

7. Does a man who issues a <u>retraction</u> refuse to take back his remarks?

8. Does a <u>gesticulating</u> speaker emphasize ideas better than a motionless speaker?

---

Group from Company A, Eighth New York State Militia in Arlington, Virginia (1861).

# Connected Readings

## The Civil War

The story and poem you have just read—"A Mystery of Heroism" and "War Is Kind"—present a literary response to the Civil War. The next five readings are nonfiction accounts written by either participants, observers, or historians of the Civil War. As you read, consider how the points of view expressed in these pieces are alike and how they are different. After you read these selections, you'll find questions on pages 518–519 asking you to compare all seven readings.

## Points *of* View

### Before You Read

In 1861, when his home state of Virginia seceded, Robert E. Lee (1807–1870) was offered command of the Union army. He chose instead to stay with his "native state" and thus with the Confederacy. Lee became commander of the Confederate army in 1862 and made a number of daring and successful raids northward. After Gettysburg, however, he gradually fell back until he was forced to surrender at Appomattox.

The American historian Bruce Catton writes, "Lee might have ridden down from the old age of chivalry, lance in hand." He was an idealistic man whose honorable behavior at Appomattox, together with that of the Union commander, Ulysses S. Grant, made reconciliation possible. This letter to his son reveals Lee's views of secession and war at a time when he still hoped war could be prevented.

*General Robert E. Lee* (c. 1865) by John Adams Elder.

LETTER

# Letter to His Son

## Robert E. Lee

January 23, 1861

I received Everett's[1] *Life of Washington* which you sent me, and enjoyed its perusal.[2] How his spirit would be grieved could he see the wreck of his mighty labors! I will not, however, permit myself to believe, until all ground of hope is gone, that the fruit of his noble deeds will be destroyed, and that his precious advice and virtuous example will so soon be forgotten by his countrymen. As far as I can judge by the papers, we are between a state of anarchy[3] and civil war. May God avert both of these evils from us! I fear that mankind will not for years be sufficiently Christianized to bear the absence of restraint and force. I see that four states[4] have declared themselves out of the Union; four more will apparently follow their example. Then, if the border states are brought into the gulf of revolution, one half of the country will be arrayed[5] against the other. I must try and be patient and await the end, for I can do nothing to hasten or retard it.

The South, in my opinion, has been aggrieved by the acts of the North, as you say. I feel the aggression and am willing to take every proper step for redress.[6] It is the principle I contend for, not individual or private benefit. As an American citizen, I take great pride in my country, her prosperity and institutions, and would defend any state if her rights were invaded. But I can anticipate no greater calamity for the country than a dissolution[7] of the Union. It would be an accumulation of all the evils we complain of, and I am willing to sacrifice everything but honor for its preservation. I hope, therefore, that all constitutional means will be exhausted before there is a resort to force. Secession is nothing but revolution. The framers of our Constitution never exhausted so much labor, wisdom, and forbearance in its formation, and surrounded it with so many guards and securities, if it was intended to be broken by every member of the Confederacy at will. It was intended for "perpetual union," so expressed in the preamble, and for the establishment of a government, not a compact,[8] which can only be dissolved by revolution or the consent of all the people in convention assembled. It is idle to talk of secession. Anarchy would have been established, and not a government, by Washington, Hamilton, Jefferson, Madison, and the other patriots of the Revolution. . . . Still, a Union that can only be maintained by swords and bayonets, and in which strife and civil war are to take the place of brotherly love and kindness, has no charm for me. I shall mourn for my country and for the welfare and progress of mankind. If the Union is dissolved, and the government disrupted, I shall return to my native state and share the miseries of my people; and, save in defense, will draw my sword on none.

*R. E. Lee*

---

1. **Everett's:** Edward Everett (1794–1865) was an American statesman and orator who spoke at Gettysburg before Abraham Lincoln delivered his famous speech.
2. **perusal** *n.:* act of reading carefully.
3. **anarchy** *n.:* complete absence of government.
4. **four states:** South Carolina, Mississippi, Florida, and Alabama.
5. **arrayed** *v.:* set up; placed in order.
6. **redress** *n.:* correction for a wrong done.

7. **dissolution** *n.:* breaking up into parts.
8. **compact** *n.:* agreement between two or more states.

In July 1861, Maj. Sullivan Ballou of Rhode Island wrote this letter to his wife, Sarah—a letter that reveals his devotion to both the Union cause and his wife and family. A week later Ballou was killed near Manassas, Virginia, in the First Battle of Bull Run.

LETTER

# Letter to Sarah Ballou
## Maj. Sullivan Ballou

> July 14, 1861
> Camp Clark, Washington

My very dear Sarah:

The indications are very strong that we shall move in a few days—perhaps tomorrow. Lest I should not be able to write again, I feel impelled to write a few lines that may fall under your eye when I shall be no more. . . .

I have no misgivings about, or lack of confidence in the cause in which I am engaged, and my courage does not halt or falter. I know how strongly American Civilization now leans on the triumph of the Government, and how great a debt we owe to those who went before us through the blood and sufferings of the Revolution. And I am willing—perfectly willing—to lay down all my joys in this life, to help maintain this Government, and to pay that debt. . . .

Sarah, my love for you is deathless; it seems to bind me with mighty cables that nothing but Omnipotence° could break; and yet my love of Country comes over me like a strong wind and bears me unresistibly on with all these chains to the battlefield.

The memories of the blissful moments I have spent with you come creeping over me, and I feel most gratified to God and to you that I have enjoyed them so long. And hard it is for me to give them up and burn to ashes the hopes of future years, when, God willing, we might still have lived and loved together, and seen our sons grown up to honorable manhood around us. I have, I know, but few and small claims upon Divine Providence, but something whispers to me—perhaps it is the wafted prayer of my little Edgar, that I shall return to my loved ones unharmed. If I do not, my dear Sarah, never forget how much I love you, and when my last breath escapes me on the battlefield, it will whisper your name. Forgive my many faults, and the many pains I have caused you. How thoughtless and foolish I have oftentimes been! How gladly would I wash out with my tears every little spot upon your happiness. . . .

But, O Sarah! If the dead can come back to this earth and flit unseen around those they loved, I shall always be near you; in the gladdest days and in the darkest nights . . . *always, always,* and if there be a soft breeze upon your cheek, it shall be my breath; as the cool air fans your throbbing temple, it shall be my spirit passing by. Sarah, do not mourn me dead; think I am gone and wait for thee, for we shall meet again. . . .

*Sullivan*

---

°**Omnipotence:** one who has unlimited power (meaning God).

## Points of View

**Before You Read**

The blood bath of Gettysburg, fought on July 1–3, 1863, was the greatest single battle of the Civil War and its turning point. The battle left 51,000 dead, wounded, captured, or missing. A few days after the battle, President Abraham Lincoln commented that he was "not prepared to make [a speech] worthy of the occasion." Several months later, at the dedication of a Gettysburg memorial cemetery on November 19, Lincoln did in fact deliver this "worthy" speech, probably the most memorable of his career.

**SPEECH**

# The Gettysburg Address
## Abraham Lincoln

Fourscore and seven[1] years ago our fathers brought forth on this continent a new nation, conceived[2] in Liberty, and dedicated to the proposition that all men are created equal.

Now we are engaged in a great civil war, testing whether that nation, or any nation so conceived and so dedicated, can long endure. We are met on a great battlefield of that war. We have come to dedicate a portion of that field as a final resting place for those who here gave their lives that that nation might live. It is altogether fitting and proper that we should do this.

But, in a larger sense, we cannot dedicate—we cannot consecrate[3]—we cannot hallow[4]—this ground. The brave men, living and dead, who struggled here, have consecrated it far above our poor power to add or detract. The world will little note nor long remember what we say here, but it can never forget what they did here. It is for us the living, rather, to be dedicated here to the unfinished work which they who fought here have thus far so nobly advanced. It is rather for us to be here dedicated to the great task remaining before us—that from these honored dead we take increased devotion to that cause for which they gave the last full measure of devotion—that we here highly resolve that these dead shall not have died in vain—that this nation, under God, shall have a new birth of freedom—and that government of the people, by the people, for the people, shall not perish from the earth.

*A. Lincoln—*

---

1. **fourscore and seven:** eighty-seven. A score is a set of twenty.
2. **conceived** *v.* used as *adj.*: developed; imagined.
3. **consecrate** *v.*: set apart as sacred or holy.
4. **hallow** *v.*: make holy.

## Points *of* View

### Before You Read

Mary Boykin Chesnut was the wife of James Chesnut, a former U.S. senator from South Carolina and an aide to Jefferson Davis, president of the Confederacy. During the course of the war, Mary Chesnut traveled from city to city in the South as the capital of the Confederacy changed. She kept up with the war news through her husband and their wide circle of knowledgeable and influential friends. Mary Chesnut was sophisticated, witty, and sensitive. Her diaries present an invaluable firsthand view of life in the South during the war.

Mary Chesnut had been in Charleston, South Carolina, in April 1861, when the attack on Fort Sumter took place, beginning the Civil War. As she had been present at the beginning of the war, Mary Chesnut was also present at its end. In Columbia, South Carolina, she received the news, increasingly discouraging, from the field.

DIARY

# *from* A Diary from Dixie
## Mary Chesnut

September 1, 1864

The battle is raging at Atlanta, our fate hanging in the balance.

September 2, 1864

Atlanta is gone. Well that agony is over. Like David, when the child was dead, I will get up from my knees, will wash my face and comb my hair.° There is no hope, but we will try to have no fear. . .

September 21, 1864

The president [of the Confederacy] has gone West. He has sent for Mr. Chesnut.

I went with Mrs. Rhett to hear Dr. Palmer [a minister]. I did not know before how utterly hopeless was our situation. This man is so eloquent; it was hard to listen and not give way. Despair was his word, and martyrdom. He offered us nothing more in this world than the martyr's crown. He is not for slavery, he says; he is for freedom, the freedom to govern our own country as we see fit. He is against foreign interference in our state matters. That is what Mr. Palmer went to war for, it appears. Every day shows that slavery is doomed the world over. For that he thanked God. He spoke of this time of our agony; and then came the cry: "Help us, Oh God! Vain is the help of man." So we came away shaken to the depths. . . .

The end has come, no doubt of the fact. . . . We are going to be wiped off the face of the earth. Now what is there to prevent Sherman taking General Lee in the rear. We have but two armies, and Sherman is between them now.

September 29, 1864

These stories of our defeats in the Valley fall like blows upon a dead body. Since Atlanta, I have felt as if all were dead within me, forever. Captain Ogden of General Chesnut's staff dined here today. Had ever a Brigadier with little or no brigade so magnificent a staff? The reserves, as somebody said, are gathered by robbing the cradle and the grave of men too old and boys too young. . . .

October 30, 1864

Every man is being hurried to the front. Today Mr. Chesnut met a poor creature coming from the surgeon's with a radiant face and a certificate. "General, see! I am exempt from service; one leg utterly useless, the other not warranted to last three months."

---

°**Like David . . . comb my hair:** Chesnut alludes to 2 Samuel 12:20–23 in the Bible, where David weeps and prays for his sick child.

## Points *of* View
### Before You Read

An acknowledged expert on the Civil War, the American historian and novelist Shelby Foote (1916–2005) was born in Mississippi and served as a captain of field artillery during World War II. Several years after that war he signed a contract to write a short history of the Civil War but soon realized that he would have to go "whole hog on the thing." In the end, Foote's classic three-volume work, *The Civil War,* ran to three thousand pages and took twenty years to complete. The questions and answers in this reading are culled from many hours of on-camera conversations with Ken Burns, maker of the documentary film series *The Civil War.*

INTERVIEW

# *from* Men at War: An Interview with Shelby Foote
## Ken Burns

### Why are we drawn to the Civil War?

Any understanding of this nation has to be based, and I mean really based, on an understanding of the Civil War. I believe that firmly. It defined us. The Revolution did what it did. Our involvement in European wars, beginning with the First World War, did what it did. But the Civil War defined us as what we are and it opened us to being what we became, good and bad things. And it is very necessary, if you're going to understand the American character in the twentieth century, to learn about this enormous catastrophe of the nineteenth century. It was the crossroads of our being, and it was a hell of a crossroads. . . .

### Did the soldiers on both sides really know what they were fighting for?

Early on in the war, a Union squad closed in on a single ragged Confederate. He didn't own any slaves and he obviously didn't have much interest in the Constitution or anything else. And they asked him, "What are you fighting for anyhow?" And he said, "I'm fighting because you're down here." Which was a pretty satisfactory answer. Lincoln had the much more difficult job of sending men out to shoot up somebody else's home. He had to unite them before he could do that, and his way of doing it was twofold. One was to say the Republic must be preserved, not split in two. That was one. And the other one he gave them as a cause: the freeing of the slaves.

But no one on either side thought it would last long. Those few individuals who said that it *would,* William Tecumseh Sherman° for instance, were actually judged to be insane for making predictions about casualties which were actually low. There was even a congressman, I believe from Alabama, who said there would be no war, and offered to wipe up all the blood that would be shed with a pocket handkerchief. I've always said someone could get a Ph.D. by calculating how many pocket handkerchiefs it would take to wipe up all the blood that was shed. It would be a lot of handkerchiefs.

### Did the South ever have a chance of winning?

I think that the North fought that war with one hand behind its back. At the same time the war

---

°**William Tecumseh Sherman** (1820–1891): Union general in the Civil War, known for his military genius.

*The Battle of Gettysburg: Pickett's Charge* (detail) by Peter F. Rothermel.
State Museum of Pennsylvania, Pennsylvania Historical and Museum Commission.

was going on, the Homestead Act was being passed, all these marvelous inventions were going on. In the spring of 1864, the Harvard-Yale boat races were going on and not a man in either crew ever volunteered for the army or the navy. They didn't need them. I think that if there had been more Southern victories, and a lot more, the North simply would have brought that other arm out from behind its back. I don't think the South ever had a chance to win that war. . . .

### How did the war change us? What did we become?

The Civil War was really one of those watershed things. There was a huge chasm between the beginning and the end of the war. The nation had come face to face with a dreadful tragedy and we reacted the way a family would do with a dreadful tragedy. It was almost inconceivable that anything that horrendous could happen. You must remember that casualties in Civil War battles were so far beyond anything we can

imagine now. If we had 10 percent casualties in a battle today, it would be looked on as a blood bath. They had 30 percent in several battles. And one after another, you see.

And yet that's what made us a nation. Before the war, people had a theoretical notion of having a country, but when the war was over, on both sides they knew they had a country. They'd been there. They had walked its hills and tramped its roads. They saw the country and they knew they had a country. And they knew the effort that they had expended and their dead friends had expended to preserve it. It did that. The war made their country an actuality.

Before the war, it was said, "The United States are. . . ." Grammatically, it was spoken that way and thought of as a collection of independent states. After the war, it was always "The United States *is* . . ."—as we say today without being self-conscious at all. And that sums up what the war accomplished. It made us an "is."

**Ken Burns and Shelby Foote** 517

# Analysis Comparing Points of View

## The Civil War

The questions on this page ask you to analyze the views on the Civil War presented in the preceding seven selections:

Stephen Crane . . . . . . . . **A Mystery of Heroism**

Stephen Crane . . . . . . . . **War Is Kind**

Robert E. Lee . . . . . . . . . **Letter to His Son**

Maj. Sullivan Ballou . . . . **Letter to Sarah Ballou**

Abraham Lincoln . . . . . . **The Gettysburg Address**

Mary Chesnut . . . . . . . . from **A Diary from Dixie**

Ken Burns . . . . . . . . . . from **Men at War: An Interview with Shelby Foote**

### Thinking Critically

1. Look back at your KWL chart (see page 498), and fill in the last column, titled "What I Learned." Considering your prior knowledge, what surprises did you find in these selections?

2. How would you characterize the overall emotional impact of these seven readings on the Civil War? As a group, how do they document and dramatize the *human* cost of the war?

3. Shelby Foote says of the Civil War, "If we'd been anything like as superior as we think we are, we would not have fought that war." Judging from the Gettysburg Address and "Letter to His Son," would Abraham Lincoln and Robert E. Lee also have preferred to avoid war? Summarize their views on this topic, as implied or stated in these readings.

4. Shelby Foote observes that before the Civil War, the usual grammatical construction was "The United States are . . ."—a construction suggesting that people thought of the states as separate, self-governing entities. Where in these selections do you find echoes of this strong sense of home state as one's personal "country"? Foote further remarks that the war "made us an 'is.'" How do you feel about this notion of union in our country today? (Look back at your Quickwrite notes from page 498.)

5. Each of the seven works in this feature implies or states political points of view on the Civil War. For you, which selection offers the *clearest* political statement? Discuss your choice with your classmates, using evidence from the text to support your choice. Discuss whether the viewpoints expressed in your choice are consistent with viewpoints expressed in the works your classmates selected.

*Mary Boykin Chesnut* (1856) by Samuel Osgood (1801–1885). Oil on canvas adhered to masonite (48″ × 30″).

National Portrait Gallery, Smithsonian Institution; © Private Collection. Courtesy Art Resource, NY.

**SKILLS FOCUS**

Pages 498–519 cover

**Literary Skills**
Analyze and compare points of view on a topic.

**Reading Skills**
Use prior knowledge.

**Writing Skills**
Write an essay comparing themes.

6. Chesnut, Lincoln, Ballou, and Lee personally experienced the Civil War, making their writings primary sources. Crane and Foote, who studied the war, provide us with secondary sources. For analyzing political views on the Civil War, which type of source proved more helpful to you? Explain your reasons.

7. Elsewhere in his interview with Ken Burns, Shelby Foote makes the following remarks on Lincoln's writing ability:

> He's knocking on the door of Mark Twain. He's a very great writer. When I was a child in Mississippi, I was required to memorize the Gettysburg Address. . . . What it said didn't have anything to do with whether or not I was required to memorize it. It was literary skill that made me memorize it. . . . His literary skill is almost unbelievable.

However, a correspondent for the London *Times,* who was present at the speech, made these remarks about Lincoln's writing:

> The ceremony was rendered ludicrous by . . . the sallies of that poor President Lincoln. . . . Anyone more dull and commonplace it would not be easy to produce.

Re-read Lincoln's address, and then state which critic you agree with and why. Be sure to back up your remarks with specific references to Lincoln's text.

## WRITING

### Tracing a Theme

The seven readings included in this Comparing Points of View feature range from fiction and poetry to a public speech, letters, a diary excerpt, and an interview. Many universal themes run through these writings, themes having to do with honor, heroism, grief, loss, idealism, and devotion to a cause. Choose one theme, and write an **essay** comparing the ways that theme is developed in two or more of the selections. Focus on the writers' ideas of that theme in the context of the Civil War.

*Guerrilla Warfare* or *Picket Duty in Virginia* (1862) by Albert Bierstadt.

# Chief Joseph
## (c. 1840–1904)

**B**orn in what is now Oregon, Chief Joseph, or In-mut-too-yah-lat-lat, has become a symbol of the heroic spirit of the Nez Perce of the Pacific Northwest. During the first half of the nineteenth century, the Nez Perce were friendly to European settlers. Many American Indians, including Joseph's father, were converted to Christianity, and Joseph attended a mission school. After 1850, however, the influx of white settlers into the Pacific Northwest motivated U.S. officials to draw up treaties removing American Indians from their lands and resettling them on small reservations. Many Nez Perce believed these treaties had been signed by chiefs who did not represent their people.

When Joseph became Nez Perce chief in 1871, he continued his father's policy and refused to sign a treaty that would send his people to a reservation. The United States responded with force, and Chief Joseph and his people were drawn into battle. In 1877, when the Nez Perce were ordered to move from their native Wallowa Valley in Oregon to the Lapwai Reservation in Idaho, Chief Joseph reluctantly agreed, hoping to avoid bloodshed. Then he learned that three of his men had killed a group of white settlers. Fearing retaliation, he attempted to escape to Canada with a few hundred warriors and their families. From June to September, Chief Joseph led a retreat of more than a thousand miles through Oregon, Washington, Idaho, and Montana, masterfully outmaneuvering and sometimes defeating U.S. troops. His caravan made it to within forty miles of the Canadian border before exhaustion and near starvation forced them to stop.

On surrender, the Nez Perce were first taken to a barren reservation in Indian Territory (now a part of Oklahoma), where many became sick and died. Chief Joseph traveled twice to Washington, D.C., to plead with President Theodore Roosevelt for the return of his people to their ancestral home.

Chief Joseph delivered the following speech when he surrendered to Gen. Nelson A. Miles of the U.S. Army on October 5, 1877. General Howard was the military commander who presented the Nez Perce with an ultimatum to give up their land and move to a reservation.

In 1885, the Nez Perce were moved to Colville Reservation in Washington State, but they were never allowed to return to the Wallowa Valley. Chief Joseph died in Colville on September 21, 1904.

# Before You Read

## "I Will Fight No More Forever"

### Make the Connection

In 1871, when Chief Joseph's father was dying, he urged his son, "You must stop your ears whenever you are asked to sign a treaty selling your home. . . . This country holds your father's body. Never sell the bones of your father and mother." As you read this speech, consider how his father's words might have affected Chief Joseph when he was surrendering.

### Literary Focus
#### American Indian Oratory

For centuries most American Indians have relied on spoken language for diplomacy, decision making, and preservation of their history and culture. In American Indian cultures, spoken language mystically links the natural and spiritual worlds and has the power to shape and control events. Thus, American Indians have often chosen their leaders in part for their eloquence. Important speeches are even memorized exactly as spoken and passed on orally for generations.

Chief Joseph was a particularly eloquent speaker. "'I Will Fight No More Forever'" is well remembered today, more than one hundred years after the delivery of the speech. As you read, pay attention to the qualities that make it so powerful, especially **repetition** and **tone**.

---

## "I Will Fight No More Forever"

### Chief Joseph

Tell General Howard I know his heart. What he told me before, I have in my heart. I am tired of fighting. Our chiefs are killed. Looking Glass is dead. Toohoolhoolzote is dead. The old men are all dead. It is the young men who say yes and no. He who led on the young men is dead. It is cold and we have no blankets. The little children are freezing to death. My people, some of them, have run away to the hills and have no blankets, no food; no one knows where they are—perhaps freezing to death. I want to have time to look for my children and see how many I can find. Maybe I shall find them among the dead. Hear me, my chiefs. I am tired; my heart is sick and sad. From where the sun now stands I will fight no more forever.

**SKILLS FOCUS**

**Literary Skills**
Understand the characteristics of American Indian oratory, including repetition and tone.

*Chief Joseph Rides to Surrender* (detail) by Howard Terpning.

Courtesy The Greenwich Workshop, Inc. © 1982.

# Response and Analysis

## Reading Check

1. In "'I Will Fight No More Forever,'" what has happened to the leaders among Chief Joseph's people?

2. What is the major reason that Chief Joseph gives for his surrender to U.S. forces?

## Thinking Critically

3. What **tone** does Chief Joseph establish by using words such as *heart, tired, freezing,* and *dead?*

4. What words are repeated frequently throughout the speech? What effect does this **repetition** create?

5. Judging by this speech, how would you describe Chief Joseph's relationship to his people? What phrases or sentences support your interpretation?

6. Does Chief Joseph's speech appeal to logic, to emotion, or to both? Explain your response.

## WRITING

### Reservations Today

Using data supplied by the U.S. Census Bureau or other sources, such as the U.S. Economic Development Administration (both of which have sites on the Internet), find out more about American Indian reservations today. You might want to find out where the Nez Perce live and the location and population of other reservations across the country. Also find out about life on a typical reservation, including such aspects as the structure and functioning of schools and local governments. Present your findings in a brief **report.** If you wish, include a map or chart with your report.

**SKILLS FOCUS**

**Literary Skills**
Analyze the characteristics of American Indian oratory, including repetition and tone.

**Writing Skills**
Write a brief research report.

# Mark Twain
## (1835–1910)

**M**ark Twain is the most celebrated humorist in American history. His ability to make us laugh has contributed to the singular popularity of his books, not just in Twain's own time but in following generations. It is even more surprising to find that Twain's appeal has traveled throughout the world.

The great humorist is also, ironically, our great realist. Behind the backwoods humor—especially in his novel *Adventures of Huckleberry Finn*—is a revelation of the illusions that exist in American life. Huck's journey on a raft with the escaped slave Jim is not a "hymn to boyhood." It is a dramatization of the grim realities of a slaveholding society.

Although Twain became remarkably successful, his later life was shadowed by disappointment and tragedy, and as he grew older, he turned into a bitter man. He once told his friend William Dean Howells, the influential novelist and editor of *The Atlantic Monthly,* "Everyone is a moon and has a dark side which he never shows to anybody."

### "Mark Twain!"

Twain was born Samuel Langhorne Clemens in the backwoods of Missouri. His father, John Clemens, a bright, ambitious, but impractical Virginian, had married Jane Lampton, a witty, dynamic woman who was also a great beauty. When John's store failed in 1839, he moved his hopes and his family to Hannibal, Missouri—the Mississippi River town that Sam, writing as Mark Twain, would later fashion into the setting of the most renowned boyhood in American literature, that of Tom Sawyer.

Sam's own carefree boyhood ended at twelve when his father died. To help support his mother and sister, he went to work setting type and editing copy for the newspaper started by his older brother Orion. At

*Mark Twain* (1935) by Frank Edwin Larson. Oil on canvas (48″ × 36″).

eighteen, Sam set out on his own. Over the next fifteen years, he worked as a printer in various towns from Missouri to the East Coast. Smitten by a love for the magical steamboats that plied the Mississippi, he apprenticed himself to the great steamboat pilot Horace Bixby. From Bixby, Sam Clemens learned the bends and shallows of the great river. It was the leadsman's cry of "Mark twain!"—announcing a water depth of two fathoms (twelve feet)—that provided Clemens with his celebrated pen name.

### A Gold Mine of Humor

For a short time during the Civil War, Twain was a soldier with a company of Confederate irregulars, but he soon abandoned the military life for that of a gold prospector in Nevada. While he found little gold there, he did discover the rich mine of storytelling within himself. With his Missouri drawl and relaxed manner, Twain captivated audiences. In pretending not to recognize the coarseness or absurdity of his material, Twain maintained a deadpan attitude that added to his material's hilarity.

Twain soon turned his comic voice to prose, working as a journalist between 1862 and 1871. In 1865, he achieved wide recognition as a humorist with the publication of his version of an old tall tale, "The Celebrated Jumping Frog of Calaveras County." Four years later, Twain's dispatches from a Mediterranean tour were published as a book titled *The Innocents Abroad*. This satirical travelogue poked fun at the traditional American pilgrimage to the monuments of European civilization. It sold well, and Twain had launched a prosperous literary career.

## An American Masterpiece

At thirty-five, with a raffish, barroom air about him, Twain was a dubious candidate for marriage, but he courted Olivia Langdon, the daughter of an affluent family from Elmira, New York. She was a delicate, proper woman, but Twain overcame all resistance, and in 1870, Livy's father gave the couple his consent and a lavish wedding. Twain embarked on a marriage of unceasing devotion.

In 1871, Twain moved to Hartford, Connecticut, where he built an enormous home that is visited today by thousands of tourists. The next year he published *Roughing It*, which drew on his experiences as a tenderfoot in the West. Then William Dean Howells invited Twain to do a series for *The Atlantic Monthly* about his days as a riverboat pilot. Those reminiscences were eventually expanded into the book *Life on the Mississippi* (1883).

By the mid-1870s, Twain was also at work on *The Adventures of Tom Sawyer* (1876). This celebration of boyhood absorbed him but presented difficulties of voice and point of view. Twain could not decide whether he was writing a book for children or for adults. Nevertheless, in writing the book he made an imaginative return to the Hannibal of his childhood and succeeded in transforming it into a compelling myth.

In *Adventures of Huckleberry Finn* (1884), Twain found the voice he had been seeking. Through Huck's natural, slangy first-person narration, Twain caused a revolution in American literature. As Ernest Hemingway (page 682), speaking through a fictional character, later put it, "All modern American literature comes from one book by Mark Twain called *Huckleberry Finn*." T. S. Eliot (page 655), a fellow Missourian, added that Twain's was "a new way of writing . . . a literary language based on American colloquial speech."

## Loss and Legacy

Twain was never able to duplicate the success of *Huckleberry Finn*, but he continued to produce popular books, including *A Connecticut Yankee in King Arthur's Court* (1889) and *Pudd'nhead Wilson* (1894). Twain's later years were marked by financial and professional disappointment as well as personal tragedy. His fascination with business and getting ahead financially, so typical of the new middle class, led him to invest, disastrously, in the Paige typesetting machine. The economic panic of 1893 bankrupted him.

Then illness overtook the close-knit Clemens family. Susy, Twain's eldest daughter, died of meningitis in 1896. His wife, who was chronically ill during her last years, died in 1904. In a final blow, Jean, his youngest daughter, died in an epileptic seizure in 1909. "Possibly," said Twain after Jean's death, "I know now what the soldier feels when a bullet crashes through his heart." Four months later he too was dead.

As loss followed loss and as the whole country seemed to lose its vitality and become more complex, Twain turned into an obsessive, embittered old man. In his final years the subject matter of his work was his own disillusionment on a grand scale; the great comic writer appeared to be at war with the entire human race.

### For Independent Reading

We recommend these books by Twain:

- *Adventures of Huckleberry Finn* (novel)
- *Life on the Mississippi* (memoir)
- *Roughing It* (travel sketches)

# Before You Read

## The Celebrated Jumping Frog of Calaveras County

### Make the Connection

Mark Twain took a story he'd heard in the mining camps and turned it into a classic of American humor. In fact, this story is famous as an example of the American **tall tale,** a humorous story characterized by outrageous exaggeration and outlandish events. Twain's story demonstrates a key aspect of all humor: It's not only *what you say* but also *how you say it* that makes people laugh.

### Literary Focus
#### Comic Devices

Why something is funny is hard to explain, but here are some commonly used devices that for some reason usually make people laugh:

- **hyperbole**—outrageous exaggeration
- **understatement**—saying less than what is really meant, usually for ironic purposes
- **comic comparisons**—similes and metaphors that surprisingly link very dissimilar things and thus create colorful, outlandish images
- **comic characters and situations**—unusual people dealing with unlikely events; probably the oldest and most reliable comic device

As you read the story, look for examples of each of these devices.

Comic devices include **hyperbole,** or outrageous exaggeration, and **understatement,** saying less than what is meant, usually for ironic purposes.
*For more on Hyperbole and Understatement, see the Handbook of Literary and Historical Terms.*

### Reading Skills
#### Understanding Vernacular

Use of the **vernacular** (the language commonly spoken by people in a particular place or region) is an essential element of Mark Twain's style. In this story it helps Twain create vivid characters and capture the flavor of a rough-and-tumble mining camp in the gold rush era. A vernacular usually includes **unique vocabulary,** characteristic **idioms** (expressions and constructions that make no literal sense, such as *raining cats and dogs*), and **dialect** forms (local variations of spoken words).

A vernacular can be difficult to understand if you are not familiar with it. Try reading aloud confusing words or phrases, especially those with unconventional spellings. Notice, for instance, that *feller'd* may look unfamiliar at first, but if you read the word aloud in its context ("but that *feller'd* offer to bet on it"), it becomes clear that the word *feller'd* means "fellow would."

### Vocabulary Development

**garrulous** (gar′ə·ləs) *adj.*: talking a great deal, especially about unimportant things.

**conjectured** (kən·jek′chərd) *v.*: guessed; predicted.

**infamous** (in′fə·məs) *adj.*: having a bad reputation.

**dilapidated** (də·lap′ə·dāt′id) *adj.*: partially ruined; in need of repair.

**interminable** (in·tʉr′mi·nə·bəl) *adj.*: endless; seeming to last forever.

**SKILLS FOCUS**

**Literary Skills**
Understand comic devices.

**Reading Skills**
Understand author's style and use of the vernacular.

**INTERNET**

**Vocabulary Practice**
•
**More About Mark Twain**
•

Keyword: LE7 11-4

# The CELEBRATED JUMPING FROG of Calaveras County

**Mark Twain**

There couldn't be no solit'ry thing mentioned but that feller'd offer to bet on it . . .

In compliance with the request of a friend of mine, who wrote me from the East, I called on good-natured, garrulous old Simon Wheeler and inquired after my friend's friend, *Leonidas W. Smiley*, as requested to do, and I hereunto append the result. I have a lurking suspicion that *Leonidas W. Smiley* is a myth; that my friend never knew such a personage; and that he only conjectured that if I asked old Wheeler about him, it would remind him of his infamous *Jim* Smiley, and he would go to work and bore me nearly to death with some infernal reminiscence[1] of him as long and tedious it should be useless to me. If that was the design, it certainly succeeded.

I found Simon Wheeler dozing comfortably by the barroom stove of the old, dilapidated tavern in the ancient mining camp of Angel's, and I noticed that he was fat and baldheaded and had an expression of winning gentleness and simplicity upon his tranquil countenance.[2] He roused up and gave me good day. I told him a friend of mine had commissioned me to make some inquiries about a cherished companion of his boyhood named *Leonidas W. Smiley—Rev. Leonidas W.* Smiley—a young minister of the gospel, who he had heard was at one time a resident of Angel's Camp. I added that if Mr. Wheeler could tell me anything about this Rev. Leonidas W. Smiley, I would feel under many obligations to him.

Simon Wheeler backed me into a corner and blockaded me there with his chair and then sat me down and reeled off the monotonous narrative which follows this paragraph. He never smiled, he never frowned, he never changed his voice from the gentle-flowing key to which he tuned the initial sentence, he never betrayed the slightest suspicion of enthusiasm; but all through the interminable narrative there ran a vein of impressive earnestness and sincerity, which showed me plainly that so far from his imagining that there was anything ridiculous or

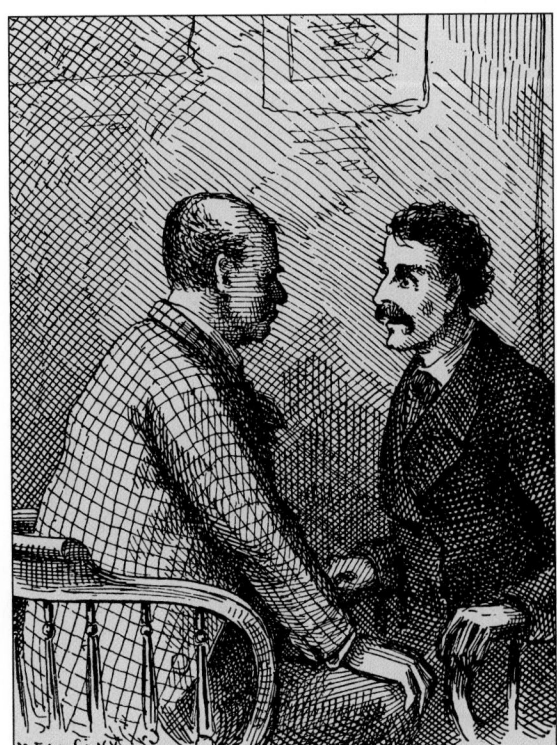

funny about his story, he regarded it as a really important matter and admired its two heroes as men of transcendent genius in finesse.[3] To me, the spectacle of a man drifting serenely along through such a queer yarn without ever smiling was exquisitely absurd. As I said before, I asked him to tell me what he knew of Rev. Leonidas W. Smiley, and he replied as follows. I let him go on in his own way, and never interrupted him once:

There was a feller here once by the name of *Jim* Smiley, in the winter of '49—or maybe it was

---

3. **transcendent genius in finesse** (fə·nes′): exceptional skill and craftiness.

---

1. **infernal reminiscence:** awful or unpleasant story of past experiences.
2. **tranquil countenance:** calm face.

the spring of '50—I don't recollect exactly, somehow, though what makes me think it was one or the other is because I remember the big flume[4] wasn't finished when he first came to the camp; but anyway, he was the curiousest man about always betting on anything that turned up you ever see, if he could get anybody to bet on the other side; and if he couldn't, he'd change sides. Any way that suited the other man would suit him—any way just so's he got a bet, *he* was satisfied. But still he was lucky, uncommon lucky; he most always come out winner. He was always ready and laying for a chance; there couldn't be no solit'ry thing mentioned but that feller'd offer to bet on it and take any side you please, as I was just telling you. If there was a horse race, you'd find him flush,[5] or you'd find him busted at the end of it; if there was a dogfight, he'd bet on it; if there was a catfight, he'd bet on it; why if there was a chicken fight, he'd bet on it; why, if there was two birds setting on a fence, he would bet you which one would fly first; or if there was a camp meeting, he would be there reg'lar, to bet on Parson Walker, which he judged to be the best exhorter[6] about here,

and so he was, too, and a good man. If he even seen a straddlebug start to go anywheres, he would bet you how long it would take him to get wherever he was going to, and if you took him up, he would foller that straddlebug to Mexico but what he would find out where he was bound for and how long he was on the road. Lots of the boys here has seen that Smiley and can tell you about him. Why, it never made no difference to *him*—he would bet on *any-thing*—the dangdest feller. Parson Walker's wife laid very sick once, for a good while, and it seemed as if they warn't going to save her; but one morning he come in, and Smiley asked how she was, and he said she was considerable bet-ter—thank the Lord for his inf'nit mercy—and coming on so smart that with the blessing of Prov'dence, she'd get well yet; and Smiley, before he thought, says, "Well, I'll risk twoandahalf that she don't, anyway."

Thish-yer Smiley had a mare—the boys called her the fifteen-minute nag, but that was only in fun, you know, because, of course, she was faster than that—and he used to win money on that horse, for all she was so slow and always had the asthma, or the distemper, or the consumption, or something of that kind. They used to give her two or three hundred yards' start and then pass her underway; but always at the end of the race she'd get excited and desper-ate-like, and come cavorting[7] and straddling up, and scattering her legs around limber, some-times in the air, and sometimes out to one side amongst the fences, and kicking up m-o-r-e dust, and raising m-o-r-e racket with her coughing and sneezing and blowing her nose—and always fetch up at the stand just about a neck ahead, as near as you could cipher it down.[8]

And he had a little small bull pup, that to look at him you'd think he wa'n't worth a cent but to set around and look ornery and lay for a chance to steal something. But as soon as money was up on him, he was a different dog; his under-

---

4. **flume** *n.:* man-made waterway.
5. **flush** *adj.:* with a lot of money.
6. **exhorter** (eg·zôrt'ər) *n.:* preacher.

---

7. **cavorting** *v.* used as *adv.:* running around playfully.
8. **cipher** (sī'fər) **it down:** calculate it.

jaw'd begin to stick out like the fo'castle[9] of a steamboat, and his teeth would uncover and shine savage like the furnaces. And a dog might tackle him, and bullyrag him, and bite him, and throw him over his shoulder two or three times, and Andrew Jackson—which was the name of the pup—Andrew Jackson would never let on but what *he* was satisfied and hadn't expected nothing else—and the bets being doubled and doubled on the other side all the time, till the money was all up; and then all of a sudden he would grab that other dog jest by the j'int of his hind leg and freeze to it—not chaw, you understand, but only jest grip and hang on till they threwed up the sponge,[10] if it was a year. Smiley always come out winner on that pup, till he harnessed a dog once that didn't have no hind legs, because they'd been sawed off by a circular saw, and when the thing had gone along far enough, and the money was all up, and he come to make a snatch for his pet holt,[11] he saw in a minute how he'd been imposed on and how the other dog had him in the door, so to speak, and he 'peared surprised, and then he looked sorter discouraged-like, and didn't try no more to win the fight, and so he got shucked out bad. He give Smiley a look, as much as to say his heart was broke, and it was *his* fault, for putting up a dog that hadn't no hind legs for him to take holt of, which was his main dependence in a fight, and then he limped off a piece and laid down and died. It was a good pup, was that Andrew Jackson, and would have made a name for hisself if he'd lived, for the stuff was in him, and

DAN'L

he had genius—I know it, because he hadn't no opportunities to speak of, and it don't stand to reason that a dog could make such a fight as he could under them circumstances, if he hadn't no talent. It always makes me feel sorry when I think of that last fight of his'n, and the way it turned out.

Well, thish-yer Smiley had rat tarriers, and chicken cocks, and tomcats, and all them kind of things, till you couldn't rest, and you couldn't fetch nothing for him to bet on but he'd match you. He ketched a frog one day, and took him home, and said he cal'klated to edercate him; and so he never done nothing for three months but set in his backyard and learn that frog to jump. And you bet you he *did* learn him, too. He'd give him a little punch behind, and the next minute you'd see that frog whirling in the air like a doughnut—see him turn one summerset, or maybe a couple, if he got a good start, and come down flat-footed and all right, like a cat. He got him up so in the matter of catching flies, and kept him in practice so constant, that he'd nail a fly every time as far as he could see him. Smiley said all a frog wanted was education, and he could do most anything—and I believe him. Why, I've seen him set Dan'l Webster down here on this floor—Dan'l Webster was the name of the frog—and sing out, "Flies, Dan'l, flies!" and quicker'n you could wink, he'd spring straight up, and snake a fly off'n the counter there, and flop down on the floor again as solid as a gob of mud, and fall to scratching the side of his head with his hind foot as indifferent as if he hadn't no idea he'd been doin' any more'n any frog might do. You never see a frog so modest and straightfor'ard as he was, for all he was so gifted. And when it come to fair-and-square jumping on a dead

---

9. **fo'castle** (fōk′səl) *n.:* forecastle, the front part of a ship's upper deck.
10. **threwed up the sponge:** gave up.
11. **pet holt:** favorite grip.

level, he could get over more ground at one straddle than any animal of his breed you ever see. Jumping on a dead level was his strong suit, you understand; and when it come to that, Smiley would ante up money on him as long as he had a red.[12] Smiley was monstrous proud of his frog, and well he might be, for fellers that had traveled and been everywheres all said he laid over any frog that ever *they* see.

Well, Smiley kept the beast in a little lattice box, and he used to fetch him downtown sometimes and lay for a bet. One day a feller—a stranger in the camp, he was—come across him with his box, and says:

"What might it be that you've got in the box?"

And Smiley says, sorter indifferent-like, "It might be a parrot, or it might be a canary, maybe, but it ain't—it's only just a frog."

And the feller took it, and looked at it careful, and turned it round this way and that, and says, "H'm—so 'tis. Well, what's *he* good for?"

"Well," Smiley says, easy and careless, "he's good enough for *one* thing, I should judge—he can outjump any frog in Calaveras County."

The feller took the box again, and took another long, particular look, and give it back to Smiley, and says, very deliberate, "Well, I don't see no p'ints[13] about that frog that's any better'n any other frog."

"Maybe you don't," Smiley says. "Maybe you understand frogs, and maybe you don't understand 'em; maybe you've had experience, and maybe you an't only a amature, as it were. Anyways, I've got *my* opinion, and I'll risk forty dollars that he can outjump any frog in Calaveras County."

And the feller studied a minute and then says, kinder sadlike, "Well, I'm only a stranger here, and I an't got no frog; but if I had a frog, I'd bet you."

And then Smiley says, "That's all right—

---

12. **red** *n.:* penny (as in *red cent*).

13. **p'ints** *n. pl.:* points, or physical qualities of an animal, used to judge breeding.

that's all right—if you'll hold my box a minute, I'll go and get you a frog." And so the feller took the box, and put up his forty dollars along with Smiley's, and set down to wait.

So he set there a good while thinking and thinking to hisself, and then he got the frog out and prized[14] his mouth open and took a teaspoon and filled him full of quail shot[15]—filled him pretty near up to his chin—and set him on the floor. Smiley he went to the swamp and slopped around in the mud for a long time, and finally he ketched a frog, and fetched him in, and give him to this feller, and says:

"Now, if you're ready, set him alongside of Dan'l, with his forepaws just even with Dan'l, and I'll give the word." Then he says, "One—two—three—jump!" and him and the feller touched up the frogs from behind, and the new frog hopped off, but Dan'l give a heave, and hysted up his shoulders—so—like a Frenchman, but it wan't no use—he couldn't budge; he was planted as solid as an anvil,[16] and he couldn't no more stir than if he was anchored out. Smiley was a good deal surprised, and he was disgusted too, but he didn't have no idea what the matter was, of course.

The feller took the money and started away; and when he was going out at the door, he sorter jerked his thumb over his shoulders—this way—at Dan'l, and says again, very deliberate, "Well, *I* don't see no p'ints about that frog that's any better'n any other frog."

Smiley he stood scratching his head and looking down at Dan'l a long time, and at last he says, "I do wonder what in the nation that frog throw'd off for—I wonder if there an't something the matter with him—he 'pears to look mighty baggy, somehow." And he ketched Dan'l by the nap of the neck and lifted him up and says, "Why, blame my cats, if he don't weigh five pound!" and turned him upside down, and he belched out a double handful of shot. And

then he see how it was, and he was the maddest man—he set the frog down and took out after that feller, but he never ketched him. And—

[Here Simon Wheeler heard his name called from the front yard and got up to see what was wanted.] And turning to me as he moved away, he said: "Just set where you are, stranger, and rest easy—I an't going to be gone a second."

But, by your leave, I did not think that a continuation of the history of the enterprising vagabond[17] *Jim* Smiley would be likely to afford me much information concerning the Rev. *Leonidas W.* Smiley, and so I started away.

At the door I met the sociable Wheeler returning, and he buttonholed[18] me and recommenced:

"Well, thish-yer Smiley had a yaller one-eyed cow that didn't have no tail, only jest a short stump like a bannanner, and—"

"Oh! hang Smiley and his afflicted cow!" I muttered, good-naturedly, and bidding the old gentleman good day, I departed. ■

---

14. **prized** *v.:* pried.
15. **shot** *n.:* metal pellets used as ammunition for a shotgun.
16. **anvil** *n.:* iron or steel block on which metal objects are hammered into shape.

17. **vagabond** *n.:* someone who wanders from place to place without a home; drifter.
18. **buttonholed** *v.:* approached aggressively and delayed in conversation.

# The Frog Jumping of the County of Calaveras

*After Twain's story appeared in a New York newspaper in 1865, it became so popular that it was soon reprinted in newspapers across the country. The story, which helped make Twain a national celebrity, was even translated into French. After reading the French version, Twain said it would bring grief and sickness to anyone who read it. He took revenge by retranslating the story into English. Here is an excerpt from "The Frog Jumping of the County of Calaveras":*

"Eh bien! This Smiley nourished some terriers à rats, and some cocks of combat, and some cats, and all sorts of things; and with his rage of betting one no had more of repose. He trapped one day a frog and him imported with him (et l'emporta chez lui), saying that he pretended to make his education. You me believe if you will, but during three months he not has nothing done but to him apprehend to jump (apprendre à sauter) in a court retired of her mansion (de sa maison). And I you respond that he have succeeded. He him gives a small blow by behind, and the instant after you shall see the frog turn in the air like a grease-biscuit, makes one summersault, sometimes two, when she was well started, and re-fall upon his feet like a cat. He him had accomplished in the art of to gobble the flies (gober des mouches), and him there exercised continually—so well that a fly at the most far that she appeared was a fly lost."

*Mark Twain*

Drawing by David Levine. Reprinted with permission from *The New York Review of Books.* Copyright © 1966 NYREV, Inc.

# Response and Analysis

## Reading Check

1. What does the narrator hope to learn from Simon Wheeler? What does he learn instead?

2. According to Wheeler, what was Jim Smiley's favorite activity?

3. Which frog wins the jumping contest? Why?

## Thinking Critically

4. "The Celebrated Jumping Frog of Calaveras County" is a story within a story—that is, it consists of a **frame story** (at the beginning and the end) and an inner story. What is the basic plot of the frame story?

5. Describe Simon Wheeler's **tone,** or attitude, toward his story. Do you think his tone adds to the humor of Mark Twain's story? Why or why not?

6. Find at least three places in the story where Twain uses the **vernacular.** Explain why the vernacular makes the story more authentic, more vivid, or more comic.

7. Find two or more examples of each of the following **comic devices:** hyperbole, comic comparisons, and comic characters and situations.

8. Compare Twain's retranslated excerpt on page 532 with the original selection, found on page 529. How does this retranslation illustrate Twain's humor and wit?

## Extending and Evaluating

9. Do you think "The Celebrated Jumping Frog of Calaveras County" is funny? Why or why not?

## Literary Criticism

10. **Tall tales,** like this story by Twain, played a major role in the imaginative life of Americans. Stretchers, whoppers, and embroidered lies became an amazingly popular form of fiction. Do you think Americans today still have this love of exaggeration? Why or why not?

## WRITING

### Tell the Tale

The narrator leaves when Wheeler starts to tell him about Smiley's "yaller one-eyed cow that didn't have no tail." What amazing story do you think Wheeler might have told about that cow? Write Wheeler's "yaller one-eyed cow" **story.** Include at least two comic devices (such as hyperbole, understatement, comic comparisons, and comic characters and situations). You may also want to try imitating the vernacular that Twain uses or another vernacular that you are familiar with. Read aloud as you write. Remember that much of the humor of this kind of story comes from its *sound.*

▶ **Use "Writing a Short Story," pages 338–345, for help with this assignment.**

---

### Vocabulary Development

#### Yes or No

Be sure you can justify your answers to these questions.

1. Would a garrulous person be a lively party guest?

2. If the man conjectured that his frog would win the contest, would he bet against it?

3. Would an infamous liar tell the absolute truth in court?

4. Is a dilapidated shack likely to be the home of a millionaire?

5. Is listening to an interminable story enjoyable?

---

# The Lowest Animal

## Make the Connection
### Quickwrite ✏️

Americans have always had a high regard for progress and self-improvement. Mark Twain couples this admirable national trait with a blistering vision of how far, in his opinion, the human race falls short of its ideals. Think about what you would like to change about human nature, and freewrite your ideas.

## Literary Focus
### Satire: The Weapon of Laughter

Mark Twain wrote that we have only "one really effective weapon—laughter. Power, money, persuasion, supplication—these can lift a colossal humbug—push it a little—weaken it a little, century by century; but only laughter can blow it to rags and atoms at a blast."

Satire uses humor to critique people or institutions with the intention of improving them. One of the favorite techniques of the satirist is **exaggeration**—overstating something to make it look ridiculous. Another technique is **irony**—stating the opposite of what's really meant.

Like many other great satires, this famous essay is clearly outrageous. Twain doesn't really mean much of what he says, but sometimes the most exaggerated and maddening pieces of writing force us to think critically.

**SKILLS FOCUS**

**Literary Skills**
Understand the characteristics of satire.

**Reading Skills**
Analyze a writer's purpose.

**go.hrw.com**

**INTERNET**

Vocabulary Practice
•
More About Mark Twain
•

Keyword: LE7 11-4

> **Satire** is a type of writing that ridicules the shortcomings of people and institutions in an attempt to bring about change.
>
> *For more on Satire, see the Handbook of Literary and Historical Terms.*

## Reading Skills
### Recognizing a Writer's Purpose

In general, a writer's **purpose** can be to describe, to inform, to narrate, to entertain, to analyze, or to persuade. Satires are usually exaggerated and humorous, but the true satirist intends to do more than simply make you laugh. Real-world change; reform; honest reexamination of values; the development of new goals, attitudes, and perspectives—these are the satirist's deeper purposes. To get to the deeper meaning of a satire, consider the following questions:

• What is the writer's philosophical position?
• What are the writer's religious, political, and social beliefs?
• Whom or what is the writer aiming to improve? What is his or her target?
• What does the writer want me to believe and—most important—to *do*?

## Vocabulary Development

**dispositions** (dis′pə·zish′ənz) *n. pl.*: natures; characters.

**allegiance** (ə·lē′jəns) *n.*: loyalty.

**caliber** (kal′ə·bər) *n.*: quality or ability.

**wantonly** (wänt′′n·lē) *adv.*: carelessly, often with ill will.

**transition** (tran·zish′ən) *n.*: passage from one condition, form, or stage to another.

**scrupled** (skrōō′pəld) *v.*: hesitated because of feelings of guilt.

**appease** (ə·pēz′) *v.*: satisfy; pacify.

**avaricious** (av′ə·rish′əs) *adj.*: greedy.

**atrocious** (ə·trō′shəs) *adj.*: evil; very bad.

**sordid** (sôr′did) *adj.*: dirty; cheap; shameful.

# The Lowest Animal

Mark Twain

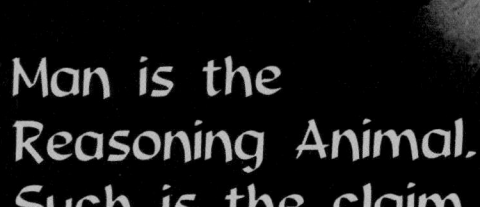

Man is the
Reasoning Animal.
Such is the claim.

I have been studying the traits and dispositions of the "lower animals" (so-called) and contrasting them with the traits and dispositions of man. I find the result humiliating to me. For it obliges me to renounce[1] my allegiance to the Darwinian theory of the Ascent of Man from the Lower Animals, since it now seems plain to me that that theory ought to be vacated[2] in favor of a new and truer one, this new and truer one to be named the *Descent* of Man from the Higher Animals.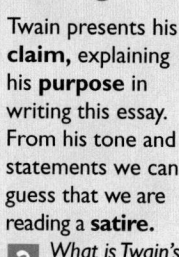

In proceeding toward this unpleasant conclusion, I have not guessed or speculated or conjectured,[3] but have used what is commonly called the scientific method.[4] That is to say, I have subjected every postulate[5] that presented itself to the crucial test of actual experiment and have adopted it or rejected it according to the result. Thus, I verified and established each step of my course in its turn before advancing to the next. These experiments were made in the London Zoological Gardens and covered many months of painstaking and fatiguing work. ❷

Before particularizing any of the experiments, I wish to state one or two things which seem to more properly belong in this place than further along. This in the interest of clearness. The massed experiments established to my satisfaction certain generalizations, to wit: ❸

1. That the human race is of one distinct species. It exhibits slight variations—in color, stature, mental caliber, and so on—due to climate, environment, and so forth; but it is a species by itself and not to be confounded with any other.

2. That the quadrupeds[6] are a distinct family, also. This family exhibits variations—in color, size, food preferences, and so on; but it is a family by itself.

3. That the other families—the birds, the fishes, the insects, the reptiles, etc.—are more or less distinct, also. They are in the procession. They are links in the chain which stretches down from the higher animals to man at the bottom.

Some of my experiments were quite curious. In the course of my reading, I had come across a case where, many years ago, some hunters on our Great Plains organized a buffalo hunt for the entertainment of an English earl—that, and to provide some fresh meat for his larder.[7] They had charming sport. They killed seventy-two of those great animals and ate part of one of them and left the seventy-one to rot. In order to determine the difference between an anaconda[8] and an earl—if any—I caused seven young calves to be turned into the anaconda's cage. The grateful reptile immediately crushed one of them and swallowed it, then lay back satisfied. It showed no further interest in the calves and no disposition to harm them. I tried this experiment with other anacondas, always with the same result. The fact stood proven that the

---

❶ Twain presents his **claim,** explaining his **purpose** in writing this essay. From his tone and statements we can guess that we are reading a **satire.**

❓ What is Twain's claim?

❷ ❓ What method does Twain use to arrive at his conclusions?

❸ Here Twain explains that experiments have led him to three main **generalizations,** which he then outlines.

---

1. **renounce** *v.:* give up; reject.
2. **vacated** *v.:* made void.
3. **conjectured** *v.:* inferred; predicted from incomplete evidence.
4. **scientific method:** research method in which a theory is tested by careful, documented experiments.
5. **postulate** (päs′chə·lit) *n.:* assumption.

---

6. **quadrupeds** (kwä′drŏŏ·pedz′) *n. pl.:* four-footed animals.
7. **larder** *n.:* supply of food or place where food supplies are kept.
8. **anaconda** (an′ə·kän′də) *n.:* long, heavy snake that crushes its prey.

---

**Vocabulary**

**dispositions** (dis′pə·zish′ənz) *n. pl.:* natures; characters.
**allegiance** (ə·lē′jəns) *n.:* loyalty.
**caliber** (kal′ə·bər) *n.:* quality or ability.

difference between an earl and an anaconda is that the earl is cruel and the anaconda isn't; and that the earl wantonly destroys what he has no use for, but the anaconda doesn't. This seemed to suggest that the anaconda was not descended from the earl. It also seemed to suggest that the earl was descended from the anaconda, and had lost a good deal in the transition. ❹

❹

**?** *According to Twain, what does the experiment with the earl and the anaconda prove?*

I was aware that many men who have accumulated more millions of money than they can ever use have shown a rabid hunger for more, and have not scrupled to cheat the ignorant and the helpless out of their poor servings in order to partially appease that appetite. I furnished a hundred different kinds of wild and tame animals the opportunity to accumulate vast stores of food, but none of them would do it. The squirrels and bees and certain birds made accumulations, but stopped when they had gathered a winter's supply and could not be persuaded to add to it either honestly or by chicane.[9] In order to bolster up a tottering reputation, the ant pretended to store up supplies, but I was not deceived. I know the ant. These experiments convinced me that there is this difference between man and the higher animals: He is avaricious and miserly, they are not. ❺

❺

Note Twain's **word choice** in this paragraph, especially his use of words such as *rabid, cheat, helpless, poor,* and *miserly.*

**?** *How do these words increase the effect of Twain's satire?*

In the course of my experiments, I convinced myself that among the animals man is the only one that harbors[10] insults and injuries, broods over them, waits till a chance offers, then takes revenge. The passion of revenge is unknown to the higher animals.

Roosters keep harems,[11] but it is by consent of their concubines;[12] therefore no wrong is done. Men keep harems, but it is by brute force, privileged by atrocious laws which the other sex was allowed no hand in making. In this matter man occupies a far lower place than the rooster.

Cats are loose in their morals, but not consciously so. Man, in his descent from the cat, has brought the cat's looseness with him but has left the unconsciousness behind—the saving grace which excuses the cat. The cat is innocent, man is not.

Indecency, vulgarity, obscenity—these are strictly confined to man; he invented them. Among the higher animals there is no trace of them. They hide nothing; they are not ashamed. Man, with his soiled mind, covers himself. He will not even enter a drawing room with his breast and back naked, so alive are he and his mates to indecent suggestion. Man is the Animal that Laughs. But so does the monkey, as Mr. Darwin pointed out, and so does the Australian bird that is called the laughing jackass. No— Man is the Animal that Blushes. He is the only one that does it—or has occasion to. ❻

❻

Twain repeats his **main idea,** that man is a lower animal.

**?** *What claim does he make here?*

At the head of this article[13] we see how "three monks were burnt to death" a few days ago and a prior was "put to death with atrocious cruelty."

---

11. **harems** *n. pl.*: groups of females who mate and live with one male.
12. **concubines** (kän′kyoo·bīnz′) *n.*: secondary wives.
13. **at the head of this article:** Twain is referring to 1897 newspaper reports of religious persecution in Crete.

---

**Vocabulary**

**wantonly** (wänt′'n·lē) *adv.*: carelessly, often with ill will.
**transition** (tran·zish′ən) *n.*: passage from one condition, form, or stage to another.
**scrupled** (skroo′pəld) *v.*: hesitated because of feelings of guilt.
**appease** (ə·pēz′) *v.*: satisfy; pacify.
**avaricious** (av′ə·rish′əs) *adj.*: greedy.
**atrocious** (ə·trō′shəs) *adj.*: evil; very bad.

---

9. **chicane** (shi·kān′) *n.*: clever deception; trickery. (*Chicanery* is the more common form.)
10. **harbors** *v.*: clings to; nourishes.

Do we inquire into the details? No; or we should find out that the prior was subjected to unprintable mutilations. Man—when he is a North American Indian—gouges out his prisoner's eyes; when he is King John,[14] with a nephew to render untroublesome, he uses a red-hot iron; when he is a religious zealot[15] dealing with heretics[16] in the Middle Ages, he skins his captive alive and scatters salt on his back; in the first Richard's[17] time, he shuts up a multitude of Jewish families in a tower and sets fire to it; in Columbus's time he captures a family of Spanish Jews and—but *that* is not printable; in our day in England, a man is fined ten shillings for beating his mother nearly to death with a chair, and another man is fined forty shillings for having four pheasant eggs in his possession without being able to satisfactorily explain how he got them. Of all the animals, man is the only one that is cruel. He is the only one that inflicts pain for the pleasure of doing it. It is a trait that is not known to the higher animals. The cat plays with the frightened mouse; but she has this excuse, that she does not know that the mouse is suffering. The cat is moderate—unhumanly moderate: She only scares the mouse, she does not hurt it; she doesn't dig out its eyes, or tear off its skin, or drive splinters under its nails—man fashion; when she is done playing with it, she makes a sudden meal of it and puts it out of its trouble. Man is the Cruel Animal. He is alone in that distinction. ❼

The higher animals engage in individual fights, but never in organized masses. Man is the only animal that deals in that atrocity[18] of atrocities, war. He is the only one that gathers his brethren about him and goes forth in cold blood and with calm pulse to exterminate his kind. He is the only animal that for sordid wages will march out, as the Hessians[19] did in our Revolution, and as the boyish Prince Napoleon did in the Zulu war,[20] and help to slaughter strangers of his own species who have done him no harm and with whom he has no quarrel.

Man is the only animal that robs his helpless fellow of his country—takes possession of it and drives him out of it or destroys him. Man has done this in all the ages. There is not an acre of ground on the globe that is in possession of its rightful owner, or that has not been taken away from owner after owner, cycle after cycle, by force and bloodshed.

Man is the only Slave. And he is the only animal who enslaves. He has always been a slave in one form or another, and has always held other slaves in bondage under him in one way or another. In our day he is always some man's slave for wages and does that man's work; and this slave has other slaves under him for minor wages, and they do *his* work. The higher animals are the only ones who exclusively do their own work and provide their own living. ❽

Man is the only Patriot. He sets himself apart in his

---

❼ Here Twain uses examples from history and then-current events to support his **main idea.**

❓ What specific trait of man is Twain **satirizing** in this paragraph?

❽ In the previous paragraphs, Twain uses **loaded words,** such as *slaughter, slave,* and *assassins,* to emphasize man's immorality.

❓ How do these loaded words increase the power of Twain's **satire?**

---

14. **King John:** King of England from 1199 to 1216, known for seizing the throne from his nephew Arthur.
15. **zealot** (zel′ət) *n.:* overly enthusiastic person; fanatic.
16. **heretics** (her′ə·tiks) *n. pl.:* people who hold beliefs opposed to those of the church.
17. **first Richard's:** refers to Richard I (1157–1199), also called Richard the Lion-Hearted, king of England from 1189 to 1199.
18. **atrocity** (ə·träs′ə·tē) *n.:* shockingly cruel and inhuman act.
19. **Hessians** (hesh′ənz): German soldiers who served for pay in the British army during the American Revolution.
20. **Prince Napoleon . . . Zulu war:** In search of adventure, Prince Napoleon, son of Napoleon III, joined the British campaign against Zululand (part of South Africa) in 1879.

**Vocabulary**

**sordid** (sôr′did) *adj.:* dirty; cheap; shameful.

own country, under his own flag, and sneers at the other nations, and keeps multitudinous uniformed assassins on hand at heavy expense to grab slices of other people's countries and keep *them* from grabbing slices of *his*. And in the intervals between campaigns, he washes the blood off his hands and works for "the universal brotherhood of man"—with his mouth.

Man is the Religious Animal. He is the only Religious Animal. He is the only animal that has the True Religion—several of them. He is the only animal that loves his neighbor as himself, and cuts his throat if his theology isn't straight. He has made a graveyard of the globe in trying his honest best to smooth his brother's path to happiness and heaven. He was at it in the time of the Caesars, he was at it in Mahomet's[21] time, he was at it in the time of the Inquisition, he was at it in France a couple of centuries, he was at it in England in Mary's day,[22] he has been at it ever since he first saw the light, he is at it today in Crete—he will be at it somewhere else tomorrow. The higher animals have no religion. And we are told that they are going to be left out, in the hereafter. I wonder why. It seems questionable taste.

Man is the Reasoning Animal. **❾** Such is the claim. I think it is open to dispute. Indeed, my experiments have proven to me that he is the Unreasoning Animal. Note his history, as sketched above. It seems plain to me that whatever he is, he is *not* a reasoning animal. His record is the fantastic record of a maniac. I consider that the strongest count against his intelligence is the fact that with that record back of him, he blandly sets himself up as the head animal of the lot;

> **❾**
> In this paragraph, Twain begins his final summation. He first presents the theory he is arguing against: that man is a reasoning animal.

whereas by his own standards, he is the bottom one.

In truth, man is incurably foolish. Simple things which the other animals easily learn he is incapable of learning. Among my experiments was this. In an hour I taught a cat and a dog to be friends. I put them in a cage. In another hour I taught them to be friends with a rabbit. In the course of two days I was able to add a fox, a goose, a squirrel, and some doves. Finally a monkey. They lived together in peace, even affectionately.

Next, in another cage I confined an Irish Catholic from Tipperary, and as soon as he seemed tame, I added a Scottish Presbyterian from Aberdeen. Next a Turk from Constantinople, a Greek Christian from Crete, an Armenian, a Methodist from the wilds of Arkansas, a Buddhist from China, a Brahman from Benares. Finally, a Salvation Army colonel from Wapping. Then I stayed away two whole days. When I came back to note results, the cage of Higher Animals was all right, but in the other there was but a chaos of gory odds and ends of turbans and fezzes and plaids and bones and flesh—not a specimen left alive. These Reasoning Animals had disagreed on a theological detail and carried the matter to a higher court. **❿** ■

> **❿**
> To wrap up his argument, Twain presents the disastrous results of the final experiment.
> **?** *Summarize those results.*

---

21. **Mahomet's:** Mohammed (c. A.D. 570–632) was an Arab prophet and founder of Islam.

22. **in Mary's day:** during the reign of Queen Mary (1553–1558), who was given the nickname "Bloody Mary" when she ordered the deaths of many Protestants.

*This article was written shortly after the terrorist attack that brought down the World Trade Center towers in New York City on September 11, 2001.*

# A Time of Gifts

## Stephen Jay Gould

Firefighters leaving rescue area near World Trade Center, September 13, 2001.

The patterns of human history mix decency and depravity in equal measure. We often assume, therefore, that such a fine balance of results must emerge from societies made of decent and depraved people in equal numbers. But we need to expose and celebrate the fallacy of this conclusion so that, in this moment of crisis, we may reaffirm an essential truth too easily forgotten and regain some crucial comfort too readily forgone. Good and kind people outnumber all others by thousands to one. The tragedy of human history lies in the enormous potential for destruction in rare acts of evil, not in the high frequency of evil people. Complex systems can only be built step by step, whereas destruction requires but an instant. Thus, in what I like to call the Great Asymmetry, every spectacular incident of evil will be balanced by ten thousand acts of kindness, too often unnoted and invisible as the "ordinary" efforts of a vast majority.

We have a duty, almost a holy responsibility, to record and honor the victorious weight of these innumerable little kindnesses when an unprecedented act of evil so threatens to distort our perception of ordinary human behavior. I have stood at ground zero, stunned by the twisted ruins of the largest human structure ever destroyed in a catastrophic moment. (I will discount the claims of a few biblical literalists for the Tower of Babel.) And I have contemplated a single day of carnage that our nation has not suffered since battles that still evoke passions and tears, nearly 150 years later: Antietam, Gettysburg, Cold Harbor. The scene is insufferably sad, but not at all depress-

Drawing found taped to a wall on Sixth Avenue and Eleventh Street in New York City, September 25, 2001.

ing. Rather, ground zero can only be described, in the lost meaning of a grand old word, as "sublime," in the sense of awe inspired by solemnity.

In human terms, ground zero is the focal point for a vast web of bustling goodness, channeling unaccountable deeds of kindness from an entire planet—the acts that must be recorded to reaffirm the overwhelming weight of human decency. The rubble of ground zero stands mute, while a beehive of human activity churns within and radiates outward as everyone makes a selfless contribution, big or tiny according to means and skills, but each of equal worth. My wife and stepdaughter established a depot on Spring Street to collect and ferry needed items in short supply, including face masks and shoe inserts, to the workers at ground zero. Word spreads like a fire of goodness, and people stream in, bringing gifts, from a pocketful of batteries to a ten-thousand-dollar purchase of hard hats, made on the spot at a local supply house and delivered right to us.

I will cite but one tiny story, among so many, to add to the count that will overwhelm the power of any terrorist's act. And by such tales, multiplied many millionfold, let those few depraved people finally understand why their vision of inspired fear cannot prevail over ordinary decency. As we left a local restaurant to make a delivery to ground zero late one evening, the cook gave us a shopping bag and said: "Here's a dozen apple brown bettys, our best dessert, still warm. Please give them to the rescue workers." How lovely, I thought, but how meaningless, except as an act of solidarity, connecting the cook to the cleanup. Still, we promised that we would make the distribution, and we put the bag of twelve apple brown bettys atop several thousand face masks and shoe pads.

Twelve apple brown bettys into the breach. Twelve apple brown bettys for thousands of workers. And then I learned something important that I should never have forgotten—and the joke turned on me. Those twelve apple brown bettys went like literal hot cakes. These trivial symbols in my initial judgment turned into little drops of gold within a rainstorm of similar offerings for the stomach and soul, from children's postcards to cheers by the roadside. We gave the last one to a firefighter, an older man in a young crowd, sitting alone in utter exhaustion as he inserted one of our shoe pads. And he said, with a twinkle and a smile restored to his face: "Thank you. This is the most lovely thing I've seen in four days—and still warm!"

—*The New York Times*
September 26, 2001

# Response and Analysis

## Reading Check

1. What are the first three **generalizations** Twain presents as a result of his experiments in the London Zoological Gardens?

2. Name four ways in which human beings are inferior to other animals, according to Twain.

3. Describe Twain's last experiment with the two cages. What are the results of the experiment?

## Thinking Critically

4. Summarize Twain's overall **purpose** in this essay. How would you characterize that purpose—as noble, childish, useless, realistic? Give reasons for your opinion.

5. What specific changes in human nature does Twain hope his **satire** will encourage? How do Twain's ideas compare with yours? (Refer to your Quickwrite notes.)

6. Find at least two examples of **exaggeration** in the essay. Do these exaggerations make the satire more effective, or are they just silly? Explain.

## Extending and Evaluating

7. Evaluate Twain's philosophical beliefs, as revealed in this essay. In your opinion, are his generalizations about people and their behavior valid, partly valid, or completely invalid? Explain.

## WRITING

### You're Wrong, Mr. Twain

Write a **rebuttal** of Twain's essay in which you defend the human race as civilized, caring beings. Your rebuttal may be in any form you like: a letter to Twain, a parody of Twain's essay, a serious essay, a poem, an anecdote, an editorial, or something else.

Support your points with specific examples, just as Twain does. Re-read the **Connection** on page 540 for ideas for your rebuttal.

---

## Vocabulary Development
### Suffixes That Form Nouns

| | | |
|---|---|---|
| dispositions | transition | atrocious |
| allegiance | scrupled | sordid |
| caliber | appease | |
| wantonly | avaricious | |

A **suffix** is a word part added to the end of a word or a **root** (word base) to create a new word. Certain suffixes change words into nouns—for example, the adjective *sordid* and the suffix *–ness* form the noun *sordidness*. Study the following noun-forming suffixes and their meanings.

| Suffix | Meaning |
|---|---|
| –tion | act, result, or state of |
| –ance | act, process, or quality of |
| –ment | result or product; means |
| –ness | quality or state of being |

**Practice.** Write down the words listed above, and indicate whether each one is a noun. If it is a noun and it contains one of the suffixes listed in the chart, circle the suffix. If the word is *not* a noun, turn it into a noun by adding one of the suffixes. (Note: For one of the words, you will have to remove a suffix before you add the noun-forming suffix. For one other word, you need only remove the suffix to form a noun.) Finally, look up the meanings of the new words in a dictionary.

---

**SKILLS FOCUS**

**Literary Skills**
Analyze satire.

**Reading Skills**
Analyze a writer's purpose.

**Writing Skills**
Write a rebuttal of an essay.

**Vocabulary Skills**
Understand noun-forming suffixes.

---

# Vocabulary Development

## Greek and Latin Roots in Math and Science

Although the Greek Parthenon and the Roman Colosseum have suffered damage through the centuries, the Greek and Latin languages are alive and well in the English that we speak every day. Thousands of English words have Greek or Latin roots, and recognizing these roots can be a great help to you in improving your vocabulary.

A **root** is a word part that carries the core meaning of a word. In most cases, roots combine with prefixes or suffixes or both to form whole words. Groups of words with the same root are called **word families.**

Many words used in math and science have Greek or Latin roots. This is due in part to the many scientific accomplishments of the Greeks and to the use of Latin as the common language of science for centuries.

In "The Lowest Animal," Mark Twain uses scientific and mathematical terms that have their origins in Greek and Latin roots—for example, *theory, scientific, zoological, verified, species,* and *quadrupeds.* In the following charts, you'll find these words and other common words from math and science that have Greek and Latin roots. (For more about mathematical and scientific terms, see page 295.)

### Greek

| Word | Root | Meaning of Root | Meaning of Word | Family Words |
|------|------|-----------------|-----------------|--------------|
| theory | –theor– | to look at, view | idea or plan that explains how something works | theoretical, theorem |
| zoological | –log–, –logy– | word, study | having to do with the study of animals | logic, biology |
| genesis | –gen– | to be born | beginning, origin | genetics, genotype |
| thermonuclear | –therm–, –thermo– | heat | using heat energy released in nuclear fusion | thermometer, thermal |

*(continued)*

SKILLS FOCUS

**Vocabulary Skills**
Identify Greek and Latin roots.

**Latin**

| Word | Root | Meaning of Root | Meaning of Word | Family Words |
|------|------|-----------------|-----------------|--------------|
| verified | –ver– | true | proved true | veracity, verdict |
| scientific | –scien– | to know | systematic and exact | conscience, scientist |
| quadrupeds | –ped– | foot | animals with four feet | biped, pedal |
| integer | –integ– | whole | positive or negative whole number or zero | integral, integrate |
| triangle | –ang– | corner, angle | figure with three angles and three sides | angular, rectangle |

**PRACTICE**

1. For each root listed in the charts, find at least one other word in the same word family. You may use a dictionary for help.

2. For the mathematical and scientific terms below, complete a chart like the one above. The root and the meaning of the root appear in parentheses following each word. Use a dictionary to find the meaning of the word. Then, find at least one family word. (You will note that several words also have common prefixes.)

| | |
|---|---|
| **orthodontist** | (–ortho–, "straight") |
| **epidermis** | (–derm–, "skin") |
| **habitat** | (–hab–, "have; hold") |
| **translucent** | (–luc–, "light") |
| **symmetry** | (–metr–, "measure") |
| **equilateral** | (–lat–, "side") |

# Jack London
## (1876–1916)

In his teens and twenties, Jack London adventured on sea and ice. Then, in the sixteen remaining years of his life, he turned out fifty volumes of essays and fiction. Known during his lifetime as a passionate socialist, London is remembered today not for his political convictions but for his exciting, fast-paced adventure stories.

London was born into a poor family in San Francisco. As a boy he was largely uncared for by his parents. He delivered newspapers, worked on an ice wagon, set up pins in a bowling alley, and worked in a cannery. "Almost the first thing I realized were responsibilities," he said. He graduated from grammar school in Oakland, across the bay from San Francisco.

Meanwhile, London read everything he could find in the public library, especially stories of real-life adventure. In his teens he plunged into danger. "I joined the oyster pirates in the bay; shipped as sailor on a schooner; took a turn at salmon fishing; shipped before the mast and sailed for the Japanese coast on a seal-hunting expedition. After sealing for seven months I came back to California, and took odd jobs. . . ."

London was still in his teens when he settled in Oakland again. He began to write, selling a few pieces to local papers. After attending high school for one year, he passed the entrance exams for the University of California at Berkeley by cramming on his own. The combination of work, school, and writing proved too much, however, and he quit halfway through his freshman year. He submerged himself in writing for the next three months. But he earned practically nothing, so in 1897 he took off to prospect for gold in the Klondike—part of the Yukon Territory in northwestern Canada.

London became sick and had to leave the Klondike in less than a year, but the experience convinced him that life is a struggle in which the strong survive and the weak do not. London's short stories and novels dramatize his belief that "civilized" beings are either destroyed or re-created in savage environments.

London's first major success was a story collection, *The Son of the Wolf* (1900). Readers were thrilled by the shocking brutality of his stories, then hooked by the action and adventure. His most famous novel, *The Call of the Wild* (1903), celebrates the escape to freedom of a sled dog named Buck.

London became a millionaire from his writings, and success greatly altered his life. In 1900, he married and had two daughters, but his wife sued him for divorce in 1905. He remarried and established his home at Glen Ellen in Sonoma County, north of San Francisco. There he intended to create a magnificent ranch estate, but he lost interest when Wolf House, his nearly completed mansion, burned down in 1913. London, for years an alcoholic, suffered in his later years from kidney disease and depression. One evening in November 1916, when the physical pain finally became unendurable, London took a lethal dose of narcotics and lapsed into a coma. He died the next evening; he was forty years old.

### For Independent Reading

One of most popular novels in America is London's tale about a sled dog:

- *The Call of the Wild*

# To Build a Fire

## Make the Connection

"To Build a Fire" must be the coldest story ever written. London draws on his own experience of prospecting for gold in the Yukon—a bleak region of northwestern Canada—to give authenticity to the story.

This is ultimately far more than a classic "person versus nature" story. It is a grimly realistic tale about a man who is "quick and alert in the things of life, but . . . not in the significances"—an innocent who is not prepared for an unforgiving environment.

## Literary Focus
### Naturalism

The naturalists were nineteenth-century writers who went beyond realism in an attempt to portray life exactly as it is. Influenced by the scientist Charles Darwin (1809–1882), who put forth the theories of natural selection and survival of the fittest, the naturalist writers believed that human behavior is determined by heredity and environment. Relying on new theories in sociology and psychology, the naturalists dissected human behavior with detachment and objectivity, like scientists dissecting laboratory specimens. Naturalism presents human beings as subject to natural forces beyond their control. This idea is at the center of "To Build a Fire."

**SKILLS FOCUS**

**Literary Skills**
Understand naturalism.
Understand philosophical ideas presented in literary works.

**Reading Skills**
Understand cause and effect.

go.
hrw
.com

**INTERNET**

**More About Jack London**

Keyword: LE7 11-4

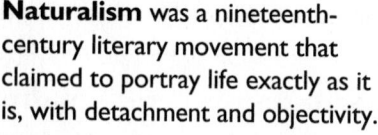

**Naturalism** was a nineteenth-century literary movement that claimed to portray life exactly as it is, with detachment and objectivity.

*For more on Naturalism, see the Handbook of Literary and Historical Terms.*

## Reading Skills
### Analyzing Text Structures: Cause and Effect

Science tells us that for every action there is a reaction. In literature we call this the relationship of **cause** and **effect.** A plot is made up of a string of causes and effects. As you read London's story, keep notes on each action the protagonist takes, and note its effect. You will find that an action as small as a misstep or the lighting of a match can take on critical importance.

## Vocabulary Development

**intangible** (in·tan'jə·bəl) *adj.*: difficult to define; vague.

**undulations** (un'jə·lā'shənz) *n. pl.*: wave-like motions.

**protruding** (prō·trood'iŋ) *v.* used as *adj.*: sticking out.

**apprehension** (ap'rē·hen'shən) *n.*: anxious or frightening feeling; dread.

**imperative** (im·per'ə·tiv) *adj.*: absolutely necessary; urgent.

**extremities** (ek·strem'ə·tēz) *n. pl.*: limbs of the body, especially hands and feet.

**recoiled** (ri·koild') *v.*: shrank away; drew back.

**excruciating** (eks·kroo'shē·āt'iŋ) *adj.*: intensely painful.

**ensued** (en·sood') *v.*: resulted.

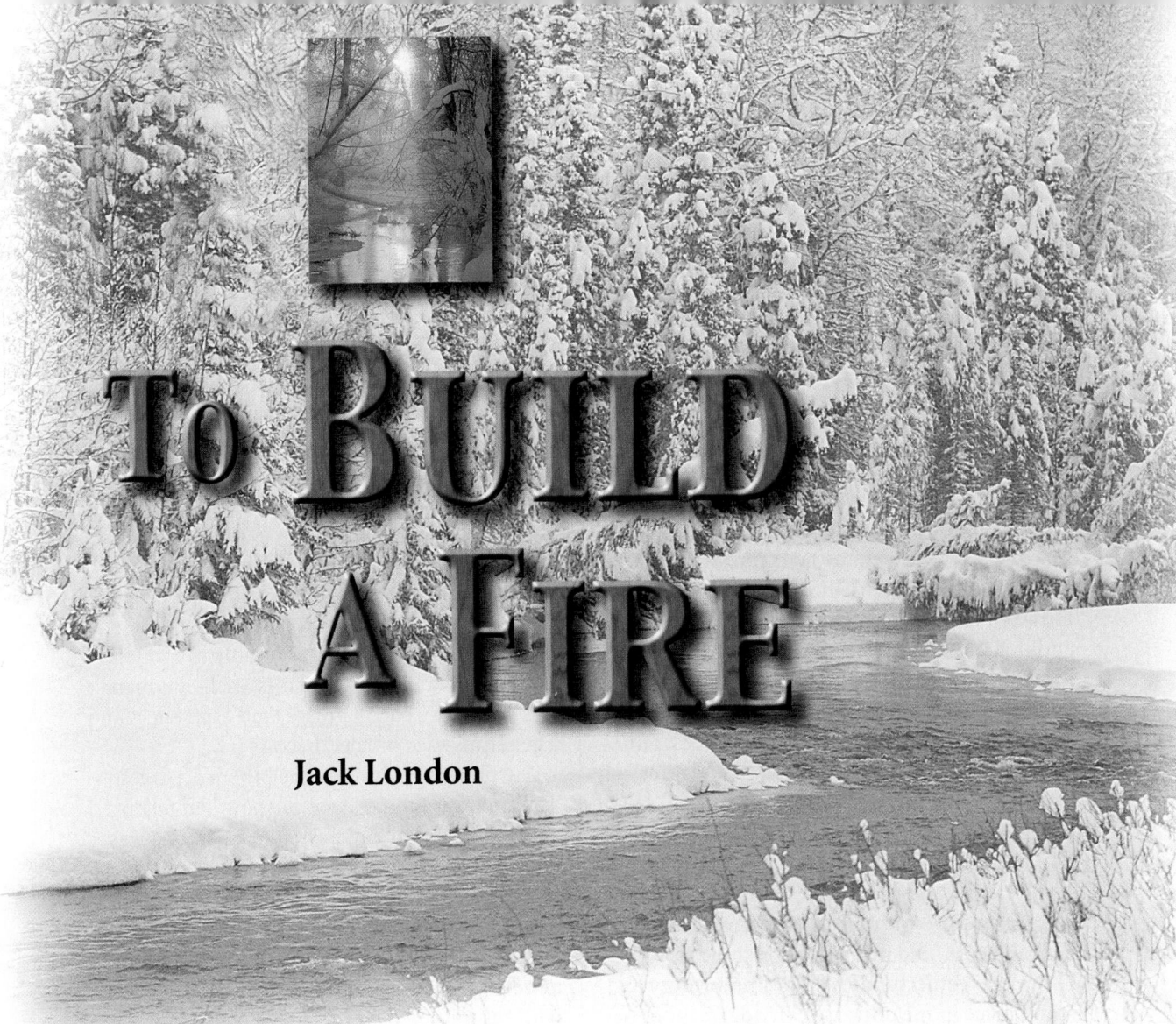

# To Build a Fire

### Jack London

**D**ay had broken cold and gray, exceedingly cold and gray, when the man turned aside from the main Yukon trail and climbed the high earth bank, where a dim and little-traveled trail led eastward through the fat spruce timberland. It was a steep bank, and he paused for breath at the top, excusing the act to himself by looking at his watch. It was nine o'clock. There was no sun or hint of sun, though there was not a cloud in the sky. It was a clear day, and yet there seemed an intangible pall[1] over the face of things, a subtle gloom that made the day dark, and that was due to the absence of sun. This fact did not worry the man. He was used to the lack of sun. It had been days since he had seen the sun, and he knew that a few more days must pass before that cheerful orb, due south, would just peep above the skyline and dip immediately from view.

The man flung a look back along the way he had come. The Yukon lay a mile wide and hidden under three feet of ice. On top of this ice were as many feet of snow. It was all pure white, rolling in gentle undulations where the ice jams of the freeze-up had formed. North and south, as far as his eye could see, it was unbroken

---

1. **pall** *n.:* overspreading atmosphere of gloom and depression.

**Vocabulary**

**intangible** (in·tan′jə·bəl) *adj.:* difficult to define; vague.
**undulations** (un′jə·lā′shənz) *n. pl.:* wavelike motions.

white, save for a dark hairline that curved and twisted from around the spruce-covered island to the south, and that curved and twisted away into the north, where it disappeared behind another spruce-covered island. This dark hairline was the trail—the main trail—that led south five hundred miles to the Chilkoot Pass, Dyea, and salt water; and that led north seventy miles to Dawson, and still on to the north a thousand miles to Nulato, and finally to St. Michael on the Bering Sea, a thousand miles and half a thousand more.

But all this—the mysterious, far-reaching hairline trail, the absence of sun from the sky, the tremendous cold, and the strangeness and weirdness of it all—made no impression on the man. It was not because he was long used to it. He was a newcomer in the land, a cheechako,[2] and this was his first winter. The trouble with him was that he was without imagination. He was quick and alert in the things of life, but only in the things, and not in the significances. Fifty degrees below zero meant eighty-odd degrees of frost. Such fact impressed him as being cold and uncomfortable, and that was all. It did not lead him to meditate upon his frailty as a creature of temperature, and upon man's frailty in general, able only to live within certain narrow limits of heat and cold, and from there on it did not lead him to the conjectural[3] field of immortality and man's place in the universe. Fifty degrees below zero stood for a bite of frost that hurt and that must be guarded against by the use of mittens, earflaps, warm moccasins, and thick socks. Fifty degrees below zero was to him just precisely fifty degrees below zero. That there should be anything more to it than that was a thought that never entered his head.

As he turned to go on, he spat speculatively. There was a sharp, explosive crackle that startled him. He spat again. And again, in the air, before it could fall to the snow, the spittle crackled. He knew that at fifty below, spittle crackled

on the snow, but this spittle had crackled in the air. Undoubtedly it was colder than fifty below—how much colder he did not know. But the temperature did not matter. He was bound for the old claim[4] on the left fork of Henderson Creek, where the boys were already. They had come over across the divide from the Indian Creek country, while he had come the roundabout way to take a look at the possibilities of getting out logs in the spring from the islands in the Yukon. He would be into camp by six o'clock; a bit after dark, it was true, but the boys would be there, a fire would be going, and a hot supper would be ready. As for lunch, he pressed his hand against the protruding bundle under his jacket. It was also under his shirt, wrapped up in a handkerchief and lying against the naked skin. It was the only way to keep the biscuits from freezing. He smiled agreeably to himself as he thought of those biscuits, each cut open and sopped in bacon grease, and each enclosing a generous slice of fried bacon.

He plunged in among the big spruce trees. The trail was faint. A foot of snow had fallen since the last sled had passed over, and he was glad he was without a sled, traveling light. In fact, he carried nothing but the lunch wrapped in the handkerchief. He was surprised, however, at the cold. It certainly was cold, he concluded, as he rubbed his numb nose and cheekbones with his mittened hand. He was a warm-whiskered man, but the hair on his face did not protect the high cheekbones and the eager nose that thrust itself aggressively into the frosty air.

At the man's heels trotted a dog, a big native husky, the proper wolf dog, gray coated and without any visible or temperamental difference from its brother, the wild wolf. The animal was depressed by the tremendous cold. It knew that it was no time for traveling. Its instinct told it a truer tale than was told to the man by the man's judgment. In reality, it was not merely colder

---

2. **cheechako** (chē·chä′kō)*n.:* Chinook jargon for "newcomer" or "tenderfoot."
3. **conjectural** *adj.:* based on guesswork or uncertain evidence.

---

4. **claim** *n.:* piece of land staked out by a miner.

---

**Vocabulary**

**protruding** (prō·trōōd′iŋ) *v.* used as *adj.:* sticking out.

than fifty below zero; it was colder than sixty below, than seventy below. It was seventy-five below zero. Since the freezing point is thirty-two above zero, it meant that one hundred and seven degrees of frost obtained. The dog did not know anything about thermometers. Possibly in its brain there was no sharp consciousness of a condition of very cold such as was in the man's brain. But the brute had its instinct. It experienced a vague but menacing apprehension that subdued it and made it slink along at the man's heels, and that made it question eagerly every unwonted[5] movement of the man, as if expecting him to go into camp or to seek shelter somewhere and build a fire. The dog had learned fire, and it wanted fire, or else to burrow under the snow and cuddle its warmth away from the air.

The frozen moisture of its breathing had settled on its fur in a fine powder of frost, and especially were its jowls, muzzle, and eyelashes whitened by its crystaled breath. The man's red beard and moustache were likewise frosted, but more solidly, the deposit taking the form of ice and increasing with every warm, moist breath he exhaled. Also, the man was chewing tobacco, and the muzzle of ice held his lips so rigidly that he was unable to clear his chin when he expelled the juice. The result was that a crystal beard of the color and solidity of amber was increasing its length on his chin. If he fell down it would shatter itself, like glass, into brittle fragments. But he did not mind the appendage.[6] It was the penalty all tobacco chewers paid in that country, and he had been out before in two cold snaps. They had not been so cold as this, he knew, but by the spirit thermometer[7] at Sixty Mile he knew they had been registered at fifty below and at fifty-five.

He held on through the level stretch of woods for several miles, crossed a wide flat, and dropped down a bank to the frozen bed of a small stream. This was Henderson Creek, and he knew he was ten miles from the forks. He looked at his watch. It was ten o'clock. He was making four miles an hour, and he calculated that he would arrive at the forks at half past twelve. He decided to celebrate that event by eating his lunch there.

The dog dropped in again at his heels, with a tail drooping discouragement, as the man swung along the creek bed. The furrow of the old sled trail was plainly visible, but a dozen inches of snow covered the marks of the last runners. In a month no man had come up or down that silent creek. The man held steadily on. He was not much given to thinking, and just then particularly, he had nothing to think about save that he would eat lunch at the forks and that at six o'clock he would be in camp with the boys. There was nobody to talk to; and, had there been, speech would have been impossible because of the ice muzzle on his mouth. So he continued monotonously to chew tobacco and to increase the length of his amber beard.

Once in a while the thought reiterated[8] itself that it was very cold and that he had never experienced such cold. As he walked along he rubbed his cheekbones and nose with the back of his mittened hand. He did this automatically, now and again changing hands. But rub as he would, the instant he stopped his cheekbones went numb, and the following instant the end of his nose went numb. He was sure to frost his cheeks; he knew that, and experienced a pang of regret that he had not devised a nose strap of the sort Bud wore in the cold snaps. Such a strap passed across the cheeks, as well, and saved them. But it didn't matter much, after all. What were frosted cheeks? A bit painful, that was all; they were never serious.

---

5. **unwonted** *adj.:* unusual.
6. **appendage** *n.:* something attached to another object.
7. **spirit thermometer** *n.:* alcohol thermometer. In places where the temperature often drops below the freezing point of mercury, alcohol is used in thermometers.

---

8. **reiterated** *v.:* repeated.

**Vocabulary**

**apprehension** (ap′rē·hen′shən) *n.:* anxious or frightening feeling; dread.

**He did not expose his fingers
more than a minute, and was
astonished at the swift
numbness that smote them.**

Empty as the man's mind was of thought, he was keenly observant, and he noticed the changes in the creek, the curves and bends and timber jams, and always he sharply noted where he placed his feet. Once, coming around a bend, he shied abruptly, like a startled horse, curved away from the place where he had been walking, and retreated several paces back along the trail. The creek, he knew, was frozen clear to the bottom—no creek could contain water in that arctic winter—but he knew also that there were springs that bubbled out from the hillsides and ran along under the snow and on top of the ice of the creek. He knew that the coldest snaps never froze these springs, and he knew likewise their danger. They were traps. They hid pools of water under the snow that might be three inches deep, or three feet. Sometimes a skin of ice half an inch thick covered them, and in turn was covered by the snow. Sometimes there were alternate layers of water and ice skin, so that when one broke through he kept on breaking through for a while, sometimes wetting himself to the waist.

That was why he had shied in such panic. He had felt the give under his feet and heard the crackle of a snow-hidden ice skin. And to get his feet wet in such a temperature meant trouble and danger. At the very least it meant delay, for he would be forced to stop and build a fire, and under its protection to bare his feet while he dried his socks and moccasins. He stood and studied the creek bed and its banks, and decided that the flow of water came from the right. He reflected awhile, rubbing his nose and cheeks, then skirted to the left, stepping gingerly and testing the footing for each step. Once clear of the danger, he took a fresh chew of tobacco and swung along at his four-mile gait.

In the course of the next two hours he came upon several similar traps. Usually the snow above the hidden pools had a sunken, candied appearance that advertised the danger. Once again, however, he had a close call; and once, suspecting danger, he compelled the dog to go on in front. The dog did not want to go. It hung back until the man shoved it forward, and then it went quickly across the white, unbroken surface. Suddenly it broke through, floundered to one side, and got away to firmer footing. It had wet its forefeet and legs, and almost immediately the water that clung to it turned to ice. It made quick efforts to lick the ice off its legs, then dropped down in the snow and began to bite out the ice that had formed between the toes. This was a matter of instinct. To permit the ice to remain would mean sore feet. It did not know this. It merely obeyed the mysterious prompting that arose from the deep crypts[9] of its being. But the man knew, having achieved a judgment on the subject, and he removed the mitten from his right hand and helped tear out the ice particles. He did not expose his fingers more than a minute, and was astonished at the swift numbness that smote[10] them. It certainly was cold. He pulled on the mitten hastily, and beat the hand savagely across his chest.

At twelve o'clock the day was at its brightest. Yet the sun was too far south on its winter journey to clear the horizon. The bulge of the earth intervened between it and Henderson Creek, where the man walked under a clear sky at noon and cast no shadow. At half past twelve, to the minute, he arrived at the forks of the creek. He was pleased at the speed he had made. If he kept it up, he would certainly be with the boys by six. He unbuttoned his jacket and shirt and drew forth his lunch. The action consumed no more than a quarter of a minute, yet in that brief moment the numbness laid hold of the exposed fingers. He did not put the mitten on, but instead struck the fingers a dozen sharp smashes against his leg. Then he sat down on a snow-covered log to eat. The sting that followed upon the striking of his fingers against his leg ceased so quickly that he was startled. He had had no chance to take a bite of biscuit. He struck the fingers repeatedly and returned them to the mitten, baring the other hand for the purpose of eating. He tried to take a mouthful, but the ice muzzle prevented. He had forgotten to build a fire and thaw out. He chuckled at his foolish-

---

9. **crypts** *n. pl.*: hidden recesses.
10. **smote** *v.* (past tense of *smite*): powerfully struck.

ness, and as he chuckled he noted the numbness creeping into the exposed fingers. Also, he noted that the stinging which had first come to his toes when he sat down was already passing away. He wondered whether the toes were warm or numb. He moved them inside the moccasins and decided that they were numb.

He pulled the mitten on hurriedly and stood up. He was a bit frightened. He stamped up and down until the stinging returned into the feet. It certainly was cold, was his thought. That man from Sulfur Creek had spoken the truth when telling how cold it sometimes got in the country. And he had laughed at him at the time! That showed one must not be too sure of things. There was no mistake about it, it *was* cold. He strode up and down, stamping his feet and threshing his arms, until reassured by the returning warmth. Then he got out matches and proceeded to make a fire. From the undergrowth, where high water of the previous spring had lodged a supply of seasoned twigs, he got his firewood. Working carefully from a small beginning, he soon had a roaring fire, over which he thawed the ice from his face and in the protection of which he ate his biscuits. For the moment the cold of space was outwitted. The dog took satisfaction in the fire, stretching out close enough for warmth and far enough away to escape being singed.

When the man had finished, he filled his pipe and took his comfortable time over a smoke. Then he pulled on his mittens, settled the earflaps of his cap firmly about his ears, and took the creek trail up the left fork. The dog was disappointed and yearned back toward the fire. This man did not know cold. Possibly all the generations of his ancestry had been ignorant of cold, of real cold, of cold one hundred and seven degrees below freezing point. But the dog knew; all its ancestry knew, and it had inherited the knowledge. And it knew that it was not good to walk abroad in such fearful cold. It was the time to lie snug in a hole in the snow and wait for a curtain of cloud to be drawn across the face of outer space whence this cold came. On the other hand, there was no keen intimacy between the dog and the man. The one was the toil slave of the other, and the only caresses it had ever received were the caresses of the whiplash and of harsh and menacing throat sounds that threatened the whiplash. So the dog made no effort to communicate its apprehension to the man. It was not concerned in the welfare of the man; it was for its own sake that it yearned back toward the fire. But the man whistled, and spoke to it with the sound of whiplashes, and the dog swung in at the man's heels and followed after.

The man took a chew of tobacco and proceeded to start a new amber beard. Also, his moist breath quickly powdered with white his moustache, eyebrows, and lashes. There did not seem to be so many springs on the left fork of the Henderson, and for half an hour the man saw no signs of any. And then it happened. At a place where there were no signs, where the soft, unbroken snow seemed to advertise solidity beneath, the man broke through. It was not deep. He wet himself halfway to the knees before he floundered out to the firm crust.

He was angry, and cursed his luck aloud. He had hoped to get into camp with the boys at six o'clock, and this would delay him an hour, for he would have to build a fire and dry out his footgear. This was imperative at that low temperature—he knew that much; and he turned aside to the bank, which he climbed. On top, tangled in the underbrush about the trunks of several small spruce trees, was a high-water deposit of dry firewood—sticks and twigs, principally, but also larger portions of seasoned branches and fine, dry, last year's grasses. He threw down several large pieces on top of the snow. This served for a foundation and prevented the young flame from drowning itself in the snow it otherwise would melt. The flame he got by touching a match to a small shred of birch bark that he took from his pocket. This burned even more readily than paper. Placing it on the foundation, he fed the young flame with wisps of dry grass and with the tiniest dry twigs.

He worked slowly and carefully, keenly aware of his danger. Gradually, as the flame grew stronger, he increased the size of the twigs with which he fed it. He squatted in the snow, pulling the twigs out from their entanglement in the brush and feeding directly to the flame. He knew there must be no failure. When it is seventy-five below zero, a man must not fail in his first attempt to build a fire—that is, if his feet are wet. If his feet are dry, and he fails, he can run along the trail for a half a mile and restore his circulation. But the circulation of wet and freezing feet cannot be restored by running when it is seventy-five below. No matter how fast he runs, the wet feet will freeze the harder.

All this the man knew. The old-timer on Sulfur Creek had told him about it the previous fall, and now he was appreciating the advice. Already all sensation had gone out of his feet. To build the fire, he had been forced to remove his mittens, and the fingers had quickly gone numb. His pace of four miles an hour had kept his heart pumping blood to the surface of his body and to all the extremities. But the instant he stopped, the action of the pump eased down. The cold of space smote the unprotected tip of the planet, and he, being on that unprotected tip, received the full force of the blow. The blood of his body recoiled before it. The blood was alive, like the dog, and like the dog it wanted to hide away and cover itself up from the fearful cold. So long as he walked four miles an hour, he pumped that blood, willy-nilly,[11] to the surface; but now it ebbed away and sank down into the recesses of his body. The extremities were the first to feel its absence. His wet feet froze the faster, and his exposed fingers numbed the faster, though they had not yet begun to freeze. Nose and cheeks were already freezing, while the skin of all his body chilled as it lost its blood.

11. **willy-nilly** *adv.:* without choice.

**Vocabulary**

**imperative** (im·per′ə·tiv) *adj.:* absolutely necessary; urgent.

**extremities** (ek·strem′ə·tēz) *n. pl.:* limbs of the body, especially hands and feet.

**recoiled** (ri·koild′) *v.:* shrank away; drew back.

But he was safe. Toes and nose and cheeks would be only touched by the frost, for the fire was beginning to burn with strength. He was feeding it twigs the size of his finger. In another minute he would be able to feed it with branches the size of his wrist, and then he could remove his wet footgear, and, while it dried, he could keep his naked feet warm by the fire, rubbing them at first, of course, with snow. The fire was a success. He was safe. He remembered the advice of the old-timer on Sulfur Creek, and smiled. The old-timer had been very serious in laying down the law that no man must travel alone in the Klondike after fifty below. Well, here he was; he had had the accident; he was alone; and he had saved himself. Those old-timers were rather womanish, some of them, he thought. All a man had to do was to keep his head and he was all right. Any man who was a man could travel alone. But it was surprising, the rapidity with which his cheeks and nose were freezing. And he had not thought his fingers could go lifeless in so short a time. Lifeless they were, for he could scarcely make them move together to grip a twig, and they seemed remote from his body and from him. When he touched a twig, he had to look and see whether or not he had hold of it. The wires were pretty well down between him and his finger ends.

All of which counted for little. There was the fire, snapping and crackling and promising life with every dancing flame. He started to untie his moccasins. They were coated with ice; the thick German socks were like sheaths of iron halfway to the knees; and the moccasin strings were like rods of steel all twisted and knotted as by some conflagration.[12] For a moment he tugged with his numb fingers, then, realizing the folly of it, he drew his sheath knife.

But before he could cut the strings it happened. It was his own fault, or, rather, his mistake. He should not have built the fire under the spruce tree. He should have built it in the open. But it had been easier to pull the twigs from the bush and drop them directly on the fire. Now the tree under which he had done this carried a weight of snow on its boughs. No wind had blown for weeks, and each bough was fully freighted. Each time he had pulled a twig he had communicated a slight agitation to the tree—an imperceptible agitation, so far as he was concerned, but an agitation sufficient to bring about the disaster. High up in the tree one bough capsized its load of snow. This fell on the boughs beneath, capsizing them. This process continued, spreading out and involving the whole tree. It grew like an avalanche, and it descended without warning upon the man and the fire, and the fire was blotted out! Where it had burned was a mantle of fresh and disordered snow.

The man was shocked. It was as though he had just heard his own sentence of death. For a moment he sat and stared at the spot where the fire had been. Then he grew very calm. Perhaps the old-timer on Sulfur Creek was right. If he had only had a trail mate, he would have been in no danger now. The trail mate could have built the fire. Well, it was up to him to build the fire over again, and this second time there must be no failure. Even if he succeeded, he would most likely lose some toes. His feet must be badly frozen by now, and there would be some time before the second fire was ready.

Such were his thoughts, but he did not sit and think them. He was busy all the time they were passing through his mind. He made a new foundation for a fire, this time in the open, where no treacherous tree could blot it out. Next he gathered dry grasses and tiny twigs from the high-water flotsam.[13] He could not bring his fingers together to pull them out, but he was able to gather them by the handful. In this way he got many rotten twigs and bits of green moss that were undesirable, but it was the best he could do. He worked methodically, even collecting an armful of the larger branches to be used later when the fire gathered strength. And all the while the dog sat and watched him, a

---

12. **conflagration** *n.*: large fire.

13. **high-water flotsam:** branches and debris washed ashore by a stream or river during the warm months, when the water is high.

certain yearning wistfulness in its eyes, for it looked upon him as the fire provider, and the fire was slow in coming.

When all was ready, the man reached in his pocket for a second piece of birch bark. He knew the bark was there, and, though he could not feel it with his fingers, he could hear its crisp rustling as he fumbled for it. Try as he would, he could not clutch hold of it. And all the time, in his consciousness, was the knowledge that each instant his feet were freezing. This thought tended to put him in a panic, but he fought against it and kept calm. He pulled on his mittens with his teeth, and threshed his arms back and forth, beating his hands with all his might against his sides. He did this sitting down, and he stood up to do it; and all the while the dog sat in the snow, its wolf brush of a tail curled around warmly over its forefeet, its sharp wolf ears pricked forward intently as it watched the man. And the man, as he beat and threshed with his arms and hands, felt a great surge of envy as he regarded the creature that was warm and secure in its natural covering.

After a time he was aware of the first faraway signals of sensation in his beaten fingers. The faint tingling grew stronger till it evolved into a stinging ache that was excruciating, but which the man hailed with satisfaction. He stripped the mitten from his right hand and fetched forth the birch bark. The exposed fingers were quickly going numb again. Next he brought out his bunch of sulfur matches. But the tremendous cold had already driven the life out of his fingers. In his effort to separate one match from the others, the whole bunch fell in the snow. He tried to pick it out of the snow, but failed. The dead fingers could neither touch nor clutch. He was very careful. He drove the thought of his freezing feet, and nose, and cheeks, out of his mind, devoting his whole soul to the matches. He watched, using the sense of vision in place of that of touch, and when he saw his fingers on each side of the bunch, he closed them— that is, he willed to close them, for the wires were down, and the fingers did not obey. He pulled the mitten on the right hand, and beat

it fiercely against his knee. Then, with both mittened hands, he scooped the bunch of matches, along with much snow, into his lap. Yet he was no better off.

After some manipulation he managed to get the bunch between the heels of his mittened hands. In this fashion he carried it to his mouth. The ice crackled and snapped when by a violent effort he opened his mouth. He drew the lower jaw in, curled the upper lip out of the way, and scraped the bunch with his upper teeth in order to separate a match. He succeeded in getting one, which he dropped on his lap. He was no better off. He could not pick it up. Then he devised a way. He picked it up in his teeth and scratched it on his leg. Twenty times he scratched before he succeeded in lighting it. As it flamed he held it with his teeth to the birch bark. But the burning brimstone went up his nostrils and into his lungs, causing him to cough spasmodically.[14] The match fell into the snow and went out.

The old-timer on Sulfur Creek was right, he thought in the moment of controlled despair that ensued: After fifty below, a man should travel with a partner. He beat his hands, but failed in exciting any sensation. Suddenly he bared both hands, removing the mittens with his teeth. He caught the whole bunch between the heels of his hands. His arm muscles, not being frozen, enabled him to press the hand heels tightly against the matches. Then he scratched the bunch along his leg. It flared into flame, seventy sulfur matches at once! There was no wind to blow them out. He kept his head to one side to escape the strangling fumes, and held the blazing bunch to the birch bark. As he so held it, he became aware of sensation in his hand. His flesh was burning. He could smell it. Deep down below the surface he could feel it.

---

14. **spasmodically** *adv.*: in a sudden, violent manner; fitfully.

---

**Vocabulary**

**excruciating** (eks·kroo′shē·āt′iŋ) *adj.*: intensely painful.
**ensued** (en·sood′) *v.*: resulted.

Even if he succeeded, he would most likely lose some toes. His feet must be badly frozen by now, and there would be some time before the second fire was ready.

The sensation developed into pain that grew acute. And still he endured it, holding the flame of matches clumsily to the bark that would not light readily because his own burning hands were in the way, absorbing most of the flame.

At last, when he could endure no more, he jerked his hands apart. The blazing matches fell sizzling into the snow, but the birch bark was alight. He began laying dry grass and the tiniest twigs on the flame. He could not pick and choose, for he had to lift the fuel between the heels of his hands. Small pieces of rotten wood and green moss clung to the twigs, and he bit them off as well as he could with his teeth. He cherished the flame carefully and awkwardly. It meant life, and it must not perish. The withdrawal of blood from the surface of his body now made him begin to shiver, and he grew more awkward. A large piece of green moss fell squarely on the little fire. He tried to poke it out with his fingers, but his shivering frame made him poke too far, and he disrupted the nucleus of the little fire, the burning grasses and tiny twigs separating and scattering. He tried to poke them together again, but in spite of the tenseness of the effort, his shivering got away with him, and the twigs were hopelessly scattered. Each twig gushed a puff of smoke and went out. The fire provider had failed. As he looked apathetically[15] about him, his eyes chanced on the dog, sitting across the ruins of the fire from him, in the snow, making restless, hunching movements, slightly lifting one forefoot and then the other, shifting its weight back and forth on them with wistful eagerness.

The sight of the dog put a wild idea into his head. He remembered the tale of the man, caught in a blizzard, who killed a steer and crawled inside the carcass, and so was saved. He would kill the dog and bury his hands in the warm body until the numbness went out of them. Then he could build another fire. He spoke to the dog, calling it to him; but in his voice was a strange note of fear that frightened the animal, who had never known the man to speak in such a way before. Something was the matter, and its suspicious nature sensed danger—it knew not what danger, but somewhere, somehow, in its brain arose an apprehension of the man. It flattened its ears down at the sound of the man's voice, and its restless, hunching movements and the liftings and shiftings of its forefeet became more pronounced; but it would not come to the man. He got on his hands and knees and crawled toward the dog. This unusual posture again excited suspicion, and the animal sidled mincingly[16] away.

The man sat up in the snow for a moment and struggled for calmness. Then he pulled on his mittens, by means of his teeth, and got up on his feet. He glanced down at first in order to assure himself that he was really standing up, for the absence of sensation in his feet left him unrelated to the earth. His erect position in itself started to drive the webs of suspicion from the dog's mind; and when he spoke peremptorily,[17] with the sound of whiplashes in his voice, the dog rendered its customary allegiance and came to him. As it came within reaching distance, the man lost his control. His arms flashed out to the dog, and he experienced genuine surprise when he discovered that his hands could not clutch, that there was neither bend nor feeling in the fingers. He had forgotten for the moment that they were frozen and that they were freezing more and more. All this happened quickly, and before the animal could get away, he encircled its body with his arms. He sat down in the snow, and in this fashion held the dog, while it snarled and whined and struggled.

But it was all he could do, hold its body encircled in his arms and sit there. He realized that he could not kill the dog. There was no way to do it. With his helpless hands he could neither draw nor hold his sheath knife nor throttle the animal. He released it, and it plunged wildly away, its tail between its legs and still snarling. It halted forty feet away and surveyed him curiously, with ears sharply pricked forward. The man looked down at his hands in order to locate them, and found them hanging on the ends of his arms. It struck him as curious that one should have to use his eyes in order to find out where his hands were. He began threshing his arms back and forth, beating the mittened hands against his sides. He did this for five minutes, violently, and his heart pumped enough blood up to the surface to put a stop to his shivering. But no sensation was aroused in his hands. He had an impression that they hung like weights on the ends of his arms, but when he tried to run the impression down, he could not find it.

A certain fear of death, dull and oppressive, came to him. This fear quickly became poignant[18] as he realized that it was no longer a mere matter of freezing his fingers and toes, or of losing his hands and feet, but that it was a matter of life and death, with the chances against him. This threw him into a panic, and he turned and ran up the creek bed along the old, dim trail. The dog joined in behind and kept up with him. He ran blindly, without in-

---

15. **apathetically** *adv.:* with little interest or concern; indifferently.
16. **sidled mincingly:** moved sideways with small steps.
17. **peremptorily** (pər·emp′tə·rə·lē) *adv.:* in a commanding way.

---

18. **poignant** *adj.:* painfully affecting feelings; touching.

**He spoke to the dog, calling it to him;**

**but in his voice was a strange note of**

**fear that frightened the animal.**

tention, in fear such as he had never known in his life. Slowly, as he plowed and floundered through the snow, he began to see things again—the banks of the creek, the old timber jams, the leafless aspens, and the sky. The running made him feel better. He did not shiver. Maybe, if he ran on, his feet would thaw out; and, anyway, if he ran far enough, he would reach the camp and the boys. Without doubt he would lose some fingers and toes and some of his face; but the boys would take care of him, and save the rest of him when he got there. And, at the same time, there was another thought in his mind that said he would never get to the camp and the boys; that it was too many miles away, that the freezing had too great a start on him, and that he would soon be stiff and dead. This thought he kept in the

background and refused to consider. Sometimes it pushed itself forward and demanded to be heard, but he thrust it back and strove to think of other things.

It struck him as curious that he could run at all on feet so frozen that he could not feel them when they struck the earth and took the weight of his body. He seemed to himself to skim along above the surface, and to have no connection with the earth. Somewhere he had once seen a winged Mercury,[19] and he wondered if Mercury felt as he felt when skimming over the earth.

His theory of running until he reached camp and the boys had one flaw in it: He lacked the

---

19. **Mercury:** in Roman mythology, messenger of the gods, who is depicted wearing winged sandals and a winged hat.

endurance. Several times he stumbled, and finally he tottered, crumpled up, and fell. When he tried to rise, he failed. He must sit and rest, he decided, and next time he would merely walk and keep on going. As he sat and regained his breath, he noted that he was feeling quite warm and comfortable. He was not shivering, and it even seemed that a warm glow had come to his chest and trunk. And yet, when he touched his nose or cheeks, there was no sensation. Running would not thaw them out. Nor would it thaw out his hands and feet. Then the thought came to him that the frozen portions of his body must be extending. He tried to keep this thought down, to forget it, to think of something else; he was aware of the panicky feeling that it caused, and he was afraid of the panic. But the thought asserted itself, and persisted, until it produced a vision of his body totally frozen. This was too much, and he made another wild run along the trail. Once he slowed down to a walk, but the thought of the freezing extending itself made him run again.

And all the time the dog ran with him, at his heels. When he fell down a second time, it curled its tail over its forefeet and sat in front of him, facing him, curiously eager and intent. The warmth and security of the animal angered him, and he cursed it till it flattened down its ears appeasingly. This time the shivering came more quickly upon the man. He was losing in this battle with the frost. It was creeping into his body from all sides. The thought of it drove him on, but he ran no more than a hundred feet when he staggered and pitched headlong. It was his last panic. When he had recovered his breath and control, he sat up and entertained in his mind the conception of meeting death with dignity. However, the conception did not come to him in such terms. His idea of it was that he had been making a fool of himself, running around like a chicken with its head cut off—such was the simile that occurred to him. Well, he was bound to freeze anyway, and he might as well take it decently. With this newfound peace of mind came the first glimmerings of drowsiness.

A good idea, he thought, to sleep off to death. It was like taking an anesthetic.[20] Freezing was not so bad as people thought. There were lots worse ways to die.

He pictured the boys finding his body next day. Suddenly he found himself with them, coming along the trail and looking for himself. And, still with them, he came around a turn in the trail and found himself lying in the snow. He did not belong with himself anymore, for even then he was out of himself, standing with the boys and looking at himself in the snow. It certainly was cold, was his thought. When he got back to the States, he could tell the folks what real cold was. He drifted on from this to a vision of the old-timer on Sulfur Creek. He could see him quite clearly, warm and comfortable, and smoking a pipe.

"You were right, old hoss; you were right," the man mumbled to the old-timer of Sulfur Creek.

Then the man drowsed off into what seemed to him the most comfortable and satisfying sleep he had ever known. The dog sat facing him and waiting. The brief day drew to a close in a long, slow twilight. There were no signs of a fire to be made, and, besides, never in the dog's experience had it known a man to sit like that in the snow and make no fire. As the twilight drew on, its eager yearning for the fire mastered it, and with a great lifting and shifting of forefeet, it whined softly, then flattened its ears down in anticipation of being chidden[21] by the man. But the man remained silent. Later, the dog whined loudly. And still later it crept close to the man and caught the scent of death. This made the animal bristle and back away. A little longer it delayed, howling under the stars that leaped and danced and shone brightly in the cold sky. Then it turned and trotted up the trail in the direction of the camp it knew, where were the other food providers and fire providers. ■

20. **anesthetic** *n.*: medication that causes loss of the sensation of pain.
21. **chidden** *v.* used as *adj.* (past participle of *chide*): scolded.

# *from* Left for Dead

## Beck Weathers

*On May 10, 1996, Dr. Seaborn ("Beck") Weathers was erroneously reported dead after lying exposed for eighteen hours in a massive blizzard high on the face of Mount Everest. A member of one of several expedition teams scaling Mount Everest at that time, Weathers never reached the summit. The high altitude affected his vision, leaving him wandering blindly and eventually unconscious. Eight climbers lost their lives during that blizzard, but Weathers determinedly clung to his life. The following excerpt tells about his struggle to return to camp after awakening from a deep coma the day after the storm.*

I thought I was inured[1] to the idea of dying on the mountain. Such a death may even have seemed to me to have a romantic and noble quality. But even though I was prepared to die, I just wasn't ready. . . .

Both my hands were completely frozen. My face was destroyed by the cold. I was profoundly hypothermic.[2] I had not eaten in three days, or taken water for two days. I was lost and I was almost completely blind.

---

1. **inured** *v.* used as *adj.*: accustomed; used to.
2. **hypothermic** *adj.*: of abnormally low body temperature.

You cannot sweat that small stuff, I said to myself. You have to *focus* on that which must be done, and do that thing.

I began to move in that same repetitive, energy-conserving motion that my body knows so well. The ground was uneven, scattered with little ledges maybe five to eight inches deep that in the flat light of late afternoon were invisible to me.

Each time I encountered one of these hidden ledges, I would fall. At first, I instinctively put out my hands to break the fall, but I didn't want to compound the effects of the frostbite by further damaging my hands, so I held them close to my body and tried to turn on my back, or on my side, each time I slipped and fell. I hit the frozen ground pretty hard. . . . Then I'd get up and start again. . . .

I was overwhelmed by an enormous, encompassing sense of melancholy.[3] That I would not say goodbye to my family, that I would never again say "I love you" to my wife, that I would never again hold my children was just not acceptable.

"Keep moving," I said to myself again and again.

I began to hallucinate[4] again, getting awfully close to losing it. Things were really moving around.

Then I saw these two odd blue rocks in front of me, and I thought for one moment, Those might be the tents! Just as quickly I said to myself, Don't! When you walk up to them and they are nothing but rocks, you're going to be discouraged and you might stop. *You cannot do that.* You are going to walk right up to them and you are going to walk right past them. It makes *no* difference.

Beck Weathers, after rescue by helicopter from Mount Everest.

I concentrated on these blue blurs, torn between believing they were camp and fearing they were not, until I got within a hundred feet of them—when suddenly a figure loomed up! It was Todd Burleson, the leader of yet another climbing expedition, who beheld a strange creature lurching toward him in the twilight.

Burleson later shared his first impression of me with a TV interviewer:

"I couldn't believe what I saw. This man had no face. It was completely black, solid black, like he had a crust over him. His jacket was unzipped down to his waist, full of snow. His right arm was bare and frozen over his head. We could not lower it. His skin looked like marble. White stone. No blood in it."

---

3. **melancholy** *n.:* sadness; gloom.
4. **hallucinate** *v.:* see what is not there; have delusions.

# Response and Analysis

## Reading Check

1. Summarize the **plot** of the story by listing its string of major **causes** and **effects.** Start by identifying the man's mission. Then, review your reading notes, and explain *why* the man builds two fires, what happens to each fire, and what results from each of these events. Be sure to include what happens to the man and to the dog by the end of the story.

## Thinking Critically

2. Several times in the story the man recalls the old-timer from Sulfur Creek. What key advice did the old-timer give him? Why, in your opinion, did the man not follow his advice?

3. Early in his story, London writes, "The animal was depressed by the tremendous cold. It knew that it was no time for traveling" (page 548). This passage alerts you to the possibility of trouble ahead. Locate four other passages that **foreshadow** events. Explain the link between each passage and the later event.

4. London does not merely tell you that it is extremely cold. He gives details that make you *feel* the cold. For example, he notes the "sharp, explosive crackle" when the man spits into the frigid air. List five other details from the story that make the cold real to you.

5. In the story a man who thinks is contrasted with a dog who reacts by instinct. How do the man and the dog differ in the ways they approach the intense cold? What point do you think London is making?

## Extending and Evaluating

6. London wrote another, more commercially acceptable ending for an earlier version of "To Build a Fire." In the first version the man survives, returns to camp, and learns an important lesson: Never travel alone. Do you think this ending improves the story or weakens it? Explain your opinion.

## Literary Criticism

7. **Philosophical approach.** Re-read the definition of **naturalism** (page 546). How does the **theme** of this story reflect key naturalist beliefs? How do you feel about the naturalist view of human beings?

Buck, an illustration by Paul Bransom for London's *The Call of the Wild* (1903).

The Granger Collection, New York.

# WRITING

## Opposing Forces

Beck Weathers, in his real-life tale of survival in the excerpt from *Left for Dead* (see the **Connection** on page 559), describes a man in a predicament similar to that of London's protagonist in "To Build a Fire." In a brief **essay,** analyze the **conflicts** in each selection. Consider questions such as these: What are the central conflicts in each? Why does Weathers manage to overcome the forces against him, but London's character does not? Is the most challenging conflict that London's character faces **internal** or **external**? Use details from the selections to support your analysis.

## Vocabulary Development
### Word Origins

intangible   apprehension recoiled
undulations  imperative   excruciating
protruding   extremities  ensued

Where do words come from? For each of the remaining Vocabulary words, fill out a word origin map like the one below. Use a dictionary for help. Some words will not have prefixes or suffixes. (Most dictionaries include prefixes, suffixes, and their meanings in the explanation of the word's origin. Sometimes the word origin in the dictionary may send you to another word.)

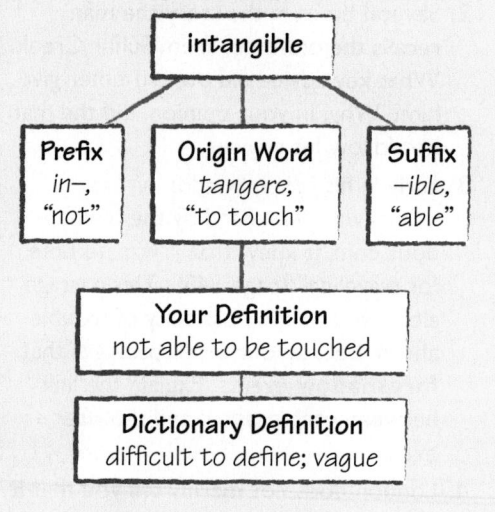

**SKILLS FOCUS**

**Writing Skills**
Write an essay analyzing the conflicts in two selections.

**Vocabulary Skills**
Understand word origins.

**Grammar Skills**
Use adverb and adjective clauses.

# Grammar Link

## Using Adverb and Adjective Clauses: Making Connections

You can improve the variety and flow of your sentences by using adjective and adverb clauses to show connections between ideas.

An **adjective clause** is a subordinate clause that follows a noun or pronoun and modifies the noun or pronoun by specifying *what kind, which one,* or *how many.* Adjective clauses begin with a **relative pronoun,** such as *who, whom, whose, which,* or *that,* or with the **relative adverb** *where* or *when.*

An **adverb clause** is a subordinate clause that modifies a verb, an adjective, or another adverb by specifying *how, when, where, why, to*

---

what extent, or under what condition. Adverb clauses begin with a **sub-ordinating conjunction,** such as *after, although, because, before, if, since, that, unless, until, when,* and *while.*

Use an adverb or adjective clause to combine two simple sentences into a single complex sentence.

Jack London began writing as a teenager. His most famous work is the novel *The Call of the Wild.*

Here, the two simple sentences are joined by an adjective clause:

Jack London, whose most famous work is the novel *The Call of the Wild,* began writing as a teenager.

In the new sentence the adjective clause modifies the proper noun *Jack London,* telling *which one.*

The man in "To Build a Fire" freezes to death. He foolishly attempts to travel alone in the Yukon during an intense cold spell.

Here the two sentences are joined by an adverb clause:

Because he foolishly attempts to travel alone in the Yukon during an intense cold spell, the man in "To Build a Fire" freezes to death.

The adverb clause modifies the verb *freezes* in the main clause, telling *why* the man freezes.

**Note:** If an adjective clause is not essential to the meaning of a sentence, it is a **non-restrictive clause** and should be set off from the rest of the sentence with a comma or commas (see the example to the left). If the clause is essential to the meaning of the sentence, it is a **restrictive clause** and should not be set off by punctuation.

**Note:** When you begin a sentence with an adverb clause, set it off from the main clause with a comma.

**PRACTICE**

Combine each pair of sentences by using an adjective clause or an adverb clause. Identify the kind of clause you have used.

1. Naturalism was a nineteenth-century literary movement. It viewed human beings as victims of natural forces beyond their control.

2. The man in "To Build a Fire" is keenly observant. He does not think about the significance of what he sees.

3. The man foolishly builds a fire under a tree. The tree drops a pile of snow and puts out the fire.

4. The dog finally abandons the man. It catches the scent of death.

## Apply to Your Writing

Look at a current writing assignment or a piece of writing that you've already completed. Are there any short, choppy sentences that you could combine into one complex sentence to make the relationship between your ideas clearer? Use adjective and adverb clauses to create smoother sentences and clearer connections.

▷ **For more help, see Clauses, 7d and 7f, in the Language Handbook.**

# Gabriela Mistral

## (1889–1957)

**A**lthough she was a respected teacher and diplomat, Gabriela Mistral is best known as the first Latin American and the first female poet to be awarded the Nobel Prize in literature. Born Lucila Godoy Alcayaga in the village of Vicuna in Chile, Lucila was a child with a dual nature—shy and withdrawn on the one hand, fiery and irrepressible on the other. When she was three years old, her father abandoned the family, and mother and daughter became very close.

Young Lucila, who was tutored at home, was an excellent student and aspired to become a teacher herself. Around the age of eleven, she started writing poems that soon appeared in local periodicals. This first flush of literary success coincided with her first romance. When Mistral was barely fifteen, she fell in love with a railroad worker named Romelio Ureta. The couple lived far apart for years and conducted most of their romance through letters and postcards. When Ureta committed suicide, in 1909, after a bitter breakup with Mistral, she was devastated. Two things sustained her: her love of teaching and her ability to translate emotions into poetry. She poured her grief and guilt into the "Sonetos de la muerte" ("Sonnets of Death"). Five years later, these poems won first place at a literary competition in Chile and were eventually included in her first collection of poetry titled *Desolación* (*Desolation*).

Because the emotional frankness and intimacy of Mistral's poetry was something new in Chilean literature, her poems created controversy. Fearing the effect such publicity could have on her teaching career, Lucila Godoy Alcayaga decided to publish her poetry under the pen name Gabriela Mistral.

Anonymity would not last long, however. Mistral gained international attention when Federico de Onis, founder of the Hispanic Institute and a teacher at Columbia University in New York City, published the first edition of *Desolación* in 1922. In the years that followed, Mistral traveled tirelessly throughout the United States and Europe, working on behalf of educational reform and women's rights. In the 1930s, she served as a lecturer at several American universities, as a Chilean consul in Italy and Spain, and as a cultural representative to the League of Nations. In the midst of this activity, she continued to write more books of poetry, winning the Nobel Prize in literature in 1945.

Gabriela Mistral was the rarest of artists: a fierce intellectual whose poems also captured the simple, strong feelings of ordinary people. Much beloved, she was often greeted on her returns to Chile by thousands of schoolchildren singing her poems. Mistral, who once described herself as "the direct voice of the poets of my race," wrote with an intimacy and a universality that ranks her not only among the greatest of Latin American poets but also among the greatest poets of the world. The inscription on her tomb reads, "What the soul does for the body so does the poet for her people."

# Before You Read

## What Do You Feel Underground?

Gabriela Mistral experienced repeated losses throughout her life, and she sometimes expressed her grief in poems addressed to the one who was gone. Have you ever wished to speak to someone who has died or gone out of your life? Have you found yourself thinking, "If only I had said how important he or she was to me"?

Jot down a few of the "if onlys" you have thought about and any other thoughts and feelings you would like to share with the person you miss.

### Literary Focus
**Imagery**

**Imagery** is the use of sensory language. Most images appeal to the sense of sight, but images can also evoke taste, smell, hearing, and touch. Imagery is used in all types of writing but is especially important in poetry. In "War Is Kind," for example, Stephen Crane appeals to the sense of hearing with the phrase "hoarse, booming drums." Watch for Mistral's rich images from nature in "What Do You Feel Underground?"

> **Imagery** is the use of sensory language to evoke a picture or a concrete sensation of a person, a thing, a place, or an experience.
>
> *For more on Imagery, see the Handbook of Literary and Historical Terms.*

**SKILLS FOCUS**

**Literary Skills**
Understand imagery.

# What Do You Feel Underground?

## Gabriela Mistral

*translated by* **Maria Giachetti**

Underground do you feel
the delicate warmth of this spring?
Does the sharp perfume of honeysuckle
reach you through the earth?

5    Do you remember the sky,
the clear jets of mountain water,
the shimmering summit?
Do you remember the deep-tapestried path,
my still hand in your trembling hand?

10   This spring perfumes and refines
the sweet liquor of veins.
If only underground your beautiful
closed mouth could savor it!

Bordering the river, to this green
15   redolence° you would come.
You might like the ambivalent° warmth
of my mouth, its soft violence.

But you are underground—
your tongue silenced by dust;
20   there is no way that you can sing with me
the sweet and fiery songs of this spring.

---

**15. redolence** *n.:* quality of being fragrant;
sweetness of scent.
**16. ambivalent** *adj.:* characterized by a mixture
of opposite feelings at the same time.

# Response and Analysis

## Thinking Critically

1. Who is the speaker of the poem, and who is being addressed? How would you characterize the relationship between the two people?

2. Find five sensory **images** in the poem, and identify the sense to which each image appeals—sight, hearing, touch, taste, or smell.

3. Describe the **tone** of the speaker's voice (for example, amused, ironic).

4. Mistral uses questions repeatedly throughout the poem. What emotional effect do these repeated questions create?

5. In a sentence, state the **theme** of the poem. What insight into life or love does it reveal? What evidence from the text supports your interpretation?

## Extending and Evaluating

6. Is it morbid and unnatural for a poet to address a dead person in a poem, or do poems like Mistral's echo what people think and feel when someone dies? (Consult your Quickwrite notes.) What would you say to someone who thinks such poems are an unnatural way to deal with loss? ✏️

## Comparing Literature

7. Compare Mistral's use of **sensory images** with Stephen Crane's in "War Is Kind." List the images you find in each poem and the senses to which they appeal. Which poet makes greater use of images evoking touch? sight? Give evidence from the poems to support your conclusions.

8. Mistral's poem was written nearly fifty years after Crane wrote "War Is Kind" (page 509). Crane's poem expresses specific ideas about war, especially about feelings toward war, in the aftermath of the Civil War. Do you think

Crane's readers at that time would have appreciated Mistral's poem and the feelings about death presented in it? Explain your answer.

## WRITING

### Comparing Poetic Echoes

Develop your comparisons of the poems of Mistral and Crane into an **essay.** Review each poem, and consider the theme, or message, each author is trying to convey. Then, consider the poems' similarities and differences in subject matter, speaker, person addressed, and tone. How successful do you think each poem is in conveying its message?

## LISTENING AND SPEAKING

### Interpreting Poetry

With one or two classmates, prepare either Crane's "War Is Kind" or Mistral's "What Do You Feel Underground?" for an oral reading. Use textual clues from the poem and insights gained from class discussions to help you orally interpret the meaning of each poem. For example, in Crane's poem, how can you use your voice to convey the speaker's ironic tone? In Mistral's poem, how can you use your voice to suggest the speaker's grief and longing? When you are satisfied that your reading enhances the meaning of the poem, perform it for the class.

Gabriela Mistral receiving the Nobel Prize from King Christian X of Denmark (1945).

**SKILLS FOCUS**

**Literary Skills**
Analyze imagery.

**Writing Skills**
Write an essay comparing and contrasting poems.

**Listening and Speaking Skills**
Present an oral interpretation of a poem.

# Kate Chopin
## (1851–1904)

**K**ate Chopin's work went unrecognized and was even scorned during her life time. Along with many other literary pioneers, Chopin never lived to see her work vindicated.

Kate Chopin was born Katherine O'Flaherty in St. Louis, Missouri, to an Irish immigrant father and a mother descended from French Creole aristocrats. (In the United States, Creoles are people of French or Spanish descent who are born in the states bordering the Gulf of Mexico but who retain their European culture.) Kate's prosperous parents encouraged her early interest in music and reading; her mother invited such a flurry of stimulating visitors to their house that Kate sometimes escaped to the attic to read. She was given lessons in French and piano for a time by her worldly great-grandmother, who stirred the child's imagination with vivid tales of old St. Louis. Kate became a witty and popular young woman with a notably independent turn of mind.

At nineteen, Kate married Oscar Chopin, a French Creole from New Orleans. The Chopins settled in Louisiana and reared a family of six children, but when Kate was thirty-one, Oscar died suddenly from swamp fever. Kate returned to St. Louis, and it was then that she began to write. She published a poem when she was thirty-eight, followed by some short stories. In 1890, she published her first novel.

Chopin's short stories concern the life of French Creoles in Louisiana. Published in national magazines and collected in two volumes called *Bayou Folk* (1894) and *A Night in Acadie* (1897), the stories were praised for their accurate portrayal of the French Creole strand in American culture. Chopin's dominant theme, however, was a much more controversial matter: the repression of women in Victorian America.

This theme was presented most dramatically in her novel *The Awakening* (1899). The novel portrays a dissatisfied New Orleans wife who breaks from the confines of her marriage and, in her quest for freedom, flagrantly defies the Victorian ideals of motherhood and domesticity. The novel was greeted with hostility by American critics, who condemned it as sordid and vulgar. The novel was removed from circulation in St. Louis libraries, some of Chopin's friends shunned her, and the local arts club denied her membership. Chopin was disheartened enough by this rejection to allow her writing to languish, and she produced little more before her death in 1904. After her death, her work fell into obscurity, and often copies of her books couldn't even be obtained.

*The Awakening* and many of Chopin's other works were rediscovered decades after her death. With the help of discerning critics and the women's movement of the 1960s and 1970s, Kate Chopin is now recognized as a novelist of skill and perception, whose work appeared half a century before its time.

## For Independent Reading

Try reading Chopin's most famous novel:
• *The Awakening* (novel)

# A Pair of Silk Stockings

## Make the Connection

From time to time, everyone feels trapped by the humdrum duties of daily life. All of us—probably even rock stars and world travelers—fantasize about escape from routines that have come to feel boring or confining. For a nineteenth-century woman of limited means trying to satisfy the needs of her family, even a brief reprieve from the demands of domestic life could be a life-changing bid for freedom and a temporary escape from day-to-day duties.

## Literary Focus
### Motivation

**Motivation** is the reasons for a character's actions. As in life the motivations of fictional characters are often complex, so for us to understand why they act the way they do, their motivations must be believable. In Chopin's story, Mrs. Sommers seems swept away in a series of actions that she has not anticipated. As you read, look for her underlying feelings and the reasons behind her unexpected behavior. Are her actions understandable?

> **Motivation** refers to the reasons for a character's behavior.
>
> *For more on Motivation, see the Handbook of Literary and Historical Terms.*

## Reading Skills
### Analyzing Historical Context

To understand fully a work of literature, you often need to evaluate how the influences from the historical period in which the work was written shape it. In the 1890s, when Chopin wrote "A Pair of Silk Stockings," women in the United States could not vote, were not financially independent, and had few opportunities for education and employment. Although women's rights activists were beginning to seek social justice, progress was slow in coming. As you read Chopin's story, note the differences in the position of women in the 1890s and women today. Consider the ways the story would change if it took place today.

## Background

As you read, be aware that nylon had not yet been invented in the 1890s; most women wore long, thick, cotton stockings. Silk stockings ranked as pure luxury. Also, as you'll see in this story, fifteen dollars in the 1890s could buy far more than two meals at a fast-food restaurant.

## Vocabulary Development

**judicious** (jōō·dish′əs) *adj.*: cautious; wise.

**appreciable** (ə·prē′shə·bəl) *adj.*: measurable.

**veritable** (ver′i·tə·bəl) *adj.*: genuine; true.

**acute** (ə·kyōōt′) *adj.*: keen; sharp.

**laborious** (lə·bôr′ē·əs) *adj.*: difficult; involving much hard work.

**reveling** (rev′əl·iŋ) *v.*: taking pleasure.

**fastidious** (fa·stid′ē·əs) *adj.*: difficult to please; critical.

**preposterous** (prē·päs′tər·əs) *adj.*: ridiculous.

**gaudy** (gô′dē) *adj.*: showy but lacking in good taste.

**poignant** (poin′yənt) *adj.*: emotionally moving.

**SKILLS FOCUS**

**Literary Skills**
Understand motivation.

**Reading Skills**
Analyze historical context, especially political and social influences of the time.

**INTERNET**

**Vocabulary Practice**

Keyword: LE7 11-4

# A Pair of Silk Stockings

**Kate Chopin**

Little Mrs. Sommers one day found herself the unexpected possessor of fifteen dollars. It seemed to her a very large amount of money, and the way in which it stuffed and bulged her worn old *porte-monnaie*[1] gave her a feeling of importance such as she had not enjoyed for years.

The question of investment was one that occupied her greatly. For a day or two she walked about apparently in a dreamy state, but really absorbed in speculation[2] and calculation. She did not wish to act hastily, to do anything she might afterward regret. But it was during the still hours of the night when she lay awake revolving plans in her mind that she seemed to see her way clearly toward a proper and judicious use of the money.

A dollar or two should be added to the price usually paid for Janie's shoes, which would ensure their lasting an appreciable time longer than they usually did. She would buy so-and-so many yards of percale[3] for new shirtwaists for the boys and Janie and Mag. She had intended to make the old ones do by skillful patching. Mag should have another gown. She had seen some beautiful patterns, veritable bargains in the shop windows. And still there would be left enough for new stockings—two pairs apiece—and what darning that would save for a while! She would get caps for the boys and sailor hats for the girls. The vision of her little brood looking fresh and dainty and new for once in their lives excited her and made her restless and wakeful with anticipation.

The neighbors sometimes talked of certain "better days" that little Mrs. Sommers had known before she had ever thought of being Mrs. Sommers. She herself indulged in no such morbid retrospection.[4] She had no time—no second of time to devote to the past. The needs of the present absorbed her every faculty. A vision of the future like some dim, gaunt monster sometimes appalled[5] her, but luckily tomorrow never comes.

Mrs. Sommers was one who knew the value of bargains; who could stand for hours making her way inch by inch toward the desired object that was selling below cost. She could elbow her way if need be; she had learned to clutch a piece of goods and hold it and stick to it with persistence and determination till her turn came to be served, no matter when it came.

But that day she was a little faint and tired. She had swallowed a light luncheon—no! when she came to think of it, between getting the children fed and the place righted, and preparing herself for the shopping bout, she had actually forgotten to eat any luncheon at all!

She sat herself upon a revolving stool before a counter that was comparatively deserted, trying to gather strength and courage to charge through an eager multitude that was besieging breastworks[6] of shirting and figured lawn. An all-gone limp feeling had come over her and she rested her hand aimlessly upon the counter. She wore no gloves. By degrees she grew aware that her hand had encountered something very soothing, very pleasant to touch. She looked down to see that her hand lay upon a pile of silk stockings. A placard nearby announced that they had been reduced in price from two dollars and fifty cents to one dollar and ninety-eight cents; and a young girl who stood behind the

---

1. *porte-monnaie* (pôrt·mô·ne′): French for "purse."
2. speculation *n.:* deep thought; meditation.
3. percale *n.:* finely woven cotton cloth.

---

4. **morbid retrospection:** brooding on things in the past.
5. **appalled** *v.:* shocked; dismayed.
6. **breastworks** *n. pl.:* low walls put up as barricades during battle. The bolts of shirting material and fine patterned cotton, or "figured lawn," are compared to barricades being stormed by shoppers.

**Vocabulary**

**judicious** (jōō·dish′əs) *adj.:* cautious; wise.
**appreciable** (ə·prē′shə·bəl) *adj.:* measurable.
**veritable** (ver′i·tə·bəl) *adj.:* genuine; true.

(Opposite) *The Cup of Tea* (1879) by Mary Cassatt. Oil on canvas ($36^3/_8'' \times 25^3/_4''$).

The Metropolitan Museum of Art, New York. From the Collection of James Stillman. Gift of Dr. Ernest G. Stillman, 1922 (22.16.17). Photograph © 1998 The Metropolitan Museum of Art.

counter asked her if she wished to examine their line of silk hosiery. She smiled, just as if she had been asked to inspect a tiara of diamonds with the ultimate view of purchasing it. But she went on feeling the soft, sheeny luxurious things—with both hands now, holding them up to see them glisten, and to feel them glide serpentlike through her fingers.

Two hectic blotches came suddenly into her pale cheeks. She looked up at the girl.

"Do you think there are any eights-and-a-half among these?"

There were any number of eights-and-a-half. In fact, there were more of that size than any other. Here was a light blue pair; there were some lavender, some all black, and various shades of tan and gray. Mrs. Sommers selected a black pair and looked at them very long and closely. She pretended to be examining their texture, which the clerk assured her was excellent.

"A dollar and ninety-eight cents," she mused aloud. "Well, I'll take this pair." She handed the girl a five-dollar bill and waited for her change and for her parcel. What a very small parcel it was! It seemed lost in the depths of her shabby old shopping bag.

Mrs. Sommers after that did not move in the direction of the bargain counter. She took the elevator, which carried her to an upper floor into the region of the ladies' waiting rooms. Here, in a retired corner, she exchanged her cotton stockings for the new silk ones which she had just bought. She was not going through any <u>acute</u> mental process or reasoning with herself, nor was she striving to explain to her satisfaction the motive of her action. She was not thinking at all. She seemed for the time to be taking a rest from that <u>laborious</u> and fatiguing function and to have <u>abandoned</u> herself to some mechanical impulse[7] that directed her actions and freed her of responsibility.

How good was the touch of the raw silk to her flesh! She felt like lying back in the cushioned chair and <u>reveling</u> for a while in the lux-

ury of it. She did for a little while. Then she replaced her shoes, rolled the cotton stockings together, and thrust them into her bag. After doing this she crossed straight over to the shoe department and took her seat to be fitted.

She was <u>fastidious</u>. The clerk could not make her out; he <u>could not reconcile</u>[8] her shoes with her stockings, and she was not too easily pleased. She held back her skirts and turned her feet one way and her head another way as she glanced down at the polished, pointed-tipped boots. Her foot and ankle looked very pretty. She could not realize that they belonged to her and were a part of herself. She wanted an excellent and stylish fit, she told the young fellow who served her, and she did not mind the difference of a dollar or two more in the price so long as she got what she desired.

It was a long time since Mrs. Sommers had been fitted with gloves. On rare occasions when she had bought a pair they were always "bargains," so cheap that it would have been <u>preposterous</u> and unreasonable to have expected them to be fitted to the hand.

Now she rested her elbow on the cushion of the glove counter, and a pretty, pleasant young creature, delicate and deft of touch, drew a long-wristed "kid" over Mrs. Sommers's hand. She smoothed it down over the wrist and buttoned it neatly, and both lost themselves for a second or two in admiring contemplation of the little symmetrical gloved hand. But there were other places where money might be spent.

There were books and magazines piled up in the window of a stall a few paces down the street. Mrs. Sommers bought two high-priced magazines such as she had been accustomed

---

8. **reconcile** *v.:* make compatible; bring into agreement.

---

**Vocabulary**

**acute** (ə·kyo͞ot′) *adj.:* keen; sharp.
**laborious** (lə·bôr′ē·əs) *adj.:* difficult; involving much hard work.
**reveling** (rev′əl·iŋ) *v.:* taking pleasure.
**fastidious** (fa·stid′ē·əs) *adj.:* difficult to please; critical.
**preposterous** (prē·päs′tər·əs) *adj.:* ridiculous.

---

7. **impulse** *n.:* sudden, driving force.

*The Fitting* (1890/1891) by Mary Cassatt.
Color print with drypoint, soft ground, and aquatint ($14^3/_4'' \times 10^1/_8''$).

**Kate Chopin**    **573**

to read in the days when she had been accustomed to other pleasant things. She carried them without wrapping. As well as she could she lifted her skirts at the crossings. Her stockings and boots and well-fitting gloves had worked marvels in her bearing—had given her a feeling of assurance, a sense of belonging to the well-dressed multitude.

She was very hungry. Another time she would have stilled the cravings for food until reaching her own home, where she would have brewed herself a cup of tea and taken a snack of anything that was available. But the impulse that was guiding her would not suffer her to entertain any such thought.

There was a restaurant at the corner. She had never entered its doors; from the outside she had sometimes caught glimpses of spotless damask and shining crystal, and soft-stepping waiters serving people of fashion.

When she entered, her appearance created no surprise, no consternation, as she had half feared it might. She seated herself at a small table alone, and an attentive waiter at once approached to take her order. She did not want a profusion;[9] she craved a nice and tasty bite—a half dozen bluepoints,[10] a plump chop with cress, a something sweet—a crème-frappé,[11] for instance; a glass of Rhine wine, and after all a small cup of black coffee.

While waiting to be served she removed her gloves very leisurely and laid them beside her. Then she picked up a magazine and glanced through it, cutting the pages with a blunt edge of her knife.[12] It was all very agreeable. The damask was even more spotless than it had seemed through the window, and the crystal more sparkling. There were quiet ladies and gentlemen, who did not notice her, lunching at the small tables like her own. A soft, pleasing strain of music could be heard, and a gentle breeze was blowing through the window. She tasted a bite, and she read a word or two, and she sipped the amber wine and wiggled her toes in the silk stockings. The price of it made no difference. She counted the money out to the waiter and left an extra coin on his tray, whereupon he bowed before her as before a princess of royal blood.

There was still money in her purse, and her next temptation presented itself in the shape of a matinée poster.

It was a little later when she entered the theater, the play had begun, and the house seemed to her to be packed. But there were vacant seats here and there, and into one of them she was ushered, between brilliantly dressed women who had gone there to kill time and eat candy and display their gaudy attire. There were many others who were there solely for the play and acting. It is safe to say there was no one present who bore quite the attitude which Mrs. Sommers did to her surroundings. She gathered in the whole—stage and players and people in one wide impression, and absorbed it and enjoyed it. She laughed at the comedy and wept—she and the gaudy woman next to her wept over the tragedy. And they talked a little together over it. And the gaudy woman wiped her eyes and sniffled on a tiny square of filmy, perfumed lace and passed little Mrs. Sommers her box of candy.

The play was over, the music ceased, the crowd filed out. It was like a dream ended. People scattered in all directions. Mrs. Sommers went to the corner and waited for the cable car.

A man with keen eyes, who sat opposite her, seemed to like the study of her small, pale face. It puzzled him to decipher what he saw there. In truth, he saw nothing—unless he were wizard enough to detect a poignant wish, a powerful longing that the cable car would never stop anywhere, but go on and on with her forever. ∎

---

9. **profusion** *n.*: abundance; great wastefulness.
10. **bluepoints** *n. pl.*: small oysters.
11. **crème-frappé** (krem·fra·pā′) *n.*: dessert similar to ice cream.
12. **cutting . . . knife:** At one time, magazines and books were often sold with folded, untrimmed pages. These outer edges had to be cut apart before one could read them.

**Vocabulary**

**gaudy** (gô′dē) *adj.*: showy but lacking in good taste.
**poignant** (poin′yənt) *adj.*: emotionally moving.

## Elegant Discomfort

INFORMATIONAL TEXT

In the 1890s, clothing was layered, hot, heavy, and expensive. Rows of buttons fastened everything from men's pants to women's long gloves. Styles followed those of London and Paris. City shops carried, at a range of prices, everything from boots to ribbons, but women's dresses were still custom-made. By today's standards, people did not own much clothing, and they often had old garments remodeled instead of buying expensive new ones. The natural fabrics—wool, silk, cotton—could be spoiled by the harsh soaps of the day, so clothes were brushed more often than they were cleaned. Men and women alike used perfumes and scents to conceal odor.

**Stepping out in style.** A well-turned-out man in the 1890s wore a derby hat and a lined suit. His shirt had a long tail and a detachable collar. His coat was buttoned so high that it sometimes concealed his cravat (tie)—the one item declaring his personal taste. His under-clothes might be knitted from wool. For outerwear, he might own an inverness (a loose overcoat with an arm-length cape) or an ulster (a long, belted coat). Men generally kept their hair trimmed above the collar, and many wore full moustaches or neat beards.

The fashionable woman of the time wore a large-brimmed hat and a full-length suit or dress. For clerical work or the new crazes of tennis and bicycling, she tucked a shirtwaist (a blouse tailored like a man's shirt) into a full skirt. At home, she could receive guests in a loosefitting tea gown adorned with pleats and lace. On formal occasions, however, she had to strap herself into a painful corset—a tightly fitting upper-body undergarment often stiffened with bone—and wear a dress that emphasized her bosom in front and hips behind. Although not so extreme as the bustles and front lifts of earlier decades, the resulting corseted shape, seen from the side, was that of a slightly tilted hourglass. Her cotton or silk underwear might be trimmed with lace, embroidery, or ribbon. For outerwear, she donned a shaped cape. She usually wore her hair swept up into a chignon (a knot of hair worn at the nape of the neck), with the sides rolled to frame her face. She finished everything off with ribbons, lace, and jewelry.

**Dressing for success.** The point of fashion, then as now, was to make a statement. The gloves Mrs. Sommers tries on, for example, would have been an expensive item and so tightfitting as to be useless for work, marking the wearer as a "lady of leisure." Women also needed to dress to attract social invitations and a good marriage. This point was clear to Lily Bart, the protagonist of *The House of Mirth*, a turn-of-the-century novel by the American writer Edith Wharton (1862–1937). As Lily puts it, "If I were shabby no one would have me: A woman is asked out as much for her clothes as for herself. The clothes are the background, the frame, if you like: They don't make success, but they are a part of it."

# Now and Then, America

## Pat Mora

Who wants to rot
beneath dry, winter grass
in a numbered grave
in a numbered row
5  in a section labeled Eternal Peace
with neighbors plagued
by limp, plastic roses
springing from their toes?
Grant me a little life now and then, America.

10  Who wants to rot
as she marches through life
in a pinstriped suit
neck chained in a soft, silk bow
in step, in style, insane.
15  Let me in
to boardrooms wearing hot
colors, my hair long and free,
maybe speaking Spanish.
Risk my difference, my surprises.
20  Grant me a little life, America.

And when I die, plant *zempasúchitl*,°
flowers of the dead, and at my head
plant organ cactus, green fleshy
fingers sprouting, like in Oaxaca.°
25  Let desert creatures hide
in the orange blooms.
Let birds nest in the cactus stems.
Let me go knowing life flower and song
will continue right above my bones.

*Iraida* (1992) by Nick Quijano.

**21. *zempasúchitl*** (sem·pä·sōō′chē·t'l) *n.*:
Mexican marigolds.

**24. Oaxaca** (wä·hä′kä): state in southeast Mexico.

# Response and Analysis

## Reading Check

1. What does Mrs. Sommers plan to do with the extra fifteen dollars?
2. What does Mrs. Sommers end up doing with the money?

## Thinking Critically

3. The author describes the main character as "little Mrs. Sommers," and we learn that she has several children, lacks the time to recall "better days," and regards the future as a "dim, gaunt monster." No mention is made of her husband or the source of her spending money. How would you describe her **character**? What other details lead you to this description?

4. Considering what the author tells us about Mrs. Sommers's earlier life, how would you explain the **motivation** for her shopping spree?

5. When Mrs. Sommers first feels the silk stockings, they "glide serpentlike through her fingers." What does a serpent often **symbolize** in Western culture? Explain why the use of "serpentlike" is significant.

## Extending and Evaluating

6. The story is more than one hundred years old. Do you think knowledge of the **historical context** of the period in which it was written makes the story more believable, or do you think the story makes sense without any understanding of its time period? Explain.

## Literary Criticism

7. **Philosophical approach.** A feminist critic might say that this story is about a woman who is striving to gain personal freedom and identity. A Marxist critic might say it is about the class struggle. The critic Barbara C. Ewell writes, "The power of money to enhance self-esteem and confidence is the core of this poignant tale." Which critic, if any, do you agree with? Why?

## WRITING

### Breaking Bonds

Both Chopin and Pat Mora, in the **Connection** on page 576, write about escape, freedom, identity, and individuality. In a brief **essay,** compare and contrast the two writers' attitudes toward these **themes.** What kinds of **images** do they use to convey their messages? What comment on life is each writer making?

---

## Vocabulary Development

### Analogies

| | | |
|---|---|---|
| judicious | laborious | gaudy |
| appreciable | reveling | poignant |
| veritable | fastidious | |
| acute | preposterous | |

An **analogy** consists of two pairs of words. The words in the first pair relate to each other in the same way as the words in the second pair. For example, a pair of words could be synonyms, or one word could describe a characteristic of the other word. Fill in each blank below with the Vocabulary word that completes the analogy.

1. CAUTIOUS : RECKLESS :: _____ : foolish
2. HUMOROUS : FUNNY :: _____ : absurd
3. SPICY : BLAND :: _____ : dull
4. DEEP : SHALLOW :: _____ : unfeeling
5. MOURNING : FUNERAL :: _____ : party
6. FALSE : IMITATION :: _____ : truth
7. RESTFUL : VACATION :: _____ : work
8. SOLID : UNFORMED :: _____ : imperceptible
9. HUMBLE : MODEST :: _____ : flamboyant
10. ATTENTIVE : DISTRACTED :: _____ : careless

---

**SKILLS FOCUS**

**Literary Skills**
Analyze motivation.

**Reading Skills**
Analyze historical context, especially political and social influences of the time.

**Writing Skills**
Write an essay comparing and contrasting poems by two writers.

**Vocabulary Skills**
Analyze word analogies.

go.
hrw
.com

**INTERNET**

Projects and Activities

Keyword: LE7 11-4

# Willa Cather

## (1873–1947)

Willa Cather (1926).
Photograph by Edward Steichen.

Willa Cather was born in rural Virginia, the first of seven children. When she was nine, her father uprooted the family and headed for the untried lands of the West, settling in Webster County, Nebraska. She would later recall that in her first encounter with the prairie she felt "a kind of erasure of personality."

Nevertheless, Cather was stimulated by the hard life she saw around her, and she absorbed the stories of the immigrant families who were her neighbors. She became an outstanding student at the school in Red Cloud, Nebraska. In her boyish clothes, Willa was an unusual figure, and her teachers recognized in her an adolescent nonconformist.

While a freshman at the University of Nebraska, Cather became a regular contributor to a Lincoln newspaper. By the time she graduated in 1895, she had already won a statewide reputation for brash, bright reviews. She moved to Pittsburgh and for a decade continued to work as a journalist. In 1903, she published her first book, a collection of verse titled *April Twilights.* This was followed in 1905 by *The Troll Garden,* a collection of short stories that includes "A Wagner Matinée."

In 1906, Cather moved to New York and joined the staff of the dynamic, muckraking magazine *McClure's.* For six years she served as a writer and editor, immersed in the social and political currents of the time; in 1912, she resigned from the magazine to dedicate herself to writing fiction.

In 1908, Cather had met the Maine writer Sarah Orne Jewett (1849–1909), who had encouraged Cather to write about what she knew best: the moral values of the hardworking immigrant families on the midwestern prairie. Cather believed that these pioneers, who had sought to cultivate this wild, new land, had a vital, earthy richness and were the heart of the so-called American dream. Cather developed these themes in *O Pioneers!* (1913) and in her novel *My Ántonia* (1918).

As Cather witnessed the decline of the agrarian ideal, her work became increasingly elegiac about the past and disillusioned with the present. *One of Ours* (1922), which was far from Cather's best novel but which won her the Pulitzer Prize, reflects Cather's dissatisfaction with the new people and machines who had betrayed the pioneer ideal.

Although Cather continued to produce finely crafted novels and stories—including the two masterpieces *The Professor's House* (1925) and *Death Comes for the Archbishop* (1927)—her creative vision remained rooted in the realities of the nineteenth century. She was uncomfortable with the modernist sensibility that swept through artistic and literary circles after World War I. "The world broke in two in 1922 or there about," Cather wrote, explaining that no one born in the twentieth century could grasp her own vision of America—a noble society of heroic pioneers. Having seen her beloved Nebraska devastated by the machine, she predicted that the new comforts of modern science would almost surely demand something of our spirit in return.

## For Independent Reading

Try these popular novels by Cather:

- *O Pioneers!*
- *Death Comes for the Archbishop*

## A Wagner Matinée

### Make the Connection
**Quickwrite** ✏️

Most people can name at least one thing they enjoy that's a source of personal bliss—something they'd rather do more than anything else in the world. Suppose, like the woman in Cather's story, you were deprived of your bliss for many years, and then you had the opportunity to experience it again, but only briefly. Write your ideas about how you would respond. Would you seize the opportunity or pass up the chance for fear that it would be too painful to realize what you had been missing?

### Literary Focus
**Setting**

As in most of Cather's works, **setting** plays a central role in this story. Here, however, there are really two settings. Rural Nebraska—in which the narrator of the story spent his formative years, like Cather—is contrasted with Boston and its thriving cultural life.

> **Setting** is the time and location in which a story takes place.
>
> *For more on Setting, see the Handbook of Literary and Historical Terms.*

### Background

Many of Cather's works are set on the Nebraska frontier that she loved. She believed that midwestern farm life fostered important values, yet she was hardly a romantic who underestimated the hardships of that life or the harsh losses that many of her stoic characters had to endure.

In addition to the frontier, music was a recurring element in Cather's work. She had a great personal passion for music and was an accomplished musician. This story's title refers to the German composer Richard Wagner (väg'nər) (1813–1883), an outstanding Romantic composer of the nineteenth century. A matinée is an afternoon performance of a play or concert.

### Vocabulary Development

**legacy** (leg'ə·sē) *n.:* inheritance.

**grotesque** (grō·tesk') *adj.:* strange; absurd.

**eluding** (ē·lood'iŋ) *v.* used as *adj.:* escaping.

**reverential** (rev'ə·ren'shəl) *adj.:* deeply respectful.

**pious** (pī'əs) *adj.:* devoted to one's religion.

**inert** (in·urt') *adj.:* inactive; dull.

**trepidation** (trep'ə·dā'shən) *n.:* anxious uncertainty.

**obliquely** (ō·blēk'lē) *adv.:* at a slant.

**deluge** (del'yooj') *n.:* rush; flood.

**myriad** (mir'ē·əd) *adj.:* countless.

**SKILLS FOCUS**

**Literary Skills**
Understand setting.

go.
hrw
.com

**INTERNET**

**Vocabulary Practice**
Keyword: LE7 11-4

Willa Cather **579**

# A Wagner Matinée

## Willa Cather

I received one morning a letter, written in pale ink on glassy, blue-lined notepaper, and bearing the postmark of a little Nebraska village. This communication, worn and rubbed, looking as though it had been carried for some days in a coat pocket that was none too clean, was from my Uncle Howard and informed me that his wife had been left a small legacy by a bachelor relative who had recently died, and that it would be necessary for her to go to Boston to attend to the settling of the estate. He requested me to meet her at the station and render her whatever services might be necessary. On examining the date indicated as that of her arrival, I found it no later than tomorrow. He had characteristically delayed writing until, had I been away from home for a day, I must have missed the good woman altogether.

The name of Aunt Georgiana called up not alone her own figure, at once pathetic and grotesque, but opened before my feet a gulf of recollection so wide and deep, that, as the letter dropped from my hand, I felt suddenly a stranger to all the present conditions of my existence, wholly ill at ease and out of place amid the familiar surroundings of my study. I became, in short, the gangling farmer boy my aunt had known, scourged[1] with chilblains[2] and bashfulness, my hands cracked and sore from the cornhusking. I felt the knuckles of my thumb tentatively, as though they were raw again. I sat again before her parlor organ, fumbling the scales with my stiff, red hands, while she, beside me, made canvas mittens for the huskers.

The next morning, after preparing my landlady somewhat, I set out for the station. When the train arrived I had some difficulty in finding my aunt. She was the last of the passengers to alight, and it was not until I got her into the carriage that she seemed really to recognize me. She had come all the way in a day coach; her linen duster had become black with soot and her black bonnet gray with dust during the journey. When we arrived at my boardinghouse the landlady put her to bed at once and I did not see her again until the next morning.

Whatever shock Mrs. Springer experienced at my aunt's appearance, she considerately concealed. As for myself, I saw my aunt's misshapen figure with that feeling of awe and respect with which we behold explorers who have left their ears and fingers north of Franz Josef Land,[3] or their health somewhere along the upper Congo.[4] My Aunt Georgiana had been a music teacher at the Boston Conservatory, somewhere back in the latter sixties. One summer, while visiting in the little village among the Green Mountains where her ancestors had dwelt for generations, she had kindled the callow[5] fancy of the most idle and shiftless of all the village lads, and had conceived for this Howard Carpenter one of those extravagant passions which a handsome country boy of twenty-one some-

---

3. **Franz Josef Land:** group of islands in the Arctic Ocean.
4. **upper Congo:** river in West Africa, also called the Zaire.
5. **callow** *adj.:* immature; inexperienced.

**Vocabulary**

**legacy** (leg'ə·sē) *n.:* inheritance.
**grotesque** (grō·tesk') *adj.:* strange; absurd.

---

1. **scourged** *v.:* afflicted; tormented.
2. **chilblains** (chil'blānz') *n. pl.:* inflammation of the hands and feet, caused by exposure to cold.

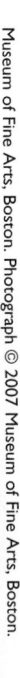

*In the Loge* (1878) by Mary Cassatt. Oil on canvas 81.28 × 66.04 cm (32 × 26 in.) The Hayden Collection-Charles Henry Hayden Fund, 10.35.

times inspires in an angular, spectacled woman of thirty. When she returned to her duties in Boston, Howard followed her, and the upshot of this inexplicable infatuation was that she eloped with him, eluding the reproaches of her family and the criticisms of her friends by going with him to the Nebraska frontier. Carpenter, who, of course, had no money, had taken a homestead in Red Willow County, fifty miles from the railroad. There they had measured off their quarter section themselves by driving across the prairie in a wagon, to the wheel of which they had tied a red cotton handkerchief, and counting off its revolutions. They built a dugout in the red hillside, one of those cave dwellings whose inmates so often reverted to primitive conditions. Their water they got from the lagoons where the buffalo drank, and their slender stock of provisions was always at the mercy of bands of roving Indians. For thirty years my aunt had not been further than fifty miles from the homestead.

But Mrs. Springer knew nothing of all this, and must have been considerably shocked at what was left of my kinswoman. Beneath the soiled linen duster which, on her arrival, was the most conspicuous feature of her costume, she wore a black stuff[6] dress, whose ornamentation showed that she had surrendered herself unquestioningly into the hands of a country dressmaker. My poor aunt's figure, however, would have presented astonishing difficulties to any dressmaker. Originally stooped, her shoulders were now almost bent together over her sunken chest. She wore no stays,[7] and her gown, which trailed unevenly behind, rose in a sort of peak over her abdomen. She wore ill-fitting false teeth, and her skin was as yellow as a Mongolian's from constant exposure to a pitiless wind and to the alkaline water which hardens the most transparent cuticle into a sort of flexible leather.

I owed to this woman most of the good that ever came my way in my boyhood, and had a reverential affection for her. During the years when I was riding herd for my uncle, my aunt, after cooking the three meals—the first of which was ready at six o'clock in the morning—and putting the six children to bed, would often stand until midnight at her ironing board, with me at the kitchen table beside her, hearing me recite Latin declensions and conjugations,[8] gently shaking me when my drowsy head sank down over a page of irregular verbs. It was to her, at her ironing or mending, that I read my first Shakespeare, and her old textbook on mythology was the first that ever came into my empty hands. She taught me my scales and exercises, too—on the little parlor organ, which her husband had bought her after fifteen years, during which she had not so much as seen any instrument, but an accordion that belonged to one of the Norwegian farmhands. She would sit beside me by the hour, darning and counting while I struggled with the "Joyous Farmer," but she seldom talked to me about music, and I understood why. She was a pious woman; she had the consolations of religion and, to her at least, her martyrdom was not wholly sordid.[9] Once when I had been doggedly[10] beating out some easy passages from an old score of *Euryanthe*[11] I had found among her music books, she came up to me and, putting her hands over my eyes, gently drew my head back upon her shoulder, saying tremulously,[12] "Don't love it so well, Clark, or it may be taken from you. Oh! dear boy, pray that whatever your sacrifice may be, it be not that."

---

8. **Latin declensions and conjugations:** different forms of nouns, pronouns, adjectives, and verbs. Students often memorize these forms when studying Latin or other languages.
9. **sordid** *adj.:* unethical; dishonest.
10. **doggedly** *adv.:* stubbornly; persistently.
11. *Euryanthe:* opera by German composer Carl Maria von Weber.
12. **tremulously** *adv.:* in a trembling or shaking manner.

**Vocabulary**
**eluding** (ē·lood′iŋ) *v.* used as *adj.:* escaping.
**reverential** (rev′ə·ren′shəl) *adj.:* deeply respectful.
**pious** (pī′əs) *adj.:* devoted to one's religion.

---

6. **stuff** *n.:* cloth, usually woolen.
7. **stays** *n. pl.:* corset, or figure-enhancing women's undergarment, stiffened as with whalebone.

When my aunt appeared on the morning after her arrival, she was still in a semisomnambulant[13] state. She seemed not to realize that she was in the city where she had spent her youth, the place longed for hungrily half a lifetime. She had been so wretchedly trainsick throughout the journey that she had no recollection of anything but her discomfort, and, to all intents and purposes, there were but a few hours of nightmare between the farm in Red Willow County and my study on Newbury Street. I had planned a little pleasure for her that afternoon, to repay her for some of the glorious moments she had given me when we used to milk together in the straw-thatched cowshed and she, because I was more than usually tired, or because her husband had spoken sharply to me, would tell me of the splendid performance of the *Huguenots*[14] she had seen in Paris, in her youth. At two o'clock the Symphony Orchestra was to give a Wagner program, and I intended to take my aunt; though, as I conversed with her, I grew doubtful about her enjoyment of it. Indeed, for her own sake, I could only wish her taste for such things quite dead, and the long struggle mercifully ended at last. I suggested our visiting the Conservatory and the Common before lunch, but she seemed altogether too timid to wish to venture out. She questioned me absently about various changes in the city, but she was chiefly concerned that she had forgotten to leave instructions about feeding half-skimmed milk to a certain weakling calf, "old Maggie's calf, you know, Clark," she explained, evidently having forgotten how long I had been away. She was further troubled because she had neglected to tell her daughter about the freshly opened kit of mackerel in the cellar, which would spoil if it were not used directly.

I asked her whether she had ever heard any of the Wagnerian operas, and found that she had not, though she was perfectly familiar with their respective situations, and had once possessed the piano score of *The Flying Dutchman*. I began to think it would have been best to get her back to Red Willow County without waking her, and regretted having suggested the concert.

From the time we entered the concert hall, however, she was a trifle less passive and inert, and for the first time seemed to perceive her surroundings. I had felt some trepidation lest she might become aware of the absurdities of her attire, or might experience some painful embarrassment at stepping suddenly into the world to which she had been dead for a quarter of a century. But, again, I found how superficially I had judged her. She sat looking about her with eyes as impersonal, almost as stony, as those with which the granite Ramses[15] in a museum watches the froth and fret[16] that ebbs and flows about his pedestal—separated from it by the lonely stretch of centuries. I have seen this same aloofness in old miners who drift into the Brown Hotel at Denver, their pockets full of bullion,[17] their linen soiled, their haggard faces unshaven; standing in the thronged corridors as solitary as though they were still in a frozen camp on the Yukon,[18] conscious that certain experiences have isolated them from their fellows by a gulf no haberdasher[19] could bridge.

We sat at the extreme left of the first balcony, facing the arc of our own and the balcony above us, veritable hanging gardens, brilliant as tulip beds. The matinée audience was made up

---

13. **semisomnambulant** (sem′ē·säm·nam′byo͞o·lənt) *adj.*: confused and unperceiving, as if sleepwalking.
14. *Huguenots* (hyo͞o′gə·näts): opera by Giacomo Meyerbeer about the violent struggle between Catholics and Protestants in sixteenth-century France.

15. **Ramses** (ram′sēz′): one of the kings of ancient Egypt.
16. **froth and fret:** agitated waters moving around obstacles.
17. **bullion** *n.*: gold.
18. **Yukon:** river in Yukon Territory in northwestern Canada.
19. **haberdasher** (hab′ər·dash′ər) *n.*: one who sells men's clothing. A men's clothing store is sometimes called a haberdashery.

---

**Vocabulary**

**inert** (in·ʉrt′) *adj.*: inactive; dull.
**trepidation** (trep′ə·dā′shən) *n.*: anxious uncertainty.

chiefly of women. One lost the contour of faces and figures, indeed any effect of line whatever, and there was only the color of bodices past counting, the shimmer of fabrics soft and firm, silky and sheer; red, mauve, pink, blue, lilac, purple, ecru, rose, yellow, cream, and white, all the colors that an impressionist[20] finds in a sunlit landscape, with here and there the dead shadow of a frock coat. My Aunt Georgiana regarded them as though they had been so many daubs of tube paint on a palette.

When the musicians came out and took their places, she gave a little stir of anticipation and looked with quickening interest down over the rail at that invariable grouping, perhaps the first wholly familiar thing that had greeted her eye since she had left old Maggie and her weakling calf. I could feel how all those details sank into her soul, for I had not forgotten how they had sunk into mine when I came fresh from plowing forever and forever between green aisles of corn, where, as in a treadmill, one might walk from daybreak to dusk without perceiving a shadow of change. The clean profiles of the musicians, the gloss of their linen, the dull black of their coats, the beloved shapes of the instruments, the patches of yellow light thrown by the green shaded lamps on the smooth, varnished bellies of the cellos and the bass viols in the rear, the restless, wind-tossed forest of fiddle necks and bows—I recalled how, in the first orchestra I had ever heard, those long bow strokes seemed to draw the heart out of me, as a conjurer's[21] stick reels out yards of paper ribbon from a hat.

The first number was the *Tannhäuser*[22] overture. When the horns drew out the first strain of the Pilgrim's chorus, my Aunt Georgiana clutched my coat sleeve. Then it was I first realized that for her this broke a silence of thirty years; the inconceivable silence of the plains. With the battle between the two motives, with

the frenzy of the Venusberg theme and its ripping of strings, there came to me an overwhelming sense of the waste and wear we are so powerless to combat; and I saw again the tall, naked house on the prairie, black and grim as a wooden fortress; the black pond where I had learned to swim, its margin pitted with sun-dried cattle tracks; the rain-gullied clay banks about the naked house, the four dwarf ash seedlings where the dishcloths were always hung to dry before the kitchen door. The world there was the flat world of the ancients; to the east, a cornfield that stretched to daybreak; to the west, a corral that reached to sunset; between, the conquests of peace, dearer bought than those of war.

The overture closed, my aunt released my coat sleeve, but she said nothing. She sat staring at the orchestra through a dullness of thirty years, through the films made little by little by each of the three hundred and sixty-five days in every one of them. What, I wondered, did she get from it? She had been a good pianist in her day I knew, and her musical education had been broader than that of most music teachers of a quarter of a century ago. She had often told me of Mozart's[23] operas and Meyerbeer's, and I could remember hearing her sing, years ago, certain melodies of Verdi's.[24] When I had fallen ill with a fever in her house she used to sit by my cot in the evening—when the cool, night wind blew in through the faded mosquito netting tacked over the window and I lay watching a certain bright star that burned red above the cornfield—and sing "Home to our mountains, O, let us return!" in a way fit to break the heart of a Vermont boy near dead of homesickness already.

I watched her closely through the prelude to *Tristan and Isolde*, trying vainly to conjecture what that seething turmoil of strings and winds might mean to her, but she sat mutely staring at

---

20. **impressionist** *n.*: one who follows impressionism, a movement in French painting emphasizing the effects of light and color.
21. **conjurer's:** magician's.
22. *Tannhäuser* (tän′hoi′zər): Wagner's opera about German minstrels in the thirteenth century.

23. **Mozart's:** Wolfgang Amadeus Mozart (1756–1791), Austrian composer.
24. **Verdi's:** Giuseppe Verdi (1813–1901), Italian composer of opera.

the violin bows that drove obliquely downward, like the pelting streaks of rain in a summer shower. Had this music any message for her? Had she enough left to at all comprehend this power which had kindled the world since she had left it? I was in a fever of curiosity, but Aunt Georgiana sat silent upon her peak in Darien.[25] She preserved this utter immobility throughout the number from *The Flying Dutchman,* though her fingers worked mechanically upon her black dress, as though, of themselves, they were recalling the piano score they had once played. Poor old hands! They had been stretched and twisted into mere tentacles to hold and lift and knead with; the palms unduly swollen, the fingers bent and knotted—on one of them a thin, worn band that had once been a wedding ring. As I pressed and gently quieted one of those groping hands, I remembered with quivering eyelids their services for me in other days.

Soon after the tenor began the "Prize Song,"[26] I heard a quick drawn breath and turned to my aunt. Her eyes were closed, but the tears were glistening on her cheeks, and I think, in a moment more, they were in my eyes as well. It never really died, then—the soul that can suffer so excruciatingly and so interminably; it withers to the outward eye only; like that strange moss which can lie on a dusty shelf half a century and yet, if placed in water, grows green again. She wept so throughout the development and elaboration of the melody.

During the intermission before the second half of the concert, I questioned my aunt and found that the "Prize Song" was not new to her. Some years before there had drifted to the farm in Red Willow County a young German, a tramp cowpuncher, who had sung the chorus at Bayreuth,[27] when he was a boy, along with the other peasant boys and girls. Of a Sunday morning he used to sit on his gingham-sheeted bed in the hands' bedroom which opened off the kitchen, cleaning the leather of his boots and saddle, singing the "Prize Song," while my aunt went about her work in the kitchen. She had hovered about him until she had prevailed upon him to join the country church, though his sole fitness for this step, in so far as I could gather, lay in his boyish face and his possession of this divine melody. Shortly afterward he had gone to town on the Fourth of July, been drunk for several days, lost his money at a faro[28] table, ridden a saddled Texan steer on a bet, and disappeared with a fractured collarbone. All this my aunt told me huskily, wanderingly, as though she were talking in the weak lapses of illness.

"Well, we have come to better things than the old *Trovatore*[29] at any rate, Aunt Georgie?" I queried, with a well-meant effort at jocularity.

Her lip quivered and she hastily put her handkerchief up to her mouth. From behind it she murmured, "And you have been hearing this ever since you left me, Clark?" Her question was the gentlest and saddest of reproaches.

The second half of the program consisted of four numbers from the *Ring,*[30] and closed with Siegfried's funeral march. My aunt wept quietly, but almost continuously, as a shallow vessel overflows in a rainstorm. From time to time her dim eyes looked up at the lights which studded the ceiling, burning softly under their dull glass globes; doubtless they were stars in truth to her. I was still perplexed as to what measure of musical comprehension was left to her, she who had heard nothing but the singing of gospel hymns at Methodist services in the square

---

25. **silent ... Darien:** allusion to John Keats's "On First Looking into Chapman's Homer," a poem about Keats's awe in the presence of a literary work of art.

26. **"Prize Song":** aria from the third act of Wagner's opera *Die Meistersinger von Nürnberg.*

27. **Bayreuth** (bī·roit′): Bavarian city that hosts an annual festival of Wagnerian music.

28. **faro** (fer′ō) *n.:* gambling game played with cards.

29. *Trovatore* (trô′vä·tô′rä): opera by the Italian composer Giuseppe Verdi.

30. *Ring:* Wagner's *Der Ring des Nibelungen,* a cycle of four operas based on traditional Germanic, Scandinavian, and Icelandic myths and legends.

**Vocabulary**
**obliquely** (ō·blēk′lē) *adv.:* at a slant.

frame schoolhouse on Section Thirteen for so many years. I was wholly unable to gauge how much of it had been dissolved in soapsuds, or worked into bread, or milked into the bottom of a pail.

The deluge of sound poured on and on; I never knew what she found in the shining current of it; I never knew how far it bore her, or past what happy islands. From the trembling of her face I could well believe that before the last numbers she had been carried out where the myriad graves are, into the gray, nameless burying grounds of the sea; or into some world of death vaster yet, where, from the beginning of the world, hope has lain down with hope and dream with dream and, renouncing,[31] slept.

The concert was over; the people filed out of the hall chattering and laughing, glad to relax and find the living level again, but my

---

31. **renouncing** *v.:* giving up.

kinswoman made no effort to rise. The harpist slipped its green felt cover over his instrument; the flute players shook the water from their mouthpieces; the men of the orchestra went out one by one, leaving the stage to the chairs and music stands, empty as a winter cornfield.

I spoke to my aunt. She burst into tears and sobbed pleadingly. "I don't want to go, Clark, I don't want to go!"

I understood. For her, just outside the door of the concert hall, lay the black pond with the cattle-tracked bluffs; the tall, unpainted house, with weather-curled boards; naked as a tower, the crookbacked ash seedlings where the dishcloths hung to dry; the gaunt, molting turkeys picking up refuse about the kitchen door. ■

---

**Vocabulary**

**deluge** (del′yōōj′) *n.:* rush; flood.
**myriad** (mir′ē·əd) *adj.:* countless.

# Response and Analysis

**SKILLS FOCUS**

**Literary Skills**
Analyze setting.

**Writing Skills**
Write an essay comparing and contrasting characters.

**Vocabulary Skills**
Use context clues.

**INTERNET**

**Projects and Activities**

Keyword: LE7 11-4

## Reading Check

1. Numerous **flashbacks** in the story provide information about Aunt Georgiana's life before and after she moved to Nebraska. In what ways does her life change as a result of her move?

2. Who is the narrator, and why does he feel he owes a great debt to Aunt Georgiana?

3. What special treat has the narrator planned for Aunt Georgiana in Boston?

## Thinking Critically

4. Locate passages in which the first-person **narrator** also functions as an omniscient, or all-knowing, narrator. How would you characterize the narrator? Why do you think Cather chose a male rather than a female narrator to tell this story?

5. The emotional effect of the music and the concert hall on Aunt Georgiana is in direct contrast to the emotional effect on her of the Nebraska frontier—the **setting** we hear about over and over again in the story. How does Cather make you feel about the Nebraska setting? What details from the story create this feeling?

6. Summarize in your own words what you think Clark understands at the end of the story.

7. What series of emotions does Aunt Georgiana experience at the concert? At the end, do you think she finds her pleasure worth the pain of reawakened longings? Why?

8. What seems to be Cather's **theme** in the story? How would you say the central episode of the concert contributes to this theme?

## Extending and Evaluating

9. Aunt Georgiana says to the narrator about music, "Don't love it so well, Clark, or it may be taken from you." Do you agree with this advice, or do you have other ideas on how to cope with losing what you love? Your Quickwrite notes may help you. ✏️

## Literary Criticism

10. If this story were written by a Romantic rather than a realist, how differently might Aunt Georgiana's visit to Boston have turned out? How do you think a Romantic writer would have described the Nebraska farm setting?

Willa Cather.
Nebraska State Historical Society Photograph Collections.

## WRITING

### Linked Lives

In what ways is Aunt Georgiana's experience at the concert like the shopping experience of Mrs. Sommers in Kate Chopin's story "A Pair of Silk Stockings" (page 570)? Write a brief essay **comparing and contrasting** the two women and their afternoons of escape. For each character, consider her life at the present and in the past, her emotional needs, and her range of reactions to her "escape" experience.

---

### Vocabulary Development

#### Diagramming Context

| | | |
|---|---|---|
| grotesque | pious | obliquely |
| eluding | inert | deluge |
| reverential | trepidation | myriad |

The diagram below shows how one reader figured out the meaning of the word *legacy* by using **context clues.** After noting this reader's strategies, study the other Vocabulary words where they appear in the story. (You'll find them underlined.) For each word, look for context clues. If you find any, list them and explain how the clues help make the word's meaning clear.

"This communication, worn and rubbed, looking as though it had been carried for some days in a coat pocket that was none too clean, was from my Uncle Howard and informed me that his wife had been left a small legacy by a bachelor relative who had recently died, and that it would be necessary for her to go to Boston to attend to the settling of the estate."

> If she was left something, it might be a gift of some kind.

> Since it was from a relative who died, *legacy* might be some sort of inheritance.

> I've heard this phrase used in reference to a will. *Legacy* is probably related to a will.

# Edwin Arlington Robinson
## (1869–1935)

By the 1890s, the vitality of the nineteenth century seemed exhausted, and the gathering forces of modernism were still scattered and obscure. Between 1890 and 1910, many poets were churning out the same old rhymes and meters of Romanticism. In those two decades, one voice spoke out in traditional forms enlivened with an authentic, contemporary American accent: the voice of Edwin Arlington Robinson.

The strengths that distinguish Robinson are his native voice and his wise and ironic view of human behavior. Robinson's bedrock realism informs even the most formal of his carefully wrought poems. In some of his poetic portraits of individuals, he anticipates by a decade the more loosely drawn portraits found in Edgar Lee Masters's *Spoon River Anthology*. In his skill with meter, Robinson foreshadows Robert Frost's gift for bending the strictly counted line to accommodate the ease and flow of vernacular speech.

Robinson was a Yankee from the rocky coast of Maine. Born at Head Tide in 1869, he lived for the next twenty-seven years in the town of Gardiner, except for the two years when he attended Harvard as a special student. Gardiner became the Tilbury Town of his poems, the home of some of his most famous characters. When he was in his late twenties, Robinson moved to New York City and published his first book. There he supported himself at various jobs, including one as a timekeeper at the construction site of the new subway system.

After a year of such work, Robinson's fortunes took a surprising turn for the better. Among the young poet's readers was none other than the president of the United States,

Theodore Roosevelt. When Roosevelt learned that the poet he admired was barely scraping by on a laborer's salary, he arranged to have the New York Custom House hire him as a clerk, a position Robinson held for almost five years. One year after Robinson resigned, he published *The Town Down the River* (1910) and dedicated the volume to Roosevelt.

Another form of assistance came in an invitation from the famous MacDowell Colony in Peterborough, New Hampshire. The colony is a center for composers, artists, and writers, established by the widow of the American composer Edward MacDowell. There Robinson spent long working summers for the greater part of his life.

Robinson became increasingly popular, and during his career he won the Pulitzer Prize in poetry three times. His traditional poetic forms link him to the nineteenth century, and his sense of irony attach him to the twentieth. At the time of Robinson's death, it was clear that even as modernism flourished, he had secured a unique and permanent place in American literature.

## Richard Cory

### Make the Connection
**Quickwrite** ✏️

One of the persistent themes of early-twentieth-century American poetry is that the conventions and behaviors common to small-town life are a facade that often obscures unpleasant realities.

Can we accurately determine the inner feelings of a person by observing his or her outward behavior? Write a few sentences stating your opinion, supported by specific reasons.

### Literary Focus
**Language and Style: Connotations**

In Robinson's famous poem an unidentified speaker tells what happened to Richard Cory, a prominent town citizen. Robinson never shows it outright, but he implies that the townspeople see Cory as a king. The poet achieves this effect by using words with connotations of royalty. Words get such **connotations,** or emotional overtones and associations, through shared usage.

It would be hard, for example, for a writer to call a character a lamb without someone familiar with English making an immediate association with innocence and docility. This would be true even for readers who have never seen a lamb; they would only have to be familiar with the Bible or with nursery rhymes to recognize these associations. As you read the poem, be alert for important word connotations.

**Literary Skills**
Understand connotations.

# Richard Cory

### Edwin Arlington Robinson

Whenever Richard Cory went downtown,
    We people on the pavement looked at him:
He was a gentleman from sole to crown,
    Clean favored, and imperially slim.

5   And he was always quietly arrayed,
    And he was always human when he talked;
But still he fluttered pulses when he said,
    "Good morning," and he glittered when he walked.

And he was rich—yes, richer than a king—
10   And admirably schooled in every grace:
In fine, we thought that he was everything
    To make us wish that we were in his place.

So on we worked, and waited for the light,
    And went without the meat, and cursed the bread;
15  And Richard Cory, one calm summer night,
    Went home and put a bullet through his head.

*Winter Twilight* (1930) by Charles Burchfield (1893–1967). Oil on composition board. 27³/₄ × 30¹/₂ in. (70.5 × 77.5 cm).

## Miniver Cheevy

### Make the Connection
**Quickwrite** ✏️

The glory and glamour of bygone days hold an irresistible charm for many of us. Sometimes, though, a longing for the past leaves people sorely disappointed with the present. On a sheet of paper, write down some reasons why a person might be drawn to splendid times in the distant past.

### Background

The title "Miniver Cheevy" contains a clue to the poem's meaning. The word *miniver* refers to the white fur trim that can be seen on the costumes of royalty in medieval and Renaissance portraits. The subjects of such portraits are usually members of rich and powerful families, such as the Medici family. Other references in the poem also evoke heroic eras of the past.

*The Sentimental Yearner* (1936) by Grant Wood. Pencil, black and white conté crayon, painted white around image.

The Minneapolis Institute of Arts; Gift of Alan Goldstein, 1980.

# Miniver Cheevy

## Edwin Arlington Robinson

Miniver Cheevy, child of scorn,
    Grew lean while he assailed the seasons;
He wept that he was ever born,
    And he had reasons.

5    Miniver loved the days of old
    When swords were bright and steeds were prancing:
The vision of a warrior bold
    Would set him dancing.

Miniver sighed for what was not,
10    And dreamed, and rested from his labors;
He dreamed of Thebes° and Camelot,°
    And Priam's° neighbors.

Miniver mourned the ripe renown
    That made so many a name so fragrant;
15    He mourned Romance, now on the town,°
    And Art, a vagrant.°

**11. Thebes** (thēbz): city in ancient Greece associated with several myths. **Camelot:** legendary site of King Arthur's court.
**12. Priam's:** In Homer's epic poem the *Iliad,* Priam (prī'əm) is the king of Troy during the Trojan War.
**15. on the town:** dependent on charity.
**16. vagrant** *n.*: wanderer; beggar.

Miniver loved the Medici,°
    Albeit° he had never seen one;
He would have sinned incessantly
20      Could he have been one.

Miniver cursed the commonplace
    And eyed a khaki suit with loathing;
He missed the medieval grace
    Of iron clothing.°

25  Miniver scorned the gold he sought,
    But sore annoyed was he without it;
Miniver thought, and thought, and thought,
    And thought about it.

Miniver Cheevy, born too late,
30    Scratched his head and kept on thinking;
Miniver coughed, and called it fate,
    And kept on drinking.

**17. Medici** (med′ə·chē): members of a powerful Italian family of the fourteenth to sixteenth centuries. They were famous for their wealth, their sponsorship of the arts, and their control of the city of Florence.
**18. albeit** (ôl·bē′it) *conj.*: even though. The word combines and condenses "although it be."

**24. iron clothing:** armor worn by medieval knights.

## PRIMARY SOURCE / LETTERS

# Robinson on Richard Cory

I 've written a nice little thing called "Richard Cory"—"Whenever Richard Cory went downtown, we people on the pavement looked at him . . . And Richard Cory, one calm summer night, went home and put a bullet through his head." There isn't any idealism in it, but there's lots of something else—humanity, maybe.

◆

Why don't you like "Richard Cory"? You say it makes you feel cold, but that statement doesn't seem to agree with my impression of your character. It can't be you are squeamish after all. If you are, don't read "Reuben Bright" or he will knock you down. I used to read about clearness, force, and elegance in the rhetoric books, but I'm afraid I go in chiefly for force. So you will not be offended if I'm not always elegant. There are too many elegant men in the world just now, and they seem to be increasing.

◆

I don't have trances, furors, or ecstasies. My poetic spells are of the most prosaic sort. I just sit down and grind it out and use a trifle more tobacco than is good for me.

◆

You may call me anything you like—anything but Eddie. I had an aunt who called me Eddie and now she doesn't call me at all.

—from *Edwin Arlington Robinson's Letters to Edith Brower*

# Response and Analysis

## Richard Cory

### Thinking Critically

1. Find at least five words or phrases in "Richard Cory" with **connotations** of kingliness or royalty. Replace each of these words or phrases with a neutral one that, in your opinion, has no strong connotations at all. How is the effect of the poem different?

2. Find other words with important **connotations** in the poem. For example, what does the word *gentleman* (line 3) suggest? What does *downtown* (line 1) suggest that *uptown* would not? How do the poet's word choices contribute to the contrast between the townspeople and Richard Cory?

3. Why is it **ironic** that Richard Cory takes his own life? What irony is there in the fact that the night is calm?

4. Does the harsh surprise ending hint that the real story is the one that remains untold? What aspects of Richard Cory's life are not mentioned? How might these hidden or overlooked areas account for his fate?

5. Read Robinson's comments on "Richard Cory" (page 591). What do you think he means when he says there is a lot of "humanity" in the poem? Why do you think the poem made Robinson's correspondent feel "cold"? How does it make you feel?

6. The poem indicates that appearances can be deceiving. Does Cory's tale have a **moral** or message for readers today? (Refer to your Quickwrite notes.)

### Extending and Evaluating

7. Is Robinson successful in suggesting how the influences of Cory's social class shaped his personality and fate? Why or why not?

## Miniver Cheevy

### Thinking Critically

1. Do Miniver Cheevy's problems really stem from his having been "born too late"? Explain. How does the disappointed Cheevy cope with his lot in life?

2. What do you think "child of scorn" means? What **connotations** does the expression have? What does it suggest about Cheevy's character?

3. Romance and Art are **personified** in the fourth stanza. What does Cheevy think has happened to romance and art in his own time?

4. How would you describe the overall **tone** of the poem prior to the last stanza? How does the tone shift in the last stanza?

5. Where might Miniver Cheevys be found today? What sorts of worlds do they mourn for?

### Literary Criticism

6. **Philosophical approach.** The poet James Dickey wrote that although Robinson has been called a "laureate of failure," he actually chronicled "the delusions necessary to sustain life." How does this statement apply to "Miniver Cheevy"? Do you agree that delusions and illusions can help people get through their lives? Why or why not?

## WRITING

### Rising Above or Mired Below?

In a brief **essay,** analyze the character of either Richard Cory or Miniver Cheevy to show whether he demonstrates the transcendentalist ideals of self-reliance and individualism championed by Emerson (page 203) and Thoreau (page 213). As the focus of your essay, choose an appropriate quotation from either of these writers.

# Reflecting *on the* Literary Period

## The Rise of Realism: The Civil War to 1914

19th century lithograph of Assabet Manufacturing Company.

## Think About...

The Civil War destroyed forever certain American illusions of innocence and isolation from the forces of history. In contrast to the Romantics' focus on the inner life of the individual or the mysteries of nature and the universe, post–Civil War writers tended to emphasize the everyday world and common human problems in social settings. This new literary writing, called **realism,** attempted to describe the life of ordinary people as it really was, revealing the realities of social conditions and ethical struggles of the times.

Along with the dramatic changes caused by the Civil War, American perceptions were also shaped by industrialization, the birth of the United States as a world power, and new scientific ideas. The process of industrialization moved the United States away from the simple agricultural economy of its early years. Large cities, new factories, and increasingly newer and better inventions were a normal part of life between 1890 and 1914. In addition, the United States became a world power in the late 1800s when it entered the Spanish-American War. The emerging sciences of biology, sociology, and psychology also played a significant role in shaping the United States. These conflicts and changes, along with the closing of the American frontier in 1890, compelled Americans to look at life differently and to seek new horizons.

**SKILLS FOCUS**

Pages 593–600 cover **Literary Skills** Evaluate the philosophical, political, religious, ethical, and social influences of a historical period.

### Focus Question

As you read each selection, keep in mind this Focus Question and take notes to help you answer it at the end of the feature:
    How did realist writers portray social issues and the struggles of ordinary people?

## The Story of an Hour

**Meet the Writer** An enigma even to those who thought they knew her best, **Kate Chopin** (1851–1904) as a child was anything but docile: Among her escapades were such things as asking cheeky questions and reading banned books. Chopin continued her eccentricities into adulthood, flirting with men, and, in general, shocking the neighbors.

Chopin suffered many losses throughout her life, beginning with the death of her father in a freak train accident in 1855. After her husband died in 1882, and her mother in 1885, Chopin began to write seriously for publication. However, most of her writings, much like her life, were baffling and unacceptable to the people of her day.

(For more information about Kate Chopin, see page 568.)

**Background** When Chopin wrote "The Story of an Hour," a woman was still looked upon as needing the protection and support of her husband. Many of Chopin's female characters, however, seek freedom from the conventional restraints of society, including marriage. Although women could own property and file for divorce when Chopin wrote this story, independent women were still frowned upon.

---

**CONNECTING TO THE**
**Focus Question**

In "The Story of an Hour," Chopin explores a wife's response to the news of her husband's death. As you read, consider this question: Does Mrs. Mallard's reaction seem typical for a grieving wife?

---

# The Story of an Hour

## Kate Chopin

Knowing that Mrs. Mallard was afflicted with a heart trouble, great care was taken to break to her as gently as possible the news of her husband's death.

It was her sister Josephine who told her, in broken sentences; veiled hints that revealed in half concealing. Her husband's friend Richards was there, too, near her. It was he who had been in the newspaper office when intelligence of the railroad disaster was received, with Brently Mallard's name leading the list of "killed." He had only taken the time to assure himself of its truth by a second telegram, and had hastened to forestall[1] any less careful, less tender friend in bearing the sad message.

She did not hear the story as many women have heard the same, with a paralyzed inability to accept its significance. She wept at once, with sudden, wild abandonment, in her sister's arms. When the storm of grief had spent itself she went away to her room alone. She would have no one follow her.

There stood, facing the open window, a comfortable, roomy armchair. Into this she sank, pressed down by a physical exhaustion that haunted her body and seemed to reach into her soul.

She could see in the open square before her house the tops of trees that were all aquiver with the new spring life. The delicious breath of rain was in the air. In the street below a peddler was crying his wares. The notes of a distant song which some one was singing reached her

---

1. **forestall** (fôr·stôl′): to stop something from happening by acting ahead of time.

faintly, and countless sparrows were twittering in the eaves.

There were patches of blue sky showing here and there through the clouds that had met and piled one above the other in the west facing her window.

She sat with her head thrown back upon the cushion of the chair, quite motionless, except when a sob came up into her throat and shook her, as a child who has cried itself to sleep continues to sob in its dreams.

She was young, with a fair, calm face, whose lines bespoke repression[2] and even a certain strength. But now there was a dull stare in her eyes, whose gaze was fixed away off yonder on one of those patches of blue sky. It was not a glance of reflection, but rather indicated a suspension of intelligent thought.

There was something coming to her and she was waiting for it, fearfully. What was it? She did not know; it was too subtle and elusive[3] to name. But she felt it, creeping out of the sky, reaching toward her through the sounds, the scents, the color that filled the air.

*The Victorian Chair* (1906) by Childe Hassam. Smithsonian American Art Museum, Washington, D.C., U.S.A. Oil on wood.

Now her bosom rose and fell tumultuously. She was beginning to recognize this thing that was approaching to possess her, and she was striving to beat it back with her will—as powerless as her two white slender hands would have been.

When she abandoned herself a little whispered word escaped her slightly parted lips. She said it over and over under her breath: "free, free, free!"

The vacant stare and the look of terror that had followed it went from her eyes. They stayed keen and bright. Her pulses beat fast, and the coursing blood warmed and relaxed every inch of her body.

She did not stop to ask if it were or were not a monstrous joy that held her. A clear and exalted perception enabled her to dismiss the suggestion as trivial.

She knew that she would weep again when she saw the kind, tender hands folded in death; the face that had never looked save with love upon her, fixed and gray and dead. But she saw beyond that bitter moment a long procession of years to come that would belong to her absolutely. And she opened and spread her arms out to them in welcome.

There would be no one to live for her during those coming years; she would live for herself. There would be no powerful will bending hers in that blind persistence with which men and women believe they have a right to impose a private will upon a fellow-creature. A kind intention or a cruel intention made the act seem no less a crime as she looked upon it in that brief moment of illumination.

And yet she had loved him—sometimes. Often she had not. What did it matter! What could love, the unsolved mystery, count for in face of this possession of self-assertion which she suddenly recognized as the strongest impulse of her being!

"Free! Body and soul free!" she kept whispering.

Josephine was kneeling before the closed door with her lips to the keyhole, imploring for admission. "Louise, open the door! I beg; open the

---

2. **repression** (ri·presh′ən): restraint.
3. **elusive** (ē·lōō′siv): difficult to understand.

*Erie Locomotive* (detail) by Richard Hayley Lever.
(1876–1958) Private Collection.

door—you will make yourself ill. What are you doing, Louise? For heaven's sake open the door."

"Go away. I am not making myself ill." No; she was drinking in a very elixir[4] of life through that open window.

Her fancy was running riot along those days ahead of her. Spring days, and summer days, and all sorts of days that would be her own. She breathed a quick prayer that life might be long. It was only yesterday she had thought with a shudder that life might be long.

She arose at length and opened the door to her sister's importunities.[5] There was a feverish triumph in her eyes, and she carried herself unwittingly like a goddess of Victory. She clasped her sister's waist, and together they descended the stairs. Richards stood waiting for them at the bottom.

Some one was opening the front door with a latchkey. It was Brently Mallard who entered, a little travel-stained, composedly carrying his grip-sack and umbrella. He had been far from the scene of accident, and did not even know there had been one. He stood amazed at Josephine's piercing cry; at Richards' quick motion to screen him from the view of his wife.

But Richards was too late.

When the doctors came they said she had died of heart disease—of joy that kills. ■

---

4. **elixir** (i·lik′sər): a remedy for every illness.
5. **importunities** (im′pôr·tōōn′i·tēz): determined requests.

# Response and Analysis

## Reading Check

**1.** What report does Richards bring to Josephine and Mrs. Mallard?

**2.** What emotions is Mrs. Mallard experiencing as she gazes out the window and thinks about her future?

## Thinking Critically

**3.** What aspects of **realist** writing are apparent in "The Story of an Hour"? Remember that realism often focuses on social issues and the accurate portrayal of human behavior.

**4.** What is **ironic** about Mrs. Mallard's death at the end of the story?

**5.** In Chopin's day, women were expected to marry and be dependent upon their husbands. How do Mrs. Mallard's dreams differ from these expectations?

**6.** Using details from the selection, respond to **Connecting to the Focus Question** on page 594.

## Extending and Evaluating

**7.** Many of Chopin's characters search for their identity by defying the social customs of their day. Are people today still searching for identity? If so, in what ways?

# Douglass
# We Wear the Mask

**Meet the Writer** During his brief life, **Paul Laurence Dunbar** (1872–1906) became one of the first African American writers to attain national prominence and to support himself wholly by his writing. Dunbar, who was born in Dayton, Ohio, was the son of former slaves. Though poor and unschooled, his parents were ambitious for their son and predicted greatness for him. The only African American student in his high school class, Dunbar was the president of the literary society, editor of the school newspaper, and class poet.

After graduation, Dunbar took a job as an elevator operator and composed poems in his spare time. During a meeting in Dayton of the Western Association of Writers, a former teacher asked him to prepare an address of welcome. Dunbar delivered a poem. Impressed, the members of the association showed some of his poems to the famous writer James Whitcomb Riley, who responded with an encouraging letter of congratulations. Within a year Dunbar published his first volume of poetry, *Oak and Ivy* (1893).

A second collection, *Majors and Minors,* appeared the following year and received a laudatory review from the most influential critic of the day, William Dean Howells. The publication of *Lyrics of Lowly Life* (1896), with an introduction by Howells, made Dunbar a famous and popular poet. In addition to writing twelve books of poetry, Dunbar wrote short stories, a play, and five novels. He once wrote that his ambition was to "be able to interpret my own people through song and story, and to prove to the many that after all we are more human than African." Dunbar's life was cut short by tuberculosis when he was only thirty-three.

> ## CONNECTING TO THE
> ## Focus Question
>
> Dunbar's poetry explores the oppression of African American people. As you read "Douglass" and "We Wear the Mask," ask yourself: What negative effects of racial conflict does Dunbar discuss or allude to in these poems?

*Library II* (1960) by Jacob Lawrence. (1917–2000) Private Collection, New York, NY, U.S.A. Egg tempera on hardboard. 23¹/₂" x 29¹/₂".

© 2005 The Jacob and Gwendolyn Lawrence Foundation, Seattle/Artists Rights Society (ARS), New York.

In 1893, Dunbar met Frederick Douglass, the famous African American lecturer, editor, and leader. Both men thought very highly of each other. In fact, Dunbar wrote several poems honoring the famous abolitionist. The poem "Douglass," published almost ten years after Douglass's death in 1895, contrasts Douglass's life with the time in which Dunbar was living. In it, the speaker laments the loss of Douglass and his leadership.

# Douglass

## Paul Laurence Dunbar

Ah, Douglass, we have fall'n on evil days,
    Such days as thou, not even thou didst know,
    When thee, the eyes of that harsh long ago
Saw, salient,° at the cross of devious ways,
5  And all the country heard thee with amaze.
    Not ended then, the passionate ebb and flow,
    The awful tide that battled to and fro;
We ride amid a tempest° of dispraise.

Now, when the waves of swift dissension° swarm,
10    And Honor, the strong pilot, lieth° stark,
Oh, for thy voice high-sounding o'er the storm,
    For thy strong arm to guide the shivering bark,
The blast-defying power of thy form,
    To give us comfort through the lonely dark.

---

  **4. salient** (sāl′yənt): prominent.
  **8. tempest** (tem′pist): a violent storm.
  **9. dissension** (di·sen′shən): disagreement.
  **10. lieth** (lī′eth): archaic form of *lies*.

Portrait of Frederick Douglass (detail).
American School, (19th century).
Frederick Douglass National Historic
Site, Washington, USA.

# We Wear the Mask

## Paul Laurence Dunbar

We wear the mask that grins and lies,
It hides our cheeks and shades our eyes,—
This debt we pay to human guile;°
With torn and bleeding hearts we smile,
5    And mouth with myriad° subtleties.

Why should the world be overwise,
In counting all our tears and sighs?
Nay, let them only see us, while
        We wear the mask.

10    We smile, but, O great Christ, our cries
To thee from tortured souls arise.
We sing, but oh the clay is vile
Beneath our feet, and long the mile;
But let the world dream otherwise,
15        We wear the mask!

---

3. **guile** (gīl): deceitfulness in dealing with others.
5. **myriad** (mir'ē·əd): innumerable.

*Three Friends* (1944–1945) by William H. Johnson. (1901–1970) Smithsonian American Art Museum, Washington, DC, U.S.A. Serigraph on paper. 15⅞" x 11⅝". Gift of the Harmon Foundation.

# Response and Analysis

## Douglass

### Thinking Critically

1. How does the poet use the **metaphor** of a boat caught in a storm and in need of a pilot to praise the strength of Frederick Douglass?

2. To what does the "awful tide that battled to and fro" (line 7) refer?

3. In the last stanza of the poem, what **images** of power and courage represent Douglass?

### Extending and Evaluating

4. What might Dunbar be saying that African Americans have lost with the death of Frederick Douglass? Do you agree or disagree with his view? Explain.

## We Wear the Mask

### Thinking Critically

1. What does the mask **symbolize**?

2. In one sentence, state the poem's **theme**.

3. Describe the **tone** of the speaker's voice. What words or phrases convey the tone?

### Extending and Evaluating

4. In "We Wear the Mask," African Americans hide "torn and bleeding hearts" (line 4) with a mask that "grins and lies" (line 1). Do you believe that hiding pain can make one stronger in the eyes of an oppressor?

• • •

Using details from the poems, respond to **Connecting to the Focus Question** on page 597.

# Reflecting *on the* Literary Period

## The Rise of Realism: The Civil War to 1914

The following questions ask you to compare and analyze the selections in this feature and respond to the Focus Question. Where possible, cite passages from the selections to support your answers.

Kate Chopin . . . . . . . . . . . . . . . . . . . . . . . . . . . . . . . . . . . . . . . **The Story of an Hour**

Paul Laurence Dunbar . . . . . . . . . . . . . . . . . . . . . . . . . . . . . . . . . . . **Douglass**

. . . . . . . . . . . . . . . . . . . . . . . . . . . . . . **We Wear the Mask**

## Comparing Literature

1. Chopin and Dunbar both grew up during a time of upheaval and change, and they both experienced many conflicts during their lifetimes. Based on the story and poems you have just read, how do you think Chopin and Dunbar responded to the turmoil in their lives and society?

2. Dunbar and Chopin present heroic or admirable **characters** in "Douglass" and "The Story of an Hour." What similarities do you see between Mrs. Mallard and Douglass?

3. In his poems "Douglass" and "We Wear the Mask," Dunbar focuses on the struggles of African Americans to achieve equality. What might Dunbar be saying about the prospects for African American people to be treated fairly? Use examples from the text to support your answer.

4. "The Story of an Hour" is about death—not only the death of a spouse but also the death of someone's dreams. How might "We Wear the Mask" also be about a kind of death?

5. Both Chopin and Dunbar talk about or allude to freedom in their works. What aspects of freedom appeal to Mrs. Mallard? What components of freedom are important to the speakers in Dunbar's poems?

**SKILLS FOCUS**

Pages 593–600 cover
**Literary Skills**
Evaluate the philosophical, political, religious, ethical, and social influences of a historical period.

### RESPONDING TO THE
### Focus Question

Review your notes and responses related to the Focus Question for this feature. Using details from the selections, write your answer to the question.

How did realist writers portray social issues and the struggles of ordinary people?

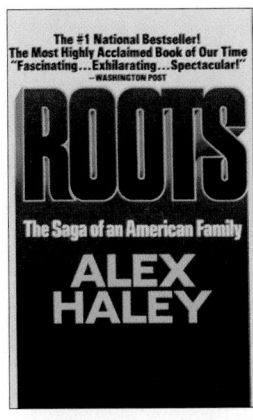

**FICTION**

## A Family Saga

When Alex Haley was a child, his grandmother told him tales of an ancestor known only as the African—a man torn from his Mandingo people and forced into slavery in America. When Haley grew up, he discovered that the African had a real name—Kunta Kinte—and a story that had the power to reach people everywhere. *Roots* is a fictionalized chronicle spanning the period between Kunta's birth in 1750 and the death of Haley's father, a college professor, in the twentieth century.

**FICTION**

## The Great American Novel

Ernest Hemingway wrote, "All modern American literature comes from one book by Mark Twain called *Huckleberry Finn*." Widely regarded as Twain's masterpiece, ***Adventures of Huckleberry Finn*** is a wise and funny novel about a young boy coming of age on the Mississippi River.

**This title is available in the HRW Library.**

**NONFICTION**

## The War Between the States

For an inside look at the most dramatic war waged on U.S. soil, consider ***The Civil War: An Illustrated History*** by Geoffrey C. Ward and others. This companion volume to the PBS series, produced by Ric and Ken Burns, features essays; interviews; and an arresting series of photographs depicting generals, soldiers, and everyday citizens from the North and the South. The historical narrative and stunning images trace the war from the first shots at Fort Sumter through the bloody battlefields and finally to General Lee's surrender at Appomattox.

**FICTION**

## The Wild Frontier

The late nineteenth century was a time in which the United States became a nation of immigrants—a time when people from many lands were drawn to the promise of the western frontier. Willa Cather's classic novel *My Ántonia* is the story of one such immigrant family—the Shimerdas of Bohemia—and their new life in Nebraska. At the center of the story is the Shimerdas's daughter Ántonia, who captures the heart and imagination of a lonely neighbor boy.

# Reporting Historical Research

**Writing Assignment**
**Write a paper investigating a historical event that intrigues you.**

Paralleling the rise of realism in American literature was a rise in realism for historians, who began to take a more scientific and objective approach to gathering and interpreting evidence about historical events. Instead of writing to glorify or justify conquerors, historians would analyze and evaluate all the available evidence about an event before drawing any conclusions. Now you will have the opportunity to **investigate a historical event** by analyzing several different historical records about it, explaining the similarities and differences among the records, and drawing conclusions about the event.

## Prewriting

### Choose and Narrow a Topic

**Travel to the Past** You investigate a historical event so you can draw your own conclusions about the event and its significance. When you read a single record of a historical event—the attack on Pearl Harbor or the assassination of President John F. Kennedy, the fall of the Berlin Wall—you are likely to be reading information that represents only one **perspective,** or point of view, on that event. To understand a historical event fully, you need to examine a wide variety of sources representing all relevant perspectives on the event.

As you consider a topic for your paper, look for a controversial event that interests you and for which you will be able to find a variety of sources. You should also make sure that the topic is narrow enough to be covered well in a paper of 1,500 words. To choose an appropriate topic, follow the example in the student model below.

| | |
|---|---|
| What historical event am I interested in? | I'm interested in the Civil War. |
| How can I narrow this topic, if necessary? | I can focus on one important event: General Sherman's march from Atlanta to Savannah. |
| Can I find a variety of sources on this topic? | Yes—records and newspaper accounts written during the war, memoirs and books written after the war are available. |
| Can I find sources representing all relevant perspectives on this topic? | Yes, there should be plenty of information representing various points of view, such as those of Northerners, Southerners, soldiers, and civilians. |

Answering the last two questions in the chart on the previous page might require some preliminary research. If you can't find information representing different perspectives on the event, pick another event that lends itself to hearty investigation.

If you're not sure what historical event you're interested in, thumb through a history book for intriguing topics or ask a history teacher to suggest interesting historical events for you to consider.

## Consider Purpose and Audience

**Cover the Basics**  Once you have narrowed your topic, you should consider your **purpose** for writing this investigative paper. Of course you want to inform your **audience**—most likely your classmates and teacher—about your topic. Avoid, however, simply compiling a collection of facts. Instead, focus on creating a historical investigation paper that synthesizes, or combines, information gathered from various sources, and include conclusions you draw about that information based on logical analysis.

> **TIP**  Adopt a formal and objective **tone**—your attitude toward your topic and your audience—in your paper. Write from the third-person point of view (avoid the pronoun *I* or *you*), and avoid slang, colloquial expressions, and contractions.

## Ask Research Questions

**What Do I Want to Know?**  Clear **research questions** will help you focus your search for sources and will lead you to analyze the different perspectives on the historical event you're investigating. The following chart shows the research questions one writer developed to focus his research on General Sherman's March.

- What are the facts of Sherman's March?
- What perspective is revealed by the written or spoken testimony of each group directly involved in or affected by the march?
- What were the perspectives of Northerners and Southerners not directly involved in or affected by the march?

## Find Answers to Research Questions

**The Search Begins**  Begin to track down the answers to your research questions with a general reference work. You'll get an overview of your topic and gain valuable background information. In addition, an article in a general reference work usually mentions other sources you can use in your research. For this initial step, consult a print or CD-ROM encyclopedia, or search the Internet for sites or pages that contain related key words.

**Follow the Leads**  Once you have an overview of your topic, move on to specific sources that can help you answer your research questions. Be creative in developing a research strategy. Avoid restricting yourself to print sources available at your school or community library. Your most valuable information might come from

**Writing Skills**
Write a historical research report. Choose a topic. Consider purpose and audience. Generate research questions, and conduct research.

an interview with a historian, a visit to a museum, a letter (or e-mail) requesting additional information, or a visit to an actual historical site. Some sources may lead you to other sources. The chart below lists some information sources in your library and community.

## INFORMATION RESOURCES

| Library Resources | Sources of Information |
|---|---|
| Card catalog or online catalog | Books and audiovisuals (separate catalogs in some libraries) |
| *Readers' Guide to Periodical Literature* or online periodical indexes | Articles from magazines and journals |
| Newspaper indexes, specialized reference books, and CD-ROMs | Newspapers (often on microfilm), dictionaries, encyclopedias, and bibliographies |
| Microfilm or microfiche and online databases | Indexes to major newspapers, back issues of some newspapers and magazines |
| **Community Resources** | **Sources of Information** |
| National, state, and local government offices | Official records |
| Museums and historical societies | Exhibits, experts |
| Schools and colleges | Libraries, experts |
| World Wide Web and online services | Articles, interviews, bibliographies, pictures, videos |

**The Hard Evidence**  Your topic may have generated so much interest that you might quickly find yourself buried under information. The following guidelines can help you avoid such a fate.

- **Choose a balance of primary and secondary sources.**  A **primary source** is firsthand, original information, such as a letter, an autobiography, a work of literature or art, a historical document, or an interview with a person who participated in the event being researched. A **secondary source** is information derived from, or about, primary sources, or even from other secondary sources. Examples include an encyclopedia or CD-ROM, a documentary film, a biography, a history book, or an interview with a historian. (Sometimes a primary source may be included in a secondary source or another primary source—called an **indirect source.** For example, a book about Sherman's March is the indirect source of a soldier's letter describing the march.)

  For a paper on Sherman's March, primary sources might include General Sherman's memoirs. Secondary sources might include a book about Sherman's March.

**Writing Skills**
Use a variety of research sources, including primary and secondary sources.

- **Choose reliable sources.** Don't assume that all sources are reliable. Memory may be faulty or selective in an autobiography or memoir, and emotions may override facts in a letter or diary. A secondary source may be biased or slanted. Research as much as possible in journals and books published by reputable institutions such as major universities and well-known publishing companies. Factual information from such sources can generally be regarded as reliable and can provide you with a good basis for deciding whether other information you uncover is accurate and objective. The reliability of interpretations of facts can be judged only through logical analysis.

- **Make sure your sources cover all relevant perspectives.** Look for sources that tell the perspectives of all the major groups involved in the event. For instance, plenty of information about Sherman's March is available from the perspectives of Northerners, Sherman and his troops, and Southerners, but less is available from Southern slaves. If information from a certain perspective is scarce, look for hints about what the group thought and felt in information written from other perspectives.

**TIP** Remember to check any Internet source that you use for its validity and reliability. Usually educational, governmental, or professional Web sites pass muster.

## Record and Organize Information

**Sources First**  Using a separate note card or a separate computer file for each source, write complete and accurate information about all the sources you consult, even if you're not sure you will use them in your paper. Include a short note describing the information contained in the source and estimating the value of the source. Such notes will turn your source cards into an **annotated bibliography.** Also, since your *Works Cited* list—the list of sources at the end of your paper—must contain specific publishing information, you will save time if you record that information on sources exactly as it will appear in the *Works Cited* list. Follow the guidelines below to make your source cards.

**Reference Note**

For sample **Works Cited entries,** see pages 611–613.

### GUIDELINES FOR MAKING SOURCE CARDS

1. **Assign each source a number.** Later, when you are taking notes, it will save time to write a number instead of the author and title. (You might also use the author's last name as a source code.)

2. **Record full publishing information.** Consult the Guidelines for Preparing the *Works Cited* List on page 611 and enter publishing information exactly as it appears for each type of entry you have.

3. **Annotate each source.** Write a short note to remind yourself of the content and value of the source.

4. **Note the call number or location.** This information will help you relocate the source quickly.

**SKILLS FOCUS**

**Writing Skills**
Record and organize your research.

**Finding the Note Worthy** Now that you have selected, evaluated, and recorded your sources, take notes to answer your research questions. To get started, read each source to be sure that you understand the overall meaning. Then, use the following guidelines for taking notes. See page 607 for sample note cards.

## GUIDELINES FOR TAKING NOTES

1. **Use a separate card, half-sheet of paper, or computer file for each source and item of information.** Separate cards or files make rearranging and organizing notes easier when you get ready to write.

2. **Record the source number.** In the upper right-hand corner of each note, write the number (or author's last name) you assigned each source to tell you exactly where you got the information.

3. **Write a label or heading.** In the upper left-hand corner of the card or file, identify the main idea of your note so that you do not have to re-read each note to remind yourself what it is about.

4. **Write the page number(s).** At the end of your note, write the page numbers from which the information comes. Page references, if available, are required for the documentation in your paper.

**Decisions, Decisions** As you take notes, decide how to record each piece of information: Will you quote the information directly? summarize it? paraphrase it? Use the following guidelines to decide.

- **Direct quotation** To capture interesting, well-phrased passages or a passage's technical accuracy, quote an author directly and exactly, including punctuation, capitalization, and spelling. Resist the urge to quote too much. Your task is to synthesize information and draw conclusions from it, not to stitch together a long series of quotations.

    Enclose the passage in quotation marks and remember to use ellipsis points to indicate omissions from quoted text. Use brackets to explain words you have changed for the sense of a sentence.

**Reference Note**

For more on the use of **ellipsis points,** see Ellipsis Points, 13e, and for more on **brackets** with quotations, see Brackets, 13n, in the Language Handbook.

- **Paraphrase** If you want to use specific ideas or information from a source without quoting the source, paraphrase the information. Paraphrasing requires completely rewriting the information in your own words and style.

- **Summary** Summarize information when you want to use the general idea presented in a source. A summary is highly condensed—typically one fourth to one third the length of the original passage.

**TIP** To avoid **plagiarizing,** or failing to give credit to an author whose words or ideas you have used, you must completely rewrite paraphrases and summaries. Simply substituting synonyms for some of the words from your source is not enough.

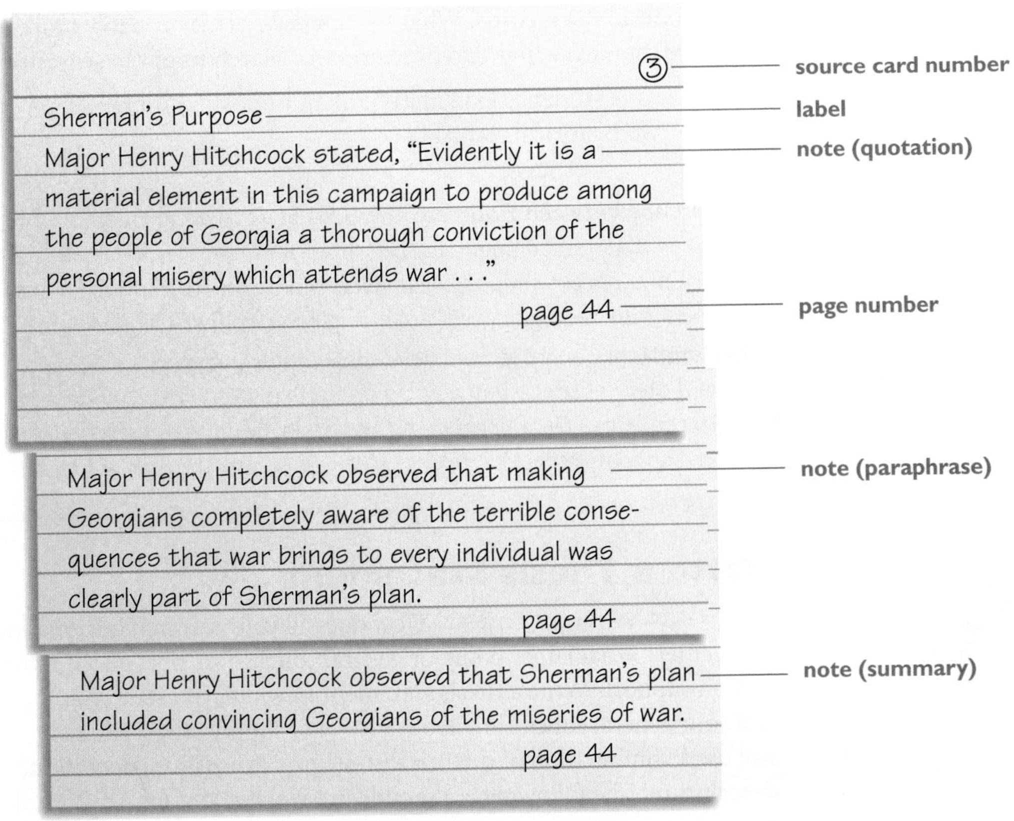

**source card number** ③

**label** Sherman's Purpose

**note (quotation)** Major Henry Hitchcock stated, "Evidently it is a material element in this campaign to produce among the people of Georgia a thorough conviction of the personal misery which attends war . . ."

**page number** page 44

**note (paraphrase)** Major Henry Hitchcock observed that making Georgians completely aware of the terrible consequences that war brings to every individual was clearly part of Sherman's plan.

page 44

**note (summary)** Major Henry Hitchcock observed that Sherman's plan included convincing Georgians of the miseries of war.

page 44

# Analyze Your Information

**Accounting for the Records** The next step in the historical investigation process is to analyze your information. Begin by separating your note cards by their headings. For example, the student writing about Sherman's March found that he had collected information from the perspectives of Northerners, General Sherman, Southerners, and slaves, and divided his note cards accordingly.

As you analyze the information you have gathered, you will probably find that your sources contain conflicting information or different interpretations of the same facts. How can you account for such differences? Here are a couple of questions you can use to analyze differences in your sources.

1. **What is the background of the author of the information?** Is his or her perspective on the event likely to be biased because of that background? For example, a descendant of a Southerner whose plantation was destroyed by General Sherman's troops might have a biased perspective on the march.

2. **When was the information recorded or the source written?** While material written at the time of an event might have the quality of "eyewitness" news, material written after an event sometimes has the advantage of objectivity. For example, a professional historian writing a century after Sherman's March has had the opportunity to

**SKILLS FOCUS**

**Writing Skills**
Analyze your research.

examine all the records. What he or she writes is probably more objective than what a victim of Sherman's March might have written.

Here is one student's explanation of an important difference between two historical records.

> **Difference between Sources:** The U.S. Senate and House of Representatives commended Sherman and his men for their "gallantry and good conduct," when Sherman himself was aware that his men had been guilty of "acts of pillage, robbery, and violence."
>
> **Explanation:** Congress commended Sherman's men not only to reward their success but also to spread political propaganda and to increase morale. Sherman, on the other hand, was speaking long after the fact, reflecting honestly on his march through Georgia.

## Write a Thesis Statement

**So, What's Your Point?** How does all your research information fit together? What larger point, or general conclusion, does all the information support? Write a **thesis statement** in which you state your topic and your general conclusion about it. As you support that statement, you will use a combination of rhetorical strategies: **exposition, narration, description.** The following is a sample thesis statement for a historical research paper.

DO THIS

> Northerners, General Sherman, Southerners, and slaves had powerful reasons for their different perspectives on Sherman's March, and the historical record supports them all.

## Develop an Outline

**Divide and Conquer** An outline provides an organizational overview of your paper, and allows you to ensure that your ideas flow in a logical progression, with adequate support for each idea.

First, sort your note cards into groups with similar labels—the information you have written in the left-hand corner of each card. The way you group the labels may immediately suggest the main sections or ideas of your paper. Then, decide how best to order these sections. You'll probably need to use a combination of **chronological order** (the order in which events occur), **logical order** (related ideas grouped together), and **order of importance** (most important idea to least important, or the reverse). Finally, decide how to order the ideas within sections and which supporting details to use.

Now, put your information in a formal outline. A **formal outline** has numerals and letters to identify headings (main ideas), subheadings (supporting ideas and evidence), and details. It provides an overview of your research paper and can serve as a table of contents.

**SKILLS FOCUS**

**Writing Skills**
Write a thesis statement.
Develop an outline.

Check with your teacher to see if you should attach a formal outline to the final draft of your paper. Here is part of a student's formal outline for his historical research paper on Sherman's March.

I. Introduction
   A. Overview of research
   B. Thesis: Northerners, General Sherman, Southerners, and slaves had powerful reasons for their different perspectives on Sherman's March, and the historical record supports them all.
II. The view from the North
   A. Military importance
      1. Grant's chief of staff's view
      2. New York Times view
      3. General Grant's view
   B. Conduct of troops
      1. Southerners' view
      2. Public Resolution No. 4

**TIP** **Headings** can be used within a research paper to make the paper easier to follow. The headings can be taken from the main ideas in your outline. Notice how the Writer's Model on pages 614–618 uses headings.

## Documenting Sources

**Give Credit Where Credit Is Due** Documenting a paper means identifying the sources of information you use in the paper, as you use them. The rules for *how* to document sources are clearly specified in whatever style guide you follow, for example, the Modern Language Association (MLA) or the American Psychological Association (APA) style guide. The rules about *what* to document are not so clear. Use the following guidelines to decide what to document.

| WHAT TO DOCUMENT | |
|---|---|
| Yes | Each direct quotation (unless it's widely known, such as John L. Swigert's famous understatement on Apollo 13: "Okay, Houston, we've had a problem here.") |
| Yes | Any original theory or opinion that is not your own, even if not directly quoted. Since ideas belong to their authors, you must give the authors credit. Otherwise, you are guilty of plagiarism, a form of cheating. |
| Yes | Data from surveys, research studies, and interviews |
| Yes | Unusual, little-known facts or questionable "facts" |
| No | Information that appears in several sources or in standard reference books, such as the fact that William Tecumseh Sherman was a general in the Union army who led a march through Georgia during the Civil War |

**Point the Way** Sources of information enclosed in parentheses and placed within the body of your paper are called **parenthetical citations.** They point the way to the complete bibliographical information in the *Works Cited* list at the end of your paper. The parenthetical citation should be placed as close as possible to the material it documents without disrupting the flow of the sentence. This means that citations are usually inserted at the ends of sentences. The following example shows two sentences that incorporate material from two sources.

> On November 12, 1864, Sherman set out with an army of 62,000 men on a 250-mile march from Atlanta to Savannah (Inglehart). His army destroyed a strip of land 60 miles wide and inflicted $100 million in damages (Holzer 172).

Parenthetical citations should also be as brief as possible. For most citations, the last name of the author and the page number are sufficient. If the author is named in the sentence, you need give only the page number in parentheses. The following chart shows the form for the most common kinds of sources.

**Quick guide!**

## BASIC CONTENT AND FORM FOR PARENTHETICAL CITATIONS

| Type of Source | Content of Citation | Example |
|---|---|---|
| Sources with one author | Author's last name and a page reference, if any | (Golay 36) |
| Separate passages in a single source | Author's last name and page references | (Derry 386, 388) |
| Sources with more than one author | All authors' last names; if over three, use first author's last name and *et al.* (and others) | (Ward, Burns, and Burns 333) |
| Multivolume source | Author's last name, plus volume and page | (Davis 1: 145–146) |
| Sources with a title only | Full title (if short) or shortened version | (March of Southern Men 38) |
| Literary sources published in many editions | Author's last name, title, and division references (act, scene, canto, book, part, or line numbers) in place of page numbers | (Shakespeare, Hamlet. 3.4.107–108) |
| Indirect sources | Abbreviation *qtd. in* (quoted in) before the source | (qtd. in Miles 175) |
| More than one source in the same citation | Citations separated with semicolons | (Miles 30; Sherman 64) |

**SKILLS FOCUS**

**Writing Skills**
Document sources in parenthetical citations and a *Works Cited* list.

**TIP** Your teacher may want you to use a documentation style different from the parenthetical citation system, such as footnotes or endnotes. A **footnote** is placed at the bottom of the same page where you used the source information, while **endnotes** are listed all together at the end of the paper.

**Follow the Forms** The *Works Cited* list contains all the sources, print and nonprint, that you credit in your paper. You may have used other sources, but if you do not credit them in your historical research paper you need not include them in a *Works Cited* list. Use the following guidelines to help you prepare your *Works Cited* list.

**TIP** A **bibliography** contains only print publications.

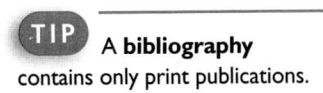

## GUIDELINES FOR PREPARING THE WORKS CITED LIST

**Center the words *Works Cited*.** Ask your teacher whether the list should begin on a new page.

**Begin each entry on a separate line.** Position the first line of the entry even with the left margin, and indent all other lines five spaces, or one-half inch if you are using a word processor. Double-space all entries.

**Alphabetize the sources by the authors' last names.** If there is no author, alphabetize by title, ignoring *A, An,* and *The* and using the first letter of the next word.

**If you use two or more sources by the same author, include the author's last name only in the first entry.** For all other entries, put three hyphens in place of the author's last name (---), followed by a period.

The following sample entries are a reference for preparing your *Works Cited* list. Notice that you include page numbers only for sources that are one part of a whole work, such as one essay in a book of essays.

## SAMPLE WORKS CITED ENTRIES

**Standard Reference Works** If an author is credited in a standard reference work, cite that person's name first in an entry. Otherwise, the title of the book or article appears first. You do not need to cite the editor. Page and volume numbers aren't needed if the work alphabetizes entries. For common reference works, use only the edition (if listed) and the year of publication.

**Print Encyclopedia Article**
Tebeau, Charlton W. "Sherman, William Tecumseh." The New Encyclopedia Britannica: Micropedia. 15th ed. 1995.
"Civil War." The World Book Encyclopedia. 1998 ed.

**Article in a Biographical Reference Book**
"Ulysses Simpson Grant." Abridged Encyclopedia of World Biography. 6 vols. Detroit: Gale, 1999.

**Books**
**One Author**
Derry, Joseph T. Story of the Confederate States. New York: Arno, 1979.

**Two Authors**
Catton, William, and Bruce Catton. Two Roads to Sumter. New York: McGraw, 1963.

**Three Authors**
Ward, Geoffrey C., Ric Burns, and Ken Burns. The Civil War: An Illustrated History. New York: Knopf, 1990.

*(continued)*

(continued)

**Four or More Authors**
Beringer, Richard E., et al. <u>Why the South Lost the Civil War</u>. Athens: U of Georgia P, 1986.

**No Author Shown**
<u>The March of the Southern Men</u>. Richmond: Dunn, 1863.

**Editor of a Collection of Writings**
Marius, Richard, ed. <u>The Columbia Book of Civil War Poetry</u>. New York: Columbia UP, 1994.

**Two or Three Editors**
Greenberg, Martin H., and Bill Pronzini, eds. <u>A Treasury of Civil War Stories</u>. New York: Bonanza, 1985.

**Bibliography Published as a Book**
Moss, William. <u>Confederate Broadside Poems: An Annotated Descriptive Bibliography</u>. Westport: Meckler, 1988.

**Translation**
Hess, Earl J., ed. <u>A German in the Yankee Fatherland: The Civil War Letters of Henry A. Kircher</u>. Trans. Ernest J. Thode. Kent: The Kent State UP, 1983.

## Selections Within Books
**From a Book of Works by One Author**
Varhola, Michael J. "The Army." <u>Everyday Life During the Civil War</u>. Cincinnati: Writer's Digest, 1999. 129.

**From a Book of Works by Several Authors**
McMurry, Richard M. "The Atlanta Campaign." <u>The South Besieged: Volume Five of the Image of War, 1861–1865</u>. Ed. William C. Davis. New York: Doubleday, 1983. 240–302.

**Introduction, Preface, Foreword, or Afterword**
Simpson, Brooks D., and Jean V. Berlin. Introduction. <u>Sherman's Civil War: Selected Correspondence of William T. Sherman, 1860–1865</u>. Chapel Hill: U of North Carolina P, 1999.

## Articles from Magazines, Newspapers, and Journals
**From a Weekly Magazine**
Ebeling, Ashlea. "Battle Cry." <u>Forbes</u>. 5 Oct. 1998: 78–80.

**From a Monthly or Quarterly Magazine**
Wert, Jeffrey D. "A Month Overrated: April, 1865 in the U.S. Civil War." <u>Civil War Times</u>. May 2001: 20.

**Anonymous Author**
"South Rises." <u>U.S. News and World Report</u>. 10 May 1999: 8.

**From a Scholarly Journal**
Brown, William O., and Richard K. Burdekin. "Turning Points in the U.S. Civil War: A British Perspective." <u>Journal of Economic History</u>. 60.1 (216–231).

**From a Daily Newspaper, with a Byline**
Horwitz, Tony. "Shades of Gray: Did Blacks Fight Freely for the Confederacy?" <u>The Wall Street Journal</u>. 8 May 1997: A1.

**From a Daily Newspaper, without a Byline**
"The Latest Battle of Gettysburg." <u>New York Times</u>. 4 July 1997: A18.

**Unsigned Editorial from a Daily Newspaper, No City in Paper's Title**
"Humanity of the War." Editorial. <u>The Christian Recorder</u>. 1 March 1862.

(continued)

*(continued)*

## Other Sources

### Personal Interview
Norton, Stewart. Personal interview. 14 Aug. 2001.

### Telephone Interview
LaRue, Patricia. Telephone interview. 23 May 2001.

### Published Interview
Burns, Ken. Interview with Alice Cary. "If Abe Lincoln Were Campaigning for President Today, He
      Wouldn't Win." TV Guide 25 Jan. 1992: 13.

### Broadcast or Recorded Interview
Burns, Ken. Interview with Terry Gross. Fresh Air. Natl. Public Radio. WHYY, Philadelphia. 29 Jan. 1997.

### Published Letter
Sherman, William T. "To John Sherman." 22 April 1862. Letter in Sherman's Civil War: Selected
      Correspondence of William T. Sherman, 1860–1865. Ed. Brooks D. Simpson and Jean V.
      Berlin. Chapel Hill: U of North Carolina P, 1999.

### Unpublished Letter or E-Mail Message
Gumble, Max. Letter to the author. 3 Sept. 2001.

Westmoreland, Margaret. E-mail to the author. 30 Dec. 2001.

### Unpublished Thesis or Dissertation
Bass, Patrick Grady. "Fall of Crisis: European Intervention and the American Civil War." Diss.
      Claremont Graduate School, 1986.

### Sound Recording
Songs of the Civil War. New World Records, 1976.

### Film or Video Recording
The Civil War. Dir. Ken Burns. Videocassette. PBS Video, 1989.

**NOTE:** Always include the title, director or producer, distributor, and year. For DVD or video recordings,
add a description of the medium (Videodisc or Videocassette) before the distributor's name.

### Material Accessed Through the Internet
"American Civil War." Britannica Online. Vers. 1994–2001. Encyclopedia Britannica. 6 June 2001.
      <http://members.eb.com/>.

### Article from a CD-ROM Reference Work
Hassler, Jr., Warren W. "Sherman, William Tecumseh." Grolier Multimedia Encyclopedia.
      CD-ROM. Grolier Inc. 2001.

### Full-Text Magazine, Newspaper, or Journal Article from a CD-ROM Database
"Here Are the 10 Civil War Battlefields Listed as 'Endangered' by Trust." Knight-Ridder/Tribune News
      Service, 27 Feb. 2001: K2031. Infotrac. CD-ROM. Gale Group, 2001.

**PRACTICE & APPLY 1** Following the guidelines in the
Prewriting section, plan your historical
research paper. Remember that accurate records of your research will
make writing and documenting your report easier. Closely follow
the guidelines for making source cards (page 605) and taking notes
(page 606) as you work.

# Writing

## Reporting Historical Research

---

## A Writer's Framework

### Introduction

- Draw readers in with an interesting opener.
- Give readers background information and an overview of your research.
- Include your thesis statement.

### Body

- Develop each main idea that supports your thesis.
- Include facts and details from a variety of primary and secondary sources.
- Arrange your ideas in a logical order.

### Conclusion

- Restate your thesis.
- Summarize your main points.
- Bring the paper to a close with a concluding thought or a thought-provoking idea.

---

## A Writer's Model

**INTRODUCTION**

*Interesting opener*

**Background information**

**Overview of research**

**Secondary source**

**Thesis statement**

**BODY/Heading: First main idea**

**Point 1: Military importance**

Sherman's March: A Civil War Controversy

General William Tecumseh Sherman's army was ready. The sick and wounded and all excess baggage had been sent away. Captain Daniel Oakley of the 2nd Massachusetts wrote, "The army was reduced, one might say, to its fighting weight, no man being retained who was not capable of a long march" (qtd. in Nevin 44). General Sherman sent out last minute dispatches before ordering the telegraph lines be cut, making it impossible for him and his army to communicate further with the Union. His last wire to General Grant reiterated the rationale for the march: "If the North can march an army right through the South, . . . it is proof positive that the North can prevail" (qtd. in Nevin 44). On November 12, 1864, Sherman set out with an army of 62,000 men on a 250-mile march from Atlanta to Savannah (Inglehart). His army destroyed a strip of land 60 miles wide and inflicted $100 million in damages (Holzer 172). While the annals of the American Civil War are filled with controversial actions, Sherman's march across Georgia remains one of the most debated. The U.S. government and many Northerners celebrated Sherman's action as a brilliant military success, but Sherman himself thought it a necessary, if harsh, part of war. Southerners whose homes were destroyed saw it as a lawless act of cruelty. Who was right? Each group had powerful reasons for its perspective, and the historical record supports them all.

The View from the North

Most historical records written from a Northern perspective concentrate on the military importance of Sherman's March. H.W.

---

Halleck, General Grant's chief of staff, called the march a "splendid success" (qtd. in Sherman, <u>Memoirs</u> 699). A <u>New York Times</u> editorial referred to it as "the most remarkable military achievement of the war" (qtd. in Miles 37). In a letter to Sherman, Grant expressed complete satisfaction with the march: "You have now destroyed the roads of the South" (qtd. in Sherman, <u>Memoirs</u> 682). To read these dry records, one would never know that the action described involved the destruction of citizens' homes. From the distance of Washington or New York, it must have been easy to see the march as a simple movement of troops.

While Northerners made much of the march's military results, few Northern records focus on how these results were accomplished. Although Southerners complained bitterly of their treatment at the hands of Sherman's troops, the official record of the United States praises their actions. Public Resolution No. 4 states: "[T]he thanks of the people and of the Congress of the United States are due and are hereby tendered to Major-General William T. Sherman, and [his] officers and men, for their gallantry and good conduct . . ." (qtd. in Sherman, <u>Memoirs</u> 706–707). The phrase "gallantry and good conduct" might have been chosen to refute Southerners' claims of abuses.

The View from the Ground: Sherman and His Troops

While the official records of the U. S. present the march as a military campaign like any other, Sherman was aware that others saw his action as unusual. "[T]he march to the sea," he wrote in his memoirs, "was generally regarded as something extraordinary, something anomalous, something out of the usual order of events . . ." (Sherman, <u>Memoirs</u> 697). However, Sherman remembers the march as a straightforward military tactic: "I considered this march as a means to an end, and not as an essential act of war. . . .[I]n fact, I simply moved from Atlanta to Savannah . . ." (Sherman, <u>Memoirs</u> 697). Sherman's memory, however, is contradicted by his field order of November 9, 1864, ordering commanders to "order and enforce a devastation more or less relentless, according to the measure of such hostility" as his army was shown (Sherman, <u>GeorgiaInfo</u>).

In fact, it is clear from Sherman's own records and those of his officers that he and his army considered their action more than the movement of troops or the destruction of supplies that Confederates might use. He clearly understood the action's effect on civilians but believed it justified because it would end the war more quickly. "War is cruelty," Sherman stated. "There is no use trying to reform it; the crueler it is, the sooner it will be over" (qtd. in <u>Brother Against Brother</u> 370). Major Henry Hitchcock stated, "Evidently it is a material element in this

*(continued)*

Marginal notes:

- Indirect source
- Direct quotation; Primary source
- Writer's conclusion
- Point 2: Conduct of troops
- Indirect source
- Writer's conclusion
- Second main idea
- Point 1: Military importance
- Direct quotation
- Point 2: Strategy
- Indirect source

campaign to produce among the people of Georgia a thorough conviction of the personal misery which attends war" (qtd. in Nevin 44). In today's terms, this is psychological warfare.

Although Sherman planned to bring war home to Southerners, the record indicates that he intended to control his troops and prevent abuses. The army was walking a fine line. They wanted to break the South's resistance but behave honorably in the process. Sherman directed his army to "forage liberally on the country" (Miles 30; Sherman, GeorgiaInfo). However, he restricted these activities to special foraging parties led by officers and stated that only corps commanders could destroy private buildings. Foragers were to be polite and to leave each family enough to eat (Sherman, GeorgiaInfo). Sherman, however, admitted in his memoirs that these rules were not always followed. "No doubt, many acts of pillage, robbery, and violence were committed by these parties of foragers . . . for I have since heard of jewelry taken from women and the plunder of articles that never reached the commissary" (Sherman, Memoirs 659). Although he sometimes contradicted himself, Sherman saw his march as a harsh but justified action against traitors to the United States who had brought the war upon themselves (Janda 16), an action calculated to bring a quick end to a destructive war. The Southerners saw it differently.

The View from the South

Southerners saw themselves not as traitors or rebels, but as citizens of a sovereign nation, the Confederate States of America. In their eyes, Sherman's march amounted to a foreign invasion. The manpower of the South had been drained, leaving women, children, and old men undefended at home. For enemy troops to come literally to their doors and take their property—including thousands of slaves who left their masters to follow Sherman's troops ("Sherman and the March to the Sea")—was an outrage. Henrietta Lee voiced the feelings of many Southerners when she wrote to Union General David Hunter: "Your name will stand on history's pages as the Hunter of weak women, and innocent children: the Hunter to destroy defenseless villages and beautiful homes" (qtd. in Clinton 125).

To Southerners, the conduct of Sherman's troops seemed anything but gallant. The following statement by the Confederate Congress expresses the Southern view of Sherman's March.

> Accompanied by every act of cruelty and pain, the
> conduct of the enemy has been destitute of [without]
> that forbearance [restraint] and magnanimity
> [generosity] which civilization and Christianity have

*Marginal annotations:*

**Writer's conclusion**

**Point 3: Conduct of troops**

**Information from two sources**

**Paraphrase**

**Third main idea**
**Point 1: Foreign invasion**

**Indirect source**

**Point 2: Conduct of troops**
**Indirect source**
**Block quotation**
**Writer's additions in brackets**

introduced to mitigate [soften] the asperities [hardships] of war. Houses are pillaged and burned, churches are defaced, towns are ransacked, clothing of women and infants is stripped from their persons, jewelry and mementoes of the dead are stolen . . . means of subsistence [survival] are wantonly [cruelly] wasted to produce beggary, . . . the last morsel of food has been taken from families." (qtd. in Clinton 111)

Doubtless fear and hatred of the advancing army gave rise to many rumors, and some accounts may have been exaggerated. However, credible testimony from Southern eyewitnesses concurs with the description above. Eliza Andrews' "The War-Time Journal of a Georgia Girl, 1864–1865," describes the destruction left by Sherman's army:

There was hardly a fence left standing. . . . The fields were trampled down and the road was lined with carcasses of horses, hogs, and cattle that the invaders, unable either to consume or to carry away with them, had wantonly shot down to starve out the people. . . . The dwellings that were standing all showed signs of pillage, and . . . here and there, lone chimney-stacks, "Sherman's Sentinels," told of homes laid in ashes. (19)

Understandably, Southern historians were anxious to keep the memory of Sherman's March alive. Story of the Confederate States, written in 1895, asserts, "Sherman's army . . . [took] everything that was valuable . . . and sometimes set fire to the house itself. Rings were taken from the fingers of ladies, and old men were hung up to make them tell where their treasures were concealed" (Derry 386). The bitterness of Southerners has not been assuaged by the passage of time. In A Ruined Land: The End of the Civil War, published in 1999, Golay describes Sherman's men as thieves and arsonists (36). Such accounts keep the bitterness alive.

Was Sherman's March a brilliant military tactic, a march for freedom, an act of psychological warfare, or a war crime? It seems likely that all these perspectives are at least partially true. Beyond a doubt, the march heightened the will and the morale of the North, demoralized the South, and hastened the end of the war. Some Southerners exaggerated the destructiveness of Sherman's troops, while the U.S. government had reason to downplay the troops' excesses. Ironically, Sherman himself may have had the most balanced view. He knew the march was cruel, but felt that victory was worth the cost. Perhaps Sherman's March is one of those historical events that defies a final, definitive judgment.

**Author named in text**

**Point 3: Continued bitterness**

**Summary**

**CONCLUSION**

**Restatement of thesis**

**Summary of main points**

**Thought-provoking idea**

*(continued)*

*(continued)*

## Works Cited

Andrews, Eliza Frances. "The War-Time Journal of a Georgia Girl, 1864–1865: Electronic Edition." <u>Documenting the American South, or The Southern Experience in 19th-century America</u>. 1997. U of North Carolina at Chapel Hill Libs. 14 May 2001 <http://docsouth.unc.edu/andrews/andrews.html>.

<u>Brother Against Brother: Time-Life Books History of the Civil War</u>. New York: Prentice, 1990.

Clinton, Catherine. <u>Tara Revisited: Women, War, and the Plantation Legend</u>. New York: Abbeville, 1995.

Derry, Joseph T. <u>Story of the Confederate States</u>. New York: Arno, 1979.

Golay, Michael. <u>A Ruined Land: The End of the Civil War</u>. New York: Wiley, 1999.

Holzer, Harold. <u>Witness to War: The Civil War: 1861–1865</u>. New York: Berkley, 1996.

Inglehart, David. <u>Fateful Lightening: A Narrative History of the Civil War</u>. CD-ROM. Troubadour Interactive. 1998.

Janda, Lance. "Shutting the Gates of Mercy: The American Origins of Total War, 1860–1880." <u>The Journal of Military History</u>. 59.1: 7–26.

Miles, Jim. <u>To the Sea: A History and Tour Guide of Sherman's March</u>. Nashville: Rutledge Hill, 1989.

Nevin, David, and the Editors of Time-Life Books. <u>The Civil War: Sherman's March: Atlanta to the Sea</u>. Alexandria: Time-Life Books, Inc., 1986.

"Sherman and the March to the Sea." <u>Civil War Journal II</u>. Prod. Greg Goldman. Videocassette. A&E Home Video, 1994.

Sherman, William Tecumseh. <u>Memoirs of General W. T. Sherman</u>. New York: Lib. of America, 1951.

---. "Special Field Orders Issued by Gen. Sherman, Nov. 9, 1864." <u>GeorgiaInfo</u>. Carl Vinson Institute of Government, U of Georgia. 14 May 2001 <http://www.cviog.uga.edu/Projects/gainfo/order2.htm>.

**TIP** Research papers and their *Works Cited* lists are normally double-spaced. Due to limited space, they are represented single-spaced here.

**INTERNET**

**More Writer's Models**

Keyword: LE7 11-4

**PRACTICE & APPLY** 2 As you write the first draft of your historical research paper, refer to the framework and the Writer's Model, including the *Works Cited* list.

# Revising

## Evaluate and Revise Content, Organization, and Style

**Twice Is Nice** To assess your writing effectively, read through your paper at least twice. The first time, evaluate and revise content and organization. Then, in your second reading, revise for style.

> **First Reading: Content and Organization** The following chart can help you determine whether you have clearly communicated your research. If you need help answering the questions in the first column, use the tips in the middle column. Then, revise your paper by making the changes suggested in the last column.

**PEER REVIEW**

Exchange your research paper with a classmate, who may have suggestions for improving the clarity of your summaries and paraphrases.

## Rubric: Reporting Historical Research

| Evaluation Questions | ▶ Tips | ▶ Revision Techniques |
|---|---|---|
| ❶ Does the introduction draw readers into the research, give an overview of the research, and state the thesis? | ▶ **Underline** the sentence that draws readers into the research; **bracket** the overview of research; **circle** the thesis statement. | ▶ **Add** a quotation or interesting detail to the opening sentence. **Add** overview information, or **elaborate** on existing information. **Add** a thesis statement. |
| ❷ Do several main ideas develop the thesis? Do facts and details support the main ideas? | ▶ In the margin, **check** each main idea that develops the thesis. In the text, **double-check** at least one piece of supporting evidence for each idea. If there are not at least three main ideas and support for each, revise. | ▶ **Add** main ideas to develop your thesis; consult your outline and note cards for ideas you may have missed. **Delete** ideas that do not support the thesis. **Elaborate** on each idea with material drawn from your research. |
| ❸ Does the paper include summaries and paraphrases in addition to direct quotations? | ▶ **Circle** all direct quotations. If direct quotations comprise more than 1/3 of the paper, revise. | ▶ **Replace** some direct quotations with paraphrases or summaries. |
| ❹ Are sources cited when necessary? Are the citations in the correct MLA format? | ▶ **Place stars** by direct quotations and by facts that are not common knowledge. | ▶ **Add** documentation for quoted, summarized, or paraphrased material. **Revise** incorrect citations. |
| ❺ Does the conclusion restate the thesis and summarize the paper's main points? Does the writer close with a concluding thought or a thought-provoking idea? | ▶ **Bracket** the restatement of the thesis. **Highlight** the summary of main ideas. **Circle** the thought-provoking ending. | ▶ **Add** a sentence that returns the reader to the thesis of the paper. **Add** a summary of main ideas. **Add** a concluding thought or a thought-provoking idea. |

▷ **Second Reading: Style** Your style, how you express your ideas, is important in a long and complex research paper. If every sentence begins the same way, such as with the subject and verb of a main clause, your paper may bore readers. You can make your paper more interesting by **varying sentence beginnings.** For example, you can begin some sentences with adverb clauses. Adverb clauses answer the questions *How? When? Where? Why?* and *To what extent?* Use the following style guidelines to evaluate and refine your sentence beginnings.

## Style Guidelines

| Evaluation Question | ▶ Tip | ▶ Revision Technique |
|---|---|---|
| ● Do many of the paper's sentences begin the same way? | ▶ **Underline** the first five words of each sentence. If most subjects and verbs are underlined, revise. | ▶ **Rearrange** and **combine** sentences to place adverb clauses at the beginning. Rephrase when necessary. |

### ANALYZING THE REVISION PROCESS
Study these revisions, and answer the questions that follow.

On November 12, 1864, Sherman set out with an army of

62,000 men on a 250-mile march from Atlanta to Savannah

(Inglehart). His army destroyed a strip of land 60 miles wide

and inflicted $100 million in damages. Sherman's march across *(Holzer 172) While the annals of the*

*American Civil War are filled with controversial actions,*

Georgia remains one of the most debated ~~action of the Civil War.~~

*add/add*

*delete*

### Responding to the Revision Process

1. Why is the information that the writer added to the second sentence necessary?
2. Why did the writer decide to change the last sentence?

**PRACTICE & APPLY** 3 Using the guidelines in the charts on these two pages, revise the content, organization, and style of your research paper. If possible, collaborate with a peer throughout the revision process.

# Publishing

## Proofread and Publish Your Paper

**Take Care of Business**  So that your readers will fully appreciate your historical research report, proofread it carefully. The last thing you want is for your readers to dismiss your work completely because they run into basic errors in grammar, usage, and mechanics. Therefore, take care to find and correct such errors. Having a peer help you proofread your paper is a good idea, too. You might be so familiar with your paper that you read over the errors.

**Everything You Wanted to Know About . . .**  Doing a research paper requires a lot of hard work. Now that you've done that hard work, don't let your accomplishment go unnoticed. Find a larger audience for your paper. Here are some ways you might share your historical research paper with others.

- Save your historical research paper as a writing sample to submit for a college or job application.

- If the topic would be of interest to students in lower grades, send your paper to a teacher who teaches a related subject to those students. Consider scanning pictures of people and places involved in the event into your document to enhance its appeal to a younger audience.

- Surf the Web to discover sites related to your historical research topic, and submit your paper for possible online publication. As you prepare your work for a wider audience, look for places where you might incorporate **visuals** and **graphics** such as maps, charts, tables, or graphs to make your information more accessible.

## Reflect on Your Paper

**Take Stock**  Writing thoughtful responses to the following questions will help you develop as a thinker, a writer, and a researcher.

- How would you describe the extent of your knowledge of your topic before you researched it?

- How did your research experience affect your understanding of your topic? How did it affect your understanding of the study of history?

- If you had to list four fundamental principles of research for a student younger than you, what would they be?

**PRACTICE & APPLY**  First, proofread your paper, paying particular attention to the placement and punctuation of your citations. Then, publish your paper for a wider reading audience. Finally, reflect on your paper by answering the reflection questions above.

**TIP**  Proofreading will help ensure that your paper follows the **conventions** of standard American English and the documenting format required by your teacher. For example, pay particular attention to the placement and punctuation of parenthetical citations.

**COMPUTER TIP**

If you have access to a computer and advanced publishing software, consider using those tools to design and format graphics and visuals to enhance the content of your research paper. For more on **graphics** and **visuals,** see Designing Your Writing in the Writer's Handbook.

**SKILLS FOCUS**

**Writing Skills**
Proofread, especially for punctuation and parenthetical citations. Use graphics and visuals to enhance a report.

# Presenting Historical Research

**Speaking Assignment**
Adapt a historical investigation report, and present it orally before an audience.

**P**rofessional historians routinely publish books and articles on the results of their research. They also present their research in oral presentations to their peers at conferences and meetings of historical organizations. To make these oral presentations interesting, historians use verbal and nonverbal techniques.

## Adapt Your Report

**Maintain Your Focus**  Your **purpose** in giving an oral report of historical research is to present your findings in a clear, concise, and interesting way. Your oral report could be shorter or longer than your written report, depending upon the time limit set by your teacher. Decide whether you need to shorten or lengthen your written report, and then use the following guidelines to adapt it.

- If your listening audience is different from your reading audience, consider revising the **introduction** by providing additional background information. Then, state your **thesis** so that it clearly communicates conclusions about the topic.

- If you have to cut your paper because of time limitations, be sure to maintain a balance of **primary** and **secondary sources** that represent relevant **perspectives** on the topic and show that you have analyzed several historical records. If you need to add information to your presentation, make sure you consider the **validity** and **reliability** of the new sources.

- Use a combination of rhetorical strategies to present your analysis of historical records. Use **exposition** to explain similarities and differences in the historical records and **persuasion** to convince readers of the validity of your conclusions. Look for places where you can effectively use **narration** and **description** because these rhetorical strategies make audiences feel as if they are listening to an exciting story rather than a dull report on research results.

- Since your audience will not have access to your *Works Cited* list, name the author and source of all quotations, statistics, important facts, and conclusions and judgments that are not your own.

- Check the **conclusion** in your paper to see if your summary of main ideas and restatement of the thesis are obvious to a listening audience. If you used long, complex sentences in the paper, simplify them so that listeners can understand you.

**SKILLS FOCUS**

**Listening and Speaking Skills**
Deliver an oral research report.

# Present Your Report

**The Natural Sound** Speakers who read a speech often sound stiff and dull. Extemporaneous speakers, on the other hand, usually have note cards or an outline to glance at as the need arises. They also rehearse their presentations until they feel confident that they know their material and that they sound natural and spontaneous.

Prepare to deliver your presentation extemporaneously by writing on note cards your thesis, the main supporting ideas, and brief reminders of details you want to include. Arrange your note cards in the same pattern you used for your paper. Then, review your presentation to see if the order is clear for a listening audience. If the order seems confusing, experiment with new arrangements until you find one that is easy to follow.

**Do a Dress Rehearsal** To learn your text and master your performance, rehearse your oral report until you feel comfortable presenting it. You might want to videotape your presentation, practice in front of a mirror, or present your report to an audience of friends or family. Refer to the following table to improve your use of **verbal and nonverbal techniques.**

**TIP** To ensure the best possible communication with your audience, use **standard American English.** Also be sure that your vocabulary is appropriate for your audience. For example, avoid terms that are likely to be unfamiliar to your audience. If your report requires the use of technical language, use the terms correctly and define them.

| VERBAL TECHNIQUES | NONVERBAL TECHNIQUES |
|---|---|
| • **Tone:** maintain a formal tone to help your audience focus on the information | • **Eye contact:** involve your audience by making eye contact with your listeners |
| • **Volume:** speak loudly enough for everyone to hear you; emphasize important words by speaking slightly louder and with more force | • **Facial expression:** allow your face to express your feelings and attitude |
| • **Pause:** pause for a moment after an important point to allow your audience to catch up with you | • **Gestures:** use natural gestures as you speak; feel free to move around, but don't pace or fidget |
| • **Rate:** speak slowly enough to allow your audience to follow you, but not so slowly that they become bored | • **Posture:** use good posture to convey a sense of confidence |

**PRACTICE & APPLY 5** Use the instruction in this workshop to adapt, rehearse, and present orally your historical investigation report. Ask your classmates for feedback on the quality of your presentation.

**SKILLS FOCUS**

**Listening and Speaking Skills**
Use effective verbal and nonverbal techniques.

**Test Practice**  The following two pieces of literature were written almost a hundred years apart. Both deal with the horrors of war.

Stephen Crane (1871–1900) was born after the Civil War, but his best-known work is *The Red Badge of Courage,* a short novel that supposedly takes place at the battle of Chancellorsville in Virginia. This classic work of fiction is told through the eyes of young Henry Fleming, a Union soldier.

The poet Yusef Komunyakaa (1947–    ) won the Pulitzer Prize in 1994 for his poetry collection *Neon Vernacular.* Much of Komunyakaa's work, including "Camouflaging the Chimera," is based on his experiences in the Vietnam War, where he served as an information specialist.

DIRECTIONS: Read the following novel excerpt and poem. Then, read each multiple-choice question that follows, and write the letter of the best response.

*This excerpt from* The Red Badge of Courage *describes a column of soldiers headed into battle. The "youth" is Henry Fleming, Crane's protagonist in the novel.*

# *from* The Red Badge of Courage

Stephen Crane

Presently the calm head of a forward-going column of infantry[1] appeared in the road. It came swiftly on. Avoiding the obstructions gave it the sinuous movement of a serpent. The men at the head butted mules with their musket stocks. They prodded teamsters[2] indifferent to all howls. The men forced their way through parts of the dense mass by strength. The blunt head of the column pushed. The raving teamsters swore many strange oaths.

The commands to make way had the ring of a great importance in them. The men were going forward to the heart of the din. They were

**SKILLS FOCUS**

Pages 624–627 cover
**Literary Skills**
Compare and contrast works from different literary periods.

---

1. **infantry** *n.:* foot soldiers.
2. **teamsters** *n. pl.:* drivers of teams of horses used for hauling.

to confront the eager rush of the enemy. They felt the pride of their onward movement when the remainder of the army seemed trying to dribble down this road. They tumbled teams about with a fine feeling that it was no matter so long as their column got to the front in time. This importance made their faces grave and stern. And the backs of the officers were very rigid.

As the youth looked at them the black weight of his woe returned to him. He felt that he was regarding a procession of chosen beings. The separation was as great to him as if they had marched with weapons of flame and banners of sunlight. He could never be like them. He could have wept in his longings.

He searched about in his mind for an adequate malediction[3] for the indefinite cause, the thing upon which men turn the words of final blame. It—whatever it was—was responsible for him, he said. There lay the fault.

The haste of the column to reach the battle seemed to the forlorn young man to be something much finer than stout fighting. Heroes, he thought, could find excuses in that long seething lane. They could retire with perfect self-respect and make excuses to the stars.

He wondered what those men had eaten that they could be in such haste to force their way to grim chances of death. As he watched his envy grew until he thought that he wished to change lives with one of them. He would have liked to have used a tremendous force, he said, throw off himself and become a better. Swift pictures of himself, apart, yet in himself, came to him—a blue desperate figure leading lurid charges with one knee forward and a broken blade high—a blue, determined figure standing before a crimson and steel assault, getting calmly killed on a high place before the eyes of all. He thought of the magnificent pathos[4] of his dead body.

These thoughts uplifted him. He felt the quiver of war desire. In his ears, he heard the ring of victory. He knew the frenzy of a rapid successful charge. The music of the trampling feet, the sharp voices, the clanking arms of the column near him made him soar on the red wings of war. For a few moments he was sublime.[5]

---

3. **malediction** *n.*: curse.
4. **pathos** *n.*: the quality in something experienced or observed, which arouses a sense of sorrow or pity.
5. **sublime** *adj.*: noble; majestic.

# Camouflaging the Chimera°

Yusef Komunyakaa

We tied branches to our helmets.
We painted our faces & rifles
with mud from a riverbank,

blades of grass hung from the pockets
5   of our tiger suits.° We wove
ourselves into the terrain,
content to be a hummingbird's target.

We hugged bamboo & leaned
against a breeze off the river,
10   slow-dragging with ghosts

from Saigon to Bangkok,
with women left in doorways
reaching in from America.
We aimed at dark-hearted songbirds.

15   In our way station of shadows
rock apes° tried to blow our cover,
throwing stones at the sunset.
        Chameleons

crawled our spines, changing from day
to night: green to gold,
20   gold to black. But we waited
till the moon touched metal,

till something almost broke
inside us. VC° struggled
with the hillside, like black silk°

25   wrestling iron through grass.
We weren't there. The river ran
through our bones. Small animals took
        refuge
against our bodies; we held our breath,

ready to spring the L-shaped
30   ambush, as a world revolved
under each man's eyelid.

---

°   **Chimera** (kī·mir′ə): a monster in Greek
mythology. The word today also refers to a
fanciful creation of the imagination.
5.   **tiger suits:** camouflage uniforms with black
and green stripes.
16.   **rock apes:** apes or tailless monkeys known to
throw rocks at humans, often scaring soldiers
in Vietnam into thinking they were being attacked by the enemy.

23.   **VC:** The Viet Cong were Communist forces
that opposed the U.S. and South Vietnamese
governments during the Vietnam War.
24.   **black silk:** The Viet Cong wore black silk to
camouflage themselves at night.

# Collection 4: Skills Review

1. Which of the following statements is *not* true, based on *The Red Badge of Courage* excerpt?
   - **A** The soldiers are proud to go to battle.
   - **B** The youth feels alienated from the soldiers leading the march.
   - **C** The soldiers are delaying their charge into battle.
   - **D** The youth imagines his own heroic death.

2. Which statement *best* represents the **situational irony** in the Crane excerpt?
   - **F** Although the youth is fearless, he does not look forward to the battle.
   - **G** The youth feels pride when looking at the enemy rather than when looking at his fellow soldiers.
   - **H** The youth feels ecstatic when he fantasizes about his death.
   - **J** Although he does not want to be a hero, the youth fights bravely.

3. Which of the animals mentioned in the Komunyakaa poem *best* **symbolizes** the soldiers?
   - **A** Hummingbirds
   - **B** Songbirds
   - **C** Rock apes
   - **D** Chameleons

4. The words that *best* describe the **tone** of Komunyakaa's poem are —
   - **F** judgmental and condemning
   - **G** adoring and extravagant
   - **H** tense and apprehensive
   - **J** bitter and sarcastic

5. Which statement accurately describes a contrast between the two selections?
   - **A** Crane's piece is bitter, whereas Komunyakaa's poem is uplifting.
   - **B** Crane's piece is written from one man's viewpoint, whereas Komunyakaa's poem uses the collective voice of a group of soldiers.
   - **C** Crane's piece focuses on events the narrator remembers from the past, whereas Komunyakaa's poem takes place in the present.
   - **D** Crane's piece emphasizes the loud sounds of the battle, whereas Komunyakaa's poem focuses on the smells of war.

6. Which of the following statements expresses a shared **theme** of these two selections?
   - **F** Peace can be obtained only through bloodshed.
   - **G** War requires ordinary people to perform extraordinary tasks.
   - **H** Soldiers are incapable of true heroism.
   - **J** Nature is ultimately ruined by war.

## Essay Question

In a brief essay, compare and contrast these two pieces of literature. Pay particular attention to the impression of war created by the imagery in each work. How does each writer use **descriptive details** and **sensory images** to enhance the realistic nature of his work? How does imagery contribute to the **tone** of each work?

# Collection 4: Skills Review
## Vocabulary Skills

**Test Practice**

**Synonyms**

DIRECTIONS: Choose the best synonym for the underlined word in each sentence.

1. Peyton Farquhar promised his allegiance to the Confederacy.
   - **A** hatred
   - **B** loyalty
   - **C** bitterness
   - **D** income

2. Stephen Crane's writing offers a candid description of the harsh reality of war.
   - **F** false
   - **G** crafty
   - **H** sincere
   - **J** critical

3. Harriet Jacobs found solace in reading the Scriptures.
   - **A** comfort
   - **B** clarity
   - **C** knowledge
   - **D** power

4. Mark Twain is known for his wit and humor, rather than for his solemnity.
   - **F** harshness
   - **G** anger
   - **H** seriousness
   - **J** informality

5. Against the advice of others, the man faced the perilous cold on his own.
   - **A** unbearable
   - **B** dangerous
   - **C** freezing
   - **D** unending

6. Aunt Georgiana was moved to tears by the bewitching music.
   - **F** repulsive
   - **G** joyful
   - **H** evil
   - **J** captivating

7. Mary Chesnut wrote the lamentable news of Atlanta's capture in her diary.
   - **A** wonderful
   - **B** distressing
   - **C** unexpected
   - **D** refreshing

8. Frederick Douglass believed the battle with Mr. Covey was inevitable.
   - **F** unlikely
   - **G** unjust
   - **H** questionable
   - **J** unavoidable

9. Richard Cory's death seemed preposterous considering all he had to live for.
   - **A** fitting
   - **B** questionable
   - **C** miraculous
   - **D** absurd

10. Abraham Lincoln had the arduous task of reuniting a divided nation.
    - **F** difficult
    - **G** important
    - **H** honorable
    - **J** remarkable

**SKILLS FOCUS**

**Vocabulary Skills**
Analyze synonyms.

# Collection 4: Skills Review

## Writing Skills

Test Practice DIRECTIONS: The following paragraph is from a draft of a student's historical research paper. Read the questions below it, and choose the best answer to each question.

Before the battle of Gettysburg, Major General J. E. B. Stuart—with General Robert E. Lee's permission—attempted to take his cavalry unit completely around the Union army of the Potomoc. Because the Union army was far more spread out than he had supposed, Stuart lost touch with Lee for ten days. General Lee was, therefore, unaware that the Union army had moved north of the Potomoc River and thus believed he had positioned the Confederate army correctly. Lee was certain Stuart would have informed him if the Union army had changed its position. When Lee found out otherwise, he hastily moved his army into positions around Gettysburg. From there he was forced to fight before he was ready—just one of the reasons the Confederates lost the battle of Gettysburg.

1. Which of the following research questions does the information in the paragraph best answer?
   A  Who was the Confederate army's leader?
   B  Why did the Confederate army lose the battle at Gettysburg?
   C  Where did Major General Stuart fight during the Civil War?
   D  How did the Civil War affect Southerners and Northerners?

2. To support the main idea, which sentence could the writer add?
   F  Stuart was supposed to inform Lee of the Union army's location.
   G  Stuart was one of the most flamboyant of Lee's subordinates.
   H  The battle of Gettysburg was an important battle of the war.
   J  The battle site in Pennsylvania is now a national park.

3. To find more information, which primary source could the writer consult?
   A  an encyclopedia article on the battle
   B  a letter written by General Stuart
   C  a journal article analyzing the battle
   D  a biography of General Robert E. Lee

4. If the writer wanted to include a visual in his paper, which would be best?
   F  a timeline showing the major battles of the Civil War
   G  a table listing the number of soldiers in each unit of the Union army
   H  a picture of the Confederate and Union soldiers' uniforms
   J  a map illustrating the movements of Stuart's cavalry

5. To present this information in an oral presentation, the speaker should
   A  use only secondary sources because they will be more reliable
   B  delete all references to sources
   C  give only one perspective
   D  weave parenthetical citation information into the speech

**SKILLS FOCUS**

**Writing Skills**
Write a historical research report.

*Welcome to Our City* (1921) by Charles Henry Demuth.
Oil on canvas (25 1/8″ × 20 1/8″).

Terra Foundation for American
Art, Chicago, U.S.A.

# THE
# MODERNS
## 1914–1939

### *Redefining the American Dream*

Men travel faster now, but I
do not know if they go to
better things.

—Willa Cather

go.
hrw
.com

**INTERNET**

Collection
Resources

Keyword: LE7 11-5

# The Moderns 1914–1939

## LITERARY EVENTS

**1910**

**1913** Ezra Pound forms imagist group

**1913** Robert Frost publishes his first poetry collection, *A Boy's Will*

**1915** Edgar Lee Masters reveals the shocking underside of small-town life in *Spoon River Anthology*

**1916** Carl Sandburg publishes *Chicago Poems*

**1920**

**1920** Sinclair Lewis publishes *Main Street*

**1922** Irish writer James Joyce publishes *Ulysses*

**1922** T. S. Eliot publishes his long poem, *The Waste Land*

**1923** Edna St. Vincent Millay wins the Pulitzer Prize in poetry

**1925** Virginia Woolf publishes *Mrs. Dalloway*

**1925** F. Scott Fitzgerald publishes his novel of the Jazz Age, *The Great Gatsby*

The Granger Collection, New York.

## POLITICAL AND SOCIAL EVENTS

**1910**

**1912** British ocean liner *Titanic* sinks after striking an iceberg off Newfoundland

**1913** Armory Show in New York City introduces modern art to United States

**1914** Panama Canal opens

**1920**

**1914** World War I begins in Europe

**1917** United States enters World War I

**1917** Russian Revolution ends czarist regime

**1919** Treaty of Versailles ends World War I

**1920** Harlem Renaissance begins

**The famous Cotton Club in Harlem.**

**1920** First commercial radio broadcast in the United States is aired

**1920** Eighteenth Amendment (prohibiting the sale of alcohol) goes into effect (repealed in 1933)

**1920** Nineteenth Amendment to Constitution grants U.S. women the right to vote

**A woman marches for voting rights, New York City (c. 1914–1918).**

**The Red Cross caring for World War I soldiers in France.**

1930                 1940

**1925** Theodore Dreiser publishes *An American Tragedy*

**1926** Langston Hughes publishes his first poetry collection, *The Weary Blues*

**1929** Ernest Hemingway publishes noted World War I novel, *A Farewell to Arms*

**1931** Eugene O'Neill's trilogy of plays, *Mourning Becomes Electra,* opens, shocking theatergoers with its stark portrayal of family rivalry

**Ernest Hemingway.**

**1937** Zora Neale Hurston publishes *Their Eyes Were Watching God*

**1939** John Steinbeck publishes *The Grapes of Wrath* and wins the Pulitzer Prize in literature

1930                 1940

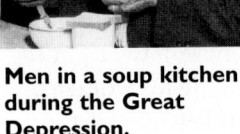

**Men in a soup kitchen during the Great Depression.**

**1927** Charles A. Lindbergh completes first transatlantic solo flight by airplane

**1927** *The Jazz Singer,* one of the first sound films with dialogue, opens

**1929** U.S. stock market crashes, leading to Great Depression

**1930** Mohandas Gandhi leads protest against British salt tax in India

**1933** Franklin D. Roosevelt becomes U.S. president; New Deal program to counter Great Depression begins

**1933** Nazi leader Adolf Hitler comes to power in Germany

**1935** Social Security Act is enacted

**1936** Spanish Civil War breaks out

**1937** Pioneering aviator Amelia Earhart disappears while flying around the world

**1939** Nationalist forces of Francisco Franco win Spanish Civil War

**1939** Germany invades Poland; World War II begins in Europe

**1939** First commercial television broadcast in United States is aired

*Guernica* (1937) by Pablo Picasso. Oil on canvas (350 cm × 782 cm).
© 2005 Estate of Pablo Picasso/Artists Rights Society (ARS), New York.

# Political and Social

## The Great War, 1914–1918

**W**orld War I, the so-called Great War, began in June 1914, when the Archduke Francis Ferdinand of Austria-Hungary was assassinated by a Serbian nationalist. That act of violence called the world to arms, and a local European conflict ultimately became the first global war. In 1917, the United States entered the conflict. The war, which was fought under the bright banners of humanity and democratic righteousness, soon became a bloodbath. In 1916, more than a half-million soldiers were killed in a ten-month-long battle near the town of Verdun in northeastern France. Nearly fifty million lives were lost by the time the armistice, or truce, was signed in November 1918. The Treaty of Versailles officially ended the war in June 1919. Although America emerged from the war as a victor, at home its values were beginning to be challenged . . .

Troops in France during World War I.

## Women's Suffrage

**I**n 1920, with the ratification of the Nineteenth Amendment, women in the United States finally won the right to vote. The battle for women's rights had taken almost 150 years from the time of Abigail Adams's original plea to her husband to "Remember the Ladies." With their newfound status and the flourish of postwar change, many women began wearing shorter skirts and bobbing their hair in a daring modern fashion. More and more women "kept up with the boys," participating in motoring parties, sports, and the arts.

# Milestones 1914–1939

Suffragist parade in New York.

## The Great Depression, 1929

The Great Depression that followed the crash of the New York stock market in 1929 brought suffering to millions of Americans—to those same hardworking people who had put their faith in the boundless capacity of America to provide them with jobs and their children with brighter futures. By 1933, the country was in the depths of the Great Depression. Anywhere from one fourth to one third of American workers were unemployed. People waited in bread lines and soup lines, hunted for food in garbage dumps, and slept in sewer pipes. Homeless families lived in tents and shacks in camps called Hoovervilles, named for President Herbert Hoover, who was reluctant to take steps to correct the economic downslide. The American dream seemed to have turned into a nightmare.

*Woman of the High Plains, Texas Panhandle* (1938). Photograph by Dorothea Lange.

Copyright the Dorothea Lange Collection, Oakland Museum of California, City of Oakland. Gift of Paul S. Taylor.

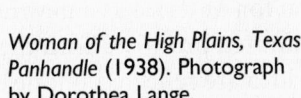

# The Moderns 1914–1939

*by* John Leggett *and* John Malcolm Brinnin

PREVIEW

## Think About ...

Life during the early part of the twentieth century was marked by tremendous change—political, social, psychological, and spiritual. Each decade seemed to bring new upheaval, and each upheaval required a new adjustment in attitude. These changes were reflected in a new period in American literature, called modernism.

As you read about this period, look for answers to these questions:

- What is the American dream?
- What happened to the American dream in the early twentieth century?
- In what ways did modernism challenge tradition—especially in what people valued in art and literature?

World War I, the so-called Great War, was one of the events that changed the American voice in fiction. The country appeared to have lost its innocence. Idealism had turned to cynicism for many Americans, who began to question the authority and tradition that was thought to be our bedrock. American writers, like their European counterparts, were also being profoundly affected by the **modernist** movement. This movement in literature, painting, music, and the other arts was swept along by disillusionment with traditions that seemed to have become spiritually empty. Modernism called for bold experimentation and wholesale rejection of traditional themes and styles.

## The American Dream: Pursuit of a Promise

Before we look at the upheavals that marked the first part of the twentieth century, we should review some of the uniquely American beliefs that had for centuries played a major role in the formation of the "American mind." There are three central assumptions, explained below, that we have come to call the **American dream.**

### ■ America as a New Eden

First, there is admiration for America as a new Eden: a land of beauty, bounty, and unlimited promise. Both the promise and the disappointment of this idea are reflected in one of the greatest American novels, *The Great Gatsby* (1925), by F. Scott Fitzgerald (page 695). This work appeared at a time when great wealth and the pursuit of pleasure had become ends in themselves for many people.

**SKILLS FOCUS**

Collection introduction (pages 636–643) covers

**Literary Skills**
Evaluate the philosophical, political, religious, ethical, and social issues of a historical period.

*The Voice of the City of New York Interpreted: The Brooklyn Bridge (The Bridge)* (1920–1922) by Joseph Stella. Oil and tempera on canvas (88¼" × 54").

The title character, Gatsby, is a self-made man whose wealth has mysterious and clearly illegal origins. Gatsby tries to woo both society and the woman he loves with lavish expenditures. His extravagant gestures are in pursuit of a dream. Unfortunately Gatsby's capacity for dreaming is far greater than any opportunity offered by the Roaring Twenties, and he meets a grotesquely violent end. But Gatsby's greatness is bound up with his tragedy: He believes in an America that has virtually disappeared under the degradations of modern life.

It is left to Nick Carraway, the narrator, to reflect at the end of the novel on the original promise of the American dream:

> 66 Gradually I became aware of the old island here that flowered once for Dutch sailors' eyes—a fresh, green breast of the new world. Its vanished trees, the trees that had made way for Gatsby's house, had once pandered in whispers to the last and greatest of all human dreams; for a transitory enchanted moment man must have held his breath in the presence of this continent, compelled into an aesthetic contemplation he neither understood nor desired, face to face for the last time in history with something commensurate to his capacity for wonder. 99

—F. Scott Fitzgerald, from *The Great Gatsby*

## A CLOSER LOOK: SOCIAL INFLUENCES

### Popular Entertainment

**Radio.** Perhaps the most popular form of entertainment during the 1930s was the radio. By 1933, two thirds of American households owned at least one radio. People also relied on radios for news, as was demonstrated by a famous Halloween broadcast of 1938. Six million listeners tuned in to Orson Welles's radio play *Invasion from Mars*—a series of convincing but fictional news bulletins about a Martian invasion near New York City, based on H. G. Wells's science fiction novel *War of the Worlds*. Believing that the broadcast was reporting a real invasion, people clogged eastern highways in an attempt to escape the alien invaders.

**Movies.** To get Americans' minds off the hardships of the Depression, Hollywood produced slapstick comedies by Laurel and Hardy and the Marx Brothers and romantic musicals with Fred Astaire. The cost of going to a movie was relatively inexpensive, and each week millions of Americans flocked to watch cartoons, newsreels, and feature films at elaborate movie palaces with romantic names like the Bijou, the Roxy, and the Ritz. To top off the decade, audiences in 1939 thronged to see Clark Gable and Vivien Leigh in the long-awaited blockbuster *Gone with the Wind*.

### ■ A Belief in Progress

The second element in the American dream is optimism, justified by the ever-expanding opportunity and abundance that many people had come to expect. Americans had come to believe in progress—that life will keep getting better and that we are always moving toward an era of greater prosperity, justice, and joy.

### ■ Triumph of the Individual

The final element in the American dream is the importance and ultimate triumph of the individual—the independent, self-reliant person. This ideal of the self-reliant individual was championed by Ralph Waldo Emerson (page 203), who probably deserves most of the credit for defining the essence of the American dream, including its roots in the promise of the "new Eden" and its faith that "things are getting better all the time." Trust the universe and trust yourself, Emerson wrote. "If the single man plant himself indomitable on his instincts, and there abide, the huge world will come round to him."

## A Crack in the World: Breakdown of Beliefs and Traditions

The devastation of World War I and the economic crash a decade later severely damaged these inherited ideas of an Edenic land, an optimism in the future, and a faith in individualism. Postwar writers became skeptical of the New England Puritan tradition and the gentility that had been central to the literary ideal. In fact, the center of American literary life finally started to shift away from New England, which had been the native region of America's most brilliant writers during the nineteenth century. Many modernist writers were born in the South, the Midwest, or the West.

In the postwar period two new intellectual theories or movements, **Marxism** and **psychoanalysis,** combined to influence previous beliefs and values.

## Marxism and the Challenge to Free Enterprise

In Russia during World War I, a Marxist revolution had toppled and even murdered an anointed ruler, the czar. The socialistic beliefs of Karl Marx (1818–1883) that had powered the Russian Revolution in 1917 conflicted with the American system of capitalism and free enterprise, and Marxists threatened to export their revolution everywhere. Some Americans, however, believed that certain elements of Marxism would provide much-needed rights to workers. After visiting Russia, the American writer and social reformer Lincoln Steffens reported, "I have seen the future and it works."

---

### Elements of Modernism

- Emphasis on bold experimentation in style and form, reflecting the fragmentation of society

- Rejection of traditional themes, subjects, and forms

- Sense of disillusionment and loss of faith in the American dream

- Rejection of sentimentality and artificiality

- Rejection of the ideal of a hero as infallible in favor of a hero who is flawed and disillusioned but shows "grace under pressure"

- Interest in the inner workings of the human mind, sometimes expressed through new narrative techniques, such as stream of consciousness

- Revolt against the spiritual debasement of the modern world

*Village Speakeasy, Closed for Violation* (c. 1934) by Ben Shahn.
Tempera on masonite (16³/₈″ × 47⁷/₈″).

Museum of the City of New York. Permanent Deposit of the Public Art Project through the Whitney Museum.
Art © Estate of Ben Shahn/Licensed by VAGA, New York, NY.

## Freud and the Unconscious Mind

In Vienna there was another ground-shaking movement. Sigmund Freud (1856–1939), the founder of psychoanalysis, had opened the workings of the unconscious mind to scrutiny and called for a new understanding of human sexuality and the role it plays in our unconscious thoughts. Throughout America there was a growing interest in this new field of psychology and a resulting anxiety about the amount of freedom an individual really had. If our actions were influenced by our subconscious and if we had no control over our subconscious, there seemed to be little room left for free will.

One literary result of this interest in the psyche was the narrative technique called **stream of consciousness.** This writing style abandoned chronology and attempted to imitate the moment-by-moment flow of a character's perceptions and memories. The Irish writer James Joyce (1882–1941) radically changed the very concept of the novel by using stream of consciousness in *Ulysses* (1922), his monumental "odyssey" set in Dublin. Soon afterward the American writers Katherine Anne Porter (page 769) and William Faulkner (page 717) used the stream-of-consciousness technique in their works.

## At Home and Abroad: The Jazz Age

In 1919, the Constitution was amended to prohibit the manufacture and sale of alcohol, which was singled out as a central social evil. But far from shoring up traditional values, Prohibition ushered in

*The liberty of the individual is no gift of civilization. It was greatest before there was any civilization.*

—Sigmund Freud
from *Civilization and Its Discontents* (1930)

an age characterized by the bootlegger, the speak-easy, the cocktail, the short-skirted flapper, the new rhythms of jazz, and the dangerous but lucrative profession of the gangster. Recording the Roaring Twenties and making the era a vivid chapter in our history, F. Scott Fitzgerald gave it its name: the Jazz Age.

During the Jazz Age, women too played a prominent role. In 1920, women won the right to vote, and they began to create a presence in artistic, intellectual, and social circles. As energetic as the Roaring Twenties were in America, the pursuit of pleasure abroad was even more attractive to some than was its enjoyment at home. F. Scott Fitzgerald was among the many American writers and artists who abandoned their own shores after the war for the expatriate life in France. After World War I, living was not only cheap in Paris and on the sunny French Riviera but also somehow better; it was more exotic, filled with more grace and luxury, and there was no need to go down a cellar stairway to get a drink. This wave of expatriates (Americans living abroad) was another signal that something had gone wrong with the American dream—with the idea that America was Eden, with our belief in progress, and especially with the conviction that America was a land of heroes.

## Grace Under Pressure: The New American Hero

The most influential of all the post–World War I writers was Ernest Hemingway (page 682). Hemingway is perhaps most famous for his literary style, which affected the style of American prose fiction for several generations. Like the Puritans, who strove for a plain style centuries earlier, Hemingway reduced the flamboyance of literary language to the bare bones of the truth it must express.

Hemingway also introduced a new kind of hero to American fiction, a character type that many readers embraced as a protagonist and a role model. This Hemingway hero is a man of action, a warrior, and a tough competitor; he has a code of honor, courage, and endurance. He shows, in Hemingway's own words, "grace under pressure." But the most important trait of this Hemingway hero is his thorough disillusionment, a quality that reflected the author's own outlook—that at the mysterious center of creation lay nothing at all.

Hemingway found his own answer to this crisis of faith in a belief in the self and in such qualities as decency, bravery, competence, and skillfulness. He clung to this conviction in spite of what he saw as the absolutely unbeatable odds waged against us all. A further part of the Hemingway code was the importance of recognizing and snatching up the rare, good, rich moments that life offers before those moments elude us.

### FAST FACTS

#### Political Highlights

- In 1917, the United States enters World War I on the side of the Allied nations.
- Women win the right to vote when the Nineteenth Amendment is passed in 1920.
- The stock market crash of 1929 ushers in the Great Depression.

#### Philosophical Views

- Marxism, which embraced socialism as the desired social structure, takes hold in Russia and finds some support in the United States.
- The science of psychoanalysis encourages exploration of the human subconscious and the meaning of dreams.

#### Social Influences

- Speak-easies and jazz clubs spring up during Prohibition. The underground social scene becomes popular.
- During the 1920s, many young women flout tradition and become more independent in thought, dress, and attitude.

# Modern Voices in Poetry:
## A Dazzling Period of Experimentation

By the second decade of the century, the last traces of British influence on American poetry were washed away, and American poets entered into their most dazzling period of experimentation. Many poets began to explore the artistic life of Europe, especially Paris. With other writers, artists, and composers from all over the world, they absorbed the lessons of modernist painters like Henri Matisse and Pablo Picasso, who were exploring new ways to see and represent reality. In the same way, poets sought to create poems that invited new ways of seeing and thinking. Ezra Pound (page 648) and T. S. Eliot (page 655) used the suggestive techniques of **symbolism** to fashion a new, modernist poetry (see page 645). Pound also spearheaded a related poetic movement called **imagism.** Exemplified by brilliant poets like E. E. Cummings (page 675), the imagist and symbolist styles would prevail in poetry until the mid–twentieth century.

## Voices of American Character

Meanwhile other American poets rejected modernist trends. While their colleagues found inspiration in Paris, these poets stayed at home, ignoring or defying the revolution of modernism. These poets preferred to say what they had to say in plain American speech. Their individual accents reveal the regional diversity of American life and character.

Of these poets the greatest was unquestionably Robert Frost (page 790). Frost's independence was grounded in his ability to handle ordinary New England speech and in his surprising skill at taking the most conventional poetic forms and giving them a twist all his own. In an era when "good" was being equated by many artists with "new," the only new thing about Robert Frost was old: individual poetic genius. Using this gift to impose his own personality on the iambic line in verse, Frost created a poetic voice that was unique and impossible to imitate.

## The Harlem Renaissance:
## Voices of the African American Experience

In the early 1920s, a group of black poets focused directly on the unique contributions of African American culture to America. Their poetry based its rhythms on spirituals and jazz, its lyrics on songs known as the blues, and its diction on the street talk of the ghettos.

Foremost among the African American lyric poets were James Weldon Johnson, Claude McKay (page 880), Langston Hughes

*Still Life of a Table* (1931) by Pablo Picasso. Oil on canvas (195 CM × 130.5 CM). Musée Picasso, Paris, France.

© 2005 Estate of Pablo Picasso/Artists Rights Society (ARS), New York.

(page 823), and Countee Cullen (page 818). These poets brought literary distinction to the broad movement of artists known as the **Harlem Renaissance** (page 816). The geographical center of the movement was Harlem, the neighborhood of New York City north of 110th Street in Manhattan. Its spiritual center, though, was a place in the consciousness of African Americans—a people too long ignored, patronized, or otherwise shuffled to the margins of American art. When African American poetry, hand in hand with the music echoing from New Orleans, Memphis, and Chicago, became part of the Jazz Age, it was a catalyst for a new appreciation of the role of black talent in American culture.

## The American Dream Revised

In some respects the modernist era is the richest period of American writing since the flowering of New England in the first half of the nineteenth century. The writers of this era—some of the best that America has produced—experimented boldly with forms and subject matter. But they were also still trying to find the answers to basic human questions: Who are we? Where are we going? What values should guide us on the search for our human identity?

**REVIEW**

## Talk About . . .

Turn back to the Think About questions at the start of this introduction to the modern period (page 636), and discuss your views.

## Write About . . .

### Contrasting Literary Periods

**The American dream, then and now.** In 1929, Gertrude Stein, a leading modernist literary figure among the American expatriates in Paris, declared, "Everything is the same and everything is different." Apply her remark to the American dream of the early twentieth century, and then apply it to today—and tomorrow. Note the ways in which the American dream remains the same and ways in which it has changed.

**War and economics, then and now.** A major war and a major economic disaster marked the first decades of the twentieth century. How do you think historians of the future will describe the past twenty years? What forces—political and economic—contributed to the way people lived, what they hoped for and feared, and what they wrote about? Write your responses, and then share them with a partner.

# Make It New!

**Pound**
**Eliot**
**Williams**
**Moore**
**Cummings**

Make it new!
Art is a joyous thing.
—Ezra Pound

go.hrw.com
**INTERNET**
**Collection Resources**
Keyword: LE7 11-5

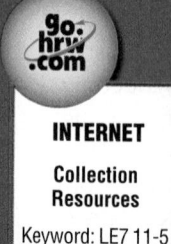

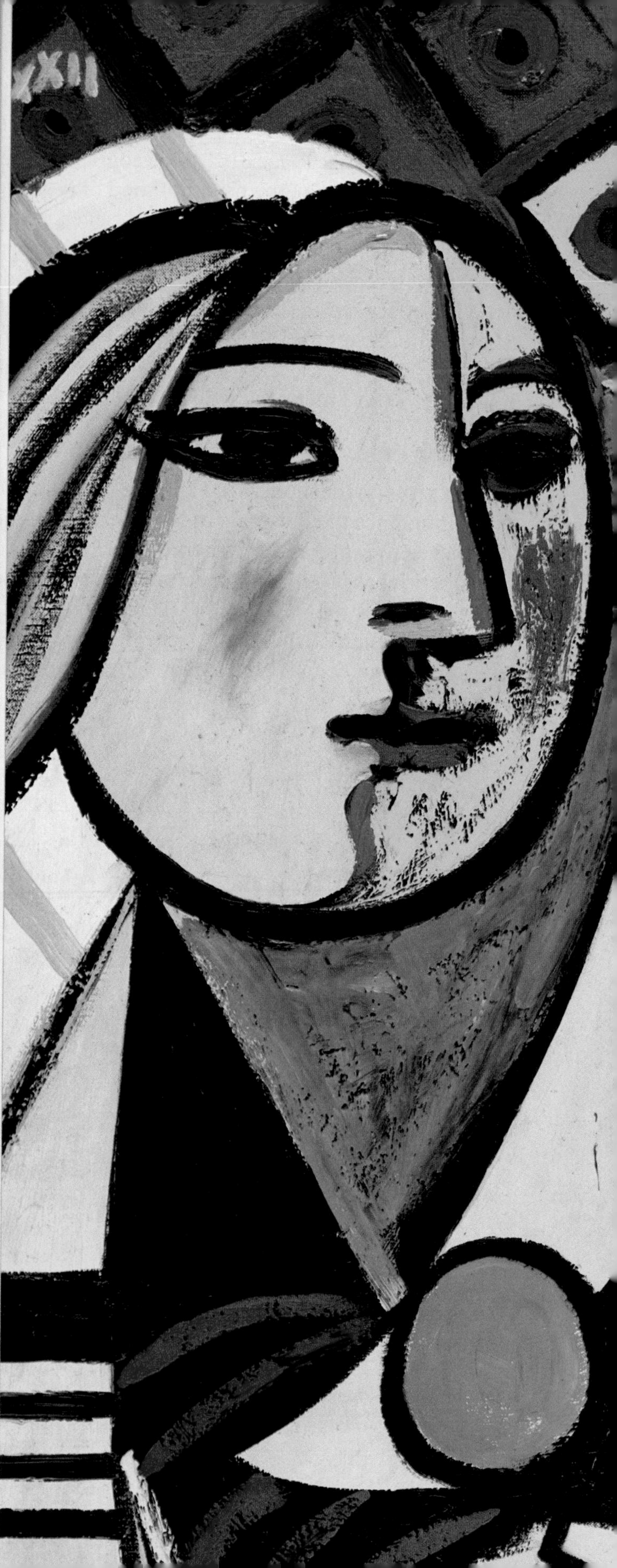

*Girl Before a Mirror* (detail) (1932) by Pablo Picasso.

# Symbolism, Imagism, and Beyond

*by* **John Malcolm Brinnin**

Sometime in the early twentieth century, Americans awoke to a sense that their own national culture had come of age. This was true in poetry and in painting, in music and in dance, even in the new architecture of the skyscraper. Ironically American poets found their new inspiration in Paris rather than their homeland. Learning from the French symbolist poets, who dominated French literature from about 1875 to 1895, Americans were able to produce a new type of poetry through which the true American genius could speak.

## Symbolism: The Search for a New Reality

**Symbolism** is a form of expression in which the world of appearances is violently rearranged by artists who seek a different and more truthful version of reality. The symbolist poets did not merely describe objects; they tried to portray the emotional effects that objects can suggest. But don't be misled by the term *symbolism*. It has nothing to do with the religious, national, or psychological symbols we are all familiar with. In fact, the symbolists were concerned with getting rid of such symbols, which they saw as having become dull and meaningless through overuse. The symbolists stressed instead the need for a trust in the nonrational. Imagination is more reliable than reason, the symbolists argued, and just as precise. With their emphasis on the mysterious and the intuitive, symbolists hoped to bring revelation—self-discovery—to the reader through poems that lead the imagination to discover truths.

Symbolism was a new manifestation of the Romanticism that had swept over Europe and the United States in the nineteenth century. The Romantics had stressed the importance of feeling and the independence of the individual, and they had made a great stand against the mechanization of human life. In the natural world the Romantics found messages that spoke to the soul and gave it strength.

The symbolists, however, could find neither solace nor spiritual renewal in nature. By the start of the twentieth century, nature had been subjected to so much scientific classification and interpretation that it had been stripped of much of its mystery. Artists now faced the onslaught of the modern world, which in spite of advances in science and technology suffered increased poverty, violence, and conflict. The symbolist poets saw this new world as spiritually corrupt, and they faced it with a distaste amounting to outrage. They knew they could not transform or erase the modern

*The Quencher (Night Fires)* (ca.1919) by Joseph Stella (American, 1877–1946). Pastel on paper. 22½ × 29 in.

Milwaukee Art Museum, Gift of Friends of Art, M1978.32.

world, though, so their revolt was spiritual. They tried to redefine what it meant to be human in a time when individualism was succumbing to the power of mass culture.

## Imagism: "The *Exact* Word"

The two Americans who first came into close contact with symbolism and introduced the techniques of the movement to the United States were Ezra Pound (page 648) and T. S. Eliot (page 655). With the help of several British poets, a group of Americans led by Pound founded a school perhaps better known and understood in the United States than symbolism itself. This was **imagism,** which flourished in the years 1912–1917.

Like the symbolists, imagists believed that poetry can be made purer by concentration on the precise, clear, unqualified image. Imagery alone, the imagists believed, could carry a poem's emotion and message. It could do this almost instantly, without all the elaborate metrics and stanza patterns that were part of poetry's traditional mode. The imagists took on the role of reformers. They would rid poetry of its prettiness, sentimentality, and artificiality, concentrating instead on the raw power of the image to communicate feeling and thought.

The imagists issued a "manifesto," or public declaration, proposing "to use the language of common speech," as well as "the *exact* word, not merely the decorative word." In the same spirit they called for a poetry "hard and clear, never blurred or indefinite." Some of the imagists' inspiration was drawn from Eastern art forms, particularly Japanese haiku, a verse form that often juxtaposes two distinct images and invites the reader to experience the emotion created by the juxtaposition.

Pound defined an image as "that which presents an intellectual and emotional complex in an instant of time." Here is a famous imagist poem that illustrates this concept:

### In a Station of the Metro

The apparition of these faces in the crowd;
Petals on a wet, black bough.

—Ezra Pound

## A New Poetic Order

Today poems with imagistic technique are commonplace. But at the time the imagists published their manifesto on poetry's nature and function, their theory created a great stir. It insisted that the range of poetic subject matter might include the kitchen sink as well as the rising of the moon, the trash can as well as the Chinese porcelain vase. The strongest opposition to the imagists was caused by their proposal "to create new rhythms—as the expression of new moods. . . . We do believe that the individuality of a poet may often be better expressed in free verse than in conventional forms." To tradition-minded poets this **free verse**—poetry without regular rhyming and metrical patterns—was deplorable. It meant a loosening of poetic standards and an assault on the very craft of poetry. These poets did not yet realize that successful free verse was at least as difficult to create as verse written in traditional forms.

Although imagism was a short-lived movement, it gave rise to some of our greatest poets. Many in the forefront of imagism went beyond the movement's limitations and expanded its insights. Besides Pound, these included William Carlos Williams (page 665), Marianne Moore (page 671), and E. E. Cummings (page 675). Eventually, imagism came to stand for a whole new order of poetry in the United States. Most Americans became familiar with the movement mainly as the school of free verse. But the imagist program was not only a call for a new method of organizing lines and stanzas; it was also an invitation to a new way of seeing and experiencing the world.

# Ezra Pound
(1885–1972)

Boris De Rachewiltz, courtesy of New Directions, used courtesy of New Directions Publishing Corp.

**E**zra Pound is remembered by many people as the man who was charged with treason during World War II and spent many years in a psychiatric hospital. This notoriety has tended to obscure Pound's impact on American poetry. But his influence is still apparent everywhere; the generations of poets who have come after Pound have kept alive a complex memory of a man whose career wavered between brilliance and episodic madness.

Pound was born in Hailey, Idaho, and grew up in Pennsylvania. He taught at a conservative religious college for a while, but his bohemian lifestyle was out of tune with his surroundings.

In search of greater personal freedom and contacts with European poets, Pound settled in London in 1908. There he became a self-appointed spokesperson for the new poetic movement known as imagism. He also became a self-exiled critic of American life and a torchbearer for any art that challenged the complacent middle class.

Pound—whose slogan was "Make it new!"—was a born teacher whose advice was sought by the most brilliant writers of the period. T. S. Eliot acknowledged Pound's valuable advice when he dedicated his great poem *The Waste Land* (1922) to him.

After World War I, Pound felt the need for even broader horizons than London offered him. He moved to Paris in 1921 and to Italy three years later, where he continued to write poetry and criticism. And now came a tragic turning point in Pound's life. His interest in economics and social theory led him to support Benito Mussolini, the Fascist dictator of Italy.

When World War II broke out, Pound stayed in Italy and turned propagandist for Mussolini's policies. In his radio broadcasts from Italy, Pound denounced the struggle of the United States and its allies against Germany, Italy, and Japan. Many of these broadcasts were viciously anti-Semitic.

When the American army advanced northward up the Italian peninsula in 1945, Pound was taken prisoner. He was confined to a cage on an airstrip near Pisa and eventually returned to the United States to be tried for treason. Psychiatrists judged him mentally incompetent, however, and in 1946 the poet was committed to St. Elizabeth's, at the time designated a hospital for the criminally insane, in Washington, D.C.

Twelve years later he was released through the intercession of writers, including Archibald MacLeish and Robert Frost, who argued that his literary contributions outweighed his disastrous lack of judgment and his notorious bigotry. Pound returned to Italy, where he lived the rest of his life. During these last years of exile, a reporter once asked Pound where he was living. "In hell," Pound answered. "Which hell?" the reporter asked. "Here," said Pound, pressing his heart. "Here."

When he died, in Venice, Pound left behind a body of work extending from the delicate lyrics he wrote at the turn of the century to *The Cantos,* an enormous epic he did not complete until well over fifty years later. He also left a public record that still uncomfortably involves scholars and historians in "the case of Ezra Pound."

# Before You Read

## The River-Merchant's Wife: A Letter

### Make the Connection

In this letter-poem, Pound assumes the voice of a Chinese river-merchant's wife as she thinks about her growing love for her husband. This poem is a tribute to Li Po (701–762), one of the greatest Chinese poets. Pound had to cross generations, cultures, continents, and genders to write the poem; its intimate tone creates a bridge for the reader. If you have ever been moved to write a letter to someone you loved and missed, you will identify at once with the feelings of this eighth-century Chinese speaker.

### Literary Focus
### Imagery

Pound's poem is not a word-for-word translation of Li Po's poem but an adaptation based on the **images** and feelings that Pound experienced when he read translations of the original. Pound's images are simple and concrete; they help the reader to see the speaker and her setting clearly and to imagine how she is feeling.

> **Imagery** is language that creates vivid sense impressions and suggests emotional states.
>
> *For more on Imagery, see the Handbook of Literary and Historical Terms.*

SKILLS FOCUS

**Literary Skills**
Understand imagery.

Wang Xizhi Watching Geese (detail) (ca.1295) by Qian Xuan (c.1235–before 1307) Yuan Dynasty. Handscroll. Ink, color, and gold on paper, 9¹/₈ × 36¹/₂ in. (23.2 × 92.7cm).

# The River-Merchant's Wife: A Letter

## Ezra Pound

While my hair was still cut straight across my forehead
Played I about the front gate, pulling flowers.
You came by on bamboo stilts, playing horse,
You walked about my seat, playing with blue plums.
5   And we went on living in the village of Chokan:
Two small people, without dislike or suspicion.

At fourteen I married My Lord you.
I never laughed, being bashful.
Lowering my head, I looked at the wall.
10   Called to, a thousand times, I never looked back.

At fifteen I stopped scowling,
I desired my dust to be mingled with yours
Forever and forever and forever.
Why should I climb the lookout?

The Metropolitan Museum of Art, Ex coll.: C. C. Wang Family, Gift of The Dillon Fund, 1973 (1973.120.6). Photograph © 1981 The Metropolitan Museum of Art.

15   At sixteen you departed
     You went into far Ku-to-yen, by the river of swirling eddies,
     And you have been gone five months.
     The monkeys make sorrowful noise overhead.

     You dragged your feet when you went out.
20   By the gate now, the moss is grown, the different mosses,
     Too deep to clear them away!
     The leaves fall early this autumn, in wind.
     The paired butterflies are already yellow with August
     Over the grass in the West garden;
25   They hurt me. I grow older.
     If you are coming down through the narrows of the river Kiang,
     Please let me know beforehand.
     And I will come out to meet you
               As far as Cho-fu-Sa.
                              *—Li T'ai Po*

## The Garden

### Make the Connection

"*En robe de parade*" is a quotation from the nineteenth-century French poet Albert Samain. It means "dressed for show" or, in military terms, "in full regalia." In this poem a beautifully dressed woman is observed walking in a London park called Kensington Gardens. Many poor children are playing nearby. As you read, use Pound's images to picture the scene.

*Lillah McCarthy* (c. 1920) by Ambrose McEvoy.
Oil on canvas (39³/₄″ × 30″).
National Portrait Gallery, London.

# The Garden

## Ezra Pound

*En robe de parade.*
—Samain

Like a skein of loose silk blown against a wall
She walks by the railing of a path in Kensington Gardens,
And she is dying piecemeal
    of a sort of emotional anemia.

5    And round about there is a rabble
Of the filthy, sturdy, unkillable infants of the very poor.
They shall inherit the earth.

In her is the end of breeding.
Her boredom is exquisite and excessive.
10   She would like someone to speak to her,
and is almost afraid that I
    will commit that indiscretion.

Youngsters in an
East End slum, London.

*Ezra Pound wrote the following "rules" for poets in an article in the March 1913 issue of* Poetry *magazine. Many of these rules are useful to all writers.*

**INFORMATIONAL TEXT**

# A Few Don'ts by an Imagiste

It is better to present one Image in a lifetime than to produce voluminous works. . . .

Pay no attention to the criticism of men who have never themselves written a notable work. Consider the discrepancies between the actual writing of the Greek poets and dramatists, and the theories of the Greco-Roman grammarians, concocted to explain their meters.

## Language

Use no superfluous word, no adjective, which does not reveal something.

Don't use such an expression as "dim lands of peace." It dulls the image. It mixes an abstraction with the concrete. It comes from the writer's not realizing that the natural object is always the *adequate* symbol.

Go in fear of abstractions. Don't retell in mediocre verse what has already been done in good prose. Don't think any intelligent person is going to be deceived when you try to shirk all the difficulties of the unspeakably difficult art of good prose by chopping your composition into line lengths. . . .

Don't imagine that the art of poetry is any simpler than the art of music, or that you can please the expert before you have spent at least as much effort on the art of verse as the average piano teacher spends on the art of music.

Be influenced by as many great artists as you can, but have the decency either to acknowledge the debt outright, or to try to conceal it. . . .

## Rhythm and Rhyme

Let the neophyte know assonance and alliteration, rhyme immediate and delayed, simple and polyphonic, as a musician would expect to know harmony and counterpoint and all the minutiae of his craft. No time is too great to give to these matters or to any one of them, even if the artist seldom have need of them. . . .

Consider the way of the scientists rather than the way of an advertising agent for a new soap.

The scientist does not expect to be acclaimed as a great scientist until he has *discovered* something. He begins by learning what has been discovered already. He goes from that point onward. He does not bank on being a charming fellow personally. He does not expect his friends to applaud the results of his freshman classwork. Freshmen in poetry are unfortunately not confined to a definite and recognizable classroom. They are "all over the shop." Is it any wonder "the public is indifferent to poetry"?

Don't chop your stuff into separate *iambs*. Don't make each line stop dead at the end, and then begin every next line with a heave. Let the beginning of the next line catch the rise of the rhythm wave, unless you want a definite longish pause. . . .

If you are using a symmetrical form, don't put in what you want to say and then fill up the remaining vacuums with slush.

*E. Z. Pound*

# Response and Analysis

## The River-Merchant's Wife: A Letter

### Thinking Critically

1. What events are referred to in the first four stanzas of "The River-Merchant's Wife"?

2. How is the third stanza a **turning point** in the poem? What do you think the river-merchant's wife means by line 14?

3. What **image** suggests that the river-merchant was reluctant to leave home?

4. What hurts the young wife in line 25, and why? In the same line, why does she say, after only five months, that she grows "older"?

5. Think of possible reasons why the river-merchant left. Do you think he will ever return? What may have delayed him?

## The Garden

### Thinking Critically

1. What **simile** in the first stanza of "The Garden" describes what the woman looks like as she walks in the park?

2. How would you explain "emotional anemia"? How might it cause the woman to die "piecemeal"?

3. What contrast to the woman is set up in the second stanza?

4. Line 7, "They shall inherit the earth," is an allusion to the Bible (Matthew 5:5). There Jesus says, "Blessed are the meek, for they shall inherit the earth." What does the statement mean in this context?

5. *Breeding* can mean "producing offspring" or "good upbringing or good training." How would you explain the double meaning of the word in line 8?

6. In line 10, what does the speaker imagine the woman wants? What is she afraid of?

7. "The Garden" is a poem about two individuals, the woman and the speaker, but it is also about something broader. What is Pound's larger subject?

## WRITING

### Imagine It

Write a very brief **poem** making use of Pound's "A Few Don'ts by an Imagiste" (see the **Primary Source** on page 653). First, choose a topic you feel strongly about, perhaps a topic from one of these poems: love, parting, the contrast between rich and poor, the need for human contact. Then, think of a single concrete image that suggests the situation and your feelings about it. Describe the image as specifically as you can. Use Pound's "In a Station of the Metro" (page 647) as a model—Pound sets a mood by describing a single, strong image.

**SKILLS FOCUS**

**Literary Skills**
Analyze imagery.

**Writing Skills**
Write a poem describing an image.

**INTERNET**

**Projects and Activities**

Keyword: LE7 11-5

# T. S. Eliot
## (1888–1965)

**A**t the time when he was regarded as America's most eminent living poet, T. S. Eliot announced that he was a "classicist in literature, royalist in politics, and Anglo-Catholic in religion." In 1927, Eliot gave up his U.S. citizenship and became a subject of the king of England. The same year he was received into the Church of England. By a kind of poetic justice, this loss to America was later to be made up for: W. H. Auden (page 979), the leading British poet of his time, became a naturalized American citizen in 1946. But residence in an adopted country does not necessarily change the philosophy or the style of a poet. Eliot continued to speak in a voice first heard in the Puritan pulpits of Massachusetts. Auden retained a British sense of language unaffected by the inroads of American speech.

Thomas Stearns Eliot's family was rooted in New England, though he was born in St. Louis, Missouri, where his grandfather had been a founder and chancellor of Washington University. Eliot's childhood awareness of his native city would show itself in his poetry, but only after he had moved far away from St. Louis. He graduated from Harvard and went on to do postgraduate work at the Sorbonne in Paris.

Just before the outbreak of World War I, Eliot took up residence in London, the city that would become his home for the rest of his life. There he worked for a time in a bank, suffered a nervous breakdown, married an emotionally troubled Englishwoman, and finally took up the business of literature. He became active as a publisher in the outstanding firm of Faber and Faber and, on his own, edited *The Criterion,* a literary magazine. As a critic he was responsible for reviving interest in many neglected poets, notably the seventeenth-century English poet John Donne.

### Complex Poetry for a Complex World

Long before he decided to live abroad permanently, Eliot had developed a taste for classical literature. He was as familiar with European and Eastern writings as he was with the masterpieces of English. But the most crucial influence on his early work came from the late-nineteenth-century French poets who, as a group, came to be known as the symbolists. (For more on the symbolists, see page 645.) When he was nineteen, Eliot came upon a book by the British critic Arthur Symons titled *The Symbolist Movement in Literature.* "I myself owe Mr. Symons a great debt," wrote Eliot. "But for having read his book, I should not . . . have heard of Laforgue and Rimbaud; I should probably not have begun to read Verlaine; and but for reading Verlaine, I should not have heard of Corbière. So the Symons book is one of those which have affected the course of my life."

The poets Eliot mentions were men of distinctly different talents. Yet they all believed in poetry as an art of suggestion rather than statement. They saw poetry as an art of re-creating states of mind and feeling, as opposed to reporting or confessing them. These beliefs became the basis of Eliot's own poetic methods. When people complained that this poetic method of suggestion was complex and diffi-cult to understand, Eliot retorted that poetry had to be complex to express the complexities of modern life. More or less ignoring the still undervalued contribution of Walt Whitman, Eliot and other American poets also believed that, divorced from British antecedents, they would once and for all bring the rhythms of their native speech into the mainstream of world literature. Eliot and these other poets are often referred to as modernists.

## Words for a Wasteland

Eliot had an austere view of poetic creativity; he disagreed with those who regarded a poem as a means of self-expression, as a source of comfort, or as a kind of spiritual pep talk. Practicing what he preached, Eliot startled his contemporaries with "The Love Song of J. Alfred Prufrock" in 1915 and "Portrait of a Lady" in 1917. Then, in 1922, with the editorial advice and encouragement of Ezra Pound, Eliot published *The Waste Land,* a long work consid-ered the most significant poem of the early twentieth century. The poem describes a civi-lization that is spiritually empty and paralyzed by indecision.

Assembled in the manner of a painter's col-lage or a moviemaker's montage, *The Waste Land* proved that it is possible to write an epic poem of classical scope in the space of 434 lines. Critics pored over the poem's complex structure and its dense network of allusions to world literature, Eastern religions, and an-thropology. A few years after *The Waste Land* appeared, Eliot published a series of notes identifying many of his key references. (He was dismayed to find that some of his more ardent admirers were more interested in the notes than in the poem itself.)

In 1925, Eliot published a kind of lyrical postscript to *The Waste Land* called "The Hollow Men," which predicted in its somber conclusion that the world would end not with a bang but with a whimper. In "The Hollow Men," Eliot repeats and expands some of the themes of his longer poem and arrives at that point of despair beyond which lie but two al-ternatives: renewal or annihilation.

## A Submission to Peace

For critics surveying Eliot's career, it has become commonplace to say that, after the spiritual dead end of "The Hollow Men," Eliot chose hope over despair and faith over the world-weary cynicism that marked his early years. But there is much evidence in his later poems to indicate that, for Eliot, hope and faith were not conscious choices. Instead, they were the consequences of a submission, even a surrender, to that "peace which passeth understanding," referred to in the last line of *The Waste Land.*

Eliot spent the remainder of his poetic career in an extended meditation on the limits of individual will and the limitless power of faith in the presence of grace.

Cited for his work as a pioneer of modern poetry, Eliot was awarded the Nobel Prize in literature in 1948. In the decades that followed, he came frequently to the United States to lecture and to read his poems, sometimes to audiences so large that he had to appear in football stadiums. Some of those who fought to buy tickets on the fifty-yard line were prob-ably unaware of the irony in all of this: that a man once regarded as the most difficult and obscure poet of his era had achieved the drawing power of a rock star.

Ezra Pound (who called Eliot "Possum") wrote a few final words on the death of his old friend, ending with this passage:

"Am I to write 'about' the poet Thomas Stearns Eliot? Or my friend 'the Possum'? Let him rest in peace, I can only repeat, but with the urgency of fifty years ago: READ HIM."

## The Love Song of J. Alfred Prufrock

### Make the Connection

In the PBS television series *The Power of Myth*, the noted scholar of myths Joseph Campbell says, "The hero is today running up against a hard world that is in no way responsive to his spiritual need." Modern society has become a "stagnation of inauthentic lives and living . . . that evokes nothing of our spiritual life, our potentialities, or even our physical courage." According to Campbell, the times we live in are hostile to heroism. Heroes are people of action, but the drudgery of modern life has made many people observers rather than participants in life's adventures. See if you agree that the protagonist of this poem is a person of profound self-absorption and passivity. Does he fit the profile of antihero, the disillusioned and ineffectual protagonist we find in much modern and contemporary literature?

### Literary Focus
#### Dramatic Monologue

This poem is written as a **dramatic monologue**—a poem in which a character speaks directly to one or more listeners. The words are being spoken by a man named Prufrock.

In a dramatic monologue we must learn everything about the setting, the situation, the other characters, and the personality of the speaker through what the speaker tells us. Sometimes Prufrock's line of reasoning is interrupted by an unexpected thought. You will often have to supply the missing connections in the speaker's stream of thoughts and associations.

A **dramatic monologue** is a poem in which a character speaks directly to one or more listeners.

*For more on Dramatic Monologue, see the Handbook of Literary and Historical Terms.*

### Reading Skills
#### Identifying Main Ideas

Read the poem through twice. The first time, aim for a general sense of Prufrock's thoughts. As you read the poem again, write down examples of how his thoughts reflect the following ideas about his own time (the poem was published in 1915, during World War I) and perhaps about our time as well: (1) people are spiritually empty, and (2) contemporary life is unromantic and unheroic.

**SKILLS FOCUS**

**Literary Skills**
Understand dramatic monologue.

**Reading Skills**
Identify main ideas.

**INTERNET**

**More About T. S. Eliot**

Keyword: LE7 11-5

# THE LOVE SONG OF J. ALFRED PRUFROCK

## T. S. Eliot

*T. S. Eliot (1930) by Powys Evans.*

*S'io credessi che mia risposta fosse*
*a persona che mai tornasse al mondo,*
*questa fiamma staria senza più scosse.*
*Ma per ciò che giammai di questo fondo*
*non tornò vivo alcun, s'i'odo il vero,*
*senza tema d'infamia ti rispondo.*

Let us go then, you and I,
When the evening is spread out against the sky
Like a patient etherized upon a table;
Let us go, through certain half-deserted streets,
5   The muttering retreats
Of restless nights in one-night cheap hotels
And sawdust restaurants with oyster-shells:
Streets that follow like a tedious argument
Of insidious intent
10   To lead you to an overwhelming question . . .
Oh, do not ask, "What is it?"
Let us go and make our visit.

In the room the women come and go
Talking of Michelangelo.°

**Epigraph.** This quotation is from Dante's epic poem *The Divine Comedy* (1321). The speaker is Guido da Montefeltro, a man sent to Hell for dispensing evil advice. He speaks from a flame that quivers when he talks: "If I thought my answer were to one who ever could return to the world, this flame should shake no more; but since none ever did return alive from this depth, if what I hear be true, without fear of infamy I answer this" (*Inferno*, Canto 27, lines 61–66). Think of Prufrock as speaking from his own personal hell.

**3.** *What is the evening compared to?*

**7.** *Where does the speaker want to take his companion? Whom could he be talking to?*

**14. Michelangelo:** Michelangelo Buonarroti (1475–1564), a great artist of the Italian Renaissance.

15 The yellow fog that rubs its back upon the window-panes,
The yellow smoke that rubs its muzzle on the window-panes,
Licked its tongue into the corners of the evening,
Lingered upon the pools that stand in drains,
Let fall upon its back the soot that falls from chimneys,
20 Slipped by the terrace, made a sudden leap,
And seeing that it was a soft October night,
Curled once about the house, and fell asleep.

And indeed there will be time
For the yellow smoke that slides along the street
25 Rubbing its back upon the window-panes;
There will be time, there will be time
To prepare a face to meet the faces that you meet;
There will be time to murder and create,
And time for all the works and days of hands
30 That lift and drop a question on your plate;
Time for you and time for me,
And time yet for a hundred indecisions,
And for a hundred visions and revisions,
Before the taking of a toast and tea.

35 In the room the women come and go
Talking of Michelangelo.

And indeed there will be time
To wonder, "Do I dare?" and, "Do I dare?"
Time to turn back and descend the stair,
40 With a bald spot in the middle of my hair—
(They will say: "How his hair is growing thin!")
My morning coat, my collar mounting firmly to the chin,
My necktie rich and modest, but asserted by a simple pin—
(They will say: "But how his arms and legs are thin!")
45 Do I dare
Disturb the universe?
In a minute there is time
For decisions and revisions which a minute will reverse.

For I have known them all already, known them all—
50 Have known the evenings, mornings, afternoons,
I have measured out my life with coffee spoons;
I know the voices dying with a dying fall°
Beneath the music from a farther room.
        So how should I presume?

**?** **22.** *What details of this setting are you given?*

**?** **27.** *How would you paraphrase this line?*

**?** **34.** *What words are repeated in this stanza for poetic effect?*

**?** **38.** *What could he want to dare to do?*

**?** **41.** *Who are "they"?*

**?** **42.** *A morning coat is formal daytime dress for men. What does Prufrock look like? Is he young, middle-aged, or elderly?*

**?** **51.** *Has a life that is measured in coffee spoons been exciting or heroic?*

**52. dying fall:** in music, notes that fade away.

55    And I have known the eyes already, known them all—
        The eyes that fix you in a formulated° phrase,
        And when I am formulated, sprawling on a pin,
        When I am pinned and wriggling on the wall,
        Then how should I begin
60    To spit out all the butt-ends of my days and ways?
            And how should I presume?

        And I have known the arms already, known them all—
        Arms that are braceleted and white and bare
        (But in the lamplight, downed with light brown hair!)
65    Is it perfume from a dress
        That makes me so digress?
        Arms that lie along a table, or wrap about a shawl.
           And should I then presume?
           And how should I begin?

            ·    ·    ·    ·

70    Shall I say, I have gone at dusk through narrow streets
        And watched the smoke that rises from the pipes
        Of lonely men in shirt-sleeves, leaning out of windows? . . .

        I should have been a pair of ragged claws
        Scuttling across the floors of silent seas.

            ·    ·    ·    ·

75    And the afternoon, the evening, sleeps so peacefully!
        Smoothed by long fingers,
        Asleep . . . tired . . . or it malingers,
        Stretched on the floor, here beside you and me.
        Should I, after tea and cakes and ices,
80    Have the strength to force the moment to its crisis?
        But though I have wept and fasted, wept and prayed,
        Though I have seen my head (grown slightly bald)
            brought in upon a platter,°
        I am no prophet—and here's no great matter;
        I have seen the moment of my greatness flicker,
        And I have seen the eternal Footman hold my coat,
85          and snicker,
        And in short, I was afraid.

        And would it have been worth it, after all,
        After the cups, the marmalade, the tea,
        Among the porcelain, among some talk of you and me,
90    Would it have been worth while,
        To have bitten off the matter with a smile,
        To have squeezed the universe into a ball
        To roll it towards some overwhelming question,

**56. formulated** *v.* used as *adj.*: reduced to a formula and made insignificant.

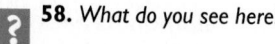 **58.** *What do you see here?*

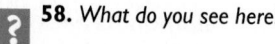 **60.** *What are his days compared to? Is this a positive or a negative image?*

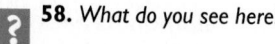 **72.** *What has Prufrock done in early evening?*

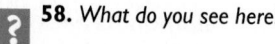 **74.** *What is the speaker comparing himself to here?*

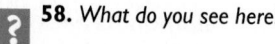 **77.** Malingers *means "pretends to be sick." How is this image of the evening connected to the one that opens the poem?*

**82. my head . . . a platter:** biblical allusion to the execution of John the Baptist (Mark 6:17–28; Matthew 14:3–11). The dancing of Salome so pleased Herod Antipas, ruler of ancient Galilee, that he offered her any reward she desired. Goaded by her mother, who hated John, Salome asked for John's head. Herod ordered the prophet beheaded and his head delivered on a serving plate.

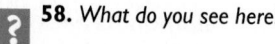 **85.** *The "eternal Footman" is death. What does this line tell you about Prufrock's confidence?*

To say: "I am Lazarus, come from the dead,

95   Come back to tell you all, I shall tell you all"—

If one, settling a pillow by her head,

    Should say: "That is not what I meant at all.

    That is not it, at all."

And would it have been worth it, after all,

100   Would it have been worth while,

After the sunsets and the dooryards and the sprinkled streets,

After the novels, after the teacups, after the skirts that trail

    along the floor—

And this, and so much more?—

It is impossible to say just what I mean!

But as if a magic lantern° threw the nerves in patterns on a

105     screen:

Would it have been worth while

If one, settling a pillow or throwing off a shawl,

And turning toward the window, should say:

    "That is not it at all,

110     That is not what I meant, at all."

    .   .   .   .   .

No! I am not Prince Hamlet, nor was meant to be;

Am an attendant lord, one that will do

To swell a progress,° start a scene or two,

Advise the prince; no doubt, an easy tool,

115   Deferential, glad to be of use,

Politic, cautious, and meticulous;

Full of high sentence,° but a bit obtuse;

At times, indeed, almost ridiculous—

Almost, at times, the Fool.

120   I grow old . . . I grow old . . .

I shall wear the bottoms of my trousers rolled.

Shall I part my hair behind? Do I dare to eat a peach?

I shall wear white flannel trousers, and walk upon the beach.

I have heard the mermaids singing, each to each.

125   I do not think that they will sing to me.

I have seen them riding seaward on the waves

Combing the white hair of the waves blown back

When the wind blows the water white and black.

We have lingered in the chambers of the sea

130   By sea-girls wreathed with seaweed red and brown

Till human voices wake us, and we drown.

---

**94.** *In the Bible a man named Lazarus is raised from the dead by Jesus (John 11:38–44). How do these lines connect to the opening quote from Dante?*

**98.** *What is he afraid would happen if he "squeezed the universe into a ball"?*

**105. magic lantern:** early type of projector that could magnify and project opaque photographs or book pages as well as transparent slides.

**110.** *Who do you think might say this to Prufrock? Is it the same person as in lines 97–98?*

**111.** *Hamlet is the hero of Shakespeare's tragedy about a prince of Denmark. What is Prufrock saying "No!" to?*

**113. swell a progress:** fill out a scene in a play or pageant by serving as an extra.

**117. high sentence:** pompous talk.

**119.** *How does Prufrock feel about himself?*

**121.** *The style of the time called for fashionable young men to turn up the cuffs of their trousers. What is Prufrock hoping for here?*

**125.** *If the mermaids do not sing to him, what will he miss in life?*

**128.** *What does he see here?*

**131.** *What breaks the romantic spell cast by the sight of the mermaids? What could "drown" mean here?*

# The Oddest Love Song

INFORMATIONAL TEXT

Of all the love songs ever written, this must be one of the oddest and most pathetic. The man who "sings" it has feelings but no one to share them with and ideas that are realized nowhere but in his own mind. Sensitive emotions and sophisticated thoughts do nothing to help him come to grips with the real world of the streets. He knows that life is "out there," but he also knows that he will never join it, and so he takes refuge in self-dramatization and heroic fantasy. Yet the man himself is not pitiful. He has sufficient knowledge of himself to control his longings and enough of a sense of humor to portray himself as a victim without being victimized.

"I am not Prince Hamlet," he says; and yet, he shares with Hamlet a breadth of vision to see two sides or more of every issue and the inability to act decisively upon any of his insights. If, in the jargon of today, we'd ask, "What's his problem?" the answer might be "self-consciousness—the egocentric trap that keeps an extraordinarily sophisticated man from enjoying the pleasures of this world that simpler men and women pursue and embrace without a thought."

One way to read the poem is to think of it as a movie—scenes follow one another immediately, without the connections or transitions that a conventional writer would provide. Consequently, the poem is demanding. What it demands is that, in the absence of logical connections, the reader must make the *psychological* connections that underlie the poem's structure and content.

"Let us go then," says the speaker, and so invites us (or someone) to join him on a "visit." But, instead of going wherever it is he has in mind, we soon find ourselves observers in the course of the man's search. Our companion seems to be looking for answers to the meaning of life and the nature of romantic love. He tries, without success, to find some place for himself even in the world he knows well. In line 10, we read that he has an "overwhelming question." But he impatiently brushes us aside before we can ask what it is.

Quick as a flash, we're confronted with something unexpected: women passing back and forth in a room and discussing Michelangelo, one of the greatest artists of all time. This little glimpse from the corner of the eye, so to speak, introduces an aspect of Prufrock's character that we'll find illustrated time and again. Focusing on one thing, he can't help thinking of something else. Everything actual has its counterpart in an image or a metaphor or a situation, by means of which Eliot can dramatize the dilemma of a man suffering a kind of emotional paralysis. As for the women who "come and go," they may be in an art gallery or in a museum or at a party or someplace else. The importance of their early and sudden appearance is to prepare us for the *method* of the poem. It is made up of a sequence of disjointed scenes that are psychologically related to the speaker's half-formed thoughts.

Time is a motif that recurs throughout the poem. Prufrock is conscious of time, and toward the end of his "love song," he makes his preoccupation clear: "I grow old . . . I grow old. . . ." Oppressed by time, he makes fun of his own obsession with it when he says, "There will be time . . . for a hundred visions." This statement might make us think of a religious revelation and the promise of salvation. But only for a moment. Prufrock soon drops us back into reality by the workaday word *revisions*—as if he is suggesting that the grandeur of imagination could be edited with a blue pencil, and that this would all take place before teatime.

# Response and Analysis

## Thinking Critically

1. The *Critical Comment* on page 662 suggests that Prufrock has some kind of problem. Now that you have shared Prufrock's thoughts, how would you describe his problem?

2. How does the famous **simile** in lines 2–3 reveal that the speaker's mind or will is paralyzed?

3. What is the speaker inviting someone to do in lines 1–12? What is suggested by the **images** of the place they are going to travel through?

4. What does the name Michelangelo contribute in lines 13–14? What would be the effect if, for instance, the women were "talking of Joe DiMaggio" or "discussing detergents"?

5. In lines 15–25, we have one of the most famous **extended metaphors** in modern poetry. What is being indirectly compared to what? How many details extend the metaphor?

6. The self-consciousness of the speaker is nowhere more evident than in lines 37–44. What do you think he is self-conscious and worried about in these lines?

7. What does line 51 imply about the way Prufrock has lived? What other measuring devices would suggest a different kind of life?

8. What references to women does Prufrock make in the poem? How do you think he feels about women and his attractiveness to them?

9. How are the **setting** and people described in lines 70–72 different from those familiar to Prufrock? What might this experience with another segment of city life tell us about Prufrock?

10. In lines 73–74, the speaker creates a **metaphor** to dramatize pointedly his alienation from the rest of the world.

Can you explain why Prufrock thinks he should have been a clawed creature on the floor of the sea?

11. Lines 87–98 echo the widely heard complaint that a lack of communication between people is the cause of misunderstanding. What do you think Prufrock would like to tell people?

12. In lines 99–104, Prufrock considers giving another person a summary of his life and reaches a point of exasperation that seems close to surrender: "It is impossible to say just what I mean!" Why does Prufrock find it so difficult to express himself to others?

13. Identify the brilliant visual **metaphor** in line 105. How does it relate to the rest of the poem? How does the speaker think people will respond to his "exposure"?

14. Read lines 120–125 closely. Explain how the speaker sees his role in life. Do you think he has overcome his doubts?

15. How would you characterize someone who worries about the part in his hair and about what he should dare to eat (line 122)?

SKILLS FOCUS

**Literary Skills**
Analyze dramatic monologue.
Analyze rhythm, rhymes, and metaphors.

**Reading Skills**
Identify main ideas.

**Writing Skills**
Write a dramatic monologue.
Write an analysis of a poem. Write an essay comparing and contrasting two texts.

I SHOULD HAVE BEEN A PAIR OF RAGGED CLAWS SCUTTLING ACROSS THE FLOORS OF SILENT SEAS.

go.
hrw
.com

**INTERNET**

Projects and Activities

Keyword: LE7 11-5

16. In lines 125–128, the speaker thinks that the mermaids are indifferent to him, yet he is held by this romantic vision. Why might he be so fascinated by these mythological creatures, and what might they represent for him? Why does he believe they will not sing to him?

17. By means of **paraphrase,** restate the meaning of lines 129–131. When "human voices wake us," what do we "drown" in?

18. Think about this poem as a journey, a quest that begins with an invitation to join the man who makes it. In your opinion, what has the journey led us to?

### Extending and Evaluating

19. Why might Eliot have called this a love song? If you were titling it, would you keep "love song" or use some other phrase?

## WRITING

### "Let Us Go Then . . ."

Write a **dramatic monologue** spoken by someone who wants to invite another person to go somewhere. Let your monologue reflect the random process of the speaker's thoughts. Try to find images that suggest the speaker's feelings and states of mind. Open with Eliot's words: "Let us go then, you and I."

### Analyzing Themes

This poem was published in 1915. How does Prufrock's love song reflect certain themes that characterize his own times? In a brief **analysis,** show how the poem reflects the following themes:

- People are spiritually empty.
- Contemporary life is unromantic and offers no opportunities for heroism.

Be sure to cite passages from the poem to support your analysis. At the end of your essay, comment on whether the themes in "Prufrock" connect to our times. Do you think that people today are spiritually empty? Does modern life offer no opportunities for

heroism? Be specific in your analysis, and offer examples from life as you know it to support your opinions. Be sure to check your reading notes before you write your response.

▶ Use "Analyzing Literature," pages 739–740, for help with this assignment.

### Comparing Texts

How do Prufrock's anxieties and uncertainties compare with those expressed by another famous character in twentieth-century poetry, Miniver Cheevy? What advice would the optimistic nineteenth-century philosopher Ralph Waldo Emerson give Prufrock? Write an **essay** in which you either compare Prufrock with Miniver Cheevy (page 590) or contrast Prufrock's paralysis with Emerson's rousing advice in "Self-Reliance" (page 209). Be sure to cite passages from each text in your essay.

### Language and Style

### Analyzing Rhythm, Rhymes, and Metaphors

"No *vers* [verse] is *libre* [free] for the man who wants to do a good job," Eliot once remarked. Though Eliot's poem is written in free verse (page 647), it makes use of rhythm, rhyme, and of course, figurative language.

- Re-read the first stanza, and identify the lines that conform to a particular **metrical pattern.**
- How does repetition in the first thirty-six lines help create **rhythm** in the poem?
- How many **end rhymes** can you find in the poem? How many **internal rhymes**?
- Make a list of at least five **metaphors** in the poem that you think are particularly original and memorable.
- Note the terms of comparison in the metaphors. Has Eliot based his comparison on items from modern life? Are his comparisons instead based mostly on elements from the world of nature?

# William Carlos Williams
## (1883–1963)

**W**illiam Carlos Williams was born in Rutherford, New Jersey, where he lived and practiced medicine as a pediatrician and obstetrician for most of his adult life. While studying medicine at the University of Pennsylvania, he came in contact with Ezra Pound (page 648). Pound's theories of imagism had a considerable influence on Williams's early verse, which was published in *Poems* (1909) and *The Tempers* (1913). During the next two decades, however, Williams went on to evolve his own distinctive poetic style, which he called objectivism.

Williams defined the source of his poetry as "the local," by which he meant a strict focus on the reality of individual life and its surroundings. Williams looked for a return to the barest essentials in poetry. In this respect he opposed such contemporaries as T. S. Eliot (page 655) and, to a certain extent, Pound himself in their frequent use of allusions to art, history, religion, and foreign cultures. (Williams and Eliot, in fact, made no secret of their dislike of each other's work.)

In addition to poetry, Williams produced novels, plays, essays, and several autobiographical memoirs. His influence on twentieth-century American poetry, especially since World War II, has been considerable, and he was awarded a Pulitzer Prize in 1963. His masterpiece is the long epic *Paterson,* a poem that appeared in five volumes over a twelve-year span (1946–1958). In this partly autobiographical epic, a poet wanders the neighborhoods of Paterson, New Jersey, an industrial town near Williams's home, and meditates on the variegated experiences of urban life.

In his insistence on local topics and colloquial speech, Williams was allying himself with the kind of poetic revolution championed by the English Romantics a century earlier. William Wordsworth, in his preface to the third edition of *Lyrical Ballads* (1802), had written that poetry should treat "incidents and situations from common life . . . in a selection of language really used by men."

Williams deliberately wrote in a spare, detached style about commonplace subjects, the very opposite of what many nineteenth-century American writers had thought of as poetic material. Using as his slogan "No ideas but in things," Williams wrote of such sights and events as animals at the zoo, schoolgirls walking down a street, a piece of paper blowing down a street, and a raid on the refrigerator. As Marianne Moore, an admirer, pointed out, Williams's topics are "American"— crowds at the movies, turkey nests, mushrooms among the trunks of fir trees, mist rising from a duck pond, a ballgame.

# Before You Read

## The Red Wheelbarrow
## The Great Figure
## This Is Just to Say

### Make the Connection

The imagists wanted to describe commonplace subjects just as they are. The imagist poets were very different from many popular poets of the nineteenth century, who believed that poetry should be about certain lofty, "poetic" subjects. Do you think there should be any limitations on the subject matter of poetry? What are poems written about today?

### Literary Focus
**Imagery**

**Imagery** is language that appeals to the senses. Most images create visual pictures, but they also can help us hear, feel, taste, or smell precisely what writers want us to experience. Imagery helps us to share, on a real sensory level, the writers' own perceptions.

> **Imagery** is language that appeals to the senses.
>
> *For more on Imagery, see the Handbook of Literary and Historical Terms.*

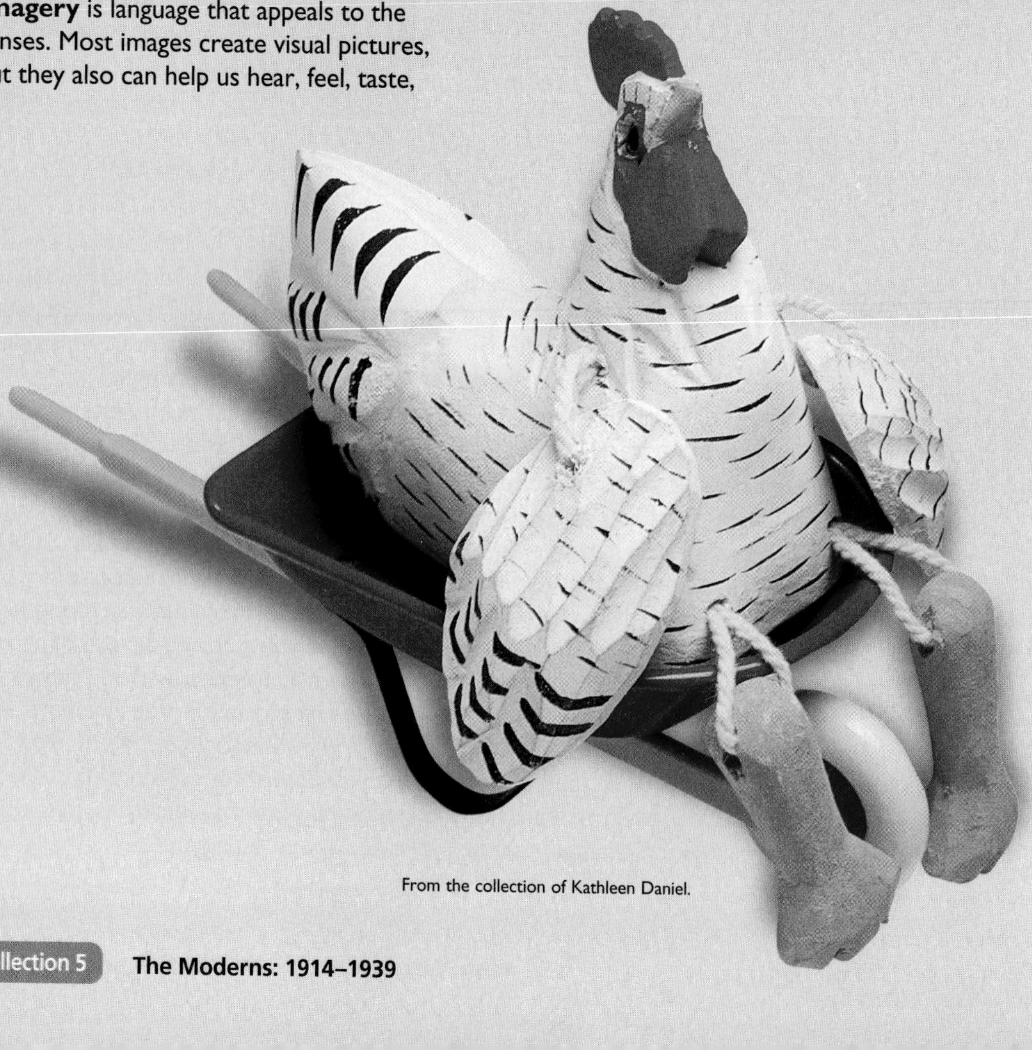

From the collection of Kathleen Daniel.

SKILLS FOCUS

**Literary Skills** Understand imagery.

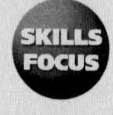

# The Red Wheelbarrow

## William Carlos Williams

so much depends
upon

a red wheel
barrow

glazed with rain
water

beside the white
chickens.

## So Much Depends

INFORMATIONAL TEXT

**W**illiams's "The Red Wheelbarrow" at first glance seems to be very slight. But it has proved to have the power that the ancient Greek inventor Archimedes spoke of when he said (to illustrate the principle of the lever), "Give me a place to stand, and I will move the world." Where William Carlos Williams stood was a place where ordinary things were *not* used as symbols or metaphors; they were simply ordinary things. The world he moved was the world of poetry. Before Williams, poets saw things not as things in themselves but as objects to be used (to be compared, to be endowed with symbolic meaning, or to be played with); in themselves things meant nothing.

How do we talk about this poem? When we consider analyzing it, where do we begin? Trying to answer these questions leads only to frustration. This poem is a composition of words so complete and simple that it denies all attempts to treat it as a poem.

And yet there is the temptation to ask what happens in the brief course of the poem that has made it so durable. It was, after all, not a typographical accident; it was composed, and as such it can be analyzed. But our analysis must be concerned with the modest premises of the poem; we must not attempt to give it meanings that it does not claim.

The first line contains a vague but enormously suggestive phrase that leads the reader to expect an answer. (*What* depends on *what*?) But except for the metaphorical lift of the word *glazed* in line 5, what the reader gets is only bare, flat reality—a moment captured as permanently as if it had been photographed. If the poem can be said to have some movement, some progress, from its first word to its last, it would be in what we call reverse action. Our yearning for what might be meant by "so much depends" is quietly checked by the simple beauty of what *is.*

# The Great Figure

## William Carlos Williams

Among the rain
and lights
I saw the figure 5
in gold
5  on a red
fire truck
moving
tense
unheeded
10  to gong clangs
siren howls
and wheels rumbling
through the dark city.

*The Figure 5 in Gold* (1928) by Charles Henry Demuth (American, 1883–1935).
Oil on cardboard. h. 35¹/₂, w. 30 in. (90.2 × 76.2 cm).

The Metropolitan Museum of Art, Alfred Stieglitz Collection, 1949 (49.59.1).
Photograph © 1986 The Metropolitan Museum of Art.

# This Is Just to Say

## William Carlos Williams

I have eaten
the plums
that were in
the icebox

5　and which
you were probably
saving
for breakfast

Forgive me
10　they were delicious
so sweet
and so cold

## This Is Just to Say

**W**hen William Carlos Williams first began to write poems like this, hardly anybody took him seriously. His lines had no meter and no rhyme, no simile or metaphor, none of the familiar elements of poetry at all except for imagery and a kind of rhythm that was entirely personal. He did not even use punctuation! But gradually readers and critics of poetry began to see that even a little note left on the refrigerator door can be poetry and that the simplest expressions of everyday life have their own special phrasing and a kind of spontaneity that is apt to be missing from more formal attempts to make them sound "poetic."

*Throwaway* is a term that was often used in the 1960s for poetry written not to be published and preserved but, like facial tissue, to be used and then tossed away. Behind this idea was the belief that poetry ought to be considered not literature but an easy part of ordinary existence. Emily Dickinson had the same idea a hundred years earlier when she would enclose a poem with the gift of a pie she'd baked or with a jar of preserves she'd put up or when a birthday or a holiday called for the kind of sentiments we nowadays find mainly on greeting cards.

Most greeting-card verse is trite because the people who are hired to write it use the same old words and rhymes over and over again. But little messages of affection or gratitude don't *have* to be trite. Both Dickinson and Williams have shown us that when our feelings are expressed honestly, we are all poets.

# Response and Analysis

## The Red Wheelbarrow
## The Great Figure
## This Is Just to Say

### Thinking Critically

1. Think about what Williams has in mind when he says, "so much depends upon a red wheel barrow." What might he be saying about poetry or art? Do you agree with him?

2. In "The Red Wheelbarrow," Williams focuses on an ordinary workday object. Are the subjects of "The Great Figure" and "This Is Just to Say" equally ordinary? Explain.

3. The painter Charles Henry Demuth (1883–1935) was so struck by the dynamic **imagery** in "The Great Figure" that he painted *The Figure 5 in Gold* (see page 668). What movement do you *see* in the painting? What do you *hear* in the poem itself?

4. What one word is used **metaphorically** to describe the fire truck as if it were a person?

5. How would the feeling of "The Great Figure" change if the colors were different? Try it and see.

6. Which one of the five senses does the **imagery** in "This Is Just to Say" primarily appeal to?

7. Whom do you think the speaker of "This Is Just to Say" is addressing? What response do you imagine he or she will receive, and why?

## WRITING
### As Is

Write a brief imagist **poem** describing some subject from your everyday life. Use sensory images to convey the sight, smell, sound, taste, and feel of what you are describing. Try to capture your subject exactly as it is, without using it as a symbol or giving it any significance beyond what it simply is. You might open with one of Williams's opening lines. (The first line of "This Is Just to Say" has been used in hundreds of other poems, many of them parodies or mockery of Williams's humble subjects and simple free verse.)

**SKILLS FOCUS**

**Literary Skills**
Analyze imagery.

**Writing Skills**
Write an imagist poem.

**INTERNET**

**Projects and Activities**

Keyword: LE7 11-5

# Marianne Moore
## (1887–1972)

**M**arianne Moore is remembered by many people as the woman who wrote a poem in 1955 celebrating the only World Series the Brooklyn Dodgers ever won. Moore spent almost half her life in Brooklyn, where she became one of the most famous supporters of the local baseball team.

She was born in Kirkwood, a suburb of St. Louis, Missouri. After graduating from Bryn Mawr College, outside Philadelphia, Moore worked as a teacher and a librarian and later served as editor of *The Dial,* a magazine that encouraged young writers. She spent a good part of her life caring for her brother and mother. When her mother died, Moore lost her best friend—and her toughest critic.

All the while, Moore was writing and publishing her poems in the prestigious journals of the time. By 1921, she was living in New York City and had just published her first collection of poetry, *Poems.* Among the literary celebrities in New York, she was easily identifiable by her antique capes and other nineteenth-century touches in costume.

Behind the costume, however, Moore was a serious poet of meticulous detail, clarity, and humor. Mixing with the literati did not mean that she endorsed their tolerance in matters of personal behavior or their embrace of anything in the arts that seemed new or bold or simply amusing.

In fact, the only thing modern about Moore was her poetry. Like a bird building an intricate nest, she carefully pieced together her poems by combining her own writing with quotations and excerpts from social-science and natural-history journals. It has been said of her that no one was ever more indebted to other writers for material and, at the same time, more original. Her poetry reflects some of the influence of the imagists, and it also makes constant use of the concrete in the tradition of William Carlos Williams. Williams himself assessed his colleague's achievement when he said, "The magic name, Marianne Moore . . . I don't think there is a better poet writing in America today or one who touches so deftly a great range of our thought."

Like the visual artists of the twentieth century, Moore was able to join apparently unrelated elements of what she observed and bring them into a picture with a single focus. In some of her poems, Moore works like a painter whose nervous strokes and jagged edges capture a hundred details in one moment stopped in time. What she says in one famous poem, "The Steeple-Jack," might apply to readers approaching her work for the first time: "It is a privilege to see so much confusion."

## Poetry

### Make the Connection
### Quickwrite ✏

Without knowing why, many people complain, "I hate poetry! I never understand it." In this poem, Moore directly and humorously explains the usefulness and characteristics of good poetry. Moore takes on the role of the critic, daring to set standards for poets and readers alike.

Before you read, jot down your thoughts about poetry. Be honest: What do you like about poetry? What don't you like?

**SKILLS FOCUS**

**Literary Skills**
Understand how imagery conveys meaning.

### Literary Focus
### Imagery and Meaning

The imagists believed that imagery alone could carry a poem's meaning. Their use of imagery was not merely to decorate, not merely to use a lot of sensory images to describe something. Instead, they wanted to find the exact image to describe the poet's perception in simple language.

### Background

Since the days of the Latin poet Horace (65–8 B.C.), poets have tried to explain what poetry is. Some poets have written poems about poetry, hoping to *show* rather than tell what the art of poetry is. Marianne Moore's "Poetry" and Archibald MacLeish's "Ars Poetica" (see the **Connection** on page 673) are in this tradition of poets writing about poetry.

# Poetry

## Marianne Moore

I, too, dislike it: there are things that are important beyond all this fiddle.°
  Reading it, however, with a perfect contempt for it, one discovers in
  it after all, a place for the genuine.
    Hands that can grasp, eyes
5    that can dilate, hair that can rise
      if it must, these things are important not because a

high-sounding interpretation can be put upon them but because they are
  useful. When they become so derivative° as to become unintelligible,
  the same thing may be said for all of us, that we
10    do not admire what
    we cannot understand: the bat
      holding on upside down or in quest of something to

---

1. **fiddle** *n.:* slang for "nonsense."
8. **derivative** *adj.:* based on the work of others; unoriginal.

eat, elephants pushing, a wild horse taking a roll, a tireless wolf under
    a tree, the immovable critic twitching his skin like a horse that feels a flea, the base-
15    ball fan, the statistician—
        nor is it valid
            to discriminate against "business documents and

school-books"; all these phenomena are important. One must make a distinction
    however: when dragged into prominence by half poets, the result is not poetry,
20    nor till the poets among us can be
        "literalists of
        the imagination"—above
            insolence and triviality and can present

for inspection, "imaginary gardens with real toads in them," shall we have
25    it. In the meantime, if you demand on the one hand,
        the raw material of poetry in
            all its rawness and
        that which is on the other hand
            genuine, then you are interested in poetry.

## CONNECTION / POEM

*Archibald MacLeish (1892–1982), an American poet and Moore's contemporary, reflects on the means and ends of poetry in the following poem. Ars poetica is Latin for "the art of poetry."*

# Ars Poetica

## Archibald MacLeish

A poem should be palpable and mute
As a globed fruit,

Dumb
As old medallions to the thumb,

5  Silent as the sleeve-worn stone
Of casement ledges where the moss has
    grown—

A poem should be wordless
As the flight of birds.

    •

A poem should be motionless in time
10  As the moon climbs,

Leaving, as the moon releases
Twig by twig the night-entangled trees,

Leaving, as the moon behind the winter
    leaves,
Memory by memory the mind—

15  A poem should be motionless in time
As the moon climbs.

    •

A poem should be equal to:
Not true.

For all the history of grief
20  An empty doorway and a maple leaf.

For love
The leaning grasses and two lights above
    the sea—

A poem should not mean
But be.

# Response and Analysis

## Thinking Critically

1. This poem suggests that someone has just made a remark to Moore. Whom do you think Moore is addressing in this poem? What **tone** does she take toward her audience?

2. According to lines 4–7, what kind of poetry does Moore like?

3. What kind of poetry, according to lines 8–11, does Moore dislike?

4. According to lines 20–25, what elements does Moore think "useful" poetry should have?

5. Moore says in lines 21–22 that poets must be "literalists of the imagination." What do you think she means? How is this idea related to her **image** of "imaginary gardens with real toads in them" (line 24)?

6. MacLeish's poem (see the *Connection* on page 673) also defines poetry, using a series of **similes.** List all the things MacLeish says poetry should be.

7. Some of MacLeish's **similes** are puzzling because they seem to be self-contradictory. For example, how can a poem, which is made of words, be "word-less"? How does MacLeish explain all his similes in the last two lines?

8. How do the two **images** in line 20 of MacLeish's poem suggest grief?

## Extending and Evaluating

9. Did Moore and MacLeish give you any new ideas about what poetry should be? (Review your Quickwrite notes before you answer.) Cite details from each poem to illustrate your evaluation (which may be positive or negative). ✏

## WRITING

### Poetry Is . . .

The most famous line in Moore's poem is the one that says that poetry should show us "imaginary gardens with real toads in them." Write your own **poem** about poetry. Use concrete images to illustrate what a poem is or can do. You may want to begin with the words "Poetry is . . ."

## LISTENING AND SPEAKING

### "Poetry" Reading

With a partner, take turns reading "Poetry" aloud. Pay attention to line and stanza breaks and to the placement of end punctuation. Note also the alternation of long and short lines. Decide where you would read quickly and where you would slow down for emphasis. Record or perform two or three readings for your class, and discuss with your audience the effects of the different readings.

Marianne Moore, a long-time Dodgers fan, tries out a boy's new baseball bat in New York City.

**SKILLS FOCUS**

**Literary Skills**
Analyze the way imagery conveys meaning.

**Writing Skills**
Write a poem with concrete images.

**Listening and Speaking Skills**
Deliver an oral interpretation of a poem.

**INTERNET**

**Projects and Activities**

Keyword: LE7 11-5

# E. E. Cummings
## (1894–1962)

*Self-Portrait* by E. E. Cummings.

**E**dward Estlin (E. E.) Cummings was born in Cambridge, Massachusetts, the son of a Unitarian minister. After a childhood spent within walking distance of Harvard, he attended the university at a time when French symbolism and free verse were major new influences on American poetry. Like other poets, Cummings found guidelines in the imagist manifesto that allowed him to experiment and to break old rules.

If there is such a thing as rugged individualism in poetry, Cummings may be its prime example. All by himself he altered conventional English syntax and made typography and the division of words part of the shape and meaning of a poem. And—in the age of celebration of the common person—he went against the grain by championing the virtues of elitism. "So far as I am concerned," he wrote, "poetry and every other art was and is and forever will be strictly and distinctly a question of individuality. . . . Poetry is being, not doing. If you wish to follow, even at a distance, the poet's calling . . . you've got to come out of the measurable doing universe into the immeasurable house of being. . . . Nobody else can be alive for you; nor can you be alive for anybody else."

Graduating from college in the midst of World War I, Cummings became part of the conflict well before American soldiers appeared on European battlefields in 1917. He volunteered for an ambulance corps privately financed by Americans and staffed by young men. Crossing to Bordeaux on a French troop ship threatened by German U-boats, Cummings had hardly begun his duties when a French censor, intercepting one of his typographically odd letters, imprisoned him on suspicion of espionage. Released within three months, Cummings drew on the experience to produce his first important book of prose, *The Enormous Room* (1922).

After World War I, Cummings returned to France. He was one of the American literary expatriates who found in Paris the freedom and inspiration they felt were denied them by the restrictive Puritan climate of their own country. During this period, Cummings refined the eccentric shifts of syntax and typography that would become his trademark. In 1923, he published his first collection of verse, *Tulips and Chimneys,* which was followed by *&* (1925), *XLI Poems* (1925), and *is 5* (1926). His poetry is often marked by jubilant lyricism as he celebrates love, nature's beauty, and an almost Transcendentalist affirmation of the individual. He reserved his mischievous wit for the satire of the "unman," by which he meant the unthinking, unfeeling temperament of urban "humans."

Back in the United States, Cummings split his time between an apartment in Greenwich Village in New York City and a house in Silver Lake, New Hampshire. He died still believing that "when skies are hanged and oceans drowned, / the single secret will still be man."

## what if a much of a which of a wind
## somewhere i have never travelled,gladly beyond

### Make the Connection

Have you ever been at a loss for words, unable to find the right way to express a deep feeling? Poets, too, search for ways of using language that will come close to conveying their complex feelings and thoughts. In a sense, therefore, a poem can be thought of as an attempt to put on paper what cannot quite be expressed in words. Think about what Cummings might be trying to say as you read the following poems.

**SKILLS FOCUS**

### Reading Skills
### Untangling Syntax

**Reading Skills**
Understand
syntax.

In all languages, words are arranged in certain ways in order to make utterances that are easily understood. The way words are arranged in a sentence is called **syntax.** Writers, particularly poets, in their search for fresh ways to express experience, sometimes experiment with syntax. Cummings is known for his unconventional syntax and usage (his punctuation is unorthodox, he uses parts of speech interchangeably, his spacing is such that sometimes words bump into one another). Reading his poems can be challenging. You may have to begin your reading process by doing something very basic: Look for where Cummings begins and ends his sentences. Then, look for the subject and predicate of each sentence. Once you have done this, half of your work will have been done.

# what if a much of a which of a wind

## E. E. Cummings

what if a much of a which of a wind
gives the truth to summer's lie;
bloodies with dizzying leaves the sun
and yanks immortal stars awry?°
5  Blow king to beggar and queen to seem
(blow friend to fiend:blow space to time)
—when skies are hanged and oceans drowned,
the single secret will still be man

what if a keen of a lean wind flays°
10  screaming hills with sleet and snow:
strangles valleys by ropes of thing
and stifles forests in white ago?
Blow hope to terror;blow seeing to blind

(blow pity to envy and soul to mind)
15  —whose hearts are mountains,roots are trees,
it's they shall cry hello to the spring

what if a dawn of a doom of a dream
bites this universe in two,
peels forever out of his grave
20  and sprinkles nowhere with me and you?
Blow soon to never and never to twice
(blow life to isn't:blow death to was)
—all nothing's only our hugest home;
the most who die,the more we live

---

4. **awry** (ə·rī′) *adv.:* out of place.
9. **flays** *v.:* here, whips; lashes.

## "Miracles are to come"

The poems to come are for you and for me and are not for mostpeople
—it's no use trying to pretend that most-people and ourselves are alike. Mostpeople have less in common with ourselves than the squarerootofminusone. You and I are human beings;mostpeople are snobs. . . .

you and I are not snobs. We can never be born enough. We are human beings;for whom birth is a supremely welcome mystery,the mystery of growing:the mystery which happens only and whenever we are faithful to ourselves. You and I wear the dangerous looseness of doom and find it becoming. Life, for eternal us,is now;and now is much too busy being a little more than everything to seem anything,catastrophic included. . . .

Miracles are to come. With you I leave a remembrance of miracles:they are by somebody who can love and who shall be continually reborn,a human being;somebody who said to those near him,when his fingers would not hold a brush "tie it into my hand"—

—from *New Poems*

# somewhere i have never travelled,gladly beyond

## E. E. Cummings

somewhere i have never travelled,gladly beyond
any experience,your eyes have their silence:
in your most frail gesture are things which enclose me,
or which i cannot touch because they are too near

5    your slightest look easily will unclose me
though i have closed myself as fingers,
you open always petal by petal myself as Spring opens
(touching skilfully,mysteriously)her first rose

or if your wish be to close me,i and
10   my life will shut very beautifully,suddenly,
as when the heart of this flower imagines
the snow carefully everywhere descending;

nothing which we are to perceive in this world equals
the power of your intense fragility:whose texture
15   compels me with the colour of its countries,
rendering death and forever with each breathing

(i do not know what it is about you that closes
and opens;only something in me understands
the voice of your eyes is deeper than all roses)
20   nobody,not even the rain,has such small hands

*The Kiss (Der Kuss)* (1907–1908) by Gustav Klimt.

Oesterreichische Galerie, Vienna, Austria. Courtesy Erich Lessing/Art Resource, NY.

# Response and Analysis

## what if a much . . .

### Thinking Critically

1. Cummings opens each stanza with a question. What are the questions? What are the answers?

2. What are the three kinds of mass destruction that Cummings refers to in the first six lines of each stanza?

3. What do you think Cummings means by the last two lines? Is he celebrating life or death? Explain your response.

4. Identify the **rhyme scheme** of the poem. Where do you hear **internal rhyme**?

5. What **tone** do you hear in Cummings's poem—is the speaker cynical, despairing, solemn, hopeful, triumphant, or something else besides?

## somewhere i have never . . .

### Thinking Critically

1. In the first three stanzas, what **figures of speech** does Cummings use to talk about how he feels about his love and how she affects him?

2. The poem rises in intensity in the fourth stanza. **Paraphrase** this stanza, making clear what you think the speaker means by "death and forever."

3. In line 2, the phrase "your eyes have their silence" is an example of **synesthesia** (sin′əs·thē′zhə)—the juxtaposition of one sensory image with another that appeals to a different sense. Where in the last stanza does Cummings use synesthesia again?

4. A **paradox** is a statement that appears contradictory but actually reveals a kind of truth. Find two paradoxes in the poem, and explain what they mean.

5. In what way could the rain be said to have small hands? What is the speaker suggesting about his love by using this beautiful and mysterious **metaphor**?

### Extending and Evaluating

6. Find examples in the poems of Cummings's unconventional **syntax,** or word order, and of words used in unusual ways. Do you think his linguistic inventions add to or detract from the effectiveness of the poems? Explain your evaluations.

## WRITING

### "for you and for me . . ."

In the comment called "Miracles are to come" (see the *Primary Source* on page 677), Cummings talks to you, the readers of his poems. Respond to Cummings in the form of a **letter** or **poem.**

### Images in Prose

Imagery is not limited to poetry. Prose writers also use imagery to make a setting or a person or an event vivid to the reader. Think back on the imagist poems you have read. Does one of them suggest a topic for a **descriptive paragraph**—in prose? You might find a topic just by thinking about the topics of these poems: a journey, a garden, a farmyard, a fire truck, plums in the refrigerator, wind, a person you love. Find a topic, and describe it in a prose paragraph. Descriptive paragraphs can be organized spatially: Where are the items located in space (front, back, side, and so on)? You can also organize a descriptive paragraph by order of importance: What is the first important thing you see, what is the second? Give your paragraph a good title.

▶ **For help with this assignment, use "Writing a Descriptive Essay," pages 679–680.**

# Writing a Descriptive Essay

The poets featured in this chapter were able to create vivid, unforgettable descriptions in just a few well-crafted lines. Like writing memorable poetry, describing a subject in an essay also requires the careful choice of details that add up to an overall impression. In this Mini-Workshop you'll write a **descriptive essay** that paints a vivid picture, helping your readers share an experience of a person, place, or thing that has been important to you.

**Choose a Subject**  A compelling essay doesn't have to describe a famous person or place. An everyday subject can be fresh, interesting, and dramatic when you choose precise details and vivid, descriptive words. Choose a subject that meets the following criteria.

- **The subject is very familiar to you.**  In other words, don't try to describe the Hoover Dam if you only rode over it in a car once. Instead, describe the small stream that flows through the woods near your school.

- **The subject holds some meaning for you.**  No matter how many details you might come up with for a subject, if you don't care about it, your readers won't either.

- **The subject has some complexity.**  Be sure you can say something fresh in your essay, either by choosing an unusual subject for your description or by choosing a subject with facets your readers might not have considered.

- **The subject is narrow.**  Pick a subject that you can examine closely in a 1,500-word essay. If you choose a large subject—a city, for example—you may not be able to describe it adequately. Instead, choose a small part of a large subject and describe this part in detail, such as one block, building, or park within a city.

**Note Details**  Observe your subject at length, and jot down notes about the following kinds of details.

- **concrete sensory details**—sights, sounds, smells, and textures

- **action details**—movements, gestures, or other specific actions related to the subject

- **details about changes,** including images that depend on specific circumstances (such as the time of day) and shifting vantage points of the subject (such as its appearance when viewed from a different angle)

    As you take notes, use **fresh, natural language** to describe the details you observe. For example, rather than saying, "The spider's web is

**Writing Assignment**
**Write a descriptive essay about a person, place, or thing that is important to you.**

**SKILLS FOCUS**

**Writing Skills**
Write a descriptive essay. Use sensory details.

difficult to see unless the sun hits it just right," you might say, "The spider's web is an invisible snare until a sunbeam catches the delicate fibers, making them gleam." The language you use to describe your details will set the **tone,** or attitude, for your essay.

**Make an Impression** Bringing your unique view of your subject to life is your **purpose** for writing your descriptive essay. To achieve this purpose, consider your **controlling impression**—the overall idea or feeling you want readers to get about your subject. Perhaps the most important thing about a beautiful downtown park is that it was a barren, dusty field before students helped with a landscaping project. A writer's controlling impression of this subject is the field's transformation for the better. The details and background information that the writer provides develop that impression.

As the **speaker** in your essay, it's your job to help readers, or your **audience,** see what *you* think makes the subject special. Even if several classmates describe the same subject, only your essay will share this unique perspective. Identify the controlling impression you want to create and choose the details for your essay, or the **form** your ideas will take. Then, write a statement of your controlling impression that prepares your audience for your ideas.

**Select and Elaborate on Details** To focus readers on a controlling impression of your subject, winnow the details down to the essentials. To decide which details to keep, answer these questions.

- Which details will help readers visualize the subject as you see it? Give readers the most important details so that they can imagine it through your eyes.

- Which details let readers know your feelings about your subject? Choose details that create the controlling impression you want—that your subject is forbidding or welcoming, pleasant or disgusting.

Delete any details that don't contribute to your controlling impression, and elaborate on those that do, clearly connecting each contributing detail to the statement of your controlling impression.

**Organize Your Ideas** Decide on the most effective arrangement of the details you will include. Most descriptions are arranged in **spatial order,** moving from left to right, top to bottom, front to back, or some other progression. However, because your description explains the subject's importance to you, you might instead arrange details in **order of importance,** moving from the least important detail to the most important detail or vice versa.

**PRACTICE & APPLY** Follow the preceding instructions to plan and write a descriptive essay about a person, place, or thing that is important to you. Then, share your finished description with your classmates.

> DO THIS ⟶

**SKILLS FOCUS**

**Writing Skills**
Elaborate on details. Organize ideas.

# Modern American Fiction

**Hemingway**

**Fitzgerald**

**Faulkner**

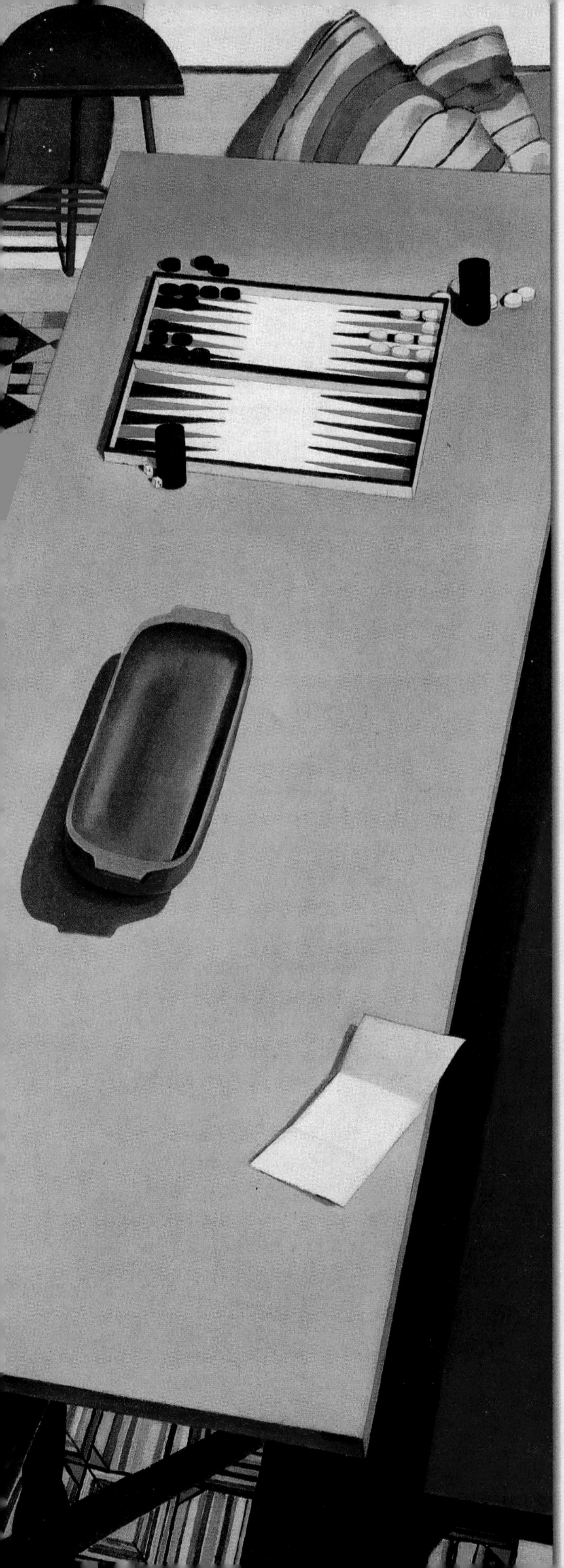

A writer's problem does not change. He himself changes, but his problem remains the same. It is always how to write truly and, having found what is true, to project it in such a way that it becomes a part of the experience of the person who reads it.

—Ernest Hemingway

go.hrw.com

**INTERNET**

Collection Resources

Keyword: LE7 11-5

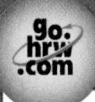

*Americana* (detail) (1931) by Charles Sheeler. (American, 1883–1965). Oil on canvas. 48 × 36 in. (121.0 × 91.4 cm).

The Metropolitan Museum of Art, Edith and Milton Lowenthal Collection, Bequest of Edith Abrahamson Lowenthal, 1991 (1992.24.8). Photograph © 1992 The Metropolitan Museum of Art.

# Ernest Hemingway
## (1899–1961)

**F**ew American authors have offered as powerful a definition of the twentieth-century hero as Ernest Hemingway has. Hemingway's fiction presents a strict code of contemporary heroism. His vision centers on disillusionment with the conventions of an optimistic, patriotic society and a belief that the essence of life is violence, from which there is no refuge. As Hemingway saw it, the only victory that can be won from life lies in a graceful stoicism, a willingness to accept gratefully life's few moments of pleasure.

Although this ideal of rugged machismo may now seem superficial, it powerfully affected generations of American readers. Moreover, Hemingway launched a new style of writing so forceful in its simplicity that it became a measure of excellence around the world.

Hemingway's life, like F. Scott Fitzgerald's, bore a notable resemblance to the lives of his fictional characters. He was born in the Chicago suburb of Oak Park on July 21, 1899. His father, a doctor, initiated him early into a love for the Michigan woods and the hunting and fishing that could be found there. Growing up, Hemingway boxed and played football devotedly, but he also wrote poetry, short stories, and a column for the school newspaper. Graduating from high school in 1917, just as the United States entered World War I, he yearned to enlist, but he was rejected by the army because of a boxing injury to his eye. He landed a job as a reporter for *The Kansas City Star.* Hemingway reached the war a year later as an ambulance driver for the Red Cross in Italy, but after six weeks he was wounded in the knee, seriously enough to require a dozen operations. This wound was a central episode in both Hemingway's real life and his creative

one. During his long convalescence in an Italian hospital, he fell in love with a nurse who became the model for the heroine of his novel *A Farewell to Arms.*

After the armistice in 1918, Hemingway returned to Michigan. His experience of coming to terms with the war is reflected in his story "Big Two-Hearted River." In the story, Nick Adams, a war veteran, camps and fishes alone in the woods, escaping from the world in order to heal himself from both a physical and a psychological shattering.

**An American in Paris**

In 1921, newly married and with a commission as a roving reporter for *The Toronto Star,* Hemingway set off for Paris. It was the era of the American expatriates, when writers and painters crowded the cafes of the Left Bank of the Seine. Here Hemingway worked at the craft of fiction and met other important writers, among them F. Scott Fitzgerald, James Joyce, and Ezra Pound. But most important, he met the American writer Gertrude Stein (1874–1946). She read all his work and advised him to prune his descriptions and to "concentrate." Hemingway took her advice and spoke fervently of writing "the truest sentence that you know" and of arriving through straight presentation of unvarnished fact at a "true, simple declarative sentence."

Hemingway's first book, *Three Stories and Ten Poems* (1923), along with *The Torrents of Spring* (1926), a parody of his friend Sherwood Anderson's work, drew scant notice. Then, late in 1926, he published *The Sun Also Rises,* a novel based on his life in Paris but transplanted to Pamplona, the Spanish town famous for its annual running of the bulls through the streets. The novel brought Hemingway widespread critical attention. Gertrude Stein's remark, "You are all a lost generation," was the novel's epigraph, and the book did reveal the postwar epoch to itself. Many readers of Hemingway's age embraced it as a portrait of their shattered lives.

Hemingway, around thirty years old and married for the second time, went on to write an even more powerful and successful novel, *A Farewell to Arms* (1929). This is the beautifully told story of Frederic Henry, a wounded ambulance driver. Disillusioned with the war, he falls in love with Catherine Barkley, an English nurse, and flees with her to Switzerland, where she dies in childbirth. Frederic's farewell to the dying Catherine is one of the great love scenes in fiction.

## Author and Adventurer

After the major success of *A Farewell to Arms,* Hemingway established himself as a worldwide adventurer, as though a heroic style was as important to his life as to his fiction.

During the early 1930s, Hemingway brought out two nonfiction books that revealed his fascination with bullfighting and big-game hunting—*Death in the Afternoon* (1932) and *Green Hills of Africa* (1935). In 1940, just as the literary world was writing Hemingway off as a has-been novelist, he presented another triumph, *For Whom the Bell Tolls.*

The outbreak of World War II drew Hemingway back into uniform. Although officially a correspondent, he gathered around himself a small army of adventurers. During one battle, Hemingway's band was sixty miles in front of the Americans' advancing line. When the Allies at last reached Paris in 1944, they found that Hemingway had already "liberated" the bar at the Ritz Hotel.

By 1952, Hemingway's celebrated literary accomplishments and his continuous pursuit of excitement and danger had made him as famous as any film star. In spite of his flamboyant exploits, he produced yet another widely acclaimed novel in that year, *The Old Man and the Sea,* which won the 1953 Pulitzer Prize. It tells of an old Cuban fisherman who hooks a giant marlin far out at sea and battles the fish for two days and nights. Although he finally succeeds in subduing the great fish and lashing it to the side of his boat, sharks tear at the carcass until the man is left with only the marlin's skeleton. The tale has been interpreted as Hemingway's metaphor for life: a vision of the hero weighed down by the years but still able to use his skill to taunt fate and so win a kind of victory from it.

In 1954, Hemingway won the Nobel Prize in literature. He now divided his time between his house in Ketchum, Idaho, and his restless travels all over the world: to Cuba, China, Venice, Spain, and Africa. His health deteriorated, and periods of elation alternated with episodes of severe depression. After a visit to the Mayo Clinic for treatment, he returned to Idaho. On the morning of July 2, 1961, he rose early, and with two charges of a double-barreled shotgun, he killed himself.

"He put life back on the page," wrote the critic Alfred Kazin, "made us see, feel, and taste the gift of life. . . . To read Hemingway was always to feel more alive."

## For Independent Reading

Try these famous novels by Hemingway:

- *A Farewell to Arms*
- *For Whom the Bell Tolls*
- *The Old Man and the Sea*

# Before You Read

## Soldier's Home

### Make the Connection

World War I was greeted as the "war to end all wars," and songs like "Over There" celebrated the heroism of hundreds of thousands of American soldiers who were shipped off to fight in the trenches of Europe. But advances in weaponry made the Great War (a name it held until World War II) devastating, both physically and psychologically. Returning soldiers sometimes couldn't readjust to life back home, which seemed to offer little they could relate to or believe in. As you can imagine, some became disillusioned, cynical, isolated, and overwhelmed by hopelessness. They became the most lost of Gertrude Stein's lost generation.

### Literary Focus
#### Protagonist: The Antihero

In literature the **protagonist** is the main actor in the plot, the one who initiates the story's action. The protagonist need not be a hero. In fact, the antihero is a type of protagonist who appears in much modern literature. The **antihero** contrasts with the hero archetype, or model, which appears over and over again in the traditional literature of many cultures. The traditional hero responds to challenges with courage and self-sacrifice. The modern antihero gives in to disillusionment, hopelessness, and inaction.

The **protagonist** is the central character of a work of literature. Heroes are protagonists, but not all protagonists are heroes. Some may be antiheroes.

*For more on Protagonist, see the Handbook of Literary and Historical Terms.*

### Reading Skills
#### Reading for Details

As you read the story, try to piece together a **character profile** of the returned soldier Harold Krebs. Take notes on Krebs's feelings, attitudes, and views on the war, his return home, his family, other people, his hometown, and his future.

### Background

Soldiers who returned home from World War I were often described as shellshocked —suffering from a mental and emotional condition of confusion, exhaustion, anxiety, and depression. In the past the condition— now termed *post-traumatic stress disorder*— was not well understood, and friends and relatives often found themselves at a loss. They could not understand why some soldiers seemed unable to plunge back into civilian life.

### Vocabulary Development

**hysteria** (hi·ster′ē·ə) *n.:* uncontrolled excitement.

**atrocity** (ə·träs′ə·tē) *n.* used as *adj.:* horrible; brutal.

**apocryphal** (ə·päk′rə·fəl) *adj.:* of questionable authority; false.

**alliances** (ə·lī′əns·iz) *n. pl.:* close associations entered into for mutual benefit.

**intrigue** (in′trēg′) *n.:* scheming; plotting.

(Pages 685–687) Photographs of Ernest Hemingway in Italy and France during World War I (1918).

# Soldier's Home

## Ernest Hemingway

Krebs went to the war from a Methodist college in Kansas. There is a picture which shows him among his fraternity brothers, all of them wearing exactly the same height and style collar. He enlisted in the Marines in 1917 and did not return to the United States until the second division returned from the Rhine[1] in the summer of 1919.

There is a picture which shows him on the Rhine with two German girls and another corporal. Krebs and the corporal look too big for their uniforms. The German girls are not beautiful. The Rhine does not show in the picture.

By the time Krebs returned to his home town in Oklahoma the greeting of heroes was over.

He came back much too late. The men from the town who had been drafted had all been welcomed elaborately on their return. There had been a great deal of hysteria. Now the reaction had set in. People seemed to think it was rather ridiculous for Krebs to be getting back so late, years after the war was over.

At first Krebs, who had been at Belleau Wood, Soissons, the Champagne, St. Mihiel and in the Argonne[2] did not want to talk about the war at all. Later he felt the need to talk but no one

---

1. **Rhine:** river that flows through Germany toward the North Sea.

2. **Belleau** (be·lō′) **Wood . . . Argonne** (är′gän′): sites of World War I battles that demonstrated the Allies' superior strength against the Germans.

**Vocabulary**
**hysteria** (hi·ster′ē·ə) *n.:* uncontrolled excitement.

wanted to hear about it. His town had heard too many atrocity stories to be thrilled by actualities. Krebs found that to be listened to at all he had to lie, and after he had done this twice he, too, had a reaction against the war and against talking about it. A distaste for everything that had happened to him in the war set in because of the lies he had told. All of the times that had been able to make him feel cool and clear inside himself when he thought of them; the times so long back when he had done the one thing, the only thing for a man to do, easily and naturally, when he might have done something else, now lost their cool, valuable quality and then were lost themselves.

His lies were quite unimportant lies and consisted in attributing to himself things other men had seen, done or heard of, and stating as facts certain apocryphal incidents familiar to all soldiers. Even his lies were not sensational at the pool room. His acquaintances, who had heard detailed accounts of German women found chained to machine guns in the Argonne forest and who could not comprehend, or were barred by their patriotism from interest in, any German machine gunners who were not chained, were not thrilled by his stories.

Krebs acquired the nausea in regard to experience that is the result of untruth or exaggeration, and when he occasionally met another man who had really been a soldier and they talked a few minutes in the dressing room at a dance he fell into the easy pose of the old soldier among other soldiers: that he had been badly, sickeningly frightened all the time. In this way he lost everything.

During this time, it was late summer, he was sleeping late in bed, getting up to walk down town to the library to get a book, eating lunch at home, reading on the front porch until he became bored and then walking down through the town to spend the hottest hours of the day in the cool dark of the pool room. He loved to play pool.

In the evening he practised on his clarinet, strolled down town, read and went to bed. He was still a hero to his two young sisters. His

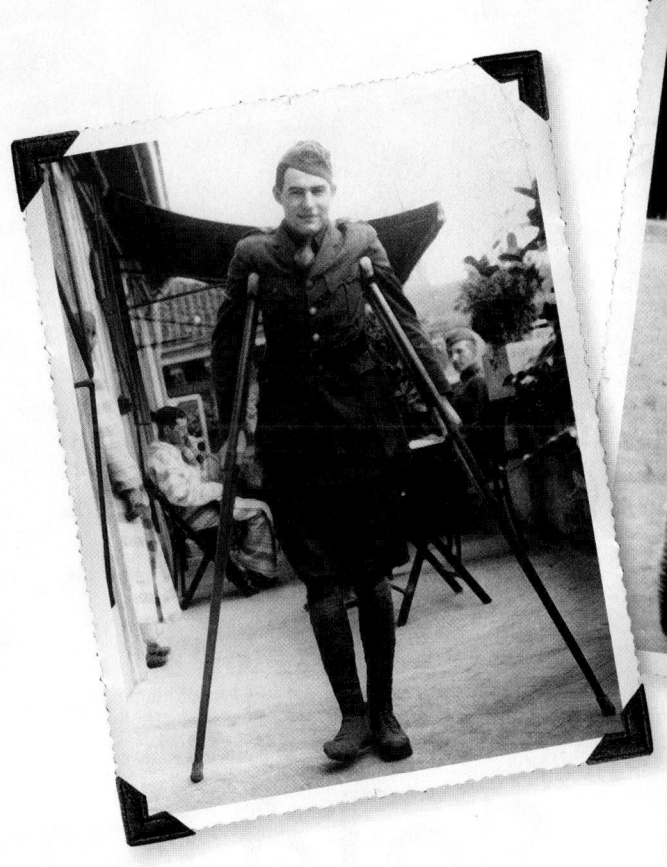

mother would have given him breakfast in bed if he had wanted it. She often came in when he was in bed and asked him to tell her about the war, but her attention always wandered. His father was non-committal.

Before Krebs went away to the war he had never been allowed to drive the family motor car. His father was in the real estate business and always wanted the car to be at his command when he required it to take clients out into the country to show them a piece of farm property. The car always stood outside the First National Bank building where his father had an office on

**Vocabulary**

**atrocity** (ə·träs′ə·tē) *n.* used as *adj.:* horrible; brutal.
**apocryphal** (ə·päk′rə·fəl) *adj.:* of questionable
authority; false.

the second floor. Now, after the war, it was still the same car.

Nothing was changed in the town except that the young girls had grown up. But they lived in such a complicated world of already defined alliances and shifting feuds that Krebs did not feel the energy or the courage to break into it. He liked to look at them, though. There were so many good-looking young girls. Most of them had their hair cut short. When he went away only little girls wore their hair like that or girls that were fast. They all wore sweaters and shirt waists with round Dutch collars. It was a pattern. He liked to look at them from the front porch as they walked on the other side of the street. He liked to watch them walking under the shade of the trees. He liked the round Dutch collars above their sweaters. He liked their silk stockings and flat shoes. He liked their bobbed hair and the way they walked.

When he was in town their appeal to him was not very strong. He did not like them when he saw them in the Greek's ice cream parlor. He did not want them themselves really. They were too complicated. There was something else. Vaguely he wanted a girl but he did not want to have to work to get her. He would have liked to have a girl but he did not want to have to spend a long time getting her. He did not want to get into the intrigue and the politics. He did not want to have to do any courting. He did not want to tell any more lies. It wasn't worth it.

He did not want any consequences. He did not want any consequences ever again. He wanted to live along without consequences. Besides he did not really need a girl. The army had taught him that. It was all right to pose as though you had to have a girl. Nearly everybody did that. But it wasn't true. You did not need a girl. That was the funny thing. First a fellow boasted how girls mean nothing to him, that he never thought of them, that they could not touch him. Then a fellow boasted that he could not get along without girls, that he had to have them all the time, that he could not go to sleep without them.

That was all a lie. It was all a lie both ways. You did not need a girl unless you thought about them. He learned that in the army. Then sooner or later you always got one. When you were really ripe for a girl you always got one. You did not have to think about it. Sooner or later it would come. He had learned that in the army.

Now he would have liked a girl if she had come to him and not wanted to talk. But here at home it was all too complicated. He knew he could never get through it all again. It was not worth the trouble. That was the thing about French girls and German girls. There was not all this talking. You couldn't talk much and you did not need to talk. It was simple and you were

---

**Vocabulary**

**alliances** (ə·lī′əns·iz) *n. pl.*: close associations entered into for mutual benefit.

**intrigue** (in′trēg′) *n.*: scheming; plotting.

friends. He thought about France and then he began to think about Germany. On the whole he had liked Germany better. He did not want to leave Germany. He did not want to come home. Still, he had come home. He sat on the front porch.

He liked the girls that were walking along the other side of the street. He liked the look of them much better than the French girls or the German girls. But the world they were in was not the world he was in. He would like to have one of them. But it was not worth it. They were such a nice pattern. He liked the pattern. It was exciting. But he would not go through all the talking. He did not want one badly enough. He liked to look at them all, though. It was not worth it. Not now when things were getting good again.

He sat there on the porch reading a book on the war. It was a history and he was reading about all the engagements he had been in. It was the most interesting reading he had ever done. He wished there were more maps. He looked forward with a good feeling to reading all the really good histories when they would come out with good detail maps. Now he was really learning about the war. He had been a good soldier. That made a difference.

One morning after he had been home about a month his mother came into his bedroom and sat on the bed. She smoothed her apron.

"I had a talk with your father last night, Harold," she said, "and he is willing for you to take the car out in the evenings."

"Yeah?" said Krebs, who was not fully awake. "Take the car out? Yeah?"

"Yes. Your father has felt for some time that you should be able to take the car out in the evenings whenever you wished but we only talked it over last night."

"I'll bet you made him," Krebs said.

"No. It was your father's suggestion that we talk the matter over."

## A CLOSER LOOK: SOCIAL INFLUENCES

### The Decade That Roared

INFORMATIONAL TEXT

Harold Krebs finds his hometown much the same as he left it before the war, except for new styles in women's hair and clothing. He especially notices girls' short, bobbed hair—a style that had marked a girl as fast only a few years earlier, when he shipped out to the trenches of France.

**The flap over flappers.** Krebs was right on target. As the slick, sophisticated ads of the era show, nothing symbolized the decade after World War I so well as the flapper—a liberated young woman who cropped her hair into a cap-like shape, wore half the amount of clothing of her Victorian-era counterpart, and boldly wore rouge and lipstick. The flapper abandoned the confines of the corset and opted instead for loose, long-waisted dresses that ended at or above the knee. She showed off her legs in the new silk or rayon stockings that were affordable at every income level. And she kicked, shim-mied, and swayed in a wild, new dance called the Charleston.

**An era of excess.** Tired of war and dis-illusioned with political and social causes, city dwellers and even small-town residents yearned for fun and excitement in the Roaring Twenties. Millions of Americans purchased automobiles and took to the road on touring vacations. Consumerism grew by leaps and bounds, fueled by abundant advertising and easy credit plans. Popular entertainment filled people's leisure time: Commercial radio and the movies changed American life by forming a national mass culture. People devoured the sensational stories of the day—vivid reports of scandals, crimes, freak disasters, and sports exploits. Young and old alike reveled in learning details of the private lives of movie stars like Rudolph Valentino, writers like Edna St. Vincent Millay (page 151), sports figures like Babe Ruth and the American Indian athlete Jim Thorpe, and celebrities like the pilot Charles Lindbergh.

"Yeah. I'll bet you made him," Krebs sat up in bed.

"Will you come down to breakfast, Harold?" his mother said.

"As soon as I get my clothes on," Krebs said.

His mother went out of the room and he could hear her frying something downstairs while he washed, shaved and dressed to go down into the dining-room for breakfast. While he was eating breakfast his sister brought in the mail.

"Well, Hare," she said. "You old sleepy-head. What do you ever get up for?"

Krebs looked at her. He liked her. She was his best sister.

"Have you got the paper?" he asked.

She handed him *The Kansas City Star* and he shucked off its brown wrapper and opened it to the sporting page. He folded *The Star* open and propped it against the water pitcher with his cereal dish to steady it, so he could read while he ate.

"Harold," his mother stood in the kitchen doorway, "Harold, please don't muss up the paper. Your father can't read his *Star* if it's been mussed."

"I won't muss it," Krebs said.

His sister sat down at the table and watched him while he read.

"We're playing indoor over at school this afternoon," she said. "I'm going to pitch."

"Good," said Krebs. "How's the old wing?"[3]

"I can pitch better than lots of the boys. I tell them all you taught me. The other girls aren't much good."

"Yeah?" said Krebs.

"I tell them all you're my beau.[4] Aren't you my beau, Hare?"

"You bet."

---

**3. wing** *n.:* arm.
**4. beau** (bō) *n.:* boyfriend.

---

Charleston endurance contest (1926).

Crazes spread throughout the country—manias for the Chinese game of mahjong, six-day bicycle races, dance marathons, and even flagpole sitting. Jazz, one of the great African American contributions to popular culture, provided the exciting soundtrack to the era.

**The young rebels.** Women and men alike, more aware of modernist thought and the psychoanalytic theories of Sigmund Freud, called for new social freedoms. Young people rebelled against the tight moral codes and even the good manners of the prewar years. They scoffed at the prohibition on alcohol by inventing the private cocktail party. With the new availability of motorcars, people roared off to dances in places where no one knew them, where they could feel free of their inhibitions. Couples danced together closer than ever before, tangoing and fox-trotting cheek to cheek to the sound of the saxophone.

The twenties' emphasis on youth and openness is recognizably modern. At the time many Americans were shocked and outraged by what they saw as the deterioration of culture and values. The 1920s were a rowdy, roisterous time—a decade that roared.

"Couldn't your brother really be your beau just because he's your brother?"

"I don't know."

"Sure you know. Couldn't you be my beau, Hare, if I was old enough and if you wanted to?"

"Sure. You're my girl now."

"Am I really your girl?"

"Sure."

"Do you love me?"

"Uh, huh."

"Will you love me always?"

"Sure."

"Will you come over and watch me play indoor?"

"Maybe."

"Aw, Hare, you don't love me. If you loved me, you'd want to come over and watch me play indoor."

Krebs's mother came into the dining-room from the kitchen. She carried a plate with two fried eggs and some crisp bacon on it and a plate of buckwheat cakes.

"You run along, Helen," she said. "I want to talk to Harold."

She put the eggs and bacon down in front of him and brought in a jug of maple syrup for the buckwheat cakes. Then she sat down across the table from Krebs.

"I wish you'd put down the paper a minute, Harold," she said.

Krebs took down the paper and folded it.

"Have you decided what you are going to do yet, Harold?" his mother said, taking off her glasses.

"No," said Krebs.

"Don't you think it's about time?" His mother did not say this in a mean way. She seemed worried.

"I hadn't thought about it," Krebs said.

"God has some work for every one to do," his mother said. "There can be no idle hands in His Kingdom."

"I'm not in His Kingdom," Krebs said.

"We are all of us in His Kingdom."

Krebs felt embarrassed and resentful as always.

"I've worried about you so much, Harold," his mother went on. "I know the temptations you must have been exposed to. I know how weak men are. I know what your own dear grandfather, my own father, told us about the Civil War and I have prayed for you. I pray for you all day long, Harold."

Krebs looked at the bacon fat hardening on his plate.

"Your father is worried, too," his mother went on. "He thinks you have lost your ambition, that you haven't got a definite aim in life. Charley Simmons, who is just your age, has a good job and is going to be married. The boys are all settling down; they're all determined to get somewhere; you can see that boys like Charley Simmons are on their way to being really a credit to the community."

Krebs said nothing.

"Don't look that way, Harold," his mother said. "You know we love you and I want to tell you for your own good how matters stand. Your father does not want to hamper your freedom. He thinks you should be allowed to drive the car. If you want to take some of the nice girls out riding with you, we are only too pleased. We want you to enjoy yourself. But you are going to have to settle down to work, Harold. Your father doesn't care what you start in at. All work is honorable as he says. But you've got to make a start at something. He asked me to speak to you this morning and then you can stop in and see him at his office."

"Is that all?" Krebs said.

"Yes. Don't you love your mother, dear boy?"

"No," Krebs said.

His mother looked at him across the table. Her eyes were shiny. She started crying.

"I don't love anybody," Krebs said.

It wasn't any good. He couldn't tell her, he couldn't make her see it. It was silly to have said it. He had only hurt her. He went over and took hold of her arm. She was crying with her head in her hands.

"I didn't mean it," he said. "I was just angry at something. I didn't mean I didn't love you."

His mother went on crying. Krebs put his arm on her shoulder.

"Can't you believe me, mother?"

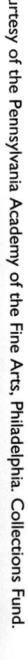

*East Wind over Weehawken* (1934) by Edward Hopper. Oil on canvas (34″ × 50¼″). Acc. no.: 1952.12.

His mother shook her head.

"Please, please, mother. Please believe me."

"All right," his mother said chokily. She looked up at him. "I believe you, Harold."

Krebs kissed her hair. She put her face up to him.

"I'm your mother," she said. "I held you next to my heart when you were a tiny baby."

Krebs felt sick and vaguely nauseated.

"I know, Mummy," he said. "I'll try and be a good boy for you."

"Would you kneel and pray with me, Harold?" his mother asked.

They knelt down beside the dining-room table and Krebs's mother prayed.

"Now, you pray, Harold," she said.

"I can't," Krebs said.

"Try, Harold."

"I can't."

"Do you want me to pray for you?"

"Yes."

So his mother prayed for him and then they stood up and Krebs kissed his mother and went out of the house. He had tried so to keep his life from being complicated. Still, none of it had touched him. He had felt sorry for his mother and she had made him lie. He would go to Kansas City and get a job and she would feel all right about it. There would be one more scene maybe before he got away. He would not go down to his father's office. He would miss that one. He wanted his life to go smoothly. It had just gotten going that way. Well, that was all over now, anyway. He would go over to the schoolyard and watch Helen play indoor baseball. ■

**Ernest Hemingway**      **691**

# Nobel Prize Acceptance Speech, 1954

**H**aving no facility for speech making and no command of oratory nor any domination of rhetoric, I wish to thank the administrators of the generosity of Alfred Nobel for this prize.

No writer who knows the great writers who did not receive the prize can accept it other than with humility. There is no need to list these writers. Everyone here may make his own list according to his knowledge and his conscience.

It would be impossible for me to ask the ambassador of my country to read a speech in which a writer said all of the things which are in his heart. Things may not be immediately discernible in what a man writes, and in this sometimes he is fortunate; but eventually they are quite clear and by these and the degree of alchemy[1] that he possesses he will endure or be forgotten.

Writing, at its best, is a lonely life. Organizations for writers palliate[2] the writer's loneliness, but I doubt if they improve his writing. He grows in public stature as he sheds his loneliness, and often his work deteriorates. For he does his work alone, and if he is a good enough writer he must face eternity, or the lack of it, each day.

For a true writer each book should be a new beginning where he tries again for something that is beyond attainment. He should always try for something that has never been

Ernest Hemingway (left) receiving the medal for the Nobel Prize in literature (1954).

done or that others have tried and failed. Then sometimes, with great luck, he will succeed.

How simple the writing of literature would be if it were only necessary to write in another way what has been well written. It is because we have had such great writers in the past that a writer is driven far out past where he can go, out to where no one can help him.

I have spoken too long for a writer. A writer should write what he has to say and not speak it. Again I thank you.

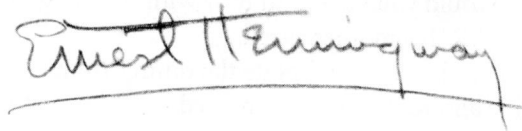

---

1. **alchemy** *n.:* magical power to transform the ordinary into the extraordinary. Alchemy was a branch of medieval science, one aim of which was to change common metals such as lead into gold.
2. **palliate** (pal′ē·āt′) *v.:* ease; lessen.

# Response and Analysis

## Reading Check

1. Describe the way Krebs spends his days.
2. What is Krebs's reaction to reading a history of the battles he fought in?
3. What makes Krebs decide to leave home?

## Thinking Critically

4. By the time Krebs returned, his hometown had quit "the greeting of heroes" and "the reaction had set in." What is this reaction? How does it affect Krebs?
5. What does Krebs mean by wanting "to live along without consequences"? Why might he feel that way?
6. What does Krebs's statement "You did not need a girl unless you thought about them" reveal about how he adapted to the hardships of war? How might such an adjustment affect his life at home?
7. Describe the **conflicts** revealed in the conversation between Mrs. Krebs and Harold at the end of the story. What losses on Harold's part does the talk reveal?
8. How would you state the **theme** of "Soldier's Home"—what does the story reveal to you about the way war can affect a young soldier?
9. How is Krebs an example of an **antihero**? How does he compare with the young **protagonists** of today's books and movies?
10. Ernest Hemingway himself was viewed as a member of the lost generation, scarred by the horrors of World War I. What details in his Nobel Prize acceptance speech (see the *Primary Source* on page 692) reflect the attitudes of a modern antihero?

## WRITING

### Krebs in Analysis

Write a **character profile** of Krebs, using the notes you took as you read the story. Be sure to support your analysis of Krebs with details from the story.

### The Tip of the Iceberg

Ernest Hemingway once remarked of his writing style, "I always try to write on the principle of the iceberg. There is seven-eighths of it underwater for every part that shows." In a brief **essay,** explain what you think he means, and use examples from "Soldier's Home" to explain the "iceberg principle." Be sure to answer the question: What parts of "Soldier's Home" are underwater?

### The Decade That . . .

On pages 688–689 is a description of the Roaring Twenties. Using this essay as a model, write a **description** of a recent decade that you know fairly well. Be sure to describe the following aspects of life in your decade: fashions; gender issues; popular entertainment; social and philosophical attitudes; and crazes, or fads.

---

## Vocabulary Development

### What If?

In a small group, discuss the possible outcomes of these scenarios:

1. What if hysteria spread through a crowd of fans at a rock concert?
2. What if an atrocity charge against the military were covered up?
3. What if an employer discovered that the work history on a résumé was apocryphal?
4. What if the United States were to pull out of all of its military alliances?
5. How could an ambitious person use intrigue to get ahead?

---

**INTERNET**

**Projects and Activities**

Keyword: LE7 11-5

# Grammar Link

## Avoiding Subject-Verb Agreement Problems: Making Things Match

One rule of grammar is that the subject and the verb in a sentence have to agree in number. Here are some situations in which it's not easy to tell whether the subject is singular or plural:

**The subject has more than one part.** If two or more subjects are joined by *and,* the verb is usually plural. If two singular subjects are joined by *or* or *nor,* the verb is singular. If both are plural, the verb is plural. But, if one subject is singular and the other is plural, the verb agrees with the physically closer subject.

PLURAL    Harold's father *and* mother **are** worried.

SINGULAR    His father *or* his mother **needs** to talk to him.

PLURAL    Neither Harold *nor* his parents **want** to talk about the war.

SINGULAR    Neither his parents *nor* his sister **understands** him.

**The subject is indefinite.** Pronouns that refer to unspecified people or things are called **indefinite pronouns.** Most such pronouns are singular (*anybody, anyone, each, either, everybody, everyone, everything, neither, no one, somebody, someone*); some are plural (*both, many, several*); and a few can be either singular or plural, depending on how they're used (*all, any, more, most, none, some*).

SOMETIMES SINGULAR    All work **is** honorable, according to Harold's father.

SOMETIMES PLURAL    All the other soldiers **return** to a hero's welcome.

**The subject is a group.** Nouns that name a group (like *audience, class, crowd, couple*) are called **collective nouns.** If the group refers to a unit, use a singular verb. If the group refers to its members as individuals, use a plural.

SINGULAR    Harold's family **is** not helping him with his trauma.

PLURAL    His family **are** the last people he would go to for help.

## Apply to Your Writing

Re-read a current writing assignment, and correct any sentences with subject-verb-agreement problems.

▶ **For more help, see Agreement of Subject and Verb, 2a–i, in the Language Handbook.**

**SKILLS FOCUS**

**Grammar Skills** Revise errors in subject-verb agreement.

---

**PRACTICE**

In each sentence, circle the subject, and choose the correct verb from the underlined pair.

1. Most of the heroes in Hemingway's fiction (is/are) wounded—physically, psychologically, or both.

2. Harold Krebs, who is the hero of one of Hemingway's stories, (returns/return) from World War I to his hometown in Oklahoma.

3. Neither his father nor his mother really (tries/try) to talk with Harold about his experiences during the war.

4. The crowd that he spends time with (has/have) heard many sensational war stories.

**Note:** *None* takes a singular verb if it refers to an amount (*none of it*) and a plural verb if it refers to individuals (*none of them*).

None of the water **is** left.

None of the dancers **are** here.

# F. Scott Fitzgerald
## (1896–1940)

If ever there was a writer whose life and fiction were one, it was F. Scott Fitzgerald. Fitzgerald—handsome, charming, and uncommonly gifted—was not only part of the crazy, wonderful, irresponsible era of the 1920s; he helped to name it the Jazz Age. He made a literary legend of it and, with his wife Zelda, lived it out in all of its excesses. He also almost certainly died of it.

### Early Failures—And a Smash Hit

Fitzgerald was born in 1896 in St. Paul, Minnesota, the son of a father with claims to an aristocratic Maryland family. Scott was named for an ancestor, Francis Scott Key, the composer of "The Star-Spangled Banner." His mother was the daughter of a rich Irish immigrant. The young Scott was a spoiled boy, a failure at schoolwork and—to his own great disappointment—at sports. But he was a success at daydreaming and, while still in his teens, at writing stories and plays.

At Princeton University, which he entered in 1913, he wrote one of the Triangle Club musical shows, contributed to a literary magazine, and befriended the writers Edmund Wilson and John Peale Bishop. When the United States entered World War I, in 1917, Fitzgerald left college for officers' training school, yearning for heroic adventure on the battlefields of France. He was never sent overseas, but in camp he began a novel, *The Romantic Egoist,* which was twice turned down by the publishing company Scribner's.

While he was stationed at Camp Sheridan in Alabama, romance of a different sort overtook him. He fell deeply in love with Zelda Sayre, a high-spirited and gorgeous woman whose escapades had scandalized her hometown of Montgomery. Like Scott, Zelda hungered for new experiences. She was sure of her appeal and felt it was bound to bring her a full measure of luxury and gaiety. Although Scott courted her persistently, he had not nearly enough money to offer her the kind of marriage she wanted, and at first she turned him down.

Now out of the army, Fitzgerald took a low-paying job he hated; he sent his novel, rewritten and retitled *This Side of Paradise,* off to Scribner's for the third time. In 1919, the company agreed to publish it.

"I was an empty bucket," he said of the experience, "so mentally blunted by the summer's writing that I'd taken a job repairing car roofs at the Northern Pacific shops. Then the postman rang, and that day I quit work and ran along the streets, stopping automobiles to tell friends and acquaintances about it—my novel *This Side of Paradise* was accepted for publication. That week the postman rang and rang, and I paid off my terrible small debts, bought a suit, and woke up every morning with a world of ineffable toploftiness and promise."

When it was published, in 1920, *This Side of Paradise* was a sensation. The old, prewar world with its Victorian code of behavior had been dumped in favor of a great, gaudy spree of new freedoms. Girls bobbed their hair and shortened their skirts while boys filled their flasks with bootleg gin. To the wail of saxophones, couples danced the Charleston across the nation's dance floors. In Fitzgerald's novel the Jazz Age had found its definition.

## Taking Aim at the American Dream

Zelda married Scott in April of that year. The newlyweds moved to New York and became the center of a round of parties while Scott turned out scores of stories. In the first years of the decade, he published two collections of stories and a second novel. After a stay in France, the Fitzgeralds returned to St. Paul, where their only child, a daughter named Frances, was born.

Scott announced to Maxwell Perkins, his editor at Scribner's, that he was going to write "something new—something extraordinary and beautiful and simple and intricately patterned." He fulfilled that ambition in *The Great Gatsby,* his nearly flawless masterpiece, which was published in 1925. It tells the story of James Gatz, a poor boy from the Middle West who dreams of success and elegance and finds their incarnation in a Louisville girl named Daisy Fay. When Gatz returns from the war, he learns that she has become Daisy Buchanan, married to a rich Chicagoan and leading a careless, sumptuous life on Long Island. The hero, now a successful bootlegger known as Jay Gatsby, hopes to win Daisy from what he believes is a loveless, unhappy marriage. The story ends with Gatsby's death, but we can see that his dreams and his feelings are admirable. The Buchanans, on the other hand, are insulated from life's possibilities by their wealth and self-indulgence.

The central triumph of *The Great Gatsby* is its revelation of the rich in all their seductive luxury and heedlessness, accompanied by an implicit condemnation of their way of life. In a remarkably concise work, Fitzgerald probed deeply the ambiguities of the American dream.

## An Epitaph for the Jazz Age

*The Great Gatsby* won some critical praise, but it was a financial disappointment. Fitzgerald had to work even harder to keep up with the high cost of his and Zelda's international lifestyle. He turned out more potboiling short stories and went to Hollywood to write movie scripts. In 1930, the tenth year of their marriage, Zelda suffered a mental breakdown and spent the rest of her life in and out of asylums. Hers was a search for both sanity and identity. She aspired to be a dancer and a writer and in 1932 produced her own novel, *Save Me the Waltz.* This was her thinly disguised account of her troubled marriage.

Scott's novel *Tender Is the Night,* published in 1934, was his rebuttal of Zelda's novel. Its hero, Dick Diver, is the protector and healer of the mad heroine, Nicole. However, the stock market crash of 1929 had put an end to Fitzgerald's era, and readers had lost interest in the problems of expatriates like Dick Diver. Still, the book displays Fitzgerald's hard-won experience of life, the commitment to early dreams, the self-destructiveness of charm, and a whole generation's craving for endless youth and irresponsibility. In its despair, *Tender Is the Night* is an epitaph for the Jazz Age.

It was Fitzgerald's epitaph as well. After its publication he struggled with mounting debts, failing health, drinking, and depression. When he could, he continued to do serious work. Through his love affair with Sheilah Graham, a British journalist, he grew interested in the work of the Hollywood producer Irving Thalberg and began to write a novel about him. He was at work on this novel, *The Last Tycoon,* in 1940 when he died of heart failure. *The Last Tycoon* was compiled and edited by his friend Edmund Wilson and was published to wide critical praise after Fitzgerald's death.

## For Independent Reading

Fitzgerald's American classic, *The Great Gatsby,* is available in many editions.

# Before You Read

## Winter Dreams

### Make the Connection

Have you ever met someone and thought, "That's the person I want to marry"? If you have had this thought—or if you ever do someday—you might find yourself facing the same kinds of problems that Dexter Green faces. In fiction as well as in life, what individuals hope and long for is not always what they get.

### Literary Focus
#### Motivation

**Motivation** refers to the reasons why characters behave as they do. Motivation can come from internal sources (ambition, insecurity, shyness) or from external factors (poverty, an ambitious parent, the crash of the stock market). In one-dimensional literature, motivation comes from a single cause. But in more sophisticated fiction, as in the complexity of life itself, motivation may come from many sources and is sometimes hard to pin down. In many stories, characters aren't even aware of their own motivation.

> **Motivation** refers to the reasons for a character's behavior.
>
> For more on Motivation, see the Handbook of Literary and Historical Terms.

### Reading Skills
#### Drawing Inferences About Characters

When you make an **inference,** you make an educated guess based on facts presented in the text and on your own life experience. As you read this story, jot down the inferences you make to answer these questions about the characters: How are Dexter's two ambitions—achieving material success and winning Judy's hand—tied together? What picture of Judy's character do you put together from what she says and does in the story? Why can't Dexter fully escape from Judy's magnetic charms?

### Background

This story is one of several that Fitzgerald wrote about the dreams and illusions that marked the Jazz Age. "Winter Dreams" was written in 1922, when Fitzgerald's stories were commanding top prices from *The Saturday Evening Post* and other popular magazines. The story opens around 1911, when fourteen-year-old Dexter is caddying for wealthy golfers, and it spans eighteen years of Dexter's life.

### Vocabulary Development

**elation** (ē·lā′shən) *n.:* celebration.

**perturbation** (pʉr′tər·bā′shən) *n.:* feeling of alarm or agitation.

**malicious** (mə·lish′əs) *adj.:* intentionally hurtful.

**reserve** (ri·zʉrv′) *n.:* self-restraint.

**petulance** (pech′ə·ləns) *n.:* irritability; impatience.

**mirth** (mʉrth) *n.:* joyfulness.

**divergence** (dī·vʉr′jəns) *n.:* variance; difference.

**turbulence** (tʉr′byə·ləns) *n.:* wild disorder.

**ludicrous** (lōō′di·krəs) *adj.:* laughable; absurd.

**plaintive** (plān′tiv) *adj.:* expressing sadness.

**SKILLS FOCUS**

**Literary Skills**
Understand motivation.

**Reading Skills**
Make inferences about characters.

**INTERNET**

Vocabulary
Practice
•
More About
F. Scott Fitzgerald

Keyword: LE7 11-5

# Winter Dreams

**F. Scott Fitzgerald**

Some of the caddies were poor as sin and lived in one-room houses with a neurasthenic[1] cow in the front yard, but Dexter Green's father owned the second best grocery store in Black Bear—the best one was "The Hub," patronized by the wealthy people from Sherry Island—and Dexter caddied only for pocket-money.

In the fall when the days became crisp and gray, and the long Minnesota winter shut down like the white lid of a box, Dexter's skis moved over the snow that hid the fairways[2] of the golf course. At these times the country gave him a feeling of profound melancholy—it offended him that the links should lie in enforced fallowness, haunted by ragged sparrows for the long season. It was dreary, too, that on the tees where the gay colors fluttered in summer there were now only the desolate sandboxes knee-deep in crusted ice. When he crossed the hills the wind blew cold as misery, and if the sun was out he tramped with his eyes squinted up against the hard dimensionless glare.

In April the winter ceased abruptly. The snow ran down into Black Bear Lake scarcely tarrying[3] for the early golfers to brave the season with red and black balls. Without elation, without an interval of moist glory, the cold was gone.

Dexter knew that there was something dismal about this Northern spring, just as he knew there was something gorgeous about the fall. Fall made him clinch his hands and tremble and repeat idiotic sentences to himself, and make brisk abrupt gestures of command to imaginary audiences and armies. October filled him with hope which November raised to a sort of ecstatic triumph, and in this mood the fleeting brilliant impressions of the summer at Sherry Island were ready grist to his mill.[4] He became a golf champion and defeated Mr. T. A. Hedrick in a marvellous match played a hundred times over the fairways of his imagination, a match each detail of which he changed about untiringly—sometimes he won with almost laughable ease, sometimes he came up magnificently from behind. Again, stepping from a Pierce-Arrow automobile, like Mr. Mortimer Jones, he strolled frigidly into the lounge of the Sherry Island Golf Club—or perhaps, surrounded by an admiring crowd, he gave an exhibition of fancy diving from the spring-board of the club raft. . . . Among those who watched him in open-mouthed wonder was Mr. Mortimer Jones.

And one day it came to pass that Mr. Jones—himself and not his ghost—came up to Dexter with tears in his eyes and said that Dexter was the—best caddy in the club, and wouldn't he decide not to quit if Mr. Jones made it worth his while, because every other—caddy in the club lost one ball a hole for him—regularly—

"No, sir," said Dexter decisively, "I don't want to caddy any more." Then, after a pause: "I'm too old."

"You're not more than fourteen. Why the devil did you decide just this morning that you

---

1. **neurasthenic** (nŏŏr′əs·then′ik) *adj.*: thin and weak, as though suffering from a nervous disorder.
2. **fairways** *n. pl.*: mowed parts of a golf course. The fairway of most holes starts at the tee and ends near the green.
3. **tarrying** *v.* used as *adj.*: waiting.

4. **grist to his mill**: something that can be used to advantage.

**Vocabulary**
**elation** (ē·lā′shən) *n.*: celebration.

wanted to quit? You promised that next week you'd go over to the State tournament with me."

"I decided I was too old."

Dexter handed in his "A Class" badge, collected what money was due him from the caddy-master, and walked home to Black Bear Village.

"The best—caddy I ever saw," shouted Mr. Mortimer Jones over a drink that afternoon. "Never lost a ball! Willing! Intelligent! Quiet! Honest! Grateful!"

The little girl who had done this was eleven—beautifully ugly as little girls are apt to be who are destined after a few years to be inexpressibly lovely and bring no end of misery to a great number of men. The spark, however, was perceptible. There was a general ungodliness in the way her lips twisted down at the corners when she smiled, and in the—Heaven help us!—in the almost passionate quality of her eyes. Vitality is born early in such women. It was utterly in evidence now, shining through her thin frame in a sort of glow.

She had come eagerly out on to the course at nine o'clock with a white linen nurse and five small new golf clubs in a white canvas bag which the nurse was carrying. When Dexter first saw her she was standing by the caddy house, rather ill at ease and trying to conceal the fact by engaging her nurse in an obviously unnatural conversation graced by startling and irrelevant grimaces from herself.

"Well, it's certainly a nice day, Hilda," Dexter heard her say. She drew down the corners of her mouth, smiled, and glanced furtively around, her eyes in transit falling for an instant on Dexter.

Then to the nurse:

"Well, I guess there aren't very many people out here this morning, are there?"

The smile again—radiant, blatantly artificial—convincing.

> There was a general ungodliness in the way her lips twisted down at the corners when she smiled, and in the—Heaven help us!—in the almost passionate quality of her eyes.

"I don't know what we're supposed to do now," said the nurse, looking nowhere in particular.

"Oh, that's all right. I'll fix it up."

Dexter stood perfectly still, his mouth slightly ajar. He knew that if he moved forward a step his stare would be in her line of vision—if he moved backward he would lose his full view of her face. For a moment he had not realized how young she was. Now he remembered having seen her several times the year before—in bloomers.[5]

Suddenly, involuntarily, he laughed, a short abrupt laugh—then, startled by himself, he turned and began to walk quickly away.

"Boy!"

Dexter stopped.

"Boy—"

Beyond question he was addressed. Not only that, but he was treated to that absurd smile, that preposterous smile—the memory of which at least a dozen men were to carry into middle age.

"Boy, do you know where the golf teacher is?"

"He's giving a lesson."

"Well, do you know where the caddy-master is?"

"He isn't here yet this morning."

"Oh." For a moment this baffled her. She stood alternately on her right and left foot.

"We'd like to get a caddy," said the nurse. "Mrs. Mortimer Jones sent us out to play golf, and we don't know how without we get a caddy."

Here she was stopped by an ominous glance from Miss Jones, followed immediately by the smile.

"There aren't any caddies here except me," said Dexter to the nurse, "and I got to stay here in charge until the caddy-master gets here."

---

5. **bloomers** *n. pl.*: baggy pants gathered at the knee, formerly worn by females for athletic activities.

"Oh."

Miss Jones and her retinue[6] now withdrew, and at a proper distance from Dexter became involved in a heated conversation, which was concluded by Miss Jones taking one of the clubs and hitting it on the ground with violence. For further emphasis she raised it again and was about to bring it down smartly upon the nurse's bosom, when the nurse seized the club and twisted it from her hands.

"You damn little mean old *thing!*" cried Miss Jones wildly.

Another argument ensued. Realizing that the elements of the comedy were implied in the scene, Dexter several times began to laugh, but each time restrained the laugh before it reached audibility. He could not resist the monstrous conviction that the little girl was justified in beating the nurse.

The situation was resolved by the fortuitous[7] appearance of the caddy-master, who was appealed to immediately by the nurse.

"Miss Jones is to have a little caddy, and this one says he can't go."

"Mr. McKenna said I was to wait here till you came," said Dexter quickly.

"Well, he's here now." Miss Jones smiled cheerfully at the caddy-master. Then she dropped her bag and set off at a haughty mince[8] toward the first tee.

"Well?" the caddy-master turned to Dexter. "What you standing there like a dummy for? Go pick up the young lady's clubs."

"I don't think I'll go out today," said Dexter.

"You don't—"

"I think I'll quit."

The enormity of his decision frightened him. He was a favorite caddy, and the thirty dollars a month he earned through the summer were not to be made elsewhere around the lake. But he had received a strong emotional shock, and his perturbation required a violent and immediate outlet.

---

6. **retinue** (ret″n·o͞o′) *n.:* group of followers or servants attending a person of rank.
7. **fortuitous** (fôr·to͞o′ə·təs) *adj.:* fortunate.
8. **mince** *v.* used as *n.:* prim, affected walk.

It is not so simple as that, either. As so frequently would be the case in the future, Dexter was unconsciously dictated to by his winter dreams.

## II

Now, of course, the quality and the seasonability of these winter dreams varied, but the stuff of them remained. They persuaded Dexter several years later to pass up a business course at the State university—his father, prospering now, would have paid his way—for the precarious[9] advantage of attending an older and more famous university in the East, where he was bothered by his scanty funds. But do not get the impression, because his winter dreams happened to be concerned at first with musings on the rich, that there was anything merely snobbish in the boy. He wanted not association with glittering things and glittering people—he wanted the glittering things themselves. Often he reached out for the best without knowing why he wanted it—and sometimes he ran up against the mysterious denials and prohibitions in which life indulges. It is with one of those denials and not with his career as a whole that this story deals.

He made money. It was rather amazing. After college he went to the city from which Black Bear Lake draws its wealthy patrons. When he was only twenty-three and had been there not quite two years, there were already people who liked to say: "Now *there's* a boy—" All about him rich men's sons were peddling bonds precariously, or investing patrimonies[10] precariously, or plodding through the two dozen volumes of the "George Washington Commercial Course," but Dexter borrowed a thousand dollars on his college degree and his confident mouth, and bought a partnership in a laundry.

---

9. **precarious** (pri·ker′ē·əs) *adj.:* uncertain.
10. **patrimonies** (pa′trə·mō′nēz) *n. pl.:* inheritances.

**Vocabulary**

**perturbation** (pʉr′tər·bā′shən) *n.:* feeling of alarm or agitation.

It was a small laundry when he went into it but Dexter made a specialty of learning how the English washed fine woolen golf stockings without shrinking them, and within a year he was catering to the trade that wore knickerbockers.[11] Men were insisting that their Shetland hose and sweaters go to his laundry just as they had insisted on a caddy who could find golf balls. A little later he was doing their wives' lingerie as well—and running five branches in different parts of the city. Before he was twenty-seven he owned the largest string of laundries in his section of the country. It was then that he sold out and went to New York. But the part of his story that concerns us goes back to the days when he was making his first big success.

When he was twenty-three Mr. Hart—one of the gray-haired men who like to say "Now there's a boy"—gave him a guest card to the Sherry Island Golf Club for a weekend. So he signed his name one day on the register, and that afternoon played golf in a foursome with Mr. Hart and Mr. Sandwood and Mr. T. A. Hedrick. He did not consider it necessary to remark that he had once carried Mr. Hart's bag over this same links, and that he knew every trap and gully with his eyes shut—but he found himself glancing at the four caddies who trailed them, trying to catch a gleam or gesture that would remind him of himself, that would lessen the gap which lay between his present and his past.

It was a curious day, slashed abruptly with fleeting, familiar impressions. One minute he had the sense of being a trespasser—in the next he was impressed by the tremendous superiority he felt toward Mr. T. A. Hedrick, who was a bore and not even a good golfer any more.

Then, because of a ball Mr. Hart lost near the fifteenth green, an enormous thing happened. While they were searching the stiff grasses of the rough there was a clear call of "Fore!"[12] from behind a hill in their rear. And as they all turned abruptly from their search a bright new ball sliced abruptly over the hill and caught Mr. T. A. Hedrick in the abdomen.

"By Gad!" cried Mr. T. A. Hedrick, "they ought to put some of these crazy women off the course. It's getting to be outrageous."

A head and a voice came up together over the hill:

"Do you mind if we go through?"

"You hit me in the stomach!" declared Mr. Hedrick wildly.

"Did I?" The girl approached the group of men. "I'm sorry. I yelled 'Fore!' "

Her glance fell casually on each of the men— then scanned the fairway for her ball.

"Did I bounce into the rough?"

It was impossible to determine whether this question was ingenuous[13] or malicious. In a moment, however, she left no doubt, for as her partner came up over the hill she called cheerfully:

"Here I am! I'd have gone on the green except that I hit something."

As she took her stance for a short mashie[14] shot, Dexter looked at her closely. She wore a blue gingham dress, rimmed at throat and shoulders with a white edging that accentuated her tan. The quality of exaggeration, of thinness, which had made her passionate eyes and downturning mouth absurd at eleven, was gone now. She was arrestingly beautiful. The color in her cheeks was centered like the color in a picture—it was not a "high" color, but a sort of fluctuating and feverish warmth, so shaded that it seemed at any moment it would recede and disappear. This color and the mobility of her mouth gave a continual impression of flux, of intense life, of passionate vitality—balanced only partially by the sad luxury of her eyes.

---

13. **ingenuous** (in·jen′yoo·əs) adj.: innocent; without guile.
14. **mashie** n.: number five iron (golf club).

---

**Vocabulary**

**malicious** (mə·lish′əs) adj.: intentionally hurtful.

---

11. **knickerbockers** n. pl.: short, loose pants gathered at the knees, formerly worn by golfers.
12. **fore** interj.: warning cry that a golfer gives before hitting a ball down the fairway.

She swung her mashie impatiently and without interest, pitching the ball into a sand-pit on the other side of the green. With a quick, insincere smile and a careless "Thank you!" she went on after it.

"That Judy Jones!" remarked Mr. Hedrick on the next tee, as they waited—some moments—for her to play on ahead. "All she needs is to be turned up and spanked for six months and then to be married off to an old-fashioned cavalry captain."

"My God, she's good-looking!" said Mr. Sandwood, who was just over thirty.

"Good-looking!" cried Mr. Hedrick contemptuously, "she always looks as if she wanted to be kissed! Turning those big cow-eyes on every calf in town!"

It was doubtful if Mr. Hedrick intended a reference to the maternal instinct.

"She'd play pretty good golf if she'd try," said Mr. Sandwood.

"She has no form," said Mr. Hedrick solemnly.

"She has a nice figure," said Mr. Sandwood.

"Better thank the Lord she doesn't drive a swifter ball," said Mr. Hart, winking at Dexter.

Later in the afternoon the sun went down with a riotous swirl of gold and varying blues and scarlets, and left the dry, rustling night of Western summer. Dexter watched from the veranda of the Golf Club, watched the even overlap of the waters in the little wind, silver molasses under the harvest moon. Then the moon held a finger to her lips and the lake became a clear pool, pale and quiet. Dexter put on his bathing suit and swam out to the farthest raft, where he stretched dripping on the wet canvas of the springboard.

There was a fish jumping and a star shining and the lights around the lake were gleaming. Over on a dark peninsula a piano was playing the songs of last summer and of summers before that—songs from "Chin-Chin" and "The Count of Luxemburg" and "The Chocolate Soldier"—and because the sound of a piano over a stretch of water had always seemed beautiful to Dexter he lay perfectly quiet and listened.

The tune the piano was playing at that moment had been gay and new five years before when Dexter was a sophomore at college. They had played it at a prom once when he could not afford the luxury of proms, and he had stood outside the gymnasium and listened. The sound of the tune precipitated in him a sort of ecstasy and it was with that ecstasy he viewed what happened to him now. It was a mood of intense appreciation, a sense that, for once, he was magnificently attuned to life and that everything about him was radiating a brightness and a glamour he might never know again.

A low, pale oblong[15] detached itself suddenly from the darkness of the Island, spitting forth the reverberate[16] sound of a racing motorboat. Two white streamers of cleft water rolled themselves out behind it and almost immediately the boat was beside him, drowning out the hot tinkle of the piano in the drone of its spray. Dexter raising himself on his arms was aware of a figure standing at the wheel, of two dark eyes regarding him over the lengthening space of water—then the boat had gone by and was sweeping in an immense and purposeless circle of spray round and round in the middle of the lake. With equal eccentricity one of the circles flattened out and headed back toward the raft.

"Who's that?" she called, shutting off her motor. She was so near now that Dexter could

> *The color in her cheeks was centered like the color in a picture—it was not a "high" color, but a sort of fluctuating and feverish warmth, so shaded that it seemed at any moment it would recede and disappear.*

---

15. **oblong** *n.:* rectangular figure longer than it is broad.
16. **reverberate** *adj.:* reflected; echoed.

see her bathing suit, which consisted apparently of pink rompers.[17]

The nose of the boat bumped the raft, and as the latter tilted rakishly, he was precipitated[18] toward her. With different degrees of interest they recognized each other.

"Aren't you one of those men we played through this afternoon?" she demanded.

He was.

"Well, do you know how to drive a motorboat? Because if you do I wish you'd drive this one so I can ride on the surfboard behind. My name is Judy Jones"—she favored him with an absurd smirk—rather, what tried to be a smirk, for, twist her mouth as she might, it was not grotesque, it was merely beautiful—"and I live in a house over there on the Island, and in that house there is a man waiting for me. When he drove up at the door I drove out of the dock because he says I'm his ideal."

There was a fish jumping and a star shining and the lights around the lake were gleaming. Dexter sat beside Judy Jones and she explained how her boat was driven. Then she was in the water, swimming to the floating surfboard with a sinuous[19] crawl. Watching her was without effort to the eye, watching a branch waving or a seagull flying. Her arms, burned to butternut, moved sinuously among the dull platinum ripples, elbow appearing first, casting the forearm back with a cadence of falling water, then reaching out and down, stabbing a path ahead.

They moved out into the lake; turning, Dexter saw that she was kneeling on the low rear of the now uptilted surfboard.

"Go faster," she called, "fast as it'll go."

> *"My name is Judy Jones"—she favored him with an absurd smirk—rather, what tried to be a smirk, for, twist her mouth as she might, it was not grotesque, it was merely beautiful . . .*

Obediently he jammed the lever forward and the white spray mounted at the bow. When he looked around again the girl was standing up on the rushing board, her arms spread wide, her eyes lifted toward the moon.

"It's awful cold," she shouted. "What's your name?"

He told her.

"Well, why don't you come to dinner tomorrow night?"

His heart turned over like the flywheel[20] of the boat, and, for the second time, her casual whim gave a new direction to his life.

### III

Next evening while he waited for her to come downstairs, Dexter peopled the soft deep summer room and the sunporch that opened from it with the men who had already loved Judy Jones. He knew the sort of men they were—the men who when he first went to college had entered from the great prep schools with graceful clothes and the deep tan of healthy summers. He had seen that, in one sense, he was better than these men. He was newer and stronger. Yet in acknowledging to himself that he wished his children to be like them he was admitting that he was but the rough, strong stuff from which they eternally sprang.

When the time had come for him to wear good clothes, he had known who were the best tailors in America, and the best tailors in America had made him the suit he wore this evening. He had acquired that particular <u>reserve</u> peculiar

---

17. **rompers** *n. pl.:* one-piece outfit with loose pants gathered at the knee.
18. **precipitated** *v.:* thrown headlong.
19. **sinuous** *adj.:* curving back and forth; snakelike.

20. **flywheel** *n.:* wheel that regulates the speed of a machine.

**Vocabulary**
**reserve** (ri·zʉrv′) *n.:* self-restraint.

to his university, that set it off from other universities. He recognized the value to him of such a mannerism and he had adopted it; he knew that to be careless in dress and manner required more confidence than to be careful. But carelessness was for his children. His mother's name had been Krimslich. She was a Bohemian of the peasant class and she had talked broken English to the end of her days. Her son must keep to the set patterns.

At a little after seven Judy Jones came downstairs. She wore a blue silk afternoon dress, and he was disappointed at first that she had not put on something more elaborate. This feeling was accentuated when, after a brief greeting, she went to the door of a butler's pantry and pushing it open called: "You can serve dinner, Martha." He had rather expected that a butler would announce dinner, that there would be a cocktail. Then he put these thoughts behind him as they sat down side by side on a lounge and looked at each other.

"Father and mother won't be here," she said thoughtfully.

He remembered the last time he had seen her father, and he was glad the parents were not to be here tonight—they might wonder who he was. He had been born in Keeble, a Minnesota village fifty miles farther north, and he always gave Keeble as his home instead of Black Bear Village. Country towns were well enough to come from if they weren't inconveniently in sight and used as footstools by fashionable lakes.

They talked of his university, which she had visited frequently during the past two years, and of the nearby city which supplied Sherry Island with its patrons, and whither Dexter would return next day to his prospering laundries.

During dinner she slipped into a moody depression which gave Dexter a feeling of uneasiness. Whatever petulance she uttered in her throaty voice worried him. Whatever she smiled at—at him, at a chicken liver, at nothing—it disturbed him that her smile could have no root in mirth, or even in amusement. When the scarlet corners of her lips curved down, it was less a smile than an invitation to a kiss.

Then, after dinner, she led him out on the dark sunporch and deliberately changed the atmosphere.

"Do you mind if I weep a little?" she said.

"I'm afraid I'm boring you," he responded quickly.

"You're not. I like you. But I've just had a terrible afternoon. There was a man I cared about, and this afternoon he told me out of a clear sky that he was poor as a church mouse. He'd never even hinted it before. Does this sound horribly mundane?"[21]

"Perhaps he was afraid to tell you."

"Suppose he was," she answered. "He didn't start right. You see, if I'd thought of him as poor—well, I've been mad about loads of poor men, and fully intended to marry them all. But in this case, I hadn't thought of him that way, and my interest in him wasn't strong enough to survive the shock. As if a girl calmly informed her fiancé that she was a widow. He might not object to widows, but—

"Let's start right," she interrupted herself suddenly. "Who are you, anyhow?"

For a moment Dexter hesitated. Then:

"I'm nobody," he announced. "My career is largely a matter of futures."

"Are you poor?"

"No," he said frankly, "I'm probably making more money than any man my age in the Northwest. I know that's an obnoxious remark, but you advised me to start right."

There was a pause. Then she smiled and the corners of her mouth drooped and an almost imperceptible sway brought her closer to him, looking up into his eyes. A lump rose in Dexter's throat, and he waited breathless for the experiment, facing the unpredictable compound that would form mysteriously from the elements of their lips. Then he saw—she communicated her excitement to him, lavishly, deeply, with kisses

---

21. **mundane** *adj.:* ordinary; everyday.

**Vocabulary**

**petulance** (pech′ə · ləns) *n.:* irritability; impatience.
**mirth** (murth) *n.:* joyfulness.

that were not a promise but a fulfillment. They aroused in him not hunger demanding renewal but surfeit[22] that would demand more surfeit . . . kisses that were like charity, creating want by holding back nothing at all.

It did not take him many hours to decide that he had wanted Judy Jones ever since he was a proud, desirous little boy.

## IV

It began like that—and continued, with varying shades of intensity, on such a note right up to the dénouement.[23] Dexter surrendered a part of himself to the most direct and unprincipled personality with which he had ever come in contact. Whatever Judy wanted, she went after with the full pressure of her charm. There was no <u>divergence</u> of method, no jockeying for position or premeditation of effects—there was a very little mental side to any of her affairs. She simply made men conscious to the highest degree of her physical loveliness. Dexter had no desire to change her. Her deficiencies were knit up with a passionate energy that transcended and justified them.

When, as Judy's head lay against his shoulder that first night, she whispered, "I don't know what's the matter with me. Last night I thought I was in love with a man and tonight I think I'm in love with you—" —it seemed to him a beautiful and romantic thing to say. It was the exquisite excitability that for the moment he controlled and owned. But a week later he was compelled to view this same quality in a different light. She took him in her roadster to a picnic supper, and after supper she disappeared, likewise in her roadster, with another man. Dexter became enormously upset and was scarcely able to be decently civil to the other people present. When she assured him that she had not kissed the other man, he knew she was lying— yet he was glad that she had taken the trouble to lie to him.

He was, as he found before the summer ended, one of a varying dozen who circulated about her. Each of them had at one time been favored above all others—about half of them still basked in the solace of occasional sentimental revivals. Whenever one showed signs of dropping out through long neglect, she granted

---

22. **surfeit** *n.:* discomfort resulting from excess or overindulgence.
23. **dénouement** (dā′nōō·mä*n*′) *n.:* final outcome.

**Vocabulary**
**divergence** (dī·vʉr′jəns) *n.:* variance; difference.

him a brief honeyed hour, which encouraged him to tag along for a year or so longer. Judy made these forays[24] upon the helpless and defeated without malice, indeed half unconscious that there was anything mischievous in what she did.

When a new man came to town every one dropped out—dates were automatically cancelled.

The helpless part of trying to do anything about it was that she did it all herself. She was not a girl who could be "won" in the kinetic[25] sense—she was proof against[26] cleverness, she was proof against charm; if any of these assailed her too strongly she would immediately resolve the affair to a physical basis, and under the magic of her physical splendor the strong as well as the brilliant played her game and not their own. She was entertained only by the gratification of her desires and by the direct exercise of her own charm. Perhaps from so much youthful love, so many youthful lovers, she had come, in self-defense, to nourish herself wholly from within.

Succeeding Dexter's first exhilaration came restlessness and dissatisfaction. The helpless ecstasy of losing himself in her was opiate rather than tonic.[27] It was fortunate for his work during the winter that those moments of ecstasy came infrequently. Early in their acquaintance it had seemed for a while that there was a deep and spontaneous mutual attraction—that first August, for example—three days of long evenings on her dusky veranda, of strange wan kisses through the late afternoon, in shadowy alcoves or behind the protecting trellises of the garden arbors, of mornings when she was fresh as a dream and almost shy at meeting him in the clarity of the rising day. There was all the ecstasy of an engagement about it, sharpened by his realization that there was no engagement. It was during those three days that, for the first time, he had asked her to marry him. She said "maybe some day," she said "kiss me," she said "I'd like to marry you," she said "I love you" —she said—nothing.

The three days were interrupted by the arrival of a New York man who visited at her house for half September. To Dexter's agony, rumor engaged them. The man was the son of the president of a great trust company. But at the end of a month it was reported that Judy was yawning. At a dance one night she sat all evening in a motorboat with a local beau, while the New Yorker searched the club for her frantically. She told the local beau that she was bored with her visitor, and two days later he left. She was seen with him at the station, and it was reported that he looked very mournful indeed.

On this note the summer ended. Dexter was twenty-four, and he found himself increasingly in a position to do as he wished. He joined two clubs in the city and lived at one of them. Though he was by no means an integral part of the stag-lines[28] at these clubs, he managed to be on hand at dances where Judy Jones was likely to appear. He could have gone out socially as

---

24. **forays** (fôr'āz) *n. pl.:* raids.
25. **kinetic** (ki·net'ik) *adj.:* coming about through action or energy.
26. **proof against:** able to withstand.
27. **opiate . . . tonic:** calming rather than stimulating.
28. **stag-lines** *n. pl.:* lines of unaccompanied men at a dance, waiting for available dance partners.

much as he liked—he was an eligible young man, now, and popular with downtown fathers. His confessed devotion to Judy Jones had rather solidified his position. But he had no social aspirations and rather despised the dancing men who were always on tap for the Thursday or Saturday parties and who filled in at dinners with the younger married set. Already he was playing with the idea of going East to New York. He wanted to take Judy Jones with him. No disillusion as to the world in which she had grown up could cure his illusion as to her desirability.

Remember that—for only in the light of it can what he did for her be understood.

Eighteen months after he first met Judy Jones he became engaged to another girl. Her name was Irene Scheerer, and her father was one of the men who had always believed in Dexter. Irene was light-haired and sweet and honorable, and a little stout, and she had two suitors whom she pleasantly relinquished when Dexter formally asked her to marry him.

Summer, fall, winter, spring, another summer, another fall—so much he had given of his active life to the incorrigible[29] lips of Judy Jones. She had treated him with interest, with encouragement, with malice, with indifference, with contempt. She had inflicted on him the innumerable little slights and indignities possible in such a case—as if in revenge for having ever cared for him at all. She had beckoned him and yawned at him and beckoned him again and he had responded often with bitterness and narrowed eyes. She had brought him ecstatic happiness and intolerable agony of spirit. She had caused him untold inconvenience and not a little trouble. She had insulted him, and she had ridden over him, and she had played his interest in her against his interest in his work—for fun.

> When autumn had come and gone again it occurred to him that he could not have Judy Jones.

She had done everything to him except to criticize him—this she had not done—it seemed to him only because it might have sullied[30] the utter indifference she manifested and sincerely felt toward him.

When autumn had come and gone again it occurred to him that he could not have Judy Jones. He had to beat this into his mind but he convinced himself at last. He lay awake at night for a while and argued it over. He told himself the trouble and the pain she had caused him, he enumerated her glaring deficiencies as a wife. Then he said to himself that he loved her, and after a while he fell asleep. For a week, lest he imagined her husky voice over the telephone or her eyes opposite him at lunch, he worked hard and late, and at night he went to his office and plotted out his years.

At the end of a week he went to a dance and cut in on her once. For almost the first time since they had met he did not ask her to sit out with him or tell her that she was lovely. It hurt him that she did not miss these things—that was all. He was not jealous when he saw that there was a new man tonight. He had been hardened against jealousy long before.

He stayed late at the dance. He sat for an hour with Irene Scheerer and talked about books and about music. He knew very little about either. But he was beginning to be master of his own time now, and he had a rather priggish[31] notion that he—the young and already fabulously successful Dexter Green—should know more about such things.

That was in October, when he was twenty-five. In January, Dexter and Irene became engaged. It was to be announced in June, and they were to be married three months later.

The Minnesota winter prolonged itself interminably, and it was almost May when the winds

---

29. **incorrigible** *adj.:* incapable of correction or reform.

30. **sullied** *v.:* tainted; soiled.
31. **priggish** *adj.:* annoyingly precise and proper.

came soft and the snow ran down into Black Bear Lake at last. For the first time in over a year Dexter was enjoying a certain tranquility of spirit. Judy Jones had been in Florida, and afterward in Hot Springs, and somewhere she had been engaged, and somewhere she had broken it off. At first, when Dexter had definitely given her up, it had made him sad that people still linked them together and asked for news of her, but when he began to be placed at dinner next to Irene Scheerer people didn't ask him about her any more—they told him about her. He ceased to be an authority on her.

May at last. Dexter walked the streets at night when the darkness was damp as rain, wondering that so soon, with so little done, so much of ecstasy had gone from him. May one year back had been marked by Judy's poignant, unforgivable, yet forgiven turbulence—it had been one of those rare times when he fancied she had grown to care for him. That old penny's worth of happiness he had spent for this bushel of content. He knew that Irene would be no more than a curtain spread behind him, a hand moving among gleaming teacups, a voice calling to children . . . fire and loveliness were gone, the magic of nights and the wonder of the varying hours and seasons . . . slender lips, downturning, dropping to his lips and bearing him up into a heaven of eyes. . . . The thing was deep in him. He was too strong and alive for it to die lightly.

In the middle of May when the weather balanced for a few days on the thin bridge that led to deep summer he turned in one night at Irene's house. Their engagement was to be announced in a week now—no one would be surprised at it. And tonight they would sit together on the lounge at the University Club and look on for an hour at the dancers. It gave him a sense of solidity to go with her—she was so sturdily popular, so intensely "great."

He mounted the steps of the brownstone house and stepped inside.

"Irene," he called.

Mrs. Scheerer came out of the living room to meet him.

"Dexter," she said, "Irene's gone upstairs with a splitting headache. She wanted to go with you but I made her go to bed."

"Nothing serious, I—"

"Oh, no. She's going to play golf with you in the morning. You can spare her for just one night, can't you, Dexter?"

Her smile was kind. She and Dexter liked each other. In the living room he talked for a moment before he said good-night.

Returning to the University Club, where he had rooms, he stood in the doorway for a moment and watched the dancers. He leaned against the doorpost, nodded at a man or two—yawned.

"Hello, darling."

The familiar voice at his elbow startled him. Judy Jones had left a man and crossed the room to him—Judy Jones, a slender enameled doll in cloth of gold: gold in a band at her head, gold in two slipper points at her dress's hem. The fragile glow of her face seemed to blossom as she smiled at him. A breeze of warmth and light blew through the room. His hands in the pockets of his dinner jacket tightened spasmodically. He was filled with a sudden excitement.

"When did you get back?" he asked casually.

"Come here and I'll tell you about it."

She turned and he followed her. She had been away—he could have wept at the wonder of her return. She had passed through enchanted streets, doing things that were like provocative music. All mysterious happenings, all fresh and quickening hopes, had gone away with her, come back with her now.

She turned in the doorway.

"Have you a car here? If you haven't, I have."

"I have a coupé."

In then, with a rustle of golden cloth. He slammed the door. Into so many cars she had stepped—like this—like that—her back against the leather, so—her elbow resting on the door—waiting. She would have been soiled long since

**Vocabulary**
turbulence (tʉr'byə·ləns) n.: wild disorder.

had there been anything to soil her—except herself—but this was her own self outpouring.

With an effort he forced himself to start the car and back into the street. This was nothing, he must remember. She had done this before, and he had put her behind him, as he would have crossed a bad account from his books.

He drove slowly downtown and, affecting abstraction, traversed the deserted streets of the business section, peopled here and there where a movie was giving out its crowd or where consumptive[32] or pugilistic[33] youth lounged in front of pool halls. The clink of glasses and the slap of hands on the bars issued from saloons, cloisters of glazed glass and dirty yellow light.

She was watching him closely and the silence was embarrassing, yet in this crisis he could find no casual word with which to profane[34] the hour. At a convenient turning he began to zigzag back toward the University Club.

"Have you missed me?" she asked suddenly.

"Everybody missed you."

He wondered if she knew of Irene Scheerer. She had been back only a day—her absence had been almost contemporaneous with his engagement.

"What a remark!" Judy laughed sadly—without sadness. She looked at him searchingly. He became absorbed in the dashboard.

"You're handsomer than you used to be," she said thoughtfully. "Dexter, you have the most rememberable eyes."

He could have laughed at this, but he did not laugh. It was the sort of thing that was said to sophomores. Yet it stabbed at him.

"I'm awfully tired of everything, darling." She called every one darling, endowing the endearment with careless, individual comraderie. "I wish you'd marry me."

The directness of this confused him. He should have told her now that he was going to marry another girl, but he could not tell her. He could as easily have sworn that he had never loved her.

"I think we'd get along," she continued, on the same note, "unless probably you've forgotten me and fallen in love with another girl."

Her confidence was obviously enormous. She had said, in effect, that she found such a thing

---

32. **consumptive** *adj.:* destructive; wasteful.
33. **pugilistic** (pyoo´jə·liz´tik) *adj.:* eager to fight.
34. **profane** *v.:* curse.

impossible to believe, that if it were true he had merely committed a childish indiscretion—and probably to show off. She would forgive him, because it was not a matter of any moment but rather something to be brushed aside lightly.

"Of course you could never love anybody but me," she continued. "I like the way you love me. Oh, Dexter, have you forgotten last year?"

"No, I haven't forgotten."

"Neither have I!"

Was she sincerely moved—or was she carried along by the wave of her own acting?

"I wish we could be like that again," she said, and he forced himself to answer:

"I don't think we can."

"I suppose not.... I hear you're giving Irene Scheerer a violent rush."

There was not the faintest emphasis on the name, yet Dexter was suddenly ashamed.

"Oh, take me home," cried Judy suddenly; "I don't want to go back to that idiotic dance—with those children."

Then, as he turned up the street that led to the residence district, Judy began to cry quietly to herself. He had never seen her cry before.

The dark street lightened, the dwellings of the rich loomed up around them, he stopped his coupé in front of the great white bulk of the Mortimer Joneses house, somnolent,[35] gorgeous, drenched with the splendor of the damp moonlight. Its solidity startled him. The strong walls, the steel of the girders, the breadth and beam and pomp of it were there only to bring out the contrast with the young beauty beside him. It was sturdy to accentuate her slightness—as if to show what a breeze could be generated by a butterfly's wing.

He sat perfectly quiet, his nerves in wild clamor, afraid that if he moved he would find her irresistibly in his arms. Two tears had rolled down her wet face and trembled on her upper lip.

"I'm more beautiful than anybody else," she said brokenly, "why can't I be happy?" Her moist eyes tore at his stability—her mouth turned slowly downward with an exquisite sadness: "I'd like to marry you if you'll have me, Dexter. I suppose you think I'm not worth having, but I'll be so beautiful for you, Dexter."

A million phrases of anger, pride, passion, hatred, tenderness fought on his lips. Then a perfect wave of emotion washed over him, carrying off with it a sediment of wisdom, of convention,[36] of doubt, of honor. This was his girl who was speaking, his own, his beautiful, his pride.

"Won't you come in?" He heard her draw in her breath sharply.

Waiting.

"All right," his voice was trembling, "I'll come in."

### V

It was strange that neither when it was over nor a long time afterward did he regret that night. Looking at it from the perspective of ten years, the fact that Judy's flare for him endured just one month seemed of little importance. Nor did it matter that by his yielding he subjected himself to a deeper agony in the end and gave serious hurt to Irene Sheerer and to Irene's parents, who had befriended him. There was nothing sufficiently pictorial about Irene's grief to stamp itself on his mind.

Dexter was at bottom hard-minded. The attitude of the city on his action was of no importance to him, not because he was going to leave the city, but because any outside attitude on the situation seemed superficial. He was completely indifferent to popular opinion. Nor, when he had seen that it was no use, that he did not possess in himself the power to move fundamentally or to hold Judy Jones, did he bear any malice toward her. He loved her, and he would love her until the day he was too old for loving—but he could not have her. So he tasted the deep pain that is reserved only for the strong, just as he had tasted for a little while the deep happiness.

---

35. **somnolent** *adj.:* sleepy.

36. **convention** *n.:* accepted practices of social behavior.

Even the ultimate falsity of the grounds upon which Judy terminated the engagement, that she did not want to "take him away" from Irene—Judy, who had wanted nothing else—did not revolt him. He was beyond any revulsion or any amusement.

He went East in February with the intention of selling out his laundries and settling in New York—but the war came to America in March and changed his plans. He returned to the West, handed over the management of the business to his partner, and went into the first officers' training camp in late April. He was one of those young thousands who greeted the war with a certain amount of relief, welcoming the liberation from webs of tangled emotion.

## VI

This story is not his biography, remember, although things creep into it which have nothing to do with those dreams he had when he was young. We are almost done with them and with him now. There is only one more incident to be related here, and it happens seven years farther on.

It took place in New York, where he had done well—so well that there were no barriers too high for him. He was thirty-two years old, and, except for one flying trip immediately after the war, he had not been West in seven years. A man named Devlin from Detroit came into his office to see him in a business way, and then and there this incident occurred, and closed out, so to speak, this particular side of his life.

"So you're from the Middle West," said the man Devlin with careless curiosity. "That's funny—I thought men like you were probably born and raised on Wall Street. You know—wife of one of my best friends in Detroit came from your city. I was an usher at the wedding."

Dexter waited with no apprehension of what was coming.

"Judy Simms," said Devlin with no particular interest; "Judy Jones she was once."

"Yes, I knew her." A dull impatience spread over him. He had heard, of course, that she was

married—perhaps deliberately he had heard no more.

"Awfully nice girl," brooded Devlin meaninglessly, "I'm sort of sorry for her."

"Why?" Something in Dexter was alert, receptive, at once.

"Oh, Lud Simms has gone to pieces in a way. I don't mean he ill-uses her, but he drinks and runs around—"

"Doesn't she run around?"

"No. Stays at home with her kids."

"Oh."

"She's a little too old for him," said Devlin.

"Too old!" cried Dexter. "Why, man, she's only twenty-seven."

He was possessed with a wild notion of rushing out into the streets and taking a train to Detroit. He rose to his feet spasmodically.

"I guess you're busy," Devlin apologized quickly. "I didn't realize—"

"No, I'm not busy," said Dexter, steadying his voice. "I'm not busy at all. Not busy at all. Did you say she was—twenty-seven? No, I said she was twenty-seven."

"Yes, you did," agreed Devlin dryly.

"Go on, then. Go on."

"What do you mean?"

"About Judy Jones."

Devlin looked at him helplessly.

"Well, that's—I told you all there is to it. He treats her like the devil. Oh, they're not going to get divorced or anything. When he's particularly outrageous she forgives him. In fact, I'm inclined to think she loves him. She was a pretty girl when she first came to Detroit."

A pretty girl! The phrase struck Dexter as ludicrous.

"Isn't she—a pretty girl, anymore?"

"Oh, she's all right."

"Look here," said Dexter, sitting down suddenly, "I don't understand. You say she was a 'pretty girl' and now you say she's 'all right.' I don't understand what you mean—Judy Jones wasn't a pretty girl, at all. She was a great beauty. Why, I knew her, I knew her. She was—"

Devlin laughed pleasantly.

"I'm not trying to start a row," he said. "I think Judy's a nice girl and I like her. I can't understand how a man like Lud Simms could fall madly in love with her, but he did." Then he added: "Most of the women like her."

Dexter looked closely at Devlin, thinking wildly that there must be a reason for this, some insensitivity in the man or some private malice.

"Lots of women fade just like *that*," Devlin snapped his fingers. "You must have seen it happen. Perhaps I've forgotten how pretty she was at her wedding. I've seen her so much since then, you see. She has nice eyes."

A sort of dullness settled down upon Dexter. For the first time in his life he felt like getting very drunk. He knew that he was laughing loudly at something Devlin had said, but he did not know what it was or why it was funny. When, in a few minutes, Devlin went, he lay down on his lounge and looked out the window at the New York skyline into which the sun was sinking in dull lovely shades of pink and gold.

He had thought that having nothing else to lose he was invulnerable at last—but he knew that he had just lost something more, as surely as if he had married Judy Jones and seen her fade away before his eyes.

> *The dream was gone. Something had been taken from him.*

The dream was gone. Something had been taken from him. In a sort of panic he pushed the palms of his hands into his eyes and tried to bring up a picture of the waters lapping on Sherry Island and the moonlit veranda, and gingham on the golf links and the dry sun and the gold color of her neck's soft down. And her mouth damp to his kisses and her eyes plaintive with melancholy and her freshness like new fine linen in the morning. Why, these things were no longer in the world! They had existed and they existed no longer.

For the first time in years the tears were streaming down his face. But they were for himself now. He did not care about mouth and eyes and moving hands. He wanted to care, and he could not care. For he had gone away and he could never go back anymore. The gates were closed, the sun was gone down, and there was no beauty but the gray beauty of steel that withstands all time. Even the grief he could have borne was left behind in the country of illusion, of youth, of the richness of life, where his winter dreams had flourished.

"Long ago," he said, "long ago, there was something in me, but now that thing is gone. Now that thing is gone, that thing is gone. I cannot cry. I cannot care. That thing will come back no more." ■

**Vocabulary**

**ludicrous** (loo′di·krəs) *adj.*: laughable; absurd.
**plaintive** (plān′tiv) *adj.*: expressing sadness.

# A Letter to His Daughter

La Paix, Rodgers' Forge,
Towson, Maryland,
August 8, 1933

Dear Pie:

I feel very strongly about you doing duty. Would you give me a little more documentation about your reading in French? I am glad you are happy—but I never believe much in happiness. I never believe in misery either. Those are things you see on the stage or the screen or the printed page, they never really happen to you in life.

All I believe in in life is the rewards for virtue (according to your talents) and the *punishments* for not fulfilling your duties, which are doubly costly. If there is such a volume in the camp library, will you ask Mrs. Tyson to let you look up a sonnet of Shakespeare's in which the line occurs "*Lilies that fester smell far worse than weeds.*"

Have had no thoughts today, life seems composed of getting up a *Saturday Evening Post* story. I think of you, and always pleasantly; but if you call me "Pappy" again I am going to take the White Cat out and beat his bottom *hard, six times for every time you are impertinent.* Do you react to that? I will arrange the camp bill.

Halfwit, I will conclude. Things to worry about:

    Worry about courage
    Worry about cleanliness
    Worry about efficiency
    Worry about horsemanship . . .

Things not to worry about:

    Don't worry about popular opinion
    Don't worry about dolls
    Don't worry about the past
    Don't worry about the future
    Don't worry about growing up
    Don't worry about anybody getting ahead of you
    Don't worry about triumph
    Don't worry about failure unless it comes through your own fault
    Don't worry about mosquitoes
    Don't worry about flies
    Don't worry about insects in general
    Don't worry about parents
    Don't worry about boys
    Don't worry about disappointments
    Don't worry about pleasures
    Don't worry about satisfactions

Things to think about:

What am I really aiming at?

How good am I really in comparison to my contemporaries in regard to:

    (a) Scholarship
    (b) Do I really understand about people and am I able to get along with them?
    (c) Am I trying to make my body a useful instrument or am I neglecting it?

    With dearest love,

—Dad

*F. Scott Fitzgerald*

F. Scott Fitzgerald with his daughter, Scottie.

# Response and Analysis

## Reading Check

1. This story is divided into six parts. Review each part of the story; then, sum up the main event or events of each part. Look for those key events that advance the plot.

2. When you finish your list of key events, indicate which event you think marks the **climax** of the story—its most emotional moment, when we know what becomes of the main character's quest.

## Thinking Critically

3. What details indicate that Dexter is an ambitious young man? What are Dexter's **motivations**?

4. In *Richard III,* Shakespeare refers to "the winter of our discontent." How do Dexter's "winter dreams" reflect discontent? Does his discontent subside when he becomes rich and respected? Explain.

5. When they meet again as adults, Dexter decides that he has "wanted Judy Jones ever since he was a proud, desirous little boy" (page 706). What does Judy represent for Dexter? Does Dexter really love her? (Be sure to refer to the notes you took while reading to explain your responses.)

6. What makes Dexter "newer and stronger" than the "careless" wealthy people he meets? Why, then, does he want his children to be like those people?

7. Compare Dexter's ambitions for his children with those expressed by Scott Fitzgerald in his letter to his daughter (see the **Primary Source** on page 714).

8. A recurring **theme** in Fitzgerald's work is the pursuit of the American dream. How would you define what Fitzgerald saw as the American dream? (Be sure to include Dexter's quest for Judy as part of your answer.)

9. Why do you think Dexter feels such a profound sense of loss when he hears about Judy at the end of the story?

10. Do you think Dexter would have been happier in the end if he had married Judy? Why or why not?

11. Do you think the **themes** of this story are universal and timeless, or is this a story that could have happened only in its specific time and place—the Jazz Age? Explain your responses with examples from stories and movies that are popular today.

**SKILLS FOCUS**

**Literary Skills**
Analyze motivation.

**Reading Skills**
Make inferences about characters.

**Writing Skills**
Write an essay analyzing a poem.

**Vocabulary Skills**
Understand synonyms and antonyms.

**INTERNET**

Projects and Activities

Keyword: LE7 11-5

# WRITING

## Fitzgerald's Fairy Tale?

In a book review of Fitzgerald's stories, the novelist and critic Jay McInerney wrote the following comment:

> The young (poor) boy's quest for the hand of the beautiful, rich princess is undoubtedly Fitzgerald's best plot, the fairy-tale skeleton of his jazz age tales. One supposes that magazine editors preferred the stories in which the quest is successful, but in the better ones, like "Winter Dreams" (1922) and "The Sensible Thing" (1924), the success is qualified or the quest ends in failure.

In a brief **essay,** analyze the ways in which "Winter Dreams" is like and unlike a fairy tale. Consider the story's **plot, characterization, tone,** and **theme.**

## Vocabulary Development
### Synonym and Antonym Mapping

| | |
|---|---|
| elation | mirth |
| perturbation | divergence |
| malicious | turbulence |
| reserve | ludicrous |
| petulance | plaintive |

**Synonyms** are words with the same or similar meanings. **Antonyms** are words with more or less opposite meanings. Make either a synonym or an antonym word map like the following one for each of the Vocabulary words (the first one has been done for you). You will have to think of either a synonym or an antonym for each word and then write sentences illustrating your understanding of the word. Feel free to consult a dictionary or a thesaurus.

| Word | Sentence |
|---|---|
| elation | Dexter's feelings of elation were directly linked to how much attention Judy paid to him. |
| Antonym<br>dejection | Dexter's dejection could be explained by the loss of his ideal. |

F. Scott and Zelda Fitzgerald (1921).

# William Faulkner
(1897–1962)

**Y**oknapatawpha County, Mississippi, is surely the hardest of American literary place-names to pronounce. Still, it is wise to learn how (yäk′nə·pə·tô′fə), for it is famous as the imagined world of William Faulkner, the scene of his most celebrated novels and stories. Imaginary Yoknapatawpha is similar in many ways to the actual impoverished farmland, with its red-clay hills, that rings Oxford, Mississippi, home of the state's main university. It was there that William's father, Murry Falkner (William added the *u* to the family name), ran a livery stable and later became the university's business manager. William Faulkner lived and wrote there throughout most of his life.

## The South Provides a Theme

Faulkner was a mediocre student and quit high school in the tenth grade, but he read widely and wrote poetry. At the outbreak of World War I, the U.S. Army rejected him because he failed to meet its height and weight requirements. However, he enlisted in the Royal Air Force of Canada and trained for flight duty, only to see the war end before he was commissioned. Returning to Oxford after the war, he took some courses at the university and did poorly in English. With neither profession nor skill and a marked distaste for regular employment, he seemed a moody and puzzling young man to his neighbors.

Faulkner took several short-lived jobs, among them that of postmaster for the university. Resigning from that job, he wrote, "I will be damned if I propose to be at the beck and call of every itinerant scoundrel who has two cents to invest in a postage stamp."

In 1924, Faulkner left Oxford for New Orleans, where he met Sherwood Anderson, who had attracted much attention with the publication of *Winesburg, Ohio* (1919), his study of small-town life. Impressed and encouraged by Anderson, Faulkner tried his hand at fiction. In five months he completed a first novel, *Soldier's Pay,* a self-conscious story about the lost generation. Thereafter, Faulkner wrote with a tireless energy.

Within the next three years, Faulkner found his great theme: the American South as a microcosm for the universal themes of time, the passions of the human heart, and the destruction of the wilderness. Faulkner saw the South as a nation unto itself, with a strong sense of its noble past and an array of myths by which it clung to its pride, despite the humiliating defeat of the Civil War and the enforced acceptance of the distasteful values of an industrial North. Faulkner started to explore these themes in *Sartoris* (the first story set in mythical Yoknapatawpha) and *The Sound and the Fury,* two novels published within months of each other in 1929. *The Sound and the Fury* was a milestone in American literature, owing to Faulkner's bold manipulation of point of view and its stream-of-consciousness narrative technique.

In the decade that followed, Faulkner produced a succession of dazzling books: *As I Lay Dying* (1930), *Sanctuary* (1931), *Light in August* (1932), *Absalom, Absalom!* (1936)—considered by many readers to be his finest work—*The Unvanquished* (1938), and *The Hamlet* (1940). These works reveal Faulkner as equally skillful in the tragic or comic mode. He portrayed the South accurately, perceptively, and with a poignant ambivalence—on the one hand affectionate, on the other critical. He once said of the South, "Well, I love it and I hate it."

## Faulkner's Fictional Families

Faulkner described his South through fictional families who often reappear from novel to novel. They resemble trees, attaining grandeur, casting much shade, and then growing old and dry, crumbling as the seedlings of social change grow up around their fallen limbs and stumps.

There are the aristocratic Sartorises, who resemble Faulkner's own ancestors. Colonel John Sartoris, for example, was patterned after Faulkner's great-grandfather, who rose from rural poverty to command the Second Mississippi Regiment, built a railroad, wrote a best-selling novel, and was murdered on the street.

There are also the Compsons, who incorporate some characteristics of the author's immediate family. They form the centerpiece of *The Sound and the Fury*, which records the decline of a once great clan, and with it the passing of a traditionally southern world.

*As I Lay Dying* tells of the poor white Bundren family and its efforts to bring the body of its matriarch, Addie, back to the town of Jefferson for burial. The novel reveals these humble people as more enduring than their social betters. *Light in August* concerns other southern families and explores the problem of racism through the character of the protagonist, Joe Christmas. Although he appears white, Joe's racial heritage is mixed. His failure to find a place in either white or black society leads to his murder.

Finally, there is Faulkner's unforgettable portrayal of the Snopeses—a sprawling clan of irresponsible, depraved, socially ambitious varmints who rise from the dust and cheat their way to respectability and wealth, destroying the old values of aristocracy and peasantry alike.

Faulkner often forces the reader to piece together events from a seemingly random and fragmentary series of impressions experienced by a variety of narrators. Faulkner's style often strains conventional syntax; he might pile up clause upon clause in an effort to capture the complexity of thought. In *The Sound and the Fury*, for example, he entrusts part of the narrative to the chaotic intelligence of Benjy Compson. But the efforts of patient readers are richly repaid, as they discover in book after book a mythical universe in which the moral dilemmas are the perennial mysteries of human existence.

## "The Dream of Perfection"

By the time he received the Nobel Prize in literature, in 1950, Faulkner's best work was behind him. After his richly productive period (1929–1942), he wrote many more stories and novels, including *Intruder in the Dust* (1948), *Requiem for a Nun* (1951), *A Fable* (1954), *The Town* (1957), *The Mansion* (1959), and *The Reivers* (1962). These works displayed his virtuosity and willingness to experiment, but his powers were clearly diminished.

Faulkner's writing surely diverged from that of his realist contemporaries—notably Ernest Hemingway, whom he put at the bottom of his own list of the best American contemporary writers. "I said we were all failures. All of us had failed to match the dream of perfection. . . . I rated Hemingway last because he stayed within what he knew. He did it fine, but he didn't try for the impossible."

Faulkner had this to say about the qualities of a novel: "The only mistake with any novel is if it fails to create pleasure. That it is not true is irrelevant; a novel is to be enjoyed. A book that fails to create enjoyment is not a good one."

Debate will always rage about the position of figures in our literary pantheon, but critics are now unanimous in their opinion that Faulkner is one of the greatest of all American novelists. There is certainly no argument over William Faulkner's preeminence among southern writers. As Flannery O'Connor once put it, "The presence alone of Faulkner in our midst makes a great difference in what the writer can and cannot permit himself to do. Nobody wants his mule and wagon stalled on the same track the Dixie Limited is roaring down."

# A Rose for Emily

## Make the Connection

Faulkner, the master of the southern Gothic tale, knew firsthand the old American South and its powerful social traditions. It's all here in "A Rose for Emily"—the small-town social castes, the changing social values, the politeness with which people go about the routine of life, and the struggles they undergo to find joy in it.

The facts of this story tell a lurid tale, as sensational as any you might see headlined in scandal sheets displayed at supermarket checkouts. What primarily turns this account of outrageous human behavior into literature, though, is the relationship between the event and its setting. As the story of one eccentric woman unfolds, we learn some important truths about the rest of her community: its loyalty to family and the past, its pride, its faithfulness to old values, its fierce independence, and its scorn for all that is newly accepted.

## Literary Focus
### Setting

**Setting** is the time and location in which a story takes place. Setting also includes the customs and social conditions of a time—including, in this case, such things as racial stereotyping. If parts of this story give off an offensive odor, it comes only in part from Miss Emily's house and her horrible deed: It comes also from the racial slurs used by some of the characters. Although we find this language offensive, we must remember that Faulkner used it to portray as realistically as possible a racially segregated town of the rural South in the early part of the twentieth century.

> **Setting** is the time and location in which a story takes place.
>
> *For more on Setting, see the Handbook of Literary and Historical Terms.*

## Reading Skills
### Making Inferences About Characters

Miss Emily has a quality we all share to some degree: a tendency to retreat from a reality we don't like into a fantasy world where we can have things our own way. Is her bizarre behavior, however, merely madness or is it an extension of qualities admired in her community? As you read the story, take notes on Miss Emily's characteristics. Include your ideas about the motives for her strange actions.

### Vocabulary Development

**remitted** (ri·mit′id) v.: canceled; refrained from enforcing payment.

**archaic** (är·kā′ik) adj.: old-fashioned.

**vindicated** (vin′də·kāt′id) v. used as adj.: proved correct.

**pauper** (pô′pər) n.: extremely poor person.

**circumvent** (sʉr′kəm·vent′) v.: avoid by cleverness or deceit.

**virulent** (vir′yoo·lənt) adj.: full of hate; venomous.

**tranquil** (traŋ′kwəl) adj.: calm; quiet.

**perverse** (pər·vʉrs′) adj.: odd; contrary.

**acrid** (ak′rid) adj.: bitter; irritating.

**inextricable** (in·eks′tri·kə·bəl) adj.: unable to be freed or disentangled from.

**SKILLS FOCUS**

**Literary Skills**
Understand setting.

**Reading Skills**
Make inferences about characters.

**INTERNET**

Vocabulary Practice
•
More About William Faulkner

Keyword: LE7 11-5

# A Rose for Emily

## William Faulkner

### I

When Miss Emily Grierson died, our whole town went to her funeral: the men through a sort of respectful affection for a fallen monument, the women mostly out of curiosity to see the inside of her house, which no one save an old manservant—a combined gardener and cook—had seen in at least ten years.

It was a big, squarish frame house that had once been white, decorated with cupolas[1] and spires and scrolled balconies in the heavily lightsome style of the seventies,[2] set on what had once been our most select street. But garages and cotton gins had encroached and obliterated even the august names of that neighborhood; only Miss Emily's house was left, lifting its stubborn and coquettish decay above the cotton wagons and the gasoline pumps—an eyesore among eyesores. And now Miss Emily had gone to join the representatives of those august names where they lay in the cedar-bemused cemetery among the ranked and anonymous graves of Union and Confederate soldiers who fell at the battle of Jefferson.

Alive, Miss Emily had been a tradition, a duty, and a care; a sort of hereditary obligation upon the town, dating from that day in 1894 when Colonel Sartoris, the mayor—he who fathered the edict that no Negro woman should appear on the streets without an apron—remitted her taxes, the dispensation dating from the death of her father on into perpetuity.[3] Not

---

1. **cupolas** (kyo͞o′pə·ləz) *n. pl.:* small, dome-shaped structures built on a roof.
2. **the seventies:** the 1870s.

3. **perpetuity** (pʉr′pə·to͞o′ə·tē) *n.:* eternity.

**Vocabulary**
**remitted** (ri·mit′id) *v.:* canceled; refrained from enforcing payment.

that Miss Emily would have accepted charity. Colonel Sartoris invented an involved tale to the effect that Miss Emily's father had loaned money to the town, which the town, as a matter of business, preferred this way of repaying. Only a man of Colonel Sartoris' generation and thought could have invented it, and only a woman could have believed it.

When the next generation, with its more modern ideas, became mayors and aldermen, this arrangement created some little dissatisfaction. On the first of the year they mailed her a tax notice. February came, and there was no reply. They wrote her a formal letter, asking her to call at the sheriff's office at her convenience. A week later the mayor wrote her himself, offering to call or to send his car for her and received in reply a note on paper of an archaic shape in a thin, flowing calligraphy in faded ink, to the effect that she no longer went out at all. The tax notice was also enclosed, without comment.

They called a special meeting of the Board of Aldermen. A deputation waited upon her, knocked at the door through which no visitor had passed since she ceased giving china-painting lessons eight or ten years earlier. They were admitted by the old Negro into a dim hall from which a stairway mounted into still more shadow. It smelled of dust and disuse—a close, dank smell. The Negro led them into the parlor. It was furnished in heavy, leather-covered furniture. When the Negro opened the blinds of one window they could see that the leather was cracked; and when they sat down, a faint dust rose sluggishly about their thighs spinning with slow motes in the single sun-ray. On a tarnished gilt easel before the fireplace stood a crayon portrait of Miss Emily's father.

They rose when she entered—a small, fat woman in black, with a thin gold chain descending to her waist and vanishing into her belt, leaning on an ebony cane with a tarnished gold head. Her skeleton was small and spare; perhaps that was why what would have been merely plumpness in another was obesity in her. She looked bloated, like a body long submerged in motionless water, and of that pallid hue. Her eyes, lost in the fatty ridges of her face, looked like two small pieces of coal pressed into a lump of dough as they moved from one face to another while the visitors stated their errand.

She did not ask them to sit. She just stood in the door and listened quietly until the spokesman came to a stumbling halt. Then they could hear the invisible watch ticking at the end of the gold chain.

Her voice was dry and cold. "I have no taxes in Jefferson. Colonel Sartoris explained it to me. Perhaps one of you can gain access to the city records and satisfy yourselves."

"But we have. We are the city authorities, Miss Emily. Didn't you get a notice from the sheriff, signed by him?"

"I received a paper, yes," Miss Emily said. "Perhaps he considers himself the sheriff . . . I have no taxes in Jefferson."

"But there is nothing on the books to show that, you see. We must go by the—"

"See Colonel Sartoris. I have no taxes in Jefferson."

"But, Miss Emily—"

"See Colonel Sartoris."

(Colonel Sartoris had been dead almost ten years.) "I have no taxes in Jefferson. Tobe!" The Negro appeared. "Show these gentlemen out."

*S he looked bloated, like a body long submerged in motionless water...*

## II

So she vanquished them, horse and foot, just as she had vanquished their fathers thirty years before about the smell. That was two years after her father's death and a short time after her sweetheart—the one we believed would marry her—had deserted her. After her father's death

---

**Vocabulary**

**archaic** (är·kā′ik) *adj.*: old-fashioned.

*My Mother* (1921) by George Wesley Bellows. Oil on canvas (210.8 cm × 124.5 cm). Frank Russell Wadsworth Memorial (1923.975).

Reproduction © The Art Institute of Chicago.

she went out very little; after her sweetheart went away, people hardly saw her at all. A few of the ladies had the temerity[4] to call, but were not received, and the only sign of life about the place was the Negro man—a young man then— going in and out with a market basket.

"Just as if a man—any man—could keep a kitchen properly," the ladies said; so they were not surprised when the smell developed. It was another link between the gross, teeming world and the high and mighty Griersons.

A neighbor, a woman, complained to the mayor, Judge Stevens, eighty years old.

"But what will you have me do about it, madam?" he said.

"Why, send her word to stop it," the woman said. "Isn't there a law?"

"I'm sure that won't be necessary," Judge Stevens said. "It's probably just a snake or a rat that nigger of hers killed in the yard. I'll speak to him about it."

The next day he received two more complaints, one from a man who came in diffident deprecation.[5] "We really must do something about it, Judge. I'd be the last one in the world to bother Miss Emily, but we've got to do something." That night the Board of Aldermen met—three graybeards and one younger man, a member of the rising generation.

"It's simple enough," he said. "Send her word to have her place cleaned up. Give her a certain time to do it in, and if she don't . . ."

"Dammit, sir," Judge Stevens said, "will you accuse a lady to her face of smelling bad?"

So the next night, after midnight, four men crossed Miss Emily's lawn and slunk about the house like burglars, sniffing along the base of

---

4. **temerity** *n.:* foolish boldness; rashness.
5. **diffident deprecation:** timid disapproval.

---

the brickwork and at the cellar openings while one of them performed a regular sowing motion with his hand out of a sack slung from his shoulder. They broke open the cellar door and sprinkled lime there, and in all the outbuildings. As they recrossed the lawn, a window that had been dark was lighted and Miss Emily sat in it, the light behind her, and her upright torso motionless as that of an idol. They crept quietly across the lawn and into the shadow of the locusts that lined the street. After a week or two the smell went away.

That was when people had begun to feel really sorry for her. People in our town, remembering how old lady Wyatt, her great-aunt, had gone completely crazy at last, believed that the Griersons held themselves a little too high for what they really were. None of the young men were quite good enough for Miss Emily and such. We had long thought of them as a tableau,[6] Miss Emily a slender figure in white in the background, her father a spraddled silhouette in the foreground, his back to her and clutching a horsewhip, the two of them framed by the back-flung front door. So when she got to be thirty and was still single, we were not pleased exactly, but vindicated; even with insanity in the family she wouldn't have turned down all of her chances if they had really materialized.

When her father died, it got about that the house was all that was left to her; and in a way, people were glad. At last they could pity Miss Emily. Being left alone, and a pauper, she had become humanized. Now she too would know the old thrill and the old despair of a penny more or less.

The day after his death all the ladies prepared to call at the house and offer condolence and aid, as is our custom. Miss Emily met them at the door, dressed as usual and with no trace of

---

6. **tableau** *n.:* striking dramatic scene, usually motionless.

**Vocabulary**

**vindicated** (vin′də·kāt′id) *v.* used as *adj.:* proved correct.
**pauper** (pô′pər) *n.:* extremely poor person.

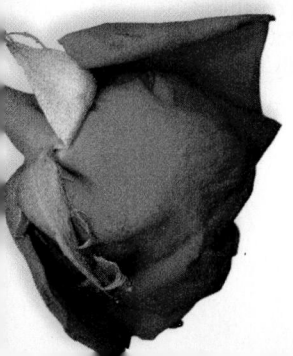

grief on her face. She told them that her father was not dead. She did that for three days, with the ministers calling on her, and the doctors, trying to persuade her to let them dispose of the body. Just as they were about to resort to law and force, she broke down, and they buried her father quickly.

We did not say she was crazy then. We believed she had to do that. We remembered all the young men her father had driven away, and we knew that with nothing left, she would have to cling to that which had robbed her, as people will.

### III

She was sick for a long time. When we saw her again, her hair was cut short, making her look like a girl, with a vague resemblance to those angels in colored church windows—sort of tragic and serene.

The town had just let the contracts for paving the sidewalks, and in the summer after her father's death they began the work. The construction company came with niggers and mules and machinery, and a foreman named Homer Barron, a Yankee—a big, dark, ready man, with a big voice and eyes lighter than his face. The little boys would follow in groups to hear him cuss the niggers, and the niggers singing in time to the rise and fall of picks. Pretty soon he knew everybody in town. Whenever you heard a lot of laughing anywhere about the square, Homer Barron would be in the center of the group. Presently we began to see him and Miss Emily on Sunday afternoons driving in the yellow-wheeled buggy and the matched team of bays from the livery stable.

At first we were glad that Miss Emily would have an interest, because the ladies all said, "Of course a Grierson would not think seriously of a Northerner, a day laborer." But there were still others, older people, who said that even grief could not cause a real lady to forget *noblesse*

*A nd as soon as the old people said, "Poor Emily," the whispering began.*

*oblige* [7]—without calling it *noblesse oblige*. They just said, "Poor Emily. Her kinsfolk should come to her." She had some kin in Alabama; but years ago her father had fallen out with them over the estate of old lady Wyatt, the crazy woman, and there was no communication between the two families. They had not even been represented at the funeral.

And as soon as the old people said, "Poor Emily," the whispering began. "Do you suppose it's really so?" they said to one another. "Of course it is. What else could . . ." This behind their hands; rustling of craned[8] silk and satin behind jalousies[9] closed upon the sun of Sunday afternoon as the thin, swift, clop-clop-clop of the matched team passed: "Poor Emily."

She carried her head high enough—even when we believed that she was fallen. It was as if she demanded more than ever the recognition of her dignity as the last Grierson; as if it had wanted that touch of earthiness to reaffirm her imperviousness. Like when she bought the rat poison, the arsenic. That was over a year after they had begun to say "Poor Emily," and while the two female cousins were visiting her.

"I want some poison," she said to the druggist. She was over thirty then, still a slight woman, though thinner than usual, with cold, haughty black eyes in a face the flesh of which was strained across the temples and about the eye-sockets as you imagine a lighthouse-keeper's face ought to look. "I want some poison," she said.

"Yes, Miss Emily. What kind? For rats and such? I'd recom—"

---

7. **noblesse oblige** (nō·bles′ ō·blēzh′): French for "nobility obliges"; that is, the supposed obligation of the upper classes to act nobly or kindly toward the lower classes.
8. **craned** *v.* used as *adj.*: stretched.
9. **jalousies** (jal′ə·sēz′) *n. pl.*: windows, shades, or doors made of overlapping, adjustable slats.

"I want the best you have. I don't care what kind."

The druggist named several. "They'll kill anything up to an elephant. But what you want is—"

"Arsenic," Miss Emily said. "Is that a good one?"

"Is . . . arsenic? Yes, ma'am. But what you want—"

"I want arsenic."

The druggist looked down at her. She looked back at him, erect, her face like a strained flag. "Why, of course," the druggist said. "If that's what you want. But the law requires you to tell what you are going to use it for."

Miss Emily just stared at him, her head tilted back in order to look him eye for eye, until he looked away and went and got the arsenic and wrapped it up. The Negro delivery boy brought her the package; the druggist didn't come back. When she opened the package at home there was written on the box, under the skull and bones: "For rats."

## IV

So the next day we all said, "She will kill herself"; and we said it would be the best thing. When she had first begun to be seen with Homer Barron, we had said, "She will marry him." Then we said, "She will persuade him yet," because Homer himself had remarked—he liked men, and it was known that he drank with the younger men in the Elks' Club—that he was not a marrying man. Later we said, "Poor Emily," behind the jalousies as they passed on Sunday afternoon in the glittering buggy, Miss Emily with her head high and Homer Barron with his hat cocked and a cigar in his teeth, reins and whip in a yellow glove.

Then some of the ladies began to say that it was a disgrace to the town and a bad example to the young people. The men did not want to interfere, but at last the ladies forced the Baptist minister—Miss Emily's people were Episcopal—to call upon her. He would never divulge what happened during that interview, but he refused to go back again. The next Sunday they again

*That Which I Should Have Done I Did Not Do* (1931–1941) by Ivan Le Lorraine Albright. Oil on canvas (246.5 cm × 91.5 cm).

**William Faulkner** 725

drove about the streets, and the following day the minister's wife wrote to Miss Emily's relations in Alabama.

So she had blood-kin under her roof again and we sat back to watch developments. At first nothing happened. Then we were sure that they were to be married. We learned that Miss Emily had been to the jeweler's and ordered a man's toilet set[10] in silver, with the letters H. B. on each piece. Two days later we learned that she had bought a complete outfit of men's clothing, including a nightshirt, and we said, "They are married." We were really glad. We were glad because the two female cousins were even more Grierson than Miss Emily had ever been.

So we were not surprised when Homer Barron—the streets had been finished some time since—was gone. We were a little disappointed that there was not a public blowing-off, but we believed that he had gone on to prepare for Miss Emily's coming, or to give her a chance to get rid of the cousins. (By that time it was a cabal,[11] and we were all Miss Emily's allies to help circumvent the cousins.) Sure enough, after another week they departed. And, as we had expected all along, within three days Homer Barron was back in town. A neighbor saw the Negro man admit him at the kitchen door at dusk one evening.

And that was the last we saw of Homer Barron. And of Miss Emily for some time. The Negro man went in and out with the market basket, but the front door remained closed. Now and then we would see her at a window for a moment, as the men did that night when they sprinkled the lime, but for almost six months she did not appear on the streets. Then we knew that this was to be expected too; as if that quality of her father which had thwarted her woman's life so many times had been too virulent and too furious to die.

When we next saw Miss Emily, she had grown fat and her hair was turning gray. During the next few years it grew grayer and grayer until it attained an even pepper-and-salt iron-gray, when it ceased turning. Up to the day of her death at seventy-four it was still that vigorous iron-gray, like the hair of an active man.

From that time on her front door remained closed, save for a period of six or seven years, when she was about forty, during which she gave lessons in china-painting. She fitted up a studio in one of the downstairs rooms, where the daughters and granddaughters of Colonel Sartoris' contemporaries were sent to her with the same regularity and in the same spirit that they were sent to church on Sundays with a twenty-five-cent piece for the collection plate. Meanwhile her taxes had been remitted.

Then the newer generation became the backbone and the spirit of the town, and the painting pupils grew up and fell away and did not send their children to her with boxes of color and tedious brushes and pictures cut from the ladies' magazines. The front door closed upon the last one and remained closed for good. When the town got free postal delivery, Miss Emily alone refused to let them fasten the metal numbers above her door and attach a mailbox to it. She would not listen to them.

Daily, monthly, yearly we watched the Negro grow grayer and more stooped, going in and out with the market basket. Each December we sent her a tax notice, which would be returned by the post office a week later, unclaimed. Now and then we would see her in one of the downstairs

*And that was the last we saw of Homer Barron. And of Miss Emily for some time.*

---

10. **toilet set:** set of grooming aids, such as a hand mirror, hairbrush, and comb.
11. **cabal** (kə·bäl′)*n.:* small group involved in a secret intrigue.

windows—she had evidently shut up the top floor of the house—like the carven torso of an idol in a niche, looking or not looking at us, we could never tell which. Thus she passed from generation to generation—dear, inescapable, impervious, tranquil, and perverse.

And so she died. Fell ill in the house filled with dust and shadows, with only a doddering Negro man to wait on her. We did not even know she was sick; we had long since given up trying to get any information from the Negro. He talked to no one, probably not even to her, for his voice had grown harsh and rusty, as if from disuse.

She died in one of the downstairs rooms, in a heavy walnut bed with a curtain, her gray head propped on a pillow yellow and moldy with age and lack of sunlight.

## V

The Negro met the first of the ladies at the front door and let them in, with their hushed, sibilant[12] voices and their quick, curious glances, and then he disappeared. He walked right through the house and out the back and was not seen again.

The two female cousins came at once. They held the funeral on the second day, with the town coming to look at Miss Emily beneath a mass of bought flowers, with the crayon face of her father musing profoundly above the bier[13] and the ladies sibilant and macabre;[14] and the very old men—some in their brushed Confederate uniforms—on the porch and the lawn, talking of Miss Emily as if she had been a contemporary of theirs, believing that they had danced with her and courted her perhaps, confusing time with its mathematical progression, as the old do, to whom all the past is not a diminishing road but, instead, a huge meadow which no winter ever quite touches, divided from them now by the narrow bottle-neck of the most recent decade of years.

---

12. **sibilant** (sibʹə·lənt) *adj.:* hissing.
13. **bier** (bir) *n.:* coffin and its supporting platform.
14. **macabre** (mə·käbʹrə) *adj.:* focused on the gruesome; horrible.

Already we knew that there was one room in that region above stairs which no one had seen in forty years, and which would have to be forced. They waited until Miss Emily was decently in the ground before they opened it.

The violence of breaking down the door seemed to fill this room with pervading dust. A thin, acrid pall as of the tomb seemed to lie everywhere upon this room decked and furnished as for a bridal: upon the valance curtains of faded rose color, upon the rose-shaded lights, upon the dressing table, upon the delicate array of crystal and the man's toilet things backed with tarnished silver, silver so tarnished that the monogram was obscured. Among them lay a collar and tie, as if they had just been removed, which, lifted, left upon the surface a pale crescent in the dust. Upon a chair hung the suit, carefully folded; beneath it the two mute shoes and the discarded socks.

The man himself lay in the bed.

For a long while we just stood there, looking down at the profound and fleshless grin. The body had apparently once lain in the attitude of an embrace, but now the long sleep that outlasts love, that conquers even the grimace of love, had cuckolded[15] him. What was left of him, rotted beneath what was left of the nightshirt, had become inextricable from the bed in which he lay; and upon him and upon the pillow beside him lay that even coating of the patient and biding dust.

Then we noticed that in the second pillow was the indentation of a head. One of us lifted something from it, and leaning forward, that faint and invisible dust dry and acrid in the nostrils, we saw a long strand of iron-gray hair. ∎

---

15. **cuckolded** (kukʹəld·id) *v.* used as *adj.:* betrayed; usually used to describe a husband whose wife has been unfaithful.

---

**Vocabulary**

**tranquil** (tranʹkwəl) *adj.:* calm; quiet.
**perverse** (pər·vʉrsʹ) *adj.:* odd; contrary.
**acrid** (akʹrid) *adj.:* bitter; irritating.
**inextricable** (in·eksʹtri·kə·bəl) *adj.:* unable to be freed or disentangled from.

# Nobel Prize Acceptance Speech, 1950

I feel that this award was not made to me as a man, but to my work—a life's work in the agony and sweat of the human spirit, not for glory and least of all for profit, but to create out of the materials of the human spirit something which did not exist before. So this award is only mine in trust. It will not be difficult to find a dedication for the money part of it commensurate with the purpose and significance of its origin. But I would like to do the same with the acclaim too, by using this moment as a pinnacle from which I might be listened to by the young men and women already dedicated to the same anguish and travail, among whom is already that one who will someday stand here where I am standing.

Our tragedy today is a general and universal physical fear so long sustained by now that we can even bear it. There are no longer problems of the spirit. There is only the question: When will I be blown up? Because of this, the young man or woman writing today has forgotten the problems of the human heart in conflict with itself which alone can make good writing because only that is worth writing about, worth the agony and the sweat.

He must learn them again. He must teach himself that the basest of all things is to be afraid; and, teaching himself that, forget it forever, leaving no room in his workshop for anything but the old verities and truths of the heart, the old universal truths lacking which any story is ephemeral and doomed—love and honor and pity and pride and compassion and sacrifice. Until he does so, he labors under a curse. He writes not of love but of lust, of defeats in which nobody loses anything of value, of victories without hope and, worst of all, without pity or compassion. His griefs grieve on no universal bones, leaving no scars. He writes not of the heart but of the glands.

Until he relearns these things, he will write as though he stood among and watched the end of man. I decline to accept the end of man. It is easy enough to say that man is immortal simply because he will endure: that when the last dingdong of doom has clanged and faded from the last worthless rock hanging tideless in the last red and dying evening, that even then there will still be one more sound: that of his puny inexhaustible voice, still talking. I refuse to accept this. I believe that man will not merely endure: he will prevail. He is immortal, not because he alone among creatures has an inexhaustible voice, but because he has a soul, a spirit capable of compassion and sacrifice and endurance. The poet's, the writer's, duty is to write about these things. It is his privilege to help man endure by lifting his heart, by reminding him of the courage and honor and hope and pride and compassion and pity and sacrifice which have been the glory of his past. The poet's voice need not merely be the record of man, it can be one of the props, the pillars to help him endure and prevail.

*William Faulkner*

# Response and Analysis

## Reading Check

1. How does Miss Emily behave after her father dies?

2. Why does the minister's wife send for Miss Emily's relations?

3. Who is Homer Barron? When does he disappear?

4. How does Miss Emily spend the last decades of her life?

5. What do people discover when they force open the door to the room above the stairs?

## Thinking Critically

6. What **conflicts** existed between Emily and her father? (For whom or what was the horsewhip intended?)

7. Colonel Sartoris's white lie to Miss Emily about her taxes is an attempt to spare her pride. Explain how Judge Stevens also takes steps to protect her. How does the townspeople's shift in attitude about the taxes reflect wider social and economic changes in the South?

8. Why do you think Faulkner emphasizes the *way* that Miss Emily's hair turns gray and the precise *time* that it begins to happen?

9. What significance do you see in the long strand of iron-gray hair on the pillow in the upstairs bedroom? What exactly do you think happened there, and why?

10. What hints or clues throughout the story **foreshadow** the gruesome ending? Did these hints prepare you for the ending, or were you surprised by it?

11. What part do you think Tobe, the African American manservant, plays in Miss Emily's history?

12. What sort of person do you think the **narrator** of this story is? Is it a man or a woman? What feelings toward Miss Emily does the narrator show?

13. Consider what roses usually **symbolize.** Then, defend the title of the story, or propose a more appropriate title.

14. Historical details in this story reveal a great deal about its **setting.** What do you learn about the times from the white townspeople's attitudes toward the African Americans who live in Jefferson? Nowadays have such attitudes changed or stayed much the same? Explain your response.

15. In his Nobel Prize acceptance speech (see the *Primary Source* on page 728), Faulkner urges young writers to tackle "the old universal truths . . . love and honor and pity and pride and compassion and sacrifice." Do you think Faulkner follows his own advice in "A Rose for Emily"? Explain your responses with details from the story.

SKILLS FOCUS

**Literary Skills**
Analyze setting.

**Reading Skills**
Make inferences about characters.

**Writing Skills**
Write a short story about a fictional character. Write a character analysis.

**Vocabulary Skills**
Demonstrate word knowledge.

go. hrw .com

**INTERNET**
Projects and Activities
Keyword: LE7 11-5

*William Faulkner.* Drawing by David Levine.

# WRITING

## Hometown Horror

Write a **short short story** (about twelve hundred words) about a fictional character, and set the story in your own neighborhood or one that you know well. Before beginning to write, think up a shocking secret that lies hidden in the character's past, and outline the plot events that will reveal the secret. Include vivid, descriptive details that create a mysterious atmosphere but a believable setting. Save the startling truth for the last sentence, as Faulkner does in "A Rose for Emily."

▶ **Use "Writing a Short Story," pages 338–345, for help with this assignment.**

## Miss Emily Up Close

Write a **character analysis** of Miss Emily. Include details from the story that reveal the following issues: what other people thought of her, what Miss Emily said and did, what the narrator tells us directly about Miss Emily, how Miss Emily's setting reflects her character. Be sure to check your reading notes. You must include your take on Miss Emily's **motive** for her crime.

▶ **Use "Analyzing Literature," pages 739–740, for help with this assignment.**

## Vocabulary Development

| | |
|---|---|
| remitted | virulent |
| archaic | tranquil |
| vindicated | perverse |
| pauper | acrid |
| circumvent | inextricable |

### Which Word?

Which of the Vocabulary words describes

1. the smell of burning rubber?
2. the speech of Shakespeare's characters?
3. a strange, stubborn person?
4. a bill that has already been paid?
5. a tangle of threads?
6. someone forced to beg for food?
7. how to avoid paying taxes by putting money in foreign banks?
8. a scientist whose groundbreaking research is finally taken seriously?
9. a rumor deliberately spread to destroy an honest person's reputation?
10. a sleeping baby in a loving parent's arms?

# Literature of the Americas

## Uruguay

### Horacio Quiroga
(1878–1937)

**H**oracio Quiroga (kē·rō′gä) was one of Latin America's finest and most celebrated short story writers, a master of the taut, suspenseful, well-crafted tale. Born in Salto, Uruguay, Quiroga was an avid admirer of Edgar Allan Poe's fiction. Like Poe, Quiroga wrote stories that blend horror with psychological suspense. Also like Poe, Quiroga developed a philosophy of short story writing. In his essay "Manual of the Perfect Short Story Writer," Quiroga presents an approach to writing not unlike Poe's theory of the "single effect": the idea that every word and detail in a story should build to a single, unified emotional effect. Quiroga felt that in the perfect short story the first few sentences are as important as the last few and inevitably lead to them. In his best stories—among which is "The Feather Pillow" (first published in 1907)—Quiroga achieves a compressed, sustained effect with every word and sentence. By the time of his death, he had written about two hundred works of fiction.

A master of dramatic technique, Quiroga was also superb at creating setting. In his stories, as in the stories of William Faulkner and other American writers who explore in depth certain real or fictionalized regions, Quiroga makes setting almost a character in itself. He spent a good portion of his life in San Ignacio, a jungle province in Misiones (in northern Argentina) that provided inspiration for his settings. In many of his stories, he deals with fundamental conflicts between human beings and the world of nature—conflicts in which nature is invariably the victor. Many of his jungle stories illustrate his uncompromising vision of life as an eternal, often brutal struggle for survival, not unlike some of the tales of Jack London, with whom Quiroga has also been compared.

Quiroga's Poe-like obsession with death and the grotesque is not surprising, given that his life was a patchwork of nightmares as disturbing as the tales he crafted. Quiroga came face to face with gruesome death early in his life. First, his father accidentally killed himself with a shotgun. When he was twenty-three, Quiroga accidentally shot to death one of his closest friends. There were more personal tragedies: Quiroga's attempts to start a business in the rugged and dangerous Argentine jungle failed; his first wife, in despair over their living conditions in the jungle, took her own life; his second marriage ended unhappily in separation. Quiroga ended his own tragic life in 1937, after discovering that he was dying of cancer.

### For Independent Reading

For more mystery, here are two story collections by Quiroga:
- *Jungle Tales*
- *The Decapitated Chicken and Other Stories*

# Before You Read

## The Feather Pillow

### Make the Connection

Be warned: The story you are about to read is one you won't soon forget. After you come to its stunning conclusion, you may never think of a feather pillow in the same way again.

### Literary Focus
#### Comparing Themes Across Cultures

The Gothic tale is well represented in the literature of the United States, going as far back as the haunted tales of Nathaniel Hawthorne in the early nineteenth century and coming to full flower with the horror stories of Edgar Allan Poe later in that same century. The tradition continued into the first half of the twentieth century in the work of the southern Gothic writers, such as William Faulkner and Flannery O'Connor, and still flourishes in the bestselling fiction of Stephen King and Anne Rice.

Gothic tales are not an American invention, however. In its most basic form the scary story is as old as fiction itself and has appeared in many times and places. Gothic horror, for example, was a staple of that new form of fiction—the novel—that developed in England in the eighteenth and nineteenth centuries.

In the hands of writers like Hawthorne, Poe, and Faulkner, the Gothic is not merely a big scare but a mirror of the dark fears and nightmares of the human mind.

**SKILLS FOCUS**

**Literary Skills**
Compare themes across cultures. Understand Gothic fiction.

go.
hrw
.com

**INTERNET**

**Vocabulary Practice**

Keyword: LE7 11-5

*The Lovers* (1928) by René Magritte. Oil on canvas. (21 3/8″ × 27 7/8″).

Richard S. Zeisler Collection, New York. © 2005 C. Herscovici, Brussels/Artists Rights Society (ARS), New York.

# The Feather Pillow

## Horacio Quiroga

*translated by* **Margaret Sayers Peden**

Her entire honeymoon gave her hot and cold shivers. A blond, angelic, and timid young girl, the childish fancies she had dreamed about being a bride had been chilled by her husband's rough character. She loved him very much, nonetheless, although sometimes she gave a light shudder when, as they returned home through the streets together at night, she cast a furtive glance at the impressive stature of her Jordan, who had been silent for an hour. He, for his part, loved her profoundly but never let it be seen.

For three months—they had been married in April—they lived in a special kind of bliss. Doubtless she would have wished less severity in the rigorous sky of love, more expansive and less cautious tenderness, but her husband's impassive manner always restrained her.

The house in which they lived influenced her chills and shuddering to no small degree. The whiteness of the silent patio—friezes,[1] columns, and marble statues—produced the wintry impression of an enchanted palace. Inside, the glacial brilliance of stucco, the completely bare walls, affirmed the sensation of unpleasant coldness. As one crossed from one room to another, the echo of his steps reverberated throughout the house, as if long abandonment had sensitized its resonance.

Alicia passed the autumn in this strange love nest. She had determined, however, to cast a veil over her former dreams and live like a sleeping beauty in the hostile house, trying not to think about anything until her husband arrived each evening.

It is not strange that she grew thin. She had a light attack of influenza that dragged on insidiously for days and days: After that Alicia's health never returned. Finally one afternoon she was able to go into the garden, supported on her husband's arm. She looked around listlessly. Suddenly Jordan, with deep tenderness, ran his hand very slowly over her head, and Alicia instantly burst into sobs, throwing her arms around his neck. For a long time she cried out all the fears she had kept silent, redoubling her weeping at Jordan's slightest caress. Then her sobs subsided, and she stood a long while, her face hidden in the hollow of his neck, not moving or speaking a word.

This was the last day Alicia was well enough to be up. On the following day she awakened feeling faint. Jordan's doctor examined her with minute attention, prescribing calm and absolute rest.

"I don't know," he said to Jordan at the street door. "She has a great weakness that I am unable to explain. And with no vomiting, nothing . . . if she wakes tomorrow as she did today, call me at once."

---

1. **friezes** (frēz'iz) *n. pl.*: decorative, ornamental bands around a room or along a wall.

---

**Vocabulary**

**furtive** (fur'tiv) *adj.*: stealthy; hidden.

**rigorous** (rig'ər·əs) *adj.*: precise; severe.

**impassive** (im·pas'iv) *adj.*: controlled; not revealing any emotions.

**reverberated** (ri·vur'bə·rāt'id) *v.*: resounded; re-echoed.

**resonance** (rez'ə·nəns) *n.*: capacity to intensify sound.

**subsided** (səb·sīd'id) *v.*: lessened.

When she awakened the following day, Alicia was worse. There was consultation. It was agreed there was an anemia of incredible progression, completely inexplicable. Alicia had no more fainting spells, but she was visibly moving toward death. The lights were lighted all day long in her bedroom, and there was complete silence. Hours went by without the slightest sound. Alicia dozed. Jordan virtually lived in the drawing room, which was also always lighted. With tireless persistence he paced ceaselessly from one end of the room to the other. The carpet swallowed his steps. At times he entered the bedroom and continued his silent pacing back and forth alongside the bed, stopping for an instant at each end to regard his wife.

Suddenly Alicia began to have hallucinations, vague images, at first seeming to float in the air, then descending to floor level. Her eyes excessively wide, she stared continuously at the carpet on either side of the head of her bed. One night she suddenly focused on one spot. Then she opened her mouth to scream, and pearls of sweat suddenly beaded her nose and lips.

"Jordan! Jordan!" she clamored, rigid with fright, still staring at the carpet.

Jordan ran to the bedroom, and, when she saw him appear, Alicia screamed with terror.

"It's I, Alicia, it's I!"

Alicia looked at him confusedly; she looked at the carpet; she looked at him once again; and after a long moment of stupefied confrontation, she regained her senses. She smiled and took her husband's hand in hers, caressing it, trembling, for half an hour.

Among her most persistent hallucinations was that of an anthropoid[2] poised on his fingertips on the carpet, staring at her.

The doctors returned, but to no avail. They saw before them a diminishing life, a life bleeding away day by day, hour by hour, absolutely without their knowing why. During their last consultation Alicia lay in a stupor while they took her pulse, passing her inert wrist from one to another. They observed her a long time in silence and then moved into the dining room.

"Phew . . ." The discouraged chief physician shrugged his shoulders. "It is an inexplicable case. There is little we can do . . ."

"That's my last hope!" Jordan groaned. And he staggered blindly against the table.

Alicia's life was fading away in the subdelirium[3] of anemia, a delirium which grew worse throughout the evening hours but which let up somewhat after dawn. The illness never worsened during the daytime, but each morning she awakened pale as death, almost in a swoon. It seemed only at night that her life drained out of her in new waves of blood. Always when she awakened she had the sensation of lying collapsed in the bed with a million-pound weight on top of her. Following the third day of this relapse she never left her bed again. She could scarcely move her head. She did not want her bed to be touched, not even to have her bedcovers arranged. Her crepuscular[4] terrors advanced now in the form of monsters that dragged themselves toward the bed and laboriously climbed upon the bedspread.

Then she lost consciousness. The final two days she raved ceaselessly in a weak voice. The lights funereally illuminated the bedroom and drawing room. In the deathly silence of the house the only sound was the monotonous delirium from the bedroom and the dull echoes of Jordan's eternal pacing.

Finally, Alicia died. The servant, when she came in afterward to strip the now empty bed, stared wonderingly for a moment at the pillow.

"Sir!" she called Jordan in a low voice. "There are stains on the pillow that look like blood."

---

3. **subdelirium** (sub·di·lir′ē·əm) *n.*: restless, feverish state in which a person hallucinates.
4. **crepuscular** (kri·pus′kyo͞o·lər) *adj.*: happening at or related to twilight.

---

**Vocabulary**

**inexplicable** (in·eks′pli·kə·bəl) *adj.*: unable to be explained.

**inert** (in·urt′) *adj.*: motionless.

---

2. **anthropoid** (an′thrə·poid′) *n.*: humanlike creature, such as an ape.

Jordan approached rapidly and bent over the pillow. Truly, on the case, on both sides of the hollow left by Alicia's head, were two small, dark spots.

"They look like punctures," the servant murmured after a moment of motionless observation.

"Hold it up to the light," Jordan told her.

The servant raised the pillow but immediately dropped it and stood staring at it, livid and trembling. Without knowing why, Jordan felt the hair rise on the back of his neck.

"What is it?" he murmured in a hoarse voice.

"It's very heavy," the servant whispered, still trembling.

Jordan picked it up; it was extraordinarily heavy. He carried it out of the room, and on the dining room table he ripped open the case and the ticking with a slash. The top feathers floated away, and the servant, her mouth opened wide, gave a scream of horror and covered her face with her clenched fists: In the bottom of the pillowcase, among the feathers, slowly moving its hairy legs, was a monstrous animal, a living, viscous ball. It was so swollen one could scarcely make out its mouth.

Night after night, since Alicia had taken to her bed, this abomination had stealthily applied its mouth—its proboscis[5] one might better say—to the girl's temples, sucking her blood. The puncture was scarcely perceptible. The daily plumping of the pillow had doubtlessly at first impeded its progress, but as soon as the girl could no longer move, the suction became vertiginous.[6] In five days, in five nights, the monster had drained Alicia's life away.

These parasites of feathered creatures, diminutive in their habitual environment, reach enormous proportions under certain conditions. Human blood seems particularly favorable to them, and it is not rare to encounter them in feather pillows. ■

---

5. **proboscis** (prō·bäs′is) *n.:* tubular mouthparts used by parasites to attach to a host and withdraw blood.
6. **vertiginous** (vər·tij′ə·nəs) *adj.:* causing vertigo; dizzying.

**Vocabulary**

**punctures** (puŋk′chərz) *n. pl.:* small holes.
**diminutive** (də·min′yōō·tiv) *adj.:* very small; tiny.

## A CLOSER LOOK: SOCIAL INFLUENCES

### Urban Legends

What makes your skin crawl? Part of what makes "The Feather Pillow" so effectively creepy is the sneaking suspicion (or fear) we all have that *something like this could really happen.*

Our tendency to half believe in the grotesque possibilities of stories about creepy creatures lurking inside feather pillows (or wigs or the linings of down jackets or even the bedroom closet) is the fuel for what anthropologists call **urban folklore,** or urban belief tales. Like all folk tales, these anecdotes travel at lightning speed simply by word of mouth, probably the way fairy tales were transmitted hundreds of years ago. And they seem all too believable.

Not all urban folk tales are scary, but many of the most memorable ones are.

INFORMATIONAL TEXT

You may have heard tales about giant alligators living in city sewers, spider eggs in bubble gum that later hatch inside a person's stomach, or earwigs that crawl into people's ears and drill right through their brains. We don't know whether Quiroga based his story on scary tales he had heard, but one thing is certain: "The Feather Pillow" plays on the same emotions of fascination, fear, and disgust that we all feel when we hear a scary story that we *know* is not true but that makes us sneak a few extra peeks in the closet or under the bed anyway.

# Response and Analysis

## Reading Check

1. Copy this story map onto a separate piece of paper. Then, fill in the map with details from the story. Put an asterisk beside the event that you think marks the story's **climax**—its most suspenseful, emotional moment, when you know how the characters' problems are worked out.

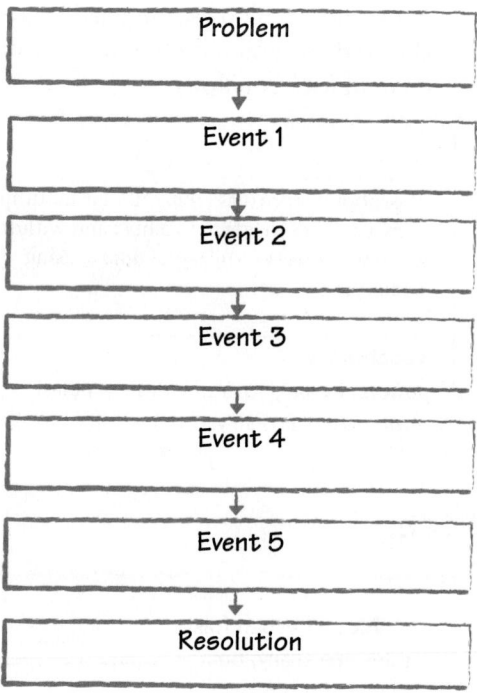

```
┌─────────────────────────────┐
│          Problem            │
└─────────────────────────────┘
              ↓
┌─────────────────────────────┐
│          Event 1            │
└─────────────────────────────┘
              ↓
┌─────────────────────────────┐
│          Event 2            │
└─────────────────────────────┘
              ↓
┌─────────────────────────────┐
│          Event 3            │
└─────────────────────────────┘
              ↓
┌─────────────────────────────┐
│          Event 4            │
└─────────────────────────────┘
              ↓
┌─────────────────────────────┐
│          Event 5            │
└─────────────────────────────┘
              ↓
┌─────────────────────────────┐
│         Resolution          │
└─────────────────────────────┘
```

## Thinking Critically

2. What **tone** is set by the very first sentence of this story?

3. In what ways are the characters of Jordan and Alicia **foils,** or opposites?

4. Re-read the description of the **setting,** the house in which Jordan and Alicia live. What **mood** do these details of the setting create?

5. On the literal level, Alicia is the victim of a parasitical creature that feeds on her blood. What **symbolic** interpretation can you make of such a death? (What else in Alicia's environment might have been sapping her vitality?)

6. The helpless woman at the mercy of a powerful man is one of the **themes** of Gothic fiction. What variations on this theme is Quiroga communicating in this strange story?

7. Do you agree with the view expressed in **A Closer Look** on page 735, that "The Feather Pillow" is effective because readers fear that something like the events in the story could really happen? Give specific reasons to support your response.

## Comparing Literature

8. Compare this story with "A Rose for Emily" (page 720). Note, for example, that both stories end on a shocking note, but Faulkner does not spell out what happened to Miss Emily and Homer Barron. Quiroga, on the other hand, reveals Alicia's fate in graphic detail. In what other ways are Faulkner's and Quiroga's stories alike and different? In your comparison, focus on these elements of Gothic fiction:

   • sinister settings
   • fantastic plot
   • grotesque character
   • use of the supernatural

## WRITING

### Seeing Is Believing

The horror movie is an outgrowth of the horror story and is a perennial favorite with audiences. Choose a horror film that you found especially effective, and write an **essay** analyzing the elements that make the movie work so well (consider plot, characters, setting, and special effects). Then, describe what the movie has in common with "The Feather Pillow." Conclude your essay with a comment on film versus print: Which medium has more powerful emotional effects?

## Vocabulary Development

| | |
|---|---|
| furtive | subsided |
| rigorous | inexplicable |
| impassive | inert |
| reverberated | punctures |
| resonance | diminutive |

### Diagramming Context

The following diagram shows how one reader figured out the meaning of *inert* by using clues in the sentences that surround the word in the story. After studying this reader's strategies, locate the context of the other vocabulary words in the story. Make a context diagram for each one.

"The doctors . . . saw before them a (diminishing) life, a life bleeding away day by day, hour by hour, . . . Alicia lay in a (stupor) while they took her pulse, passing her (inert) wrist from one to another."

A *diminishing* life is one that is losing strength and vigor.

A *stupor* is "a motionless state."

*Inert* might mean "still; barely moving."

## Vocabulary Development

### Greek and Latin Roots in Math and Science

Many English words are built from Greek or Latin roots. Becoming familiar with these roots can help you improve your vocabulary. A **root** is a word part that carries the core meaning of a word. Groups of words with the same root are called **word families.**

Words used in science and math are often based on Greek and Latin roots. Horacio Quiroga uses some of those words in his story "The Feather Pillow." In the charts on the next page you'll find some of Quiroga's words and related words that have applications in math and science. (For more about mathematical and scientific terms, see page 295.)

**SKILLS FOCUS**

**Vocabulary Skills**
Understand Greek and Latin roots.

## Greek

| Word | Root | Meaning of Root | Meaning of Word | Family Words |
|------|------|-----------------|-----------------|--------------|
| anthropoid | –anthropo– | human being | resembling a human | anthropology, anthropocentric |
| monotonous | –mono– | one | one tone; lacking variety | monad, monolith |
| physician | –physic– | of nature | doctor of medicine | physics, physiology |

## Latin

| Word | Root | Meaning of Root | Meaning of Word | Family Words |
|------|------|-----------------|-----------------|--------------|
| influenced | –flu– | flow | affected | fluid, confluence |
| perceptible | –cept– | take hold | grasped by the senses | concept, precept |
| produced | –duc–, –duct– | lead; draw | brought forth | reduce, induction |
| progression | –grad–, –gress– | step; degree | advancement by steps | gradation, regression |
| subsided | –sed–, –sid–, –sess– | settle; sit | settled; became less active | sediment, sedate |

**PRACTICE**

1. For each root listed in the charts, find one additional word in the same word family. You may use a dictionary for help.

2. Make a chart like the ones above for the following mathematical and scientific terms. Find the root and the meaning of the root given in parentheses for each word. Use a dictionary to find the meaning of the word. Then, find at least one family word. (You will note that several words also have common prefixes.)

**astronomy**    (–aster–, –astro–, "star")
**monograph**    (–graph–, "write; draw; record")
**psychiatry**    (–psych–, "mind; soul; spirit")
**illuminate**    (–luc–, –lumin–, "light")
**telescope**    (–scop–, "see")
**television**    (–vis–, –vid–, "see; look")

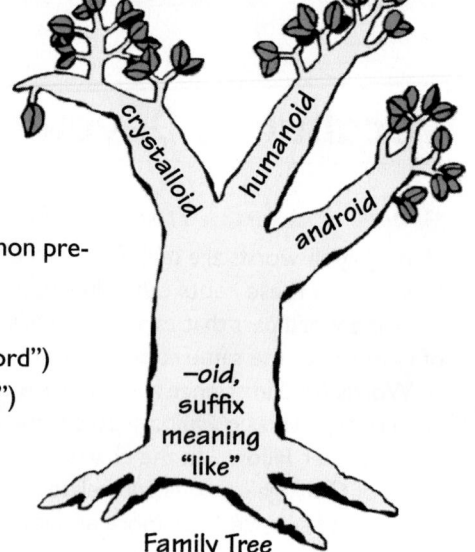

crystalloid
humanoid
android

–oid, suffix meaning "like"

Family Tree

# Analyzing Literature

As you've seen from the works in this section, modern short stories pack a lot of ideas into just a few pages. Short story writers don't say *everything* they want to communicate. They also depend on their readers to figure out some ideas. To delve into a writer's meaning, you must **analyze** a story, breaking it down into its parts and examining how those parts work together to produce an overall effect. In this workshop you will write an essay that does just that.

**Writing Assignment**
**Write a literary analysis of a short story.**

**Choose a Story**  You may choose to analyze a short story you already know and like. If you prefer to choose something new, look through anthologies or this textbook to find a complex, interesting story. Check with your teacher to make sure your choice is appropriate.

**Analyze the Story**  Analyzing a literary work is like taking apart an engine to see how it works. First, read the story to become familiar with the plot and to understand the story's significant ideas. Then, use the questions in the left-hand column of the chart below to analyze specific elements of the story. The sample answers are for an analysis of Ernest Hemingway's story "Soldier's Home" (page 685).

## ANALYZING A LITERARY WORK

| Analysis Questions | Sample Answers |
| --- | --- |
| What happens in the **plot?** How is the main conflict resolved? | A young soldier returns from war and finds himself alienated from his family. The soldier ends up living a lie. |
| What changes take place within the main **character?** | At the beginning of the story, the soldier wants to talk about his experiences, but he soon learns to lie or avoid discussing them at all. |
| What mood does the **setting** convey? Does the setting affect the plot? | The setting is an ordinary small town. The ordinariness of the town contrasts with the soldier's experiences in war and creates a mood of understated anxiety. |
| What **universal themes** are addressed in the story? | The story addresses the theme of alienation. |
| Does the story contain any **symbols** (objects or characters that have meanings of their own but also stand for something else)? | The girls that the soldier watches symbolize the normal life he cannot have. |
| Are there any **ambiguities** (things that can be understood in more than one way), **nuances** (fine shades of meaning), or **complexities** (interrelated ideas) in the text? | Hemingway never tells exactly what happened to the soldier during the war—he allows the reader to infer this information from the effects the experiences have had on the character. |

*(continued)*

| | |
|---|---|
| What **stylistic devices,** such as repetition, figurative language (similes and metaphors), and sentence patterns, does the writer use? How are they appropriate for the story? | Hemingway uses short, declarative sentences and repeats key words, such as "consequences." The short sentences mirror the main character's apparent lack of feeling, and the repetition of key words shows their importance for him. |
| What kind of **language** does the writer use? Is it straightforward? poetic? complicated? | Hemingway's language is simple, factual, and unemotional. |
| What feelings are suggested by the story's **imagery** (descriptions that evoke sounds, tastes, textures, and smells)? | Hemingway uses mostly visual imagery in the story. The lack of other imagery makes the reader feel like the main character—cut off from the town's life. |

**TIP** In addition to the elements in the chart, look for **unique aspects of the text** you have chosen. For instance, E. E. Cummings used unconventional punctuation, capitalization, and line breaks for effect in his poetry.

**TIP** Remember that your essay must be coherent and focused, with a **well-defined perspective** and **tightly reasoned argument.** Make sure to explain how the evidence relates to your thesis.

**Write a Thesis Statement** Read your answers to the analysis questions, and ask yourself which literary element, boldfaced in the chart above, seems most important in the story. Write a preliminary **thesis statement**—a sentence or two stating the point you want to make about that element. As you develop details for your analysis, you may need to refine your thesis. Here is one student's thesis statement focusing on the element of language.

In "Soldier's Home," Ernest Hemingway uses simple, repetitive, unemotional language to express the soldier's feeling of alienation from his family and hometown.

**Use Literary Evidence** Now that you have stated a point about the short story, you must prove it with **literary evidence**—accurate and detailed references to the text. To document quotations from the story, include the page number in parentheses following the quotation and before the period. You may supplement your literary evidence with quotations from secondary sources such as published literary criticism, but most of your evidence should come from the text itself. If you do use information from a secondary source, be sure to credit the source.

**Organize Your Essay** You may arrange your essay in **chronological order,** tracing the development of the literary element from its first appearance in the work until its last, or in **order of importance,** saving your most important piece of evidence for last.

**SKILLS FOCUS**

**Writing Skills**
Write an essay analyzing a short story. Analyze literary elements and the author's style.

**PRACTICE & APPLY** Choose a complex, interesting short story, and use the guidelines in this Mini-Workshop to write an essay analyzing it.

Collection 5: The Moderns

# Midcentury Voices

**Steinbeck**
**Welty**
**Porter**
**Thurber**
**Frost**

Listening children know stories are there. When their elders sit and begin, children are just waiting and hoping for one to come out, like a mouse from its hole.

—Eudora Welty

go.hrw.com

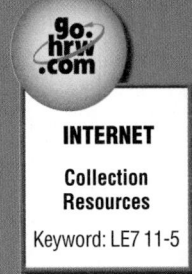

**INTERNET**

**Collection Resources**

Keyword: LE7 11-5

*Compartment C, Car 293* (detail) (1938) by Edward Hopper.

# John Steinbeck
## (1902–1968)

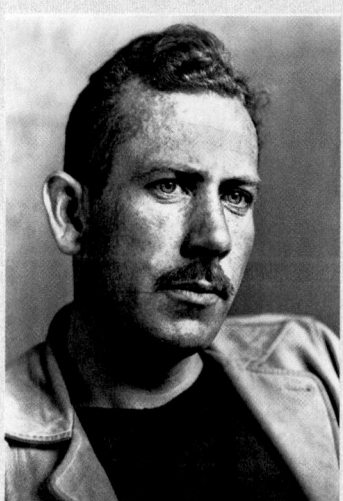

**M**ost writers would probably agree that fiction that delivers a political message may be effective propaganda but it is unlikely to be art. John Steinbeck would *not* have agreed with this precept, and he is a notable exception to it.

During the 1930s, the Great Depression cost millions of people their jobs and shook their faith in the American dream. But big business and the corporate farm seemed untouched by hard times; they were angrily perceived by many as impersonal and indifferent to human hardship.

Many novelists of the time were moved by this sense of injustice and turned their pens to a byproduct of the Depression known as the protest novel. Among these writers, John Steinbeck was the most widely praised.

Steinbeck was born in California's Salinas Valley in 1902, the son of a county treasurer and a schoolteacher. Although he graduated from high school and spent some time at Stanford University, he took more pride in the many jobs he held as a young man than in his formal education. He worked as a mason's assistant, fruit picker, apprentice painter, laboratory assistant, caretaker, surveyor, and journalist. He also wrote seventeen novels, in addition to stories, plays, and screenplays.

Steinbeck's first major success came in 1937 with *Of Mice and Men,* a short, bestselling novel that Steinbeck himself adapted for the Broadway theater. It is a tale of two itinerant farmhands: George and the powerful but simple-minded Lennie. Steinbeck took a pathetic situation and transformed it into an affirmative acceptance of life's brutal conflicts, along with life's possibilities for fellowship and courage.

He followed this success by living and working with some Oklahoma farmers—known as Okies—over the next two years. The result was his strongest and most enduring novel, *The Grapes of Wrath* (1939). This novel tells of the Joad family and their forced migration from the Dust Bowl of Oklahoma to California, the region that promised work at decent wages and a chance to buy land. Once in California, however, the Joads find only the exploitation and poverty of labor camps. Gradually they learn what *Okies* really means—people who never even had a chance.

*The Grapes of Wrath* is an angry book that speaks out on behalf of the migrant workers. Steinbeck sharply criticizes a system that bankrupted thousands of farmers and turned them from their own land, making them into paid help for the big growers. When the novel appeared, it was both praised and condemned, and it became the most widely read of all the novels of the 1930s.

*The Grapes of Wrath* won a Pulitzer Prize in 1940. After this major success, however, Steinbeck's eminence waned. In 1962, Steinbeck was awarded the Nobel Prize in literature and published *Travels with Charley,* a nostalgic account of his odyssey across America with his aged poodle, Charley. But Steinbeck's reputation is grounded on those earlier novels that portray California as the land of American promise.

## For Independent Reading

These works by Steinbeck are recommended:

- *Of Mice and Men* (novel)
- *The Grapes of Wrath* (novel)
- *Travels with Charley* (nonfiction)

# Before You Read

## The Leader of the People

### Make the Connection
#### Quickwrite ✏️

It seems that in every generation there are older people who say, "It was different in my day." These people feel nostalgic about their past, remembering it as a golden age when everything was somehow better, happier, more heroic. In fact, some people end up living mainly in memories of a past that no longer exists and may never have been as they remember it.

Do you believe that the time of heroes is long past? Who are today's heroes, or are there none worthy of the label? What opportunities do you see for heroism today? Quickwrite your thoughts.

### Literary Focus
#### Conflict

"The Leader of the People" shows three generations of a family in conflict because of differences in age, gender, personal histories, and the roles they play on the family ranch. Some conflicts in the story are **external conflicts:** They occur between two or more people. Others are **internal conflicts:** Those occur inside a person's mind. To understand one of the conflicts in the story, take a close look at the recurring dream of a more heroic American past.

> **Conflict** is a struggle between opposing forces or characters in a story.
>
> Conflict can be **internal** (a character struggles with conscience, for example) or **external** (a character struggles against a force of nature, another character, or a whole society).
>
> *For more on Conflict, see the Handbook of Literary and Historical Terms.*

### Background

In "The Leader of the People," John Steinbeck explores the conflict between dream and reality at the heart of so much American fiction. This story appears as the fourth and final part of Steinbeck's novel *The Red Pony* (1945). Each part of this novel was published as a complete story. The stories, all connected by their characters and settings, are "The Gift," "The Great Mountains," "The Promise," and "The Leader of the People."

### Vocabulary Development

**arrogant** (ar′ə·gənt) *adj.*: proud and overly confident.

**immune** (i·myōōn′) *adj.*: protected.

**cleft** (kleft) *n.*: opening or crack in something.

**contemptuously** (kən·temp′chōō·əs·lē) *adv.*: scornfully.

**judiciously** (jōō·dish′əs·lē) *adv.*: wisely, like a judge.

**rancor** (raŋ′kər) *n.*: anger.

**convened** (kən·vēnd′) *v.*: assembled.

**listlessly** (list′lis·lē) *adv.*: wearily; without energy or interest in anything.

**retract** (ri·trakt′) *v.*: take back; draw back.

**disconsolately** (dis·kän′sə·lit·lē) *adv.*: unhappily.

**SKILLS FOCUS**

**Literary Skills**
Understand internal and external conflict.

**INTERNET**

**Vocabulary Practice**
•
**More About John Steinbeck**

Keyword: LE7 11-5

# The Leader of the People

## John Steinbeck

**O**n Saturday afternoon Billy Buck, the ranch-hand, raked together the last of the old year's haystack and pitched small forkfuls over the wire fence to a few mildly interested cattle. High in the air small clouds like puffs of cannon smoke were driven eastward by the March wind. The wind could be heard whishing in the brush on the ridge crests, but no breath of it penetrated down into the ranch-cup.

The little boy, Jody, emerged from the house eating a thick piece of buttered bread. He saw Billy working on the last of the haystack. Jody tramped down scuffing his shoes in a way he had been told was destructive to good shoe-leather. A flock of white pigeons flew out of the black cypress tree as Jody passed, and circled the tree and landed again. A half-grown tortoise-shell[1] cat leaped from the bunkhouse porch, galloped on stiff legs across the road, whirled and galloped back again. Jody picked up a stone to help the game along, but he was too late, for the cat was under the porch before the stone could be discharged. He threw the stone into the cypress tree and started the white pigeons on another whirling flight.

Arriving at the used-up haystack, the boy leaned against the barbed wire fence. "Will that be all of it, do you think?" he asked.

The middle-aged ranch-hand stopped his careful raking and stuck his fork[2] into the ground. He took off his black hat and smoothed down his hair. "Nothing left of it that isn't soggy from ground moisture," he said. He replaced his hat and rubbed his dry leathery hands together.

"Ought to be plenty mice," Jody suggested.

---

1. **tortoise-shell** *n.* used as *adj.*: having a pattern of brown and yellow markings, as commonly seen on the shell of a tortoise.
2. **fork** *n.*: pitchfork.

*Ranch Near San Luis Obispo, Evening Light* (c. 1935) by Phil Paradise. Oil on canvas (28″ × 34″).

The Buck Collection, Laguna Beach, California.

"Lousy with them," said Billy. "Just crawling with mice."

"Well, maybe, when you get all through, I could call the dogs and hunt the mice."

"Sure, I guess you could," said Billy Buck. He lifted a forkful of the damp ground-hay and threw it into the air. Instantly three mice leaped out and burrowed frantically under the hay again.

Jody sighed with satisfaction. Those plump, sleek, arrogant mice were doomed. For eight months they had lived and multiplied in the haystack. They had been immune from cats, from traps, from poison and from Jody. They had grown smug in their security, overbearing and fat. Now the time of disaster had come; they would not survive another day.

Billy looked up at the top of the hills that surrounded the ranch. "Maybe you better ask your father before you do it," he suggested.

"Well, where is he? I'll ask him now."

"He rode up to the ridge ranch after dinner. He'll be back pretty soon."

Jody slumped against the fence post. "I don't think he'd care."

As Billy went back to his work he said ominously, "You'd better ask him anyway. You know how he is."

Jody did know. His father, Carl Tiflin, insisted upon giving permission for anything that was done on the ranch, whether it was important or not. Jody sagged farther against the post until he was sitting on the ground. He looked up at the little puffs of wind-driven cloud. "Is it like to rain, Billy?"

"It might. The wind's good for it, but not strong enough."

"Well, I hope it don't rain until after I kill those damn mice." He looked over his shoulder to see whether Billy had noticed the mature profanity. Billy worked on without comment.

Jody turned back and looked at the side-hill where the road from the outside world came down. The hill was washed with lean March sunshine. Silver thistles, blue lupins[3] and a few poppies bloomed among the sage bushes. Halfway up the hill Jody could see Doubletree Mutt, the black dog, digging in a squirrel hole. He paddled for a while and then paused to kick bursts of dirt out between his hind legs, and he dug with an earnestness which belied the knowledge he must have had that no dog had ever caught a squirrel by digging in a hole.

Suddenly, while Jody watched, the black dog stiffened, and backed out of the hole and looked up the hill toward the cleft in the ridge where the road came through. Jody looked up too. For a moment Carl Tiflin on horseback stood out against the pale sky and then he moved down the road toward the house. He carried something white in his hand.

The boy started to his feet. "He's got a letter," Jody cried. He trotted away toward the ranch house, for the letter would probably be read aloud and he wanted to be there. He reached the house before his father did, and ran in. He heard Carl dismount from his creaking saddle and slap the horse on the side to send it to the barn where Billy would unsaddle it and turn it out.

Jody ran into the kitchen. "We got a letter!" he cried.

His mother looked up from a pan of beans. "Who has?"

"Father has. I saw it in his hand."

Carl strode into the kitchen then, and Jody's mother asked, "Who's the letter from, Carl?"

He frowned quickly. "How did you know there was a letter?"

She nodded her head in the boy's direction. "Big-Britches Jody told me."

Jody was embarrassed.

His father looked down at him contemptuously. "He *is* getting to be a Big-Britches," Carl

---

3. **lupins** (lo͞o′pinz) *n. pl.:* flowering plants of the bean family; more often spelled *lupines*.

---

**Vocabulary**

**arrogant** (ar′ə·gənt) *adj.:* proud and overly confident.
**immune** (i·myo͞on′) *adj.:* protected.
**cleft** (kleft) *n.:* opening or crack in something.
**contemptuously** (kən·temp′cho͞o·əs·lē) *adv.:* scornfully.

said. "He's minding everybody's business but his own. Got his big nose into everything."

Mrs. Tiflin relented a little. "Well, he hasn't enough to keep him busy. Who's the letter from?"

Carl still frowned on Jody. "I'll keep him busy if he isn't careful." He held out a sealed letter. "I guess it's from your father."

Mrs. Tiflin took a hairpin from her head and slit open the flap. Her lips pursed judiciously. Jody saw her eyes snap back and forth over the lines. "He says," she translated, "he says he's going to drive out Saturday to stay for a little while. Why, this is Saturday. The letter must have been delayed." She looked at the postmark. "This was mailed day before yesterday. It should have been here yesterday." She looked up questioningly at her husband, and then her face darkened angrily. "Now what have you got that look on you for? He doesn't come often."

Carl turned his eyes away from her anger. He could be stern with her most of the time, but when occasionally her temper arose, he could not combat it.

"What's the matter with you?" she demanded again.

In his explanation there was a tone of apology Jody himself might have used. "It's just that he talks," Carl said lamely. "Just talks."

"Well, what of it? You talk yourself."

"Sure I do. But your father only talks about one thing."

"Indians!" Jody broke in excitedly. "Indians and crossing the plains!"

Carl turned fiercely on him. "You get out, Mr. Big-Britches! Go on, now! Get out!"

Jody went miserably out the back door and closed the screen with elaborate quietness. Under the kitchen window his shamed, downcast eyes fell upon a curiously shaped stone, a stone of such fascination that he squatted down and picked it up and turned it over in his hands.

The voices came clearly to him through the open kitchen window. "Jody's damn well right," he heard his father say. "Just Indians and crossing the plains. I've heard that story about how the horses got driven off about a thousand times. He just goes on and on, and he never changes a word in the things he tells."

When Mrs. Tiflin answered her tone was so changed that Jody, outside the window, looked up from his study of the stone. Her voice had become soft and explanatory. Jody knew how her face would have changed to match the tone. She said quietly, "Look at it this way, Carl. That was the big thing in my father's life. He led a wagon train clear across the plains to the coast, and when it was finished, his life was done. It was a big thing to do, but it didn't last long enough. Look!" she continued, "it's as though he was born to do that, and after he finished it, there wasn't anything more for him to do but think about it and talk about it. If there'd been any farther west to go, he'd have gone. He's told me so himself. But at last there was the ocean. He lives right by the ocean where he had to stop."

She had caught Carl, caught him and entangled him in her soft tone.

"I've seen him," he agreed quietly. "He goes down and stares off west over the ocean." His voice sharpened a little. "And then he goes up to the Horseshoe Club in Pacific Grove, and he tells people how the Indians drove off the horses."

She tried to catch him again. "Well, it's everything to him. You might be patient with him and pretend to listen."

Carl turned impatiently away. "Well, if it gets too bad, I can always go down to the bunkhouse and sit with Billy," he said irritably. He walked through the house and slammed the front door after him.

Jody ran to his chores. He dumped the grain to the chickens without chasing any of them. He gathered the eggs from the nests. He trotted into the house with the wood and interlaced it so carefully in the wood-box that two armloads seemed to fill it to overflowing.

His mother had finished the beans by now.

---

**Vocabulary**

**judiciously** (jōo·dish′əs·lē) *adv.*: wisely, like a judge.

She stirred up the fire and brushed off the stove-top with a turkey wing. Jody peered cautiously at her to see whether any rancor toward him remained. "Is he coming today?" Jody asked.

"That's what his letter said."

"Maybe I better walk up the road to meet him."

Mrs. Tiflin clanged the stove-lid shut. "That would be nice," she said. "He'd probably like to be met."

"I guess I'll just do it then."

Outside, Jody whistled shrilly to the dogs. "Come on up the hill," he commanded. The two dogs waved their tails and ran ahead. Along the roadside the sage had tender new tips. Jody tore off some pieces and rubbed them on his hands until the air was filled with the sharp wild smell. With a rush the dogs leaped from the road and yapped into the brush after a rabbit. That was the last Jody saw of them, for when they failed to catch the rabbit, they went back home.

Jody plodded on up the hill toward the ridge top. When he reached the little cleft where the road came through, the afternoon wind struck him and blew up his hair and ruffled his shirt. He looked down on the little hills and ridges below and then out at the huge green Salinas Valley. He could see the white town of Salinas far out in the flat and the flash of its windows under the waning sun. Directly below him, in an oak tree, a crow congress had convened. The tree was black with crows all cawing at once.

Then Jody's eyes followed the wagon road down from the ridge where he stood, and lost it behind a hill, and picked it up again on the other side. On that distant stretch he saw a cart slowly pulled by a bay[4] horse. It disappeared behind the hill. Jody sat down on the ground and watched the place where the cart would reappear again. The wind sang on the hilltops and the puff-ball clouds hurried eastward.

Then the cart came into sight and stopped. A man dressed in black dismounted from the seat and walked to the horse's head. Although it was

so far away, Jody knew he had unhooked the check-rein, for the horse's head dropped forward. The horse moved on, and the man walked slowly up the hill beside it. Jody gave a glad cry and ran down the road toward them. The squirrels bumped along off the road, and a road-runner flirted its tail and raced over the edge of the hill and sailed out like a glider.

Jody tried to leap into the middle of his shadow at every step. A stone rolled under his foot and he went down. Around a little bend he raced, and there, a short distance ahead, were his grandfather and the cart. The boy dropped from his unseemly[5] running and approached at a dignified walk.

The horse plodded stumble-footedly up the hill and the old man walked beside it. In the lowering sun their giant shadows flickered darkly behind them. The grandfather was dressed in a black broadcloth suit and he wore kid congress gaiters[6] and a black tie on a short, hard collar. He carried his black slouch hat in his hand. His white beard was cropped close and his white eyebrows overhung his eyes like mustaches. The blue eyes were sternly merry. About the whole face and figure there was a granite dignity, so that every motion seemed an impossible thing. Once at rest, it seemed the old man would be stone, would never move again. His steps were slow and certain. Once made, no step could ever be retraced; once headed in a direction, the path would never bend nor the pace increase nor slow.

When Jody appeared around the bend, Grandfather waved his hat slowly in welcome, and he called, "Why, Jody! Come down to meet me, have you?"

Jody sidled[7] near and turned and matched

---

4. **bay** *adj.:* reddish brown.

5. **unseemly** *adj.:* improper.
6. **kid congress gaiters:** high leather (kid) boots with elastic inserts in each side.
7. **sidled** (sīd′'ld) *v.:* approached sideways.

---

**Vocabulary**

**rancor** (raŋ′kər) *n.:* anger.
**convened** (kən·vēnd′) *v.:* assembled.

his step to the old man's step and stiffened his body and dragged his heels a little. "Yes, sir," he said. "We got your letter only today."

"Should have been here yesterday," said Grandfather. "It certainly should. How are all the folks?"

"They're fine, sir." He hesitated and then suggested shyly, "Would you like to come on a mouse hunt tomorrow, sir?"

"Mouse hunt, Jody?" Grandfather chuckled. "Have the people of this generation come down to hunting mice? They aren't very strong, the new people, but I hardly thought mice would be game for them."

"No, sir. It's just play. The haystack's gone. I'm going to drive out the mice to the dogs. And you can watch, or even beat the hay a little."

The stern, merry eyes turned down on him. "I see. You don't eat them, then. You haven't come to that yet."

Jody explained, "The dogs eat them, sir. It wouldn't be much like hunting Indians, I guess."

"No, not much—but then later, when the troops were hunting Indians and shooting children and burning teepees, it wasn't much different from your mouse hunt."

They topped the rise and started down into the ranch cup, and they lost the sun from their shoulders. "You've grown," Grandfather said. "Nearly an inch, I should say."

"More," Jody boasted. "Where they mark me on the door, I'm up more than an inch since Thanksgiving even."

Grandfather's rich throaty voice said, "Maybe you're getting too much water and turning to pith and stalk. Wait until you head out, and then we'll see."[8]

Jody looked quickly into the old man's face to see whether his feelings should be hurt, but there was no will to injure, no punishing nor putting-in-your-place light in the keen blue eyes. "We might kill a pig," Jody suggested.

"Oh, no! I couldn't let you do that. You're just humoring me. It isn't the time and you know it."

"You know Riley, the big boar, sir?"

"Yes. I remember Riley well."

"Well, Riley ate a hole into that same haystack, and it fell down on him and smothered him."

"Pigs do that when they can," said Grandfather.

"Riley was a nice pig, for a boar, sir. I rode him sometimes, and he didn't mind."

A door slammed at the house below them, and they saw Jody's mother standing on the porch waving her apron in welcome. And they saw Carl Tiflin walking up from the barn to be at the house for the arrival.

The sun had disappeared from the hills by now. The blue smoke from the house chimney hung in flat layers in the purpling ranch-cup. The puff-ball clouds, dropped by the falling wind, hung listlessly in the sky.

Billy Buck came out of the bunkhouse and

---

8. **Maybe . . . we'll see:** Like an overwatered plant, Jody may grow tall but not be very productive. Not until he "heads out" will anyone know what he is capable of.

**Vocabulary**

**listlessly** (list′lis·lē) *adv.:* wearily; without energy or interest in anything.

*Pioneers of the West* (1934) by Helen Lundeberg. Oil on canvas (40″ × 50¼″).
National Museum of American Art, Washington D.C./Courtesy Art Resource, New York.

flung a wash basin of soapy water on the ground. He had been shaving in mid-week, for Billy held Grandfather in reverence, and Grandfather said that Billy was one of the few men of the new generation who had not gone soft. Although Billy was in middle age, Grandfather considered him a boy. Now Billy was hurrying toward the house too.

When Jody and Grandfather arrived, the three were waiting for them in front of the yard gate.

Carl said, "Hello, sir. We've been looking for you."

Mrs. Tiflin kissed Grandfather on the side of his beard, and stood still while his big hand patted her shoulder. Billy shook hands solemnly, grinning under his straw mustache. "I'll put up your horse," said Billy, and he led the rig away.

Grandfather watched him go, and then, turning back to the group, he said as he had said a hundred times before, "There's a good boy. I knew his father, old Mule-tail Buck. I never knew why they called him Mule-tail except he packed mules."

Mrs. Tiflin turned and led the way into the house. "How long are you going to stay, Father? Your letter didn't say."

"Well, I don't know. I thought I'd stay about two weeks. But I never stay as long as I think I'm going to."

In a short while they were sitting at the white oilcloth table eating their supper. The lamp with the tin reflector hung over the table. Outside the dining-room windows the big moths battered softly against the glass.

Grandfather cut his steak into tiny pieces and chewed slowly. "I'm hungry," he said. "Driving out here got my appetite up. It's like when we were crossing. We all got so hungry every night we could hardly wait to let the meat get done. I could eat about five pounds of buffalo meat every night."

"It's moving around does it," said Billy. "My father was a government packer. I helped him when I was a kid. Just the two of us could about clean up a deer's ham."

"I knew your father, Billy," said Grandfather. "A fine man he was. They called him Mule-tail Buck. I don't know why except he packed mules."

"That was it," Billy agreed. "He packed mules."

Grandfather put down his knife and fork and looked around the table. "I remember one time we ran out of meat—" His voice dropped to a curious low sing-song, dropped into a tonal groove the story had worn for itself. "There was no buffalo, no antelope, not even rabbits. The hunters couldn't even shoot a coyote. That was the time for the leader to be on the watch. I was the leader, and I kept my eyes open. Know why? Well, just the minute the people began to get hungry they'd start slaughtering the team oxen. Do you believe that? I've heard of parties that just ate up their draft cattle. Started from the middle and worked toward the ends. Finally they'd eat the lead pair, and then the wheelers. The leader of a party had to keep them from doing that."

In some manner a big moth got into the room and circled the hanging kerosene lamp. Billy got up and tried to clap it between his hands. Carl struck with a cupped palm and caught the moth and broke it. He walked to the window and dropped it out.

"As I was saying," Grandfather began again, but Carl interrupted him. "You'd better eat some more meat. All the rest of us are ready for our pudding."

Jody saw a flash of anger in his mother's eyes. Grandfather picked up his knife and fork. "I'm pretty hungry, all right," he said. "I'll tell you about that later."

When supper was over, when the family and Billy Buck sat in front of the fireplace in the other room, Jody anxiously watched Grandfather. He saw the signs he knew. The bearded head leaned forward; the eyes lost their sternness and looked wonderingly into the fire; the big lean fingers laced themselves on the black knees. "I wonder," he began, "I just wonder whether I ever told you how those thieving Piutes[9] drove off thirty-five of our horses."

"I think you did," Carl interrupted. "Wasn't it just before you went up into the Tahoe country?"

Grandfather turned quickly toward his son-in-law. "That's right. I guess I must have told you that story."

"Lots of times," Carl said cruelly, and he avoided his wife's eyes. But he felt the angry eyes on him, and he said, " 'Course I'd like to hear it again."

Grandfather looked back at the fire. His fingers unlaced and laced again. Jody knew how he felt, how his insides were collapsed and empty. Hadn't Jody been called a Big-Britches that very afternoon? He arose to heroism and opened himself to the term Big-Britches again. "Tell about Indians," he said softly.

Grandfather's eyes grew stern again. "Boys

---

9. **Piutes** (pī′yo͞ots′): usually spelled *Paiutes.* The Paiutes are an American Indian people who originally lived in Utah, Arizona, Nevada, and California.

always want to hear about Indians. It was a job for men, but boys want to hear about it. Well, let's see. Did I ever tell you how I wanted each wagon to carry a long iron plate?"

Everyone but Jody remained silent. Jody said, "No. You didn't."

"Well, when the Indians attacked, we always put the wagons in a circle and fought from between the wheels. I thought that if every wagon carried a long plate with rifle holes, the men could stand the plates on the outside of the wheels when the wagons were in the circle and they would be protected. It would save lives and that would make up for the extra weight of the iron. But of course the party wouldn't do it. No party had done it before and they couldn't see why they should go to the expense. They lived to regret it, too."

Jody looked at his mother, and knew from her expression that she was not listening at all. Carl picked at a callus on his thumb and Billy Buck watched a spider crawling up the wall.

Grandfather's tone dropped into its narrative groove again. Jody knew in advance exactly what words would fall. The story droned on, speeded up for the attack, grew sad over the wounds, struck a dirge[10] at the burials on the great plains. Jody sat quietly watching Grandfather. The stern blue eyes were detached. He looked as though he were not very interested in the story himself.

When it was finished, when the pause had been politely respected as the frontier of the story, Billy Buck stood up and stretched and hitched his trousers. "I guess I'll turn in," he said. Then he faced Grandfather. "I've got an old powder horn and a cap and ball pistol down to the bunkhouse. Did I ever show them to you?"

Grandfather nodded slowly. "Yes, I think you did, Billy. Reminds me of a pistol I had when I was leading the people across." Billy stood po-

---

10. **dirge** (dʉrj) *n.:* sad song that accompanies a funeral or expresses grief.

## A CLOSER LOOK: SOCIAL INFLUENCES

### The West: Its Mythmakers and Archetypes

*"This is the West, sir. When the legend becomes fact, print the legend."*

—*from* "The Man Who Shot Liberty Valance" *by* Dorothy Johnson

INFORMATIONAL TEXT

When Jody lies in bed thinking of "the impossible world of Indians and buffaloes" that he has heard about from his grandfather's tales, he muses that "a race of giants had lived then, fearless men, men of a staunchness unknown in this day." Jody's idealized vision of the West is a vision firmly entrenched in the popular imagination. Hollywood filmmakers played a major role in creating this larger-than-life vision. Starting with silent films such as *The Great Train Robbery* (1903), western movies have presented a world of heroes, evildoers, epic cattle drives, and heart-stopping action, all against a backdrop of spectacular scenery.

**The archetypal hero.** Dominating the action in western films is the western hero: self-reliant, solitary, often shadowed by a mysterious or tragic past, and ever ready to take matters into his hands. He is fearless, possessed of awesome skills, at home with nature and animals (especially his horse), in command of people as well as things. He usually is awkward with women. He routinely punishes evildoers and rescues the good (usually women). Above all, he displays integrity and honor. This character of the heroic, solitary man who emerges from a mysterious past to save a threatened people is an **archetype**—a model for countless heroes, ranging from the ancient superhero Beowulf to the latest *Star Wars* hero.

Western screen heroes have been played by such stars as Gary Cooper (most notably in *High Noon,* 1952); Alan Ladd, who was perhaps

litely until the little story was done, and then he said, "Good night," and went out of the house.

Carl Tiflin tried to turn the conversation then. "How's the country between here and Monterey? I've heard it's pretty dry."

"It is dry," said Grandfather. "There's not a drop of water in the Laguna Seca. But it's a long pull from '87. The whole country was powder then, and in '61 I believe all the coyotes starved to death. We had fifteen inches of rain this year."

"Yes, but it all came too early. We could do with some now." Carl's eye fell on Jody. "Hadn't you better be getting to bed?"

Jody stood up obediently. "Can I kill the mice in the old haystack, sir?"

"Mice? Oh! Sure, kill them all off. Billy said there isn't any good hay left."

Jody exchanged a secret and satisfying look with Grandfather. "I'll kill every one tomorrow," he promised.

Jody lay in his bed and thought of the impossible world of Indians and buffaloes, a world that had ceased to be forever. He wished he could have been living in the heroic time, but he knew he was not of heroic timber.[11] No one living now, save possibly Billy Buck, was worthy to do the things that had been done. A race of giants had lived then, fearless men, men of a staunchness unknown in this day. Jody thought of the wide plains and of the wagons moving across like centipedes. He thought of Grandfather on a huge white horse, marshaling[12] the people. Across his mind marched the great phantoms, and they marched off the earth and they were gone.

He came back to the ranch for a moment, then. He heard the dull rushing sound that space and silence make. He heard one of the dogs, out in the doghouse, scratching a flea and bumping his elbow against the floor with every

---

11. **timber** *n.:* character.
12. **marshaling** *v.* used as *adj.:* leading; guiding.

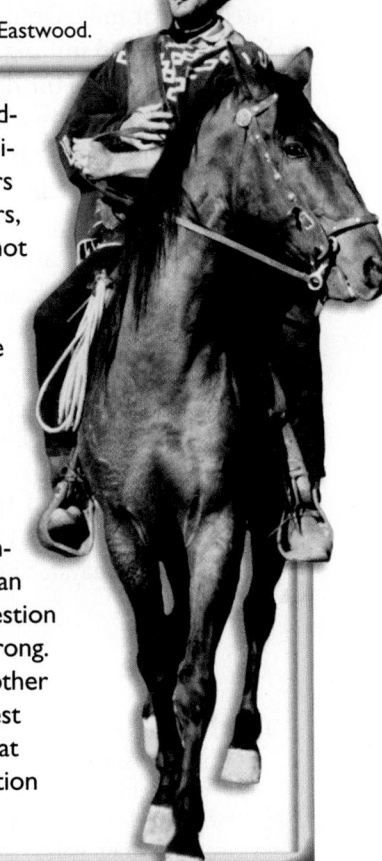

Clint Eastwood.

the most archetypal western hero in *Shane* (1953); and John Wayne, the actor who became *the* rugged western hero in many Americans' minds in films like *She Wore a Yellow Ribbon* (1949) and *True Grit* (1969). Clint Eastwood has become John Wayne's successor as the archetype of the lone western hero.

**Revising the myth.** But historians tell us that the West—and the western hero—was a far cry from movie depictions. The myth tells of a land where rugged individualists lived in harmony with nature, where men settled scores with shootouts on the town's main street. But in the historical West, eastern investors and federal government programs played major roles in land development. Certain farming practices created environmental catastrophes, and the some-times terrifying loneliness and hardships of the prairie tore apart families and drove some homesteaders mad. (Also, cattle rustlers, burglars, and other criminals were often shot unceremoniously in the back, not in well-orchestrated shootouts.)

If we know the truth about the West, why do most of us still prefer the legend? Perhaps because the myth shows us the people we wish we were and the world we wish we lived in. The world of the mythic West is a simpler, much more romantic one than ours, one in which there's no question about distinguishing right from wrong. Indeed, filmmakers, writers, and other mythmakers of the American West have always found an audience that eagerly embraces the transformation of reality into legend.

stroke. Then the wind arose again and the black cypress groaned and Jody went to sleep.

He was up half an hour before the triangle sounded for breakfast. His mother was rattling the stove to make the flames roar when Jody went through the kitchen. "You're up early," she said. "Where are you going?"

"Out to get a good stick. We're going to kill the mice today."

"Who is 'we'?"

"Why, Grandfather and I."

"So you've got him in it. You always like to have someone in with you in case there's blame to share."

"I'll be right back," said Jody. "I just want to have a good stick ready for after breakfast."

He closed the screen door after him and went out into the cool blue morning. The birds were noisy in the dawn and the ranch cats came down from the hill like blunt snakes. They had been hunting gophers in the dark, and although the four cats were full of gopher meat, they sat in a semi-circle at the back door and mewed piteously for milk. Doubletree Mutt and Smasher moved sniffing along the edge of the brush, performing the duty with rigid ceremony, but when Jody whistled, their heads jerked up and their tails waved. They plunged down to him, wriggling their skins and yawning. Jody patted their heads seriously, and moved on to the weathered scrap pile. He selected an old broom handle and a short piece of inch-square scrap wood. From his pocket he took a shoelace and tied the ends of the sticks loosely together to make a flail.[13] He whistled his new weapon through the air and struck the ground experimentally, while the dogs leaped aside and whined with apprehension.

Jody turned and started down past the house toward the old haystack ground to look over

---

13. **flail** *n.:* farm tool for hand-threshing grain. A flail is made of a short stick fastened with a leather strap to a longer handle. The user lets the short stick swing freely from the handle to knock the heads from the grain stalks.

the field of slaughter, but Billy Buck, sitting patiently on the back steps, called to him, "You better come back. It's only a couple of minutes till breakfast."

Jody changed his course and moved toward the house. He leaned his flail against the steps. "That's to drive the mice out," he said. "I'll bet they're fat. I'll bet they don't know what's going to happen to them today."

"No, nor you either," Billy remarked philosophically, "nor me, nor anyone."

Jody was staggered by this thought. He knew it was true. His imagination twitched away from the mouse hunt. Then his mother came out on the back porch and struck the triangle, and all thoughts fell in a heap.

Grandfather hadn't appeared at the table when they sat down. Billy nodded at his empty chair. "He's all right? He isn't sick?"

"He takes a long time to dress," said Mrs. Tiflin. "He combs his whiskers and rubs up his shoes and brushes his clothes."

Carl scattered sugar on his mush. "A man that's led a wagon train across the plains has got to be pretty careful how he dresses."

Mrs. Tiflin turned on him. "Don't do that, Carl! Please don't!" There was more of threat than of request in her tone. And the threat irritated Carl.

"Well, how many times do I have to listen to the story of the iron plates, and the thirty-five horses? That time's done. Why can't he forget it, now it's done?" He grew angrier while he talked, and his voice rose. "Why does he have to tell them over and over? He came across the plains. All right! Now it's finished. Nobody wants to hear about it over and over."

The door into the kitchen closed softly. The four at the table sat frozen. Carl laid his mush spoon on the table and touched his chin with his fingers.

Then the kitchen door opened and Grandfather walked in. His mouth smiled tightly and his eyes were squinted. "Good morning," he said, and he sat down and looked at his mush dish.

Carl could not leave it there. "Did—did you hear what I said?"

Grandfather jerked a little nod.

"I don't know what got into me, sir. I didn't mean it. I was just being funny."

Jody glanced in shame at his mother, and he saw that she was looking at Carl, and that she wasn't breathing. It was an awful thing that he was doing. He was tearing himself to pieces to talk like that. It was a terrible thing to him to retract a word, but to retract it in shame was infinitely worse.

Grandfather looked sidewise. "I'm trying to get right side up," he said gently. "I'm not being mad. I don't mind what you said, but it might be true, and I would mind that."

"It isn't true," said Carl. "I'm not feeling well this morning. I'm sorry I said it."

"Don't be sorry, Carl. An old man doesn't see things sometimes. Maybe you're right. The crossing is finished. Maybe it should be forgotten, now it's done."

Carl got up from the table. "I've had enough to eat. I'm going to work. Take your time, Billy!" He walked quickly out of the dining-room. Billy gulped the rest of his food and followed soon after. But Jody could not leave his chair.

"Won't you tell any more stories?" Jody asked.

"Why, sure I'll tell them, but only when—I'm sure people want to hear them."

"I like to hear them, sir."

"Oh! Of course you do, but you're a little boy. It was a job for men, but only little boys like to hear about it."

Jody got up from his place. "I'll wait outside for you, sir. I've got a good stick for those mice."

He waited by the gate until the old man came out on the porch. "Let's go down and kill the mice now," Jody called.

"I think I'll just sit in the sun, Jody. You go kill the mice."

"You can use my stick if you like."

"No, I'll just sit here a while."

Jody turned disconsolately away, and walked down toward the old haystack. He tried to whip up his enthusiasm with thoughts of the fat juicy mice. He beat the ground with his flail. The dogs coaxed and whined about him, but he could not go. Back at the house he could see Grandfather sitting on the porch, looking small and thin and black.

Jody gave up and went to sit on the steps at the old man's feet.

"Back already? Did you kill the mice?"

"No, sir. I'll kill them some other day."

The morning flies buzzed close to the ground and the ants dashed about in front of the steps. The heavy smell of sage slipped down the hill. The porch boards grew warm in the sunshine.

Jody hardly knew when Grandfather started to talk. "I shouldn't stay here, feeling the way I do." He examined his strong old hands. "I feel as though the crossing wasn't worth doing." His eyes moved up the side-hill and stopped on a motionless hawk perched on a dead limb. "I tell those old stories, but they're not what I want to tell. I only know how I want people to feel when I tell them.

"It wasn't Indians that were important, nor adventures, nor even getting out here. It was a whole bunch of people made into one big crawling beast. And I was the head. It was westering and westering. Every man wanted something for himself, but the big beast that was all of them wanted only westering. I was the leader, but if I hadn't been there, someone else would have been the head. The thing had to have a head.

"Under the little bushes the shadows were black at white noonday. When we saw the mountains at last, we cried—all of us. But it wasn't getting here that mattered, it was movement and westering.

"We carried life out here and set it down the way those ants carry eggs. And I was the leader. The westering was as big as God, and the slow steps that made the movement piled up and piled up until the continent was crossed.

"Then we came down to the sea, and it was done." He stopped and wiped his eyes until the rims were red. "That's what I should be telling instead of stories."

When Jody spoke, Grandfather started and looked down at him. "Maybe I could lead the people some day," Jody said.

---

**Vocabulary**

**retract** (ri·trakt') *v.*: take back; draw back.

**disconsolately** (dis·kän′sə·lit·lē) *adv.*: unhappily.

The old man smiled. "There's no place to go. There's the ocean to stop you. There's a line of old men along the shore hating the ocean because it stopped them."

"In boats I might, sir."

"No place to go, Jody. Every place is taken. But that's not the worst—no, not the worst. Westering has died out of the people. Westering isn't a hunger any more. It's all done. Your father is right. It is finished." He laced his fingers on his knee and looked at them.

Jody felt very sad. "If you'd like a glass of lemonade I could make it for you."

Grandfather was about to refuse, and then he saw Jody's face. "That would be nice," he said. "Yes, it would be nice to drink a lemonade."

Jody ran into the kitchen where his mother was wiping the last of the breakfast dishes. "Can I have a lemon to make a lemonade for Grandfather?"

His mother mimicked—"And another lemon to make a lemonade for you."

"No, ma'am. I don't want one."

"Jody! You're sick!" Then she stopped suddenly. "Take a lemon out of the cooler," she said softly. "Here, I'll reach the squeezer down to you." ■

# Response and Analysis

## Reading Check

1. How does Jody feel about his grandfather's visit?

2. Why does Jody's father dread the visit?

3. What are Grandfather's stories about?

4. In what way was Grandfather "the leader of the people"?

## Thinking Critically

5. What seems to have been the significance of "the crossing" for Jody's grandfather?

6. This story centers on several **conflicts**—some external, between members of the family, and some internal, existing in a character's mind. Describe the conflicts in the story, and explain how each conflict is resolved by the story's conclusion. (*Are all the conflicts resolved?*) Do you think the story is more about the stresses of family life than it is about the changing attitudes of each new generation? Explain your responses.

7. Re-read *A Closer Look* (pages 752–753). How does Jody's grandfather in his prime resemble the **archetypal**

**character** of the western hero? (Do you think Grandfather's view of the past reflects more myth than reality or vice versa?)

8. There is another **archetype** in this story, one that is also found in many other stories through the ages and in actual life as well. The archetype is not a character but an attitude: It involves a conviction that there was a time and place in the past that was more perfect, more heroic than the present. Some people call this a yearning for a golden age. (A Greek myth tells us that the first people lived in a golden age, a time of perfect happiness.) How is this archetypal longing for a past golden age expressed in Steinbeck's story? Where do you hear or see this longing for a more perfect past expressed in actual life? Think of stories, TV shows, films, and even commercials.

9. The story is full of **ironies,** or surprising departures from what is expected. How does Steinbeck use the mouse hunt ironically, to contrast the modern age with the heroic past?

**Literary Skills**
Analyze internal and external conflict and archetypes.

**Writing Skills**
Write an essay comparing and contrasting a story and a poem. Write an essay comparing and contrasting the themes from a novel and a story.

**Vocabulary Skills**
Clarify word meanings.

10. Think about the **theme** of the story. What does the story reveal about the relationship between dreams and reality and the loss of the heroic ideal?

11. Look back at your Quickwrite notes. Do you believe, as Jody's grandfather does, that there are no longer any worlds for young people to conquer? If not, where do you see opportunities for Jody and other young people to prove themselves as heroes? ✎

12. In your opinion, is Jody right to want to listen to Grandfather's stories over and over again, or is Carl right in wanting to forget the past and concentrate on the future? Are there, perhaps, ways in which both characters are right? Give reasons to support your views.

## WRITING

### Comparing Literature

In an **essay,** compare and contrast Steinbeck's story with Whitman's poem "I understand the large hearts of heroes" (page 370). Focus on three of these topics for your points of comparison:

- main theme in each text
- what each text says about heroism
- what each text says about America
- tone of each text (positive, negative, cynical, sad, uplifting)
- view of life in each text
- how each text's historical context affects its theme and tone

Be sure to use passages from each text to support your points.

### Variations on a Theme

Review the major **theme** of Steinbeck's story as you see it. You may want to focus on the contrast between dream and reality, on the loss of heroism, on the conflicts between generations, on disillusionment, or on the limitations of the American dream. Then, choose a novel from your own reading that deals with a similar theme. Write an **essay** comparing and contrasting the ways in which the novel and the story develop the theme. In your essay, focus on what the characters in the story and in the novel discover as they work out their conflicts.

▷ **Use "Analyzing a Novel," pages 870–877, for help with this assignment.**

### Vocabulary Development

#### What's the Difference?

To show that you understand the meaning of each Vocabulary word, answer the following questions. Use a dictionary for help.

1. How is *arrogant* different from *ignorant*?
2. How is *immune* different from *immure*?
3. How is *cleft* different from *cliff*?
4. How is *contemptuously* different from *contemporaneously*?
5. How is *judiciously* different from *judgmentally*?
6. How is *rancor* different from *rigor*?
7. How is *convened* different from *convinced*?
8. How is *listlessly* different from *liberally*?
9. How is *retract* different from *repeat*?
10. How is *disconsolately* different from *discontinuously*?

# Eudora Welty
## (1909–2001)

**E**udora Welty was born in the quintessentially Southern city of Jackson, Mississippi, where she lived almost her whole life. As the daughter of an insurance man and a schoolteacher, she enjoyed a conventional girlhood. She recalled pleading with her brothers to teach her golf, sharing their enthusiasm for baseball, and bicycling to the library in *two* petticoats to forestall the librarian's sarcastic remark, "I can practically see through you."

Welty attended Mississippi State College for Women, graduated from the University of Wisconsin, and did graduate work at Columbia University, anticipating a career in advertising. However, the Depression sent her home to Jackson with a belief, which did not fail her, that she would succeed as a writer of fiction.

Among those who shared Welty's belief was the writer Katherine Anne Porter, who befriended her when Welty was sending out stories and getting back rejection slips. Another person who shared Welty's confidence in her writing abilities was her literary agent Diarmuid Russell. He not only took her on as a client, but also said of a certain Welty story that if the editor didn't accept it, the two ought to "horsewhip the offending editor for his insult to literature." (The editor in question bought the story.)

Welty's first collections of stories, *A Curtain of Green* and *The Wide Net,* appeared in the 1940s. These were followed by *The Golden Apples* (1949), one of her best-known volumes of short stories. Then came a novella, *The Ponder Heart* (1954), which was made into a Broadway play. *Losing Battles,* Welty's fine comic novel about a family reunion in the rural South, was published in 1970. Two years later Welty produced *The Optimist's Daughter,* an emotionally gripping short novel about family conflicts; this book won her the Pulitzer Prize.

Welty's widely recognized triumph is painstaking accuracy in colloquial, or everyday, speech. She was always fascinated by words, by the way people say things, by snatches of overheard dialogue. She was once delighted to hear a country woman confess to "a gnawing and a craving" for something. Telling a friend about it, Welty added, "Wasn't that a wonderful way of putting it? A gnawing and a craving!"

Welty admitted to being blessed with a visual mind, and she said that this gift makes for "the best shorthand a writer can have." She once wrote, "To watch everything about me I regarded grimly and possessively as a need." Clearly, that need became an enviable artistic vision.

## For Independent Reading

For a glimpse into a writer's young life, read this memoir by Welty:

- *One Writer's Beginnings*

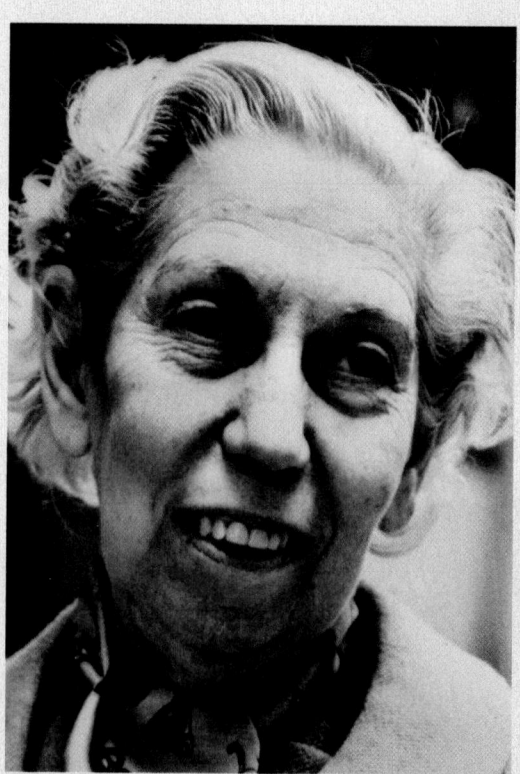

# A Worn Path

## Make the Connection
### Quickwrite 🖉

From earliest times, mythmakers and storytellers have used the perilous journey as an example, or **archetype,** of life itself. When we think of a perilous journey, we might think of a steely, larger-than-life hero or heroine who endures incredible hardships and faces monstrous adversaries. But a perilous journey can be a much more ordinary—even everyday—affair, on a road as modest and simple as a worn path.

Take a moment to write about a journey that you or someone you know undertook. Describe the purpose of the journey, any hardships encountered, and the journey's outcome.

## Literary Focus
### Theme

**Theme** is the truth about life that gives meaning to a story. Theme is almost never directly stated. Instead, the writer hopes that we will enter into the experiences of the characters and share the discoveries they make as they face their conflicts.

When you think about the theme of a story—about what it *means*—think about what happens to the main character. Does the main character discover something or learn something? Does the main character accomplish something important?

Then, think about how that character is like people you know or maybe even like yourself. For example, after you read this story, think about how following this old woman on her worn path might help you understand your own path in life or the path of someone you know.

Theme is not the subject of a story. The subject of this story is a journey. But the story's theme is so vital and interesting that it cannot be stated in a single word; it must be stated in at least one sentence.

> **Theme** is the insight into human life revealed in a story.
>
> *For more on Theme, see the Handbook of Literary and Historical Terms.*

## Background

"A Worn Path" takes place during the Depression of the 1930s. This was a time when one fourth to one third of America's workers were unemployed. As a result, many people were forced to rely on charity for food and medicine, and even shelter. As you read this story, look for clues to the hard life lived by America's poor during this time period.

## Vocabulary Development

**persistent** (pər·sist′ənt) *adj.:* continuing.

**illumined** (i·lōō′mənd) *v.:* lighted up.

**intent** (in·tent′) *adj.:* purposeful.

**appointed** (ə·point′id) *v.* used as *adj.:* assigned.

**solemn** (säl′əm) *adj.:* serious.

**SKILLS FOCUS**

**Literary Skills**
Understand theme and archetype.

go.hrw.com

**INTERNET**

**Vocabulary Practice**

Keyword: LE7 11-5

# A Worn Path

**Eudora Welty**

It was December—a bright frozen day in the early morning. Far out in the country there was an old Negro woman with her head tied in a red rag, coming along a path through the pinewoods. Her name was Phoenix Jackson. She was very old and small and she walked slowly in the dark pine shadows, moving a little from side to side in her steps, with the balanced heaviness and lightness of a pendulum in a grandfather clock. She carried a thin, small cane made from an umbrella, and with this she kept tapping the frozen earth in front of her. This made a grave and <u>persistent</u> noise in the still air, that seemed meditative like the chirping of a solitary little bird.

She wore a dark striped dress reaching down to her shoe tops, and an equally long apron of bleached sugar sacks, with a full pocket: all neat and tidy, but every time she took a step she might have fallen over her shoelaces, which dragged from her unlaced shoes. She looked straight ahead. Her eyes were blue with age. Her skin had a pattern all its own of numberless branching wrinkles and as though a whole little tree stood in the middle of her forehead, but a golden color ran underneath, and the two knobs of her cheeks were <u>illumined</u> by a yellow burning under the dark. Under the red rag her hair came down on her neck in the frailest of ringlets, still black, and with an odor like copper.

Now and then there was a quivering in the thicket. Old Phoenix said, "Out of my way, all you foxes, owls, beetles, jack rabbits, coons, and

**Vocabulary**

**persistent** (pər·sist′ənt) *adj.*: continuing.
**illumined** (i·loo′mənd) *v.*: lighted up.

A woman of the thirties, Hinds County (1935).
Photograph by Eudora Welty.

wild animals! . . . Keep out from under these feet, little bobwhites. . . . Keep the big wild hogs out of my path. Don't let none of those come running in my direction. I got a long way." Under her small black-freckled hand her cane, limber as a buggy whip, would switch at the brush as if to rouse up any hiding things.

On she went. The woods were deep and still. The sun made the pine needles almost too bright to look at, up where the wind rocked. The cones dropped as light as feathers. Down in the hollow was the mourning dove—it was not too late for him.

The path ran up a hill. "Seem like there is chains about my feet, time I get this far," she said, in the voice of argument old people keep to use with themselves. "Something always take a hold of me on this hill—pleads I should stay."

After she got to the top she turned and gave a full, severe look behind her where she had come. "Up through pines," she said at length. "Now down through oaks."

Her eyes opened their widest, and she started down gently. But before she got to the bottom of the hill a bush caught her dress.

Her fingers were busy and intent, but her skirts were full and long, so that before she could pull them free in one place they were caught in another. It was not possible to allow the dress to tear. "I in the thorny bush," she said. "Thorns, you doing your appointed work. Never want to let folks pass, no sir. Old eyes thought you was a pretty little green bush."

Finally, trembling all over, she stood free, and after a moment dared to stoop for her cane.

"Sun so high!" she cried, leaning back and looking, while the thick tears went over her eyes. "The time getting all gone here."

At the foot of this hill was a place where a log was laid across the creek.

"Now comes the trial," said Phoenix.

Putting her right foot out, she mounted the log and shut her eyes. Lifting her skirt, leveling her cane fiercely before her, like a festival figure in some parade, she began to march across. Then she opened her eyes and she was safe on the other side.

"I wasn't as old as I thought," she said.

But she sat down to rest. She spread her skirts on the bank around her and folded her hands over her knees. Up above her was a tree in a pearly cloud of mistletoe. She did not dare to close her eyes, and when a little boy brought her a plate with a slice of marble cake on it she spoke to him. "That would be acceptable," she said. But when she went to take it there was just her own hand in the air.

So she left that tree, and had to go through a barbed-wire fence. There she had to creep and crawl, spreading her knees and stretching her fingers like a baby trying to climb the steps. But she talked loudly to herself: She could not let her dress be torn now, so late in the day, and she could not pay for having her arm or her leg sawed off if she got caught fast where she was.

At last she was safe through the fence and risen up out in the clearing. Big dead trees, like black men with one arm, were standing in the purple stalks of the withered cotton field. There sat a buzzard.

"Who you watching?"

In the furrow[1] she made her way along.

"Glad this not the season for bulls," she said, looking sideways, "and the good Lord made his snakes to curl up and sleep in the winter. A pleasure I don't see no two-headed snake coming around that tree, where it come once. It took a while to get by him, back in the summer."

> Finally, trembling all over, she stood free, and after a moment dared to stoop for her cane.

---

1. **furrow** *n.*: groove in the land made by a plow.

---

**Vocabulary**

**intent** (in·tent′) *adj.*: purposeful.
**appointed** (ə·point′id) *v.* used as *adj.*: assigned.

She passed through the old cotton and went into a field of dead corn. It whispered and shook and was taller than her head. "Through the maze now," she said, for there was no path.

Then there was something tall, black, and skinny there, moving before her.

At first she took it for a man. It could have been a man dancing in the field. But she stood still and listened, and it did not make a sound. It was as silent as a ghost.

"Ghost," she said sharply, "who be you the ghost of? For I have heard of nary death close by."

But there was no answer—only the ragged dancing in the wind.

She shut her eyes, reached out her hand, and touched a sleeve. She found a coat and inside that an emptiness, cold as ice.

"You scarecrow," she said. Her face lighted. "I ought to be shut up for good," she said with laughter. "My senses is gone. I too old. I the oldest people I ever know. Dance, old scarecrow," she said, "while I dancing with you."

She kicked her foot over the furrow, and with mouth drawn down, shook her head once or twice in a little strutting way. Some husks blew down and whirled in streamers about her skirts.

Then she went on, parting her way from side to side with the cane, through the whispering field. At last she came to the end, to a wagon track where the silver grass blew between the red ruts. The quail were walking around like pullets, seeming all dainty and unseen.

"Walk pretty," she said. "This the easy place. This the easy going."

She followed the track, swaying through the quiet bare fields, through the little strings of trees silver in their dead leaves, past cabins silver from weather, with the doors and windows boarded shut, all like old women under a spell sitting there. "I walking in their sleep," she said, nodding her head vigorously.

In a ravine she went where a spring was silently flowing through a hollow log. Old Phoenix bent and drank. "Sweet gum makes the water sweet," she said, and drank more. "Nobody know who made this well, for it was here when I was born."

The track crossed a swampy part where the moss hung as white as lace from every limb. "Sleep on, alligators, and blow your bubbles." Then the track went into the road.

Deep, deep the road went down between the high green-colored banks. Overhead the live oaks met, and it was as dark as a cave.

A black dog with a lolling tongue came up out of the weeds by the ditch. She was meditating, and not ready, and when he came at her she only hit him a little with her cane. Over she went in the ditch, like a little puff of milkweed.

Down there, her senses drifted away. A dream visited her, and she reached her hand up, but nothing reached down and gave her a pull. So she lay there and presently went to talking. "Old woman," she said to herself, "that black dog come up out of the weeds to stall you off, and now there he sitting on his fine tail, smiling at you."

A white man finally came along and found her—a hunter, a young man, with his dog on a chain. "Well, Granny!" he laughed. "What are you doing there?"

"Lying on my back like a June bug waiting to be turned over, mister," she said, reaching up her hand.

He lifted her up, gave her a swing in the air, and set her down. "Anything broken, Granny?"

"No sir, them old dead weeds is springy enough," said Phoenix, when she had got her breath. "I thank you for your trouble."

"Where do you live, Granny?" he asked, while the two dogs were growling at each other.

"Away back yonder, sir, behind the ridge. You can't even see it from here."

"On your way home?"

"No sir, I going to town."

"Why, that's too far! That's as far as I walk when I come out myself, and I get something for my trouble." He patted the stuffed bag he carried, and there hung down a little closed claw. It was one of the bobwhites, with its beak hooked bitterly to show it was dead. "Now you go on home, Granny!"

"I bound to go to town, mister," said Phoenix. "The time come around."

He gave another laugh, filling the whole landscape. "I know you old colored people! Wouldn't miss going to town to see Santa Claus!"

But something held old Phoenix very still. The deep lines in her face went into a fierce and different radiation.[2] Without warning, she had seen with her own eyes a flashing nickel fall out of the man's pocket onto the ground.

"How old are you, Granny?" he was saying.

"There is no telling, mister," she said, "no telling."

Then she gave a little cry and clapped her hands and said, "Git on away from here, dog! Look! Look at that dog!" She laughed as if in admiration. "He ain't scared of nobody. He a big black dog." She whispered, "Sic him!"

"Watch me get rid of that cur," said the man. "Sic him, Pete! Sic him!"

Phoenix heard the dogs fighting, and heard the man running and throwing sticks. She even heard a gunshot. But she was slowly bending forward by that time, further and further forward, the lids stretched down over her eyes, as if she were doing this in her sleep. Her chin was lowered almost to her knees. The yellow palm of her hand came out from the fold of her apron. Her fingers slid down and along the ground under the piece of money with the grace and care they would have in lifting an egg from under a setting hen. Then she slowly straightened up, she stood erect, and the nickel was in her apron pocket. A bird flew by. Her lips moved. "God watching me the whole time. I come to stealing."

The man came back, and his own dog panted about them. "Well, I scared him off that time," he said, and then he laughed and lifted his gun and pointed it at Phoenix.

She stood straight and faced him.

"Doesn't the gun scare you?" he said, still pointing it.

"No, sir, I seen plenty go off closer by, in my day, and for less than what I done," she said holding utterly still.

---

2. **radiation** *n.*: pattern.

He smiled, and shouldered the gun. "Well, Granny," he said, "you must be a hundred years old, and scared of nothing. I'd give you a dime if I had any money with me. But you take my advice and stay home, and nothing will happen to you."

"I bound to go on my way, mister," said Phoenix. She inclined her head in the red rag. Then they went in different directions, but she could hear the gun shooting again and again over the hill.

She walked on. The shadows hung from the oak trees to the road like curtains. Then she smelled woodsmoke, and smelled the river, and she saw a steeple and the cabins on their steep steps. Dozens of little black children whirled around her. There ahead was Natchez shining. Bells were ringing. She walked on.

In the paved city it was Christmas time. There were red and green electric lights strung and crisscrossed everywhere, and all turned on in the daytime. Old Phoenix would have been lost if she had not distrusted her eyesight and depended on her feet to know where to take her.

She paused quietly on the sidewalk where people were passing by. A lady came along in the crowd, carrying an armful of red-, green-, and silver-wrapped presents; she gave off perfume like the red roses in hot summer, and Phoenix stopped her.

"Please, missy, will you lace up my shoe?" She held up her foot.

"What do you want, Grandma?"

"See my shoe," said Phoenix. "Do all right for out in the country, but wouldn't look right to go in a big building."

"Stand still then, Grandma," said the lady. She put her packages down on the sidewalk beside her and laced and tied both shoes tightly.

"Can't lace 'em with a cane," said Phoenix. "Thank you, missy. I doesn't mind asking a nice lady to tie up my shoe, when I gets out on the street."

Moving slowly and from side to side, she went into the big building, and into a tower of steps, where she walked up and around and around until her feet knew to stop.

She entered a door, and there she saw nailed up on the wall the document that had been stamped with the gold seal and framed in the gold frame, which matched the dream that was hung up in her head.

"Here I be," she said. There was a fixed and ceremonial stiffness over her body.

"A charity case, I suppose," said an attendant who sat at the desk before her.

But Phoenix only looked above her head. There was sweat on her face, the wrinkles in her skin shone like a bright net.

"Speak up, Grandma," the woman said. "What's your name? We must have your history, you know. Have you been here before? What seems to be the trouble with you?"

Old Phoenix only gave a twitch to her face as if a fly were bothering her.

"Are you deaf?" cried the attendant.

But then the nurse came in.

"Oh, that's just old Aunt Phoenix," she said. "She doesn't come for herself—she has a little grandson. She makes these trips just as regular as clockwork. She lives away back off the Old Natchez Trace." She bent down. "Well, Aunt Phoenix, why don't you just take a seat? We won't keep you standing after your long trip." She pointed.

The old woman sat down, bolt upright in the chair.

"Now, how is the boy?" asked the nurse.

Old Phoenix did not speak.

"I said, how is the boy?"

But Phoenix only waited and stared straight ahead, her face very <u>solemn</u> and withdrawn into rigidity.

"Is his throat any better?" asked the nurse. "Aunt Phoenix, don't you hear me? Is your grandson's throat any better since the last time you came for the medicine?"

With her hands on her knees, the old woman waited, silent, erect and motionless, just as if she were in armor.

"You mustn't take up our time this way, Aunt Phoenix," the nurse said. "Tell us quickly about your grandson, and get it over. He isn't dead, is he?"

At last there came a flicker and then a flame of comprehension across her face, and she spoke.

"My grandson. It was my memory had left me. There I sat and forgot why I made my long trip."

"Forgot?" The nurse frowned. "After you came so far?"

Then Phoenix was like an old woman begging a dignified forgiveness for waking up frightened in the night. "I never did go to school, I was too old at the Surrender," she said in a soft voice. "I'm an old woman without an education. It was my memory fail me. My little grandson, he is just the same, and I forgot it in the coming."

"Throat never heals, does it?" said the nurse, speaking in a loud, sure voice to old Phoenix. By now she had a card with something written on it, a little list. "Yes. Swallowed lye. When was it?—January—two-three years ago—"

Phoenix spoke unasked now. "No, missy, he not dead, he just the same. Every little while his throat begin to close up again, and he not able to swallow. He not get his breath. He not able to help himself. So the time come around, and I go on another trip for the soothing medicine."

"All right. The doctor said as long as you came to get it, you could have it," said the nurse. "But it's an obstinate case."

"My little grandson, he sit up there in the house all wrapped up, waiting by himself," Phoenix went on. "We is the only two left in the world. He suffer and it don't seem to put him back at all. He got a sweet look. He going to last. He wear a little patch quilt and peep out holding his mouth open like a little bird. I remembers so plain now. I not going to forget him again, no, the whole enduring time. I could tell him from all the others in creation."

"All right." The nurse was trying to hush her now. She brought her a bottle of medicine. "Charity," she said, making a check mark in a book.

**Vocabulary**

**solemn** (säl′əm) *adj.:* serious.

**Old Phoenix held the bottle close to her eyes, and then carefully put it into her pocket.**

Courthouse town, Grenada (1935). Photograph by Eudora Welty.

Old Phoenix held the bottle close to her eyes, and then carefully put it into her pocket.

"I thank you," she said.

"It's Christmas time, Grandma," said the attendant. "Could I give you a few pennies out of my purse?"

"Five pennies is a nickel," said Phoenix stiffly.

"Here's a nickel," said the attendant.

Phoenix rose carefully and held out her hand. She received the nickel and then fished the other nickel out of her pocket and laid it beside the new one. She stared at her palm closely, with her head on one side.

Then she gave a tap with her cane on the floor.

"This is what come to me to do," she said. "I going to the store and buy my child a little windmill they sells, made out of paper. He going to find it hard to believe there such a thing in the world. I'll march myself back where he waiting, holding it straight up in this hand."

She lifted her free hand, gave a little nod, turned around, and walked out of the doctor's office. Then her slow step began on the stairs, going down. ■

Fayette (1930s). Photograph by Eudora Welty.

The path is
the thing
that matters.
—Eudora Welty

# "Is Phoenix Jackson's Grandson Really Dead?"

INFORMATIONAL TEXT

A story writer is more than happy to be read by students; the fact that these serious readers think and feel something in response to his work he finds life-giving. At the same time he may not always be able to reply to their specific questions in kind. I wondered if it might clarify something, for both the questioners and myself, if I set down a general reply to the question that comes to me most often in the mail, from both students and their teachers, after some classroom discussion. The unrivaled favorite is this: "Is Phoenix Jackson's grandson really dead?"

. . . I had not meant to mystify readers by

withholding any fact; it is not a writer's business to tease. The story is told through Phoenix's mind as she undertakes her errand. As the author at one with the character as I tell it, I must assume that the boy is alive. As the reader, you are free to think as you like, of course: The story invites you to believe that no matter what happens, Phoenix for as long as she is able to walk and can hold to her purpose will make her journey. The possibility that she would keep on even if he were dead is there in her devotion and its single-minded, single-track errand. Certainly the artistic truth, which should be good enough for the fact, lies in Phoenix's own answer to that question. When the nurse asks, "He isn't dead, is he?" she speaks for herself: "He still the same. He going to last."

The grandchild is the incentive. But it is the journey, the going of the errand, that is the story, and the question is not whether the grandchild is in reality alive or dead. It doesn't affect the outcome of the story or its meaning from start to finish. But it is not the question itself that has struck me as much as the idea, almost without exception implied in the asking, that for Phoenix's grandson to be dead would somehow make the story "better."

. . . The grandson's plight was real and it made the truth of the story, which is the story of an errand of love carried out. If the child no longer lived, the truth would persist in the "wornness" of the path. But his being dead can't increase the truth of the story, can't affect it one way or the other. I think I signal this, because the end of the story has been reached before old Phoenix gets home again: she simply starts back. To the question "Is the grandson really dead?" I could reply that it doesn't make any difference. I could also say that I did not make him up in order to let him play a trick on Phoenix. But my best answer would be: "Phoenix is alive."

The origin of a story is sometimes a trustworthy clue to the author—or can provide him with the clue—to its key image; maybe in this case it will do the same for the reader. One day I saw a solitary old woman like Phoenix. She was walking; I saw her, at middle distance, in a winter country landscape, and watched her slowly make her way across my line of vision. That sight of her made me write the story. I invented an errand for her, but that only seemed a living part of the figure she was herself: What errand other than for someone else could be making her go? And her going was the first thing, her persisting in her landscape was the real thing, and the first and the real were what I wanted and worked to keep. I brought her up close enough, by imagination, to describe her face, make her present to the eyes, but the full-length figure moving across the winter fields was the indelible one and the image to keep, and the perspective extending into the vanishing distance the true one to hold in mind.

I invented for my character, as I wrote, some passing adventures—some dreams and harassments and a small triumph or two, some jolts to her pride, some flights of fancy to console her, one or two encounters to scare her, a moment that gave her cause to feel ashamed, a moment to dance and preen—for it had to be a journey, and all these things belonged to that, parts of life's uncertainty.

. . . What I hoped would come clear was that in the whole surround of this story, the world it threads through, the only certain thing at all is the worn path. The habit of love cuts through confusion and stumbles or contrives its way out of difficulty, it remembers the way even when it forgets, for a dumbfounded moment, its reason for being. The path is the thing that matters.

*Eudora Welty*

# Response and Analysis

## Reading Check

1. What is the purpose of Phoenix Jackson's journey?

2. List several of the obstacles Phoenix overcomes.

3. What is the result of Phoenix's long and perilous journey? Does she get what she wants? Explain.

## Thinking Critically

4. In mythology a phoenix is a bird that lives for five hundred years and then is reborn from its own ashes. Why is *Phoenix* an appropriate name for the main character?

5. How do Welty's descriptions of Phoenix's appearance, speech, and behavior identify her with the world of nature and with time itself?

6. Describe what Phoenix's encounters with the little boy, the buzzard, the scarecrow, the thorny bush, and the hunter tell about her **character.**

7. How would you state Welty's major **theme** in "A Worn Path"? Put another way, what "worn path" is open to us all? Refer to your Quickwrite notes for ideas. ✏️

8. In the *Primary Source* on page 766, Welty says that the "worn path" is a **metaphor** for the habit of love. Explain what Welty means by "the habit of love," and tell why this habit might be compared to a worn path (and not to a new road, or the shining path of a rocket, or a crystal stairway).

9. Is Phoenix Jackson a heroine in the traditional sense of the word? Explain, giving examples of other heroines you have encountered in literature, television, or film.

## Extending and Evaluating

10. Many readers leave "A Worn Path" wondering whether or not Phoenix's grandson is actually alive. In light of this, do you believe that Welty has provided a satisfying end to this story? Why or why not? (See the *Primary Source* on page 766.)

11. Which of the people Phoenix encounters treat her in a condescending manner? Given the time period in which the story is set, are the characters' actions and behavior realistic? Explain.

## WRITING

### A Perilous Journey

Writers through the ages have used the **archetype** of a journey to make larger observations about life. Phoenix Jackson's walk on the "worn path" follows this literary tradition. Examine Phoenix's journey. In an **essay,** draw parallels between stages of her journey and life itself. Where does Phoenix encounter problems, triumphs, shame, and joy?

## LISTENING AND SPEAKING

### Interpret Dialogue

With two other classmates, cast and rehearse the scene involving Phoenix, the nurse, and the attendant. Use text clues to interpret your lines. When you are satisfied with the scene, perform it for the class.

**SKILLS FOCUS**

**Literary Skills**
Analyze theme and archetype.

**Writing Skills**
Write an essay analyzing an archetype.

**Listening and Speaking Skills**
Perform a scene from a story.

**Vocabulary Skills**
Use words in context.

go.
hrw
.com

**INTERNET**

Projects and Activities

Keyword: LE7 11-5

## Vocabulary Development

### Sentence Completion

Fill in each blank with the appropriate Vocabulary word from the list below.

| persistent | intent | solemn |
|---|---|---|
| illumined | appointed | |

At the hour ____ by the agency, hundreds of citizens, driven by ____ hunger, lined up for food. The hall was dark and poorly ____, but the people, ____ on getting something to eat, barely noticed. The atmosphere was quiet and ____ .

# Katherine Anne Porter

(1890–1980)

Katherine Anne Porter was born in a Texas log cabin. She was raised, mostly by her grandmother, as a member of a sprawling family on close terms with hardship and deprivation. Her schooling was fragmentary. In later life, Porter tended to embroider these plain origins with romantic details, as though her past could be revised like a novel in progress.

The first of Porter's four marriages took place when she was sixteen. She was consistently impatient with lasting marital relationships, and yet she disliked being alone. Her early years were a struggle to define herself as an individual, as a southern woman, and as the writer that, so very slowly, she was becoming.

After her Texas youth, Porter traveled widely, living at various times in the West, New York City's Greenwich Village, New England, Washington, Mexico, Paris, and Berlin. She supported herself as a newspaper reporter and a translator.

As a creative writer, Porter was largely self-taught. She became well-read and had a natural talent for clear, flowing language. She could tell a story effortlessly, combining a searching intelligence, honesty, sound psychology, a flawless memory, and a vivid sense of scene. The grace of her objective style concealed the labor that went into it. Porter worked slowly and painstakingly, and she did not begin publishing until she was over thirty. Her first book of stories, *Flowering Judas* (1930), grew out of her experiences in Mexico immediately after World War I. This collection won her a critical reputation as a stylist.

Much of Porter's work presents southern women caught up in a web of custom and obligation. Her main themes include the burden of past evil and the strain with which that evil holds us captive in the present. Miranda, the clearly autobiographical central figure of so many of Porter's stories, is forever trying to separate the fictions of family legend from objective truth. Miranda knows that people do not always tell the truth, and she is skeptical of the romantic sheen with which they disguise the realities of poverty and sexuality.

With the publication of her finest story collection, *Pale Horse, Pale Rider* (1939), Porter's growing audience eagerly awaited a promised novel. In 1941, Porter began her novel, titled *Ship of Fools*. The novel takes place during the early days of Hitler's rise to power and chronicles the passage of a steamer ship whose passengers, to escape their loneliness, search for fantasy rather than friendship or love. *Ship of Fools* is really about the seeds of World War II—a bitter portrait of the Nazi state and the human race's capacity for cruelty. The novel took twenty years to write. When it finally appeared in 1962, it enjoyed a wide popular success. *Ship of Fools* was followed by the many awards and tributes (including the National Book Award and the Pulitzer Prize) that embellished the final years of Porter's long life.

# The Jilting of Granny Weatherall

## Make the Connection

Most people, even those in middle or old age, look forward to what life has in store for them. They ask, "What's the weather going to be tomorrow? Where shall we go on vacation next year?" Some older persons, however, start to look backward more than forward. Events from long ago seem more vivid than events from yesterday or the recent past. That is surely true of Ellen Weatherall, the nearly eighty-year-old narrator of this story. Granny Weatherall has little interest in the future, of which she knows she has very little. But the past! Now *there's* something to think about, and she does.

The point of this story is what Granny Weatherall recalls most vividly of all. It happened sixty years ago, Granny tells us, and the memory still hurts.

## Literary Focus
### Stream of Consciousness

Although Porter uses some dialogue in this story, she mostly uses the modernist narrative technique called **stream of consciousness.** This technique gives readers the impression that they are listening in on the main character's thoughts and memories as they flow randomly through that person's mind. In this story the thoughts and memories of Granny Weatherall come and go in no special order. They shift back and forth, from what is happening in her present to what happened in her life long ago.

Since the thoughts that stream freely through the mind are often irrational and contradictory, stream-of-consciousness narratives often contain many **ambiguities,** or meanings that are unclear or open to more than one interpretation.

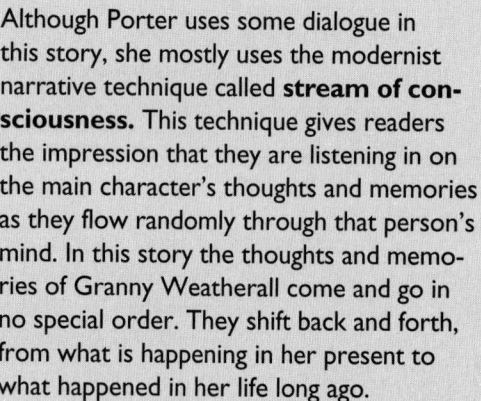

**Stream of consciousness** is a style of writing that conveys the inner—and sometimes chaotic—workings of a character's mind.

*For more on Stream of Consciousness, see the Handbook of Literary and Historical Terms.*

## Reading Skills
### Reading Closely

Like a good detective, you will have to sift clues carefully as you share Granny's stream of consciousness. Here are some suggestions: Pay careful attention to tenses of verbs, since they help distinguish past from present. Also, pay attention to quotation marks. They enclose words actually spoken aloud as opposed to unspoken thoughts. Finally, be patient. If the identity of a character is not immediately clear, keep reading until you have enough clues to figure out who he or she is.

## Vocabulary Development

**tactful** (takt′fəl) *adj.*: skilled in saying the right thing.

**clammy** (klam′ē) *adj.*: cold and damp.

**plague** (plāg) *v.*: annoy.

**vanity** (van′ə·tē) *n.*: excessive pride.

**jilted** (jilt′id) *v.*: rejected (as a lover).

**disputed** (di·spyo͞ot′id) *v.*: contested.

**nimbus** (nim′bəs) *n.*: aura; halo.

**dwindled** (dwin′dəld) *v.*: diminished.

**SKILLS FOCUS**

**Literary Skills**
Understand stream of consciousness and ambiguity.

**Reading Skills**
Read closely for clues to meaning.

go.
hrw
.com

**INTERNET**

**Vocabulary Practice**

Keyword: LE7 11-5

*New England Woman*
(1895) by Cecilia Beaux.
Oil on canvas. 43 ×
24¼ in. Acc. no.: 1896.1.

The Pennsylvania Academy
of the Fine Arts, Philadelphia.
Joseph E. Temple Fund.

# The Jilting of Granny Weatherall

## Katherine Anne Porter

She flicked her wrist neatly out of Doctor Harry's pudgy careful fingers and pulled the sheet up to her chin. The brat ought to be in knee breeches. Doctoring around the country with spectacles on his nose! "Get along now, take your schoolbooks and go. There's nothing wrong with me."

Doctor Harry spread a warm paw like a cushion on her forehead where the forked green vein danced and made her eyelids twitch. "Now, now, be a good girl, and we'll have you up in no time."

"That's no way to speak to a woman nearly eighty years old just because she's down. I'd have you respect your elders, young man."

"Well, Missy, excuse me." Doctor Harry patted her cheek. "But I've got to warn you, haven't I? You're a marvel, but you must be careful or you're going to be good and sorry."

"Don't tell me what I'm going to be. I'm on my feet now, morally speaking. It's Cornelia. I had to go to bed to get rid of her."

Her bones felt loose, and floated around in her skin, and Doctor Harry floated like a balloon around the foot of the bed. He floated and pulled down his waistcoat and swung his glasses on a cord. "Well, stay where you are, it certainly can't hurt you."

"Get along and doctor your sick," said Granny Weatherall. "Leave a well woman alone. I'll call for you when I want you. . . . Where were you forty years ago when I pulled through milk leg[1] and double pneumonia? You weren't even born. Don't let Cornelia lead you on," she shouted, because Doctor Harry appeared to float up to the ceiling and out. "I pay my own bills, and I don't throw my money away on nonsense!"

She meant to wave goodbye, but it was too much trouble. Her eyes closed of themselves, it was like a dark curtain drawn around the bed. The pillow rose and floated under her, pleasant as a hammock in a light wind. She listened to the leaves rustling outside the window. No,

somebody was swishing newspapers: No, Cornelia and Doctor Harry were whispering together. She leaped broad awake, thinking they whispered in her ear.

"She was never like this, *never* like this!" "Well, what can we expect?" "Yes, eighty years old. . . ."

Well, and what if she was? She still had ears. It was like Cornelia to whisper around doors. She always kept things secret in such a public way. She was always being tactful and kind. Cornelia was dutiful; that was the trouble with her. Dutiful and good: "So good and dutiful," said Granny, "that I'd like to spank her." She saw herself spanking Cornelia and making a fine job of it.

"What'd you say, Mother?"

Granny felt her face tying up in hard knots.

"Can't a body think, I'd like to know?"

"I thought you might want something."

"I do. I want a lot of things. First off, go away and don't whisper."

She lay and drowsed, hoping in her sleep that the children would keep out and let her rest a minute. It had been a long day. Not that she was tired. It was always pleasant to snatch a minute now and then. There was always so much to be done, let me see: tomorrow.

Tomorrow was far away and there was nothing to trouble about. Things were finished somehow when the time came; thank God there was always a little margin over for peace: Then a person could spread out the plan of life and tuck in the edges orderly. It was good to have everything clean and folded away, with the hairbrushes and tonic bottles sitting straight on the white embroidered linen: the day started without fuss and the pantry shelves laid out with rows of jelly glasses and brown jugs and white stone-china jars with blue whirligigs and words painted on them: coffee, tea, sugar, ginger, cinnamon, allspice: and the bronze clock with the lion on top nicely dusted off. The dust that lion

---

1. **milk leg:** painful swelling of the leg, usually as a result of an infection during childbirth.

**Vocabulary**

**tactful** (takt′fəl) *adj.*: skilled in saying the right thing.

could collect in twenty-four hours! The box in the attic with all those letters tied up, well, she'd have to go through that tomorrow. All those letters—George's letters and John's letters and her letters to them both—lying around for the children to find afterward made her uneasy. Yes, that would be tomorrow's business. No use to let them know how silly she had been once.

While she was rummaging around she found death in her mind and it felt clammy and unfamiliar. She had spent so much time preparing for death there was no need for bringing it up again. Let it take care of itself now. When she was sixty she had felt very old, finished, and went around making farewell trips to see her children and grandchildren, with a secret in her mind: This is the very last of your mother, children! Then she made her will and came down with a long fever. That was all just a notion like a lot of other things, but it was lucky too, for she had once for all got over the idea of dying for a long time. Now she couldn't be worried. She hoped she had better sense now. Her father had lived to be one hundred and two years old and had drunk a noggin[2] of strong hot toddy[3] on his last birthday. He told the reporters it was his daily habit, and he owed his long life to that. He had made quite a scandal and was very pleased about it. She believed she'd just plague Cornelia a little.

"Cornelia! Cornelia!" No footsteps, but a sudden hand on her cheek. "Bless you, where have you been?"

"Here, Mother."

"Well, Cornelia, I want a noggin of hot toddy."

"Are you cold, darling?"

"I'm chilly, Cornelia. Lying in bed stops the circulation. I must have told you that a thousand times."

Well, she could just hear Cornelia telling her husband that Mother was getting a little childish and they'd have to humor her. The thing that most annoyed her was that Cornelia thought she was deaf, dumb, and blind. Little hasty glances and tiny gestures tossed around her and over her head saying, "Don't cross her, let her have her way, she's eighty years old," and she sitting there as if she lived in a thin glass cage. Sometimes Granny almost made up her mind to pack up and move back to her own house where nobody could remind her every minute that she was old. Wait, wait, Cornelia, till your own children whisper behind your back!

In her day she had kept a better house and had got more work done. She wasn't too old yet for Lydia to be driving eighty miles for advice when one of the children jumped the track, and Jimmy still dropped in and talked things over: "Now, Mammy, you've a good business head, I want to know what you think of this? . . ." Old. Cornelia couldn't change the furniture around without asking. Little things, little things! They had been so sweet when they were little. Granny wished the old days were back again with the children young and everything to be done over. It had been a hard pull, but not too much for her. When she thought of all the food she had cooked, and all the clothes she had cut and sewed, and all the gardens she had made—well, the children showed it. There they were, made out of her, and they couldn't get away from that. Sometimes she wanted to see John again and point to them and say, Well, I didn't do so badly, did I? But that would have to wait. That was for tomorrow. She used to think of him as a man, but now all the children were older than their father, and he would be a child beside her if she saw him now. It seemed strange and there was something wrong in the idea. Why, he couldn't possibly recognize her. She had fenced in a hundred acres once, digging the postholes herself and clamping the wires with just a Negro boy to help. That changed a woman. John would be looking for a young woman with the peaked Spanish comb in her hair and the painted fan. Digging postholes changed a woman. Riding

---

2. **noggin** *n.*: mug.
3. **hot toddy:** drink made of liquor mixed with hot water, sugar, and spices.

**Vocabulary**
**clammy** (klam′ē) *adj.*: cold and damp.
**plague** (plāg) *v.*: annoy.

country roads in the winter when women had their babies was another thing: sitting up nights with sick horses and sick Negroes and sick children and hardly ever losing one. John, I hardly ever lost one of them! John would see that in a minute, that would be something he could understand, she wouldn't have to explain anything!

It made her feel like rolling up her sleeves and putting the whole place to rights again. No matter if Cornelia was determined to be everywhere at once, there were a great many things left undone on this place. She would start tomorrow and do them. It was good to be strong enough for everything, even if all you made melted and changed and slipped under your hands, so that by the time you finished you almost forgot what you were working for. What was it I set out to do? she asked herself intently, but she could not remember. A fog rose over the valley, she saw it marching across the creek swallowing the trees and moving up the hill like an army of ghosts. Soon it would be at the near edge of the orchard, and then it was time to go in and light the lamps. Come in, children, don't stay out in the night air.

Lighting the lamps had been beautiful. The children huddled up to her and breathed like little calves waiting at the bars in the twilight. Their eyes followed the match and watched the flame rise and settle in a blue curve, then they moved away from her. The lamp was lit, they didn't have to be scared and hang on to mother any more. Never, never, never more. God, for all my life I thank Thee. Without Thee, my God, I could never have done it. Hail, Mary, full of grace.

I want you to pick all the fruit this year and see that nothing is wasted. There's always someone who can use it. Don't let good things rot for want of using. You waste life when you waste good food. Don't let things get lost. It's bitter to lose things. Now, don't let me get to thinking, not when I am tired and taking a little nap before supper. . . .

The pillow rose about her shoulders and pressed against her heart and the memory was being squeezed out of it: Oh, push down the pillow, somebody: It would smother her if she tried to hold it. Such a fresh breeze blowing and such a green day with no threats in it. But he had not come, just the same. What does a woman do when she has put on the white veil and set out the white cake for a man and he doesn't come? She tried to remember. No, I swear he never harmed me but in that. He never harmed me but in that . . . and what if he did? There was the day, the day, but a whirl of dark smoke rose and covered it, crept up and over into the bright field where everything was planted so carefully in orderly rows. That was hell, she knew hell when she saw it. For sixty years she had prayed against remembering him and against losing her soul in the deep pit of hell, and now the two things were mingled in one and the thought of him was a smoky cloud from hell that moved and crept in her head when she had just got rid of Doctor Harry and was trying to rest a minute. Wounded vanity, Ellen, said a sharp voice in the top of her mind. Don't let your wounded vanity get the upper hand of you. Plenty of girls get jilted. You were jilted, weren't you? Then stand up to it. Her eyelids wavered and let in streamers of blue-gray light like tissue paper over her eyes. She must get up and pull the shades down or she'd never sleep. She was in bed again and the shades were not down. How could that happen? Better turn over, hide from the light, sleeping in the light gave you nightmares. "Mother, how do you feel now?" and a stinging wetness on her forehead. But I don't like having my face washed in cold water!

Hapsy? George? Lydia? Jimmy? No, Cornelia, and her features were swollen and full of little puddles. "They're coming, darling, they'll all be here soon." Go wash your face, child, you look funny.

Instead of obeying, Cornelia knelt down and put her head on the pillow. She seemed to be talking but there was no sound. "Well, are you

**Vocabulary**

**vanity** (van′ə·tē) *n.*: excessive pride.
**jilted** (jilt′id) *v.*: rejected (as a lover).

*Evening Light* (1908) by Frank Benson. Oil on canvas (25¼″ × 30½″).

tongue-tied? Whose birthday is it? Are you going to give a party?"

Cornelia's mouth moved urgently in strange shapes. "Don't do that, you bother me, daughter."

"Oh, no, Mother. Oh, no . . ."

Nonsense. It was strange about children. They <u>disputed</u> your every word. "No what, Cornelia?"

"Here's Doctor Harry."

"I won't see that boy again. He just left five minutes ago."

"That was this morning, Mother. It's night now. Here's the nurse."

"This is Doctor Harry, Mrs. Weatherall. I never saw you look so young and happy!"

"Ah, I'll never be young again—but I'd be happy if they'd let me lie in peace and get rested."

She thought she spoke up loudly, but no one answered. A warm weight on her forehead, a warm bracelet on her wrist, and a breeze went on whispering, trying to tell her something. A shuffle of leaves in the everlasting hand of God, He blew on them and they danced and rattled.

"Mother, don't mind, we're going to give you a little hypodermic."[4] "Look here, daughter, how do ants get in this bed? I saw sugar ants yesterday." Did you send for Hapsy too?

It was Hapsy she really wanted. She had to go a long way back through a great many rooms to find Hapsy standing with a baby on her arm. She seemed to herself to be Hapsy also, and the baby on Hapsy's arm was Hapsy and himself and herself, all at once, and there was no surprise in the meeting. Then Hapsy melted from within and turned flimsy as gray gauze and the baby was a gauzy shadow, and Hapsy came up close and said, "I thought you'd never come," and looked at her very searchingly and said, "You haven't changed a bit!" They leaned forward to kiss, when Cornelia began whispering from a long way off, "Oh, is there anything you want to tell me? Is there anything I can do for you?"

---

4. **hypodermic** *n.*: injection of medicine.

**Vocabulary**

**disputed** (di·spyo͞ot′id) *v.*: contested.

Yes, she had changed her mind after sixty years and she would like to see George. I want you to find George. Find him and be sure to tell him I forgot him. I want him to know I had my husband just the same and my children and my house like any other woman. A good house too and a good husband that I loved and fine children out of him. Better than I hoped for even. Tell him I was given back everything he took away and more. Oh, no, oh, God, no, there was something else besides the house and the man and the children. Oh, surely they were not all? What was it? Something not given back. . . . Her breath crowded down under her ribs and grew into a monstrous frightening shape with cutting edges; it bored up into her head, and the agony was unbelievable: Yes, John, get the Doctor now, no more talk, my time has come.

When this one was born it should be the last. The last. It should have been born first, for it was the one she had truly wanted. Everything came in good time. Nothing left out, left over. She was strong, in three days she would be as well as ever. Better. A woman needed milk in her to have her full health.

"Mother, do you hear me?"

"I've been telling you—"

"Mother, Father Connolly's here."

"I went to Holy Communion only last week. Tell him I'm not so sinful as all that."

"Father just wants to speak to you."

He could speak as much as he pleased. It was like him to drop in and inquire about her soul as if it were a teething baby, and then stay on for a cup of tea and a round of cards and gossip. He always had a funny story of some sort, usually about an Irishman who made his little mistakes and confessed them, and the point lay in some absurd thing he would blurt out in the confessional showing his struggles between native piety and original sin.[5] Granny felt easy about her soul. Cornelia, where are your manners?

---

5. **original sin:** in Christian theology, the sin of disobedience committed by Adam and Eve, the first man and first woman, which is passed on to all persons.

Give Father Connolly a chair. She had her secret comfortable understanding with a few favorite saints who cleared a straight road to God for her. All as surely signed and sealed as the papers for the new Forty Acres. Forever . . . heirs and assigns forever. Since the day the wedding cake was not cut, but thrown out and wasted. The whole bottom dropped out of the world, and there she was blind and sweating with nothing under her feet and the walls falling away. His hand had caught her under the breast, she had not fallen, there was the freshly polished floor with the green rug on it, just as before. He had cursed like a sailor's parrot and said, "I'll kill him for you." Don't lay a hand on him, for my sake leave something to God. "Now, Ellen, you must believe what I tell you. . . ."

So there was nothing, nothing to worry about any more, except sometimes in the night one of the children screamed in a nightmare, and they both hustled out shaking and hunting for the matches and calling, "There, wait a minute, here we are!" John, get the doctor now, Hapsy's time has come. But there was Hapsy standing by the bed in a white cap. "Cornelia, tell Hapsy to take off her cap. I can't see her plain."

Her eyes opened very wide and the room stood out like a picture she had seen somewhere. Dark colors with the shadows rising toward the ceiling in long angles. The tall black dresser gleamed with nothing on it but John's picture, enlarged from a little one, with John's eyes very black when they should have been blue. You never saw him, so how do you know how he looked? But the man insisted the copy was perfect, it was very rich and handsome. For a picture, yes, but it's not my husband. The table by the bed had a linen cover and a candle and a crucifix. The light was blue from Cornelia's silk lampshades. No sort of light at all, just frippery. You had to live forty years with kerosene lamps to appreciate honest electricity. She felt very strong and she saw Doctor Harry with a rosy nimbus around him.

---

**Vocabulary**

**nimbus** (nim′bəs) *n.*: aura; halo.

"You look like a saint, Doctor Harry, and I vow that's as near as you'll ever come to it."

"She's saying something."

"I heard you, Cornelia. What's all this carrying-on?"

"Father Connolly's saying—"

Cornelia's voice staggered and bumped like a cart in a bad road. It rounded corners and turned back again and arrived nowhere. Granny stepped up in the cart very lightly and reached for the reins, but a man sat beside her and she knew him by his hands, driving the cart. She did not look in his face, for she knew without seeing, but looked instead down the road where the trees leaned over and bowed to each other and a thousand birds were singing a Mass. She felt like singing too, but she put her hand in the bosom of her dress and pulled out a rosary, and Father Connolly murmured Latin in a very solemn voice and tickled her feet.[6] My God, will you stop that nonsense? I'm a married woman. What if he did run away and leave me to face the priest by myself? I found another a whole world better. I wouldn't have exchanged my husband for anybody except St. Michael[7] himself, and you may tell him that for me with a thank you in the bargain.

Light flashed on her closed eyelids, and a deep roaring shook her. Cornelia, is that lightning? I hear thunder. There's going to be a storm. Close all the windows. Call the children in. . . . "Mother, here we are, all of us." "Is that you, Hapsy?" "Oh, no, I'm Lydia. We drove as fast as we could." Their faces drifted above her, drifted away. The rosary fell out of her hands and Lydia put it back. Jimmy tried to help, their hands fumbled together, and Granny closed two fingers around Jimmy's thumb. Beads wouldn't do, it must be something alive. She was so amazed her thoughts ran round and round. So, my dear Lord, this is my death and I wasn't even thinking about it. My children have come to see me die. But I can't, it's not time. Oh, I always hated surprises. I wanted to give Cornelia the amethyst[8] set—Cornelia, you're to have the amethyst set, but Hapsy's to wear it when she wants, and, Doctor Harry, do shut up. Nobody sent for you. Oh, my dear Lord, do wait a minute. I meant to do something about the Forty Acres, Jimmy doesn't need it and Lydia will later on, with that worthless husband of hers. I meant to finish the altar cloth and send six bottles of wine to Sister Borgia for her dyspepsia.[9] I want to send six bottles of wine to Sister Borgia, Father Connolly, now don't let me forget.

Cornelia's voice made short turns and tilted over and crashed. "Oh, Mother, oh, Mother, oh, Mother . . ."

"I'm not going, Cornelia. I'm taken by surprise. I can't go."

You'll see Hapsy again. What about her? "I thought you'd never come." Granny made a long journey outward, looking for Hapsy. What if I don't find her? What then? Her heart sank down and down, there was no bottom to death, she couldn't come to the end of it. The blue light from Cornelia's lampshade drew into a tiny point in the center of her brain, it flickered and winked like an eye, quietly it fluttered and dwindled. Granny lay curled down within herself, amazed and watchful, staring at the point of light that was herself; her body was now only a deeper mass of shadow in an endless darkness and this darkness would curl around the light and swallow it up. God, give a sign!

For the second time there was no sign. Again no bridegroom and the priest in the house. She could not remember any other sorrow because this grief wiped them all away. Oh, no, there's nothing more cruel than this—I'll never forgive it. She stretched herself with a deep breath and blew out the light. ■

---

6. **murmured . . . feet:** The priest is performing the sacramental last rites of the Roman Catholic Church, which include anointing the dying person's feet with oil.
7. **Michael:** most powerful of the four archangels in Jewish and Christian doctrine. In Christian art he is usually depicted as a handsome knight in white armor.

---

8. **amethyst** (am′i·thist) *n*.: purple or violet quartz gemstone, used in jewelry.
9. **dyspepsia** (dis·pep′sē·ə) *n*.: indigestion.

---

**Vocabulary**

**dwindled** (dwin′dəld) *v*.: diminished.

# Response and Analysis

## Reading Check

1. Where is Granny Weatherall in the beginning of the story? What is happening to her?

2. Who is with Granny Weatherall, and what kind of a relationship does she seem to have with these characters?

3. What past incident does Granny keep returning to in her thoughts?

4. Who is it that Granny wishes most to see? Where does that person appear in the story?

## Thinking Critically

5. Review the notes you made as you read the story. What are the names of Granny's children, and what do you learn about each one? Which child was Granny's favorite? Who are George and John?

6. When Granny recalls George, she thinks, "Find him and be sure to tell him I forgot him" (page 776). What is **ironic** about this statement? How did George really affect Granny's life?

7. The **stream-of-consciousness** technique is totally subjective and based on free association. This means the character thinks of one thing, and that thought reminds him or her of something else, perhaps totally unrelated. Trace some of Granny's thoughts in her stream of consciousness. What revelations come out as we share her random thoughts and associations?

8. **Ambiguity** is a technique in which a writer deliberately suggests two or more different, possibly conflicting, meanings in a work. Granny feels that she was "given back everything" that was taken away by the jilting. Yet then she says that something was "not given back." Discuss what that something might be.

9. What other **ambiguities** can you find in the story?

10. What is **ambiguous** about the character Hapsy? What does her name suggest about her identity?

11. What does Granny mean when she thinks, "That was hell, she knew hell when she saw it" (page 774)? How does she feel about heaven?

12. The end of the story suggests that Granny is jilted once again. Who jilts her this time? How does Granny feel at this moment of revelation?

## Extending and Evaluating

13. Granny's last thoughts revolve around a rejection that occurred six decades earlier. Do you find this believable? Why or why not?

*Evening Light* (detail) (1908) by Frank Benson. Oil on canvas (25¹/₄″ × 30¹/₂″).

Cincinnati Art Museum, Kate Banning Fund.

*Miss Blanche Hurlbert* (c. 1892) by Thomas Eakins.

a person's thoughts and associations during a critical time. You will first have to decide what your character's situation is. You might try a moment in a series of events that take place during a sports event, the minutes before an exam, or a meeting with a new person. Tell your story in the third person, as Porter does—in other words, refer to your main character as "he" or "she." ("He saw that the hands of the clock had just ticked off one more minute." "She saw the exams on the desk and thought she would faint.")

### The Light Fails

In a brief **essay,** compare this story with Dickinson's poem "I heard a Fly buzz—when I died" (page 403). In your comparison, consider the **tone** each writer reveals in her description of a person facing death and the **images** she uses to help you share the scene.

## WRITING

### Portrait of Granny

Write a **biographical narrative** that tells Granny Weatherall's life story, based on the information in Porter's story. Include an analysis of Granny's character. Before you write, organize the information about Granny's life in a chart like this one:

| | |
|---|---|
| Key events in Granny's life | |
| Kind of life she led | |
| Her attitude toward other people | |
| Her feelings about death | |

▶ Use "Writing a Biographical Narrative," pages 813–814, for help with this assignment.

### Stream of Consciousness

Write a short **narrative** in a stream-of-consciousness style, in which you record

### Vocabulary Development
#### Back to the Story

Answer the following questions based on evidence from the story:

1. Do you think Cornelia was really a tactful person? Why does Granny describe her as such?
2. How would the ailing Granny be likely to explain her clammy hands?
3. Why do you think Granny wanted to plague Cornelia?
4. Why do you think George jilted Granny? Does the story offer any clues?
5. What else besides Granny's vanity might have been injured by the jilting?
6. What is disputed between Granny and Doctor Harry?
7. Why does Granny see a nimbus around Doctor Harry's head?
8. At the end of the story, what has dwindled, in addition to the light from the lampshade?

# James Thurber
## (1894–1961)

James Thurber is generally acknowledged to be the foremost American humorist of the twentieth century. He was a supremely gifted cartoonist and a writer of essays, sketches, and stories. He once mocked the typical puffed-up biographies of literary figures by presenting this self-portrait:

> James Thurber was born in Columbus Ohio, where so many awful things happened to him, on December 8, 1894. He was unable to keep anything on his stomach until he was seven years old, but grew to six feet one and a quarter inches tall and to weigh a hundred and fifty-four pounds fully dressed for winter. He began to write when he was ten years old . . . and to draw when he was fourteen. . . . Quick to arouse, he is very hard to quiet and people often just go away. . . . He never listens when anybody else is talking, preferring to keep his mind a blank until they get through, so he can talk. His favorite book is *The Great Gatsby*. His favorite author is Henry James. He wears excellent clothes very badly and can never find his hat. . . .

He is Sagittarius with the moon in Aries and gets along fine with persons born between the 20th and 24th of August.

Thurber did grow up in Columbus, where he attended Ohio State University. He worked as a reporter in Columbus and Chicago for a number of years. He moved east, went to work for *The New Yorker* magazine in 1927, and remained on the staff for the rest of his life. Thurber's literary career peaked in the 1940s, even as his eyesight, damaged in a boyhood accident, worsened. In addition to many collections of essays, stories, and children's books, he collaborated on a successful Broadway play.

His humor often turned on the chaos of contemporary American life. Thurber focused on the "little man," who cannot quite assert himself in a confusing world where women seem surer of their way. Walter Mitty, the antihero of Thurber's most famous story, seeks in fantasy a release from a wife who overwhelms him.

While Thurber claimed to hope the feminist movement would seize power and prevent men from blowing the world to bits, he viewed women with a certain ambivalence—as intimidating to their mates, and as mother figures rather than partners.

Thurber defined humor as "a kind of emotional chaos told about calmly and quietly in retrospect." The writer Mark Van Doren, a friend of Thurber's, said of him: "He was an extraordinary man . . . with so many quick changes: gentle and fierce, fascinating and boring, sophisticated and boorish, kind and cruel, broad-minded and parochial. You can't explain Thurber."

## For Independent Reading

Here are more Thurber titles that will make you laugh:

- *The Thurber Carnival* (stories, drawings, and poems)
- *James Thurber: Writings and Drawings* (edited by Garrison Keillor)

## The Secret Life of Walter Mitty

### Make the Connection

The name *Walter Mitty* has entered the language as a description of the little guy who is dominated by an overbearing wife. In fact, the term is defined in *Webster's Third New International Dictionary* as "a commonplace unadventurous person who seeks escape from reality through daydreaming and typically imagines himself leading a glamorous life and becoming famous." Although Thurber's Mitty is based on the age-old stereotype of the henpecked husband, Thurber's character is also an original—no one else dreams his dreams in quite the same way as Mitty dreams them.

### Literary Focus
#### Parody

A **parody** makes fun of another work by imitating or exaggerating aspects of its style and contents. You've probably encountered parodies of shows, songs, and films in humor magazines, TV sitcoms, commercials, and movies. After you've read the first paragraph of this story, ask yourself what kind of movie it parodies.

> A **parody** is a work that ridicules another work by imitating some aspect of its style or content.
>
> *For more on Parody, see the Handbook of Literary and Historical Terms.*

### Reading Skills
#### Analyzing Cause and Effect

In this famous story, James Thurber uses the basic plot structure of **cause** and **effect** in a highly original way. He creates a pattern of free association in which trivial details from Mitty's everyday life trigger grand adventures in Mitty's imagination. Thus, what is momentous and imaginary is the effect of a mundane and trivial cause, giving Mitty at least a temporary triumph over reality. As you read the story a second time, jot down the unheroic detail that triggers each heroic daydream. Note also the subjects of the daydreams and what snaps Mitty out of each fantasy.

### Vocabulary Development

**rakishly** (rāk′ish·lē) *adv.*: in a casual, stylish manner.

**distraught** (di·strôt′) *adj.*: troubled.

**haggard** (hag′ərd) *adj.*: wasted or worn in appearance.

**craven** (krā′vən) *adj.*: very fearful; cowardly.

**insolent** (in′sə·lənt) *adj.*: boldly disrespectful.

**bickering** (bik′ər·iŋ) *v.* used as *adj.*: quarreling over something unimportant; squabbling.

**pandemonium** (pan′də·mō′nē·əm) *n.*: wild confusion.

**bedlam** (bed′ləm) *n.*: place or condition of great noise and confusion.

**rending** (rend′iŋ) *v.* used as *n.*: violent ripping apart.

**inscrutable** (in·skrōōt′ə·bəl) *adj.*: mysterious.

**SKILLS FOCUS**

**Literary Skills**
Understand parody.

**Reading Skills**
Analyze cause and effect.

**INTERNET**

**Vocabulary Practice**

Keyword: LE7 11-5

# The Secret Life of Walter Mitty

## James Thurber

"We're going through!" The commander's voice was like thin ice breaking. He wore his full-dress uniform, with the heavily braided white cap pulled down rakishly over one cold gray eye. "We can't make it, sir. It's spoiling for[1] a hurricane, if you ask me." "I'm not asking you, Lieutenant Berg," said the commander. "Throw on the power lights! Rev her up to 8,500! We're going through!"

The pounding of the cylinders increased: ta-pocketa-pocketa-pocketa-*pocketa-pocketa*. The commander stared at the ice forming on the pilot window. He walked over and twisted a row of complicated dials. "Switch on No. 8 auxiliary!" he shouted. "Switch on No. 8 auxiliary!" repeated Lieutenant Berg. "Full strength in No. 3 turret!" shouted the commander. "Full

---

1. **it's spoiling for:** slang for "conditions are right for."

**Vocabulary**
**rakishly** (rāk′ish·lē) *adv.*: in a casual, stylish manner.

strength in No. 3 turret!" The crew, bending to their various tasks in the huge, hurtling eight-engined navy hydroplane, looked at each other and grinned. "The Old Man'll get us through," they said to one another. "The Old Man ain't afraid of Hell!" . . .

"Not so fast! You're driving too fast!" said Mrs. Mitty. "What are you driving so fast for?"

"Hmm?" said Walter Mitty. He looked at his wife, in the seat beside him, with shocked astonishment. She seemed grossly unfamiliar, like a strange woman who had yelled at him in a crowd. "You were up to fifty-five," she said. "You know I don't like to go more than forty. You were up to fifty-five." Walter Mitty drove on toward Waterbury in silence, the roaring of the SN202 through the worst storm in twenty years of navy flying fading in the remote, intimate airways of his mind. "You're tensed up again," said Mrs. Mitty. "It's one of your days. I wish you'd let Dr. Renshaw look you over."

Walter Mitty stopped the car in front of the building where his wife went to have her hair done. "Remember to get those overshoes while I'm having my hair done," she said. "I don't need overshoes," said Mitty. She put her mirror back into her bag. "We've been all through that," she said, getting out of the car. "You're not a young man any longer." He raced the engine a little. "Why don't you wear your gloves? Have you lost your gloves?" Walter Mitty reached in a pocket and brought out the gloves. He put them on, but after she had turned and gone into the building and he had driven on to a red light, he took them off again. "Pick it up, brother!" snapped a cop as the light changed, and Mitty hastily pulled on his gloves and lurched ahead. He drove around the streets aimlessly for a time, and then he drove past the hospital on his way to the parking lot.

. . . "It's the millionaire banker, Wellington McMillan," said the pretty nurse. "Yes?" said Walter Mitty, removing his gloves slowly. "Who has the case?" "Dr. Renshaw and Dr. Benbow, but there are two specialists here, Dr. Remington from New York and Mr. Pritchard-Mitford from London. He flew over." A door opened down a long, cool corridor and Dr. Renshaw came out. He looked distraught and haggard. "Hello, Mitty," he said. "We're having the devil's own time with McMillan, the millionaire banker and close personal friend of Roosevelt. Obstreosis of the ductal tract. Tertiary. Wish you'd take a look at him." "Glad to," said Mitty.

In the operating room there were whispered introductions: "Dr. Remington, Dr. Mitty. Mr. Pritchard-Mitford, Dr. Mitty." "I've read your book on streptothricosis," said Pritchard-Mitford, shaking hands. "A brilliant performance, sir." "Thank you," said Walter Mitty. "Didn't know you were in the States, Mitty," grumbled Remington. "Coals to Newcastle,[2] bringing Mitford and me up here for a tertiary." "You are very kind," said Mitty. A huge, complicated machine, connected to the operating table, with many tubes and wires, began at this moment to go pocketa-pocketa-pocketa. "The new anesthetizer is giving way!" shouted an intern. "There is no one in the East who knows how to fix it!" "Quiet, man!" said Mitty, in a low, cool voice. He sprang to the machine, which was now going pocketa-pocketa-queep-pocketa-queep. He began fingering delicately a row of glistening dials. "Give me a fountain pen!" he snapped. Someone handed him a fountain pen. He pulled a faulty piston out of the machine and inserted the pen in its place. "That will hold for ten minutes," he said. "Get on with the operation." A nurse hurried over and whispered to Renshaw, and Mitty saw the man turn pale. "Coreopsis has set in," said Renshaw nervously. "If you would take over, Mitty?" Mitty looked at him and at the craven figure of Benbow, who drank, and at the grave, uncertain faces of the two great specialists. "If you wish," he said. They slipped a white gown on him; he adjusted a

---

2. **coals to Newcastle:** unnecessary effort. Newcastle, England, was a major coal-producing city.

---

**Vocabulary**

**distraught** (di·strôt′) *adj.:* troubled.
**haggard** (hag′ərd) *adj.:* wasted or worn in appearance.
**craven** (krā′vən) *adj.:* very fearful; cowardly.

mask and drew on thin gloves; nurses handed him shining . . .

"Back it up, Mac! Look out for that Buick!" Walter Mitty jammed on the brakes. "Wrong lane, Mac," said the parking-lot attendant, looking at Mitty closely. "Gee. Yeh," muttered Mitty. He began cautiously to back out of the lane marked "Exit Only." "Leave her sit there," said the attendant. "I'll put her away." Mitty got out of the car. "Hey, better leave the key." "Oh," said Mitty, handing the man the ignition key. The attendant vaulted into the car, backed it up with insolent skill, and put it where it belonged.

They're so damn cocky, thought Walter Mitty, walking along Main Street; they think they know everything. Once he had tried to take his chains[3] off, outside New Milford, and he had got them wound around the axles. A man had had to come out in a wrecking car and unwind them, a young, grinning garageman. Since then Mrs. Mitty always made him drive to a garage to have the chains taken off. The next time, he thought, I'll wear my right arm in a sling; they won't grin at me then. I'll have my right arm in a sling, and they'll see I couldn't possibly take the chains off myself. He kicked at the slush on the sidewalk. "Overshoes," he said to himself, and he began looking for a shoe store.

When he came out into the street again, with the overshoes in a box under his arm, Walter Mitty began to wonder what the other thing was his wife had told him to get. She had told him, twice, before they set out from their house for Waterbury. In a way he hated these weekly trips to town—he was always getting something wrong. Kleenex, he thought, Squibb's,[4] razor blades? No. Toothpaste, toothbrush, bicarbonate, carborundum, initiative and referendum? He gave it up. But she would remember it.

"Where's the what's-its-name?" she would ask. "Don't tell me you forgot the what's-its-name." A newsboy went by shouting something about the Waterbury trial.

. . . "Perhaps this will refresh your memory." The district attorney suddenly thrust a heavy automatic at the quiet figure on the witness stand. "Have you ever seen this before?" Walter Mitty took the gun and examined it expertly. "This is my Webley-Vickers 50.80," he said calmly. An excited buzz ran around the courtroom. The judge rapped for order. "You are a crack shot with any sort of firearms, I believe?" said the district attorney, insinuatingly. "Objection!" shouted Mitty's attorney. "We have shown that the defendant could not have fired the shot. We have shown that he wore his right arm in a sling on the night of the fourteenth of July." Walter Mitty raised his hand briefly and the bickering attorneys were stilled. "With any known make of gun," he said evenly, "I could have killed Gregory Fitzhurst at three hundred feet *with my left hand*." Pandemonium broke loose in the courtroom. A woman's scream rose above the bedlam and suddenly a lovely, dark-haired girl was in Walter Mitty's arms. The district attorney struck at her savagely. Without rising from his chair, Mitty let the man have it on the point of the chin. "You miserable cur!"[5] . . .

"Puppy biscuit," said Walter Mitty. He stopped walking and the buildings of Waterbury rose up out of the misty courtroom and surrounded him again. A woman who was passing laughed. "He said 'Puppy biscuit,'" she said to her companion. "That man said 'Puppy biscuit' to himself." Walter Mitty hurried on. He

---

5. **cur** *n.:* cowardly or contemptible person; also, a mongrel dog.

**Vocabulary**

**insolent** (in'sə·lənt) *adj.:* boldly disrespectful.

**bickering** (bik'ər·iŋ) *v.* used as *adj.:* quarreling over something unimportant; squabbling.

**pandemonium** (pan'də·mō'nē·əm) *n.:* wild confusion.

**bedlam** (bed'ləm) *n.:* place or condition of great noise and confusion.

---

3. **chains** *n. pl.:* chains attached to automobile tires to increase traction in snow and ice.
4. **Squibb's:** Squibb (now part of Bristol-Myers Squibb) was a U.S. pharmaceutical company, established in 1858, that manufactured a variety of prescription drugs and healthcare products, such as cough and cold medicines and vitamins. It is not clear which product Mitty is thinking about.

went into an A & P, not the first one he came to but a smaller one farther up the street. "I want some biscuit for small, young dogs," he said to the clerk. "Any special brand, sir?" The greatest pistol shot in the world thought a moment. "It says 'Puppies Bark for It' on the box," said Walter Mitty.

His wife would be through at the hairdresser's in fifteen minutes, Mitty saw in looking at his watch, unless they had trouble drying it; sometimes they had trouble drying it. She didn't like to get to the hotel first; she would want him to be there waiting for her as usual. He found a big leather chair in the lobby, facing a window, and he put the overshoes and the puppy biscuit on the floor beside it. He picked up an old copy of *Liberty* and sank down into the chair. "Can Germany Conquer the World Through the Air?" Walter Mitty looked at the pictures of bombing planes and of ruined streets.

. . . "The cannonading has got the wind up in young Raleigh, sir," said the sergeant. Captain Mitty looked up at him through tousled hair. "Get him to bed," he said wearily. "With the others. I'll fly alone." "But you can't, sir," said the sergeant anxiously. "It takes two men to handle that bomber and the Archies[6] are pounding hell out of the air. Von Richtman's circus[7] is between here and Saulier." "Somebody's got to get to that ammunition dump," said Mitty. "I'm going over. Spot of brandy?" He poured a drink for the sergeant and one for himself. War thundered and whined around the dugout and battered at the door. There was a <u>rending</u> of wood and splinters flew through the room. "A bit of a near thing," said Captain Mitty carelessly. "The box barrage is closing in," said the sergeant. "We only live once, Sergeant," said Mitty, with his faint, fleeting smile. "Or do we?" He poured another brandy and tossed it off. "I never see a man could hold his brandy like you, sir," said the sergeant. "Begging your pardon, sir." Captain Mitty stood up and strapped on his huge Webley-Vickers automatic. "It's forty kilometers through hell, sir," said the sergeant. Mitty finished one last brandy. "After all," he said softly, "what isn't?" The pounding of the cannon increased; there was the rat-tat-tatting of machine guns, and from somewhere came the menacing pocketa-pocketa-pocketa of the new flamethrowers. Walter Mitty walked to the door of the dugout humming "Auprès de Ma Blonde."[8] He turned and waved to the sergeant. "Cheerio!" he said. . . .

Something struck his shoulder. "I've been looking all over this hotel for you," said Mrs. Mitty. "Why do you have to hide in this old chair? How did you expect me to find you?" "Things close in," said Walter Mitty vaguely. "What?" Mrs. Mitty said. "Did you get the what's-its-name? The puppy biscuit? What's in that box?" "Overshoes," said Mitty. "Couldn't you have put them on in the store?" "I was thinking," said Walter Mitty. "Does it ever occur to you that I am sometimes thinking?" She looked at him. "I'm going to take your temperature when I get you home," she said.

They went out through the revolving doors that made a faintly derisive whistling sound when you pushed them. It was two blocks to the parking lot. At the drugstore on the corner she said, "Wait here for me. I forgot something. I won't be a minute." She was more than a minute. Walter Mitty lighted a cigarette. It began to rain, rain with sleet in it. He stood up against the wall of the drugstore, smoking. . . . He put his shoulders back and his heels together. "To hell with the handkerchief," said Walter Mitty scornfully. He took one last drag on his cigarette and snapped it away. Then, with that faint, fleeting smile playing about his lips, he faced the firing squad; erect and motionless, proud and disdainful, Walter Mitty the Undefeated, <u>inscrutable</u> to the last. ■

---

8. **Auprès de Ma Blonde** (ō·prā′ də mä blônd): French song. The title means "Near My Blonde."

**Vocabulary**
**rending** (rend′iŋ) *v.* used as *n.*: violent ripping apart.
**inscrutable** (in·skroōt′ə·bəl) *adj.*: mysterious.

---

6. **Archies:** German antiaircraft guns or gunners in World War I.
7. **circus** *n.*: squadron of planes.

**James Thurber** 785

*Thurber's longtime associate at* The New Yorker, *E. B. White, wrote this parting tribute to his friend on November 11, 1961.*

# The New Yorker's Farewell

I am one of the lucky ones; I knew him before blindness hit him, before fame hit him, and I tend always to think of him as a young artist in a small office in a

From *The Owl in the Attic.*

big city, with all the world still ahead. It was a fine thing to be young and at work in New York for a new magazine when Thurber was young and at work, and I will always be glad that this happened to me.

It was fortunate that we got on well; the office we shared was the size of a hall bedroom. There was just room enough for two men, two typewriters, and a stack of copy paper. The copy paper disappeared at a scandalous rate—not because our production was high (although it was) but because Thurber used copy paper as the natural receptacle for discarded sorrows, immediate joys, stale dreams, golden prophecies, and messages of good cheer to the outside world and to fellow workers. His mind was never at rest, and his pencil was connected to his mind by the best conductive tissue I have ever seen in action. The whole world knows what a funny man he was, but you had to sit next to him day after day to understand the extravagance of his clowning, the wildness and subtlety of his thinking, and the intensity of his interest in others and his sympathy for their dilem-

mas—dilemmas that he instantly enlarged, put in focus, and made immortal, just as he enlarged and made immortal the strange goings-on in the Ohio home of his boyhood. His waking dreams and his sleeping dreams commingled shamelessly and uproariously. Ohio was never far from his thoughts, and when he received a medal from his home state in 1953, he wrote, "The clocks that strike in my dreams are often the clocks of Columbus." It is a beautiful sentence and a revealing one.

He was both a practitioner of humor and a defender of it. The day he died, I came upon a letter from him, dictated to a secretary and signed in pencil with his sightless and enormous "Jim." "Every time is a time for humor," he wrote. "I write humor the way a surgeon operates, because it is a livelihood, because I have a great urge to do it, because many interesting challenges are set up, and because I have the hope it may do some good." Once, I remember, he heard someone say that humor is a shield, not a sword, and it made him mad. He wasn't going to have anyone beating his sword into a shield. That "surgeon," incidentally, is pure Mitty. During his happiest years, Thurber did not write the way a surgeon operates, he wrote the way a child skips rope, the way a mouse waltzes.

Although he is best known for "Walter Mitty" and *The Male Animal,* the book of his I like best is *The Last Flower.* In it you will find his faith in the renewal of life, his feeling for the beauty and fragility of life on earth. Like all good writers, he fashioned his own best obituary notice. Nobody else can add to the record, much as he might like to. And of all the flowers, real and figurative, that will find their way to Thurber's last resting place, the one that will remain fresh and wiltproof is the little flower he himself drew, on the last page of that lovely book.

*E B White*

# Response and Analysis

## Reading Check

1. List the errands Mitty is doing in real life.

2. Who sends Mitty on these errands? How does he feel about doing them?

3. In contrast to his errands, what deeds does Mitty perform in fantasy?

4. What sort of person is Mitty in each of his fantasies?

## Thinking Critically

5. Thurber uses the psychological technique of free association, in which words, sounds, and events from Mitty's real life inspire elements of his daydreams. Review the notes you made while reading. What causes Mitty to lapse into each daydream? What decidedly unheroic event snaps him out of each fantasy?

6. **Irony** involves a discrepancy between what we *expect* to happen—or what we think is appropriate—and what really *does* happen. When a firehouse burns down, we sense irony. When a big dog cowers in front of a mouse, we sense irony. Irony is one of the key elements of modern fiction. What is the central irony of Mitty's life—in other words, how is his actual life different from his daydreams?

7. Mitty's daydreams **parody,** or make fun of, movies and novels with their stereotyped characters and dialogue. Where does Thurber make fun of movies and stories about war heroes, doctor heroes, and courtroom dramas? (Do you find these stereotypes in movies and TV shows today?)

8. Could Mitty be a disappointed romantic? Explain your response.

9. Walter Mitty and the formidable Mrs. Mitty are like many **stock characters** in popular culture. Brainstorm a list of popular movies and TV sitcoms in which similar husband and wife characters can be found. Why do you think these character types endure? Do you think changing views of gender roles will eventually make these stock characters seem out of date? Explain.

## WRITING

### Her Secret Dreams

All people have fantasies in which they escape from their everyday lives. What do you think Mrs. Mitty daydreams about? Brainstorm a list of elements you would include in an episode about Mrs. Mitty's daydreams as contrasted with her everyday reality. Use your list to write a **story** called "The Secret Life of Mrs. Mitty."

### Analyzing Humor

In his tribute to Thurber (see the **Primary Source** on page 786), E. B. White recalls Thurber's belief that humor "may do some good." In a brief **essay,** analyze the effects of humor in "The Secret Life of Walter Mitty." What good can come out of reading this story? What insight into human nature does the story reveal?

**SKILLS FOCUS**

**Literary Skills**
Analyze parody.

**Reading Skills**
Analyze cause and effect.

**Writing Skills**
Write a story. Write an essay analyzing a story's humor.

**Vocabulary Skills**
Analyze connotations.

"Why don't you let me know what it is, if it's so pleasant?"

Cartoons on pages 786–789 are by James Thurber.

**INTERNET**

Projects and Activities

Keyword: LE7 11-5

## Vocabulary Development

### Word Ratings: Connotations

**Connotations** are the feelings and associations that have come to be attached to some words. Connotations go beyond a word's strict dictionary definition, or **denotation.** Often a word's connotations affect its shades of meaning or intensity. Use the symbols + or – to show how the words in each of the following pairs compare in intensity. Use + if the word on the left seems stronger; use – if it seems weaker. Consult a dictionary, and discuss the connotations with a partner. The first pair has been rated for you.

| | | |
|---|---|---|
| 1. rakishly | flamboyantly | ( + ) |
| 2. distraught | upset | ( ) |
| 3. haggard | tired | ( ) |
| 4. craven | reluctant | ( ) |
| 5. insolent | impolite | ( ) |
| 6. bickering | disagreeing | ( ) |
| 7. pandemonium | noise | ( ) |
| 8. bedlam | disorder | ( ) |
| 9. rending | tearing | ( ) |
| 10. inscrutable | puzzling | ( ) |

# Vocabulary Development

### Analogies

Standardized tests often include a type of logic problem called an **analogy.** In order to solve the analogy, you must first identify the relationship between a given pair of words. Then you must select another pair of words that has the same relationship as that expressed by the first pair. In an analogy the symbol : means "is to." The symbol :: means "as." The analogy that follows would be read: "*Joyful* is to *happy* as . . . ?" You have to pick the pair of words that has the same relationship that *joyful* has to *happy*.

He always half suspected that something would get him.

JOYFUL : HAPPY ::

a. depressed : cheerful
b. melancholy : sad
c. tired : energized
d. tiny : huge

The only answer choice which completes the analogy is b. "*Joyful* is related to *happy* in the same way that *melancholy* is related to *sad*." Each word pair expresses a relationship between synonyms.

In Collection 2, you examined analogies showing these relationships: similar in meaning (synonym), opposite in meaning (antonym), and characteristic of. The chart on the next page presents three more types of relationship that may be used in analogies:

**SKILLS FOCUS**

**Vocabulary Skills**
Analyze word analogies.

| Type | Relationship | Example |
|------|-------------|---------|
| Classification | is a type of | ANGER : EMOTION |
| Cause and effect | is a cause (or effect) of | TRAGEDY: SORROW |
| Degree | is a smaller (or larger) | CHUCKLE : LAUGH |

**Test-taking strategies.** Keep these guidelines in mind when taking analogy tests:

- Know the precise meanings of the words.
- Identify the way in which the first pair of words is related.
- Look for another pair that shows the same relationship.

**PRACTICE 1**

Using the categories in the chart, identify the type of analogy in each of the following word pairs:

1. SPARK : FIRE
2. LINEN : FABRIC
3. THIN : EMACIATED
4. WARM : BOILING
5. PERSIAN : CAT
6. VIRUS : SICKNESS

**PRACTICE 2**

Select the lettered pair that best expresses the same relationship as the one in the capitalized pair. The relationship may be any of the six types you have studied: synonym, antonym, characteristic of, classification, cause and effect, or degree.

1. SHOWER : HURRICANE ::
   a. snow : sleet
   b. umbrella : coat
   c. flurry : blizzard
   d. rain : ice

2. SORROW : TEARS ::
   a. mirth : joy
   b. fear : hope
   c. pain : scream
   d. help : accident

3. SONNET : POEM ::
   a. story : narrator
   b. joke : comedian
   c. tragedy : drama
   d. movie : script

4. ANGRY : FURIOUS ::
   a. upset : ill
   b. hurt : healthy
   c. immediately : now
   d. happy : ecstatic

Some nights she threw them all.

James Thurber   **789**

# Robert Frost

## (1874–1963)

**A**lthough Robert Frost is most closely identified with New England, he was actually born in San Francisco, California. Frost was about ten years old before he first saw the New England landscapes and knew the changing seasons that he would later describe with the familiarity of a native son. The boy's move across the country was the result of his father's early death and his mother's decision to settle in the industrial town of Lawrence, Massachusetts. After high school in Lawrence, Frost entered Dartmouth College in New Hampshire. He decided after a few months

that he was not yet ready for higher education, and he returned to Lawrence to work in the cotton mills and to write. His verse, however, found little favor with magazine editors.

Married and with a growing family, Frost in his early twenties finally began to feel the need for a more formal education than his random reading could provide. He took his family to Cambridge, Massachusetts, where he entered Harvard and stayed for less than two years. He later wrote of his decision to leave: "Harvard had taken me away from the question of whether I could write or not."

Frost earned a living as a schoolteacher and as an editor before deciding to try farming. For ten years, Frost tilled the stony New Hampshire soil on thirty acres that his grandfather had bought for him. But he decided that the concentration necessary for writing poetry did not mix with the round-the-clock physical effort of working the land. Discouraged, he returned to teaching full time for a few years; then, in 1912, he sought a complete change of scene by taking his family to England.

### From Scribbler to Scribe

The move turned out to be a wise one. Stimulated by meeting English poets, Frost continued to write poetry, though he found his subjects in New England. In the three years he spent in England, he completed the two volumes that would make him famous—*A Boy's Will* (1913) and *North of Boston* (1914). These collections included several poems that would stand among Frost's best-known works: "The Tuft of Flowers," "In Hardwood Groves," "Mending Wall," "The Death of the Hired Man," and "After Apple-Picking." These poems were marked by a flinty realism and an impressive mastery of iambic rhythm, narrative dialogue, and the dramatic monologue.

When Frost returned to New Hampshire in 1915, he was no longer an obscure scribbler intent on turning New England folkways into poetry; he was an accomplished writer who had already extended the scope and character of American literature into the twentieth century. In 1916, the publication of *Mountain Interval*—a collection that included such favorites as "The Road Not Taken," " 'Out, Out—,' " and "Birches" —solidified his fame. Rewarded with many prizes (including four Pulitzer Prizes and a Congressional Medal), numerous honorary degrees, and the faithful attention of a wide readership, Frost spent the rest of his life as a lecturer at a number of colleges and as a public performer who, as he put it, liked to "say" rather than to recite his poetry.

### Poet of the People

Onstage Frost in his later years became a character of his own creation—a lovable, fumbling old gent who could nevertheless pierce the minds and hearts of those able to see beyond his playacting. In private, he was apt to put aside this guileless character and become a sometimes wicked commentator on the pretensions of rival poets; and he could be just as cutting to gushing devotees, who were unaware that he held in contempt the very flattery he demanded.

On Inauguration Day, 1961, standing bareheaded in a bright, cold wind beside President John F. Kennedy on the Capitol steps in Washington, D.C., Frost recited "The Gift Outright." His art with words had brought him not only the friendship of a president (who was half his age) but also, by means of radio and television, the largest single audience in history for a poet up until that time.

In a period when poetry was being changed by verbal experiment and by exotic influences from abroad, Frost remained devoted to traditional forms and firmly rooted in American soil. If, at the time of his death, he seemed to belong more to the past than to the present, his reputation today is secure. Neither the cranky realism nor the homely philosophy of self-reliance and spiritual independence that mark his work have been forgotten. He was an artist who developed his talents with stubborn persistence, and he created a unique voice that remained unaffected by the clamor of modernism.

## Common Diction

It has been a long time since I used any word not common in everyday speech. For example, I would never think of using the word "casement" for window in general. Whenever I have used that word, which I have occasionally, it was because I was writing about *that* kind of a window—never for window as such. In this, perhaps, I have unconsciously tried to do just what Chaucer did when the language was young and untried and virile. I have sought only those words I have met up with as a boy in New Hampshire, working on farms during the summer vacations. I listened to the men with whom I worked, and found that I could make out their conversation as they talked together out of ear-shot, even when I had not plainly heard the words they spoke. When I started to carry their conversation over into poetry, I could hear their voices, and the sound posture differentiated between one and the other. It was the sense of sound I have been talking about. In some sort of way like this I have been able to write poetry, where characters talk, and, though not without infinite pains, to make it plain to the reader which character is saying the lines, without having to place his name before it, as is done in the drama.

*Robert Frost*

# Before You Read

## Design

### Make the Connection

Anyone who has had a direct experience of nature knows that sudden violence and destruction are facts of life: The strong devour the weak; the quick overtake the slow; the young and healthy ultimately die and decay. By human standards, nature can be cold and merciless. To paraphrase Frost in this poem, nature can be "appalling." Think for a few minutes of how you regard the natural world. Do you think of it as predominately brutal? or as a source of comfort and support?

### Literary Focus
#### Sonnet

The **sonnet** is a specific type of lyric poem, one that consists of fourteen lines, usually written in iambic pentameter (see page 197), and is characterized by a fixed rhyme scheme. There are two main sonnet structures. In the **Petrarchan,** or Italian, sonnet, a question is asked or a problem is posed in the first eight lines, which are called the **octave.** An answer or solution is proposed in the last six lines, the **sestet.** In the **Shakespearean,** or English, sonnet, three four-line units, called **quatrains,** are followed by a concluding **couplet** (two lines of rhyming verse).

### Background

Frost was particularly proud of his sonnets, which are considered among the finest in the English language. He often expressed regret that more of them were not reprinted in the hundreds of anthologies in which his work appeared. "Design" reveals how densely packed with ideas his sonnets can be. (If you need more evidence, look at the number of questions we ask on page 794 about only fourteen lines of verse!)

SKILLS FOCUS

**Literary Focus**
Understand characteristics of sonnets.

**INTERNET**

**More About Robert Frost**

Keyword: LE7 11-5

> A **sonnet** is a fourteen-line lyric poem that is usually written in a fixed meter and with a regular rhyme scheme.
>
> *For more on Sonnet, see the Handbook of Literary and Historical Terms.*

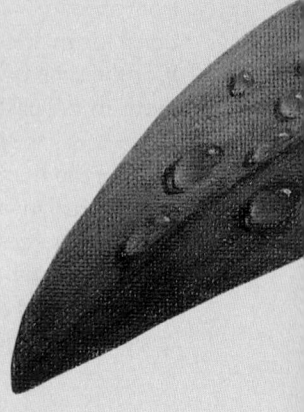

# Design

## Robert Frost

I found a dimpled spider, fat and white,
On a white heal-all,° holding up a moth
Like a white piece of rigid satin cloth—
Assorted characters of death and blight
5    Mixed ready to begin the morning right,
Like the ingredients of a witches' broth—
A snowdrop spider, a flower like a froth,°
And dead wings carried like a paper kite.

What had that flower to do with being white,
10    The wayside blue and innocent heal-all?
What brought the kindred spider to that height,
Then steered the white moth thither° in the night?
What but design of darkness to appall?—
If design govern in a thing so small.

---

2. **heal-all** *n.:* flowering plant of the mint family. The
flowers, leaves, and stems are used in folk medicine
to treat sore throats and other minor ailments.
7. **froth** *n.:* foam.
12. **thither** *adv.:* archaic for "there."

# Response and Analysis

## Thinking Critically

1. Describe the scene set up in the first stanza. What are the three characters in the poem, and what is happening to each one?

2. What color is each character? What justifies the poet's description of them as "characters of death and blight"?

3. **Tone** refers to the writer's attitude toward a subject or toward life in general. Tone can be described as sarcastic, cynical, awed, tender, and so on. Tone is created by language. What **similes** are used in the poem's octave (its first eight lines)? How do they affect the **tone** of the poem?

4. What questions does the speaker ask in the **sestet**?

5. What is the answer in the final **couplet**? How would you explain what the "design of darkness" is?

6. Always look for **ambiguity** in Frost: His poems often suggest several meanings or contain contradictory details. In line 14, at the poem's end, what reservation or doubt remains in his mind?

7. How does this last line affect the whole **tone** and meaning of the poem?

8. Describe the rhyme scheme of this sonnet. In your view, what key words or concepts do the rhyming sounds emphasize?

9. Look at what Frost says about his **diction,** or word choice, in the *Primary Source* on page 791. Do you find his views about common speech reflected in this poem? Cite details from the poem to support your response.

## Literary Criticism

10. **Philosophical approach.** The critic Laurence Perrine said that although Frost's brief poem seems innocent enough, in it the poet "chillingly poses the problem of evil." If you agree that this is the problem posed in the poem, give reasons for your opinion. If you disagree, state what you think is the poem's central theme.

11. How do you think a Puritan writer would answer the questions Frost asks in this poem? How do you think an eighteenth-century rationalist or deist would answer them?

CALVIN AND HOBBES © 1993 Watterson. Dist. by UNIVERSAL PRESS SYNDICATE. Reprinted with permission. All rights reserved.

## Nothing Gold Can Stay

### Make the Connection

*Gold,* whether it refers to the metal or the color, conjures up many images and meanings. Over the centuries, writers and artists have used gold as a symbol of perfection. What specific associations do you make with the word *gold*?

### Literary Focus
**Allusion**

Some writers' styles are marked by the frequent use of allusions. An **allusion** is a reference, direct or indirect, to someone or something outside a literary work. Allusions can refer to another work of literature or to events or persons in history, art, or contemporary life. When writers make allusions, they expect their readers to recognize the reference. To understand "Nothing Gold Can Stay," you need to recognize two references Frost is making to other literary accounts. The first allusion is to the biblical story of Adam and Eve's expulsion from the Garden of Eden. The second allusion is to the Greek myth about the loss of the Golden Age, a time of innocent happiness that, like Eden, did not last.

> An **allusion** is a reference to someone or something known from any branch of knowledge, culture, or history.
>
> *For more on Allusion, see the Handbook of Literary and Historical Terms.*

**SKILLS FOCUS**

**Literary Focus**
Understand
allusion.

**INTERNET**

More About
Robert Frost

Keyword: LE7 11-5

# Nothing Gold Can Stay

## Robert Frost

Nature's first green is gold,
Her hardest hue to hold.
Her early leaf's a flower;
But only so an hour.
Then leaf subsides to leaf.
So Eden sank to grief,
So dawn goes down to day.
Nothing gold can stay.

# Trying to Name What Doesn't Change

## Naomi Shihab Nye

Roselva says the only thing that doesn't change
is train tracks. She's sure of it.
The train changes, or the weeds that grow up spidery
by the side, but not the tracks.
5   I've watched one for three years, she says,
and it doesn't curve, doesn't break, doesn't grow.

Peter isn't sure. He saw an abandoned track
near Sabinas, Mexico, and says a track without a train
is a changed track. The metal wasn't shiny anymore.
10   The wood was split and some of the ties were gone.

Every Tuesday on Morales Street
butchers crack the necks of a hundred hens.
The widow in the tilted house
spices her soup with cinnamon.
15   Ask her what doesn't change.

Stars explode.
The rose curls up as if there is fire in the petals.
The cat who knew me is buried under the bush.

The train whistle still wails its ancient sound
20   but when it goes away, shrinking back
from the walls of the brain,
it takes something different with it every time.

(Opposite)
*Expulsion from the Garden
of Eden* (detail) (1828) by
Thomas Cole. Oil on
canvas. 100.96 × 138.43 cm
(39³/₄ × 54¹/₂ in.).

Museum of Fine Arts, Boston. Gift
of Mrs. Martha C. Karolik for the
M. and M. Karolik Collection of
American Paintings, 1815–1865.
47.1188. Photograph © 2007
Museum of Fine Arts, Boston.

# Response and Analysis

## Thinking Critically

1. Identify four specific things in "Nothing Gold Can Stay" that the speaker says cannot, or did not, "stay."

2. Think of what the very first buds of leaves look like in spring, and then explain what line 1 means.

3. What natural process is described in line 5?

4. Explain the biblical **allusion** in line 6.

5. **Symbols** are things that function as themselves in a piece of literature and that have a broader meaning as well. What state of mind or human situation might "Eden" **symbolize** here?

6. What different ideas might gold **symbolize** in the poem? Why can't gold stay—or do you think it can?

7. Take the poem apart to see how tightly its forty words are put together. Describe its **rhyme scheme,** its **meter,** and its use of **alliteration.** Be sure to read the poem aloud to hear its sound effects.

8. In the poem by Naomi Shihab Nye (see the **Connection** on page 796), a speaker tries to name things that do not change. How are her poem and Frost's poem alike and different in **tone** and **theme?** Identify the central point each poet is trying to convey about change and loss.

9. Compare Frost's "Nothing Gold Can Stay" with "Eldorado" by Edgar Allan Poe (page 305). Think about each poem's **theme,** its use of gold as an **image** and **symbol,** and its poetic structure.

**SKILLS FOCUS**

**Literary Focus**
Analyze allusion.

# Before You Read

## Birches

**SKILLS FOCUS**

**Reading Skills**
Understand the use of sound and punctuation in poetry.

**go. hrw .com**

**INTERNET**
More About Robert Frost

Keyword: LE7 11-5

### Make the Connection

Many poems start with a speaker who is looking at a scene in nature. As the speaker observes the scene, some personal experience is recalled, and ultimately that personal experience reveals a universal truth about life. What sights have you observed, or merely glimpsed for a few seconds, which have reminded you of something far larger than the scene itself?

### Reading Skills
**Reading Poetry**

Frost's poems are written in a form that is very close to conversational English. (See the **Primary Source** on page 791 and the descriptions of **blank verse** on page 812.)

Read this poem aloud to hear the rise and fall of the speaker's voice. When you come to a period, whether at the end of a line or in the middle of a line, make a full stop. When you come to a comma, semicolon, or dash, pause slightly. If there is no mark of punctuation at the end of a line, read right on to the next line without pausing.

### Background

As spindly and awkward as a giraffe's legs, the birch trees of Robert Frost's New England have white bark ringed with black. Their trunks are remarkably pliable—a fact that gives this poem its realistic base. Children do, in fact, climb and swing on birch trees.

# Birches

## Robert Frost

When I see birches bend to left and right
Across the lines of straighter darker trees,
I like to think some boy's been swinging them.
But swinging doesn't bend them down to stay
5    As ice storms do. Often you must have seen them
Loaded with ice a sunny winter morning
After a rain. They click upon themselves
As the breeze rises, and turn many-colored
As the stir cracks and crazes their enamel.
10   Soon the sun's warmth makes them shed crystal shells
Shattering and avalanching on the snow crust—
Such heaps of broken glass to sweep away
You'd think the inner dome of heaven had fallen.
They are dragged to the withered bracken° by the load,
15   And they seem not to break; though once they are bowed

---

**14. bracken** *n.*: large, coarse fern.

So low for long, they never right themselves:
You may see their trunks arching in the woods
Years afterwards, trailing their leaves on the ground
Like girls on hands and knees that throw their hair
20　Before them over their heads to dry in the sun.
But I was going to say when Truth broke in
With all her matter of fact about the ice storm,
I should prefer to have some boy bend them
As he went out and in to fetch the cows—
25　Some boy too far from town to learn baseball,
Whose only play was what he found himself,
Summer or winter, and could play alone.
One by one he subdued his father's trees
By riding them down over and over again
30　Until he took the stiffness out of them,
And not one but hung limp, not one was left
For him to conquer. He learned all there was
To learn about not launching out too soon
And so not carrying the tree away
35　Clear to the ground. He always kept his poise°
To the top branches, climbing carefully
With the same pains you use to fill a cup
Up to the brim, and even above the brim.
Then he flung outward, feet first, with a swish,
40　Kicking his way down through the air to the ground.
So was I once myself a swinger of birches.
And so I dream of going back to be.
It's when I'm weary of considerations,
And life is too much like a pathless wood
45　Where your face burns and tickles with the cobwebs
Broken across it, and one eye is weeping
From a twig's having lashed across it open.
I'd like to get away from earth awhile
And then come back to it and begin over.
50　May no fate willfully misunderstand me
And half grant what I wish and snatch me away
Not to return. Earth's the right place for love:
I don't know where it's likely to go better.
I'd like to go by climbing a birch tree,
55　And climb black branches up a snow-white trunk
*Toward* heaven, till the tree could bear no more,
But dipped its top and set me down again.
That would be good both going and coming back.
One could do worse than be a swinger of birches.

---

**35. poise** *n.*: balance.

# Response and Analysis

## Thinking Critically

1. Describe the scenario the speaker imagines when he sees the bent birch trees.

2. What realistic objection to his idea does the speaker recognize in lines 4–5? What "matter of fact" does "Truth" break in with in lines 5–20?

3. According to lines 23–40, what does the speaker prefer to believe about the bent birches? What lessons would this young boy learn about life as he subdues his father's trees?

4. In lines 41–49, what does the speaker say he wishes he could do now when life is "like a pathless wood"?

5. How does the speaker correct himself in lines 50–53? What does he say he wants to do in lines 54–57?

6. What does the playful activity of birch swinging seem to **symbolize** in the poem?

7. Summarize in your own words what you think is the **moral,** or message, of Frost's poem.

8. Two strong **similes** give the poem a richness that is both imaginative and the result of close observation. Find these similes in lines 18–20 and lines 44–47, and explain what is being compared with what. What does each simile help you *see?*

**SKILLS FOCUS**

**Reading Skills**
Analyze the use of sound and punctuation in poetry.

9. "Birches" is composed in **blank verse,** which is unrhymed iambic pentameter. That means that each line of the poem has five **iambs**—an iamb being an unaccented syllable followed by an accented syllable. Here is how the first two lines work out when scanned:

˘  ′  ˘  ′  ˘  ′  ˘  ′  ˘  ′
When I see birches bend to left and right

˘  ′  ˘  ′  ˘  ′  ˘  ′  ˘  ′
Across the lines of straighter darker trees

Continue marking stressed and unstressed syllables for the first nine lines. Does Frost vary his use of iambic pentameter? (To hear and feel the effects of blank verse, you have to read the poem aloud.)

## Extending and Evaluating

10. In a famous remark about the nature of poetry, Frost said that a poem "begins in delight and ends in wisdom." Do you think that this formula applies to "Birches"? Explain your view, including what you think Frost means by *delight* and *wisdom.*

# Before You Read

## Mending Wall

**SKILLS FOCUS**

**Literary Skills**
Understand ambiguity.

### Make the Connection
#### Quickwrite ✏️

People who live in cold climates know that freezing water can shift stone walls, crack sidewalks, and push underground boulders up through the earth. The wall Frost describes in this poem is made up of large stones piled one on another by hand. Although low, such a wall can effectively mark the boundary between neighbors.

List all the different kinds of walls and boundaries you can think of. What's good about boundaries—and what's bad about them?

### Literary Focus
#### Ambiguity

This is one of Frost's most controversial poems because of its **ambiguity**—that is, it is open to opposing interpretations. The poem presents two mind-sets, and it is unclear which of the two is being endorsed. The neighbor expresses the view that walls are useful, while the speaker sees them as barriers that should be torn down. There are also other ambiguities: For example, if the speaker dislikes walls, why does he begin the wall mending each spring?

> **Ambiguity** in literature is the quality of being open to two or more, sometimes conflicting, interpretations.
>
> *For more on Ambiguity, see the Handbook of Literary and Historical Terms.*

**INTERNET**

**More About Robert Frost**

Keyword: LE7 11-5

# Mending Wall

## Robert Frost

Something there is that doesn't love a wall,
That sends the frozen-ground-swell under it
And spills the upper boulders in the sun,
And makes gaps even two can pass abreast.
5  The work of hunters is another thing:
I have come after them and made repair
Where they have left not one stone on a stone,
But they would have the rabbit out of hiding,
To please the yelping dogs. The gaps I mean,
10  No one has seen them made or heard them made,
But at spring mending-time we find them there.
I let my neighbor know beyond the hill;
And on a day we meet to walk the line
And set the wall between us once again.
15  We keep the wall between us as we go.
To each the boulders that have fallen to each.
And some are loaves and some so nearly balls

We have to use a spell to make them balance:
"Stay where you are until our backs are turned!"
20 We wear our fingers rough with handling them.
Oh, just another kind of outdoor game,
One on a side. It comes to little more:
There where it is we do not need the wall:
He is all pine and I am apple orchard.
25 My apple trees will never get across
And eat the cones under his pines, I tell him.
He only says, "Good fences make good neighbors."
Spring is the mischief in me, and I wonder
If I could put a notion in his head:
30 "*Why* do they make good neighbors? Isn't it
Where there are cows? But here there are no cows.
Before I built a wall I'd ask to know
What I was walling in or walling out,
And to whom I was like to give offense.
35 Something there is that doesn't love a wall,
That wants it down." I could say "Elves" to him,
But it's not elves exactly, and I'd rather
He said it for himself. I see him there,
Bringing a stone grasped firmly by the top
40 In each hand, like an old-stone savage armed.
He moves in darkness as it seems to me,
Not of woods only and the shade of trees.
He will not go behind his father's saying,
And he likes having thought of it so well
45 He says again, "Good fences make good neighbors."

*This poem was written by a teacher in Lakeside, California.*

# Mending Test

### (Apologies to Robert Frost)

## Penelope Bryant Turk

Something there is that doesn't love a test,
That sends the frozen mind-set under it
And spills the grade objectives in the room,
And makes gaps students often fall between.
5   No one has seen them made or heard them made
But at spring testing time we find them here.
I let my classes know within my room
And on a day we meet to take the test
And set the norms between us once again.
10  We wear our minds quite rough with handling them.
Oh, just another kind of indoor game,
One on a side. It comes to little more.
There where it is, we do not need the test.
The teachers can assess their goals, I tell him,
15  The district's high inquisitor, once more.
He only says, "Good tests will make good students."
Spring is the mischief in me, and I wonder
If I could put a notion in his head.
"Why do they make good students?" I inquire.
20  "Before I gave a test, I'd ask to know
What I was testing in or testing out.
And to whom I was like to do some good.
Something there is that doesn't love a test,
That wants it done." I could say this to him
25  But it's not politic, and then I'd rather
He said it for himself. I see him there
Bringing a test grasped firmly in each hand,
With pencils like an old-time pedant° armed.
He moves in darkness as it seems to me,
30  Not of woods only and the shade of trees.
He will not go behind the state's command,
And he likes having thought of it so well,
He says again, "Good tests will make good students."

---

**28. pedant** (ped′nt) *n.*: fussy, narrow-minded teacher.

---

*In a 1995 opinion written for the Supreme Court, Justice Antonin Scalia justified a "high wall" separating the levels of government by quoting the neighbor in Frost's poem. The* New York Times *published an editorial reminding Justice Scalia that Frost did not think good fences made good neighbors. Here is one letter about the controversy:*

To the Editor:
Robert Frost's "Mending Wall" has been subjected to many conflicting interpretations, but your April 22 editorial gives the correct one. The "pro-wall" speaker was Frost's French Canadian neighbor, Napoleon Guay. In the opening lines,

*Something there is that doesn't
      love a wall,
That sends the frozen-ground-
      swell under it*

the "something," a natural force that breaks down the wall and indicates the poet's point of view, is frost. Frost liked to pun on his name, calling his satire "frostbite."

When this poem was translated into Russian and printed in the newspapers for Frost's official visit to the Soviet Union in 1962, many writers and intellectuals saw a negative reference to the Berlin Wall put up by East Germany in 1961. So the Soviet translators jump-started the poem with line two.

—Jeffrey Meyers
April 22, 1995

# Response and Analysis

## Thinking Critically

1. What makes the speaker say that "something" doesn't love a wall? Besides this "something," who else sometimes knocks down walls?

2. Describe what is happening in lines 13–16. According to the speaker, why is rebuilding the wall merely a game (lines 23–26)?

3. What questions does the speaker think should be settled before building a wall, according to lines 32–34?

4. Why would the speaker say "Elves" (line 36)?

5. From whom did the neighbor get his saying: "Good fences make good neighbors"?

6. Frost creates two characters in this poem, and we come to know them by what they say and do and think. What persons or points of view in contemporary life do Frost's characters reflect?

7. What do you think the word *darkness* means in line 41? What could the **simile** in line 40 have to do with darkness?

8. What might the wall in the poem **symbolize**?

9. How do you explain the fact that the man who doesn't see the need for a wall is the one who, every spring, is the first to call upon his neighbor and so make sure the wall is rebuilt? Might he want something more from his neighbor than merely a hand with repair work? Explain your response.

10. This poem is **ambiguous**—it presents opposing views about the wall. Do you think Frost favors the view of the speaker or of the neighbor? Which details from the poem lead you to this interpretation?

11. What historical walls or boundaries have separated neighbors? (Be sure to check your Quickwrite notes.)

## Extending and Evaluating

12. Do you believe that "Good fences make good neighbors"? Do you think the generalization could apply in some situations but not all? Give your reasons. (See the **Connection** on page 803 for Justice Antonin Scalia's position on walls.)

13. The poem "Mending Test" (see the **Connection** on page 803) is a **parody** (a work that makes fun of another work) of Frost's poem. Do you think Penelope Turk makes a serious point about test-taking, or is her poem just a clever imitation of Frost's form and style? Explain the reasons for your evaluation.

Women walking next to the Berlin Wall (1985).

# Before You Read

## The Death of the Hired Man

### Make the Connection
#### Quickwrite 🖉

One of Frost's most famous lines is from this poem: "Home is the place where, when you have to go there, / They have to take you in." The poem also offers another definition of home: "Something you somehow haven't to deserve." To some people, home is a definite place; to others, it is a state of mind, a sense of connectedness and belonging. Quickwrite your definition of home.

### Literary Focus
#### A Narrative Poem

A **narrative poem** is a poem that tells a story—a series of related events. Most of this narrative poem consists of **dialogue** written in **blank verse** (see page 812). The poem's main character, Silas the hired man, does not speak for himself, yet his presence dominates the poem. By the last line we have heard enough about Silas's background, habits, and attitudes to feel we know him. In gradually learning about him, we also come to know the husband and wife whose dialogue tells the poem's story.

> A **narrative poem** is a poem that tells a story—a series of related events with a beginning, a middle, and an end. A narrative poem also features characters and, frequently, dialogue.
>
> *For more on Narrative Poem, see the Handbook of Literary and Historical Terms.*

### Reading Skills 📚
#### Drawing Inferences About Characters

Read this poem as if it were a short story. As you read, make notes about the feelings you sense between Warren and Mary. Think too about the feelings each of them has toward Silas. Note your own responses to each of these characters. Do your feelings change as you read on through the poem?

**SKILLS FOCUS**

**Literary Skills**
Understand the characteristics of a narrative poem.

**Reading Skills**
Make inferences about characters.

**INTERNET**

**More About Robert Frost**

Keyword: LE7 11-5

---

# The Death of the Hired Man

## Robert Frost

Mary sat musing on the lamp-flame at the table,
Waiting for Warren. When she heard his step,
She ran on tiptoe down the darkened passage
To meet him in the doorway with the news
5  And put him on his guard. "Silas is back."
She pushed him outward with her through the door
And shut it after her. "Be kind," she said.

She took the market things from Warren's arms
And set them on the porch, then drew him down
10    To sit beside her on the wooden steps.

"When was I ever anything but kind to him?
But I'll not have the fellow back," he said.
"I told him so last haying, didn't I?
If he left then, I said, that ended it.
15    What good is he? Who else will harbor° him
At his age for the little he can do?
What help he is there's no depending on.
Off he goes always when I need him most.
He thinks he ought to earn a little pay,
20    Enough at least to buy tobacco with,
So he won't have to beg and be beholden.°
'All right,' I say, 'I can't afford to pay
Any fixed wages, though I wish I could.'
'Someone else can.' 'Then someone else will have to.'
25    I shouldn't mind his bettering himself
If that was what it was. You can be certain,
When he begins like that, there's someone at him
Trying to coax him off with pocket money—
In haying time, when any help is scarce.
30    In winter he comes back to us. I'm done."

"Sh! not so loud: He'll hear you," Mary said.

"I want him to: He'll have to soon or late."

"He's worn out. He's asleep beside the stove.
When I came up from Rowe's I found him here,
35    Huddled against the barn door fast asleep,
A miserable sight, and frightening, too—
You needn't smile—I didn't recognize him—
I wasn't looking for him—and he's changed.
Wait till you see."

                    "Where did you say he'd been?"

40    "He didn't say. I dragged him to the house,
And gave him tea and tried to make him smoke.
I tried to make him talk about his travels.
Nothing would do: He just kept nodding off."

"What did he say? Did he say anything?"

"But little."

45                "Anything? Mary, confess
He said he'd come to ditch° the meadow for me."

"Warren!"

**15. harbor** *v.:* provide safe shelter for.

**21. beholden** *adj.:* indebted.

**46. ditch** *v.:* dig drainage channels in.

"But did he? I just want to know."

"Of course he did. What would you have him say?
Surely you wouldn't grudge the poor old man
50  Some humble way to save his self-respect.
He added, if you really care to know,
He meant to clear the upper pasture, too.
That sounds like something you have heard before?
Warren, I wish you could have heard the way
55  He jumbled everything. I stopped to look
Two or three times—he made me feel so queer°—
To see if he was talking in his sleep.
He ran on° Harold Wilson—you remember—
The boy you had in haying four years since.
60  He's finished school, and teaching in his college.
Silas declares you'll have to get him back.
He says they two will make a team for work:
Between them they will lay this farm as smooth!
The way he mixed that in with other things.
65  He thinks young Wilson a likely lad, though daft
On education—you know how they fought
All through July under the blazing sun,
Silas up on the cart to build the load,
Harold along beside to pitch it on."

70  "Yes, I took care to keep well out of earshot."

"Well, those days trouble Silas like a dream.
You wouldn't think they would. How some things linger!
Harold's young college-boy's assurance piqued° him.
After so many years he still keeps finding
75  Good arguments he sees he might have used.
I sympathize. I know just how it feels
To think of the right thing to say too late.
Harold's associated in his mind with Latin.
He asked me what I thought of Harold's saying
80  He studied Latin, like the violin,
Because he liked it—that an argument!
He said he couldn't make the boy believe
He could find water with a hazel prong°—
Which showed how much good school had ever done him.
85  He wanted to go over that. But most of all
He thinks if he could have another chance
To teach him how to build a load of hay—"

"I know, that's Silas' one accomplishment.
He bundles every forkful in its place,
90  And tags and numbers it for future reference,
So he can find and easily dislodge it

---

**56. queer** *adj.:* uncomfortable; ill at ease.

**58. ran on:** kept talking in a rambling way about.

**73. piqued** *v.:* provoked.

**83. hazel prong:** forked branch used to find water underground.

In the unloading. Silas does that well.
He takes it out in bunches like big birds' nests.
You never see him standing on the hay
95  He's trying to lift, straining to lift himself."

"He thinks if he could teach him that, he'd be
Some good perhaps to someone in the world.
He hates to see a boy the fool of books.
Poor Silas, so concerned for other folk,
100  And nothing to look backward to with pride,
And nothing to look forward to with hope,
So now and never any different."

Part of a moon was falling down the west,
Dragging the whole sky with it to the hills.
105  Its light poured softly in her lap. She saw it
And spread her apron to it. She put out her hand
Among the harplike morning-glory strings,
Taut with the dew from garden bed to eaves,
As if she played unheard some tenderness
110  That wrought° on him beside her in the night.                    **110. wrought** *v.:* worked.
"Warren," she said, "he has come home to die:
You needn't be afraid he'll leave you this time."

"Home," he mocked gently.

                                   "Yes, what else but home?
It all depends on what you mean by home.
115  Of course he's nothing to us, any more
Than was the hound that came a stranger to us
Out of the woods, worn out upon the trail."

"Home is the place where, when you have to go there,
They have to take you in."

                                   "I should have called it
120  Something you somehow haven't to deserve."

Warren leaned out and took a step or two,
Picked up a little stick, and brought it back
And broke it in his hand and tossed it by.
"Silas has better claim on us you think
125  Than on his brother? Thirteen little miles
As the road winds would bring him to his door.
Silas has walked that far no doubt today.
Why doesn't he go there? His brother's rich,
A somebody—director in the bank."

"He never told us that."

130                                   "We know it, though."

"I think his brother ought to help, of course.
I'll see to that if there is need. He ought of right
To take him in, and might be willing to—
He may be better than appearances.
135 But have some pity on Silas. Do you think
If he had any pride in claiming kin
Or anything he looked for from his brother,
He'd keep so still about him all this time?"

"I wonder what's between them."

                            "I can tell you.
140 Silas is what he is—we wouldn't mind him—
But just the kind that kinsfolk can't abide.
He never did a thing so very bad.
He don't know why he isn't quite as good
As anybody. Worthless though he is,
145 He won't be made ashamed to please his brother."

"*I* can't think Si ever hurt anyone."

"No, but he hurt my heart the way he lay
And rolled his old head on that sharp-edged chair-back.
He wouldn't let me put him on the lounge.
150 You must go in and see what you can do.
I made the bed up for him there tonight.
You'll be surprised at him—how much he's broken.
His working days are done; I'm sure of it."

"I'd not be in a hurry to say that."

155 "I haven't been. Go, look, see for yourself.
But, Warren, please remember how it is:
He's come to help you ditch the meadow.
He has a plan. You mustn't laugh at him.
He may not speak of it, and then he may.
160 I'll sit and see if that small sailing cloud
Will hit or miss the moon."

                            It hit the moon.
Then there were three there, making a dim row,
The moon, the little silver cloud, and she.

Warren returned—too soon, it seemed to her—
165 Slipped to her side, caught up her hand and waited.

"Warren?" she questioned.
                            "Dead," was all he answered.

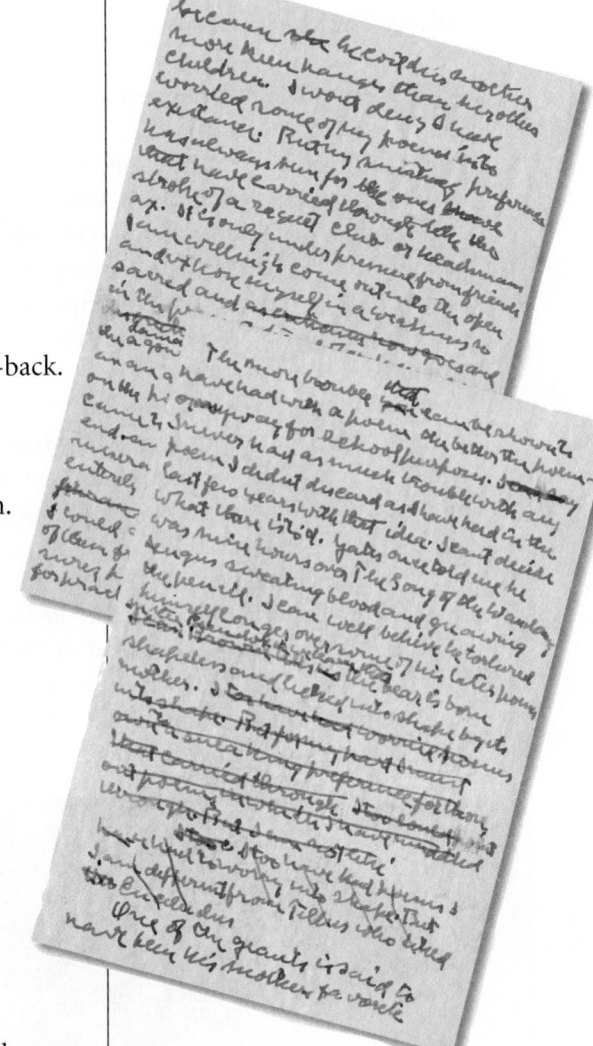

Frost's notes on "The Death of the Hired Man."

**Robert Frost**    **809**

# "I must have the pulse beat of rhythm . . ."

*These comments are from an interview in* The New York Times *in 1917. Here Frost has been talking about American poetry.*

We're still a bit afraid. America, for instance, was afraid to accept Walt Whitman when he first sang the songs of democracy. His influence on American poetry began to be felt only after the French had hailed him as a great writer, a literary revolutionist. Our own poet had to be imported from France before we were sure of his strength.

Today almost every man who writes poetry confesses his debt to Whitman. Many have gone very much further than Whitman would have traveled with them. They are the people who believe in wide straddling.

I, myself, as I said before, don't like it for myself. I do not write free verse; I write blank verse. I must have the pulse beat of rhythm, I like to hear it beating under the things I write.

That doesn't mean I do not like to read a bit of free verse occasionally. I do. It some-times succeeds in painting a picture that is very clear and startling. It's good as something created momentarily for its sudden startling effect; it hasn't the qualities, however, of something lastingly beautiful.

And sometimes my objection to it is that it's a pose. It's not honest. When a man sets out consciously to tear up forms and rhythms and measures, then he is not interested in giving you poetry. He just wants to perform; he wants to show you his tricks. He will get an effect; nobody will deny that, but it is not a harmonious effect.

Sometimes it strikes me that the free-verse people got their idea from incorrect proof sheets. I have had stuff come from the printers with lines half left out or positions changed about. I read the poems as they stood, distorted and half finished, and I confess I get a rather pleasant sensation from them. They make a sort of nightmarish half-sense. . . .

*Robert Frost*

Robert Frost at John F. Kennedy's inauguration, January 20, 1961.

# Response and Analysis

## Thinking Critically

1. All stories are built around conflict. Sum up the basic problem facing Warren, Mary, and Silas as it unfolds in the dialogue between Mary and Warren. Some might say that Mary sees the hired man's situation in an emotional sense and Warren views it in a business sense. Do you agree? Explain.

2. Based on their dialogue, what **inferences** can you make about the relationship between Warren and Mary and about the way in which each relates to Silas?

3. Identify the details in lines 103–110 that create a vivid image of the **setting** of this narrative poem. What does this passage tell you about Mary's **character**?

4. Do any of the main characters change in the course of the narrative? Quote passages to support your answer.

5. Does the conclusion of this narrative poem strike you as inevitable, or unavoidable? Why or why not? What would your feelings have been if Warren, instead of answering "Dead" to Mary's question, had answered "Asleep" or "Sharpening his scythe"?

6. Find the two definitions of *home* offered in the poem. A critic has said that one definition is based on law and duty, and the other on mercy. Identify each. Do you agree with the critic's observation? Which definition is closer to yours? Be sure to refer to your Quickwrite notes. 🖉

7. State in your own words the poem's **theme,** or what it reveals to you about our lives. How could its theme apply to social issues faced in both rural and urban areas today?

## Extending and Evaluating

8. In the **Primary Source** on page 810, Frost says he aimed to give the speech of each character in his poetry a distinct sound, just as people's voices sound different in real life. Does he successfully differentiate Warren's and Mary's dialogue? Give reasons for your opinion.

## WRITING

### Frost Bites

The critic Louise Bogan pointed out the "tensions, dark conflicts, and passionate involvements" that appear in Frost's poetry and "pervade certain poems with almost nightmare intensity." In a brief **essay,** explore examples of the "dark conflicts" in the Frost poems you have read here. What attitudes does Frost share with the Dark Romantics (page 172)?

### Accident or Design?

In a brief essay, **compare and contrast** Frost's "Design" with Emily Dickinson's "Apparently with no surprise" (page 398). Before you write, gather your data in a chart like the one below:

|  | Dickinson | Frost |
|---|---|---|
| Message |  |  |
| Symbols |  |  |
| Rhyme and rhythm |  |  |
| Imagery |  |  |

**SKILLS FOCUS**

**Literary Skills**
Analyze a narrative poem and blank verse.

**Reading Skills**
Make inferences about characters.

**Writing Skills**
Write an essay analyzing a poem. Write an essay comparing and contrasting two poems.

**Listening and Speaking Skills**
Perform an oral interpretation of a poem.

**INTERNET**

Projects and Activities

Keyword: LE7 11-5

*The Veteran in a New Field* (detail) (1865) by Winslow Homer (American 1836–1910). Oil on canvas. 24¹/₈ × 38¹/₈ in. (61.3 × 96.8 cm).

The Metropolitan Museum of Art, Bequest of Miss Adelaide Milton de Groot, (1876–1967), 1967 (67.187.131). Photograph © 1995, The Metropolitan Museum of Art.

## LISTENING AND SPEAKING

### Dynamic Dialogue

With a partner, prepare an oral reading of "The Death of the Hired Man." Begin by thoroughly discussing the characters of Warren and Mary. Be sure you know what each character wants. How can their different personalities be conveyed by varying the speed, volume, and tone of their speech? Practice these variations along with appropriate gestures and movements. When you are satisfied with your interpretation, perform it for your class or group.

## Literary Focus
### Blank Verse

"The poet goes in like a rope skipper to make the most of his opportunities," Frost wrote in an essay called "The Constant Symbol." "If he trips himself he stops the rope. He is of our stock and has been brought up by ear to choice of two meters, strict iambic and loose iambic (not to count varieties of the latter)." Like most of Frost's poems, "The Death of the Hired Man" is written in **blank verse,** which is unrhymed iambic pentameter. It is called *blank verse* because the lines do not have end rhymes. Iambic pentameter means that there are five iambs to each line; an iamb is an unaccented syllable followed by an accented syllable:

da DUM ( ˘ ′ )

- Scan the first ten lines, and recite them aloud to hear the meter. (For help scanning a poem, see page 195.)
- Look over the poem, and find examples of strict iambic and loose iambic meter.
- Do you think Frost ever "trips" himself in this poem?
- Take ten lines from this poem, and rewrite them in the free verse style of Walt Whitman (for more on free verse, see page 367). Where will you break the lines? What rearrangement of words will have to be made to break the iambic meter?
- Look at Frost's comments on free verse in the **Primary Source** on page 810. What is *your* opinion of Frost's ideas?

# Writing a Biographical Narrative

**Writing Assignment**
**Write a biographical narrative about an incident that shows another person's character.**

"There's more there than meets the eye" is an expression you could apply to Granny Weatherall and Walter Mitty, two of the interesting characters you encountered in the preceding literature section. Like fictional characters, real people also have stories—stories that writers like you can tell. In this workshop you'll tell another person's story by writing a **biographical narrative,** a true story based on an incident in the life of someone you know.

**Choose a Subject** As you consider a subject for your biographical narrative—a person to write about—choose someone you already know well or someone you can interview if you need extra information. Make sure you have specific knowledge of at least one incident that reveals that person's character. If necessary, interview your subject to learn more details about the incident.

**Add Details** To make the **characterization** of your subject vivid and to bring the incident you're describing to life, use narrative and descriptive details.

- **Narrative details** tell what happened; they are the sequence of events that make up the incident. Narrative details also provide information about the specific actions, movements, gestures, and feelings of the people involved in the incident.

- **Descriptive details** give information about the subject's **appearance** and personality. Descriptive details also explain the setting or **specific places** where the incident occurs.

Take notes on the narrative and descriptive details you want to include in your paper. Then, add **concrete sensory details**—details that appeal to the senses of touch, taste, smell, sight, and hearing—to create specific **images** in the reader's mind of each part of the incident.

**Use Stylistic Devices** One technique you can use to portray your subject as a unique, fully developed individual is **interior monologue,** in which your subject "thinks out loud." Interior monologue allows the reader to experience your subject's thoughts directly. Use interior monologue for thoughts that the subject has told you about, such as the one below.

> Benny carefully picked the sparrow up from the ground. "Come on, little bird," he thought, "you're going to be fine."

**SKILLS FOCUS**

**Writing Skills**
Write a
biographical
narrative.
Include
narrative and
descriptive
details.

DO THIS ➤

**TIP** The words you choose and the way you arrange those words in sentences make up the **style** of your paper. Sometimes those words and sentences can be used to convey **irony,** a contrast between what is expected and what is real, as in the towering and gruff appearance of a caring and gentle person.

**Establish a Point of View** You'll generally write from your own **point of view** to show readers how you see your subject. Occasionally, however, it may be helpful to include someone else's point of view. Changing from one point of view to another and back again is called **shifting perspectives.** As you write, make sure any transitions between perspectives are clear to readers. Notice how the student shifts perspectives in the example below to show a different view of her subject.

> Because of Benny's enormous build and somber nature, my friend Janis thought of him as a stereotypical athlete who cared only about himself and lifting weights. She was surprised to learn that Benny helped rescue a sparrow that had fallen from its nest.

**Organize and Pace Your Narrative** Once you've gathered all the details for your biographical narrative, plan its organization and pace. In general, your biography should be in **chronological order.** Within this framework, however, you may need to use other organizational strategies. For instance, you might use **spatial order** to describe your subject's appearance or the setting of an important event.

The **pace** of your biographical narrative—the rate at which you relate events—should vary to accommodate spatial (place) changes, temporal (time) changes, and dramatic mood changes. Look at the following chart to see how the student writer plans to accommodate spatial, temporal, and mood changes.

> **Spatial changes:** I'll describe our walk in the woods in detail to slow the pace and give readers time to absorb the setting.
>
> **Temporal changes:** Because Benny and I attended a wildlife camp, I'll include a flashback to explain why I knew what to do with the sparrow.
>
> **Mood changes:** I'll add details about Benny's difficulty in climbing the tree to increase the pace gradually and show our growing anticipation at replacing the baby bird in its nest.

**Explain the Meaning** The events and details you include in your narrative will show your subject's character. Save any direct statement about the person's character until the last paragraph, after your readers have had a chance to draw conclusions about the subject for themselves.

**SKILLS FOCUS**

**Writing Skills**
Organize the narrative.

**PRACTICE & APPLY** Using the information on these two pages, plan and write a biographical narrative. Then, share your biographical narrative with your classmates.

# The Harlem Renaissance

**Cullen**

**Hughes**

**Hurston**

I, too, sing America.

—Langston Hughes

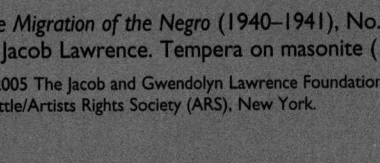

**INTERNET**

Collection
Resources

Keyword: LE7 11-5

*The Migration of the Negro* (1940–1941), No. 1,
by Jacob Lawrence. Tempera on masonite (12" × 18").

© 2005 The Jacob and Gwendolyn Lawrence Foundation,
Seattle/Artists Rights Society (ARS), New York.

# The Harlem Renaissance

In the early 1920s, African American artists, writers, musicians, and performers were part of a great cultural movement known as the Harlem Renaissance. The huge migration to the north after World War I brought African Americans of all ages and walks of life to the thriving New York City neighborhood called Harlem. Doctors, singers, students, musicians, shopkeepers, painters, and writers congregated, forming a vibrant mecca of cultural affirmation and inspiration.

As Langston Hughes wrote, "It was the period when the Negro was in vogue." Marcus Garvey's "Back to Africa" movement was in full swing. The blues were vibrantly alive; jazz was just beginning. An all-black show, *Shuffle Along,* opened on Broadway in 1921, with music composed by Eubie Blake and lyrics by Noble Sissle. *Shuffle Along* introduced audiences to three performers soon to become famous: Josephine Baker, Paul Robeson, and Florence Mills. Meanwhile, mainstream America was developing a new respect for African art and culture, thanks in part to its reflection in the work of the modernist artists Pablo Picasso and Georges Braque.

Against this backdrop, Harlem Renaissance artists insisted that the African American be accepted as "a collaborator and participant in American civilization," in the words of the educator and critic Alain Locke. Writers such as Jean Toomer and Zora Neale Hurston (page 836) wrote about the African American experience. Artists such as Aaron Douglas and William H. Johnson painted it. The photographer James Van Der Zee recorded it with his camera. The trumpeter Louis Armstrong and the pianist Fletcher Henderson set it to music, and the vocalists Bessie Smith and Ma Rainey sang it.

Bessie Smith.

Harlem newspapers and journals, such as *Crisis* and *Opportunity*, published the work of both new and established African American writers. To promote and support intellectually gifted young people, the journals sponsored literary contests that encouraged creative writing and rewarded it with cash prizes and social introductions to the top writers of the time.

In autobiographies, poetry, short stories, novels, and folklore, African American writers affirmed the role of black talent in American culture and focused on different aspects of black life in Harlem, the South, Europe, the Caribbean, and even Russia. They addressed issues of race, class, religion, and gender. Some writers focused entirely on black characters, while others addressed relationships among people of different races. Some writers attacked racism; others addressed issues within black communities. A byproduct of African American writing was the affirmation that black dialects were as legitimate as standard English.

Unfortunately, by the early 1930s, the Great Depression had depleted many of the funds that had provided financial support to individual African American writers, institutions, and publications. Nevertheless, Harlem and African American culture were forever changed. The foundation was laid for Ralph Ellison, James Baldwin, Gwendolyn Brooks, Alice Walker, Toni Morrison, Maya Angelou, Terry McMillan, Rita Dove, and thousands of other African American writers, painters, composers, and singers to make their feelings and experiences part of American artistic expression: "I, too, sing America."

Louis Armstrong.

# Countee Cullen
## (1903–1946)

Countee Cullen grew up in New York City as the adopted son of Rev. and Mrs. Frederick Cullen. He was a brilliant student, and during high school he was already writing accomplished poems in traditional forms. He graduated Phi Beta Kappa from New York University in 1925. While in college, Cullen won the Witter Bynner Poetry Prize; that same year, *Color,* his first volume of poetry, was published. This collection won a gold medal from the Harmon Foundation and established the young poet's reputation.

After earning his master's degree from Harvard in 1926, Cullen worked as an assistant editor of the important African American magazine *Opportunity.* His poems were published in such influential periodicals as *Harper's, Poetry,* and *Crisis.* In 1927, he published *Copper Sun,* a collection of poems, and *Caroling Dusk,* an anthology of poetry by African Americans. *Caroling Dusk* was a significant contribution to the Harlem Renaissance, but the introduction Cullen wrote for the book was controversial. He called for black poets to write traditional verse and to avoid the restrictions of solely racial themes.

At the peak of his career, Cullen married the daughter of the famous black writer W.E.B. Du Bois and published a third collection of poems, *The Ballad of the Brown Girl.* In 1929, he published a fourth volume, *The Black Christ.* Although he continued to write prose until the end of his life, this was his last collection of poetry. During the Great Depression of the 1930s, unable to make a living solely from writing, he began teaching in Harlem public schools, a job that he held until his early death.

*Countee Porter Cullen* (c. 1925) by Winold Reiss. Pastel on artist board ($30^{1}/_{16}'' \times 21^{1}/_{2}''$).

Cullen's verse was heavily influenced by the poetry of the English Romantics, especially John Keats. He thought of himself primarily as a lyric poet in the Romantic tradition, not as a black poet writing about social and racial themes. Nevertheless, Cullen found himself repeatedly drawn to such themes: "Somehow or other I find my poetry of itself treating of the Negro, of his joys and his sorrows— mostly of the latter—and of the heights and depths of emotion which I feel as a Negro."

# Before You Read

## Tableau

### Make the Connection

The history of race relations in the United States is long and tragic, the cause of much pain and misunderstanding. Knowledge of the great public confrontations such as the Civil War and the civil rights movement can illuminate that history, but in the end, it may be the personal experiences of individual blacks and whites that provide us with the deepest understanding of our past and of our possible future. As you read the following two poems by Cullen, think about the impact of the encounters on the individuals involved—and on the society in which they lived.

A *tableau* is "a scene or an action stopped cold," like a still picture in a reel of film.

### Literary Focus
#### Metaphor

A **metaphor** is a **figure of speech,** an imaginative comparison between two unlike things. Some metaphors are stated directly, using a linking verb: *That boy is a streak of lightning.* Often they are more indirect. This poem uses four metaphors to reveal the way the poet feels about the sight of two boys crossing a street. Watch for the metaphors that end the first and last stanzas.

A **metaphor** is a figure of speech that makes a comparison between two unlike things without the use of a specific word of comparison.

*For more on Metaphor, see the Handbook of Literary and Historical Terms.*

**Literary Skills**
Understand metaphor.

# Tableau

*(For Donald Duff)*

## Countee Cullen

Locked arm in arm they cross the way,
    The black boy and the white,
The golden splendor of the day,
    The sable pride of night.

5  From lowered blinds the dark folk stare,
    And here the fair folk talk,
Indignant that these two should dare
    In unison to walk.

Oblivious to look and word
10    They pass, and see no wonder
That lightning brilliant as a sword
    Should blaze the path of thunder.

# Before You Read

## Incident

### Make the Connection
**Quickwrite** ✏

The power of a word to taunt, to criticize, to dehumanize can't be underestimated. You might be shaken by the offensive word in this poem—imagine how it would affect a child.

   Before you read "Incident," quickwrite your response to the poem's title. Does it suggest something serious, or something relatively minor? How would you react if the title were "Catastrophe"?

# Incident

## Countee Cullen

Once, riding in old Baltimore,
   Heart-filled, head-filled with glee,
I saw a Baltimorean
   Keep looking straight at me.

5   Now I was eight and very small,
   And he was no whit bigger,
And so I smiled, but he poked out
   His tongue, and called me "Nigger."

I saw the whole of Baltimore
10   From May until December;
Of all the things that happened there
   That's all that I remember.

*Passengers* (1953) by Raphael Soyer. Oil on canvas.

© Estate of Raphael Soyer, Forum Gallery, New York. Image courtesy of Sotheby's.

# Response and Analysis

## Tableau

### Thinking Critically

1. What exactly are the two boys in the tableau doing?

2. Why are "the dark folk" and "the fair folk" indignant? How do the boys respond?

3. What **metaphor** in the first stanza describes the black boy? the white boy?

4. Two more **metaphors** are used in the third stanza. Who or what is "lightning brilliant as a sword"? Who or what is "the path of thunder"?

5. How do the metaphors make you feel about the boys?

6. What do you have to know about the social context of the poem in order to understand why such a commonplace thing as a friendship between two boys could evoke such a dramatic response?

## Incident

### Thinking Critically

1. Who are the two people in this poem, and what exactly happens between them?

2. What do you think leads the "Baltimorean" to act as he does? Are his actions more disturbing or less disturbing because he is a child? Explain your responses.

3. What does the word *incident* suggest to you? Why do you think Cullen chose this as his title? Be sure to refer to your Quickwrite notes. 🖉

4. The speaker never directly states his emotional response to the experience. How does the last stanza indirectly make clear the impact the encounter had on him?

### Extending and Evaluating

5. Do you think that the content and messages of "Tableau" and "Incident" are relevant only to the time in which Cullen wrote? Or are the incidents described in these poems still occurring today? Explain.

## WRITING

### Analyzing Literature

When you analyze a piece of literature, you take it apart to see how its elements work together to create meaning. In an **essay,** analyze these two poems, "Incident" and "Tableau." Before you start to write, gather your details in a chart like the following one:

|  | Tableau | Incident |
|---|---|---|
| Message |  |  |
| Tone |  |  |
| Images or figures of speech |  |  |
| Use of rhyme |  |  |
| Use of meter |  |  |

Analyze each poem separately, first "Tableau" and then "Incident." At the end of your analysis, include a comment that describes your response to each poem. Which element of the poem has the strongest impact on your response?

▶ **Use "Analyzing Literature," pages 739–740, for help with this assignment.**

**SKILLS FOCUS**

**Literary Skills**
Analyze metaphor.

**Writing Skills**
Write an essay analyzing two poems.

**INTERNET**

**Projects and Activities**

Keyword: LE7 11-5

# Langston Hughes
## (1902–1967)

One evening toward the end of 1925, the poet Vachel Lindsay was eating dinner in the Wardman Park Hotel in Washington, D.C. The busboy, a twenty-three-year-old African American, left three poems near Lindsay's plate. Lindsay was so impressed by the poems that he presented them in his reading that night, telling the audience that he had discovered a true poet—a young black man who was working as a busboy in the hotel restaurant. Over the next few days, articles about the "busboy poet" appeared in newspapers up and down the East Coast.

The busboy, Langston Hughes, was no beginning writer. In fact, when he shyly approached Lindsay, Hughes's first book of poetry, *The Weary Blues,* was about to be published by a prestigious New York company, and individual poems had appeared in numerous places. Lindsay warned the young poet about literary "lionizers" who might exploit him for their own purpose: "Hide and write and study and think. I know what factions do. Beware of them. I know what lionizers do. Beware of them." In response to Lindsay, Hughes wrote back: "If anything is important, it is my poetry, not me. I do not want folks to know me, but if they know and like some of my poems I am glad. Perhaps the mission of an artist is to interpret beauty to the people—the beauty within themselves. That is what I want to do, if I consciously want to do anything with poetry."

Before this encounter, Hughes had attended Columbia University and worked his way to Africa and back as a crew member on an ocean freighter. Ambitious and energetic, Hughes had learned early to rely on himself. He spoke German and Spanish; he had lived in Mexico, France, and Italy. In the years that followed his "overnight" celebrity, he earned his degree at Lincoln University, wrote fifteen volumes of poetry, six novels, three books of short stories, eleven plays, and a variety of nonfiction works.

Born in Joplin, Missouri, Hughes spent most of his childhood in Lawrence, Kansas, with his grandmother. When he was thirteen, she died, and he moved to Lincoln, Illinois, and then to Cleveland, Ohio, to live with his mother and stepfather.

Hughes began writing poems in the eighth grade, and he began publishing his work as a high school student in his school literary magazine. He read voraciously and greatly admired the work of Edgar Lee Masters, Vachel Lindsay, Amy Lowell, Carl Sandburg, and Walt Whitman.

*Portrait of Langston Hughes by Winold Reiss.*

The most important influences on Hughes's poetry were Walt Whitman and Carl Sandburg. Both poets broke from traditional poetic forms and used free verse to express the humanity of all people regardless of their age, gender, race, and class. Encouraged by the examples of Whitman and Sandburg, Hughes celebrated the experiences of African Americans, often using jazz rhythms and the repetitive structure of the blues in his poems. Toward the end of his life, he wrote poems specifically for jazz accompaniment. He was also responsible for the founding of several black theater companies, and he wrote and translated a number of dramatic works. His work, he said, was an attempt to "explain and illuminate the Negro condition in America." It succeeded in doing that with both vigor and compassion.

## The Weary Blues

### Make the Connection
#### Quickwrite 🖉

Among the great contributions from American culture to the world is the music created by African Americans: orchestral, blues, ragtime, soul, rap, and new musical expressions that are being developed every day.

The music known as the blues started to attract attention at the turn of the twentieth century. Eventually the blues became widely popular in the United States and abroad, making stars of such singers as Bessie Smith and Ethel Waters. In this poem, Hughes describes his experience of listening to "a sad raggy tune" and captures some of its rhythms in words.

Jot down your associations with the word *blues* and the music it describes. What feelings or words are associated with blues music? Is there any blues influence on the music you like?

### Literary Focus
#### Rhythm

**Rhythm** in poetry is the rise and fall of the voice, produced by alternating stressed and unstressed syllables. Langston Hughes uses several kinds of rhythms in "The Weary Blues." As he says in the first line, he uses the "syncopated tune" of a piano. He also uses the rhythm of everyday speech, the soulful rhythm of the blues, and even the formal meter of traditional poetry. His poems are true originals.

**SKILLS FOCUS**

**Literary Skills**
Understand rhythm.

> **Rhythm** is the alternation of stressed and unstressed syllables in a line of prose or poetry.
>
> *For more on Rhythm, see the Handbook of Literary and Historical Terms.*

**INTERNET**

**More About Langston Hughes**

Keyword: LE7 11-5

### Background

On a March night in 1922, Langston Hughes sat in a small Harlem cabaret and wrote "The Weary Blues." In this poem, Hughes incorporated the many elements of his life—the music of Southern black speech, the lyrics of the first blues he ever heard, and conventional poetic forms he learned in school. While the body of the poem took shape quickly, it took the poet two years to get the ending right: "I could not achieve an ending I liked, although I worked and worked on it." When he at last completed the poem, "The Weary Blues" marked the beginning of his literary career.

*Solo Sax* by Phoebe Beasley.

The Block (1971) by Romare Bearden (American, 1914–1988)
cut and pasted papers on masonite, overall: H. 4 ft. W. 18 ft.

The Metropolitan Museum of Art, Gift of Mr. and Mrs. Samuel Shore, 1978
(178.61.1-6). Photograph © 1992 The Metropolitan Museum of Art.
Art © Romare Bearden Foundation/Licensed by VAGA, New York, NY.

# The Weary Blues

## Langston Hughes

Droning a drowsy syncopated tune,°
Rocking back and forth to a mellow croon,
   I heard a Negro play.
Down on Lenox Avenue° the other night
5  By the pale dull pallor of an old gas light
   He did a lazy sway . . .
   He did a lazy sway . . .
To the tune o' those Weary Blues.
With his ebony hands on each ivory key
10  He made that poor piano moan with melody.
   O Blues!
Swaying to and fro on his rickety stool
He played that sad raggy tune like a musical fool.
   Sweet Blues!
15  Coming from a black man's soul.
   O Blues!
In a deep song voice with a melancholy tone
I heard that Negro sing, that old piano moan—
   "Ain't got nobody in all this world,
20   Ain't got nobody but ma salf.
   I's gwine to quit ma frownin'
   And put ma troubles on the shelf."
Thump, thump, thump, went his foot on the floor.
He played a few chords then he sang some more—
25   "I got the Weary Blues
   And I can't be satisfied.
   Got the Weary Blues
   And can't be satisfied—
   I ain't happy no mo'
30   And I wish that I had died."
And far into the night he crooned that tune.
The stars went out and so did the moon.
The singer stopped playing and went to bed
While the Weary Blues echoed through his head.
35  He slept like a rock or a man that's dead.

**1. syncopated tune:** melody in which accents
are placed on normally unaccented beats.

**4. Lenox Avenue:** street in Harlem.

*Lazy Sway* by Phoebe Beasley.

*Out Chorus* (1979–1980) by Romare Bearden (1911–1988). Color silkscreen. 12 ⅜ × 16 ⅜ in.

New Britain Museum of Art, New Britain, Connecticut. Friends Purchase Fund 1981.41. Photo by E. Irving Blomstrann.
© Romare Bearden Foundation/Licensed by VAGA, New York, New York.

## Birth of the Blues

INFORMATIONAL TEXT

When asked about the origins of the blues, a veteran New Orleans fiddler once said: "The blues? Ain't no first blues! The blues always been." The first form of blues, country blues, developed in several parts of the United States, most notably the Mississippi Delta, around 1900. Country blues tunes were typically sung by men—usually share-croppers. The subject was often the relationship between men and women. As the contemporary blues singer B. B. King once said, the blues is about a man losing his woman.

From the start, blues music was improvisational—it changed with every singer and performance. Parts of lyrics were freely borrowed from other songs or based on folk songs or figures of speech. Lines might be repeated two or three times, with different accents and emphases, then answered or completed by a rhyming line:

> Black cat on my doorstep, black cat on my window sill. (repeat)
> If some black cat don't cross me, some other black cat will.
>
> —Ma Rainey

**The blues catch on.** The earliest blues singers, among them Charley Patton, Robert Johnson, and Blind Lemon Jefferson, played at country stores, at Friday- and Saturday-night dances, at cafes, and at picnics. The first popular blues recordings, made in the 1920s, featured female singers such as Ma Rainey and Bessie Smith backed by a piano or a jazz band.

When rural Southern African Americans migrated after World War I to cities like Chicago, New York, Detroit, St. Louis, and Memphis, the blues sound evolved further. Musicians sang about their experiences in the city, adding the electric guitar, amplified harmonica, bass, and drums to blues ensembles. Musicians such as Sunnyland Slim, T-Bone Walker, and Memphis Minnie pioneered the urban blues sound in the 1930s and 1940s; the next generation included the blues greats Muddy Waters, Howlin' Wolf, and B. B. King. Since then, blues music has influenced virtually every genre of music, including folk, country and western, and—most profoundly—rock. Elvis Presley, Bob Dylan, the Rolling Stones, Eric Clapton, and Bonnie Raitt have all borrowed freely from the blues tradition. Today, blues music is still being played and created by such artists as Buddy Guy, Otis Rush, Koko Taylor, Keb' Mo', and Robert Cray. They are carrying on a musical tradition that was invented at a particular time and place—the American South in the early 1900s—to express the African American experience. The genius of the blues is that it has honored its origins even as it expresses universal hopes, fears, and sorrows.

# Before You Read

## Harlem

**SKILLS FOCUS**

**Literary Skills**
Understand mood.

**INTERNET**

**More About Langston Hughes**

Keyword: LE7 11-5

### Make the Connection
### Quickwrite ✐

The Harlem Renaissance writers responded to the oppression and feelings of powerlessness that pervaded the lives of their Harlem neighbors. Hughes himself wrote several poems called "Harlem." This one is set during the Great Depression of the 1930s, a time when even a one-cent increase in the price of bread could be disastrous, a time also when being black usually meant being poor with little opportunity to earn more.

How does it feel to be a victim of discrimination? Jot down some notes.

### Literary Focus
### Mood

In literature, **mood** refers to the feelings aroused by words and by sounds. A poem, for example, might make a reader feel sad or amused or thoughtful. Poems can create more than one feeling, but often they have one dominant mood. (Often, in talking about a work of literature, the words *mood* and *atmosphere* are used interchangeably.) As you read "Harlem," look for words and images that create a particular mood.

> **Mood** is the overall feeling created in a piece of writing.
>
> *For more on Mood, see the Handbook of Literary and Historical Terms.*

# Harlem

## Langston Hughes

Here on the edge of hell
Stands Harlem—
Remembering the old lies,
The old kicks in the back,
5   The old "Be patient"
They told us before.

Sure, we remember.
Now when the man at the corner store
Says sugar's gone up another two cents,
10  And bread one,
And there's a new tax on cigarettes—
We remember the job we never had,

Never could get,
And can't have now
15  Because we're colored.

So we stand here
On the edge of hell
In Harlem
And look out on the world
20  And wonder
What we're gonna do
In the face of what
We remember.

*Harlem Street Scene* (1975) by Jacob Lawrence. Serigraph (27" × 24").

*Jockey Club* (1929) by Archibald John Motley, Jr. Oil on canvas.

# Heyday in Harlem

*Langston Hughes describes the vigor and excitement of Harlem in the 1920s and 1930s.*

White people began to come to Harlem in droves. For several years they packed the expensive Cotton Club on Lenox Avenue. But I was never there, because the Cotton Club was a Jim Crow club[1] for gangsters and monied whites. They were not cordial to Negro patronage, unless you were a celebrity like Bojangles.[2] So Harlem Negroes did not like the Cotton Club and never appreciated its Jim Crow policy in the very heart of their dark community. . . .

It was a period when, at almost every Harlem upper-crust dance or party, one would be introduced to various distinguished white celebrities there as guests. It was a period when almost any Harlem Negro of any social importance at all would be likely to say casually: "As I was remarking the other day to Heywood—," meaning Heywood Broun.[3] Or: "As I said to George—," referring to George

**INFORMATIONAL TEXT**

---

1. **Jim Crow club:** segregated nightclub.
2. **Bojangles:** Bill "Bojangles" Robinson (1879–1949), star of black musical comedies and vaudeville.

3. **Heywood Broun** (1888–1939): American journalist during the 1920s and 1930s.

Gershwin.[4] It was a period when local and visiting royalty were not at all uncommon in Harlem. And when the parties of A'Lelia Walker, the Negro heiress, were filled with guests whose names would turn any Nordic[5] social climber green with envy. . . . It was a period when every season there was at least one hit play on Broadway acted by a Negro cast. And when books by Negro authors were being published with much greater frequency and much more publicity than ever before or since in history. It was a period when white writers wrote about Negroes more successfully (commercially speaking) than Negroes did about themselves. It was the period (God help us!) when Ethel Barrymore[6] appeared in blackface in *Scarlet Sister Mary*! It was the period when the Negro was in vogue. . . .

Then it was that house-rent parties began to flourish—and not always to raise the rent either. But, as often as not, to have a get-together of one's own, where you could do the black-bottom[7] with no stranger behind you trying to do it, too. Nontheatrical, non-intellectual Harlem was an unwilling victim of its own vogue. It didn't like to be stared at by white folks. But perhaps the downtowners never knew this—for the cabaret owners, the entertainers, and the speakeasy[8] proprietors treated them fine—as long as they paid.

The Saturday night rent parties that I attended were often more amusing than any night club, in small apartments where God knows who lived—because the guests seldom did—but where the piano would often be augmented by a guitar, or an odd cornet, or somebody with a pair of drums walking in off the street. And where awful bootleg whiskey and good fried fish or steaming chitterling[9] were sold at very low prices. And the dancing and singing and impromptu entertaining went on until dawn came in at the windows.

These parties, often termed whist[10] parties or dances, were usually announced by brightly colored cards stuck in the grille of apartment house elevators. Some of the cards were highly entertaining in themselves:

---

*Some wear pajamas, some wear pants, what does it matter just so you can dance, at*

## A Social Whist Party

GIVEN BY

MR. & MRS. BROWN

AT 258 W. 115TH STREET, APT. 9

SATURDAY EVE., SEPT. 14, 1929

*The music is sweet and everything good to eat!*

---

Almost every Saturday night when I was in Harlem I went to a house-rent party. I wrote lots of poems about house-rent parties, and ate thereat many a fried fish and pig's foot—with liquid refreshments on the side. I met ladies' maids and truck drivers, laundry workers and shoeshine boys, seamstresses and porters. I can still hear their laughter in my ears, hear the soft slow music, and feel the floor shaking as the dancers danced.

*Langston Hughes*

from "When the Negro Was in Vogue"

---

4. **George Gershwin** (1898–1937): great American composer of both popular and serious music.
5. **Nordic**: white.
6. **Ethel Barrymore** (1879–1959): American stage and movie actress.
7. **black-bottom** *n.*: popular dance of the late 1920s.
8. **speakeasy** *n.*: club where alcoholic drinks were sold illegally during Prohibition.

9. **chitterling** (chit'lin) *n.*: food made from small intestines of pigs, deep-fried in hot oil.
10. **whist** *n.*: card game.

# Response and Analysis

## The Weary Blues

### Thinking Critically

1. What **scene** do you see as you read this poem?

2. How does the message of the blues singer's first verse contrast with that of the second verse?

3. What **similes** in the poem's last line describe how the singer sleeps? What do you think the last five words suggest?

4. Think of how the blues singer, the listener, and you feel as you hear the blues song. How would you describe the overall **mood** of the poem? What words help to create this mood? (Be sure to check your Quickwrite notes.) ✏️

5. Describe how the poem's structure suggests the **rhythms** of blues music.

6. Hughes also uses alliteration and onomatopoeia to create his music. **Alliteration** is the repetition of similar consonant sounds in words that are close together. **Onomatopoeia** is the use of words that actually *sound* like what they name (*swish*, *slap*, and *pop* are examples). Read aloud examples of **alliteration** and **onomatopoeia** that add to the musical effect of "The Weary Blues."

## Harlem

### Thinking Critically

1. What **mood** does the speaker immediately create with this description of the poem's **setting:** "Here on the edge of hell / Stands Harlem—"?

2. Name the specific hardships and injustices that the people of Harlem remember, according to the speaker.

3. What is the effect of the **repetition** of the word *remember?*

4. How do you interpret the poem's final stanza? Is it an expression of powerlessness, of opposition, or of something else? Be sure you can defend your interpretation.

5. Did any adjectives in your Quickwrite describe the feelings expressed in this poem? If not, what adjective would you use to describe the overall **mood** of the poem? ✏️

## WRITING

### An Investigation into the Harlem Renaissance

Find out more about some of the writers and artists of the Harlem Renaissance. You may want to read more of Hughes's poetry or research some of the musicians mentioned in his essay "Heyday in Harlem." (See the *Primary Source* on page 830 Alternatively, you could investigate the works of other writers of that time, such as Claude McKay or Paul Laurence Dunbar. You might investigate one of the great Harlem Renaissance artists, such as Aaron Douglas or William H. Johnson. Write a brief **research report** on some topic related to the Harlem Renaissance. Share your findings with the rest of the class.

▶ **Use "Reporting Historical Research," pages 602–621, for help with this assignment.**

## LISTENING AND SPEAKING

### From the Soul

Paying careful attention to punctuation and line breaks, read "The Weary Blues" and "Harlem" aloud to express each poem's unique **rhythm** and **mood.** Let another group of students evaluate your performance.

**SKILLS FOCUS**

**Literary Skills**
Analyze rhythm and mood.

**Writing Skills**
Write a historical research report.

**Listening and Speaking Skills**
Perform an oral interpretation of a poem.

**INTERNET**

**Projects and Activities**

Keyword: LE7 11-5

# Before You Read

## The Negro Speaks of Rivers

### Make the Connection

**Imagery** is the use of language to create pictures. Images can appeal not only to our sense of sight but also to our senses of hearing, smell, taste, and touch. Some images appear again and again in art. There seems to be no end to the capacity of these images to stir our imaginations and move our emotions. In this poem by Langston Hughes and in the poem that follows by the contemporary writer Lucille Clifton, the recurring image is that of a river. What do you think of when you see or imagine a mighty river?

### Literary Focus
#### Repetition

Poets create rhythm and musical effects by using **repetition**—of sounds, words, phrases, or even entire lines. A repeated line in a poem or song is called a **refrain**. Repetition not only affects the sound of a poem; it also emphasizes important ideas and builds up certain feelings and expectations.

> **Repetition** is the recurrence of certain sounds, words, phrases, or lines in a poem to achieve rhythmic or emotional effects. A repeated line is called a **refrain.**
>
> *For more on Refrain, see the Handbook of Literary and Historical Terms.*

**Literary Skills**
Understand repetition.

**INTERNET**

More About
Langston Hughes

Keyword: LE7 11-5

# The Negro Speaks of Rivers

## Langston Hughes

I've known rivers:
I've known rivers ancient as the world and older than the flow
    of human blood in human veins.

My soul has grown      deep like rivers.

    I bathed in the Euphrates when dawns were young.
5    I built my hut near the Congo and it lulled me to sleep.
    I looked upon the Nile and raised the pyramids above it.
    I heard the singing of the Mississippi when Abe Lincoln went
        down to New Orleans, and I've seen its muddy bosom turn
        all golden in the sunset.

I've known rivers:
Ancient, dusky rivers.

10    My soul has grown      deep like rivers.

*When They Speak of Rivers* by Phoebe Beasley.

# the mississippi river empties into the gulf

## Lucille Clifton

and the gulf enters the sea and so forth,
none of them emptying anything,
all of them carrying yesterday
forever on their white tipped backs,
5   all of them dragging forward tomorrow.
it is the great circulation
of the earth's body, like the blood
of the gods, this river in which the past
is always flowing. every water
10   is the same water coming round.
everyday someone is standing on the edge
of this river, staring into time,
whispering mistakenly:
only here. only now.

# Response and Analysis

## Thinking Critically

1. What specific rivers does the speaker name?

2. Like Whitman (see page 361), this speaker speaks for a multitude. Who or what does the poet imagine is the "I" in this poem? (The title provides one clue.)

3. What special connections may African Americans have with each of these rivers? (Note the verbs that follow the word "I" at the beginning of each line in the third stanza.)

4. In the last line, what comparison does the speaker make?

5. What instances of **repetition** occur in the poem? What line acts as a **refrain**? What is the emotional effect of this repetition?

6. After you read Hughes's poem aloud, think about the **tone** you hear. Which word best describes that tone: sad? bitter? thoughtful? joyful? Give details from the poem to support your response.

7. In the **Connection** on this page, Lucille Clifton also writes about a river. What river is she describing? What does the river remind this speaker of, according to lines 6–10? How do both Clifton's speaker and Hughes's speaker identify rivers with human life?

**SKILLS FOCUS**

**Literary Skills**
Analyze repetition.

# Zora Neale Hurston

## (c. 1891–1960)

**A**lthough she claimed to have been born in Eatonville, Florida, in 1901, Zora Neale Hurston was actually born ten years earlier in Notsaluga, Alabama. Her family moved to the all-black town of Eatonville when she was very young. Her father was a preacher, and her mother, a schoolteacher, urged her talented daughter to "jump at the sun."

In her autobiography, Hurston recalls that as a young girl, "I used to climb to the top of one of the huge chinaberry trees which guarded our front gate and look out over the world. The most interesting thing that I saw was the horizon. . . . It grew upon me that I ought to walk out to the horizon and see what the end of the world was like."

When Hurston was about fourteen, her mother died, and Zora was passed among relatives and family friends, supporting herself from her early teens on. Eventually, she enrolled at Howard University in Washington, D.C., where she published her first story in 1921.

Four years later, she set out for New York City to attend Barnard College, arriving with a dollar and a half in her pocket. Hurston was soon in the midst of the Harlem Renaissance, writing stories and plays that celebrated her African American heritage. She wore big hats and turbans, danced, gave parties, and sometimes shocked other African American artists.

At Barnard, Hurston met the anthropologist Franz Boas, who believed that Hurston's interest was in his field, the study of human social and cultural behavior. Indeed, Hurston, who became his protégé, did eventually make her reputation not just as a fiction writer but also as a folklorist. She traveled through Alabama, Florida, and Louisiana to gather material, using a scholar's eye to evaluate oral tales. Eventually, she gathered enough folklore to fill two groundbreaking collections, *Mules and Men* (1935) and *Tell My Horse* (1938). Alice Walker (page 1102) says that the stories in *Mules and Men* gave back to her own relatives in the South all the stories they'd forgotten or grown ashamed of.

Hurston also wrote musical revues portraying black folk culture, and these brought her initial success. But it was *Story* magazine's publication of her short story "The Gilded Six Bits" that launched her literary career. When the Philadelphia publisher J. B. Lippincott asked if she had a novel, Hurston promptly sat down and wrote *Jonah's Gourd Vine,* published in 1934. Three years later Hurston published her best novel, *Their Eyes Were Watching God,* the story of a young African American woman who strikes out for a life beyond a conventional marriage, much as Hurston herself had done.

Throughout the last twenty years of her life, Hurston continued to produce fiction and nonfiction, including her autobiography, *Dust Tracks on a Road.* But she began to have difficulty finding a market for her work, some of which was criticized in the African American community for celebrating the life of black people in the United States rather than confronting the white community for its discrimination.

In the late 1940s, Hurston left New York and returned to Florida. In 1960, she died, broke, in a Florida welfare home. A collection had to be taken up to pay for her funeral. Ironically, in the years since her death, much of her work has been brought back into print, and Hurston is now recognized as the forerunner of such celebrated contemporary writers as Toni Morrison and Alice Walker.

## *from* Dust Tracks on a Road

### Make the Connection

It's no surprise that autobiographies of writers often include lovingly detailed memories of childhood experiences that paved the way for the adult's embrace of the writing profession. In her autobiography, *One Writer's Beginnings,* Eudora Welty states, "Writing fiction has developed in me . . . a sense of where to look for the threads, how to follow, how to connect, find in the thick of the tangle what clear line persists. The strands are all there: To the memory nothing is ever really lost." In this excerpt from her autobiography, Zora Neale Hurston connects some of her own threads by recounting what surely was one of the great experiences of her life: the discovery of her passion for reading.

### Literary Focus
#### Autobiography

An **autobiography** is an account of a writer's own life (from the prefix *auto–,* meaning "self," and the word *biography,* meaning "story of a life"). When a published writer tells the story of his or her own life, we expect to learn how that person became a writer, what experiences the writer drew from to produce his or her poems or novels. In autobiographies we also look for **subjective details**—we want to know how the writer felt about his or her family, friends, and experiences. It is these authentic, firsthand, subjective details that distinguish autobiography from biography.

> An **autobiography** is a written account of a person's own life.
>
> *For more on Autobiography, see the Handbook of Literary and Historical Terms.*

### Background

Zora Neale Hurston's *Dust Tracks on a Road* is rich with cultural and historical meaning, as well as personal insights. Woven through these recollections of Hurston's childhood are her impressions of racial segregation, economic conditions, education, and social customs in the South at the turn of the century.

### Vocabulary Development

**hail** *v.:* greet.

**brazenness** (brā′zən·nis) *n.:* boldness.

**caper** (kā′pər) *n.:* foolish prank.

**exalted** (eg·zôlt′id) *v.:* lifted up.

**realm** (relm) *n.:* kingdom.

**avarice** (av′ə·ris) *n.:* greed.

**tread** (tred) *n.:* step; walk.

**profoundly** (prō·found′lē) *adv.:* deeply.

**resolved** (ri·zälvd′) *v.:* made a decision; determined.

**conceive** (kən·sēv′) *v.:* think; imagine.

SKILLS
FOCUS

**Literary Skills**
Understand the characteristics of autobiography. Understand the political and social influences of a historical period.

**INTERNET**

**Vocabulary Practice**
•
**More About Zora Neale Hurston**

Keyword: LE7 11-5

*from* **Dust Tracks on a Road**

# Zora Neale Hurston

**My grandmother worried about my forward ways a great deal.**

I used to take a seat on top of the gatepost and watch the world go by. One way to Orlando ran past my house, so the carriages and cars would pass before me. The movement made me glad to see it. Often the white travelers would hail me, but more often I hailed them, and asked, "Don't you want me to go a piece of the way with you?"

They always did. I know now that I must have caused a great deal of amusement among them, but my self-assurance must have carried the point, for I was always invited to come along. I'd ride up the road for perhaps a half-mile, then walk back. I did not do this with the permission of my parents, nor with their foreknowledge. When they found out about it later, I usually got a whipping. My grandmother worried about my forward ways a great deal. She had known slavery and to her my brazenness was unthinkable.

"Git down offa dat gatepost! You li'l sow, you! Git down! Setting up dere looking dem white

**Vocabulary**

**hail** *v.:* greet.
**brazenness** (brā'zən·nis) *n.:* boldness.

*Dunbar High School,* Quincy, Florida (pages 837–839, 841, 842).

Florida State Archives.

folks right in de face! They's gowine[1] to lynch you, yet. And don't stand in dat doorway gazing out at 'em neither. Youse too brazen to live long."

Nevertheless, I kept right on gazing at them, and "going a piece of the way" whenever I could make it. The village seemed dull to me most of the time. If the village was singing a chorus, I must have missed the tune.

Perhaps a year before the old man[2] died, I came to know two other white people for myself. They were women.

It came about this way. The whites who came down from the North were often brought by their friends to visit the village school. A Negro school was something strange to them, and while they were always sympathetic and kind, curiosity must have been present, also. They came and went, came and went. Always, the room was hurriedly put in order, and we were threatened with a prompt and bloody death if we cut one caper while the visitors were present. We always sang a spiritual, led by Mr. Calhoun himself. Mrs. Calhoun always stood in the back, with a palmetto switch[3] in her hand as a squelcher. We were all little angels for the duration, because we'd better be. She would cut her eyes[4] and give us a glare that meant trouble, then turn her face toward the visitors and beam as much as to say it was a great privilege and pleasure to teach lovely children like us. They couldn't see that palmetto hickory in her hand behind all those benches, but we knew where our angelic behavior was coming from.

Usually, the visitors gave warning a day ahead and we would be cautioned to put on shoes, comb our heads, and see to ears and fingernails. There was a close inspection of every one of us before we marched in that morning. Knotty heads, dirty ears, and fingernails got hauled out

of line, strapped, and sent home to lick the calf[5] over again.

This particular afternoon, the two young ladies just popped in. Mr. Calhoun was flustered, but he put on the best show he could. He dismissed the class that he was teaching up at the front of the room, then called the fifth grade in reading. That was my class.

So we took our readers and went up front. We stood up in the usual line, and opened to the lesson. It was the story of Pluto and Persephone.[6] It was new and hard to the class in general, and Mr. Calhoun was very uncomfortable as the readers stumbled along, spelling out words with their lips, and in mumbling undertones before they exposed them experimentally to the teacher's ears.

Then it came to me. I was fifth or sixth down the line. The story was not new to me, because I had read my reader through from lid to lid, the first week that Papa had bought it for me.

That is how it was that my eyes were not in the book, working out the paragraph which I knew would be mine by counting the children ahead of me. I was observing our visitors, who held a book between them, following the lesson. They had shiny hair, mostly brownish. One had a looping gold chain around her neck. The other one was dressed all over in black and white with a pretty finger ring on her left hand. But the thing that held my eyes were their fingers. They were long and thin, and very white, except up near the tips. There they were baby pink. I had never seen such hands. It was a fascinating discovery for me. I wondered how they felt. I would have given those hands more attention, but the child before me was almost

---

1. **gowine:** dialect for "going."
2. **old man:** white farmer who knew Hurston's family, took her fishing, and gave her advice.
3. **palmetto switch:** whip made from the stem of a large, fanlike leaf of a kind of palm tree. Teachers sometimes used these switches to discipline students.
4. **cut her eyes:** slang for "look scornfully."
5. **lick the calf:** slang for "wash up."
6. **Pluto and Persephone** (pər·sef′ə·nē): In classical mythology, Pluto, or Hades, is the god who rules the underworld; Persephone, also known as Proserpina, is his wife, queen of the underworld. In this version of the origin of the seasons, Hurston uses the names of Roman and Greek gods interchangeably.

**Vocabulary**

**caper** (kā′pər) *n.:* foolish prank.

through. My turn next, so I got on my mark, bringing my eyes back to the book and made sure of my place. Some of the stories I had reread several times, and this Greco-Roman myth was one of my favorites. I was <u>exalted</u> by it, and that is the way I read my paragraph.

"Yes, Jupiter[7] had seen her (Persephone). He had seen the maiden picking flowers in the field. He had seen the chariot of the dark monarch pause by the maiden's side. He had seen him when he seized Persephone. He had seen the black horses leap down Mount Aetna's[8] fiery throat. Persephone was now in Pluto's dark <u>realm</u> and he had made her <u>his wife</u>."

The two women looked at each other and then back to me. Mr. Calhoun broke out with a proud smile beneath his bristly moustache, and instead of the next child taking up where I had ended, he nodded to me to go on. So I read the story to the end, where flying Mercury, the messenger of the Gods, brought Persephone back to the sunlit earth and restored her to the arms of Dame Ceres, her mother, that the world might have springtime and summer flowers, autumn and harvest. But because she had bitten the pomegranate while in Pluto's kingdom, she must return to him for three months of each year, and be his queen. Then the world had winter, until she returned to earth.

The class was dismissed and the visitors smiled us away and went into a low-voiced conversation with Mr. Calhoun for a few minutes. They glanced my way once or twice and I began to worry. Not only was I barefooted, but my feet and legs were dusty. My hair was more uncombed than usual, and my nails were not shiny clean. Oh, I'm going to catch it now. Those ladies saw me, too. Mr. Calhoun is promising to 'tend to me. So I thought.

Then Mr. Calhoun called me. I went up thinking how awful it was to get a whipping before company. Furthermore, I heard a snicker run over the room. Hennie Clark and Stell Brazzle did it out loud, so I would be sure to hear them. The smart aleck was going to get it. I slipped one hand behind me and switched my dress tail at them, indicating scorn.

"Come here, Zora Neale," Mr. Calhoun cooed as I reached the desk. He put his hand on my shoulder and gave me little pats. The ladies smiled and held out those flower-looking fingers toward me. I seized the opportunity for a good look.

"Shake hands with the ladies, Zora Neale," Mr. Calhoun prompted and they took my hand one after the other and smiled. They asked me if I loved school, and I lied that I did. There was *some* truth in it, because I liked geography and reading, and I liked to play at recess time. Whoever it was invented writing and arithmetic got no thanks from me. Neither did I like the arrangement where the teacher could sit up there with a palmetto stem and lick me whenever he saw fit. I hated things I couldn't do anything about. But I knew better than to bring that up right there, so I said yes, I *loved* school.

"I can tell you do," Brown Taffeta gleamed. She patted my head, and was lucky enough not to get sandspurs in her hand. Children who roll and tumble in the grass in Florida are apt to get sandspurs in their hair. They shook hands with me again and I went back to my seat.

The ladies smiled and held out those flower-looking fingers toward me.

---

7. **Jupiter:** in Roman mythology, king of the gods.
8. **Mount Aetna's:** Mount Aetna (also spelled *Etna*) is a volcanic mountain in eastern Sicily.

**Vocabulary**

**exalted** (eg·zôlt′id) *v.:* lifted up.
**realm** (relm) *n.:* kingdom.

When school let out at three o'clock, Mr. Calhoun told me to wait. When everybody had gone, he told me I was to go to the Park House, that was the hotel in Maitland, the next afternoon to call upon Mrs. Johnstone and Miss Hurd. I must tell Mama to see that I was clean and brushed from head to feet, and I must wear shoes and stockings. The ladies liked me, he said, and I must be on my best behavior.

The next day I was let out of school an hour early, and went home to be stood up in a tub of suds and be scrubbed and have my ears dug into. My sandy hair sported a red ribbon to match my red and white checked gingham dress, starched until it could stand alone. Mama saw to it that my shoes were on the right feet, since I was careless about left and right. Last thing, I was given a handkerchief to carry, warned again about my behavior, and sent off, with my big brother John to go as far as the hotel gate with me.

First thing, the ladies gave me strange things, like stuffed dates and preserved ginger, and encouraged me to eat all that I wanted. Then they showed me their Japanese dolls and just talked. I was then handed a copy of *Scribner's Magazine*, and asked to read a place that was pointed out to me. After a paragraph or two, I was told with smiles, that that would do.

I was led out on the grounds and they took my picture under a palm tree. They handed me what was to me then a heavy cylinder done up in fancy paper, tied with a ribbon, and they told me goodbye, asking me not to open it until I got home.

My brother was waiting for me down by the lake, and we hurried home, eager to see what was in the thing. It was too heavy to be candy or anything like that. John insisted on toting it for me.

My mother made John give it back to me and let me open it. Perhaps, I shall never experience such joy again. The nearest thing to that moment was the telegram accepting my first book. One hundred goldy-new pennies rolled out of the cylinder. Their gleam lit up the world. It was not avarice that moved me. It was the beauty of the thing. I stood on the mountain. Mama let me play with my pennies for a while, then put them away for me to keep.

That was only the beginning. The next day I received an Episcopal hymnbook bound in white leather with a golden cross stamped into the front cover, a copy of *The Swiss Family Robinson*, and a book of fairy tales.

I set about to commit the song words to memory. There was no music written there, just the words. But there was to my consciousness music in between them just the same. "When I survey the Wondrous Cross" seemed the most beautiful to me, so I committed that to memory first of all. Some of them seemed dull and without life, and I pretended they were not there. If white people liked trashy singing like that, there must be something funny about them that I had not noticed before. I stuck to the pretty ones where the words marched to a throb I could feel.

A month or so after the two young ladies returned to Minnesota, they sent me a huge box packed with clothes and books. The red coat with a wide circular collar and the red tam pleased me more than any of the other things. My chums pretended not to like anything that I had, but even then I knew that they were jealous. Old Smarty had gotten by them again. The clothes were not new, but they were very good. I shone like the morning sun.

But the books gave me more pleasure than

Perhaps, I shall never experience such joy again.

**Vocabulary**
**avarice** (av'ə·ris) *n.*: greed.

the clothes. I had never been too keen on dressing up. It called for hard scrubbings with Octagon soap suds getting in my eyes, and none too gentle fingers scrubbing my neck and gouging in my ears.

In that box were *Gulliver's Travels, Grimm's Fairy Tales, Dick Whittington, Greek and Roman Myths,* and best of all, *Norse Tales.* Why did the Norse tales strike so deeply into my soul? I do not know, but they did. I seemed to remember seeing Thor swing his mighty short-handled hammer as he sped across the sky in rumbling thunder, lightning flashing from the <u>tread</u> of his steeds and the wheels of his chariot. The great and good Odin, who went down to the well of knowledge to drink, and was told that the price of a drink from that fountain was an eye. Odin drank deeply, then plucked out one eye without a murmur and handed it to the grizzly keeper, and walked away. That held majesty for me.

Of the Greeks, Hercules moved me most. I followed him eagerly on his tasks. The story of the choice of Hercules as a boy when he met Pleasure and Duty, and put his hand in that of Duty and followed her steep way to the blue hills of fame and glory, which she pointed out at the end, moved me <u>profoundly</u>. I <u>resolved</u> to be like him. The tricks and turns of the other gods and goddesses left me cold. There were other thin books about this and that sweet and gentle little girl who gave up her heart to Christ and good works. Almost always they died from it, preaching as they passed. I was utterly indifferent to their deaths. In the first place I could not <u>conceive</u> of death, and in the next place they never had any funerals that amounted to a hill of beans, so I didn't care how soon they rolled up their big, soulful, blue eyes and kicked the bucket. They had no meat on their bones.

But I also met Hans Andersen[9] and Robert Louis Stevenson.[10] They seemed to know what I wanted to hear and said it in a way that tingled me. Just a little below these friends was Rudyard Kipling in his Jungle Books.[11] I loved his talking snakes as much as I did the hero.

I came to start reading the Bible through my mother. She gave me a licking one afternoon for repeating something I had overheard a neighbor telling her. She locked me in her room after the whipping, and the Bible was the only thing in there for me to read. I happened to open to the place where David was doing some mighty smiting, and I got interested. David went here and he went there, and no matter where he went, he smote 'em hip and thigh. Then he sung songs to his harp awhile, and went out and smote some more. Not one time did David stop and preach about sins and things. All David wanted to know from God was who to kill and when. He took care of the other details himself. Never a quiet moment. I liked him a lot. So I read a great deal more in the Bible, hunting for some more active people like David. Except for the beautiful language of Luke and Paul, the New Testament still plays a poor second to the Old Testament for me. The Jews had a God who laid about Him[12] when they needed Him. I could see no use waiting till Judgment Day to see a man who was just crying for a good killing, to be told to go and roast.[13] My idea was to give him a good killing first, and then if he got roasted later on, so much the better. ■

---

9. **Hans Andersen:** Hans Christian Andersen (1805–1875), Danish writer known primarily for his fairy tales.
10. **Robert Louis Stevenson** (1850–1894): Scottish writer of adventure stories such as *Kidnapped* and *Treasure Island.*

11. **Rudyard Kipling . . . Books:** Kipling (1865–1936) was an English writer born in India. His *Jungle Book* and *Second Jungle Book* contain stories of the adventures of Mowgli, a boy raised by animals in the jungles of India.
12. **laid about Him:** slang for "struck blows in every direction."
13. **roast:** slang for "burn in hell."

---

**Vocabulary**

**tread** (tred) *n.:* step; walk.

**profoundly** (prō·found′lē) *adv.:* deeply.

**resolved** (ri·zälvd′) *v.:* made a decision; determined.

**conceive** (kən·sēv′) *v.:* think; imagine.

# Response and Analysis

## Reading Check

1. Why is Hurston's grandmother afraid of her granddaughter's boldness?
2. Who visits Zora's school?
3. What do the visitors send from Minnesota?
4. What are the narrator's favorite books?

## Thinking Critically

5. Why do you think the two visitors come to Zora's school?
6. What does Zora feel about the two visitors? How do you know?
7. What do the visitors think of Zora? How do you know?
8. What do you think is the most lasting effect of Zora's encounter with the visitors? Do you think her life might have taken a different direction if this meeting had not taken place? Explain.
9. How would you describe the **character** of the narrator? Cite examples from the text that support your analysis, especially the passages in which Hurston talks about her favorite books.
10. What details from this **autobiography** shed light on why Zora became a writer when she grew up?
11. Hurston's unmistakable voice comes through very clearly in this autobiography. What **tone** do you hear in her story of the white visitors?

## Literary Criticism

12. **Philosophical approach.** Some of Hurston's contemporaries criticized her for not emphasizing in her writing the oppression of African Americans by the white community. Using references from this excerpt, explain whether or not you think this is a valid criticism. Would the quality of Hurston's work have been improved by comments on those political and social issues? Explain your response.

**SKILLS FOCUS**

**Literary Skills**
Analyze an autobiography. Analyze the political and social influences of a historical period.

**Writing Skills**
Write an essay analyzing a title.

**Vocabulary Skills**
Create semantic maps.

go.
hrw
.com

**INTERNET**

**Projects and Activities**

Keyword: LE7 11-5

## WRITING

### Judging a Book by Its Cover

The title of an autobiography can reveal a great deal about how the writer views his or her own life. Write an **essay** in which you give your reactions to Hurston's title, *Dust Tracks on a Road*. Use what you learned about Hurston from the biography on page 836 and from this autobiographical excerpt to speculate about why she chose this title. What does it reveal about Hurston's life experiences and her responses to them?

### Vocabulary Development

#### Mapping an Unfamiliar Word

| | |
|---|---|
| hail | avarice |
| brazenness | tread |
| caper | profoundly |
| exalted | resolved |
| realm | conceive |

One way to own a word is to think of examples of how it is used. Take the word *caper*, for example. Filling out a word map like the one that follows will help you know the word better. Study this map for *caper*, and then make word maps of your own for the other Vocabulary words. If you prefer, use the base form of each word (*brazen*, not *brazenness*; *profound*, not *profoundly*).

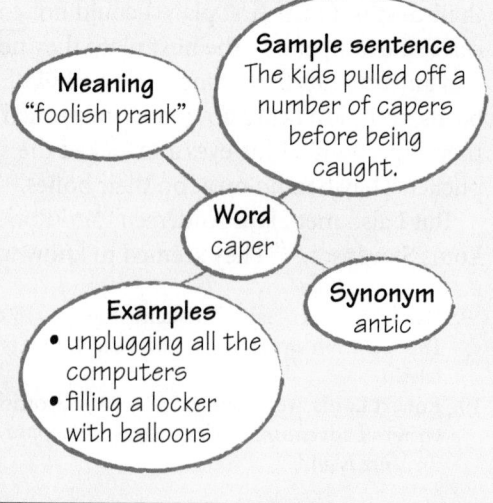

# Grammar Link

## Avoiding Misplaced and Dangling Modifiers: Saying What You Mean

**A single-word modifier.** A **modifier** is a word, a phrase, or a clause that makes the meaning of another word more specific. (The two kinds of modifiers are **adjectives** and **adverbs**.) A **misplaced modifier** is one that accidentally attaches itself to the wrong word in a sentence, usually because it's too far away from the right word. Although your readers *might* understand what you're trying to say, you're expecting them to do a lot of extra work to figure out your meaning.

Single-word modifiers, such as *only, always, often, almost, even,* and *nearly,* should go directly in front of or after the words or phrases they're intended to describe. Sometimes the meaning of the sentence changes depending on where you place this type of word.

| | |
|---|---|
| MISPLACED | Zora Neale only rode part of the way with the travelers she hailed. |
| CLEAR | Zora Neale rode only part of the way with the travelers she hailed. |

**Phrases and clauses.** Modifying phrases and clauses should also go as close as possible to the words they modify. Otherwise, the sentence can be confusing or even ridiculous. Sometimes the best way to fix a misplaced phrase or clause is to move it closer to the right word; other sentences require more tinkering to solve the problem.

| | |
|---|---|
| MISPLACED | Zora Neale Hurston was the daughter of a minister and a teacher who published her first story in 1921. [It was Zora Neale, not her mother, who published the story.] |
| CLEAR | The daughter of a minister and a teacher, Zora Neale Hurston published her first story in 1921. |

**Dangling modifiers.** While a misplaced modifier attaches itself to the wrong word, a **dangling modifier** doesn't logically modify *any* word in the sentence. The most common example is called a **dangling participle.** An introductory **participial phrase** (a word group beginning with an *–ing* or an *–ed* verb form) should modify the noun or the pronoun that comes directly after it. If that word doesn't make sense as the "doer" of the action described in the participial phrase, then the phrase is dangling. You can fix the problem by (1) naming the doer immediately after the participial phrase, (2) turning the phrase into a clause that names the doer as its subject, or (3) rewriting the whole sentence.

| | |
|---|---|
| DANGLING | Sitting on the gatepost, the carriages and cars passed by Zora Neale's house. [It was Zora Neale who was sitting on the gatepost, not the carriages and cars.] |

**SKILLS FOCUS**

**Grammar Skills**
Avoid misplaced and dangling modifiers.

| CLEAR | Sitting on the gatepost, Zora Neale watched the carriages and cars pass by her house. |
|---|---|
| CLEAR | While Zora Neale was sitting on the gatepost, the carriages and cars passed by her house. |

## PRACTICE

In the following sentences, correct any misplaced or dangling modifiers. You may need to add or change words or rewrite sentences.

1. Afraid she would be punished, Mr. Calhoun called Zora Neale up to his desk.
2. Zora Neale only received a box of clothes and books from the two white women who visited her class.
3. Zora Neale loved the books from the two women that she received.
4. Scrubbed and warned about her behavior, Zora Neale's mother sent her to the hotel.
5. Resolving to be like Hercules, the other Greek gods and goddesses were ignored by Zora Neale.

## Apply to Your Writing

Re-read a current writing assignment or one that you've already completed. Correct any misplaced or dangling modifiers.

▷ **For more help, see Placement of Modifiers, 5f–5g, in the Language Handbook.**

Zora Neale Hurston.

# Reflecting *on the* Literary Period

## The Moderns: 1914–1939

> The selections in this feature were written during the same literary period as the other selections in Collection 5, and they share many of the same ideas and concerns. The Focus Question will guide your reading and help you reflect on important aspects of the period.
>

## Think About...

Ralph Waldo Emerson (page 203) is given the most credit for defining the essence of the American dream. Trust the universe and trust yourself, he wrote. "If the single man plant himself indomitable on his instincts and there abide, the huge world will come around to him." The American dream had optimistically promised boundless potential for the hardworking individual.

Only a few decades after Emerson's death in 1882, the American dream seemed to be a thing of the past. With the rise of industrialization and with millions of people living in cities that were fast becoming slums, it was hard to see the United States as a green and innocent Eden. When World War I officially ended in 1919, many Americans had begun to take a dim view of the human condition. By the 1930s, as the economic devastation of the Great Depression created bread lines and massive unemployment, it was equally difficult to see America as a land of heroes—of independent, self-reliant people. Instead of promoting Emerson's optimism, American writers were, for the most part, dealing with deep disillusionment, even cynicism, about the changing face of the American dream.

*Unemployment* by Ben Shahn (1898–1969) (tempera on paper).

Private Collection. Art © Estate of Ben Shahn/Licensed by VAGA, New York, NY.

SKILLS FOCUS

Pages 847–868 cover **Literary Skills** Evaluate the philosophical, political, religious, ethical, and social issues of a historical period.

---

### Focus Question

As you read each selection, keep in mind this Focus Question and take notes to help you answer it at the end of the feature:

How do the poems and stories of modern writers express disillusionment with the American dream and, in particular, loss of faith in the possibility of individual heroism?

# Chicago

**Meet the Writer  Carl Sandburg**
(1878–1967) was already an American legend
when he died in his ninetieth year. Sandburg's
craggy features and his boyish shock of hair had
been familiar to Americans for more than fifty
years. As the author of two of the most popular
poems of the century—"Chicago" (1914) and
"Fog" (1916)—and of a six-volume biography of
Abraham Lincoln (1926–1939), Sandburg had
carved a place for himself in modern literature. As
a poetic spokesman for the American worker toil-
ing under industrialization, he had become part of
the folklore from which he drew his inspiration.

While he seemed on the page to be the
roughest of American poets, Sandburg was
actually a gentle and thoughtful man. He found
his most characteristic voice in the vernacular—
in slang, street talk, and common speech, with all
its clichés and plain expressions.

A descendant of Swedes who had settled in
Galesburg, Illinois, where he was born, Sandburg
was not schooled so much in a classroom as in the
proverbial school of hard knocks. Before he was
twenty, he had ranged the Midwest from
Illinois to Nebraska, supporting himself with odd
jobs. The field and factory laborers that he met in
his travels would one day people his own poetic
landscape.

Sandburg volunteered, more from restlessness
than from patriotism, to fight in the Spanish-
American War that broke out in 1898. Eventually
he went to college in his hometown, and there he
began to think of himself as a writer. This self-
image became a reality when Sandburg was
thirty-six; that year the influential magazine *Poetry*
published some of his shorter poems, including
"Chicago."

Sandburg—who has been compared with Walt
Whitman (page 360)—uses free verse and colloquial speech, which some critics disliked
but which have established him as a major literary

figure. Sandburg's strong affirmation of American
democracy and of the inherent nobility of labor
and the working person resulted in one of his
best-known collections of poems, *The People,
Yes* (1936).

**Background**  In this poem, Sandburg addresses
an entire city as though it were a person. This
person has many jobs—hog butcher, toolmaker,
railroad engineer, freight handler.

---

**CONNECTING TO THE
Focus Question**

Carl Sandburg—somewhat like Walt
Whitman—spent his life praising ordinary
people and celebrating a new kind of
American hero. As you read, consider this
question: How does the poem reveal a new
take on the American dream?

---

*Chicago* (1923) by Louis Lozowick. Oil on canvas.
Private Collection, Washington, D.C. Mary Ryan Gallery.

# Chicago

## Carl Sandburg

Hog Butcher for the World,
Tool Maker, Stacker of Wheat,
Player with Railroads and the Nation's Freight Handler;
Stormy, husky, brawling,
5  City of the Big Shoulders:

They tell me you are wicked and I believe them, for I have seen your
     painted women under the gas lamps luring the farm boys.
And they tell me you are crooked and I answer: Yes, it is true I have seen
     the gunman kill and go free to kill again.
And they tell me you are brutal and my reply is: On the faces of women
     and children I have seen the marks of wanton hunger.
And having answered so I turn once more to those who sneer at this my
     city, and I give them back the sneer and say to them:
10  Come and show me another city with lifted head singing so proud to be
     alive and coarse and strong and cunning.
Flinging magnetic curses amid the toil of piling job on job, here is a tall
     bold slugger set vivid against the little soft cities;
Fierce as a dog with tongue lapping for action, cunning as a savage pitted
     against the wilderness,
        Bareheaded,
        Shoveling,
15          Wrecking,
        Planning,
        Building, breaking, rebuilding.
Under the smoke, dust all over his mouth, laughing with white teeth,
Under the terrible burden of destiny laughing as a young man laughs,
20  Laughing even as an ignorant fighter laughs who has never lost a battle,
Bragging and laughing that under his wrist is the pulse, and under his
     ribs the heart of the people,
          Laughing!
Laughing the stormy, husky, brawling laughter of Youth, half-naked,
     sweating, proud to be Hog Butcher, Tool Maker, Stacker of Wheat,
     Player with Railroads and Freight Handler to the Nation.

# Response and Analysis

## Thinking Critically

**1.** Sandburg opens with a series of **epithets,** or descriptive phrases, about Chicago. What does each epithet tell you about the city and its economy?

**2.** What do the people tell the speaker about Chicago? How does the speaker answer the city's critics?

**3.** To what kind of person is Chicago being compared?

**4.** What **images** in the poem make Chicago the very embodiment of the rugged American individual who bows to no one?

**5.** Using details from the selection, respond to **Connecting to the Focus Question** on page 848.

## Extending and Evaluating

**6.** What features of Chicago do you think have changed since this poem was written in 1914? Which features mentioned in the poem might still be part of the city?

# Richard Bone
# "Butch" Weldy
# Mrs. George Reece

**Meet the Writer** **Edgar Lee Masters**
(1869–1950), like his contemporary Carl Sandburg, was a product of the Midwest, also known as the "corn belt" or "Bible Belt." Masters was born in Garnett, Kansas, and when he was still a boy, his family moved to Illinois.

As a young man with literary ambitions, Masters found small-town life oppressive. After studying law at his father's office in Lewistown, Illinois, Masters moved to Chicago, where he became the partner of a leading criminal lawyer. In his spare time, he wrote poems, plays, and essays, but none of his work attracted much attention.

In 1914, an editor friend of Masters gave him a copy of *Epigrams from the Greek Anthology,* a collection of short Greek poems and **epitaphs,** or brief statements that sum up an individual's life. These poems gave Masters the idea of writing their Midwestern counterparts, uncovering the lives he had known in the small towns of southern Illinois. Instead of the traditional forms and meters he had used in his previous poetry, Masters chose to write his epitaphs in free verse.

Just as Sandburg had done, Masters found his voice in the free verse that characterized the second decade of the twentieth century. Though he published a great deal, Masters is primarily known today for just one book, *Spoon River Anthology* (1915), which became a landmark in American literature and made Masters famous. It is a collection of almost 250 epitaphs spoken by the ordinary inhabitants of a cemetery in the fictional town of Spoon River. Drawing upon his memories, Masters uses the epitaphs to show the hidden underside of American life.

**Background** In *Spoon River Anthology,* the deceased inhabitants of Spoon River tell their stories, freed by death to talk without fear of consequences. Bit by bit, they fill in a picture of small-town life vastly different from the folksy, sentimental magazine cover images of the time. Masters's speakers from beyond the grave bring buried truth into the daylight and, at the same time, a new kind of realism to poetry.

---

**CONNECTING TO THE**
**Focus Question**

As you read these poems, think about the American dream and what it meant for earlier Americans. Ask yourself: What do the people of Spoon River, speaking from the second decade of the twentieth century, reveal about the possibility of heroism—even individual integrity—in their own time?

---

*Richard Bone, like many other departed citizens of the town, is troubled by his conscience. Bone confesses hypocrisy in quietly accepting false appearances. The name Masters gives this speaker is itself a clue to his profession and to his nature. As a stonecutter in life, he engraved words that would identify skeletons; as a spokesman for his own conscience, he speaks words that "cut to the bone."*

# Richard Bone

## Edgar Lee Masters

When I first came to Spoon River
I did not know whether what they told me
Was true or false.
They would bring me the epitaph
5      And stand around the shop while I worked
And say "He was so kind," "He was wonderful,"
"She was the sweetest woman," "He was a consistent Christian."
And I chiseled for them whatever they wished,
All in ignorance of its truth.
10    But later, as I lived among the people here,
I knew how near to the life
Were the epitaphs that were ordered for them as they died.
But still I chiseled whatever they paid me to chisel
And made myself party to the false chronicles°
15    Of the stones,
Even as the historian does who writes
Without knowing the truth,
Or because he is influenced to hide it.

**14. chronicles:** historical accounts.

*Many of the stories told in* Spoon River Anthology *are interlocking. The villain of the whole book is Deacon Thomas Rhodes, who "ran the church as well as the store and the bank." We hear about Rhodes from a number of his victims, including "Butch" Weldy. Butch also refers to Jack the Fiddler, a blind man who is buried in the Spoon River cemetery. Jack was killed when Butch, who had been drinking, drove a carriage into a ditch.*

# "Butch" Weldy

## Edgar Lee Masters

After I got religion and steadied down
They gave me a job in the canning works,
And every morning I had to fill
The tank in the yard with gasoline,
5    That fed the blow-fires in the sheds
To heat the soldering irons.
And I mounted a rickety ladder to do it,
Carrying buckets full of the stuff.
One morning, as I stood there pouring,
10   The air grew still and seemed to heave,
And I shot up as the tank exploded,
And down I came with both legs broken
And my eyes burned crisp as a couple of eggs,
For someone left a blow-fire going,
15   And something sucked the flame in the tank.
The Circuit Judge said whoever did it
Was a fellow-servant of mine, and so
Old Rhodes' son didn't have to pay me.
And I sat on the witness stand as blind
20   As Jack the Fiddler, saying over and over,
"I didn't know him at all."

*Factories at Night—New Jersey*
(1929) by Joseph Stella
(1879–1946). Oil on canvas.
The Newark Museum.

*This epitaph refers to a real-life bank failure in Lewistown, Illinois, in 1894, which Masters blamed on Henry Phelps (here renamed Thomas Rhodes) and Phelps's son. The bank collapse caused enormous hardships for the town's citizens, and Masters's father, a lawyer, helped prosecute the bank officials. None of the bank officials were sent to prison.*

# Mrs. George Reece

## Edgar Lee Masters

To this generation I would say:
Memorize some bit of verse of truth or beauty.
It may serve a turn in your life.
My husband had nothing to do
5   With the fall of the bank—he was only cashier.
The wreck was due to the president, Thomas Rhodes,
And his vain, unscrupulous son.
Yet my husband was sent to prison,
And I was left with the children,
10   To feed and clothe and school them.
And I did it, and sent them forth
Into the world all clean and strong,
And all through the wisdom of Pope, the poet:°
"Act well your part, there all the honor lies."

**13. Pope, the poet:** the English poet Alexander Pope (1688–1744), whose wise sayings are often quoted.

# Response and Analysis

### Richard Bone • "Butch" Weldy • Mrs. George Reece

#### Thinking Critically

1. What does Richard Bone, the stone carver, come to realize about the people of Spoon River? What does he realize about himself?

2. What happened to Butch Weldy? Why do you think the judge decided that Old Rhodes's son didn't have to compensate Butch for the accident that ruined his life?

3. What is **ironic,** or contradictory, about all these terrible things happening to Butch Weldy after he got religion and settled down?

4. What happened to Mrs. George Reece? How does Pope's advice relate to the way Mrs. Reece responded to her tragedy?

5. Using details from the poems, respond to **Connecting to the Focus Question** on page 851.

#### Extending and Evaluating

6. Could the situations and life experiences described in these poems be found in our society today? Explain.

7. Do you find qualities to admire in any of the speakers of these **epitaphs**? Explain your response.

# A Black Man Talks of Reaping

**Meet the Writer  Arna Bontemps**
(1902–1973), born in Louisiana and brought up in California, lived through periods in the history of the United States when discrimination against African Americans was widespread. In the 1930s, trials in the infamous Scottsboro case, in which an all-white jury convicted nine African American youths of rape, took place not far from the junior college in Alabama where Bontemps was teaching.

With racial tensions at a high pitch, the college asked Bontemps to prove he was not a political radical by burning books in his private library. (In the Scottsboro case, members of the Communist Party were aiding in the youths' defense). Instead of destroying his books—by such great African American writers as James Weldon Johnson, W.E.B. Du Bois, and Frederick Douglass—Bontemps moved with his family back to California.

Bontemps produced only one book of poetry, *Personals* (1963), but he published, along with Langston Hughes, valuable collections of African American writings, including *The Poetry of the Negro* (1949) and *The Book of Negro Folklore* (1958). Bontemps also edited a popular anthology, *American Negro Poetry* (1963), published during the revival of African American literature in the 1960s.

Disappointed that his novels for adults met with minimal success, Bontemps wrote children's books as well as very popular biographies of George Washington Carver, Frederick Douglass, and Booker T. Washington. Some critics think Bontemps's finest work in any genre is *Black Thunder* (1936), the true story of the failed slave rebellion led by Gabriel Prosser near Richmond, Virginia, in 1800.

**Background**  The speaker in this poem talks about his life in terms of farming: *Reaping* literally refers to the gathering of a crop, usually grain. In another sense, *reaping* refers to what one gets as a reward for some action or work. In writing this poem, Bontemps might have had in mind the verse from the New Testament: "For whatever a man sows, this he will also reap" (Galatians 6:7). For the speaker of Bontemps's poem, this promise is turned on its head.

---

### CONNECTING TO THE
### Focus Question

As you read, keep in mind that the American dream in the early decades of the twentieth century had bitter significance for many people in the United States. African Americans, in particular, felt excluded from the promise of endless opportunities and progress for the hardworking person. According to this poem, what results could a hardworking black man expect to attain?

---

*Plowing* (1940) by
Aiden Lassell Ripley
(1896–1969).
Watercolor,
21 x 30 inches.

Collection of the
Greenville County
Museum of Art.

# A Black Man Talks of Reaping

## Arna Bontemps

I have sown beside all waters in my day.
I planted deep, within my heart the fear
that wind or fowl would take the grain away.
I planted safe against this stark, lean year.

5   I scattered seed enough to plant the land
in rows from Canada to Mexico
but for my reaping only what the hand
can hold at once is all that I can show.

Yet what I sowed and what the orchard yields
10  my brother's sons are gathering stalk and root;
small wonder then my children glean in fields
they have not sown, and feed on bitter fruit.

## Response and Analysis

### Thinking Critically

1. According to the first stanza, what has this speaker taken care to do?

2. According to the second stanza, how much seed has he planted? What has he got to show for it?

3. In the third stanza, who are "my brother's sons"? What do you think he means by saying that his children "feed on bitter fruit"?

4. Is the speaker referring literally to himself and his children, or is he speaking on behalf of a group of people? Explain.

5. Using details from the poem, respond to **Connecting to the Focus Question** on page 855.

### Extending and Evaluating

6. What social and political situations in the United States in the early years of the twentieth century could explain why the American dream has not worked for the speaker of this poem?

# The Life You Save May Be Your Own

**Meet the Writer** **Flannery O'Connor** (1925–1964) was born in Savannah, Georgia, and spent almost all of her short life in nearby Milledgeville, where her family had lived since the Civil War. Although she limited herself to a rural, Southern literary terrain and the body of her work is small, her place in American literature is secure.

O'Connor graduated from the Georgia State College for Women and then went to the Writers' Workshop at the University of Iowa. She wrote steadily from 1948 until her early death sixteen years later. For many years, she suffered from lupus, a painful wasting disease of the immune system that had also killed her father. The illness kept her more confined and immobile as the years went on. "I have never been anywhere but sick," O'Connor wrote. "In a sense sickness is a place, more instructive than a long trip to Europe, and it's always a place where there's no company, where nobody can follow. Sickness before death is a very appropriate thing, and I think those who don't have it miss one of God's mercies."

From the first, O'Connor was recognized as a satirist of astonishing originality and energy, whose targets were smugness, optimism, and self-righteousness. The essential element of her life and work is that she remained a Roman Catholic without the slightest wavering of faith. A thunder-and-lightning Christian belief fills every story and novel she wrote. Her attraction to the grotesque and the violent puts off some readers who fail to appreciate that the violent motifs in her short stories and novels grow from her passionate Christian vision of secular society.

What O'Connor wants to tell us is that, in our rationality, we have lost the one essential—a spiritual center for our lives. O'Connor seems to be saying that we have become so accustomed to the lack of God in our lives that a writer must use violent means to make a point.

*Lilacs* (detail) (1927) by Charles Ephraim Burchfield (1893–1967). Oil on canvas mounted on board.

**Background** The characters in this story, though peculiar, make up a masterful portrait from the rural South. With all their peculiarity, O'Connor's characters are disturbingly familiar. They are homespun figures, as real as anyone in a Georgia barnyard or roadside cafe, drawn with a kind of humor that balances on the edge of terror. Just as we are made to feel comfortable, enjoying O'Connor's carnival show, the comedy is miraculously transcended and we realize the situation has a philosophical meaning.

---

**CONNECTING TO THE
Focus Question**

As you read this story, think about the hard-working, self-reliant hero who has long been a part of American idealism. Ask yourself: How do the characters in this story distort the idea of the self-reliant, unconquerable hero? What does the American dream mean to them?

---

© Delaware Art Museum, Wilmington, USA.

*Lilacs* (1927) by Charles Ephraim Burchfield (1893–1967). Oil on canvas mounted on board.
© Delaware Art Museum, Wilmington, USA.

# The Life You Save May Be Your Own

## Flannery O'Connor

The old woman and her daughter were sitting on their porch when Mr. Shiftlet came up their road for the first time. The old woman slid to the edge of her chair and leaned forward, shading her eyes from the piercing sunset with her hand. The daughter could not see far in front of her and continued to play with her fingers. Although the old woman lived in this desolate spot with only her daughter and she had never seen Mr. Shiftlet before, she could tell, even from a distance, that he was a tramp and no one to be afraid of. His left coat sleeve was folded up to show there was only half an arm in it and his gaunt figure listed[1] slightly to the side as if the breeze were pushing him. He had on a black town suit and a brown felt hat that was turned up in the front and down in the back and he carried a tin toolbox by a handle. He came on, at an amble,[2] up her road, his face turned toward the sun which appeared to be balancing itself on the peak of a small mountain.

The old woman didn't change her position until he was almost into her yard; then she rose

---

1. **listed** (list′id): tilted.
2. **amble** (am′bəl): leisurely pace.

with one hand fisted on her hip. The daughter, a large girl in a short blue organdy dress, saw him all at once and jumped up and began to stamp and point and make excited speechless sounds.

Mr. Shiftlet stopped just inside the yard and set his box on the ground and tipped his hat at her as if she were not in the least afflicted; then he turned toward the old woman and swung the hat all the way off. He had long black slick hair that hung flat from a part in the middle to beyond the tips of his ears on either side. His face descended in forehead for more than half its length and ended suddenly with his features just balanced over a jutting steel-trap jaw. He seemed to be a young man but he had a look of composed dissatisfaction as if he understood life thoroughly.

"Good evening," the old woman said. She was about the size of a cedar fence post and she had a man's gray hat pulled down low over her head.

The tramp stood looking at her and didn't answer. He turned his back and faced the sunset. He swung both his whole and his short arm up slowly so that they indicated an expanse of sky and his figure formed a crooked cross. The old woman watched him with her arms folded across her chest as if she were the owner of the sun, and the daughter watched, her head thrust forward and her fat helpless hands hanging at the wrists. She had long pink-gold hair and eyes as blue as a peacock's neck.

He held the pose for almost fifty seconds and then he picked up his box and came on to the porch and dropped down on the bottom step. "Lady," he said in a firm nasal voice, "I'd give a fortune to live where I could see me a sun do that every evening."

"Does it every evening," the old woman said and sat back down. The daughter sat down too and watched him with a cautious sly look as if he were a bird that had come up very close. He leaned to one side, rooting in his pants pocket, and in a second he brought out a package of chewing gum and offered her a piece. She took it and unpeeled it and began to chew without taking her eyes off him. He offered the old woman a piece but she only raised her upper lip to indicate she had no teeth.

Mr. Shiftlet's pale sharp glance had already passed over everything in the yard—the pump near the corner of the house and the big fig tree that three or four chickens were preparing to roost in—and had moved to a shed where he saw the square rusted back of an automobile. "You ladies drive?" he asked.

"That car ain't run in fifteen year," the old woman said. "The day my husband died, it quit running."

"Nothing is like it used to be, lady," he said. "The world is almost rotten."

"That's right," the old woman said. "You from around here?"

"Name Tom T. Shiftlet," he murmured, looking at the tires.

"I'm pleased to meet you," the old woman said. "Name Lucynell Crater and daughter Lucynell Crater. What you doing around here, Mr. Shiftlet?"

He judged the car to be about a 1928 or '29 Ford. "Lady," he said, and turned and gave her his full attention, "lemme tell you something. There's one of these doctors in Atlanta that's taken a knife and cut the human heart—the human heart," he repeated, leaning forward, "out of a man's chest and held it in his hand," and he held his hand out, palm up, as if it were slightly weighted with the human heart, "and studied it like it was a day-old chicken, and lady," he said, allowing a long significant pause in which his head slid forward and his clay-colored eyes brightened, "he don't know no more about it than you or me."

"That's right," the old woman said.

"Why, if he was to take that knife and cut into every corner of it, he still wouldn't know no more than you or me. What you want to bet?"

"Nothing," the old woman said wisely. "Where you come from, Mr. Shiftlet?"

He didn't answer. He reached into his pocket and brought out a sack of tobacco and a package of cigarette papers and rolled himself a cigarette, expertly with one hand, and attached it in a hanging position to his upper lip. Then he took a box of wooden matches from his pocket and struck one on his shoe. He held the burning match as if he were studying the mystery of flame while it traveled dangerously toward his skin. The daughter began to make loud noises and to point to his hand and shake her finger at him, but when the flame was just before touching him, he leaned down with his hand cupped over it as if he were going to set fire to his nose and lit the cigarette.

He flipped away the dead match and blew a stream of gray into the evening. A sly look came over his face. "Lady," he said, "nowadays, people'll do anything anyways. I can tell you my name is Tom T. Shiftlet, and I come from Tarwater, Tennessee, but you never have seen me before: How you know I ain't lying? How you know my name ain't Aaron Sparks, lady, and I come from Singleberry, Georgia, or how you know it's not George Speeds and I come from Lucy, Alabama, or how you know I ain't Thompson Bright from Toolafalls, Mississippi?"

"I don't know nothing about you," the old woman muttered, irked.[3]

"Lady," he said, "people don't care how they lie. Maybe the best I can tell you is, I'm a man; but listen lady," he said and paused and made his tone more ominous still, "what is a man?"

The old woman began to gum a seed. "What you carry in that tin box, Mr. Shiftlet?" she asked.

"Tools," he said, put back. "I'm a carpenter."

"Well, if you come out here to work, I'll be able to feed you and give you a place to sleep but I can't pay. I'll tell you that before you begin," she said.

There was no answer at once and no particular expression on his face. He leaned back against the two-by-four that helped support the porch roof. "Lady," he said slowly, "there's some men that some things mean more to them than money." The old woman rocked without comment and the daughter watched the trigger that

moved up and down in his neck. He told the old woman then that all most people were interested in was money, but he asked what a man was made for. He asked her if a man was made for money, or what. He asked her what she thought she was made for but she didn't answer, she only sat rocking and wondered if a one-armed man could put a new roof on her garden house. He asked a lot of questions that she didn't answer. He told her that he was twenty-eight years old and had lived a varied life. He had been a gospel singer, a foreman on the railroad, an assistant in an undertaking parlor, and he come over the radio for three months with Uncle Roy and his Red Creek Wranglers. He said he had fought and bled in the Arm Service of his country and visited every foreign land and that everywhere he had seen people that didn't care if they did a thing one way or another. He said he hadn't been raised thataway.

A fat yellow moon appeared in the branches of the fig tree as if it were going to roost there with the chickens. He said that a man had to escape to the country to see the world whole and that he wished he lived in a desolate place like this where he could see the sun go down every evening like God made it to do.

"Are you married or are you single?" the old woman asked.

There was a long silence. "Lady," he asked finally, "where would you find you an innocent woman today? I wouldn't have any of this trash I could just pick up."

The daughter was leaning very far down, hanging her head almost between her knees watching him through a triangular door she had made in her overturned hair; and she suddenly fell in a heap on the floor and began to whimper. Mr. Shiftlet straightened her out and helped her get back in the chair.

"Is she your baby girl?" he asked.

"My only," the old woman said, "and she's the sweetest girl in the world. I would give her up for nothing on earth. She's smart too. She can sweep the floor, cook, wash, feed the chickens, and hoe. I wouldn't give her up for a casket of jewels."

---

**3. irked** (ʉrkt): annoyed; irritated.

"No," he said kindly, "don't ever let any man take her away from you."

"Any man come after her," the old woman said, "'ll have to stay around the place."

Mr. Shiftlet's eye in the darkness was focused on a part of the automobile bumper that glittered in the distance. "Lady," he said, jerking his short arm up as if he could point with it to her house and yard and pump, "there ain't a broken thing on this plantation that I couldn't fix for you, one-arm jackleg[4] or not. I'm a man," he said with a sullen dignity, "even if I ain't a whole one. I got," he said, tapping his knuckles on the floor to emphasize the immensity of what he was going to say, "a moral intelligence!" and his face pierced out of the darkness into a shaft of doorlight and he stared at her as if he were astonished himself at this impossible truth.

The old woman was not impressed with the phrase. "I told you you could hang around and work for food," she said, "if you don't mind sleeping in that car yonder."

"Why listen, lady," he said with a grin of delight, "the monks of old slept in their coffins!"

"They wasn't as advanced as we are," the old woman said.

The next morning he began on the roof of the garden house while Lucynell, the daughter, sat on a rock and watched him work. He had not been around a week before the change he had made in the place was apparent. He had patched the front and back steps, built a new hog pen, restored a fence, and taught Lucynell, who was completely deaf and had never said a

word in her life, to say the word "bird." The big rosy-faced girl followed him everywhere, saying "Burrttddt ddbirrrttdt," and clapping her hands. The old woman watched from a distance, secretly pleased. She was ravenous for a son-in-law.

Mr. Shiftlet slept on the hard narrow back seat of the car with his feet out the side window. He had his razor and a can of water on a crate that served him as a bedside table and he put up a piece of mirror against the back glass and kept his coat neatly on a hanger that he hung over one of the windows.

In the evenings he sat on the steps and talked while the old woman and Lucynell rocked violently in their chairs on either side of him. The old woman's three mountains were black against the dark blue sky and were visited off and on by various planets and by the moon after it had left the chickens. Mr. Shiftlet pointed out that the reason he had improved this plantation was because he had taken a personal interest in it. He said he was even going to make the automobile run.

He had raised the hood and studied the mechanism and he said he could tell that the car had been built in the days when cars were really built. You take now, he said, one man puts in one bolt and another man puts in another bolt and another man puts in another bolt so that it's a man for a bolt. That's why you have to pay so much for a car: you're paying all those men. Now if you didn't have to pay but one man, you could get you a cheaper car and one that had had a personal interest taken in it, and it would be a better car. The old woman agreed with him that this was so.

Mr. Shiftlet said that the trouble with the world was that nobody cared, or stopped and took any trouble. He said he never would have been able to teach Lucynell to say a word if he hadn't cared and stopped long enough.

> In the evenings he sat on the steps and talked while the old woman and Lucynell rocked violently in their chairs on either side of him.

---

4. **jackleg:** amateur; someone not correctly trained. O'Connor is probably playing with the other meaning of *jackleg*, "a dishonest person."

"Teach her to say something else," the old woman said.

"What you want her to say next?" Mr. Shiftlet asked.

The old woman's smile was broad and toothless and suggestive. "Teach her to say 'sugarpie,'" she said.

Mr. Shiftlet already knew what was on her mind.

The next day he began to tinker with the automobile and that evening he told her that if she would buy a fan belt, he would be able to make the car run.

The old woman said she would give him the money. "You see that girl yonder?" she asked, pointing to Lucynell who was sitting on the floor a foot away, watching him, her eyes blue even in the dark. "If it was ever a man wanted to take her away, I would say, 'No man on earth is going to take that sweet girl of mine away from me!' but if he was to say, 'Lady, I don't want to take her away, I want her right here,' I would say, 'Mister, I don't blame you none. I wouldn't pass up a chance to live in a permanent place and get the sweetest girl in the world myself. You ain't no fool,' I would say."

"How old is she?" Mr. Shiftlet asked casually.

"Fifteen, sixteen," the old woman said. The girl was nearly thirty but because of her innocence it was impossible to guess.

"It would be a good idea to paint it too," Mr. Shiftlet remarked. "You don't want it to rust out."

"We'll see about that later," the old woman said.

The next day he walked into town and returned with the parts he needed and a can of gasoline. Late in the afternoon, terrible noises issued from the shed and the old woman rushed out of the house, thinking Lucynell was somewhere having a fit. Lucynell was sitting on a chicken crate, stamping her feet and screaming, "Burrddttt! bddurrddtttt!" but her fuss was drowned out by the car. With a volley of blasts it emerged from the shed, moving in a fierce and stately way. Mr. Shiftlet was in the driver's seat, sitting very erect. He had an expression of serious modesty on his face as if he had just raised the dead.

That night, rocking on the porch, the old woman began her business, at once. "You want you an innocent woman, don't you?" she asked sympathetically. "You don't want none of this trash."

"No'm, I don't," Mr. Shiftlet said.

"One that can't talk," she continued, "can't sass you back or use foul language. That's the kind for you to have. Right there," and she pointed to Lucynell sitting cross-legged in her chair, holding both feet in her hands.

"That's right," he admitted. "She wouldn't give me any trouble."

"Saturday," the old woman said, "you and her and me can drive into town and get married."

Mr. Shiftlet eased his position on the steps.

"I can't get married right now," he said. "Everything you want to do takes money and I ain't got any."

"What you need with money?" she asked.

"It takes money," he said. "Some people'll do anything anyhow these days, but the way I think, I wouldn't marry no woman that I couldn't take on a trip like she was somebody. I mean take her to a hotel and treat her. I wouldn't marry the Duchesser Windsor,[5] he said firmly, "unless I could take her to a hotel and giver something good to eat.

"I was raised thataway and there ain't a thing I can do about it. My old mother taught me how to do."

"Lucynell don't even know what a hotel is," the old woman muttered. "Listen here, Mr. Shiftlet," she said, sliding forward in her chair, "you'd be getting a permanent house and a deep

---

5. **Duchesser Windsor:** the duchess of Windsor, the American woman whom King Edward VIII of England gave up his throne to marry. The duchess of Windsor was one of the most elegant women of her time. The very idea that Mr. Shiftlet would imagine himself escorting her to a hotel for dinner is hilarious.

well and the most innocent girl in the world. You don't need no money. Lemme tell you something: there ain't any place in the world for a poor disabled friendless drifting man."

The ugly words settled in Mr. Shiftlet's head like a group of buzzards in the top of a tree. He didn't answer at once. He rolled himself a cigarette and lit it and then he said in an even voice, "Lady, a man is divided into two parts, body and spirit."

The old woman clamped her gums together.

"A body and a spirit," he repeated. "The body, lady, is like a house: it don't go anywhere; but the spirit, lady, is like a automobile: always on the move, always . . ."

"Listen, Mr. Shiftlet," she said, "my well never goes dry and my house is always warm in the winter and there's no mortgage on a thing about this place. You can go to the courthouse and see for yourself. And yonder under that shed is a fine automobile." She laid the bait carefully. "You can have it painted by Saturday. I'll pay for the paint."

In the darkness, Mr. Shiftlet's smile stretched like a weary snake waking up by a fire. After a second he recalled himself and said, "I'm only saying a man's spirit means more to him than anything else. I would have to take my wife off for the weekend without no regards at all for cost. I got to follow where my spirit says to go."

"I'll give you fifteen dollars for a weekend trip," the old woman said in a crabbed voice. "That's the best I can do."

"That wouldn't hardly pay for more than the gas and the hotel," he said. "It wouldn't feed her."

"Seventeen-fifty," the old woman said. "That's all I got so it isn't any use you trying to milk me. You can take a lunch."

Mr. Shiftlet was deeply hurt by the word "milk." He didn't doubt that she had more money sewed up in her mattress but he had already told her he was not interested in her money. "I'll make that do," he said and rose and walked off without treating[6] with her further.

---

6. **treating:** dealing; negotiating.

On Saturday the three of them drove into town in the car that the paint had barely dried on and Mr. Shiftlet and Lucynell were married in the Ordinary's office[7] while the old woman witnessed. As they came out of the courthouse, Mr. Shiftlet began twisting his neck in his collar. He looked morose[8] and bitter as if he had been insulted while someone held him. "That didn't satisfy me none," he said. "That was just something a woman in an office did, nothing but paperwork and blood tests. What do they know about my blood? If they was to take my heart and cut it out," he said, "they wouldn't know a thing about me. It didn't satisfy me at all."

"It satisfied the law," the old woman said sharply.

"The law," Mr. Shiftlet said and spit. "It's the law that don't satisfy me."

He had painted the car dark green with a yellow band around it just under the windows. The three of them climbed in the front seat and the old woman said, "Don't Lucynell look pretty? Looks like a baby doll." Lucynell was dressed up in a white dress that her mother had uprooted from a trunk and there was a Panama hat on her head with a bunch of red wooden cherries on the brim. Every now and then her placid expression was changed by a sly isolated little thought like a shoot of green in the desert. "You got a prize!" the old woman said.

Mr. Shiftlet didn't even look at her.

They drove back to the house to let the old woman off and pick up the lunch. When they were ready to leave, she stood staring in the window of the car, with her fingers clenched around the glass. Tears began to seep sideways out of her eyes and run along the dirty creases in her face. "I ain't ever been parted with her for two days before," she said.

Mr. Shiftlet started the motor.

"And I wouldn't let no man have her but you because I seen you would do right. Good-bye, Sugarbaby," she said, clutching at the sleeve of

---

7. **Ordinary's office:** judge's office.
8. **morose** (mə·rōs′): gloomy.

*Death on Ridge Road* (1935) by Grant Wood (American, 1892–1942). Oil on masonite. Frame H: 99.00 cm, frame W: 117.00 cm.

the white dress. Lucynell looked straight at her and didn't seem to see her there at all. Mr. Shiftlet eased the car forward so that she had to move her hands.

The early afternoon was clear and open and surrounded by pale blue sky. Although the car would go only thirty miles an hour, Mr. Shiftlet imagined a terrific climb and dip and swerve that went entirely to his head so that he forgot his morning bitterness. He had always wanted an automobile but he had never been able to afford one before. He drove very fast because he wanted to make Mobile by nightfall.

Occasionally he stopped his thoughts long enough to look at Lucynell in the seat beside him. She had eaten the lunch as soon as they were out of the yard and now she was pulling the cherries off the hat one by one and throwing them out the window. He became depressed in spite of the car. He had driven about a hundred miles when he decided that she must be hungry again and at the next small town they came to, he stopped in front of an aluminum-painted eating place called The Hot Spot and took her in and ordered her a plate of ham and grits. The ride had made her sleepy

and as soon as she got up on the stool, she rested her head on the counter and shut her eyes. There was no one in The Hot Spot but Mr. Shiftlet and the boy behind the counter, a pale youth with a greasy rag hung over his shoulder. Before he could dish up the food, she was snoring gently.

"Give it to her when she wakes up," Mr. Shiftlet said. "I'll pay for it now."

The boy bent over her and stared at the long pink-gold hair and the half-shut sleeping eyes. Then he looked up and stared at Mr. Shiftlet. "She looks like an angel of Gawd," he murmured.

"Hitchhiker," Mr. Shiftlet explained. "I can't wait. I got to make Tuscaloosa."

The boy bent over again and very carefully touched his finger to a strand of the golden hair and Mr. Shiftlet left.

He was more depressed than ever as he drove on by himself. The late afternoon had grown hot and sultry and the country had flattened out. Deep in the sky a storm was preparing very slowly and without thunder as if it meant to drain every drop of air from the earth before it broke. There were times when Mr. Shiftlet preferred not to be alone. He felt too that a man with a car had a responsibility to others and he kept his eye out for a hitchhiker. Occasionally he saw a sign that warned: "Drive carefully. The life you save may be your own."

The narrow road dropped off on either side into dry fields and here and there a shack or a filling station stood in a clearing. The sun began to set directly in front of the automobile. It was a reddening ball that through his windshield was slightly flat on the bottom and top. He saw a boy in overalls and a gray hat standing on the edge of the road and he slowed the car down and stopped in front of him. The boy didn't

> # Occasionally he saw a sign that warned: "Drive carefully. The life you save may be your own."

have his hand raised to thumb the ride, he was only standing there, but he had a small cardboard suitcase and his hat was set on his head in a way to indicate that he had left somewhere for good. "Son," Mr. Shiftlet said, "I see you want a ride."

The boy didn't say he did or he didn't but he opened the door of the car and got in, and Mr. Shiftlet started driving again. The child held the suitcase on his lap and folded his arms on top of it. He turned his head and looked out the window away from Mr. Shiftlet. Mr. Shiftlet felt oppressed. "Son," he said after a minute, "I got the best old mother in the world so I reckon you only got the second best."

The boy gave him a quick dark glance and then turned his face back out the window.

"It's nothing so sweet," Mr. Shiftlet continued, "as a boy's mother. She taught him his first prayers at her knee, she give him love when no other would, she told him what was right and what wasn't, and she seen that he done the right thing. Son," he said, "I never rued[9] a day in my life like the one I rued when I left that old mother of mine."

The boy shifted in his seat but he didn't look at Mr. Shiftlet. He unfolded his arms and put one hand on the door handle.

"My mother was a angel of Gawd," Mr. Shiftlet said in a very strained voice. "He took her from heaven and giver to me and I left her." His eyes were instantly clouded over with a mist of tears. The car was barely moving.

The boy turned angrily in the seat. "You go to the devil!" he cried. "My old woman is a fleabag and yours is a stinking polecat!" and with that he flung the door open and jumped out with his suitcase into the ditch.

---

9. **rued** (rood): regretted.

Mr. Shiftlet was so shocked that for about a hundred feet he drove along slowly with the door still open. A cloud, the exact color of the boy's hat and shaped like a turnip, had descended over the sun, and another, worse looking, crouched behind the car. Mr. Shiftlet felt that the rottenness of the world was about to engulf him. He raised his arm and let it fall again to his breast. "Oh Lord!" he prayed. "Break forth and wash the slime from this earth!"

The turnip continued slowly to descend. After a few minutes there was a guffawing[10] peal of thunder from behind and fantastic raindrops, like tin-can tops, crashed over the rear of Mr. Shiftlet's car. Very quickly he stepped on the gas and with his stump sticking out the window he raced the galloping shower into Mobile. ■

---

10. **guffawing** (gu·fô′iŋ): like a loud burst of laughter.

# Response and Analysis

## Reading Check

1. Explain how Mr. Shiftlet seems to want to exploit the Craters. How does the older Lucynell want to exploit Mr. Shiftlet?

2. What has become of young Lucynell and Mr. Shiftlet by the story's end?

## Thinking Critically

3. What is the significance of the narrator's saying that Mr. Shiftlet's figure formed "a crooked cross" (page 860) and later that his smile "stretched like a weary snake" (page 864)? What **images** do these descriptions bring to mind? How does the narrator want us to regard Mr. Shiftlet?

4. What does the hitchhiker say to Mr. Shiftlet just before he leaps from the car? How do the remarks affect Mr. Shiftlet?

5. At the end of the story, Mr. Shiftlet feels that "the rottenness of the world was about to engulf him" (page 867). What other remarks does Mr. Shiftlet make throughout the story that suggest he feels he is morally superior to

most other people? What **irony**, or contradictions, do you sense in Mr. Shiftlet's view of his own morality?

6. Where do you find the **title** used in the story? What do you think it means?

7. Are there any heroes in this story? Do you think the story's **theme** involves innocence versus evil, or is it a story about a world in which everyone is morally questionable? Explain your response using details from the text.

8. Using details from the selection, respond to **Connecting to the Focus Question** on page 857.

## Extending and Evaluating

9. O'Connor said that her aunt did not like the way the story ends and was happy when a teleplay changed the ending, having Mr. Shiftlet return to The Hot Spot and drive away with Lucynell. What do you think of the way the story ends?

# Reflecting *on the* Literary Period

## The Moderns: 1914–1939

The following questions ask you to compare and analyze the selections in this feature and respond to the Focus Question. Where possible, cite passages from the selections to support your answers.

Carl Sandburg . . . . . . . . . . . . . . . . . . . . . . . . . . . . . . . . . . . . . . . . . . **Chicago**

Edgar Lee Masters . . . . . . . . . . . . . . . . . . . . . . . . . . . . . . . . . . . **Richard Bone**

. . . . . . . . . . . . . . . . . . . . . . . . . . . . . . . . . . . . **"Butch" Weldy**

. . . . . . . . . . . . . . . . . . . . . . . . . . . . . . . **Mrs. George Reece**

Arna Bontemps . . . . . . . . . . . . . . . . . . . . . . **A Black Man Talks of Reaping**

Flannery O'Connor . . . . . . . . . . . . . **The Life You Save May Be Your Own**

### Comparing Literature

1. Both Sandburg's "Chicago" and Masters's poems are written in **free verse**—poetry that does not conform to a regular **meter** or **rhyme scheme.** What effects does this create in the poems? In what ways is this spare style well-suited to each poet's subject matter?

2. What do the speakers in "'Butch' Weldy" and "A Black Man Talks of Reaping" have in common? How would you describe their outlook on life?

3. Both speakers in "Chicago" and "Richard Bone" talk about negative sides of their communities. What viewpoints might these two speakers share about their neighbors? How do you think the speakers differ in the way they see their communities?

4. The speaker in "Harlem" (page 828), as in "A Black Man Talks of Reaping," is an African American. What similarities do you find in these two poems?

5. Both O'Connor's "The Life You Save May Be Your Own" and Masters's "Mrs. George Reece" discuss people who have been victims. What **tone,** or attitude, do O'Connor and Masters take toward victims and being victimized?

**SKILLS FOCUS**

Pages 847–868 cover **Literary Skills** Evaluate the philosophical, political, religious, ethical, and social issues of a historical period.

### RESPONDING TO THE
## Focus Question

Review your notes and responses related to the Focus Question for this feature. Using details from the selections, write your answer to the question.

How do the poems and stories of modern writers express disillusionment with the American dream and, in particular, loss of faith in the possibility of individual heroism?

**FICTION**

## Strange Twists of Fate

Winters in Starkville, Massachusetts, are harsh and lonely, and no one feels this loneliness more than Ethan Frome, who is stuck in his broken-down farmhouse with a sick and unpleasant wife. When his wife's attractive cousin, Mattie, comes to stay with the Fromes, Ethan feels a sense of hope and renewal that he hasn't felt in years, and he's overjoyed to learn that Mattie feels the same way. *Ethan Frome,* by Edith Wharton, is a classic story of an ill-fated romance that ends with a shocking twist.

**This title is available in the HRW Library.**

**FICTION**

## Lifestyles of the Rich and Famous

He's rich, he's handsome, he throws great parties—so why does Jay Gatsby stand outside his opulent Long Island mansion, gazing longingly at a light across the water? The narrator, Nick Carraway, tries to unlock the puzzle in *The Great Gatsby,* F. Scott Fitzgerald's novel of American dreams and disappointments during the Jazz Age.

**This title is available in the HRW Library.**

**FICTION**

## Wounds of War

Ernest Hemingway is famous for his realistic, almost journalistic accounts of the triumphs and tragedies of warfare. In *A Farewell to Arms,* he sets a tragic romance against the backdrop of World War I Italy. In *For Whom the Bell Tolls,* the backdrop changes to the Spanish civil war.

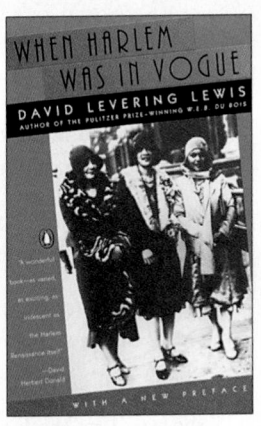

**NONFICTION**

## Take the "A" Train

From about 1919 to 1932, New York City experienced a blossoming of African American culture known as the Harlem Renaissance (see page 816). Langston Hughes, Zora Neale Hurston, and James Weldon Johnson are just three of the many creative talents featured in *When Harlem Was in Vogue,* a highly readable social history by David Levering Lewis.

# Analyzing a Novel

**Writing Assignment**
Write a literary analysis that focuses on a literary element of a novel.

The works of Harlem Renaissance writers can be appreciated more deeply when you look below the surface to analyze their messages and techniques. Similarly, literary analysis adds depth to your understanding of a great novel. To develop your unique viewpoint about a novel, analyze the themes and techniques the author uses. By writing a **literary analysis,** you can help others discover deeper layers of meaning in a novel and add to their appreciation of it.

# Prewriting

## Read and Analyze

**Once Is Not Enough** First, choose an appropriate novel—one that is complex enough for you to analyze in a 1,500-word essay—and read it for enjoyment and general understanding. (If you need help choosing a novel to analyze, ask your teacher or librarian for suggestions.) Then, review your novel, and make notes about the significant ideas presented in it. To develop a **comprehensive understanding** of the author's ideas, consider the literary elements of your novel by answering the analysis questions in the right-hand column of the chart below.

| QUESTIONS FOR LITERARY ANALYSIS | |
|---|---|
| **Literary Element** | **Analysis Questions** |
| Characters | How do the important characters in the novel think, talk, and act? In what ways do their actions or attitudes change over the course of the novel? |
| Setting | What is the time and place of the novel? How does the setting affect the mood or the development of the plot? |
| Plot | What is the central conflict, or problem, of the story? How does the outcome of the story relate to the theme? |
| Point of View | Is the story told by a first-person or a third-person narrator? What does the narrator think about the characters and events in the story? |
| Theme | What universal truths does the novel express about human nature, experiences, problems, or relationships? What details reflect this theme? |
| Symbolism | Do any objects or elements show up repeatedly? Does any person, place, or thing seem to represent an abstract idea? If so, what? |

*(continued)*

(continued)

**Stylistic Devices**

| | |
|---|---|
| **Imagery** | What feelings do sensory descriptions of people, places, events, and ideas suggest? What effects are created through the use of imagery? |
| **Diction** | Is the author's word choice straightforward, or is the language connotative (having meaning beyond a simple definition)? What is the novel's tone? How does the word choice affect the tone of the story? |
| **Figurative Language** | Does the author use similes and metaphors? If so, what effects do these comparisons create? |

**TIP** As you analyze these elements in your novel, consider **unique aspects of the text,** such as an author's unusual use of point of view, language, or plot structure. For example, you might focus on how J. D. Salinger's use of a first-person narrator with a distinct attitude and way of speaking affects a reader's impression of *The Catcher in the Rye.*

## Write a Thesis Statement

**Zoom In**   To plan your essay, focus on analyzing a single element over the entire course of the novel. Look at your notes to decide which element seems most important or interesting. Identify a few major points that make that element so strong—for example, the most surprising plot events or the characters whose lives point out the theme. Then, write a sentence that presents your perspective about the novel—a conclusion based on the major points about your chosen element. This sentence, your working **thesis statement,** will serve as a guide. If necessary, you can revise this statement later. Here is how one student expressed a viewpoint in a working thesis statement.

| | |
|---|---|
| Through the empty lives of three <u>characters</u> from this novel— <u>George Wilson</u>, <u>Jay Gatsby</u>, and <u>Daisy Buchanan</u>—<u>Fitzgerald</u> <u>shows that chasing hollow dreams leads only to misery.</u> | Literary element<br>Major points<br>Conclusion about the novel |

## Gather Evidence

**Get the Facts**   Find and make notes of evidence to support your working thesis statement. Your most important support will be **literary evidence**—detailed references to the text of the novel. Literary evidence includes quotations, paraphrases, and summaries of specific details and passages in the text. Although most of your evidence will come from the **primary source,** the novel itself, you might also find evidence in **secondary sources**—reference materials such as encyclopedias, periodicals, biographies of authors, or literary criticism. Such sources can bolster your major points and provide background information your readers may need to understand the context of the novel.

**SKILLS FOCUS**

**Writing Skills**
Write an analysis of a novel. Analyze literary elements and the author's style. Write a thesis statement.

**Spell It Out** Explain how each piece of evidence supports your thesis and develops your major points. To do this, elaborate on the importance of each idea and its connection to your thesis. As part of your elaboration, explain how the author uses ambiguities, nuances, and complexities, and how those devices relate to your thesis.

- **ambiguities:** language or situations that can be interpreted in more than one way or have more than one meaning

- **nuances:** fine shades of meaning, especially any changes in the way the author expresses a recurring idea

- **complexities:** details in the novel that at first seem self-contradictory, requiring some thought to understand thoroughly

One student gathered evidence for her thesis using the notes below.

> **Thesis:** Through the empty lives of three characters from <u>The Great Gatsby</u>, Fitzgerald shows that chasing hollow dreams leads only to misery.
>
> **Major point:** Jay Gatsby's shallow pursuit of wealth and Daisy
>
> **Evidence:** Daisy says to Gatsby: "Oh, you want too much!" (133)
>
> **Elaboration:** Gatsby's desire to have it all—money, class, power, and Daisy, no matter the cost—has corrupted his spirit.

**TIP** Document quotations from the novel by enclosing the words in quotation marks and including the page number, as shown to the right. When you use material from secondary sources to support your thesis, identify the author and title in your essay to avoid **plagiarism**—using other authors' words or ideas without giving proper credit. Also, be sure to copy the quotation exactly as it appears in the original source.

**DO THIS**

## Arrange Your Ideas

**Map the Course** How you organize your ideas will depend on your thesis. For example, if you were examining how a character changes over time, you would use **chronological order.** Then again, if you were examining the importance of individual characters to a novel's theme, you could discuss them in **order of importance.** Once you've picked an order, map or outline your ideas. Here is one student's plan in order of importance.

| | | |
|---|---|---|
| Show how Wilson chases empty dreams as first support. Use his attempt to buy a car and his weak marriage as examples. | Use Gatsby's shallow life as second support. Use as examples the wealth he gained illegally and his attempt to get Daisy back. | Use Daisy as the most important support of thesis. Use the examples of her marriage and her love for Gatsby to show the hollowness of her life. |

**SKILLS FOCUS**

**Writing Skills** Organize your ideas.

**PRACTICE & APPLY 1** Read and analyze an appropriate novel. Develop a thesis that states a conclusion about the novel, gather evidence, and organize your ideas.

# Writing

## Analyzing a Novel

## A Writer's Framework

### Introduction

- Present background information that provides a context for your analysis.
- Give the novel's author and title.
- Include a clear thesis statement.

### Body

- Organize major points in a logical order.
- Include literary evidence from the text or secondary sources.
- Elaborate on how evidence supports major points.

### Conclusion

- Restate your thesis and summarize your major points.
- End your analysis with a memorable statement—an idea your readers can ponder.

## A Writer's Model

### Hollow Dreams—Empty Lives

After World War I, America seemed to promise unlimited financial and social opportunities for anyone willing to work hard—an American Dream. For some, however, striving for and realizing that dream corrupted them, as they acquired wealth only to pursue pleasure. Even though the characters in F. Scott Fitzgerald's <u>The Great Gatsby</u> appear to relish the freedom of the 1920s, their lives demonstrate the emptiness that results when wealth and pleasure become ends in themselves. Specifically, the empty lives of three characters from this novel—George Wilson, Jay Gatsby, and Daisy Buchanan—show that chasing hollow dreams results only in misery.

One character who chases an empty dream is George Wilson, the owner of a garage. Wilson has gone into business with the hope of becoming rich, but he has not been successful. Wilson thinks that if Tom Buchanan, Daisy's wealthy husband, will sell him a fancy car, he can then turn a profit by reselling it. When Tom and the narrator Nick Carraway meet Wilson at his garage, Nick says that there is a "damp gleam of hope" in Wilson's eyes (25). Wilson complains that the sale is going slowly, and Tom replies, "[I]f you feel that way about it, maybe I'd better sell it somewhere else after all" (25). Wilson instantly backs down. This exchange suggests that Wilson has no chance of either making a profit off Tom's car or realizing his dream of wealth. His hope for economic security is doomed to failure.

*(continued)*

**INTRODUCTION**
**Background information**

**Author and title**

**Thesis statement**

**BODY**
**Major point #1**

**Evidence**

**Elaboration**

*(continued)*

Major point #2

Background information

Evidence

Elaboration

Another character who holds tightly to an illusion is the title character, Jay Gatsby. Before the war, Gatsby and Daisy fell deeply in love. However, Daisy's family prevented her from marrying Gatsby because, as a young soldier, he was penniless. As a result, he spent his years after the war becoming very rich, but he did so by engaging in illegal activities. Having made his fortune, he moves near Daisy and puts on lavish parties in the hope that Daisy might leave her husband for him. Unfortunately, his newfound wealth does not earn him respect or acceptance into a higher social class. Rumors about his tainted past circulate, even as the partygoers devour the extravagant food and drink he provides. Gatsby is an outsider, and even when Daisy comes back to him, their love is tainted by money. In a final conversation, Daisy cries out to Gatsby: "Oh, you want too much!" (133) She is right: Gatsby's desire to have it all—money, class, power, and Daisy, no matter the cost—has corrupted his spirit.

Major point #3

Evidence

Elaboration

Unlike Gatsby, Daisy Buchanan seems perfectly at ease in her wealthy social circle. Money, rather than love, has determined her choice of husbands. Despite her love for Gatsby, she married Tom Buchanan, who gave her "a string of pearls valued at three hundred and fifty thousand dollars" for a wedding gift (77). Betraying Gatsby's love for Buchanan's money, Daisy is herself betrayed by her husband for another woman. Daisy returns to Gatsby, but she is still unable to free herself from the constraints of her wealthy society, particularly from her husband, who sneers at Gatsby's background and newfound wealth. The dream of happiness—the love she and Gatsby once shared—is doomed, because she believes that money is more important.

CONCLUSION

Restatement of thesis and major points

Memorable statement

Throughout the novel, F. Scott Fitzgerald portrays a society that has corrupted the true meaning of the American Dream through Wilson, Gatsby, and Daisy's hollow pursuit of wealth. If the characters in The Great Gatsby come from various classes of American society, then a major theme of The Great Gatsby is that no one in 1920s America was safe from vacant dreams and their negative results.

**INTERNET**

**More Writer's Models**

Keyword: LE7 11-5

**TIP** When you incorporate a quotation into a sentence, use capitalization appropriate to the sentence, even if the capitalization is different in the source. To indicate that you have made such a change, put brackets around the letter that has been changed, as shown in the second paragraph of the Writer's Model.

**PRACTICE & APPLY 2** Write the first draft of your literary analysis of a novel, using the framework on page 873 and the Writer's Model above as guides.

# Revising

## Evaluate and Revise Your Analysis

**Do a Double Take** Your analysis isn't complete until you've revised it carefully. Read through your draft at least twice. Use the first-reading guidelines below to look critically at content and organization. Then, use the style guidelines on page 876 to evaluate and revise the style of your analysis.

> **First Reading: Content and Organization** Using the chart below, evaluate and revise the content and organization of your literary analysis.

**PEER REVIEW**

Before you revise, trade papers with a peer and ask for input on where you need to integrate literary evidence more smoothly in your paper.

### Rubric: Analyzing a Novel

| Evaluation Questions | ▶ Tips | ▶ Revision Techniques |
|---|---|---|
| ❶ Does the introduction include background information to give the analysis context? Does it include the author's name and the novel's title? | ▶ **Circle** the information that provides context for the analysis. **Underline** the name of the author and the title of the novel. | ▶ **Add** information that provides context, such as details about the author's life or the novel's historical setting. **Add** the name of the author or the novel's title. |
| ❷ Does a clear thesis statement present a conclusion about the novel based on a literary element? | ▶ **Bracket** the element identified in the thesis and the writer's conclusion about the novel. | ▶ **Add** a conclusion about the novel or a clearer statement of the literary element on which the analysis focuses. |
| ❸ Does each body paragraph develop a major point that supports the thesis? | ▶ **Label** the major point of each body paragraph in the margin next to the paragraph. | ▶ **Replace** sentences or paragraphs that don't support the thesis. |
| ❹ Does evidence support each major point? | ▶ **Draw a jagged line** under each piece of evidence. If a paragraph includes little evidence or evidence that doesn't clearly support its point, revise. | ▶ **Add** quotations, paraphrases, or summaries from the novel or other sources. **Elaborate** on how the evidence supports the paragraph's point. |
| ❺ Are the paper's major points organized effectively? | ▶ **Number** ideas in sequence for chronological order. For order of importance, **underline** the most important point. | ▶ **Reorder** a chronological essay in correct time order. For order of importance, **reorder** to place the most important point first or last. |
| ❻ Does the conclusion restate the thesis and sum up the major points? Does it close the essay with a memorable statement? | ▶ **Circle** the sentences that restate the essay's thesis and sum up major points. **Double underline** a memorable concluding statement. | ▶ **Add** a sentence or two restating the thesis and summarizing major points. **Elaborate** with a memorable statement. |

> **Second Reading: Style** To improve the style of your literary analysis, look at how you **introduce quotations.** To weave quotations smoothly into your sentences, introduce them with a brief clause. Look at these examples:

**Original:** A "damp gleam of hope" is what the narrator, Nick, says the character Wilson has in his eyes (25).

**Revision:** Nick says that there is a "damp gleam of hope" in Wilson's eyes (25).

Use the guidelines below to evaluate your style.

## Style Guidelines

| Evaluation Question | ▶ Tip | ▶ Revision Technique |
|---|---|---|
| ● Are quotations woven into the structure of the sentence? Does each quotation have an introduction? | ▶ **Draw a box** around each sentence that includes a quotation. **Underline** the introduction of each quotation. | ▶ **Reword** sentences that are confusing by using a brief clause before quotations to introduce them. |

### ANALYZING THE REVISION PROCESS
Study these revisions, and answer the questions that follow.

reword

Wilson complains that the sale is going slowly, *, and Tom replies,* "[I]f you feel

that way about it, maybe I'd better sell it somewhere else after

elaborate

all" ~~is what Tom says~~ (25). Wilson instantly backs down. His

hope for economic security is doomed to failure.

*This exchange suggests that Wilson has no chance of either making a profit off Tom's car or realizing his dream of wealth.*

### Responding to the Revision Process

1. How does the revision of the first two sentences make the paragraph easier to follow?

2. Why did the writer add a sentence? How does the new sentence explain the literary evidence?

**SKILLS FOCUS**

**Writing Skills**
Revise for content and style.

**PRACTICE & APPLY** 3 Use the guidelines on pages 875 and 876 to evaluate and revise your essay's content, organization, and style. Consider peer comments as well.

# Publishing

## Proofread and Publish Your Analysis

**To Err Is Human** All writers make mistakes. A good writer catches and corrects mistakes before the work is published. Carefully check your draft—individually and collaboratively—for grammar, usage, spelling, and punctuation errors before you submit the final copy.

**Get the Word Out** Your analysis presents your unique perspective on a literary work. Don't limit the audience for that perspective to just your classmates and teacher. Here are some ways you might share your literary analysis with a wider audience.

- Collaborate with other students on a booklet of related analyses. You might collect analyses that discuss various works by the same author or works by authors from the same era, or you could group essays that analyze the same literary element in different works or that examine similar themes. Bind your booklet, and add it to a class or library display of student work.

- Create a bulletin board for your class. Arrange your literary analysis next to a photo of the novel's author. Add other supplementary material related to the novel or its author to catch a reader's eye.

- Find a Web site about the author of the novel you analyzed. Send an e-mail message to ask the producers of the site if they will publish your analysis there.

## Reflect on Your Literary Analysis

**Get Some Perspective** Now that your literary analysis is complete, take time to reflect on your writing. Writing responses to the following questions will help you identify and build on what you learned in this workshop.

- How did you choose the focus of your analysis? What other elements of the novel or major points might you have analyzed instead?

- How has writing the analysis deepened your understanding of the literary work?

- What important revisions did you make to your draft? How did they improve it?

- What will you do differently if you write another literary analysis?

**PRACTICE & APPLY** 4 Proofread your revised analysis to correct any errors in grammar, usage, or mechanics. Then, publish your analysis using one of the suggestions above. Finally, answer the questions above, and attach your responses to your analysis.

**TIP** Proofread carefully for English-language **conventions.** One convention writers of literary analyses use is the literary present tense. Because the events in a novel are constantly unfolding for new readers, use the present tense to refer to events that occur in the novel you analyze. For more on the **literary present tense,** see Tenses and Their Uses, 3b, in the Language Handbook.

**SKILLS FOCUS**

**Writing Skills**
Proofread, especially for use of the literary present tense.

# Presenting a Literary Analysis

**Speaking Assignment**
Adapt your written literary analysis into an oral response to literature, and deliver it your class.

**W**riting an essay isn't the only way for you to share your analysis of a novel. You can also tell a group of listeners your ideas in an **oral response to literature.** You'll use slightly different ideas and techniques in your oral presentation, though. This workshop will help you adapt your written ideas and present them to a listening audience.

## Adapt Your Analysis

**Think Out Loud**  You crafted your written literary analysis for an audience of classmates and teachers. Even if you have the same audience for your presentation, you'll need to adjust your analysis to fit their needs as listeners rather than readers. Use the following tips.

**Keep It Short**  If you have a time limit, make sure you can deliver your presentation within it. Even without a time limit, focus on a limited number of points and evidence to hold your listeners' interest.

**Plan Content**  Your **thesis statement** will show your comprehensive understanding of the significant ideas in the work. Adapt your written thesis statement by shortening or simplifying it to make it easier for listeners to understand, and summarize your points up front to prepare listeners for the ideas you will present.

Focus your speech on the most important points about the element you analyzed in your essay. Remember that these points can include descriptions and explanations of other literary elements, including **universal themes,** point of view, symbolism, **stylistic devices** such as **imagery** and the author's choice of **language,** and other **unique aspects** of the text.

Support your thesis and each major point you discuss with evidence in the form of accurate and detailed references to the text or to other works. Identify the title and author of any secondary source you quote. Elaborate on the evidence by showing how it relates to the assertion your thesis makes about the work. If appropriate, explain any significant **ambiguities, nuances,** or **complexities** in the work to help you develop your major points or your elaboration.

**Use Rhetorical Techniques**  To make your presentation easier for listeners to understand and remember, try using the following techniques.

- **rhetorical questions,** or questions with debatable answers asked for effect—for example, the student analyzing *The Great Gatsby* might begin by asking, "Which is more important, love or money?"

- **parallel structure,** or using the same grammatical form for similar ideas—for example, "While *Gatsby has loved* only Daisy, *Daisy has loved* Tom and his money as well as Gatsby."

**Listening and Speaking Skills**
Present an oral response to a literary work. Use effective rhetorical techniques.

# Homework

*Homage Kenneth Koch*

Allen Ginsberg

If I were doing my Laundry I'd wash my dirty Iran
I'd throw in my United States, and pour on the Ivory Soap, scrub
    up Africa, put all the birds and elephants back in
    the jungle,
I'd wash the Amazon river and clean the oily Carib & Gulf of
    Mexico,
Rub that smog off the North Pole, wipe up all the pipelines in
    Alaska,
Rub a dub dub for Rocky Flats and Los Alamos, Flush that
    sparkly Cesium out of Love Canal
Rinse down the Acid Rain over the Parthenon & Sphinx,
    Drain the Sludge out of the Mediterranean basin &
    make it azure again,
Put some blueing back into the sky over the Rhine, bleach the
    little Clouds so snow return white as snow,
Cleanse the Hudson Thames & Neckar, Drain the Suds out
    of Lake Erie
Then I'd throw big Asia in one giant Load & wash out the
    blood & Agent Orange,
Dump the whole mess of Russia and China in the wringer,
    squeeze out the tattletail Gray of U.S. Central American
    police state,
& put the planet in the drier & let it sit 20 minutes or an Aeon
    till it came out clean.

*April 26, 1980*

# Collection 5: Skills Review
## Comparing Literature

1. In the first four lines of McKay's poem, what does he confess about his feelings for America?
   - **A** He dislikes her.
   - **B** He loves her.
   - **C** He does not understand her.
   - **D** He wishes to leave her.

2. In the first four lines, what does McKay **personify** America as?
   - **F** A tiger
   - **G** A mother
   - **H** A nurse
   - **J** A nightmare

3. Consider McKay's background and the time he wrote this poem. How would you explain what he means by "her hate" in line 6?
   - **A** He refers to America's size.
   - **B** He refers to racism.
   - **C** He refers to prejudice against poets.
   - **D** He refers to hatred of the poor.

4. Which words *best* describe the **tone** of lines 11–14 of "America"?
   - **F** Defiant and sad
   - **G** Terrified and mocking
   - **H** Admiring and triumphant
   - **J** Bitter and angry

5. The central **conflict** in "America" takes place between —
   - **A** the speaker's contradictory feelings
   - **B** the king and the rebel
   - **C** the tiger and the poet
   - **D** America and her tragic fate

6. In lines 8–10 of "America," the speaker does not revolt against America because —
   - **F** time will destroy America
   - **G** he loves his country
   - **H** he moves to Europe
   - **J** he feels powerless

7. In "America," what does the speaker see as the future of the country?
   - **A** America will be overcome by violence.
   - **B** America will lead the world.
   - **C** America's glory will not endure.
   - **D** America will no longer exist.

8. In the laundry **metaphor** that runs throughout "Homework," what does the speaker want cleaned up?
   - **F** Urban decay and rural poverty
   - **G** Pornographic books and films
   - **H** Scandals in Washington, D.C.
   - **J** Political and environmental problems

9. In Ginsberg's poem, how long does the speaker say he'll wait for the wash to come "out clean"?
   - **A** Until the end of time
   - **B** A minute or two
   - **C** Twenty minutes or an aeon
   - **D** Half an hour

**10.** Which word *best* describes Ginsberg's **tone**?

**F**  Tragic

**G**  Threatening

**H**  Playful

**J**  Bitter

**11.** Which statement would the speaker of "Homework" most likely agree with?

**A**  America's problems are easy to solve.

**B**  The speaker has a responsibility to help America.

**C**  America's problems are unsolvable.

**D**  America is not a good place to live.

**12.** Which statement is true of *both* "America" and "Homework"?

**F**  The speakers of both poems describe their love of America.

**G**  Both poets refer to America as a female.

**H**  Both poets have a negative outlook for America's future.

**J**  Both poets use metaphors to describe their feelings.

**13.** With which of the following statements about the United States do you think McKay and Ginsberg would agree?

**A**  America and the world are not perfect and need reform.

**B**  We should not let the natural world become polluted.

**C**  Individuals are powerless in society today.

**D**  This is the best of all possible worlds.

**14.** What do McKay and Ginsberg have in common with other twentieth-century American writers, such as Hemingway and Fitzgerald?

**F**  They prefer lyrical, romantic language.

**G**  They have a critical attitude toward modern life.

**H**  They all have amusing tones.

**J**  They think that American society is perfect.

## Essay Question

Speaking from different eras and different experiences, Claude McKay and Allen Ginsberg present personal visions of the modern world. Write an essay in which you first summarize each poet's main message. Then, compare the views of these poets with the reality of the world as you see it today.

**Test Practice**

**Analogies**

DIRECTIONS: For each of the following items, choose the lettered pair of words that expresses a relationship that is most similar to the relationship between the capitalized pair of words.

1. LUDICROUS : ABSURD ::
   A  pure : filthy
   B  quick : unmoving
   C  ill : healthy
   D  peaceful : undisturbed

2. PAUPER : POOR ::
   F  criminal : respectable
   G  professor : ignorant
   H  painter : trustworthy
   J  comedian : funny

3. HAIL : GREET ::
   A  avoid : dodge
   B  deny : give
   C  destroy : restore
   D  find : lose

4. ARCHAIC : MODERN ::
   F  immature : novice
   G  shy : timid
   H  violent : peaceful
   J  wild : untamed

5. BEDLAM : WAR ::
   A  order : beach
   B  quiet : library
   C  comfort : court
   D  distress : supermarket

6. CONVENED : DISPERSED ::
   F  retreated : repelled
   G  welcomed : accepted
   H  froze : melted
   J  imagined : created

7. DISTRAUGHT : TROUBLED ::
   A  giddy : bored
   B  injured : well
   C  excited : lethargic
   D  confused : bewildered

8. DIMINUTIVE : SMALL ::
   F  complicated : easy
   G  gorgeous : good-looking
   H  dull : brilliant
   J  fancy : elaborate

9. CRAVEN : COWARD ::
   A  biased : judge
   B  stingy : miser
   C  frightening : scary
   D  braggart : bully

10. PANDEMONIUM : RIOT ::
    F  illness : virus
    G  sorrow : excitement
    H  environment : pollution
    J  verdict : guilty

**SKILLS FOCUS**

**Vocabulary Skills**
Analyze word analogies.

# Collection 5: Skills Review

## Writing Skills

**Test Practice**   DIRECTIONS: Read the following paragraph from a literary analysis. Mark on your own paper the best answer to each question.

(1) In the novel *Passing,* the two main characters are masked. (2) The novel proved Nella Larsen one of the most influential writers of the Harlem Renaissance. (3) Although the characters in *Passing,* Clare and Irene, come from African American families, both are able to "pass" as white women. (4) Early in the novel, Irene describes Clare's face as an "ivory mask" which she uses to break away "from all that was familiar and friendly to take [her] chance in another environment" (24). (5) Irene also passes, and at the end of the novel "her face ha[s] become a mask" that she uses to hide her emotions (99). (6) While masking themselves allows Clare and Irene entrance into other social spheres, they soon learn the greater consequences of not being true to themselves.

1. Which sentence could replace sentence 1 to express a clearer perspective?
   - **A** *Passing* uses the metaphor of a mask to show how characters hide their true identities.
   - **B** *Passing* contrasts Clare and Irene's lifestyles and families.
   - **C** *Passing* explains how and why light-skinned African Americans entered white society.
   - **D** *Passing,* a Harlem Renaissance novel, explores issues of race.

2. Which sentence would explain the quotations in sentence 4?
   - **F** Passing causes Clare to lose family, friends, and heritage.
   - **G** Irene passes because she enjoys fooling others.
   - **H** Through passing, Clare experiences white society.
   - **J** Clare doesn't miss the friends and family she leaves behind.

3. To further support his viewpoint, the student could
   - **A** summarize his major points
   - **B** include more detailed and accurate references to the text
   - **C** analyze in this paragraph other elements of the novel
   - **D** ignore ambiguities and complexities within the text

4. Which sentence should be moved to another paragraph to improve organization?
   - **F** 2       **H** 5
   - **G** 4       **J** 6

5. To present this analysis orally, the student should
   - **A** make the thesis statement longer and more complex
   - **B** read the entire analysis aloud from note cards
   - **C** rehearse one time only
   - **D** focus on the strongest main points and evidence

SKILLS FOCUS

**Writing Skills**
Write an analysis of a novel.

*Ocean Park No. 31* by Richard Diebenkorn.

# Contemporary Literature

## 1939 to Present

### *New Voices, New Visions*

You can't say it that way
any more.

—John Ashbery

**INTERNET**

Collection
Resources

Keyword: LE7 11-6

# Contemporary Literature
## 1939 to Present

## LITERARY EVENTS

**1940**    **1950**

**1940** Richard Wright publishes his brutal novel *Native Son*

**1945** Tennessee Williams's memory play *The Glass Menagerie* opens on Broadway

Tennessee Williams.

**1946** William Carlos Williams publishes the first part of his long poem *Paterson*

**1948** William Faulkner publishes *Intruder in the Dust,* about the growing moral awareness of a white boy in the South

**1949** Arthur Miller's tragedy *Death of a Salesman* opens

**1951** J. D. Salinger publishes his novel *The Catcher in the Rye*

**1952** Ralph Ellison publishes his novel *Invisible Man*

**1959** Lorraine Hansberry's play *A Raisin in the Sun* opens

**1960** Harper Lee publishes her novel *To Kill a Mockingbird*

**1962** John Steinbeck wins the Nobel Prize in literature

**1965** *The Autobiography of Malcolm X* is published

**1966** Truman Capote publishes his "nonfiction novel," *In Cold Blood*

**1967** Colombian writer Gabriel García Márquez publishes *One Hundred Years of Solitude*

## POLITICAL AND SOCIAL EVENTS

**1940**    **1960**

**1941** U.S. enters World War II after Japan attacks Pearl Harbor, Hawaii

**1944** Allies begin final drive against German forces on D-day, June 6

**May 1945** Germany surrenders

**1945** United States explodes atomic bombs over Hiroshima (August 6) and Nagasaki (August 9); Japan surrenders (August 14)

**1945** United Nations is established

**1950** Senator Joseph McCarthy charges that 205 Communists have infiltrated the State Department

**1953** Korean War ends with division of the country into North Korea and South Korea

**1954** U.S. Supreme Court rules that segregation in public schools is unconstitutional

**1957** Soviet Union launches first artificial satellite, *Sputnik I,* beginning the "space race" with the United States

**1961** U.S. invasion of Bay of Pigs, in Cuba, fails

**1963** Martin Luther King, Jr., delivers "I Have a Dream" speech during the March on Washington

**1963** President John F. Kennedy is assassinated

**1964** An estimated 73 million viewers tune in to *The Ed Sullivan Show* to watch the North American debut of the Beatles

**1965** U.S. involvement in the Vietnam War escalates

**1969** Two U.S. astronauts become the first human beings to walk on the moon

Edwin "Buzz" Aldrin, Jr. (July 20, 1969).

## 1980

**1970** Maya Angelou publishes her autobiography *I Know Why the Caged Bird Sings*

**1975** E. L. Doctorow publishes *Ragtime,* a novel mixing fictional and real characters

**1976** Alex Haley publishes *Roots,* a fictional history of his family, beginning with its African origins

**1981** John Updike publishes his third "Rabbit" novel, *Rabbit Is Rich*

**1982** Alice Walker publishes her novel *The Color Purple*

**1983** Raymond Carver publishes *Cathedral,* a collection of short stories

**1989** Amy Tan publishes *The Joy Luck Club*

**1990** Tim O'Brien publishes *The Things They Carried*

**1991** Sandra Cisneros publishes a story collection called *Woman Hollering Creek*

**1993** Toni Morrison wins the Nobel Prize in literature

## 2000

**2000** Jhumpa Lahiri wins the Pulitzer Prize for her short story collection *Interpreter of Maladies*

**2005** American playwright Arthur Miller dies

American soldiers in Vietnam.

## 1980

**1973** Peace treaty provides for a cease-fire in Vietnam and with-drawal of U.S. forces

**1974** Watergate scandal forces Richard M. Nixon to resign as president of the United States

**1979** Iranian militants seize the U.S. embassy in Tehran and take fifty-two American hostages, beginning a 444-day "hostage crisis"

**1979** Soviet Union invades Afghanistan

**1985** Era of great change in the Soviet Union begins as Mikhail Gor-bachev rises to power

**1986** U.S. space shuttle *Challenger* explodes soon after liftoff

**1987** U.S. and Soviet Union sign a treaty reducing medium-range nuclear weapons

**1989** Berlin Wall is knocked down

**1989** Pro-democracy demonstrations are crushed in Tiananmen Square, Beijing

**1990** West Germany and East Germany unite

**1991** Soviet Union is dissolved

**1995** Bomb explosion kills 168 at the Murrah Federal Building in Oklahoma City, Oklahoma

**2001** Terrorist attacks at the World Trade Center in New York, at the Pentagon in Washington, D.C., and on a plane over Pennsylvania kill thousands

## 2000

**2003** U.S., Britain, and Spain go to war with Iraq

**2004** Earthquake in Indian Ocean triggers massive tsunami, leaving over 250,000 people missing or dead

# Political and Social

## World War II, 1939–1945

The second great war of the twentieth century officially began in 1939, when Britain and France declared war on Germany after Hitler's armies invaded Poland. The United States was drawn into the conflict in 1941, when Japan bombed the U.S. naval base at Pearl Harbor, in Hawaii. By the time the war ended, in 1945 (after the United States dropped atomic bombs that wasted two Japanese cities), the conflict had become global.

Hiroshima, Japan, after the atomic bombing (1945).

## The Cold War, 1945–1991

The United States emerged from World War II an economic and political powerhouse, but U.S. dominance did not go unchallenged for long. Soon after the war ended, the Soviet Union seized control of most of Eastern Europe and installed one-party Communist governments behind what Winston Churchill called an "iron curtain."

With the Soviet Union's development of nuclear weapons in the 1950s and 1960s, the ideological conflict between the United States and the Soviet Union hardened into a long and expensive arms race. Smaller countries, such as Korea and Vietnam, became bloody battlegrounds on which the great powers played out their rivalries in a standoff dubbed the cold war.

In the late 1980s, the Soviet Union began to unravel. In 1991, under the combined weight of Western pressure and internal failures, it collapsed. A new Russian republic with democratic aspirations (and plenty of domestic problems) took its place. Suddenly all over Eastern Europe the iron curtain lifted.

# Milestones 1939 to Present

## The Digital Revolution and Economic Prosperity

In the second half of the twentieth century, life for the average American may well have been most profoundly changed by the introduction of computer technology into daily life. In the 1950s and 1960s, business and government were revolutionized by giant mainframe computers, which made quick electronic storage and retrieval of vast amounts of data possible for the first time. Then, in the 1980s and 1990s, desktop computers began to appear in offices, schools, and homes. Yet more changes came in the late 1990s, when Internet communication and wireless technology promised to keep Americans constantly connected. All of these innovations fueled a surge in the stock market in the 1990s, which, like all giddy upturns, ended with a thud in the spring of 2000. The greatest period of economic prosperity was sputtering out when, on September 11, 2001, foreign terrorists carried out the worst attack on American soil in our history.

President Reagan, a bust of Lenin behind him, speaks at Moscow State University (1988).

# Contemporary Literature
## 1939 to Present

*by* John Leggett, Susan Allen Toth, John Malcolm Brinnin,
*and* Thomas Hernacki

**P R E V I E W**

## Think About ...

During the second half of the twentieth century, the United States emerged victorious from two wars, one hot and one cold. In the final decades of the century, however, when the United States was the undisputed military and economic leader of the world, American culture seemed unwilling to identify exclusively with any one group or class. America's emphasis on cultural and ethnic inclusion is reflected in the postmodern literature of the period.

As you read this introduction to the contemporary period, look for answers to these questions:

- How did rapid developments in technology after World War II affect everyday life?
- What does *postmodern* mean?
- How did political and economic development shape people's lives in the second half of the twentieth century?

SKILLS FOCUS

Collection introduction (pages 892–905) covers **Literary Skills** Evaluate genres and traditions in American literature.

On August 6, 1945, at 8:15 A.M., an atomic bomb was dropped on the Japanese city of Hiroshima from the U.S. airplane *Enola Gay.* Within seconds the center of Hiroshima had disappeared. The bomb in effect ended World War II, and its mushroom cloud has cast a shadow over every generation since.

Although many Americans disapproved of the use of the atomic bomb to end World War II, most agreed with the purpose of the war itself. They were fighting against tyranny, against regimes that would destroy the American way of life. Only twenty years later, however, the United States became deeply involved in another overseas war—this time in Vietnam—that would sharply divide the nation. In the 1960s, demonstrations against the government, both peaceful and violent, became commonplace.

To some writers the madness of the war-torn world was an inescapable condition of modern life, and the only appropriate response was hard-edged laughter at life's tragic ironies. The term *gallows humor*—ironic humor arising from an acknowledgment of

*War Series: Victory* (1947) by Jacob Lawrence (1917–2000). Egg tempera on composition board 20 × 16 in. (50.8 × 40.64 cm).

Toppled statue of the Soviet dictator Joseph Stalin, Russia (1991).

*At all times, an old world is collapsing and a new world arising; we have better eyes for the collapse than the rise, for the old one is the world we know. The artist, in focusing on his creation, finds, and offers, relief from the tension and sadness of being burdened not just with consciousness but with historical consciousness.*

—John Updike,
from *Hugging the Shore*

the absurd or grotesque—was often used to describe the work of writers who flourished after World War II. In the works of writers like Tim O'Brien (page 961), madness and war are inextricably mixed, not because madness is a result of war but because war is the result of madness.

The 1970s saw the winding down of the Vietnam War, but another focus of disillusionment filled the news: the Watergate scandal, which in 1974 forced the only resignation of a U.S. president, Richard M. Nixon.

Then came the 1980s, which many Americans now regard as the time of the "me generation," when individual enjoyment and material success seemed to overshadow other concerns. As the 1980s ended, so did the cold war, the struggle between the United States and the Soviet Union that had dominated international politics since shortly after the end of World War II. The Soviet Union collapsed as its republics and satellite nations declared independence. The end of the cold war reduced but did not end the threat of nuclear violence.

## A CLOSER LOOK: SOCIAL INFLUENCES

### Atomic Anxiety

INFORMATIONAL TEXT

Things are probably going to look different when you get outside.

—from *How to Survive an Atomic Bomb* (1950)

Americans testing a bomb-shelter escape hatch (1952), Bronxville, New York.

Nuclear explosion in the Nevada desert (1955).

In many ways the nuclear bomb is the dramatic symbol of the last half of the twentieth century. Its infamous mushroom cloud represents the triumph of science and technology, the purpose of which was, ironically enough, to benefit humankind, to make life richer and easier for all.

*Peace Today* by Rube Goldberg.
The Granger Collection, New York.

**A**t the end of World War II, Americans confronted two new, unsettling facts of life: the atomic bomb and the cold war with the Soviet Union. U.S. scientists published chilling calculations of what would happen if atomic (and, later, hydrogen) bombs were dropped on American cities. Meanwhile, a vivid image of a malignant Soviet leadership, with its collective finger poised over the red button that would launch a nuclear attack, was created in the American psyche—an image memorably evoked in the 1963 film *Dr. Strangelove or: How I Learned to Stop Worrying and Love the Bomb*. Politicians warned that war would come, in the words of New York's governor Thomas E. Dewey, "whenever the fourteen evil men in Moscow decide to have it break out." It was high time, experts of various stripes agreed, to devise a new national civil-defense plan.

The possible options in response to nuclear attack were succinctly described by one U.S. government official as "dig, die, or get out." The second option aside, getting out meant leaving big cities, which presumably would be targets of Soviet bombs. Some policymakers urged that major cities be relocated under mountain ranges or in thirty-foot strips alongside highways. Government officials ultimately rejected these and other relocation schemes. Even the less ambitious idea of evacuating cities drove planners to despair as they pondered maps of New York City and Los Angeles.

What was left but to dig? The notion of burrowing underground took root partly because it allowed every citizen a personal response to nuclear war: Build a bomb shelter. Companies selling shelters proliferated in the 1950s, and marketing creativity soared. Using fictitious "protection factor" ratings, shelter ads promised blastproof rooms; one ad featured a decontamination room for latecomers. Bomb shelters generated so much enthusiasm that by the end of 1960, industrious Americans had constructed about one million of them.

The fears that inspired those bunkers are now, sadly, entirely understandable to twenty-first-century Americans facing new threats to their security.

*Counter Intelligence* (1996) by
Mark Kostabi. Oil on canvas
(84″ × 132″).

© Mark Kostabi.

# The Promise and Peril of Technology

In some ways, science and technology have fulfilled their promise.
They have increased the life spans of many people and have better
fed and housed many. They have moved us faster from place to
place—even allowing a few of us to stroll on the surface of the
moon.

Large segments of our society still live in poverty, however. Computer technology has made many jobs obsolete, especially in the

TGV Atlantique, a French high-speed train, seats 485 passengers and travels at 188 mph (1993).

manufacturing sector, even though it has opened up employment in the white-collar and service sectors. The era of the computer chip has also threatened Ralph Waldo Emerson's ideal of the rugged individual. Many Americans feel that they have become anonymous consumers, known only by a computer password or credit card number. They worry, too, that their privacy is unprotected and that their thoughts and even their dreams are being shaped by mass advertising, mass journalism, and mass entertainment.

# Contemporary Fiction: Diversity and Vitality

One of the words most commonly used to describe contemporary American culture is ***postmodern,*** a term that, like our age, is still in the process of being defined. Postmodernism sees contemporary culture as a change—a development or a departure—from modernism, the dominant movement in the arts from about 1890 to 1945. In literature the great American modernists—notably Ezra Pound, T. S. Eliot, William Carlos Williams, Marianne Moore, Wallace Stevens, Katherine Anne Porter, William Faulkner, and Ernest Hemingway—forged new styles and new forms with which to express the sensibility of the early twentieth century. Postmodern writers build with many of the tools the modernists provided, but they are constructing a body of literature that is strikingly different from that produced by the modernists.

## ■ Perspectives in Postmodern Fiction

Postmodern writers of fiction allow for multiple meanings and multiple worlds in their works. Realistic and literal worlds, past worlds, and dreamlike metaphorical worlds may merge, as they do in Toni Morrison's novel *Beloved.* Narrators and characters may tell different versions of a story, or a story may deliberately accommodate several valid interpretations. The postmodernist asks, "Why choose only one version? Why limit ourselves?"

Writers of our time often structure their works in a variety of nontraditional forms. They do not abide by conventional rules for shaping fiction. Donald Barthelme's story "Sentence," for example, is a nine-page tale that consists entirely of one sentence. In Walter Abish's novel *Alphabetical Africa* (1974) every word in the first chapter begins with the letter *a,* every word in the second chapter begins with *a* or *b,* and so on through the alphabet to *z* and then, in reverse, all the way back to *a.*

Some postmodern works are also intensely self-conscious: They comment on themselves, criticize themselves, take themselves apart, and encourage us to put them together again. In his novel *Operation Shylock* (1993), the author Philip Roth meets a character named Philip Roth and wonders which one of them is real. In other words, postmodern literature is aware of itself as literature and encourages the reader's self-awareness as well. (An example of a self-conscious postmodern point of view in a nonfiction title is Dave Eggers's *A Heartbreaking Work of Staggering Genius.*)

The vitality of contemporary fiction lies in its cultural diversity, in its enthusiasm for blending fiction with nonfiction, and in its extraordinary sense of play. It also demonstrates a typically American ability to invigorate the old by means of the new.

Václav Havel, president of the Czech Republic, said this about

> *The past is not a terrible burden to be sustained but a box of images to be resorted to for pleasure.*
>
> —Denis Donoghue

postmodernism at Independence Hall on July 4, 1994, after receiving the Philadelphia Liberty Medal:

> ❝There are good reasons for suggesting that the modern age has ended. Many things indicate that we are going through a transitional period, when it seems that something is on the way out and something else is painfully being born. It is as if something were crumbling, decaying, and exhausting itself, while something else, still indistinct, were arising from the rubble.
>
> The distinguishing features of transitional periods are a mixing and blending of cultures and plurality or parallelism of intellectual and spiritual worlds. These are periods when all consistent value systems collapse, when cultures distant in time and space are discovered or rediscovered. New meaning is gradually born from the encounter, or the intersection, of many different elements.
>
> Today, this state of mind, or of the human world, is called postmodernism.❞

## Characteristics of Postmodern Literature

- Allows for multiple meanings and multiple worlds
- Structures works in nontraditional forms
- Comments on itself
- Can be intensely personal
- Features cultural diversity
- Blends fiction and nonfiction
- Uses the past fearlessly

Student with poster of Václav Havel, celebrating the arrival of democracy in Czechoslovakia (1989).

# Contemporary Nonfiction: Breaking the Barriers

Until fairly recently *nonfiction* meant whatever was *not* fiction—suggesting that nonfiction was not a literary form and not art. Nonfiction writers were lumped together with journalists, who in turn were defined as nonliterary folk whose work was quickly written, read, and discarded. Critics tended to concentrate on the search for the elusive Great American Novel, which was thought to be more important than anything a nonfiction writer could produce.

Since the 1970s, however, nonfiction has come into its own. Featured reviews now discuss the art (not just the factual content) of books on computers, architecture, travel, history, film, and other subjects. Lists of bestsellers, which have always included self-help books, cookbooks, and exercise manuals, now regularly feature memoirs, biographies, and histories as well.

## ■ Does It Have to Be Accurate?

Critics, however, are still uncertain about the terminology we should apply to nonfiction. For instance, when discussing fiction, we can talk about point of view, character, plot, theme, and setting; in discussing more complex fiction, we can analyze irony, metaphors, symbols, and levels of meaning. These traditional literary terms don't always apply to nonfiction, however.

More troubling is the problem of accuracy. Truth or accuracy is often a test applied to nonfiction, with frequently unsatisfactory results. For example, a class read Peter Matthiessen's *The Snow Leopard* (1978), a travel memoir about wildlife

Peter Matthiessen.

in the Himalayas and the writer's search for the meaning of life. The class praised the book for its penetrating observations, philosophical depth, and narrative technique. Students were then asked whether they would like it just as much if they learned that it was fiction, that Matthiessen had done extensive research in a library but had never gone to the Himalayas at all. (This, of course, is *not* the case.) No, many students said; they would not like the book as well. It would no longer be true. Wasn't truth what distinguished nonfiction from fiction?

### ■ The New Journalism

This question was often raised in the 1960s, when the new journalism (also called literary journalism) began to appear. Truman Capote, Tom Wolfe, Joan Didion, Norman Mailer, and others attracted attention by describing contemporary culture and actual events in strongly individual voices. They used many of the devices of fiction, including complex characterization, plot, suspense, setting, symbolism, and irony.

A new journalist did not feel obliged to keep his or her opinion and presence out of the writing; in fact, presence and participation were often crucial. Joan Didion bought a dress for a defendant in a trial she was covering as a journalist. Truman Capote befriended the murderers he was writing about in *In Cold Blood,* which he called a nonfiction novel—a perfect example of the overlapping of genres. Readers wanted to know just what the writer was thinking or feeling about the subject, and so the tone of a book became nearly as important as its facts.

If facts alone do not distinguish nonfiction from fiction, what does? No one is sure. What readers *are* sure about is their interest in nonfiction that uses the traditional attractions of accomplished fiction: characters to care about, suspense, and compelling use of language. Many readers, eager for literature that will illuminate their lives, enrich their knowledge, and entertain them, have become as willing to turn to nonfiction as to fiction.

Joan Didion visiting the closed Alcatraz Prison (1967).

## Contemporary Poetry: Varied and Intensely Personal

In recent years more Americans have been writing poetry than ever before. It is a special challenge to determine which poets and movements will last.

### ■ The Decline of Modernism

There are a number of clear, significant differences between American poetry written before World War II and poetry written in the decades since. The twenty years between the two world wars marked the flowering and near monopoly of modernist poetry. That was the kind of poetry defined by and large by the theories and practices of T. S. Eliot, Ezra Pound, and, somewhat later, W. H. Auden.

In 1917, Eliot had called for an impersonal, objective poetry that was not concerned with the subjective emotions of the poet. The poem, said Eliot, should be impersonal, allusive (it should make references, or allusions, to other works), and intellectually challenging.

Modernist writers followed Pound's insistence that the image was all-important and that any unnecessary words should be omitted; but in doing this, they often eliminated material that could have made their poetry more understandable to more people.

By the early 1950s, there was a growing sense that modernism was somehow played out, that it was no longer appropriate for the times. The era itself may have had something to do with the shift away from modernism. A generation had returned from war to a country where conformity and material success were the main values. The Soviet Union and the atomic bomb worried Americans in the late 1940s and early 1950s, but acquiring a house and a car and making money were generally of more immediate importance. "These are the tranquilized *Fifties,*" Robert Lowell wrote in a poem toward the end of that decade, as he ironically described the conformity he saw around him:

> I hog a whole house on Boston's
> "hardly passionate Marlborough Street,"
> where even the man
> scavenging filth in the back alley trash cans,
> has two children, a beach wagon, a helpmate,
> and is a "young Republican."
>
> —Robert Lowell,
>     from "Memories of West Street and Lepke"

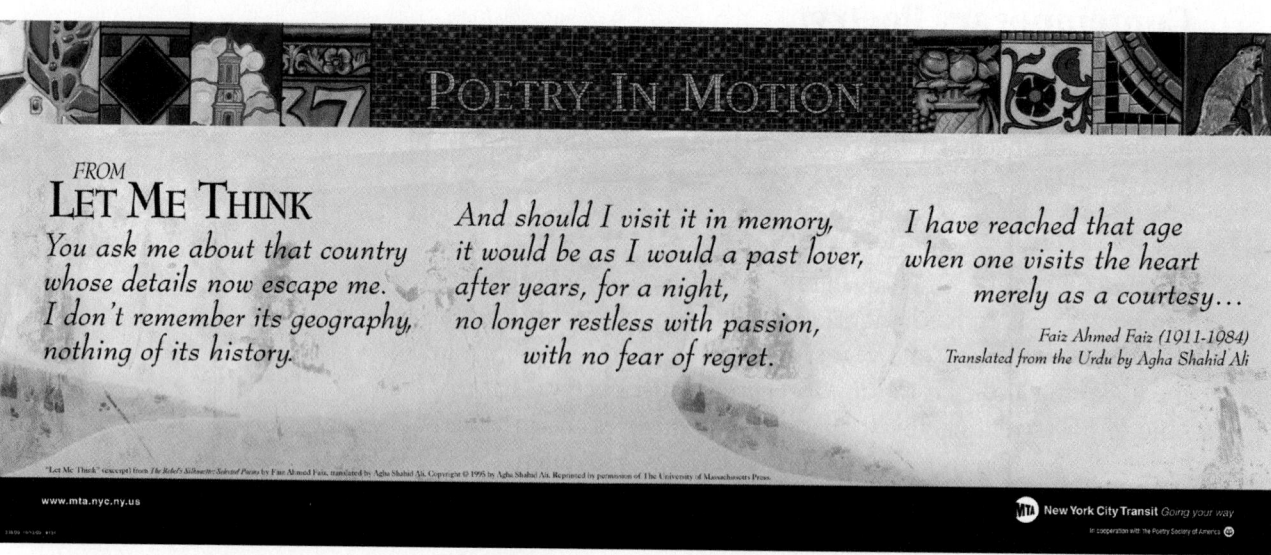

**POETRY IN MOTION**

*FROM*
## LET ME THINK

*You ask me about that country whose details now escape me. I don't remember its geography, nothing of its history.*

*And should I visit it in memory, it would be as I would a past lover, after years, for a night, no longer restless with passion, with no fear of regret.*

*I have reached that age when one visits the heart merely as a courtesy...*

*Faiz Ahmed Faiz (1911-1984)*
*Translated from the Urdu by Agha Shahid Ali*

"Let Me Think" (excerpt) from *The Rebel's Silhouette: Selected Poems* by Faiz Ahmed Faiz, translated by Agha Shahid Ali. Copyright © 1995 by Agha Shahid Ali. Reprinted by permission of The University of Massachusetts Press.

www.mta.nyc.ny.us

**New York City Transit** *Going your way*
In cooperation with The Poetry Society of America

Courtesy Metropolitan Transportation Authority/New York City Transit Authority in cooperation with Poetry Society of America. Copyright © 1991 by University of Massachusetts Press.

## ■ The Beat Poets

In 1956, a long poem called *Howl* was published by Allen Ginsberg, a writer who could by no stretch of the imagination be described as dull. A cry of outrage against the conformity of the 1950s, *Howl* was far removed from the safe confines of modernism. *Howl* begins, "I saw the best minds of my generation destroyed by madness, starving hysterical naked," and it continues at the same intense pitch for hundreds of lines.

Beatnik poet reading to the accompaniment of a musician in New York's Greenwich Village (1959).

Together with *On the Road* (1957), Jack Kerouac's novel celebrating the bohemian life, *Howl* quickly became a kind of bible for the young nonconformists who made up what became known as the beat generation. Beat poetry and the beat lifestyle—marked by poetry readings, jazz performances, and the appearance of late-night coffeehouses in San Francisco and New York's Greenwich Village—had an immediate impact on American popular culture.

*Howl* provided the first clear alternative to poetry that seemed to be written for analysis in the classroom. *Howl* addressed the concerns of contemporary life. Many of Ginsberg's concerns—the injustices of modern life, the importance of the imagination—would become the principal themes of the next decade's poetry.

## ■ Poetry and Personal Experience

In 1959, Robert Lowell published *Life Studies,* one of the most important and influential volumes of verse to appear since World War II. These poems are about personal experiences that modernist poets had avoided dealing with directly: emotional distress, alcoholism, illness, and depression. In *Life Studies,* Lowell clearly and decisively broke with Eliot's theory that poetry should be impersonal. In doing so, he helped to reunite, for himself and for other writers, "the man who suffers and the mind which creates."

Shortly after *Life Studies* appeared, a critic described Lowell's poems as "confessional." The label stuck, and the **confessional school** of poets, mostly friends or students of Lowell's, was officially born. Those poets—including Sylvia Plath, Anne Sexton, and John Berryman—wrote frank, sometimes brutal poems about their private lives.

Poetry reading at Nuyorican Poets Café in New York City (1995).

## Social Influences

- The counterculture movement of the late 1960s rejects conformity in politics and art in favor of dissent and experimentation.

- During the first part of the twenty-first century, continuing technological advancements and faster Internet services make possible unprecedented access to information and new ways to communicate using computers, cell phones, and hand-held wireless devices.

## ■ History of the Human Heart

Today American poetry is characterized by diversity. The extraordinary variety in style and attitude has attracted large new audiences. Poetry performances have sprung up throughout America, with live poetry slams at such places as the Nuyorican Poets Café in New York City. Technology has made available thousands of readings on audiotape and videotape, and television broadcasts and numerous Web sites are devoted to poetry.

Much contemporary poetry reflects a democratic quality, often influenced by the works of Walt Whitman and William Carlos Williams. Poetry lives in the people, contemporary poets seem to say, and any walk of life, any experience, any style of expression can result in authentic poetry. Contemporary poets often write in the language of common speech, and they do not hesitate to surprise or even shock with their language, their attitudes, and the details of their private lives. Poetry today is anything but impersonal.

Will today's poetry reach audiences a hundred years from now? The answer by the poet laureate Billy Collins suggests that it will: "It's the only history of the human heart we have," he says.

## Where the Present Meets the Past on the Way to the Future

The literature that captures a wide audience often does so by offering a fresh voice and a new attitude, for those are the powerful needs of each new generation. Yet much of contemporary American literature deals with the same themes that concerned our greatest writers of the nineteenth century: Poe, Hawthorne, Whitman, Dickinson, Melville, Emerson, and Thoreau. The characters created by the novelist John Updike, for example, seek spiritual revelations in ordinary life. "The invariable mark of wisdom," Emerson wrote, "is to find the miraculous in the common." It is more difficult, however, to find transcendent spiritual values in the cheap clutter of modern life than it was in the woods around Emerson's Concord. Still, Updike's characters continue the search. "I find myself . . . circling back to man's religious nature," Updike has written of his own work, "and the real loss to man and art alike when that nature has nowhere to plug itself in." Those words could serve to describe the work of a great number of contemporary writers whose intellectual roots can be traced to the Transcendentalists of the nineteenth century and perhaps even further back, to those hardy, practical Puritans who braved the two-month voyage across the Atlantic in small wooden ships.

> *Everything is connected in the end.*
>
> —Don DeLillo, from *Underworld*

## REVIEW

# Talk About . . .

Turn back to the Think About questions at the start of this essay (page 892), and discuss your views.

# Write About . . .

### Contrasting Literary Periods

**Today versus the past.** On page 899, Václav Havel says that he thinks we are in an age of transition, that something is on the way out and something new is being born. In a paragraph, explain your response to Havel's comment. From what you know of the past, tell what you think is on the way out. From what you know of the present, tell what you think might be on the way in. Try to focus on the old and the new in terms of things like books, dance, music, values, dress.

Collection 6:
Contemporary Literature

# Comparing Points of View:

# World War II

**Jarrell**
**Wiesel**
**Hersey**
**Jackson**
**Frank**
**Whitehead**
**Bourke-White**

I hate war as only a soldier who has lived it can, only as one who has seen its brutality, its futility, its stupidity.

—Gen. Dwight D. Eisenhower

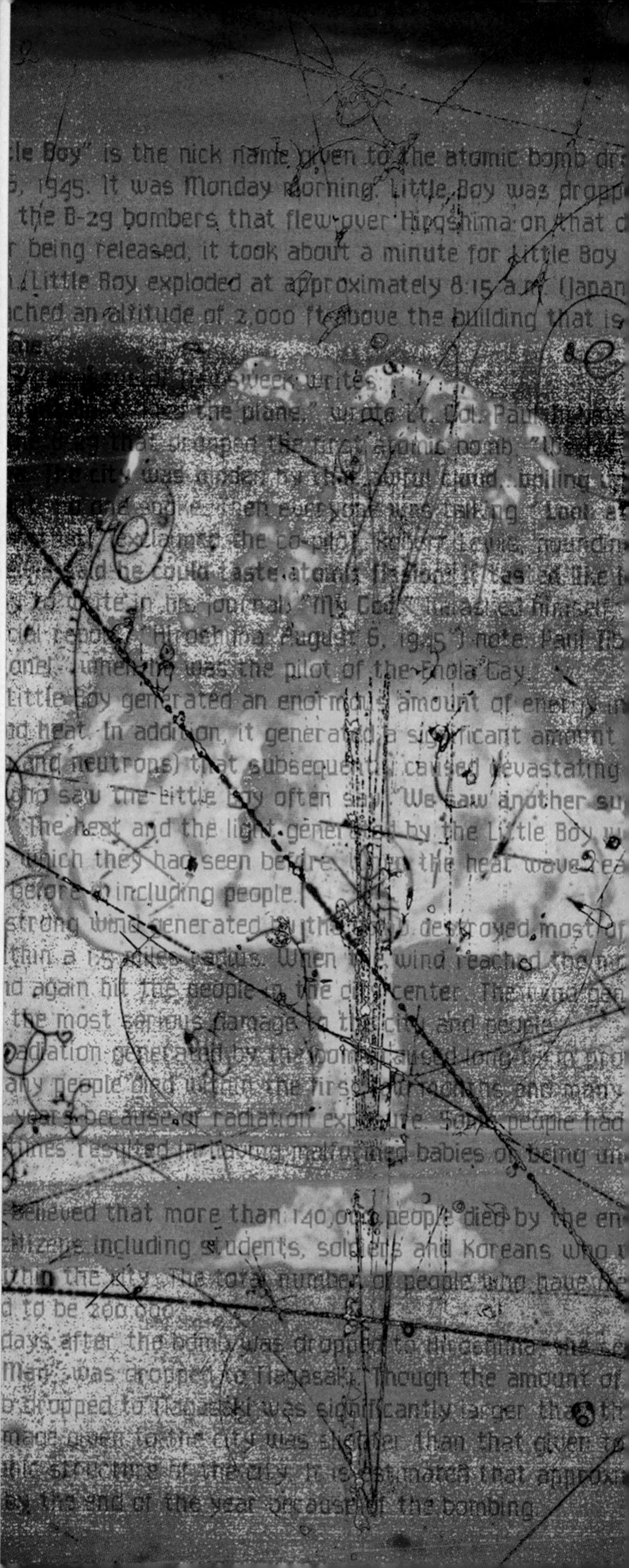

# Introduction Comparing Points *of* View

## World War II

### Main Readings



### Connected Readings



The seven selections listed above are included in this Comparing Points of View feature on World War II. In the top corner of the pages in this feature, you'll find three stars. Smaller versions of the stars appear next to the questions on pages 911, 923, 924, 939, and 948 that focus on World War II. At the end of the feature (page 958), you'll compare the various points of view expressed in these selections—points of view about war, about responsibility, about the effects of evil, about the impulse toward good.

### Examining the Issue: World War II

The twentieth century might become known as the Century of War. Only twenty-one years after the end of the so-called Great War, the world was plunged into another horror. World War II began on a September morning in 1939 when an enormous German army invaded Poland.

On December 7, 1941, Japanese forces bombed America's Pacific fleet as it lay at anchor in Pearl Harbor in the Hawaiian Islands. The next day the United States declared war on Japan. By December 11, the United States was also at war in Europe.

The war in Europe ended with the fall of Berlin and the surrender of Germany on May 8, 1945. The Japanese emperor surrendered on August 14, 1945, but only after the Japanese cities of Hiroshima and Nagasaki were devastated by atomic bombs.

(Opposite) *Nuclear Holocaust* by J. B. Weekes. Digital composite.

**SKILLS FOCUS**

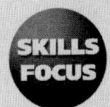

Pages 907–959 cover
**Literary Skills** Analyze points of view on a topic.

**Reading Skills** Evaluate credibility.

The exact number of casualties of World War II is not known. It is estimated that Russia alone lost about eighteen million people in the war. When Gen. Dwight D. Eisenhower and the U.S. military entered Germany after its surrender, they found the concentration camps abandoned by the Nazis. Millions of Jews and members of other persecuted groups had perished in those camps.

## Reading Skills
### Evaluating Credibility

When you read about historical events, it is important to evaluate the credibility of your sources. There are two types of sources. **Primary sources** are firsthand, original accounts, such as interviews, autobiographies, letters, diaries, memoirs, and newsreels. Primary sources provide reliable eyewitness information. **Secondary sources** are materials like newspaper articles, biographies, history books, and encyclopedia articles. The credibility of secondary sources depends on their authorship and on the dates they were written. In other words, you want reliable and up-to-date secondary sources.

U.S. warships on fire in Pearl Harbor after a surprise Japanese attack (December 7, 1941).

Prisoners in the concentration camp at Dachau, Germany, cheering their liberators, the U.S. Army (May 1945).

# Randall Jarrell
## (1914–1965)

**O**ne of the most careful and learned readers of contemporary poetry, Randall Jarrell was, at the same time, both an abrasive critic and a generous promoter of the art of poetry.

Born in Nashville, Tennessee, Jarrell was brought up in California. His childhood experiences included close observation of the gaudy remnants of the old Hollywood, a personal acquaintance with the MGM lion, and an appreciation of the difference between fantasy and fact—between life and myths about life—that would provide him with themes for poetry for years to come.

After graduating from Vanderbilt University in his native city, Jarrell began a career that led to positions in the English departments of many colleges and universities from Texas to New York. In 1942, he joined the Army Air Corps and served for a time as a pilot and then, for a longer time, as celestial navigation trainer of pilots assigned to fly the famous B-29 bombers of World War II. Out of this experience came two notable books of poetry, *Little Friend, Little Friend* (1945) and *Losses* (1948). Many critics say these books rank among the best American contributions to the literature of World War II.

A man of extraordinary wit, Jarrell gave full play to his gifts in his often caustic and devastating critical articles and essays, particularly in the collection *A Sad Heart at the Supermarket* (1962). In poetry, however, his faculty for contemptuous criticism is kept under wraps: His wit shows itself only in mellow good humor ("I feel like the first men who read Wordsworth. / It's so simple I can't understand it") and in a resigned toleration of the more absurd aspects of American life.

Jarrell died when struck by a car while walking on a North Carolina highway in 1965. His tragic death raised a question: Was it actually a suicide? But of the loss to American letters and to the poets who had counted upon him to explain, judge, and celebrate their art there was no question at all.

### Points of View

**Quickwrite** ✏️

These five lines, written in 1945, make up the most famous poem to come out of World War II. Before you read, write your thoughts on these questions: What attitude toward war do you expect to find in a poem written in 1945? What attitude toward war do you find in most literature and films about war produced today?

### Literary Focus
**Implied Metaphor**

**SKILLS FOCUS**

**Literary Skills**
Analyze points of view on a topic. Understand implied metaphor.

Some metaphors are directly stated. Emily Dickinson uses a direct metaphor when she says, "Hope is the thing with feathers." Other metaphors are implied; that is, they are not directly stated. We recognize an **implied metaphor** from the language the writer uses. If Dickinson had written, "Hope nests in my soul and warms me with its feathers," she would have used an implied metaphor. The words *nest* and *feathers* provide clues that the poet is comparing hope to a bird. What metaphor is implied in this poem by Jarrell?

> An **implied metaphor** is a comparison between two unlike things that is implied, or suggested, but not directly stated.
>
> *For more on Metaphor, see the Handbook of Literary and Historical Terms.*

# The Death of the Ball Turret Gunner

## Randall Jarrell

From my mother's sleep I fell into the State,
And I hunched in its belly till my wet fur froze.
Six miles from earth, loosed from its dream of life,
I woke to black flak and the nightmare fighters.
When I died they washed me out of the turret with a hose.

A Czech fighter pilot in England (1940).

# The Ball Turret

**A** ball turret was a plexi-
glass sphere set into the
belly of a B-17 or B-24, and
inhabited by two .50 caliber
machine guns and one man,
a short, small man. When this gunner
tracked with his machine guns a fighter
attacking his bomber from below, he
revolved with the turret; hunched upside down in his little sphere, he
looked like the fetus in the womb. The fighters which attacked him were
armed with cannon firing explosive shells. The hose was a steam hose.

—Randall Jarrell

# Response and Analysis

## Thinking Critically

1. Who is speaking in this poem?

2. What is the temperature like in the ball turret?

3. What happens to the speaker?

4. How do you know that the speaker didn't enter the army on the basis of a rational decision?

5. "Belly" in line 2 of the poem can be read on two levels. What is the literal meaning? What is the **metaphoric** meaning?

6. What is the speaker's "wet fur"? Why do you think he compares himself to an animal?

7. Explain the **implied metaphor** in the poem. (In other words, what is the ball turret gunner compared to?) What specific words develop the metaphor?

8. What details in Jarrell's explanation of the ball turret (see the **Primary Source** above) add levels of meaning to his poem?

9. How would you describe the emotional effect of Randall's metaphor?

10. What is this poem really about? What statement about war is made in only five lines? Explain your views, and provide details from the text to support them.

## Extending and Evaluating

11. Review your Quickwrite notes. How well did you predict Jarrell's attitude toward war? Did you find his attitude old-fashioned or surprisingly contemporary? Explain.

**SKILLS FOCUS**

**Literary Skills**
Analyze points of view on a topic. Analyze implied metaphor.

# Elie Wiesel
## (1928–        )

In March of 1944, when Elie Wiesel (el'ē vē·zel') was fifteen, his life changed forever. At the time, Wiesel was living in the little town where he was born—Sighet, a remote village in the Carpathian Mountains of Hungary (now Romania). Raised in the Jewish mystical tradition of Hasidism, Wiesel had spent his childhood years immersed in the heritage of his extended family and in intense religious study. But in March 1944, the German army invaded Hungary. Soon Wiesel, his family, and some fifteen thousand other Jews from his region were rounded up and deported to extermination camps in Nazi-occupied Poland.

What Wiesel experienced in the camps was an unremitting horror. He saw his mother and youngest sister sent to die in a gas chamber, he saw his father succumb to dysentery and senseless violence, and he saw great numbers of fellow prisoners, many of them children, tortured and murdered by the Nazis.

After Wiesel was liberated from Buchenwald concentration camp in April 1945, he could not bring himself to write of the Holocaust for a decade, for fear "that words might betray it." Yet he also remembered the promise he had made to himself: "If, by some miracle, I survive, I will devote my life to testifying on behalf of all those whose shadows will be bound to mine forever." The result of this promise was *Night,* Wiesel's devastating memoir of his experiences under the Nazi terror, originally published in Yiddish as *Un di velt hot geshvign* (*And the World Kept Silent*) in 1956. In the same year he came to the United States to cover the United Nations as a reporter. He became a U.S. citizen in 1963 and is now a professor at Boston University.

For over four decades, Wiesel has continued to be a powerful advocate for human dignity—as a novelist, dramatist, journalist, religious scholar, and international activist. Seeking to maintain global awareness of the Nazi atrocities and to prevent similar crimes against humanity, he has spoken out against human-rights abuses in Cambodia, the former Soviet Union, Bosnia and Herzegovina, and South Africa under the apartheid regime. Such work earned Wiesel a Nobel Peace Prize in 1986. In his acceptance speech he reflected on his past and his purpose in life.

"This is what I say to the young Jewish boy wondering what I have done with his years. It is in his name that I speak to you and that I express to you my deepest gratitude. No one is as capable of gratitude as one who has emerged from the Kingdom of Night. We know that every moment is a moment of grace, every hour an offering; not to share them would mean to betray them. Our lives no longer belong to us alone; they belong to all those who need us desperately."

# Before You Read

## *from* Night

### Points *of* View

Wiesel's memoir takes us inside the Nazi concentration camps of World War II. Part of Wiesel's power as a writer is his ability to make us feel enormous empathy and deep fear. When a writer fulfills his responsibility as a witness, what is your responsibility as a reader?

### Reading Skills
#### Analyzing a Writer's Message

Wiesel's *Night* is a **memoir,** which means it is a true account of a personal experience. Wiesel is a moralist, yet he does not directly state any message to us in this part of his memoir. Instead, he allows the horror of the experience and the responses of different people to their suffering to speak for themselves. As you read, think about what Wiesel's writing reveals about the power of faith, the power of evil, the power of art. What implicit philosophical beliefs underlie Wiesel's message?

### Background

World War II forced people to face not only battlefield atrocities but also the grim reality that an industrialized, civilized society was capable of profound evil. The Nazis of Germany deliberately tortured, starved, and murdered millions who posed no military threat. In the Holocaust, or Shoah, the Nazis and their collaborators made a systematic attempt to implement a "Final Solution" that would destroy all the Jews of Europe. By the end of the war in 1945, the Nazis had killed more than six million Jews. They had also killed five million other civilians whom they deemed undesirable—Romany (Gypsies), homosexuals, and "non-Aryans"—as well as political opponents and resistance fighters.

On the following pages you will find three excerpts from Wiesel's memoir about his personal experience of the Holocaust. The events described in the first excerpt occurred on a train headed for Auschwitz (ͻush′vits′), the most notorious Nazi concentration camp. Wiesel, who was fifteen at the time, and his family had been forced into a railroad car with eighty other Hungarian Jews.

---

## Vocabulary Development

**abyss** (ə·bis′) *n.:* bottomless gulf or void.

**pestilential** (pes′tə·len′shəl) *adj.:* dangerous and harmful, like a deadly infection.

**abominable** (ə·bäm′ə·nə·bəl) *adj.:* nasty and disgusting.

**encumbrance** (en·kum′brəns) *n.:* hindrance; burden.

**semblance** (sem′bləns) *n.:* appearance; likeness.

**conscientiously** (kän′shē·en′shəs·lē) *adv.:* carefully; painstakingly; thoroughly.

**apathy** (ap′ə·thē) *n.:* indifference; lack of emotion.

---

**Literary Skills**
Analyze points of view on a topic.

**Reading Skills**
Understand a writer's message.

**INTERNET**

Vocabulary Practice

Keyword: LE7 11-6

---

Elie Wiesel    **913**

# *from* Night

## Elie Wiesel

*translated by* **Stella Rodway**

Identity card and yellow star for a Jew living in Amsterdam in 1943.

The train stopped at Kaschau,[1] a little town on the Czechoslovak frontier. We realized then that we were not going to stay in Hungary. Our eyes were opened, but too late.

The door of the car slid open. A German officer, accompanied by a Hungarian lieutenant-interpreter, came up and introduced himself.

"From this moment, you come under the authority of the German army. Those of you who still have gold, silver, or watches in your possession must give them up now. Anyone who is later found to have kept anything will be shot on the spot. Secondly, anyone who feels ill may go to the hospital car. That's all."

The Hungarian lieutenant went among us with a basket and collected the last possessions from those who no longer wished to taste the bitterness of terror.

"There are eighty of you in this wagon," added the German officer. "If anyone is missing, you'll all be shot, like dogs. . . ."

They disappeared. The doors were closed. We were caught in a trap, right up to our necks. The doors were nailed up; the way back was finally cut off. The world was a cattle wagon hermetically sealed.[2]

We had a woman with us named Madame Schächter.[3] She was about fifty; her ten-year-old son was with her, crouched in a corner. Her husband and two eldest sons had been deported with the first transport by mistake. The separation had completely broken her.

I knew her well. A quiet woman with tense, burning eyes, she had often been to our house. Her husband, who was a pious man, spent his days and nights in study, and it was she who worked to support the family.

Madame Schächter had gone out of her mind. On the first day of the journey she had already begun to moan and to keep asking why she had been separated from her family. As time went on, her cries grew hysterical.

On the third night, while we slept, some of us sitting one against the other and some standing, a piercing cry split the silence:

"Fire! I can see a fire! I can see a fire!"

There was a moment's panic. Who was it who had cried out? It was Madame Schächter. Standing in the middle of the wagon, in the pale light from the windows, she looked like a withered tree in a cornfield. She pointed her arm toward the window, screaming:

"Look! Look at it! Fire! A terrible fire! Mercy! *Oh, that fire!*"

Some of the men pressed up against the bars. There was nothing there; only the darkness.

The shock of this terrible awakening stayed with us for a long time. We still trembled from it. With every groan of the wheels on the rail, we felt that an abyss was about to open beneath our bodies. Powerless to still our own anguish, we tried to console ourselves:

"She's mad, poor soul. . . ."

Someone had put a damp cloth on her brow, to calm her, but still her screams went on:

"Fire! Fire!"

---

1. **Kaschau** (kä′shou′); also called Košice (kô′shē·tse).
2. **hermetically** (hər·met′ik·lē) **sealed:** airtight.
3. **Schächter** (shekh′tər).

---

**Vocabulary**

**abyss** (ə·bis′) *n.*: bottomless gulf or void.

Arriving at Auschwitz from Hungary (spring 1944).

Her little boy was crying, hanging onto her skirt, trying to take hold of her hands. "It's all right, Mummy! There's nothing there. . . . Sit down. . . ." This shook me even more than his mother's screams had done.

Some women tried to calm her. "You'll find your husband and your sons again . . . in a few days. . . ."

She continued to scream, breathless, her voice broken by sobs. "Jews, listen to me! I can see a fire! There are huge flames! It is a furnace!"

It was as though she were possessed by an evil spirit which spoke from the depths of her being.

We tried to explain it away, more to calm ourselves and to recover our own breath than to comfort her. "She must be very thirsty, poor thing! That's why she keeps talking about a fire devouring her."

But it was in vain. Our terror was about to burst the sides of the train. Our nerves were at breaking point. Our flesh was creeping. It was as though madness were taking possession of us all. We could stand it no longer. Some of the young men forced her to sit down, tied her up, and put a gag in her mouth.

Silence again. The little boy sat down by his mother, crying. I had begun to breathe normally again. We could hear the wheels churning out that monotonous rhythm of a train traveling through the night. We could begin to doze, to rest, to dream. . . .

An hour or two went by like this. Then another scream took our breath away. The woman had broken loose from her bonds and was crying out more loudly than ever:

"Look at the fire! Flames, flames everywhere. . . ."

Once more the young men tied her up and gagged her. They even struck her. People encouraged them:

"Make her be quiet! She's mad! Shut her up! She's not the only one. She can keep her mouth shut. . . ."

They struck her several times on the head—blows that might have killed her. Her little boy clung to her; he did not cry out; he did not say a word. He was not even weeping now.

An endless night. Toward dawn, Madame Schächter calmed down. Crouched in her corner, her bewildered gaze scouring[4] the emptiness, she could no longer see us.

She stayed like that all through the day, dumb, absent, isolated among us. As soon as night fell, she began to scream: "There's a fire over there!" She would point at a spot in space, always the same one. They were tired of hitting her. The heat, the thirst, the pestilential stench, the suffocating lack of air—these were as nothing compared with these screams which tore us to shreds. A few days more and we should all have started to scream too.

But we had reached a station. Those who were next to the windows told us its name:

"Auschwitz."

No one had ever heard that name.

The train did not start up again. The afternoon passed slowly. Then the wagon doors slid

---

4. **scouring** v. used as *adj.*: roaming about; searching.

**Vocabulary**

**pestilential** (pes'tə·len'shəl) *adj.*: dangerous and harmful, like a deadly infection.

Elie Wiesel    **915**

open. Two men were allowed to get down to fetch water.

When they came back, they told us that, in exchange for a gold watch, they had discovered that this was the last stop. We would be getting out here. There was a labor camp. Conditions were good. Families would not be split up. Only the young people would go to work in the factories. The old men and invalids would be kept occupied in the fields.

The barometer of confidence soared. Here was a sudden release from the terrors of the previous nights. We gave thanks to God.

Madame Schächter stayed in her corner, wilted, dumb, indifferent to the general confidence. Her little boy stroked her hand.

As dusk fell, darkness gathered inside the wagon. We started to eat our last provisions. At ten in the evening, everyone was looking for a convenient position in which to sleep for a while, and soon we were all asleep. Suddenly:

"The fire! The furnace! Look, over there! . . ."

Waking with a start, we rushed to the window. Yet again we had believed her, even if only for a moment. But there was nothing outside save the darkness of night. With shame in our souls, we went back to our places, gnawed by fear, in spite of ourselves. As she continued to scream, they began to hit her again, and it was with the greatest difficulty that they silenced her.

The man in charge of our wagon called a German officer who was walking about on the platform, and asked him if Madame Schächter could be taken to the hospital car.

"You must be patient," the German replied. "She'll be taken there soon."

Toward eleven o'clock, the train began to move. We pressed against the windows. The convoy was moving slowly. A quarter of an hour later, it slowed down again. Through the windows we could see barbed wire; we realized that this must be the camp.

We had forgotten the existence of Madame Schächter. Suddenly, we heard terrible screams:

"Jews, look! Look through the window! Flames! Look!"

And as the train stopped, we saw this time that flames were gushing out of a tall chimney into the black sky.

Madame Schächter was silent herself. Once more she had become dumb, indifferent, absent, and had gone back to her corner.

We looked at the flames in the darkness. There was an <u>abominable</u> odor floating in the air. Suddenly, our doors opened. Some odd-looking characters, dressed in striped shirts and black trousers, leapt into the wagon. They held electric torches[5] and truncheons.[6] They began to strike out to right and left, shouting:

"Everybody get out! Everyone out of the wagon! Quickly!"

We jumped out. I threw a last glance toward Madame Schächter. Her little boy was holding her hand.

In front of us flames. In the air that smell of burning flesh. It must have been about midnight. We had arrived—at Birkenau,[7] reception center for Auschwitz. . . .

---

*The following section of* Night *takes place in Buna* (bōō′nə), *another camp in Poland, where Wiesel and his father were sent from Auschwitz. It documents the horrifying process of selection, in which the Nazis separated those prisoners judged fit to perform slave labor from those who were to be killed immediately. It was after such a selection that Wiesel's mother and sister were murdered in the Auschwitz gas chamber.*

---

The head of our block had never been outside concentration camps since 1933. He had already been through all the slaughterhouses, all the

---

5. **electric torches:** flashlights.
6. **truncheons** (trun′chənz) *n. pl.:* short, thick clubs.
7. **Birkenau** (bir′kə·nou).

**Vocabulary**
**abominable** (ə·bäm′ə·nə·bəl) *adj.:* nasty and disgusting.

factories of death. At about nine o'clock, he took up his position in our midst:

"Achtung!"[8]

There was instant silence.

"Listen carefully to what I am going to say." (For the first time, I heard his voice quiver.) "In a few moments the selection will begin. You must get completely undressed. Then one by one you go before the SS[9] doctors. I hope you will all succeed in getting through. But you must help your own chances. Before you go into the next room, move about in some way so that you give yourselves a little color. Don't walk slowly, run! Run as if the devil were after you! Don't look at the SS. Run, straight in front of you!"

He broke off for a moment, then added:

"And, the essential thing, don't be afraid!"

Here was a piece of advice we should have liked very much to be able to follow.

I got undressed, leaving my clothes on the bed. There was no danger of anyone stealing them this evening.

Tibi and Yossi, who had changed their unit at the same time as I had, came up to me and said:

"Let's keep together. We shall be stronger."

Yossi was murmuring something between his teeth. He must have been praying. I had never realized that Yossi was a believer. I had even always thought the reverse. Tibi was silent, very pale. All the prisoners in the block stood naked between the beds. This must be how one stands at the last judgment.

"They're coming!"

There were three SS officers standing round the notorious Dr. Mengele,[10] who had received

us at Birkenau. The head of the block, with an attempt at a smile, asked us:

"Ready?"

Yes, we were ready. So were the SS doctors. Dr. Mengele was holding a list in his hand: our numbers.[11] He made a sign to the head of the block: "We can begin!" As if this were a game!

The first to go by were the "officials" of the block: *Stubenaelteste*,[12] Kapos,[13] foremen, all in perfect physical condition of course! Then came the ordinary prisoners' turn. Dr. Mengele took stock of them from head to foot. Every now and then, he wrote a number down. One single thought filled my mind: not to let my number be taken; not to show my left arm.

There were only Tibi and Yossi in front of me. They passed. I had time to notice that Mengele had not written their numbers down. Someone pushed me. It was my turn. I ran without looking back. My head was spinning: You're too thin, you're weak, you're too thin, you're good for the furnace. . . . The race seemed interminable. I thought I had been running for years. . . . You're too thin, You're too weak. . . . At last I had arrived exhausted. When I regained my breath, I questioned Yossi and Tibi:

"Was I written down?"

"No," said Yossi. He added, smiling: "In any case, he couldn't have written you down, you were running too fast. . . ."

I began to laugh. I was glad. I would have liked to kiss him. At that moment, what did the others matter! I hadn't been written down.

Those whose numbers had been noted stood apart, abandoned by the whole world. Some were weeping in silence. . . .

---

8. **achtung** (äkh′tooŋ): German for "attention."

9. **SS:** Abbreviation for *Schutzstaffel* (shoots′shtə′fəl), German for "protection squad," the elite Nazi guards who oversaw the operation of the concentration camps.

10. **Dr. Mengele:** Josef Mengele (yō′zef′meŋ′ə·lə) (1911–1979) was a Nazi doctor and SS officer infamous for torturing camp prisoners, often children, sometimes in pseudoscientific experiments.

11. **our numbers:** Concentration camp prisoners were identified by a number, which was usually tattooed on the left arm shortly after arrival.

12. *Stubenaelteste* (shtoob′ən·el′təst·ə): German for "barracks leaders" or "room leaders."

13. **Kapos** (kä′pōz): prisoners appointed by the Nazis to head work gangs, often in exchange for better treatment.

Several days had elapsed. We no longer thought about the selection. We went to work as usual, loading heavy stones into railway wagons. Rations had become more meager: This was the only change.

We had risen before dawn, as on every day. We had received the black coffee, the ration of bread. We were about to set out for the yard as usual. The head of the block arrived, running.

"Silence for a moment. I have a list of numbers here. I'm going to read them to you. Those whose numbers I call won't be going to work this morning; they'll stay behind in the camp."

And, in a soft voice, he read out about ten numbers. We had understood. These were numbers chosen at the selection. Dr. Mengele had not forgotten.

The head of the block went toward his room. Ten prisoners surrounded him, hanging onto his clothes:

"Save us! You promised . . . ! We want to go to the yard. We're strong enough to work. We're good workers. We can . . . we will. . . ."

He tried to calm them, to reassure them about their fate, to explain to them that the fact that they were staying behind in the camp did not mean much, had no tragic significance.

"After all, I stay here myself every day," he added.

It was a somewhat feeble argument. He realized it, and without another word went and shut himself up in his room.

The bell had just rung.

"Form up!"

It scarcely mattered now that the work was hard. The essential thing was to be as far away as possible from the block, from the crucible of death, from the center of hell.

I saw my father running toward me. I became frightened all of a sudden.

"What's the matter?"

Out of breath, he could hardly open his mouth.

"Me, too . . . me, too . . . ! They told me to stay behind in the camp."

They had written down his number without his being aware of it.

"What will happen?" I asked in anguish.

But it was he who tried to reassure me.

"It isn't certain yet. There's still a chance of escape. They're going to do another selection today . . . a decisive selection."

I was silent.

He felt that his time was short. He spoke quickly. He would have liked to say so many things. His speech grew confused; his voice choked. He knew that I would have to go in a few moments. He would have to stay behind alone, so very alone.

"Look, take this knife," he said to me. "I don't need it any longer. It might be useful to you. And take this spoon as well. Don't sell them. Quickly! Go on. Take what I'm giving you!"

The inheritance.

"Don't talk like that, Father." (I felt that I would break into sobs.) "I don't want you to say that. Keep the spoon and knife. You need them as much as I do. We shall see each other again this evening, after work."

He looked at me with his tired eyes, veiled with despair. He went on:

"I'm asking this of you. . . . Take them. Do as I ask, my son. We have no time. . . . Do as your father asks."

Our Kapo yelled that we should start.

The unit set out toward the camp gate. Left, right! I bit my lips. My father had stayed by the block, leaning against the wall. Then he began to run, to catch up with us. Perhaps he had forgotten something he wanted to say to me. . . . But we were marching too quickly. . . . Left, right!

We were already at the gate. They counted us, to the din of military music. We were outside.

The whole day, I wandered about as if sleepwalking. Now and then Tibi and Yossi would throw me a brotherly word. The Kapo, too, tried to reassure me. He had given me easier work today. I felt sick at heart. How well they were treating me! Like an orphan! I thought: Even now, my father is still helping me.

I did not know myself what I wanted—for the day to pass quickly or not. I was afraid of finding myself alone that night. How good it would be to die here!

At last we began the return journey. How I longed for orders to run!

The military march. The gate. The camp.

I ran to Block 36.

Were there still miracles on this earth? He was alive. He had escaped the second selection. He had been able to prove that he was still useful. . . . I gave him back his knife and spoon.

Akiba Drumer left us, a victim of the selection. Lately, he had wandered among us, his eyes glazed, telling everyone of his weakness: "I can't go on. . . . It's all over. . . ." It was impossible to raise his morale. He didn't listen to what we told him. He could only repeat that all was over for him, that he could no longer keep up the struggle, that he had no strength left, nor faith. Suddenly his eyes would become blank, nothing but two open wounds, two pits of terror.

He was not the only one to lose his faith during those selection days. I knew a rabbi from a little town in Poland, a bent old man, whose lips were always trembling. He used to pray all the time, in the block, in the yard, in the ranks. He would recite whole pages of the Talmud from memory, argue with himself, ask himself questions and answer himself. And one day he said to me: "It's the end. God is no longer with us."

And, as though he had repented of having spoken such words, so clipped, so cold, he added in his faint voice:

"I know. One has no right to say things like that. I know. Man is too small, too humble and inconsiderable to seek to understand the mysterious ways of God. But what can I do? I'm not a sage, one of the elect, nor a saint. I'm just an ordinary creature of flesh and blood. I've got eyes, too, and I can see what they're doing here. Where is the divine Mercy? Where is God? How

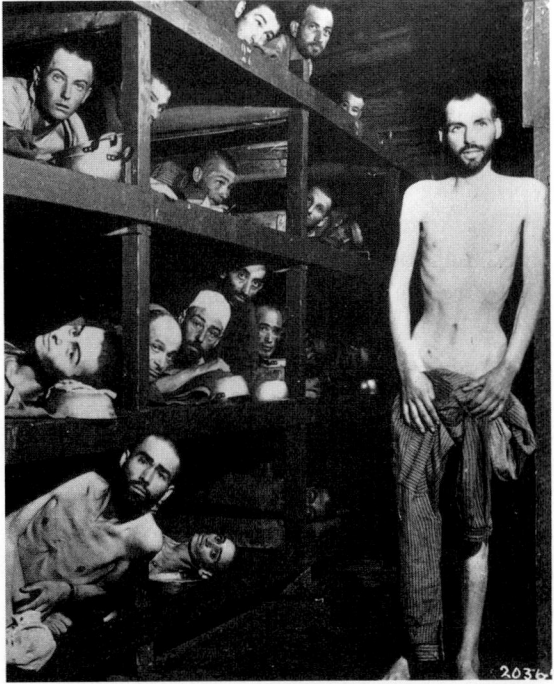

Slave laborers in the barracks of Buchenwald concentration camp (April 16, 1945). Elie Wiesel is the man whose face can be seen on the far right of the center bunk.

can I believe, how could anyone believe, in this merciful God?"

Poor Akiba Drumer, if he could have gone on believing in God, if he could have seen a proof of God in this Calvary,[14] he would not have been taken by the selection. But as soon as he felt the first cracks forming in his faith, he had lost his reason for struggling and had begun to die.

When the selection came, he was condemned in advance, offering his own neck to the executioner. All he asked of us was:

"In three days I shall no longer be here. . . . Say the Kaddish[15] for me."

We promised him. In three days' time, when we saw the smoke rising from the chimney, we

---

14. **Calvary:** Wiesel compares Drumer's tragedy to the crucifixion of Jesus, which took place at the site near Jerusalem called Golgotha, or Calvary.

15. **Kaddish** (käd′ish): Jewish prayer in praise of God, one form of which is recited to mourn a death.

would think of him. Ten of us would gather together and hold a special service. All his friends would say the Kaddish.

Then he went off toward the hospital, his step steadier, not looking back. An ambulance was waiting to take him to Birkenau.

These were terrible days. We received more blows than food; we were crushed with work. And three days after he had gone, we forgot to say the Kaddish. . . .

---

*The next section of* Night *occurs toward the end of Wiesel's eleven months in the concentration camps. It opens during a brutal march toward a new camp, Gleiwitz (glī'vits). The Nazi guards have forced the prisoners to run for miles in the snow without adequate rest or clothing. As a result, hundreds will die before they reach the dangerously overcrowded barracks.*

---

The door of the shed opened. An old man appeared, his moustache covered with frost, his lips blue with cold. It was Rabbi Eliahou,[16] the rabbi of a small Polish community. He was a very good man, well loved by everyone in the camp, even by the Kapos and the heads of the blocks. Despite the trials and privations, his face still shone with his inner purity. He was the only rabbi who was always addressed as "Rabbi" at Buna. He was like one of the old prophets, always in the midst of his people to comfort them. And, strangely, his words of comfort never provoked rebellion; they really brought peace.

He came into the shed and his eyes, brighter than ever, seemed to be looking for someone:

"Perhaps someone has seen my son somewhere?"

He had lost his son in the crowd. He had looked in vain among the dying. Then he had scratched up the snow to find his corpse. Without result.

For three years they had stuck together. Al-

ways near each other, for suffering, for blows, for the ration of bread, for prayer. Three years, from camp to camp, from selection to selection. And now—when the end seemed near—fate had separated them. Finding himself near me, Rabbi Eliahou whispered:

"It happened on the road. We lost sight of one another during the journey. I had stayed a little to the rear of the column. I hadn't any strength left for running. And my son didn't notice. That's all I know. Where has he disappeared? Where can I find him? Perhaps you've seen him somewhere?"

"No, Rabbi Eliahou, I haven't seen him."

He left then as he had come: like a wind-swept shadow.

He had already passed through the door when I suddenly remembered seeing his son running by my side. I had forgotten that, and I didn't tell Rabbi Eliahou!

Then I remembered something else: his son had seen him losing ground, limping, staggering back to the rear of the column. He had seen him. And he had continued to run on in front, letting the distance between them grow greater.

A terrible thought loomed up in my mind: He had wanted to get rid of his father! He had felt that his father was growing weak, he had believed that the end was near and had sought this separation in order to get rid of the burden, to free himself from an <u>encumbrance</u> which could lessen his own chances of survival.

I had done well to forget that. And I was glad that Rabbi Eliahou should continue to look for his beloved son.

And, in spite of myself, a prayer rose in my heart, to that God in whom I no longer believed.

My God, Lord of the Universe, give me strength never to do what Rabbi Eliahou's son has done.

Shouts rose outside in the yard, where dark-

---

16. **Eliahou** (el·ē·ä'hōō').

**Vocabulary**

**encumbrance** (en·kum'brəns) *n.:* hindrance; burden.

ness had fallen. The SS ordered the ranks to form up.

The march began again. The dead stayed in the yard under the snow, like faithful guards assassinated, without burial. No one had said the prayer for the dead over them. Sons abandoned their fathers' remains without a tear.

On the way it snowed, snowed, snowed endlessly. We were marching more slowly. The guards themselves seemed tired. My wounded foot no longer hurt me. It must have been completely frozen. The foot was lost to me. It had detached itself from my body like the wheel of a car. Too bad. I should have to resign myself; I could live with only one leg. The main thing was not to think about it. Above all, not at this moment. Leave thoughts for later.

Our march had lost all <u>semblance</u> of discipline. We went as we wanted, as we could. We heard no more shots. Our guards must have been tired.

But death scarcely needed any help from them. The cold was <u>conscientiously</u> doing its work. At every step someone fell and suffered no more.

From time to time, SS officers on motorcycles would go down the length of the column to try and shake us out of our growing <u>apathy</u>:

"Keep going! We are getting there!"

"Courage! Only a few more hours!"

"We're reaching Gleiwitz."

These words of encouragement, even though they came from the mouths of our assassins, did us a great deal of good. No one wanted to give up now, just before the end, so near to the goal. Our eyes searched the horizon for the barbed wire of Gleiwitz. Our only desire was to reach it as quickly as possible.

The night had now set in. The snow had ceased to fall. We walked for several more hours before arriving.

We did not notice the camp until we were just in front of the gate.

Some Kapos rapidly installed us in the barracks. We pushed and jostled one another as if

this were the supreme refuge, the gateway to life. We walked over pain-racked bodies. We trod on wounded faces. No cries. A few groans. My father and I were ourselves thrown to the ground by this rolling tide. Beneath our feet someone let out a rattling cry:

"You're crushing me . . . mercy!"

A voice that was not unknown to me.

"You're crushing me . . . mercy! mercy!"

The same faint voice, the same rattle, heard somewhere before. That voice had spoken to me one day. Where? When? Years ago? No, it could only have been at the camp.

"Mercy!"

I felt that I was crushing him. I was stopping his breath. I wanted to get up. I struggled to disengage myself, so that he could breathe. But I was crushed myself beneath the weight of other bodies. I could hardly breathe. I dug my nails into unknown faces. I was biting all round me, in order to get air. No one cried out.

Suddenly I remembered. Juliek![17] The boy from Warsaw who played the violin in the band at Buna. . . .

"Juliek, is it you?"

"Eliezer[18] . . . the twenty-five strokes of the whip. Yes . . . I remember."

He was silent. A long moment elapsed.

"Juliek! Can you hear me, Juliek?"

"Yes . . . ," he said, in a feeble voice. "What do you want?"

He was not dead.

"How do you feel, Juliek?" I asked, less to know the answer than to hear that he could speak, that he was alive.

"All right, Eliezer. . . . I'm getting on all

---

17. **Juliek** (yo͞o'lē·ek).
18. **Eliezer** (ā·lē·ā'zər).

---

**Vocabulary**

**semblance** (sem'bləns) n.: appearance; likeness.

**conscientiously** (kän'shē·en'shəs·lē) adv.: carefully; painstakingly; thoroughly.

**apathy** (ap'ə·thē) n.: indifference; lack of emotion.

Concentration Camp (1944) by Ben Shahn. Tempera (24" × 24").
© Estate of Ben Shahn/Licensed by VAGA, New York. Courtesy Sotheby's New York.

right . . . hardly any air . . . worn out. My feet are swollen. It's good to rest, but my violin . . ."

I thought he had gone out of his mind. What use was the violin here?

"What, your violin?"

He gasped.

"I'm afraid . . . I'm afraid . . . that they'll break my violin. . . . I've brought it with me."

I could not answer him. Someone was lying full length on top of me, covering my face. I was unable to breathe, through either mouth or nose. Sweat beaded my brow, ran down my spine. This was the end—the end of the road. A silent death, suffocation. No way of crying out, of calling for help.

I tried to get rid of my invisible assassin. My whole will to live was centered in my nails. I scratched. I battled for a mouthful of air. I tore at decaying flesh which did not respond. I could not free myself from this mass weighing down my chest. Was it a dead man I was struggling against? Who knows?

I shall never know. All I can say is that I won. I succeeded in digging a hole through this wall of dying people, a little hole through which I could drink in a small quantity of air.

"Father, how are you?" I asked, as soon as I could utter a word.

I knew he could not be far from me.

"Well!" answered a distant voice, which

seemed to come from another world. I tried to sleep.

He tried to sleep. Was he right or wrong? Could one sleep here? Was it not dangerous to allow your vigilance to fail, even for a moment, when at any minute death could pounce upon you?

I was thinking of this when I heard the sound of a violin. The sound of a violin, in this dark shed, where the dead were heaped on the living. What madman could be playing the violin here, at the brink of his own grave? Or was it really an hallucination?

It must have been Juliek.

He played a fragment from Beethoven's concerto. I had never heard sounds so pure. In such a silence.

How had he managed to free himself? To draw his body from under mine without my being aware of it?

It was pitch-dark. I could hear only the violin, and it was as though Juliek's soul were the bow. He was playing his life. The whole of his life was gliding on the strings—his lost hopes, his charred past, his extinguished future. He played as he would never play again.

I shall never forget Juliek. How could I forget that concert, given to an audience of dying and dead men! To this day, whenever I hear Beethoven played my eyes close and out of the dark rises the sad, pale face of my Polish friend, as he said farewell on his violin to an audience of dying men.

I do not know for how long he played. I was overcome by sleep. When I awoke, in the daylight, I could see Juliek, opposite me, slumped over, dead. Near him lay his violin, smashed, trampled, a strange overwhelming little corpse. ■

# Response and Analysis

## Reading Check

1. What does Madame Schächter see on the journey? How do her cries affect her son? her fellow prisoners?

2. When the prisoners arrive at Auschwitz, what do they see that proves Madame Schächter's visions were tragically accurate?

3. In the second excerpt, what does the head of Wiesel's block advise the prisoners to do before the selection process? Why?

4. What is Akiba Drumer's last request?

5. In the third excerpt, what does Juliek play at Gleiwitz? Who is his audience?

## Thinking Critically

6. In the first excerpt, what do you think causes Madame Schächter's terrible visions?

7. In the second excerpt, how has Akiba Drumer "begun to die" when he starts to lose his faith in God? What do you think kept Wiesel from giving up?

8. In the third excerpt, why is it **ironic** that Rabbi Eliahou will "continue to look for his beloved son"? Why is Wiesel glad that he will keep looking?

9. At the end of the third excerpt, why do you think Wiesel uses the **metaphor** of "a strange overwhelming little corpse" to describe Juliek's violin? What might the violin **symbolize** for Wiesel?

10. What **message** is Wiesel communicating to us in telling these stories of terrible human suffering? Think of what these stories say about the power of faith, the power of evil, and the power of art.

**SKILLS FOCUS**

**Literary Skills**
Analyze points of view on a topic.

**Reading Skills**
Analyze a writer's message.

**Writing Skills**
Write an essay comparing and connecting texts.

**Vocabulary Skills**
Understand connotations of synonyms.

## Literary Criticism

**11. Political approach.** When Wiesel accepted the Nobel Peace Prize, he said that "indifference" is the "greatest source of evil and danger in the world." He also said that if humanity ever forgets the Holocaust, "we are guilty, we are accomplices." What do you think he meant? Do you agree with this political point of view? Explain your position.

## WRITING

### Comparing Texts

The following comment was made by a German Lutheran pastor named Martin Niemöller, who found the courage to resist the Nazis during World War II. Read Niemöller's cautionary tale carefully. In a brief **essay,** explain the main point of the tale, and tell how it connects with Wiesel's experiences. How might the tale also connect with world events today?

In Germany, the Nazis first came for the Communists and I didn't speak up because I wasn't a Communist. Then they came for the Jews and I did not speak up because I was not a Jew. Then they came for the trade unionists and I didn't speak up because I was not a trade unionist. Then they came for the Catholics and I was a Protestant so I didn't speak up. Then they came for me: By that time there was no one left to speak up.

—Martin Niemöller

## Vocabulary Development
### Precise Meanings

Wiesel's memoir was written in French and translated into English. Go back to the sections reprinted here, and locate each Vocabulary word. Fill out a chart like the following one for each word. Has the translator chosen her words carefully? If a synonym were substituted, would the emotional impact of the sentence be affected?

pestilential    semblance
abominable    conscientiously
encumbrance    apathy

| Word |
| --- |
| abyss |

| Synonyms |
| --- |
| chasm; hole |

| Could synonyms be substituted in the sentence and have the same impact? |
| --- |
| chasm (yes); hole (no) |

Elie Wiesel accepting the Nobel Peace Prize (October 14, 1986).

# John Hersey
## (1914–1993)

**W**hat book was considered so extraordinary that the great scientist Albert Einstein ordered one thousand copies? What book was thought so compelling that the Book-of-the-Month Club distributed free copies because no book "could be of more importance at this moment to the human race"? The book is *Hiroshima* by John Hersey.

Hersey was born in China, where he lived until he was ten. He later graduated from Yale and studied at Cambridge University in England, served as private secretary to the American novelist Sinclair Lewis, and reported from the South Pacific and the Mediterranean during World War II for *Time* and *Life* magazines.

But journalism (if that means objective, factual reporting) could not contain Hersey's passionate concern about contemporary events. In 1945, he won a Pulitzer Prize for his novel *A Bell for Adano,* based on what he had seen of American military government in Italy. Some critics saw this novel as a troubling examination of democracy and its ideals and the difficulties of putting it into practice.

In 1946, Hersey published *Hiroshima.* Combining techniques of a novel and the factual air of journalism to describe a real event, *Hiroshima* began what some critics call the genre of the "nonfiction novel." (Other examples include Truman Capote's *In Cold Blood* [1966] and Norman Mailer's *The Executioner's Song* [1979].) Hersey took an almost incomprehensible act, the dropping of an atomic bomb on a civilian population, and showed how it affected the lives of six survivors. Through their eyes, Americans could experience this catastrophe as if it were happening to them and to their friends and neighbors.

Through Hersey's vivid narrative and his gift for characterization, the unimaginable became horrifyingly real.

*Hiroshima* became a national event, a precursor of the kind of celebrity status that bestsellers often enjoy today, with attention paid to the authors on talk shows and in interviews in magazines and newspapers. *Hiroshima* first appeared in *The New Yorker,* which devoted an entire issue to the book—a startling commitment for a magazine. The American Broadcasting Company had the book read aloud on its radio stations. *Hiroshima* has since been called the most significant piece of reportage in modern times.

After *Hiroshima,* Hersey became famous as a writer who could make history understandable. While serving as a teacher and mentor at Yale, he continued to dramatize issues and events, dealing with the Holocaust, racism, fascism, and other evils of modern life. He called his type of fiction "the novel of contemporary history" and wrote that "this kind of novel should make anyone who reads it better able to meet life in his generation—whenever that generation may be." He produced books in a steady stream from the 1940s to the 1990s, sending his publisher a manuscript of new short stories, *Key West Tales,* six weeks before his death. His books include the highly acclaimed novel *The Wall* (1950), about the annihilation of Polish Jews in the Warsaw ghetto, and *Blues* (1987), a brilliant meditation on Hersey's favorite sport, fishing. (The book, of course, turns out to be about much more than fly-casting and trolling.)

None of Hersey's other works achieved the impact of *Hiroshima.* The book continues to force readers to face the horrifying realities of nuclear war. To this day no book on nuclear warfare has come close to *Hiroshima's* impact on our moral and ethical sensibilities.

# Before You Read

## A Noiseless Flash

### Points *of* View

Modern war, waged with highly sophisticated weapons, is often described in terms of numbers: how many missiles fired, how many targets annihilated, how many people killed. It takes artists and writers and photographers to restore our awareness of the *personal* element of war—the fact that wars, first and foremost, bring devastation to human beings.

### Literary Focus

**Subjective and Objective Reporting**

In **subjective reporting** a writer openly expresses personal emotions and attitudes toward the events and characters he or she is writing about. In **objective reporting** a writer's emotions are kept at a distance, and he or she focuses on observable, verifiable facts. Objective reporting focuses so tightly on observable data that, often, the only way we can discover how a writer feels about an event is to analyze closely the *kinds* of details the writer chooses to include or to omit.

Why do you think Hersey's slim book has been seen as a political document?

> **Subjective** writing openly expresses a writer's feelings and attitudes about a subject. **Objective** writing keeps emotion at a distance by focusing on observable, verifiable facts.
>
> *For more on Subjective and Objective Writing, see the Handbook of Literary and Historical Terms.*

### Reading Skills

**Reading Closely for Details**

Hersey describes the effects of the atomic bombing of Hiroshima by focusing on six people in that city. As you read, note the many precise details Hersey uses to lend his account authenticity. Skim the account before you begin to read it. Notice the six sections, each set off by extra space, one for each person Hersey names. As you read, pick one of the six people, and take notes on the key details Hersey gives you about that person.

A scene in Hiroshima after the atomic bomb was dropped.

## Background

War erupted between the United States and Japan on December 7, 1941, when Japanese bombers broke the stillness of a Sunday morning and blasted the U.S. naval base at Pearl Harbor in Hawaii. By August 1945, the war in Europe had ended, but the United States and its allies had not yet defeated Japan. To bring the long war to a close, the United States used its newest and most lethal weapon. The atomic bombs struck twice—first hit was the Japanese city of Hiroshima and then, three days later, the city of Nagasaki. It was the world's first—and to date the last—use of atomic weapons in war. Between 70,000 and 80,000 people were killed in Hiroshima. In Nagasaki, 35,000 to 40,000 people perished.

# A Noiseless Flash

*from* Hiroshima

John Hersey

927

At exactly fifteen minutes past eight in the morning, on August 6, 1945, Japanese time, at the moment when the atomic bomb flashed above Hiroshima, Miss Toshiko Sasaki, a clerk in the personnel department of the East Asia Tin Works, had just sat down at her place in the plant office and was turning her head to speak to the girl at the next desk. At that same moment, Dr. Masakazu Fujii was settling down cross-legged to read the Osaka *Asahi*[1] on the porch of his private hospital, overhanging one of the seven deltaic rivers which divide Hiroshima; Mrs. Hatsuyo Nakamura, a tailor's widow, stood by the window of her kitchen, watching a neighbor tearing down his house because it lay in the path of an air-raid-defense fire lane; Father Wilhelm Kleinsorge, a German priest of the Society of Jesus,[2] reclined in his underwear on a cot on the top floor of his order's three-story mission house, reading a Jesuit magazine, *Stimmen der Zeit;*[3] Dr. Terufumi Sasaki, a young member of the surgical staff of the city's large, modern Red Cross Hospital, walked along one of the hospital corridors with a blood specimen for a Wassermann test[4] in his hand; and the Reverend Mr. Kiyoshi Tanimoto, pastor of the Hiroshima Methodist Church, paused at the door of a rich man's house in Koi, the city's western suburb, and prepared to unload a handcart full of things he had evacuated from town in fear of the massive B-29 raid which everyone expected Hiroshima to suffer. A hundred thousand people were killed by the atomic bomb, and these six were among the survivors. They still wonder why they lived when so many others died. Each of them counts many small items of chance or volition—a step taken in time, a decision to go indoors, catching one streetcar instead of the next—that spared him. And now each knows that in the act of survival he lived a dozen lives and saw more death than he ever thought he would see. At the time, none of them knew anything.

The Reverend Mr. Tanimoto got up at five o'clock that morning. He was alone in the parsonage, because for some time his wife had been commuting with their year-old baby to spend nights with a friend in Ushida, a suburb to the north. Of all the important cities of Japan, only two, Kyoto[5] and Hiroshima, had not been visited in strength by *B-san,* or Mr. B, as the Japanese, with a mixture of respect and unhappy familiarity, called the B-29; and Mr. Tanimoto, like all his neighbors and friends, was almost sick with anxiety. He had heard uncomfortably detailed accounts of mass raids on Kure, Iwakuni, Tokuyama, and other nearby towns; he was sure Hiroshima's turn would come soon. He had slept badly the night before, because there had been several air-raid warnings. Hiroshima had been getting such warnings almost every night for weeks, for at that time the B-29s were using Lake Biwa, northeast of Hiroshima, as a rendezvous point, and no matter what city the Americans planned to hit, the Superfortresses streamed in over the coast near Hiroshima. The frequency of the warnings and the continued abstinence of Mr. B with respect to Hiroshima had made its citizens jittery; a rumor was going around that the Americans were saving something special for the city.

Mr. Tanimoto is a small man, quick to talk, laugh, and cry. He wears his black hair parted in

---

1. *Asahi:* Japanese for "morning sun." The Osaka *Asahi* is the city newspaper.
2. **Society of Jesus:** Roman Catholic religious order of priests and brothers, also known as the Jesuit (jezh′ oo·it) order.
3. *Stimmen der Zeit* (shtim′ən der tsīt): German for "Voices of the Times."
4. **Wassermann test:** blood test used to diagnose syphilis.

5. **Kyoto:** city some two hundred miles east of Hiroshima.

**Vocabulary**

**rendezvous** (rän′dā·voo′) *n.* used as *adj.:* meeting.
**abstinence** (ab′stə·nəns) *n.:* staying away.

the middle and rather long; the prominence of the frontal bones just above his eyebrows and the smallness of his moustache, mouth, and chin give him a strange, old-young look, boyish and yet wise, weak and yet fiery. He moves nervously and fast, but with a restraint which suggests that he is a cautious, thoughtful man. He showed, indeed, just those qualities in the uneasy days before the bomb fell. Besides having his wife spend the nights in Ushida, Mr. Tanimoto had been carrying all the portable things from his church, in the close-packed residential district called Nagaragawa, to a house that belonged to a rayon manufacturer in Koi, two miles from the center of town. The rayon man, a Mr. Matsui, had opened his then unoccupied estate to a large number of his friends and acquaintances, so that they might evacuate whatever they wished to a safe distance from the probable target area. Mr. Tanimoto had had no difficulty in moving chairs, hymnals, Bibles, altar gear, and church records by pushcart himself, but the organ console and an upright piano required some aid. A friend of his named Matsuo had, the day before, helped him get the piano out to Koi; in return, he had promised this day to assist Mr. Matsuo in hauling out a daughter's belongings. That is why he had risen so early.

Mr. Tanimoto cooked his own breakfast. He felt awfully tired. The effort of moving the piano the day before, a sleepless night, weeks of worry and unbalanced diet, the cares of his parish—all combined to make him feel hardly adequate to the new day's work. There was another thing, too: Mr. Tanimoto had studied theology at Emory College, in Atlanta, Georgia; he had graduated in 1940; he spoke excellent English; he dressed in American clothes; he had corresponded with many American friends right up to the time the war began; and among a people obsessed with a fear of being spied upon—perhaps almost obsessed himself—he found himself growing increasingly uneasy. The police had questioned him several times, and just a few

days before, he had heard that an influential acquaintance, a Mr. Tanaka, a retired officer of the Toyo Kisen Kaisha steamship line, an anti-Christian, a man famous in Hiroshima for his showy philanthropies and notorious for his personal tyrannies, had been telling people that Tanimoto should not be trusted. In compensation, to show himself publicly a good Japanese, Mr. Tanimoto had taken on the chairmanship of his local *tonarigumi*, or Neighborhood Association, and to his other duties and concerns this position had added the business of organizing air-raid defense for about twenty families.

Before six o'clock that morning, Mr. Tanimoto started for Mr. Matsuo's house. There he found that their burden was to be a *tansu*, a large Japanese cabinet, full of clothing and household goods. The two men set out. The morning was perfectly clear and so warm that the day promised to be uncomfortable. A few minutes after they started, the air-raid siren went off—a minute-long blast that warned of approaching planes but indicated to the people of Hiroshima only a slight degree of danger, since it sounded every morning at this time, when an American weather plane came over. The two men pulled and pushed the handcart through the city streets. Hiroshima was a fan-shaped city, lying mostly on the six islands formed by the seven estuarial[6] rivers that branch out from the Ota River; its main commercial and residential districts, covering about four square miles in the center of the city, contained three-quarters of its population, which had been reduced by several evacuation programs from a wartime peak of 380,000 to about 245,000. Factories and other residential

---

**6. estuarial** (es′tyōō·er′ē·əl) *adj.*: on the estuary, or mouth of a river, where freshwater meets saltwater.

---

**Vocabulary**
**notorious** (nō·tôr′ē·əs) *adj.*: known widely and usually unfavorably.

First photograph taken of Hiroshima after the atomic explosion (August 6, 1945).

districts, or suburbs, lay compactly around the edges of the city. To the south were the docks, an airport, and the island-studded Inland Sea. A rim of mountains runs around the other three sides of the delta. Mr. Tanimoto and Mr. Matsuo took their way through the shopping center, already full of people, and across two of the rivers to the sloping streets of Koi, and up them to the outskirts and foothills. As they started up a valley away from the tight-ranked houses, the all-clear sounded. (The Japanese

radar operators, detecting only three planes, supposed that they comprised a reconnaissance.)[7] Pushing the handcart up to the rayon man's house was tiring, and the men, after they had maneuvered their load into the driveway and to the front steps, paused to rest awhile. They stood with a wing of the house between them and the city. Like most homes in this part of Japan, the house consisted of a wooden frame and wooden walls supporting a heavy tile roof. Its front hall, packed with rolls of bedding and clothing, looked like a cool cave full of fat cushions. Opposite the house, to the right of the front door, there was a large, finicky rock gar-

---

7. **reconnaissance** (ri·kän′ə·səns) *n.:* exploratory mission.

one of them. As his face was against the stone, he did not see what happened. He felt a sudden pressure, and then splinters and pieces of board and fragments of tile fell on him. He heard no roar. (Almost no one in Hiroshima recalls hearing any noise of the bomb. But a fisherman in his sampan[8] on the Inland Sea near Tsuzu, the man with whom Mr. Tanimoto's mother-in-law and sister-in-law were living, saw the flash and heard a tremendous explosion; he was nearly twenty miles from Hiroshima, but the thunder was greater than when the B-29s hit Iwakuni, only five miles away.)

When he dared, Mr. Tanimoto raised his head and saw that the rayon man's house had collapsed. He thought a bomb had fallen directly on it. Such clouds of dust had risen that there was a sort of twilight around. In panic, not thinking for the moment of Mr. Matsuo under the ruins, he dashed out into the street. He noticed as he ran that the concrete wall of the estate had fallen over—toward the house rather than away from it. In the street, the first thing he saw was a squad of soldiers who had been burrowing into the hillside opposite, making one of the thousands of dugouts in which the Japanese apparently intended to resist invasion, hill by hill, life for life; the soldiers were coming out of the hole, where they should have been safe, and blood was running from their heads, chests, and backs. They were silent and dazed.

Under what seemed to be a local dust cloud, the day grew darker and darker.

At nearly midnight, the night before the bomb was dropped, an announcer on the city's radio station said that about two hundred B-29s were approaching southern Honshu[9] and advised the population of Hiroshima to evacuate to their designated "safe areas." Mrs. Hatsuyo

den. There was no sound of planes. The morning was still; the place was cool and pleasant.

Then a tremendous flash of light cut across the sky. Mr. Tanimoto has a distinct recollection that it traveled from east to west, from the city toward the hills. It seemed a sheet of sun. Both he and Mr. Matsuo reacted in terror—and both had time to react (for they were 3,500 yards, or two miles, from the center of the explosion). Mr. Matsuo dashed up the front steps into the house and dived among the bedrolls and buried himself there. Mr. Tanimoto took four or five steps and threw himself between two big rocks in the garden. He bellied up very hard against

---

8. **sampan** *n.:* small, flat-bottomed boat.
9. **Honshu:** largest island of Japan. Hiroshima is in southern Honshu.

Nakamura, the tailor's widow, who lived in the section called Noboricho and who had long had a habit of doing as she was told, got her three children—a ten-year-old boy, Toshio, an eight-year-old girl, Yaeko, and a five-year-old girl, Myeko—out of bed and dressed them and walked with them to the military area known as the East Parade Ground, on the northeast edge of the city. There she unrolled some mats and the children lay down on them. They slept until about two, when they were awakened by the roar of the planes going over Hiroshima.

As soon as the planes had passed, Mrs. Nakamura started back with her children. They reached home a little after two-thirty and she immediately turned on the radio, which, to her distress, was just then broadcasting a fresh warning. When she looked at the children and saw how tired they were, and when she thought of the number of trips they had made in past weeks, all to no purpose, to the East Parade Ground, she decided that in spite of the instructions on the radio, she simply could not face starting out all over again. She put the children in their bedrolls on the floor, lay down herself at three o'clock, and fell asleep at once, so soundly that when the planes passed over later, she did not waken to their sound.

The siren jarred her awake at about seven. She arose, dressed quickly, and hurried to the house of Mr. Nakamoto, the head of her Neighborhood Association, and asked him what she should do. He said that she should remain at home unless an urgent warning—a series of intermittent blasts of the siren—was sounded. She returned home, lit the stove in the kitchen, set some rice to cook, and sat down to read that morning's Hiroshima *Chugoku*.[10] To her relief, the all-clear sounded at eight o'clock. She heard the children stirring, so she went and gave each of them a handful of peanuts and told them to stay on their bedrolls, because they were tired from the night's walk. She had hoped that they would go back to sleep, but the man in the house directly to the south began to make a terrible hullabaloo of hammering, wedging, ripping, and splitting. The prefectural government,[11] convinced, as everyone in Hiroshima was, that the city would be attacked soon, had begun to press with threats and warnings for the completion of wide fire lanes, which, it was hoped, might act in conjunction with the rivers to localize any fires started by an incendiary[12] raid; and the neighbor was reluctantly sacrificing his home to the city's safety. Just the day before, the prefecture had ordered all able-bodied girls from the secondary schools to spend a few days helping to clear these lanes, and they started work soon after the all-clear sounded.

Mrs. Nakamura went back to the kitchen, looked at the rice, and began watching the man next door. At first, she was annoyed with him for making so much noise, but then she was moved almost to tears by pity. Her emotion was specifically directed toward her neighbor, tearing down his home, board by board, at a time when there was so much unavoidable destruction, but undoubtedly she also felt a generalized, community pity, to say nothing of self-pity. She had not had an easy time. Her husband, Isawa, had gone into the Army just after Myeko was born, and she had heard nothing from or of him for a long time, until, on March 5, 1942, she received a seven-word telegram: "Isawa died an honorable death at Singapore." She learned later that he had died on February 15th, the day Singapore fell, and that he had been a corporal. Isawa had been a not particularly prosperous tailor, and his only capital was a Sankoku sewing machine. After his death, when his allotments stopped coming, Mrs. Nakamura got out the machine and began to

---

10. *Chugoku:* newspaper named for the region where Hiroshima is located.
11. **prefectural government:** regional administration of each Japanese district, called a prefecture.
12. **incendiary** (in·sen'dē·er'ē) *adj.:* designed to cause fires.

take in piecework[13] herself, and since then had supported the children, but poorly, by sewing.

As Mrs. Nakamura stood watching her neighbor, everything flashed whiter than any white she had ever seen. She did not notice what happened to the man next door; the reflex of a mother set her in motion toward her children. She had taken a single step (the house was 1,350 yards, or three-quarters of a mile, from the center of the explosion) when something picked her up and she seemed to fly into the next room over the raised sleeping platform, pursued by parts of her house.

Timbers fell around her as she landed, and a shower of tiles pummeled her; everything became dark, for she was buried. The debris did not cover her deeply. She rose up and freed herself. She heard a child cry, "Mother, help me!," and saw her youngest—Myeko, the five-year-old—buried up to her breast and unable to move. As Mrs. Nakamura started frantically to claw her way toward the baby, she could see or hear nothing of her other children.

In the days right before the bombing, Dr. Masakazu Fujii, being prosperous, hedonistic, and at the time not too busy, had been allowing himself the luxury of sleeping until nine or nine-thirty, but fortunately he had to get up early the morning the bomb was dropped to see a house guest off on a train. He rose at six, and half an hour later walked with his friend to the station, not far away, across two of the rivers. He was back home by seven, just as the siren sounded its sustained warning. He ate breakfast and then, because the morning was already hot, undressed down to his underwear and went out on the porch to read the paper. This porch—in fact, the whole building—was curiously constructed. Dr. Fujii was the proprietor of a peculiarly Japanese institution: a private, single-doctor hospital. This building, perched beside

and over the water of the Kyo River, and next to the bridge of the same name, contained thirty rooms for thirty patients and their kinfolk—for, according to Japanese custom, when a person falls sick and goes to a hospital, one or more members of his family go and live there with him, to cook for him, bathe, massage, and read to him, and to offer incessant familial sympathy, without which a Japanese patient would be miserable indeed. Dr. Fujii had no beds—only straw mats—for his patients. He did, however, have all sorts of modern equipment: an X-ray machine, diathermy[14] apparatus, and a fine tiled laboratory. The structure rested two-thirds on the land, one-third on piles over the tidal waters of the Kyo. This overhang, the part of the building where Dr. Fujii lived, was queer-looking, but it was cool in summer and from the porch, which faced away from the center of the city, the prospect of the river, with pleasure boats drifting up and down it, was always refreshing. Dr. Fujii had occasionally had anxious moments when the Ota and its mouth branches rose to flood, but the piling was apparently firm enough and the house had always held.

Dr. Fujii had been relatively idle for about a month because in July, as the number of untouched cities in Japan dwindled and as Hiroshima seemed more and more inevitably a target, he began turning patients away, on the ground that in case of a fire raid he would not be able to evacuate them. Now he had only two patients left—a woman from Yano, injured in the shoulder, and a young man of twenty-five recovering from burns he had suffered when the steel factory near Hiroshima in which he worked had been hit. Dr. Fujii had six nurses to tend his patients. His wife and children were

---

14. **diathermy** *n.* used as *adj.:* heat treatment.

**Vocabulary**

**debris** (də·brē′) *n.:* rubble; broken pieces.

**hedonistic** (hē′də·nis′tik) *adj.:* pleasure-loving; self-indulgent.

**sustained** (sə·stānd′) *v.* used as *adj.:* prolonged.

---

13. **piecework** *n.:* work paid at a fixed rate for each piece completed.

safe; his wife and one son were living outside Osaka, and another son and two daughters were in the country on Kyushu.[15] A niece was living with him, and a maid and a manservant. He had little to do and did not mind, for he had saved some money. At fifty, he was healthy, <u>convivial</u>, and calm, and he was pleased to pass the evenings drinking whiskey with friends, always sensibly and for the sake of conversation. Before the war, he had affected brands imported from Scotland and America; now he was perfectly satisfied with the best Japanese brand, Suntory.

Dr. Fujii sat down cross-legged in his underwear on the spotless matting of the porch, put on his glasses, and started reading the Osaka *Asahi*. He liked to read the Osaka news because his wife was there. He saw the flash. To him—faced away from the center and looking at his paper—it seemed a brilliant yellow. Startled, he began to rise to his feet. In that moment (he was 1,550 yards from the center), the hospital leaned behind his rising and, with a terrible ripping noise, toppled into the river. The doctor, still in the act of getting to his feet, was thrown forward and around and over; he was buffeted and gripped; he lost track of everything, because things were so speeded up; he felt the water.

Dr. Fujii hardly had time to think that he was dying before he realized that he was alive, squeezed tightly by two long timbers in a V across his chest, like a morsel suspended between two huge chopsticks—held upright, so that he could not move, with his head miraculously above water and his torso and legs in it. The remains of his hospital were all around him in a mad assortment of splintered lumber and materials for the relief of pain. His left shoulder hurt terribly. His glasses were gone.

Father Wilhelm Kleinsorge, of the Society of Jesus, was, on the morning of the explosion, in rather frail condition. The Japanese wartime diet had not sustained him, and he felt the strain of being a foreigner in an increasingly xenophobic[16] Japan; even a German, since the defeat of the Fatherland,[17] was unpopular. Father Kleinsorge had, at thirty-eight, the look of a boy growing too fast—thin in the face, with a prominent Adam's apple, a hollow chest, dangling hands, big feet. He walked clumsily, leaning forward a little. He was tired all the time. To make matters worse, he had suffered for two days, along with Father Cieslik, a fellow-priest, from a rather painful and urgent diarrhea, which they blamed on the beans and black ration bread they were obliged to eat. Two other priests then living in the mission compound, which was in the Noboricho section—Father Superior LaSalle and Father Schiffer—had happily escaped this affliction.

Father Kleinsorge woke up about six the morning the bomb was dropped, and half an hour later—he was a bit tardy because of his sickness—he began to read Mass in the mission chapel, a small Japanese-style wooden building which was without pews, since its worshipers knelt on the usual Japanese matted floor, facing an altar graced with splendid silks, brass, silver, and heavy embroideries. This morning, a Monday, the only worshipers were Mr. Takemoto, a theological student living in the mission house; Mr. Fukai, the secretary of the diocese;[18] Mrs. Murata, the mission's devoutly Christian housekeeper; and his fellow-priests. After Mass, while Father Kleinsorge was reading the Prayers of Thanksgiving, the siren sounded. He stopped the service and the missionaries retired across

---

16. **xenophobic** (zen′ō·fō′bik) *adj.:* fearing or disliking foreigners.
17. **defeat of the Fatherland:** Germany surrendered to the Allies on May 7, 1945, approximately three months before the bombing of Hiroshima.
18. **diocese** (dī′ə·sis) *n.:* church district administered by a bishop.

---

**Vocabulary**

**convivial** (kən·viv′ē·əl) *adj.:* jovial; sociable.

---

15. **Kyushu** (kyōō′shōō′): southernmost of the principal islands of Japan.

the compound to the bigger building. There, in his room on the ground floor, to the right of the front door, Father Kleinsorge changed into a military uniform which he had acquired when he was teaching at the Rokko Middle School in Kobe and which he wore during air-raid alerts.

After an alarm, Father Kleinsorge always went out and scanned the sky, and in this instance, when he stepped outside, he was glad to see only the single weather plane that flew over Hiroshima each day about this time. Satisfied that nothing would happen, he went in and breakfasted with the other Fathers on substitute coffee and ration bread, which, under the circumstances, was especially repugnant to him. The Fathers sat and talked awhile, until, at eight,

they heard the all-clear. They went then to various parts of the building. Father Schiffer retired to his room to do some writing. Father Cieslik sat in his room in a straight chair with a pillow over his stomach to ease his pain, and read. Father Superior LaSalle stood at the window of his room, thinking. Father Kleinsorge went up to a room on the third floor, took off all his clothes except his underwear, and stretched out on his right side on a cot and began reading his *Stimmen der Zeit*.

After the terrible flash—which, Father Kleinsorge later realized, reminded him of something he had read as a boy about a large meteor colliding with the earth—he had time (since he was 1,400 yards from the center) for

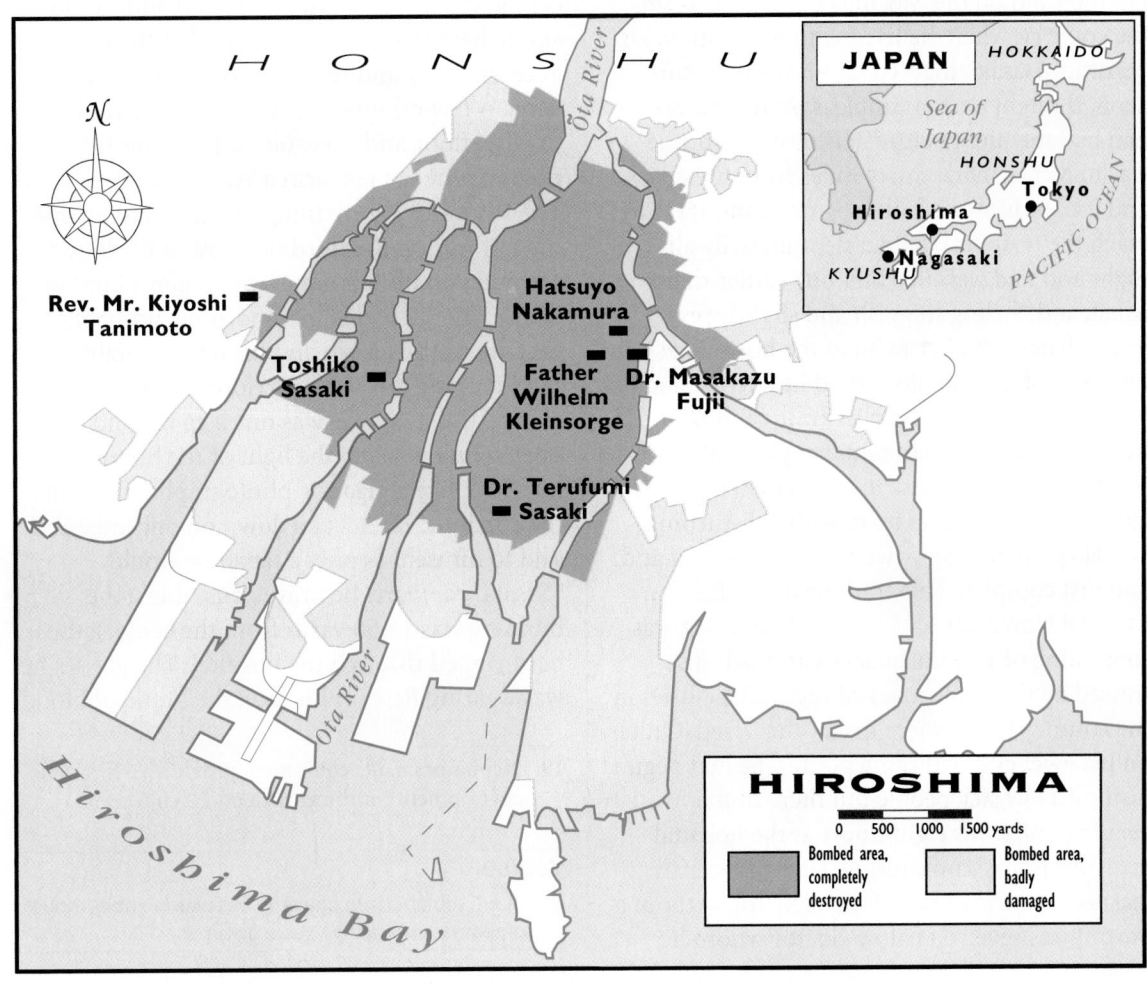

one thought: A bomb has fallen directly on us. Then, for a few seconds or minutes, he went out of his mind.

Father Kleinsorge never knew how he got out of the house. The next things he was conscious of were that he was wandering around in the mission's vegetable garden in his underwear, bleeding slightly from small cuts along his left flank; that all the buildings round about had fallen down except the Jesuits' mission house, which had long before been braced and double-braced by a priest named Gropper, who was terrified of earthquakes; that the day had turned dark; and that Murata-*san*, the housekeeper, was nearby, crying over and over, *"Shu Jesusu, awaremi tamai!* Our Lord Jesus, have pity on us!"

On the train on the way into Hiroshima from the country, where he lived with his mother, Dr. Terufumi Sasaki, the Red Cross Hospital surgeon, thought over an unpleasant nightmare he had had the night before. His mother's home was in Mukai-hara, thirty miles from the city, and it took him two hours by train and tram to reach the hospital. He had slept uneasily all night and had wakened an hour earlier than usual, and, feeling sluggish and slightly feverish, had debated whether to go to the hospital at all; his sense of duty finally forced him to go, and he had started out on an earlier train than he took most mornings. The dream had particularly frightened him because it was so closely associated, on the surface at least, with a disturbing actuality. He was only twenty-five years old and had just completed his training at the Eastern Medical University, in Tsingtao, China. He was something of an <u>idealist</u> and was much distressed by the inadequacy of medical facilities in the country town where his mother lived. Quite on his own, and without a permit, he had begun visiting a few sick people out there in the evenings, after his eight hours at the hospital and four hours' commuting. He had recently learned that the penalty for practicing without a permit was severe; a fellow-doctor whom he had asked about it had given him a serious scolding. Nevertheless, he had continued to practice. In his dream, he had been at the bedside of a country patient when the police and the doctor he had consulted burst into the room, seized him, dragged him outside, and beat him up cruelly. On the train, he just about decided to give up the work in Mukai-hara, since he felt it would be impossible to get a permit, because the authorities would hold that it would conflict with his duties at the Red Cross Hospital.

At the terminus, he caught a streetcar at once. (He later calculated that if he had taken his customary train that morning, and if he had had to wait a few minutes for the streetcar, as often happened, he would have been close to the center at the time of the explosion and would surely have perished.) He arrived at the hospital at seven-forty and reported to the chief surgeon. A few minutes later, he went to a room on the first floor and drew blood from the arm of a man in order to perform a Wassermann test. The laboratory containing the incubators[19] for the test was on the third floor. With the blood specimen in his left hand, walking in a kind of distraction he had felt all morning, probably because of the dream and his restless night, he started along the main corridor on his way toward the stairs. He was one step beyond an open window when the light of the bomb was reflected, like a gigantic photographic flash, in the corridor. He ducked down on one knee and said to himself, as only a Japanese would, "Sasaki, *gambare!* Be brave!" Just then (the building was 1,650 yards from the center), the blast ripped through the hospital. The glasses he was wearing flew off his face; the bottle of blood

---

19. **incubators** *n. pl.:* equipment providing a favorable environment for the growth of cell cultures.

---

**Vocabulary**

**idealist** (ī·dē′əl·ist) *n.:* one who believes in noble, though sometimes impractical, goals; dreamer.

Hiroshima after the atomic-bomb blast (October 1945).

crashed against one wall; his Japanese slippers zipped out from under his feet—but otherwise, thanks to where he stood, he was untouched.

Dr. Sasaki shouted the name of the chief surgeon and rushed around to the man's office and found him terribly cut by glass. The hospital was in horrible confusion: Heavy partitions and ceilings had fallen on patients, beds had overturned, windows had blown in and cut people, blood was spattered on the walls and floors, instruments were everywhere, many of the patients were running about screaming, many more lay dead. (A colleague working in the laboratory to which Dr. Sasaki had been walking was dead; Dr. Sasaki's patient, whom he had just left and who a few moments before had been dreadfully afraid of syphilis, was also dead.) Dr. Sasaki found himself the only doctor in the hospital who was unhurt.

Dr. Sasaki, who believed that the enemy had hit only the building he was in, got bandages and began to bind the wounds of those inside the hospital; while outside, all over Hiroshima, maimed and dying citizens turned their unsteady steps toward the Red Cross Hospital to begin an invasion that was to make Dr. Sasaki forget his private nightmare for a long, long time.

Miss Toshiko Sasaki, the East Asia Tin Works clerk, who is not related to Dr. Sasaki, got up at three o'clock in the morning on the day the bomb fell. There was extra housework to do. Her eleven-month-old brother, Akio, had come down the day before with a serious stomach upset; her mother had taken him to the Tamura Pediatric Hospital and was staying there with him. Miss Sasaki, who was about twenty, had to cook breakfast for her father, a brother, a sister, and herself, and—since the hospital, because of the war, was unable to provide food—to prepare a whole day's meals for her mother and the baby, in time for her father, who worked in a factory making rubber earplugs for artillery crews, to take the food by on his way to the plant. When she had finished and had cleaned and put away the cooking things, it was nearly seven. The family lived in Koi, and she had a forty-five-minute trip to the tin works, in the section of town called Kannon-machi. She was in charge of the personnel records in the

factory. She left Koi at seven, and as soon as she reached the plant, she went with some of the other girls from the personnel department to the factory auditorium. A prominent local Navy man, a former employee, had committed suicide the day before by throwing himself under a train—a death considered honorable enough to warrant a memorial service, which was to be held at the tin works at ten o'clock that morning. In the large hall, Miss Sasaki and the others made suitable preparations for the meeting. This work took about twenty minutes.

Miss Sasaki went back to her office and sat down at her desk. She was quite far from the windows, which were off to her left, and behind her were a couple of tall bookcases containing all the books of the factory library, which the personnel department had organized. She settled herself at her desk, put some things in a drawer, and shifted papers. She thought that before she began to make entries in her lists of new employees, discharges, and departures for the Army, she would chat for a moment with the girl at her right. Just as she turned her head away from the windows, the room was filled with a blinding light. She was paralyzed by fear, fixed still in her chair for a long moment (the plant was 1,600 yards from the center).

Everything fell, and Miss Sasaki lost consciousness. The ceiling dropped suddenly and the wooden floor above collapsed in splinters and the people up there came down and the roof above them gave way; but principally and first of all, the bookcases right behind her swooped forward and the contents threw her down, with her left leg horribly twisted and breaking underneath her. There, in the tin factory, in the first moment of the atomic age, a human being was crushed by books. ∎

## PRIMARY SOURCE / COMMENT

### Unforgettable Fire

*Some thirty years later, the horror of the bombing of Hiroshima remained etched in the mind of Yasuko Yamagata, a survivor. She explains her painting, at the right:*

"About 8:00 A.M., August 7, on the street in front of the former Hiroshima Broadcasting Station.

"Since I was at school in Ujina I had been exposed to radiation separately from my parents. The next morning at 7:30 I started from school toward the ruins of my house in Nobori-cho. I passed by Hijiyama. There were few people to be seen in the scorched field. I saw for the first time a pile of burned bodies in a water tank by the entrance to the broadcasting station. Then I was suddenly frightened by a terrible sight on the street 40 to 50 meters from Shukkeien Garden. There was a charred body of a woman standing frozen in a running position with one leg lifted and her baby tightly clutched in her arms. Who on earth could she be? This cruel sight still vividly remains in my mind."

—Yasuko Yamagata

Yasuko Yamagata, age forty-nine.

From *Unforgettable Fire: Pictures Drawn by Atomic Bomb Survivors*, edited by the Japan Broadcasting Corporation. Copyright © 1977 by NHK. Reprinted by permission of Pantheon Books, a division of Random House, Inc.

# Response and Analysis

## Reading Check

1. List the six people presented in this excerpt from *Hiroshima*. Besides surviving the explosion of the atomic bomb, what do they have in common?

2. What simple **images** does Hersey use to help us imagine the actual physical impact of the bomb? For example, what words does he use to describe the flash as seen by each survivor?

3. How does Hersey explain the **ironic** fact that an all-clear signal sounded just before the bomb was dropped?

4. What small, commonplace human-interest details does Hersey give about these six people to make them come alive as people we might know?

## Thinking Critically

5. What **ironies** can you find in each character's story—including the tragic irony of the final image?

6. Although Hersey mostly cites facts **objectively,** he communicates a **subjective** attitude toward war. What details communicate his assumptions and beliefs about the Japanese people? about the United States?

7. During World War II, most Americans felt that the Japanese, like their German allies, were enemies to be destroyed no matter what the cost. How do you respond to Hersey's treatment of the Japanese in this account? How do you think readers in 1946—one year after the war had ended—responded?

8. From what you know of history and from what you have read here, tell, in human and political terms, why the explosion at Hiroshima was a crucial event of the twentieth century. Do you think this distant event has affected our lives even today? Explain.

## Literary Criticism

9. **Political approach.** Why do you think Hersey chooses not to give any details in this excerpt to suggest the reasons why the bomb was dropped? How does this affect your reading of the text?

## WRITING

### Analyzing Suspense

Readers of Hersey's *Hiroshima* know the outcome of the narrative before they even open the book. In a brief **essay,** explain how in this excerpt Hersey manages, nevertheless, to create suspense. In your essay, cite the questions Hersey plants in your mind. When does he answer them?

## Vocabulary Development

### Yes or No?

Be sure you can justify your response to each question below:

1. Would the middle of a busy street be a good place for a rendezvous point?

2. If a dinner guest told you of her abstinence of alcohol, would you serve her a glass of wine?

3. If a gangster is notorious, are the police probably on the lookout for him?

4. Would a park full of debris be a good place for children to play?

5. Is a hedonistic person likely to be self-centered?

6. Does a sustained alarm continue to ring for a long time?

7. Would you invite a convivial person to a party?

8. Does an idealist have many negative plans?

**SKILLS FOCUS**

**Literary Skills**
Analyze points of view on a topic. Analyze subjective and objective reporting.

**Reading Skills**
Read closely for details.

**Writing Skills**
Write an essay analyzing suspense.

**Vocabulary Skills**
Demonstrate word knowledge.

# Robert H. Jackson
## (1892–1954)

From his rural roots in Pennsylvania, Robert Houghwout Jackson eventually became the chief prosecutor of one of the most notorious trials in recent history. Although he attended law school for one year in his late teens, Jackson was primarily self-educated. A precocious scholar, he needed special permission to plead his first case because he was still a minor at the time. At the age of twenty-one, he was admitted to the bar as an attorney.

A strong supporter of President Franklin D. Roosevelt, Jackson was appointed to several positions in the legal arena of the New Deal government. In February 1941, Roosevelt named Jackson to the U.S. Supreme Court. (Jackson was the last justice to have become a lawyer by "reading law" rather than by means of a formal education.) Appointed by President Truman in May 1945 to the War Crimes Commission, Jackson took a leave from the Supreme Court to serve as chief U.S. prosecutor of the Nuremberg trials.

Jackson was largely responsible for the legal document (the Charter of the International Military Tribunal) that provided the basis for the trials. He stated: "This trial represents mankind's desperate effort to apply the discipline of the law to statesmen who have used their powers of state to attack the foundations of the world's peace and to commit aggressions against the rights of their neighbors." Jackson's successful case against the Nazi war criminals set new standards in international law.

# Before You Read

## "The Arrogance and Cruelty of Power"

### Points *of* View

#### Quickwrite ✎

During its twelve years in power in Germany, the Nazi party murdered at least eleven *million* people. The following words by the philosopher George Santayana are now posted on a tablet at the entrance to the Dachau concentration camp: "Those who cannot remember the past are condemned to repeat it." Write briefly about a societal tragedy—either a current event or a historical one—that should not be forgotten. What lessons should society learn from it?

### Literary Focus

#### Persuasion and Argument

**Persuasion** is the use of language that appeals to both our reason and our emotion in order to persuade us to act or think in a certain way. Strictly speaking, **argument** is a form of persuasion that appeals only to our reason, not to our emotions. In this opening speech and throughout the trial, Jackson used all the methods of persuasion to convince the members of the International Military Tribunal of the defendants' guilt. By citing facts, showing statistics, and displaying evidence, Jackson used logic to appeal to the listeners' **reason.** However, like the best persuasive speakers, Jackson also used powerful language to appeal to his listeners' **emotions** and to their **ethics,** or sense of morality.

> **Persuasion** is the use of reason and emotional appeals to convince the listener to think or act in a certain way.
>
> *For more on Persuasion, see the Handbook of Literary and Historical Terms.*

### Background

In 1945, at a court in the ruined city of Nuremberg, Germany, twenty-one men listened through headphones to a translation of charges against them. These men were the most important Nazi leaders known to have survived World War II. They had helped Adolf Hitler in his plan to build a German empire. Their ambition had led to the deaths of six million Jews in concentration camps and to the deaths of millions of other human beings in those camps as well—including homosexuals, Romany (Gypsies), Polish Catholics, and resistance fighters.

The ambition of Robert H. Jackson, the U.S. Supreme Court justice who had organized the case against them, was more honorable: to hold "the first trial in history for crimes against the peace of the world." Jackson delivered the opening speech of the trial on November 21, 1945, on behalf of the Allies (the United States, Great Britain, France, and Russia) and seventeen other countries.

Some critics claimed that the International Military Tribunal, organized to conduct the trial, was acting on shaky legal grounds. The critics said that many of the Nazis' crimes were not declared illegal until after they were committed, and, furthermore, that an individual should not be tried for the crimes of a government. In October 1946, however, after the consideration of hundreds of thousands of pieces of evidence, the court convicted nineteen of the defendants of war crimes. Twelve were condemned to death. Of these twelve, ten were hanged in a messy execution, and one escaped the hangman by swallowing poison. The twelfth was missing and was tried and convicted *in absentia.*

**Literary Skills**
Analyze points of view. Understand persuasion and argument.

**INTERNET**

Vocabulary Practice

Keyword: LE7 11-6

## Vocabulary Development

**malignant** (mə·lig′nənt) *adj.*: destructive; evil.

**vengeance** (ven′jəns) *n.*: revenge; punishment in return for a wrongdoing.

**vindicate** (vin′də·kāt′) *v.*: prove correct; justify.

**magnitude** (mag′nə·to͞od′) *n.*: importance; greatness of scope.

**reproached** (ri·prōcht′) *v.*: blamed; disgraced.

**precariously** (pri·ker′ē·əs·lē) *adv.*: in a shaky or unstable way.

**arrogance** (ar′ə·gəns) *n.*: overbearing pride; self-importance.

**invincible** (in·vin′sə·bəl) *adj.*: unconquerable.

**prostrate** (präs′trāt′) *adj.*: helpless; overcome.

**dissident** (dis′ə·dənt) *adj.*: disagreeing; differing in belief or opinion.

(Photographs, pages 942–945)
Among the Nazis on trial at Nuremberg were top leaders Hermann Goering (far left), the designated successor to Adolf Hitler, and Rudolf Hess (seated next to Goering), Hitler's deputy. The Nazis wearing headphones are listening to a German translation of the proceedings.

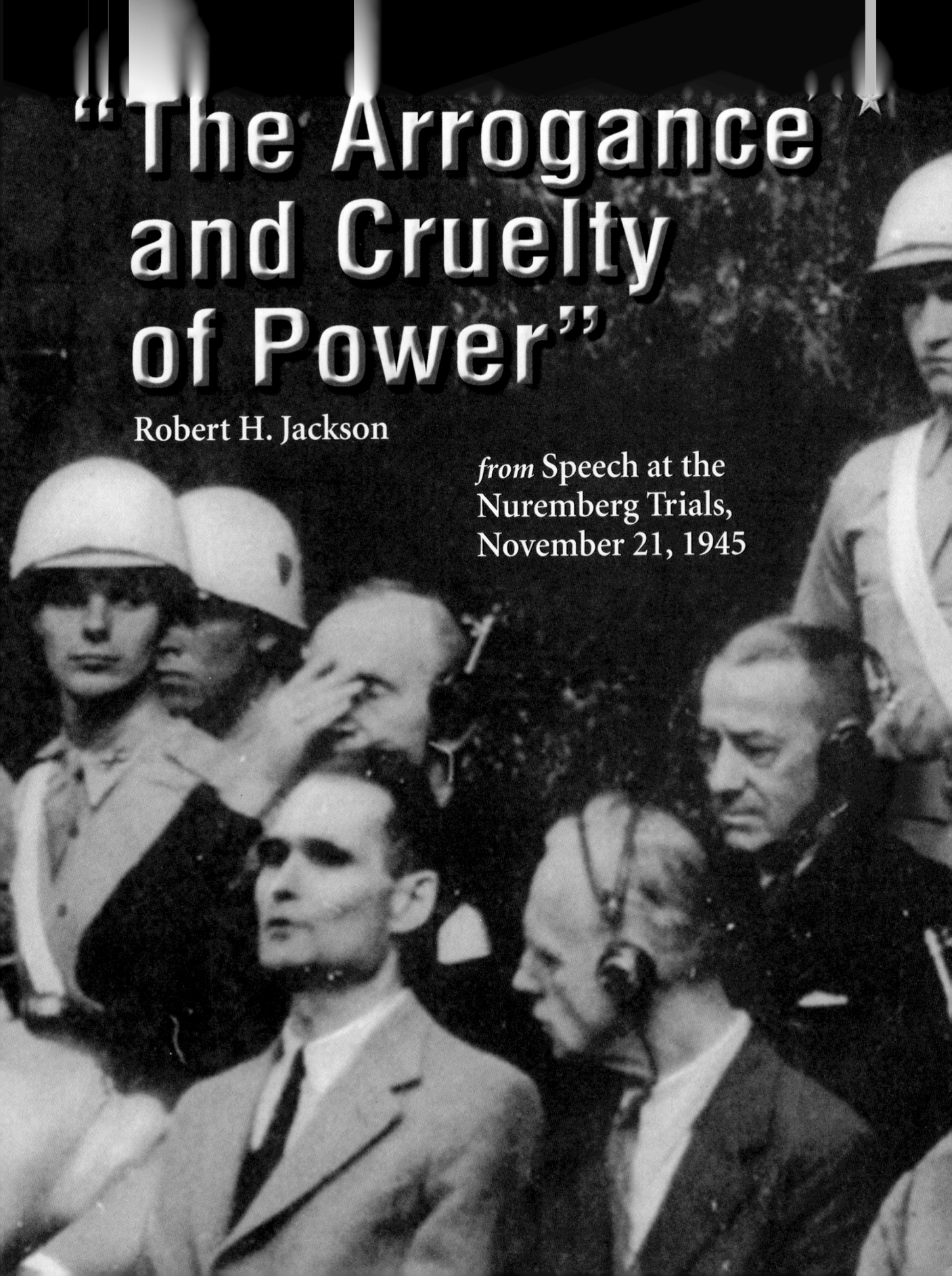

# "The Arrogance and Cruelty of Power"

Robert H. Jackson

*from* Speech at the
Nuremberg Trials,
November 21, 1945

The privilege of opening the first trial in history for crimes against the peace of the world imposes a grave responsibility. The wrongs which we seek to condemn and punish have been so calculated, so malignant, and so devastating that civilization cannot tolerate their being ignored, because it cannot survive their being repeated. That four great nations, flushed with victory and stung with injury, stay the hand of vengeance and voluntarily submit their captive enemies to the judgment of the law is one of the most significant tributes that Power has ever paid to Reason.

This Tribunal, while it is novel and experimental, is not the product of abstract speculations, nor is it created to vindicate legalistic theories. This inquest represents the practical effort of four of the most mighty of nations, with the support of seventeen more, to utilize international law to meet the greatest menace of our times—aggressive war. The common sense of mankind demands that law shall not stop with the punishment of petty crimes by little people. It must also reach men who possess themselves of great power and make deliberate and concerted use of it to set in motion evils which leave no home in the world untouched. It is a cause of that magnitude that the United Nations will lay before Your Honors.

In the prisoners' dock sit twenty-odd broken men. Reproached by the humiliation of those they have led almost as bitterly as by the deso-

In opening, Jackson explains the need for this trial of major war criminals. Such evils must never be repeated, he says.

Jackson states that people in power must be held responsible for their actions, especially when that power is used for evil and destructive ends.

---

**Vocabulary**

**malignant** (mə·lig′nənt) *adj.*: destructive; evil.

**vengeance** (ven′jəns) *n.*: revenge; punishment in return for a wrongdoing.

**vindicate** (vin′də·kāt′) *v.*: prove correct; justify.

**magnitude** (mag′nə·tōōd′) *n.*: importance; greatness of scope.

**reproached** (ri·prōcht′) *v.*: blamed; disgraced.

lation of those they have attacked, their personal capacity for evil is forever past. It is hard now to perceive in these men as captives the power by which as Nazi leaders they once dominated much of the world and terrified most of it. Merely as individuals their fate is of little consequence to the world.

What makes this inquest significant is that these prisoners represent sinister influences that will lurk in the world long after their bodies have returned to dust. We will show them to be living symbols of racial hatreds, of terrorism and violence, and of the arrogance and cruelty of power. They are symbols of fierce nationalisms and of militarism, of intrigue and war making which have embroiled Europe generation after generation, crushing its manhood, destroying its homes, and impoverishing its life. They have so identified themselves with the philosophies they conceived and with the forces they directed that any tenderness to them is a victory and an encouragement to all the evils which are attached to their names. Civilization can afford no compromise with the social forces which would gain renewed strength if we deal ambiguously or indecisively with the men in whom those forces now precariously survive.

What these men stand for we will patiently and temperately[1] disclose. We will give you undeniable proofs of incredible events. The catalog of crimes will omit nothing that could be conceived by a pathological[2]

> The prisoners are important not as individuals but for what they represent.
>
> **?** *What is the main thing the prisoners represent?*

> This paragraph of Jackson's speech emphasizes the immoral and corrupt nature of the Nazis' actions.
>
> **?** *What did their actions eventually lead to?*

---

1. **temperately** *adj.:* dispassionately; in a calm, restrained way.
2. **pathological** *adj.:* diseased; here, morally harmful or corrupt.

---

**Vocabulary**
**precariously** (pri·ker′ē·əs·lē) *adv.:* in a shaky or unstable way.

pride, cruelty, and lust for power. These men created in Germany, under the "Führerprinzip,"[3] a National Socialist despotism[4] equaled only by the dynasties of the ancient East. They took from the German people all those dignities and freedoms that we hold natural and inalienable rights in every human being. The people were compensated by inflaming and gratifying hatreds toward those who were marked as "scapegoats."[5] Against their opponents, including Jews, Catholics, and free labor, the Nazis directed such a campaign of <u>arrogance</u>, brutality, and annihilation as the world has not witnessed since the pre-Christian ages. They excited the German ambition to be a "master race," which of course implies serfdom[6] for others. They led their people on a mad gamble for domination. They diverted social energies and resources to the creation of what they thought to be an <u>invincible</u> war machine. They overran their neighbors. To sustain the "master race" in its war making, they enslaved millions of human beings and brought them into Germany, where these hapless creatures now wander as "displaced persons." At length, bestiality and bad faith reached such excess that they aroused the sleeping strength of imperiled Civilization. Its united efforts have ground the German war machine to fragments. But the struggle has left Europe a liberated yet <u>prostrate</u> land where a demoralized society struggles to survive. These are the fruits of the sinister forces that sit with these defendants in the prisoners' dock. . . .

In general, our case will disclose these defendants all uniting at some time with the Nazi party in a plan which they well knew could be accomplished only by an outbreak of war in Europe. Their seizure of the German state, their subjugation[7] of the German people, their terrorism and extermination of <u>dissident</u> elements, their planning and waging

Jackson states that his case will focus on the conspiracy that brought about the war and its horrors, rather than on individuals' criminal behavior.

---

3. **Führerprinzip** (fü′rər·prin·tsēp′): German for "leader principle"; principle vesting absolute authority in the Führer, or Nazi leader, Adolf Hitler.
4. **despotism** *n.:* rule by one with absolute power; tyranny.
5. **scapegoats** *n. pl.:* people blamed unjustly. The Nazis used Jews, Catholics, Communists, and other groups as scapegoats for Germany's troubles after World War I.
6. **serfdom** *n.:* servitude; bondage. Strictly speaking, a serf is someone who is compelled to work a piece of land for the benefit of the landowner and can be transferred along with the land to a new owner.
7. **subjugation** *n.:* act of crushing or subduing.

---

**Vocabulary**

**arrogance** (ar′ə·gəns) *n.:* overbearing pride; self-importance.
**invincible** (in·vin′sə·bəl) *adj.:* unconquerable.
**prostrate** (präs′trāt′) *adj.:* helpless; overcome.
**dissident** (dis′ə·dənt) *adj.:* disagreeing; differing in belief or opinion.

of war, their calculated and planned ruthlessness in the conduct of warfare, their deliberate and planned criminality toward conquered peoples—all these are ends for which they acted in concert; and all these are phases of the conspiracy, a conspiracy which reached one goal, only to set out for another and more ambitious one. We shall also trace for you the intricate web of organizations which these men formed and utilized to accomplish these ends. We will show how the entire structure of offices and officials was dedicated to the criminal purposes and committed to the use of the criminal methods planned by these defendants and their co-conspirators, many of whom war and suicide have put beyond reach.

It is my purpose to open the case, particularly under Count One of the Indictment, and to deal with the Common Plan or Conspiracy to achieve ends possible only by resort to Crimes Against Peace, War Crimes, and Crimes Against Humanity.[8] My emphasis will not be on individual barbarities and perversions which may have occurred independently of any central plan. One of the dangers ever present is that this trial may be protracted[9] by details of particular wrongs and that we will become lost in a "wilderness of single instances." Nor will I now dwell on the activity of individual defendants except as it may contribute to exposition of the common plan.

The case as presented by the United States will be concerned with the brains and authority back of all the crimes. These defendants were men of a station and rank which does not soil its own hands with blood. They were men who knew how to use lesser folk as tools. We want to reach the planners and designers, the inciters and leaders, without whose evil architecture the world would not have been for so long scourged with the violence and lawlessness, and wracked with the agonies and convulsions, of this terrible war. ■

*What will the case presented by the United States focus on? Whom does Jackson want to reach?*

---

8. **Count One of the Indictment . . . Against Humanity:** The accused were charged with four counts: crimes against peace; crimes against humanity; war crimes; and the conspiracy to commit all of these crimes.

9. **protracted** *v.*: prolonged; extended unnecessarily.

General view of the Nuremberg Trials (1946).

# Response and Analysis

## Reading Check

1. To see how logically organized Jackson's argument is, make a simple outline of his opening statement. The main headings of the outline follow. You will have to fill in the subheads. Remember that when you add subheads to an outline, you must add at least two.

   I. Need for trial
   II. Purpose of inquest
   III. What defendants represent
   IV. What prosecutor will show about the defendants
   V. Conspiracy of defendants
   VI. What prosecutor will not emphasize
   VII. What case will be concerned with

   The sidenotes in the text will help you create your outline.

## Thinking Critically

2. What **appeals to reason** do you find in Jackson's speech?

3. What **appeals to emotion** do you find in Jackson's speech? List, especially, all the **word choices** you can find that denote or connote evil or wickedness. How does this buildup of emotionally loaded language affect you?

4. In the third paragraph, Jackson describes the defendants as "broken men." Why do you think Jackson uses this emotionally loaded description?

5. What does Jackson say might happen if the defendants are dealt with "ambiguously or indecisively"? How might this statement make an **ethical appeal** to the audience?

6. Jackson addresses the crimes of war that were committed by Nazi leaders during World War II. Do you think that the Nazi leaders considered their actions honorable during the war? after the war?

7. Review your Quickwrite notes and the quotation by Santayana on page 941, and then answer this question: Some people might say that executing these war criminals on the spot when they were first captured would have saved time and trouble. Why was it important to bring these leaders to trial before an international tribunal?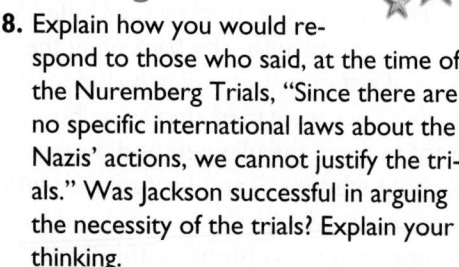

## Extending and Evaluating

8. Explain how you would respond to those who said, at the time of the Nuremberg Trials, "Since there are no specific international laws about the Nazis' actions, we cannot justify the trials." Was Jackson successful in arguing the necessity of the trials? Explain your thinking.

# WRITING

## The Arrogance and Cruelty of Power

Since 1945, many other people on the world stage have abused their power and brought untold suffering on their people and on other people in the world. Take one of Jackson's statements in this speech, and show how it could apply to another leader or leaders who abused their authority. Have any leaders "set in motion evils" that affected the whole world? In your **essay,** name the leader you are writing about, cite Jackson's words that apply to that person, tell what the person did, and describe what eventually happened to him or her.

**SKILLS FOCUS**

**Literary Skills**
Analyze points of view. Analyze persuasion and argument.

**Writing Skills**
Write an essay extending a statement from a text.

**Vocabulary Skills**
Understand denotations and connotations.

## Vocabulary Development

### Exploring Connotations

| malignant | reproached | invincible |
|-----------|------------|------------|
| vengeance | precariously | prostrate |
| vindicate | arrogance | dissident |
| magnitude | | |

**Denotation** is the strict dictionary definition of a word; **connotation** refers to the emotions and associations that have come to be attached to the word. Words may be positive, negative, or fairly neutral in connotation. For example, *slender* carries positive connotations, *skinny* carries negative connotations, and *thin* is fairly neutral. Fill out a chart like the one that follows for each Vocabulary word. Categorize each word as either **positive, negative,** or **neutral** in connotation. You may use a dictionary for help. Be sure to compare your charts in class.

| Word | Positive | Negative | Neutral |
|------|----------|----------|---------|
| arrogance | | X | |

## Vocabulary Development

### Terms Used in Political Science and History

Many terms used in law, government, political science, and history derive from French: for example, *acquit, defendant, judge, verdict, council, court,* and *power.* When you read a public document like the speech Robert H. Jackson delivered at the opening of the Nuremberg Trials (page 943), you can expect to encounter many political terms derived from French. Since the French language itself evolved from Latin and the English language has always freely adapted useful words from any source, be alert to the possibility of other origins as well.

**Tracing a word's origins.** The history of a word's origin and development is called its **etymology.** Most dictionaries give the etymology of a word in brackets after its pronunciation and the abbreviation for its part of speech. Check the introduction of your dictionary for an explanation of how it organizes entries and what symbols and abbreviations it uses. Even when you already know a word and some of its related words, exploring its etymology can enrich your

**SKILLS FOCUS**

**Vocabulary Skills**
Understand etymologies of words used in political science and history.

understanding. Here's the beginning of a dictionary entry for *conspiracy*, a term used in Jackson's speech:

> **conspiracy** (kən·spir′ə·sē) *n.* [[ME *conspiracie*, prob. via ML *conspirancia* < L *conspirare:* see CONSPIRE]]

The etymology of *conspiracy* shows that it comes from a Middle English word, probably via a Middle Latin word that goes back to the Latin word *conspirare*. For more on that word, you must consult the entry for *conspire*.

> **conspire** (kən·spīr′) *vi.* [[ME *conspiren* < OFr *conspirer* < L *conspirare*, to breathe together, agree, unite < *com–*, together + *spirare*, to breathe: see SPIRIT]]

The etymology of *conspire* leads you to the Latin word *conspirare*, which means "to breathe together," from the prefix *com–*, "together," and *spirare*, "to breathe." Knowing the story behind terms used in political science and history can lead you to even more words, those related to the original term (*inspire, spirit,* even *perspire*).

## PRACTICE

Working with a partner, use a dictionary to research the etymologies and meanings of the following political or historical terms. Then, try to find at least one related word. Double-check the etymology of the related word in a dictionary to make sure both words have the same origin. Remember that you may sometimes need to refer to an earlier entry to learn the full story of an etymology. Record your information in a chart like the one below.

**despot**          **inquest**
**domination**      **philosophy**
**dynasty**         **subjugation**
**extermination**   **terrorism**
**force**           **warfare**

| Word | Etymology | Meaning | Related Words |
|------|-----------|---------|---------------|
| serfdom | Old French from Latin *servus,* "slave" | state or condition of being enslaved | servant, servitude, service, serve |

# Connected Readings

## World War II

Anne Frank . . . . . . . . . . . . . . *from* **The Diary of a Young Girl**

John Whitehead . . . . . . . . . **"The Biggest Battle of All History"** *from* The Greatest Generation Speaks *by* Tom Brokaw

Margaret Bourke-White . . . *from* **April in Germany**

You have just read four main selections and considered the views each expresses about World War II. The next three selections you will be reading present additional firsthand points of view on World War II. As you read, ask yourself how these views are alike and how they are different. After you read these selections, you'll find questions on page 958 asking you to compare all seven readings.

## Points *of* View

### Before You Read

On June 12, 1942, Anne Frank, a young Jewish girl living in Amsterdam, received a diary for her thirteenth birthday. Less than two months later, Anne, her parents, and her older sister, Margot, along with four other Jews, went into hiding from the Nazis. For two years, the eight people lived in what Anne called the "Secret Annex"—a back office and attic in the warehouse of her father's spice business in Amsterdam. Dutch friends took great risks to smuggle food and other supplies to the fugitives—until someone tipped off the Gestapo, the Nazi secret police. In August 1944, the Gestapo raided the building and sent its hidden occupants to concentration camps. Miep Gies and Bep Voskuijl, the two secretaries working in the building at the time, found Anne's diaries among the scattered papers the Gestapo left behind. Anne died of typhus in March 1945 at a camp in Germany called Bergen-Belsen. She was fifteen years old.

Anne's father, Otto, was the only member of the Secret Annex to survive the camps. Gies and Voskuijl returned Anne's diaries to her father after the war. Mr. Frank had the diaries published in 1947, and the book rapidly became a classic of war literature. Since 1947, it has been translated into more than fifty languages.

Anne Frank's diary.

The English translation, *The Diary of a Young Girl* by Anne Frank (1929–1945), was republished in 1995 with added material that had been removed from the original version. The diary reveals a bright, sensitive young woman who speaks to "Kitty," her diary, as a trusted friend. The following excerpt, from the revised edition, describes how the British Broadcasting Company (BBC) broadcasts of D-day raised the family's hopes of surviving the war. The liberation of Europe came too late for Anne. Nine months after listening to this triumphant news, she was dead.

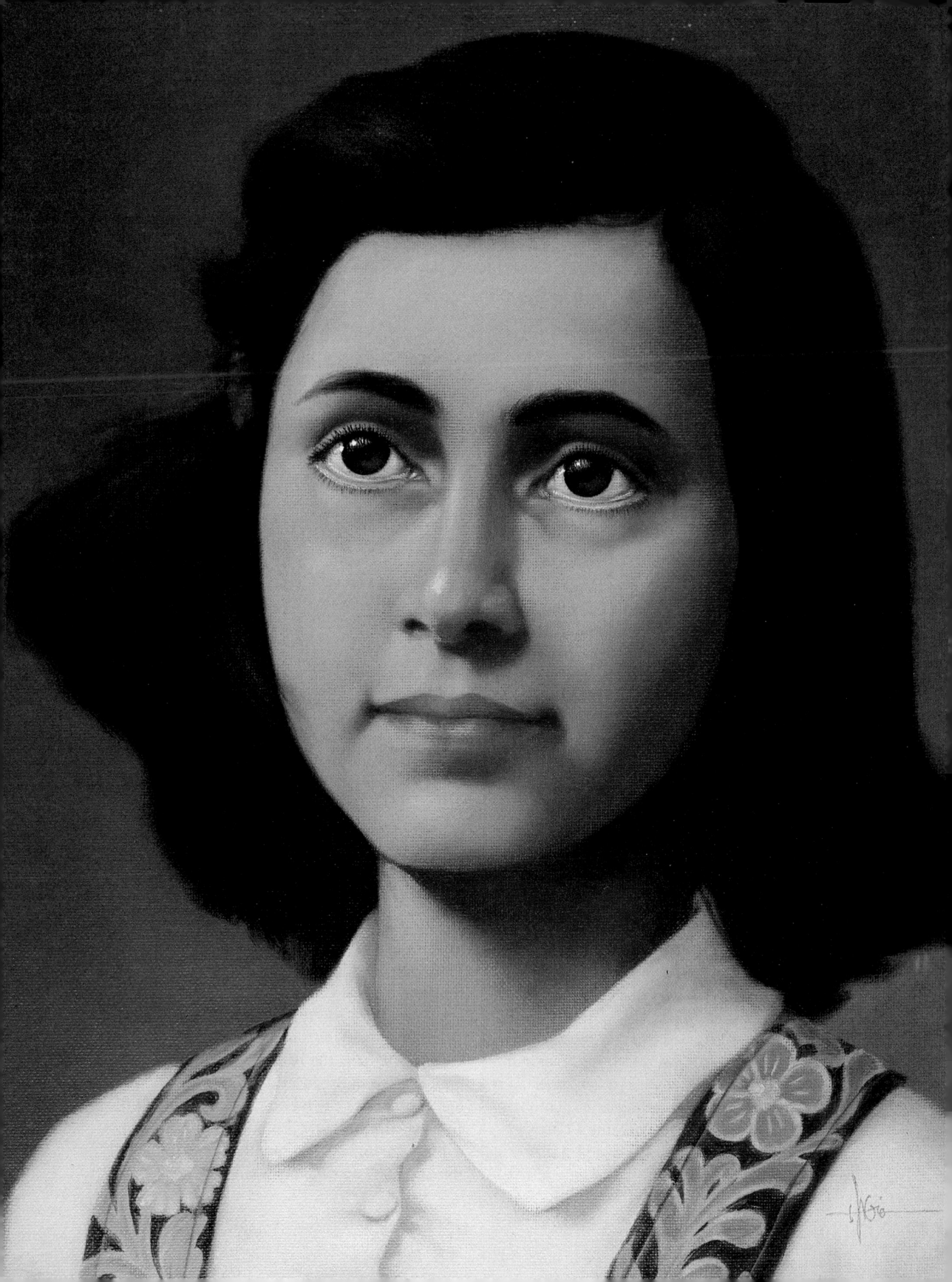

# *from* The Diary of a Young Girl

## Anne Frank

Tuesday, June 6, 1944

My dearest Kitty,

"This is D-day," the BBC announced at twelve. "This is *the* day." The invasion has begun!

This morning at eight the British reported heavy bombing of Calais, Boulogne, Le Havre and Cherbourg, as well as Pas de Calais[1] (as usual). Further, as a precautionary measure for those in the occupied territories, everyone living within a zone of twenty miles from the coast was warned to prepare for bombardments. Where possible, the British will drop pamphlets an hour ahead of time.

According to the German news, British paratroopers have landed on the coast of France. "British landing craft are engaged in combat with German naval units," according to the BBC.

Conclusion reached by the Annex while breakfasting at nine: this is a trial landing, like the one two years ago in Dieppe.

BBC broadcast in German, Dutch, French and other languages at ten: The invasion has begun! So this is the "real" invasion. BBC broadcast in German at eleven: speech by Supreme Commander General Dwight Eisenhower.

BBC broadcast in English: "This is D-day." General Eisenhower said to the French people: "Stiff fighting will come now, but after this the victory. The year 1944 is the year of complete victory. Good luck!"

BBC broadcast in English at one: Eleven thousand planes are shuttling back and forth or standing by to land troops and bomb behind enemy lines; four thousand landing craft and small boats are continually arriving in the area between Cherbourg and Le Havre. English and American troops are already engaged in heavy combat. Speeches by Gerbrandy, the Prime Minister of Belgium, King Haakon of Norway, de Gaulle of France, the King of England and, last but not least, Churchill.[2]

A huge commotion in the Annex! Is this really the beginning of the long-awaited liberation? The liberation we've all talked so much about, which still seems too good, too much of a fairy tale ever to come true? Will this year, 1944, bring us victory? We don't know yet. But where there's hope, there's life. It fills us with fresh courage and makes us strong again. We'll need to be brave to endure the many fears and hardships and the suffering yet to come. It's now a matter of remaining calm and steadfast, of gritting our teeth and keeping a stiff upper lip! France, Russia, Italy, and even Germany, can cry out in agony, but we don't yet have that right!

Oh, Kitty, the best part about the invasion is that I have the feeling that friends are on the way. Those terrible Germans have oppressed and threatened us for so long that the thought of friends and salvation means everything to us! Now it's not just the Jews, but Holland and all of occupied Europe. Maybe, Margot says, I can even go back to school in September or October.

Yours,

*Anne*

P.S. I'll keep you informed of the latest news!

---

1. **Calais ... Pas de Calais:** All of the places Anne mentions lie in Normandy, a region on the northern coast of France.

2. **Churchill:** Sir Winston Churchill (1874–1965), British statesman and historian who was Great Britain's prime minister during World War II.

## Points of View

### Before You Read

The television journalist Tom Brokaw (1940–    ) walked the beaches of Normandy in northern France on the fortieth and fiftieth anniversaries of D-day—the June 6, 1944, Allied invasion of Nazi-occupied France that signaled the beginning of the final stage of World War II in Europe. As Brokaw walked, he began to realize how much he owed the generation who had fought World War II. It was his parents' generation, people shaped by the Great Depression of the 1930s and the war years of the 1940s—a generation little known or under-stood by people coming of age in the 1980s and 1990s, an era of prosperity. He decided to thank that generation for its legacy of "duty and honor, sacrifice and accomplishment" by telling its stories in a book he called *The Greatest Generation* (1998).

Response proved so enthusiastic that Brokaw compiled a second book. *The Greatest Generation Speaks* (1999) contains letters and reflections by men and women who directly experienced World War II. The excerpt you are about to read comes from a letter written by John Whitehead, who served in the U.S. Navy as a supply officer on the U.S.S. *Thomas Jefferson.* World War II "was a long war," Whitehead said earlier in his letter, but one that was "universally accepted by all of us who par-ticipated as a 'just war.' . . . It was a war that had to be won and we would willingly stay the course."

For the D-day mission on June 6, 1944, White-head was assigned to be a boat officer. The fol-lowing excerpt begins after Whitehead and his crew had landed two thousand soldiers on the beaches of Normandy, France, for the planned attack.

U.S. infantrymen wading ashore during D-day landing.

Allied forces at the beach in Normandy.

# "The Biggest Battle of All History"

## John Whitehead

*from* **The Greatest Generation Speaks**
*by* **Tom Brokaw**

There was one moment of D-day which, rather strangely, remains more vivid in my mind than anything else. It was a quiet moment, a moment of peace and introspection after a very long day of noise and fear, of chaos and seasickness, of little acts of courage, and of death.

It was about 3:00 and we had made our second landing of the day and would soon be starting again the two-hour trip back to the *T.J.*[1] The beach was now secure. My five little boats had all made it in without serious problems and we were actually a little ahead of schedule. The ship's crew had only had two casualties from the landing. The Army lieutenant from my boat was now busy trying to get ashore a large machine gun and, for the first time since 2:00 A.M., I had a free moment.

I clambered off the boat—we were stuck on a little shoal in about two feet of water—and walked a few yards up the beach. I took a few deep breaths and looked around me. The dead and wounded had been moved up to the first dune and were being cared for. Equipment— guns and food and ammunition—was being unloaded, along with more troops. As far as I could see, in both directions, LCVPs[2] were landing, unloading, and withdrawing, and I realized that what I could see was less than 5 percent of the landing beaches. It wasn't orderly, but it wasn't chaos either. I got the sense that it was going to work, that what had looked like such a disaster only a few hours earlier was beginning to look like it had a chance.

I felt thankful, of course, that I seemed to have survived the worst part. I took a few deep breaths and felt suddenly elated, proud to be having even a tiny part in what was maybe the biggest battle of all history. At that moment, soaked to the skin, seasick, dead tired, cold, still scared, I would not have wanted to be anywhere else.

---

1. ***T.J.:*** Whitehead's abbreviation for the U.S.S. *Thomas Jefferson.*
2. **LCVPs:** plural form of the acronym for "landing craft, vehicle, personnel," small U.S. Navy boats designed to carry personnel from ship to shore.

## Points *of* View

### Before You Read

Photojournalist Margaret Bourke-White (1906–1971) gained a reputation for photographing scenes that no other photographers had dared to attempt. Bourke-White covered World War II for *Life* magazine, and she personally shared hardships with the American military troops. She experienced everything from shipwreck and battle-front duty to the chaos of postwar Germany. At the end of the war, her photographs of corpses and emaciated survivors in the Nazi concentration camps stunned the world.

   In the excerpt you are about to read, Bourke-White described her reactions and those of German civilians on seeing an enormous pile of corpses in the courtyard of the Buchenwald camp.

People salvaging bricks and boards from bomb-damaged German buildings.

Photographs on pages 956–957 are by Margaret Bourke-White.

Prisoners of Buchenwald (April 1945).

MEMOIR

# *from* April in Germany
## Margaret Bourke-White

Concentration-camp survivor weeping.

"**W**e didn't know! We didn't know!"
I first heard these words on a sunny afternoon in mid-April, 1945. They were repeated so often during the weeks to come, and all of us heard them with such monotonous frequency, that we came to regard them as a kind of national chant for Germany.

There was an air of unreality about that April day in Weimar,[1] a feeling to which I found myself stubbornly clinging. I kept telling myself that I would believe the indescribably horrible sight in the courtyard before me only when I had a chance to look at my own photographs. Using the camera was almost a relief; it interposed a slight barrier between myself and the white horror in front of me.

This whiteness had the fragile translucence[2] of snow, and I wished that under the bright April sun which shone from a clean blue sky it would all simply melt away. I longed for it to disappear, because while it was there I was reminded that men actually had done this thing—men with arms and legs and eyes and hearts not so very unlike our own. And it made me ashamed to be a member of the human race.

The several hundred other spectators who filed through the Buchenwald[3] courtyard on that sunny April afternoon were equally unwilling to admit association with the human beings who had perpetrated these horrors. But their reluctance had a certain tinge of self-interest; for these were the citizens of Weimar, eager to plead their ignorance of the outrages.

When Third Army troops had occupied Buchenwald two days before, that tough old soldier, General Patton,[4] had been so incensed at what he saw that he ordered his police to go through Weimar, of which Buchenwald is a suburb, and bring back one thousand civilians to make them see with their own eyes what their leaders had done. The MPs[5] were so enraged that they brought back two thousand.

The newly freed inmates of the camp, dressed in their blue and white striped prison suits, scrambled to the top of the fences around the courtyard. From here these slave laborers and political prisoners waited to see German people forced to view the heap of their dead comrades. Woman fainted or wept. Men covered their faces and turned their heads away. It was when the civilians began repeating, "We didn't know! We didn't know!" that the ex-prisoners were carried away with wrath.

"You did know," they shouted. "Side by side we worked with you in the factories. At the risk of our lives we told you. But you did nothing."

Of course they knew, as did almost all Germans.

---

1. **Weimar** (vī′mär′): city in east central Germany.
2. **translucence** *n.:* semitransparency.
3. **Buchenwald** (boo′kən·vält′): village near Weimar and the site of one of the largest of the Nazi concentration camps. Buchenwald's prisoners worked as slave laborers. Although Buchenwald did not have gas chambers, hundreds of prisoners died there each month from disease, malnutrition, beatings, and executions. The wife of the Nazi commandant was known as the Witch of Buchenwald because of her cruelty.

---

4. **Patton:** Gen. George S. Patton (1885–1945), who commanded the U.S. Third Army at the defeat of Germany in 1945.
5. **MPs:** military police.

# Analysis **Comparing Points** *of* **View**

## World War II

The questions on this page ask you to analyze the views expressed in the preceding seven selections:

Randall Jarrell . . . . . . . . . . . **The Death of the Ball Turret Gunner**

Elie Wiesel . . . . . . . . . . . . . *from* **Night**

John Hersey . . . . . . . . . . . . **A Noiseless Flash** *from* Hiroshima

Robert H. Jackson . . . . . . . . "**The Arrogance and Cruelty of Power**" *from* Speech at the Nuremberg Trials, November 21, 1945

Anne Frank . . . . . . . . . . . . . *from* **The Diary of a Young Girl**

John Whitehead . . . . . . . . . "**The Biggest Battle of All History**" *from* The Greatest Generation Speaks *by* Tom Brokaw

Margaret Bourke-White . . . *from* **April in Germany**

### Thinking Critically

1. Which of the selections in this feature are **primary sources**? Which are **secondary sources**?

2. How would you rate the **credibility** of the secondary sources? What accounts for your evaluation of their credibility?

3. Six of these selections deal with Germany's role in World War II in Europe. What underlying attitudes toward this war can you find in each selection? Are the assumptions in agreement, or do some selections profess different points of view? Consider these issues:
   • how human beings can be reduced to statistics during war
   • how suffering can dehumanize people
   • how people's response to war and suffering can be courageous
   • how civilization must constantly struggle against impulses toward destruction, hatred, and violence

4. Do you find contradicting attitudes in some of these selections? For example, how do the attitudes of the speaker in "The Death of the Ball Turret Gunner" (page 910) and John Whitehead's experiences on D-day (page 955) differ? How do you account for such differences?

5. What words of Jackson's in the speech at Nuremberg could apply to the military rulers of Japan who caused the war that led to the terrible suffering of their own people at Hiroshima? How does John Hersey feel about the Japanese victims? How can you tell?

Margaret Bourke-White.

# WRITING

## Preparing a Multimedia Report

Select a topic related to World War II that intrigues you, perhaps the war in the Pacific, the postwar recovery in Japan or in Europe, Holocaust memorials, or individual leaders such as Franklin Delano Roosevelt, Winston Churchill, Joseph Stalin, or Adolf Hitler. Use print, Internet, and media resources to learn more about your topic. Obtain still pictures or videos to accompany the **report** you research, write, and present to your class.

▶ **Use "Analyzing and Using Media," pages 1314–1321, for help with this assignment.**

## Arguing a Case

Choose a topic from World War II that still arouses debate, such as the right of the International Military Tribunal to try Nazi leaders for war crimes; President Harry S. Truman's decision to use the atomic bomb; or the problems with the Soviet Union's control of Berlin after the war. Research the issues on both sides of the debate, and write a **report** that summarizes the arguments and presents your own conclusions.

▶ **Use "Reporting Historical Research," pages 602–621, for help with this assignment.**

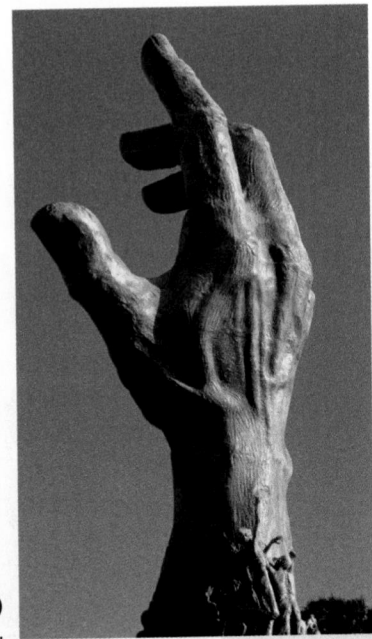

Bronze sculpture (detail) (1990)
by Kenneth Treister.

Women rebuilding a wall
in Dresden, Germany (1940s).

# Contemporary Fiction

**O'Brien**

**Barthelme**

**Carver**

**Alvarez**

**Tan**

**Lahiri**

**Danticat**

Write about the stuff that isn't quite comfortable inside you, the things that are hard to get at and say.

—Julia Alvarez

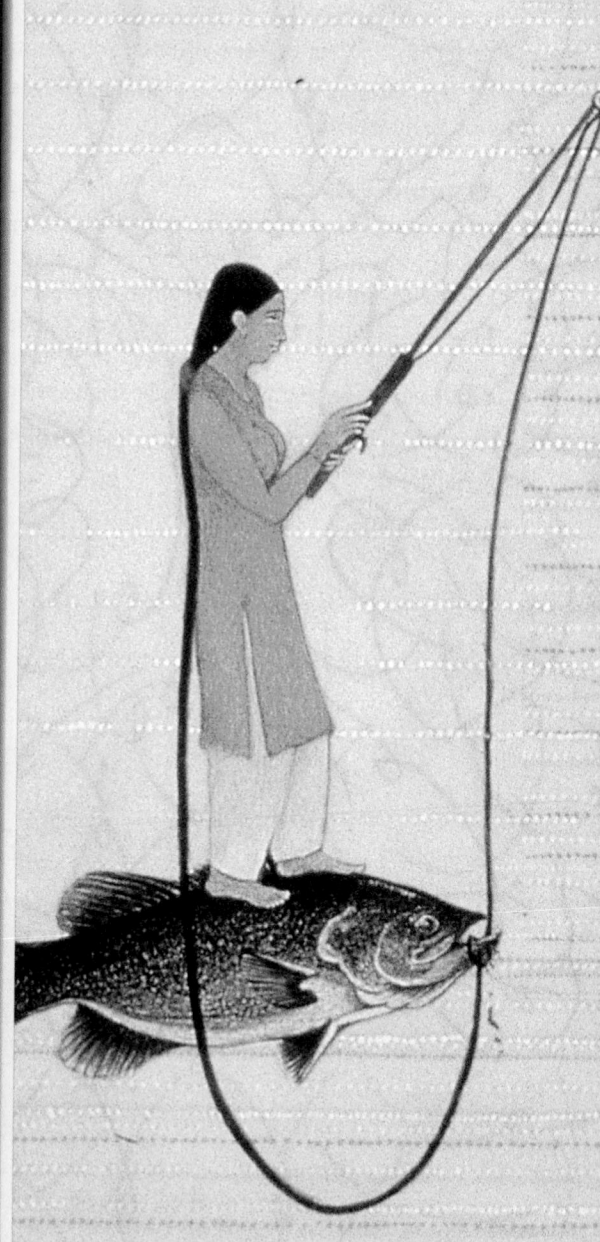

From *Bed of My Own Making* (1999), a series of paintings by Ambreen Butt. Watercolor, gouache, and thread on Mylar and paper.

# Tim O'Brien

## (1946–    )

"All my work has been somewhat political in that it's been directed at big issues," Tim O'Brien once said. "My concerns have to do with the abstractions: What's courage and how do you get it? What's justice and how do you achieve it? How does one do right in an evil situation?" O'Brien turned those questions into powerful artistic tools in his gripping war novel *Going After Cacciato* (1978).

O'Brien was born in Austin, Minnesota, and graduated from Macalester College. In 1968, he was drafted and served with the U.S. Army in Vietnam, where he attained the rank of sergeant. Returning from the war, he went to Harvard for graduate work in English. A summer internship at *The Washington Post* led to a job as national affairs reporter for that newspaper.

O'Brien had been writing stories since childhood, and even in the midst of his academic work, he knew he wanted to write full time. It was his military experience in Vietnam that provided much of the material for his fiction and personal narratives. *If I Die in a Combat Zone, Box Me Up and Ship Me Home* (1973) is a collection of anecdotes and observations of his duty in Vietnam. The book drew widespread praise, particularly from veterans, as an authentic re-creation of the foot soldier's experience in an unpopular war.

O'Brien's first novel, *Northern Lights,* appeared in 1974 and dealt with a veteran returned to civilian life. *Going After Cacciato,* his second novel, followed four years later. This novel returned to the jungle war and depicted a soldier's fantasy of quitting the battle and walking off across the mountains to find Paris. *Cacciato* was acclaimed as one of the few novels to have captured the essence of the Vietnam experience, and it won the prestigious National Book Award in 1979. O'Brien has said of his novel, "It's not really Vietnam that I was concerned about when I wrote *Cacciato;* rather it was to have readers care about what's right and wrong and about the difficulty of doing right, the difficulty of saying no to a war."

In 1990, O'Brien published *The Things They Carried,* a remarkable fictional memoir about the Vietnam War and its human effects. The book is made up of interconnected stories narrated by a character named Tim O'Brien, who, the author says, is not himself. The title story deals with the physical objects a soldier carries into battle, such as weapons and letters from home, as well as the intangible things, like fears and memories. At publication, O'Brien told an interviewer, "My life is storytelling. I believe in stories, in their incredible power to keep people alive, to keep the living alive, and the dead. . . . In Vietnam, men were constantly telling one another stories about the war."

O'Brien's Vietnam experience also lies at the core of his psychological thriller, *In the Lake of the Woods* (1994). The book focuses on a politician who tries to conceal his past involvement in the massacre of Vietnamese civilians by American soldiers at My Lai in 1968.

## For Independent Reading

If you'd like to read more O'Brien short stories about Vietnam, try

- "The Things They Carried"
- "Calling Home"

# Before You Read

## Speaking of Courage

### Make the Connection
#### Quickwrite

What is courage? Can it be measured by awards and medals? In this story, Paul Berlin looks back, wishing he had *really* been courageous in war—especially during one particular incident. He finds himself unable to discuss with his father what happened. Why might it be difficult for a young soldier to speak with a parent about a war experience? Write down reasons why such conversations might be strained.

### Literary Focus
#### Conflict

A **conflict** is a struggle between opposing forces or characters. An **external conflict** can involve two people, or a person and a natural or artificial force. An **internal conflict** involves opposing forces within a person's mind. "Speaking of Courage" focuses mainly on an internal conflict within the mind of Paul Berlin.

> **Conflict** is a struggle between opposing forces or characters.
>
> *For more on Conflict, see the Handbook of Literary and Historical Terms.*

### Reading Skills
#### Identifying Historical Context

The setting of a story includes not only its time and place but also its historical context—the social and political environment unique to that time and place. Atmosphere, characterization, and the central conflicts of a story often flow directly from historical context, as they do in "Speaking of Courage." As you read, take notes on contrasts between the attitudes and values of small-town Iowa, Paul Berlin's home, and the realities of jungle warfare in Vietnam, which Paul has just experienced.

### Background

Before O'Brien completed his war novel, *Going After Cacciato*, he published earlier versions of some sections as short stories. This story, which appears in a different form in the novel, was named one of the O. Henry Prize Stories of 1978.

The novel describes the war as experienced by a young soldier named Paul Berlin. In "Speaking of Courage," Paul has recently returned home from battle duty in Vietnam. Like many other veterans of that war, Paul is vaguely dissatisfied and confused about the meaning of his experiences.

### Vocabulary Development

**affluent** (af'lo͞o·ənt) *n.*: well-to-do people.

**tepid** (tep'id) *adj.*: lukewarm.

**mesmerizing** (mez'mər·īz'iŋ) *v.* used as *adj.*: hypnotic.

**drone** *n.*: steady hum.

**recede** (ri·sēd') *v.*: become more distant and indistinct.

**valor** (val'ər) *n.*: great courage.

**municipal** (myo͞o·nis'ə·pəl) *adj.*: belonging to a city or town.

**profundity** (prō·fun'də·tē) *n.*: intellectual depth.

**tactile** (tak'təl) *adj.*: able to be perceived by touch.

# SPEAKING OF COURAGE

Tim O'Brien

His father would not talk. His father had been in another war, so he knew the truth already, and there was no one left to talk with.

The war was over, and there was no place in particular to go. Paul Berlin followed the tar road in its seven-mile loop around the lake, then he started all over again, driving slowly, feeling safe inside his father's big Chevy, now and again looking out onto the lake to watch the boats and waterskiers and scenery. It was Sunday and it was summer, and things seemed pretty much the same. The lake was the same. The houses were the same, all low-slung and split level and modern, porches and picture windows facing the water. The lots were spacious. On the lake-side of the road, the houses were handsome and set deep in, well-kept and painted, with docks jutting out into the lake, and boats moored and covered with canvas, and gardens, and sometimes even gardeners, and stone patios with barbecue spits and grills, and wooden shingles saying who lived where. On the other side of the road, to his left, the houses were also handsome, though less expensive and on a smaller scale and with no docks or boats or wooden shingles. The road was a sort of boundary between the affluent and the almost affluent, and to live on the lake-side of the road was one of the few natural privileges in a town of the prairie—the difference between watching the sun set over cornfields or over the lake.

It was a good-sized lake. In high school he'd driven round and round and round with his friends and pretty girls, talking about urgent matters, worrying eagerly about the existence of God and theories of causation,[1] or wondering whether Sally Hankins, who lived on the lake-side of the road, would want to pull into the shelter of Sunset Park. Then, there had not been a war. But there had always been the lake. It had been dug out by the southernmost advance of the Wisconsin glacier. Fed by neither springs nor streams, it was a tepid, algaed lake that depended on fickle prairie rains for replenishment. Still, it was the town's only lake, the only one in twenty-six miles, and at night the moon made a white swath across its waters, and on sunny days it was nice to look at, and that evening it would dazzle with the reflections of fireworks, and it was the center of things from the very start, always there to be driven around, still mesmerizing and quieting and a good audience for silence, a seven-mile flat circumference that could be traveled by slow car in twenty-five minutes. It was not such a good lake for swimming. After college, he'd caught an ear infection that had almost kept him out of the war. And the lake had drowned Max Arnold, keeping him out of the war entirely. Max had been one who liked to talk about the existence of God. "No, I'm not saying *that*," he would say carefully against the drone of the engine. "I'm saying it is possible as an idea, even necessary as an idea, a final cause in the whole structure of causation." Now he knew, perhaps. Before the war, they'd driven around the lake as friends, but now Max was dead and most of the others were living in Des Moines or Sioux City, or going to school somewhere, or holding down jobs. None of the girls was left. Sally Hankins was married. His father would not talk. His father had been in another war, so he knew the truth already, and he would not talk about it, and there was no one left to talk with.

He turned on the radio. The car's big engine fired machinery that blew cold air all over him. Clockwise, like an electron spinning forever around its nucleus, the big Chevy circled the lake, and he had little to do but sit in the air-conditioning, both hands on the wheel, letting the car carry him in orbit. It was a lazy Sunday. The town was small. Out on the lake, a man's motorboat had stalled, and the fellow was bent over the silver motor with a wrench and a frown, and beyond him there were waterskiers and smooth July waters and two mud hens.

---

1. **theories of causation:** philosophical theories holding that events are connected through cause-and-effect relationships.

**Vocabulary**

**affluent** (af'loo·ənt) *n.*: well-to-do people.
**tepid** (tep'id) *adj.*: lukewarm.
**mesmerizing** (mez'mər·īz'iŋ) *v.* used as *adj.*: hypnotic.
**drone** *n.*: steady hum.

The road curved west. The sun was low in front of him, and he figured it was close to five o'clock. Twenty after, he guessed. The war had taught him to figure time. Even without the sun, waking from sleep, he could usually place it within fifteen minutes either way. He wished his father were there beside him, so he could say, "Well, looks about five-twenty," and his father would look at his watch and say, "Hey! How'd you do that?" "One of those things you learn in the war," he would say. "I know exactly what you mean," his father would then say, and the ice would be broken, and then they would be able to talk about it as they circled the lake.

He drove past Slater Park and across the causeway and past Sunset Park. The radio announcer sounded tired. He said it was five-thirty. The temperature in Des Moines was eighty-one degrees, and "All you on the road, drive carefully now, you hear, on this fine Fourth of July." Along the road, kicking stones in front of them, two young boys were hiking with knapsacks and toy rifles and canteens. He honked going by, but neither boy looked up. Already he'd passed them six times, forty-two miles, nearly three hours. He watched the boys recede in his rearview mirror. They turned purply colored, like clotted blood, before finally disappearing.

"How many medals did you win?" his father might have asked.

"Seven," he would have said, "though none of them were for valor."

"That's all right," his father would have answered, knowing full well that many brave men did not win medals for their bravery, and that others won medals for doing nothing. "What are the medals you won?"

And he would have listed them, as a kind of starting place for talking about the war: the Combat Infantryman's Badge, the Air Medal, the Bronze Star (without a V-device for valor),

**"Though none of them were for valor."**

the Army Commendation Medal, the Vietnam Campaign Medal, the Good Conduct Medal, and the Purple Heart, though it wasn't much of a wound, and there was no scar, and it didn't hurt and never had. While none of them was for valor, the decorations still looked good on the uniform in his closet, and if anyone were to ask, he would have explained what each signified, and eventually he would have talked about the medals he did not win, and why he did not win them, and how afraid he had been.

"Well," his father might have said, "that's an impressive list of medals, all right."

"But none were for valor."

"I understand."

And that would have been the time for telling his father that he'd almost won the Silver Star, or maybe even the Medal of Honor.

"I almost won the Silver Star," he would have said.

"How's that?"

"Oh, it's just a war story."

"What's wrong with war stories?" his father would have said.

"Nothing, except I guess nobody wants to hear them."

"Tell me," his father would have said.

And then, circling the lake, he would have started the story by saying what a crazy hot day it had been when Frenchie Tucker crawled like a snake into the clay tunnel and got shot in the neck, going on with the story in great detail, telling how it smelled and what the sounds had been, everything, then going on to say how he'd almost won the Silver Star for valor.

"Well," his father would have said, "that's not a very pretty story."

"I wasn't very brave."

"You have seven medals."

---

**Vocabulary**

**recede** (ri·sēd′) v.: become more distant and indistinct.
**valor** (val′ər) n.: great courage.

Vietnam Veterans Memorial (detail), Washington, D.C.

"True, true," he would have said, "but I might have had eight," but even so, seven medals was pretty good, hinting at courage with their bright colors and heavy metals. "But I wasn't brave," he would have admitted.

"You weren't a coward, either," his father would have said.

"I might have been a hero."

"But you weren't a coward," his father would have insisted.

"No," Paul Berlin would have said, holding the wheel slightly right of center to produce the constant clockwise motion, "no, I wasn't a coward, and I wasn't brave, but I had the chance." He would have explained, if anyone were there to listen, that his most precious medal, except for the one he did not win, was the Combat Infantryman's Badge. While not strictly speaking a genuine medal—more an insignia of soldierdom—the CIB meant that he had seen the war as a real soldier, on the ground. It meant he'd had the opportunity to be brave, it meant that. It meant, too, that he'd . . . seen Frenchie Tucker crawl into the tunnel so that just his feet were

left showing, and heard the sound when he got shot in the neck. With its crossed rifles and silver and blue colors, the CIB was really not such a bad decoration, not as good as the Silver Star or Medal of Honor, but still evidence that he'd once been there with the chance to be very brave. "I wasn't brave," he would have said, "but I might have been."

The road descended into the outskirts of town, turning northwest past the junior college and tennis courts, then past the city park where tables were spread with sheets of colored plastic as picnickers listened to the high school band, then past the municipal docks where a fat woman stood in pedal-pushers and white socks, fishing for bullheads.[2] There were no other fish in the lake, excepting some perch and a few

---

2. **bullheads** *n. pl.:* type of freshwater catfish with hornlike growths near its mouth.

**Vocabulary**
**municipal** (myo͞o·nis′ə·pəl) *adj.:* belonging to a city or town.

worthless carp. It was a bad lake for swimming and fishing both.

He was in no great hurry. There was no place in particular to go. The day was very hot, but inside the Chevy the air was cold and oily and secure, and he liked the sound of the big engine and the radio and the air-conditioning. Through the windows, as though seen through one-way glass, the town shined like a stop-motion photograph, or a memory. The town could not talk, and it would not listen, and it was really a very small town anyway. "How'd you like to hear about the time I almost won the Silver Star for valor?" he might have said. The Chevy seemed to know its way around the lake.

It was late afternoon. Along an unused railway spur, four men were erecting steel launchers for the evening fireworks. They were dressed alike in khaki trousers, work shirts, visored caps and black boots. They were sweating. Two of them were unloading crates of explosives from a city truck, stacking the crates near the steel launchers. They were talking. One of them was laughing. "How'd you like to hear about it?" he might have murmured, but the men did not look up. Later they would blow color into the sky. The lake would be like a mirror, and the picnickers would sigh. The colors would open wide. "Well, it was this crazy hot day," he would have said to anyone who asked, "and Frenchie Tucker took off his helmet and pack and crawled into the tunnel with a forty-five and a knife, and the whole platoon stood in a circle around the mouth of the tunnel to watch him go down. 'Don't get blowed away,' said Stink Harris, but Frenchie was already inside and he didn't hear. You could see his feet wiggling, and you could smell the dirt and clay, and then, when he got shot through the neck, you could smell the gunpowder and you could see Frenchie's feet jerk, and that was the day I could have won the Silver Star for valor."

The Chevy rolled smoothly across the old railroad spur. To his right, there was only the open lake. To his left, the lawns were scorched dry like October corn. Hopelessly, round and round, a rotating sprinkler scattered water into Doctor Mason's vegetable garden. In August it would get worse. The lake would turn green, thick with bacteria and decay, and the golf course would dry up, and dragonflies would crack open for lack of good water. The summer seemed permanent.

The big Chevy curled past the A&W[3] and Centennial Beach, and he started his seventh revolution around the lake.

He followed the road past the handsome low-slung houses. Back to Slater Park, across the causeway, around to Sunset Park, as though riding on tracks.

Out on the lake, the man with the stalled motorboat was still fiddling with the engine.

The two boys were still trudging on their hike. They did not look up when he honked.

The pair of mud hens floated like wooden decoys. The waterskiers looked tan and happy, and the spray behind them looked clean.

It was all distant and pretty.

Facing the sun again, he figured it was nearly six o'clock. Not much later the tired announcer in Des Moines confirmed it, his voice seeming to rock itself into a Sunday afternoon snooze.

Too bad, he thought. If Max were there, he would say something meaningful about the announcer's fatigue, and relate it to the sun low and red now over the lake, and the war, and courage. Too bad that all the girls had gone away. And his father, who already knew the difficulties of being brave, and who preferred silence.

Circling the lake, with time to talk, he would have told the truth. He would not have faked it. Starting with the admission that he had not been truly brave, he would have next said he hadn't been a coward, either. "I almost won the Silver Star for valor," he would have said, and, even so, he'd learned many important things in the war. Like telling time without a watch. He had learned to step lightly. He knew, just by the sound, the difference between friendly and enemy mortars,[4] and with time to talk and with an audience, he could explain the difference in

---

3. **A&W:** chain of drive-in fast-food restaurants.
4. **mortars** *n. pl.*: cannons used to fire explosive shells.

great detail. He could tell people that the enemy fired 82-millimeter mortar rounds, while we fired 81's, and that this was a real advantage to the enemy since they could steal our rounds and shoot them from their own weapons. He knew many lies. Simple, unprofound things. He knew it is a lie that only stupid men are brave. He knew that a man can die of fright, literally, because it had happened just that way to Billy Boy Watkins after his foot had been blown off. Billy Boy had been scared to death. Dead of a heart attack caused by fright, according to Doc Peret, who would know. He knew, too, that it is a lie, the old saying that you never hear the shot that gets you, because Frenchie Tucker was shot in the neck, and after they dragged him out of the tunnel he lay there and told everyone his great discovery; he'd heard it coming the whole way, he said excitedly; and then he raised his thumb and bled through his mouth, grinning at the great discovery. So the old saying was surely a lie, or else Frenchie Tucker was lying himself, which under the circumstances was hard to believe. He knew a lot of things. They were not new or profound, but they were true. He knew that he might have won a Silver Star, like Frenchie, if he'd been able to finish what Frenchie started in the foul tunnel. He knew many war stories, a thousand details, smells and the confusion of the senses, but nobody was there to listen, and nobody knew a damn about the war because nobody believed it was really a war at all. It was not a war for war stories, or talk of valor, and nobody asked questions about the details, such as how afraid you can be, or what the particular sounds were, or whether it hurts to be shot, or what you think about and hear and see on ambush, or whether you can really tell in a firefight which way to shoot, which you can't, or how you become brave enough to win the Silver Star, or how it smells of sulfur against your cheek after firing eighteen fast rounds, or how you crawl on hands and knees without knowing direction, and how, after crawling into the red-mouthed tunnel, you close your eyes like a mole and follow the tunnel walls and smell Frenchie's fresh blood and know

a bullet cannot miss in there, and how there is nowhere to go but forward or backward, eyes closed, and how you can't go forward, and lose all sense, and are dragged out by the heels, losing the Silver Star. All the details, without profundity, simple and age old, but nobody wants to hear war stories because they are age old and not new and not profound, and because everyone knows already that it hadn't been a war like other wars. If Max or his father were ever to ask, or anybody, he would say, "Well, first off, it was a war the same as any war," which would not sound profound at all, but which would be the truth. Then he would explain what he meant in great detail, explaining that, right or wrong or win or lose, at root it had been a real war, regardless of corruption in high places or politics or sociology or the existence of God. His father knew it already, though. Which was why he didn't ask. And Max could not ask. It was a small town, but it wasn't the town's fault, either.

He passed the sprawling ranch-style homes. He lit a cigarette. He had learned to smoke in the war. He opened the window a crack but kept the air-conditioner going full, and again he circled the lake. His thoughts were the same. Out on the lake, the man was frantically yanking the cord to his stalled outboard motor. Along the causeway, the two boys marched on. The pair of mud hens sought sludge at the bottom of the lake, heads under water and tails bobbing.

Six-thirty, he thought. The lake had divided into two halves. One half still glistened. The other was caught in shadow. Soon it would be dark. The crew of workers would shoot the sky full of color, for the war was over, and the town would celebrate independence. He passed Sunset Park once again, and more houses, and the junior college and tennis courts, and the picnickers and the high school band, and the municipal docks where the fat woman patiently waited for fish.

**Vocabulary**

**profundity** (prō·fun′də·tē) *n.*: intellectual depth.

Already, though it wasn't quite dusk, the A&W was awash in neon lights.

He maneuvered his father's Chevy into one of the parking slots, let the engine idle, and waited. The place was doing a good holiday business. Mostly kids in their fathers' cars, a few farmers in for the day, a few faces he thought he remembered, but no names. He sat still. With the sound of the engine and air-conditioning and radio, he could not hear the kids laughing, or the cars coming and going and burning rubber. But it didn't matter, it seemed proper, and he sat patiently and watched while mosquitoes and June bugs swarmed off the lake to attack the orange-colored lighting. A slim, hipless, deft young blonde delivered trays of food, passing him by as if the big Chevy were invisible, but he waited. The tired announcer in Des Moines gave the time, seven o'clock. He could trace the fall of dusk in the orange lights which grew brighter and sharper. It was a bad war for medals. But the Silver Star would have been nice. Nice to have been brave. The tactile, certain substance of the Silver Star, and how he could have rubbed his fingers over it, remembering the tunnel and the smell of clay in his nose, going forward and not backward in simple bravery. He waited patiently. The mosquitoes were electrocuting themselves against a Pest-Rid machine. The slim young carhop ignored him, chatting with four boys in a Firebird, her legs in nylons even in mid-summer.

He honked once, a little embarrassed, but she did not turn. The four boys were laughing. He could not hear them, or the joke, but he could see their bright eyes and the way their heads moved. She patted the cheek of the driver.

He honked again, twice. He could not hear the sound. The girl did not hear, either.

He honked again, this time leaning on the horn. His ears buzzed. The air-conditioning shot cold air into his lap. The girl turned slowly, as though hearing something very distant, not at all sure. She said something to the boys, and they laughed, then she moved reluctantly toward him. EAT MAMA BURGERS said the orange and brown button on her chest. "How'd you like to hear about the war," he whispered, feeling vengeful. "The time I almost won the Silver Star."

She stood at the window, straight up so he could not see her face, only the button that said, EAT MAMA BURGERS. "Papa Burger, root beer, and french fries," he said, but the girl did not move or answer. She rapped on the window.

"Papa Burger, root beer, and french fries," he said, rolling it down.

She leaned down. She shook her head dumbly. Her eyes were as lovely and fuzzy as cotton candy.

"Papa Burger, root beer, and french fries," he said slowly, pronouncing the words separately and distinctly for her.

She stared at him with her strange eyes. "You blind?" she chirped suddenly. She gestured toward an intercom attached to a steel post. "You blind or something?"

"Papa Burger, root beer, and french fries."

"Push the button," she said, "and place your order." Then, first punching the button for him, she returned to her friends in the Firebird.

"Order," commanded a tinny voice.

"Papa Burger, root beer, and french fries."

"Roger-dodger," the voice said. "Repeat: one Papa, one beer, one fries. Stand by. That's it?"

"Roger," said Paul Berlin.

"Out," said the voice, and the intercom squeaked and went dead.

"Out," said Paul Berlin.

When the slim carhop brought him his tray,

**"I almost won the Silver Star."**

---

**Vocabulary**

**tactile** (tak′təl) *adj.:* able to be perceived by touch.

he ate quickly, without looking up, then punched the intercom button.

"Order," said the tinny voice.

"I'm done."

"That's it?"

"Yes, all done."

"Roger-dodger, over n' out," said the voice.

"Out."

On his ninth revolution around the lake he passed the hiking boys for the last time. The man with the stalled motorboat was paddling toward shore. The mud hens were gone. The fat woman was reeling in her line. The sun had left a smudge of watercolor on the horizon, and the bandshell[5] was empty, and Doctor Mason's sprinkler went round and round.

On his tenth revolution, he switched off the air-conditioning, cranked open a window, and rested his elbow comfortably on the sill, driving with one hand. He could trace the contours of the tunnel. He could talk about the scrambling sense of being lost, though he could not describe it even in his thoughts. He could talk about the terror, but he could not describe it or even feel it anymore. He could talk about emerging to see sunlight, but he could not feel the warmth, or see the faces of the men who looked away, or talk about his shame. There was no one to talk to, and nothing to say.

On his eleventh revolution, the sky went crazy with color.

He pulled into Sunset Park and stopped in the shadow of a picnic shelter. After a time, he got out and walked down to the beach and stood with his arms folded and watched the fireworks. For a small town, it was a pretty good show. ∎

---

5. **bandshell** *n.:* open-air stage with a rear sounding board shaped like the shell of a scallop.

# Response and Analysis

**Literary Skills**
Analyze external and internal conflict.

**Reading Skills**
Analyze historical context.

**Writing Skills**
Write an essay comparing and contrasting two characters. Write an essay explaining the use of contrast in a story.

**Vocabulary Skills**
Use context clues.

## Reading Check

1. Describe both **settings** of the story—the one in which Paul Berlin finds himself on July 4 and the scene he keeps remembering from Vietnam.

2. What does Paul wish his father would do?

3. List the things Paul has learned as a result of the war.

4. According to Paul, why don't people want to hear about the war?

5. What does Paul wish he had done in Vietnam? What does he want to tell his father?

## Thinking Critically

6. Explain why it is so difficult for Paul and his father to talk. What do you think Paul means when he says that his father "knew the truth already"? (Be sure to check your Quickwrite notes.)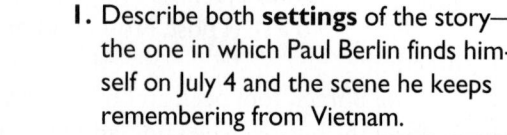

7. Discuss the **symbolic** meaning of the repeated circular actions in the story and the repeated references to time.

8. Considering the historical context of the story, what is **symbolic** about the date on which these events take place?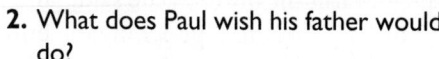

9. Given Paul's experiences, what is **ironic** about the military language used over the intercom at the A&W drive-in?

10. Find the passages in which Paul mentions conversations about God. What purpose do you think these passages serve?

11. What is Paul's **internal conflict**? Has it been resolved by the end of the story? Explain.

12. Is Paul being too hard on himself? Do you think he is a courageous person? Explain your responses to Paul's character.

**13.** How could a greater awareness of historical context—specifically, knowledge of the Vietnam War and American attitudes toward the war—help explain why Paul has a hard time finding anyone who is willing to talk about the war?

# WRITING

## Comparing Stories

In a brief **essay,** compare and contrast the situation and character of Paul Berlin with those of Harold Krebs in Ernest Hemingway's "Soldier's Home" (page 685). What can you infer about the similarities and differences in the experiences of soldiers returning from World War I and those returning from Vietnam?

## War and Peace

"Speaking of Courage" deals indirectly with the horror of warfare by contrasting war with small-town life. In a brief **essay,** explain how the story uses contrast to present a picture of war versus peace.

## Vocabulary Development
### Using Context Clues

Define each underlined word, and identify the **context clues** that give hints to its meaning. Then, go back to "Speaking of Courage," and see if O'Brien provides context clues for each word.

**1.** The veteran had earned a Purple Heart for his bravery, but dreams of greater valor continued to haunt him, even as the war itself continued to recede into the past.

**2.** Though the car salesman's pitch lacked profundity, his charming, rapid-fire delivery proved mesmerizing to the man who kept staring at the new car.

**3.** The coffee proved to be tepid, not hot, when the woman gave it a quick tactile test by dipping her finger into it.

**4.** We were alerted to the power outage by the sudden silencing of the usual drone of lights, fans, and household appliances.

**5.** Anyone in town could use the municipal parks and piers, but only the affluent could lounge on the private beaches of their exclusive lakeside estates.

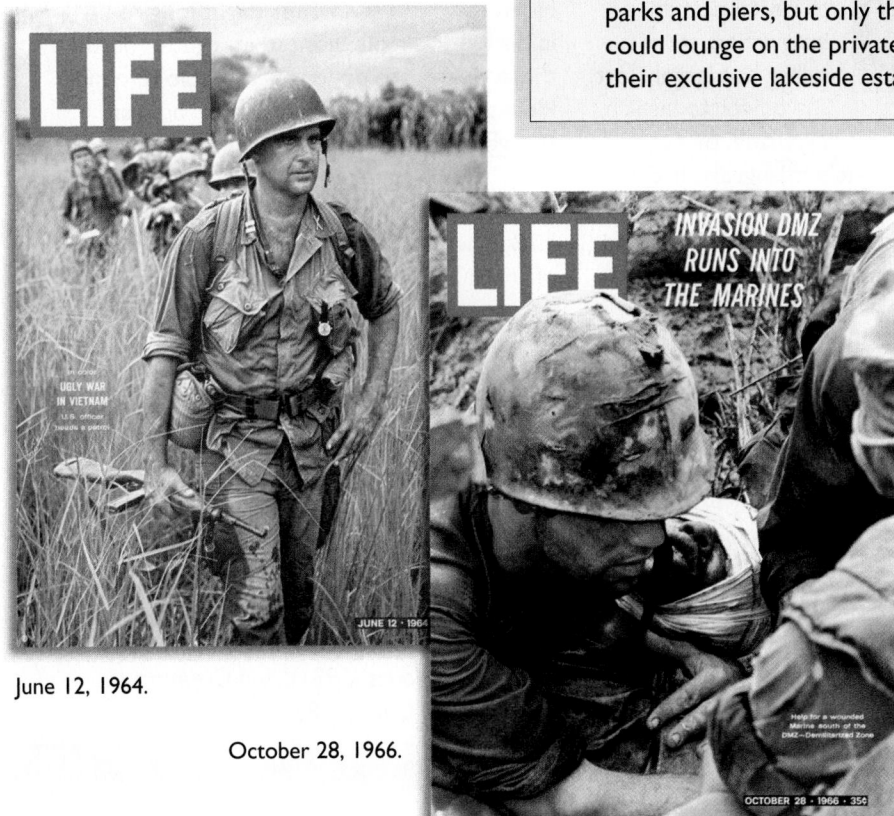

June 12, 1964.

October 28, 1966.

# Donald Barthelme
## (1931–1989)

© Nancy Crampton.

**D**onald Barthelme (bär'thəl·mē) was an experimenter in fiction and a true member of the avant-garde. Sometimes known as a postmodernist, he is widely regarded as one of the ablest and most versatile American stylists—witty, adventurous, and profound.

In broad terms, Barthelme believed that while literature of the past functioned to revitalize the imagination, storytelling had largely lost the power to inspire, persuade, or even entertain us. He felt that our language had gone bankrupt. Since words no longer effectively communicated feelings, he said, they had lost the power to move us. Contemporary language, Barthelme asserted, is thick with sludge and stuffing. Its use of clichés and its wordiness obscure truth rather than reveal it. As Snow White, the title character of Barthelme's 1967 novel, says, "Oh I wish there were some words in the world that were not the words I always hear!"

Barthelme saw the problems with language as a reflection of a society so dehumanized, so lacking in quality, that it could no longer sustain the kinds of myths that once gave us our identity. Thus, he felt, the whole point of storytelling was lost.

In his fiction, Barthelme set out to create a banal world that fails to make distinctions of quality in people, things, and ideas. Then, since he felt it was no longer possible to write about real life or the real world, he took writing itself for his subject—the art of making art out of language. His interest lay in the form and sound of language, and he tended to play with words, to make art out of fragments, much as some contemporary sculptors fashion works out of everyday objects and some pop artists transform cartoons into art.

Barthelme's plots are also unconventional. They are episodic, a clutter of styles, absurdities, and slapstick. "Fragments are the only forms I trust," says one of his narrators. His characters are types rather than fully developed individuals.

In Barthelme's hands, myth may turn into realism and realism into absurdity; readers can lose their way as they try to identify with the proceedings and wonder about the writer's point. Barthelme explained to the puzzled: "Art is not difficult because it wishes to be difficult, rather because it wishes to be art. However much the writer might long to be, in his work, simple, honest, straightforward, these virtues are no longer available to him. He discovers that in being simple, honest, straightforward, nothing much happens. . . . We are looking for the as yet unspeakable, the as yet unspoken."

Barthelme was born in Philadelphia, the son of an avant-garde architect, and was raised and educated in Texas. After serving with the U.S. Army, he worked as a reporter for the *Houston Post,* as a museum director, as the editor of an art and literature review, as a professor of English at the City University of New York, and as a teacher of creative writing at the University of Houston. He was a regular contributor to *The New Yorker* magazine. Collections of his stories include *Come Back, Dr. Caligari* (1964), *Unspeakable Practices, Unnatural Acts* (1968), in which "Game" appears, *Sixty Stories* (1981), and *Overnight to Many Distant Cities* (1983).

# Before You Read

## Game

### Make the Connection

How we view the world determines in large measure how we live our lives and how we react to the people with whom we live. The following story offers a disturbing view of our times. "Game" won't give you a clear picture of your world, but it may start you thinking.

### Literary Focus
#### Theme and Title

Think about the word *game*. How many meanings can you identify? What does *game* mean to a child? to an athlete? to a hunter? Does the word suggest something serious or something frivolous? As you read Barthelme's story, jot down each new meaning of *game* that seems to apply. Then, think about how Barthelme's title reveals a theme of the story.

> **Theme** is the insight into human life that is communicated by a work as a whole. The **title** of a story often suggests or supports the theme.
>
> *For more on Theme, see the Handbook of Literary and Historical Terms.*

### Vocabulary Development

**sated** (sāt′id) *v.*: satisfied.

**simultaneously** (sī′məl·tā′nē·əs·lē) *adv.*: at the same time.

**ruse** (ro͞oz) *n.*: trick; deception.

**scrupulously** (skro͞op′yə·ləs·lē) *adv.*: painstakingly; with great care.

**precedence** (pres′ə·dəns) *n.*: priority because of superiority in rank.

**exemplary** (eg·zem′plə·rē) *adj.*: serving as a model; worth imitating.

**acrimoniously** (ak′ri·mō′nē·əs·lē) *adv.*: bitterly; harshly.

**stolidly** (stäl′id·lē) *adv.*: in a way that shows little emotion; impassively.

SKILLS FOCUS

**Literary Skills**
Understand theme and title.

**INTERNET**

Vocabulary Practice

Keyword: LE7 11-6

**Donald Barthelme** 973

# If I behave strangely Shotwell is supposed to shoot me.

# Game

Donald Barthelme

**S**hotwell keeps the jacks and the rubber ball in his attaché case and will not allow me to play with them. He plays with them, alone, sitting on the floor near the console[1] hour after hour, chanting "onesies, twosies, threesies, foursies" in a precise, well-modulated voice, not so loud as to be annoying, not so soft as to allow me to forget. I point out to Shotwell that two can derive more enjoyment from playing jacks than one, but he is not interested. I have asked repeatedly to be allowed to play by myself, but he simply shakes his head. "Why?" I ask. "They're mine," he says. And when he has finished, when he has <u>sated</u> himself, back they go into the attaché case.

It is unfair but there is nothing I can do about it. I am aching to get my hands on them.

Shotwell and I watch the console. Shotwell and I live under the ground and watch the console. If certain events take place upon the console, we are to insert our keys in the appropriate locks and turn our keys. Shotwell has a key and I have a key. If we turn our keys <u>simultaneously</u> the bird flies, certain switches are activated and the bird flies. But the bird never flies. In one hundred thirty-three days the bird has not flown. Meanwhile Shotwell and I watch each other. We each wear a .45 and if Shotwell behaves strangely I am supposed to shoot him. If I behave strangely Shotwell is supposed to shoot me. We watch the console and think about shooting each other and think about the bird. Shotwell's behavior with the jacks is strange. Is it strange? I do not know. Perhaps he is merely

---

1. **console** (kän′sōl′) *n.*: desklike control panel.

---

**Vocabulary**
**sated** (sāt′id) *v.*: satisfied.
**simultaneously** (sī′məl·tā′nē·əs·lē) *adv.*: at the same
   time.

selfish . . . perhaps his character is flawed, perhaps his childhood was twisted. I do not know.

Each of us wears a .45 and each of us is supposed to shoot the other if the other is behaving strangely. How strangely is strangely? I do not know. In addition to the .45 I have a .38 which Shotwell does not know about concealed in my attaché case, and Shotwell has a .25 caliber Beretta which I do not know about strapped to his right calf. Sometimes instead of watching the console I pointedly watch Shotwell's .45, but this is simply a <u>ruse</u>, simply a maneuver, in reality I am watching his hand when it dangles in the vicinity of his right calf. If he decides I am behaving strangely he will shoot me not with the .45 but with the Beretta. Similarly, Shotwell pretends to watch my .45 but he is really watching my hand resting idly atop my attaché case, my hand resting idly atop my attaché case, my hand. My hand resting idly atop my attaché case.

In the beginning I took care to behave normally. So did Shotwell. Our behavior was painfully normal. Norms of politeness, consideration, speech, and personal habits were <u>scrupulously</u> observed. But then it became apparent that an error had been made, that our relief was not going to arrive. Owing to an oversight. Owing to an oversight we have been here for one hundred thirty-three days. When it became clear that an error had been made, that we were not to be relieved, the norms were relaxed. Definitions of normality were redrawn in the agreement of January 1, called by us, The Agreement. Uniform regulations were relaxed, and mealtimes are no longer rigorously scheduled. We eat when we are hungry and sleep when we are tired. Considerations of rank and <u>precedence</u> were temporarily put aside, a handsome concession on the part of Shotwell, who is a captain, whereas I am only a first lieutenant. One of us watches the console at all times rather than two of us watching the console at all times, except when we are both on our feet. One of us watches the console at all times and if the bird flies then that one wakes the other and we turn our keys in the locks simultaneously and the

bird flies. Our system involves a delay of perhaps twelve seconds but I do not care because I am not well, and Shotwell does not care because he is not himself. After the agreement was signed Shotwell produced the jacks and the rubber ball from his attaché case, and I began to write a series of descriptions of forms occurring in nature, such as a shell, a leaf, a stone, an animal. On the walls.

Shotwell plays jacks and I write descriptions of natural forms on the walls.

Shotwell is enrolled in a USAFI[2] course which leads to a master's degree in business administration from the University of Wisconsin (although we are not in Wisconsin, we are in Utah, Montana or Idaho). When we went down it was in either Utah, Montana or Idaho, I don't remember. We have been here for one hundred thirty-three days owing to an oversight. The pale green reinforced concrete walls sweat and the air conditioning zips on and off erratically and Shotwell reads *Introduction to Marketing* by Lassiter and Munk, making notes with a blue ballpoint pen. Shotwell is not himself but I do not know it, he presents a calm aspect and reads *Introduction to Marketing* and makes his <u>exemplary</u> notes with a blue ballpoint pen, meanwhile controlling the .38 in my attaché case with one-third of his attention. I am not well.

We have been here one hundred thirty-three days owing to an oversight. Although now we are not sure what is oversight, what is plan. Perhaps the plan is for us to stay here permanently, or if not permanently at least for a year, for

---

2. **USAFI:** United States Armed Forces Information, an organization that supervises courses taken by service members.

---

### Vocabulary

**ruse** (ro͞oz) *n.*: trick; deception.

**scrupulously** (skro͞op′yə·ləs·lē) *adv.*: painstakingly; with great care.

**precedence** (pres′ə·dəns) *n.*: priority because of superiority in rank.

**exemplary** (eg·zem′plə·rē) *adj.*: serving as a model; worth imitating.

three hundred sixty-five days. Or if not for a year for some number of days known to them and not known to us, such as two hundred days. Or perhaps they are observing our behavior in some way, sensors[3] of some kind, perhaps our behavior determines the number of days. It may be that they are pleased with us, with our behavior, not in every detail but in sum. Perhaps the whole thing is very successful, perhaps the whole thing is an experiment and the experiment is very successful. I do not know. But I suspect that the only way they can persuade sun-loving creatures into their pale green sweating reinforced concrete rooms under the ground is to say that the system is twelve hours on, twelve hours off. And then lock us below for some number of days known to them and not known to us. We eat well although the frozen enchiladas are damp when defrosted and the frozen devil's food cake is sour and untasty. We sleep uneasily and acrimoniously. I hear Shotwell shouting in his sleep, objecting, denouncing, cursing sometimes, weeping sometimes, in his sleep. When Shotwell sleeps I try to pick the lock on his attaché case, so as to get at the jacks. Thus far I have been unsuccessful. Nor has Shotwell been successful in picking the locks on my attaché case so as to get at the .38. I have seen the marks on the shiny surface. I laughed, in the latrine, pale green walls sweating and the air conditioning whispering, in the latrine.

I write descriptions of natural forms on the walls, scratching them on the tile surface with a diamond. The diamond is a two and one-half carat solitaire I had in my attaché case when we went down. It was for Lucy. The south wall of the room containing the console is already

---

3. **sensors** (sen′sərz) *n. pl.:* detecting devices.

covered. I have described a shell, a leaf, a stone, animals, a baseball bat. I am aware that the baseball bat is not a natural form. Yet I described it. "The baseball bat," I said, "is typically made of wood. It is typically one meter in length or a little longer, fat at one end, tapering to afford a comfortable grip at the other. The end with the handhold typically offers a slight rim, or lip, at the nether[4] extremity, to prevent slippage." My description of the baseball bat ran to 4500 words, all scratched with a diamond on the south wall. Does Shotwell read what I have written? I do not know. I am aware that Shotwell regards my writing-behavior as a little strange. Yet it is no stranger than his jacks-behavior, or the day he appeared in black bathing trunks with the .25 caliber Beretta strapped to his right calf and stood over the console, trying to span with his two arms outstretched the distance between the locks. He could not do it, I had already tried, standing over the console with my two arms outstretched, the distance is too great. I was moved to comment but did not comment, comment would have provoked counter-comment,

---

4. **nether** (ne*th*′ər) *adj.:* lower.

**Vocabulary**
**acrimoniously** (ak′ri·mō′nē·əs·lē) *adv.:* bitterly; harshly.

**Donald Barthelme** 977

comment would have led God knows where. They had in their infinite patience, in their infinite foresight, in their infinite wisdom already imagined a man standing over the console with his two arms outstretched, trying to span with his two arms outstretched the distance between the locks.

Shotwell is not himself. He has made certain overtures. The burden of his message is not clear. It has something to do with the keys, with the locks. Shotwell is a strange person. He appears to be less affected by our situation than I. He goes about his business stolidly, watching the console, studying *Introduction to Marketing*, bouncing his rubber ball on the floor in a steady, rhythmical, conscientious manner. He appears to be less affected by our situation than I am. He is stolid. He says nothing. But he has made certain overtures, certain overtures have been made. I am not sure that I understand them. They have something to do with the keys, with the locks. Shotwell has something in mind. Stolidly he shucks the shiny silver paper from the frozen enchiladas, stolidly he stuffs them into the electric oven. But he has something in mind. But there must be a quid pro quo.[5] I insist on a quid pro quo. I have something in mind.

I am not well. I do not know our target. They do not tell us for which city the bird is targeted. I do not know. That is planning. That is not my responsibility. My responsibility is to watch the console and when certain events take place upon the console, turn my key in the lock. Shotwell bounces the rubber ball on the floor in a steady, stolid, rhythmical manner. I am aching

___
5. **quid pro quo:** Latin for "something for something." The phrase is used here to mean an even exchange.

to get my hands on the ball, on the jacks. We have been here one hundred thirty-three days owing to an oversight. I write on the walls. Shotwell chants "onesies, twosies, threesies, foursies" in a precise, well-modulated voice. Now he cups the jacks and the rubber ball in his hands and rattles them suggestively. I do not know for which city the bird is targeted. Shotwell is not himself.

Sometimes I cannot sleep. Sometimes Shotwell cannot sleep. Sometimes when Shotwell cradles me in his arms and rocks me to sleep, singing Brahms' "Guten Abend, gute Nacht,"[6] or I cradle Shotwell in my arms and rock him to sleep, singing, I understand what it is Shotwell wishes me to do. At such moments we are very close. But only if he will give me the jacks. That is fair. There is something he wants me to do with my key, while he does something with his key. But only if he will give me my turn. That is fair. I am not well. ∎

___
6. **Guten Abend, gute Nacht** (go͞ot′'n ä′bənt go͞ot′ə näkht): German for "good evening, good night." This line is from the musical composition popularly known as "Brahms's Lullaby" by Johannes Brahms (1833–1897).

**Vocabulary**
**stolidly** (stäl′id·lē) *adv.*: in a way that shows little emotion; impassively.

# The Unknown Citizen

## W. H. Auden

*To JS/07/M/378*
*This Marble Monument Is Erected by the State*

Social Programs (detail) by
Robert Graham. Sculpture
at the Franklin D.
Roosevelt Memorial in
Washington, D.C.

He was found by the Bureau of Statistics to be
One against whom there was no official complaint,
And all the reports on his conduct agree
That, in the modern sense of an old-fashioned word,
    he was a saint,
5    For in everything he did he served the Greater Community.
Except for the War till the day he retired
He worked in a factory and never got fired,
But satisfied his employers, Fudge Motors Inc.
Yet he wasn't a scab or odd in his views,
10   For his Union reports that he paid his dues,
(Our report on his Union shows it was sound)
And our Social Psychology workers found
That he was popular with his mates and liked a drink.
The Press are convinced that he bought a paper every day
15   And that his reactions to advertisements were normal in every way.
Policies taken out in his name prove that he was fully insured,
And his Health-card shows he was once in hospital but left it cured.
Both Producers Research and High-Grade Living declare
He was fully sensible to the advantages of the Installment Plan
20   And had everything necessary to the Modern Man,
A gramophone, a radio, a car, and a frigidaire.
Our researchers into Public Opinion are content
That he held the proper opinions for the time of year;
When there was peace, he was for peace; when there was war, he went.
25   He was married and added five children to the population,
Which our Eugenist says was the right number for a parent of his generation,
And our teachers report that he never interfered with their education.
Was he free? Was he happy? The question is absurd:
Had anything been wrong, we should certainly have heard.

# The Absurd World of "Game"

**A**lmost every element of Barthelme's story contributes to its satirical, absurdist tone. As in the plays of the Theater of the Absurd, such as those composed by Samuel Beckett and Eugene Ionesco, statements either do not follow logically from each other, or are connected by false logic. The narrator's constant repetition suggests someone on the brink of a precipice, desperately trying to hold on to words as symbols of reality and sanity.

The two characters, Shotwell and the unnamed narrator, are confined underground for an indefinite period. We never learn the exact details of the mission they may be called on to carry out, but it seems to involve nuclear warfare and so could result in world destruction.

The first-person narration underscores the horror, as we know only what the speaker can tell us about his situation. Both he and Shotwell have been reduced to a state of infancy as they wait for the signals that may or may not appear on the console: Childish pastimes alternate with petty jealousies and disturbing nightmares. The two men's gradual dehumanization is relieved only when they rock each other to sleep. The men's eccentric behavior is portrayed as a desperate attempt to blot out the horror of their circumstances, but both are clearly on the edge of madness: Note that Shotwell seems determined to activate the two locks and thereby launch what will apparently be a catastrophic event.

As you read Barthelme's tale of life in the nuclear age, it may be easy to dismiss the particulars of his vision as exaggerated or surrealistic. But consider that a serious theme may underlie this apparently absurdist story. Our modern methods of warfare, Barthelme seems to be suggesting, are horrible not only because of their potential for physical destruction, but also because of the way their very existence corrodes and perverts humanity.

# Response and Analysis

**SKILLS FOCUS**

**Literary Skills**
Analyze theme and title.

**Writing Skills**
Write an essay analyzing two literary characters.

**Vocabulary Skills**
Recognize synonyms.

## Reading Check

**1.** Despite his experimentation, Barthelme continues to use some essential elements of fiction. Who is the **narrator** of this story? What is the **setting**?

**2.** What is the narrator's problem, or **conflict**? Is the conflict ever resolved? If so, describe the resolution.

## Thinking Critically

**3.** Which details in the first paragraph suggest the mental states of Shotwell and the narrator?

**4.** How would you explain the men's strange behavior? What do you think happened before the story begins?

**5.** What is the "bird"? How did you arrive at your conclusion?

**6.** What "oversight" could have led to the men's confinement?

**7.** The narrator is concerned that Shotwell may have "something in mind." What might that something be? How can you tell?

**8.** Barthelme uses a great deal of **repetition** in the story. What phrases are repeated most often? How does the repetition contribute to the **characterization** of Shotwell and the narrator?

9. What denotations and connotations does the word *game* have in this story? How does the word's use as a title point toward a **theme** of the story?

10. Do you think the story "Game" applies to the modern world in general? Explain your response using details from the story and from real life.

### Extending and Evaluating

11. Review the **Critical Comment** on page 980. Do you agree with the entire comment, or do you find any problems with the critic's take on the story? Explain.

## WRITING

### The World According to You

In "The Unknown Citizen," W. H. Auden (1907–1973) describes a citizen of the modern world. (See the **Connection** on page 979.) In a brief **essay,** tell whether you think Barthelme's characters and Auden's citizen live in the same *kind* of world. Has modern society taken away their freedom and ignored their humanity? Do these views of the world relate to life as we know it today? Use details from the story and poem and from life today to support your responses.

## Vocabulary Development

### Recognizing Synonyms

Choose the best synonym for each word in capital letters, as it is used in "Game."

1. SATED:
   a. satisfied  c. sedated
   b. angered  d. seated

2. SIMULTANEOUSLY:
   a. presently  c. at the same time
   b. swiftly  d. securely

3. RUSE:
   a. rush  c. trick
   b. joke  d. game

4. SCRUPULOUSLY:
   a. carelessly  c. skillfully
   b. carefully  d. scratchily

5. PRECEDENCE:
   a. privilege  c. presence
   b. principle  d. priority

6. EXEMPLARY:
   a. model  c. inefficient
   b. exhaustive  d. easy

7. ACRIMONIOUSLY:
   a. criminally  c. bitterly
   b. mournfully  d. piteously

8. STOLIDLY:
   a. forcefully  c. angrily
   b. peacefully  d. unemotionally

*"But that's the beauty of the game. At this very moment your absurd vicarious defeat is being perfectly counterbalanced by some opposing fan's absurd vicarious triumph."*

## Literary Focus

### Satire

A **satire**—a literary work in which human foolishness or wrongdoing is ridiculed—ultimately holds a moral. The sting of satire is meant to cure us of our pretensions and delusions. While a realistic, ironic writer wants us to come to terms with the world as it is, a satirist wants to reform that world. The satirist's premise is that exposing unacceptable situations to ridicule and laughter will bring about change.

**The tools of satire.** Satire requires two ingredients to be successful: (1) humor and (2) a target.

The humor of the satirist almost always involves **irony**—a discrepancy between what is said and what is actually meant, or between what we expect and what actually happens. Satirists also use **hyperbole,** or exaggeration, and **incongruity,** a kind of irony that brings together two ideas (or events or people) that do not belong together (*incongruous* means "not fitting together"). Donald Barthelme uses all three devices in "Game."

**Fantasy and the collapse of common sense.** Another device sometimes used in satire is **fantasy,** the creation of a world in which common sense has collapsed. Two of the most famous fantasies in the English language are Lewis Carroll's *Alice's Adventures in Wonderland* (1865) and *Through the Looking-Glass* (1871). In these books, reality is turned on its head. Even language itself no longer means what we think it means. "When *I* use a word," proclaims Humpty Dumpty, "it means just what I choose it to mean—neither more nor less."

**Satire and the absurd.** At times, a satirist's fantasy turns to the absurd or grotesque, producing a grim, cynical kind of humor known as *gallows humor* (the term means literally "humor displayed by someone facing the executioner").

**Satire in American literature.** Satire has a long history in American literature. The shrewd counsels of prudence we hear from Benjamin Franklin's Poor Richard (page 76) are a kind of satire, in which the writer suggests practical ways to succeed in a less-than-ideal world. Mark Twain (page 523) was more of a satirist than is generally recognized; his satire "The Lowest Animal" (page 535) is an amusing and bitter critique of the whole human race. James Thurber created in Walter Mitty (page 782) an American version of the man bullied by a woman, an archetypal character popular in satire since the days of ancient Rome. And, of course, the daily newspapers are filled with biting editorial cartoons built on satire.

**"Game" as satire.** Write an **analysis** of "Game," showing how it uses the techniques of satire. Use details from the story to show how Barthelme uses irony, hyperbole, and incongruity to hit his target. Be sure to specify his exact target. In other words, what does Barthelme want to reform?

*"You said a moment ago that everybody you look at seems to be a rabbit. Now just what do you mean by that, Mrs. Sprague?"*

Drawing by James Thurber. © 1937 The New Yorker Magazine, Inc.

**SKILLS FOCUS**

**Literary Skills**
Understand satire.

# Raymond Carver
## (1938–1988)

"We didn't have any youth," Raymond Carver remembered in a 1983 interview. He was thinking of the tough days he spent growing up in a working-class family in the Pacific Northwest. Carver was born in Oregon and raised in Yakima, Washington, where his father worked in a lumber mill and his mother worked periodically as a waitress and a clerk. Carver married soon after graduating from high school, and by the time he turned twenty he and his wife were raising two children. To support his family, he worked at a variety of blue-collar jobs: pumping gas, sweeping hospital corridors, picking tulips.

Given Carver's experiences, it is no surprise that in his stories—as the critic Thomas R. Edwards has commented—"people worry about whether their old cars will start, [and] unemployment or personal bankruptcy are present dangers." Carver's characters typically work as mechanics, factory workers, waitresses, or door-to-door salespeople in an America where making a living can be difficult and uncertain. Characters often survive their difficulties, however, and there is a sense of hope in many Carver stories. "I have a great deal of sympathy with [characters in my stories]," Carver once said. "They're my people. I know them. I could never write down to them."

In the late 1950s, the Carvers moved to California, where Raymond enrolled in college, taking a course in fiction writing with the novelist John Gardner. In 1963, he earned a college degree and then attended the University of Iowa's highly regarded Writers' Workshop.

In the 1960s and early 1970s, Carver published stories and poems, some dealing with favorite topics like hunting and fishing. A breakthrough came in 1976 with the publication of a collection of his stories, *Will You Please Be Quiet, Please?* The lavish praise bestowed upon this book earned Carver wide recognition as a hugely talented writer. The critic Margo Johnson noted that the stories "are filled with glass-sharp details, images and conversations, meticulously arranged." In 1977, Carver won a prestigious Guggenheim fellowship. Yet as he succeeded professionally, his personal life deteriorated, and his marriage ended.

In 1981, Carver published another collection of stories, *What We Talk About When We Talk About Love,* and in 1983, his story collection *Cathedral* enjoyed enormous critical and popular success. By then critics were talking of Carver's permanent place in American literature. The critic Irving Howe compared his work to that of Stephen Crane and Ernest Hemingway. *The Washington Post* book reviewer Jonathan Yardley called Carver "a writer of astonishing compassion and honesty, utterly free of pretense and affectation, his eye set only on describing and revealing the world as he sees it. His eye is so clear, it almost breaks your heart."

Carver's personal life brightened in the years before his early death from lung cancer. He formed a close relationship with the poet and short-story writer Tess Gallagher, who eventually became his wife. Since his death, and despite recent revelations about the significant role one editor played in shaping his stories, Carver's reputation as an important poet and short-story writer has remained firm.

# Everything Stuck to Him

## Make the Connection

If we think in simple terms about human feelings, reducing them to clear-cut patterns, we may trick ourselves into believing that feelings themselves are simple. Great fiction, no matter how simple on the surface, enables us to discover the depths of feelings. We respond to such fiction because we recognize in it the give-and-take of real experience, the gains and the losses, and the complex interactions of people who defy stereotyping.

## Literary Focus
### Style

One of the most striking elements of Raymond Carver's writing is his **style,** the unique way in which he uses language. Carver's prose has a chiseled quality, as if he has chipped away every unnecessary word. His style includes some oddities, however. He uses no quotation marks around dialogue, and he often doesn't give his characters names. These are not mere tricks, however. Each element of Carver's style has a purpose.

*L* (1986) by Mike and Doug Starn. Toned silver print on polyester, tape, wood (48″ × 48″).

Image courtesy Leo Castelli Photo Archives. © 2005 Mike and Doug Starn/Artists Rights Society (ARS), New York.

> **Style** is the unique way in which a writer uses language.
>
> *For more on Style, see the Handbook of Literary and Historical Terms.*

## Reading Skills
### Learning Through Questioning

As you read "Everything Stuck to Him," make a list of questions that occur to you about the characters. You might ask about their feelings, for instance, or what they are *not* saying to each other.

## Vocabulary Development

**coincide** (kō′in·sīd′) *v.*: occur at the same time.

**striking** *adj.*: impressive; attractive.

**fitfully** *adv.*: irregularly; in stops and starts.

# Everything Stuck to Him

**Raymond Carver**

They were kids themselves, but they were crazy in love.

She's in Milan[1] for Christmas and wants to know what it was like when she was a kid. Tell me, she says. Tell me what it was like when I was a kid. She sips Strega,[2] waits, eyes him closely.

She is a cool, slim, attractive girl, a survivor from top to bottom.

That was a long time ago. That was twenty years ago, he says.

You can remember, she says. Go on.

What do you want to hear? he says. What else can I tell you? I could tell you about something that happened when you were a baby. It involves you, he says. But only in a minor way.

Tell me, she says. But first fix us another so you won't have to stop in the middle.

He comes back from the kitchen with drinks, settles into his chair, begins.

They were kids themselves, but they were crazy in love, this eighteen-year-old boy and this seventeen-year-old girl when they married. Not all that long afterwards they had a daughter.

The baby came along in late November during a cold spell that just happened to coincide with the peak of the waterfowl season. The boy loved to hunt, you see. That's part of it.

The boy and girl, husband and wife, father and mother, they lived in a little apartment under a dentist's office. Each night they cleaned the dentist's place upstairs in exchange for rent and utilities. In summer they were expected to maintain the lawn and the flowers. In winter the boy shoveled snow and spread rock salt on the walks. Are you still with me? Are you getting the picture?

I am, she says.

That's good, he says. So one day the dentist finds out they were using his letterhead for their personal correspondence. But that's another story.

He gets up from his chair and looks out the window. He sees the tile rooftops and the snow that is falling steadily on them.

Tell the story, she says.

The two kids were very much in love. On top of this they had great ambitions. They were always talking about the things they were going to do and the places they were going to go.

Now the boy and girl slept in the bedroom, and the baby slept in the living room. Let's say the baby was about three months old and had only just begun to sleep through the night.

---

1. **Milan** (mi·lan′): city in northwestern Italy.
2. **Strega:** sweet Italian liqueur.

**Vocabulary**
**coincide** (kō′in·sīd′) v.: occur at the same time.

On this one Saturday night after finishing his work upstairs, the boy stayed in the dentist's office and called an old hunting friend of his father's.

Carl, he said when the man picked up the receiver, believe it or not, I'm a father.

Congratulations, Carl said. How is the wife?

She's fine, Carl. Everybody's fine.

That's good, Carl said, I'm glad to hear it. But if you called about going hunting, I'll tell you something. The geese are flying to beat the band. I don't think I've ever seen so many. Got five today. Going back in the morning, so come along if you want to.

I want to, the boy said.

The boy hung up the telephone and went downstairs to tell the girl. She watched while he laid out his things. Hunting coat, shell bag, boots, socks, hunting cap, long underwear, pump gun.

What time will you be back? the girl said.

Probably around noon, the boy said. But maybe as late as six o'clock. Would that be too late?

It's fine, she said. The baby and I will get along fine. You go and have some fun. When you get back, we'll dress the baby up and go visit Sally.

The boy said, Sounds like a good idea.

Sally was the girl's sister. She was striking. I don't know if you've seen pictures of her. The boy was a little in love with Sally, just as he was a little in love with Betsy, who was another sister the girl had. The boy used to say to the girl, If we weren't married, I could go for Sally.

What about Betsy? the girl used to say. I hate to admit it, but I truly feel she's better looking than Sally and me. What about Betsy?

Betsy too, the boy used to say.

After dinner he turned up the furnace and helped her bathe the baby. He marveled again at the infant who had half his features and half the girl's. He powdered the tiny body. He powdered between fingers and toes.

He emptied the bath into the sink and went upstairs to check the air. It was overcast and cold. The grass, what there was of it, looked like canvas, stiff and gray under the street light.

Snow lay in piles beside the walk. A car went by. He heard sand under the tires. He let himself imagine what it might be like tomorrow, geese beating the air over his head, shotgun plunging against his shoulder.

Then he locked the door and went downstairs.

In bed they tried to read. But both of them fell asleep, she first, letting the magazine sink to the quilt.

It was the baby's cries that woke him up.

The light was on out there, and the girl was standing next to the crib rocking the baby in her arms. She put the baby down, turned out the light, and came back to the bed.

He heard the baby cry. This time the girl stayed where she was. The baby cried fitfully and stopped. The boy listened, then dozed. But the baby's cries woke him again. The living-room light was burning. He sat up and turned on the lamp.

I don't know what's wrong, the girl said, walking back and forth with the baby. I've changed her and fed her, but she keeps on crying. I'm so tired I'm afraid I might drop her.

You come back to bed, the boy said. I'll hold her for a while.

He got up and took the baby, and the girl went to lie down again.

Just rock her for a few minutes, the girl said from the bedroom. Maybe she'll go back to sleep.

The boy sat on the sofa and held the baby. He jiggled it in his lap until he got its eyes to close, his own eyes closing right along. He rose carefully and put the baby back in the crib.

It was a quarter to four, which gave him forty-five minutes. He crawled into bed and dropped off. But a few minutes later the baby

---

**Vocabulary**

**striking** *adj.*: impressive; attractive.

**fitfully** *adv.*: irregularly; in stops and starts.

was crying again, and this time they both got up.

The boy did a terrible thing. He swore.

For God's sake, what's the matter with you? the girl said to the boy. Maybe she's sick or something. Maybe we shouldn't have given her the bath.

The boy picked up the baby. The baby kicked its feet and smiled.

Look, the boy said, I really don't think there's anything wrong with her.

How do you know that? the girl said. Here, let me have her. I know I ought to give her something, but I don't know what it's supposed to be.

The girl put the baby down again. The boy and the girl looked at the baby, and the baby began to cry.

The girl took the baby. Baby, baby, the girl said with tears in her eyes.

Probably it's something on her stomach, the boy said.

The girl didn't answer. She went on rocking the baby, paying no attention to the boy.

The boy waited. He went to the kitchen and put on water for coffee. He drew his woolen underwear on over his shorts and T-shirt, buttoned up, then got into his clothes.

What are you doing? the girl said.

Going hunting, the boy said.

I don't think you should, she said. I don't want to be left alone with her like this.

Carl's planning on me going, the boy said. We've planned it.

I don't care about what you and Carl

*Couple in Open Doorway* (1977) by George Segal.
Painted plaster, wood, and metal (96″ × 69″ × 52″).

© The George and Helen Segal Foundation/Licensed by VAGA, New York.

planned, she said. And I don't care about Carl, either. I don't even know Carl.

You've met Carl before. You know him, the boy said. What do you mean you don't know him?

That's not the point and you know it, the girl said.

What is the point? the boy said. The point is we planned it.

The girl said, I'm your wife. This is your baby. She's sick or something. Look at her. Why else is she crying?

I know you're my wife, the boy said.

The girl began to cry. She put the baby back in the crib. But the baby started up again. The girl dried her eyes on the sleeve of her night-gown and picked the baby up.

The boy laced up his boots. He put on his shirt, his sweater, his coat. The kettle whistled on the stove in the kitchen.

You're going to have to choose, the girl said. Carl or us. I mean it.

What do you mean? the boy said.

You heard what I said, the girl said. If you want a family, you're going to have to choose.

They stared at each other. Then the boy took up his hunting gear and went outside. He started the car. He went around to the car windows and, making a job of it, scraped away the ice.

He turned off the motor and sat awhile. And then he got out and went back inside.

The living-room light was on. The girl was asleep on the bed. The baby was asleep beside her.

The boy took off his boots. Then he took off everything else. In his socks and his long under-wear, he sat on the sofa and read the Sunday paper.

The girl and the baby slept on. After a while, the boy went to the kitchen and started frying bacon.

The girl came out in her robe and put her arms around the boy.

Hey, the boy said.

I'm sorry, the girl said.

It's all right, the boy said.

I didn't mean to snap like that.

It was my fault, he said.

You sit down, the girl said. How does a waffle sound with bacon?

Sounds great, the boy said.

She took the bacon out of the pan and made waffle batter. He sat at the table and watched her move around the kitchen.

She put a plate in front of him with bacon, a waffle. He spread butter and poured syrup. But when he started to cut, he turned the plate into his lap.

I don't believe it, he said, jumping up from the table.

If you could see yourself, the girl said.

The boy looked down at himself, at every-thing stuck to his underwear.

I was starved, he said, shaking his head.

You were starved, she said, laughing.

He peeled off the woolen underwear and threw it at the bathroom door. Then he opened his arms and the girl moved into them.

We won't fight anymore, she said.

The boy said, We won't.

He gets up from his chair and refills their glasses.

That's it, he says. End of story. I admit it's not much of a story.

I was interested, she says.

He shrugs and carries his drink over to the window. It's dark now but still snowing.

Things change, he says. I don't know how they do. But they do without your realizing it or wanting them to.

Yes, that's true, only—But she does not finish what she started.

She drops the subject. In the window's reflec-tion he sees her study her nails. Then she raises her head. Speaking brightly, she asks if he is going to show her the city, after all.

He says, Put your boots on and let's go.

But he stays by the window, remembering. They had laughed. They had leaned on each other and laughed until the tears had come, while everything else—the cold, and where he'd go in it—was outside, for a while anyway. ∎

*This is an excerpt from an article on Raymond Carver.*

# A Still, Small Voice

## Jay McInerney

The recurring image I associate with Raymond Carver is one of people leaning toward him, working very hard at the act of listening. He mumbled. T. S. Eliot once described Ezra Pound, qua mentor, as "a man trying to convey to a very deaf person the fact that the house is on fire." Raymond Carver had precisely the opposite manner. The smoke could be filling the room, flames streaking across the carpet, before Carver would ask, "Is it, uh, getting a little hot in here, maybe?" And you would be sitting in your chair, bent achingly forward at the waist, saying, "Beg pardon, Ray?" Never insisting, rarely asserting, he was an unlikely teacher. I once sat in and listened while Carver was interviewed for two and a half hours. The writer conducting the interview moved the tape recorder closer and closer and finally asked if Carver would put it in his lap. A few days later the interviewer called up, near despair: Ray's voice on the tapes was nearly inaudible. The word "soft-spoken" hardly begins to do justice to his speech; this condition was aggravated whenever he was pressed into the regions of generality or prescription. . . .

One aspect of what Carver seemed to say to us—even to someone who had never been inside a lumber mill or a trailer park—was that literature could be fashioned out of strict observation of real life, whenever and however it was lived, even if it was lived with a bottle of Heinz ketchup on the table and the television set droning. This was news at a time when academic metafiction was the regnant° mode. His example reinvigorated realism as well as the short-story form. . . .

Having fallen under Carver's spell on reading his first collection, *Will You Please Be Quiet, Please?,* a book I would have bought on the basis of the title alone, I was lucky enough to meet him a few years later and

---

°**regnant** *adj.:* ruling.

eventually to become his student at Syracuse University in the early 80s. . . .

My first semester, Ray somehow forgot to enter my grade for workshop. I pointed this out to him, and we went together to the English office to rectify the situation. "You did some real good work," he said, informing me that I would get an A. I was very pleased with myself, but perhaps a little less so when Ray opened the grade book and wrote an A next to my name underneath a solid column of identical grades. Everybody did good work, apparently. In workshop he approached every story with respect—treating each as if it were a living entity, a little sick, possibly, or lame, but something that could be nursed and trained to health.

Though Ray was always encouraging, he could be rigorous if he knew criticism was welcome. Fortunate students had their stories subjected to the same process he employed on his own numerous drafts. Manuscripts came back thoroughly ventilated with Carver deletions, substitutions, question marks and chicken-scratch queries. I took one story back to him seven times; he must have spent fifteen or twenty hours on it. He was a meticulous, obsessive line editor. One on one, in his office, he almost became a tough guy, his voice gradually swelling with conviction.

Once we spent some ten or fifteen minutes debating my use of the word *earth*. Carver felt it had to be *ground*, and he felt it was worth the trouble of talking it through. That one exchange was invaluable; I think of it constantly when I'm working. Carver himself used the same example later in an essay he wrote that year, in discussing the influence of his mentor, John Gardner. "Ground is ground, he'd say, it means ground, dirt, that kind of stuff. But if you say *earth*, that's something else, that word has other ramifications." . . .

For someone who claimed he didn't love to teach, he made a great deal of difference to a great many students. He certainly changed my life irrevocably and I have heard others say the same thing.

I'm still leaning forward with my head cocked to one side, straining to hear his voice.

—from *The New York Times* August 6, 1989

Raymond Carver giving a lecture at Syracuse University (early 1980s).
Rare Books and Manuscripts Library of the Ohio State University Libraries.

# Response and Analysis

## Reading Check

1. This story has a frame story and an inner story. A **frame story** is just that: a "frame" for an inner story. What is the **setting,** and who are the **characters** in the frame story (the introductory narrative within which a character proceeds to tell the inner story)?

2. In the inner story (the one told by one of the characters), what is the **setting,** and who are the **characters**? Which characters appear in both stories?

3. What happened during the night when the baby kept crying?

4. What promise did the couple make on Sunday morning?

## Thinking Critically

5. What is the main **conflict** between the husband and wife in the inner story?

6. What thoughts and emotions do you think the boy experienced as he "sat awhile" in the car?

7. After telling the inner story, the man says that "things change." What do you think has changed since the time of the inner story? What has the man learned?

8. Near the end of the frame story, the woman replies, "Yes, that's true, only—" She does not finish. What do you think she intended to say, and why did she stop?

9. The **title** of the story refers to an incident in the inner story. Explain how the title also refers to something much more important to the man.

10. What is the **theme** of the story—what does the story reveal about the human condition? How does the theme relate to the story's title?

11. One aspect of Carver's **style** in this story is the omission of names for his main characters. Why do you think he did this? Why do you think he uses the terms *boy* and *girl* instead of *man* and *woman* or *father* and *mother*?

## Literary Criticism

12. In the **Connection** on page 989, Jay McInerney says, "One aspect of what Carver seemed to say to us . . . was that literature could be fashioned out of strict observation of real life, whenever and however it was lived. . . ." Do you agree with this statement? Use details from this story and from other stories or novels you have read to support your response.

# WRITING

## Major or Minor?

Early on, the man says that the inner story involves the woman, "but only in a minor way." Do you agree with this comment, or was the man using **understatement,** a manner of speaking that downplays the importance of something? In a brief **essay,** explain how important the woman's role is in the inner story. Defend your interpretation with evidence from the story.

## Writing an Interior Monologue

Write an **interior monologue** that reveals the unspoken thoughts and feelings of one of the characters in "Everything Stuck to Him." Write your monologue from the first-person point of view, using the pronoun "I." Choose one of the following scenes: (1) the girl sitting up alone with the baby, (2) the boy sitting alone in the car, or (3) the woman looking at her fingernails after hearing the story.

---

### Vocabulary Development
#### Using Words in Context

Write a short paragraph that uses all three of the Vocabulary words and provides clues to their meaning: *coincide, striking, fitfully.*

---

# Grammar Link

## Avoiding Shifts in Verb Tense: Keeping Things Consistent

In "Everything Stuck to Him," Raymond Carver tells two stories: an outer frame story about a father and his twenty-year-old daughter and an inner story that takes place when the father was much younger. One of the ways Carver signals the switch between the two stories is by shifting verb tenses—using the present tense for the frame story and the past tense for the inner story.

| PRESENT | He <u>gets</u> up from the chair and <u>looks</u> out the window. |
|---|---|

| PAST | The two kids <u>were</u> very much in love. |
|---|---|

The **tense** of a verb indicates the time of the action or state of being that is expressed by the verb. Sometimes you have to shift tenses within a passage or even a single sentence. For example, when you're describing events that took place at different times, you may need to use different tenses to show the correct sequence in time. In the following example the writer needs to shift from the present tense to the past tense.

| NECESSARY SHIFT | The father <u>tells</u> his adult daughter a story about an incident that <u>happened</u> when she was a baby. |
|---|---|

Problems occur when a writer shifts verb tenses arbitrarily. Unless you have a good reason for switching tenses, you should stick to one consistent tense.

| INCONSISTENT | At first the boy <u>decides</u> to go hunting, but then he <u>changed</u> his mind. |
|---|---|

| CONSISTENT | At first the boy <u>decides</u> to go hunting, but then he <u>changes</u> his mind. |
|---|---|

Use the present tense when you're writing about what happens in a work of literature. This is called the *literary present.*

| PRESENT | In "Everything Stuck to Him," the young father accidentally <u>spills</u> his breakfast onto his lap. |
|---|---|

## Apply to Your Writing

Re-read a current writing assignment or one that you've already competed. Underline every verb, and then check each one to make sure that you've used the correct tense.

▶ **For more help, see Tenses and Their Uses, 3b–3c, in the Language Handbook.**

**SKILLS FOCUS**

**Grammar Skills**
Use verb tenses correctly.

**PRACTICE**

Rewrite the following sentences, and correct any unnecessary shifts in verb tenses or incorrect use of tenses. If you think the verb tenses are correct, write *OK*. (There may be more than one error in a sentence.)

1. Carver's first collection of stories was nominated for a National Book Award in 1976, and he goes on to publish four more collections of stories and five volumes of poetry before he died in 1988.

2. In "Everything Stuck to Him," the frame story suggested that the father was no longer married to the mother in the inner story.

3. In the inner story the girl is furious that her husband wanted to go hunting when their baby was sick.

4. Carver revised many of his earlier, minimalist stories; for example, "A Small, Good Thing" is a fleshed-out version of "The Bath."

# Julia Alvarez
## (1950–      )

"All my childhood I had dressed like an American, eaten American foods, and befriended American children. I had gone to an American school and spent most of the day speaking and reading English. At night, my prayers were full of blond hair and blue eyes and snow. . . . All my childhood I had longed for this moment of arrival. And here I was, an American girl, coming home at last."

With these words, Julia (pronounced hoo'lē·ä) Alvarez describes stepping back into America. Although born in New York City, Alvarez spent her early childhood in the Dominican Republic. In 1960, just before her father was to be arrested for his involvement in a secret plot to overthrow the dictator Rafael Trujillo Molina, Alvarez and her family were tipped off by an American agent and escaped to the United States.

Paradoxically, her homecoming was filled with all the difficulties of adjusting to a brand-new life. Learning contemporary American English was only part of the adjustment. Alvarez also had to learn to compromise in order to resolve conflicts between American customs and her parents' more traditional views. This theme is at the heart of her fiction—particularly her short stories and her best-known work, the novel *How the Garcia Girls Lost Their Accents* (1991).

Before concentrating on writing fiction, Alvarez taught courses in poetry for twelve years in schools in Kentucky, California, Vermont, Illinois, and Washington, D.C. Her first collection of poems, appropriately titled *Homecoming,* was published in 1984. Alvarez has also won the American Academy of Poetry Prize, but it is as a novelist that she has received the most notice.

*How the Garcia Girls Lost Their Accents* is a novel of fifteen interlocking stories with engaging and memorable characters. The Garcia family, with its four daughters, struggles to overcome a variety of cultural and generational conflicts, and comparisons with Alvarez's own family make it clear that the novel is highly autobiographical. Her 1994 novel, *In the Time of the Butterflies,* is a fictionalized account of the lives and deaths of three sisters, Patria, Minerva, and María Teresa Mirabal, the wives of political prisoners in the Dominican Republic. The women, who had been visiting their husbands, were murdered in 1960 by thugs connected to the Trujillo regime. Alvarez's 1997 novel *¡Yo!* is populated by some of the *Garcia Girls* characters.

It is clear that Alvarez has forged, out of memory and imagination, a novelist's sensibility. As one critic said about *Garcia Girls,* Alvarez has "beautifully captured the threshold experience of the new immigrant, where the past is not yet a memory and the future remains an anxious dream."

## For Independent Reading

For more about the characters in the following story, read

• *How the Garcia Girls Lost Their Accents* (novel)

# Before You Read

## Daughter of Invention

### Make the Connection

From the biblical parable of the prodigal son to a short story written this morning, literature will probably always tell stories of children and parents struggling to understand one another. "Experience is the greatest teacher, so trust us," says the older generation. "We want to live our own lives, not yours," say the children. What are some other phrases, sayings, or typical pieces of advice that parents use when they talk to their children?

### Literary Focus
#### Conflict

Stories run on **conflict,** and this story is no exception. It takes its strength and much of its fun from the clash between the anxious values of Latin American parents and the liberated values of their New York–raised daughter. Each major character experiences both **external conflict** (clashes with other people, a government, or society in general) and **internal conflict** (problems that exist within his or her own mind).

**SKILLS FOCUS**

**Literary Skills**
Understand external and internal conflict.

**Reading Skills**
Make inferences about characters.

**INTERNET**

**Vocabulary Practice**
•
**More About Julia Alvarez**

Keyword: LE7 11-6

**External conflict** is a clash of opposing forces, which can exist between two people, between a person and a force of nature, or between a person and society.
**Internal conflict** is a clash between opposing forces that exist within a person's mind.

*For more on Conflict, see the Handbook of Literary and Historical Terms.*

### Reading Skills
#### Making Inferences About Characters

"Daughter of Invention" is one of the fifteen interwoven stories in *How the Garcia Girls Lost Their Accents.* It is fascinating to watch how the characters in this story adapt so differently to the liberty the family enjoys in its new country. As a skilled reader, you will want to go beneath the surface events of the story and try to understand why these characters respond to new social customs in such different ways. In other words, you'll make **inferences,** or educated guesses, about the psychology of the characters, based on clues provided in the story and on your own experience with people.

### Vocabulary Development

**disembodied** (dis′im·bäd′ēd) *v.* used as *adj.:* separated from the body.

**labyrinth** (lab′ə·rinth′) *n.:* place full of complex passageways; maze.

**communal** (kə·myo͞on′əl) *adj.:* belonging to an entire group (in this case, Mami's daughters).

**eulogy** (yo͞o′lə·jē) *n.:* public speech of praise.

**noncommittal** (nän′kə·mit′'l) *adj.:* neutral; giving no clear indication of feeling or attitude.

**florid** (flôr′id) *adj.:* showy.

**ultimatum** (ul′tə·māt′əm) *n.:* last offer; final proposition.

**vengeful** (venj′fəl) *adj.:* intent on revenge.

**reconcile** (rek′ən·sīl′) *v.:* make peace.

# Daughter of Invention

Julia Alvarez

She always invented at night, after settling her house down.

She wanted to invent something, my mother. There was a period after we arrived in this country, until five or so years later, when my mother was inventing. They were never pressing, global needs she was addressing with her pencil and pad. She would have said that was for men to do, rockets and engines that ran on gasoline and turned the wheels of the world. She was just fussing with little house things, don't mind her.

She always invented at night, after settling her house down. On his side of the bed my father would be conked out for an hour already, his Spanish newspaper draped over his chest, his glasses, propped up on his bedside table, looking out eerily at the darkened room like a disembodied guard. But in her lighted corner, like some devoted scholar burning the midnight oil, my mother was inventing, sheets pulled to her lap, pillows propped up behind her, her reading glasses riding the bridge of her nose like a schoolmarm's. On her lap lay one of those innumerable pads of paper my father always brought home from his office, compliments of some pharmaceutical company, advertising tranquilizers or antibiotics or skin cream; in her other hand, my mother held a pencil that looked like a pen with a little cylinder of lead inside. She would work on a sketch of something familiar, but drawn at such close range so she could attach a special nozzle or handier handle, the thing looked peculiar. Once, I mistook the spiral of a corkscrew for a nautilus shell, but it could just as well have been a galaxy forming.

It was the only time all day we'd catch her sitting down, for she herself was living proof of the *perpetuum mobile*[1] machine so many inventors had sought over the ages. My sisters and I would seek her out now when she seemed to have a moment to talk to us: We were having

We wanted to become Americans and my father—and my mother, at first—would have none of it.

trouble at school or we wanted her to persuade my father to give us permission to go into the city or to a shopping mall or a movie—in broad daylight! My mother would wave us out of her room. "The problem with you girls . . ." I can tell you right now what the problem always boiled down to: We wanted to become Americans and my father—and my mother, at first—would have none of it.

"You girls are going to drive me crazy!" She always threatened if we kept nagging. "When I end up in Bellevue,[2] you'll be safely sorry!"

She spoke in English when she argued with us, even though, in a matter of months, her daughters were the fluent ones. Her English was much better than my father's, but it was still a mishmash of mixed-up idioms and sayings that showed she was "green behind the ears," as she called it.

If my sisters and I tried to get her to talk in Spanish, she'd snap, "When in Rome, do unto the Romans . . ."

I had become the spokesman for my sisters, and I would stand my ground in that bedroom. "We're not going to that school anymore, Mami!"

"You have to." Her eyes would widen with worry. "In this country, it is against the law not to go to school. You want us to get thrown out?"

"You want us to get killed? Those kids were throwing stones today!"

"Sticks and stones don't break bones . . ." she chanted. I could tell, though, by the look on her face, it was as if one of those stones the kids had aimed at us had hit her. But she always pretended we were at fault. "What did you do to provoke them? It takes two to tangle, you know."

---

1. *perpetuum mobile* (per·pe′tōō·əm mō′bi·lā): Latin for "perpetual motion."

2. **Bellevue:** large New York City hospital known for its psychiatric department.

**Vocabulary**

**disembodied** (dis′im·bäd′ēd) v. used as *adj.*: separated from the body.

"Thanks, thanks a lot, Mom!" I'd storm out of that room and into mine. I never called her *Mom* except when I wanted her to feel how much she had failed us in this country. She was a good enough Mami, fussing and scolding and giving advice, but a terrible girlfriend parent, a real failure of a Mom.

Back she'd go to her pencil and pad, scribbling and tsking and tearing off paper, finally giving up, and taking up her *New York Times*. Some nights, though, she'd get a good idea, and she'd rush into my room, a flushed look on her face, her tablet of paper in her hand, a cursory knock on the door she'd just thrown open: "Do I have something to show you, Cukita!"

This was my time to myself, after I'd finished my homework, while my sisters were still downstairs watching TV in the basement. Hunched over my small desk, the overhead light turned off, my lamp shining poignantly on my paper, the rest of the room in warm, soft, uncreated darkness, I wrote my secret poems in my new language.

"You're going to ruin your eyes!" My mother would storm into my room, turning on the overly bright overhead light, scaring off whatever shy passion I had just begun coaxing out of a labyrinth of feelings with the blue thread of my writing.

"Oh Mami!" I'd cry out, my eyes blinking up at her. "I'm writing."

"Ay, Cukita." That was her communal pet name for whoever was in her favor. "Cukita, when I make a million, I'll buy you your very own typewriter." (I'd been nagging my mother for one just like the one father had bought her to do his order forms at home.) "Gravy on the turkey" was what she called it when someone was buttering her up. She'd butter and pour. "I'll hire you your very own typist."

Down she'd plop on my bed and hold out her pad to me. "Take a guess, Cukita?" I'd study her rough sketch a moment: soap sprayed from the nozzle head of a shower when you turned the knob a certain way? Coffee with creamer already mixed in? Time-released water capsules for your plants when you were away? A key chain with a timer that would go off when your parking meter was about to expire? (The ticking would help you find your keys easily if you mislaid them.) The famous one, famous only in hindsight, was the stick person dragging a square by a rope—a suitcase with wheels? "Oh, of course," we'd humor her. "What every household needs: a shower like a car wash, keys ticking like a bomb, luggage on a leash!" By now, as you can see, it'd become something of a family joke, our Thomas Edison Mami, our Benjamin Franklin Mom.

Her face would fall. "Come on now! Use your head." One more wrong guess, and she'd tell me, pressing with her pencil point the different highlights of this incredible new wonder. "Remember that time we took the car to Bear Mountain, and we re-ah-lized that we had forgotten to pack an opener with our pick-a-nick?" (We kept correcting her, but she insisted this is how it should be said.) "When we were ready to eat we didn't have any way to open the refreshments cans?" (This before fliptop lids, which she claimed had crossed her mind.) "You know what this is now?" A shake of my head. "Is a car bumper, but see this part is a removable can opener. So simple and yet so necessary, no?"

"Yeah, Mami. You should patent it." I'd shrug. She'd tear off the scratch paper and fold it, carefully, corner to corner, as if she were going to save it. But then, she'd toss it in the wastebasket on her way out of the room and give a little laugh like a disclaimer.[3] "It's half of one or two dozen of another . . ."

I suppose none of her daughters was very encouraging. We resented her spending time on those dumb inventions. Here, we were trying to fit in America among Americans; we needed

---

3. **disclaimer** *n.*: refusal to accept responsibility; denial.

---

### Vocabulary

**labyrinth** (lab′ə·rinth′) *n.*: place full of intricate passageways; maze.

**communal** (kə·myoon′əl) *adj.*: belonging to an entire group (in this case, Mami's daughters).

help figuring out who we were, why these Irish kids whose grandparents were micks two generations ago, why they were calling us spics. Why had we come to the country in the first place? Important, crucial, final things, you see, and here was our own mother, who didn't have a second to help us puzzle any of this out, inventing gadgets to make life easier for American moms. Why, it seemed as if she were arming our own enemy against us!

One time, she did have a moment of triumph. Every night, she liked to read *The New York Times* in bed before turning off her light, to see what the Americans were up to. One night, she let out a yelp to wake up my father beside her, bolt upright, reaching for his glasses which, in his haste, he knocked across the room. *"Que pasa? Que pasa?"*[4] What is wrong? There was terror in his voice, fear she'd seen in his eyes in the Dominican Republic before we left. We were being watched there; he was being followed; he and mother had often exchanged those looks. They could not talk, of course, though they must have whispered to each other in fear at night in the dark bed. Now in America, he was safe, a success even; his Centro Medico in Brooklyn was thronged with the sick and the homesick. But in dreams, he went back to those awful days and long nights, and my mother's screams confirmed his secret fear: We had not gotten away after all; they had come for us at last.

"Ay, Papi, I'm sorry. Go back to sleep, Cukito. It's nothing, nothing really." My mother held up the *Times* for him to squint at the small print, back page headline, one hand tapping all over the top of the bedside table for his glasses, the other rubbing his eyes to wakefulness.

They could not talk, of course, though they must have whispered to each other in fear at night in the dark bed.

"Remember, remember how I showed you that suitcase with little wheels so we would not have to carry those heavy bags when we traveled? Someone stole my idea and made a million!" She shook the paper in his face. She shook the paper in all our faces that night. "See! See! This man was no *bobo!*[5] He didn't put all his pokers on a back burner. I kept telling you, one of these days my ship would pass me by in the night!" She wagged her finger at my sisters and my father and me, laughing all the while, one of those eerie laughs crazy people in movies laugh. We had congregated in her room to hear the good news she'd been yelling down the stairs, and now we eyed her and each other. I suppose we were all thinking the same thing: Wouldn't it be weird and sad if Mami did end up in Bellevue as she'd always threatened she might?

"*Ya, ya!* Enough!" She waved us out of her room at last. "There is no use trying to drink spilt milk, that's for sure."

It was the suitcase rollers that stopped my mother's hand; she had weather vaned a minor brainstorm. She would have to start taking herself seriously. That blocked the free play of her ingenuity. Besides, she had also begun working at my father's office, and at night, she was too tired and busy filling in columns with how much money they had made that day to be fooling with gadgets!

She did take up her pencil and pad one last time to help me out. In ninth grade, I was chosen by my English teacher, Sister Mary Joseph, to deliver the teacher's day address at the school assembly. Back in the Dominican Republic, I was a terrible student. No one could ever get me to sit down to a book. But in New York, I needed to settle somewhere, and the natives were unfriendly, the country inhospitable, so I took root in the language. By high school, the nuns were reading my stories and compositions

---

4. *Que pasa?* (kä pä'sä): Spanish for "What's going on?"

(Opposite) *Madre e hija* (1995) by Oscar Pardo. Pastel on paper (19" × 12½").
Courtesy of the artist.

---

5. *bobo:* Spanish for "fool."

out loud to my classmates as examples of imagination at work.

This time my imagination jammed. At first I didn't want and then I couldn't seem to write that speech. I suppose I should have thought of it as a "great honor," as my father called it. But I was mortified. I still had a pronounced lilt to my accent, and I did not like to speak in public, subjecting myself to my classmates' ridicule. Recently, they had begun to warm toward my sisters and me, and it took no great figuring to see that to deliver a eulogy for a convent full of crazy, old overweight nuns was no way to endear myself to the members of my class.

But I didn't know how to get out of it. Week after week, I'd sit down, hoping to polish off some quick, noncommittal little speech. I couldn't get anything down.

The weekend before our Monday morning assembly I went into a panic. My mother would just have to call in and say I was in the hospital, in a coma. I was in the Dominican Republic. Yeah, that was it! Recently, my father had been talking about going back home to live.

My mother tried to calm me down. "Just remember how Mister Lincoln couldn't think of anything to say at the Gettysburg, but then, Bang! 'Four score and once upon a time ago,'" she began reciting. Her version of history was half invention and half truths and whatever else she needed to prove a point. "Something is going to come if you just relax. You'll see, like the Americans say, 'Necessity is the daughter of invention.' I'll help you."

All weekend, she kept coming into my room with help. "Please, Mami, just leave me alone, please," I pleaded with her. But I'd get rid of the goose only to have to contend with the gander. My father kept poking his head in the door just to see if I had "fulfilled my obligations," a phrase he'd used when we were a little younger, and he'd check to see whether we had gone to the bathroom before a car trip. Several times that

weekend around the supper table, he'd recite his valedictorian speech from when he graduated from high school. He'd give me pointers on delivery, on the great orators and their tricks. (Humbleness and praise and falling silent with great emotion were his favorites.)

My mother sat across the table, the only one who seemed to be listening to him. My sisters and I were forgetting a lot of our Spanish, and my father's formal, florid diction was even harder to understand. But my mother smiled softly to herself, and turned the Lazy Susan at the center of the table around and around as if it were the prime mover,[6] the first gear of attention.

That Sunday evening, I was reading some poetry to get myself inspired: Whitman in an old book with an engraved cover my father had picked up in a thrift shop next to his office a few weeks back. "I celebrate myself and sing myself . . ." "He most honors my style who learns under it to destroy the teacher." The poet's words shocked and thrilled me. I had gotten used to the nuns, a literature of appropriate sentiments, poems with a message, expurgated texts. But here was a flesh and blood man, belching and laughing and sweating in poems. "Who touches this book touches a man."

That night, at last, I started to write, recklessly, three, five pages, looking up once only to see my father passing by the hall on tiptoe. When I was done, I read over my words, and my eyes filled. I finally sounded like myself in English!

When I was done, I read over my words, and my eyes filled. I finally sounded like myself in English!

---

6. **prime mover:** in philosophy, the self-moved being that is the source of all motion; in machinery, the source of power, such as a windmill or an engine.

**Vocabulary**

**eulogy** (yōō′lə·jē) *n.*: public speech of praise.
**noncommittal** (nän′kə·mit″l) *adj.*: neutral; giving no clear indication of feeling or attitude.
**florid** (flôr′id) *adj.*: showy.

As soon as I had finished that first draft, I called my mother to my room. She listened attentively, as she had to my father's speech, and in the end, her eyes were glistening too. Her face was soft and warm and proud. "That is a beautiful, beautiful speech, Cukita. I want for your father to hear it before he goes to sleep. Then I will type it for you, all right?"

Down the hall we went, the two of us, faces flushed with accomplishment. Into the master bedroom where my father was propped up on his pillows, still awake, reading the Dominican papers, already days old. He had become interested in his country's fate again. The dictatorship had been toppled. The interim government was going to hold the first free elections in thirty years. There was still some question in his mind whether or not we might want to move back. History was in the making, freedom and hope were in the air again! But my mother had gotten used to the life here. She did not want to go back to the old country where she was only a wife and a mother (and a failed one at that, since she had never had the required son). She did not come straight out and disagree with my father's plans. Instead, she fussed with him about reading the papers in bed, soiling those sheets with those poorly printed, foreign tabloids. "*The Times* is not that bad!" she'd claim if my father tried to humor her by saying they shared the same dirty habit.

The minute my father saw my mother and me, filing in, he put his paper down, and his face brightened as if at long last his wife had delivered a son, and that was the news we were bringing him. His teeth were already grinning from the glass of water next to his bedside lamp, so he lisped when he said, "Eh-speech, eh-speech!"

"It is so beautiful, Papi," my mother previewed him, turning the sound off on his TV. She sat down at the foot of the bed. I stood before both of them, blocking their view of the soldiers in helicopters landing amid silenced gun reports and explosions. A few weeks ago it had been the shores of the Dominican Republic. Now it was the jungles of Southeast Asia they were saving. My mother gave me the nod to begin reading.

I didn't need much encouragement. I put my nose to the fire, as my mother would have said, and read from start to finish without looking up. When I was done, I was a little embarrassed at my pride in my own words. I pretended to quibble with a phrase or two I was sure I'd be talked out of changing. I looked questioningly to my mother. Her face was radiant. She turned to share her pride with my father.

But the expression on his face shocked us both. His toothless mouth had collapsed into a dark zero. His eyes glared at me, then shifted to my mother, accusingly. In barely audible Spanish, as if secret microphones or informers were all about, he whispered, "You will permit her to read *that*?"

My mother's eyebrows shot up, her mouth fell open. In the old country, any whisper of a challenge to authority could bring the secret police in their black V.W.'s. But this was America. People could say what they thought. "What is wrong with her speech?" my mother questioned him.

"What ees wrrrong with her eh-speech?" My father wagged his head at her. His anger was always more frightening in his broken English. As if he had mutilated the language in his fury—and now there was nothing to stand between us and his raw, dumb anger. "What is wrong? I will tell you what is wrong. It shows no gratitude. It is boastful. 'I celebrate myself'? 'The best student learns to destroy the teacher'?" He mocked my plagiarized words. "That is insubordinate. It is improper. It is disrespecting of her teachers—" In his anger he had forgotten his fear of lurking spies: Each wrong he voiced was a decibel higher than the last outrage. Finally, he was yelling at me, "As your father, I forbid you to say that eh-speech!"

My mother leapt to her feet, a sign always that she was about to make a speech or deliver an <u>ultimatum</u>. She was a small woman, and she

**Vocabulary**

**ultimatum** (ul′tə·māt′əm) *n.*: last offer; final proposition.

spoke all her pronouncements standing up, either for more protection or as a carry-over from her girlhood in convent schools where one asked for, and literally took, the floor in order to speak. She stood by my side, shoulder to shoulder; we looked down at my father. "That is no tone of voice, Eduardo—" she began.

By now, my father was truly furious. I suppose it was bad enough I was rebelling, but here was my mother joining forces with me. Soon he would be surrounded by a house full of independent American women. He too leapt from his bed, throwing off his covers. The Spanish newspapers flew across the room. He snatched my speech out of my hands, held it before my panicked eyes, a vengeful, mad look in his own, and then once, twice, three, four, countless times, he tore my prize into shreds.

"Are you crazy?" My mother lunged at him. "Have you gone mad? That is her speech for tomorrow you have torn up!"

"Have *you* gone mad?" He shook her away. "You were going to let her read that . . . that insult to her teachers?"

"Insult to her teachers!" My mother's face had crumpled up like a piece of paper. On it was written a love note to my father. Ever since they had come to this country, their life together was a constant war. "This is America, Papi, America!" she reminded him now. "You are not in a savage country any more!"

I was on my knees, weeping wildly, collecting all the little pieces of my speech, hoping that I could put it back together before the assembly tomorrow morning. But not even a sibyl[7]

---

7. **sibyl** (sib′əl) *n.:* in ancient Greece and Rome, a woman who foretold the future.

---

**Vocabulary**
**vengeful** (venj′fəl) *adj.:* intent on revenge.

## A CLOSER LOOK: SOCIAL INFLUENCES

### Patently American Inventions

INFORMATIONAL TEXT

Have an invention of your own you'd like to protect? Consider patenting it. A U.S. patent gives you the right to exclude all others from making, using, or selling your invention within the United States for a limited number of years. To start, put your idea in writing, illustrate your device or process, and sign and date the document (use indelible ink). But before you reach for pad and pen, you might want to learn a little more about patents and inventions.

Patents are granted by the U.S. Patent and Trademark Office, in Arlington, Virginia. The Patent Office is flooded with over 150,000 applications a year, each of which takes about two years to process. If you can convince the patent officer that your invention is (1) new, (2) useful, and (3) original, a patent is yours. But be warned: You'll need deep pockets, since patent fees typically exceed $1,000.

**Patented inventions we haven't seen in stores.** Anyone wanting an afternoon's—or a lifetime's—entertainment could do worse than browse through the five million patents on record at the Patent Office. Ideas on record include these:

- eye protectors for chickens
- a device combining a plow and a gun
- a locket for storing used chewing gum
- a wake-up device consisting of suspended wood blocks that fall on the sleeper's face
- a device to create or maintain dimples
- balloons powered by large birds
- farms that rest on giant saucers floating in the sea

**Did you know . . . ?** The narrator's mother in "Daughter of Invention" is one in a long list of female American inventors. Since 1793, U.S. patents have been granted to women for inventions ranging from the brown paper bag, the modern coffeepot, and the disposable diaper to

could have made sense of all those scattered pieces of paper. All hope was lost. "He broke it, he broke it," I moaned as I picked up a handful of pieces.

Probably, if I had thought a moment about it, I would not have done what I did next. I would have realized my father had lost brothers and comrades to the dictator Trujillo.[8] For the rest of his life, he would be haunted by blood in the streets and late night disappearances. Even after he had been in the states for years, he jumped if a black Volkswagen passed him on the street. He feared anyone in uniform: the meter maid giving out parking tickets, a museum guard

approaching to tell him not to touch his favorite Goya at the Metropolitan.[9]

I took a handful of the scraps I had gathered, stood up, and hurled them in his face. "Chapita!" I said in a low, ugly whisper. "You're just another Chapita!"

It took my father only a moment to register the hated nickname of our dictator, and he was after me. Down the halls we raced, but I was quicker than he and made it to my room just in time to lock the door as my father threw his weight against it. He called down curses on my head, ordered me on his authority as my father to open that door this very instant! He throttled that doorknob, but all to no avail. My mother's love of gadgets saved my hide that night. She

---

8. **Trujillo** (trōō·hē′yō): Rafael Leonidas Trujillo Molina, general who took over as president of the Dominican Republic and ruled oppressively from 1930 to 1938 and from 1942 until 1961, when he was assassinated.

9. **Goya . . . Metropolitan:** painting by the Spanish artist Francisco José de Goya y Lucientes at the Metropolitan Museum of Art in New York City.

---

the first computer program, cancer treatments, and construction methods for dams and reservoirs. Here are some other patently interesting facts:

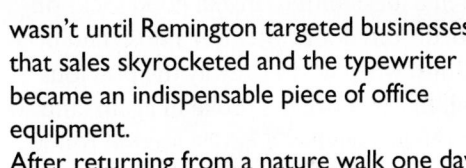

- The U.S. patent code forbids the patenting of devices with "no utility"—loosely speaking, no evident usefulness. One interesting category under the "no utility" banner is devices that defy the laws of nature. Inventors of antigravity boots, flying saucers, and other sci-fi devices needn't bother to apply for patents.
- The typewriter bombed when it was first brought out by E. Remington and Sons in 1874. Some recipients of typewritten letters felt insulted, and others, assuming the letters were junk mail, threw them away. And who could tell if typed letters had been forged? It wasn't until Remington targeted businesses that sales skyrocketed and the typewriter became an indispensable piece of office equipment.
- After returning from a nature walk one day, a Swiss inventor noticed that the cockleburs clinging to his jacket had tiny hooks that attached themselves to the fabric. He imitated the design in the first version of Velcro™ (from velvet and crochet).
- One day in 1958, Willy Higinbotham, a physicist bored with his work, devised a game involving two players and a tiny five-inch screen that displayed a net along with a ball each player could control with a button and a knob: video tennis. Despite the fact that people literally stood in line to play his game, Higinbotham saw no commercial value in it. The holder of twenty patents, he didn't bother to patent a device that launched the billion-dollar video-game industry.

*Uno* (1920) by Alejandro Xul Solar. Watercolor and pencil on paper on card (5⁹/₃₂″ × 7¹/₂″).

© Private Collection. Image courtesy Rachel Adler Gallery.

had hired a locksmith to install good locks on all the bedroom doors after our house had been broken into while we were away the previous summer. In case burglars broke in again, and we were in the house, they'd have a second round of locks to contend with before they got to us.

"Eduardo," she tried to calm him down. "Don't you ruin my new locks."

He finally did calm down, his anger spent. I heard their footsteps retreating down the hall. I heard their door close, the clicking of their lock. Then, muffled voices, my mother's peaking in anger, in persuasion, my father's deep murmurs of explanation and of self-defense. At last, the house fell silent, before I heard, far off, the gun blasts and explosions, the serious, self-important voices of newscasters reporting their TV war.

A little while later, there was a quiet knock at my door, followed by a tentative attempt at the doorknob. "Cukita?" my mother whispered. "Open up, Cukita."

"Go away," I wailed, but we both knew I was glad she was there, and I needed only a mo-

ment's protest to save face before opening that door.

What we ended up doing that night was putting together a speech at the last moment. Two brief pages of stale compliments and the polite commonplaces on teachers, wrought by necessity without much invention by mother for daughter late into the night in the basement on the pad of paper and with the same pencil she had once used for her own inventions, for I was too upset to compose the speech myself. After it was drafted, she typed it up while I stood by, correcting her misnomers and mis-sayings.

She was so very proud of herself when I came home the next day with the success story of the assembly. The nuns had been flattered, the audience had stood up and given "our devoted teachers a standing ovation," what my mother had suggested they do at the end of my speech.

She clapped her hands together as I re-created the moment for her. "I stole that from your father's speech, remember? Remember how he put that in at the end?" She quoted him in

Spanish, then translated for me into English.

That night, I watched him from the upstairs hall window where I'd retreated the minute I heard his car pull up in front of our house. Slowly, my father came up the driveway, a grim expression on his face as he grappled with a large, heavy cardboard box. At the front door, he set the package down carefully and patted all his pockets for his house keys—precisely why my mother had invented her ticking key chain. I heard the snapping open of the locks downstairs. Heard as he struggled to maneuver the box through the narrow doorway. Then, he called my name several times. But I would not answer him.

"My daughter, your father, he love you very much," he explained from the bottom of the stairs. "He just want to protect you." Finally, my mother came up and pleaded with me to go down and reconcile with him. "Your father did not mean to harm. You must pardon him. Always it is better to let bygones be forgotten, no?"

I guess she was right. Downstairs, I found him setting up a brand new electric typewriter on the kitchen table. It was even better than the one I'd been begging to get like my mother's. My father had outdone himself with all the extra features: a plastic carrying case with my initials, in decals, below the handle, a brace to lift the paper upright while I typed, an erase cartridge, an automatic margin tab, a plastic hood like a toaster cover to keep the dust away. Not even my mother, I think, could have invented such a machine!

But her inventing days were over just as mine were starting up with my schoolwide success. That's why I've always thought of that speech my mother wrote for me as her last invention rather than the suitcase rollers everyone else in the family remembers. It was as if she had passed on to me her pencil and pad and said, "Okay, Cukita, here's the buck. You give it a shot." ■

---

**Vocabulary**

**reconcile** (rek′ən·sīl′) v.: make peace

# Response and Analysis

## Reading Check

1. Which of the mother's ideas for an invention is a huge success for somebody else?
2. Why did the daughters resent the time their mother spent on inventions?
3. The narrator's mother uses many English-language **aphorisms** (af′ə·riz′əmz)—brief, wise sayings—but she gets them slightly wrong. Give the correct version of two or three of her sayings.
4. How does the daughter insult her father after he destroys her speech?
5. How do the father and daughter become reconciled?

## Thinking Critically

6. The narrator wants to use Whitman's words, "He most honors my style who learns under it to destroy the teacher" (page 1000). How does her father interpret the words? What do you think Whitman really meant?
7. The narrator says that her mother was "a good enough Mami" but "a terrible girlfriend parent, a real failure of a Mom" (page 997). What does the narrator mean? What do you think of her conflicting feelings for her mother? Are these typical American responses, or are they found in many cultures? Explain.
8. What **conflicts** does the father face in the story? How does the narrator deal with these conflicts?

**SKILLS FOCUS**

**Literary Skills**
Analyze external and internal conflict.

**Reading Skills**
Make inferences about characters.

**Writing Skills**
Write an essay analyzing conflict in a story.

**Vocabulary Skills**
Demonstrate word knowledge.

9. What inferences can you make about the **characters** based on the ways they have adapted (or failed to adapt) to their new country?

10. A good **title** has what is sometimes called resonance (rez′ə·nəns). That means that the title resounds or echoes with meanings. Think of how and why Alvarez's title works. In what ways does it relate to the story's **theme**? How do you feel about her choice of title?

11. In this story the father's experience with authority in his home country influences his behavior in the United States. Do you think this is a realistic portrayal of a person who has come to America from a country with an oppressive government? How does it compare with the experiences of immigrants you know or have heard about? Explain your responses.

# WRITING

## Analyzing Conflicts

"Daughter of Invention" builds upon a variety of **external** and **internal conflicts.** Make a four-column chart like the one below to organize your thoughts about the conflicts in the story. In the first column, list all the types of conflicts you can identify, such as social, interpersonal, cultural, and political conflicts. In the second column, tell who is involved in each conflict: for example, mother-daughter, father-daughter, husband-wife. In the third column, describe how the conflict is—or is not—resolved in the story. In the fourth column, evaluate each conflict's power to hold your interest and to evoke reactions. Finally, use your chart as the basis of an **essay** analyzing the conflicts in "Daughter of Invention."

| Type of Conflict | Who Is Involved | Resolution | Evaluation |
|---|---|---|---|
| Social | | | |
| Interpersonal | | | |
| Cultural | | | |
| Political | | | |

## Vocabulary Development

### What If?

In a small group, discuss the possible outcomes of these scenarios.

1. What if a disembodied hand gripped your shoulder?

2. What if you found yourself in a labyrinth?

3. What if a communal meeting hall was off-limits to teenagers?

4. What if a eulogy said negative things about its subject?

5. What if your date suddenly became noncommittal about going to the prom?

6. What if a teacher said you wrote florid prose?

7. What if you were given a tough ultimatum?

8. What if a vengeful victim confronted her attacker?

9. What if you could not reconcile with an old friend?

# Gabriel García Márquez
## (1928–        )

**G**abriel García Márquez (gä′brē·el′ gär·sē′ä mär′kes) was born in Aracataca, Colombia, the town that became the model for the fictional village of Macondo in his popular novel *One Hundred Years of Solitude* (1967). He spent his early years with his maternal grandparents, whom he regards as "wonderful beings." According to García Márquez, "They had an enormous house, full of ghosts. They were people of great imagination and superstitions. In every corner there were dead people and memories, and after six o'clock in the [evening] the house was untraversable. It was a world prodigious with terror. There were conversations in code."

Gabriel García Márquez at his desk.

After attending universities in Bogotá and Cartagena, García Márquez worked as a journalist in Colombia and in Rome, Paris, Barcelona, Caracas, and New York. Newspaper work helped García Márquez (like Ernest Hemingway) develop a style of writing fiction. Even after ending his newspaper career in 1965, García Márquez considered himself to be at heart a journalist, which is one reason for the factual or realistic basis for his fiction. It also accounts for his occasional nonfiction books, such as *News of a Kidnapping* (1997). Because of serious political differences with the Colombian government, he lives in Mexico City.

García Márquez has achieved international renown mainly for his fiction, which includes, besides *One Hundred Years of Solitude, The Autumn of the Patriarch* (1976), *Love in the Time of Cholera* (1988), *Strange Pilgrims* (1993), and *Of Love and Other Demons* (1995).

García Márquez's novels have often been compared with those of William Faulkner, who created a mythical county in Mississippi as the background for bizarre and sometimes hilarious events that reflect exaggerated historical reality. Faulkner's influence can also be seen in García Márquez's use of long, rhythmic sentences and shifting points of view. However, it is the rich storytelling traditions and the unique imaginative fantasies of Latin America that García Márquez has found most valuable. Awarded the Nobel Prize for literature in 1982, García Márquez deplored, in his acceptance speech, the way many Latin American writers ignore their own heritage and accept the hand-me-downs of European history and culture.

# Before You Read

## The Handsomest Drowned Man in the World

### Make the Connection

Archetypes sound complicated but they are only very basic patterns that you probably first encountered in stories from childhood. **Archetype** (är′kə·tīp′) means "an original pattern or a basic pattern." Archetypes have recurred in writing throughout the centuries; they can be plots, characters, events, or just things. An example of an archetype is the superhuman hero. The comic-strip hero Superman is an example of that archetype, still alive and well today. Another example of an archetype is a metamorphosis, a marvelous transformation from one form to another. You have read about metamorphoses in myths and fairy tales: In a version of the Cinderella story, for example, a pumpkin is magically transformed into a fabulous carriage. What other superheroes can you name? What metamorphoses can you remember from the stories you have read?

### Literary Focus
#### Magic Realism

**Magic realism** is a literary style that combines incredible events with realistic details and relates them all in a matter-of-fact tone. The style was invented in Latin America around the middle of the twentieth century and has since gained worldwide popularity. Magic realism blurs the lines that usually separate what seems real from what seems imagined or fantastic. Its incorporation of magic, myth, imagination, and religious elements into literature aims to expand rigid notions of what constitutes reality. You can find echoes of magic realism in works by such noted American authors as Donald Barthelme (page 972), Thomas Pynchon, and Kurt Vonnegut, as well as in the novels of Günter Grass of Germany and John Fowles of England.

> **Magic realism** is a literary style that combines incredible events with realistic details and relates them all in a matter-of-fact tone.
>
> *For more on Magic Realism, see the Handbook of Literary and Historical Terms.*

### Vocabulary Development

**bountiful** (boun′tə·fəl) *adj.*: generous.

**haggard** (hag′ərd) *adj.*: gaunt; worn out.

**virile** (vir′əl) *adj.*: manly; masculine.

**destitute** (des′tə·to͞ot′) *adj.*: poverty-stricken.

**frivolity** (fri·väl′ə·tē) *n.*: silliness.

**mortified** (môrt′ə·fīd′) *v.* used as *adj.*: humiliated; deeply embarrassed.

**SKILLS FOCUS**

**Literary Skills**
Understand characteristics of magic realism.

**go. hrw .com**

**INTERNET**

**Vocabulary Practice**

Keyword: LE7 11-6

# The Handsomest Drowned Man in the World

## Gabriel García Márquez

*translated by* **Gregory Rabassa**

### A Tale for Children

The first children who saw the dark and slinky bulge approaching through the sea let themselves think it was an enemy ship. Then they saw it had no flags or masts and they thought it was a whale. But when it was washed up on the beach, they removed the clumps of seaweed, the jellyfish tentacles, and the remains of fish and flotsam, and only then did they see that it was a drowned man.

They had been playing with him all afternoon, burying him in the sand and digging him up again, when someone chanced to see them and spread the alarm in the village. The men who carried him to the nearest house noticed that he weighed more than any dead man they had ever known, almost as much as a horse, and they said to each other that maybe he'd been floating too long and the water had got into his bones. When they laid him on the floor they said he'd been taller than all other men because there was barely enough room for him in the house, but they thought that

maybe the ability to keep on growing after death was part of the nature of certain drowned men. He had the smell of the sea about him and only his shape gave one to suppose that it was the corpse of a human being, because the skin was covered with a crust of mud and scales.

They did not even have to clean off his face to know that the dead man was a stranger. The village was made up of only twenty-odd wooden houses that had stone courtyards with no flowers and which were spread about on the end of a desertlike cape. There was so little land that mothers always went about with the fear that the wind would carry off their children and the few dead that the years had caused among them had to be thrown off the cliffs. But the sea

Art on pages 1007, 1009, 1010, and 1014 by Sergio Bustamente/Photos by Clint Clemens.

was calm and <u>bountiful</u> and all the men fit into seven boats. So when they found the drowned man they simply had to look at one another to see that they were all there.

That night they did not go out to work at sea. While the men went to find out if anyone was missing in neighboring villages, the women stayed behind to care for the drowned man. They took the mud off with grass swabs, they removed the underwater stones entangled in his hair, and they scraped the crust off with tools used for scaling fish. As they were doing that they noticed that the vegetation on him came from faraway oceans and deep water and that his clothes were in tatters, as if he had sailed through labyrinths of coral. They noticed too that he bore his death with pride, for he did not have the lonely look of other drowned men who came out of the sea or that <u>haggard</u>, needy look of men who drowned in rivers. But only when they finished cleaning him off did they become aware of the kind of man he was and it left them breathless. Not only was he the tallest, strongest, most <u>virile</u>, and best-built man they had ever seen, but even though they were looking at him there was no room for him in their imagination.

They could not find a bed in the village large enough to lay him on nor was there a table solid enough to use for his wake. The tallest men's holiday pants would not fit him, not the fattest ones' Sunday shirts, nor the shoes of the one with the biggest feet. Fascinated by his huge size and his beauty, the women then decided to make him some pants from a large piece of sail and a shirt from some bridal brabant linen[1] so that he could continue through his death with dignity. As they sewed, sitting in a circle and gazing at the corpse between stitches, it seemed to them that the wind had never been so steady nor the sea so restless as on that night and they supposed that the change had something to do with the dead man. They thought that if that magnificent man had lived in the village, his house would have had the widest doors, the highest ceiling, and the strongest floor, his bedstead would have been made from a midship frame held together by iron bolts, and his wife would have been the happiest woman. They thought that he would have had so much authority that he could have drawn fish out of the sea simply by calling their names and that he would have put so much work into his land that springs would have burst forth from among the rocks so that he would have been able to plant flowers on the cliffs. They secretly compared him to their own men, thinking that for all their lives theirs were incapable of doing what he could do in one night, and they ended up dismissing them deep in their hearts as the weakest, meanest, and most useless creatures on earth. They were wandering through that maze of fantasy when the oldest woman, who as the oldest had looked upon the drowned man with more compassion than passion, sighed:

---

1. **brabant** (brə·bant′) **linen:** linen from Brabant, a province of Belgium known for its fine lace and cloth.

**Vocabulary**
**bountiful** (boun′tə·fəl) *adj.:* generous.
**haggard** (hag′ərd) *adj.:* gaunt; worn out.
**virile** (vir′əl) *adj.:* manly; masculine.

"He has the face of someone called Esteban."[2]

It was true. Most of them had only to take another look at him to see that he could not have any other name. The more stubborn among them, who were the youngest, still lived for a few hours with the illusion that when they put his clothes on and he lay among the flowers in patent leather shoes his name might be Lautaro.[3] But it was a vain illusion. There had not been enough canvas, the poorly cut and worse sewn pants were too tight, and the hidden strength of his heart popped the buttons on his shirt. After midnight the whistling of the wind died down and the sea fell into its Wednesday drowsiness.[4] The silence put an end to any last doubts: he was Esteban. The women who had dressed him, who had combed his hair, had cut his nails and shaved him were unable to hold back a shudder of pity when they had to resign themselves to his being dragged along the ground. It was then that they understood how unhappy he must have been with that huge body since it bothered him even after death. They could see him in life, condemned to going through doors sideways, cracking his head on crossbeams, remaining on his feet during visits, not knowing what to do with his soft, pink, sea lion hands while the lady of the house looked for her most resistant chair and begged him, frightened to death, sit here, Esteban, please, and he, leaning against the wall, smiling, don't bother, ma'am, I'm fine where I am, his heels raw and his back roasted from having done the same thing so many times whenever he paid a visit, don't bother, ma'am, I'm fine where I am, just to avoid the embarrassment of breaking up the chair, and never knowing perhaps that the ones who said don't go, Esteban, at least wait till the coffee's ready, were the ones who later on would whisper the big boob finally left, how nice, the handsome fool has gone. That was what the women were thinking beside the body a little before dawn. Later, when they covered his face with a handkerchief so that the light would not bother him, he looked so forever dead, so defenseless, so much like their men that the first furrows of tears opened in their hearts. It was one of the younger ones who began the weeping. The others, coming to, went from sighs to wails, and the more they sobbed the more they felt like weeping, because the drowned man was becoming all the more Esteban for them, and so they wept so much, for he was the most destitute, most peaceful, and most obliging man on earth, poor Esteban. So when the men returned with the news that the drowned man was not from the neighboring villages either, the women felt an opening of jubilation in the midst of their tears.

"Praise the Lord," they sighed, "he's ours!"

The men thought the fuss was only womanish frivolity. Fatigued because of the difficult nighttime inquiries, all they wanted was to get rid of the bother of the newcomer once and for all before the sun grew strong on that arid, windless day. They improvised a litter with the remains of foremasts and gaffs,[5] tying it together with rigging so that it would bear the weight of the body until they reached the cliffs. They wanted to tie the anchor from a cargo ship to him so that he would sink easily into the deepest waves, where fish are blind and divers die of nostalgia, and bad currents would not bring him back to shore, as had happened with

---

2. **Esteban** (es·te′bän): Spanish equivalent of "Stephen." In Christian tradition, Stephen was the first martyr. He was stoned to death because of his beliefs.

3. **Lautaro** (lou·tä′rð): leader of the Araucanian Indian people who resisted the Spanish conquistadors entering their land, in what is now Chile, during the sixteenth century. Lautaro is now seen as a Chilean national hero.

4. **Wednesday drowsiness** (and later **Wednesday meat** and **Wednesday dead body**): *Wednesday* is a colloquial expression for "tiresome." In many fishing villages, fishers returned from the sea on Thursday, so by Wednesday, people began running out of food and were generally weary and bored.

5. **gaffs** *n. pl.*: poles used on a boat to support a sail.

**Vocabulary**

**destitute** (des′tə·toot′) *adj.*: poverty-stricken.
**frivolity** (fri·väl′ə·tē) *n.*: silliness.

other bodies. But the more they hurried, the more the women thought of ways to waste time. They walked about like startled hens, pecking with the sea charms[6] on their breasts, some interfering on one side to put a scapular[7] of the good wind on the drowned man, some on the other side to put a wrist compass on him, and after a great deal of *get away from there, woman, stay out of the way, look, you almost made me fall on top of the dead man,* the men began to feel mistrust in their livers and started grumbling about why so many main-altar decorations for a stranger, because no matter how many nails and holy-water jars he had on him, the sharks would chew him all the same, but the women kept piling on their junk relics, running back and forth, stumbling, while they released in sighs what they did not in tears, so that the men finally exploded with *since when has there ever been such a fuss over a drifting corpse, a drowned nobody, a piece of cold Wednesday meat.* One of the women, mortified by so much lack of care, then removed the handkerchief from the dead man's face and the men were left breathless too.

He was Esteban. It was not necessary to repeat it for them to recognize him. If they had been told Sir Walter Raleigh, even they might have been impressed with his gringo accent, the macaw[8] on his shoulder, his cannibal-killing blunderbuss,[9] but there could be only one Esteban in the world and there he was, stretched out like a sperm whale, shoeless, wearing the pants of an undersized child, and with those stony nails that had to be cut with a knife. They only had to take the handkerchief off his face to see that he was ashamed, that it was not his fault that he was so big or so heavy or so handsome, and if he had known that this was going to hap-

pen, he would have looked for a more discreet place to drown in, seriously, I even would have tied the anchor off a galleon around my neck and staggered off a cliff like someone who doesn't like things in order not to be upsetting people now with this Wednesday dead body, as you people say, in order not to be bothering anyone with this filthy piece of cold meat that doesn't have anything to do with me. There was so much truth in his manner that even the most mistrustful men, the ones who felt the bitterness of endless nights at sea fearing that their women would tire of dreaming about them and begin to dream of drowned men, even they and others who were harder still shuddered in the marrow of their bones at Esteban's sincerity.

That was how they came to hold the most splendid funeral they could conceive of for an abandoned drowned man. Some women who had gone to get flowers in the neighboring villages returned with other women who could not believe what they had been told, and those women went back for more flowers when they saw the dead man, and they brought more and more until there were so many flowers and so many people that it was hard to walk about. At the final moment it pained them to return him to the waters as an orphan and they chose a father and mother from among the best people, and aunts and uncles and cousins, so that through him all the inhabitants of the village became kinsmen. Some sailors who heard the weeping from a distance went off course and people heard of one who had himself tied to the mainmast, remembering ancient fables about sirens.[10] While they fought for the privilege of

----

6. **sea charms:** magic charms worn to protect the wearer from dangers at sea.
7. **scapular** (skap′yə·lər) *n.:* pair of small cloth squares showing images of saints, joined by string and worn under clothing by some Roman Catholics as a symbol of religious devotion.
8. **macaw** *n.:* large, brightly colored parrot.
9. **blunderbuss** *n.:* now-outdated gun with a short, flaring muzzle.

----

10. **sirens** *n. pl.:* In Greek mythology, the sirens are sea maidens whose seductive singing lures men to wreck their boats on coastal rocks. Odysseus, hero of Homer's *Odyssey,* fills his crew's ears with wax so that they can pass the sirens safely. Odysseus, however, has his crew tie him to the ship's mast so that he can listen to the sirens' songs without plunging into the sea.

----

**Vocabulary**

**mortified** (môrt′ə·fīd′) *v.* used as *adj.:* humiliated; deeply embarrassed.

----

carrying him on their shoulders along the steep escarpment by the cliffs, men and women became aware for the first time of the desolation of their streets, the dryness of their courtyards, the narrowness of their dreams as they faced the splendor and beauty of their drowned man. They let him go without an anchor so that he could come back if he wished and whenever he wished, and they all held their breath for the fraction of centuries the body took to fall into the abyss. They did not need to look at one another to realize that they were no longer all present, that they would never be. But they also knew that everything would be different from then on, that their houses would have wider doors, higher ceilings, and stronger floors so that Esteban's memory could go everywhere without bumping into beams and so that no one in the future would dare whisper the big boob finally died, too bad, the handsome fool has finally died, because they were going to paint their house fronts gay colors to make Esteban's memory eternal and they were going to break their backs digging for springs among the stones and planting flowers on the cliffs so that in future years at dawn the passengers on great liners would awaken, suffocated by the smell of gardens on the high seas, and the captain would have to come down from the bridge in his dress uniform, with his astrolabe,[11] his polestar, and his row of war medals and, pointing to the promontory of roses on the horizon, he would say in fourteen languages, look there, where the wind is so peaceful now that it's gone to sleep beneath the beds, over there, where the sun's so bright that the sunflowers don't know which way to turn, yes, over there, that's Esteban's village. ■

---

11. **astrolabe** (as'trō·lāb') *n.*: instrument used to find a star's altitude and to help navigators determine their position at sea.

# Response and Analysis

## Reading Check

1. How is the drowned man discovered?

2. What is unusual about the drowned man? How do the villagers explain these characteristics?

3. What name do the villagers give the drowned man? Why?

4. What do the villagers do with the body of the drowned man?

5. How does the drowned man transform the people and their village?

## Thinking Critically

6. Where is the story set? What details about the setting are examples of **magic realism**?

7. A strong **theme** of this story concerns the human need for dreams and heroes. What does this story say about our need for heroes, about how heroes are created, and about how heroes can transform societies? Use details from the text to support your statement of theme.

8. In Homer's *Odyssey*, the hero, Odysseus, who has been away from home for twenty years, is washed up from the sea onto the shores of his own kingdom. What echoes of this myth can you find in this story?

9. Where do you find these **archetypes** in the story: the superhuman hero; metamorphoses; a hope for a hero who will transform our everyday lives?

10. **Satire** is the kind of writing that is critical of some aspect of society. Satire often uses humor and exaggeration to make its points. Do you find any hints in this story that García Márquez is making fun of some aspects of human nature? Explain your responses.

SKILLS FOCUS

**Literary Skills**
Analyze the use of magic realism.

**Writing Skills**
Write an expository essay. Write an essay analyzing the use of magic realism in a story.

**Vocabulary Skills**
Demonstrate word knowledge.

Drowned Man in the World," you could refer to "Miniver Cheevy" (page 590); "Soldier's Home" (page 685); "The Leader of the People" (page 745); "The Secret Life of Walter Mitty" (page 782); or "Speaking of Courage" (page 963). In your essay, explain why you think we need heroes.

## Analyzing Magic Realism

In a brief **essay**, analyze García Márquez's use of **magic realism** in this story. Before you write, review the story to locate some particularly realistic details. Then, locate some of the story's fantastic elements. You might organize your details on a chart like the one below. At the end of your essay, state your general response to the use of magic realism. Do you like this blending of fantasy and reality? Or do you prefer either pure fantasy or pure realism?

| Fantastic Events | Realistic Details |
| --- | --- |
| | |

## Literary Criticism

11. The literary critic David Young says this about magic realism:

> One way to understand magic realism is as a kind of pleasant joke on realism. . . . [Magic realism] manages to combine the truthful and verifiable aspects of realism with the magical effects we associate with myth, folk tale, tall story, and that being in all of us—our childhood self, perhaps—who loves the spell that narrative casts even when it is perfectly implausible.

Which passages of García Márquez's story remind you of myth, legend, folk tale, or tall tale? How well does the story as a whole exemplify Young's definition of magic realism?

## WRITING

### Do We Need Heroes?

Answer that question in a brief **essay**. In your answer, refer to García Márquez's story and to one other story in this book that also focuses on the topic of heroism. Note how heroism can transform the world (or, if it is absent, how that absence can affect it). In addition to "The Handsomest

### Vocabulary Development
**True or False?**

Each sentence that follows makes a statement about García Márquez's story. Show your understanding of the underlined words by labeling each sentence true or false. Be able to explain the reason for your choice.

1. The villagers made their living fishing the bountiful sea.
2. The drowned man looked sickly and haggard.
3. Esteban appeared destitute, yet handsome and exceptionally virile.
4. The women were annoyed with the frivolity of the men's businesslike attitudes toward the body.
5. The women imagined that, in life, Esteban often felt mortified about his great size.

# Amy Tan
## (1952–     )

Amy Tan had not planned to become a fiction writer. In fact, for years she worked as a freelance writer for high-technology companies, a career in which flights of imagination are not permitted. To ease the pressures of her job, she decided to take jazz piano lessons—and she began writing fiction. The result was the release of a dazzling new storyteller.

Tan's parents had fled Communist China and had come to the United States shortly before she was born in Oakland, California. Her mother, a nurse, was originally from Shanghai; her father, an engineer and a Baptist minister, came from Beijing.

After her father and young brother both died of brain tumors when Amy Tan was just fifteen, her mother took her away from the "diseased" house to Switzerland, where she finished high school. Her mother expected her talented daughter to become a neurosurgeon, as well as a pianist, in her spare time. When they returned to the United States, Tan enrolled as a pre-med student at Linfield College, a Baptist school in Oregon, which had been selected by her mother. But she defied her mother by leaving Linfield to join her boyfriend at San Jose State University, where she changed her major from pre-med to English. Tan's mother took this defiance as a sort of death between them, and mother and daughter did not speak for six months.

Tan was well aware of her mother's narrative gift, a gift that may have prompted her own desire to write. However, Tan was thirty-three before she wrote her first story, "Endgame" (retitled "Rules of the Game"). This story and others were collected in 1989 into a bestselling volume, *The Joy Luck Club* (also made into a popular movie). The collection interweaves stories about four Chinese American young women with stories of their mothers, born in China, who are members of a mah-jongg club in San Francisco.

In Tan's 1991 novel, *The Kitchen God's Wife,* a mother tells her grown daughter about life in China during World War II—and the daughter begins to see both her mother and herself with new eyes. A third novel, *The Hundred Secret Senses* (1995), explores another familial relationship—one between two sisters whose lives are transformed during a visit to a small village in China.

Tan's mother died in 1999, and the final days of her life helped shape Tan's fourth bestseller, *The Bonesetter's Daughter* (2001). The novel, moving between San Francisco of today and a Chinese village of the past, tells the story of a mother and daughter who find themselves through their dreams and their histories. Her mother, Tan said, will continue to serve as her muse. "She is a voice. A voice that can do all kinds of things. . . . She'll insist that she has a role in the next book. She's not done with me yet."

## Rules of the Game

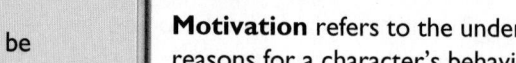

### Make the Connection
### Quickwrite ✏️

At first the following story appears to be about a Chinese American girl who stumbles into the forbidding world of championship chess and becomes an absolute whiz at it. Soon, however, we come to understand that the story is about something far more familiar to us: the clash between a mother's authority over her children and her ambitions for them and a child's need to find his or her own way.

Before you read "Rules of the Game," think about the rules of chess or another game you know. Then, write down some ways in which the rules of the game might parallel rules of human relationships, especially relations between children and parents. Could the title of this story have more than one meaning?

### Literary Focus
### Motivation

**Motivation** refers to the reasons for a character's behavior. A writer can reveal motivation directly by telling us what makes a character tick. More often, however, a writer describes characters through their speech and actions, without telling us exactly why they behave as they do: We must sift through the details and infer their motivation. Tan's story fits into this second category. Pay particular attention to how the beat-up chess set arrives in the Jong family, how Waverly becomes interested in the game while her brothers play, and how her interest grows as theirs wanes. Then, ask yourself, "What's really going on in that final match between Waverly and her true coach and adversary?"

> **Motivation** refers to the underlying reasons for a character's behavior.
>
> *For more on Motivation, see the Handbook of Literary and Historical Terms.*

### Vocabulary Development

**ancestral** (an·ses′trəl) *adj.:* inherited.

**intricate** (in′tri·kit) *adj.:* complicated; detailed.

**obscured** (əb·skyoord′) *v.:* concealed; hidden.

**retort** (ri·tôrt′) *n.:* quick, sharp answer.

**touted** (tout′id) *v.:* highly praised.

**prodigy** (präd′ə·jē) *n.:* extremely gifted person.

**malodorous** (mal·ō′dər·əs) *adj.:* bad-smelling.

**concessions** (kən·sesh′ənz) *n. pl.:* acts of giving in.

**careened** (kə·rēnd′) *v.:* lurched sideways.

**successive** (sək·ses′iv) *adj.:* consecutive.

**SKILLS FOCUS**

**Literary Skills**
Understand motivation.

**INTERNET**

**More About Amy Tan**

Keyword: LE7 11-6

# Rules of the Game

## from The Joy Luck Club

### Amy Tan

I was six when my mother taught me the art of invisible strength. It was a strategy for winning arguments, respect from others, and eventually, though neither of us knew it at the time, chess games.

"Bite back your tongue," scolded my mother when I cried loudly, yanking her hand toward the store that sold bags of salted plums. At home, she said, "Wise guy, he not go against wind. In Chinese we say, Come from South, blow with wind—poom!—North will follow. Strongest wind cannot be seen."

The next week I bit back my tongue as we entered the store with the forbidden candies. When my mother finished her shopping, she quietly plucked a small bag of plums from the rack and put it on the counter with the rest of the items.

My mother imparted her daily truths so she could help my older brothers and me rise above our circumstances. We lived in San Francisco's Chinatown. Like most of the other Chinese children who played in the back alleys of restaurants and curio shops, I didn't think we were poor. My bowl was always full, three five-course meals every day, beginning with a soup full of mysterious things I didn't want to know the names of.

We lived on Waverly Place, in a warm, clean, two-bedroom flat that sat above a small Chinese bakery specializing in steamed pastries and dim sum. In the early morning, when the alley was still quiet, I could smell fragrant red beans as they were cooked down to a pasty sweetness. By daybreak, our flat was heavy with the odor of fried sesame balls and sweet curried chicken crescents. From my bed, I would listen as my father got ready for work, then locked the door behind him, one-two-three clicks.

At the end of our two-block alley was a small sandlot playground with swings and slides well-shined down the middle with use. The play area was bordered by wood-slat benches where old-country people sat cracking roasted watermelon seeds with their golden teeth and scattering the husks to an impatient gathering of gurgling pigeons. The best playground, however, was the dark alley itself. It was crammed with daily mysteries and adventures. My brothers and I would peer into the medicinal herb shop, watching old Li dole out onto a still sheet of white paper the right amount of insect shells, saffron-colored seeds, and pungent leaves for his ailing customers. It was said that he once cured a woman dying of an ancestral curse that had eluded the best of American doctors. Next to the pharmacy was a printer who specialized in gold-embossed wedding invitations and festive red banners.

---

**Vocabulary**

**ancestral** (an·ses′trəl) *adj.*: inherited.

Farther down the street was Ping Yuen Fish Market. The front window displayed a tank crowded with doomed fish and turtles struggling to gain footing on the slimy green-tiled sides. A handwritten sign informed tourists, "Within this store, is all for food, not for pet." Inside, the butchers with their bloodstained white smocks deftly gutted the fish while customers cried out their orders and shouted, "Give me your freshest," to which the butchers always protested, "All are freshest." On less crowded market days, we would inspect the crates of live frogs and crabs which we were warned not to poke, boxes of dried cuttlefish, and row upon row of iced prawns, squid, and slippery fish. The sanddabs made me shiver each time; their eyes lay on one flattened side and reminded me of my mother's story of a careless girl who ran into a crowded street and was crushed by a cab. "Was smash flat," reported my mother.

At the corner of the alley was Hong Sing's, a four-table café with a recessed stairwell in front that led to a door marked "Tradesmen." My brothers and I believed the bad people emerged from this door at night. Tourists never went to Hong Sing's, since the menu was printed only in Chinese. A Caucasian man with a big camera once posed me and my playmates in front of the restaurant. He had us move to the side of the picture window so the photo would capture the roasted duck with its head dangling from a juice-covered rope. After he took the picture, I told him he should go into Hong Sing's and eat dinner. When he smiled and asked me what they served, I shouted, "Guts and duck's feet and octopus gizzards!" Then I ran off with my friends, shrieking with laughter as we scampered across the alley and hid in the entryway grotto of the China Gem Company, my heart pounding with hope that he would chase us.

My mother named me after the street that we lived on: Waverly Place Jong, my official name for important American documents. But my family called me Meimei, "Little Sister." I was the youngest, the only daughter. Each morning before school, my mother would twist and yank on my thick black hair until she had formed two tightly wound pigtails. One day, as she struggled to weave a hard-toothed comb through my disobedient hair, I had a sly thought.

I asked her, "Ma, what is Chinese torture?" My mother shook her head. A bobby pin was wedged between her lips. She wetted her palm and smoothed the hair above my ear, then pushed the pin in so that it nicked sharply against my scalp.

"Who say this word?" she asked without a trace of knowing how wicked I was being. I shrugged my shoulders and said, "Some boy in my class said Chinese people do Chinese torture."

"Chinese people do many things," she said simply. "Chinese people do business, do medicine, do painting. Not lazy like American people. We do torture. Best torture."

My older brother Vincent was the one who actually got the chess set. We had gone to the annual Christmas party held at the First Chinese Baptist Church at the end of the alley. The missionary ladies had put together a Santa bag of gifts donated by members of another church. None of the gifts had names on them. There were separate sacks for boys and girls of different ages.

One of the Chinese parishioners had donned a Santa Claus costume and a stiff paper beard with cotton balls glued to it. I think the only children who thought he was the real thing were too young to know that Santa Claus was not Chinese. When my turn came up, the Santa man asked me how old I was. I thought it was a trick question; I was seven according to the American formula and eight by the Chinese calendar. I said I was born on March 17, 1951. That seemed to satisfy him. He then solemnly asked if I had been a very, very good girl this year and did I believe in Jesus Christ and obey my parents. I knew the only answer to that. I nodded back with equal solemnity.

Having watched the other children opening their gifts, I already knew that the big gifts were not necessarily the nicest ones. One girl my age got a large coloring book of biblical characters, while a less greedy girl who selected a smaller box received a glass vial of lavender toilet water.[1] The sound of the box was also important. A ten-year-old boy had chosen a box that jangled when he shook it. It was a tin globe of the world with a slit for inserting money. He must have thought it was full of dimes and nickels, because when he saw that it had just ten pennies, his face fell with such undisguised disappointment that his mother slapped the side of his head and led him out of the church hall, apologizing to the crowd for her son who had such bad manners he couldn't appreciate such a fine gift.

As I peered into the sack, I quickly fingered the remaining presents, testing their weight, imagining what they contained. I chose a heavy, compact one that was wrapped in shiny silver foil and a red satin ribbon. It was a twelve-pack of Life Savers and I spent the rest of the party arranging and rearranging the candy tubes in the order of my favorites. My brother Winston chose wisely as well. His present turned out to be a box of <u>intricate</u> plastic parts; the instructions on the box proclaimed that when they were properly assembled he would have an authentic miniature replica of a World War II submarine.

Vincent got the chess set, which would have been a very decent present to get at a church Christmas party, except it was obviously used and, as we discovered later, it was missing a black pawn and a white knight. My mother graciously thanked the unknown benefactor, saying, "Too good. Cost too much." At which point, an old lady with fine white, wispy hair nodded toward our family and said with a whistling whisper, "Merry, merry Christmas."

When we got home, my mother told Vincent to throw the chess set away. "She not want it. We not want it," she said, tossing her head stiffly to the side with a tight, proud smile. My brothers had deaf ears. They were already lining up the chess pieces and reading from the dog-eared instruction book.

I watched Vincent and Winston play during Christmas week. The chessboard seemed to hold elaborate secrets waiting to be untangled. The chessmen were more powerful than Old Li's magic herbs that cured ancestral curses. And my brothers wore such serious faces that I was sure something was at stake that was greater than avoiding the tradesmen's door to Hong Sing's.

"Let me! Let me!" I begged between games when one brother or the other would sit back with a deep sigh of relief and victory, the other annoyed, unable to let go of the outcome. Vincent at first refused to let me play, but when I offered my Life Savers as replacements for the buttons that filled in for the missing pieces, he relented. He chose the flavors: wild cherry for the black pawn and peppermint for the white knight. Winner could eat both.

As our mother sprinkled flour and rolled out small doughy circles for the steamed dumplings that would be our dinner that night, Vincent explained the rules, pointing to each piece. "You have sixteen pieces and so do I. One king and queen, two bishops, two knights, two castles, and eight pawns. The pawns can only move forward one step, except on the first move. Then they can move two. But they can only take men by moving crossways like this, except in the beginning, when you can move ahead and take another pawn."

"Why?" I asked as I moved my pawn. "Why can't they move more steps?"

"Because they're pawns," he said.

"But why do they go crossways to take other men? Why aren't there any women and children?"

"Why is the sky blue? Why must you always ask stupid questions?" asked Vincent. "This is a game. These are the rules. I didn't make them up. See. Here. In the book." He jabbed a page

---

1. **toilet water:** perfumed after-bath skin freshener.

**Vocabulary**

**intricate** (in'tri·kit) *adj.:* complicated; detailed.

with a pawn in his hand. "Pawn. P-A-W-N. Pawn. Read it yourself."

My mother patted the flour off her hands. "Let me see book," she said quietly. She scanned the pages quickly, not reading the foreign English symbols, seeming to search deliberately for nothing in particular.

"This American rules," she concluded at last. "Every time people come out from foreign country, must know rules. You not know, judge say, Too bad, go back. They not telling you why so you can use their way go forward. They say, Don't know why, you find out yourself. But they knowing all the time. Better you take it, find out why yourself." She tossed her head back with a satisfied smile.

I found out about all the whys later. I read the rules and looked up all the big words in a dictionary. I borrowed books from the Chinatown library. I studied each chess piece, trying to absorb the power each contained.

I learned about opening moves and why it's important to control the center early on; the shortest distance between two points is straight down the middle. I learned about the middle game and why tactics between two adversaries are like clashing ideas; the one who plays better has the clearest plans for both attacking and getting out of traps. I learned why it is essential in the endgame to have foresight, a mathematical understanding of all possible moves, and patience; all weaknesses and advantages become evident to a strong adversary and are obscured to a tiring opponent. I discovered that for the whole game one must gather invisible strengths and see the endgame before the game begins.

I also found out why I should never reveal "why" to others. A little knowledge withheld is a great advantage one should store for future use. That is the power of chess. It is a game of secrets in which one must show and never tell.

I loved the secrets I found within the sixty-four black and white squares. I carefully drew a handmade chessboard and pinned it to the wall next to my bed, where at night I would stare for hours at imaginary battles. Soon I no longer lost any games or Life Savers, but I lost my adver-

saries. Winston and Vincent decided they were more interested in roaming the streets after school in their Hopalong Cassidy[2] cowboy hats.

On a cold spring afternoon, while walking home from school, I detoured through the playground at the end of our alley. I saw a group of old men, two seated across a folding table playing a game of chess, others smoking pipes, eating peanuts, and watching. I ran home and grabbed Vincent's chess set, which was bound in a cardboard box with rubber bands. I also carefully selected two prized rolls of Life Savers. I came back to the park and approached a man who was observing the game.

"Want to play?" I asked him. His face widened with surprise and he grinned as he looked at the box under my arm.

"Little sister, been a long time since I play with dolls," he said, smiling benevolently. I quickly put the box down next to him on the bench and displayed my retort.

Lau Po, as he allowed me to call him, turned out to be a much better player than my brothers. I lost many games and many Life Savers. But over the weeks, with each diminishing roll of candies, I added new secrets. Lau Po gave me the names. The Double Attack from the East and West Shores. Throwing Stones on the

---

2. **Hopalong Cassidy:** cowboy hero of movies and television from the 1930s through the early 1950s.

**Vocabulary**

**obscured** (əb·skyoord′) v.: concealed; hidden.
**retort** (ri·tôrt′) n.: quick, sharp answer.

(Opposite) Scene from the movie *The Joy Luck Club.*
© Buena Vista Distribution, Inc.

Drowning Man. The Sudden Meeting of the Clan. The Surprise from the Sleeping Guard. The Humble Servant Who Kills the King. Sand in the Eyes of Advancing Forces. A Double Killing Without Blood.

There were also the fine points of chess etiquette. Keep captured men in neat rows, as well-tended prisoners. Never announce "Check" with vanity, lest someone with an unseen sword slit your throat. Never hurl pieces into the sandbox after you have lost a game, because then you must find them again, by yourself, after apologizing to all around you. By the end of the summer, Lau Po had taught me all he knew, and I had become a better chess player.

A small weekend crowd of Chinese people and tourists would gather as I played and defeated my opponents one by one. My mother would join the crowds during these outdoor exhibition games. She sat proudly on the bench, telling my admirers with proper Chinese humility, "Is luck."

A man who watched me play in the park suggested that my mother allow me to play in local chess tournaments. My mother smiled graciously, an answer that meant nothing. I desperately wanted to go, but I bit back my tongue. I knew she would not let me play among strangers. So as we walked home I said in a small voice that I didn't want to play in the local tournament. They would have American rules. If I lost, I would bring shame on my family.

"Is shame you fall down nobody push you," said my mother.

During my first tournament, my mother sat with me in the front row as I waited for my turn. I frequently bounced my legs to unstick them from the cold metal seat of the folding chair. When my name was called, I leapt up. My mother unwrapped something in her lap. It was her *chang*, a small tablet of red jade which held the sun's fire. "Is luck," she whispered, and tucked it into my dress pocket. I turned to my opponent, a fifteen-year-old boy from Oakland. He looked at me, wrinkling his nose.

As I began to play, the boy disappeared, the color ran out of the room, and I saw only my white pieces and his black ones waiting on the other side. A light wind began blowing past my ears. It whispered secrets only I could hear.

"Blow from the South," it murmured. "The wind leaves no trail." I saw a clear path, the traps to avoid. The crowd rustled. "Shhh! Shhh!" said the corners of the room. The wind blew stronger. "Throw sand from the East to distract him." The knight came forward ready for the sacrifice. The wind hissed, louder and louder. "Blow, blow, blow. He cannot see. He is blind now. Make him lean away from the wind so he is easier to knock down."

"Check," I said, as the wind roared with laughter. The wind died down to little puffs, my own breath.

My mother placed my first trophy next to a new plastic chess set that the neighborhood Tao society had given to me. As she wiped each piece with a soft cloth, she said, "Next time win more, lose less."

"Ma, it's not how many pieces you lose," I said. "Sometimes you need to lose pieces to get ahead."

"Better to lose less, see if you really need."

At the next tournament, I won again, but it was my mother who wore the triumphant grin.

"Lost eight piece this time. Last time was eleven. What I tell you? Better off lose less!" I was annoyed, but I couldn't say anything.

I attended more tournaments, each one farther away from home. I won all games, in all divisions. The Chinese bakery downstairs from our flat displayed my growing collection of trophies in its window, amidst the dust-covered cakes that were never picked up. The day after

I won an important regional tournament, the window encased a fresh sheet cake with whipped-cream frosting and red script saying, "Congratulations, Waverly Jong, Chinatown Chess Champion." Soon after that, a flower shop, headstone engraver, and funeral parlor offered to sponsor me in national tournaments. That's when my mother decided I no longer had to do the dishes. Winston and Vincent had to do my chores.

"Why does she get to play and we do all the work," complained Vincent.

"Is new American rules," said my mother. "Meimei play, squeeze all her brains out for win chess. You play, worth squeeze towel."

By my ninth birthday, I was a national chess champion. I was still some 429 points away from grand-master status,[3] but I was <u>touted</u> as the Great American Hope, a child <u>prodigy</u> and a girl to boot. They ran a photo of me in *Life* magazine next to a quote in which Bobby Fischer[4] said, "There will never be a woman grand master." "Your move, Bobby," said the caption.

The day they took the magazine picture I wore neatly plaited braids clipped with plastic barrettes trimmed with rhinestones. I was playing in a large high school auditorium that echoed with phlegmy coughs and the squeaky rubber knobs of chair legs sliding across freshly waxed wooden floors. Seated across from me was an American man, about the same age as Lau Po, maybe fifty. I remember that his sweaty brow seemed to weep at my every move. He wore a dark, <u>malodorous</u> suit. One of his pockets was stuffed with a great white kerchief on which he wiped his palm before sweeping his hand over the chosen chess piece with great flourish.

In my crisp pink-and-white dress with scratchy lace at the neck, one of two my mother had sewn for these special occasions, I would clasp my hands under my chin, the delicate points of my elbows poised lightly on the table in the manner my mother had shown me for posing for the press. I would swing my patent leather shoes back and forth like an impatient child riding on a school bus. Then I would pause, suck in my lips, twirl my chosen piece in midair as if undecided, and then firmly plant it in its new threatening place, with a triumphant smile thrown back at my opponent for good measure.

I no longer played in the alley of Waverly Place. I never visited the playground where the pigeons and old men gathered. I went to school, then directly home to learn new chess secrets, cleverly concealed advantages, more escape routes.

But I found it difficult to concentrate at home. My mother had a habit of standing over me while I plotted out my games. I think she thought of herself as my protective ally. Her lips would be sealed tight, and after each move I made, a soft "Hmmmmph" would escape from her nose.

"Ma, I can't practice when you stand there like that," I said one day. She retreated to the kitchen and made loud noises with the pots and pans. When the crashing stopped, I could see out of the corner of my eye that she was standing in the doorway. "Hmmmph!" Only this one came out of her tight throat.

My parents made many <u>concessions</u> to allow

---

3. **grand-master status:** top rank in international chess competition.
4. **Bobby Fischer** (1943–    ): American chess master, the youngest player in the world to attain the rank of grand master, in 1958.

me to practice. One time I complained that the bedroom I shared was so noisy that I couldn't think. Thereafter, my brothers slept in a bed in the living room facing the street. I said I couldn't finish my rice; my head didn't work right when my stomach was too full. I left the table with half-finished bowls and nobody complained. But there was one duty I couldn't avoid. I had to accompany my mother on Saturday market days when I had no tournament to play. My mother would proudly walk with me, visiting many shops, buying very little. "This my daughter Wave-ly Jong," she said to whoever looked her way.

One day, after we left a shop I said under my breath, "I wish you wouldn't do that, telling everybody I'm your daughter." My mother stopped walking. Crowds of people with heavy bags pushed past us on the sidewalk, bumping into first one shoulder, then another.

"Aiii-ya. So shame be with mother?" She grasped my hand even tighter as she glared at me.

I looked down. "It's not that, it's just so obvious. It's just so embarrassing."

"Embarrass you be my daughter?" Her voice was cracking with anger.

"That's not what I meant. That's not what I said."

"What you say?"

I knew it was a mistake to say anything more, but I heard my voice speaking. "Why do you have to use me to show off? If you want to show off, then why don't you learn to play chess?"

My mother's eyes turned into dangerous black slits. She had no words for me, just sharp silence.

I felt the wind rushing around my hot ears. I jerked my hand out of my mother's tight grasp and spun around, knocking into an old woman. Her bag of groceries spilled to the ground.

"Aii-ya! Stupid girl!" my mother and the woman cried. Oranges and tin cans careened down the sidewalk. As my mother stooped to help the old woman pick up the escaping food, I took off.

I raced down the street, dashing between people, not looking back as my mother screamed shrilly, "Meimei! Meimei!" I fled down an alley, past dark, curtained shops and merchants washing the grime off their windows. I sped into the sunlight, into a large street crowded with tourists examining trinkets and souvenirs. I ducked into another dark alley, down another street, up another alley. I ran until it hurt and I realized I had nowhere to go, that I was not running from anything. The alleys contained no escape routes.

My breath came out like angry smoke. It was cold. I sat down on an upturned plastic pail next to a stack of empty boxes, cupping my chin with my hands, thinking hard. I imagined my mother, first walking briskly down one street or another looking for me, then giving up and returning home to await my arrival. After two hours, I stood up on creaking legs and slowly walked home.

The alley was quiet and I could see the yellow lights shining from our flat like two tiger's eyes in the night. I climbed the sixteen steps to the door, advancing quietly up each so as not to make any warning sounds. I turned the knob; the door was locked. I heard a chair moving, quick steps, the locks turning—click! click! click!—and then the door opened.

"About time you got home," said Vincent. "Boy, are you in trouble."

He slid back to the dinner table. On a platter were the remains of a large fish, its fleshy head still connected to bones swimming upstream in vain escape. Standing there waiting for my punishment, I heard my mother speak in a dry voice.

"We not concerning this girl. This girl not have concerning for us."

Nobody looked at me. Bone chopsticks clinked against the inside of bowls being emptied into hungry mouths.

I walked into my room, closed the door, and lay down on my bed. The room was dark, the

**Vocabulary**

**careened** (kə·rēnd′) v.: lurched sideways.

ceiling filled with shadows from the dinnertime lights of neighboring flats.

In my head, I saw a chessboard with sixty-four black and white squares. Opposite me was my opponent, two angry black slits. She wore a triumphant smile. "Strongest wind cannot be seen," she said.

Her black men advanced across the plane, slowly marching to each successive level as a single unit. My white pieces screamed as they scurried and fell off the board one by one. As her men drew closer to my edge, I felt myself growing light. I rose up into the air and flew out the window. Higher and higher, above the alley, over the tops of tiled roofs, where I was gathered up by the wind and pushed up toward the night sky until everything below me disappeared and I was alone.

I closed my eyes and pondered my next move. ■

---

**Vocabulary**
**successive** (sək·ses′iv) *adj.*: consecutive.

# Response and Analysis

## Reading Check

1. Describe where Waverly lives.
2. How do the Jongs acquire their first chess set?
3. How does Waverly persuade her brothers to let her play chess too?
4. What are some ways in which Waverly's mother shows she is ambitious for her daughter and proud of her accomplishments?
5. As a result of Waverly's success at chess, what **conflicts** arise between her and her mother?

## Thinking Critically

6. What does Waverly's mother mean on page 1019 when she says about the used chess set, "She not want it. We not want it"? How does the boys' reaction show cultural and generational **conflicts** between the mother and her children?
7. Review your Quickwrite notes. How do the rules of chess relate to the relationship between Waverly and her mother? 🖉
8. What do you see as Mrs. Jong's **motivation** for showing off her daughter? Why does Waverly resent her mother's actions?

9. Toward the end of the story, Waverly's imaginary opponent says, "Strongest wind cannot be seen." Where else in the story is that statement used? What do you think it means?
10. What do you think Waverly's fantasy at the end of the story means? What do you predict as her "next move"?
11. Find passages in the story where rules of various sorts are talked about. What multiple meanings might the **title** have?

## Literary Criticism

12. In a review of *The Joy Luck Club,* the critic Susan Dooley wrote the following comment:

> These women from China find trying to talk to their daughters like trying to plug a foreign appliance into an American outlet. The current won't work. Impulses collide and nothing flows through the wires except anger and exasperation.

How does this comment apply to "The Rules of the Game"? Use specific examples from the story to support your conclusions.

**SKILLS FOCUS**

**Literary Skills**
Analyze motivation.

**Writing Skills**
Write an essay describing two literary characters in another context. Write an autobiographical narrative.

**Vocabulary Skills**
Demonstrate word knowledge.

## WRITING

### Visitors from Other Stories

In a brief **essay,** tell what you think would happen if Mrs. Jong and Mrs. Garcia (the narrator's mother from "Daughter of Invention" by Julia Alvarez, page 995) were to enter each other's story. If Mrs. Jong could be brought into Alvarez's story, whose side would she take—that of Mrs. Garcia or that of the narrator's father? If Mrs. Garcia from "Daughter of Invention" could be introduced to Mrs. Jong, what advice would she give Mrs. Jong? Write one paragraph about each mother. Be sure to explain *why* you think each character would behave the way she does.

### Rules of Your Game

Have you ever had an experience like Waverly has had in this story? Think back to a time when you learned about the rules of life. What happened? Whose rules did you break? In a few paragraphs, write a **narrative** about this incident.

▶ **Use "Writing an Autobiographical Narrative," pages 1060–1061, for help with this assignment.**

---

### Vocabulary Development

**Own It**

1. Give an example of an <u>ancestral</u> trait.
2. Describe an <u>intricate</u> object.
3. Explain how something might be <u>obscured.</u>
4. Write a few lines of dialogue, with an example of a <u>retort.</u>
5. Describe something you have been <u>touted</u> for.
6. Use the word *prodigy* in a sentence.
7. Write a brief description of a <u>malodorous</u> person.
8. Look in the dictionary to find another meaning for the word *concessions.*
9. Describe an incident with the word *careened.*
10. List five numbers in <u>successive</u> order.

---

# Grammar Link

## Using Transitional Expressions: Making Things Coherent

**Transitional expressions** are words or phrases that provide a smooth flow from one idea to the next, making your writing more coherent and logical. Transitional expressions help the reader follow your train of thought and see connections within sentences or between sentences or paragraphs. Transitional expressions often show **chronological** or **spatial** relationships. They may also show connections based on **comparison and contrast, cause and effect,** or **exemplification-restatement.** In the following passages from Amy Tan's "Rules of the Game," notice the transitional words that connect the sentences:

> "I knew she would not let me play among strangers. So as we walked home I said in a small voice that I didn't want to play in the local tournament." [**So** indicates a cause-and-effect relationship.]

**SKILLS FOCUS**

**Grammar Skills**
Use transitional expressions to connect ideas.

"One time I complained that the bedroom I shared was so noisy that I couldn't think. <u>Thereafter</u>, my brothers slept in a bed in the living room facing the street."

[**Thereafter** indicates a chronological relationship.]

In the first example the transitional word *so* explains why Waverly says what she does to her mother—her motivation. In the second example the word *thereafter* tells the order in which these two linked events occurred—and by implication, that the change in sleeping arrangements occurred as a result of Waverly's complaint.

Transitional words and phrases are like the string that holds together a beaded necklace, keeping it from scattering into separate pieces. Whenever your writing sounds choppy or disjointed, consider adding a transitional word or phrase that clarifies the connection between your ideas.

| Transitional Words and Phrases | | | |
|---|---|---|---|
| **Chronological** | then | first | meanwhile |
| | finally | before | eventually |
| | soon | at last | after |
| | next | later | afterward |
| **Spatial** | above | across | next to |
| | below | inside | over |
| | near | outside | under |
| | there | here | around |
| **Comparison** | also | like | likewise |
| | similarly | too | moreover |
| **Contrast** | yet | still | nevertheless |
| | however | although | in spite of |
| | unlike | in contrast | on the other hand |
| **Cause and Effect** | because | so that | consequently |
| | since | therefore | as a result |
| | thus | since | for this reason |
| **Exemplification-Restatement** | specifically | for example | for instance |
| | that is | in fact | in other words |

## Apply to Your Writing

Re-read a current writing assignment or one that you've already completed. Are there any passages that seem choppy or confusing because your ideas don't flow smoothly together? See if you can clarify the coherence of your writing by adding a transitional expression.

▶ **For more help, see Combining Sentences for Variety, 10a–d, in the Language Handbook.**

In the following passages, add transitional expressions to create a smoother flow and to strengthen the connection between ideas. You may choose to combine sentences or keep them separate.

1. In Amy Tan's story "Rules of the Game," Waverly's brother Vincent gets a chess set at a church Christmas party. Their mother tells him to throw it away.

2. Waverly learns to play chess better than her brothers. They lose interest in playing with her.

3. Waverly becomes a chess champion. Her mother is proud of her. Waverly is uncomfortable with her mother's way of showing her pride.

4. Waverly sees her conflict with her mother in terms of chess. She runs away from her mother after their fight. She says that the alley contains "no escape routes," a term she previously used to describe "chess secrets."

# Jhumpa Lahiri
## (1967– )

**M**ost young writers can only dream of the success that Jhumpa Lahiri has found. Propelled by a stint at the Provincetown Fine Arts Work Center in Provincetown, Massachusetts, her career took off. "It was something of a miracle. In seven months I got an agent, sold a book, and had a story published in *The New Yorker*. I've been extremely lucky." Behind that luck lies a great deal of searching, uncertainty, and writing, writing, writing.

Born in London to parents who had emigrated from Calcutta, India, Lahiri grew up in Rhode Island. Her experience as an Indian American has been essential in forging her identity as a writer. "One of the things I was always aware of growing up was conflicting expectations. I was expected to be Indian by Indians and American by Americans. I didn't feel equipped even as a child to fully participate in things. . . . In the act of writing, it was more justified to withdraw into myself and have that be a vital experience, rather than just feeling neglected or left out." As a child she filled her notebooks with "novels," which she sometimes wrote together with friends.

Lahiri graduated from Barnard College in New York City with a degree in English literature and has since gained a doctorate in Renaissance studies. Nonetheless, she admits that scholarship does not fill her with the love and satisfaction she finds in writing fiction. The Provincetown experience changed her life. Her first collection of stories, *Interpreter of Maladies*, won the Pulitzer Prize in fiction in 2000, a rare honor for a first book.

As Lahiri explains, the title story of *Interpreter of Maladies* grew out of an encounter with a man who worked as a translator for a doctor whose patients did not speak English. The man's occupation intrigued her, and she came to see his role as a metaphor for her own life as a writer. "I think it best expresses the predicament at the heart of the book: the dilemma, the difficulty and often the impossibil-ity of communicating emotional pain to others, as well as expressing it to ourselves. In some senses I view my position as a writer, insofar as I attempt to articulate these emotions, as an interpreter as well."

"When Mr. Pirzada Came to Dine," another story in *Interpreter of Maladies*, depicts characters near to Lahiri's heart and experience—Indians and Indian Americans dealing with the "maladies," the difficulties and limits, of commitment, compassion, and communication. Mr. Pirzada, Lahiri remarked in an interview, "is a man who actually came to our home, but I was four then, not ten. I had seen photos of him in the family album but knew only that he was a Muslim. I had no details. Our relationship is imagined." Nevertheless, it is a relationship fraught with intense but unspoken feeling. "The characters I'm drawn to all face some barrier of communication. I like to write about people who think in a way they can't fully express."

# When Mr. Pirzada Came to Dine

## Make the Connection

Hundreds of news photographs flash before our eyes every day—in newspapers, on round-the-clock news television, and even on the Internet. It is easy to ignore the fact that the distant events they capture are affecting the lives of people just like us. Refugees fleeing a war-torn country and survivors of an earthquake—all are individuals whose lives are disrupted, perhaps ruined. What does it take to learn to have compassion for other people?

## Literary Focus
### Theme

A **theme** is an insight about human life that is revealed in a literary work. In good literature a theme is almost never stated directly. After all, the writer of imaginative fiction does not want to preach to us, or moralize. Instead, the writer wants us, along with the characters, to recognize some truth about human existence. The writer wants to bring alive some segment of human life. When the writer's task is done well, theme arises naturally from the story, so that by the end of the story we think we have discovered something—or rediscovered a truth we had forgotten.

To get to the theme of a story, it is better to ask, "What does this story reveal to me?" than to ask, "What does this story teach me?"

The ability to state a theme is a test of our understanding of a story. Although there is no one way to find a theme, one of the best ways is by asking how the main character has changed in the course of the story and what he or she has discovered or learned from the experience. Sometimes, though not always, the title provides a clue. Sometimes a key statement in the story points to its theme.

When you state a theme, you must state it as a generalization about life. The statement of a theme must be a sentence—one word or a phrase can express a topic, but it takes a subject and verb to express a theme.

> A **theme** is an insight about human life that is revealed in a literary work.
>
> *For more on Theme, see the Handbook of Literary and Historical Terms.*

## Background

After ruling India for almost two hundred years, in 1947 the British agreed to a transfer of power. Because the Muslim minority demanded a separate state, the British partitioned the Indian subcontinent into predominantly Hindu India and predominantly Muslim Pakistan. This division resulted in violent killings and the displacement of millions of people. Pakistan itself was divided into two geographically, ethnically, and linguistically separate parts. Other than sharing a common religion, the people of East Pakistan and West Pakistan had little in common. They spoke different languages and had different cultures, traditions, and physical traits.

By the autumn of 1971, when this story takes place, East Pakistan, led by Sheikh Mujib Rahman, was demanding independence. The West Pakistan government, directed by Yahyah Kahn, reacted with brutal force, driving ten million refugees into India. As a result, India intervened, quickly forcing the Pakistani army to surrender. In mid-December 1971, Bangladesh, the former East Pakistan, was established as an independent state.

**SKILLS FOCUS**

**Literary Skills**
Understand theme.

**INTERNET**

**More About Jhumpa Lahiri**

Keyword: LE7 11-6

In this story a family gathers to watch the grim and confusing nightly news about the conflict in Pakistan. They live in a quiet New England community, but the young narrator soon finds that their emotional lives are intertwined with the violent birth of a new nation, half a world away.

## Vocabulary Development

**ascertaining** (as'ər·tān'iŋ) *v.:* finding out with certainty.

**autonomy** (ô·tän'ə·mē) *n.:* independence; self-government.

**austere** (ô·stir') *adj.:* very plain.

**impeccably** (im·pek'ə·blē) *adv.:* perfectly; without error or defect.

**imperceptible** (im'pər·sep'tə·bəl) *adj.:* unnoticeable; so slight as not to be noticed.

**rotund** (rō·tund') *adj.:* round; plump.

**coveted** (kuv'it·id) *v.:* longed for; wanted badly.

**deplored** (dē·plôrd') *v.:* condemned as wrong; disapproved of.

**reiteration** (rē·it'ə·rā'shən) *n.:* repetition.

**placid** (plas'id) *adj.:* peaceful; quiet.

*Pushpak Viman (Chariot of Lord Rama)* by Vinod Dave. Mixed media on canvas.

# When Mr. Pirzada Came to Dine

**Jhumpa Lahiri**

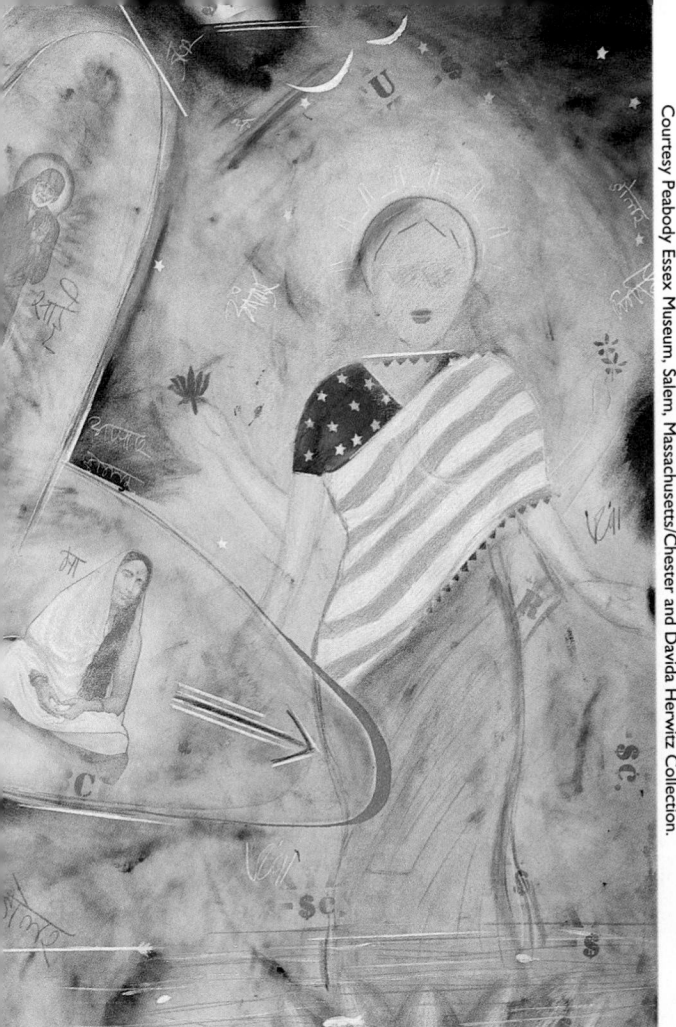

versity, a wife of twenty years, and seven daughters between the ages of six and sixteen whose names all began with the letter *A*. "Their mother's idea," he explained one day, producing from his wallet a black-and-white picture of seven girls at a picnic, their braids tied with ribbons, sitting cross-legged in a row, eating chicken curry off of banana leaves. "How am I to distinguish? Ayesha, Amira, Amina, Aziza, you see the difficulty."

Each week Mr. Pirzada wrote letters to his wife, and sent comic books to each of his seven daughters, but the postal system, along with most everything else in Dacca, had collapsed, and he had not heard word of them in over six months. Mr. Pirzada, meanwhile, was in America for the year, for he had been awarded a grant from the government of Pakistan to study the foliage[2] of New England. In spring and summer he had gathered data in Vermont and Maine, and in autumn he moved to a university north of Boston, where we lived, to write a short book about his discoveries. The grant was a great honor, but when converted into dollars it was not generous. As a result, Mr. Pirzada

Dacca, East Pakistan (1962).

lived in a room in a graduate dormitory, and did not own a proper stove or a television set of his own. And so he came to our house to eat dinner and watch the evening news.

At first I knew nothing of the reason for his visits. I was ten years old, and was not surprised that my parents, who were from India, and had a number of Indian acquaintances at the university, should ask Mr. Pirzada to share our

In the autumn of 1971 a man used to come to our house, bearing confections[1] in his pocket and hopes of ascertaining the life or death of his family. His name was Mr. Pirzada, and he came from Dacca, now the capital of Bangladesh, but then a part of Pakistan. That year Pakistan was engaged in civil war. The eastern frontier, where Dacca was located, was fighting for autonomy from the ruling regime in the west. In March, Dacca had been invaded, torched, and shelled by the Pakistani army. Teachers were dragged onto streets and shot, women dragged into barracks and raped. By the end of the summer, three hundred thousand people were said to have died. In Dacca Mr. Pirzada had a three-story home, a lectureship in botany at the uni-

---

1. **confections** *n. pl.:* candies and other sweet things.

---

2. **foliage** *n.:* leaves, as on a plant or tree.

---

**Vocabulary**

**ascertaining** (as′ər·tān′iŋ) *v.:* finding out with certainty.
**autonomy** (ô·tän′ə·mē) *n.:* independence; self-government.

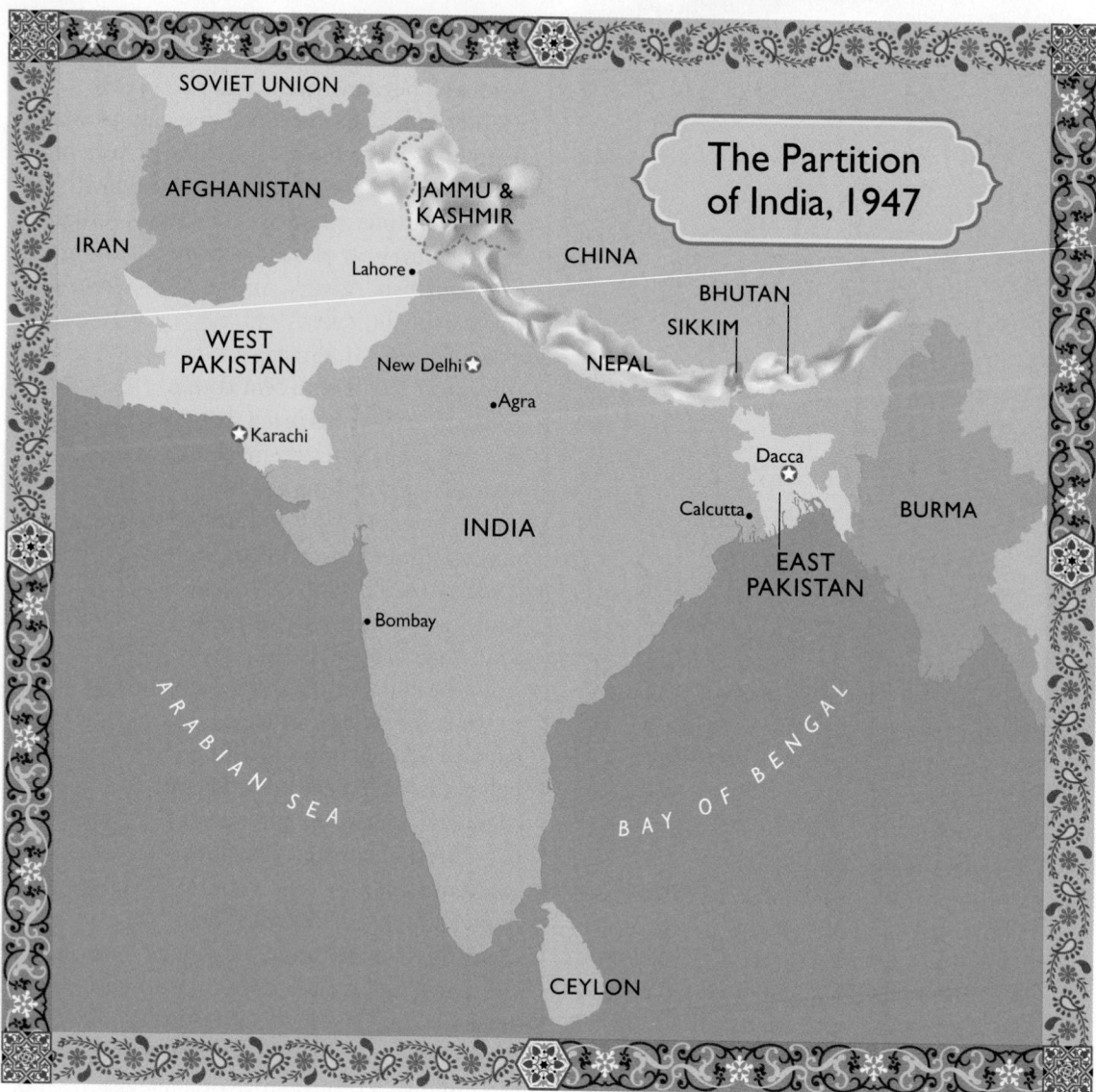

The Partition
of India, 1947

SOVIET UNION

AFGHANISTAN

IRAN

JAMMU &
KASHMIR

CHINA

Lahore

BHUTAN

SIKKIM

WEST
PAKISTAN

New Delhi

NEPAL

Agra

Karachi

Dacca

Calcutta

BURMA

INDIA

EAST
PAKISTAN

Bombay

ARABIAN SEA

BAY OF BENGAL

CEYLON

meals. It was a small campus, with narrow brick walkways and white pillared buildings, located on the fringes of what seemed to be an even smaller town. The supermarket did not carry mustard oil, doctors did not make house calls, neighbors never dropped by without an invitation, and of these things, every so often, my parents complained. In search of compatriots,[3] they used to trail their fingers, at the start of each new semester, through the columns of the university directory, circling surnames familiar to their part

of the world. It was in this manner that they discovered Mr. Pirzada, and phoned him, and invited him to our home.

I have no memory of his first visit, or of his second or his third, but by the end of September I had grown so accustomed to Mr. Pirzada's presence in our living room that one evening, as I was dropping ice cubes into the water pitcher, I asked my mother to hand me a fourth glass from a cupboard still out of my reach. She was busy at the stove, presiding over a skillet of fried spinach with radishes, and could not hear me because of the drone of the exhaust fan and

---

3. **compatriots** *n. pl.:* people from the same country.

the fierce scrapes of her spatula. I turned to my father, who was leaning against the refrigerator, eating spiced cashews from a cupped fist.

"What is it, Lilia?"

"A glass for the Indian man."

"Mr. Pirzada won't be coming today. More importantly, Mr. Pirzada is no longer considered Indian," my father announced, brushing salt from the cashews out of his trim black beard. "Not since Partition.[4] Our country was divided. 1947."

When I said I thought that was the date of India's independence from Britain, my father said, "That too. One moment we were free and then we were sliced up," he explained, drawing an *X* with his finger on the countertop, "like a pie. Hindus here, Muslims there. Dacca no longer belongs to us." He told me that during Partition Hindus and Muslims had set fire to each other's homes. For many, the idea of eating in the other's company was still unthinkable.

It made no sense to me. Mr. Pirzada and my parents spoke the same language, laughed at the same jokes, looked more or less the same. They ate pickled mangoes with their meals, ate rice every night for supper with their hands. Like my parents, Mr. Pirzada took off his shoes before entering a room, chewed fennel seeds after meals as a digestive, drank no alcohol, for dessert dipped austere biscuits into successive cups of tea. Nevertheless my father insisted that I understand the difference, and he led me to a map of the world taped to the wall over his desk. He seemed concerned that Mr. Pirzada might take offense if I accidentally referred to him as an Indian, though I could not really imagine Mr. Pirzada being offended by much of anything. "Mr. Pirzada is Bengali, but he is a Muslim," my father informed me. "Therefore he lives in East Pakistan, not India." His finger trailed across the Atlantic, through Europe, the Mediterranean, the Middle East, and finally to the sprawling orange diamond that my mother once told me resembled a woman wearing a sari with her left arm extended. Various cities had been circled with lines drawn between them to indicate my parents' travels, and the place of their birth, Calcutta, was signified by a small silver star. I had been there only once and had no memory of the trip. "As you see, Lilia, it is a different country, a different color," my father said. Pakistan was yellow, not orange. I noticed that there were two distinct parts to it, one much larger than the other, separated by an expanse of Indian territory; it was as if California and Connecticut constituted a nation apart from the U.S.

My father rapped his knuckles on top of my head. "You are, of course, aware of the current situation? Aware of East Pakistan's fight for sovereignty?"[5]

I nodded, unaware of the situation.

We returned to the kitchen, where my mother was draining a pot of boiled rice into a colander. My father opened up the can on the counter and eyed me sharply over the frames of his glasses as he ate some more cashews. "What exactly do they teach you at school? Do you study history? geography?"

"Lilia has plenty to learn at school," my mother said. "We live here now, she was born here." She seemed genuinely proud of the fact, as if it were a reflection of my character. In her estimation, I knew, I was assured a safe life, an easy life, a fine education, every opportunity. I would never have to eat rationed food, or obey curfews, or watch riots from my rooftop, or hide neighbors in water tanks to prevent them from being shot, as she and my father had. "Imagine having to place her in a decent school. Imagine her having to read during power failures by the light of kerosene lamps. Imagine the pressures,

---

4. **Partition:** division of the British-ruled Indian subcontinent in 1947, creating the independent dominions of India and Pakistan. Pakistan was further divided into two parts—West Pakistan and East Pakistan.

5. **sovereignty** (säv′rən·tē) *n.*: independent political authority.

**Vocabulary**

**austere** (ô·stir′) *adj.*: very plain.

Refugees from the Indian-Pakistani civil war.

the tutors, the constant exams." She ran a hand through her hair, bobbed to a suitable length for her part-time job as a bank teller. "How can you possibly expect her to know about Partition? Put those nuts away."

"But what does she learn about the world?" My father rattled the cashew can in his hand. "What is she learning?"

We learned American history, of course, and American geography. That year, and every year, it seemed, we began by studying the Revolutionary War. We were taken in school buses on field trips to visit Plymouth Rock, and to walk the Freedom Trail, and to climb to the top of the Bunker Hill Monument. We made dioramas out of colored construction paper depicting George Washington crossing the choppy waters of the Delaware River, and we made puppets of King George wearing white tights and a black bow in his hair. During tests we were given blank maps of the thirteen colonies, and asked to fill in names, dates, capitals. I could do it with my eyes closed.

The next evening Mr. Pirzada arrived, as usual, at six o'clock. Though they were no longer strangers, upon first greeting each other, he and my father maintained the habit of shaking hands.

"Come in, sir. Lilia, Mr. Pirzada's coat, please."

He stepped into the foyer, <u>impeccably</u> suited and scarved, with a silk tie knotted at his collar. Each evening he appeared in ensembles[6] of plums, olives, and chocolate browns. He was a compact man, and though his feet were perpetually splayed,[7] and his belly slightly wide, he nevertheless maintained an efficient posture, as if balancing in either hand two suitcases of equal weight. His ears were insulated by tufts of

graying hair that seemed to block out the unpleasant traffic of life. He had thickly lashed eyes shaded with a trace of camphor,[8] a generous moustache that turned up playfully at the ends, and a mole shaped like a flattened raisin in the very center of his left cheek. On his head he wore a black fez made from the wool of Persian lambs, secured by bobby pins, without which I was never to see him. Though my father always offered to fetch him in our car, Mr. Pirzada preferred to walk from his dormitory to our neighborhood, a distance of about twenty minutes on foot, studying trees and shrubs on his way, and when he entered our house, his knuckles were pink with the effects of crisp autumn air.

"Another refugee, I am afraid, on Indian territory."

"They are estimating nine million at the last count," my father said.

Mr. Pirzada handed me his coat, for it was my job to hang it on the rack at the bottom of the stairs. It was made of finely checkered gray-and-blue wool, with a striped lining and horn buttons, and carried in its weave the faint smell of limes. There were no recognizable tags inside, only a hand-stitched label with the phrase "Z. Sayeed, Suitors" embroidered on it in cursive with glossy black thread. On certain days a birch or maple leaf was tucked into a pocket. He unlaced his shoes and lined them against the baseboard; a golden paste clung to the toes and heels, the result of walking through our damp, unraked lawn. Relieved of his trappings, he grazed my throat with his short, restless fingers, the way a person feels for solidity behind a wall before driving in a nail. Then he followed my father to the living room, where the television was tuned to the local news. As soon as they were seated, my mother appeared from

---

6. **ensembles** *n. pl.:* outfits; costumes.
7. **splayed** *v.* used as *adj.:* spread out; turned outward.

8. **camphor** *n.:* fragrant substance made from the camphor tree. Camphor is often used for medicinal purposes.

---

**Vocabulary**

**impeccably** (im·pek′ə·blē) *adv.:* perfectly; without error or defect.

the kitchen with a plate of mincemeat kebabs with coriander chutney. Mr. Pirzada popped one into his mouth.

"One can only hope," he said, reaching for another, "that Dacca's refugees are as heartily fed. Which reminds me." He reached into his suit pocket and gave me a small plastic egg filled with cinnamon hearts. "For the lady of the house," he said with an almost <u>imperceptible</u> splay-footed bow.

"Really, Mr. Pirzada," my mother protested. "Night after night. You spoil her."

"I only spoil children who are incapable of spoiling."

It was an awkward moment for me, one which I awaited in part with dread, in part with delight. I was charmed by the presence of Mr. Pirzada's <u>rotund</u> elegance, and flattered by the faint theatricality of his attentions, yet unsettled by the superb ease of his gestures, which made me feel, for an instant, like a stranger in my own home. It had become our ritual, and for several weeks, before we grew more comfortable with one another, it was the only time he spoke to me directly. I had no response, offered no comment, betrayed no visible reaction to the steady stream of honey-filled lozenges, the raspberry truffles, the slender rolls of sour pastilles. I could not even thank him, for once, when I did, for an especially spectacular peppermint lollipop wrapped in a spray of purple cellophane, he had demanded, "What is this thank-you? The lady at the bank thanks me, the cashier at the shop thanks me, the librarian thanks me when I return an overdue book, the overseas operator thanks me as she tries to connect me to Dacca and fails. If I am buried in this country, I will be thanked, no doubt, at my funeral."

It was inappropriate, in my opinion, to consume the candy Mr. Pirzada gave me in a casual manner. I <u>coveted</u> each evening's treasure as I would a jewel, or a coin from a buried kingdom, and I would place it in a small keepsake box made of carved sandalwood beside my bed, in which, long ago in India, my father's mother used to store the ground areca nuts she ate after her morning bath. It was my only memento of a grandmother I had never known, and until Mr. Pirzada came to our lives, I could find nothing to put inside it. Every so often before brushing my teeth and laying out my clothes for school the next day, I opened the lid of the box and ate one of his treats.

That night, like every night, we did not eat at the dining table, because it did not provide an unobstructed view of the television set. Instead we huddled around the coffee table, without conversing, our plates perched on the edges of our knees. From the kitchen my mother brought forth the succession of dishes: lentils with fried onions, green beans with coconut, fish cooked with raisins in a yogurt sauce. I followed with the water glasses, and the plate of lemon wedges, and the chili peppers, purchased on monthly trips to Chinatown and stored by the pound in the freezer, which they liked to snap open and crush into their food.

Before eating, Mr. Pirzada always did a curious thing. He took out a plain silver watch without a band, which he kept in his breast pocket, held it briefly to one of his tufted ears, and wound it with three swift flicks of his thumb and forefinger. Unlike the watch on his wrist, the pocket watch, he had explained to me, was set to the local time in Dacca, eleven hours ahead. For the duration of the meal the watch rested on his folded paper napkin on the coffee table. He never seemed to consult it.

Now that I had learned Mr. Pirzada was not an Indian, I began to study him with extra care, to try to figure out what

East Pakistanis fleeing to India (1971).

---

**Vocabulary**

**imperceptible** (im′pər·sep′tə·bəl) *adj.:* unnoticeable; so slight as not to be noticed.

**rotund** (rō·tund′) *adj.:* round; plump.

**coveted** (kuv′it·id) *v.:* longed for; wanted badly.

made him different. I decided that the pocket watch was one of those things. When I saw it that night, as he wound it and arranged it on the coffee table, an uneasiness possessed me; life, I realized, was being lived in Dacca first. I imagined Mr. Pirzada's daughters rising from sleep, tying ribbons in their hair, anticipating breakfast, preparing for school. Our meals, our actions, were only a shadow of what had already happened there, a lagging ghost of where Mr. Pirzada really belonged.

At six-thirty, which was when the national news began, my father raised the volume and adjusted the antennae. Usually I occupied myself with a book, but that night my father insisted that I pay attention. On the screen I saw tanks rolling through dusty streets, and fallen buildings, and forests of unfamiliar trees into which East Pakistani refugees had fled, seeking safety over the Indian border. I saw boats with fan-shaped sails floating on wide coffee-colored rivers, a barricaded university, newspaper offices burned to the ground. I turned to look at Mr. Pirzada; the images flashed in miniature across his eyes. As he watched, he had an immovable expression on his face, composed but alert, as if someone were giving him directions to an unknown destination.

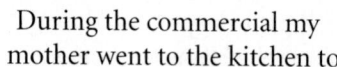

East Pakistani soldiers (1970).

During the commercial my mother went to the kitchen to get more rice, and my father and Mr. Pirzada deplored the policies of a general named Yahyah Khan.[9] They discussed intrigues I did not know, a catastrophe I could not comprehend. "See, children your age, what they do to survive," my father said as he served me another piece of fish. But I could no longer eat. I could only steal glances at Mr. Pirzada, sitting beside me in his olive-green jacket, calmly creating a well in his rice to make room for a second helping of lentils. He was not my notion of a man burdened by such grave concerns. I wondered if the reason he was always so smartly dressed was in preparation to endure with dignity whatever news assailed him, perhaps even to attend a funeral at a moment's notice. I wondered, too, what would happen if suddenly his seven daughters were to appear on television, smiling and waving and blowing kisses to Mr. Pirzada from a balcony. I imagined how relieved he would be. But this never happened.

That night when I placed the plastic egg filled with cinnamon hearts in the box beside my bed, I did not feel the ceremonious satisfaction I normally did. I tried not to think about Mr. Pirzada, in his lime-scented overcoat, connected to the unruly, sweltering world we had viewed a few hours ago in our bright, carpeted living room. And yet for several moments that was all I could think about. My stomach tightened as I worried whether his wife and seven daughters were now members of the drifting, clamoring[10] crowd that had flashed at intervals on the screen. In an effort to banish the image, I looked around my room, at the yellow canopied bed with matching flounced curtains, at framed class pictures mounted on white-and-violet papered walls, at the penciled inscriptions by the closet door where my father recorded my height on each of my birthdays. But the more I tried to distract myself, the more I began to convince myself that Mr. Pirzada's family was in all likelihood dead. Eventually I took a square of white chocolate out of the box, and unwrapped it, and then I did something I had never done before. I put the chocolate in my mouth, letting it soften until the last possible moment, and then as I chewed it slowly, I prayed that Mr. Pirzada's family was safe and sound. I had never prayed for anything before, had never been taught or

10. **clamoring** v. used as *adj.*: noisy; demanding.

**Vocabulary**

**deplored** (dē·plôrd′) v.: condemned as wrong; disapproved of.

9. **Yahyah Khan** (1917–1980): president of Pakistan from 1969 to 1971. Khan used brutal force to try to upset East Pakistan's bid for independence.

told to, but I decided, given the circumstances, that it was something I should do. That night when I went to the bathroom, I only pretended to brush my teeth, for I feared that I would somehow rinse the prayer out as well. I wet the brush and rearranged the tube of paste to prevent my parents from asking any questions, and fell asleep with sugar on my tongue.

No one at school talked about the war followed so faithfully in my living room. We continued to study the American Revolution, and learned about the injustices of taxation without representation, and memorized passages from the Declaration of Independence. During recess the boys would divide in two groups, chasing each other wildly around the swings and seesaws, Redcoats against the colonies. In the classroom our teacher, Mrs. Kenyon, pointed frequently to a map that emerged like a movie screen from the top of the chalkboard, charting the route of the *Mayflower,* or showing us the location of the Liberty Bell. Each week two members of the class gave a report on a particular aspect of the Revolution, and so one day I was sent to the school library with my friend Dora to learn about the surrender at Yorktown. Mrs. Kenyon handed us a slip of paper with the names of three books to look up in the card catalog. We found them right away, and sat down at a low round table to read and take notes. But I could not concentrate. I returned to the blond-wood shelves, to a section I had noticed labeled "Asia." I saw books about China, India, Indonesia, Korea. Eventually I found a book titled *Pakistan: A Land and Its People.* I sat on a footstool and opened the book. The laminated[11] jacket crackled in my grip. I began turning the pages, filled with photos of rivers and rice fields and men in military uniforms. There was a chapter about Dacca, and I began to read about its rainfall, and its jute production. I was studying a population chart when Dora appeared in the aisle.

"What are you doing back here? Mrs. Kenyon's in the library. She came to check up on us."

I slammed the book shut, too loudly. Mrs. Kenyon emerged, the aroma of her perfume filling up the tiny aisle, and lifted the book by the tip of its spine as if it were a hair clinging to my sweater. She glanced at the cover, then at me.

East Pakistani soldiers (1970).

"Is this book a part of your report, Lilia?"

"No, Mrs. Kenyon."

"Then I see no reason to consult it," she said, replacing it in the slim gap on the shelf. "Do you?"

As weeks passed, it grew more and more rare to see any footage from Dacca on the news. The report came after the first set of commercials, sometimes the second. The press had been censored, removed, restricted, rerouted. Some days, many days, only a death toll was announced, prefaced by a reiteration of the general situation. More poets were executed, more villages set ablaze. In spite of it all, night after night, my parents and Mr. Pirzada enjoyed long, leisurely meals. After the television was shut off, and the dishes washed and dried, they joked, and told stories, and dipped biscuits in their tea. When they tired of discussing political matters, they discussed, instead, the progress of Mr. Pirzada's book about the deciduous trees of New England, and my father's nomination for tenure, and the peculiar eating habits of my mother's American coworkers at the bank. Eventually I was sent upstairs to do my homework, but through the carpet I heard them as they drank more tea, and listened to cassettes of Kishore Kumar,[12] and played Scrabble on the coffee table, laughing

---

11. **laminated** *adj.:* covered with a thin sheet of plastic.

12. **Kishore Kumar:** popular Indian singer.

**Vocabulary**
**reiteration** (rē·it′ə·rā′shən) *n.:* repetition.

and arguing long into the night about the spellings of English words. I wanted to join them, wanted, above all, to console Mr. Pirzada somehow. But apart from eating a piece of candy for the sake of his family and praying for their safety, there was nothing I could do. They played Scrabble until the eleven o'clock news, and then, sometime around midnight, Mr. Pirzada walked back to his dormitory. For this reason I never saw him leave, but each night as I drifted off to sleep, I would hear them, anticipating the birth of a nation on the other side of the world.

One day in October Mr. Pirzada asked upon arrival, "What are these large orange vegetables on people's doorsteps? A type of squash?"

"Pumpkins," my mother replied. "Lilia, remind me to pick one up at the supermarket."

"And the purpose? It indicates what?"

"You make a jack-o'-lantern," I said, grinning ferociously. "Like this. To scare people away."

"I see," Mr. Pirzada said, grinning back. "Very useful."

The next day my mother bought a ten-pound pumpkin, fat and round, and placed it on the dining table. Before supper, while my father and Mr. Pirzada were watching the local news, she told me to decorate it with markers, but I wanted to carve it properly like others I had noticed in the neighborhood.

"Yes, let's carve it," Mr. Pirzada agreed, and rose from the sofa. "Hang the news tonight." Asking no questions, he walked into the kitchen, opened a drawer, and returned, bearing a long serrated knife. He glanced at me for approval. "Shall I?"

I nodded. For the first time we all gathered around the dining table, my mother, my father, Mr. Pirzada, and I. While the television aired unattended, we covered the tabletop with newspa-

pers. Mr. Pirzada draped his jacket over the chair behind him, removed a pair of opal cuff links, and rolled up the starched sleeves of his shirt.

"First go around the top, like this," I instructed, demonstrating with my index finger.

He made an initial incision and drew the knife around. When he had come full circle, he lifted the cap by the stem; it loosened effortlessly, and Mr. Pirzada leaned over the pumpkin for a moment to inspect and inhale its contents. My mother gave him a long metal spoon with which he gutted the interior until the last bits of string and seeds were gone. My father, meanwhile, separated the seeds from the pulp and set them out to dry on a cookie sheet, so that we could roast them later on. I drew two triangles against the ridged surface for the eyes, which Mr. Pirzada dutifully carved, and crescents for eyebrows, and another triangle for the nose. The mouth was all that remained, and the teeth posed a challenge. I hesitated.

"Smile or frown?" I asked.

"You choose," Mr. Pirzada said.

As a compromise I drew a kind of grimace, straight across, neither mournful nor friendly. Mr. Pirzada began carving, without the least bit of intimidation,[13] as if he had been carving jack-o'-lanterns his whole life. He had nearly finished when the national news began. The reporter mentioned Dacca, and we all turned to listen: An Indian official announced that unless the world helped to relieve the burden of East Pakistani refugees, India would have to go to war against Pakistan. The reporter's face dripped with sweat as he relayed the information. He did not wear a tie or a jacket, dressed instead as if he himself were about to take part in the battle. He shielded his scorched face as he hollered things to the cameraman. The knife slipped from Mr. Pirzada's hand and made a gash dipping toward the base of the pumpkin.

"Please forgive me." He raised a hand to one side of his face, as if someone had slapped him there. "I am—it is terrible. I will buy another. We will try again."

---

13. **intimidation** *n.:* fear; timidity.

"Not at all, not at all," my father said. He took the knife from Mr. Pirzada, and carved around the gash, evening it out, dispensing altogether with the teeth I had drawn. What resulted was a disproportionately large hole the size of a lemon, so that our jack-o'-lantern wore an expression of placid astonishment, the eyebrows no longer fierce, floating in frozen surprise above a vacant, geometric gaze.

For Halloween I was a witch. Dora, my trick-or-treating partner, was a witch too. We wore black capes fashioned from dyed pillowcases and conical hats with wide cardboard brims. We shaded our faces green with a broken eye shadow that belonged to Dora's mother, and my mother gave us two burlap sacks that had once contained basmati rice, for collecting candy. That year our parents decided that we were old enough to roam the neighborhood unattended. Our plan was to walk from my house to Dora's, from where I was to call to say I had arrived safely, and then Dora's mother would drive me home. My father equipped us with flashlights, and I had to wear my watch and synchronize it with his. We were to return no later than nine o'clock.

When Mr. Pirzada arrived that evening, he presented me with a box of chocolate-covered mints.

"In here," I told him, and opened up the burlap sack. "Trick or treat!"

"I understand that you don't really need my contribution this evening," he said, depositing the box. He gazed at my green face, and the hat secured by a string under my chin. Gingerly he lifted the hem of the cape, under which I was wearing a sweater and a zipped fleece jacket. "Will you be warm enough?"

I nodded, causing the hat to tip to one side.

He set it right. "Perhaps it is best to stand still."

The bottom of our staircase was lined with baskets of miniature candy, and when Mr. Pirzada removed his shoes, he did not place them there as he normally did, but inside the closet instead. He began to unbutton his coat, and I waited to take it from him, but Dora

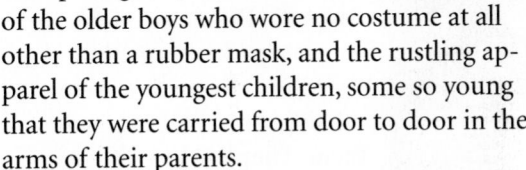

called me from the bathroom to say that she needed my help drawing a mole on her chin. When we were finally ready, my mother took a picture of us in front of the fireplace, and then I opened the front door to leave. Mr. Pirzada and my father, who had not gone into the living room yet, hovered in the foyer. Outside it was already dark. The air smelled of wet leaves, and our carved jack-o'-lantern flickered impressively against the shrubbery by the door. In the distance came the sounds of scampering feet, and the howls of the older boys who wore no costume at all other than a rubber mask, and the rustling apparel of the youngest children, some so young that they were carried from door to door in the arms of their parents.

"Don't go into any of the houses you don't know," my father warned.

Mr. Pirzada knit his brows together. "Is there any danger?"

"No, no," my mother assured him. "All the children will be out. It's a tradition."

"Perhaps I should accompany them?" Mr. Pirzada suggested. He looked suddenly tired and small, standing there in his splayed, stockinged feet, and his eyes contained a panic I had never seen before. In spite of the cold I began to sweat inside my pillowcase.

"Really, Mr. Pirzada," my mother said, "Lilia will be perfectly safe with her friend."

"But if it rains? If they lose their way?"

"Don't worry," I said. It was the first time I had uttered those words to Mr. Pirzada, two simple words I had tried but failed to tell him for weeks, had said only in my prayers. It shamed me now that I had said them for my own sake.

---

**Vocabulary**

**placid** (plas'id) *adj.*: peaceful; quiet.

He placed one of his stocky fingers on my cheek, then pressed it to the back of his own hand, leaving a faint green smear. "If the lady insists," he conceded, and offered a small bow.

We left, stumbling slightly in our black pointy thrift-store shoes, and when we turned at the end of the driveway to wave good-bye, Mr. Pirzada was standing in the frame of the doorway, a short figure between my parents, waving back.

"Why did that man want to come with us?" Dora asked.

"His daughters are missing." As soon as I said it, I wished I had not. I felt that my saying it made it true, that Mr. Pirzada's daughters really were missing, and that he would never see them again.

"You mean they were kidnapped?" Dora continued. "From a park or something?"

"I didn't mean they were missing. I meant, he misses them. They live in a different country, and he hasn't seen them in a while, that's all."

We went from house to house, walking along pathways and pressing doorbells. Some people had switched off all their lights for effect, or strung rubber bats in their windows. At the McIntyres' a coffin was placed in front of the door, and Mr. McIntyre rose from it in silence, his face covered with chalk, and deposited a fistful of candy corns into our sacks. Several people told me that they had never seen an Indian witch before. Others performed the transaction without comment. As we paved our way with the parallel beams of our flashlights, we saw eggs cracked in the middle of the road, and cars covered with shaving cream, and toilet paper garlanding the branches of trees. By the time we reached Dora's house, our hands were chapped from carrying our bulging burlap bags, and our feet were sore and swollen. Her mother gave us bandages for our blisters and served us warm cider and

Crowd cheering the independence of Bangladesh (1972).

caramel popcorn. She reminded me to call my parents to tell them I had arrived safely, and when I did, I could hear the television in the background. My mother did not seem particularly relieved to hear from me. When I replaced the phone on the receiver, it occurred to me that the television wasn't on at Dora's house at all. Her father was lying on the couch, reading a magazine, with a glass of wine on the coffee table, and there was saxophone music playing on the stereo.

After Dora and I had sorted through our plunder,[14] and counted and sampled and traded until we were satisfied, her mother drove me back to my house. I thanked her for the ride, and she waited in the driveway until I made it to the door. In the glare of her headlights I saw that our pumpkin had been shattered, its thick shell strewn in chunks across the grass. I felt the sting of tears in my eyes, and a sudden pain in my throat, as if it had been stuffed with the sharp tiny pebbles that crunched with each step under my aching feet. I opened the door, expecting the three of them to be standing in the foyer, waiting to receive me, and to grieve for our ruined pumpkin, but there was no one. In the living room Mr. Pirzada, my father, and mother were sitting side by side on the sofa. The television was turned off, and Mr. Pirzada had his head in his hands.

What they heard that evening, and for many evenings after that, was that India and Pakistan were drawing closer and closer to war. Troops from both sides lined the border, and Dacca was insisting on nothing short of independence. The war was to be waged on East Pakistani soil. The United States was siding with West Pakistan, the Soviet Union with India and what was soon to be Bangladesh. War was declared officially on December 4, and twelve days later, the Pakistani army, weakened by having to fight three thousand miles from their source of supplies, surrendered in Dacca. All of these facts I know only now, for they are available to me in any history book, in any library. But then it remained, for

---

14. **plunder** *n.:* loot.

the most part, a remote mystery with haphazard clues. What I remember during those twelve days of the war was that my father no longer asked me to watch the news with them, and that Mr. Pirzada stopped bringing me candy, and that my mother refused to serve anything other than boiled eggs with rice for dinner. I remember some nights helping my mother spread a sheet and blankets on the couch so that Mr. Pirzada could sleep there, and high-pitched voices hollering in the middle of the night when my parents called our relatives in Calcutta to learn more details about the situation. Most of all I remember the three of them operating during that time as if they were a single person, sharing a single meal, a single body, a single silence, and a single fear.

In January, Mr. Pirzada flew back to his three-story home in Dacca, to discover what was left of it. We did not see much of him in those final weeks of the year; he was busy finishing his manuscript, and we went to Philadelphia to spend Christmas with friends of my parents. Just as I have no memory of his first visit, I have no memory of his last. My father drove him to the airport one afternoon while I was at school. For a long time we did not hear from him. Our evenings went on as usual, with dinners in front of the news. The only difference was that Mr. Pirzada and his extra watch were not there to accompany us. According to reports Dacca was repairing itself slowly, with a newly formed parliamentary government. The new leader, Sheikh Mujib Rahman,[15] recently re-

Dacca residents celebrating the homecoming of Sheikh Mujib Rahman (1972).

leased from prison, asked countries for building materials to replace more than one million houses that had been destroyed in the war. Countless refugees returned from India, greeted, we learned, by unemployment and the threat of famine. Every now and then I studied the map above my father's desk and pictured Mr. Pirzada on that small patch of yellow, perspiring heavily, I imagined, in one of his suits, searching for his family. Of course, the map was outdated by then.

Finally, several months later, we received a card from Mr. Pirzada commemorating the Muslim New Year, along with a short letter. He was reunited, he wrote, with his wife and children. All were well, having survived the events of the past year at an estate belonging to his wife's grandparents in the mountains of Shillong. His seven daughters were a bit taller, he wrote, but otherwise they were the same, and he still could not keep their names in order. At the end of the letter he thanked us for our hospitality, adding that although he now understood the meaning of the words "thank you," they still were not adequate to express his gratitude. To celebrate the good news, my mother prepared a special dinner that evening, and when we sat down to eat at the coffee table, we toasted our water glasses, but I did not feel like celebrating. Though I had not seen him for months, it was only then that I felt Mr. Pirzada's absence. It was only then, raising my water glass in his name, that I knew what it meant to miss someone who was so many miles and hours away, just as he had missed his wife and daughters for so many months. He had no reason to return to us, and my parents predicted, correctly, that we would never see him again. Since January, each night before bed, I had continued to eat, for the sake of Mr. Pirzada's family, a piece of candy I had saved from Halloween. That night there was no need to. Eventually, I threw them away. ■

---

15. **Sheikh Mujib Rahman** (1920–1975): Bengali leader who demanded independence for East Pakistan. He became the first prime minister of Bangladesh in 1972 and its president in 1975.

# The Ravaged People of East Pakistan

## Alvin S. Toffler

East Pakistani refugees taking shelter near Calcutta, India (1971).

**A**planetary catastrophe is taking place in Asia, a human disaster so massive that it could bathe the future in blood, not just for Asians, but for those of us in the West as well. Yet the response of the global community has been minimal at best. In the United States, the official response has been worse than minimal and morally numb.

I have just returned from Calcutta and the border of East Pakistan, where I conducted interviews with refugees avalanching into India as a result of the West Pakistanis' genocidal attack on them. Since March 25, West Pakistani troops have bombed, burned, looted, and murdered the citizens of East Pakistan in what can only be a calculated campaign to decimate them or to drive them out of their villages and over the border into India.

Part of the time I traveled with a Canadian parliamentary delegation. We saw babies' skin stretched tight, bones protruding, weeping women who told us they would rather die today in India than return to East Pakistan after the tragedies they had witnessed, the total wretchedness of refugee camps, and the unbelievable magnitude of this forced human migration—6.7 million refugees pouring into India within a matter of four months.

I saw Indian villages deluged by masses of destitute refugees, every available inch crammed with bodies seeking shelter from the blistering sun and the torrential rain. I saw refugees still streaming along the roads unable to find even a resting place. I saw miserable Indian villagers sharing their meager food with the latest frightened and hungry arrivals. I saw thousands of men, women, and babies lined up, waiting patiently under the sun for hours to get their rations. These pitiful few ounces of rice, wheat, and dhal provide a level of nutrition so low that it will inevitably create protein breakdown, liver illness, and a variety of other diseases in addition to the cholera, pneumonia, and bronchitis that are already rampant. I saw Indian relief officials struggling heroically, and with immense personal sympathy, to cope with the human tidal wave—and to do so on a budget of one rupee a day—about 13 cents per human.

It is now clear that famine will further devastate East Pakistan this fall, and that millions more will seek refuge in an India already staggering under the burden.

—from *The New York Times*
August 5, 1971

# Response and Analysis

## Reading Check

1. To review the basic elements of the plot of the story, fill out a chart like the following one:

| |
|---|
| Narrator: |
| Other characters: |
| Settings (times, places): |
| Conflicts:<br>   Exterior (between people):<br>   Interior (inside a person's mind): |
| Climax: |
| Resolution: |
| Key passages: |

## Thinking Critically

2. What does Mr. Pirzada mean when he says on page 1034, "Another refugee, I am afraid, on Indian territory"?

3. What important realization does Lilia come to after seeing Mr. Pirzada wind his pocket watch one night?

4. One night after watching the news report from East Pakistan for the first time, Lilia does something she has never done before. What does she do, and why does she do it?

5. Why is Mr. Pirzada nervous when the girls are about to go out on Halloween? What does his concern for the girls reveal about his state of mind?

6. This is a story that focuses on a clash of cultures, but it involves several conflicts, and some are subtle.

   • What **conflict** exists in Lilia's father's mind between his native culture (India) and the culture of his daughter's native country (America)?

   • What internal **conflict** does Mr. Pirzada face when he remains in America while the news from India and Pakistan worsens?

   • What wider, tragic **conflict** forms a backdrop to the entire story?

7. The narrator learns about another war for independence in her fourth-grade class. What contrast do you feel between what the children learn about that war and the reality of the war raging in Pakistan?

8. The writer spends time describing the American setting of the story, including its Halloween customs. What contrast does she set up between the make-believe horror of the American holiday and the reality of the situation in India and Pakistan? How does the writer use food to establish a further contrast between America and India?

9. Point of view refers to the vantage point from which a story is told. This story is told in the first-person point of view, by a ten-year-old girl. This means we know only what Lilia knows. What else would we know if the story had been told by Mr. Pirzada?

10. Think of what Lilia discovered about lives beyond her own. What, in your own words, is the **theme** of the story?

# WRITING

## Looking into History

Write an **investigative report** about one of the historical events in Lahiri's story. You might consider writing about the colonization of India by the British, the partition of India, or the foundation of Bangladesh. Before you write, narrow your topic, making sure it is manageable. Also be sure to state your main idea clearly and directly. In doing your research, analyze several historical records of the event you have chosen, and include information or opinions from different perspectives. Evaluate your sources carefully, and don't forget to include a bibliography. (For research ideas, refer to the **Connection** on page 1043.)

▶ **Use "Reporting Historical Research," pages 602–621, for help with this assignment.**

## Comparing Selections

Communicating what we think and feel is a universal human impulse, and often it is an equally universal source of uncertainty and frustration. Write an **essay** comparing the experience of Lilia in "When Mr. Pirzada Came to Dine" with the experience of the narrator in Amy Tan's "Rules of the Game" (page 1017). Even though these stories were written by people of different cultures, you will find connections between them. Before you write, fill out a chart like the following one to gather details for your comparison:

|  | "Rules of the Game" | "When Mr. Pirzada Came to Dine" |
|---|---|---|
| Narrator |  |  |
| Conflicts |  |  |
| Discoveries |  |  |

## Vocabulary Development
### Map It!

| | |
|---|---|
| ascertaining | rotund |
| autonomy | coveted |
| austere | deplored |
| impeccably | reiteration |
| imperceptible | placid |

You can learn a great deal about a word by studying its origin. Usually the origin, or history, of a word is given in a dictionary, set off in brackets before the definition. For each of the remaining Vocabulary words, fill out a word map like the one below. You will have to use a dictionary.

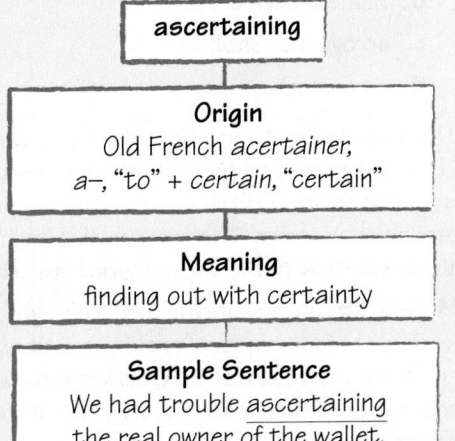

ascertaining

**Origin**
Old French *acertainer,*
*a–,* "to" + *certain,* "certain"

**Meaning**
finding out with certainty

**Sample Sentence**
We had trouble ascertaining the real owner of the wallet.

# Vocabulary Development

## Analogies

Standardized tests often include a type of comparison or logic problem called an **analogy.** An analogy begins by offering a pair of words. First you must determine how the words in the pair are related. Then you must select another pair of words whose relationship is the same as the one expressed by the first pair. The analogy that follows would be read "*Loyalty* is to *patriot* as . . . " You have to pick the pair of words that has the same relationship as *loyalty* has to *patriot.*

LOYALTY : PATRIOT ::

**a.** friendliness : foe

**b.** sadness : celebrant

**c.** arrogance : snob

**d.** tiny : small

The only answer choice that completes the analogy is *c*: "*Loyalty* is related to *patriot* in the same way that *arrogance* is related to *snob.*" Each pair of words expresses a characteristic relationship. The first word in each pair describes a characteristic of the second word in each pair.

**Making the connection.** In Collections 2 and 5, you learned these six types of analogy relationships: synonym, antonym, characteristic of, classification, cause and effect, and degree. The following chart presents four more types of relationships that may be used in analogies:

### Types of Analogy Relationships

| Type | Relationship | Example |
| --- | --- | --- |
| Object and performer | is the tool of | baton : conductor |
| Part and whole | is a part of | floor : building |
| Performer and action | does/performs | artist : painting |
| Use | is used for | pencil : writing |

**Test-taking strategies.** Keep these guidelines in mind when you take analogy tests:

1. Know and use the precise meanings of words.
2. Identify the way in which the words in the first pair are related.
3. Look for another pair of words that shows the same relationship.

**SKILLS FOCUS**

**Vocabulary Skills**
Understand and use word analogies.

**PRACTICE 1**

Using the categories in the chart, identify the type of analogy in each of the following word pairs:

**1.** hammer : carpenter

**2.** room : house

**3.** lawyer : defends

**4.** razor : shaving

**5.** refugee : flee

**6.** player : team

**7.** fork : eating

**8.** actor : play

**PRACTICE 2**

Select the answer that *best* expresses the same relationship as the one in the capitalized pair.

**1.** AUTUMN : SEASON ::

  **a.** snow : sleet

  **b.** thunder : lightning

  **c.** dog : mammal

  **d.** hunting : rifle

**2.** CRAYON : DRAW ::

  **a.** health : doctor

  **b.** midwife : nurse

  **c.** artist : studio

  **d.** shovel : dig

**3.** LEAVES : PLANT ::

  **a.** smile : frown

  **b.** finger : hand

  **c.** glove : mitten

  **d.** salt : shaker

**4.** CHEF : COOKS ::

  **a.** rabbit : hops

  **b.** frog : toad

  **c.** eat : dine

  **d.** sailor : swimmer

# Edwidge Danticat
## (1969–     )

**I**n Haiti a storyteller asks *"Krik?,"* meaning "Are you ready for a story?" The circle of listeners answers *"Krak!,"* meaning "Yes, we are ready to listen!" In this way, stories begin, take shape, and play their role in community life. In her own way, Edwidge Danticat, a Haitian American novelist and short story writer, keeps that tradition alive.

Edwidge Danticat (ed′wēj′ dän·ti·käh′) came to the United States from Haiti when she was twelve, joining her parents, who had emigrated years earlier. She remembers the shock: "It was all so very different. I didn't speak the language. I felt very lost and I withdrew into myself, became much more shy than I already was. I sought solace in books, read a lot, and kept journals written in fragmented Creole, French, and English. I think it's very difficult for every child who comes here from another culture."

Danticat went to high school in Brooklyn, New York, where she struggled with feelings of isolation and began to write stories. She earned a degree in French from Barnard College in New York City and received a master's of fine arts in writing at Brown University. Her thesis, *Breath, Eyes, Memory,* became her first novel. Published in 1994, it is the gripping story of a Haitian immigrant girl deeply bonded to the generations of women who have come before her yet facing her arrival at adulthood as an independent woman in the United States.

*Breath, Eyes, Memory* was followed by *Krik? Krak!* (1995), a collection of short stories that was nominated for the National Book Award. Poverty, dreams, love, migration, social and emotional barriers, the delights and disappointments of family life—Danticat's themes are universal, yet her stories reflect firsthand experience. The critic Jordana Hart commented that the stories in *Krik? Krak!* "are tex-tured and deeply personal, as if the twenty-six-year-old Haitian American author had spilled her own tears over each."

Danticat's second novel, *The Farming of Bones* (1998), takes a courageous step back into Haitian history. Set in 1937, this chronicle of long struggle and ironic triumph centers on the massacre of Haitian citizens by the Dominican Republic dictator Rafael Trujillo. The grim title refers to the backbreaking work done in the fields by thousands of Caribbean sugar-cane workers.

Danticat continues to develop as a weaver of vibrant tales. "When you write, it's like braiding your hair. Taking a handful of coarse unruly strands and attempting to bring them to unity. . . . Some of the braids are long, others are short. Some are thick, others are thin. Some are heavy. Others are light."

## The Book of the Dead

### Make the Connection

Have you ever made a discovery that changed your perception of someone you thought you knew? The discovery may have been good or bad, small or large, but it forced you to see the person in a new light.

### Literary Focus
#### Irony

In general, **irony** is a discrepancy between what is expected and what happens. A speaker who uses **verbal irony** says one thing but means another. In **situational irony** an event turns out differently from what we expected or from what we think is appropriate. We feel **dramatic irony** when we know something that a character does not know. Keep an eye out for all three uses of irony as you read "The Book of the Dead."

> **Irony** is a discrepancy between appearance and reality. **Verbal irony** occurs when someone says one thing but means something else. **Situational irony** takes place when what is expected is different from what happens. **Dramatic irony** occurs when the reader knows more than a character does.
>
> *For more on Irony, see the Handbook of Literary and Historical Terms.*

**SKILLS FOCUS**

**Literary Skills**
Understand irony, including verbal, situational, and dramatic irony.

go. hrw .com

**INTERNET**

**Vocabulary Practice**

Keyword: LE7 11-6

### Background

Haiti, a country in the West Indies, occupies the western portion of the island of Hispaniola, which lies between Cuba and Puerto Rico in the Caribbean Sea. Beautiful, tropical, mountainous, and very poor, Haiti has a long history of political instability. The period most relevant to "The Book of the Dead" is the time when Haiti was ruled by the op-pressive Duvalier regime, which ran Haiti during the time the narrator's father was a young man. In 1957, François Duvalier, a country doctor known as Papa Doc, was elected president of Haiti. In 1964, he declared himself president for life, or dictator. In 1971, when Duvalier died, his nineteen-year-old son, Jean-Claude, known as Baby Doc, took over, using the hated secret police (the Tonton Macoutes, or "bogeymen") to shore up his authority. Many Haitians fled the grinding poverty, police brutality, and political oppression.

Baby Doc was overthrown in 1986. A free election was held, but a series of military dictators took over. Some order finally came to the country in the mid-1990s, after the United Nations, supported by U.S. troops and a trade boycott by the Organization of American States, forced the military to accept the rule of a formerly elected president, Jean Bertrand Aristide. The last U.S. troops left Haiti in 1996. Although some positive developments have been made under Aristide, the opposition claims that the elections were fraudulent and human rights are still being violated.

### Vocabulary Development

**gaudy** (gô′dē) *adj.:* showy but lacking in good taste.

**vulnerability** (vul′nər·ə·bil′ə·tē) *n.:* capability of being hurt.

**eradicated** (ē·rad′i·kāt′id) *v.:* wiped out; destroyed.

(Background, opposite) Hieroglyphs from the Egyptian Book of the Dead.
(Inset, opposite) Prisoners in Haiti.

# The
# BOOK
# of the
# DEAD

**Edwidge Danticat**

My father is gone. I am slouched in a cast-aluminum chair across from two men, one the manager of the hotel where we're staying and the other a policeman. They are waiting for me to explain what has become of him, my father.

The manager—"Mr. Flavio Salinas," the plaque on his office door reads—has the most striking pair of chartreuse[1] eyes I have ever seen on a man with an island-Spanish lilt to his voice.

The officer is a baby-faced, short white Floridian with a pot belly.

"Where are you and your daddy from, Ms. Bienaimé?" he asks.

I answer "Haiti," even though I was born and raised in East Flatbush, Brooklyn, and have never visited my parents' birthplace. I do this because it is one more thing I have longed to have in common with my parents.

The officer plows forward. "You down here in Lakeland from Haiti?"

"We live in New York. We were on our way to Tampa."

I find Manager Salinas's office gaudy. The walls are covered with orange-and-green wallpaper, briefly interrupted by a giant gold-leaf-bordered print of a Victorian cottage that somehow resembles the building we're in. Patting his light-green tie, he whispers reassuringly, "Officer Bo and I will do the best we can to help you find your father."

We start out with a brief description: "Sixty-four, five feet eight inches, two hundred and twenty pounds, moon-faced, with thinning salt-and-pepper hair. Velvet-brown eyes—"

"Velvet-brown?" says Officer Bo.

"Deep brown—same color as his complexion."

My father has had partial frontal dentures for ten years, since he fell off his and my mother's bed when his prison nightmares began. I mention that, too. Just the dentures, not the nightmares. I also bring up the claw-shaped marks that run from his left ear down along his cheek to the corner of his mouth—the only visible reminder of the year he spent at Fort Dimanche,

the Port-au-Prince prison ironically named after the Lord's Day.

"Does your daddy have any kind of mental illness, senility?" asks Officer Bo.

"No."

"Do you have any pictures of your daddy?"

I feel like less of a daughter because I'm not carrying a photograph in my wallet. I had hoped to take some pictures of him on our trip. At one of the rest stops I bought a disposable camera and pointed it at my father. No, no, he had protested, covering his face with both hands like a little boy protecting his cheeks from a slap. He did not want any more pictures taken of him for the rest of his life. He was feeling too ugly.

"That's too bad," says Officer Bo. "Does he speak English, your daddy? He can ask for directions, et cetera?"

"Yes."

"Is there anything that might make your father run away from you—particularly here in Lakeland?" Manager Salinas interjects. "Did you two have a fight?"

I had never tried to tell my father's story in words before now, but my first sculpture of him was the reason for our trip: a two-foot-high mahogany figure of my father, naked, crouching on the floor, his back arched like the curve of a crescent moon, his downcast eyes fixed on his short stubby fingers and the wide palms of his hands. It was hardly revolutionary, minimalist at best, but it was my favorite of all my attempted representations of him. It was the way I had imagined him in prison.

The last time I had seen my father? The previous night, before falling asleep. When we pulled into the pebbled driveway, densely lined with palm and banana trees, it was almost midnight. All the restaurants in the area were closed. There was nothing to do but shower and go to bed.

---

1. **chartreuse** (shär·trōoz′) *adj.:* pale yellowish green.

**Vocabulary**

**gaudy** (gô′dē) *adj.:* showy but lacking in good taste.

"It is like a paradise here," my father said when he saw the room. It had the same orange-and-green wallpaper as Salinas's office, and the plush green carpet matched the walls. "Look, Annie," he said, "it is like grass under our feet." He was always searching for a glimpse of paradise, my father.

He picked the bed closest to the bathroom, removed the top of his gray jogging suit, and unpacked his toiletries. Soon after, I heard him humming, as he always did, in the shower.

After he got into bed, I took a bath, pulled my hair back in a ponytail, and checked on the sculpture—just felt it a little bit through the bubble padding and carton wrapping to make sure it wasn't broken. Then I slipped under the covers, closed my eyes, and tried to sleep.

I pictured the client to whom I was delivering the sculpture: Gabrielle Fonteneau, a young woman about my age, an actress on a nationally syndicated television series. My friend Jonas, the principal at the East Flatbush elementary school where I teach drawing to fifth-graders, had shown her a picture of my *Father* sculpture, and, the way Jonas told it, Gabrielle Fonteneau had fallen in love with it and wished to offer it as a gift to her father on his birthday.

Since this was my first big sale, I wanted to make sure that the piece got there safely. Besides, I needed a weekend away, and both my mother and I figured that my father, who watched a lot of television, both in his barbershop and at home, would enjoy meeting Gabrielle, too. But when I woke up the next morning, my father was gone.

I showered, put on my driving jeans and a T-shirt, and waited. I watched a half hour of mid-morning local news, smoked three mentholated cigarettes even though we were in a nonsmoking room, and waited some more. By noon, four hours had gone by. And it was only then that I noticed that the car was still there but the sculpture was gone.

I decided to start looking for my father: in the east garden, the west garden, the dining room, the exercise room, and in the few guest rooms cracked open while the maid changed the sheets; in the little convenience store at the Amoco gas station nearby; even in the Salvation Army thrift shop that from a distance seemed to blend into the interstate. All that waiting and looking actually took six hours, and I felt guilty for having held back so long before going to the front desk to ask, "Have you seen my father?"

I feel Officer Bo's fingers gently stroking my wrist. Up close he smells like fried eggs and gasoline, like breakfast at the Amoco. "I'll put the word out with the other boys," he says. "Salinas here will be in his office. Why don't you go back to your room in case he shows up there?"

I return to the room and lie in the unmade bed, jumping up when I hear the click from the electronic key in the door. It's only the housekeeper. I turn down the late-afternoon cleaning and call my mother at the beauty salon where she perms, presses, and braids hair, next door to my father's barbershop. But she isn't there. So I call my parents' house and leave the hotel number on their machine. "Please call me as soon as you can, Manman. It's about Papi."

Once, when I was twelve, I overheard my mother telling a young woman who was about to get married how she and my father had first met on the sidewalk in front of Fort Dimanche the evening that my father was released from jail. (At a dance, my father had fought with a soldier out of uniform who had him arrested and thrown in prison for a year.) That night, my mother was returning home from a sewing class when he stumbled out of the prison gates and collapsed into her arms, his face still bleeding from his last beating. They married and left for New York a year later. "We were like two seeds planted in a rock," my mother had told the young woman, "but somehow when our daughter, Annie, came, we took root."

My mother soon calls me back, her voice staccato[2] with worry.

---

2. **staccato** (stə·kät′ō) *adj.*: made up of abrupt, distinct sounds.

"Where is Papi?"

"I lost him."

"How you lost him?"

"He got up before I did and disappeared."

"How long he been gone?"

"Eight hours," I say, almost not believing myself that it's been that long.

My mother is clicking her tongue and humming. I can see her sitting at the kitchen table, her eyes closed, her fingers sliding up and down her flesh-colored stockinged legs.

"You call police?"

"Yes."

"What they say?"

"To wait, that he'll come back."

My mother is thumping her fingers against the phone's mouthpiece, which is giving me a slight ache in my right ear.

"Tell me where you are," she says. "Two more hours and he's not there, call me, I come."

I dial Gabrielle Fonteneau's cellular-phone number. When she answers, her voice sounds just as it does on television, but more silken and seductive without the sitcom laugh track.

"To think," my father once said while watching her show, "Haitian-born actresses on American television."

"And one of them wants to buy my stuff," I'd added.

When she speaks, Gabrielle Fonteneau sounds as if she's in a place with cicadas,[3] waterfalls, palm trees, and citronella candles to keep the mosquitoes away. I realize that I, too, am in such a place, but I can't appreciate it.

"So nice of you to come all this way to deliver the sculpture," she says. "Jonas tell you why I like it so much? My papa was a journalist in Port-au-Prince. In 1975, he wrote a story criticizing the dictatorship, and he was arrested and put in jail."

"Fort Dimanche?"

"No, another one," she says. "Caserne. Papa kept track of days there by scraping lines with his fingernails on the walls of his cell. One of the guards didn't like this, so he pulled out all his fingernails with pliers."

I think of the photo spread I saw in the *Haitian Times* of Gabrielle Fonteneau and her parents in their living room in Tampa. Her father was described as a lawyer, his daughter's manager; her mother a court stenographer. There was no hint in that photograph of what had once happened to the father. Perhaps people don't see anything in my father's face, either, in spite of his scars.

"We celebrate his birthday on the day he was released from prison," she says. "It's the hands I love so much in your sculpture. They're so strong."

I am drifting away from Gabrielle Fonteneau when I hear her say, "So when will you get here? You have instructions from Jonas, right? Maybe we can make you lunch. My mother makes great *lanbi*."[4]

"I'll be there at twelve tomorrow," I say. "My father is with me. We are making a little weekend vacation of this."

My father loves museums. When he isn't working in his barbershop, he's often at the Brooklyn Museum. The ancient Egyptian rooms are his favorites.

"The Egyptians, they was like us," he likes to say. The Egyptians worshiped their gods in many forms and were often ruled by foreigners. The pharaohs were like the dictators he had fled. But what he admires most about the Egyptians is the way they mourned.

"Yes, they grieve," he'll say. He marvels at the mummification that went on for weeks, resulting in bodies that survived thousands of years.

My whole adult life, I have struggled to find the proper manner of sculpting my father, a man who learned about art by standing with me most of the Saturday mornings of my

---

3. **cicadas** (si•kā′dəz) *n. pl.:* cricketlike insects that make loud, shrill sounds.

(Opposite) *Agoue and His Wife* (1945) by Hector Hyppolite. (Agoue is the Voodoo god of the sea.)

---

4. *lanbi n.:* Creole for "conch," a type of shellfish.

Prisoners in Haiti.

childhood, mesmerized by the golden masks, the shawabtis,[5] and Osiris, ruler of the underworld.

When my father finally appears in the hotel-room doorway, I am awed by him. Smiling, he looks like a much younger man, further bronzed after a long day at the beach.

"Annie, let your father talk to you." He walks over to my bed, bends down to unlace his sneakers. "*On ti koze,* a little chat."

"Where were you? Where is the sculpture, Papi?" I feel my eyes twitching, a nervous reaction I inherited from my mother.

"That's why we need to chat," he says. "I have objections with your statue."

He pulls off his sneakers and rubs his feet with both hands.

"I don't want you to sell that statue," he says.

Then he picks up the phone and calls my mother.

"I know she called you," he says to her in Creole. "Her head is so hot. She panics so easily. I was just out walking, thinking."

I hear my mother lovingly scolding him and telling him not to leave me again. When he hangs up the phone, he picks up his sneakers and puts them back on.

"Where is the sculpture?" My eyes are twitching so hard now that I can barely see.

"Let us go," he says. "I will take you to it."

As my father maneuvers the car out of the parking lot, I tell myself he might be ill, mentally ill, even though I have never detected anything wrong beyond his prison nightmares. I am trying to piece it together, this sudden yet familiar picture of a parent's vulnerability. When I was ten years old and my father had the chicken pox, I overheard him say to a friend on

---

5. **shawabtis** *n. pl.:* figures that are buried with ancient Egyptian mummies. *Shawabtis* contain passages from the Book of the Dead and are meant to represent a mummy's servants in the afterlife.

**Vocabulary**

**vulnerability** (vul′nər·ə·bil′ ə·tē) *n.:* capability of being hurt.

the phone, "The doctor tells me that at my age chicken pox can kill a man." This was the first time I realized that my father could die. I looked up the word *kill* in every dictionary and encyclopedia at school, trying to comprehend what it meant, that my father could be <u>eradicated</u> from my life.

My father stops the car on the side of the highway near a man-made lake, one of those artificial creations of the modern tropical city, with curved stone benches surrounding stagnant water. There is little light to see by except a half-moon. He heads toward one of the benches, and I sit down next to him, letting my hands dangle between my legs.

"Is this where the sculpture is?" I ask.

"In the water," he says.

"OK," I say. "But please know this about yourself. You are an especially harsh critic."

My father tries to smother a smile.

"Why?" I ask.

He scratches his chin. Anger is a wasted emotion, I've always thought. My parents got angry at unfair politics in New York or Port-au-Prince, but they never got angry at my grades—at all the B's I got in everything but art classes—or at my not eating vegetables or occasionally vomiting my daily spoonful of cod-liver oil. Ordinary anger, I thought, was a weakness. But now I am angry. I want to hit my father, beat the craziness out of his head.

"Annie," he says. "When I first saw your statue, I wanted to be buried with it, to take it with me into the other world."

"Like the ancient Egyptians," I say.

He smiles, grateful, I think, that I still recall his passions.

"Annie," he asks, "do you remember when I read to you from the Book of the Dead?"

"Are you dying?" I say to my father. "Because I can only forgive you for this if you are. You can't take this back."

He is silent for a moment too long.

I think I hear crickets, though I cannot imagine where they might be. There is the highway, the cars racing by, the half-moon, the lake dug

---

**Vocabulary**

**eradicated** (ē·rad′i·kāt′id) *v.:* wiped out; destroyed.

up from the depths of the ground, the allée[6] of royal palms beyond. And there is me and my father.

"You remember the judgment of the dead," my father says, "when the heart of a person is put on a scale. If it is heavy, then this person cannot enter the other world."

It is a testament to my upbringing that I am not yelling at him.

"I don't deserve a statue," he says, even while looking like one: the Madonna of Humility, for example, contemplating her losses in the dust.

"Annie, your father was the hunter," he says. "He was not the prey."

"What are you saying?" I ask.

"We have a proverb," he says. " 'One day for the hunter, one day for the prey.' Your father was the hunter. He was not the prey." Each word is hard won as it leaves my father's mouth, balanced like those hearts on the Egyptian scale.

"Annie, when I saw your mother the first time, I was not just out of prison. I was a guard in the prison. One of the prisoners I was questioning had scratched me with a piece of tin. I went out to the street in a rage, blood all over my face. I was about to go back and do something bad, very bad. But instead comes your mother. I smash into her, and she asks me what I am doing there. I told her I was just let go from prison and she held my face and cried in my hair."

"And the nightmares, what are they?"

"Of what I, your father, did to others."

"Does Manman know?"

"I told her, Annie, before we married."

I am the one who drives back to the hotel. In the car, he says, "Annie, I am still your father, still your mother's husband. I would not do these things now."

When we get back to the hotel room, I leave a message for Officer Bo, and another for Manager Salinas, telling them that I have found my father. He has slipped into the bathroom, and now he runs the shower at full force. When it seems that he is never coming out, I call my mother at home in Brooklyn.

"How do you love him?" I whisper into the phone.

My mother is tapping her fingers against the mouthpiece.

"I don't know, Annie," she whispers back, as though there is a chance that she might also be overheard by him. "I feel only that you and me, we saved him. When I met him, it made him stop hurting the people. This is how I see it. He was a seed thrown into a rock, and you and me, Annie, we helped push a flower out of the rock."

When I get up the next morning, my father is already dressed. He is sitting on the edge of his bed with his back to me, his head bowed, his face buried in his hands. If I were sculpting him, I would make him a praying mantis, crouching motionless, seeming to pray while waiting to strike.

With his back still turned, my father says, "Will you call those people and tell them you have it no more, the statue?"

"We were invited to lunch there. I believe we should go."

He raises his shoulders and shrugs. It is up to me.

The drive to Gabrielle Fonteneau's house seems longer than the twenty-four hours it took to drive from New York: the ocean, the palms along the road, the highway so imposingly neat. My father fills in the silence in the car by saying, "So now you know, Annie, why your mother and me, we have never returned home."

The Fonteneaus' house is made of bricks of white coral, on a cul-de-sac[7] with a row of banyans[8] separating the two sides of the street.

Silently, we get out of the car and follow a concrete path to the front door. Before we can knock, an older woman walks out. Like Gabrielle, she has stunning midnight-black eyes

---

6. **allée** *n.:* walkway between two rows of evenly planted trees.

7. **cul-de-sac** *n.:* dead-end street; blind alley.
8. **banyans** *n. pl.:* tropical fig trees.

and skin the color of sorrel,[9] with spiraling curls brushing the sides of her face. When Gabrielle's father joins her, I realize where Gabrielle Fonteneau gets her height. He is more than six feet tall.

Mr. Fonteneau extends his hands, first to my father and then to me. They're large, twice the size of my father's. The fingernails have grown back, thick, densely dark, as though the past had nestled itself there in black ink.

We move slowly through the living room, which has a cathedral ceiling and walls covered with Haitian paintings—Obin, Hyppolite, Tiga, Duval-Carrié. Out on the back terrace, which towers over a nursery of orchids and red dracaenas, a table is set for lunch.

---

9. **sorrel** *n.:* light reddish brown.

Mr. Fonteneau asks my father where his family is from in Haiti, and my father lies. In the past, I thought he always said a different province because he had lived in all those places, but I realize now that he says this to keep anyone from tracing him, even though twenty-six years and eighty more pounds shield him from the threat of immediate recognition.

When Gabrielle Fonteneau makes her entrance, in an off-the-shoulder ruby dress, my father and I stand up.

"Gabrielle," she says, when she shakes hands with my father, who blurts out spontaneously, "You are one of the flowers of Haiti."

Gabrielle Fonteneau tilts her head coyly.

"We eat now," Mrs. Fonteneau announces, leading me and my father to a bathroom to wash up before the meal. Standing before a pink

*Village Scene* (20th century) by Yves Phonard.

seashell-shaped sink, my father and I dip our hands under the faucet flow.

"Annie," my father says, "we always thought, your mother and me, that children could raise their parents higher. Look at what this girl has done for her parents."

During the meal of conch, plantains, and mushroom rice, Mr. Fonteneau tries to draw my father into conversation. He asks when my father was last in Haiti.

"Twenty-six years," my father replies.

"No going back for you?" asks Mrs. Fonteneau.

"I have not had the opportunity," my father says.

"We go back every year to a beautiful place overlooking the ocean in the mountains in Jacmel," says Mrs. Fonteneau.

"Have you ever been to Jacmel?" Gabrielle Fonteneau asks me.

I shake my head no.

"We are fortunate," Mrs. Fonteneau says, "that we have another place to go where we can say our rain is sweeter, our dust is lighter, our beach is prettier."

"So now we are tasting rain and weighing dust," Mr. Fonteneau says, and laughs.

"There is nothing like drinking the sweet juice from a green coconut you fetched yourself from your own tree, or sinking your hand in sand from the beach in your own country," Mrs. Fonteneau says.

"When did you ever climb a coconut tree?" Mr. Fonteneau says, teasing his wife.

I am imagining what my father's nightmares might be. Maybe he dreams of dipping his hands in the sand on a beach in his own country and finds that what he comes up with is a fist full of blood.

After lunch, my father asks if he can have a closer look at the Fonteneaus' backyard garden. While he's taking the tour, I confess to Gabrielle Fonteneau that I don't have the sculpture.

"My father threw it away," I say.

Gabrielle Fonteneau frowns.

"I don't know," she says. "Was there even a sculpture at all? I trust Jonas, but maybe you fooled him, too. Is this some scam, to get into our home?"

"There was a sculpture," I say. "Jonas will tell you that. My father just didn't like it, so he threw it away."

She raises her perfectly arched eyebrows, perhaps out of concern for my father's sanity or my own.

"I'm really disappointed," she says. "I wanted it for a reason. My father goes home when he looks at a piece of art. He goes home deep inside himself. For a long time, he used to hide his fingers from people. It's like he was making a fist all the time. I wanted to give him this thing so that he knows we understand what happened to him."

"I am truly sorry," I say.

Over her shoulders, I see her parents guiding my father through rows of lemongrass. I want to promise her that I will make her another sculpture, one especially modeled on her father. But I don't know when I will be able to work on anything again. I have lost my subject, the father I loved as well as pitied.

In the garden, I watch my father snap a white orchid from its stem and hold it out toward Mrs. Fonteneau, who accepts it with a nod of thanks.

"I don't understand," Gabrielle Fonteneau says. "You did all this for nothing."

I wave to my father to signal that we should perhaps leave now, and he comes toward me, the Fonteneaus trailing slowly behind him.

With each step he rubs the scars on the side of his face.

Perhaps the last person my father harmed had dreamed this moment into my father's future—his daughter seeing those marks, like chunks of warm plaster still clinging to a cast, and questioning him about them, giving him a chance to either lie or tell the truth. After all, we have the proverb, as my father would say: "Those who give the blows may try to forget, but those who carry the scars must remember." ∎

# Response and Analysis

## Reading Check

1. Why are Annie and her father in Florida?

2. Where does Annie's father go when he leaves the motel, and what does he do?

3. What surprising information does Annie's father give her about his past?

4. Why does Annie hold back from promising to make another statue for Gabrielle Fonteneau?

## Thinking Critically

5. How does a particular historical period shape the events of this story? Could you imagine similar events happening in the lives of people who lived in another period of history, even in the present? Explain your response.

6. What basic **irony** is at the heart of this story—how is Annie's father the opposite of the heroic figure she admired?

7. At the beginning of the story, what does the sculpture **symbolize** for Annie? What does the same sculpture symbolize for Gabrielle Fonteneau?

8. Explain the **dramatic irony** that builds during the luncheon at the Fonteneau's house. In other words, what do we know that the Fonteneaus do not know?

9. What conclusion can you draw about Annie's father from his throwing the statue away? What is the significance of his rubbing the scars on his face after the luncheon?

10. In the story, Annie first loses her father and then her sculpture. What deeper loss does Annie experience?

11. What does the **title** of the story refer to literally?

12. On another level, what does the title mean? How would you state the story's **theme**—what truth about life does the story reveal?

## WRITING

### Analyzing a Theme

In an **essay,** take this story apart to show how it reveals a theme—a revelation about life. Think about what the story reveals about guilt, repentance, and forgiveness. Before you begin to write, review the discussion of theme on page 1029. Then, fill out a chart like the one below, in which you gather details from the story that help you interpret the theme. At the beginning of the essay, state the theme you find in the story. Use the rest of the essay to elaborate on that statement of theme and to cite passages of the story that support your interpretation. If you quote directly from the story, be sure to use quotation marks.

| Main character: |
| --- |
| Character's conflict: |
| Resolution: |
| What character discovers: |
| Key passages: |

## Vocabulary Development

### What's Wrong?

Explain what's wrong with each sentence below:

1. The lawyer was tastefully dressed in a <u>gaudy</u> pinstriped suit.

2. The firemen displayed their <u>vulnerability</u> by rescuing the victims from the burning building.

3. Because their food source has been <u>eradicated</u>, the squirrels are getting plump.

SKILLS FOCUS

**Literary Skills**
Analyze irony, including verbal, situational, and dramatic irony.

**Writing Skills**
Write an essay analyzing theme in a story.

**Vocabulary Skills**
Demonstrate word knowledge.

# Writing an Autobiographical Narrative

**Writing Assignment**
**Write an essay of at least 1,500 words in which you narrate a meaningful experience from your life and tell why it is important to you.**

A memoir such as *Night*, which you read beginning on page 914, is based on the life of the writer. The events of your life can become the basis for your own **autobiographical narrative,** a type of writing in which you relate a meaningful experience from your life and reveal to readers why that event is significant to you.

**Choose an Experience** Any experience that has meaning for you—no matter how large or small—is important enough to be a topic for your autobiographical narrative. You might look in a journal or diary to recall experiences you've had, or you might jot down responses to statements such as *I'll never forget when . . .* or *Somehow I felt different after . . . .* The experience that you choose should be one that you remember well, that will interest your readers, and that you'll feel comfortable sharing.

**Consider Purpose and Audience** Your dual **purposes** for writing an autobiographical narrative are to share your experience and its meaning with others and to explore and express your own thoughts and feelings about the experience.

How can you enable your **audience** to understand and share in your experience? Ask yourself the following questions.

- **What background information do my readers need?** Provide a context for the events that follow. For example, if you're writing about the first time you completed a ten-kilometer run, readers will appreciate that accomplishment more if you first discuss your years of being a couch potato.

- **How can I make my readers truly participate in my experience?** Describe your experience so vividly that readers can clearly imagine themselves in your place. Try to connect the events and details of the experience to something that will be familiar to most of your readers.

- **How can I convey to my readers the meaning of my experience?** Your readers will need to know what you thought and felt during the events as well as what you think about the experience now.

**Recall and Record Details** If you need help recalling the details of your experience, go "back in time" by mentally visualizing the experience, talking about it with someone else who was involved, or looking through old photographs, yearbooks, scrapbooks, awards, and so on.

**SKILLS FOCUS**

**Writing Skills**
Write an autobiographical narrative. Choose an experience. Consider purpose and audience. Record details.

The large details in your narrative will be the separate events that made up the experience you're describing. You can't stop with just this "skeleton," though; you must also provide **narrative and descriptive** details to flesh out the sequence of events. Include the following kinds of details.

## NARRATIVE AND DESCRIPTIVE DETAILS

- Tell your readers where and when **specific events and incidents** of your experience occurred.

- Use **concrete sensory details** to communicate the sights, sounds, and smells associated with each event.

- Include descriptions of the **appearances, movements, gestures, expressions,** and **feelings** of the people in the experience.

- Include **dialogue** to make the narrative more real and to give it a sense of immediacy.

**DO THIS**

To record the events and details of your experience, create a three-column chart. List each **event** of the experience in one column, the narrative and descriptive **details** about that event in a second column, and your **thoughts and feelings** about that event in a third column.

Put the events and details in an **order** appropriate to your story. Most autobiographical narratives explain events in chronological order, moving from the first event to the last. You may jump back or forward in time with a flashback or a flash-forward. Within this chronological order, arrange your details by spatial order or by order of importance. Make sure you use transitions to clarify any changes in time, sequence, location, or actions. You can also signal these changes by adjusting the **pace** of events—slowing down during a flashback, for example.

**Think About Meaning**   To examine what the experience means to you, ask yourself these questions:

- What did I learn about myself or others from this experience?

- How did the experience cause me to change or to think differently?

Keep the significance of your experience in mind as you draft your narrative. In the **introduction,** hint at—but don't fully reveal—the meaning of the experience. In the **body,** relate the main events and details of your experience. In the **conclusion,** state the significance of your experience directly, and explain or elaborate to make its importance clear to your readers.

**SKILLS FOCUS**

**PRACTICE & APPLY**   Follow the instructions in this section to plan and write an autobiographical narrative. Then, share your narrative with your classmates.

**Writing Skills**
Develop clear structure. Think about meaning.

# Contemporary Nonfiction

**Wright**
**Kingston**
**Momaday**
**Walker**
**Baldwin**
**Cisneros**

I would hurl words into the darkness and wait for an echo. If an echo sounded, no matter how faintly, I would send other words to tell, to march, to fight, to create a sense of the hunger for life that gnaws in us all, to keep alive in our hearts a sense of the inexpressibly human.

—Richard Wright

*Lucas/Woodcut* (detail) (1993) by Chuck Close.
Woodcut with pochoir (46¹/₄" × 36").

Courtesy Pace Editions, New York.

# Richard Wright
## 1908–1960

"It had been only through books—at best, no more than vicarious cultural transfusions—that I had managed to keep myself alive. . . ." Richard Wright *did* keep himself alive, and he became a writer with a gift for conveying the intensity of his struggle. He is typically described as the first African American writer to expose American racism to a large white audience. But this cool academic assessment fails to capture the angry, relentless drive of his most famous novel, *Native Son* (1940), or of his autobiography *Black Boy* (1945).

Critics have labored to justify Wright's membership in the Communist party and explain his self-exile in Paris for the last fourteen years of his life. Full of contradictions, Wright is hard to label, yet it is clear that African American writers who have followed him have had to emerge from his shadow.

When the University of Mississippi organized a symposium on Wright in 1985, it was front-page news. Part of the poignancy of such posthumous recognition comes from the fact that Wright had remembered his home state of Mississippi with "ambivalence." We can only speculate on how Wright might have reacted to an authority on Southern culture who told *The New York Times:* "Faulkner is considered the top Mississippi writer, but I would put Wright with Eudora Welty and Tennessee Williams in their international reputation."

Wright's life began in poverty. His father, a Mississippi sharecropper, abandoned his family when Wright was five; when the boy was twelve, his mother could no longer support the family. Raised by various relatives, Wright early learned the bitter lessons of survival on ghetto streets. He remembered living with "the sustained expectation of violence." By borrowing a white man's library card, he was finally able to gain access to books.

Before he was twenty, Wright fled the South forever, moving to Chicago and then to New York. He joined the WPA Federal Writers Project, a Depression-era government organization that provided a livelihood for unemployed writers. He explored Marxism and eventually joined the Communist party at a time when many people thought it offered hope for a better society (and before the horrors of the Stalinist purges of the 1930s became public). Finally disillusioned, Wright left the party in 1944.

Wright achieved his first real recognition with *Native Son,* a tale of a victimized black man, Bigger Thomas, who accidentally kills once, then murders again to avoid betrayal. *Black Boy* secured Wright's fame and became a bestseller. But in the fifteen years between its publication and his death, Wright wrote no other book that equaled its success. He struggled to understand the historical and cultural place of African Americans in modern life, visiting Africa and recording his observations. But he felt as much an alien in Africa as anywhere else. He died in Paris, where he had found as much of a home as he could.

## For Independent Reading

For more about Richard Wright, read his autobiography *Black Boy*.

# Before You Read

*from* Black Boy

## Make the Connection

What does it mean to grow up and to participate in the world as mature and responsible adults? What elements of childhood do we carry with us forever? The discoveries we make as children, awakening to what the world is like, can be harsh or sweet, shocking or gradual, depending on the specific circumstances of our lives. Through our individual experiences, we are each deeply affected by our childhood awakenings.

## Literary Focus
### Dialogue and Nonfiction

We often associate **dialogue,** the directly quoted words of people speaking to one another, with drama and fiction. Nowadays dialogue also plays an important part in nonfiction, particularly in autobiography and journalism. Dialogue in nonfiction, however, can become controversial. Reporters, for instance, have been challenged in court to prove that the words they put in quotation marks were the actual words spoken by the people they interviewed.

In Wright's autobiography, most of the scenes are dramatized by means of dialogue. Wright's use of dialogue gives his autobiography the feel of a novel, even though he is writing about actual events. The passage you are about to read provides a good example of how nonfiction writers often use the elements of fiction to make their texts come alive. As a critical reader you have to decide if the extensive use of dialogue, which the writer could not possibly have recalled accurately, affects the veracity, or truthfulness, of his text. Does Wright use the dialogue to reveal the essence of the characters he is presenting to us? Could he have brought his mother and father to life without the use of dialogue?

**SKILLS FOCUS**

**Literary Skills**
Understand dialogue in nonfiction.

**INTERNET**

**Vocabulary Practice**
•
**More About Richard Wright**

Keyword: LE7 11-6

> **Dialogue** is the directly quoted words of two or more people in conversation.
>
> *For more on Dialogue, see the Handbook of Literary and Historical Terms.*

## Vocabulary Development

**enthralled** (en·thrôld′) *v.*: fascinated.

**clamor** (klam′ər) *n.*: loud noise; loud demand or complaint.

**dispirited** (di·spir′it·id) *adj.*: discouraged.

**frenzy** (fren′zē) *n.*: frantic behavior; wildness.

**ardently** (är′dənt·lē) *adv.*: intensely; eagerly.

**copiously** (kō′pē·əs·lē) *adv.*: abundantly.

**futile** (fyo͞ot′l) *adj.*: useless; pointless.

**eluded** (ē·lo͞od′id) *v.*: escaped detection or notice.

**withering** (with′ər·iŋ) *v.* used as *adj.*: drying up; weakening.

# *from* Black Boy

## Richard Wright

Where was I going? I did not know. The farther I walked the more frantic I became.

One day my mother told me that we were going to Memphis on a boat, the *Kate Adams,* and my eagerness thereafter made the days seem endless. Each night I went to bed hoping that the next morning would be the day of departure.

"How big is the boat?" I asked my mother.

"As big as a mountain," she said.

"Has it got a whistle?"

"Yes."

"Does the whistle blow?"

"Yes."

"When?"

"When the captain wants it to blow."

"Why do they call it the *Kate Adams*?"

"Because that's the boat's name."

"What color is the boat?"

"White."

"How long will we be on the boat?"

"All day and all night."

"Will we sleep on the boat?"

"Yes, when we get sleepy, we'll sleep. Now, hush."

For days I had dreamed about a huge white boat floating on a vast body of water, but when my mother took me down to the levee on the day of leaving, I saw a tiny, dirty boat that was not at all like the boat I had imagined. I was disappointed and when time came to go on board I cried and my mother thought that I did not want to go with her to Memphis, and I could not tell her what the trouble was. Solace came when I wandered about the boat and gazed at Negroes throwing dice, drinking whiskey, playing cards, lolling on boxes, eating, talking, and singing. My father took me down into the engine room and the throbbing machines enthralled me for hours.

In Memphis we lived in a one-story brick tenement. The stone buildings and the concrete pavements looked bleak and hostile to me. The absence of green, growing things made the city seem dead. Living space for the four of us—my mother, my brother, my father, and me—was a kitchen and a bedroom. In the front and rear were paved areas in which my brother and I could play, but for days I was afraid to go into the strange city streets alone.

It was in this tenement that the personality of my father first came fully into the orbit of my concern. He worked as a night porter in a Beale Street drugstore and he became important and forbidding to me only when I learned that I could not make noise when he was asleep in the daytime. He was the lawgiver in our family and I never laughed in his presence. I used to lurk timidly in the kitchen doorway and watch his huge body sitting slumped at the table. I stared at him with awe as he gulped his beer from a tin bucket, as he ate long and heavily, sighed, belched, closed his eyes to nod on a stuffed belly. He was quite fat and his bloated stomach always lapped over his belt. He was always a stranger to me, always somehow alien and remote. . . .

Hunger stole upon me so slowly that at first I was not aware of what hunger really meant. Hunger had always been more or less at my elbow when I played, but now I began to wake up at night to find hunger standing at my bedside, staring at me gauntly. The hunger I had known before this had been no grim, hostile stranger; it had been a normal hunger that had made me beg constantly for bread, and when I ate a crust or two I was satisfied. But this new hunger baffled me, scared me, made me angry and insistent. Whenever I begged for food now my mother would pour me a cup of tea which would still the clamor in my stomach for a moment or two; but a little later I would feel hunger nudging my ribs, twisting my empty guts until they ached. I would grow dizzy and my vision would dim. I became less active in my play, and for the first time in my life I had to pause and think of what was happening to me.

"Mama, I'm hungry," I complained one afternoon.

"Jump up and catch a kungry," she said, trying to make me laugh and forget.

"What's a *kungry*?"

"It's what little boys eat when they get hungry," she said.

"What does it taste like?"

"I don't know."

"Then why do you tell me to catch one?"

"Because you said that you were hungry," she said, smiling.

I sensed that she was teasing me and it made me angry.

"But I'm hungry. I want to eat."

"You'll have to wait."

"But I want to eat now."

"But there's nothing to eat," she told me.

"Why?"

"Just because there's none," she explained.

"But I want to eat," I said, beginning to cry.

"You'll just have to wait," she said again.

"But why?"

"For God to send some food."

"When is He going to send it?"

"I don't know."

"But I'm hungry!"

She was ironing and she paused and looked at me with tears in her eyes.

"Where's your father?" she asked me.

I stared in bewilderment. Yes, it was true that my father had not come home to sleep for many days now and I could make as much noise as I wanted. Though I had not known why he was absent, I had been glad that he was not there to

---

**Vocabulary**

**enthralled** (en·thrôld′) v.: fascinated.

**clamor** (klam′ər) n.: loud noise; loud demand or complaint.

shout his restrictions at me. But it had never occurred to me that his absence would mean that there would be no food.

"I don't know," I said.

"Who brings food into the house?" my mother asked me.

"Papa," I said. "He always brought food."

"Well, your father isn't here now," she said.

"Where is he?"

"I don't know," she said.

"But I'm hungry," I whimpered, stomping my feet.

"You'll have to wait until I get a job and buy food," she said.

As the days slid past, the image of my father became associated with my pangs of hunger, and whenever I felt hunger I thought of him with a deep biological bitterness.

My mother finally went to work as a cook and left me and my brother alone in the flat each day with a loaf of bread and a pot of tea. When she returned at evening she would be tired and dispirited and would cry a lot. Sometimes, when she was in despair, she would call us to her and talk to us for hours, telling us that we now had no father, that our lives would be different from those of other children, that we must learn as soon as possible to take care of ourselves, to dress ourselves, to prepare our own food; that we must take upon ourselves the responsibility of the flat while she worked. Half frightened, we would promise solemnly. We did not understand what had happened between our father and our mother and the most that these long talks did to us was to make us feel a vague dread. Whenever we asked why father had left, she would tell us that we were too young to know.

One evening my mother told me that thereafter I would have to do the shopping for food. She took me to the corner store to show me the way. I was proud; I felt like a grownup. The next afternoon I looped the basket over my arm and went down the pavement toward the store. When I reached the corner, a gang of boys grabbed me, knocked me down, snatched the basket, took the money, and sent me running

home in panic. That evening I told my mother what had happened, but she made no comment; she sat down at once, wrote another note, gave me more money, and sent me out to the grocery again. I crept down the steps and saw the same gang of boys playing down the street. I ran back into the house.

"What's the matter?" my mother asked.

"It's those same boys," I said. "They'll beat me."

"You've got to get over that," she said. "Now, go on."

"I'm scared," I said.

"Go on and don't pay any attention to them," she said.

I went out of the door and walked briskly down the sidewalk, praying that the gang would not molest me. But when I came abreast of them someone shouted.

"There he is!"

They came toward me and I broke into a wild run toward home. They overtook me and flung me to the pavement. I yelled, pleaded, kicked, but they wrenched the money out of my hand. They yanked me to my feet, gave me a few slaps, and sent me home sobbing. My mother met me at the door.

"They b-beat m-me," I gasped. "They t-t-took the m-money."

I started up the steps, seeking the shelter of the house.

"Don't you come in here," my mother warned me.

I froze in my tracks and stared at her.

"But they're coming after me," I said.

"You just stay right where you are," she said in a deadly tone. "I'm going to teach you this night to stand up and fight for yourself."

She went into the house and I waited, terrified, wondering what she was about. Presently she returned with more money and another note; she also had a long heavy stick.

"Take this money, this note, and this stick,"

---

**Vocabulary**

**dispirited** (di·spir′it·id) *adj.:* discouraged.

she said. "Go to the store and buy those groceries. If those boys bother you, then fight."

I was baffled. My mother was telling me to fight, a thing that she had never done before.

"But I'm scared," I said.

"Don't you come into this house until you've gotten those groceries," she said.

"They'll beat me; they'll beat me," I said.

"Then stay in the streets; don't come back here!"

I ran up the steps and tried to force my way past her into the house. A stinging slap came on my jaw. I stood on the sidewalk, crying.

"Please, let me wait until tomorrow," I begged.

"No," she said. "Go now! If you come back into this house without those groceries, I'll whip you!"

She slammed the door and I heard the key turn in the lock. I shook with fright. I was alone upon the dark, hostile streets and gangs were after me. I had the choice of being beaten at home or away from home. I clutched the stick, crying, trying to reason. If I were beaten at home, there was absolutely nothing that I could do about it; but if I were beaten in the streets, I had a chance to fight and defend myself. I walked slowly down the sidewalk, coming closer to the gang of boys, holding the stick tightly. I was so full of fear that I could scarcely breathe. I was almost upon them now.

"There he is again!" the cry went up.

They surrounded me quickly and began to grab for my hand.

"I'll kill you!" I threatened.

They closed in. In blind fear I let the stick fly, feeling it crack against a boy's skull. I swung again, lamming another skull, then another. Realizing that they would retaliate if I let up for but a second, I fought to lay them low, to knock them cold, to kill them so that they could not strike back at me. I flayed with tears in my eyes, teeth clenched, stark fear making me throw every ounce of my strength behind each blow. I hit again and again, dropping the money and the grocery list. The boys scattered, yelling, nursing their heads, staring at me in utter disbe-

lief. They had never seen such frenzy. I stood panting, egging them on, taunting them to come on and fight. When they refused, I ran after them and they tore out for their homes, screaming. The parents of the boys rushed into the streets and threatened me, and for the first time in my life I shouted at grownups, telling them that I would give them the same if they bothered me. I finally found my grocery list and the money and went to the store. On my way back I kept my stick poised for instant use, but there was not a single boy in sight. That night I won the right to the streets of Memphis. . . .

After my father's desertion, my mother's ardently religious disposition dominated the household and I was often taken to Sunday school where I met God's representative in the guise of a tall, black preacher. One Sunday my mother invited the tall, black preacher to a dinner of fried chicken. I was happy, not because the preacher was coming but because of the chicken. One or two neighbors also were invited. But no sooner had the preacher arrived than I began to resent him, for I learned at once that he, like my father, was used to having his own way. The hour for dinner came and I was wedged at the table between talking and laughing adults. In the center of the table was a huge platter of golden-brown fried chicken. I compared the bowl of soup that sat before me with the crispy chicken and decided in favor of the chicken. The others began to eat their soup, but I could not touch mine.

"Eat your soup," my mother said.

"I don't want any," I said.

"You won't get anything else until you've eaten your soup," she said.

The preacher had finished his soup and had asked that the platter of chicken be passed to him. It galled me. He smiled, cocked his head this way and that, picking out choice pieces. I

**Vocabulary**
**frenzy** (fren′zē) *n.*: frantic behavior; wildness.
**ardently** (är′dənt·lē) *adv.*: intensely; eagerly.

forced a spoonful of soup down my throat and looked to see if my speed matched that of the preacher. It did not. There were already bare chicken bones on his plate, and he was reaching for more. I tried eating my soup faster, but it was no use; the other people were now serving themselves chicken and the platter was more than half empty. I gave up and sat staring in despair at the vanishing pieces of fried chicken.

"Eat your soup or you won't get anything," my mother warned.

I looked at her appealingly and could not answer. As piece after piece of chicken was eaten, I was unable to eat my soup at all. I grew hot with anger. The preacher was laughing and joking and the grownups were hanging on his words. My growing hate of the preacher finally became more important than God or religion and I could no longer contain myself. I leaped up from the table, knowing that I should be ashamed of what I was doing, but unable to stop, and screamed, running blindly from the room.

"That preacher's going to eat *all* the chicken!" I bawled.

The preacher tossed back his head and roared with laughter, but my mother was angry and told me that I was to have no dinner because of my bad manners.

When I awakened one morning my mother told me that we were going to see a judge who would make my father support me and my brother. An hour later all three of us were sitting in a huge crowded room. I was overwhelmed by the many faces and the voices which I could not understand. High above me was a white face which my mother told me was the face of the judge. Across the huge room sat my father, smiling confidently, looking at us. My mother warned me not to be fooled by my father's friendly manner; she told me that the judge might ask me questions, and if he did I must tell him the truth. I agreed, yet I hoped that the judge would not ask me anything.

For some reason the entire thing struck me as being useless; I felt that if my father were going

That night I won the right to the streets of Memphis . . .

*Boy with Tire* (1952) by Hughie Lee-Smith. Oil on prestwood panel (60.3 cm × 82.6 cm).

to feed me, then he would have done so regardless of what a judge said to him. And I did not want my father to feed me; I was hungry, but my thoughts of food did not now center about him. I waited, growing restless, hungry. My mother gave me a dry sandwich and I munched and stared, longing to go home. Finally I heard my mother's name called; she rose and began weeping so <u>copiously</u> that she could not talk for a few moments; at last she managed to say that her husband had deserted her and two children, that her children were hungry, that they stayed hungry, that she worked, that she was trying to raise them alone. Then my father was called; he came forward jauntily, smiling. He tried to kiss my mother, but she turned away from him. I only heard one sentence of what he said.

"I'm doing all I can, Your Honor," he mumbled, grinning.

It had been painful to sit and watch my mother crying and my father laughing and I was glad when we were outside in the sunny streets. Back at home my mother wept again and talked complainingly about the unfairness of the judge who had accepted my father's word. After the court scene, I tried to forget my father; I did not hate him; I simply did not want to think of him. Often when we were hungry my mother would beg me to go to my father's job and ask him for a dollar, a dime, a nickel . . . But I would never consent to go. I did not want to see him.

My mother fell ill and the problem of food became an acute, daily agony. Hunger was with us always. Sometimes the neighbors would feed us or a dollar bill would come in the mail from my grandmother. It was winter and I would buy a dime's worth of coal each morning from the corner coalyard and lug it home in paper bags. For a time I remained out of school to wait upon my mother, then Granny came to visit us and I returned to school.

At night there were long, halting discussions about our going to live with Granny, but

**Vocabulary**
**copiously** (kō′pē·əs·lē) *adv.*: abundantly.

nothing came of it. Perhaps there was not enough money for railroad fare. Angered by having been hauled into court, my father now spurned us completely. I heard long, angrily whispered conversations between my mother and grandmother to the effect that "that woman ought to be killed for breaking up a home." What irked me was the ceaseless talk and no action. If someone had suggested that my father be killed, I would perhaps have become interested; if someone had suggested that his name never be mentioned, I would no doubt have agreed; if someone had suggested that we move to another city, I would have been glad. But there was only endless talk that led nowhere and I began to keep away from home as much as possible, preferring the simplicity of the streets to the worried, futile talk at home.

Finally we could no longer pay the rent for our dingy flat; the few dollars that Granny had left us before she went home were gone. Half sick and in despair, my mother made the rounds of the charitable institutions, seeking help. She found an orphan home that agreed to assume the guidance of me and my brother provided my mother worked and made small payments. My mother hated to be separated from us, but she had no choice.

The orphan home was a two-story frame building set amid trees in a wide, green field. My mother ushered me and my brother one morning into the building and into the presence of a tall, gaunt, mulatto woman who called herself Miss Simon. At once she took a fancy to me and I was frightened speechless; I was afraid of her the moment I saw her and my fear lasted during my entire stay in the home.

The house was crowded with children and there was always a storm of noise. The daily routine was blurred to me and I never quite grasped it. The most abiding feeling I had each day was hunger and fear. The meals were skimpy and there were only two of them. Just before we went to bed each night we were given a slice of bread smeared with molasses. The children were silent, hostile, vindictive, continuously complaining of hunger. There was an overall atmosphere of nervousness and intrigue, of children telling tales upon others, of children being deprived of food to punish them.

The home did not have the money to check the growth of the wide stretches of grass by having it mown, so it had to be pulled by hand. Each morning after we had eaten a breakfast that seemed like no breakfast at all, an older child would lead a herd of us to the vast lawn and we would get to our knees and wrench the grass loose from the dirt with our fingers. At intervals Miss Simon would make a tour of inspection, examining the pile of pulled grass beside each child, scolding or praising according to the size of the pile. Many mornings I was too weak from hunger to pull the grass; I would grow dizzy and my mind would become blank and I would find myself, after an interval of unconsciousness, upon my hands and knees, my head whirling, my eyes staring in bleak astonishment at the green grass, wondering where I was, feeling that I was emerging from a dream . . .

During the first days my mother came each night to visit me and my brother, then her visits stopped. I began to wonder if she, too, like my father, had disappeared into the unknown. I was rapidly learning to distrust everything and everybody. When my mother did come, I asked her why had she remained away so long and she told me that Miss Simon had forbidden her to visit us, that Miss Simon had said that she was spoiling us with too much attention. I begged my mother to take me away; she wept and told me to wait, that soon she would take us to Arkansas. She left and my heart sank.

Miss Simon tried to win my confidence; she asked me if I would like to be adopted by her if my mother consented and I said no. She would take me into her apartment and talk to me, but her words had no effect. Dread and mistrust had already become a daily part of my being and my memory grew sharp, my senses more

**Vocabulary**
**futile** (fyo͞ot′'l) *adj.*: useless; pointless.

impressionable; I began to be aware of myself as a distinct personality striving against others. I held myself in, afraid to act or speak until I was sure of my surroundings, feeling most of the time that I was suspended over a void. My imagination soared; I dreamed of running away. Each morning I vowed that I would leave the next morning, but the next morning always found me afraid.

One day Miss Simon told me that thereafter I was to help her in the office. I ate lunch with her and, strangely, when I sat facing her at the table, my hunger vanished. The woman killed something in me. Next she called me to her desk where she sat addressing envelopes.

"Step up close to the desk," she said. "Don't be afraid."

I went and stood at her elbow. There was a wart on her chin and I stared at it.

"Now, take a blotter from over there and blot each envelope after I'm through writing on it," she instructed me, pointing to a blotter that stood about a foot from my hand.

I stared and did not move or answer.

"Take the blotter," she said.

I wanted to reach for the blotter and succeeded only in twitching my arm.

"Here," she said sharply, reaching for the blotter and shoving it into my fingers.

She wrote in ink on an envelope and pushed it toward me. Holding the blotter in my hand, I stared at the envelope and could not move.

"Blot it," she said.

I could not lift my hand. I knew what she had said; I knew what she wanted me to do; and I had heard her correctly. I wanted to look at her and say something, tell her why I could not move; but my eyes were fixed upon the floor. I could not summon enough courage while she sat there looking at me to reach over the yawning space of twelve inches and blot the wet ink on the envelope.

"Blot it!" she spoke sharply.

Still I could not move or answer.

"Look at me!"

I could not lift my eyes. She reached her hand to my face and I twisted away.

"What's wrong with you?" she demanded.

I began to cry and she drove me from the room. I decided that as soon as night came I would run away. The dinner bell rang and I did not go to the table, but hid in a corner of the hallway. When I heard the dishes rattling at the table, I opened the door and ran down the walk to the street. Dusk was falling. Doubt made me stop. Ought I go back? No; hunger was back there, and fear. I went on, coming to concrete sidewalks. People passed me. Where was I going? I did not know. The farther I walked the more frantic I became. In a confused and vague way I knew that I was doing more running *away* from than running *toward* something. I stopped. The streets seemed dangerous. The buildings were massive and dark. The moon shone and the trees loomed frighteningly. No, I could not go on. I would go back. But I had walked so far and had turned too many corners and had not kept track of the direction. Which way led back to the orphan home? I did not know. I was lost.

I stood in the middle of the sidewalk and cried. A "white" policeman came to me and I wondered if he was going to beat me. He asked me what was the matter and I told him that I was trying to find my mother. His "white" face created a new fear in me. I was remembering the tale of the "white" man who had beaten the "black" boy. A crowd gathered and I was urged to tell where I lived. Curiously, I was too full of fear to cry now. I wanted to tell the "white" face that I had run off from an orphan home and that Miss Simon ran it, but I was afraid. Finally I was taken to the police station where I was fed. I felt better. I sat in a big chair where I was surrounded by "white" policemen, but they seemed to ignore me. Through the window I could see that night had completely fallen and that lights now gleamed in the streets. I grew sleepy and dozed. My shoulder was shaken gently and I opened my eyes and looked into a "white" face of another policeman who was sitting beside me. He asked me questions in a quiet, confidential tone, and quite before I knew it he was not "white" any more. I told him that I had run

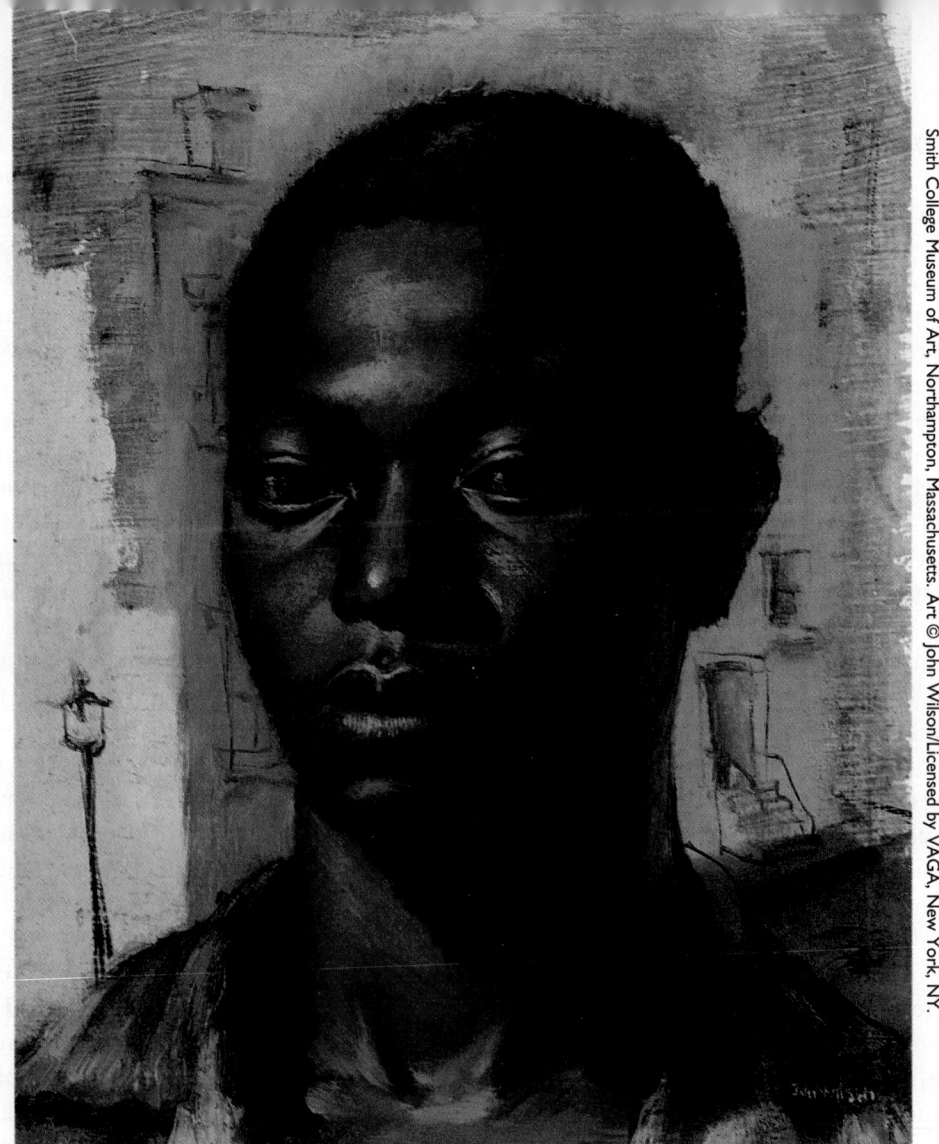

*My Brother* (1942) by John Wilson (American 1922–    ). Oil on panel. (12″ × 10⅝″).

away from an orphan home and that Miss Simon ran it.

It was but a matter of minutes before I was walking alongside a policeman, heading toward the home. The policeman led me to the front gate and I saw Miss Simon waiting for me on the steps. She identified me and I was left in her charge. I begged her not to beat me, but she yanked me upstairs into an empty room and lashed me thoroughly. Sobbing, I slunk off to bed, resolved to run away again. But I was watched closely after that.

My mother was informed upon her next visit that I had tried to run away and she was terribly upset.

"Why did you do it?" she asked.

"I don't want to stay here," I told her.

"But you must," she said. "How can I work if I'm to worry about you? You must remember that you have no father. I'm doing all I can."

"I don't want to stay here," I repeated.

"Then, if I take you to your father . . ."

"I don't want to stay with him either," I said.

"But I want you to ask him for enough money for us to go to my sister's in Arkansas," she said.

Again I was faced with choices I did not like, but I finally agreed. After all, my hate for my father was not so great and urgent as my hate for the orphan home. My mother held to her idea and one night a week or so later I found myself standing in a room in a frame house. My father and a strange woman were sitting before a bright fire that blazed in a grate. My mother and I were standing about six feet away, as though we were afraid to approach them any closer.

"It's not for me," my mother was saying. "It's for your children that I'm asking you for money."

"I ain't got nothing," my father said, laughing.

"Come here, boy," the strange woman called to me.

I looked at her and did not move.

"Give him a nickel," the woman said. "He's cute."

"Come here, Richard," my father said, stretching out his hand.

I backed away, shaking my head, keeping my eyes on the fire.

"He is a cute child," the strange woman said.

"You ought to be ashamed," my mother said to the strange woman. "You're starving my children."

"Now, don't you-all fight," my father said, laughing.

"I'll take that poker and hit you!" I blurted at my father.

He looked at my mother and laughed louder.

"You told him to say that," he said.

"Don't say such things, Richard," my mother said.

"You ought to be dead," I said to the strange woman.

The woman laughed and threw her arms about my father's neck. I grew ashamed and wanted to leave.

"How can you starve your children?" my mother asked.

"Let Richard stay with me," my father said.

"Do you want to stay with your father, Richard?" my mother asked.

"No," I said.

"You'll get plenty to eat," he said.

"I'm hungry now," I told him. "But I won't stay with you."

"Aw, give the boy a nickel," the woman said.

My father ran his hand into his pocket and pulled out a nickel.

"Here, Richard," he said.

"Don't take it," my mother said.

"Don't teach him to be a fool," my father said. "Here, Richard, take it."

I looked at my mother, at the strange woman, at my father, then into the fire. I wanted to take the nickel, but I did not want to take it from my father.

"You ought to be ashamed," my mother said, weeping. "Giving your son a nickel when he's hungry. If there's a God, He'll pay you back."

"That's all I got," my father said, laughing again and returning the nickel to his pocket.

We left. I had the feeling that I had had to do with something unclean. Many times in the years after that the image of my father and the strange woman, their faces lit by the dancing flames, would surge up in my imagination so vivid and strong that I felt I could reach out and touch it; I would stare at it, feeling that it possessed some vital meaning which always eluded me.

A quarter of a century was to elapse between the time when I saw my father sitting with the strange woman and the time when I was to see him again, standing alone upon the red clay of a Mississippi plantation, a sharecropper,° clad in ragged overalls, holding a muddy hoe in his gnarled, veined hands—a quarter of a century during which my mind and consciousness had become so greatly and violently altered that when I tried to talk to him I realized that, though ties of blood made us kin, though I could see a shadow of my face in his face, though there was an echo of my voice in his voice, we were forever strangers, speaking a different language, living on vastly distant planes

---

°**sharecropper** *n.*: farmer who works a piece of land for its owner and gets a small portion of the crop in return.

**Vocabulary**

**eluded** (ē·loōd′id) *v.*: escaped detection or notice.

of reality. That day a quarter of a century later when I visited him on the plantation—he was standing against the sky, smiling toothlessly, his hair whitened, his body bent, his eyes glazed with dim recollection, his fearsome aspect of twenty-five years ago gone forever from him—I was overwhelmed to realize that he could never understand me or the scalding experiences that had swept me beyond his life and into an area of living that he could never know. I stood before him, poised, my mind aching as it embraced the simple nakedness of his life, feeling how completely his soul was imprisoned by the slow flow of the seasons, by wind and rain and sun, how fastened were his memories to a crude and raw past, how chained were his actions and emotions to the direct, animalistic impulses of his withering body . . .

From the white landowners above him there had not been handed to him a chance to learn the meaning of loyalty, of sentiment, of tradition. Joy was as unknown to him as was despair.

As a creature of the earth, he endured, hearty, whole, seemingly indestructible, with no regrets and no hope. He asked easy, drawling questions about me, his other son, his wife, and he laughed, amused, when I informed him of their destinies. I forgave him and pitied him as my eyes looked past him to the unpainted wooden shack. From far beyond the horizons that bound this bleak plantation there had come to me through my living the knowledge that my father was a black peasant who had gone to the city seeking life, but who had failed in the city; a black peasant whose life had been hopelessly snarled in the city, and who had at last fled the city—that same city which had lifted me in its burning arms and borne me toward alien and undreamed-of shores of knowing. ∎

**Vocabulary**

**withering** (with′ər·iŋ) v. used as *adj.*: drying up; weakening.

# Response and Analysis

**SKILLS FOCUS**

**Literary Skills**
Analyze dialogue in nonfiction.

**Writing Skills**
Write an essay analyzing a character.

**Vocabulary Skills**
Understand synonyms.

## Reading Check

1. What was life like for Richard and his family when they arrived in Memphis?

2. What happened when Richard went to buy groceries?

3. How did Richard's father behave in the courtroom scene and when Richard and his mother went to see him at home?

4. How did Richard feel about his father during most of his childhood?

## Thinking Critically

5. What **details** does Wright use to make the reader feel the physical and emotional hunger he experienced as a boy?

6. When Richard's mother sent him back to face the boys who robbed him, what lesson was she trying to teach him? What else could she have done?

7. Why couldn't Richard eat his soup while the preacher was devouring the chicken? What does this incident reveal about the boy's **character**?

8. Wright uses vivid **dialogue** to dramatize scenes of great emotional conflict between Richard and people he was forced to depend on. Find and read two of these scenes aloud, and then discuss what they reveal about Richard's emotions.

9. On page 1073, Wright describes his feelings about the white policeman who took him to the police station. At first Wright was scared but then he remarks, ". . . before I knew it he was not 'white' any more." What does his initial fear of the policeman and then this later comment reveal about Wright's beliefs about white people at the time?

10. Remembering his father and the strange woman, "their faces lit by the dancing flames," Wright says this **image** "possessed some vital meaning which always eluded me" (page 1075). What do you think he means?

11. When Wright saw his father again after twenty-five years, what did he realize about his father? How was the city's effect on his father different from its effect on Wright himself?

### Extending and Evaluating

12. Review Wright's use of **dialogue** in this portion of his autobiography. Does the use of dialogue Wright could not possibly have accurately recalled detract from the power or authority of his story? Discuss your responses in class.

## WRITING

### "The Simple Nakedness of His Life . . ."

In a short **essay,** analyze the **character** of Wright's father as Wright presents him. Consider the father when he lived in Memphis and, twenty-five years later, when he lived as a sharecropper in rural Mississippi. Had the father changed a great deal over the years? Had Wright himself changed? What assessment did Wright make of his father at the end? Do you think his evaluation fits the facts of his father's life? Before you write, collect details for your analysis in a chart like the following one:

|  | Details from Text |
| --- | --- |
| Father's words and actions in Memphis |  |
| Father's words and actions 25 years later |  |
| General assessment of father |  |

▶ Use "Analyzing Literature," pages 739–740, for more help with this assignment.

House in rural Tennessee (1945).

### Vocabulary Development

#### Synonym Maps

| enthralled | frenzy | futile |
| --- | --- | --- |
| clamor | ardently | eluded |
| dispirited | copiously | withering |

Use a dictionary or a thesaurus to find a synonym for each Vocabulary word. Then, go back to the text, and replace each Vocabulary word with the synonym you have found. For each word, decide whether the synonym works as well, or not as well, in the context of the sentence. See the following example:

```
      clamor

     Synonym
      noise
```

**Sentence**

Whenever I begged for food now my mother would pour me a cup of tea which would still the **noise** in my stomach for a moment or two.

**Judgment**

*Noise* could also work, but *clamor* suggests a person complaining loudly and is more powerful.

# Grammar Link

## Using Parallel Structure: Keeping Things in Balance

You create **parallel structure** when you state equal, or parallel, ideas in the same grammatical form. In this sentence from *Black Boy,* notice how Richard Wright uses parallelism. All the underlined phrases start with the preposition *of* and end with a noun.

| PARALLEL | "From the white landowners above him there had not been handed to him a chance to learn the meaning of loyalty, of sentiment, of tradition." |
|---|---|

If Wright had written the following sentence, he would have created a grammatical error. The underlined words are not in parallel grammatical form.

| NOT PARALLEL | From the white landowners above him there had not been handed to him a chance to learn the meaning of loyalty, sentiment, of having tradition. |
|---|---|

The key to parallel structure is balance: You must pair a noun with a noun, a verb with a verb, a prepositional phrase with a prepositional phrase, a clause with the same kind of clause. In the following sentence the underlined elements are *not* parallel in structure:

| NOT PARALLEL | To read *Black Boy* will teach people more about the African American experience than listening to rap music. [*To read* is an infinitive paired with *listening,* a gerund.] |
|---|---|

*To read* is an infinitive, but *listening* is a gerund. You can correct the error and make the verbs parallel by using the same grammatical form for both verbs.

| PARALLEL | Reading *Black Boy* will teach people more about the African American experience than listening to rap music. [gerund paired with gerund] |
|---|---|

**SKILLS FOCUS**

**Grammar Skills**
Use parallel structure.

Drafts of Wright's writings.

(Above and right) Yale Collection of American Literature, Beinecke Rare Book and Manuscript Library.

Following are some situations in which you'll want to check your sentences for parallel structure:

- Linking ideas by using **coordinating conjunctions** (such as *and, but, or, nor,* and *yet*)

  Wright's mother tells the judge <u>that her husband has deserted his family</u> **and** <u>that their children are hungry.</u> [noun clause paired with noun clause]

- Connecting several ideas in a series

  The boys were <u>yelling,</u> <u>nursing</u> their heads, and <u>staring</u> at Wright in disbelief. [three verbs in the present progressive]

- Linking ideas by using **correlative conjunctions** (pairs of words such as *either . . . or, neither . . . nor,* and *both . . . and*)

  Wright **not only** <u>threatens</u> to hit his father with a poker **but also** <u>tells</u> his companion that she ought to be dead. [verb paired with verb]

### Apply to Your Writing

Re-read a current writing assignment or one that you've already completed. Correct any examples of faulty parallelism, paying particular attention to the situations discussed above.

▶ **For more help, see Using Parallel Structure, 9c, in the Language Handbook.**

PRACTICE

In the following sentences, correct any examples of faulty parallelism:

1. Richard Wright is most famous for the novel *Native Son* and for having written the autobiography *Black Boy.*

2. In this excerpt from *Black Boy,* Wright decides that it would be worse to get beaten at home than if he got beat up on the streets.

3. Wright's father is neither generous nor does he show remorse.

4. When Wright visits his father twenty-five years later, he feels forgiveness, pity, and that he understands the old man.

# Maxine Hong Kingston

## (1940–    )

Maxine Hong Kingston burst onto the literary scene in 1976 with an extraordinary and innovative book—*The Woman Warrior: Memoirs of a Girlhood Among Ghosts.* Kingston, who was born in California of Chinese immigrant parents, uses a mixture of autobiography, myth, poetic meditation, and fiction to convey her memories and feelings about growing up in a strange world (the United States) populated by what she and her family thought of as white-skinned "ghosts."

The book received immediate acclaim. William McPherson of *The Washington Post* wrote: "*The Woman Warrior* is a strange, sometimes savagely terrifying and, in the literal sense, wonderful story about growing up caught between two highly sophisticated and utterly alien cultures, both vivid, often menacing, and equally mysterious." Paul Gray said in *Time:* "Exiles and refugees tell sad stories of the life they left behind. Even sadder, sometimes, is the muteness of their children. They are likely to find the old ways and old language excess baggage, especially if their adopted homeland is the United States, where the race is to the swift and the adaptable. Thus a heritage of centuries can die in a generation of embarrassed silence. *The Woman Warrior* gives that silence a voice."

When *The Woman Warrior* won the National Book Critics Circle Award for general nonfiction in 1976, Kingston gained national attention. The suddenness of her appearance as an important literary figure was startling.

Where had Kingston been until the age of thirty-six? Named for an American woman in the gambling house where her father worked for a time, Maxine Hong grew up in the Chinatown of Stockton, California. She earned a B.A. from the University of California at Berkeley in 1962 and married the actor Earll Kingston. After their son was born, the Kingstons lived in Hawaii for a time, where Maxine taught English at the high school and college levels, before returning to California.

In 1980, Kingston published a companion piece to *The Woman Warrior,* a kind of ancestral history called *China Men.* The critic Susan Currier has described this book as "a sort of vindication of all the Chinese who helped build America but who were rewarded with abuse and neglect." In 1988, Kingston published an extravagant novel called *Tripmaster Monkey: His Fake Book,* blending Chinese history and myth and vivid storytelling in the adventures of a young Chinese American named Wittman Ah Sing. The noted novelist Anne Tyler called *Tripmaster Monkey* "a novel of satisfying complexity and bite and verve." In the 1990s, Kingston taught creative writing at the University of California at Berkeley and worked on a book of nonfiction.

Despite the attention given to her books, Kingston has remained relatively private. She seldom gives interviews or appears at public readings. In her two memoirs she does not answer all of the personal questions raised by her writing. In the selection that follows, even a careful reader will not be able to decide what is truth, what is fiction, and what is simply left unsaid. This ambiguity gives Kingston's work much of its haunting quality.

# The Girl Who Wouldn't Talk

## Make the Connection

It happens just about every day to all of us. For one reason or another, we don't tell others what we really think or feel about something important. Out of self-doubt, politeness, fear, or even because we are trying to keep the truth from ourselves, we are silent. Sometimes we act out what we don't say in ways that hurt ourselves and others, but at other times we find positive ways that express our feelings in writing, painting, music, or some other art form.

## Literary Focus
### Characterization

Just like fiction writers, nonfiction writers use all the devices of **characterization** to bring the people in their texts to life. It is the expert use of these fictional devices that sometimes makes us feel as if we are reading fiction—when what we are reading is supposed to be factually true.

Maxine Hong Kingston reveals the personalities of her narrator and of the other characters in her **memoir** (mem′wär′) by describing how they look, dress, act, and speak (including *if* they speak). She also shows us how her characters affect other people and what other people think of them. Since Kingston writes in the first person, we are also given access to the private thoughts and feelings of the narrator.

> **Characterization** is the process by which a writer reveals the personality of a character.
>
> *For more on Character, see the Handbook of Literary and Historical Terms.*

## Reading Skills
### Drawing Inferences About Characters

As you read, take notes on how the writer characterizes the narrator and the silent girl. Look for clues that reveal how the narrator views her white American classmates and how she feels about them. Then, stop near the top of page 1088, and write down what you think the silent girl is *not* saying—that is, what are her unexpressed thoughts and feelings? You might also jot down what you think the narrator is not saying.

## Background

The Chinese American family in this excerpt from *The Woman Warrior* lives in Stockton, California. Just before the episode starts, the narrator describes Chinese voices, which she says are louder than American voices. Describing her own voice, the narrator says, "You could hear splinters in my voice, bones rubbing jagged against one another. I was loud, though. I was glad I didn't whisper."

The "ghosts" mentioned by the narrator are white Americans, who seemed so strange to this Chinese family.

> ## Vocabulary Development
>
> **loitered** (loit′ərd) *v.*: spent time; hung around.
>
> **nape** *n.*: back of the neck.
>
> **habitually** (hə·bich′ oo·ə·lē) *adv.*: usually; by habit.
>
> **sarcastic** (sär·kas′tik) *adj.*: scornful; mocking.
>
> **temples** (tem′pəlz) *n. pl.*: sides of the forehead, just above and in front of the ears.

**SKILLS FOCUS**

**Literary Skills**
Understand characterization.

**Reading Skills**
Make inferences about characters.

**INTERNET**

Vocabulary Practice

Keyword: LE7 11-6

# The Girl Who Wouldn't Talk

*from* **The Woman Warrior**

Maxine Hong Kingston

Normal Chinese women's voices are strong and bossy. We American-Chinese girls had to whisper to make ourselves American-feminine. Apparently we whispered even more softly than the Americans. Once a year the teachers referred my sister and me to speech therapy, but our voices would straighten out, unpredictably normal, for the therapists. Some of us gave up, shook our heads, and said nothing, not one word. Some of us could not even shake our heads. At times shaking my head no is more self-assertion than I can manage. Most of us eventually found some voice, however faltering. We invented an American-feminine speaking personality, except for that one girl who could not speak up even in Chinese school.

She was a year older than I and was in my class for twelve years. During all those years she read aloud but would not talk. Her older sister was usually beside her; their parents kept the older daughter back to protect the younger one. They were six and seven years old when they began school. Although I had flunked kindergarten, I was the same age as most other students in our class; my parents had probably lied about my age, so I had had a head start and came out even. My younger sister was in the class below me; we were normal ages and normally separated. The parents of the quiet girl, on the other hand, protected both daughters. When it sprinkled, they kept them home from school. The girls did not work for a living the way we did. But in other ways we were the same.

We were similar in sports. We held the bat on our shoulders until we walked to first base. (You got a strike only when you actually struck at the ball.) Sometimes the pitcher wouldn't bother to throw to us. "Automatic walk," the other children would call, sending us on our way. By fourth or fifth grade, though, some of us would try to hit the ball. "Easy out," the other kids would say. I hit the ball a couple of times. Baseball was nice in that there was a definite spot to run to after hitting the ball. Basketball confused me because when I caught the ball I didn't know whom to throw it to. "Me. Me," the kids would

be yelling. "Over here." Suddenly it would occur to me I hadn't memorized which ghosts were on my team and which were on the other. When the kids said, "Automatic walk," the girl who was quieter than I kneeled with one end of the bat in each hand and placed it carefully on the plate. Then she dusted her hands as she walked to first base, where she rubbed her hands softly, fingers spread. She always got tagged out before second base. She would whisper-read but not talk. Her whisper was as soft as if she had no muscles. She seemed to be breathing from a distance. I heard no anger or tension.

I joined in at lunchtime when the other students, the Chinese too, talked about whether or not she was mute, although obviously she was not if she could read aloud. People told how *they* had tried *their* best to be friendly. *They* said hello, but if she refused to answer, well, they didn't see why they had to say hello anymore. She had no friends of her own but followed her sister everywhere, although people and she herself probably thought I was her friend. I also followed her sister about, who was fairly normal. She was almost two years older and read more than anyone else.

I hated the younger sister, the quiet one. I hated her when she was the last chosen for her team and I, the last chosen for my team. I hated her for her China doll hair cut. I hated her at music time for the wheezes that came out of her plastic flute.

One afternoon in the sixth grade (that year I was arrogant with talk, not knowing there were going to be high school dances and college seminars to set me back), I and my little sister and the quiet girl and her big sister stayed late after school for some reason. The cement was cooling, and the tetherball poles made shadows across the gravel. The hooks at the rope ends were clinking against the poles. We shouldn't have been so late; there was laundry work to do and Chinese school to get to by 5:00. The last time we had stayed late, my mother had phoned the police and told them we had been kidnapped by bandits. The radio stations broadcast our descriptions. I had to get home before she did that again. But sometimes if you loitered long enough in the schoolyard, the other children would have gone home and you could play with the equipment before the office took it away. We were chasing one another through the playground and in and out of the basement, where the playroom and lavatory were. During air raid drills (it was during the Korean War, which you knew about because every day the front page of the newspaper printed a map of Korea with the top part red and going up and down like a window shade), we curled up in this basement. Now everyone was gone. The playroom was army green and had nothing in it but a long trough with drinking spigots in rows. Pipes across the ceiling led to the drinking fountains and to the toilets in the next room. When someone flushed you could hear the water and other matter, which the children named, running inside the big pipe above the drinking spigots. There was one playroom for girls next to the girls' lavatory and one playroom for boys next to the boys' lavatory. The stalls were open and the toilets had no lids, by which we knew that ghosts have no sense of shame or privacy.

Inside the playroom the lightbulbs in cages had already been turned off. Daylight came in x-patterns through the caging at the windows. I looked out and, seeing no one in the school-yard, ran outside to climb the fire escape upside down, hanging on to the metal stairs with fin-gers and toes.

I did a flip off the fire escape and ran across the schoolyard. The day was a great eye, and it was not paying much attention to me now. I could disappear with the sun; I could turn quickly sideways and slip into a different world. It seemed I could run faster at this time, and by evening I would be able to fly. As the afternoon wore on we could run into the forbidden places—the boys' big yard, the boys' playroom. We could go into the boys' lavatory and look at the urinals. The only time during school hours I had crossed the boys' yard was when a flatbed truck with a giant thing covered with canvas and tied down with ropes had parked across the

street. The children had told one another that it was a gorilla in captivity; we couldn't decide whether the sign said "Trail of the Gorilla" or "Trial of the Gorilla." The thing was as big as a house. The teachers couldn't stop us from hys-terically rushing to the fence and clinging to the wire mesh. Now I ran across the boys' yard clear to the Cyclone fence and thought about the hair that I had seen sticking out of the canvas. It was going to be summer soon, so you could feel that freedom coming on too.

I ran back into the girls' yard, and there was the quiet sister all by herself. I ran past her, and she followed me into the girls' lavatory. My foot-steps rang hard against cement and tile because of the taps I had nailed into my shoes. Her foot-steps were soft, padding after me. There was no one in the lavatory but the two of us. I ran all around the rows of twenty-five open stalls to make sure of that. No sisters. I think we must have been playing hide-and-go-seek. She was not good at hiding by herself and usually followed her sister; they'd hide in the same place. They must have gotten separated. In this growing twi-light, a child could hide and never be found.

I stopped abruptly in front of the sinks, and she came running toward me before she could stop herself, so that she almost collided with me. I walked closer. She backed away, puzzle-ment, then alarm in her eyes.

"You're going to talk," I said, my voice steady and normal, as it is when talking to the familiar, the weak, and the small. "I am going to make you talk, you sissy-girl." She stopped backing away and stood fixed.

I looked into her face so I could hate it close up. She wore black bangs, and her cheeks were pink and white. She was baby-soft. I thought that I could put my thumb on her nose and push it bonelessly in, indent her face. I could poke dimples into her cheeks. I could work her face around like dough. She stood still, and I did not want to look at her face anymore; I hated

---

**Vocabulary**

**loitered** (loit'ərd) v.: spent time; hung around.

fragility. I walked around her, looked her up and down the way the Mexican and Negro girls did when they fought, so tough. I hated her weak neck, the way it did not support her head but let it droop; her head would fall backward. I stared at the curve of her nape. I wished I was able to see what my own neck looked like from the back and sides. I hoped it did not look like hers; I wanted a stout neck. I grew my hair long to hide it in case it was a flower-stem neck. I walked around to the front of her to hate her face some more.

I reached up and took the fatty part of her cheek, not dough, but meat, between my thumb and finger. This close, and I saw no pores. "Talk," I said. "Are you going to talk?" Her skin was fleshy, like squid out of which the glassy blades of bones had been pulled. I wanted tough skin, hard brown skin. I had callused my hands; I had scratched dirt to blacken the nails, which I cut straight across to make stubby fingers. I gave her face a squeeze. "Talk." When I let go, the pink rushed back into my white thumbprint on her skin. I walked around to her side. "Talk!" I shouted into the side of her head. Her straight hair hung, the same all these years, no ringlets or braids or permanents. I squeezed her other cheek. "Are you? Huh? Are you going to talk?" She tried to shake her head, but I had hold of her face. She had no muscles to jerk away. Her skin seemed to stretch. I let go in horror. What if it came away in my hand? "No, huh?" I said, rubbing the touch of her off my fingers. "Say 'No,' then," I said. I gave her another pinch and a twist. "Say 'No.'" She shook her head, her straight hair turning with her head, not swinging side to side like the pretty girls'. She was so neat. Her neatness bothered me. I hated the way she folded the wax paper from her lunch; she did not wad her

brown paper bag and her school papers. I hated her clothes—the blue pastel cardigan, the white blouse with the collar that lay flat over the cardigan, the homemade flat, cotton skirt she wore when everybody else was wearing flared skirts. I hated pastels; I would wear black always. I squeezed again, harder, even though her cheek had a weak rubbery feeling I did not like. I squeezed one cheek, then the other, back and forth until the tears ran out of her eyes as if I had pulled them out. "Stop crying," I said, but although she habitually followed me around, she did not obey. Her eyes dripped; her nose dripped. She wiped her eyes with her papery fingers. The skin on her hands and arms seemed powdery-dry, like tracing paper, onion paper. I hated her fingers. I could snap them like breadsticks. I pushed her hands down. "Say 'Hi,'" I said. "'Hi.' Like that. Say your name. Go ahead. Say it. Or are you stupid? You're so stupid, you don't know your own name, is that it? When I say, 'What's your name?' you just blurt it out, O.K.? What's your name?" Last year the whole class had laughed at a boy who couldn't fill out a form because he didn't know his father's name. The teacher sighed, exasperated and was very sarcastic, "Don't you notice things? What does your mother call him?" she said. The class laughed at how dumb he was not to notice things. "She calls him father of me," he said. Even we laughed although we knew that his mother did not call his father by name, and a son does not

> "You're going to talk," I said, my voice steady and normal, as it is when talking to the familiar, the weak, and the small. "I am going to make you talk . . ."

---

**Vocabulary**

**nape** *n.:* back of the neck.
**habitually** (hə·bich'ōō·ə·lē) *adv.:* usually; by habit.
**sarcastic** (sär·kas'tik) *adj.:* scornful; mocking.

know his father's name. We laughed and were relieved that our parents had had the foresight to tell us some names we could give the teachers. "If you're not stupid," I said to the quiet girl, "what's your name?" She shook her head, and some hair caught in the tears; wet black hair stuck to the side of the pink and white face. I reached up (she was taller than I) and took a strand of hair. I pulled it. "Well, then, let's honk your hair," I said. "Honk. Honk." Then I pulled the other side—"ho-o-n-nk"—a long pull; "ho-o-n-n-nk"—a longer pull. I could see her little white ears, like white cutworms curled underneath the hair. "Talk!" I yelled into each cutworm.

I looked right at her. "I know you talk," I said. "I've heard you." Her eyebrows flew up. Something in those black eyes was startled, and I pursued it. "I was walking past your house when you didn't know I was there. I heard you yell in English and in Chinese. You weren't just talking.

You were shouting. I heard you shout. You were saying, 'Where are you?' Say that again. Go ahead, just the way you did at home." I yanked harder on the hair, but steadily, not jerking. I did not want to pull it out. "Go ahead. Say, 'Where are you?' Say it loud enough for your sister to come. Call her. Make her come help you. Call her name. I'll stop if she comes. So call. Go ahead."

She shook her head, her mouth curved down, crying. I could see her tiny white teeth, baby teeth. I wanted to grow big strong yellow teeth. "You do have a tongue," I said. "So use it." I pulled the hair at her temples, pulled the tears out of her eyes. "Say, 'Ow'" I said. "Just 'Ow.' Say, 'Let go.' Go ahead. Say it. I'll honk you again

---

**Vocabulary**

**temples** (tem′pəlz) *n. pl.*: sides of the forehead, just above and in front of the ears.

---

## A CLOSER LOOK: CULTURAL INFLUENCES

### The Chinese American Family

In her story, Maxine Hong Kingston mentions that the girl who wouldn't talk was supported and protected by her family. This isn't surprising, given the importance of family relationships in Chinese culture. As the Chinese American writer Leslie Li notes, solitude is not a coveted state among most Chinese people. "They love their family and friends and want them around, along with the *renao* they bring, the heat and noise of human relationships."

**Family ties.** In Chinese culture, one's name does not so much signify individual identity as relationship to others, such as daughter, son, aunt, uncle, and so on. In Chinese tradition the family name is given first—for example, "Chan Jackie," not the Americanized "Jackie Chan"—and family members are often introduced not by their names but by their family relationships. Children may address family members not by name but as Aunt, Second Older Brother, Grandfather, and so on. In Kingston's story a boy is laughed at in class because he doesn't know his father's name; at home, he says, his father is called only "father of me." In the story "Rules of the Game" by the Chinese American writer

**INFORMATIONAL TEXT**

if you don't say, 'Let me alone.' Say, 'Leave me alone,' and I'll let you go. I will. I'll let go if you say it. You can stop this anytime you want to, you know. All you have to do is tell me to stop. Just say, 'Stop.' You're just asking for it, aren't you? You're just asking for another honk. Well then, I'll have to give you another honk. Say, 'Stop.'" But she didn't. I had to pull again and again.

Sounds did come out of her mouth, sobs, chokes, noises that were almost words. Snot ran out of her nose. She tried to wipe it on her hands, but there was too much of it. She used her sleeve. "You're disgusting," I told her. "Look at you, snot streaming down your nose, and you won't say a word to stop it. You're such a nothing." I moved behind her and pulled the hair growing out of her weak neck. I let go. I stood silent for a long time. Then I screamed, "Talk!" I would scare the words out of her. If she had had

little bound feet, the toes twisted under the balls, I would have jumped up and landed on them—crunch!—stomped on them with my iron shoes. She cried hard, sobbing aloud. "Cry, 'Mama,'" I said. "Come on. Cry, 'Mama.' Say, 'Stop it.'"

I put my finger on her pointed chin. "I don't like you. I don't like the weak little toots you make on your flute. Wheeze. Wheeze. I don't like the way you don't swing at the ball. I don't like the way you're the last one chosen. I don't like the way you can't make a fist for tetherball. Why don't you make a fist? Come on. Get tough. Come on. Throw fists." I pushed at her long hands; they swung limply at her sides. Her fingers were so long, I thought maybe they had an extra joint. They couldn't possibly make fists like other people's. "Make a fist," I said. "Come on. Just fold those fingers up; fingers on the inside, thumbs on the outside. Say some-

Amy Tan (page 1017), the character Waverly is called "Waverly" for the benefit of outsiders, but at home she is "Meimei" (Little Sister).

**Bridging two worlds.** Ultimately many Chinese Americans choose to integrate the cultures of both China and the United States in their family life. They embrace some traditional beliefs of their immigrant parents or grandparents, but they also take part in mainstream American traditions. They may celebrate both Chinese and American holidays, for example, or enjoy traditional Chinese foods one day, grilled steak the next. They may use American names with outsiders but their Chinese middle names at home. In addition to attending regular public or private school all day, some Chinese American children spend three or four hours at Chinese school (often held on Saturdays), where their parents expect them to learn Chinese language, literature, history, and philosophy.

thing. Honk me back. You're so tall, and you let me pick on you.

"Would you like a hanky? I can't get you one with embroidery on it or crocheting along the edges, but I'll get you some toilet paper if you tell me to. Go ahead. Ask me. I'll get it for you if you ask." She did not stop crying. "Why don't you scream, 'Help'?" I suggested. "Say, 'Help.' Go ahead." She cried on. "O.K. O.K. Don't talk. Just scream, and I'll let you go. Won't that feel good? Go ahead. Like this." I screamed not too loudly. My voice hit the tile and rang it as if I had thrown a rock at it. The stalls opened wider and the toilets wider and darker. Shadows leaned at angles I had not seen before. It was very late. Maybe a janitor had locked me in with this girl for the night. Her black eyes blinked and stared, blinked and stared. I felt dizzy from hunger. We had been in this lavatory to-gether forever. My mother would call the police again if I didn't bring my sister home soon. "I'll let you go if you say just one word," I said. "You can even say 'a' or 'the,' and I'll let you go. Come on. Please." She didn't shake her head anymore, only cried steadily, so much water coming out of her. I could see the two duct holes where the tears welled out. Quarts of tears but no words. I grabbed her by the shoul-der. I could feel bones. The light was coming in queerly through the frosted glass with the chicken wire embedded in it. Her crying was like an animal's—a seal's—and it echoed around the basement. "Do you want to stay here all night?" I asked. "Your mother is wondering what happened to her baby. You wouldn't want to have her mad at you. You'd better say some-thing." I shook her shoulder. I pulled her hair again. I squeezed her face. "Come on! Talk! Talk! Talk!" She didn't seem to feel it anymore when I pulled her hair. "There's nobody here but you

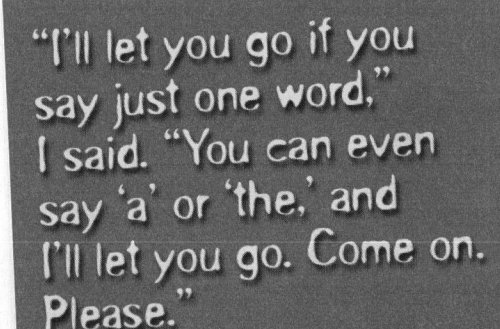

"I'll let you go if you say just one word," I said. "You can even say 'a' or 'the,' and I'll let you go. Come on. Please."

and me. This isn't a classroom or a playground or a crowd. I'm just one person. You can talk in front of one person. Don't make me pull harder and harder until you talk." But her hair seemed to stretch; she did not say a word. "I'm going to pull harder. Don't make me pull anymore, or your hair will come out and you're going to be bald. Do you want to be bald? You don't want to be bald, do you?"

Far away, coming from the edge of town, I heard whistles blow. The cannery was changing shifts, letting out the afternoon people, and still we were here at school. It was a sad sound— work done. The air was lonelier after the sound died.

"Why won't you talk?" I started to cry. What if I couldn't stop, and everyone would want to know what happened? "Now look what you've done," I scolded. "You're going to pay for this. I want to know why. And you're going to tell me why. You don't see I'm try-ing to help you out, do you? Do you want to be like this, dumb (do you know what dumb means?), your whole life? Don't you ever want to be a cheerleader? Or a pom-pom girl? What are you going to do for a living? Yeah, you're going to have to work because you can't be a housewife. Somebody has to marry you before you can be a housewife. And you, you are a plant. Do you know that? That's all you are if you don't talk. If you don't talk, you can't have a personality. You'll have no personal-ity and no hair. You've got to let people know you have a personality and a brain. You think somebody is going to take care of you all your stupid life? You think you'll always have your big sister? You think somebody's going to marry you, is that it? Well, you're not the type that gets dates, let alone gets married. Nobody's going to notice you. And you have to talk for interviews, speak right up in front of the boss. Don't you know that? You're so dumb. Why do I waste my time on you?" Sniffling and snorting, I couldn't stop crying and talking at the same time. I kept wiping my nose on my arm, my sweater lost somewhere (probably not worn because my mother said to wear a sweater). It seemed as if I had spent my life in that basement, doing the worst thing I had yet done to another person. "I'm doing this for your own good," I said. "Don't you dare tell anyone I've been bad to you. Talk. Please talk."

I was getting dizzy from the air I was gulping. Her sobs and my sobs were bouncing wildly off the tile, sometimes together, sometimes alternating. "I don't understand why you won't say just one word," I cried, clenching my teeth. My knees were shaking, and I hung on to her hair to stand up. Another time I'd stayed too late, I had had to walk around two Negro kids who were bonking each other's head on the concrete. I went back later to see if the concrete had cracks in it. "Look. I'll give you something if you talk. I'll give you my pencil box. I'll buy you some candy. O.K.? What do you want? Tell me. Just say it, and I'll give it to you. Just say, 'yes,' or, 'O.K.,' or, 'Baby Ruth.'" But she didn't want anything.

I had stopped pinching her cheek because I did not like the feel of her skin. I would go crazy if it came away in my hands. "I skinned her," I would have to confess.

Suddenly I heard footsteps hurrying through the basement, and her sister ran into the lavatory calling her name. "Oh, there you are," I said. "We've been waiting for you. I was only trying to teach her to talk. She wouldn't cooperate, though." Her sister went into one of the stalls and got handfuls of toilet paper and wiped her off. Then we found my sister, and we walked home together. "Your family really ought to force her to speak," I advised all the way home. "You mustn't pamper her."

The world is sometimes just, and I spent the next eighteen months sick in bed with a mysterious illness. There was no pain and no symptoms, though the middle line in my left palm broke in two. Instead of starting junior high school, I lived like the Victorian recluses° I read about. I had a rented hospital bed in the living room, where I watched soap operas on TV, and my family cranked me up and down. I saw no one but my family, who took good care of me. I could have no visitors, no other relatives, no villagers. My bed was against the west window, and I watched the seasons change the peach tree. I had a bell to ring for help. I used a bedpan. It was the best year and a half of my life. Nothing happened.

But one day my mother, the doctor, said, "You're ready to get up today. It's time to get up and go to school." I walked about outside to get my legs working, leaning on a staff I cut from the peach tree. The sky and trees, the sun were immense—no longer framed by a window, no longer grayed with a fly screen. I sat down on the sidewalk in amazement—the night, the stars. But at school I had to figure out again how to talk. I met again the poor girl I had tormented. She had not changed. She wore the same clothes, hair cut, and manner as when we were in elementary school, no make-up on the pink and white face, while the other Asian girls were starting to tape their eyelids. She continued to be able to read aloud. But there was hardly any reading aloud anymore, less and less as we got into high school.

I was wrong about nobody taking care of her. Her sister became a clerk-typist and stayed unmarried. They lived with their mother and father. She did not have to leave the house except to go to the movies. She was supported. She was protected by her family, as they would normally have done in China if they could have afforded it, not sent off to school with strangers, ghosts, boys. ■

---

°**Victorian recluses:** characters in Victorian novels who, because of some illness or incapacity, lived shut away from the world.

# Response and Analysis

## Reading Check

1. What reasons does the narrator give for hating the silent girl? What do the other students think of the silent one?

2. How does the narrator try to make the silent girl talk? How does the girl respond?

3. What happens to the narrator to make her say that "the world is sometimes just"?

## Thinking Critically

4. The narrator's intense anger seems directed solely at the silent girl, but why is she so angry with her? Perhaps she is angry for other reasons and not admitting her feelings. Is she affected by an **internal conflict**—a struggle occurring in her own mind? Explain your response, using details from the text.

5. The author **characterizes** the narrator by showing us what she says, does, thinks, and feels, but we can also make inferences about her character based on what she does *not* express. What, for example, do you think the narrator does *not* say about her white American classmates? (Check your reading notes.)

6. **Imagery** is the use of language to evoke a picture of a person, a place, or a thing. Find the images that Kingston uses to help us imagine the silent girl's skin, her fingers, her ears, and her crying. What do these images reveal about the narrator's feelings toward the silent girl? What can you infer about the narrator from her description of the girl?

7. The silent girl is obviously able to speak. Why do you think she does not speak? (Review the notes you made while reading.) What do you imagine she is thinking and feeling—but not saying?

8. What inference can you draw from the fact that the narrator says that her time in bed "was the best year and a half of my life"? What discoveries about herself or about the silent girl might she have made during that time?

9. Review *A Closer Look* on pages 1086–1087 about the Chinese American family. Do any details in this feature connect with details in Kingston's memoir? How do you think the story would have differed if the narrator had been a member of a different culture?

## Extending and Evaluating

10. A character's **motivation** is what causes him or her to act the way he or she does. Motivation can come from needs, fears, and desires. What do you think is the motivation behind the narrator's wanting to make the silent girl speak? Do her feelings and actions strike you as believable? Give reasons for your evaluation based on your own experiences.

## WRITING

### Tortured Character

Write a brief **character analysis** of the narrator. (Be sure to review your reading notes.) Focus on how this character is revealed through her words, actions, appearance, private thoughts, and influence on others. Before you write, gather details from the text in a cluster diagram like the one below:

Conclude your analysis by discussing your own assessment of the narrator with a classmate.

# N. Scott Momaday
## (1934–      )

**A**mong American voices, one that has made itself heard at long last is that of the Native American. Previously American Indians were presented in literature and the other arts as the crudest of stereotypes, either as noble, primitive warriors or as fearsome, ignorant savages. One has only to look at westerns—movies from the 1940s and 1950s—to see how blatant the stereotypes were. Even American history textbooks seldom questioned the popular view that the white settlers' gradual "winning" of the West was a virtuous struggle against the unwarranted resistance of American Indians. Few Americans gave much thought either to the moral basis on which the United States expanded or to the history of the American Indians.

When the civil rights movement of the 1950s and 1960s brought discrimination against African Americans to the forefront of public discussion, other minority groups began to demand a fairer social and political standing for themselves. Native Americans spoke loudly and clearly of loss, injustice, and prejudice.

Navarre Scott Momaday was born in Lawton, Oklahoma, of Kiowa ancestry on his father's side, and some Cherokee on his mother's. After receiving an undergraduate degree from the University of New Mexico, Momaday studied creative writing at Stanford University, where he earned a doctorate.

But Momaday broke loose from the standard academic mold with three works grounded in his knowledge of American Indian life: a Pulitzer Prize–winning novel, *House Made of Dawn* (1968), and two memoirs, *The Way to Rainy Mountain* (1969) and *The Names* (1976).

*The Way to Rainy Mountain* is part legend, part history, and part poetry, with striking illustrations by Momaday's father, Alfred Momaday. Following the introduction, Momaday describes Kiowa history in a form that is associative and imagistic; it works on the reader's imagination in subtle ways that do not depend on a straightforward narrative. On one page he sets down a Kiowa myth or legend; on the facing page he places a short excerpt from a traditional history and then a personal memory of his own. In the mind of the reader, the inner truth blends with the outer; emotion mixes with fact.

The Kiowas' journey to Rainy Mountain begins in the hidden mists of time, when a tribe of unknown origin descends from the headwaters of the Yellowstone River eastward to the Black Hills (in present-day South Dakota) and south to the Wichita Mountains. It ends in a cemetery where many of Momaday's Kiowa relatives are buried. Momaday says that "the journey is an evocation of three things in particular: a landscape that is incomparable, a time that is gone forever, and the human spirit, which endures."

The incomparable landscape is the Great Plains, wind-swept and lonely, in turn brilliant with summer sun and buried in winter snows. Momaday's love of the land where he grew up suffuses everything he writes. He reminds us of both the spiritual richness and the rigors of living close to the land, under a wide, open sky, in harmony with the changing seasons. In his work, Momaday has looked at his own particular landscape from so many angles that his pictures often shimmer like prisms.

## *from* The Way to Rainy Mountain

### Make the Connection

Why do we honor the generations that preceded us? Perhaps it's because we realize that not only did they build civilizations and give us life—but also that they *knew* something. We search in thousands of ways for the secrets of what they must have known. We search in history, archaeology, anthropology, art, linguistics, architecture, music, mythology, literature. In many ways, what we are doing as we search for the past is searching for knowledge of ourselves.

### Literary Focus
#### Setting

Like a storyteller, Momaday is a master at describing **setting,** the time and location in which events occur or in which characters are placed. The following excerpt from Momaday's memoir contains descriptions of several settings. In some cases, Momaday's description is made up of just one or two well-chosen images. Note how these settings are used to create mood, or atmosphere.

> **Setting** is the time and location in which events occur or in which characters are placed.
>
> *For more on Setting, see the Handbook of Literary and Historical Terms.*

### Reading Skills
#### Identifying Main Ideas and Supporting Details

As you read (or as you re-read), take notes on Momaday's **main ideas** and their **supporting details.** Use the following format for your notes:

> **Main idea:**
>
> Supporting detail:
>
> Supporting detail:

### Background

This excerpt from *The Way to Rainy Mountain* is not a straightforward narrative. Momaday uses frequent **flashbacks** to earlier times, and he often omits transitional passages. The text is like a poem in which the narrator traces, in his imagination, the heroic and ultimately tragic history of his people, the Kiowas.

### Vocabulary Development

**infirm** (in·fʉrm′) *adj.*: physically weak.

**preeminently** (prē·em′ə·nənt·lē) *adv.*: above all else.

**luxuriant** (lug·zhoor′ē·ənt) *adj.*: rich; abundant.

**tenuous** (ten′yoo·əs) *adj.*: slight; insubstantial; not firm.

**wariness** (wer′ē·nis) *n.*: carefulness; caution.

**disperse** (di·spʉrs′) *v.*: scatter.

**opaque** (ō·pāk′) *adj.*: not transparent; not letting light pass through.

**vital** (vīt′′l) *adj.*: filled with life.

**enmities** (en′mə·tēz) *n. pl.*: hatreds.

**indulge** (in·dulj′) *v.*: satisfy; please; humor.

**INTERNET**

**Vocabulary Practice**

Keyword: LE7 11-6

Kosahn, a blind Kiowa woman, at Carnegie, Oklahoma, powwow (1946). Photo by Pierre Tartoue.

Tartoue Negative Collection, 20912.14.150. Research Division of the Oklahoma Historical Society.

*from*

# THE WAY TO RAINY MOUNTAIN

## N. Scott Momaday

A single knoll rises out of the plain in Oklahoma north and west of the Wichita Range. For my people, the Kiowas, it is an old landmark, and they gave it the name Rainy Mountain. The hardest weather in the world is there. Winter brings blizzards, hot tornadic winds arise in the spring, and in summer the prairie is an anvil's edge. The grass turns brittle and brown, and it cracks beneath your feet. There are green belts along the rivers and creeks, linear groves of hickory and pecan, willow and witch hazel. At a distance in July or August the steaming foliage seems almost to writhe in fire. Great green and yellow grasshoppers are everywhere in the tall grass, popping up like corn to sting the flesh, and tortoises crawl about on the red earth, going nowhere in the plenty of time. Loneliness is an aspect of the land. All things in the plain are isolate; there is no confusion of objects in the eye, but *one* hill or *one* tree or *one* man. To look upon that landscape in the early morning, with the sun at your back, is to lose the sense of proportion. Your imagination comes to life, and this, you think, is where Creation was begun. ❶

Devils Tower, Wyoming.

**❶** Why is Rainy Mountain so important to the writer?

I returned to Rainy Mountain in July. My grandmother had died in the spring, and I wanted to be at her grave. She had lived to be very old and at last infirm. Her only living daughter was with her when she died, and I was told that in death her face was that of a child.

I like to think of her as a child. When she was born, the Kiowas were living that last great moment of their history. For more than a hundred years they had controlled the open range from the Smoky Hill River to the Red, from the headwaters of the Canadian to the fork of the Arkansas and Cimarron. In alliance with the Comanches, they had ruled the whole of the southern Plains. War was their sacred business, and they were among the finest horsemen the world has ever known. But warfare for the Kiowas was preeminently a matter of disposition rather than of survival, and they never understood the grim, unrelenting advance of the U.S. Cavalry. When at last, divided and ill-provisioned, they were driven onto the Staked Plains in the cold rains of autumn, they fell into panic. In Palo Duro Canyon they abandoned their crucial stores to pillage[1] and had nothing then but their lives. In order to save themselves, they surrendered to the soldiers at Fort Sill and were imprisoned in the old stone corral that now stands as a military museum. My grandmother was spared the humiliation of those high gray walls by eight or ten years, but she must have known from birth the affliction of defeat, the dark brooding of old warriors. ❷

**❷** Why did the Kiowas surrender to the U.S. Cavalry?

Her name was Aho, and she belonged to the last culture to evolve in North America. Her forebears came down from the high country in western Montana nearly three centuries ago. They were a mountain people, a mysterious tribe of hunters whose language has never been positively classified in any major group. In the late seventeenth century they began a long migration to the south and east. It was a journey toward the dawn, and it led to a golden age. Along the way the Kiowas were befriended by the Crows, who gave them the culture and religion of the Plains. They acquired horses, and their ancient nomadic spirit was suddenly free

---

1. **pillage** *n.*: loot; that which is stolen.

---

**Vocabulary**

**infirm** (in·furm′) *adj.*: physically weak.
**preeminently** (prē·em′ə·nənt·lē) *adv.*: above all else.

of the ground. They acquired Tai-me, the sacred Sun Dance doll, from that moment the object and symbol of their worship, and so shared in the divinity of the sun. Not least, they acquired the sense of destiny, therefore courage and pride. When they entered upon the southern Plains they had been transformed. No longer were they slaves to the simple necessity of survival; they were a lordly and dangerous society of fighters and thieves, hunters and priests of the sun. According to their origin myth, they entered the world through a hollow log. From one point of view, their migration was the fruit of an old prophecy, for indeed they emerged from a sunless world. ❸

> ❸
> **?** How did the Kiowas become transformed as a result of their long migration south and east?

Although my grandmother lived out her long life in the shadow of Rainy Mountain, the immense landscape of the continental interior lay like memory in her blood. She could tell of the Crows, whom she had never seen, and of the Black Hills, where she had never been. I wanted to see in reality what she had seen more perfectly in the mind's eye, and traveled fifteen hundred miles to begin my pilgrimage. ❹

> ❹
> **?** Why did the narrator decide to return to Rainy Mountain?

Yellowstone, it seemed to me, was the top of the world, a region of deep lakes and dark timber, canyons and waterfalls. But, beautiful as it is, one might have the sense of confinement there. The skyline in all directions is close at hand, the high wall of the woods and deep cleavages of shade. There is a perfect freedom in the mountains, but it belongs to the eagle and the elk, the badger and the bear. The Kiowas reckoned their stature by the distance they could see, and they were bent and blind in the wilderness.

Descending eastward, the highland meadows are a stairway to the plain. In July the inland slope of the Rockies is luxuriant with flax and buckwheat, stonecrop and larkspur. The earth unfolds and the limit of the land recedes. Clus-

ters of trees, and animals grazing far in the distance, cause the vision to reach away and wonder to build upon the mind. The sun follows a longer course in the day, and the sky is immense beyond all comparison. The great billowing clouds that sail upon it are shadows that move upon the grain like water, dividing light. Farther down, in the land of the Crows and Blackfeet, the plain is yellow. Sweet clover takes hold of the hills and bends upon itself to cover and seal the soil. There the Kiowas paused on their way; they had come to the place where they must change their lives. The sun is at home on the plains. Precisely there does it have the certain character of a god. When the Kiowas came to the land of the Crows, they could see the dark lees[2] of the hills at dawn across the Bighorn River, the profusion of light on the grain shelves, the oldest deity ranging after the solstices.[3] Not yet would they veer southward to the caldron of the land that lay below; they must wean their blood from the northern winter and hold the mountains a while longer in their view. They bore Tai-me in procession to the east. ❺

> ❺
> **?** What does this paragraph tell you about the Kiowas' religious beliefs?

A dark mist lay over the Black Hills, and the land was like iron. At the top of a ridge I caught sight of Devils Tower upthrust against the gray sky as if in the birth of time the core of the earth had broken through its crust and the motion of the world was begun. There are things in nature that engender[4] an awful quiet in the heart of man; Devils Tower is one of them. Two centuries ago, because they could not do otherwise, the Kiowas made a legend at the base of the rock. My grandmother said:

---

2. **lees** *n. pl.*: shelters.
3. **solstices** *n. pl.*: The solstices are the points where the sun is farthest north and farthest south of the celestial equator, creating the longest day (June 21) and the shortest day (December 21) of sunlight in the Northern Hemisphere.
4. **engender** *v.*: cause; produce.

**Vocabulary**
**luxuriant** (lug·zhoor′ē·ənt) *adj.*: rich; abundant.

*Eight children were there at play, seven sisters and their brother. Suddenly the boy was struck dumb; he trembled and began to run upon his hands and feet. His fingers became claws, and his body was covered with fur. Directly there was a bear where the boy had been. The sisters were terrified; they ran, and the bear after them. They came to the stump of a great tree, and the tree spoke to them. It bade them climb upon it, and as they did so it began to rise into the air. The bear came to kill them, but they were just beyond its reach. It reared against the tree and scored the bark all around with its claws. The seven sisters were borne into the sky, and they became the stars of the Big Dipper.*

From that moment, and so long as the legend lives, the Kiowas have kinsmen in the night sky. Whatever they were in the mountains, they could be no more. However tenuous their well-being, however much they had suffered and would suffer again, they had found a way out of the wilderness. ❻

> ❻
> **?** What does it mean that the Kiowas "have kinsmen in the night sky"?

My grandmother had a reverence for the sun, a holy regard that now is all but gone out of mankind. There was a <u>wariness</u> in her, and an ancient awe. She was a Christian in her later years, but she had come a long way about, and she never forgot her birthright. As a child she had been to the Sun Dances; she had taken part in those annual rites, and by them she had learned the restoration of her people in the presence of Tai-me. She was about seven when the last Kiowa Sun Dance was held in 1887 on the Washita River above Rainy Mountain Creek. The buffalo were gone. In order to consummate[5] the ancient sacrifice—to impale the head of a buffalo bull upon the medicine tree—a delegation of old men journeyed into Texas, there to beg and barter for an animal from the Goodnight herd. She was ten when the Kiowas came together for the last time as a living Sun Dance culture. They could find no buffalo; they had to hang an old hide from the sacred tree. Before the dance could begin, a company of soldiers rode out from Fort Sill under orders to <u>disperse</u> the tribe. Forbidden without cause the essential act of their faith, having seen the wild herds slaughtered and left to rot upon the ground, the Kiowas backed away forever from the medicine tree. That was July 20, 1890, at the great bend of the Washita. My grandmother was there. Without bitterness, and for as long as she lived, she bore a vision of deicide.[6] ❼

> ❼
> **?** In what sense had his grandmother witnessed deicide, the murder of a god?

Now that I can have her only in memory, I see my grandmother in the several postures that

---

5. **consummate** *v.*: finish; make complete.
6. **deicide** (dē′ə·sīd′) *n.*: murder of a god.

---

**Vocabulary**

**tenuous** (ten′yo͞o·əs) *adj.*: slight; insubstantial; not firm.
**wariness** (wer′ē·nis) *n.*: carefulness; caution.
**disperse** (di·spʉrs′) *v.*: scatter.

were peculiar to her: standing at the wood stove on a winter morning and turning meat in a great iron skillet; sitting at the south window, bent above her beadwork, and afterwards, when her vision failed, looking down for a long time into the fold of her hands; going out upon a cane, very slowly as she did when the weight of age came upon her; praying. I remember her most often at prayer. She made long, rambling prayers out of suffering and hope, having seen many things. I was never sure that I had the right to hear, so exclusive were they of all mere custom and company. The last time I saw her she prayed standing by the side of her bed at night, naked to the waist, the light of a kerosene lamp moving upon her dark skin. Her long, black hair, always drawn and braided in the day, lay upon her shoulders and against her breasts like a shawl. I do not speak Kiowa, and I never understood her prayers, but there was something inherently sad in the sound, some merest hesitation upon the syllables of sorrow. She began in a high and descending pitch, exhausting her breath to silence; then again and again—and always the same intensity of effort, of something that is, and is not, like urgency in the human voice. Transported so in the dancing light among the shadows of her room, she seemed beyond the reach of time. But that was illusion; I think I knew then that I should not see her again. **8**

**8**
? In her old age, what was his grandmother's life like?

Houses are like sentinels in the plain, old keepers of the weather watch. There, in a very little while, wood takes on the appearance of great age. All colors wear soon away in the wind and rain, and then the wood is burned gray and the grain appears and the nails turn red with rust. The windowpanes are black and opaque; you imagine there is nothing within, and indeed there are many ghosts, bones given up to the land. They stand here and there against the sky, and you approach them for a longer time than you expect. They belong in the distance; it is their domain.

Once there was a lot of sound in my grandmother's house, a lot of coming and going, feasting and talk. The summers there were full of excitement and reunion. The Kiowas are a summer people; they abide the cold and keep to themselves, but when the season turns and the land becomes warm and vital they cannot hold still; an old love of going returns upon them. The aged visitors who came to my grandmother's house when I was a child were made of lean and leather, and they bore themselves upright. They wore great black hats and bright ample shirts that shook in the wind. They rubbed fat upon their hair and wound their braids with strips of colored cloth. Some of them painted their faces and carried the scars of old and cherished enmities. They were an old council of warlords, come to remind and be reminded of who they were. Their wives and daughters served them well. The women might indulge themselves; gossip was at once the mark and compensation of their servitude. They made loud and elaborate talk among themselves, full of jest and gesture, fright and false alarm. They went abroad in fringed and flowered shawls, bright beadwork and German silver. They were at home in the kitchen, and they prepared meals that were banquets.

There were frequent prayer meetings, and great nocturnal feasts. When I was a child I played with my cousins outside, where the lamplight fell upon the ground and the singing of the old people rose up around us and carried away into the darkness. There were a lot of good things to eat, a lot of laughter and surprise. And afterwards, when the quiet returned, I lay down with my grandmother and could hear the frogs away by the river and feel the motion of the air. **9**

**9**
? What **main idea** is the writer expressing about his grandmother's house when he was a child?

**Vocabulary**

**opaque** (ō·pāk′) *adj.*: not transparent; not letting light pass through.
**vital** (vīt′′l) *adj.*: filled with life.
**enmities** (en′mə·tēz) *n. pl.*: hatreds.
**indulge** (in·dulj′) *v.*: satisfy; please; humor.

Now there is a funeral silence in the rooms, the endless wake of some final word. The walls have closed in upon my grandmother's house. When I returned to it in mourning, I saw for the first time in my life how small it was. It was late at night, and there was a white moon, nearly full. I sat for a long time on the stone steps by the kitchen door. From there I could see out across the land; I could see the long row of trees by the creek, the low light upon the rolling plains, and the stars of the Big Dipper. Once I looked at the moon and caught sight of a strange thing. A cricket had perched upon the handrail, only a few inches away from me. My line of vision was such that the creature filled the moon like a fossil.[7] It had gone there, I thought, to live and die, for there, of all places, was its small definition made whole and eternal.

---

7. **fossil** *n.:* hardened remains of plant or animal life from a previous geological time period.

A warm wind rose up and purled[8] like the longing within me. ⑩

The next morning I awoke at dawn and went out on the dirt road to Rainy Mountain. It was already hot, and the grasshoppers began to fill the air. Still, it was early in the morning, and the birds sang out of the shadows. The long yellow grass on the mountain shone in the bright light, and a scissortail[9] hied above the land. There, where it ought to be, at the end of a long and legendary way, was my grandmother's grave. Here and there on the dark stones were ancestral names. Looking back once, I saw the mountain and came away. ■

---

8. **purled** (purld) *v.:* moved in ripples.
9. **scissortail** *n.:* species of flycatcher bird. The bird's distinctive tail is an average of thirteen inches long and is divided like scissors near its end.

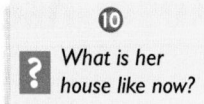

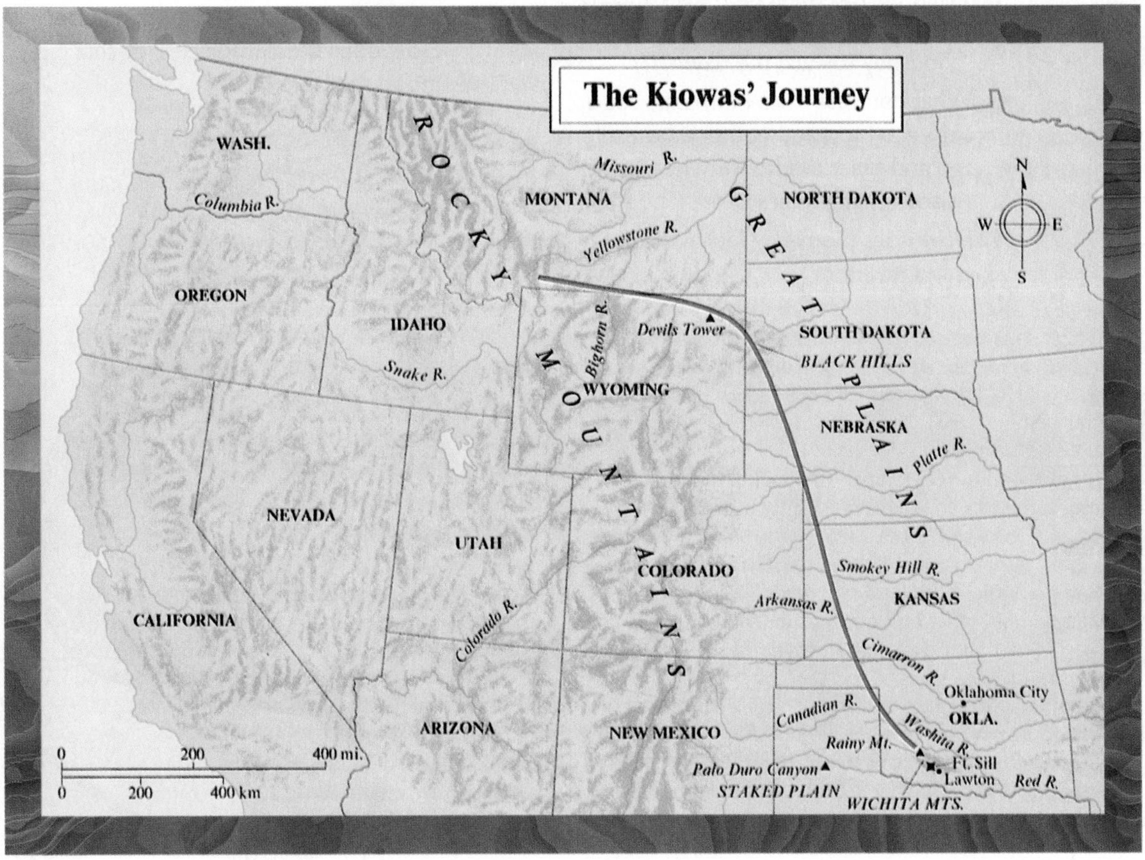

⑩
**?** What is her house like now?

---

**The Kiowas' Journey**

WASH.
Columbia R.
OREGON
IDAHO
Snake R.
NEVADA
UTAH
CALIFORNIA
Colorado R.
ARIZONA
NEW MEXICO
Palo Duro Canyon ▲
STAKED PLAIN

R O C K Y   M O U N T A I N S
MONTANA
Missouri R.
Yellowstone R.
Bighorn R.
Devils Tower ▲
WYOMING
COLORADO
Arkansas R.
Cimarron R.
Canadian R.
Rainy Mt.
Washita R.

NORTH DAKOTA
G R E A T   P L A I N S
SOUTH DAKOTA
BLACK HILLS
NEBRASKA
Platte R.
Smokey Hill R.
KANSAS
Oklahoma City
OKLA.
Ft. Sill
Lawton    Red R.
WICHITA MTS.

N
W       E
S

0      200      400 mi.
0    200    400 km

# Response and Analysis

**Reading Check**

1. What is Rainy Mountain?

2. What is the weather like on Rainy Mountain?

3. What does the memoir tell us about the Kiowas' religion and the role of the sun in their rituals?

4. According to Kiowa legend, what is the origin of the Big Dipper?

5. Devils Tower (pictured on page 1095) is a strange rock formation in Wyoming. The sides of the tower look as if a huge bear has clawed its sides. How does the myth on page 1097 explain the formation of Devils Tower?

6. What eventually happened to the Kiowas?

## Thinking Critically

7. What do you think Momaday means when he calls the Kiowa migration "a journey toward the dawn"?

8. What contrast does Momaday set up between his grandmother's house long ago and the same house when he visited it many years later?

9. How does Momaday feel about his grandmother?

10. Momaday's evocative poetic prose re-creates several **settings.** On page 1096, re-read the paragraph that begins "Descending eastward . . ." Identify at least three descriptive details that help you visualize the plains of the Rockies.

11. What do you think the cricket that Momaday sees outlined against the moon at the end of the excerpt might **symbolize** (page 1099)?

12. Momaday's book *The Way to Rainy Mountain* is in part an elegy. Strictly speaking, an **elegy** is a funeral song or a poem praising a dead person. What does Momaday praise about the Kiowas? What does he mourn?

13. **Mood** is the overall feeling created in a piece of writing. What feeling or feelings does this excerpt create in you—does it make you feel sad, joyful, frightened, awed, or something else? How does the author convey that mood to you?

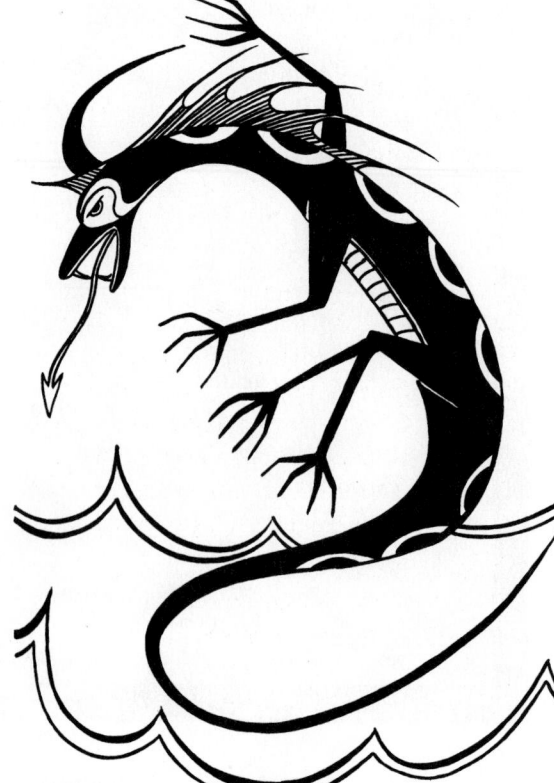

**SKILLS FOCUS**

**Literary Skills**
Analyze setting.

**Reading Skills**
Analyze main ideas and supporting details.

**Writing Skills**
Write a description of a setting.

**Vocabulary Skills**
Demonstrate word knowledge.

The illustrations on pages 1100 and 1101 are by Alfred Momaday for his son's memoir, *The Way to Rainy Mountain.*

Courtesy of N. Scott Momaday.

## Extending and Evaluating

**14.** Go back to the text, and find two places where Momaday uses a **flash-back.** Do these glimpses of life at an earlier time provide you with a clearer picture of the Kiowas? Did you find the shifting of time confusing? Explain.

**15.** Which text do you think would give you a more powerful understanding of Kiowa history—a history textbook written in factual prose or Momaday's poetic memoir? Give reasons for your response.

## WRITING

### The Remembered Earth

For Momaday the land around Rainy Mountain is associated with childhood and ancestral traditions. Think of a place you associate with your childhood—a store, a park, a play area. Write a **description** of this place, using vivid imagery to describe what it looked like and to suggest what it meant to you.

▶ **Use "Writing a Descriptive Essay," pages 679–680, for help with this assignment.**

## Vocabulary Development
### What's Wrong with This Picture?

Explain what's wrong with each sentence below:

**1.** The climber was feeling so infirm that she decided to climb another thousand feet.

**2.** The miser was preeminently interested in spending as much money as possible.

**3.** The fields were luxuriant because of the lack of rain.

**4.** Married fifty years, the couple celebrated their tenuous relationship.

**5.** Soldiers must display wariness in peaceful territory.

**6.** High-rise housing will disperse the population over a broad area.

**7.** You could see everything through the opaque screen.

**8.** The deserted town appeared vital in the setting sun.

**9.** Because of their long-standing enmities, the two nations lived in peace.

**10.** The parents indulge their child by refusing to buy him sweets and toys.

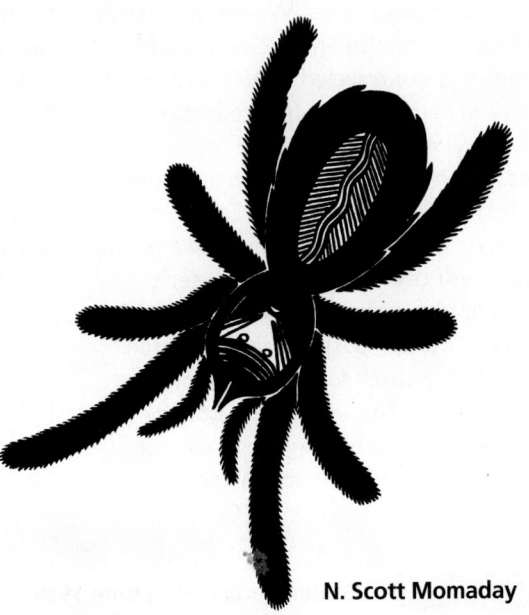

# Alice Walker

## (1944– )

In her poetry, essays, and novels, Alice Walker has celebrated the endurance, the strength, and the creativity of African American women like her mother—unsung women who carried immense familial and social burdens even as they struggled against low status and a complete lack of recognition.

Walker was born in Eatonton, Georgia, and grew up on a succession of farms in the area. Her father was a sharecropper, and her mother labored side-by-side with him in the fields, cared for their eight children, and still never failed, wherever they were living, to cultivate a large and beautiful flower garden. Her mother's hard work and determination to enrich her own life have served as an inspiration to Walker throughout her career.

A childhood accident that blinded Walker in one eye made her feel for a time disfigured and outcast. Seeking solace, she turned to writing poetry and reading, and also to closely observing people around her. Walker later attended Spelman College in Atlanta for two and a half years, before transferring to Sarah Lawrence College, near New York City. There she studied with the noted poet Muriel Rukeyser before graduating in 1965.

During her college years, Walker was active in the civil rights movement in Georgia and Mississippi, and she traveled in Africa. Many of the poems in her first published collection, *Once: Poems* (1968), were inspired by these activities. The poems were written in a burst of creativity while Walker was at Sarah Lawrence. As quickly as she completed a poem, she would rush over to Muriel Rukeyser's classroom (a converted gardener's cottage in the center of the campus) and shove it under the door, then go back to her own room and write some more. This immense outpouring of creative energy continued night and day for the short period it lasted, but Walker didn't

even care what Rukeyser did with the poems —the point was the creative surge of expression, not the end goal of publication. But the result was that Rukeyser gave the poems to her agent, and *Once: Poems* was published a few years later.

After graduating from college, Walker began a career of teaching and writing. She was among the first to teach university courses on the work of African American women writers, and she has since brought an understanding of their work to a wider audience. Walker edited an important collection of the writings of Zora Neale Hurston (page 836) called *I Love Myself When I Am Laughing . . .* (1979). In addition to poetry, short stories, and essays, Walker has written a number of well-received novels, including the Pulitzer Prize–winning *The Color Purple* (1982).

According to the critic Donna Haisty Winchell, Walker "comes across in her writing from the 1980s and 1990s as a woman at peace with herself and with the universe. Some of the anger of her youth remains, but it is more tempered and more focused." This mellowing is evident in her 1983 collection of essays, *In Search of Our Mothers' Gardens*. In 1996, Walker published *The Same River Twice*, a memoir about the filming of her novel *The Color Purple*.

## *from* In Search of Our Mothers' Gardens

### Make the Connection

The selection that follows is the second part of an essay about the creative spirit of African American women. In this section of her personal essay, Walker attempts to answer some questions she raises earlier: What did it mean for black women of previous generations to be artists? How were black women able to be creative despite limited opportunity and freedom? Walker explores these questions by examining her mother's own life.

### Literary Focus
#### Personal Essay

There are two types of essays, formal essays, such as Thomas Paine's *The Crisis* (see page 89), and informal essays, sometimes called personal essays. A **personal essay** is a short prose work of nonfiction that explores a topic in a personal way. Some of the best personal essays show how the individual experience of the writer connects with larger, more universal concerns. Such essays typically tap deeply into the emotional life of a writer.

> A **personal,** or **informal, essay** is a short prose work of nonfiction that takes a personal look at some topic.
>
> *For more on the Essay, see the Handbook of Literary and Historical Terms.*

### Reading Skills
#### Identifying the Main Idea: Outlining

Personal essays are often discursive, even rambling—that is, they are not as tightly organized as more formal essays. For that reason, it may be harder to recognize the main idea in a personal essay. When you read Walker's essay for the first time, note each time she introduces a new topic. When you have finished your first reading, go back over the text, and expand your notes into an outline. First, write each main idea you find in her essay on a separate line. Then in an indented list under each main idea, provide details, examples, or anecdotes from the text that support and illustrate each main idea. Review your notes to see if you can find one general, overriding idea that covers *all* these separate ideas. Note also any key passages that seem to point to or support your statement of a main idea. Be sure to consider the significance of the essay's unusual title.

> ### Vocabulary Development
>
> **vibrant** (vī′brənt) *adj.:* full of energy.
>
> **medium** (mē′dē·əm) *n.:* material for an artist.
>
> **profusely** (prō·fyōōs′lē) *adv.:* in great quantities.
>
> **conception** (kən·sep′shən) *n.:* mental formation of ideas.
>
> **ingenious** (in·jēn′yəs) *adj.:* clever.

**SKILLS FOCUS**

**Literary Skills**
Understand a personal, or informal, essay.

**Reading Skills**
Identify the main idea by outlining.

**INTERNET**

**More About Alice Walker**

Keyword: LE7 11-6

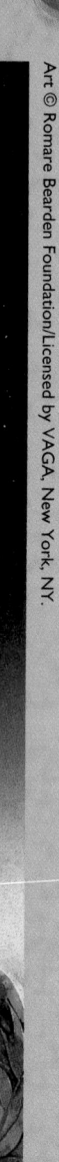

*Sunset and Moonrise with Maudell Sleet* (1978) by Romare Bearden. From the *Profile/ Part 1: The Twenties* series (Mecklenburg County). Collage on board (41" × 29").

*from*

# IN SEARCH OF Our Mothers' Gardens

## Alice Walker

In the late 1920s my mother ran away from home to marry my father. Marriage, if not running away, was expected of seventeen-year-old girls. By the time she was twenty, she had two children and was pregnant with a third. Five children later, I was born. And this is how I came to know my mother: She seemed a large, soft, loving-eyed woman who was rarely impatient in our home. Her quick, violent temper was on view only a few times a year, when she battled with the white landlord who had the misfortune to suggest to her that her children did not need to go to school.

She made all the clothes we wore, even my brothers' overalls. She made all the towels and sheets we used. She spent the summers canning vegetables and fruits. She spent the winter evenings making quilts enough to cover all our beds.

During the "working" day, she labored beside—not behind—my father in the fields. Her day began before sunup, and did not end until late at night. There was never a moment for her to sit down, undisturbed, to unravel her own private thoughts; never a time free from interruption— by work or the noisy inquiries of her many children. And yet, it is to my mother— and all our mothers who were not famous—

that I went in search of the secret of what has fed that muzzled and often mutilated, but vibrant, creative spirit that the black woman has inherited, and that pops out in wild and unlikely places to this day.

But when, you will ask, did my overworked mother have time to know or care about feeding the creative spirit?

The answer is so simple that many of us have spent years discovering it. We have constantly looked high, when we should have looked high—and low.

For example: In the Smithsonian Institution in Washington, D.C., there hangs a quilt unlike any other in the world. In fanciful, inspired, and yet simple and identifiable figures, it portrays the story of the Crucifixion. It is considered rare, beyond price. Though it follows no known pattern of quilt-making, and though it is made of bits and pieces of worthless rags, it is obviously the work of a person of powerful imagination and deep spiritual feeling. Below this quilt I saw a note that says it was made by "an anonymous Black woman in Alabama, a hundred years ago."

**Vocabulary**
**vibrant** (vī′brənt) *adj.:* full of energy.

If we could locate this "anonymous" black woman from Alabama, she would turn out to be one of our grandmothers—an artist who left her mark in the only materials she could afford, and in the only <u>medium</u> her position in society allowed her to use.

As Virginia Woolf[1] wrote further, in *A Room of One's Own:*

> Yet genius of a sort must have existed among women as it must have existed among the working class. [Change this to "slaves" and "the wives and daughters of sharecroppers."] Now and again an Emily Brontë[2] or a Robert Burns[3] [change this to "a Zora Hurston or a Richard Wright"] blazes out and proves its presence. But certainly it never got itself on to paper. When, however, one reads of a witch being ducked, of a woman possessed by devils [or "Sainthood"[4]], of a wise woman selling herbs [our root workers], or even a very remarkable man who had a mother, then I think we are on the track of a lost novelist, a suppressed poet, of some mute and inglorious Jane Austen. . . .[5] Indeed, I would venture to guess that Anon, who wrote so many poems without signing them, was often a woman. . . .

And so our mothers and grandmothers have, more often than not anonymously, handed on the creative spark, the seed of the flower they themselves never hoped to see: or like a sealed letter they could not plainly read.

And so it is, certainly, with my own mother. Unlike "Ma" Rainey's[6] songs, which retained their creator's name even while blasting forth from Bessie Smith's[7] mouth, no song or poem will bear my mother's name. Yet so many of the stories that I write, that we all write, are my mother's stories. Only recently did I fully realize this: that through years of listening to my mother's stories of her life, I have absorbed not only the stories themselves, but something of the manner in which she spoke, something of the urgency that involves the knowledge that her stories—like her life—must be recorded. It is probably for this reason that so much of what I have written is about characters whose counterparts in real life are so much older than I am.

But the telling of these stories, which came from my mother's lips as naturally as breathing, was not the only way my mother showed herself as an artist. For stories, too, were subject to being distracted, to dying without conclusion. Dinners must be started, and cotton must be gathered before the big rains. The artist that was and is my mother showed itself to me only after many years. This is what I finally noticed:

> Like Mem, a character in *The Third Life of Grange Copeland,*[8] my mother adorned with flowers whatever shabby house we were forced to live in. And not just your typical straggly country stand of zinnias, either. She planted ambitious gardens—and still does—with over

---

1. **Virginia Woolf:** English novelist and critic. In *A Room of One's Own* (1929), Woolf says that, in order to write, a woman must have a room of her own (privacy) and the means to support herself (money).
2. **Emily Brontë:** English novelist and poet, best known for her novel *Wuthering Heights* (1847).
3. **Robert Burns:** eighteenth-century Scottish poet.
4. **"Sainthood":** In the early part of this essay, Walker talks about certain black women in the South called Saints. Intensely spiritual, these women were driven to madness by their creativity, for which they could find no release.
5. **Jane Austen:** English novelist, best known for *Pride and Prejudice* (1813).

6. **"Ma" Rainey:** nickname of Gertrude Malissa Nix Pridgett Rainey. She was the first great African American professional blues vocalist and is considered to be the mother of the blues.
7. **Bessie Smith:** One of the greatest of blues singers, Smith was helped to professional status by Ma Rainey. She became known in her lifetime as "Empress of the Blues."
8. ***The Third Life of Grange Copeland:*** Alice Walker's first novel, published in 1970.

---

**Vocabulary**
**medium** (mē′dē·əm) *n*.: material for an artist.

fifty different varieties of plants that bloom <u>profusely</u> from early March until late November. Before she left home for the fields, she watered her flowers, chopped up the grass, and laid out new beds. When she returned from the fields she might divide clumps of bulbs, dig a cold pit,[9] uproot and replant roses, or prune branches from her taller bushes or trees—until night came and it was too dark to see.

Whatever she planted grew as if by magic, and her fame as a grower of flowers spread over three counties. Because of her creativity with her flowers, even my memories of poverty are seen through a screen of blooms—sunflowers, petunias, roses, dahlias, forsythia, spirea, delphiniums, verbena . . . and on and on.

And I remember people coming to my mother's yard to be given cuttings from her flowers; I hear again the praise showered on her because whatever rocky soil she landed on, she turned into a garden. A garden so brilliant with colors, so original in its design, so magnificent with life and creativity, that to this day people drive by our house in Georgia—perfect strangers and imperfect strangers—and ask to stand or walk among my mother's art.

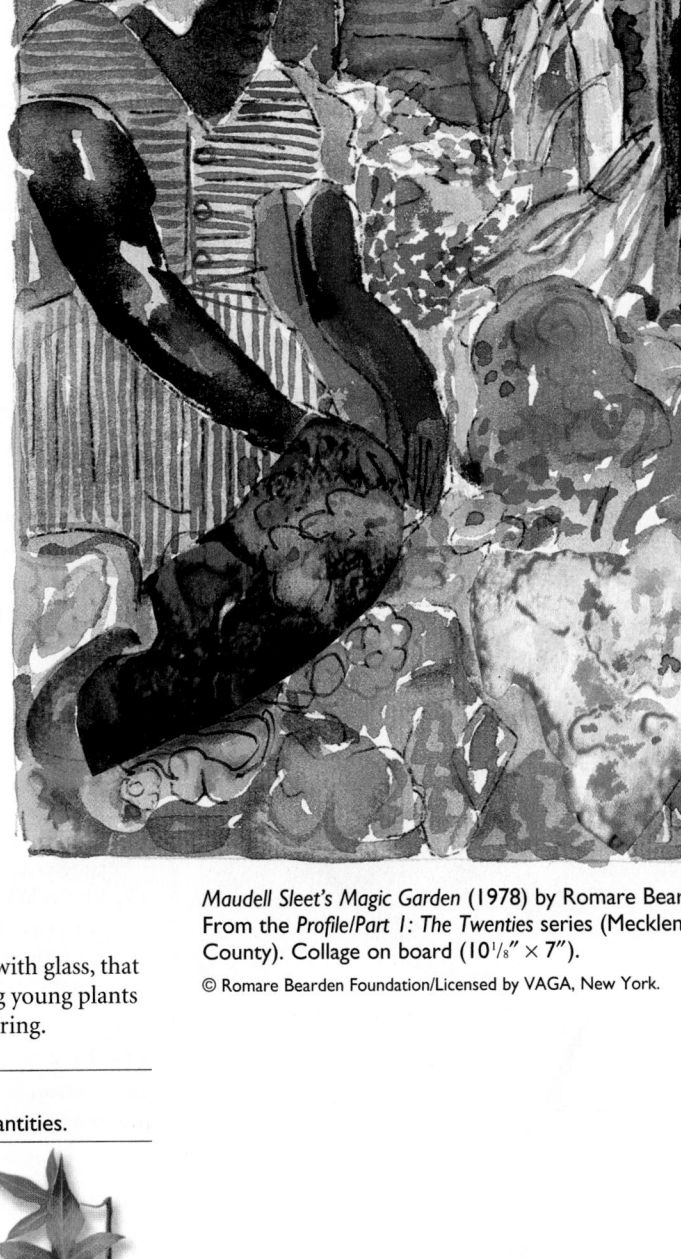

*Maudell Sleet's Magic Garden* (1978) by Romare Bearden. From the *Profile/Part 1: The Twenties* series (Mecklenburg County). Collage on board (10¹⁄₈″ × 7″).

© Romare Bearden Foundation/Licensed by VAGA, New York.

---

9. **cold pit:** shallow pit, usually covered with glass, that is used for rooting plants or sheltering young plants from temperature variations in the spring.

---

**Vocabulary**

**profusely** (prō·fyōōs′lē) *adv.:* in great quantities.

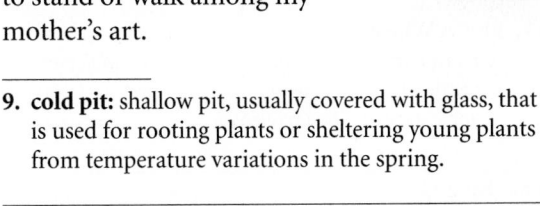

I notice that it is only when my mother is working in her flowers that she is radiant, almost to the point of being invisible—except as Creator: hand and eye. She is involved in work her soul must have. Ordering the universe in the image of her personal conception of Beauty.

Her face, as she prepares the Art that is her gift, is a legacy of respect she leaves to me, for all that illuminates and cherishes life. She has handed down respect for the possibilities—and the will to grasp them.

For her, so hindered and intruded upon in so many ways, being an artist has still been a daily part of her life. This ability to hold on, even in very simple ways, is work black women have done for a very long time.

This poem is not enough, but it is something, for the woman who literally covered the holes in our walls with sunflowers:

> They were women then
> My mama's generation
> Husky of voice—Stout of
> Step
> With fists as well as
> Hands
> How they battered down
> Doors
> And ironed
> Starched white
> Shirts
> How they led
> Armies

> Headragged Generals
> Across mined
> Fields
> Booby-trapped
> Kitchens
> To discover books
> Desks
> A place for us
> How they knew what we
> *Must* know
> Without knowing a page
> Of it
> Themselves.

Guided by my heritage of a love of beauty and a respect for strength—in search of my mother's garden, I found my own.

And perhaps in Africa over two hundred years ago, there was just such a mother; perhaps she painted vivid and daring decorations in oranges and yellows and greens on the walls of her hut; perhaps she sang—in a voice like Roberta Flack's[10]—*sweetly* over the compounds of her village; perhaps she wove the most stunning mats or told the most ingenious stories of all the village storytellers. Perhaps she was herself a poet—though only her daughter's name is signed to the poems that we know.

Perhaps Phillis Wheatley's[11] mother was also an artist.

Perhaps in more than Phillis Wheatley's biological life is her mother's signature made clear. ∎

---

10. **Roberta Flack:** popular African American singer-songwriter.
11. **Phillis Wheatley** (1753?–1783): American poet, born in Africa and brought to America in slavery. Wheatley is often referred to as the first African American poet. (See page 62.)

---

**Vocabulary**

**conception** (kən·sep′shən) *n.:* mental formation of ideas.
**ingenious** (in·jēn′yəs) *adj.:* clever.

# Response and Analysis

## Reading Check

1. Describe the kind of life Walker's mother led while Walker was growing up.

2. What secret does Walker wish to discover by examining her mother's life and the lives of other women like her?

3. In what two ways does Walker's mother express her creativity?

4. What happens to Walker's mother when she works in her garden?

## Thinking Critically

5. In this **personal essay,** Walker relates her personal experience to a larger, universal issue. What is that issue?

6. In a key passage on page 1106, Walker uses a **metaphor** and a **simile** to describe how African American women handed down their "creative spark" over the generations. What are these imaginative comparisons between two very different things? (Can you think of others she might have used?)

7. What do you think Walker the writer has learned from her mother the storyteller? from her mother the gardener?

8. In the last five lines of the poem on the opposite page, Walker presents a **paradox,** an apparent contradiction. State the paradox in your own words, and tell what kind of knowledge you think Walker is talking about.

9. What do you think Walker means when she says she found her own "garden" in her process of searching for her mother's?

## WRITING

### A Personal Essay

Imitating Walker's style and choice of subject, write a **personal essay** in which you recall a person who means a great deal to you. It could be a family member or a teacher, a friend, or a neighbor. Use descriptive details to capture the way the person looks and talks, and use personal anecdotes to bring your subject's character to life. Before you write, think about the main idea you want to convey about your important person.

### A Personal Response

Refer to the outline you made of Walker's text, then write two paragraphs **summarizing** and **evaluating** the essay. In the first paragraph, summarize Walker's main idea and the details that support that idea. What are her philosophical beliefs about women as artists? In the second paragraph, give your response to Walker's main idea. Use your own personal experiences to either support or challenge Walker's conclusions.

## Vocabulary Development

### Word Histories

| vibrant | conception |
|---------|------------|
| medium | profusely |

Use a good dictionary to research the origin, or **etymology,** of each Vocabulary word. This information usually appears in brackets or parentheses following the word's pronunciation. A dictionary will also provide a key to the abbreviations used in its etymologies. Fill out a chart like the one below to organize your findings:

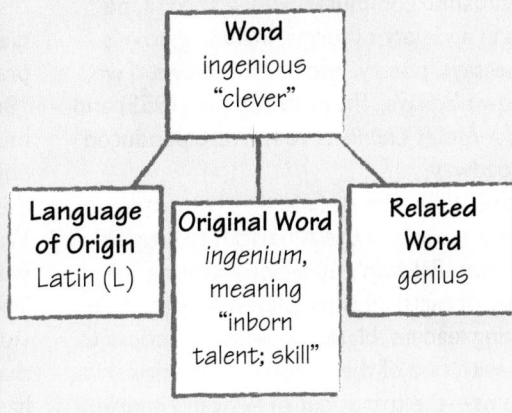

**SKILLS FOCUS**

**Literary Skills**
Analyze a personal, or informal, essay.

**Reading Skills**
Analyze the main idea.

**Writing Skills**
Write a personal essay. Write a summary evaluating a personal essay.

**Vocabulary Skills**
Create semantic maps.

# James Baldwin

## (1924–1987)

James Baldwin felt compelled to write at length about being an African American "because it was the gate I had to unlock before I could hope to write about anything else." His essays flow from his conviction that a writer's duty is "to examine attitudes, to go beneath the surface, to tap the source."

One of the most controversial and stirring writers of the twentieth century, James Baldwin was born and raised in New York City's Harlem, where his stepfather was the minister of a small evangelical church. As a young man, Baldwin read voraciously and served as a junior minister for a few years at the Fireside Pentecostal Assembly. At the age of twenty-four, he used funds from a fellowship to move to Europe. While living in Paris, he completed his first—and some say best—novel, *Go Tell It on the Mountain* (1953). *Notes of a Native Son,* a collection of autobiographical essays published in 1955, established Baldwin as an American writer of the first rank. The critic Irving Howe said Baldwin was among "the two or three greatest essayists this country has ever produced."

Although he lived much of his life in France, Baldwin never relinquished his U.S. citizenship, and in later years he traveled back to his homeland so often that he considered himself a transatlantic commuter. While abroad, he wrote in a variety of forms, including novels, plays, essays, poetry, and book reviews. Two of Baldwin's plays, *The Amen Corner* (1955) and *Blues for Mister Charlie* (1964), were produced on Broadway.

In the 1950s, the decade that witnessed the early growth of the American civil rights movement, Baldwin's audacious, searing scrutiny of racial injustice played a major role in forcing leaders, black and white, to come to terms with one of the nation's most anguishing problems—the treatment of African Americans. He saw himself as a "disturber of the peace," and some chided him for his unrelenting criticism. For instance, Benjamin DeMott wrote in the *Saturday Review,* "To function as a voice of outrage month after month for a decade and more strains heart and mind, and rhetoric as well; the consequence is a writing style ever on the edge of being winded by too many summonses to intensity."

In the early sixties, Baldwin's reputation grew with the publication of additional essays, *Nobody Knows My Name: More Notes of a Native Son* (1961) and *The Fire Next Time* (1963), a groundbreaking book on race relations that had wide influence. He later published several novels, participated in TV documentaries, and remained a prominent, humane advocate of racial justice in American life.

At the time of his death in France, Baldwin was working on a biography of the Reverend Martin Luther King, Jr. Soon after Baldwin died, two noted African American writers praised his lifework. Orde Coombs wrote, "Because he existed we felt that the racial miasma that swirled around us would not consume us, and it is not too much to say that this man saved our lives." Juan Williams of *The Washington Post* said, "America and the literary world are far richer for [Baldwin's] witness. The proof of a shared humanity across the divides of race, class, and more is the testament that the preacher's son, James Arthur Baldwin, has left us."

# Autobiographical Notes

## Make the Connection

The ancient Greek philosopher Socrates believed that only an examined life is worth living. What exactly does it mean to live an examined life? At the least it means stepping back from the whirl of daily activities and gaining some perspective on who you are, where you have been, and where you are heading. It means creating new angles of vision, asking questions, proposing answers. It means making self-assessment a part of self-creation. As you will see, James Baldwin certainly took Socrates' words to heart. The autobiographical notes that follow first appeared as a preface to Baldwin's acclaimed *Notes of a Native Son.*

## Literary Focus
### Tone

Since Baldwin is writing his autobiography, his main subject is himself and his life experience. Therefore, when we speak of his **tone,** we mean his attitude toward himself and the world in which he lived. We sense that attitude by the words he chooses and by the style or manner in which he arranges those words. Tone can often by summed up in a single adjective, such as *ironic* or *light-hearted;* the way in which that tone is achieved must be examined by detailed analysis.

> The **tone** of a literary work is the attitude the writer takes toward the subject and the audience.
>
> *For more on Tone, see the Handbook of Literary and Historical Terms.*

## Reading Skills
### Evaluating an Author's Arguments

In this essay, Baldwin assesses his life experience. He tells us what conclusions he has drawn about a number of important subjects, such as the racial divide in American society and the dilemma of the African American writer. Often, he explicitly states his beliefs and gives reasons for his assertions. As you read, jot down statements that reveal Baldwin's beliefs and the reasons he gives for making those assertions. After you read, think about your own responses to Baldwin's text. What assertions will *you* make about Baldwin's beliefs?

## Vocabulary Development

**bleak** *adj.:* cheerless.

**censored** (sen′sərd) *v.:* cut or changed to remove material deemed objectionable.

**assess** (ə·ses′) *v.:* evaluate; judge the value of.

**conundrum** (kə·nun′drəm) *n.:* riddle.

**coherent** (kō·hir′ənt) *adj.:* clear, logical, and consistent.

**crucial** (kro͞o′shəl) *adj.:* critical; decisive.

**interloper** (in′tər·lō′pər) *n.:* intruder; meddler.

**appropriate** (ə·prō′prē·āt′) *v.:* take over.

**explicit** (eks·plis′it) *adj.:* clear; definite.

**pulverized** (pul′vər·īzd′) *v.:* crushed; destroyed.

**SKILLS FOCUS**

**Literary Skills**
Understand tone.

**Reading Skills**
Understand an author's arguments.

THIS IS THE ONLY REAL CONCERN OF THE ARTIST, TO RECREATE OUT OF THE DISORDER OF LIFE THAT ORDER WHICH IS ART.

# Autobiographical Notes

James Baldwin

I was born in Harlem thirty-one years ago. I began plotting novels at about the time I learned to read. The story of my childhood is the usual bleak fantasy, and we can dismiss it with the restrained observation that I certainly would not consider living it again. In those days my mother was given to the exasperating[1] and mysterious habit of having babies. As they were born, I took them over with one hand and held a book with the other. The children probably suffered, though they have since been kind enough to deny it, and in this way I read *Uncle Tom's Cabin* and *A Tale of Two Cities* over and over and over again; in this way, in fact, I read just about everything I could get my hands on—except the Bible, probably because it was the only book I was encouraged to read. I must also confess that I wrote—a great deal—and my first professional triumph, in any case, the first effort of mine to be seen in print, occurred at the age of twelve or thereabouts, when a short story I had written about the Spanish revolution won some sort of a prize in an extremely short-lived church newspaper. I remember the story was censored by the lady editor, though I don't remember why, and I was outraged.

Also wrote plays, and songs, for one of which I received a letter of congratulations from Mayor La Guardia,[2] and poetry, about which the less said, the better. My mother was delighted by all these goings-on, but my father wasn't; he wanted me to be a preacher. When I was fourteen I became a preacher, and when I was seventeen I stopped. Very shortly thereafter I left home. For God knows how long I struggled with the world of commerce and industry—I guess they would say they struggled with *me*—and when I was about twenty-one I had enough done of a novel to get a Saxton Fellowship. When I was twenty-two the fellowship was over, the novel turned out to be unsalable, and I started waiting on tables in a Village[3] restaurant and writing book reviews—mostly, as it turned out, about the Negro problem, concerning which the color of my skin made me automatically an expert. Did another book, in company with photographer Theodore Pelatowski, about the store-front churches in Harlem. This book met exactly the same fate as my first—fellowship, but no sale. (It was a Rosenwald Fellowship.) By the time I was twenty-four I had decided to stop reviewing books about the Negro problem—which, by this time, was only slightly less horrible in print than it was in life—and I packed my bags and went to France, where I finished, God knows how, *Go Tell It on the Mountain.*

Any writer, I suppose, feels that the world into which he was born is nothing less than a conspiracy against the cultivation of his talent—which attitude certainly has a great deal to support it. On the other hand, it is only because the world looks on his talent with such a frightening indifference that the artist is compelled to make his talent important. So that any writer, looking back over even so short a span of time as I am here forced to assess, finds that the things which hurt him and the things which helped him cannot be divorced from each other; he could be helped in a certain way only because he was hurt in a certain way; and his help is simply to be enabled to move from one conundrum to the next—one is tempted to say that he moves from one disaster to the next. When one begins looking for influences one finds them by the

---

1. **exasperating** *adj.*: irritating; very annoying.
2. **Mayor La Guardia:** Fiorello La Guardia, mayor of New York City from 1934 to 1945.
3. **Village:** Greenwich Village, a section of Manhattan noted as a center for writers and other artists.

---

**Vocabulary**

**bleak** *adj.*: cheerless.
**censored** (sen′sərd) *v.*: cut or changed to remove material deemed objectionable.
**assess** (ə·ses′) *v.*: evaluate; judge the value of.
**conundrum** (kə·nun′drəm) *n.*: riddle.

---

score. I haven't thought much about my own, not enough anyway; I hazard that the King James Bible, the rhetoric of the store-front church, something ironic and violent and perpetually understated in Negro speech—and something of Dickens' love for bravura[4]—have something to do with me today; but I wouldn't stake my life on it. Likewise, innumerable people have helped me in many ways; but finally, I suppose, the most difficult (and most rewarding) thing in my life has been the fact that I was born a Negro and was forced, therefore, to effect some kind of truce with this reality. (Truce, by the way, is the best one can hope for.)

One of the difficulties about being a Negro writer (and this is not special pleading, since I don't mean to suggest that he has it worse than anybody else) is that the Negro problem is written about so widely. The bookshelves groan under the weight of information, and everyone therefore considers himself informed. And this information, furthermore, operates usually (generally, popularly) to reinforce traditional attitudes. Of traditional attitudes there are only two—For or Against—and I, personally, find it difficult to say which attitude has caused me the most pain. I am speaking as a writer; from a social point of view I am perfectly aware that the change from ill-will to good-will, however motivated, however imperfect, however expressed, is better than no change at all.

But it is part of the business of the writer—as I see it—to examine attitudes, to go beneath the surface, to tap the source. From this point of view the Negro problem is nearly inaccessible. It is not only written about so widely; it is written about so badly. It is quite possible to say that the price a Negro pays for becoming articulate is to find himself, at length, with nothing to be articulate about. ("You taught me language," says Caliban to Prospero,[5] "and my profit on't is I know how to curse.") Consider: the tremendous social

activity that this problem generates imposes on whites and Negroes alike the necessity of looking forward, of working to bring about a better day. This is fine, it keeps the waters troubled; it is all, indeed, that has made possible the Negro's progress. Nevertheless, social affairs are not generally speaking the writer's prime concern, whether they ought to be or not; it is absolutely necessary that he establish between himself and these affairs a distance which will allow, at least, for clarity, so that before he can look forward in any meaningful sense, he must first be allowed to take a long look back. In the context of the Negro problem neither whites nor blacks, for excellent reasons of their own, have the faintest desire to look back; but I think that the past is all that makes the present coherent, and further, that the past will remain horrible for exactly as long as we refuse to assess it honestly.

I know, in any case, that the most crucial time in my own development came when I was forced to recognize that I was a kind of bastard of the West; when I followed the line of my past I did not find myself in Europe but in Africa. And this meant that in some subtle way, in a really profound way, I brought to Shakespeare, Bach, Rembrandt, to the stones of Paris, to the cathedral at Chartres, and to the Empire State Building, a special attitude. These were not really my creations, they did not contain my history; I might search in them in vain forever for any reflection of myself. I was an interloper; this was not my heritage. At the same time I had no other heritage which I could possibly hope to use—I had certainly been unfitted for the jungle or the tribe. I would have to appropriate these white centuries, I would have to make them mine—I would have to accept my special attitude, my special place in this scheme—otherwise I would have no place in *any* scheme. What was the most difficult was the fact that I was forced to admit

---

4. **bravura** (brə·vyŏŏr'ə) *n.:* florid, brilliant style.
5. **Caliban to Prospero:** In *The Tempest* by William Shakespeare, Caliban, a rough creature, is Prospero's slave, whom Prospero tries to civilize. The quotation is from Act I, Scene 2.

**Vocabulary**

**coherent** (kō·hir'ənt) *adj.:* clear, logical, and consistent.
**crucial** (krōō'shəl) *adj.:* critical; decisive.
**interloper** (in'tər·lō'pər) *n.:* intruder; meddler.
**appropriate** (ə·prō'prē·āt') *v.:* take over.

something I had always hidden from myself, which the American Negro has had to hide from himself as the price of his public progress; that I hated and feared white people. This did not mean that I loved black people; on the contrary, I despised them, possibly because they failed to produce Rembrandt. In effect, I hated and feared the world. And this meant, not only that I thus gave the world an altogether murderous power over me, but also that in such a self-destroying limbo[6] I could never hope to write.

One writes out of one thing only—one's own experience. Everything depends on how relentlessly one forces from this experience the last drop, sweet or bitter, it can possibly give. This is the only real concern of the artist, to recreate out of the disorder of life that order which is art. The difficulty then, for me, of being a Negro writer was the fact that I was, in effect, prohibited from examining my own experience too closely by the tremendous demands and the very real dangers of my social situation.

I don't think the dilemma outlined above is uncommon. I do think, since writers work in the disastrously explicit medium of language, that it goes a little way toward explaining why, out of the enormous resources of Negro speech and life, and despite the example of Negro music, prose written by Negroes has been generally speaking so pallid[7] and so harsh. I have not written about being a Negro at such length because I expect that to be my only subject, but only because it was the gate I had to unlock before I could hope to write about anything else. I don't think that the Negro problem in America can be even discussed coherently without bearing in mind its context; its context being the history, traditions, customs, the moral assumptions and preoccupations of the country; in short, the general social fabric. Appearances to the contrary, no one in America escapes its effects and everyone in America bears some responsibility for it. I believe this the more firmly because it is the overwhelming tendency to

speak of this problem as though it were a thing apart. But in the work of Faulkner, in the general attitude and certain specific passages in Robert Penn Warren, and, most significantly, in the advent of Ralph Ellison, one sees the beginnings—at least—of a more genuinely penetrating search. Mr. Ellison, by the way, is the first Negro novelist I have ever read to utilize in language, and brilliantly, some of the ambiguity and irony of Negro life.

About my interests: I don't know if I have any, unless the morbid desire to own a sixteen-millimeter camera and make experimental movies can be so classified. Otherwise, I love to eat and drink—it's my melancholy conviction that I've scarcely ever had enough to eat (this is because it's *impossible* to eat enough if you're worried about the next meal)—and I love to argue with people who do not disagree with me too profoundly, and I love to laugh. I do *not* like bohemia,[8] or bohemians, I do not like people whose principal aim is pleasure, and I do not like people who are *earnest* about anything. I don't like people who like me because I'm a Negro; neither do I like people who find in the same accident grounds for contempt. I love America more than any other country in the world, and, exactly for this reason, I insist on the right to criticize her perpetually. I think all theories are suspect, that the finest principles may have to be modified, or may even be pulverized by the demands of life, and that one must find, therefore, one's own moral center and move through the world hoping that this center will guide one aright. I consider that I have many responsibilities, but none greater than this: to last, as Hemingway says, and get my work done.

I want to be an honest man and a good writer. ∎

8. **bohemia** *n.*: any nonconformist, unconventional community, often made up of writers and other artists.

6. **limbo** *n.*: borderland state of uncertainty and oblivion.
7. **pallid** *adj.*: dull; lacking in vitality.

**Vocabulary**

**explicit** (eks·plis′it) *adj.*: clear; definite.
**pulverized** (pul′vər·īzd′) *v.*: crushed; destroyed.

*Toni Morrison (1931–    ) was awarded the Nobel Prize in literature in 1993. She is noted for her novels* Song of Solomon *(1977) and* Beloved *(1987). She delivered this eulogy at Baldwin's memorial service at the Cathedral of St. John the Divine in New York City on December 8, 1987.*

PUBLIC · DOCUMENT

# *from* On James Baldwin

## Toni Morrison

Jimmy, there is too much to think about you, and too much to feel. The difficulty is your life refuses summation—it always did—and invites contemplation instead. Like many of us left here I thought I knew you. Now I discover that in your company it is myself I know. That is the astonishing gift of your art and your friendship: You gave us ourselves to think about, to cherish. We are like Hall Montana[1] watching "with new wonder" his brother saints, knowing the song he sang is us, "He is us."

I never heard a single command from you, yet the demands you made on me, the challenges you issued to me, were nevertheless unmistakable, even if unenforced: that I work and think at the top of my form, that I stand on moral ground but know that ground must

be shored up by mercy, that "the world is before [me] and [I] need not take it or leave it as it was when [I] came in."

Well, the season was always Christmas with you there and, like one aspect of that scenario, you did not neglect to bring at least three gifts. You gave me a language to dwell in, a gift so perfect it seems my own invention. I have been thinking your spoken and written thoughts for so long I believed they were mine. I have been seeing the world through your eyes for so long, I believed that clear clear view was my own. Even now, even here, I need you to tell me what I am feeling and how to articulate it. So I have pored again through the 6,895 pages of your published work to acknowledge the debt and thank you for the credit. No one possessed or inhabited language for me the way you did. You made American English honest— genuinely international. . . .

The second gift was your courage, which you let us share: the courage of one who could go as a stranger in the village and transform the distances between people into intimacy with the whole world; courage to understand that experience in ways that made it a personal revelation for each of us. It was you who gave us the courage to appropriate an alien, hostile, all-white geography because you had discovered that "this world [meaning history] is white no longer and it will never be white again." Yours was the courage to live life in and from its belly as well as beyond its edges, to see and say what it was, to recognize and identify evil but never fear or stand in awe of it. It is a courage that came from a ruthless intelligence married to a pity so profound it could convince anyone who cared to know that those who despised us "need the moral

---

1. **Hall Montana:** character in Baldwin's novel *Just Above My Head.*

authority of their former slaves, who are the only people in the world who know anything about them and who may be indeed, the only people in the world who really care anything about them." . . .

The third gift was hard to fathom and even harder to accept. It was your tenderness—a tenderness so delicate I thought it could not last, but last it did and envelop me it did. In the midst of anger it tapped me lightly like the child in Tish's[2] womb. . . .

You knew, didn't you, how I needed your language and the mind that formed it? How I relied on your fierce courage to tame wildernesses for me? How strengthened I was by the certainty that came from knowing you would never hurt me? You knew, didn't you, how I loved your love? You knew. This then is no calamity. No. This is jubilee. "Our crown," you said, "has already been bought and paid for. All we have to do," you said, "is wear it."

And we do, Jimmy. You crowned us.

---

2. **Tish:** character in Baldwin's novel *If Beale Street Could Talk.*

# Response and Analysis

## Reading Check

1. What was Baldwin's childhood like?

2. What does Baldwin see as the business of a writer?

3. According to the essay, what was the most crucial time in Baldwin's development? What did he learn about himself then?

4. What does Baldwin say is his greatest responsibility?

## Thinking Critically

5. According to Baldwin, how does a writer make use of his or her experience? Do you think Baldwin practices what he preaches in this essay? Support your response with details from the text.

6. Why does Baldwin say his "social situation" as an African American creates a dilemma for him as a writer?

7. What **tone** does Baldwin take toward his subject matter? What specific words or details help you to identify his tone?

## Extending and Evaluating

8. Do you agree with Baldwin's statement that "the world looks on [the artist's] talent with such a frightening indifference"? Back up your opinion with examples of contemporary writers, painters, musicians, or other artists.

9. What do you think were Baldwin's main goals in writing these autobiographical notes? Do you think he achieved his goals? Explain.

10. By the end of the essay, has Baldwin convinced you to accept his view of the role of the writer in society, especially the African American writer? (Go back over your reading notes.) Use details from the text to defend your stance.

11. Toni Morrison is an African American writer who says she received three gifts from Baldwin. (See the **Connection** on page 1116.) What are those gifts? How would you interpret Baldwin's statement about the crown, quoted at the end of Morrison's eulogy?

**SKILLS FOCUS**

**Literary Skills**
Analyze tone.

**Reading Skills**
Evaluate an author's arguments.

**Writing Skills**
Write an essay containing an assertion.

**Vocabulary Skills**
Demonstrate word knowledge.

# WRITING

## Presenting Your Own Argument

An **assertion** is a statement of opinion about some issue. An assertion is not a factual statement; it cannot be proved true. To persuade your audience to accept your assertions, you must back them up with facts, examples, or anecdotes.

Write a brief **essay** in which you make an assertion about one of the opinions Baldwin expresses in this essay. Open with the statement from Baldwin's essay that you want to focus on. Then, state your assertion. Support your assertion with facts, with examples, or with a personal story. Here are some of Baldwin's assertions that you might want to respond to. Remember, Baldwin wrote this essay a long time ago, in 1955.

- "I think that the past is all that makes the present coherent, and further, that the past will remain horrible for exactly as long as we refuse to assess it honestly. . . ." (page 1114)

- "Everyone in America bears some responsibility for it [the Negro problem]. . . ." (page 1115)

- "I love America more than any other country in the world, and, exactly for this reason, I insist on the right to criticize her perpetually." (page 1115)

## Vocabulary Development
### Back to the Text

How would you answer these questions about Baldwin's "Autobiographical Notes"? The underlined words are Vocabulary words and are defined in the essay.

1. What were some of the bleak aspects of Baldwin's childhood?

2. How did Baldwin feel about writing being censored?

3. How did Baldwin assess the relationship of African Americans to Western culture?

4. According to Baldwin, what conundrum does the African American writer face?

5. Where would Baldwin look for a coherent view of life?

6. What moral quality does Baldwin view as crucial when evaluating himself as a man?

7. Why did Baldwin feel he was an interloper in Western civilization?

8. Why does Baldwin feel it is necessary for him to appropriate Western culture?

9. What explicit attitude toward America does Baldwin express?

10. What social and political situations might have pulverized James Baldwin?

*James Baldwin.* Drawing by David Levine.
Copyright © 1963–2002 NYREV, Inc. All rights reserved.

# Sandra Cisneros
(1954–    )

**S**andra Cisneros remembers her Chicago childhood as solitary, even though, she says, her parents would be hard pressed to remember it that way. The nine members of her Mexican American family lived in cramped apartments where the only room with any privacy was the bathroom. But as the only female child in a family of six sons, Cisneros often felt as solitary as an only child.

To Cisneros, solitude proved important. If she had had a sister or a best friend, Cisneros thinks, she would not have buried herself in books. She read voraciously—lives of the saints, Horatio Alger's office-boy-makes-good stories, Doctor Doolittle books, *Alice in Wonderland,* and fairy tales.

Cisneros received a bachelor's degree from Loyola University, in Chicago, and then earned a master's at The Writers' Workshop at the University of Iowa. There she began writing in earnest. Finding her own voice did not come easily or quickly for Cisneros; she did not realize for a long time that her best writer's voice was the voice of the home she grew up in, a voice that was a combination of her mother's South Side Chicago "tough" street English and her father's gentle, lulling Spanish. The result is a style that suggests a unique synthesis of the disparate languages of her childhood. Cisneros writes in an English often heavily informed by Spanish diction and grammatical structure.

Cisneros's first novel, *The House on Mango Street* (1983), won the American Book Award of the Before Columbus Foundation. In 1991, she published *Woman Hollering Creek and Other Stories.* In 1995, she was awarded a prestigious long-term fellowship by the John D. and Catherine T. MacArthur Foundation.

Growing up and attending college in Chicago, Cisneros led a circumscribed life and, like many young people (not just writers), desperately yearned to break away. She took comfort from thinking of Emily Dickinson (page 389), who seldom left her house, let alone her hometown, but still managed to create a magnificent legacy of creative work. Dickinson became Cisneros's source of inspiration, the image to which she hitched her dreams of becoming a professional writer. Only years later did Cisneros, all too aware of the struggles of working-class people (especially women), realize that Dickinson lived a uniquely privileged existence in circumstances any aspiring writer would envy: She had money, a fine education, her own room in her own house, and even household help to take care of time-consuming chores. Cisneros, growing up, had none of these advantages. Yet, like Dickinson, Cisneros has been able to take both the possibilities and the constraints of her unique situation and weave them into art.

## For Independent Reading

Here are two books by Cisneros you should enjoy:

- *The House on Mango Street* (novel)
- *Woman Hollering Creek and Other Stories*

## Straw into Gold

### Make the Connection

One of the oldest bits of advice to an aspiring writer is simply "write about what you know." Taking that advice, just about every good writer discovers that personal experience is what gives vitality and authenticity to literature. Some of the best writers have an uncanny ability to discover the essential that is hidden in the everyday, the universal that is hidden in the local. In the following autobiographical essay, Sandra Cisneros tells about some of the raw material she has transformed into literature.

### Literary Focus
#### Allusion

An **allusion** is a reference to someone or something that is known from history, literature, religion, politics, sports, science, or some other branch of culture. Writers expect readers to understand their allusions—a confidence based on the assumption of the shared culture. Cisneros builds an allusion into the title of this essay: Do you recognize the old folk tale she is referring to? As you read, think about what she is suggesting through this allusion.

> An **allusion** is a reference to someone or something known from history, literature, the arts, politics, or some other branch of culture.
>
> For more on Allusion, see the Handbook of Literary and Historical Terms.

### Reading Skills
#### Understanding a Writer's Background

Since personal experience is such an important resource for writers, understanding a writer's cultural background can be a key to understanding and appreciating his or her writing. Cultural background includes where and when a writer grew up as well as the racial, ethnic, religious, and political traditions and values of the writer's family and neighborhood. Although writers usually move beyond their beginnings and make value choices of their own, they are never untouched by the culture they came from. As you read, jot down the elements of Cisneros's background that she says have influenced her writing.

### Vocabulary Development

**subsisting** (səb·sist′iŋ) v. used as an adj.: staying alive.

**intuitively** (in·tōō′i·tiv·lē) adv.: without conscious reasoning.

**edible** (ed′ə·bəl) adj.: capable of being eaten.

**ventured** (ven′chərd) v.: dared or risked going.

**taboo** (tə·bōō′) n.: social restriction.

**nomadic** (nō·mad′ik) adj.: wandering.

**nostalgia** (nä·stal′jə) n.: longing.

**flourished** (flʉr′ishd) v.: thrived; prospered.

**prestigious** (pres·tij′əs) adj.: impressive; having distinction.

(Opposite) *Woman Making Tortillas* (1945) by Diego Rivera. Watercolor (12″ × 15¾″).

Courtesy of Mary-Anne Martin/Fine Art, New York. Reproducción autorizada por el Instituto Nacional de Bellas Artes y Literatura.

**SKILLS FOCUS**

**Literary Skills**
Understand allusion.

**Reading Skills**
Understand a writer's background.

# STRAW INTO GOLD

## The Metamorphosis of the Everyday

Sandra Cisneros

When I was living in an artists' colony in the south of France, some fellow Latin-Americans who taught at the university in Aix-en-Provence invited me to share a home-cooked meal with them. I had been living abroad almost a year then on an NEA[1] grant, subsisting mainly on French bread and lentils so that my money could last longer. So when the invitation to dinner arrived, I accepted without hesitation. Especially since they had promised Mexican food.

---

1. **NEA:** National Endowment for the Arts, a federal agency that grants money to selected organizations and individuals so they may engage in creative pursuits.

What I didn't realize when they made this invitation was that I was supposed to be involved in preparing the meal. I guess they assumed I knew how to cook Mexican food because I am Mexican. They wanted specifically tortillas, though I'd never made a tortilla in my life.

It's true I had witnessed my mother rolling the little armies of dough into perfect circles, but my mother's family is from Guanajuato; they are *provincianos,* country folk. They only know how to make flour tortillas. My father's

*La Llorona* (*The Crying Woman*) by Carmen Lomas Garza. Gouache (18″ × 26″).
© 1989 Carmen Lomas Garza. Photo by Wolfgang Dietze. Collection of Sonia Saldivar-Hull and Felix Hull, Austin, Texas.

family, on the other hand, is *chilango*[2] from Mexico City. We ate corn tortillas but we didn't make them. Someone was sent to the corner tortilleria to buy some. I'd never seen anybody make corn tortillas. Ever.

Somehow my Latino hosts had gotten a hold of a packet of corn flour, and this is what they tossed my way with orders to produce tortillas. *Así como sea.* Any ol' way, they said and went back to their cooking.

Why did I feel like the woman in the fairy tale who was locked in a room and ordered to spin straw into gold? I had the same sick feeling when I was required to write my critical essay for the MFA[3] exam—the only piece of noncreative writing necessary in order to get my graduate degree. How was I to start? There were rules involved here, unlike writing a poem or story, which I did intuitively. There was a step by step process needed and I had better know it. I felt as if making tortillas—or writing a critical paper, for that matter—were tasks so impossible I wanted to break down into tears.

Somehow though, I managed to make tortillas—crooked and burnt, but edible nonetheless. My hosts were absolutely ignorant when it came to Mexican food; they thought my tortillas were delicious. (I'm glad my mama wasn't there.) Thinking back and looking at an old photograph documenting the three of us consuming those lopsided circles I am amazed. Just as I am amazed I could finish my MFA exam.

I've managed to do a lot of things in my life I didn't think I was capable of and which many others didn't think I was capable of either. Especially be-cause I am a woman, a Latina, an only daughter in a family of six men. My father would've liked to have seen me married long ago. In our culture men and women don't leave their father's house except by way of marriage. I crossed my father's threshold with nothing carrying me but my own two feet. A woman whom no one came for and no one chased away.

To make matters worse, I left before any of my six brothers had ventured away from home. I broke a terrible taboo. Somehow, looking back at photos of myself as a child, I wonder if I was aware of having begun already my own quiet war.

I like to think that somehow my family, my Mexicanness, my poverty, all had something to do with shaping me into a writer. I like to think my parents were preparing me all along for my life as an artist even though they didn't know it. From my father I inherited a love of wandering. He was born in Mexico City but as a young man he traveled into the U.S. vagabonding. He eventually was drafted and thus became a citizen. Some of the stories he has told about his first months in the U.S. with little or no English surface in my stories in *The House on Mango Street* as well as others I have in mind to write in the future. From him I inherited a sappy heart. (He still cries when he watches Mexican soaps—especially if they deal with children who have forsaken their parents.)

My mother was born like me—in Chicago but of Mexican descent. It would be her tough streetwise voice that would haunt all my stories and poems. An amazing woman who loves to draw and read books and can sing an opera. A smart cookie.

When I was a little girl we traveled to Mexico City so much I thought my grandparents' house on La Fortuna, number 12, was home. It was the

---

2. **chilango:** variation of "*Shilango,*" name used by people of coastal Veracruz for those who live inland, especially the poor people of Mexico.
3. **MFA:** master of fine arts.

**Vocabulary**

**intuitively** (in·tōō′i·tiv·lē) *adv.*: without conscious reasoning.
**edible** (ed′ə·bəl) *adj.*: capable of being eaten.
**ventured** (ven′chərd) *v.*: dared or risked going.
**taboo** (tə·bōō′) *n.*: social restriction.

CARMEN
LOMAS
GARZA
©1989
LaLlorona

**Sandra Cisneros**     **1123**

only constant in our <u>nomadic</u> ramblings from one Chicago flat to another. The house on Destiny Street, number 12, in the colonia Tepeyac would be perhaps the only home I knew, and that <u>nostalgia</u> for a home would be a theme that would <u>obsess</u> me.

My brothers also figured greatly in my art. Especially the older two; I grew up in their shadows. Henry, the second oldest and my favorite, appears often in poems I have written and in stories which at times only borrow his nickname, Kiki. He played a major role in my childhood. We were bunk-bed mates. We were co-conspirators. We were pals. Until my oldest brother came back from studying in Mexico and left me odd woman out for always.

What would my teachers say if they knew I was a writer now? Who would've guessed it? I wasn't a very bright student. I didn't much like school because we moved so much and I was always new and funny looking. In my fifth-grade report card I have nothing but an avalanche of C's and D's, but I don't remember being that stupid. I was good at art and I read plenty of library books and Kiki laughed at all my jokes. At home I was fine, but at school I never opened my mouth except when the teacher called on me.

When I think of how I see myself it would have to be at age eleven. I know I'm thirty-two on the outside, but inside I'm eleven. I'm the girl in the picture with skinny arms and a crumpled skirt and crooked hair. I didn't like school because all they saw was the outside me. School was lots of rules and sitting with your hands folded and being very afraid all the time. I liked looking out the window and thinking. I liked staring at the girl across the way writing her name over and over again in red ink. I wondered why the boy with the dirty collar in front of me didn't have a mama who took better care of him.

I think my mama and papa did the best they could to keep us warm and clean and never hungry. We had birthday and graduation parties and things like that, but there was another hunger that had to be fed. There was a hunger I didn't even have a name for. Was this when I began writing?

In 1966 we moved into a house, a real one, our first real home. This meant we didn't have to change schools and be the new kids on the block every couple of years. We could make friends and not be afraid we'd have to say goodbye to them and start all over. My brothers and the flock of boys they brought home would become important characters eventually for my stories—Louie and his cousins, Meme Ortiz and his dog with two names, one in English and one in Spanish.

My mother <u>flourished</u> in her own home. She took books out of the library and taught herself to garden—to grow flowers so envied we had to put a lock on the gate to keep out the midnight flower thieves. My mother has never quit gardening.

This was the period in my life, that slippery age when you are both child and woman and neither, I was to record in *The House on Mango Street*. I was still shy. I was a girl who couldn't come out of her shell.

How was I to know I would be recording and documenting the women who sat their sadness on an elbow and stared out a window? It would be the city streets of Chicago I would later record, as seen through a child's eyes.

I've done all kinds of things I didn't think I could do since then. I've gone to a <u>prestigious</u> university, studied with famous writers, and taken an MFA degree. I've taught poetry in schools in Illinois and Texas. I've gotten an NEA grant and run away with it as far as my courage would take me. I've seen the bleached and bitter mountains of the Peloponnesus.[4] I've lived on an island. I've been to Venice twice. I've lived in

---

4. **Peloponnesus** (pel′ə·pə·nē′səs): large peninsula on the mainland of Greece.

---

**Vocabulary**

**nomadic** (nō·mad′ik) *adj.*: wandering.
**nostalgia** (nä·stal′jə) *n.*: longing.
**flourished** (flʉr′ishd) *v.*: thrived; prospered.
**prestigious** (pres·tij′əs) *adj.*: impressive; having distinction.

J. Frank Dobie's Paisano ranch.

Yugoslavia. I've been to the famous Nice[5] flower market behind the opera house. I've lived in a village in the pre-Alps and witnessed the daily parade of promenaders.

I've moved since Europe to the strange and wonderful country of Texas, land of polaroid-blue skies and big bugs. I met a mayor with my last name. I met famous Chicana and Chicano artists and writers and *políticos*.

Texas is another chapter in my life. It brought with it the Dobie-Paisano Fellowship, a six-month residency on a 265-acre ranch. But most important, Texas brought Mexico back to me.

In the days when I would sit at my favorite people-watching spot, the snakey Woolworth's counter across the street from the Alamo (the Woolworth's which has since been torn down to make way for progress), I couldn't think of anything else I'd rather be than a writer. I've traveled and lectured from Cape Cod to San Francisco, to Spain, Yugoslavia, Greece, Mexico, France, Italy, and now today to Texas. Along the way there has been straw for the taking. With a little imagination, it can be spun into gold. ■

---

5. **Nice** (nēs): port city in southern France.

# Response and Analysis

## Reading Check

1. What similarities does Cisneros see between making the tortillas and writing the critical essay for her MFA exam? How does she feel about doing both?

2. Describe Cisneros's experiences at elementary school.

3. Why does Cisneros think that wanting a home is a **theme** that obsesses her?

## Thinking Critically

4. Think of the metamorphoses characters undergo in myths and fairy tales. How would you interpret the essay's subtitle, "The Metamorphosis of the Everyday"?

5. Look back at your reading notes, and describe how Cisneros believes her family helped to shape her as a writer. What other qualities as a person and a writer has she developed from her childhood background?

6. What do you think Cisneros means when she says she found herself "documenting the women who sat their sadness on an elbow and stared out a window" (page 1124)?

7. A writer's **style** is the distinctive way in which he or she uses language. Identify some fresh **images** and **figures of speech** in the essay that reveal Cisneros as an accomplished writer. How would you describe her style? (Is it formal, conversational, poetic?)

8. The title of the essay includes an **allusion** to the folk tale about Rumpelstiltskin. In the essay itself, how does Cisneros use that magical story as a **metaphor** for her writing? How does the title point to the essay's **main idea**?

9. On page 1124, Cisneros describes "a hunger I didn't even have a name for." In the excerpt from *Black Boy* (page 1065), Richard Wright describes physical and emotional hunger. How would you compare Cisneros's hunger with Wright's? How do their cultures and backgrounds influence their experiences?

## WRITING
### Women of Culture

Like Cisneros's writings, the works of Alice Walker (page 1102) and Amy Tan (page 1015) have been greatly influenced by each author's family and cultural background. All three women have also transformed their experiences into meaningful literature. Research the background of Cisneros, Walker, or Tan, and then write an **essay** in which you explore one way in which the writer's work has been shaped by her background.

---

### Vocabulary Development
#### Which Word?

| | | |
|---|---|---|
| subsisting | ventured | nostalgia |
| intuitively | taboo | flourished |
| edible | nomadic | prestigious |

Use a Vocabulary word to answer each question below. Use each word only once.

1. Which word would you use to describe what last year's bumper crop did?

2. Which word might be used in a book about mushrooms?

3. Which word describes how a dog is living if it eats only what it finds on the street?

4. Which word might a DJ use to describe her audience's longing for oldies?

5. Which word could you use to describe the most influential law firm in the country?

6. Which word can be used to describe the lifestyle of wandering sheepherders?

7. Which word refers to forbidden behavior?

8. Which word describes what a person who has left the safety of the known has done?

9. Which word is the opposite of *consciously*?

---

**SKILLS FOCUS**

**Literary Skills**
Analyze allusion.

**Reading Skills**
Analyze a writer's background.

**Writing Skills**
Write an essay exploring the impact of a writer's background on her work.

**Vocabulary Skills**
Demonstrate word knowledge.

# Analyzing Nonfiction

**Writing Assignment**
Write an essay analyzing how a writer of nonfiction uses literary elements to achieve specific rhetorical and aesthetic purposes.

The contemporary works you've read in this section are classified as nonfiction because they're based on fact. Nonfiction, when in the hands of skilled writers, has literary qualities as lively and compelling as those in fiction. By analyzing a work of **literary nonfiction,** you can learn how the writer uses language to convey significant ideas both effectively and artistically.

**Choose a Nonfiction Work** You may already know of an interesting work of literary nonfiction, such as an essay, a memoir, or a letter. If not, scan this book's table of contents or anthologies of nonfiction for ideas, or ask your teachers or school librarian to recommend works in current magazines or newspapers or on the Internet.

**Consider Purpose, Audience, and Form** When you compose an analysis of nonfiction, keep in mind that the **purpose** of your analysis is to explain how the nonfiction writer uses literary elements to achieve specific **rhetorical** and **aesthetic goals.** In other words, you'll explain what makes the writing effective and artistically appealing. Your immediate **audience** will be your teacher and classmates, and the **form** in which you'll present your analysis will be a written essay.

**Survey the Work** During your first reading of the work, identify the writer's purpose, and develop a general understanding of the work's ideas. During your second reading, use the questions in the chart below to analyze which literary elements the writer uses and what effect they have on the work. The sample answers are for an analysis of Alice Walker's essay "In Search of Our Mothers' Gardens" (page 1105).

## ANALYSIS QUESTIONS AND SAMPLE ANSWERS

| | |
|---|---|
| What **theme,** or insight about human life, is revealed in the work? | African American women have always found ways to sustain their creative spirits. |
| What is the work's **tone**—the writer's attitude toward the subject and audience? | The writer's tone is respectful and determined. |
| What emotional state, or **mood,** does the work evoke? | The work evokes pride and respect for all African American women, especially for the writer's mother. |

**Style,** a writer's distinct use of language, is another important literary element. To analyze the **stylistic devices** writers use, look for the devices listed in the chart on the next page, and try to determine what effect the device has on the work you've selected.

**TIP** Keep in mind that not every work will necessarily include all of the stylistic devices listed below. Writers often use one or two devices more than the others, or use several of them sparingly to achieve their intended effect.

## STYLISTIC DEVICES AND EXAMPLES

| | |
|---|---|
| **Irony**—a contrast or discrepancy between expectation and reality | The writer's mother, although "hindered and intruded upon" (1108), made art a daily part of her life. |
| **Diction**—choice of words; can be neutral and objective, or emotionally charged | Strong verbs, such as "battled" and "labored" (1105), reflect the strength of the writer's mother. |
| **Imagery**—language that appeals to the senses; can evoke emotions | The vivid images of the Smithsonian quilt, the mother's garden, and the determined woman described in the poem make the reader feel a sense of awe. |
| **Sound effects**—such as the **repetition** of vowel or consonant sounds **(assonance, alliteration)**, sound patterns **(rhythm)**, or words and phrases | Repeating "She" as the subject of four consecutive sentences strongly reinforces the mother's endless tasks (1105). Highlighting her creative spirit are the phrases "so brilliant," "so original," and "so magnificent" (1107). |
| Other stylistic devices include **allusions, figurative language, parallelism,** and **sentence structure.** | The writer's mother is metaphorically described as "Creator." Her garden is the universe she made. |

**State and Support Your Thesis** Choose the literary elements that contribute most to making the work effective and appealing. Then, write a **thesis statement** that identifies the elements and expresses your main idea about them. Next, support your thesis statement with **precise and relevant examples.** Use direct quotations, paraphrases, and summaries of the text to support the ideas in your analysis. Provide at least two examples for each element you select. Document your direct quotations with parenthetical citations.

| **DO THIS** →

**Organize Your Essay** Finally, make sure the organization of your essay is clear and logical by using the following two common organizational patterns for analyses.

**SKILLS FOCUS**

**Writing Skills**
Write an essay analyzing nonfiction. Choose a nonfiction work. Consider purpose, audience, and form. Survey the work. State and support your thesis. Organize your essay.

- **Chronological order** traces the writer's use of one literary element from its first appearance in the work until its last.

- **Order of importance** arranges discussion of more than one element from most important to least important, or vice versa.

**PRACTICE & APPLY** Using the guidelines in this workshop, plan and write an essay that analyzes how a writer uses literary elements in a nonfiction work. Then, share your analysis with your classmates.

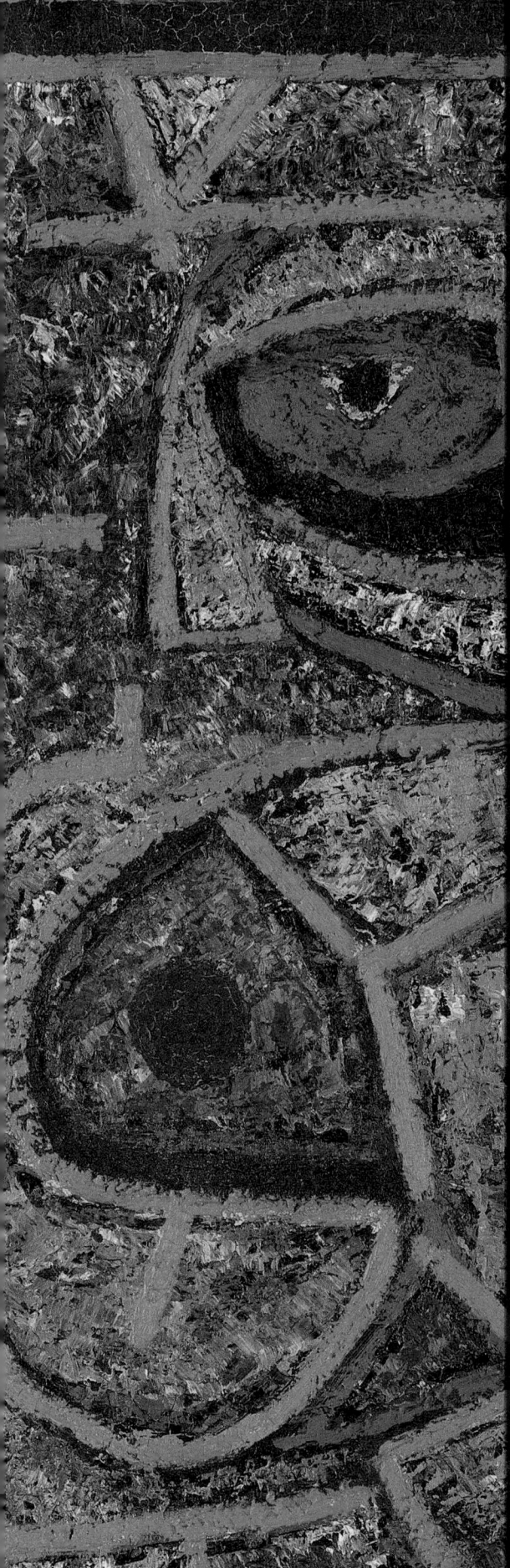

# Contemporary Poetry

| | |
|---|---|
| Roethke | Forché |
| Wilbur | Cofer |
| Bishop | Dove |
| Plath | Doty |
| Sexton | Lee |
| Brooks | Ali |
| Walcott | Collins |

If we are looking for something which is new and something which is vital, we must look first into the chaos within ourselves. That will help us in the directions that we need to go—that's why our poetry is so essential, so vital.

—Audre Lorde

*Untitled* (detail) (1952) by Kenneth Noland.
Oil on fiberboard mounted on wood: plywood, (21³/₈″ × 13¹/₈″).

Smithsonian American Art Museum, Washington, D.C. Art © Kenneth Noland, Licensed by VAGA, New York, NY.

# Theodore Roethke

## (1908–1963)

"**E**verything that lives is holy: I call upon these holy forms of life." These words of Theodore Roethke's, which sound like the words of a religious ceremony, are at the core of his intense vision. For Roethke (ret′kē) the function of poetry is to represent in words the sanctified forms and experiences of life.

A native of Saginaw, Michigan, Roethke grew up in a family that had an enormous influence on his poetry. His father owned the largest greenhouse complex in the state, and Roethke's childhood was spent close to nature, nurturing cuttings and small plants and walking in the vast acres of woodlands owned by his family. This childhood world provided the foundation for much of his poetry, which often looks at the smallest aspects of nature—worms, snails, tiny seedlings—through the eyes of a child. "I have a genuine love of nature," he wrote when he was a sophomore in college. "When I get alone under an open sky where man isn't too evident—then I'm tremendously exalted and a thousand vivid ideas and sweet visions flood my consciousness."

Roethke studied law and worked in public relations for some time after graduating from college, but his desire to become a writer finally led him to graduate school. He began a teaching career at Lafayette College in Easton, Pennsylvania (where he also coached the tennis team); taught at Pennsylvania State University; and, from 1947 until his death, taught at the University of Washington.

A passionate and dedicated teacher, Roethke brought the same energy to the classroom that he brought to poetry. In teaching he sought the same rewards he searched for in his writing: transcendence and illumination.

The search for illumination and ecstasy was a fundamental concern for Roethke in life as well as in poetry. This search brought with it a

psychological imbalance that he tried to face openly and employ honestly in his verse. "My heart keeps open house," he wrote in an early poem.

Between 1947 and 1958, Roethke published four volumes of poetry and received a number of honors, including a Pulitzer Prize, a National Book Award, and a Bollingen Prize. A poet of both pain and joy, the dark and the light, Roethke tried to find in both extremes the same transcendent moment, "a consciousness beyond the mundane," as he once put it, "a purity, a final innocence."

### For Independent Reading

Try these poems by Roethke:

- "The Bat"
- "My Papa's Waltz"
- "Elegy for Jane"

Railroad Sunset (1929) by Edward Hopper (1882–1967). Oil on canvas. 29¼ × 48 in. (74.3 × 121.92 cm).

# Before You Read

## Night Journey

### Make the Connection

A cross-country train ride is a real journey. From coast to coast, a train ride takes about three days. Today we can fly across the country in about five hours. What once had to be a journey can now be merely a trip. What would we experience during a train ride that we would miss while we were thousands of feet up in a plane?

*Pullman berth* in line 3 refers to a car with sleeping arrangements. The Pullman car was named after its inventor, G. M. Pullman.

### Literary Focus
#### Rhyme and Rhythm

**Rhyme** is the repetition of vowel sounds in accented syllables and in all succeeding syllables (*wonder/thunder*). Rhymes can be **internal** (appearing within lines), or they can be **end rhymes** (coming at the ends of lines). Not all poets use rhyme; some poets use it so subtly that unless you listen closely, you may miss the rhyme altogether.

**Rhythm** is the alternation of stressed and unstressed syllables in oral and written language. Rhythm occurs in all uses of language, but it is most obvious in poetry.

> **Rhyme** is the repetition of vowel sounds in accented syllables and in all succeeding syllables.
>
> **Rhythm** is the alternation of stressed and unstressed syllables in oral and written language.
>
> *For more on Rhyme and Rhythm, see the Handbook of Literary and Historical Terms.*

**SKILLS FOCUS**

**Literary Skills**
Understand rhyme and rhythm.

# Night Journey

## Theodore Roethke

Now as the train bears west,
Its rhythm rocks the earth,
And from my pullman berth
I stare into the night
5  While others take their rest.
Bridges of iron lace,
A suddenness of trees,
A lap of mountain mist
All cross my line of sight,
10  Then a bleak wasted place,
And a lake below my knees.
Full on my neck I feel
The straining at the curve;
My muscles move with steel,

15  I wake in every nerve.
I watch a beacon swing
From dark to blazing bright;
We thunder through ravines
And gullies washed with light.
20  Beyond the mountain pass
Mist deepens on the pane;
We rush into the rain
That rattles double glass.
Wheels shake the roadbed stone,
25  The pistons jerk and shove.
I stay up half the night
To see the land I love.

# Response and Analysis

## Thinking Critically

1. Roethke uses **metaphors,** imaginative comparisons between two unlike things, to share his experiences. What metaphors in lines 6–8 help you imagine the bridges, the trees, and the mist in new ways?

2. Roethke also uses **images,** descriptive words that help you see, hear, taste, smell, or touch something. In lines 16–24, what images help you see and hear what the speaker sees and hears from his berth?

3. What is the speaker's **attitude** toward the train and toward the land? Which line gives you the answer?

4. What words at the ends of the lines **rhyme**? Which end-of-line words have no matching rhyming sounds in the poem?

## WRITING

### Comparing Literature

Carl Sandburg also wrote a poem about train travel. His poem "Limited" appears below. Many trains are still called Limited— they are fast trains that make few stops. As you read this poem, think about all the meanings *limited* can have.

### Limited

I am riding on a limited express,
    one of the crack trains of the
    nation.
Hurtling across the prairie into
    blue haze and dark air go
    fifteen all-steel coaches holding
    a thousand people.
(All the coaches shall be scrap and
    rust and all the men and women
    laughing in the diners and sleep-
    ers shall pass to ashes.)
I ask a man in the smoker where
    he is going and he answers:
    "Omaha."

                —Carl Sandburg

In an **essay,** compare Sandburg's poem with Roethke's. Before you begin writing, gather details for a comparison, using a chart like the following one:

|  | Roethke | Sandburg |
|---|---|---|
| Subject |  |  |
| What poem says about subject |  |  |
| Images |  |  |
| Rhythm and rhymes |  |  |
| Significance of title |  |  |
| Tone of poem |  |  |

## LISTENING AND SPEAKING

### Night Journey Alive

Perform "Night Journey" aloud. In planning your performance, re-read the poem. Notice how the poem's **rhythm** helps create the feeling of riding on a train. Is the rhythm metrically regular—that is, does the poet use a strong, steady pattern of stressed and unstressed syllables? Or is the poem written loosely, without regard for meter? You can find the answers to these questions by reading the poem aloud and listening to its beat.

**SKILLS FOCUS**

**Literary Skills**
Analyze rhyme and rhythm.

**Writing Skills**
Write an essay comparing two poems.

**Listening and Speaking Skills**
Perform an oral recitation of a poem.

# Richard Wilbur

## (1921–    )

"**N**o poetry can have any strength unless it continually bashes itself against the reality of things." This poetic credo of Richard Wilbur's has given us some of the strongest poems of our time—rock hard at the center, subtle and delicate on the edges.

From the time of his first book, *The Beautiful Changes and Other Poems* (1947), Wilbur has been recognized as one of the most graceful and technically adept poets of his generation. His poetry reminds us of the meters and natural speech of Robert Frost and of the metaphysical elegance and emotional reticence of Wallace Stevens.

The influences of Frost and Stevens are merely overtones, however. Wilbur's poetic character is forged of his own unassertive religious devotion, his political liberalism, and his irrepressible delight in "the things of this world." Wilbur writes at a time when poetry has often been marked by self-promotion and seeming formlessness, as well as by uneasy borrowings from the paintings of minimalists and surrealists. But Wilbur has continued to write lyrics demanding scrupulous care and skill. His inward vision of delight finds expression in measured speech and indelible metaphor.

Wilbur was born in New York City but grew up in suburban New Jersey. He attended Amherst College in Massachusetts, served with combat troops during World War II, and went to graduate school at Harvard. There he prepared for the illustrious teaching career that has taken him to long-term appointments at Wellesley, Wesleyan (in Connecticut), and Smith. During 1987–1988, Wilbur served as poet laureate of the United States.

When Wilbur is not on reading tours that take him across the continent, he divides his time between Cummington, Massachusetts— the Berkshire village where he lives within a stone's throw of the homestead where William Cullen Bryant (page 189) lived—and Key West, Florida.

In addition to poetry, Wilbur has produced sparkling translations of the plays of Molière, including *The Misanthrope* (1955) and *Tartuffe* (1963). These rhymed-verse versions of the seventeenth-century French playwright's work are both elegant and earthy, as well as practical enough to be successfully produced on stage.

Two of Wilbur's poetry collections, *Things of This World: Poems* (1956) and *New and Collected Poems* (1988), won Pulitzer Prizes. He has also published several noted books for children, including four witty books about synonyms and antonyms. The fourth is called *Opposites, More Opposites, and a Few Differences* (2000).

### For Independent Reading

For a closer look at Wilbur, try these poems:

- "Boy at the Window"
- "The Writer"

## The Beautiful Changes

### Make the Connection

Think of all the beautiful things in the world. How do you feel when you look at a clear blue lake or a starry sky or an insect so intricate that it too strikes you as beautiful? What effect does beauty have on you?

Then, think about love. How does love change the world? Have you ever felt that all things great and small become beautiful because *you* are in love?

### Literary Focus
#### Ambiguity

The title of Wilbur's poem presents us with an **ambiguity**—that is, the statement in the title can mean several things. Does "the beautiful changes" mean that beautiful things change? Does it mean, perhaps, that all changes are beautiful? Or does it mean that our *idea* of what is beautiful changes? Could all these meanings apply to the poem's title?

> **Ambiguity** is a technique whereby a writer deliberately suggests two or more different meanings.
>
> *For more on Ambiguity, see the Handbook of Literary and Historical Terms.*

### Background

Queen Anne's lace (or wild carrot) is a common weed. Its flower looks like a crocheted doily with a tiny ruby at its center. "Lucernes" (loo·surnz') is a reference to the beautiful glacier-fed Lake of Lucerne in Switzerland.

**SKILLS FOCUS**

**Literary Skills**
Understand ambiguity.

*Approaching Thunderstorm* (1859) by Martin Johnson Heade. Oil on canvas. (28″ × 44″).

The Metropolitan Museum of Art, Gift of Erving Wolfe Foundation and Mr. and Mrs. Erving Wolfe, 1975. (1975.160) Photograph © 1992 The Metropolitan Museum of Art.

# The Beautiful Changes

## Richard Wilbur

One wading a Fall meadow finds on all sides
The Queen Anne's Lace lying like lilies
On water; it glides
So from the walker, it turns
5    Dry grass to a lake, as the slightest shade of you
Valleys my mind in fabulous blue Lucernes.

The beautiful changes as a forest is changed
By a chameleon's tuning his skin to it;
As a mantis, arranged
10   On a green leaf, grows
Into it, makes the leaf leafier, and proves
Any greenness is deeper than anyone knows.

Your hands hold roses always in a way that says
They are not only yours; the beautiful changes
15   In such kind ways,
Wishing ever to sunder
Things and things' selves for a second finding, to lose
For a moment all that it touches back to wonder.

# Response and Analysis

## Thinking Critically

1. According to the speaker, how does Queen Anne's lace change a meadow of dry grass?

2. Who could be "you" in line 5?

3. How does "you" affect the speaker?

4. How does a chameleon change a forest? How does a mantis change a green leaf?

5. What is "you" doing in the last stanza?

6. To understand what the speaker says about the beautiful changes, paraphrase the last stanza. (The verb *sunder* in line 16 means "separate; break apart.")

7. In your own words, explain the **ambiguity** of the title. Does the poem as a whole support just one meaning or all meanings?

8. Is this a love poem? If so, whom or what does the speaker love? Pick out the lines that support your answer.

## WRITING

### "Glorious Energy"

In an interview, Wilbur made this statement:

> To put it simply, I feel that the universe is full of glorious energy, that the energy tends to take pattern and shape, and that the ultimate character of things is comely and good.

In a brief **essay,** discuss how "The Beautiful Changes" supports Wilbur's statement. Do you agree with him? Why or why not?

### The Beautiful Changes

Write three lines of a **poem** in which you tell how *you* think the beautiful changes. You could structure your verse with these words: "The beautiful changes as . . . is changed into . . ."

**SKILLS FOCUS**

**Literary Skills**
Analyze ambiguity.

**Writing Skills**
Write an essay evaluating a writer's comment. Write three lines of a poem.

# Elizabeth Bishop
## (1911–1979)

**A** "poet's poet," Elizabeth Bishop has been, for many important poets of our time, an acknowledged master of the highest art and most meticulous craft. She has also been an unacknowledged inspiration for many other poets who are still trying to solve the mystery of her impenetrable simplicity. Her poetry has won wide formal recognition, including a Pulitzer Prize for *Poems: North and South—A Cold Spring* (1955) and a National Book Award for *Complete Poems* (1969).

Born in Worcester, Massachusetts, Bishop spent her early years in a Nova Scotia village—a childhood marked by the early death of her father and darkened by the long illness of her mother. These circumstances in effect made her an orphan whose upbringing was entrusted to relatives.

At the time of her mother's death in a psychiatric hospital, Bishop was a student at Vassar College. After graduation she embarked on a career quietly devoted to poetry and, by means of a private income, travel. In her travels she discovered two places congenial enough to detain her for years—Key West, Florida, and Rio de Janeiro, Brazil. *Questions of Travel* (1965), the title she gave to one of her books, might serve as an index to the story of a life told in poems that are always "letters from abroad." In these poems, places—near or far—provide temporary settings for an endless inquiry into the nature of perception and reality.

In the final years of her life, Bishop lived in a condominium on a Boston Harbor wharf and spent her summers on an island off the coast of Maine. These changes of scene came about when her close friend the poet Robert Lowell became ill and Harvard University invited her to take over the classes he had been scheduled to teach. She continued to teach at Harvard until her death.

A shy woman with a taste for the exotic as well as a love of the ordinary, Bishop surrounded herself with artifacts acquired in the course of her travels. She conducted herself with a scrupulous conventionality much at odds with the audacity and profundity of her imagination. Her poems most truly reveal her character: a combination of the conservatism and moral rectitude many associate with the North and the casual sensuousness and cheerfully untidy sprawl many associate with nature and the everyday outdoor life of the South. For Elizabeth Bishop, geography was less a matter of maps and place-names than of states of mind and areas of feeling.

## The Fish

### Make the Connection

Since ancient times, people have observed things from the natural world and seen all aspects of human behavior reflected in them—from the heroic to the most foolish. Have you ever looked at some animal and felt great sympathy for it? Or have you ever sensed something heroic about an animal or even a tree—some courage or "humanity" that surprised you?

### Literary Focus
#### Symbol

A **symbol** is a person, a place, a thing, or an event that has meaning in itself and also stands for something much more than itself. Often symbols stand for abstract ideas or qualities. The dove, for instance, is used as a symbol of peace. A skull symbolizes death. A red rose symbolizes love. A flag symbolizes an entire country. These are all public symbols; everyone agrees on what they mean. Writers may make up private symbols. As you read this poem, think about what this old fish might symbolize to the speaker.

> A **symbol** is a person, a place, a thing, or an event that has meaning in itself and also stands for something much more than itself.
>
> *For more on Symbol, see the Handbook of Literary and Historical Terms.*

**SKILLS FOCUS**

**Literary Skills**
Understand symbols.

**Elizabeth Bishop    1139**

# The Fish

## Elizabeth Bishop

I caught a tremendous fish
and held him beside the boat
half out of water, with my hook
fast in a corner of his mouth.
5   He didn't fight.
He hadn't fought at all.
He hung a grunting weight,
battered and venerable°
and homely. Here and there
10  his brown skin hung in strips
like ancient wall-paper,
and its pattern of darker brown
was like wall-paper:
shapes like full-blown roses
15  stained and lost through age.
He was speckled with barnacles,
fine rosettes° of lime,
and infested
with tiny white sea-lice,
20  and underneath two or three
rags of green weed hung down.
While his gills were breathing in
the terrible oxygen
—the frightening gills
25  fresh and crisp with blood,
that can cut so badly—
I thought of the coarse white flesh
packed in like feathers,
the big bones and the little bones,
30  the dramatic reds and blacks
of his shiny entrails,
and the pink swim-bladder
like a big peony.
I looked into his eyes
35  which were far larger than mine

*Leaping Trout* (1889) by Winslow Homer.
Watercolor on paper ($14^{1}/_{16}$″ × $20^{1}/_{16}$″).

but shallower, and yellowed,
the irises backed and packed
with tarnished tinfoil
seen through the lenses
40  of old scratched isinglass.°
They shifted a little, but not
to return my stare.
—It was more like the tipping
of an object toward the light.
45  I admired his sullen face,
the mechanism of his jaw,
and then I saw

---

**8. venerable** *adj.:* old and respected.
**17. rosettes** *n. pl.:* formations resembling roses.

---

**40. isinglass** (ī′zin‧glas′) *n.:* mica, a glasslike
mineral that crystallizes in thin layers.

that from his lower lip
—if you could call it a lip—
50 grim, wet, and weapon-like,
hung five old pieces of fish-line,
or four and a wire leader
with the swivel still attached,
with all their five big hooks
55 grown firmly in his mouth.
A green line, frayed at the end
where he broke it, two heavier lines,
and a fine black thread
still crimped from the strain and snap
60 when it broke and he got away.
Like medals with their ribbons
frayed and wavering,
a five-haired beard of wisdom
trailing from his aching jaw.

65 I stared and stared
and victory filled up
the little rented boat,
from the pool of bilge°
where oil had spread a rainbow
70 around the rusted engine
to the bailer rusted orange,
the sun-cracked thwarts,°
the oarlocks on their strings,
the gunnels°—until everything
75 was rainbow, rainbow, rainbow!
And I let the fish go.

---

**68. bilge** *n.:* dirty water that gathers in the bottom of a boat.
**72. thwarts** *n. pl.:* seats on a boat.
**74. gunnels** *n. pl.:* gunwales, the upper edges of the sides of a boat.

**Elizabeth Bishop    1141**

# Before You Read

## One Art

### Make the Connection
**Quickwrite** 🖉

We all lose things—a favorite cap, our keys, a pair of sunglasses. Take a few minutes to write down some of the losses everyone must face in life—from silly losses to tragic ones.

### Literary Focus
**Villanelle**

A **villanelle** (vil'ə·nel') is an intricately patterned, nineteen-line lyric poem. The traditional format for this type of poem follows these guidelines:

- The poem consists of five three-line stanzas and a final four-line stanza.
- The first line of the poem is repeated as the last line of the second and fourth stanzas.
- The third line of the poem is repeated as the last line of the third and fifth stanzas.
- These two repeated, or refrain, lines also make up the two final lines of the poem.
- The rhyme scheme is *aba*, except in the last stanza, where it is *abaa*.

This complex form of poetry presents many challenges: maintaining a steady rhythm, finding enough rhyming words for the *a* or *b* endings of all nineteen lines, and, especially, constructing the poem in such a way that the emotional intensity reaches a crescendo in the final stanza.

> A **villanelle** is an intricately patterned, nineteen-line lyric poem.
>
> *For more on Villanelle, see the Handbook of Literary and Historical Terms.*

**SKILLS FOCUS**

**Literary Skills**
Understand the characteristics of a villanelle.

# One Art

## Elizabeth Bishop

The art of losing isn't hard to master;
so many things seem filled with the intent
to be lost that their loss is no disaster.

Lose something every day. Accept the fluster
5   of lost door keys, the hour badly spent.
The art of losing isn't hard to master.

Then practice losing farther, losing faster:
places, and names, and where it was you meant
to travel. None of these will bring disaster.

10   I lost my mother's watch. And look! my last, or
next-to-last, of three loved houses went.
The art of losing isn't hard to master.

I lost two cities, lovely ones. And, vaster,
some realms I owned, two rivers, a continent.
15   I miss them, but it wasn't a disaster.

—Even losing you (the joking voice, a gesture
I love) I shan't have lied. It's evident
the art of losing's not too hard to master
though it may look like (*Write* it!) like disaster.

*Lovers with Flowers* (1927) by Marc Chagall.
Israel Museum, Jerusalem, Israel, © 2005 Artists Rights
Society (ARS), New York/ADAGP, Paris.

# Response and Analysis

## The Fish

### Thinking Critically

1. Describe the setting of "The Fish."

2. Why is the oxygen "terrible" in line 23?

3. This speaker describes the fish in a series of **similes** and **metaphors.** Find at least six **figures of speech,** or imaginative comparisons, in lines 1–40 that help you visualize the fish.

4. Identify the two figures of speech in lines 61–64 that **personify** the fish—that make the fish seem human. What type of person do these comparisons suggest?

5. What are the "medals" in line 61 and the "five-haired beard of wisdom" in line 63?

6. As the speaker stared at the fish, "victory filled up" the boat. Whose victory is it? Who or what is the enemy?

7. Why do you think she lets the fish go?

8. What clues suggest that the fish might have a **symbolic** meaning? What could the rainbow at the end mean? Explain.

### Extending and Evaluating

9. Writers can be criticized for being too sentimental when they write about the natural world. Is Bishop being sentimental about this fish, or is she realistic in her re-creation of her experience? Explain your evaluation of the poem.

## One Art

### Thinking Critically

1. List, by stanza, the things the speaker has lost. What progression do you see in the importance of the things lost? Refer to your Quickwrite notes to compare your list of losses with those in the poem.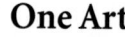

2. What is the **tone** of the first stanza—how does the speaker feel about losing things? Use different adjectives to describe the tone of each succeeding stanza. How has the tone changed by the final stanza?

3. The poem reaches its emotional climax in the last stanza. How might the speaker really feel about losing "you"?

4. In the final line of the poem, whom is the speaker addressing when she orders, "*Write* it!" Do you think the speaker believes what she is saying, or is she just putting up a good front? Use details from the poem to support your answer.

### Extending and Evaluating

5. Review the characteristics of the **villanelle** form (see the Literary Focus on page 1142). How closely does Bishop follow the form? What do you think of her variations—especially in the very last line?

## WRITING

### Analyzing a Poem

The first line of "The Fish" is a simple statement: "I caught a tremendous fish." So is the last line: "And I let the fish go." What happens in between? Write a brief **narration** telling what happens in the poem, using chronological order. In addition to citing external actions, explain what is happening inside the speaker's mind. Be sure to identify the moment at which the speaker decides to give up something that other anglers would have kept.

### Accept the Challenge

Try writing a **villanelle** of your own. First, write the lines you will be repeating. Remember that you can make slight variations in the form, as Bishop has done with "One Art." Be sure to share your villanelle with the rest of the class.

# Sylvia Plath
(1932–1963)

**U**ntil her death, Sylvia Plath was, to most appearances, a model of achievement. Her success, however, could neither fully mask nor calm a fearsome inner turmoil.

Plath was born in Boston and spent her early years in the nearby seaside town of Winthrop. Her father, a professor of biology, was from Poland; her mother, a teacher of office skills, was from Austria. Plath later seemed convinced that the reason for her emotional suffering as an adult was her father's death, from diabetes, when she was only eight.

Plath started writing poems and stories in elementary school, and she first published a poem, in a Boston newspaper, around the time of her father's death. From an early age she was persistent in finding a publisher for her work: She persevered through forty-five rejection slips from *Seventeen* magazine before landing a story there in 1950. Plath was awarded a scholarship to Smith College, and she won a much-coveted fiction prize from *Mademoiselle* magazine in her junior year, spending the summer as a guest editor in the magazine's New York office.

The first sign of dangerous turbulence in Plath's emotional life came at the end of that seemingly storybook summer, when she was overcome by depression and attempted suicide, an experience that became the basis for her novel, *The Bell Jar.* After psychiatric treatment and electroshock therapy—"the painful agony of slow rebirth and psychic regeneration," as she called it—Plath returned to college. Unfortunately she was ill with bipolar disorder—years before effective drug therapy was available.

After graduating from Smith, Plath attended Cambridge University in England on a Fulbright fellowship. At Cambridge she met the noted English poet Ted Hughes, whom she married in 1956. They lived in Boston during most of the late 1950s and moved to London at the end of 1959. The following year, Plath's first book of poetry, *The Colossus,* was published, and their daughter, Frieda, was born; their son, Nicholas, was born in 1962.

In January 1963, Plath's famous autobiographical novel, *The Bell Jar,* was published. In the months just before its publication, Plath wrote at a furious pace—sometimes two or three poems a day. The subject matter and style of these poems, published posthumously in *Ariel* (1965), were different from her earlier work. Most poems in *The Colossus* were relatively restrained and formal, influenced by a number of poetic styles. The *Ariel* poems, especially the bitter poems about her father and her attempts at suicide, showed a violence and a frankness absent from her earlier work. The Pulitzer Prize–winning poet Robert Lowell wrote in the book's foreword, "These poems are playing Russian roulette with six cartridges in the cylinder, a game of 'chicken,' the wheels of both cars locked and unable to swerve." The poems were, he said, an "appalling and triumphant fulfillment" of her talents.

In 1963, Plath was separated from her husband and caring for their two young children in an unheated London flat. In February, during a very cold London winter, Plath's depression returned. She attempted suicide again. This time she succeeded.

In 1998, to mark what would have been Plath's sixty-fifth birthday, Hughes published *Birthday Letters,* a series of poems about Plath and their passionate but troubled relationship.

## Mirror

### Make the Connection

We all do it: We check our appearance in a mirror, partly to make sure we are appropriately groomed, partly to discover and polish our self-image. What might a mirror think or say about the people peering into or passing by it?

### Literary Focus
#### Speaker

When we read lyric poetry, we hear a voice speaking to us. Often we identify that voice as the poet's. At other times, though, the voice talking to us in the poem is identifiable as someone or something else. In the following two poems by Sylvia Plath, the speakers are things that in reality have no voice at all. The poet imagines what these things—a mirror and mushrooms—would share with us if they had a voice.

> The **speaker** of a poem is the person (or thing) addressing the reader directly, using the pronoun *I*.
>
> *For more on Speaker, see the Handbook of Literary and Historical Terms.*

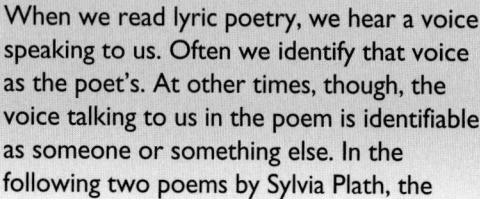

## Sylvia Plath

I am silver and exact. I have no preconceptions.°
Whatever I see I swallow immediately
Just as it is, unmisted by love or dislike.
I am not cruel, only truthful—
5   The eye of a little god, four-cornered.
Most of the time I meditate on the opposite wall.
It is pink, with speckles. I have looked at it so long
I think it is a part of my heart. But it flickers.
Faces and darkness separate us over and over.
10  Now I am a lake. A woman bends over me,
Searching my reaches for what she really is.
Then she turns to those liars, the candles or the moon.
I see her back, and reflect it faithfully.
She rewards me with tears and an agitation° of hands.
15  I am important to her. She comes and goes.
Each morning it is her face that replaces the darkness.
In me she has drowned a young girl, and in me an old woman
Rises toward her day after day, like a terrible fish.

**1. preconceptions** *n. pl.:* ideas or opinions formed before having enough information.

**14. agitation** *n.:* violent motion.

*Mirror IV* (1976–1979) by George Tooker. Egg tempera on gesso panel (24″ × 20″).

# Before You Read

## Mushrooms

### Make the Connection

Have you ever thought about the power of nature—how flowers can appear out of nowhere after a rainstorm? how trees can slice through a sidewalk? how mushrooms can multiply silently overnight? What do such natural events make you think about? Could your reactions range from awe to horror?

### Literary Focus
### Tone

**Tone** is the attitude a writer takes toward the subject of a work, the characters in the work, or the audience. Tone, which results from the complex interplay of diction and style, can often be described in one word (*playful, sarcastic, tragic*). As you read "Mushrooms," listen for its tone.

> **Tone** is the attitude a writer takes toward the subject of a work, the characters in the work, or the audience.
>
> *For more on Tone, see the Handbook of Literary and Historical Terms.*

**SKILLS FOCUS**

**Literary Skills**
Understand tone.

go.
hrw
.com

**INTERNET**

**More About Sylvia Plath**

Keyword: LE7 11-6

# MUSHROOMS

## Sylvia Plath

Overnight, very
Whitely, discreetly,
Very quietly

Our toes, our noses
5   Take hold on the loam,
Acquire the air.

Nobody sees us,
Stops us, betrays us;
The small grains make room.

10  Soft fists insist on
Heaving the needles,
The leafy bedding,

Even the paving.
Our hammers, our rams,
15  Earless and eyeless,

Perfectly voiceless,
Widen the crannies,
Shoulder through holes. We

Diet on water,
20  On crumbs of shadow,
Bland-mannered, asking

Little or nothing.
So many of us!
So many of us!

25  We are shelves, we are
Tables, we are meek,
We are edible,

Nudgers and shovers
In spite of ourselves.
30  Our kind multiplies:

We shall by morning
Inherit the earth.
Our foot's in the door.

# Response and Analysis

## Mirror

### Thinking Critically

1. Identify the **speaker** of the poem—who is the "I"?

2. What qualities does the speaker claim to possess? What does the speaker imply by saying it is "the eye of a little god" (line 5)?

3. Why would the speaker refer to the candles and the moon as "liars" (line 12)?

4. The last line of "Mirror" contains the striking **image** of "a terrible fish." How would you explain this last image? What associations and emotional overtones does the image of a terrible fish have for you?

5. What would you say is the real subject of this poem? (It is not really about a mirror.) What *is* it about?

## Mushrooms

### Thinking Critically

1. Who are the speakers of this poem?

2. What natural process do the speakers describe? How does the poet use **personification**—a figure of speech in which an object or an animal is given human characteristics—to help you visualize what is happening in the poem?

3. "Blessed are the meek, for they shall inherit the earth" is a well-known expression from Matthew 5:5 in the Bible. Where do the speakers of the poem allude to this saying? Are the speakers truly meek? Explain your responses to this stanza.

4. What kind of people do you think the mushrooms **symbolize**? Explain.

5. You have read two poems by Plath. What **tones** do you hear in these poems? (Are the tones similar?)

## WRITING

### Mirror Poem

Write your own **poem** in which you give a mirror a voice. Let your mirror speak as "I." Make clear to the reader what kind of mirror is speaking (wall mirror, hand mirror, car mirror, and so on). What does *your* mirror think about the people and events it reflects?

### Comparing Texts

In a brief **essay,** compare Plath's attitude toward nature in "Mushrooms" with the attitude toward nature revealed in another text, such as Emerson's *Nature* (page 206), Thoreau's *Walden* (page 216), Dickinson's "Apparently with no surprise" (page 398), or Bishop's "The Fish" (page 1140). Focus on these points for your comparison of the writers' ideas:

- attitude toward nature
- view of the universe as benign, hostile, or indifferent
- tone in each text

# Anne Sexton

## (1928–1974)

From the very beginning of her literary career, Anne Sexton was recognized as a spirit in turmoil. The writer James Dickey put it this way: "Anne Sexton's poems so obviously come out of deep, painful sections of the author's life that one's literary opinions scarcely seem to matter; one feels tempted to drop them furtively into the nearest ashcan, rather than be caught with them in the presence of so much naked suffering."

Sexton's poetry was an eruption of her stormy emotional life into art. The titles of her most gripping volumes indicate a preoccupation with bouts of anxiety and mental illness and with the need to confront ultimate questions: *To Bedlam and Part Way Back* (1960), *Live or Die* (1966), *The Death Notebooks* (1974), and *The Awful Rowing Toward God* (1975).

Anne Gray Harvey was born in Newton, Massachusetts, and attended the public schools in nearby Wellesley. In 1947, she enrolled in the Garland School, a finishing school for women, and in 1948 married Alfred Sexton. Anne Sexton worked for a time as a fashion model, gave birth to two daughters, and then, at age twenty-eight, began writing poetry.

Sexton studied with Robert Lowell in his graduate writing seminar at Boston University and developed friendships with other important poets, including Sylvia Plath (page 1145), Maxine Kumin, and George Starbuck. One of the strongest influences on her was the work of her friend W. D. Snodgrass, whose volume of poetry, *Heart's Needle* (1959), traced the emotional consequences of a difficult midlife divorce.

Sexton traveled to Europe and Africa, taught at Boston University, gave readings, and earned numerous prizes for her poetry, including a Pulitzer Prize for *Live or Die*. In 1968, she formed a rock-music group called Anne Sexton and Her Kind: Sexton read her poems to the accompaniment of guitar, flute, saxophone, drums, bass, and keyboards.

Sexton's poetry was intended to be, as she said, "a shock to the senses." In her second book, *All My Pretty Ones* (1962), she quoted Franz Kafka: "The books we need are the kind that act upon us like a misfortune, that make us suffer like the death of someone we love more than ourselves. . . . [A] book should serve as the ax for the frozen sea within us." Her books were personal axes, but they also opened up a wider vision of contemporary women. Many of her poems portray women in moments of crisis.

The general public as well as other poets responded enthusiastically to Sexton's poems. Artistic success did not strengthen her fragile personality, though. As her close friend Robert Lowell remembered: "At a time when poetry readings were expected to be boring, no one ever fell asleep at Anne's. I see her as having the large, transparent, breakable, and increasingly ragged wings of a dragonfly—her poor, shy, driven life, the blind terror behind her bravado, her deadly increasing pace . . . her bravery while she lasted."

### For Independent Reading

These poems by Sexton are comic and ironic takeoffs of popular fairy tales:

- "Snow White and the Seven Dwarfs"
- "Rumpelstiltskin"
- "Rapunzel"
- "Cinderella"

# Before You Read

## The Bells
## Young

### Make the Connection
### Quickwrite

Some events, major or minor at the time, stick in our minds many years later. A parade, a kiss, a summer night, a song—it could be anything that brings back the past for us and reminds us of our younger selves. Jot down an experience from the past that makes you feel joy. What images or sounds prompt your memory of the experience?

### Literary Focus
### Imagery

**Imagery** is the use of language to evoke a picture or a concrete sensation of a person, a place, a thing, or an experience. Most images appeal to our sense of sight. An image can, however, also appeal to our senses of taste, smell, hearing, and touch. In poetry, imagery is used to help us participate in an experience and evoke emotional responses. Imagery is so important in poetry that we can even make distinctions among poets based purely on the images they use.

> **Imagery** is the use of language to evoke a picture or a concrete sensation of a person, a place, a thing, or an experience.
>
> *For more on Imagery, see the Handbook of Literary and Historical Terms.*

**SKILLS FOCUS**

**Literary Skills**
Understand imagery.

# THE BELLS

## Anne Sexton

Today the circus poster
is scabbing off the concrete wall
and the children have forgotten
if they knew at all.
5    Father, do you remember?
Only the sound remains,
the distant thump of the good elephants,
the voice of the ancient lions
and how the bells
10   trembled for the flying man.
I, laughing,
lifted to your high shoulder
or small at the rough legs of strangers,
was not afraid.
15   You held my hand
and were instant to explain
the three rings of danger.
Oh see the naughty clown
and the wild parade
20   while love love
love grew rings around me.
This was the sound where it began;
our breath pounding up to see
the flying man breast out
25   across the boarded sky
and climb the air.
I remember the color of music
and how forever
all the trembling bells of you
30   were mine.

*Circus (Le Cirque)* by Marc Chagall.
© 2005 Artists Rights Society (ARS), New York/ADAGP, Paris.

*Anne Sexton said that "Young" should be "said in one breath" and that the poem is composed of a single sentence in order to capture a single moment in time.*

# Young

## Anne Sexton

A thousand doors ago
when I was a lonely kid
in a big house with four
garages and it was summer
5    as long as I could remember,
I lay on the lawn at night,
clover wrinkling under me,
the wise stars bedding over me,
my mother's window a funnel
10   of yellow heat running out,
my father's window, half shut,
an eye where sleepers pass,
and the boards of the house
were smooth and white as wax
15   and probably a million leaves
sailed on their strange stalks
as the crickets ticked together
and I, in my brand new body,
which was not a woman's yet,
20   told the stars my questions
and thought God could really see
the heat and the painted light,
elbows, knees, dreams, goodnight.

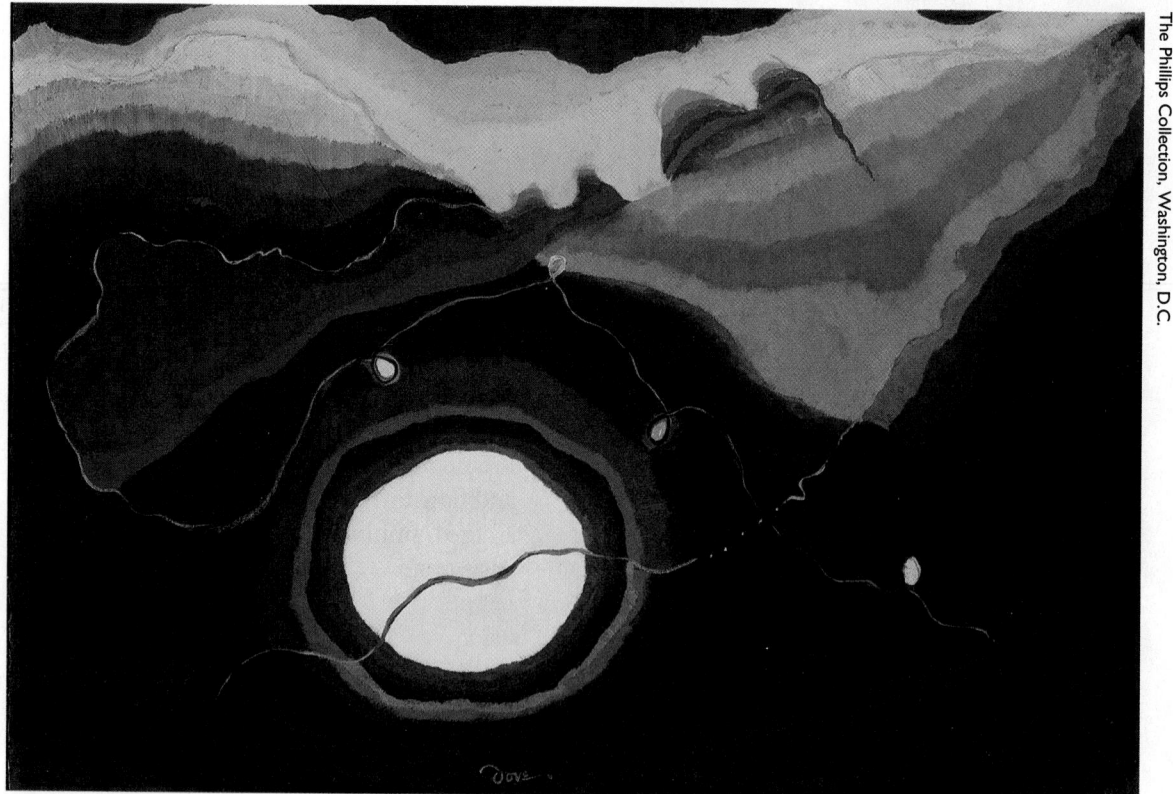

*Me and the Moon* (1937) by Arthur G. Dove.
Wax emulsion on canvas (18″ × 26″).

# Response and Analysis

## The Bells

### Thinking Critically

1. What prompts the speaker to remember the scene from her past?

2. In line 5, whom do we learn the speaker is talking to?

3. According to line 6, what "remains"?

4. How does the speaker feel about her father? What lines give you the answer?

5. Rings are mentioned twice in the poem. What are the "rings of danger"? What are the other rings?

6. Describing a perception of one sense in terms of another sense is called **synesthesia** (sin′əs·thē′zhə). What senses does Sexton mix in line 27?

7. One **theme** of the poem is conveyed with childlike simplicity in lines 28–30. How would you paraphrase these lines—that is, how would you state their message in your own words?

## Young

### Thinking Critically

1. "Young" overflows with visual **imagery.** Make a list of all the images that this poem helps you see. What image helps you *hear* a sound?

2. Sexton reminds us that this poem is one long sentence. A sentence always contains a doer and an action. What did the speaker do "a thousand doors ago" when she was a lonely kid? What did she tell the stars? What did she think God could really see?

3. Why might the speaker say that her youth took place "a thousand doors ago"?

4. What **metaphors** does the poet use to describe the windows of her house? How could these metaphors reflect the speaker's different feelings for her mother and her father?

5. Describe the **tone** of the poem—the attitude the speaker conveys toward that summer night long ago.

## WRITING

### Respond to a Critic

Sexton believed that a book "should serve as the ax for the frozen sea within us" (see page 1151). In a brief **essay,** write a response to that statement. Address these questions in your essay:

- How would you explain this quotation in your own words?
- How could these two poems break a reader's "frozen sea"?

### Writing a Description

Write a **poem** or a **paragraph** in which you use visual images to re-create an experience from your childhood that made you feel joy. You might try to model your poem after Sexton's and write just one long sentence. Be sure to refer to your Quickwrite notes.

## LISTENING AND SPEAKING

### Oral Performance

Perform "Young" aloud, as Sexton recommends. Where must you pause slightly for breath? Where is it a good idea to pause slightly for emphasis? How could you use your voice to make the poem sound as if a young girl were speaking?

# Gwendolyn Brooks
## (1917–2000)

**B**orn in Kansas, Gwendolyn Brooks grew up in Chicago, the city whose African American community she celebrated as Bronzeville in her poetry. Brooks was honored not only for her literary achievement but also for her efforts on behalf of young black writers, to whom she gave practical advice and tireless encouragement. For many of these young writers, Brooks, as a teacher and an editor, opened doors to self-realization and professional careers.

Gwendolyn Brooks established her credentials early. In her first two volumes of poetry—*A Street in Bronzeville* (1945) and *Annie Allen* (1949), for which she was awarded the Pulitzer Prize—she used conventional poetic forms to present portraits of black city dwellers. After that, Brooks turned to more open forms and more extensive use of common speech. This transition was sparked by the insistence of young black poets that their poetry use the rhythms and the vernacular of urban black speech and culture. In her work, Brooks also reflected the expansion of black consciousness in the embattled years of the 1950s and 1960s, when the civil rights movement renewed pride among the followers of Martin Luther King, Jr.

Brooks's most widely known work of fiction, *Maud Martha* (1953), is the story of a young black woman forging her identity in the face of self-doubt, racism, and disillusion. One critic wrote, "It is a powerful, beautiful dagger of a book, as generous as it can possibly be. It teaches more, more quickly, more lastingly, than a thousand pages of protest."

At the age of sixty-eight, Gwendolyn Brooks became the first black woman to serve as Poet Laureate Consultant in Poetry to the Library of Congress. Known for her generosity, Brooks often sponsored literary awards and gave prizes out of her own funds. She received numerous honorary degrees, yet she never let praise cloud her vision. In the first volume of her autobiography, *Report from Part One* (1972), Gwendolyn Brooks summed herself up this way: "I—who have 'gone the gamut' from an almost angry rejection of my dark skin by some of my brainwashed brothers and sisters to a surprised queenhood in the new Black sun—am qualified to enter at least the kindergarten of new consciousness now. New consciousness and trudge-toward-progress. I have hopes for myself."

## For Independent Reading

For more by Brooks, read

• *Maud Martha* (novel)

*Waiting Room* (detail) (1984) by Phoebe Beasley.
© Phoebe Beasley/Omni-Photo Communications.

# Before You Read

## The Bean Eaters

### Make the Connection

According to a popular saying, you are what you eat. Think about how often writers and moviemakers set scenes during meals in order to display personal conflicts and family tensions. The circumstances and details of a dinner can reveal a great deal about, for example, people's social conditions, their attitudes toward one another, and even their outlook on the future. What do you immediately think of when you read the title of this poem, "The Bean Eaters"?

### Literary Focus
### The Uses of Rhyme

In years past, a poet's use of rhyme was a matter of following rules and conventions and staying within traditional verse forms. Contemporary poets use rhyme more freely. It can be ironic or comic, quietly elegant or intentionally surprising. A poet can use rhyme to suggest a sense of control and order, calm balance, or even grim finality. When you read a poem that rhymes, ask yourself why the poet made the choice: How does the use of rhyme support the ideas or feelings the poem is trying to convey? How does rhyme create music in the poem?

> **Rhyme** is the repetition of vowel sounds in accented syllables and all succeeding syllables.
>
> *For more on Rhyme, see the Handbook of Literary and Historical Terms.*

SKILLS FOCUS

**Literary Skills**
Understand the uses of rhyme.

*Waiting Room* (1984) by Phoebe Beasley.
Collage (36" × 36").
© Phoebe Beasley

# THE BEAN EATERS

## Gwendolyn Brooks

They eat beans mostly, this old yellow pair.
Dinner is a casual affair.
Plain chipware on a plain and creaking wood,
Tin flatware.

5    Two who are Mostly Good.
Two who have lived their day,
But keep on putting on their clothes
and putting things away.

And remembering . . .
10   Remembering, with twinklings and twinges,
As they lean over the beans in their rented back room that
      is full of beads and receipts and dolls and cloths, tobacco
      crumbs, vases and fringes.

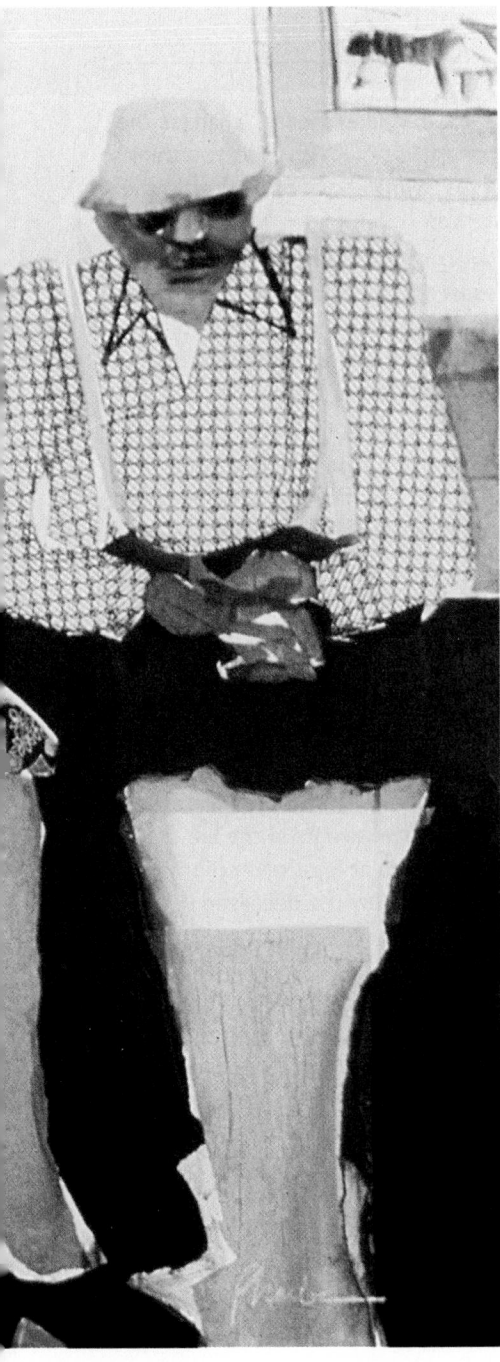

## In Honor of David Anderson Brooks, My Father

What is the appropriate way to react when someone we know dies? It's a question we all have faced or will face eventually. Brooks wrote the following poem after the death of her father. As you read, think about her attitude toward death—and toward the father she honors in this poem.

# In Honor of David Anderson Brooks, My Father

## Gwendolyn Brooks

*July 30, 1883–November 21, 1959*

A dryness is upon the house
My father loved and tended.
Beyond his firm and sculpted door
His light and lease have ended.

5   He walks the valleys, now—replies
To sun and wind forever.
No more the cramping chamber's chill,
No more the hindering fever.

Now out upon the wide clean air
10  My father's soul revives,
All innocent of self-interest
And the fear that strikes and strives.

He who was Goodness, Gentleness,
And Dignity is free,
15  Translates to public Love
Old private Charity.

# Response and Analysis

## The Bean Eaters

### Thinking Critically

1. Which details of the **setting** tell you the most about this old couple?

2. What can you infer about the couple based on their usual meal and their habitual actions?

3. Why might Brooks make a point of saying that the couple is "Mostly Good"? (Is she suggesting that they deserve more than the life they have?)

4. In line 10, what does the phrase *twinklings and twinges* reveal about the couple's emotional life?

5. What words in the poem rhyme? Look for **internal rhymes** as well as **end rhymes.** Why might the poet have made the last sentence so long?

6. This is a poem, not a historical account, but the poem still reflects several social conditions of its time and place. What social influences do you think helped shape the characters and the setting of the poem?

## In Honor of David Anderson Brooks, My Father

### Thinking Critically

1. How does the speaker feel about her father?

2. In line 1, what do you think is the "dryness" upon the father's house?

3. In the second stanza, what differences does the poet imagine between her father in life and her father in death? Is the speaker's tone in this stanza sad, bitter, or triumphant? Explain your response.

4. In line 15, *translates* means "changes the form or nature of." What do you think Brooks is saying about her father in the last stanza?

5. The **theme** of a poem is the revelation it gives us about a particular truth about our lives. In your own words, state what you think is the theme of the poem. What details in the poem support your interpretation?

6. What words **rhyme** in this poem? When do you hear **alliteration**—the repetition of consonant sounds?

## WRITING

### A Life

Write a fictional newspaper **obituary** for either the man or the woman in "The Bean Eaters" or for Brooks's father. Incorporate some of the information given or suggested in the poems. You may want to invent significant and appropriate events in the life of your subject. Include at least one comment by someone who knew the deceased.

## LISTENING AND SPEAKING

### Oral Performance

Get together with two or more classmates, and plan and rehearse a reading of these poems by Gwendolyn Brooks. You may want to alternate individual and group readers, and you may consider using appropriate background music. Before you perform the poems, be sure you are aware of how the poet uses rhyme, alliteration, and meter to create music in each poem. Perform the reading for the class.

**SKILLS FOCUS**

**Literary Skills**
Analyze the uses of rhyme.

**Writing Skills**
Write a fictional newspaper obituary.

**Listening and Speaking Skills**
Perform a group recitation of poems.

# Derek Walcott
## (1930–    )

**W**hen he was eighteen years old, Derek Walcott borrowed two hundred dollars to print his first book of poems, and then he stood on the street corners of Saint Lucia, in the West Indies, in order to sell it. Decades later, after forging a unique style that blends English and Caribbean elements with his own remarkable perspective, he won the 1992 Nobel Prize in literature. The distance from street corner to Nobel podium reveals the contrasting yet complementary qualities of his poetry: intimate and formal, lyrical and political, folklike and almost classical.

Derek Walcott was born and raised in the former British colony of Saint Lucia. His parents were educators, but the island was his greatest teacher. Lush valleys, plantations, rolling volcanic landscapes, and—most important—the sea provided him with endless imagery. He absorbed the music, art, and languages of the mix of African, French, and English cultures around him, and he fell in love with the English classics he read in school. Walcott went on to study at the University of the West Indies in Jamaica and then moved to Trinidad, where he still lives. He often travels to the United States and teaches writing at Boston University.

Walcott's poems—gathered in such collections as *Sea Grapes* (1976) and *Midsummer* (1984)—convey passionate intensity in precise and elegant language. Classical mythology, historical allusions, and complex extended metaphors move naturally through his lines. He has also tried, particularly in his plays, to capture the vocal rhythm, diction, and dialect of the speech of the islands. Walcott's style is as multifaceted as his heritage and his outlook.

Honored as a poet, Walcott has also built a career as a playwright. His best-known plays include *Ti-Jean and His Brothers* (1957) and *Dream on Monkey Mountain* (1967). He founded the Trinidad Theatre Workshop, where many of his plays premiered. Walcott is a gifted painter too. His book-length poem *Tiepolo's Hound* (2000) is illustrated with dozens of his vibrant watercolors.

It is his poems, however, that best embody his spirit. They combine the experiences of the many varied inhabitants of the West Indies: those who have victimized and those who have endured injustice. Walcott writes as much about those who find daily delight in the natural world as he does about those who search angrily for identity in a new world of shared cultures. One of his most remarkable books, *Omeros* (1990), uses Homer's *Iliad* and *Odyssey* as the basis for a West Indian story, fusing themes of wandering and exile, culture and history, identity and justice. "Elsewhere," reprinted here, is a powerful appeal to moral vision. It insists that oppression and censorship affect us all, no matter where in the world they take place.

# Before You Read

## Elsewhere

### Make the Connection

Terrible events that occur in faraway places—wars, revolutions, earthquakes, famines, political oppression—can seem so removed that we cannot empathize with those affected by them. Despite graphic television news coverage that we witness in our living rooms, catastrophes in the lives of other people can seem remote. What can we do about other people's tragedies?

### Literary Focus
#### Repetition

In a poem, repetition can be much more than a sound effect. Poets can also use repetition to convey meaning, emphasize ideas, clarify images, build rhythms, create moods, and evoke emotional responses. When you read a poem aloud, listen for the repetition. What is the writer trying to achieve by repeating certain sounds, words, images, ideas?

> **Repetition** is the repeated use of the same sound, word, image, or idea to enhance a poem's meaning and overall effect.
>
> *For more on Repetition, see the Handbook of Literary and Historical Terms.*

### Reading Skills
#### Determining Meaning

Sometimes asking a series of questions can help you to clarify meaning. As you read a poem, ask yourself the following questions:

- What does the writer want me to *see*? (What **images** are presented and emphasized?)
- What **figures of speech** are used in the poem?
- What does the writer want me to *feel*? (What **mood** is created by the images and figures of speech?)
- What does the writer want me to *understand*? (What is the main **theme** or message of the poem?)

### Background

Derek Walcott's *The Arkansas Testament* (1987) is divided into two sections: "Here" and "Elsewhere." In the first section the poems focus on Saint Lucia—its landscape, language, and culture. In the second section (in which the poem "Elsewhere" appears), the poems encompass a worldwide vision. Walcott moves beyond his concern about Caribbean colonialism to the effects of political and cultural oppression around the globe. "Elsewhere" is dedicated to Sir Stephen Spender (1909–1995), a British writer noted for his poems of social protest and his eloquent sympathy for victims of war and oppression, especially during the Spanish Civil War and World War II. For Walcott, Spender is a model of creativity and activism.

**SKILLS FOCUS**

**Literary Skills**
Understand repetition.

**Reading Skills**
Determine meaning.

# Elsewhere

## Derek Walcott

*(For Stephen Spender)*

Somewhere a white horse gallops with its
    mane
plunging round a field whose sticks
are ringed with barbed wire, and men
break stones or bind straw into ricks.°

5  Somewhere women tire of the shawled sea's
weeping, for the fishermen's dories°
still go out. It is blue as peace.
Somewhere they're tired of torture stories.

That somewhere there was an arrest.
10  Somewhere there was a small harvest
of bodies in the truck. Soldiers rest
somewhere by a road, or smoke in a forest.

Somewhere there is the conference rage
at an outrage. Somewhere a page
15  is torn out, and somehow the foliage
no longer looks like leaves but camouflage.

Somewhere there is a comrade,
a writer lying with his eyes wide open
on a mattress ticking,° who will not read
20  this, or write. How to make a pen?

And here we are free for a while, but
elsewhere, in one-third, or one-seventh
of this planet, a summary° rifle butt
breaks a skull into the idea of a heaven

25  where nothing is free, where blue air
is paper-frail, and whatever we write
will be stamped twice, a blue letter,
its throat slit by the paper knife of the state.

Through these black bars
30  hollowed faces stare. Fingers
grip the cross bars of these stanzas
and it is here, because somewhere else

their stares fog into oblivion
thinly, like the faceless numbers
35  that bewilder you in your telephone
diary. Like last year's massacres.

The world is blameless. The darker crime
is to make a career of conscience,
to feel through our own nerves the silent
    scream
40  of winter branches, wonders read as signs.

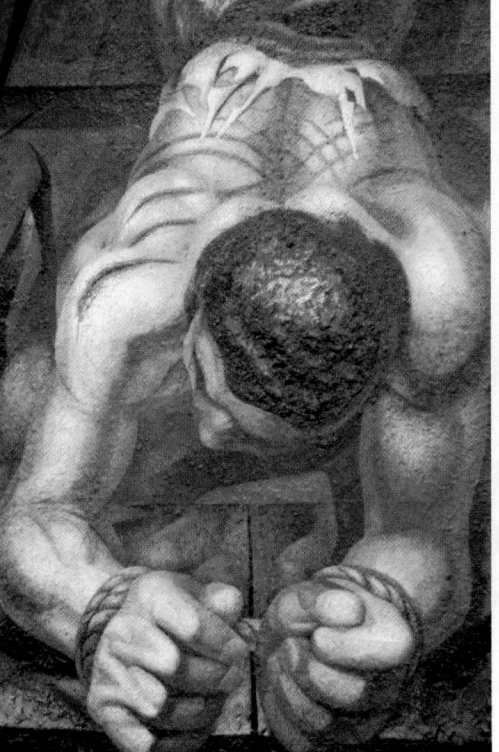

*Victim of Fascism* (1944) (detail) by David Alfaro
Siqueiros. Palacio de Bellas Artes, Mexico City, D.F.,
Mexico.

---

**4. ricks** *n. pl.*: stacks of hay.
**6. dories** *n. pl.*: rowboats.
**19. ticking** *n.*: strong fabric, usually striped, used for
mattress covers.
**23. summary** *adj.*: quickly executed.

Murdered victims of the Khmer Rouge (1970s).

Tuol Sleng Museum, Phnom Penh, Cambodia.

# Response and Analysis

## Thinking Critically

1. In the first five stanzas of "Elsewhere," Walcott presents a series of **images** of oppression. Identify at least three of these images, and tell what they help you to visualize. Which one do you think is the most powerful? Why?

2. The poem changes dramatically at line 21. What is the world like "here"? What images of violence break into this stanza?

3. Describe in your own words the extraordinary **image** presented in the eighth and ninth stanzas. What are the "cross bars"? What can be seen through them?

4. What is the shocking **simile** Walcott uses in lines 34–36?

5. The poem rises to its most direct statement of **theme** in the final stanza. What do you think it means "to make a career of conscience"? How does Walcott believe a sympathetic person should respond to the world's suffering?

6. What words does Walcott keep repeating? What emotional effect does this **repetition** have on you?

7. Express in your own words Walcott's meaning in "Elsewhere." What does he want you to see, to feel, to understand?

## Literary Criticism

8. **Philosophical approach.** In his book on Derek Walcott, the critic John Thieme says that "Elsewhere" is "less concerned with attacking political injustice than exposing the inadequacy of armchair liberalism." Why might Thieme come to this conclusion? Do you agree? Explain why or why not, using specific references to the text to support your response.

## WRITING

### A Poetic Response

Write a **poem** in Walcott's style about the problems that exist in the world today—in some "elsewhere." Use exact images to help your readers see the situations you describe. Open your poem with the word *somewhere,* and repeat that word often. At some point in your poem, describe what things are like "here"—wherever here is for you.

**SKILLS FOCUS**

**Literary Skills**
Analyze repetition.

**Reading Skills**
Analyze meaning.

**Writing Skills**
Write a poem in a poet's style.

**1164**   Collection 6   **Contemporary Literature: 1939 to Present**

# Carolyn Forché
(1950–        )

**C**arolyn Forché writes about people who have been silenced by political oppression. She is a voice for those who have disappeared.

Born in Detroit, Forché (fôr′shā) grew up in rural Michigan. Her early poems, collected in *Gathering the Tribes* (1976), focus on themes of nature and kinship, inspired by the lives of her Slovak ancestors and her experiences among Native Americans in the Southwest. After that first book, however, her life and poetry changed. When she was a teacher in San Diego, Forché began to translate the poems of the Salvadoran poet Claribel Alegría (see page 1170). Later she worked as a journalist and human-rights activist in El Salvador during that country's civil war. Forché's experiences transformed her. She says that at first she "tried not to write about El Salvador in poetry, because I thought it might be better to do so in journalistic circles. But I couldn't—the poems just came."

The result was *The Country Between Us* (1981), a collection of scorching poems about El Salvador that have been described as having "the immediacy of war correspondence, postcards from the volcano of twentieth-century barbarism."

In addition to teaching and writing, Forché has worked in Lebanon as a correspondent for National Public Radio and as a human-rights liaison in South Africa. She has also been a member of the Commission on United States–Central American Relations, a rare position for a poet.

## For Independent Reading

You may appreciate these poems by Forché:

- "Message"
- "The Testimony of Light"

## The Memory of Elena

### Make the Connection

There was a time when the nasty details of real-world politics did not enter poetry, especially poetry written by women. Emily Dickinson, for example, was writing poetry throughout the years of the American Civil War, but she did not deal with the war in her poems. Today is different. As the following poem shows, poetry can absorb everything in the human world, even terrible suffering and violence. Moreover, the writer of this poem is a woman.

How do you get your information about the world? Do you depend totally on television for news and commentary? Have you ever thought that a poem can make violence and injustice more memorable than live images on TV?

### Literary Focus
#### Imagery

The story in this poem is told in a series of images. We, the readers, must fill in the gaps between the images so that the entire story is apparent to us.

**Imagery** refers to the use of language that appeals to our senses: sight, hearing, taste, smell, and touch. In the past, poets as well as writers of prose avoided details that would shock their readers. In poems today, imagery evoking pictures of violence and horror is commonplace. In fact, a writer's choice of imagery may provide clues to the poem's message.

In this poem the writer combines images of a dinner of paella with images of torture and suffering. Notice how the images are linked by the speaker's memory.

> **Imagery** is the use of language that appeals to our senses of sight, hearing, taste, smell, and touch.
>
> *For more on Imagery, see the Handbook of Literary and Historical Terms.*

### Background

Forché's poem is set during the violent political upheaval that overtook Argentina during the 1970s. Amid kidnappings, riots, and terrorist attacks, various political groups vied for control of the government. In 1976, after seizing control of the government, the military began a campaign to end terrorism. In the process, thousands of people were arrested and imprisoned without trials, and some twenty thousand to thirty thousand people vanished. These people have been called *los desaparecidos* (the disappeared ones).

Hebe de Bonafini, the leader of the mothers of "the disappeared ones" of Argentina (2001).

**SKILLS FOCUS**

**Literary Skills**
Understand imagery.

# THE MEMORY OF ELENA

## Carolyn Forché

We spend our morning
in the flower stalls counting
the dark tongues of bells
that hang from ropes waiting
5   for the silence of an hour.
We find a table, ask for *paella,*°
cold soup and wine, where a calm
light trembles years behind us.

In Buenos Aires only three
10   years ago, it was the last time his hand
slipped into her dress, with pearls
cooling her throat and bells like
these, chipping at the night—

As she talks, the hollow
15   clopping of a horse, the sound
of bones touched together.
The *paella* comes, a bed of rice
and *camarones,*° fingers and shells,
the lips of those whose lips
20   have been removed, mussels
the soft blue of a leg socket.

This is not *paella,* this is what
has become of those who remained
in Buenos Aires. This is the ring
25   of a rifle report on the stones,
her hand over her mouth,
her husband falling against her.

These are the flowers we bought
this morning, the dahlias tossed
30   on his grave and bells
waiting with their tongues cut out
for this particular silence.

---

**6.** *paella* (pä·e′lyä) *n.:* Spanish dish of rice prepared
with seafood and flavored with saffron.
**18.** *camarones* (kä·mä·rȏn′·əs) *n. pl.:* Spanish for "shrimp."

## Bearing Witness: An Interview with Carolyn Forché

*The following excerpt is from an interview of Carolyn Forché by the broadcast journalist Bill Moyers. When this excerpt begins, Moyers has just asked Forché about "The Memory of Elena." In the interview, Forché mentions Claribel Alegría (see page 1170).*

**Forché:** That poem ["The Memory of Elena"] is about a woman whose husband was a very prominent journalist in Argentina. The night of their wedding anniversary they went out to dinner, and after dinner they took a walk along the Río de la Plata and then hailed a taxicab to take them home. When they climbed into the taxicab, they gave the address but apparently somehow the police were in communication with that cab because when they pulled in front of the house her husband was machine-gunned to death and she was wounded in the mouth. She was taken to police detention for twenty-four hours and then so many people in Buenos Aires followed her husband's coffin during his funeral that she was saved, she was allowed to leave the country and go into exile. Elena is a very close friend of Claribel's.

**Moyers:** *Why a poem about a subject so grim?*

**Forché:** Because I was a human-rights person taking the histories and testimonies of people from all over Latin America who have suffered under dictatorships and political oppression, and sometimes I would be taking these histories in a setting so very different from the story that was being told to me. In this case, a café in a calm European country where I made the mistake of ordering food before hearing a very brutal, very difficult story. So I began not to write about her story but about how her story affected the listener.

One of the things that I believe happens when poets bear witness to historical events is that everyone they tell becomes a witness too, everyone they tell also becomes responsible for what they have heard and what they now know. So the poem began in my puzzlement over the enigma of having a calm, civilized lunch and talking about something as horrible as the twenty-four hours she spent in detention after her husband's murder.

—from *The Language of Life* by Bill Moyers

A demonstrator displays a relative's picture during a protest march demanding a full accounting of missing prisoners (2001).

# Response and Analysis

## Thinking Critically

1. Who is speaking in the poem? Whose story is the narrator telling?

2. Write a sentence or two summing up what happens in each stanza.

3. The **visual imagery** of the poem is deliberately shocking. Which images do you see most clearly? How do they link past and present events?

4. Find three **images of sound** in the poem and three instances of silence. Why does the speaker emphasize silence?

5. What details of Elena's identity and her experiences in Buenos Aires are spelled out in Bill Moyers's interview with Forché? (See the **Primary Source** on page 1168.) Do you need to know these details in order to understand the poem? Would you have preferred the poem to include all the details Forché gives in the interview? Why or why not?

## Extending and Evaluating

6. Do you think writing a poem is an effective way to "bear witness to historical events"? Explain.

## WRITING

### Comparing Poems

Both Derek Walcott and Carolyn Forché write poems about contemporary social problems. In a brief **essay,** compare Walcott's poem (page 1163) with Forché's. Before you write, gather your details in a chart like the following one:

|  | Walcott | Forché |
|---|---|---|
| Subject |  |  |
| Theme |  |  |
| Images |  |  |
| Tone |  |  |
| Style |  |  |
| Shock value |  |  |

Write your essay in the block style: First, discuss Walcott's poem, and then discuss Forché's. Organize your essay around the elements you listed in your chart.

Mothers of "the disappeared ones" in Buenos Aires, Argentina (1977).

SKILLS FOCUS

**Literary Skills**
Analyze imagery.

**Writing Skills**
Write an essay comparing two poems.

# Literature of the Americas

## El Salvador

### Claribel Alegría
**(1924–    )**

Claribel Alegría is El Salvador's most renowned poet and one of the most versatile of contemporary Central American writers. In her poetry, novels, short stories, children's books, essays, and powerful works of nonfiction, she confronts the complex truths of Latin American life.

Born in Nicaragua, Alegría grew up in exile in El Salvador and considers herself to be Salvadoran. She has since returned to Nicaragua and has also lived in the United States, Mexico, Chile, Uruguay, and Spain. A graduate of George Washington University, she married D. J. Flakoll, a writer who became her closest collaborator and who translated most of her works into English. However, it was the 1982 translation of *Flowers from the Volcano* by her friend and fellow poet Carolyn Forché (see page 1165) that opened the ears of North Americans to Alegría's remarkable voice.

Readers around the world recognize her authenticity. She is, as the title of one of her books puts it, "on the front line."

#### For Independent Reading

For an interesting perspective on Alegría, read "The Island," a poem about Claribel Alegría in Carolyn Forché's book *The Country Between Us.*

## Ars Poetica

### Make the Connection

What is a poet? What are the rewards of being a poet? Does a poet lead a dull life, devoid of action? Or is there action in observing life and finding the words to report on it truly? Consider what Alegría said about her poem "Ars Poetica," Latin for "the art of poetry":

> ❝ I wrote that poem when there was war in El Salvador—it was terrible, destruction and death everywhere—but I always thought that there was something behind all that, and I thought that if I didn't keep in mind what was behind all that horror I would surely go crazy. Now I feel the same way for the whole world. ❞

### Literary Focus
#### Allusion

An **allusion** is a reference to someone or something from literature, music, history, current events, religion, or science. In the hands of a good writer, a well-placed allusion can help convey a central theme, set a tone, evoke a series of images, or lead to new ideas and associations.

> An **allusion** is a reference to someone or something that is known from history, literature, religion, politics, sports, science, or some other branch of culture.
>
> *For more on Allusion, see the Handbook of Literary and Historical Terms.*

### Background

The Venus de Milo is a famous marble statue from ancient Greece, housed in the Louvre Museum in Paris. The statue is of Aphrodite, the goddess of love and beauty. Venus is the Roman name for the goddess. (*Milo* is a form of Melos, the name of a Greek island.)

(Background) El Salvador (2001).

**SKILLS FOCUS**

**Literary Skills**
Understand allusion.

# Ars Poetica

## Claribel Alegría

*translated by* **D. J. Flakoll**

I,
poet by trade,
condemned so many times
to be a crow,
5   would never change places
with the Venus de Milo:
while she reigns in the Louvre
and dies of boredom
and collects dust

10   I discover the sun
each morning
and amid valleys
volcanos
and debris of war
15   I catch sight of the promised land.

# Response and Analysis

## Thinking Critically

1. At the beginning of the poem, the poet says that she has been condemned to be a crow. What do you think she means by being a crow?

2. Why does the poet say she would never change places with the Venus de Milo? What does this statement reveal about her values?

3. What do you think she means, as a poet, that she discovers the sun each morning?

4. In line 15, the poet refers to the "promised land." This is an **allusion** to the homeland sought by the ancient Israelites in the Book of Exodus in the Bible. The phrase *promised land* has come to signify any ultimate reward, goal, or time of prosperity. How does Alegría's use of this allusion relate to the **theme** of her poem?

5. The **title** of the poem "Ars Poetica" means "the art of poetry." Based on the final six lines of the poem, summarize Alegría's view of what poetry is or should be.

## Comparing Literature

### Ars Poetica

Marianne Moore's "Poetry" (page 672) and Archibald MacLeish's "Ars Poetica" (page 673) offer two other perspectives on the art of poetry. Select one of these poems to **compare** with Alegría's "Ars Poetica." Make at least one statement about poetry on which you think Alegría and Moore or MacLeish would agree. Then, make a statement about poetry on which you think they would disagree. Briefly explain your responses, using examples from the poems.

**SKILLS FOCUS**

**Literary Skills**
Analyze allusion.

# Judith Ortiz Cofer

## (1952–    )

**A**ccording to Judith Ortiz Cofer, "My family is one of the main topics of my poetry; the ones left behind on the island of Puerto Rico, and the ones who came to the United States. In tracing their lives, I discover more about mine." This impulse toward self-discovery and self-definition emerges in Cofer's stories, essays, and poems. By delving into her past, she clarifies her place in the present; by writing of those who shaped her life, she shapes her own life.

"We lived in Puerto Rico until my brother was born in 1954," Cofer has written. "Soon after, because of economic pressures on our growing family, my father joined the United States Navy. He was assigned to duty on a ship in Brooklyn [Navy] Yard . . . that was to be his home base in the States until his retirement more than twenty years later." Subsequently Cofer's childhood was divided between a mainland American urban environment and Puerto Rico. She lived mostly in Paterson, New Jersey, but moved temporarily to Puerto Rico with her mother and brother when her father was at sea.

Cofer earned a master's degree in English and has taught at the University of Miami and the University of Georgia, conducting poetry workshops on the side. Her first publication, *Latin Women Pray,* appeared in 1980. Since then she has published several additional volumes of poetry, including *Peregrina* (1986) and *Terms of Survival* (1987). Her semiautobiographical first novel, *The Line of the Sun* (1989), traces a family that moves from Puerto Rico to Paterson and is then caught between two cultural heritages. A reviewer of the novel describes Cofer as "a prose writer of evocatively lyrical authority." She has also published a volume of personal essays called *Silent Dancing: A Partial Remembrance of a Puerto Rican Childhood* (1990); *An Island Like You: Stories from the Barrio*

(1995); and *The Year of Our Revolution: Selected and New Stories and Poems* (1998).

Some consider Cofer's *The Latin Deli* (1993), a collection of poetry and prose, her most powerful book. It is a mosaic of responses to cultural differences and an engaging blend of poetry and lyrical prose. As Cofer has said, "The place of birth itself becomes a metaphor for the things we all must leave behind; the assimilation of a new culture is the coming into maturity by accepting the terms necessary for survival. My poetry is a study of this process of change, assimilation, and transformation."

Language, of course, plays a major role in such a transformation. In one interview, Cofer summed up what the dynamic force of language has meant to her: "The 'infinite variety' and power of language interest me. I never cease to experiment with it. As a native Puerto Rican, my first language was Spanish. It was a challenge, not only to learn English, but to master it enough to teach it and—the ultimate goal—to write poetry in it."

## For Independent Reading

For more by Cofer, try one of her prose works:

- *Silent Dancing* (essays)
- *The Line of the Sun* (novel)

Photo of Judith Ortiz Cofer is reprinted with permission from the publisher— APP Archive Files (Houston: Arte Público Press, University of Houston).

## The Latin Deli: An Ars Poetica

### Make the Connection

Language is the most common tool of self-expression. Hidden in our words, beneath their obvious meanings, are layers of personal associations and even cultural histories. This is especially true for immigrants, who are adjusting to a new country and a new language. People new to America and new to English as well will tell you that their language is one of the things they miss profoundly. Language, to most people, is part of *home*.

### Literary Focus
#### Concrete and Abstract Language

**Concrete language** is language that uses sensory details to describe a particular subject. **Abstract language** deals with generalities and intangible concepts. A *warm puppy* is concrete; *happiness* is abstract. In concrete language, details are everything; in abstract language they rarely play a role. Cofer's poem is a striking example of the effective use of concrete language.

> **Concrete language** uses sensory details to describe a particular subject. **Abstract language** deals with generalities and intangible concepts.
>
> *For more on Concrete and Abstract Language, see the Handbook of Literary and Historical Terms.*

### Background

*Ars poetica* is a Latin term meaning "the art of poetry." On pages 672, 673, and 1172, you'll find three other poems about the art of poetry. Cofer sees the art of poetry operating in a very unusual place—not in a literary magazine or classroom but in a delicatessen.

*Un diá a la vez (One Day at a Time)* by Joe Villareal.

# The Latin Deli:
## An Ars Poetica

### Judith Ortiz Cofer

Presiding over a formica counter,
plastic Mother and Child magnetized
to the top of an ancient register,
the heady mix of smells from the open bins
5    of dried codfish, the green plantains°
hanging in stalks like votive offerings,°
she is the Patroness of Exiles,
a woman of no-age who was never pretty,
who spends her days selling canned memories
10   while listening to the Puerto Ricans complain
that it would be cheaper to fly to San Juan
than to buy a pound of Bustelo coffee here,
and to Cubans perfecting their speech
of a "glorious return" to Havana—where no one
15   has been allowed to die and nothing to change until then;
to Mexicans who pass through, talking lyrically
of *dólares* to be made in El Norte—
                              all wanting the comfort
of spoken Spanish, to gaze upon the family portrait
20   of her plain wide face, her ample bosom
resting on her plump arms, her look of maternal interest
as they speak to her and each other
of their dreams and their disillusions—
how she smiles understanding,
25   when they walk down the narrow aisles of her store
reading the labels of packages aloud, as if
they were the names of lost lovers: *Suspiros,*°
*Merengues,*° the stale candy of everyone's childhood.
                              She spends her days
30   slicing *jamón y queso*° and wrapping it in wax paper
tied with string: plain ham and cheese
that would cost less at the A&P, but it would not satisfy
the hunger of the fragile old man lost in the folds
of his winter coat, who brings her lists of items
35   that he reads to her like poetry, or the others,
whose needs she must divine, conjuring up products
from places that now exist only in their hearts—
closed ports she must trade with.

**5. plantains** *n. pl.*: type of banana.

**6. votive offerings:** sacrifices made to fulfill a vow or offered in devotion.

**27. *suspiros*** (so̅o̅s·pē′r ōs): type of small spongecake.

**28. *merengues*** (mā·rān′gās): candy made of meringue (mixture of egg whites and sugar).

**30. *jamón y queso*** (khä·mōn′ ē kā′sō): Spanish for "ham and cheese."

*El Mercado Juarez (Juarez Market)* by Hal Marcus.

# Response and Analysis

## Thinking Critically

1. How does the poet describe the woman who runs the deli? What details in the poem make her seem almost like a religious figure?

2. Describe in your own words the feelings of the customers who come to the deli. Why do they choose this particular deli?

3. The poem contains many **sensory images.** Identify at least one image that appeals to each of the senses—sight, hearing, taste, smell, and touch.

4. What examples of **concrete language** help make this poem very specific? Which of these details also root the poem in one particular time and place?

5. In ancient Rome the poet Horace (65–8 B.C.) wrote a treatise called *Ars Poetica,* or *The Art of Poetry.* In it he set forth his own rules for writing poetry. Since Horace's time many poets have explored ideas about what poetry is or should be. What details in this poem suggest that Cofer believes the Spanish words spoken and loved by the deli customers are a kind of beautiful poetry?

## WRITING

### Comparing Poems

"Poetry" by Marianne Moore (page 672) and "Ars Poetica" by Archibald MacLeish

(page 673) deal directly with the nature of poetry. Cofer, in contrast, makes no direct statements about poetry; we must infer her beliefs about poetry from what she *says* in her poem. How do you think Cofer would define poetry? (For some hints, see lines 16–17, 26–27, and 34–35.) How does her art of poetry compare with the opinions offered by Moore and MacLeish? In an **essay,** cover these points:

- definition of poetry
- what poetry does for us
- importance of images in poetry
- importance of sounds in poetry

## Visual Arts

### A Collage

Cofer uses many images to craft this poem. Transfer her technique to the visual arts by making a collage or a painting that unites a number of concrete images of your own choice. You may want to follow Cofer's lead and use a deli as your subject, but you could also assemble images of a restaurant, a ballgame, a city, or another memory. Before you finalize your choice of images, be sure you know what mood you want your images to create (peaceful, scary, funny, fantastic, and so on).

# Rita Dove
## (1952–    )

**R**ita Dove's Pulitzer Prize–winning sequence of poems, *Thomas and Beulah* (1986), is loosely based on the lives of her maternal grandparents. Dove described the poems in an interview:

> I know that when I was writing the poems that went into *Thomas and Beulah* . . . I realized that what I was trying to tell, let's say, was not a narrative as we know narratives but actually the moments that matter most in our lives. I began to think, how do we remember our lives? How do we think of our lives or shape our lives in our own consciousnesses, and I realized that we don't actually think of our lives in very cohesive strands but we remember as beads on a necklace, moments that matter to us, come to us in flashes, and the connections are submerged.

This statement expresses the central concern of much of Dove's poetry: how memory shapes who we are—in other words, how we become ourselves.

In addition to *Thomas and Beulah,* Dove's books of poetry include *The Other Side of the House* (1988), *Grace Notes* (1989), *Selected Poems* (1993), *Mother Love* (1995), and *On the Bus with Rosa Parks: Poems* (1999). From 1993 to 1995, Dove served as poet laureate of the United States.

Born and raised in Akron, Ohio, Dove graduated *summa cum laude* from Miami University (in Ohio), studied literature at the University of Tübingen in Germany, and attended the noted Writers' Workshop at the University of Iowa, where she received a master's degree in 1977. After teaching at several universities, Dove became a professor of English at the University of Virginia, Charlottesville, in 1989.

The joys and trials of raising a family play as large a part in Dove's life, as they do in her writing. Dove says that after her daughter, Aviva, was born, she felt she was living "the story of many women who all have three full-time jobs: You teach, you do parenting, and you try to write, too. I just was tired all the time. I remember days when I came back home and fell asleep over dessert."

Besides writing on personal subjects, Dove weaves historical themes, including race relations, into her verse. As she told *The Washington Post,* "Obviously, as a black woman, I am concerned with race. But certainly not every poem of mine mentions the fact of being black. They are poems about humanity, and sometimes humanity happens to be black. I cannot run from, I *won't* run from any kind of truth."

## For Independent Reading

For more poems by Rita Dove, read

- "Adolescence III"
- "The Satisfaction Coal Company"

## Before You Read

# Testimonial

## Make the Connection

Testimonials are usually written to thank and celebrate people. You most often hear testimonials read at retirement parties, birthdays, and graduation ceremonies. Testimonials are also used to praise something—a new book, perhaps, or a new restaurant.

Rita Dove read this poem, called "Testimonial," at a commencement ceremony at Howard University, where she was being honored. The poem was part of her speech to the graduates. As you read, think about what she is giving testimony to.

## Literary Focus
### Sound Effects

Some **sound effects** in poetry are obvious and hard to miss. Others don't call much attention to themselves. Skillful poets use a wide range of sound effects to create rich and surprising verbal music. **Rhyme,** for example, especially end rhyme, is the sound effect most listeners usually notice first. **Onomatopoeia**—the use of language to imitate sounds, such as *hiss, slap, buzz*—is also easy to spot. **Alliteration**—the repetition of consonant sounds—can require more attention. **Assonance**—the repetition of vowel sounds—can be even more subtle, yet it can produce the most memorable music. Read the poem aloud to hear its sound effects, and note how they make you feel.

> **Sound effects** refer to the use of sounds—including **rhythm, rhyme, meter, alliteration, onomatopoeia, assonance,** and **repetition**—to create specific effects.
>
> *For more on Sound Effects, see the Handbook of Literary and Historical Terms.*

**SKILLS FOCUS**

**Literary Skills**
Understand sound effects.

# Testimonial

## Rita Dove

Back when the earth was new
and heaven just a whisper,
back when the names of things
hadn't had time to stick;

5    back when the smallest breezes
melted summer into autumn,
when all the poplars quivered
sweetly in rank and file . . .

the world called, and I answered.
10    Each glance ignited to a gaze.
I caught my breath and called that life,
swooned between spoonfuls of lemon sorbet.

I was pirouette and flourish,
I was filigree and flame.
15    How could I count my blessings
when I didn't know their names?

Back when everything was still to come,
luck leaked out everywhere.
I gave my promise to the world,
20    and the world followed me here.

Rita Dove in front of Thomas Jefferson's home,
Monticello.

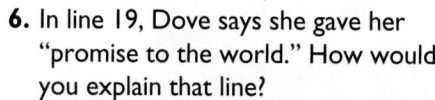

# Response and Analysis

*Fatima* (1994) by Elizabeth Barakah Hodges.

## Thinking Critically

1. Describe in your own words the time that Dove evokes in lines 1–8.

2. What could be the "call" that the world makes in line 9?

3. Could the narrator be talking about falling in love in the third stanza? Why or why not?

4. Dove uses **metaphors** to compare herself to four things in lines 13–14. How would you picture a girl who is "pirouette and flourish" and "filigree and flame"?

5. How would you describe the **tone** of lines 13–16? Explain your response.

6. In line 19, Dove says she gave her "promise to the world." How would you explain that line?

7. What do you think Dove means by the last line, "and the world followed me here"?

8. In "Testimonial," who or what is Dove thanking, honoring, or celebrating? In other words, what is the main point or **theme** of the poem?

9. Read aloud lines 10 and 12, and find examples of **alliteration**. Which line uses both alliteration and **assonance**? What other instances of alliteration and assonance can you find?

## WRITING

### Responding to a Poem

What do you think of this poem? In an **essay**, explain your response to "Testimonial." Before you write, review the poem to be sure you can answer these questions. The answers to these questions can form your response:

- What is the poem about? What is its **main idea**?

- What images do you see in the poem?

- Do you fully understand the poem? Are there **ambiguities** in the poem that puzzle you?

- Is the poem effective—that is, does it work for you? Give at least one reason for your answer.

Be sure to use passages from the poem to support your main points. Also be sure to cite the author of the poem and its title at the beginning of your essay. At the end of your essay, tell whether you think this was a good poem to read at a commencement ceremony (remember that *commencement* means "beginning").

▶ **Use "Analyzing Literature," pages 739–740, for help with this assignment.**

**SKILLS FOCUS**

**Literary Skills**
Analyze sound effects.

**Writing Skills**
Write an essay responding to a poem.

# Mark Doty

## (1953– )

**M**ark Doty makes poems out of everyday scenes—riding on a bus, watching a building being torn down, seeing people he doesn't really know. He is an alert and sympathetic observer of quickly passing moments, and in poetry he makes those moments his own. Doty notes, "Poems are always made alone, somewhere out on the edge of things, and if they succeed they are saturated with the texture of the uniquely felt life."

Mark Doty, whose father was an army engineer, grew up in Tennessee, Florida, Arizona, and California. He attended Drake University in Iowa and earned a master's degree in creative writing from Goddard College in Vermont. His first two books—*Turtle, Swan* (1987) and *Bethlehem in Broad Daylight* (1991)—contain poems of intimate lyricism and deceptive simplicity. They established the style that he has continued to develop, a voice that is both reflective and simple, reserved yet warmly casual.

It was Doty's third book—*My Alexandria* (1993)—that opened critics' eyes. The collection won the National Poetry Series contest and the National Book Critics Circle Award, and it was a finalist for the National Book Award. *My Alexandria* finds strength and beauty in moments of pain and loss, such as those caused by the plague of AIDS. *My Alexandria* transformed Doty into one of America's leading poets.

All poets respond in one way or another to those who have come before them, and Doty has been particularly influenced by Robert Lowell, Elizabeth Bishop, and James Merrill. In his work, Doty displays a similar gift for painterlike imagery and a fearless awareness of tragedy. Doty's poems in *Atlantis* (1995) and *Sweet Machine* (1998) continue his journey into the self. Doty summed it up this way:

> Perhaps the signal characteristic of American poetry is our desire to put the self at the center—whether it be Whitman's expansive, inclusive "I" or Dickinson's microcosmic, endlessly doubting examination. Our way of knowing the world is through the study of our own feelings and perceptions. . . . Through its bold curiosity about the self, its willingness to investigate perception, thought, and feeling with a relentless intensity, American poetry in our century has evolved into a vibrant and diverse endeavor. . . .

### For Independent Reading

For another poem by Mark Doty, read

- "Golden Retrievals" (in *Sweet Machine*)

# Before You Read

## Coastal

### Make the Connection

Have you ever thought someone was foolish yet admired him or her at the same time? Is it possible to laugh at someone publicly yet respect the person privately? When do simple actions generate complex responses?

### Literary Focus
#### Tone

**Tone**—a writer's attitude toward a subject or an audience—can reveal a great deal about the writer's values. You can sometimes infer a writer's philosophical stance on life's basic issues from the tone of his or her work. For example, if a writer's work takes a consistently lighthearted tone, we can infer a positive attitude toward life, a sense that the world is not to be taken too seriously. If a writer reveals a consistently ironic tone— a sense that life is never quite what it should be—we can infer a questioning attitude, a sense that life is not always fair.

Remember, too, that tone may change as a work proceeds. Although tone is often described with one word—such as *objective, lighthearted,* or *ironic*—more than one tone may be heard in a single work.

> **Tone** is the attitude a writer takes toward the subject of a work, the characters in it, or the audience.
>
> *For more about Tone, see the Handbook of Literary and Historical Terms.*

SKILLS
FOCUS

**Literary Skills**
Understand tone.

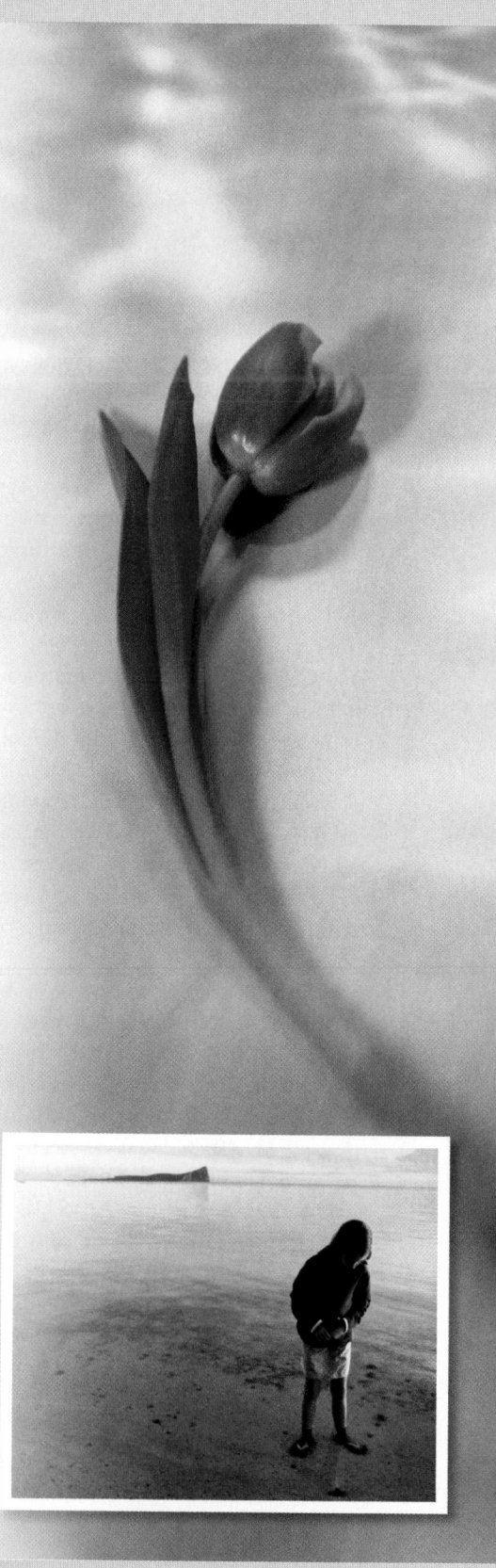

# Coastal

## Mark Doty

Cold April and the neighbor girl
   —our plumber's daughter—
     comes up the wet street

from the harbor carrying,
5     in a nest she's made
      of her pink parka,

a loon. *It's so sick,*
    she says when I ask.
     Foolish kid,

10  does she think she can keep
    this emissary of air?
     Is it trust or illness

that allows the head
    —sleek tulip—to bow
15     on its bent stem

across her arm?
    Look at the steady,
     quiet eye. She is carrying

the bird back from indifference,
20    from the coast
     of whatever rearrangement

the elements intend,
    and the loon allows her.
     She is going to call

25  the Center for Coastal Studies,
    and will swaddle the bird
     in her petal-bright coat

until they come.
    She cradles the wild form.
30     Stubborn girl.

# Response and Analysis

## Thinking Critically

1. What does the speaker of the poem see?

2. In line 9, what is the **tone** of the speaker's initial reaction to the girl?

3. What **image** in lines 13–16 does the speaker use to describe the sick bird? What does this image suggest about the way the speaker feels about the bird?

4. Although the narrative of the poem takes place in a coastal town, lines 18–23 refer to another "coast." Explain this figurative coast.

5. What does the poet's choice of the word *swaddle* in line 26 suggest about his feelings toward the girl?

6. By the time the speaker makes his final comment in line 30, the **tone** of the poem has shifted. Compare lines 9 and 30, and explain the shift of tone.

7. In your own words, state the **theme** of the poem.

## WRITING

### Stubborn Girl Speaks

How do you think the girl in this poem might respond to the speaker? What **tone** would she use to express her reasons for trying to save the loon? Write a brief **response** to the speaker of "Coastal" either in verse or in prose.

# Li-Young Lee
(1957–    )

**S**eeing and re-seeing, interpreting and reinterpreting, are the driving forces in Li-Young Lee's poetry. As someone who has had to adjust to different countries and cultural contexts, Lee is a poet profoundly aware that life is what we make—and remake—of it.

Li-Young Lee was born in Jakarta, Indonesia, to Chinese parents. In China his father had been one of Mao Tse-tung's personal physicians. Caught in the turmoil of the Chinese Revolution, the family moved to Indonesia, where Lee's father was imprisoned by former President Sukarno's government for almost two years, most of the time in a leper colony. The family fled to Hong Kong in 1959, then to Macau, then to Japan, and in 1964 to the United States.

Lee went to colleges in Pennsylvania, Arizona, and New York. He published his first book of poems, *Rose,* in 1986. Four years later his second book, *The City in Which I Love You,* was the Lamont Poetry Selection of the Academy of American Poets. Lee has taught at several universities, including Northwestern and the University of Iowa, and now lives with his wife and children in Chicago. His prose memoir, *The Winged Seed: A Remembrance* (1995), recalls the touching and tumultuous history of his family.

Li-Young Lee's poems often shuttle between dream and reality. Whether he is writing about personal experience or his family's past, Lee presents history as a combination of memory, dream, and invention. As he says in one poem, "memory revises me," and his poems offer multiple perspectives on "truth." Li-Young Lee is in close touch with his past, yet he cannot ever be quite sure what occurred there. In his poem "Arise, Go Down," he describes the art of creative uncertainty:

> For years now I have come to conclusions
> without my father's help, discovering
> on my own what I know, what I don't know,
>
> and seeing how one cancels the other.
> I've become a scholar of cancellations.

## For Independent Reading
You might also read these poems by Lee:
- "The Gift" (in *Rose*)
- "For a New Citizen of These United States" (in *The City in Which I Love You*)

# Before You Read

## Visions and Interpretations

### Make the Connection

Most of us know how it feels to relate a story or a memory or a dream that is so complex that the telling of it falls short. The words just don't seem equal to the experience. Then we try to tell it again. Each version of our dream or memory seems more or less truthful, more or less complete than the others. Each version, however, is satisfying in its own way.

### Literary Focus
#### Theme

A poem's **theme** is the insight about life that it reveals to us. A theme is different from a subject or topic. The subject of the poem that follows is stated in its title: visions and interpretations. The theme is what the poem says or reveals to us about our visions and interpretations.

Poets, like other writers, rarely state their themes directly. Instead, they hope that the experience of the poem will provide us with a revelation about human life that we call theme.

Poems don't necessarily reveal something *new* to us. More often a poem will remind us of something we had always known deep in our hearts was true.

> **Theme** is the insight about human life that is revealed in a literary work.
>
> *For more on Theme, see the Handbook of Literary and Historical Terms.*

*Lotus and Bird* (1700) by Bada Shanren.

# Visions and Interpretations

## Li-Young Lee

Because this graveyard is a hill,
I must climb up to see my dead,
stopping once midway to rest
beside this tree.

5   It was here, between the anticipation
of exhaustion, and exhaustion,
between vale and peak,
my father came down to me

and we climbed arm in arm to the top.
10  He cradled the bouquet I'd brought,
and I, a good son, never mentioned his grave,
erect like a door behind him.

And it was here, one summer day, I sat down
to read an old book. When I looked up
15 from the noon-lit page, I saw a vision
of a world about to come, and a world about to go.

Truth is, I've not seen my father
since he died, and, no, the dead
do not walk arm in arm with me.

20 If I carry flowers to them, I do so without their help,
the blossoms not always bright, torch-like,
but often heavy as sodden newspaper.

Truth is, I came here with my son one day,
and we rested against this tree,
25 and I fell asleep, and dreamed

a dream which, upon my boy waking me, I told.
Neither of us understood.
Then we went up.

Even this is not accurate.
30 Let me begin again:

Between two griefs, a tree.
Between my hands, white chrysanthemums, yellow
chrysanthemums.

The old book I finished reading
I've since read again and again.

35 And what was far grows near,
and what is near grows more dear,

and all of my visions and interpretations
depend on what I see,

and between my eyes is always
40 the rain, the migrant rain.

*Pavilion in Tall Mountains* (late 15th century)
by Wen Zhengming.

# Response and Analysis

## Thinking Critically

1. Lee's poem relates an experience in three ways. Lines 1–16 might be called the dream version. What happens in the speaker's dream?

   **a.** Why might Lee use the words *my dead* in line 2? Whom is he referring to?

   **b.** In line 10, the speaker's father "cradled the bouquet." What **image** does the word *cradled* bring to mind?

   **c.** In lines 15–16, the speaker sees a vision. Could this vision represent the speaker's world at the time of his father's death? Explain.

2. Lines 17–29 might be called the real-world version of the poem. According to this version, what was the speaker's experience?

   **a.** Why might the blossoms in lines 20–21 be "often heavy"?

   **b.** Do you think it's important that the speaker says that neither he nor his son understood his dream? Why or why not?

3. Lines 30–40 might be called the poetic version. How do you explain what happens in this version?

   **a.** Which **image** in this version do you find most moving or meaningful? Why?

   **b.** What do you think the poet means in the last two lines? What might the "migrant rain" represent?

4. A **symbol** is something that has a meaning deeper than its straightforward, literal meaning. A tree, flowers, and an old book appear repeatedly in the poem. What do you think each of these things symbolizes?

5. The subject of the poem is dealing with a father's death. The occasion of the poem is visiting the cemetery. How would you state the **theme** of the poem—what does it reveal to you about the longings and sorrows of human life?

## Extending and Evaluating

6. In your opinion, has the speaker of the poem succeeded in coming to terms with the death of his father? Is it ever possible to come to terms with death and loss? Why or why not?

## WRITING

### Your Own Words

When you paraphrase a poem, you restate it using your own words. Use the following techniques:

- Substitute simple words for long, complex ones.
- Explain figures of speech to make clear exactly what is being compared.
- State ideas in complete sentences.

Write a **paraphrase** of Lee's poem. The first verse might be paraphrased like this:

> This graveyard is on a hill, so I must climb up to see the graves of my dead relatives. I stop once halfway up the hill to rest beside a tree.

Paraphrasing a poem helps you see if you understand the poem. When you hit a snag in your paraphrase, you probably have hit on a part of the poem you do not fully understand.

**SKILLS FOCUS**

**Literary Skills**
Analyze theme.

**Writing Skills**
Write a paraphrase of a poem.

# Agha Shahid Ali
## (1949–2001)

**B**orn in New Delhi, India, Agha Shahid Ali lived, studied, and taught in the United States for more than twenty-five years. His poems, which embrace multiple heritages and cross literary traditions, sound simultaneously ancient and modern, Eastern and Western. As he explained in an interview,

> The point is you are a universe. You are the product of immense historical forces. There is the Muslim in me, there is the Hindu in me, there is the Western in me. It is there because I have grown up in three cultures and various permutations of those cultures.

Ali grew up in Kashmir, a beautiful region that is still a source of friction between India and Pakistan. Kashmir forms the background— geographical, political, emotional—of many of Ali's poems. His family, he recalled, recited poetry in Persian, Urdu, Hindi, and English. Ali attended colleges in India and in 1984 earned a doctorate in English at Pennsylvania State University. The winner of numerous poetry awards, Ali taught English and creative writing at the University of Utah and the University of Massachusetts. He was a popular teacher, though he could be tough. "This line should be put against a wall and shot," he once told a student in his poetry class.

Ali's collections include *The Half-Inch Himalayas* (1987), *A Nostalgist's Map of America* (1991), *The Country Without a Post Office* (1997), and *Rooms Are Never Finished* (2001), which was a finalist for the National Book Award. His poems often blend history, myth, popular culture, and personal memory into dreamlike scenes. "I see everything in a very elegiac way," he remarked. "It's not something morbid, but it's part of my emotional coloring." His poems bridge cultures and centuries and like all nostalgists, he finds the past very much alive in the present.

A joyful, brilliant poet, a man blessed with many friends and honors, Ali died from a brain tumor at the age of fifty-two.

## For Independent Reading

For more poems by Ali, read

- "Snow on the Desert" (in *A Nostalgist's Map of America*)
- "The Wolf's Postscript to Little Red Riding Hood" (in *A Walk Through the Yellow Pages*)

## Medusa

### Make the Connection

Literature abounds with stories of transformation. Characters change both outside and inside, physically and emotionally. They change what they look *like* and what they look *for*. They change the people they love and the people they hate.

### Literary Focus
### Archetypes

**Archetypes** are repeated patterns that help us tell ourselves the stories of our own lives. We have all encountered in our reading archetypal characters (like the superhero), archetypal plots (like the perilous journey or the Cinderella story), archetypal places (like the monster's cave), and archetypal images (like snakes and lambs).

Metamorphosis—a marvelous change in shape or form—is also an archetype. You might recall the old Greek myths in which people metamorphose into animals, flowers, rivers, and constellations. Today special effects in film can morph anybody into anything. As long as caterpillars continue to metamorphose into butterflies and tadpoles into frogs, we will probably continue to find metamorphosis a powerful archetype in storytelling.

> An **archetype** is an original or fundamental imaginative pattern that is repeated through the ages. **Metamorphosis**—a marvelous change in shape or form—is a common archetype.
>
> *For more on Archetype, see the Handbook of Literary and Historical Terms.*

*Medusa* (1598–1599) by Caravaggio. Oil on canvas mounted on wood. (60 cm × 50 cm).

### Background

In Greek mythology, Medusa was one of three beautiful sisters called the Gorgons. The sisters were turned into monsters by Athena, the goddess of wisdom, who was angry at the destruction of one of her temples. Medusa was turned into a horrific creature with a gaping mouth, hypnotic eyes, and hair made of writhing snakes. Anyone who looked at Medusa was immediately turned into stone.

The hero Perseus, with the help of winged sandals, a shield polished like a mirror, and a helmet of invisibility, managed to behead the hideous Medusa as she slept.

In this poem, Medusa is given a voice and allowed to speak.

**Literary Skills**
Understand archetypes and metamorphosis.

# MEDUSA

## Agha Shahid Ali

"I must be beautiful.
Or why would men be speechless
at my sight? I have populated the countryside
with animals of stone
5   and put nations painlessly to sleep.

I too was human, I who now live here
at the end of the world
with two aging sisters, spinsters
massaging poisons into our scalps
10   and sunning our ruffled snakes,

and dreading the night, when
under the warm stars
we recall men we have loved,
their gestures now forever refusing us.

15   Then why let anything remain
when whatever we loved
turned instantly to stone?
I am waiting for the Mediterranean
to see me: It will petrify.
20   And as caravans from Africa begin to cross it,
I will freeze their cargo of slaves.

Soon, soon, the sky will have eyes:
I will fossilize its dome into cracked blue,
I who am about to come
25   into God's full view
from the wrong side of the mirror
into which He gazes."

And so she dreams
till the sun-crimsoned shield
30   blinds her into nightmare:
her locks, falling from their roots,
crawl into rocks to die.
Perseus holds the sword above her neck.
Restless in her sleep, she,
35   for the last time, brushes back
the hissing curls from her forehead.

# Response and Analysis

## Thinking Critically

1. The poem opens with a surprising statement. Who is speaking? What is **ironic** about what she is saying?

2. Medusa is both a victim of **metamorphosis** and one of its greatest agents. What do you think is the **tone** of line 6—"I too was human"? How does Medusa feel about her own metamorphosis?

3. Humans dread Medusa, yet Medusa herself dreads something. According to lines 11–14, what does she dread, and why?

4. Lines 15–27 delve deeply into Medusa's character. What does Medusa threaten to do? What is her **motivation**—the reason for her plans?

5. In the final stanza, what is about to happen, unknown to Medusa?

6. How does the poet's use of the **first-person point of view** affect your feelings about Medusa?

## WRITING

### Revisiting a Myth

Many contemporary writers have enjoyed telling old stories from new perspectives. Agha Shahid Ali, for example, wrote a poem from the point of view of the wolf in "Little Red Riding-Hood." Choose a character from a fairy tale, a myth, or a movie, and write a **poem** from that character's point of view. Let the character speak as "I." Be sure to let your reader understand who the character is and what makes him or her tick. Before you write, decide how you want readers to feel about your character. If you let the one-eyed Cyclops from the *Odyssey* speak, for example, will you want your readers to fear him or feel sorry for him? Open your poem with the pronoun *I*.

SKILLS
FOCUS

**Literary Skills**
Analyze archetypes and metamorphosis.

**Writing Skills**
Write a poem from the point of view of a character from a fairy tale, a myth, or a movie.

# Billy Collins
## (1941–    )

**W**hen Billy Collins was named poet laureate of the United States in 2001, he said, "It came completely out of the blue, like a soft wrecking ball from outer space." This contradictory image of a soft wrecking ball is characteristic of Collins's poetry—surprising, playful, almost casual, but with a hint of danger.

Born in New York City, Billy Collins has been a professor of English at the City University of New York for more than thirty years—as he modestly puts it, a "lifter of chalk in the Bronx." During his career he has won many poetry awards, including fellowships from the National Endowment for the Arts and the Guggenheim Foundation. He has also won wide popularity—some have called him the most popular poet in America—largely because his poems are anything but dry, heavy, or academic. Collins tries to be reader friendly:

> I have one reader in mind, someone who is in the room with me, and who I'm talking to, and I want to make sure I don't talk too fast, or too glibly. Usually I try to create a hospitable tone at the beginning of a poem. Stepping from the title to the first lines is like stepping into a canoe. A lot of things can go wrong.

Billy Collins's collections include *The Apple That Astonished Paris* (1988); *Questions About Angels* (1991), which was selected for the National Poetry Series; *The Art of Drowning* (1995); and *Sailing Alone Around the Room* (2001). He conducts poetry workshops during the summer and has recorded many of his poems. Collins's poems may at first seem deceptively low-key, but they usually convey a subtle message. As his fellow poet Edward

Hirsch says: "Billy Collins is an American original, a metaphysical poet with a funny bone and a sly questioning intelligence. . . . His poems —witty, playful, and beautifully turned—bump up against the deepest human mysteries."

## For Independent Reading

For more by Billy Collins, read these poems from *The Art of Drowning*:

- "Center"
- "Sunday Morning with the Sensational Nightingales"

## Man Listening to Disc

### Make the Connection

Here's what Billy Collins has to say about the poem you're about to read, "Man Listening to Disc":

❝ I am usually not one of those people who walks around town with earphones on his head. I prefer to listen to the unpredictable noises of the city—people talking to themselves, a metal grate being thrown open, the sound of a messenger-bike with no brakes bearing down on me. But this day, I was wired to a metallic-blue Discman I had tucked in my coat pocket. The music sounded so intimate and immediate as I walked up one street and down another, I could not help feeling that I was in the physical company of the musicians. ❞

So put on the headphones, turn up the volume, and take a stroll with Billy Collins.

### Literary Focus
#### Style

When we talk about **style** in literature, we refer to the way a writer uses language. Style can be ornate, slangy, plain, informal, elegant, personal, complex, and so on. People in many professions—athletes and politicians, for example—are sometimes criticized for having more style than substance. In literature and the arts, however, style and substance are deeply intertwined. In fact, the best writers make style part of the substance of their works. The Puritan plain style reflected an entire community's faith in the saving power of simplicity. Whitman's free verse embodied his wide-ranging democratic energy. Hemingway's

muscular, sculptured prose conveyed his belief in the value of strength and grace in both literature and life.

In twenty-first-century American literature many different styles coexist. They range from formal and objective to informal and immediate.

> **Style** is the distinctive way in which a writer uses language.
>
> *For more on Style, see the Handbook of Literary and Historical Terms.*

### Background

As he bops down the street, Collins is listening to a classic jazz CD, *Thelonious Monk/ Sonny Rollins*. The disc features Thelonious Monk on piano, Sonny Rollins on tenor saxophone, Tommy Potter on bass, and Arthur Taylor on drums, along with several other musicians. Their vibrant version of the popular romantic song "The Way You Look Tonight," by Jerome Kern and Dorothy Fields, was recorded in 1954.

Thelonious Monk (1960).

SKILLS FOCUS

**Literary Skills**
Understand style.

# Man Listening to Disc

## Billy Collins

This is not bad—
ambling along 44th Street
with Sonny Rollins for company,
his music flowing through the soft calipers
5    of these earphones,

as if he were right beside me
on this clear day in March,
the pavement sparkling with sunlight,
pigeons fluttering off the curb,
10    nodding over a profusion of bread crumbs.

In fact, I would say
my delight at being suffused
with phrases from his saxophone—
some like honey, some like vinegar—
15    is surpassed only by my gratitude

to Tommy Potter for taking the time
to join us on this breezy afternoon
with his most unwieldy bass
and to the esteemed Arthur Taylor
20    who is somehow managing to navigate

this crowd with his cumbersome drums.
And I bow deeply to Thelonious Monk
for figuring out a way
to motorize—or whatever—his huge piano
25    so he could be with us today.

The music is loud yet so confidential
I cannot help feeling even more
like the center of the universe
than usual as I walk along to a rapid
30    little version of "The Way You Look Tonight,"

and all I can say to my fellow pedestrians,
to the woman in the white sweater,
the man in the tan raincoat and the heavy glasses,
who mistake themselves for the center of the universe—
35    all I can say is watch your step

because the five of us, instruments
    and all,
are about to angle over
to the south side of the street
and then, in our own tightly knit
    way,
40    turn the corner at Sixth Avenue.

And if any of you are curious
about where this aggregation,
this whole battery-powered crew,
is headed, let us just say
45    that the real center of the universe,

the only true point of view,
is full of the hope that he,
the hub of the cosmos
with his hair blown sideways,
will eventually make it all the way
50    downtown.

(Opposite) *Summer Madness* (1993) by Michael Escoffery. Mixed media. Private Collection.

# Response and Analysis

## Thinking Critically

1. Where is the poem set?

2. What does the speaker imagine is happening in lines 1–25?

3. How does the music make the speaker feel? Find lines of the poem that describe his feelings.

4. What makes the music "loud yet so confidential" (line 26)?

5. What does the speaker want to say to the other pedestrians?

6. In the last verse, who is the "hub of the cosmos" who hopes he'll make it downtown?

7. Which of these words best describes Collins's **style**? More than one descriptive word can be correct.

   - formal
   - informal
   - complex
   - elegant
   - personal
   - humorous

8. Collins says, "Poetry is my cheap form of transportation. By the end of the poem, the reader should be in a different place from where he started. I would like him to be slightly disoriented at the end, like I drove him outside of town at night and dropped him off in a cornfield." Did "Man Listening to Disc" work on you the way Collins hoped it would? Explain your response to the poem.

## WRITING

### Ars Poetica

Some critics wonder if Collins's work belongs on the shelf with the work of the best living American poets. To think about that question, review two famous poems on pages 672 and 673 that talk about the art of poetry. Then, select one of these poems, and relate what it says to Collins's poem. In a brief **essay,** tell whether Collins's poem qualifies as a genuine poem, based on what Moore or MacLeish says a poem should be. Use at least two specifics from Moore's or MacLeish's poem to apply to Collins's.

### "Listening to . . . "

Choose a song or a CD that might be *your* own private soundtrack. Write an **essay** or a **poem** about the experience of listening to the music most meaningful to you. Be sure to explain *why* the music moves you. Feel free to experiment with a style that matches your thoughts and feelings.

**SKILLS FOCUS**

**Literary Skills**
Analyze style.

**Writing Skills**
Write an essay evaluating a poem. Write an essay or a poem about a song.

**D**rama is probably the most difficult form of writing; it certainly seems to take the longest to learn. According to a saying, young poets are eighteen, young novelists are twenty-four, and young playwrights are thirty.

George S. Kaufman, a noted American writer of comedies during the 1920s and 1930s, said that writing plays was not an art but a trick. Art or trick, it is difficult, possibly because when a play is written, it is not finished in the same way that a poem or novel is. There remains the painful and pleasurable process of bringing the play to life on stage, with the help of a director, actors, set designer, costume designer, lighting technician, stagehands, musicians— and a responsive audience. Producing a play is a team effort, and much can go wrong. A beautifully written and acted scene, for example, can be ruined if the lighting technician dims the lights too rapidly.

Another difference between drama and other literary forms is that movement and gesture are essential elements in drama. Some of the high points in a play may even be nonverbal. In *The Diary of Anne Frank,* for example, Mr. Frank realizes that the Nazis are downstairs and that the family's hiding place is about to be discovered. He turns to his family and friends and spreads his hands in resignation. This heartbreaking moment is conceived by the playwright, but its achievement on the stage—the exact gesture—requires the close and creative cooperation of actor and director.

Young writers are often drawn to the stage by the theatrical trappings: the gestures, the colorful sets, and the magical effects that drama can achieve. But playwrights soon learn that theatrical effects are rarely enough in themselves. The effects and gestures are there only to serve a story, and it must be a story that engages the passions of the collaborators—the director, the actors, and dozens of others who work to produce a play. Stage technicians may dazzle our senses with intricate and fascinating effects, but if a play doesn't have a significant story, we find nothing moving in the end, because our emotions have not been touched.

> . . . [W]hile I am working I toss papers right and left; at the end of each day I gather them helter-skelter and pile them together. So that the ultimate arrangement is a colossal job, which I do with actual groans and muttered curses, sitting on the floor with papers all about me, gradually going into little separate stacks, some order finally emerging, but not till I have died a thousand deaths. . . . Writing is not a happy profession.
>
> —Tennessee Williams

## Structure: Organizing Our Emotions

When a play goes wrong, it is almost always because the writer has failed to conceive the story in dramatic terms. There are, of course, some plays (such as Thornton Wilder's *Our Town*) that work in the theater even though they ignore the usual principles of drama. But over the centuries certain principles have developed, and they are usually observed by playwrights who want to catch, hold, and reward the attention of an audience.

The analogy is slightly oversimplified, but we respond to a play in very much the way we respond to a sports event. Let's assume that one summer evening you go to a professional baseball game. For some reason, you take a liking to one of the pitchers. Then someone sitting next to you says that the pitcher has been out for several weeks with an injured elbow and is trying to make a comeback. If he fails in this game, he is finished. You start rooting for him. He gets some bad calls from the plate umpire, and you boo or whistle. Then your neighbor tells you that the pitcher is not pitching his best. Unless he stops protecting his injured elbow and starts putting more speed in his pitches, he will not win.

Most plays have more psychological complexity than this situation does. With a little imagination, however, we can add to the pitcher's problems. Suppose, for instance, that the pitcher's wife is afraid that if he throws too hard, he will ruin his elbow and be unable to play. She tells him that if he damages his elbow further, she will leave him; but, to him, the glory of winning transcends practical matters. To his wife, he is a ball-playing "boy," careless and immature. And so forth. . . . What has happened in this scenario is what happens in almost every play. Early on, the playwright organizes our emotions behind some character or group of characters: We are "for" them. The playwright has placed these characters in a situation involving **conflict** and then has made us understand that it is not just any conflict: The character or characters have something vital at stake. They want to win, and they need to win in order to survive. In the baseball game, the situation is made difficult for the pitcher, who is the **protagonist** (the major character who wants something and who drives the action forward). The pitcher struggles against

You have to hit the public when it is not looking . . . you have to make it real to them the way the subway is real. You can't depend on their embracing your work because it is art, but only because it somehow reaches into the part of them that is still alive and questing.

—Arthur Miller

EMANUEL AZENBERG, WAYNE M. ROGERS, RADIO CITY MUSIC HALL PRODUCTIONS in association with CENTER THEATRE GROUP/AHMANSON present

**NEIL SIMON'S** New Comedy

**BRIGHTON BEACH MEMOIRS**

Starring (in alphabetical order)
MATTHEW BRODERICK
ELIZABETH FRANZ
PETER MICHAEL GOETZ
MANDY INGBER
ŽELJKO IVANEK
JODI THELEN
JOYCE VAN PAT

Setting designed by DAVID MITCHE

JED HARRIS presents

**OUR TOWN** A PLAY BY THORNTON WILDER

**PLAYBILL** a weekly magazine for theatregoers

Winter Garden

WEST SIDE STORY

both **external conflict** (the opposing side) and **internal conflict** (his fears of damaging his arm, his feelings about the pressure from his wife). The fan sitting next to you has given us the background information, or **exposition** (who the pitcher is, what he wants to do, and what he has at stake). The story of a character who, against the odds, wants something meaningful has been set in motion. The tension mounts as the innings pass; we are witnessing, or participating in and enjoying, a drama.

The word *participation* is important. We have all heard ballplayers say how encouraged they are by the response of the spectators. Actors, too, may say as they come offstage after a scene, "That's a wonderful audience out there tonight!" And because of the audience, performances often rise to a higher level. It has often been said that a play exists halfway between the stage and the audience. What an audience gets from a performance is directly related to what it brings to the performance, not only in the way of understanding and feeling but also in enthusiasm. In successful dramatic performances, a note is sounded onstage, and a chord of recognition or responsiveness echoes back from the audience. A play performed in an empty theater is not a play.

> ... I would say that the whole notion of going into a theater and sitting with a lot of other people and watching a spectacle, especially now when you can watch television or the movies with greater convenience, tells me that, apart from the fact that it's a little more exciting to see a live actor on the stage, it's also exciting to sit next to human beings.
>
> —Arthur Miller

*The basic elements of drama include exposition, which gives us information, and a protagonist, the major character who struggles against internal conflict and external conflict.*

## How a Play Is Produced (It's a Miracle!)

The English plays of the late Middle Ages were called miracle plays because they often dealt with stories of miracles from the Bible or the lives of the saints. Any modern-day American play might also be called a miracle play, because it is a miracle that it was written and even more of a miracle that it was produced. In the United States today, drama is dependent on money. Only a few institutional theaters are able to present plays with little or no regard for profit. Most of the plays that are produced (and that therefore stand a chance of becoming part of our dramatic literature) are put on with the idea that they will make money.

To produce any writer's new play on Broadway costs a minimum of half a million dollars (at this writing). The **producers** (people who advance the money) willing to take such a risk are rare, although such risks *are* taken every season. Even though it operates in a very costly manner, the professional Broadway theater, to its credit, has been the launching pad for most of the distinguished plays in American dramatic literature.

Recently, regional theaters throughout the country have been presenting new plays by both new and established playwrights. The Broadway producers often visit, look, and take whatever they want for production. For the most part, only a successful Broadway production gives a playwright enough income to plunge in and take the years necessary to write the next play. For that reason, Broadway remains the goal of most playwrights.

There are many stops on the way to New York, some of which become full stops. Over ten thousand plays are copyrighted every year; this probably represents only half of the plays that are actually written. Perhaps several hundred new plays are produced onstage *somewhere* around the country; maybe ten appear on Broadway.

Producers could not hope to cope with reading thousands and thousands of plays, so playwrights must generally find an **agent** who will handle their work. The agent is the producer's first line of defense. Knowing their various tastes, the agent submits a play to likely producers, who may take three months to a year to read it. They may admire the play but still be unwilling to produce it. One playwright used to say, "If they take you to lunch, they're not going to invest in your play." A good lunch is a consolation prize, and many playwrights have eaten very well off plays that were never produced.

But if the producer should decide to finance the play, he or she then sits down with the playwright to go over changes suggested for the script or ideas for directors and actors. Authors maintain control over their scripts, and the playwright is very much involved in the selection of the director and the actors. Of course, since theater is a collaborative medium, the playwright tries to get along with the producer. But if the playwright and producer discover during these preliminary talks that they have incompatible ideas, they can shake hands and part.

The director becomes the playwright's surrogate at rehearsals. In a sense, the director takes the play away from the playwright, and, finally, the actors take it away from both of them.

Rehearsals involve both pleasure and tension. Many temperaments must mesh as the actors move forward to the climactic moment of opening night. (Note that all the elements of drama itself are also present at play rehearsals: striving for a goal, having something at stake, dealing with internal and external conflicts, etc.)

A manuscript page of *The Glass Menagerie*, by Tennessee Williams, with alterations in the playwright's hand.

To a certain extent I imagine a play is completely finished in my mind—in my case, at any rate—without my knowing it, before I sit down to write. So in that sense, I suppose, writing a play is *finding out* what the play is.

—Edward Albee

Scenes from 1989 production
of *A Raisin in the Sun* by Lorraine Hansberry.

© Mitzi Trumbo for PBS
American Playhouse,
KCET Los Angeles.

The play opens in a smaller city for a tryout run or in New York for previews. Sometimes all goes well, and the production needs only some refining and sharpening. More often, the play needs work—rewriting, new sets, new costumes, sometimes a new director or a new star. Chaos reigns until opening night, when all the cast will suddenly come down with laryngitis, intestinal upsets, sinus trouble, or splitting headaches. Somehow, the curtain rises, and the show goes on.

The day after the opening, there may or may not be a line of eager theatergoers at the box office. If there is, the playwright has created what may later be called an American classic, which will be performed around the world and will find its way into the anthologies you study in school. If there isn't a line, the playwright will quickly look around for a way to make a living while writing the next play—if he or she has the courage. The second instance is the more usual. The theater has been called the "fabulous invalid," always teetering on the edge of extinction. If so, playwrights themselves might be called the walking wounded—working, barely surviving, but finally enduring to try once again.

***The production of a play depends on a successful working relationship between the playwright, the producer, the director, and the actors.***

. . . [T]he final evaluation of a play has nothing to do with immediate audience or critical response. The playwright, along with any writer, composer, painter in this society, has got to have a terribly private view of his own value, of his own work. He's got to listen to his own voice primarily.
—Edward Albee

# The History of American Drama: The Caboose of Literature

Eugene O'Neill (1888–1953) is generally considered the first important figure in American drama. It is significant that decades after the 1920 production of his first full-length play, *Beyond the Horizon,* he is still regarded as the most important playwright the United States has produced.

American drama before O'Neill consisted mostly of shows and entertainments. These wildly theatrical spectacles often featured such delights as chariot races and burning cities, staged by means of special effects that dazzled audiences. Melodramas and farces were also written for famous actors, much as television shows today are created to display the personalities and talents of popular performers. In fact, O'Neill's own father, James O'Neill, spent the better part of his life touring in a spectacular melodrama based on Alexandre Dumas's *The Count of Monte Cristo.*

There was great theatrical activity in the United States in the nineteenth century, a time when there were no movies, radio, or television. Every town of any size had its theater or "opera house" in which touring companies performed. Given the hunger for entertainment, one may wonder why no significant American drama was staged in the century that produced, among others, Melville, Emerson, Whitman, Dickinson, and Twain.

> Playwrights are either intuitively keen analytical psychologists—or they aren't good playwrights.
> —Eugene O'Neill

A scene from the original Broadway production of *The Piano Lesson* by August Wilson.

PLAYBILL

WALTER KERR THEATRE

THE PIANO LESSON

One explanation is that theater has usually followed the other arts, rather than pointing the way toward new directions. Robert Sherwood, one of a group of notable American playwrights between 1920 and 1940, once said, "Drama travels in the caboose of literature." Theater seems to take up new attitudes, subject matter, and forms only after they have been explored in the other arts. For the most part, theater tends to dramatize accepted attitudes and values.

The reason for this is that theater is a social art, one we attend as part of a large group; we seem to respond to something new much more slowly as a group than we do as individuals. When you laugh or cry in the theater, your response is noticed. You are, in a sense, giving your approval, and this approval may be subject to criticism or condemnation by those sitting around you who are not laughing or crying. Furthermore, you may not be shocked to *read* about your secret thoughts, dreams, and desires; but if you *see* them shown on stage as you sit among a thousand people, you may refuse to respond, refuse to acknowledge them. You may even rise up and stalk out of the theater.

Thus, the novel and, to some extent, the poetry of the nineteenth and early twentieth centuries were more daring than the theater in giving us a record of experience, in showing us life as it *is* lived rather than as it *should be* lived.

> **During the period before Eugene O'Neill, American drama tended to be mild and sentimental, rarely questioning the life and attitudes it depicted, almost never challenging the accepted traditions of its times.**

## The Influence of Europe: Psychology and Taboo Subjects

European drama, which was to influence modern American drama profoundly, matured in the last third of the nineteenth century with the achievements of three playwrights: the Norwegian Henrik Ibsen, the Swede August Strindberg, and the Russian Anton Chekhov. Ibsen deliberately tackled subjects such as guilt, sexuality, and mental illness— subjects that had never before been so realistically and disturbingly portrayed on stage. Strindberg brought to his characterizations an unprecedented level of psychological complexity. And Chekhov, along with Ibsen and Strindberg, shifted the subject matter of drama from wildly theatrical displays of external action to inner action and emotions and the concerns of everyday life. Chekhov once remarked, "People don't go to the North Pole and fall off icebergs. They go to the office and quarrel with their wives and eat cabbage soup."

> **Ibsen, Strindberg, and Chekhov bequeathed to their American heirs plays about life as it is actually lived. They presented characters and situations more or less realistically, in what has been called the "slice-of-life" dramatic technique.**

# Realism and Eugene O'Neill: Putting American Drama on the Map

**Realistic drama** is based on the illusion that when we watch a play, we are looking at life through a "fourth wall" that has been removed so that we can see the action. Soon after the beginning of the twentieth century, realism became the dominant mode of American drama.

As with all theatrical revolutions, the movement toward realism began apart from the commercial theater. But very soon after the new drama succeeded in the little theaters off Broadway (about 1916), the commercial theater adopted realism, too.

In 1916 and 1917, two small theater groups in New York—the Provincetown Players and the Washington Square Players—began to produce new American plays. They provided a congenial home for new American playwrights, notably Eugene O'Neill, whose first one-act plays about the sea were produced by the Provincetown Players in Greenwich Village in 1916. (New movements in the theater have often begun with one-act plays. In addition to O'Neill, Tennessee Williams, Clifford Odets, and Edward Albee all started with short plays.)

These theater groups seemed to have no program. They were not sure what they were for, but they were sure what they were against: the established commercial theater. They would produce any play, in any style, that commercial theater would not touch.

O'Neill gravitated there naturally. Well aware of Sigmund Freud and his new theories about the complex self, O'Neill tried especially hard to reveal more than realism—or Naturalism—could normally reveal. "The old naturalism," he wrote, "no longer applies. We have taken too many snapshots of each other in every graceless position; we have endured too much from the banality of surfaces."

In *The Great God Brown* (1926), O'Neill experimented with using masks to differentiate between two sides of a personality. In *Days Without End* (1934), he had two actors play one character to achieve the same end. And in *Strange Interlude* (1928), characters spoke in asides to the audience, revealing thoughts and feelings that could not be expressed in dialogue to other characters.

Goodspeed Opera House, East Haddam, Connecticut.

Inge Morath/Magnum.

Sure, I'll write about happiness if I ever happen to meet up with that luxury and find it sufficiently dramatic and in harmony with any deep rhythm of life. But happiness is a word. What does it mean? Exaltation, an intensified feeling of the significant worth of man's being and becoming? Well, if it means that—and not a mere smirking contentment with one's lot—I know that there is more of it in one real tragedy than in all the happy ending plays ever written.

—Eugene O'Neill

Scene from *Death of a Salesman* by Arthur Miller.

With his experimental flair, his enormous output, and his high aspirations for the theater, Eugene O'Neill dominated American drama in his generation; he can be said to have put it on the map. His plays were widely produced abroad, and he was awarded the Nobel Prize in literature in 1936.

Americans fancy themselves . . . to be openhanded, on the side of justice, a little bit careless about what they buy, wasteful, but essentially good guys, optimistic. But under that level of awareness there is another one, which gets expressed in very few movies and very few plays, but in more plays in proportion than in the movies: the level which confronts our bewilderment, our lonely naïveté, our hunger for purpose.

—Arthur Miller

## Arthur Miller: Playwright of Our Social Conscience

The post–World War II years brought two important figures to prominence in American drama: Arthur Miller (1915–2005) and Tennessee Williams (1911–1983). Although other playwrights, such as William Inge (1913–1973), have contributed striking and effective plays, Miller and Williams remain the dominant figures of the second half of the century. Miller and Williams represent the two principal movements in modern American drama: realism, and realism combined with an attempt at something more imaginative. From the beginning, American playwrights have tried to break away from realism or to blend it with more poetic expression, as in Miller's *Death of a Salesman* (1949), Williams's *The Glass Menagerie* (1944), and Thornton Wilder's *Our Town* (1938) and *The Skin of Our Teeth* (1942).

death of a **Salesman**

*The*

**PLAYBILL** *for the Morosco Theatre*

Arthur Miller's best work, *Death of a Salesman,* is one of the most successful in fusing the realistic and the imaginative; in all of his other plays, however, Miller is the master of realism. He is a true disciple of Henrik Ibsen, not only in his realistic technique but also in his concern about society's impact on his characters' lives.

In Miller's plays, the course of the action and the development of characters depend not only on the characters' psychological makeup but also on the social, philosophical, and economic atmosphere of their times. Miller's most notable character, Willy Loman in *Death of a Salesman,* is a self-deluded man; but he is also a product of the American dream of success and a victim of the American business machine, which disposes of him when he has outlived his usefulness.

Miller is a writer of high moral seriousness, whether he is dealing with personal versus social responsibility, as in *All My Sons* (1947), or with witch hunts past and present, as in *The Crucible* (1953), which you are about to read. Miller writes a plain and muscular prose that under the force of emotion often becomes eloquent, as in Linda Loman's famous speech in *Death of a Salesman,* in which she talks to her two sons about their father:

> I don't say he's a great man. Willy Loman never made a lot of money. His name was never in the paper. He's not the finest character that ever lived. But he's a human being, and a terrible thing is happening

to him. So attention must be paid. He's not to be allowed to fall into his grave like an old dog. Attention, attention must finally be paid to such a person.

—Arthur Miller,
*from Death of a Salesman*

## Tennessee Williams: Playwright of Our Souls

Although Tennessee Williams was Miller's contemporary, his concern was not with social matters, but with personal ones. If Miller was often the playwright of our social conscience, then Williams was the playwright of our souls. In play after play, he probed the psychological complexities of his characters, especially of his female characters: Amanda and Laura in *The Glass Menagerie* (1944), Blanche in *A Streetcar Named Desire* (1947), and Alma in *Summer and Smoke* (1948).

In contrast to Miller's spare, plain language, Williams's writing is delicate and sensuous; it is often colored with lush imagery and evocative rhythms. Miller's characters are, by and large, ordinary people with whom we identify because they are caught up in the social tensions of our times. Williams's characters are often women who are lost ladies, drowning in their own neuroses, but somehow mirroring a part of our own complex psychological selves.

The actual scenes in Williams's plays are usually purely realistic, even though these scenes may deal with colorful and extreme characters. But Williams usually theatricalized the realism with "music in the wings" or symbolic props, such as Laura's unicorn in *The Glass Menagerie* or the looming statue of Eternity in *Summer and Smoke.* He always conceived his plays in visually arresting, colorful, theatrical environments— an effort in which he was aided by the

**Scene from *The Glass Menagerie* by Tennessee Williams. Long Wharf Theater, New Haven, Connecticut, 1986.**

imaginative designer Jo Mielziner, who designed the sets for many of his plays.

*In the works of Arthur Miller and Tennessee Williams, we see the two strongest strands in American drama: pure realism, and realism blended with an imaginative, poetic sensibility.*

## The Revolt Against Realism: Theater of Fragmentation

In the mid–nineteenth century, realism in drama was conceived as a revolt against crude theatricalism. Currently, there is a revolt against realism itself in American drama. Naturally, the movement is toward theatricalism again, with its emphasis on stage effects and imaginative settings. This revolt does not confine itself to a particular manner of staging; instead, it extends to the texture of language and plot in the scripts themselves.

The moral and religious certainties that once bound people together exert little or no force on many modern audiences. Some people believe that survival itself depends on a willingness to accept life as formless or meaningless.

Some American playwrights found this new outlook on life impossible to express in the orderly "beginning, middle, end" format of realism. They borrowed, again from Europe, a theater of fragmentation, impressions, and stream of consciousness that was called "expressionist." **Expressionist drama** aimed at the revelation of characters' interior consciousness without reference to a logical sequence of surface actions. Many writers who used expressionist techniques in drama came to be called playwrights of the Theater of the Absurd. Samuel Beckett (1906-1989) and Eugene Ionesco (1912-1994) were among the founders of the Theater of the Absurd. The drama critic Martin Esslin has written this about the Absurdists:

> The action of a play of the Theater of the Absurd is not intended to tell a story but to communicate a pattern of poetic images. To give but one example: Things happen in [Samuel Beckett's] *Waiting for Godot,* but these things do not constitute a plot or a story; they are an image of Beckett's intuition that *nothing really ever happens* in man's existence.
>
> —Martin Esslin

Scene from *Happy Days* by Samuel Beckett. The entire play takes place while the actors are half buried in a pile of sand.

The trouble with a static play that mirrors a static life is that it is static. It is an image, a picture; and a picture can absorb our interest for only so long because it lacks the progression and development of a dramatic story. We can observe a situation without development for about the length of a one-act play. Perhaps this is why so many of the Absurdist plays *are* only one act, such as Beckett's *Krapp's Last Tape* and Ionesco's *The Bald Soprano*.

The most significant Absurdist in the United States has been Edward Albee (1928–    ). Albee is not a pure Absurdist, since, like all innovative playwrights, he experiments with many forms. From 1959 to 1970, Albee produced a play a year. These works ranged from his startling one-act debut, *The Zoo Story* (1959), through the Absurdist play *The American Dream* (1961), to the savage and electrifying domestic drama *Who's Afraid of Virginia Woolf?* (1962), which made Albee world famous.

Experimental drama has increased the options that are open to playwrights. There are practically no conventions in the theater anymore; there is simply a stage and an audience. Playwrights are free to load the stage with scenery, lights, and special effects; but they are equally free—as the playwright was in the age of Shakespeare—to have an actor gesture toward one side of an utterly bare stage and say, "This is the Forest of Arden."

*Dramatists now have the freedom to express their deepest feelings in almost any form they choose—provided that their approach can be made comprehensible to an audience and touch their emotions.*

### Quickwrite 🖉

What do you predict will happen to American drama in the next ten years? Consider subject matter, sets and costume design, popularity, and competition with movies, television, and the Internet. Jot down your thoughts, and then compare notes with your classmates.

# Arthur Miller

## (1915–2005)

*by* Robert Anderson

Arthur Miller, considered by many to be the pre-eminent American playwright of the second half of the twentieth century, was born in New York City. His father manufactured women's coats, and his mother was a schoolteacher. In high school, Arthur was more involved with sports than with literature. "Until the age of seventeen," Miller said, "I can safely say that I never read a book weightier than *Tom Swift* and *The Rover Boys,* and only verged on literature with some Dickens."

On graduation from high school, Miller applied to the University of Michigan, but his grades were not good enough for a scholarship, and the Depression left his father unable to finance his tuition. To earn money for college, Miller worked for two years in an automobile parts plant, where, incidentally, he read Tolstoy's *War and Peace.* The experience in the parts plant later supplied him with the material for his 1955 play *A Memory of Two Mondays.*

Miller eventually enrolled in the University of Michigan. To help finance his education, he took on various jobs. More important, he started to write plays. After graduation, Miller returned to New York and earned a living by writing radio scripts.

Miller's first Broadway success, *All My Sons,* was produced in 1947 and won The New York Drama Critics' award for Best Play. That play struck a note that was to become familiar in Miller's work: the need for moral responsibility in families and society.

In 1949, with the production of his masterpiece, *Death of a Salesman* (written in a small studio he built with his own hands on his property in northwestern Connecticut), all promises were fulfilled. Miller instantly joined the pantheon of the great American playwrights.

It was totally in character that Miller's next play, produced in 1953, should be *The Crucible*—about a witch hunt that took place in 1692 in Salem, Massachusetts. In that witch hunt, Miller found parallels to the "Red hunt" being conducted in the 1950s in Washington, D.C., by Senator Joseph McCarthy. Writers, actors, politicians—and all kinds of other people—were summoned to appear before McCarthy to answer the question: "Are you now or were you ever a Communist?" Those summoned were required to inform on neighbors and friends or be sent to jail.

Three years after the production of *The Crucible* in New York, Miller was summoned before a congressional committee. He spoke freely about himself and his occasional attendance, years before, as a guest at Communist meetings; but he refused to name names of other people in attendance. Miller was found in contempt of Congress, but his conviction was later overturned by the Supreme Court.

*The Crucible* was not successful in its first production. Some critics questioned the comparison between the old witch hunts and the contemporary hunt for Communists in government. In a later production, supervised by Miller himself, the play ran for over six hundred performances. It is now Miller's most produced play.

# Why I Wrote *The Crucible*
## An artist's answer to politics

### *by* Arthur Miller

As I watched *The Crucible* taking shape as a movie over much of the past year, the sheer depth of time that it represents for me kept returning to mind. As those powerful actors blossomed on the screen, and the children and the horses, and the crowds and the wagons, I thought again about how I came to cook all this up nearly fifty years ago, in an America almost nobody I know seems to remember clearly. . . .

I remember those years—they formed *The Crucible's* skeleton—but I have lost the dead weight of the fear I had then. Fear doesn't travel well; just as it can warp judgment, its absence can diminish memory's truth. What terrifies one generation is likely to bring only a puzzled smile to the next. . . .

[Senator] McCarthy's power to stir fears of creeping Communism was not entirely based on illusion, of course. . . . From being our wartime ally, the Soviet Union rapidly became an expanding empire. In 1949, Mao Zedong took power in China. Western Europe also seemed ready to become Red, especially Italy, where the Communist Party was the largest outside Russia, and was growing. . . . McCarthy—brash and ill-mannered but to many authentic and true—boiled it all down to what anyone could understand: We had "lost China" and would soon lose Europe as well, because the State Department—staffed, of course, under Democratic presidents—was full of treasonous pro-Soviet intellectuals. It was as simple as that. . . .

*The Crucible* was an act of desperation. . . . By 1950 when I began to think of writing about the hunt for Reds in America, I was motivated in some great part by the paralysis that had set in among many liberals who, despite their discomfort with the inquisitors' violations of civil rights, were fearful, and with good reason, of being identified as covert Communists if they should protest too strongly. . . .

I visited Salem for the first time on a dismal spring day in 1952. . . . In the gloomy courthouse there I read the transcripts of the witchcraft trials of 1692, as taken down in a primitive shorthand by ministers who were spelling each other. But there was one entry in Upham° in which the thousands of pieces I had come across were jogged into place. It was from a report written by the Reverend Samuel Parris, who was one of the chief instigators of the witch-hunt. "During the examination of Elizabeth Proctor, Abigail Williams, and Ann Putnam"—the two were "afflicted" teen-age accusers, and Abigail was Parris's niece—"both made offer to strike at said Proctor; but when Abigail's hand came near, it opened, whereas it was made up, into a fist before, and came down exceeding lightly as it drew near to said Proctor, and at length, with open and extended fingers, touched Proctor's hood very lightly. Immediately Abigail cried out her fingers, her fingers, her fingers burned. . . ."

In this remarkably observed gesture of a troubled young girl, I believed, a play became possible. Elizabeth Proctor had been the orphaned Abigail's mistress, and they had lived together in the same small house until Elizabeth fired the girl. By this time, I was sure, John Proctor had bedded Abigail, who had to be dismissed most likely to appease Elizabeth. There was bad blood between the two women now. That Abigail started, in effect, to condemn Elizabeth to death with her touch, then stopped her hand, then went through with it, was quite suddenly the human center of all this turmoil.

All this I understood. I had not approached the witchcraft out of nowhere or from purely social and political considerations. My own marriage of twelve years was teetering and I knew more than I wished to know about where the blame lay. That John Proctor the sinner might overturn his paralyzing personal guilt and become the most forthright voice against the madness around him was a reassurance to me, and, I suppose, an inspiration: It demonstrated that a clear moral outcry could still spring even from an ambiguously unblemished soul. Moving crabwise across the profusion of evidence, I sensed that I had at last found something of myself in it, and a play began to accumulate around this man.

—from *The New Yorker,*
October 21 and 28, 1996

°Charles W. Upham, a mayor of Salem, published a two-volume study of the trials in 1867.

# Before You Read

## The Crucible

### Make the Connection
#### Quickwrite ✏️

Most of us recognize the difference between our public and private selves. Sometimes, however, those selves come into conflict. Then, we must make a choice. These choices may simply be to avoid embarrassment, prevent hurt feelings, or confess dishonesty. Sometimes, however, they have much more serious consequences.

Based on your own experiences, how do you think most people resolve conflicts between their public and private lives? If your private and public selves were in conflict, which would you choose to reveal?

### Literary Focus
#### Motivation

Motivation is what moves people to act the way they do. Just like real people, fictional characters often have complex motivations, and their actions can result from several motivating factors. In *The Crucible,* Miller shows that every person in Salem had at least one reason for acting the way he or she did—psychological, sexual, financial, theological, or political.

> **Motivation** is the reason for a character's behavior.
>
> *For more on Motivation, see the Handbook of Literary and Historical Terms.*

### Reading Skills 📖
#### Interpreting a Text

To understand a complex dramatic work like *The Crucible,* you need to **interpret** it. In other words, you should offer your own explanations of who the characters really are, why they behave the way they do, and what the larger meaning of their situation might be.

As you read *The Crucible,* jot down your interpretation of what the dialogue and actions reveal about the characters' values, emotions, motivations, and personal histories. You may need to monitor your reading by going back over the play and re-reading sections to find more information about the characters and their actions.

### Background

*The Crucible* is based on the witch trials that took place in 1692, in Salem, Massachusetts. Elizabeth Parris, daughter of Reverend Samuel Parris, and Abigail Williams, his niece, began acting strangely. Since no medical cause for their behavior could be found, doctors concluded that the girls were bewitched. Soon other girls began exhibiting the same behavior, crying out the names of women they knew and sparking the witch hunt. Over the next eight months, twenty-seven people were convicted, nineteen were hanged, one was pressed to death, and more than one hundred were imprisoned.

go.hrw.com

**INTERNET**

**More About Arthur Miller**

Keyword: LE7 11-6

# The Crucible
## Arthur Miller

They believed that they held in their steady hands the candle that would light the world.

The Crucible *was first presented by Kermit Bloomgarden at the Martin Beck Theatre, New York City, January 22, 1953, with the following cast.*

*(in order of appearance)*

**Reverend Parris** . . . . . . . . . . . . . . .Fred Stewart
**Betty Parris** . . . . . . . . . . . . . .Janet Alexander
**Tituba** . . . . . . . . . . . . . . . . . . .Jacqueline Andre
**Abigail Williams** . . . . . . . .Madeleine Sherwood
**Susanna Walcott** . . . . . . . . . . .Barbara Stanton
**Mrs. Ann Putnam** . . . . . . . . . . . .Jane Hoffman
**Thomas Putnam** . . . . . . . . . . .Raymond Bramley
**Mercy Lewis** . . . . . . . . . . . . . .Dorothy Joliffe
**Mary Warren** . . . . . . . . . . . . . . .Jennie Egan
**John Proctor** . . . . . . . . . . . . . .Arthur Kennedy
**Rebecca Nurse** . . . . . . . . . . . . . . .Jean Adair
**Giles Corey** . . . . . . . . . . . . . .Joseph Sweeney
**Reverend John Hale** . . . . . . . . .E. G. Marshall
**Elizabeth Proctor** . . . . . . . . . . .Beatrice Straight
**Francis Nurse** . . . . . . . . . . . . . .Graham Velsey
**Ezekiel Cheever** . . . . . . . . . . . . .Don McHenry
**Marshal Herrick** . . . . . . . . . . .George Mitchell
**Judge Hathorne** . . . . . . . . . . . .Philip Coolidge
**Deputy Governor Danforth** . . .Walter Hampden
**Sarah Good** . . . . . . . . . . . . . . . .Adele Fortin
**Hopkins** . . . . . . . . . . . . . . . . .Donald Marye

**Staged by** Jed Harris

**Settings by** Boris Aronson

**Costumes made and designed by** Edith Lutyens

*The play is set in Salem, Massachusetts, in 1692.*

**Act One (An Overture)**
Home of Rev. Samuel Parris.

**Act Two**
John Proctor's house, eight days later.

**Act Three**
Salem meeting house, serving as the General Court.

**Act Four**
A cell in Salem jail, fall 1692.

# Act One

## (An Overture)

*A small upper bedroom in the home of* REVEREND SAMUEL PARRIS, *Salem, Massachusetts, in the spring of the year 1692.*

*There is a narrow window at the left. Through its leaded panes the morning sunlight streams. A candle still burns near the bed, which is at the right. A chest, a chair, and a small table are the other furnishings. At the back a door opens on the landing of the stairway to the ground floor. The room gives off an air of clean spareness. The roof rafters are exposed, and the wood colors are raw and unmellowed.*

*As the curtain rises,* REVEREND PARRIS *is discovered kneeling beside the bed, evidently in prayer. His daughter,* BETTY PARRIS, *aged ten, is lying on the bed, inert.*

At the time of these events Parris was in his middle forties. In history he cut a villainous path, and there is very little good to be said for him. He believed he was being persecuted wherever he went, despite his best efforts to win people and God to his side. In meeting, he felt insulted if someone rose to shut the door without first asking his permission. He was a widower with no interest in children, or talent with them. He regarded them as young adults, and until this strange crisis he, like the rest of Salem, never conceived that the children were anything but thankful for being permitted to walk straight, eyes slightly lowered, arms at the sides, and mouths shut until bidden to speak.

His house stood in the "town"—but we today would hardly call it a village. The meeting house was nearby, and from this point outward—toward the bay or inland—there were a few small-windowed, dark houses snuggling against the raw Massachusetts winter. Salem had been established hardly forty years before. To the European world the whole province was a barbaric frontier inhabited by a sect of fanatics who, nevertheless, were shipping out products of slowly increasing quantity and value.

No one can really know what their lives were like. They had no novelists—and would not have permitted anyone to read a novel if one were handy. Their creed forbade anything resembling a theater or "vain enjoyment." They did not celebrate Christmas, and a holiday from work meant only that they must concentrate even more upon prayer.

Which is not to say that nothing broke into this strict and somber way of life. When a new farmhouse was built, friends assembled to "raise the roof," and there would be special foods cooked and probably some potent cider passed around. There was a good supply of ne'er-do-wells in Salem, who dallied at the shovelboard in Bridget Bishop's tavern. Probably more than the creed, hard work kept the morals of the place from spoiling, for the people were forced to fight the land like heroes for every grain of corn, and no man had very much time for fooling around.

That there were some jokers, however, is indicated by the practice of appointing a two-man patrol whose duty was to "walk forth in the time of God's worship to take notice of such as either lye about the meeting house, without attending to the word and ordinances, or that lye at home or in the fields without giving good account thereof, and to take the names of such persons, and to present them to the magistrates, whereby they may be accordingly proceeded against." This predilection for minding other people's business was time-honored among the people of Salem, and it undoubtedly created many of the suspicions which were to feed the coming madness. It was also, in my opinion, one of the things that a John Proctor would rebel against, for the time of the armed camp had almost passed, and since the country was reasonably—although not wholly— safe, the old disciplines were beginning to rankle. But, as in all such matters, the issue was not clear-cut, for danger was still a possibility, and in unity still lay the best promise of safety.

The edge of the wilderness was close by. The American continent stretched endlessly west, and it was full of mystery for them. It stood, dark and threatening, over their shoulders night and day, for out of it Indian tribes marauded from time to time, and Reverend Parris had parishioners who had lost relatives to these heathen.

The parochial snobbery of these people was partly responsible for their failure to convert the Indians. Probably they also preferred to take land from heathens rather than from fellow Christians. At any rate, very few Indians were converted, and the Salem folk believed that the virgin forest was the Devil's last preserve, his home base and the citadel of his final stand. To the best of their knowledge the American forest was the last place on earth that was not paying homage to God.

For these reasons, among others, they carried about an air of innate resistance, even of persecution. Their fathers had, of course, been persecuted in England. So now they and their church found it necessary to deny any other sect its freedom, lest their New Jerusalem[1] be defiled and corrupted by wrong ways and deceitful ideas.

They believed, in short, that they held in their steady hands the candle that would light the world. We have inherited this belief, and it has helped and hurt us. It helped them with the discipline it gave them. They were a dedicated folk, by and large, and they had to be to survive the life they had chosen or been born into in this country.

The proof of their belief's value to them may be taken from the opposite character of the first Jamestown settlement, farther south, in Virginia. The Englishmen who landed there were motivated mainly by a hunt for profit. They had thought to pick off the wealth of the new country and then return rich to England. They were a band of individualists, and a much more ingratiating group than the Massachusetts men. But Virginia destroyed them. Massachusetts tried to kill off the Puritans, but they combined; they set up a communal society which, in the beginning, was little more than an armed camp with an autocratic and very devoted leadership. It was, however, an autocracy by consent, for they were united from top to bottom by a commonly held ideology whose perpetuation was the reason and justification for all their sufferings. So their self-denial, their purposefulness, their suspicion of all vain pursuits, their hard-handed justice were altogether perfect instruments for the conquest of this space so antagonistic to man.

But the people of Salem in 1692 were not quite the dedicated folk that arrived on the *Mayflower.*

1. **New Jerusalem:** in the Bible (Revelations 21), the holy city of heaven.

A vast differentiation had taken place, and in their own time a revolution had unseated the royal government and substituted a junta which was at this moment in power. The times, to their eyes, must have been out of joint, and to the common folk must have seemed as insoluble and complicated as do ours today. It is not hard to see how easily many could have been led to believe that the time of confusion had been brought upon them by deep and darkling forces. No hint of such speculation appears on the court record, but social disorder in any age breeds such mystical suspicions, and when, as in Salem, wonders are brought forth from below the social surface, it is too much to expect people to hold back very long from laying on the victims with all the force of their frustrations.

The Salem tragedy, which is about to begin in these pages, developed from a paradox. It is a paradox in whose grip we still live, and there is no prospect yet that we will discover its resolution. Simply, it was this: for good purposes, even high purposes, the people of Salem developed a theocracy, a combine of state and religious power whose function was to keep the community together, and to prevent any kind of disunity that might open it to destruction by material or ideological enemies. It was forged for a necessary purpose and accomplished that purpose. But all organization is and must be grounded on the idea of exclusion and prohibition, just as two objects cannot occupy the same space. Evidently the time came in New England when the repressions of order were heavier than seemed warranted by the dangers against which the order was organized. The witch-hunt was a perverse manifestation of the panic which set in among all classes when the balance began to turn toward greater individual freedom.

When one rises above the individual villainy displayed, one can only pity them all, just as we shall be pitied someday. It is still impossible for man to organize his social life without repressions, and the balance has yet to be struck between order and freedom.

The witch-hunt was not, however, a mere repression. It was also, and as importantly, a long overdue opportunity for everyone so inclined to express publicly his guilt and sins, under the cover of accusations against the victims. It suddenly became possible—and patriotic and holy—for a man to say that Martha Corey had come into his bedroom at night, and that, while his wife was sleeping at his side, Martha laid herself down on his chest and "nearly suffocated him." Of course it was her spirit only, but his satisfaction at confessing himself was no lighter than if it had been Martha herself. One could not ordinarily speak such things in public.

Long-held hatreds of neighbors could now be openly expressed, and vengeance taken, despite the Bible's charitable injunctions. Land-lust, which had been expressed by constant bickering over boundaries and deeds, could now be elevated to the arena of morality; one could cry witch against one's neighbor and feel perfectly justified in the bargain. Old scores could be settled on a plane of heavenly combat between Lucifer and the Lord; suspicions and the envy of the miserable toward the happy could and did burst out in the general revenge.

REVEREND PARRIS *is praying now, and, though we cannot hear his words, a sense of his confusion hangs about him. He mumbles, then seems about to weep; then he weeps, then prays again; but his daughter does not stir on the bed.*

*The door opens, and his Negro slave enters.* TITUBA *is in her forties.* PARRIS *brought her with him from Barbados, where he spent some years as a merchant before entering the ministry. She enters as one does who can no longer bear to be barred from the sight of her beloved, but she is also very frightened because her slave sense has warned her that, as always, trouble in this house eventually lands on her back.*

**Tituba,** *already taking a step backward:* My Betty be hearty soon?
**Parris:** Out of here!
**Tituba,** *backing to the door:* My Betty not goin' die . . .
**Parris,** *scrambling to his feet in a fury:* Out of my sight! *She is gone.* Out of my— *He is overcome with sobs. He clamps his teeth against them and closes the door and leans against it, exhausted.* Oh, my God! God help me! *Quaking with fear, mumbling to himself through his sobs, he goes to the bed and gently takes* BETTY's *hand.*

Betty. Child. Dear child. Will you wake, will you open up your eyes! Betty, little one . . .

*He is bending to kneel again when his niece,* ABIGAIL WILLIAMS, *seventeen, enters—a strikingly beautiful girl, an orphan, with an endless capacity for dissembling. Now she is all worry and apprehension and propriety.*

**Abigail:** Uncle? *He looks to her.* Susanna Walcott's here from Doctor Griggs.
**Parris:** Oh? Let her come, let her come.
**Abigail,** *leaning out the door to call to* SUSANNA, *who is down the hall a few steps:* Come in, Susanna.

SUSANNA WALCOTT, *a little younger than* ABIGAIL, *a nervous, hurried girl, enters.*

**Parris,** *eagerly:* What does the doctor say, child?
**Susanna,** *craning around* PARRIS *to get a look at* BETTY: He bid me come and tell you, reverend sir, that he cannot discover no medicine for it in his books.
**Parris:** Then he must search on.
**Susanna:** Aye, sir, he have been searchin' his books since he left you, sir. But he bid me tell you, that you might look to unnatural things for the cause of it.
**Parris,** *his eyes going wide:* No—no. There be no unnatural cause here. Tell him I have sent for Reverend Hale of Beverly, and Mr. Hale will surely confirm that. Let him look to medicine and put out all thought of unnatural causes here. There be none.
**Susanna:** Aye, sir. He bid me tell you. *She turns to go.*
**Abigail:** Speak nothin' of it in the village, Susanna.
**Parris:** Go directly home and speak nothing of unnatural causes.
**Susanna:** Aye, sir. I pray for her. *She goes out.*
**Abigail:** Uncle, the rumor of witchcraft is all about; I think you'd best go down and deny it yourself. The parlor's packed with people, sir. I'll sit with her.
**Parris,** *pressed, turns on her:* And what shall I say to them? That my daughter and my niece I discovered dancing like heathen in the forest?
**Abigail:** Uncle, we did dance; let you tell them I confessed it—and I'll be whipped if I must be. But they're speakin' of witchcraft. Betty's not witched.

**Parris:** Abigail, I cannot go before the congregation when I know you have not opened with me. What did you do with her in the forest?
**Abigail:** We did dance, uncle, and when you leaped out of the bush so suddenly, Betty was frightened and then she fainted. And there's the whole of it.
**Parris:** Child. Sit you down.
**Abigail,** *quavering, as she sits:* I would never hurt Betty. I love her dearly.
**Parris:** Now look you, child, your punishment will come in its time. But if you trafficked with spirits in the forest I must know it now, for surely my enemies will, and they will ruin me with it.
**Abigail:** But we never conjured spirits.
**Parris:** Then why can she not move herself since midnight? This child is desperate! ABIGAIL *lowers her eyes.* It must come out—my enemies will bring it out. Let me know what you done there. Abigail, do you understand that I have many enemies?
**Abigail:** I have heard of it, uncle.
**Parris:** There is a faction that is sworn to drive me from my pulpit. Do you understand that?
**Abigail:** I think so, sir.
**Parris:** Now then, in the midst of such disruption, my own household is discovered to be the very center of some obscene practice. Abominations are done in the forest—
**Abigail:** It were sport, uncle!
**Parris,** *pointing at* BETTY: You call this sport? *She lowers her eyes. He pleads:* Abigail, if you know something that may help the doctor, for God's sake tell it to me. *She is silent.* I saw Tituba waving her arms over the fire when I came on you. Why was she doing that? And I heard a screeching and gibberish coming from her mouth. She were swaying like a dumb beast over that fire!
**Abigail:** She always sings her Barbados songs, and we dance.
**Parris:** I cannot blink what I saw, Abigail, for my enemies will not blink it. I saw a dress lying on the grass.
**Abigail,** *innocently:* A dress?
**Parris**—*it is very hard to say:* Aye, a dress. And I thought I saw—someone naked running through the trees!
**Abigail,** *in terror:* No one was naked! You mistake yourself, uncle!

**Parris,** *with anger:* I saw it! *He moves from her. Then, resolved:* Now tell me true, Abigail. And I pray you feel the weight of truth upon you, for now my ministry's at stake, my ministry and perhaps your cousin's life. Whatever abomination you have done, give me all of it now, for I dare not be taken unaware when I go before them down there.

**Abigail:** There is nothin' more. I swear it, uncle.

**Parris,** *studies her, then nods, half convinced:* Abigail, I have fought here three long years to bend these stiff-necked people to me, and now, just now when some good respect is rising for me in the parish, you compromise my very character. I have given you a home, child, I have put clothes upon your back—now give me upright answer. Your name in the town—it is entirely white, is it not?

**Abigail,** *with an edge of resentment:* Why, I am sure it is, sir. There be no blush about my name.

**Parris,** *to the point:* Abigail, is there any other cause than you have told me, for your being discharged from Goody[2] Proctor's service? I have

---

2. **Goody:** formerly a title (short for *goodwife*) for a woman, especially a housewife or older woman.

---

heard it said, and I tell you as I heard it, that she comes so rarely to the church this year for she will not sit so close to something soiled. What signified that remark?

**Abigail:** She hates me, uncle, she must, for I would not be her slave. It's a bitter woman, a lying, cold, sniveling woman, and I will not work for such a woman!

**Parris:** She may be. And yet it has troubled me that you are now seven month out of their house, and in all this time no other family has ever called for your service.

**Abigail:** They want slaves, not such as I. Let them send to Barbados for that. I will not black my face for any of them! *With ill-concealed resentment at him:* Do you begrudge my bed, uncle?

**Parris:** No—no.

**Abigail,** *in a temper:* My name is good in the village! I will not have it said my name is soiled! Goody Proctor is a gossiping liar!

*Enter* MRS. ANN PUTNAM. *She is a twisted soul of forty-five, a death-ridden woman, haunted by dreams.*

**Parris,** *as soon as the door begins to open:* No—no, I cannot have anyone. *He sees her, and a certain deference springs into him, although his*

Samuel Parris "believed he was being persecuted wherever he went."

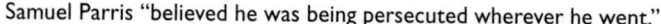

*worry remains.* Why, Goody Putnam, come in.

**Mrs. Putnam,** *full of breath, shiny-eyed:* It is a marvel. It is surely a stroke of hell upon you.

**Parris:** No, Goody Putnam, it is—

**Mrs. Putnam,** *glancing at* BETTY: How high did she fly, how high?

**Parris:** No, no, she never flew—

**Mrs. Putnam,** *very pleased with it:* Why, it's sure she did. Mr. Collins saw her goin' over Ingersoll's barn, and come down light as bird, he says!

**Parris:** Now, look you, Goody Putnam, she never— *Enter* THOMAS PUTNAM, *a well-to-do, hard-handed landowner, near fifty.* Oh, good morning, Mr. Putnam.

**Putnam:** It is a providence the thing is out now! It is a providence. *He goes directly to the bed.*

**Parris:** What's out, sir, what's—?

MRS. PUTNAM *goes to the bed.*

**Putnam,** *looking down at* BETTY: Why, *her* eyes is closed! Look you, Ann.

**Mrs. Putnam:** Why, that's strange. *To* PARRIS: Ours is open.

**Parris,** *shocked:* Your Ruth is sick?

**Mrs. Putnam,** *with vicious certainty:* I'd not call it sick; the Devil's touch is heavier than sick. It's death, y'know, it's death drivin' into them, forked and hoofed.

**Parris:** Oh, pray not! Why, how does Ruth ail?

**Mrs. Putnam:** She ails as she must—she never waked this morning, but her eyes open and she walks, and hears naught, sees naught, and cannot eat. Her soul is taken, surely.

PARRIS *is struck.*

**Putnam,** *as though for further details:* They say you've sent for Reverend Hale of Beverly?

**Parris,** *with dwindling conviction now:* A precaution only. He has much experience in all demonic arts, and I—

**Mrs. Putnam:** He has indeed; and found a witch in Beverly last year, and let you remember that.

**Parris:** Now, Goody Ann, they only thought that were a witch, and I am certain there be no element of witchcraft here.

**Putnam:** No witchcraft! Now look you, Mr. Parris—

**Parris:** Thomas, Thomas, I pray you, leap not to witchcraft. I know that you—you least of all, Thomas, would ever wish so disastrous a charge laid upon me. We cannot leap to witchcraft. They will howl me out of Salem for such corruption in my house.

A word about Thomas Putnam. He was a man with many grievances, at least one of which appears justified. Some time before, his wife's brother-in-law, James Bayley, had been turned down as minister of Salem. Bayley had all the qualifications, and a two-thirds vote into the bargain, but a faction stopped his acceptance, for reasons that are not clear.

Thomas Putnam was the eldest son of the richest man in the village. He had fought the Indians at Narragansett, and was deeply interested in parish affairs. He undoubtedly felt it poor payment that the village should so blatantly disregard his candidate for one of its more important offices, especially since he regarded himself as the intellectual superior of most of the people around him.

His vindictive nature was demonstrated long before the witchcraft began. A former Salem minister, George Burroughs, had had to borrow money to pay for his wife's funeral, and, since the parish was remiss in his salary, he was soon bankrupt. Thomas and his brother John had Burroughs jailed for debts the man did not owe. The incident is important only in that Burroughs succeeded in becoming minister where Bayley, Thomas Putnam's brother-in-law, had been rejected; the motif of resentment is clear here. Thomas Putnam felt that his own name and the honor of his family had been smirched by the village, and he meant to right matters however he could.

Another reason to believe him a deeply embittered man was his attempt to break his father's will, which left a disproportionate amount to a stepbrother. As with every other public cause in which he tried to force his way, he failed in this.

So it is not surprising to find that so many accusations against people are in the handwriting of Thomas Putnam, or that his name is so often found as a witness corroborating the supernatural testimony, or that his daughter led the crying-out at the most opportune junctures of the trials, especially when—But we'll speak of that when we come to it.

**Putnam**—*at the moment he is intent upon getting* PARRIS, *for whom he has only contempt, to move toward the abyss:* Mr. Parris, I have taken your part in all contention here, and I would continue; but I cannot if you hold back in this. There are hurtful, vengeful spirits layin' hands on these children.

**Parris:** But, Thomas, you cannot—

**Putnam:** Ann! Tell Mr. Parris what you have done.

**Mrs. Putnam:** Reverend Parris, I have laid seven babies unbaptized in the earth. Believe me, sir, you never saw more hearty babies born. And yet, each would wither in my arms the very night of their birth. I have spoke nothin', but my heart has clamored intimations. And now, this year, my Ruth, my only— I see her turning strange. A secret child she has become this year, and shrivels like a sucking mouth were pullin' on her life too. And so I thought to send her to your Tituba—

**Parris:** To Tituba! What may Tituba—?

**Mrs. Putnam:** Tituba knows how to speak to the dead, Mr. Parris.

**Parris:** Goody Ann, it is a formidable sin to conjure up the dead!

**Mrs. Putnam:** I take it on my soul, but who else may surely tell us what person murdered my babies?

**Parris,** *horrified:* Woman!

**Mrs. Putnam:** They were murdered, Mr. Parris! And mark this proof! Mark it! Last night my Ruth were ever so close to their little spirits; I know it, sir. For how else is she struck dumb now except some power of darkness would stop her mouth? It is a marvelous sign, Mr. Parris!

**Putnam:** Don't you understand it, sir? There is a murdering witch among us, bound to keep herself in the dark. PARRIS *turns to* BETTY, *a frantic terror rising in him.* Let your enemies make of it what they will, you cannot blink it more.

**Parris,** *to* ABIGAIL: Then you were conjuring spirits last night.

**Abigail,** *whispering:* Not I, sir—Tituba and Ruth.

**Parris,** *turns now, with new fear, and goes to* BETTY, *looks down at her, and then, gazing off:* Oh, Abigail, what proper payment for my charity! Now I am undone.

**Putnam:** You are not undone! Let you take hold here. Wait for no one to charge you—declare it yourself. You have discovered witchcraft—

**Parris:** In my house? In my house, Thomas? They will topple me with this! They will make of it a—

*Enter* MERCY LEWIS, *the* PUTNAMS' *servant, a fat, sly, merciless girl of eighteen.*

**Mercy:** Your pardons. I only thought to see how Betty is.

**Putnam:** Why aren't you home? Who's with Ruth?

**Mercy:** Her grandma come. She's improved a little, I think—she give a powerful sneeze before.

**Mrs. Putnam:** Ah, there's a sign of life!

**Mercy:** I'd fear no more, Goody Putnam. It were a grand sneeze; another like it will shake her wits together, I'm sure. *She goes to the bed to look.*

**Parris:** Will you leave me now, Thomas? I would pray a while alone.

**Abigail:** Uncle, you've prayed since midnight. Why do you not go down and—

**Parris:** No—no. *To* PUTNAM: I have no answer for that crowd. I'll wait till Mr. Hale arrives. *To get* MRS. PUTNAM *to leave:* If you will, Goody Ann . . .

**Putnam:** Now look you, sir. Let you strike out against the Devil, and the village will bless you for it! Come down, speak to them—pray with them. They're thirsting for your word, Mister! Surely you'll pray with them.

**Parris,** *swayed:* I'll lead them in a psalm, but let you say nothing of witchcraft yet. I will not discuss it. The cause is yet unknown. I have had enough contention since I came; I want no more.

**Mrs. Putnam:** Mercy, you go home to Ruth, d'y'hear?

**Mercy:** Aye, mum.

MRS. PUTNAM *goes out.*

**Parris,** *to* ABIGAIL: If she starts for the window, cry for me at once.

**Abigail:** I will, uncle.

**Parris,** *to* PUTNAM: There is a terrible power in her arms today. *He goes out with* PUTNAM.

**Abigail,** *with hushed trepidation:* How is Ruth sick?

**Mercy:** It's weirdish, I know not—she seems to walk like a dead one since last night.

**Abigail,** *turns at once and goes to* BETTY, *and now, with fear in her voice:* Betty? BETTY *doesn't move. She shakes her.* Now stop this! Betty! Sit up now!

> ## "Let either of you breathe a word about the other things, and I will bring a pointy reckoning that will shudder you."

BETTY *doesn't stir.* MERCY *comes over.*

**Mercy:** Have you tried beatin' her? I gave Ruth a good one and it waked her for a minute. Here, let me have her.

**Abigail,** *holding* MERCY *back:* No, he'll be comin' up. Listen, now; if they be questioning us, tell them we danced—I told him as much already.

**Mercy:** Aye. And what more?

**Abigail:** He knows Tituba conjured Ruth's sisters to come out of the grave.

**Mercy:** And what more?

**Abigail:** He saw you naked.

**Mercy,** *clapping her hands together with a frightened laugh:* Oh, Jesus!

*Enter* MARY WARREN, *breathless. She is seventeen, a subservient, naïve, lonely girl.*

**Mary Warren:** What'll we do? The village is out! I just come from the farm; the whole country's talkin' witchcraft! They'll be callin' us witches, Abby!

**Mercy,** *pointing and looking at* MARY WARREN: She means to tell, I know it.

**Mary Warren:** Abby, we've got to tell. Witchery's a hangin' error, a hangin' like they done in Boston two year ago! We must tell the truth, Abby! You'll only be whipped for dancin', and the other things!

**Abigail:** Oh, *we'll* be whipped!

**Mary Warren:** I never done none of it, Abby. I only looked!

**Mercy,** *moving menacingly toward* MARY: Oh, you're a great one for lookin', aren't you, Mary Warren? What a grand peeping courage you have!

BETTY, *on the bed, whimpers.* ABIGAIL *turns to her at once.*

**Abigail:** Betty? *She goes to* BETTY. Now, Betty, dear, wake up now. It's Abigail. *She sits* BETTY *up and furiously shakes her.* I'll beat you, Betty! BETTY *whimpers.* My, you seem improving. I talked to your papa and I told him everything. So there's nothing to—

**Betty,** *darts off the bed, frightened of* ABIGAIL, *and flattens herself against the wall:* I want my mama!

**Abigail,** *with alarm, as she cautiously approaches* BETTY: What ails you, Betty? Your mama's dead and buried.

**Betty:** I'll fly to Mama. Let me fly! *She raises her arms as though to fly, and streaks for the window, gets one leg out.*

**Abigail,** *pulling her away from the window:* I told him everything; he knows now, he knows everything we—

**Betty:** You drank blood, Abby! You didn't tell him that!

**Abigail:** Betty, you never say that again! You will never—

**Betty:** You did, you did! You drank a charm to kill John Proctor's wife! You drank a charm to kill Goody Proctor!

**Abigail,** *smashes her across the face:* Shut it! Now shut it!

**Betty,** *collapsing on the bed:* Mama, Mama! *She dissolves into sobs.*

**Abigail:** Now look you. All of you. We danced. And Tituba conjured Ruth Putnam's dead sisters. And that is all. And mark this. Let either of you breathe a word, or the edge of a word, about the other things, and I will come to you in the black of some terrible night and I will bring a pointy reckoning that will shudder you. And you know I can do it; I saw Indians smash my dear parents' heads on the pillow next to mine, and I have seen some reddish work done at night, and I can make you wish you had never seen the sun go down! *She goes to* BETTY *and roughly sits her up.* Now, you— sit up and stop this!

*But* BETTY *collapses in her hands and lies inert on the bed.*

**Mary Warren,** *with hysterical fright:* What's got her? ABIGAIL *stares in fright at* BETTY. Abby, she's going to die! It's a sin to conjure, and we—

**Abigail,** *starting for* MARY: I say shut it, Mary Warren!

*Enter* JOHN PROCTOR. *On seeing him,* MARY WARREN *leaps in fright.*

Proctor was a farmer in his middle thirties. He need not have been a partisan of any faction in the town, but there is evidence to suggest that he had a sharp and biting way with hypocrites. He was the kind of man—powerful of body, even-tempered, and not easily led—who cannot refuse support to partisans without drawing their deepest resentment. In Proctor's presence a fool felt his foolishness instantly—and a Proctor is always marked for calumny therefore.

But as we shall see, the steady manner he displays does not spring from an untroubled soul. He is a sinner, a sinner not only against the moral fashion of the time, but against his own vision of decent conduct. These people had no ritual for the washing away of sins. It is another trait we inherited from them, and it has helped to discipline us as well as to breed hypocrisy among us. Proctor, respected and even feared in Salem, has come to regard himself as a kind of fraud. But no hint of this has yet appeared on the surface, and as he enters from the crowded parlor below it is a man in his prime we see, with a quiet confidence and an unexpressed, hidden force. Mary Warren, his servant, can barely speak for embarrassment and fear.

**Mary Warren:** Oh! I'm just going home, Mr. Proctor.

**Proctor:** Be you foolish, Mary Warren? Be you deaf? I forbid you leave the house, did I not? Why shall I pay you? I am looking for you more often than my cows!

**Mary Warren:** I only come to see the great doings in the world.

**Proctor:** I'll show you a great doin' on your arse one of these days. Now get you home; my wife is waitin' with your work! *Trying to retain a shred of dignity, she goes slowly out.*

**Mercy Lewis,** *both afraid of him and strangely titillated:* I'd best be off. I have my Ruth to watch. Good morning, Mr. Proctor.

MERCY *sidles out. Since* PROCTOR'*s entrance,* ABIGAIL *has stood as though on tiptoe, absorbing his presence, wide-eyed. He glances at her, then goes to* BETTY *on the bed.*

**Abigail:** Gah! I'd almost forgot how strong you are, John Proctor!

**Proctor,** *looking at* ABIGAIL *now, the faintest suggestion of a knowing smile on his face:* What's this mischief here?

**Abigail,** *with a nervous laugh:* Oh, she's only gone silly somehow.

**Proctor:** The road past my house is a pilgrimage to Salem all morning. The town's mumbling witchcraft.

**Abigail:** Oh, posh! *Winningly she comes a little closer, with a confidential, wicked air.* We were dancin' in the woods last night, and my uncle leaped in on us. She took fright, is all.

**Proctor,** *his smile widening:* Ah, you're wicked yet, aren't y'! *A trill of expectant laughter escapes her, and she dares come closer, feverishly looking into his eyes.* You'll be clapped in the stocks before you're twenty.

*He takes a step to go, and she springs into his path.*

**Abigail:** Give me a word, John. A soft word. *Her concentrated desire destroys his smile.*

**Proctor:** No, no, Abby. That's done with.

**Abigail,** *tauntingly:* You come five mile to see a silly girl fly? I know you better.

**Proctor,** *setting her firmly out of his path:* I come to see what mischief your uncle's brewin' now. *With final emphasis:* Put it out of mind, Abby.

**Abigail,** *grasping his hand before he can release her:* John—I am waitin' for you every night.

**Proctor:** Abby, I never give you hope to wait for me.

**Abigail,** *now beginning to anger—she can't believe it:* I have something better than hope, I think!

**Proctor:** Abby, you'll put it out of mind. I'll not be comin' for you more.

**Abigail:** You're surely sportin' with me.

**Proctor:** You know me better.

**Abigail:** I know how you clutched my back behind your house and sweated like a stallion when ever I come near! Or did I dream that? It's she put me out, you cannot pretend it were you. I saw your face when she put me out, and you loved me then and you do now!

**Proctor:** Abby, that's a wild thing to say—

**Abigail:** A wild thing may say wild things. But not so wild, I think. I have seen you since she put me out; I have seen you nights.

**Proctor:** I have hardly stepped off my farm this sevenmonth.

**Abigail:** I have a sense for heat, John, and yours has drawn me to my window, and I have seen you looking up, burning in your loneliness. Do you tell me you've never looked up at my window?

**Proctor:** I may have looked up.

**Abigail,** *now softening:* And you must. You are no wintry man. I know you, John. I *know* you. *She is weeping.* I cannot sleep for dreamin'; I cannot dream but I wake and walk about the house as though I'd find you comin' through some door. *She clutches him desperately.*

**Proctor,** *gently pressing her from him, with great sympathy but firmly:* Child—

**Abigail,** *with a flash of anger:* How do you call me child!

**Proctor:** Abby, I may think of you softly from time to time. But I will cut off my hand before I'll ever reach for you again. Wipe it out of mind. We never touched, Abby.

**Abigail:** Aye, but we did.

**Proctor:** Aye, but we did not.

**Abigail,** *with a bitter anger:* Oh, I marvel how such a strong man may let such a sickly wife be—

**Proctor,** *angered—at himself as well:* You'll speak nothin' of Elizabeth!

**Abigail:** She is blackening my name in the village! She is telling lies about me! She is a cold, sniveling woman, and you bend to her! Let her turn you like a—

**Proctor,** *shaking her:* Do you look for whippin'?

*A psalm is heard being sung below.*

**Abigail,** *in tears:* I look for John Proctor that took me from my sleep and put knowledge in my heart! I never knew what pretense Salem was, I never knew the lying lessons I was taught by all these Christian women and their covenanted men! And now you bid me tear the light out of my eyes? I will not, I cannot! You loved me, John Proctor,

"We never touched, Abby."

and whatever sin it is, you love me yet! *He turns abruptly to go out. She rushes to him.* John, pity me, pity me!

*The words "going up to Jesus" are heard in the psalm, and* BETTY *claps her ears suddenly and whines loudly.*

**Abigail:** Betty? *She hurries to* BETTY, *who is now sitting up and screaming.* PROCTOR *goes to* BETTY *as* ABIGAIL *is trying to pull her hands down, calling "Betty!"*

**Proctor,** *growing unnerved:* What's she doing? Girl, what ails you? Stop that wailing!

*The singing has stopped in the midst of this, and now* PARRIS *rushes in.*

**Parris:** What happened? What are you doing to her? Betty! *He rushes to the bed, crying, "Betty, Betty!"* MRS. PUTNAM *enters, feverish with curiosity, and with her* THOMAS PUTNAM *and* MERCY LEWIS. PARRIS, *at the bed, keeps lightly slapping* BETTY's *face, while she moans and tries to get up.*

**Abigail:** She heard you singin' and suddenly she's up and screamin'.

**Mrs. Putnam:** The psalm! The psalm! She cannot bear to hear the Lord's name!

**Parris:** No, God forbid. Mercy, run to the doctor! Tell him what's happened here! MERCY LEWIS *rushes out.*

**Mrs. Putnam:** Mark it for a sign, mark it!

REBECCA NURSE, *seventy-two, enters. She is white-haired, leaning upon her walking-stick.*

**Putnam,** *pointing at the whimpering* BETTY: That is a notorious sign of witchcraft afoot, Goody Nurse, a prodigious sign!

**Mrs. Putnam:** My mother told me that! When they cannot bear to hear the name of—

**Parris,** *trembling:* Rebecca, Rebecca, go to her, we're lost. She suddenly cannot bear to hear the Lord's—

GILES COREY, *eighty-three, enters. He is knotted with muscle, canny, inquisitive, and still powerful.*

**Rebecca:** There is hard sickness here, Giles Corey, so please to keep the quiet.

**Giles:** I've not said a word. No one here can testify I've said a word. Is she going to fly again? I hear she flies.

**Putnam:** Man, be quiet now!

*Everything is quiet.* REBECCA *walks across the room to the bed. Gentleness exudes from her.* BETTY *is quietly whimpering, eyes shut.* REBECCA *simply stands over the child, who gradually quiets.*

And while they are so absorbed, we may put a word in for Rebecca. Rebecca was the wife of Francis Nurse, who, from all accounts, was one of those men for whom both sides of the argument had to have respect. He was called upon to arbitrate disputes as though he were an unofficial judge, and Rebecca also enjoyed the high opinion most people had for him. By the time of the delusion, they had three hundred acres, and their children were settled in separate homesteads within the same estate. However, Francis had originally rented the land, and one theory has it that, as he gradually paid for it and raised his social status, there were those who resented his rise.

Another suggestion to explain the systematic campaign against Rebecca, and inferentially against Francis, is the land war he fought with his neighbors, one of whom was a Putnam. This squabble grew to the proportions of a battle in the woods between partisans of both sides, and it is said to have lasted for two days. As for Rebecca herself, the general opinion of her character was so high that to explain how anyone dared cry her out for a witch—and more, how adults could bring themselves to lay hands on her—we must look to the fields and boundaries of that time.

As we have seen, Thomas Putnam's man for the Salem ministry was Bayley. The Nurse clan had been in the faction that prevented Bayley's taking office. In addition, certain families allied to the Nurses by blood or friendship, and whose farms were contiguous with the Nurse farm or close to it, combined to break away from the Salem town authority and set up Topsfield, a new and independent entity whose existence was resented by old Salemites.

That the guiding hand behind the outcry was Putnam's is indicated by the fact that, as soon as it began, this Topsfield-Nurse faction absented themselves from church in protest and disbelief. It was Edward and Jonathan Putnam who signed the first complaint against Rebecca; and Thomas Putnam's little daughter was the one who fell into a fit at the hearing and pointed to Rebecca as her attacker. To top it all, Mrs. Putnam—who is now staring at the bewitched child on the bed—soon accused Rebecca's spirit of "tempting her to iniquity," a charge that had more truth in it than Mrs. Putnam could know.

**Mrs. Putnam,** *astonished:* What have you done?

REBECCA, *in thought, now leaves the bedside and sits.*

**Parris,** *wondrous and relieved:* What do you make of it, Rebecca?

**Putnam,** *eagerly:* Goody Nurse, will you go to my Ruth and see if you can wake her?

**Rebecca,** *sitting:* I think she'll wake in time. Pray calm yourselves. I have eleven children, and I am twenty-six times a grandma, and I have seen them all through their silly seasons, and when it come on them they will run the Devil bowlegged keeping up with their mischief. I think she'll wake when she tires of it. A child's spirit is like a child, you can never catch it by running after it; you must stand still, and, for love, it will soon itself come back.

**Proctor:** Aye, that's the truth of it, Rebecca.

**Mrs. Putnam:** This is no silly season, Rebecca. My Ruth is bewildered, Rebecca; she cannot eat.

**Rebecca:** Perhaps she is not hungered yet. *To* PARRIS: I hope you are not decided to go in search of loose spirits, Mr. Parris. I've heard promise of that outside.

**Parris:** A wide opinion's running in the parish that the Devil may be among us, and I would satisfy them that they are wrong.

**Proctor:** Then let you come out and call them wrong. Did you consult the wardens before you called this minister to look for devils?

**Parris:** He is not coming to look for devils!

**Proctor:** Then what's he coming for?

**Putnam:** There be children dyin' in the village, Mister!

**Proctor:** I seen none dyin'. This society will not be a bag to swing around your head, Mr. Putnam. *To* PARRIS: Did you call a meeting before you—?

**Putnam:** I am sick of meetings; cannot the man turn his head without he have a meeting?

**Proctor:** He may turn his head, but not to Hell!

**Rebecca:** Pray, John, be calm. *Pause. He defers to her.* Mr. Parris, I think you'd best send Reverend Hale back as soon as he come. This will set us all to arguin' again in the society, and we thought to have peace this year. I think we ought rely on the doctor now, and good prayer.

**Mrs. Putnam:** Rebecca, the doctor's baffled!

**Rebecca:** If so he is, then let us go to God for the cause of it. There is prodigious danger in the seeking of loose spirits. I fear it, I fear it. Let us rather blame ourselves and—

**Putnam:** How may we blame ourselves? I am one of nine sons; the Putnam seed have peopled this province. And yet I have but one child left of eight—and now she shrivels!

**Rebecca:** I cannot fathom that.

**Mrs. Putnam,** *with a growing edge of sarcasm:* But I must! You think it God's work you should never lose a child, nor grandchild either, and I bury all but one? There are wheels within wheels in this village, and fires within fires!

**Putnam,** *to* PARRIS: When Reverend Hale comes, you will proceed to look for signs of witchcraft here.

**Proctor,** *to* PUTNAM: You cannot command Mr. Parris. We vote by name in this society, not by acreage.

**Putnam:** I never heard you worried so on this society, Mr. Proctor. I do not think I saw you at Sabbath meeting since snow flew.

**Proctor:** I have trouble enough without I come five mile to hear him preach only hellfire and bloody damnation. Take it to heart, Mr. Parris.

There are many others who stay away from church these days because you hardly ever mention God any more.

**Parris,** *now aroused:* Why, that's a drastic charge!

**Rebecca:** It's somewhat true; there are many that quail to bring their children—

**Parris:** I do not preach for children, Rebecca. It is not the children who are unmindful of their obligations toward this ministry.

**Rebecca:** Are there really those unmindful?

**Parris:** I should say the better half of Salem village—

**Putnam:** And more than that!

**Parris:** Where is my wood? My contract provides I be supplied with all my firewood. I am waiting since November for a stick, and even in November I had to show my frostbitten hands like some London beggar!

**Giles:** You are allowed six pound a year to buy your wood, Mr. Parris.

**Parris:** I regard that six pound as part of my salary. I am paid little enough without I spend six pound on firewood.

**Proctor:** Sixty, plus six for firewood—

**Parris:** The salary is sixty-six pound, Mr. Proctor! I am not some preaching farmer with a book under my arm; I am a graduate of Harvard College.

**Giles:** Aye, and well instructed in arithmetic!

**Parris:** Mr. Corey, you will look far for a man of my kind at sixty pound a year! I am not used to this poverty; I left a thrifty business in the Barbados to serve the Lord. I do not fathom it, why am I persecuted here? I cannot offer one proposition but there be a howling riot of argument. I have often wondered if the Devil be in it somewhere; I cannot understand you people otherwise.

**Proctor:** Mr. Parris, you are the first minister ever did demand the deed to this house—

**Parris:** Man! Don't a minister deserve a house to live in?

**Proctor:** To live in, yes. But to ask ownership is like you shall own the meeting house itself; the last meeting I were at you spoke so long on deeds and mortgages I thought it were an auction.

**Parris:** I want a mark of confidence, is all! I am your third preacher in seven years. I do not wish to be put out like the cat whenever some majority feels the whim. You people seem not to comprehend that a minister is the Lord's man in the parish; a minister is not to be so lightly crossed and contradicted—

**Putnam:** Aye!

**Parris:** There is either obedience or the church will burn like Hell is burning!

**Proctor:** Can you speak one minute without we land in Hell again? I am sick of Hell!

**Parris:** It is not for you to say what is good for you to hear!

**Proctor:** I may speak my heart, I think!

**Parris,** *in a fury:* What, are we Quakers?[3] We are not Quakers here yet, Mr. Proctor. And you may tell that to your followers!

**Proctor:** My followers!

**Parris**—*now he's out with it:* There is a party in this church. I am not blind; there is a faction and a party.

**Proctor:** Against you?

**Putnam:** Against him and all authority!

**Proctor:** Why, then I must find it and join it.

*There is shock among the others.*

**Rebecca:** He does not mean that.

**Putnam:** He confessed it now!

**Proctor:** I mean it solemnly, Rebecca; I like not the smell of this "authority."

**Rebecca:** No, you cannot break charity with your minister. You are another kind, John. Clasp his hand, make your peace.

**Proctor:** I have a crop to sow and lumber to drag home. *He goes angrily to the door and turns to* COREY *with a smile.* What say you, Giles, let's find the party. He says there's a party.

**Giles:** I've changed my opinion of this man, John. Mr. Parris, I beg your pardon. I never thought you had so much iron in you.

**Parris,** *surprised:* Why, thank you, Giles!

**Giles:** It suggests to the mind what the trouble be among us all these years. *To all:* Think on it. Wherefore is everybody suing everybody else? Think on it now, it's a deep thing, and dark as a pit. I have been six time in court this year—

**Proctor,** *familiarly, with warmth, although he knows he is approaching the edge of* GILES' *tolerance with this:* Is it the Devil's fault that a man cannot say you good morning without you clap him for defamation? You're old, Giles, and you're not hearin' so well as you did.

**Giles**—*he cannot be crossed:* John Proctor, I have only last month collected four pound damages for you publicly sayin' I burned the roof off your house, and I—

**Proctor,** *laughing:* I never said no such thing, but I've paid you for it, so I hope I can call you deaf without charge. Now come along, Giles, and help me drag my lumber home.

**Putnam:** A moment, Mr. Proctor. What lumber is that you're draggin', if I may ask you?

**Proctor:** My lumber. From out my forest by the riverside.

**Putnam:** Why, we are surely gone wild this year. What anarchy is this? That tract is in my bounds, it's in my bounds, Mr. Proctor.

**Proctor:** In your bounds! *Indicating* REBECCA: I bought that tract from Goody Nurse's husband five months ago.

**Putnam:** He had no right to sell it. It stands clear in my grandfather's will that all the land between the river and—

**Proctor:** Your grandfather had a habit of willing land that never belonged to him, if I may say it plain.

**Giles:** That's God's truth; he nearly willed away my north pasture but he knew I'd break his fingers before he'd set his name to it. Let's get your lumber home, John. I feel a sudden will to work coming on.

**Putnam:** You load one oak of mine and you'll fight to drag it home!

**Giles:** Aye, and we'll win too, Putnam—this fool and I. Come on! *He turns to* PROCTOR *and starts out.*

**Putnam:** I'll have my men on you, Corey! I'll clap a writ on you!

*Enter* REVEREND JOHN HALE *of Beverly.*

Mr. Hale is nearing forty, a tight-skinned, eager-eyed intellectual. This is a beloved errand for him; on being called here to ascertain witchcraft he felt the pride of the specialist whose unique knowledge has at last been publicly called for. Like almost all men of learning, he spent a good deal of his time pondering the invisible world, especially

---

**3. Quakers:** Most Quakers believe that no rite or formally trained priest is needed to commune with God; instead, divine truth can be found in one's "inner light."

since he had himself encountered a witch in his parish not long before. That woman, however, turned into a mere pest under his searching scrutiny, and the child she had allegedly been afflicting recovered her normal behavior after Hale had given her his kindness and a few days of rest in his own house. However, that experience never raised a doubt in his mind as to the reality of the underworld or the existence of Lucifer's many-faced lieutenants. And his belief is not to his discredit. Better minds than Hale's were—and still are—convinced that there is a society of spirits beyond our ken. One cannot help noting that one of his lines has never yet raised a laugh in any audience that has seen this play; it is his assurance that "We cannot look to superstition in this. The Devil is precise." Evidently we are not quite certain even now whether diabolism is holy and not to be scoffed at. And it is no accident that we should be so bemused.

Like Reverend Hale and the others on this stage, we conceive the Devil as a necessary part of a respectable view of cosmology. Ours is a divided empire in which certain ideas and emotions and actions are of God, and their opposites are of Lucifer. It is as impossible for most men to conceive of a morality without sin as of an earth without "sky." Since 1692 a great but superficial change has wiped out God's beard and the Devil's horns, but the world is still gripped between two diametrically opposed absolutes. The concept of unity, in which positive and negative are attributes of the same force, in which good and evil are relative, ever-changing, and always joined to the same phenomenon—such a concept is still reserved to the physical sciences and to the few who have grasped the history of ideas. When it is recalled that until the Christian era the underworld was never regarded as a hostile area, that all gods were useful and essentially friendly to man despite occasional lapses; when we see the steady and methodical inculcation into humanity of the idea of man's worthlessness—until redeemed—the necessity of the Devil may become evident as a weapon, a weapon designed and used time and time again in every age to whip men into a surrender to a particular church or church-state.

Our difficulty in believing the—for want of a better word—political inspiration of the Devil is due in great part to the fact that he is called up and damned not only by our social antagonists but by our own side, whatever it may be. The Catholic Church, through its Inquisition,[4] is famous for cultivating Lucifer as the arch-fiend, but the Church's enemies relied no less upon the Old Boy to keep the human mind enthralled. Luther[5] was himself accused of alliance with Hell, and he in turn accused his enemies. To complicate matters further, he believed that he had had contact with the Devil, and had argued theology with him. I am not surprised at this, for at my own university a professor of history—a Lutheran, by the way—used to assemble his graduate students, draw the shades, and commune in the classroom with Erasmus.[6] He was never, to my knowledge, officially scoffed at for this, the reason being that the university officials, like most of us, are the children of a history which still sucks at the Devil's teats. At this writing, only England has held back before the temptations of contemporary diabolism. In the countries of the Communist ideology, all resistance of any import is linked to the totally malign capitalist succubi,[7] and in America any man who is not reactionary in his views is open to the charge of alliance with the Red hell. Political opposition, thereby, is given an inhumane overlay which then justifies the abrogation of all normally applied customs of civilized intercourse. A political policy is equated with moral right, and opposition to it with diabolical malevolence. Once such an equation is effectively made, society becomes a congerie of plots and counterplots, and the main role of government changes from that of the arbiter to that of the scourge of God.

The results of this process are no different now from what they ever were, except sometimes in the degree of cruelty inflicted, and not always

**4. Inquisition:** suppression and punishment, begun in the thirteenth century by the Roman Catholic Church, of people thought to hold heretical beliefs.
**5. Luther:** Martin Luther (1483–1546), a German theologian and leader of the Protestant Reformation.
**6. Erasmus** (i·raz′məs) (c. 1466–1536): Dutch scholar and humanist, who came into conflict with Luther over predestination. (Erasmus believed in free will.)
**7. succubi** (suk′yōō·bī): plural of *succubus,* a female evil spirit or demon thought in medieval times to have sexual intercourse with sleeping men.

even in that department. Normally the actions and deeds of a man were all that society felt comfortable in judging. The secret intent of an action was left to the ministers, priests, and rabbis to deal with. When diabolism rises, however, actions are the least important manifests of the true nature of a man. The Devil, as Reverend Hale said, is a wily one, and, until an hour before he fell, even God thought him beautiful in Heaven.

The analogy, however, seems to falter when one considers that, while there were no witches then, there are Communists and capitalists now, and in each camp there is certain proof that spies of each side are at work undermining the other. But this is a snobbish objection and not at all warranted by the facts. I have no doubt that people *were* communing with, and even worshiping, the Devil in Salem, and if the whole truth could be known in this case, as it is in others, we should discover a regular and conventionalized propitiation of the dark spirit. One certain evidence of this is the confession of Tituba, the slave of Reverend Parris, and another is the behavior of the children who were known to have indulged in sorceries with her.

There are accounts of similar *klatches* in Europe, where the daughters of the towns would assemble at night and, sometimes with fetishes, sometimes with a selected young man, give themselves to love, with some bastardly results. The Church, sharp-eyed as it must be when gods long dead are brought to life, condemned these orgies as witchcraft and interpreted them rightly, as a resurgence of the Dionysiac[8] forces it had crushed long before. Sex, sin, and the Devil were early linked, and so they continued to be in Salem, and are today. From all accounts there are no more puritanical mores in the world than those enforced by the Communists in Russia, where women's fashions, for instance, are as prudent and all-covering as any American Baptist would desire. The divorce laws lay a tremendous responsibility on the father for the care of his children. Even the laxity of divorce regulations in the early years of the revolution was undoubtedly a revulsion from the nineteenth-century Victorian immobility of

marriage and the consequent hypocrisy that developed from it. If for no other reasons, a state so powerful, so jealous of the uniformity of its citizens, cannot long tolerate the atomization of the family. And yet, in American eyes at least, there remains the conviction that the Russian attitude toward women is lascivious. It is the Devil working again, just as he is working within the Slav who is shocked at the very idea of a woman's disrobing herself in a burlesque show. Our opposites are always robed in sexual sin, and it is from this unconscious conviction that demonology gains both its attractive sensuality and its capacity to infuriate and frighten.

Coming into Salem now, Reverend Hale conceives of himself much as a young doctor on his first call. His painfully acquired armory of symptoms, catchwords, and diagnostic procedures is now to be put to use at last. The road from Beverly is unusually busy this morning, and he has passed a hundred rumors that make him smile at the ignorance of the yeomanry in this most precise science. He feels himself allied with the best minds of Europe—kings, philosophers, scientists, and ecclesiasts of all churches. His goal is light, goodness and its preservation, and he knows the exaltation of the blessed whose intelligence, sharpened by minute examinations of enormous tracts, is finally called upon to face what may be a bloody fight with the Fiend himself.

*He appears loaded down with half a dozen heavy books.*

**Hale:** Pray you, someone take these!
**Parris,** *delighted:* Mr. Hale! Oh! it's good to see you again! *Taking some books:* My, they're heavy!
**Hale,** *setting down his books:* They must be; they are weighted with authority.
**Parris,** *a little scared:* Well, you do come prepared!
**Hale:** We shall need hard study if it comes to tracking down the Old Boy. *Noticing* REBECCA: You cannot be Rebecca Nurse?
**Rebecca:** I am, sir. Do you know me?
**Hale:** It's strange how I knew you, but I suppose you look as such a good soul should. We have all heard of your great charities in Beverly.
**Parris:** Do you know this gentleman? Mr. Thomas Putnam. And his good wife Ann.

---

8. **Dionysiac** (dī′ə·nis′ē·ak′): like Dionysus (dī′ə·nī′səs), the ancient Greek god of wine and revelry.

**Hale:** Putnam! I had not expected such distinguished company, sir.

**Putnam,** *pleased:* It does not seem to help us today, Mr. Hale. We look to you to come to our house and save our child.

**Hale:** Your child ails too?

**Mrs. Putnam:** Her soul, her soul seems flown away. She sleeps and yet she walks . . .

**Putnam:** She cannot eat.

**Hale:** Cannot eat! *Thinks on it. Then, to* PROCTOR *and* GILES COREY: Do you men have afflicted children?

**Parris:** No, no, these are farmers. John Proctor—

**Giles Corey:** He don't believe in witches.

**Proctor,** *to* HALE: I never spoke on witches one way or the other. Will you come, Giles?

**Giles:** No—no, John, I think not. I have some few queer questions of my own to ask this fellow.

**Proctor:** I've heard you to be a sensible man, Mr. Hale. I hope you'll leave some of it in Salem.

PROCTOR *goes.* HALE *stands embarrassed for an instant.*

**Parris,** *quickly:* Will you look at my daughter, sir? *Leads* HALE *to the bed.* She has tried to leap out the window; we discovered her this morning on the highroad, waving her arms as though she'd fly.

**Hale,** *narrowing his eyes:* Tries to fly.

**Putnam:** She cannot bear to hear the Lord's name, Mr. Hale; that's a sure sign of witchcraft afloat.

**Hale,** *holding up his hands:* No, no. Now let me instruct you. We cannot look to superstition in this. The Devil is precise; the marks of his presence are definite as stone, and I must tell you all that I shall not proceed unless you are prepared to believe me if I should find no bruise of Hell upon her.

**Parris:** It is agreed, sir—it is agreed—we will abide by your judgment.

**Hale:** Good then. *He goes to the bed, looks down at* BETTY. *To* PARRIS: Now, sir, what were your first warning of this strangeness?

**Parris:** Why, sir—I discovered her—*indicating* ABIGAIL—and my niece and ten or twelve of the other girls, dancing in the forest last night.

**Hale,** *surprised:* You permit dancing?

**Parris:** No, no, it were secret—

**Mrs. Putnam,** *unable to wait:* Mr. Parris's slave has knowledge of conjurin', sir.

**Parris,** *to* MRS. PUTNAM: We cannot be sure of that, Goody Ann—

**Mrs. Putnam,** *frightened, very softly:* I know it, sir. I sent my child—she should learn from Tituba who murdered her sisters.

**Rebecca,** *horrified:* Goody Ann! You sent a child to conjure up the dead?

**Mrs. Putnam:** Let God blame me, not you, not you, Rebecca! I'll not have you judging me any more! *To* HALE: Is it a natural work to lose seven children before they live a day?

**Parris:** Sssh!

REBECCA, *with great pain, turns her face away. There is a pause.*

**Hale:** Seven dead in childbirth.

**Mrs. Putnam,** *softly:* Aye. *Her voice breaks; she looks up at him. Silence.* HALE *is impressed.* PARRIS *looks to him. He goes to his books, opens one, turns pages, then reads. All wait, avidly.*

**Parris,** *hushed:* What book is that?

**Mrs. Putnam:** What's there, sir?

**Hale,** *with a tasty love of intellectual pursuit:* Here is all the invisible world, caught, defined, and calculated. In these books the Devil stands stripped of all his brute disguises. Here are all your familiar spirits—your incubi and succubi; your witches that go by land, by air, and by sea; your wizards of the night and of the day. Have no fear now—we shall find him out if he has come among us, and I mean to crush him utterly if he has shown his face! *He starts for the bed.*

**Rebecca:** Will it hurt the child, sir?

**Hale:** I cannot tell. If she is truly in the Devil's grip we may have to rip and tear to get her free.

**Rebecca:** I think I'll go, then. I am too old for this. *She rises.*

**Parris,** *striving for conviction:* Why, Rebecca, we may open up the boil of all our troubles today!

**Rebecca:** Let us hope for that. I go to God for you, sir.

> "I mean to crush him utterly . . ."

**Parris,** *with trepidation—and resentment:* I hope you do not mean we go to Satan here! *Slight pause.*

**Rebecca:** I wish I knew. *She goes out; they feel resentful of her note of moral superiority.*

**Putnam,** *abruptly:* Come, Mr. Hale, let's get on. Sit you here.

**Giles:** Mr. Hale, I have always wanted to ask a learned man—what signifies the readin' of strange books?

**Hale:** What books?

**Giles:** I cannot tell; she hides them.

**Hale:** Who does this?

**Giles:** Martha, my wife. I have waked at night many a time and found her in a corner, readin' of a book. Now what do you make of that?

**Hale:** Why, that's not necessarily—

**Giles:** It discomfits me! Last night—mark this—I tried and tried and could not say my prayers. And then she close her book and walks out of the house, and suddenly—mark this—I could pray again!

Old Giles must be spoken for, if only because his fate was to be so remarkable and so different from that of all the others. He was in his early eighties at this time, and was the most comical hero in the history. No man has ever been blamed for so much. If a cow was missed, the first thought was to look for her around Corey's house; a fire blazing up at night brought suspicion of arson to his door. He didn't give a hoot for public opinion, and only in his last years—after he had married Martha—did he bother much with the church. That she stopped his prayer is very probable, but he forgot to say that he'd only recently learned any prayers and it didn't take much to make him stumble over them. He was a crank and a nuisance, but withal a deeply innocent and brave man. In court, once, he was asked if it were true that he had been frightened by the strange behavior of a hog and had then said he knew it to be the Devil in an animal's shape. "What frighted you?" he was asked. He forgot everything but the word "frighted," and instantly replied, "I do not know that I ever spoke that word in my life."

**Hale:** Ah! The stoppage of prayer—that is strange. I'll speak further on that with you.

**Giles:** I'm not sayin' she's touched the Devil, now, but I'd admire to know what books she reads and why she hides them. She'll not answer me, y' see.

**Hale:** Aye, we'll discuss it. *To all:* Now mark me, if the Devil is in her you will witness some frightful wonders in this room, so please to keep your wits about you. Mr. Putnam, stand close in case she flies. Now, Betty, dear, will you sit up? PUTNAM *comes in closer, ready-handed.* HALE *sits* BETTY *up, but she hangs limp in his hands.* Hmmm. *He observes her carefully. The others watch breathlessly.* Can you hear me? I am John Hale, minister of Beverly. I have come to help you, dear. Do you remember my two little girls in Beverly? *She does not stir in his hands.*

**Parris,** *in fright:* How can it be the Devil? Why would he choose my house to strike? We have all manner of licentious people in the village!

**Hale:** What victory would the Devil have to win a soul already bad? It is the best the Devil wants, and who is better than the minister?

**Giles:** That's deep, Mr. Parris, deep, deep!

**Parris,** *with resolution now:* Betty! Answer Mr. Hale! Betty!

**Hale:** Does someone afflict you, child? It need not be a woman, mind you, or a man. Perhaps some bird invisible to others comes to you—perhaps a pig, a mouse, or any beast at all. Is there some figure bids you fly? *The child remains limp in his hands. In silence he lays her back on the pillow. Now, holding out his hands toward her, he intones:* In nomine Domini Sabaoth sui filiique ite ad infernos.⁹ *She does not stir. He turns to* ABIGAIL, *his eyes narrowing.* Abigail, what sort of dancing were you doing with her in the forest?

**Abigail:** Why—common dancing is all.

**Parris:** I think I ought to say that I—I saw a kettle in the grass where they were dancing.

**Abigail:** That were only soup.

**Hale:** What sort of soup were in this kettle, Abigail?

**Abigail:** Why, it were beans—and lentils, I think, and—

**Hale:** Mr. Parris, you did not notice, did you, any living thing in the kettle? A mouse, perhaps, a spider, a frog—?

9. **In nomine Domini Sabaoth sui filiique ite ad infernos:** Latin for "In the name of the Lord of Hosts and his son, get thee to hell."

**Parris,** *fearfully:* I—do believe there were some movement—in the soup.

**Abigail:** That jumped in, we never put it in!

**Hale,** *quickly:* What jumped in?

**Abigail:** Why, a very little frog jumped—

**Parris:** A frog, Abby!

**Hale,** *grasping* ABIGAIL: Abigail, it may be your cousin is dying. Did you call the Devil last night?

**Abigail:** I never called him! Tituba, Tituba . . .

**Parris,** *blanched:* She called the Devil?

**Hale:** I should like to speak with Tituba.

**Parris:** Goody Ann, will you bring her up? MRS. PUTNAM *exits.*

**Hale:** How did she call him?

**Abigail:** I know not—she spoke Barbados.

**Hale:** Did you feel any strangeness when she called him? A sudden cold wind, perhaps? A trembling below the ground?

**Abigail:** I didn't see no Devil! *Shaking* BETTY: Betty, wake up. Betty! Betty!

**Hale:** You cannot evade me, Abigail. Did your cousin drink any of the brew in that kettle?

**Abigail:** She never drank it!

**Hale:** Did you drink it?

**Abigail:** No, sir!

**Hale:** Did Tituba ask you to drink it?

**Abigail:** She tried, but I refused.

**Hale:** Why are you concealing? Have you sold yourself to Lucifer?

**Abigail:** I never sold myself! I'm a good girl! I'm a proper girl!

MRS. PUTNAM *enters with* TITUBA, *and instantly* ABIGAIL *points at* TITUBA.

**Abigail:** She made me do it! She made Betty do it!

**Tituba,** *shocked and angry:* Abby!

**Abigail:** She makes me drink blood!

**Parris:** Blood!!

**Mrs. Putnam:** My baby's blood?

**Tituba:** No, no, chicken blood. I give she chicken blood!

**Hale:** Woman, have you enlisted these children for the Devil?

**Tituba:** No, no, sir, I don't truck with no Devil!

**Hale:** Why can she not wake? Are you silencing this child?

**Tituba:** I love me Betty!

**Hale:** You have sent your spirit out upon this child, have you not? Are you gathering souls for the Devil?

**Abigail:** She sends her spirit on me in church; she makes me laugh at prayer!

**Parris:** She have often laughed at prayer!

**Abigail:** She comes to me every night to go and drink blood!

**Tituba:** You beg *me* to conjure! She beg *me* make charm—

**Abigail:** Don't lie! *To* HALE: She comes to me while I sleep; she's always making me dream corruptions!

**Tituba:** Why you say that, Abby?

**Abigail:** Sometimes I wake and find myself standing in the open doorway and not a stitch on my body! I always hear her laughing in my sleep. I hear her singing her Barbados songs and tempting me with—

**Tituba:** Mister Reverend, I never—

**Hale,** *resolved now:* Tituba, I want you to wake this child.

**Tituba:** I have no power on this child, sir.

**Hale:** You most certainly do, and you will free her from it now! When did you compact with the Devil?

**Tituba:** I don't compact with no Devil!

**Parris:** You will confess yourself or I will take you out and whip you to your death, Tituba!

**Putnam:** This woman must be hanged! She must be taken and hanged!

**Tituba,** *terrified, falls to her knees:* No, no, don't hang Tituba! I tell him I don't desire to work for him, sir.

**Parris:** The Devil?

**Hale:** Then you saw him! TITUBA *weeps.* Now Tituba, I know that when we bind ourselves to Hell it is very hard to break with it. We are going to help you tear yourself free—

**Tituba,** *frightened by the coming process:* Mister Reverend, I do believe somebody else be witchin' these children.

**Hale:** Who?

**Tituba:** I don't know, sir, but the Devil got him numerous witches.

**Hale:** Does he! *It is a clue.* Tituba, look into my eyes. Come, look into me. *She raises her eyes to his fearfully.* You would be a good Christian woman, would you not, Tituba?

**Tituba:** Aye, sir, a good Christian woman.

**Hale:** And you love these little children?

**Tituba:** Oh, yes, sir, I don't desire to hurt little children.

**Hale:** And you love God, Tituba?

**Tituba:** I love God with all my bein'.

**Hale:** Now, in God's holy name—

**Tituba:** Bless Him. Bless Him. *She is rocking on her knees, sobbing in terror.*

**Hale:** And to His glory—

**Tituba:** Eternal glory. Bless Him—bless God . . .

**Hale:** Open yourself, Tituba—open yourself and let God's holy light shine on you.

**Tituba:** Oh, bless the Lord.

**Hale:** When the Devil comes to you does he ever come—with another person? *She stares up into his face.* Perhaps another person in the village? Someone you know.

**Parris:** Who came with him?

**Putnam:** Sarah Good? Did you ever see Sarah Good with him? Or Osburn?

**Parris:** Was it man or woman came with him?

**Tituba:** Man or woman. Was—was woman.

**Parris:** What woman? A woman, you said. What woman?

**Tituba:** It was black dark, and I—

**Parris:** You could see him, why could you not see her?

**Tituba:** Well, they was always talking; they was always runnin' round and carryin' on—

**Parris:** You mean out of Salem? Salem witches?

**Tituba:** I believe so, yes, sir.

*Now* HALE *takes her hand. She is surprised.*

**Hale:** Tituba. You must have no fear to tell us who they are, do you understand? We will protect you. The Devil can never overcome a minister. You know that, do you not?

**Tituba**—*she kisses* HALE's *hand:* Aye, sir, oh, I do.

**Hale:** You have confessed yourself to witchcraft, and that speaks a wish to come to Heaven's side. And we will bless you, Tituba.

**Tituba,** *deeply relieved:* Oh, God bless you, Mr. Hale!

**Hale,** *with rising exaltation:* You are God's instrument put in our hands to discover the Devil's agents among us. You are selected, Tituba, you are chosen to help us cleanse our village. So speak utterly, Tituba, turn your back on him and face God—face God, Tituba, and God will protect you.

**Tituba,** *joining with him:* Oh, God, protect Tituba!

**Hale,** *kindly:* Who came to you with the Devil? Two? Three? Four? How many?

TITUBA *pants and begins rocking back and forth again, staring ahead.*

**Tituba:** There was four. There was four.

**Parris,** *pressing in on her:* Who? Who? Their names, their names!

**Tituba,** *suddenly bursting out:* Oh, how many times he bid me kill you, Mr. Parris!

**Parris:** Kill me!

**Tituba,** *in a fury:* He say Mr. Parris must be kill! Mr. Parris no goodly man, Mr. Parris mean man and no gentle man, and he bid me rise out of my bed and cut your throat! *They gasp.* But I tell him "No! I don't hate that man. I don't want kill that man." But he say, "You work for me, Tituba, and I make you free! I give you pretty dress to wear, and put you way high up in the air, and you gone fly back to Barbados!" And I say, "You lie, Devil, you lie!" And then he come one stormy night to me, and he say, "Look! I have *white* people belong to me." And I look—and there was Goody Good.

**Parris:** Sarah Good!

**Tituba,** *rocking and weeping:* Aye, sir, and Goody Osburn.

**Mrs. Putnam:** I knew it! Goody Osburn were midwife to me three times. I begged you, Thomas, did I not? I begged him not to call Osburn because I feared her. My babies always shriveled in her hands!

**Hale:** Take courage, you must give us all their names. How can you bear to see this child suffering? Look at her, Tituba. *He is indicating* BETTY *on the bed.* Look at her God-given innocence; her soul is so tender; we must protect her, Tituba; the Devil is out and preying on her like a beast upon the flesh of the pure lamb. God will bless you for your help.

ABIGAIL *rises, staring as though inspired, and cries out.*

**Abigail:** I want to open myself! *They turn to her, startled. She is enraptured, as though in a pearly light.* I want the light of God, I want the sweet love of Jesus! I danced for the Devil; I saw him; I wrote in his book; I go back to Jesus; I kiss His hand. I saw Sarah Good with the Devil! I saw Goody Osburn with the Devil! I saw Bridget Bishop with the Devil!

*As she is speaking,* BETTY *is rising from the bed, a fever in her eyes, and picks up the chant.*

**Betty,** *staring too:* I saw George Jacobs with the Devil! I saw Goody Howe with the Devil!
**Parris:** She speaks! *He rushes to embrace* BETTY. She speaks!
**Hale:** Glory to God! It is broken, they are free!
**Betty,** *calling out hysterically and with great relief:* I saw Martha Bellows with the Devil!
**Abigail:** I saw Goody Sibber with the Devil! *It is rising to a great glee.*

**Putnam:** The marshal, I'll call the marshal!

PARRIS *is shouting a prayer of thanksgiving.*

**Betty:** I saw Alice Barrow with the Devil!

*The curtain begins to fall.*

**Hale,** *as* PUTNAM *goes out:* Let the marshal bring irons!
**Abigail:** I saw Goody Hawkins with the Devil!
**Betty:** I saw Goody Bibber with the Devil!
**Abigail:** I saw Goody Booth with the Devil!

*On their ecstatic cries*

> *The curtain falls*

# Response and Analysis

## Act One

### Reading Check

1. When Abigail is alone with Proctor, what claim does she make?

2. Whom has Parris invited to Salem?

3. Why are both Mrs. Putnam and Abigail interested in Tituba's "conjuring"?

### Thinking Critically

4. Why is Reverend Parris so terrified by the events in Salem? What possible result does he fear?

5. How would you explain the "illnesses" of Betty and Ruth?

6. Re-read sections of Act One, including the background information Miller provides about the history of Salem, in order to find out when important events occurred. Then make a **time line** that places in rough **chronological order** events such as the murder of Abigail's parents, the dispute over the election of the minister, the battle over Francis Nurse's land, and the death of Mrs. Putnam's babies.

7. How would you **interpret** Abigail's relationship with the other girls and her relationship with Proctor? Be sure to check your reading notes.

8. Summarize Hale's view of his mission in Salem. What does he mean when he says the Devil is "precise"?

9. At the end of the act, what do you think is Abigail's **motivation** to "open" herself and begin naming names?

10. A **static character** changes little or not at all during a story. A **dynamic character** changes in an important way as a result of the story's action. Among the characters from Act One, which do you think have potential for change?

### Extending and Evaluating

11. When someone is accused of a crime today, do people still have a tendency to side with the accusers? Explain your answer.

**Literary Skills**
Analyze motivation.

**Reading Skills**
Interpret a dramatic work. Monitor reading by re-reading the text.

# Act Two

*The common room of* PROCTOR'*s house, eight days later.*

*At the right is a door opening on the fields outside. A fireplace is at the left, and behind it a stairway leading upstairs. It is the low, dark, and rather long living room of the time. As the curtain rises, the room is empty. From above,* ELIZABETH *is heard softly singing to the children. Presently the door opens and* JOHN PROCTOR *enters, carrying his gun. He glances about the room as he comes toward the fireplace, then halts for an instant as he hears her singing. He continues on to the fireplace, leans the gun against the wall as he swings a pot out of the fire and smells it. Then he lifts out the ladle and tastes. He is not quite pleased. He reaches to a cupboard, takes a pinch of salt, and drops it into the pot. As he is tasting again, her footsteps are heard on the stair. He swings the pot into the fireplace and goes to a basin and washes his hands and face.* ELIZABETH *enters.*

**Elizabeth:** What keeps you so late? It's almost dark.

**Proctor:** I were planting far out to the forest edge.

**Elizabeth:** Oh, you're done then.

**Proctor:** Aye, the farm is seeded. The boys asleep?

**Elizabeth:** They will be soon. *And she goes to the fireplace, proceeds to ladle up stew in a dish.*

**Proctor:** Pray now for a fair summer.

**Elizabeth:** Aye.

**Proctor:** Are you well today?

**Elizabeth:** I am. *She brings the plate to the table, and, indicating the food:* It is a rabbit.

**Proctor,** *going to the table:* Oh, is it! In Jonathan's trap?

**Elizabeth:** No, she walked into the house this afternoon; I found her sittin' in the corner like she come to visit.

**Proctor:** Oh, that's a good sign walkin' in.

**Elizabeth:** Pray God. It hurt my heart to strip her, poor rabbit. *She sits and watches him taste it.*

**Proctor:** It's well seasoned.

**Elizabeth,** *blushing with pleasure:* I took great care. She's tender?

**Proctor:** Aye. *He eats. She watches him.* I think

we'll see green fields soon. It's warm as blood beneath the clods.

**Elizabeth:** That's well.

PROCTOR *eats, then looks up.*

**Proctor:** If the crop is good I'll buy George Jacobs' heifer. How would that please you?

**Elizabeth:** Aye, it would.

**Proctor,** *with a grin:* I mean to please you, Elizabeth.

**Elizabeth**—*it is hard to say:* I know it, John.

*He gets up, goes to her, kisses her. She receives it. With a certain disappointment, he returns to the table.*

**Proctor,** *as gently as he can:* Cider?

**Elizabeth,** *with a sense of reprimanding herself for having forgot:* Aye! *She gets up and goes and pours a glass for him. He now arches his back.*

**Proctor:** This farm's a continent when you go foot by foot droppin' seeds in it.

**Elizabeth,** *coming with the cider:* It must be.

**Proctor,** *he drinks a long draught, then, putting the glass down:* You ought to bring some flowers in the house.

**Elizabeth:** Oh! I forgot! I will tomorrow.

**Proctor:** It's winter in here yet. On Sunday let you come with me, and we'll walk the farm together; I never see such a load of flowers on the earth. *With good feeling he goes and looks up at the sky through the open doorway.* Lilacs have a purple smell. Lilac is the smell of nightfall, I think. Massachusetts is a beauty in the spring!

**Elizabeth:** Aye, it is.

*There is a pause. She is watching him from the table as he stands there absorbing the night. It is as though she would speak but cannot. Instead, now, she takes up his plate and glass and fork and goes with them to the basin. Her back is turned to him. He turns to her and watches her. A sense of their separation rises.*

**Proctor:** I think you're sad again. Are you?

**Elizabeth**—*she doesn't want friction, and yet she must:* You come so late I thought you'd gone to Salem this afternoon.

**Proctor:** Why? I have no business in Salem.

**Elizabeth:** You did speak of going, earlier this week.

**Proctor**—*he knows what she means:* I thought better of it since.

**Elizabeth:** Mary Warren's there today.

**Proctor:** Why'd you let her? You heard me forbid her to go to Salem any more!

**Elizabeth:** I couldn't stop her.

**Proctor,** *holding back a full condemnation of her:* It is a fault, it is a fault, Elizabeth—you're the mistress here, not Mary Warren.

**Elizabeth:** She frightened all my strength away.

**Proctor:** How may that mouse frighten you, Elizabeth? You—

**Elizabeth:** It is a mouse no more. I forbid her go, and she raises up her chin like the daughter of a prince and says to me, "I must go to Salem, Goody Proctor; I am an official of the court!"

**Proctor:** Court! What court?

**Elizabeth:** Aye, it is a proper court they have now. They've sent four judges out of Boston, she says, weighty magistrates of the General Court, and at the head sits the Deputy Governor of the Province.

**Proctor,** *astonished:* Why, she's mad.

**Elizabeth:** I would to God she were. There be fourteen people in the jail now, she says. PROCTOR *simply looks at her, unable to grasp it.* And they'll be tried, and the court have power to hang them too, she says.

**Proctor,** *scoffing, but without conviction:* Ah, they'd never hang—

**Elizabeth:** The Deputy Governor promise hangin' if they'll not confess, John. The town's gone wild, I think. She speak of Abigail, and I thought she were a saint, to hear her. Abigail brings the other girls into the court, and where she walks the crowd will part like the sea for Israel. And folks are brought before them, and if they scream and howl and fall to the floor—the person's clapped in the jail for bewitchin' them.

**Proctor,** *wide-eyed:* Oh, it is a black mischief.

**Elizabeth:** I think you must go to Salem, John. *He turns to her.* I think so. You must tell them it is a fraud.

**Proctor,** *thinking beyond this:* Aye, it is, it is surely.

**Elizabeth:** Let you go to Ezekiel Cheever—he knows you well. And tell him what she said to you last week in her uncle's house. She said it had naught to do with witchcraft, did she not?

**Proctor,** *in thought:* Aye, she did, she did. *Now a pause.*

**Elizabeth,** *quietly, fearing to anger him by prodding:* God forbid you keep that from the court, John. I think they must be told.

**Proctor,** *quietly, struggling with his thought:* Aye, they must, they must. It is a wonder they do believe her.

**Elizabeth:** I would go to Salem now, John—let you go tonight.

**Proctor:** I'll think on it.

**Elizabeth,** *with her courage now:* You cannot keep it, John.

**Proctor,** *angering:* I know I cannot keep it. I say I will think on it!

**Elizabeth,** *hurt, and very coldly:* Good, then, let you think on it. *She stands and starts to walk out of the room.*

**Proctor:** I am only wondering how I may prove what she told me, Elizabeth. If the girl's a saint now, I think it is not easy to prove she's fraud, and the town gone so silly. She told it to me in a room alone—I have no proof for it.

**Elizabeth:** You were alone with her?

**Proctor,** *stubbornly:* For a moment alone, aye.

**Elizabeth:** Why, then, it is not as you told me.

**Proctor,** *his anger rising:* For a moment, I say. The others come in soon after.

**Elizabeth,** *quietly—she has suddenly lost all faith in him:* Do as you wish, then. *She starts to turn.*

**Proctor:** Woman. *She turns to him.* I'll not have your suspicion any more.

**Elizabeth,** *a little loftily:* I have no—

**Proctor:** I'll not have it!

**Elizabeth:** Then let you not earn it.

**Proctor,** *with a violent undertone:* You doubt me yet?

**Elizabeth,** *with a smile, to keep her dignity:* John, if it were not Abigail that you must go to hurt, would you falter now? I think not.

**Proctor:** Now look you—

**Elizabeth:** I see what I see, John.

**Proctor,** *with solemn warning:* You will not judge me more, Elizabeth. I have good reason to think before I charge fraud on Abigail, and I will think on it. Let you look to your own improvement before you go to judge your husband any more. I have forgot Abigail, and—

**Elizabeth:** And I.

**Proctor:** Spare me! You forget nothin' and forgive nothin.' Learn charity, woman. I have gone tiptoe in this house all seven month since she is gone. I have not moved from there to there without I think to please you, and still an everlasting funeral marches round your heart. I cannot speak but I am doubted, every moment judged for lies, as though I come into a court when I come into this house!

**Elizabeth:** John, you are not open with me. You saw her with a crowd, you said. Now you—

**Proctor:** I'll plead my honesty no more, Elizabeth.

**Elizabeth**—*now she would justify herself:* John, I am only—

**Proctor:** No more! I should have roared you down when first you told me your suspicion. But I wilted, and, like a Christian, I confessed. Confessed! Some dream I had must have mistaken you for God that day. But you're not, you're not, and let you remember it! Let you look sometimes for the goodness in me, and judge me not.

**Elizabeth:** I do not judge you. The magistrate sits in your heart that judges you. I never thought you but a good man, John—*with a smile*—only somewhat bewildered.

**Proctor,** *laughing bitterly:* Oh, Elizabeth, your justice would freeze beer! *He turns suddenly toward a sound outside. He starts for the door as* MARY WARREN *enters. As soon as he sees her, he goes directly to her and grabs her by her cloak, furious.* How do you go to Salem when I forbid it? Do you mock me? *Shaking her:* I'll whip you if you dare leave this house again!

*Strangely, she doesn't resist him but hangs limply by his grip.*

**Mary Warren:** I am sick, I am sick, Mr. Proctor. Pray, pray, hurt me not. *Her strangeness throws him off, and her evident pallor and weakness. He frees her.* My insides are all shuddery; I am in the proceedings all day, sir.

**Proctor,** *with draining anger—his curiosity is draining it:* And what of these proceedings here?

When will you proceed to keep this house, as you are paid nine pound a year to do—and my wife not wholly well?

*As though to compensate,* MARY WARREN *goes to* ELIZABETH *with a small rag doll.*

**Mary Warren:** I made a gift for you today, Goody Proctor. I had to sit long hours in a chair, and passed the time with sewing.

**Elizabeth,** *perplexed, looking at the doll:* Why, thank you, it's a fair poppet.[1]

**Mary Warren,** *with a trembling, decayed voice:* We must all love each other now, Goody Proctor.

**Elizabeth,** *amazed at her strangeness:* Aye, indeed, we must.

**Mary Warren,** *glancing at the room:* I'll get up early in the morning and clean the house. I must sleep now. She turns and starts off.

**Proctor:** Mary. *She halts.* Is it true? There be fourteen women arrested?

**Mary Warren:** No, sir. There be thirty-nine now— *She suddenly breaks off and sobs and sits down, exhausted.*

**Elizabeth:** Why, she's weepin'! What ails you, child?

**Mary Warren:** Goody Osburn—will hang! *There is a shocked pause, while she sobs.*

**Proctor:** Hang! *He calls into her face.* Hang, y'say?

**Mary Warren,** *through her weeping:* Aye.

**Proctor:** The Deputy Governor will permit it?

**Mary Warren:** He sentenced her. He must. *To ameliorate it:* But not Sarah Good. For Sarah Good confessed, y'see.

**Proctor:** Confessed! To what?

**Mary Warren:** That she—*in horror at the memory*—she sometimes made a compact with Lucifer, and wrote her name in his black book—with her blood—and bound herself to torment Christians till God's thrown down—and we all must worship Hell forevermore.

*Pause.*

**Proctor:** But—surely you know what a jabberer she is. Did you tell them that?

**Mary Warren:** Mr. Proctor, in open court she near to choked us all to death.

**Proctor:** How, choked you?

**Mary Warren:** She sent her spirit out.

1. **poppet:** doll; puppet.

The girls of Salem "scream and howl and fall to the floor . . ."

**Elizabeth:** Oh, Mary, Mary, surely you—

**Mary Warren,** *with an indignant edge:* She tried to kill me many times, Goody Proctor!

**Elizabeth:** Why, I never heard you mention that before.

**Mary Warren:** I never knew it before. I never knew anything before. When she come into the court I say to myself, I must not accuse this woman, for she sleep in ditches, and so very old and poor. But then—then she sit there, denying and denying, and I feel a misty coldness climbin' up my back, and the skin on my skull begin to creep, and I feel a clamp around my neck and I cannot breathe air; and then—*entranced*—I hear a voice, a screamin' voice, and it were my voice— and all at once I remember everything she done to me!

**Proctor:** Why? What did she do to you?

**Mary Warren,** *like one awakened to a marvelous secret insight:* So many time, Mr. Proctor, she come to this very door, beggin' bread and a cup of cider—and mark this: whenever I turned her away empty, she *mumbled.*

**Elizabeth:** Mumbled! She may mumble if she's hungry.

**Mary Warren:** But *what* does she mumble? You must remember, Goody Proctor. Last month—a Monday, I think—she walked away, and I thought my guts would burst for two days after. Do you remember it?

**Elizabeth:** Why—I do, I think, but—

**Mary Warren:** And so I told that to Judge Hathorne, and he asks her so. "Goody Osburn," says he, "what curse do you mumble that this girl must fall sick after turning you away?" And then she replies—*mimicking an old crone*—"Why, your excellence, no curse at all. I only say my commandments; I hope I may say my commandments," says she!

**Elizabeth:** And that's an upright answer.

**Mary Warren:** Aye, but then Judge Hathorne say, "Recite for us your commandments!"—*leaning avidly toward them*—and of all the ten she could not say a single one. She never knew no commandments, and they had her in a flat lie!

**Proctor:** And so condemned her?

**Mary Warren,** *now a little strained, seeing his stubborn doubt:* Why, they must when she condemned herself.

**Proctor:** But the proof, the proof!

**Mary Warren,** *with greater impatience with him:* I told you the proof. It's hard proof, hard as rock, the judges said.

**Proctor**—*he pauses an instant, then:* You will not go to court again, Mary Warren.

**Mary Warren:** I must tell you, sir, I will be gone every day now. I am amazed you do not see what weighty work we do.

**Proctor:** What work you do! It's strange work for a Christian girl to hang old women!

**Mary Warren:** But, Mr. Proctor, they will not hang them if they confess. Sarah Good will only sit in jail some time—*recalling*—and here's a wonder for you; think on this. Goody Good is pregnant!

**Elizabeth:** Pregnant! Are they mad? The woman's near to sixty!

**Mary Warren:** They had Doctor Griggs examine her, and she's full to the brim. And smokin' a pipe all these years, and no husband either! But she's safe, thank God, for they'll not hurt the innocent child. But be that not a marvel? You must see it, sir, it's God's work we do. So I'll be gone every day for some time. I'm—I am an official of the court, they say, and I— *She has been edging toward offstage.*

**Proctor:** I'll official you! *He strides to the mantel, takes down the whip hanging there.*

**Mary Warren,** *terrified, but coming erect, striving for her authority:* I'll not stand whipping any more!

**Elizabeth,** *hurriedly, as* PROCTOR *approaches:* Mary, promise now you'll stay at home—

**Mary Warren,** *backing from him, but keeping her erect posture, striving, striving for her way:* The Devil's loose in Salem, Mr. Proctor; we must discover where he's hiding!

**Proctor:** I'll whip the Devil out of you! *With whip raised he reaches out for her, and she streaks away and yells.*

**Mary Warren,** *pointing at* ELIZABETH: I saved her life today!

*Silence. His whip comes down.*

**Elizabeth,** *softly:* I am accused?

**Mary Warren,** *quaking:* Somewhat mentioned. But I said I never see no sign you ever sent your

spirit out to hurt no one, and seeing I do live so closely with you, they dismissed it.

**Elizabeth:** Who accused me?

**Mary Warren:** I am bound by law, I cannot tell it. *To* PROCTOR: I only hope you'll not be so sarcastical no more. Four judges and the King's deputy sat to dinner with us but an hour ago. I—I would have you speak civilly to me, from this out.

**Proctor,** *in horror, muttering in disgust at her:* Go to bed.

**Mary Warren,** *with a stamp of her foot:* I'll not be ordered to bed no more, Mr. Proctor! I am eighteen and a woman, however single!

**Proctor:** Do you wish to sit up? Then sit up.

**Mary Warren:** I wish to go to bed!

**Proctor,** *in anger:* Good night, then!

**Mary Warren:** Good night. *Dissatisfied, uncertain of herself, she goes out. Wide-eyed, both* PROCTOR *and* ELIZABETH *stand staring.*

**Elizabeth,** *quietly:* Oh, the noose, the noose is up!

**Proctor:** There'll be no noose.

**Elizabeth:** She wants me dead. I knew all week it would come to this!

**Proctor,** *without conviction:* They dismissed it. You heard her say—

**Elizabeth:** And what of tomorrow? She will cry me out until they take me!

**Proctor:** Sit you down.

**Elizabeth:** She wants me dead, John, you know it!

**Proctor:** I say sit down! *She sits, trembling. He speaks quietly, trying to keep his wits.* Now we must be wise, Elizabeth.

**Elizabeth,** *with sarcasm, and a sense of being lost:* Oh, indeed, indeed!

**Proctor:** Fear nothing. I'll find Ezekiel Cheever. I'll tell him she said it were all sport.

**Elizabeth:** John, with so many in the jail, more than Cheever's help is needed now, I think. Would you favor me with this? Go to Abigail.

**Proctor,** *his soul hardening as he senses . . . :* What have I to say to Abigail?

**Elizabeth,** *delicately:* John—grant me this. You have a faulty understanding of young girls. There is a promise made in any bed—

**Proctor,** *striving against his anger:* What promise!

**Elizabeth:** Spoke or silent, a promise is surely made. And she may dote on it now—I am sure she does—and thinks to kill me, then to take my place.

PROCTOR's *anger is rising; he cannot speak.*

**Elizabeth:** It is her dearest hope, John, I know it. There be a thousand names; why does she call mine? There be a certain danger in calling such a name—I am no Goody Good that sleeps in ditches, nor Osburn, drunk and half-witted. She'd dare not call out such a farmer's wife but there be monstrous profit in it. She thinks to take my place, John.

**Proctor:** She cannot think it! *He knows it is true.*

**Elizabeth,** *"reasonably":* John, have you ever shown her somewhat of contempt? She cannot pass you in the church but you will blush—

**Proctor:** I may blush for my sin.

**Elizabeth:** I think she sees another meaning in that blush.

**Proctor:** And what see you? What see you, Elizabeth?

**Elizabeth,** *"conceding":* I think you be somewhat ashamed, for I am there, and she so close.

**Proctor:** When will you know me, woman? Were I stone I would have cracked for shame this seven month!

**Elizabeth:** Then go and tell her she's a whore. Whatever promise she may sense—break it, John, break it.

**Proctor,** *between his teeth:* Good, then. I'll go. *He starts for his rifle.*

**Elizabeth,** *trembling, fearfully:* Oh, how unwillingly!

**Proctor,** *turning on her, rifle in hand:* I will curse her hotter than the oldest cinder in hell. But pray, begrudge me not my anger!

**Elizabeth:** Your anger! I only ask you—

**Proctor:** Woman, am I so base? Do you truly think me base?

**Elizabeth:** I never called you base.

**Proctor:** Then how do you charge me with such a promise? The promise that a stallion gives a mare I gave that girl!

**Elizabeth:** Then why do you anger with me when I bid you break it?

**Proctor:** Because it speaks deceit, and I am honest! But I'll plead no more! I see now your spirit twists around the single error of my life, and I will never tear it free!

**Elizabeth,** *crying out:* You'll tear it free—when you come to know that I will be your only wife, or no wife at all! She has an arrow in you yet, John Proctor, and you know it well!

*Quite suddenly, as though from the air, a figure appears in the doorway. They start slightly. It is* MR. HALE. *He is different now—drawn a little, and there is a quality of deference, even of guilt, about his manner now.*

**Hale:** Good evening.

**Proctor,** *still in his shock:* Why, Mr. Hale! Good evening to you, sir. Come in, come in.

**Hale,** *to* ELIZABETH: I hope I do not startle you.

**Elizabeth:** No, no, it's only that I heard no horse—

**Hale:** You are Goodwife Proctor.

**Proctor:** Aye; Elizabeth.

**Hale,** *nods, then:* I hope you're not off to bed yet.

**Proctor,** *setting down his gun:* No, no. HALE *comes further into the room. And* PROCTOR, *to explain his nervousness:* We are not used to visitors after dark, but you're welcome here. Will you sit you down, sir?

**Hale:** I will. *He sits.* Let you sit, Goodwife Proctor.

*She does, never letting him out of her sight. There is a pause as* HALE *looks about the room.*

**Proctor,** *to break the silence:* Will you drink cider, Mr. Hale?

**Hale:** No, it rebels my stomach; I have some further traveling yet tonight. Sit you down, sir. PROCTOR *sits.* I will not keep you long, but I have some business with you.

**Proctor:** Business of the court?

**Hale:** No—no, I come of my own, without the court's authority. Hear me. *He wets his lips.* I know not if you are aware, but your wife's name is—mentioned in the court.

**Proctor:** We know it, sir. Our Mary Warren told us. We are entirely amazed.

**Hale:** I am a stranger here, as you know. And in my ignorance I find it hard to draw a clear opinion of them that come accused before the court. And so this afternoon, and now tonight, I go from house to house—I come now from Rebecca Nurse's house and—

**Elizabeth,** *shocked:* Rebecca's charged!

**Hale:** God forbid such a one be charged. She is, however—mentioned somewhat.

> ## "The powers of the dark are gathered in monstrous attack upon this village."

**Elizabeth,** *with an attempt at a laugh:* You will never believe, I hope, that Rebecca trafficked with the Devil.

**Hale:** Woman, it is possible.

**Proctor,** *taken aback:* Surely you cannot think so.

**Hale:** This is a strange time, Mister. No man may longer doubt the powers of the dark are gathered in monstrous attack upon this village. There is too much evidence now to deny it. You will agree, sir?

**Proctor,** *evading:* I—I have no knowledge in that line. But it's hard to think so pious a woman be secretly a Devil's bitch after seventy year of such good prayer.

**Hale:** Aye. But the Devil is a wily one, you cannot deny it. However, she is far from accused, and I know she will not be. *Pause.* I thought, sir, to put some questions as to the Christian character of this house, if you'll permit me.

**Proctor,** *coldly, resentful:* Why, we—have no fear of questions, sir.

**Hale:** Good, then. *He makes himself more comfortable.* In the book of record that Mr. Parris keeps, I note that you are rarely in the church on Sabbath Day.

**Proctor:** No, sir, you are mistaken.

**Hale:** Twenty-six time in seventeen month, sir. I must call that rare. Will you tell me why you are so absent?

**Proctor:** Mr. Hale, I never knew I must account to that man for I come to church or stay at home. My wife were sick this winter.

**Hale:** So I am told. But you, Mister, why could you not come alone?

**Proctor:** I surely did come when I could, and when I could not I prayed in this house.

**Hale:** Mr. Proctor, your house is not a church; your theology must tell you that.

**Proctor:** It does, sir, it does; and it tells me that a minister may pray to God without he have golden candlesticks upon the altar.

**Hale:** What golden candlesticks?

**Proctor:** Since we built the church there were pewter candlesticks upon the altar; Francis Nurse made them, y'know, and a sweeter hand never touched the metal. But Parris came, and for twenty week he preach nothin' but golden candlesticks until he had them. I labor the earth from dawn of day to blink of night, and I tell you true, when I look to heaven and see my money glaring at his elbows—it hurt my prayer, sir, it hurt my prayer. I think, sometimes, the man dreams cathedrals, not clapboard meetin' houses.

**Hale,** *thinks, then:* And yet, Mister, a Christian on Sabbath Day must be in church. *Pause.* Tell me— you have three children?

**Proctor:** Aye. Boys.

**Hale:** How comes it that only two are baptized?

**Proctor,** *starts to speak, then stops, then, as though unable to restrain this:* I like it not that Mr. Parris should lay his hand upon my baby. I see no light of God in that man. I'll not conceal it.

**Hale:** I must say it, Mr. Proctor; that is not for you to decide. The man's ordained, therefore the light of God is in him.

**Proctor,** *flushed with resentment but trying to smile:* What's your suspicion, Mr. Hale?

**Hale:** No, no, I have no—

**Proctor:** I nailed the roof upon the church, I hung the door—

**Hale:** Oh, did you! That's a good sign, then.

**Proctor:** It may be I have been too quick to bring the man to book, but you cannot think we ever desired the destruction of religion. I think that's in your mind, is it not?

**Hale,** *not altogether giving way:* I—have—there is a softness in your record, sir, a softness.

**Elizabeth:** I think, maybe, we have been too hard with Mr. Parris. I think so. But sure we never loved the Devil here.

**Hale,** *nods, deliberating this. Then, with the voice of one administering a secret test:* Do you know your Commandments, Elizabeth?

**Elizabeth,** *without hesitation, even eagerly:* I surely do. There be no mark of blame upon my life, Mr. Hale. I am a covenanted Christian woman.

**Hale:** And you, Mister?

**Proctor,** *a trifle unsteadily:* I—am sure I do, sir.
**Hale,** *glances at her open face, then at* JOHN, *then:* Let you repeat them, if you will.
**Proctor:** The Commandments.
**Hale:** Aye.
**Proctor,** *looking off, beginning to sweat:* Thou shalt not kill.
**Hale:** Aye.
**Proctor,** *counting on his fingers:* Thou shalt not steal. Thou shalt not covet thy neighbor's goods, nor make unto thee any graven image. Thou shalt not take the name of the Lord in vain; thou shalt have no other gods before me. *With some hesitation:* Thou shalt remember the Sabbath Day and keep it holy. *Pause. Then:* Thou shalt honor thy father and mother. Thou shalt not bear false witness. *He is stuck. He counts back on his fingers, knowing one is missing.* Thou shalt not make unto thee any graven image.
**Hale:** You have said that twice, sir.
**Proctor,** *lost:* Aye. *He is flailing for it.*
**Elizabeth,** *delicately:* Adultery, John.
**Proctor,** *as though a secret arrow had pained his heart:* Aye. *Trying to grin it away—to* HALE: You see, sir, between the two of us we do know them all. HALE *only looks at* PROCTOR, *deep in his attempt to define this man.* PROCTOR *grows more uneasy.* I think it be a small fault.
**Hale:** Theology, sir, is a fortress; no crack in a fortress may be accounted small. *He rises; he seems worried now. He paces a little, in deep thought.*
**Proctor:** There be no love for Satan in this house, Mister.
**Hale:** I pray it, I pray it dearly. *He looks to both of them, an attempt at a smile on his face, but his misgivings are clear.* Well, then—I'll bid you good night.
**Elizabeth,** *unable to restrain herself:* Mr. Hale. *He turns.* I do think you are suspecting me somewhat? Are you not?
**Hale,** *obviously disturbed—and evasive:* Goody Proctor, I do not judge you. My duty is to add what I may to the godly wisdom of the court. I pray you both good health and good fortune. *To* JOHN: Good night, sir. *He starts out.*
**Elizabeth,** *with a note of desperation:* I think you must tell him, John.
**Hale:** What's that?

**Elizabeth,** *restraining a call:* Will you tell him?

*Slight pause.* HALE *looks questioningly at* JOHN.

**Proctor,** *with difficulty:* I—I have no witness and cannot prove it, except my word be taken. But I know the children's sickness had naught to do with witchcraft.
**Hale,** *stopped, struck:* Naught to do—?
**Proctor:** Mr. Parris discovered them sportin' in the woods. They were startled and took sick.

*Pause.*

**Hale:** Who told you this?
**Proctor,** *hesitates, then:* Abigail Williams.
**Hale:** Abigail!
**Proctor:** Aye.
**Hale,** *his eyes wide:* Abigail Williams told you it had naught to do with witchcraft!
**Proctor:** She told me the day you came, sir.
**Hale,** *suspiciously:* Why—why did you keep this?
**Proctor:** I never knew until tonight that the world is gone daft with this nonsense.
**Hale:** Nonsense! Mister, I have myself examined Tituba, Sarah Good, and numerous others that have confessed to dealing with the Devil. They have *confessed* it.
**Proctor:** And why not, if they must hang for denyin' it? There are them that will swear to anything before they'll hang; have you never thought of that?
**Hale:** I have. I—I have indeed. *It is his own suspicion, but he resists it. He glances at* ELIZABETH, *then at* JOHN. And you—would you testify to this in court?
**Proctor:** I—had not reckoned with goin' into court. But if I must I will.
**Hale:** Do you falter here?
**Proctor:** I falter nothing, but I may wonder if my story will be credited in such a court. I do wonder on it, when such a steady-minded minister as you will suspicion such a woman that never lied, and cannot, and the world knows she cannot! I may falter somewhat, Mister; I am no fool.
**Hale,** *quietly—it has impressed him:* Proctor, let you open with me now, for I have a rumor that troubles me. It's said you hold no belief that there may even be witches in the world. Is that true, sir?
**Proctor**—*he knows this is critical, and is*

*striving against his disgust with* HALE *and with himself for even answering:* I know not what I have said, I may have said it. I have wondered if there be witches in the world—although I cannot believe they come among us now.

**Hale:** Then you do not believe—

**Proctor:** I have no knowledge of it; the Bible speaks of witches, and I will not deny them.

**Hale:** And you, woman?

**Elizabeth:** I—I cannot believe it.

**Hale,** *shocked:* You cannot!

**Proctor:** Elizabeth, you bewilder him!

**Elizabeth,** *to* HALE: I cannot think the Devil may own a woman's soul, Mr. Hale, when she keeps an upright way, as I have. I am a good woman, I know it; and if you believe I may do only good work in the world, and yet be secretly bound to Satan, then I must tell you, sir, I do not believe it.

**Hale:** But, woman, you do believe there are witches in—

**Elizabeth:** If you think that I am one, then I say there are none.

**Hale:** You surely do not fly against the Gospel, the Gospel—

**Proctor:** She believe in the Gospel, every word!

**Elizabeth:** Question Abigail Williams about the Gospel, not myself!

HALE *stares at her.*

**Proctor:** She do not mean to doubt the Gospel, sir, you cannot think it. This be a Christian house, sir, a Christian house.

**Hale:** God keep you both; let the third child be quickly baptized, and go you without fail each Sunday in to Sabbath prayer; and keep a solemn, quiet way among you. I think—

GILES COREY *appears in doorway.*

**Giles:** John!

**Proctor:** Giles! What's the matter?

**Giles:** They take my wife.

FRANCIS NURSE *enters.*

**Giles:** And his Rebecca!

**Proctor,** *to* FRANCIS: Rebecca's in the *jail!*

**Francis:** Aye, Cheever come and take her in his wagon. We've only now come from the jail, and they'll not even let us in to see them.

**Elizabeth:** They've surely gone wild now, Mr. Hale!

**Francis,** *going to* HALE: Reverend Hale! Can you not speak to the Deputy Governor? I'm sure he mistakes these people—

**Hale:** Pray calm yourself, Mr. Nurse.

**Francis:** My wife is the very brick and mortar of the church, Mr. Hale—*indicating* GILES—and Martha Corey, there cannot be a woman closer yet to God than Martha.

**Hale:** How is Rebecca charged, Mr. Nurse?

**Francis,** *with a mocking, half-hearted laugh:* For murder, she's charged! *Mockingly quoting the warrant:* "For the marvelous and supernatural murder of Goody Putnam's babies." What am I to do, Mr. Hale?

**Hale,** *turns from* FRANCIS, *deeply troubled, then:* Believe me, Mr. Nurse, if Rebecca Nurse be tainted, then nothing's left to stop the whole green world from burning. Let you rest upon the justice of the court; the court will send her home, I know it.

**Francis:** You cannot mean she will be tried in court!

**Hale,** *pleading:* Nurse, though our hearts break, we cannot flinch; these are new times, sir. There is a misty plot afoot so subtle we should be criminal to cling to old respects and ancient friendships. I have seen too many frightful proofs in court—the Devil is alive in Salem, and we dare not quail to follow wherever the accusing finger points!

**Proctor,** *angered:* How may such a woman murder children?

**Hale,** *in great pain:* Man, remember, until an hour before the Devil fell, God thought him beautiful in Heaven.

**Giles:** I never said my wife were a witch, Mr. Hale; I only said she were reading books!

**Hale:** Mr. Corey, exactly what complaint were made on your wife?

**Giles:** That bloody mongrel Walcott charge her. Y'see, he buy a pig of my wife four or five year ago, and the pig died soon after. So he come dancin' in for his money back. So my Martha, she says to him, "Walcott, if you haven't the wit to feed a pig properly, you'll not live to own many," she says. Now he goes to court and claims that from that day to this he cannot keep a pig alive for more than four weeks because my Martha be-witch them with her books!

*Enter* EZEKIEL CHEEVER. *A shocked silence.*

**Cheever:** Good evening to you, Proctor.
**Proctor:** Why, Mr. Cheever. Good evening.
**Cheever:** Good evening, all. Good evening, Mr. Hale.
**Proctor:** I hope you come not on business of the court.
**Cheever:** I do, Proctor, aye. I am clerk of the court now, y'know.

*Enter* MARSHAL HERRICK, *a man in his early thirties, who is somewhat shamefaced at the moment.*

**Giles:** It's a pity, Ezekiel, that an honest tailor might have gone to Heaven must burn in Hell. You'll burn for this, do you know it?
**Cheever:** You know yourself I must do as I'm told. You surely know that, Giles. And I'd as lief[2] you'd not be sending me to Hell. I like not the sound of it, I tell you; I like not the sound of it. *He fears* PROCTOR, *but starts to reach inside his coat.* Now believe me, Proctor, how heavy be the law, all its tonnage I do carry on my back tonight. *He takes out a warrant.* I have a warrant for your wife.
**Proctor,** *to* HALE: You said she were not charged!
**Hale:** I know nothin' of it. *To* CHEEVER: When were she charged?
**Cheever:** I am given sixteen warrant tonight, sir, and she is one.
**Proctor:** Who charged her?
**Cheever:** Why, Abigail Williams charge her.
**Proctor:** On what proof, what proof?
**Cheever,** *looking about the room:* Mr. Proctor, I have little time. The court bid me search your house, but I like not to search a house. So will you hand me any poppets that your wife may keep here?
**Proctor:** Poppets?
**Elizabeth:** I never kept no poppets, not since I were a girl.
**Cheever,** *embarrassed, glancing toward the mantel where sits* MARY WARREN's *poppet:* I spy a poppet, Goody Proctor.
**Elizabeth:** Oh! *Going for it:* Why, this is Mary's.

2. **lief:** gladly.

**Cheever,** *shyly:* Would you please to give it to me?
**Elizabeth,** *handing it to him, asks* HALE: Has the court discovered a text in poppets now?
**Cheever,** *carefully holding the poppet:* Do you keep any others in this house?
**Proctor:** No, not this one either till tonight. What signifies a poppet?
**Cheever:** Why, a poppet—*he gingerly turns the poppet over*—a poppet may signify— Now, woman, will you please to come with me?
**Proctor:** She will not! *To* ELIZABETH: Fetch Mary here.
**Cheever,** *ineptly reaching toward* ELIZABETH: No, no, I am forbid to leave her from my sight.
**Proctor,** *pushing his arm away:* You'll leave her out of sight and out of mind, Mister. Fetch Mary, Elizabeth. ELIZABETH *goes upstairs.*
**Hale:** What signifies a poppet, Mr. Cheever?
**Cheever,** *turning the poppet over in his hands:* Why, they say it may signify that she— *He has lifted the poppet's skirt, and his eyes widen in astonished fear.* Why, this, this—
**Proctor,** *reaching for the poppet:* What's there?
**Cheever:** Why—*he draws out a long needle from the poppet*—it is a needle! Herrick, Herrick, it is a needle!

HERRICK *comes toward him.*

**Proctor,** *angrily, bewildered:* And what signifies a needle!
**Cheever,** *his hands shaking:* Why, this go hard with her, Proctor, this—I had my doubts, Proctor, I had my doubts, but here's calamity. *To* HALE, *showing the needle:* You see it, sir, it is a needle!
**Hale:** Why? What meanin' has it?
**Cheever,** *wide-eyed, trembling:* The girl, the Williams girl, Abigail Williams, sir. She sat to dinner in Reverend Parris's house tonight, and

without word nor warnin' she falls to the floor. Like a struck beast, he says, and screamed a scream that a bull would weep to hear. And he goes to save her, and, stuck two inches in the flesh of her belly, he draw a needle out. And demandin' of her how she come to be so stabbed, she—*to* PROCTOR *now*—testify it were your wife's familiar spirit pushed it in.

**Proctor:** Why, she done it herself! *To* HALE: I hope you're not takin' this for proof, Mister!

HALE, *struck by the proof, is silent.*

**Cheever:** 'Tis hard proof! *To* HALE: I find her a poppet Goody Proctor keeps. I have found it, sir. And in the belly of the poppet a needle's stuck. I tell you true, Proctor, I never warranted to see such proof of Hell, and I bid you obstruct me not, for I—

*Enter* ELIZABETH *with* MARY WARREN. PROCTOR, *seeing* MARY WARREN, *draws her by the arm to* HALE.

**Proctor:** Here now! Mary, how did this poppet come into my house?

**Mary Warren,** *frightened for herself, her voice very small:* What poppet's that, sir?

**Proctor,** *impatiently, pointing at the doll in* CHEEVER'*s hand:* This poppet, this poppet.

**Mary Warren,** *evasively, looking at it:* Why, I—I think it is mine.

**Proctor:** It is your poppet, is it not?

**Mary Warren,** *not understanding the direction of this:* It—is, sir.

**Proctor:** And how did it come into this house?

**Mary Warren,** *glancing about at the avid faces:* Why—I made it in the court, sir, and—give it to Goody Proctor tonight.

**Proctor,** *to* HALE: Now, sir—do you have it?

**Hale:** Mary Warren, a needle have been found inside this poppet.

**Mary Warren,** *bewildered:* Why, I meant no harm by it, sir.

**Proctor,** *quickly:* You stuck that needle in yourself?

**Mary Warren:** I—I believe I did, sir, I—

**Proctor,** *to* HALE: What say you now?

**Hale,** *watching* MARY WARREN *closely:* Child, you are certain this be your natural memory? May it be, perhaps, that someone conjures you even now to say this?

**Mary Warren:** Conjures me? Why, no, sir, I am entirely myself, I think. Let you ask Susanna Walcott—she saw me sewin' it in court. *Or better still:* Ask Abby, Abby sat beside me when I made it.

**Proctor,** *to* HALE, *of* CHEEVER: Bid him begone. Your mind is surely settled now. Bid him out, Mr. Hale.

**Elizabeth:** What signifies a needle?

**Hale:** Mary—you charge a cold and cruel murder on Abigail.

**Mary Warren:** Murder! I charge no—

**Hale:** Abigail were stabbed tonight; a needle were found stuck into her belly—

**Elizabeth:** And she charges me?

**Hale:** Aye.

**Elizabeth,** *her breath knocked out:* Why—! The girl is murder! She must be ripped out of the world!

**Cheever,** *pointing at* ELIZABETH: You've heard that, sir! Ripped out of the world! Herrick, you heard it!

**Proctor,** *suddenly snatching the warrant out of* CHEEVER'*s hands:* Out with you.

**Cheever:** Proctor, you dare not touch the warrant.

**Proctor,** *ripping the warrant:* Out with you!

**Cheever:** You've ripped the Deputy Governor's warrant, man!

**Proctor:** Damn the Deputy Governor! Out of my house!

**Hale:** Now, Proctor, Proctor!

**Proctor:** Get y'gone with them! You are a broken minister.

**Hale:** Proctor, if she is innocent, the court—

**Proctor:** If *she* is innocent! Why do you never wonder if Parris be innocent, or Abigail? Is the accuser always holy now? Were they born this morning as clean as God's fingers? I'll tell you what's walking Salem—vengeance is walking Salem. We are what we always were in Salem, but now the little crazy children are jangling the keys of the kingdom, and common vengeance writes the law! This warrant's vengeance! I'll not give my wife to vengeance!

**Elizabeth:** I'll go, John—

**Proctor:** You will not go!

**Herrick:** I have nine men outside. You cannot keep her. The law binds me, John, I cannot budge.

**Proctor,** *to* HALE, *ready to break him:* Will you see her taken?

**Hale:** Proctor, the court is just—

**Proctor:** Pontius Pilate![3] God will not let you wash your hands of this!

**Elizabeth:** John—I think I must go with them. *He cannot bear to look at her.* Mary, there is bread enough for the morning; you will bake, in the afternoon. Help Mr. Proctor as you were his daughter—you owe me that, and much more. *She is fighting her weeping. To* PROCTOR: When the children wake, speak nothing of witchcraft—it will frighten them. *She cannot go on.*

**Proctor:** I will bring you home. I will bring you soon.

**Elizabeth:** Oh, John, bring me soon!

**Proctor:** I will fall like an ocean on that court! Fear nothing, Elizabeth.

**Elizabeth,** *with great fear:* I will fear nothing. *She looks about the room, as though to fix it in her mind.* Tell the children I have gone to visit someone sick.

*She walks out the door,* HERRICK *and* CHEEVER *behind her. For a moment,* PROCTOR *watches from the doorway. The clank of chain is heard.*

**Proctor:** Herrick! Herrick, don't chain her! *He rushes out the door. From outside:* Damn you, man, you will not chain her! Off with them! I'll not have it! I will not have her chained!

*There are other men's voices against his.* HALE, *in a fever of guilt and uncertainty, turns from the door to avoid the sight;* MARY WARREN *bursts into tears and sits weeping.* GILES COREY *calls to* HALE.

**Giles:** And yet silent, minister? It is fraud, you know it is fraud! What keeps you, man?

PROCTOR *is half braced, half pushed into the room by two deputies and* HERRICK.

**Proctor:** I'll pay you, Herrick, I will surely pay you!

**Herrick,** *panting:* In God's name, John, I cannot help myself. I must chain them all. Now let you keep inside this house till I am gone! *He goes out with his deputies.*

PROCTOR *stands there, gulping air. Horses and a wagon creaking are heard.*

3. **Pontius Pilate** (pun′chəs pī′lət) (1st century A.D.): Roman official who unwillingly condemned Christ to death. Pilate is said to have declared, "I am innocent of the blood of this just man" (Matthew 27:24).

**Hale,** *in great uncertainty:* Mr. Proctor—

**Proctor:** Out of my sight!

**Hale:** Charity, Proctor, charity. What I have heard in her favor, I will not fear to testify in court. God help me, I cannot judge her guilty or innocent—I know not. Only this consider: the world goes mad, and it profit nothing you should lay the cause to the vengeance of a little girl.

**Proctor:** You are a coward! Though you be ordained in God's own tears, you are a coward now!

**Hale:** Proctor, I cannot think God be provoked so grandly by such a petty cause. The jails are packed—our greatest judges sit in Salem now—and hangin's promised. Man, we must look to cause proportionate. Were there murder done, perhaps, and never brought to light? Abomination? Some secret blasphemy that stinks to Heaven? Think on cause, man, and let you help me to discover it. For there's your way, believe it, there is your only way, when such confusion strikes upon the world. *He goes to* GILES *and* FRANCIS. Let you counsel among yourselves; think on your village and what may have drawn from heaven such thundering wrath upon you all. I shall pray God open up our eyes.

HALE *goes out.*

**Francis,** *struck by* HALE's *mood:* I never heard no murder done in Salem.

**Proctor**—*he has been reached by* HALE's *words:* Leave me, Francis, leave me.

**Giles,** *shaken:* John—tell me, are we lost?

**Proctor:** Go home now, Giles. We'll speak on it tomorrow.

**Giles:** Let you think on it. We'll come early, eh?

**Proctor:** Aye. Go now, Giles.

**Giles:** Good night, then.

GILES COREY *and* FRANCIS NURSE *go out. After a moment:*

**Mary Warren,** *in a fearful squeak of a voice:* Mr. Proctor, very likely they'll let her come home once they're given proper evidence.

**Proctor:** You're coming to the court with me, Mary. You will tell it in the court.

**Mary Warren:** I cannot charge murder on Abigail.

**Proctor,** *moving menacingly toward her:* You will tell the court how that poppet come here and who stuck the needle in.

**Mary Warren:** She'll kill me for sayin' that! PROC-TOR *continues toward her.* Abby'll charge lechery on you, Mr. Proctor!

**Proctor,** *halting:* She's told you!

**Mary Warren:** I have known it, sir. She'll ruin you with it, I know she will.

**Proctor,** *hesitating, and with deep hatred of himself:* Good. Then her saintliness is done with. MARY *backs from him.* We will slide together into our pit; you will tell the court what you know.

**Mary Warren,** *in terror:* I cannot, they'll turn on me—

PROCTOR *strides and catches her, and she is repeating, "I cannot, I cannot!"*

**Proctor:** My wife will never die for me! I will bring your guts into your mouth but that goodness will not die for me!

**Mary Warren,** *struggling to escape him:* I cannot do it, I cannot!

**Proctor,** *grasping her by the throat as though he would strangle her:* Make your peace with it! Now Hell and Heaven grapple on our backs, and all our old pretense is ripped away—make your peace! *He throws her to the floor, where she sobs, "I cannot, I cannot . . ." And now, half to himself, staring, and turning to the open door:* Peace. It is a providence, and no great change; we are only what we always were, but naked now. *He walks as though toward a great horror, facing the open sky.* Aye, naked! And the wind, God's icy wind, will blow!

*And she is over and over again sobbing, "I cannot, I cannot, I cannot," as*

*The curtain falls*

# Response and Analysis

## Act Two

### Reading Check

1. At the beginning of the act, why does Elizabeth want John to go to Salem?

2. What gift does Mary Warren give Elizabeth?

3. According to Elizabeth, what is Abigail's true objective in court?

4. Why is Rebecca Nurse in jail?

5. What does John Proctor want Mary to testify?

### Thinking Critically

6. Describe the relationship between John and Elizabeth Proctor. Explain the **metaphor** of the "everlasting funeral" that John sees in Elizabeth's heart.

7. Based on Mary's statements, what do you **infer** is the real reason Mary gives Elizabeth the gift?

8. How do you **interpret** Mary's visions and accusations? What clues does Miller give for her **motivation**?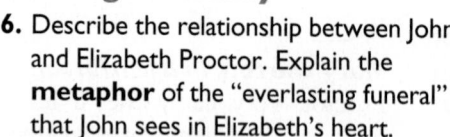

9. Why does Hale become suspicious of the Proctors? What is the **irony** in Hale's urging Proctor to show "charity"?

10. The **protagonist** is the central character who drives the action and is usually considered the hero or heroine. The **antagonist** struggles against the protagonist, often with cruel or destructive intent. At this point in the play, which character seems to be the protagonist, and which is the antagonist?

11. Describe Proctor's **internal conflict.** How could it relate to a broader conflict in the play—between public and private selves?

## WRITING

### Analyzing Abby

Write a **character analysis** of Abigail Williams. Include details from Acts One and Two that reveal the following information about her character: what others think of her, what she does and says, and how she sees herself. Be sure to include your take on Abigail's motives for her actions.

# Act Three

*The vestry room of the Salem meeting house, now serving as the anteroom of the General Court.*

*As the curtain rises, the room is empty, but for sunlight pouring through two high windows in the back wall. The room is solemn, even forbidding. Heavy beams jut out, boards of random widths make up the walls. At the right are two doors leading into the meeting house proper, where the court is being held. At the left another door leads outside.*

*There is a plain bench at the left, and another at the right. In the center a rather long meeting table, with stools and a considerable armchair snugged up to it.*

*Through the partitioning wall at the right we hear a prosecutor's voice,* JUDGE HATHORNE'S, *asking a question; then a woman's voice,* MARTHA COREY'S, *replying.*

**Hathorne's Voice:** Now, Martha Corey, there is abundant evidence in our hands to show that you have given yourself to the reading of fortunes. Do you deny it?

**Martha Corey's Voice:** I am innocent to a witch. I know not what a witch is.

**Hathorne's Voice:** How do you know, then, that you are not a witch?

**Martha Corey's Voice:** If I were, I would know it.

**Hathorne's Voice:** Why do you hurt these children?

**Martha Corey's Voice:** I do not hurt them. I scorn it!

**Giles' Voice,** *roaring:* I have evidence for the court!

*Voices of townspeople rise in excitement.*

**Danforth's Voice:** You will keep your seat!

**Giles' Voice:** Thomas Putnam is reaching out for land!

**Danforth's Voice:** Remove that man, Marshal!

**Giles' Voice:** You're hearing lies, lies!

*A roaring goes up from the people.*

**Hathorne's Voice:** Arrest him, Excellency!

**Giles' Voice:** I have evidence. Why will you not hear my evidence?

*The door opens and* GILES *is half carried into the vestry room by* HERRICK. FRANCIS NURSE *enters, trailing anxiously behind* GILES.

**Giles:** Hands off, damn you, let me go!

**Herrick:** Giles, Giles!

**Giles:** Out of my way, Herrick! I bring evidence—

**Herrick:** You cannot go in there, Giles; it's a court!

*Enter* HALE *from the court.*

**Hale:** Pray be calm a moment.

**Giles:** You, Mr. Hale, go in there and demand I speak.

**Hale:** A moment, sir, a moment.

**Giles:** They'll be hangin' my wife!

JUDGE HATHORNE *enters. He is in his sixties, a bitter, remorseless Salem judge.*

**Hathorne:** How do you dare come roarin' into this court! Are you gone daft, Corey?

**Giles:** You're not a Boston judge yet, Hathorne. You'll not call me daft!

*Enter* DEPUTY GOVERNOR DANFORTH *and, behind him,* EZEKIEL CHEEVER *and* PARRIS. *On his appearance, silence falls.* DANFORTH *is a grave man in his sixties, of some humor and sophistication that do not, however, interfere with an exact loyalty to his position and his cause. He comes down to* GILES, *who awaits his wrath.*

**Danforth,** *looking directly at* GILES: Who is this man?

**Parris:** Giles Corey, sir, and a more contentious—

**Giles,** *to* PARRIS: I am asked the question, and I am old enough to answer it! *To* DANFORTH, *who impresses him and to whom he smiles through his strain:* My name is Corey, sir, Giles Corey. I have six hundred acres, and timber in addition. It is my wife you be condemning now. *He indicates the courtroom.*

**Danforth:** And how do you imagine to help her cause with such contemptuous riot? Now be gone. Your old age alone keeps you out of jail for this.

**Giles,** *beginning to plead:* They be tellin' lies about my wife, sir, I—

**Danforth:** Do you take it upon yourself to determine what this court shall believe and what it shall set aside?

**Giles:** Your Excellency, we mean no disrespect for—

**Danforth:** Disrespect indeed! It is disruption, Mister. This is the highest court of the supreme government of this province, do you know it?

**Giles,** *beginning to weep:* Your Excellency, I only said she were readin' books, sir, and they come and take her out of my house for—

**Danforth,** *mystified:* Books! What books?

**Giles,** *through helpless sobs:* It is my third wife, sir; I never had no wife that be so taken with books, and I thought to find the cause of it, d'y'see, but it were no witch I blamed her for. *He is openly weeping.* I have broke charity with the woman, I have broke charity with her. *He covers his face, ashamed.* DANFORTH *is respectfully silent.*

**Hale:** Excellency, he claims hard evidence for his wife's defense. I think that in all justice you must—

**Danforth:** Then let him submit his evidence in proper affidavit.[1] You are certainly aware of our procedure here, Mr. Hale. *To* HERRICK: Clear this room.

**Herrick:** Come now, Giles. *He gently pushes* COREY *out.*

**Francis:** We are desperate, sir; we come here three days now and cannot be heard.

**Danforth:** Who is this man?

**Francis:** Francis Nurse, Your Excellency.

**Hale:** His wife's Rebecca that were condemned this morning.

**Danforth:** Indeed! I am amazed to find you in such uproar. I have only good report of your character, Mr. Nurse.

**Hathorne:** I think they must both be arrested in contempt, sir.

**Danforth,** *to* FRANCIS: Let you write your plea, and in due time I will—

**Francis:** Excellency, we have proof for your eyes; God forbid you shut them to it. The girls, sir, the girls are frauds.

**Danforth:** What's that?

**Francis:** We have proof of it, sir. They are all deceiving you.

DANFORTH *is shocked, but studying* FRANCIS.

1. **affidavit** (af′ə·dā′vit): written statement made under oath before a legal authority.

**Hathorne:** This is contempt, sir, contempt!

**Danforth:** Peace, Judge Hathorne. Do you know who I am, Mr. Nurse?

**Francis:** I surely do, sir, and I think you must be a wise judge to be what you are.

**Danforth:** And do you know that near to four hundred are in the jails from Marblehead to Lynn, and upon my signature?

**Francis:** I—

**Danforth:** And seventy-two condemned to hang by that signature?

**Francis:** Excellency, I never thought to say it to such a weighty judge, but you are deceived.

*Enter* GILES COREY *from left. All turn to see as he beckons in* MARY WARREN *with* PROCTOR. MARY *is keeping her eyes to the ground;* PROCTOR *has her elbow as though she were near collapse.*

**Parris,** *on seeing her, in shock:* Mary Warren! *He goes directly to bend close to her face.* What are you about here?

**Proctor,** *pressing* PARRIS *away from her with a gentle but firm motion of protectiveness:* She would speak with the Deputy Governor.

**Danforth,** *shocked by this, turns to* HERRICK: Did you not tell me Mary Warren were sick in bed?

**Herrick:** She were, Your Honor. When I go to fetch her to the court last week, she said she were sick.

**Giles:** She has been strivin' with her soul all week, Your Honor; she comes now to tell the truth of this to you.

**Danforth:** Who is this?

**Proctor:** John Proctor, sir. Elizabeth Proctor is my wife.

**Parris:** Beware this man, Your Excellency, this man is mischief.

**Hale,** *excitedly:* I think you must hear the girl, sir, she—

**Danforth,** *who has become very interested in* MARY WARREN *and only raises a hand toward* HALE: Peace. What would you tell us, Mary Warren?

PROCTOR *looks at her, but she cannot speak.*

**Proctor:** She never saw no spirits, sir.

**Danforth,** *with great alarm and surprise, to* MARY: Never saw no spirits!

**Giles,** *eagerly:* Never.

**Proctor,** *reaching into his jacket:* She has signed a deposition, sir—

**Danforth,** *instantly:* No, no, I accept no depositions. *He is rapidly calculating this; he turns from her to* PROCTOR. Tell me, Mr. Proctor, have you given out this story in the village?

**Proctor:** We have not.

**Parris:** They've come to overthrow the court, sir! This man is—

**Danforth:** I pray you, Mr. Parris. Do you know, Mr. Proctor, that the entire contention of the state in these trials is that the voice of Heaven is speaking through the children?

**Proctor:** I know that, sir.

**Danforth,** *thinks, staring at* PROCTOR, *then turns to* MARY WARREN: And you, Mary Warren, how came you to cry out people for sending their spirits against you?

**Mary Warren:** It were pretense, sir.

**Danforth:** I cannot hear you.

**Proctor:** It were pretense, she says.

**Danforth:** Ah? And the other girls? Susanna Walcott, and—the others? They are also pretending?

**Mary Warren:** Aye, sir.

**Danforth,** *wide-eyed:* Indeed. *Pause. He is baffled by this. He turns to study* PROCTOR's *face.*

**Parris,** *in a sweat:* Excellency, you surely cannot think to let so vile a lie be spread in open court!

**Danforth:** Indeed not, but it strike hard upon me that she will dare come here with such a tale. Now, Mr. Proctor, before I decide whether I shall hear you or not, it is my duty to tell you this. We burn a hot fire here; it melts down all concealment.

**Proctor:** I know that, sir.

**Danforth:** Let me continue. I understand well, a husband's tenderness may drive him to extravagance in defense of a wife. Are you certain in your conscience, Mister, that your evidence is the truth?

**Proctor:** It is. And you will surely know it.

**Danforth:** And you thought to declare this revelation in the open court before the public?

**Proctor:** I thought I would, aye—with your permission.

**Danforth,** *his eyes narrowing:* Now, sir, what is your purpose in so doing?

**Proctor:** Why, I—I would free my wife, sir.

**Danforth:** There lurks nowhere in your heart, nor hidden in your spirit, any desire to undermine this court?

**Proctor,** *with the faintest faltering:* Why, no, sir.

**Cheever,** *clears his throat, awakening:* I— Your Excellency.

**Danforth:** Mr. Cheever.

**Cheever:** I think it be my duty, sir—*Kindly, to* PROCTOR: You'll not deny it, John. *To* DANFORTH: When we come to take his wife, he damned the court and ripped your warrant.

**Parris:** Now you have it!

**Danforth:** He did that, Mr. Hale?

**Hale,** *takes a breath:* Aye, he did.

**Proctor:** It were a temper, sir. I knew not what I did.

**Danforth,** *studying him:* Mr. Proctor.

**Proctor:** Aye, sir.

**Danforth,** *straight into his eyes:* Have you ever seen the Devil?

**Proctor:** No, sir.

**Danforth:** You are in all respects a Gospel Christian?

**Proctor:** I am, sir.

**Parris:** Such a Christian that will not come to church but once in a month!

**Danforth,** *restrained—he is curious:* Not come to church?

**Proctor:** I—I have no love for Mr. Parris. It is no secret. But God I surely love.

**Cheever:** He plow on Sunday, sir.

**Danforth:** Plow on Sunday!

**Cheever,** *apologetically:* I think it be evidence, John. I am an official of the court, I cannot keep it.

**Proctor:** I—I have once or twice plowed on Sunday. I have three children, sir, and until last year my land give little.

**Giles:** You'll find other Christians that do plow on Sunday if the truth be known.

**Hale:** Your Honor, I cannot think you may judge the man on such evidence.

**Danforth:** I judge nothing. *Pause. He keeps watching* PROCTOR, *who tries to meet his gaze.* I tell you straight, Mister—I have seen marvels in this court. I have seen people choked before my eyes by spirits; I have seen them stuck by pins and slashed by daggers. I have until this moment not the slightest reason to suspect that the children may be deceiving me. Do you understand my meaning?

**Proctor:** Excellency, does it not strike upon you that so many of these women have lived so long with such upright reputation, and—

**Parris:** Do you read the Gospel, Mr. Proctor?

**Proctor:** I read the Gospel.

**Parris:** I think not, or you should surely know that Cain were an upright man, and yet he did kill Abel.[2]

**Proctor:** Aye, God tells us that. *To* DANFORTH: But who tells us Rebecca Nurse murdered seven babies by sending out her spirit on them? It is the children only, and this one will swear she lied to you.

DANFORTH *considers, then beckons* HATHORNE *to him.* HATHORNE *leans in, and he speaks in his ear.* HATHORNE *nods.*

**Hathorne:** Aye, she's the one.

**Danforth:** Mr. Proctor, this morning, your wife send me a claim in which she states that she is pregnant now.

**Proctor:** My wife pregnant!

**Danforth:** There be no sign of it—we have examined her body.

**Proctor:** But if she say she is pregnant, then she must be! That woman will never lie, Mr. Danforth.

**Danforth:** She will not?

**Proctor:** Never, sir, never.

**Danforth:** We have thought it too convenient to be credited. However, if I should tell you now that I will let her be kept another month; and if she begin to show her natural signs, you shall have her living yet another year until she is delivered—what say you to that? JOHN PROCTOR *is struck silent.* Come now. You say your only purpose is to save your wife. Good, then, she is saved at least this year, and a year is long. What say you, sir? It is done now. *In conflict,* PROCTOR *glances at* FRANCIS *and* GILES. Will you drop this charge?

**Proctor:** I—I think I cannot.

**Danforth,** *now an almost imperceptible hardness in his voice:* Then your purpose is somewhat larger.

**Parris:** He's come to overthrow this court, Your Honor!

**Proctor:** These are my friends. Their wives are also accused—

**Danforth,** *with a sudden briskness of manner:* I judge you not, sir. I am ready to hear your evidence.

**Proctor:** I come not to hurt the court; I only—

**Danforth,** *cutting him off:* Marshal, go into the court and bid Judge Stoughton and Judge Sewall declare recess for one hour. And let them go to the tavern, if they will. All witnesses and prisoners are to be kept in the building.

**Herrick:** Aye, sir. *Very deferentially:* If I may say it, sir, I know this man all my life. It is a good man, sir.

**Danforth**—*it is the reflection on himself he resents:* I am sure of it, Marshal. HERRICK *nods, then goes out.* Now, what deposition do you have for us, Mr. Proctor? And I beg you be clear, open as the sky, and honest.

**Proctor,** *as he takes out several papers:* I am no lawyer, so I'll—

**Danforth:** The pure in heart need no lawyers. Proceed as you will.

**Proctor,** *handing* DANFORTH *a paper:* Will you read this first, sir? It's a sort of testament. The people signing it declare their good opinion of Rebecca, and my wife, and Martha Corey. DANFORTH *looks down at the paper.*

**Parris,** *to enlist* DANFORTH*'s sarcasm:* Their good opinion! *But* DANFORTH *goes on reading, and* PROCTOR *is heartened.*

**Proctor:** These are all landholding farmers, members of the church. *Delicately, trying to point out a paragraph:* If you'll notice, sir—they've known the women many years and never saw no sign they had dealings with the Devil.

PARRIS *nervously moves over and reads over* DANFORTH*'s shoulder.*

**Danforth,** *glancing down a long list:* How many names are here?

**Francis:** Ninety-one, Your Excellency.

**Parris,** *sweating:* These people should be summoned. DANFORTH *looks up at him questioningly.* For questioning.

**Francis,** *trembling with anger:* Mr. Danforth, I gave them all my word no harm would come to them for signing this.

**Parris:** This is a clear attack upon the court!

2. **Cain . . . Abel:** According to the Book of Genesis, Cain, the oldest son of Adam and Eve, killed his brother Abel.

**Hale,** *to* PARRIS, *trying to contain himself:* Is every defense an attack upon the court? Can no one—?

**Parris:** All innocent and Christian people are happy for the courts in Salem! These people are gloomy for it. *To* DANFORTH *directly:* And I think you will want to know, from each and every one of them, what discontents them with you!

**Hathorne:** I think they ought to be examined, sir.

**Danforth:** It is not necessarily an attack, I think. Yet—

**Francis:** These are all covenanted Christians, sir.

**Danforth:** Then I am sure they may have nothing to fear. *Hands* CHEEVER *the paper.* Mr. Cheever, have warrants drawn for all of these—arrest for examination. *To* PROCTOR: Now, Mister, what other information do you have for us? FRANCIS *is still standing, horrified.* You may sit, Mr. Nurse.

**Francis:** I have brought trouble on these people; I have—

**Danforth:** No, old man, you have not hurt these people if they are of good conscience. But you must understand, sir, that a person is either with this court or he must be counted against it, there be no road between. This is a sharp time, now, a precise time—we live no longer in the dusky afternoon when evil mixed itself with good and befuddled the world. Now, by God's grace, the shining sun is up, and them that fear not light will surely praise it. I hope you will be one of those. MARY WARREN *suddenly sobs.* She's not hearty, I see.

**Proctor:** No, she's not, sir. *To* MARY, *bending to her, holding her hand, quietly:* Now remember what the angel Raphael said to the boy Tobias.[3] Remember it.

**Mary Warren,** *hardly audible:* Aye.

**Proctor:** "Do that which is good, and no harm shall come to thee."

**Mary Warren:** Aye.

**Danforth:** Come, man, we wait you.

MARSHAL HERRICK *returns, and takes his post at the door.*

**Giles:** John, my deposition, give him mine.

**Proctor:** Aye. *He hands* DANFORTH *another paper.* This is Mr. Corey's deposition.

**Danforth:** Oh? *He looks down at it. Now*

HATHORNE *comes behind him and reads with him.*

**Hathorne,** *suspiciously:* What lawyer drew this, Corey?

**Giles:** You know I never hired a lawyer in my life, Hathorne.

**Danforth,** *finishing the reading:* It is very well phrased. My compliments. Mr. Parris, if Mr. Putnam is in the court, will you bring him in? HATHORNE *takes the deposition, and walks to the window with it.* PARRIS *goes into the court.* You have no legal training, Mr. Corey?

**Giles,** *very pleased:* I have the best, sir—I am thirty-three time in court in my life. And always plaintiff, too.

**Danforth:** Oh, then you're much put-upon.

**Giles:** I am never put-upon; I know my rights, sir, and I will have them. You know, your father tried a case of mine—might be thirty-five year ago, I think.

**Danforth:** Indeed.

**Giles:** He never spoke to you of it?

**Danforth:** No, I cannot recall it.

**Giles:** That's strange, he give me nine pound damages. He were a fair judge, your father. Y'see, I had a white mare that time, and this fellow come to borrow the mare— *Enter* PARRIS *with* THOMAS PUTNAM. *When he sees* PUTNAM, GILES' *ease goes; he is hard.* Aye, there he is.

**Danforth:** Mr. Putnam, I have here an accusation by Mr. Corey against you. He states that you coldly prompted your daughter to cry witchery upon George Jacobs that is now in jail.

**Putnam:** It is a lie.

**Danforth,** *turning to* GILES: Mr. Putnam states your charge is a lie. What say you to that?

**Giles,** *furious, his fists clenched:* A fart on Thomas Putnam, that is what I say to that!

**Danforth:** What proof do you submit for your charge, sir?

**Giles:** My proof is there! *Pointing to the paper.* If Jacobs hangs for a witch he forfeit up his property—that's law! And there is none but Putnam with the coin to buy so great a piece. This man is killing his neighbors for their land!

**Danforth:** But proof, sir, proof.

**Giles,** *pointing at his deposition:* The proof is there! I have it from an honest man who heard Putnam say it! The day his daughter cried out on Jacobs, he said she'd given him a fair gift of land.

---

3. **Raphael...Tobias:** In the Old Testament Apocrypha, the archangel Raphael guides Tobias, an exiled Jew.

**Hathorne:** And the name of this man?

**Giles,** *taken aback:* What name?

**Hathorne:** The man that give you this information.

**Giles,** *hesitates, then:* Why, I—I cannot give you his name.

**Hathorne:** And why not?

**Giles,** *hesitates, then bursts out:* You know well why not! He'll lay in jail if I give his name!

**Hathorne:** This is contempt of the court, Mr. Danforth!

**Danforth,** *to avoid that:* You will surely tell us the name.

**Giles:** I will not give you no name. I mentioned my wife's name once and I'll burn in hell long enough for that. I stand mute.

**Danforth:** In that case, I have no choice but to arrest you for contempt of this court, do you know that?

**Giles:** This is a hearing; you cannot clap me for contempt of a hearing.

**Danforth:** Oh, it is a proper lawyer! Do you wish me to declare the court in full session here? Or will you give me good reply?

**Giles,** *faltering:* I cannot give you no name, sir, I cannot.

**Danforth:** You are a foolish old man. Mr. Cheever, begin the record. The court is now in session. I ask you, Mr. Corey—

**Proctor,** *breaking in:* Your Honor—he has the story in confidence, sir, and he—

**Parris:** The Devil lives on such confidences! *To* DANFORTH: Without confidences there could be no conspiracy, Your Honor!

**Hathorne:** I think it must be broken, sir.

**Danforth,** *to* GILES: Old man, if your informant tells the truth let him come here openly like a decent man. But if he hide in anonymity I must know why. Now sir, the government and central church demand of you the name of him who reported Mr. Thomas Putnam a common murderer.

**Hale:** Excellency—

**Danforth:** Mr. Hale.

**Hale:** We cannot blink it more. There is a prodigious fear of this court in the country—

**Danforth:** Then there is a prodigious guilt in the country. Are *you* afraid to be questioned here?

**Hale:** I may only fear the Lord, sir, but there is fear in the country nevertheless.

**Danforth,** *angered now:* Reproach me not with the fear in the country; there is fear in the country because there is a moving plot to topple Christ in the country!

**Hale:** But it does not follow that everyone accused is part of it.

**Danforth:** No uncorrupted man may fear this court, Mr. Hale! None! *To* GILES. You are under arrest in contempt of this court. Now sit you down and take counsel with yourself, or you will be set in the jail until you decide to answer all questions.

GILES COREY *makes a rush for* PUTNAM. PROCTOR *lunges and holds him.*

**Proctor:** No, Giles!

**Giles,** *over* PROCTOR's *shoulder at* PUTNAM: I'll cut your throat, Putnam, I'll kill you yet!

**Proctor,** *forcing him into a chair:* Peace, Giles, peace. *Releasing him.* We'll prove ourselves. Now we will. *He starts to turn to* DANFORTH.

**Giles:** Say nothin' more, John. *Pointing at* DANFORTH: He's only playin' you! He means to hang us all!

MARY WARREN *bursts into sobs.*

**Danforth:** This is a court of law, Mister. I'll have no effrontery here!

**Proctor:** Forgive him, sir, for his old age. Peace, Giles, we'll prove it all now. *He lifts up* MARY's *chin.* You cannot weep, Mary. Remember the angel, what he say to the boy. Hold to it, now; there is your rock. MARY *quiets. He takes out a paper, and turns to* DANFORTH. This is Mary Warren's deposition. I—I would ask you remember, sir, while you read it, that until two week ago she were no different than the other children are today. *He is speaking reasonably, restraining all his fears, his anger, his anxiety.* You saw her scream, she howled, she swore familiar spirits choked her; she even testified that Satan, in the form of women now in jail, tried to win her soul away, and then when she refused—

**Danforth:** We know all this.

**Proctor:** Aye, sir. She swears now that she never saw Satan; not any spirit, vague or clear, that Satan may have sent to hurt her. And she declares her friends are lying now.

PROCTOR *starts to hand* DANFORTH *the deposition,*

*and* HALE *comes up to* DANFORTH *in a trembling state.*

**Hale:** Excellency, a moment. I think this goes to the heart of the matter.

**Danforth,** *with deep misgivings:* It surely does.

**Hale:** I cannot say he is an honest man; I know him little. But in all justice, sir, a claim so weighty cannot be argued by a farmer. In God's name, sir, stop here; send him home and let him come again with a lawyer—

**Danforth,** *patiently:* Now look you, Mr. Hale—

**Hale:** Excellency, I have signed seventy-two death warrants; I am a minister of the Lord, and I dare not take a life without there be a proof so immaculate no slightest qualm of conscience may doubt it.

**Danforth:** Mr. Hale, you surely do not doubt my justice.

**Hale:** I have this morning signed away the soul of Rebecca Nurse, Your Honor. I'll not conceal it, my hand shakes yet as with a wound! I pray you, sir, *this* argument let lawyers present to you.

**Danforth:** Mr. Hale, believe me; for a man of such terrible learning you are most bewildered—I hope you will forgive me. I have been thirty-two year at the bar, sir, and I should be confounded were I called upon to defend these people. Let you consider, now— *To* PROCTOR *and the others:* And I bid you all do likewise. In an ordinary crime, how does one defend the accused? One calls up witnesses to prove his innocence. But witchcraft is *ipso facto,*[4] on its face and by its nature, an invisible crime, is it not? Therefore, who may possibly be witness to it? The witch and the victim. None other. Now we cannot hope the witch will accuse herself; granted? Therefore, we must rely upon her victims—and they do testify, the children certainly do testify. As for the witches, none will deny that we are most eager for all their confessions. Therefore, what is left for a lawyer to bring out? I think I have made my point. Have I not?

**Hale:** But this child claims the girls are not truthful, and if they are not—

**Danforth:** That is precisely what I am about to consider, sir. What more may you ask of me? Unless you doubt my probity?[5]

4. *ipso facto:* by that very fact.
5. **probity:** integrity.

**Hale,** *defeated:* I surely do not, sir. Let you consider it, then.

**Danforth:** And let you put your heart to rest. Her deposition, Mr. Proctor.

PROCTOR *hands it to him.* HATHORNE *rises, goes beside* DANFORTH, *and starts reading.* PARRIS *comes to his other side.* DANFORTH *looks at* JOHN PROCTOR, *then proceeds to read.* HALE *gets up, finds position near the judge, reads too.* PROCTOR *glances at* GILES. FRANCIS *prays silently, hands pressed together.* CHEEVER *waits placidly, the sublime official, dutiful.* MARY WARREN *sobs once.* JOHN PROCTOR *touches her head reassuringly. Presently* DANFORTH *lifts his eyes, stands up, takes out a kerchief and blows his nose. The others stand aside as he moves in thought toward the window.*

**Parris,** *hardly able to contain his anger and fear:* I should like to question—

**Danforth**—*his first real outburst, in which his contempt for* PARRIS *is clear:* Mr. Parris, I bid you be silent! *He stands in silence, looking out the window. Now, having established that he will set the gait:* Mr. Cheever, will you go into the court and bring the children here? CHEEVER *gets up and goes out upstage.* DANFORTH *now turns to* MARY. Mary Warren, how came you to this turnabout? Has Mr. Proctor threatened you for this deposition?

**Mary Warren:** No, sir.

**Danforth:** Has he ever threatened you?

**Mary Warren,** *weaker:* No, sir.

**Danforth,** *sensing a weakening:* Has he threatened you?

**Mary Warren:** No, sir.

**Danforth:** Then you tell me that you sat in my court, callously lying, when you knew that people would hang by your evidence? *She does not answer.* Answer me!

**Mary Warren,** *almost inaudibly:* I did, sir.

**Danforth:** How were you instructed in your life? Do you not know that God damns all liars? *She cannot speak.* Or is it now that you lie?

**Mary Warren:** No, sir—I am with God now.

**Danforth:** You are with God now.

**Mary Warren:** Aye, sir.

**Danforth,** *containing himself:* I will tell you this—you are either lying now, or you were lying in the court, and in either case you have committed perjury and you will go to jail for it. You cannot lightly say you lied, Mary. Do you know that?

**Mary Warren:** I cannot lie no more. I am with God, I am with God.

*But she breaks into sobs at the thought of it, and the right door opens, and enter* SUSANNA WALCOTT, MERCY LEWIS, BETTY PARRIS, *and finally* ABIGAIL. CHEEVER *comes to* DANFORTH.

**Cheever:** Ruth Putnam's not in the court, sir, nor the other children.

**Danforth:** These will be sufficient. Sit you down, children. *Silently they sit.* Your friend, Mary Warren, has given us a deposition. In which she swears that she never saw familiar spirits, apparitions, nor any manifest of the Devil. She claims as well that none of you have seen these things either. *Slight pause.* Now, children, this is a court of law. The law, based upon the Bible, and the Bible, writ by Almighty God, forbid the practice of witchcraft, and describe death as the penalty thereof. But likewise, children, the law and Bible damn all bearers of false witness. *Slight pause.* Now then. It does not escape me that this deposition may be devised to blind us; it may well be that Mary Warren has been conquered by Satan, who sends her here to distract our sacred purpose. If so, her neck will break for it. But if she speak true, I bid you now drop your guile and confess your pretense, for a quick confession will go easier with you. *Pause.* Abigail Williams, rise. ABIGAIL *slowly rises.* Is there any truth in this?

**Abigail:** No, sir.

**Danforth,** *thinks, glances at* MARY, *then back to* ABIGAIL: Children, a very augur bit[6] will now be turned into your souls until your honesty is proved. Will either of you change your positions now, or do you force me to hard questioning?

**Abigail:** I have naught to change, sir. She lies.

**Danforth,** *to* MARY: You would still go on with this?

**Mary Warren,** *faintly:* Aye, sir.

**Danforth,** *turning to* ABIGAIL: A poppet were discovered in Mr. Proctor's house, stabbed by a needle. Mary Warren claims that you sat beside her in the court when she made it, and that you saw her make

---

6. **augur bit:** drilling tool with pointed end and spiral grooves. (The conventional spelling is *auger.*)

---

it and witnessed how she herself stuck her needle into it for safe-keeping. What say you to that?

**Abigail,** *with a slight note of indignation:* It is a lie, sir.

**Danforth,** *after a slight pause:* While you worked for Mr. Proctor, did you see poppets in that house?

**Abigail:** Goody Proctor always kept poppets.

**Proctor:** Your Honor, my wife never kept no poppets. Mary Warren confesses it was her poppet.

**Cheever:** Your Excellency.

**Danforth:** Mr. Cheever.

**Cheever:** When I spoke with Goody Proctor in that house, she said she never kept no poppets. But she said she did keep poppets when she were a girl.

**Proctor:** She has not been a girl these fifteen years, Your Honor.

**Hathorne:** But a poppet will keep fifteen years, will it not?

**Proctor:** It will keep if it is kept, but Mary Warren swears she never saw no poppets in my house, nor anyone else.

**Parris:** Why could there not have been poppets hid where no one ever saw them?

**Proctor,** *furious:* There might also be a dragon with five legs in my house, but no one has ever seen it.

**Parris:** We are here, Your Honor, precisely to discover what no one has ever seen.

**Proctor:** Mr. Danforth, what profit this girl to turn herself about? What may Mary Warren gain but hard questioning and worse?

**Danforth:** You are charging Abigail Williams with a marvelous cool plot to murder, do you understand that?

**Proctor:** I do, sir. I believe she means to murder.

**Danforth,** *pointing at* ABIGAIL, *incredulously:* This child would murder your wife?

**Proctor:** It is not a child. Now hear me, sir. In the sight of the congregation she were twice this year put out of this meetin' house for laughter during prayer.

**Danforth,** *shocked, turning to* ABIGAIL: What's this? Laughter during—!

**Parris:** Excellency, she were under Tituba's power at that time, but she is solemn now.

**Giles:** Aye, now she is solemn and goes to hang people!

**Danforth:** Quiet, man.

**Hathorne:** Surely it have no bearing on the question, sir. He charges contemplation of murder.

**Danforth:** Aye. *He studies* ABIGAIL *for a moment, then:* Continue, Mr. Proctor.

**Proctor:** Mary. Now tell the Governor how you danced in the woods.

**Parris,** *instantly:* Excellency, since I come to Salem this man is blackening my name. He—

**Danforth:** In a moment, sir. *To* MARY WARREN, *sternly, and surprised:* What is this dancing?

**Mary Warren:** I— *She glances at* ABIGAIL, *who is staring down at her remorselessly. Then, appealing to* PROCTOR: Mr. Proctor—

**Proctor,** *taking it right up:* Abigail leads the girls to the woods, Your Honor, and they have danced there naked—

**Parris:** Your Honor, this—

**Proctor,** *at once:* Mr. Parris discovered them himself in the dead of night! There's the "child" she is!

**Danforth**—*it is growing into a nightmare, and he turns, astonished, to* PARRIS: Mr. Parris—

**Parris:** I can only say, sir, that I never found any of them naked, and this man is—

**Danforth:** But you discovered them dancing in the woods? *Eyes on* PARRIS, *he points at* ABIGAIL. Abigail?

**Hale:** Excellency, when I first arrived from Beverly, Mr. Parris told me that.

**Danforth:** Do you deny it, Mr. Parris?

**Parris:** I do not, sir, but I never saw any of them naked.

**Danforth:** But she have *danced?*

**Parris,** *unwillingly:* Aye, sir.

DANFORTH, *as though with new eyes, looks at* ABIGAIL.

**Hathorne:** Excellency, will you permit me? *He points at* MARY WARREN.

**Danforth,** *with great worry:* Pray, proceed.

**Hathorne:** You say you never saw no spirits, Mary, were never threatened or afflicted by any manifest of the Devil or the Devil's agents.

**Mary Warren,** *very faintly:* No, sir.

**Hathorne,** *with a gleam of victory:* And yet, when people accused of witchery confronted you in court, you would faint, saying their spirits came out of their bodies and choked you—

**Mary Warren:** That were pretense, sir.

**Danforth:** I cannot hear you.

**Mary Warren:** Pretense, sir.

**Parris:** But you did turn cold, did you not? I myself picked you up many times, and your skin were icy. Mr. Danforth, you—

**Danforth:** I saw that many times.

**Proctor:** She only pretended to faint, Your Excellency. They're all marvelous pretenders.

**Hathorne:** Then can she pretend to faint now?

**Proctor:** Now?

**Parris:** Why not? Now there are no spirits attacking her, for none in this room is accused of witchcraft. So let her turn herself cold now, let her pretend she is attacked now, let her faint. *He turns to* MARY WARREN. Faint!

**Mary Warren:** Faint?

**Parris:** Aye, faint. Prove to us how you pretended in the court so many times.

**Mary Warren,** *looking to* PROCTOR: I—cannot faint now, sir.

**Proctor,** *alarmed, quietly:* Can you not pretend it?

**Mary Warren:** I— *She looks about as though searching for the passion to faint.* I—have no sense of it now, I—

**Danforth:** Why? What is lacking now?

**Mary Warren:** I—cannot tell, sir, I—

**Danforth:** Might it be that here we have no afflicting spirit loose, but in the court there were some?

**Mary Warren:** I never saw no spirits.

**Parris:** Then see no spirits now, and prove to us that you can faint by your own will, as you claim.

**Mary Warren,** *stares, searching for the emotion of it, and then shakes her head:* I—cannot do it.

**Parris:** Then you will confess, will you not? It were attacking spirits made you faint!

**Mary Warren:** No, sir, I—

**Parris:** Your Excellency, this is a trick to blind the court!

**Mary Warren:** It's not a trick! *She stands.* I—I used to faint because I—I thought I saw spirits.

**Danforth:** *Thought* you saw them!

**Mary Warren:** But I did not, Your Honor.

**Hathorne:** How could you think you saw them unless you saw them?

**Mary Warren:** I—I cannot tell how, but I did. I—I heard the other girls screaming, and you, Your Honor, you seemed to believe them, and I— It were only sport in the beginning, sir, but then the whole world cried spirits, spirits, and I—I promise you, Mr. Danforth, I only thought I saw them but I did not.

DANFORTH *peers at her.*

**Parris,** *smiling, but nervous because* DANFORTH *seems to be struck by* MARY WARREN*'s story:* Surely Your Excellency is not taken by this simple lie.

**Danforth,** *turning worriedly to* ABIGAIL: Abigail. I bid you now search your heart and tell me this— and beware of it, child, to God every soul is precious and His vengeance is terrible on them that take life without cause. Is it possible, child, that the spirits you have seen are illusion only, some deception that may cross your mind when—

**Abigail:** Why, this—this—is a base question, sir.

**Danforth:** Child, I would have you consider it—

**Abigail:** I have been hurt, Mr. Danforth; I have seen my blood runnin' out! I have been near to murdered every day because I done my duty pointing out the Devil's people—and this is my reward? To be mistrusted, denied, questioned like a—

**Danforth,** *weakening:* Child, I do not mistrust you—

**Abigail,** *in an open threat:* Let *you* beware, Mr. Danforth. Think you to be so mighty that the power of Hell may not turn *your* wits? Beware of it! There is— *Suddenly, from an accusatory attitude, her face turns, looking into the air above— it is truly frightened.*

**Danforth,** *apprehensively:* What is it, child?

**Abigail,** *looking about in the air, clasping her arms about her as though cold:* I—I know not. A wind, a cold wind, has come. *Her eyes fall on* MARY WARREN.

**Mary Warren,** *terrified, pleading:* Abby!

**Mercy Lewis,** *shivering:* Your Honor, I freeze!

**Proctor:** They're pretending!

**Hathorne,** *touching* ABIGAIL*'s hand:* She is cold, Your Honor, touch her!

**Mercy Lewis,** *through chattering teeth:* Mary, do you send this shadow on me?

**Mary Warren:** Lord, save me!

**Susanna Walcott:** I freeze, I freeze!

**Abigail,** *shivering visibly:* It is a wind, a wind!

**Mary Warren:** Abby, don't do that!

"Do you witch her?"

**Danforth,** *himself engaged and entered by* ABIGAIL: Mary Warren, do you witch her? I say to you, do you send your spirit out?

*With a hysterical cry* MARY WARREN *starts to run.* PROCTOR *catches her.*

**Mary Warren,** *almost collapsing:* Let me go, Mr. Proctor, I cannot, I cannot—

**Abigail,** *crying to Heaven:* Oh, Heavenly Father, take away this shadow!

*Without warning or hesitation,* PROCTOR *leaps at* ABIGAIL *and, grabbing her by the hair, pulls her to her feet. She screams in pain.* DANFORTH, *astonished, cries, "What are you about?" and* HATHORNE *and* PARRIS *call, "Take your hands off her!" and out of it all comes* PROCTOR*'s roaring voice.*

**Proctor:** How do you call Heaven! Whore! Whore!

HERRICK *breaks* PROCTOR *from her.*

**Herrick:** John!
**Danforth:** Man! Man, what do you—
**Proctor,** *breathless and in agony:* It is a whore!
**Danforth,** *dumfounded:* You charge—?
**Abigail:** Mr. Danforth, he is lying!
**Proctor:** Mark her! Now she'll suck a scream to stab me with, but—
**Danforth:** You will prove this! This will not pass!
**Proctor,** *trembling, his life collapsing about him:* I have known her, sir. I have known her.
**Danforth:** You—you are a lecher?
**Francis,** *horrified:* John, you cannot say such a—
**Proctor:** Oh, Francis, I wish you had some evil in you that you might know me! *To* DANFORTH: A man will not cast away his good name. You surely know that.
**Danforth,** *dumfounded:* In—in what time? In what place?
**Proctor,** *his voice about to break, and his shame great:* In the proper place—where my beasts are bedded. On the last night of my joy, some eight months past. She used to serve me in my house, sir. *He has to clamp his jaw to keep from weeping.* A man may think God sleeps, but God sees everything, I know it now. I beg you, sir, I beg you—see her what she is. My wife, my dear good wife, took this girl soon after, sir, and put her

out on the highroad. And being what she is, a lump of vanity, sir— *He is being overcome.* Excellency, forgive me, forgive me. *Angrily against himself, he turns away from the Governor for a moment. Then, as though to cry out is his only means of speech left:* She thinks to dance with me on my wife's grave! And well she might, for I thought of her softly. God help me, I lusted, and there *is* a promise in such sweat. But it is a whore's vengeance, and you must see it; I set myself entirely in your hands. I know you must see it now.

**Danforth,** *blanched, in horror, turning to* ABIGAIL: You deny every scrap and tittle of this?
**Abigail:** If I must answer that, I will leave and I will not come back again!

DANFORTH *seems unsteady.*

**Proctor:** I have made a bell of my honor! I have rung the doom of my good name—you will believe me, Mr. Danforth! My wife is innocent, except she knew a whore when she saw one!
**Abigail,** *stepping up to* DANFORTH: What look do you give me? DANFORTH *cannot speak.* I'll not have such looks! *She turns and starts for the door.*
**Danforth:** You will remain where you are! HERRICK *steps into her path. She comes up short, fire in her eyes.* Mr. Parris, go into the court and bring Goodwife Proctor out.
**Parris,** *objecting:* Your Honor, this is all a—
**Danforth,** *sharply to* PARRIS: Bring her out! And tell her not one word of what's been spoken here. And let you knock before you enter. PARRIS *goes out.* Now we shall touch the bottom of this swamp. *To* PROCTOR: Your wife, you say, is an honest woman.
**Proctor:** In her life, sir, she have never lied. There are them that cannot sing, and them that cannot weep—my wife cannot lie. I have paid much to learn it, sir.
**Danforth:** And when she put this girl out of your house, she put her out for a harlot?
**Proctor:** Aye, sir.
**Danforth:** And knew her for a harlot?
**Proctor:** Aye, sir, she knew her for a harlot.
**Danforth:** Good then. *To* ABIGAIL: And if she tell me, child, it were for harlotry, may God spread His mercy on you! *There is a knock. He calls to the door.* Hold! *To* ABIGAIL: Turn your back. Turn your

back. *To* PROCTOR: Do likewise. *Both turn their backs—* ABIGAIL *with indignant slowness.* Now let neither of you turn to face Goody Proctor. No one in this room is to speak one word, or raise a gesture aye or nay. *He turns toward the door, calls:* Enter! *The door opens.* ELIZABETH *enters with* PARRIS. PARRIS *leaves her. She stands alone, her eyes looking for* PROCTOR. Mr. Cheever, report this testimony in all exactness. Are you ready?

**Cheever:** Ready, sir.

**Danforth:** Come here, woman. ELIZABETH *comes to him, glancing at* PROCTOR'*s back.* Look at me only, not at your husband. In my eyes only.

**Elizabeth,** *faintly:* Good, sir.

**Danforth:** We are given to understand that at one time you dismissed your servant, Abigail Williams.

**Elizabeth:** That is true, sir.

**Danforth:** For what cause did you dismiss her? *Slight pause. Then* ELIZABETH *tries to glance at* PROCTOR. You will look in my eyes only and not at your husband. The answer is in your memory and you need no help to give it to me. Why did you dismiss Abigail Williams?

**Elizabeth,** *not knowing what to say, sensing a situation, wetting her lips to stall for time:* She— dissatisfied me. *Pause.* And my husband.

**Danforth:** In what way dissatisfied you?

**Elizabeth:** She were— *She glances at* PROCTOR *for a cue.*

**Danforth:** Woman, look at me! ELIZABETH *does.* Were she slovenly? Lazy? What disturbance did she cause?

**Elizabeth:** Your Honor, I—in that time I were sick. And I—My husband is a good and righteous man. He is never drunk as some are, nor wastin' his time at the shovelboard, but always at his work. But in my sickness—you see, sir. I were a long time sick after my last baby, and I thought I saw my husband somewhat turning from me. And this girl— *She turns to* ABIGAIL.

**Danforth:** Look at me.

**Elizabeth:** Aye, sir. Abigail Williams— *She breaks off.*

**Danforth:** What of Abigail Williams?

**Elizabeth:** I came to think he fancied her. And so one night I lost my wits, I think, and put her out on the highroad.

**Danforth:** Your husband—did he indeed turn from you?

**Elizabeth,** *in agony:* My husband—is a goodly man, sir.

**Danforth:** Then he did not turn from you.

**Elizabeth,** *starting to glance at* PROCTOR: He—

**Danforth,** *reaches out and holds her face, then:* Look at me! To your own knowledge, has John Proctor ever committed the crime of lechery? *In a crisis of indecision she cannot speak.* Answer my question! Is your husband a lecher!

**Elizabeth,** *faintly:* No, sir.

**Danforth:** Remove her, Marshal.

**Proctor:** Elizabeth, tell the truth!

**Danforth:** She has spoken. Remove her!

**Proctor,** *crying out:* Elizabeth, I have confessed it!

**Elizabeth:** Oh, God! *The door closes behind her.*

**Proctor:** She only thought to save my name!

**Hale:** Excellency, it is a natural lie to tell; I beg you, stop now before another is condemned! I may shut my conscience to it no more—private vengeance is working through this testimony! From the beginning this man has struck me true. By my oath to Heaven, I believe him now, and I pray you call back his wife before we—

**Danforth:** She spoke nothing of lechery, and this man has lied!

**Hale:** I believe him! *Pointing at* ABIGAIL: This girl has always struck me false! She has—

ABIGAIL, *with a weird, wild, chilling cry, screams up to the ceiling.*

**Abigail:** You will not! Begone! Begone, I say!

**Danforth:** What is it, child? *But* ABIGAIL, *pointing with fear, is now raising up her frightened eyes, her awed face, toward the ceiling—the girls are doing the same—and now* HATHORNE, HALE, PUTNAM, CHEEVER, HERRICK, *and* DANFORTH *do the same.* What's there? *He lowers his eyes from the ceiling, and now he is frightened; there is real tension in his voice.* Child! *She is transfixed—with all the girls, she is whimpering open-mouthed, agape at the ceiling.* Girls! Why do you—?

**Mercy Lewis,** *pointing:* It's on the beam! Behind the rafter!

**Danforth,** *looking up:* Where!

**Abigail:** Why—? *She gulps.* Why do you come, yellow bird?

**Proctor:** Where's a bird? I see no bird!

**Abigail,** *to the ceiling:* My face? My face?

**Proctor:** Mr. Hale—

**Danforth:** Be quiet!

**Proctor,** *to* HALE: Do you see a bird?

**Danforth:** Be quiet!!

**Abigail,** *to the ceiling, in a genuine conversation with the "bird," as though trying to talk it out of attacking her:* But God made my face; you cannot want to tear my face. Envy is a deadly sin, Mary.

**Mary Warren,** *on her feet with a spring, and horrified, pleading:* Abby!

**Abigail,** *unperturbed, continuing to the "bird":* Oh, Mary, this is a black art to change your shape. No, I cannot, I cannot stop my mouth; it's God's work I do.

**Mary Warren:** Abby, I'm *here*!

**Proctor,** *frantically:* They're pretending, Mr. Danforth!

**Abigail**—*now she takes a backward step, as though in fear the bird will swoop down momentarily:* Oh, please, Mary! Don't come down.

**Susanna Walcott:** Her claws, she's stretching her claws!

**Proctor:** Lies, lies.

**Abigail,** *backing further, eyes still fixed above:* Mary, please don't hurt me!

**Mary Warren,** *to* DANFORTH: I'm not hurting her!

**Danforth,** *to* MARY WARREN: Why does she see this vision?

**Mary Warren:** She sees nothin'!

**Abigail,** *now staring full front as though hypnotized, and mimicking the exact tone of* MARY WARREN'*s cry:* She sees nothin'!

**Mary Warren,** *pleading:* Abby, you mustn't!

**Abigail and All the Girls,** *all transfixed:* Abby, you mustn't!

**Mary Warren,** *to all the girls:* I'm here, I'm here!

**Girls:** I'm here, I'm here!

**Danforth,** *horrified:* Mary Warren! Draw back your spirit out of them!

**Mary Warren:** Mr. Danforth!

**Girls,** *cutting her off:* Mr. Danforth!

**Danforth:** Have you compacted with the Devil? Have you?

**Mary Warren:** Never, never!

**Girls:** Never, never!

**Danforth,** *growing hysterical:* Why can they only repeat you?

**Proctor:** Give me a whip—I'll stop it!

**Mary Warren:** They're sporting. They—!

**Girls:** They're sporting!

**Mary Warren,** *turning on them all hysterically and stamping her feet:* Abby, stop it!

**Girls,** *stamping their feet:* Abby, stop it!

**Mary Warren:** Stop it!

**Girls:** Stop it!

**Mary Warren,** *screaming it out at the top of her lungs, and raising her fists:* Stop it!!

**Girls,** *raising their fists:* Stop it!!

MARY WARREN, *utterly confounded, and becoming overwhelmed by* ABIGAIL'*s—and the girls'—utter conviction, starts to whimper, hands half raised, powerless, and all the girls begin whimpering exactly as she does.*

**Danforth:** A little while ago you were afflicted. Now it seems you afflict others; where did you find this power?

**Mary Warren,** *staring at* ABIGAIL: I—have no power.

**Girls:** I have no power.

**Proctor:** They're gulling you, Mister!

**Danforth:** Why did you turn about this past two weeks? You have seen the Devil, have you not?

**Hale,** *indicating* ABIGAIL *and the girls:* You cannot believe them!

**Mary Warren:** I—

**Proctor,** *sensing her weakening:* Mary, God damns all liars!

**Danforth,** *pounding it into her:* You have seen the Devil, you have made compact with Lucifer, have you not?

**Proctor:** God damns liars, Mary!

MARY *utters something unintelligible, staring at* ABIGAIL, *who keeps watching the "bird" above.*

**Danforth:** I cannot hear you. What do you say? MARY *utters again unintelligibly.* You will confess yourself or you will hang! *He turns her roughly to face him.* Do you know who I am? I say you will hang if you do not open with me!

**Proctor:** Mary, remember the angel Raphael—do that which is good and—

**Abigail,** *pointing upward:* The wings! Her wings are spreading! Mary, please, don't, don't—!

**Hale:** I see nothing, Your Honor!

**Danforth:** Do you confess this power! *He is an inch from her face.* Speak!

**Abigail:** She's going to come down! She's walking the beam!

**Danforth:** Will you speak!

**Mary Warren,** *staring in horror:* I cannot!

**Girls:** I cannot!

**Parris:** Cast the Devil out! Look him in the face! Trample him! We'll save you, Mary, only stand fast against him and—

**Abigail,** *looking up:* Look out! She's coming down!

*She and all the girls run to one wall, shielding their eyes. And now, as though cornered, they let out a gigantic scream, and* MARY, *as though infected, opens her mouth and screams with them. Gradually* ABIGAIL *and the girls leave off, until only* MARY *is left there, staring up at the "bird," screaming madly. All watch her, horrified by this evident fit.* PROCTOR *strides to her.*

**Proctor:** Mary, tell the Governor what they— *He has hardly got a word out, when, seeing him coming for her, she rushes out of his reach, screaming in horror.*

**Mary Warren:** Don't touch me—don't touch me! *At which the girls halt at the door.*

**Proctor,** *astonished:* Mary!

**Mary Warren,** *pointing at* PROCTOR: You're the Devil's man!

*He is stopped in his tracks.*

**Parris:** Praise God!

**Girls:** Praise God!

**Proctor,** *numbed:* Mary, how—?

**Mary Warren:** I'll not hang with you! I love God, I love God.

**Danforth,** *to* MARY: He bid you do the Devil's work?

**Mary Warren,** *hysterically, indicating* PROCTOR: He come at me by night and every day to sign, to sign, to—

**Danforth:** Sign what?

**Parris:** The Devil's book? He come with a book?

**Mary Warren,** *hysterically, pointing at* PROCTOR, *fearful of him:* My name, he want my name. "I'll murder you," he says, "if my wife hangs! We must go and overthrow the court," he says!

DANFORTH's *head jerks toward* PROCTOR, *shock and horror in his face.*

**Proctor,** *turning, appealing to* HALE: Mr. Hale!

**Mary Warren,** *her sobs beginning:* He wake me every night, his eyes were like coals and his fingers claw my neck, and I sign, I sign . . .

**Hale:** Excellency, this child's gone wild!

**Proctor,** *as* DANFORTH's *wide eyes pour on him:* Mary, Mary!

**Mary Warren,** *screaming at him:* No, I love God; I go your way no more. I love God, I bless God. *Sobbing, she rushes to* ABIGAIL. Abby, Abby, I'll never hurt you more! *They all watch, as* ABIGAIL, *out of her infinite charity, reaches out and draws the sobbing* MARY *to her, and then looks up to* DANFORTH.

**Danforth,** *to* PROCTOR: What are you? PROCTOR *is beyond speech in his anger.* You are combined with anti-Christ,[7] are you not? I have seen your power; you will not deny it! What say you, Mister?

**Hale:** Excellency—

**Danforth:** I will have nothing from you, Mr. Hale! *To* PROCTOR: Will you confess yourself befouled with Hell, or do you keep that black allegiance yet? What say you?

**Proctor,** *his mind wild, breathless:* I say—I say— God is dead!

**Parris:** Hear it, hear it!

**Proctor,** *laughs insanely, then:* A fire, a fire is burning! I hear the boot of Lucifer, I see his filthy face! And it is my face, and yours, Danforth! For them that quail to bring men out of ignorance, as I have quailed, and as you quail now when you know in all your black hearts that this be fraud— God damns our kind especially, and we will burn, we will burn together!

**Danforth:** Marshal! Take him and Corey with him to the jail!

**Hale,** *starting across to the door:* I denounce these proceedings!

**Proctor:** You are pulling Heaven down and raising up a whore!

**Hale:** I denounce these proceedings, I quit this court! *He slams the door to the outside behind him.*

**Danforth,** *calling to him in a fury:* Mr. Hale! Mr. Hale!

*The curtain falls*

**7. anti-Christ:** in the Bible, Christ's great enemy, expected to spread evil before Christ conquers him and the world ends (1 John 2:18).

# Response and Analysis

## Act Three

### Reading Check

1. How does Mary respond when Danforth asks her to explain the "crying out"?

2. What does Danforth do with the list of people supporting Rebecca and Martha?

3. What test does Danforth devise to determine why Abigail was put out of the Proctor house?

4. What is Abigail's "vision"?

### Thinking Critically

5. Serious dramatic works often include **comic relief**—the inclusion of a comic episode or element to relieve emotional tension. Do you think Giles Corey's eccentric and earthy **dialogue** provides comic relief in *The Crucible*? Support your answer with specific examples from the play.

6. What does Hale mean when he asks if every defense is an attack upon the court? By the end of this act, would you say Hale is a **dynamic** or **static character**? Use details from the play to support your response.

7. When John reveals his true relationship to Abigail, what do you think he also reveals about his **character** and his **motivation**?

### Extending and Evaluating

8. In sports, in politics, and in war, people often demonize their opponents—that is, they portray their enemies as incarnations of evil. Can you think of an example? Why do you think people do this? What effect do you think such behavior has on society as a whole?

**SKILLS FOCUS**

**Literary Skills**
Analyze motivation.

**Reading Skills**
Interpret a dramatic work.

# Act Four

*A cell in Salem jail, that fall.*

*At the back is a high barred window; near it, a great, heavy door. Along the walls are two benches.*

*The place is in darkness but for the moonlight seeping through the bars. It appears empty. Presently footsteps are heard coming down a corridor beyond the wall, keys rattle, and the door swings open.* MARSHAL HERRICK *enters with a lantern.*

*He is nearly drunk, and heavy-footed. He goes to a bench and nudges a bundle of rags lying on it.*

**Herrick:** Sarah, wake up! Sarah Good! *He then crosses to the other bench.*

**Sarah Good,** *rising in her rags:* Oh, Majesty! Comin', comin'! Tituba, he's here, His Majesty's come!

**Herrick:** Go to the north cell; this place is wanted now. *He hangs his lantern on the wall.* TITUBA *sits up.*

**Tituba:** That don't look to me like His Majesty; look to me like the marshal.

**Herrick,** *taking out a flask:* Get along with you now, clear this place. *He drinks, and* SARAH GOOD *comes and peers up into his face.*

**Sarah Good:** Oh, is it you, Marshal! I thought sure you be the Devil comin' for us. Could I have a sip of cider for me goin'-away?

**Herrick,** *handing her the flask:* And where are you off to, Sarah?

**Tituba,** *as* SARAH *drinks:* We goin' to Barbados, soon the Devil gits here with the feathers and the wings.

**Herrick:** Oh? A happy voyage to you.

**Sarah Good:** A pair of bluebirds wingin' southerly, the two of us! Oh, it be a grand transformation, Marshal! *She raises the flask to drink again.*

**Herrick,** *taking the flask from her lips:* You'd best give me that or you'll never rise off the ground. Come along now.

**Tituba:** I'll speak to him for you, if you desires to come along, Marshal.

**Herrick:** I'd not refuse it, Tituba; it's the proper morning to fly into Hell.

**Tituba:** Oh, it be no Hell in Barbados. Devil, him be pleasureman in Barbados, him be singin' and dancin' in Barbados. It's you folks—you riles him up 'round here; it be too cold 'round here for that Old Boy. He freeze his soul in Massachusetts, but in Barbados he just as sweet and— *A bellowing cow is heard, and* TITUBA *leaps up and calls to the window:* Aye, sir! That's him, Sarah!

**Sarah Good:** I'm here, Majesty! *They hurriedly pick up their rags as* HOPKINS, *a guard, enters.*

**Hopkins:** The Deputy Governor's arrived.

**Herrick,** *grabbing* TITUBA: Come along, come along.

**Tituba,** *resisting him:* No, he comin' for me. I goin' home!

**Herrick,** *pulling her to the door:* That's not Satan, just a poor old cow with a hatful of milk. Come along now, out with you!

**Tituba,** *calling to the window:* Take me home, Devil! Take me home!

**Sarah Good,** *following the shouting* TITUBA *out:* Tell him I'm goin', Tituba! Now you tell him Sarah Good is goin' too!

*In the corridor outside* TITUBA *calls on—"Take me home, Devil; Devil take me home!" and* HOPKINS' *voice orders her to move on.* HERRICK *returns and begins to push old rags and straw into a corner. Hearing footsteps, he turns, and enter* DANFORTH *and* JUDGE HATHORNE. *They are in greatcoats and wear hats against the bitter cold. They are followed in by* CHEEVER, *who carries a dispatch case and a flat wooden box containing his writing materials.*

**Herrick:** Good morning, Excellency.

**Danforth:** Where is Mr. Parris?

**Herrick:** I'll fetch him. *He starts for the door.*

**Danforth:** Marshal. HERRICK *stops.* When did Reverend Hale arrive?

**Herrick:** It were toward midnight, I think.

**Danforth,** *suspiciously:* What is he about here?

**Herrick:** He goes among them that will hang, sir. And he prays with them. He sits with Goody Nurse now. And Mr. Parris with him.

**Danforth:** Indeed. That man have no authority to enter here, Marshal. Why have you let him in?

**Herrick:** Why, Mr. Parris command me, sir. I cannot deny him.

**Danforth:** Are you drunk, Marshal?

**Herrick:** No, sir; it is a bitter night, and I have no fire here.

**Danforth,** *containing his anger:* Fetch Mr. Parris.

**Herrick:** Aye, sir.

**Danforth:** There is a prodigious stench in this place.

**Herrick:** I have only now cleared the people out for you.

**Danforth:** Beware hard drink, Marshal.

**Herrick:** Aye, sir. *He waits an instant for further orders. But* DANFORTH, *in dissatisfaction, turns his back on him, and* HERRICK *goes out. There is a pause.* DANFORTH *stands in thought.*

**Hathorne:** Let you question Hale, Excellency; I should not be surprised he have been preaching in Andover lately.

**Danforth:** We'll come to that; speak nothing of Andover. Parris prays with him. That's strange. *He blows on his hands, moves toward the window, and looks out.*

**Hathorne:** Excellency, I wonder if it be wise to let Mr. Parris so continuously with the prisoners. DANFORTH *turns to him, interested.* I think, sometimes, the man has a mad look these days.

**Danforth:** Mad?

**Hathorne:** I met him yesterday coming out of his house, and I bid him good morning—and he wept and went his way. I think it is not well the village sees him so unsteady.

**Danforth:** Perhaps he have some sorrow.

**Cheever,** *stamping his feet against the cold:* I think it be the cows, sir.

**Danforth:** Cows?

**Cheever:** There be so many cows wanderin' the highroads, now their masters are in the jails, and much disagreement who they will belong to now. I know Mr. Parris be arguin' with farmers all yesterday—there is great contention, sir, about the cows. Contention make him weep, sir; it were always a man that weep for contention. *He turns, as do* HATHORNE *and* DANFORTH, *hearing someone coming up the corridor.* DANFORTH *raises his head as* PARRIS *enters. He is gaunt, frightened, and sweating in his greatcoat.*

**Parris,** *to* DANFORTH, *instantly:* Oh, good morning, sir, thank you for coming, I beg your pardon wakin' you so early. Good morning, Judge Hathorne.

**Danforth:** Reverend Hale have no right to enter this—

**Parris:** Excellency, a moment. *He hurries back and shuts the door.*

**Hathorne:** Do you leave him alone with the prisoners?

**Danforth:** What's his business here?

**Parris,** *prayerfully holding up his hands:* Excellency, hear me. It is a providence. Reverend Hale has returned to bring Rebecca Nurse to God.

**Danforth,** *surprised:* He bids her confess?

**Parris,** *sitting:* Hear me. Rebecca have not given me a word this three month since she came. Now she sits with him, and her sister and Martha Corey and two or three others, and he pleads with them, confess their crimes and save their lives.

**Danforth:** Why—this is indeed a providence. And they soften, they soften?

**Parris:** Not yet, not yet. But I thought to summon you, sir, that we might think on whether it be not wise, to— *He dares not say it.* I had thought to put a question, sir, and I hope you will not—

**Danforth:** Mr. Parris, be plain, what troubles you?

**Parris:** There is news, sir, that the court—the court must reckon with. My niece, sir, my niece—I believe she has vanished.

**Danforth:** Vanished!

**Parris:** I had thought to advise you of it earlier in the week, but—

**Danforth:** Why? How long is she gone?

**Parris:** This be the third night. You see, sir, she told me she would stay a night with Mercy Lewis. And next day, when she does not return, I send to Mr. Lewis to inquire. Mercy told him she would sleep in *my* house for a night.

**Danforth:** They are both gone?!

**Parris,** *in fear of him:* They are, sir.

**Danforth,** *alarmed:* I will send a party for them. Where may they be?

**Parris:** Excellency, I think they be aboard a ship. DANFORTH *stands agape.* My daughter tells me how she heard them speaking of ships last week, and tonight I discover my—my strongbox is broke into. *He presses his fingers against his eyes to keep back tears.*

**Hathorne,** *astonished:* She have robbed you?

**Parris:** Thirty-one pound is gone. I am penniless. *He covers his face and sobs.*

**Danforth:** Mr. Parris, you are a brainless man! *He walks in thought, deeply worried.*

**Parris:** Excellency, it profit nothing you should

blame me. I cannot think they would run off except they fear to keep in Salem any more. *He is pleading.* Mark it, sir, Abigail had close knowledge of the town, and since the news of Andover has broken here—

**Danforth:** Andover is remedied. The court returns there on Friday, and will resume examinations.

**Parris:** I am sure of it, sir. But the rumor here speaks rebellion in Andover, and it—

**Danforth:** There is no rebellion in Andover!

**Parris:** I tell you what is said here, sir. Andover has thrown out the court, they say, and will have no part of witchcraft. There be a faction here, feeding on that news, and I tell you true, sir, I fear there will be riot here.

**Hathorne:** Riot! Why at every execution I have seen naught but high satisfaction in the town.

**Parris:** Judge Hathorne—it were another sort that hanged till now. Rebecca Nurse is no Bridget that lived three year with Bishop before she married him. John Proctor is not Isaac Ward that drank his family to ruin. *To* DANFORTH: I would to God it were not so, Excellency, but these people have great weight yet in the town. Let Rebecca stand upon the gibbet[1] and send up some righteous prayer, and I fear she'll wake a vengeance on you.

**Hathorne:** Excellency, she is condemned a witch. The court have—

**Danforth,** *in deep concern, raising a hand to* HATHORNE: Pray you. *To* PARRIS: How do you propose, then?

**Parris:** Excellency, I would postpone these hangin's for a time.

**Danforth:** There will be no postponement.

**Parris:** Now Mr. Hale's returned, there is hope, I think—for if he bring even one of these to God, that confession surely damns the others in the public eye, and none may doubt more that they are all linked to Hell. This way, unconfessed and claiming innocence, doubts are multiplied, many honest people will weep for them, and our good purpose is lost in their tears.

**Danforth,** *after thinking a moment, then going to* CHEEVER: Give me the list.

1. **gibbet** (jib'it): gallows, or structure from which a person is executed by hanging.

CHEEVER *opens the dispatch case, searches.*

**Parris:** It cannot be forgot, sir, that when I summoned the congregation for John Proctor's excommunication there were hardly thirty people come to hear it. That speak a discontent, I think, and—

**Danforth,** *studying the list:* There will be no postponement.

**Parris:** Excellency—

**Danforth:** Now, sir—which of these in your opinion may be brought to God? I will myself strive with him till dawn. *He hands the list to* PARRIS, *who merely glances at it.*

**Parris:** There is not sufficient time till dawn.

**Danforth:** I shall do my utmost. Which of them do you have hope for?

**Parris,** *not even glancing at the list now, and in a quavering voice, quietly:* Excellency—a dagger— *He chokes up.*

**Danforth:** What do you say?

**Parris:** Tonight, when I open my door to leave my house—a dagger clattered to the ground. *Silence.* DANFORTH *absorbs this. Now* PARRIS *cries out:* You cannot hang this sort. There is danger for me. I dare not step outside at night!

REVEREND HALE *enters. They look at him for an instant in silence. He is steeped in sorrow, exhausted, and more direct than he ever was.*

**Danforth:** Accept my congratulations, Reverend Hale; we are gladdened to see you returned to your good work.

**Hale,** *coming to* DANFORTH *now:* You must pardon them. They will not budge.

HERRICK *enters, waits.*

**Danforth,** *conciliatory:* You misunderstand, sir; I cannot pardon these when twelve are already hanged for the same crime. It is not just.

**Parris,** *with failing heart:* Rebecca will not confess?

**Hale:** The sun will rise in a few minutes. Excellency, I must have more time.

**Danforth:** Now hear me, and beguile yourselves no more. I will not receive a single plea for pardon or postponement. Them that will not confess will hang. Twelve are already executed; the names of these seven are given out, and the village expects to see them die this morning. Postponement now speaks a floundering on my part; reprieve or pardon must cast doubt upon the guilt of them that died till now. While I speak God's law, I will not crack its voice with whimpering. If retaliation is your fear, know this—I should hang ten thousand that dared to rise against the law, and an ocean of salt tears could not melt the resolution of the statutes. Now draw yourselves up like men and help me, as you are bound by Heaven to do. Have you spoken with them all, Mr. Hale?

**Hale:** All but Proctor. He is in the dungeon.

**Danforth,** *to* HERRICK: What's Proctor's way now?

**Herrick:** He sits like some great bird; you'd not know he lived except he will take food from time to time.

**Danforth,** *after thinking a moment:* His wife—his wife must be well on with child now.

**Herrick:** She is, sir.

**Danforth:** What think you, Mr. Parris? You have closer knowledge of this man; might her presence soften him?

**Parris:** It is possible, sir. He have not laid eyes on her these three months. I should summon her.

**Danforth,** *to* HERRICK: Is he yet adamant? Has he struck at you again?

**Herrick:** He cannot, sir, he is chained to the wall now.

**Danforth,** *after thinking on it:* Fetch Goody Proctor to me. Then let you bring him up.

**Herrick:** Aye, sir. HERRICK *goes. There is silence.*

**Hale:** Excellency, if you postpone a week and publish to the town that you are striving for their confessions, that speak mercy on your part, not faltering.

**Danforth:** Mr. Hale, as God have not empowered me like Joshua to stop this sun from rising,[2] so I cannot withhold from them the perfection of their punishment.

**Hale,** *harder now:* If you think God wills you to raise rebellion, Mr. Danforth, you are mistaken!

**Danforth,** *instantly:* You have heard rebellion spoken in the town?

---

2. **Joshua . . . rising:** In the Bible, Joshua, the successor of Moses, commands the sun and moon to stand still while his people take vengeance on their enemies.

---

**Hale:** Excellency, there are orphans wandering from house to house; abandoned cattle bellow on the highroads, the stink of rotting crops hangs everywhere, and no man knows when the harlots' cry will end his life—and you wonder yet if rebellion's spoke? Better you should marvel how they do not burn your province!

**Danforth:** Mr. Hale, have you preached in Andover this month?

**Hale:** Thank God they have no need of me in Andover.

**Danforth:** You baffle me, sir. Why have you returned here?

**Hale:** Why, it is all simple. I come to do the Devil's work. I come to counsel Christians they should belie themselves. *His sarcasm collapses.* There is blood on my head! Can you not see the blood on my head!!

**Parris:** Hush! *For he has heard footsteps. They all face the door.* HERRICK *enters with* ELIZABETH. *Her wrists are linked by heavy chain, which* HERRICK *now removes. Her clothes are dirty; her face is pale and gaunt.* HERRICK *goes out.*

**Danforth,** *very politely:* Goody Proctor. *She is silent.* I hope you are hearty?

**Elizabeth,** *as a warning reminder:* I am yet six month before my time.

**Danforth:** Pray be at your ease, we come not for your life. We—*uncertain how to plead, for he is not accustomed to it.* Mr. Hale, will you speak with the woman?

**Hale:** Goody Proctor, your husband is marked to hang this morning.

*Pause.*

**Elizabeth,** *quietly:* I have heard it.

**Hale:** You know, do you not, that I have no connection with the court? *She seems to doubt it.* I come of my own, Goody Proctor. I would save your husband's life, for if he is taken I count myself his murderer. Do you understand me?

**Elizabeth:** What do you want of me?

**Hale:** Goody Proctor, I have gone this three month like our Lord into the wilderness. I have sought a Christian way, for damnation's doubled on a minister who counsels men to lie.

**Hathorne:** It is no lie, you cannot speak of lies.

**Hale:** It is a lie! They are innocent!

**Danforth:** I'll hear no more of that!

**Hale,** *continuing to* ELIZABETH: Let you not mistake your duty as I mistook my own. I came into this village like a bridegroom to his beloved, bearing gifts of high religion; the very crowns of holy law I brought, and what I touched with my bright confidence, it died; and where I turned the eye of my great faith, blood flowed up. Beware, Goody Proctor—cleave to no faith when faith brings blood. It is mistaken law that leads you to sacrifice. Life, woman, life is God's most precious gift; no principle, however glorious, may justify the taking of it. I beg you, woman, prevail upon your husband to confess. Let him give his lie. Quail not before God's judgment in this, for it may well be God damns a liar less than he that throws his life away for pride. Will you plead with him? I cannot think he will listen to another.

**Elizabeth,** *quietly:* I think that be the Devil's argument.

**Hale,** *with a climactic desperation:* Woman, before the laws of God we are as swine! We cannot read His will!

**Elizabeth:** I cannot dispute with you, sir; I lack learning for it.

**Danforth,** *going to her:* Goody Proctor, you are not summoned here for disputation. Be there no wifely tenderness within you? He will die with the sunrise. Your husband. Do you understand it? *She only looks at him.* What say you? Will you contend with him? *She is silent.* Are you stone? I tell you true, woman, had I no other proof of your unnatural life, your dry eyes now would be sufficient evidence that you delivered up your soul to Hell! A very ape would weep at such calamity! Have the Devil dried up any tear of pity in you? *She is silent.* Take her out. It profit nothing she should speak to him!

**Elizabeth,** *quietly:* Let me speak with him, Excellency.

**Parris,** *with hope:* You'll strive with him? *She hesitates.*

**Danforth:** Will you plead for his confession or will you not?

**Elizabeth:** I promise nothing. Let me speak with him.

*A sound—the sibilance of dragging feet on stone. They turn. A pause.* HERRICK *enters with* JOHN PROCTOR. *His wrists are chained. He is* another man, bearded, filthy, his eyes misty as though webs had overgrown them. He halts inside the doorway, his eye caught by the sight of ELIZABETH. *The emotion flowing between them prevents anyone from speaking for an instant. Now* HALE, *visibly affected, goes to* DANFORTH *and speaks quietly.*

**Hale:** Pray, leave them, Excellency.

**Danforth,** *pressing* HALE *impatiently aside:* Mr. Proctor, you have been notified, have you not? PROCTOR *is silent, staring at* ELIZABETH. I see light in the sky, Mister; let you counsel with your wife, and may God help you turn your back on Hell. PROCTOR *is silent, staring at* ELIZABETH.

**Hale,** *quietly:* Excellency, let—

DANFORTH *brushes past* HALE *and walks out.* HALE *follows.* CHEEVER *stands and follows,* HATHORNE *behind.* HERRICK *goes.* PARRIS, *from a safe distance, offers:*

**Parris:** If you desire a cup of cider, Mr. Proctor, I am sure I— PROCTOR *turns an icy stare at him, and he breaks off.* PARRIS *raises his palms toward* PROCTOR. God lead you now. PARRIS *goes out.*

*Alone.* PROCTOR *walks to her, halts. It is as though they stood in a spinning world. It is beyond sorrow, above it. He reaches out his hand as though toward an embodiment not quite real, and as he touches her, a strange soft sound, half laughter, half amazement, comes from his throat. He pats her hand. She covers his hand with hers. And then, weak, he sits. Then she sits, facing him.*

**Proctor:** The child?

**Elizabeth:** It grows.

**Proctor:** There is no word of the boys?

**Elizabeth:** They're well. Rebecca's Samuel keeps them.

**Proctor:** You have not seen them?

**Elizabeth:** I have not. *She catches a weakening in herself and downs it.*

**Proctor:** You are a—marvel, Elizabeth.

**Elizabeth:** You—have been tortured?

**Proctor:** Aye. *Pause. She will not let herself be drowned in the sea that threatens her.* They come for my life now.

**Elizabeth:** I know it.

*Pause.*

**Proctor:** None—have yet confessed?

**Elizabeth:** There be many confessed.

**Proctor:** Who are they?

**Elizabeth:** There be a hundred or more, they say. Goody Ballard is one; Isaiah Goodkind is one. There be many.

**Proctor:** Rebecca?

**Elizabeth:** Not Rebecca. She is one foot in Heaven now; naught may hurt her more.

**Proctor:** And Giles?

**Elizabeth:** You have not heard of it?

**Proctor:** I hear nothin', where I am kept.

**Elizabeth:** Giles is dead.

*He looks at her incredulously.*

**Proctor:** When were he hanged?

**Elizabeth,** *quietly, factually:* He were not hanged. He would not answer aye or nay to his indictment; for if he denied the charge they'd hang him surely, and auction out his property. So he stand mute, and died Christian under the law. And so his sons will have his farm. It is the law, for he could not be condemned a wizard without he answer the indictment, aye or nay.

**Proctor:** Then how does he die?

**Elizabeth,** *gently:* They press him, John.

**Proctor:** Press?

**Elizabeth:** Great stones they lay upon his chest until he plead aye or nay. *With a tender smile for the old man:* They say he give them but two words. "More weight," he says. And died.

**Proctor,** *numbed—a thread to weave into his agony:* "More weight."

**Elizabeth:** Aye. It were a fearsome man, Giles Corey.

*Pause.*

**Proctor,** *with great force of will, but not quite looking at her:* I have been thinking I would confess to them, Elizabeth. *She shows nothing.* What say you? If I give them that?

**Elizabeth:** I cannot judge you, John.

*Pause.*

**Proctor,** *simply—a pure question:* What would you have me do?

**Elizabeth:** As you will, I would have it. *Slight pause.* I want you living, John. That's sure.

**Proctor**—*he pauses, then with a flailing of hope:* Giles' wife? Have she confessed?

**Elizabeth:** She will not.

*Pause.*

**Proctor:** It is a pretense, Elizabeth.

**Elizabeth:** What is?

**Proctor:** I cannot mount the gibbet like a saint. It is a fraud. I am not that man. *She is silent.* My honesty is broke, Elizabeth; I am no good man. Nothing's spoiled by giving them this lie that were not rotten long before.

**Elizabeth:** And yet you've not confessed till now. That speak goodness in you.

**Proctor:** Spite only keeps me silent. It is hard to give a lie to dogs. *Pause, for the first time he turns directly to her.* I would have your forgiveness, Elizabeth.

**Elizabeth:** It is not for me to give, John, I am—

**Proctor:** I'd have you see some honesty in it. Let them that never lied die now to keep their souls. It is pretense for me, a vanity that will not blind God nor keep my children out of the wind. *Pause.* What say you?

**Elizabeth,** *upon a heaving sob that always threatens:* John, it come to naught that I should forgive you, if you'll not forgive yourself. *Now he turns away a little, in great agony.* It is not my soul, John, it is yours. *He stands, as though in physical pain, slowly rising to his feet with a great immortal longing to find his answer. It is difficult to say, and she is on the verge of tears.* Only be sure of this, for I know it now: Whatever you will do, it is a good man does it. *He turns his doubting, searching gaze upon her.* I have read my heart this three month, John. *Pause.* I have sins of my own to count. It needs a cold wife to prompt lechery.

> "Only be sure of this:
> Whatever you will do,
> it is a good man does it."

**Proctor,** *in great pain:* Enough, enough—

**Elizabeth,** *now pouring out her heart:* Better you should know me!

**Proctor:** I will not hear it! I know you!

**Elizabeth:** You take my sins upon you, John—

**Proctor,** *in agony:* No, I take my own, my own!

**Elizabeth:** John, I counted myself so plain, so poorly made, no honest love could come to me! Suspicion kissed you when I did; I never knew how I should say my love. It were a cold house I kept! *In fright, she swerves, as* HATHORNE *enters.*

**Hathorne:** What say you, Proctor? The sun is soon up.

PROCTOR, *his chest heaving, stares, turns to* ELIZABETH. *She comes to him as though to plead, her voice quaking.*

**Elizabeth:** Do what you will. But let none be your judge. There be no higher judge under Heaven than Proctor is! Forgive me, forgive me, John—I never knew such goodness in the world! *She covers her face, weeping.*

PROCTOR *turns from her to* HATHORNE; *he is off the earth, his voice hollow.*

**Proctor:** I want my life.

**Hathorne,** *electrified, surprised:* You'll confess yourself?

**Proctor:** I will have my life.

**Hathorne,** *with a mystical tone:* God be praised! It is a providence! *He rushes out the door, and his voice is heard calling down the corridor:* He will confess! Proctor will confess!

**Proctor,** *with a cry, as he strides to the door:* Why do you cry it? *In great pain he turns back to her.* It is evil, is it not? It is evil.

**Elizabeth,** *in terror, weeping:* I cannot judge you, John, I cannot!

**Proctor:** Then who will judge me? *Suddenly clasping his hands:* God in Heaven, what is John Proctor, what is John Proctor? *He moves as an animal, and a fury is riding in him, a tantalized search.* I think it is honest, I think so; I am no saint. *As though she had denied this he calls angrily at her:* Let Rebecca go like a saint; for me it is fraud!

*Voices are heard in the hall, speaking together in suppressed excitement.*

**Elizabeth:** I am not your judge, I cannot be. *As though giving him release:* Do as you will, do as you will!

**Proctor:** Would you give them such a lie? Say it. Would you ever give them this? *She cannot answer.* You would not; if tongs of fire were singeing you you would not! It is evil. Good, then—it is evil, and I do it!

HATHORNE *enters with* DANFORTH, *and, with them,* CHEEVER, PARRIS, *and* HALE. *It is a businesslike, rapid entrance, as though the ice had been broken.*

**Danforth,** *with great relief and gratitude:* Praise to God, man, praise to God; you shall be blessed in Heaven for this. CHEEVER *has hurried to the bench with pen, ink, and paper.* PROCTOR *watches him.* Now then, let us have it. Are you ready, Mr. Cheever?

**Proctor,** *with a cold, cold horror at their efficiency:* Why must it be written?

**Danforth:** Why, for the good instruction of the village, Mister; this we shall post upon the church door! *To* PARRIS, *urgently:* Where is the marshal?

**Parris,** *runs to the door and calls down the corridor:* Marshal! Hurry!

**Danforth:** Now, then, Mister, will you speak slowly, and directly to the point, for Mr. Cheever's sake. *He is on record now, and is really dictating to* CHEEVER, *who writes.* Mr. Proctor, have you seen the Devil in your life? PROCTOR*'s jaws lock.* Come, man, there is light in the sky; the town waits at the scaffold; I would give out this news. Did you see the Devil?

**Proctor:** I did.

**Parris:** Praise God!

**Danforth:** And when he come to you, what were his demand? PROCTOR *is silent.* DANFORTH *helps.* Did he bid you to do his work upon the earth?

**Proctor:** He did.

**Danforth:** And you bound yourself to his service? DANFORTH *turns, as* REBECCA NURSE *enters, with* HERRICK *helping to support her. She is barely able to walk.* Come in, come in, woman!

**Rebecca,** *brightening as she sees* PROCTOR: Ah, John! You are well, then, eh?

PROCTOR *turns his face to the wall.*

**Danforth:** Courage, man, courage—let her witness your good example that she may come to God herself. Now hear it, Goody Nurse! Say on, Mr. Proctor. Did you bind yourself to the Devil's service?

**Rebecca,** *astonished:* Why, John!

**Proctor,** *through his teeth, his face turned from* REBECCA: I did.

**Danforth:** Now, woman, you surely see it profit nothin' to keep this conspiracy any further. Will you confess yourself with him?

**Rebecca:** Oh, John—God send his mercy on you!

**Danforth:** I say, will you confess yourself, Goody Nurse?

**Rebecca:** Why, it is a lie, it is a lie; how may I damn myself? I cannot, I cannot.

**Danforth:** Mr. Proctor. When the Devil came to you did you see Rebecca Nurse in his company? PROCTOR *is silent.* Come, man, take courage—did you ever see her with the Devil?

**Proctor,** *almost inaudibly:* No.

DANFORTH, *now sensing trouble, glances at* JOHN *and goes to the table, and picks up a sheet—the list of condemned.*

**Danforth:** Did you ever see her sister, Mary Easty, with the Devil?

**Proctor:** No, I did not.

**Danforth,** *his eyes narrow on* PROCTOR: Did you ever see Martha Corey with the Devil?

**Proctor:** I did not.

**Danforth,** *realizing, slowly putting the sheet down:* Did you ever see anyone with the Devil?

**Proctor:** I did not.

**Danforth:** Proctor, you mistake me. I am not empowered to trade your life for a lie. You have most certainly seen some person with the Devil. PROCTOR *is silent.* Mr. Proctor, a score of people have already testified they saw this woman with the Devil.

**Proctor:** Then it is proved. Why must I say it?

**Danforth:** Why "must" you say it! Why, you should rejoice to say it if your soul is truly purged of any love for Hell!

**Proctor:** They think to go like saints. I like not to spoil their names.

**Danforth,** *inquiring, incredulous:* Mr. Proctor, do you think they go like saints?

**Proctor,** *evading:* This woman never thought she done the Devil's work.

**Danforth:** Look you, sir. I think you mistake your duty here. It matters nothing what she thought—she is convicted of the unnatural murder of children, and you for sending your spirit out upon Mary Warren. Your soul alone is the issue here, Mister, and you will prove its whiteness or you cannot live in a Christian country. Will you tell me now what persons conspired with you in the Devil's company? PROCTOR *is silent.* To your knowledge was Rebecca Nurse ever—

**Proctor:** I speak my own sins; I cannot judge another. *Crying out, with hatred:* I have no tongue for it.

**Hale,** *quickly to* DANFORTH: Excellency, it is enough he confess himself. Let him sign it, let him sign it.

**Parris,** *feverishly:* It is a great service, sir. It is a weighty name; it will strike the village that Proctor confess. I beg you, let him sign it. The sun is up, Excellency!

**Danforth,** *considers; then with dissatisfaction:* Come, then, sign your testimony. *To* CHEEVER: Give it to him. CHEEVER *goes to* PROCTOR, *the confession and a pen in hand.* PROCTOR *does not look at it.* Come, man, sign it.

**Proctor,** *after glancing at the confession:* You have all witnessed it—it is enough.

**Danforth:** You will not sign it?

**Proctor:** You have all witnessed it; what more is needed?

**Danforth:** Do you sport with me? You will sign your name or it is no confession, Mister! *His breast heaving with agonized breathing,* PROCTOR *now lays the paper down and signs his name.*

**Parris:** Praise be to the Lord!

PROCTOR *has just finished signing when* DANFORTH *reaches for the paper. But* PROCTOR *snatches it up, and now a wild terror is rising in him, and a boundless anger.*

**Danforth,** *perplexed, but politely extending his hand:* If you please, sir.

**Proctor:** No.

**Danforth,** *as though* PROCTOR *did not understand:* Mr. Proctor, I must have—

> ## "How may I live without my name? I have given you my soul; leave me my name!"

**Proctor:** No, no. I have signed it. You have seen me. It is done! You have no need for this.

**Parris:** Proctor, the village must have proof that—

**Proctor:** Damn the village! I confess to God, and God has seen my name on this! It is enough!

**Danforth:** No, sir, it is—

**Proctor:** You came to save my soul, did you not? Here! I have confessed myself; it is enough!

**Danforth:** You have not con—

**Proctor:** I have confessed myself! Is there no good penitence but it be public? God does not need my name nailed upon the church! God sees my name; God knows how black my sins are! It is enough!

**Danforth:** Mr. Proctor—

**Proctor:** You will not use me! I am no Sarah Good or Tituba, I am John Proctor! You will not use me! It is no part of salvation that you should use me!

**Danforth:** I do not wish to—

**Proctor:** I have three children—how may I teach them to walk like men in the world, and I sold my friends?

**Danforth:** You have not sold your friends—

**Proctor:** Beguile me not! I blacken all of them when this is nailed to the church the very day they hang for silence!

**Danforth:** Mr. Proctor, I must have good and legal proof that you—

**Proctor:** You are the high court, your word is good enough! Tell them I confessed myself; say Proctor broke his knees and wept like a woman; say what you will, but my name cannot—

**Danforth,** *with suspicion:* It is the same, is it not? If I report it or you sign to it?

**Proctor**—*he knows it is insane:* No, it is not the same! What others say and what I sign to is not the same!

**Danforth:** Why? Do you mean to deny this confession when you are free?

**Proctor:** I mean to deny nothing!

**Danforth:** Then explain to me, Mr. Proctor, why you will not let—

**Proctor,** *with a cry of his whole soul:* Because it is my name! Because I cannot have another in my life! Because I lie and sign myself to lies! Because I am not worth the dust on the feet of them that hang! How may I live without my name? I have given you my soul; leave me my name!

**Danforth,** *pointing at the confession in* PROC-TOR's *hand:* Is that document a lie? If it is a lie I will not accept it! What say you? I will not deal in lies, Mister! PROCTOR *is motionless.* You will give me your honest confession in my hand, or I cannot keep you from the rope. PROCTOR *does not reply.* Which way do you go, Mister?

*His breast heaving, his eyes staring,* PROCTOR *tears the paper and crumples it, and he is weeping in fury, but erect.*

**Danforth:** Marshal!

**Parris,** *hysterically, as though the tearing paper were his life:* Proctor, Proctor!

**Hale:** Man, you will hang! You cannot!

**Proctor,** *his eyes full of tears:* I can. And there's your first marvel, that I can. You have made your magic now, for now I do think I see some shred of goodness in John Proctor. Not enough to weave a banner with, but white enough to keep it from such dogs. ELIZABETH, *in a burst of terror, rushes to him and weeps against his hand.* Give them no tear! Tears pleasure them! Show honor now, show a stony heart and sink them with it! *He has lifted her, and kisses her now with great passion.*

**Rebecca:** Let you fear nothing! Another judgment waits us all!

**Danforth:** Hang them high over the town! Who weeps for these, weeps for corruption! *He sweeps out past them.* HERRICK *starts to lead* REBECCA, *who*

almost collapses, but PROCTOR *catches her, and she glances up at him apologetically.*
**Rebecca:** I've had no breakfast.
**Herrick:** Come, man.

HERRICK *escorts them out,* HATHORNE *and* CHEEVER *behind them.* ELIZABETH *stands staring at the empty doorway.*

**Parris,** *in deadly fear, to* ELIZABETH: Go to him, Goody Proctor! There is yet time!

*From outside a drumroll strikes the air.* PARRIS *is startled.* ELIZABETH *jerks about toward the window.*

**Parris:** Go to him! *He rushes out the door, as though to hold back his fate.* Proctor! Proctor!

*Again, a short burst of drums.*

"He have his goodness now."

**Hale:** Woman, plead with him! *He starts to rush out the door, and then goes back to her.* Woman! It is pride, it is vanity. *She avoids his eyes, and moves to the window. He drops to his knees.* Be his helper! What profit him to bleed? Shall the dust praise him? Shall the worms declare his truth? Go to him, take his shame away!

**Elizabeth,** *supporting herself against collapse, grips the bars of the window, and with a cry:* He have his goodness now. God forbid I take it from him!

*The final drumroll crashes, then heightens violently.* HALE *weeps in frantic prayer, and the new sun is pouring in upon her face, and the drums rattle like bones in the morning air.*

*The curtain falls*

# Response and Analysis

## Act Four

### Reading Check

1. Why has Reverend Hale returned to Salem?

2. What news about Abigail does Parris give Danforth?

3. What two things does Elizabeth say she is unable to do for John?

4. Why does Danforth want a written confession from Proctor?

### Thinking Critically

5. Why does Hale say he has come "to do the Devil's work"? What **motivates** his action?

6. What events precede the sudden disappearance of Abigail and Mercy?

7. What does Parris fear about the response of the people in Andover?

8. Why does Hale counsel Elizabeth to persuade John Proctor to lie? Do you think he is right to do so?

9. How do you interpret Arthur Miller's statement that John and Elizabeth inhabit a world "beyond sorrow, above it" (page 1268)?

10. What **motivation** does Proctor have for confessing? At the same time, why does he see his confession as deeply **ironic?**

11. In the play's **climax**, Proctor destroys his own confession. Why does he ultimately choose his "goodness"? Review your reading notes about Proctor's character.

## The Play as a Whole

12. Read the dictionary definition of *crucible* at the top of the next column, and explain the **title** of the play. Why do you think Miller chose this title?

**cru·ci·ble** (krōō′sə bəl) *n.*
[ML *crucibulum,* lamp, crucible, prob. < Gmc, as in OE *cruce,* pot, jug, MHG *kruse,* earthen pot (see CRUSE) + L suffix *-ibulum* (as in *thuribulum,* censer), but assoc. by folk etym. with L *crux,* CROSS, as if lamp burning before cross] **1** a container made of a substance that can resist great heat, for melting, fusing, or calcining ores, metals, etc. **2** the hollow at the bottom of an ore furnace, where the molten metal collects **3** a severe test or trial

13. Miller said he wrote *The Crucible* with the conviction that "there were moments when an individual conscience was all that could keep the world from falling apart." Do you agree with him? Do you think the play actually demonstrates a triumph of individual conscience? Explain your response.

14. What, in your opinion, is the difference between the way Proctor and Hale resolve the **conflicts** between their public and their private lives? Whose solution is better? Could their conflicts be found in people today? Support your answers with examples from the text and from life.

15. Miller has called *The Crucible* a **tragedy.** Do you think it is a tragedy? Why or why not?

**SKILLS FOCUS**

**Literary Skills**
Analyze motivation.

**Reading Skills**
Interpret a dramatic work.

### Extending and Evaluating

**16.** The writer of a literary work may have responsibilities not only to readers and publishers but also to the people he or she chooses to write about. Do you think Miller had a responsibility to portray the Salem witch trials accurately? Is his use of "artistic license" with respect to some of the historical facts justifiable? To what extent should a writer, artist, or filmmaker be accurate when basing a work of fiction on historical events? Explain your responses.

**17.** Some critics have claimed that Miller's play is really a vehicle for his own political viewpoints. How do you feel about these criticisms? Miller's lengthy commentary throughout the play is certainly unusual. How do you feel about his commentary? Be specific in your answers.

## WRITING

Choose from among the following assignments to respond to the play.

### 1. The Breaking of Charity

In his **autobiography**, *Timebends,* Arthur Miller writes that "the real story" of the Salem witch trials is to be found in "the breaking of charity" within a human community. Write a brief **essay** explaining what you think Miller means by this interesting statement, and support your opinion with evidence from *The Crucible.* Conclude your essay with your reflection on whether "the breaking of charity" could destroy a community today.

### 2. Characters in Conflict

In a brief essay, write a **character analysis** of one of the characters in *The Crucible.* (You can use the notes you took about the characters as you read the play.) In your essay, focus on these aspects of the character:

- conflicts
- motivation
- significant actions or decisions
- changes or discoveries

Include at the end of the essay your response to the character: Did you find the character believable? Did he or she do the right thing? Did you admire this person? Were your feelings negative? Or was your response mixed or complex?

### 3. Comparing History and Drama

Write an **essay** in which you **compare** details of the actual Salem witch trials with details presented in *The Crucible.* You'll find information on the trials in A Closer Look on pages 10–11 in Collection 1. Use this feature and other resources, including libraries and the Internet, to gather data on the trials. Before looking further, formulate questions that will guide your research.

▶ **Use "Reporting Historical Research" on pages 602–621 for help with this assignment.**

### 4. Naming Names

Research the 1950s Congressional hearings into "un-American activities," and write a **persuasive essay** analyzing the relationship of Miller's play to this painful American event. Examine Miller's own comments about his intentions (see the playwright's essay "Why I Wrote *The Crucible,*" on page 1213), as well as the reactions of contemporary literary and social critics. Include your own point of view on how effectively a work of fiction can comment on a real-life political or social situation.

▶ **Use "Reporting Historical Research" on pages 602–621 for help with this assignment.**

**SKILLS FOCUS**

**Writing Skills**
Write an essay interpreting theme. Write a character analysis. Write an essay comparing a dramatic work to historical fact. Write a persuasive essay analyzing the relationship between literature and historical context. Write a comparison-contrast essay.

### 5. Tales of Horror

In an **essay** about Nathaniel Hawthorne called "Hawthorne in Salem," critic Van Wyck Brooks describes Salem and the past that still hung over the town when Hawthorne lived there in the early 1800s. Judge Hathorne, a character in *The Crucible*, is Hawthorne's ancestor.

> Salem bristled with old wives' tales and old men's legends. One heard of locked closets in haunted houses where skeletons had been found. One heard of walls that resounded with knocks where there had once been doorways, now bricked up. One heard of poisonous houses and blood-stained houses. . . .

Is this view of Salem and its dark past reflected in *The Crucible*? How might reading Miller's play change the popular perception of Salem as the scene of a supernatural horror story? Write an **essay** in which you **compare** Brooks's description of Salem with the Salem that Miller presents in *The Crucible*. In your essay consider what each writer suggests about the sources of the town's disastrous events and "skeletons in the closet."

# Reflecting *on the* Literary Period

## Contemporary Literature: 1939 to Present

The selections in this feature were written during the same literary period as the other selections in Collection 6, and they share many of the same ideas and concerns. The Focus Question will guide your reading and help you reflect on important aspects of the period.

### Think About...

Characterizing contemporary American literature is difficult because it is in a continuous state of change. Despite this ambiguous nature, American literature today is distinct from that of other literary periods in its focus on the private lives of individuals. Contemporary writers often explore personal issues, the pains and joys of life, and, sometimes, the redemptive power of love.

Another unique feature of contemporary literature is the explosion of new voices. American voices now come from African Americans, Latinos, Asian Americans, Native Americans; from Protestants, Catholics, Jews, Muslims, Buddhists, Hindus, and from people with no religious affiliation at all. These voices are insistent, talented, honest—and they *will* be heard.

Today's writers are producing what Ralph Waldo Emerson called for over a century and a half ago: a diverse and truly national literature. When that true literature is produced, he said, the sign of it will be that the complete revelation of the most private self will be universally recognized and accepted by all people everywhere.

*Family Group* (1951) by John Koch (1909–1978).

Smithsonian American Art Museum, Washington, DC, U.S.A.

### Focus Question

As you read each selection, keep in mind this Focus Question and take notes to help you answer it at the end of the feature:

What do these contemporary writers, who represent a range of American voices, say about the human condition and our very personal needs for love, family, community, and freedom?

**SKILLS FOCUS**

Pages 1277–1312 cover **Literary Skills** Evaluate genres and traditions in American literature.

## The Magic Barrel

**Meet the Writer** Although **Bernard Malamud** (1914–1986) crafted tales that draw on the experiences of Jewish people, Malamud preferred not to be pigeonholed. He did write *about* Jews, but he wrote *for* all people.

Malamud's characters usually live at a level of bare physical subsistence. Though we feel compassion for them, they do not display the least self-pity. Even if their lives are sad, Malamud's characters are triumphant because they survive heroically against the odds we all face.

Malamud's own upbringing was bleak. He was the older of two sons of a Russian immigrant storekeeper. His mother died when he was fourteen. He grew up in Brooklyn in a household without books, music, or pictures on the walls. In particular, it was the suffering of European Jews during World War II that convinced Malamud he had something to say as a writer. "Somebody has to cry," he said, "even if it's just a writer, twenty years later."

Malamud's stories are spun out of the commonplace, the tragicomedy of survival in a brutal world. But his stories are always informed by love, and indeed, his characters are largely redeemed by love.

Many writers in the last half of the twentieth century broke with earlier traditions in storytelling and experimented with forms and style. Their characters are adrift in a world that seems devoid of meaning. Malamud was different. In his carefully plotted stories, a reader might hear echoes of the nineteenth-century storyteller and moralist Nathaniel Hawthorne, whose characters live in a world where good and evil are forces to contend with.

---

**CONNECTING TO THE**
**Focus Question**

As you read "The Magic Barrel," ask yourself this question: What does Leo Finkle discover about himself, about love, and about the possibility of personal redemption?

---

# The Magic Barrel

## Bernard Malamud

Not long ago there lived in uptown New York, in a small, almost meager[1] room, though crowded with books, Leo Finkle, a rabbinical student in the Yeshivah University.[2] Finkle, after six years of study, was to be ordained in June and had been advised by an acquaintance that he might find it easier to win himself a congregation if he were married. Since he had no present prospects of marriage, after two tormented days of turning it over in his mind, he called in Pinye Salzman, a marriage broker whose two-line advertisement he had read in the *Forward*.[3]

The matchmaker appeared one night out of the dark fourth-floor hallway of the graystone rooming house where Finkle lived, grasping a black, strapped portfolio that had been worn thin with use. Salzman, who had been long in the business, was of slight but dignified build,

---

1. **meager** (mē′gər): poor. The room probably has little furniture.
2. **Yeshivah** (yə·shē′və) **University:** school in New York City that is a general college and a seminary for the training of Orthodox Jewish rabbis.

3. ***Forward:*** the *Jewish Daily Forward*, a Yiddish newspaper in New York City.

*Birthday (L'Anniversaire)* (1915) by Marc Chagall. Oil on cardboard.

Acquired through the Lillie P. Bliss Bequest. (275.1949). Digital Image © The Museum of Modern Art/Licensed by SCALA/ Art Resource, NY. © 2005 Artists Rights Society (ARS), New York/ADAGP, Paris.

wearing an old hat, and an overcoat too short and tight for him. He smelled frankly of fish, which he loved to eat, and although he was missing a few teeth, his presence was not displeasing, because of an amiable manner curiously contrasted with mournful eyes. His voice, his lips, his wisp of beard, his bony fingers were animated, but give him a moment of repose and his mild blue eyes revealed a depth of sadness, a characteristic that put Leo a little at ease although the situation, for him, was inherently tense.

He at once informed Salzman why he had asked him to come, explaining that his home was in Cleveland, and that but for his parents, who had married comparatively late in life, he was alone in the world. He had for six years devoted himself almost entirely to his studies, as a result of which, understandably, he had found himself without time for a social life and the company of young women. Therefore he thought it the better part of trial and error—of embarrassing fumbling—to call in an experienced person to advise him on these matters. He remarked in passing that the function of the marriage broker was ancient and honorable, highly approved in the Jewish community, because it made practical

the necessary without hindering joy. Moreover, his own parents had been brought together by a matchmaker. They had made, if not a financially profitable marriage—since neither had possessed any worldly goods to speak of—at least a successful one in the sense of their everlasting devotion to each other. Salzman listened in embarrassed surprise, sensing a sort of apology. Later, however, he experienced a glow of pride in his work, an emotion that had left him years ago, and he heartily approved of Finkle.

The two went to their business. Leo had led Salzman to the only clear place in the room, a table near a window that overlooked the lamp-lit city. He seated himself at the matchmaker's side but facing him, attempting by an act of will to suppress[4] the unpleasant tickle in his throat. Salzman eagerly unstrapped his portfolio and removed a loose rubber band from a thin packet of much-handled cards. As he flipped through them, a gesture and sound that physically hurt Leo, the student pretended not to see and gazed steadfastly out the window. Although it was still February, winter was on its last legs, signs of which he had for the first time in years begun to notice. He now observed the round white moon, moving high in the sky through a cloud menagerie,[5] and watched with half-open mouth as it penetrated a huge hen, and dropped out of her like an egg laying itself. Salzman, though pretending through eyeglasses he had just slipped on, to be engaged in scanning the writing on the cards, stole occasional glances at the young man's distinguished face, noting with pleasure the long, severe scholar's nose, brown eyes heavy with learning, sensitive yet ascetic[6] lips, and a certain, almost hollow quality of the dark cheeks. He gazed around at shelves upon shelves of books and let out a soft, contented sigh.

When Leo's eyes fell upon the cards, he counted six spread out in Salzman's hand.

"So few?" he asked in disappointment.

"You wouldn't believe me how much cards I got in my office," Salzman replied. "The drawers are already filled to the top, so I keep them now in a barrel, but is every girl good for a new rabbi?"

Leo blushed at this, regretting all he had revealed of himself in a curriculum vitae[7] he had sent to Salzman. He had thought it best to acquaint him with his strict standards and specifications, but in having done so, felt he had told the marriage broker more than was absolutely necessary.

He hesitantly inquired, "Do you keep photographs of your clients on file?"

"First comes family, amount of dowry,[8] also what kind promises," Salzman replied, unbuttoning his tight coat and settling himself in the chair. "After comes pictures, rabbi."

"Call me Mr. Finkle. I'm not yet a rabbi."

Salzman said he would, but instead called him doctor, which he changed to rabbi when Leo was not listening too attentively.

Salzman adjusted his horn-rimmed spectacles, gently cleared his throat and read in an eager voice the contents of the top card:

"Sophie P. Twenty four year. Widow one year. No children. Educated high school and two years college. Father promises eight thousand dollars. Has wonderful wholesale business. Also real estate. On the mother's side comes teachers, also one actor. Well known on Second Avenue."

Leo gazed up in surprise. "Did you say a widow?"

"A widow don't mean spoiled, rabbi. She lived with her husband maybe four months. He was a sick boy she made a mistake to marry him."

"Marrying a widow has never entered my mind."

"This is because you have no experience. A widow, especially if she is young and healthy like

---

4. **suppress:** check or hold back.
5. **menagerie** (mə·naj′ər·ē): collection of animals. The clouds look like animals.
6. **ascetic** (ə·set′ik): severe.
7. **curriculum vitae** (kə·rik′yo͞o·ləm vīt′ē): Latin for "course of life"; a résumé.
8. **dowry** (dou′rē): money or goods that a bride brings to a marriage.

this girl, is a wonderful person to marry. She will be thankful to you the rest of her life. Believe me, if I was looking now for a bride, I would marry a widow."

Leo reflected, then shook his head.

Salzman hunched his shoulders in an almost imperceptible[9] gesture of disappointment. He placed the card down on the wooden table and began to read another:

"Lily H. High school teacher. Regular. Not a substitute. Has savings and new Dodge car. Lived in Paris one year. Father is successful dentist thirty-five years. Interested in professional man. Well Americanized family. Wonderful opportunity.

"I knew her personally," said Salzman. "I wish you could see this girl. She is a doll. Also very intelligent. All day you could talk to her about books and theater and what not. She also knows current events."

"I don't believe you mentioned her age?"

"Her age?" Salzman said, raising his brows. "Her age is thirty-two years."

Leo said after a while, "I'm afraid that seems a little too old."

Salzman let out a laugh. "So how old are you, rabbi?"

"Twenty-seven."

"So what is the difference, tell me, between twenty-seven and thirty-two? My own wife is seven years older than me. So what did I suffer?—Nothing. If a Rothschild's[10] daughter wants to marry you, would you say on account her age, no?"

"Yes," Leo said dryly.

Salzman shook off the no in the yes. "Five years don't mean a thing. I give you my word that when you will live with her for one week you will forget her age. What does it mean five years—that she lived more and knows more than somebody who is younger? On this girl,

God bless her, years are not wasted. Each one that it comes makes better the bargain."

"What subject does she teach in high school?"

"Languages. If you heard the way she speaks French, you will think it is music. I am in the business twenty-five years, and I recommend her with my whole heart. Believe me, I know what I'm talking, rabbi."

"What's on the next card?" Leo said abruptly.

Salzman reluctantly turned up the third card:

"Ruth K. Nineteen years. Honor student. Father offers thirteen thousand cash to the right bridegroom. He is a medical doctor. Stomach specialist with marvelous practice. Brother-in-law owns own garment business. Particular people."

Salzman looked as if he had read his trump card.

"Did you say nineteen?" Leo asked with interest.

"On the dot."

"Is she attractive?" He blushed. "Pretty?"

Salzman kissed his finger tips. "A little doll. On this I give you my word. Let me call the father tonight and you will see what means pretty."

But Leo was troubled. "You're sure she's that young?"

"This I am positive. The father will show you the birth certificate."

"Are you positive there isn't something wrong with her?" Leo insisted.

"Who says there is wrong?"

"I don't understand why an American girl her age should go to a marriage broker."

A smile spread over Salzman's face.

"So for the same reason you went, she comes."

Leo flushed. "I am pressed for time."

Salzman, realizing he had been tactless, quickly explained. "The father came, not her. He wants she should have the best, so he looks around himself. When we will locate the right boy he will introduce him and encourage. This makes a better marriage than if a young girl without experience takes for herself. I don't have to tell you this."

"But don't you think this young girl believes in love?" Leo spoke uneasily.

---

9. **imperceptible** (im′pər·sep′tə·bəl): not plain or distinct; not noticeable.
10. **Rothschild's daughter:** The Rothschilds are a wealthy banking family.

Salzman was about to guffaw but caught himself and said soberly, "Love comes with the right person, not before."

Leo parted dry lips but did not speak. Noticing that Salzman had snatched a glance at the next card, he cleverly asked, "How is her health?"

"Perfect," Salzman said, breathing with difficulty. "Of course, she is a little lame on her right foot from an auto accident that it happened to her when she was twelve years, but nobody notices on account she is so brilliant and also beautiful."

Leo got up heavily and went to the window. He felt curiously bitter and upbraided[11] himself for having called in the marriage broker. Finally, he shook his head.

"Why not?" Salzman persisted, the pitch of his voice rising.

"Because I detest stomach specialists."

"So what do you care what is his business? After you marry her do you need him? Who says he must come every Friday night in your house?"

Ashamed of the way the talk was going, Leo dismissed Salzman, who went home with heavy, melancholy eyes.

Though he had felt only relief at the marriage broker's departure, Leo was in low spirits the next day. He explained it as arising from Salzman's failure to produce a suitable bride for him. He did not care for his type of clientele.[12] But when Leo found himself hesitating whether to seek out another matchmaker, one more polished than Pinye, he wondered if it could be— his protestations to the contrary, and although he honored his father and mother—that he did not, in essence, care for the matchmaking institution? This thought he quickly put out of mind yet found himself still upset. All day he ran around in the woods—missed an important appointment, forgot to give out his laundry, walked out of a Broadway cafeteria without paying and had to run back with the ticket in his hand; had even not recognized his landlady in the street when she passed with a friend and courteously called out, "A good evening to you, Doctor Finkle." By nightfall, however, he had regained sufficient calm to sink his nose into a book and there found peace from his thoughts.

Almost at once there came a knock on the door. Before Leo could say enter, Salzman, commercial cupid, was standing in the room. His face was gray and meager, his expression hungry, and he looked as if he would expire[13] on his feet. Yet the marriage broker managed, by some trick of the muscles, to display a broad smile.

"So good evening. I am invited?"

Leo nodded, disturbed to see him again, yet unwilling to ask the man to leave.

Beaming still, Salzman laid his portfolio on the table. "Rabbi, I got for you tonight good news."

"I've asked you not to call me rabbi. I'm still a student."

"Your worries are finished. I have for you a first-class bride."

"Leave me in peace concerning this subject." Leo pretended lack of interest.

"The world will dance at your wedding."

"Please, Mr. Salzman, no more."

"But first must come back my strength," Salzman said weakly. He fumbled with the portfolio straps and took out of the leather case an oily paper bag, from which he extracted a hard, seeded roll and a small, smoked whitefish. With a quick motion of his hand he stripped the fish out of its skin and began ravenously to chew. "All day in a rush," he muttered.

Leo watched him eat.

"A sliced tomato you have maybe?" Salzman hesitantly inquired.

"No."

The marriage broker shut his eyes and ate. When he had finished he carefully cleaned up the crumbs and rolled up the remains of the fish, in the paper bag. His spectacled eyes roamed the room until he discovered, amid some piles of books, a one-burner gas stove. Lifting his hat he humbly asked, "A glass tea you got, rabbi?"

---

11. **upbraided** (up·brād′id): criticized.
12. **clientele** (klī′ən·tel′): customers.

13. **expire** (ek·spīr′): die.

*The Rabbi* by Marc Chagall.
Kunstmuseum, Basel, Switzerland.
SCALA/Art Resource, NY.
© 2005 Artists Rights Society
(ARS), New York/ADAGP, Paris.

Conscience-striken, Leo rose and brewed the tea. He served it with a chunk of lemon and two cubes of lump sugar, delighting Salzman.

After he had drunk his tea, Salzman's strength and good spirits were restored.

"So tell me, rabbi," he said amiably, "you considered some more the three clients I mentioned yesterday?"

"There was no need to consider."

"Why not?"

"None of them suits me."

"What then suits you?"

Leo let it pass because he could give only a confused answer.

Without waiting for a reply, Salzman asked, "You remember this girl I talked to you—the high school teacher?"

"Age thirty-two?"

But, surprisingly, Salzman's face lit in a smile. "Age twenty-nine."

Leo shot him a look. "Reduced from thirty-two?"

"A mistake," Salzman avowed. "I talked today with the dentist. He took me to his safety deposit box and showed me the birth certificate. She was twenty-nine years last August. They made her a party in the mountains where she went for her vacation. When her father spoke to me the first

time I forgot to write the age and I told you thirty-two, but now I remember this was a different client, a widow."

"The same one you told me about? I thought she was twenty-four?"

"A different. Am I responsible that the world is filled with widows?"

"No, but I'm not interested in them, nor for that matter, in school teachers."

Salzman pulled his clasped hands to his breast. Looking at the ceiling he devoutly exclaimed, "Yiddishe kinder,[14] what can I say to somebody that he is not interested in high school teachers? So what then you are interested?"

Leo flushed but controlled himself.

"In what else will you be interested," Salzman went on, "if you not interested in this fine girl that she speaks four languages and has personally in the bank ten thousand dollars? Also her father guarantees further twelve thousand. Also she has a new car, wonderful clothes, talks on all subjects, and she will give you a first-class home and children. How near do we come in our life to paradise?"

"If she's so wonderful, why wasn't she married ten years ago?"

"Why?" said Salzman with a heavy laugh. "—Why? Because she is *partikiler*. This is why. She wants the *best*."

Leo was silent, amused at how he had entangled himself. But Salzman had aroused his interest in Lily H., and he began seriously to consider calling on her. When the marriage broker observed how intently Leo's mind was at work on the facts he had supplied, he felt certain they would soon come to an agreement.

Late Saturday afternoon, conscious of Salzman, Leo Finkle walked with Lily Hirschorn along Riverside Drive. He walked briskly and erectly, wearing with distinction the black fedora he had that morning taken with trepidation[15] out of the dusty hat box on his closet shelf, and the heavy black Saturday coat he had thoroughly whisked clean. Leo also owned a walking stick, a present from a distant relative, but quickly put temptation aside and did not use it. Lily, petite and not unpretty, had on something signifying the approach of spring. She was au courant,[16] animatedly, with all sorts of subjects, and he weighed her words and found her surprisingly sound—score another for Salzman, whom he uneasily sensed to be somewhere around, hiding perhaps high in a tree along the street, flashing the lady signals with a pocket mirror; or perhaps a cloven-hoofed Pan,[17] piping nuptial[18] ditties as he danced his invisible way before them, strewing wild buds on the walk and purple grapes in their path, symbolizing fruit of a union, though there was of course still none.

Lily startled Leo by remarking, "I was thinking of Mr. Salzman, a curious figure, wouldn't you say?"

Not certain what to answer, he nodded.

She bravely went on, blushing, "I for one am grateful for his introducing us. Aren't you?"

He courteously replied, "I am."

"I mean," she said with a little laugh—and it was all in good taste, or at least gave the effect of being not in bad—"do you mind that we came together so?"

He was not displeased with her honesty, recognizing that she meant to set the relationship aright, and understanding that it took a certain amount of experience in life, and courage, to want to do it quite that way. One had to have some sort of past to make that kind of beginning.

He said that he did not mind. Salzman's function was traditional and honorable—valuable for what it might achieve, which, he pointed out, was frequently nothing.

---

14. **Yiddishe kinder:** Yiddish for "Jewish children."
15. **trepidation** (trep′ə·dā′shən): fearful uneasiness; anxiety.
16. **au courant** (ō kōō·rä*n*): French for "in the current," meaning up-to-date on news or events.
17. **Pan:** Greek god of the woodlands, often shown with the feet and horns of a goat. Pan was a merry god who played the pipes and was always in love with one nymph or another.
18. **nuptial** (nup′shəl): having to do with weddings or marriage.

Lily agreed with a sigh. They walked on for a while and she said after a long silence, again with a nervous laugh, "Would you mind if I asked you something a little bit personal? Frankly, I find the subject fascinating." Although Leo shrugged, she went on half embarrassedly, "How was it that you came to your calling? I mean was it a sudden passionate inspiration?"

Leo, after a time, slowly replied, "I was always interested in the Law."[19]

"You saw revealed in it the presence of the Highest?"

He nodded and changed the subject. "I understand that you spent a little time in Paris, Miss Hirschorn?"

"Oh, did Mr. Salzman tell you, Rabbi Finkle?" Leo winced but she went on, "It was ages ago and almost forgotten. I remember I had to return for my sister's wedding."

And Lily would not be put off. "When," she asked in a trembly voice, "did you become enamored of God?"

He stared at her. Then it came to him that she was talking not about Leo Finkle, but of a total stranger, some mystical figure, perhaps even passionate prophet that Salzman had dreamed up for her—no relation to the living or dead. Leo trembled with rage and weakness. The trickster had obviously sold her a bill of goods, just as he had him, who'd expected to become acquainted with a young lady of twenty-nine, only to behold, the moment he laid eyes upon her strained and anxious face, a woman past thirty-five and aging rapidly. Only his self-control had kept him this long in her presence.

"I am not," he said gravely, "a talented religious person," and in seeking words to go on, found himself possessed by shame and fear. "I think," he said in a strained manner, "that I came to God not because I loved Him, but because I did not."

This confession he spoke harshly because its unexpectedness shook him.

Lily wilted. Leo saw a profusion of loaves of bread go flying like ducks high over his head, not unlike the winged loaves by which he had counted himself to sleep last night. Mercifully, then, it snowed, which he would not put past Salzman's machinations.[20]

He was infuriated with the marriage broker and swore he would throw him out of the room the minute he reappeared. But Salzman did not come that night, and when Leo's anger had subsided, an unaccountable despair grew in its place. At first he thought this was caused by his disappointment in Lily, but before long it became evident that he had involved himself with Salzman without a true knowledge of his own intent. He gradually realized—with an emptiness that seized him with six hands—that he had called in the broker to find him a bride because he was incapable of doing it himself. This terrifying insight he had derived as a result of his meeting and conversation with Lily Hirschorn. Her probing questions had somehow irritated him into revealing—to himself more than her—the true nature of his relationship to God, and from that it had come upon him, with shocking force, that apart from his parents, he had never loved anyone. Or perhaps it went the other way, that he did not love God so well as he might, because he had not loved man. It seemed to Leo that his whole life stood starkly revealed and he saw himself for the first time as he truly was—unloved and loveless. This bitter but somehow not fully unexpected revelation brought him to a point of panic, controlled only by extraordinary effort. He covered his face with his hands and cried.

The week that followed was the worst of his life. He did not eat and lost weight. His beard darkened and grew ragged. He stopped attending seminars and almost never opened a book. He seriously considered leaving the Yeshivah, although he was deeply troubled at the thought of

---

19. **the Law:** the first five books of the Jewish scriptures, also called the Torah. These books along with all the commentary written on them make up the Jewish Law.

20. **machinations** (mak′ə·nā′shənz): plots; schemes.

the loss of all his years of study—saw them like pages torn from a book, strewn over the city—and at the devastating effect of this decision upon his parents. But he had lived without knowledge of himself, and never in the Five Books and all the Commentaries—mea culpa[21]—had the truth been revealed to him. He did not know where to turn, and in all this desolating loneliness there was no *to whom,* although he often thought of Lily but not once could bring himself to go downstairs and make the call. He became touchy and irritable, especially with his landlady, who asked him all manner of personal questions; on the other hand, sensing his own disagreeableness, he waylaid her on the stairs and apologized abjectly, until mortified, she ran from him. Out of this, however, he drew the consolation that he was a Jew and that a Jew suffered. But gradually, as the long and terrible week drew to a close, he regained his composure and some idea of purpose in life: to go on as planned. Although he was imperfect, the ideal was not. As for his quest of a bride, the thought of continuing afflicted him with anxiety and heartburn, yet perhaps with this new knowledge of himself he would be more successful than in the past. Perhaps love would now come to him and a bride to that love. And for this sanctified seeking who needed a Salzman?

The marriage broker, a skeleton with haunted eyes, returned that very night. He looked, withal, the picture of frustrated expectancy—as if he had steadfastly waited the week at Miss Lily Hirschorn's side for a telephone call that never came.

Casually coughing, Salzman came immediately to the point: "So how did you like her?"

Leo's anger rose and he could not refrain from chiding the matchmaker: "Why did you lie to me, Salzman?"

Salzman's pale face went dead white, the world had snowed on him.

"Did you not state that she was twenty-nine?" Leo insisted.

"I give you my word—"

"She was thirty-five, if a day. *At least* thirty-five."

"Of this don't be too sure. Her father told me—"

"Never mind. The worst of it was that you lied to her."

"How did I lie to her, tell me?"

"You told her things about me that weren't true. You made me out to be more, consequently less than I am. She had in mind a totally different person, a sort of semi-mystical Wonder Rabbi."

"All I said, you was a religious man."

"I can imagine."

Salzman sighed. "This is my weakness that I have," he confessed. "My wife says to me I shouldn't be a salesman, but when I have two fine people that they would be wonderful to be married, I am so happy that I talk too much." He smiled wanly.[22] "This is why Salzman is a poor man."

Leo's anger left him. "Well, Salzman, I'm afraid that's all."

The marriage broker fastened hungry eyes on him.

"You don't want any more a bride?"

"I do," said Leo, "but I have decided to seek her in a different way. I am no longer interested in an arranged marriage. To be frank, I now admit the necessity of premarital love. That is, I want to be in love with the one I marry."

"Love?" said Salzman, astounded. After a moment he remarked, "For us, our love is our life, not for the ladies. In the ghetto they—"

"I know, I know," said Leo. "I've thought of it often. Love, I have said to myself, should be a by-product of living and worship rather than its own end. Yet for myself I find it necessary to establish the level of my need and fulfill it."

Salzman shrugged but answered, "Listen, rabbi, if you want love, this I can find for you also. I have such beautiful clients that you will love them the minute your eyes will see them."

___

21. **mea culpa** (mā′ä kōōl′pä): Latin for "by my fault."

___

22. **wanly** (wän′lē): feebly.

Leo smiled unhappily. "I'm afraid you don't understand."

But Salzman hastily unstrapped his portfolio and withdrew a manila packet from it.

"Pictures," he said, quickly laying the envelope on the table.

Leo called after him to take the pictures away, but as if on the wings of the wind, Salzman had disappeared.

March came. Leo had returned to his regular routine. Although he felt not quite himself yet—lacked energy—he was making plans for a more active social life. Of course it would cost something, but he was an expert in cutting corners; and when there were no corners left he would make circles rounder. All the while Salzman's pictures had lain on the table, gathering dust. Occasionally as Leo sat studying, or enjoying a cup of tea, his eyes fell on the manila envelope, but he never opened it.

The days went by and no social life to speak of developed with a member of the opposite sex—it was difficult, given the circumstances of his situation. One morning Leo toiled up the stairs to his room and stared out the window at the city. Although the day was bright his view of it was dark. For some time he watched the people in the street below hurrying along and then turned with a heavy heart to his little room. On the table was the packet. With a sudden relentless gesture he tore it open. For a half-hour he stood by the table in a state of excitement, examining the

photographs of the ladies Salzman had included. Finally, with a deep sigh he put them down. There were six, of varying degrees of attractiveness, but look at them long enough and they all became Lily Hirschorn: all past their prime, all starved behind bright smiles, not a true personality in the lot. Life, despite their frantic yoohooings, had passed them by; they were pictures in a briefcase that stank of fish. After a while, however, as Leo attempted to return the photographs into the envelope, he found in it another, a snapshot of the type taken by a machine for a quarter. He gazed at it a moment and let out a cry.

Her face deeply moved him. Why, he could at first not say. It gave him the impression of youth—spring flowers, yet age—a sense of having been used to the bone, wasted; this came from the eyes, which were hauntingly familiar, yet absolutely strange. He had a vivid impression

*Phyllis Seated* (1952) by Moses Soyer. Oil on canvas. 42 × 36 inches.

ACA Galleries.

that he had met her before, but try as he might he could not place her although he could almost recall her name, as if he had read it in her own handwriting. No, this couldn't be; he would have remembered her. It was not, he affirmed, that she had an extraordinary beauty—no, though her face was attractive enough; it was that *something* about her moved him. Feature for feature, even some of the ladies of the photographs could do better; but she leaped forth to his heart—had *lived,* or wanted to—more than just wanted, perhaps regretted how she had lived—had somehow deeply suffered: It could be seen in the depths of those reluctant eyes, and from the way the light enclosed and shone from her, and within her, opening realms of possibility: This was her own. Her he desired. His head ached and eyes narrowed with the intensity of his gazing, then as if an obscure fog had blown up in the mind, he experienced fear of her and was aware that he had received an impression, somehow, of evil. He shuddered, saying softly, it is thus with us all. Leo brewed some tea in a small pot and sat sipping it without sugar, to calm himself. But before he had finished drinking, again with excitement he examined the face and found it good: good for Leo Finkle. Only such a one could understand him and help him seek whatever he was seeking. She might, perhaps, love him. How she had happened to be among the discards in Salzman's barrel he could never guess, but he knew he must urgently go find her.

Leo rushed downstairs, grabbed up the Bronx[23] telephone book, and searched for Salzman's home address. He was not listed, nor was his office. Neither was he in the Manhattan book. But Leo remembered having written down the address on a slip of paper after he had read Salzman's advertisement in the "personals" column of the *Forward.* He ran up to his room and tore through his papers, without luck. It was exasperating. Just when he needed the matchmaker he was nowhere to be found. Fortunately Leo remembered to look in his wallet. There on a card he found his name written and a Bronx address.

> **O**nly such a one could understand him and help him seek whatever he was seeking. She might, perhaps, love him.

No phone number was listed, the reason—Leo now recalled—he had originally communicated with Salzman by letter. He got on his coat, put a hat on over his skullcap and hurried to the subway station. All the way to the far end of the Bronx he sat on the edge of his seat. He was more than once tempted to take out the picture and see if the girl's face was as he remembered it, but he refrained, allowing the snapshot to remain in his inside coat pocket, content to have her so close. When the train pulled into the station he was waiting at the door and bolted out. He quickly located the street Salzman had advertised.

The building he sought was less than a block from the subway, but it was not an office building, nor even a loft, nor a store in which one could rent office space. It was a very old tenement house. Leo found Salzman's name in pencil on a soiled tag under the bell and climbed three dark flights to his apartment. When he knocked, the door was opened by a thin, asthmatic, gray-haired woman, in felt slippers.

"Yes?" she said, expecting nothing. She listened without listening. He could have sworn he had seen her, too, before but knew it was an illusion.

"Salzman—does he live here? Pinye Salzman," he said, "the matchmaker?"

She stared at him a long minute. "Of course."

---

23. **the Bronx:** one of the five boroughs of New York City. The others are Manhattan, Queens, Brooklyn, and Staten Island.

He felt embarrassed. "Is he in?"

"No." Her mouth, though left open, offered nothing more.

"The matter is urgent. Can you tell me where his office is?"

"In the air." She pointed upward.

"You mean he has no office?" Leo asked.

"In his socks."

He peered into the apartment. It was sunless and dingy, one large room divided by a half-open curtain, beyond which he could see a sagging metal bed. The near side of the room was crowded with rickety chairs, old bureaus, a three-legged table, racks of cooking utensils, and all the apparatus of a kitchen. But there was no sign of Salzman or his magic barrel, probably also a figment of the imagination. An odor of frying fish made Leo weak to the knees.

"Where is he?" he insisted. "I've got to see your husband."

At length she answered, "So who knows where he is? Every time he thinks a new thought he runs to a different place. Go home, he will find you."

"Tell him Leo Finkle."

She gave no sign she had heard.

He walked downstairs, depressed.

But Salzman, breathless, stood waiting at his door.

Leo was astounded and overjoyed. "How did you get here before me?"

"I rushed."

"Come inside."

They entered. Leo fixed tea, and a sardine sandwich for Salzman. As they were drinking he reached behind him for the packet of pictures and handed them to the marriage broker.

Salzman put down his glass and said expectantly, "You found somebody you like?"

"Not among these."

The marriage broker turned away.

"Here is the one I want." Leo held forth the snapshot.

Salzman slipped on his glasses and took the picture into his trembling hand. He turned ghastly and let out a groan.

"What's the matter?" cried Leo.

"Excuse me. Was an accident this picture. She isn't for you."

Salzman frantically shoved the manila packet into his portfolio. He thrust the snapshot into his pocket and fled down the stairs.

Leo, after momentary paralysis, gave chase and cornered the marriage broker in the vestibule. The landlady made hysterical outcries but neither of them listened.

"Give me back the picture, Salzman."

"No." The pain in his eyes was terrible.

"Tell me who she is then."

"This I can't tell you. Excuse me."

He made to depart, but Leo, forgetting himself, seized the matchmaker by his tight coat and shook him frenziedly.

"Please," sighed Salzman. "*Please.*"

Leo ashamedly let him go. "Tell me who she is," he begged. "It's very important for me to know."

"She is not for you. She is a wild one—wild, without shame. This is not a bride for a rabbi."

"What do you mean wild?"

"Like an animal. Like a dog. For her to be poor was a sin. This is why to me she is dead now."

"In God's name, what do you mean?"

"Her I can't introduce to you," Salzman cried.

"Why are you so excited?"

"Why, he asks," Salzman said, bursting into tears. "This is my baby, my Stella, she should burn in hell."

Leo hurried up to bed and hid under the covers. Under the covers he thought his life through. Although he soon fell asleep he could not sleep her out of his mind. He woke, beating his breast. Though he prayed to be rid of her, his prayers went unanswered. Through days of torment he endlessly struggled not to love her; fearing success, he escaped it. He then concluded to convert her to goodness, himself to God. The idea alternately nauseated and exalted him.

He perhaps did not know that he had come to a final decision until he encountered Salzman in

a Broadway cafeteria. He was sitting alone at a rear table, sucking the bony remains of a fish. The marriage broker appeared haggard, and transparent to the point of vanishing.

Salzman looked up at first without recognizing him. Leo had grown a pointed beard and his eyes were weighted with wisdom.

"Salzman," he said, "love has at last come to my heart."

"Who can love from a picture?" mocked the marriage broker.

"It is not impossible."

"If you can love her, then you can love anybody. Let me show you some new clients that they just sent me their photographs. One is a little doll."

"Just her I want," Leo murmured.

"Don't be a fool, doctor. Don't bother with her."

"Put me in touch with her, Salzman," Leo said humbly. "Perhaps I can be of service."

Salzman had stopped eating and Leo understood with emotion that it was now arranged.

Leaving the cafeteria, he was, however, afflicted by a tormenting suspicion that Salzman had planned it all to happen this way.

Leo was informed by letter that she would meet him on a certain corner, and she was there one spring night, waiting under a street lamp. He appeared, carrying a small bouquet of violets and rosebuds. Stella stood by the lamppost, smoking. She wore white with red shoes, which fitted his expectations, although in a troubled moment he had imagined the dress red, and only the shoes white. She waited uneasily and shyly. From afar he saw that her eyes—clearly her father's—were filled with desperate innocence. He pictured, in her, his own redemption. Violins and lit candles revolved in the sky. Leo ran forward with flowers outthrust.

Around the corner, Salzman, leaning against a wall, chanted prayers for the dead. ■

# Response and Analysis

## Reading Check

1. Who is Finkle, and who is Salzman? What does each character want?

2. Why does Finkle fall in love with the woman in the photograph?

3. By the end of the story, have Finkle and Salzman both gotten what they want? Explain.

## Thinking Critically

4. According to Finkle's confession to Lily, why did he come to God? How would you explain the **paradox**—or seeming contradiction—in his statement?

5. Why do you think Finkle pictures in Stella his own redemption? What does he want to be redeemed *from*?

6. Why do you think Salzman is chanting prayers for the dead at the end of the story?

7. Do you think Salzman arranged the match between Finkle and Stella after all? Explain your answer.

8. Using details from the selection, respond to **Connecting to the Focus Question** on page 1278.

## Extending and Evaluating

9. What do you think will happen to Leo and Stella once they learn more about each other? Why?

# Son

**Meet the Writer** **John Updike** (1932– ), who grew up in the small town of Shillington, Pennsylvania, is gifted with what seems like a total recall of American middle-class life. Updike also displays a skill with language that can evoke responses to the most ordinary and familiar events, endowing them with importance.

After graduating *summa cum laude* from Harvard University in 1954, Updike studied drawing in England for a year, and on his return to the United States went to work for *The New Yorker* magazine. After two years, he made the courageous decision to support his young family entirely by writing. He left New York for Massachusetts and has since produced a long shelf of impressive novels, stories, poems, memoirs, and critical essays.

Among his most famous and probably most enduring works is the "Rabbit" series—*Rabbit, Run* (1960), *Rabbit Redux* (1971), *Rabbit Is Rich* (1981; Pulitzer Prize), and *Rabbit at Rest* (1990). These novels chronicle the life of Harry "Rabbit" Angstrom, a former high school star athlete who feels trapped by small-town life. In these novels, Updike portrays forty years of American social behavior.

**Background** The story that follows is about fathers and sons, several generations of them. Updike's own father was a teacher. Updike's son, who probably provided the inspiration for the story, became a writer like his father. As you read, you may want to create a time line to keep track of the different generations of fathers and sons.

---

**CONNECTING TO THE**
**Focus Question**

As you read "Son," consider these questions: Are generational conflicts like the ones in this story unique to contemporary American society today? Why or why not?

---

# Son

## John Updike

He is often upstairs, when he has to be home. He prefers to be elsewhere. He is almost sixteen, though beardless still, a man's mind indignantly captive in the frame of a child. I love touching him, but don't often dare. The other day, he had the flu, and a fever, and I gave him a back rub, marvelling at the symmetrical[1] knit of muscle, the organic tension. He is high-strung. Yet his sleep is so solid he sweats like a stone in the wall of a well. He wishes for perfection. He would like to destroy us, for we are, variously, too fat, too jocular,[2] too sloppy, too affectionate, too grotesque and heedless in our ways. His mother smokes too much. His younger brother chews with his mouth open. His older sister leaves unbuttoned the top button of her blouses. His younger sister tussles with the dogs, getting them overexcited, avoiding doing her homework. Everyone in the house talks nonsense. He would be a better father than his father. But time has tricked him, has made him a son. After a quarrel, if he cannot go outside and kick a ball, he retreats to a corner of the house and reclines on the beanbag chair in an attitude of strange—infantile or leonine[3]—torpor.[4] We exhaust him, without meaning to. He takes an interest in the

---

1. **symmetrical** (si·me′tri·kəl): balanced.
2. **jocular** (jäk′yōō·lər): jolly; joking.
3. **leonine** (lē′ə·nīn): like a lion.
4. **torpor** (tôr′pər): sluggishness; dullness.

newspaper now, the front page as well as the sports, in this tiring year of 1973.

He is upstairs, writing a musical comedy. It is a Sunday in 1949. He has volunteered to prepare a high-school assembly program; people will sing. Songs of the time go through his head, as he scribbles new words. *Up in de mornin', down at de school, work like a debil for my grades.* Below him, irksome voices grind on, like machines working their way through tunnels. His parents each want something from the other. "Marion, you don't understand that man like I do; he has a heart of gold." His father's charade[5] is very complex: the world, which he fears, is used as a flail[6] on his wife. But from his cringing attitude he would seem to an outsider the one being flailed. With burning red face, the woman accepts the role of aggressor as penance for the fact, the incessant shameful fact, that *he* has to wrestle with the world while she hides here, in solitude, at home. This is normal, but does not seem to them to be so. Only by convolution[7] have they arrived at the dominant/submissive relationship society has assigned them. For the man is maternally kind and with a smile hugs to himself his jewel, his certainty of being victimized; it is the mother whose tongue is sharp, who sometimes strikes. "Well, he gets you out of the house, and I guess that's gold to you." His answer is "Duty calls," pronounced mincingly.[8] "The social contract is a balance of compromises." This will infuriate her, the son knows; as his heart thickens, the downstairs overflows with her hot voice. "*Don't* wear that smile at me! And *take* your hands off your hips; you look like a sissy!" Their son tries not to listen. When he does, visual details of the downstairs flood his mind: the two antagonists, circling with their coffee cups; the shabby mismatched furniture; the hopeful

books; the docile framed photographs of the dead, docile and still like cowed students. This matrix[9] of pain that bore him—he feels he is floating above it, sprawled on the bed as on a cloud, stealing songs as they come into his head *(Across the hallway from the guidance room / Lives a French instructor called Mrs. Blum)*, contemplating the view from the upstairs window (last summer's burdock[10] stalks like the beginnings of an alphabet, an apple tree holding three rotten apples as if pondering why they failed to fall), yearning for Monday, for the ride to school with his father, for the bell that calls him to homeroom, for the excitements of class, for Broadway, for fame, for the cloud that will carry him away, out of this, out.

He returns from his paper-delivery route and finds a few Christmas presents for him on the kitchen table. I must guess at the year. 1913? Without opening them, he knocks them to the floor, puts his head on the table, and falls asleep. He must have been consciously dramatizing his plight: His father was sick, money was scarce, he had to work, to win food for the family when he was still a child. In his dismissal of Christmas, he touched a nerve: his love of anarchy, his distrust of the social contract. He treasured this moment of revolt; else why remember it, hoard a memory so bitter, and confide it to his son many Christmases later? He had a teaching instinct, though he claimed that life miscast him as a schoolteacher. I suffered in his classes, feeling the confusion as a persecution of him, but now wonder if his rebellious heart did not court confusion, not as Communists do, to intrude their own order, but, more radical still, as an end pleasurable in itself, as truth's very body. Yet his handwriting (an old pink permission slip recently fluttered from a book where it had been marking a page for twenty years) was always

---

5. **charade** (shə·rād): act.
6. **flail** (flāl): kind of whip.
7. **convolution** (kän′və·loo′shən): process that is extremely involved and complicated.
8. **mincingly** (mins′iŋ·lē): in an artificially dainty manner.

---

9. **matrix** (mā′triks): origin; here, some event or situation from which his pain originates.
10. **burdock:** plant with large leaves and prickly, purple flower heads.

*Laurence Typing* (1952) by Fairfield Porter. Oil on canvas (40″ x 30⅛″).

The Parrish Art Museum, Southampton, New York. Gift of the Estate of Fairfield Porter. Photo by Noel Rowe.

considerately legible, and he was sitting up doing arithmetic the morning of the day he died.

And letters survive from that yet prior son, written in brown ink, in a tidy tame hand, home to his mother from the Missouri seminary where he was preparing for his vocation. The dates are 1887, 1888, 1889. Nothing much happened: He missed New Jersey, and was teased at a church social for escorting a widow. He wanted to do the right thing, but the little sheets of faded penscript exhale a dispirited calm, as if his heart already knew he would not make a successful minister, or live to be old. His son, my father, when old, drove hundreds of miles out of his way to visit the Missouri town from which those letters had been sent. Strangely, the town had not changed; it looked just as he had imagined, from his father's descriptions: tall wooden houses, rain-soaked, stacked on a bluff. The town was a sepia[11] postcard mailed homesick home and preserved in an attic. My father cursed: His father's old sorrow bore him down into depression, into hatred of life. My mother claims his decline in health began at that moment.

He is wonderful to watch, playing soccer. Smaller than the others, my son leaps, heads, dribbles, feints, passes. When a big boy knocks him down, he tumbles on the mud, in his green-and-black school uniform, in an ecstasy of falling. I am envious. Never for me the jaunty pride of the school uniform, the solemn ritual of the coach's pep talk, the camaraderie[12] of shook hands and slapped backsides, the shadow-striped hush of late afternoon and last quarter, the solemn vaulted universe of official combat, with its cheering mothers and referees exotic as zebras and the bespectacled timekeeper alert with his claxon.[13] When the boy scores a goal, he runs

into the arms of his teammates with upraised arms and his face alight as if blinded by triumph. They lift him from the earth in a union of muddy hugs. What spirit! What valor! What skill! His father, watching from the sidelines, inwardly registers only one complaint: He feels the boy, with his talent, should be more aggressive.

They drove across the Commonwealth of Pennsylvania to hear their son read in Pittsburgh. But when their presence was announced to the audience, they did not stand; the applause groped for them and died. My mother said afterwards she was afraid she might fall into the next row if she tried to stand in the dark. Next morning was sunny, and the three of us searched for the house where once they had lived. They had been happy there; I imagined, indeed, that I had been conceived there, just before the slope of the Depression steepened and fear gripped my family. We found the library where she used to read Turgenev,[14] and the little park where the bums slept close as paving stones in the summer night; but their street kept eluding us, though we circled in the car. On foot, my mother found the tree. She claimed she recognized it, the sooty linden tree she would gaze into from their apartment windows. The branches, though thicker, had held their pattern. But the house itself, and the entire block, was gone. Stray bricks and rods of iron in the grass suggested that the demolition had been recent. We stood on the empty spot and laughed. They knew it was right, because the railroad tracks were the right distance away. In confirmation, a long freight train pulled itself east around the curve, its great weight gliding as if on a river current; then a silver passenger train came gliding as effortlessly in the other direction. The curve of the tracks tipped the cars slightly toward us. The Golden Triangle,[15] gray and hazed, was off to our

---

11. **sepia** (sē′pē·ə): reddish brown in color, as in old photographs.
12. **camaraderie**(kam′ə·räd′ə·rē): feeling of being friends.
13. **claxon** (klaks′ən): more correctly, Klaxon, the trademark for a type of electric horn used in sporting events to mark ends of time periods.

---

14. **Turgenev** (tŏŏr·gän′əf): Ivan Turgenev (1818–1883), Russian writer, author of a novel called *Fathers and Sons*.
15. **Golden Triangle:** triangular piece of land formed by the junction of the Allegheny and Monongahela rivers.

*Eli* by Alex Katz (b. 1927). Oil on canvas. Overall (canvas): 73¹/₂ × 95¹/₂ in. (186.7 × 242.6 cm). Framed: 74⁷/₈ × 97 × 1³/₅ in. (190.2 × 246.4 × 4.4 cm).

Whitney Museum of American Art, New York. Gift of Mr. and Mrs. Herbert Fischbach (64.37). Photograph © 1998 Whitney Museum of American Art. Art © Alex Katz/Licensed by VAGA, New York, NY.

left, beyond a forest of bridges. We stood on the grassy rubble that morning, where something once had been, beside the tree still there, and were intensely happy. Why? We knew.

"'No,' Dad said to me, 'the Christian ministry isn't a job you choose, it's a vocation for which you got to receive a call.' I could tell he wanted me to ask him. We never talked much, but we understood each other, we were both scared devils, not like you and the kid. I asked him, Had he ever received the call? He said No. He said No, he never had. Received the call. That was a terrible thing, for him to admit. And I was the one he told. As far as I knew he never admitted it to anybody, but he admitted it to me. He felt like hell about it, I could tell. That was all we ever said about it. That was enough."

He has made his younger brother cry, and justice must be done. A father enforces justice. I corner the rat in our bedroom; he is holding a cardboard mailing tube like a sword. The challenge flares white-hot; I roll my weight toward him like a rock down a mountain, and knock the weapon from his hand. He smiles. Smiles! Because my facial expression is silly? Because he is glad that he can still be overpowered, and hence is still protected? Why? I do not hit him. We stand a second, father and son, and then as nimbly as on the soccer field he steps around me and out the door. He slams the door. He shouts obscenities in the hall, slams all the doors he can find on the way to his room. Our moment of smilingly shared silence was the moment of compression; now the explosion. The whole house rocks with it. Downstairs, his siblings and

mother come to me and offer advice and psychological analysis. I was too aggressive. He is spoiled. What they can never know, my grief alone to treasure, was that lucid many-sided second of his smiling and my relenting, before the world's wrathful pantomime of power resumed.

As we huddle whispering about him, my son takes his revenge. In his room, he plays his guitar. He has greatly improved this winter; his hands getting bigger is the least of it. He has found in the guitar an escape. He plays the Romanza[16] wherein repeated notes, with a sliding like the heart's valves, let themselves fall along the scale:

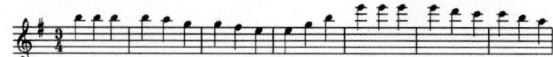

The notes fall, so gently he bombs us, drops feathery notes down upon us, our visitor, our prisoner. ■

---

16. **Romanza** (rō·män′zə): very romantic piece of music.

# Response and Analysis

## Reading Check

1. Identify the time period and the characters that appear in each of the story's eight sections.

2. What test does the father-narrator face in the last section?

3. How does the son respond to the father's discipline?

## Thinking Critically

4. Are there common causes for the sorrow and friction that exist between each son and his father in these stories? Explain.

5. How would you describe the narrator's **tone,** or attitude, in telling this story? How does he feel about the people in his family? Give details from the story to support your response.

6. What **thematic** thread unifies each section of the story? How does the time frame relate to the story's meaning?

7. What is the significance of the father's calling his son "our visitor, our prisoner" at the story's end?

8. Using details from the selection, respond to **Connecting to the Focus Question** on page 1291.

## Extending and Evaluating

9. The "social contract" is mentioned twice in the story. A social contract sets forth the responsibilities that people in a society have toward one another; social contracts deal with the tension between the private good and the social good. The U.S. Constitution, for example, is a social contract. Do you think a social contract exists in most families everywhere today, or are they unique to American families? What terms do you think should be included in such a contract? Explain your answer.

# What For

**Meet the Writer** **Garrett Hongo**
(1951–    ) hopes that his poems "might help produce and reveal our 'better nature.'" Hongo was born in Volcano, Hawaii, and grew up on Oahu and in the Los Angeles area. He graduated from Pomona College in California and earned a master of fine arts degree from the University of California at Irvine in 1980.

Garrett Hongo says he writes for his father, Albert Kazuyoshi Hongo. "I want to be his witness," Hongo says of his father, "to testify to his great and noble life, in struggle against anger, in struggle against his own loneliness and isolation for being a Hawaiian Japanese who emigrated to Los Angeles without much family or community. He was a great example to me of a man who refused to hate, or, being different himself, to be afraid of difference, who accepted the friendship of all the strange and underprivileged ostracized by the rest of 'normal' society—Vietnamese, Mexicans, Southern blacks, reservation Indians relocated to the city—and I want my poems to be equal to his heart."

Hongo's first poetry collection was *Yellow Light* (1982), which includes homages to Japanese American history and to the laborers who helped build this country, people like his grandfather and father. But it was his second collection, *The River of Heaven* (1988), that captured the attention of the critics and was a finalist for a Pulitzer Prize. His memories of growing up are found in *Volcano: A Memoir of Hawaii* (1995).

---

**CONNECTING TO THE**
**Focus Question**

In this poem, Hongo expresses a common desire of many poets—the desire to connect with others. As you read "What For," think about this question: How does the speaker want to connect with his grandfather, grandmother, and father?

---

# What For

### Garrett Hongo

At six I lived for spells:
how a few Hawaiian words could call
up the rain, could hymn like the sea
in the long swirl of chambers
5   curling in the nautilus of a shell,
how Amida's° ballads of the Buddhaland
in the drone of the priest's liturgy
could conjure money from the poor
and give them nothing but mantras,°
10  the strange syllables that healed desire.

I lived for stories about the war
my grandfather told over *hana* cards,°
slapping them down on the mats
with a sharp Japanese *kiai.*°

**6. Amida's:** *Amida* is Japanese for "Amitōbha," Sanskrit for "infinite light." Amida is the great savior worshiped by members of the Pure Land sect, one of the most popular forms of Buddhism in eastern Asia.

**9. mantras:** hymns or other portions of sacred Hindu text, chanted or intoned as incantations or prayers.

**12. *hana* cards:** cards used in a Japanese game in which players attempt to match pairs of flower patterns. *Hana* is Japanese for "flower."

**14. *kiai*:** a Japanese onomatopoeic word for the sound made by slapping down *hana* cards.

Hana Fuda playing cards.

Japanese American Archival Collection, Department of Special Collections and University Archives Library, California State University, Sacramento.

15   I lived for songs my grandmother sang
      stirring curry into a thick stew,
      weaving a calligraphy of Kannon's° love
      into grass mats and straw sandals.

      I lived for the red volcano dirt
20   staining my toes, the salt residue
      of surf and sea wind in my hair,
      the arc of a flat stone skipping
      in the hollow trough of a wave.

      I lived a child's world, waited
25   for my father to drag himself home,
      dusted with blasts of sand, powdered rock,
      and the strange ash of raw cement,
      his deafness made worse by the clang
      of pneumatic drills, sore in his bones
30   from the buckings of a jackhammer.
      He'd hand me a scarred lunchpail,
      let me unlace the hightop G.I. boots,
      call him the new name I'd invented
      that day in school, write it for him
35   on his newspaper. He'd rub my face
      with hands that felt like gravel roads,
      tell me to move, go play, and then he'd
      walk to the laundry sink to scrub,
      rinse the dirt of his long day
40   from a face brown and grained as koa° wood.

**17. Kannon's:** In Japanese Buddhism, Kannon is the bodhisattva ("Buddha to be") of infinite compassion and mercy.

**40. koa:** Hawaiian mimosa tree valued for its wood and bark.

I wanted to take away the pain
in his legs, the swelling in his joints,
give him back his hearing,
clear and rare as crystal chimes,
45  the fins of glass that wrinkled
and sparked the air with their sound.

I wanted to heal the sores that work
and war had sent to him,
let him play catch in the backyard
50  with me, tossing a tennis ball
past papaya trees without the shoulders
of pain shrugging back his arms.

I wanted to become a doctor of pure magic,
to string a necklace of sweet words
55  fragrant as pine needles and plumeria,°
fragrant as the bread my mother baked,
place it like a lei of cowrie shells
and *pikake*° flowers around my father's neck,
and chant him a blessing, a sutra.°

**55. plumeria:** classification of fragrant, flowering, tropical American trees.

**58. *pikake*:** Hawaiian for "Arabian jasmine."

**59. sutra:** in general, one of the sacred scriptures of Buddhism.

# Response and Analysis

## Thinking Critically

1. According to the speaker, what did he live for as a child?

2. What did the speaker wait for as a child? What did he want to do for his father?

3. What do you think the speaker means by "I wanted to become a doctor of pure magic" (line 53)?

4. What **images** in this poem help you to visualize the speaker's father? How do these images contrast with images that the speaker remembers in the first four stanzas?

5. What do you think the **title** of the poem means?

6. Using details from the selection, respond to **Connecting to the Focus Question** on page 1297.

## Extending and Evaluating

7. In a personal essay, Garrett Hongo writes about how his grandfather's stories shaped his life and work. Hongo remembers holding his grandfather's "testimony" in his mind "like it was an heirloom." Do you think the testimony of previous generations is important to hold and pass along? Explain your response.

# Reflecting *on the* Literary Period • Before You Read

## Teenage Wasteland

**Meet the Writer** **Anne Tyler** (1941–    ) thinks that her attraction to writing came from her sense of being set apart from others—she was born in Minneapolis but as a child lived in various Quaker communities in the United States. Tyler graduated from Duke University, did postgraduate work in Russian studies at Columbia University, and has lived most of her adult life in Baltimore, which is also the setting for many of her novels.

Tyler's favorite theme in fiction is the small-scale dramas of family life. In the family, she says, with all its conflicts, lies a "perfect breeding ground for plot." Discussing characterization, Tyler once said that many novels lack "quiet, gentle, basically good people." A reviewer commented on this observation: "Her fiction is a quiet, gentle reminder of the goodness to be found in most ordinary lives. In a noisy, violent world, this is surely not to be sniffed at—and neither is her extremely fine writing."

Tyler has published over fifteen novels. Her most popular novel is *The Accidental Tourist* (1985), about a travel writer who writes guides for people who hate to travel. His family life is horribly torn apart when his son is murdered in a fast-food restaurant. The book was made into an Oscar-winning movie in 1988. In 1989, Tyler won the Pulitzer Prize for *Breathing Lessons,* the story of a married couple with yearnings to repair their son's broken marriage.

**Background** In this story about a troubled American family, Tyler explores the world of Matt and Daisy Coble, who are enduring the alienation of their teenage son. But Tyler's story also examines another conflict—one considered all-too-typical of late twentieth-century America: the conflict between differing value systems.

---

**CONNECTING TO THE
Focus Question**

As you read, consider this question: What value systems collide in this story about parents trying to save—and to understand—their teenager?

---

# Teenage Wasteland

## Anne Tyler

He used to have very blond hair—almost white—cut shorter than other children's so that on his crown a little cowlick always stood up to catch the light. But this was when he was small. As he grew older, his hair grew darker, and he wore it longer—past his collar even. It hung in lank, taffy-colored ropes around his face, which was still an endearing face, fine-featured, the eyes an unusual aqua blue. But his cheeks, of course, were no longer round, and a sharp new Adam's apple jogged in his throat when he talked.

In October, they called from the private school he attended to request a conference with his parents. Daisy went alone; her husband was at work. Clutching her purse, she sat on the principal's couch and learned that Donny was noisy, lazy, and disruptive, always fooling around with his friends, and he wouldn't respond in class.

In the past, before her children were born, Daisy had been a fourth-grade teacher. It shamed her now to sit before this principal as a parent, a delinquent parent, a parent who struck Mr. Lanham, no doubt, as unseeing or uncaring. "It isn't that we're not concerned," she said. "Both of us

*Yellow Pitcher* by Pam Ingalls.

are. And we've done what we could, whatever we could think of. We don't let him watch TV on school nights. We don't let him talk on the phone till he's finished his homework. But he tells us he doesn't *have* any homework or he did it all in study hall. How are we to know what to believe?"

From early October through November, at Mr. Lanham's suggestion, Daisy checked Donny's assignments every day. She sat next to him as he worked, trying to be encouraging, sagging inwardly as she saw the poor quality of everything he did—the sloppy mistakes in math, the illogical leaps in his English themes, the history questions left blank if they required any research.

Daisy was often late starting supper, and she couldn't give as much attention to Donny's younger sister. "You'll never guess what happened at . . ." Amanda would begin, and Daisy would have to tell her, "Not now, honey."

By the time her husband Matt came home, she'd be snappish. She would recite the day's hardships—the fuzzy instructions in English, the botched history map, the morass[1] of unsolvable algebra equations. Matt would look surprised and confused, and Daisy would gradually wind down. There was no way, really, to convey how exhausting all this was.

In December, the school called again. This time, they wanted Matt to come as well. She and Matt had to sit on Mr. Lanham's couch like two bad children and listen to the news: Donny had improved only slightly, raising a D in history to a C, and a C in algebra to a B-minus. What was worse, he had developed new problems. He had cut classes on at least three occasions. Smoked in the furnace room. Helped Sonny Barnett break into a freshman's locker. And last week, during athletics, he and three friends had been seen off the school grounds; when they returned, the coach had smelled beer on their breath.

Daisy and Matt sat silent, shocked. Matt rubbed his forehead with his fingertips. Imagine, Daisy thought, how they must look to Mr.

---

1. **morass** (mə·ras′): something troublesome or puzzling; a difficult mess.

Lanham: an overweight housewife in a cotton dress and a too-tall, too-thin insurance agent in a baggy, frayed suit. Failures, both of them—the kind of people who are always hurrying to catch up, missing the point of things that everyone else grasps at once. She wished she'd worn nylons instead of knee socks.

It was arranged that Donny would visit a psychologist for testing. Mr. Lanham knew just the person. He would set this boy straight, he said.

When they stood to leave, Daisy held her stomach in and gave Mr. Lanham a firm, responsible handshake.

Donny said the psychologist was a jackass and the tests were really dumb; but he kept all three of his appointments, and when it was time for the follow-up conference with the psychologist and both parents, Donny combed his hair and seemed unusually sober and subdued. The psychologist said Donny had no serious emotional problems. He was merely going through a difficult period in his life. He required some academic help and a better sense of self-worth. For this reason, he was suggesting a man named Calvin Beadle, a tutor with considerable psychological training.

In the car going home, Donny said he'd be damned if he'd let them drag him to some stupid dork tutor. His father told him to watch his language in front of his mother.

That night, Daisy lay awake pondering the term "self-worth." She had always been free with her praise. She had always told Donny he had talent, was smart, was good with his hands. She had made a big to-do over every little gift he gave her. In fact, maybe she had gone too far, although, Lord knows, she had meant every word. Was that his trouble?

She remembered when Amanda was born. Donny had acted lost and bewildered. Daisy had been alert to that, of course, but still, a new baby keeps you so busy. Had she really done all she could have? She longed—she ached—for a time machine. Given one more chance, she'd do it perfectly—hug him more, praise him more, or

Traveling (Mark) (1975) by Harvey Dinnerstein. Pastel on Board.

perhaps praise him less. Oh, who can say . . .

The tutor told Donny to call him Cal. All his kids did he said. Daisy thought for a second that he meant his own children, then realized her mistake. He seemed too young, anyhow, to be a family man. He wore a heavy brown handlebar mustache. His hair was as long and stringy as Donny's, and his jeans as faded. Wire-rimmed spectacles slid down his nose. He lounged in a canvas director's chair with his fingers laced across his chest, and he casually, amiably[2] questioned Donny, who sat upright and glaring in an armchair.

"So they're getting on your back at school," said Cal. "Making a big deal about anything you do wrong."

"Right," said Donny.

"Any idea why that would be?"

"Oh, well, you know, stuff like homework and all," Donny said.

"You don't do your homework?"

"Oh, well, I might do it sometimes but not just exactly like they want it." Donny sat forward and said, "It's like a prison there, you know? You've got to go to every class, you can never step off the school grounds."

"You cut classes sometimes?"

"Sometimes," Donny said, with a glance at his parents.

Cal didn't seem perturbed.[3] "Well," he said, "I'll tell you what. Let's you and me try working together three nights a week. Think you could handle that? We'll see if we can show that school of yours a thing or two. Give it a month; then if you don't like it, we'll stop. If *I* don't like it, we'll stop. I mean, sometimes people just don't get along, right? What do you say to that?"

"Okay," Donny said. He seemed pleased.

"Make it seven o'clock till eight, Monday, Wednesday, and Friday," Cal told Matt and Daisy. They nodded. Cal shambled[4] to his feet, gave them a little salute, and showed them to the door.

This was where he lived as well as worked, evidently. The interview had taken place in the dining room, which had been transformed into a kind of office. Passing the living room, Daisy winced at the rock music she had been hearing,

2. **amiably** (ā′mē·ə·blē): in a friendly way.
3. **perturbed** (pər·tʉrb′′d): used as *adj.*: troubled.

4. **shambled** (sham′bəld): moved in a clumsy or awkward way.

without registering it, ever since she had entered the house. She looked in and saw a boy about Donny's age lying on a sofa with a book. Another boy and a girl were playing Ping-Pong in front of the fireplace. "You have several here together?" Daisy asked Cal.

"Oh, sometimes they stay on after their sessions, just to rap. They're a pretty sociable group, all in all. Plenty of goof-offs like young Donny here."

He cuffed Donny's shoulder playfully. Donny flushed and grinned.

Climbing into the car, Daisy asked Donny, "Well? What did you think?"

But Donny had returned to his old evasive[5] self. He jerked his chin toward the garage. "Look," he said. "He's got a basketball net."

Now on Mondays, Wednesdays, and Fridays, they had supper early—the instant Matt came home. Sometimes, they had to leave before they were really finished. Amanda would still be eating her dessert. "Bye, honey. Sorry," Daisy would tell her.

Cal's first bill sent a flutter of panic through Daisy's chest, but it was worth it, of course. Just look at Donny's face when they picked him up: alight and full of interest. The principal telephoned Daisy to tell her how Donny had improved. "Of course, it hasn't shown up in his grades yet, but several of the teachers have noticed how his attitude's changed. Yes sir, I think we're onto something here."

At home, Donny didn't act much different. He still seemed to have a low opinion of his parents. But Daisy supposed that was unavoidable—part of being fifteen. He said his parents were too "controlling"—a word that made Daisy give him a sudden look. He said they acted like wardens. On weekends, they enforced a curfew. And any time he went to a party, they always telephoned first to see if adults would be supervising. "For God's sake!" he said. "Don't you trust me?"

"It isn't a matter of trust, honey . . ." But there was no explaining to him.

His tutor called one afternoon. "I get the sense," he said, "that this kid's feeling . . . underestimated, you know? Like you folks expect the worst of him. I'm thinking we ought to give him more rope."

"But see, he's still so suggestible," Daisy said. "When his friends suggest some mischief—smoking or drinking or such—why, he just finds it very hard not to go along with them."

"Mrs. Coble," the tutor said, "I think this kid is hurting. You know? Here's a serious, sensitive kid, telling you he'd like to take on some grown-up challenges, and you're giving him the message that he can't be trusted. Don't you understand how that hurts?"

"Oh," said Daisy.

"It undermines his self-esteem—don't you realize that?"

"Well, I guess you're right," said Daisy. She saw Donny suddenly from a whole new angle: his pathetically poor posture, that slouch so forlorn[6] that his shoulders seemed about to meet his chin . . . oh, wasn't it awful being young? She'd had a miserable adolescence herself and had always sworn no child of hers would ever be that unhappy.

They let Donny stay out later, they didn't call ahead to see if the parties were supervised, and they were careful not to grill him about his evening. The tutor had set down so many rules! They were not allowed any questions at all about any aspect of school, nor were they to speak with his teachers. If a teacher had some complaint, she should phone Cal. Only one teacher disobeyed—the history teacher, Miss Evans. She called one morning in February. "I'm a little concerned about Donny, Mrs. Coble."

"Oh, I'm sorry, Miss Evans, but Donny's tutor handles these things now . . ."

"I always deal directly with the parents. You are the parent," Miss Evans said, speaking very slowly and distinctly. "Now, here is the problem. Back when you were helping Donny with his

5. **evasive** (ē·vā'siv): not straightforward; hard to pin down.

6. **forlorn** (fôr·lôrn'): miserable or hopeless looking.

**1304**   Collection 6   **Contemporary Literature: 1939 to Present**

homework, his grades rose from a D to a C, but now they've slipped back, and they're closer to an F."

"They are?"

"I think you should start overseeing his homework again."

"But Donny's tutor says . . ."

"It's nice that Donny has a tutor, but you should still be in charge of his homework. With you, he learned it. Then he passed his tests. With the tutor, well, it seems the tutor is more of a crutch. 'Donny,' I say, 'a quiz is coming up on Friday. Hadn't you better be listening instead of talking?' 'That's okay, Miss Evans,' he says. 'I have a tutor now.' Like a talisman![7] I really think you ought to take over, Mrs. Coble."

"I see," said Daisy. "Well, I'll think about that. Thank you for calling."

Hanging up, she felt a rush of anger at Donny. A talisman! For a talisman, she'd given up all luxuries, all that time with her daughter, her evenings at home!

She dialed Cal's number. He sounded muzzy. "I'm sorry if I woke you," she told him, "but Donny's history teacher just called. She says he isn't doing well."

"She should have dealt with me."

"She wants me to start supervising his homework again. His grades are slipping."

"Yes," said the tutor, "but you and I both know there's more to it than mere grades, don't we? I care about the *whole* child—his happiness, his self-esteem. The grades will come. Just give them time."

When she hung up, it was Miss Evans she was angry at. What a narrow woman!

It was Cal this, Cal that, Cal says this, Cal and I did that. Cal lent Donny an album by the Who. He took Donny and two other pupils to a rock concert. In March, when Donny began to talk endlessly on the phone with a girl named Miriam, Cal even let Miriam come to one of the tutoring sessions. Daisy was touched that Cal would grow so involved in Donny's life, but she was also a little hurt, because she had offered to have Miriam to dinner and Donny had refused. Now he asked them to drive her to Cal's house without a qualm.[8]

This Miriam was an unappealing girl with blurry lipstick and masses of rough red hair. She wore a short, bulky jacket that would not have been out of place on a motorcycle. During the trip to Cal's she was silent, but coming back, she was more talkative. "What a neat guy, and what a house! All those kids hanging out, like a club. And the stereo playing rock . . . gosh, he's not like a grown-up at all! Married and divorced and everything, but you'd think he was our own age."

"Mr. Beadle was married?" Daisy asked.

"Yeah, to this really controlling lady. She didn't understand him a bit."

"No, I guess not," Daisy said.

Spring came, and the students who hung around at Cal's drifted out to the basketball net above the garage. Sometimes, when Daisy and Matt arrived to pick up Donny, they'd find him there with the others—spiky and excited, jittering on his toes beneath the backboard. It was staying light much longer now, and the neighboring fence cast narrow bars across the bright grass. Loud music would be spilling from Cal's windows. Once it was the Who, which Daisy recognized from the time that Donny had borrowed the album. *"Teenage Wasteland,"*[9] she said aloud, identifying the song, and Matt gave a short, dry laugh. "It certainly is," he said. He'd misunderstood; he thought she was commenting on the scene spread before them. In fact, she might have been. The players looked like hoodlums, even her son. Why, one of Cal's students had recently been knifed in a tavern. One had been shipped off to boarding school in midterm; two had been withdrawn by their parents. On the other hand, Donny had mentioned someone who'd been

---

7. **talisman** (tal′is·mən): charm thought to have magical powers.

8. **qualm** (kwäm): uneasy feeling; doubt.

9. **"Teenage Wasteland":** words repeated in the song "Baba O'Riley" from a 1971 album by the British rock group The Who. The song is often referred to as "Teenage Wasteland."

studying with Cal for five years. "Five years!" said Daisy. "Doesn't anyone ever stop needing him?"

Donny looked at her. Lately, whatever she said about Cal was read as criticism. "You're just feeling competitive," he said. "And controlling."

She bit her lip and said no more.

In April, the principal called to tell her that Donny had been expelled. There had been a locker check, and in Donny's locker they found five cans of beer and half a pack of cigarettes. With Donny's previous record, this offense meant expulsion.

Daisy gripped the receiver tightly and said, "Well, where is he now?"

"We've sent him home," said Mr. Lanham. "He's packed up all his belongings, and he's coming home on foot."

Daisy wondered what she would say to him. She felt him looming closer and closer, bringing this brand-new situation that no one had prepared her to handle. What other place would take him? Could they enter him in a public school? What were the rules? She stood at the living room window, waiting for him to show up. Gradually, she realized that he was taking too long. She checked the clock. She stared up the street again.

When an hour had passed, she phoned the school. Mr. Lanham's secretary answered and told her in a grave, sympathetic voice that yes, Donny Coble had most definitely gone home. Daisy called her husband. He was out of the office. She went back to the window and thought a while, and then she called Donny's tutor.

"Donny's been expelled from school," she said, "and now I don't know where he's gone. I wonder if you've heard from him?"

There was a long silence. "Donny's with me, Mrs. Coble," he finally said.

"With you? How'd he get there?"

"He hailed a cab, and I paid the driver."

"Could I speak to him, please?"

There was another silence. "Maybe it'd be better if we had a conference," Cal said.

"I don't *want* a conference. I've been standing at the window picturing him dead or kidnapped

or something, and now you tell me you want a—"

"Donny is very, very upset. Understandably so," said Cal. "Believe me, Mrs. Coble, this is not what it seems. Have you asked Donny's side of the story?"

"Well, of course not, how could I? He went running off to you instead."

"Because he didn't feel he'd be listened to."

"But I haven't even—"

"Why don't you come out and talk? The three of us," said Cal, "will try to get this thing in perspective."

"Well, all right," Daisy said. But she wasn't as reluctant as she sounded. Already she felt soothed by the calm way Cal was taking this.

Cal answered the doorbell at once. He said, "Hi, there," and led her into the dining room. Donny sat slumped in a chair, chewing the knuckle of one thumb. "Hello, Donny," Daisy said. He flicked his eyes in her direction.

"Sit here, Mrs. Coble," said Cal, placing her opposite Donny. He himself remained standing, restlessly pacing. "So," he said.

Daisy stole a look at Donny. His lips were swollen, as if he'd been crying.

"You know," Cal told Daisy, "I kind of expected something like this. That's a very punitive[10] school you've got him in—you realize that. And any half-decent lawyer will tell you they've violated his civil rights. Locker checks! Where's their search warrant?"

"But if the rule is—" Daisy said.

"Well, anyhow, let him tell you his side."

She looked at Donny. He said, "It wasn't my fault. I promise."

"They said your locker was full of beer."

"It was a put-up job! See, there's this guy that doesn't like me. He put all these beers in my locker and started a rumor going, so Mr. Lanham ordered a locker check."

"What was the boy's name?" Daisy asked. "Huh?"

"Mrs. Coble, take my word, the situation is not

---

10. **punitive** (pyo͞o′ni·tiv): focused on punishment.

*Woman with a Newspaper* by Richard Diebenkorn (1922–1993).

"Doesn't *Donny* ever get blamed?"

"Now, Mrs. Coble, you heard what he—"

"Forget it," Donny told Cal. "You can see she doesn't trust me."

Daisy drew in a breath to say that of course she trusted him—a reflex. But she knew that bold-faced, wide-eyed look of Donny's. He had worn that look when he was small, denying some petty misdeed with the evidence plain as day all around him. Still, it was hard for her to accuse him outright. She temporized[13] and said, "The only thing I'm sure of is that they've kicked you out of school, and now I don't know what we're going to do."

"We'll fight it," said Cal.

"We can't. Even you must see we can't."

"I could apply to Brantly," Donny said.

Cal stopped his pacing to beam down at him. "Brantly! Yes. They're really onto where a kid is coming from, at Brantly. Why, *I* could get you into Brantly. I work with a lot of their students."

Daisy had never heard of Brantly, but already she didn't like it. And she didn't like Cal's smile, which struck her now as feverish and avid[14]—a smile of hunger.

so unusual," Cal said. "You can't imagine how vindictive[11] kids can be sometimes."

"What was the boy's *name*," said Daisy, so that I can ask Mr. Lanham if that's who suggested he run a locker check."

"You don't believe me," Donny said.

"And how'd this boy get your combination in the first place?"

"Frankly," said Cal, "I wouldn't be surprised to learn the school was in on it. Any kid that marches to a different drummer,[12] why, they'd just love an excuse to get rid of him. The school is where I lay the blame."

---

11. **vindictive** (vin·dik**'**tiv): looking for revenge.

12. **different drummer:** reference to a passage from Henry David Thoreau's *Walden*: "If a man does not keep pace with his companions, perhaps it is because he hears a different drummer. Let him step to the music which he hears, however measured or far away."

13. **temporized** (tem**'**pə·rīzd): evaded making a decision in order to buy time.

14. **avid** (av**'**id): greedy; having an intense desire for something.

On the fifteenth of April, they entered Donny in a public school, and they stopped his tutoring sessions. Donny fought both decisions bitterly. Cal, surprisingly enough, did not object. He admitted he'd made no headway with Donny and said it was because Donny was emotionally disturbed.

Donny went to his new school every morning, plodding off alone with his head down. He did his assignments, and he earned average grades, but he gathered no friends, joined no clubs. There was something exhausted and defeated about him.

The first week in June, during final exams, Donny vanished. He simply didn't come home one afternoon, and no one at school remembered seeing him. The police were reassuring, and for the first few days, they worked hard. They combed Donny's sad, messy room for clues; they visited Miriam and Cal. But then they started talking about the number of kids who ran away every year. Hundreds, just in this city. "He'll show up, if he wants to," they said. "If he doesn't, he won't."

Evidently, Donny didn't want to.

It's been three months now and still no word. Matt and Daisy still look for him in every crowd of awkward, heartbreaking teenage boys. Every time the phone rings, they imagine it might be Donny. Both parents have aged. Donny's sister seems to be staying away from home as much as possible.

At night, Daisy lies awake and goes over Donny's life. She is trying to figure out what went wrong, where they made their first mistake. Often, she finds herself blaming Cal, although she knows he didn't begin it. Then at other times she excuses him, for without him, Donny might have left earlier. Who really knows? In the end, she can only sigh and search for a cooler spot on the pillow. As she falls asleep, she occasionally glimpses something in the corner of her vision. It's something fleet[15] and round, a ball—a basketball. It flies up, it sinks through the hoop, descends, lands in a yard littered with last year's leaves and striped with bars of sunlight as white as bones, bleached and parched and cleanly picked. ■

---

15. **fleet:** swift; fast.

# Response and Analysis

## Reading Check

1. Describe the problem that exists in the Coble family at the start of the story. What does the principal suggest the parents do with Donny?

2. Why is Donny expelled from school?

3. What effect does Donny's running away have on the rest of the family?

## Thinking Critically

4. How would you describe Daisy's **character**? Does she change during the course of the story, or does she stay the same?

5. What information does the writer give us about Cal's house? What does this information say about the type of person Cal is?

6. Why do you think Donny left? Do you think anything could have been done to prevent him from running away? Explain your responses.

7. At the end of the story, Daisy visualizes a basketball going through a hoop. What might this image **symbolize** for her? Where else has a basketball been mentioned in the story?

8. Using details from the selection, respond to **Connecting to the Focus Question** on page 1300.

## Extending and Evaluating

9. Do you think the writer takes sides in the conflict between Donny's parents and Cal? Cite details from the story to support your response.

# Reflecting *on the* Literary Period • **Before You Read**

## The Beep Beep Poem

**Meet the Writer** **Nikki Giovanni**
(1943–    ) has, at last count, been awarded
twenty-one honorary doctorates; written more
than two dozen books; and had her *Nikki Giovanni
Poetry Collection,* a spoken-word CD, rank as a
finalist for a 2003 Grammy award. Also in 2003,
she published *The Collected Poetry of Nikki Giovanni:
1968–1998.*

Giovanni, whose given names are Yolande
Cornelia, was born in Knoxville, Tennessee, and
grew up in Cincinnati, Ohio. She graduated from
Fisk University in Nashville and did graduate work
at the University of Pennsylvania and Columbia
University School of Fine Arts.

Giovanni is affectionately called the Princess
of Black Poetry because of the large, enthusiastic
crowds she attracts whenever she gives public
readings of her work. Behind all of Giovanni's
poetry, according to one critic, are "the creation
of racial pride and the communication of

individual love." Giovanni says of her writing,
"I write out of my own experiences—which
also happen to be the experiences of
my people."

Nikki Giovanni is a University Distinguished
Professor at Virginia Tech, where she has taught
writing and literature since 1987. Not flattered
when her students write poems that sound like
hers, she says, "I already sound like me. I want my
students to hear their own voices."

---

**CONNECTING TO THE
Focus Question**

The image of this poet passing the moon and
hollering to the stars as she is "coming
through" in her car helps us look forward to
the next century of American voices. As you
read, ask yourself: What does the poem
have to say about individuality and freedom?

---

# The Beep Beep Poem

## Nikki Giovanni

I should write a poem
but there's almost nothing
that hasn't been said
and said and said
5  beautifully, ugly, blandly
excitingly
        stay in school
        make love not war
        death to all tyrants
10       where have all the flowers gone
and don't they understand at kent state
the troopers° will shoot . . . again

**12. kent state . . . troopers:**
Kent State University in Ohio
was the scene of a tragic confrontation between troops in
the National Guard and students protesting the movement of U. S. troops into
Cambodia during the Vietnam
War. On May 4, 1970, four
students were killed and nine
wounded when Guard troops
opened fire during a noontime
demonstration.

i could write a poem
because i love walking
15  in the rain
and the solace of my naked
body in a tub of warm water
cleanliness may not be next
to godliness but it sure feels
20  good

i wrote a poem
for my father but it was so constant
i burned it up
he hates change
25  and i'm baffled by sameness

i composed a ditty
about encore american and worldwide news
but the editorial board
said no one would understand it
30    as if people have to be tricked
into sensitivity
though of course they do

i love to drive my car
hours on end
35    along back country roads
i love to stop for cider and apples and acorn squash
three for a dollar
i love my CB when the truckers talk
and the hum of the diesel in my ear
40    i love the aloneness of the road
when I ascend descending curves
the power within my toe delights me
and i fling my spirit down the highway
i love the way i feel
45    when i pass the moon and i holler to the stars
i'm coming through

Beep Beep

# Response and Analysis

## Thinking Critically

1. In the first stanza, why does the speaker think she can't write a poem?

2. What poems could she write? What poems are rejected?

3. After rejecting several ideas for poems in the first stanzas, what has she written a poem about in the final stanza?

4. What words and phrases are repeated in the poem? How do they contribute to the poem's **rhythm** and **mood?**

5. What details show the speaker's sense of individuality?

6. In the last stanza, what **images** convey how the speaker feels about driving her car? What is it about this experience that makes her feel this way?

7. Using details from the selection, respond to **Connecting to the Focus Question** on page 1309.

## Extending and Evaluating

8. In this poem Giovanni says that people have to be "tricked / into sensitivity" (lines 30–31). Do you agree or disagree with this idea? Explain your response.

REVIEW

# Reflecting *on the* Literary Period

## Contemporary Literature: 1939 to Present

The following questions ask you to compare and analyze the selections in this feature and respond to the Focus Question. Where possible, cite passages from the selections to support your answers.

Bernard Malamud . . . . . . . . . . . . . . . . . . . . . . . . . . **The Magic Barrel**

John Updike . . . . . . . . . . . . . . . . . . . . . . . . . . . . . . . . . . . **Son**

Garrett Hongo . . . . . . . . . . . . . . . . . . . . . . . . . . . . . . **What For**

Anne Tyler . . . . . . . . . . . . . . . . . . . . . . . . . . . . **Teenage Wasteland**

Nikki Giovanni . . . . . . . . . . . . . . . . . . . . . . **The Beep Beep Poem**

### Comparing Literature

**1.** Four of these selections deal with a search for love—with its redemptive power, problems, and sometimes heartbreaking futility. Compare the works of Malamud, Updike, Tyler, and Hongo in terms of what they reveal about the power and pain of love—both lost and found.

**2.** John Updike in "Son" explores father-son relationships, while Amy Tan in "Rules of the Game" (page 1017) deals with relationship issues between a mother and daughter. Based on these two stories, what issues do both types of relationships have in common? In what ways do they differ?

**3.** What similarities and differences do you see in Hongo's use of language in "What For" and the language Giovanni uses in "The Beep Beep Poem"? Cite specific examples from the poems.

**4.** Updike's "Son" and Tyler's "Teenage Wasteland" deal with parent-child relationships. What do both writers seem to be saying about parents' responsibilities and the problems they encounter raising teenagers?

**5.** Compare Leo Finkle in "The Magic Barrel" and Cal in "Teenage Wasteland." How do their personalities differ? What might these two men agree and disagree about?

**SKILLS FOCUS**

Pages 1277–1312 cover **Literary Skills** Evaluate genres and traditions in American literature.

### RESPONDING TO THE
### Focus Question

Review your notes and responses related to the Focus Question for this feature. Using details from the selections, write your answer to the question.

What do these contemporary writers, who represent a range of American voices, say about the human condition and our very personal needs for love, family, community, and freedom?

Many works of contemporary literature use realistic language and graphic descriptions. Be sure to check with your teacher and a parent or guardian before reading any of the following books.

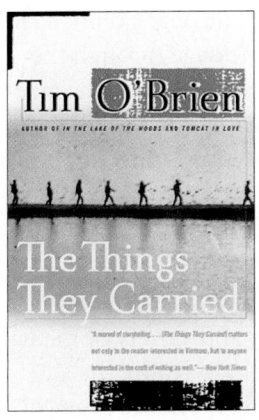

### FICTION
## Objects of War

A Bible used as a pillow, a pebble kept under the tongue, a can of peaches—these objects may puzzle us, but they mean the world to the young soldiers depicted in Tim O'Brien's *The Things They Carried.* This work of interconnected short stories straddles the line between reality and imagination, relating the stories of soldiers both on and off the battlefield.

### FICTION
## Both Sides of the Story

Toni Morrison (page 1116) writes of the debilitating effects of the oppression of African Americans on victim and perpetrator alike; she also explores the other side of the coin: the richness of the African American community and its traditions. Her novel *Beloved* tells the story of a mother's desperate attempt to save her children from slavery.

### NONFICTION
## Irrational Acts

*Into the Wild* and *Into Thin Air,* both by the journalist Jon Krakauer, are examples of nonfiction writing at its best. *Into the Wild* is the tragic story of a young man who set off to experience the wilderness. His adventure ended in an abandoned school bus in Denali National Park in Alaska. *Into Thin Air* is Krakauer's account of his guided ascent of Mount Everest.

### POETRY
## A Nation of Poets

More people are writing poetry than ever before, and happily, the audience for poetry is also growing. *Unsettling America: An Anthology of Contemporary Multicultural Poetry,* edited by Maria M. Gillan and Jennifer Gillan, contains thematically grouped poems by American poets of many cultures. To explore the more recent work of poets such as Charles Olson, Denise Levertov, and Jimmy Santiago Baca, see *Postmodern American Poetry,* edited by Paul Hoover.

# Analyzing and Using Media

**S**ometimes what you think and how you feel about a poem can be affected by the **medium,** or form, in which it is presented. When you read poems such as Sylvia Plath's "Mirror" or Billy Collins's "Man Listening to Disc," you experience the poet's message through the medium of print. You may be affected differently if you experience the poem through other **media,** such as film, video, radio, television, or the Internet. You can change how your own messages affect others by using different media as well. In this workshop you'll convey a message through words, images, and sounds in a **multimedia presentation.**

## Analyzing Media

**Media Sources** Think about the number and variety of media messages you receive every day, and you'll begin to realize the significant part that media play in everyday life. From the time you wake up in the morning with the radio blaring, to the advertising billboards you pass on the way to school, to the last Web site you surf before going to bed, media messages are interwoven into your daily life. Individual media messages like songs, advertisements, and Web sites are placed in **media sources** so that the messages come in contact with their intended audiences—which includes *you.* **Print media sources** include books, newspapers, magazines, pamphlets, advertising fliers, billboards, and posters. **Electronic media sources** include documentaries, films, television, the Internet, radio, and CD-ROMs.

**Media Literacy Concepts** Critical viewers of media use media literacy concepts to analyze, interpret, and evaluate media messages. Below are explanations of five key concepts of media literacy, as well as questions you can ask yourself to analyze media messages.

### MEDIA LITERACY CONCEPTS

| Concept | Analysis Questions |
|---|---|
| **1. All messages are made by someone.** Every media message is written, edited, selected, illustrated, or composed by one or more individuals who make decisions about what to include in the message, what to leave out, and how to sequence the chosen elements. | What words, images, or sounds were used to create the message? What may have been left out of the message? |
| **2. Media messages are not reality.** They are *representations* of reality that shape people's ideas of the world. Even a message that may seem real, such as an eyewitness news account of a robbery, reflects only one person's point of view, edited down to a few images and words for the nightly news. | What is the point of view or experience of the message maker? How does this message affect the way I think about this topic? |

*(continued)*

*(continued)*

| | |
|---|---|
| **3. Each person interprets media messages differently.** You interpret a media message based on your knowledge of the world in which you live. | How does the message make me feel? What does the message make me think of? |
| **4. People have a wide range of purposes for creating media messages.** Those purposes include informing, persuading, entertaining, gaining power, expressing ideas, transmitting culture, and making money. | Who created this message? What is the purpose of this message? Is there more than one purpose? |
| **5. Each mass medium has unique characteristics.** Media producers tailor their work to take full advantage of a particular medium's strengths. For example, TV news favors visual messages that involve movement, while newspapers favor still photographs that can be studied at length. | What medium delivers the message? How does the form affect the message? How would a different medium present the message? |

**Media Strategies** Media producers and visual image-makers, such as graphic artists, documentary filmmakers, and news photographers, use certain strategies—singly or in combination—to shape their messages for their intended audiences. Being able to **interpret and evaluate** the ways these strategies accomplish their purposes will enable you as a media consumer to make conscious and informed decisions about how you use media and how you let media influence you. The chart below describes some of the most common media strategies.

## MEDIA STRATEGIES

| Strategy | Example |
|---|---|
| **Language**—tailored to suit any purpose, audience, or message—is the main strategy used to accomplish a media purpose. | A film documentary might use precise, informational language to inform viewers of a social problem and persuasive, emotional language to convince them to help fix the problem. |
| **Stereotypes** are generalized beliefs based on misinformation or insufficient evidence about an entire group of individuals. | A television comedy might use stereotypes, such as a smart-aleck younger brother or sister, to entertain. A political advertisement might use the stereotype that all older people depend on Social Security to persuade voters to support legislation concerning the welfare of older Americans. |
| **Special effects,** including graphics, lighting, and sound and visual effects, enhance media messages' impact. | An Internet site dedicated to a pop star might blend computer-generated graphics and sound effects to give information about the star while also entertaining the viewer to keep his or her interest. |
| **Visual representations,** such as art, photographs, charts, and maps, can create a powerful effect either alone or combined with language. | A map in a newspaper might give information about a country where important current events are taking place. An advertisement with a fashion-model photo might use the model's beauty to influence the viewer's feelings about a product. |

**Media Effects** The high profile of television, movies, music, and the Internet may lead you to think primarily in terms of entertainment when you think of media messages. However, there are more significant and serious reasons why you should be able to analyze and evaluate media messages. Media have a powerful and direct impact on the democratic process at the local, state, and national levels, exerting influence on elections, creating images of leaders and candidates, and shaping attitudes about important issues. Learning to decode and analyze media messages will help you make informed decisions as a voter and as a citizen.

Here are some of the ways media affect the democratic process.

● **Influencing elections** Because of the media's power to reach the voter directly, candidates for public office must use media skillfully and effectively to present their messages. Candidates solicit votes as well as campaign donations with television and radio advertisements and direct mailings to voters' homes. Errors in the use of media can be devastating to a campaign. For example, many people believe that Richard Nixon's performance in the nationally televised 1960 presidential debates with John F. Kennedy cost Nixon the election.

● **Creating images of leaders** Campaign advertisements are often designed to create a certain image of a candidate. For example, by showing the candidate relaxing with his or her family, working hard at a desk full of papers, and listening carefully to "common people," an advertisement attempts to create an image of the candidate as a hard-working person who cares about his or her family and who is in touch with the average voter.

● **Shaping attitudes** The amount of attention an issue receives in the media can shape people's attitudes about that issue. For example, the more that the media cover a certain issue, the more importance people begin to attach to it. In a famous example of how media shaped public attitudes, graphic news coverage of the Vietnam War greatly influenced public opinion against the war and eventually led the United States to withdraw troops from Vietnam sooner than planned.

**PRACTICE & APPLY** **1** Select a topic that you've seen covered in many different media sources. For example, choose a topic of national importance, such as transportation issues or biodiversity. Find four media messages on that topic: two each from print sources and electronic sources. Then, analyze each message and take notes on

• how it fulfills its purpose or purposes

• how it has been shaped for its intended audience

• how it uses media strategies

**Writing Skills**
Create a multimedia presentation. Analyze media sources, concepts, strategies, and effects.

Finally, evaluate the effectiveness of each message—how well it achieves its purposes. Which message would you recommend to someone interested in the topic? Why?

# Using Media

**Choose a Topic** Now that you've studied the uses and impact of various media, you'll create an impact of your own by planning and producing a multimedia presentation. **Multimedia presentations** combine a spoken part with text, images, and sound. Like speeches and oral presentations, multimedia presentations rely on the spoken word. Speeches might incorporate some text, images, or sounds to support the spoken part; however, the use of all three—text, images, and sound—is an *essential* part of multimedia presentations. Find a topic that interests you and that also holds possibilities for a presentation incorporating text, images, and sound. You might consider

- topics related to history or current events, such as women's suffrage, the civil rights movement, or environmental protection

- topics from fields such as science, sports, or the arts

- topics from literature, such as an exploration of a literary period or of an author whose work you enjoy

   In this workshop you'll see examples based on one student's research for a multimedia presentation on Elizabeth Bishop, whose poems you read on pages 1140 and 1143.

> **TIP** When thinking of a topic, consider your **purpose** and **audience**. Focus your thoughts, and establish a direction for your presentation by thinking carefully about why you are creating it and who will view your work. Knowing your purpose and audience can also help you select appropriate and effective media.

**Research Your Topic** Begin by searching for information on your topic. This information will comprise the spoken part—the core—of your presentation and will be complemented by the text, images, and sound that you find later. Consult both print and electronic sources for facts, examples, relevant quotations, and other material to use in your presentation, and take notes on all the information that you believe might be useful. Keep a list of all the sources you consult since you might want to return to them later. (For more on **making source cards,** see page 605.)

**Write a Thesis Statement** Review your notes and pull together all your information to decide on three to five key points you'll make about your topic. Then, write a clear **thesis statement** that encompasses these key points and states the focus of your presentation. (For more on **writing a thesis statement,** see page 608.) Here's one student's thesis for her presentation on Elizabeth Bishop.

> Elizabeth Bishop's background, her poetry, and her poetic style— all reflect her independent nature.

**SKILLS FOCUS**

**Writing Skills**
Choose and research a topic. Write a thesis statement.

**Select Media** The text, images, and sound that you use should **elaborate** on the presentation's content and should add to your presentation's **aesthetic appeal** and **effectiveness.**

| DO THIS →

To achieve these two purposes, search for and select material from a variety of sources, such as magazines and newspapers, videotapes and television broadcasts, and CD-ROMs and Internet Web sites. As you review these sources, consider what medium is appropriate for each part of your presentation. The following chart shows ways you can use text, images, and sound to support your key points and enhance your presentation. The right-hand column of the chart shows examples from the student creating a presentation on Elizabeth Bishop.

## USING MEDIA

| Media | Uses | Student Examples |
|---|---|---|
| **Text**—any text that will appear on an overhead projector, a video screen, or a computer slide | to illustrate or enhance your key points or their support, such as by showing quotations from literary works | • show a quotation from "The Fish"<br>• add the caption *Elizabeth Bishop (1911–1979)* under her photo |
| **Images**—charts, maps, graphs, photos, illustrations, paintings, video or film clips, and computer-generated animation | to provide images of people, places, and things relevant to the topic, and to appeal to the audience's emotions | • show a photo of Elizabeth Bishop<br>• include an illustration of a realistic-looking fish<br>• show a video clip of people fishing |
| **Sound**—sound files or other recordings of music, speeches, literary readings, and sound effects | to enhance and support a key point, to create a mood, and to appeal to the audience's emotions | • play a recording of Elizabeth Bishop reading "The Fish"<br>• play the sound of waves<br>• play light, relaxing music |

Before the student selected the specific medium to fit each part of the presentation, she had to think about questions such as these:

- What kind of caption (text) would complement the photograph of Bishop?

- Would a key point and its support be better illustrated by a video clip or an excerpt from a newspaper?

- Which would be more interesting for an audience: a still image of a photograph or a graphic from a Web site?

- How can a sound file or recording be effectively combined with an image?

**SKILLS FOCUS**

**TIP** Remember that using someone else's words, images, or sounds without giving proper credit is **plagiarism,** a serious academic offense. Document your media sources so that audience members can refer to them for further information. For more on **documenting sources,** see page 609.

**Writing Skills**
Select media based on aesthetic appeal and effectiveness.

**Maximize Your Impact** Pay attention to the quality of the material you choose. Equally important is how you incorporate your audiovisuals into your presentation. Remember that audiovisuals should elaborate upon the spoken part of your presentation. They should not dominate or distract. Use the following design principles to create the maximum impact on your audience.

● **Text** Limit the amount of text you show on slides, overhead transparencies, or a screen. Use a maximum of six lines of text, with six words per line. To aid your text's readability, write large and plainly, or, if you are using a computer program, choose a plain font and a large font size (36 to 48 points). You may also wish to use italics, capital letters, underscore, and boldface to emphasize words, but don't combine too many of these treatments.

**COMPUTER TIP**

For more on **fonts**, see Designing Your Writing in the Writer's Handbook.

● **Images** Visuals should complement the spoken material in your presentation, so don't use more than you need. Make sure images are large enough to be seen by people sitting in the back of the room. Edit film clips so that only the most important material is shown. For example, include an important excerpt of a videotaped speech rather than the entire speech.

● **Sound** Sounds, such as a recording or sound file of a speech or literary recitation, should be clear and easily heard by everyone in the audience. Background music or sounds that contribute to mood should be somewhat quiet so they don't compete with your voice for the audience's attention.

**Organize Your Presentation** Plan the organization of your presentation effectively to combine the spoken content and the text, images, and sound that will elaborate and enhance your words. To plan the organization of your content and the integration of the multimedia elements you've chosen, follow the steps in the chart below.

### ORGANIZING A MULTIMEDIA PRESENTATION

1. Create **note cards** for the key points and supporting details in the spoken part of your presentation (as you would do when presenting a speech).

2. Group cards for key points and details together, and arrange the groups by **order of importance.** Begin with the most important key point and end with the least important one, or vice versa.

3. Make a note card for each piece of multimedia support you plan to use. Use a different color from the note cards for your spoken content so that you can see how much media support you are using. You might even use a different color for each type of support, such as peach for text, blue for images, and yellow for sound.

4. Insert each media card before the spoken content card that it will support.

5. Use your note cards to create an **outline** of your presentation. Check that your organization makes sense and that media support is properly integrated into the presentation.

The chart below shows one student's outline for her presentation on Elizabeth Bishop. The information in brackets highlights the media support she plans to use in her presentation.

I. Introduction of Elizabeth Bishop as an independent woman
   [Show photo of Elizabeth Bishop with caption, play audiotape of light, relaxing background music]
   A. Experienced death of father when she was a child; observed mother's long illness; raised by relatives
   B. Always felt like a guest
   C. Didn't take part in any current literary movement
II. Characteristics of Bishop's poetry
   [Show text of "The Fish" excerpt, alternate with realistic illustration of fish to clarify images expressed in the poem]
   A. Incorporates meaning, but not obviously
   B. Makes symbols of everyday things
   C. Focuses outward instead of inward on the poet's feelings
III. Characteristics of Bishop's style
   [Play recording of Bishop reading "The Fish," follow with video of people fishing (with sound turned off) while playing audiotape of the sound of waves as I discuss style]
   A. Uses vivid description
   B. Has internal rhyme
   C. Uses rhythm more like prose than poetry
IV. Conclusion

If you find places in your outline where you need to locate and include more text, images, or sound to support or enhance your spoken words, create new cards and insert them into your stack. Use these cards as cues during your multimedia presentation.

> **TIP** **Transitions** are essential to a multimedia presentation. Guide your audience from one idea to the next and from oral content to media support. For example, one student provided the following transition to introduce the audio recording of the poet Elizabeth Bishop reading her work: **"As Bishop reads her work,** listen to her vivid descriptions and use of internal rhyme. **Also notice** how her rhythm is more like prose than poetry."

**SKILLS FOCUS**

**Writing Skills**
Design and organize a presentation.

**PRACTICE & APPLY 2** Use the information on page 1317 to choose and research a topic for a multimedia presentation. Write a thesis statement, and select text, images, and sounds to enhance the information in the presentation. Organize your presentation by creating note cards and an outline. Finally, revise the content of your presentation to make it as clear as possible.

**Practice Your Presentation**  You can get a pretty good idea of an essay's likely effect on its audience just by reading it through. In a multimedia presentation, however, many different elements have to come together to create an effect. You can look at your note cards and outline to imagine the effect you hope to achieve, but the only way to make sure all the elements of your multimedia presentation work together is by rehearsing. Gather a group of friends or family members and deliver your presentation exactly as you would for the intended audience of your final presentation. If you need to use your school's audiovisual equipment, ask your teacher if you can do a practice presentation before or after school.

As you rehearse, don't forget that the most important element of your multimedia presentation is you. After all, your **delivery** holds it all together. As you rehearse, use natural hand gestures; don't put your hands behind your back or in your pockets. Face your audience and make eye contact with audience members; don't turn your back on your audience when showing a supporting image. Speak clearly and carefully, avoiding voiced pauses such as *um* or *ah*.

After your rehearsal, ask for **feedback** from your audience. The following chart shows sample feedback questions you can ask your practice audience for their responses.

| AUDIENCE FEEDBACK |
| --- |
| **Questions** |
| Which part of the presentation was most memorable? Why did it succeed? |
| Which of the multimedia elements of the presentation was most effective? Why do you think so? |
| How well did I combine the spoken content of the presentation with text, images, and sound? Explain. |
| What parts of the presentation, if any, did you find confusing? What confused you? How could I make those parts clearer? |
| How did my delivery affect the presentation? Explain. |

Use the responses from your practice audience to **revise** both the content and delivery of your presentation. Then, rehearse your delivery again with all your audiovisual equipment to make sure that you have eliminated all the problems before giving your final presentation.

**PRACTICE & APPLY  3**  Rehearse your presentation for friends or family, and then solicit feedback. Use your sample audience's responses to improve your presentation. Finally, deliver your revised presentation to your classmates.

SKILLS FOCUS

**Listening and Speaking Skills**
Rehearse and deliver a presentation.

# Reciting Literature

**Speaking Assignment**
**Prepare and perform a recitation of a literary work.**

**O**ne of the possible purposes of a multimedia presentation is to entertain. Acclaimed authors such as Elizabeth Bishop often have entertained crowds of admiring listeners by reciting their works aloud. You can deepen your own and others' understanding of a literary work you admire by bringing it to life through the spoken word.

**Select a Text**  Choose a poem, a speech, or a dramatic soliloquy that seems to speak directly to—or for—you. It may be one you've read for school or one you've found in another print source, on the Internet, or on radio or television. Make sure the selection you choose is relevant and suitable for your audience.

**Analyze the Text**  Reciting a text from memory shows your **interpretation** of it—the special meaning it has for you. First, clarify your understanding by analyzing the text thoroughly so that you can make sound decisions about your performance.

- Check the **definitions** and **pronunciations** of any unfamiliar words.

- **Research** to clarify material you don't understand. Use an encyclopedia for historical allusions and an unabridged or specialized dictionary for classical or literary allusions.

- Think of how you can use **performance details,** such as gestures and vocal techniques, to enhance your interpretation.

- **Paraphrase** the text—restate it in your own words—for clarity.

- Identify the images and sound devices that contribute to the selection's **mood,** or atmosphere.

- Analyze the **punctuation** of the text to understand the author's intent.

**Create and Rehearse Your Presentation**  To achieve command of the text, rehearse your performance, and try various ways of using your voice and body to express the meaning you find in the work. Watch videos of professional recitations, or attend a speech, play, or poetry reading. Notice how the speaker uses gestures, movement, and vocalization to make his or her presentation clear, forceful, and aesthetically pleasing. Some speakers use **characterization** (giving voice to the characters in their texts), **dialect** (individual speech characteristics), correct **pronunciation,** and clear, distinct **enunciation.** You, too, should incorporate these performance details into your own recitation.

If equipment is available, record your practice sessions on a videotape or ask a friend to watch your rehearsals and offer feedback. To polish your vocal delivery and demonstrate your understanding of the text, pay attention to the performance details listed on the next page.

**SKILLS FOCUS**

**Listening and Speaking Skills**
Perform an oral recitation of literature. Select and analyze a text. Create and rehearse a presentation.

- **Emphasize** a word or phrase by stressing it or by pausing slightly after you deliver it.

- Reveal the speaker's feelings by varying the **pitch** and **tone** of your voice. For example, to suggest uncertainty, try speaking with a rising tone; to express conviction, use a falling tone.

- Convey the mood of the selection by varying your **rate** of speech. Speak more slowly to signal hesitation or reflection, and speed up your pace slightly to suggest excitement, joy, nervousness, or anger.

- Consider where **visuals, music, sound effects,** or **graphics** might contribute to the effectiveness of your recitation. For example, add background music to your delivery of a historical speech.

Also, when reviewing your rehearsals, pay close attention to your **nonverbal language** for the overall artistic staging of your recitation. Evaluate your facial expressions, gestures, and movements carefully.

To remember the decisions you make as you plan your recitation, prepare a double-spaced copy of the text to use during rehearsals. Use the following chart to mark your copy of the text. Then, use the interpretive techniques for an effective recitation.

## MARKING TEXT FOR DELIVERY

| Textual Cues | Markings | Interpretive Techniques |
|---|---|---|
| **Commas, semicolons, colons, dashes, and periods** | **Draw a single slash** (/) after each comma or semicolon; **draw a double slash** (//) after each colon, dash, and period. | Pause for each single slash; pause longer for each double slash. |
| **Words in parentheses** | **Circle** words in parentheses. | Pause and speak more softly. |
| **Italicized words** | **Underline** italicized words. | Stress or speak these words more loudly. |
| **Question marks** | **Draw an arrow** with a rising curve over each question mark ( ⤴ ). | Speak with a rising tone. |
| **Especially important words, phrases, or lines** | **Highlight** significant words, phrases, or lines. | Adjust pitch, volume, or rate for emphasis. |

**Introduce Your Presentation**  A brief introduction will interest your listeners. Include the title of the selection and its writer's name. Also, provide background information about the writer, the work, or both. For a dramatic soliloquy, outline earlier events in the play from which the soliloquy is taken.

**SKILLS FOCUS**

**PRACTICE & APPLY** 4  Use the guidelines in this workshop to prepare a recitation of a poem, speech, or dramatic soliloquy. Rehearse your selection, and then perform it.

**Listening and Speaking Skills**
Deliver a presentation.

# Collection 6: Skills Review

## Comparing Literature

**Test Practice**

Each of the following poems was written by an American woman in time of war. Julia Alvarez's poem "How I Learned to Sweep" recalls how television brought the violent images of jungle warfare in Vietnam into American living rooms during the 1960s and 1970s. "September, 1918" was written by Amy Lowell when the final, horrific battles of World War I were claiming tens of thousands of lives in France.

DIRECTIONS: Read the following poems. Then, read each multiple-choice question that follows, and write the letter of the best response.

## How I Learned to Sweep

Julia Alvarez

My mother never taught me
        sweeping. . . .
One afternoon she found me watching
TV. She eyed the dusty floor
boldly, and put a broom before
me, and said she'd like to be able
to eat her dinner off that table,
and nodded at my feet, then left.
I knew right off what she expected
and went at it. I stepped and swept;
the TV blared the news; I kept
my mind on what I had to do,
until in minutes, I was through.
Her floor was as immaculate
as a just-washed dinner plate.
I waited for her to return
and turned to watch the President,
live from the White House, talk of war:
in the Far East our soldiers were
landing in their helicopters

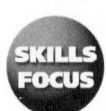

**SKILLS FOCUS**

Pages 1324–1327 cover **Literary Skills** Compare and contrast works from different literary periods.

20    into jungles their propellers
     swept like weeds seen underwater
     while perplexing shots were fired
     from those beautiful green gardens
     into which these dragonflies
25    filled with little men descended.
     I got up and swept again
     as they fell out of the sky.
     I swept all the harder when
     I watched a dozen of them die . . .
30    as if their dust fell through the screen
     upon the floor I had just cleaned.
     She came back and turned the dial;
     The screen went dark. *That's beautiful,*
     she said, and ran her clean hand through
35    my hair, and on, over the window-
     sill, coffee table, rocker, desk,
     and held it up—I held my breath—
     *That's beautiful,* she said, impressed,
     she hadn't found a speck of death.

# September, 1918

Amy Lowell

This afternoon was the color of water falling through sunlight;
The trees glittered with the tumbling of leaves;
The sidewalks shone like alleys of dropped maple leaves;
And the houses ran along them laughing out of square, open windows.
5   Under a tree in the park,
Two little boys, lying flat on their faces,
Were carefully gathering red berries
To put in a pasteboard box.
Some day there will be no war.
10  Then I shall take out this afternoon
And turn it in my fingers,
And remark the sweet taste of it upon my palate,
And note the crisp variety of its flights of leaves.
Today I can only gather it
15  And put it into my lunch-box,
For I have time for nothing
But the endeavor to balance myself
Upon a broken world.

# Collection 6: Skills Review

1. What **mood** is created by the images in the first eight lines of "September, 1918"?
   A Deep longing
   B Looming dread
   C Carefree innocence
   D Quiet sadness

2. How would you describe the speaker's **attitude** in lines 9–18 of "September, 1918"?
   F Losing hope
   G Troubled but hopeful
   H Disillusioned and angry
   J Frightened of the future

3. In the implied comparison in lines 10–13 of "September, 1918," the afternoon is compared to a —
   A glass globe
   B leaf from a tree
   C child's ball
   D piece of fruit

4. The **irony** at the center of Lowell's poem is the contrast between the —
   F beautiful fall day and the reality of war
   G boys' innocence and the speaker's despair
   H present and the past
   J boys at home and the boys at war

5. In addition to the dust on the floor, what else is the speaker of "How I Learned to Sweep" trying to sweep away?
   A Her mother's presence
   B Her dislike of housework
   C Her fear of dying
   D The deaths of the soldiers

6. What is the **tone** of the last two lines of Alvarez's poem?
   F Angry
   G Ironic
   H Hopeful
   J Disappointed

7. By the end of Alvarez's poem, the dust on the floor has become identified with —
   A the garden on television
   B the dragonflies
   C the dead soldiers
   D weeds underwater

8. Both poems make a statement about war by —
   F directly stating their opposition to war
   G showing how war hurts innocent people
   H contrasting war with ordinary life
   J graphically describing the horrors of war

## Essay Question

Both of these poems were written by women in the United States who were experiencing war thousands of miles away from the actual battlefields. Write an essay in which you analyze the ways each poet responds to a war raging abroad. What contrasts do you find in each poem? Consider how war news would have reached the United States at the time each poet was writing.

# Collection 6: Skills Review
## Vocabulary Skills

**Test Practice**

**Analogies**

DIRECTIONS: For each of the following items, choose the lettered pair of words that expresses a relationship that is most similar to the relationship between the pair of capitalized words.

1. INTERLOPER : INTRUDES ::
   A   plumber : toilet
   B   burglar : steals
   C   leader : follows
   D   drives : rides

2. TEPID : BOILING ::
   F   happy : ecstatic
   G   freezing : cold
   H   smooth : bumpy
   J   drenched : damp

3. VIRILE : FEMININE ::
   A   beautiful : gorgeous
   B   strong : courageous
   C   gentle : aggressive
   D   violent : demanding

4. MEDIUM : ARTIST ::
   F   painting : draw
   G   photographer : camera
   H   wood : carpenter
   J   hammer : nail

5. MORTIFIED : EMBARRASSED ::
   A   drizzled : flurried
   B   forgetful : regretful
   C   faithful : disloyal
   D   arrogant : proud

6. INGENIOUS : SKILLFUL ::
   F   rich : wealthy
   G   stubborn : easygoing
   H   irritated : pleased
   J   sweet : sour

7. MALODOROUS : SKUNK ::
   A   robin : bird
   B   deceitful : cheater
   C   fair : tyrant
   D   teacher : faculty

8. ABOMINABLE : DISGUSTING ::
   F   ferocious : tame
   G   accident : blame
   H   mistaken : correct
   J   horrifying : scary

9. EULOGY : SPEECH ::
   A   envelope : letter
   B   comedy : play
   C   death : burial
   D   writer : typist

10. AUSTERE : LUXURIOUS ::
    F   harsh : severe
    G   secure : safe
    H   restful : vacation
    J   elegant : plain

**SKILLS FOCUS**

**Vocabulary Skills**
Analyze word analogies.

# Collection 6: Skills Review
## Writing Skills

DIRECTIONS: Read the following paragraph from a draft of a student's autobiographical narrative. Then, answer the questions below it.

(1) When my mother told me I'd have to spend my winter break taking care of my sick grandmother, I was disappointed. (2) I wanted to spend my vacation hanging out with friends, going to movies, and shopping at the mall, but instead I was going to be driving to doctor appointments, cooking meals, and dosing out medication. (3) I thought nothing could be more boring, but my opinion quickly changed. (4) It took me three hours to drive to the town where my grandmother lived. (5) During my stay, my grandmother and I talked about everything. (6) I heard interesting stories I'd never known about my family, and I learned just how much my grandmother had experienced in her seventy-five years of life.

1.  Which sentence could be added to the end of the passage to relate the significance of the experience?

    A   I wished I could have stayed at home with my friends.

    B   I couldn't believe my grandmother wanted to be an actress.

    C   All families have some secrets hidden in their pasts.

    D   You can enjoy spending time with someone older.

2.  To improve how she characterizes herself, the writer could

    F   use dialogue to communicate the grandmother's stories

    G   describe her drive to the town with sensory details

    H   describe the facial expressions of the grandmother

    J   use interior monologue to depict her changing feelings

3.  Which sentence could the writer include to add sensory details?

    A   My grandmother's house brought fond memories to my mind.

    B   My friends were just as disappointed as I was.

    C   A warm, golden light from the fire flickered across our faces as we talked.

    D   My grandmother pulled out several photo albums that I had never seen before.

4.  To locate the incident in a specific place, the writer could add

    F   a description of the room where she and her grandmother talked

    G   a description of the mall where she shops

    H   a description of her grandmother's doctor's office

    J   a description of her grandmother's childhood home

5.  Which sentence should be deleted in order to improve the organization?

    A   1

    B   3

    C   4

    D   6

**SKILLS FOCUS**

**Writing Skills**
Write an autobiographical narrative.

# Resource Center

*The Parisian Novels (The Yellow Books),* Vincent van Gogh, 1888.

## When the Text Is Tough

Remember the reading you did back in first, second, and third grades? Big print. Short texts. Easy words. In high school, however, the texts you read are often filled with small print, long chapters, and complicated plots or topics. Also, you now find yourself reading a variety of material—from your driver's-ed handbook to college applications, from job applications to income-tax forms, from e-mail to e-zines, from classics to comics, from textbooks to checkbooks.

Doing something every day that you find difficult and tedious isn't much fun—and that includes reading. So this section of this book is designed to show you what to do when the text gets tough. Let's begin to look at some reading matters.

### READING UP CLOSE: HOW TO USE THIS SECTION

- **This section is for you.** Turn to it whenever you need to remind yourself about what to do when the text gets tough. Don't wait for your teacher to assign this section for you to read. It's your handbook. Use it.

- **Read the sections that you need.** You don't have to read every word. Skim the headings, and find the information you need.

- **Use this information to help you with reading for other classes,** not just for the reading you do in this book.

- **Don't be afraid to *re-read* the information** you find in Reading Matters. The best readers constantly re-read information.

- **If you need more help, then check the index.** The index will direct you to other pages in this book with information on reading skills and strategies.

# Improving Your Comprehension

Comprehension, your ability to understand what you read, is a critical part of the reading process. Your comprehension can be affected by many factors. Think about each of the following types of texts, and rate your comprehension of each from 1 (*never understand*) to 5 (*always understand*):

A. notes from your friends
B. e-mail messages from friends
C. college applications
D. job applications
E. magazines
F. computer manuals
G. Internet sites
H. school textbooks
I. novels you choose
J. novels your teachers choose for you

You probably didn't rate yourself the same for each type of text. Factors such as your interest level and the text's vocabulary level will cause your ratings to differ from text to text. Now, go back, and look specifically at items H, I, and J. How did you rate there? If you think your comprehension of those materials is low, then you'll want to study the next few pages carefully. They are filled with tips to help you improve your comprehension.

## READING UP CLOSE

### ▶ Monitoring Your Comprehension

Skilled readers often pay more attention to what they don't understand than to what they do understand. Here are some symbols you could put on self-sticking notes and place on texts as you are reading so that you can keep up with what's confusing you. Decide how you would use each symbol.

**Visualizing the text.** The ability to visualize—or see in your mind—what you are reading is important for comprehension. To understand how visualizing makes a difference, try this quick test. At home, watch a television show you enjoy. Then, turn your back to the television set. How long will you keep "watching" the program that way? Probably not long. Why not? Because it would be boring if you couldn't see what was happening. The same is true of reading: If you can't see in your mind what is happening on the page, then you probably will tune out of reading quickly. You can improve your ability to visualize a text by practicing the following strategies:

1. **Read a few sentences; then pause, and describe what is happening on the page.** Forcing yourself to describe the scene will take some time at first, but doing that will help in the long run.

2. **On a sheet of paper or a stick-on note, make a graphic representation of what is happening as you are reading.** For instance, if two characters are talking, draw two stick figures with arrows pointing from one to the other to show yourself that they are talking.

3. **Discuss a scene or a part of a chapter with a buddy.** Talk about what you "saw" as you were reading.

4. **Read aloud.** You might be having troubling visualizing the text because you aren't "hearing" it. Try reading a portion of your text aloud, using good expression and phrasing. As you hear the words, you may find it easier to see the scenes.

---

### READING UP CLOSE

▶ **Visualizing What You Read**

Read the following excerpt from "The Minister's Black Veil" (page 263), and discuss what you "see":

> The sexton stood in the porch of Milford meetinghouse, pulling lustily at the bell rope. The old people of the village came stooping along the street. Children, with bright faces, tripped merrily beside their parents, or mimicked a graver gait, in the conscious dignity of their Sunday clothes. Spruce bachelors looked sidelong at the pretty maidens, and fancied that the Sabbath sunshine made them prettier than on weekdays. When the throng had mostly streamed into the porch, the sexton began to toll the bell, keeping his eye on the Reverend Mr. Hooper's door.

**How's your metacognition?** Your attention wanders for a moment as you are reading something, but your eyes don't quit moving from word to word. After a few minutes you realize you are several pages beyond the last point at which you can remember thinking about what you were reading. Then you know you need to back up and start over. This ability to think about your thinking—or, in this case, your lack of thinking—is called **metacognition.**

Metacognition refers to your ability to analyze what you are doing as you try to make sense of texts. A critical part of metacognition is paying attention to what you are reading. It's normal to find that your attention *sometimes* wanders while reading. If it always wanders, though, then try one of the following activities: (1) Keep paper and pen close, and jot down notes as you read; (2) read for a set amount of time (five minutes), and then stop and review what's happened since the last time you stopped. Lengthen this time as you find yourself able to focus longer. Take the quiz below to see what your metacognition level is.

---

## READING UP CLOSE

### ▶ Measuring Your Attention Quotient

The lower the score, the less you pay attention to what you are reading. The higher the score, the more you pay attention.

**When I read, I**

**A. let my mind wander a lot**

| 1 | 2 | 3 |
|---|---|---|
| most of the time | sometimes | almost never |

**B. forget what I'm reading**

| 1 | 2 | 3 |
|---|---|---|
| most of the time | sometimes | almost never |

**C. get confused and stay confused or don't even realize I am confused**

| 1 | 2 | 3 |
|---|---|---|
| most of the time | sometimes | almost never |

**D. discover I've turned lots of pages and don't have a clue as to what I've read**

| 1 | 2 | 3 |
|---|---|---|
| most of the time | sometimes | almost never |

**E. rarely finish whatever I'm supposed to be reading**

| 1 | 2 | 3 |
|---|---|---|
| most of the time | sometimes | almost never |

**Try Think-Aloud.** Comprehension problems don't appear only after you *finish* reading. Confusion occurs *as* you read. Therefore, don't wait until you complete your reading assignment to try to understand the text; instead, work on comprehending while reading by becoming an active reader.

Active readers **predict, connect, clarify, question,** and **visualize** as they read. If you don't do those things, you need to pause while you read to

- make **predictions**

- make **connections**

- **clarify** in your own thoughts what you are reading

- **question** what you don't understand

- **visualize** the text

Use the Think-Aloud strategy to practice your active-reading skills. Read a selection of text aloud to a partner. As you read, pause to make comments and ask questions. Your partner's job is to tally your comments and classify each one according to the list above.

> ## READING UP CLOSE
>
> ▶ **One Student's Think-Aloud**
>
> Here's José's Think-Aloud for "The Jilting of Granny Weatherall" (page 771):
>
> Page 772: The doctor is visiting her at her house? This must be set long ago. (**Connection/Prediction**)
>
> Page 773: Who are George and John? Maybe they are children that moved away? or friends? oh, maybe old boyfriends? (**Question/Prediction**)
>
> Page 773 So John was her husband. It says he'd be a child beside her, so . . . ? Oh, he died, so now she's much older than he was when he died. (**Clarification**)
>
> Page 776: See, George stood her up—that's who jilted her. This part here—it says she wants to tell him she forgot him—I don't think so! I think she'll be angry till she dies. (**Clarification/Prediction**)

**Question the text.** This scenario may be familiar: You've just finished reading one of the selections in this book. Then you look at the questions that you'll be discussing tomorrow in class. You realize that you don't know the answers. In frustration you decide to give up on the questions.

While giving up is one way to approach the problem, it's not the best approach. In fact, what you need to do is focus *more* on questions—and focus on them while reading. This doesn't mean memorizing study questions and looking for specific answers as you read. It means constantly asking yourself questions about characters, plot, point of view, setting, conflict, and even vocabulary while reading. The more you question the text while reading, the more prepared you'll be to answer the questions at the end of the text.

## READING UP CLOSE

▶ **Asking Questions While Reading**

Here is a list of questions you can use as you read literary selections. You should recopy this list on note cards and keep it close as you read.

**Character Questions**

1. Who is the central character? Is this character the narrator? What are the greatest strengths and greatest weaknesses of this character?

2. Is the narrator telling the story while it is happening or while looking back? Can you trust this narrator? What if the narrator were a different character? How would the story change? What point of view does the narrator have—first person, third-person limited, omniscient—and how does that point of view affect the narrator's authority?

3. Who are the other characters? What makes them important to the central character? What do their actions reveal about their personalities? How do your thoughts about the characters change as you read the story? Can you find specific points in the text where your feelings about characters shift? Could any character have been omitted from the story?

4. Which character do you like the best? What do you have in common with this character?

**Plot, Setting, and Conflict Questions**

1. What are the major events in the plot? Which events are mandatory in order for the story to reach the conclusion it does? What prior knowledge is necessary for understanding this plot?

2. How does the setting affect the story? Could you change the location or the historical context and have the same story? How does the author situate the reader in the setting? Is the setting believable?

3. What event creates the conflict? How does the central character react to the conflict? How do other characters react? How is the conflict resolved?

**Re-reading and rewording.** The best way to improve your comprehension is simply to **re-read.** The first time you read something, you get the basic idea of the text. The next time you read it, you revise your understanding. Try thinking of your first reading as a draft—like the first draft of an essay. As you revise your essay, you are improving your writing. As you revise your reading, you are improving your comprehension.

Sometimes as you re-read, you find some specific sentences or even passages that you just don't understand. When that's the case, you need to spend some time closely studying those sentences. One effective way to tackle tough text is to **reword** the text:

1. On a piece of paper, write down the sentences that confuse you.

2. Leave a few blank lines between each line that you write.

3. Then, choose the difficult words, and reword them in the space above.

While you wouldn't want to reword every line of a long text—or even of a short one—this is a powerful way to help you understand key sentences.

## READING UP CLOSE

▶ **One Student's Rewording**

Regina created this rewording for parts of *The Autobiography* by Benjamin Franklin (page 69). Notice how the third rewording is a bit different from the first two. You might prefer to reword the entire sentence rather than just change the difficult words.

*thought of the brave     difficult task*

1. It was about this time I ~~conceived the bold~~ and ~~arduous project~~ of
*reaching*
~~arriving at~~ moral perfection (page 71).

*reason     consequently arranged*

2. For this ~~purpose,~~ I ~~therefore contrived~~ the following method (page 71).

3. My intention being to acquire the *habitude* of all these virtues, I judged it would be well not to distract my attention by attempting the whole at once (page 72): *Since I planned on making each of these a habit, I thought I'd do better by not trying to do all at one time.*

**Summarizing narrative text.** Understanding a long piece of text is easier if you can summarize chunks of it. If you are reading a **narrative,** or a story (including a biography or an autobiography), then use a strategy called **Somebody Wanted But So (SWBS)** for help writing summaries of what you are reading.

SWBS is a powerful way to think about the characters in or subjects of a narrative and note what each did, what conflict each faced, and what the resolution was. As you write an SWBS statement for different characters or subjects within the same narrative, you are forcing yourself to rethink the narrative from different **points of view.**

Here are the steps for writing SWBS statements:

1. Write the words *Somebody, Wanted, But,* and *So* across four columns.
2. Under the "Somebody" column, write a character's name.
3. Then, under the "Wanted" column, write what that character wanted to do.
4. Next, under the "But" column, explain what happened that kept the character from doing what he or she wanted.
5. Finally, under the "So" column, explain the eventual outcome.

If you're making an SWBS chart for a long story or novel, you might need to write several statements at different points in the story.

## READING UP CLOSE

▶ **One Student's SWBS Chart**

Read Keisha's SWBS chart for the last paragraph of "Phillis Wheatley: A Revolutionary Woman" (page 63), and then write your own for the first three paragraphs.

| Somebody | Wanted | But | So |
|---|---|---|---|
| Phillis | wanted recognition for her work | but the culture of her time valued her work only as a curiosity and soon forgot about her | so she died poor and alone. |

**Summarizing expository text.** If summarizing the information in a text is difficult, try a strategy called GIST.

1. Choose three or four sections of text you want to summarize.
2. Read the first section of text.
3. Draw twenty blank lines on a sheet of paper.
4. Write a summary of the first section of text using exactly twenty words—one word for each blank.
5. Read the next section of text.
6. Now, in your next set of twenty blanks, write a new summary statement that combines your first summary with whatever you want to add from this second section of text. You still have only twenty blanks to fill in, not forty.

Repeat this process one or two more times, depending on how many more sections of text you have to read. When you are finished, you'll have a twenty-word statement that gives you the gist, or overall idea, of what the entire text was about.

## READING UP CLOSE

▶ **One Student's GIST**

After reading "The City, Grim and Gray" (pages 164–165), Eric wrote the following GIST statements:

GIST 1 (for the first paragraph)
<u>New York</u>, <u>America's</u> <u>largest</u> <u>city</u>, <u>more</u> <u>than</u> <u>doubled</u> <u>its</u> <u>population</u> <u>from</u> <u>1820</u> <u>to</u> <u>1840</u>, <u>as</u> <u>people</u> <u>crammed</u> <u>into</u> <u>overcrowded</u> <u>tenements</u>.

GIST 2 (adding the second paragraph of information)
<u>Overcrowding</u> <u>and</u> <u>unsanitary</u> <u>conditions</u> <u>in</u> <u>New</u> <u>York</u>, <u>America's</u> <u>largest</u> <u>city</u>, <u>caused</u> <u>a</u> <u>deadly</u> <u>cholera</u> <u>epidemic</u> <u>in</u> <u>the</u> <u>summer</u> <u>of</u> <u>1832</u>.

___  ___  ___  ___  ___  ___  ___  ___  ___  ___

___  ___  ___  ___  ___  ___  ___  ___  ___  ___

**Using question maps.** Most readers at some point will struggle with a text. Some readers find reading poetry a struggle, but they can breeze through computer magazines. Others find the technical language in computer magazines difficult but read poetry easily. It's not whether you struggle with texts that matters; instead, what matters is what you *do* when you struggle.

If you are an independent reader, then you know how to find the answers on your own—independently—to whatever causes you to struggle. If you are a dependent reader, you expect others to do the explaining for you. Dependent readers often say, "I don't get it," and give up. Independent readers, by contrast, know what they don't get and then figure out how to get it.

If you think you are a dependent reader, try using a Question Map like the one below. As you complete the chart, you'll be mapping your way toward independent reading.

1. In the first column, **list your questions** as you are reading.

2. In the second column, **make notes about each question.** For instance, jot down what made you think about the question or what page you are on in the text.

3. In the third column, **list possibilities for finding answers.** Remember that re-reading the text is always a good idea. Other places to find answers include dictionaries (especially if you have questions about vocabulary), your own mind (sometimes the text gives you part of the information, and you must figure out the rest), or other parts of the book (especially if you are reading a science, math, or history book).

4. In the final column, **jot down answers to your questions** only after you've made notes about them and thought out where to find answers to them. If you can't answer your question at this point, then it's time to see your teacher.

## READING UP CLOSE

▶ **One Student's Question Map**

Here is Easton's question map for *Walden* (page 216):

| Questions | Notes | Places to find answers | Answers |
|---|---|---|---|
| 1. What's a sojourner? | page 217 | dictionary | traveler |
| 2. Who are poor students? | page 217 | in my mind | could be money poor or not good in school |
| 3. Did Thoreau really do this? | page 218 | encyclopedia on Thoreau or biography | Yes! He did! |

**Some smart words.** Sometimes you understand what you've read, but you can't find the words you want to use to discuss the characters, theme, plot, or style of writing. Here's a list of words and phrases that can serve as a springboard to discussion. They are beginning points—you still must be able to explain why you chose these words or phrases.

### Words and Phrases to Describe the Plot

| Positive | Negative |
|---|---|
| realistic | unrealistic |
| good pace from scene to scene | plodding |
| suspenseful | predictable |
| well-developed ideas | sketchy ideas |

### Words and Phrases to Describe the Characters

| Positive | Negative |
|---|---|
| original | stereotyped |
| believable | unbelievable |
| well-rounded | flat |
| dynamic; able to change | static; unable to change |

### Words to Describe the Theme

| Positive | Negative |
|---|---|
| important | trivial |
| subtle | overbearing |
| unique | overworked |
| powerful | ineffective |

### Words and Phrases to Describe the Author's Style of Writing

| Positive | Negative |
|---|---|
| descriptive; filled with figurative language | boring; lacking imagery |
| original | filled with clichés |
| lively; full of action | slow-moving |
| poetic; lyrical | plodding; jumpy |

## READING UP CLOSE

### ▶ Using Smart Words

Choose one of the selections you've read in *Elements of Literature* this semester, and using some of the words above, describe the plot, character, theme, and author's writing style. Remember to support your word choices with examples from the story.

# Improving Your Reading Rate

If your reading concerns are more about getting through the words than figuring out the meaning, then this part of Reading Matters is for you.

If you think you are a slow reader, then reading can seem overwhelming. However, you can change your **reading rate**—the pace at which you read. All you have to do is practice. The point isn't to read so that you just rush over words—the I'mgoingtoreadsofastthatallthewordsrun-together approach. Instead, the goal is to find a pace that keeps you moving comfortably through the pages. Why is it important to establish a good reading rate? Let's do a little math to see why your silent reading rate counts. Try working out the math problem in the box above. Then, compare your answers with the answers in the chart to the right.

> **MATH PROBLEM!**
> If you read 40 words per minute (wpm) and there are 400 words on a page, how long will it take you to read 1 page? 5 pages? 10 pages? How long will it take if you read 80 wpm? 100 wpm? 200 wpm?

| Words per Minute (wpm) | 1 page @400 words/page | 5 pages @400 words/page | 10 pages @400 words/page |
|---|---|---|---|
| 40 wpm | 10 minutes | 50 minutes | 100 minutes |
| 80 wpm | 5 minutes | 25 minutes | 50 minutes |
| 100 wpm | 4 minutes | 20 minutes | 40 minutes |
| 200 wpm | 2 minutes | 10 minutes | 20 minutes |

**Reading rate and homework.** Now, assume that with literature homework, science homework, and social studies homework, you have forty pages to read in one night. If you are reading at 40 wpm, you are spending more than six *hours* just reading the information; but at 100 wpm, you would spend only two hours and forty minutes. At 200 wpm, you'd finish in one hour and twenty minutes.

## READING UP CLOSE

### ▶ Tips on Varying Your Reading Rate

- Increasing your rate doesn't matter if your comprehension goes down.

- Don't rush to read fast if that means understanding less. Plus, remember, your rate will vary as your purpose for reading varies.

- You'll read more slowly when you are studying for a test than when you are skimming a text.

## Figuring Out Your Reading Rate

To determine your silent-reading rate, you'll need three things: a watch or clock with a second hand, a book, and someone to watch the time for you. Then, complete the following steps:

1. Have your friend time you as you begin reading to yourself.

2. Read at your normal rate. Don't speed just because you're being timed.

> **Example**
>
> 1st minute     180 words
> 2nd minute    215 words
> 3rd minute    190 words
>
> 585 words ÷ 3 = 195 wpm

3. Stop when your friend tells you one minute is up.

4. Record the number of words you read in that minute.

5. Repeat this process several more times, using different passages.

6. Then, add the number of words together, and divide by the number of times you timed yourself. That's your average number of words per minute.

### Reading Rate Reminders

1. **Make sure you aren't reading one word at a time with a pause between each word.** Practice phrasing words in your mind as you read. For instance, read the following rhyme. The first time you read it, pause between each word; the second time, pause only where you see the slash marks. Hear the difference the phrasing makes?

> Mary had a little lamb, / Its fleece was white as snow. / Everywhere that Mary went, / The lamb was sure to go. /

Word-at-a-time reading is much slower than phrase reading. If you are reading a word at a time, you'll want to practice reading by phrases. You can hear good phrasing by listening to a book on tape.

2. **Make sure when you are reading silently that you really are silent.** As you read, avoid moving your lips or reading aloud softly. These habits slow you down!

3. **Don't use your finger to point to words as you read.** If you find that you always use your finger to point to words as you read, then you are probably reading one word at a time. Instead, use a bookmark to stay on the correct line while you practice your phrase reading.

4. **As you practice your fluency, remember that the single best way to improve your reading rate is simply to read more.** So start reading more, and use the tips listed above. Soon you'll find that reading too slowly isn't a problem anymore.

# Vocabulary Development

**F**luency, reading rate, and comprehension are all connected to how quickly you recognize words and know what they mean. No matter how many words you study in school, you can't learn all the words you'll ever encounter. So you need to understand how words work—what *prefixes, suffixes,* and *roots* mean—so that when you encounter new words, you can see their components and figure out their meanings.

## LATIN AND GREEK ROOTS, PREFIXES, AND SUFFIXES

| Prefix | Meaning | Examples |
|---|---|---|
| ad– | to | adapt, addict, adhere, admit |
| amphi– | both; around | amphibian, amphitheater |
| an– | without | anarchy, anesthesia, anonymous, anorexia |
| auto– | self | autobiography, autograph, automatic, automobile |
| co– | together | coauthor, cognate, coincide, cooperate |
| de– | opposite | deactive, deform, degrade, deplete, descend |
| dis– | opposite | disagree, disarm, discontinue, disgust, dishonest |
| for– | not | forbid, forget, forgo |
| il– | not | illegal, illegible, illegitimate, illiterate, illogical |
| im– | not | imbalance, immaculate, immature |
| in– | not | inaccurate, inactive, inadvertent, incognito |
| ir– | not | irreconcilable, irregular, irresponsible |
| mal– | bad | maladjusted, malaise, malevolent, malice |
| pro– | before | progeny, prognosis, program, prologue |
| pro– | forward | proceed, produce, proficient, progress |
| re– | again | reappear, redistribute, redo, repaint, rewrite |
| sub– | under | subcontract, subject, submarine, subordinate |
| trans– | across | transatlantic, transcend, transcribe, transfer |
| un– | not | unable, uncertain, uncomfortable, unhappy |

| Root | Meaning | Examples |
|---|---|---|
| –act– | do | action, actor, enact, react, transact |
| –aud– | hear | audible, audience, audition, auditorium |
| –cred– | believe | credit, credulous, discredit, incredible |
| –dic– | speak | contradict, dictate, diction, predict, verdict |
| –graph– | write | autograph, paragraph, phonograph, photograph |
| –loc– | place | allocate, dislocate, locate, location |
| –man– | hand | manipulate, manual, manufacture, manuscript |

*(continued)*

| | | |
|---|---|---|
| —mot— | move | demote, motion, motor, promote |
| —ped— | foot | pedal, pedestal, pedestrian |
| —pop— | people | populace, popular, population |
| —port— | carry | export, import, portable, porter, transport |
| —sign— | mark | insignia, signal, signature, significant |
| —spec— | see | inspect, respect, spectacle, spectator, suspect |
| —tract— | pull; drag | attract, contract, detract, subtract, traction, tractor |
| —vid— | see | evidence, provide, providence, video |
| —volve— | roll | evolve, involve, revolution, revolve, revolver |

| Suffixes | Meaning | Examples |
|---|---|---|
| —ade | action or process | blockade, escapade, parade |
| —age | action or process | marriage, pilgrimage, voyage |
| —ant | one who | assistant, defendant, immigrant, merchant, servant |
| —cle | small | corpuscle, cubicle, particle |
| —dom | state or quality of | boredom, freedom, martyrdom, wisdom |
| —ent | one who | parent, resident, regent, superintendent |
| —ful | full of | careful, fearful, joyful, thoughtful |
| —ic | relating to | comic, historic, poetic, public |
| —less | without | ageless, careless, thoughtless, tireless |
| —let | small | islet, leaflet, owlet, rivulet, starlet |
| —ly | resembling | fatherly, helpfully, motherly, scholarly |
| —ly | every | daily, monthly, weekly, yearly |
| —ment | action or process | development, embezzlement, government |
| —ment | state or quality of | amazement, amusement, predicament |
| —ment | product or thing | fragment, instrument, ornament |
| —or | one who | actor, auditor, doctor, donor |

# The World of Work

You will use reading and writing skills almost every day of your life. For example, a police officer must write coherent reports. A parent must understand school policies. A car buyer must understand the contract. A dissatisfied employee must document unfair treatment in an effective memo. In your life and in the world of work, you will use reading and writing skills to learn new information, to communicate effectively, and to get the results you want.

## Reading

Reading is an important decision-making tool that helps you analyze information, weigh arguments, and make informed choices. Much of the real-life reading you will do will come from **informative documents** and **persuasive documents.**

**Informative Documents** Informative documents focus on providing facts and information, and they can be good places to check when you want to verify or clarify information from other sources. For example, suppose a co-worker sends you an e-mail complaining about a new vacation policy. Before responding, you can read the memo that explains the policy to see if your co-worker has understood the information correctly. Informative documents include **consumer documents** and **workplace documents.**

**Consumer Documents** As a consumer, you will face thousands of buying decisions. Maybe you've heard the warning: "Let the buyer beware!" That warning means that buyers are responsible for reading and understanding information about products and services. This information can be found in consumer documents, which spell out details about products and the legal rights and responsibilities of the buyer and the companies that produce and sell the product. Consumer documents you're likely to see include **warranties, contracts, product information,** and **instruction manuals.**

- **Warranties** describe what happens if the product breaks down or doesn't work properly. Warranties such as the one below note how long the product is covered for repair or replacement, which repairs the warranty does and does not cover, and how to receive repair service.

The MovieBuff DVD player is guaranteed to be free of defects in material or workmanship under normal use for a period of one (1) year from the date of purchase. Equipment covered by the warranty will be repaired by MovieBuff merchants WITHOUT CHARGE, except for insurance, transportation, and handling charges. A copy of this warranty card and proof of purchase must be enclosed when returning equipment for warranty service. The warranty does not apply in the following cases:

- if loss or damage to the equipment is due to abuse
- if the equipment is defective due to leaking batteries or liquid damage
- if the equipment has been serviced by unauthorized repair technicians

● **Contracts** give details about an agreement that the buyer enters into with a company. For example, a buyer might sign a membership contract at a local gym. The contract defines the terms of the agreement, the length of the membership, the benefits of membership, and the responsibilities of the buyer and the gym. Both parties must sign a contract to show that they understand and agree to its terms.

---

**BodyFitness Membership Contract**

A one-year membership, effective the date of this signed contract, to BodyFitness Gym includes the following services:

1. Unlimited access to the equipment, classes, and locker room facilities
2. Three sessions with a personal trainer to develop a fitness plan
3. Assistance by staff in operating equipment

Member agrees to the following terms:

1. The monthly membership fee will be paid by the tenth of each month for a full year. A charge of 5 percent will be added to late payments.
2. Members who discontinue membership will be required to pay all past-due charges and the remaining months of the membership.
3. After one year, membership may be renewed on a month-to-month basis.

_____          _____
BodyFitness representative                Member signature and date

---

● **Product information** describes the basic features and materials of a product. Product information on a laptop computer box would give the processor speed, hard-drive space, monitor size, and other specifications of the computer.

● **Instruction manuals** tell the owner how to set up, operate, and troubleshoot problems with the product. Instruction manuals also include safety precautions, diagrams, and descriptions of the product's features.

**Workplace Documents** When you work, you want to know what's expected of you, when changes are made in procedures, and when important meetings are being held. This information comes in workplace documents, such as **memos** and **procedure manuals.** Knowing how to read these documents can make you an informed and effective worker.

● **Memos** are the standard form of communication in many businesses. They provide direct, concise, and clearly organized messages to announce or summarize meetings, request action, or provide important information. To read a memo effectively, first check the subject line at the top to learn the topic of the memo. As you read, notice headings or bullets that indicate the main ideas, and pay attention to the purpose of the memo: Is it summarizing information, requesting action, or providing facts, such as dates and prices? You will know whether and how to respond by understanding the purpose of the memo.

● **Procedure manuals** detail the steps to follow for conducting business, operating machinery, reporting problems, or requesting vacation time—anything a company wants done in a certain way. Procedure manuals are often used to train new employees and to clarify procedures for existing employees so the company runs in a smooth and predictable way. As you read a procedure manual, pay attention to the step-by-step instructions so you know exactly how to carry out the procedures.

**Persuasive Documents** Some persuasive documents may sound informative. For example, a policy statement by a city commission on changing the curfew is persuasive. Its purpose is to persuade citizens to support the changes, even though it may rely heavily on facts to make its argument. Learning to recognize and analyze the features and rhetorical devices used in a persuasive public document can help you learn about what is happening in your community and watch out for your own interests. Common persuasive public documents include **policy statements, political platforms, speeches,** and **debates.**

- A **policy statement** outlines a group's position on an issue and sometimes provides the rationale for its position. For example, the school board might issue a policy statement explaining why it supports or rejects allowing soft-drink machines in schools. The policy statement gives the major points for the school board's position and may make a logical appeal or use rhetorical devices, such as an analogy, to support its position. A policy statement may also include a call to action. Many groups issue policy statements to endorse upholding or changing specific laws. The audience for a policy statement is the public who must vote on the issue or the lawmakers who are creating legislation concerning it.

- A **political platform** describes the direction a political candidate or party wants to take if elected. It details specific positions and goals on a variety of issues and describes the principles that guide these positions, often through ethical appeals. The positions and goals are known as the **planks** of the platform. Some platforms also address opposing viewpoints, although the audience for a platform is usually friendly to the candidate.

A platform is intended to arouse support and to persuade undecided voters. Here is an excerpt concerning recycling from a mayoral candidate's platform.

```
Greenville is a community that has
long deserved its name—it is a
place of tree-lined streets, clear
lakes, and green meadows. It is
time to preserve this beauty for
our children and grandchildren by
instituting a recycling program.
Our landfills are near capacity,
and statistics show that we are
collecting 28 percent more garbage
than we did just five years ago.
A recycling program may be expen-
sive to implement, but I believe
Greenville's citizens are willing
to make small sacrifices for long-
term gains. If elected, I would
push the city council to begin a
recycling program and explore ways
to fund this program.
```

- A persuasive **speech** may establish a fact, strengthen or change a person's belief, or move a person to action. A persuasive speaker may use a variety of logical, emotional, and ethical appeals to make arguments, address listener concerns, and rebut counterclaims. Logical appeals, based on facts and solid reasoning, give a speaker the strongest credibility. However, emotional and ethical appeals, which may target a listener's sympathy or sense of duty, may be even more persuasive to a listener who is not carefully analyzing the message. (For more on **persuasive speeches,** see page 146.)

- A **debate** involves two teams who systematically discuss a controversial topic to determine which side has the stronger argument. The issue is called the **proposition,** and the **case** includes the reasons and evidence a side uses for its position. After both sides present their cases, they may **refute** each other's arguments, attacking or trying to disprove the opposing side's points.

## Critiquing Persuasive Public Documents

Learning to critique the validity and truthfulness of the various arguments and appeals that are used in persuasive documents can help you avoid being easily misled. Here are some questions to guide you.

- To whom does the document appeal—a friendly or a hostile audience? Are that audience's concerns and counterclaims addressed in a convincing and appropriate way?

- What kinds of appeals does the document make? Does it appeal primarily to logic and reason, to emotions such as sympathy and anger, or to ethics and authority? How powerful are the appeals that are used?

- Can you distinguish between facts and opinions? Can factual claims be confirmed through other sources, including informative public documents? Can any statements of opinion be analyzed for meaning?

- Is the writer or speaker credible and knowledgeable? Are respectable and credible sources of information being used?

**PRACTICE & APPLY 1** Choose a persuasive public document, and critique it. Analyze the document's features, rhetorical devices, and appeals, and identify the call to action, if any. Consult at least one informative public document, such as a city ordinance or the minutes from a city council meeting, to verify information presented in the persuasive document.

## Writing

In the adult world, to win your dream job you'll have to write a letter and a résumé. To help your company improve quality, you'll have to write a memo outlining your plan. Effective writing makes things happen in the world of work, from getting hired to sharing ideas.

**Job Applications and Résumés** Your ticket to the world of work usually comes in the form of a job application or résumé. A **job application** is a form that asks for specific information. To complete a job application completely and accurately, read the instructions carefully. Type or write neatly in blue or black ink. Include all information requested. If a question does not apply to you, write *N/A* or *not applicable* in the blank. Proofread your completed form, and neatly correct errors. Avoid cross-outs. Finally, submit the form to the correct person.

A **résumé** summarizes your background and experience in an easy-to-read format. It should be written with your potential employer in mind. That means you should use the appropriate tone, level, and type of language for the employer and highlight skills that would appeal to him or her. An advertising company, for example, might enjoy a creative approach. A lawyer's office, however, would probably appreciate a serious tone with formal language. Here are some more tips to help you create an effective résumé.

- Give complete information about work experience, including job title, dates of employment, company, and location.

- Do not use *I*; instead, use short, parallel phrases that describe duties and activities.

- Proofread carefully. Mistakes on a résumé make the writer seem careless.

**Workplace Documents** Writing effectively on the job includes knowing how to write concise, easy-to-understand memos. Standard memo format includes the date, the recipient, the sender, and the subject at the top of the document. In a professional and courteous tone, the memo should answer *who, what, when, where, why,* and *how* for the reader. The following memo gets right to the point, communicating clearly and directly.

Date: October 8, 2003

To: Isabel Gutierrez

From: David Fossi

Subject: Internship Program

The Human Resources Department met yesterday to plan an internship program for high school students. These recommendations were made:

1. Internships will last nine weeks to fit the school calendar.

2. No more than one intern at a time may be assigned to a department.

3. Interns will be selected based on an application letter, teacher recommendations, and grade-point average. Each department will be responsible for interviewing and selecting candidates.

Please let me know by November 20th if your department is interested in participating in this program. I will also need a brief description of the kinds of duties an intern would participate in during the internship.

**Word-Processing Features** Creating clear content for documents is essential, but presenting that content in a predictable, easy-to-read way is just as important. Give your ideas greater impact and add to the readability of your documents by using word-processing features. Use the following suggestions to format documents correctly and to integrate databases, graphics, or spreadsheets.

**Formatting Documents** Presenting workplace information effectively involves formatting documents by setting the **margins, fonts,** and **spacing** to enhance impact and readability.

- **Margins** are the blank space that surrounds the text on a page. Most word-processing programs automatically set margins, but you can adjust these default margins as needed.

- A **font** is a complete set of characters (including letters, numbers, and punctuation marks) in a particular size and design. Choose a font that suits your purpose and is businesslike and easy to read. To maintain a professional appearance, avoid mixing several fonts in one document. For more on **fonts,** see page 1360.

- **Line spacing** is the white space between lines of text. Most word processors allow

you to choose single- or double-space measurements. Most letters and memos are single-spaced to conserve space, but longer reports are often double-spaced to allow room for handwritten edits and comments.

**Integrating Databases, Graphics, and Spreadsheets** Suppose you are writing a memo summarizing sales figures for each salesperson in a company. To make this information clear, you might include a bar graph or a spreadsheet that lists the figures. Integrate databases, graphics, or spreadsheets into documents when they will support your ideas or help readers grasp information. These features should be placed close to the related text and be clearly explained. For help in integrating databases, graphics, and spreadsheets into documents, consult the Help feature of your word-processing program or ask your teacher to help you.

**A Model Résumé** Word-processing features can help you create a winning résumé. Follow these guidelines to format a résumé effectively.

- Make sure the résumé is not cluttered. Use wide margins for the top, bottom, and sides, and use double-spacing between sections to make the résumé easy to scan for information.

- Use a font size of at least ten points. Consider using a different font, boldface, and a larger point size for your name and headings. Be sure all fonts are easy to read.

This example uses a typical résumé format.

---

**MALIK MILLER**
489 Oceanside Drive
San Pedro, CA 90731
(310) 555-0162
E-mail: mmiller@sbahs.k12.ca.us

**Education:**
Junior: Susan B. Anthony High School
Grade-point average: 3.0 (B)
Major studies: Writing and computer graphics courses

**Work Experience:**
Summer 2003    **Public Relations Volunteer**
Habitat for Humanity, San Pedro
- Helped write and design layout for newsletter
- Input data for mailing list

Summer 2002    **Office Assistant**
Saunders Realty, Rancho Palos Verdes
- Proofread letters and documents
- Answered phones and greeted customers

**Skills:**
Typing:    50 words per minute
Computers: Word processing, publication layout, graphics

**Activities:**
Copyeditor, yearbook; member of Future Business Leaders of America

**References:**
Dr. Shavonne Newman, Principal    Scott Saunders, Owner
Susan B. Anthony High School    Saunders Realty
(310) 555-0029    (310) 555-0196

---

**PRACTICE & APPLY 2** Create a résumé for your dream job. Include experiences and skills you have that would appeal to your potential employer. Then, present this information in a clear, concise, and eye-catching way.

# Writer's Handbook

## The Writing Process

You have a writing assignment due tomorrow. Your plan was to dash something off quickly and turn it in, so why are you stuck? What is keeping your ideas from flowing effortlessly onto the page? Realizing that writing is a process requiring many steps can help you get unstuck. The chart below explains the stages of the writing process.

### STAGES OF THE WRITING PROCESS

**Prewriting**
- Choose and narrow a topic, and choose a form.
- Identify your purpose and audience.
- Gather information about the topic.
- Begin to organize the information.
- Draft a sentence that expresses your main point and your perspective on the topic.

**Writing**
- Draft an introduction that gets your readers' attention.
- Provide background information.
- Follow a plan or an organizational pattern that makes sense.
- State your main points, and elaborate on them.
- Wrap things up with a conclusion.

**Revising**
- Evaluate your draft.
- Revise the draft's content, organization, and style.

**Publishing**
- Proofread for spelling, punctuation, and grammar mistakes.
- Share your finished writing with readers.
- Reflect on your writing experience.

This process is **recursive,** which means you have the flexibility to jump forward to another stage of the process, go back, or start all over again. Suppose you are drafting a report and discover that you need additional facts to elaborate on a point. Simply go back to the prewriting task of gathering information. Then, pick up where you left off, insert the new information, and continue the process.

As you progress through each stage in the writing process, make sure you do the following.

- **Keep your ideas coherent and focused.** Present a tightly reasoned argument that will help you achieve your specific purpose. Every idea should focus on the point you make in your thesis statement.

- **Share your own perspective.** Give readers a piece of your mind by clearly communicating your viewpoint on the topic. Leave no doubt about who is the speaker in your writing, whether that person is you as a writer or a character you create to narrate a fictional piece.

- **Keep your audience in mind.** Use your understanding of your specific audience's backgrounds and interests to make your writing speak directly to them. If you have the option, choose a form that will be familiar or appealing to your readers—for example, a song, poem, memoir, editorial, screenplay, pamphlet, or letter.

- **Plan to publish.** Develop every piece as if it might be submitted for publication. When you proofread, work with a classmate who can help you find errors and inconsistencies. Use the following questions to guide you. The numbers in parentheses indicate the sections in which instruction on each topic begins in the Language Handbook.

### QUESTIONS FOR PROOFREADING

**1.** Is every sentence complete, not a fragment or run-on? (9d, e)

**2.** Are punctuation marks used correctly? (12a–r, 13a–n, 14n)

**3.** Do sentences and proper nouns and adjectives begin with a capital letter? (11a, c)

**4.** Does each verb agree in number with its subject? (2a) Are verb forms and tenses used correctly? (3a–c)

**5.** Are subject and object forms of personal pronouns used correctly? (4a–d) Does every pronoun agree with a clear antecedent in number and gender? (4j)

To mark corrections, use the following symbols.

### SYMBOLS FOR REVISING AND PROOFREADING

| Symbol | Example | Meaning of Symbol |
|---|---|---|
| ≡ | Spence college | Capitalize a lowercase letter. |
| / | our Best friend | Lowercase a capital letter. |
| ∧ | on *the* fourth of July | Insert a missing word, letter, or punctuation mark. |
| — | the capital of *Ohio* Iowa | Replace a word. |
| ∿ | hoped for to go | Delete a word, letter, or punctuation mark. |

# Paragraphs

## The Parts of a Paragraph

Paragraphs come in all sorts of shapes and sizes. They can be as short as one sentence or as long as many pages; they can seamlessly connect several items or develop a single idea.

In works of nonfiction, including essays that you write for school, paragraphs usually develop one main idea. These main-idea paragraphs are often made up of a **topic sentence, supporting sentences,** and a **clincher sentence,** as explained in the chart below.

### PARTS OF PARAGRAPHS

**Topic Sentence**
- states the main idea, or central focus, of the paragraph
- is often the first or second sentence of a paragraph
- can be placed at or near the end of a paragraph to create surprise or to summarize ideas

**Supporting Sentences**
- support or prove the main idea in the topic sentence
- use the following kinds of details:

  *sensory details*—images of sight, sound, taste, smell, and texture

  *facts*—statements that can be proved true

  *examples*—specific instances or illustrations of a general idea; examples must be relevant to the main idea and precise rather than general

  *anecdotes*—brief biographical or autobiographical stories used to illustrate a main idea

  *analogies*—comparisons between ideas familiar to readers and unfamiliar concepts being explained

**Clincher Sentence**
- is a final sentence that emphasizes or summarizes the main idea
- can help readers grasp the main idea of a longer paragraph

**TIP** Many paragraphs—even those that develop a main idea—do not use a clincher sentence. Use clinchers sparingly in your writing to avoid boring readers by restating an obvious main idea.

**TIP** Not all paragraphs have or need topic sentences. In fiction, paragraphs rarely include topic sentences. Paragraphs in nonfiction works that relate a sequence of events or steps frequently do not contain topic sentences. In much of the writing you do for school, however, you'll find topic sentences useful. They provide a focus for readers, and they keep you from straying off the topic as you develop the rest of your paragraph.

**Putting the Parts Together** Look carefully at the parts of the following paragraph. Notice that the topic sentence at the beginning expresses the main idea.

**Topic Sentence**

**Supporting Sentences**

**Clincher Sentence**

> In the past forty years, however, anthropologists have done some very thorough digging into the life of the North American Indians and have discovered a bewildering variety of cultures and societies beyond anything the schoolbooks have taught. There were Indian societies that dwelt in permanent settlements, and others that wandered; some were wholly democratic, and others had very rigid class systems based on property. Some were ruled by gods carried around on litters; some had judicial systems; to some the only known punishment was torture. Some lived in caves, others in tepees of bison skins, others in cabins. There were tribes ruled by warriors or by women, by sacred elders or by councils. . . .There were tribes who worshiped the bison or a matriarch or the maize they lived by. There were tribes that had never heard of war, and there were tribes debauched by centuries of fighting. In short, there was a great diversity of Indian nations, speaking over five hundred languages.
>
> Alistair Cooke, *Alistair Cooke's America*

## Qualities of Paragraphs

You wouldn't build a house without thinking about how the boards, bricks, and shingles fit together. Paragraphs need to be just as carefully constructed. A well-written paragraph has **unity** and **coherence.**

**Unity** Unity simply means that a paragraph "hangs together." In other words, all the supporting sentences work together to develop a focused main idea. A paragraph should have unity whether the main idea is directly stated or merely suggested. Unity is achieved when all sentences relate to a stated or implied main idea or when all sentences relate to a sequence of events. In paragraphs that relate a series of actions or events, you can achieve unity by providing all the steps in the sequence, with no digressions.

**Coherence** In a coherent paragraph, the relationship between ideas is clear—the paragraph flows smoothly. You can go a long way toward making paragraphs coherent by paying attention to two things:

- the structure, or **order,** you use to arrange your ideas

- the **connections** you make between ideas

## TYPES OF ORDER

| Order | When To Use | How It Works |
|-------|-------------|--------------|
| Chronological | • to tell a story<br>• to explain a process<br>• to show cause and effect | shows how things change over time |
| Spatial | • to describe | provides details according to their location—near to far, top to bottom, left to right, and so on |
| Order of Importance | • to inform<br>• to persuade | arranges ideas and details from most important to least or vice versa, depending on which order the writer considers most effective |
| Logical | • to explain or classify— often by defining, dividing a subject into parts, or comparing and contrasting | groups ideas together in a way that shows the relationships between them |

**TIP** At times, you may need to use multiple orders. In explaining an effect, for example, you may trace it **chronologically** from its cause. If one effect has four simultaneous causes, you would place these causes in **logical order** or **order of importance.** To avoid confusing your readers, use multiple orders in a sustained way and only when necessary.

In addition to presenting details in an order that makes sense, a paragraph that has coherence also shows how these details are connected. You can show connections by using **direct references** (or repetition of ideas), **transitional expressions,** and **parallelism.**

## CONNECTING IDEAS

| Connecting Strategy | How To Use It |
|---------------------|---------------|
| Direct References, or Repetition of Ideas | • Refer to a noun or pronoun used earlier in the paragraph.<br>• Repeat a word used earlier.<br>• Use a word or phrase that means the same thing as one used earlier. |

**TIP** Direct references and transitional expressions can also build coherence in longer compositions, leading readers from one sentence, paragraph, or idea to another. Try not to overuse these connecting strategies in your writing, though, as doing so can result in writing that sounds artificial and stilted.

*(continued)*

*(continued)*

| | |
|---|---|
| **Transitional Expressions** | • Compare ideas *(also, and, another, just as, like, likewise, moreover, similarly, too)*. |
| | • Contrast ideas *(although, but, however, in spite of, instead, nevertheless, on the other hand, still, yet)*. |
| | • Show cause and effect *(as a result, because, consequently, since, so that, therefore)*. |
| | • Show time *(after, at last, at once, before, eventually, finally, first, later, meanwhile, next, soon, then, thereafter, when, while)*. |
| | • Show place *(above, across, around, before, beyond, down, here, in, inside, into, next, over, there, to, under)*. |
| | • Show importance *(first, last, mainly, more important, then, to begin with)*. |
| **Parallelism** | • Use the same grammatical forms or structures to balance related ideas in a sentence. |
| | • Sparingly, use the same sentence structures to show connections between related ideas in a paragraph or composition. |

**PRACTICE & APPLY**  Choose a broad topic that interests you, and then use the instruction in this section to develop two paragraphs on the topic, following these steps:

• Think of two ways to organize ideas about the topic—for example, you could organize ideas about school in chronological order to narrate the events in a typical school day or in spatial order to describe the campus.

• Plan a topic sentence, a variety of supporting details (see page 1353), and a clincher sentence for each of the two paragraphs you will write.

• Draft your paragraphs, following the organizational patterns you have chosen. Eliminate any ideas that detract from your focus, and connect ideas using direct references, transitional expressions, and parallelism.

# The Writer's Language

After your ideas are on paper, complete and organized, revise your writing for **style**—the way you communicate those ideas. Consider your **voice** and **tone, word choice, sentence variety,** and your use of **rhetorical devices** to develop a style that will fit your audience and purpose and the type of writing you have chosen.

**A Sound All Its Own**  Revise to give your writing a natural **voice** and an appropriate **tone.**

**Voice**  A writer's voice reveals his or her personality. A writer's voice should sound distinctive and natural, never stilted or forced. Read your own writing aloud to decide whether it sounds like you. Make sure your natural voice comes through loud and clear.

**Tone**  Tone reveals the writer's attitude toward a given topic and audience. As with voice, tone can be revealed through word choice and sentence structure. Select a tone that fits your **purpose.** For example, if your main purpose is to entertain, you won't use a serious tone because that could interfere with your goal. Also, consider how formal or informal your tone should be, based on your audience. Are you addressing your friends, classmates, and family members? In that case, your tone will probably be informal. If you are addressing your teacher or a group of strangers, it is best to use a formal tone.

Notice the differences in the following sentences.

FORMAL TONE  Going for a difficult run at dawn prepares me for the challenges of the day.

INFORMAL TONE  Nothing gets me ready to slay the day's dragons like a tough run at dawn.

**Precisely My Point**  To make your writing fresh and vivid, revise your word choice. Replace vague language with **precise verbs, nouns,** and **adjectives.** Instead of dull verbs, like *talk,* use more precise verbs, such as *mumble* or *chatter.* Isn't "Second Avenue, choked with honking taxis and stalled delivery trucks" more vivid than "a noisy, crowded street"? Create a clear, striking picture of your subject.

Many words have special **connotations**—that is, they create a particular emotional effect. For example, the word *cowardly* has a negative connotation. The word *frightened* expresses the same idea in a more positive way. Notice connotations as you revise.

**Variety Is the Spice of Life**  Aim for a variety of sentence lengths in your writing—a short, simple sentence here, and a longer, more complex one there. Review each piece to give it a mix of simple, compound, and complex sentences and to vary the beginnings of your sentences. For example, if most of your sentences start with a subject, occasionally move a phrase from later in the sentence to the beginning.

**A Rhetorical Point**   To make your writing more effective, use the **rhetorical devices** of parallelism, repetition, and analogy.

**Parallelism**   Use the same grammatical forms to connect related ideas within a sentence. Also, consider linking two ideas that appear in different sentences by using the same sentence structure. Use this latter technique sparingly to create an "echo" in readers' minds that will help them see the connections between important points.

**Repetition**   Repeating words or phrases can cement important ideas in readers' minds and make your writing more coherent. Significant words, when repeated, can also create an emotional response, as in Martin Luther King, Jr.'s famous "I Have a Dream" speech.

**Analogy**   An analogy is an extended comparison between two things. You can use an analogy to explain something unfamiliar to readers in terms they will understand, or you can enhance your tone through an analogy, such as this one: "The island emerged from the ocean in the same way that movie monsters suddenly appear from the darkness."

**A Descriptive Model**   As you read the following passage, notice its voice and tone, word choice, sentence variety, and rhetorical devices.

## A Writer's Model

Analogy
Precise language

Voice and tone

Repetition

Tone

The day I went to Alcatraz was as bleak as the island prison's past. It was cold and windy, and the waters of the bay were gunmetal gray. Along with the other tourists, my family and I crowded onto the ferry to the island, and the boat set out. Alcatraz loomed out of the waters of the bay, its peak crowned with concrete prison buildings and an old lighthouse. Gray, gray, everything looked gray. Later I would notice that wildflowers grew all over the island. At that moment, though, there was no color to be seen.

**PRACTICE & APPLY**   Revise the following paragraph to improve its style.

I went to the Muir Woods last Saturday with my friend. We saw a big cross section of a redwood tree that showed that the tree was very old. We walked in the forest all day. The trees were tall. There were lots of other people walking in the forest. Afterward we went to the gift shop. I bought a bracelet made of redwood. It reminds me of the forest.

# Designing Your Writing

A poorly designed document won't communicate even strong information effectively. In a well-designed document, the design supports the content, making it easy for readers to navigate through ideas and using visuals to share information that is difficult to communicate in words. You can create effective design and visuals by hand, or you can use advanced publishing software and graphics programs to design pages and to integrate databases, graphics, and spreadsheets into your documents.

## Page Design

**User-Friendly**  As a reader, you know that some document designs make text look inviting and others make you want to turn the page. As a writer, design your documents to be as appealing and easy to read as possible. Use these design elements to improve readability:

**Columns and Blocks**  **Columns** arrange text in separate sections printed side by side. A **block** is a rectangle of text shorter than a page separated from other text by white space. The text in advertisements is usually set in blocks so that it may be read quickly. Text in reference books and newspapers usually appears in columns.

**Bullets**  A **bullet** (•) is a symbol used to separate information into lists like the one on the next page. Bullets attract attention and help readers remember the information included in the lists.

**Headings and Subheadings**  A **heading** at the beginning of a section of text, such as a chapter, gives a general idea of what that section will be about. A **subheading** indicates a new idea within the section. Several subheadings often appear under one heading. Headings and subheadings are usually set in larger type or in a different style than the rest of the text.

**Pull-quotes**  Many magazine articles catch your attention with pull-quotes. A **pull-quote** is a significant sentence from the text that is printed in a large font and set in a box.

**White Space**  **White space** is any area on a page where there is little or no text, visuals, or graphics. Usually, white space is limited to the margins and the spaces between words, lines, columns, and blocks. Advertisements usually have more white space than do books or articles.

**Captions**  **Captions** are lines of text that explain the meaning or importance of photographs or illustrations and connect them to the main text. Captions may appear in italics or in smaller type than the main text.

**Contrast** Contrast refers to the balance of light and dark areas on a page. Dark areas are those that contain blocks of text or graphics. Light areas have little type. A page with high contrast, or roughly balanced light and dark areas, is easier to read than a page with low contrast, such as one that is filled with text and images.

**Emphasis** Emphasis is how a page designer indicates which information on a page is important. For example, the front page of a newspaper uses photographs and large headlines to place emphasis on a particular story. Because readers' eyes are drawn naturally to color, large print, and graphics, these elements are often used to create emphasis.

# Type

**Just My Type** The kind of type you choose affects the readability of your documents. You can use type to provide emphasis and interest by varying the case and the font of your letters.

**Case** You can vary case in your documents in the following ways.

- **Uppercase letters** Words in all uppercase, or capital, letters attract readers' attention and may be used in headings or titles. Text in all capital letters can be difficult to read. Therefore, use it sparingly.

- **Initial letter** An initial letter is a large first letter used to draw readers into an essay. You can draw your initial letter by hand, or you can enlarge a letter using a word-processing program.

- **Small caps** Small caps are uppercase letters reduced in size. They appear in abbreviations of time, such as 9:00 A.M. and A.D. 1500. Small caps may be combined with capitals for an artistic effect.

**Font** A **font** is one complete set of characters (such as letters, numbers, and punctuation marks) of a given size and design. All fonts belong to one of the three categories shown in the chart below.

| CATEGORIES OF FONTS | | |
| --- | --- | --- |
| **Category** | **Explanation** | **Uses** |
| **decorative,** or **script** | elaborately designed characters that convey a distinct mood or feeling | Decorative fonts are difficult to read and should be used in small amounts for an artistic effect. |
| **serif** | characters with small strokes (serifs) attached at each end | Because the strokes on serif characters help guide the reader's eyes from letter to letter, serif type is often used for large bodies of text. |
| **sans serif** | characters formed of straight lines, with no serifs (*sans serif* means "without strokes") | Sans serif fonts are easy to read and are used for headings, subheadings, callouts, and captions. |

- **Font size** The size of the type in a document is called the font size or point size. Many newspapers use type measured at 12 points, with larger type for headings and smaller type for captions.

- **Font style** Most text is set in *roman* ("not slanted") style. *Italic,* or slanted, style has special uses, as for captions or book titles. Underscored or boldface type can be used for emphasis.

## Visuals

**Get Visual** Some ideas can be communicated more effectively visually than as part of the text. For instance, a line graph showing how your club's membership has grown over the last four years would be more effective than simply writing about the information. If available, use technology, such as computer software and graphics programs, to create visuals and to integrate databases, graphics, and spreadsheets into documents. Whether you create them with software or by hand, the following types of visuals can help you effectively share ideas.

**Graphs** A **bar graph** can compare quantities at a glance or indicate the parts of a whole. A **line graph** such as the example below can compare trends or show how two or more variables interact. Both kinds of graphs can show trends or changes over time.

**TIP** You can copy databases or spreadsheets and paste them into word-processed documents. For example, imagine that you are writing a letter to your school administration asking for more money for the prom. Your letter will be more effective if you include in the letter a spreadsheet showing the budget and estimated expenses for the prom.

EXAMPLE

**Tables** use rows and columns to provide detailed information arranged in an accessible, organized way. A **spreadsheet** is a special kind of table created on a computer. The cells of a spreadsheet are associated with mathematical equations. Spreadsheets are especially useful for budgets or schedules in which the numbers are variables in an equation. In the spreadsheet on the next page, the last row totals the figures in each column.

| Club Account Balances by Month | | | | |
|---|---|---|---|---|
| Month | September | October | November | December |
| deposit (dues) | 150.00 | 150.00 | 165.00 | 165.00 |
| deposit (other) | 75.00 | 38.00 | 17.75 | 119.00 |
| total | 225.00 | 188.00 | 182.75 | 284.00 |

**Pictures** You may scan a drawing or photograph into your document on the computer or paste it in manually. Place a picture as close as possible to the reference in the text, and use a caption.

**Charts** Charts show relationships among ideas or data. Two types of charts you are likely to use are flowcharts and pie charts. A **flowchart** uses geometric shapes linked by arrows to show the sequence of events in a process. A **pie chart** is a circle that is divided into wedges. Each wedge represents a certain percentage of the total, and a legend tells what concept each wedge color represents.

EXAMPLE

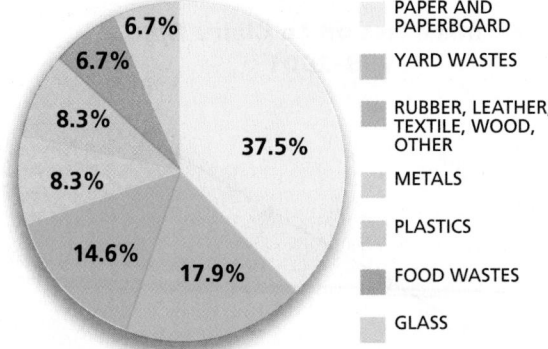

**What Creates Solid Wastes?**
**(Percentage of solid waste)**

6.7%
6.7%
8.3%
8.3%
14.6%
17.9%
37.5%

PAPER AND PAPERBOARD
YARD WASTES
RUBBER, LEATHER, TEXTILE, WOOD, OTHER
METALS
PLASTICS
FOOD WASTES
GLASS

**Time Lines** Time lines identify the events dealing with a particular subject that have taken place over a given period of time. (See page 2 for an example of a time line.)

**PRACTICE & APPLY** Use the instructions in this section to choose and create the visual you think would most effectively communicate the following information.

Last year, the total production cost for the Eureka High yearbook was $2,000. Paper cost $400, printing cost $1,000, and binding cost $600. This year, production costs have gone up. Paper will cost $500, printing will cost $1,250, and binding will cost $725, for a total of $2,475.

# Test Smarts

## by Flo Ota De Lange *and* Sheri Henderson

# Strategies for Taking Multiple-Choice Tests

You have now reached your junior year and are almost at the end of your high school career. To graduate, however, you still need to pass a lot of tests. You'll have plenty of quizzes, midterm exams, and finals to get through. You'll take the state's standardized tests, and if you plan to go on to college, you'll need to tackle the *Scholastic Assessment Test (SAT)* or the *American College Testing Program (ACT)*.

The following pages can help you prepare for all your standardized tests. They are designed to help you meet three goals:

- to become familiar with the different types of questions you will be asked
- to learn some strategies for approaching the questions
- to discover the kinds of questions that give you trouble

Once you have met those goals, you will want to practice answering the kinds of questions that give you trouble until you feel comfortable with them. Here are some basic strategies that will help you approach your multiple-choice tests with confidence:

## Stay Calm

You have studied the material, and you know your stuff, but you're still nervous. That's OK. A little nervousness helps you focus, but so does a calm body. **Take a few deep breaths** before you begin.

## Track Your Time

First, take a few minutes to estimate how much time you have for each question. Then, set checkpoints for yourself—how many questions should be completed at a quarter of the time, half the time, and so on. That way you can **pace yourself** as you work through the test. If you're behind, you can speed up. If you're ahead, you can—and should—slow down.

## Master the Directions

**Read the directions carefully** to be sure you know exactly what to do and how to do it. If you are supposed to fill in a bubble, fill it in cleanly and carefully. Be careful to match each question's number to the number on the answer sheet.

## Study the Questions

**Read each question once, twice, three times**—until you are absolutely certain you know what the question is asking you. Watch out for words like *not* and *except:* They tell you to look for choices that are false, different, or opposite.

## Anticipate Answers

Once you are sure you understand the question, **anticipate the answer** before you read the choices. If the answer you guessed is there, it is probably correct. To be sure, though, check out each choice. If you understand the question but don't know the answer, eliminate any choices you think are wrong. Then, make an educated—not a wild—guess. Take care to **avoid distracters,** choices that are true but don't fit the question.

## Don't Give Up

If you are having a hard time with a test, take a deep breath, and **keep on going.** On most tests the questions do not get more difficult as you go, and an easier question is probably coming up soon. The last question on a test is worth just as many points as the first, so give your all—all the way to the end.

## Types of Test Questions

You will feel more confident if you are familiar with the kinds of questions given on a test. Following are examples of and tips for taking the different types of questions on many standardized tests.

# Critical-Reading Questions

The critical-reading section of a test seeks to determine how well you think analytically about what you read. This is not news to you. That is the purpose of every reading test you have ever taken. Although challenging tests may give you long, difficult readings and complicated questions, it helps to remember that you will find everything you need—including the answers—right there on the page.

## Strategies for Answering Critical-Reading Questions

Here are some tips for answering critical-reading questions:

- **Look for main ideas.** In this kind of test, pay special attention to the **introductory and concluding paragraphs,** in which writers often state their main idea. Read all footnotes or margin notes. As you read the passage, look for **key words, phrases, and ideas.** If you are allowed to write on the test, circle or underline them.
- **Look for structure.** Try to determine how the logic of a passage is developed by paying attention to **transition words** and the **pattern of organization.** Does the author build an argument brick by brick, using words and phrases such as *also, and, as well as, furthermore*? Does the author instead offer an argument with contrasts, using words and phrases such as *however, although, in spite of, nevertheless*? Finally, **what is the writer's point?**
- **Eliminate obviously wrong choices.** If the questions are long and complicated, it often helps to translate them into plain English to be sure you understand what's being asked. Then, anticipate the possible answers. When you have eliminated the obviously wrong choices, put your finger on the choice you think is correct, and go back to the passage. **Check it.** Do not rely on memory. This is particularly important for vocabulary in context questions.
- **Watch out for traps.** Be wary of choices that use extreme words, like *always* and *never*. Look out for choices that are true but do not correctly answer a question—these are called *distracters*. Remember that questions using *except* or *least* or *not* are asking you to find the false answer. Trust your common sense.

We'll use the reading selection below to discuss a few of the most common kinds of critical-reading questions:

**DIRECTIONS:** Read the passage below. Then, read the questions that follow, and write the letter of the best answer.

1　During the 1870s, Americans across the nation became enthralled by the West in general and cowboys in particular. Craving an authentic taste of
5　life on the range, they traveled west for "working" vacations on ranches.
　　These tourists sported spanking-new western fashions as eagerly as the ranch workers donned their usual worn,
10　dusty garb. Ranch workers could not help but mock their wealthy imitators. No doubt Buffalo Bill would have done the same. They called fake cowhands dudes; this derogatory label is believed
15　to be derived from the German dialect word—*dude,* meaning "fool."
　　In the 1870s, ranchers in Colorado became the first to charge dudes fees for the privilege of experiencing the
20　Wild West. During the next decade wealthy men from Great Britain began journeying to the American West to hunt wildlife. Excited by the prospect of luring such prosperous customers,
25　one entrepreneur created a ranch for tourists only. The "dude ranch" was born.
　　Dude ranches eventually offered affordable vacations not only for the
30　rich but also for ordinary Americans. The ranches had a surge of success during World War I: Tourists couldn't travel to Europe, so they trekked west instead, surging in like the wagon

*(continued)*

*(continued)*

35 trains of the 1800s. When cattle prices plummeted in the 1920s, visiting dudes became the only means of support for many ranches.

40 Still popular today, dude ranches offer tourists treats like television and air conditioning—amenities that an exhausted 1870s cowpoke would have relished.

## VOCABULARY-IN-CONTEXT

**QUESTIONS** ask you to define words within the context of the reading. If the word is fairly common, look out! A word's meaning in the reading may be an unusual or uncommon one. If it is a really tough word, read several lines above and several lines below the line in which the word is found. Whatever you do, **always go back and check the reading** for vocabulary-in-context questions. Always.

> 1. The word *prospect* in line 23 means —
>
>    **A** a broad, scenic view
>
>    **B** the outlook from a particular place
>
>    **C** something hoped for or expected
>
>    **D** income
>
>    **E** a place in the earth where minerals are deposited

*Answer:* All of the choices except **D** are real meanings of the word *prospect,* but only **C** ("something hoped for or expected") is the meaning of the word as it is used in the passage. **A** doesn't make sense in the context. You might be tempted by a metaphorical use of **B,** but that's a stretch, so keep looking. **D** doesn't work because it's not a meaning of *prospect.* **The answer is C.**

## PARAPHRASING or RESTATING

**QUESTIONS** ask you to choose the best restatement of an idea, detail, or fact in the selection. You are not asked to make any judgments about the idea; you are simply asked to report what the writer said. If the question is complex, put it in your own words **before** you read the choices. The answer is easier to find if you know what is being asked.

> 2. According to the writer, dude ranches became popular in the 1870s because —
>
>    **A** tourists couldn't travel to Europe
>
>    **B** the price of cattle fell
>
>    **C** Americans wanted to experience the West and the life of the cowboy
>
>    **D** wealthy men who owned the ranches wanted to open them to the public
>
>    **E** advertisers wanted to sell western fashions to easterners

*Answer:* **C is the correct answer,** a paraphrase of the first paragraph. **A** and **B** are distracters—true statements that apply to a later time period, not to the 1870s. **D** and **E** are clearly wrong; those statements are not mentioned in the passage.

## INFERENCE QUESTIONS ask you to read

between the lines to connect clues from the ideas in the selections. You compile hints and key bits of information to arrive at the answer. Inference questions require careful reading in order to glean what is implied rather than stated outright.

> 3. The writer compares ranch workers with tourists in order to —
>
>    **A** create sympathy for the tourists
>
>    **B** point out their similarities
>
>    **C** explain the decline of ranching
>
>    **D** illustrate that the tourists were only pretending
>
>    **E** show that tourists hurt productivity

*Answer:* This question asks you to make an inference about the author's purpose in using a particular rhetorical device—comparison-contrast. First, determine whether a choice is true according to the known facts in the reading. **A** is clearly not true: No special sympathy is shown for the tourists. **B** is also clearly wrong: No similarities are pointed out in the passage. You can eliminate choice **C**, the decline of ranching, because although it is mentioned in the passage, the tourists surely didn't cause it. The passage doesn't say anything about **E**. Therefore, **D is the best answer.**

**TONE or MOOD QUESTIONS** ask you to infer the writer's attitude toward the subject. Pay attention to the descriptions of the subject. Are they positive, neutral, or negative? Is the writer hopeful, sad, admiring, wishy-washy, sarcastic? (A standardized test might use more difficult vocabulary words for those same moods: *sanguine, melancholy, reverent, ambivalent, sardonic.*)

> 4. The tone of this selection about dude ranches is *best* described as —
>
> **A** objective and somewhat humorous
>
> **B** objective and critical
>
> **C** extremely critical and angry
>
> **D** subjective and opinionated
>
> **E** very admiring and somewhat objective

*Answer:* All right. What is the tone of most history-based readings? Yes, objective. Does that hold true for this reading? Yes, mostly. So choices **A, B,** and **E** are possible because they contain the word *objective.* Let's see which choices can be eliminated. You can eliminate **D:** The writer's tone isn't subjective or opinionated. Nor is it critical or angry, so eliminate **C.** Choice **A** seems to fit, but check out the rest. The reading seems neither critical **(B)** nor very admiring **(E). That leaves A as the best answer.** Mention of Buffalo Bill and the passage's last sentence give it a "somewhat humorous" tone.

**MAIN-IDEA or BEST-TITLE QUESTIONS** ask you to consider the big picture, much as you might do when you step back from a beautiful garden to focus on the entire effect rather than zoom in on the individual plants that create that effect. Ask yourself:

- What is the subject?
- What aspect of the subject does the writer address?
- What does the writer want me to understand about this aspect?

**Main ideas are often found at the beginning or end of a selection.** In choosing your answers, be wary of those that may be true but are either too specific or too general to reflect the message of *this* selection.

> 5. The writer's main idea is that dude ranches were —
>
> **A** a significant, if humorous, development in the history of the West
>
> **B** a place for wealthy tourists only
>
> **C** bad for the ranches and ranchers
>
> **D** an embarrassing development that had no value and should never have happened
>
> **E** successful because of wars

*Answer:* First, eliminate the obviously wrong choices—**B** and **E.** Remember that you're looking for the *main* idea. Choice **C** is clearly wrong: The dude ranches were helpful in providing income, especially when cattle prices dropped. **D** is wrong because it presupposes a critical tone that the passage doesn't have. **Choice A is the best answer.**

**EVALUATING-THE-WRITER'S-CRAFT QUESTIONS** ask you to look at the selection's organization, logic, and argumentative techniques. An example is on the next page.

**6.** The relationship between the first and second paragraphs can best be described as —

**A** introductory to supporting paragraph

**B** introductory to concluding paragraph

**C** supporting to concluding paragraph

**D** primary to secondary supporting paragraph

**E** secondary supporting paragraph to concluding paragraph

*Answer:* **A is the best answer** because the first paragraph clearly introduces the subject of dude ranches and the second paragraph elaborates on (supports) that theme. There are no secondary supporting paragraphs in the selection, so eliminate **D** and **E;** and the concluding paragraph would be the fifth paragraph, so cross out **B** and **C.**

# Vocabulary Questions

You will encounter several types of vocabulary questions on standardized tests. They all test your understanding of word meanings, both in and out of context.

**SENTENCE-COMPLETION, or FILL-IN-THE-BLANK, QUESTIONS** look easy, but they require your full attention. Here's a step-by-step way to approach each question:

- **Cover up the choices, and read the entire sentence carefully.** Most sentences will contain clues to the intended meaning and thus to the word you want. Ask yourself, "What is this blank about?" and "What else does the sentence say about the subject of the blank?"
- **Look for clue words.** Pay special attention to words that change the direction of a sentence. Look for words that **reverse** the sentence's main idea, such as *no, not, although, however, but.* Look also for words that indicate that a **synonym** is wanted: *and, also, in addition, likewise, moreover.* Finally, look for words that suggest **cause and effect:** *thus, therefore, because, since, so.*
- **Anticipate answers.** Think of words that might best fill the blank.

- **Look at the choices.** If the word you guessed is there, it is probably the correct choice. You can double-check by eliminating any choices that are obviously wrong. Then, try *each* choice in the blank, and re-read the sentence *each* time to find the best fit. Take no shortcuts on this step. Following are three fill-in-the-blank questions:

**7.** If a human track star wanted to try to beat a racehorse, her success would depend on the _____ of the race because horses take longer than humans to attain top speed.

**A** adversity

**B** brevity

**C** location

**D** obstacles

**E** importance

*Answer:* You will be looking for a word that means *shortness* or *length.* How do you know that? Your clue lies after the word *because,* where you learn that horses take awhile to get going. That tells you that humans have the advantage before the horse hits its stride. Of course, a difficult test like the SAT will not give you a common word like *shortness* for a choice. Choice **B is correct.** Choices **A** (which means "difficulty") **C, D,** and **E** don't make sense in the sentence.

**8.** The odds are quite _____ that a human can beat a crocodile in a foot race, since the crocodile can attain a top speed of only eight to ten miles per hour.

**A** nebulous

**B** noxious

**C** partial

**D** intractable

**E** auspicious

*Answer:* Even if you do not know the speed a human can attain, you have a great clue word (*only*) in the cause-and-effect section of the sentence, which begins with the word *since.* *Only* clearly tells you that a human can do more than the crocodile.

Thus, you are looking for a word that means "good." **E is your best choice.**

But let's imagine for a moment that the choices are all unfamiliar words. (What? You say they *are* unfamiliar words?) You can still think them through. **Use what you know to eliminate incorrect choices.** For instance, you know that a nebula is a hazy cloud of dust and gas in space, so choice **A** (*nebulous*—like a nebula) probably means "hazy" too.

Choice **B** (*noxious*) may be an unfamiliar word, but you can guess it's related to *obnoxious,* which means "totally unpleasant." **C** (*partial*) gives its meaning away in its root word: *part.* However, you may have heard someone say he or she is partial to chocolate, as in liking it. That *could* be a match, but it's a stretch. Keep looking for a better choice.

**D** (*intractable*) has a familiar prefix (*in–,* meaning "not") and suffix (*able*). Not able to *tract.* Hmmm. A word that means "not able to do something" isn't going to fit the blank.

So what's left? Bingo! You might even have connected the ancient tradition of augury (telling the future) with the modern word *auspicious* in **E.**

### Two Blanks to Fill In

Some sentence-completion questions contain two blanks. The trick is to find the choice that fits both blanks correctly—in the order given. **As a shortcut, determine the choices that fit *one* blank, whichever blank seems easier to you.** Cross out all the choices that don't fit. **Then, consider *only* the remaining choices when filling in the other blank.**

> **9.** Comprehending that a million is a truly _____ quantity to visualize, the professor _____ to the class that one million dollar bills stacked atop one another would reach more than four hundred feet high and weigh one ton.
>
> **A** knotty, pontificated
>
> **B** prodigious, explained
>
> **C** immense, refused
>
> **D** cuboid, lampooned
>
> **E** scant, illuminated

*Answer:* Before you look at the choices, make sense of the sentence. You know from the sentence that the first blank will reflect a *large* quantity, because the second half describes its considerable height and weight. Now, look at the choices. **You can immediately eliminate any first-blank choices that do not reflect the sentence's meaning.** Eliminate **A** (*knotty*) and **D** (*cuboid*) as irrelevant. Eliminate **E** (*scant*) because it's an antonym for the word you want. That leaves **B** (*prodigious*) and **C** (*immense*). Even if you don't know the definitions of those words, consider them. **Now, go on to the second blank, checking only the choices that fit the first blank**—in this case **B** and **C**. The second blank describes what the professor did. Of the two choices left, **B** (*explained to the class*) fits well, but **C** (*refused to the class*) makes no sense. **Thus, the best answer is B.**

**ANALOGY QUESTIONS** require that you figure out the relationship between one pair of words and then select another pair with the same relationship. Analogies use many kinds of relationships, among them, **classification, degree, cause and effect, part and whole, object and performer, performer and action, characteristic, synonym, antonym,** and **use.** For more about analogies, see pages 187, 788, and 1046.

The more comprehensive your vocabulary, the better off you will be when you face an analogy question. If you are stumped, try breaking an unfamiliar word into its prefix, suffix, and root. In some tests the analogy questions get harder as you go, but don't give up. Everyone's vocabulary is different, and a word that seems difficult to others may be easy for you. Let's try one out:

> **10.** CHEAPSKATE : STINGINESS ::
>
> **A** donor : generosity
>
> **B** grouch : cheerfulness
>
> **C** bully : merriment
>
> **D** beggar : excess
>
> **E** flatterer : truthfulness

Begin by turning the first pair of words (the stem words) into a sentence that defines their relationship. Your sentence should begin with the first word in the pair and end with the second word; you fill in the middle. A sentence for item 10 might be *A characteristic of a cheapskate is stinginess.* Now, try out each choice in that sentence: A characteristic of a donor is generosity? A characteristic of a grouch is cheerfulness? A characteristic of a bully is merriment? A characteristic of a beggar is excess? A characteristic of a flatterer is truthfulness?

*Answer:* **A is the best answer** because it preserves the same relationship in both word pairs, which in this case is a person and a characteristic. Both a cheapskate and a donor are kinds of people. Both stinginess and generosity are characteristics of people, and each is, indeed, a characteristic of its paired type of person. All other choices—**B, C, D,** and **E**—mismatch people and characteristics. Oh, there's just one more thing about the words in item 10. On the *SAT* the words would be much more difficult, like this:

> **11.** MISER : PARSIMONY ::
>
> **A** philanthropist : largesse
>
> **B** curmudgeon : felicity
>
> **C** lout : joviality
>
> **D** mendicant : surfeit
>
> **E** sycophant : verity

*Answer:* **The correct answer is still A.** In item 11, every word is a synonym of the corresponding word in item 10.

You may have already noticed that words in vocabulary questions are anything but commonplace. What's a student to do in the face of such *egregious, inordinate,* and *maliciously pedantic* word choices? Study them. Study them. Study them. The best way, though, to learn vocabulary words is to read. Read many different kinds of materials. Don't just skim over words you don't know: Look them up. Then, think about the meaning they add to the passage you are reading. If you follow those suggestions, you'll increase your vocabulary *exponentially,* and questions on vocabulary tests will be much less *formidable.*

Here are two more analogy questions—the kind with easy words:

> **12.** LYRICS : SONG ::
>
> **A** table : lamp
>
> **B** dialogue : script
>
> **C** poetry : prose
>
> **D** trial : judgment
>
> **E** plow : tractor

*Answer:* To define the relationship in the stem words, you might make up this sentence: *Lyrics are part of a song.* (The relationship is that of part and whole.) Then, try out that same sentence with all of the choices. You can eliminate **A, C,** and **E** because they don't make sense in your sentence. **B** makes sense: The dialogue *is* part of a script. **D** would have made sense if the words were in reverse order (a judgment is part of a trial)—but they're not. **So B is the correct answer.**

> **13.** PAINTER : CANVAS ::
>
> **A** experiment : science
>
> **B** concentration : distraction
>
> **C** athlete : spine
>
> **D** dentist : molars
>
> **E** cathedral : architect

*Answer:* **The answer is D.** The relationship in this analogy is that of a performer (the doer) and object: *A painter works on a canvas.* You can quickly eliminate **B** (the words are antonyms) and **C** (spine doesn't fit; if the choice were *race,* that might work). **A** doesn't make sense in your sentence, and **E** gives the words in the wrong order. The only choice that fits is **D**: A dentist works on molars.

# Multiple-Choice Writing Questions

Multiple-choice writing questions are designed to test your knowledge of standard written English. Some questions ask you to spot errors in a sentence's grammar or punctuation. Some ask you to spot the best written form of a sentence. Some ask when a paragraph is (or isn't) properly developed. You will need to know the rules of punctuation and grammar. Here are some question formats you might encounter:

## IDENTIFYING-SENTENCE-ERROR QUESTIONS

ask you to look at underlined sections of a sentence and choose the section that includes an error. You are *not* expected to correct the error.

> 14. When Daniel P. Mannix, a sword
>     swallower, <u>being accused</u> of using retract-
>             A
>
>     ing swords to fool his <u>audience, Mannix</u>
>                       B
>
>     swallowed a neon <u>tube and then</u> turned
>                    C
>
>     it on, bringing new meaning to the old
>     <u>adage</u> "Light of my life." <u>No error.</u>
>      D                      E

*Answer:* **The correct answer is A.** Replace the participle *being* with the verb *was*. Remember, however, that that kind of question asks you only to *find* the error, *not* to correct it. By the way, don't try Daniel's trick at home.

## IMPROVING-SENTENCES QUESTIONS

ask you to correct an underlined section by choosing the best version offered. It is helpful to find the error before you look at the choices. Then, anticipate how it could best be corrected. The answers to questions like these are often confusing to read because they are long and very poorly written (remember that all but one of them are wrong). Take some time with such questions.

**Directions:** Read the sentence below. Then, choose the answer that best improves the underlined portion of the sentence. Remember: The answers do not replace the whole sentence; they replace only the underlined part.

> 15. The water strider is a <u>type of insect, it walks
>     on water</u> with padlike feet that skate over
>     the water's surface tension.
>
>     **A** The water strider is a type of insect, which it is able to walk on water
>
>     **B** To walk on water, a type of insect called the water strider walks on water
>
>     **C** The water strider, a type of insect, walks on water
>
>     **D** Walking on water, the water strider, a type of insect, walks on water
>
>     **E** The water strider, which has the ability to walk on water, is a type of insect that walks on water

*Answer:* **C is the best answer.** It corrects the run-on in the original sentence by creating an appositive, *a type of insect.* Choice **A** is grammatically incorrect because the word *it* follows *which.* Choices **B** and **D** are grammatically correct, but they're unnecessarily repetitious. The introductory infinitive phrase in **B** (*To walk on water*) and the introductory participial phrase in **D** (*Walking on water*) create sentences that awkwardly repeat *walks on water* later in the sentence. **E** is grammatically correct and would be a good choice except for the repetition of *walk/walks on water.* Notice that the correct answer, **C,** wastes no words—it's streamlined, clear, and direct.

## IMPROVING-THE-PARAGRAPH QUESTIONS

present a paragraph followed by questions. You may be asked to pick a choice that combines or rewrites portions of sentences. You may be asked to decide which sentences could be added or removed from the paragraph. You may be asked which sentence could be used to strengthen the argument of the writer or to pick a thesis statement for the paragraph.

**Directions:** Read the paragraph below. Then, find the best answer to the following questions.

(1) A professional baseball pitcher's fast ball crosses the plate in about .4 seconds from the time it is thrown. (2) You could literally blink and miss it. (3) And a swing that is 7/1,000$^{th}$ of a second too early or too late will foul out. (4) The best spot on the bat to hit a ball is really small. (5) It is only about as big as a tube of lipstick. (6) If the batter doesn't hit that spot, the ball doesn't go all that far, and the vibration up the bat stings like crazy. (7) A professional baseball player swings the bat at about 70 mph with a force of about three horse-power. (8) When everything lines up just right, that swing at 70 mph meets the ball with about four tons of pressure, which flattens it for a split second to about half its diameter and then sets it flying at 110 mph over the fence.

**16.** Which of the following statements represents the best way to combine sentences 4 and 5?

**A** The best spot on the bat to hit a ball is really small, it is only about as big as a tube of lipstick.

**B** The best spot on the bat to hit a ball is really small, only about as big as a tube of lipstick.

**C** The best spot on the bat to hit a ball is really small like a tube of lipstick is really small.

**D** The best spot on the bat to hit a ball is only about as big as a tube of lipstick.

**E** The best spot on the bat to hit a ball is only a tube of lipstick.

*Answer:* You are looking for the sentence that contains all of the important information with the *least* amount of repetition. **A** is a run-on sentence, so that clearly won't work. **C** is awkwardly repetitious, and **E** is just plain silly. **B** is a good possibility, but **D** says it in fewer words. **Your best answer is D,** which cuts the repetitious *really small* since you have preserved *only about as big*.

**17.** You want to add the following sentences to the paragraph on the left. Where is the best place to put them?

So you think baseball is easy to play? Think again.

**A** Before sentence 1

**B** After sentence 8

**C** Between sentences 2 and 3

**D** Between sentences 5 and 6

**E** Between sentences 7 and 8

*Answer:* If you try out the two sentences in the places mentioned, you'll quickly discover that **C, D,** and **E** are wrong. The two sentences interrupt the thought—the logic—of the paragraph and ruin the paragraph's coherence. Both **A** (at the beginning) and **B** (at the end) seem possible, but the sentence *Think again* suggests that information will follow that will contradict your notion that baseball is easy to play. **Therefore, A is the best answer.**

# Strategies for Taking Writing Tests

 ## Writing a Response to Literature

On a test you may be asked to respond in writing to a poem. To do so effectively, you must not only understand the poem on the surface but also draw conclusions that lead you to understand the poem's deeper meaning. Follow the steps below. The sample responses provided are based on the prompt to the right.

### Prompt

In an essay, explain the meaning of the following poem by Emily Dickinson. Support your ideas with examples from the poem and from your own knowledge.

> Tell all the Truth but tell it slant—
> Success in Circuit lies
> Too bright for our infirm Delight
> The Truth's superb surprise
> As Lightning to the Children eased
> With Explanation kind
> The Truth must dazzle gradually
> Or every man be blind —

**THINKING IT THROUGH**

## Writing a Response to Literature

**STEP 1** **First, read the prompt carefully; then, read the selection.** Decide what tasks the prompt calls for, and read the selection for understanding.

This poem talks about telling the whole truth, but not telling it all right away.

**STEP 2** **Draw a conclusion about the deeper meaning of the piece.** Base your conclusion on your own knowledge and on details that seem important in the selection.

I think the poet is saying that the really important truths in life can't be understood unless you learn them indirectly or gradually. She's talking about important, life-and-death things, because Truth with a capital "T"(which appears 3 times) doesn't mean something small, like admitting you forgot your homework.

**STEP 3** **Gather support for your thesis.** Choose strong details and examples, and elaborate on those details and examples using your own knowledge and experience.

Capitalized words: Truth (3 times), Circuit, Delight, Lightning, Explanation, Children
Repetition: Truth, images of bright lights (Too bright, Lightning, dazzle)
The Truth is the bright light.

**STEP 4** **Develop a thesis statement for your essay.** Your thesis statement will sum up your main points and state your conclusion about the piece.

Dickinson's poem suggests that the only way to help someone understand an important truth in life is to reveal it gradually or indirectly.

**STEP 5** **Write your essay.** Make clear how examples you use from the text relate to your thesis. As you draft your essay, maintain a serious, objective tone. Proofread your finished draft, and correct any errors in grammar, usage, and mechanics.

## Writing a Response to Expository Text

You read **expository** text, such as instructions for a task, a chapter in a textbook, or a magazine article, to gain information. Such text is usually clearly organized to help you learn from it. When you write a response to expository text, you must demonstrate what you have learned and show that you understand how that information is organized. Use the steps below. ("The Most Remarkable Woman of This Age" begins on page 484.)

**Prompt**

The article "The Most Remarkable Woman of This Age" was first published during the Civil War. What do you think the author hoped to achieve by writing the article? In an essay, note details from the article that support the purpose you identify.

**Test Smarts**

### THINKING IT THROUGH  Writing a Response to Expository Text

**STEP 1** **First, read the prompt carefully. Then, read the text.** Decide what tasks the prompt calls for, and get an overview of the selection.

I need to read the article looking for clues about the author's purpose, keeping in mind that the article was published during the Civil War.

**STEP 2** **Decide on your general answer, and identify your main supporting points.** Skim the selection to identify the main points you will make to support your answer to the prompt.

Even though it isn't a persuasive piece, I think the author wants people to admire Harriet Tubman and support her cause. The article discusses her difficult life, her efforts toward helping people to freedom, and her personal outlook.

**STEP 3** **Develop a thesis statement for your essay.** Your thesis statement will sum up your main points and draw a conclusion about your topic.

Although it isn't stated directly, the author probably supports the abolition of slavery based on the ideas in the article and on what I know about the Civil War. My thesis will be: This article was written to win support for Harriet Tubman's efforts and for the larger cause of abolishing slavery in the United States.

**STEP 4** **Gather support for your thesis.** Choose details and examples that will provide strong support, and elaborate on those details and examples by drawing on your own knowledge and experience.

Details such as Tubman's head injury, the sedated infant, and Tubman's statement about the lengths necessary to avoid betrayal point out the evils of slavery and the difficulty involved in finding freedom. The final paragraph shows that the writer feels that God supports Harriet Tubman's cause.

**STEP 5** **Write your essay.** Begin with an attention-getter, such as a question or a surprising statement. Organize ideas clearly and logically, using transitions to show readers the links among those ideas. Then, find and correct any errors in English-language conventions in your draft.

# Writing a Biographical Narrative

An effective **biographical narrative** relates an event in someone's life so vividly that readers feel that they, too, have experienced it. It also presents a conclusion about the person involved in the event, helping readers learn something more about him or her. To write a biographical narrative in response to a test prompt, follow the steps below.

## Prompt

Heroic deeds come in many forms, from acts that make front-page news to those that affect only one person. Think of something you consider heroic that someone you know has done, and write a narrative describing the event.

## THINKING IT THROUGH
## Writing a Biographical Narrative

▶ **STEP 1  Carefully read the prompt, and choose a subject.**

I have to describe a heroic act by someone I know. I'll tell about the time when my brother saved a dog that was caught in a storm sewer during a thunderstorm.

▶ **STEP 2  Identify the parts of the event you will relate.** Jot down in sequence the smaller events that make up your chosen event.

1. We were excited, listening to the thunder and watching the radar on TV, when we heard a faint howling.
2. We went out with a flashlight and found the dog a few yards back from where the storm sewer opens to the creek behind our house.
3. My brother waded into the knee-deep water that was pouring out of the storm sewer and carried the dog out.
4. We took care of it and let it sleep in the garage, then found its owner the next day.

▶ **STEP 3  Identify important details about the people, events, and setting.** Details should be relevant and specific to bring the incident to life.

Important details include the flashes of lightning, the way the water roaring out of the storm sewer sounded and looked, the determined look on my brother's face, and the sound and appearance of the bedraggled dog.

▶ **STEP 4  Draw a conclusion based on the details.** Decide why the incident is significant; this conclusion will be the basis for your narrative's thesis.

Despite his discomfort and the possible dangers of wading into deep, fast-moving water, my brother was a hero to a helpless animal that night.

▶ **STEP 5  Write a draft of your biographical narrative.** Include an introduction to provide context for readers. Make sure you consistently relate the event from your own point of view, not from your subject's, and check that every detail you include helps support your thesis or bring the event to life. Finally, correct any errors in grammar, usage, and mechanics.

# Writing an Expository Composition

When you write an **expository composition,** you provide information to an audience of curious readers. To help readers understand your ideas, answer questions they might have about your topic and clear up any potential misunderstandings or biases about the topic. Use the steps below to write an effective expository composition for a test. The sample responses provided are based on the prompt to the right.

## Prompt

There is a wide variety of after-school activities in which you might participate. Choose two of your favorite activities, and write an essay in which you explain how they are similar and different—not only in *what* you do, but in *why* you participate and what you get out of them.

## THINKING IT THROUGH · Writing an Expository Composition

**STEP 1** **Carefully read the prompt, and choose a topic you know well.**

*I need to explain the similarities and differences between two after-school activities I participate in, including what I get out of participating. I'll compare and contrast my two favorite activities—drama club and track.*

**STEP 2** **Divide the topic into parts.** Note the main categories of information you will provide about your topic.

*Similarities: In both I challenge myself, try new things, and represent the school.*
*Differences: Track is more physical, while drama is more mental. Also, in track I usually race alone, while in drama I work as part of a cast.*

**STEP 3** **Brainstorm details about each part of the topic.** Details should answer the *5W-How?* questions *(Who? What? Where? When? Why? How?).*

*People already know the obvious details about these activities, so I'll focus on the kinds of challenges and on details about mental preparation and teamwork. For example, my comparison can note how much time I spend practicing alone for both activities. My contrast can explain the importance of other cast members' actions to my performance in drama, as well as how my track performance is independent of how my teammates do.*

**STEP 4** **Synthesize your ideas to plan a thesis.** Draft a thesis sentence explaining the point made by all of your information about your topic.

*While track and drama seem on the surface to be very different activities, they also share similarities in how they affect me personally.*

**STEP 5** **Write a draft of your expository composition.** To provide clear, useful information for readers, avoid simply stringing together obvious ideas about your topic. Instead, include striking or unusual ideas and explain them thoroughly for readers. Organize all of your ideas in an easy-to-follow way. Finally, proofread to correct any errors in grammar, usage, and mechanics.

# Writing a Persuasive Composition

Standardized writing tests often ask you to write a **persuasive composition** in which you state an opinion and provide support in response to a prompt. The prompt consists of two parts: introduction of the topic and directions for responding to the topic. Use the following steps to develop a convincing and clear response to a persuasive test prompt. The sample responses provided are based on the prompt to the right.

## Prompt

Your school is debating whether to have a closed campus (no one allowed off campus during school hours) or an open campus. Consider each option's effects on students, teachers, and the school's atmosphere, and choose the option you prefer. In an essay, support your opinion with evidence.

## THINKING IT THROUGH • Writing a Persuasive Composition

**STEP 1** **Carefully read the prompt, analyzing the situation and the task.**

I have to choose between an open campus, where students are allowed to leave for lunch, and a closed campus, where they can't. I need to consider the effects on the students, teachers, and school atmosphere, and provide evidence for my choice.

**STEP 2** **State your opinion.** Write a rough opinion statement on the topic.

I think our school should continue to have a closed campus.

**STEP 3** **Identify reasons and evidence for your opinion using the acronym _FACE_ (Fact, Anecdote, Cause/Effect, Example).**

Cause/Effect: An open campus might weaken the sense of unity students feel. Now we spend free time together in the quad or the cafeteria, but an open campus would separate us from each other at restaurants, the mall, and other areas. (Reason = atmosphere)

Anecdote: When my brother was in high school, truancy and tardiness dropped when his school switched from an open to a closed campus. (Reason = discipline)

Fact: After Wilson High changed to an open campus, the number of students involved in off-campus traffic accidents increased. (Reason = student safety)

Example: The cafeteria would lose money, like it did when we briefly allowed a fast-food vendor on campus. (Reason = financial burden on school)

**STEP 4** **Decide which of your reasons are strongest and best supported.** Choose reasons that are relevant to your opinion and to the prompt.

My first three reasons fit the prompt and have strong evidence.

**STEP 5** **Write a draft.** To maintain a convincing, knowledgeable voice, develop reasons and evidence with details you thoroughly understand. Organize your ideas in order of importance, and address the main concern a reader might have for opposing your opinion. Then, proofread your draft and correct any errors.

# Writing an Analytical Composition

Writing an **analytical composition** requires you to analyze a statement, idea, or situation and support a generalization about it with evidence. To develop an insightful response to such a test prompt, follow the steps below. The sample responses provided are based on the prompt to the right.

## Prompt

In the eighteenth century, Voltaire wrote, "I disapprove of what you say, but I will defend to the death your right to say it." Write an essay in which you explain why you feel that this quotation is or is not relevant today.

---

**THINKING IT THROUGH**

## Writing an Analytical Composition

**STEP I** **Read the prompt, and form a generalization.** Consider examples that apply to the prompt, and form a generalization based on them.

This quotation is very relevant today. It applies to the First Amendment of the Constitution and to political speech on TV and in newspapers.

**STEP 2** **Identify your strongest support.** Examples from history or literature usually provide stronger support than examples from your life.

These examples show the quotation is relevant: our First Amendment right to freedom of speech, a TV comedian and a newspaper columnist who got into trouble for saying unpopular things, and our history of welcoming people from all over the world who hold a variety of opinions.

**STEP 3** **Synthesize your ideas to plan a thesis statement.** Draft a sentence or two explaining how your examples prove your generalization.

Voltaire's quotation may be more relevant now than ever, especially in the U.S. While our nation has long welcomed people with opposing viewpoints and set forth a right to free speech in the Constitution, recent responses to unpopular statements made by members of the media emphasize the importance of defending freedom of expression.

**STEP 4** **Organize your supporting ideas.** Depending on your topic, you might organize ideas using order of importance, comparison and contrast, cause and effect, chronological order, or a combination of orders.

I'll organize my support by order of importance, first explaining our national history of welcoming all people (in chronological order starting with the Pilgrims), then discussing the First Amendment, and ending with specific, recent examples to drive the point home.

**STEP 5** **Write your analytical composition.** Begin by explaining what you think quotations or important ideas in the prompt mean, and state your thesis clearly and forcefully. Connect your supporting ideas with transitional expressions. Conclude by restating your thesis, and close with a memorable comment. Proofread your essay to correct any errors in English-language conventions.

# Handbook of Literary and Historical Terms

You will find more information about the terms in this Handbook on the pages given at the ends of the entries. To learn more about **Ambiguity,** for example, turn to pages 770, 801, and 1135 in this book.

Cross-references at the ends of some entries refer to other entries in the Handbook containing related information. For instance, at the end of **Antagonist,** you are referred to **Protagonist.**

**ABSTRACT LANGUAGE** **A term used to describe language that deals with generalities and intangible concepts.** Words such as *happiness, despair, hope, beauty,* and *evil* are examples of the abstract. Abstract language is useful in dealing with philosophical ideas.

See page 1174.
See also *Concrete Language.*

**ALLEGORY** **A story or poem in which characters, settings, and events stand for other people or events or for abstract ideas or qualities.** An allegory can be read on one level for its literal meaning and on a second level for its symbolic, or allegorical, meaning. The most famous allegory in the English language is *The Pilgrim's Progress* (1678) by the English Puritan writer John Bunyan, in which Christian, on his journey to the Celestial City, meets such personages as Mr. Worldly Wiseman, Hopeful, and Giant Despair and travels to such places as the Slough of Despond, the Valley of Humiliation, and Doubting Castle. Puritans were trained to see their own lives as allegories of biblical experiences. Nathaniel Hawthorne's and Edgar Allan Poe's fictions are often called allegorical.

See page 251.

**ALLITERATION** **The repetition of the same or similar consonant sounds in words that are close together.** Alliteration is used to create musical effects and to establish mood. In the following line from "The Tide Rises, the Tide Falls" (Collection 2) by Henry Wadsworth Longfellow, the repetition of the *s* sound is an example of alliteration:

> But the sea, the sea in darkness calls

See pages 195, 303, 367, 1178.
See also *Assonance, Onomatopoeia, Rhyme.*

**ALLUSION** **A reference to someone or something that is known from history, literature, religion, politics, sports, science, or some other branch of culture.** T. S. Eliot drew on his knowledge of the Bible when he alluded to the raising of Lazarus from the dead in "The Love Song of J. Alfred Prufrock" (Collection 5). The title of Sandra Cisneros's essay "Straw into Gold" (Collection 6) is an allusion to the folk tale about Rumpelstiltskin.

You won't understand the cartoon below unless you recognize the fairy tale it alludes to.

See pages 36, 657, 795, 1120, 1171.

*"They're offering a deal—you can pay court costs and damages, they drop charges of breaking and entering."*

**AMBIGUITY** **A technique by which a writer deliberately suggests two or more different, and sometimes conflicting, meanings in a work.**

Langston Hughes's poem "Harlem" (Collection 5) has an ambiguous ending. The title of Richard Wilbur's poem "The Beautiful Changes" (Collection 6) is also deliberately ambiguous.

See pages 770, 801, 1135.

**AMERICAN DREAM A uniquely American vision of the country consisting of three central ideas.** The American dream consists of a belief in America as a new Eden—a land of beauty, bounty, and unlimited promise; a feeling of optimism, created by ever expanding opportunity; and a confidence in triumph of the individual. Aspects of the American dream are reflected in the literature of all periods in American history.

See page 636.

**ANALOGY A comparison made between two things to show how they are alike.** In "The Crisis, No. I" (Collection I), Thomas Paine draws an analogy between a thief breaking into a house and the king of England interfering in the affairs of the American Colonies.

See pages 88, 94.

**ANAPEST A metrical foot that has two unstressed syllables followed by one stressed syllable.** The word *coexist* (˘ ˘ ʹ) is an example of an anapest.

See also *Dactyl, Foot, Iamb, Iambic Pentameter, Meter, Spondee, Trochee.*

**ANECDOTE A very brief story, told to illustrate a point or serve as an example of something.** In Thomas Paine's "The Crisis, No. I" (Collection I), the tale of the Tory tavern keeper and his child is an anecdote.

See page 88.

**ANTAGONIST The opponent who struggles against or blocks the hero, or protagonist, in a story.** In *The Narrative of the Life of Frederick Douglass* (Collection 4), Mr. Covey is Douglass's antagonist. Mrs. Mitty is Mr. Mitty's antagonist in Thurber's story "The Secret Life of Walter Mitty" (Collection 5).

See also *Protagonist.*

**ANTHROPOMORPHISM Attributing human characteristics to an animal or inanimate object.** Writers often anthropomorphize animals

or objects in order to achieve humorous or satirical effects.

See also *Personification.*

**APHORISM** (afʹə·rizʹəm) **A brief, cleverly worded statement that makes a wise observation about life.** Benjamin Franklin's *Poor Richard's Almanack* (Collection I) is a book of aphorisms. Ralph Waldo Emerson's style is **aphoristic**—he incorporates many pithy sayings into his essays (which is why he is so quotable).

See pages 75, 212, 1005.
See also *Proverb.*

**ARCHETYPE** (ärʹkə·tīpʹ) **A very old imaginative pattern that appears in literature across cultures and is repeated through the ages. An archetype can be a character, a plot, an image, a theme, or a setting.** The plot in which a man sells his soul to the devil, as in "The Devil and Tom Walker" (Collection 2), is a recurring pattern in folk tales and other literature from around the world. The tragic hero is an example of an archetypal character that appears again and again in literature. The pattern of the journey, or quest, is a plot that recurs repeatedly in American literature.

See pages 21, 261, 304, 753, 756, 1008, 1191.

**ARGUMENT A form of persuasion that appeals to reason, rather than emotion, to convince an audience to think or act in a certain way.** The Declaration of Independence (Collection I) is a famous example of a closely reasoned argument.

See pages 98, 941.
See also *Persuasion.*

**ASSONANCE The repetition of similar vowel sounds followed by different consonant sounds, especially in words close together.** Notice the repeated sounds of *i* in these lines from "The Tide Rises, the Tide Falls" (Collection 2) by Henry Wadsworth Longfellow. Read the lines aloud to hear the verbal music created by assonance.

> The tide rises, the tide falls,
> The twilight darkens, the curlew calls

See pages 367, 1178.
See also *Alliteration, Onomatopoeia, Rhyme.*

**ATMOSPHERE** **The mood or feeling created in a piece of writing.** A story's atmosphere might be peaceful, festive, menacing, melancholy, and so on. Elie Wiesel's *Night* (Collection 6), for example, creates an atmosphere of terror and sadness.

> See also *Mood, Setting.*

**AUTOBIOGRAPHY** **An account of the writer's own life.** Benjamin Franklin's *Autobiography* (Collection 1) is one of the most famous autobiographies in American literature. An excerpt from Richard Wright's autobiography, *Black Boy,* is on page 1065.

> See pages 53, 472, 837.

**BALLAD** **A song or poem that tells a story.** The typical ballad tells a tragic story in the form of a monologue or dialogue. Ballads usually have a simple, steady rhythm, a simple rhyme pattern, and a refrain, all of which make them easy to memorize. Ballads composed by unknown singers and passed on orally from one generation to the next are called **folk ballads. Literary ballads** are written to imitate the sounds and subjects of folk ballads. A strong tradition of folk ballads and literary ballads exists in the United States. Country-and-western music, for example, frequently features songs written to imitate the older ballads. Here is the start of a favorite ballad, telling the story of Betsy and Ike:

> Oh don't you remember sweet Betsy from Pike,
> Who crossed the big mountains with her lover Ike,
> With two yoke of oxen, a big yellow dog,
> A tall Shanghai rooster, and one spotted hog?
> *Chorus*
> Singing dang fol dee dido,
> Singing dang fol dee day.

**BIOGRAPHY** **An account of someone's life written by another person.** One of the most famous biographies in American literature is Carl Sandburg's multivolume life of Abraham Lincoln. A more recent, bestselling biography is David McCullough's *John Adams,* about one of our nation's founders and presidents.

**BLANK VERSE** **Poetry written in unrhymed iambic pentameter.** Blank verse has a long history in English literature. It was used notably by such poets as Shakespeare and Milton in the sixteenth and seventeenth centuries and by Robert Frost in the twentieth.

> See pages 800, 805, 812.
> See also *Iambic Pentameter.*

**CADENCE** **The natural, rhythmic rise and fall of a language as it is normally spoken.** Cadence is different from **meter,** in which stressed and unstressed syllables of a poetic line are carefully counted to conform to a regular pattern. Walt Whitman was a master of imitating the cadence of spoken American English in his free verse.

> See pages 98, 358, 367, 372.
> See also *Free Verse, Meter, Rhythm.*

**CAESURA** (si·zyoor'ə) **A pause or break within a line of poetry.** Some pauses are indicated by punctuation; others are suggested by phrasing or meaning. In the lines below, the caesuras are marked by double vertical lines. These pauses are indicated by punctuation.

> Announced by all the trumpets of the sky,
> Arrives the snow, || and, || driving o'er the fields,
> Seems nowhere to alight: || the whited air
> Hides hills and woods . . .
>
> —Ralph Waldo Emerson, from "The Snow-Storm"

**CATALOG** **A list of things, people, or events.** Cataloging was a favorite device of Walt Whitman, who included long, descriptive lists throughout *Leaves of Grass.*

> See page 364.

**CHARACTER** **An individual in a story or play.** A character always has human traits, even if the character is an animal, as in Aesop's fables, or a god, as in the Greek and Roman myths. The process by which the writer reveals the personality of a character is called **characterization.** A writer can reveal a character in the following ways:
- by telling us directly what the character is like: sneaky, generous, mean to pets, and so on
- by describing how the character looks and dresses
- by letting us hear the character speak
- by revealing the character's private thoughts and feelings

- by revealing the character's effect on other people—showing how other characters feel or behave toward the character
- by showing the character in action

The first method of revealing a character is called **direct characterization.** When a writer uses this method, we do not have to figure out what a character's personality is like—the writer tells us directly. The other five methods of revealing a character are known as **indirect characterization.** When a writer uses these methods, we have to exercise our own judgment, putting clues together to infer what a character is like—just as we do in real life when we are getting to know someone.

Characters are often classified as static or dynamic. A **static character** is one who does not change much in the course of a story. A **dynamic character,** on the other hand, changes in some important way as a result of the story's action. Characters can also be classified as flat or round. **Flat characters** have few personality traits. They can be summed up by a single phrase: the loyal sidekick, the buffoon, the nosy neighbor. In contrast, **round characters** have more dimension to their personalities—they are complex, just as real people are.

See pages 787, 1081.
See also *Motivation, Stereotype.*

**CLICHÉ A word or phrase, often a figure of speech, that has become lifeless because of overuse.** Some examples of clichés are "green with envy," "quiet as a mouse," and "pretty as a picture."

**CLIMAX That point in a plot that creates the greatest intensity, suspense, or interest.** The climax is usually the point at which the conflict in the story is resolved.

See page 736.

**COMEDY In general, a story that ends with a happy resolution of the conflicts faced by the main character or characters.** In many comedies the conflict is provided when a young couple who wish to marry are blocked by adults. In many comedies the main character at the end has moved into a world of greater freedom. In literature the word *comedy* is not synonymous with *humor.* Some comedies are humorous; some are not.

See also *Tragedy.*

**CONCEIT An elaborate metaphor or other figure of speech that compares two things that are startlingly different.** Often a conceit is also a very lengthy comparison. The conceit was a popular figure of speech in seventeenth-century English metaphysical poetry. In American literature the poems of Emily Dickinson (Collection 3) are known for their conceits. In more recent literary history, T. S. Eliot (Collection 5) also used conceits.

See also *Figure of Speech, Metaphor.*

**CONCRETE LANGUAGE A term for language that uses specific words and details to describe a particular subject.** Concrete language deals with the specifics of a subject. Words that engage the senses of hearing, touch, sight, smell, and taste are important examples of concrete language. *A fuzzy puppy with a round belly* is an example of concrete language.

See page 1174.
See also *Abstract Language.*

**CONFESSIONAL SCHOOL A group of poets who wrote in the 1950s.** Confessional poets include Robert Lowell, Sylvia Plath, Anne Sexton, and John Berryman. The confessional poets wrote frank and sometimes brutal poems about their personal lives.

See page 903.

**CONFLICT The struggle between opposing forces or characters in a story.** A conflict can be **internal,** involving opposing forces within a person's mind. In James Thurber's "The Secret Life of Walter Mitty" (Collection 5), for example, the title character has a comical internal conflict between his desire for heroism and his cowardice in the face of a formidable spouse. **External** conflicts can exist between two people, between a person and a force of nature or a machine, or between a person and a whole society. In one segment of Julia Alvarez's "Daughter of Invention" (Collection 6), the narrator is in conflict with both her father and mother. Many stories have both internal and external conflicts.

See pages 472, 743, 962, 994.
See also *Setting.*

**CONNOTATION The associations and emotional overtones that have become attached to a word or phrase, in addition to its strict**

**dictionary definition.** The words *determined, firm, rigid, stubborn,* and *pigheaded* have similar dictionary definitions, or **denotations,** but widely varying connotations, or overtones of meaning. *Determined* and *firm* both suggest an admirable kind of resoluteness; *rigid* suggests an inability to bend and a kind of mindless refusal to change. *Stubborn* and *pigheaded,* on the other hand, have even more negative connotations. *Stubborn* has associations with a mule, and *pigheaded* with the pig, which, wrongly or not, is an animal often associated with mindless willfulness. Here are some other words that are more or less synonymous but which have vastly different connotations: *fastidious* and *fussy; daydreamer* and *escapist; scent, odor, smell,* and *stink.* Words with strong connotations are often called **loaded** words or **suggestive** words.

See page 589.

**CONSONANCE The repetition of the same or similar final consonant sounds on accented syllables or in important words.** The words *ticktock* and *singsong* contain examples of consonance. Some modern poets use consonance in place of rhyme.

**COUPLET Two consecutive rhyming lines of poetry.** If the two rhyming lines express a complete thought, they are called a **closed couplet.** The following lines are from a poem built on a series of closed couplets:

> If ever wife was happy in a man,
> Compare with me, ye women, if you can.
>
> —Anne Bradstreet, from
> "To My Dear and Loving Husband"

**DACTYL A metrical foot of three syllables in which the first syllable is stressed and the next two are unstressed.** The word *tendency* ($'\breve{}\,\breve{}$) is a dactyl.

See also *Anapest, Foot, Iamb, Iambic Pentameter, Meter, Spondee, Trochee.*

**DARK ROMANTICS A group of nineteenth-century writers who explored the dark side of human nature.** The Dark Romantics include Nathaniel Hawthorne, Herman Melville, and Edgar Allan Poe. In contrast to the optimistic nature of the Transcendentalist writers, the Dark Romantics explored the potentially evil side of humanity. Often their writings explored the psychological effects of guilt, sin, and madness.

See page 172.

**DEISM An eighteenth-century philosophy based on rationalism.** Deists believed that God created the world and its natural laws, but takes no other part in it. In contrast to the Puritans, deists believed in humanity's innate goodness and perfectibility. Many of the founders of the United States were deists.

See page 18.

**DENOUEMENT** (dā'nōō·män') **The conclusion (or resolution) of a story.** In French the word means "unraveling." At this point in a story, all the mysteries are unraveled, the conflicts are resolved, and all the questions raised by the plot are answered. Much modern fiction ends without a denouement, leaving the reader with a sense of incompleteness—just as life itself often offers only incomplete or ambiguous resolutions to problems.

See also *Plot, Resolution.*

**DESCRIPTION One of the four major forms of discourse, in which language is used to create a mood or emotion.** Description does this by using words that appeal to our senses: sight, hearing, touch, smell, and taste. Walt Whitman gives a vivid description of a Civil War battlefield in *Specimen Days* (Collection 3). N. Scott Momaday gives a wonderful description of a unique landmark in the opening paragraph of the selection from *The Way to Rainy Mountain* (Collection 6). The other three major forms of discourse are **exposition, narration,** and **persuasion.**

**DIALECT A way of speaking that is characteristic of a certain social group or of the inhabitants of a certain geographical area.** Dialects may differ from one another in vocabulary, pronunciation, and grammar. The dialect that has become dominant in America is known as Standard English. This is the dialect used most often on national radio news and television news broadcasts. Many writers try to capture dialects to give their stories local color, humor, or an air of authenticity. Some writers who are known for their skilled use of dialect are Mark Twain, Eudora Welty, William Faulkner, and Langston Hughes.

See page 525.
See also *Vernacular*.

**DIALOGUE** **The directly quoted words of people speaking to one another.** Writers use dialogue to advance the plot and develop characters.

See pages 805, 1064.
See also *Dialect, Diction, Tone*.

**DICTION** **A speaker's or writer's choice of words.** Diction can be formal, informal, colloquial, full of slang, poetic, ornate, plain, abstract, concrete, and so on. Diction depends on the writer's subject, purpose, and audience. Some words, for example, are suited to informal conversations but are inappropriate in a formal speech. Diction has a powerful effect on the **tone** of a piece of writing.

See also *Tone*.

**DRAMATIC MONOLOGUE** **A poem in which a character speaks to one or more listeners whose responses are not known.** The reactions of the listener must be inferred by the reader. From the speaker's words the reader learns about the setting, the situation, the identity of the other characters, and the personality of the speaker. The outstanding dramatic monologue in American literature is T. S. Eliot's "The Love Song of J. Alfred Prufrock" (Collection 5).

See page 657.

**ELEGY** **A poem of mourning, usually about someone who has died.** Most elegies are written to mark a particular person's death, but some extend their subject to reflect on life, death, and the fleeting nature of beauty. William Cullen Bryant's poem "Thanatopsis" (Collection 2) is an elegy. The excerpt from N. Scott Momaday's *The Way to Rainy Mountain* (Collection 6) is partly elegiac in that it mourns the death of a particular person and, by extension, the passing of an entire way of life.

See page 1100.

**ENJAMBMENT** **The running on of sense from the end of one line of verse into the next, without a punctuated pause.** Poets often use enjambment to add rhythmic diversity. Enjambment is contrasted

with an end-stopped line (a line that is a grammatical unit and ends with punctuation). Enjambed lines allow the poet to create a pause in the middle of a sentence. This mental and physical "breath" creates an unexpected moment for the reader.

**EPIC** **A long narrative poem, written in heightened language, which recounts the deeds of a heroic character who embodies the values of a particular society.** Epics in English include *Beowulf* (c. 700) and John Milton's *Paradise Lost* (1667). Some critics of Walt Whitman's *Leaves of Grass* see his collection as an American epic in which the hero is the questing poet.

**EPITHET** **A descriptive word or phrase that is frequently used to characterize a person or a thing.** The epithet "the father of our country" is often used to characterize George Washington. New York City's popular epithet, "the Big Apple," is frequently used by advertisers. Epics such as Homer's *Odyssey* and *Illiad* frequently use **stock epithets** over and over again to describe certain characters or places: "patient Penelope," "wily Odysseus," and "earthshaker" for Poseidon.

**ESSAY** **A short piece of nonfiction prose in which the writer discusses some aspect of a subject.** The word *essay* come from French *essai*, meaning "to try," a derivation that suggests that the essay form is not an exhaustive treatment of a subject. Essays are sometimes classified as **formal** or **informal** (or personal). The essay form was especially popular in the twentieth century, particularly among American writers. Some famous American essayists of the past include Thomas Paine (Collection 1), Ralph Waldo Emerson (Collection 2), and Henry David Thoreau (Collection 2). More recent essayists include E. B. White, Alice Walker (Collection 6), James Baldwin (Collection 6), Annie Dillard, and Joan Didion.

See page 1103.

**EXPOSITION** **One of the four major forms of discourse, in which something is explained or set forth.** Exposition is most commonly used in nonfiction. The word *exposition* also refers to that part of a plot in which the reader is given important background information on the characters, their setting, and their problems. Such exposition is usually provided at the opening of a story or play. See the opening paragraph of Nathaniel Hawthorne's "The Minister's Black Veil" (Collection 2) for an example. The other three major forms of discourse are **description, narration,** and **persuasion.**

See also *Plot.*

**FABLE A very short story told in prose or poetry that teaches a practical lesson about how to succeed in life.** In many fables the characters are animals that behave like people. The most ancient fabulist is the Greek Aesop; the most famous American fabulist is James Thurber (Collection 5), who wrote *Fables for Our Time* and *Further Fables for Our Time.*

**FARCE A type of comedy in which ridiculous and often stereotyped characters are involved in silly far-fetched situations.** The humor in a farce is often physical and slapstick, with characters being hit in the face with pies or running into closed doors. American cinema has produced many farces, including those starring Laurel and Hardy, Abbott and Costello, and the Marx Brothers.

**FIGURE OF SPEECH A word or phrase that describes one thing in terms of something else and that is not meant to be taken literally.** Figures of speech almost always involve a comparison of two things that are basically very dissimilar. Hundreds of figures of speech have been identified by scholars; the most common ones are **simile, metaphor, personification,** and **symbol.** Figures of speech, also called, more generally, **figurative language,** are basic to everyday speech. Statements like "She is a tower of strength" and "He is a pain in the neck" are figures of speech.

See pages 45, 208, 215.
See also *Conceit, Metaphor, Personification, Simile, Symbol.*

**FIRESIDE POETS A group of nineteenth-century poets from Boston including Henry Wadsworth Longfellow, John Greenleaf Whittier, Oliver Wendell Holmes, and James Russell Lowell.** Their poems were often read by the fireside as family entertainment and memorized and recited by students in classrooms. They were also known as the Schoolroom Poets.

See page 170.

**FLASHBACK A scene that interrupts the normal chronological sequence of events in a story to depict something that happened at an earlier time.** Although the word was coined to describe a technique used by moviemakers, the technique itself is at least as old as ancient Greek literature. Much of Homer's epic poem the *Odyssey* is a flashback. Willa Cather uses frequent flashbacks to reveal the past of Georgiana in "A Wagner Matinée" (Collection 4).

See page 1093.

**FOIL A character who acts as a contrast to another character.** In Maxine Hong Kingston's "The Girl Who Wouldn't Talk" (Collection 6), the quiet girl who takes refuge in her Chinese family is a foil for the narrator who is aggressively trying to fit into American society.

**FOOT A metrical unit of poetry.** A foot always contains at least one stressed syllable and, usually, one or more unstressed syllables. An **iamb** is a common foot in English poetry: It consists of an unstressed syllable followed by a stressed syllable ($\smallsmile$ $\prime$).

See also *Anapest, Blank Verse, Dactyl, Iamb, Iambic Pentameter, Meter, Spondee, Trochee.*

**FORESHADOWING The use of hints and clues to suggest what will happen later in a plot.** A writer might use foreshadowing to create suspense or to prefigure later events. In "To Build a Fire" (Collection 4), for example, Jack London places hints throughout the text that foreshadow the story's conclusion.

**FRAME STORY A literary device in which a story is enclosed in another story, a tale within a tale.** The best-known example of a frame story is the Persian collection *The Thousand and One Nights* (also known as *Arabian Nights*). Raymond Carver uses the frame device in "Everything Stuck to Him" (Collection 6). His story begins and ends with a frame in which an unnamed man tells a woman a story. The story that the man tells is the main body of Carver's tale.

**FREE ENTERPRISE The practice of allowing private businesses to operate competitively for profit with little government regulation.** Free enterprise was threatened by Marxist beliefs. Several novelists of the 1920s and 1930s satirized the free-enterprise system and the gross materialism of American business of the time. Sinclair Lewis's *Babbitt* (1922) is a major example.

See page 639.

**FREE VERSE** **Poetry that does not conform to regular meter or rhyme scheme.** Poets who write in free verse try to reproduce the natural rhythms of spoken language. Free verse uses the traditional poetic elements of **imagery, figures of speech, repetition, internal rhyme, alliteration, assonance,** and **onomatopoeia.** The first American practitioner of free verse was Walt Whitman (Collection 3). Some of Whitman's heirs are William Carlos Williams (Collection 5), Carl Sandburg (Collection 5), and Allen Ginsberg (Collection 5).

See pages 367, 647.
See also *Cadence, Meter, Rhythm.*

**HAIKU** **A short, unrhymed poem developed in Japan in the fifteenth century.** A haiku consists of three unrhymed lines and a total of seventeen syllables. The first and third lines of a traditional haiku have five syllables each, and the middle line has seven syllables. Haiku often convey feelings through a descriptive snapshot of a natural object or scene. Imagists like Ezra Pound were influenced by the haiku form.

**HARLEM RENAISSANCE** **A cultural movement of the early 1920s led by African American artists, writers, musicians, and performers, located in Harlem.** After World War I, vast numbers of African Americans migrated north and settled in the New York City neighborhood called Harlem. Important contributors to the Harlem Renaissance were the writers Langston Hughes and Countee Cullen, the artists Jacob Lawrence and Aaron Douglas, and the performers Paul Robeson and Josephine Baker.

See pages 642, 815.

**HYPERBOLE** (hī·pʉr′bə·lē) **A figure of speech that uses an incredible exaggeration, or overstatement, for effect.** In "The Celebrated Jumping Frog of Calaveras County" (Collection 4), Mark Twain uses hyperbole for comic effect. In his poetry, Walt Whitman often uses overstatement to create a larger-than-life persona, or speaker, as in the line below.

> I sound my barbaric yawp over the roofs of the world.
>
> —Walt Whitman,
> from *Song of Myself*, 54

See page 525.
See also *Understatement.*

**IAMB** **A metrical foot in poetry that has an unstressed syllable followed by a stressed syllable, as in the word** *protect.* The iamb (˘ ′) is a common foot in poetry written in English.

See pages 195, 197.
See also *Anapest, Blank Verse, Dactyl, Foot, Iambic Pentameter, Meter, Spondee, Trochee.*

**IAMBIC PENTAMETER** **A line of poetry that contains five iambic feet.** The iambic pentameter line is most common in English and American poetry. Shakespeare and John Milton, among others, used iambic pentameter in their major works. So did such American poets as William Cullen Bryant, Ralph Waldo Emerson, Robert Frost, and Wallace Stevens. Here, for example is the opening line of a poem by Emerson:

> ˘ ′ ˘ ′ ˘ ′ ˘ ′ ˘ ′˘ ′
> In May, when sea-winds pierced our solitudes
>
> —Ralph Waldo Emerson, from "The Rhodora"

See page 197.
See also *Blank Verse, Foot, Iamb, Meter, Scanning.*

**IDIOM** **An expression particular to a certain language that means something different from the literal definitions of its parts.** "Falling in love" is an American idiom, as is "I lost my head."

See also *Figure of Speech.*

**IMAGERY** **The use of language to evoke a picture or a concrete sensation of a person, a thing, a place, or an experience.** Although most images appeal to the sense of sight, they may appeal to the sense of taste, smell, hearing, and touch as well.

See pages 205, 565, 649, 666, 672, 1152, 1166.

**IMAGISM** **A twentieth-century movement in European and American poetry that advocated the creation of hard, clear images, concisely expressed in everyday speech.** The leading Imagist poets in America were Ezra Pound, Amy Lowell, H. D. [Hilda Doolittle], and William Carlos Williams.

See pages 642, 646.

**IMPRESSIONISM** **A nineteenth-century movement in literature and art that advocated recording one's personal impressions of the world, rather than attempting a strict representa-**

**tion of reality.** Some famous American impressionists in art are Mary Cassatt, Maurice Prendergast, and William Merritt Chase. In fiction, Stephen Crane pioneered a kind of literary impressionism in which he portrayed not objective reality but one character's impressions of reality. Crane's impressionistic technique is best seen in his novel *The Red Badge of Courage.*

**INCONGRUITY** (in´kän·groo´i·tē) **The deliberate joining of opposites or of elements that are not appropriate to each other.** T. S. Eliot's famous opening simile in "The Love Song of J. Alfred Prufrock" (Collection 5) joins two incongruous elements: a sunset and a patient knocked out by ether on an operating table. Incongruity can also be used for humor: We laugh at the sight of an elephant dressed in a pink tutu because the two elements are incongruous. Writers also use incongruity for dramatic effect. In Donald Barthelme's "Game" (Collection 6), the childish actions of the characters are in sharp contrast with the devastation they can cause by turning a key.

**INTERIOR MONOLOGUE** **A narrative technique that records a character's internal flow of thoughts, memories, and associations.** Parts of James Joyce's *Ulysses* and William Faulkner's *The Sound and the Fury* are written as interior monologues.

See also *Stream of Consciousness.*

**INTERNAL RHYME** **Rhyme that occurs within a line of poetry or within consecutive lines.** The first line of the following couplet includes an internal rhyme.

> And so, all the night-**tide,** I lie down by the **side**
> Of my darling—my darling—my life and my
>   bride. . . .
>
>   —Edgar Allan Poe, from "Annabel Lee"

See also *Rhyme.*

**INVERSION** **The reversal of the normal word order in a sentence or phrase.** An English sentence is normally built on subject-verb-complement, in that order. An inverted sentence reverses one or more of those elements. In poetry written many years ago, writers often inverted word order as a matter of course, in order to have words conform to the meter, or to create rhymes. The poetry of Anne Bradstreet

contains many inversions, as in the first line of the poem on the burning of her house:

> In silent night when rest I took

In prose, inversion is often used for emphasis, as when Patrick Henry, in his fiery speech to the Virginia Convention (Collection 1), thundered "Suffer not yourselves to be betrayed with a kiss" (instead of "Do not suffer [allow] yourselves," and so on).

See pages 28, 190.

**IRONY** **In general, a discrepancy between appearances and reality.** There are three main types of irony:

1. **Verbal irony** occurs when someone says one thing but really means something else. The first line of Stephen Crane's poem "War Is Kind" is an example of verbal irony: "Do not weep, maiden, for war is kind." The speaker really believes that war is *not* kind and warrants weeping.

2. **Situational irony** takes place when there is a discrepancy between what is expected to happen, or what would be appropriate to happen, and what really does happen. A famous use of situational irony is in Stephen Crane's "A Mystery of Heroism" (Collection 4), in which a soldier risks his life to get water that is then spilled.

3. **Dramatic irony** is so called because it is often used on stage. In this kind of irony a character in the play or story thinks one thing is true, but the audience or reader knows better. In Edwin Arlington Robinson's "Miniver Cheevy" (Collection 4), Miniver thinks he is too refined for his time, but to the reader he seems foolish and somewhat pathetic.

See pages 401, 500, 508, 1048.

**LYRIC POEM** **A poem that does not tell a story but expresses the personal feelings or thoughts of a speaker.** The many lyric poems in this textbook include "Thanatopsis" by William Cullen Bryant (Collection 2) and the optimistic "what of a much of a which of a wind" by E. E. Cummings (Collection 5).

**MAGIC REALISM** **A genre developed in Latin America that juxtaposes the everyday with the marvelous or magical.** Myths, folk tales, religious beliefs, and tall tales are the raw material for many magic realist writers. Gabriel García Márquez's work, particularly his novel *One Hundred Years of Solitude* (1967), established him as a master of the genre. Other prominent Latin American magic realists include Jorge Luis Borges, Julio Cortázar, and Isabel Allende. Among American writers, Donald Barthelme (Collection 6) and Thomas Pynchon have been influenced by magic realism.

See page 1008.

**MARXISM  The political and economic philosophy developed by Karl Marx and his followers in the mid-nineteenth century.** In contrast to capitalists, Marxists believe greater economic unity can be reached by a classless society.

See page 639.

**MEMOIR  A type of autobiography that often focuses on a specific time period or historical event.** Elie Wiesel's *Night* (Collection 6) is a memoir about the author's harrowing experience in a concentration camp.

See page 913.
See also *Autobiography.*

**METAPHOR  A figure of speech that makes a comparison between two unlike things without the use of such specific words of comparison as *like, as, than, or resembles.* There are several kinds of metaphor:**

1. A **directly stated metaphor** states the comparison explicitly: "Fame is a bee" (Emily Dickinson).
2. An **implied metaphor** does not state explicitly the two terms of the comparison: "I like to see it lap the Miles" (Emily Dickinson) contains an implied metaphor in which the verb *lap* implies a comparison between "it," which is a train, and some animal that "laps" up water.
3. An **extended metaphor** is a metaphor that is extended or developed over a number of lines or with several examples. Dickinson's poem beginning "Fame is a bee" is an extended metaphor: the comparison of fame to a bee is extended for four lines:

> Fame is a bee.
> It has a song—
> It has a sting—
> Ah, too, it has a wing.

4. A **dead metaphor** is a metaphor that has been used so often that the comparison is no longer vivid: "The head of the house," "the seat of government," and a "knotty problem" are all dead metaphors.
5. A **mixed metaphor** is a metaphor that fails to make a logical comparison because its mixed terms are visually or imaginatively incompatible. If you say, "The president is a lame duck who is running out of gas," you've lost control of your metaphor and have produced a statement that is ridiculous (ducks do not run out of gas).

See pages 215, 464, 819, 910.
See also *Conceit, Figure of Speech, Simile.*

**METER  A pattern of stressed and unstressed syllables in poetry.** The meter of a poem is commonly indicated by using the symbol (ˊ) for stressed syllables and the symbol (˘) for unstressed syllables. This is called **scanning** the poem.

Meter is described as **iambic, trochaic, dactylic, or anapestic.** These scanned lines from "Richard Cory" (Collection 4) are iambic: They are built on iambs— unstressed syllables followed by stressed syllables.

> ˘ ˊ ˘ ˊ ˘ ˊ ˘ ˊ ˘ ˊ
> And he was always quietly arrayed
> ˘ ˊ ˘ ˊ ˘ ˊ ˘ ˊ ˘ ˊ
> And he was always human when he talked

See page 195.
See also *Anapest, Cadence, Dactyl, Foot, Free Verse, Iamb, Iambic Pentameter, Rhythm, Scanning, Spondee, Trochee.*

**METONYMY** (mə·tän′ə·mē) **A figure of speech in which a person, place, or thing is referred to by something closely associated with it.** Referring to a king or queen as "the crown" is an example of metonymy, as is calling a car "wheels."

See also *Synecdoche.*

**MODERNISM  A term for the bold new experimental styles and forms that swept the arts during the first third of the twentieth century.** Modernism called for changes in subject matter, in fictional styles, in poetic forms, and in attitudes. T. S. Eliot and Ezra Pound are associated with the modernist movement in poetry. Their aim was to rid poetry of its nineteenth-century prettiness and sentimentality.

See page 636.
See also *Imagism, Symbolism.*

**MOOD** **The overall emotion created by a work of literature.** Mood can usually be described with one or two adjectives such as *bittersweet, playful,* or *scary.* All the elements of literature, including sound effects, rhythm, and word choice, contribute to a work's mood. The mood of Horacio Quiroga's "The Feathered Pillow" (Collection 5) is cold and menacing.

See pages 175, 828.
See also *Atmosphere, Setting.*

**MOTIVATION** **The reasons for a character's behavior.** In order for us to understand why characters act the way they do, their motivation has to be believable, at least in terms of the story. At times a writer directly reveals motivation; in subtler fiction we must use details from the story to infer motivation.

See pages 569, 697, 1016, 1090, 1214.
See also *Character.*

**MYTH** **An anonymous traditional story that is basically religious in nature and that usually serves to explain a belief, ritual, or mysterious natural phenomenon.** Most myths have grown out of religious rituals, and almost all of them involve the exploits of gods and humans. Works of magic realism often draw on myths or mythlike tales.

See pages 24, 25.

**NARRATIVE** **The form of discourse that tells about a series of events.** Narration is used in all kinds of literature: fiction, nonfiction, and poetry. Usually a narrative is told in **chronological order**—in the order in which events occurred. The other three major forms of discourse are **description, exposition,** and **persuasion.**

**NARRATIVE POEM** **A poem that tells a story—a series of related events with a beginning, a middle, and an end.** A narrative poem also features characters and, frequently, dialogue. Henry Wadsworth Longfellow is famous for his long narrative poems based on figures from myth and from European and American history. *The Song of Hiawatha* and *Evangeline* are major examples of his narrative poems.

See page 805.

**NARRATOR** **In fiction the one who tells the story.** Narrators differ in their degree of participation in the story: (1) **Omniscient narrators** are all-knowing and outside the action; they can take us into minds and hearts of all the characters and behind all the events unfolding in the story; (2) **first-person narrators** are either witnesses to or participants in the story; (3) **third-person-limited narrators** are omniscient narrators too, but they zoom in on one character and allow us to experience the story through this one character's perceptions.

See also *Point of View.*

**NATURALISM** **A nineteenth-century literary movement that was an extension of realism and that claimed to portray life exactly as if it were being examined through a scientist's microscope.** The naturalists relied heavily on the new fields of psychology and sociology. They tended to dissect human behavior with complete objectivity, the way a scientist would dissect a specimen in the laboratory. The naturalists were also influenced by Darwinian theories of the survival of the fittest. Naturalists believed that human behavior is determined by heredity and environment; they felt that people have no recourse to supernatural forces and that human beings, like animals, are subject to laws of nature beyond their control. The outstanding naturalists among American writers are Theodore Dreiser, Jack London, and Frank Norris. Some people consider John Steinbeck's *The Grapes of Wrath* a naturalistic novel, in which characters are the pawns of economic conditions.

See pages 460, 546.
See also *Realism.*

**OCTAVE** **An eight-line poem, or the first eight lines of a Petrarchan, or Italian, sonnet.** In a Petrarchan sonnet the octave states the subject of the sonnet or poses a problem or question.

See also *Sestet, Sonnet.*

**ODE** **A lyric poem, usually long, on a serious subject and written in dignified language.** In ancient Greece and Rome, odes were written to be read in public at ceremonial occasions. In modern literature, odes tend to be more private, informal, and reflective.

**ONOMATOPOEIA** (än′ō·mat′ō·pē′ə) **The use of a word whose sound imitates or suggests its meaning.** The word *buzz* is onomatopoeic; it imitates the sound it names.

**OXYMORON** (äk′si·môr′än′) **A figure of speech that combines opposite or contradictory terms in a brief phrase.** *Sweet sorrow, deafening silence,* and *living death* are common oxymorons. (Some jokesters claim that phrases such as *jumbo shrimp, congressional leadership,* and *limited nuclear war* are also oxymorons.)

**PARABLE A relatively short story that teaches a moral, or lesson, about how to lead a good life.** The most famous parables are those told by Jesus in the Bible.

See pages 230, 273.

**PARADOX A statement that appears self-contradictory but reveals a kind of truth.** Many writers like to use paradox because it allows them to express the complexity of life by showing how opposing ideas can be both contradictory and true. Emily Dickinson often used paradoxes, as in "I taste a liquor never brewed" and "Much Madness is divinest Sense" (Collection 3).

See pages 234, 404.

**PARALLEL STRUCTURE The repetition of words or phrases that have similar grammatical structures (also called** *parallelism*). Lincoln, in his Gettysburg Address (Collection 4), uses several memorable parallel structures, as when he refers to "government of the people, by the people, for the people."

See pages 98, 367.

**PARODY A work that makes fun of another work by imitating some aspect of the writer's style.** Parodies often achieve their effects by humorously exaggerating certain features in the original work.

See page 781.

**PASTORAL A type of poem that depicts country life in idyllic, idealized terms.** The term *pastoral* comes from the Latin word for "shepherd" (the word survives today in our word *pastor*). Originally, in the Latin verse of ancient Rome, pastorals were about the loves of shepherds and nymphs and the simple idealized pleasures of country life. (Any work of literature that treats rural life as it really is would not be pastoral.) Today the term has a looser meaning, referring to any poem that portrays an idyllic rural setting or expresses nostalgia for an age or place of lost innocence. England has a long pastoral tradition; America has almost no pastoral tradition at all. The term *pastoral* is often used, misleadingly, to refer to poets who write about rural life. Robert Frost, for example, has been called a pastoral poet. No poet's work could be further from the idealized pastoral tradition. Frost is a deeply ironic, even dark poet.

**PERSONIFICATION A figure of speech in which an object or animal is given human feelings, thoughts, or attitudes.** Personification is a type of metaphor in which two dissimilar things are compared. In "Apparently with no surprise" (Collection 3), Emily Dickinson personifies the frost as a heedless killer and a flower as a playful child.

See pages 395, 1150.
See also *Anthropomorphism,*
*Figure of Speech.*

**PERSUASION One of the four forms of discourse, which uses reason and emotional appeals to convince a reader to think or act in a certain way.** Persuasive techniques are used in the Declaration of Independence (Collection 1), in Patrick Henry's "Give me liberty, or give me death" speech (Collection 1), and in Thomas Paine's *The Crisis, No. 1* (Collection 1). Persuasion is almost exclusively used in nonfiction, particularly in essays and speeches. The other three major forms of discourse are **description, exposition,** and **narration.**

See pages 81, 88, 232, 941.
See also *Argument.*

**PLAIN STYLE A way of writing that stresses simplicity and clarity of expression.** The plain style was favored by most Puritan writers, who avoided unnecessary ornamentation in all aspects of their lives, including church ritual and even the style of church structures. Simple sentences, everyday words from common speech, and clear and direct statements characterize the plain style. This style can be seen in Anne Bradstreet's works. One of the chief exponents of the plain style in recent American literature was Ernest Hemingway.

See page 28.
See also *Style.*

**PLOT** **The series of related events in a story or play, sometimes called the story line.** Most short story plots contain the following elements: **exposition,** which tells us who the characters are and introduces their conflict; **complications,** which arise as the characters take steps to resolve their conflicts; the **climax,** that exciting or suspenseful moment when the outcome of the conflict is imminent; and a **resolution** or **denouement,** when the story's problems are all resolved and the story ends.

The plots of dramas and novels are more complex because of their length. A schematic representation of a typical dramatic plot is shown below. It is based on a pyramid developed by the nineteenth-century German critic Gustav Freitag. The **rising action** refers to all the actions that take place before the **turning point** (sometimes called the **crisis**). The turning point is the point at which the hero experiences a decisive reversal of fortune: In a comedy, things begin to work out well at that turning point; in a tragedy they get worse and worse. (In Shakespeare's plays the turning point takes place in the third act. In *Romeo and Juliet,* for example, after he kills Tybalt in the third act, Romeo's fate is sealed and he experiences one disaster after another.) All the action after the turning point is called **falling action** because it leads to the final resolution (happy or unhappy) of the conflict. The major **climax** in most plays and novels takes place just before the ending; in Shakespeare's plays the final climax takes place in the fifth, or last, act. (In *Romeo and Juliet* the major climax takes place in the last act when the two young people kill themselves.)

**Dramatic Plot**

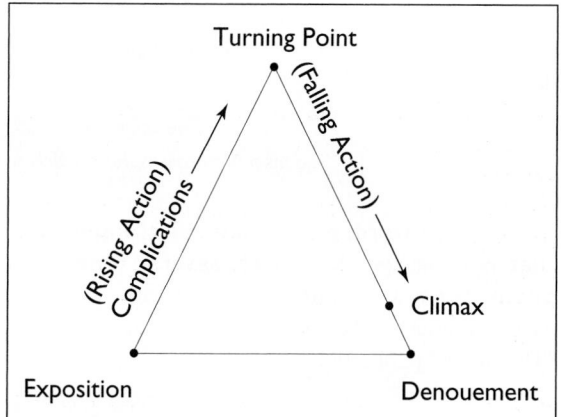

See page 186.
See also *Climax, Denouement, Exposition, Resolution.*

**POINT OF VIEW** **The vantage point from which the writer tells a story.** In broad terms, there are four main points of view: **first person, third person limited, omniscient,** and **objective.**

1. In the **first-person point of view,** one of the characters in the story tells the story, using first-person pronouns such as *I* and *we.* With this point of view, we can know only what the narrator knows. Mark Twain's novel *Adventures of Huckleberry Finn* is told from the first-person point of view, by the novel's main character, a boy named Huck Finn. One of the great pleasures of that novel, in fact, is that its point of view allows us to hear Huck's very distinct voice and dialect. It also allows us to see the complex adult world through the eyes of a young boy who is often victimized by that world.

2. In the **third-person-limited point of view,** an unknown narrator (usually thought of as the author) tells the story, but this narrator zooms in to focus on the thoughts and feelings of only one character. (This point of view gets its name because the narrator refers to all the characters as *he, she,* and *they;* this narrator does not refer to himself or herself with the first-person pronoun *I.*) Like the first-person point of view, however, this point of view also limits us to the perceptions of one character, but in this case the narrator can tell us many things that the character is unaware of. For example, Eudora Welty tells "A Worn Path" (Collection 5) from the third-person-limited point of view, which zooms in on her protagonist, an old woman named Phoenix Jackson. At one point, Welty's narrator tells us that Phoenix was "like an old woman begging a dignified forgiveness."

3. In the **omniscient point of view,** an omniscient, or all-knowing, narrator tells the story, also using the third-person pronouns. However, this narrator, instead of focusing on one character only, often tells us everything about many characters: their motives, weaknesses, hopes, childhoods, and sometimes even their futures. This narrator can also comment directly on the characters' actions. Nathaniel Hawthorne's "The Minister's Black Veil" (Collection 2) is told from the omniscient point of view.

4. In the **objective point of view,** a narrator who is totally impersonal and objective tells the story, with no comment on any characters or events. The objective point of view is like the point of view of a movie camera; it is totally impersonal, and what we know is only what the camera might see. This narrator never gives any direct revelation of the characters' thoughts

or motives. Ernest Hemingway uses this objective point of view, which is why his stories often seem so puzzling to readers. "What happened?" we ask. The *reader* must infer what happens in Hemingway's stories, just as in real life we have to infer the motives, thoughts, and feelings of people we meet.

See page 489.

**POSTMODERNISM A term for the dominant trend in the arts since 1945 characterized by experiments with nontraditional forms and the acceptance of multiple meanings.** The lines between real and imaginary worlds are often blurred in post-modern texts, as is the boundary between fiction and nonfiction. Other characteristics of postmodern texts are cultural diversity and an often playful self-consciousness, which is an acknowledgment that literature is not a mirror that accurately reflects the world, but a created world unto itself. Some well-known postmodern writers are Donald Barthelme, Toni Morrison, and Philip Roth.

See page 898.

**PROTAGONIST The central character in a story, the one who initiates or drives the action.** The protagonist might or might not be the story's hero; some protagonists are actually the villains in the story.

See page 684.
See also *Antagonist.*

**PROVERB A short, pithy statement that expresses a common truth or experience.** Many of Benjamin Franklin's sayings, such as "Fish and visitors smell in three days," have become proverbs in American culture.

See also *Aphorism.*

**PSYCHOANALYSIS A method of examining the unconscious mind, developed primarily by the Austrian physician Sigmund Freud (1865–1939).** Psychoanalysis is based on the assumption that many mental and emotional disorders are the result of the conscious mind repressing factors that persist in the unconscious and can cause conflicts. Modern writers often use the techniques of psychoanalysis. In "The Secret Life of Walter Mitty" (Collection 5), James Thurber uses the psychoanalytic technique of free association to give us a picture of a man with (comically) repressed desires.

See page 640.

**PUN A play on words based on the multiple meanings of a single word or on words that sound alike but mean different things.** An example of the first type of pun is a singer explaining her claim that she was locked out of an audition because she couldn't find the right key. The second kind of pun can be found in the opening lines of Shakespeare's *Julius Caesar,* where a man who repairs shoes claims to be a mender of men's souls (soles). Puns are often used for humor, but some puns are a serious element in poetry.

**QUATRAIN A poem consisting of four lines, or four lines of a poem that can be considered as a unit.** The typical ballad stanza, for example, is a quatrain.

**RATIONALISM The belief that human beings can arrive at truth by using reason, rather than by relying on the authority of the past, on religious faith, or on intuition.** The Declaration of Independence (Collection 1) is a document based on rationalist principles.

See page 14.

**REALISM A style of writing, developed in the nineteenth century, that attempts to depict life accurately, as it really is, without idealizing or romanticizing it.** Instead of writing about the long ago or far away, the realists concentrated on contemporary life and on middle- and lower-class lives in particular. Among the outstanding realistic novelists in America are Stephen Crane, Willa Cather, and John Steinbeck. European playwrights who wrote realistic dramas, including Henrik Ibsen, August Strindberg, and Anton Chekhov, discarded artificial plots in favor of themes centering on contemporary society. They also rejected extravagant language in favor of simple, everyday diction.

See pages 455, 459.
See also *Naturalism, Romanticism.*

**REFRAIN A word, phrase, line, or group of lines that is repeated, for effect, several times in a poem.** Refrains are often used in ballads and other narrative poems. "Nevermore" is a refrain in Poe's "The Raven" (Collection 2).

See page 833.

**REGIONALISM Literature that emphasizes a specific geographic setting and that reproduces the speech, behavior, and attitudes of the people**

who live in that region. Among the great regional writers of the twentieth century are Sinclair Lewis (Midwest); John Steinbeck (California); and William Faulkner, Flannery O'Connor, and Eudora Welty (South).

See page 457.

**REPETITION A unifying property of repeated words, sounds, syllables, and other elements that appear in a work.** Repetition occurs in most poetry and in some prose. Repetition is used to create rhythm, to reinforce a message, and to enhance a mood or emotional affect. **Rhyme, refrain, assonance, dissonance,** and other literary devices are all based on the repetition of certain sounds.

See pages 833, 1162.
See also *Assonance, Consonance, Refrain, Rhyme.*

**RESOLUTION The conclusion of a story, when all or most of the conflicts have been settled.** The resolution is also often called the *denouement.*

See also *Denouement, Plot.*

**RHETORICAL QUESTION A question that is asked for effect and that does not actually require an answer.** In his speech to the Virginia Convention (Collection 1), Patrick Henry asks several rhetorical questions. Such questions presume the audience agrees with the speaker on the answers.

**RHYME The repetition of vowel sounds in accented syllables and all succeeding syllables.** *Listen* and *glisten* rhyme, as do *chime* and *sublime.* When words within the same line of poetry have repeated sounds, we have an example of **internal rhyme. End rhyme** refers to rhyming words at the end of lines.

The pattern of rhymes in a poem is called a **rhyme scheme.** Rhyme scheme is commonly indicated with letters of the alphabet, each rhyming sound represented by a different letter of the alphabet. For example, the rhyme scheme of the following lines is *abab.*

| | |
|---|---|
| Tell me not, in mournful numbers, | *a* |
| Life is but an empty dream!— | *b* |
| For the soul is dead that slumbers, | *a* |
| And things are not what they seem. | *b* |

—Henry Wadsworth Longfellow,
from "A Psalm of Life"

**Approximate rhymes** (also called **off rhymes, half rhymes, imperfect rhymes,** or **slant rhymes**) are words that have some correspondence in sound but not an exact one. Examples of approximate rhymes are often found in Emily Dickinson's poems. *Flash* and *flesh* are approximate rhymes, as are *stream* and *storm,* and *early* and *barley.* Approximate rhyme has the effect of catching the reader off guard: Where you expect a perfect rhyme, you get only an approximation. The emotional effect is something like that of the sound of a sharp or flat note in music.

See pages 1131, 1157.
See also *Internal Rhyme, Rhythm, Slant Rhyme.*

**RHYTHM The alternation of stressed and unstressed syllables in language.** Rhythm occurs naturally in all forms of spoken and written English. The most obvious kind of rhythm is produced by **meter,** the regular pattern of stressed and unstressed syllables found in some poetry. Writers can also create less structured rhythms by using rhyme, repetition, pauses, and variations in line length and by balancing long and short words or phrases.

See pages 824, 1131.
See also *Cadence, Free Verse, Meter, Rhyme.*

**ROMANCE In general, a story in which an idealized hero or heroine undertakes a quest and is successful.** In a romance, beauty, innocence, and goodness usually prevail over evil. Romances are traditionally set in the distant past and use a great deal of fantasy. The laws of nature are often suspended in a romance, so that the hero often has supernatural powers, as we see in the adventures of King Arthur and his knights. Stories set in the American West are in the romance mode, except that the supernatural elements are eliminated (though the sheriff-hero usually has a nearly magical skill with his gun). Today we also use the word *romance* to refer to a kind of popular escapist love story, which often takes place in an exotic setting. A popular contemporary romance in the traditional sense is the bestselling trilogy by J.R.R. Tolkien, *The Lord of the Rings.*

**ROMANTICISM A revolt against rationalism that affected literature and the other arts, beginning in the late eighteenth century and remaining strong throughout most of the nineteenth century.** Romanticism is marked by these characteristics: (1) a conviction that intuition, imagination, and emotion are superior to reason; (2) a conviction that poetry is superior to science; (3) a belief that contemplation of the natural world is a means of discovering the truth that lies behind mere reality; (4) a distrust of industry and city life and an idealization of rural life and of the wilderness; (5) an interest in the more "natural" past and in the supernatural. Romanticism affected so many creative people that it was bound to take many different forms; the result is that it is difficult to define the word in a way that includes everyone who might be called a Romantic. In the nineteenth century, for example, Romantics were outspoken in their love of nature and contempt for technology. In the twentieth century, however, as nature was taken over by real-estate developers and highways, some writers took a romantic view of machines, buildings, and other products of technology.

See pages 164, 167, 168.

See also *Realism.*

**ROMANTIC NOVEL A novel with a happy ending that presents readers with characters engaged in adventures filled with courageous acts, daring chases, and exciting escapes.** James Fenimore Cooper is known for novels such as *The Last of the Mohicans* (1826) and *The Deerslayer* (1841), which are filled with romantic adventures.

See page 455.

**SATIRE A type of writing that ridicules the shortcomings of people or institutions in an attempt to bring about a change.** Satire can cover a wide range of tones, from gentle spoofing to savage mockery. In "The Secret Life of Walter Mitty" (Collection 5), for example, James Thurber pokes fun at the domesticated American male's tendency to escape into heroic fantasies. In Donald Barthelme's "Game" (Collection 6), the satire is harsh, as it points out the absurdity and illogic of nuclear war games. Satire is always intensely moral in its purpose. Mark Twain, in his essay "The Lowest Animal" (Collection 4), satirizes the moral infirmity of the entire human race by ironically comparing the behavior of humans with that of the animals and finding the latter to be morally superior.

See pages 186, 534, 982.

**SCANNING The analysis of a poem to determine its meter.** When you scan a poem, you describe the pattern of stressed and unstressed syllables in each line. Stresses or accents are indicated by the symbol (ˈ) and unstressed syllables by the symbol (˘).

> Tŏ hím whŏ ín thĕ lóve ŏf Náture hŏlds
> Commúnion wíth hĕr vísiblĕ forms, shĕ spéaks
> Ă várĭoŭs lánguăge: fŏr hĭs gáyĕr hoŭrs
> Shĕ hás ă voíce ŏf gládnĕss, ănd ă smíle.
>
> —William Cullen Bryant, from "Thanatopsis"

See also *Anapest, Blank Verse, Dactyl, Foot, Iamb, Iambic Pentameter, Meter, Spondee, Trochee.*

**SESTET Six lines of poetry, especially the last six lines of a Petrarchan, or Italian, sonnet.** In the Petrarchan sonnet the sestet offers a comment on the subject or problem presented in the first eight lines, or the octave, of the poem.

See pages 197, 202.

See also *Octave, Sonnet.*

**SETTING The time and location in which a story takes place.** Setting can have several functions in fiction:

1. Setting is often used to create **conflict.** In the purest and often simplest form of a story, a character is in conflict with some element of a setting. The narrator in Jack London's "To Build a Fire" (Collection 4), for example, is in conflict with extreme cold (the cold wins).
2. Often the setting helps to create **atmosphere** or **mood.** Edgar Allan Poe's setting of a dungeon in "The Pit and the Pendulum" (Collection 2) creates a mood of horror.
3. Setting can also create and delineate **character.** In William Faulkner's "A Rose for Emily" (Collection 5), Miss Emily Grierson's old-fashioned house with its musty rooms reflects her refusal to live in the present.

See pages 579, 719, 1093.

**SHORT STORY A brief work of prose fiction.** A short story has a simpler plot than a novel and is not long enough to be published as a volume of its own. Short stories usually focus on a few characters and one major event. Edgar Allan Poe has often been called one of the originators and masters of the modern short story. Some of the great American short story writers include Nathaniel Hawthorne, Flannery O'Connor, Eudora Welty, and Raymond Carver.

**SIMILE** **A figure of speech that makes an explicit comparison between two unlike things, using a word such as** *like, as, than,* **or** *resembles.*

> Helen, thy beauty is to me
> Like those Nicéan barks of yore
>
> —Edgar Allan Poe, from "To Helen"

See also *Figure of Speech, Metaphor.*

**SLANT RHYME** **A rhyming sound that is not exact.** *Follow/fellow* and *mystery/mastery* are examples of slant or approximate rhyme. Emily Dickinson frequently uses the subtleties of slant rhyme.

See pages 391, 395.
See also *Rhyme.*

**SOLILOQUY** **A long speech made by a character in a play while no other characters are onstage.** A soliloquy is different from a monologue in that the speaker appears to be thinking aloud, not addressing a listener.

**SONNET** **A fourteen-line poem, usually written in iambic pentameter, that has one of two basic structures.** The **Petrarchan sonnet,** also called the **Italian sonnet,** is named after the fourteenth-century Italian poet Petrarch. Its first eight lines, called the **octave,** ask a question or pose a problem. These lines have a rhyme scheme of *abba, abba.* The last six lines, called the **sestet,** respond to the question or problem. These lines have a rhyme scheme of *cde, cde.*

The form used to such perfection by William Shakespeare is known as the **English, Elizabethan,** or **Shakespearean sonnet.** It has three four-line units, or **quatrains,** and it concludes with a **couplet.** The most common rhyme scheme for the Shakespearean sonnet is *abab, cdcd, efef, gg.*

Longfellow wrote many sonnets, such as "The Cross of Snow" (Collection 2), as did Edna St. Vincent Millay, Robert Frost, and E. E. Cummings.

See pages 32, 197, 202, 792.
See also *Octave, Sestet.*

**SOUND EFFECTS** **The use of sounds to create specific literary effects.** Writers use devices such as **rhythm, rhyme, meter, alliteration, onomatopoeia, assonance, consonance,** and **repetition** to make the sounds of a work convey and enhance its meaning.

See pages 297, 303, 1178.

**SPEAKER** **The voice that addresses the reader in a poem.** The speaker may be the poet or a persona, a character whose voice and concerns do not necessarily reflect those of the poet. The speaker of T. S. Eliot's "The Love Song of J. Alfred Prufrock" (Collection 5) is one of the most famous personas in literature. The speaker in Sylvia Plath's poem "Mirror" (Collection 6) is the personified mirror itself.

See page 1146.

**SPEECH** **A formal address delivered to an audience, or the printed version of the same address.** Speeches are most commonly delivered by politicians, political activists, and other types of public figures. "The Arrogance and Cruelty of Power" from the Nuremberg Trials (Collection 6), delivered by Robert H. Jackson, is an example of a speech given to open a trial.

**SPONDEE** **A metrical foot consisting of two syllables, both of which are stressed.** The words *true-blue* and *nineteen* are made of spondees. When Walt Whitman writes "Beat! beat! drums," he uses spondees. Spondaic feet are rarely used extensively because of their *thump-thump* sound. However, poets sometimes use spondees to provide a brief change from an iambic or trochaic beat or to provide emphasis.

See also *Anapest, Dactyl, Foot, Iamb, Iambic Pentameter, Meter, Trochee.*

**STANZA** **A group of consecutive lines that forms a structural unit in a poem.** Stanzas come in varying numbers of lines, though four is the most common. On the page, stanzas are separated by spaces. Stanza patterns are determined by the number of lines, the kind of feet in each line, and metrical and rhyme schemes, if any.

**STEREOTYPE** **A fixed idea or conception of a character or a group of people that does not allow for any individuality and is often based on religious, social, or racial prejudices.** Some common stereotypes are the unsophisticated farmer, the socially inept honor student, the dumb athlete, and the lazy teenager. Stereotypes, also called **stock characters,** are often deliberately used in comedies and in melodramas, where they receive instant recognition from the audience and make fully fleshed characterization unnecessary. In Thurber's "The Secret Life of Walter Mitty" (Collection 5), Walter and Mrs. Mitty are stock characters—the henpecked husband and the domineering wife.

See also *Character.*

**STREAM OF CONSCIOUSNESS** **A style of writing that portrays the inner (and often chaotic) workings of a character's mind.** The stream-of-consciousness technique usually consists of a recording of the random flow of ideas, memories, associations, images, and emotions, as they arise spontaneously in a character's mind. This flow of the contents of a character's mind is called an **interior monologue.** William Faulkner, in his novel *The Sound and the Fury,* uses a stream-of-consciousness technique. Two other great writers that successfully use a stream-of-consciousness technique are the Irish writer James Joyce and the English writer Virginia Woolf.

See pages 640, 770.

**STYLE** **The distinctive way in which a writer uses language.** Style can be plain, ornate, metaphorical, spare, descriptive, and so on. Style is determined by such factors as sentence length and complexity, syntax, use of figurative language and imagery, and diction.

See pages 88, 589, 984, 1193.
See also *Plain Style, Stream of Consciousness, Tone.*

**SUBJECTIVE AND OBJECTIVE WRITING** **Subjectivity, in terms of writing, suggests that the writer's primary purpose is to express personal experiences, feelings, and ideas. Objectivity suggests that the writer's purpose is to report facts, avoiding personal judgments and feelings.** Subjective writing is typified by autobiographies and memoirs. Objective writing is used mostly in news reporting and other types of journalism. This is not to say that all writing must be one or the other. In fact, most writing will have elements of subjective and objective writing.

See page 926.

**SURREALISM** **A movement in art and literature that started in Europe during the 1920s. Surrealists wanted to replace conventional realism with the full expression of the unconscious mind, which they considered to be more real than the "real" world of appearances.** Surrealists, influenced by the psychoanalytic theories of Sigmund Freud, tried not to censor the images that came from their dreams or to impose logical connections on these images. This resulted in surprising combinations of "inner" and "outer" reality—a "suprareality." Surrealism affected writers as diverse as T. S. Eliot and Donald Barthelme. Two famous surrealist artists are the Spaniard Salvador Dali (1904–1989) and the Belgian René Magritte (1898–1967).

**SUSPENSE** **A feeling of uncertainty and curiosity about what will happen next in a story.** A key element in fiction and drama, suspense is one of the hooks a writer uses to keep the audience interested.

**SYMBOL** **A person, a place, a thing, or an event that has meaning in itself and that also stands for something more than itself.** We can distinguish between **public** and **personal symbols.** The dove, for example, is a public symbol of peace—that is, it is widely accepted the world over as such a symbol. The bald eagle is a public symbol that stands for the United States; a picture of a skull and crossbones is a public symbol of death; two snakes coiled around a staff is a widely accepted symbol of the medical profession.

Most symbols used in literature are personal symbols; even though a symbol may be widely used, a writer will usually adapt it in some imaginative, personal way so that it can suggest not just one, but a myriad of meanings. One of the most commonly used symbols in literature, for example, is the journey, which can stand for a search for truth, for redemption from evil, or for discovery of the self and freedom.

The writers known as the Dark Romantics—Poe, Hawthorne, and Melville—used symbolism heavily in their works. One of American literature's most famous symbols is Melville's white whale, Moby-Dick, used to symbolize the inexpressible nature of evil.

See pages 262, 279, 375, 1139.
See also *Figure of Speech.*

**SYMBOLISM A literary movement that originated in late-nineteenth-century France, in which writers rearranged the world of appearances in order to reveal a more truthful version of reality.** The symbolists believed that direct statements of feeling were inadequate. Instead, they called for new and striking imaginative images to evoke complexities of meaning and mood. The French symbolists were influenced by the poetry and critical writings of the American writer Edgar Allan Poe. The poetry of Ezra Pound, T. S. Eliot, and Wallace Stevens is in the symbolist tradition.

See pages 642, 645.

**SYNECDOCHE** (si·nek′də·kē) **A figure of speech in which a part represents the whole.** The capital city of a nation, for example, is often spoken of as though it were the government: *Washington and Moscow are both claiming popular support for their positions.* In "The Love Song of J. Alfred Prufrock" (Collection 5), T. S. Eliot writes "And I have known the arms already. . . ." *Arms* stands for all the women he has known.

See also *Metonymy.*

**SYNESTHESIA** (sin′əs·thē′zhə) **The juxtaposition of one sensory image with another image that appeals to an unrelated sense.** In synesthesia an image of sound might be conveyed in terms of an image of taste as in "sweet laughter," or an image that appeals to the sense of touch might be combined with an image that appeals to the sense of sight, as in the example from Emily Dickinson: "golden touch."

**TALL TALE An outrageously exaggerated, humorous story that is obviously unbelievable.** Tall tales are part of folk literature of many countries, including the United States. Perhaps the most famous tall tale in American literature is Mark Twain's "The Celebrated Jumping Frog of Calaveras County" (Collection 4).

See page 533.

**THEME The insight about human life that is revealed in literary work.** Themes are rarely stated directly in literature. Most often, a reader has to infer the theme of a work after considerable thought. Theme is different from **subject.** A story's subject might be stated as "growing up," "love," "heroism," or "fear." The theme is the statement the writer wants to make about that subject: "For most young people, growing up is a process that involves the pain of achieving self-knowledge." Theme must be stated in at least one sentence; most themes are complex enough to require several sentences, or even an essay.

See pages 190, 759, 973, 1029, 1185.

**TONE The attitude a writer takes toward the subject of a work, the characters in it, or the audience.** In speaking we use voice inflections and even body language to show how we feel about what we are saying. Writers manipulate language in an attempt to achieve the same effect. For example, John Hersey takes an objective tone in telling about the nuclear explosion in *Hiroshima* (see "A Noiseless Flash," Collection 6). In contrast, the tone in Patrick Henry's speech to the Virginia Convention (Collection 1) is subjective, even impassioned. Tone is dependent on **diction** and **style,** and we cannot say we have understood any work of literature until we have sensed the writer's tone. Tone can usually be described in a single word: objective, solemn, playful, ironic, sarcastic, critical, reverent, irreverent, philosophical, cynical, and so on.

See pages 398, 1111, 1148, 1182.
See also *Diction, Style.*

**TRAGEDY In general, a story in which a heroic character either dies or comes to some other unhappy end.** In most tragedies the main character is in an enviable, even exalted, position when the story begins (in classical tragedies and in Shakespeare's plays, the tragic hero is of noble origin, often a king or queen, prince or princess). The character's downfall generally occurs because of some combination of fate, an error in judgment, or a personality failure known as a **tragic flaw** (Creon's stubbornness in *Antigone* or Hamlet's indecision, for example). The tragic character has usually gained wisdom at the end of the story, in spite of suffering defeat or even death. Our feeling on reading or viewing a tragedy is usually exaltation—despite the unhappy ending—because we have witnessed the best that human beings are capable of.

See also *Comedy.*

**TRANSCENDENTALISM A nineteenth-century movement in the Romantic tradition, which held that every individual can reach ultimate truths through spiritual intuition, which transcends reason and sensory experience.** The Transcendental movement was centered in Concord, Massachusetts, home of its leading exponents, Ralph Waldo Emerson and Henry David Thoreau. The basic tenets of the Transcendentalists were (1) a belief that God is present in every aspect of nature, including every human being; (2) the conviction that everyone is capable of apprehending God through the use of intuition; (3) the belief that all of nature is symbolic of the spirit. A corollary of these beliefs was an optimistic view of the world as good and evil as nonexistent.

See pages 170, 171.

**TROCHEE A metrical foot made up of an accented syllable followed by an unaccented syllable, as in the word _taxi_.** A trochee, the opposite of an iamb, is sometimes used to vary iambic rhythm.

See also _Anapest, Dactyl, Foot, Iamb, Iambic Pentameter, Meter, Spondee._

**UNDERSTATEMENT A statement that says less than what is meant.** Understatement, paradoxically, can make us recognize the truth of something by saying that just the opposite is true. If you are sitting down to enjoy a ten-course meal and say, "Ah! A little snack before bedtime," you are using an understatement to emphasize the tremendous amount of food you are about to eat. Understatement is often used to make an ironic point; it can also be used for humor.

See page 525.
See also _Hyperbole._

**VERNACULAR The language spoken by the people who live in a particular locality.** Regionalist writers try to capture the vernacular of their area.

See page 525.
See also _Dialect._

**VILLANELLE A nineteen-line poem consisting of five tercets (three-line stanzas) with the rhyme scheme _aba_ and with a final quatrain (four-line stanza) of _abaa_.** Two well-known villanelles in the English language are Dylan Thomas's "Do Not Go Gentle into That Good Night" and Elizabeth Bishop's "One Art" (Collection 6).

See page 1142.

# Language Handbook

## CONTENTS

# Language Handbook

| PART OF SPEECH | DEFINITION | EXAMPLES |
|---|---|---|
| **NOUN** | Names person, place, thing, or idea | poet, Sylvia Plath, city, Chicago, awards, Nobel Prize, *Of Mice and Men,* books, crew, herd, Harlem Renaissance, realism |
| **PRONOUN** | Takes place of one or more nouns or pronouns | |
| **Personal** | Refers to one(s) speaking (first person), spoken to (second person), spoken about (third person) | I, me, my, mine, we, us, our, ours you, your, yours he, him, his, she, her, hers, it, its, they, them, their, theirs |
| **Reflexive** | Refers to subject and directs action of verb back to subject | myself, ourselves, yourself, yourselves, himself, herself, itself, themselves |
| **Intensive** | Refers to and emphasizes noun or another pronoun | (same as examples for Reflexive) |
| **Demonstrative** | Refers to specific one(s) of group | this, that, these, those |
| **Interrogative** | Introduces question | what, which, who, whom, whose |
| **Relative** | Introduces subordinate clause | that, which, who, whom, whose |
| **Indefinite** | Refers to one(s) not specifically named | all, any, anyone, both, each, either, everybody, many, none, nothing, someone |
| **ADJECTIVE** | Modifies noun or pronoun by telling *what kind, which one, how many,* or *how much* | **a large black** box, **an able-bodied** worker, **that** one, **the five Iroquois** nations, **enough** time, **less** money, **many** choices |
| **VERB** | Shows action or state of being | |
| **Action** | Expresses physical or mental activity | write, receive, run, think, imagine, understand |
| **Linking** | Connects subject with word identifying or describing it | appear, be, seem, become, feel, look, smell, sound, taste |
| **Helping (Auxiliary)** | Assists another verb to express time, voice, or mood | be, have, may, can, shall, will, would |
| **ADVERB** | Modifies verb, adjective, or adverb by telling *how, when, where,* or *to what extent* | speaks **clearly, quite** interesting, **rather** calmly, arrived **there late** |
| **PREPOSITION** | Relates noun or pronoun to another word | about, at, by, for, of, in, on, through, according to, in front of, out of |

*(continued)*

| PART OF SPEECH | DEFINITION | EXAMPLES |
|---|---|---|
| **CONJUNCTION** | Joins words or word groups | |
| **Coordinating** | Joins words or word groups used in same way | and, but, for, nor, or, so, yet |
| **Correlative** | A pair of conjunctions that joins parallel words or word groups | both . . . and, not only . . . but (also), either . . . or, neither . . . nor |
| **Subordinating** | Begins subordinate clause and connects it to independent clause | although, as if, because, since, so that, unless, when, where, while |
| **INTERJECTION** | Expresses emotion | hey, oh, ouch, wow, well, hooray |

# 2 AGREEMENT

## AGREEMENT OF SUBJECT AND VERB

**2a.** **A verb should agree in number with its subject. Singular subjects take singular verbs. Plural subjects take plural verbs.**

SINGULAR   The **character lives** on a farm in Yoknapatawpha County.

PLURAL   **Both** of the stories **were written** by William Faulkner.

**2b.** **The number of the subject is not changed by a phrase or a clause following the subject.**

SINGULAR   **Langston Hughes,** who wrote several books of poetry, **was** a major figure in the Harlem Renaissance.

PLURAL   **The students,** as well as Ms. Ramos, **are** eager to use the new software.

**2c.** **Indefinite pronouns may be singular, plural, or either.**

(1) The following indefinite pronouns are singular: *anybody, anyone, anything, each, either, one, everybody, everyone, everything, neither, nobody, no one, nothing, somebody, someone,* and *something.*

**EXAMPLE**
**Neither** of the books **contains** that story.

(2) The following indefinite pronouns are plural: *both, few, many,* and *several.*

**EXAMPLE**
**Both** of the poems **were written** by Claude McKay.

(3) The indefinite pronouns *all, any, most, none,* and *some* are singular when they refer to singular words and are plural when they refer to plural words.

SINGULAR   **Some** of her artwork **is** beautiful.
   [*Some* refers to *artwork.*]

PLURAL   **Some** of her paintings **are** beautiful.
   [*Some* refers to *paintings.*]

**2d.** **A *compound subject,* which is two or more subjects that have the same verb, may be singular or plural.**

(1) Subjects joined by *and* usually take a plural verb.

**EXAMPLE**
**Hemingway, Steinbeck, and Morrison are** Nobel Prize winners.

A compound subject that names only one person or thing takes a singular verb.

**EXAMPLE**
Roderick Usher's **sister and** sole **companion is** Madeline.

(2) Singular subjects joined by *or* or *nor* take a singular verb.

**EXAMPLES**
**Either Amy or Eric plans** to report on William Byrd.
**Neither** the **rain nor** the **wind has stopped**.

(3) When a singular subject and a plural subject are joined by *or* or *nor,* the verb agrees with the subject nearer the verb.

**EXAMPLE**
**Neither** the **performers nor** the **director was** eager to rehearse.

**NOTE** Whenever possible, revise the sentence to avoid this awkward construction.

**EXAMPLE**
The **director was** not eager to rehearse the scene again, and neither **were** the **performers.**

**2e.** **The verb agrees with its subject even when the verb precedes the subject, such as in sentences beginning with *here*, *there*, or *where*.**

**EXAMPLES**
Here **is** [*or* here's] a **copy** of the Declaration of Independence.
Here **are** [*not* here's] two **copies** of the Declaration of Independence.

**2f.** **A *collective noun* (such as *class*, *herd*, or *jury*) is singular in form but names a group of persons or things. A collective noun takes a singular verb when the noun refers to the group as a unit and takes a plural verb when the noun refers to the parts or members of the group.**

SINGULAR | The **cast** of *A Raisin in the Sun* **is made** up entirely of juniors. [The cast as a unit is made up of juniors.]
PLURAL | After the play, the **cast are joining** their families for a celebration. [The members of the cast are joining their families.]

**2g.** **An expression of an amount (a length of time, a statistic, or a fraction, for example) is singular when the amount is thought of as a unit or when it refers to a singular word. An amount is plural when it is thought of as many parts or when it refers to a plural word.**

SINGULAR | **Twenty years was** a long time for Rip Van Winkle to sleep. [one unit]
PLURAL | **Fifty percent** of the students **have** already **read** *Walden*. [The percentage refers to *students*.]

Expressions of measurement (length, weight, capacity, area) are usually singular.

**EXAMPLES**
**Seventy-five degrees below zero was** the air temperature in "To Build a Fire."
**Four and a half miles was** how far the man walked in an hour.

**2h.** **The title of a creative work (such as a book, song, film, or painting) or the**

name of an organization, a country, or a city (even if the name is plural in form) takes a singular verb.

**EXAMPLES**
"Birches" **was written** by Robert Frost.
The **United States calls** its flag Old Glory.

**2i.** **A verb agrees with its subject, not with its predicate nominative.**

SINGULAR | One **symptom** of flu **is** sore muscles.
PLURAL | Sore **muscles are** one symptom of flu.

## AGREEMENT OF PRONOUN AND ANTECEDENT

A pronoun usually refers to a noun or another pronoun. The word to which a pronoun refers is called its *antecedent.*

**2j.** **A pronoun agrees with its antecedent in number and gender. Singular pronouns refer to singular antecedents. Plural pronouns refer to plural antecedents. A few singular pronouns indicate gender (neuter, feminine, masculine).**

**EXAMPLES**
**Marianne Moore** published **her** first book of poems in 1921. [singular, feminine]
**Peyton Farquhar** thinks **he** has escaped. [singular, masculine]
Benjamin Franklin wrote, "**Three** may keep a secret if two of **them** are dead." [plural]

**2k.** **Indefinite pronouns may be singular, plural, or either.**

**(1)** Singular pronouns are used to refer to the indefinite pronouns *anybody, anyone, anything, each, either, everybody, everyone, everything, neither, nobody, no one, nothing, one, somebody, someone,* and *something.* The gender of any of these pronouns is often determined by a word in a phrase following the pronoun.

**EXAMPLES**
**Each** of the **girls** has already memorized **her** part.
**One** of the **boys** gave **his** interpretation of "Nothing Gold Can Stay."

If the antecedent may be either masculine or feminine, use both the masculine and feminine pronouns to refer to it.

**EXAMPLE**
**Anyone** who is qualified for the job may submit **his** or **her** application.

**NOTE** Whenever possible, revise the sentence to avoid this awkward construction.

**EXAMPLE**

Anyone who is qualified for the job may submit an application.

**(2)** Plural pronouns are used to refer to the indefinite pronouns *both, few, many,* and *several.*

**EXAMPLE**

**Both** of the finalists played **their** best.

**(3)** Singular or plural pronouns may be used to refer to the indefinite pronouns *all, any, most, none,* and *some.* These indefinite pronouns are singular when they refer to singular words and are plural when they refer to plural words.

| SINGULAR | **All** of our **planning** achieved **its** purpose. |
| PLURAL | **All** of your **suggestions** had **their** good points. |

**2l.** A plural pronoun is used to refer to two or more singular antecedents joined by *and.*

**EXAMPLE**

**Jerry and Francesca** read the sonnets **they** wrote about Olaudah Equiano.

**2m.** A singular pronoun is used to refer to two or more singular antecedents joined by *or* or *nor.*

**EXAMPLE**

Neither **Cindy nor Carla** thinks **she** is ready to write the final draft.

**2n.** When a singular and a plural antecedent are joined by *or* or *nor,* the pronoun agrees with the nearer antecedent.

**EXAMPLE**

Either **Jerry or** the **twins** will bring **their** stereo.

**Revising Misleading Sentences**

Sentences with antecedents joined by *or* or *nor* can be misleading when the antecedents are of different genders or numbers. Revise the sentences to avoid such constructions.

| MISLEADING | Either Christopher or Tiffany will give her report on Transcendentalism. [The sentence suggests that Christopher may give Tiffany's report.] |
| REVISED | Either **Christopher** will give **his** report on Transcendentalism, or **Tiffany** will give **hers**. |

**2o.** A collective noun (such as *audience, family,* or *team*) takes a singular pronoun when the noun refers to the group as a unit and takes a plural pronoun when the noun refers to the parts or members of the group.

| SINGULAR | The **debate club** elected **its** new officers. |
| PLURAL | The **debate club** will practice **their** speeches in this week's workshop. |

**2p.** The title of a creative work (such as a book, song, film, or painting) or the name of an organization, a country, or a city (even if it is plural in form) takes a singular pronoun.

**EXAMPLES**

The teacher read **"Mushrooms"** and then asked me to interpret **it.**

**Anderson Outfitters** advertises **itself** as "the first step in getting away from it all."

# 3 USING VERBS

## REGULAR AND IRREGULAR VERBS

Every verb has four basic forms called the **principal parts:** the *base form,* the *present participle,* the *past,* and the *past participle.* A verb is classified as *regular* or *irregular* depending on the way it forms the past and past participle.

**3a.** A *regular verb* forms the past and past participle by adding *–d* or *–ed* to the base form. An *irregular verb* forms the past and the past participle in some other way.

The following examples include *is* and *have* in parentheses to show that helping verbs are used with the present participle and past participle forms.

## COMMON REGULAR AND IRREGULAR VERBS

| BASE FORM | PRESENT PARTICIPLE | PAST | PAST PARTICIPLE |
|---|---|---|---|
| **REGULAR** | | | |
| ask | (is) asking | asked | (have) asked |
| attack | (is) attacking | attacked | (have) attacked |
| drown | (is) drowning | drowned | (have) drowned |
| plan | (is) planning | planned | (have) planned |
| try | (is) trying | tried | (have) tried |
| use | (is) using | used | (have) used |
| **IRREGULAR** | | | |
| be | (is) being | was, were | (have) been |
| begin | (is) beginning | began | (have) begun |
| catch | (is) catching | caught | (have) caught |
| drink | (is) drinking | drank | (have) drunk |
| drive | (is) driving | drove | (have) driven |
| go | (is) going | went | (have) gone |
| lend | (is) lending | lent | (have) lent |
| shake | (is) shaking | shook | (have) shaken |
| swim | (is) swimming | swam | (have) swum |
| tear | (is) tearing | tore | (have) torn |
| throw | (is) throwing | threw | (have) thrown |

Before adding the suffix *–ing* or *–ed* to form the present participle or the past or past participle of a verb, double the final consonant if the base form satisfies both of these conditions:

(1) It has only one syllable or has the accent on the last syllable.

(2) It ends in a single consonant preceded by a single vowel.

**EXAMPLES**

grin + -ing = grin**ning**

refer + -ed = refer**red**

See 14m for exceptions.

**NOTE** If you are not sure about the principal parts of a verb, look in a current dictionary. Entries for irregular verbs give the principal parts. If no principal parts are listed, the verb is a regular verb.

## TENSES AND THEIR USES

**3b.** The *tense* of a verb indicates the time of the action or the state of being expressed by the verb.

(1) The *present tense* is used mainly to express an action or a state of being that is occurring now.

**EXAMPLE**

We **understand** now.

The present tense is also used

- to show a customary or habitual action or state of being
- to convey a general truth—something that is always true
- to make a historical event seem current (such use is called the *historical present*)
- to summarize the plot or subject matter of a literary work or to refer to an author's relationship to his or her work (such use is called the *literary present*)
- to express future time

**EXAMPLES**

For breakfast I **eat** cereal and **drink** orange juice. [customary action]

The earth **revolves** once around the sun each year. [general truth]

Several of the *Mayflower* passengers **die** before the ship **reaches** Plymouth. [historical present]

*Moby-Dick* **tells** the story of a man who **pursues** a white whale. [literary present]

The workshop **begins** tomorrow. [future time]

(2) The *past tense* is used to express an action or a state of being that occurred in the past but did not continue into the present.

**EXAMPLES**

Pepe **grabbed** his rifle and **crawled** into the brush.

(3) The *future tense* (*will* or *shall* + base form) is used to express an action or a state of being that will occur.

**EXAMPLES**

Elisa **will play** the part of Beneatha Younger.

I **will** [*or* shall] **serve** as her understudy.

(4) The *present perfect tense* (*have* or *has* + past participle) is used mainly to express an action or a state of being that occurred at some indefinite time in the past.

**EXAMPLE**

**Have** you **read** any stories by Sandra Cisneros?

The present perfect tense is also used to express an action or a state of being that began in the past and continues into the present.

**EXAMPLE**

My sister **has been** a Girl Scout for two years.

**(5)** The *past perfect tense* (*had* + past participle) is used to express an action or a state of being that was completed in the past before another action or state of being occurred.

**EXAMPLE**

Miss Emily returned the tax notice that she **had received.**

 **NOTE** Use the past perfect tense in "if" clauses that express the earlier of two past actions.

**EXAMPLE**

If he **had taken** [*not* would have taken *or* took] more time, he would have won.

**(6)** The *future perfect tense* (*will have* or *shall have* + past participle) is used to express an action or a state of being that will be completed in the future before some other future occurrence.

**EXAMPLE**

By the time Rip Van Winkle returns to his village, the Revolutionary War **will have occurred.**

**3c.** **Avoid unnecessary shifts in tense.**

| INCONSISTENT | Shiftlet marries Lucynell and then abandoned her. |
| CONSISTENT | Shiftlet **marries** Lucynell and then **abandons** her. |
| CONSISTENT | Shiftlet **married** Lucynell and then **abandoned** her. |

When describing events that occur at different times, use verbs in different tenses to show the order of events.

**EXAMPLE**

She now **works** for *The New York Times,* but she **worked** for *The Wall Street Journal* last year.

## ACTIVE VOICE AND PASSIVE VOICE

**3d.** *Voice* **is the form a verb takes to indicate whether the subject of the verb performs or receives the action.**

A verb is in the *active voice* when its subject performs the action.

**ACTIVE VOICE**  Julia Alvarez **wrote** "Daughter of Invention."

A verb is in the *passive voice* when its subject receives the action. A passive voice verb is always a verb phrase that includes a form of *be* and the past participle of an action verb.

**PASSIVE VOICE**  "Daughter of Invention" **was written** by Julia Alvarez.

**3e.** **Use the passive voice sparingly.**

In general, the passive voice is less direct and less forceful than the active voice. In some cases, the passive voice may sound awkward.

| AWKWARD PASSIVE | A memorable speech was delivered by William Faulkner when the Nobel Prize was accepted by him in 1950. |
| ACTIVE | William Faulkner delivered a memorable speech when he accepted the Nobel Prize in 1950. |

The passive voice is useful
1. when you do not know the performer of the action
2. when you do not want to reveal the performer of the action
3. when you want to emphasize the receiver of the action

**EXAMPLES**

Hemingway **was** severely **wounded** during the war.

Many careless errors **were made** in some of the essays about Amy Tan.

Madeline Usher **had been buried** alive!

# 4 USING PRONOUNS

## CASE

*Case* is the form that a noun or a pronoun takes to indicate its use in a sentence. In English, there are three cases: *nominative, objective,* and *possessive.*

The form of a noun is the same for both the nominative case and the objective case. A noun changes form only in the possessive case. Unlike nouns, most personal pronouns have one form for each case. The form a pronoun takes depends on its function in a sentence.

## The Nominative Case

**4a.** A subject of a verb is in the nominative case.

**EXAMPLES**
**They** were happy that **he** was home from the war. [*They* is the subject of *were,* and *he* is the subject of *was.*]

**4b.** A predicate nominative is in the nominative case.

**EXAMPLE**
The one who jilts Granny Weatherall is **he.** [*He* follows *is* and identifies the subject *one.*]

## The Objective Case

**4c.** An object of a verb is in the objective case.

**EXAMPLES**
My stepbrother and stepsister don't have driver's licenses yet, so I usually give **them** a ride to school. [*Them* is the direct object of the verb *give.*]
The Jazz Age collage earned **Donna and him** blue ribbons. [*Donna and him* is a compound indirect object of the verb *earned.*]

**4d.** An object of a preposition is in the objective case.

**EXAMPLES**
Did you send copies of *Blue Highways* to **her and him**? [*Her and him* is a compound object of the preposition *to.*]

## The Possessive Case

**4e.** A noun or a pronoun preceding a gerund is in the possessive case.

**EXAMPLE**
Warren did not appreciate **Silas's** [*or* **his**] leaving during haying time. [*Silas's* (or *his*) modifies *leaving,* a gerund used as a direct object telling what Warren did not appreciate.]

### SPECIAL PRONOUN PROBLEMS

**4f.** An appositive is in the same case as the noun or pronoun to which it refers.

**EXAMPLES**
The Ushers, **Madeline and he,** live in a gloomy mansion. [The appositive, *Madeline and he,* refers to the subject, *Ushers,* which is in the nominative case.]
Tom T. Shiftlet deceives both of them, **Mrs. Crater and her.** [The appositive, *Mrs. Crater and her,* refers to the object of the preposition, *them,* which is in the objective case.]

**4g.** The pronoun *who* (*whoever*) is in the nominative case. The pronoun *whom* (*whomever*) is in the objective case.

**EXAMPLES**
**Who** wrote *Dangling Man*? [*Who* is the subject of *wrote.*]
With **whom** did Moss Hart write the play? [*Whom* is the object of *with.*]

### PERSONAL PRONOUNS

#### SINGULAR

| | NOMINATIVE | OBJECTIVE | POSSESSIVE |
| --- | --- | --- | --- |
| FIRST PERSON | I | me | my, mine |
| SECOND PERSON | you | you | your, yours |
| THIRD PERSON | he, she, it | him, her, it | his, her, hers, its |

#### PLURAL

| | NOMINATIVE | OBJECTIVE | POSSESSIVE |
| --- | --- | --- | --- |
| FIRST PERSON | we | us | our, ours |
| SECOND PERSON | you | you | your, yours |
| THIRD PERSON | they | them | their, theirs |

**NOTE** Notice in the chart that *you* and *it* have the same forms for the nominative and the objective cases. All other personal pronouns have different forms for each case. Notice also that only third-person singular pronouns indicate gender.

For more information about possessive pronouns, see *its, it's* on page 1435, *their, there, they're* on page 1436, and *who's, whose* and *your, you're* on page 1437.

**4h.** A pronoun ending in *–self* or *–selves* should not be used in place of a personal pronoun.

**EXAMPLE**

Lupe and I [*not* myself] went to the ballet.

**4i.** A pronoun following *than* or *as* in an elliptical construction is in the same case as it would be if the construction were completed.

An **elliptical construction** is a clause from which words have been omitted. Notice how the meaning of each of the following sentences depends on the pronoun form in the elliptical construction.

| | |
|---|---|
| **NOMINATIVE CASE** | I have known Leigh longer **than she.** [I have known Leigh longer than she has known Leigh.] |
| **OBJECTIVE CASE** | I have known Leigh longer **than her.** [I have known Leigh longer than I have known her.] |

## CLEAR PRONOUN REFERENCE

**4j.** A pronoun should refer clearly to its antecedent. Avoid an ambiguous, a general, a weak, or an indefinite reference by (1) rephrasing the sentence, (2) replacing the pronoun with a noun, or (3) giving the pronoun a clear antecedent.

| | |
|---|---|
| **AMBIGUOUS** | Jody talked to Billy Buck while he was working. [*He* refers to either antecedent, *Jody* or *Billy Buck.*] |
| **CLEAR** | While Billy Buck was working, Jody talked to him. |
| **CLEAR** | While Jody was working, he talked to Billy Buck. |
| **GENERAL** | The wind rose, and dark clouds descended on the House of Usher. This seemed to bewilder Roderick. [*This* has no specific antecedent.] |
| **CLEAR** | The wind rose, and dark clouds descended on the House of Usher. These ominous conditions seemed to bewilder Roderick. |
| **CLEAR** | The rising wind and dark clouds that descended on the House of Usher seemed to bewilder Roderick. |
| **WEAK** | He was superstitious. One of these was that walking under a ladder brings bad luck. [The antecedent of *these* is not expressed.] |
| **CLEAR** | He was superstitious. One of his superstitions was that walking under a ladder brings bad luck. |
| **CLEAR** | He believed in many superstitions, one of which was that walking under a ladder brings bad luck. |
| **INDEFINITE** | In this history book, it refers to the American Civil War as the War Between the States. [*It* is unnecessary to the meaning of the sentence.] |
| **CLEAR** | This history book refers to the American Civil War as the War Between the States. |

# 5 USING MODIFIERS

## WHAT IS A MODIFIER?

A **modifier** is a word or group of words that limits the meaning of another word or group of words. The two kinds of modifiers are *adjectives* and *adverbs*.

## COMPARISON OF MODIFIERS

**5a.** *Comparison* refers to the change in the form of an adjective or an adverb to show increasing or decreasing degrees in the quality the modifier expresses.

The three degrees of comparison are *positive, comparative,* and *superlative.*

(1) Most one-syllable modifiers form the comparative and superlative degrees by adding *–er* (*less*) and *–est* (*least*).

(2) Some two-syllable modifiers form the comparative and superlative degrees by adding *–er* and *–est*; others form the comparative and superlative degrees by using *more* and *most*. All two-syllable modifiers form decreasing comparisons by using *less* and *least.*

(3) Modifiers of more than two syllables form the comparative and superlative degrees by using *more* (*less*) and *most* (*least*).

| POSITIVE | COMPARATIVE | SUPERLATIVE |
|---|---|---|
| neat | neater | neatest |
| simple | less simple | least simple |
| calmly | more calmly | most calmly |
| optimistic | less optimistic | least optimistic |

**(4)** Some modifiers form the comparative and superlative degrees in other ways.

| POSITIVE | COMPARATIVE | SUPERLATIVE |
|---|---|---|
| bad | worse | worst |
| far | farther (further) | farthest (furthest) |
| good (well) | better | best |
| little | less | least |
| many (much) | more | most |

**5b.** Use the comparative degree when comparing two things. Use the superlative degree when comparing more than two.

**COMPARATIVE**   Although both puppies look cute, the **more active** one seems **healthier.**

**SUPERLATIVE**   Of the four plays that we saw, I think *Death of a Salesman* was the **most moving.**

**5c.** Avoid a double comparison or a double negative. A *double comparison* is the use of two comparative forms (usually –*er* and *more*) or two superlative forms (usually –*est* and *most*) to modify the same word. A *double negative* is the use of two negative words when one is enough.

**EXAMPLES**
Samuel Clemens is **better** [*not* more better] known as Mark Twain.
She did**n't** say **anything** [*not* nothing].

**5d.** Include the word *other* or *else* when comparing one member of a group with the rest of the group.

**EXAMPLE**
Esteban is taller than anyone **else** on the team.

**5e.** Avoid comparing items that cannot logically be compared.

**ILLOGICAL**   Hemingway's style is perhaps more imitated than any other American writer. [illogical comparison between a style and a writer]

**LOGICAL**   Hemingway's style is perhaps more imitated than any other American writer's (style). [logical comparison of styles]

## PLACEMENT OF MODIFIERS

**5f.** Avoid using a *misplaced modifier*—a modifying word, phrase, or clause that sounds awkward because it modifies the wrong word or group of words.

To correct a misplaced modifier, place the word, phrase, or clause as close as possible to the word or words you intend it to modify.

**MISPLACED**   Thoreau listened intently to the song of a distant robin looking at the glittering pond. [Was the robin or Thoreau looking at the pond?]

**CLEAR**   **Looking at the glittering pond,** Thoreau listened intently to the song of a distant robin.

For information about phrases, see 6a–g. For more on clauses, see 7a–g.

**5g.** Avoid using a *dangling modifier*—a modifying word, phrase, or clause that does not sensibly modify any word or words in a sentence.

You may correct a dangling modifier by
- adding a word or words that the dangling word, phrase, or clause can sensibly refer to
- adding a word or words to the dangling word, phrase, or clause
- rewording the sentence

**DANGLING**   Alone, the mountain is virtually impossible to climb. [Who or what is alone?]

**CLEAR**   **For a person alone,** the mountain is virtually impossible to climb.

**CLEAR**   The mountain is virtually impossible **for a person** to climb **alone.**

**DANGLING**   After winning the Pulitzer Prize, the novel *Maud Martha* was written. [Who won the Pulitzer Prize?]

**CLEAR**   After winning the Pulitzer Prize, **Gwendolyn Brooks wrote** the novel *Maud Martha.*

**CLEAR**   After **Gwendolyn Brooks won** the Pulitzer Prize, **she wrote** the novel *Maud Martha.*

## 6a.
A *phrase* is a group of related words that is used as a single part of speech and that does not contain a verb and its subject.

**EXAMPLES**
**At two o'clock** [adverb phrase], the event **of the year** [adjective phrase], the company picnic, **will commence** [verb phrase].

## THE PREPOSITIONAL PHRASE

## 6b.
A *prepositional phrase* begins with a preposition and ends with the *object of the preposition,* a word or word group that functions as a noun.

**EXAMPLES**
**On the pillow** was a strand **of gray hair.** [The noun *pillow* is the object of the preposition *on.* The noun *hair* is the object of the preposition *of.*]
*Brian's Song* is an inspiring story **about friendship and courage.** [Both *friendship* and *courage* are objects of the preposition *about.*]

**(1)** An *adjective phrase* is a prepositional phrase that modifies a noun or a pronoun. An adjective phrase usually follows the word it modifies. That word may be the object of another preposition.

**EXAMPLES**
Cassie Soldierwolf made a batch **of fry bread,** using a recipe very similar to that **of her ancestors.** [*Of fry bread* modifies the noun *batch. Of her ancestors* modifies the pronoun *that.*]
Sarah Kemble Knight kept a journal **of her trip to New York.** [*Of her trip* modifies the noun *journal. To New York* modifies *trip,* which serves as the object of the preposition *of.*]

More than one adjective phrase may modify the same word.

**EXAMPLE**
Sarah Kemble Knight's journey **on horseback from Boston to New York** was long and difficult. [*On horseback, from Boston,* and *to New York* modify the noun *journey.*]

**(2)** An *adverb phrase* is a prepositional phrase that modifies a verb, an adjective, or an adverb. An adverb phrase tells *how, when, where, why,* or *to what extent* (*how long* or *how far*).

More than one adverb phrase can modify the same word. Also, an adverb phrase can precede or follow the word it modifies.

**EXAMPLES**
**During the Civil War,** Louisa May Alcott worked **in a hospital as a nurse for six weeks.** [Each phrase modifies the verb *worked. During the Civil War* tells *when, in a hospital* tells *where, as a nurse* tells *how,* and *for six weeks* tells *how long.*]

## VERBALS AND VERBAL PHRASES

A *verbal* is a form of a verb used as a noun, an adjective, or an adverb. A *verbal phrase* consists of a verbal and any of its modifiers or complements.

# Participles and Participial Phrases

## 6c.
A *participle* is a verb form that is used as an adjective. A *participial phrase* consists of a participle and all words related to the participle.

There are two kinds of participles—the *present participle* and the *past participle.*

**(1)** **Present participles** end in *–ing.*

**EXAMPLES**
The explorer could hear something **moving in the brush.** [The participial phrase modifies the pronoun *something. In the brush* is an adverb phrase modifying the present participle *moving.*]
A mountain lion stood there **watching him.** [The participial phrase modifies the noun *mountain lion.* The pronoun *him* is the direct object of the present participle *watching.*]

**(2)** Most **past participles** end in *–d* or *–ed.* Others are irregularly formed.

**EXAMPLES**
**Obsessed with revenge,** Captain Ahab pursued the white whale. [The participial phrase modifies the noun *Captain Ahab.* The adverb phrase *with revenge* modifies the past participle *obsessed.*]
Samuel Clemens, **better known as Mark Twain,** was born in Florida, Missouri, in 1835. [The participial phrase modifies the noun *Samuel Clemens.* The adverb *better* and the adverb phrase *as Mark Twain* modify the past participle *known.*]

Do not confuse a participle used as an adjective with a participle used as part of a verb phrase.

**ADJECTIVE** The Vietnam Veterans Memorial, **designed** by Maya Ying Lin, is made of black granite.

**VERB PHRASE** The Vietnam Veterans Memorial, which **was designed** by Maya Ying Lin, is made of black granite.

 For information about misplaced participial phrases, see 5f.

## Gerunds and Gerund Phrases

**6d.** A *gerund* is a verb form ending in *–ing* that is used as a noun. A *gerund phrase* consists of a gerund and all words related to the gerund.

**EXAMPLES**
**Exercising regularly** is important for maintaining good health. [The gerund phrase is the subject of the verb *is*. The adverb *regularly* modifies the gerund *exercising*.]

Dexter enjoyed **working at the golf club.** [The gerund phrase is the direct object of the verb *enjoyed*. The adverb phrase *at the golf club* modifies the gerund *working*.]

Walter Mitty daydreamed of **being a pilot.** [The gerund phrase is the object of the preposition *of*. The noun *pilot* is a predicate nominative completing the meaning of the gerund *being*.]

One way to build your vocabulary is **reading good literature.** [The gerund phrase is a predicate nominative explaining the subject *way*. *Literature* is the direct object of the gerund *reading*.]

Do not confuse a gerund with a present participle used as an adjective or as part of a verb phrase.

**GERUND** I enjoy **reading** at night. [direct object of the verb *enjoy*]

**PRESENT PARTICIPLE** I sometimes fall asleep **reading** at night. [adjective modifying the pronoun *I*]

**PRESENT PARTICIPLE** Sometimes, I listen to classical music while I am **reading** at night. [part of the verb phrase *am reading*]

 **NOTE** A noun or pronoun directly before a gerund takes the possessive case.

**EXAMPLES**
**Grandad's** cooking tastes great.
The bandleader said that he was pleased with **our** marching.

## Infinitives and Infinitive Phrases

**6e.** An *infinitive* is a verb form that can be used as a noun, an adjective, or an adverb. An infinitive usually begins with *to*. An *infinitive phrase* consists of an infinitive and all words related to the infinitive.

### NOUNS
**To find Moby-Dick** was Ahab's burning ambition. [The infinitive phrase is the subject of *was. Moby-Dick* is the direct object of the infinitive *to find*.]

Ahab's burning ambition was **to find Moby-Dick.** [The infinitive phrase is a predicate nominative identifying the subject *ambition*.]

### ADJECTIVES
Napoleon's plan **to conquer the world** failed. [The infinitive phrase modifies the noun *plan. World* is the direct object of the infinitive *to conquer*.]

The one **to ask** is your guidance counselor. [The infinitive modifies the pronoun *one*.]

### ADVERBS
With his dog Wolf, Rip Van Winkle went into the woods **to hunt squirrels.** [The infinitive phrase modifies *went. Squirrels* is the direct object of the infinitive *to hunt*.]

Nearly everyone was reluctant **to speak to her.** [The infinitive phrase modifies *reluctant*. The adverb phrase *to her* modifies the infinitive *to speak*.]

The word *to*, the sign of the infinitive, is sometimes omitted.

**EXAMPLE**
Will you help [to] dry the dishes?

 **NOTE** Do not confuse an infinitive with a prepositional phrase that begins with *to*.

**INFINITIVES** **To have** a friend, you need **to be** a friend.

**PREPOSITIONAL PHRASES** Give one sample **to each** of the customers, and return the rest **to Rhonda.**

## The Infinitive Clause

**6f.** Unlike other verbals, an infinitive may have a subject. Such a construction is called an *infinitive clause*.

**EXAMPLE**
Our teacher asked **us to read "Thanatopsis."** [*Us* is the subject of the infinitive *to read*. The entire infinitive clause is the direct object of *asked*.]

## APPOSITIVES AND APPOSITIVE PHRASES

**6g.** An *appositive* is a noun or a pronoun placed beside (usually after) another noun or pronoun to identify or explain it. An *appositive phrase* consists of an appositive and its modifiers.

An appositive or appositive phrase usually follows the word it identifies or explains.

### EXAMPLES

We went to the Navajo Gallery in Taos, New Mexico, to see R. C. Gorman's artwork *Freeform Lady.* [The appositive *Freeform Lady* identifies the noun *artwork.*]

Can you believe that I **myself** plan to become a writer? [The pronoun *myself* refers to the pronoun *I.*]

For emphasis, however, an appositive or appositive phrase may come at the beginning of a sentence.

### EXAMPLE

**A young painter,** Jaune Quick-to-See Smith shows a deep awareness of her French, Shoshone, and Cree heritage.

Appositives are sometimes introduced by a colon or by the expressions *or, namely, such as, for example, i.e.,* or *e.g.*

### EXAMPLES

The homeless shelter is accepting donations of the following items: canned **foods, blankets,** and winter **coats.**

Beneficial insects, **such as ladybugs** and **praying mantises,** can help control the population of harmful insects in a garden.

 For information on how to punctuate appositives, see 12k.

# 7 CLAUSES

**7a.** A *clause* is a group of words that contains a verb and its subject and that is used as part of a sentence. There are two kinds of clauses: the *independent clause* and the *subordinate clause.*

## THE INDEPENDENT CLAUSE

**7b.** An *independent* (or *main*) *clause* expresses a complete thought and can stand by itself as a sentence.

### EXAMPLE

    SUBJECT       VERB

**Emily Dickinson wrote** nearly eighteen hundred poems.

## THE SUBORDINATE CLAUSE

**7c.** A *subordinate* (or *dependent*) *clause* does not express a complete thought and cannot stand alone as a sentence.

### EXAMPLE

    SUBJECT   VERB

that   **we**    **read**

The thought expressed by a subordinate clause becomes complete when the clause is combined with an independent clause.

### EXAMPLE

The last book **that we read** was *Blue Highways.*

## The Adjective Clause

**7d.** An *adjective clause* is a subordinate clause that modifies a noun or a pronoun.

An adjective clause follows the word or words that it modifies. Usually, an adjective clause begins with a relative pronoun, which (1) relates the adjective clause to the word or words the clause modifies and (2) performs a function within the adjective clause.

### EXAMPLE

Li recommends every poem **that Denise Levertov has written.** [The relative pronoun *that* relates the adjective clause to the noun *poem* and serves as the direct object of the verb *has written.*]

An adjective clause may begin with a relative adverb, such as *when* or *where.*

### EXAMPLE

From 1914 to 1931, Isak Dinesen lived in Kenya, **where she operated a coffee plantation.**

Sometimes the relative pronoun or relative adverb is not expressed.

**EXAMPLE**
The book [that] **I am reading** is a biography.

## The Noun Clause

**7e.** A *noun clause* is a subordinate clause that may be used as a subject, a predicate nominative, a direct object, an indirect object, or an object of a preposition.

Words commonly used to introduce noun clauses include *how, that, what, whether, who,* and *why.*

**EXAMPLES**
A catchy slogan is **what we will need for this campaign.** [predicate nominative]
Emerson liked **what Whitman wrote.** [direct object]
The director will give **whoever does best in this audition** the lead role. [indirect object]

The word that introduces a noun clause may or may not have another function in the clause.

**EXAMPLES**
Do any of you know **who wrote *Spoon River Anthology*?** [The word *who* introduces the noun clause and serves as subject of the verb *wrote.*]
She told Walter **that he was driving too fast and should slow down.** [The word *that* introduces the noun clause but does not have any function within the noun clause.]

The word that introduces a noun clause is not always expressed.

**EXAMPLE**
I think [that] **I've read all of Langston Hughes's poetry.**

## The Adverb Clause

**7f.** An *adverb clause* is a subordinate clause that modifies a verb, an adjective, or an adverb.

An adverb clause, which may come before or after the word or words it modifies, tells *how, when, where, why, to what extent,* or *under what condition.* An adverb clause is introduced by a **subordinating conjunction**—a word or word group that relates the adverb clause to the word or words the clause modifies.

**EXAMPLES**
William Cullen Bryant wrote the first version of "Thanatopsis" **when he was a teenager.** [The adverb clause modifies the verb *wrote,* telling *when* Bryant wrote the first version.]
Zoë can explain naturalism to you better **than I can.** [The adverb clause modifies the adverb *better,* telling *to what extent* Zoë can better explain naturalism.]

**NOTE** An adverb clause that begins a sentence is always set off by a comma.

## The Elliptical Clause

**7g.** Part of a clause may be left out when the meaning can be understood from the context of the sentence. Such a clause is called an *elliptical clause.*

**EXAMPLES**
Roger knew the rules better **than Elgin [did].**
**While [he was] living at Walden Pond,** Thoreau wrote his first book.

 For information about using pronouns in elliptical clauses, see 4i.

# 8 SENTENCE STRUCTURE

## SENTENCE OR FRAGMENT?

**8a.** A *sentence* is a group of words that has a subject and a verb and expresses a complete thought.

**EXAMPLE**
Benjamin Franklin lived in London and in Paris.

Only a sentence should begin with a capital letter and end with either a period, a question mark, or an exclamation point. A group of words that either does not contain a subject and a verb or does not express a complete thought is called a **sentence fragment.**

| | |
|---|---|
| **FRAGMENT** | Collapses during a storm. |
| **SENTENCE** | The House of Usher collapses during a storm. |

For information about how to correct sentence fragments, see 9d. For information about using end marks with sentences, see 12a–e.

## SUBJECT AND PREDICATE

**8b.** A sentence consists of two parts: a subject and a predicate. A *subject* tells *whom* or *what* the sentence is about. A *predicate* tells something about the subject.

In the following examples, all the words labeled *subject* make up the **complete subject,** and all the words labeled *predicate* make up the **complete predicate.**

| SUBJECT | PREDICATE |
|---|---|
| Walt Whitman | wrote *Leaves of Grass.* |

| PREDICATE | SUBJECT | PREDICATE |
|---|---|---|
| Why did | Phoenix | walk to town? |

## The Simple Subject

**8c.** A *simple subject* is the main word or group of words that tells *whom* or *what* the sentence is about.

### EXAMPLE
**Harold Krebs,** the protagonist of the story, returns home from the war. [The complete subject is *Harold Krebs, the protagonist of the story.*]

## The Simple Predicate

**8d.** A *simple predicate* is a verb or verb phrase that tells something about the subject.

### EXAMPLE
**Did** Judy **marry** Dexter? [The complete predicate is *did marry Dexter.*]

## The Compound Subject and the Compound Verb

**8e.** A *compound subject* consists of two or more subjects that are joined by a conjunction—usually *and* or *or*—and that have the same verb.

### EXAMPLE
**Reuben** and **I** are preparing a report on "A Wagner Matinée."

**8f.** A *compound verb* consists of two or more verbs that are joined by a conjunction—usually *and, but,* or *or*—and that have the same subject.

### EXAMPLE
Kendra **recognized** the song but **had forgotten** its title.

## How to Find the Subject of a Sentence

**8g.** To find the subject of a sentence, ask *Who?* or *What?* before the verb.

**(1)** The subject of a sentence is never within a prepositional phrase.

### EXAMPLE
On the quarter-deck stood **Captain Ahab.** [Who stood? Captain Ahab stood. *Quarter-deck* is the object of the preposition *on.*]

**(2)** The subject of a sentence expressing a command or a request is always understood to be *you,* although *you* may not appear in the sentence.

**COMMAND** Identify two of the most striking characteristics of E. E. Cummings's poetry. [Who is being told to identify? *You* is understood.]

The subject of a command or a request is *you* even when a sentence contains a **noun of direct address**—a word naming the one or ones spoken to.

**REQUEST** Jordan, [you] please read aloud Jimmy Santiago Baca's "Fall."

**(3)** The subject of a sentence expressing a question usually follows the verb or a part of the verb phrase. Turning the question into a statement will often help you find the subject.

**QUESTION** Was Pearl Buck awarded the Nobel Prize in literature in 1938? [Who was awarded?]

**STATEMENT** **Pearl Buck** was awarded the Nobel Prize in literature in 1938.

**QUESTION** Where is the dog's leash? [Where is what?]

**STATEMENT** The dog's **leash** is where.

**(4)** The word *there* or *here* is never the subject of a sentence.

### EXAMPLE
Here are your **gloves.** [What are here? Gloves are.]

## COMPLEMENTS

**8h.** A *complement* is a word or a group of words that completes the meaning of a verb. There are four main kinds of complements: *direct object, indirect object, objective complement,* and *subject complement.*

## The Direct Object and the Indirect Object

**8i.** A *direct object* is a noun, a pronoun, or a word group that functions as a noun and tells *who* or *what* receives the action of a transitive verb.

**EXAMPLES**
Kerry called **me** at noon. [called whom? me]
Captain Ahab sacrifices his **ship** and almost **all** of his crew. [sacrifices what? ship and all—compound direct object]

**8j.** An *indirect object* is a word or word group that comes between a transitive verb and a direct object. An indirect object, which may be a noun, a pronoun, or a word group that functions as a noun, tells *to whom* or *to what* or *for whom* or *for what* the action of the verb is done.

**EXAMPLES**
Emily Dickinson sent **Thomas Wentworth Higginson** four poems. [sent to whom? Thomas Wentworth Higginson]
Ms. Cruz showed **José** and **me** pictures of her trip to Walden Pond. [showed to whom? José and me—compound indirect object]

**NOTE** A sentence that has an indirect object must always have a direct object as well.

 For more information about verbs, see 3a–e.

## The Objective Complement

**8k.** An *objective complement* is a word or word group that helps complete the meaning of a transitive verb by identifying or modifying the direct object. An objective complement, which may be a noun, a pronoun, an adjective, or a word group that functions as a noun or adjective, almost always follows the direct object.

**EXAMPLES**
Everyone considered her **dependable.** [The adjective *dependable* modifies the direct object *her.*]
Many literary historians call Poe **the master of the macabre.** [The word group *the master of the macabre* modifies the direct object *Poe.*]

## The Subject Complement

**8l.** A *subject complement* is a word or word group that completes the meaning of a linking verb and identifies or modifies the subject. There are two kinds of subject complements: the *predicate nominative* and the *predicate adjective.*

**(1)** A *predicate nominative* is the word or group of words that follows a linking verb and refers to the same person or thing as the subject of the verb.

A predicate nominative may be a noun, a pronoun, or a word group that functions as a noun.

**EXAMPLES**
Of the three applicants, Carlos is the most competent **one.** [The pronoun *one* refers to the subject *Carlos.*]
The main characters are **Aunt Georgiana** and **Clark.** [The nouns *Aunt Georgiana* and *Clark* refer to the subject *characters.*]

**(2)** A *predicate adjective* is an adjective that follows a linking verb and modifies the subject of the verb.

**EXAMPLES**
Eben Flood felt very **lonely.** [The adjective *lonely* modifies the subject *Eben Flood.*]
Shiftlet is **sly** and **scheming.** [The adjectives *sly* and *scheming* modify the subject *Shiftlet.*]

### SENTENCES CLASSIFIED ACCORDING TO STRUCTURE

**8m.** According to structure, sentences are classified as *simple, compound, complex,* and *compound-complex.*

**(1)** A *simple sentence* has one independent clause and no subordinate clauses.

**EXAMPLE**
Thornton Wilder's *Our Town* is one of my favorite plays.

**(2)** A *compound sentence* has two or more independent clauses but no subordinate clauses.

**EXAMPLE**
Jack London was a prolific writer; he wrote nearly fifty books in less than twenty years. [two independent clauses joined by a semicolon]

**NOTE** Do not confuse a simple sentence that has a compound subject or a compound verb with a compound sentence.

**(3)** A *complex sentence* has one independent clause and at least one subordinate clause.

**EXAMPLE**
Before we read *The Great Gatsby,* let's talk about the Jazz Age. [The independent clause is *let's talk about the Jazz Age.* The subordinate clause is *before we read* The Great Gatsby.]

**(4)** A *compound-complex* sentence has two or more independent clauses and at least one subordinate clause.

**EXAMPLE**
The two eyewitnesses told the police officer what they saw, but their accounts of the accident were quite different. [The two independent clauses are *the two eyewitnesses told the police officer* and *their accounts of the accident were quite different.* The subordinate clause is *what they saw.*]

## SENTENCES CLASSIFIED ACCORDING TO PURPOSE

**8n.** Sentences may be classified according to purpose.

**(1)** A *declarative sentence* makes a statement. It is followed by a period.

**EXAMPLE**
Swimming fast toward the ship was the white whale.

**(2)** An *interrogative sentence* asks a question. It is followed by a question mark.

**EXAMPLE**
Have you ever read *Blue Highways*?

**(3)** An *imperative sentence* makes a request or gives a command. It is usually followed by a period. A strong command, however, is followed by an exclamation point.

**EXAMPLES**
Please give me the dates for the class meetings.
Read Act I of *A Raisin in the Sun* by tomorrow.
Help me!

**(4)** An *exclamatory sentence* expresses strong feeling or shows excitement. It is followed by an exclamation point.

**EXAMPLE**
What a noble leader he was!

# 9 SENTENCE STYLE

## WAYS TO ACHIEVE CLARITY

### Coordinating Ideas

**9a.** To *coordinate* two or more ideas, or to give them equal emphasis, link them with a connecting word, an appropriate mark of punctuation, or both.

**EXAMPLE**
Edgar Allan Poe wrote "The Raven"; Edgar Lee Masters wrote *Spoon River Anthology.*

### Subordinating Ideas

**9b.** To *subordinate* an idea, or to show that one idea is related to but less important than another, use an adverb clause or an adjective clause.

An *adverb clause* begins with a subordinating conjunction, which shows how the adverb clause relates to the main clause. Usually, the relationship is *time, cause or reason, purpose or result,* or *condition.*

**EXAMPLES**
**Whenever I think of Boston,** I think of the Lowells. [time]
Janet got a lead role in *Our Town* **because she is one of the best actors in our school.** [cause]
Let's finish now **so that we won't have to come back tomorrow.** [purpose]

An *adjective clause* usually begins with *who, whom, whose, which, that,* or *where.*

**EXAMPLE**
Tamisha is the one **whose essay won first prize.**

 For more about adjective clauses and adverb clauses, see 7d and f.

### Using Parallel Structure

**9c.** Use the same grammatical form (*parallel structure*) to express ideas of equal weight.

1. Use parallel structure when you link coordinate ideas.

**EXAMPLE**
The company guaranteed **that salaries would be increased and that working days would be shortened.** [noun clause paired with noun clause]

2. Use parallel structure when you compare or contrast ideas.

**EXAMPLE**
**Thinking** logically is as important as **calculating** accurately. [gerund compared with gerund]

3. Use parallel structure when you link ideas with correlative conjunctions (such as *both . . . and, either . . . or, neither . . . nor,* and *not only . . . but also*).

**EXAMPLE**
With *Ship of Fools,* Katherine Anne Porter proved she was talented not only **as a short-story writer** but also **as a novelist.** [Note that the correlative conjunctions come directly before the parallel terms.]

When you revise for parallel structure, you may need to repeat an article, a preposition, or a pronoun before each of the parallel terms.

| UNCLEAR | Through Kate Chopin's stories, we can learn almost as much about the author as the social condition of women in her era. |
| CLEAR | Through Kate Chopin's stories, we can learn almost as much **about** the author as **about** the social condition of women in her era. |

## OBSTACLES TO CLARITY

### Sentence Fragments

**9d.** Avoid using a *sentence fragment*— a word or word group that either does not contain a subject and a verb or does not express a complete thought.

Attach the fragment to the sentence that comes before or after it, or add words to or delete words from the fragment to make it a complete sentence.

| FRAGMENT | Nina Otero was one of the first Mexican American women. To hold a major public post in New Mexico. |
| SENTENCE | Nina Otero was one of the first Mexican American women **to hold a major public post in New Mexico.** |

☞ For more information about sentence fragments, see 8a.

### Run-on Sentences

**9e.** Avoid using a *run-on sentence*—two or more complete thoughts that run together as if they were one complete thought.

There are two kinds of run-on sentences.

- A *fused sentence* has no punctuation at all between the complete thoughts.
- A *comma splice* has just a comma between the complete thoughts.

| FUSED SENTENCE | Emerson praised Whitman's poetry most other poets sharply criticized it. |
| COMMA SPLICE | Emerson praised Whitman's poetry, most other poets sharply criticized it. |

You may correct a run-on sentence in one of the following ways. Depending on the relationship you want to show between ideas, facts, and other information, one method will often prove to be more effective than another.

1. Make two sentences.

**EXAMPLE**
Emerson praised Whitman's poetry**.** **M**ost other poets sharply criticized it.

2. Use a comma and a coordinating conjunction.

**EXAMPLE**
Emerson praised Whitman's poetry**,** **but** most other poets sharply criticized it.

3. Change one of the independent clauses to a subordinate clause.

**EXAMPLE**
Emerson praised Whitman's poetry, **while most other poets sharply criticized it.**

4. Use a semicolon.

**EXAMPLE**
Emerson praised Whitman's poetry**;** most other poets sharply criticized it.

5. Use a semicolon and a conjunctive adverb followed by a comma.

**EXAMPLE**
Emerson praised Whitman's poetry**; however,** most other poets sharply criticized it.

## Unnecessary Shifts in Sentences

**9f.** Avoid making unnecessary shifts in subject, in verb tense, and in voice.

| | |
|---|---|
| **AWKWARD** | Athletes should be at the parking lot by 7:00 so that you can leave by 7:15. [shift in subject] |
| **BETTER** | **Athletes** should be at the parking lot by 7:00 so that **they** can leave by 7:15. |
| **AWKWARD** | She walked into the room, and she says, "The lights of the car outside are on." [shift in verb tense] |
| **BETTER** | She **walked** into the room, and she **said,** "The lights of the car outside are on." |
| **AWKWARD** | Russell Means starred as Chingachgook in *The Last of the Mohicans,* and an outstanding performance was delivered. [shift in voice] |
| **BETTER** | Russell Means **starred** as Chingachgook in *The Last of the Mohicans* and **delivered** an outstanding performance. |

## REVISING FOR VARIETY

**9g.** Use a variety of sentence beginnings.

The following examples show how a writer can revise sentences to avoid beginning with the subject every time.

| | |
|---|---|
| **SUBJECT FIRST** | *Billy Budd* was published in 1924 and helped revive an interest in Melville's other works. |
| **PARTICIPIAL PHRASE FIRST** | **Published in 1924,** *Billy Budd* helped revive an interest in Melville's other works. |
| **PREPOSITIONAL PHRASE FIRST** | **In 1924,** *Billy Budd* was published and helped revive interest in Melville's other works. |
| **ADVERB CLAUSE FIRST** | **When *Billy Budd* was published in 1924,** it helped revive interest in Melville's other works. |

## Varying Sentence Structure

**9h.** Use a mix of simple, compound, complex, and compound-complex sentences in your writing.

The following paragraph shows a mix of sentence structures.

San Francisco is famous for its scenic views. [simple] Because the city sprawls over forty-two hills, driving through San Francisco is like riding a roller coaster. [complex] Atop one of San Francisco's hills is Chinatown; atop another is Coit Tower. [compound] The most popular place to visit is the San Francisco Bay area, where the Golden Gate Bridge and Fisherman's Wharf attract a steady stream of tourists. [complex]

 For information about the four types of sentence structure, see 8m.

## Revising to Reduce Wordiness

**9i.** Avoid using unnecessary words in your writing.

The following guidelines suggest some ways to revise wordy sentences.

**1.** Take out a whole group of unnecessary words.

| | |
|---|---|
| **WORDY** | After climbing down to the edge of the river, we boarded a small houseboat that was floating there on the surface of the water. |
| **BETTER** | After climbing down to the edge of the river, we boarded a small houseboat. |

**2.** Replace pretentious words and expressions with straightforward ones.

| | |
|---|---|
| **WORDY** | The young woman, who was at some indeterminate point in her teenage years, sported through her hair a streak of pink dye that could be considered extremely garish. |
| **BETTER** | The **teenager** sported a streak of **shocking**-pink dye in her hair. |

**3.** Reduce a clause to a phrase.

| | |
|---|---|
| **WORDY** | Emily Dickinson fell in love with Charles Wadsworth, who was a Presbyterian minister. |
| **BETTER** | Emily Dickinson fell in love with Charles Wadsworth, **a Presbyterian minister.** |

**4.** Reduce a phrase or a clause to one word.

| | |
|---|---|
| **WORDY** | One of the writers from the South was William Faulkner. |
| **BETTER** | One of the **Southern** writers was William Faulkner. |

# 10 SENTENCE COMBINING

## COMBINING SENTENCES FOR VARIETY

## Combining by Inserting Words and Phrases

**10a.** Combine related sentences by taking a key word (or using another form of the word) from one sentence and inserting it into another.

ORIGINAL  Jack London describes the man's attempt to build a fire. The description is vivid.

COMBINED  Jack London **vividly** describes the man's attempt to build a fire. [The adjective *vivid* becomes the adverb *vividly.*]

**10b.** Combine related sentences by taking (or creating) a phrase from one sentence and inserting it into another.

ORIGINAL  Our class is reading "Everyday Use." It is by Alice Walker.

COMBINED  Our class is reading "Everyday Use" **by Alice Walker.** [prepositional phrase]

## Combining by Coordinating Ideas

**10c.** Combine related sentences whose ideas are equally important by using coordinating conjunctions (*and, but, or, nor, for, yet*) or correlative conjunctions (*both . . . and, either . . . or, neither . . . nor, not only . . . but also*).

The relationship of the ideas determines which connective will work best. When joined, the coordinate ideas form compound elements.

ORIGINAL  Robert Frost did not receive the Nobel Prize. Carl Sandburg never received it, either.

COMBINED  **Neither Robert Frost nor Carl Sandburg** received the Nobel Prize.

You can also form a compound sentence by linking independent clauses with a semicolon and a conjunctive adverb or with just a semicolon.

EXAMPLE
We planned to go swimming**; however,** the weather did not oblige.

## Combining by Subordinating Ideas

**10d.** Combine related sentences whose ideas are not equally important by placing the less important idea in a subordinate clause.

ORIGINAL  The National Air and Space Museum is in Washington, D.C. It contains exhibits on the history of aeronautics.

COMBINED  The National Air and Space Museum, **which contains exhibits on the history of aeronautics,** is in Washington, D.C. [adjective clause]

ORIGINAL  Shiftlet married Lucynell. He wanted her mother's car.

COMBINED  Shiftlet married Lucynell **because he wanted her mother's car.** [adverb clause]

ORIGINAL  Judy Jones was married. Devlin told Dexter this.

COMBINED  Devlin told Dexter **that Judy Jones was married.** [noun clause]

# 11 CAPITALIZATION

**11a.** Capitalize the first word in every sentence.

EXAMPLES
The author Leslie Marmon Silko was born in Albuquerque, New Mexico.
Stop!

(1) Capitalize the first word of a sentence following a colon.

EXAMPLE
The police commissioner issued a surprising statement: **I**n light of new evidence, the investigation of the Brooks burglary will be reopened.

**(2)** Capitalize the first word of a direct quotation that is a complete sentence.

**EXAMPLE**
When he finally surrendered in 1877, Chief Joseph declared, "From where the sun now stands I will fight no more forever."

When quoting from another writer's work, capitalize the first word of the quotation only if the writer has capitalized it in the original work.

**EXAMPLE**
When he finally surrendered in 1877, Chief Joseph declared that he would "fight no more forever."

 For more information about using capital letters in quotations, see 13c.

**(3)** Traditionally, the first word of a line of poetry is capitalized.

**EXAMPLES**
I placed a jar in Tennessee,
And round it was, upon a hill.
— Wallace Stevens, from "Anecdote of the Jar"

 **NOTE** Some writers, for reasons of style, do not follow this rule. When you quote from a writer's work, always use capital letters exactly as the writer uses them.

**11b.** Capitalize the first word in the salutation and the closing of a letter.

**EXAMPLES**
Dear Maria,    Dear Sir or Madam:    Sincerely,

| TYPE OF NAME | EXAMPLES | |
|---|---|---|
| **Countries** | Mozambique | Costa Rica |
| **Continents** | North America | Asia |
| **Islands** | Catalina Island | Isle of Pines |
| **Mountains** | Blue Ridge Mountains | Mount McKinley |
| **Other Land Forms and Features** | Cape Cod<br>Mojave Desert | Isthmus of Panama<br>Horse Cave |
| **Bodies of Water** | Great Lakes<br>Amazon River | Strait of Hormuz<br>Lake Huron |
| **Parks** | Mississippi Headwaters State Forest<br>Gates of the Arctic National Park | |
| **Roads, Highways, Streets** | Route 30<br>Interstate 55<br>Pennsylvania Turnpike | Michigan Avenue<br>Thirty-first Street<br>Morningside Drive |

*(continued)*

**11c.** Capitalize proper nouns and proper adjectives.

A **common noun** is a general name for a person, place, thing, or idea. A **proper noun** is the specific name of a particular person, place, thing, or idea. A **proper adjective** is formed from a proper noun. Common nouns are capitalized only if they begin a sentence (also, in most cases, a line of poetry) or a direct quotation or are part of a title.

| COMMON NOUNS | PROPER NOUNS | PROPER ADJECTIVES |
|---|---|---|
| poet | Homer | Homeric epithet |
| country | Russia | Russian diplomat |
| state | Hawaii | Hawaiian climate |

In most proper nouns made up of two or more words, do *not* capitalize articles (*a, an, the*), short prepositions (those with fewer than five letters, such as *at, of, for, to, with*), the mark of the infinitive (*to*), and coordinating conjunctions (*and, but, for, nor, or, so, yet*).

**EXAMPLES**
Army of the Potomac    "Writing to Persuade"

**(1)** Capitalize the names of most persons and animals.

| GIVEN NAMES | Julia | Richard |
|---|---|---|
| **SURNAMES** | Alvarez | Wright |
| **ANIMALS** | Moby-Dick | White Fang |

**(2)** Capitalize geographical names.

 **NOTE** The second word in a hyphenated number begins with a lowercase letter.

**EXAMPLES**
Forty-second Street
Eighty-ninth District

 In addresses, abbreviations such as *St., Ave., Dr.,* and *Blvd.* are capitalized. For more about abbreviations, see 12e.

| TYPE OF NAME | EXAMPLES | |
|---|---|---|
| **Towns, Cities** | **B**oston<br>**S**outh **B**end | **R**io de **J**aneiro<br>**St. P**etersburg |
| **Counties, Townships, Provinces** | **Y**oknapatawpha<br>**C**ounty | **L**awrence<br>**T**ownship |
| **States and Territories** | **W**isconsin<br>**Y**ukon **T**erritory | **N**uevo **L**eón<br>**T**he **V**irgin **I**slands |
| **Regions** | **N**ew **E**ngland<br>the **S**unbelt | the **W**est **C**oast<br>the **S**outhwest |

**NOTE** Words such as *north* and *western* are not capitalized when they indicate direction.

**EXAMPLES**

east of the river      driving southeast

☞ The abbreviations of names of states are always capitalized. For more about using and punctuating such abbreviations, see 12e.

**(3)** Capitalize the names of organizations, teams, business firms, institutions, buildings and other structures, and government bodies.

| TYPE OF NAME | EXAMPLES | |
|---|---|---|
| **Organizations** | **N**ational **S**cience **F**oundation<br>**G**uide **D**og **F**oundation for the **B**lind | **F**uture **F**armers of **A**merica<br>**D**isabled **A**merican **V**eterans |
| **Teams** | **D**etroit **P**istons<br>**H**arlem **G**lobetrotters | **C**edar **H**ill **B**ulldogs<br>**S**an **D**iego **P**adres |
| **Business Firms** | **G**eneral **E**lectric<br>**U**niversity **S**quare **M**all | **H**ip-**H**op **M**usic, **I**nc.<br>**L**a **F**iesta **R**estaurant |
| **Institutions** | **U**niversity of **C**alifornia, **L**os **A**ngeles<br>the **L**ibrary of **C**ongress | **M**ayo **C**linic<br>**H**abitat for **H**umanity |
| **Buildings and Other Structures** | **M**eadowlawn **J**unior **H**igh **S**chool<br>the **P**yramid of **K**hufu | the **G**olden **G**ate **B**ridge<br>**R**ialto **T**heater |
| **Government Bodies** | **A**tomic **E**nergy **C**ommission<br>**F**ederal **B**ureau of **I**nvestigation | **U**nited **S**tates **M**arine **C**orps<br>**H**ouse of **R**epresentatives |

**(4)** Capitalize the names of historical events and periods, special events, holidays and other calendar items, and time zones.

| TYPE OF NAME | EXAMPLES | |
|---|---|---|
| **Historical Events and Periods** | **B**oston **T**ea **P**arty<br>**B**attle of **S**aratoga<br>**M**iddle **A**ges | **R**oaring **T**wenties<br>**F**rench **R**evolution<br>**M**esozoic **E**ra |
| **Special Events** | **O**lympics<br>**E**arth **S**ummit | **O**hio **S**tate **F**air<br>**S**unshine **F**estival |
| **Holidays and Other Calendar Items** | **W**ednesday<br>**S**eptember | **F**ourth of **J**uly<br>**H**ispanic **H**eritage **M**onth |
| **Time Zones** | **M**ountain **S**tandard **T**ime (**MST**)<br>**E**astern **D**aylight **T**ime (**EDT**) | |

**NOTE** Do not capitalize the name of a season unless the season is being personified or unless it is used as part of a proper noun.

**EXAMPLES**

The winter was unusually warm.

Overnight, **W**inter crept in, trailing her snowy veil.

We plan to attend the school's **W**inter **C**arnival.

**(5)** Capitalize the brand names of business products.

**EXAMPLES**

Borden milk     Colonial bread     Zenith television

Notice in these examples that the noun that follows a brand name is not capitalized. Also, over time, some brand names become common nouns. To find out if a name is a brand name, consult a current dictionary.

| TYPE OF NAME | EXAMPLES | |
|---|---|---|
| **Ships** | *Cunard Princess* | **U.S.S.** *Forrestal* |
| **Trains** | *Orient Express* | **North Coast Limited** |
| **Aircraft** | *Spirit of St. Louis* | **Air Force One** |
| **Spacecraft** | *Atlantis* | *Apollo 11* |
| **Monuments** | **Lincoln Memorial** | **Statue of Liberty** |
| **Awards** | **Academy Award** | **Pulitzer Prize** |
| **Planets, Stars, Constellations** | **Jupiter** <br> **Ursa Minor** | **Orion** <br> the **Milky Way** |
| **Other Particular Things, Places, and Events** | **Underground Railroad** <br> **Silk Route** <br> **Hurricane Andrew** | **Treaty Oak** <br> **Valkyries** <br> **Marshall Plan** |

**11d.** Do not capitalize the names of school subjects, except for names of languages and course names followed by a number.

**EXAMPLES**

Spanish     chemistry     Chemistry II

**11e.** Capitalize titles.

**(1)** Capitalize a title belonging to a particular person when it comes before the person's name. Also capitalize abbreviations such as *Jr., M.D.,* and *Ph.D.* after a name.

**EXAMPLES**

General Davis     Ms. Diaz     President Kennedy
Rev. Martin Luther King, **Jr.**     Dr. Kerry Jones, **M.D.**

In general, do not capitalize a title used alone or following a name. Some titles, however, are by tradition

**(6)** Capitalize the names of nationalities, races, and peoples.

**EXAMPLES**

Chinese     Jewish     Hopi     Caucasian

**(7)** Capitalize the names of ships, trains, aircraft, spacecraft, monuments, awards, planets, and any other particular places, things, or events.

**NOTE** Do not capitalize the words *sun* and *moon*. Do not capitalize the word *earth* unless it is used along with the names of other heavenly bodies that are capitalized.

**EXAMPLES**

This orchid grows wild in only one place on earth.
Venus is closer to the sun than Earth is.

capitalized. If you are unsure of whether or not to capitalize a title, check in a dictionary.

**EXAMPLE**

Who is the **g**overnor of Kansas?

A title is usually capitalized when it is used alone in direct address.

**EXAMPLE**

Have you reached your decision, **Governor**?

**(2)** Capitalize words showing family relationships except when preceded by a possessive.

**EXAMPLES**

Aunt Amy     my **a**unt     Mother     Bill's **m**other

**(3)** Capitalize the names of religions and their followers, holy days and celebrations, holy writings, and specific deities and venerated beings.

| TYPE OF NAME | EXAMPLES | |
|---|---|---|
| **Religions and Followers** | Islam | **Roman Catholic** |
| **Holy Days and Celebrations** | Epiphany | **Rosh Hashanah** |
| **Holy Writings** | Bible | **U**panishads |
| **Specific Deities and Venerated Beings** | **G**od <br> the **P**rophet (**M**ohammed) | |

**NOTE** The words *god* and *goddess* are not capitalized when they refer to the deities of mythology. The names of specific mythological deities are capitalized, however.

**EXAMPLES**

The Greek **g**od of war was **A**res.

**(4)** Capitalize the first and last words and all important words in titles of books, periodicals, poems, stories, essays, speeches, plays, historical documents, movies, radio and television programs, works of art, musical compositions, and cartoons.

Unimportant words in a title include articles (*a, an, the*), short prepositions (those with fewer than five letters, such as *of, to, in, for, from, with*), and coordinating conjunctions (*and, but, for, nor, or, so, yet*).

| TYPE OF NAME | EXAMPLES |
|---|---|
| Books | *The Call of the Wild* |
| Periodicals | *Car and Driver* |
| Poems | "Once by the Pacific" |
| Stories | "The Fall of the House of Usher" |
| Essays and Speeches | "The Lost Worlds of Ancient America" "I Have a Dream" |
| Plays | *A Raisin in the Sun* |
| Historical Documents | Declaration of Independence |
| Movies | *Raiders of the Lost Ark* |
| Radio and TV Programs | *Star Trek: The Next Generation* |
| Works of Art | *Double Dutch on the Golden Gate Bridge* |
| Musical Compositions | "Lift Every Voice and Sing" |
| Cartoons | *Where I'm Coming From* |

 **NOTE** The article *the* before a title is not capitalized unless it is part of the official title. The official title of a book is found on the title page. The official title of a newspaper or periodical is found on the masthead (usually on the editorial page).

**EXAMPLES**
the *Odyssey*
the *Boston Herald*

*The Wall Street Journal*
*The Man in the Iron Mask*

 For information about which titles should be italicized and which should be enclosed in quotation marks, see 13a and d.

---

# 12 PUNCTUATION

## END MARKS

 For information about how sentences are classified according to purpose, see 8n.

**12a.** A statement (or declarative sentence) is followed by a period.

**EXAMPLE**
Felipe asked whether Edgar Allan Poe was primarily a poet, an essayist, or a short-story writer.

**12b.** A question (or interrogative sentence) is followed by a question mark.

**EXAMPLE**
Have you read any of Edgar Allan Poe's poetry?

**12c.** A request or command (or imperative sentence) is followed by either a period or an exclamation point.

**EXAMPLES**
Answer the phone, please.
Turn the music down now!

**12d.** An exclamation (or exclamatory sentence) is followed by an exclamation point.

**EXAMPLE**
What an imagination Edgar Allan Poe had!

 **NOTE** An exclamation point may be used after a single word (especially an interjection) as well as after a sentence.

**EXAMPLE**
Hey! Wait for me!

**12e.** An abbreviation is usually followed by a period.

(See the chart at the top of the next page for examples.)

Some common abbreviations, including many for units of measurement, are written without periods.

**EXAMPLES**
AM/FM, FBI, IOU, MTV, PC, ROTC, SOS, cc, db, ft, lb, kw, ml, psi, rpm [Use a period with the abbreviation *in.* (*inch*) to avoid confusion with the word *in.*]

| TYPE OF ABBREVIATION | EXAMPLES |
|---|---|
| **Personal Names** | N. Scott Momaday   E. A. Robinson |
| **Organizations and Companies** | Assn.   Co.   Corp.   Ltd.   Inc. |
| **Titles Used with Names** | Dr.   Jr.   Ms.   Ph.D. |
| **Times of Day** | A.M. (*or* a.m.)   P.M. (*or* p.m.) |
| **Years** | B.C. (*written after the date*)<br>A.D. (*written before the date*) |
| **Addresses** | Ave.   Blvd.   Dr.   St.   P.O. Box |
| **States** | Ark.   Fla.   R.I.   N. Mex. |

**NOTE** If an abbreviation has a period, do not place a period after it at the end of a sentence.

**NOTE** Two-letter state abbreviations without periods are used only when the ZIP Code is included.

**EXAMPLE**
Springfield, **MA** 01101

## COMMAS

**12f.** **Use commas to separate items in a series.**

**EXAMPLE**
The main characters are Huck, Tom, and Jim.

If all the items in a series are linked by *and, or,* or *nor,* do not use commas to separate them.

**EXAMPLE**
Saul Bellow **and** Isaac Bashevis Singer **and** Toni Morrison won Nobel Prizes.

**12g.** **Use a comma to separate two or more adjectives preceding a noun.**

**EXAMPLE**
Lincoln was a noble, compassionate, wise leader.

**12h.** **Use a comma before *and, but, or, nor, for, so,* and *yet* when they join independent clauses.**

**EXAMPLE**
I read an excerpt from Amy Tan's *The Joy Luck Club,* and now I want to read the entire book.

You may omit the comma before *and, but, or,* or *nor* if the clauses are very short and there is no chance of misunderstanding.

**12i.** **Use commas to set off nonessential clauses and nonessential participial phrases.**

A *nonessential* clause or phrase is one that can be left out without changing the meaning of the sentence.

| NONESSENTIAL CLAUSE | Eudora Welty, **who was born in Mississippi,** uses her home state in many of her stories. |
|---|---|
| NONESSENTIAL PHRASE | Lee, **noticing my confusion,** rephrased her question. |

An *essential* clause or phrase is one that can't be left out without changing the meaning of the sentence. Essential clauses and phrases are *not* set off by commas.

| ESSENTIAL CLAUSE | Material **that is quoted verbatim** should be placed in quotation marks. |
|---|---|
| ESSENTIAL PHRASE | The only word **spoken by the raven** is *nevermore.* |

**12j.** **Use a comma after certain introductory elements.**

**(1)** Use a comma after a one-word adverb such as *first, yes,* or *no* and after any mild exclamation such as *well* or *why* at the beginning of a sentence.

**EXAMPLE**
**Yes,** Hemingway is my favorite author.

**(2)** Use a comma after an introductory participial phrase or introductory adverb clause.

**EXAMPLES**
**Standing on the quarter-deck,** Captain Ahab spoke to his crew. [participial phrase]
**After he had driven around the lake several times,** he decided to go to the drive-in restaurant. [adverb clause]

**(3)** Use a comma after two or more introductory prepositional phrases.

**EXAMPLE**
**At the end of the story,** Walter Mitty imagines that he is facing a firing squad.

**12k.** **Use commas to set off elements that interrupt a sentence.**

**(1)** Appositives and appositive phrases are usually set off by commas.

**EXAMPLE**
My favorite book by Claude McKay, *Banjo,* was first published in 1929.

Sometimes an appositive is so closely related to the word or words it refers to that it should not be set off by commas.

**EXAMPLE**
The poet **Maya Angelou** read one of her poems on Inauguration Day.

**(2)** Words used in direct address are set off by commas.

**EXAMPLE**
Your essay, **Theo,** was well organized.

**(3)** Parenthetical expressions are set off by commas.

*Parenthetical expressions* are remarks that add incidental information or that relate ideas to each other.

**EXAMPLE**
Simón Bolívar liberated much of South America from Spanish rule; he went on, **moreover,** to become the most powerful person on the continent.

**12l.** Use a comma in certain conventional situations.

**(1)** Use a comma to separate items in dates and addresses.

**EXAMPLES**
On Friday, October 23, 1994, my niece Leslie was born.
Please address all further inquiries to 92 Keystone Crossings, Indianapolis, IN 46240. [Notice that a comma is not used between a state abbreviation and a ZIP Code.]

**(2)** Use a comma after the salutation of a friendly letter and after the closing of any letter.

**EXAMPLES**
Dear Rosa,       Sincerely yours,

**(3)** Use a comma to set off an abbreviation such as *Jr., Sr., RN, M.D., Ltd.,* or *Inc.*

**EXAMPLE**
Is Juan Fuentes, Jr., your cousin?

## SEMICOLONS

**12m.** Use a semicolon between independent clauses that are closely related in thought and are not joined by *and, but, for, nor, or, so,* or *yet.*

**EXAMPLE**
"Tart words make no friends; a spoonful of honey will catch more flies than a gallon of vinegar."
       —Benjamin Franklin, *Poor Richard's Almanack*

**12n.** Use a semicolon between independent clauses joined by a conjunctive adverb or a transitional expression.

A *conjunctive adverb* (such as *consequently, however,* or *therefore*) or a *transitional expression* (such as *as a result, for example,* or *in other words*) indicates the relationship of the independent clauses that it joins. Notice in the following example that a comma is placed after the conjunctive adverb.

**EXAMPLE**
Dexter knew that Judy was selfish and insensitive; **nevertheless,** he continued to adore her.

**12o.** Use a semicolon (rather than a comma) before a coordinating conjunction to join independent clauses that contain commas.

**EXAMPLE**
During the nineteenth century—the era of such distinguished poets as Longfellow, Whittier, and Holmes—most poetry was written in traditional metrical patterns; but one poet, Walt Whitman, rejected the conventional verse forms.

**12p.** Use a semicolon between items in a series if the items contain commas.

**EXAMPLE**
The summer reading list includes *Behind the Trail of Broken Treaties,* by Vine Deloria, Jr.; *House Made of Dawn,* by N. Scott Momaday; and *Blue Highways: A Journey into America,* by William Least Heat-Moon.

## COLONS

**12q.** Use a colon to mean "note what follows."

**(1)** Use a colon before a list of items, especially after expressions such as *as follows* and *the following.*

**EXAMPLE**
The magazine article profiles the following famous American authors of the nineteenth century: Edgar Allan Poe, Nathaniel Hawthorne, and Herman Melville.

 **NOTE**    Do not use a colon before a list that directly follows a verb or a preposition.

**EXAMPLE**
The anthology includes "The Raven," "Richard Cory," and "Thanatopsis." [The list directly follows the verb *includes.*]

**(2)** Use a colon before a quotation that lacks a speaker tag such as *he said* or *she remarked*.

**EXAMPLE**
Dad's orders were loud and clear**:** "Everybody up and at 'em."

**(3)** Use a colon before a long, formal statement or quotation.

**EXAMPLE**
Patrick Henry concluded his fiery speech before the Virginia House of Burgesses with these words**:** "Is life so dear, or peace so sweet, as to be purchased at the price of chains and slavery? Forbid it, Almighty God! I know not what course others may take; but as for me, give me liberty, or give me death!"

**12r.** Use a colon in certain conventional situations.

**EXAMPLES**
5**:**20 P.M. [between the hour and the minute]
Deuteronomy 5**:**6–21 [between chapter and verse in referring to passages from the Bible]
Dear Sir or Madam**:** [after the salutation of a business letter]
"Cold Kills**:** Hypothermia" [between a title and a subtitle]

# 13 PUNCTUATION

## ITALICS

*Italics* are printed characters that slant to the right. To indicate italics in handwritten or typewritten work, use underlining.

**PRINTED** Who wrote *Black Boy?*
**HANDWRITTEN** *Who wrote Black Boy?*

**13a.** Use italics (underlining) for titles of books, plays, long poems, periodicals, newspapers, works of art, films, television series, long musical compositions, recordings, comic strips, computer software, court cases, trains, ships, aircraft, and spacecraft.

| TYPE OF NAME | EXAMPLES | |
| --- | --- | --- |
| **Books** | *The Scarlet Letter* | *Fifth Chinese Daughter* |
| **Plays** | *The Crucible* | *West Side Story* |
| **Long Poems** | *I Am Joaquín* | the *Epic of Gilgamesh* |
| **Periodicals** | *Reader's Digest* | *Newsweek* |
| **Newspapers** | *The Wall Street Journal* | the *Austin American-Statesman* |
| **Works of Art** | *The Kiss* | *The Starry Night* |
| **Films** | *Forrest Gump* | *Stand and Deliver* |
| **TV Series** | *Jeopardy!* | *Star Trek: The Next Generation* |
| **Long Musical Compositions** | *Liverpool Oratorio* | *Hiawatha's Wedding Feast* |
| **Recordings** | *Achtung Baby* | *Sketches of Spain* |
| **Comic Strips** | *Peanuts* | *Calvin and Hobbes* |
| **Computer Software** | *WordPerfect* | *Paintbrush* |
| **Court Cases** | *Plessy v. Ferguson* | *Bailey v. Alabama* |
| **Trains, Ships** | *Empire Builder* | *Queen Mary* |
| **Aircraft, Spacecraft** | *Solar Challenger* | *Apollo 11* |

**NOTE** The article *the* before the title of a book, periodical, or newspaper is not italicized or capitalized unless it is part of the official title. The official title of a book appears on the title page. The official title of a periodical or newspaper is the name given on the masthead, which usually appears on the editorial page.

**EXAMPLES**
The article appeared in both the *Philadelphia Inquirer* and *The New York Times.*

☞ For examples of titles that are not italicized but that are enclosed in quotation marks, see 13d.

**13b.** **Use italics (underlining) for words, letters, numerals, and symbols referred to as such and for foreign words that have not been adopted into English.**

**EXAMPLES**

Should the use of *their* for *there* be considered a spelling error or a usage error?

The teacher couldn't tell whether I had written a script *S*, the number *5*, or an *&*.

All U.S. coins are now stamped with the inscription *e pluribus unum.*

## QUOTATION MARKS

**13c.** **Use quotation marks to enclose a** *direct quotation*—**a person's exact words.**

**EXAMPLE**

Chief Joseph said, "The earth is the mother of all people, and all people should have equal rights upon it."

Notice that a direct quotation begins with a capital letter. However, if the quotation is only part of a sentence, it does not begin with a capital letter.

**EXAMPLE**

Chief Joseph called the earth "the mother of all people."

**(I)** When the expression identifying the speaker divides a quoted sentence, the second part begins with a lowercase letter.

**EXAMPLE**

"I really have to leave now," said Gwen, "so that I will be on time." [Notice that each part of a divided quotation is enclosed in quotation marks.]

When the second part of a divided quotation is a new sentence, it begins with a capital letter.

**EXAMPLE**

"Teddy Roosevelt was the first U.S. President to express concern about the depletion of the nation's natural resources," explained Mr. Fuentes. "He established a conservation program that expanded the national park system."

**(2)** When used with quotation marks, other marks of punctuation are placed according to the following rules.

● Commas and periods are always placed inside the closing quotation marks.

**EXAMPLES**

"On the other hand," he said, "your decision may be correct."

● Semicolons and colons are always placed outside the closing quotation marks.

**EXAMPLES**

My neighbor said, "Sure, I'll buy a subscription"; it was lucky that I asked her on payday.

Edna St. Vincent Millay uses these devices in her poem "Spring": alliteration, slant rhyme, and personification.

● Question marks and exclamation points are placed inside the closing quotation marks if the quotation itself is a question or an exclamation. Otherwise, they are placed outside.

**EXAMPLES**

Was it you who wrote the poem "Upon Turning Seventeen"?

"What a tortured soul Reverend Dimmesdale is!" said Mr. Klein.

**(3)** When quoting a passage that consists of more than one paragraph, put quotation marks at the beginning of each paragraph and at the end of only the last paragraph.

**EXAMPLE**

"As he neared the house, each detail of the scene became vivid to him. He was aware of some bricks of the vanished chimney lying on the sod. There was a door which hung by one hinge.

"Rifle bullets called forth by the insistent skirmishers came from the far-off bank of foliage. They mingled with the shells and the pieces of shells until the air was torn in all directions by hootings, yells, howls. The sky was full of fiends who directed all their wild rage at his head."

—Stephen Crane, "A Mystery of Heroism"

**(4)** Use single quotation marks to enclose a quotation within a quotation.

**EXAMPLES**

The teacher requested, "Jorge, please explain what Emerson meant when he said, 'To be great is to be misunderstood.'"

"Have you read 'Rip Van Winkle'?" Jill asked.

**(5)** When writing *dialogue* (a conversation), begin a new paragraph every time the speaker changes, and enclose the speaker's words in quotation marks.

**EXAMPLE**

"How far is it to the Owl Creek bridge?" Farquhar asked.

"About thirty miles."

"Is there no force on this side the creek?"

"Only a picket post half a mile out, on the railroad, and a single sentinel at this end of the bridge."

—Ambrose Bierce, "An Occurrence at Owl Creek Bridge"

**13d.** Use quotation marks to enclose titles of short works, such as short stories, poems, essays, articles, songs, episodes of television series, and chapters and other parts of books.

| TYPE OF NAME | EXAMPLES | |
|---|---|---|
| Short Stories | "The Magic Barrel" | "The Tell-Tale Heart" |
| Poems | "The Latin Deli" | "Thanatopsis" |
| Essays | "On the Mall" | "The Creative Process" |
| Articles | "Old Poetry and Modern Music" | |
| Songs | "On Top of Old Smoky" | |
| TV Episodes | "The Flight of the Condor" | |
| Chapters and Parts of Books | "The World Was New" "The Colonies' Struggle for Freedom" | |

**NOTE** Neither italics nor quotation marks are used for titles of major religious works or titles of legal or historical documents.

**EXAMPLES**
Bible       Bill of Rights

☞ For a list of titles that are italicized rather than placed in quotation marks, see 13a.

## ELLIPSIS POINTS

**13e.** Use three spaced periods called *ellipsis points* (. . .) to mark omissions from quoted material and pauses in a written passage.

**ORIGINAL**    The second half of the program consisted of four numbers from the *Ring,* and closed with Siegfried's funeral march. My aunt wept quietly, but almost continuously, as a shallow vessel overflows in a rainstorm. From time to time her dim eyes looked up at the lights which studded the ceiling, burning softly under their dull glass globes; doubtless they were stars in truth to her. I was still perplexed as to what measure of musical comprehension was left to her, she who had heard nothing but the singing of gospel hymns at Methodist services in the square frame schoolhouse on Section Thirteen for so many years. I was wholly unable to gauge how much of it had been dissolved in soapsuds, or worked into bread, or milked into the bottom of a pail.
—Willa Cather, "A Wagner Matinée"

**(1)** If the quoted material that comes before the ellipsis points is not a complete sentence, use three ellipsis points with a space before the first point.

**EXAMPLE**
The narrator notes, "The second half of the program . . . closed with Siegfried's funeral march."

**(2)** If the quoted material that comes before or after the ellipsis points is a complete sentence, use an end mark before the ellipsis points.

**EXAMPLE**
The narrator observes, "My aunt wept quietly. . . . "

**(3)** If one sentence or more is omitted, ellipsis points follow the end mark that precedes the omitted material.

**EXAMPLE**
Recalling the experience, the narrator says, "My aunt wept quietly, but almost continuously, as a shallow vessel overflows in a rainstorm. . . . I was still perplexed as to what measure of musical comprehension was left to her, she who had heard nothing but the singing of gospel hymns at Methodist services in the square frame schoolhouse on Section Thirteen for so many years."

**(4)** To show that a full line or more of poetry has been omitted, use an entire line of spaced periods.

**ORIGINAL**    If you were coming in the Fall,
I'd brush the Summer by
With half a smile, and half a spurn,
As Housewives do, a Fly.
—Emily Dickinson, "If you were coming in the Fall"

**WITH OMISSION**    If you were coming in the Fall,
I'd brush the Summer by
. . . . . . . . . . . . . . . .
As Housewives do, a Fly.

## APOSTROPHES

**13f.** Use an apostrophe in forming the possessive of nouns and indefinite pronouns.

**(1)** To form the possessive of a singular noun, add an apostrophe and an *s.*

**EXAMPLES**
the minister's veil       Ross's opinion

**NOTE** When forming the possessive of a singular noun ending in an *s* sound, add only an apostrophe if the addition of *'s* will make the noun awkward to pronounce. Otherwise, add *'s*.

**EXAMPLES**
Douglass's autobiography     Texas' population

**(2)** To form the possessive of a plural noun ending in *s*, add only the apostrophe. If the plural noun does not end in *s*, add an apostrophe and an *s*.

**EXAMPLES**
the authors' styles     the Ushers' house
men's fashions     children's toys

**(3)** To form the possessive of an indefinite pronoun, add an apostrophe and an *s*.

**EXAMPLES**
each one's time     everybody's opinion

**NOTE** In such forms as *anyone else* and *somebody else*, the correct possessives are *anyone else's* and *somebody else's*.

**(4)** Form the possessive of only the last word in a compound word, in the name of an organization or business firm, or in a word group showing joint possession.

**EXAMPLES**
father-in-law's gloves     Roz and Denise's idea
Taylor, Sanders, and Weissman's law office

**(5)** Form the possessive of each noun in a word group showing individual possession of similar items.

**EXAMPLE**
Baldwin's and Ellison's writings

When a possessive pronoun is part of a word group showing joint possession, each noun in the word group is also possessive.

**EXAMPLE**
Walter Mitty's and **her** relationship

**(6)** When used in the possessive form, words that indicate time (such as *hour, week,* and *year*) and words that indicate amounts of money require apostrophes.

**EXAMPLES**
a week's vacation     five dollars' worth

**13g.** Use an apostrophe to show where letters, words, or numbers have been omitted in a contraction.

**EXAMPLES**
they had . . . **they'd**     Kerry is . . . **Kerry's**
let us . . . **let's**     of the clock . . . **o'clock**
where is . . . **where's**     1997 . . . **'97**

The word *not* can be shortened to *–n't* and added to a verb, usually without any change in the spelling of the verb.

**EXAMPLES**
is not . . . **isn't**     has not . . . **hasn't**

**EXCEPTION**
will not . . . **won't**

**13h.** Use an apostrophe and an *s* to form the plurals of all lowercase letters, some uppercase letters, numerals, and some words referred to as words.

**EXAMPLES**
There are two *r*'s and two *s*'s in *embarrassed*.
Soon after Tom and Lucynell said their *I do*'s, he
     abandoned her.

You may add only an *s* to form the plurals of such items—except lowercase letters—if the plural forms will not cause misreading.

**EXAMPLES**
Compact discs (**CDs**) were introduced in the
     **1980s.**
On her report card were three **A's** and three **C's.**

## HYPHENS

**13i.** Use a hyphen to divide a word at the end of a line.

When dividing a word at the end of a line, remember the following rules:

**(1)** Do not divide a one-syllable word.

**EXAMPLE**
Peyton Farquhar was captured, and he was finally
**hanged** from the bridge.

**(2)** Divide a word only between syllables.

**EXAMPLE**
Ernest Hemingway's *A Farewell to Arms* was **published** in 1929.

**(3)** Divide an already hyphenated word at the hyphen.

**EXAMPLE**
Stephen Crane died in Germany at the age of **twenty-
eight.**

**(4)** Do not divide a word so that one letter stands alone.

**EXAMPLE**
One fine autumn day, Rip Van Winkle fell fast
**asleep** in the mountains.

**13j.** Use a hyphen with compound numbers from twenty-one to ninety-nine and with fractions used as modifiers.

**EXAMPLES**

six hundred **twenty-five**

a **three-fourths** quorum [*but* three fourths of the audience]

## DASHES

**13k.** Use dashes to set off abrupt breaks in thoughts.

**EXAMPLE**

The poor condition of this road—it really needs to be paved—makes this route unpopular.

**13l.** Use dashes to set off an appositive or a parenthetical expression that contains commas.

**EXAMPLE**

Several of the nineteenth-century American poets—Poe, Dickinson, and Whitman, for example—led remarkable lives.

## PARENTHESES

**13m.** Use parentheses to enclose informative or explanatory material of minor importance.

**EXAMPLES**

Harriet Tubman (c. 1820-1913) is remembered for her work in the Underground Railroad.

On our vacation we visited Natchitoches (it's pronounced nak′ə·täsh′), Louisiana.

Thoreau lived at Walden Pond for two years. (See the map on page 350.)

## BRACKETS

**13n.** Use brackets to enclose an explanation within quoted or parenthetical material.

**EXAMPLE**

I think that Hilda Doolittle (more commonly known as H. D. [1886-1961]) is best remembered for her Imagist poetry.

# 14 SPELLING

## UNDERSTANDING WORD STRUCTURE

Many English words are made up of roots and affixes (prefixes and suffixes).

## Roots

**14a.** The *root* of a word is the part that carries the word's core meaning.

| ROOTS | MEANINGS | EXAMPLES |
|---|---|---|
| –bio– | life | biology, symbiotic |
| –duc–, –duct– | lead | educate, conductor |
| –mit–, –miss– | send | remit, emissary |
| –port– | carry, bear | transport, portable |

**NOTE** To find the meaning of a root or an affix, look in a dictionary. Most dictionaries have individual entries for word parts.

## Prefixes

**14b.** A *prefix* is one or more letters or syllables added to the beginning of a word or word part to create a new word.

| PREFIXES | MEANINGS | EXAMPLES |
|---|---|---|
| a– | lacking, without | amorphous, apolitical |
| dia– | through, across, apart | diagonal, diameter, diagnose |
| inter– | between, among | intercede, international |
| mis– | badly, wrongly | misfire, misspell |

## Suffixes

**14c.** A *suffix* is one or more letters or syllables added to the end of a word or word part to create a new word.

| SUFFIXES | MEANINGS | EXAMPLES |
|---|---|---|
| –ation, –ition | action, result | repetition, starvation |
| –er | doer, native of | baker, westerner |
| –ible | able, likely, fit | edible, possible, divisible |
| –or | doer, office, action | director, juror, error |

## SPELLING RULES

### ie and ei

**14d.** Write *ie* when the sound is long e, except after c.

**EXAMPLES**
believe    field    **cei**ling    rece**i**ve
**EXCEPTIONS**
**ei**ther    le**i**sure    se**i**ze    prote**i**n

**14e.** Write *ei* when the sound is not long e.

**EXAMPLES**
e**i**ght    n**ei**ghbor    we**i**gh    fore**i**gn
**EXCEPTIONS**
anc**i**ent    v**i**ew    fr**i**end    effic**i**ent

### –cede, –ceed, and –sede

**14f.** The only English word ending in *–sede* is *supersede*. The only words ending in *–ceed* are *exceed, proceed,* and *succeed.* Most other words with this sound end in *–cede.*

**EXAMPLES**
ac**cede**    con**cede**    inter**cede**    re**cede**

## Adding Prefixes

**14g.** When adding a prefix, do not change the spelling of the root.

**EXAMPLES**
mis + spell = **mis**spell
inter + national = **inter**national

## Adding Suffixes

**14h.** When adding the suffix *–ness* or *–ly,* do not change the spelling of the original word.

**EXAMPLES**
plain + ness = plain**ness**    casual + ly = casual**ly**
**EXCEPTIONS**
For most words ending in y, change the y to i before adding *-ness* or *-ly.*
empty + ness = empt**iness**    busy + ly = bus**ily**

**NOTE** One-syllable adjectives ending in y generally follow rule 14h.

**EXAMPLES**
dry + ness = dry**ness**    shy + ly = shy**ly**

**14i.** Drop the final silent e before a suffix beginning with a vowel.

**EXAMPLES**
care + ing = car**ing**    dose + age = dos**age**
**EXCEPTIONS**
Keep the final silent e
- in a word ending in *ce* or *ge* before a suffix beginning with *a* or *o*: peac**eable**, courag**eous**
- in *dye* and in *singe* before *–ing*: dy**eing**, sing**eing**
- in *mile* before *–age*: mil**eage**

**NOTE** When adding *–ing* to words that end in *ie,* drop the e and change the i to y.

**EXAMPLES**
die + ing = d**ying**    lie + ing = l**ying**

**14j.** Keep the final silent e before a suffix beginning with a consonant.

**EXAMPLES**
hope + ful = hop**eful**    love + ly = lov**ely**
**EXCEPTIONS**
awe + ful = aw**ful**    whole + ly = whol**ly**
nine + th = nin**th**    argue + ment = argu**ment**

**14k.** For words ending in y preceded by a consonant, change the y to i before any suffix that does not begin with i.

**EXAMPLES**
thirsty + est = thirst**iest**    plenty + ful = plent**iful**

**14l.** For words ending in y preceded by a vowel, keep the y when adding a suffix.

**EXAMPLES**
joy + ful = joy**ful**    obey + ing = obey**ing**
**EXCEPTIONS**
day—da**ily**    lay—la**id**    pay—pa**id**    say—sa**id**

**14m.** **Double the final consonant before a suffix that begins with a vowel if the word both**

**(1)** has only one syllable or has the accent on the last syllable

*and*

**(2)** ends in a single consonant preceded by a single vowel.

**EXAMPLES**
thin + est = thi**nnest**      occur + ed = occu**rred**
**EXCEPTIONS**

● For words ending in *w* or *x*, do not double the final consonant.

new + er = new**er**  relax + ing = relax**ing**

● For words ending in *c*, add *k* before the suffix instead of doubling the *c*.

picnic + k + ed = picnic**ked**

 **NOTE**  The final consonant of some words may or may not be doubled, such as *traveled/travelled*. If you are unsure about doubling a final consonant, consult a dictionary.

## Forming the Plurals of Nouns

**14n.** **Remembering the following rules will help you spell the plural forms of nouns.**

**(1)** For most nouns, add *–s*.

**EXAMPLES**
players    islands    Jeffersons

**(2)** For nouns ending in *s, x, z, ch,* or *sh,* add *–es*.

**EXAMPLES**
class**es**    match**es**    tax**es**    Cháve**zes**

**(3)** For nouns ending in *y* preceded by a vowel, add *–s*.

**EXAMPLES**
monkeys    alloys    McKays

**TIPS FOR SPELLING**  In some names, diacritical marks (marks that show pronunciation) are as essential to correct spelling as the letters themselves. If you are not sure about the spelling of a name, check with the person whose name it is or consult a reference source.

**EXAMPLES**
Abolfat'h    Hélène    Bashō    Da 'Shawn

**(4)** For nouns ending in *y* preceded by a consonant, change the *y* to *i* and add *–es*.

**EXAMPLES**
fl**ies**    countr**ies**    troph**ies**
**EXCEPTIONS**
For proper nouns, add *–s*: Kennedys

**(5)** For some nouns ending in *f* or *fe,* add *–s*. For others, change the *f* or *fe* to *v* and add *–es*. For proper nouns, add *–s*.

**EXAMPLES**
gulfs    roofs    lea**ves**    kni**ves**    wol**ves**
Tallchiefs    Wolfes

**(6)** For nouns ending in *o* preceded by a vowel, add *–s*.

**EXAMPLES**
studios    stereos    Ignacios

**(7)** For nouns ending in *o* preceded by a consonant, add *–es*.

**EXAMPLES**
tomato**es**    hero**es**    veto**es**

For some common nouns ending in *o* preceded by a consonant, especially those referring to music, and for proper nouns, add only an *–s*.

**EXAMPLES**
tacos    pianos    altos    Suros

 **NOTE**  For some nouns ending in *o* preceded by a consonant, either *–s* or *–es* may be added.

**EXAMPLES**
zeros *or* zeroes    mosquitos *or* mosquitoes

**(8)** The plurals of a few nouns are formed in irregular ways.

**EXAMPLES**
teeth    women    m**ice**    geese

**(9)** For a few nouns, the singular and the plural forms are the same.

**EXAMPLES**
sheep    trout    aircraft    Japanese    Sioux

**(10)** For most compound nouns, form the plural of only the last word of the compound.

**EXAMPLES**
bookshel**ves**    baby sitters    ten-year-olds

**(11)** For compound nouns in which one of the words is modified by the other word or words, form the plural of the noun modified.

**EXAMPLES**
sisters-in-law    runners-up    mountain goats

**(12)** For some nouns borrowed from other languages, the plural is formed as in the original languages.

**EXAMPLES**
alga—alg**ae**      hypothesis—hypothes**es**
ellipsis—ellips**es**      phenomenon—phenomen**a**

**(13)** To form the plurals of figures, most uppercase letters, signs, and words used as words, add an *–s* or both an apostrophe and an *–s.*

**EXAMPLES**
1990—1990**s** *or* 1990**'s**      *C*—*C*s *or* *C*'s
*and*—*and*s *or* *and*'s      *&*—*&*s *or* *&*'s

To prevent confusion, add both an apostrophe and an *–s* to form the plural of all lowercase letters, certain uppercase letters, and some words used as words.

**EXAMPLES**
The word *Mississippi* contains four *s*'s and four *i*'s. [Without an apostrophe, the plural of *i* could be confused with *is.*]
Because I mistakenly thought Flannery O'Connor was a man, I used *his*'s instead of *her*'s in my paragraph. [Without an apostrophe, the plural of *his* would look like the word *hiss,* and the plural of *her* would look like the pronoun *hers.*]

# 15 GLOSSARY OF USAGE

The **Glossary of Usage** is an alphabetical list of words and expressions with definitions, explanations, and examples. Some examples in this list are labeled *standard, nonstandard, formal,* or *informal.* The labels **standard** and **formal** identify usage that is appropriate in serious writing and speaking (such as in compositions and speeches). The label *informal* indicates standard English commonly used in conversation and in everyday writing such as personal letters. The label **nonstandard** identifies usage that does not follow the guidelines of standard English usage.

---

**accept, except**   *Accept* is a verb meaning "to receive." *Except* may be either a verb meaning "to leave out" or a preposition meaning "excluding."

**EXAMPLES**
I will **accept** another yearbook assignment. [verb]
Should the military services **except** women from combat duty? [verb]
I have read all of Willa Cather's novels **except** *My Ántonia.* [preposition]

**affect, effect**   *Affect* is a verb meaning "to influence." *Effect* may be either a verb meaning "to bring about or accomplish" or a noun meaning "the result [of an action]."

**EXAMPLES**
How did the House of Usher **affect** the narrator?
Renewed interest in *Moby-Dick* during the 1920s **effected** a change in Melville's reputation.
What **effect** did the war have on Paul Berlin?

**all ready, already**   *All ready* means "all prepared." *Already* means "previously."

**EXAMPLES**
Are you **all ready** to give your report?
We have **already** read that story.

**all the farther, all the faster**   Avoid using these expressions in formal situations. Use *as far as* or *as fast as.*

**EXAMPLE**
The first act was **as far as** [*not* all the farther] we had read in *A Raisin in the Sun.*

**all together, altogether**   *All together* means "everyone or everything in the same place." *Altogether* means "entirely."

**EXAMPLES**
My family will be **all together** for the holidays this year.
The president is **altogether** opposed to the bill.

**allusion, illusion**   An *allusion* is an indirect reference to something. An *illusion* is a mistaken idea or a misleading appearance.

**EXAMPLES**
In her stories, Flannery O'Connor makes numerous **allusions** to the Bible.
**Illusions** of success haunt Willy Loman.
Makeup can be used to create an **illusion.**

**almost, most**   Avoid using *most* for *almost* in all writing other than dialogue.

**EXAMPLE**
**Almost** [*not* most] everyone in class was surprised by the outcome in Ambrose Bierce's story "An Occurrence at Owl Creek Bridge."

**a lot**   Avoid this expression in formal situations by using *many* or *much.*

**already**   See **all ready, already.**

**altogether**   See **all together, altogether.**

**among**  See **between, among.**

**amount, number**  Use *amount* to refer to a singular word. Use *number* to refer to a plural word.

**EXAMPLES**

The library has a large **amount** of resource material about the Harlem Renaissance. [*Amount* refers to *material.*]

The library has a large **number** of books about the Harlem Renaissance. [*Number* refers to *books.*]

**and, but**  In general, avoid beginning a sentence with *and* or *but* in formal writing.

**and etc.**  *Etc.* stands for the Latin words *et cetera,* meaning "and others" or "and so forth." Always avoid using *and* before *etc.* In general, avoid using *etc.* in formal situations. Use an unabbreviated English expression instead.

**EXAMPLE**

We are studying twentieth-century American novelists: Ernest Hemingway, Margaret Walker, Jean Toomer, **and others** [*or* etc., *but not* and etc.].

**and/or**  Avoid using this confusing construction. Decide which alternative, *and* or *or,* expresses what you mean, and use it alone.

**any more, anymore**  The expression *any more* specifies a quantity. *Anymore* means "now; nowadays."

**EXAMPLES**

Do you know **any more** Caddo folk tales?
Kam doesn't work at the record store **anymore.**

**any one, anyone**  The expression *any one* specifies one member of a group. *Anyone* is a pronoun meaning "one person, no matter which."

**EXAMPLES**

**Any one** of you can play the part.
**Anyone** can try out for the part.

**anyways, anywheres**  Omit the final *s* from these words and others like them (*everywheres, nowheres, somewheres*).

**EXAMPLE**

I can't go **anywhere** [*not* anywheres] until I finish.

**as**  See **like, as.**

**as if**  See **like, as if.**

**at**  Avoid using *at* after a construction beginning with *where.*

**EXAMPLE**

**Where** was Chief Joseph [*not* where was Chief Joseph at] when he delivered his surrender speech?

**a while, awhile**  *A while* means "a period of time." *Awhile* means "for a short time."

**EXAMPLES**

Let's wait here **awhile**.
Let's sit here for **a while** and listen to the band.

**bad, badly**  *Bad* is an adjective. *Badly* is an adverb. In standard English, *bad* should follow a sense verb, such as *feel, look, sound, taste,* or *smell,* or other linking verb.

| NONSTANDARD | If the cole slaw smells badly, don't eat it. |
| STANDARD | If the cole slaw smells **bad,** don't eat it. |

**because**  In formal situations, do not use the construction *reason . . . because.* Instead, use *reason . . . that.*

**EXAMPLE**

The **reason** for the eclipse is **that** [*not* because] the moon has come between the Earth and the sun.

**being as, being that**  Avoid using either of these expressions in place of *since* or *because.*

**EXAMPLE**

**Because** [*not* being as *or* being that] Ms. Ribas is a gemologist, she may know what these stones are.

**beside, besides**  *Beside* is a preposition meaning "by the side of" or "next to." *Besides* may be either a preposition meaning "in addition to" or "other than" or an adverb meaning "moreover."

**EXAMPLES**

Rip Van Winkle laid his rifle **beside** him on the ground. [preposition]
No one **besides** Lurleen has read all of *Leaves of Grass.* [preposition]
I'm not in the mood to go shopping; **besides,** I have an English test tomorrow. [adverb]

**between, among**  Use *between* to refer to only two items or to more than two when comparing each item individually to each of the others.

**EXAMPLES**

The money from the sale of the property was evenly divided **between** Sasha and Antonio.
Don't you know the difference **between** a simile, a metaphor, and an analogy? [Each figure of speech is compared individually to each of the others.]

Use *among* to refer to more than two items when you are not considering each item in relation to each other item individually.

**EXAMPLE**

The money from the sale of the property was evenly divided **among** the four relatives.

**bring, take** *Bring* means "to come carrying something." *Take* means "to go carrying something."

**EXAMPLES**

I'll **bring** my Wynton Marsalis tapes when I come over.

When he went hunting, Rip Van Winkle **took** his gun and dog.

**but** See **and, but.**

**cannot (can't) help but** Avoid using *but* followed by the infinitive form of a verb after the expression *cannot (can't) help.* Instead, use a gerund after the expression.

| NONSTANDARD | I can't help but tap my foot whenever I hear mariachi music. |
| STANDARD | I can't help **tapping** my foot whenever I hear mariachi music. |

**compare, contrast** Used with *to, compare* means "to look for similarities between." Used with *with, compare* means "to look for similarities and differences between." *Contrast* is always used to point out differences.

**EXAMPLES**

Write a simile **comparing** a manufactured product **to** something in nature.

How do the haiku of Taniguchi Buson **compare with** those of Matsuo Bashō?

The teacher **contrasted** the writing styles of Walt Whitman and Emily Dickinson.

**could of** See **of.**

**double subject** Do not use an unnecessary pronoun after the subject of a sentence.

**EXAMPLE**

**Judy Jones** [*not* Judy Jones she] fascinates Dexter Green.

**due to** Avoid using *due to* for "because of" or "owing to."

**EXAMPLE**

The game was postponed **because of** [*not* due to] rain.

**each and every** The expression *each and every* is redundant. Instead, use either *each* or *every* alone.

**EXAMPLE**

**Every** [*not* each and every] resident of Jefferson attended Miss Emily Grierson's funeral.

**effect** See **affect, effect.**

**either, neither** *Either* usually means "one or the other of two." *Neither* usually means "not one or the other of two." Avoid using *either* or *neither* when referring to more than two.

**EXAMPLE**

Consider writing about the Jazz Age, the Harlem Renaissance, or the Great Depression; **any one** [*not* either] of those topics would be interesting.

**emigrate, immigrate** *Emigrate* means "to leave a country or a region to settle elsewhere." *Immigrate* means "to come into a country or a region to settle there."

**EXAMPLES**

Claude McKay **emigrated** from Jamaica in 1912.

Claude McKay **immigrated** to the United States in 1912.

**etc.** See **and etc.**

**every** See **each and every.**

**every day, everyday** *Every day* means "each day." *Everyday* means "daily" or "usual."

**EXAMPLES**

Parson Hooper wore the black veil **every day.**

Walking the dog is one of my **everyday** chores.

**every one, everyone** *Every one* specifies every person or thing of those named. *Everyone* means "every person; everybody."

**EXAMPLES**

**Every one** of these poems was written by Anne Sexton.

Has **everyone** read "The Bells"?

**except** See **accept, except.**

**farther, further** Use *farther* to express physical distance. Use *further* to express abstract relationships of degree or quantity.

**EXAMPLES**

We swam **farther** than we usually do.

After discussing "The Road Not Taken" **further**, we agreed with Karl's interpretation of the poem.

**fewer, less** Use *fewer* to modify a plural noun and *less* to modify a singular noun.

**EXAMPLES**

Later in life, Emily Dickinson entertained even **fewer** guests.

Later in life, Emily Dickinson spent **less** time entertaining guests.

**further** See **farther, further.**

**good, well** Do not use the adjective *good* to modify a verb. Instead, use the adverb *well,* meaning "capably" or "satisfactorily." As an adjective, *well* means "in good health" or "satisfactory in appearance or condition."

**EXAMPLES**
The school orchestra played **well** [adverb].
He says that he feels quite **well** [adjective].
It's midnight, and all is **well** [adjective].

**had of** See **of.**

**had ought, hadn't ought** Do not use *had* or *hadn't* with *ought.*

**EXAMPLE**
His scores **ought** [*not* had ought] to be back by now.

**half** Avoid using an indefinite article (*a* or *an*) both before and after *half.*

**EXAMPLE**
We've waited for **half an hour** [*or* a half hour].

**if, whether** Avoid using *if* for *whether* in indirect questions and in expressions of doubt.

**EXAMPLE**
Dickinson wanted to know **whether** [*not* if] her poems were "alive."

**illusion** See **allusion, illusion.**

**immigrate** See **emigrate, immigrate.**

**imply, infer** *Imply* means "to suggest indirectly." *Infer* means "to interpret" or "to draw a conclusion."

**EXAMPLES**
The speaker of "Thanatopsis" **implies** that nature can allay one's fear of death.
I **infer** from the poem that nature can cure many ills.

**in, into** *In* generally shows location. *Into* generally shows direction.

**EXAMPLES**
Randall Jarrell was born **in** Nashville, Tennessee.
When Rip walked **into** the village, everybody stared.

**irregardless, regardless** *Irregardless* is nonstandard. Use *regardless* instead.

**EXAMPLE**
**Regardless** [*not* irregardless] of the children's pleas, their father said they had to go to bed.

**its, it's** *Its* is the possessive form of *it. It's* is the contraction of *it is* or *it has.*

**EXAMPLES**
The crew prepares for **its** fight with Moby-Dick.
**It's** [it is] Captain Ahab's obsession.
**It's** [it has] been many years since Ahab lost his leg.

**kind of, sort of** In formal situations, avoid using these terms for the adverb *somewhat* or *rather.*

| INFORMAL | Roderick became kind of agitated. |
| FORMAL | Roderick became **rather** agitated. |

**kind of a(n), sort of a(n)** In formal situations, omit the *a(n).*

| INFORMAL | What kind of an essay is Baldwin's "The Creative Process"? |
| FORMAL | What **kind of** essay is Baldwin's "The Creative Process"? |

**kind(s), sort(s), type(s)** With the singular form of each of these nouns, use *this* or *that.* With the plural form, use *these* or *those.*

**EXAMPLE**
**This kind** of gas is safe, but **those kinds** aren't.

**lay, lie** See **lie, lay.**

**learn, teach** *Learn* means "to gain knowledge." *Teach* means "to provide with knowledge."

**EXAMPLE**
The more you **teach** someone else, the more you **learn** yourself.

**less** See **fewer, less.**

**lie, lay** The verb *lie* means "to rest" or "to stay, to recline, or to remain in a certain state or position." Its principal parts are *lie, lying, lay,* and *lain. Lie* never takes an object. The verb *lay* means "to put [something] in a place." Its principal parts are *lay, laying, laid,* and *laid. Lay* usually takes an object.

**EXAMPLES**
Their land **lay** in the shadow of Rainy Mountain. [no object]
Eduardo **laid** the strips of grilled meat on the tortilla. [*Strips* is the object of *laid.*]

**like, as** In formal situations, do not use *like* for the conjunction *as* to introduce a subordinate clause.

| INFORMAL | Plácido Domingo sings like Caruso once did. |
| FORMAL | Plácido Domingo sings **as** Caruso once did. |

**like, as if** In formal situations, avoid using the preposition *like* for the conjunction *as if* or *as though* to introduce a subordinate clause.

| INFORMAL | The singers sounded like they had not rehearsed. |
| FORMAL | The singers sounded **as if** [*or* as though] they had not rehearsed. |

**might of, must of** See **of.**

**most** See **almost, most.**

**neither** See **either, neither.**

**nor** See **or, nor.**

**number** See **amount, number.**

**of** *Of* is a preposition. Do not use *of* in place of *have* after verbs such as *could, should, would, might, must,* and *ought* [*to*]. Also, do not use *had of* for *had.*

**EXAMPLES**
You ought to **have** [*not* of] studied harder.
If he **had** [*not* had of] remembered the name of the
    author of "Mending Wall," he **would have** [*not*
    would of] made a perfect score.

Avoid using *of* after other prepositions such as
*inside, off,* and *outside.*

**EXAMPLE**
Chian-Chu dived **off** [*not* off of] the side of the pool
into the water.

**on to, onto** In the expression *on to, on* is an adverb
and *to* is a preposition. *Onto* is a preposition.

**EXAMPLES**
Dexter held **on to** his winter dreams.
The cat leapt gracefully **onto** the windowsill.

**or, nor** Use *or* with *either;* use *nor* with *neither.*

**EXAMPLES**
On Tuesdays the school cafeteria offers a choice of
    **either** a taco salad **or** a pizza.
I wonder why **neither** Ralph Ellison **nor** Robert
    Frost was given the Nobel Prize in literature.

**ought** See **had ought, hadn't ought.**

**ought to of** See **of.**

**reason . . . because** See **because.**

**regardless** See **irregardless, regardless.**

**rise, raise** The verb *rise* means "to go up" or "to get
up." Its principal parts are *rise, rising, rose,* and *risen. Rise*
never takes an object. The verb *raise* means "to cause
[something] to rise" or "to lift up." Its principal parts
are *raise, raising, raised,* and *raised. Raise* usually takes an
object.

**EXAMPLES**
The queen **rose** from her throne. [no object]
The movers **raised** the boxes onto their shoulders.
    [*Boxes* is the object of *raised.*]

**should of** See **of.**

**sit, set** The verb *sit* means "to rest in an upright,
seated position." Its principal parts are *sit, sitting, sat,*
and *sat. Sit* seldom takes an object. The verb *set* means
"to put [something] in a place." Its principal parts are
*set, setting, set,* and *set. Set* usually takes an object.

**EXAMPLES**
The raven **sat** on the bust of Pallas above the door.
    [no object]
Eben **set** the jug down. [*Jug* is the object of *set.*]

**some, somewhat** In formal situations, use *somewhat* instead of *some* to mean "to some extent."

**EXAMPLE**
My grades have improved **somewhat** [*not* some].

**sort(s)** See **kind(s), sort(s), type(s)** and **kind of
a(n), sort of a(n).**

**sort of** See **kind of, sort of.**

**take** See **bring, take.**

**teach** See **learn, teach.**

**than, then** *Than* is a conjunction used in comparisons. *Then* is an adverb meaning "at that time" or
"next."

**EXAMPLES**
Tyrone is more studious **than** I am.
First, mix the wet ingredients; **then,** add the flour
    and other dry ingredients.

**that** See **who, which, that.**

**their, there, they're** *Their* is a possessive form of
*they.* As an adverb, *there* means "at that place." *There*
can also be used to begin a sentence. *They're* is the
contraction of *they are.*

**EXAMPLES**
The performers are studying **their** lines.
I will be **there** after rehearsal. [adverb]
**There** will be four acts in the play. [expletive]
**They're** performing a play by Lorraine Hansberry.

**theirs, there's** *Theirs* is a possessive form of the
pronoun *they. There's* is the contraction for *there is*
or *there has.*

**EXAMPLES**
These posters are ours; **theirs** are the ones on the
    opposite wall.
**There's** [there is] a biography of W.E.B. DuBois
    in the library.
**There's** [there has] been a change in plans.

**them** Do not use *them* as an adjective. Use *those.*

**EXAMPLE**
**Those** [*not* them] lines illustrate Poe's use of internal rhyme.

**then** See **than, then.**

**this here, that there** Avoid using *here* or *there* after *this* or *that.*

**EXAMPLE**
**This** [*not* this here] magazine has an article about Andrea Lee.

**try and, try to** Use *try to,* not *try and.*

**EXAMPLE**
I will **try to** [*not* try and] finish my report on John Updike.

**type, type of** Avoid using the noun *type* as an adjective. Add *of* after *type.*

**EXAMPLE**
I prefer this **type of** [*not* type] shirt.

**type(s)** See **kind(s), sort(s), type(s).**

**ways** Use *way,* not *ways,* when referring to distance.

**EXAMPLE**
My home in Wichita is a long **way** [*not* ways] from Tokyo, where my pen pal lives.

**well** See **good, well.**

**when, where** Avoid using *when* or *where* to begin a definition.

| NONSTANDARD | A predicament is where you are in an embarrassing situation. |
|---|---|
| STANDARD | A predicament is **an embarrassing situation.** |

**where** Avoid using *where* for *that.*

**EXAMPLE**
I read **that** [*not* where] the Smithsonian Institution has preserved a great many of William H. Johnson's paintings.

**where . . . at** See **at.**

**whether** See **if, whether.**

**who, which, that** *Who* refers to persons only. *Which* refers to things only. *That* may refer to either persons or things.

**EXAMPLES**
Wasn't Beethoven the composer **who** [*or* that] continued to write music after he lost his hearing?
First editions of Poe's first book, **which** is titled *Tamerlane and Other Poems,* are worth thousands of dollars.
Is this the only essay **that** James Baldwin wrote?
I've never met or even seen the person **that** delivers our newspaper each morning.

**who's, whose** *Who's* is the contraction of *who is* or *who has. Whose* is the possessive form of *who.*

**EXAMPLES**
**Who's** [who is] going to portray the Navajo detective in the play?
**Who's** [who has] been using my computer?
**Whose** artwork is this?

**would of** See **of.**

**your, you're** *Your* is a possessive form of *you. You're* is the contraction of *you are.*

**EXAMPLES**
Is this **your** book?
I hope **you're** able to come to my graduation.

# Glossary

The glossary that follows is an alphabetical list of words found in the selections in this book. Use this glossary just as you would use a dictionary—to find out the meanings of unfamiliar words. (Some technical, foreign, and more obscure words in this book are not listed here but instead are defined for you in the footnotes that accompany many of the selections.)

Many words in the English language have more than one meaning. This glossary gives the meanings that apply to the words as they are used in the selections in this book. Words closely related in form and meaning are usually listed together in one entry (for instance, *compassion* and *compassionate*), and the definition is given for the first form.

The following abbreviations are used:

| | |
|---|---|
| *adj.* | adjective |
| *adv.* | adverb |
| *n.* | noun |
| *v.* | verb |

Each word's pronunciation is given in parentheses. A guide to the pronunciation symbols appears at the bottom of the odd-numbered pages. For more information about the words in this glossary or for information about words not listed here, consult a dictionary.

## A

**abdicate** (ab′di·kāt′) *v.*: give up responsibility for.

**abhor** (ab·hôr′) *v.*: scorn; hate.

**abominable** (ə·bäm′ə·nə·bəl) *adj.*: nasty and disgusting.

**abrasion** (ə·brā′zhən) *n.*: scrape.

**abstinence** (ab′stə·nəns) *n.*: staying away.

**abyss** (ə·bis′) *n.*: bottomless gulf or void.

**acquiesce** (ak′wē·es′) *v.*: accept quietly.

**acrid** (ak′rid) *adj.*: bitter; irritating.

**acrimonious** (ak′ri·mō′nē·əs) *adj.*: bitter; harsh. —**acrimoniously** *adv.*

**acute** (ə·kyo͞ot′) *adj.*: keen; sharp.

**admonish** (ad·män′ish) *v.*: warn mildly. —**admonishing** *v.* used as *adj.*

**adversary** (ad′vər·ser′ē) *n.*: opponent.

**affliction** (ə·flik′shən) *n.*: pain; hardship.

**affluent** (af′lo͞o·ənt) *n.*: well-to-do people.

**afford** (ə·fôrd′) *v.*: give; provide.

**alacrity** (ə·lak′rə·tē) *n.*: promptness in responding; eagerness.

**allegiance** (ə·lē′jəns) *n.*: loyalty.

**alleviate** (ə·lē′vē·āt′) *v.*: relieve; reduce.

**alliance** (ə·lī′əns) *n.*: close association entered into for mutual benefit.

**ancestral** (an·ses′trəl) *adj.*: inherited.

**antipathy** (an·tip′ə·thē) *n.*: strong dislike.

**apathy** (ap′ə·thē) *n.*: indifference; lack of emotion.

**apocryphal** (ə·päk′rə·fəl) *adj.*: of questionable authority; false.

**appalling** (ə·pôl′iŋ) *adj.*: frightful.

**appease** (ə·pēz′) *v.*: calm; satisfy; pacify.

**appoint** (ə·point′) *v.*: assign. —**appointed** *v.* used as *adj.*

**appreciable** (ə·prē′shə·bəl) *adj.*: measurable.

**apprehension** (ap′rē·hen′shən) *n.*: anxious or frightening feeling; dread.

**appropriate** (ə·prō′prē·āt′) *v.*: take over.

**archaic** (är·kā′ik) *adj.*: old-fashioned.

**ardent** (är′dənt) *adj.*: intense; eager. —**ardently** *adv.*

**arduous** (är′jo͞o·əs) *adj.*: difficult.

**arrogance** (ar′ə·gəns) *n.*: overbearing pride; self-importance. —**arrogant** *adj.*

**ascertain** (as′ər·tān′) *v.*: find out with certainty.

**ascribe** (ə·skrīb′) *v.*: regard as coming from a certain cause.

**assailant** (ə·sāl′ənt) *n.*: attacker.

**assess** (ə·ses′) *v.*: evaluate; judge the value of.

**atrocious** (ə·trō′shəs) *adj.*: evil; very bad.

**atrocity** (ə·träs′ə·tē) *n.*: horror; brutality. —**atrocity** *n.* used as *adj.*

**attribute** (ə·trib′yo͞ot) *v.*: think of as resulting from.

---

at, āte, cär; ten, ēve; is, īce; gō, hôrn, look, to͞ol; oil, out; up, fʉr; ə *for unstressed vowels, as* a *in* ago, u *in* focus; ′ *as in* Latin (lat′'n); chin; she; thin; *the*; zh *as in* azure (azh′ər); ŋ *as in* ring (riŋ)

---

**austere** (ô·stir′) *adj.*: very plain.

**autonomy** (ô·tän′ə·mē) *n.*: independence; self-government.

**avarice** (av′ə·ris) *n.*: greed. —**avaricious** *adj.*

**avert** (ə·vʉrt′) *v.*: prevent; turn away.

## B

**bedlam** (bed′ləm) *n.*: place or condition of great noise and confusion.

**bewitch** (bē·wich′) *v.*: entice; make someone or something irresistible. —**bewitching** *v.* used as *adj.*

**bicker** (bik′ər) *v.*: quarrel over something unimportant; squabble. —**bickering** *v.* used as *adj.*

**blanch** (blanch) *v.*: drain of color. —**blanched** *v.* used as *adj.*

**bleak** *adj.*: cheerless.

**blithe** (blīth) *adj.*: carefree.

**bountiful** (bɔun′tə·fəl) *adj.*: generous.

**brazenness** (brā′zən·nis) *n.*: boldness.

## C

**caliber** (kal′ə·bər) *n.*: quality or ability.

**candid** (kan′did) *adj.*: unbiased; fair.

**caper** (kā′pər) *n.*: foolish prank.

**careen** (kə·rēn′) *v.*: lurch sideways.

**celestial** (sə·les′chəl) *adj.*: divine; perfect.

**censor** (sen′sər) *v.*: cut or change to remove material deemed objectionable.

**circumvent** (sʉr′kəm·vent′) *v.*: avoid by cleverness or deceit.

**clammy** (klam′ē) *adj.*: cold and damp.

**clamor** (klam′ər) *n.*: loud noise; loud demand or complaint.

**cleft** (kleft) *n.*: opening or crack in something.

**coherent** (kō·hir′ənt) *adj.*: clear, logical, and consistent.

**coincide** (kō′in·sīd′) *v.*: occur at the same time.

**commodious** (kə·mō′dē·əs) *adj.*: spacious.

**communal** (kə·myōōn′əl) *adj.*: belonging to an entire group.

**compel** (kəm·pel′) *v.*: drive; force.

**comply** (kəm·plī′) *v.*: obey; agree to a request.

**conceive** (kən·sēv′) *v.*: think; imagine.

**conception** (kən·sep′shən) *n.*: mental formation of ideas.

**concession** (kən·sesh′ən) *n.*: act of giving in.

**confiscation** (kän′fis·kā′shən) *n.*: seizure of property by authority.

**conflagration** (kän′flə·grā′shən) *n.*: huge fire.

**conjecture** (kən·jek′chər) *v.*: guess; predict.

**conscientious** (kän′shē·en′shəs) *adj.*: careful; painstaking; thorough. —**conscientiously** *adv.*

**consolation** (kän′sə·lā′shən) *n.*: comfort.

**consternation** (kän′stər·nā′shən) *n.*: confusion resulting from fear or shock.

**constitution** (kän′stə·tōō′shən) *n.*: physical condition.

**constrain** (kən·strān′) *v.*: force.

**contemptuous** (kən·temp′chōō·əs) *adj.*: scornful. —**contemptuously** *adv.*

**contrivance** (kən·trī′vəns) *n.*: scheme; plan.

**conundrum** (kə·nun′drəm) *n.*: riddle.

**convene** (kən·vēn′) *v.*: assemble.

**conviction** (kən·vik′shən) *n.*: fixed or strong belief.

**convivial** (kən·viv′ē·əl) *adj.*: jovial; sociable.

**copious** (kō′pē·əs) *adj.*: abundant. —**copiously** *adv.*

**covet** (kuv′it) *v.*: long for; want badly.

**craven** (krā′vən) *adj.*: very fearful; cowardly.

**crucial** (krōō′shəl) *adj.*: critical; decisive.

**cunning** (kun′iŋ) *adj.*: sly or crafty.

## D

**debris** (də·brē′) *n.*: rubble; broken pieces.

**deference** (def′ər·əns) *n.*: respect.

**deferential** (def′ər·en′shəl) *adj.*: showing respect or courteous regard.

**deluge** (del′yōōj′) *n.*: rush; flood.

**delusion** (di·lōō′zhən) *n.*: false belief or opinion.

**deplore** (dē·plôr′) *v.*: condemn as wrong; disapprove of.

**derision** (di·rizh′ən) *n.*: ridicule; contempt.

**destitute** (des′tə·tōōt′) *adj.*: poverty-stricken.

**dilapidated** (də·lap′ə·dāt′id) *adj.*: partially ruined; in need of repair.

**diminutive** (də·min′yōō·tiv) *adj.*: very small; tiny.

**disconsolate** (dis·kän′sə·lit) *adj.*: unhappy. —**disconsolately** *adv.*

**disembody** (dis′im·bäd′ē) *v.*: separate from the body. —**disembodied** *v.* used as *adj.*

**disperse** (di·spʉrs′) *v.*: scatter.

**dispirited** (di·spir′it·id) *adj.*: discouraged.

**disposition** (dis′pə·zish′ən) *n.*: nature; character.

**dispute** (di·spyōōt′) *v.*: contest.

**dissident** (dis′ə·dənt) *adj.*: disagreeing; differing in belief or opinion.

**distraction** (di·strak′shən) *n.*: mental disturbance or distress.

**distraught** (di·strôt′) *adj.*: troubled.

**distressed** (di·strest′) *adj.*: suffering; troubled.

**divergence** (dī·vʉr′jəns) *n.*: variance; difference.

**dominion** (də·min′yən) *n.:* rule.

**drone** *n.:* steady hum.

**dwindle** (dwin′dəl) *v.:* diminish.

# E

**edible** (ed′ə·bəl) *adj.:* capable of being eaten.

**efface** (ə·fās′) *v.:* erase; wipe out.

**effectual** (e·fek′chōō·əl) *adj.:* productive; efficient.

**effervescent** (ef′ər·ves′ənt) *adj.:* bubbling up; foaming.

**effete** (e·fēt′) *adj.:* sterile; unproductive.

**elation** (ē·lā′shən) *n.:* celebration.

**eloquence** (el′ə·kwəns) *n.:* forceful, fluent, and graceful speech.

**elude** (ē·lōōd′) *v.:* escape detection or notice. —**eluding** *v. used as adj.*

**encompass** (en·kum′pəs) *v.:* surround; enclose. —**encompassed** *v. used as adj.*

**encumbrance** (en·kum′brəns) *n.:* burden; hindrance.

**enmity** (en′mə·tē) *n.:* hatred.

**ensue** (en·sōō′) *v.:* result.

**enthrall** (en·thrôl′) *v.:* fascinate.

**entreat** (en·trēt′) *v.:* ask sincerely; beg.

**eradicate** (ē·rad′i·kāt′) *v.:* eliminate; wipe out; destroy.

**eradication** (ē·rad′i·kā′shən) *n.:* utter destruction; obliteration.

**ethereal** (ē·thir′ē·əl) *adj.:* not earthly; spiritual.

**eulogy** (yōō′lə·jē) *n.:* public speech of praise.

**exalt** (eg·zôlt′) *v.:* lift up.

**excruciating** (eks·krōō′shē·āt′iŋ) *adj.:* intensely painful.

**exemplary** (eg·zem′plə·rē) *adj.:* serving as a model; worth imitating.

**expedient** (ek·spē′dē·ənt) *n.:* convenience; means to an end.

**expire** (ek·spīr′) *v.:* die. —**expiring** *v. used as adj.*

**explicit** (eks·plis′it) *adj.:* clear; definite.

**expunge** (ek·spunj′) *v.:* erase; remove.

**extremity** (ek·strem′ə·tē) *n.:* limb of the body, especially a hand or foot. —**extremities** *n. pl.*

# F

**facilitate** (fə·sil′ə·tāt′) *v.:* make easier.

**fastidious** (fa·stid′ē·əs) *adj.:* difficult to please; critical.

**fervent** (fur′vənt) *adj.:* having intense feeling. —**fervently** *adv.*

**fitful** *adj.:* irregular; in stops and starts. —**fitfully** *adv.*

**florid** (flôr′id) *adj.:* showy.

**flourish** (flur′ish) *v.:* thrive; prosper.

**frenzy** (fren′zē) *n.:* frantic behavior; wildness.

**frivolity** (fri·väl′ə·tē) *n.:* silliness.

**furtive** (fur′tiv) *adj.:* stealthy; hidden.

**futile** (fyōōt′′l) *adj.:* useless; pointless.

# G

**garrulous** (gar′ə·ləs) *adj.:* talking a great deal, especially about unimportant things.

**gaudy** (gô′dē) *adj.:* showy but lacking in good taste.

**gesticulate** (jes·tik′yōō·lāt′) *v.:* gesture, especially with the hands and arms. —**gesticulating** *v. used as adj.*

**grotesque** (grō·tesk′) *adj.:* strange; absurd.

**gyration** (jī·rā′shən) *n.:* circular movement; whirling.

# H

**habitual** (hə·bich′ōō·əl) *adj.:* usual; by habit. —**habitually** *adv.*

**haggard** (hag′ərd) *adj.:* gaunt; wasted or worn in appearance.

**hail** *v.:* greet.

**hedonistic** (hē′də·nis′tik) *adj.:* pleasure-loving; self-indulgent.

**hysteria** (hi·ster′ē·ə) *n.:* uncontrolled excitement.

# I

**idealist** (ī·dē′əl·ist) *n.:* one who believes in noble though sometimes impractical goals; dreamer.

**illumine** (i·lōō′mən) *v.:* light up.

**immune** (i·myōōn′) *adj.:* protected.

**impart** (im·pärt′) *v.:* reveal.

**impassive** (im·pas′iv) *adj.:* controlled; not revealing any emotions.

**impeccable** (im·pek′ə·bəl) *adj.:* perfect; without error or defect. —**impeccably** *adv.*

**imperative** (im·per′ə·tiv) *adj.:* absolutely necessary; urgent.

---

at, āte, cär; ten, ēve; is, īce; gō, hôrn, look, tōol; oil, out; up, fur; ə *for unstressed vowels, as* a *in* ago, u *in focus;* ′ *as in* Latin (lat′′n); chin; she; thin; *the;* zh *as in* azure (azh′ər); ŋ *as in* ring (riŋ)

**imperceptible** (im′pər·sep′tə·bəl) *adj.*: unnoticeable; so slight as not to be noticed; not clear or obvious to the senses or mind.

**impervious** (im·pʉr′vē·əs) *adj.*: resistant; incapable of being penetrated.

**impetuous** (im·pech′o͞o·əs) *adj.*: impulsive.

**impious** (im′pē·əs) *adj.*: irreverent.

**impregnable** (im·preg′nə·bəl) *adj.*: impossible to capture or enter by force.

**improvident** (im·präv′ə·dənt) *adj.*: careless; not providing for the future.

**impulse** (im′puls′) *n.*: sudden desire or urge.

**impute** (im·pyo͞ot′) *v.*: credit; assign.

**incessant** (in·ses′ənt) *adj.*: without stopping. —**incessantly** *adv.*

**inconceivable** (in′kən·sēv′ə·bəl) *adj.*: unimaginable; beyond understanding.

**indolent** (in′də·lənt) *adj.*: lazy.

**induce** (in·do͞os′) *v.*: persuade; force; cause.

**indulge** (in·dulj′) *v.*: satisfy; please; humor.

**inert** (in·ʉrt′) *adj.*: inactive; dull; motionless.

**inevitable** (in·ev′i·tə·bəl) *adj.*: not avoidable.

**inexplicable** (in·eks′pli·kə·bəl) *adj.*: unable to be explained.

**inextricable** (in·eks′tri·kə·bəl) *adj.*: unable to be freed or disentangled from.

**infamous** (in′fə·məs) *adj.*: having a bad reputation; disgraceful.

**infirm** (in·fʉrm′) *adj.*: physically weak.

**ingenious** (in·jēn′yəs) *adj.*: clever.

**inherent** (in·hir′ənt) *adj.*: inborn; built-in.

**iniquity** (i·nik′wi·tē) *n.*: wickedness.

**inscrutable** (in·skro͞ot′ə·bəl) *adj.*: mysterious.

**insidious** (in·sid′ē·əs) *adj.*: sly; sneaky.

**insolent** (in′sə·lənt) *adj.*: boldly disrespectful.

**insuperable** (in·so͞o′pər·ə·bəl) *adj.*: incapable of being overcome.

**insurrection** (in′sə·rek′shən) *n.*: rebellion; revolt.

**intangible** (in·tan′jə·bəl) *adj.*: difficult to define; vague.

**integrate** (in′tə·grāt′) *v.*: unify.

**integrity** (in·teg′rə·tē) *n.*: sound moral principles; honesty.

**intent** (in·tent′) *adj.*: purposeful.

**interloper** (in′tər·lō′pər) *n.*: intruder; meddler.

**interminable** (in·tʉr′mi·nə·bəl) *adj.*: endless; seeming to last forever.

**interpose** (in′tər·pōz′) *v.*: put forth in order to interfere.

**intersperse** (in′tər·spʉrs′) *v.*: place at intervals. —**interspersed** *v.* used as *adj.*

**intimate** (in′tə·māt′) *v.*: state indirectly; hint.

**intricate** (in′tri·kit) *adj.*: complicated; detailed.

**intrigue** (in′trēg′) *n.*: scheming; plotting.

**intuitive** (in·to͞o′i·tiv) *adj.*: without conscious reasoning. —**intuitively** *adv.*

**invincible** (in·vin′sə·bəl) *adj.*: unconquerable.

**inviolate** (in·vī′ə·lit) *adj.*: uncorrupted.

## J

**jilt** (jilt) *v.*: reject (as a lover).

**judicious** (jo͞o·dish′əs) *adj.*: cautious; wise, like a judge. —**judiciously** *adv.*

## L

**laborious** (lə·bôr′ē·əs) *adj.*: difficult; involving much hard work.

**labyrinth** (lab′ə·rinth′) *n.*: place full of complex passageways; maze.

**lamentable** (lə·men′tə·bəl) *adj.*: regrettable; distressing.

**legacy** (leg′ə·sē) *n.*: inheritance.

**lethargy** (leth′ər·jē) *n.*: abnormal drowsiness.

**listless** (list′lis) *adj.*: weary; without energy or interest in anything. —**listlessly** *adv.*

**loiter** (loit′ər) *v.*: spend time; hang around.

**lucid** (lo͞o′sid) *adj.*: clearheaded; not confused.

**ludicrous** (lo͞o′di·krəs) *adj.*: laughable; absurd.

**luxuriant** (lug·zhoor′ē·ənt) *adj.*: rich; abundant.

## M

**magnanimity** (mag′nə·nim′ə·tē) *n.*: nobility of spirit.

**magnitude** (mag′nə·to͞od′) *n.*: importance; greatness of scope.

**malice** (mal′is) *n.*: deliberate ill will; desire to harm. —**malicious** *adj.*

**malign** (mə·līn′) *adj.*: harmful; evil.

**malignant** (mə·lig′nənt) *adj.*: destructive; evil.

**malodorous** (mal·ō′dər·əs) *adj.*: bad-smelling.

**manifest** (man′ə·fəst′) *adj.*: plain; clear.

**martial** (mär′shəl) *adj.*: warlike.

**medium** (mē′dē·əm) *n.*: material for an artist.

**melancholy** (mel′ən·käl′ē) *adj.*: sad; gloomy; sorrowful.

**mesmerize** (mez′mər·īz) *v.*: hypnotize. —**mesmerizing** *v.* used as *adj.*

**mirth** (mʉrth) *n.*: joyfulness.

**mortify** (môrt′ə·fī′) *v.*: humiliate; deeply embarrass. —**mortified** *v.* used as *adj.*

**municipal** (myoo·nis′ə·pəl) *adj.*: belonging to a city or town.

**myriad** (mir′ē·əd) *adj.*: countless.

# N

**nape** *n.*: back of the neck.

**nimbus** (nim′bəs) *n.*: aura; halo.

**nomadic** (nō·mad′ik) *adj.*: wandering.

**noncommittal** (nän′kə·mit′′l) *adj.*: neutral; giving no clear indication of feeling or attitude.

**nostalgia** (nä·stal′jə) *n.*: longing.

**notorious** (nō·tôr′ē·əs) *adj.*: known widely and usually unfavorably.

# O

**oblique** (ō·blēk′) *adj.*: slanted. —**obliquely** *adv.*

**obliterate** (ə·blit′ər·āt) *v.*: erase or destroy.

**obscure** (əb·skyoor′) *v.*: conceal; hide.

**obscurity** (əb·skyoor′ə·tē) *n.*: darkness.

**occult** (ə·kult′) *adj.*: hidden.

**ominous** (äm′ə·nəs) *adj.*: threatening; menacing.

**omnipotent** (äm·nip′ə·tənt) *adj.*: all-powerful.

**opaque** (ō·pāk′) *adj.*: not transparent; not letting light pass through.

**oscillation** (äs′ə·lā′shən) *n.*: regular back-and-forth movement.

**ostentatious** (äs′tən·tā′shəs) *adj.*: deliberately attracting notice.

# P

**pandemonium** (pan′də·mō′nē·əm) *n.*: wild confusion.

**parsimony** (pär′sə·mō′nē) *n.*: stinginess.

**pauper** (pô′pər) *n.*: extremely poor person.

**penitent** (pen′i·tənt) *adj.*: sorry for doing wrong.

**pensive** (pen′siv) *adj.*: deeply thoughtful. —**pensively** *adv.*

**perennial** (pə·ren′ē·əl) *adj.*: persistent; constant.

**perilous** (per′ə·ləs) *adj.*: dangerous.

**perseverance** (pur′sə·vir′əns) *n.*: persistence.

**persistent** (pər·sist′ənt) *adj.*: continuing.

**pertinent** (purt′′n·ənt) *adj.*: to the point; applying to the situation.

**perturbation** (pur′tər·bā′·shən) *n.*: feeling of alarm or agitation.

**perverse** (pər·vurs′) *adj.*: odd; contrary.

**pervert** (pər·vurt′) *v.*: misdirect; corrupt.

**pestilential** (pes′tə·len′shəl) *adj.*: dangerous and harmful, like a deadly infection.

**petulance** (pech′ə·ləns) *n.*: irritability; impatience.

**pious** (pī′əs) *adj.*: devoted to one's religion.

**pivotal** (piv′ət·′l) *adj.*: central; acting as a point around which other things turn.

**placid** (plas′id) *adj.*: peaceful; quiet.

**plague** (plāg) *v.*: annoy.

**plaintive** (plān′tiv) *adj.*: expressing sadness.

**plausibility** (plô′zə·bil′ə·tē) *n.*: believability.

**plunder** (plun′dər) *n.*: goods seized, especially during wartime.

**poignant** (poin′yənt) *adj.*: emotionally moving.

**ponder** (pän′dər) *v.*: think deeply.

**ponderous** (pän′dər·əs) *adj.*: very heavy.

**portend** (pôr·tend′) *v.*: signify.

**posterity** (päs·ter′ə·tē) *n.*: generations to come.

**potent** (pōt′′nt) *adj.*: powerful or effective.

**precarious** (pri·ker′ē·əs) *adj.*: uncertain; insecure; risky; unstable. —**precariously** *adv.*

**precedence** (pres′ə·dəns) *n.*: priority because of superiority in rank.

**preeminent** (prē·em′ə·nənt) *adj.*: above all else. —**preeminently** *adv.*

**preposterous** (prē·päs′tər·əs) *adj.*: ridiculous.

**prestigious** (pres·tij′əs) *adj.*: impressive; having distinction.

**pretense** (prē·tens′) *n.*: false claim.

**prevalent** (prev′ə·lənt) *adj.*: widely existing; frequent.

**prodigy** (präd′ə·jē) *n.*: extremely gifted person.

**profound** (prō·found′) *adj.*: deep. —**profoundly** *adv.*

**profundity** (prō·fun′də·tē) *n.*: intellectual depth.

**profuse** (prō·fyoos′) *adj.*: in great quantities. —**profusely** *adv.*

**prostrate** (präs′trāt′) *adj.*: **1.** lying flat. **2.** helpless; overcome.

**protrude** (prō·trood′) *v.*: stick out. —**protruding** *v.* used as *adj.*

---

at, āte, cär; ten, ēve; is, īce; gō, hôrn, look, tool; oil, out; up, fur; ə *for unstressed vowels, as* a *in* ago, u *in focus;* ′ *as in* Latin (lat′′n); chin; she; thin; *the*; zh *as in* azure (azh′ər); ŋ *as in* ring (riŋ)

**provisional** (prə·vizh'ə·nəl) *adj.*: temporary; serving for the time being.

**provocation** (präv'ə·kā'shən) *n.*: something that stirs up action or feeling.

**provoke** (prə·vōk') *v.*: anger. —**provoked** *v.* used as *adj.*

**proximity** (präk·sim'ə·tē) *n.*: nearness.

**prudence** (prōō'dəns) *n.*: sound judgment.

**pulverize** (pul'vər·īz') *v.*: crush; destroy.

**puncture** (puŋk'chər) *n.*: small hole.

# R

**rakish** (rāk'ish) *adj.*: casual; stylish. —**rakishly** *adv.*

**rancor** (raŋ'kər) *n.*: anger.

**ravage** (rav'ij) *n.*: violent destruction.

**realm** (relm) *n.*: kingdom.

**recede** (ri·sēd') *v.*: become more distant and indistinct.

**recoil** (ri·koil') *v.*: shrink away; draw back.

**reconcile** (rek'ən·sīl') *v.*: make peace.

**rectitude** (rek'tə·tōōd') *n.*: correctness.

**reiteration** (rē·it'ə·rā'shən) *n.*: repetition.

**relinquish** (ri·liŋ'kwish) *v.*: give up.

**remit** (ri·mit') *v.*: cancel; refrain from enforcing payment.

**rend** (rend) *v.*: violently rip apart. —**rending** *v.* used as *n.*

**render** (ren'dər) *v.*: make.

**rendezvous** (rän'dā·vōō') *n.*: meeting. —**rendezvous** *n.* used as *adj.*

**renounce** (ri·nouns') *v.*: give up.

**reproach** (ri·prōch') *v.*: blame; disgrace.

**reserve** (ri·zʉrv') *n.*: self-restraint.

**resolute** (rez'ə·lōōt') *adj.*: determined; resolved; unwavering.

**resolve** (ri·zälv') *v.*: make a decision; determine.

**resonance** (rez'ə·nəns) *n.*: capacity to intensify sound.

**retort** (ri·tôrt') *n.*: quick, sharp answer.

**retract** (ri·trakt') *v.*: take back; draw back.

**retraction** (ri·trak'shən) *n.*: withdrawal.

**revel** (rev'əl) *v.*: take pleasure.

**reverberate** (ri·vʉr'bə·rāt') *v.*: resound; re-echo.

**reverential** (rev'ə·ren'shəl) *adj.*: deeply respectful.

**rigorous** (rig'ər·əs) *adj.*: precise; severe.

**rotund** (rō·tund') *adj.*: round; plump.

**ruse** (rōōz) *n.*: trick; deception.

# S

**sagacious** (sə·gā'shəs) *adj.*: wise; keenly perceptive.

**sarcastic** (sär·kas'tik) *adj.*: scornful; mocking.

**sate** (sāt) *v.*: satisfy.

**savory** (sā'vər·ē) *adj.*: appetizing; tasty.

**scruple** (skrōō'pəl) *v.*: hesitate because of feelings of guilt.

**scrupulous** (skrōōp'yə·ləs) *adj.*: painstaking; with great care. —**scrupulously** *adv.*

**semblance** (sem'bləns) *n.*: outward appearance; likeness.

**sentinel** (sent''n·əl) *n.*: guard; sentry.

**simultaneous** (sī'məl·tā'nē·əs) *adj.*: at the same time. —**simultaneously** *adv.*

**singular** (siŋ'gyə·lər) *adj.*: remarkable.

**solace** (säl'is) *v.*: comfort.

**solemnity** (sə·lem'nə·tē) *n.*: seriousness. —**solemn** *adj.*

**sordid** (sôr'did) *adj.*: dirty; cheap; shameful.

**spurn** (spʉrn) *v.*: reject.

**stagnant** (stag'nənt) *adj.*: not flowing or moving.

**stolid** (stäl'id) *adj.*: showing little emotion; impassive. —**stolidly** *adv.*

**stolidity** (stə·lid'ə·tē) *n.*: absence of emotional reactions.

**striking** *adj.*: impressive; attractive.

**subsequent** (sub'si·kwənt) *adj.*: following.

**subside** (səb·sīd') *v.*: lessen.

**subsist** (səb·sist') *v.*: stay alive. —**subsisting** *v.* used as *adj.*

**successive** (sək·ses'iv) *adj.*: consecutive.

**superficial** (sōō'pər·fish'əl) *adj.*: not profound; shallow.

**superfluous** (sə·pʉr'flōō·əs) *adj.*: more than is needed or wanted; useless.

**supplication** (sup'lə·kā'shən) *n.*: plea; prayer.

**sustain** (sə·stān') *v.*: prolong. —**sustained** *v.* used as *adj.*

# T

**taboo** (tə·bōō') *n.*: social restriction.

**tactful** (takt'fəl) *adj.*: skilled in saying the right thing.

**tactile** (tak'təl) *adj.*: able to be perceived by touch.

**tedious** (tē'dē·əs) *adj.*: tiring; dreary.

**temple** (tem'pəl) *n.*: side of the forehead, just above and in front of the ear.

**temporal** (tem'pə·rəl) *adj.*: temporary.

**tenuous** (ten′yoo·əs) *adj.:* slight; insubstantial; not firm.

**tepid** (tep′id) *adj.:* lukewarm.

**tout** (tout) *v.:* praise highly.

**tranquil** (traŋ′kwəl) *adj.:* calm; quiet.

**transcendent** (tran·sen′dənt) *adj.:* excelling; surpassing.

**transient** (tran′shənt) *adj.:* temporary; passing quickly or soon.

**transition** (tran·zish′ən) *n.:* passage from one condition, form, or stage to another.

**tread** (tred) *n.:* step; walk.

**trepidation** (trep′ə·dā′shən) *n.:* anxious uncertainty.

**tumultuous** (too·mul′choo·əs) *adj.:* violent; noisy and disorderly; greatly agitated or disturbed; stormy.

**turbulence** (tʉr′byə·ləns) *n.:* wild disorder.

**tyranny** (tir′ə·nē) *n.:* cruel use of power.

# U

**ultimatum** (ul′tə·māt′əm) *n.:* last offer; final proposition.

**undulation** (un′jə·lā′shən) *n.:* wavelike motion.

**unnerve** (un·nʉrv′) *v.:* cause to lose one's courage.

# V

**valor** (val′ər) *n.:* great courage.

**vanity** (van′ə·tē) *n.:* excessive pride.

**venerable** (ven′ər·ə·bəl) *adj.:* worthy of respect, usually by reason of age.

**vengeance** (ven′jəns) *n.:* revenge; punishment in return for a wrongdoing.

**vengeful** (venj′fəl) *adj.:* intent on revenge.

**venture** (ven′chər) *v.:* dare or risk going.

**veracious** (və·rā′shəs) *adj.:* honest; truthful.

**veritable** (ver′i·tə·bəl) *adj.:* genuine; true.

**vibrant** (vi′brənt) *adj.:* full of energy.

**vigilant** (vij′ə·lənt) *adj.:* watchful. —**vigilant** *adj.* used as *n.*

**vindicate** (vin′də·kāt′) *v.:* prove correct; justify. —**vindicated** *v.* used as *adj.*

**virile** (vir′əl) *adj.:* manly; masculine.

**virulent** (vir′yoo·lənt) *adj.:* full of hate; venomous.

**vital** (vīt′'l) *adj.:* filled with life.

**vulnerability** (vul′nər·ə·bil′ə·tē) *n.:* capability of being hurt.

# W

**wanton** (wänt′'n) *adj.:* careless, often with deliberate ill will. —**wantonly** *adv.*

**wariness** (wer′ē·nis) *n.:* carefulness; caution.

**wither** (with′ər) *v.:* dry up; weaken. —**withering** *v.* used as *adj.*

---

at, āte, cär; ten, ēve; is, īce; gō, hôrn, look, tool; oil, out; up, fʉr; ə *for unstressed vowels, as* a *in* ago, u *in focus;* ′ *as in* Latin (lat′'n); chin; she; thin; *the*; zh *as in* azure (azh′ər); ŋ *as in* ring (riŋ)

# Spanish Glossary

## A

**abiding/duradero** *adj.* perpetuo; perdurable; respetuoso de las leyes.

**abhor/aborrecer** *v.* despreciar; odiar algo en particular.

**abominable/abominable** *adj.* espantoso; detestable; horrible.

**abrasion/abrasión** *s.* rozadura; frote; raspadura.

**abstinence/abstinencia** *s.* privación; abstención.

**abyss/abismo** *s.* precipicio; barranco.

**acquiesce/consentir** *v.* asentir en; conformarse con; aceptar o consentir sin protestar.

**acrid/acre** *adj.* corrosivo; áspero.

**acrimonious/mordaz** *adj.* enojoso; cáustico.

**acute/agudo** *adj.* penetrante; afilado.

**admonish/amonestar** *v.* reprender; advertir; aconsejar.

**adversary/adversario** *s.* enemigo; contrincante; antagonista.

**adorn/adornar** *v.* embellecer; decorar.

**affliction/aflicción** *s.* pesar; angustia; consternación.

**affluent/próspero** *adj.* acaudalado; rico; opulento.

**afford/dar** *v.* 1. proporcionar; conceder; facilitar. 2. permitirse o costearse algo.

**alacrity/diligencia** *s.* prontitud; alacridad; esmero.

**allegiance/lealtad** *s.* devoción; fidelidad.

**alleviate/aliviar** *v.* mitigar; calmar; tranquilizar.

**alliance/alianza** *s.* coalición; liga; asociación convenida por beneficio mutuo.

**ancestral/ancestral** *adj.* patrimonial; hereditario.

**antipathy/antipatía** *s.* hostilidad; repugnancia; aversión.

**apathy/apatía** *s.* indolencia; abandono; indiferencia; falta de emoción.

**aprocyphal/apócrifo** *s.* falso; de veracidad dudosa; ficticio.

**appaling/espantoso** *adj.* horrible; aterrador; grotesco; temible.

**appease/apaciguar** *v.* tranquilizar; sosegar; satisfacer; calmar.

**appreciable/apreciable** *adj.* estimable; respetable; importante; considerable.

**apprehension/aprensión** *s.* recelo; temor del futuro.

**appropriate/apropiarse** *v.* captar; adaptar; adecuar.

**archaic/arcaico** *adj.* antiguo; vetusto; prehistórico.

**ardent/ardiente** *adj.* intenso; ávido; vivo.

**arduous/arduo** *adj.* espinoso; difícil.

**arrogance/arrogancia** *s.* soberbia; presunción; orgullo.

**ascertain/comprobar** *v.* verificar; cotejar; constatar.

**ascribe/atribuir** *v.* imputar; dedicar; considerar que proviene de una causa cierta.

**assailant/asaltante** *s.* atracador; agresor.

**assess/evaluar** *v.* valorar; calcular el valor de.

**atrocious/atroz** *adj.* cruel; horrible; feo.

**atrocity/atrocidad** *s.* crueldad; barbaridad.

**attribute/imputar** *v.* atribuir, pensar que resulta de.

**austere/austero** *adj.* sobrio; riguroso; serio; sin adornos.

**autonomy/autonomía** *s.* independencia; emancipación; soberanía.

**avarice/avaricia** *s.* codicia; egoísmo.

**avert/apartar** *v.* alejar; evitar; desviar.

## B

**bedlam/alboroto** *s.* tumulto; agitación; algarabía; bulla.

**bewitch/hechizar** *v.* fascinar; embrujar; cautivar; encantar; hacer que algo o alguien sea irresistible.

**bicker/discutir** *v.* reñir; pelear; lidiar sobre algo que no es muy importante.

**blanch/palidecer** *v.* perder el color; demacrar.

**bleak/desolado** *adj.* un paisaje desierto; un futuro poco prometedor.

**blithe/alegre** *adj.* sin preocupaciones; lozano; fresco.

**bountiful/generoso** *adj.* una cosecha abundante; copioso; exuberante.

**brazenness/descaro** *s.* frescura; atrevimiento; osadía; audacia.

## C

**caliber/calibre** *s.* calidad o capacidad; característica.

**candid/sincero** *s.* franco; imparcial; ingenuo.

**caper/travesura** *s.* diablura; fechoría.

**careen/volcar** *v.* inclinar; invertir; tumbar.

**celestial/celeste** *adj.* divino; perfecto; glorioso; etéreo.

**censor/censurar** *v.* eliminar o modificar material que se estima inaceptable.

**circumvent/embaucar** *v.* evitar algo mediante el engaño; timar; enredar.

**clammy/pegajoso** *adj.* frío y húmedo.

**clamor/clamor** *s.* estruendo; ruido; fragor.

**cleft/grieta** *s.* hendidura; abertura.

**coherent/coherente** *adj.* lógico; claro; razonable.

**coincide/coincidir** *v.* ocurrir al mismo tiempo; concordar; armonizar; concurrir.

**commodious/espacioso** *adj.* ancho.

**communal/comunal** *adj.* público; colectivo; general; que pertenece a un grupo entero.

**compel/compeler** *v.* obligar; forzar; imponer.

**comply/cumplir** *v.* obedecer; acatar.

**conceive/concebir** *v.* imaginar; pensar; creer.

**conception/concepción** *s.* idea; pensamiento; concepto.

**concession/concesión** *s.* consentimiento; indulgencia; aprobación.

**confiscation/confiscación** *s.* apropiación; retención; requisa de propiedad por las autoridades.

**conflagration/conflagración** *s.* incendio enorme; fuego.

**conjecture/conjetura** *s.* suposición; hipótesis; sospecha.

**conscientious/concienzudo** *adj.* esmerado; escrupuloso.

**consolation/consuelo** *s.* alivio; desahogo; remedio.

**consternation/consternación** *s.* abatimiento; aturdimiento tras un susto o un disgusto.

**constitution/constitución** *s.* condición física; temperamento.

**constrain/constreñir** *v.* obligar; imponer; exigir.

**contemptuous/despreciativo** *adj.* peyorativo; frío; indiferente.

**contrivance/invención** *s.* ardid; artificio.

**conundrum/enigma** *s.* misterio; adivinanza.

**convene/convenir** *v.* coincidir; concurrir; acudir.

**conviction/convicción** *s.* persuasión; certeza; creencia.

**convivial/sociable** *adj.* jovial; alegre; comunicativo.

**copious/copioso** *adj.* abundante; generoso; cuantioso.

**covet/codiciar** *v.* ambicionar, desear con fuerte anhelo.

**craven/cobarde** *adj.* pávido; temeroso.

**crucial/crucial** *adj.* decisivo; capital.

**cunning/astuto** *adj.* ingenuo; listo; avisado.

## D

**debris/escombros** *s.* escorias; desechos; sobras.

**deference/deferencia** *s.* atención; respeto; educación.

**deferential/deferente** *adj.* atento; respetuoso; considerado.

**deluge/diluvio** *s.* inundación; torrente.

**delusion/engaño** *s.* error; confusión; espejismo.

**deplore/deplorar** *v.* lamentar; condenar.

**derision/mofa** *s.* burla; broma; desprecio.

**destitute/indigente** *adj.* desvalido; pobre; desdichado.

**dilapidated/derruido** *adj.* desvencijado; muy estropeado, en malas condiciones.

**diminutive/diminuto** *adj.* minúsculo; pequeño.

**disconsolate/desconsolado** *adj.* que causa tristeza o depresión, afligido, dolorido.

**disembody/separar** *v.* escindir del cuerpo.

**disperse/dispersar** *v.* separar y diseminar; dividir.

**dispirited/desalentado** *adj.* desanimado; abatido;

deprimido.

**disposition/disposición** *s.* inclinación; carácter; tendencia.

**dispute/disputa** *s.* altercado; querella; contienda.

**dissident/disidente** *adj.* disconforme; contrario; discordante.

**distraction/distracción** *s.* 1. diversión; entretenimiento. 2. aturdimiento; confusión.

**distraught/turbado** *adj.* loco; enloquecido; trastornado.

**distressed/afligido** *adj.* desolado; angustiado.

**divergence/divergencia** *s.* discrepancia; variación.

**dominion/dominio** *s.* mando; autoridad.

**drone/zumbido** *s.* ronroneo; sonido; rumor.

**dwindle/disminuir** *v.* menguar; reducir.

# E

**edible/comestible** *adj.* que se puede comer; alimenticio.

**efface/borrar** *v.* suprimir; anular.

**effectual/eficaz** *adj.* válido; eficiente; productivo.

**effervescent/efervescente** *adj.* espumoso; exaltado; agitado.

**effete/agotado** *adj.* exhausto; infructífero; poco fértil.

**elation/júbilo** *s.* gran alegría; regocijo; deleite.

**eloquence/elocuencia** *adj.* persuasión; palabra convincente y persuasiva.

**elude/eludir** *v.* evitar; esquivar; rodear.

**encompass/abarcar** *v.* englobar; abrazar; incorporar.

**encumbrance/estorbo** *s.* contrariedad; inconveniente; obstáculo.

**enmity/enemistad** *s.* hostilidad; odio; antipatía.

**ensue/resultar** *v.* producir; manifestar.

**enthrall/cautivar** *v.* fascinar; hechizar; encantar.

**entreat/suplicar** *v.* implorar; rogar; invocar.

**eradicate/erradicar** *v.* desarraigar plantas; extirpar una mala costumbre; eliminar; arrancar.

**eradication/erradicación** *s.* desarraigue; extirpación; eliminación; arranque.

**ethereal/etéreo** *adj.* celeste; que no es de la tierra; espiritual.—**ether/éter** *s.* esfera celeste

aparente que rodea a la Tierra.

**eulogy/elogio** *s.* encomio; aplauso; aclamación; discurso laudatorio público.

**exalt/exaltar** *v.* enaltecer; ensalzar; celebrar.

**excrutiating/intolerable** *adj.* insoportable; inaguantable; intensamente doloroso.

**exemplary/ejemplar** *adj.* intachable; excelente; que sirve de modelo; que merece copiarse.

**expedient/conveniencia** *s.* utilidad.

**expire/expirar** *v.* morir; fallecer; caducar.

**explicit/explícito** *adj.* claro; manifiesto; evidente.

**expunge/borrar** *v.* tachar; suprimir.

**extremity/extremidad** *s.* miembro del cuerpo, en particular los pies y las manos.

# F

**facilitate/facilitar** *v.* proveer; allanar; posibilitar; simplificar.

**fastidious/melindroso** *adj.* delicado; quisquilloso; caprichoso.

**fervent/ardiente** *adj.* ferviente; vehemente; apasionado.

**fitful/espasmódico** *adj.* convulsivo; crispado.

**florid/florido** *adj.* adornado; estilo elocuente; labrado.

**flourish/florecer** *v.* brotar; prosperar.

**frenzy/frenesí** *s.* arrebato; delirio; agitación.

**frivolity/frivolidad** *s.* futilidad; trivialidad; superficialidad.

**furtive/furtivo** *adj.* 1. que actúa a escondidas. 2. que se hace en secreto.

**futile/vano** *adj.* inútil; frívolo; pueril.

# G

**garrulous/locuaz** *adj.* parlanchín; indiscreto; que habla mucho de temas poco importantes.

**gaudy/chillón** *adj.* llamativo; vistoso; sobrecargado.

**gesticulate/gesticular** *v.* menear; moverse mucho especialmente con las manos y los brazos.

**grotesque/grotesco** *adj.* extraño; absurdo.

**gyration/giro** *s.* vuelta; rotación.

# H

**habitual/habitual** *adj.* acostumbrado; inveterado; habituado.

**haggard/ojeroso** *adj.* pálido; exangüe; agotado; marchito.

**hail/saludar** *v.* llamar; aclamar.

**hedonistic/hedonista** *adj.* gozador; sensualista; indulgente consigo mismo.

**hysteria/histeria** *s.* nerviosismo; excitación fuera de control.

# I

**idealist/idealista** *s.* persona guiada por sus ideales o sus principios de perfección.

**illumine/iluminar** *v.* alumbrar; encender; brillar.

**immune/inmune** *adj.* exento; libre; protegido.

**impart/impartir** *v.* revelar; inculcar; comunicar.

**impassive/impasible** *adj.* inalterable; inmutable.

**impeccable/impecable** *adj.* perfecto; correcto; sin error o defecto.

**imperative/imperativo** *adj.* absolutamente necesario; obligado; urgente.

**imperceptible/imperceptible** *adj.* gradual; paulatino, inapreciable.

**impervious/insensible** *adj.* indiferente; impasible; resistente; impenetrable.

**impetuous/impetuoso** *adj.* impulsivo; precipitado.

**impious/impío** *adj.* incrédulo; ateo; irreverente.

**impregnable/invulnerable** *adj.* inexpugnable; que no se puede capturar o penetrar.

**improvident/gastador** *adj.* derrochador; que no ahorra para el futuro.

**impulse/impulso** *s.* deseo repentino; estímulo.

**impute/imputar** *v.* hacer responsable; atribuir; asignar.

**incessant/incesante** *adj.* constante; continuo; perpetuo.

**inconceivable/inconcebible** *adj.* sorprendente; extraordinario; que no se puede comprender.

**indolent/indolente** *adj.* apático; perezoso.

**induce/inducir** *v.* persuadir; convencer; incitar.

**indulge/mimar** *v.* consentir; permitir.

**inert/inerte** *adj.* inactivo; inmóvil; quieto.

**inevitable/inevitable** *adj.* necesario; irremediable; fijo.

**inextricable/inextricable** *adj.* confuso; enredado; complicado.

**infamous/infame** *adj.* de mala fama; disoluto.

**infirm/enfermizo** *adj.* débil; enclenque; achacoso.

**ingenous/ingenuo** *adj.* cándido; inocente; sencillo; demasiado confiado.

**inherent/inherente** *adj.* congénito; innato; propio.

**iniquity/iniquidad** *s.* perversidad; maldad; perfidia.

**inscrutable/inescrutable** *adj.* insondable; recóndito; misterioso.

**insidious/insidioso** *adj.* pérfido; traidor; espía.

**insolent/insolente** *adj.* desvergonzado; fresco; ofensivo.

**insuperable/insuperable** *adj.* excelente; óptimo; impar; que no se puede mejorar.

**insurrection/insurrección** *s.* sedición; motín; revuelta.

**intangible/intangible** *adj.* impalpable; invisible; sutil.

**integrate/integrar** *v.* completar; suplir; añadir; reunir.

**intent/atento** *adj.* considerado; galante; dispuesto; vigilante.

**interloper/intruso** *s.* indiscreto; impostor; fisgón.

**interminable/interminable** *adj.* sin fin; imperecedero; eterno; perpetuo.

**interpose/interponer** *v.* intercalar; insertar; mezclar.

**intersperse/esparcir** *v.* entremezclar; diseminar.

**intimate/insinuar** *v.* sugerir; aludir; indicar.

**intricate/intrincado** *adj.* complicado; enredado; equívoco.

**intrigue/intriga** *s.* maquinación; complot; ardid.

**intuitive/intuitivo** *adj.* instintivo; automático; sin razonamiento consciente.

**invincible/invencible** *adj.* invulnerable; inmune.

**inviolate/intacto** *adj.* ileso, incorrupto.

# L

**laborious/laborioso** *adj.* trabajoso; penoso; costoso.

**labyrinth/laberinto** *s.* lugar lleno de enredos; caos.

**lamentable/lamentable** *adj.* triste; deplorable; calamitoso.

**legacy/legado** s. herencia; cesión; dote.

**lethargy/letargo** s. sopor; modorra; somnolencia.

**listless/decaído** adj. indiferente; sin energía ni interés.

**loiter/rezagarse** v. vagar; deambular.

**lucid/lúcido** adj. consciente; claro; penetrante; fino.

**ludicrous/absurdo** adj. ridículo; irracional; incoherente.

**luxuriant/exuberante** adj. copioso; generoso; abundante.

## M

**magnanimity/magnanimidad** s. generosidad; nobleza; altruismo.

**magnitude/magnitud** s. dimensión; importancia; alcance.

**malice/malicia** s. picardía; perfidia; deseo de hacer el mal.

**malign/calumniar** v. difamar; hablar mal de otro.

**malignant/maligno** adj. perverso; malo; destructivo.

**malodorous/maloliente** adj. fétido; hediondo; que hule mal.

**manifest/manifiesto** adj. evidente; notorio; ostensible.

**martial/marcial** adj. guerrero; bélico; valiente.

**medium/medio** s. instrumento; material para un artista.

**melancholy/melancólico** adj. triste; sombrío.

**mesmerize/hipnotizar** v. hechizar; magnetizar.

**mirth/alegría** s. regocijo; júbilo.

**mortify/mortificar** v. apesadumbrar; afligir; apenar.

**municipal/municipal** adj. comunal; administrativo; que pertenece a una comunidad.

**myriad/miríada** s. multitud; infinidad.

## N

**nape/nuca** s. cogote; cerviz.

**nimbus/nimbo** s. aureola; corona; halo.

**nomadic/nómada** adj. errante; ambulante; vagabundo.

**noncommittal/evasivo** adj. ambiguo; impreciso.

**nostalgia/nostalgia** s. añoranza; recuerdo; melancolía.

**notorious/célebre** adj. famoso; popular; conocido; un criminal notorio.

## O

**oblique/oblicuo** adj. inclinado; diagonal; torcido.

**obliterate/obliterar** v. impedir; eliminar; tachar.

**obscure/oscurecer** v. ocultar; disimular; esconder.

**obscurity/oscuridad** s. noche; tinieblas; sombra.

**occult/oculto** adj. recóndito; clandestino; escondido.

**ominous/siniestro** adj. inquietante; adverso.

**omnipotent/omnipotente** adj. todopoderoso; supremo; soberano.

**opaque/opaco** adj. oscuro; mate; turbio.

**oscillation/oscilación** s. vaivén; fluctuación; flujo.

**ostentatious/ostentoso** adj. aparatoso; teatral; grandioso.

## P

**pandemonium/caos** s. gran confusión; anarquía; jaleo.

**parsimony/parsimonia** s. parquedad; frugalidad.

**pauper/pobre** s. persona indigente.

**penitent/penitente** adj. mortificado; arrepentido; contrito.

**pensive/pensativo** adj. meditabundo; ensimismado; absorto.

**perennial/eterno** adj. continuo; perenne.

**perilous/peligroso** adj. arriesgado; azaroso.

**perseverance/perseverancia** s. constancia; persistencia; firmeza.

**persistent/persistente** adj. continuo; constante.

**pertinent/pertinente** adj. oportuno; acertado; apto; una observación referente al tema.

**perturbation/perturbación** s. inquietud; nerviosismo.

**perverse/perverso** adj. perjudicial; contrario; nocivo.

**pervert/pervertir** v. trastornar; perturbar; depravar; corromper.

pestilential/pestilente *adj.* peligroso o dañino, como una infección mortal.

petulance/petulancia *s.* irritabilidad; impaciencia.

pious/piadoso *adj.* devoto; religioso; practicante; creyente.

pivotal/esencial *adj.* fundamental; que actúa como eje.

placid/plácido *adj.* apacible; tranquilo; sosegado.

plague/plaga *s.* calamidad; catástrofe; desastre.

plaintive/quejumbroso *adj.* lastimero; triste; apenado.

plausibility/plausibilidad *s.* veracidad; certeza; factible.

plunder/saqueo *s.* pillaje; botín.

poignant/conmovedor *adj.* patético; triste; melancólico; dolor agudo; mordaz.

ponder/considerar *v.* examinar; reflexionar; pensar.

ponderous/laborioso *adj.* pesado, que se mueve con lentitud.

portend/presagiar *v.* predecir; profetizar; pronosticar; augurar algo malo; vaticinar.

posterity/posteridad *s.* futuro; porvenir; futuras generaciones.

potent/potente *adj.* un argumento poderoso, un remedio eficaz; fuerte.

precarious/precario *adj.* inestable; inseguro.

precedence/precedencia *s.* primacía; prioridad debida al rango o a la edad.

preeminent/preeminente *adj.* relevante; de mayor importancia.

preposterous/absurdo *adj.* ridículo; extravagante.

prestigious/prestigioso *adj.* acreditado; famoso; popular; distinguido.

pretense/pretensión *s.* petición falsa.

prevalent/predominante *adj.* preponderante; frecuente.

prodigy/prodigio *s.* fenómeno; niño dotado de un talento extraordinario.

profound/profundo *adj.* hondo; penetrante; intenso.

profundity/profundidad *s.* fondo intelectual.

profuse/profuso *adj.* abundante; pródigo; copioso.

protrude/sobresalir *v.* resaltar; despuntar; predominar.

provisional/provisional *adj.* temporal; transitorio.

provocation/provocación *s.* desafío; reto; incitación.

provoke/provocar *v.* suscitar; irritar; excitar.

proximity/proximidad *s.* cercanía; vecindad; contacto.

prudence/prudencia *s.* sensatez; moderación; cautela.

pulverize/pulverizar *v.* machacar; destruir; demoler.

puncture/pinchazo *s.* punzada; perforación.

## R

rakish/desenvuelto *adj.* resuelto; original.

rancor/rencor *s.* odio; resentimiento; aversión.

ravage/destrozar *v.* asolar; desfigurar; causar estragos; arrasar.

realm/reino *s.* terreno; esfera.

recede/retroceder *v.* retirarse; volverse atrás.

recoil/rechazar *v.* echarse atrás; sentir repugnancia por; tener horror.

reconcile/reconciliar *v.* interceder; mediar; arreglar; poner fin a una disputa.

rectitude/rectitud *s.* integridad; dignidad.

reiteration/reiteración *s.* repetición; confirmación; reincidencia.

relinquish/renunciar *v.* desistir; dimitir.

remit/remitir *v.* realizar un pago; enviar; expedir; facturar.

rend/rasgar *v.* rajar; hender; desgarrar.

render/rendir *v.* dar gracias a Dios; presentar; dar cuenta de; entregar.

rendez-vous/cita *s.* convocatoria; reunión.

renounce/renunciar *v.* desistir; dimitir; declinar.

reproach/reprender *v.* condenar; criticar; censurar.

reserve/reserva *s.* prudencia; discreción; reticencia.

resolute/resuelto *adj.* determinado; decidido; audaz; temerario.

resolve/resolución *s.* decisión; propósito; valor.

resonance/resonancia *s.* repercusión; eco; capacidad de intensificar un sonido.

retort/réplica *s.* argumento; objeción.

retract/retractar *v.* retirar; revocar; rescindir; anular.

retraction/retractación *s.* rescisión; anulación;

revocación.

**revel/deleitarse** *v.* gozar; divertirse; disfrutar.

**reverberate/reverberar** *v.* repercutir; resonar; retumbar.

**reverential/reverencial** *adj.* que actúa con un gran respeto.

**rigorous/riguroso** *adj.* duro; preciso; severo.

**rotund/rotundo** *adj.* redondo; corpulento; grueso.

**ruse/ardid** *s.* astucia; treta.

## S

**sagacious/sagaz** *adj.* perspicaz; prudente; sensato.

**sarcastic/sarcástico** *adj.* punzante; que se burla de algo o de alguien; satírico.

**sate/saciar** *v.* hartar; satisfacer; colmar.

**savory/sabroso** *adj.* suculento; gustoso; apetitoso.

**scruple/escrúpulo** *s.* miramiento; recato; duda.

**scrupulous/escrupuloso** *adj.* cuidadoso; esmerado; aplicado.

**semblance/semblante** *s.* aspecto exterior; fisonomía; parecer.

**sentinel/centinela** *s.* guardián; vigilante.

**simultaneous/simultáneo** *adj.* sincrónico; paralelo; presente; que ocurre al mismo tiempo.

**singular/singular** *adj.* único; extraño; original.

**solace/consuelo** *s.* alivio; desahogo.

**solemnity/solemnidad** *s.* ceremonia; protocolo; seriedad.

**sordid/sórdido** *adj.* mezquino; indecoroso; vil.

**spurn/despreciar** *v.* rechazar; menospreciar; desfavorecer; desdeñar.

**stagnant/estancado** *adj.* estacionario; sin movimiento.

**stolid/impasible** *adj.* imperturbable; impávido.

**stolidity/impasibilidad** *s.* imperturbabilidad; equilibrio; serenidad.

**striking/sorprendente** *adj.* impresionante; admirable.

**subsequent/subsiguiente** *adj.* sucesivo.

**subside/disminuir** *v.* 1. hundirse una estructura o terreno. 2. dejarse caer.

**subsist/subsistir** *v.* perdurar; vivir; aguantar.

**successive/sucesivo** *adj.* continuo; repetido; cíclico.

**superficial/superficial** *adj.* frívolo; que solamente toca la superficie; somero.

**superfluous/superfluo** *adj.* prolijo; sobrante; redundante; más de lo necesario.

**supplication/súplica** *s.* ruego; demanda humilde; solicitud.

**sustain/mantener** *v.* sostener; conservar; alimentar; nutrir.

## T

**taboo/tabú** *s.* prohibición; restricción social.

**tactful/discreto** *adj.* lleno de tacto; que sabe decir lo correcto.

**tactile/táctil** *adj.* palpable; tangible; que se percibe tocando.

**tedious/tedioso** *adj.* aburrido; pesado; fastidioso.

**temple/sien** *s.* lado de la frente, justo encima y en frente de los oídos.

**temporal/temporal** *adj.* transitorio; pasajero.

**tenous/tenue** *adj.* sutil; frágil; delicado.

**tepid/tibio** *adj.* templado; ni caliente ni frío.

**tout/alabar** *v.* ensalzar; vender algo.

**tranquil/tranquilo** *adj.* sereno; sosegado; apacible.

**transcendent/trascendente** *adj.* eminente; excelente; culminante.

**transient/transitorio** *adj.* temporal; provisorio; provisional.

**transition/transición** *s.* metamorfosis; evolución; etapa entre una condición a la otra.

**tread/pisar** *v.* andar; pasar; marcar.

**trepidation/trepidación** *s.* estremecimiento; conmoción; incertidumbre ansiosa; ansiedad.

**tumultous/tumultuoso** *adj.* disturbado; alborotado; turbulento; revuelto.

**turbulence/turbulencia** *s.* perturbación; revuelta; disturbio.

**tyranny/tiranía** *s.* opresión; despotismo; absolutismo; abuso de poder.

## U

**ultimatum/ultimátum** *s.* exigencia; proposición final.

**undulation/ondulación** *s.* pulsación; onda.

**unnerve/desconcertar** *v.* turbar; desanimar; acobardar.

## V

**valor/valor** *s.* valentía; coraje; audacia.

**vanity/vanidad** *s.* engreimiento; presunción; orgullo desmesurado.

**venerable/venerable** *adj.* respetable; honorable; noble; digno.

**vengeance/venganza** *s.* represalia; punición; castigo.

**vengeful/vengativo** *adj.* rencoroso; resentido; vengador.

**venture/arriesgar** *v.* emprender; aventurar; osar.

**veracious/veraz** *adj.* cierto; sincero; honesto.

**veritable/verdadero** *adj.* exacto; vigente; que es verdad.

**vibrant/vibrante** *adj.* excitante; apasionante; lleno de energía.

**vigilant/vigilante** *adj.* alerta; precavido; cuidadoso.

**vindicate/vindicar** *v.* justificar; rehabilitar.

**virile/viril** *adj.* varonil; masculino.

**virulent/virulento** *adj.* venenoso; mordaz; maligno.

**vital/vital** *adj.* enérgico; vigoroso; lleno de vida.

**vulnerability/vulnerabilidad** *s.* fragilidad; delicadeza.

## W

**wanton/desenfrenado** *adj.* sin miramientos, ni precaución; negligente.

**wariness/cautela** *s.* precaución; recelo.

**wither/marchitar** *v.* debilitar; languidecer.

# Acknowledgments

*For permission to reprint copyrighted material, grateful acknowledgment is made to the following sources:*

**Agencia Literaria Carmen Balcells, S.A.:** "Plenos Poderes" from *Plenos Poderes* by Pablo Neruda. Copyright © 1962 by Pablo Neruda and Fundación Pablo Neruda.

**American Documentaries:** From "Men at War: An Interview with Shelby Foote" from *The Civil War* by Ken Burns, Rick Burns, and Geoffrey Ward. Copyright © 1990 by American Documentaries Inc.

**Andrews McMeel Universal:** "Coyote Finishes His Work" from *Giving Birth to Thunder, Sleeping with His Daughter* by Barry Holstun Lopez. Copyright © 1977 by Barry Holstun Lopez. All rights reserved.

**Arte Público Press**: "The Latin Deli: An Ars Poetica" by Judith Ortiz Cofer from *The Americas Review*, vol. 19, no. 1. Copyright © 1991 by Judith Ortiz Cofer. Published by Arte Público Press–University of Houston, 1991. From *Silent Dancing: A Partial Remembrance of a Puerto Rican Childhood* by Judith Ortiz Cofer. Copyright © 1990 by Judith Ortiz Cofer. Published by Arte Público Press–University of Houston, 1990. "Now and Then, America" from *Borders* by Pat Mora. Copyright © 1986 by Pat Mora. Published by Arte Público Press–University of Houston, 1986.

**Elizabeth Barnett, Literary Executor:** "Sonnet XXX" of *Fatal Interview* from *Collected Poems* by Edna St. Vincent Millay. Copyright © 1931, 1958 by Edna St. Vincent Millay and Norma Millay Ellis. Published by HarperCollins. All rights reserved.

**Beacon Press, Boston:** "Autobiographical Notes" and excerpts from *Notes of a Native Son* by James Baldwin. Copyright © 1955 and renewed © 1983 by James Baldwin.

**Susan Bergholz Literary Services, New York:** From "An American Childhood in the Dominican Republic" by Julia Alvarez from *The American Scholar*, vol. 56, no. 1, Winter 1987. Copyright © 1987 by Julia Alvarez. "Daughter of Invention" from *How the Garcia Girls Lost Their Accents* by Julia Alvarez. Copyright © 1991 by Julia Alvarez. Published by Plume, an imprint of Dutton Signet, a division of Penguin Group (USA). Originally published in hardcover by Algonquin Books of Chapel Hill. All rights reserved. "How I Learned to Sweep" from *Homecoming* by Julia Alvarez. Copyright © 1984, 1996 by Julia Alvarez. Published by Plume, an imprint of Dutton Signet, a division of Penguin Group (USA). Originally published by Grove Press. All rights reserved. "Straw into Gold" by Sandra Cisneros. Copyright © 1987 by Sandra Cisneros. First published in *The Texas Observer*, September 1987. All rights reserved.

**BOA Editions, Ltd:** "the mississippi river empties into the gulf" from *the terrible stories* by Lucille Clifton. Copyright © 1996 by Lucille Clifton. From "Furious Versions" and from "Arise, Go Down" from *The City in Which I Love You* by Li-Young Lee. Copyright © 1990 by Li-Young Lee. "Visions and Interpretations" from *Rose* by Li-Young Lee. Copyright © 1986 by Li-Young Lee.

**Estate of Margaret Bourke-White:** From "April in Germany" from *Dear Fatherland, Rest Quietly* by Margaret Bourke-White. Copyright © 1946 by Margaret Bourke-White; copyright renewed © 1974 by the Estate of Margaret Bourke-White.

**Brooks Permissions:** "In Honor of David Anderson Brooks, My Father" and "The Bean Eaters" from *Blacks* by Gwendolyn Brooks. Copyright © 1991 by Gwendolyn Brooks. Published by Third World Press, Chicago, 1991.

**Grace Cavalieri:** From "Rita Dove: An Interview" by Grace Cavalieri from *American Poetry Review*, March/April 1995. Copyright © 1995 by Grace Cavalieri.

**Condé Nast Publications for the Estate of E. B. White:** From "James Thurber" [retitled "The New Yorker's Farewell"] from *E. B. White: Writings from "The New Yorker," 1927–1976*. Copyright © 1961, 1989 by E. B. White. Originally appeared in *The New Yorker*. Published by HarperCollins.

**Curbstone Press:** "Ars Poetica" from *Fugues* by Claribel Alegría, translated by Darwin J. Flakoll. Copyright © 1993 by Curbstone Press. Distributed by Consortium. "Who Understands Me but Me" from *What's Happening* by Jimmy Santiago Baca. Copyright © 1982 by Jimmy Santiago Baca. Distributed by Consortium.

**Denis Donoghue:** From "The Promiscuous Cool of Postmodernism" by Denis Donoghue from *The New York Times Book Review*, June 22, 1986. Copyright © 1986 by Denis Donoghue.

**Mark Doty:** From "What is American about American Poetry?" by Mark Doty from *Poetry Society of America* Web site accessed December 11, 2001, at http://www.poetrysociety.org/doty.html. Copyright © 2001 by Mark Doty.

**Doubleday, a division of Random House, Inc.:** From *The Diary of a Young Girl: The Definitive Edition* by Anne Frank, edited by Otto H. Frank and Mirjam Pressler, translated by Susan Massotty. Copyright © 1995 by Doubleday, a division of Random House, Inc. From "Carolyn Forché" from *The Language of Life: A Festival of Poets* by Bill Moyers. Copyright © 1995 by Public Affairs Television, Inc. and David Grubin Productions, Inc. "Night Journey" from *The Collected Poems of Theodore Roethke*. Copyright 1940 by Theodore Roethke.

**Rita Dove:** Quote by Rita Dove from *Washington Post*, April 17, 1987. Copyright © 1987 by Rita Dove.

**Faber and Faber Ltd.:** From *The Criterion*, vol. IX, by T. S. Eliot. Copyright © 1967 by Faber and Faber Ltd.

**Far Corner Books:** "Trying to Name What Doesn't Change" from *Words Under the Words: Selected Poems* by Naomi Shihab Nye. Copyright © 1995 by Naomi Shihab Nye. Published by Far Corner Books, Portland, OR.

**Farrar, Straus & Giroux, LLC:** "The Fish" and "One Art" from *The Complete Poems 1927–1979* by Elizabeth Bishop. Copyright © 1979, 1983 by Alice Helen Methfessel. "The Death of the Ball Turret Gunner" and from Introduction (retitled "The Ball Turret") from *The Complete Poems* by Randall Jarrell. Copyright © 1969 and renewed © 1997 by Mary von S. Jarrell. From "Memories of West Street and Lepke" from *Life Studies* by Robert Lowell. Copyright © 1959 by Robert Lowell; copyright renewed © 1987 by Caroline Lowell, Sheridan Lowell, and Harriet Lowell. From "The Murdered Albatross" from *Passions and Impressions* by Pablo Neruda, translated by Margaret Sayers Peden. Translation copyright © 1983 by Farrar, Straus & Giroux, Inc. From "Some Aspects of the Grotesque in Southern Fiction" from *Mystery and Manners* by Flannery O'Connor. Copyright © 1969 by the Estate of Mary Flannery O'Connor. "Elsewhere" from *The Arkansas Testament* by Derek Walcott. Copyright © 1987 by Derek Walcott.

**Farrar, Straus & Giroux, Inc.** and electronic format by permission of **Russell & Volkening, Inc. as agents for the author:** "The Magic Barrel" from *The Magic Barrel* by Bernard Malamud. Copyright © 1950, 1958 and renewed © 1977, 1986 by Bernard Malamud.

**Fulcrum Publishing:** "The Sky Tree" by Joseph Bruchac from *Keepers of Life: Discovering Plants Through Native American Stories and Earth Activities for Children* by Michael J. Caduto and Joseph Bruchac. Copyright © 1994 by Fulcrum Publishing.

**The Gale Group:** Quotes by Judith Ortiz Cofer from *Contemporary Authors, New Revision Series*, vol. 32, edited by James G. Lesniak. Copyright © 1991 by The Gale Group.

**Tess Gallagher:** "Everything Stuck to Him" from *What We Talk About When We Talk About Love* by Raymond Carver. Copyright © 1977, 1983, 1988 by Raymond Carver; copyright © 1989, 2005 by Tess Gallagher.

**The Estate of Stephen Jay Gould:** "A Time of Gifts" by Stephen Jay Gould from *The New York Times*, September 26, 2001. Copyright © 2001 by Stephen Jay Gould.

**GRM Associates, Inc., Agents for the Estate of Ida M. Cullen:** "Incident" and "Tableau" from *Color* by Countee Cullen. Copyright © 1925 by Harper & Brothers; copyright renewed © 1953 by Ida M. Cullen.

**Grove/Atlantic, Inc.:** "Full Powers" from *A New Decade (Poems: 1958–1967)* by Pablo Neruda, translated by Alastair Reid. English translation copyright © 1969 by Alastair Reid.

**Harcourt, Inc.:** "The Life You Save May Be Your Own" from *A Good Man Is Hard to Find and Other Stories* by Flannery O'Connor. Copyright 1950 by Flannery O'Connor; copyright renewed © 1981 by Regina O'Connor. "The Beautiful Changes" from *The Beautiful Changes and Other Poems* by Richard Wilbur. Copyright 1947 and renewed © 1975 by Richard Wilbur.

**Harcourt, Inc.** and electronic format by permission of **The Permissions Company:** "The Jilting of Granny Weatherall" from *Flowering Judas and Other Stories* by Katherine Anne Porter. Copyright 1930 and renewed © 1958 by Katherine Anne Porter.

**Harcourt, Inc.** and electronic format by permission of **Russell & Volkening, Inc., as agents for Eudora Welty:** "A Worn Path" from *A Curtain of Green and Other Stories* by Eudora Welty. Copyright 1941 and renewed © 1969 by Eudora Welty.

**Harcourt, Inc.** and electronic format by permission of **Wendy Weil Agency, Inc.:** "Women" (as it appears in "In Search of Our Mothers' Gardens") from *Revolutionary Petunias & Other Poems* by Alice Walker. Copyright © 1970 and renewed © 1998 by Alice Walker. From "In Search of Our Mothers' Gardens" from *In Search of Our Mothers' Gardens: Womanist Prose* by Alice Walker. Copyright © 1974 by Alice Walker.

**HarperCollins Publishers, Inc.:** "The Memory of Elena" from *The Country Between Us* by Carolyn Forché. Copyright © 1981 by Carolyn Forché. "Coastal" from *Atlantis* by Mark Doty. Copyright © 1995 by Mark Doty. "Homework" and "Howl" from *Collected Poems 1947–1980* by Allen Ginsberg. Copyright © 1955, 1984 by Allen Ginsberg. "The Beep Beep Poem" from *Cotton Candy on a Rainy Day* by Nikki Giovanni. Copyright © 1978 by Nikki Giovanni. From *Dust Tracks on a Road* by Zora Neale Hurston. Copyright 1942 by Zora Neale Hurston; copyright renewed © 1970 by John C. Hurston. "The Handsomest Drowned Man in the World" from *Leaf Storm and Other Stories* by Gabriel García Márquez. Copyright © 1971 by Gabriel García Márquez. "Mirror" from *Crossing the Water* by Sylvia Plath. Copyright © 1963 by Ted Hughes. Originally appeared in *The New Yorker*. From "The Lowest Animal" from *Letters from the Earth* by Mark Twain, edited by Bernard DeVoto. Copyright 1938, 1944, 1946, © 1959, 1962 by The Mark Twain Company. Copyright 1942 by The President and Fellows of Harvard College. From page 135 from *American Hunger* by Richard Wright. Copyright © 1944 by Richard Wright; copyright © 1977 by Ellen Wright. From *Black Boy* by Richard Wright. Copyright 1937, 1942, 1944, 1945 by Richard Wright; copyright renewed © 1973 by Ellen Wright.

**Harvard University Press:** From *i: Six Nonlectures*, p. 24, by E. E. Cummings. Copyright © 1923, 1925, 1927, 1931, 1933, 1935, 1938, 1939, 1940, 1944, 1946, 1947, 1948, 1950, 1951, 1953 by E. E. Cummings; copyright © 1926 by Horace Liveright; copyright © 1934 by Modern Library, Inc.; copyright © 1940 by Gotham Book Mart; copyright © 1945 by Oscar Williams; copyright © 1948 by Charles Norman; copyright © 1951 by Wake Editions. Published by Harvard University Press, Cambridge, MA. "World, in hounding me, what do you gain?" by Sor Juana Inés de la Cruz, pp. 95 and 97, from *A Sor Juana Anthology*, translated by Alan S. Trueblood. Copyright © 1988 by the President and Fellows of Harvard College. Published by Harvard University Press, Cambridge, MA. From pp. 97–105 from *The Narrative of the Life of Frederick Douglass: An American Slave Written by Himself*, edited by Benjamin Quarles. Copyright © 1960, 1988 by the President and Fellows of Harvard College. Published by The Belknap Press of Harvard University Press, Cambridge, MA. From *Sor Juana: Or, The Traps of Faith* by Octavio Paz, translated by Margaret Sayers Peden, pp. 1–2. Copyright © 1988 by the President and Fellows of Harvard College. Published by The Belknap Press of Harvard University Press, Cambridge, MA.

**Harvard University Press and the Trustees of Amherst College:** "1624: Apparently with no surprise," "712: Because I could not stop for Death," "1763: Fame is a bee," "465: I heard a Fly buzz—when I died," "288: I'm Nobody! Who are you?," "303: The Soul selects her own Society," and "1129: Tell all the Truth but tell it slant—" from *The Poems of Emily Dickinson*, edited by Thomas H. Johnson. Copyright © 1951, 1955, 1979 by the President and Fellows of Harvard College. Published by The Belknap Press of Harvard University Press, Cambridge, MA.

**Václav Havel:** From speech by Václav Havel accepting Philadelphia Freedom Medal, July 4, 1994. Copyright © 1994 by Václav Havel.

**Hill and Wang, a division of Farrar, Straus & Giroux, LLC** and electronic format by permission of **Georges Borchardt, Inc. for Elie Wiesel:** From *Night* by Elie Wiesel, translated by Stella Rodway. Copyright © 1960 by MacGibbon & Kee; copyright renewed © 1988 by The Collins Publishing Group.

**Hill and Wang, a division of Farrar, Straus & Giroux, LLC** and electronic by permission of **Harold Ober Associates Incorporated:** From "When the Negro Was in Vogue" from *The Big Sea* by Langston Hughes. Copyright © 1940 by Langston Hughes; copyright renewed © 1968 by Arna Bontemps and George Houston Bass.

**The Johns Hopkins University Press:** Quote by Tim O'Brien from "Two Interviews: Talks with Tim O'Brien and Robert Stone" by Eric James Schroeder from *Modern Fiction Studies*, 30 Spring 1984. Copyright © 1984 by Purdue Research Foundation.

**Houghton Mifflin Company:** "When Mr. Pirzada Came to Dine" from *Interpreter of Maladies* by Jhumpa Lahiri. Copyright © 1999 by Jhumpa Lahiri. All rights reserved. "Ars Poetica" from *Collected Poems 1917–1982*, by Archibald MacLeish. Copyright © 1985 by The Estate of Archibald MacLeish. All rights reserved.

**Houghton Mifflin Company** and electronic format by permission of **SLL/Sterling Lord Literistic, Inc.:** "Young" from *All My Pretty Ones* by Anne Sexton. Copyright © 1962 by Anne Sexton; copyright renewed © 1990 by Linda G. Sexton. All rights reserved. "The Bells" from *To Bedlam and Part Way Back* by Anne Sexton. Copyright © 1960 by Anne Sexton; copyright renewed © 1988 by Linda G. Sexton. All rights reserved.

**International Creative Management, Inc.:** From "On James Baldwin" by Toni Morrison from *The New York Times Book Review*, December 20, 1987. Copyright © 1987 by Toni Morrison. From quote by Arthur Miller from *Michigan Quarterly Review*, 6, pp. 153–163. Copyright © 1967 by Arthur Miller.

**Mary Von S. Jarrell:** "The One Who Was Different" from *The Lost World* by Randall Jarrell. Copyright © 1965 by Randall Jarrell. Reprinted in *The Complete Poems of Randall Jarrell*, published by Farrar, Straus & Giroux, 1969.

**Alfred Kazin:** From *Contemporaries* by Alfred Kazin. Copyright 1924, 1946, 1952, 1955, © 1956, 1957, 1958, 1959, 1960, 1961, 1962, 1982 by Alfred Kazin.

**The Estate of Martin Luther King, Jr., c/o Writers House, LLC, as agent for the proprietor, New York, NY:** From "Letter from Birmingham City Jail" by Martin Luther King, Jr. Copyright © 1963 by Martin Luther King, Jr.; copyright renewed © 1991 by Coretta Scott King.

**Alfred A. Knopf, Inc., a division of Random House, Inc.:** From *Alistair Cooke's America*. Copyright © 1973 by Alistair Cooke. "Anecdote of the Jar" from *The Collected Poems of Wallace Stevens*. Copyright © 1954 by Wallace Stevens; copyright renewed © 1982 by Holly Stevens. From Appendix from *Hugging the Shore* by John Updike. Copyright © 1983 by John Updike. "Son" from *Problems and Other Stories* by John Updike. Copyright © 1976 by John Updike.

**Alfred A. Knopf, a division of Random House, Inc.** and electronic format by permission of **Edwidge Danticat and Aragi, Inc.:** "The Book of the Dead" from *The Dew Breaker* by Edwidge Danticat. Copyright © 2004 by Edwidge Danticat. Originally published in *The New Yorker*, June 1999.

**Alfred A. Knopf, a division of Random House, Inc.** and electronic format by permission of **Maxine Hong Kingston and the Sandra Dijkstra Literary Agency:** "The Girl Who Wouldn't Talk" from *The Woman Warrior* by Maxine Hong Kingston. Copyright © 1975, 1976 by Maxine Hong Kingston.

**Alfred A. Knopf, a division of Random House, Inc.** and electronic format by permission of **Faber & Faber Ltd.:** "Mushrooms" from *The Colossus and Other Poems* by Sylvia Plath. Copyright © 1962 by Sylvia Plath.

**Alfred A. Knopf, a division of Random House, Inc.** and electronic format by permission of **Brook Hersey:** "A Noiseless Flash" from *Hiroshima* by John Hersey. Copyright 1946 and renewed © 1974 by John Hersey.

**Alfred A. Knopf, a division of Random House, Inc.** and electronic format by permission of **Harold Ober Associates Incorporated:** "Harlem" and "The Weary Blues" from *The Selected Poems of Langston Hughes*. Copyright 1926 by Alfred A. Knopf, Inc.; copyright renewed 1954 by Langston Hughes. Copyright © 1994 by The Estate of Langston Hughes.

**Liveright Publishing Corporation:** From Introduction to *New Poems* (from *Collected Poems 1904–1962* ) by E. E. Cummings, edited by George J. Firmage. Copyright 1938, © 1966, 1991 by the Trustees for the E. E. Cummings Trust. "somewhere i have never travelled, gladly beyond" and "what if a much of a which of a wind" from *Complete Poems: 1904–1962* by E. E. Cummings, edited by George J. Firmage. Copyright 1944, © 1972, 1991 by the Trustees for the E. E. Cummings Trust; copyright © 1979 by George James Firmage.

**Lotus Press:** "Emily Dickinson" from *Songs for My Fathers* by Gary Smith. Copyright © 1984 by Gary Smith.

**Macmillan, a division of Simon & Schuster, Inc.:** "Chapter 19: The Indians' Hospitality before and after a New Calamity" from *Adventures in the Unknown Interior of America* by Cabeza de Vaca, translated and edited by Cyclone Covey. Copyright © 1961 by Cyclone Covey.

**Jeffrey Meyers:** "Foe of Walls," letter to the editor by Jeffrey Meyers from *The New York Times*, April 27, 1995. Copyright © 1995 by Jeffrey Meyers.

**National Council of Teachers of English:** "Mending Test" by Penelope Bryant Turk from *English Journal*, January 1993. Copyright © 1993 by the National Council of Teachers of English.

**Navajivan Trust:** From "Readiness for Satyagraha" from *The Essential Writings of Mahatma Gandhi*, edited by Raghavan Iyer. Copyright © 1990 by Navajivan Trust.

**New Directions Publishing Corporation:** "Helen" from *Collected Poems 1912–1944* (Hilda Doolittle). Copyright © 1982 by The Estate of Hilda Doolittle. "A Pact," "The Garden," "In a Station of the Metro," and "The River Merchant's Wife: A Letter" from *Personae: The Collected Poems of Ezra Pound*. Copyright © 1926 by Ezra Pound. "The Great Figure," "The Red Wheelbarrow," and "This is Just to Say" from *Collected Poems: 1909–1939*, vol. I, by William Carlos Williams. Copyright © 1938 by New Directions Publishing Corporation.

**New Directions Publishing Corporation** and electronic format by permission of **Harold Ober Associates Incorporated:** From "Early Success" from *The Crack-up* by F. Scott Fitzgerald. Copyright © 1945 by New Directions Publishing Corporation.

**The New York Review of Books:** From "Fitzgerald Revisited" by Jay McInerney from *The New York Review of Books*, August 15, 1991. Copyright © 1991 by NYREV, Inc.

**The New York Times Company:** From "Mississippi Honors a 'Native Son' Who Fled" by Edwin McDowell from *The New York Times*, November 23, 1985. Copyright © 1985 by The New York Times Company. From "Raymond Carver: A Still, Small Voice" by Jay McInerney from *The New York Times*, August 16, 1989. Copyright © 1989 by The New York Times Company. Quote by Tim O'Brien from "A Storyteller for the War That Won't End" by D.J.R. Bruckner from *The New York Times*, April 3, 1990. Copyright © 1990 by The New York Times Company. From "Honoring African Heritage" by Halimah Abdullah from *The New York Times*, June 22, 1997. Copyright © 1997 by The New York Times Company.

**The Nobel Foundation:** Acceptance speech by William Faulkner from *Nobel Lectures in Literature: 1901–1967*, edited by Horst Frenz. Copyright 1949 by The Nobel Foundation. Acceptance speech by Ernest Hemingway from *Nobel Lectures in Literature: 1901–1967*, edited by Horst Frenz. Copyright © 1954 by The Nobel Foundation. From Nobel Prize acceptance speech by Elie Wiesel. Copyright © 1986 by The Nobel Foundation.

**W. W. Norton & Company, Inc.:** "Medusa" from *A Nostalgist's Map of America* by Agha Shahid Ali. Copyright © 1991 by Agha Shahid Ali.

**W. W. Norton & Company, Inc.** and electronic format by permission of **Rita Dove:** "Testimonial" from *On the Bus With Rosa Parks* by Rita Dove. Copyright © 1999 by Rita Dove.

**W. W. Norton & Company, Inc.** and electronic format by permission of **Jean V. Naggar Literary Agency:** "Emily Dickinson" from *PM/AM: New and Selected Poems* by Linda Pastan. Copyright © 1971 by Linda Pastan.

**Tim O'Brien:** "Speaking of Courage" from *The Things They Carried* by Tim O'Brien. Copyright © 1979, 1990 by Tim O'Brien.

**Harold Ober Associates Incorporated:** "A Black Man Talks of Reaping" from *Personals* by Arna Bontemps. Copyright © 1963 by Arna Bontemps.

**Teresa Palomo Acosta:** "In the season of change" by Teresa Palomo Acosta. Copyright © 1994 by Teresa Palomo Acosta.

**G. P. Putnam's Sons, a division of Penguin Group (USA) Inc.** and electronic format by permission of **Amy Tan and the Sandra Dijkstra Literary Agency:** From "Rules of the Game" from *The Joy Luck Club* by Amy Tan. Copyright © 1989 by Amy Tan.

**Random House, Inc.** and electronic format by permission of **Curtis Brown Ltd.:** "The Unknown Citizen" from *W. H. Auden: The Collected Poems*, edited by Edward Mendelson. Copyright © 1940 and renewed © 1968 by W. H. Auden.

**Random House, Inc.** and electronic format by permission of **Faulkner Literary Estate:** "A Rose for Emily" from *Collected Stories of William Faulkner*. Copyright 1930 and renewed © 1958 by William Faulkner.

**Random House, Inc.** and electronic format by permission of **Russell & Volkening, Inc., as agents for Eudora Welty:** "Is Phoenix Jackson's Grandson Really Dead?" from *The Eye of the Story: Selected Essays* by Eudora Welty. Copyright © 1978 by Eudora Welty.

**Random House, Inc.** and electronic format by permission of **SLL/Sterling Lord Literistic, Inc.:** "Man Listening to Disc" from *Sailing Alone Around the Room* by Billy Collins. Copyright © 1999, 2001 by Billy Collins.

**Russell & Volkening, Inc.:** "Teenage Wasteland" by Anne Tyler from *Seventeen Magazine*, November 1983. Copyright © 1983 by Anne Tyler.

**Scribner, an imprint of Simon & Schuster Adult Publishing Group:** "Chapter 19: The Indians' Hospitality before and after a New Calamity" from *Adventures in the Unknown Interior of America* by Cabeza de Vaca, translated and annotated by Cyclone Covey. Copyright © 1961 by Macmillan Publishing. "Soldier's Home" from *In Our Time* by Ernest Hemingway. Copyright 1925 by Charles Scribner's Sons; copyright renewed 1953 by Ernest

Drinking Gourd" by H. B. Parks from *Follow de Drinkin' Gou'd, Publications of the Texas Folklore Society*, no. VII, edited by J. Frank Dobie. Copyright 1928 by the Texas Folklore Society.

**Rosemary A. Thurber and The Barbara Hogenson Agency:** From "A Biographical Sketch of James Thurber" from *Collecting Himself* by James Thurber. Copyright © 1989 by Rosemary A. Thurber. Originally published by HarperCollins Publishers. "The Secret Life of Walter Mitty" from *My World—and Welcome to It* by James Thurber. Copyright © 1942 and copyright renewed © 1970 by Rosemary A. Thurber. All rights reserved.

**Time Inc.:** From "Book of Changes" by Paul Gray from *Time*, December 6, 1976. Copyright © 1976 by Time Inc.

**Alvin Toffler:** From "The Ravaged People of East Pakistan" by Alvin Toffler from *The New York Times*, August 5, 1971. Copyright © 1971 by Alvin Toffler.

**The University of New Mexico Press:** From Introduction and excerpt from *The Way to Rainy Mountain* by N. Scott Momaday. Copyright © 1969 by The University of New Mexico Press. First published in *The Reporter*, January 26, 1967.

**University of North Carolina Press:** From *The Invasion of America* by Francis Jennings. Copyright © 1975 by the University of North Carolina Press.

**University of Oklahoma Press:** Quote by Robert Frost from *Robert Frost: Life and Talks-Walking* by Louis Mertins. Copyright © 1965 by the University of Oklahoma Press.

**University of Texas Press:** "The Feather Pillow," pp. 3–8, from *The Decapitated Chicken and Other Stories* by Horacio Quiroga, translated by Margaret Sayers Peden. Copyright © 1976 by the University of Texas Press.

**University Press of New England:** "What For" from *Yellow Light* by Garrett Kaoru Hongo. Copyright © 1982 by Garrett Kaoru Hongo. Published by Wesleyan University Press.

**Viking Penguin, a division of Penguin Group (USA) Inc.:** *The Crucible* by Arthur Miller. Copyright 1952, 1953, 1954, renewed © 1980, 1981, 1982 by Arthur Miller. "The Leader of the People" from *The Red Pony* by John Steinbeck. Copyright 1933, 1937, 1938 and renewed © 1961, 1965, 1966 by John Steinbeck.

**Villard Books, a division of Random House, Inc.** and electronic format by permission of **Cynthia Cannell Literary Agency:** From *Left for Dead* by Beck Weathers. Copyright © 2000 by S. Beck Weathers.

**Villard Books, a division of Random House, Inc.** and electronic format by permission of **Van der Leun and Associates:** From *All I Really Need to Know I Learned in Kindergarten* by Robert L. Fulghum. Copyright © 1986, 1988 by Robert L. Fulghum.

**Walden Woods Project, an Activity of The Isis Fund:** From Preface by Don Henley from *Heaven Is Under Our Feet*, edited by Don Henley and Dave Marsh. Copyright © 1991 by The Isis Fund.

**The Washington Post :** From William McPherson's review of Maxine Hong Kingston's *The Woman Warrior* from *Washington Post Book World*, October 10, 1976. Copyright © 1976 by The Washington Post. From Jonathan Yardley's review of Raymond Carver's *Cathedral* from *Washington Post Book World*, September 20, 1983. Copyright © 1983 by The Washington Post. Quote by Juan Williams from *The Washington Post*, December 2, 1987. Copyright © 1987 by The Washington Post.

**Wesleyan University Press:** "Camouflaging the Chimera" from *Neon Vernacular: New and Selected Poems* by Yusef Komunyakaa. Copyright © 1993 by Yusef Komunyakaa.

**White Pine Press:** "What Do You Feel Underground?" by Gabriela Mistral from *A Gabriela Mistral Reader*, translated by Maria Giachetti, edited by Marjorie Agosin. Translation copyright © 1993 by Maria Giachetti.

**John C. Whitehead:** Comments on war experience from *The Greatest Generation Speaks: Letters and Reflections* by Tom Brokaw. Copyright © 1999 by John Whitehead.

**The H. W. Wilson Company:** From "Gabriel García Márquez" from *Spanish American Authors: The Twentieth Century* by Angel Flores. Copyright © 1992 by Angel Flores.

**The Wylie Agency, Inc.:** "Game" from *Unspeakable Practices, Unnatural Acts* by Donald Barthelme. Copyright © 1968 by Donald Barthelme. From "Return to Gitche Gumee" by J. D. McClatchy from *The New York Times*, October 22, 2000. Copyright © 2000 by J. D. McClatchy.

**David Young:** From Introduction from *Magical Realist Fiction*, edited by David Young and Keith Hollaman. Copyright © 1984 by David Young.

***Sources Cited:***

From "Not-Knowing" by Donald Barthelme.

From "20 Questions: Jhumpa Lahiri" by Baiutra Bahadur from *Philadelphia City Paper*, September 16–23, 1999. Published by CP Communications, 1999.

Quote by Martin Niemöller from *Their Brothers' Keepers* by Philip Friedman. Published by Crown Publishers, New York, 1957.

Quote by Diarmuid Russell from *Author and Agent: Eudora Welty and Diarmuid Russell* by Michael Kreyling. Published by Farrar, Straus & Giroux, Inc., New York, 1999.

From "Nonfiction as Literature" from *On Writing Well*, Fifth Edition, by William K. Zinsser. Published by HarperPerennial, New York, 1995.

Quote by Jhumpa Lahiri from "Booked for Success" by Naresh Fernandes from *India Times*, June 13, 1999, http://www.indiatimes.com/culture/literate/jlahiri.html.

From *Death Comes for the Archbishop* by Willa Cather. Published by A. A. Knopf, New York, 1927.

From "I, Too" from *Selected Poems* by Langston Hughes Published by Alfred A. Knopf, Inc., New York, 1959.

From Galatians 6:7 from *New American Standard Bible*. Published by Lockman Foundation, 1995.

From *Selected Prose 1909–1965* by Ezra Pound, edited by William Cookson. Published by New Directions Publishing Corporation, New York, 1973.

From "Interview with Jhumpa Lahiri" by Vibhuti Patel from *Newsweek International*, September 20, 1999.

From "10. One True Sentence" from *Ernest Hemingway: A Life Story* by Carlos Baker. Published by Scribner, a division of Simon & Schuster, Inc., New York, 1969.

Quote by Billy Collins on "Man Listening to Disc" from *The Best American Poetry 2000*. Published by Scribner, New York, 2000.

From "Notes Toward A Biography" by Lois Ames from *TriQuarterly*, no. 7, Fall 1966. Published by Tri-Quarterly Books, Northwestern University, 1966.

From "Some Self-Analysis" from *On the Poet and His Craft: Selected Prose of Theodore Roethke*, edited by Ralph J. Mills, Jr. Published by University of Washington Press, 1965.

From the James Weldon Johnson Collection: Quotations from "Draft Ideas," December 3, 1964, by Langston Hughes, as they appear in *The Life of Langston Hughes, Volume II: 1941–1967, I Dream a World*. Yale Collection of American Literature, Beinecke Rare Book and Manuscript Library, Yale University.

# Picture Credits

**Page A5:** *The Declaration of Independence, 4 July 1776* (detail) by John Trumbull (1756–1843). Oil on canvas. Yale University Art Gallery, Trumbull Collection; **A12:** *Home, Sweet Home* (1863) by Winslow Homer. Oil on canvas. Image © 2005 Board of Trustees, National Gallery of Art, Washington, D. C. Patrons' Permanent Fund; **3:** (top) © Bettmann/CORBIS; (center) Kirchoff/Wohlberg; (bottom right) © CORBIS; **4:** © Geoffrey Clemens/CORBIS; **4–5:** © Burnstein Collection/CORBIS; **5:** © Bettmann/CORBIS; **11:** Culver Pictures, Inc.; **13** (right): John Carter Brown Library/Brown University, Providence, Rhode Island; **16–17:** Library of Congress; **22:** Theo Westenberger; **24:** Jerry Jacka Photography; **25:** Courtesy Gallery 10, Scottsdale, AZ/Jerry Jacka Photography; **26:** Courtesy of Fifth Generation Trading Company/Jerry Jacka Photography; **30:** © CORBIS; **33:** Courtesy of The Sor Juana Ines de la Cruz Project/Dartmouth College Library; **37:** North Wind Picture Archives; **46:** Sinclair Hamilton Collection, Graphic Arts Collections, Visual Materials Division, Department of Rare Books and Special Collections, Princeton University Libraries; **49:** © Lee Snider/Photo Images/CORBIS; **54–55** (background): Marc and Evelyn Bernheim/Woodfin Camp & Associates; **58:** © Bettmann/CORBIS; **64:** AP/Wide World Photos; **68, 73:** From the Frankliniana Collection of the Franklin Institute, Philadelphia, Pennsylvania; **74:** B. Timmons/The Image Bank; **79:** The New York Public Library/Art Resource, NY; **89:** (inset left) North Wind Picture Archives; (center), **92:** Joe Viesti/Viesti Associates; **94:** Courtesy National Park Service, Museum Management Program, and Guilford Courthouse National Military Park; **95:** Painting by Don Troiani; **103:** © Bettmann/CORBIS; **104:** Joe Viesti/Viesti Associates; **108:** © Smithsonian American Art Museum/Art Resource, NY; **111, 113:** © Bettmann/CORBIS; **116:** © Bettmann/CORBIS; **117:** © Lowe Art Museum/SuperStock; **119:** © Joseph Sohm; ChromoSohm Inc./CORBIS; **131:** © Giraudon/Art Resource, NY; **134:** The New York Public Library/Art Resource, NY; **137:** (top left) Archie Ferguson, *Hope Leslie* by Catherine Maria Sedgwick. Copyright © 1987 by Rutgers, The State University of New Jersey. Reprinted by permission of Rutgers University Press; (top right) Cover illustration from *Africans in America: America's Journey Through Slavery,* copyright © 1998 by WGGH Educational Foundation, with the exception of the fictional material by Charles Johnson. Fictional material copyright © 1998 by Charles Johnson, reprinted by permission of Harcourt, Inc.; (bottom left) Jacket design from *In the Trail of the Wind* by John Bierhorst. Cover illustration: *A Blackfoot Indian on Horseback,* aquatint engraving after Karl Bodmer. From *Travels in the Interior of North America* by Maximillian, Prince of Wied. Published in 1843 (Joselyn Art Museum, Omaha, Nebraska). Reprinted by permission of Farrar, Straus and Giroux, LLC; (bottom right) © HRW, cover embroidery by Zelda Sperber; **158:** (top) Hurd-LaRinconada Gallery, San Patricio, New Mexico; (bottom) Woolaroc Museum, Bartlesville, Oklahoma; **159:** (top and bottom) © Bettmann/CORBIS; (center right) © HRW, cover embroidery by Zelda Sperber; **160:** National Archives; **160–161, 161** (left): Collection of Matthew R. Isenburg, Oakland Museum of California Art of the Gold Rush; **161** (right): © Bettmann/CORBIS; **164:** Culver Pictures, Inc.; **165:** Courtesy Schweitzer Gallery, New York;

**166–167:** From *The Illustrated Edgar Allan Poe* by Wilfred Satty. Copyright © 1976 by Wilfred Satty and Edgar Allan Poe. Picture Collection. The New York Public Library/Art Resource, NY; **168:** Reprinted by permission of Atheneum Books for Young Readers, an imprint of Simon & Schuster Children's Publishing Division from *The Deerslayer* by James Fenimore Cooper, illustrated by N. C. Wyeth. Copyright © 1925 and renewed © 1953, Charles Scribner's Sons; **169:** (top right) Photofest; (bottom left) 20th Century Fox courtesy of The Kobal Collection; **172:** Courtesy of the artist; **190–193:** Kirchoff/Wohlberg; **194:** Courtesy George Eastman House; **195:** MS Am 1340 (134). By permission of the Houghton Library, Harvard University. © The President and Fellows of Harvard College; **197:** Courtesy of Houghton Mifflin Company; **198:** Courtesy Colorado Historical Society; **199–201:** © Bettmann/CORBIS; **202:** Jerry Cooke/TimePix; **206–207:** (background) Douglas Pulsipher/The Stock Solution; **211:** MS Am 1506, By permission of the Houghton Library, Harvard University. © The President and Fellows of Harvard College; **212:** © Smithsonian American Art Museum/Art Resource, NY. Gift of Thomas M. Evans and Museum Purchase through the Smithsonian Collections Acquisition Program; **213:** National Portrait Gallery/Smithsonian Institution/Art Resource, NY; **216:** © Getty Images; **217, 219, 220:** Kirchoff/Wohlberg; **230, 231:** The Pierpont Morgan Library/Art Resource, NY; **235:** © Robert Essel/CORBIS Stock Market; **242:** Courtesy of the Concord Free Public Library; **243:** © Getty Images; **244:** TimePix; **245:** Charles Moore/Black Star/stockphoto.com; **246:** © Bettmann/CORBIS; **248** (top) Reproduced by permission of the Norman Rockwell Family Agency, Inc.; (bottom): © UPI/Bettmann/CORBIS; **250:** © HRW, cover embroidery by Zelda Sperber; **263:** Tom Hopkins; **266:** National Museum of American Art, Bequest of Henry Ward Ranger through the National Academy of Design. Courtesy Art Resource, NY; **269, 272:** Tom Hopkins; **274:** Houghton Mifflin Company; **277:** © Bettmann/CORBIS; **280–281, 291:** Mary Evans Picture Library/The Image Works, Inc.; **294:** From *The Illustrated Edgar Allan Poe* by Wilfred Satty. Copyright © 1976 by Wilfred Satty and Edgar Allan Poe. Used by permission of Warner Books. Image courtesy of the New York Public Library; **304:** Loren McIntyre/Woodfin Camp & Associates; **305:** Loren McIntyre/Woodfin Camp & Associates; **306:** © Archivo Iconografico, S.A./CORBIS; **307:** Art Resource/NY; **308:** (top) Courtesy of the Massachusetts Historical Society; (bottom) Courtesy of The Atlantic Monthly; **309:** Scott Camazine/Photo Researchers, Inc.; **329:** Bridgeman Art Library; **337:** (top left) Cover from *Moby-Dick* by Herman Melville. Used by permission of Barnes & Noble Publishing. Cover art: *The Great Shroud* (detail) by Bill Sienkiewicz. Used by permission of the artist; (top right) *Wuthering Heights* by Emily Brontë. Cover © HRW. Cover art by © Joe Comish/Getty Images and © Lois Romei Schlowsky/Getty Images; (bottom left) Used by permission of the publisher, Little, Brown and Company; (bottom right) Cover from *Silent Spring* by Rachel Carson. Copyright © 1962 by Rachel L. Carson, renewed 1990 by Roger Christie. Reprinted by permission of Houghton Mifflin Company. All rights reserved; **352:** Julie Habel/Woodfin Camp & Associates; **354:** (top left) By permission of the Houghton Library, Harvard University, Cambridge, Massachusetts; (top right) Library of Congress; (center left) © HRW, cover embroidery by Zelda Sperber; (center right) © Bettmann/CORBIS; (bottom left) Amherst College Archives and Special Collections; (bottom center) National Archives; (bottom right) Library of Congress; **355:** (top left) Courtesy of the Emily Dickinson Museum, Amherst, Massachusetts; (top right) Walt Whitman Birthplace State Historic Site, c. 1819. Photo by Dee Craft, courtesy of the Walt Whitman Birthplace Association; (bottom) National Archives; **357:** (top and background) The Pierpont Morgan Library/Art Resource, NY; (center) Library of Congress; (bottom) MS Am 1118.3 (183). By permission of the Houghton Library, Harvard University. © The President and Fellows of Harvard College; **360:** Walt Whitman, ca. 1863, MSS 829-h, Clifton Waller Barrett Library of American Literature, Special Collections, University of Virginia Library; **363:** Jeff Zelevansky/AP/Wide World Photos; **364–365:** (top) © Smithsonian American Art Museum/Art Resource, NY; (bottom) Julie Habel/Woodfin Camp & Associates; **368:** From the David T. Vernon Collection of Native American Indian Art, Colter Bay Indian Arts Museum, Grand Teton National Park, Wyoming. Photo by J. Oldenkamp; **373:** © Mary Ann McDonald/CORBIS; **374:** © Francis G. Mayer/CORBIS; **375:** © CORBIS; **377:** Denver Public Library/ Western History Department; **378:** TimePix; **379:** © Bettmann/ CORBIS; **380:** The Granger Collection, New York; **384–385:** (background) © Galen Rowell/CORBIS; (inset) © Getty Images; **386:** © Wolfgang Kaehler/CORBIS; **394** (background): Stephen P. Parker/Photo Researchers, Inc.; **398:** Jim Zipp/Photo Researchers, Inc.; **402–403:** © Images.com/CORBIS; **404:** Burnstein Collection/CORBIS; **405:** The Granger Collection, New York; **406:** Collection of the artist; **408:** SuperStock; **409:** (top) MS 1118.7. By permission of the Houghton Library, Harvard University. © The President and Fellows of Harvard College; **410, 411, 412:** © Jerome Liebling; **413:** Bridgeman Art Library; **414:** Terra Foundation for American Art, Chicago/Art Resource, NY; **417:** Jerry Schad/Photo Researchers, Inc.; **418:** © Michael Maconachie; Papilio/CORBIS; **425:** Cover of *Versos Sencillos/Simple Verses* by Raymond Ortiz Godfrey is reprinted with permission from the publisher of *Versos Sencillos/Simple Verses* by Jose Martí (Houston: Arte Público Press, University of Houston, ©1991). (top right) Cover from *Little Women* by Louisa May Alcott. Illustration by M. E. Gray/Hodder and Stroughton. Reproduced by permission of Hodder and Stroughton Limited; (bottom left) Book cover from PILGRIM AT TINKER CREEK by ANNIE DILLARD. Copyright © 1974 by Annie Dillard. Reprinted by permission of HarperCollins Publishers; (bottom right) Cover art by © 1986 Barry Moser. Reprinted from *Visiting Emily* by the permission of University of Iowa Press. Edited by Sheila Coghill and Thom Tammaro; **444:** (top right) © Bettmann/CORBIS; (bottom) Library of Congress; **445:** (top) *The Red Badge of Courage*, Clifton Waller Barrett Library of American Literature, Special Collections, University of Virginia Library; (center right) Photograph of Paul Laurence Dunbar, MSS 6323-a, Clifton Waller Barrett Library of American Literature, Special Collections, University of Virginia Library; (bottom right) National Museum of American Art, Washington, D.C./Art Resource, NY; (bottom) © Dallas and John Heaton/ CORBIS; **446–447:** © Bettmann/ CORBIS; **447:** Christie's Images/The Bridgeman Art Library, London/New York; **450:** Denver Public Library, Western History Collection, X-22175; **452** (bottom): Culver Pictures, Inc.; **453:** Civil War Photograph Collection, Library of Congress; **455:** Madison Bay Company; **459** (right): Culver Pictures, Inc.; **471:** Harvard University Press; **474:** © CORBIS; **478:** Culver Pictures, Inc.; **481:** "Go Down Moses, Moses Let My People Go." Item #: Music #708, Historic American Sheet Music. Rare Book, Manuscript, and Special Collections Library, Duke University (http://scriptorium.lib.duke.edu/sheetmusic/); **482:** (bottom left)

"Negro Spiritual Song, Swing Low, Sweet Chariot", Item #: Music #570, no.10, Historic American Sheet Music. (bottom center) "De Day of Liberty's Comin," Item #: Music B-1062, Historic American Sheet Music. (bottom right) "Swing Low, Sweet Chariot", Item #: Music #697, Historic American Sheet Music. All from Rare Book, Manuscript, and Special Collections Library, Duke University (http://scriptorium.lib.duke.edu/sheetmusic/); **482–483:** © Bettmann/CORBIS; **483:** © CORBIS; **484:** © Getty Images; **486:** AP/Wide World Photos; **487:** © Bettmann/CORBIS; **490:** © Daniel Nichols; **493:** © Bret Baunton/Getty Images; **494:** Allen Russell/Index Stock Imagery; **499:** © UPI/ Bettmann/CORBIS; **501:** © Bettmann/CORBIS; (background) University of Virginia Library; **508:** © The Stapleton Collection/CORBIS; **510:** Civil War Photograph Collection, Library of Congress; **511:** © The Corcoran Gallery of Arts/CORBIS; **512:** The Granger Collection, New York; **513:** Library of Congress; **514:** © CORBIS (bottom) Library of Congress; **519:** © Geoffrey Clements/CORBIS; **520:** University of Washington Libraries, Special Collections, NA189; **532:** The Granger Collection, New York; **535, 539:** © Bettmann/CORBIS; **540:** © Roberto Schmidt/AFP/Getty Images; **541:** © Paul Sahre; **545:** © Bettmann/CORBIS; **547:** © 2001 Michael DeYoung/Alaska Stock; **550:** © 2001 Don Pitcher/Alaska Stock; **555:** (inset) © 2001 Jeff Schultz/Alaska Stock; (background) © 2001 Johnny Johnson/Alaska Stock; **557:** (inset) © 2001 Jeff Schultz/Alaska Stock; (background) © 2001 Jeff Schultz/Alaska Stock; **559:** © Wild Country/CORBIS; **560:** AP/Wide World Photos; **564:** © Craig Lovell/CORBIS; **565:** © CORBIS; **566:** © Mike Zens/CORBIS; **567, 575:** © Bettmann/CORBIS; **579:** © Getty Images; **580:** © Getty Images; **588:** AP/Wide World Photos; **593:** © Bettmann/CORBIS; **595:** Smithsonian American Art Museum, Washington, DC/Art Resource, NY; **596:** © Christie's Images/Bridgeman Art Library; **597:** Photograph courtesy of Gwendolyn Knight Lawrence/Art Resource, NY; **598:** Bridgeman Art Library; **599:** Smithsonian American Art Museum, Washington, DC/Art Resource, NY; **601:** (top left) From *Roots* (jacket cover) by Alex Haley. Used by permission of Dell Publishing, a division of Random House, Inc.; (top right) *Adventures of Huckleberry Finn* by Mark Twain. Cover © Clint Farlinger; (bottom left) Cover from THE CIVIL WAR by Ken Burns, Rick Burns, and Geoffrey Ward. Used by permission of Alfred A. Knopf, a division of Random House, Inc.; (bottom right) Cover from *My Ántonia* by Willa Cather (Boston: Houghton Mifflin, 1995). Reprinted by permission of Houghton Mifflin Company. All rights reserved; **630:** Terra Foundation for American Art, Chicago/Art Resource, NY; **632:** (center) © Underwood and Underwood/ CORBIS; (bottom) © Bettmann/CORBIS; **633:** (top left) Karsh/ Woodfin Camp & Associates; (top right) Robert Goynes; (center) © Bettmann/ CORBIS; (bottom) John Bigelow Taylor/Art Resource, NY; **634:** IFS/US Army/National Military/TimePix; **634–635:** © Bettmann/ CORBIS; The Newark Museum/Art Resource, NY; **638:** © Getty Images; **640:** (bottom): © Bettmann/ CORBIS; **642:** Réunion des Musées Nationaux/Art Resource, NY; **644:** © SuperStock; **645–647** (background): Picture Perfect, USA; **652** (bottom): © Hulton-Deutsch Collection/CORBIS; **653:** Beinecke Rare Book and Manuscript Library, Yale University; **654:** © Roger Tidman/ CORBIS; **655:** © UPI/ Bettmann/ CORBIS; **657, 658:** Mary Evans Picture Library/The Image Works, Inc.; **665:** © Pach/Bettmann/CORBIS; **666:** Courtesy J. B. Weekes; **669, 670:** PhotoAlto; **671:** © Esther Bubley/TimePix; **673:** © David A. Northcott/CORBIS; **674:** Esther Bubley/ TimePix; **675:** © Bettmann/CORBIS; **677:** (top): By permission of the Houghton Library, Harvard University, Cambridge, Massachusetts; **682:** Karsh/Woodfin Camp & Associates; **684:** Karsh/Woodfin Camp & Associates; **685:** (left center) Department of Rare Books and Special Collections/Princeton University Libraries; (right) Madison

Bay Company; **686:** Ernest Hemingway Photograph Collection, John F. Kennedy Presidential Library and Museum, Boston; **687:** Department of Rare Books and Special Collections/Princeton University Libraries; **689:** © Hulton Archive/Getty Images; **692** (bottom): Beinecke Rare Book and Manuscript Library, Yale University; **695:** © Bettmann/CORBIS; **698, 699, 706, 707, 710, 712:** © Liberty Library Corporation/Getty Images; **714:** The Granger Collection, New York; **715:** Culver Pictures, Inc.; **716:** Mansell/TimePix; **717:** Brown Brothers; **720, 722:** Kirchoff/Wohlberg; **728:** The Granger Collection, New York; **729:** Kirchoff/Wohlberg; **730:** Mary Evans/Exploron Archives; **731:** (inset) Courtesy of the Consulate of Uruguay, New York; (background) © Hubert Stadler/CORBIS; **737:** Dwight Kuhn/Bruce Coleman, Inc.; **738:** Kirchoff/Wohlberg; **741:** © Geoffrey Clements/CORBIS; **742:** © UPI/Bettmann/CORBIS; **749:** Culver Pictures, Inc.; **753:** © Bettmann/CORBIS; **757:** Culver Pictures, Inc.; **758:** © Bettman/Corbis; **760, 765, 766, 767:** Reprinted by permission of Russell & Volkening as agents for the author. © Eudora Welty LLC; Eudora Welty Collection, Mississippi Department of Archives and History; **769:** © Hulton Archive/Getty Images; **771** (inset): Getty Images; **779:** © Philadelphia Museum of Art/CORBIS; **780:** © Bettmann/CORBIS; **782:** Photofest; **786:** (top left) Copyright © 1931 by James Thurber. Copyright renewed © 1959 by James Thurber. Reprinted by arrangement with Rosemary A. Thurber and the Barbara Hogenson Agency; (bottom right) Division of Rare Books and Manuscript Collections/Cornell University Library; **787:** From *Men, Women and Dogs.* Copyright © 1943 by James Thurber. Copyright renewed © 1971 by Helen Thurber and Rosemary A. Thurber. Reprinted by arrangement with Rosemary A. Thurber and the Barbara Hogenson Agency; **788:** From "The Night the Ghost Got In." Copyright © 1933 by James Thurber. Copyright renewed © 1961 by Helen and Rosemary Thurber. Reprinted by arrangement with Rosemary A. Thurber and the Barbara Hogenson Agency. All rights reserved; **789:** From "The Night the Bed Fell" from *My Life and Hard Times.* Copyright © 1933 by James Thurber. Copyright renewed © 1961 by James Thurber. Reprinted by arrangement with Rosemary A. Thurber and the Barbara Hogenson Agency; **790:** © Bettmann/CORBIS; **791:** Beinecke Rare Book and Manuscript Library, Yale University; **792–793:** Kunio Hagio; **795:** © Niall Benvie/CORBIS; **796:** © Rick Schafer Photography, LLC; **798:** © Niall Benvie/CORBIS; **799:** © Dewitt Jones/CORBIS; **800:** © Eric Ergenbright/CORBIS; **801, 802:** © Getty Images; **804:** © Robert Maass/CORBIS; **805:** C. Bradley Simmons/Bruce Coleman, Inc.; **809:** Dartmouth College Library; **810:** (top) Beinecke Rare Book and Manuscript Library, Yale University; (bottom) Jim Brown/Black Star/stockphoto.com; **816:** Brown Brothers; **816–817** (background): Phototone; **817:** Brown Brothers; **818:** National Portrait Gallery/Smithsonian Institution. Gift of Lawrence A. Fleischman and Howard Garfinkle with a matching grant from the National Endowment for the Arts. Courtesy Art Resource, NY; **819:** Tony Galindo; **823:** National Portrait Gallery, Smithsonian Institution/Art Resource, NY; **824, 825** (bottom): © Phoebe Beasley. Courtesy of the artist; **831:** Beinecke Rare Book and Manuscript Library, Yale University; **834:** © Phoebe Beasley. Courtesy of the artist; **835:** © Nathan Benn/CORBIS; **837, 839, 841, 842:** Florida State Archives; **846:** Library of Congress; **847:** © Christie's Images/Bridgeman Art Library; **848:** Mary Ryan Gallery after D.C.; **850:** Flip Chalfant/The Image Bank/Getty Images; **851–852:** Robert Shafer/Brand X Pictures/Getty Images; **853:** Art Resource, NY; **855:** © Robertstock; **857:** Bridgeman Art Library; **858–859:** Bridgeman Art Library; **869:** (top left) *Ethan Frome* cover © HRW. Cover art: *Mountain Winter,* woodcut © Sabra Field; (top right) Jacket cover for THE GREAT GATSBY

by F. Scott Fitzgerald. Copyright © 1925 by Charles Scribner's Sons. Copyright renewed © 1953 by Frances Scott Fitzgerald Lanahan. Reprinted by permission of Simon & Schuster Adult Publishing Group. (bottom left) Book cover for A FAREWELL TO ARMS by Ernest Hemingway. Copyright © 1929 by Charles Scribner's Sons. Copyright renewed © 1957 by Ernest Hemingway. Reprinted by permission of Simon & Schuster Adult Publishing Group; (bottom right) Cover design and logo by Maggie Payette, from *When Harlem Was in Vogue* by David Levering Lewis, copyright © 1979, 1981, 1997 by David Levering Lewis. Used by permission of Penguin, a division of Penguin Group (USA) Inc.; **886:** Christie's Images; **888** (top left): © Baldwin Ward/ CORBIS; (bottom right) © NASA/Getty Images; **889:** (top) Kirchoff/Wohlberg; (center) Larry Burrows/TimePix; (bottom) © CORBIS/Sygma; **890:** © Bettmann/CORBIS; **890–891:** Dirck Halstead/TimePix; **891:** Frank Chmura/Alamy; **894:** (top) © David and Peter Turnley/ CORBIS; (bottom) © Bettmann/CORBIS; **895:** © CORBIS; **897:** © Pitchal Frederic/CORBIS; **899:** © David and Peter Turnley/CORBIS; **900:** (left) Copyright: Peter Matthiessen, 1978. Design: Gail Belenson. Photo: George B. Schaller, 1974, Shey Monastery. All rights reserved. Courtesy Penguin Books; (right) Mario Ruiz/TimePix; **901:** © Ted Streshinsky/CORBIS; **903:** © Bettmann/CORBIS; **904:** © Kevin Fleming/CORBIS; **908:** © Getty Images; **909:** © Elliot Erwitt E/Magnum Photos; **910:** © Getty Images; **911:** Madison Bay Company; **912:** © E. Adams /CORBIS/Sygma; **914:** Private Collection/Bridgeman Art Library, London/New York; **919:** © Bettmann/CORBIS; **924:** AP/Wide World Photos; **925:** Brown Brothers; **926:** J R Eyerman/TimePix; **927:** © Getty Images; **930–931:** © Matsushige/CORBIS/Sygma; **937:** Bernard Hoffman; **940:** Associated Press; **942–945:** © Getty Images; **947:** © Bettmann/CORBIS; **951:** © Getty Images; **952:** Kunio Hagio; **953:** © Getty Images; **954:** AP/Wide World Photos; **954–955, 958, 959:** © Bettmann/CORBIS; **959** (inset): Holocaust Memorial, Miami, Florida. Photograph by Patrick Ward; **960:** Courtesy Bernard Toale Gallery, Boston, Massachusetts; **961:** © Jerry Bauer; **963:** John Gordon/Black Star/stockphoto.com; **965, 969:** © Bettmann/CORBIS; **966:** Bill Hickey; **971:** Larry Burrows/Life Magazine. © Time, Inc.; **974–975:** © Bob Elsdale; **973, 975–978:** © Gary Buss/Getty Images; **979:** © William Koplitz/Index Stock Imagery, Inc./Jupiter Images; **981, 982:** © cartoonbank.com; **982:** Barbara Hogenson Agency, Inc.; **983:** AP/Wide World Photos; **984:** Image courtesy Leo Castelli Photo Archives. © 2003 Mike and Doug Starn/Artists Rights Society (ARS), New York; **993:** © Theo Westenberger/Getty Images; **995, 996, 999, 1000:** © Getty Images; **1003:** © Bettmann/CORBIS; **1007:** Ben Martin/Time Life Pictures/Getty Images; (background) Art by Sergio Bustamante/Photo by Clint Clemens; **1008:** (top) "Adventures of Superman #599" © 2002 DC Comics. All rights reserved. Used with permission. (bottom) Mary Evans Picture Library/The Image Works, Inc.; **1009, 1010, 1014:** Art by Sergio Bustamante, photo © 1999 Clint Clemens. All rights reserved; **1015:** Reuters/Bettmann/CORBIS; **1017:** (top) © CORBIS; (center) Lawrence Manning/CORBIS; **1020, 1022, 1023:** © CORBIS; **1028:** AP Photo/Suzanne Plunkett; **1030:** © Getty Image; **1031:** © Roger Wood/CORBIS; **1032:** Eve Steccati; **1034–1037:** © Bettmann/CORBIS; **1038:** © Phil Schermeister/ CORBIS; **1039:** © Richard T. Nowitz/CORBIS; **1040:** © Annie Griffiths Belt/CORBIS; **1040–1041, 1042:** © Bettmann/CORBIS; **1043:** © Getty Images; **1047, 1049:** AP/Wide World Photos; **1049** (background): © Gianni Dagli Orti/CORBIS; **1052:** © Archivo Iconographico, S.A./CORBIS; **1054–1055:** AP/Wide World Photos; **1057:** Manu Sassoonian/Art Resource, NY; **1063:** National Portrait Gallery, Washington, D.C./Art Resource, NY/Van Vechten Trust; **1065,**

1069: Mississippi Valley Collection, University of Memphis Libraries; 1077: Ed Clark/ TimePix; 1079: © Bettmann/CORBIS; 1080: AP/Wide World Photos; 1082: Leon Sun Photography; 1086: Michael Newman/ Photoedit; 1087: (left) © Phil Schermeister/CORBIS; (right) Richard Hutchings/Photoedit; 1091: Jaye Phillips/Image Stock Imagery; 1092: © Sophie Bassouls/CORBIS/Sygma; 1095: © James Barnett/CORBIS Stock Market; 1097: © John Stevens/The Stock Solution; 1102: Jeff Reinking; 1104: Photo Courtesy ACA Galleries, New York; 1106–1107, 1108: Kirchoff/Wohlberg; 1110: © Y. Coatsaliou/ CORBIS/Sygma; 1112–1113: © Steve Schapiro/Black Star/stockphoto.com; 1116: Brian Lanker; 1119: Rubén Guzmán; 1121: © 2006 Banco de México Diego Rivera & Frida Kahlo Museums Trust. Av. Cinco de Mayo No. 2, Col. Centro, Del. Cuauhtémoc 06059, México, D.F.; 1125: © Alan Pogue/Texas Center for Documentary Photography/University of Texas, Austin; 1128–1129: Smithsonian American Art Museum, Washington, D.C./Art Resource, NY; 1130: © UPI/Bettmann/CORBIS; 1132: National Geographic Image Collection/Medford Taylor; 1136–1137: © Michael S. Yamashita/CORBIS; 1138: © UPI/ Bettmann/CORBIS; 1139: © Walter Lopez/CORBIS; 1142–1143: Bridgeman-Giraudon/Art Resource, NY; 1145: AP/Wide World Photos; 1147: S. Rannels/Grant Heilman Photography, Inc.; 1148–1149: S. Rannels/Grant Heilman Photography, Inc.; 1150: © Bruce Robinson/CORBIS; 1151: © Bettmann/Corbis; 1152–1153: Christie's Images/CORBIS; 1156: © Getty Images; 1159: © Scott Morgan/Getty Images; 1161: © Reuters NewMedia, Inc./CORBIS; 1163: Schalkwijk/Art Resource, NY; 1164: © Bohemian Nomad Picturemakers/CORBIS; 1165: © 1993 Harry Mattison; 1166: © Reuters NewMedia, Inc./CORBIS; 1167: (top) AP/Wide World Photos; (center) SuperStock; (bottom)

© Davies & Starr/Getty Images; 1168: © AFP/Getty Images; 1169: AP/Wide World Photos; 1170–1171: Curbstone Press; (background) AP/Wide World Photos; 1172: © Getty Images; 1174: © Joe Villareal; 1175: PhotoDisc/Getty Images; 1176: © Hal Marcus; 1177: Robert Severi/Gamma Liaison; 1178–1179: © Ted Thai/Time Pix/Getty Images; 1180: © Elizabeth Barakah Hodges/ SuperStock; 1181: Ted Rosenberg; 1182: (inset) © Clarissa Leahy/Getty Images; (background) © Getty Images; 1184: Arthur Furst; 1185, 1186: © Christie's Images/CORBIS; 1189: Caravaggio/ Wood River Gallery/ PictureQuest; 1190–1191: Mary Evans Picture Library/The Image Works, Inc.; 1191: © Getty Images; 1193: Herb Snitzer/TimePix; 1194: Michael Escoffery/Art Resource, NY; 1196: © Getty Images; 1197: © Joan Marcus; 1200: The New York Public Library/Art Resource, NY; 1202: Harry Ransom Humanities Research Center. The University of Texas at Austin; 1209: © T. Charles Erickson; 1210: © Martha Swope; 1273: © 20th Century Fox/Shooting Star International; 1276: © Joan Marcus; 1277: Smithsonian American Art Museum, Washington, DC/Art Resource, NY; 1299: © 2001 Douglas Peebles; 1301: © Pam Ingalls/CORBIS; 1303: Harvey Dinnerstein; 1307: Bridgeman Art Library; 1310: © Ron Watts/CORBIS; 1313: (top left) from *The Things They Carried* (jacket cover) by Tim O'Brien, copyright. Used by permission of Broadway Books, a division of Random House, Inc.; (top right) *Beloved* cover art © Thomas Blackshear; (bottom left) *Into Thin Air* by Jon Krakauer, copyright © 1997 by Jon Krakauer. Used by permission of Villard Books, a division of Random House, Inc.; (bottom right) From UNSETTLING AMERICA by Maria Mazziotti Gillan and Jennifer Gillan, copyright © 1994 by Maria Mazziotti Gillan and Jennifer Gillan. Used by permission of Viking Penguin a division of Penguin Group (USA) Inc.

# Illustrations

# Maps

**Program Staff Credits:** Kristen Azzara, Julie Beckman-Key, Tom Browne, Matt Bucher, Susan Cakars, Kimberly Cammerata, Melissa Ciano, Gail Coupland, Grant Davidson, Nina Degollado, Scott Deneroff, Christine Devall, Liz Dickson, Lydia Doty, Amy Fleming, Emily Force, Betty Gabriel, Jeff Galvez, Mikki Gibson, Guy Guidici, Leora Harris, Sally Hartin-Young, Anne Heausler, Sean Henry, Eric Higgerson, Julie Hill, Julie Hoover, Julia Hu, Liz Huckestein, Rodney Jester, Stephanie Jones, Dolores Keller, Marcia Kelley, Juliana Koenig, Karen Kolar, Jane Kominek, Cathy Kuhles, Elizabeth LaManna, Jamie Lane, Carolyn Logan, Belinda Lopez, Mary Malone, Kris Marshall, Carol Marunas, Pat McCambridge, Mark McDonald, Dick Metzger, Betty Mintz, Mary Monaco, Laura Mongello, Victoria Moreland, Cynthia Muñoz, Michael Neibergall, Steve Oelenberger, Karen Peterfreund, Marie Price, Jeff Raun, Amber Rigney, Mike Rinella, Kathryn Rogers, Beth Sample, Susan Sato, Annette Saunders, Peter Sawchuk, Kathleen Scheiner, Gloria Shahan, Mary Shaw, Dakota Smith, Emily R. Stern, Jeff Streber, Ralph Tachuk, Jennifer Tench, Carol Trammel, Lisa Vecchione, Katie Vignery, Ken Whiteside, Tamesa Williams, Evan Wilson, Sari Wilson, Richard Wright, Michael Zakhar, Sara Zettner

# Index of Skills

The boldface page numbers indicate an extensive treatment of the topic.

## LITERARY SKILLS

Abstract language, **1174, 1379**
Allegory, **251**, 327, **1379**
Alliteration, 201, 303, 367, 797, 832, 1160, 1178, 1180, **1379**
Allusion, **36**, 43, 85, **795**, 797, **1120**, 1126, **1171**, 1172, **1379**
Ambiguity, 306, 770, 778, 794, **801**, 804, **1135**, 1137, 1180, **1379**
American Indian oratory, **521**
Analogy, 88, 94, 419, **1380**
Analysis questions (Interpretations), 26, 30, 34, 43, 51, 65, 77, 85–86, 94, 106, 186, 193, 201, 202, 211, 230, 241, 261, 273, 293, 303, 306, 366, 372, 374, 381, 387, 395, 400, 406, 407, 470, 477, 497, 509, 510, 522, 533, 542, 561, 567, 577, 586, 592, 654, 663–664, 670, 674, 678, 693, 715, 719, 729, 736, 756–757, 768, 778, 787, 794, 797, 800, 804, 811, 822, 832, 835, 844, 911, 923, 939, 948, 970–971, 980–981, 991, 1005–1006, 1013, 1025, 1044, 1059, 1076–1077, 1090, 1100, 1109, 1117, 1126, 1133, 1137, 1144, 1150, 1155, 1160, 1164, 1169, 1172, 1176, 1180, 1183, 1187, 1191, 1196
Anapest, **1380**
Anecdote, 88, 238, **1380**
Antagonist, 1248, **1380**
Anthropomorphism, **1380**
Antihero, **684**, 693
Aphorism, **75**, 1005, 1380
Apostrophe, 308
Archetype, **21**, 26, **175**, 261, **304**, 306, **752–753**, 756, 759, **1008**, 1013, **1189, 1380**
Argument, 941, **1380**
Assertion, 86, 1118
Assonance, 367, 1178, 1180, 1380, 1393
Atmosphere, 311, **1381**, 1394
Autobiography, **53**, 65, **837**, 844, **1381**
Ballad, **1381**
Biography, **1381**
Blank verse, 798, 800, 805, **812, 1381**
Cadence, 98, 358, **367**, 372, 419, **1381**

Caesura, **1381**
Catalog, **364**, 366, **1381**
Character, 186, 261, 273, 477, 577, 756, 768, 811, 844, 1076, 1081, 1235, **1381**, 1394
  archetypal, 756
  comic, **525**, 533
  dynamic, 1235, **1382**
  flat, **1382**
  inferences about, **697, 719**, 805, 811, **994**, 1006, 1081, 1090
  round, **1382**
  static, 1235, **1382**
  stock, 787
Characterization, **1081**, 1090, **1381**
Chronological order, 489, 497, 1389
Cliché, **1382**
Climax, 259, 272, 715, 736, **1382**
Coda, 373
Comedy, **1382**
Comic devices, **525**, 533
Comic relief, 1263
Comparing Points of View, 96, 232, 462, 498, 907
Conceit, **1382**
Concrete language, **1174**, 1176, **1382**
Conflict, **472**, 693, 729, **743**, 756, **962**, 980, 991, **994**, 1005, 1025, 1044, 1090, **1382**
  external, **472**, 477, **743**, 756, 962, **994**
  internal, **472**, 477, **743**, 756, 962, 970, **994**, 1044, 1090
Connotation, 43, **589**, 592, **1382**, 1394
Consonance, **1383**
Couplet, **197**, 792, 794, **1383**
Dactyl, **1383**
Denouement, **1383**
Dialect, 525, **1383**
Dialogue, 805, **1064**, 1076, 1077, **1384**
Diction, 794, **1384**
Dramatic irony, **1048**, 1059, **1387**
Dramatic monologue, **657**, **1384**
Elegy, 1100, **1384**
Elizabethan (Shakespearean) sonnet, **197**, 202, 792, 1395
End rhyme, **1131**, 1160, 1393
English sonnet. See Elizabethan (Shakespearean) sonnet.
Enjambment, **1384**
Epic, **1384**

Epitaph, 851
Epithet, 850, **1384**
Essay, 1103, 1109, **1384**
Evaluation questions, 30, 34, 43, 51, 65, 77, 86, 94, 187, 193, 211, 212, 230, 241, 273, 293, 303, 306, 400, 477, 497, 533, 542, 561, 567, 577, 587, 592, 664, 674, 678, 768, 778, 800, 804, 811, 822, 911, 948, 981, 1077, 1090, 1101, 1117, 1144, 1169, 1187
Exact rhyme, **391**
Exaggeration, **508**, 534, 542
Exposition, **1384**
Extended metaphor, 30, 663, **1388**
External conflict, **472**, 477, **743**, 756, 962, **994**, 1382
Fable, **1385**
Fantasy, 982
Farce, **1385**
Figures of speech (figurative language), **45**, 51, **208**, 392, 664, 678, 819, 1126, 1144, 1162, **1385**
  personification, 34, 193, 201, 395, 400, 406, 509, 592, 1144, 1150
  simile, 51, 395, 525, 654, 663, 674, 794, 800, 804, 832, 1109, 1144, 1164
  *See also* Metaphor.
Flashback, 586, 1093, 1101, **1385**
Foil, 736, **1385**
Foot, **195, 1385**
Foreshadowing, 175, 561, 729, **1385**
Formal essay, 1103
Frame story, 533, 991, **1385**
Free verse, 358, **367**, 372, 868, **1386**
Gothic tale, **732**
Haiku, **1386**
Hero, 168, 173, 372, 684, 1013
  antihero, **684**, 693
  archetypal, **752–753**
Historical context, **569**, 577, **962**
Hyperbole, **525**, 982, **1386**
Iamb, **195**, 197, 800, **1386**
Iambic pentameter, 197, 202, **1386**
Idiom, 525, **1386**
Imagery, 201, 202, **205**, 211, 367, 392, 400, 509, **565**, 567, **649**, 654, **666**, 670, 1077, 1090, 1126, 1133, **1152**, 1155, **1166**, 1169, 1176, 1187, **1386**

## LISTENING AND SPEAKING SKILLS

## INDEPENDENT READING

# Index of Art